LITERATURE

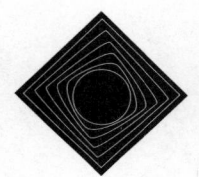

LITERATURE

LITERATURE

READING AND RESPONDING
TO FICTION, POETRY, DRAMA,
AND THE ESSAY

JOEL WINGARD
MORAVIAN COLLEGE

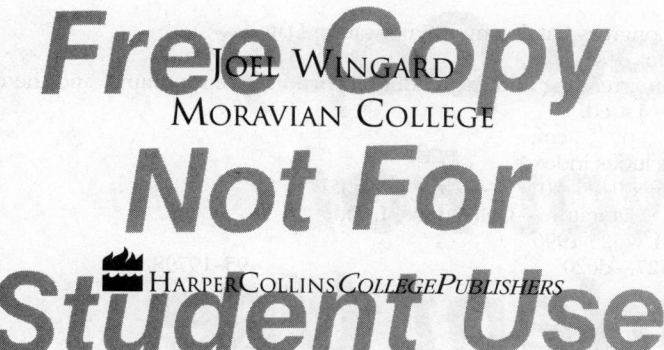

HARPERCOLLINS COLLEGE PUBLISHERS

Acquisitions Editor: Lisa Moore
Developmental Editor: Leslie Taggart
Project Coordination and Text Design: Ruttle Graphics, Inc.
Cover Designer: Kay Petronio
Cover Illustration: Lithograph by Henri Matisse. "Icarus, from the Jazz series." ARS, New
    York. Ecole des Beaux Arts, Paris, France.
Electronic Production Manager: Angel Gonzalez Jr.
Manufacturing Manager: Willie Lane
Electronic Page Makeup: Ruttle Graphics, Inc.
Printer and Binder: R R Donnelley & Sons Company
Cover Printer: Phoenix Color Corp.

For permission to use copyrighted material, grateful acknowledgment is made to the copyright holders on pp. 1717–1730, which are hereby made part of this copyright page.

Literature: Reading and Responding to Fiction, Poetry, Drama, and the Essay

Library of Congress Cataloging-in-Publication Data
Wingard, Joel, 1946-
    Literature, reading and responding to fiction, poetry, drama, and the essay / Joel
Wingard. — 1st ed.
            p.   cm.
    Includes index.
    ISBN 0-06-501735-8 (free copy ISBN)
        1.   Literature—Collections. I. Title.
PN6014.W525 1996
808'.0427—dc20   95-19798
                                                            CIP

*This book is dedicated
to John Finlay (1941–1991)
and Tom Utley (1940–1994):
friends, poets, scholars,
teachers, gentlemen.*

BRIEF CONTENTS

DETAILED CONTENTS

3 ◈ READING AND RESPONDING TO POETRY   503

6 ◈ RESEARCH AND WRITING   1631

PREFACE

It was my attendance at the first National Council of Teacher's of English Summer Institute on Teaching Literature to Undergraduates in 1987 that really transformed my teaching. That NCTE Institute allowed me to converse with such thinkers as Jane Tompkins, Houston Baker, Stanley Fish, and Steven Mailloux, as well as colleagues from around the country. Through these discussions (and through my own reading of books like Louise Rosenblatt's *Literature as Exploration*, Robert Scholes' *Textual Power*, David Bleich's *Subjective Criticism*, C. Douglas Atkins and Michael L. Johnson's *Writing and Reading Differently*, and Leslie Fiedler and Houston Baker's *Opening Up the Canon*), we explored the implications of reader-response and cultural criticism for our courses back home, and these discussions helped me to see a way to bring reader-response and cultural criticism into my classroom. More important, application of these critical approaches changed the way my students saw literature and themselves as readers and the way they wrote about both. My classroom, on both sides of the lectern, came alive with energy and a sense of discovery. That energy has resulted in this book — a book that is designed to address students' actual experience of reading and writing about literature in introductory literature and composition courses.

Empowering Readers

Literature: Reading and Responding to Fiction, Poetry, Drama, and the Essay is markedly different from other introductory literature textbooks in two fundamental ways. First, it emphasizes and empowers the reader, whereas other literature textbooks, even those that gesture in the direction of reader-response, emphasize and empower the text. To this end this book discusses formal literary elements in the context of the expectations readers bring to texts in different genres, rather than in terms of texts containing or illustrating those elements. The elements of literature are considered as text strategies: moves, maneuvers, and actions that a text puts into play. For example, most books, even those that claim to be reader oriented, approach "theme" as an element *in* or *of* the text (or as the text's relation to the larger world). In contrast, this book discusses theme as something readers *create* as they read.

In fact, each genre section offers a variety of texts that both conform to and challenge traditional literary conventions. In this way, students can see for themselves how text strategies are deployed and how their own reading strategies are affected by their awareness of and expectations for literary conventions. Furthermore, reading is described in this book as an interactive process. In the interactive model of reading, readers are active; they make their own moves in the form of reading strategies. Much of the instruction in this book is devoted to increasing students' awareness of and facility with reading strategies.

Another way this book empowers readers is that it extends the implications of the process approach to writing, emphasizing the dynamic interaction between reading and writing. It teaches students to write about themselves as readers, to be aware that they continue to read and learn as they write. Two special focus chapters in the fiction section particularly emphasize the roles culture and gender play in making meaning of what we read. *Literature* emphasizes writing to explore as individuals and as part of the world. In so doing, it emphasizes revision as an ongoing procedure in both reading and writing. This leaves the way open for students to consider that a reading is no more fixed and final than the text itself.

Expanding the Canon

The texts offered here range from "high art" to "low," from canonical to transitory, from "serious" to "popular," from literary to mass culture, and across ethnic and national cultures. The general introduction and each genre section highlights a text from mass culture: popular song lyrics, a music video, a television screenplay, and a magazine advertisement. Such texts deserve consideration for several reasons: they are an important part of students' lives; they may be read as cultural signs; and the reading strategies that students already have for them may be brought to consciousness and applied to the reading of literary texts.

I take the canon to be lively, shifting, and various, not fossilized or absolute. In addition to time-honored works by Sophocles, Shakespeare, Dickinson, Faulkner, Frost, and others, this book features contemporary writing in all four genres by a wide variety of writers, such as John Edgar Wideman, Carolyn Chute, Jamaica Kincaid, Wyatt Prunty, Sandra Cisneros, and Michelle Cliff. As the twenty-first century approaches and as the cultural mix of the classroom continues to change, I accordingly include a strong representation here of multicultural writers and multicultural experiences: Chinua Achebe, Rosario Castellanos, Mahmoud Darwish, Ved Mehta. A range of selections from various cultures helps students see that they read literature and construct reality from the perspectives of their own cultural situations.

Reader-response and cultural criticism recognize the varied responses an increasingly diverse student population are likely to have. Through representation of multicultural and women's voices, the inclusion of popular art forms, and an examination of the influence culture has on how we read texts, this book is committed to the ongoing cultural project of expanding the canon of what is read and taught in colleges and universities—and seeks to call into question the designation of "major" and "minor" writer—while encouraging students to become more aware of their own standards, aesthetic and cultural, for excellence in literature.

Building Confidence

This book sets out to build students' confidence in themselves as people with something to say about literature and to reduce the intimidation students sometimes feel about the study of "great" or "serious" literature. First, each section encourages active reading by discussing a variety of possible reading strategies. In the reading process, students can see how their decisions as readers affect the meaning of the texts they read. In addition, sharing responses in small groups or in whole class discussions is encouraged throughout the genre sections. Such discussions not only help students to articulate or try out their own emerging readings, but to also compare their readings to those of others — not so much to forge consensus as to recognize diversity.

This interactive, student-centered approach is also central to the emphasis on writing and the approach toward student writing throughout the book. Reading and meaning-making as active, conscious processes are reinforced through the emphasis on writing in both the general introduction and the genre sections. The introduction gives detailed instruction in writing response statements and all the writing discussions in the book help students expand and elaborate on these responses. A range of innovative and traditional writing assignments encourage students to tap the potential of their responses, and most reading selections in the instructional chapters are followed by response statement questions.

Exploring Writing

Response statement writing is at the heart of this book. In my classes, I have found discussions are livelier and students more interested (and student writing more interest*ing*) because of this activity. I believe the claims I am making here about student writing are borne out in the numerous samples of actual student writings and readings that appear throughout *Literature*. Five full chapters show students how to develop a formal paper, from an initial writer-based response to a piece of public prose, and a brief chapter in Part 6 explores how to compare and contrast texts. Each of these chapters features a student's writing process from response statement through multiple drafts toward a formal paper.

The work of a student who has followed a careful process is featured in each writing chapter; these six student papers demonstrate that reader-response and cultural criticism can be applied to the traditional academic aims of discovering and stating a thesis and developing that thesis by means of explanatory detail. In general, these student papers are devoted to self-conscious analysis; the students are writing about themselves as readers constructing meaning, not about literary texts as stable, aesthetic objects.

The writing is not purely subjective or personal, however, because it does take into account an audience that wants to know about the interaction between the reader and the text, not just one or the other in isolation. A caveat against purely personal association in public writing in Chapter 14 provides a negative example of a piece of student writing that ignores the interaction with the text to talk solely about the reader. However, the positive models of student writing in every genre show student readers interacting with the texts in order to explore their own beliefs and expectations and to raise questions about and offer perspectives on their interpretations of texts. These papers are typical of what the reader-response method can produce in conjunction with a process approach to writing.

In addition to reader-response versions of the traditional academic expository essay, the book offers a number of alternative assignments at the end of most chapters. These "Reading and Writing Projects for Creative and Critical Thinking" assignments move beyond the usual expository parameters toward more creative writing activities. I have gathered these assignments from discussions with colleagues at conferences and through their published descriptions in the professional literature. All are classroom tested, and several are illustrated by lively pieces of student writing.

A full chapter on research writing includes library research to help students broaden their literary experience and knowledge about any text, its author, the historical or cultural context in which a text was produced, or any issue with which a text my be concerned. This chapter will also prove useful for instructors assigning the conventional research paper or any of the alternative or reader-based projects suggested in the book. It includes up-to-the-minute coverage of computerized research resources, such as CD-ROM, as well traditional forms such as bound subject bibliographies and specialized encyclopedias, and follows the 1995 MLA documentation guidelines. In addition to particular resources, the appendix offers a search strategy that students may apply to virtually any academic library or academic discipline. In addition, Chapter 23, "Writing About Drama," shows the entire research and writing process of a student writing on Albee's *The Sandbox*. Here students can see decisions being made about quoting, paraphrasing, and summarizing, as well as read the entire text of a fully documented research paper.

Creating Critical Readers and Writers

The general introduction offers a critical thinking model—Question-Answer-Question ("QAQ")—as a way for students to explore their response writing and to keep their thinking and writing open and active. In addition to the QAQ model, the instructional chapters engage the student through frequent interactive exercises. "Share and Compare" gives students a chance to converse with the running discussion and encourages dialogue with other students in the classroom, and "Connect" invites students to discover intertextual connections.

Most stories, poems, plays, and essays are paired with response statement questions that tap into students' reading actions and cultural situations. These are not "study questions" whose "answers" may be found in the literary text or in the instructor's manual. They are open-ended questions to promote students' ongoing interaction with the texts. This active, critical approach extends to the "Reading and Writing Projects for Creative and Critical Thinking" at the end of most chapters. These assignments challenge students to think and write in ways that exercise their imaginations and emotions, and then to comment on their choices and activities in expository prose.

Teaching and Learning

This book is divided into six major sections (Part 1: An Introduction to Reading and Responding to Literature; Part 2: Reading and Responding to Fiction; Part 3: Reading and Responding to Poetry; Part 4: Reading and Responding to Drama; Part 5 Reading and Responding to the Essay; Part 6: Research and Writing) and concludes with a section on "Lives of the Writers" (biographical sketches of each author whose work is included in the book), a glossary of terms, and an index. The book is organized this way to make it useful for both introductory literature courses and for composition courses that use literary texts as readings. Instructors may assign the genre sections in any order and the introduction may be assigned and read as a whole or parceled out as a class goes through the genre sections. However an instructor decides to organize the course, I hope the following features of this book make it compatible for use in a variety of classrooms in both literature and composition.

- Reader-Centered Approach
- Cultural Connections
- Canon Expansion
- Extensive Writing Coverage
- Student Writing
- Critical Thinking Emphasis

Having (Some Serious) Fun

I believe that these features and the models on which they are built will make a difference in the classroom, in instructors' practices, in the discipline as a whole, and in students' lives. I said at the outset that reader-response and cultural criticism had made a difference for me as a teacher and for my students over the past eight years. It is that difference that compelled me to write this book. It is a serious book; it takes literature, texts, students, and teaching seriously. Its theoretical bases demand that the reader be taken as seriously as the text. But the book is also playful at times. Indeed, play itself is taken seriously, in sections like "The Reader at Play" (in poetry) and the "Reading and Writing Projects for Creative and Critical Thinking" throughout the book. In that sense, this book has been fun to write. I hope that it will also be fun to read and teach.

Joel Wingard

ACKNOWLEDGMENTS

I wish to thank the following people who reviewed portions of this manuscript and helped me revise it and those people who responded to questionnaires and surveys about their courses, their preferences for selections to be included, and their thoughts on what constitutes a good and useful textbook:

Carolyn Baker, San Antonio College
Bob Baron, Mesa Community College
Anis Bawarshi, University of Kansas
Lois Birky, Illinois Central College
Wendy Bishop, The Florida State University
Tony Boyle, State University of New York—Potsdam
Roger Brown, Laredo Community College
John Clifford, University of North Carolina—Wilmington
Patricia Connors, Memphis State University
Marcel Cornis-Pope, Virginia Commonwealth University
Ned Cummings, Commonwealth College
John L. Davis, University of Texas—San Antonio
Charles Dean, Middle Tennessee State University
Robert Dees, Orange Coast College
Kathleen A. Dooley, Tidewater Community College
David B. Downing, Indiana University of Pennsylvania
Walter J. Dudek, Fullerton College
Gail F. Duffy, Dean Junior College
Russell Durst, University of Cincinnati
Truman Eddy, Harrisburg Area Community College
Toni Empringham, El Camino College
Craig Etchison, Glenville State College
Elaine M. Fitzpatrick, Massasoit Community College
Claudia Fonda-Bonardi, Los Angeles Harbor College
Ray Foster, Scottsdale Community College
Bruce French, University of New Haven
Marilyn Gaull, New York University
Gabrielle Gautreaux, University of New Orleans
John Getz, Xavier University
Brent Gowen, Palomar College
Jackie Gray, North Carolina State University
Nicole H. M. Greene, University of Southwestern Louisiana
Iris Rose Hart, Sante Fe Community College
Denise Heikinen, Michigan Technological University
Gloria J. Hochstein, University of Wisconsin

Bill Howard, Eastern Michigan University
Linda T. Humphrey, Citrus Community College
Randy Ingram, Emory University
Ted E. Johnston, El Paso Community College
Lee Brewer Jones, DeKalb College
Edwina Jordan, Illinois Central College
Lynn Levy, Washington State University
Mary Maddock, Texas Tech University
Joseph Maiolo, University of Minnesota—Duluth
Don McClure, Indiana University of Pennsylvania
Fred Mench, Stockton State University
Charles W. Nelson, Michigan Technological University
Joe Ng, Inver Hills Community College
Larry Olpin, Central Missouri State University
Melissa Pennell, University of Massachusetts—Lowell
Betty Jo Peters, Morehead State University
Janis Rowell, North Shore Community College
Gail Rung, Black Hawk College
Beverly Schneller, Millersville University of Pennsylvania
Patrick Scott, University of South Carolina
Mary Segall, Quinnipiac College
Jill L. Sessoms, Coastal Carolina College
Pamela K. Shaffer, Fort Hays State University
Perri Shalman, City University of New York—York College
Mary Shaner, University of Massachusetts—Boston
Daniel Sheridan, University of North Dakota
Kay Smith, Valencia Community College
Louise Z. Smith, University of Massachusetts—Boston
Rebecca Stephens, Carlow College
Christina Stough, California State University—Long Beach
Willene Taylor, Southern University at New Orleans
Susan Tilka, Southwest Texas State University
Virginia Tyson, Arkansas Technical University
Robert Umphrey, University of Central Florida
Michael Vivion, University of Missouri—Kansas City
Steven Walker, Brigham Young University
Laurence Wiland, Colorado State University
David Zwonitzer, Laramie County Community College

I wish to thank the following students who allowed me to use their writing in this book, and for their writing that is honest, insightful, and self-conscious: Shirin Arastu, Catherine Bachochin, Stephanie Beacher, Tim Blangger, Carole Cockerill, Heather Colgan, Norris Daniels, Kelly DeWalt, Sharon DiBiagio, Jack Dudley, Melissa Dugan, Cluny Erickson, Wendy Gordon, Diane Gretta, Carl Hill, Justine Johnson, Gretchen Jones, Elaine Kaplowe, Tom Karabinus, Maeve Kelly, Nicholas Khan, Gina Koonce, Bill McGouldrick, Tonia McKelvie, Katerina Minakakis, Robert Moses, Marie Murphy, Gail Nagy, Victoria Napoli, Barabara Nelson, Sam Norwood, Miguel Olivares, Melanie Polak, Beth Rohn,

Alison Sebzda, Caroline Smith, Janell Snyder, Jody Strausser, Steve T., Carla Thomas, Mike Williams, and Derrick Wright.

I wish to thank the following people for their help and active support: Elaine Kaplowe, Greg Skutches, Justine Johnson, Nancy Wilson, Mickey Ortiz, Ashley Stewart, Kim Baenziger, Stephen Cook, Jack Ramsey, Curt Keim, Dennis Glew, Dorothy Glew, Scott Moore, Francine McDougall, Charles Moran, Elizabeth Penfield, and the Moravian College Faculty Development and Research Committee; the staff at HarperCollins for their wisdom and guidance: Leslie Taggart, Lisa Moore, and Kathy Smeilis; for her patience and the Tootsie rolls: Eleanor Millspaugh; and for their emotional support, their ears, and their minds: Leslie Taggart, Elaine Kaplowe, Karla Morales, and Wyatt Prunty.

Publisher's Note

The *Instructor's Manual* to accompany *Literature: Reading and Responding to Fiction, Poetry, Drama, and the Essay,* by Joel Wingard and Greg Skutches, intended for the new and experienced instructors alike, includes sections on

- the applications and benefits of reader-response theory
- how to engage students in reading and responding to literature
- how to integrate the processes of reading and writing about literature
- chapter-by-chapter teaching suggestions
- notes, questions, and comments about each literary selection

Available in fall 1995, the *Instructor's Manual* can be ordered through your local HarperCollins representative, or by calling 1-800-828-6000.

The *Writer's Workshop,* developed by the Daedalus Group, is a software program with series of heuristic questions to help students write about literature. Segments include

- Prereading: Text, Reader, and Reading Situation
- Response Statements
- Forms of Public Writing: Expository and Alternative Forms
- Incorporating Library Sources into Your Paper
- Grammar and Style Handbook
- Documentor, an electronic bibliography and notes module for MLA and APA documentation styles

The *Writer's Workshop* demonstration disk is available in fall 1995. Contact your local representative for a copy.

The *HarperCollins LitLetter,* edited by Elaine Kaplowe, is a newsletter by and for literature and composition instructors. *LitLetter* promotes the exchange of ideas, teaching tips and assignments, and suggestions for exploring intertextual links between serious literature and popular culture texts. It is also a place to share your students' writing, from response statements to more formal pieces. Submit your queries, suggestions, syllabuses, articles, or student writing to Elaine Kaplowe at ek6843@cnsvax.albany.edu or to Joel Wingard at mejdw01@moravian.edu. To receive a copy of the newsletter, call your local HarperCollins representative.

Part
ONE

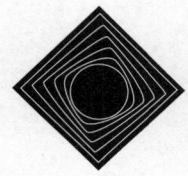

Reading
and
Responding
to
Literature

1 ◈ WHAT IS LITERATURE?

Asking what literature is may seem needless or silly, especially to college students taking a literature course. You and your literature classmates bring with you a variety of ideas about literature and experiences with literary study, and you and they may begin a course looking for answers rather than questions. But often the questions that don't seem to need to be asked are exactly the ones that should be asked. Real learning comes from that kind of interrogative activity, from going beneath or behind what seems obvious or is taken for granted. This book is full of questions. Some have definite answers, many do not. For someone seeking to learn, a questioning procedure is at least as important as finding answers, and *a* question is the best starting point. In John Fowles' novel *The Magus*, a mysterious magician-like character, Maurice Conchis, leads the protagonist, Nicholas, through a series of open-ended, puzzling, and deeply disturbing experiences. He makes Nicholas' life a series of questions with no certain answers. Finally, Nicholas is told that Conchis believes, "an answer is always a form of death" because of its finality. But a question keeps things alive and percolating. "What is literature?" is an important first question to be asked by students in a literature course, whether you know a lot or a little about literature as you begin your study.

This investigation can start with some answers you may already have to this question. Perhaps you would say literature is "works written by great authors" or, in the formulation of the nineteenth-century English critic and poet Matthew Arnold, "the best that has been thought and said." Or you might say it's "writing that expresses someone's thoughts or feelings on a subject he or she considers important." Perhaps literature is "writing such as stories, poems, or plays that deal with imaginary people, places, and situations." Other definitions may come to mind, but these are the kinds of answers many people give to the question asked above. This chapter will take a questioning look at what lies behind these various answers.

Besides questioning, another crucial procedure for learning is writing. Of course you will have to read as you work through this book, but you will also be asked to write frequently. Writing and reading are inseparable activities. As you read this book, you should have a pen or pencil in your hand. Use it. Write with it. Do what the Irish poet Seamus Heaney says he'll do with his pen: "dig with it."

To get started on both approaches—questioning and writing—take a few minutes now to jot down your definition of "literature." Use the box shown or a page in your notebook. Don't worry about being "correct" in your definition;

just take a stab at it. You can refine your understanding of the term as you read, think, and question your way through this chapter.

> **MY DEFINITION OF LITERATURE**
> Literature is ...

"Works written by great authors"

The statement that "literature is works written by great authors" is a common thumbnail definition of literature. A definition like this is probably based on experience with studying literature in school, where the emphasis often is on the great authors of the past (William Shakespeare, John Milton, Emily Dickinson, Virginia Woolf) and on some of the best-known works they have produced. If you think about this definition for a minute, you may see that it's just a bit too simple or circular: great authors make great literature; great literature is what is made by great authors. Still, this definition is useful as a start toward some deeper thinking on the subject. If you reject its simple circularity, you have sharpened your thinking already.

If you look at this definition a minute longer, you may see that the key word is "great." But who or what determines when an author is "great" or which pieces of writing are really "the best that has been thought and said"? What do words like "great" and "best" mean here? Clearly, they are subjective terms, yet this definition asks that they be taken as objective criteria. If "great" is really shorthand for a set of standards, fine, but those standards should be spelled out. Doing so would still mean that subjective judgments underlie the definition of literature, but at least they would be available for examination—your own and other people's.

Those standards don't have to be merely personal or idiosyncratic to be subjective; there might be a set of criteria that many people agree constitute greatness in literature or any other art. And if those people happen to be authority figures in the field, critics, professors, editors, "serious" readers, then that set of criteria may gain even wider acceptance. Most college students have been trained to respect authority figures and to play the game by their rules. To try to be a "serious" and "successful" student is to understand and play by those rules. So you may be conditioned to accept the standards of "greatness," in literature as well as in other areas, that people vested with academic or intellectual authority offer to you. But college might also be an opportunity like no other to question such authorities and to try to establish some standards for judgment of your own.

"Great" might also mean something like "time-honored," as in the case of authors such as those mentioned above. The works of such authors, the kind of literature that has often been the basis for whole courses in school and college, constitutes the **canon.** In fact, a definition of canon in this context is precisely those works that have come to be considered great, or at least important enough to be read, taught, and studied in college classrooms.

In recent years, however, the literary canon has come under some serious scrutiny (just as I am asking you to subject your definition(s) of literature to some scrutiny). One revelation of this scrutiny is that the canon is not carved in stone, but has in fact always been in flux. Many educated readers today would nominate Mississippian William Faulkner as one of the greatest novelists and short story writers of modern times. He was awarded the Nobel Prize for literature in 1949, yet just a few years before that happened, nearly all of his books were out of print. He wasn't much read, let alone taught and studied in schools. The seventeenth-century English poet John Donne is another canonized writer who was generally disregarded until another poet and critic, T. S. Eliot, helped "revive" him in the 1920s. Henry Wadsworth Longfellow's poetry was a staple of American schools in the early part of this century, but changes in critical taste have moved him out of the canon of "major" writers, so Longfellow is not widely read in schools and colleges today.

You may think that greatness in literature has something to do with general agreement as to quality, or that greatness in any art is at least partly determined by those who have the credentials to identify it: critics, professors, and reviewers. As long as some basic matters have been called into question here, this might as well be questioned too. The point of such questioning is not necessarily to destroy authoritative definitions of literature or attack the authority of those who assert those definitions, but to begin to exercise your own powers of aesthetic evaluation. What are your own standards for greatness in literature? Asking—and answering—such a question is to begin to see that you have, indeed, each individual reader has, some say in defining not only greatness in literary or artistic works but literature or art itself.

SHARE AND COMPARE: What is your response to this discussion of "greatness" in literature? Can you list any standards for greatness? Where do these standards come from: authorities, history, yourself? Name a poem, play, or short story that qualifies as "great" literature. Take a few minutes to jot down some of your thoughts on these questions. Compare your notes with your classmates' to see the variety of opinions a group of readers has.

"Writing that expresses someone's thoughts or feelings on a subject he or she considers important"

Saying "literature is writing that expresses someone's thoughts or feelings on a subject he or she considers important" places the emphasis very differently than the first definition. By not focusing on "greatness," it would recognize works by noncanonical authors as literature. In that way, perhaps, it improves on the first definition by broadening what could be called literature. Another challenge to the prevailing canon is the idea that works *not* written by great authors—anonymous works, for instance, or examples of "folk art"—may nevertheless be great in terms of their power to affect readers, or to express the lives of the individual people who wrote them, or to depict the historical and social circumstances that helped produce them. Do you have a favorite piece of literature, something that has really moved or spoken to you at some time in your life? Can you recall a selection that seems strongly expressive of a person in a particular situation, that really speaks for or reveals that person? Was it written by a "major" author? If so, and if it's a favorite of yours, is that *because* of who wrote it? If not, you may be able to see the inadequacy in the standard of great authors as the basis for defining literature.

SHARE AND COMPARE: How important do you think it is to consider the writer's expression in defining literature? Does your own personal canon of literature include any works primarily because of their expressiveness? What are they? Take a few minutes now to jot down your thoughts on these questions. What other perspectives emerge from sharing your ideas with your classmates?

Perhaps a closer look would reveal an aspect of this "expressive" definition of literature that you might quibble with, a way in which this definition does not depart all that much from the first definition. This second definition still puts the emphasis on the writer, who could, after all, try very hard and even succeed at expressing his or her thoughts and feelings, but still leave you more or less cold when you read it. This is not to say that such writing could not be categorized as literature, but the effect on the reader is an important factor in defining literature that should not be left out of consideration, as this definition seems to do. The emphasis on authors leaves little room for other considerations, such as whether you enjoy or can relate to those works. Perhaps the next definition avoids that problem.

"Writing such as stories, poems, or plays that deal with imaginary people, places, and situations"

By now, if you've been following this discussion carefully, you should be able to pretty easily question this definition. Right? One problem with saying "literature is writing such as stories, poems, or plays that deal with imaginary people, places, and situations" was hinted at earlier. It may be too narrow or restrictive, leaving out pieces of writing that don't fall into the usual literary categories or **genres**. How about another, related objection? The literary works you usually encounter actually do deal with imaginary people, places, and situations, even if they often seem real because of the way they are presented. But is that criterion absolutely necessary? Does the writing have to be fictional in this sense? Can't history or journalistic writing be literary? What about essays or letters? Perhaps you can think of some examples of nonfiction writing that you have found to be literary in one way or another: their ability to transport you in *your* imagination to another place and time, for instance, or their ability to "paint a picture" with words, or their effective use of such "literary" devices as simile or metaphor.

One such piece in the Essays section of this book is "Am I Blue?" by the novelist and short story writer Alice Walker. In fact, several great authors have written essays that have entered the canon: Jonathan Swift, author of *Gulliver's Travels*, also published "A Modest Proposal"; Virginia Woolf, who wrote several serious novels, has contributed "A Room of One's Own"; the poet Percy Shelley argued the importance of his craft in "A Defence of Poetry." Also in the Essays section of this book, you will find the Rev. Martin Luther King's "A Letter from Birmingham Jail," which is a combination of genres: an essay in letter form. In eighteenth-century England, in fact, letters were considered a legitimate literary form, and throughout the literary history of the Western world, the letters of numerous authors have been read for their literary merit by a much wider audience than the person for whom they were initially written.

Also, in the late 1960s and early 1970s, a subgenre of prose emerged under the name of "the New Journalism." This writing was journalism in the sense that its subjects were actual people or events, not imaginary constructions, but it deliberately used many of the artistic qualities of fiction and dropped the conventional objectivity that journalistic writing is supposed to have. A leading practitioner of this kind of writing is Tom Wolfe, whom you may know more recently as the author of the best-seller *The Bonfire of the Vanities*. Another was Truman Capote, whose "nonfiction novel" *In Cold Blood* told the story of an actual multiple murder in Kansas in 1959, but treated it not as straight reporting but in novelistic style. Then there is the writing of the notorious "gonzo journalist" Hunter S. Thompson, whose reporting on the Kentucky Derby for *Scanlan's Monthly* magazine went way beyond the boundaries of accepted journalistic practice in focusing on the high jinks of the writer himself and his illustrator/partner at the Derby. The blurring of the line between nonfiction and fiction in such works and the possibility that some nonfiction genres may have literary qualities tend to undermine "imaginary" as a criterion for literature.

Perhaps you have spotted another problem in the third tentative definition of literature, one that may not be so obvious as the question of genre but might be raised anyway: Does literature have to be writing?

Does this question go too far? If literature isn't at least writing, you may say, how can it be anything at all? There certainly is validity to that objection. But just for the sake of argument, entertain for the moment the notion that written language itself as the basis for literature may be called into question. One consequence of this would be to collapse the distinctions among all the arts, allowing literature and painting and music and dance to overlap or become confused with one another. That probably wouldn't do; some distinctions seem to be necessary and useful. But consider: music *is* usually written as a score before it is performed and heard by an audience in its usual medium of sound. It is not written in words primarily, but in musical notes, although it may often include verbal notations about tempo: *andante* (moderately slow), *allegro* (brisk, lively), and so forth. Dance is choreographed, a word that breaks down as "writing" (graph) for a "chorus," in this case dancers rather than singers. Admittedly, considering music and dance as literary arts does stretch the limits of "literature" pretty far, but such a stretching exercise can contribute to greater understanding of a term because knowing what it does *not* mean often helps clarify what it does mean.

SHARE AND COMPARE: Just for fun, take a few minutes to stretch this definition of literature beyond the usual boundaries. What specific examples can you and your classmates cite of "nonliterary" works that might qualify, by some other criteria, as "literature"? What objections might anyone raise to this stretching of the definitions of "literature"?

Having briefly tested the limits of the third definition of literature, music, dance, and other arts (painting, photography) may be left out of the question. A more limited definition can be offered.

"Verbal compositions produced to be read"

Wouldn't it be safe to define literature as "verbal compositions produced to be read"? And it would not be overly restrictive, as the earlier definitions seemed to be in one way or another. Except that what does "read" mean? Put into a visual medium so that someone's eyes and brain can process it? Or rendered into language so that someone's mouth can speak it? Or both, as with poetry and drama? But before you abandon altogether the consideration of nonverbal texts as literature, perhaps you should consider the consequences or the importance of nonverbal elements in certain texts that might be considered literary.

One genre I am thinking of here is film. Movies are dramas, which puts them into one of the usual literary categories. They are made from screenplays, which are written much like a stage drama is, even though screenplays are very rarely available for reading. Like stage plays, performance is essential to film as it is experienced by an audience. This is true of a play in a theater, a film in a public movie house, or a movie on videotape played on your VCR at home. Certainly you can read a screenplay just as you can read any other kind of drama: in print, on a page. But for it to be fully realized, a screenplay, just as any other kind of dramatic script, needs to be performed, its language spoken by human voices, its actions carried out by human bodies. In this way, the definition of literature as "verbal compositions," while not exactly wrong, is not wholly adequate.

Similarly, poetry has an aural dimension to it; that is, it uses language at least partly for its sound value: **rhyme** (words or syllables that sound alike, especially at the ends of lines), **alliteration** (repeated consonant sounds in adjacent or nearby words), **meter** (a pattern of stressed and unstressed syllables). And although you usually don't experience poetry through the medium of sound (more commonly you read it with your eyes only as words on a page) that doesn't deny its aural dimension. Historically, some forms of poetry such as the epic predate the development of writing, and other kinds of oral literature such as folktales have a long literary tradition of their own. You probably have been taught at one time or another to read poems out loud to yourself as you are studying them. You probably have heard your teacher or classmates read poems aloud. Perhaps you have even been called upon to do so yourself. Maybe you have been to poetry readings, where poets read from their own works. In this case, poetry gets closest to music: the audience doesn't usually have the "score," or "script," or written version of the poetry to look at while the "performer" or poet reads it; all the audience has is the experience of hearing the words spoken by the poet. In some cases, there may be accompaniment by musical instruments.

Considering the aural dimension of poetry and the performance dimension of drama could lead to the inclusion of another subgenre among literary categories: popular songs. Taking this step embraces the moves made earlier to break down or enlarge the boundaries that separate canonical and noncanonical works. Almost by definition, any works designated as "popular" are not great works in the sense of high-art masterpieces, and certainly popular songs are not written by people generally called great authors. And while popular songs may express strong thoughts and feelings on a subject important to the writer, they do seem to fall outside the usual literary genres. But at the same time, your interrogation of those genres should lead you to the point where you can legitimately consider popular songs as literature. They are written, both the words and the music; they are often if not always written in **verse,** as is poetry. Without a doubt, they have an aural dimension, and, as you commonly experience them, a performance dimension. In fact, the performance dimension is so strong that you may forget the other features that popular songs share with what is usually called poetry. By a curious twist, furthermore, regarding popular songs as poetry may make you a little more conscious of the performance and aural dimensions of more conventional poetry. Indeed the Poetry section of this book asks you to consider in more detail the ways in which popular song lyrics may be read as poetry and how some of the ways you "read" popular songs may be applied to reading canonical poems.

At this point, however, I should point out the absence from all the definitions considered so far of one characteristic that distinguishes literature from other kinds of writing: its aesthetic quality—whatever makes it "beautiful," "artistic," or "literary" as opposed to routinely communicative. The discussion of some types of nonfiction that might qualify as literature did talk about the literary qualities of such writing, but some of the larger implications of those qualities were left aside. So, to get at what literature is from this angle, consider one more tentative definition.

"Writing that exists primarily to please through its use of certain distinctively artistic qualities"

Clearly, "please" in this definition is meant in the aesthetic sense: the pleasure that may be derived from examining and contemplating any carefully made object, even if its subject matter or effect may be sad or tragic. This definition seems to avoid some of the pitfalls of the other tentative definitions. For one thing, it seems to allow you to include, without too much straining or contortion, nonfiction writing in the category of literature. Such writing may not "exist primarily to please"; essays, letters, and journalism may have more overtly **rhetorical** purposes, such as to inform or persuade. But such a purpose does not necessarily exclude an aesthetic purpose or effect. Indeed, sometimes the best way to achieve rhetorical ends is through aesthetic means. In the late sixteenth century, Sir Philip Sidney argued that poetry was valuable as "a medicine of cherries": good for the reader (in a moral or educational sense) and tasty too. And if what you are reading somehow provides aesthetic pleasure—even while you recognize another purpose for the writing—you may very well consider it in aesthetic terms. Similarly, this definition seems to avoid the problem of "greatness" mentioned earlier because it uses purpose or effect, not authorship, as the defining quality. It's a matter of what the writing is or does, not who wrote it.

What other virtues does this definition have? For one thing, including aesthetic considerations puts the focus on literature as an art form. For academic purposes, this is very useful. It makes available lots of aspects, features, or elements that you can study, discuss in class, be lectured on, and write papers about. Your own experience as a student may have made you familiar with this: You may have participated in class discussions or attended lectures on, say, the imagery in one of Emily Dickinson's poems. You may have studied, in assigned reading and in class, how various elements such as rhyme, meter, and syntax work together in a poem by Dylan Thomas.

This definition lends itself perfectly well to reading in order to **interpret;** that is, to find a meaning *in* the literary text. In fact, it may be argued, this definition even creates a certain way of reading, aesthetic analysis, which in turn has fostered a large industry of literary criticism and promoted an approach to classroom teaching and study in which literary works are regarded as artistic objects that have their own principles of organization. Through analysis or **close reading,** the details of a literary work are examined to discover these principles and make them available for other readers to recognize and understand. If these organizational principles can be related to **theme** in a literary work, that is, if what a work is "about" or what it "means" can be seen as the basis for the presence of other organizational principles in that work, then a literary work may be interpreted and that interpretation made available for other readers to recognize and understand.

SHARE AND COMPARE: What aesthetic criteria for literature are you aware of? That is, what qualities make literature more artistic than other kinds of writing? Don't try to be exhaustive, and, again, don't worry about being "correct." Just take a few minutes here to list a) elements of literature, b) purposes for literature, or c) effects of literature that you have encountered in specific works you have read. Share your list with your classmates to see what variety or commonality of aesthetic criteria exists among a group of readers.

In these two closely related activities of analysis and interpretation, the study of literature sometimes approaches the kind of empirical investigation of phenomena that has long dominated the natural sciences and that has helped to create the social sciences. These activities are the experimental or scientific method: testing ideas by direct, controlled observation. Such investigation seems to have academic merit that is beyond question. Furthermore, close reading of literary works for analytical or interpretive purposes tends to promote a kind of critical thinking that is also widely regarded as an important academic goal. For such academic reasons, the definition of and approach to literature in aesthetic terms have dominated American classrooms for the past 40 to 50 years. It may even seem that there is no other way to approach literature, and so the aesthetic definition of literature must be the best. However, in keeping with the questioning approach that I have invited you to take toward the other tentative definitions of literature, this definition should be investigated as well. And precisely because this aesthetic definition is so powerful, you should subject it to some especially careful scrutiny.

SHARE AND COMPARE: Can your class as a whole or in small groups suggest any problems with the aesthetic definition of literature? Try to list some. Even if you or other students subscribe to this definition, play devil's advocate for a few minutes. You may discover some ideas or strengthen ones you already have.

My own scrutiny suggests a number of problems inherent to the aesthetic definition of literature. First, along with privileging a certain way of reading, the aesthetic definition of literature also assumes a certain kind of trained reader, which not all real readers may actually be or try to be on every reading occasion. Regarding a literary work strictly as an aesthetic object assumes the actual presence in it of certain aesthetic qualities, which it is the job of the reader to locate, make sense of, discuss, or perhaps write about. What student hasn't had the experience of being "guided through" a text by a teacher, presumably a more highly trained reader than the student, and seeing an amazing number of things in the text that he or she had not realized were there?

Through such experience, no doubt, some students learn to become more skilled analytical readers; they emulate the techniques and habits of their teachers. At the same time, however, the aesthetic definition of literature tends to perpetuate the notion of a hierarchy of readers, with students generally at the lower end and teachers higher up, according to their familiarity with aesthetic features and their skill at "spotting" them in what they read. Students may be rightly considered, of course, apprentice readers, and teachers are more experienced. But that doesn't mean that one way of reading has to be so dominant, a way that depends so much on technical expertise and tends to overlook other kinds of valuable knowledge that all readers have.

In addition to ranking readers, the definition of literature in aesthetic terms tends to rank readings. If a literary text is primarily an art object, with its supposed complexities, aesthetic elements, and thematic unity, then analyses and interpretations might be ranked according to their "correctness." In quasi-scientific fashion, readers, especially in the academic context, would form an interpretive hypothesis that they would then test against available "data" from the text. The greater the "match" between the data and the hypothesis, the better or more correct the interpretation, or reading. If you carry this out to its (absurdly) logical conclusion, a reasonably sophisticated computer, properly programmed with the relevant aesthetic data, could produce a better reading than a human being. But that, like problems in some of the other definitions, is unsatisfactory in terms of readers' actual experience with different kinds of literary texts. Yes, some texts, a Shakespearean sonnet, for instance, are like scientific or intellectual puzzles that demand solution through careful mental scrutiny. But not all are. Others, perhaps a poem by Dylan Thomas, just to stay within the canon of "major" writers, seem more a matter of emotional outpourings; perhaps they even resist aesthetic analysis to some degree. So one way of reading may not always be best for all literary works.

A third kind of ranking tends to come out of the aesthetic definition of literature: a hierarchy of literary works. In discussing the first tentative definition of literature as "great" works, I touched on the idea that there might be some fairly widely agreed upon criteria for greatness, apart from authorship itself, that would qualify only some writing as literature. In addition to separating literary from nonliterary writing, by this same logic, you might even be able to rank the writing you called literary on a scale of merit. Other kinds of rankings—within the works of an individual author, for instance, or within subgenres such as epic poems—could also be possible. If you apply the aesthetic standards discussed earlier to a definition of literature broad enough to include both William Shakespeare and Andrew Lloyd Webber, Virginia Woolf and Tom Robbins, you might set up a hierarchy with "serious" literature at the high end of the scale and "popular" works at the low. This hierarchy leads back to the notion of the canon as just such a ranking: works that have been judged best by qualified readers and that have "stood the test of time" to prove the judgments of earlier readers. The greatness of the works, and perhaps of the authors who produced them, is thus established in the crucible of considered judgment of careful readers over time.

Neat as this seems, it is not without its problems. In reality, it turns out that the very aesthetic criteria used to separate the great works from the not-so-great, and to make finer distinctions among the great, are not all that objective and enduring after all. They are and have been subject to local conditions. This can be seen in the case of the reputation of the works of John Donne, who led a whole group of seventeenth-century "metaphysical poets" into the canon. The door was opened in this century, after T. S. Eliot, an influential reader who had his own and at the time quite revolutionary aesthetic criteria for poetry, argued for the canonical status of Donne and his "school." Later, a group of powerful academics, who became known as the New Critics, came to the fore in literary critical circles. After World War II, the New Critics came to dominate numerous critical journals and the English departments in leading universities. Their aesthetic standards affected college course offerings, syllabuses, and textbooks. In turn, generations of readers who took those courses in which those textbooks were assigned were trained to recognize certain qualities as more literary than others and certain authors as more literary than others. In this way, not only have some authors and works been canonized, but so, in effect, have some kinds of readers and ways of reading. At the same time, other authors have been excluded from the canon because those influential readers either ignored their work or slighted it. Often, these excluded or "minor" writers have been women or people of color. Recently, some scholars have been working to broaden the canon to include previously excluded authors; two twentieth-century American writers whose work is now increasingly available to students are the poet H. D. (Hilda Doolittle) and the fiction writer Zora Neale Hurston.

Finally, thinking of literature so much in aesthetic terms tends to disregard literature's connections to anything outside itself. The very feature of this definition that lends literature so well to academic study seems to close it within the proverbial "ivory tower" where it is sheltered from concerns of "the real world." But isn't literature, like any other human product, something that has very real and significant connections to the real world: to a time, place, and situation of production; to a particular kind of audience or public?

To answer "yes" to these questions may be to oversimplify matters, but to ask the question is to complicate yet another apparently obvious answer to the question "What is literature?" Each of the tentative definitions I have been asking you to consider as answers to that question is itself an oversimplification; surely anything as complicated, complex, and dense as literature cannot be adequately defined in a phrase or a sentence. Because of this, it is fairly easy to expose the flaws or inadequacies in those definitions, perhaps easier than it is to see their strengths or virtues, even though each of these definitions has its strengths and virtues and degrees of usefulness.

Points in the foregoing discussion or ideas raised in discussion with your classmates may have persuaded you to reject one or more of these tentative definitions. Or perhaps you have stuck by your first definition in spite of that discussion. In a way, it doesn't really matter whether your own definition of literature has been confirmed or challenged. What does matter is that you investigate the question, and not just in overly simple terms. What do *you* think literature is? As you start work in this book or in the course in which it is being used, or even in a systematic study that might lead to a major in English, it is important that you give some sustained thought to what literature is. You might find it useful to follow the approach I have taken here: write a (tentative) definition and then consider both its shortcomings and its strengths. In this way you should be able to avoid oversimplification and begin to realize a richer, more complex understanding of what this word means.

SHARE AND COMPARE: Now that you have read through this chapter, write your own definition of literature again. Justify it briefly, in a paragraph or two. Then compare your rough definition with those of your classmates. Try to keep your definition open to question or modification as your thinking develops. Keep in mind that it's not as important to determine a ruling definition of literature as much as it is that you think about what the term means.

2 ◈ THE READER'S ROLE

As part of the investigation of the question "What is Literature?" the concept of text or textuality might prove helpful. The French critic Roland Barthes offered a distinction between regarding an instance of writing as a *work,* which could be understood as a closed, finished, stable, aesthetic object with a definite reference to something "real" outside itself, and as a *text,* which could be understood as fluid, in process, volatile, indefinite. Works and texts are not so much different literary "things" as they are different ways of looking at the amorphous phenomenon "literature." Now that you have questioned and examined some different notions of "literature," you will probably find it useful and valuable to think more in terms of texts than of works.

Reading Texts

One reason for accepting this shift is that it would reveal as arbitrary the apparent separation of certain kinds of cultural products from those that a more traditional definition considers to be literature. Remember our discussion earlier of film, music, and popular songs? If you were uneasy calling these efforts literature, perhaps you would be less uneasy calling them—as well as products such as poems, plays, and stories—texts. The notion of **textuality** does not eliminate the canon or exclude canonical texts in favor of other kinds of texts. Instead, it is inclusive; it regards everything from "high art" pieces firmly ensconced in the canon to such transitory productions as commercial jingles and graffiti as related to each other in a network or web of language and culture. Thinking this way, you can overcome the problem posed by the separation of "high" and "low" cultural products, and you can bring important popular cultural forms as well as "the classics" into the same discussion. As you will see, this chapter will discuss a canonized poem and a popular song lyric—both being texts—in relation to one another.

This idea of textuality also helps move the role of the reader to the foreground in the consideration of what literature is. It empowers the reader as the agent who activates a particular network of textual associations when she or he encounters a piece of literature. This chapter will also look into how this activation happens.

Texts as Verbal Symbols

With reference to written products (rather than paintings, for instance), recent literary theory has defined text in terms of signs that may be interpreted as linguistic symbols, symbols not so much in the specialized critical sense of the

17

word, but in the broader sense in which so much of what you encounter in daily life stands *for* something else. In nonverbal terms, a red light at an intersection stands for the idea "stop"; it is a symbol for that idea. In verbal terms, the word *apple* stands for the red, green, or yellow, firm, tree-grown fruit with a sweet and tart taste. The word is a symbol; it is not the thing itself.

By this definition, we may regard a text as more than simply the marks on a page or the sound waves in the air. Those visual or auditory signs become verbal symbols, or words, when the conscious mind of a reader acts upon them to make them so. At a higher level of cognition, a reader may make certain texts into literary works. A "poem," for instance, is what a reader makes of his or her responses to a particular set of verbal symbols; it exists in terms of what the theorist Louise Rosenblatt calls the "live circuit" set up between the reader and the text. The poem is not so much the words themselves, but the reader's cognitive and emotional response to those words.

At this point, you may throw up a red flag (another symbol, couched here in a metaphor, for "stop") and object that if anybody constructs a poem, it is the poet, not the reader. Yes, of course, there is a sense in which poets construct or make poems, but remember the metaphor of the electrical circuit: completion of the construction "poem" requires the recognizing reader; without the reader, the circuit is incomplete. To look at it another way, consider what would happen if you put some lines of rhymed verse before an imaginary person from some culture whose vocabulary does not include the word or idea "poem" and who is also unaware of that word or idea as it operates in other cultures. In effect, the lines would not be a poem, author or no author, because this person would not be able to construct, or perhaps it is better to say "construe" or "understand," those signs as a poem.

Texts as Processes

The idea of texts as verbal symbols that require the presence of an activating reader suggests a model of reading in which a text is not so much a thing as a process, something that really occurs in time more than in space, during the relationship between a reader and a text. This model emphasizes the dynamic nature of reading, it recognizes the importance of both reader and text, and it situates the reader in the crucial position.[1] With respect to the attempts in Chapter 1 to define literature, you might now consider what literature would be without a reader: nowhere, nothing. And the reader I am talking about here is not necessarily one with advanced training or special expertise; the only training necessary is whatever it takes to construe a text as literature. For the most part, this comes down to experience with such texts in the past, which virtually all college students have, even if they don't all consider themselves experts.

You might wonder at this point how much freedom or latitude this reader of ours has. She or he is free to construe as a literary text not just a series of

---

[1]This model of reading derives from the pioneering work of Louise Rosenblatt, in her books *Literature as Exploration* (New York: Noble and Noble, 1938) and *The Reader, the Text, the Poem* (Carbondale: Southern Illinois University Press, 1978).

lines of rhymed verse printed in a textbook, but also graffiti scrawled on a wall or a desktop. And what's to stop this reader, you may ask, from construing even a scientific formula as literature? Nothing, really, although the practical limits of such a construction might quickly be reached if no one else could make the same construction, so the reader would have no one with whom to share or discuss his or her "poem." At the same time, however, thinking in terms of the more fluid and temporal *texts* instead of the more fixed and permanent *works* encourages readers to see relationships among various kinds of cultural products—literary, canonical, popular, transitory, what have you—in the whole network or web of textuality.

With this kind of reader freedom also comes the possibility of readings that may seem highly individualistic or "far-fetched" as well as instances of "reading into" a text ideas that do not, to others, seem to be there. An approach to literature that operates primarily in terms of supposedly stable aesthetic qualities would disqualify such readings. The model of reading as an interactive circuit, however, allows them, with certain qualifications. First, such readings should be shared with others, on paper or orally, so that they can be explained, defended, and refined. Second, the explanation of such readings must take into account the effect of the reader and the reading situation. Neither of those requirements may be easy to meet at first, but with practice and a willingness to increase your awareness of yourself as a reader—and other readers, too—you should see progress.

The Reader's Contribution

Because the notion of textuality helps to make the reader visible and to emphasize his or her importance in the interactivity of reading, it would now be a good idea to look into the matter of who or what the reader is. Chapter 1 engaged somewhat in complicating the question of what literature is. At this point, it might be useful to complicate—or problematize—"the reader."

One way of looking at the reader, derived from recent theory in a number of academic fields, *decenters* him or her: the reader is really many different selves, rather than an integrated or unified personality. Perhaps you can see the validity of this concept from your own experience: you are one self with your parents, another with your teachers (perhaps even varying this self from teacher to teacher), another with your friends, still another with strangers, and someone else again to yourself. Not that these selves are necessarily wildly different; you're probably not that schizophrenic. It's more like different emphases, more or less subtle shadings of difference. All these different selves depend to a large extent on the contexts that activate them. Different selves—or different aspects of "yourself," if you prefer, or different **persona,** to use the literary term—dominate in different reading situations, too.

In addition to the kinds of reader freedom mentioned above, the idea of textuality also allows the reader to be considered as a text, a text that has been "written" by larger forms of discourse—**ideologies**, or systems of beliefs and values—in the cultural environment. Thus, the reader can be considered in relation to his or her background, both as a person in general and specifically as a reader, and to the variety of situations in which he or she reads. There is a paradox or a tension here between the reader as free agent and as socially constructed; however, the dynamic model of reading should help you begin to see the ways in which you as a reader both *act* to make meaning out of your encounters with texts and are *acted upon* by larger cultural and situational forces.

The Reading Situation: The Academic Context

So even though you have a degree of freedom as a reader, you operate under several constraints, too. For one thing, you don't read in a vacuum; you always read in some kind of context. Even pure pleasure reading—at the beach or in a hammock in your backyard or in your favorite chair by the fireplace—is done in a context that might seem like no context: no pressure, no quiz, no discussion to be prepared for a teacher. But what you pick for pleasure reading, the kind of attention you pay to that text, the kinds of things you look at and for as you read, even whether you think very consciously about "theme" in such reading, all are context dependent. The situation or context in which you read contributes both to how you read and what you read.

The contribution of context to how you read may not need much elaboration here; what has already been said about pleasure reading vs. school reading should suggest that. You have no doubt already found that reading in the pleasure mode isn't too successful in the context of reading school assignments. But how does the reading situation affect what you read, apart from choice of subject matter? (Unless you hide it in the pages of your economics textbook, you wouldn't read a comic book in school, and you probably wouldn't take your economics textbook to the beach for pleasure reading.) The reading situation affects what you read because you construct certain kinds of texts when you begin to read them. We can illustrate this by referring to F. Scott Fitzgerald's story "Basil and Cleopatra" (see pages 405–417 below). This story first appeared in a popular, general-interest magazine, *The Saturday Evening Post,* in April 1929. You will read it here in a textbook assigned in a college literature course. The immediate context in which you encounter a text—the kind of book or magazine in which it appears, the kind of situation in which those books or magazines are available to you, the larger "reasons" for the reading—all affect the likelihood that you will construe a text as a piece of "popular fiction" or a work of "serious literature."

Or take the instance of a popular song, such as Tracy Chapman's "Fast Car." When you encounter this text in its usual context (on the radio or someone's stereo) you probably don't read it as much more than a popular song, even if your aesthetic standards for this subgenre may consider it a great song. You may like it for Chapman's plaintive vocals and her guitar playing. But the lyrics of "Fast Car" are included in the poetry section of this book (pages 560–561), and that context invites you to consider it as a poem or as "serious literature." If you read it as literature, you may pay more attention to the words, reading it in terms of images of poverty, desperation, and hope. In that context or that way of reading, you could practice the same kind of close reading that you might otherwise apply only to texts generally considered literature, a poem, for instance.

The Reading Situation: The Personal Context

There is also a personal context to be considered: Who is the person who reads a text? Or which aspect of his or her personality connects most directly in the circuitry of reader-and-text? A person who sees herself as "going nowhere" with "no plans," working a menial job to support herself and take care of a sick parent, will likely read "Fast Car" differently from a person who sees herself on the fast track to success. A person who sees himself as secure and successful in both his athletic life and his love life will read "Basil and Cleopatra" as a different story than a person who hasn't had much time for sports and dating because he's been working two part-time jobs to pay his way through college. Such personal factors, however, do not exist out of context. They are affected by the larger cultural categories that people belong to and are shaped by, and by the ideologies that people are subject to. Understanding this will allow you to move beyond or see the deeper implications of "identifying" with a character in a literary text.

The Reading Situation: The Cultural Context

There is a still broader context than either the personal or the curricular/ extracurricular. You might call this the *cultural context* in which a reading occurs, with "cultural" covering a range of possibilities: family, peer group, socioeconomic class, gender, region, nationality, race, and so forth. Your position in any of these cultural categories affects your values, beliefs, opinions, or attitudes with respect to anything you encounter in life. In this context you may consider yourself "written" by larger forms of discourse, the ideologies of those cultures and subcultures. Any culture subscribes to and inscribes into its members ideas and values such as "It is desirable to better yourself through education" and "It is possible to better yourself through education" and "Love is worth having; it fulfills some of our deeper needs" and "Love makes us do foolish things sometimes."

Put into statements like these, such ideas and values may seem merely commonsensical or even universal. But are they? Not all cultures at all times in human history have believed in or valued self-fulfillment or self-improvement. As late as the eighteenth century in England, in a time period and a cultural situation that has become known as "The Enlightenment," it was possible for a leading humanist to argue, as Alexander Pope did in his "Essay on Man," that all life from the lowliest crawling creatures to the most exalted angelic forms existed in a rigidly unchanging and divinely ordered "great chain of being," in which the harmony of the whole system and the happiness of every individual within it depended on each recognizing and accepting his or her particular station. So if you were born to poor farmers, for instance, you should forget about—or, more accurately, not even think about—improving your mind and circumstances through education in order to lift yourself and your children beyond a subsistence living eked out of a small quarter of ground. And in cultures past and present in which arranged marriages are practiced, the modern Western idea of romantic love leading to a freely chosen marriage in which personal fulfillment may be achieved is not part of the dominant ideology.

Culture and ideology also influence such matters as how much reading you do at all, whether for school or for pleasure. Not all families or socioeconomic groups encourage reading as part of their cultural values. A lot of young Americans spend more time watching television than reading or doing homework. Does your family or peer group foster a climate in which "serious," "careful" reading is encouraged or expected, or does it subtly suggest that reading is a necessary evil to be endured only as long as you are going to school? Do any of the cultural categories to which you belong tell you, in one way or another, that certain kinds of behaviors—careful reading, for instance, or taking ideas, and your own capacity to have them, seriously—are important, valuable, or appropriate for you, or not?

SHARE AND COMPARE: What are your beliefs concerning any of these topics: education, love, or work? Write three or four ideological statements on any one of these. (You may find some models on page 21.)

1.

2.

3.

4.

In a group with three or four classmates, share these statements. Then consider their cultural sources by tracing them to categories each of you may belong to, such as peer group, family, ethnicity, race, religion, and nationality.

These contexts of "academic," "personal," and "cultural" overlap more than they are distinct, so it is difficult to separate the personal from the cultural, the social, or the historical. Who you are as an individual person, as well as the individual readings different readers construct upon encountering various kinds of texts, depends on many contributing factors that really can't be isolated or accurately ranked in importance. Paradoxically, however, that doesn't mean you should regard as useless any attempt to account for the role of context and ideology on the readings you produce. To the contrary, the approach of this textbook invites you to consider yourself, indeed any reader, as the product of contextual or cultural forces and to try to sort among those various causative factors as you look deeper into the interactive circuit involved in reading literature.

The Reader: Life Experience

Whenever you encounter a text and become a reader of it, many aspects of your makeup as a reader are involved. You have all your years of life experience with you—you might say the "narrative" of your life—in the form not just of events but also of memories, associations, likes and dislikes, feelings, knowledge, beliefs, assumptions, thoughts, facts, myths, hopes, fears, expectations, neuroses, prejudices, and so forth. You also have your historical or cultural situation—your age, social class, gender, race, ethnic background, peer group(s), sexual orientation, physical circumstances, and so on—as well as what any of these means according to the ideologies you are subject to.

Every aspect of your life experience may not come to bear on any or every reading encounter. Certain aspects may be more prevalent than others on any given occasion, or, in the way of the "circuit" running between reader and text, certain "cues" that you perceive in a given text may connect more directly with or activate more strongly certain aspects of your life experience.

Look around your literature classroom. You might have 20 or 30 classmates. No doubt you and they have several attributes in common. Roughly half of your classmates probably are the same gender as you; it's probably still safe to say that most college students are "middle class." However, once you scratch the surface of that category, you find many subtle and not so subtle differences among people—the kinds of communities they grew up in; their family situation and home life; their debt load as college students, which is related to family circumstances; the career choices of family members; political or religious affiliation; special interests or "hobbies"; and so on. The fact that you and your classmates are together in college implies something about shared assumptions of your developing social roles and your futures.

The traits that are more or less common among a classroom population are relatively easy to notice. Some differences are easy too: race, ethnicity, and age, for instance. Other differences may be harder to recognize: Someone is the child of alcoholic parents; someone is particularly close to an aunt, uncle, or grandparent who may share the family home; someone is afraid of the dark; someone has very strong ideas about men's and women's roles in American life; someone is a political "green"; someone is gay; someone is playful, even with ideas; someone really lives to compete in sports; someone has music on the brain; someone is a no-nonsense person, driven to succeed; someone is HIV-positive; someone has been the victim of a crime or of racial discrimination; someone has been fighting with his or her best friend. You get the idea. These descriptive phrases may apply individually to a dozen different people, or several of them may apply to one person. Even as an individual, you really have many selves; which "one," which persona, dominates any time you read a particular text is variable. But the key point here is that such

factors that constitute a reader's life experience are vitally important to reading: They work in combination with what we might consider the "raw materials" of a text to produce the actual story, poem, or play you read.

SHARE AND COMPARE: List the particular cultural categories that you belong to; i.e., your race, your gender, your age group, and so forth. In
what ways do any of these categories affect your reading of different
kinds of texts; e.g., a canonized poem such as "Dover Beach" (reprinted
on pages 24–25), graffiti, a popular song lyric such as "Cover Me"
(reprinted on page 31), or the American Declaration of Independence?

Approaching Texts Actively

You will find that a particular text, perhaps in combination with a particular
mood or state of mind you're in, calls forth certain aspects of your life experience and not others. Consider Matthew Arnold's poem "Dover Beach,"
reprinted below. Read it and take a few minutes to respond to it in writing in
your notebook or journal. In doing so, try to focus on the aspects of your life
experience that are called forth by reading the poem.

Matthew Arnold   1822–1888

Dover Beach   1867

The sea is calm tonight.
The tide is full, the moon lies fair
Upon the straits;° on the French coast the light   the English Channel

Gleams and is gone; the cliffs of England stand,
Glimmering and vast, out in the tranquil bay.   5
Come to the window, sweet is the night-air!
Only, from the long line of spray
Where the sea meets the moon-blanched° land,   whitened
Listen! you hear the grating roar
Of pebbles which the waves draw back, and fling,   10
At their return, up the high strand,°   beach
Begin, and cease, and then again begin,
With tremulous cadence° slow, and bring   rhythm
The eternal note of sadness in.

Sophocles° long ago   Greek playwright   15
Heard it on the Aegean,° and it brought   sea east of Greece
Into his mind the turbid° ebb and flow   confused
Of human misery; we
Find also in the sound a thought,
Hearing it by this distant northern sea.   20

The Sea of Faith
Was once, too, at the full, and round° earth's shore   around
Lay like the folds of a bright girdle° furled.   sash, belt
But now I only hear
Its melancholy, long, withdrawing roar,   25
Retreating, to the breath
Of the night-wind, down the vast edges drear
And naked shingles° of the world.   pebbly beaches

Ah, love, let us be true
To one another! for the world, which seems   30
To lie before us like a land of dreams,
So various, so beautiful, so new,
Hath really neither joy, nor love, nor light,
Nor certitude, nor peace, nor help for pain;
And we are here as on a darkling° plain   in the dark   35
Swept with confused alarms of struggle and flight,
Where ignorant armies clash by night.

The Dynamics of Response

As you read the first stanza of this poem, perhaps you recall memories or associations of being someplace similar to where this speaker is: with another
person at the seashore on a moonlit night. Perhaps your recollection, together
with the atmosphere created by the slow pace of this speaker's phrases and
the descriptive images he or she uses, builds a mood for you. If so, is that
mood one of "sadness," as it is for the speaker in this poem (line 14)? Or is it
romance or mystery or peacefulness or fear or something else?

As you read on through the poem's second and third stanzas, do your associations of the sound of waves washing over the shore allow you also to "find a thought"? If so, perhaps that thought is similar to the speaker's thought that the "Sea of Faith" is receding, if, when you consider the world's troubles, that is your experience or judgment. Or perhaps your thought is of the majesty of eternal nature, which transcends people's problems and is therefore soothing. More than 100 years separate your world from this speaker's; do your experiences and associations suggest an even greater decline in "Faith" than that which the speaker in the poem describes, or have you seen a reversal of what the speaker refers to? Maybe when you recall hearing the waves break on a moonlit stretch of beach you also recall a sense of oneness with all creation, not a spiritual isolation.

In the last stanza of the poem, the scene the speaker has been contemplating leads him or her to some pretty strong assertions about what the world "seems" to be and "really" is. The speaker tells his or her "love" that they must "be true to one another" in the face of such an uncertain and confusing world (lines 29–30). Do your beliefs and experiences confirm this speaker's apparently pessimistic emphasis? Perhaps if you are a person of the usual college age, you prefer to believe that the world really does "lie before [you] ... like a land of dreams" (31). Sentiments like that are often expressed in commencement addresses, at any rate. Or perhaps if you belong to "Generation X," Americans born in the 1970s, and share that age group's reputed disillusionment with promises and prospects for the future, you find the closing lines of the poem an accurate and striking assessment of the world. In any case—and there are certainly countless other ones that will actually arise when different readers encounter this text—the causes of your response can be traced to what you bring to the text in the way of life experience in terms of associations, memories, beliefs, and values.

Perhaps the simplest way to understand the effect of the reader's life experience on her or his response is in terms of liking or disliking a text. If you like, for instance, Scott Fitzgerald's story "Basil and Cleopatra," a good deal of that response has to do with the reader you are or become when you encounter that text. Are you a young man, perhaps a college freshman or sophomore, who plays or follows football? Do you have "dreams of glory" in terms of success in some public endeavor? Do you enjoy the attention or admiration of your peers? These factors or ones like them may account for your liking the story, regardless of certain features of the story that you may downplay or ignore, such as the differences between the way football was played 65 years ago and today; the rather formal behavior of teenagers toward one another; and the language in which the characters think and talk.

On the other hand, the same reason applies if you disliked the story. Are you a woman who has never understood men's infatuation with competitive sports? Have you had to pay your own way into a public college, and do you resent "preppies" or "yuppies" who seem to have social and economic advantages (like going to Yale) that you don't have? Do you want more action and less introspection on the part of the main character? I don't mean to suggest that liking or disliking "Basil and Cleopatra" is simply or automatically caused by your gender or social class. It isn't. But perhaps these responses point most clearly to the role of what a reader brings to a text: Initially, you may judge a story "good" or "poor" according to your own background.

The Dynamics of Interpretation

What a text is "about" is also influenced by the reader. Is "Basil and Cleopatra" about romantic success and failure? Is that issue a metaphor, so that the story is really about professional and social success and failure? Is it a portrayal of a pathetic jock wannabe, or of a young man at a critical breakthrough moment in the process of his maturity? Is it a critique of people who put too much stock into trivial accomplishments such as social popularity or athletic success? Is it a story that avoids or ignores more important issues such as the political repression and racism that flourished in American society in the 1920s? Is it simply an entertaining yarn about a young guy who wants to be a football star and campus hero?

Is the poem "Dover Beach" about the decline of faith or the need for personal romantic commitment in troubled times? Is it an elaborate seduction routine on the part of the speaker, who sets a mood mainly to suggest a romantic liaison? "Thematic" issues or interpretive possibilities like any of these for "Dover Beach" or "Basil and Cleopatra" are to a large degree set by whoever reads the text on what occasion, bringing with him or her the whole complex of attitudes, beliefs, experiences, and so forth that constitute his or her life experience. Interpreting a text is not so much a matter of digging into it to "get out" of it some meaning or the meaning it presumably already has. If that "digging" metaphor is to be applied at all, you should think about what you dig with, not just what you dig into, and who the person is who is doing the digging. Interpretation is a *dynamic* excavation, a two-way street (to use another metaphor), a live circuit between the text and the reader.

The Reader: Literary Experience

In similar fashion to the way you bring to a reading your life experience, you also bring your literary experience—your experiences with and attitudes, ideas, and beliefs about specifically literary matters. This experience also includes a set of **reading strategies** that you employ when you read: the way you process information from a text; how and why you put that information together the way you do; the expectations you have as you begin to read a text. Like your life experience, certain aspects of your literary experience are activated according to what you encounter in a text.

The reference to theme in "Basil and Cleopatra" provides an example: In all likelihood, your experience as a reader and as a student (perhaps it is more accurate to say as a "student-reader") has taught you that short stories have themes, so that it's natural enough for there to be a reference to theme in the context of a discussion of a short story. Or, from another angle, it's natural for you to expect to find a theme in a text you recognize as a short story. If so, one reading strategy you probably employ is to look for a theme as you read, or to read to *interpret* the story.

On the other hand, it would not be so natural to talk about a theme in a music video, your college catalog, or the Super Bowl. You have probably not been a student-reader of such texts; that is, you probably haven't read them as part of your academic studies, and when you encounter them in the contexts in which you usually encounter them, theme seems either irrelevant to the genres to which those texts belong or not especially worthy of consideration. But that's not to say you couldn't look for and find a theme in one of these texts. With a little effort and study, you probably could. (In fact, in Chapter 5 you will be invited to think about theme in a music video, Tom Petty and the Heartbreakers' "Mary Jane's Last Dance.")

Your experience as a reader affects how you approach—even how you define—different kinds of texts. Like your life experience, your literary experience should be scrutinized as you work to become a more sophisticated reader and as you work toward a fuller understanding of what's involved in the reading process.

The Reader's Expectations   Your experience as a reader shapes the expectations you bring to a particular reading. You are usually not conscious of them, but they do affect how you read and the strategies with which you read. For instance, suppose you are assigned to read a poem. Suppose further that you don't really like to read poems; you rarely read them on your own. Although you do encounter them more often than you may think you do, the context of a school assignment to read a poem may raise expectations that it will be difficult, that you'll have to be able to talk about it in poetic terminology that you've never quite grasped, and that the teacher will point out certain "things in it" that you didn't see when you read it. You'll wind up with a reinforced sense of your own inadequacy as a reader of poetry, which you will carry with you to the next occasion of reading a poem for class. If the first lines of the poem are "I caught this morning morning's minion / Kingdom of daylight's dauphin, ..." there's a good chance that the reading interaction will confirm those expectations, merely because those expectations were so strong.[2]

But what if the poem turns out to be a rock lyric? Maybe it's not especially "difficult," or learned, or full of complex grammatical constructions that make the line of thought hard to follow. Maybe it starts out, "I took the time to write to my old friend / I walked across that burning bridge."[3] Now perhaps different expectations are aroused; you may even forget the text is "a poem" with what that term usually means for you and go on to have a different kind of reading experience. Or it could work the other way around: You could be full of anticipation for some juicy intellectual work and find the first example cited here something you can really sink your teeth into, or find the second example crude and superficial.

Let's take another example: The text you are about to read is supposed to be a short story. You bring to the reading certain expectations for fiction. You

---

[2]The lines are from Gerard Manley Hopkins' "The Windhover." The poem is reprinted in full in Chapter 11, page 537.
[3]The lines are from Michelle Shocked's "Anchorage," which is reprinted in full in Chapter 10, pages 523–524.

don't read too far before you find those expectations foiled: "Voices are a river you step in once and again never the same Bubba here you are dead boy dead dead dead nigger with spooky Boris Karloff powder caked on your face boy skin lightener...."[4] This text seems to lack features you've come to expect from "normal" English prose, such as internal sentence punctuation, or from fiction, such as quotation marks indicating speech and a narrator to orient you as to the setting, characters, and who's saying or thinking what. What to do? Certainly your expectations and reading strategies combining with certain text strategies makes for a very volatile mix. Consequently you get a different response than you would from a text that starts out, "The thousand injuries of Fortunato I had borne as I best could, but when he ventured upon insult I vowed revenge."[5] That at least seems like the beginning of a short story.

You could also consider the progressive nature of expectations: It's quite likely you revise them as you go along. Reading may be thought of as a process of having then changing and reformulating expectations as you read. We will look at this process in greater detail in succeeding chapters.

The Reader's Knowledge of Literary Conventions   Another aspect of your literary experience is your awareness of **conventions,** which is another term for those features or elements of literature, any of its genres, or any patterned human activity, that we recognize as regularly or usually occurring. Applauding a performance or a speaker, for instance, is a convention. Language is full of conventions such as punctuation and phrases uttered on certain occasions ("Hello," instead of some other word, when you answer the phone). Language itself is a convention: English doesn't have to be the way it is. Conventions change somewhat over time because they are subject to changing taste or fashion, but they change slowly enough that they establish or maintain a pattern. Recognizing the pattern of conventions allows you to understand something as belonging to a certain category or genre, and that understanding, in turn, affects your expectations and reading strategies. Among the conventions of realistic drama, for instance, is the pretense that the action carried out on the stage is "really" happening and that the audience just happens to be witnessing it, so the actors disregard the presence of the audience until the play is over. On the other hand, it's *un*conventional in drama for there to be a narrator, a mediator between the action and the audience. Yet in fiction, mediating narrators are an accepted convention.

Two points could be made here. The first is that when texts do things in a certain way often enough, those things become conventional; they are usually taken for granted, assumed to be "natural" features of that kind of text, and not really questioned. Take the dramatic convention of the **soliloquy,** for instance: a speech by a single character, often alone on stage or on camera, that is supposed to reveal his or her inner thoughts to the audience. Because the audience can't read a character's mind, and because drama usually does not

---

[4]John Edgar Wideman, "everybody knew bubba riff." This story is reprinted in Chapter 6, beginning on page 191.
[5]Edgar Allan Poe, "The Cask of Amontillado." This story is reprinted in Chapter 6, beginning on page 133.

use the convention of a mediating narrator, something like a soliloquy becomes necessary if such thoughts are to be revealed. If you are familiar with this convention, you don't think it odd or unnatural for a character to be talking out loud to no one in particular. But in "real" life, if someone saw you exhibiting the same behavior you'd be thought of as odd. Soliloquizing is just not conventional in most human cultures.

The second point about conventions is that, if you often don't notice their presence as anything out of the ordinary, you often do notice their absence from a particular genre, or instances where they have been turned around or altered in some way. In the 1920s and 1930s in Europe and the United States, a kind of fiction developed called **stream of consciousness.** This was a version of **realism** that attempted to render the consciousness of a character or characters directly to the reader, without the convention of a mediating narrator. Virginia Woolf, James Joyce, and William Faulkner pioneered the technique in some of their novels, and contemporary writers such as John Edgar Wideman have also worked with it. This kind of fiction got a reputation for being difficult from readers whose expectations and reading strategies were shaped by the convention of a "third-person" narrator saying things about a character, or of a "first-person" narrator saying things about herself or himself. But with stream-of-consciousness fiction, the reader is plunged more or less immediately into the mind of a character without any of the conventional signposts ("she thought" or "I remembered," or even time-sequence words such as "then" or "afterwards") to provide orientation. Such fiction is still difficult for readers because of the dominance of the more usual narrative conventions, which shapes their expectations of fiction.

The Reader's Storehouse of Texts   Another aspect of your literary experience is your storehouse of texts. Everyone today is continually bombarded by messages. And of course these messages are texts, in the form of advertisements in all media, television news and programs, music videos, movies, songs and talk on the radio, articles in newspapers and magazines, cartoons, posters, and class lectures; in short, anything you see, hear, and read, including literary texts. You don't remember all of this, of course, but you do remember some of it. A lot of it is stored in your memory to be recalled both when it's needed and when it isn't.

Earlier I said that textuality was a web or network connecting all these individual texts. Whenever you are conscious of a particular connection—a particular strand in the web—this is an instance of **intertextuality.** In considering how your literary experience operates in your reading, one thing you can do is try to be conscious of the intertextual connections that occur to you as you read. This opportunity presents itself sometimes in the form of **allusions,** indirect references in one text to another, such as the allusions to ancient Greek tragedies in "Dover Beach." But it also happens whenever *you* see a connection from a text you are reading to any of the other myriad texts that make up the network of textuality. Often, one text in an intertextual relation with another sheds light on the other or gives you a handle on it. Sometimes there's a contrast that helps you understand the text you're reading. Sometimes you can see common themes or approaches to a topic. For example, according to your literary storehouse, you may find Arnold's "Dover Beach," a poem from the canon of English literature, to be intertextual with a text from popular culture: Bruce Springsteen's "Cover Me."

Bruce Springsteen   b. 1949

Cover Me   *1984*

The times are tough now
Just getting tougher
This old world is rough
It's just getting rougher
Cover me   5
Come on baby, cover me
Well I'm looking for a lover who will
come on in and cover me

Promise me baby you won't let them find us
Hold me in your arms
Let's let our love blind us   10
Cover me
Shut the door and cover me
Well I'm looking for a lover who will
come on in and cover me   15

Outside's the rain, the driving snow
I can hear the wild wind blowing
Turn out the light
Bolt the door
I ain't going out there no more
This whole world is out there just trying to score   20
I've seen enough I don't want to see any more
Cover me
Come on and cover me
I'm looking for a lover who will come on in and cover me   25
Looking for a lover who will come on in and cover me

Certainly, having "Dover Beach" in my literary storehouse allowed me to regard "Cover Me" as thematically similar almost the first time I heard it. I see the vision of the world depicted in both texts as pessimistic, even though the language through which that vision is described is different. And in both texts I hear the speaker expressing a wish to turn away from a threatening, uncertain world to the more concrete pleasure a love partner may provide.

There are other ways in which, for me, each of these texts sheds light on the other. The main thing to keep in mind about intertextuality is that you establish the connections according to your literary experience. In doing so you are intervening in the text you are reading, playing an active role, and creating meaning for the text and for yourself.[6]

SHARE AND COMPARE: After carefully re-reading "Dover Beach" and "Cover Me," what other connections can you find between these two texts? Share your findings with some of your classmates: Are their findings similar to yours or different?

The Text's Contribution

Some of what has been discussed above in terms of the literary experience of readers—the language of particular poems, for instance, or the characters and setting of certain short stories, or dramatic or narrative conventions—may be considered aspects of texts as well. It doesn't make much sense to speak of the literary experience of a text, so I will borrow a term from the critic Wolfgang Iser and refer to the specifically literary qualities of a text as its **literary repertoire** instead. It also seems inappropriate to talk about the life experience of a text, even though there are numerous parallels between a text and a reader in terms of values, beliefs, and assumptions. The term *ideology* will serve as shorthand for all the cultural values inscribed in a text, active in the reading dynamic, and subject to analysis by readers.

The Text: The Literary Context

The literary repertoire of a text comprises any of its generic conventions (or its violation of conventions) and its techniques, methods, or literary elements;

---

[6]For another example of intertextuality with "Dover Beach," see Anthony Hecht's poem "The Dover Bitch," on page 702.

that is, any of the things a text "does" or any of the means by which it does what it does. Analogous to the reading strategies that are part of a reader's literary experience, technical matters such as rhyme or imagery in poetry or characters and a narrator in fiction constitute **text strategies** that are part of the literary repertoire of a text.

Analyzing the literary repertoire of a text is close to if not identical with, in slightly different terminology, the analytical practices that have dominated literature classrooms in the United States for decades. That approach was discussed in Chapter 1 as the way of reading promoted by an aesthetic definition of literature. The approach of this book, by comparison, is not so much to downplay or ignore the text's literary repertoire as it is to situate that repertoire in the whole dynamic of the reading transaction. That being the case, little more need be said about the literary repertoire of texts at this point. But perhaps a few words should be devoted to the subject of another aspect of the text's contribution: its ideology.

The Text: The Cultural Context

A text may be written by an author, in the usual sense in which we take the word "written." But it is certainly also written by a culture; by historical, social, and economic circumstances; by the possibilities and constraints of language. Its author is affected by these circumstances, too. Those larger contexts inscribe ideologies in a text (just as they do in you as a reader): values, beliefs, assumptions with respect to the world, human experience, even the nature of literature. Sometimes those ideologies are explicit, as in the case of "propaganda" or argumentative nonfiction prose or religious **allegory.** Often they are more subtle, as with the rhetorical pattern of **symbolism** in poetry, fiction, or drama. Sometimes they can't even be detected until years or generations later, when a reader with a particular ideologic perspective sees them there. In other cases, a text's situation within a cultural context very different from your own (historically, racially, nationally, and so on) allows you to see its ideology—and your own—fairly easily.

In terms of the texts presented in this chapter, I would suggest that both "Dover Beach" and "Cover Me" bear the inscriptions of the cultural contexts in which they were produced. The sense of a hostile world necessitating two people's clinging together spiritually, romantically, or physically was not the exclusive idea of either Matthew Arnold in 1860s England or Bruce Springsteen in the United States in the 1980s; it was part of the ideology that both writers were subject to and hence found its way into poems they wrote.

Interactions Between Readers and Texts

Earlier, I said a reader activates a text into a poem or other literary genre. But in terms of the model of reading as a circuit, you must remember that a text also activates or triggers certain aspects of a reader. It's a give-and-take between the two; the reading dynamic may be restated as an interaction that can be examined in either of two areas: the literary or the ideological. In the first area, you would look at how your literary experience interacts with the literary repertoire of a text. In the second area, you would analyze how your life experience interacts with the cultural context of a text. The diagram that follows is an attempt to represent the interactive model graphically.

The Reading Interaction

THE TEXT   THE READER
Literary Repertoire   Literary Experience

A Reading

Cultural Context   Life Experience
(Ideology)   (Ideology)

Sometimes, depending on the nature of a particular reader encountering a particular text (or vice versa), the circuit is completed in such a way that resistance is negligible; this could be called a *harmonious* interaction. Other times, all there seems to be is resistance from one or the other of the parties to the interaction; this could be called a *clashing* interaction. I don't mean to suggest that polar opposites are the only possibilities for the reading interaction. Most readings aren't that simple; they involve some mixture of harmony and clash. But having terms to characterize the extremes of a reading interaction will help you see the range of possibilities.

In the case of a harmonious interaction in terms of literary matters, it may be said that certain elements exist in the literary repertoire of the text and the literary experience of the reader virtually simultaneously, so that it's hard to separate the reader's contribution to the interaction from the text's. In the case of a clashing interaction, it is often clearer that one of the two parties to the interaction "doesn't have" some element to complement the corresponding element in the other: The reader's expectations for a short story don't include the possibility that the text he or she is reading as a short story will not be structured around plot; the language of a text features words used in senses unfamiliar to a reader who doesn't know 1950s street slang.

The ideological interaction may be clashing or harmonious also. If the ideology of a text seems to confirm your own regarding a certain issue—the decline of faith in the Western world, for instance—the interaction is harmonious. If the ideology of a text challenges your own, there is a clash. What matters most for the interactive model of reading is not the cultural context of a text as it exists "objectively" or in isolation, as much as those aspects of the ideology of a text that engage a reader or that a reader engages as she or he reads. In the case of "Dover Beach," for instance, it's not essential that a reader know about the widespread religious doubt that bothered English writers and intellectuals in the late nineteenth century as a result of the scientific theories of Charles Darwin and others. That aspect of the cultural context of "Dover Beach" can be investigated, with consequences that may enrich a reader's response to that poem, as a separate topic in English literary or cultural history. But a reader can have an equally rich interaction with "Dover Beach" without knowing all that. If he or she sees a concern with truth or faith of any kind, or with the importance of lovers' commitment to each other, as an idea raised by that poem, and if that idea is important to that reader, he or she can interact meaningfully with the text on the ideological level.

A problem may seem to arise here regarding a reader's lack of knowledge with respect to the cultural context of a text. What if a reader's expectations include nothing about the author or the time period in which the text was written? What if he or she doesn't know about, say, Arnold's career as a poet and English cultural critic and his struggles with religious doubt or Fitzgerald's experiences as a "preppie" youth from the midwestern United States who fell hard in love with a "southern belle" and who had an insatiable desire for fame? How can a reader respond to or interpret such texts "correctly" without having all the necessary background or contextual knowledge? These are legitimate questions for students, but they should become less urgent if you consider a few ideas.

One is the relativity of "correct" interpretation and response. As I hope you have seen from the examination of various definitions of "literature" in Chapter 1 and from the discussion of "literature" vs. "texts" in this chapter, only one definition of literature and one model of reading insist on "correctness" in interpretation. That definition is not absolute, and that model is not the one operating in this book. Deciding "objectively" on the "correct" interpretation of a text does not have to be the emphasis or purpose of reading— not, at any rate, if reading and learning are to be centered in the reader.

Second, your sense of the meaning or effect of a text does not have to be determined by faithfulness to historical circumstances of a text or an author's life or intentions. The question of an author's purpose or **intention** is an open and problematic one. To what extent, if at all, did the writer intend to please in the aesthetic sense? To what extent, if at all, did he or she intend to do something else: instruct, enlighten, preach, move to action? How sure can you ever be about these intentions, especially if the writer is dead or unavailable for any reason? (And even if an author *is* available—via interviews, lectures, or just in the phone book—at least two questions still arise: Will she or he say anything at all reliable about intentions, and, if so, to what extent must you read what the author has written in those terms?) To be sure, the general purpose of some pieces of writing can be fairly reliably determined: an advertisement, for instance, or a sermon, or John Milton's *Paradise Lost,* which states the intention to "justify the ways of God to man." But other texts are not so clear-cut. Does a novel or short story try mainly to entertain (to "please," as this definition has it)? If it is "realistic" or "political" fiction, to what extent does it seek to promote real-world action and understanding on the part of readers?

You may be familiar with the controversy in the news media, in the wake of the spring 1992 disturbances in Los Angeles, over the rock song "Cop Killer" by Ice-T. Some readers (or listeners) thought it intended to promote or even cause the killing of police. Ice-T himself disclaimed that intention, saying the song was the expression of a fictional character, a black man from the inner city who felt like killing a police officer. Ice-T seemed to be arguing for an aesthetic intention: the creation of a fictional character or **voice** that had a kind of life of its own, separate from his identity as author. This kind of character, in the situation he "lived" in, could be realistically expected to have the kind of attitude expressed in the song. Ice-T's disclaimers, however, did little to mollify certain readers, who urged a boycott of the album, the record label that distributed it, and even of all products of Time Warner, the media conglomerate that owned the record label. And some of Ice-T's concerts had to be canceled for the rest of that year because local police refused to provide security. In this case, the choice of some readers to respond contrary to the author's professed intentions suggests that the intentions of authors in general are a weak standard and need not be considered the final arbiter of meaning or determinant of "correctness" in interpretation.

A third idea to keep in mind is that knowledge of a text's cultural context can contribute to a reader's response and interpretation, but at an introductory or undergraduate level of study, it is not essential. Such knowledge can indeed enhance, deepen, or otherwise modify your response and interpretation, and depending on how important greater knowledge of a text's cultural context is for you, there are ways to get it, ways valuable both in themselves and for the ends they serve. Library research is an option you may engage in, looking into the background or contexts of a particular text. Or you may read more widely in the works of a particular writer or "school" of writers to see more about what he, she, or they are up to. Or you may even take further courses devoted to the study of a particular writer, literary movement, or historical period. In these courses you may read a particular text again, anew—in light of more or at least different information from when you encountered it for the first time.

For the moment, however, it matters more what you already know, think, or believe about the contexts in which a given text was produced. You can tap into your knowledge and make use of it to strengthen yourself as a reader.

Thinking Critically About the Reader's Role

In general, you should work to become a self-conscious reader. Consider self-consciousness both a goal and a method; the way to the goal *is* the goal; the goal *is* the way. If you become a self-conscious reader, you will learn much more than can be tested by the traditional classroom methods, which seek to measure what you know about texts as objects. Even essay tests usually ask you to write about the text as a discrete, static object separate from yourself and analyzable in quasi-scientific fashion. If you study hard and focus your mind on the test questions, you may demonstrate that you know a lot about the texts you read. Fine. But if you aim at and practice self-consciousness as a reader, you will learn about yourself and your culture as well as about the texts you read.

An even greater benefit of self-consciousness is that you will teach yourself, which is a lasting and effective way to learn. You will learn how and why you read as you do, both in general and on specific occasions. You will learn about your likes and dislikes, your feelings and experiences, your memories and associations. You will learn how you think and interpret, not just with respect to literature, but with respect to all the myriad texts you encounter in the world. You will learn about how and why you are constructed as you are by the cultural forces to which you are subject. You will begin to tease apart the complex fabric of culture, to distinguish some of its separate strands.

In a classroom full of others working the same way toward the same goal, the chance to share your labor and some of its fruits will increase your learning because your ideas or values may be transformed by your interactions with others. Paradoxically, as you become self-conscious, you will become more aware of a diversity of conscious selves around you, and of what makes them tick. It is important to share your responses in a community of readers and learners, to make at least some of your readings public, to offer them in the marketplace of ideas that a college or university is supposed to be. To do all this is to become a stronger reader, and again, not just of literary texts but of any cultural texts you encounter. The next chapter will look at some practical ways of realizing that latent power within you.

3 ◆ READING LITERATURE ACTIVELY

In addition to being self-conscious, a strong reader is a deliberately *active* reader. Reading is an activity, of course, as much as playing tennis or dancing, except that you exercise your mind more than your body. This chapter will present some techniques and strategies you can practice before and while you read. If you think of yourself as entering into a dialogue with texts, you can begin to make yourself aware of your activity as a reader. Some of these "activating strategies" you may have heard of before, some you may have practiced before or practice now, some may be new, and some may seem strange and unnatural. I encourage you to try them all in a more or less systematic fashion. Eventually you should see which ones are most helpful to you, and you should find yourself more comfortable with practicing what might at first seem awkward.

Creating a Dialogue with a Text

Chapter 4 will demonstrate in detail the process of turning active reading into a piece of public or formal writing. Diane Gretta, the student whose work serves as the model for that demonstration, practiced several of the methods this chapter will advocate. To get in step with her reading and writing, you will shortly be asked to read a short story, Ernest Hemingway's "Hills Like White Elephants." You will also be asked to activate a dialogue with that text by practicing some particular reading and writing activities, as follows.

Writing in Your Book

Read with a pen or pencil in your hand, and use it. Mark up your book. Write in it. Talk back to the words on the page. Make notes as you are reading.

Notes don't have to be extensive; they might not even always be much more than underlines, highlights, stars, or marginal marks of some kind, although writing occasional words and phrases of your own requires a little more in the way of activity on your part. Don't think of this technique as a way of marking important lines or passages that you'll have to go back to when you study for a test on the material. Think of it as one way to make a text your own, to insert your voice into it, to conduct a dialogue with it. At the same time, this marking of a text does have the practical application of making it easier to find what you consider to be significant passages when, later on, you may choose or be assigned to write something on your reading of the text.

Students sometimes think they shouldn't mark up a textbook. Are you such a person? Perhaps you think books, especially textbooks, are sacred objects and that to write in them is to defile them. Such a belief is related to the ideology that knowledge is information, that students are supplicants at the temple, that teachers and their instruments (e.g., textbooks) are not to be tampered with or disturbed. To the contrary, I would suggest a model of teaching and learning that is much more self-driven. If you are to interact with ideas, not just or primarily with the containers they come in, you must give yourself some credit for being worthy of those ideas. This is your book now. Make it your own. Make your education your own. Make your life your own. And you can start by doing something you may have always felt forbidden to do: writing in your school book. Diane did that, and below are two brief sections of the Hemingway story showing her interaction with the text. Notice the questions among Diane's marginal notes; Diane's active reading was not limited to making statements about what she read, but included indicating her uncertainty and tentativeness as well.

"They look like white elephants," she said. *referring to the hills*
"I've never seen one," the man drank his beer.
"No, you wouldn't have." *pessimistic/disappointed*
"I might have," the man said. "Just because you say I wouldn't have doesn't prove anything." *defensive*
The girl looked at the bead curtain. "They've painted something on it," she said. "What does it say?" *quick change of subject*
"Anis del Toro. It's a drink."
"Could we try it?" *asking for permission?*
The man called "Listen" through the curtain. The woman came out from the bar.

* * *

The warm wind blew the bead curtain against the table.
"The beer's nice and cool," the man said.
"It's lovely," the girl said.
"It's really an awfully simple operation, Jig," the man said. "It's not really an operation at all." *not really an operation at all—abortion is the 1st thing to come to mind. Seems*
The girl looked at the ground the table legs rested on.
"I know you wouldn't mind it, Jig. It's really not anything. It's just to let the air in." *he's trying to talk her into something (convince her).*
The girl did not say anything.
"I'll go with you and I'll stay with you all the time. They just let the air in and then it's all perfectly natural."
"Then what will we do afterward?" *She's worried about the future of*
"We'll be fine afterward. Just like we were before." *the relationship. Will he*
"What makes you think so?" *dump her when it's over?*
"That's the only thing that bothers us. It's the only thing that's made us unhappy."
The girl looked at the bead curtain, put her hand out and took hold of two of the strings of beads.

"And you think then we'll be all right and be happy."

"I know we will. You don't have to be afraid. I've known lots of people that have done it." *He seems so confident.*

"So have I," said the girl. "And afterward they were all so happy."

Writing Outside Your Book

Writing is thinking, or at least a certain kind of writing is: writing in which you talk to yourself, rather than to a teacher; writing in which you let your mind go where it will (within certain limits), as opposed to writing that is supposed to stick to a thesis; writing that may not be especially polished or grammatically correct or even very neat; writing that makes itself up as it goes along; writing that creates or stimulates thoughts and ideas, rather than just "records" them. Eventually, you will probably be asked to do some writing that will be read by others—your teacher or your classmates. This is writing that comes after your reading, which is the sequence of activities you may be most familiar with. In that situation, you will have to polish your writing, fine-tune some of your thoughts and the way you express them, and state a thesis and develop it in coherent fashion.

But that kind of writing will not be the first you will do in response to your reading, nor will it constitute the majority of the writing you do. To make your writing more interactive with your reading, to the benefit of both, you should do some writing *before* you read and a lot of different kinds of writing *while* you read. Writing and reading cannot be exactly simultaneous, of course, but those two activities can be more closely integrated than is allowed by the usual model of writing only after you have read a text. As you integrate these activities, think of your writing as a way to learn about yourself, as a reader and as a person, and about the texts you encounter and what you make of them as you read.

Writing Before You Read

If you free yourself from the notion that, in college, writing is always something done after reading is completed, for the purpose of showing the teacher what you know, you can open yourself to some new possibilities. For instance, sometimes you may profitably write before you begin to read, with the profit coming primarily to you as the writing helps you understand the dynamics of your own reading.

A useful prereading exercise in this regard is to list some of the expectations you bring with you to a text, expectations that might be raised by the genre to which the text belongs, the time period in which it was produced, or the author by whom it was written—and by what you know, think, or believe about any of those. These expectations could be vague, as in "I think I might like this but we'll see," or quite specific, as in "There's going to be some difficult language here that I'm going to have to really think hard about" or "A story by Edgar Allan Poe is going to be spooky and chilling. I can't wait!" Diane's response statement to "Hills Like White Elephants" in Chapter 4 was not written before she read that story, but the first paragraph of her response statement does refer to expectations she brought with her to the reading, based on previous experiences with stories by Hemingway. Here's some of what she wrote:

> I have read Hemingway before and I like his style of writing. He writes beautifully; the words flow when being read and I like the descriptive quality he utilizes. He makes the story seem very realistic.

Try your hand at this now, before you begin to read "Hills Like White Elephants" for yourself. This story was first published in 1927. As a first activity, use the box below or a page in your notebook to list your expectations for this short story, based on anything you know, think, or believe about it *before* you start reading it.

PREREADING EXPECTATIONS FOR "HILLS LIKE WHITE ELEPHANTS"

1.

2.

3.

4.

5.

6.

In expanding a bit on this list, you could act self-consciously by asking yourself where these expectations come from or why you have these expectations and not others. Is it the assignment itself or anything else having to do with context in which you are about to read this text? The author's name? The category or genre the text is supposedly a part of? The text's title? The opening lines or paragraph?

Writing While You Read

Writing *while* you are reading can help you see the process nature of reading because it allows you to watch yourself construct interpretation as you develop and revise your responses and expectations. One technique is to read a text in bits or chunks and immediately write down your reactions to each chunk, your expectations or predictions for the next chunk, and what happens to those predictions when you actually get to that next part. You can read poems by lines or by stanzas this way; short stories by paragraphs, pages, or scenes; plays by scenes or acts. This is admittedly artificial, and it may seem really awkward at first, but it's a good way to develop reading strategies other than just following the plot, in fiction or drama, because you allow yourself to build up or alter responses as you go along and not just wait to see how it all turns out before you decide what your response is.

Try this method now with "Hills Like White Elephants." Reprinted below is the first paragraph of that story. Read it, then take a few minutes to jot down the following:

- Your first responses to the opening of the story
- Your expectations for the story, as raised by the opening paragraph
- Your predictions for what will happen next in the story.

> *The hills across the valley of the Ebro were long and white. On this side there was no shade and no trees and the station was between two lines of rails in the sun. Close against the side of the station there was the warm shadow of the building and a curtain, made of strings of bamboo beads, hung across the open door into the bar, to keep out flies. The American and the girl with him sat at a table in the shade, outside the building. It was very hot and the express from Barcelona would come in forty minutes. It stopped at this junction for two minutes and went on to Madrid.*

Now do the same with this next chunk of the story, all dialogue between "the American" and "the girl," that follows immediately after the opening paragraph. This time, before you state your expectations or predictions for what will follow, say something about how any of the expectations or predictions you stated after reading the opening paragraph worked out.

> *"What should we drink?" the girl asked. She had taken off her hat and put it on the table.*
> *"It's pretty hot," the man said.*
> *"Let's drink beer."*
> *"Dos cervezas," the man said into the curtain.*
> *"Big ones?" a woman asked from the doorway.*
> *"Yes. Two big ones."*
> *The woman brought two glasses of beer and two felt pads. She put the felt pads and the beer glasses on the table and looked at the man and the girl. The girl was looking off at the line of hills. They were white in the sun and the country was brown and dry.*
> *"They look like white elephants," she said.*
> *"I've never seen one," the man said.*
> *"No, you wouldn't have."*
> *"I might have," the man said. "Just because you say I wouldn't have doesn't prove anything."*
> *The girl looked at the bead curtain. "They've painted something on it," she said. "What does it say?"*
> *"Anis del Toro. It's a drink."*
> *"Could we try it?"*
> *The man called "Listen" through the curtain. The woman came out from the bar.*
> *"Four reales."*
> *"We want two Anis del Toro."*
> *"With water?"*
> *"Do you want it with water?"*

"I don't know," the girl said. "Is it good with water?"
"It's all right."
"You want them with water?" asked the woman.
"Yes, with water."

Paying attention to your expectations and predictions and to whatever happens to them, whether they are confirmed or foiled and whether they apply to an entire text or smaller chunks of it, is good practice in reading self-consciously. You could go on through the rest of "Hills Like White Elephants" in this way. Just interrupt your reading for a bit whenever you come to what feels like a good place to stop and write some more about your responses and your expectations. Here is "Hills like White Elephants" in its entirety.

Ernest Hemingway   1899–1961

Hills Like White Elephants   *1927*

The hills across the valley of the Ebro* were long and white. On this side there was no shade and no trees and the station was between two lines of rails in the sun. Close against the side of the station there was the warm shadow of the building and a curtain, made of strings of bamboo beads, hung across the open door into the bar, to keep out flies. The American and the girl with him sat at a table in the shade, outside the building. It was very hot and the express from Barcelona would come in forty minutes. It stopped at this junction for two minutes and went on to Madrid.

"What should we drink?" the girl asked. She had taken off her hat and put it on the table.

"It's pretty hot," the man said.

"Let's drink beer."

"Dos cervezas," the man said into the curtain.

"Big ones?" a woman asked from the doorway.   5

"Yes. Two big ones."

The woman brought two glasses of beer and two felt pads. She put the felt pads and the beer glasses on the table and looked at the man and the girl. The girl was looking off at the line of hills. They were white in the sun and the country was brown and dry.

"They look like white elephants," she said.

"I've never seen one," the man drank his beer.   10

"No, you wouldn't have."

"I might have," the man said. "Just because you say I wouldn't have doesn't prove anything."

The girl looked at the bead curtain. "They've painted something on it," she said. "What does it say?"

"Anis del Toro. It's a drink."

"Could we try it?"   15

---

*Ebro – river flowing through northeastern Spain into the Mediterranean Sea.

The man called "Listen" through the curtain. The woman came out from the bar.

"Four reales."

"We want two Anis del Toro."

"With water?"

"Do you want it with water?"

"I don't know," the girl said. "Is it good with water?"

"It's all right."

"You want them with water?" asked the woman.

"Yes, with water."

"It tastes like licorice," the girl said and put the glass down.

"That's the way with everything."

"Yes," said the girl. "Everything tastes of licorice. Especially all the things you've waited so long for, like absinthe."

"Oh, cut it out."

"You started it," the girl said. "I was being amused. I was having a fine time."

"Well, let's try and have a fine time."

"All right. I was trying. I said the mountains looked like white elephants. Wasn't that bright?"

"That was bright."

"I wanted to try this new drink. That's all we do, isn't it—look at things and try new drinks?"

"I guess so."

The girl looked across at the hills.

"They're lovely hills," she said. "They don't really look like white elephants. I just meant the coloring of their skin through the trees."

"Should we have another drink?"

"All right."

The warm wind blew the bead curtain against the table.

"The beer's nice and cool," the man said.

"It's lovely," the girl said.

"It's really an awfully simple operation, Jig," the man said. "It's not really an operation at all."

The girl looked at the ground the table legs rested on.

"I know you wouldn't mind it, Jig. It's really not anything. It's just to let the air in."

The girl did not say anything.

"I'll go with you and I'll stay with you all the time. They just let the air in and then it's all perfectly natural."

"Then what will we do afterward?"

"We'll be fine afterward. Just like we were before."

"What makes you think so?"

"That's the only thing that bothers us. It's the only thing that's made us unhappy."

The girl looked at the bead curtain, put her hand out and took hold of two of the strings of beads.

"And you think then we'll be all right and be happy."

"I know we will. You don't have to be afraid. I've known lots of people that have done it."

"So have I," said the girl. "And afterward they were all so happy."

"Well," the man said, "if you don't want to you don't have to. I wouldn't   55
have you do it if you didn't want to. But I know it's perfectly simple."

"And you really want to?"

"I think it's the best thing to do. But I don't want you to do it if you don't really want to."

"And if I do it you'll be happy and things will be like they were and you'll love me?"

"I love you now. You know I love you."

"I know. But if I do it, then it will be nice again if I say things are like   60
white elephants, and you'll like it?"

"I'll love it. I love it now but I just can't think about it. You know how I get when I worry."

"If I do it you won't ever worry?"

"I won't worry about that because it's perfectly simple."

"Then I'll do it. Because I don't care about me."

"What do you mean?"   65

"I don't care about me."

"Well, I care about you."

"Oh, yes. But I don't care about me. And I'll do it and then everything will be fine."

"I don't want you to do it if you feel that way."

The girl stood up and walked to the end of the station. Across on the   70
other side, were fields of grain and trees along the banks of the Ebro. Far away, beyond the river, were mountains. The shadow of a cloud moved across the field of grain and she saw the river through the trees.

"And we could have all this," she said. "And we could have everything and every day we make it more impossible."

"What did you say?"

"I said we could have everything."

"We can have everything."

"No, we can't."

"We can have the whole world."

"No, we can't."   75

"We can go everywhere."

"No, we can't. It isn't ours any more."

"It's ours."   80

"No, it isn't. And once they take it away, you never get it back."

"But they haven't taken it away."

"We'll wait and see."

"Come on back in the shade," he said. "You mustn't feel that way."

"I don't feel any way," the girl said. "I just know things."   85

"I don't want you to do anything that you don't want to do—"

"Nor that isn't good for me," she said. "I know. Could we have another beer?"

"All right. But you've got to realize—"

"I realize," the girl said. "Can't we maybe stop talking?"

They sat down at the table and the girl looked at the hills on the dry side   90
of the valley and the man looked at her and at the table.

"You've got to realize," he said, "that I don't want you to do it if you don't
want to. I'm perfectly willing to go through with it if it means anything to you."

"Doesn't it mean anything to you? We could get along."

"Of course it does. But I don't want anybody but you. I don't want any
one else. And I know it's perfectly simple."

"Yes, you know it's perfectly simple."

"It's all right for you to say that, but I do know it."   95

"Would you do something for me now?"

"I'd do anything for you."

"Would you please please please please please please please stop talking?"

He did not say anything but looked at the bags against the wall of the station. There were labels on them from all the hotels where they had spent nights.

"But I don't want you to," he said, "I don't care anything about it."   100

"I'll scream," the girl said.

The woman came out through the curtains with two glasses of beer and put
them down on the damp felt pads. "The train comes in five minutes," she said.

"What did she say?" asked the girl.

"That the train is coming in five minutes."

The girl smiled brightly at the woman, to thank her.   105

"I'd better take the bags over to the other side of the station," the man
said. She smiled at him.

"All right. Then come back and we'll finish the beer."

He picked up the two heavy bags and carried them around the station to
the other tracks. He looked up the tracks but could not see the train. Coming
back, he walked through the barroom, where people waiting for the train
were drinking. He drank an Anis at the bar and looked at the people. They
were all waiting reasonably for the train. He went out through the bead curtain. She was sitting at the table and smiled at him.

"Do you feel better?" he asked.

"I feel fine," she said. "There's nothing wrong with me. I feel fine."   110

Reading and Writing Critically

As you involve writing with your reading—whether that writing is done before, during, or after you read—I want to stress two points. The first is *general
method* for your writing; the second is a particular *form* for your writing.

Thinking Critically: Question-Answer-Question

QAQ is not a word from Maori or Maltese. It's an acronym for Question-
Answer-Question, which is a method or procedure you should use as you
write about texts and your responses to them. Think of your writing as a kind
of looping progression: it, and your thinking, goes around and upward or

onward at the same time. It's not linear. It's not the shortest distance between two points. Pose yourself a question or questions. Try to work in an answering mode for a while. Then question your own answers. Keep your writing and your thoughts open; don't always look for closure.

You can get a start on this method by putting some of the notations you write in your book in question form. If you look back at pages 39–40, which contains a section of "Hills Like White Elephants" with Diane's notes reproduced, you can see that Diane made some of those notes in a questioning mode.

Response Statements

Response statements are a kind of writing developed by teacher and literary theorist David Bleich in his courses at Indiana University and the University of Rochester. In writing them, you focus on yourself and your reading of a text rather than on the text as an object. You record and develop your emotional and cognitive responses to a text. In the process, you begin to work out a reading, a making-meaning, of the text. In the next chapter, you will see a response statement Diane wrote after her first reading of "Hills Like White Elephants." Writing your own response statements regularly in a journal or notebook adds a little systematization to the interactive reading process and gives you something a little more substantial and permanent to hold on to.

Response statements use the QAQ method, starting with three basic questions:

- **What is my response to this text?**
- **What accounts for my response, in terms of the text and myself?**
- **What does my response tell me about myself or my culture?**

These questions are **heuristics,** or discovery procedures, that lead to "answers" (the quotation marks indicating their tentative, contingent nature), that lead to other questions, and so on. Occasionally in this textbook, you will be asked more specific heuristic questions to generate writing about particular texts, or your teacher may devise such questions for you. But in their absence, you can always use the three basic questions listed above to generate a response statement. Let's now look at each one in a little more depth.

The question **"What is my response to this text?"** could also be asked as "How do I feel about this text?" or "What do I think about this text?" As first answers, perhaps a menu of responses would help:

I:
like
dislike
hate
love
this text.

I find it:

interesting	*admirable*	*ironic*
puzzling	*despicable*	*complicated*
stimulating	*sexist*	*naive*
confusing	*ageist*	*powerful*
boring	*racist*	*weak*
maddening	*classist*	*gruesome*
annoying	*classic*	*grim*
satisfying	*trite*	*funny*
frightening	*innovative*	*absurd*
disturbing	*awesome*	*sick*
erotic	*heavy*	*bizarre*
romantic	*superficial*	
exciting	*ambiguous*	

Keep in mind that any of these words, or combinations, describes your response to the text, not the text itself. Remind yourself of this. Be willing to revise your thoughts as you write. Having started out saying a text is one thing, you haven't committed yourself to that position to the extent that you can't change it or even discard it as you go. That's what happens sometimes.

Also, these one-word response answers are just starting points. As such, they're fine, but their limitation is that they're just one word. They need elaboration, exploration. Follow them to wherever they lead: backward to their source and forward to new thoughts. There's no real learning going on in one-word responses. You should complicate or problematize all the time, question your answers, probe deeper.

There are several ways to do this. One is to write more in a response statement, using the second and third basic questions listed on page 47. Those will be discussed in more detail later. Another way is to freewrite: Once you have down one word that names your response, just keep writing without stopping for a set period of time—10 or 15 minutes, for instance—using that word as a starting point. Don't worry about the correctness of any aspect of your writing (grammar, punctuation, spelling); don't try to be logical or coherent, just let the words flow. When your time is up, read back over what you've written and see if you can pull out (summarize in a sentence or two) one or two points that seem worth pursuing further.

A third way to complicate a one-word first response is to work with a branching or cluster diagram. Branches suggest logical connections from your first response, either going backward to the source of that response or forward to its implications. Clusters allow you to list ideas you associate with any of those in the branches. In your notebook, make a replica of the box that follows so you can have a chance to try this with "Hills like White Elephants." Put your initial one-word response in the circle in the center. To the left of that, the branches connect to other circles where you can enter

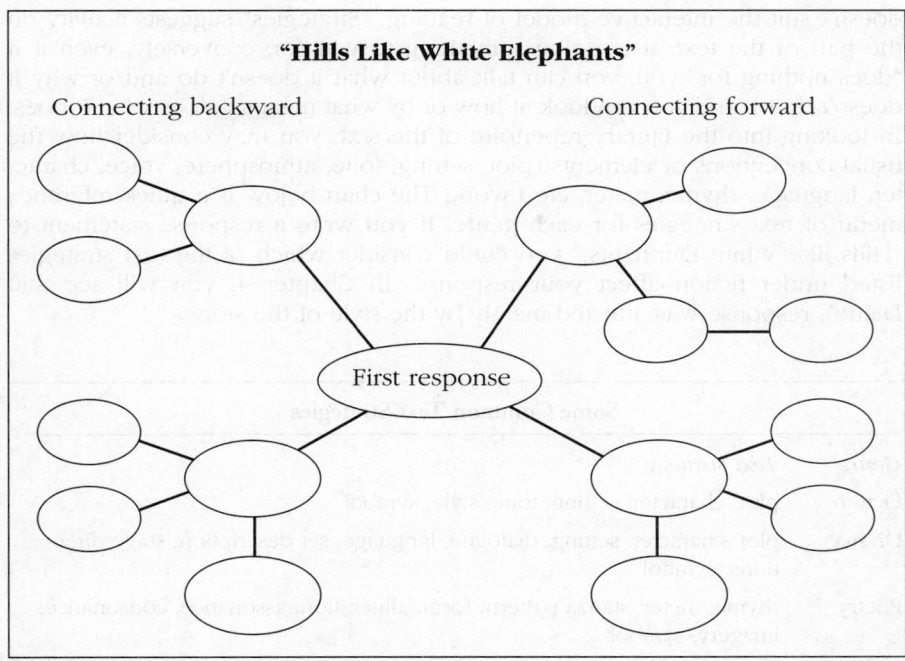

words or brief phrases that trace your first response backward into the text or yourself. The circles on the right are areas where you can follow the implications of your first response in terms of what it tells you about yourself or your culture.

The second basic response statement question, **"What accounts for my response?"** could also be phrased as "What has produced or contributed to my response?" Following our interactive model of the reading process, there are two complementary parts to this question: yourself and the text. So this question can be divided into two subquestions:

- How or in what ways does the text contribute to my response?
- How or in what ways do I contribute to my response?

Each of these two subquestions has two subquestions of its own, so that when you ask what accounts for your response to a text you are opening up four areas for exploration: the literary repertoire and cultural context of the text and your own literary and life experience.

Text Strategies   In pursuing the first of the two subquestions, you can look into text strategies. This term is preferable to words like "features" or "elements," because those suggest a static, stable, objective nature to the text that doesn't suit the interactive model of reading. "Strategies" suggests activity on the part of the text; it is doing something to you (or, conversely, even if it "does nothing for" you, you can talk about what it doesn't do and/or why it doesn't do it), and you can look at how or by what means it does what it does. In looking into the literary repertoire of the text, you may consider how the usual conventions or elements (plot, setting, tone, atmosphere, voice, character, language, rhyme, meter, etc.) work. The chart below is a quick-reference menu of text strategies for each genre. If you write a response statement to "Hills like White Elephants," you could consider which of the text strategies listed under fiction affect your response. In Chapter 4, you will see that Diane's response was affected mainly by the style of the story.

Some Common Text Strategies

Genre	Text Strategy
Fiction	plot, character, setting, tone, style, symbol
Drama	plot, character, setting, dialogue, language, set description, stage directions, symbol
Poetry	rhyme, meter, stanza pattern, form, alliteration, assonance, consonance, imagery, symbol
Essay	language, structure, rhetoric, imagery, tone

The emphasis in your writing here should be on whatever strategies or conventions you notice or are affected by; it's not a matter of your running through a checklist of features that have to be discussed. Remember, you're not trying to show your teacher that you know about certain textual conventions and can cite examples of them in the text; you're trying to explore, primarily for yourself, the dynamics of the interaction between you and the text in terms of text strategies.

Reading Strategies   Text strategies, remember, aren't effective at all until they're activated by a reader, and different readers activate, notice, or are affected by different text strategies. This complementary relationship means that different reading strategies both emphasize and are engaged by different text strategies. For instance, if you're reading a short story primarily to find out what happens, you're going to be largely concerned with plot and you may downplay or ignore certain other strategies such as atmosphere, tone, or character. Have you ever found yourself well into a novel that you didn't really like, but you just couldn't put it aside for good without flipping to the end to find out how it all comes out? That experience is an exaggerated form of a reading strategy that focuses on or emphasizes plot, pretty much to the exclusion of other text strategies. Or how about reading a story for the second time? You already know the outcome of the plot, so now your reading strategy is necessarily different, and you notice different text strategies than you did the first time you read the story.

Here are some other reading strategies with brief descriptions of each.

- *Reading quickly to get the gist.* Perhaps a good "orientation" strategy for your first encounter with a new text. Diane did this with "Hills Like White Elephants," as her response statement in Chapter 4 indicates.

- *Identifying with a character.* Emphasizing the similarities you see between your situation and a character's.

- *Creating theme.* Theme was not listed among any of the text strategies on page 50 because the interactive model of the reading process emphasizes the reader's role in making meaning; accordingly, theme is not objectively "in" a text as much as it is created by a reader who brings certain ideas and concerns to a text. This activity is illustrated in Diane's response statement to "Hills Like White Elephants" in Chapter 4.

- *Noticing gaps or indeterminacies.* Another activity of a reader may be identifying places in a text where something appears to be "missing" (**gaps**) or where meaning seems to be indefinite (**indeterminacies**). For instance, the gender of the speaker in "Dover Beach" (Chapter 2, pages 24–25) may be seen as a gap, and the particular "operation" being considered by the characters in "Hills Like White Elephants" may be considered an indeterminacy. Related reading strategies are *filling in gaps* or *resolving indeterminacies.* If you think of a gap or an indeterminacy as a "question," your action in filling in or resolving it is an attempt at an "answer."

- *Naturalizing.* This strategy involves ignoring the fact that a text strategy may be conventional and accepting it as "natural" within that text or a genre: the dramatic soliloquy, for instance.

- *Putting closure on a text.* Deciding, more or less definitely, what a text means or how it should be read; excluding other possible readings.

- *Playing with a text.* This strategy is roughly the opposite of putting closure on it; it involves keeping your interpretive options open.

- *Building consistency.* The process of deciding on meaning as you read; "collating data" or information from a text; tying things together.

- *Adopting a wandering viewpoint.* This strategy is roughly the opposite of but also complementary to building consistency; it is the process of entertaining different "hypotheses" as to meaning as you read.

This list is not exhaustive; some additional reading strategies will be discussed in the separate genre sections of this book. For now, however, just two points need to be made: one, you can *become conscious* of the reading strategies you already tend to employ or that are triggered by certain text strategies in what you read; and two, you can *consciously control* your use of particular reading strategies. Both will help make you a more active reader.

The Interaction Between Readers and Texts   In trying to account for your response to a text, you should also inquire into the **interaction of ideologies** that went on. What ideas, values, beliefs, assumptions, or articles of faith of yours were confirmed by the text? Which were challenged? Conversely, what ideas, values, and so forth that the text seems to hold (explicitly or implicitly) can you endorse or challenge? Put differently, to what extent did the text and you harmonize in these areas, or to what extent did you and the text clash? Your analysis here may help account for, or even modify, your initial response, as you will see from Diane's response statement to "Hills Like White Elephants" in Chapter 4. Liking a text, for instance, may have a good deal to do with your "finding in it" attractive values or ideas, and disliking a text may depend on your "finding in it" repellent values or ideas. One reviewer of James Dickey's novel *Deliverance,* while admiring it on other grounds, condemned the book for its "moral insensitivity." He thought it was "all too patently the concoction of a situation in which it will be morally permissible . . . to kill men with a bow and arrow." For him, the text's apparent valuation of such killing was enough to cause a strongly clashing interaction of ideologies, and that overrode all the other things he found to like about the book.[1]

Looking at how aspects of your ideology interact with that of the text can get you into what has been called **reading against the grain.** "The grain" in this instance is something like the moral, ethical, or value direction the text seems to take. Going against it means resisting that direction, objecting to it, fighting it off, saying "No" when the text would have you say "Yes." Sometimes this kind of reading comes pretty much unforced, as in the case of Ricks' response to *Deliverance.* Another is Chinua Achebe's response to Joseph Conrad's novella *Heart of Darkness,* which the Nigerian Achebe read as a text revealing racist attitudes on the part of white Europeans toward black Africans, in spite of many other readings that found *Heart of Darkness* to be a critique of nineteenth-century European imperialism and the racist attitudes that went with it.[2]

In being self-conscious about your responses, there are two things you can do concerning a reading against the grain: you can look closely at your ideological differences with a text and try to explore them, rather than just consigning them to the vague territory of uneasiness or disquietude; or you can force such ideological differences by changing the perspective from which you may be first inclined to read. The first of these options does not necessarily mean condemning the text in its entirety; Achebe and Ricks both found grounds for praising the texts they otherwise objected to. The second of these choices often does mean a conscious decision on your part to read differently, or to read as a different person, or to let a certain aspect of your personality come to the foreground as you respond. Here you consider the effect of your gender, age, race, class, sexual preference, physical or mental condition, and

---

[1]Christopher Ricks. rev. of *Deliverance.* by James Dickey. *The New York Review of Books* 23 April, 1970.
[2]Chinua Achebe. "An Image of Africa: Racism in Conrad's *Heart of Darkness." The Massachusetts Review* 18 (1977): 782–94.

so forth on whether you accept or reject some aspect of the text's ideology, or what would happen if you changed your situation with regard to any of these and approached this text accordingly.

Asking questions like these can reveal significant things about your situation as a reader and the relation of that situation to the text. It can also reveal the fluid or plastic nature of texts, which appear different to different readers according to how they are situated with respect to any of these categories. Think of jokes, for instance: how many of them exclude certain people according to what categories they fall into; how you might not want to tell certain jokes to certain people; how if you were a different kind of person, you might be offended by a joke you have just laughed at, or vice versa. It's the same with all texts: they, or many of them, assume a certain kind of audience or reader and perhaps in the process exclude others. Choosing to adopt a resisting stance toward a text means you are going to experience a clash between some aspect of its ideology and your own. You should also see from this discussion that reading against the grain, resisting or contesting a text, is another reading strategy. It is an active stance you can adopt as you interact with a text, and it proceeds from self-consciousness on your part.

The third basic response statement question mentioned earlier, **"What does my response tell me about myself or my culture?"** takes you still further toward self-consciousness. Asking this question is a way to look at how your own **cognitive processes** work or at the **cultural processes** that make you the kind of responding reader you are. How does your mind work as you read a text, or how does your culture work to construct the you who in turn constructs a text? This kind of question and the "answers" that proceed from it take you into an analysis of the wider implications of your reading of a text.

Analytical Approaches   Looking at your own cognitive processes goes back to—or proceeds from—an analysis of your reading strategies as they interact with certain text strategies. That interaction, your mind working in a particular instance, shows something about how your mind works in general: how and why you construct the outer world, or at least certain instances of it, as you do. This kind of analysis can give you a chance to reflect on whether and why you are able to tolerate ambiguity or confusion, for instance, or whether and why you want loose ends to be tied up or closure to be achieved in intellectual problems.

Critical perspective of this kind can have further consequences: If you see something in your own thinking processes that you don't like, you may have made the first move toward changing it. If you see something there that you do like, you may have given yourself reason to strengthen it. But at the very least, the self-knowledge that is made available through this approach is worth pursuing.

Analyzing your response in terms of how it is culturally produced, on the other hand, gives you a still wider critical perspective. You can begin to see exactly how you are in certain ways socially constructed; you can see where some of your attitudes and habits of mind and heart come from in terms of the ideological contexts you operate in and that operate on you. You can begin to examine, for instance, the role your gender, race, or class plays in making you the kind of responding person you are. It can be very revealing and instructive to discover how powerful those and other categories can be, not just in the more obvious areas like who you would consent to date, but in shaping your assumptions and values. As is the case with understanding your cognitive processes, cultural analysis can be a tool for change—of yourself if, for instance, you don't like the effect some cultural category is having on you, or even of the larger cultural categories, if you have the energy and motivation to begin that effort. Social change often starts with conscious individual people.

In these ways, then, working to become self-conscious as you read and respond also helps you become a more active reader. You should feel strength and the confidence that comes with it in your literature class as you see how literary texts depend on you for their meaning and their very life. You should also begin to feel it in other areas of study as well as beyond the college walls. Remember, self-consciousness is a goal and a method. As a method, it is transportable, applicable wherever there are texts to be encountered and read.

4 ◈ Writing About Literature

An essential way to become a stronger reader is to involve writing with your reading. Chapter 3 suggested some methods for doing this. In further consideration of the relationship between reading and writing, this chapter will look at some more public or formal kinds of writing you can do and some different purposes and occasions for such writing. It will also outline a suggested progression in moving from reading a text to developing a formal paper about your reading of it. That progression will cover the essential stages of *prewriting, drafting, revising,* and *editing* that constitute the writing process for formal papers. Finally, this chapter will illustrate one student's process of moving from a first response to a text toward a formal paper.

Forms of Writing

In the academic context, it is common practice to write about literature in more public forms: essays, themes, compositions, or papers. These forms of writing have both benefits and drawbacks, which I would like to examine briefly here. Assignments for these kinds of writing typically ask you to approach a text as if it were a more-or-less self-contained object and to analyze it in order to develop a hypothesis that you can then "test" by returning to the text for confirming evidence. Your paper then takes the form of an argument in which you state your interpretive thesis and support it through textual evidence culled from analysis. You try to get your reader to look at the text with the same dispassionate glance as you have employed.

Argumentative writing of this kind is not without value. Leading your reader to see or understand what you have already seen and understood is a legitimate purpose for writing, if that understanding has indeed already been accomplished. Carefully marshaling evidence and logic to support and explain a point is a valuable academic skill because it promotes careful thinking on the part of the student/writer and because it takes a form that lends itself to relatively easy grading for the teacher/reader.

At the same time, this model of writing, and the model of reading that goes along with it, is built on a number of questionable assumptions. One assumption is that texts are stable and can best be approached in an objective manner. Another is that the actual practice of readers is to approach texts that way, or that it should be for the sake of the academic benefits. A third is that coherent, unified interpretations, the kind that can be presented in argumentative writing, really are the product of reading. A fourth is that most if not all writing in an academic context is produced to be graded.

These assumptions are questionable in at least three ways. First, they ignore the role of the reader and suppress his or her voice. Second, they allow for only one sequence between reading and writing; they ignore that reading and interpretation constitute a *process*, one that does not necessarily end as writing begins. Third, they take the purpose of writing to be to explain or argue only. Those assumptions, leading to assignments of the kind sketched out above, need to be challenged if your public writing is to be a more accurate indicator of what happens in your reading and if doing that kind of writing is to play a more active role in your learning.

There are a number of alternatives to the standard academic essay. These may be graded or ungraded, depending on your teacher's agenda or whatever he or she negotiates with the class. But in all cases they have proven value as ways to learn, not just as records of what you have already learned. I will not elaborate on all of them here; I will just mention some of them. You could try any of these approaches with "Hills Like White Elephants," so it might be useful to think about that text as you read the following discussion.

Some Alternative Forms for Public Writing

- You can write imitations or **parodies** of texts or parts of texts; these forms can help you "get inside the skin" of the original writer a bit or go against the grain of a text in a form other than the analytical essay.
- You can do rewrites of a text or parts of a text; not necessarily to change it completely, but, for instance, to make a new ending, to give voice to a "silenced" character, or to add or continue a scene left out. Rewrites allow you to work with gaps in a text and to insert something of your ideology into a text. In these ways, they demonstrate the plastic nature of texts and demolish the notion that they are stable.
- You can write **prologues** or **epilogues**—narratives or scenes preceding or following the action—for fiction or drama.
- You can write background sketches for characters in which, again, you can creatively fill in gaps with ideas of your own.
- You can invent dreams for characters, giving yourself a chance to play with a text and with literary symbols. You can invent other scenarios, such as a character having to plead his or her case before some kind of high tribunal, that enable you to have some fun as well as assume a point of view different from your own.

For any of these, you can also provide an essay portion discussing why you did certain things you did, both in terms of your own ideology and the effective strategies of the text.

Other writing forms—perhaps a bit less "creative," perhaps a bit more "tried and true,"—include **personal narrative, description, explanation,** and **letter.** All may serve as alternatives to the standard argumentative essay. You can, for instance, tell your own story or part of it in response to a text. You can describe or explain something in your own life experience that influences or is affected by your reading of a text. You can write directly to, say, a character, an author, or someone in your own life, past or present, who is in some way implicated in your reading of a text.

These kinds of writing may seem to take you away from the text itself and you may object to this direction. However, it would be wise to remember that once a reader encounters it, the text is more than just the marks on the page; it really exists in the circuitry established between the marks on the page and the reader. And that circuitry is more like a very complex board, not just a string run between two tin cans. A text may be most important as a doorway to valuable learning about yourself and your culture. To allow for that learning in academic writing, you shouldn't limit yourself to writing just about the text.

Further suggestions for alternative writing ideas are provided at the ends of most chapters in the genre sections of this book, under the heading Reading and Writing Projects for Creative and Critical Thinking. Beginning on page 126 in the Fiction section is a piece of student writing that illustrates one such suggestion by changing the ending of a short story and briefly explaining the writer's reasons for rewriting the ending as she did.

Expository Essay Assignments

I hope the discussion in the preceding pages has broadened your horizons a bit as to the kinds of writing you might do in relation to your reading of literary texts. Now I want to focus on one particular kind of such writing—an expository essay form, not one of the more "creative" kinds mentioned above. This kind of writing does presume that your teacher will read and grade it, but it is not the standard kind of objective analytical paper that the foregoing discussion has sought to challenge. It is writing that develops from one or more response statements on a given text, so it is different in that way. And it is about your reading of that text, not about the text itself or in isolation from you as an active reader. It has explanation as a goal, but rather than explaining the internal workings of a text, it seeks to explain how or why a reading was produced and what that reading may reveal in cognitive or cultural terms. In these ways, it simply develops (in greater detail, with more attention to the reader, and ultimately with appropriate attention to the conventions of surface correctness that academic writing is supposed to observe) the material generated by the original response-statement questions.

This essay does have a thesis, but that thesis is not about the text—how the text works or is unified, or what it means in some objective sense. The thesis takes you and your reading as its subject and predicates something about that subject along the lines of analyzing the reading transaction. Areas for such analysis may include:

- The ways in which your reading strategies interact with certain text strategies: What happens when you read as you do, encountering the text strategies that you do?
- How your assumptions about literature in general or a genre in particular influence you to read a text in a certain way.
- How some aspect of your ideology clashes or harmonizes with some aspect of the text's ideology.

- How the text is open to different interpretive options according to the perspective from which it is read.

In none of these cases do you have to marshal evidence from the text to support an "objective" thesis statement. Yes, you may very well cite specific passages from the text—as examples of particular text strategies that you may want to talk about, for instance. But you will also refer to your own role in the reading transaction: to certain reading strategies or other aspects of your literary experience, for instance, or to aspects of your life experience, such as associations that arise in your reading of the text, beliefs of yours that enable a harmonious or clashing interaction, or your situation with respect to any or several cultural categories that affect how or why you interpret the text as you do.

You don't have to be conclusive in such a paper, either. Your writing can acknowledge conflict and contradiction within yourself if elements of your repertoire clash. It can admit doubt and uncertainty about interpretations or their bases. It should at least tacitly acknowledge that your reading, like any reading, is only one of many possible; that it doesn't claim to settle matters of interpretation once and for all, despite the tempting rhetorical power of such a move, especially in a graded situation.

The Writing Process

Good writing—defined for our purposes here as writing that teaches the writer something about his or her interaction with a text and is interesting to read—takes time. It does not, like the mythical Athena from the head of Zeus, spring fully grown from your brain, pen, or word processor. The following discussion of the writing process assumes that you will allow sufficient time to nurture and cultivate your thoughts and the expression of them as you move from reading a text to writing about that reading. Accordingly, we will consider the entire writing process in terms of four areas or stages: prewriting, drafting, revising, and editing. These stages do not necessarily occur in linear succession; for most writers, there is considerable overlap among them. But any discussion of the writing process has to be laid out in sequential fashion, so the following pages will take up each of those stages separately.

Prewriting

Prewriting or *planning* covers a multitude of activities that come before you begin to give shape to your thoughts in the form of a first draft. If you have a formal writing assignment before you read a text, then your reading would constitute a prewriting activity. So would any of the writing activities you might do before or while you read, as suggested in Chapter 3. But whether you have a formal writing assignment before you read a text or not, the approach advocated here considers a response statement as one possible prewriting element.

Response Statements If you have a formal paper assignment when you sit down to read "Hills Like White Elephants," for example, writing a response statement will give you some rough prewriting that you can use as a resource for further prewriting and drafting. If you do not have such an assignment when you read a particular text, writing a response statement will serve the same purpose whenever you do: You can go back to that record of your first response and work from there.

Each of the four options listed on pages 57–58 for analyzing your interaction with a text grows out of the three basic response statement questions that were discussed in greater detail in Chapter 3. Those questions are as follows:

- What is my response to this text?
- What accounts for my response, in terms of the text and myself?
- What does my response tell me about myself or my culture?

Because a response statement may be in effect prewriting for a formal paper, you should be careful and thorough in writing a response statement—even if the response statement itself is not public writing. Do not, for instance, just "free associate" from your initial response (or, if you do, be sure to come back from that detour and write something in response to the second and third basic questions). If time allows or if it seems helpful, don't write a response statement all at once but on separate occasions, perhaps saving the third or second and third basic questions for the second occasion of writing. Again, if you have a writing assignment of any one or more of the four options before you read a text and write a response to it, you can start to concentrate on one of the options as you write your response statement. If your writing assignment comes along later, there are still ways to go back to a response statement and read it analytically for the potential it holds in any of those four areas.

For instance, suppose you were assigned to read "Hills Like White Elephants" in order to develop a formal paper about how your reading strategies interact with text strategies in that story. Suppose further that your first response to that story was something like "confusion" as to the main characters' relationship and the topic of their conversation. This is certainly possible considering two aspects of the text: the indirectness of the characters' conversation and the absence of a narrative voice to fill in the gaps. Your response statement in this situation could concentrate on how your "confusion" was produced by those (and perhaps other) text strategies *and* your own reading strategies, which may have been to read for plot, to look for some pattern of action in terms of conflict and resolution, and to expect some explanation from an authoritative narrator.

On the other hand, Diane Gretta was assigned a formal paper only after she had first read and responded to "Hills Like White Elephants," so she had to go back to her response statement to see what was there that might be developed in terms of any of those analytical options. You should now read Diane's response statement for yourself. It would be good practice to pretend Diane is your classmate and that you are reading her response statement to suggest to her how she might develop it into a formal paper. As you do so, look for statements that might be expanded in terms of any of the options for a formal paper listed earlier.

A college sophomore, Diane read and responded to "Hills Like White Elephants" in the first few weeks of an introductory literature course. She used the three basic questions to generate her writing. Her response statement is brief, as it should be, and she wasn't especially concerned with developing ideas or with editing for surface correctness. Here is what she wrote.

Student Writing

Diane Gretta: Response to "Hills Like White Elephants"

I enjoyed reading this short story. I have read Hemingway before and I like his style of writing. He writes beautifully; the words flow when being read and I like the descriptive quality he utilizes. He makes the story seem very realistic. I read the story once at a more superficial level, so as to enjoy it as an entertaining story. Then I proceeded to read it again and attempted to "figure out" the meaning.

I concluded that the girl is pregnant and that the man is trying to talk her into getting an abortion. She is young, innocent, and perhaps even a little naive. I think she wants to keep the baby, but is persuaded by the man's comments. He talks about how other people had this done and were happy afterward. The woman puts her own feelings aside and wants to do what the man thinks is best; she wants to make sure he will still love her afterwards. Also, the girl is very pessimistic and this is evident when she responds, "Once they take it away, you never get it back."

I think this story can be expanded to a broader, more universal scope concerning the relationship between men and women. The story is short, but it says a lot. The story shows the male-dominant character persuading the woman on something that should be her own decision. It seems that the man has his mind made up about what he wants her to do; I think the girl has different feelings, yet she is not strong enough to voice her opinion. This angers me because I believe that women should not feel subservient to men and should be an equal contributor to the relationship. Times are much different today than they were at the time the story was written, but I think Hemingway was subtly expressing the idea that women should not belittle themselves or stifle their feelings. A real relationship cannot be strong this way.

I think that my reaction to the story shows my individualism and my ideals of equality in relationships. The fact that I am a female who grew up in the 1980s probably has an impact on my beliefs. Communication is the key to *any* relationship. The man and the woman in the story talk *at* each other, not *with* each other. I also believe that society's views have drastically changed for the better in the past 30–40 years concerning women and their roles in society. It is socially acceptable for a woman to voice her feelings and to make decisions. It is also acceptable for the woman to tell that man what to do! I could just imagine revising this story to fit in with today's society and ideals. It would be very different, I am sure.

Sharing Responses During a workshop session in class not long after Diane had read "Hills Like White Elephants," she shared her response statement with a small group of her classmates who had also read and responded to that story. Talking with those other readers helped Diane in two ways when she chose to develop a paper on her response to "Hills Like White Elephants": (1) It gave her the opportunity to compare her response to the story to the responses of other readers, thereby giving her some perspective on herself as a reader and on her reading of the story; and (2) Other readers' comments on her original response statement helped her focus on certain aspects of her response as she continued her prewriting and began to draft her paper. You will see some of those comments below. In your own class, you should have a variety of opportunities to share your responses to any text you read. General class discussion is one such opportunity; working in small groups or one-on-one with other readers is another. Your teacher may set up panel discussions so that one group of readers can offer their perspectives to the whole class. Chapter 9 offers an example of a formal paper describing how different reading perspectives generate multiple interpretive options for the same text, a paper that grew not only out of the writer's initial response to a short story but also from sharing her response statement with a classmate.

Analyzing Your Response Writing a response statement and sharing your response may be the first step in prewriting a formal paper. Analyzing your response statement is an important next step. To try to be systematic about that analysis, here are some things you can do.

Thinking Critically: Question-Answer-Question First, you can take the QAQ approach to your own response statements; you can question them. Ask yourself this general question: "What have I written here that might be developed toward a formal paper?" Ask yourself these specific questions corresponding to the larger writing options:

1. What reading strategies did I use with this text? Why those? What happened when those reading strategies encountered certain text strategies? (Some reading strategies are listed on page 51 in Chapter 3; others will be discussed in the genre sections. A brief list of text strategies appears in a chart in Chapter 3, page 50.)
2. What was I assuming or expecting as I began reading this text? How were my expectations or assumptions influenced by my literary experience in

terms of the genre a particular text belongs to? How were my assumptions or expectations influenced by previous experiences with reading, in any way? How did these expectations or assumptions cause me to read the way I did?

3. What kind of ideological interaction did I experience with this text? What seems to be the ideology of the text? How do I know this? What is my own ideology in relation to the same issue or idea? Does the text confirm or challenge my beliefs or values?

4. From what perspective did I read this text? What was the effect of reading from that perspective? In the text, what harmonized or clashed with a reading from that perspective? What different perspectives might this text be read from? What would happen then?

It's a good idea to write these questions down, not just hold them in your mind. The physical act of writing, whether with a pen or pencil or at a keyboard, helps to get your brain in gear. Similarly, you should write your answers to these questions. But do remember that these answers should not be considered in terms of "right" and "wrong." In the prewriting stage especially, you should not inhibit the flow of thought and words by correcting, judging, or editing yourself. In applying the QAQ method to your own response statements, it may be helpful to practice freewriting, which is a style of writing in which you do not stop to edit or correct yourself in any way. A variation of freewriting that is helpful for some writers who work on a word processor is to turn the screen down so that the typed words are not visible. This strategy can help the words and thoughts to flow because if you can't see them, you may be less likely to change or correct them at a time when you should be concentrating on just churning them out. In any case, remember that when you do freewriting you are not producing something that anyone else will read and judge you on. You are not even writing a first draft at this point, so coherence, organization, logic, and so forth really do not matter.

Branch Diagrams Productive prewriting can also be accomplished in the form of a branch or cluster diagram. One of these was illustrated in Chapter 3 (page 49) as a way to complicate a one-word first response to a text. If you made such a diagram while writing a response statement, you could go back to it when you are prewriting a paper. Perhaps a second look would suggest new branches or clusters you could now add, or perhaps some of the branches that seemed fairly barren then may bear fruit now. If you did not make such a diagram before, try it at this point in your writing process, using one word from your first response as the central "kernel." Or make several diagrams—a sort of orchard—from several different response words as kernels. Or use this way to represent in graphic terms your reading strategies, text strategies, or elements of your life experience or the text's ideology.

Some people work better in the prewriting stage by taking a more graphic approach to representing ideas, not trying to discuss their ideas in words just yet. One of my students, Miguel Olivares, made the following diagram when he went back to a response statement he had written earlier on "Dover Beach." He used the word "interest" to describe his first response, although that

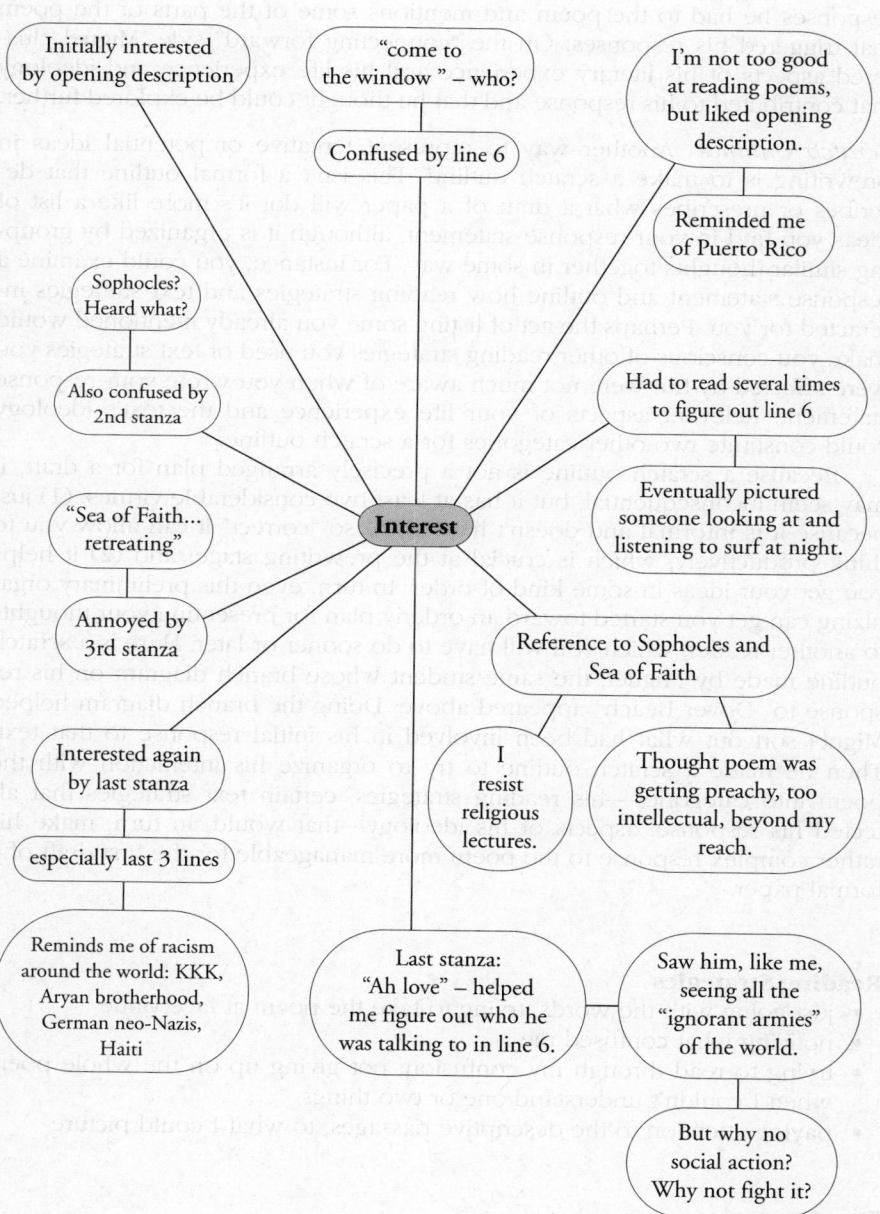

Initially interested by opening description

"come to the window" – who?

Confused by line 6

I'm not too good at reading poems, but liked opening description.

Reminded me of Puerto Rico

Sophocles? Heard what?

Also confused by 2nd stanza

"Sea of Faith... retreating"

Annoyed by 3rd stanza

Interest

Had to read several times to figure out line 6

Eventually pictured someone looking at and listening to surf at night.

Reference to Sophocles and Sea of Faith

Interested again by last stanza

especially last 3 lines

Reminds me of racism around the world: KKK, Aryan brotherhood, German neo-Nazis, Haiti

I resist religious lectures.

Thought poem was getting preachy, too intellectual, beyond my reach.

Last stanza: "Ah love" – helped me figure out who he was talking to in line 6.

Saw him, like me, seeing all the "ignorant armies" of the world.

But why no social action? Why not fight it?

response was a bit more complicated than that word may suggest. On the "connecting backward" side, Miguel's branch diagram shows other, secondary responses he had to the poem and mentions some of the parts of the poem that triggered his responses. On the "connecting forward" side, Miguel clustered aspects of his literary experience and his life experience and ideology that contributed to his response and that he thought could be explored further.

Scratch Outlines Another way to represent tentative or potential ideas in prewriting is to make a scratch outline. This isn't a formal outline that describes or prescribes what a draft of a paper will do; it's more like a list of ideas you find in your response statement, although it is organized by grouping similar thoughts together in some way. For instance, you could examine a response statement and outline how reading strategies and text strategies interacted for you. Perhaps the act of listing some you already mentioned would make you conscious of other reading strategies you used or text strategies you were affected by but were not much aware of when you wrote your response statement. Relevant aspects of your life experience and the text's ideology could constitute two other categories for a scratch outline.

Because a scratch outline is not a precisely arranged plan for a draft, it may seem inconsequential, but it has at least two considerable virtues: (1) just because it is informal and doesn't have to be so "correct" it can allow you to think productively, which is crucial at the prewriting stage; and (2) it helps you get your ideas in some kind of order. In turn, even this preliminary organizing can get you started toward an orderly plan for presenting your thoughts to another reader, which you will have to do sooner or later. Here is a scratch outline made by Miguel, the same student whose branch diagram on his response to "Dover Beach" appeared above. Doing the branch diagram helped Miguel sort out what had been involved in his initial response to that text. Then he made a scratch outline to try to organize his interaction with the poem into categories—his reading strategies, certain text strategies that affected his response, aspects of his ideology—that would, in turn, make his rather complex response to the poem more manageable for the first draft of a formal paper.

Reading Strategies
- just going with the words, trying to take the poem at face value
- noticing what confused me
- trying to read through my confusion; not giving up on the whole poem when I couldn't understand one or two things
- paying attention to the descriptive passages, to what I could picture

Text Strategies
- good descriptions in first 12 lines
- plain language there too
- references to Sophocles, the Aegean: I'm not sure about these

- seems to go way off from hearing surf: "Sea of Faith" (?)
- gets back to reality in last stanza: "ignorant armies clash by night"

My Ideology
- my childhood in P.R. and later visits there
- racism I have seen as a minority in U.S.A.
- racism, ignorance I am aware of elsewhere
- how these make me pay attention to final stanza of poem
- when I reread the poem, I understand this man's feeling that the tide of ignorance is high and the world is dark
- I understand his wanting to cling to his "love," but think that political action is more important in fighting against "ignorant armies"

Tentative Thesis The goal of all your prewriting, whichever tactic(s) you use, is to arrive at a tentative **thesis statement.** This is a sentence that does several things at once: It pulls together and gives focus to the thinking you have done informally in writing a response statement and doing other prewriting activities. And it sums up, for you and your early draft readers, what your draft will elaborate and explain.

Just as a reminder at this point, a thesis statement for a formal paper following any of the options listed on pages 57–58 should be about *your reading* of a text, not about the text itself. Go ahead and name yourself "I" and make a statement about that "I" as a reading subject interacting with a text. For instance, if you are working on the first option with "Hills Like White Elephants," your prewriting might lead to a tentative thesis statement like this: "When I read 'Hills Like White Elephants' using the reading strategy of trying to follow the plot, I was frustrated because the text strategy of a fairly plotless story did not conform to my way of reading." Such a thesis statement may be rough and in need of polish and revision; it is, after all, tentative. But it is on the right track because it is a statement about *reading* the text, not about something the text is or seems to be doing in isolation from a reader. Here is a thesis statement that may sound better as a sentence but that excludes the reader or ignores his or her contribution to the interaction: "'Hills Like White Elephants' is a fairly plotless story that is difficult to understand." Do you see the difference in emphasis? A tentative thesis statement sets the course for your first draft; it need not be a polished gem at this point as long as it gets you going.

When Diane Gretta was given the assignment to develop a paper on her reading of a short story, she went back to her response statement to "Hills Like White Elephants" to analyze its potential for development. In doing so, she noticed that her first response featured her attempt to figure out what the couple were discussing and what the larger implications of that discussion were. She saw that she had been an active reader who had attempted to resolve an indeterminacy in the text by bringing her life experience to bear. So by subjecting her initial response statement to some analysis in terms of one of the writing options, Diane was able to decide on a direction for her paper and begin to plan how she would draft a paper in that direction.

Drafting

Once you have in mind and down on paper a tentative thesis statement (a summary of the main idea your paper will explain and develop), there are basically two ways you can proceed. One way is to just start writing, almost in a freewriting mode but not so nonstop. If you have been conscientious in your prewriting, you should have a tentative thesis statement that roughly organizes what your first draft will say. The tentative thesis statement offered above for a reading of "Hills Like White Elephants" suggests an organization along the lines of a description of the person's reading strategies—probably including why he or she used those strategies, what aspects of his or her literary experience suggested he or she read the story that way—followed by a description of the text strategies that constitute "a fairly plotless story," and then an explanation of the clash that resulted from the encounter of the one strategy with the other. That's enough of an organizational plan for someone with that tentative thesis to write a first draft.

The other way to proceed would be to make another outline. Again, this need not be formal, with every topic sentence and supporting detail planned out. It could be a scratch outline similar to one you produced in prewriting, but this time laying out the sections of your first draft in the order in which you want them to occur. Then you can use this sketch plan as a basis for writing your first draft. Either way, you should consider a first draft as an opportunity to verbalize your thoughts primarily for yourself, to see how (well or poorly) they hang together, to have something you can look at critically and revise. It is not ready to go public, to be presented to your reader, although you may offer it to a surrogate reader who will give you some feedback and help you gain critical perspective on your work.

In writing a first draft, it's often a good idea to concentrate just on the body of your paper. Introductory and concluding paragraphs can easily be saved until later, when you attack your first draft again in revision. It's hard, after all, to introduce a discussion that you have yet to write. In laying out your thoughts in the body of a first draft, an important concern should be to offer explanatory support for your thesis. This support can be broken down into two levels. First are a few statements that serve to directly explain your thesis; organizationally, each of these would head up a major section of your draft. Second are details that indirectly support your thesis but directly explain the first-level statements. According to the purpose option you have chosen or been assigned, these details will be drawn variously from the four areas of the reading dynamic: your literary or life experience, the literary repertoire or the ideology of the text.

Discussing *both* the text and yourself is essential because both contribute to the reading interaction that your draft is explaining. Talking only about the text may be traditionally and academically acceptable, but only according to a model of reading and writing that leaves the reader out of consideration. Talking only about yourself may be interesting to you, but it leaves the text out of consideration. It is the *interaction* of you and the text that should be presented for the consideration, understanding, and interest of another reader or a public audience.

Below are some suggestions for organizing support for each of the four purpose options outlined earlier, assuming "Hills Like White Elephants" as the text with which you interacted. These are not exactly scratch outlines themselves, but if you plug in the particulars from your reading interaction, you can generate a scratch outline of your own.

Option 1   The ways in which your reading strategies interact with certain text strategies: what happens when you read as you do, encountering the text strategies that you do?

Tentative Thesis   Reading "Hills Like White Elephants" as if the resolution of plot would suggest a meaning to the story proved unsatisfactory for me because of the story's relative plotlessness.

Primary divisions of draft, with supporting details for each
  I. My literary experience concerning short stories.
      A. my experience with reading short stories in the past;
      B. what I expected before reading "Hills";
      C. how I expected to read it.
 II. My strategy of reading to follow plot.
      A. how I started reading "Hills": how I looked for a plot.
III. The text strategies of "Hills Like White Elephants."
      A. how I didn't find a plot;
      B. how I was surprised by the sudden ending of the story and the sense that nothing really happened.
 IV. The interaction of my reading strategies and the text strategies of the story.
      A. my feelings of frustration that I couldn't tell what the story meant.

Option 2   How your assumptions about literature in general or a genre in particular influence you to read a text in a certain way.

Tentative Thesis   My assumption that an author writes a short story in order to make a point about some aspect of life caused me to look between the lines as I read "Hills Like White Elephants."

Primary divisions and supporting details
  I. My beliefs about what literature is.
      A. literature exists to express an author's views on life or some aspect of it;
      B. a successful reading of a literary work consists of understanding the author's point.
 II. My beliefs about short stories in particular.
      A. in short stories in particular, the plot structure usually allows me to see the author's point;
      B. if the plot doesn't reveal a point, then some other text strategy, like symbolism, will.
III. My initial experience with "Hills."
      A. my first reading of "Hills" showed that plot structure and narration did not help me understand a point.

IV. How I reread the story in a different way.
   A. in my second reading, I dug between the lines and analyzed the characters' comments and movements to decide on Hemingway's point.
V. The result of this way of reading.
   A. my decision of what that point was.

You might notice that each of these approaches lends itself to a kind of narrative organization: in both cases the writer can describe her or his reading interaction as it happened through time, beginning with reference to reading experiences that preceded the encounter with "Hills Like White Elephants" and moving through a roughly chronological account of his or her reading or readings of that story. A narrative or chronological organization is useful because the draft pretty much organizes itself if the writer just recounts what happened in the order in which it happened.

Option 3   How some aspect of your life experience clashes or harmonizes with some aspect of the text's ideology.

Tentative Thesis   My beliefs about relationships between men and women clash with the relationship depicted in "Hills Like White Elephants."

Primary divisions and supporting details
   I. My experience with respect to relationships.
      A. my family situation;
      B. my gender and feminist consciousness;
      C. my relationship with my boyfriend.
   II. The text's apparent ideology.
      A. the relationship depicted in the text;
      B. the condescension of "the man";
      C. the submissiveness of "the girl";
      D. the self-denial of "the girl."
   III. The clash that results when these different values encounter each other.
      A. how the relationship depicted in the text violates my sense of the equality and open communication that I believe should exist in a relationship.

Option 4   How the text is open to different interpretive options according to the perspective from which it is read.

Tentative Thesis   "Hills Like White Elephants" takes on different meanings depending on the gender perspective of the reader and his or her position on abortion.

Primary divisions and supporting details
   I. A masculinist interpretation.
      A. the threats to the man's freedom and independence;
      B. the man's directness in pushing the issue;
      C. the woman's indirectness and avoidance of the issue.

   II. A feminist interpretation.
      A. the threats to the woman's self-determination;
      B. the man's manipulativeness;
      C. the woman's relative powerlessness.
  III. An abortion-rights interpretation.
      A. the woman's right to reproductive freedom;
      B. the couple's right to choose;
      C. the possibilities for safe and legal abortion in Europe in the 1920s.
  IV. An anti-abortion interpretation.
      A. the immorality of the couple's discussion;
      B. the immorality of their lifestyle;
      C. the selfishness of the couple.
   V. The relativity of interpretation to the perspective of the reader.
      A. how the different readings made possible by viewing the text from
         different perspectives shows the relativity of interpretation.

Combinations of these purposes are possible. Diane's paper, for example, involves an analysis of her reading strategies and the interaction of her ideology with that of the text. Rather than feel strictly limited to any one of these purposes, you should think about using your paper to describe your actual reading, whatever that may have entailed. The individual purpose options do, however, offer ways to narrow and focus your discussion so that you don't try to do too much in a relatively short paper.

Sharing and Analyzing   As mentioned above, Diane's prewriting included sharing her response statement to "Hills Like White Elephants" with two classmates who had also read the story. They wrote notes to her in the margins and at the end of her response statement. By taking part in the QAQ method, those readers helped Diane develop her response. Where Diane said she concluded that "the girl is pregnant and . . . the man is trying to talk her into getting an abortion," one classmate asked "Why do you think so?" In the same paragraph, where Diane said the woman in the story "puts her feelings aside and wants to do what the man thinks is best . . . to make sure he will still love her afterward," another reader asked, "Isn't that the classic sex talk?" One student responded to Diane's remark that "The man and the woman . . . talk *at* each other, not *with* each other" by saying "Good point!" This reader, a male, added a final comment that Diane's response seemed to be "one-sided, from the woman's view," but that her response statement "could easily be expanded" into a paper.

In undertaking that expansion, Diane used her classmates' comments and the QAQ method to analyze her response statement to see how she constructed meaning from "Hills Like White Elephants." In that analysis, Diane looked at three aspects of her first response. First, she examined her assessment of "the girl" in the story as "young, innocent, and . . . naive" and the man as "male-dominant," asking herself "Why do I say this?" This process led her to a closer examination of the dialogue in the text. Second, she questioned her statement that ". . . the girl is pregnant and . . . the man is trying to talk her into getting an abortion." This took her back to the text again to see how she constructed a certain kind of relationship within the couple. Third, she tried to analyze her first response that "this story can be expanded to a broader . . . scope concerning the relationship between men and women." It is worth noting that Diane did not try to hide her "one-sided" reading; instead, she tried to locate that reading in her experience with and beliefs about male-female relationships.

Here is Diane's first attempt at drafting a paper from her response statement. Diane did not make a scratch outline for this draft, but notice her tentative thesis at the end of the first paragraph and how its three-part structure provides a rough organization for this draft.

STUDENT WRITING
Diane Gretta: First Draft

"Hills Like White Elephants," by Ernest Hemingway, can be read two ways: first, it is an entertaining story at face value with a harmonious flow to it that makes it enjoyable to read; second, although it is quite short in length, it figuratively says a lot concerning important issues. My reading strategies followed both of these paths. I read it lightly the first time, enjoying the descriptive beauty of the passages. I then proceeded to read it again, paying more attention to it and analyzing the situation. The story has one major indeterminacy—the author does not explicitly reveal what the couple is discussing. In this paper, I will discuss the conclusions of my interpretations, how and why I derived them, and will analyze the universality of the theme in relation to our society.

By analyzing the conversation between the two characters, I concluded that the male is older than the female because he is referred to as "the man," while she is "the girl." From the very beginning, it appears that the girl is innocent, perhaps a bit naive, and a "dreamer." She looks off to the hills with the bright sun shining off of them and says, "They look like white elephants." This statement shows her imaginative and ingenuous perspective. The man shatters her creativity by his cynical response that he has never seen one. She replies, almost despondently, "No, you wouldn't have." This brief exchange of words says much about the personalities of the two characters. It is further displayed when soon after the girl attempts a playful jest; the man again shoots it down by telling her to "cut it out." In addition, it seems as if the girl is trying to impress the man, but has to ask for reinforcement from him: "I said the mountains looked like white elephants. Wasn't that bright?" If she felt confident in herself, she could say what is on her mind without asking his approval. This reminds me of a little girl searching for never-ending acceptance from her father.

It is evident that the couple has a communication problem. As soon as the one begins to talk about something meaningful, the other interrupts with a comment about a drink. Their conversation never gets anywhere because neither of them allows it to do so. The girl even reluctantly states, "That's all we do, isn't it—look at things and try new drinks?" The man does not defend this statement, which right there shows his agreement. Then the girl rationalizes her previous statement about the hills by explaining herself. She probably felt she had to do this in order to rectify herself in the man's eyes. The man replies to her statement with "Should we have another drink?"

Then the man abruptly shifts the conversation to a more serious topic. The two discuss an "operation" but never refer to exactly what kind of operation. I resolved this indeterminacy through my own interpretation. The ramifications of the conversation led me to believe that the girl is pregnant and that the man is trying to persuade her to have an abortion. The girl's innocence is greatly portrayed in this segment. It appears that the man has an answer for everything—her fears, her apprehensions. Since it appeared from the beginning of the story that the couple is not very close, I concluded that the man wants her to have an abortion because he does not want to deal with the problems of her keeping the baby; he feels this is an easy solution. He assures her that they will be happy afterward, that he has known "lots of people" who have done it, and that he "knows it's perfectly simple." It is obvious that the girl is hesitant, but she trusts this older man and want to make sure that "things will be like they were and you'll love me?" The girl puts her feelings aside and wants to do what the man thinks is best. She says she will do it "because I don't care about me." This is a very selfless act on her part, but she probably trusts the man so much and wants to please him.

Throughout the rest of the conversation, the girl responds to the man with what I perceive to contain an underlying bite of sarcasm. For example, when the man reiterates that he knows the operation is perfectly simple, the girl replies sarcastically, "Yes, you know it's perfectly simple." This shows her growing defiance toward the man. She even suggests that they stop talking; this could be resulting from the anger building inside her. Maybe she wants to stop talking before she says something she will regret. The conversation is ended; a waitress informs them that the train will arrive in five minutes. The end of the story is not very definite and left me wondering. It is as if it does not really end; it leaves much opportunity for the reader to make his/her own assumptions. I thought the girl is pretending to feel fine just to get the man to leave her alone and she did not want to talk anymore.

I think this story can be expanded to a broader, more universal scope concerning the relationship between men and women. The story shows the male-dominant character persuading the girl about something which she should have an equal part in deciding. It seems that the man has his mind made up about what he wants her to do; I think the girl has different feelings, yet is afraid to voice them. This angers me because I believe that women should not feel inferior to men and should be an equal contributor to the relationship. Times are much different today than they were at the time the story was written, but I think Hemingway was subtly expressing the idea that women should not stifle their feelings because of a man. A real relationship cannot be strong this way.

I think that my reaction to the story shows my individualism and my ideals of equality in relationships. The fact that I am a female who grew up in the 1980s probably has an impact on my beliefs. Communication is the key to *any* relationship. The man and the girl talk *at* each other, not *with* each other. I also believe that society's values have drastically changed for the better in the past 30 years concerning women and their roles in society. It is socially acceptable for a woman to voice her feelings and to make decisions. *Especially* if the decision concerns the woman's own body. It is no wonder the divorce rate is so high today. People get married prematurely; a man and a woman need to communicate their feelings, thoughts, and desires to each other. The man and the girl in "Hills Like White Elephants" lacked

the communication necessary for a successful and meaningful relationship. I think

the man persuaded the girl into having sex when the girl is obviously not ready for

it. The man should not have used his age to persuade the naive girl. Stereotypically,

he was probably only interested in the sexual aspect of the "relationship." In con-

clusion, the story depicts many themes of society concerning relationships; despite

its brevity, it covers many aspects that I am sure many readers of various ages can

relate to.

I hope you can see a couple of basic things about this draft, in relation to the earlier discussion about different purposes in academic papers. One, Diane has tried to foreground herself as reader, at least at a couple of places in this draft. This comes from working from a response statement as a form of prewriting and from realizing that her formal paper should be about her *reading* of the text, not about the story itself. Two, at the same time, she has not been able to keep her reading consistently in the foreground; she has talked a lot about the text as if it were a stable entity in which certain facts could be seen by any objective reader. On the whole, however, Diane has accomplished the major purpose of a first draft: to get her ideas down on paper in an organized fashion and to have a rough version of her paper that can be refined through revision.

Revising

The suggestions for prewriting and generating a first draft are intended to make those parts of the writing process a little easier than they might otherwise be, to reduce the anxiety that students sometimes have when confronted with the blank page that must be filled up with words and ideas, and to help avoid writer's block. Thinking of a first draft in terms of writing for yourself is one big way to accomplish those goals. But the time inevitably comes when your rough writing has to be transformed for another reader; it has to be made into a more public piece. That's what *revising* is all about. In terms of successfully communicating an analysis of your reading to a public, an audience, this phase is the most important aspect of the entire writing process. Two things will work in your favor as you revise: time and consciousness.

Time can be your ally because letting a couple of days pass between writing a first draft and starting to revise allows you to gain a little perspective on your first draft. You can look at it somewhat objectively; you can play the role of reader of your own writing, which is a step toward seeing it the way your eventual other reader will. Time also allows for the intervention of surrogate readers in your writing process. Your classmates in writing workshops, peer tutors in your campus writing center, your teacher—any or all may provide you with feedback to guide your revisions.

Being conscious of revision as a phase that transforms your rough writing into a form that satisfies another reader's needs helps you gain control over your own writing. You can manage it to achieve the goals you want it to accomplish—in this case explaining to another reader how and why you read a text the way you did or the consequences of your actions as a reader. Putting yourself in the place of that other reader is helpful, but it is crucial to get feedback from another person who can act as a temporary or surrogate reader.

You should ask the person who serves as a reviewer of your first draft several specific, other-reader-oriented questions about it. Here are some questions that should apply to any draft of a paper that uses any of the four options discussed earlier.

- What seems to be the main idea in this draft? How easy or hard is it for you to identify it?
- What parts of this draft are particularly clear? Why are they that way?
- In what parts of this draft do you need more information to understand the point being made? What kind(s) of information would you like to hear there?
- What do you particularly like about this draft?
- What two or three specific suggestions for revision might you make?

Other questions for reviewers, written with the specific purpose of your paper in mind, can be devised. It's often helpful to list specific problems you need help in solving as you revise, and to ask your reviewer's advice on those questions. Specific questions or statements are more valuable than general ones in eliciting practical feedback. Don't ask a reviewer, for instance, something like "Tell me what you think of this draft" or "Am I doing this well enough?" Make statements like "Please help me find some good places to cite the text," or ask questions like "Does the last half of the third page seem out of place? How might I integrate it more smoothly with what I was saying just before that?" Even the act of devising questions that are specific to your draft, your purpose, helps you to gain conscious control over your revision efforts.

Notice two things about the questions for reviewers offered here: (1) None of them asks a reviewer to evaluate the content of your first draft; each focuses on the practical aspects of your writing. As you revise, it is the practical matters you should attend to—how you are explaining your ideas, not the merit of the ideas themselves. (2) The questions ask reviewers to comment on the larger elements of the draft instead of on "micro" aspects of your writing such as grammar, punctuation, spelling, and word choice. Those matters that deal with the surface of your writing can be attended to when you edit; revision should be dedicated to the deeper elements of organization and development.

As you work on a revised draft of your paper, you may find that you can use some sections—paragraphs, sentences—of your first draft in their entirety. Other sections may have to be rewritten, merged, moved around, or even discarded. Feedback comments from reviewers will help you decide what kind of revision moves to make and will get you thinking in terms of the needs of another person reading your paper. With that other person in mind, here are some other questions you can ask of your first draft and attend to as you revise it.

- Is the logical relationship between your thesis and its supporting points clear?
- Does your thesis itself need to be refined, recast, modified?
- What kind of introduction will best lead up to the statement of your thesis? How much background or preliminary information about you, the text, or the reading situation does your reader need in order to see where your paper is going?
- Will your reader be able to move smoothly from one part of the body of your paper to the next or from one idea to the next? What kinds of transitional words and phrases would help your reader do this?
- Are quotations from the text integrated smoothly into your writing? Are they offered at appropriate places?
- What kind of concluding paragraph will round out your paper and best reinforce your main point or purpose in your reader's mind? Do you want to try to achieve closure on your discussion or leave it open to further consideration? Either way, what kind of conclusion will accomplish this?

In Diane's writing process, Diane got feedback on two occasions—once when her two classmates read her first response statement, as you have seen above, and again when her teacher read her first draft. In his questions and notes, Diane's instructor urged her to explain her role as a reader in deciding two particular issues that her first draft mentioned: How or why did she decide the couple in the story was discussing an abortion, as opposed to some other kind of "operation" such as cosmetic surgery or shock therapy? And how or why did she draw the conclusions she did about the kind of people these two were and their relationship? As she revised her first draft, Diane tried consciously to explain her role as reader (both her reading strategies and what she contributed from her experience and beliefs) in making meaning of her encounter with this text. Here is her revised draft, with her substantive additions in italics and annotated:

STUDENT WRITING
Diane Gretta: Revised Draft

"Hills Like White Elephants," by Ernest Hemingway, can be read

two ways. First, it is an entertaining short story at face value that is

enjoyable to read. Second, although it is short in length, it is quite

complicated when read analytically. My reading strategies followed

both of these paths. I read it the first time with the sole purpose of

my own enjoyment. I usually incorporate this reading strategy when reading a new piece of literature. Doing this also familiarizes me with the work before I attempt to analyze it. I then proceeded to read it a second time. This is when I read a work slower, pay closer attention to details, and analytically try to comprehend the story. *Because of the indeterminacies I identified in this story, I was forced to supply my own interpretations and ideas. My own beliefs about relationships were extremely active in allowing me to do this.*

By analyzing the conversation between the two characters, I concluded that the male is older than the female because in the text he is referred to as "the man" and she is "the girl." *I then proceeded to categorize these two labels according to my experience and the societal stereotypes that accompany the labels. Doing this helped me to formulate the characters' personalities and to build images of them in my mind.* I pictured the man as being strong, stilted, prudent, cynical, and sophisticated. I imagined the girl as being carefree, innocent, naive, and a dreamer. *This aided me in interpreting the way in which sentences were said by the characters.* For example, the girl looks off to the hills and says, "They look like white elephants" (43). The man seems to shatter her imaginative remark by the cynical response that he has never seen one. She replies almost despondently, "No, you wouldn't have" (43). This brief exchange of words in my opinion says a great deal about the personalities of the two characters. It is further displayed when the girl attempts a playful jest; the man again shoots it down by telling her to "cut it out" (44). *It seems that the characters do fit in with the stereotypes that I brought to the story. I derived these interpretations of personality from my life experience and stereotypes I see in our culture. The views and opinions that are set in my mind are what led me to interpret the story as I do.*

Diane's thesis has been revised to emphasize her reading of the text.

Diane acknowledges her experience as a factor in constructing the relationship between the characters.

She mentions the interaction between the dialog and her developing construction of the characters.

This passage shows her awareness of the role of her experience in interpretation.

While I attempted to build my interpretations of the characters, I became very involved in trying to understand the conflict situation between the man and the girl. *My opinions concerning relationships come from personal experience, listening to friends' experiences, television, movies, and novels. From this diverse group of sources I have developed opinions about what I believe to be a good relationship between a man and a woman. I used these beliefs to aid me in establishing the relationship between the man and the girl in the story.* I think that their relationship is not a very strong one because of their communication problem. I believe you cannot have a solid relationship unless both partners are open and honest about their feelings. The conversation between the man and the girl seems to be superficial and they do not appear to be very close. I took the information that I brought to the text and compared the man and the girl's relationship to that information; it was not consistent. The girl states, "That's all we do, isn't it—look at things and try new drinks?" (44).

I tried to utilize the reading strategy of consistency building in figuring out the relationship between the two characters. I thought I had formed my interpretation until I arrived at the section where the man says, "I love you" and "I care about you" (45). Also, he says, "I don't want you to do it if you don't want to" (45). In the latter part of the story the man seems to be showing support for the girl and expressing emotion towards her. This is quite different from my first interpretations. I concluded that maybe they did love each other but did not know how to express themselves. I again referred to my prior experience in order to arrive at these conclusions.

The next text strategy that I tried to conquer was the indeterminacy that I noticed in the text. The man and the girl begin discussing some operation, but neither one ever explicitly says what

This passage shows her recognition of some of the sources of her beliefs.

Diane acknowledges a reading strategy.

kind of operation. The first thought that came into my mind was that the girl is pregnant with the man's baby and they are contemplating abortion. Even though I do not think the man and the girl have a close relationship, I believe they engaged in sexual activity. This could be part of what keeps them together. *People who are not close still have sex. The cues I received from the text, combined with my previous experience, led me to this conclusion. Abortion is such a current issue that it was readily available in my mind to consider it as a possibility.*

I used consistency building to reinforce my first idea of resolving the indeterminacy. I feel that the story is consistent with my interpretation that the girl is pregnant and that the man wants her to get an abortion. First, the man talks of an operation that is "not really an operation at all" (44). The girl at first is obviously uncomfortable with the conversation because at first she stares at the ground and says nothing. "I'll go with you and stay with you the whole time" implies that it is the girl who will be operated on and that the man could stay with her while she gets it done (44). *I know that when a female gets an abortion, she is allowed to have a person stay with her while she is getting the abortion performed. I think this is what the man is referring to.* Next, the man tries to persuade the girl even more by telling her that he knows "lots of people who have done it" (45). Finally, I got the impression that the decision being discussed was one of absolute importance that would affect both of their lives. They speak of how it is the best thing to do and of what their relationship will be like afterwards. The girl asks, "And if I do it you'll be happy and things will be like they were and you'll love me?" (45). These factors reinforced my original interpretation of the abortion issue.

Diane recognizes a cultural source for her interpretation.

She recognizes the combined effect of this cultural source and her primary reading strategy.

Diane's prior knowledge is mentioned again.

Because of the closeness in age between the girl and myself and because of the fact that I am also a female, I feel that I can relate to the girl from a more personal level. I think this greatly influenced my interpretation of the story because I can easily put myself in the girl's position and know how I would react or feel in the same situation. I suppose this could be considered a reading strategy. I can understand how the girl must trust this older man and how she just wants to make him happy. She sees how much he wants her to get an abortion and she trusts him and his opinions.

Diane admits to the situational perspective from which she reads and acknowledges its effect.

I think that the girl was persuaded by the man in making her decision. This idea was reinforced by several factors in the text. First, the man does most of the talking when they discuss their decision. This shows his dominance while it shows her reluctance and indecision. Second, he refers to "other people" that have gotten it done in order to back up his argument. This probably makes her think, "Well, if other people did it and were happy afterward, then maybe it is the right thing to do." Finally, he talks about how "perfectly simple" the procedure is. He does this to ease the girl's apprehensions about pain and possibly even moral and ethical concerns. For these reasons, which I inferred from consistency building and character analysis, I feel that the man persuaded the girl. But the girl allowed this to happen because she did not voice her opinion and true feelings. All in all, the man puts up a solid argument and the girl ultimately gives in.

There was one final piece of information that I came across that reinforced my idea that the girl is pregnant and is contemplating an abortion. *I found in my thesaurus that a "white elephant" is a nuisance, embarrassment, burden, or impediment.* If a couple really does not want to have a child, these words are exactly what the baby could become to the parents. Therefore, I think that the author intentionally used this term not just to describe the sun shining on the hills, but for symbolic reasons. *This just reinforced my original interpretation.*

I think this story can be expanded to a broader, more universal scope concerning the relationship between men and women. The story shows the male-dominant character persuading the girl about something which she should have an equal part in deciding. It seems that the man has his mind made up about what he wants her to do. I think the girl has different feelings, yet is afraid to voice them. This angers me because I believe that women should not feel inferior to men and should be an equal contributor to the relationship. *The values that I was brought up with and any cohort effects combined to form my beliefs.*

I think that my reaction to the story shows my individualism and my ideals of equality in relationships. The fact that I am a female who grew up in the 1980s had an impact on my beliefs. Communication is the key to any relationship. The man and the girl talk **at** each other, not **with** each other. I also believe that society's views have drastically changed in the right direction concerning women and their role in society. It is socially acceptable for a woman to voice her feelings and to make decisions. **Especially** if the decision concerns the woman's own body. The man and the girl in the story lacked the communication necessary for a successful and meaningful relationship.

Never before when reading a text have I encountered such an interaction between the text and my prior experience and beliefs. Because of the indeterminacy in the text, I was free to analyze the characters and to interpret the situation. My experience and the reading strategy of consistency building helped me in forming these interpretations.

Diane tacitly admits another reading strategy and sees its effect.

She mentions again the role of beliefs she brought to the text.

She concludes with a concise summary of her interaction with the text, which involved both her reading strategies and the operation of her prior beliefs and experiences.

A conscientiously revised version of your paper should, like Diane's revised draft, begin to assume the shape of a piece of public writing, even if it has not yet been edited for surface correctness. It should also be a separate document from your first draft, both to emphasize revision as a discrete operation in the overall writing process and to provide a relatively "clean" version of your paper that can be edited for surface correctness.

Editing

As your writing process nears completion, you can turn your attention to polishing up the surface of your writing so that it is presentable for public display. *Editing* your revised draft means reading it again, this time with an eye toward its conformity to the conventions of correctness in academic writing: grammatically correct sentences, standard usage and spelling, punctuation that helps your reader see how the parts of your sentences relate to one another. Gaps and indeterminacies may be interesting text strategies in a literary text, but if those are created in a formal paper by erratic punctuation, nonstandard spelling, and incorrect grammar, they only inhibit your reader's understanding of what you are trying to say.

The editing phase of the writing process is also a time for you to look at the efficiency of your prose style. If you are writing an expository essay, one quality of your writing you might try to ensure is tightness. Try to make every word count; look for places where you might eliminate redundancies and wordiness. You can use time profitably again here by asking a peer to edit your revised draft—not actually to make surface changes in your writing, but to call potential trouble spots to your attention so you can make the changes. If you must edit your own writing, it can help to read it once from back to front, a paragraph at a time, so as to avoid getting swept along by the flow of your prose and thus missing some surface errors. Referring to a good style handbook and a dictionary is appropriate here too.

Saving this kind of editing for last in the writing process also allows you to attend to more substantive matters first. Making your writing correct in terms of grammar, punctuation, and spelling is important, but that effort should not interfere with letting your thoughts flow in a first draft and then shaping and strengthening the communication of them in revision.

Toward Further Revision

Diane's paper is clearly moving in the direction of a self-conscious analysis, although there are several areas where it could go further and deeper. She does mention the role of her prior experience and beliefs in her interpretation of the text, but that analysis tends to be superficial. Reading this text, Diane appears to be what is sometimes called "written by contradictory discourses" from her cultural situation. This is evident in her conflicting responses to "the girl" in the story. On the one hand, Diane says, because of her own position as a female she can relate to the girl's giving in to "the man" on the abortion question: the girl trusts the man and wants to make him happy. On the other, Diane says she is angered by the girl's inability to voice her feelings about the abortion and about the couple's relationship because Diane believes women should not feel inferior and should have an equal voice in matters that concern them. She says that growing up in the 1980s probably contributed to her feelings about what a relationship should be in this regard, but she seems unaware that growing up in the 1980s for most American women also still means making concessions to traditional stereotypes. It's not that Diane should necessarily resolve this contradiction one way or the other, but a more careful cultural analysis on her part might have allowed her to become conscious of this contradiction and acknowledge it.

There may be a clue as to why Diane left this stone unturned in her statement that she adopted *consistency building* as a reading strategy: that would tend to downplay or ignore inconsistencies and conflicts, both in Diane's own experience and in her interpretation of the characters. At one point, she does admit a problem in her reading strategy when it appears the man really may love the girl, but she lets that drop without further analysis. She could consider how her reading strategy tends to smooth over inconsistencies, or she could try to confront this apparent inconsistency in her response and subject it to analysis of her cognitive style. Does she generally prefer to dismiss rather than tolerate contradictions? Again, it is not a matter of the rightness or wrongness of whatever Diane might say, but simply her becoming more aware of the dynamic of her reading.

To look for a moment at some editing Diane might do, I would suggest she could tighten her writing and liven up her style at the same time by cutting out many of the "I think" and "I feel that" phrases that dot the body of this draft. Her acknowledgment of herself as reader in her introductory paragraph and her references to her particular reading strategies and her ideology are enough to foreground herself in her paper. She doesn't need to repeatedly qualify her statements with those tag phrases.

Editing aside, however, Diane's revised draft is rich in possibilities for further development. Sometimes writing comes close to fulfilling its potential, sometimes it doesn't. It's often in the nature of academic assignments to put arbitrary closure on a project: it's due on a certain day, and Diane, like most students, has other demands on her time. Perhaps someday she will come back to "Hills Like White Elephants," even if not to write a school assignment on it. Her response may be different. Her awareness of what's involved in her response may be richer. She is in process; her reading and writing are in process. The text too may seem very different to her after some time has gone by.

Part
Two

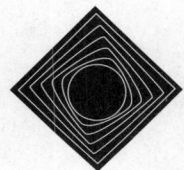

Reading
and
Responding
to
Fiction

5 ◊ WHAT IS FICTION?

It may not be justified to say that most art or literary forms are universal, but it is probably safe to say that everybody, regardless of cultural background or literary **ideology**, likes stories—likes to hear them and likes to tell them, even if everyone doesn't always like or have experience with reading them. But certainly if you have gone through a Western or Westernized educational system to the point of college, you have a good deal of familiarity with reading stories (and probably less with hearing them told by a storyteller).

The Appeal of Stories

Outside the academic context, stories are common in your life in the sense that you often recount, and hear others' accounts of, events or episodes in life in **narrative** form. Just the "and then, and then, and then . . ." sequence in which you often experience events as well as retell them to others puts something of a narrative structure over what is called reality, and in that way makes narratives that you encounter in reading seem natural enough, perhaps even **realistic.** So when you consider fiction, part of what makes it comfortable for you is this resemblance to certain actual practices in your life. Of course, you also are probably aware that fiction, as distinguished from real life, is made up, even if you don't think of the chronological sequence in which fictional events may be narrated as especially artificial.

The category of fiction to be considered in this part is the **short story,** a kind of writing that has its roots in oral traditions going back thousands of years. In many preliterate ancient societies, oral narratives were a way of passing on and teaching religious and cultural understandings of the world. The **didactic,** or instructional, purpose of these tales of racial heroes and divine personages was enhanced because the stories were entertaining to hear. Narratives such as the ancient Greek Homer's tales of the Trojan War and the subsequent wanderings of Odysseus (*The Iliad* and *The Odyssey*) were written down in verse rather than in prose because in preliterate societies storytellers used rhyme and rhythm as memorization aids. The Babylonian *Epic of Gilgamesh* and the Anglo-Saxon *Beowulf* are other examples of very early mythological stories that have survived because eventually they were recorded in writing. The Bible also contains ancient narratives such as the accounts of the creation of the world, the temptation and fall of Adam and Eve, Cain's killing of Abel, and the stories of Ruth and Jonah. You may also be familiar with the fables recorded by the Greek slave Aesop, which date back to the sixth century B.C. These stories, both much shorter and less monumental in scope and cultural implication than the epics, also took advantage of narrative's capacity to please in order to instruct by attaching an explicit moral to the end of a brief narrative, usually concerning animal characters. Similarly, the parables of Jesus recorded in the New Testament use narrative to teach a moral or religious lesson.

In the European Middle Ages, the French Marie de France (writing in England), the Italian Giovanni Boccaccio, and the English Geoffrey Chaucer adapted existing tales and fashioned new versions of them. Marie's *lais* and Chaucer's *The Canterbury Tales* were written in verse, Boccaccio's *Decameron* in prose. The work of all three writers reflects the increasing secularization of literature in the late Middle Ages; none of the three was especially concerned with overtly teaching or reinforcing ideological beliefs, an important function of the earlier story types mentioned above. Chaucer's tales also represent an advance in narrative by their introduction of moral ambiguity and complexity similar to that in stories of the present day. By putting the tales in the mouths of his fictional pilgrims, Chaucer achieved a degree of distance from the moral implications of any of the tales, thus making the moral authority of the whole text indeterminate. It's hard to say for sure where Chaucer the author stood because he even fictionalized himself as one of the pilgrims who is repeating to his reader everything he heard the other pilgrims say. And this pilgrim-Chaucer adds a disclaimer to the effect that anyone finding any of the stories to be immoral or indecent should not blame him because he is merely telling what he heard!

As a prose form, the short story got a boost in both artistic status and popularity in nineteenth-century Europe and the United States. The rise to economic and cultural dominance of an industrial middle class in that era created a larger, more affluent, and more widely literate audience than had been known before.

The development of the novel had accompanied the growth of the middle class from the eighteenth century, but the spread of magazines in the nineteenth century promoted a kind of short fiction that could be written for and published by that medium. The American writer and critic Edgar Allan Poe was the first modern theorist of the short story. He promoted the short story as a discrete genre, which he called the "tale." Poe was not especially interested in realism as an end in itself or as a style, but neither was he a proponent of didactic or moralistic fiction. He argued that a tale should create a unified "effect or impression" on the reader and that economy of treatment was essential to this. His influential criticism in the 1840s emphasized the artistic craft of short story writing to achieve the kinds of effects he thought were essential to the genre.[1]

Poe's ideas and his own stories, along with those of other nineteenth-century Western writers such as Nathaniel Hawthorne, Sarah Orne Jewett, and Henry James in the United States; Alphonse Daudet and Guy de Maupassant in

---

[1]Perhaps the best single source for Poe's theories of the short story is his review of Nathaniel Hawthorne's *Twice-Told Tales*, which appeared originally in *Graham's Magazine* in 1842. It has been widely reprinted.

France; and Aleksandr Pushkin and Nikolay Gogol in Russia, helped to make the short story as much of a serious or high art form as poetry or drama. In contrast to the earlier forms of narratives surveyed above, the nineteenth-century short story concerned itself less with legendary, fabulous, or aristocratic personages and more with ordinary, middle-class people; less with making a moral point and more with creating an effect or impression or with presenting a slice of daily life.

In the 1880s, another influential critic, the American novelist and short story writer William Dean Howells, said that "fidelity to experience and probability of motive" were "essential conditions of a great imaginative literature." In saying this, Howells was basically making realism synonymous with fiction as art.[2] Whatever short stories you have read in English classes in high school or college probably come from this high art tradition, the **canon** of Western literature, and are no older than roughly 150 years.

You may have read or at least heard of such twentieth-century writers of short stories as James Joyce, Ernest Hemingway, F. Scott Fitzgerald, Eudora Welty, Joyce Carol Oates, and Bobbie Ann Mason. They and others have continued the tradition of the realistic short story as a serious art form. At the same time, the twentieth century has seen the development of the *experimental* story, which, to generalize, plays against the **conventions** of the genre as established in the realist tradition. Writers such as Donald Barthelme, Jorge Luis Borges, Angela Carter, Gabriel García Márquez, Gertrude Stein, and Ronald Sukenick have challenged such traditional practices as plot, character, point of view, and psychological or physical probability. In so doing they have also challenged the expectations of readers and demonstrated the continuing evolution of the short story form.

But even outside of the canon of art stories, you are probably comfortable with narrative as a way of representing reality because virtually everyone uses it to recount experiences to friends, parents, children, coworkers, and so on. You can't literally relive an experience, for yourself or someone else, so you convert it into narrative form. And in doing so, you often use many of the following **text strategies** that have become conventional with fictional stories.

- a **plot** or structure to the sequence of related events, including perhaps the common plot elements of **conflict** and **resolution**
- a **setting** or location in space and time where the related events occurred
- **characters** in your version of the people involved in the related events
- **point of view** from which the events are related to your listener
- a **style** of language in which the events are related, perhaps marked by a certain **tone** or attitude toward the events themselves, the people involved in them, your listener, or all three
- a **theme,** if your story has a moral or ethical point to it or even just an aesthetic resolution

---

[2]Howells' comments first appeared in his column for *Harper's Monthly* magazine, "The Editor's Study," in 1887. Like Poe's review of Hawthorne, cited above, this essay has been widely reprinted. It is included in a collection of Howells' work titled *Criticism and Fiction,* published in 1891.

READING CULTURE Narratives in Other Media: A Music Video

In addition to narrating your own experiences and hearing others narrate theirs, you may be used to "reading" narratives in other media, such as movies and television. These nonliterary texts use text strategies similar to those listed just above as conventions of short stories, although you may not be conscious of them as such. You may also not be aware of your strategies for processing such texts as narratives, but I think you do use some of the same cognitive strategies for music videos as you do for short stories.

To illustrate this and to indicate something of the **intertextuality** across the genres of short story and music video, I will refer to a music video: Tom Petty and the Heartbreakers' "Mary Jane's Last Dance," produced by Maria Gallagher and directed by Keir McFarlane. To follow this discussion, it's not necessary for you to have seen this video, although obviously your understanding will be enhanced if you have it in your storehouse of texts. Whether you do or not, I will provide a brief synopsis.

Tom Petty appears as an attendant in a morgue. One night at work, he discovers the body of a beautiful woman, presumably "Mary Jane," among the corpses being prepared for autopsy. Apparently overcome by an attraction for her beauty, he slips out of the morgue with this body and carries it home, where he prepares an intimate dinner for two. He dresses up in his best formal clothes and outfits the body in a party dress and makes up her face. They "dance" (presumably the "last dance" of the song's title) before he carries her out of his house and down to the sea. Laying her down in the water, he bids her farewell and turns to walk back to dry land. The last shot in the video shows the submerged body open her eyes.

To refresh your memory if you have seen the video, or to help you envision it if you have not, pages 90–91 show some still photographs of the video. The first group is from the early part of the video, as Tom Petty's character is leaving the morgue's examining room with the woman's body on a gurney. The second group of photographs shows him preparing the corpse for their formal dinner, and the third shows him carrying her to the sea.

Even though music video is not usually considered a literary genre, this particular one may be analyzed as a narrative. Doing so should reveal its use of several text strategies that will be discussed in connection with short stories in the following chapters. It will also suggest some of the **reading strategies,** similar to those used with short stories, that are involved in watching it. On another level, this analysis may call into question the distinction often insisted upon in Western culture between popular or "low" art on the one hand and serious or "high" art on the other.

First, the video establishes characters: Tom (the mortician) and Mary Jane. A viewer may become interested in those characters, particularly Tom, as people and tend to forget they are fictional creations. This effect is likely to be enhanced by your ability to actually see the characters in this medium. Second, the video has a setting or settings: the morgue, Tom's house, the seashore. Seeing the characters in these settings may work in two contrary ways; it enhances their believability as people and reveals **gaps** concerning them. Who is

"Mary Jane," or who was she when alive? What is the motivation for Tom's actions? How or why did Tom come to live in that house if he, presumably, makes a minimum salary as an attendant at the morgue? Third, the video has a plot: Tom apparently "falls in love" with the beautiful dead woman; "kidnaps" her body from the morgue; takes her home for dinner and dancing; and returns her to the sea, where, perhaps, she revives. This sequence of events loosely follows the usual structure of a narrative plot: conflict → rising action → climax → denouement. The "perhaps" I attached to the corpse's "revival" indicates an **indeterminacy** in the ending of the story: Has she come back to life from the dead, was she ever dead at all, or has Tom's love saved her in a spiritual way?

Some of the gaps I cited above may be filled by viewers reading certain text strategies as **symbols:** Perhaps the woman is Venus or an embodiment of romantic love, not so much a real person. Perhaps the sea is not so much a physical thing or place as it is an elemental or eternal principle—life and death together in one. Viewers may also create a theme as they read the video. Perhaps it is about how (obsessive or redeeming) love conquers all, or, less in terms of a moral, how a lonely man has his rather pathetic moment of true love.

Whatever tendency you have to see an idea such as any of these unifying or explaining the other text strategies in the video reveals **consistency building** as a reading strategy. Your tendency to entertain different, even contradictory, explanations for the characters or what they do or mean indicates **wandering viewpoint** as a reading strategy.

Finally, the video may be read as intertextual, according to the literary or textual experience a reader brings to it. *Intertextuality* is the implicit reference in one text to another or the influence of one text on another, whether the texts are "high" art or "low" art. For me, this video refers to William Faulkner's short story "A Rose for Emily" (reprinted on pages 399–405) and to Edgar Allan Poe's poem "The Sleeper" (reprinted on pages 755–756). I'm not saying that Tom Petty or the producer or director of the video was consciously referring to either of those canonical texts. Maybe they were, maybe they weren't. But the presence of the Faulkner story and the Poe poem in my storehouse of texts allows me to see connections between the video and them, and that intertextuality makes no cultural distinctions between "high" and "low" art.

Like any music video, this one is also intertextual with the song it uses and interprets. As a song, "Mary Jane's Last Dance" belongs to a different genre. (The lyrics appear below.) As an interpretation, the video is a **strong reading** of that song. If you can recall the video, comparing it with the song lyrics should indicate the differences in emphases or even in theme in the two texts. If you have not seen the video, perhaps the synopsis given earlier will help you see these differences. As with other strong readings such as film treatments of novels or short stories or theatrical productions of plays, music videos' capacity to close down interpretive options of the songs they treat sometimes raises objections among viewers. If that is the case with you and "Mary Jane's Last Dance," may I suggest you sketch out your own video of that song? That action would be one way of asserting your own reading of that text

Frame enlargements taken from
the video "Mary Jane's Last Dance."
Greatest Hits. Tom Petty and the
Heartbreakers. © 1992 MCA

7

8

9

10

11

12

and of working out that strong reading in a creative medium. It would also give you another perspective on intertextuality, as the text you create is influenced by and refers to the existing text of the song.

Tom Petty   b. 1953

Mary Jane's Last Dance   *1993*

She grew up in an Indiana town
Had a good-looking mama who never was around.
But she grew up tall and she grew up right
With them Indiana boys on an Indiana night.

Well, she moved down here at the age of eighteen.   5
She blew the boys away, was more than they had seen.
I was introduced and we first started grooving,
She said "I dig you, baby, but I gotta keep moving."
(. . . on, keep moving on.)

Chorus
Last dance with Mary Jane   10
One more time to kill the pain.
I feel summer creeping in
And I'm tired of this town again.

Well, I don't know, but I been told
You never slow down, you never grow old.   15
Tired of screwing up, tired of going down,
Tired of myself, tired of this town.

Oh my my, oh hell, yes!
Honey put on that party dress!
Buy me a drink, sing me a song.   20
Take me as I come, 'cause I can't stay long.
Chorus

There's pigeons now on market square.
She's standing in her underwear
Looking down from her hotel room.
Nightfall will be coming soon.   25

Oh my my, oh hell, yes!
You got to put on that party dress.
It was too cold to cry when I woke up alone,
I hit the last number. I walked to the road.
Chorus

With those ideas about narrative as applied to a music video in mind, it's time to turn to a narrative in a more traditional genre: a short story.

Reading Strategies

As a start, consider a text from one of the nineteenth-century fiction writers mentioned above: Guy de Maupassant. Before you read his story "The Necklace," take a few minutes to write down, in the box provided or in your journal, some answers to the following questions, in order to heighten your consciousness of your **literary experience** with respect to short fiction. Be prepared to share your notes with others as part of class discussion.

- What do you expect a short story to be or to have? Based on your experience with short stories, what features, elements, conventions, etc., have you come to expect?
- What do you expect to do as a reader? What will you look for? What kind of mental operations will you probably undertake as you read?

MY EXPECTATIONS FOR A SHORT STORY

The text	Myself as a reader
1.	1.
2.	2.
3.	3.
4.	4.
5.	5.

As you read through "The Necklace," also make some brief notes, in the box on page 94 or in your journal, about what's actually happening in the process of your reading of this text. The following questions will help you focus your thoughts.

- When and why do you start to predict what will happen next? Do your predictions change as you read on? If so, when and why?
- When do you start to form any judgments of the characters? Why do you make the judgments you make? Do your judgments change as you read on? If so, when and why?
- Do you ever make any interpretations, draw any conclusions about theme? If you do, how easy or hard is it to do this? What helps or hinders you in doing this?

> ### What happens as I read "The Necklace"
>
> Predictions:
>
>
> Judgments:
>
>
> Interpretations:

Guy de Maupassant   1850–1893

The Necklace   *1884*

Translated by Edgar V. Roberts

She was one of those pretty and charming women, born, as if by an error of destiny, into a family of clerks and copyists. She had no dowry, no prospects, no way of getting known, courted, loved, married by a rich and distinguished man. She finally settled for a marriage with a minor clerk in the Ministry of Education.

She was a simple person, without the money to dress well, but she was as unhappy as if she had gone through bankruptcy, for women have neither rank nor race. In place of high birth or important family connections, they can rely only on their beauty, their grace, and their charm. Their inborn finesse, their elegant taste, their engaging personalities, which are their only power, make working-class women the equals of the grandest ladies.

She suffered constantly, feeling herself destined for all delicacies and luxuries. She suffered because of her grim apartment with its drab walls, threadbare furniture, ugly curtains. All such things, which most other women in her situation would not even have noticed, tortured her and filled her with despair. The sight of the young country girl who did her simple housework awakened in her only a sense of desolation and lost hopes. She daydreamed of large, silent anterooms, decorated with oriental tapestries and lighted by high bronze floor lamps, with two elegant valets in short culottes dozing in large armchairs under the effects of forced-air heaters. She visualized large drawing rooms draped in the most expensive silks, with fine end tables on which were placed knickknacks of inestimable value. She dreamed of the perfume of dainty private rooms, which were designed only for intimate tête-à-têtes with the closest friends, who because of their achievements and fame would make her the envy of all other women.

When she sat down to dinner at her round little table covered with a cloth that had not been washed for three days, in front of her husband who opened the kettle while declaring ecstatically, "Ah, good old boiled beef! I don't know anything better," she dreamed of expensive banquets with shining place settings, and wall hangings depicting ancient heroes and exotic birds in an enchanted forest. She imagined a gourmet-prepared main course carried on the most exquisite trays and served on the most beautiful dishes, with whispered gallantries which she would hear with a sphinxlike smile as she dined on the pink meat of a trout or the delicate wing of a quail.

She had no decent dresses, no jewels, nothing. And she loved nothing but these; she believed herself born only for these. She burned with the desire to please, to be envied, to be attractive and sought after.

She had a rich friend, a comrade from convent days, whom she did not want to see anymore because she suffered so much when she returned home. She would weep for the entire day afterward with sorrow, regret, despair, and misery.

Well, one evening, her husband came home glowing and carrying a large envelope.

"Here," he said, "this is something for you."

She quickly tore open the envelope and took out a card engraved with these words:

> *The Chancellor of Education and Mrs. George Ramponneau request that Mr. and Mrs. Loisel do them the honor of coming to dinner at the Ministry of Education on the evening of January 8.*

Instead of being delighted, as her husband had hoped, she threw the invitation spitefully on the table, muttering:

"What do you expect me to do with this?"

"But honey, I thought you'd be glad. You never get to go out, and this is a special occasion! I had a lot of trouble getting the invitation. Everyone wants one; the demand is high and not many clerks get invited. Everyone important will be there."

She looked at him angrily and stated impatiently:

"What do you want me to wear to go there?"

He had not thought of that. He stammered:

"But your theater dress. That seems nice to me ..."

He stopped, amazed and bewildered, as his wife began to cry. Large tears fell slowly from the corners of her eyes to her mouth. He said falteringly:

"What's wrong? What's the matter?"

But with a strong effort she had recovered, and she answered calmly as she wiped her damp cheeks:

"Nothing, except that I have nothing to wear and therefore can't go to the party. Give your invitation to someone else at the office whose wife will have nicer clothes than mine."

Distressed, he responded:

"Well, all right, Mathilde. How much would a new dress cost, something you could use at other times, but not anything fancy?"

She thought for a few minutes, adding things up and thinking also of an amount that she could ask without getting an immediate refusal and a frightened outcry from the frugal clerk.

Finally she responded tentatively:

"I don't know exactly, but it seems to me that I could get by on four hundred francs."   25

He blanched slightly at this, because he had set aside just that amount to buy a shotgun for Sunday lark-hunts the next summer with a few friends in the Plain of Nanterre.

However, he said:

"All right, you've got four hundred francs, but make it a pretty dress."

As the day of the party drew near, Mrs. Loisel seemed sad, uneasy, anxious, even though her gown was all ready. One evening her husband said to her:

"What's the matter? You've been acting funny for several days."   30

She answered:

"It's awful, but I don't have any jewels to wear, not a single gem, nothing to dress up my outfit. I'll look like a beggar. I'd almost rather not go to the party."

He responded:

"You can wear a corsage of cut flowers. This year it's all the rage. For only ten francs you can get two or three gorgeous roses."

She was not convinced.   35

"No . . . there's nothing more humiliating than looking shabby in the company of rich women."

But her husband exclaimed:

"God, but you're silly! Go to your friend Mrs. Forrestier, and ask her to lend you some jewelry. You know her well enough to do that."

She uttered a cry of joy:

"That's right. I hadn't thought of that."   40

The next day she went to her friend's house and described her problem.

Mrs. Forrestier went to her mirrored wardrobe, took out a large jewel box, opened it, and said to Mrs. Loisel:

"Choose, my dear."

She saw bracelets, then a pearl necklace, then a Venetian cross of finely worked gold and gems. She tried on the jewelry in front of a mirror, and hesitated, unable to make up her mind about each one. She kept asking:

"Do you have something else?"   45

"Certainly. Look to your heart's content. I don't know what will please you most."

Suddenly, she found, in a black satin box, a superb diamond necklace, and her heart throbbed with desire for it. Her hands shook as she picked it up. She fastened it around her neck, watched it gleam at her throat, and looked at herself ecstatically.

Then she asked, haltingly and anxiously:

"Could you lend me this, nothing but this?"

"Why yes, certainly."

She jumped up, hugged her friend joyfully, then hurried away with her treasure.

The day of the party came. Mrs. Loisel was a success. She was prettier than anyone else, stylish, graceful, smiling, and wild with joy. All the men saw her, asked her name, sought to be introduced. All the important administrators stood in line to waltz with her. The Chancellor himself eyed her.

She danced joyfully, passionately, intoxicated with pleasure, thinking of nothing but the moment, in the triumph of her beauty, in the glory of her success, on cloud nine with happiness made up of all the admiration, of all the aroused desire, of this victory so complete and so sweet to the heart of any woman.

She did not leave until four o'clock in the morning. Her husband, since midnight, had been sleeping in a little empty room with three other men whose wives had also been enjoying themselves.

He threw over her shoulders the shawl that he had brought for the trip home, a modest everyday wrap, the poverty of which contrasted sharply with the elegance of her evening gown. She felt it and hurried away to avoid being noticed by the other women who luxuriated in rich furs.

Loisel tried to hold her back:

"Wait a minute. You'll catch cold outdoors. I'll call a cab."

But she paid no attention and hurried down the stairs. When they reached the street they found no carriages. They began to look for one, shouting at cabmen passing by at a distance.

They walked toward the Seine, desperate, shivering. Finally, on a quay, they found one of those old night-going buggies that are seen in Paris only after dark, as if they were ashamed of their wretched appearance in daylight.

It took them to their door, on the Street of Martyrs, and they sadly climbed the stairs to their flat. For her, it was finished. As for him, he could think only that he had to begin work at the Ministry of Education at ten o'clock.

She took the shawl off her shoulders, in front of the mirror, to see herself once more in her glory. But suddenly she cried out. The necklace was no longer around her neck!

Her husband, already half undressed, asked:

"What's wrong?"

She turned toward him frantically:

"I . . . I . . . I no longer have Mrs. Forrestier's necklace."

He stood up bewildered:

"What! . . . How! . . . It's not possible!"

And they looked in the folds of the gown, in the folds of the shawl, in the pockets, everywhere. The found nothing.

He asked:

"You're sure you still had it when you left the party?"

"Yes. I checked it in the vestibule of the Ministry."

"But if you had lost it in the street, we would have heard it fall. It must be in the cab."

"Yes, probably. Did you notice the number?"

"No. Did you see it?"

"No."

Overwhelmed, they looked at each other. Finally, Loisel got dressed again:

"I'm going out to retrace all our steps," he said, "to see if I can find the necklace that way."

And he went out. She stayed in her evening dress, without the energy to get ready for bed, stretched out in a chair, drained of strength and thought.

Her husband came back at about seven o'clock. He had found nothing.

He went to Police Headquarters and to the newspapers to announce a reward. He went to the small cab companies, and finally he followed up even the slightest hopeful lead.

She waited the entire day, in the same enervated state, in the face of this frightful disaster.

Loisel came back in the evening, his face pale and haggard. He had found nothing.

"You'll have to write to your friend," he said, "that you broke a clasp on her necklace and that you are having it fixed. That will give us time to look around."

She wrote as he dictated.

At the end of a week they had lost all hope.

And Loisel, looking five years older, declared:

"We'll have to see about replacing the jewels."

The next day they took the case which had contained the necklace and went to the jeweler whose name was inside. He looked at his books:

"I wasn't the one, Madam, who sold the necklace. I only made the case."

Then they went from jeweler to jeweler, searching for a necklace like the other one, racking their memories, both of them sick with worry and anguish.

In a shop in the Palais-Royal, they found a necklace of diamonds that seemed to them exactly like the one they were looking for. It was priced at forty thousand francs. They could buy it for thirty-six thousand.

They got the jeweler to promise not to sell it for three days. And they made an agreement that he would buy it back for thirty-four thousand francs if the original was recovered before the end of February.

Loisel had saved eighteen thousand francs that his father had left him. He would have to borrow the rest.

He borrowed, asking a thousand francs from one, five hundred from another, five louis[1] here, three louis there. He wrote promissory notes, undertook ruinous obligations, did business with finance companies and the whole tribe of loan sharks. He compromised himself for the remainder of his days, risked his signature without knowing whether he would be able to honor it, and, terrified by anguish over the future, by the black misery that was about to descend on him, by the prospect of all kinds of physical deprivations and mortal tortures, he went to get the new necklace, and put down thirty-six thousand francs on the jeweler's counter.

Mrs. Loisel took the necklace back to Mrs. Forrestier, who said with an offended tone:

"You should have brought it back sooner; I might have needed it."

---

[1]louis—coin equal to 20 francs.

She did not open the case, as her friend feared she might. If she had noticed the substitution, what would she have thought? What would she have
said? Would she not have taken her for a thief?

Mrs. Loisel soon discovered the horrible life of the needy. She did her
share, however, completely, heroically. That horrifying debt had to be paid.
She would pay. They dismissed the maid; they changed their address; they
rented an attic flat.

She learned to do the heavy housework, dirty kitchen jobs. She washed
the dishes, wearing away her manicured fingernails on greasy pots and encrusted baking dishes. She handwashed dirty linen, shirts, and dish towels that
she hung out on the line to dry. Each morning, she took the garbage down to
the street, and she carried up water, stopping at each floor to catch her breath.
And, dressed in cheap house dresses, she went to the fruit dealer, the grocer,
the butchers, with her basket under her arms, haggling, insulting, defending
her measly cash penny by penny.

They had to make installment payments every month, and, to buy more
time, to refinance loans.

The husband worked evenings to make fair copies of tradesmen's accounts, and late into the night he made copies at five cents a page.

And this life lasted ten years.

At the end of ten years, they had paid back everything—everything—including the extra charges imposed by loan sharks and the accumulation of
compound interest.

Mrs. Loisel looked old now. She had become the strong, hard, and rude
woman of poor households. Her hair unkempt, with uneven skirts and rough,
red hands, she spoke loudly, washed floors with large buckets of water. But
sometimes, when her husband was at work, she sat down near the window,
and she dreamed of that evening so long ago, of that party, where she had
been so beautiful and so admired.

What would life have been like if she had not lost that necklace? Who
knows? Who knows? Life is so peculiar, so uncertain. How little a thing it takes
to destroy you or to save you!

Well, one Sunday, when she had gone for a stroll along the Champs-
Elysées to relax from the cares of the week, she suddenly noticed a woman
walking with a child. It was Mrs. Forrestier, still youthful, still beautiful, still
attractive.

Mrs. Loisel felt moved. Would she speak to her? Yes, certainly. And now
that she had paid, she could tell all. Why not?

She walked closer.

"Hello, Jeanne."

The other gave no sign of recognition and was astonished to be addressed
so familiarly by this working-class woman. She stammered:

"But . . . Madam! . . . I don't know . . . You must have made a mistake."

"No. I'm Mathilde Loisel."

Her friend cried out.

"Oh! . . . My poor Mathilde, you've changed so much."

"Yes. I've had some tough times since I saw you last; in fact, hardships . . .   115
and all because of you! . . ."

"Of me . . . how so?"

"You remember the diamond necklace that you lent me to go to the party
at the Ministry of Education?"

"Yes. What then?"

"Well, I lost it."

"How, since you gave it back to me?"   120

"I returned another exactly like it. And for ten years we've been paying for
it. You understand that this wasn't easy for us, who have nothing. . . . Finally
it's over, and I'm damned glad."

Mrs. Forrestier stopped her.

"You say that you bought a diamond necklace to replace mine?"

"Yes, you didn't notice it, eh? It was exactly like yours."

And she smiled with proud and childish joy.   125

Mrs. Forrestier, deeply moved, took both her hands.

"Oh, my poor Mathilde! But mine was only costume jewelry. At most, it
was worth only five hundred francs! . . ."

Now take a few minutes to answer these questions in the box below or in
your journal. To what extent did "The Necklace" conform to your expectations
for it as a short story? To what extent was it easy to read? Were your usual
strategies for reading a short story applicable to this text? Did you "get out of
it" what you thought you would in terms of what you "put into it"?

My Experience Reading "The Necklace"

How are your responses to the questions about your expectations meeting the reality of reading "The Necklace" similar to or different from those of your classmates? What accounts for the similarity or difference, in terms of the *literary* experience different readers bring to this story?

Some Literary Conventions

One of my students wrote in her journal after reading "The Necklace," "This short story was basically what I believed a short story would be. It was very easy to read." Her comment is typical, I think, of what most people who read "The Necklace" in the context of a literature classroom would say. This text seems to have most if not all of the features most people have come to expect of a short story. It has well-defined characters (Mathilde Loisel, her husband, her friend, Mrs. Forrestier) in a particular place and time (late nineteenth-century Paris) called a setting. An episode from those characters' lives is related by a narrator who has knowledge about what happened to those characters and who chooses to tell you certain things and not others.

> *She was one of those pretty and charming women, born, as if by an error of destiny, into a family of clerks and copyists. She had no dowry, no prospects, no way of getting known, courted, loved, married by a rich and distinguished man. She finally settled for a marriage with a minor clerk in the Ministry of Education.*

You may be used to describing this text strategy of a short story in terms of point of view. Depending on the vocabulary your literary experience provides for such things, you may further define the point of view in "The Necklace" as **third-person** (according to the pronouns used to refer to the characters—"she," "he," "they"), or **omniscient** (because the story is not narrated by a character), or **reliable** (because you have little or no reason to doubt what the narrator says). To consider point of view in relation to a narrator, however, is to conceive of a "person" or a **voice** that "speaks" to you or tells you the story as you read it.

The episode the narrator relates assumes the structure of a plot, which involves a conflict (Mathilde's desire to be a social sensation versus her actual situation), **rising action** (her preparations for the party and the party itself), a **climax** (Mathilde's discovery that she has lost the necklace), and **falling action** (the couple's efforts to work off their debt for the replacement necklace), or a **denouement** or resolution of the action (in this case, Mrs. Forrestier's revelation that the lost necklace was "only costume jewelry"). In "The Necklace," this resolution features an ending with an **ironic** twist. The language of the whole story exhibits a **style** of writing in terms of the kind of sentences and choice of words in which it is told.

> *Mrs. Loisel soon discovered the horrible life of the needy. She did her share, however, completely, heroically. That horrifying debt had to*

be paid. She would pay. They dismissed the maid; they changed their address; they rented an attic flat.

Perhaps you would describe this style as "straightforward," "plain," "objective," or "simple."

Most of this—the plot, the characters, and the setting at any rate—seem believable, as if it could have really happened. Fiction that seems true-to-life in these ways is said to have a high degree of **verisimilitude**, or true-seemingness. So most people would call this story realistic. Finally, it seems possible to state a theme along the lines of the folly of vanity, the dangers of self-delusion, or the importance of honesty; something like that appears to be the purpose or point of the story in ethical or moral terms. Even if the narrator doesn't state a theme explicitly, the shape of the plot and its resolution may seem to suggest such a theme. Or perhaps you read the necklace as a symbol of material possessions in general, so that Mathilde's desire for the necklace, her loss of it, and her subsequent need to work to pay for it mean something fairly definite about the error of greed. One of my students described a theme in "The Necklace" this way:

> I interpreted the loss of the necklace to be a punishment for Mrs. Loisel's life-time of greed. She needed to see the error of her ways; unfortunately, it took something as drastic as ten years of debt to get the point across.

It may appear, then, that "The Necklace" is cut-and-dried, open-and-shut, a thoroughly conventional story about which little more need be said. But at the same time, its very conventionality offers a chance for you to begin to consider how expectations from your literary experience, interacting harmoniously with conventional text strategies, produce the kind of reading experience I am assuming you had with "The Necklace." And as you do that, perhaps you may see something new about those very conventions that make texts like "The Necklace" both easy to read *and* contrived, both realistic *and* artificial.

Character

Before you read the discussion of character below, take a few minutes to briefly describe your sense of Mathilde, her husband, and/or Mrs. Forrestier as people. Then share and compare your ideas with your classmates. What makes for any differences that arise in different readers' judgments of these characters?

"The Necklace" seems to me to be a story in which depth of character is not a particularly strong concern. At least for the first part of the story, I think Mathilde Loisel is not a very complex person; she is a dreamer and a status-seeker. She sees her life and the symbols of her status as inadequate to her

SHARE AND COMPARE:

Mathilde is

Mr. Loisel is

Mrs. Forrestier is

image of herself and longs for what she does not have. Her husband, whose first name is never given, is even less of a complex character. He seems to function in the story mainly to provide plausible reasons for Mathilde to want a more richly material life than she has and to have the opportunity to go to the party, for which she will need jewels, and to indicate what degree of sacrifice the couple has to make to replace the lost necklace. Mathilde's wealthy friend, Mrs. Forrestier, seems plainly to be a purely functional character, first to provide the necklace, the loss of which will be an issue, and then to provide the story's final twist. Functional characters like Mr. Loisel and Mrs. Forrestier are sometimes called "flat" characters, as opposed to characters who have more "depth" and who may "grow" or "develop" over the course of a story.

In spite of the relative flatness of these characters, the story seems to have an air of plausibility about it, so that most readers, like me, are probably willing to believe such people could exist and could get into such a situation. The one-dimensionality of Mrs. Loisel, for instance, leaves a gap as to the rest of her personality. In the process of believing in her as a real-seeming person and not merely a symbol for an abstract quality such as greed, a reader must fill in this gap; he or she must sketch in the outline of her character from his or her own experience. This does not seem hard for most readers to do. For instance, one of my students wrote this in his response journal: "I immediately made a harsh judgment on [Mathilde], . . . for I have no patience with people who are not happy with what they have, yet will not work hard to get where they want to go." Most of my students made similar negative judgments of Mathilde, at least at first, as "a woman who . . ." or "a person who. . . ." Such language indicates their perception of her as a character who conforms to their experience with actual people; they do not doubt her verisimilitude.

Yet consider: Do you know any real people who are as one-dimensional or flat as Mrs. Loisel or the other characters in this story? Even obsessive people like Mathilde apply their energies and their obsessiveness to more than one thing. Of course, you may object, this is a short story; there's not room or time for the characters to be developed in more depth. That's precisely the point: it is a *convention* of short fiction to present characters who aren't really true-to-life, but just enough so that readers don't ask too many questions of them. And—this is a key point about what readers bring to such experiences—if you are at all used to reading stories like this—or to seeing hour-long dramas on television or music videos in which characters are no more well-rounded than these—you accept the relative *un*reality of such characters as "natural" to the genre. You don't ask too many questions, not because you're a poor or weak reader, but because of what you've come to accept as natural or normal for this kind of text.

> **CONNECT:**   For an example of a story with characters that are presented in greater depth and complexity, see "Teenage Wasteland" in Chapter 7. In that story, in contrast to "The Necklace," complexity of character seems to take precedence over a plainly moral theme. (See the discussion of theme beginning on page 108.)

Setting

Your sense of the realism of the characters in "The Necklace" may also derive in part from the setting in which they are presented: middle-class Paris of the late nineteenth century. It is probably easy to imagine or picture someone like Mathilde Loisel: "one of those pretty and charming women" who are unhappy with their economic and social situation and long for a more luxurious lifestyle. The specific date of January 8 for the party at the Ministry of Education and the reference to Mathilde possibly catching cold in the night air after the party add a bit more believability. Other details appropriate to this time and place, such as the reference to the cab the Loisels find to carry them home ("one of those old night-going buggies that are seen in Paris only after dark") and the mention of Paris locations such as the Palais-Royal and the Champs-Elysées, lend plausibility as well. If you imagine the characters' behavior or motivation as believable in terms of what people living in that time and place would do and why, then character and setting work together to enhance the verisimilitude of the story. At the same time, your sense of the "realism" of these people in this place and time depends on your own imagination too, because your lived experience does not include time spent with middle-class nineteenth-century Parisians. In fact, it may be that your lived experience and your values are so different from the situation and the ideology of the characters in this story that they seem unreal to you. In any case, as a reader of this or any story, really, you must engage in what the poet and critic Samuel Taylor Coleridge called a "willing suspension of disbelief" in order to accept the story as at all believable or realistic. The closer your experience is to the circumstances of the characters in "The Necklace" or the more you know about that "reality," the easier this "suspension" will be.

Without trying to claim that the setting of "The Necklace" is unrealistic, I will point out that a true-seeming setting is a convention of short stories that many readers are used to. For the sake of economy in "The Necklace," just enough about setting is suggested or sketched that you can fill in the rest to imagine the Loisels as real-seeming people, even if you have no firsthand experience with nineteenth-century Paris. Their apartment is described as "grim . . . with its drab walls, threadbare furniture, [and] ugly curtains," but no more detail is given. Were the walls "drab" because of their dull color, their old paint, their faded wallpaper? How many pieces, of what style, did their "threadbare furniture" consist of? Why and how were their curtains "ugly"? All these matters of setting could have been described in much greater detail, and if so the story might seem even more true-to-life, accurate down to the scuffs on the Loisels' tables and chairs.

On the other hand, the whole story could have been told without reference to a specific place and the characters not given plausible names, and the effect might have been very different. What if it opened with a sentence that said "Once upon a time there was a pretty and charming young woman who was born into a poor and humble family"? What if the invitation were not to a dinner party at the Ministry of Education but to a ball at the palace of the prince? What if instead of a "rich friend, a comrade from convent days," the main character obtained the necklace from an old hag in the forest? Features of setting such as these would make the story seem quite different, considerably less "realistic." Such features are conventions too, of course—conventions of what has come to be called the "fairy tale." In such a story, you might still predict that the main character would lose the necklace and her moment of happiness, but you might also expect a "happy" ending in which the character's problems are resolved in some way that satisfies her and you, instead of one that provides the ironic surprise of "The Necklace."

CONNECT: For a story in which setting is handled very differently from the realistic manner of "The Necklace," see "The Snow Child" beginning on page 332.

Plot

How about the plot of "The Necklace"? It too may seem believable and realistic enough, given the kinds of people who are involved in it and the time and place in which it occurs. If you accept the descriptions of Mathilde in the first six paragraphs of the story, then two important things, probably, start to happen: (1) having to do with your reading strategies, you anticipate that her dreams of a luxurious life will involve her in some kind of complication related to those dreams; and (2) having to do with text strategies, when the plot is advanced through her husband's coming home with the party invitation, what follows next seems believable. Even if her initial rejection of the chance to go to such an important gala is a setback to your expectations, that rejection just provides more impetus for the plot when she persuades her husband to buy her a nice dress and makes plausible her desire to have fancy jewels to go with that dress. It would violate realism at this point for the Loisels to be able to buy such jewels, or for them to have a necklace suddenly willed to them by a long lost relative, or to find one in, say, a magic loaf of bread. But since Mathilde's wealthy friend has already been mentioned in the process of setting up Mathilde's character, when Mr. Loisel suggests Mathilde borrow jewels from her, it probably seems perfectly plausible.

And so does the rest of it: her losing the necklace; the couple's frantic scramble first to find it then to cover up the loss by replacing it; what they have to go through to pay for something priced way beyond their means; the physical toll the years of hard work and sacrifice have on Mathilde; even, perhaps, her final encounter with her old friend Jeanne. With respect to that final encounter, perhaps you did momentarily put aside your "willing suspension of disbelief" at the end of the story and consider, just for a moment, Mathilde's chance encounter with Mrs. Forrestier to be just a little too neat. But then again, chance encounters with people you have not seen in many years do happen, and it's probable enough that Mathilde, having on her mind the recent satisfaction of the debt for the diamond necklace, would make a point of speaking to Mrs. Forrestier about it. Even if a grain of doubt did enter your mind as you read the end of the story, you may very well have quickly dismissed it in order to go along with what appears to be the purpose of the story as a moral tale.

Even assuming a fairly high degree of realism to this plot, however, you might consider now whether this plot or any plot can really be realistic. Real life, as it is lived day-to-day by most people in Western society anyway, does not have a tidy plot to it: It's sloppy and free-form, in contrast to a short story (or even a novel) that may structure something resembling real life or actual experience into a plot. But you are so used to stories having plots that you overlook the artificiality or contrivance of this structuring and take plot as natural, not conventional, or realistic, not artificial. Yes, you have conflicts and complications in real life (Sometimes life may seem to be nothing but conflicts and complications!), and yes, those conflicts may get increasingly intense and eventually resolve themselves in some way, but a fictional plot focuses, artificially, on just one aspect of people's or characters' lives, to the exclusion of others, and that's not like real life, where you usually have dozens (at least) of things going on at once.

In "The Necklace," the focus is on one aspect of the Loisels' social life, so that a whole host of other possible aspects of their lives is left out: their children, or why they don't have any; their other amusements; his job or career; what she does all day at home; their relationships with their neighbors; their extended family relationships. All these things, more instances of gaps in the story, potentially and probably involve dozens of conflicts and complications—stories in themselves—but of course to bring those into the story would destroy the economy of focus of "The Necklace." To do so would make the story more realistic in the sense of like life, but less realistic in the sense of a particular combination of literary conventions.

CONNECT: The story "everybody knew bubba riff," in the Stories for Exploration section following Chapter 6, treats the text strategy of plot in a different way. If you read it, you might consider whether it or "The Necklace" is the more "realistic" story. You might also consider the extent to which the realism or unrealism of either story is produced by text strategies or by the sense of social reality you bring to the text.

The absence of information about these other aspects of the Loisels' lives constitutes gaps in the text. Now that this has been pointed out to you, perhaps you may wonder a bit about the larger lives of Mathilde and her husband. And if you do that, you may start to question the supposed realism of the story. But a gap such as this in "The Necklace" is probably not something most readers would be aware of as they are reading (were you?) because they are used to going along with the conventions of realistic fiction, which in this case means accepting the text's focus on just one aspect of the characters' lives.

CONNECT: The video of "Mary Jane's Last Dance" offered gaps concerning the characters' lives analogous to those I have pointed out in "The Necklace." If you have seen the video, or drawing on your experience with music videos in general, in which text are you more likely to notice or identify such gaps? In which text are you more likely to overlook them? In either case, why?

As you try to develop a more self-conscious approach to reading fiction, however, you should be aware that a reader may notice or emphasize gaps of many kinds and significance in any text he or she reads. A reader's freedom to do so demonstrates again the interactive nature of the reading dynamic, and it is one way that he or she can move toward becoming a stronger reader. That will be considered in more depth in the concluding section in this chapter. For now, take a look at another of the conventions most readers expect in association with short stories: theme.

Theme

Assuming your literary experience includes familiarity with different kinds of narratives—short stories, novels, even films and television dramas—you are probably used to considering what the whole story is "about" in some larger terms. This is another gap because usually—and especially in "realistic" fiction—no authoritative voice in the narrative actually tells what it is about or what it means. The reader has to decide, although with a story like "The Necklace" that may not be too difficult; it may even seem that virtually all its text strategies are arranged so as to point or lead a reader toward a particular interpretive conclusion.

So perhaps the story is about something more general than just this unfortunate episode in the lives of a couple of anonymous Parisians. Some of my students who read "The Necklace" offered interpretations such as these:

> "I feel the theme here is money hunger and just the simple statement, 'You always want what you can't get.'"

> "The theme, I believe, is plainly 'tell the truth.'"

> "The themes you could find in this story are 'Don't be greedy'; 'Honesty is the best policy'; 'Be satisfied with what you have, it could be worse.'"

Such thematic interpretations probably are not too much of a stretch for most readers to get to. The way the plot works out—both through Mathilde's losing her friend's necklace and her final discovery that it wasn't very valuable after all—seems to lead to some such conclusions as to theme. Similarly, reading the necklace itself as symbolic of some abstract concept such as greed would allow you to interpret the story in more general terms than just one particular woman's experiences. Or perhaps whatever ways the story sacrifices verisimilitude to allow a moral point to emerge help you decide on a theme. If you thought that was happening as you read, you would be already starting to concede a disjunction—a disharmonious difference—between theme and realism: a true "slice of life" as most people experience it would not be so neatly arranged to allow a moral point or theme to emerge.

As with plot, theme is purely a matter of literary convention and readers' expectations. As with plot, life as it is actually lived does not take shape so as to point to a theme. Yes, you may draw conclusions from your experiences or those of other people, and yes, you may learn lessons from episodes in your life, but if you do that's entirely up to you. According to the dominant ideology of Western culture at any rate, it seems very unlikely that episodes of lived experience exist in order to point to a theme, teach you a lesson, force you to draw a conclusion. Yet it is common for people to accept and expect themes in fiction, and at the same time to consider at least some pieces of fiction to be realistic.

> **CONNECT:** For a story whose title seems to make theme explicit, but in which theme may be much less obvious than in "The Necklace," see "Theme of the Traitor and the Hero" in the Stories for Exploration section following Chapter 6.

Style

Usually, the realism of a short story seems to be a matter of those text strategies that most nearly approximate external reality: the action, the characters, the setting. The story's style—its diction, the types and length of its sentences, its use of figurative language—may contribute to an impression of verisimilitude also, even though language is usually thought of as the means or the channel through which the content of the story (in terms of action, character, and setting) is conveyed. The kind of language in which "The Necklace" is written may contribute to the story's air of realism by being straightforward, unobtrusive, or transparent. When my students called "The Necklace" easy to read, I surmise they were saying in part that the style made no extra demands on them or did not call attention to itself. For this very reason readers may be better able to momentarily forget they are actually reading a story, a fictional creation, and not a factual report of an episode in some people's lives. Readers' "willing suspension of disbelief" is also part of the interaction that creates a sense of verisimilitude, but readers' ability to suspend disbelief is facilitated by a style that is not especially noticeable as such. The apparently objective tone of the narrative portions of the story (the nonjudgmental attitude of the narrator) and the ordinary language in which the characters' **dialogue** is rendered, both of which are part of the overall style of "The Necklace," help readers construe the characters and their situation as lifelike, not as the artificial contrivances they really are.

On this note, it may be appropriate to quote de Maupassant himself. "To make things seem real on the page," he wrote in an essay called "The Writer's Goal," "consists in giving the complete *illusion* of reality." And from this statement he concluded that "writers who call themselves realists should more accurately call themselves illusionists." Part of the illusion of reality that readers may experience with "The Necklace" is attributable to its style.

> **CONNECT:** For an example of a story that also employs a realistic style but that presents a highly unrealistic premise, see "A Very Old Man with Enormous Wings," in the Stories for Exploration section following this chapter.

This discussion on the conventions of the short story has attempted to destabilize a reading of "The Necklace" as a realistic story; that is, to demonstrate that reading "The Necklace" as realistic derives from expectations in a reader's literary experience interacting harmoniously with conventional text strategies. Now go back to the first two questions you answered about your expectations for short stories, on page 93. Look at your answers again before you read "Continuity of Parks," below. Also, as you read this short story, do as you did with "The Necklace" and keep track of your predictions for where the plot is going. When you finish reading "Continuity of Parks," record your responses to the questions that follow it.

Julio Cortázar   1914–1984

Continuity of Parks   *1963*

He had begun to read the novel a few days before. He had put it down because of some urgent business conferences, opened it again on his way back to the estate by train; he permitted himself a slowly growing interest in the plot, in the characterizations. That afternoon, after writing a letter giving his power of attorney and discussing a matter of joint ownership with the manager of his estate, he returned to the book in the tranquillity of his study which looked out upon the park with its oaks. Sprawled in his favorite armchair, its back toward the door—even the possibility of an intrusion would have irritated him, had he thought of it—he let his left hand caress repeatedly the green velvet upholstery and set to reading the final chapters. He remembered effortlessly the names and his mental image of the characters; the novel spread its glamor over him almost at once. He tasted the almost perverse pleasure of disengaging himself line by line from the things around him, and at the same time feeling his head rest comfortably on the green velvet of the chair with its high back, sensing that the cigarettes rested within reach of his hand, that beyond the great windows the air of afternoon danced under the oak trees in the park. Word by word, licked up by the sordid dilemma of the hero and heroine, letting himself be absorbed to the point where the images settled down and took on color and movement, he was witness to the final encounter in the mountain cabin. The woman arrived first, apprehensive; now the lover came in, his face cut by the backlash of a branch. Admirably, she stanched the blood with her kisses, but he rebuffed her caresses, he had not come to perform again the ceremonies of a secret passion, protected by a world of dry leaves and furtive paths through the forest. The dagger warmed itself against his chest, and underneath liberty pounded, hidden close. A lustful, panting dialogue raced down the pages like a rivulet of snakes, and one felt it had all been decided from eternity. Even to those caresses which writhed about the lover's body, as though wishing to keep him there, to dissuade him from it; they sketched abominably the frame of that other body it was necessary to destroy. Nothing had been forgotten: alibis, unforeseen hazards, possible mistakes. From this hour on, each instant had its use minutely assigned. The cold-blooded, twice-gone-over reexamination of the details was barely broken off so that a hand could caress a cheek. It was beginning to get dark.

Not looking at one another now, rigidly fixed upon the task which awaited them, they separated at the cabin door. She was to follow the trail that led north. On the path leading in the opposite direction, he turned for a moment to watch her running, her hair loosened and flying. He ran in turn, crouching among the trees and hedges until, in the yellowish fog of dusk, he could distinguish the avenue of trees which led up to the house. The dogs were not supposed to bark, they did not bark. The estate manager would not be there at this hour, and he was not there. He went up the three porch steps and entered. The woman's words reached him over the thudding of blood in his ears: first a blue chamber, then a hall, then a carpeted stairway. At the top, two doors. No one in the first room, no one in the second. The door of the salon, and then, the knife in hand, the light from the great windows, the high back of an armchair covered in green velvet, the head of the man in the chair reading a novel.

Response Statement Questions

- To what extent did "Continuity of Parks" conform to your expectations for it as a short story? To what extent did it defy those expectations? What new text strategies or unusual treatment of familiar ones are you aware of?

- Was the story easy to read? Were your usual strategies for reading a short story applicable to this text? Did you "get out of it" what you thought you would in terms of what you "put into it"?

- Do you ever make any interpretations, draw any conclusions about theme? If you do, how easy or hard is it to do this? What helps or hinders you in doing this?

- To what extent is "Continuity of Parks" a realistic story? To what extent is it artificial?

- *Share and Compare* How are your responses to these questions similar to or different from those of your classmates? What accounts for the similarity or difference, in terms of the literary experience different readers bring to this story and the reading strategies they might adopt in reading it?

Challenging Conventions

"Continuity of Parks" is an interesting story for many reasons, but what I'd like you to notice especially now is the way in which it first conforms to, then challenges readers' expectations for a short story. In that way, it acts as a reminder of just how active readers usually are in collaborating with texts to produce the "normal" kinds of reading experiences. "The Necklace" seems easy to read because it harmonizes with the expectations that most readers bring to it; "Continuity of Parks" is startling because at a crucial moment it turns those expectations upside down. Still, this story is probably not a difficult one to read. Even though it is unconventional in some of its text strategies, it works with and within conventional text strategies to surprise readers. Now I invite you to take a closer look at how some of these conventions are handled in this story.

Setting

"Continuity of Parks" is not as specific as "The Necklace" as to where and when the action occurs. There are no specific geographical, local, or historical references. As to time, it could take place just about any time since the invention of the railroad and the popularity of the novel, say in the last 175 years. Perhaps the reference to the man's cigarettes suggests a somewhat later time frame, sometime after machine-made and packaged cigarettes were first made available. Despite this lack of specificity, however, the setting seems familiar enough to qualify the story as realistic. As one of my students wrote in her journal, "Early on in the story I judge the man in the chair to be a successful business man who desired some rest ... [after] his busy day," a situation that seems believable in terms of contemporary reality.

Plot and Structure

The structure of a short story plot is often described in terms of a conflict arising out of the initial situation, producing rising action and suspense, leading to a climax, and finally letting the tension down again through falling action. "Continuity of Parks" presents an initial situation as described above, and in the opening few sentences it observes the convention of a sequential order of events as told by an omniscient narrator. But the action moves so quickly to a climax that part of the surprise may be just that it ends so abruptly, before you even know what conflict arises out of the initial situation.

Rising action and other conventional structural aspects of plot seem to be in the novel the man is reading, not in the narrated action of the "outer" story. At the same time, there is a structure to the narrative. It presents a man reading, describes what he's reading (which contains its own structure: the couple's rendezvous, the discussion of their plan, their parting, and the execution of their plan), and then merges what the man is reading and the situation of him reading in the simultaneous climax of both the plot of the novel and the structure of the narrative.

Conflict, like plot structure, seems limited to the novel, but recognizing it even there requires you to fill gaps as to who these characters are, why they are meeting in secret, what's driven them to, apparently, plan a murder, and whom they intend to kill. Of course you may **naturalize** or dismiss the strangeness of much of those characters' situations by referring to your own experience with popular novels, if those are in your literary experience. You may just accept that, given the kind of "trashy" novel the man is reading, these are the kinds of characters and "sordid dilemma" you would expect. As one of my students commented, "The woman and her lover were, to me, the 'classic' heroine and hero. This judgment was probably due to the fact that they were introduced as novel characters." If the person whom the woman and her lover are planning to kill is a gap for you, it is filled in, probably to your surprise, at the climactic moment of the story. Here's what a student of mine said about her predictions as she read:

> I first began to predict that some violent act could be about to occur with the
>
> mention of the dagger and lover—as opposed to husband. It made me think of a
>
> love triangle and murder. My suspicions began to be confirmed; death was in-
>
> volved. The surprise at the end of the story shocked me. I had no idea the man in
>
> the chair was the one about to be killed.

The surprise effect depends at least in part on how the conventional text strategy of plot—and readers' expectations regarding the unfolding direction of plot—are manipulated in this story.

Character

In this very short story, the nameless characters are even flatter than the characters in "The Necklace"; that is, they don't have the depth or complexity that you may expect of characters who more closely resemble real people. (Perhaps the story just doesn't go on long enough for the man who is reading to assume much depth of character.) All the same, at least for the first half dozen sentences or so, the man seems believable enough as a real person. You may be able to relate what is said in those sentences about his reading experience to your own: as one of my students commented, "I became engrossed in 'Continuity of Parks' because, like the man in the green chair, I often become overly involved in my reading." The other two characters are specifically literary ("the 'classic' heroine and hero," as my student called them) and as such they may be believable or realistic enough. But then their literary status is violated when the male of the pair enters the "real" world of the man in the green chair.

At the same time, the man reading, who seems "real" initially, becomes fictional as his reality merges with the fictionality he is reading about. My student who had accepted the woman and her lover as "the 'classic' heroine and hero ...[because] they were introduced as novel characters," said that "at the end... the man in the chair gained an added air of fiction—since he became part of the novel—and the characters became more real—because they entered the world which I had thought to be real." The distinction readers are used to maintaining between "fiction" and "reality"—even while they pretend that fictional characters are real or real-seeming—is seriously challenged if not shattered at the end of "Continuity of Parks." That too is part of its shock effect.

Theme

Some of my students who read "Continuity of Parks" answered the third response statement question by saying:

> I don't see a theme. It was just enjoyable to read because of its fluid transition
>
> between two possible (or maybe one?) plots.

It was very hard for me to arrive at a theme. I thought of the story as just a sur-

prising tale.... I think becoming so involved with the plot hindered me from seeing

other aspects such as theme.

To me, the theme seems to be one which says, "Don't get too engrossed with

literature (fiction)—it can prove to be 'deadly.'"

Perhaps, like the first two students quoted here, you found it difficult to identify a theme to "Continuity of Parks," or you found yourself preoccupied by other text strategies so that interpretation didn't seem to be a reading goal for you. If so, that's understandable: unlike "The Necklace," "Continuity of Parks" does not seem to be a text that carries a theme with it, at least in terms of a point or moral.

Consider again for a moment, however, the kinds of thematic statements my students offered about "The Necklace" (page 108) and your own and those of your classmates. Based on those readings, it can be said that theme in general seems to be an application of a story to something outside itself, some matter of external reality or a reader's life. Or, conversely, theme may be considered as the application of some value from a reader's life or external reality to the text. However, because "Continuity of Parks" seems to call into question the usual or conventional separation of fictional and external reality, it seems to problematize theme too, to the extent that identifying or creating theme depends on a difference between the created reality of a fictional world and the "objective" reality of the external world. In this regard, it would seem worthwhile to recall the words of Guy de Maupassant that "to make things seem real on the page consists in giving the complete *illusion* of reality." "Continuity of Parks" gives this illusion of reality and then reminds you that it is an illusion, something that readers of conventional short stories are not used to.

Style

A few points are worth observing, I think, about style in "Continuity of Parks." This story begins, in the same general manner as the conventionally realistic "The Necklace," with an "objective" or "detached" tone as it matter-of-factly describes the situation of the man settling down to read the final chapters of his novel. The air of verisimilitude promoted by this style continues, even as the style itself changes somewhat, as the narration moves from the man sitting in the green chair reading, into a rendition of what he is reading. Even though the novel is not quoted directly, the language in which it is summarized becomes more heated, the word choice appropriate to a novel that concerns a "sordid dilemma": "A lustful, panting dialogue raced down the pages like a rivulet of snakes," and "caresses ... writhed about the lover's body, as though wishing to keep him there." Perhaps you found it easy to believe that the man reading could become "licked up" and "absorbed" by such a book, or even that he as a reader was supplying some of the qualities of lustfulness and panting to the dialogue. At any rate, the heightened artificiality of the language of the story as it moves from the supposedly real world of the man in the green chair to the imaginative world of the novel seems both realistically appropriate and effective in pulling the reader into the fictional world of the novel, from which, in a sense, he never emerges.

As an element of style here, a final consideration might be this story's title. A title *is* a text strategy, after all, even though it too may be overlooked as such or taken for granted. Can you recall what you thought of the title "Continuity of Parks" before you read the story itself? Perhaps, if anything, it seemed just slightly obscure, perhaps more appropriate to an essay than to a short story? (I didn't mention the title among the response statement questions above because I didn't want to call special attention to it.) What do you think of it now? Does it seem now to be more obviously a text strategy, one that contributes to any interpretation you might construct? The status of any title as a text strategy might be revealed more clearly if you try substituting another title. What about, in this case, "The Man in the Green Chair"? or "Preoccupations"? or "The Deadly Novel"? or "A Möbius Strip"?

> **SHARE AND COMPARE:** Can you say what difference the presence of a different title—one of those I suggested or another that seems appropriate—would have on your expectations concerning "Continuity of Parks"? What ideas for "alternative" titles do your classmates have? Of all possibilities, which is the "best" title, and why?

Stories for Exploration

Here are three more short stories that you can read to expand your awareness of how your literary experience influences your response. The prereading questions listed below can help you inventory your expectations for short stories in general. Thus, they can be applied in any reading situation in which you want to focus on the **literary interaction** you have with a short story. You should make some notes, at least, in answer to those questions before you start to read the stories reprinted below. The response statement questions provide follow-up to the notes you make for the prereading questions. They too can be used to guide your responsive writing on any story—those reprinted below or others—for which you want to begin to analyze the literary interaction you experienced.

Critical Reading Questions

- What do you expect a short story to be or to have? Based on your experience with short stories, what features, elements, conventions, etc. have you come to expect?
- What do you expect to do as a reader? What will you look for? What kind of mental operations will you probably undertake as you read?

- After having read "The Necklace" and "Continuity of Parks" and the accompanying discussion in this chapter, how, if at all, are your answers to the above questions different from what they were earlier?

Response Statement Questions

- How well does this story match your expectations for it as a short story? What reading experiences are those expectations based on?
- Is this story realistic? If so, what text strategies or conventions contribute to its realism? If not, what text strategies challenge its realism?
- What reading strategies do you use to read this story? How or why might you read this story as symbolic?
- What gaps exist in this text? How or why are you able to fill in any of those gaps?
- How, if at all, are you able to decide on a theme for this story? What text strategies and reading strategies help you to do this?
- How does your life experience interact with whatever "reality" is presented in the story? What do you know, think, or believe that helps or hinders your ability to believe in what the story presents?
- *Share and Compare*   Discuss your responses to the above questions with your classmates, as a whole or in a small group. What differences exist among you as far as expectations and reading strategies are concerned? How did different reading strategies meet with text strategies to produce harmonious or clashing interactions at the literary level? In addition to text strategies, how did differences in readers' senses of reality contribute to their deciding the story was realistic or not?

Gabriel García Márquez   b. 1928

A Very Old Man with Enormous Wings   1971

Translated by Gregory Rabassa

A Tale for Children

On the third day of rain they had killed so many crabs inside the house that Pelayo had to cross his drenched courtyard and throw them into the sea, because the newborn child had a temperature all night and they thought it was due to the stench. The world had been sad since Tuesday. Sea and sky were a single ash-gray thing and the sands of the beach, which on March nights glimmered like powdered light, had become a stew of mud and rotten shellfish. The light was so weak at noon that when Pelayo was coming back to the house after throwing away the crabs, it was hard for him to see what is was that was moving and groaning in the rear of the courtyard. He had to go very close to see that it was an old man, a very old man, lying face down in the mud, who, in spite of his tremendous efforts, couldn't get up, impeded by his enormous wings.

Frightened by that nightmare, Pelayo ran to get Elisenda, his wife, who was putting compresses on the sick child, and he took her to the rear of the courtyard. They both looked at the fallen body with mute stupor. He was dressed like a ragpicker. There were only a few faded hairs left on his bald skull and very few teeth in his mouth, and his pitiful condition of a drenched great-grandfather had taken away any sense of grandeur he might have had. His huge buzzard wings, dirty and half-plucked, were forever entangled in the mud. They looked at him so long and so closely that Pelayo and Elisenda very soon overcame their surprise and in the end found him familiar. Then they dared speak to him, and he answered in an incomprehensible dialect with a strong sailor's voice. That was how they skipped over the inconvenience of the wings and quite intelligently concluded that he was a lonely castaway from some foreign ship wrecked by the storm. And yet, they called in a neighbor woman who knew everything about life and death to see him, and all she needed was one look to show them their mistake.

"He's an angel," she told them. "He must have been coming for the child, but the poor fellow is so old that the rain knocked him down."

On the following day everyone knew that a flesh-and-blood angel was held captive in Pelayo's house. Against the judgment of the wise neighbor woman, for whom angels in those times were the fugitive survivors of a celestial conspiracy, they did not have the heart to club him to death. Pelayo watched over him all afternoon from the kitchen, armed with his bailiff's club, and before going to bed he dragged him out of the mud and locked him up with the hens in the wire chicken coop. In the middle of the night, when the rain stopped, Pelayo and Elisenda were still killing crabs. A short time afterward the child woke up without a fever and with a desire to eat. Then they felt magnanimous and decided to put the angel on a raft with fresh water and provisions for three days and leave him to his fate on the high seas. But when they went out into the courtyard with the first light of dawn, they found the whole neighborhood in front of the chicken coop having fun with the angel, without the slightest reverence, tossing him things to eat through the openings in the wire as if he weren't a supernatural creature but a circus animal.

Father Gonzaga arrived before seven o'clock, alarmed at the strange news. By that time onlookers less frivolous than those at dawn had already arrived and they were making all kinds of conjectures concerning the captive's future. The simplest among them thought that he should be named mayor of the world. Others of sterner mind felt that he should be promoted to the rank of five-star general in order to win all wars. Some visionaries hoped that he could be put to stud in order to implant on earth a race of winged wise men who could take charge of the universe. But Father Gonzaga, before becoming a priest, had been a robust woodcutter. Standing by the wire, he reviewed his catechism in an instant and asked them to open the door so that he could take a close look at that pitiful man who looked more like a huge decrepit hen among the fascinated chickens. He was lying in a corner drying his open wings in the sunlight among the fruit peels and breakfast leftovers that the early risers had thrown him. Alien to the impertinences of the world, he only lifted his antiquarian eyes and murmured something in his dialect when Father Gonzaga went into the chicken coop and said good morning to him in Latin. The parish priest had his first suspicion of an imposter when he saw that he did not understand the language of God or know how to greet His ministers.

Then he noticed that seen close up he was much too human: he had an unbearable smell of the outdoors, the back side of his wings was strewn with
parasites and his main feathers had been mistreated by terrestrial winds, and
nothing about him measured up to the proud dignity of angels. Then he came
out of the chicken coop and in a brief sermon warned the curious against the
risks of being ingenuous. He reminded them that the devil had the bad habit
of making use of carnival tricks in order to confuse the unwary. He argued
that if wings were not the essential element in determining the difference between a hawk and an airplane, they were even less so in the recognition of
angels. Nevertheless, he promised to write a letter to his bishop so that the latter would write to his primate so that the latter would write to the Supreme
Pontiff[1] in order to get the final verdict from the highest courts.

His prudence fell on sterile hearts. The news of the captive angel spread
with such rapidity that after a few hours the courtyard had the bustle of a marketplace and they had to call in troops with fixed bayonets to disperse the
mob that was about to knock the house down. Elisenda, her spine all twisted
from sweeping up so much marketplace trash, then got the idea of fencing in
the yard and charging five cents admission to see the angel.

The curious came from far away. A traveling carnival arrived with a flying
acrobat who buzzed over the crowd several times, but no one paid any attention to him because his wings were not those of an angel but, rather, those of
a sidereal bat. The most unfortunate invalids on earth came in search of
health: a poor woman who since childhood had been counting her heartbeats
and had run out of numbers; a Portuguese man who couldn't sleep because
the noise of the stars disturbed him; a sleepwalker who got up at night to
undo the things he had done while awake; and many others with less serious
ailments. In the midst of that shipwreck disorder that made the earth tremble,
Pelayo and Elisenda were happy with fatigue, for in less than a week they had
crammed their rooms with money and the line of pilgrims waiting their turn to
enter still reached beyond the horizon.

The angel was the only one who took no part in his own act. He spent his
time trying to get comfortable in his borrowed nest, befuddled by the hellish
heat of the oil lamps and sacramental candles that had been placed along the
wire. At first they tried to make him eat some mothballs, which, according to
the wisdom of the wise neighbor woman, were the food prescribed for angels.
But he turned them down, just as he turned down the papal lunches that the
penitents brought him, and they never found out whether it was because he
was an angel or because he was an old man that in the end he ate nothing but
eggplant mush. His only supernatural virtue seemed to be patience. Especially
during the first days, when the hens pecked at him, searching for the stellar
parasites that proliferated in his wings, and the cripples pulled out feathers to
touch their defective parts with, and even the most merciful threw stones at
him, trying to get him to rise so they could see him standing. The only time
they succeeded in arousing him was when they burned his side with an iron
for branding steers, for he had been motionless for so many hours that they

---

[1]Supreme Pontiff—the pope.

thought he was dead. He awoke with a start, ranting in his hermetic language and with tears in his eyes, and he flapped his wings a couple of times, which brought on a whirlwind of chicken dung and lunar dust and a gale of panic that did not seem to be of this world. Although many thought that his reaction had been one not of rage but of pain, from then on they were careful not to annoy him, because the majority understood that his passivity was not that of a hero taking his ease but that of a cataclysm in repose.

Father Gonzaga held back the crowd's frivolity with formulas of maidservant inspiration while awaiting the arrival of a final judgment on the nature of the captive. But the mail from Rome showed no sense of urgency. They spent their time finding out if the prisoner had a navel, if his dialect had any connection with Aramaic, how many times he could fit on the head of a pin, or whether he wasn't just a Norwegian with wings. Those meager letters might have come and gone until the end of time if a providential event had not put an end to the priest's tribulations.

It so happened that during those days, among so many other carnival at-   10
tractions, there arrived in town the traveling show of the woman who had been changed into a spider for having disobeyed her parents. The admission to see her was not only less than the admission to see the angel, but people were permitted to ask her all manner of questions about her absurd state and to examine her up and down so that no one would ever doubt the truth of her horror. She was a frightful tarantula the size of a ram and with the head of a sad maiden. What was most heart-rending, however, was not her outlandish shape but the sincere affliction with which she recounted the details of her misfortune. While still practically a child she had sneaked out of her parents' house to go to a dance, and while she was coming back through the woods after having danced all night without permission, a fearful thunderclap rent the sky in two and through the crack came the lightning bolt of brimstone that changed her into a spider. Her only nourishment came from the meatballs that charitable souls chose to toss into her mouth. A spectacle like that, full of so much human truth and with such a fearful lesson, was bound to defeat without even trying that of a haughty angel who scarcely deigned to look at mortals. Besides, the few miracles attributed to the angel showed a certain mental disorder, like the blind man who didn't recover his sight but grew three new teeth, or the paralytic who didn't get to walk but almost won the lottery, and the leper whose sores sprouted sunflowers. Those consolation miracles, which were more like mocking fun, had already ruined the angel's reputation when the woman who had been changed into a spider finally crushed him completely. That was how Father Gonzaga was cured forever of his insomnia and Pelayo's courtyard went back to being as empty as during the time it had rained for three days and crabs walked through the bedrooms.

The owners of the house had no reason to lament. With the money they saved they built a two-story mansion with balconies and gardens and high netting so that crabs wouldn't get in during the winter, and with iron bars on the windows so that angels wouldn't get in. Pelayo also set up a rabbit warren close to town and gave up his job as bailiff for good, and Elisenda bought some satin pumps with high heels and many dresses of iridescent silk, the kind worn on Sunday by the most desirable women in those times. The chicken coop was the only thing that didn't receive any attention. If they washed it down with creolin[2] and burned tears of myrrh[3] inside it every so often, it was not in homage to the angel but to drive away the dungheap stench that still hung everywhere like a ghost and was turning the new house into an old one. At first, when the child learned to walk, they were careful that he not get too close to the chicken coop. But then they began to lose their fears and got used to the smell, and before the child got his second teeth he'd gone inside the chicken coop to play, where the wires were falling apart. The angel was no less standoffish with him than with other mortals, but he tolerated the most ingenious infamies with the patience of a dog who had no illusions. They both came down with chicken pox at the same time. The doctor who took care of the child couldn't resist the temptation to listen to the angel's heart, and he found so much whistling in the heart and so many sounds in his kidneys that it seemed impossible for him to be alive. What surprised him most, however, was the logic of his wings. They seemed so natural on that completely human organism that he couldn't understand why other men didn't have them too.

When the child began school it had been some time since the sun and rain had caused the collapse of the chicken coop. The angel went dragging himself about here and there like a stray dying man. They would drive him out of the bedroom with a broom and a moment later find him in the kitchen. He seemed to be in so many places at the same time that they grew to think that he'd been duplicated, that he was reproducing himself all through the house, and the exasperated and unhinged Elisenda shouted that it was awful living in that hell full of angels. He could scarcely eat and his antiquarian eyes had also become so foggy that he went about bumping into posts. All he had left were the bare cannulae[4] of his last feathers. Pelayo threw a blanket over him and extended him the charity of letting him sleep in the shed, and only then did they notice that he had a temperature at night, and was delirious with the tongue twisters of an old Norwegian. That was one of the few times they became alarmed, for they thought he was going to die and not even the wise neighbor woman had been able to tell them what to do with dead angels.

And yet he not only survived his worst winter, but seemed improved with the first sunny days. He remained motionless for several days in the farthest corner of the courtyard, where no one would see him, and at the beginning of December some large, stiff feathers began to grow on his wings, the feathers of a scarecrow, which looked more like another misfortune of decrepitude. But he must have known the reason for those changes, for he was quite careful that no one should notice them, that no one should hear the sea chanteys that he sometimes sang under the stars. One morning Elisenda was cutting some bunches of onions for lunch when a wind that seemed to come from the high seas blew into the kitchen. Then she went to the window and caught the angel in his first attempts at flight. They were so clumsy that his fingernails

---

[2]creolin—disinfectant made from wood tar.
[3]myrrh—aromatic resin.
[4]cannulae—tubes.

opened a furrow in the vegetable patch and he was on the point of knocking the shed down with the ungainly flapping that slipped on the light and couldn't get a grip on the air. But he did manage to gain altitude. Elisenda let out a sigh of relief, for herself and for him, when she saw him pass over the last houses, holding himself up in some way with the risky flapping of a senile vulture. She kept watching him even when she was through cutting the onions and she kept on watching until it was no longer possible for her to see him, because then he was no longer an annoyance in her life but an imaginary dot on the horizon of the sea.

Chinua Achebe   b. 1930

Dead Men's Path   1972

Michael Obi's hopes were fulfilled much earlier than he expected. He was appointed headmaster of Ndume Central School in January 1949. It had always been an unprogressive school, so the Mission authorities decided to send a young and energetic man to run it. Obi accepted this responsibility with enthusiasm. He had many wonderful ideas and this was an opportunity to put them into practice. He had had sound secondary school education which designated him a "pivotal teacher" in the official records and set him apart from the other headmasters in the mission field. He was outspoken in his condemnation of the narrow views of these older and often less-educated ones.

"We shall make a good job of it, shan't we?" he asked his young wife when they first heard the joyful news of his promotion.

"We shall do our best," she replied. "We shall have such beautiful gardens and everything will be just *modern* and delightful ..." In their two years of married life she had become completely infected by his passion for "modern methods" and his denigration of "these old and superannuated people in the teaching field who would be better employed as traders in the Onitsha market." She began to see herself already as the admired wife of the young headmaster, the queen of the school.

The wives of the other teachers would envy her position. She would set the fashion in everything ... Then, suddenly, it occurred to her that there might not be other wives. Wavering between hope and fear, she asked her husband, looking anxiously at him.

"All our colleagues are young and unmarried," he said with enthusiasm which for once she did not share. "Which is a good thing," he continued.

"Why?"

"Why? They will give all their time and energy to the school."

Nancy was downcast. For a few minutes she became sceptical about the new school; but it was only for a few minutes. Her little personal misfortune could not blind her to her husband's happy prospects. She looked at him as he sat folded up in a chair. He was stoop-shouldered and looked frail. But he sometimes surprised people with sudden bursts of physical energy. In his present posture, however, all his bodily strength seemed to have retired behind his

5

deep-set eyes, giving them an extraordinary power of penetration. He was only twenty-six, but looked thirty or more. On the whole, he was not unhandsome.

"A penny for your thoughts, Mike," said Nancy after a while, imitating the woman's magazine she read.

"I was thinking what a grand opportunity we've got at last to show these 10 people how a school should be run."

Ndume School was backward in every sense of the word. Mr. Obi put his whole life into the work, and his wife hers too. He had two aims. A high standard of teaching was insisted upon, and the school compound was to be turned into a place of beauty. Nancy's dream-gardens came to life with the coming of the rains, and blossomed. Beautiful hibiscus and allamanda hedges in brilliant red and yellow marked out the carefully tended school compound from the rank neighbourhood bushes.

One evening as Obi was admiring his work he was scandalized to see an old woman from the village hobble right across the compound, through a marigold flower-bed and the hedges. On going up there he found faint signs of an almost disused path from the village across the school compound to the bush on the other side.

"It amazes me," said Obi to one of his teachers who had been three years in the school, "that you people allowed the villagers to make use of this foot-path. It is simply incredible." He shook his head.

"The path," said the teacher apologetically, "appears to be very important to them. Although it is hardly used, it connects the village shrine with their place of burial."

"And what has that got to do with the school?" asked the headmaster. 15

"Well, I don't know," replied the other with a shrug of the shoulders. "But I remember there was a big row some time ago when we attempted to close it."

"That was some time ago. But it will not be used now," said Obi as he walked away. "What will the Government Education Officer think of this when he comes to inspect the school next week? The villagers might, for all I know, decide to use the schoolroom for a pagan ritual during the inspection."

Heavy sticks were planted closely across the path at the two places where it entered and left the school premises. These were further strengthened with barbed wire.

Three days later the village priest of *Ani* called on the headmaster. He was an old man and walked with a slight stoop. He carried a stout walking-stick which he usually tapped on the floor, by way of emphasis, each time he made a new point in his argument.

"I have heard," he said after the usual exchange of cordialities, "that our 20 ancestral footpath has recently been closed . . ."

"Yes," replied Mr. Obi. "We cannot allow people to make a highway of our school compound."

"Look here, my son," said the priest bringing down his walking-stick, "this path was here before you were born and before your father was born. The whole life of this village depends on it. Our dead relatives depart by it and our ancestors visit us by it. But most important, it is the path of children coming in to be born . . ."

Mr. Obi listened with a satisfied smile on his face.

"The whole purpose of our school," he said finally, "is to eradicate just such beliefs as that. Dead men do not require footpaths. The whole idea is just fantastic. Our duty is to teach your children to laugh at such ideas."

"What you say may be true," replied the priest, "but we follow the prac-   25
tices of our fathers. If you re-open the path we shall have nothing to quarrel about. What I always say is: let the hawk perch and let the eagle perch." He rose to go.

"I am sorry," said the young headmaster. "But the school compound cannot be a thoroughfare. It is against our regulations. I would suggest your constructing another path, skirting our premises. We can even get our boys to help in building it. I don't suppose the ancestors will find the little detour too burdensome."

"I have no more words to say," said the old priest, already outside.

Two days later a young woman in the village died in childbed. A diviner was immediately consulted and he prescribed heavy sacrifices to propitiate ancestors insulted by the fence.

Obi woke up next morning among the ruins of his work. The beautiful hedges were torn up not just near the path but right round the school, the flowers trampled to death and one of the school buildings pulled down . . . That day, the white Supervisor came to inspect the school and wrote a nasty report on the state of the premises but more seriously about the "tribal-war situation developing between the school and the village, arising in part from the misguided zeal of the new headmaster."

Gertrude Stein   1874–1946

Preciosilla   *1913*

Cousin to Clare washing.

In the win all the band beagles which have cousin lime sign and arrange a weeding match to presume a certain point to exstate to exstate a certain pass lint to exstate a lean sap prime lo and shut shut is life.

Bait, bait, tore, tore her clothes, toward it, toward a bit, to ward a sit, sit down in, in vacant surely lots, a single mingle, bait and wet, wet a single establishment that has a lily lily grow. Come to the pen come in the stem, come in the grass grown water.

Lily wet lily wet while. This is so pink so pink in stammer, a long bean which shows bows is collected by a single curly shady, shady get, get set wet bet.

It is a snuff a snuff to be told and have can wither, can is it and sleep sleep   5
knot, it is a lily scarf the pink and blue yellow, not blue not odour sun, nobles are bleeding bleeding two seats two seats on end. Why is grief. Grief is strange black. Sugar is melting. We will not swim.

Preciosilla

Please be please be get, please get wet, wet naturally, naturally in weather. Could it be fire more firier. Could it be so in ate struck. Could it be gold up, gold up stringing, in it while while which is hanging, hanging in dingling, dingling in pinning, not so. Not so dots large dressed dots, big sizes, less laced, less laced diamonds, diamonds white, diamonds bright, diamonds in the in the light, diamonds light diamonds door diamonds hanging to be four, two four, all before, this bean, lessly, all most, a best, willow, vest, a green guest, guest, go go go go go go, go. Go go. Not guessed. Go go.

Toasted susie is my ice-cream.

READING AND WRITING PROJECTS

FOR CREATIVE AND CRITICAL THINKING

Your own writing is important as you try to learn more about yourself as a reader—both what you do cognitively and what is done to you culturally—to produce the kind of reader you are when you interact with any particular text. In addition to response statements and the formal expository paper that may grow out of them, there are other ways to use writing to learn. What follows are suggestions for integrating your reading of and writing about literary texts in various ways. These suggestions include exploratory writing, playing with texts and language, creative efforts in various genres, and other writing exercises designed to strengthen your awareness of the cognitive and cultural processes involved in your reading.

If you produce any "creative" pieces of your own (stories, poems, dramatic scenes, nonverbal displays, and so on) think of them as instances of intertextuality: Directly or indirectly, they refer to and are part of the textual network that includes other texts already written. If you work on any of the more "expository" or "discursive" projects, think of what you're doing as joining a conversation with other texts and other voices.

▶ Write imaginatively to add another episode to any short story. (An example might be, from "The Necklace," another of the attempts the Loisels made to raise money to pay for the replacement necklace or, from "everybody knew bubba riff," another voice in the chorus of voices talking about something Bubba had done when he was alive.)

▶ Write to continue the action of any short story. (In "The Necklace," for instance, how would you see the conversation between Mrs. Loisel and Mrs. Forrestier continuing after Mrs. Forrestier tells Mathilde that the original necklace was "costume jewelry"? An interesting variation of this kind of writing would be to try it with "Continuity of Parks." It would seem to be impossible to do within the "world" of that story because the action ends simultaneously with the ending of the story the man in the green armchair is reading. If you find this to be so, discuss why the action of such a story as "Continuity of Parks" cannot be continued but the action of a story such as "The Necklace" can.)

▶ As another variation on the above project, add a dream to the end of a story. (Perhaps this would work with a story like "Continuity of Parks": What would happen if you imagined the man in the green armchair was dreaming that he was stabbed? What would happen if the feel of the knife plunging into him woke him? What would his waking reality be like? With a story like "The Necklace," suppose you added a dream of Mrs. Loisel the night after her encounter with Mrs. Forrestier on the boulevard.)

▶ Rewrite the ending of any short story. Pick up the action at any point you choose and change the direction of the action.

▶ Work out the shots for a video of any short story. This can be done with sketches or with photographs of actors whom you choose and direct. In addition to the plot or storyline, you should consider details of setting and characters' clothes, their movements and facial expressions that would matter more in a visual medium and less on the page. A project such as this could be undertaken individually or by a small group working together. Either way, if more than one such project is done in your class, compare the different concepts that are created.

As an example of what can be done in terms of creatively playing with a short story, consider the following writing by a student. Tonia McKelvie, a freshman in an introductory literature class, took an assignment much like the fourth one listed above and developed her own sense of how "The Necklace" should end. That assignment also asked her to write a brief explanation of her reasons for changing the ending the way she did.

Tonia's writing developed out of her first response to the story, in which she expressed some disappointment at the "unhappy" ending of de Maupassant's story. That response resulted from her interaction, on both the literary and the ideologic levels, with the text strategy of de Maupassant's ending.

To indicate something of her writing process in this project, I have reproduced below Tonia's prewriting notes about what she wanted to do. As you can see, she first considered two ways of providing Mathilde with "moral growth," as well as the possibilities for each of those approaches. Then she decided to "stick with a happy ending" and sketched out some ideas for that ending.

Alternate Routes to First Draft

Not satisfied with Mathilde's moral growth in the original ending.

1. See that she is punished by some destructive measure to herself or the others. (She may or may not gain any moral growth even at this point.)
2. She reflects upon her life and realizes that she got what she deserves. (She may accept it or not.)

Stick with a Happy Ending
- New-found moral growth
- Mr. Loisel has nothing to do with the diamonds. Jeanne keeps the secret to herself.
- Mrs. Loisel is told, but reacts differently. Her eyes are opened by Jeanne's actions.

Idea for New Ending
- They meet, talk, and discuss the necklace.
- Mrs. Forrestier has a secret as well.
- Mrs. Loisel tells her of the dilemma.
- Mrs. Forrestier invites her to her home for a talk.
- Mrs. Forrestier surprises her w/ two diamond necklaces. Explains her original was given back the day after the ball.
- If Mrs. Loisel would have been honest, none of this would have happened.
- One last surprise: Mr. Loisel knew of the returned necklace all along.

Now here is Tonia's new ending of "The Necklace," followed by her expository discussion of why she changed it the way she did.

STUDENT WRITING
Tonia McKelvie: The Altered "Necklace"

"Oh, my poor Mathilde! How you are changed." (Maupassant, paragraph 114)

"Yes, I have had days hard enough, since I have seen you, days wretched enough—and that because of you!"

"Of me? How so?"

"Do you remember that diamond necklace which you lent me to wear at the ministerial ball?"

"Yes. Well?"

"Well, I lost it." (Maupassant, 119)

"Mathilde, after ten years, why now do you tell me of this?"

"I thought you must know what I went through the last ten years, all because of you!"

"Again you say because of me, but I must say that it is not I that caused you such misfortune. Mathilde, you brought this all on yourself. You are the only one to blame."

"Me! Why do you make such wild accusations?"

"We must talk. Come to my home at noon where we may sit and discuss this."

Mrs. Forrestier went home and prepared for a nice lunch. She had been waiting for this day to come for ten years. She must now tell Mrs. Loisel of her secret.

There was a knock at the front door. Mrs. Forrestier took a deep breath and realized that this was something that had to be done. She reassured herself that everything was going to be fine, opened the door, and welcomed Mrs. Loisel.

"Please come in and have a seat. I have prepared trout for lunch. I know that is your favorite."

"Yes, it looks wonderful. Before I begin eating, would you please consider telling me what it is that is so important?"

"If you wish."

Mrs. Forrestier left the room and returned with two beautiful diamond necklaces.

"I do not understand, Jeanne. Why do you now have two identical necklaces?"

"One, my dear, is the original one that you borrowed. The other is the one you returned."

"What? How could that be?"

"I left the ball shortly after you."

"Yes?"

"I went into one of the anterooms where I had left my fur safely deserted and noticed the string of diamonds on the floor that looked like my own. I checked the small silver clasp on which the initials J.F. were engraved. Yes, it certainly was my diamond necklace. It must have slipped off when you went to wake Mr. Loisel."

"Yes."

"I was very surprised to see your letter explaining that the clasp had been broken, and you would return it just as soon as it was fixed. Very odd, I thought, very odd indeed."

"Why did you not tell me? That was so wrong of you!"

"Of me, my dear? You were the one who was wrong. Your entire life, if I may say so."

"Oh! I could just tear those diamonds from you and watch each and every one of them shatter to the ground!"

"My dear Mathilde, do you not hear yourself? What is it that makes you so evil? Didn't you ever learn to appreciate the things that you have? Your wonderful husband. That loving man. Can you understand anything that I am saying?"

"A bit."

"He helped you through all of this grief, and not once did you ever tell him that you loved him, did you? Nobody owes you anything, not I, not your husband, and certainly not the world."

A single tear fell from Mathilde's eye.

"You have lived your every day unsatisfied, unhappy. There is only one thing that you must do to change that, and it has nothing to do with money."

Sincerely, with questioning eyes, Mathilde raised her head.

"What is it, my friend?"

"Love."

"Love?"

"Yes, Mathilde. Let go of the evil, the greed, the want. You have the only thing you could ever want. Only you were too naive to see it."

"It is my husband, isn't it?"

"Yes, my dear. I am sorry for the hard words, but I could not stand to see you this way anymore."

"I do not know what to say."

"Please don't say anything; just go to him and remember that I will always be here for you."

"I will."

"One thing before you go. This belongs to you."

"Oh, no."

"Yes, I insist. The diamonds are yours. Now you may have one of your luxuries as well."

"Thank you, Jeanne. You have given me a new life. Everything you said, it was all true. How could I have been so cruel?"

"Do not worry about the past now; just worry about changing it."

They kissed each other and Mathilde rushed home.

"What is it, my dear Mathilde? Such a big smile."

"I am sorry for what I have done."

"Done?"

"Yes, my entire life with you. I was so miserable. I am almost embarrassed to admit it."

"Oh, my dear."

"You are the only gem I need. I love you."

"I love you, Mathilde. What is this you have brought back from Mrs. Forrestier's?"

"The diamonds, the diamonds that we bought."

"What?"

"It is a long story, but they are ours now. Mrs. Forrestier has her original necklace."

"Is this true?"

"Yes, from now on our lives will change for the better. I will do my best to change completely as fast as I can."

"Did Mrs. Forrestier have anything to do with this?"

"A bit."

"Mathilde, let me put these on you. Oh, look how beautiful they are! What a beautiful treasure for you to have!"

"No, they are ours. I want you to sell them."

"Sell them?"

"Yes, I need to give you a wonderful life after all you have done."

"Are you certain?"

"Please, right away. I want to start our wonderful life as soon as possible."

"First we will buy you a new home, Mathilde."

"Certainly not. First we will buy you a gun for your shooting."

Mr. Loisel smiled, and the more than happy little lady smiled back.

The Rationale for My New Ending

I enjoyed "The Necklace" very much, but the ending was a tad unsatisfying for me. I did not feel that Mrs. Loisel had gained any moral growth after all the hardship that she put both herself and her husband through.

Despite my original feelings that the ending should be negative, I decided to go with a happy one. My problem was that I did not like the fact that Mrs. Loisel had not changed her cruel ways. I wanted her to not only change her ways, but realize the way she had been all of her life. With this embarrassment in mind, I also wanted Mrs. Forrestier and Mr. Loisel to gain from her improvement.

I like Jeanne in the original story, so I decided to use her as more of a main character in my story. She did do the ultimate job of opening Mrs. Loisel's eyes by making her realize her cruel ways of life. I liked the story better with a new-found moral growth on Mrs. Loisel's part. In this happy ending everybody got a chance to gain something good. Now that's a happy ending!

6 ◇ READING FICTION ACTIVELY

The brief survey of the background and history of the short story in Chapter 5 occasionally used the term *narrative* as a synonym for *story;* that is, both terms denote an account of events or an episode in the life of some imaginary person, a character. This chapter will consider short stories in the more specific sense as *narratives;* that is, as accounts *told* by a specific person or voice, by a **narrator**.

A Brief History of Narration

In the earliest days of storytelling, the narrator was basically identical with the poet who was reciting the account. The **literary repertoires** of those ancient societies were relatively narrow in this regard. But once literature began to be reconceived as the imaginative product of individual poets and fiction writers (in Western history, this took place in the late Middle Ages) new possibilities arose. As considered briefly in Chapter 5, Chaucer's *The Canterbury Tales* represented a step toward greater complexity because Chaucer used the text strategy of a fictionalized narrator: an unnamed pilgrim who accompanies the others on their journey to the shrine of Thomas á Becket at Canterbury and who recounts some of what happened among the pilgrims on the way. In terms of the literary experience of a twentieth-century reader, *The Canterbury Tales* may seem quite modern in this respect, in spite of the obvious antiquity of the characters in the poem and the language in which it is written. If this is so, it is because the literary experience of most twentieth-century readers has been shaped by their experience with short stories and novels written since the middle of the nineteenth century. And as the brief historical survey in Chapter 5 also pointed out, fiction in Western culture really began to be regarded and developed as a form of serious or high literary art roughly 150 years ago. With the more self-consciously artistic efforts of fiction writers in the West after about 1840, there developed greater attention to narrator as a text strategy, not merely as a necessary function of getting a story told.

It is true that in many modern short stories ("The Necklace" and "Continuity of Parks" in Chapter 5 are examples) narrator may not be especially obvious or important as a text strategy. In general, in realistic fiction the narrator has tended to be "invisible." In what is called real life, you don't experience anything like a narrator telling you what's going on, so many writers in the realistic mode have attempted to tell stories with the narrator having as low a profile as possible. (Even "Continuity of Parks," a story that seems consciously to challenge some of the conventions of realistic fiction, uses a low-profile or invisible narrator in order to seem realistic at first.) At the same time, however, numerous other stories from the middle nineteenth century on have used more visible or involved narrators, thus making point of view more obvious as a text strategy. This chapter will continue the consideration of the literary interaction that happens when you read short stories. But because narration is such an essential text strategy of fiction, it will be the focus of this chapter.

Narrative Voice

As you did in Chapter 5, try to heighten your awareness of what you bring to the reading interaction by taking a look at your literary experience before you begin to read a short story. Take a few minutes to write down, in the box provided or in your journal, some answers to the following questions. Be prepared to share your notes with others as part of class discussion.

- What do you expect a short story to have in the way of a narrator? What different possibilities for point of view are you familiar with? How do you think the narrator might affect your response to other text strategies in a story?
- What do you expect to do as a reader as you interact with the narrator in a short story? For instance, will you regard the narrator as a character? Will you believe what the narrator is telling you? What reading strategies do you expect will interact most logically with narrator as a text strategy?

My Expectations for a Narrator in a Short Story	
Text Strategies	Reading Strategies
1.	1.
2.	2.
3.	3.
4.	4.
5.	5.

Also, as you read through the selection that follows, make some brief notes, in the box provided or in your journal, about what's actually happening in your processing of this text, such as:

- When and how do you know who is telling the story? Are you able to construct a "person" behind the narrative voice? If so, how and why are you able to do this? What kind of person does he seem to be?
- How do you feel as the audience being addressed by the narrative voice? For instance, are you offended? flattered? insulted? compromised?

- How and why does your interaction with the narrator affect your response to other text strategies (for instance plot, character, theme, and so on?)

WHAT HAPPENS AS I READ "THE CASK OF AMONTILLADO"

Identifying the narrator:

Responding as audience:

Affecting my response to other text strategies:

Edgar Allan Poe   1809–1849

The Cask of Amontillado   1846

The thousand injuries of Fortunato I had borne as I best could; but when he ventured upon insult; I vowed revenge. You, who so well know the nature of my soul, will not suppose, however, that I gave utterance to a threat. *At length* I would be avenged; this was a point definitely settled—but the very definititiveness with which it was resolved precluded the idea of risk. I must not only punish, but punish with impunity. A wrong is unredressed when retribution overtakes its redresser. It is equally unredressed when the avenger fails to make himself felt as such to him who has done the wrong.

It must be understood, that neither by word nor deed had I given Fortunato cause to doubt my good-will. I continued, as was my wont, to smile in his face, and he did not perceive that my smile *now* was at the thought of his immolation.

He had a weak point—this Fortunato—although in other regards he was a man to be respected and even feared. He prided himself on his connoisseurship in wine. Few Italians have the true virtuoso spirit. For the most part their enthusiasm is adopted to suit the time and opportunity—to practise imposture upon the British and Austrian *millionnaires*. In painting and gemmary Fortunato, like his countrymen, was a quack—but in the matter of old wines he was sincere. In this respect I did not differ from him materially: I was skilful in the Italian vintages myself, and bought largely whenever I could.

It was about dusk, one evening during the supreme madness of the carnival season, that I encountered my friend. He accosted me with excessive warmth, for he had been drinking much. The man wore motley. He had on a tight-fitting parti-striped dress, and his head was surmounted by the conical cap and bells. I was so pleased to see him, that I thought I should never have done wringing his hand.

I said to him: "My dear Fortunato, you are luckily met. How remarkably well you are looking to-day! But I have received a pipe[1] of what passes for Amontillado,[2] and I have my doubts."

"How?" said he. "Amontillado? A pipe? Impossible! And in the middle of the carnival!"

"I have my doubts," I replied; "and I was silly enough to pay the full Amontillado price without consulting you in the matter. You were not to be found, and I was fearful of losing a bargain."

"Amontillado!"

"I have my doubts."

"Amontillado!"

"And I must satisfy them."

"Amontillado!"

"As you are engaged, I am on my way to Luchesi. If any one has a critical turn, it is he. He will tell me——"

"Luchesi cannot tell Amontillado from Sherry."

"And yet some fools will have it that his taste is a match for your own."

"Come, let us go."

"Whither?"

"To your vaults."

"My friend, no; I will not impose upon your good nature. I perceive you have an engagement. Luchesi——"

"I have no engagement;—come."

"My friend, no. It is not the engagement, but the severe cold with which I perceive you are afflicted. The vaults are insufferably damp. They are encrusted with nitre."

"Let us go, nevertheless. The cold is merely nothing. Amontillado! You have been imposed upon. And as for Luchesi, he cannot distinguish Sherry from Amontillado."

Thus speaking, Fortunato possessed himself of my arm. Putting on a mask of black silk, and drawing a *roquelaire*[3] closely about my person, I suffered him to hurry me to my palazzo.

There were no attendants at home; they had absconded to make merry in honor of the time. I had told them that I should not return until the morning, and had given them explicit orders not to stir from the house. These orders were sufficient, I well knew, to insure their immediate disappearance, one and all, as soon as my back was turned.

---

[1]pipe—cask, barrel.
[2]Amontillado—a type of Spanish sherry.
[3]roquelaire—knee-length cape.

I took from their sconces two flambeaux, and giving one to Fortunato,   25
bowed him through several suites of rooms to the archway that led into the
vaults. I passed down a long and winding staircase, requesting him to be cautious as he followed. We came at length to the foot of the descent, and stood
together on the damp ground of the catacombs of the Montresors.

The gait of my friend was unsteady, and the bells upon his cap jingled as
he strode.

"The pipe?" said he.

"It is farther on," said I; "but observe the white web-work which gleams
from these cavern walls."

He turned toward me, and looked into my eyes with two filmy orbs that
distilled the rheum of intoxication.

"Nitre?" he asked, at length.   30

"Nitre," I replied. "How long have you had that cough?"

"Ugh! ugh! ugh!—ugh! ugh! ugh!—ugh! ugh! ugh!—ugh! ugh! ugh!—ugh!
ugh! ugh!"

My poor friend found it impossible to reply for many minutes.

"It is nothing," he said, at last.

"Come," I said, with decision, "we will go back; your health is precious.   35
You are rich, respected, admired, beloved; you are happy, as once I was. You
are a man to be missed. For me it is no matter. We will go back; you will be
ill, and I cannot be responsible. Besides, there is Luchesi—"

"Enough," he said; "the cough is a mere nothing; it will not kill me. I shall
not die of a cough."

"True—true," I replied; "and, indeed, I had no intention of alarming you
unnecessarily; but you should use all proper caution. A draught of this
Medoc⁴ will defend us from the damps."

Here I knocked off the neck of a bottle which I drew from a long row of
its fellows that lay upon the mould.

"Drink," I said, presenting him the wine.

He raised it to his lips with a leer. He paused and nodded to me familiarly,   40
while his bells jingled.

"I drink," he said, "to the buried that repose around us."

"And I to your long life."

He again took my arm, and we proceeded.

"These vaults," he said, "are extensive."

"The Montresors," I replied, "were a great and numerous family."

"I forget your arms."   45

"A huge human foot d'or,⁵ in a field azure; the foot crushes a serpent rampant whose fangs are imbedded in the heel."

"And the motto?"

*Nemo me impune lacessit.*⁶

"Good!" he said.   50

---

⁴Medoc—a French red wine.
⁵d'or—French: of gold.
⁶*Nemo me impune lacessit*—Latin: "No one wounds me with impunity."

The wine sparkled in his eyes and the bells jingled. My own fancy grew warm with the Medoc. We had passed through walls of piled bones, with casks and puncheons intermingling, into the inmost recesses of the catacombs. I paused again, and this time I made bold to seize Fortunato by an arm above the elbow.

"The nitre!" I said; "see, it increases. It hangs like moss upon the vaults. We are below the river's bed. The drops of moisture trickle among the bones. Come, we will go back ere it is too late. Your cough——"

"It is nothing," he said; "let us go on. But first, another draught of the Medoc."

I broke and reached him a flagon of De Grâve.[7] He emptied it at a breath. His eyes flashed with a fierce light. He laughed and threw the bottle upward with a gesticulation I did not understand.

I looked at him in surprise. He repeated the movement—a grotesque one.   55

"You do not comprehend?" he said.

"Not I," I replied.

"Then you are not of the brotherhood."

"How?"

"You are not of the masons."[8]   60

"Yes, yes," I said; "yes, yes."

"You? Impossible! A mason?"

"A mason," I replied.

"A sign," he said.

"It is this," I answered, producing a trowel from beneath the folds of my   65
roquelaire.

"You jest," he exclaimed, recoiling a few paces. "But let us proceed to the Amontillado."

"Be it so," I said, replacing the tool beneath the cloak, and again offering him my arm. He leaned upon it heavily. We continued our route in search of the Amontillado. We passed through a range of low arches, descended, passed on, and descending again, arrived at a deep crypt, in which the foulness of the air caused our flambeaux rather to glow than flame.

At the most remote end of the crypt there appeared another less spacious. Its walls had been lined with human remains, piled to the vault overhead, in the fashion of the great catacombs of Paris. Three sides of this interior crypt were still ornamented in this manner. From the fourth the bones had been thrown down, and lay promiscuously upon the earth, forming at one point a mound of some size. Within the wall thus exposed by the displacing of the bones, we perceived a still interior recess, in depth about four feet, in width three, in height six or seven. It seemed to have been constructed for no especial use within itself, but formed merely the interval between two of the colossal supports of the roof of the catacombs, and was backed by one of their circumscribing walls of solid granite.

It was in vain that Fortunato, uplifting his dull torch, endeavored to pry into the depth of the recess. Its termination the feeble light did not enable us to see.

---

[7]De Grâve—a French white wine.
[8]masons—the Freemasons, a fraternal order.

"Proceed," I said, "herein is the Amontillado. As for Luchesi—" ₇₀

"He is an ignoramus," interrupted my friend, as he stepped unsteadily forward, while I followed immediately at his heels. In an instant he had reached the extremity of the niche, and finding his progress arrested by the rock, stood stupidly bewildered. A moment more and I had fettered him to the granite. In its surface were two iron staples, distant from each other about two feet, horizontally. From one of these depended a short chain, from the other a padlock. Throwing the links about his waist, it was but the work of a few seconds to secure it. He was too much astounded to resist. Withdrawing the key I stepped back from the recess.

"Pass your hand," I said, "over the wall; you cannot help feeling the nitre. Indeed it is *very* damp. Once more let me *implore* you to return. No? Then I must positively leave you. But I must first render you all the little attentions in my power."

"The Amontillado!" ejaculated my friend, not yet recovered from his astonishment.

"True," I replied; "the Amontillado."

As I said these words I busied myself among the pile of bones of which I ₇₅ have before spoken. Throwing them aside, I soon uncovered a quantity of building stone and mortar. With these materials and with the aid of my trowel, I began vigorously to wall up the entrance of the niche.

I had scarcely laid the first tier of the masonry when I discovered that the intoxication of Fortunato had in a great measure worn off. The earliest indication I had of this was a low moaning cry from the depth of the recess. It was *not* the cry of a drunken man. There was then a long and obstinate silence. I laid the second tier, and the third, and the fourth; and then I heard the furious vibrations of the chain. The noise lasted for several minutes, during which, that I might hearken to it with the more satisfaction, I ceased my labors and sat down upon the bones. When at last the clanking subsided, I resumed the trowel, and finished without interruption the fifth, the sixth, and the seventh tier. The wall was now nearly upon a level with my breast. I again paused, and holding the flambeaux over the masonwork, threw a few feeble rays upon the figure within.

A succession of loud and shrill screams, bursting suddenly from the throat of the chained form, seemed to thrust me violently back. For a brief moment I hesitated—I trembled. Unsheathing my rapier, I began to grope with it about the recess; but the thought of an instant reassured me. I placed my hand upon the solid fabric of the catacombs, and felt satisfied. I reapproached the wall. I replied to the yells of him who clamored. I re-echoed—I aided—I surpassed them in volume and in strength. I did this, and the clamorer grew still.

It was now midnight, and my task was drawing to a close. I had completed the eighth, the ninth, and the tenth tier. I had finished a portion of the last and the eleventh; there remained but a single stone to be fitted and plastered in. I struggled with its weight; I placed it partially in its destined position. But now there came from out the niche a low laugh that erected the hairs upon my head. It was succeeded by a sad voice, which I had difficulty in recognizing as that of the noble Fortunato. The voice said—

"Ha! ha! ha!—he! he!—a very good joke indeed—an excellent jest. We will have many a rich laugh about it at the palazzo—he! he! he!—over our wine—he! he! he!"

"The Amontillado!" I said.   80

"He! he! he—he! he! he—yes, the Amontillado. But is it not getting late? Will not they be awaiting us at the palazzo, the Lady Fortunato and the rest? Let us be gone."

"Yes," I said, "let us be gone."

"For the love of God, Montresor!"

"Yes," I said, "for the love of God!"

But to these words I hearkened in vain for a reply. I grew impatient. I   85
called aloud:

"Fortunato!"

No answer. I called again:

"Fortunato!"

No answer still. I thrust a torch through the remaining aperture and let it fall within. There came forth in return only a jingling of the bells. My heart grew sick—on account of the dampness of the catacombs. I hastened to make an end of my labor. I forced the last stone into its position; I plastered it up. Against the new masonry I re-erected the old rampart of bones. For the half of a century no mortal has disturbed them. *In pace requiescat!*[9]

Interacting with the Narrator

Depending on what you have in your literary experience, you may have described point of view in "The Cask of Amontillado" as **first-person**. That should have been easy to spot from the very first sentence, where the first-person singular pronoun, "I," appears, outside of quotation marks. The chart below shows one way of differentiating kinds of narrators, according to grammatical person.

Short Story Narrators	
Type	*Pronoun Used to Refer to Narrator*
First-person	I, We*
Second-person	You**
Third-person	He, She, It, They*

*Plural narration is rarely used.
**Second-person narration is theoretically possible but rarely if ever used.

This convention of fiction pretends that the narrative is being related by someone who is "speaking" to you as a reader. Although you may not be accustomed to reading a first-person narrator this way, you could identify sev-

---

[9]*In pace requiescat*—Latin: May he rest in peace.

eral gaps in association with this "I": Who is this person? Why is she or he speaking on this occasion? What is he or she going to tell about?

Actually, you may be aware of asking that third question as you begin to read "The Cask of Amontillado" or any story that opens with the words of a first-person narrator. According to the conventions of short stories, you may expect the gap concerning what you're about to be told to be filled fairly soon as you read on in the text. But you may not be so conscious of the other gaps. If so, that just shows how unquestioned is the place of first-person narration in your literary experience. Because there's nothing really strange or unconventional about this text strategy, it's easy to naturalize this speaking voice as a character recounting some experience he's been through. Even the details he does *not* provide may not seem to be terribly problematic gaps; you probably expect him to tell you soon enough what he decides you need to know.

Character

As you read on in "The Cask of Amontillado" for three or four paragraphs, you are probably able to fill in the first two gaps identified above. This narrator is someone who feels he has been insulted by someone named Fortunato, a person whom the narrator has apparently known for some time, long enough to have "borne … [a] thousand injuries" from him. This narrator says that he "vowed revenge," and so is speaking apparently in order to tell you about this revenge. As you read on through the first few paragraphs, do you also begin to construct a person behind this narrative voice, a person who could be described in terms like "cool-headed," "calculating," and "deceptive"? He says not only that he "vowed revenge" but several other things that, if you notice them, might help you construct a person behind the narrative voice. For instance, he says he was in no great hurry to enact his revenge; he intended not to be caught but to make his victim aware that vengeance was being carried out; he "continued . . . to smile in . . . [Fortunato's] face" so as not to arouse suspicion even that he had grounds for revenge; and he identified a "weak point" in Fortunato that he could use in his revenge.

In addition to *what* a first-person narrator says, *how* he or she says it may help you construct him or her as a person behind the narrative voice. The narrator's implied attitude toward what he or she is talking about, toward himself or herself, and toward his or her audience constitutes **tone** in a narrative, and tone may be used to create a picture of a person speaking through the narrative voice. Based on your reading of the opening paragraphs of "The Cask of Amontillado," how might you describe this narrator's implied attitude toward his audience, himself, or the subject of his narrative? Might you use words like "calm" or "cold" for his tone regarding his revenge plan? How about "scornful" or "steely" for his attitude toward Fortunato? Does his tone seem "candid" or "remorseless" as he addresses his audience? And perhaps his attitude about himself can be described as "self-assured" or "egotistical"? Whether or not you or your classmates identified qualities like these regarding the narrator's tone in "The Cask of Amontillado," the attitudes that he projects about himself, his audience, and the subject of his discourse should help you construct him as a person through his narrative voice. The chart below offers another way, besides grammar of pronouns, of defining narrator—by considering the narrator's status as a character or person.

Short Story Narrators

Type	Status as Character	Variations, Pronouns
Involved or limited	Is a character in the story.	Dramatized narrator: I Narrative focus: He, She
Omniscient	Stands outside the action he or she recounts.	Privileged: Takes reader "inside" characters; may reveal their thoughts and feelings; may provide his/her own thoughts and feelings. May or may not refer to himself/herself as "I"; in the most common formulation, is a narrative *voice*, not a person.
		Not privileged: Stays "distant" from characters; withholds his/her thoughts and feelings. May or may not refer to himself/herself as "I"; in the most common formulation, is a narrative *voice*, not a person.

Constructing the narrator as a person is possible, of course, with an **involved** narrator because an involved narrator is a character in the story he or she tells. But it is much easier with a first-person or **dramatized** narrator, who speaks, as it were, in his or her own voice, rather than with a third-person **narrative focus**.

A first-person narrator may also digress from recounting his or her story to describe himself or herself as a character, but the narrator in "The Cask of Amontillado" reveals things about himself, through both what he says and how he says it, while he moves the action of his story along. (If you recall what Chapter 5 said about Poe's belief in economy in the short story, you have a basis in your literary experience for appreciating why this narrator does not digress or why the **exposition** of this story is so brief.) Because the narrator's exposition is so brief and self-revealing, you may become more interested in him as a person, not just as a functional device to relate the action. Furthermore, your sense of his personality may affect your interest in the plot of this story as early as the third paragraph: How will he—or how *did* he, inasmuch as he is recounting events from his past—exact his calculated revenge? Will it be merely some public embarrassment of Fortunato, or something more evil and cruel?

In similar economical fashion, what this narrator says in the first few paragraphs about Fortunato may help you get a sense of him as a character too, while the narrator is getting the plot under way. Fortunato is someone who has injured and insulted the narrator, and so may be a nasty and sarcastic person. He appears to be blindly egotistical: Perhaps you may infer from what the narrator says about Fortunato never doubting the narrator's good will that Fortunato was unable to conceive of the narrator being insulted enough to gain revenge. And Fortunato is proud of "his connoisseurship in wine," so proud that the narrator sees this as a "weak point" he can use in carrying out his revenge. These aspects of Fortunato's personality, in turn, may reveal something else about the narrator as a character: that he either is or thinks he is smarter than Fortunato, although Fortunato apparently thinks he is smarter than the narrator. And the narrator uses this final aspect of Fortunato's character to set the trap of the narrator's revenge *and* to advance the plot.

> CONNECT: Both stories in Chapter 5, "The Necklace" and "Continuity of Parks," are narrated from a third-person omniscient point of view. Consequently, in neither story is it possible to develop a sense of the narrator as a *character* because in both stories the narrator is just a *voice*.

Plot

The initial conflict has been established by the third paragraph of the story. That conflict is between the narrator and Fortunato, although of the two of them only the narrator is aware of it. That he lets the reader in on it and that he says relatively few things about himself as the story opens suggest that the plot structure of this story will be twofold: it will recount how the narrator got his revenge on Fortunato and at the same time it will gradually reveal to the reader more of the personality of the narrator as a character.

Beginning with the fifth paragraph, the narrator presents most of the rest of the story in dialogue rather than in narrative. Because this text strategy has the effect of showing the reader the action more or less as it unfolds—whereas direct narration would tell by summarizing the action—this text strategy may be considered *dramatic* presentation. This is, after all, the way a stage drama advances its action: by having characters act out situations in front of the audience, with no intervening narrator. This kind of dramatic presentation suits the kind of dramatized or involved narrator "The Cask of Amontillado" has. It also suits the plot interest of gradual revelation of character that accompanies the narrator's and Fortunato's progress through the catacombs of the Montresors.

An aspect of plot in a story such as "The Cask of Amontillado" is **suspense**, which is produced in the reader from the interaction of reader and text. That is, the text offers enough information as the plot unfolds to allow the reader to make guesses as to where the plot is heading, what will happen next or ultimately, but not so much information all at once to prevent these guesses from being made in the first place. In other words, some information is dispensed bit by bit by the text while at the same time some information is withheld. But the information that is provided gradually narrows the initially

wide gap of how the plot will be resolved, allowing the reader the pleasure—
even the pleasure of horror—of coming closer and closer to the understanding
that she anticipates achieving when the plot as a whole, or even a certain
movement within it, is resolved. This gap-narrowing procedure is closely related to the reading strategy of consistency building, in which the reader
makes some kind of interpretive guess and proceeds to select information
from the text that is consistent with this guess, and perhaps to disregard other
information that challenges this consistency. The pleasurable tension involved
in this process of narrowing down the possibilities of where the plot is headed
is expressed in the cliché that a suspenseful plot "keeps you on the edge of
your seat."

In "The Cask of Amontillado," the plot allows the suspense of seeing the
action build gradually but inevitably toward the final accomplishment of Montresor's revenge. The text strategy of the dramatized narrator contributes to
this suspense through what he does *not* tell you as a reader as well as through
what he does. By not telling you certain things but letting you guess at them
through what the dialogue reveals, the narrator involves you in the unfolding
action. Perhaps the best example of this is Montresor's waving a trowel at Fortunato when Fortunato asks him for a sign that he is a mason. At this point in
your reading, did you begin to make a more educated guess as to the kind of
revenge Montresor had planned? A reader who brought to the story knowledge of different senses of the word "mason" and of the use to which one
kind of mason puts a trowel would be drawn further into the action here than
a reader whose experience does not include such knowledge.

This kind of detail could contribute to suspense just as well if the story
were told through a third-person point of view. But first-person narration allows for the same kind of detail to provide greater revelation of the character
of the narrator too. Perhaps as you read "The Cask of Amontillado," you felt a
sense of horror mounting when Montresor says he "produc[ed] ... a trowel
from beneath the folds of my *roquelaire*" because of the guess it enabled you
to make about Montresor's specific plans. But perhaps your sense of horror
and suspense were heightened because Montresor himself recounts this detail,
and because he makes no commentary upon it either to Fortunato or to you
as reader.

Irony

Irony may be defined broadly as a difference between appearance and reality;
in fiction, irony may take verbal form as words that seem to mean one thing
but actually mean something different from or even the opposite of their apparent meaning. The moment in "The Cask of Amontillado" when Montresor
produces a trowel from beneath his cloak as a sign that he is a "mason" may
be considered ironic because Montresor understands the word "mason" in a
different sense from the way Fortunato has just used it. Fortunato had referred
to the fraternal order, known colloquially as "masons"; Montresor has in mind
a meaning of "mason" closer to "bricklayer." If this incident helped you guess

the means of Montresor's revenge (to entomb Fortunato alive in the cata-combs) then you may also read this exchange between the two men as ironic because of what you guessed Montresor's intentions to be and your recogni-tion that Fortunato does not guess.

The exchange about the trowel and the word "mason" could also be ironic, just as it could help build suspense, if this story were told by a third-person narrator; changing the first-person pronoun to "Montresor" and the third-person pronoun to "Fortunato" would not necessarily change the differ-ence in understanding that exists between the two characters. But the text strategy of a first-person, involved narrator does deepen the irony in this ex-change—and elsewhere in the story—because that text strategy allows a reader to get closer to the person Montresor who is speaking through the nar-rative voice, closer than third-person narration would allow. To go back for a moment to the opening paragraphs of the story, the first-person narrator tends to take you as a reader into his confidence—partly by confessing that he "vowed revenge" but also by addressing "you" directly and asserting that you "so well know the nature of . . . [his] soul." At this point in your reading of the story, you probably don't know the nature of his soul, but perhaps the narra-tor's saying that you do induces you to drop your guard, so to speak, and go along with him. As you are taken into Montresor's confidence, you become, in effect, his ally against Fortunato: you and Montresor know, when Montresor invites Fortunato to inspect his newly acquired Amontillado, that Fortunato is being led into a trap. And you know that Fortunato does not know this. If you were aware of that difference in understanding at the point in the story when Montresor first mentions the Amontillado to Fortunato, you may have been alert to an ironic level of language and action on Montresor's part as the action moves deeper into the catacombs.

This awareness of irony, however, may also differ from reader to reader according to their ideologies: some readers, indeed some people, have a more active sensitivity to irony than others. If you did not notice irony while reading "The Cask of Amontillado" the first time—in the exchange about "mason" or elsewhere—you almost certainly will if you read it again soon. In a second reading, you should find that the level of suspense decreases be-cause you already know the outcome of the plot, but that your awareness of irony increases for the very same reason. (If you have ever watched a video-tape of a sports event—a basketball or football game, for instance—the out-come of which you already know, you will know what I mean here: certain "triumphant" actions and celebrations on the part of the ultimately losing side or their fans become ironic because of your now-greater knowledge of the outcome.)

Whether on first or second reading, however, you may have read Montre-sor's professed concern for Fortunato's health and Montresor's suggestions that they turn back as ironic because Montresor's plans are exactly the oppo-site of what he is saying. And how about Montresor's reply of "True—true" to Fortunato's statement "I shall not die of a cough" and Montresor's subsequent toast to Fortunato's "long life"?

CONNECT: Involved narration in "The Cask of Amontillado" allows *verbal* irony to arise, whereas the omniscient narration in "The Necklace" permits *dramatic* irony: You may have seen Mathilde's fall into poverty as a result of her desire to seem wealthy as ironic; the same with the final revelation that the necklace she and her husband had worked so hard to replace was merely costume jewelry. Such irony is a matter of events rather than words.

Unreliable Narrators

In all these instances, Fortunato is the victim of Montresor's irony, which is deepened, as I have said, by the first-person narration that tends to align you with Montresor against Fortunato. Your ideology does not have to value revenge, much less cruel and murderous revenge, for this to happen, either. To the contrary, some of the horrifying effect of "The Cask of Amontillado" comes from your sense of participation in a cold-blooded, premeditated murder and your experiencing it through the point of view of a remorseless, even gloating, murderer. You are carried along in spite of yourself. Or your literary experience draws you along as the suspense builds toward the resolution of the plot, while your ideology is trying to hold you back, saying, in effect, "No, no! This can't be happening!"

My intention here is not to go too deeply into the psychology of this response, but to suggest that your ideology may interact with the first-person, involved narrator in "The Cask of Amontillado" in another way as well. If you do react with repulsion toward Montresor at the same time as you are drawn into his mind, you may read him as the victim of his own verbal irony. For instance, his superior and rather sneering reference to Fortunato as a proud man may turn around on him, in your eyes, if you see Montresor as even more proud. Doesn't he, after all, come close to boasting about his criminal revenge against Fortunato? Doesn't he invoke his family motto, *Nemo me impune lacessit* ("No one wounds me with impunity") with a particular, perhaps even damning, pride? Your answers to these questions are, of course, a matter of interpretation, which probably varies from reader to reader, according to the ideology of each. But I raise the possibility of reading "against" Montresor in order to introduce the concept of the **unreliable** narrator. This chapter has already presented two ways of defining short story narrators—according to grammatical person and according to their status as characters. The chart on page 145 shows yet another way, according to their reliability.

Short Story Narrators

Type	Other Characteristics
Reliable	Usually *omniscient;* does not refer to him/herself as "I"; maintains "objectivity" about people and events related in narrative.
Unreliable	Usually *involved,* whether first- or third-person; does not have to be a total or consistent "liar" or "insane"; may just have a limited, subjective perspective.

Note: Reliability/unreliability of narrators is a matter of degree; it is rarely absolute.

"Unreliable" in this sense does not necessarily mean that the narrator is lying to you, although some narrators may be unreliable in that way, but it does mean that some narrators cannot be trusted. They may not speak truth to another character or characters. (Certainly Montresor is unreliable in what he says to Fortunato, but only you are able to recognize this; poor Fortunato cannot.) They may not speak truth to themselves. They may think they are truthful but you see them as inaccurate, misguided, out of touch with reality. They may not be an accurate representation of the ideology of the text in a larger sense or of its author, although their unreliability does not necessarily mean their values are exactly opposite to those of the text. More nearly, the relation of the values of most unreliable narrators to those of the text or its author is indeterminate—a matter of degree, not absolutely identical or opposite.[1]

What is more certain, however, is that only first-person involved narrators can be unreliable. This is not to say that they all necessarily are unreliable, but that an omniscient narrator is not; omniscience—knowing everything—is antithetical to unreliability, which is a matter of limited knowledge or perspective. In "The Cask of Amontillado," Montresor apparently doesn't know or doesn't care that his words to his audience may damn him in their eyes. Either way, his reliability as a "normal," "sane," or "trustworthy" person is called into question. And the possibility of irony reflecting back on the narrator is another text strategy that is made possible by narration in the first-person, involved point of view.

CONNECT: Think back to the narrators of "The Necklace" and "Continuity of Parks." Were they unreliable in the same sense that Montresor is in "The Cask of Amontillado"? Conventionally, omniscient narrators have to be trustworthy.

---

[1]Because of Edgar Allan Poe's reputation in popular culture, however (which is not necessarily a matter of historical fact), it may be especially difficult to differentiate the values of one of his numerous "mad" narrators from those of Poe himself or from those of the "Poe" he created through writing such stories. "Poe" too is a text that culture asks be read in a certain way.

Style

In Chapter 5, style in a short story was presented as the overall impression created by the language choices a writer makes, an impression built up by more
particular choices about diction and sentence construction. It is possible to
describe the style of any short story as the author's or to arrive at some conclusions about an author's style in general by looking at several of her stories,
essays, poems, or plays. In the case of a short story that features the text
strategy of an involved, first-person narrator, however, it would also be appropriate to consider style to be the narrator's. After all, the convention of first-
person, involved narration pretends that the words and sentences you read
are being spoken or written by a particular person. You can get a better sense
of that person if the style with which he addresses you is consistent.

In order for "The Cask of Amontillado" to have the concentrated effect on
a reader that it apparently wants to have—what you might name "horrifying"
or "thrilling"—it seems that a consistent style that helps a reader define the
narrative voice is necessary. What you might call the "formal" style of this
story—based on the narrator's avoidance of contractions, for instance, and his
careful and apparently educated diction—may seem to contribute to your
sense of the kind of person this narrator is. It may also contribute to the text's
apparently desired effect if the formality of the narrator's language suits his
methodically executed revenge plan and belies what you may perceive to be
the depravity of his soul. The narrator's apparent fastidiousness with language
as he arranges the death of Fortunato may help you construct him as a cold-
blooded, merciless killer.

Cultural Context

Much of what I have asked you to consider in this discussion of the first-person narrator in "The Cask of Amontillado" has an ideological assumption underlying it, which now needs to be exposed. Not to contradict the above
points about the narrator as a character and the person you perceive speaking
through the narrative voice, but all of that—indeed the very convention of
first-person point of view itself—is based in the idea of the *unified self.* In the
process of problematizing "literature" in Chapter 2, I asked you to consider the
idea of the *decentered* self. I suggested that the former idea was part of the
dominant ideology of Western culture, but that the latter idea offered another
model for understanding people as several different selves, various ones of
which come to the fore in different situations. If the goal of presenting a unified effect or impression in the short story was important in Poe's literary
repertoire, and if he found first-person, involved narration to be an effective
text strategy toward that goal, it seems logical that he would subscribe to the
ideology of the unified self. That belief certainly aids economy in the short
story, as this discussion of point of view in "The Cask of Amontillado" has
tried to show. At any rate, what has been considered through much of this
chapter as a text strategy, a literary matter, also has an ideological dimension

to it.[2] That thought should prove useful again when you consider narrative voice in a different short story, as I will ask you to do shortly.

A Reading Strategy: Building Consistency

If you found "The Cask of Amontillado" an easy story to read, I would suggest that that ease reflects a harmonious literary interaction between you and the text not only in terms of the conventionality of text strategies. "The Cask of Amontillado" is easy to read because the unity of effect or impression that its author apparently sought to achieve meshes nicely with your tendency to look for and find consistency in this or any short story. Certainly the text strategy of first-person, involved point of view in "The Cask of Amontillado" contributes to a reader's sense that the story is consistent in mood, plot, and theme. Although theme has not been explicitly considered in the study of "The Cask of Amontillado" in this chapter, it seems easy to say that the story is about revenge or the mind-set of an obsessively vengeful man. If you are able to interpret "The Cask of Amontillado" easily, it may seem that theme or meaning is *in* the text and not a matter of your *interaction* with the text. The model of the reading process outlined in the introduction of this book, however, holds that theme is created through the interaction, and consistency building is a reading strategy by which you are able to select information from the text to confirm your sense that it has a coherent meaning of some kind.

Also, if you found "The Cask of Amontillado" an easy story to make sense of as you read, that ease probably hides the presence of consistency building as a reading strategy in your literary experience, even if you don't have that name for a way in which you read. Becoming a stronger reader, however, involves becoming conscious of how and why you read the way you do, so that you can adapt your reading strategies according to the different text strategies you may encounter. Not all stories are as conventional as "The Cask of Amontillado," as you are about to see.

Challenging Narrative Conventions

Before you read the story that follows, take a minute to look again at the notes you made in response to the first set of questions preceding "The Cask of Amontillado," about narrator and point of view in your literary experience and about reading strategies you would expect to adopt as you interact with these text strategies. After you do so, you may use the box on page 148 or a page in

---

[2]Two other aspects of the idea of the unified self as it relates to Poe are worth mentioning here: First, he probably couldn't have conceived of the decentered self, psychologically speaking, because that twentieth-century idea was not available when he lived; second—and perhaps ironically—Poe's biography seems to reveal him as a good nineteenth-century example of the decentered self, one that had considerable trouble reconciling his different selves.

your journal to modify what you wrote earlier, if necessary, in light of your reading and the subsequent discussion of "The Cask of Amontillado."

MODIFICATIONS TO MY EXPECTATIONS FOR NARRATOR IN A SHORT STORY

1.

2.

3.

4.

Now keep track of what actually happens as you read this text, in terms of:

- When and how do you know who is telling the story? Are you able to construct a "person" behind the narrative voice? If so, how and why are you able to do this? What kind of person does he seem to be?
- How do you feel as the audience being addressed by the narrative voice? For instance, are you offended? flattered? insulted? compromised?
- How and why does your interaction with the narrator affect your response to other text strategies (for instance plot, character, theme, and so on?)

WHAT HAPPENS AS I READ "THE BIRDS"

Recognizing point of view:

Developing interest in the narrator:

Affecting my response to other text strategies:

After you have read the story, write a response statement, referring to the questions that follow the story.

Ronald Sukenick   b. 1932

The Birds   *1969*

The the the
> Nuthatch walks up the tree a Prussian soldier pivots walks back

down

>   birds

the

>   Nuthatch slick arctic acrobat seal bullets through blank air silence of page the stream carries mainly on its glassy surface rippled clouds inventing themselves from minute to minute toss in a stone

The the I want to tell you the story about "ear-tree." It was on Icelandic[1] that eighteen-hour flight from Luxemburg where your feet swell up. We cruised among fantastic shapes, formations piling shifting flowing, distortions of distortions of distortions at all altitudes. The plane skimmed across a kind of ocean of streaming transformations, the wings clipped white cumuli, and on the actual ocean waves were ripples were wrinkles, viscid metal crawling across the earth, the land itself a slower lava, somewhat thicker, especially that of Iceland, where that was what it was. I was looking out over the wing as I watched a wisp of white blew back from the engine, then another, another, and after a pause, a band of grey I looked up the aisle for the stewardess when I looked back the smoke was roiling from the engine a greasy black plume with suddenly red at its root . . .

>   Wings pulled in it allowed itself to fall, a stroke of scarlet from green to green.

>   It began in '62 a Chinese restaurant naturally midtown I remember very well because that was the phase when I had a thing with fortune cookies I am always interested in any overt confrontation

---

[1]Icelandic—airline company.

with chance though if you stop to think about it every moment is such a confrontation for each of us as likely to provide the cue for something tasty an adventure something other than sex a coincidence in any case one was tired of sex I mean of thinking about it preferably a

coincidence such things renew my faith in the unknown however the fortune merely said, "You will soon plan another oriental meal" but that wasn't the interesting thing.

Corrosive chatter. Starlings are a bore despite iridescences. They're too precocious, and have no intelligence. "We put the snake live into the freezer it was at least two feet long and when we took it out it was frozen into this really interesting shape stiff as a board but then we hung it up and it began to smell. What ever happened to Phillip Morris? And mockies? There always used to be a lot of mockies. I had an aunt who always used to smoke Phillip Morris. She got lung cancer though. She was a mockie. She's dead now. I guess that's what happens to them."

The Yellow-shafted Flicker appears around April. The male has   5
a black "mustache." Its strange laugh haunts the woods but seems to be a courtship cry. Lovemaking involves reciprocal undulations of the long necks like oriental dancers. The underwing is an astonishing pink-gold. Note the pure white rump in flight.

The dress was made of clinging white nylon jersey of a thinness that in certain angles of light would outline the thighs or reveal the curve of a breast and which, when taut against the skin, assumed something of the warm flesh tone. The loose ankle-length curtain of skirt was slit at the side to the top of the thigh. The backless halter scooped down to the point at which the swell and division of the buttocks become apparent, and was slashed to the waist in front, baring both the inner and outer curves of the breasts, leaving the nipples free to poke and bob through the material.

"A pattern was seen in the use of females to bite and kick the policemen" *New York Times* 5/7/68.

Its drumming, distinct from other peckers, resembles the sound of a muffled machine gun, a soft, hollow automatic weapon.

He came stumbling up in Tompkins square[2] with his red scabby face and clapped a hand on my shoulder: "Say buddy I'm a junkie no I mean not a junkie a wino." That was how I met Sparrow. Oh nobody knew what his name really was we called him Sparrow. After the saying, "Hot as a Sparrow." He used to say things to me like, "The salient fact about American culture is that we all have to get back to nipples and start over again. Whole cockamanie country." He's also the one who said "I wuz-a fuck 'is-a wife." When he talked like that we used to call him "the Cardinal" because he seemed so intellectual. Like a Cardinal I mean, if you really look at one.

---

[2]Tompkins Square—in Manhattan's Lower East Side.

With one stroke rose half an arc then wings pulled in allowed itself to fall like diving over a wave.

I want to write a story that does a
lot of infolding and outfolding. Majestic infolding and outfolding. No petty in-
vective and venom. No comic bits, no noodgy satire like Shawanga Lodge
casino. Calm, slow exfoliations. The life cycle of Whistling Swans. Inexorable
curves of passion. Rise and fall of continents. Concrete. Innocent. Beautiful.
No meaning.

> 30 million Americans living in poverty
> it says in I. F. Stone[3]
> in the richest country in the world
> people eat clay to still the pains of an empty belly
> children come to school too hungry to learn
> and the infants of the poor suffer
> irreversible brain damage from protein deprivation
> the 42.7% of our farmers
> with incomes of less than $2,500 a year
> received only 4.5% of total farm subsidies
> while the top 10%
> many of them farm corporations or vertical trusts
> received 64.5%
> with a budget allocated 80% to the Pentagon
> and 10% to health education and welfare

This is what I call pure poetry. This is the New American Poetry, the poetry of
pure fact. This is the purity that has been missing from our poems.

Red-winged 10
Black-birds floating in like Piper Cubs, suns on shoulders. Phoebe brooding
on her egg. Towhee, Picasso camouflage, comic butler in tails. Catbird chat.
Brown Thrasher variations. Oriole riff. Pheasants waltz across the road. In the
field a Crow barks. A Hawk hangs in the air, absolutely still. Grouse explode
in the underbrush. Doves at their vespers. Invisible, huge in the night sky, a
train of Canada Geese goes honking and gabbling full five minutes from engine to caboose.

There was an item on the menu and the Chinese was translated as "Ear-tree." It was right between Shar Ding Op (chickens, Chinese
frankfurter, water chestnut) and Hong Hong Duk (lobster tails, pig flesh, Chinese vegetable). Myself I was all for getting the "Ten Ingredient." I felt expan-
sive and experimental. But Phoebe, who was a big girl, tended toward "Mile
High Rice," with maybe an order of "Stopped Duck," or "Blistered Beef," whatever that was. So then we asked ourselves, well, what would "the Sparrow"
do? Our eyes met for an instant. There was no doubt about it: "Ear-tree." We
didn't even have to speak.

"Seen as how I'm a nice guy, I'll give you a tip. We
like to stop guys with long hair, especially in old cars. They look like students.
You're a teacher. Teach and be taught."

---

[3]I. F. Stone—publisher of an investigative newspaper.

I put the ticket in my pocket. "Yeah. Well I didn't know driving with stud-
ded snow tires was illegal in this state after May first as of ten days ago." I
opened my car door.

"Hey. Come 'ere."

I walked back to the patrol car.   15

"It's not illegal."

"No?"

"No, it's unlawful."

"Oh."

I walked back to my car and opened the door.   20

"Hey. Come 'ere."

I walked back to the patrol car.

"Ya know what illegal is?"

"No, what?"

"It's a sick bird. Hah hah hah."   25

Q. When does a bird break the law?

A. When it's a Robin.

Q. What characteristic distinguishes the Bald Eagle?

A. Its balls.

Q. When is a bird not a bird?

A. When it's a horse.

> poor Americans are four times as likely to die
> before the age of 35 as the average citizen
> Negro women in Mississippi die
> six times as often in childbirth as white women
> in some urban ghettos of the North
> one child in ten dies in infancy
> the health gap between rich and poor is growing
> in 1940 the infant mortality rate for non-whites
> was 70% higher than that for whites
> in 1962 the rate was 90% greater
> the life expectancy of an American Negro is 61 years
> that of a white American
> is 68
> it says
> in the *Sunday*
> *Times*

The Downy Woodpecker, in his prison outfit, is easily confused with the
Hairy, which in fact is almost identical. However the Downy is smaller than
the Hairy, and its call, *pik*, is softer than Hairy's. The Black-capped Chickadee
is the friendliest of acrobats. The Bobwhite is a gallinaceous bird, very henny
in other words, and acts it. But let us ascend from the ridiculous to the majestic. The Whistling Swan is common. It has a wingspan of over seven feet. Like
other swans, it has a deep, ponderous flight, neck extended. When swimming
neck is stiff and straight; secondaries are not raised.

Q. What bird would you be glad to see if you were out of gas?

A. The Petrel.

Q. What birds can't fly straight?

A. Terns.
Q. What birds are often run over by trains?
A. Rails.
Q. What bird's ass would you not want to sit on?
A. The Pintail's.
Q. Which-a bird is not-a-yours-a?
A. Myna.
Q. When does a bird make a sacrifice?
A. When it's a Bunting.
Q. What bird blows his whistle?
A. Old Dickcissel, old Dickcissel.

30

birds

the

what do they say
through the empty air
keep-back keep-back
peter-peter-peter
tea-cher tea-cher
o-say mari-a
hurry worry flurry blurry
drink-your-tea drink-your-tea
old sam peabodypeabodypeabody
ticket-ticket-ticket-ticket
wide-a-wake
rounde-lay rounde-lay
trees trees if you please
witchery-witchery-witchery
whip-three-beers
chicky-tucky-tuck
chicky-tucky-tuck

We are all, of course, familiar with that kind of anthropomorphic slop. What do the birds really say when you listen hard and understand what they are saying? They say k-a-a-a. They say kwrrk. They say

kow-kow-kow
keeur   kleep
kzrrt
prrrp   bzee
plick

rronk   tlu-tlu

                                    krr-oww

zrurrr   wheet

                                      peent

tsweep   cuh-cuh

                                     churree

che-bunk   kraaa

                                     che-bek

jeet   hooah

                                    tschizzik

kirrik   ssllick

                                    karr-reek

kwuririp   kek-kek-kek

                                      kee-oo

auw   churweeoo

                               ooah-ooo-oo-oo

pchip ee pcheewee   breep

But then again, what does it matter what they say? What matters is that they carve shapes from nothingness, decorate the silence, make melodious distinctions to distinguish one moment finely from the next.

I call waiter. What thisee here, I say, He says, That is "ear-tree," a delicious Oriental specialty. But Phoebe no likee. What is? she ask. She little girl, no muchee eatee. "Ear-tree" is a popular and delicious Cantonese dish, say waiter. He Chinee fella. It is highly recommended, he say. But what is? I say. Waiter shrug and stare to other sidee room with inscrutable Chinee face. No likee, Phoebe say. You got Chicken Chow Mein. Waiter nod. I order Chop Suey. Then other customer come. They order "ear-tree." Waiter go in Kitchen, we hear yellee to cook: Two spaghettis! I callee waiter. What this "ear-tree," I say. I pointee at menu. You say is Canton dish. Then waiter answer: It doesn't matter what you say. What matters is to hurl the words at the silence of the page like hand grenades. With feeling. Look out! someone screamed. He's got a gun!

"But why 'ear-tree'?" asked Phoebe, wide-eyed. She was a slim, light-haired pale face on summer vacation from Bryn Mawr College, but with very big boobs.

"Ah, these ees the ow-you-say question my young chérie," answered Spar-row. She was at the same time flattered and offended by his insistence that she use his first name, for it implied both a compliment and an impropriety. Why, she wondered, as she stared out the porthole and watched the clouds transform themselves from moment to moment, feeling the touch of his sharkskin on her bare microskirted thigh, did her parents allow a trip to Europe in the company of this strange, dark, manly business acquaintance of her father's, with his profile, his greying sideburns, and his carriage and skin texture that reminded her so much of an erect cock? She quivered a bit in her seat, and fastened her safety belt. He was mainly Latin in descent, from a Franco-Italian Spanish family with an intermixture of Greco-Moorish blood, that settled on

35

the island of Malta some centuries ago in the wake of the conquest of Jerusalem. Sparrow. Spiro? Ero? She wondered if it was his real name. He was the kind of person that might be incognito. The jetliner shuddered through a cumulonimbus. She pulled a lever easing her seat into a reclining position that thrust her long full firm young thighs up and forward from the pelvis where the thin stuff of her microgarb caught and bunched under her seatbelt.

"But why 'ear-tree'?" asked Phoebe.

"My charming eediot," rejoined his vibrant basso, "if we knew these ..." His middle and index fingers grazed her thigh confidentially, and came to rest near the hem of her skirt. She pretended not to notice, since she didn't know what else to do, and turned to look through the porthole where she saw a sheep running across the wing, no not a sheep a puff of smoke, another, another then after a pause a band of grey a plume of roiling black with suddenly red at its root ...

"Built entirely without design precedent or orderly planning, created bit by bit on sheer impulse, a natural artist's instinct, and the fantasy of the moment": Simone Rodia's Watts Towers. Connections proliferate, meanings drop away.

Sparrow left England traveling as a young Greek sailor named George and Nick. I found him easily before the ship had cleared harbor leaning against the starboard rail in tight white pants and striped blue shirt. The day was blue with white clouds, whitecaps, gulls dove and hung above the churning stern. The gulls of Dover scream like Harpies and fly on wings of rusty iron. Sparrow was traveling as a young Greek sailor named George and Nick, but he spoke with a thick Italian accent. "'owza da boy?" he greeted me. His theory was that from his Italian accent he would be taken for a notorious Neapolitan intellectual known as "the Cardinal" who was inclined to proletarian dress and argot as a disguise. If however he were recognized as the Greek sailor boy George and Nick masquerading as the Cardinal in proletdrag, he would still be ahead of the game. This was the evasive measure known as bifurcation. While the authorities are interrogating George and Nick, Sparrow slips out between the two of them. Or if they settle on George, Nick sidles off and meantime George subdivides into Sparrow-Spiro-Ero. The principle here is progressive fission as in certain microorganisms. They never catch up with you, whoever you are. But this, ironically, is the hang-up of the method, since some agents have been left stranded in a maze of sloughed identities nursing a king-size identity problem. Often you will see an old hand slap a green agent on the back, wink, and growl avuncularly, "Say kid, what you say we go fission?" This is the process referred to, so beware.

Sparrow pointed toward a couple standing on the bridge next to the skipper, and slipped a homing pigeon out of his attaché case. The man was tall and slender, suntanned, and of a distinguished allure in the French sense. The woman was tall and slender, suntanned, and also of a distinguished allure, etc. At this distance it was a little difficult to tell them apart, though they were both quite distinct from the skipper, who was pale and

40

squat and emanated banality. The bird ruffled and fluttered, happy to escape its confinement. Sparrow set it on his wrist, raised it high in the air, and whispered "Dai! Dai!" The pigeon flapped off while Sparrow began reciting the Paolo and Francesca episode from the fifth canto of the *Commedia*. We watched as the bird hovered over the woman's head for a moment, then perched on her shoulder. We watched as she reached up and removed the message from the bird's leg, still looking straight ahead. We watched as she swallowed the note, took the pigeon, twisted its neck, and let it flop to the deck. Then the suntanned man was standing alone on the bridge, near the squat skipper, still looking straight ahead. Sparrow pointed to the man and shrugged. "I wuz-a fuck 'iz-a wife," he said in explanation. Just then said lady appeared at the rail near us and stood there looking straight ahead. "Beh!" said Sparrow. Was he as surprised as I was to recognize Phoebe? There was probably no telling. She looked straight ahead, her eyes on the horizon. The gulls dipped and hung in our wake. Sparrow cleared his throat. "Ear-tree," he said. Phoebe turned to him, her charcoal eyes smoldering in her olive face: "Millions of people are starving. A sixth of the population lives in poverty. In the richest nation in the world, in the history of the world. Abroad we practice mass murder, at home slow genocide. How long can we continue to regard as democratic a nation run like a company town for corporate profit, built-in poverty, endemic racism? Starving children suffer irreversible brain damage while Senators get rich. Soldiers die while profits soar. Democracy by tear gas, Mace, and political assassination. What are we going to do?"

"We like to stop guys with long hair and old cars," he said. "First of all old cars are a drug on the market like. I mean seen as how you got an old car it means you ain't got a new car right. And if all you was to pay is a few bucks on an old car you ain't puttin much back into the system are yiz? And that breaks the law of the market which is free enterprise.

"Now we ain't got nothin against long hair see. But what about all these guys that set up shop as barbers, they gotta make their profit, right? That breaks the law of supply and demand.

"Now another thing is long hair ain't neat like. And if it ain't neat it's unruly. And if it's unruly it's unlawful in this state according to a law on the books as of ten days ago by which appearance can be considered an extension of overt behavior during periods of national emergency such as for example now.

"Now seen as how guys with long hair and old cars don't fit in a system for guys with old hair and long cars, what that means is you're a troublemaker which is an offense by the new law that considers mental attitude an extension of overt behavior during times of national emergency 063589 state penal code and authorizes the arresting officer to put certain questions to the accused according to the mental stop-and-search provision on grounds of reasonable suspicion like long hair and old cars. Wrong answers are considered grounds for perjury.

Part I *Short Answer* (10 points)   45
1. How would you define "illegal"?
2. What characteristic distinguishes the Bald Eagle?
3. When does a bird break the law?
4. What birds can't fly straight?
5. What bird's ass would you not want to sit on?

Part II *Essay* (90 points)
Choose *one* of the following:

a) This story is "entirely without design precedent or orderly planning, created bit by bit on sheer impulse, a natural artist's instinct, and the fantasy of the moment." Why do you think the police don't like that? Discuss.

b) What is "ear-tree"? Give examples.

In Part II, I answered b). This was my answer: "Connections proliferate, meanings disperse. The painter studies his nude, his landscape."

IN SPIRIT OF JOY AND REVOLUTIONARY EXULTATION, THOUSANDS OF STUDENTS OCCUPIED THE SORBONNE TODAY.

THE STUDENTS STARTED MOVING INTO THE UNIVERSITY LATE LAST   50
NIGHT. AFTER COMPLETING THEIR JOINT PROTEST MARCH WITH THE WORKERS OF PARIS AND SPENDING THE EVENING DANCING ON THE COBBLED STREETS OF THE LATIN QUARTER.

IN THE GRANDIOSE COBBLED COURTYARD OF THE MAIN BUILDING A SMALL JAZZ BAND PLAYED ALL THROUGH THE NIGHT.

AFTER 10 DAYS OF BLOODY CLASHES WITH THE POLICE, NOT A SINGLE POLICEMAN WAS IN SIGHT. STUDENTS IN WHITE HELMETS DIRECTED TRAFFIC. THE GOVERNMENT HAD SURRENDERED THIS PART OF THE CITY TO THE STUDENTS.

HUNDREDS OF THOUSANDS OF STUDENTS TOOK TO THE STREETS NOT ONLY IN PARIS BUT IN MOST PROVINCIAL CITIES.

MANY HAD A FEAR THAT GOVERNMENTAL POWER HAD BROKEN DOWN.

THE STUDENTS THEMSELVES DELIBERATELY HARKED BACK TO THE   55
BATTLE CRIES THAT HAD SERVED EARLIER FRENCH REVOLUTIONARIES.

TWO THOUSAND WORKERS, IMITATING THE REBELLIOUS STUDENTS OF THE SORBONNE, HAVE OCCUPIED THE AIRCRAFT CONSTRUCTION PLANT OF SUD-AVIATION AT NANTES, ON THE ATLANTIC COAST, AND ARE HOLDING THE PLANT MANAGER AND HIS PRINCIPAL AIDES PRISONERS.

THE WORKERS, WHO WERE ALREADY ON STRIKE, MOVED INTO THE PLANT EARLY LAST NIGHT AND WELDED THE MAIN GATE CLOSED, THEY THREW UP BARRICADES ON THE ROADS LEADING TO THE PLANT. THEY CLOSED DOWN THE NANTES AIRPORT, WHICH IS ADJACENT TO THE FACTORY.

FRANCE's SOCIAL REVOLT SPREAD AND CHANGED IN NATURE TODAY AS AN ESTIMATED 100,000 STRIKERS OCCUPIED DOZENS OF FACTORIES IN ALL PARTS OF THE COUNTRY.

THE STRIKE MOVEMENT SPREAD SO SWIFTLY THAT, WITHIN HALF AN HOUR EARLY THIS EVENING, REPORTS REACHED PARIS THAT SEVEN MAJOR INDUSTRIAL PLANTS AND SHIPYARDS HAD BEEN TAKEN OVER IN LE HAVRE ALONE.

PRODUCERS AND DIRECTORS OF THE GOVERNMENT'S TELEVISION AND RADIO SYSTEM WENT ON STRIKE AND THE SYSTEM'S NEWSMEN VOTED TO REFUSE TO ACCEPT ANY FURTHER DIRECTIVES FROM THE IN-FORMATION MINISTRY OR OTHER GOVERNMENT AGENCIES ON THEIR NEWS REPORTS.   60

WORKERS SEIZED THE GOLD-DOMED OPERA AND THE OPERA COMIQUE.

THE SPEECHES AT THE NATIONAL ASSEMBLY SEEMED STRANGELY IR-RELEVANT. FRANCOIS MITTERAND, THE OPPOSITION LEADER, AND WALDECK ROCHET, THE HEAD OF THE COMMUNIST PARTY, WERE AS HOPELESSLY OUT OF TOUCH AS PREMIER GEORGES POMPIDOU. THEY WERE ALL PART OF THE "ESTABLISHMENT."

ONE OF THE STUDENT LEADERS, DANIEL COHN-BENDIT, CALLED THE COMMUNISTS "STALINIST CREEPS." MR. COHN-BENDIT, CALLED DANNY THE RED, APPEARS TO HOLD VIEWS CLOSE TO ANARCHISM.

THE BLACK FLAG OF THE ANARCHISTS MADE ITS APPEARANCE DUR-ING THE MASSIVE PARADE OF STUDENTS AND WORKERS YESTERDAY.

THE RED FLAG WAS HOISTED OVER SEVERAL PLANTS.   65

THE RED AND THE BLACK FLAGS APPEARED TOGETHER, AN ABNOR-MAL SITUATION BECAUSE THE COMMUNISTS AND ANARCHISTS HAVE LONG BEEN ENEMIES. THE JOINT APPEARANCE WAS ONE OF THE MANY SIGNS THAT SOMETHING NEW HAD HAPPENED.

IF THE MOVEMENT IS AN UNCONTROLLED REVOLUTIONARY UP-SURGE, THE COUNTRY MAY BE PLUNGED INTO ANARCHY.

THE DECISION OF THE WORKERS APPEARS TO HAVE BEEN A SPON-TANEOUS MOVE BY THE RANK-AND-FILE STRIKERS, WHO ACTED WITH-OUT ORDERS FROM POLITICAL PARTIES OR LABOR UNIONS.

THE STUDENT REVOLT WAS SIMILARLY UNOFFICIAL IN ITS ORIGIN.

IT IS THIS POPULAR AND REVOLUTIONARY CHARACTER OF THE MOVEMENT THAT LEADS MANY OBSERVERS TO FEEL THAT THE STU-DENTS MAY HAVE UNLEASHED FORCES THAT CANNOT BE HARNESSED OR TAMED BY CONVENTIONAL MEANS, EITHER BY THE GOVERNMENT OR THE TRADITIONAL OPPOSITION PARTIES. INCLUDING THE COMMUNISTS.   70

JUST WHAT CAUSED THE STUDENTS' AND WORKERS' REVOLT TO AS-SUME SUCH EXPLOSIVE DIMENSIONS IS STILL A MYSTERY TO MOT OB-SERVER HERE.

MANY HAVE LINKED THE DISILLUSION OF THE FRENCH STUDENT TO A GLOBAL STUDENT MALAISE.

THE GAULLIST ADMINISTRATION, LIKE MANY PRIVATE CITIZENS, IS CONVINCED THAT A TRULY REVOLUTIONARY SITUATION EXISTS AND THAT THE DEMOCRATIC INSTITUTIONS OF FRANCE ARE THREATENED.

THE PRINCIPAL THREAT LIES IN THE SPONTANEOUS, POPULAR AND UTTERLY UNCONTROLLED NATURE OF THE MOVEMENT.

THE REVOLT, BY ITS SPONTANEOUS, TOTALLY UNCONTROLLED AND UNCONTROLLABLE NATURE HAD BECOME A TRULY REVOLUTIONARY EVENT.

75

IF THE COMMUNIST PARTY HAS MANAGED TO TAKE OVER THE MOVEMENT, THEN, IRONICALLY, THE INSTITUTIONS ARE SAFE AND THE POLITICAL CONTEST IS LIKELY TO MOVE BACK INTO THE NATIONAL ASSEMBLY, WITH VOTES OF CONFIDENCE AND VOTES OF CENSURE AND TRADITIONAL SPEECHES—AND SOONER OR LATER A NEW ELECTION.

SOMETHING HAS BEEN CREATED THAT IS IRREVERSIBLE. THERE WILL BE NO GOING BACK TO THE STATUS QUO.

The police want an end to this disorder and that depends on one question and one question only: What is "ear-tree"? This in turn leads us to the matter of the identity of the man called "Ero." Destroy this as you read. It is printed in a soluble ink which you can lick off the page sentence by sentence. The ink has various flavors depending on the parts of speech to make this easier to understand and swallow.

To get to the point, the police suspect a plot, yet all they see is disorder. They suspect that disorder is part of the plot, if not the point of it. They imagine that they merely have to figure out the plot to put an end to the disorder. But they don't understand the plot and believe the explanation lies with the meaning of the word "ear-tree." In turn they believe that this meaning will lead them to a man called Ero. In real life Ero is an eminent ornithologist, but the police believe that he is the leader of an international liberation conspiracy, and that only in his mind are all the connections coherently held together, the whole matter fully understood. To make matters worse, they aren't even sure whether Ero is dead or alive, or for that matter whether that is his right name.

I first met Ero in Tompkins Square Park. He was disguised as a bum. Although he was given to a kind of banal chattering—he sometimes compared himself to a Starling—I soon realized that this was a mere verbal subterfuge, so to speak, which could not prevent the escape of sudden flashes of the profoundest insight. For example he once remarked, almost as a nonsequitur, that the whole country had to get back to nipples. It was not long before I was captivated by his brilliance and charisma. At about that point I met another of his admirers, an English "bird" named Phoebe. Though she attended an American college, she was married, however, she had an ambiguous relation with her husband, and while she traveled with him a good deal, she spent much of the time in the protection of her parents. Ero once indicated to me quite clearly that there had been something between them, but then, she was beautiful and he—he was Ero.

80

To continue, at that time Phoebe and I used to frequent Chinese restaurants. That was because it used to be Ero's way to plant his messages in fortune cookies and leave strictly to chance whether you received them or not— Ero favored chance because he said we must remain open to the unknown. They say that he still does this, and that you might for all you know receive a message from him yourself in your very next fortune cookie—a message that might change your life. Anyway we were sitting in this Cantonese place in midtown, speaking Pigeon English to put the natives at ease and to confuse the police. The waiter recommended "ear-tree"—could he have been Ero?—but when he ordered it for someone else called it "spaghetti."

At first I thought that "ear-tree" had something to do with birds—a kind of tree that birds liked to sing in, or to. Ero was of course filled with bird lore. Birds were something special for him. He said that bird songs constituted a kind of code which, when correctly deciphered, turned out to have absolutely no meaning. On the other hand he had a whole system of private symbolism worked out on the basis of what the various species meant to him, and would often express himself in its terms. This was a code the police never cracked, though God knows they tried. For example, he once sent me a message composed completely of bird images. These involved the Red-winged Blackbird, the Phoebe, the Rufous sided Towhee, the Catbird, the Brown Thrasher, the Oriole (Orchard), the Pheasant, the Crow, the Hawk, the Grouse, the Dove, the Canada Goose, in that order. Knowing his system based on his emotional response to different birds, I worked the symbols out as follows:

> Red-winged Blackbird = calm dash
> Phoebe = domestic
> Rufous-sided Towhee = human comedy
> Catbird = eccentric relativism
> Brown Thrasher = rich
> Oriole (Orchard) = hot butter
> Pheasant = beautiful fortune, pathetic sacrifice
> Crow = wisdom floats intensely
> Hawk = kill with grace
> Grouse = explosion
> Dove = dumb animals
> Canada Goose = away, away

Decoded and allowing for variation in the given images in which the birds appeared, this means, roughly: "The *calm dash* of our once *domestic* culture has faded along with our old *human comedy*. In its place we have an *eccentric relativism* that is as *rich* as experience itself, yet as slippery as *hot butter*. Today's tragic hero is a man of *beautiful fortune, pathetic sacrifice*—his role as rich as the flux itself, and his denouement as meaningless. But in this streaming chaos *wisdom floats intensely* could one but be deadly enough with the fine net of intelligence. For wisdom and art mean precisely to kill the quick of our experience as it races past, but to *kill with grace* so that the victim may be preserved, as if alive, from oblivion. The universe is a long, an infinite *explosion* in which we are driven for an instant like *dumb animals* as it rushes *away, away*."

Unfortunately, when I showed this interpretation to Ero, he got very angry and tore it up. When I asked what his system of bird symbolism meant to him he replied: "Nothing. A feather here and there, a color, a squawk, disconnected, opaque, totally self-contained, ending in a triumph of birdness, song and soar, itself opaque and without equivalent, but the feeling ordered and defined—like that of a bird's song, or of its flight."

That was my last encounter with Ero, as such. Immediately after that he assumed the guise of Spiro the spy, then of the Cardinal, then of George and Nick, and then literally disappeared in a welter of dividing and subdividing identities—Orson, Chet Nexus, the Beach Boy, Madame Lafayette, the Light-fingered Trio—to name just a few. Originally intended as an evasive measure against an assassination plot, this frenzy of transformations, some believe, may have made him a victim of terminal identity fission, a malignant psychological disorder which progressively rarefies the ego so that it ultimately loses con-sciousness of itself and in effect ceases to exist. Some say that he was seized and murdered in one of his ephemeral metamorphoses—thrown overboard by the squat skipper and the pimply homosexual second mate as George and Nick, on board a plane that crashed in mysterious circumstances off Iceland, shot dead in a Chinese restaurant by a Cuban exile who ordered "ear-tree" and got spaghetti. No one really knows.

What we do know definitely, or at least what I know and you will in thirty seconds, is the meaning of "ear-tree." Shhh. It was on Icelandic that eighteen-hour flight from Luxemburg where your feet swell up when the insight came to me. Three A.M. and I couldn't sleep. We had been traveling maybe nine, ten hours. Nothing could have been further from my mind than that old riddle. I leaned back against my pillow and thought *oreiller*, French for pillow. I had been in France. Then I thought *pommier*, apple tree, *cerisier*, cherry tree, *pêcher*, peach tree, *oranger*, orange tree. Then I thought *oreille*, ear. Then I thought voila! *oreiller*, "ear-tree." But why "ear-tree" on a Chinese menu? Of course! Spaghetti. In Chinese restaurants in France, *lo-mein*, which as we know was brought from China to Italy as *spaghetti*, is often called *pilaf* or *pilaw*, from the Arabic, because it is used as a pillow for some kind of ragout or sauce. So some Chinese who knew neither French nor English nor Arabic very well, translated *lo-mein* to *pilaw*, *pilaw* to *oreiller*, and *oreiller* from French to English as "ear-tree." I immediately dropped off into a profound slumber from which I awoke next morning completely refreshed.

When I arrived in New York, I went back to that same Chinese restaurant and ordered a large "ear-tree." It was of excellent quality, at least three stars, and I polished it off with tremendous satisfaction. The message in my fortune cookie read: "Connections proliferate, meanings are dispelled. The traveler studies out his map."

"Je suis réellement désolé I'm really sorry to have waited so long before answering you but I am totally caught up in the events that have taken place in May and in June in France. You've undoubtedly had some echoes but it's difficult to imagine the extraordinary enthusiasm that sustained the young people during the month of May."

"To form a perfect conception of the beauty and elegance of these Swans, you must observe them when they are not aware of your proximity ... the neck, which at other times is held stiffly up-right, moves in graceful curves ... with a sudden effort a flood of water is thrown over the back and wings, when it is seen rolling off in sparkling globules, like so many large pearls. The bird then shakes its wings, beats the water, and as if giddy with delight shoots away, gliding … with surprising agility and grace. Imagine, reader, that a flock of fifty Swans are thus sporting before you, as they have more than once in my sight, and you will feel, as I have felt, more happy and void of care than I can describe."

The dress was made of clinging white nylon jersey of a thinness that in certain angles of light outline the thighs or reveal the curve of a breast and which, when taut against the skin, assumed something of the warm flesh tone. Slashed to the waist, it left the nipples free to poke and bob through the material.

in the richest country   90
in the world/people eat clay to still the pains of an empty belly/children come to school too hungry to learn/and the infants of the poor suffer/irreversible brain damage from protein deprivation

JUST WHAT CAUSED THE STUDENTS' AND WORKERS' REVOLT TO AS-SUME SUCH EXPLOSIVE DIMENSIONS IS STILL A MYSTERY TO MOT OB-SERVER HERE MANY HAVE LINKED THE DISILLUSION OF THE FRENCH STUDENT TO A GLOBAL STUDENT MALAISE

Ero is an eminent ornithologist, but the police believe that he is the leader of an international liberation conspiracy, and that only in his mind are all the connections coherently held together

"A pattern was seen in the use of fe-males to bite and kick the policemen" *New York Times* 5/7/68. Its drumming, distinct from other peckers, resembles the sound of a muffled machine gun, a soft, hollow automatic weapon.

"Les manifestations sur les barricades the demonstrations on the barri-cades were only one aspect, perhaps secondary, of this surprising movement, much more astonishing was the climate in the streets. We organized every day and during the month of May all-day meetings each of which gathered up to a hundred people sometimes until two in the morning."

THE REVOLT BY ITS   95
SPONTANEOUS TOTALLY UNCONTROLLED AND UNCONTROLLABLE NA-TURE HAD BECOME A TRULY REVOLUTIONARY EVENT

"Spontanément spontaneously, the people raised the real problems, confusedly felt and it was this, exactly that was extraordinary—it was not a question of the usual politi-cal theories struggling but of notions as vague as human dignity, the responsi-bility of each man, the infinite resources of the emotion of enthusiasm facing efficiency, the power of technology—"

IF THE MOVEMENT IS AN UNCON-TROLLED REVOLUTIONARY UPSURGE THE COUNTRY MAY BE PLUNGED INTO ANARCHY

"entirely without design precedent or orderly planning, cre-ated bit by bit on sheer impulse"

coincidence such things renew my faith in the unknown I am always interested in any overt confrontation with chance though if you stop to think about it every moment is such a confrontation for each of us Ero favored chance because he said we must remain open to the unknown

the stream carries mainly on its glassy surface rippled clouds in- ₁₀₀
venting themselves from minute to minute, fantastic shapes, formations piling
shifting flowing, distortions of distortions of distortions

"Nous attendons we
await November, December but also the movements that cannot fail to appear
in Italy, Germany perhaps the United States ..."

in the richest country in the
world

an international liberation conspiracy

the children of the poor

caused
the revolt to assume such explosive spontaneous totally uncontrolled and
uncontrollable

a soft hollow automatic weapon

left the nipples free to poke and bob
much more astonishing was

the climate in the streets

a small jazz band played
all through the night

the infinite resources of the emotion of enthusiasm
created bit by bit on sheer impulse

we await November December

formations
piling shifting flowing

we must remain open to the unknown

the bird then
shakes its wings beats the water and shoots away gliding like other Swans it
has a deep ponderous flight the underwing is an astonishing pink-gold stroke
of scarlet from green to green Nuthatch bullets through blank air Red-winged
Blackbirds floating in in the field a Crow barks

Pheasants waltz across the road
Grouse explode in the underbrush
a Hawk

hangs
in the air

birds

Response Statement Questions

- What is your overall response to the experience of reading "The
  Birds"? Was it easy to read? Were your usual strategies for reading a short

story applicable to this text? Did you have to adopt any new, different, or seldom-used reading strategies to read this text?

- To what extent did "The Birds" conform to your expectations for it as a short story? To what extent did it defy those expectations? What new text strategies or unusual treatment of familiar ones are you aware of?

- Do you ever make any interpretations, draw any conclusions about theme? If you do, how easy or hard is it to do this? What helps or hinders you in doing this?

- To what extent is "The Birds" a realistic story? To what extent is it an artificial story?

- *Share and Compare* With an unconventional story such as "The Birds," it may be especially valuable to hear the responses and the reports on successful or failed reading strategies of your classmates. Who in your classroom found "The Birds" a disastrous reading experience, and why? Who found it a more harmonious experience, and why?

Perhaps you or certainly someone in your class responded initially to reading "The Birds" the way several of my students did:

"As soon as I began to read "The Birds," I could see it was going to [make] . . . very little sense. As I kept reading on, I became more and more frustrated by the unrelated ideas. . . . I felt there were just words on paper [that] . . . did not come together to form any sort of general idea."

"I can't recall ever being confronted with a piece quite like this one . . .—literally a menagerie of random thoughts and scattered ideas which don't seem to contribute to any apparent storyline."

"Strange. That is the first response I had to this story. . . . I am accustomed to reading stories with a plot, with a few developed characters, and with some sort of message. . . . I had great difficulty understanding what it meant and trying to decipher the somewhat scattered references the author made to people and places and, most of all, birds."

Those are some of the milder negative responses I have seen from students; others have used earthier language in expressing their clashing literary interactions with "The Birds." If your class had any discussion of this story before you read this commentary, similar responses were probably reported. Clearly, it is an unconventional short story and not an easy one for most readers to process using reading strategies that are successful with a more conventional short story like "The Cask of Amontillado." If "making sense" or otherwise building an interpretation ranks high among your goals for reading, at least when you are reading for class, then you may have been as frustrated as were the students quoted above.

On the other hand, I have known students who had more successful experiences with this text. Some of them had negative initial responses but were able to adapt their reading strategies in one way or another in subsequent readings to produce a more harmonious interaction. Others were able to make some adjustments "on the fly," while they were reading the first time, to at least begin to build an interpretation. Still others were willing or able to leave aside their usual kind of interpretative or theme-making purpose of reading. They read "The Birds" not so much as a short story at all but as another genre of text, for which a successful reading does not seem to require making sense.

I do want you to consider some more and less successful reading strategies, but first you should try to get a grip on some of the text strategies that make "The Birds" so unconventional and difficult to process.

Narrator

As you began reading "The Birds," unusual as the opening is, did you identify point of view as a text strategy in the second paragraph? The first-person singular pronoun, "I," appears there, outside quotation marks, which was the same indicator of point of view identified in "The Cask of Amontillado." The next sentence refers to a trans-Atlantic flight on Icelandic Airlines and uses the informal "your" for "one's" or "a person's." The sentence after that begins, "We cruised, . . ." and the first-person plural there seems sensible enough in terms of idiomatic English for a plane full of people, one of whom is the narrator.

But did you also notice something different from the similar text strategy in "The Cask of Amontillado"? When the first-person narrator speaks, his first comment is about the story he wants to tell you, not about himself or some situation that he is about to relate. Does this make the first-person pronoun seem more nearly a name for the author than for an involved narrator? If that is so, "The Birds" is already challenging the conventional use of first-person narration in fiction. But if the "I" is close to if not synonymous with the author, what are you to make of the unconventional punctuation and grammar in the rest of that paragraph? The long fourth sentence ends in confusion: " ... where that was what it was." And the following sentence seems actually to be at least four sentences fused together, the last of which trails off without ending at a period. Perhaps your literary experience includes involved narrators who are not terribly competent with the English language (Huck Finn, for instance?), but a published *author* who is not competent? After a one-sentence paragraph that seems to refer to a bird (although it could be the airliner, considering that the previous paragraph seemed to be describing the prelude to a plane crash), the narrative voice says, "It began in '62 . . ." and names itself "I" again. "*What* began in '62," you may well ask, "the story of 'ear-tree' or something else?" If it is the story of "ear-tree," why does the narrator digress or get off track again right away? If the narrator is identical with the author, just what the heck is going on here?

The two paragraphs beginning "Corrosive chatter" (paragraph 4) and "The Yellow-shafted Flicker . . ." (paragraph 5) seem to be about birds in some kind of loose way. But a direct quotation appears in the first of those with no indication as to who is speaking those words. There is an "I" within that quotation, but it is hard to tell if that pronoun stands for the narrator, the author, or someone else. The paragraph beginning "The dress was made . . ." seems to introduce an entirely different topic. There may also seem to be at least two different narrative voices within those three paragraphs. In the two paragraphs about birds, the voice in the first, outside of the quoted comments, seems personal; the voice in the second sounds like an ornithology textbook or a field guide to birds. Then in the third of these paragraphs, the voice seems objective but also vaguely pornographic. The difference in these narrative voices seems indicated by the differences in style among these three paragraphs. Certainly a conventional treatment of point of view does not allow for the kind of abrupt shifts that seem to be going on here. Can there be different narrators in the same short story? If so, can or should they shift so quickly, without warning?

The first-person singular pronoun appears again in the paragraph beginning "He came stumbling. . . ." Again you might wonder who is narrating this passage, and yet again soon after in the statement "I want to write a story that does a lot of infolding and outfolding." Who is this "I"? The same one who says he met "Sparrow"? The same one who "had an aunt who always used to smoke Phillip Morris"? The same half-dozen other ones preceding that? The same who said he wanted to "tell you the story about 'ear-tree'"? If you or anyone in your class had questions like these when you read "The Birds," that indicates what a major gap narration in this text is.

If you do read the two first-person singular voices who say things about wanting to write or tell a story as the same, and as identical with the author, that kind of narrator could be considered *author*itative, even if he does seem to be unconventional in certain ways, perhaps even reliable as a voice for the author. But that possibility is unconventional itself for fiction, where a first-person point of view is usually that of an involved narrator, a character, not the author speaking in his or her own voice. In an essay, it's not at all unusual to identify "I" with the author, but "The Birds" doesn't seem to be an essay, does it? Before you get too comfortable with the possibility that it is, you should consider the numerous other text strategies that defy essay conventions too, such as the bits of dialogue, the lists, and the same sudden shifts from topic to topic, voice to voice, and style to style that make "The Birds" problematic as a short story.

CONNECT: For another story that problematizes the relationship of narrator to author, see "Theme of the Traitor and the Hero" in the Stories for Exploration section following this chapter. In which story does the narrator seem more reliable?

Plot

In the discussion of "The Cask of Amontillado," the relation of narrative voice to other conventional text strategies of fiction was considered. In that story, it seems easy to become interested in the narrator as a person or character. Indeed because Montresor is the central character, and because the story is apparently about him, his function as narrator also serves to advance the plot. But what about the narrator in "The Birds"? If the narrator is a gap in the text, is it possible to become interested in the narrator as a person? What did you say about that when you were making notes on your experience of reading the story?

Assuming for a moment that the story is about "ear-tree," as an apparent narrative voice says at the beginning, does that subject constitute a plot here? Eventually, after pages of digressions into other subjects—some fictional, some not—the matter of "ear-tree" is finally settled. But as another of my students who found "The Birds" to violate her expectations for short fiction wrote, "There was no rising action, climax, and then falling action. There simply was no sequence of events leading up to the ... [resolution] of a plot." And if there is any conflict in this story, it may likely involve the story's disharmony with your literary experience instead of a fictional situation within an overall plot structure.

Character

The text strategy of character also presents gaps in "The Birds." Conventionally, characters have names to help a reader identify them and keep them straight, or, as in "Continuity of Parks," they have consistent identities: the man in the green chair, the woman and her lover in the novel that man is reading (and the lover, at least, is a character on two levels at once!). It's conventional to say some characters develop or change as the plot carries them along. That's true, at least, of Mathilde Loisel in "The Necklace." But even those characters who do develop are relatively stable: you know their identity even as or after they change.

In "The Birds," there are characters in the sense of named people (Phoebe, Ero, perhaps an involved narrator) but are they stable characters? Phoebe, for instance, is apparently a college-age woman at one point—"on summer vacation from Bryn Mawr College"—and a child at another—"She little girl." She is referred to as a little girl in one scene at the Chinese restaurant, but in another, she is called "a big girl." Ero may or may not be identical with

"Sparrow" and "the Cardinal." At one point, Ero/Sparrow seems to be a spy or
secret agent traveling in disguise. In itself, that kind of double identity is conventional enough in certain kinds of stories, espionage thrillers, for instance,
but Sparrow's disguise seems to be double identity taken to absurdity: "a
young Greek sailor named George and Nick." And then even that already
skewed convention is problematized further through "the evasive measure
known as bifurcation," in which the character's identity subdivides. This
process, says whichever narrator is speaking at that point, can result in "a
king-size identity problem." Apparently so.

Style

Style was mentioned under the discussion of narrator, where I observed that
in the course of just three paragraphs on one page early in the story there
seemed to be two or three different styles in evidence. You may have noticed
still other distinct styles at other points in the story, for instance the second
Chinese restaurant scene (paragraph 33) where the narrative voice retells the
incident in Pidgin English (later referred to as "Pigeon English"). Conventionally, narration in a short story—whether it is omniscient or limited, reliable or
not, third person or first—is stylistically consistent. If you think back for a
minute to your reading of "The Necklace," "Continuity of Parks," or "The Cask
of Amontillado," you can see how any of these stories illustrates that point. In
the last of these stories, it seems, the consistency of style is related to Poe's interest in achieving a unified effect in the story as a whole. The author of "The
Birds," Ronald Sukenick, seems to be interested in something different, or else
he was mentally unstable, on drugs, incompetent, or showing off when he
wrote this story—as some of my students have remarked in their response
statements. At any rate, the presence of diverse styles in "The Birds" is one
more unconventional text strategy that makes the story difficult to process according to the conventional reading strategies and most readers' expectations
for short fiction.

Toward a Strong Reading

You may recall my saying at the beginning of this discussion of "The Birds"
that, in addition to numerous frustrated readers among my students, there
have been several who found or adapted alternative reading strategies to help
them process this text more successfully. Perhaps this was the case with your
own reading, or perhaps one or more of your classmates have reported in discussion some kind of harmonious literary interaction. I would like to turn now
to a consideration of some unconventional reading strategies that have helped
some of my students overcome or at least reduce the problems this unconventional text presents.

A clashing literary interaction results not only from the text's violation of
the conventions of a short story but also from a reader's attempt to read it
the same way she or he would read a conventional story like "The Cask of

Amontillado." In the academic setting at least, most readers emphasize the reading strategy of consistency building. This involves a reader making a guess about where the plot is headed, what the story is about, or what the whole story means. In the process, a reader focuses on information from the text that is consistent with this guess and perhaps disregards other information that challenges this developing sense of consistency. At least on a first reading of "The Birds," this reading strategy is very likely to be frustrated by the gaps and *in*consistencies of the text. The first student response statement I quoted earlier illustrates this:

> As soon as I began to read "The Birds," I could see it was going to [make] . . . very little sense. As I kept reading on, I became more and more frustrated by the unrelated ideas. . . . I felt there were just words on paper [that] . . . did not come together to form any sort of general idea.

Here's a bit more of what that student, Cluny Erickson, wrote:

> At times I thought I was beginning to understand, especially . . . [the text's] comparison of birds to people. . . . But then, all of a sudden, there would be random words, statistics, jokes, and fragments of ideas that distracted me. I found this very annoying and [it] added nothing, only took away from the story.

Although she doesn't name it, Cluny's attempt to build consistency as she read is evident in her use of phrases such as "unrelated ideas," "come together to form any sort of general idea," and "beginning to understand."

Consistency building has a "partner" as a reading strategy: **wandering viewpoint.** The two are complementary, and most readers actually read with both at different times. If consistency building is the process of selecting information from a text that is consistent with a reader's predictions and guesses, wandering viewpoint is what sets up in the reader's mind a range of possible predictions or guesses from which one can be selected for emphasis. "Wandering" really doesn't mean "without direction"; wandering viewpoint is more nearly *explorative*, reading with an "open" mind, if you will, keeping your interpretive options open. Accordingly, consistency building is choosing one path to follow out of the many your mind makes available to you, narrowing your options, usually to a single interpretation. "The Birds" is a text that seems to almost force wandering viewpoint to predominate as a reading strategy because, as Cluny put it, it does not "come together to form any sort of general idea."

The response statement that another student, Alison Sebzda, wrote to her first reading of "The Birds" shows her awareness of the problems the text presents to a reader who may be too rigidly committed to consistency building as a reading strategy. Here is part of what she wrote:

If I were to try to read . . . ["The Birds"] like the conventional short story, there are literary and ideological assumptions . . . that would make comprehension of it difficult. Usually in a story I would expect to find it all connected under a common theme or main idea. In a short story there is usually a distinct . . . plot and setting. "The Birds" completely deviates from these assumptions. There are different ideas that seem to have no connection to make a story. Furthermore, the words are not even set up on the pages in the usual fashion.

In her reading of "The Birds," Alison's recognition of the unconventionality of the text prompted her to de-emphasize "comprehension" or consistency building as a reading strategy. More of what she wrote in her response statement reveals her move to let wandering viewpoint predominate:

When I started reading . . . ["The Birds"], I thought that I would be annoyed like I was with "As a Wife Has a Cow." [3] However, I found it was fun to read all the different parts and sections of the story. . . . I broke it into pieces and took each part separately. I almost immediately dropped my expectations of finding a theme as with other short stories and simply read it for fun. I noticed that the types of strategies I used were similar to when I read the comics, flip through a magazine, go through the channels on the T.V. or the different songs on the radio. My attention, in these cases, isn't really focused and my environment is permeated by many different phrases and ideas.

Like Alison, another student, Carla Thomas, was willing to keep her options open as she read and did not try to move too quickly to a consistent interpretation. In her response statement, Carla said:

When I read ["The Birds"] the first time, I found that I didn't try to note any of the scattered details, yet I fared pretty well on the in-text quiz. I think Sukenick uses the quiz to show the reader that he or she was alert to details despite the unconventional method . . . [of the story]. It was almost embarrassing to find that I remembered the punch lines of such inane jokes. From the beginning of the story, I predicted that the author was using a sort of collage strategy, although I didn't call it that. I suspected that he was introducing the reader to potentially important details and characters, but I didn't dwell on them. Luckily, the author used repetition,

---

[3]A short story by Gertrude Stein—another unconventional text her class had read previously.

and I was able to piece together some sort of logical sequence for the story—at least the story about the "ear-tree."

At the same time as she allowed her wandering viewpoint to work for her, Carla adopted other reading strategies too, and in the process did move toward building consistency in her interpretation. Here's more of her response statement:

Concerning the deeper meaning of the story, I used the strategy of rereading the text a few days later and writing down some ideas. Through a bit of skimming of only some pages (in no specific order), the answer jumped out at me in bold print: ANARCHY, REVOLT, STRIKERS—the solution to the author's poetry of poverty and oppression. This key to the story can be qualified: a reader who dislikes the disorder in the story is like the police officer who pulls over the long-haired narrator and shows distaste for social nonconformity. Sukenick's work is "unruly" and "unlawful" because it does not conform to literary conventions. The author seems to desire to change and reform story-telling norms, just as the French students and workers protest for social reform. The police combat these protests because they fear anarchy.

Furthermore, the narrator suggests that the police are convinced that Sparrow uses disorder as part of his plot to establish a completely free world. Sukenick anticipates that the reader will be like a policeman in that he or she will believe ... [the author's] method to contain a link to the story's plot. While thinking we are all dying to find out the definition of "ear-tree," Sukenick perhaps believes that we view "The Birds" as an exercise in literary anarchy. My strategy of letting the story sink in and then later examining the poetry, statistics, and bold type made the disorder interesting, not frustrating. Despite the fact that "The Birds" avoids chronology and an obvious plot, some meaning remains apparent—even if Sukenick wanted to create something meaningless.

Carla's response is a good example of the complementary nature of wandering viewpoint and consistency building. Because she was able to be flexible or innovative in her reading strategies and not rely too exclusively on consistency building, Carla was able to begin to construct an interpretation of this text, to create some meaning even with a text that seems to want to appear "meaningless."

SHARE AND COMPARE: Put the responses of Cluny and Carla into your class's discussion of reading "The Birds." Which readers in your class read primarily in terms of consistency building or wandering viewpoint? What effects of their reading strategies do these students report?

Another reader who was initially frustrated in her attempts to build consistency was able to work this reading strategy more successfully on a subsequent reading by taking a cue from the concept of intertextuality. If you recall from Chapter 2 in the introduction, intertextuality is the idea that texts in one genre—fiction, for instance—share text strategies or ideas with texts in other, not necessarily literary, genres. A reader may become aware of such a connection when an **allusion** (an indirect reference to another text) occurs in a text or when she or he establishes such a connection herself or himself. In either case, the reader's literary—or should I say *textual?*—experience is tapped into. In reading "The Birds," a class was given the suggestion that a remark by the short story writer Donald Barthelme, to the effect that collage is one of the most important art forms of the twentieth century, might be usefully applied to this story. One student who did find it useful and who commented on it in her response statement was Carole Cockerill. What she wrote might suggest to you how comparing text strategies, for instance, across genres can allow you to put your awareness of something with which you are familiar—in this case, collage—to good use in processing something which at first seems strange—like an unconventional short story.

The unconventional nature of . . . "The Birds" . . . pressured me into applying various reading strategies in order to . . . understand the story. My first attempt at reading the story established frustration because I was not able to find meaning or purpose. . . . My first reading suggested that the author simply wrote on random subjects ranging from birds to Chinese food and had pasted these random recordings together to create a literary collage. Therefore, my reading goal for the second reading was to play detective and figure out the common link or connections that made this collage stick.

Since the author included passages on a revolutionary movement and a student protest march, I thought it represented a message of fighting for rights or freedom. . . . I tried to apply the theme of freedom to the text in order to give myself hope of understanding . . . [it]. . . . I tried to strengthen my theory by attaching the birds to this theme. Birds are animals which can symbolize freedom because they have wings which allow them to fly. The author also highlights certain aspects of a man named Ero. It is mentioned that the police believe Ero is the leader of an international liberation conspiracy. The author is presenting a human character accused of being in a movement that is fighting for freedom. This assumption based on freedom is one way I . . . . [tried to comprehend the story].

The author writes, "To get to the point, the police suspect a plot, yet all they see is disorder. They suspect that disorder is part of the plot, if not the point of it. They imagine that they merely have to figure out the plot to put an end to the disorder." In this passage, I thought the author was explaining how readers look for plot in a story. The reader is like the police because they [too] are looking for a plot. However, both the police . . . and the reader . . . of this story encounter disorder. . . . [T]he reader and the police try to find plot in the disorder . . . to feel more in control. A reader wants to feel comfortable with a text so she might try to uncover a plot in this disorder. Therefore, as a reader I will stick with my belief about freedom because I think the author is showing a collage of disorder which caters to the freedom of any reader's interpretation.

The ideological interaction between reader and text is a topic that the next two chapters will look at in more detail. Here I just want to mention that ideas, beliefs, or life experiences you bring to a text about matters outside of literature may be a resource for helping you smooth out an initially rough literary interaction with a story like "The Birds." For instance, in terms of the problematic text strategy of narrator in "The Birds," the concept of the decentered self may be helpful. Earlier, in the discussion of the first-person involved narrator in "The Cask of Amontillado," I suggested that that text strategy rested on the ideological assumption of the unified self, a conception of personality that was part of the dominant ideology of Poe's time, the first half of the nineteenth century. The idea of the unified self was harmonious with that aspect of Poe's literary ideology that believed unity of effect or impression should be the aim of the short story writer, which in turn seems to have affected his decision to narrate so many of his stories, like "The Cask of Amontillado," from the first-person, involved point of view.

In Ronald Sukenick's time (the second half of the twentieth century), however, the idea of the decentered self has entered the ideologies of many people in the Western world. If for no other reason than reading about it in this book, it has entered your ideology now too. That being the case, you might apply it to the narrator(s) in "The Birds" and perhaps begin to reduce some of the difficulty of that text. If at first there seems to be a first-person narrator in that text but then there seem to be several narrators or narrative voices, regarding this disunity as indicative of the modern idea of the decentered self may help to bring some order out of the apparent chaos of the text. This process might also be extended to the "bifurcated" characters Phoebe and Sparrow/Ero/Spiro/the Cardinal/Nick and George. If the latter can have all those different identities and still be "one" person, you might read him as an instance of a decentered character. That would still make this text strategy unconventional in literary terms, but it might also do two other things. First, it might make this character a little less unconventional in ideological terms. Second, it might remind you that character as a text strategy is, after all, a convention, and as such it is subject to manipulation by both authors and readers.

If you could just entertain the idea of the decentered self for the sake of reading a story such as "The Birds," even if you didn't completely accept it as a model for describing the way real people are, that might be a way that you could draw on ideology to help you read this strange text more successfully. Comparing the text with your own sense of reality in the larger sense, or with any concept of reality that you might hold in mind just for the purposes of reading this story, might help also. This is a reading strategy you can apply to almost any short story if your literary experience includes the idea that fiction generally, whether "realistic" or not, *represents* some aspect or version of "reality" in imaginative form.[4]

In terms of "The Birds," I would like to offer you one more response statement as an example of how this reading strategy of relating the text to a reader's conception of reality can help turn an initial clashing literary interaction into a more harmonious one. The writer is Kelly DeWalt, a first-year student in an introductory literature course. I quoted from her response statement earlier to the effect that she found the story "strange" at first. Here is the rest of that response statement. Passages in which Kelly relates the text to her sense of reality are italicized:

> I am accustomed to reading stories with a plot, with a few developed characters, and with some sort of message. During my first reading of ["The Birds"], . . . I had great difficulty understanding what it meant and trying to decipher the somewhat scattered references the author made to people and places and, most of all, birds. The author went from discussing the way a plane was flying to protests in France to a discussion of a Chinese dish that, in the end, turned out to be spaghetti.

---

[4]This reading strategy applies to plays, too, because the literary ideology of theater in the Western world also assumes a relationship between the created world presented on the stage and the "real" world outside. See Chapter 15 for a discussion.

He makes references to peculiar people in his life like the philosophical man with a thousand names who had a code for birds and the woman he often had dinner with who traveled with her husband. Where were they all supposed to fit? What did it all mean? I believe that by attempting to define a plot for the story, I ruined my first reading of it. Instead of attempting to view the story with an open mind and something of an imagination, I shut my mind and stuck to my preconceived and conventional knowledge of what a short story should be.

On subsequent readings of the story, I must admit I enjoyed it much more, although my initial response was not favorable. I specifically liked the author's intensity, the way he used the repetition of certain phrases to confuse, to baffle the reader. *He chose to show how there really was no real formula for short stories or for life in general. I interpreted the story as a map for the chaotic, a response to the imposed order we as a society futilely attempt to live by.* I really do not know if that . . . was [what] . . . the author intended, but I believe he is a writer who takes creative risks and breaks conventional boundaries in writing.

The author's passages on birds probably were the clearest and most literally perceivable . . . in the entire story. Birds are constant, like the currents of air they fly on. They are majestic, beautiful, and can soar above us. All the other concepts are presented in random order with little explanation. *In the end, though, no explanation is needed; the world is a confusing place, is it not? It has random patterns and casual acquaintances, events which confuse and enlighten us.* In summary, the story had an almost calculated chaos that enthralled me and made me read it in a new and different way.

With the exception of thinking about the possible intertextuality of "The Birds" and collage, these particular reading strategies were not, by the way, suggested or prompted by me in my own classes; they were adapted by students much like you who were trying to be strong readers when they found themselves confronted with a cantankerous text such as "The Birds." Among them, Cluny and Carla developed their first response statements into very good formal papers of **cognitive analysis** in which they pursued self-consciousness as a goal and a method in their reading of "The Birds." Carla's paper explained why and how she was able to do a strong reading of "The

Birds"—finding meaning in it in defiance of its apparent desire to be meaningless—because of the reading strategies she used. Cluny's paper attempted to account for why she had a clashing literary interaction with the text because of her expectations for what a short story should be or do. Space does not permit the reproduction of both their papers, but the excerpts reprinted below include the *thesis statements* that each student wrote.

Carla Thomas

A writer can only provide the reader with half of a literary or artistic experience; the text becomes meaningful only when the reader contributes his or her own experiences, knowledge, and values. Even chaos, like random splatters of paint on a canvas, can become meaningful and possibly beautiful if the reader is able to relate his or her own experiences to the text to make connections between the abstract and reality. [Ronald] Sukenick provides such an opportunity to make connections in a text that may initially appear disorderly, menacing, and deliberately meaningless. After several readings that were nearly as unconventional as the writing itself, I created my own meaning of "The Birds."

Cluny Erickson

Reading so many short stories has fostered in me . . . some general expectations of short stories. In addition, I have come to use certain strategies when reading them. . . . "The Birds" violates almost every quality I look to find in a short story.

While it may be desirable to achieve a harmonious literary interaction with every text you encounter, it is not always possible. But neither is it always necessary to put aside a clashing literary interaction to learn something about yourself as a reader.

Stories for Exploration

Reprinted below are three twentieth-century short stories that may be read to provide you with further opportunities for examining your interaction with the text strategy of narrator and how that text strategy affects others. The prereading questions should help you heighten your awareness of certain aspects of your literary experience that interact with narrator as a text strategy. You should make some notes as answers to those questions before you read any story below. You may profitably ask yourself those same questions before you read any short story when you want to look at your response to narrator.

A set of response statement questions follows each of these stories. These questions should generate writing in which you begin a cognitive analysis of your response.

Critical Reading Questions

- What do you expect a short story to have in the way of a narrator? What different possibilities for point of view are you familiar with? How might the narrator affect other text strategies in a story?
- What do you expect to do as a reader as you interact with the narrator in a short story? What reading strategies might interact most logically with narrator as a text strategy?

Jorge Luis Borges   1899–1986

Theme of the Traitor and the Hero   1944

> So the Platonic year
> Whirls out new right and wrong,
> Whirls in the old instead;
> All men are dancers and their tread
> Goes to the barbarous clangour of a gong.
>   W. B. Yeats: *The Tower*

Under the notable influence of Chesterton[1] (contriver and embellisher of elegant mysteries) and the palace counselor Leibniz[2] (inventor of the pre-established harmony), in my idle afternoons I have imagined this story plot which I shall perhaps write some-day and which already justifies me somehow. Details, rectifications, adjustments are lacking; there are zones of the story not yet revealed to me; today, January 3rd, 1944, I seem to see it as follows:

The action takes place in an oppressed and tenacious country: Poland, Ireland, the Venetian Republic, some South American or Balkan state . . . Or rather it has taken place, since, though the narrator is contemporary, his story occurred towards the middle or the beginning of the nineteenth century. Let us say (for narrative convenience) Ireland; let us say in 1824. The narrator's name is Ryan; he is the great-grandson of the young, the heroic, the beautiful, the assassinated Fergus Kilpatrick, whose grave was mysteriously violated, whose name illustrated the verses of Browning[3] and Hugo,[4] whose statue presides over a gray hill amid red marshes.

Kilpatrick was a conspirator, a secret and glorious captain of conspirators: like Moses, who from the land of Moab glimpsed but could not reach the promised land, Kilpatrick perished on the eve of the victorious revolt which

---

[1]Chesterton, G. K. (1874–1936): English author.
[2]Leibniz, Gottfried Wilhelm (1646–1716): German philosopher.
[3]Browning, Robert (1812–1889): English poet.
[4]Hugo, Victor (1802–1885): French poet and novelist.

he had premeditated and dreamt of. The first centenary of his death draws near; the circumstances of the crime are enigmatic; Ryan, engaged in writing a biography of the hero, discovers that the enigma exceeds the confines of a simple police investigation. Kilpatrick was murdered in a theater; the British police never found the killer; the historians maintain that this scarcely soils their good reputation, since it was probably the police themselves who had him killed. Other facets of the enigma disturb Ryan. They are of a cyclic nature: they seem to repeat or combine events of remote regions, or remote ages. For example, no one is unaware that the officers who examined the hero's body found a sealed letter in which he was warned of the risk of attending the theater that evening; likewise Julius Caeser, on his way to the place where his friends' daggers awaited him, received a note he never read, in which the treachery was declared along with the traitors' names. Caesar's wife, Calpurnia, saw in a dream the destruction of a tower decreed him by the Senate; false and anonymous rumors on the eve of Kilpatrick's death publicized throughout the country that the circular tower of Kilgarvan had burned, which could be taken as a presage, for he had been born in Kilgarvan. These parallelisms (and others) between the story of Caesar and the story of an Irish conspirator lead Ryan to suppose the existence of a secret form of time, a pattern of repeated lines. He thinks of the decimal history conceived by Condorcet, of the morphologies proposed by Hegel, Spengler and Vico, of Hesiod's men, who degenerate from gold to iron. He thinks of the transmigration of souls, a doctrine that lends horror to Celtic literature and that Caesar himself attributed to the British druids: he thinks that, before having been Fergus Kilpatrick, Fergus Kilpatrick was Julius Caesar. He is rescued from these circular labyrinths by a curious finding, a finding which then sinks him into other, more inextricable and heterogeneous labyrinths: certain words uttered by a beggar who spoke with Fergus Kilpatrick the day of his death were prefigured by Shakespeare in the tragedy *Macbeth*. That history should have copied history was already sufficiently astonishing; that history should copy literature was inconceivable. . . . Ryan finds that, in 1814, James Alexander Nolan, the oldest of the hero's companions, had translated the principal dramas of Shakespeare into Gaelic; among these was *Julius Caesar*. He also discovers in the archives the manuscript of an article by Nolan on the Swiss *Festspiele:* vast and errant theatrical representations which require thousands of actors and repeat historical episodes in the very cities and mountains where they took place. Another unpublished document reveals to him that, a few days before the end, Kilpatrick, presiding over the last meeting, had signed the order for the execution of a traitor whose name had been deleted from the records. This order does not accord with Kilpatrick's merciful nature. Ryan investigates the matter (this investigation is one of the gaps in my plot) and manages to decipher the enigma.

Kilpatrick was killed in a theater, but the entire city was a theater as well, and the actors were legion, and the drama crowned by his death extended over many days and many nights. This is what happened:

On the 2nd of August, 1824, the conspirators gathered. The country was   5
ripe for revolt; something, however, always failed: there was a traitor in the group. Fergus Kilpatrick had charged James Nolan with the responsibility of

discovering the traitor. Nolan carried out his assignment: he announced in the very midst of the meeting that the traitor was Kilpatrick himself. He demonstrated the truth of his accusations with irrefutable proof; the conspirators condemned their president to die. He signed his own sentence, but begged that his punishment not harm his country.

It was then that Nolan conceived his strange scheme. Ireland idolized Kilpatrick; the most tenuous suspicion of his infamy would have jeopardized the revolt; Nolan proposed a plan which made of the traitor's execution an instrument for the country's emancipation. He suggested that the condemned man die at the hands of an unknown assassin in deliberately dramatic circumstances which would remain engraved in the imagination of the people and would hasten the revolt. Kilpatrick swore he would take part in the scheme, which gave him the occasion to redeem himself and for which his death would provide the final flourish.

Nolan, urged on by time, was not able to invent all the circumstances of the multiple execution; he had to plagiarize another dramatist, the English enemy William Shakespeare. He repeated scenes from *Macbeth*, from *Julius Caesar*. The public and secret enactment comprised various days. The condemned man entered Dublin, discussed, acted, prayed, reproved, uttered words of pathos, and each of these gestures, to be reflected in his glory, had been pre-established by Nolan. Hundreds of actors collaborated with the protagonist; the role of some was complex; that of others momentary. The things they did and said endure in the history books, in the impassioned memory of Ireland. Kilpatrick, swept along by this minutely detailed destiny which both redeemed him and destroyed him, more than once enriched the text of his judge with improvised acts and words. Thus the populous drama unfolded in time, until on the 6th of August, 1824, in a theater box with funereal curtains prefiguring Lincoln's, a long-desired bullet entered the breast of the traitor and hero, who, amid two effusions of sudden blood, was scarcely able to articulate a few foreseen words.

In Nolan's work, the passages imitated from Shakespeare are the *least* dramatic; Ryan suspects that the author interpolated them so that in the future someone might hit upon the truth. He understands that he too forms part of Nolan's plot.... After a series of tenacious hesitations, he resolves to keep his discovery silent. He publishes a book dedicated to the hero's glory; this too, perhaps, was foreseen.

Response Statement Questions

- What is your response to the narrator in this story? Do you consider him reliable or unreliable, and why?
- This story (or the story "Ryan" will tell) seems to mix fact and fiction. Which, for you, is more believable: the fictional or the historical aspects?
- Do you believe that history can influence or prefigure literature? Do you believe that literature can influence history? What is the effect of your beliefs on your reading of this story?
- Is this story realistic? If not, why not? If so, how? Is it more or less realistic, more or less artificial, than "The Necklace" or "The Birds"?

- Is it possible to derive a theme from this story? The title seems to announce one: Is that theme the same as whatever you take the story to mean?
- *Share and Compare*   How does the literary experience of anyone in your class allow him or her to interact harmoniously with this story? How does the ideology of anyone in your class with respect to the relationship of fiction to reality allow him or her to interact harmoniously with this story? For anyone in your class who is unable to interact harmoniously with this story, what would it take for them to have that kind of interaction?

Raymond Carver   1939–1988

Cathedral   1981

This blind man, an old friend of my wife's, he was on his way to spend the night. His wife had died. So he was visiting the dead wife's relatives in Connecticut. He called my wife from his in-laws'. Arrangements were made. He would come by train, a five-hour trip, and my wife would meet him at the station. She hadn't seen him since she worked for him one summer in Seattle ten years ago. But she and the blind man had kept in touch. They made tapes and mailed them back and forth. I wasn't enthusiastic about his visit. He was no one I knew. And his being blind bothered me. My idea of blindness came from the movies. In the movies, the blind moved slowly and never laughed. Sometimes they were led by seeing-eye dogs. A blind man in my house was not something I looked forward to.

That summer in Seattle she had needed a job. She didn't have any money. The man she was going to marry at the end of the summer was in officers' training school. He didn't have any money, either. But she was in love with the guy, and he was in love with her, etc. She'd seen something in the paper: HELP WANTED—*Reading to Blind Man,* and a telephone number. She phoned and went over, was hired on the spot. She'd worked with this blind man all summer. She read stuff to him, case studies, reports, that sort of thing. She helped him organize his little office in the county social-service department. They'd become good friends, my wife and the blind man. How do I know these things? She told me. And she told me something else. On her last day in the office, the blind man asked if he could touch her face. She agreed to this. She told me he touched his fingers to every part of her face, her nose—even her neck! She never forgot it. She even tried to write a poem about it. She was always trying to write a poem. She wrote a poem or two every year, usually after something really important had happened to her.

When we first started going out together, she showed me the poem. In the poem, she recalled his fingers and the way they had moved around over her face. In the poem, she talked about what she had felt at the time, about what went through her mind when the blind man touched her nose and lips. I can remember I didn't think much of the poem. Of course, I didn't tell her that. Maybe I just don't understand poetry. I admit it's not the first thing I reach for when I pick up something to read.

Anyway, this man who'd first enjoyed her favors, the officer-to-be, he'd been her childhood sweetheart. So okay. I'm saying that at the end of the summer she let the blind man run his hands over her face, said good-bye to him, married her childhood etc., who was now a commissioned officer, and she moved away from Seattle. But they'd kept in touch, she and the blind man. She made the first contact after a year or so. She called him up one night from an Air Force base in Alabama. She wanted to talk. They talked. He asked her to send him a tape and tell him about her life. She did this. She sent the tape. On the tape, she told the blind man about her husband and about their life together in the military. She told the blind man she loved her husband but she didn't like it where they lived and she didn't like it that he was a part of the military–industrial thing. She told the blind man she'd written a poem and he was in it. She told him that she was writing a poem about what it was like to be an Air Force officer's wife. The poem wasn't finished yet. She was still writing it. The blind man made a tape. He sent her the tape. She made a tape. This went on for years. My wife's officer was posted to one base and then another. She sent tapes from Moody AFB, McGuire, McConnell, and finally Travis, near Sacramento, where one night she got to feeling lonely and cut off from people she kept losing in that moving-around life. She got to feeling she couldn't go it another step. She went in and swallowed all the pills and capsules in the medicine chest and washed them down with a bottle of gin. Then she got into a hot bath and passed out.

But instead of dying, she got sick. She threw up. Her officer—why should   5
he have a name? he was the childhood sweetheart, and what more does he want?—came home from somewhere, found her, and called the ambulance. In time, she put it all on a tape and sent the tape to the blind man. Over the years, she put all kinds of stuff on tapes and sent the tapes off lickety-split. Next to writing a poem every year, I think it was her chief means of recreation. On one tape, she told the blind man she'd decided to live away from her officer for a time. On another tape, she told him about her divorce. She and I began going out, and of course she told her blind man about it. She told him everything, or so it seemed to me. Once she asked me if I'd like to hear the latest tape from the blind man. This was a year ago. I was on the tape, she said. So I said okay, I'd listen to it. I got us drinks and we settled down in the living room. We made ready to listen. First she inserted the tape into the player and adjusted a couple of dials. Then she pushed a lever. The tape squeaked and someone began to talk in this loud voice. She lowered the volume. After a few minutes of harmless chitchat, I heard my own name in the mouth of this stranger, this blind man I didn't even know! And then this: "From all you've said about him, I can only conclude—" But we were interrupted, a knock at the door, something, and we didn't ever get back to the tape. Maybe it was just as well, I'd heard all I wanted to.

Now this same blind man was coming to sleep in my house.

"Maybe I could take him bowling," I said to my wife. She was at the draining board doing scalloped potatoes. She put down the knife she was using and turned around.

"If you love me," she said, "you can do this for me. If you don't love me, okay. But if you had a friend, any friend, and the friend came to visit, I'd make him feel comfortable." She wiped her hands with the dish towel.

"I don't have any blind friends," I said.

"You don't have *any* friends," she said. "Period. Besides," she said, "god-damn it, his wife's just died! Don't you understand that? The man's lost his wife!"   10

I didn't answer. She'd told me a little about the blind man's wife. Her name was Beulah, Beulah! That's a name for a colored woman.

"Was his wife a Negro?" I asked.

"Are you crazy?" my wife said. "Have you just flipped or something?" She picked up a potato. I saw it hit the floor, then roll under the stove. "What's wrong with you?" she said. "Are you drunk?"

"I'm just asking," I said.

Right then my wife filled me in with more detail than I cared to know. I   15
made a drink and sat at the kitchen table to listen. Pieces of the story began to fall into place.

Beulah had gone to work for the blind man the summer after my wife had stopped working for him. Pretty soon Beulah and the blind man had them-selves a church wedding. It was a little wedding—who'd want to go to such a wedding in the first place?—just the two of them, plus the minister and the minister's wife. But it was a church wedding just the same. It was what Beulah had wanted, he'd said. But even then Beulah must have been carrying the cancer in her glands. After they had been inseparable for eight years—my wife's word, *inseparable*—Beulah's health went into a rapid decline. She died in a Seattle hospital room, the blind man sitting beside the bed and holding on to her hand. They'd married, lived and worked together, slept together—had sex, sure—and then the blind man had to bury her. All this without his having ever seen what the goddamned woman looked like. It was beyond my under-standing. Hearing this, I felt sorry for the blind man for a little bit. And then I found myself thinking what a pitiful life this woman must have led. Imagine a woman who could never see herself as she was seen in the eyes of her loved one. A woman who could go on day after day and never receive the smallest compliment from her beloved. A woman whose husband could never read the expression on her face, be it misery or something better. Someone who could wear makeup or not—what difference to him? She could, if she wanted, wear green eye-shadow around one eye, a straight pin in her nostril, yellow slacks and purple shoes, no matter. And then to slip off into death, the blind man's hand on her hand, his blind eyes streaming tears—I'm imagining now—her last thought maybe this: that he never even knew what she looked like, and she on an express to the grave. Robert was left with a small insurance policy and half of a twenty-peso Mexican coin. The other half of the coin went into the box with her. Pathetic.

So when the time rolled around, my wife went to the depot to pick him up. With nothing to do but wait—sure, I blamed him for that—I was having a drink and watching the TV when I heard the car pull into the drive. I got up from the sofa with my drink and went to the window to have a look.

I saw my wife laughing as she parked the car. I saw her get out of the car and shut the door. She was still wearing a smile. Just amazing. She went around to the other side of the car to where the blind man was already starting to get out. This blind man, feature this, he was wearing a full beard! A beard on a blind man! Too much, I say. The blind man reached into the back seat and dragged out a suitcase. My wife took his arm, shut the car door, and, talking all the way, moved him down the drive and then up the steps to the front porch. I turned off the TV. I finished my drink, rinsed the glass, dried my hands. Then I went to the door.

My wife said, "I want you to meet Robert. Robert, this is my husband. I've told you all about him." She was beaming. She had this blind man by his coat sleeve.

The blind man let go of his suitcase and up came his hand.   20

I took it. He squeezed hard, held my hand, and then he let it go.

"I feel like we've already met," he boomed.

"Likewise," I said. I didn't know what else to say. Then I said, "Welcome. I've heard a lot about you." We began to move then, a little group, from the porch into the living room, my wife guiding him by the arm. The blind man was carrying his suitcase in his other hand. My wife said things like, "To your left here, Robert. That's right. Now watch it, there's a chair. That's it. Sit down right here. This is the sofa. We just bought this sofa two weeks ago."

I started to say something about the old sofa. I'd liked that old sofa. But I didn't say anything. Then I wanted to say something else, small-talk, about the scenic ride along the Hudson. How going *to* New York, you should sit on the right-hand side of the train, and coming *from* New York, the left-hand side.

"Did you have a good train ride?" I said. "Which side of the train did you   25 sit on, by the way?"

"What a question, which side!" my wife said. "What's it matter which side?" she said.

"I just asked," I said.

"Right side," the blind man said. "I hadn't been on a train in nearly forty years. Not since I was a kid. With my folks. That's been a long time. I'd nearly forgotten the sensation. I have winter in my beard now," he said. "So I've been told, anyway. Do I look distinguished, my dear?" the blind man said to my wife.

"You look distinguished, Robert," she said. "Robert," she said. "Robert, it's just so good to see you."

My wife finally took her eyes off the blind man and looked at me. I had   30 the feeling she didn't like what she saw. I shrugged.

I've never met, or personally known, anyone who was blind. This blind man was late forties, a heavy-set, balding man with stooped shoulders, as if he carried great weight there. He wore brown slacks, brown shoes, a light-brown shirt, a tie, a sports coat. Spiffy. He also had this full beard. But he didn't use a cane and he didn't wear dark glasses. I'd always thought dark glasses were a must for the blind. Fact was, I wished he had a pair. At first glance, his eyes looked like anyone else's eyes. But if you looked close, there was something different about them. Too much white in the iris, for one thing, and the pupils seemed to move around in the sockets without his knowing it or being able to stop it. Creepy. As I stared at his face, I saw the left pupil turn in toward his nose while the other made an effort to keep in one place. But it was only an effort, for that eye was on the roam without his knowing it or wanting it to be.

I said, "Let me get you a drink. What's your pleasure? We have a little of everything. It's one of our pastimes."

"Bub, I'm a Scotch man myself," he said fast enough in this big voice.

"Right," I said. Bub! "Sure you are. I knew it."

He let his fingers touch his suitcase, which was sitting alongside the sofa.   35
He was taking his bearings. I didn't blame him for that.

"I'll move that up to your room," my wife said.

"No, that's fine," the blind man said loudly. "It can go up when I go up."

"A little water with the Scotch?" I said.

"Very little," he said.

"I knew it," I said.   40

He said, "Just a tad. The Irish actor, Barry Fitzgerald? I'm like that fellow. When I drink water, Fitzgerald said, I drink water. When I drink whiskey, I drink whiskey." My wife laughed. The blind man brought his hand up under his beard. He lifted his beard slowly and let it drop.

I did the drinks, three big glasses of Scotch with a splash of water in each. Then we made ourselves comfortable and talked about Robert's travels. First the long flight from the West Coast to Connecticut, we covered that. Then from Connecticut up here by train. We had another drink concerning that leg of the trip.

I remembered having read somewhere that the blind didn't smoke because, as speculation had it, they couldn't see the smoke they exhaled. I thought I knew that much and that much only about blind people. But this blind man smoked his cigarette down to the nubbin and then lit another one. This blind man filled his ashtray and my wife emptied it.

When we sat down at the table for dinner, we had another drink. My wife heaped Robert's plate with cube steak, scalloped potatoes, green beans. I buttered him up two slices of bread. I said, "Here's bread and butter for you." I swallowed some of my drink. "Now let us pray," I said, and the blind man lowered his head. My wife looked at me, her mouth agape. "Pray the phone won't ring and the food doesn't get cold," I said.

We dug in. We ate everything there was to eat on the table. We ate like   45
there was no tomorrow. We didn't talk. We ate. We scarfed. We grazed that table. We were into serious eating. The blind man had right away located his foods, he knew just where everything was on his plate. I watched with admiration as he used his knife and fork on the meat. He'd cut two pieces of meat, fork the meat into his mouth, and then go all out for the scalloped potatoes, the beans next, and then he'd tear off a hunk of buttered bread and eat that. He'd follow this up with a big drink of milk. It didn't seem to bother him to use his fingers once in a while, either.

We finished everything, including half a strawberry pie. For a few moments, we sat as if stunned. Sweat beaded on our faces. Finally, we got up from the table and left the dirty plates. We didn't look back. We took ourselves into the

living room and sank into our places again. Robert and my wife sat on the sofa.
I took the big chair. We had us two or three more drinks while they talked about
the major things that had come to pass for them in the past ten years. For the
most part, I just listened. Now and then I joined in. I didn't want him to think I'd
left the room, and I didn't want her to think I was feeling left out. They talked
of things that had happened to them—to them!—these past ten years. I waited
in vain to hear my name on my wife's sweet lips: "And then my dear husband
came into my life"—something like that. But I heard nothing of the sort. More
talk of Robert. Robert had done a little of everything, it seemed, a regular blind
jack-of-all-trades. But most recently he and his wife had had an Amway distrib-
utorship, from which, I gathered, they'd earned their living, such as it was. The
blind man was also a ham radio operator. He talked in his loud voice about
conversations he'd had with fellow operators in Guam, in the Philippines, in
Alaska, and even in Tahiti. He said he'd have a lot of friends there if he ever
wanted to go visit those places. From time to time, he'd turn his blind face toward me, put his hand under his beard, ask me something. How long had I
been in my present position? (Three years.) Did I like my work? (I didn't.) Was I
going to stay with it? (What were the options?) Finally, when I thought he was
beginning to run down, I got up and turned on the TV.

My wife looked at me with irritation. She was heading toward a boil. Then
she looked at the blind man and said, "Robert, do you have a TV?"

The blind man said, "My dear, I have two TVs. I have a color set and a
black-and-white thing, an old relic. It's funny, but if I turn the TV on, and I'm
always turning it on, I turn on the color set. It's funny, don't you think?"

I didn't know what to say to that. I had absolutely nothing to say to that.
No opinion. So I watched the news program and tried to listen to what the announcer was saying.

"This is a color TV," the blind man said. "Don't ask me how, but I can tell."   50

"We traded up a while ago," I said.

The blind man had another taste of his drink. He lifted his beard, sniffed
it, and let it fall. He leaned forward on the sofa. He positioned his ashtray on
the coffee table, then put the lighter to his cigarette. He leaned back on the
sofa and crossed his legs at the ankles.

My wife covered her mouth, and then she yawned. She stretched. She
said, "I think I'll go upstairs and put on my robe. I think I'll change into something else. Robert, you make yourself comfortable," she said.

"I'm comfortable," the blind man said.

"I want you to feel comfortable in this house," she said.   55

"I am comfortable," the blind man said.

After she'd left the room, he and I listened to the weather report and then
to the sports roundup. By that time, she'd been gone so long I didn't know if
she was going to come back. I thought she might have gone to bed. I wished
she'd come back downstairs. I didn't want to be left alone with a blind man. I
asked him if he wanted another drink, and he said sure. Then I asked if he
wanted to smoke some dope with me. I said I'd just rolled a number. I hadn't,
but I planned to do so in about two shakes.

"I'll try some with you," he said.

"Damn right," I said. "That's the stuff."

I got our drinks and sat down on the sofa with him. Then I rolled us two fat   60
numbers. I lit one and passed it. I brought it to his fingers. He took it and inhaled.

"Hold it as long as you can," I said. I could tell he didn't know the first
thing.

My wife came back downstairs wearing her pink robe and her pink slippers.

"What do I smell?" she said.

"We thought we'd have us some cannabis," I said.

My wife gave me a savage look. Then she looked at the blind man and   65
said, "Robert, I didn't know you smoked."

He said, "I do now, my dear. There's a first time for everything. But I don't
feel anything yet."

"This stuff is pretty mellow," I said. "This stuff is mild. It's dope you can
reason with," I said. "It doesn't mess you up."

"Not much it doesn't, bub," he said, and laughed.

My wife sat on the sofa between the blind man and me. I passed her the
number. She took it and toked and then passed it back to me

"Which way is this going?" she said. Then she said, "I shouldn't be smok-   70
ing this. I can hardly keep my eyes open as it is. That dinner did me in. I
shouldn't have eaten so much."

"It was the strawberry pie," the blind man said. "That's what did it," he
said, and he laughed his big laugh. Then he shook his head.

"There's more strawberry pie," I said.

"Do you want some more, Robert?" my wife said.

"Maybe in a little while," he said.

We gave our attention to the TV. My wife yawned again. She said, "Your   75
bed is made up when you feel like going to bed, Robert. I know you must
have had a long day. When you're ready to go to bed, say so." She pulled his
arm. "Robert?"

He came to and said, "I've had a real nice time. This beats tapes, doesn't it?"

I said, "Coming at you," and I put the number between his fingers. He inhaled, held the smoke, and then let it go. It was like he'd been doing it since
he was nine years old.

"Thanks, bub," he said. "But I think this is all for me. I think I'm beginning
to feel it," he said. He held the burning roach out for my wife.

"Same here," she said. "Ditto. Me, too." She took the roach and passed it
to me. "I may just sit here for a while between you two guys with my eyes
closed. But don't let me bother you, okay? Either one of you. If it bothers you,
say so. Otherwise, I may just sit here with my eyes closed until you're ready to
go to bed," she said. "Your bed's made up, Robert, when you're ready. It's
right next to our room at the top of the stairs. We'll show you up when you're
ready. You wake me up now, you guys, if I fall asleep." She said that and then
she closed her eyes and went to sleep.

The news program ended. I got up and changed the channel. I sat back   80
down on the sofa. I wished my wife hadn't pooped out. Her head lay across
the back of the sofa, her mouth open. She'd turned so that her robe had

slipped away from her legs, exposing a juicy thigh. I reached to draw her robe back over her, and it was then that I glanced at the blind man. What the hell! I flipped the robe open again.

"You say when you want some strawberry pie," I said.

"I will," he said.

I said, "Are you tired? Do you want me to take you up to your bed? Are you ready to hit the hay?"

"Not yet," he said. "No, I'll stay up with you, bub. If that's all right. I'll stay up until you're ready to turn in. We haven't had a chance to talk. Know what I mean? I feel like me and her monopolized the evening." He lifted his beard and he let it fall. He picked up his cigarettes and his lighter.

"That's all right," I said. Then I said, "I'm glad for the company."   85

And I guess I was. Every night I smoked dope and stayed up as long as I could before I fell asleep. My wife and I hardly ever went to bed at the same time. When I did go to sleep, I had these dreams. Sometimes I'd wake up from one of them, my heart going crazy.

Something about the church and the Middle Ages was on the TV. Not your run-of-the-mill TV fare. I wanted to watch something else. I turned to the other channels. But there was nothing on them, either. So I turned back to the first channel and apologized.

"Bub, it's all right," the blind man said. "It's fine with me. Whatever you want to watch is okay. I'm always learning something. Learning never ends. It won't hurt me to learn something tonight. I got ears," he said.

We didn't say anything for a time. He was leaning forward with his head turned at me, his right ear aimed in the direction of the set. Very disconcerting. Now and then his eyelids drooped and then they snapped open again. Now and then he put his fingers into his beard and tugged, like he was thinking about something he was hearing on the television.

On the screen, a group of men wearing cowls was being set upon and tormented by men dressed in skeleton costumes and men dressed as devils. The men dressed as devils wore devil masks, horns, and long tails. This pageant was part of a procession. The Englishman who was narrating the thing said it took place in Spain once a year. I tried to explain to the blind man what was happening.   90

"Skeletons," he said. I know about skeletons," he said, and he nodded.

The TV showed this one cathedral. Then there was a long, slow look at another one. Finally, the picture switched to the famous one in Paris, with its flying buttresses and its spires reaching up to the clouds. The camera pulled away to show the whole of the cathedral rising above the skyline.

There were times when the Englishman who was telling the thing would shut up, would simply let the camera move around over the cathedrals. Or else the camera would tour the countryside, men in fields walking behind oxen. I waited as long as I could. Then I felt I had to say something. I said, "They're showing the outside of this cathedral now. Gargoyles. Little statues carved to look like monsters. Now I guess they're in Italy. Yeah, they're in Italy. There's paintings on the walls of this one church."

"Are those fresco paintings, bub?" he asked, and he sipped from his drink.

I reached for my glass. But it was empty. I tried to remember what I could 95 remember. "You're asking me are those frescoes?" I said. "That's a good question. I don't know."

The camera moved to a cathedral outside Lisbon. The differences in the Portuguese cathedral compared with the French and Italian were not that great. But they were there. Mostly the interior stuff. Then something occurred to me, and I said, "Something has occurred to me. Do you have any idea what a cathedral is? What they look like, that is? Do you follow me? If somebody says cathedral to you, do you have any notion what they're talking about? Do you know the difference between that and a Baptist church, say?"

He let the smoke dribble from his mouth. "I know they took hundreds of workers fifty or a hundred years to build," he said. "I just heard the man say that, of course. I know generations of the same families worked on a cathedral. I heard him say that, too. The men who began their life's work on them, they never lived to see the completion of their work. In that wise, bub, they're no different from the rest of us, right?" He laughed. Then his eyelids drooped again. His head nodded. He seemed to be snoozing. Maybe he was imagining himself in Portugal. The TV was showing another cathedral now. This one was in Germany. The Englishman's voice droned on. "Cathedrals," the blind man said. He sat up and rolled his head back and forth. "If you want the truth, bub, that's about all I know. What I just said. What I heard him say. But maybe you could describe one to me? I wish you'd do it. I'd like that. If you want to know, I really don't have a good idea."

I stared hard at the shot of the cathedral on the TV. How could I even begin to describe it? But say my life depended on it. Say my life was being threatened by an insane guy who said I had to do it or else.

I stared some more at the cathedral before the picture flipped off into the countryside. There was no use. I turned to the blind man and said, "To begin with, they're very tall." I was looking around the room for clues. "They reach way up. Up and up. Toward the sky. They're so big, some of them, they have to have these supports. To help hold them up, so to speak. These supports are called buttresses. They remind me of viaducts, for some reason. But maybe you don't know viaducts, either? Sometimes the cathedrals have devils and such carved into the front. Sometimes lords and ladies. Don't ask me why this is," I said.

He was nodding. The whole upper part of his body seemed to be moving 100 back and forth.

"I'm not doing so good, am I?" I said.

He stopped nodding and leaned forward on the edge of the sofa. As he listened to me, he was running his fingers through his beard. I wasn't getting through to him, I could see that. But he waited for me to go on just the same. He nodded, like he was trying to encourage me. I tried to think what else to say. "They're really big," I said. "They're massive. They're built of stone. Marble, too, sometimes. In those olden days, when they built cathedrals, men wanted to be close to God. In those olden days, God was an important part of everyone's life. You could tell this from their cathedral-building. I'm sorry," I said, "but it looks like that's the best I can do for you. I'm just no good at it."

"That's all right, bub," the blind man said. "Hey, listen. I hope you don't mind my asking you: Can I ask you something? Let me ask you a simple question, yes or no. I'm just curious and there's no offense. You're my host. But let me ask if you are in any way religious? You don't mind my asking?"

I shook my head. He couldn't see that, though. A wink is the same as a nod to a blind man. "I guess I don't believe in it. In anything. Sometimes it's hard. You know what I'm saying?"

"Sure, I do," he said.   105

"Right," I said.

The Englishman was still holding forth. My wife sighed in her sleep. She drew a long breath and went on with her sleeping.

"You'll have to forgive me," I said. "But I can't tell you what a cathedral looks like. It just isn't in me to do it. I can't do any more than I've done."

The blind man sat very still, his head down, as he listened to me. I said, "The truth is, cathedrals don't mean anything special to me. Nothing. Cathedrals. They're something to look at on late-night TV. That's all they are."

It was then that the blind man cleared his throat. He brought something 110
up. He took a handkerchief from his back pocket. Then he said, "I get it, bub. It's okay. It happens. Don't worry about it," he said. "Hey, listen to me. Will you do me a favor? I got an idea. Why don't you find us some heavy paper? And a pen. We'll do something. We'll draw one together. Get us a pen and some heavy paper. Go on, bub, get the stuff," he said.

So I went upstairs. My legs felt like they didn't have any strength in them. They felt like they did after I'd done some running. In my wife's room, I looked around. I found some ballpoints in a little basket on her table. And then I tried to think where to look for the kind of paper he was talking about.

Downstairs, in the kitchen, I found a shopping bag with onion skins in the bottom of the bag. I emptied the bag and shook it. I brought it into the living room and sat down with it near his legs. I moved some things, smoothed the wrinkles from the bag, spread it out on the coffee table.

The blind man got down from the sofa and sat next to me on the carpet.

He ran his hands over the paper. He went up and down the sides of the paper. The edges, even the edges. He fingered the corners.

"All right," he said. "All right, let's do her."   115

He found my hand, the hand with the pen. He closed his hand over my hand. "Go ahead, bub, draw," he said. "Draw. You'll see. I'll follow along with you. It'll be okay. Just begin now like I'm telling you. You'll see. Draw," the blind man said.

So I began. First I drew a box that looked like a house. It could have been the house I lived in. Then I put a roof on it. At either end of the roof, I drew spires. Crazy.

"Swell," he said. "Terrific. You're doing fine," he said. "Never thought anything like this could happen in your lifetime, did you, bub? Well, it's a strange life, we all know that. Go on now. Keep it up."

I put in windows with arches. I drew flying buttresses. I hung great doors.
I couldn't stop. The TV station went off the air. I put down the pen and closed
and opened my fingers. The blind man felt around over the paper. He moved
the tips of his fingers over the paper, all over what I had drawn, and he nodded.

"Doing fine," the blind man said.   120

I took up the pen again, and he found my hand. I kept at it. I'm no artist.
But I kept drawing just the same.

My wife opened up her eyes and gazed at us. She sat up on the sofa, her
robe hanging open. She said, "What are you doing? Tell me, I want to know."

I didn't answer her.

The blind man said, "We're drawing a cathedral. Me and him are working
on it. Press hard," he said to me. "That's right. That's good," he said. "Sure.
You got it, bub. I can tell. You didn't think you could. But you can, can't you?
You're cooking with gas now. You know what I'm saying? We're going to
really have us something here in a minute. How's the old arm?" he said. "Put
some people in there now. What's a cathedral without people?"

My wife said "What's going on? Robert, what are you doing? What's   125
going on?"

"It's all right," he said to her. "Close your eyes now," the blind man said to
me.

I did it. I closed them just like he said.

"Are they closed?" he said. "Don't fudge."

"They're closed," I said.

"Keep them that way," he said. He said, "Don't stop now. Draw."   130

So we kept on with it. His fingers rode my fingers as my hand went over
the paper. It was like nothing else in my life up to now.

Then he said, "I think that's it. I think you got it," he said. "Take a look.
What do you think?"

But I had my eyes closed. I thought I'd keep them that way for a little
longer. I thought it was something I ought to do.

"Well?" he said. "Are you looking?"

My eyes were still closed. I was in my house. I knew that. But I didn't feel   135
like I was inside anything.

"It's really something," I said.

Response Statement Questions

- What is your response to the narrator in this story? to what he says about
  himself? to how he says what he says? How does your response affect
  your acceptance of what he says about his interaction with Robert?
- The narrator's reasons for telling this story are a gap. How or why are you
  able to decide why the narrator is telling this story? What do your answers
  to that question tell you about yourself as a reader?
- How, if at all, are you able to decide on a theme in this story? What text
  strategies, if any, help you build consistency in terms of theme?
- *Share and Compare*   How many readers in your class found "Cathedral"
  a hard story to read? How many found it easy? In either case, what text

strategies, conventional or otherwise, contributed to readers' experience
of difficulty or ease?

John Edgar Wideman   b. 1941

everybody knew bubba riff   *1992*

Voices are a river you step in once and again never the same Bubba here
you are dead boy dead dead dead nigger with spooky Boris Karloff[1] powder
caked on your face boy skin lightener skin brightener and who did it to you
I'm talking to you boy don't roll your eyes at me don't suckee teeth and cutee
eye look how that boy's grown come here baby gimme some sugar baby look
at the feet on him they say you know the size of the dog by the puppy's feet
his long feet this one be a giant some day I swear some man's long feet and
his Mama's curly eyes Mama's baby Daddy's maybe I wonder if Bubba's feet
bare if his big ass and gorilla thighs and donkey dick are naked down inside
the coffin under the snow white satin naked as the day he was born a big   10
bouncy boy on his mama's knee touch him touch him he won't bite he's yours
now too man boy your daddy brought you into this world but I can take you
out the man wags a finger in the boy's face the boy sees the yellowed long
john top three undone buttons at the chewed neck and bagged about the
man's middle he's scared them funky pants slide down the man's hips man be
standing there fussing at him in his long johns his behind hanging out the
holes his knees bagged out like the baggy middle what he wants to do is put
his thumbs in the suspenders and hike them back on the trifling runty little
man's narrow shoulders here you are that's better ain't it little fellow you was
about to lose your britches now go play sit back on down where you was sit-   20
ting drinking your wine before you got all up in my face about nothing cause
you ain't my real daddy and you can wave your finger and holler all you want
but if you ever lay a hand on me again I'ma break you in half old man don't
care how much my mama need the shit you bring around here no more whipping on me you touch me or put a hand on her ever again it's rumble time
mano a mano motherfucker me and you on the green and if you can't stand
the heat get out the kitchen this ain't no Papa Bear Mama Bear and li'l Sugar
Baby Bear jam no more I'm grown now ain't taking your whiskeyhead shit no
more hit my mama hit me Ima bust you up my sweet Bubba how I loved that
boy seem like he came out smiling like he arrived here knowing something   30
that made him the grinningest baby you ever seen he was easy easy girl my
first and the only easy one I ever had I didn't know better I thought pain and
blood and walking the floor all night the way it spozed to be you know stuff
you spozed to learn growing up to be a woman so you mize well go ahead
and get on with what you got to do no way round it like falling off roller
skates when you little learning to skate and scuffed up knees bloody elbow
you climb back up off the ground ain't nothing the matter with you girl you

---

[1]Boris Karloff—actor famed for playing Frankenstein's monster.

sneak back up on your feet and look around hope nobody saw you down on
the pavement wipe the tears out your eyes make sure your clothes ain't ripped
and go ahead about your business you know you learning a lesson you know   40
how it is dues you got to pay Mama Mama look at you boy look what a mess
you made out the side of your face it always hurt you worse than it hurts them
you bound to fall once twice three times falling falling and tear up your ass as
many falls as you need to learn your lesson then you starts understanding you
know better you know ain't no lesson and ain't no learning you just keep on
falling your babies keep falling you pick yourself up pick up that boy put him
down he's big enough to be carrying you around woman look at where he bit
me little devil he's too young to start him on a bottle the falling ain't teaching
nobody nothing you keep on falling because falling down's what you born to
do all the days of your life amen till one time thank you Father amen you can't   50
stand back up no more little devil knows when he's biting me he look up all
cutie-pie wide-eyed and I'm seeing stars think the bloods trickling down my
chest boy oh boy next time Ima smack you balder headed than you already is
you know good and well you ain't spozed to be biting your Mama like that
got the nerve to have teeth little bitty nubs pushing up I rub his gums help his
teeth come in rub a ice cube on his gums when he frets please don't lose your
little smile now ain't no time to take back my titty let him nibble if he needs to
nibble he needs me now I rock him and rub his tummy he grin up at me I lifts
him and wiggle him he shakes like a bowl of jelly my little old man him diaper droopy and creases in him thighs him knees wobble shake him bake him   60
paddy cake him sing him froggy went a courtin and he did ride this room uh
huh these walls uh huh she lifts the dumpling baby uh huh uh huh tastes its
rubbery flesh she is dressed in black beside the coffin her face veiled her
gloved hands somewhere out of sight the music winds on she must not stand
too long the others behind her prop her ease her along the line fed from rows
of benches into the center aisle Amazing Grace you would think they'd get
their fill of young black men's bodies but no no end to it she must not hover
too long over the crib because the others are lined up for their turn passing
passing down the rows of benches onto the carpeted aisle then down towards
the flower-decked altar flowers flowers everywhere who pays for so many   70
flowers pays for the dope nobody around here has nothing not one red cent
so he stands there in them yellow past patching long johns trembling like a
rattle snake he would break the boy apart if he could but Bubba too big for
that bullshit now I can't do nothing with him find me a stick break a board upside his big hard nappy head maybe he start to listening to someone no no no
that's not the way Bubba's a good boy just needs a man to talk to him tell him
wildness not the only way to be a man please help me I try try I talk till I'm
blue in the face snapped a broom handle over his back he laughed and ran
out the kitchen big old boy like that he should be carrying you around put
him down woman you got a muscle in your arm big as mine it ain't nothing   80
it's a pimple look big cause my arm's skinny put that boy down on his own
two feet feets big as mine already his shoes cost as much as mine already put
that boy down boy you got teeth in them feet boy chewing out the toes of
your shoes they ain't a week old look like dogshit already I ain't made of
money smack some sense he's just a boy don't mean no harm let him be

Bubba Bubba too late for crying he's gone gone gone the others push out their hard wooden seats the rows empty one by one Amazing Grace how sweet the sound his cold cold eye on the sparrow the mourners shuffle they squeeze past ancient knees the ones too tired too old who keep their places on the benches too weary to move they sit alone left behind while the others are a river flowing to the altar and the waters part and rise again two streams returning up the side aisles to the rear of Homewood African Methodist Episcopal Zion Church where the ushers stand in white and once upon a time one of them my first love dimple-cheeked almost old as my mama she smiled at me and melted every hard leg dusty butt knucklehead I don't want to be here in church in the first place anger fear and awkwardness of being a boy force-marched Sunday morning every Sunday morning to this woman-haunted place their cries and prayers and wet-eyed singing and hats and moans and veils and bosoms Jesus help me legs Jesus in love and the loneliness beneath those closets of noisy clothes they packed their bodies in Jesus help me the organ when church finally had one when we chased out the white people and moved into their big church on Homewood Avenue first thing you hear the organ when you come in think it is some old sister humming in the amen corner as you tiptoe you always tiptoed you always stumbled or shuffled or slid like on ice because your feet would tattle on you how much you didn't want to be in church how much you wanted to fly back out the door and you'd be long gone if it wasn't for your mama dragging you in dragging you away from Bubba and them and what they into Sunday morning you set down one foot after the other careful as rain pitta patta look at the dogs on that boy Bubba you gonna be a big man pardner when you grows into them dogs must cost a pretty penny just keeping you in shoes I'd rather clothe him than feed him on his stoop we ate two dozen hot dogs and drank a gallon of grape Kool-Aid Bubba'd wait till his mama watching then cram a whole hot dog bun wiener and mustard in his mouth shove the end till it disappeared like a train in a tunnel you do that again boy Ima smack you bald-headed but she smiled when he tricked her into catching him in the act same smile on my first love's face greeting me as I crossed the threshold of A.M.E. Zion but her skin shades lighter and not as old and blemishless and warm to the touch of my eyes and her smile sliced me melted me undressed us both her smile crackling like her swift white uniform so white I could see her brownskin sealskin underneath and her smooth cheeks and dark lips part swelling the rustle of wings of power of furled wings behind her back as she handed me a Sunday program and I tripped onto the purple carpet falling head over heels in love with everything I'd set my jaw against Sunday mornings being gathered being plucked from where I was happily minding my own business dreaming of Bubba and them free as birds somewhere they shouldn't be I'm back again in line pushing forward in stiff new shoes the soles still slick I'm slipping I glide feel static electricity charging my body the green worm of flame that will spit if my fingers touch the metal-edged fountain in the church lobby who's in such a hurry this morning why do I feel the push the rush can't stop for a drink of water somebody's breath on my neck she peers down at Bubba is he sleeping is he dead babies die sometimes just lay there dead a cat suckee breath steal breath a fat white cat in her dream in his crib a green-eyed Chessy

90

100

110

120

130

cat grin too late too late cat got his tongue all his sweet breath sweet smile got
it and gone gone don't you hear me talking to you boy Sunday morning the
bells stroll up and down Homewood Avenue black hands ring them our bells
now telling time for all Homewood the biggest church on the block on the
corner ours now the pretty stained-glass windows till some junky steals them
an organ high-domed ceiling we must wash white as snow again tall scaffolds
and ladders for the men to climb Bubba won't be there it's Wednesday your   140
mother promised you'd help the men Wednesday evening old deacons and
ushers and trustees ancient monkeys in the web of pipe and board rising to
the arched ceiling jack be monkey quick angels they are lighter and faster than
you've ever seen them in these work clothes they never wear to church I
climb one foot after the other into heaven through the door she guards in
white welcoming me each finger in white and I love every one her touch
veiled but warmer washed white as snow in white glove softness the white
that sighs and stretches and must abide her brown body within its shape her
fullness her secret scents and white teeth perched within the blackness of her
lips her heavy lashes bowing as if she's been waiting shy and puzzled too as   150
the smile sinks back into her entering and warming the ebb returning as sure
as the outward flow if you were a spider high up in the tit of swelling vault
you would see the pattern how rows empty one by one and the mourners file
towards the coffin and the line breaks on the rock of the flower-draped altar
returning them in two streams to the source the rear aisle and street door narrow and straight where she nods and smiles at you and touches your cheek
once once more gentle scratch than touch more of a tracing her pointy nail inside the glove some bright winged humming insect testing the field of your
cheek faint brush of its breathy legs a path with no destination just there an instant then gone back to wildness as if your face is a flower as if your whole   160
life has been nothing till now nothing before nothing after just this quick
brush this kiss you wish now as you remember it you wish the world would
go away again as it did when she lifted her white winged hand touched her
lips teeth breath on your cheek Bubba how long how long behind me beyond
me over yonder on the bank one of the old ones too stiff and ridden to shuffle down the aisle shouts like that rock did crying out no hiding place don't
leave me this morning weak and desperate as Old Charley Rackett's voice in
that down home story I told you Bubba about my people you said you never
had no people your Mama found you in the trash you said you liked that
Charley Rackett story tell it again man that tough old nigger got some Bubba   170
in him weak and feeble and old but they knew he'd push hisself out his chair
and crawl after them to the fields how old was he then my great-great-Bubba
grandfather maybe a hundred maybe more they called him the African because when he first landed in this wilderness he spoke a bubba dubba language no one understood not one word of English and even after he *could*
speak most days he *wouldn't* speak Charley Rackett whipped till he'd answer
to that Charley Charley Charley shit a language of blows and animal noises as
if he was the beast not them in those old time slavery days then it was Freedom and my people working our own briar patch of land in South Carolina
and Charley he's too old go to the fields every morning we sit him in his chair   180
by the door so's he can look out and little Bubba one the gran kids his job to

mind the old man from can to cain't from sunup to sundown in that chair by the door then one morning old rusty black Charley Rackett said him say don't leave me behind this morning I gwine wit youall this godblasted morning and up he stood and bram down he tumble out his chair and Oh my God Oh my Blessed Savior they's running around hollering and pull bag of bones Charley off the floor and stuff him back in the chair but he flies right out again quick as a grasshopper and bram hits the floor again his nose bleeding lip cut ain't nobody seen him rise out that chair for years he's hollering and nobody don't know what to do help me Jesus Charley Rackett's mind made up he'll drag be-   190
hind them on his bloody elbows bloody knees so they gathers him up and ties him on the mule and that's what happens every day till he dies one night after supper in his bed Charley Bubba Rackett riding on the mule with them to the fields he worked a hundred hundred years slavery days and the slaving days after and they couldn't keep him down I was Bubba the boy left behind with him I follow Charley Rackett's stare through the open doorway across the scraped-clean place our cabin sits on like a turned-over bucket study rolling hills and broccoli tops of trees that rise from a crease where the creek runs to a river and river to delta fanning draining to the dark sea where her teeth flash like waves at night my job to fetch him coolish water shoo flies and plow his   200
dinner from the skillet I left too long on the stove fasten scraps of button at the neck of his long johns tend his knobby hands the color of turned earth wipe the corner of his mouth always the silvery web the slobber the grunts groans wheezes of words he can't twist his mouth around he grinds them on the stumps of his teeth chews and spits them at me I sit much of the time as far away as I'm able in the space we occupy him in his pew me scattered in a cor- ner on the floor sucking a tit of cane worrying a hard kernel of something any- thing caught in my teeth playing funny little tunes in my brain bird cries train thunder lightning crickets the women washing snap beans crack crack drum- ming in a tin bowl he coughs the walls shake I wipe sweat from his brow wet   210
from his chin it's broad daylight flies buzz I tuck him in pull up his suspenders he calls my name a word a sound nobody else in the whole world knows Bubba and next morning he tries to stand hits the floor and steals from me the long peace of day after day alone with him listening learning my name be- cause next morning they take him and I trail the mule's mulish stink mulish swish of its shitty tail its pitta pat clomp to the fields that morning lost to me unremembered until Bubba lying up there like you sleeping like you ain't got a care in the world boy and you say tell it one more time the old timey story I like and your mama looking down at you her little brown bouncing baby bro- ken boy Bubba I hear one of those stones behind me send up your name in a   220
prayer like Charley Rackett hollered Take me goddammit take me this god- blasted morning saying Bubba to myself the sound before the sense of it Bubba Bubba Bubba everybody knew Bubba how old was he was he was he was the sound of it before the sense Big Bubba that's the way we talk we say it make the sound the sense of what we're talking about when I return home I walk up Susquehanna Street the people if people had been outside on their porches would have been close enough to touch their voices loud in my ear if I'd have stopped and squatted on one of these stoops we would rap about Bubba you know Big Bubba yeah oh yeah that was some sorry shit man you

know how they did him some evil cold blood shit sure enough man you   230
know I must be getting old because it don't bother me that much anymore I
mean you know for a minute or two I want to wring a million motherfuckers'
necks but then I let it go got to let it go got to chill out I seen too much be
crazy if I don't chill out brothers cut down every day shit it don't mean a thing
everybody got to go one day you know like a shooting gallery or some moth-
erfucking evil ass lottery we all got a number just a matter of sooner or later
today or tomorrow all the brother's got a chain round they necks and a number on the chain and somebody pulling numbers daily bang bang down you
go it's just a matter of time bloods be extinct you know like them endangered
species and shit don't laugh it's true we ought to fire up a campaign shit they   240
got one for elephants and whales and ring-tailed sap-sucking woody wood-
peckers why not posters and TV ads and buttons and T-shirts *S.O.N. Save Our
Niggers* go on man you crazy man I pass by on the sidewalk listening but nobody on their stoops maybe everybody knew I was coming up Susquehanna
Street with my sad self and ran inside shut their windows shut their doors hiding till I pass with my mournful lost-my-best-friend self I wish for voices hear
empty porches hear my own feet on the pavement hear a car pass at the intersection of Braddock half a block away the oldest Homewood streets Albion
Tioga Finance these streets where Bubba's known where they say his names
Junior June Juney Junebug JB J Bub Bub Bubby Bubba all the silent names hid-   250
den behind curtains and blinds the darkness of old walls and tight corners and
lids and hoods and secrets you can't tell without giving their power up Bubba
Big Bubba I thought when I returned home one time it would be different I
didn't know exactly how but maybe better somehow things supposed to
change I'm older and heavier and slower now can't disappear down an alley
streak like a panther part of black night when I need to rendezvous with my
kind who once ruled here talking trash knocking heads the fly arch rulers and
kings of pussy and bullshit and smoke Bubba June-Boy Sonny Bo sitting high
up on the wall of our pretty where nothing no one could touch us one time it
will surely be different these empty porches and empty footsteps and lights of   260
empty cars whizzing by on Braddock but the only difference now Bubba Big
Bubba gone they say the junkies tired of him dealers tired of him cops tired of
him stealing and muscling people carried a baseball bat and you know Bubba
never could play no baseball what he look like carrying around a bat he
wouldn't listen that hard head still hard as brick man couldn't nobody never
tell Bubba nothing he'd bogart and stomp people take their shit and walk off
like dudes don't be remembering like you can do shit to people today and just
walk on away and like it's over like all you got to do is get yours today and
turn your back and walk away like ain't nothing happened like tomorrow ain't
another day yeah he was stone crazy Bubba leave me alone now I'm not for   270
no play today Bubba say fuck you punk and your mama too and snatch people's shit like he's Superman or Br'er Bear with that tree slung over his shoulder that was Big Bubba man big as he was ain't never growed up your boy
your old time boon coon and cruising cut-buddy main man yeah we go back
don't we bro way back to the olden days you me Bubba the Golden Knights
and badass Laredos those banging gangs we runned wit runned from we was
bad in our day but it's a new day out here cats ain't seeking glory punching

some bad dude's lights out no way see everybody carries these days mess wit my shit I blow you away in a minute see Bubba living in the past Bubba a throwback man like them old time big hat eldorado Iceberg Slim pimps beat they women with coathangers and shit it's all business today dude making it on the street today got to have computers and beepers no time for cowboys and indins and gorillaing people's dope that two-bit King Kong gangster jive ain't what's happening out here today it's business business build yourself an organization man power to the people good product good distribution good vibes spread a little change round keep the boy off your back everybody gets what they want plenty to go round if your shits tight it's these free-lance Rambo motherfuckers fucking things up just a matter of time before somebody waste Bubba don't care how big he is how many bad brothers he busted up with his bare hands his big bat Bubba go down just like anybody else you bust a cap in his chest no man the word on the set is nobody knows who did it but nobody in business don't care neither cause he was way out of line overdue for getting done man cause everybody knows the way it goes moving west mister moving on out bro up and out to star time don't fuck with the product product won't fuck wit you you got to remember today's today and yesterday shit yesterday's long gone we was kids back then you and me and Bubba playing kid games then time runs out it's spozed to run out things spozed to change and we sure ain't babies no more Big Bubba a dinosaur man wasn't even in the right century man living by the wrong clock man he was Bubba all right your man Bubba Bubba Bubba everybody knew Bubba.   300

Response Statement Questions

- When and how do you recognize point of view as a text strategy? How and why are you able to construct a "person" behind the narrative voice?
- What aspects of your literary experience does this story challenge? Are there any elements of your literary experience with which it harmonizes? Consider such matters as point of view, narrative voice, plot, character, even grammar and punctuation.
- What is the effect of your reading strategies on your response to this text? Are you able to adapt any alternative or unusual reading strategies in order to process this text?
- Consider the title as a text strategy, particularly the word "riff": How do you read that word, as "Bubba's" last name or as something else? If something else, what life experience or knowledge of yours allows you to decide what "riff" means? How does your decision about this affect the way you read the text?
- *Share and Compare* How many readers in your class found "everybody knew bubba riff" a hard story to read? How many found it easy? In either case, what text strategies, conventional or otherwise, contributed to readers' experience of difficulty or ease? In either case, what life experience on the part of individual readers helped or hindered their understanding of the story?

READING AND WRITING PROJECTS
FOR CREATIVE AND CRITICAL THINKING

Your own writing is important as you try to learn more about yourself as a reader—both what you do cognitively and what is done to you culturally—to produce the kind of reader you are when you interact with any particular text. In addition to response statements and the formal expository paper that may grow out of them, there are other ways to use writing to learn. What follows are suggestions for integrating your reading of and writing about literary texts in various ways. These suggestions include exploratory writing, playing with texts and language, creative efforts in various genres, and other writing exercises designed to strengthen your awareness of the cognitive and cultural processes involved in your reading.

If you produce any "creative" pieces of your own—stories, poems, dramatic scenes, nonverbal displays, and so on—think of them as instances of intertextuality: Directly or indirectly, they refer to and are part of the textual network that includes other texts already written. If you work on any of the more "expository" or "discursive" projects, think of what you're doing as joining a *conversation* with other texts and other voices.

► Identify a gap in any short story and write imaginatively to fill it in. (An example might be, from "The Cask of Amontillado," the antecedent action: what happened before the story opens. How did Fortunato "insult" Montresor?)

► Rewrite a scene from any short story from a different point of view from that in which the scene is presented in the text. (An example, from "The Cask of Amontillado," retell any of the scenes in the catacombs from Fortunato's point of view. What is going through *his* mind as Montresor leads him onward?)

► Transform any short story into a text in another genre: poetry, drama, or essay. Your transformation need not match the length of the original text, nor need it try to include every detail from the original. A narrated scene in a short story, for instance, could be rewritten as a dramatic script. A story could be retold as a descriptive essay or perhaps more thoroughly transformed into a poem.

► Add a character to any short story. This character could be one you invent, or it could be one you import from another story. Rewrite a scene from the story with attention to the way the new character changes things. (For example, what would happen if Montresor were somehow to become involved in the action of "The Birds"? Or what if he were to become one of the narrative voices in that story?)

► Go back to the story "The Birds" in this chapter. Assuming you found it a difficult text to process, go back to it and begin to reread it, this time pausing to record, in writing or on audio tape, what happens to you as you read: What expectations as to such conventions as plot, character, narrative voice, setting, and so forth are raised in you by the language of the text? How and why are these expectations satisfied or frustrated as you continue to read (even the first page or so)? How or why are you able to begin to "make sense" or "build consistency" as you read? (This project of reading and writing is especially useful for unconventional or "incoherent" texts such as "The Birds.")

▶ As a group project, try mounting a reader's theater production of "everybody knew bubba riff." A reader's theater, in contrast to stage theater, involves different people reading parts aloud, not acting out roles through movement on a stage. With "everybody knew bubba riff" as a script, identify where different voices speak and assign those voices to different class members.

7 ◈ SPECIAL FOCUS IN FICTION: CULTURAL PERSPECTIVES

The preceding two chapters have considered, for the most part, literary matters: the transaction between readers and texts at the literary level. But of course that's not all that's involved in the reading dynamic. In addition to expectations about what stories should be like and what they should do—in literary terms—readers bring a whole complex of attitudes, assumptions, beliefs, memories, opinions, and values on ethical, moral, religious, political, social, historical, and economic issues to a reading experience. In a manner analogous to the literary interaction discussed in the previous chapter, readers and texts interact in this world of values as well: their ideologies interact. Diane Gretta's response to "Hills Like White Elephants" in Chapter 4 was an illustration of this. And, like the literary interaction between reader and text, this interaction involving values, beliefs, and experiences may be harmonious or clashing.

This chapter will take a look at some of what's involved in the ideological interaction between reader and text. Specifically, it will explore some of the issues concerning the relationships between young people and their parents that are raised in two short stories, one by the early twentieth-century Irish author James Joyce, the other by the contemporary American writer Anne Tyler. It will also look at how the handling of certain text strategies in each of these stories helps to emphasize or reveal ideological positions with respect to these issues. And you will be invited to examine your own ideology as far as some of these issues are concerned.

The Culture of Family

To get a start on responding self-consciously to Joyce's "Eveline" and Tyler's "Teenage Wasteland," take a few moments to reflect on the questions below and to jot down some answers.

- What are your experiences and beliefs about the relations between teenage children and their parents, particularly on the issue of children's freedom versus parents' control? When and under what circumstances should a teenager leave home for good? Is this by mutual consent of parents and child, or does one or the other decide when it's time?
- How does your own family situation—as a teenager or young person not yet completely "on your own," as a college student going through a gradual transition out of your parents' home, as a parent yourself, as a single

person, or any related situation—influence your beliefs on the aforementioned issue?

When you read these stories, refer to what you have said in answer to these questions.

James Joyce   1882–1941

Eveline   1914

She sat at the window watching the evening invade the avenue. Her head was leaned against the window curtains and in her nostrils was the odor of dusty cretonne. She was tired.

Few people passed. The man out of the last house passed on his way home; she heard his footsteps clacking along the concrete pavement and afterwards crunching on the cinder path before the new red houses. One time there used to be a field there in which they used to play every evening with other people's children. Then a man from Belfast bought the field and built houses in it—not like their little brown houses but bright brick houses with shining roofs. The children of the avenue used to play together in that field— the Devines, the Waters, the Dunns, little Keogh the cripple, she and her brothers and sisters. Ernest, however, never played: he was too grown up. Her father used often to hunt them in out of the field with his blackthorn stick; but usually little Keogh used to keep *nix* and call out when he saw her father coming. Still they seemed to have been rather happy then. Her father was not so bad then; and besides, her mother was alive. That was a long time ago; she and her brothers and sisters were all grown up; her mother was dead. Tizzie Dunn was dead, too, and the Waters had gone back to England. Everything changes. Now she was going to go away like the others, to leave her home.

Home! She looked round the room, reviewing all its familiar objects which she had dusted once a week for so many years, wondering where on earth all the dust came from. Perhaps she would never see again those familiar objects from which she had never dreamed of being divided. And yet during all those years she had never found out the name of the priest whose yellowing photograph hung on the wall above the broken harmonium beside the colored print of the promises made to Blessed Margaret Mary Alacoque. He had been a school friend of her father. Whenever he showed the photograph to a visitor her father used to pass it with a casual word:

—He is in Melbourne now.

She had consented to go away, to leave her home. Was that wise? She tried to weigh each side of the question. In her home anyway she had shelter and food; she had those whom she had known all her life about her. Of course she had to work hard both in the house and at business. What would they say of her in the Stores when they found out that she had run away with a fellow? Say she was a fool, perhaps; and her place would be filled up by advertisement. Miss Gavan would be glad. She had always had an edge on her, especially whenever there were people listening.

—Miss Hill, don't you see these ladies are waiting?

—Look lively, Miss Hill, please.

She would not cry many tears at leaving the Stores.

But in her new home, in a distant unknown country, it would not be like that. Then she would be married—she, Eveline. People would treat her with respect then. She would not be treated as her mother had been. Even now, though she was over nineteen, she sometimes felt herself in danger of her father's violence. She knew it was that that had given her the palpitations. When they were growing up he had never gone for her, like he used to go for Harry and Ernest, because she was a girl; but latterly he had begun to threaten her and say what he would do to her only for her dead mother's sake. And now she had nobody to protect her. Ernest was dead and Harry, who was in the church decorating business, was nearly always down somewhere in the country. Besides, the invariable squabble for money on Saturday nights had begun to weary her unspeakably. She always gave her entire wages—seven shillings—and Harry always sent up what he could but the trouble was to get any money from her father. He said she used to squander the money, that she had no head, that he wasn't going to give her his hard-earned money to throw about the streets, and much more, for he was usually fairly bad of a Saturday night. In the end he would give her the money and ask her had she any intention of buying Sunday's dinner. Then she had to rush out as quickly as she could and do her marketing, holding her black leather purse tightly in her hand as she elbowed her way through the crowds and returning home late under the load of provisions. She had hard work to keep the house together and to see that the two young children who had been left to her charge went to school regularly and got their meals regularly. It was hard work—a hard life—but now that she was about to leave it she did not find it a wholly undesirable life.

She was about to explore another life with Frank. Frank was very kind, manly, open-hearted. She was to go away with him by the night-boat to be his wife and to live with him in Buenos Aires where he had a home waiting for her. How well she remembered the first time she had seen him; he was lodging in a house on the main road where she used to visit. It seemed a few weeks ago. He was standing at the gate, his peaked cap pushed back on his head and his hair tumbled forward over a face of bronze. Then they had come to know each other. He used to meet her outside the Stores every evening and see her home. He took her to see *The Bohemian Girl* and she felt elated as she sat in an unaccustomed part of the theater with him. He was awfully fond of music and sang a little. People knew that they were courting and, when he sang about the lass that loves a sailor, she always felt pleasantly confused. He used to call her Poppens out of fun. First of all it had been an excitement for her to have a fellow and then she had begun to like him. He had tales of distant countries. He had started as a deck boy at a pound a month on a ship of the Allan Line going out to Canada. He told her the names of the ships he had been on and the names of the different services. He had sailed through the

10

Straits of Magellan and he told her stories of the terrible Patagonians. He had fallen on his feet in Buenos Aires, he said, and had come over to the old country just for a holiday. Of course, her father had found out the affair and had forbidden her to have anything to say to him.

—I know these sailor chaps, he said.

One day he had quarreled with Frank and after that she had to meet her lover secretly.

The evening deepened in the avenue. The white of two letters in her lap grew indistinct. One was to Harry; the other was to her father. Ernest had been her favorite but she liked Harry too. Her father was becoming old lately, she noticed; he would miss her. Sometimes he could be very nice. Not long before, when she had been laid up for a day, he had read her out a ghost story and made toast for her at the fire. Another day, when their mother was alive, they had all gone for a picnic to the Hill of Howth. She remembered her father putting on her mother's bonnet to make the children laugh.

Her time was running out but she continued to sit by the window, leaning her head against the window curtain, inhaling the odor of dusty cretonne. Down far in the avenue she could hear a street organ playing. She knew the air. Strange that it should come that very night to remind her of the promise to her mother, her promise to keep the home together as long as she could. She remembered the last night of her mother's illness; she was again in the close dark room at the other side of the hall and outside she heard a melancholy air of Italy. The organ-player had been ordered to go away and given sixpence. She remembered her father strutting back into the sickroom saying:

—Damned Italians! coming over here!

As she mused the pitiful vision of her mother's life laid its spell on the very quick of her being—that life of commonplace sacrifices closing in final craziness. She trembled as she heard again her mother's voice saying constantly with foolish insistence:

—Derevaun Seraun! Derevaun Seraun!*

She stood up in a sudden impulse of terror. Escape! She must escape! Frank would save her. He would give her life, perhaps love, too. But she wanted to live. Why should she be unhappy? She had a right to happiness. Frank would take her in his arms, fold her in his arms. He would save her.

She stood among the swaying crowd in the station at the North Wall. He held her hand and she knew that he was speaking to her, saying something about the passage over and over again. The station was full of soldiers with brown baggages. Through the wide doors of the sheds she caught a glimpse of the black mass of the boat, lying in beside the quay wall, with illumined portholes. She answered nothing. She felt her cheek pale and cold and, out of a maze of distress, she prayed to God to direct her, to show her what was her duty. The boat blew a long mournful whistle into the mist. If she went, tomorrow she would be on the sea with Frank, steaming toward Buenos Aires. Their passage had been booked. Could she still draw back after all he had

15

*Derevaun Seraun—Gaelic phrase: "The end of pleasure is pain."

done for her? Her distress awoke a nausea in her body and she kept moving
her lips in silent fervent prayer.

A bell clanged upon her heart. She felt him seize her hand: 20
—Come!

All the seas of the world tumbled about her heart. He was drawing her into
them: he would drown her. She gripped with both hands at the iron railing.
—Come!

No! No! No! It was impossible. Her hands clutched the iron in frenzy.
Amid the seas she sent a cry of anguish!
—Eveline! Evvy!   25

He rushed beyond the barrier and called to her to follow. He was shouted
at to go on but he still called to her. She set her white face to him, passive, like
a helpless animal. Her eyes gave him no sign of love or farewell or recognition.

Response Statement Questions

- What is your estimation of Eveline's home life? Given that, do you think
  she should leave? If so, should she leave with Frank? Why do you think
  she decided to remain behind? Do you think she made the right decision?
  Why?
- Do you think the text "wants" you to identify with Eveline? Does it seem to
  present her decision at the end of the story as the right one or the wrong
  one? How can you tell which way the text is leaning on this question?
- *Share and Compare*   What variety of opinion about Eveline's situation is
  there in your class? Exchange response statements with several classmates,
  or discuss responses in small groups or in your class as a whole. How are
  any differences in opinion related to different family experiences?

Now you may go on and read "Teenage Wasteland," but before you
begin, glance back at the notes you made about your family position and your
experience and beliefs about control and freedom between parents and their
teenage children. Consider how these elements of your ideology influence
your response to this text.

Anne Tyler   b. 1941

Teenage Wasteland   *1984*

He used to have very blond hair—almost white—cut shorter than other
children's so that on his crown a little cowlick always stood up to catch the
light. But this was when he was small. As he grew older, his hair grew darker,
and he wore it longer—past his collar even. It hung in lank, taffy-colored
ropes around his face, which was still an endearing face, fine-featured, the
eyes an unusual aqua blue. But his cheeks, of course, were no longer round,
and a sharp new Adam's apple jogged in his throat when he talked.

In October, they called from the private school he attended to request a
conference with his parents. Daisy went alone; her husband was at work.
Clutching her purse, she sat on the principal's couch and learned that Donny

was noisy, lazy, and disruptive; always fooling around with his friends, and he wouldn't respond in class.

In the past, before her children were born, Daisy had been a fourth-grade teacher. It shamed her now to sit before this principal as a parent, a delinquent parent, a parent who struck Mr. Lanham, no doubt, as unseeing or uncaring. "It isn't that we're not concerned," she said. "Both of us are. And we've done what we could, whatever we could think of. We don't let him watch TV on school nights. We don't let him talk on the phone till he's finished his homework. But he tells us he doesn't *have* any homework or he did it all in study hall. How are we to know what to believe?"

From early October through November, at Mr. Lanham's suggestion, Daisy checked Donny's assignments every day. She sat next to him as he worked, trying to be encouraging, sagging inwardly as she saw the poor quality of everything he did—the sloppy mistakes in math, the illogical leaps in his English themes, the history questions left blank if they required any research.

Daisy was often late starting supper, and she couldn't give as much attention to Donny's younger sister. "You'll never guess what happened at …" Amanda would begin, and Daisy would have to tell her, "Not now, honey." 5

By the time her husband, Matt, came home, she'd be snappish. She would recite the day's hardships—the fuzzy instructions in English, the botched history map, the morass of unsolvable algebra equations. Matt would look surprised and confused, and Daisy would gradually wind down. There was no way, really, to convey how exhausting all this was.

In December, the school called again. This time, they wanted Matt to come as well. She and Matt had to sit on Mr. Lanham's couch like two bad children and listen to the news: Donny had improved only slightly, raising a D in history to a C, and a C in algebra to a B-minus. What was worse, he had developed new problems. He had cut classes on at least three occasions. Smoked in the furnace room. Helped Sonny Barnett break into a freshman's locker. And last week, during athletics, he and three friends had been seen off the school grounds; when they returned, the coach had smelled beer on their breath.

Daisy and Matt sat silent, shocked. Matt rubbed his forehead with his fingertips. Imagine, Daisy thought, how they must look to Mr. Lanham: an overweight housewife in a cotton dress and a too-tall, too-thin insurance agent in a baggy, frayed suit. Failures, both of them—the kind of people who are always hurrying to catch up, missing the point of things that everyone else grasps at once. She wished she'd worn nylons instead of knee socks.

It was arranged that Donny would visit a psychologist for testing. Mr. Lanham knew just the person. He would set this boy straight, he said.

When they stood to leave, Daisy held her stomach in and gave Mr. Lanham a firm, responsible handshake. 10

Donny said the psychologist was a jackass and the tests were really dumb; but he kept all three of his appointments, and when it was time for the follow-up conference with the psychologist and both parents, Donny combed his hair and seemed unusually sober and subdued. The psychologist said Donny had no serious emotional problems. He was merely going through a difficult period in his life. He required some academic help and a better sense of self-worth. For this reason, he was suggesting a man named Calvin Beadle, a tutor with considerable psychological training.

In the car going home, Donny said he'd be damned if he'd let them drag him to some stupid fairy tutor. His father told him to watch his language in front of his mother.

That night, Daisy lay awake pondering the term "self-worth." She had always been free with her praise. She had always told Donny he had talent, was smart, was good with his hands. She had made a big to-do over every little gift he gave her. In fact, maybe she had gone too far, although, Lord knows, she had meant every word. Was that his trouble?

She remembered when Amanda was born. Donny had acted lost and bewildered. Daisy had been alert to that, of course, but still, a new baby keeps you so busy. Had she really done all she could have? She longed—she ached—for a time machine. Given one more chance, she'd do it perfectly—hug him more, praise him more, or perhaps praise him less. Oh, who can say...

The tutor told Donny to call him Cal. All his kids did, he said. Daisy thought for a second that he meant his own children, then realized her mistake. He seemed too young, anyhow, to be a family man. He wore a heavy brown handlebar mustache. His hair was as long and stringy as Donny's, and his jeans as faded. Wire-rimmed spectacles slid down his nose. He lounged in a canvas director's chair with his fingers laced across his chest, and he casually, amiably questioned Donny, who sat upright and glaring in an armchair. 15

"So they're getting on your back at school," said Cal. "Making a big deal about anything you do wrong."

"Right," said Donny.

"Any idea why that would be?"

"Oh, well, you know, stuff like homework and all," Donny said.

"You don't do your homework?" 20

"Oh, well, I might do it sometimes but not just exactly like they want it." Donny sat forward and said, "It's like a prison there, you know? You've got to go to every class, you can never step off the school grounds."

"You cut classes sometimes?"

"Sometimes," Donny said, with a glance at his parents.

Cal didn't seem perturbed. "Well," he said, "I'll tell you what. Let's you and me try working together three nights a week. Think you can handle that? We'll see if we can show that school of yours a thing or two. Give it a month; then if you don't like it, we'll stop. If *I* don't like it, we'll stop. I mean, sometimes people just don't get along, right? What do you say to that?"

"Okay," Donny said. He seemed pleased. 25

"Make it seven o'clock till eight, Monday, Wednesday, and Friday." Cal told Matt and Daisy. They nodded. Cal shambled to his feet, gave them a little salute, and showed them to the door.

This was where he lived as well as worked, evidently. The interview had taken place in the dining room, which had been transformed into a kind of office. Passing the living room, Daisy winced at the rock music she had been hearing, without registering it, ever since she had entered the house. She looked in and saw a boy about Donny's age lying on a sofa with a book. Another boy and a girl were playing Ping-Pong in front of the fireplace. "You have several here together?" Daisy asked Cal.

"Oh, sometimes they stay on after their sessions, just to rap. They're a pretty sociable group, all in all. Plenty of goof-offs like young Donny here." He cuffed Donny's shoulder playfully. Donny flushed and grinned.

Climbing into the car, Daisy asked Donny, "Well, what do you think?"   30

But Donny had returned to his old evasive self. He jerked his chin toward the garage. "Look," he said. "He's got a basketball net."

Now on Mondays, Wednesdays, and Fridays, they had supper early—the instant Matt came home. Sometimes, they had to leave before they were really finished. Amanda would still be eating her dessert. "Bye, honey. Sorry," Daisy would tell her.

Cal's first bill sent a flutter of panic through Daisy's chest, but it was worth it, of course. Just look at Donny's face when they picked him up: alight and full of interest. The principal telephoned Daisy to tell her how Donny had improved. "Of course, it hasn't shown up in his grades yet, but several of the teachers have noticed how his attitude's changed. Yes, sir, I think we're onto something here."

At home, Donny didn't act much different. He still seemed to have a low opinion of his parents. But Daisy supposed that was unavoidable—part of being fifteen. He said his parents were too "controlling"—a word that made Daisy give him a sudden look. He said they acted like wardens. On weekends, they enforced a curfew. And any time he went to a party, they always telephoned first to see if adults would be supervising. "For God's sake!" he said. "Don't you trust me?"

"It isn't a matter of trust, honey. . ." But there was no explaining to him.   35

His tutor called one afternoon. "I get the sense," he said, "that this kid's feeling . . . underestimated, you know? Like you folks expect the worst of him. I'm thinking we ought to give him more rope."

"But see, he's still so suggestible," Daisy said. "When his friends suggest some mischief—smoking or drinking or such—why, he just finds it hard not to go along with them."

"Mrs. Coble," the tutor said, "I think this kid is hurting. You know? Here's a serious, sensitive kid, telling you he'd like to take on some grown-up challenges, and you're giving him the message that he can't be trusted. Don't you understand how that hurts?"

"Oh," said Daisy.

"It undermines his self-esteem—don't you realize that?"   40

"Well, I guess you're right," said Daisy. She saw Donny suddenly from a whole new angle: his pathetically poor posture, that slouch so forlorn that his shoulders seemed about to meet his chin ... oh, wasn't it awful being young? She'd had a miserable adolescence herself and had always sworn no child of hers would ever be that unhappy.

They let Donny stay out later, they didn't call ahead to see if the parties were supervised, and they were careful not to grill him about his evening. The tutor had set down so many rules! They were not allowed any questions at all about any aspect of school, nor were they to speak with his teachers. If a

teacher had some complaint, she should phone Cal. Only one teacher disobeyed—the history teacher, Miss Evans. She called one morning in February.
"I'm a little concerned about Donny, Mrs. Coble."

"Oh, I'm sorry, Miss Evans, but Donny's tutor handles these things now. . ."

"I always deal directly with the parents. You are the parent," Miss Evans
said, speaking very slowly and distinctly. "Now, here is the problem. Back
when you were helping Donny with his homework, his grades rose from a D
to a C, but now they've slipped back, and they're closer to an F."

"They are?"   45

"I think you should start overseeing his homework again."

"But Donny's tutor says. . ."

"It's nice that Donny has a tutor, but you should still be in charge of his
homework. With you, he learned it. Then he passed his tests. With the tutor,
well, it seems the tutor is more of a crutch. 'Donny,' I say, 'a quiz is coming up
on Friday. Hadn't you better be listening instead of talking?' 'That's okay, Miss
Evans,' he says. 'I have a tutor now.' Like a talisman! I really think you ought
to take over, Mrs. Coble."

"I see," said Daisy. "Well, I'll think about that. Thank you for calling."

Hanging up, she felt a rush of anger at Donny. A talisman! For a talisman,   50
she'd given up all luxuries, all that time with her daughter, her evenings at home!

She dialed Cal's number. He sounded muzzy. "I'm sorry if I woke you," she
told him, "but Donny's history teacher just called. She says he isn't doing well."

"She should have dealt with me."

"She wants me to start supervising his homework again. His grades are
slipping."

"Yes," said the tutor, "but you and I both know there's more to it than
mere grades, don't we? I care about the *whole* child—his happiness, his self-
esteem. The grades will come. Just give them time."

When she hung up, it was Miss Evans she was angry at. What a narrow   55
woman!

It was Cal this, Cal that, Cal says this, Cal and I did that. Cal lent Donny an
album by the Who. He took Donny and two other pupils to a rock concert. In
March, when Donny began to talk endlessly on the phone with a girl named
Miriam, Cal even let Miriam come to one of the tutoring sessions. Daisy was
touched that Cal would grow so involved in Donny's life, but she was also a
little hurt, because she had offered to have Miriam to dinner and Donny had
refused. Now he asked them to drive her to Cal's house without a qualm.

This Miriam was an unappealing girl with blurry lipstick and masses of
rough red hair. She wore a short, bulky jacket that would not have been out
of place on a motorcycle. During the trip to Cal's she was silent, but coming
back, she was more talkative. "What a neat guy, and what a house! All those
kids hanging out, like a club. And the stereo playing rock … gosh, he's not
like a grown-up at all! Married and divorced and everything, but you'd think
he was our own age."

"Mr. Beadle was married?" Daisy asked.

"Yeah, to this really controlling lady. She didn't understand him a bit."

"No, I guess not," Daisy said.

Spring came, and the students who hung around at Cal's drifted out to the basketball net above the garage. Sometimes, when Daisy and Matt arrived to pick up Donny, they'd find him there with the others—spiky and excited, jittering on his toes beneath the backboard. It was staying light much longer now, and the neighboring fence cast narrow bars across the bright grass. Loud music would be spilling from Cal's windows. Once it was the Who, which Daisy recognized from the time that Donny had borrowed the album. *"Teenage Wasteland,"** she said aloud, identifying the song, and Matt gave a short, dry laugh. "It certainly is," he said. He'd misunderstood; he thought she was commenting on the scene spread before them. In fact, she might have been. The players looked like hoodlums, even her son. Why, one of Cal's students had recently been knifed in a tavern. One had been shipped off to boarding school in midterm; two had been withdrawn by their parents. On the other hand, Donny had mentioned someone who'd been studying with Cal for five years. "Five years!" said Daisy. "Doesn't anyone ever stop needing him?"

Donny looked at her. Lately, whatever she said about Cal was read as criticism. "You're just feeling competitive," he said. "And controlling."

She bit her lip and said no more.

In April, the principal called to tell her that Donny had been expelled. There had been a locker check, and in Donny's locker they found five cans of beer and half a pack of cigarettes. With Donny's previous record, his offense meant expulsion.

Daisy gripped the receiver tightly and said, "Well, where is he now?"

"We've sent him home," said Mr. Lanham. "He's packed up all his belongings, and he's coming home on foot."

Daisy wondered what she would say to him. She felt him looming closer and closer, bringing this brand-new situation that no one had prepared her to handle. What other place would take him? Could they enter him in public school? What were the rules? She stood at the living room window, waiting for him to show up. Gradually, she realized that he was taking too long. She checked the clock. She stared up the street again.

When an hour had passed, she phoned the school. Mr. Lanham's secretary answered and told her in a grave, sympathetic voice that yes, Donny Coble had most definitely gone home. Daisy called her husband. He was out of the office. She went back to the window and thought awhile, and then she called Donny's tutor.

"Donny's been expelled from school," she said, "and now I don't know where he's gone. I wonder if you've heard from him?"

There was a long silence. "Donny's with me, Mrs. Coble," he finally said.

"With you? How'd he get there?"

"He hailed a cab, and I paid the driver."

"Could I speak to him, please?"

There was another silence. "Maybe it'd be better if we had a conference," Cal said.

---

*"Teenage Wasteland"—the song's actual title is "Baba O'Riley."

"I don't *want* a conference. I've been standing at the window picturing   75
him dead or kidnapped or something, and now you tell me you want a—"

"Donny is very, very upset. Understandably so," said Cal. "Believe me, Mrs.
Coble, this is not what it seems. Have you asked Donny's side of the story?"

"Well, of course not, how could I? He went running off to you instead."

"Because he didn't feel he'd be listened to."

"But I haven't even—"

"Why don't you come out and talk? The three of us," said Cal, "will try to   80
get this thing in perspective."

"Well, all right," Daisy said. But she wasn't as reluctant as she sounded. Already, she felt soothed by the calm way Cal was taking this.

Cal answered the doorbell at once. He said, "Hi, there," and led her into
the dining room. Donny sat slumped in a chair, chewing the knuckle of one
thumb. "Hello, Donny," Daisy said. He flicked his eyes in her direction.

"Sit here, Mrs. Coble," said Cal, placing her opposite Donny. He himself
remained standing, restlessly pacing. "So," he said.

Daisy stole a look at Donny. His lips were swollen, as if he'd been crying.

"You know," Cal told Daisy, "I kind of expected something like this. That's   85
a very punitive school you've got him in—you realize that. And any half-
decent lawyer will tell you they've violated his civil rights. Locker checks!
Where's their search warrant?"

"But if the rule is—" Daisy said.

"Well, anyhow, let him tell you his side."

She looked at Donny. He said, "It wasn't my fault. I promise."

"They said your locker was full of beer."

"It was a put-up job! See, there's this guy that doesn't like me. He put all   90
these beers in my locker and started a rumor going, so Mr. Lanham ordered a
locker check."

"What was the boy's name?" Daisy asked.

"Huh?"

"Mrs. Coble, take my word, the situation is not so unusual," Cal said. "You
can't imagine how vindictive kids can be sometimes."

"What was the boy's *name*," said Daisy, "so that I can ask Mr. Lanham if
that's who suggested he run a locker check."

"You don't believe me," Donny said.   95

"And how'd this boy get your combination in the first place?"

"Frankly," said Cal, "I wouldn't be surprised to learn the school was in on
it. Any kid that marches to a different drummer, why, they'd just love an excuse to get rid of him. The school is where I lay the blame."

"Doesn't *Donny* ever get blamed?"

"Now, Mrs. Coble, you heard what he—"

"Forget it," Donny told Cal. "You can see she doesn't trust me."   100

Daisy drew in a breath to say that of course she trusted him—a reflex. But
she knew that bold-faced, wide-eyed look of Donny's. He had worn that look
when he was small, denying some petty misdeed with the evidence plain as
day all around him. Still, it was hard for her to accuse him outright. She tem-

porized and said, "The only thing I'm sure of is that they've kicked you out of school, and now I don't know what we're going to do."

"We'll fight it," said Cal.

"We can't. Even you must see we can't."

"I could apply to Brantly," Donny said.

Cal stopped his pacing to beam down at him. "Brantly! Yes. They're really onto where a kid is coming from, at Brantly. Why, *I* could get you into Brantly. I work with a lot of their students." 105

Daisy had never heard of Brantly, but already she didn't like it. And she didn't like Cal's smile, which struck her now as feverish and avid—a smile of hunger.

On the fifteenth of April, they entered Donny in a public school, and they stopped his tutoring sessions. Donny fought both decisions bitterly. Cal, surprisingly enough, did not object. He admitted he'd made no headway with Donny and said it was because Donny was emotionally disturbed.

Donny went to his new school every morning, plodding off alone with his head down. He did his assignments, and he earned average grades, but he gathered no friends, joined no clubs. There was something exhausted and defeated about him.

The first week in June, during final exams, Donny vanished. He simply didn't come home one afternoon, and no one at school remembered seeing him. The police were reassuring, and for the first few days, they worked hard. They combed Donny's sad, messy room for clues; they visited Miriam and Cal. But then they started talking about the number of kids who ran away every year. Hundreds, just in this city. "He'll show up, if he wants to," they said. "If he doesn't, he won't."

Evidently, Donny didn't want to. 110

It's been three months now and still no word. Matt and Daisy still look for him in every crowd of awkward, heartbreaking teenage boys. Every time the phone rings, they imagine it might be Donny. Both parents have aged. Donny's sister seems to be staying away from home as much as possible.

At night, Daisy lies awake and goes over Donny's life. She is trying to figure out what went wrong, where they made their first mistake. Often, she finds herself blaming Cal, although she knows he didn't begin it. Then at other times she excuses him, for without him, Donny might have left earlier. Who really knows? In the end, she can only sigh and search for a cooler spot on the pillow. As she falls asleep, she occasionally glimpses something in the corner of her vision. It's something fleet and round, a ball—a basketball. It flies up, it sinks through the hoop, descends, lands in a yard littered with last year's leaves and striped with bars of sunlight as white as bones, bleached and parched and cleanly picked.

Response Statement Questions

• Where do your sympathies lie as you read this story: mainly with, or against, Donny, Daisy, or Cal? Do you agree or disagree that Donny is trapped in his home life and in school? Do you agree or disagree that Daisy doesn't trust him and is too controlling of him? What is your feeling about Donny's leaving at the end of the story?

- Do you think the text "wants" you to identify with one character and against another? If so, which way does that go? How can you tell which way the text is leaning with respect to the issues of parental trust and control and teenagers' freedom?
- *Share and Compare*   What variety of opinion about Donny's situation is there in your class? Exchange response statements with several classmates, or discuss responses in small groups or in your class as a whole. How are any differences in opinion related to different family experiences?

Texts and Contexts, Literary and Cultural

The way you respond to the issues referred to in the questions on pages 211–212 is affected by text strategies that are part of the literary repertoire of each text, but that may also indicate something of the ideology of each text. Let's take a look at how this works with three particular text strategies.

Point of View

Both stories follow the convention of **third-person limited narration,** with the key word being "limited." That is, both stories are told through the consciousness of a single character—Eveline, Daisy—and in neither does the narration adopt the convention of omniscience, which might allow readers access to the thoughts of, say, Eveline's father or Donny or Cal. Omniscient narration might also permit "authoritative" or "reliable" statements by a **narrative voice.** The effect of the text strategy of third-person limited narration may be to attract your identification as a reader with the character through whose consciousness the story is told. Is that what happened to you as you read each of these stories?

> CONNECT: The two stories in Chapter 5, "The Necklace" and "Continuity of Parks," also featured third-person point of view, but in those stories the narration was *omniscient.* And neither story seemed to attract identification with the main character, as both "Eveline" and "Teenage Wasteland" tend to do.

The identification with the point-of-view character that third-person limited narration tends to create shows how text strategies can influence your responses to questions of the "rightness" or "wrongness" of Eveline's decision not to run away with Frank, Donny's decision to run away from home and school, or any of Daisy's decisions in handling her son's situation. Because the narration in "Eveline" is limited to Eveline's point of view, for instance, you don't know "objectively" about how her father feels about life in their home. What you do know about her father's feelings comes only through Eveline's thoughts. These reveal that he threatened her and disapproved of sailors in general as suitors for his daughter and of Frank in particular, but you don't get the chance to hear his side of the story, or to hear the story from his side. The effect of that may be to incline you to sympathize with Eveline's desire to leave her home and to feel that her apparent last-minute decision not to leave with Frank is the wrong one. So the text, you may have said, seems to want you to see Eveline as trapped in a situation she has every good reason to want to escape from, trapped not just by her father's demands but by the inertia that her situation promotes in her. As one of my students wrote in his response journal, "The text does seem to 'want' me to feel sympathy for Evvy. The text also seems to lean toward the belief that she made the wrong decision, because her home life is depicted almost entirely negatively, while Frank's option is basically romanticized."

In "Teenage Wasteland," a similar text strategy concerning point of view perhaps inclines your identification toward Daisy. What you know of Donny's troubles comes only through Daisy's thoughts about them; the text does not allow you to see Donny's situation as he sees it, although Donny is present in "Teenage Wasteland" more often than Eveline's father is in that story. So you may have said that the text wants you to identify more with Daisy against Donny and Cal and to view Donny's running away as a sad mistake that hurts Daisy, even makes her the victim of Donny's confusion and Cal's bad influence. One student wrote in her response journal as follows:

> I think that I sympathized with Daisy because I got to know her the most as I was reading the story. I learned how caring and protective Daisy was, how she'd do anything for Donny. And Donny ignored all of this, but I don't know how he was *really* feeling. I wasn't allowed the chance to become more than mere acquaintances with him.
>
> But maybe by not letting the reader into the minds of other characters, the text is trying to emphasize parental control. This makes the mind of the teenager even more of a mystery, since readers never see how teenagers' minds work. The text isn't being completely fair here.[*]

Irony

But there is another possibility: The same text strategy of third-person limited narration could enforce some **aesthetic distance** between a reader and the point-of-view character. The limitedness of this kind of narration does tend to attract reader identification to the point-of-view character, but at the same time the third-person orientation still keeps that character at a certain distance from

---

[*]Elsewhere, this student wrote, "I *love* Anne Tyler. . . . I trust her more than . . . any other author I know of." So her sense of the "unfairness" of the text's presentation of its ideology with respect to parental control versus teenagers' desire for freedom does not come from any negative prejudgment.

the reader. A first-person narrator, by contrast, would tend to invite closer identification on a reader's part. This distance may allow **irony** to operate as a text strategy. That is, in reading either of these stories, you may have had sufficient distance to feel an important difference between, say, what Eveline or Daisy thinks and what is actually going on in their worlds. Maybe you felt Eveline was kidding herself all along about her intentions to leave home, and that you knew that and she did not. The third-person limited mode of narration does not allow for any direct or authoritative statements to that effect, nor does it present any other character thinking it and thereby raising the possibility for you. But the "objectivity" with which Eveline's thoughts are presented, even though they are presented as she thinks them, may allow you to emphasize her nostalgia and downplay her determination to escape. If this happened as you read "Eveline," you may have felt less sympathetic toward her—not so much toward her unhappy home situation, but toward her apparent decision not to go away with Frank. And you might condemn her for being weak or for missing her chance at a better life—and so see her as trapped by her own choice, not by her circumstances. One reader in my class called her final decision "cowardice." In such a reading, Eveline's thoughts about freedom and escape become ironic in light of her inability or unwillingness to act on her desires. An ironic reading like this also depends on a greater degree of aesthetic distance between reader and character than what operates in a more sympathetic reading of Eveline.

Similarly, maybe you felt that everything Daisy did in relation to Donny was really the opposite of what she should have done and, again, that you were able to recognize this and she was not—even though the text strategy of limited narration does not allow you to be told this reliably by a narrative voice. This way, you may have felt, as one of my students did, angry with her because she didn't seem able to do anything to change her circumstances, that she was well-meaning and concerned, but too quick to do what other people suggested about Donny: take him to a psychologist, place him with a tutor. This reading views Daisy ironically because of the difference between what she says she wants to do for Donny and what she actually does, in effect. It is considerably less sympathetic toward Daisy, without necessarily taking Donny's side or seeing the text as "wanting" the reader to sympathize with Donny against his mother.

CONNECT: Consider the discussion in Chapters 5 and 6 about the kinds of judgment you seem invited to make against the main characters in "The Necklace" and "The Cask of Amontillado." In the former story, the distance from Mathilde afforded by the omniscient narration enables this judgment; in the latter, the irony made possible by the first-person involved narration is the enabling factor.

Title

In Chapter 5, the **title** of "Continuity of Parks" was briefly considered as a text strategy, in relation to the reading strategy of creating theme. A reader who is trying to decide what a short story is about in terms of larger or thematic concerns may regard the title as a clue to this kind of meaning. With the two stories in this chapter, the title "Eveline" seems to offer little more than a description of the narrative focus. If it were titled "A Missed Opportunity," or "A Foolish Decision," or "A Matter of Loyalty," for instance, the ideology of the text toward the episode related in it would be clearer (even if any of those proposed titles might seem heavy-handed).

SHARE AND COMPARE: Can you say what difference the presence of a different title—one of those I suggested or another that seems appropriate—would have on your expectations concerning "Eveline"? What ideas for "alternative" titles do your classmates have? Of all the possibilities, which is the "best" title, and why?

On the other hand, perhaps the title "Teenage Wasteland" does provide a clue to that text's ideology. On one level, that title seems to refer to the song by the Who that Daisy and Matt hear playing when they visit Cal's house one day. Furthermore, in that passage, Matt misunderstands Daisy's reference (actually *mis*reference) to the song's title as a description of the scene at Cal's place. And the narrator does say at that point that Daisy's saying "'*Teenage Wasteland*'" aloud "might have been" a commentary on "the scene spread before them." If you are a reader who is looking for an anchor in the text of the text's ideology, you could interpret the title as a kind of "editorial" or authorial commentary on Donny's position with respect to his parents.

For the sake of discussion, I have oversimplified the range of responses readers could have to Eveline and Daisy in these two stories. But the point is that because of the way point of view or other text strategies are handled, you may be able to construct something of either text's ideology with respect to the issues of teenagers' freedom versus parents' control. Whether you take the narration in these stories as ironic or straightforward, you may infer textual values, one way or the other, as a result.

SHARE AND COMPARE: What varieties of opinion exist in your class as to how "Eveline" or "Teenage Wasteland" should be read? How are these opinions related to text strategies such as point of view? How are they related to the ideologies readers bring to the texts?

Interactions Between Readers and Texts

Listen to what some of my students wrote in response to the questions on pages 204 and 211-212, about how "Eveline" and "Teenage Wasteland," respectively, seem to "want" them to feel.

On "Eveline"

I think . . . . [Eveline] should definitely leave home, but . . . continue to live at home is what I think she'll do. So I do think the text "wants" me to feel sympathy for her. She's confused and afraid. . . . I think the text presents Eveline's final decision as the right one. . . . (*Melanie Polak*)

The text does seem to "want" me to feel sympathy for Evvy. The text also seems to lean toward the belief that she made the wrong decision, because her home life is depicted almost entirely negatively, while Frank's option is basically romanticized. (*Sam Norwood*)

I think the text "wants" you to feel for Eveline, but not sympathy. There is no reason to pity her; she is strong and she will get through what she has to. . . . I think that her decision at the end of the story is presented as the right one. (*Caroline Smith*)

On "Teenage Wasteland"

To me, the text sides with the young and confused Donny. His parents seem willing enough to help him with his troubles, but they falter several times. They often appear misunderstanding and indifferent toward Donny's plight even though they do love him. (*Mike Williams*)

The text "wants" me to sympathize with Daisy. She is portrayed as a loving mother who is trying to give her son the best, but she just doesn't know how. (*Norris Daniels*)

My sympathies strongly change throughout the story. . . . I'm not really sure how . . . [the text wants me to feel]. I think, perhaps, the text leans toward Donny—because it portrays him as misunderstood and tortured. (*Marie Murphy*)

Perhaps discussion in your class has revealed similar variation in how different readers think either text "wants to be read" or what its ideology is with respect to either character or to the issue of children's freedom versus parents' control. If that is the case, it may be caused by and at the same time indicate an important indeterminacy in either story.

Indeterminacy, or a quality of undecidability, means that something about a text cannot be conclusively determined or decided. In the case of these two stories, the text strategy of limited point of view makes it hard to determine the extent to which either text "wants" you to sympathize with or judge Eveline or Daisy, whether you are being invited to regard either of them ironically or not. Compared with "The Necklace," it seems these stories have deliberately backed away from a moral position with respect to their main characters (and so "The Necklace" may seem less indeterminate in that regard). Indeterminacy of this sort in a text may annoy some readers who are inclined to want or who have been trained to read for "the author's intention" in order to resolve questions of interpretation. As you read in Chapter 2, however, the author's intention is very likely indeterminate itself and is certainly not relevant to a reading model that emphasizes the reader's role in making meaning of texts. So let me make two points here about readers and indeterminacy. One is that noticing indeterminacy at any point in a text is as much the reader's doing as the author's: Readers decide what is undecidable, just as they decide what is decidable! Even though there may be general agreement in your classroom that the ideology of "Eveline" toward the title character is indeterminate, for instance, some readers may think that the text is pretty definite in suggesting a condemnation of Eveline for not having the courage to leave with Frank.

The second point is that you don't *have* to read with the goal of pinning down indeterminacies; you may leave them indeterminate. You may not want to do that; you may consider it a cop-out, if your literary experience contains the idea that the goal or purpose of reading is to decide conclusively what a text means, or if your ideology doesn't have much tolerance for ambiguity in any area of life. But on the other hand, you may not only tolerate but actually like ambiguity, especially in artistic texts. Or your attitude toward that may vary from time to time, from issue to issue, from text to text. For now, at any rate, just consider that undecidability is neither the mark of a weak text nor of a weak reader.

The Role of the Reader's Cultural Context

Consider the effect of *your* ideology on your response to these stories. Your own experience, beliefs, opinions, or attitudes regarding those issues of freedom and control play a role too. And so does your own age and your family and social circumstances. If you are close in age to Eveline, for instance, or if your own family circumstances are at all similar to hers, you may sympathize all the more with her wish to get free. At the same time, and perhaps paradoxically, you may blame her for her inability to break free, thinking that she traps herself in her situation by not having the courage to go with Frank when the opportunity actually comes. Or if you feel that way, it may be because you have gotten away from your home or are in the process of doing so gradually by going to college. A response like this would involve a *harmonious* ideological interaction between reader and text. Your tendency may be to attribute to the text alone any sympathy with Eveline or judgment against her decision to stay, and indeed traditional ways of teaching or analyzing "Eveline" would also do that, ignoring or downplaying the role of the reader in producing that effect. But a reader who could go against the grain of this text—either because of his or her own values or situation or because he chose to "resist" it in reading it—might approve of Eveline's final decision not to go with Frank on the grounds that her duty to her father and her promise to her mother dictate that she put the welfare of others above her own. Along these lines, look at what one of my students wrote in her response journal about "Eveline":

> I thought that . . . [Eveline's] character, though it may have seemed weak at the
>
> end of the story, was, in actuality, very strong. I think had she run away from her
>
> family with Frank she would have simply been taking the easy way out. By staying,
>
> she was forced to be responsible for her mother's dying wish and she also had to
>
> endure hardships with her father. She chose this life instead of one with Frank
>
> which could have led to contentment (and I don't say happiness because I don't
>
> think she really loved Frank).
>
> Maybe I am associating Eveline's action not to leave too much with my own
>
> circumstances this summer. I was very reluctant to leave home for school, but now,
>
> looking back, I realize that if I hadn't left I would have simply been taking the easy
>
> way out. Yet Eveline is not me. I had a secure home to turn to and she had nothing
>
> but memories and hardships to go back to. That fact is what leads me to believe
>
> that her choice was the noble and brave one. (Gretchen Jones)

Gretchen's response to Eveline's decision recognizes how her own situation contributes to it (even though she worries that her association of Eveline's decision to her own situation may be "too much").

In similar fashion, perhaps you can see how your family situation influences your response to "Teenage Wasteland." More and more people with growing or grown children are returning to the classroom these days. If you are one of those people yourself, or if you are a person of the traditional college age who has enjoyed a relatively smooth negotiation of your own freedom against your parents' desire for control, you may have had a harmonious ideological interaction with "Teenage Wasteland" when you read it. Your sympathies may lie with Daisy, even if you see her as not always acting effectively in her handling of Donny's problems. In fact, you may feel her ineffectiveness inclines your sympathy toward her even more, if you see that ineffectiveness as caused at least partly by her lack of helpful information from Donny and Cal about how she could help.

For instance, one student of mine who read "Teenage Wasteland" as a 21-year-old senior, described her beliefs about the relations between teenage children and their parents, particularly on the issue of children's freedom versus parents' control, in the following terms:

> Children who have been kept on a tight rein are the ones who tend to overem-
>
> phasize the freedoms to which they feel they are entitled. On the other hand, chil-
>
> dren who grow up with less parental control seem to have a better sense of their

freedom. My parents let me make my own decisions—that gives me more freedom

now. (*Maeve Kelly*)

In two different response journal entries, Maeve expressed strong sympathy for Daisy. Some of what she wrote may suggest this sympathy comes partly from her own gender. At one point she wrote:

I also felt sorry for Daisy because she had to face "rejection" whenever Donny

went to Cal. As a mother, if I were one, I'd be very jealous of Cal. Because as a

hired, outside person he doesn't hold the responsibilities of a parent. So he can

allow the children to enjoy themselves, but he doesn't have to discipline them or

make sure they grow up "right."

Another time, she wrote:

Daisy is a woman who makes me afraid to have my own children. What if my son

turns out like Donny did? I would act just as Daisy did, proud of my son yet confused by

his actions. My sympathies lie totally with Daisy, and I don't think I'll change my mind.

This same student commented that:

But just because I sympathize with [Daisy] . . . doesn't mean I can't criticize her.

She tried way too hard with Donny. She tried so hard that she wasn't "cool" any-

more. She was too much of a mother and not enough of a friend.

It seems to me that Maeve's experience in her own family situation and her beliefs about parental control versus teenagers' desire for freedom contributes to her mixed response to Daisy.

What if your own situation is closer to Donny's than to Daisy's? There's a good chance that you are closer to him in age and cultural situation than you are to Daisy. If so, while your status as a college student probably means you have not run away from home and high school, you may very well have fresh memories of situations similar to Donny's in your own relationship with your parents: being at odds with them over questions of freedom, responsibility, and trust. If so, your sympathies may be inclined toward Donny and against Daisy, in opposition to what the text apparently would have you feel. If that's the case, or if you can self-consciously adopt such a position for the sake of a strong reading of "Teenage Wasteland," you may have had a *clashing* ideological interaction with the text. That was the case with another of my students, a 20-year-old junior, who wrote this in his response journal:

Although I can't relate entirely to Donny's dilemma, I do understand his use of

the phrase, "You don't trust me!" I know that I gave such a response to my parents

on several occasions. . . . I remember so well feeling an indifference between myself and my parents; I questioned if they were indeed ever my age. Their response was similar to Daisy's: "It's not that we don't trust you . . ." Well, then, what is it?

Perhaps I'm still too young and naive to understand the meaning behind my parents' seemingly excessive care and concern. I too, like Donny, have felt the pressures of home life values and expectations. . . . When Donny left home, he succumbed to the utter despair and hopelessness he seemed to exhibit throughout most of the story. I consider it tragic that Donny found no other means of resolving his problems. However, there's a definite communication problem between Donny and his parents; they both mean well, but they don't seem to give Donny the constant support he deserves. (*Bill McGouldrick*)

Bill had indicated some of his "independent" stance toward children's freedom versus parental control in his own family situation when he wrote:

As the "baby" of my family, at age 20, I feel that I have received some privileges that my siblings have not. However, I also feel that I have worked just as hard (if not more) than some of them in my life. I feel that I should indeed be regarded as a "young adult." Also, I'm working toward an independent life; when I feel the time is right, I'll listen to my family's/friends' opinions, but I will ultimately decide for myself if I want to move on (or out).

Toward a Strong Reading

I would like to remind you at this point that a clashing interaction—at the literary or the ideological level—does not mean an incorrect or unsuccessful reading. To the contrary, it can actually lead toward a strong reading because you already have a position from which you can read against the grain of the text. It's also usually easier to read that way when you bring an oppositional or problematizing stance to the interaction from your ideology, when you don't have to choose to adopt such a stance for the sake of the exercise. In any case, the belief that your task as a reader is to interpret a text in the terms in which it apparently seeks to be interpreted is a culturally conditioned one, not an absolute. The same is true of the belief that you should put aside an initial negative response to any aspect of a text in order to "dig deeper" in it until you discover the hidden meaning or the author's purpose. A negative initial response—a problematic interaction—can lead to a strong reading in which you learn more about text strategies and your own reading strategies, your cognitive style, or your cultural situation than you can learn by pursuing the traditional analysis/interpretation approach to reading.

Maeve, the student whose responses to "Teenage Wasteland" I quoted earlier, recognized the problematical nature of her response at the end of her second journal entry. What she wrote there may also suggest the potential of that response for further exploration in a strong reading in which she would examine the disharmony she was beginning to recognize. After she wrote, "I trust [Anne Tyler] ... more than ... any other author I know of," she said, "I don't think she liked Cal. That made me not want to like him either.... As a reader, I didn't like him, but as a teenager I would have loved him. I think. I can't be sure, because I don't know much about him." Then she indicated her recognition that she was "having problems responding to this text." Her "trust and love for Anne Tyler's works," she said, were clashing with her beliefs about teens and parents and her sense that the mode of narration in "Teenage Wasteland" privileged Daisy at the expense of Donny and Cal. "I guess I need to think this out some more," she said.

She did not actually do that in the course in which she read "Teenage Wasteland"; for a formal paper assignment in that course, she chose to develop her response to a different story. But your own recognition of problematic readings, responses that you too "need to think ... out some more,"— whether to "Teenage Wasteland," "Eveline," or any other short story—ought to be pursued, explored, and developed toward strong readings, not put aside as "incorrect" or "weak" or out of line with what you may suppose to be the author's intention.

Stories for Exploration

The three reprinted short stories that follow—Tillie Olsen's "I Stand Here Ironing," Nadine Gordimer's "The Train from Rhodesia," and Joyce Carol Oates' "Where Are You Going, Where Have You Been?"—provide further opportunities for you to analyze the interaction of your ideology with that of a text. The questions that precede each story are designed to heighten your awareness of your experience, beliefs, opinions, and values with respect to particular issues of contemporary life. You should jot down some answers to those questions before you begin reading any of the stories and use those answers to gain some consciousness of yourself as you are read each story. A set of response statement questions follows each story.

Critical Reading Questions

- What is your own family situation in terms of being or having a single parent? being or having a "latchkey" child? using institutional resources such as day care or boarding school to help with child rearing, or having been reared in part by such institutions?

- If you are a parent with more than one child, what is your experience regarding sibling relations? As a child yourself, what is or was your experience in terms of your parent's or parents' relationships to you *vis á vis* your siblings?

- What qualities make for a good mother, in your opinion or experience as either a child or a parent?

Tillie Olsen   b. 1912

I Stand Here Ironing   *1961*

I stand here ironing, and what you asked me moves tormented back and forth with the iron.

"I wish you would manage the time to come in and talk with me about your daughter. I'm sure you can help me understand her. She's a youngster who needs help and whom I'm deeply interested in helping."

"Who needs help." . . . Even if I came, what good would it do? You think because I am her mother I have a key, or that in some way you could use me as a key? She has lived for nineteen years. There is all that life that has happened outside of me, beyond me.

And when is there time to remember, to sift, to weigh, to estimate, to total? I will start and there will be an interruption and I will have to gather it all together again. Or I will become engulfed with all I did or did not do, with what should have been and what cannot be helped.

She was a beautiful baby. The first and only one of our five that was beautiful at birth. You do not guess how new and uneasy her tenancy in her now-loveliness. You did not know her all those years she was thought homely, or see her poring over her baby pictures, making me tell her over and over how beautiful she had been—and would be, I would tell her—and was now, to the seeing eye. But the seeing eyes were few or nonexistent. Including mine.

I nursed her. They feel that's important nowadays. I nursed all the children, but with her, with all the fierce rigidity of first motherhood, I did like the books then said. Though her cries battered me to trembling and my breasts ached with swollenness, I waited till the clock decreed.

Why do I put that first? I do not even know if it matters, or if it explains anything.

She was a beautiful baby. She blew shining bubbles of sound. She loved motion, loved light, loved color and music and textures. She would lie on the floor in her blue overalls patting the surface so hard in ecstasy her hands and feet would blur. She was a miracle to me, but when she was eight months old I had to leave her daytimes with the woman downstairs to whom she was no miracle at all, for I worked or looked for work and for Emily's father, who "could no longer endure" (he wrote in his good-bye note) "sharing want with us."

I was nineteen. It was the pre-relief, pre-WPA[1] world of the depression. I would start running as soon as I got off the streetcar, running up the stairs, the place smelling sour, and awake or asleep to startle awake, when she saw me she would break into a clogged weeping that could not be comforted, a weeping I can hear yet.

5

---

[1] WPA—Works Progress Administration: a federal program to hire the unemployed.

After a while I found a job hashing at night so I could be with her days, and
it was better. But it came to where I had to bring her to his family and leave her.

It took a long time to raise the money for her fare back. Then she got
chicken pox and I had to wait longer. When she finally came, I hardly knew
her, walking quick and nervous like her father, looking like her father, thin,
and dressed in a shoddy red that yellowed her skin and glared at the pock-
marks. All the baby loveliness gone.

She was two. Old enough for nursery school they said, and I did not
know then what I know now—the fatigue of the long day, and the lacerations
of group life in the kinds of nurseries that are only parking places for children.

Except that it would have made no difference if I had known. It was the
only place there was. It was the only way we could be together, the only way
I could hold a job.

And even without knowing, I knew. I knew the teacher that was evil because all these years it has curdled into my memory, the little boy hunched in
the corner, her rasp, "why aren't you outside, because Alvin hits you? that's no
reason, go out, scaredy." I knew Emily hated it even if she did not clutch and
implore "don't go Mommy" like the other children, mornings.

She always had a reason why we should stay home. Momma, you look
sick. Momma, I feel sick. Momma, the teachers aren't there today, they're sick.
Momma, we can't go, there was a fire there last night. Momma, it's a holiday
today, no school, they told me.

But never a direct protest, never rebellion. I think of our others in their
three-, four-year-oldness—the explosions, the tempers, the denunciations, the
demands—and I feel suddenly ill. I put the iron down. What in me demanded
that goodness in her? And what was the cost, the cost to her of such goodness?

The old man living in the back once said in his gentle way: "You should
smile at Emily more when you look at her." What *was* in my face when I
looked at her? I loved her. There were all the acts of love.

It was only with the others I remembered what he said, and it was the
face of joy, and not of care or tightness or worry I turned to them—too late for
Emily. She does not smile easily, let alone almost always as her brothers and
sisters do. Her face is closed and sombre, but when she wants, how fluid. You
must have seen it in her pantomimes, you spoke of her rare gift for comedy
on the stage that rouses laughter out of the audience so dear they applaud and
applaud and do not want to let her go.

Where does it come from, that comedy? There was none of it in her when
she came back to me that second time, after I had had to send her away
again. She had a new daddy now to learn to love, and I think perhaps it was
a better time.

Except when we left her alone nights, telling ourselves she was old enough.
"Can't you go some other time, Mommy, like tomorrow?" she would ask.
"Will it be just a little while you'll be gone? Do you promise?"

The time we came back, the front door open, the clock on the floor in the
hall. She rigid awake. "It wasn't just a little while. I didn't cry. Three times I called
you, just three times, and then I ran downstairs to open the door so you could
come faster. The clock talked loud. I threw it away, it scared me what it talked."

10

15

20

She said the clock talked loud again that night I went to the hospital to have Susan. She was delirious with the fever that comes before red measles, but she was fully conscious all the week I was gone and the week after we were home when she could not come near the new baby or me.

She did not get well. She stayed skeleton thin, not wanting to eat, and night after night she had nightmares. She would call for me, and I would rouse from exhaustion to sleepily call back: "You're all right, darling, go to sleep, it's just a dream," and if she still called, in a sterner voice, "now go to sleep, Emily, there's nothing to hurt you." Twice, only twice, when I had to get up for Susan anyhow, I went in to sit with her.

Now when it is too late (as if she would let me hold and comfort her like I do the others) I get up and go to her at once at her moan or restless stirring. "Are you awake, Emily? Can I get you something?" And the answer is always the same: "No, I'm all right, go back to sleep, Mother."   25

They persuaded me at the clinic to send her away to a convalescent home in the country where "she can have the kind of food and care you can't manage for her, and you'll be free to concentrate on the new baby." They still send children to that place. I see pictures on the society page of sleek young women planning affairs to raise money for it, or dancing at the affairs, or decorating Easter eggs or filling Christmas stockings for the children.

They never have a picture of the children so I do not know if the girls still wear those gigantic red bows and the ravaged looks on the every other Sunday when parents can come to visit "unless otherwise notified"—as we were notified the first six weeks.

Oh it is a handsome place, green lawns and tall trees and fluted flower beds. High up on the balconies of each cottage the children stand, the girls in their red bows and white dresses, the boys in white suits and giant red ties. The parents stand below shrieking up to be heard and the children shriek down to be heard, and between them the invisible wall: "Not to Be Contaminated by Parental Germs or Physical Affection."

There was a tiny girl who always stood hand in hand with Emily. Her parents never came. One visit she was gone. "They moved her to Rose Cottage," Emily shouted in explanation. "They don't like you to love anybody here."

She wrote once a week, the labored writing of a seven-year-old. "I am fine. How is the baby. If I write my leter nicly I will have a star. Love." There never was a star. We wrote every other day, letters she could never hold or keep but only hear read—once. "We simply do not have room for children to keep any personal possessions," they patiently explained when we pieced one Sunday's shrieking together to plead how much it would mean to Emily, who loved so to keep things, to be allowed to keep her letters and cards.   30

Each visit she look frailer. "She isn't eating," they told us.

(They had runny eggs for breakfast or mush with lumps, Emily said later, I'd hold it in my mouth and not swallow. Nothing ever tasted good, just when they had chicken.)

It took us eight months to get her released home, and only the fact that she gained back so little of her seven lost pounds convinced the social worker.

I used to try to hold and love her after she came back, but her body would stay stiff, and after a while she'd push away. She ate little. Food sickened her, and I think much of life too. Oh she had physical lightness and brightness, twinkling by on skates, bouncing like a ball up and down up and down over the jump rope, skimming over the hill; but these were momentary.

She fretted about her appearance, thin and dark and foreign-looking at a time when every little girl was supposed to look or thought she should look a chubby blonde replica of Shirley Temple.[2] The doorbell sometimes rang for her, but no one seemed to come and play in the house or be a best friend. Maybe because we moved so much.

There was a boy she loved painfully through two school semesters. Months later she told me how she had taken pennies from my purse to buy him candy. "Licorice was his favorite and I brought him some every day, but he still liked Jennifer better'n me. Why, Mommy?" The kind of question for which there is no answer.

School was a worry to her. She was not glib or quick in a world where glibness and quickness were easily confused with ability to learn. To her over-worked and exasperated teachers she was an overconscientious "slow learner" who kept trying to catch up and was absent entirely too often.

I let her be absent, though sometimes the illness was imaginary. How different from my now-strictness about attendance with the others. I wasn't working. We had a new baby, I was home anyhow. Sometimes, after Susan grew old enough, I would keep her home from school, too, to have them all together.

Mostly Emily had asthma, and her breathing, harsh and labored, would fill the house with a curiously tranquil sound. I would bring the two old dresser mirrors and her boxes of collections to her bed. She would select beads and single earrings, bottle tops and shells, dried flowers and pebbles, old post-cards and scraps, all sorts of oddments; then she and Susan would play King-dom, setting up landscapes and furniture, peopling them with action.

Those were the only times of peaceful companionship between her and Susan. I have edged away from it, that poisonous feeling between them, that terrible balancing of hurts and needs I had to do between the two, and did so badly, those earlier years.

Oh there are conflicts between the others too, each one human, needing, demanding, hurting, taking—but only between Emily and Susan, no, Emily to-ward Susan that corroding resentment. It seems so obvious on the surface, yet it is not obvious. Susan, the second child, Susan, golden- and curly-haired and chubby, quick and articulate and assured, everything in appearance and man-ner Emily was not; Susan, not able to resist Emily's precious things, losing or sometimes clumsily breaking them; Susan telling jokes and riddles to company for applause while Emily sat silent (to say to me later: that was *my* riddle, Mother, I told it to Susan); Susan, who for all the five years' difference in age was just a year behind Emily in developing physically.

I am glad for that slow physical development that widened the difference between her and her contemporaries, though she suffered over it. She was too vulnerable for that terrible world of youthful competition, of preening and parading, of constant measuring of yourself against every other, of envy, "If I had that copper hair," "If I had that skin. . . ." She tormented herself enough

[2]Shirley Temple—child actress.

about not looking like the others, there was enough of the unsureness, the having to be conscious of words before you speak, the constant caring—what are they thinking of me? without having it all magnified by the merciless physical drives.

Ronnie is calling. He is wet and I change him. It is rare there is such a cry now. That time of motherhood is almost behind me when the ear is not one's own but must always be racked and listening for the child cry, the child call. We sit for a while and I hold him, looking out over the city spread in charcoal with its soft aisles of light. *"Shoogily,"* he breathes and curls closer. I carry him back to bed, asleep. *Shoogily.* A funny word, a family word, inherited from Emily, invented by her to say: *comfort.*

In this and other ways she leaves her seal, I say aloud. And startle at my saying it. What do I mean? What did I start to gather together, to try and make coherent? I was at the terrible, growing years. War years. I do not remember them well. I was working, there were four smaller ones now, there was not time for her. She had to help be a mother, and housekeeper, and shopper. She had to set her seal. Mornings of crisis and near hysteria trying to get lunches packed, hair combed, coats and shoes found, everyone to school or Child Care on time, the baby ready for transportation. And always the paper scribbled on by a smaller one, the book looked at by Susan then mislaid, the homework not done. Running out to that huge school where she was one, she was lost, she was a drop; suffering over the unpreparedness, stammering and unsure in her classes.

There was so little time left at night after the kids were bedded down. She would struggle over books, always eating (it was in those years she developed her enormous appetite that is legendary in our family) and I would be ironing, or preparing food for the next day, or writing V-mail to Bill, or tending the baby. Sometimes, to make me laugh, or out of her despair, she would imitate happenings or types at school.   45

I think I said once: "Why don't you do something like this in the school amateur show?" One morning she phoned me at work, hardly understandable through the weeping: "Mother, I did it. I won, I won; they gave me first prize; they clapped and clapped and wouldn't let me go."

Now suddenly she was Somebody, and as imprisoned in her difference as she had been in anonymity.

She began to be asked to perform at other high schools, even in colleges, then at city and statewide affairs. The first one we went to, I only recognized her that first moment when thin, shy, she almost drowned herself into the curtains. Then: Was this Emily? The control, the command, the convulsing and deadly clowning, the spell, then the roaring, stamping audience, unwilling to let this rare and precious laughter out of their lives.

Afterwards: You ought to do something about her with a gift like that—but without money or knowing how, what does one do? We have left it all to her, and the gift has as often eddied inside, clogged and clotted, as been used and growing.

She is coming. She runs up the stairs two at a time with her light graceful   50
step, and I know she is happy tonight. Whatever it was that occasioned your call did not happen today.

"Aren't you ever going to finish the ironing, Mother? Whistler painted his mother in a rocker. I'd have to paint mine standing over an ironing board." This is one of her communicative nights and she tells me everything and nothing as she fixes herself a plate of food out of the icebox.

She is so lovely. Why did you want me to come in at all? Why were you concerned? She will find her way.

She starts up the stairs to bed. "Don't get me up with the rest in the morning." "But I thought you were having midterms." "Oh, those," she comes back in, kisses me, and says quite lightly, "in a couple of years when we'll all be atom-dead they won't matter a bit."

She has said it before. She *believes* it. But because I have been dredging the past, and all that compounds a human being is so heavy and meaningful in me, I cannot endure it tonight.

I will never total it all. I will never come in to say: She was a child seldom smiled at. Her father left me before she was a year old. I had to work her first six years when there was work, or I sent her home and to his relatives. There were years she had care she hated. She was dark and thin and foreign-looking in a world where the prestige went to blondeness and curly hair and dimples, she was slow where glibness was prized. She was a child of anxious, not proud, love. We were poor and could not afford for her the soil of easy growth. I was a young mother, I was a distracted mother. There were other children pushing up, demanding. Her younger sister seemed all that she was not. There were years she did not want me to touch her. She kept too much in herself, her life was such she had to keep too much in herself. My wisdom came too late. She has much to her and probably little will come of it. She is a child of her age, of depression, of war, of fear.

Let her be. So all that is in her will not bloom—but in how many does it? There is still enough left to live by. Only help her to know—help make it so there is cause for her to know—that she is more than this dress on the ironing board, helpless before the iron.

Response Statement Questions for "I Stand Here Ironing"

- What is your response to the characters in this story? Is the narrator a good mother to Emily? Why or why not, according to your ideology? Is Emily the kind of child who is easy to be a good mother to? Why or why not?

- Does your own life experience allow you to identify with either the narrator or Emily? Family circumstances that might be relevant include single parenthood, "latchkey" children, and children raised by institutional caretakers.

- How do your age, race, gender, or social class influence the way you respond to this story?

- *Share and Compare* What different responses to the family situation depicted in "I Stand Here Ironing" emerge from your class or discussion group? How are these differences related to individual readers' own family situations and/or their ideologies concerning what constitutes good parenting?

Critical Reading Questions for "The Train from Rhodesia"

- What experience do you have as a tourist buying "native" crafts or art-work, in the United States or abroad? If you have bought such pieces as souvenirs of a visit, just what are you buying? Is either party in such a commercial transaction exploiting the other?

- What do you know, think, or believe about the relationship between English-speaking white people living in Africa and the native black people?

- What experience do you have, in a romantic relationship, of first find-ing out that any of your partner's values are different from your own? If you do have such experience, what was its effect on your view of the relationship after you found it out?

Nadine Gordimer   b. 1923

The Train from Rhodesia¹   *1952*

The train came out of the red horizon and bore down towards them over the single straight track.

The stationmaster came out of his little brick station with its pointed chalet roof, feeling the creases in his serge uniform in his legs as well. A stir of pre-paredness rippled through the squatting native vendors waiting in the dust; the face of a carved wooden animal, eternally surprised, stuck out of a sack. The stationmaster's barefoot children wandered over. From the grey mud huts with the untidy heads that stood within a decorated mud wall, chickens, and dogs with their skin stretched like parchment over their bones, followed the piccanins² down to the track. The flushed and perspiring west cast a reflec-tion, faint, without heat, upon the station, upon the tin shed marked "Goods," upon the walled kraal,³ upon the grey tin house of the stationmaster and upon the sand, that lapped all around, from sky to sky, cast little rhythmical cups of shadow, so that the sand became the sea, and closed over the chil-dren's black feet softly and without imprint.

The stationmaster's wife sat behind the mesh of her veranda. Above her head the hunk of a sheep's carcass moved slightly, dangling in a current of air.

They waited.

The train called out, along the sky; but there was no answer; and the cry   5
hung on: I'm coming . . . I'm coming. . . .

The engine flared out now, big, whisking a dwindling body behind it; the track flared out to let it in.

Creaking, jerking, jostling, gasping, the train filled the station.

---

¹Rhodesia—former name of Zimbabwe, country north of South Africa.
²piccanins—Native African children.
³kraal—enclosure where animals are kept.

Here, let me see that one—the young woman curved her body farther out of the corridor window. Missus? smiled the old man, looking at the creatures he held in his hand. From a piece of string on his grey finger hung a tiny woven basket; he lifted it, questioning. No, no, she urged, leaning down towards him, across the height of the train towards the man in the piece of old rug; that one, that one, her hand commanded. It was a lion, carved out of soft dry wood that looked like spongecake; heraldic, black and white, with impressionistic detail burnt in. The old man held it up to her still smiling, not from the heart, but at the customer. Between its vandyke teeth, in the mouth opened in an endless roar too terrible to be heard, it had a black tongue. Look, said the young husband, if you don't mind! And round the neck of the thing, a piece of fur (rat? rabbit? meerkat?); a real mane, majestic, telling you somehow that the artist had delight in the lion.

All up and down the length of the train in the dust the artists sprang, walking bent, like performing animals, the better to exhibit the fantasy held towards the faces on the train. Buck, startled and stiff, staring with round black and white eyes. More lions, standing erect, grappling with strange, thin, elongated warriors who clutched spears and showed no fear in their slits of eyes. How much, they asked from the train, how much?

Give me penny, said the little ones with nothing to sell. The dogs went and sat, quite still, under the dining car, where the train breathed out the smell of meat cooking with onion.   10

A man passed beneath the arch of reaching arms meeting grey-black and white in the exchange of money for the staring wooden eyes, the stiff wooden legs sticking up in the air; went along under the voices and the bargaining, interrogating the wheels. Past the dogs; glancing up at the dining car where he could stare at the faces behind glass, drinking beer, two by two, on either side of a uniform railway vase with its pale dead flower. Right to the end, to the guard's van, where the stationmaster's children had just collected their mother's two loaves of bread, to the engine itself, where the stationmaster and the driver stood talking against the steaming complaint of the resting beast.

The man called out to them, something loud and joking. They turned to laugh, in a twirl of steam. The two children careened over the sand, clutching the bread, and burst through the iron gate and up the path through the garden in which nothing grew.

Passengers drew themselves in at the corridor windows and turned into compartments to fetch money, to call someone to look. Those sitting inside looked up: suddenly different, caged faces, boxed in, cut off after the contact of outside. There was an orange a piccanin would like . . . What about that chocolate? It wasn't very nice. . . .

A girl had collected a handful of the hard kind, that no one liked, out of the chocolate box, and was throwing them to the dogs, over at the dining car. But the hens darted in and swallowed the chocolates, incredibly quick and accurate, before they had even dropped in the dust, and the dogs, a little bewildered, looked up with their brown eyes, not expecting anything.

—No, leave it, said the young woman, don't take it. . . .   15

Too expensive, too much, she shook her head and raised her voice to the old man, giving up the lion. He held it high where she had handed it to him.

No, she said, shaking her head. Three-and-six?[4] insisted her husband, loudly. Yes baas! laughed the old man. *Three-and-six?*—the young man was incredulous. Oh leave it—she said. The young man stopped. Don't you want it? he said, keeping his face closed to the old man. No, never mind, she said, leave it. The old native kept his head on one side, looking at them sideways, holding the lion. Three-and-six, he murmured, as old people repeat things to themselves.

The young woman drew her head in. She went into the coupé[5] and sat down. Out of the window, on the other side, there was nothing; sand and bush; a thorn tree. Back through the open doorway, past the figure of her husband in the corridor, there was the station, the voices, wooden animals waving, running feet. Her eye followed the funny little valance of scrolled wood that outlined the chalet roof of the station; she thought of the lion and smiled. That bit of fur round the neck. But the wooden buck, the hippos, the elephants, the baskets that already bulked out of their brown paper under the seat and on the luggage rack! How will they look at home? Where will you put them? What will they mean away from the places you found them? Away from the unreality of the last few weeks? The young man outside. But he is not part of the unreality; he is for good now. Odd ... somewhere there was an idea that he, that living with him, was part of the holiday, the strange places.

Outside, a bell rang. The stationmaster was leaning against the end of the train, green flag rolled in readiness. A few men who had got down to stretch their legs sprang on to the train, clinging to the observation platforms, or perhaps merely standing on the iron step, holding the rail; but on the train, safe from the one dusty platform, the one tin house, the empty sand.

There was a grunt. The train jerked. Through the glass the beer drinkers looked out, as if they could not see beyond it. Behind the fly-screen, the stationmaster's wife sat facing back at them beneath the darkening hunk of meat.

There was a shout. The flag drooped out. Joints not yet coordinated, the segmented body of the train heaved and bumped back against itself. It began to move; slowly the scrolled chalet moved past it, the yells of the natives, running alongside, jetted up into the air, fell back at different levels. Staring wooden faces waved drunkenly, there, then gone, questioning for the last time at the windows. Here, one-and-six baas!—As one automatically opens a hand to catch a thrown ball, a man fumbled wildly down his pocket, brought up the shilling and sixpence and threw them out; the old native, gasping, his skinny toes splaying the sand, flung the lion.   20

The piccanins were waving, the dogs stood, tails uncertain, watching the train go; past the mud huts, where a woman turned to look up from the smoke of the fire, her hand pausing on her hip.

The stationmaster went slowly in under the chalet.

The old native stood, breath blowing out the skin between his ribs, feet tense, balanced in the sand, smiling and shaking his head. In his opened palm, held in the attitude of receiving, was the retrieved shilling and sixpence.

---

[4]three-and-six—Three shillings, sixpence in the pre–1970 British monetary system.
[5]coupé—private compartment in the railway carriage.

The blind end of the train was being pulled helplessly out of the station.

The young man swung in from the corridor, breathless. He was shaking his head with laughter and triumph. Here! he said. And waggled the lion at her. One-and-six!

What? she said.

He laughed. I was arguing with him for fun, bargaining—when the train had pulled out already, he came tearing after.... One-and-six Baas! So there's your lion.

She was holding it away from her, the lion with the open jaws, the pointed teeth, the black tongue, the wonderful ruff of fur facing her. She was looking at it with an expression of not seeing, of seeing something different. Her face was drawn up, wryly, like the face of a discomforted child. Her mouth lifted nervously at the corner. Very slowly, cautious, she lifted her finger and touched the mane, where it was joined to the wood.

But how could you, she said. He was shocked by the dismay of her face.

Good Lord, he said, what's the matter?

If you wanted the thing, she said, her voice rising and breaking with the shrill impotence of anger, why didn't you buy it in the first place? If you wanted it, why didn't you pay for it? Why didn't you take it decently, when he offered it? Why did you have to wait for him to run after the train with it, and give him one-and-six? One-and-six!

She was pushing it at him, trying to force him to take the lion. He stood astonished, his hands hanging at his sides.

But you wanted it! You liked it so much!

—It's a beautiful piece of work, she said fiercely, as if to protect it from him. You liked it so much! You said yourself it was too expensive—

Oh *you*—she said, hopeless and furious. *You* ... She threw the lion onto the seat.

He stood looking at her.

She sat down again in the corner and, her face slumped in her hands, stared out of the window. Everything was turning round inside her. One-and-six. One-and-six. One-and-six for the wood and the carving and the sinews of the legs and the switch of the tail. The mouth open like that and the teeth. The black tongue, rolling, like a wave. The mane round the neck. To give one-and-six for that. The heat of shame mounted through her legs and body and sounded in her ears like the sound of sand pouring. Pouring, pouring. She sat there, sick. A weariness, a tastelessness, the discovery of a void made her hands slacken their grip, atrophy emptily, as if the hour was not worth their grasp. She was feeling like this again. She had thought it was something to do with singleness, with being alone and belonging too much to oneself.

She sat there not wanting to move or speak, or to look at anything even; so that the mood should be associated with nothing, no object, word or sight that might recur and so recall the feeling again.... Smuts blew in grittily, settled on her hands. Her back remained at exactly the same angle, turned against the young man sitting with his hands dropping between his sprawled legs, and the lion, fallen on its side in the corner.

The train had cast the station like a skin. It called out to the sky, I'm coming,   40
I'm coming; and again, there was no answer.

Response Statement Questions for "The Train from Rhodesia"

- Can you relate the action of this story to any experience of your own with buying "native" crafts or artwork, in the United States or abroad? What's involved in this *cultural interaction*, as opposed to the commercial transaction? What are you "buying"? Are you exploiting or being exploited? How do your experiences and beliefs influence the way you respond to this story?

- What do you decide this story is really about? Is it the relationship of blacks and whites in Africa? the relationship between "the young woman" and her husband? middle-class white couples in general? "the young woman" herself? If you think it is any of the last three, how does the *setting* of the story help or hinder you in reading the story in those terms?

- What is the role of your *race* and *class* in your response to any of the above questions?

- *Share and Compare*   What role does the race, gender, or social class of anyone in your class or discussion group have in producing a response to the situation depicted in this story?

Critical Reading Questions for "Where Are You Going, Where Have You Been?"

What does your life experience lead you to think, believe, or feel about any of the following?

- teenagers being out socially at night

- teenagers having sex, either with other teens or with adults

- popular music and its effects on teenagers' attitudes about peer relations, sex, themselves as people.

Joyce Carol Oates   b. 1938

Where Are You Going, Where Have You Been?   1970

For Bob Dylan

Her name was Connie. She was fifteen and she had a quick nervous giggling habit of craning her neck to glance into mirrors, or checking other people's faces to make sure her own was all right. Her mother, who noticed everything and knew everything and who hadn't much reason any longer to look at her own face, always scolded Connie about it. "Stop gawking at yourself, who are you? You think you're so pretty?" she would say. Connie would raise her eyebrows at these familiar complaints and look right through her mother, into a shadowy vision of herself as she was right at that moment: she knew she was pretty and that was everything. Her mother had been pretty once too, if you could believe those old snapshots in the album, but now her looks were gone and that was why she was always after Connie.

"Why don't you keep your room clean like your sister? How've you got your hair fixed—what the hell stinks? Hair spray? You don't see your sister using that junk."

Her sister June was twenty-four and still lived at home. She was a secretary in the high school Connie attended, and if that wasn't bad enough—with her in the same building—she was so plain and chunky and steady that Connie had to hear her praised all the time by her mother and her mother's sisters. June did this, June did that, she saved money and helped clean the house and cooked and Connie couldn't do a thing, her mind was all filled with trashy daydreams. Their father was away at work most of the time and when he came home he wanted supper and he read the newspaper at supper and after supper he went to bed. He didn't bother talking much to them, but around his bent head Connie's mother kept picking at her until Connie wished her mother was dead and she herself was dead and it was all over. "She makes me want to throw up sometimes," she complained to her friends. She had a high, breathless, amused voice which made everything she said sound a little forced, whether it was sincere or not.

There was one good thing: June went places with girl friends of hers, girls who were just as plain and steady as she, and so when Connie wanted to do that her mother had no objections. The father of Connie's best friend drove the girls the three miles to town and left them off at a shopping plaza, so that they could walk through the stores or go to a movie, and when he came to pick them up again at eleven he never bothered to ask what they had done.

They must have been familiar sights, walking around that shopping plaza in their shorts and flat ballerina slippers that always scuffed the sidewalk, with charm bracelets jingling on their thin wrists; they would lean together to whisper and laugh secretly if someone passed by who amused or interested them. Connie had long dark blond hair that drew anyone's eye to it, and she wore part of it pulled up on her head and puffed out and the rest of it she let fall down her back. She wore a pull-over jersey blouse that looked one way when she was at home and another way when she was away from home. Everything about her had two sides to it, one for home and one for anywhere that was not home: her walk that could be childlike and bobbing, or languid enough to make anyone think she was hearing music in her head, her mouth which was pale and smirking most of the time, but bright and pink on these evenings out, her laugh which was cynical and drawling at home—"Ha, ha, very funny"—but high-pitched and nervous anywhere else, like the jingling of the charms on her bracelet.

Sometimes they did go shopping or to a movie, but sometimes they went across the highway, ducking fast across the busy road, to a drive-in restaurant where older kids hung out. The restaurant was shaped like a big bottle, though squatter than a real bottle, and on its cap was a revolving figure of a grinning boy who held a hamburger aloft. One night in mid-summer they ran across, breathless with daring, and right away someone leaned out a car window and invited them over, but it was just a boy from high school they didn't like. It made them feel good to be able to ignore him. They went up through the maze of parked and cruising cars to the bright-lit, fly-infested restaurant, their faces pleased and expectant as if they were entering a sacred building that loomed out of the night to give them what haven and what blessing they yearned for. They sat at the counter and crossed their legs at the ankles, their thin shoulders rigid with excitement, and listened to the music that made everything so good: the music was always in the background like music at a church service, it was something to depend upon.

A boy named Eddie came in to talk with them. He sat backwards on his stool, turning himself jerkily around in semi-circles and then stopping and turning again, and after a while he asked Connie if she would like something to eat. She said she did and so she tapped her friend's arm on her way out— her friend pulled her face up into a brave droll look—and Connie said she would meet her at eleven, across the way. "I just hate to leave her like that," Connie said earnestly, but the boy said that she wouldn't be alone for long. So they went out to his car and on the way Connie couldn't help but let her eyes wander over the windshields and faces all around her, her face gleaming with a joy that had nothing to do with Eddie or even this place; it might have been the music. She drew her shoulders up and sucked in her breath with the pure pleasure of being alive, and just at that moment she happened to glance at a face just a few feet from hers. It was a boy with shaggy black hair, in a convertible jalopy painted gold. He stared at her and then his lips widened into a grin. Connie slit her eyes at him and turned away, but she couldn't help glancing back and there he was still watching her. He wagged a finger and laughed and said, "Gonna get you, baby," and Connie turned away again without Eddie noticing anything.

She spent three hours with him, at the restaurant where they ate hamburgers and drank Colas in wax cups that were always sweating, and then down an alley a mile or so away, and when he left her off at five to eleven only the movie house was still open at the plaza. Her girl friend was there, talking with a boy. When Connie came up the two girls smiled at each other and Connie said, "How was the movie?" and the girl said, "*You* should know." They rode off with the girl's father, sleepy and pleased, and Connie couldn't help but look at the darkened shopping plaza with its big empty parking lot and its signs that were faded and ghostly now, and over at the drive-in restaurant where cars were still circling tirelessly. She couldn't hear the music at this distance.

Next morning June asked her how the movie was and Connie said, "So-so."

She and that girl and occasionally another girl went out several times a week that way, and the rest of the time Connie spent around the house—it was summer vacation—getting in her mother's way and thinking, dreaming, about the boys she met. But all the boys fell back and dissolved into a single face that was not even a face, but an idea, a feeling, mixed up with the urgent insistent pounding of the music and the humid night air of July. Connie's mother kept dragging her back to the daylight by finding things for her to do or saying, suddenly, "What's this about the Pettinger girl?"

And Connie would say nervously, "Oh, her. That dope." She always drew thick clear lines between herself and such girls, and her mother was simple and kindly enough to believe her. Her mother was so simple, Connie thought, that it was maybe cruel to fool her so much. Her mother went scuffling around the house in old bedroom slippers and complained over the telephone to one

10

sister about the other, then the other called up and the two of them complained about the third one. If June's name was mentioned her mother's tone was approving, and if Connie's name was mentioned it was disapproving. This did not really mean she disliked Connie and actually Connie thought that her mother preferred her to June because she was prettier, but the two of them kept up a pretense of exasperation, a sense that they were tugging and struggling over something of little value to either of them. Sometimes, over coffee, they were almost friends, but something would come up—some vexation that was like a fly buzzing suddenly around their heads—and their faces went hard with contempt.

One Sunday Connie got up at eleven—none of them bothered with church—and washed her hair so that it could dry all day long, in the sun. Her parents and sister were going to a barbecue at an aunt's house and Connie said no, she wasn't interested, rolling her eyes to let her mother know just what she thought of it. "Stay home alone then," her mother said sharply. Connie sat out back in a lawn chair and watched them drive away, her father quiet and bald, hunched around so that he could back the car out, her mother with a look that was still angry and not at all softened through the windshield, and in the back seat poor old June all dressed up as if she didn't know what a barbecue was, with all the running yelling kids and the flies. Connie sat with her eyes closed in the sun, dreaming and dazed with the warmth about her as if this were a kind of love, the caresses of love, and her mind slipped over onto thoughts of the boy she had been with the night before and how nice he had been, how sweet it always was, not the way someone like June would suppose but sweet, gentle, the way it was in movies and promised in songs; and when she opened her eyes she hardly knew where she was, the back yard ran off into weeds and a fence-line of trees and behind it the sky was perfectly blue and still. The asbestos "ranch house" that was now three years old startled her—it looked small. She shook her head as if to get awake.

It was too hot. She went inside the house and turned on the radio to drown out the quiet. She sat on the edge of her bed, barefoot, and listened for an hour and a half to a program called XYZ Sunday Jamboree, record after record of hard, fast, shrieking songs she sang along with, interspersed by exclamations from "Bobby King": "An' look here you girls at Napoleon's—Son and Charley want you to pay real close attention to this song coming up!"

And Connie paid close attention herself, bathed in a glow of slow-pulsed joy that seemed to rise mysteriously out of the music itself and lay languidly about the airless little room, breathed in and breathed out with each gentle rise and fall of her chest.

After a while she heard a car coming up the drive. She sat up at once, startled, because it couldn't be her father so soon. The gravel kept crunching all the way in from the road—the driveway was long—and Connie ran to the window. It was a car she didn't know. It was an open jalopy, painted a bright gold that caught the sunlight opaquely. Her heart began to pound and her fingers snatched at her hair, checking it, and she whispered "Christ. Christ," wondering how bad she looked. The car came to a stop at the side door and the horn sounded four short taps as if this were a signal Connie knew.

15

She went into the kitchen and approached the door slowly, then hung out the screen door, her bare toes curling down off the step. There were two boys in the car and now she recognized the driver: he had shaggy, shabby black hair that looked crazy as a wig and he was grinning at her.

"I ain't late, am I?" he said.

"Who the hell do you think you are?" Connie said.

"Toldja I'd be out, didn't I?"

"I don't even know who you are." 20

She spoke sullenly, careful to show no interest or pleasure, and he spoke in a fast bright monotone. Connie looked past him to the other boy, taking her time. He had fair brown hair, with a lock that fell onto his forehead. His sideburns gave him a fierce, embarrassed look, but so far he hadn't even bothered to glance at her. Both boys wore sunglasses. The driver's glasses were metallic and mirrored everything in miniature.

"You wanta come for a ride?" he said.

Connie smirked and let her hair fall loose over one shoulder.

"Don'tcha like my car? New paint job," he said. "Hey."

"What?" 25

"You're cute."

She pretended to fidget, chasing flies away from the door.

"Don'tcha believe me, or what?" he said.

"Look, I don't even know who you are," Connie said in disgust.

"Hey, Ellie's got a radio, see. Mine's broke down." He lifted his friend's arm 30 and showed her the little transistor the boy was holding, and now Connie began to hear the music. It was the same program that was playing inside the house.

"Bobby King?" she said.

"I listen to him all the time. I think he's great."

"He's kind of great," Connie said reluctantly.

"Listen, that guy's *great*. He knows where the action is."

Connie blushed a little, because the glasses made it impossible for her to 35 see just what this boy was looking at. She couldn't decide if she liked him or if he was just a jerk, and so she dawdled in the doorway and wouldn't come down or go back inside. She said, "What's all that stuff painted on your car?"

"Can'tcha read it?" He opened the door very carefully, as if he was afraid it might fall off. He slid out just as carefully, planting his feet firmly on the ground, the tiny metallic world in his glasses slowing down like gelatin hardening and in the midst of it Connie's bright green blouse. "This here is my name, to begin with," he said. ARNOLD FRIEND was written in tarlike black letters on the side, with a drawing of a round grinning face that reminded Connie of a pumpkin, except it wore sunglasses. "I wanta introduce myself, I'm Arnold Friend and that's my real name and I'm gonna be your friend, honey, and inside the car's Ellie Oscar, he's kinda shy." Ellie brought his transistor radio up to his shoulder and balanced it there. "Now these numbers are a secret code, honey," Arnold Friend explained. He read off the numbers 33, 19, 17 and raised his eyebrows at her to see what she thought of that, but she didn't think much of it. The left rear fender had been smashed and around it was written, on the gleaming gold background: DONE BY CRAZY WOMAN DRIVER. Connie had to laugh at that. Arnold Friend was pleased at her laughter and looked up at her. "Around the other side's a lot more—you wanta come and see them?"

"No."

"Why not?"

"Why should I?"

"Don'tcha wanta see what's on the car? Don'tcha wanta go for a ride?"   40

"I don't know."

"Why not?"

"I got things to do."

"Like what?"

"Things."   45

He laughed as if she had said something funny. He slapped his thighs. He was standing in a strange way, leaning back against the car as if he were balancing himself. He wasn't tall, only an inch or so taller than she would be if she came down to him. Connie liked the way he was dressed, which was the way all of them dressed: tight faded jeans stuffed into black, scuffed boots, a belt that pulled his waist in and showed how lean he was, and a white pullover shirt that was a little soiled and showed the hard small muscles of his arms and shoulders. He looked as if he probably did hard work, lifting and carrying things. Even his neck looked muscular. And his face was a familiar face, somehow: the jaw and chin and cheeks slightly darkened, because he hadn't shaved for a day or two, and the nose long and hawk-like, sniffing as if she were a treat he was going to gobble up and it was all a joke.

"Connie, you ain't telling the truth. This is your day set aside for a ride with me and you know it," he said, still laughing. The way he straightened and recovered from his fit of laughing showed that it had been all fake.

"How do you know what my name is?" she said suspiciously.

"It's Connie."

"Maybe and maybe not."   50

"I know my Connie," he said, wagging his finger. Now she remembered him even better, back at the restaurant, and her cheeks warmed at the thought of how she sucked in her breath just at the moment she passed him—how she must have looked to him. And he had remembered her. "Ellie and I come out here especially for you," he said. "Ellie can sit in back. How about it?"

"Where?"

"Where what?"

"Where're we going?"

He looked at her. He took off the sunglasses and she saw how pale the   55 skin around his eyes was, like holes that were not in shadow but instead in light. His eyes were chips of broken glass that catch the light in an amiable way. He smiled. It was as if the idea of going for a ride somewhere, to some place, was a new idea to him.

"Just for a ride, Connie sweetheart."

"I never said my name was Connie," she said.

"But I know what it is. I know your name and all about you, lots of things," Arnold Friend said. He had not moved yet but stood still leaning back against the side of his jalopy. "I took a special interest in you, such a pretty girl, and found out all about you like I know your parents and sister are gone somewheres and I know where and how long they're going to be gone, and I know who you were with last night, and your best girl friend's name is Betty. Right?"

He spoke in a simple lilting voice, exactly as if he were reciting the words to a song. His smile assured her that everything was fine. In the car Ellie turned up the volume on his radio and did not bother to look around at them.

"Ellie can sit in the back seat," Arnold Friend said. He indicated his friend with a casual jerk of his chin, as if Ellie did not count and she should not bother with him.   60

"How'd you find out all that stuff?" Connie said.

"Listen: Betty Schultz and Tony Fitch and Jimmy Pettinger and Nancy Pettinger," he said, in a chant. "Raymond Stanley and Bob Hutter—"

"Do you know all those kids?"

"I know everybody."

"Look, you're kidding. You're not from around here."   65

"Sure."

"But—how come we never saw you before?"

"Sure you saw me before," he said. He looked down at his boots, as if he were a little offended. "You just don't remember."

"I guess I'd remember you," Connie said.

"Yeah?" He looked up at this, beaming. He was pleased. He began to mark time with the music from Ellie's radio, tapping his fists lightly together.   70
Connie looked away from his smile to the car, which was painted so bright it almost hurt her eyes to look at it. She looked at that name, ARNOLD FRIEND. And up at the front fender was an expression that was familiar—MAN THE FLYING SAUCERS. It was an expression kids had used the year before, but didn't use this year. She looked at it for a while as if the words meant something to her that she did not yet know.

"What're you thinking about? Huh?" Arnold Friend demanded. "Not worried about your hair blowing around in the car, are you?"

"No."

"Think I maybe can't drive good?"

"How do I know?"

"You're a hard girl to handle. How come?" he said. "Don't you know I'm   75
your friend? Didn't you see me put my sign in the air when you walked by?"

"What sign?"

"My sign." And he drew an X in the air, leaning out toward her. They were maybe ten feet apart. After his hand fell back to his side the X was still in the air, almost visible. Connie let the screen door close and stood perfectly still inside it, listening to the music from her radio and the boy's blend together. She stared at Arnold Friend. He stood there so stiffly relaxed, pretending to be relaxed, with one hand idly on the door handle as if he were keeping himself up that way and had no intention of ever moving again. She recognized most things about him, the tight jeans that showed his thighs and buttocks and the greasy leather boots and the tight shirt, and even that slippery friendly smile of his, that sleepy dreamy smile that all the boys used to get across ideas they didn't want to put into words. She recognized all this and also the singsong way he talked, slightly mocking, kidding, but serious and a little melancholy, and she recognized the way he tapped one fist against the other in homage to the perpetual music behind him. But all these things did not come together.

She said suddenly, "Hey, how old are you?"

His smile faded. She could see then that he wasn't a kid, he was much older—thirty, maybe more. At this knowledge her heart began to pound faster.

"That's a crazy thing to ask. Can'tcha see I'm your own age?"

"Like hell you are."   80

"Or maybe a coupla years older, I'm eighteen."

"Eighteen?" she said doubtfully.

He grinned to reassure her and lines appeared at the corners of his mouth. His teeth were big and white. He grinned so broadly his eyes became slits and she saw how thick the lashes were, thick and black as if painted with a black tar-like material. Then he seemed to become embarrassed, abruptly, and looked over his shoulder at Ellie. "*Him,* he's crazy," he said. "Ain't he a riot, he's a nut, a real character." Ellie was still listening to the music. His sunglasses told nothing about what he was thinking. He wore a bright orange shirt unbuttoned halfway to show his chest, which was a pale, bluish chest and not muscular like Arnold Friend's. His shirt collar was turned up all around and the very tips of the collar pointed out past his chin as if they were protecting him. He was pressing the transistor radio up against his ear and sat there in a kind of daze, right in the sun.

"He's kinda strange," Connie said.   85

"Hey, she says you're kinda strange! Kinda strange!" Arnold Friend cried. He pounded on the car to get Ellie's attention. Ellie turned for the first time and Connie saw with shock that he wasn't a kid either—he had a fair, hairless face, cheeks reddened slightly as if the veins grew too close to the surface of his skin, the face of a forty-year-old baby. Connie felt a wave of dizziness rise in her at this sight and she stared at him as if waiting for something to change the shock of the moment, make it all right again. Ellie's lips kept shaping words, mumbling along, with the words blasting in his ear.

"Maybe you two better go away," Connie said faintly.

"What? How come?" Arnold Friend cried. "We come out here to take you for a ride. It's Sunday." He had the voice of the man on the radio now. It was the same voice, Connie thought. "Don'tcha know it's Sunday all day and honey, no matter who you were with last night today you're with Arnold Friend and don't you forget it!—Maybe you better step out here," he said, and this last was in a different voice. It was a little flatter, as if the heat was finally getting to him.

"No, I got things to do."

"Hey."   90

"You two better leave."

"We ain't leaving until you come with us."

"Like hell I am—"

"Connie, don't fool around with me. I mean, I mean, don't fool *around,*" he said, shaking his head. He laughed incredulously. He placed his sunglasses on top of his head, carefully, as if he were indeed wearing a wig, and brought the stems down behind his ears. Connie stared at him, another wave of dizziness and fear rising in her so that for a moment he wasn't even in focus but was just a blur, standing there against his gold car, and she had the idea that he had driven up the driveway all right but had come from nowhere before that and belonged nowhere and that everything about him and even about the music that was so familiar to her was only half real.

"If my father comes and sees you—"   95

"He ain't coming. He's at the barbecue."

"How do you know that?"

"Aunt Tillie's. Right now they're—uh—they're drinking. Sitting around," he said vaguely, squinting as if he were staring all the way to town and over to Aunt Tillie's backyard. Then the vision seemed to get clear and he nodded energetically. "Yeah. Sitting around. There's your sister in a blue dress, huh? And high heels, the poor sad bitch—nothing like you, sweetheart! And your mother's helping some fat woman with the corn, they're cleaning the corn—husking the corn—"

"What fat woman?" Connie cried.

"How do I know what fat woman. I don't know every goddam fat woman   100 in the world!" Arnold Friend laughed.

"Oh, that's Mrs. Hornby. . . . Who invited her?" Connie said. She felt a little light-headed. Her breath was coming quickly.

"She's too fat. I don't like them fat. I like them the way you are, honey," he said, smiling sleepily at her. They stared at each other for a while, through the screen door. He said softly, "Now what you're going to do is this: you're going to come out that door. You're going to sit up front with me and Ellie's going to sit in the back, the hell with Ellie, right? This isn't Ellie's date. You're my date. I'm your lover, honey."

"What? You're crazy—"

"Yes, I'm your lover. You don't know what that is but you will," he said. "I know that too. I know all about you. But look: it's real nice and you couldn't ask for nobody better than me, or more polite. I always keep my word. I'll tell you how it is, I'm always nice at first, the first time. I'll hold you so tight you won't think you have to try to get away or pretend anything because you'll know you can't. And I'll come inside you where it's all secret and you'll give in to me and you'll love me—"

"Shut up! You're crazy!" Connie said. She backed away from the door. She   105 put her hands against her ears as if she'd heard something terrible, something not meant for her. "People don't talk like that, you're crazy," she muttered. Her heart was almost too big now for her chest and its pumping made sweat break out all over her. She looked out to see Arnold Friend pause and then take a step toward the porch lurching. He almost fell. But, like a clever drunken man, he managed to catch his balance. He wobbled in his high boots and grabbed hold of one of the porch posts.

"Honey?" he said. "You still listening?"

"Get the hell out of here!"

"Be nice, honey. Listen."

"I'm going to call the police—"

He wobbled again and out of the side of his mouth came a fast spat curse,   110 an aside not meant for her to hear. But even his "Christ!" sounded forced. Then he began to smile again. She watched this smile come, awkward as if he were smiling from inside a mask. His whole face was a mask, she thought wildly, tanned down onto his throat but then running out as if he had plastered make-up on his face but had forgotten about his throat.

"Honey—? Listen, here's how it is. I always tell the truth and I promise you this: I ain't coming in that house after you."

"You better not! I'm going to call the police if you—if you don't—"

"Honey," he said, talking right through her voice, "honey, I'm not coming in there but you are coming out here. You know why?"

She was panting. The kitchen looked like a place she had never seen before, some room she had run inside but which wasn't good enough, wasn't going to help her. The kitchen window had never had a curtain, after three years, and there were dishes in the sink for her to do—probably—and if you ran your hand across the table you'd probably feel something sticky there.

"You listening, honey? Hey?"

"—going to call the police—"

"Soon as you touch the phone I don't need to keep my promise and can come inside. You won't want that."

She rushed forward and tried to lock the door. Her fingers were shaking. "But why lock it," Arnold Friend said gently, talking right into her face. "It's just a screen door. It's just nothing." One of his boots was at a strange angle, as if his foot wasn't in it. It pointed out to the left, bent at the ankle. "I mean, anybody can break through a screen door and glass and wood and iron or anything else if he needs to, anybody at all and specially Arnold Friend. If the place got lit up with a fire honey you'd come running out into my arms, right into my arms and safe at home—like you knew I was your lover and'd stopped fooling around. I don't mind a nice shy girl but I don't like no fooling around." Part of those words were spoken with a slight rhythmic lilt, and Connie somehow recognized them—the echo of a song from last year, about a girl rushing into her boy friend's arms and coming home again—

Connie stood barefoot on the linoleum floor, staring at him. "What do you want?" she whispered.

"I want you," he said.

"What?"

"Seen you that night and thought, that's the one, yes sir. I never needed to look any more."

"But my father's coming back. He's coming to get me. I had to wash my hair first—" She spoke in a dry, rapid voice, hardly raising it for him to hear.

"No, your daddy is not coming and yes, you had to wash your hair and you washed it for me. It's nice and shining and all for me, I thank you, sweetheart," he said with a mock bow, but again he almost lost his balance. He had to bend and adjust his boots. Evidently his feet did not go all the way down; the boots must have been stuffed with something so that he would seem taller. Connie stared out at him and behind him Ellie in the car, who seemed to be looking off toward Connie's right, into nothing. This Ellie said, pulling the words out of the air one after another as if he were just discovering them, "You want me to pull out the phone?"

"Shut your mouth and keep it shut," Arnold Friend said, his face red from bending over or maybe from embarrassment because Connie had seen his boots. "This ain't none of your business."

115

120

125

"What—what are you doing? What do you want?" Connie said. "If I call the police they'll get you, they'll arrest you—"

"Promise was not to come in unless you touch that phone, and I'll keep that promise," he said. He resumed his erect position and tried to force his shoulders back. He sounded like a hero in a movie, declaring something important. He spoke too loudly and it was as if he were speaking to someone behind Connie. "I ain't made plans for coming in that house where I don't belong but just for you to come out to me, the way you should. Don't you know who I am?"

"You're crazy," she whispered. She backed away from the door but did not want to go into another part of the house, as if this would give him permission to come through the door. "What do you ... You're crazy, you ..."

"Huh? What're you saying, honey?"

Her eyes darted everywhere in the kitchen. She could not remember what it was, this room.   130

"This is how it is, honey: you come out and we'll drive away, have a nice ride. But if you don't come out we're gonna wait till your people come home and then they're all going to get it."

"You want that telephone pulled out?" Ellie said. He held the radio away from his ear and grimaced, as if without the radio the air was too much for him.

"I toldja shut up, Ellie," Arnold Friend said, "you're deaf, get a hearing aid, right? Fix yourself up. This little girl's no trouble and's gonna be nice to me, so Ellie keep to yourself, this ain't your date—right? Don't hem in on me. Don't hog. Don't crush. Don't bird dog. Don't trail me," he said in a rapid meaningless voice, as if he were running through all the expressions he'd learned but was no longer sure which one of them was in style, then rushing on to new ones, making them up with his eyes closed, "Don't crawl under my fence, don't squeeze in my chipmunk hole, don't sniff my glue, suck my popsicle, keep your own greasy fingers on yourself!" He shaded his eyes and peered in at Connie, who was backed against the kitchen table. "Don't mind him honey he's just a creep. He's a dope. Right? I'm the boy for you and like I said you come out here nice like a lady and give me your hand, and nobody else gets hurt, I mean, your nice old bald-headed daddy and your mummy and your sister in her high heels. Because listen: why bring them in this?"

"Leave me alone," Connie whispered.

"Hey, you know that old woman down the road, the one with the chick-   135
ens and stuff—you know her?"

"She's dead!"

"Dead? What? You know her?" Arnold Friend said.

"She's dead—"

"Don't you like her?"   140

"She's dead—she's— she isn't here any more—"

"But don't you like her, I mean, you got something against her? Some grudge or something?" Then his voice dipped as if he were conscious of a rudeness. He touched the sunglasses perched on top of his head as if to make sure they were still there. "Now you be a good girl."

"What are you going to do?"

"Just two things, or maybe three," Arnold Friend said. "But I promise it won't last long and you'll like me that way you get to like people you're close to. You will. It's all over for you here, so come on out. You don't want your people in any trouble, do you?"

She turned and bumped against a chair or something, hurting her leg, but she ran into the back room and picked up the telephone. Something roared in her ear, a tiny roaring, and she was so sick with fear that she could do nothing but listen to it—the telephone was clammy and very heavy and her fingers groped down to the dial but were too weak to touch it. She began to scream into the phone, into the roaring. She cried out, she cried for her mother, she felt her breath start jerking back and forth in her lungs as if it were something Arnold Friend were stabbing her with again and again with no tenderness. A noisy sorrowful wailing rose all about her and she was locked inside it the way she was locked inside the house.

After a while she could hear again. She was sitting on the floor with her wet back against the wall.   145

Arnold Friend was saying from the door, "That's a good girl. Put the phone back."

She kicked the phone away from her.

"No, honey. Pick it up. Put it back right."

She picked it up and put it back. The dial tone stopped.

"That's a good girl. Now come outside."   150

She was hollow with what had been fear, but what was now just an emptiness. All that screaming had blasted it out of her. She sat, one leg cramped under her, and deep inside her brain was something like a pinpoint of light that kept going and would not let her relax. She thought, I'm not going to see my mother again. She thought, I'm not going to sleep in my bed again. Her bright green blouse was all wet.

Arnold Friend said, in a gentle-loud voice that was like a stage voice, "The place where you came from ain't there any more, and where you had in mind to go is cancelled out. This place you are now—inside your daddy's house—is nothing but a cardboard box I can knock down any time. You know that and always did know it. You hear me?"

She thought, I have got to think. I have to know what to do.

"We'll go out to a nice field, out in the country here where it smells so nice and it's sunny," Arnold Friend said. "I'll have my arms around you so you won't need to try to get away and I'll show you what love is like, what it does. The hell with this house! It looks solid all right," he said. He ran a fingernail down the screen and the noise did not make Connie shiver, as it would have the day before. "Now put your hand on your heart, honey. Feel that? That feels solid too but we know better, be nice to me, be sweet like you can because what else is there for a girl like you but to be sweet and pretty and give in?—and get away before her people come back?"

She felt her pounding heart. Her hand seemed to enclose it. She thought   155
for the first time in her life that it was nothing that was hers, that belonged to her, but just a pounding, living thing inside this body that wasn't really hers either.

"You don't want them to get hurt," Arnold Friend went on. "Now get up, honey. Get up all by yourself."

She stood up.

"Now turn this way. That's right. Come over here to me—Ellie, put that away, didn't I tell you? You dope. You miserable creepy dope," Arnold Friend said. His words were not angry but only part of an incantation. The incantation was kindly. "Now come out through the kitchen to me honey and let's see a smile, try it, you're a brave sweet little girl and now they're eating corn and hotdogs cooked to bursting over an outdoor fire, and they don't know one thing about you and never did and honey you're better than them because not a one of them would have done this for you."

Connie felt the linoleum under her feet; it was cool. She brushed her hair back out of her eyes. Arnold Friend let go of the post tentatively and opened his arms for her, his elbows pointing in toward each other and his wrists limp, to show that this was an embarrassed embrace and a little mocking, he didn't want to make her self-conscious.

She put out her hand against the screen. She watched herself push the door slowly open as if she were safe back somewhere in the other doorway, watching this body and this head of long hair moving out into the sunlight where Arnold Friend waited. 160

"My sweet little blue-eyed girl," he said, in a half-sung sigh that had nothing to do with her brown eyes but was taken up just the same by the vast sunlit reaches of the land behind him and on all sides of him, so much land that Connie had never seen before and did not recognize except to know that she was going to it.

Response Statement Questions for "Where Are You Going, Where Have You Been?"

- How does your age or gender influence your response to this story? How does your situation within your own family (e.g., in relation to your parents or children) influence your response?

- Does this text suggest that by trying to be "pretty" or "attractive," women invite sexual aggressiveness or rape? If you think so, does such a suggestion confirm or challenge ideas in your ideology?

- Does the ideology of this text seem to have specific beliefs about the effect of popular music in the lives of young Americans? If so, do those beliefs confirm or challenge your own?

- This story is dedicated to Bob Dylan. Depending on your literary experience, do you find intertextuality between the story and any of Dylan's songs (for instance, "Like a Rolling Stone," "It's All Over Now, Baby Blue," or "Mr. Tambourine Man")? If so, how does this intertextuality influence your interpretation of the story?

- *Share and Compare* What differences in age, gender, or ideology among readers in your class or discussion group account for different responses to the character of Connie and to what happens to her with Arnold Friend?

READING AND WRITING PROJECTS
FOR CREATIVE AND CRITICAL THINKING

Your own writing is important as you try to learn more about yourself as a reader—both what you do cognitively and what is done to you culturally—to produce the kind of reader you are when you interact with any particular text. In addition to response statements and the formal expository paper that may grow out of them, there are other ways to use writing to learn. What follows are suggestions for integrating your reading of and writing about literary texts in various ways. These suggestions include exploratory writing, playing with texts and language, creative efforts in various genres, and other writing exercises designed to strengthen your awareness of the cognitive and cultural processes involved in your reading.

If you produce any "creative" pieces of your own—stories, poems, dramatic scenes, nonverbal displays, and so on—think of them as instances of intertextuality: Directly or indirectly, they refer to and are part of the textual network that includes other texts already written. If you work on any of the more "expository" or "discursive" projects, think of what you're doing as joining a conversation with other texts and other voices.

▶ If you experience a clashing ideological interaction with any short story you read, focus as narrowly as you can on the site—word, phrase, or sentence—within that text or its ideology where this "resistance" happens. Explore the disharmony in writing: What causes it to happen, in terms of the ideologies of both you and the text?

▶ Select a character from any story and write a letter to or from him or her discussing any problem that character may have. If you write to the character, perhaps you could offer some advice from your perspective. If you want to write a letter as the character, try having him or her address you, trying to explain things as he or she sees them. Other variations of this project are possible; for instance, you could have one character write a letter to another, or you could write to an author, or have the author write to you. You could also work with a classmate: One of you writes a letter from one person to another; the other replies in the role of the person addressed by the first letter.

▶ Select a significant passage from any story. Write away from this passage in a personal narrative describing any similar experience or memory or association you may have. (For example, maybe you consider Eveline's decision not to get on the boat with Frank significant for you because of a similar decision of yours not to take a big step that might have changed your life.)

▶ Write about what you consider to be the most important word, phrase, image, or sentence in any story. Why do you consider this element so important? That question may be answered in terms of *both* the text and your ideology.

▶ Select any story and cast it as a movie, choosing the actors who would take each part. The actors could be actual contemporary film actors or your friends and acquaintances. Write an explanation of why you cast the parts as you did: What characteristics of the parts could be brought out in what ways by your choices of actors?

8 ◈ SPECIAL FOCUS IN FICTION: A CASE STUDY IN GENDER

The stories "Eveline" and "Teenage Wasteland" that you read in the preceding chapter seem to intersect with readers' ideologies on the issue of relations between teenagers and their parents. Your beliefs and experiences about that issue are part of your ideology. Another aspect of your ideology is your gender, which is not so much a biological matter as it is a whole host of cultural conventions and expectations. Even though Western cultures have seen considerable "gender-bending" in the last 20 or 30 years, most people are still influenced by cultural ideology about gender roles, relations between the sexes, and relations between marital partners. This chapter will look at the ideological interaction of readers and texts on the specific issue of gender relations.

The two stories reprinted and discussed in this chapter afford opportunities for you to examine how your position with respect to *the culture of gender* influences your response to issues related to conventional or stereotypical gender-specific and marriage-role-specific behaviors and attitudes. As a prereading activity to focus your self-awareness with respect to some of these issues, you might briefly list, in the box below, behaviors that seem particularly appropriate—conventionally and stereotypically—to men and women and to husbands and wives. You might also start to reflect on which of these behaviors are "natural" and which are "learned."

| PREREADING INVENTORY | Behavior | |
	Conventional	Stereotypical
Men		
Women		
Husbands		
Wives		

247

The Culture of Gender: Women and Men

Certain behaviors for women and men are physiological, having to do with the physical differences in their respective bodies. The most obvious difference is that women bear children and men do not, but men and women tend to walk differently, too, because of structural differences in their pelvises related to their different capacities for childbearing. Also, because men are generally physically larger and have more muscle mass than women, men may perform certain kinds of physical work that women do not do.

Certain behaviors are conventional, having to do with socially constructed patterns that have come to be regarded as appropriate for one gender or the other. Differences in clothing, hair styles, and facial makeup are among these conventions. In spite of changing conceptions of appropriate gender-specific social behavior, many Western men still practice social "courtesies" such as holding doors open for women, allowing women to enter and exit elevators first, and helping women with their chairs in restaurants—and many women permit or even expect men to do these things. In some non-Western cultures, conventional behaviors include some Islamic women veiling their faces in public. All such conventional gender-specific behaviors, whether specifically religious or not, are produced by ideologies that involve specific conceptions of appropriate conduct for men and women.

Certain behaviors are stereotypical. These relate to cultural conventions but perhaps oversimplify them. In Western cultures, women are supposed to be emotional, like domestic activities such as cooking and sewing, and be relatively inept at mechanical tasks; men are supposed to be emotionless, like outdoor activities such as hunting and fishing, and be relatively competent at mechanical tasks. It may be easy to find exceptions to such stereotypical gender-specific behaviors, but the stereotypes do still exist, and they too reveal cultural ideologies that lie behind them and produce them.

In addition to your gender, therefore, your ideology includes your beliefs, opinions, and values about and experience with conventional and stereotypical behavior for women and men, girls and boys. Even more particularly, part of your ideology is your beliefs, opinions, and values about and experience with conventions and stereotypes of married men and women, husbands and wives. This ideology involves, possibly, your belief that husbands, conventionally or stereotypically, do home repairs, work on cars, work long hours at their jobs, have little time for their children, are major breadwinners, and take care of family finances. Or your ideology may involve your belief that wives, conventionally or stereotypically, stay at home, cook, clean, watch the children, do the shopping, and plan the family social calendar.

SHARE AND COMPARE: What differences of opinion with respect to the conventional and stereotypical behaviors of men and women and husbands and wives does a discussion with your whole class or a small group reveal? What are the ideological bases of these differences, in terms of the lived experience of different students?

Now go ahead and read James Thurber's "The Secret Life of Walter Mitty" and Carolyn Chute's "Tall Woman Love" and answer the questions that follow each story.

James Thurber   1894–1961

The Secret Life of Walter Mitty   1942

"We're going through!" The Commander's voice was like thin ice break-ing. He wore his full-dress uniform, with the heavily braided white cap pulled down rakishly over one cold gray eye. "We can't make it, sir. It's spoiling for a hurricane, if you ask me." "I'm not asking you, Lieutenant Berg," said the Commander. "Throw on the power lights! Rev her up to 8,500! We're going through!" The pounding of the cylinders increased: ta-pocketa-pocketa-pock-eta-*pocketa-pocketa*. The Commander stared at the ice forming on the pilot window. He walked over and twisted a row of complicated dials. "Switch on No. 8 auxiliary!" he shouted. "Switch on No. 8 auxiliary!" repeated Lieutenant Berg. "Full strength in No. 3 turret!" shouted the Commander. "Full strength in No. 3 turret!" The crew, bending to their various tasks in the huge, hurtling eight-engined Navy hydroplane, looked at each other and grinned. "The Old Man'll get us through," they said to one another. "The Old Man ain't afraid of Hell!" . . .

"No so fast! You're driving too fast!" said Mrs. Mitty. "What are you driving so fast for?"

"Hmm?" said Walter Mitty. He looked at his wife, in the seat beside him, with shocked astonishment. She seemed grossly unfamiliar, like a strange woman who had yelled at him in a crowd. "You were up to fifty-five," she said. "You know I don't like to go more than forty. You were up to fifty-five." Walter Mitty drove on toward Waterbury in silence, the roaring of the SN202 through the worst storm in twenty years of Navy flying fading in the remote, intimate airways of his mind. "You're tensed up again," said Mrs. Mitty. "It's one of your days. I wish you'd let Dr. Renshaw look you over."

Walter Mitty stopped the car in front of the building where his wife went to have her hair done. "Remember to get those overshoes while I'm having my hair done," she said. "I don't need overshoes," said Mitty. She put her mirror back into her bag. "We've been all through that," she said, getting out of the car. "You're not a young man any longer." He raced the engine a little. "Why don't you wear your gloves? Have you lost your gloves?" Walter Mitty reached in a pocket and brought out the gloves. He put them on, but after she had turned and gone into the building and he had driven on to a red light, he took them off again. "Pick it up, brother!" snapped a cop as the light changed, and Mitty hastily pulled on his gloves and lurched ahead. He drove around the streets aimlessly for a time, and then he drove past the hospital on his way to the parking lot.

. . . "It's the millionaire banker, Wellington McMillan," said the pretty nurse. "Yes?" said Walter Mitty, removing his gloves slowly. "Who has the case?" "Dr. Renshaw and Dr. Benbow, but there are two specialists here, Dr. Remington from New York and Mr. Pritchard-Mitford from London. He flew over." A door

5

opened down a long, cool corridor and Dr. Renshaw came out. He looked distraught and haggard. "Hello, Mitty," he said. "We're having the devil's own time with McMillan, the millionaire banker and close personal friend of Roosevelt. Obstreosis of the ductal tract. Tertiary. Wish you'd take a look at him." "Glad to," said Mitty.

In the operating room there were whispered introductions: "Dr. Remington, Dr. Mitty. Mr. Pritchard-Mitford, Dr. Mitty." "I've read your book on streptothricosis," said Pritchard-Mitford, shaking hands. "A brilliant performance, sir." "Thank you," said Walter Mitty. "Didn't know you were in the States, Mitty," grumbled Remington. "Coals to Newcastle, bringing Mitford and me here for a tertiary." "You are very kind," said Mitty. A huge, complicated machine, connected to the operating table, with many tubes and wires, began at this moment to go pocketa-pocketa-pocketa. "The new anesthetizer is giving way!" shouted an interne. "There is no one in the East who knows how to fix it!" "Quiet, man!" said Mitty, in a low, cool, voice. He sprang to the machine, which was now going pocketa-pocketa-queep-pocketa-queep. He began fingering delicately a row of glistening dials. "Give me a fountain pen!" he snapped. Someone handed him a fountain pen. He pulled a faulty piston out of the machine and inserted the pen in its place. "That will hold for ten minutes," he said. "Get on with the operation." A nurse hurried over and whispered to Renshaw, and Mitty saw the man turn pale. "Coreopsis has set in," said Renshaw nervously. "If you would take over, Mitty?" Mitty looked at him and at the craven figure of Benbow, who drank, and at the grave, uncertain faces of the two great specialists. "If you wish," he said. They slipped a white gown on him; he adjusted a mask and drew on thin gloves; nurses handed him shining. . . .

"Back it up, Mac! Look out for that Buick!" Walter Mitty jammed on the brakes. "Wrong lane, Mac," said the parking-lot attendant, looking at Mitty closely. "Gee. Yeh," muttered Mitty. He began cautiously to back out of the lane marked "Exit Only." "Leave her sit there," said the attendant. "I'll put her away." Mitty got out of the car. "Hey, better leave the key." "Oh," said Mitty, handing the man the ignition key. The attendant vaulted into the car, backed it up with insolent skill, and put it where it belonged.

They're so damn cocky, thought Walter Mitty, walking along Main Street; they think they know everything. Once he had tried to take his chains off, outside New Milford, and he had got them wound around the axles. A man had had to come out in a wrecking car and unwind them, a young, grinning garageman. Since then Mrs. Mitty always made him drive to a garage to have the chains taken off. The next time, he thought, I'll wear my right arm in a sling; they won't grin at me then. I'll have my right arm in a sling and they'll see I couldn't possibly take the chains off myself. He kicked at the slush on the sidewalk. "Overshoes," he said to himself, and he began looking for a shoe store.

When he came out into the street again, with the overshoes in a box under his arm, Walter Mitty began to wonder what the other thing was his wife had told him to get. She had told him twice, before they set out from their house for Waterbury. In a way he hated these weekly trips to town—he was always getting something wrong. Kleenex, he thought, Squibb's, razor blades? No. Toothpaste, toothbrush, bicarbonate, carborundum, initiative and referendum? He gave it up. But she would remember it. "Where's the what's-its-name?" she would ask. "Don't tell me you forgot the what's-its-name?" A newsboy went by shouting something about the Waterbury trial.

. . . "Perhaps this will refresh your memory." The District Attorney sud- 10 denly thrust a heavy automatic at the quiet figure on the witness stand. "Have you ever seen this before?" Walter Mitty took the gun and examined it ex-pertly. "This is my Webley-Vickers 50.80," he said calmly. An excited buzz ran around the courtroom. The judge rapped for order. "You are a crack shot with any sort of firearms, I believe?" said the District Attorney, insinuatingly. "Ob-jection!" shouted Mitty's attorney. "We have shown that the defendant could not have fired the shot. We have shown that he wore his right arm in a sling on the night of the fourteenth of July." Walter Mitty raised his hand briefly and the bickering attorneys were stilled. "With any known make of gun," he said evenly, "I could have killed Gregory Fitzhurst at three hundred feet *with my left hand.*" Pandemonium broke loose in the courtroom. A woman's scream rose above the bedlam and suddenly a lovely, dark-haired girl was in Walter Mitty's arms. The District Attorney struck at her savagely. Without rising from his chair, Mitty let the man have it on the point of the chin. "You miserable cur!" . . .

"Puppy biscuit," said Walter Mitty. He stopped walking and the buildings of Waterbury rose up out of the misty courtroom and surrounded him again. A woman who was passing laughed. "He said 'Puppy biscuit,'" she said to her companion. "That man said 'Puppy biscuit' to himself." Walter Mitty hur-ried on. He went into an A & P, not the first one he came to but a smaller one farther up the street. "I want some biscuit for small, young dogs," he said to the clerk. "Any special brand, sir?" The greatest pistol shot in the world thought a moment. "It says 'Puppies Bark for It' on the box," said Walter Mitty.

His wife would be through at the hairdresser's in fifteen minutes, Mitty saw in looking at his watch, unless they had trouble drying it; sometimes they had trouble drying it. She didn't like to get to the hotel first; she would want him to be there waiting for her as usual. He found a big leather chair in the lobby, facing a window, and he put the overshoes and the puppy biscuit on the floor beside it. He picked up an old copy of *Liberty* and sank down into the chair. "Can Germany Conquer the World Through the Air?" Walter Mitty looked at the pictures of bombing planes and of ruined streets.

. . . "The cannonading has got the wind up in young Raleigh, sir," said the sergeant. Captain Mitty looked up at him through tousled hair. "Get him to bed," he said wearily. "With the others. I'll fly alone." "But you can't, sir," said the sergeant anxiously. "It takes two men to handle that bomber and the Archies are pounding hell out of the air. Von Richtman's circus is between here and Saulier." "Somebody's got to get that ammunition dump," said Mitty. "I'm going over. Spot of brandy?" He poured a drink for the sergeant and one for himself. War thundered and whined around the dugout and battered at the door. There was a rending of wood and splinters flew through the room. "A bit of a near thing," said Captain Mitty carelessly. "The box barrage is closing in," said the sergeant. "We only live once, Sergeant," said Mitty, with his faint, fleeting smile. "Or do we?" He poured another brandy and tossed it off. "I never see a man could hold his brandy like you, sir," said the sergeant. "Begging your pardon, sir." Captain Mitty stood up and strapped on his huge Webley-Vickers automatic. "It's forty kilometers through hell, sir," said the sergeant. Mitty finished one last brandy. "After all," he said softly, "what isn't?" The pounding of the cannon increased; there was the rat-tat-tatting of machine guns, and from somewhere came the menacing pocketa-pocketa-pocketa of the new flame-throwers. Walter Mitty walked to the door of the dugout humming "Auprès de Ma Blonde." He turned and waved to the sergeant. "Cheerio!" he said. . . .

Something struck his shoulder. "I've been looking all over this hotel for you," said Mrs. Mitty. "Why do you have to hide in this old chair? How did you expect me to find you?" "Things close in," said Walter Mitty vaguely. "What?" Mrs. Mitty said. "Did you get the what's-its-name? The puppy biscuit? What's in the box?" "Overshoes," said Mitty. "Couldn't you have put them on in the store?" "I was thinking," said Walter Mitty. "Does it ever occur to you that I am sometimes thinking?" She looked at him. "I'm going to take your temperature when I get you home," she said.

They went out through the revolving doors that made a faintly derisive   15 whistling sound when you pushed them. It was two blocks to the parking lot. At the drugstore on the corner she said, "Wait here for me. I forgot something. I won't be a minute." She was more than a minute. Walter Mitty lighted a cigarette. It began to rain, rain with sleet in it. He stood up against the wall of the drugstore, smoking. . . . He put his shoulders back and his heels together. "To hell with the handkerchief," said Walter Mitty scornfully. He took one last drag on his cigarette and snapped it away. Then, with that faint, fleeting smile playing about his lips, he faced the firing squad; erect and motionless, proud and disdainful, Walter Mitty the Undefeated, inscrutable to the last.

Response Statement Questions

- Did you find this story funny? Did it annoy you in any way?
- How do you respond to the character of Walter Mitty? To his wife?
- How do your own gender and your ideology about the behaviors of marriage partners affect your response to these characters?
- Do you believe that married men in general have or tend to have "secret lives" at all like Walter Mitty's? If not married men in general, what kind of married men do, if any? Do you believe that married women have such fantasies?
- Do you believe that married women in general tend to "nag," "browbeat," or "henpeck" their husbands? If not married women in general, what kind of married women do, if any? Do you believe that married men "browbeat" their wives?
- If you are or have been married, does your own experience as a married person influence your response to this story?
- Who emerges as the winner in the psychological contest between Walter and Mrs. Mitty in this story? On what grounds does that person win, or the other lose? What exactly is at stake in this contest? What is won or lost?

- What seems to be the ideology of the text with respect to the above four questions? What kind of interaction of ideologies occurred between you and the text in this regard?
- *Share and Compare*   What variety of opinion exists in your class with respect to the above questions? How are any differences related to readers' gender and ideological positions?

Refer again to the lists you made before you read "The Secret Life of Walter Mitty." Could you now add to or subtract from the behaviors you listed there? Keep these ideas in mind as you begin reading the next story.

Carolyn Chute   b. 1947

Tall Woman Love   *1985*

The door opens and the new neighbor, March Goodspeed, the celebrated highway engineer, hurries down the hot-top path to the hot-top driveway in his pointy dress-up shoes and asphalt-color suit.

Across the road, the tall woman, Roberta Bean, is dressed in a man's ribbed undershirt and green wool pants. She is circling a piece of bare ground with an axe, her babies in yellow raincoats. The babies ornament her ankles, dangle from her pant legs. Thwank! Thwank! Thwank! Her axe beats upon the chopping block.

March Goodspeed picks open the door of his forest-green Lincoln. He lays a folder of papers on the seat. He does not say good morning to Roberta Bean. He quickly dives into his car. The tall woman circles the chopping block, her babies moving as she moves.

Roberta Bean has the smallest head of all Beans, her head being about the size of a fifteen-cent turnip with a blue knit cap stretched over the top of it. The hat has a chrome-yellow cuff. Nowhere does her black black hair show.

March Goodspeed shuts the door of his Lincoln.

Roberta Bean's axe goes Thwank! Thwank! Thwank!   5

March was to be in Portland by ten . . . a site walk for a new shopping center. It is 10:03. He turns the key. The Lincoln breathes almost like a human being. March pats the folder of papers on the seat. He clicks on the news. He starts to back out of the yard.

The tall woman is so tall she divides March's rearview mirror into two clean halves, white grass to the left, white grass to the right. And everywhere, shuffling and darting, are babies and the tall woman's peach-color hens.

The Lincoln stalls partway into the road. March twists the key.

Out of the openings of the undershirt, Roberta Bean's assiduous, straining,   10
bony neck and scarry long long arms work the axe on the stringy wood. Faster. Faster. Now and then one of her dark eyes turns onto the Lincoln Continental.

The Lincoln whispers, "A-herm hm hm hm" . . . little burps, little giggles. "Start, damn you!" the highway engineer demands.

Some of the peach-color hens have come to his lawn, poke in his short grass. March rubs his eyes.

The tall woman moves all over the Lincoln's rearview mirror as a prize-fighter moves around the ring. The white wood is spewed into the pile . . . faster, faster. Her back is to March now. She seems to ignore him.

March checks his watch. 10:09. He twists the key. "Start!" he commands. The Lincoln only laughs.

The man slumps in his seat, his heart scrambling inside his dress shirt like a pillowcase full of puppies.

The babies seem unconvinced of the possibility of being stepped upon by one of the tall woman's mighty boots. Dazed by their love, they keep in step.

March squints at the mirror.

Roberta puts down her axe. She looks at March Goodspeed.

March can smell gas.

Roberta Bean crosses the road. With her flutters an army of boots and yellow raincoats, a hollow tromp tromp tromp tromp.

"Why is this happening?" March breathes. He picks a ballpoint pen from his breast pocket and snaps it fast. He takes a breath of his Lincoln's rich interior.

Roberta Bean's tiny head is smiling at him through the glass.

March has blond hair, the color of faded newspapers. You'd never know he had been a redhead as a child; you'd never have known he had been a child. His eyes show leadership, are fibrous as salad olives. Green.

Her eyes look tired.

Reluctantly he scratches at the button. The window glass disappears as naturally as a lake thaws.

March says, "It's just flooded. It'll be all right in a few moments."

Roberta Bean redistributes her stature, somewhat to the left, and simultaneously there's the rumble of ten oversized boots, each boot to the left.

Long feelerlike noses sniff up at March. He looks down just in time to see one baby pick up a small piece of broken glass and aim it at his Lincoln. "Make that child behave!" March shouts.

Roberta's dark, close-together eyes move onto the child.

The baby puts the glass in its raincoat pocket.

Another baby spits. The foamy wob slides down the door of the Lincoln.

"You need a jump," the tall woman says. Then her mouth opens for a smile, the teeth like the far-apart teeth of a Doberman, long, fat, yellow, sharp.

March says, "It's flooded. That's all."

Roberta says, "Eyup . . . gas stinks." She puts both hands on the window frame and rocks the Lincoln so that March and the Lincoln move in great waves on the luxurious springs. "Ain't she a dandy!" the tall woman says.

March's eyes rest on the front of her undershirt, its rapt, fat flowers of spilled coffee, and some year-old blood shaped like the paw of a cat.

She says, "You set there, mistah, an' I'll getcha some help."

"No. In a few moments the gas will dry out. You just go back to what you were doing." He is as commanding as a trainer to a huge but humble dog.

"Yes-suh," she sneers, withdrawing her hands. "If it was just flooded. But you cranked on your throttle till she don't hardly turn over ... does she? ... You've run your batt'ry down. I'll getcha some help." And she veers away in the horrible scuffing of many boots.

He hangs his head.

One of the peach-color hens steps up and hammers with her beak on her reflection in the Lincoln's hubcap. 40

On the same side of the road as Roberta Bean's wee blue house is Bean's Variety Store. With sweaty dread, March anticipates four or five of those woolly, squinting Egypt, Maine, men over on the piazza of the store—fluorescent vests, black nails, wagging beards—loping toward him, hailed by Roberta Bean. And they would study him frankly through the tinted windshield, the way visitors to hospitals gape through Plexiglas at newborns.

But no. She returns without them.

Her black truck is parked by the front steps of her wee blue house like you tie a dog out to pee. She and her babies get into this truck, and she backs it out onto the pavement with a clanging like a half-dozen cowbells. The yellow-raincoated shapes of her children bounce around beside her on the seat.

She lines up her hood with his hood.

March closes his eyes, opens them slowly. 45

He turns in his seat and there's the tall woman, hurrying, helpful, steam rising out of her like what rises on the backs of straining spotted oxen. He squares his shoulders, pats the knot of his asphalt-color necktie.

"Shit!" he cries as his folder of many papers slips to the floor, covering the pedals and his pointy, shiny shoes.

Roberta flings up both hoods and uncoils jumper cables from around her neck and shoulders, cables which she carries there with the exuberance of one who wields pet snakes. He opens his eyes to see her fingers strum the cables' silken skins. And how gracefully she capers between the vehicles, her eyes misting in a joy March cannot fathom.

A half-dozen hens are now pecking at the bright hubcaps. 50

Meanwhile, the babies storm out of the black fenderless truck, three of them fastening to one of the tall woman's calves, two the other.

March sweeps open the door of his Lincoln, authority written on his face, knotting him up hard.

She is clasping the cables onto the terminals as he drives his own arms through her long long bare ones. "I'll do that now," he says.

But she is done.

The babies glare up at him. One is looking at March's left pointy black shoe. 55

March's arms are still parallel with the tall woman's bare ones. He is drawing back in slow motion, in disbelief. His heart is just one of the babies' oversized boots . . . tromp tromp tromp tromp. Roberta Bean's smell is in his face, a smell he is convinced is the smell of the inside of her wee blue house. Because of this smell, he sees the long fingers worrying the rubber from a Mason jar of cloudy green beans, boiling them hard, doling out baggy white yeast rolls, everything of a hotness that is injurious to the lips and gums, while this brood with crew cuts and long noses, like a bizarre litter of moles, tries even at the table to get close to her, forever close, madly close.

He backs onto the short grass of his yard. His necktie flounces.

With curling lips, the babies stare at March Goodspeed's pointy black shoes. "YUKK!" one of them says.

A small hen sees her reflection in his heel, jabs at it.

March re-enters his Lincoln.   60

In a matter of moments he is shifting into reverse, giving the Lincoln the gas. It lurches over the road, backwards. Hens squawk. The babies look up at the tall woman, their eyes wrinkled up with love. The big car lunges up the grade and springs into the sun.

Response Statement Questions

- Did you find this story funny? Did it annoy you in any way?
- How did you respond to Roberta Bean? How does your gender influence your response to her? How does your ideology influence your response?
- How did you respond to March Goodspeed? How does your gender influence your response to him? How does your ideology influence your response?
- Who emerges as the winner in the psychological contest between Roberta and March? On what grounds does that person win, or the other lose? What exactly is at stake in this contest? What is won or lost?
- What seems to be the ideology of the text with respect to the above four questions? What kind of interaction of ideologies occurred between you and the text in this regard?
- *Share and Compare*   What variety of opinion exists in your class with respect to the above questions? How are any differences related to readers' gender and ideological positions?

Culture and Gender Stereotypes

You are probably aware of the stereotypes in Western culture of the henpecked husband and the henpecking wife, even if you didn't think to include those in the lists you made at the beginning of this chapter. Of course, the metaphor of a married woman as a hen carries with it certain cultural stereotypes. Rarely are married women considered henpecked and their husbands hens (although commonly enough married women are beaten or otherwise physically abused by their husbands, yet English seems to have no common metaphor, mildly humorous or otherwise, for this feature of some marital relationships). Beneath this stereotype seems to lie the understanding that married men, or some of them at any rate, must endure the nagging and fault-finding of their wives and that if married men are subjected to too much of this from their wives without reasserting power over them, those men put their masculinity at risk. Besides "henpecked," "browbeaten," "nag," and "shrew," there are other, more vulgar metaphors in English for these men-victims and women-victimizers that express in direct language this threat to masculinity. This stereotype of the henpecked husband also (perhaps paradoxically in view of what I have just said) privileges the male point of view in defining the marital relationship. If for a husband to be henpecked is not the way things should be in a marriage, the flaw is in the man's status or strength: He should "control" or "master" his wife's tendencies to "peck" him.

In "The Secret Life of Walter Mitty," this stereotypical marital relationship seems to be played for humor. Perhaps you found the story funny or amusing as you read it. Perhaps you saw it as a slight exaggeration or parody of the stereotypical henpecked husband. In terms of text strategies, the dominant ones here seem to be character and point of view, with the latter helping you to construct your sense of the former. But just in terms of character alone for a moment, how do you respond to Walter Mitty's name? That's certainly a text strategy within the text strategy of character. Does it seem to "fit" the kind of man he is? Does his name help you to harmonize with the portrayal of this man as weak in relation to his wife? Does it make it easier for you to accept that his only power and effectiveness would come in his "secret life"?

The story is narrated from Walter Mitty's point of view; as a reader, you are invited to travel with him through his day of errands while his wife is having "her hair done." And the text's strategy of switching in and out of Mitty's secret life allows you to measure his fantasies against his reality, especially when Mitty is so powerful, controlling, and effective in the one and so weak, docile, and ineffective in the other. This text strategy invites you to get some aesthetic distance from Mitty, even while you travel with him. That, in turn, makes it possible for irony to work against him because of the difference you can see between his real life and his secret one.

The third-person limited point of view also makes it easy to see Mrs. Mitty as henpecking, browbeating, and so forth. Because the point of view is exclusively Walter's, his wife is presented only in relation to him; you can't get to know her from her own perspective. Everything she says to Walter is critical and nagging. One of my students wrote in his journal that Mrs. Mitty "is the woman that I have nightmares about. She is the woman that I fear marrying." Although he stopped short of calling the story funny, this same student said the story was "very interesting and entertaining."

CONNECT: "The Secret Life of Walter Mitty," "The Cask of Amontillado," "Eveline," and "Teenage Wasteland" show some of the variety of possibilities for aesthetic distance from, identification with, and irony towards point-of-view characters, depending on how the text strategy of narration is handled.

If "The Secret Life of Walter Mitty" is humorous in its apparent intention or in its actual effect, it seems its ideology must include the stereotypes of the henpecked husband and the nagging wife and must regard the relationship between such people as potentially if not always humorous. If you look into that a little further, you might observe that the joke here is really on Mitty. If the text seems to regard him ironically, it also seems to ask you to laugh at him, at the almost ludicrous difference between what he imagines himself to be in his secret life and what he actually is in his real life. Much of humor, after all, derives from a difference between how things are and how they should be, according to people's perceptions. The laughter the text seems to invite against Mitty seems to be gentle laughter, a chuckle, from an implied perspective of superiority to a man as wimpy as Mitty.

If you look a little further still into the ideology behind the humor in "The Secret Life of Walter Mitty," however, you might find that Mitty's ridiculousness suggests he's not really a man, as the dominant ideology in Western culture defines men—not just physiologically, but behaviorally. After all, in Mitty's fantasies there is no question as to his manliness, his being in charge, his gestures of control, bravado, and "grace under pressure." In this way, the irony and the laughter directed against him seem to have a bit of an edge; Mitty may be not just wimpy but rather contemptible, a failure as a male.

I would suggest that if you found yourself chuckling inwardly or audibly as you read this story and laughing at Walter Mitty, in your mind or out loud, it is because your ideology harmonized with the text's on these matters of male or husbandly behavior and is evidence of a **consoling reading**. Whether you actually know any "Walter Mittys" or not, you are aware of the stereotype and of the ideology that holds such men to be ridiculous.

But if, on the other hand, you did not find the story to be funny—or if you "saw through" or "went behind" the humor—you pretty obviously had a clashing interaction of ideologies with the text. This might involve a resistance on your part to accepting the text's apparent terms that being henpecked is stereotypical of husbands, that nagging is stereotypical of wives, and that a husband who lets his wife browbeat him and has to resort to a fantasy life to act out his masculinity is somehow less than a real man.

Such a response might also be the start of a strong reading or a **resisting reading** of this text. If your ideology clashes with the text's on these issues of the conventional or stereotypical behavior of "henpecked" husbands and "browbeating" wives, you may be able to identify a gap in the text's handling of point of view and to use your ideology as a sort of crowbar to pry the text open at that gap and expose the ideology that underlies the humor. This story probably could not have created whatever degree of sympathy and contempt you have for Walter Mitty if it did not present his point of view exclusively. Mrs. Mitty's thoughts about her husband, as opposed to just her nagging remarks to him, *have* to be excluded, it seems, if the story is going to focus on Walter's secret life and derive humor from that focus. The limited point of view is necessarily "unfair" to Mrs. Mitty, but the limited point of view is what makes the story the "interesting and entertaining" piece it is. Although "The Secret Life of Walter Mitty" is perhaps a light and humorous story, it is also a powerful text in its insistence on stereotypes that many readers recognize or believe in from other texts in Western culture: television shows and commercials, movies, jokes, gossip. To resist it, therefore, to read it **against the grain** in the way I have suggested in this discussion, may not be easy, but you might consider the relation of value to effort expended.

CONNECT: Another story that is concerned with the relation of wives and husbands is "Cooking Lesson," in the Stories for Exploration section near the end of this chapter. If you read it and are able to decide on its apparent ideology, you might try to do a resisting reading of it. See how easy or hard it is to do that, according to your own gender and ideology about marriage relationships.

Turning to "Tall Woman Love," perhaps you find another text that puts accepted ideas of gender behavior on the table, perhaps in humorous fashion. What male and female stereotypes are involved here? Any similar to those in "The Secret Life of Walter Mitty," even though March Goodspeed and Roberta Bean are not marital partners and apparently don't even really know each other? Does the story seem to call into question men's being in control, especially in situations involving mechanical matters and cars? Does it question women's yielding control to men, especially in such situations? Unlike "The Secret Life of Walter Mitty," this story seems to reverse or play with the stereotypic male and female roles, instead of emphasizing or insisting on them.

If you found this story funny, is it because of that reversal? If you also found "The Secret Life of Walter Mitty" funny, did you find "Tall Woman Love" funny for different reasons? Is the first story funny because it exaggerates stereotypical gender roles, and this one is funny because it turns those roles upside down? Certainly March Goodspeed doesn't seem to find the situation he's in all that funny. Do you sense that Roberta Bean does? That she's having fun with Goodspeed as a "typical" controlling male?

Also by way of comparison to "The Secret Life of Walter Mitty," consider the text strategies of point of view and character in "Tall Woman Love." Instead of third-person *limited* as in the Thurber story, point of view here, while also third-person, continually shifts focus from March to Roberta and back again. In the process, March seems to be revealed as a character in stereotypical male terms: he's self-important; he works outside the home; he's used to being in control, used to having power; he dresses like a business*man*. But what about Roberta? The same point of view presents her as *un*feminine in conventional terms. Her attire and manner are masculine. Although she does seem to be domestically oriented instead of working outside the home, what she is shown as doing here is stereotypically a man's job: chopping wood. And although she has "babies," she does not seem to be raising them with typically maternal habits.

Roberta seems to take pleasure in her competence at solving March's mechanical problem. Of course that competence itself, like March's relative incompetence, violates conventional gender-specific behavior. But Roberta's attitude toward her role in this little incident seems to be indeterminate. As Roberta is arranging to jump-start March's car, the narrator says she

flings up both hoods and uncoils jumper cables from around her neck and shoulders, cables which she carries there with the exuberance of one who wields pet snakes. [March] . . . opens his eyes to see her fingers strum the cables' silken skins. And how gracefully she capers between the vehicles, her eyes misting in a joy March cannot fathom.

Are Roberta's "exuberance" and "joy" due to her awareness that she is teasing March, making him uncomfortable as a man who must cede control to a woman, or merely due to her enjoyment of the chance to be helpful, no matter what the gender politics of the situation? Both readings, it seems to me, are possible.

Beyond these strategies, the ideology of the text also seems indeterminate in terms of appropriate or conventional gender roles. By constantly shifting the narrative focus and by presenting Roberta Bean as an unconventional woman, does the text seem to hold the idea that stereotypical gender roles themselves are ridiculous? Or do the text strategies of point of view, character, and plot add up to an implicit criticism of March and, by extension, all stereotypically controlling males? The plot may indeed seem to resolve itself in Roberta's triumph and March's humiliation: As one of my students wrote,

> To me, Roberta won this contest. If she hadn't intervened with her "unwomanly" skills, March would still be parked in the driveway. . . . March's pride and "dominant" male role [are] . . . at stake here; the only problem is, he chokes on both of them. (*Wendy Gordon*)

Yet another student, focusing on Roberta's uncouth dress and looks as well as on the resolution of the plot, said that

> She's not a monster or an animal, . . . and contrary to popular belief . . . March isn't a "villain" or "bad man"; he's just another guy with a male superiority complex. What is interesting is that at the end of the story it seems as if that Bean woman might have opened his eyes a little and helped him to see that women aren't just cooks and maids and baby factories, but are just like men except for biological and chemical differences. (*Robert Moses*)

That such different readings are possible without either reader especially trying to read against the grain of the text indicates the indeterminacy of the text's ideology concerning conventional or stereotypical gender roles. "Tall Woman Love," it seems, is more indeterminate than "The Secret Life of Walter Mitty" is on the same issue. The Thurber story seems to take a more definite ideological position with respect to its characters.

> **CONNECT:** Although the issues are different, the indeterminacy of "Tall Woman Love" with respect to gender roles may be similar to the indeterminacy of "Eveline" or "Teenage Wasteland" with respect to family roles.

In any case and with either "The Secret Life of Walter Mitty" or "Tall Woman Love," your response to the behaviors exhibited by the male and female characters will depend to a large degree on several elements of your own ideology: your gender, your beliefs about conventional or stereotypical gender-appropriate behavior, and your sense of the humor or seriousness of those behaviors as they appear in those stories. Whether you experience a harmonious or a clashing interaction of ideologies with either text also depends on your reading of its ideology. Exploring in writing or in class discussion either kind of ideological interaction with either text would be worthwhile, for that effort would involve a self-conscious **cultural analysis**, which can help you learn more about the cultural ideologies that have an important role in constructing both you and the texts you read.

The next chapter will look in some detail at how one student developed the ideological interaction he had with a story in his original response statement into a formal paper of self-conscious analysis.

Stories for Exploration

The three short stories reprinted below—Rosario Castellanos' "Cooking Lesson," Lynne Barrett's "Inventory," and Bharati Mukherjee's "A Wife's Story"—provide further opportunities for you to analyze the interaction of your ideology with that of a text. The questions that precede each story are designed to heighten your awareness of your experience, beliefs, opinions, and values with respect to some particular issues of contemporary life. You should jot down some answers to those questions before you begin reading either story and use those answers to gain some consciousness of yourself as you are reading each story. A set of response statement questions follows each story below.

Critical Reading Questions for "Cooking Lesson"

- What are your beliefs about a woman's "place"? When a woman marries, should she give up her job or career in order to become a homemaker? Should a man?
- Who makes the meals, especially the evening meal, in your household? Why that person and not another?
- Do you know how to cook? Why or why not? Does your gender mean you should learn how to cook?
- *Share and Compare* What are your beliefs about the progression of acquaintanceship with a person of the other sex to marriage? Does this progression follow certain distinct steps or stages? How are your beliefs related to your social class, your religion, or your ethnicity?

Rosario Castellanos   1925–1974

Cooking Lesson   1971

Translated by Maureen Ahern

The kitchen is shining white. It's a shame to have to get it dirty. One ought to sit down and contemplate it, describe it, close one's eyes, evoke it.

Looking closely, this spotlessness, this pulchritude lacks the glaring excess that causes chills in hospitals. Or is it the halo of disinfectants, the rubber-cushioned steps of the aides, the hidden presence of sickness and death? What do I care? My place is here. I've been here from the beginning of time. In the German proverb woman is synonymous with *Küche, Kinder, Kirche.** I wandered astray through classrooms, streets, offices, cafés, wasting my time on skills that now I must forget in order to acquire others. For example, choosing the menu. How could one carry out such an arduous task without the cooperation of society—of all history? On a special shelf, just right for my height, my guardian spirits are lined up, those acclaimed jugglers that reconcile the most irreducible contradictions among the pages of their recipe books: slimness and gluttony, pleasing appearance and economy, speed and succulence. With their infinite combinations: slimness and economy, speed and pleasing appearance, succulence and . . . What can you suggest to me for today's meal, O experienced housewife, inspiration of mothers here and gone, voice of tradition, clamoring secret of the supermarkets? I open a book at random and read: "Don Quijote's Dinner." Very literary but not very satisfying, because Don Quijote was not famous as a gourmet but as a bumbler. Although a more profound analysis of the text reveals etc., etc., etc. Ugh! More ink has flowed about that character than water under bridges. "Fowl Center-Face." Esoteric. Whose face? Does the face of some one or something have a center? If it does, it must not be very appetizing. "Bigos Roumanian." Well, just who do you think you're talking to? If I knew what tarragon or *ananas* were I wouldn't be consulting this book, because I'd know a lot of other things, too. If you had the slightest sense of reality, you yourself or any of your colleagues would take the trouble to write a dictionary of technical terms, edit a few prolegomena, invent a propaedeutic to make the difficult culinary art accessible to the lay person. But you all start from the assumption that we're all in on the secret and you limit yourselves to stating it. I, at least, solemnly declare that I am not, and never have been, in on either this or any other secret you share. I never understood anything about anything. You observe the symptoms: I stand here like an imbecile, in an impeccable and neutral kitchen, wearing the apron that I usurp in order to give a pretense of efficiency and of which I will be shamefully but justly stripped.

I open the refrigerator drawer that proclaims "Meat" and extract a package that I cannot recognize under its icy coating. I thaw it in hot water, revealing the title without which I never would have identified the contents: Fancy Beef Broil. Wonderful. A plain and wholesome dish. But since it doesn't mean resolving an antimony or proposing an axiom, it doesn't appeal to me.

Moreover, it's not simply an excess of logic that inhibits my hunger. It's also the appearance of it, frozen stiff; it's the color that shows now that I've ripped open the package. Red, as if it were just about to start bleeding.

Our backs were that same color, my husband and I, after our orgiastic sunbathing on the beaches of Acapulco. He could afford the luxury of "behaving like the man he is" and stretch out face down to avoid rubbing his painful skin . . . But I, self-sacrificing little Mexican wife, born like a dove to

---

*Küche, Kinder, Kirche—kitchen, children, church.

the nest, smiled like Cuauhtémoc under torture on the rack when he said, "My bed is not made of roses," and fell silent. Face up, I bore not only my own weight but also his on top of me. The classic position for making love. And I moaned, from the tearing and the pleasure. The classic moan. Myths, myths.

The best part (for my sunburn at least) was when he fell asleep. Under my fingertips—not very sensitive due to prolonged contact with typewriter keys— the nylon of my bridal nightgown slipped away in a fraudulent attempt to look like lace. I played with the tips of the buttons and those other ornaments that make whoever wears them seem so feminine in the late night darkness. The whiteness of my clothes, deliberate, repetitive, immodestly symbolic, was temporarily abolished. Perhaps at some moment it managed to accomplish its purpose beneath the light and the glance of those eyes that are now overcome by fatigue.

Eyelids close and behold, once again, exile. An enormous sandy expanse with no juncture other than the sea, whose movement suggests paralysis, with no invitation except that of the cliff to suicide.

But that's a lie. I'm not the dream that dreams in a dream that dreams; I'm not the reflection of an image in a glass; I'm not annihilated by the closing off of a consciousness or of all possible consciousness. I go on living a dense, viscose, turbid life even though the man at my side and the one far away ignore me, forget me, postpone me, abandon me, fall out of love with me.

I, too, am a consciousness that can close itself off, abandon someone, and expose him to annihilation. I . . . . The meat, under the sprinkling of salt, has toned down some of its offensive redness and now it seems more tolerable, more familiar to me. It's that piece I saw a thousand times without realizing it, when I used to pop in to tell the cook that . . .

We weren't born together. Our meeting was due to accident. A happy one? It's still too soon to say. We met by chance at an exhibition, a lecture, a film. We ran into each other in the elevator; he gave me his seat on the tram; a guard interrupted our perplexed and parallel contemplation of the giraffe because it was time to close the zoo. Someone, he or I, it's all the same, asked the stupid but indispensable question: Do you work or study? A harmony of interests and of good intentions, a show of "serious" intentions. A year ago I hadn't the slightest idea of his existence and now I'm lying close to him with our thighs entwined, damp with sweat and semen. I could get up without waking him, walk barefoot to the shower. To purify myself? I feel no revulsion. I prefer to believe that what links him to me is something as easy to wipe away as a secretion and not as terrible as a sacrament.

So I remain still, breathing rhythmically to imitate drowsiness, my insomnia the only spinster's jewel I've kept and I'm inclined to keep until death.

Beneath the brief deluge of pepper the meat seems to have gone gray. I banish this sign of aging by rubbing it as though I were trying to penetrate the surface and impregnate its thickness with flavors, because I lost my old name and I still can't get used to the new one, which is not mine either. When some employee pages me in the lobby of the hotel I remain deaf with that vague uneasiness that is the prelude to recognition. Who could that person be who doesn't answer? It could be something urgent, serious, a matter of life or death. The caller goes away without leaving a clue, a message, or even the possibility of another meeting. Is it anxiety that presses against my heart? No, it's his hand pressing on my shoulder and his lips smiling at me in benevolent mockery, more like a sorcerer than a master.

So then, I accept, as we head toward the bar (my peeling shoulder feels like it's on fire) that it's true that in my contact or collision with him I've undergone a profound metamorphosis. I didn't know and now I know; I didn't feel and now I do feel; I wasn't and now I am.

It should be left to sit for a while. Until it reaches room temperature, until it's steeped in the flavors that I've rubbed into it. I have the feeling I didn't know how to calculate very well and that I've bought a piece that's too big for the two of us—for me, because I'm lazy, not a carnivore; for him, for aesthetic reasons because he's watching his waistline. Almost all of it will be left over! Yes, I already know that I shouldn't worry: one of the good fairies that hovers over me is going to come to my rescue and explain how one uses leftovers. It's a mistake, anyhow. You don't start married life in such a sordid way. I'm afraid that you also don't start it with a dish as dull as broiled beef.

Thanks, I murmur, while I wipe my lips with a corner of the napkin. Thanks for the transparent cocktail glass, and for the submerged olive. Thanks for letting me out of the cage of one sterile routine only to lock me into the cage of another, a routine which according to all purposes and possibilities must be fruitful. Thanks for giving me the chance to show off a long gown with a train, for helping me walk up the aisle of the church, carried away by the organ music. Thanks for . . .

How long will it take to be done? Well, that shouldn't worry me too much because it has to be put on the grill at the last minute. It takes very little time, according to the cookbook. How long is little? Fifteen minutes? Ten? Five? Naturally the text doesn't specify. It presupposes an intuition which, according to my sex, I'm supposed to possess but I don't, a sense I was born without that would allow me to gauge the precise minute the meat is done.

And what about you? Don't you have anything to thank me for? You've specified it with a slightly pedantic solemnity and a precision that perhaps were meant to flatter but instead offended: my virginity. When you discovered it I felt like the last dinosaur on a planet where the species was extinct. I longed to justify myself, to explain that if I was intact when I met you it was not out of virtue or pride or ugliness but simply out of adherence to a style. I'm not baroque. The tiny imperfection in the pearl is unbearable to me. The only alternative I have is the neoclassic one, and its rigidity is incompatible with the spontaneity needed for making love. I lack that ease of the person who rows or plays tennis or dances. I don't play any sports. I comply with the ritual but my move to surrender petrifies into a statue.

Are you monitoring my transit to fluidity? Do you expect it, do you need it? Or is this hieraticism that sanctifies you, and that you interpret as the passivity natural to my nature, enough for you? So if you are voluble it will ease your mind to think that I won't hinder your adventures. It won't be necessary—thanks to my temperament—for you to fatten me up, tie me down hand and foot with children, gag me on the thick honey of resignation. I'll stay the same as I am. Calm. When you throw your body on top of mine I feel as

15

though a gravestone were covering me, full of inscriptions, strange names, memorable dates. You moan unintelligibly and I'd like to whisper my name in your ear to remind you who it is you are possessing.

I'm myself. But who am I? Your wife, of course. And that title suffices to distinguish me from past memories or future projects. I bear an owner's brand, a property tag, and yet you watch me suspiciously. I'm not weaving a web to trap you. I'm not a praying mantis. I appreciate your believing such a hypothesis, but it's false.

This meat has a toughness and consistency that is not like beef. It must be mammoth. One of those that have been preserved since prehistoric times in the Siberian ice, that the peasants thaw out and fix for food. In that terribly boring documentary they showed at the Embassy, so full of superfluous details, there wasn't the slightest mention of how long it took to make them edible. Years, months? And I only have so much time . . .

Is that a lark? Or is it a nightingale? No, our schedule won't be ruled by such winged creatures as those that announced the coming of dawn to Romeo and Juliet but by a noisy and unerring alarm clock. And you will not descend to day by the stairway of my tresses but rather on the steps of detailed complaints: you've lost a button off your jacket; the toast is burned; the coffee is cold.

I'll ruminate my resentment in silence. All the responsibilities and duties of a servant are assigned to me for everything. I'm supposed to keep the house impeccable, the clothes ready, mealtimes exact. But I'm not paid any salary; I don't get one day a week off; I can't change masters. On the other hand, I'm supposed to contribute to the support of the household and I'm expected to efficiently carry out a job where the boss is demanding, my colleagues conspire, and my subordinates hate me. In my free time I transform myself into a society matron who gives luncheons and dinners for her husband's friends, attends meetings, subscribes to the opera season, watches her weight, renews her wardrobe, cares for her skin, keeps herself attractive, keeps up on all the gossip, stays up late and gets up early, runs the monthly risk of maternity, believes the evening executive meetings, the business trips and the arrival of unexpected clients; who suffers from olfactory hallucinations when she catches a whiff of French perfume (different from the one she uses) on her husband's shirts and handkerchiefs and on lonely nights refuses to think why or what so much fuss is all about and fixes herself a stiff drink and reads a detective story with the fragile mood of a convalescent.

Shouldn't it be time to turn on the stove? Low flame so the broiler will start warming up gradually, "which should be greased first so the meat will not stick." That did occur to me; there was no need to waste pages on those recommendations.

I'm very awkward. Now it's called awkwardness, but it used to be called innocence and you loved it. But I've never loved it. When I was single I used to read things on the sly, perspiring from the arousal and shame. I never found out anything. My breasts ached, my eyes got misty, my muscles contracted in a spasm of nausea.

The oil is starting to get hot. I let it get too hot, heavy handed that I am, and now it's spitting and spattering and burning me. That's how I'm going to fry in those narrow hells, through my fault, through my fault, through my most grievous fault. But child, you're not the only one. All your classmates do the same thing or worse. They confess in the confessional, do their penance, are forgiven and fall into it again. All of them. If I had continued going around with them they'd be questioning me now, the married ones to find things out for themselves, the single ones to find out how far they can go. Impossible to let them down. I would invent acrobatics, sublime fainting spells, transports as they're called in the Thousand and One Nights—records! If you only heard me then, you'd never recognize me, Casanova!

I drop the meat onto the grill and instinctively step back against the wall.   25
What a noise! Now it's stopped. The meat lies there silently, faithful to its deceased state. I still think it's too big.

It's not that you've let me down. It's true that I didn't expect anything special. Gradually we'll reveal ourselves to one another, discover our secrets, our little tricks, learn to please each other. And one day you and I will become a pair of perfect lovers and then, right in the middle of an embrace, we'll disappear and the words, "The End," will appear on the screen.

What's the matter? The meat is shrinking. No, I'm not seeing things; I'm not wrong. You can see the mark of its original size by the outline that it left on the grill. It was only a little bit bigger. Good! Maybe it will be just the right size for our appetites.

In my next movie I'd like them to give me a different part. The white sorceress in a savage village? No, today I don't feel much inclined to either heroism or danger. Better a famous woman (a fashion designer or something like that), rich and independent, who lives by herself in an apartment in New York, Paris, or London. Her occasional *affaires* entertain her but do not change her. She's not sentimental. After a breakup scene she lights a cigarette and surveys the urban scenery through the picture window of her studio.

Ah, the color of the meat looks much better now, only raw in a few obstinate places. But the rest is browned and gives off a delicious aroma. Will it be enough for two of us? It looks very small to me.

If I got dressed up now I'd try on one of those dresses from my trousseau   30
and go out. What would happen, hmmmm? Maybe an older man with a car would pick me up. Mature. Retired. The only kind who can afford to be on the make at this time of day.

What the devil's going on? This damned meat is starting to give off horrible black smoke! I should have turned it over! Burned on one side. Well, thank goodness it has another one.

Miss, if you will allow me . . . Mrs.! And I'm warning you, my husband is very jealous. . . . Then he shouldn't let you go out alone. You're a temptation to any passerby. Nobody in this world says passerby. Pedestrian? Only the newspapers when they report accidents. You're a temptation for anyone. Mean-ing-ful silence. The glances of a sphinx. The older man is following me at a safe distance. Better for him. Better for me, because on the corner—uh, oh—my husband, who's spying on me and who never leaves me alone morning, noon, or night, who suspects everything and everybody. Your Honor. It's impossible to live this way, I want a divorce.

Now what? This piece of meat's mother never told it that it was meat and ought to act like it. It's curling up like a corkscrew pastry. Anyhow, I don't know where all that smoke can be coming from if I turned the stove off ages ago. Of course, Dear Abby, what one must do now is open the window, plug in the ventilator so it won't be smelly when my husband gets here. And I'll so cutely run right out to greet him at the door with my best dress on, my best smile, and my warmest invitation to eat out.

It's a thought. We'll look at the restaurant menu while that miserable piece of charred meat lies hidden at the bottom of the garbage pail. I'll be careful not to mention the incident because I'd be considered a somewhat irresponsible wife, with frivolous tendencies but not mentally retarded. This is the initial public image that I project and I've got to maintain it even though it isn't accurate.

There's another possibility. Don't open the window, don't turn on the ventilator, don't throw the meat in the garbage. When my husband gets here let him smell it like the ogres in all the stories and tell him that no, it doesn't smell of human flesh here, but of useless woman. I'll exaggerate my compunction so he can be magnanimous. After all, what's happened is so normal! What newlywed doesn't do the same thing that I've done? When we visit my mother-in-law, who is still at the stage of not attacking me because she doesn't know my weak points yet, she'll tell me her own experiences. The time, for example, when her husband asked her to fix coddled eggs and she took him literally . . . ha, ha. Did that stop her from becoming a fabulous widow, I mean a fabulous cook? Because she was widowed much later and for other reasons. After that she gave free rein to her maternal instincts and spoiled everything with all her pampering . . .

No, he's not going to find it the least bit amusing. He's going to say that I got distracted, that it's the height of carelessness and, yes, condescendingly, I'm going to accept his accusations.

But it isn't true, it isn't. I was watching the meat all the time, watching how a series of very odd things happened to it. Saint Theresa was right when she said that God is in the stewpots. Or matter is energy or whatever it's called now.

Let's backtrack. First there's the piece of meat, one color, one shape, one size. Then it changes, looks even nicer and you feel very happy. Then it starts changing again and now it doesn't look so nice. It keeps changing and changing and changing and you just can't tell when you should stop it. Because if I leave this piece of meat on the grill indefinitely, it will burn to a crisp till nothing is left of it. So that piece of meat that gave the impression of being so solid and real no longer exists.

So? My husband also gives the impression of being solid and real when we're together, when I touch him, when I see him. He certainly changes and I change too, although so slowly that neither of us realizes it. Then he goes off and suddenly becomes a memory and . . . Oh, no, I'm not going to fall into that trap; the one about the invented character and the invented narrator and the invented anecdote. Besides, it's not the consequence that licitly follows from the meat episode.

35

The meat hasn't stopped existing. It has undergone a series of metamor- 40
phoses. And the fact that it ceases to be perceptible for the senses does not
mean that the cycle is concluded but that it has taken the quantum leap. It will
go on operating on other levels. On the level of my consciousness, my memory, my will, changing me, defining me, establishing the course of my future.

From today on, I'll be whatever I choose to be at the moment. Seductively
unbalanced, deeply withdrawn, hypocritical. From the very beginning I will
impose, just a bit insolently, the rules of the game. My husband will resent the
appearance of my dominance, which will widen like the ripples on the surface
of the water when someone has skipped a pebble across it. I'll struggle to prevail and, if he gives in, I'll retaliate with my scorn, and, if he doesn't give in,
I'll simply be unable to forgive him.

If I assume another attitude, if I'm the typical case, femininity that begs indulgence for her errors, the balance will tip in favor of my antagonist and I
will be running the race with a handicap, which, apparently, seals my defeat,
and which, essentially, guarantees my triumph by the winding path that my
grandmothers took, the humble ones, the ones who didn't open their mouths
except to say yes and achieved an obedience foreign to even their most irrational whims. The recipe of course is ancient and its efficiency is proven. If I
still doubt, all I have to do is ask my neighbor. She'll confirm my certainty.

It's just that it revolts me to behave that way. This definition is not applicable to me, the former one either; neither corresponds to my inner truth,
or safeguards my authenticity. Must I grasp some one of them and bind myself to its terms only because it is a cliché accepted by the majority and intelligible to everyone? And it's not because I'm a *rara avis*. You can say about
me what Pfandl said about Sor Juana, that I belong to the class of hesitant
neurotics. The diagnosis is very easy, but what consequences does the assumption hold?

If I insist on affirming my version of the facts my husband is going to look
at me suspiciously; he's going to live in continual expectation that I'll be declared insane.

Our life together could not be more problematic! He doesn't want con- 45
flicts of any kind, much less such abstract, absurd, metaphysical conflicts as
the one I would present him with. His home is a haven of peace where he
takes refuge from all the storms of life. Agreed. I accepted that when I got
married and I was even ready to accept sacrifice for the sake of marital harmony. But I counted on the fact that the sacrifice, the complete renunciation
of what I am, would only be demanded of me on The Sublime Occasion, at
The Time of Heroic Solutions, at The Moment of the Definitive Decision. Not
in exchange for what I stumbled on today, which is something very insignificant and very ridiculous. And yet . . .

Response Statement Questions for "Cooking Lesson"

- What is your response to the narrator as a character? What kind of person
  does she seem to be? How close to or far from your own attitudes about
  cooking, marriage, and sex are hers?

- What do you suppose it would be like to be married to this narrator? Do you think her marriage will last? Will it thrive? In terms of what you learn about her marriage from her narration, what might work against her marriage enduring? What will have to happen for it to endure?
- Should this story be read literally or figuratively? What happens to the text if you read the narrator's references to her kitchen and the "Fancy Beef Broil" as figurative rather than literal?
- *Share and Compare* How are responses to the narrator in this story related to readers' own situations with respect to gender, age, marital status, or social class?

Critical Reading Questions for "Inventory"

- What opinions, beliefs, attitudes, or values do you have about any of the following?
- teenagers holding part-time or summer jobs
- teenagers interacting with adults in the workplace
- teenagers having sex, either with other teens or with adults
- What is your attitude toward or experience with sexual harassment in the workplace?

Lynne Barrett   b. 1950

Inventory   *1983*

"What do you think?" said the Appliances manager. "Cotton?"

"Nylon," said the other man. "The skinny ones wear little nylon bikinis. Maybe with 'Tuesday' embroidered on them."

They stood right below me looking up through the iron mesh deck of the Appliances stockroom. I had my thighs clenched. I relaxed; I kept counting transistor radios.

"This one's a kid though. What are you honey, seventeen? A baby. White cotton spankies."

I mouthed, "twennytwotwennythreetwennyfour," and marked 24 on the line for SKU 37079 in the book. They really couldn't see much looking up through the grid. And I decided long ago that looking doesn't count. I closed my big notebook and backed down the steps, my sandals going clink clonk clink, while the men watched.

"What are you, Patty?" the Appliances manager said, "seventeen?"

"Eighteen in September." I reached the floor. I glanced over at the other man, a delivery guy, a greaser.

"And anyway," I said, walking away, "anyway they're pink cotton stretch lace. You can see all of them you want over in Lingerie, you know?"

The Appliances manager laughed his little laugh like a snore.

That's what they like, when you talk back. If I told them at home, my father would holler, my mother would cry. But you just can't bother to get upset; I learned that the first week when Mrs. Grissing taught me the job. "The store makes you wear skirts and climb all over God's little acres to count the crap they haven't sold," Mrs. Grissing said. "And when you've got your fanny up in the air crawling into those bins, of course they'll peek. Big deal." Mrs. Grissing had worked for S. Kotch nineteen years. Every day her bra cut a deeper crevice into the fat of her back.

As I walked out through Appliances, all the color t.v.'s announced "Jeopardy. Jeopardy. Jeopardy." The clock radios agreed on 10:30. I'd quit Appliances early.

I crossed the main aisle into Paints, but Eddie wasn't there. No one in Paints or Hardware. In Automotive I found Eddie cutting a key for a customer. The manager of Hardware and Automotive drank, so Eddie pretty much had to cover. Eddie was supposed to be his assistant in charge of Paints, but, as Eddie said, no one bought paint at S. Kotch. People just aren't cheap about paint. Eddie was sixteen, still in high school in Singac, a tall kid with bad skin, but he was the only halfway cool person in the store as far as I was concerned.

Another customer lined up holding spark plugs. Eddie shrugged. So I decided to take off and tour the store. Over on the Softgoods side I could look at the Fall clothes just in, though I really didn't want to go off to college in clothes from S. Kotch.

As I passed Giftware, I said hello to Mrs. Sabatez, who was dusting. Mrs. Sabatez, a thin Cuban woman, dusted all day.

"I think somebody looked for you," she said.   15

"Oh? Who?"

"A pretty girl," said Mrs. Sabatez. "The girl was pretty." She nodded at her lambswool duster.

Maybe Eddie was right. He said that Mrs. Sabatez did downers. I smiled at her and moved on.

The hardest part of the job was killing time. Mrs. Grissing and her sidekick Mrs. Main were union reps and they landed themselves the easiest job in the store. Every three weeks we were supposed to count all the Hardgoods, floor and stockroom. At the start of the summer I counted as fast as I could until Mrs. Grissing took me aside: "Babes, you'll hurt yourself, climbing those shelves like an orangoutang. Three weeks is what it takes so take three weeks."

Not that Mrs. Grissing ever climbed anything. She and Mrs. Main might   20
estimate, might guess, might never look at all. If the count last time in the book was 12 they just put 6 and three weeks later 0. Once it was 0 it was always 0. They never seemed to grasp that our boss, Cherrybeth, and her boss, Mr. Wold, ordered from the books. Like the fishhooks. Cherrybeth sent me to Sporting Goods my first day counting on my own, and the book began with fishhooks. Every SKU showed 0 on the floor/0 in stock, 0/0, 0/0, 0/0 for pages. I found hundreds of fishhooks tangled on the shelves and cartons of thousands jamming Sporting Goods storage. And you should have seen the lures.

Anyway, after she got a load of my counts in Sporting Goods, Cherrybeth explained that, as union reps, Mrs. Grissing and Mrs. Main would be difficult to fire. She relied on me. Now the two old bags mostly used their Basic Books as lap trays for games of Go Fish in the Paperbacks and Records stockroom. I did inventory, which still meant slowing to stretch the books over three weeks. Usually I worked all morning and then hung out with Eddie in Paints mixing weird colors on the mixing machine.

Or, like now, I shopped. I'd crossed Jewelry and Accessories to the center of Softgoods, Juniors A Go Go, where all day tapes played and a sort of mini-lightshow cast pink and purple amoeba shapes onto the clothes. In June I bought three psychedelic nylon dresses with front zippers here on my discount, to wear to work. They were cheap, and at the end of the summer, as my mother said, I could just throw them out.

Suede minis had come in, not bad if they were real. I touched them "hunntwothreefurfi—" This job got me counting everything. Even reading, I would find myself turning the pages, just counting them. Numbers blurred through my mouth "leven twel thirdeen furdeen fideen." I counted in my sleep. I dreamed "furdysevenfurdyeightfurdyniiiiiine fiddy" till I woke myself and lay restless and ready to cry.

I used to be the only one in my family who didn't talk in my sleep. If I woke at night the house was full of noises. My older sister Maureen, before she ran away, would sing, my mother would cough and mutter, my father was always swearing, always angry, "Bastards all you bastards get you bastards!" But I slept quietly, until now, barely moving.

"Finished Appliances already, babes?" asked Mrs. Grissing.   25

I jumped. She stood under the slide projector, shifting back and forth to the music. I tried to think of a good reason to be over here, but she went on, "Well great, because Mr. Wold wants to see you before lunchbreak."

She moved away from Juniors A Go Go and I followed. "Mr. Wold? What for?"

"Cherrybeth didn't come in today."

"I know. I thought she was sick." Cherrybeth hadn't come in today or Monday, but I knew she'd gone to the shore for the weekend, and Cherrybeth usually got a one or two day sunburn when she went to the shore.

"She's sick all right," Mrs. Grissing said. "She got married."   30

"Really? Which guy? The VW or the Mustang?"

"I didn't know you and Miss S. Kotch were so close." Last year Cherrybeth was Miss S. Kotch of New Jersey; Mrs. Grissing thought it was funny to call her that. Mrs. Grissing, as she put it, "didn't care for Cherrybeth."

Now, in the main aisle, I realized Mrs. Grissing was wearing a different dress than she started out with. This time I was sure. Mrs. Grissing was gradually trading her wardrobe for clothes from the store. We had to check our coats and purses at the Employees' Desk so we couldn't sneak things out, but the system didn't prevent outright exchanges. Mrs. Grissing had on some blue thing that morning—I'd guessed it was a housecoat—and now she wore a new check dress.

We passed Mrs. Sabatez, dusting.

"Keep up the good work, Senora," Mrs. Grissing told her.   35

"Anyway," I said, "so she got married, huh?"

Mrs. Grissing led the way up the interior staircase next to Cameras.

"So why does Mr. Wold want to see me?"

She put on her all-informed look and said, "I'll let him tell you, babes."

She led the way past Complaints, past Credit, to the Hardgoods office. 40
Our office, Basic Books, was near the time clock and Personnel, but Mr. Wold
was with all the big deals. Mrs. Grissing took the Appliances book, tapped on
Mr. Wold's door, stuck her head in and said, "Here she is, Jeff."

I knew Mr. Wold by sight well enough to try and look busy when he
walked by. Now he jiggled a chair close to the side of his desk for me.

He was thirtyish, with the kind of dip and roll to his light hair that was
popular when I was a kid, like Troy Donahue. There was a combined baseball
coach-and-math teacher in my high school who looked like him and some
girls had crushes on him but I didn't. And Mr. Wold's nose was too little.

"Patty, as you know," he said, "Miss Jennings has resigned her position as
manager of Basic Books."

I tried to look like I knew.

"I'm going to miss her—very much." He looked at me hard, then away. 45
He started unbuttoning the cuffs of his long sleeve blue shirt and rolling them
up. He said, "I'm offering you a promotion to that managerial position."

"You are?" I'd worked there two months. I said, "I'm not very experienced."

"Cherrybeth—" He paused. I thought, there *can't* have been anything
going on with him and Cherrybeth. "Cherrybeth recommended you. She
praised your initiative. This will be a real boost to your career in merchandizing."

"Oh yes." My career in merchandizing was the line I used to get the job.
No one wanted to hire for the summer so I stopped saying I was going to col-
lege, figuring I could just quit in September. I still could. It didn't look like
Cherrybeth gave all that much notice.

"It's going to be tough," he said, "to replace you in inventory and I may
ask you to help out with the counts for a while. This is our light season in
Hardgoods, so I'll be able to break you in gradually with the order forms.
Cherrybeth—" By now he had his sleeves rolled and he compared to see that
they were exactly even. "She said you had done some forms for her?"

"Yes." 50

"So that's fine," he said. "If you'll stop in at Personnel they'll give you your
manager's badge."

I started to stand up and saw that he expected to shake hands, so I did—
his hand was warm and small— and kept standing. He said, "I'll be looking
forward to working with you Patty." I pulled my hand away.

"Oh my eye," he said, "my eye! I have something in my eye." He winked
his right eye shut open shut and held it. "Patty, I've got something in my eye."
I stepped over. His eye was squinched up so tight a fan of wrinkles ran up
across his nose. "Ow," he said. "Will you look and see? Get it out. Ow!"

I tried to see. I smelled coffee. "Open your eye," I said, "and roll it
around."

He took his hand away and opened his eye wide.

It was bloodshot near the corner, but I couldn't see anything in it. His 55
irises were light light blue.

"Ow," he said, "don't you see it?"

As I leaned over, his right hand waved around and came to rest on my shoulder as if for balance. He rolled his eye and whenever my finger got close he shut it.

"I don't see anything in there," I said.

"I *feel* it. Must be an eyelash. Look close, I'll hold still." He opened his eye and looked way to the left, into his nose. And his hand wandered down to my breast. I thought it must be accidental, but as I tried to shift away he found my nipple and pulled at it.

I said, "Oh, I see it," and jabbed my finger sharp into the corner of his eye.

"Ouchouch*shit!*" Mr. Wold clapped both hands to his head.

"Got it," I said, looking at my fingertip which had nothing on it. I shook it over the trash basket and backed around the desk. Mr. Wold had his hands over his face. I suspected he was laughing.

"I better get over to Personnel," I said, and closed the door behind me.

Only as I wrote for the fifth time, Tierney, Partricia K., on the Withdrawal From Union Form SK-A-47, did I see: I had to be the one they promoted, because neither Mrs. Grissing nor Mrs. Main would quit being union rep to become a manager. I heard myself telling Mr. Wold, "I'm not very experienced." Stupid, stupid. "So stupid," I said.

Neither secretary appeared to hear me. The younger one was trying to get green tape to feed straight through her letter gun so she could punch out my name for my badge. The older one, opposite, was putting my forms into files as I finished them.

"Do I get my union membership fee back?" I asked the younger. "I only joined in June."

The older one looked up. "The grace period for withdrawal from union is two weeks."

"But it was $35."

"I'm sorry. But you won't have dues taken from your paycheck anymore; that's just like a raise."

"It doesn't seem fair," said the younger. She clicked the gun a few times, then broke the tape off.

"Don't I get a raise when I become a manager?" I asked.

"You'll be eligible for a raise at the end of the first six month employment period. That's the union schedule."

"But she's not in the union anymore," said the younger.

"Right, which means she isn't really entitled to their protection. They could make her wait a year. But the store honors the union schedule anyway. And meanwhile," the elder said to me, "you don't have to pay union dues anymore, which is just like a raise."

"I see," I said.

The younger one said, "EA or IE?"

I spelled, "T I E R N E Y," as she twisted the dial for each letter. She lifted the tape delicately between long white fingernails and attached it to the badge.

"Here you go," she said.

I took the badge and started to pin it on, but I got a weird feeling when I   80
touched my chest, so I switched and put the badge higher up, near my shoulder, hoping they hadn't seen.

The older secretary read, "Miss Tierney MANAGER Basic Books. Very good," she said to the younger, "congratulations," to me.

"Congratulations," said the younger, giving me a look.

When I left Personnel I punched out for lunch and from the refrigerator behind the Employees' Desk the guard handed me my paper bag. I bought a Wink from the machine and took lunch into Cherrybeth's office. Mrs. Grissing had left the Appliances book on the desk. Then I saw that Cherrybeth's Puerto Rico and Bermuda posters were gone. The office looked bare and new. Of course, the store was new; S. Kotch moved the branch here in March. Cherrybeth told me how, last summer at the old Newark store during the riots, all the men took hunting guns from Sporting Goods and held the store until the National Guard came to convoy them out. I pictured Mr. Wold holding a shotgun, his sleeves rolled up.

I unwrapped my tuna sandwich and found it had been mushed. Mayonnaise saturated the white bread. I couldn't eat it. I threw it out. I sipped my Wink and sat at the desk. My desk. I started opening drawers. Order forms, carbon paper, blank pages to replace full pages in the inventory books. In the bottom drawer I found a cardigan sweater Cherrybeth must have left, and under it a pair of pantyhose with nail polish daubed around a hole in the heel attempting but failing to stop a run. Also a sample size can of White Rain hairspray and a roll of butterscotch lifesavers with only three left and they'd crystallized. I threw out the hairspray, candy, pantyhose, and a broken comb I found in the center drawer. There was a hairbrush, too, and I started to pull Cherrybeth's yellow hair from it, then threw the whole thing out.

Then I got up, locked the door, turned out the light, huddled up in the   85
desk chair. They always turned the air conditioning in the store so high the offices were freezing. I shivered and shivered, so I put Cherrybeth's cardigan around me. I could smell in it the old grapefruit smell of her sweat.

Then, testing, I touched my breast, to see if I'd feel weird again, and when I brushed lightly I did. Then I grabbed myself hard and it went away. No big deal, I told myself. Lots of guys had touched me. Mr. Wold was just the oldest. It would have mattered when I was fourteen, but not now. It seemed to me my life had been a progression of abandoned defenses, giving myself up in stages, kissing, frenchkissing, touching through clothes, touching under clothes, and when I went steady with Nick, everything. Which I'd thought was a big deal, but now that we were broken up, was it really? Just like kissing. When I was twelve I thought it was the greatest thing in the world that Barry Super kissed me, that he'd always be important. Well, kissing didn't mean much after a while, you could be kissed by just about anyone and take it. There were the slobbering kissers, the teeth on teeth ones, the guys who dug their tongues into the root of yours so it hurt, the nibblers, the lickers, the guys who started to talk and drooled down your throat; oh, I knew all about kissing. And how many guys had squeezed my breast? One two three ... seven, and two weeks ago at that party Kerry Sterling, who hadn't called since, and Mr. Wold. Nine. What did it matter.

The thing is, if you're a girl, people touch you and think they've gotten something. Taken something away.

Certainly that's what my father went so nuts over, when Maureen took off. He took it out on me, wouldn't let me have the car, waited up. Just the other night after that party he grabbed my arms as I came in the front door. I thought he was going to check for needle marks—since he went to the police lecture on runaways he learned ten signs of drug addiction he always checked me for—but instead he hollered, "Do they touch you? Do you let the little bastards get their hands on you?"

The thing about Maureen was, she never dated. She was a groupie from the word go. Even early on, she would rather go into New York to greet groups at the airport than go out with an ordinary boy. So my father thought she was safe. And then she went to a Hollies concert and never came back. She sent a postcard from L.A. saying she was the girlfriend of one of the guys who *really* played the Monkees music and then she went to San Francisco and last time she wrote she said she was changing her name to Tenth Cloud. Which drove my father even crazier. But he always blamed some long-haired demon who had taken her while it was clear to me that she'd done it herself.

One time I went with Maureen to a monster concert in the Village: fourteen groups. It went on for hours with long waits for set-ups. Maureen flirted with musicians during sound checks and then while they played she danced in front of them, touching her hair, biting her lips. One singer with a platinum ponytail got her frantic: she bit and bit so close I thought she'd bite his crotch and I saw he was the pursued, the girl. In the months before she ran away, Maureen would come home from sneaking into discotheques and we'd sit on her bed while she told me that she'd kissed one or rubbed two's arm and look, here was three's sleeve, four's roach, she'd boast and boast, fisicksevunateniiine.

God it was cold. So cold I was hugging myself, shivering. I got up and opened the office and punched back in: exactly thirty minutes. I could always tell now when lunch was over. I took the Hardware and Automotive book downstairs and went back to Juniors A Go Go, where I'd been when Mrs. Grissing interrupted. It was chilly here, too. Maybe it was true that they lowered the thermostat when Fall clothes came in.

In Juniors A Go Go I picked out one of the suede minis and a vest to match, together $26, and then a yellow crinkly gauze blouse, $12, which came to $38, with my store discount minus $3.80: $34.20, pretty close to my union membership fee. So I didn't feel too bad.

I took them into the dressing room and went to the far end, past the garment racks of layaways, and found a corner. I changed into my new outfit. The skirt was shorter than my usual, but heavy so it wouldn't ride up. It had its own chain belt, too; it was pretty nice for S. Kotch. I transferred my manager's badge to my new blouse, then pulled all the tags off and rolled them up with my old dress and Cherrybeth's sweater and stuffed them in a waste bin. I wondered where Mrs. Grissing got rid of her old outfits; I should ask her.

Instead of going back out I went through to the dock where Softgoods were unloaded. This was the core of the store, where all the stuff came into the departments. There were some guys down at one end eating sandwiches

90

and listening to a transistor; they waved to me as I picked my way across. I climbed onto the Appliances dock on the Hardgoods side and went through the stockroom. My heart was slamming so hard I could see it lift and drop my badge, but no one would catch me.

When I came out onto Appliances carrying my book, I could have been   95
just finishing the count there, as I had in the morning, as if nothing had happened. When I looked at my reflection in the silver top of a stove I looked okay. It was a tough outfit, and my hair was finally getting long.

The clock radios said 2:00. The color t.v.'s showed nothing going on, just newsmen talking.

When I crossed the main aisle, I looked down through the departments. Only Mrs. Sabatez, way down in Clocks dusting, moved. No one else among the displays of Hardware, Houseware, Giftware, Cameras; all the inventory spread out waiting, cheap and unbought. The store was dead.

I crossed into Automotive. I didn't see Eddie so I sat in the Test Your Reaction Time display. It was a set-up like we had in Driver Ed. with red and green lights and a timer to measure how fast you moved your foot from the gas to the brake pedal at the signal. But here they'd installed it in a mock front seat, with a dial on the dash to read out your reaction time and a chart that told you what that was in car lengths at different speeds. They'd fitted it with S. Kotch car decor items: foot pedals shaped like bare feet, leopard terry slipcovers, a leatherette wrap for the steering wheel. Kids liked to sit in it and pretend to drive while their parents shopped, though they were disappointed it didn't move like those kiddie cars they have in front of supermarkets, that jiggle a while for a nickel.

I plugged in the cord to start the timer and tested myself. I was always very fast. But then it's easy when you know a signal's coming.

After a while Eddie came out of Paints stockroom and noticed me. He said   100
hi and came over and started playing with the am/fm car radios on their display. "What do you want to hear?" he asked. "Do you know I found a teensy little country and western station from up in Mahwah the other day?"

"Piss," I said. I'd gotten distracted and missed the signal. If I'd been going 40 m.p.h. my stopping distance would have been fourteen car lengths. I said, "Country and western in New Jersey?"

He started turning the display. The sample car radios were hung on a tall rack that had wiring down the middle of it so that they could be plugged in. Eddie was forever trying to catch some shy station with a 10 watt signal or pull in soul from Detroit, which meant he would move the display around Automotive, dragging the extension cords along.

"Where's your boss?" I asked.

"He's still out to yesterday's lunch."

Eddie was getting the Temptations. He started tuning all the radios in the   105
same way. I looked at him: A tall kid with bad skin—or rather it was obvious that he had bad skin in winter. Eddie always went out at lunchbreak and stood against the concrete wall of the store and took the sun in his face, so now he was tan to the collar of his shirt and the scars only showed at his temples. He'd brought some barbells from Sporting Goods to "build up his pecs" as he

said, but he was still just as skinny as in June, in the white button-down shirt and khaki pants they made him wear to work.

It occurred to me that this was how I always looked at Eddie, and yet he was the only halfway cool person in the store. Early in the summer I'd suspected he liked me; he'd mentioned movies, but I'd kept it an on-the-job friendship. How silly, when I'd go off to a party and make out with Kerry Sterling, who never called. I thought, if I were a man and Eddie a girl, I'd look at him differently. The Appliances manager was turned on identifying underwear; Mr. Wold put on his act to fool me, just to feel me up; they'd think a kid of sixteen was meant to peek at. I tried peeking at Eddie. If I looked as he lifted I could see the damp shadow of his underarm. Was he wearing an undershirt? No. There was the line of his spine, clear through his shirt. He had a flat little ass. And when he turned I could tell his cock lay to the left. Oh, you could do it to anyone, I thought. Why not Eddie?

Eddie said, "You'd probably rather listen to Cream or something."

I said, "Jefferson Airplane."

He smiled. "Maybe Grace Slick is one of your sister's friends by now."

I'd told Eddie about Maureen. He thought the name Tenth Cloud was great; he suggested cloud names for my whole family, Storm Cloud for my father and Rain Cloud for Mom and I should be Fog or Mist or Haze because I was all over the store.

"Oh, hey," I said, remembering, "I got promoted. I'm manager of Basic Books." I showed him my badge.

He asked what happened.

"Cherrybeth got married and quit."

"She was here this morning," he said. "Did she find you?"

"Cherrybeth?"

"Yeah, she came in when we were busy. She asked if you were counting Hardware."

"Mrs. Sabatez said someone was looking for me. I wonder what she would have said."

Eddie went to the counter. "Wait," he said, "she asked me—" He looked around the register and then went into Paints. "I was busy so—yeah, here. Good thing you reminded me."

He brought over an S. Kotch bag, the smallest size. Cherrybeth had written on it:

Dear Patty,
Chuck and I are getting married this Sat, but I told them I already was so they couldn't hassel me. He's the one I told you about remember? So now you'll be the only one in the store who can do fractions. You're one in a zillion, kiddo. Take no shit.

                                            Cherrybeth Russo (to be)
P.S. Don't run for Miss S. Kotch it's fixed.

I showed the note to Eddie. I felt better thinking she had tried to see me. Maybe she would have warned me about Mr. Wold. Sometimes she called him "Mr. Mold" I remembered. I wondered if he'd fixed the contest for her.

110

115

120

I said to Eddie, "Don't you think we should celebrate?"

"Your promotion?"

"Yes, my promotion. How often does a seventeen-year-old get to manage Basic Books or anything, huh?"

"Okay," he said. "Let's have a drink."

"Sure, a drink," I said. "But what can we drink?" I got out of the display   125
car and started hunting around. "Quaker oil? Anti-freeze? Does Mr. Ellicott get into the anti-freeze much?"

"No," he said, "but he's got—come on." He led me over into Paints, into the storeroom, into the far back. "Did you forget these?" he said. "Mr. Ellicott's rock-n-rye."

We had found them a month or so before, a set of four pint bottles hidden behind a row of S. Kotch Interior Enamel. Mr. Ellicott had filled them with rye and put in rock candy crystals. Eddie said he knew other people who made it, it was a liqueur. We figured Mr. Ellicott had put them there in better days, then forgotten them.

So we sat where we always sat, on the bench by the mixing machine, and Eddie opened a bottle and we drank. It was rough and sweet and mixed with the smell of Paints stockroom, like the smell of everybody's basement on a rainy day, the smell of glue sniffing when I was twelve, before they took the high out of glue. We took turns swigging the rock-n-rye and toasting:

"To Basic Books."

"To Miss Tierney, Manager of Basic Books."   130

"To Cherrybeth Jennings Russo-to-be."

We toasted Mrs. Grissing, Mrs. Main, Mr. Ellicott, S. Kotch, Mrs. Sabatez. I had it in my head to toast Mr. Wold but couldn't quite say it. Eddie got up and put a gallon can on the mixing machine, just so we could watch it shake. He took a pair of paint mixing sticks and started drumming on cans of paint with the mixer as back beat. He played around the stockroom, rapping on my head as he passed by. Once Eddie and I talked about what would be the best song to have played at your funeral and he said he wanted "Knock on Wood" or "Grapevine," something with such a beat that no one would be able to keep from moving, including, maybe, him. Now he finished with a wipe-out solo on some primer and flopped down beside me on the bench and opened the next bottle of rock-n-rye. I found myself studying his khaki thigh.

"To Eddie DeSantis," I said. "To your career in merchandizing."

"My career," Eddie said, and drank. "Hey," he said, "maybe they'll fire El-licott and make me head of Hardware and Automotive. I'm sixteen, after all."

"Maybe they'll fire all the old guys and put kids in charge."   135

"To the first teenage-run discount department store."

"We can take over—"

"—have splash parties in the Children's wading pools—"

"—rock concerts in Juniors A Go Go—"

"When I'm Branch Manager," Eddie began his campaign speech.   140

"Let me tell your fortune," I said, and took his hand. He jerked in surprise, and as I held his palm and concentrated, I could feel a quiver in his knuckles, though he held still. I tried to recall, of all the guys I dated, whether I had ever touched one first. I had, when attracted, talked to them, waited near them, willed them towards me, but that first touch, crossing the distance, had never been mine.

"Well," I said, "what a nice long lifeline you have here."

"Oh good," said Eddie.

"And," I twisted his hand and looked at the side, "two marriages."

"Two?"

"One short and unhappy, one long and unhappy."

"Great," said Eddie.

"Well, maybe those are the lines for children, I'm not sure, I only studied this for a while when I was thirteen or so."

"So maybe it's two children, one short and unhappy, one long and unhappy?"

Eddie is cool, I thought. "It's not just the lines, either," I said. "It's the mounds."

"The mounds?"

"All the fleshy parts." I rubbed his hand, which was thin and calloused and had some light green paint on it. "There are ones for scientific and mathematic and artistic, but I don't remember which is which. But this," I squeezed the outer part of his hand, "is the mound of the moon. That's imagination."

"Do I have imagination?"

"You're very imaginative. And this is the mound of Aphrodite. Venus." I touched the flesh below his thumb. His hand was sweating lightly. Oh, this was fun. "It shows sensuality." I brushed his wrist.

"Patty?" he said. "Do you want to go out after work?"

"Oh," I said, "no. Let's not go out after work. Let's not date, no phoning or not phoning, let's just do stuff the way, you know, you hear music, you move, you don't have to think about it."

"Patty?" he said. "Are you okay? Are you going to get sick on that stuff?"

"No, no, I'm fine," I said, running my hand along his spine, each vertebra, through cloth, distinct enough to number, reaching down to where his shirt would end and I'd find skin.

Response Statement Questions for "Inventory"

- What is your judgment of Patty? Do you see her, for instance, as a victim? as a "slut"? as assertive and self-possessed? How is your judgment of her related to values in your ideology? to your gender?
- What is your response to Patty's interactions with males in the story? Does she behave appropriately? On what do you base this response?
- Consider writing another scene, showing what happens in Patty's life immediately following the last sentence in the story or at some time in her future. If you do that, how does your literary experience or your ideology influence your decisions to write this scene the way you do? How does the text of "Inventory" influence you?
- *Share and Compare*   If readers in your class or discussion group differ in their judgments of Patty or their assessments of the appropriateness of her interactions with male characters, how are these differences related to cultural categories (for instance, to gender or age)?

Critical Reading Questions for "A Wife's Story"

- What is your family's history with respect to immigration to North America? If you, your parents, or your grandparents are immigrants, how easy or difficult has the adjustment to North American culture been? What factors made this adjustment easy or difficult?
- If no one in your family today immigrated to North America, what is your attitude toward immigrants? What is your ideology concerning immigration to North America?
- What is your ideology concerning two-career married couples? In terms of deciding where such a couple will live, whose career is more important and why?

Bharati Mukherjee   b. 1940

A Wife's Story   1987

Imre says forget it, but I'm going to write David Mamet.[1] So Patels are hard to sell real estate to. You buy them a beer, whisper Glengarry Glen Ross,[2] and they smell swamp instead of sun and surf. They work hard, eat cheap, live ten to a room, stash their savings under futons in Queens, and before you know it they own half of Hoboken. You say, where's the sweet gullibility that made this nation great?

Polish jokes, Patel jokes: that's not why I want to write Mamet:

Seen their women?

Everybody laughs. Imre laughs. The dozing fat man with the Barnes & Noble sack between his legs, the woman next to him, the usher, everybody. The theater isn't so dark that they can't see me. In my red silk sari I'm conspicuous. Plump, gold paisleys sparkle on my chest.

The actor is just warming up. *Seen their women?* He plays a salesman, he's   5 had a bad day and now he's in a Chinese restaurant trying to loosen up. His face is pink. His wool-blend slacks are creased at the crotch. We bought our tickets at half-price, we're sitting in the front row, but at the edge, and we see things we shouldn't be seeing. At least I do, or think I do. Spittle, actors goosing each other, little winks, streaks of makeup.

Maybe they're improvising dialogue too. Maybe Mamet's provided them with insult kits, Thursdays for Chinese, Wednesdays for Hispanics, today for Indians. Maybe they get together before curtain time, see an Indian woman settling in the front row off to the side, and say to each other: "Hey, forget Friday. Let's get *her* today. See if she cries. See if she walks out." Maybe, like the salesmen they play, they have a little bet on.

Maybe I shouldn't feel betrayed.

---

[1]David Mamet—American playwright.
[2]Glengarry Glen Ross—play by David Mamet in which real estate hustlers make fun of an imaginary Indian family named Patel.

Their women, he goes again. *They look like they've just been fucked by a dead cat.*

The fat man hoots so hard he nudges my elbow off our shared armrest.

"Imre. I'm going home." But Imre's hunched so far forward he doesn't hear. English isn't his best language. A refugee from Budapest, he has to listen hard. "I didn't pay eighteen dollars to be insulted."

I don't hate Mamet. It's the tyranny of the American dream that scares me. First, you don't exist. Then you're invisible. Then you're funny. Then you're disgusting. Insult, my American friends will tell me, is a kind of acceptance. No instant dignity here. A play like this, back home, would cause riots. Communal, racist, and antisocial. The actors wouldn't make it off stage. This play, and all these awful feelings, would be safely locked up.

I long, at times, for clear-cut answers. Offer me instant dignity, today, and I'll take it.

"What?" Imre moves toward me without taking his eyes off the actor. "Come again?"

Tears come. I want to stand, scream, make an awful scene. I long for ugly, nasty rage.

The actor is ranting, flinging spittle. *Give me a chance. I'm not finished, I can get back on the board. I tell that asshole, give me a real lead. And what does that asshole give me? Patels. Nothing but Patels.*

This time Imre works an arm around my shoulders. "Panna, what is Patel? Why are you taking it all so personally?"

I shrink from his touch, but I don't walk out. Expensive girls' schools in Lausanne and Bombay have trained me to behave well. My manners are exquisite, my feelings are delicate, my gestures refined, my moods undetectable. They have seen me through riots, uprootings, separation, my son's death.

"I'm not taking it personally."

The fat man looks at us. The woman looks too, and shushes.

I stare back at the two of them. Then I stare, mean and cool, at the man's elbow. Under the bright blue polyester Hawaiian shirt sleeve, the elbow looks soft and runny. "Excuse me," I say. My voice has the effortless meanness of well-bred displaced Third World women, though my rhetoric has been learned elsewhere. "You're exploiting my space."

Startled, the man snatches his arm away from me. He cradles it against his breast. By the time he's ready with comebacks, I've turned my back on him. I've probably ruined the first act for him. I know I've ruined it for Imre.

It's not my fault; it's the *situation.* Old colonies wear down. Patels—the new pioneers—have to be suspicious. Idi Amin's lesson is permanent. AT&T wires move good advice from continent to continent. Keep all assets liquid. Get into 7–11s, get out of condos and motels. I know how both sides feel, that's the trouble. The Patel sniffing out scams, the sad salesmen on the stage: postcolonialism has made me their referee. It's hate I long for; simple, brutish, partisan hate.

After the show Imre and I make our way toward Broadway. Sometimes he holds my hand; it doesn't mean anything more than that crazies and drunks are crouched in doorways. Imre's been here over two years, but he's stayed very old-world, very courtly, openly protective of women. I met him in a seminar on special ed. last semester. His wife is a nurse somewhere in the Hungarian countryside. There are two sons, and miles of petitions for their emigration. My husband manages a mill two hundred miles north of Bombay. There are no children.

"You make things tough on yourself," Imre says. He assumed Patel was a Jewish name or maybe Hispanic; everything makes equal sense to him. He found the play tasteless, he worried about the effect of vulgar language on my sensitive ears. "You have to let go a bit." And as though to show me how to let go, he breaks away from me, bounds ahead with his head ducked tight, then dances on amazingly jerky legs. He's a Magyar, he often tells me, and deep down, he's an Asian too. I catch glimpses of it, knife-blade Attila cheekbones, despite the blondish hair. In his faded jeans and leather jacket, he's a rock video star. I watch MTV for hours in the apartment when Charity's working the evening shift at Macy's. I listen to WPLJ on Charity's earphones. Why should I be ashamed? Television in India is so uplifting.

Imre stops as suddenly as he'd started. People walk around us. The sum-   25
mer sidewalk is full of theatergoers in seersucker suits; Imre's year-round jacket is out of place. European. Cops in twos and threes huddle, lightly tap their thighs with night sticks and smile at me with benevolence. I want to wink at them, get us all in trouble, tell them the crazy dancing man is from the Warsaw Pact. I'm too shy to break into dance on Broadway. So I hug Imre instead.

The hug takes him by surprise. He wants me to let go, but he doesn't re-ally expect me to let go. He staggers, though I weigh no more then 104 pounds, and with him, I pitch forward slightly. Then he catches me, and we walk arm in arm to the bus stop. My husband would never dance or hug a woman on Broadway. Nor would my brothers. They aren't stuffy people, but they went to Anglican boarding schools and they have a well-developed sense of what's silly.

"Imre." I squeeze his big, rough hand. "I'm sorry I ruined the evening for you."

"You did nothing of the kind." He sounds tired. "Let's not wait for the bus. Let's splurge and take a cab instead."

Imre always has unexpected funds. The Network, he calls it, Class of '56.

In the back of the cab, without even trying, I feel light, almost free. Mem-   30
ories of Indian destitutes mix with the hordes of New York street people, and they float free, like astronauts, inside my head. I've made it. I'm making some-thing of my life. I've left home, my husband, to get a Ph.D. in special ed. I have a multiple-entry visa and a small scholarship for two years. After that, we'll see. My mother was beaten by her mother-in-law, my grandmother, when she'd registered for French lessons at the Alliance Française. My grand-mother, the eldest daughter of a rich zamindar, was illiterate.

Imre and the cabdriver talk away in Russian. I keep my eyes closed. That way I can feel the floaters better. I'll write Mamet tonight. I feel strong, reck-less. Maybe I'll write Steven Spielberg too; tell him that Indians don't eat mon-key brains.

We've made it. Patels must have made it. Mamet, Spielberg: they're not condescending to us. Maybe they're a little bit afraid.

Charity Chin, my roommate, is sitting on the floor drinking Chablis out of a plastic wineglass. She is five foot six, three inches taller than me, but weighs a kilo and a half less than I do. She is a "hands" model. Orientals are supposed to have a monopoly in the hands-modelling business, she says. She had her eyes fixed eight or nine months ago and out of gratitude sleeps with her plastic surgeon every third Wednesday.

"Oh, good," Charity says. "I'm glad you're back early. I need to talk."

She's been writing checks. MCI, Con Ed, Bonwit Teller. Envelopes, already   35
stamped and sealed, form a pyramid between her shapely, knee-socked legs. The checkbook's cover is brown plastic, grained to look like cowhide. Each time Charity flips back the cover, white geese fly over sky-colored checks. She makes good money, but she's extravagant. The difference adds up to this shared, rent-controlled Chelsea one-bedroom.

"All right. Talk."

When I first moved in, she was seeing an analyst. Now she sees a nutritionist.

"Eric called. From Oregon."

"What did he want?"

"He wants me to pay half the rent on his loft for last spring. He asked me   40
to move back, remember? He *begged* me."

Eric is Charity's estranged husband.

"What does your nutritionist say?" Eric now wears a red jumpsuit and tills the soil in Rajneeshpuram.

"You think Phil's a creep too, don't you? What else can he be when creeps are all I attract?"

Phil is a flutist with thinning hair. He's very touchy on the subject of *flautists* versus *flutists*. He's touchy on every subject, from music to books to foods to clothes. He teaches at a small college upstate, and Charity bought a used blue Datsun ("Nissan," Phil insists) last month so she could spend weekends with him. She returns every Sunday night, exhausted and exasperated. Phil and I don't have much to say to each other—he's the only musician I know; the men in my family are lawyers, engineers, or in business—but I like him. Around me, he loosens up. When he visits, he bakes us loaves of pumpernickel bread. He waxes our kitchen floor. Like many men in this country, he seems to me a displaced child, or even a woman, looking for something that passed him by, or for something that he can never have. If he thinks I'm not looking, he sneaks his hands under Charity's sweater, but there isn't too much there. Here, she's a model with high ambitions. In India, she'd be a flat-chested old maid.

I'm shy in front of the lovers. A darkness comes over me when I see them   45
horsing around.

"It isn't the money," Charity says. Oh? I think. "He says he still loves me. Then he turns around and asks me for five hundred."

What's so strange about that, I want to ask. She still loves Eric, and Eric, red jumpsuit and all, is smart enough to know it. Love is a commodity, hoarded like any other. Mamet knows. But I say, "I'm not the person to ask about love." Charity knows that mine was a traditional Hindu marriage. My parents, with the help of a marriage broker, who was my mother's cousin, picked out a groom. All I had to do was get to know his taste in food.

It'll be a long evening, I'm afraid. Charity likes to confess. I unpleat my silk sari—it no longer looks too showy—wrap it in muslin cloth and put it away in a dresser drawer. Saris are hard to have laundered in Manhattan, though there's a good man in Jackson Heights. My next step will be to brew up a pot of chrysanthemum tea. It's a very special tea from the mainland. Charity's uncle gave it to us. I like him. He's a humpbacked, awkward, terri-fied man. He runs a gift store on Mott Street, and though he doesn't speak much English, he seems to have done well. Once upon a time he worked for the railways in Chengdu, Szechwan Province, and during the Wuchang Upris-ing, he was shot at. When I'm down, when I'm lonely for my husband, when I think of our son, or when I need to be held, I think of Charity's uncle. If I hadn't left home, I'd never have heard of the Wuchang Uprising. I've broad-ened my horizons.

Very late that night my husband calls me from Ahmadabad, a town of tex-tile mills north of Bombay. My husband is a vice president at Lakshmi Cotton Mills. Lakshmi is the goddess of wealth, but LCM (Priv.), Ltd., is doing poorly. Lockouts, strikes, rock-throwings. My husband lives on digitalis, which he calls the food for our *yuga* of discontent.

"We had a bad mishap at the mill today." Then he says nothing for seconds. 50

The operator comes on. "Do you have the right party, sir? We're trying to reach Mrs. Butt."

"Bhatt," I insist. "*B* for Bombay, *H* for Haryana, *A* for Ahmadabad, double *T* for Tamil Nadu." It's a litany. "This is she."

"One of our lorries was firebombed today. Resulting in three deaths. The driver, old Karamchand, and his two children."

I know how my husband's eyes look this minute, how the eye rims sag and the yellow corneas shine and bulge with pain. He is not an emotional man—the Ahmadabad Institute of Management has trained him to cut losses, to look on the bright side of economic catastrophes—but tonight he's feeling low. I try to remember a driver named Karamchand, but can't. That part of my life is over, the way *trucks* have replaced *lorries* in my vo-cabulary, the way Charity Chin and her lurid love life have replaced inher-ited notions of marital duty. Tomorrow he'll come out of it. Soon he'll be eating again. He'll sleep like a baby. He's been trained to believe in turnovers. Every morning he rubs his scalp with cantharidine oil so his hair will grow back again.

"It could be your car next." Affection, love. Who can tell the difference in 55
a traditional marriage in which a wife still doesn't call her husband by his first name?

"No. They know I'm a flunky, just like them. Well paid, maybe. No need for undue anxiety, please."

Then his voice breaks. He says he needs me, he misses me, he wants me to come to him damp from my evening shower, smelling of sandalwood soap, my braid decorated with jasmines.

"I need you too."

"Not to worry, please," he says. "I am coming in a fortnight's time. I have already made arrangements."

Outside my window, fire trucks whine, up Eighth Avenue. I wonder if he can hear them, what he thinks of a life like mine, led amid disorder.   60

"I am thinking it'll be like a honeymoon. More or less."

When I was in college, waiting to be married, I imagined honeymoons were only for the more fashionable girls, the girls who came from slightly racy families, smoked Sobranies in the dorm lavatories and put up posters of Kabir Bedi, who was supposed to have made it as a big star in the West. My husband wants us to go to Niagara. I'm not to worry about foreign exchange. He's arranged for extra dollars through the Gujarati Network, with a cousin in San Jose. And he's bought four hundred more on the black market. "Tell me you need me. Panna, please tell me again."

I change out of the cotton pants and shirt I've been wearing all day and put on a sari to meet my husband at JFK. I don't forget the jewelry; the marriage necklace of *mangalsutra,* gold drop earrings, heavy gold bangles. I don't wear them every day. In this borough of vice and greed, who knows when, or whom, desire will overwhelm.

My husband spots me in the crowd and waves. He had lost weight, and changed his glasses. The arm, uplifted in a cheery wave, is bony, frail, almost opalescent.

In the Carey Coach, we hold hands. He strokes my fingers one by one.   65
"How come you aren't wearing my mother's ring?"

"Because muggers know about Indian women," I say. They know with us it's 24-karat. His mother's ring is showy, in ghastly taste anywhere but India: a blood-red Burma ruby set in a gold frame of floral sprays. My mother-in-law got her guru to bless the ring before I left for the States.

He looks disconcerted. He's used to a different role. He's the knowing, suspicious one in the family. He seems to be sulking, and finally he comes out with it. "You've said nothing about my new glasses." I compliment him on the glasses, how chic and Western-executive they make him look. But I can't help the other things, necessities until he learns the ropes. I handle the money, buy the tickets. I don't know if this makes me unhappy.

Charity drives her Nissan upstate, so for two weeks we are to have the apartment to ourselves. This is more privacy than we ever had in India. No parents, no servants, to keep us modest. We play at housekeeping. Imre has lent us a hibachi, and I grill saffron chicken breasts. My husband marvels at the size of the Perdue hens. "They're big like peacocks, no? These Americans, they're really something!" He tries out pizzas, burgers, McNuggets. He chews. He explores. He judges. He loves it all, fears nothing, feels at home in the summer odors, the clutter of Manhattan streets. Since he thinks that the

American palate is bland, he carries a bottle of red peppers in his pocket. I wheel a shopping cart down the aisles of the neighborhood Grand Union, and he follows, swiftly, greedily. He picks up hair rinses and high-protein diet powders. There's so much I already take for granted.

One night, Imre stops by. He wants us to go with him to a movie. In his work shirt and red leather tie, he looks arty or strung out. It's only been a week, but I feel as though I am really seeing him for the first time. The yellow hair worn very short at the sides, the wide, narrow lips. He's a good-looking man, but self-conscious, almost arrogant. He's picked the movie we should see. He always tells me what to see, what to read. He buys the *Voice*. He's a natural avant-gardist. For tonight he's chosen *Numéro Deux*.

"Is it a musical?" my husband asks. The Radio City Music Hall is on his list   70
of sights to see. He's read up on the history of the Rockettes. He doesn't catch Imre's sympathetic wink.

Guilt, shame, loyalty. I long to be ungracious, not ingratiate myself with both men.

That night my husband calculates in rupees the money we've wasted on Godard. "That refugee fellow, Nagy, must have a screw loose in his head. I paid very steep price for dollars on the black market."

Some afternoons we go shopping. Back home we hated shopping; but now it is a lovers' project. My husband's shopping list startles me. I feel I am just getting to know him. Maybe, like Imre, freed from the dignities of old-world culture, he too could get drunk and squirt Cheez Whiz on a guest. I watch him dart into stores in his gleaming leather shoes. Jockey shorts on sale in outdoor bins on Broadway entrance him. White tube socks with different bands of color delight him. He looks for microcassettes, for anything small and electronic and smuggleable. He needs a garment bag. He calls it a "wardrobe," and I have to translate.

"All of New York is having sales, no?"

My heart speeds watching him this happy. It's the third week in August,   75
almost the end of summer, and the city smells ripe, it cannot bear more heat, more money, more energy.

"This is so smashing! The prices are so excellent!" Recklessly, my prudent husband signs away traveller's checks. How he intends to smuggle it all back I don't dare ask. With a microwave, he calculates, we could get rid of our cook.

This has to be love, I think. Charity, Eric, Phil: they may be experts on sex. My husband doesn't chase me around the sofa, but he pushes me down on Charity's battered cushions, and the man who has never entered the kitchen of our Ahmadabad house now comes toward me with a dish tub of steamy water to massage away the pavement heat.

Ten days into his vacation my husband checks out brochures for sightseeing tours. Shortline, Grayline, Crossroads: his new vinyl briefcase is full of schedules and pamphlets. While I make pancakes out of a mix, he comparison-shops. Tour number one costs $10.95 and will give us the World Trade Center, Chinatown, and the United Nations. Tour number three would take us both uptown *and* downtown for $14.95, but my husband is absolutely sure he doesn't want to see Harlem. We settle for tour number four: Downtown and the Dame. It's offered by a new tour company with a small, dirty office at Eighth and Forty-eighth.

The sidewalk outside the office is colorful with tourists. My husband sends me in to buy the tickets because he has come to feel Americans don't understand his accent.

The dark man, Lebanese probably, behind the counter comes on too 80 friendly. "Come on, doll, make my day!" He won't say which tour is his. "Number four? Honey, no! Look, you've wrecked me! Say you'll change your mind." He takes two twenties and gives back change. He holds the tickets, forcing me to pull. He leans closer. "I'm off after lunch."

My husband must have been watching me from the sidewalk. "What was the chap saying?" he demands. "I told you not to wear pants. He thinks you are Puerto Rican. He thinks he can treat you with disrespect."

The bus is crowded and we have to sit across the aisle from each other. The tour guide begins his patter on Forty-sixth. He looks like an actor, his hair bleached and blow-dried. Up close he must look middle-aged, but from where I sit his skin is smooth and his cheeks faintly red.

"Welcome to the Big Apple, folks." The guide uses a microphone. "Big Apple. That's what we native Manhattan degenerates call our city. Today we have guests from fifteen foreign countries and six states from this U. S. of A. That makes the Tourist Bureau real happy. And let me assure you that while we may be the richest city in the richest country in the world, it's okay to tip your charming and talented attendant." He laughs. Then swings his hip out into the aisle and sings a song.

"And it's mighty fancy on old Delancey Street, you know. . . ."

My husband looks irritable. The guide is, as expected, a good singer. "The 85 bloody man should be giving us histories of buildings we are passing, no?" I pat his hand, the mood passes. He cranes his neck. Our window seats have both gone to Japanese. It's the tour of his life. Next to this, the quick business trips to Manchester and Glasgow pale.

"And tell me what street compares to Mott Street, in July. . . ."

The guide wants applause. He manages a derisive laugh from the Americans up front. He's working the aisles now. "I coulda been somebody, right? I coulda been a star!" Two or three of us smile, those of us who recognize the parody. He catches my smile. The sun is on his harsh, bleached hair. "Right, your highness? Look, we gotta maharani with us! Couldn't I have been a star?"

"Right!" I say, my voice coming out in a squeal. I've been trained to adapt; what else can I say?

We drive through traffic past landmark office buildings and churches. The guide flips his hands. "Art deco," he keeps saying. I hear him confide to one of the Americans: "Beats me. I went to a cheap guide's school." My husband wants to know more about this Art Deco, but the guide sings another song.

"We made a foolish choice," my husband grumbles. "We are sitting in 90 the bus only. We're not going into famous buildings." He scrutinizes the pamphlets in his jacket pocket. I think, at least it's air-conditioned in here. I could sit here in the cool shadows of the city forever.

Only five of us appear to have opted for the "Downtown and the Dame" tour. The others will ride back uptown past the United Nations after we've been dropped off at the pier for the ferry to the Statue of Liberty.

An elderly European pulls a camera out of his wife's designer tote bag. He takes pictures of the boats in the harbor, the Japanese in kimonos eating popcorn, scavenging pigeons, me. Then, pushing his wife ahead of him, he climbs back on the bus and waves to us. For a second I feel terribly lost. I wish we were on the bus going back to the apartment. I know I'll not be able to describe any of this to Charity, or to Imre. I'm too proud to admit I went on a guided tour.

The view of the city from the Circle Line is seductive, unreal. The skyline wavers out of reach, but never quite vanishes. The summer sun pushes through fluffy clouds and dapples the glass of office towers. My husband looks thrilled, even more than he had on the shopping trips down Broadway. Tourists and dreamers, we have spent our life's savings to see this skyline, this statue.

"Quick, take a picture of me!" my husband yells as he moves toward a gap of railings. A Japanese matron has given up her position in order to change film. "Before the Twin Towers disappear!"

I focus, I wait for a large Oriental family to walk out of my range. My husband holds his pose tight against the railing. He wants to look relaxed, an international businessman at home in all the financial markets.   95

A bearded man slides across the bench toward me. "Like this," he says and helps me get my husband in focus. "You want me to take the photo for you?" His name, he says, is Goran. He is Goran from Yugoslavia, as though that were enough for tracking him down. Imre from Hungary. Panna from India. He pulls the old Leica out of my hand, signaling the Orientals to beat it, and clicks away. "I'm a photographer," he says. He could have been a camera thief. That's what my husband would have assumed. Somehow, I trusted. "Get you a beer?" he asks.

"I don't. Drink, I mean. Thank you very much." I say those last words very loud, for everyone's benefit. The odd bottles of Soave with Imre don't count.

"Too bad." Goran gives back the camera.

"Take one more!" my husband shouts from the railing. "Just to be sure!"   100

The island itself disappoints. The Lady has brutal scaffolding holding her in. The museum is closed. The snack bar is dirty and expensive. My husband reads out the prices to me. He orders two french fries and two Cokes. We sit at picnic tables and wait for the ferry to take us back.

"What was that hippie chap saying?"

As if I could say. A day-care center has brought its kids, at least forty of them, to the island for the day. The kids, all wearing name tags, run around us. I can't help noticing how many are Indian. Even a Patel, probably a Bhatt if I looked hard enough. They toss hamburger bits at pigeons. They kick styrofoam cups. The pigeons are slow, greedy, persistent. I have to shoo one off the table top. I don't think my husband thinks about our son.

"What hippie?"

"The one on the boat. With the beard and the hair."

My husband doesn't look at me. He shakes out his paper napkin and tries to protect his french fries from pigeon feathers.

"Oh, him. He said he was from Dubrovnik." It isn't true, but I don't want trouble.

"What did he say about Dubrovnik?"

I know enough about Dubrovnik to get by. Imre's told me about it. And about Mostar and Zagreb. In Mostar white Muslims sing the call to prayer. I would like to see that before I die: white Muslims. Whole peoples have moved before me; they've adapted. The night Imre told me about Mostar was also the night I saw my first snow in Manhattan. We'd walked down to Chelsea from Columbia. We'd walked and talked and I hadn't felt tired at all.

"You're too innocent," my husband says. He reaches for my hand. "Panna," he cries with pain in his voice, and I am brought back from perfect, floating memories of snow, "I've come to take you back. I have seen how men watch you."

"What?"

"Come back, now. I have tickets. We have all the things we will ever need. I can't live without you."

A little girl with wiry braids kicks a bottle cap at his shoes. The pigeons wheel and scuttle around us. My husband covers his fries with spread-out fingers. "No kicking," he tells the girl. Her name, Beulah, is printed in green ink on a heart-shaped name tag. He forces a smile, and Beulah smiles back. Then she starts to flap her arms. She flaps, she hops. The pigeons go crazy for fries and scraps.

"Special ed. course is two years," I remind him. "I can't go back."

My husband picks up our trays and throws them into the garbage before I can stop him. He's carried disposability a little too far. "We've been taken," he says, moving toward the dock, though the ferry will not arrive for another twenty minutes. "The ferry costs only two dollars round-trip per person. We should have chosen tour number one for $10.95 instead of tour number four for $14.95."

With my Lebanese friend, I think. "But this way we don't have to worry about cabs. The bus will pick us up at the pier and take us back to midtown. Then we can walk home."

"New York is full of cheats and whatnot. Just like Bombay." He is not accusing me of infidelity. I feel dread all the same.

That night, after we've gone to bed, the phone rings. My husband listens, then hands the phone to me. "What is this woman saying?" He turns on the pink Macy's lamp by the bed. "I am not understanding these Negro people's accents."

The operator repeats the message. It's a cable from one of the directors of Lakshmi Cotton Mills. "Massive violent labor confrontation anticipated. Stop. Return posthaste. Stop. Cable flight details. Signed Kantilal Shah."

"It's not your factory," I say. "You're supposed to be on vacation."

"So, you are worrying about me? Yes? You reject my heartfelt wishes but   120
you worry about me?" He pulls me close, slips the straps of my nightdress off
my shoulder. "Wait a minute."

I wait, unclothed, for my husband to come back to me. The water is running in the bathroom. In the ten days he has been here he has learned American rites: deodorants, fragrances. Tomorrow morning he'll call Air India; tomorrow evening he'll be on his way back to Bombay. Tonight I should make
up to him for my years away, the gutted trucks, the degree I'll never use in
India. I want to pretend with him that nothing has changed.

In the mirror that hangs on the bathroom door, I watch my naked body
turn, the breasts, the thighs glow. The body's beauty amazes. I stand here
shameless, in ways he has never seen me. I am free, afloat, watching somebody else.

Response Statement Questions for "A Wife's Story"

- Are you or your parents or grandparents immigrants? If so, how does that
  affect your response? Are there differences in the experiences of immigrants of different races or national origin?
- If neither you nor your parents or grandparents is an immigrant, what is
  your attitude toward ethnic immigrants? How does your ideology influence your response to this story?
- The narrator of this story is an educated woman, in the United States to
  pursue a Ph.D. How does your social class influence your response to the
  narrator as a character?
- What is your ideological position with respect to the issue of traditional
  marriages or to a prolonged separation from a spouse or significant other?
  How does this aspect of your ideology influence your response to the
  Bhatts' situation in the story?
- *Share and Compare* How does the ideological position of anyone in
  your class or discussion group with respect to the issue of traditional marriages or to a prolonged separation from a spouse or significant other
  influence his or her response to Bhatts' situation in this story?

READING AND WRITING PROJECTS

FOR CREATIVE AND CRITICAL THINKING

Your own writing is important as you try to learn more about yourself as a
reader—both what you do cognitively and what is done to you culturally—to
produce the kind of reader you are when you interact with any particular text.
In addition to response statements and the formal expository paper that may
grow out of them, there are other ways to use writing to learn. What follows
are suggestions for integrating your reading of and writing about literary texts

in various ways. These suggestions include exploratory writing, playing with texts and language, creative efforts in various genres, and other writing exercises designed to strengthen your awareness of the cognitive and cultural processes involved in your reading.

If you produce any "creative" pieces of your own—stories, poems, dramatic scenes, nonverbal displays, and so on—think of them as instances of intertextuality: Directly or indirectly, they refer to and are part of the textual network that includes other texts already written. If you work on any of the more "expository" or "discursive" projects, think of what you're doing as joining a *conversation* with other texts and other voices.

▶ As an exercise in reading against the grain of a text, play the "double trouble" game, as described by Professor Sheree L. Meyer of California State University, Sacramento: Select a significant passage from any short story. Fold a sheet of paper in half. On one side of the page, describe briefly what you think the passage says or means, as if you're certain of your reading or the author's intentions. On the other side, begin a description with the words "But something bothers me." On this side be hesitant, questioning the confident assertions and certainties you wrote on the first side. Think about contradictions, about "what ifs," about what the text passage does not say directly. Explore double meanings and alternative interpretations. Don't censor the outrageous or the improbable.

▶ Imagine this scenario (adapted from an assignment by Professor Sylvia Rogers of Stanford University): You are the head of a large corporation. Three situations develop—you are starting a new plant on Mars; there's trouble in the plant in Taiwan; there's labor unrest in Antarctica. You have three vice-presidents to send out as troubleshooters. Select three characters from a story or stories you have read to take these assignments, and describe how they would handle them. (For example, what if you sent Roberta Bean to Taiwan? or Walter Mitty to Mars?) In a collaborative variation, a group of three or four could play the role of the board of trustees or the top brain trust of the corporation and work out the decision as a group.

▶ Select a character from any story and create an advertisement in which this character endorses a product or service. Write some copy for this character to "say" or be quoted as saying. (For example, March Goodspeed might be a good choice to endorse a car phone.) This project could be extended or modified by writing an explanation of why you chose this character for this product or service. This project could also be done in a small group; advertising agencies often assign a team to a campaign: some members work in words, others in visual elements.

▶ Change the gender (or age, or race, or sexual orientation) of a character or characters from any story and rewrite the story or a selected scene accordingly. This entails more deep revisions than merely changing pronoun gender, of course; you will have to rethink the situation in which the original character is involved in terms of its gender-specific nature. (For example, what if Roberta Bean were a man? or Walter Mitty a woman?) This project could be modified or extended by including an explanation of the gender issues, for instance, that are raised by the change you bring about.

▶ Create a nonverbal text or display that expresses your response to or understanding of any short story. This could take the form of a collage, a drawing or painting, a sculpture, a diorama, and so forth; it could be literal or representational, or symbolic or abstract. Perhaps a brief prose note or introduction would be helpful in orienting viewers of your display to its contents. This project also lends itself well to small-group efforts.

9 ◈ Writing About Fiction

In Chapter 4, you were asked to reconsider some of the traditional ideas about turning your reading of literary texts into writing. The response statements you have been practicing as you have read short stories in this section involve one kind of nontraditional academic writing about literature because they focus on reading as an interactive process between reader and text. I hope you have seen for yourself that response statements can be a powerful tool for you to learn about what you read as well as how and why you read the way you do when you encounter certain texts. Part of that power derives from the informal nature of response statement writing. Because they are exploratory, not definitive; somewhat rough, not polished; relatively personal, not quite so public as other kinds of academic writing, response statements allow you to take some risks as a writer, and to grow and to learn as you do so.

From another angle, response statements may be considered merely the first stage of a larger writing process, a process that may lead to more public forms of writing about your interactions with literary texts. Writing of this kind can also be a valuable learning tool because when you try to explain your reading to someone else, you have to concentrate, analyze, and describe in concrete terms what is involved in your interaction with a particular text. These intellectual operations are not always easy, but think of them like a whetstone and your intellectual and verbal skills as the two edges of a knife blade: You sharpen those skills as you would sharpen a knife by applying them to the rough surface of the whetstone/discipline of writing. More public forms of writing about your responses also provide a channel through which you can communicate what you have learned about yourself and literary texts to another person. And because most learning in human culture occurs through language, it is important that *your* ideas, insights, and understandings be communicated through this verbal channel to others.

From Response Statement to Formal Paper

The process of moving from response statement to formal paper involves writing as both a way for you to learn and a means for you to tell others what you have learned or are learning. And because you as a reader are a crucial component of this writing, this process also involves self-consciousness as a goal and a method once again.

This chapter will present one student's writing process from response statement to formal paper. That sequence will illustrate all the points made

293

above. The student whose work you will read in this chapter learned about himself as a reader during the course of this process, and he was able to communicate successfully to a public something of the dynamics of his interaction with a short story. Along the way, he revised and sharpened his verbal and intellectual skills on his own and through the feedback he received from his instructor and a classmate, both of whom read a draft of his paper while it was in process.

The story this student read and responded to was Charlotte Perkins Gilman's "The Yellow Wall-Paper," which you will find reprinted below. To better appreciate this student's work, you should first read that story yourself. It would also be a good idea to write your own response to that story. When this student's class was assigned to read "The Yellow Wall-Paper," among the response statement questions they were asked to consider were ones that asked how their beliefs about madness influenced the way they read the story, specifically in terms of their identification with the narrator or other characters, and how their society's dominant ideology about mental illness influenced their responses.

Charlotte Perkins Gilman   1860–1935

The Yellow Wall-Paper   *1899*

It is very seldom that mere ordinary people like John and myself secure ancestral halls for the summer.

A colonial mansion, a hereditary estate. I would say a haunted house, and reach the height of romantic felicity—but that would be asking too much of fate!

Still I will proudly declare that there is something queer about it.

Else, why should it be let so cheaply? And why have stood so long untenanted?

John laughs at me, of course, but one expects that in marriage.   5

John is practical in the extreme. He has no patience with faith, an intense horror of superstition, and he scoffs openly at any talk of things not to be felt and seen and put down in figures.

John is a physician, and *perhaps*—(I would not say it to a living soul, of course, but this is dead paper and a great relief to my mind—) *perhaps* that is one reason I do not get well faster.

You see he does not believe I am sick!

And what can one do?

If a physician of high standing, and one's own husband, assures friends   10
and relatives that there is really nothing the matter with one but temporary nervous depression—a slight hysterical tendency—what is one to do?

My brother is also a physician, and also of high standing, and he says the same thing.

So I take phosphates or phosphites—whichever it is, and tonics, and journeys, and air, and exercise, and am absolutely forbidden to "work" until I am well again.

Personally, I disagree with their ideas.

Personally, I believe that congenial work, with excitement and change, would do me good.

But what is one to do?

I did write for a while in spite of them; but it *does* exhaust me a good deal—having to be so sly about it, or else meet with heavy opposition.

I sometimes fancy that in my condition if I had less opposition and more society and stimulus—but John says the very worst thing I can do is to think about my condition, and I confess it always makes me feel bad.

So I will let it alone and talk about the house.

The most beautiful place! It is quite alone, standing well back from the road, quite three miles from the village. It makes me think of English places that you read about, for there are hedges and walls and gates that lock, and lots of separate little houses for the gardeners and people.

There is a *delicious* garden! I never saw such a garden—large and shady, full of box-bordered paths, and lined with long grape-covered arbors with seats under them.

There were greenhouses, too, but they are all broken now.

There was some legal trouble, I believe, something about the heirs and co-heirs; anyhow, the place has been empty for years.

That spoils my ghostliness, I am afraid, but I don't care—there is something strange about the house—I can feel it.

I even said so to John one moonlight evening, but he said what I felt was a *draught*, and shut the window.

I get unreasonably angry with John sometimes. I'm sure I never used to be so sensitive. I think it is due to this nervous condition.

But John says if I feel so, I shall neglect proper self-control; so I take pains to control myself—before him, at least, and that makes me very tired.

I don't like our room a bit. I wanted one downstairs that opened on the piazza and had roses all over the window, and such pretty old-fashioned chintz hangings! but John would not hear of it.

He said there was only one window and not room for two beds, and no near room for him if he took another.

He is very careful and loving, and hardly lets me stir without special direction.

I have a schedule prescription for each hour in the day; he takes all care from me, and so I feel basely ungrateful not to value it more.

He said we came here solely on my account, that I was to have perfect rest and all the air I could get. "Your exercise depends on your strength, my dear," said he, "and your food somewhat on your appetite; but air you can absorb all the time." So we took the nursery at the top of the house.

It is a big, airy room, the whole floor nearly, with windows that look all ways, and air and sunshine galore. It was nursery first and then playroom and gymnasium, I should judge; for the windows are barred for little children, and there are rings and things in the walls.

The paint and paper look as if a boys' school had used it. It is stripped off—the paper—in great patches all around the head of my bed, about as far as I can reach, and in a great place on the other side of the room low down. I never saw a worse paper in my life.

One of those sprawling flamboyant patterns committing every artistic sin.

It is dull enough to confuse the eye in following, pronounced enough to constantly irritate and provoke study, and when you follow the lame uncertain curves for a little distance they suddenly commit suicide—plunge off at outrageous angles, destroy themselves in unheard of contradictions.

The color is repellent, almost revolting; a smouldering unclean yellow, strangely faded by the slow-turning sunlight.

It is a dull yet lurid orange in some places, a sickly sulphur tint in others.

No wonder the children hated it! I should hate it myself if I had to live in this room long.

There comes John, and I must put this away,—he hates to have me write a word.

* * *

We have been here two weeks, and I haven't felt like writing before, since that first day.

I am sitting by the window now, up in this atrocious nursery, and there is nothing to hinder my writing as much as I please, save lack of strength.

John is away all day, and even some nights when his cases are serious.

I am glad my case is not serious!

But these nervous troubles are dreadfully depressing.

John does not know how much I really suffer. He knows there is no *reason* to suffer, and that satisfies him.

Of course it is only nervousness. It does weigh on me so not to do my duty in any way!

I meant to be such a help to John, such a real rest and comfort, and here I am a comparative burden already!

Nobody would believe what an effort it is to do what little I am able—to dress and entertain, and order things.

It is fortunate Mary is so good with the baby. Such a dear baby!

And yet I *cannot* be with him, it makes me so nervous.

I suppose John never was nervous in his life. He laughs at me so about this wall-paper!

At first he meant to repaper the room, but afterwards he said that I was letting it get the better of me, and that nothing was worse for a nervous patient than to give way to such fancies.

He said that after the wall-paper was changed it would be the heavy bedstead, and then the barred windows, and then that gate at the head of the stairs, and so on.

"You know the place is doing you good," he said, "and really, dear, I don't care to renovate the house just for a three months' rental."

"Then do let us go downstairs," I said, "there are such pretty rooms there."

Then he took me in his arms and called me a blessed little goose, and said he would go down cellar, if I wished, and have it whitewashed into the bargain.

But he is right enough about the beds and windows and things.

It is as airy and comfortable a room as any one need wish, and, of course, I would not be so silly as to make him uncomfortable just for a whim.

I'm really getting quite fond of the big room, all but that horrid paper.

Out of one window I can see the garden, those mysterious deep-shaded arbors, the riotous old-fashioned flowers, and bushes and gnarly trees.

Out of another I get a lovely view of the bay and a little private wharf belonging to the estate. There is a beautiful shaded lane that runs down there from the house. I always fancy I see people walking in these numerous paths and arbors, but John has cautioned me not to give way to fancy in the least. He says that with my imaginative power and habit of storymaking, a nervous weakness like mine is sure to lead to all manner of excited fancies, and that I ought to use my will and good sense to check the tendency. So I try.

I think sometimes that if I were only well enough to write a little it would relieve the press of ideas and rest me.

But I find I get pretty tired when I try.

It is so discouraging not to have any advice and companionship about my work. When I get really well, John says we will ask Cousin Henry and Julia down for a long visit; but he says he would as soon put fireworks in my pillow-case as to let me have those stimulating people about now.

I wish I could get well faster.

But I must not think about that. This paper looks to me as if it *knew* what a vicious influence it had!

There is a recurrent spot where the pattern lolls like a broken neck and two bulbous eyes stare at you upside down.

I get positively angry with the impertinence of it and the everlastingness. Up and down and sideways they crawl, and those absurd, unblinking eyes are everywhere. There is one place where two breadths didn't match, and the eyes go all up and down the line, one a little higher than the other.

I never saw so much expression in an inanimate thing before, and we all know how much expression they have! I used to lie awake as a child and get more entertainment and terror out of blank walls and plain furniture than most children could find in a toy-store.

I remember what a kindly wink the knobs of our big, old bureau used to have, and there was one chair that always seemed like a strong friend.

I used to feel that if any of the other things looked too fierce I could always hop into that chair and be safe.

The furniture in this room is no worse than inharmonious, however, for we had to bring it all from downstairs. I suppose when this was used as a playroom they had to take the nursery things out, and no wonder! I never saw such ravages as the children have made here.

The wall-paper, as I said before, is torn off in spots, and it sticketh closer than a brother—they must have had perseverance as well as hatred.

Then the floor is scratched and gouged and splintered, the plaster itself is dug out here and there, and this great heavy bed which is all we found in the room, looks as if it had been through the wars.

But I don't mind it a bit—only the paper.

There comes John's sister. Such a dear girl as she is, and so careful of me! I must not let her find me writing.

She is a perfect and enthusiastic housekeeper, and hopes for no better profession. I verily believe she thinks it is the writing which made me sick!

But I can write when she is out, and see her a long way off from these windows.

There is one that commands the road, a lovely shaded winding road, and one that just looks off over the country. A lovely country, too, full of great elms and velvet meadows.

This wall-paper has a kind of sub-pattern in a different shade, a particularly irritating one, for you can only see it in certain lights, and not clearly then.

But in the places where it isn't faded and where the sun is just so—I can see a strange, provoking, formless sort of figure, that seems to skulk about behind that silly and conspicuous front design.

There's sister on the stairs!

* * *

Well, the Fourth of July is over! The people are all gone and I am tired out. John thought it might do me good to see a little company, so we just had mother and Nellie and the children down for a week.

Of course I didn't do a thing. Jennie sees to everything now.

But it tired me all the same.

John says if I don't pick up faster he shall send me to Weir Mitchell[1] in the fall.

But I don't want to go there at all. I had a friend who was in his hands once, and she says he is just like John and my brother, only more so!

Besides, it is such an undertaking to go so far.

I don't feel as if it was worth while to turn my hand over for anything, and I'm getting dreadfully fretful and querulous.

I cry at nothing, and cry most of the time.

Of course I don't when John is here, or anybody else, but when I am alone.

And I am alone a good deal just now. John is kept in town very often by serious cases, and Jennie is good and lets me alone when I want her to.

So I walk a little in the garden or down that lovely lane, sit on the porch under the roses, and lie down up here a good deal.

I'm getting really fond of the room in spite of the wall-paper. Perhaps *because* of the wall-paper.

It dwells in my mind so!

I lie here on this great immovable bed—it is nailed down, I believe—and follow that pattern about by the hour. It is as good as gymnastics, I assure you. I start, we'll say, at the bottom, down in the corner over there where it has not been touched, and I determine for the thousandth time that I *will* follow that pointless pattern to some sort of a conclusion.

I know a little of the principle of design, and I know this thing was not arranged on any laws of radiation, or alternation, or repetition, or symmetry, or anything else that I ever heard of.

It is repeated, of course, by the breadths, but not otherwise.

Looked at in one way each breadth stands alone, the bloated curves and flourishes—a kind of "debased Romanesque" with *delirium tremens*[2] go waddling up and down in isolated columns of fatuity.

---

[1]Silas Weir-Mitchell (1829–1914): American doctor and psychologist.
[2]*delirium tremens*—hallucinations and trembling.

But, on the other hand, they connect diagonally, and the sprawling out- 100
lines run off in great slanting waves of optic horror, like a lot of wallowing
seaweeds in full chase.

The whole thing goes horizontally, too, at least it seems so, and I exhaust
myself in trying to distinguish the order of its going in that direction.

They have used a horizontal breadth for a frieze, and that adds wonderfully to the confusion.

There is one end of the room where it is almost intact, and there, when
the cross-lights fade and the low sun shines directly upon it, I can almost
fancy radiation after all,—the interminable grotesques seem to form around a
common centre and rush off in headlong plunges of equal distraction.

It makes me tired to follow it. I will take a nap I guess.

* * *

I don't know why I should write this.   105

I don't want to.

I don't feel able.

And I know John would think it absurd. But I *must* say what I feel and
think in some way—it is such a relief!

But the effort is getting to be greater than the relief.

Half the time now I am awfully lazy, and lie down ever so much.   110

John says I mustn't lose my strength, and has me take cod liver oil and
lots of tonics and things, to say nothing of ale and wine and rare meat.

Dear John! He loves me very dearly, and hates to have me sick. I tried to
have a real earnest reasonable talk with him the other day, and tell him how I
wish he would let me go and make a visit to Cousin Henry and Julia.

But he said I wasn't able to go, nor able to stand it after I got there; and I
did not make out a very good case for myself, for I was crying before I had
finished.

It is getting to be a great effort for me to think straight. Just this nervous
weakness I suppose.

And dear John gathered me up in his arms, and just carried me upstairs   115
and laid me on the bed, and sat by me and read to me till it tired my head.

He said I was his darling and his comfort and all he had, and that I must
take care of myself for his sake, and keep well.

He says no one but myself can help me out of it, and that I must use my
will and self-control and not let any silly fancies run away with me.

There's one comfort, the baby is well and happy, and does not have to
occupy this nursery with the horrid wall-paper.

If we had not used it, the blessed child would have! What a fortunate escape! Why, I wouldn't have a child of mine, an impressionable little thing, live
in such a room for worlds.

I never thought of it before, but it is lucky that John kept me here after all, 120
I can stand it so much easier than a baby, you see.

Of course, I never mention it to them any more—I am too wise,—but I
keep watch of it all the same.

There are things in that paper that nobody knows but me, or ever will.

Behind that outside pattern the dim shapes get clearer every day.

It is always the same shape, only very numerous.

And it is like a woman stooping down and creeping about behind that   125
pattern. I don't like it a bit. I wonder—I begin to think—I wish John would
take me away from here!

*   *   *

It is so hard to talk with John about my case, because he is so wise, and
because he loves me so.

But I tried it last night.

It was moonlight. The moon shines in all around just as the sun does.

I hate to see it sometimes, it creeps so slowly, and always comes in by
one window or another.

John was asleep and I hated to waken him, so I kept still and watched the   130
moonlight on that undulating wall-paper till I felt creepy.

The faint figure behind seemed to shake the pattern, just as if she wanted
to get out.

I got up softly and went to feel and see if the paper *did* move, and when
I came back John was awake.

"What is it, little girl?" he said. "Don't go walking about like that—you'll
get cold."

I thought it was a good time to talk, so I told him that I really was not
gaining here, and I wished he would take me away.

"Why, darling!" he said, "our lease will be up in three weeks, and I can't   135
see how to leave before.

"The repairs are not done at home, and I cannot possibly leave town just
now. Of course if you were in any danger, I could and would, but you really
are better, dear, whether you can see it or not. I am a doctor, dear, and I
know. You are gaining flesh and color, your appetite is better, I feel really
much easier about you."

"I don't weigh a bit more," said I, "nor as much; and my appetite may be
better in the evening when you are here, but it is worse in the morning when
you are away!"

"Bless her little heart!" said he with a big hug, "she shall be as sick as she
pleases! But now let's improve the shining hours by going to sleep, and talk
about it in the morning!"

"And you won't go away?" I asked gloomily.

"Why, how can I, dear? It is only three weeks more and then we will take   140
a nice little trip of a few days while Jennie is getting the house ready. Really
dear you are better!"

"Better in body perhaps—" I began, and stopped short, for he sat up
straight and looked at me with such a stern, reproachful look that I could not
say another word.

"My darling," said he, "I beg of you, for my sake and for our child's sake,
as well as for your own, that you will never for one instant let that idea enter
your mind! There is nothing so dangerous, so fascinating, to a temperament
like yours. It is a false and foolish fancy. Can you not trust me as a physician
when I tell you so?"

So of course I said no more on that score, and we went to sleep before
long. He thought I was asleep first, but I wasn't, and lay there for hours trying

to decide whether that front pattern and the back pattern really did move together or separately.

* * *

On a pattern like this, by daylight, there is a lack of sequence, a defiance of law, that is a constant irritant to a normal mind.

The color is hideous enough, and unreliable enough, and infuriating enough, but the pattern is torturing. 145

You think you have mastered it, but just as you get well underway in following, it turns a back-somersault and there you are. It slaps you in the face, knocks you down, and tramples upon you. It is like a bad dream.

The outside pattern is a florid arabesque, reminding one of a fungus. If you can imagine a toadstool in joints, an interminable string of toadstools, budding and sprouting in endless convolutions—why, that is something like it.

That is, sometimes!

There is one marked peculiarity about this paper, a thing nobody seems to notice but myself, and that is that it changes as the light changes.

When the sun shoots in through the east window—I always watch for that first long, straight ray—it changes so quickly that I never can quite believe it. 150

That is why I watch it always.

By moonlight—the moon shines in all night when there is a moon—I wouldn't know it was the same paper.

At night in any kind of light, in twilight, candlelight, lamplight, and worst of all by moonlight, it becomes bars! The outside pattern I mean, and the woman behind it is as plain as can be.

I didn't realize for a long time what the thing was that showed behind, that dim sub-pattern, but now I am quite sure it is a woman.

By daylight she is subdued, quiet. I fancy it is the pattern that keeps her so still. It is so puzzling. It keeps me quiet by the hour. 155

I lie down ever so much now. John says it is good for me, and to sleep all I can.

Indeed he started the habit by making me lie down for an hour after each meal.

It is a very bad habit I am convinced, for you see I don't sleep.

And that cultivates deceit, for I don't tell them I'm awake—O no!

The fact is I am getting a little afraid of John. 160

He seems very queer sometimes, and even Jennie has an inexplicable look.

It strikes me occasionally, just as a scientific hypothesis,—that perhaps it is the paper!

I have watched John when he did not know I was looking, and come into the room suddenly on the most innocent excuses, and I've caught him several times *looking at the paper!* And Jennie too. I caught Jennie with her hand on it once.

She didn't know I was in the room, and when I asked her in a quiet, a very quiet voice, with the most restrained manner possible, what she was doing with the paper—she turned around as if she had been caught stealing, and looked quite angry—asked me why I should frighten her so!

Then she said that the paper stained everything it touched, that she had 165
found yellow smooches on all my clothes and John's, and she wished we
would be more careful!

Did not that sound innocent? But I know she was studying that pattern,
and I am determined that nobody shall find it out but myself!

* * *

Life is very much more exciting now than it used to be. You see I have
something more to expect, to look forward to, to watch. I really do eat better,
and am more quiet than I was.

John is so pleased to see me improve! He laughed a little the other day,
and said I seemed to be flourishing in spite of my wall-paper.

I turned it off with a laugh. I had no intention of telling him it was *be-cause* of the wall-paper—he would make fun of me. He might even want to
take me away.

I don't want to leave now until I have found it out. There is a week more, 170
and I think that will be enough.

* * *

I'm feeling ever so much better! I don't sleep much at night, for it is so in-teresting to watch developments; but I sleep a good deal in the daytime.

In the daytime it is tiresome and perplexing.

There are always new shoots on the fungus, and new shades of yellow all
over it. I cannot keep count of them, though I have tried conscientiously.

It is the strangest yellow, that wall-paper! It makes me think of all the yel-low things I ever saw—not beautiful ones like buttercups, but old foul, bad
yellow things.

But there is something else about that paper—the smell! I noticed it the 175
moment we came into the room, but with so much air and sun it was not bad.
Now we have had a week of fog and rain, and whether the windows are open
or not, the smell is here.

It creeps all over the house.

I find it hovering in the dining-room, skulking in the parlor, hiding in the
hall, lying in wait for me on the stairs.

It gets into my hair.

Even when I go to ride, if I turn my head suddenly and surprise it—there
is that smell!

Such a peculiar odor, too! I have spent hours in trying to analyze it, to find 180
what it smelled like.

It is not bad—at first, and very gentle, but quite the subtlest, most endur-ing odor I ever met.

In this damp weather it is awful. I wake up in the night and find it hang-ing over me.

It used to disturb me at first. I thought seriously of burning the house—to
reach the smell.

But now I am used to it. The only thing I can think of that it is like is the
color of the paper! A yellow smell.

There is a very funny mark on this wall, low down, near the mopboard. A   185
streak that runs around the room. It goes behind every piece of furniture, except
the bed, a long, straight, even *smooch,* as if it had been rubbed over and over.

I wonder how it was done and who did it, and what they did it for. Round
and round and round—round and round and round!—it makes me dizzy!

* * *

I really have discovered something at last.

Through watching so much at night, when it changes so, I have finally
found out.

The front pattern *does* move—and no wonder! The woman behind shakes it!

Sometimes I think there are a great many women behind, and sometimes   190
only one, and she crawls around fast, and her crawling shakes it all over.

Then in the very bright spots she keeps still, and in the very shady spots
she just takes hold of the bars and shakes them hard.

And she is all the time trying to climb through. But nobody could climb
through that pattern—it strangles so; I think that is why it has so many heads.

They get through, and then the pattern strangles them off and turns them
upside down, and makes their eyes white!

If those heads were covered or taken off it would not be half so bad.

* * *

I think that woman gets out in the daytime!

And I'll tell you why—privately—I've seen her!   195

I can see her out of every one of my windows!

It is the same woman, I know, for she is always creeping, and most
women do not creep by daylight.

I see her in that long shaded lane, creeping up and down. I see her in
those dark grape arbors, creeping all around the garden.

I see her on that long road under the trees, creeping along, and when a   200
carriage comes she hides under the blackberry vines.

I don't blame her a bit. It must be very humiliating to be caught creeping
by daylight!

I always lock the door when I creep by daylight. I can't do it at night, for
I know John would suspect something at once.

And John is so queer now, that I don't want to irritate him. I wish he
would take another room! Besides, I don't want anybody to get that woman
out at night but myself.

I often wonder if I could see her out of all the windows at once.

But, turn as fast as I can, I can only see out of one at one time.

And though I always see her, she *may* be able to creep faster than I can turn!   205

I have watched her sometimes away off in the open country, creeping as
fast as a cloud shadow in a high wind.

* * *

If only that top pattern could be gotten off from the under one! I mean to
try it, little by little.

I have found out another funny thing, but I shan't tell it this time! It does not do to trust people too much.

There are only two more days to get this paper off, and I believe John is beginning to notice. I don't like the look in his eyes. 210

And I heard him ask Jennie a lot of professional questions about me. She had a very good report to give.

She said I slept a good deal in the daytime.

John knows I don't sleep very well at night, for all I'm so quiet!

He asked me all sorts of questions, too, and pretended to be very loving and kind.

As if I couldn't see through him!

Still, I don't wonder he acts so, sleeping under this paper for three months. 215

It only interests me, but I feel sure John and Jennie are secretly affected by it.

* * *

Hurrah! This is the last day, but it is enough. John is to stay in town over night, and won't be out until this evening.

Jennie wanted to sleep with me—the sly thing! but I told her I should undoubtedly rest better for a night all alone.

That was clever, for really I wasn't alone a bit! As soon as it was moonlight and that poor thing began to crawl and shake the pattern, I got up and ran to help her.

I pulled and she shook, I shook and she pulled, and before morning we had peeled off yards of that paper. 220

A strip about as high as my head and half around the room.

And then when the sun came and that awful pattern began to laugh at me, I declared I would finish it to-day!

We go away to-morrow, and they are moving all my furniture down again to leave things as they were before.

Jennie looked at the wall in amazement, but I told her merrily that I did it out of pure spite at the vicious thing.

She laughed and said she wouldn't mind doing it herself, but I must not get tired. 225

How she betrayed herself that time!

But I am here, and no person touches this paper but me,—not *alive!*

She tried to get me out of the room—it was too patent! But I said it was so quiet and empty and clean now that I believed I would lie down again and sleep all I could; and not to wake me even for dinner—I would call when I woke.

So now she is gone, and the servants are gone, and the things are gone, and there is nothing left but that great bedstead nailed down, with the canvas mattress we found on it.

We shall sleep downstairs to-night, and take the boat home to-morrow. 230

I quite enjoy the room, now it is bare again.

How those children did tear about here!

This bedstead is fairly gnawed!

But I must get to work.

I have locked the door and thrown the key down into the front path. 235

I don't want to go out, and I don't want to have anybody come in, till John comes.

I want to astonish him.

I've got a rope up here that even Jennie did not find. It that woman does get out, and tries to get away, I can tie her!

But I forgot I could not reach far without anything to stand on!

This bed will *not* move!

I tried to lift and push it until I was lame, and then I got so angry I bit off a little piece at one corner—but it hurt my teeth.

Then I peeled off all the paper I could reach standing on the floor. It sticks horribly and the pattern just enjoys it! All those strangled heads and bulbous eyes and waddling fungus growths just shriek with derision!

I am getting angry enough to do something desperate. To jump out of the window would be admirable exercise, but the bars are too strong even to try.

Besides I wouldn't do it. Of course not. I know well enough that a step like that is improper and might be misconstrued.

I don't like to *look* out of the windows even—there are so many of those creeping women, and they creep so fast.

I wonder if they all come out of that wall-paper as I did?

But I am securely fastened now by my well-hidden rope—you don't get *me* out in the road there!

I suppose I shall have to get back behind the pattern when it comes night, and that is hard!

It is so pleasant to be out in this great room and creep around as I please!

I don't want to go outside. I won't, even if Jennie asks me to.

For outside you have to creep on the ground, and everything is green instead of yellow.

But here I can creep smoothly on the floor, and my shoulder just fits in that long smooch around the wall, so I cannot lose my way.

Why there's John at the door!

It is no use, young man, you can't open it!

How he does call and pound!

Now he's crying for an axe.

It would be a shame to break down that beautiful door!

"John dear!" said I in the gentlest voice, "the key is down by the front steps, under a plantain leaf!"

That silenced him for a few moments.

Then he said—very quietly indeed, "Open the door, my darling!"

"I can't," said I. "The key is down by the front door under a plantain leaf!"

And then I said it again, several times, very gently and slowly, and said it so often that he had to go and see, and he got it of course, and came in. He stopped short by the door.

"What is the matter?" he cried. "For God's sake, what are you doing!"

I kept on creeping just the same, but I looked at him over my shoulder.

"I've got out at last," said I, "in spite of you and Jane. And I've pulled off most of the paper, so you can't put me back!"

Now why should that man have fainted? But he did, and right across my path by the wall, so that I had to creep over him every time!

Tom Karabinus' first response statement follows. In it, he concentrated mostly on the question of sympathy for the narrator and her husband. He said little explicitly about his beliefs about madness or his society's dominant ideology about it, but his last paragraph does suggest some of his own ideology regarding mental illness. The highlighted portions will be explained later.

The following paragraphs from the first page of "The Yellow Wall-Paper" show some annotations Tom made while reading. His marginal notes suggest how he began to formulate a response by noticing certain aspects of the text.

John is a physician, and perhaps—*(I would not say it to a living soul, of course, but this is dead paper and a great relief to my mind—)* perhaps *that is one reason I do not get well faster.*

* * * * *

If a physician of high standing, and one's own husband, assures friends and relatives that there is really nothing the matter with one but temporary nervous depression—a slight hysterical tendency—what is one to do?   } he shouldn't!

* * * * *

I sometimes fancy that in my condition if I had less opposition and more society and stimulus—but John says the very worst thing I can do is to think about my condition, and I confess it always makes me feel bad.   helping her?

STUDENT WRITING

Tom Karabinus: A First Response to "The Yellow Wall-Paper"

Sympathizing with all the characters involved is the attitude I take when dealing with this story. The narrator is the "mad" one but why? It is obviously not because of the wall-paper. Wall-paper, I feel, is the symbol of her insanity. The setting of the story is peculiar but I guess it shows the success of her husband, the doctor. All the characters are placed in strange predicaments by this illness, or was it the wall-paper?

The narrator knows that there is something wrong with her, but is afraid to come to terms with it or is unable to come to terms with it. The wall-paper is her release from reality. I must sympathize with her because everyone has their release but hers is taking her further from reality. I feel as though she is trapped not only by her mind but also by her husband. He makes her relax and stay in bed without anything to keep her occupied but the wall-paper.

John is trying to help his wife. I think he knows that she is going insane but does not tell her and gives her false hope or even encourages the insanity by keeping her away from the public. I believe he hides her on purpose. As a doctor it would not look good to have a wife that he could not cure. He also keeps her in the most undesired room in the house that stresses her more than anything but this is the point to the role of the wall-paper.

The wall-paper seems to drive her mad. In all actuality I believe that she would have gone mad anyway. The point of the wall-paper is that no matter how far one removes a person from society if they are going mad, it doesn't matter where they are. Like my grandfather, although he was not insane, resembles the same point. He retired and felt that no one needed him and within a year he fell ill. Separation from a common place or role probably does not help a person from becoming less mad, it probably just hurries it along. The narrator said that she could get more entertainment out of plain walls than most children got out of toys. This was said to convey this thought of no matter where she was, she would have had the same delusions. The wall-paper was just a symbol of her feeling trapped in her own mind.

No one but Tom read this response statement. Class discussion of "The Yellow Wall-Paper," for the most part, revolved around the unreliability of the narrator and the effect of that text strategy on different readers. Because of this, Tom did not share his ideas about madness, although when the question of sympathy came up he did mention his grandfather's experience as something that allowed him to relate somewhat to the narrator.

A Formal Paper Assignment

A week or so after Tom's class read "The Yellow Wall-Paper," they were assigned to begin work on a formal paper on their reading of a short story. Their assignment said that a formal paper should follow the guidelines already established for writing response statements. This instruction meant that no writer had to determine and argue the meaning of any short story. Instead, they were reminded, each writer was to pursue the goal of analyzing *how* he or she constructed meaning through the interaction with the text.

Students were also reminded that they had already done some significant prewriting for the paper in the response statements they had written for a dozen short stories by that point in the semester. As further prewriting, they were told, they could go back to one or more of those response statements and revise and expand one toward a formal paper. They would have to read back over that response statement—and perhaps the text as well—and see what they had said that could profit from further exploration.

The class was also advised that a formal paper should be written for the eyes of others (as mentioned in Chapter 4). That means it should have a clearly stated thesis near the beginning to give shape to the entire discussion that follows and to afford the paper's reader a glimpse of what the paper is going to say. But they were reminded that this thesis statement did not have to pretend to say something "objective" about what the text means, as a paper of traditional interpretation would do. They were told that a formal paper should have some kind of orderly organization of the discussion, or body. It should also refer to particular examples, from both the text and the reader, to help explain points about the reading experience.

Finally, the class was advised, a formal paper should be relatively free of its own gaps and indeterminacies, such as grammatical errors. Adherence to standard practice in terms of grammar, punctuation, and spelling and organizational matters, they were reminded, could be addressed in the revising and editing stages of the writing process. They were told their papers should probably be four to six typed pages in length. The class was given about a week to select a short story, do further prewriting as necessary, and bring a first draft of a formal paper to class.

Prewriting

Taking this information and advice into account, Tom chose to work with his response to "The Yellow Wall-Paper." He prepared a first draft in which he attempted a self-conscious analysis of the role of one aspect of his ideology in his reading of that story. First, though, Tom went back to his response statement and highlighted certain sentences and phrases that he wanted to focus and expand on. Those are the highlighted portions that appear in the response statement above. Among those, please notice, is the question "but why?" in relation to his assertion that "the narrator is the 'mad' one." Much of Tom's original response statement was his attempt to answer this question. The instructions that accompanied the formal paper assignment that Tom's class was given generally asked students to think in a questioning mode again, to interrogate their response statements and their interactions with short stories, in order to develop some further answers that they would present in their papers. And as you will see, two people who read Tom's first draft tried to move Tom back into a questioning mode as he undertook revision. The point is just to remind you that the QAQ method is integral to the writing process, in response statement writing but also in developing a first response into a formal paper.

Tom's prewriting also included a scratch outline of points he intended to cover in his draft. Tom used the highlighted portions of his response statement as well as answers from his own self-questioning to generate points in his outline, which appears below.

- reading from sociological approach
- Progressive Era story—mental illness blamed on person; morality, not treatable illness
- isolation of patients—what narrator's husband does to her

- my awareness of mental illness now, my sympathy for narrator
- narrator is trapped—wall-paper is symbol

Drafting

When the due date for first drafts arrived, students were asked to write a brief descriptive statement about their drafts and to attach them as "cover notes" to their first drafts. In this note, they were to briefly describe their purposes as writers in the draft, to summarize their tentative thesis or main idea, and to mention any problems they had encountered in preparing the draft and any questions they wished a reader of their draft to pay special attention to. Here is what Tom put in his "cover note":

> My purpose in this draft is to give a strong reading response from the stand-
>
> point of a sociologist. Although many interpretations can be given, I chose this one
>
> because I saw many of the sociological mistakes as I read.
>
> My tentative thesis/main idea is to bring an understanding to the story through
>
> a contemporary sociological approach and to contrast it with the antiquated tactics
>
> of the Progressive Era in which the story was written.
>
> The problems I am experiencing now are finding a main sentence that will de-
>
> fine my thesis clearly. I am also having trouble with avoiding too much plot summary.
>
> Questions I have are: Am I getting too far away from what a response paper is
>
> supposed to be by bringing in the sociological aspect? Am I ignoring the actual oc-
>
> currences in the story? Is my thesis along the line of a strong reading?

Tom's descriptive statement indicates how he was trying to draw on his ideology as a sociology major in responding to "The Yellow Wall-Paper" and how he was trying to show how the perspective from which he chose to read (or actually *re*read) the story influenced his interpretation. Tom did not consider himself a strong writer, but he was aware enough of his own writing process and the requirements of a formal academic paper to be able to define a problem he was having with a focused thesis sentence. From his own experience as a writer and from his understanding of the assignment, he also knew that his paper should summarize elements of the plot only to illustrate points he wanted to make about his reading.

For a writer to be able to describe such problems is important in two ways: it helps anyone who would read a draft focus his or her attention on those areas, instead of responding in more general or vague terms that might not be so practically useful to the writer in revision; it also helps the writer because getting some distance from the piece of writing in order to define specific problems is the first step to solving those problems. The same is true of the specific questions Tom asked. Instead of asking his teacher something general like "Is this OK?" or "Is this what you want?" Tom asked questions that allowed his instructor or anyone who might read his draft (a classmate or a peer tutor) to focus on specific matters so as to give him some practical advice for revising. His questions also show that he had gotten a little distance from his writing and was regarding it analytically in terms of what the assignment asked.

Peer and Instructor Reviews of the First Draft

What happened next was that Tom's instructor read his first draft. That draft is reproduced below. Tom's teacher's comments are written in the margin. Tom's instructor wrote those comments on a separate page that he attached to Tom's first draft before returning it.

Tom's class also spent some time in a peer workshop, in which students who were working on a common text in their papers were paired up to read and respond to each other's drafts. Tom's peer partner wrote her comments in the margins of the first draft. In the workshop, the peer readers did not see their teacher's comments on the draft they were reading, so they were able to provide their partners with feedback entirely from their perspective, uninfluenced by what the instructor had said. Peer reviewers were also reminded of four principles of giving first draft feedback: (1) to offer no negative criticism of the writer or the writing; (2) to address specific issues the writer sought help on; (3) to offer practical suggestions for revision, not just general evaluative comments; and (4) to avoid "nit-picking" comments on surface features of the writing that should not concern the writer until the editing stage. Between the instructor's reading and the peer workshop, each writer got two independent commentaries on his or her draft before going off to revise.

Take a look now at Tom's first draft and try to notice two things about it: one, how he had expanded his original response in the direction of a strong, self-aware reading; two, how his reviewers made suggestions based on his own statement of purpose, problems, and questions. Keep in mind that this was a *rough* draft.

STUDENT WRITING

Tom Karabinus: A First Draft

"The Yellow Wall-Paper" is a short story that I would like to

deal with from a sociological aspect. Trying to understand the story

from this aspect entails applying my social beliefs along with some

knowledge of sociological history. The date in which Charlotte

Perkins Gilman, the author of the story, was alive was during the

Progressive Era. During this time period in history social reform was

at somewhat of a standstill in its dealing with mental illness. There

was no cure, no study, just blame. The blame was placed on the in-

dividual and their morality instead of dealing with it as an illness. I can not believe that one person could feel so trapped by society and at the same time so aware of her environment through her writing.

I believe that the mentally ill were looked at as the illness being their own fault and that there was not much that could be done for the insane. Treatment of illness was about as much as can be described by the narrator in the story. To sit in a room, alone with her thoughts with nothing but time and boredom to heal her was the mind set of treating the mentally ill. This concept is portrayed in the story. The narrator sits in a room generally alone except for a few occasions when her husband, a doctor, stays with her.

This treatment to me is immoral. Being of the late twentieth century, I like to feel as though I have a better understanding of the mentally ill. It is not some sociopathic behavior that the victim can control, it is the contrary. I believe that a mentally ill person feels trapped inside of a body that will not do their mind's bidding. From this the mentally ill become preoccupied with thoughts that would not enter the average person's mind. I use the belief to understand the narrator's feelings because her thoughts seemed to be trapped in the wall-paper.°

Her husband being a doctor leads me to believe that mental illness was not considered an illness but it was rather just looking at a person as being insane in the past. Her husband never seemed to know what to do for her. The reason for this is that "insanity" was not looked at as being treatable by a doctor because psychiatry was

[Peer Comment]
Possibly a thesis? with expansion — maybe combine this idea with the symbol of the woman trapped in the wall-paper?

[Peer Comment]
Another good point.

[Instructor Comment]
...whereas if you were situated like John, a contemporary of when the story was set or written, you would feel some way different? more sympathy with him? less with the "rebellious" patient?

[Peer Comment]
Why the wall-paper and not something else?

°[Instructor Comment]
Whereas previously you seemed to be consciously enforcing some distance between your time and that of the story-and consequently sympathizing with the narrator as a victim of unenlightened practices-here you seem to be collapsing that distance, and so sympathizing with John as "doing the best he can." I think that's an interesting maneuver, and I wonder if you could analyze why you made it-or at least observe that you made it and the effect of that reading strategy on your response to these two characters.

a budding science that was not widely known of or accepted. Her husband being wise in the ways of medicine would have more than likely heard of better treatments if they had existed. I do not feel a reason for negligence on the part of her husband for keeping her out in the country, away from the public, and bedridden in a room because he was giving her the best treatment available at that date.

I sympathize with the narrator because she knows that there is something wrong with her. Her husband tells her that it is just her nerves but that is just a cover because if you tell someone that they are going crazy it will just hurry the process. She feels compelled to do more than just lie there and let her over-active imagination run wild. Here I believe her mind is telling her that something is wrong. While she is writing, I believe that she is trying to figure out what her mind is telling her. She imagines these odd things that I believe are the symbols of her problems. She feels as though a woman is trapped in the pattern of the wall-paper. This is a symbol of how the mentally ill were trapped in the pattern that society had set for the mentally ill of that time, just locking them away with no help or treatment. She feels as though she wants to get out but once labeled as disturbed, there is no getting out of the pattern.

Separating a person from a common environment probably was not the best treatment. I can't understand putting a person in a strange environment that would actually stress the person more. I think it would be better if she would have stayed with her family and friends that could talk to her and help her deal with her problems. I know this was not the case because in the past mentally ill were looked at as dirty, different, and dangerous. Her husband shouldn't have separated her in such a manner just to keep her from public

[Peer Comment]
Good observation.

[Peer Comment]
Great observation! Expand on this maybe.

[Peer Comment]
Was she labeled as disturbed? Her husband really didn't understand or acknowledge her problem?

[Peer Comment]
Wouldn't she get better without these societal restraints? I don't quite understand.

[Instructor Comment]
Now you've moved back to your awareness of yourself in one time and John, at least, in another — and you judge him again from your modern perspective.

[Peer Comment]
Good correlation of your prior knowledge with the text. Very interesting sociological and psychological approach. Beginning of a strong reading.

view because here he has removed the restraints that society places
on individuals that act along with the conscience to keep a person
within the boundaries of society. Removing these societal restraints
and her being in the state of mind that she is in allows her to act in
a way that encourages the behavior that would normally be repressed by social expectations.

Clearly, Tom's classmate made more extensive notes on the draft than Tom's instructor did. I think there are two reasons for this: first, Tom's peer partner had only one draft to read, while Tom's instructor had 25 or so (every-one in the class); second, Tom's peer partner was probably thinking of the Golden Rule: She hoped that the care she applied in reading her partner's draft would be reciprocated. Indeed, if every peer partner in a workshop reads with this thorough and helping approach, every writer would benefit. In addition to these notes on or attached to the draft itself, each of Tom's readers responded specifically to statements Tom had made on his "cover note." Tom's classmate commented about his concern that he was "having trouble avoiding too much plot summary" by writing, "I thought that this was not a problem." And Tom's instructor wrote a longer note about Tom's statement of purpose, as follows:

> Your purpose: *I don't see you really doing what you say here, al-though you may _want_ to do that (and that would be fine). You don't do enough to emphasize why and how you read from the standpoint of a (late twentieth-century) sociologist. And how reading from that standpoint produces a response or interpretation _different from_ what would happen if you read from a perspective closer to that of, say, John in the story. But you may very well come closer to achieving that pur-pose if you work on the first two comments I wrote on your draft.*

Revising: Using Reviewers' Comments, Maintaining Control of Your Own Writing

When you read Tom's revised draft, reprinted below, I hope you will notice that Tom took the comments from both readers into account. Doing so en-abled him to come closer to realizing the purpose of analyzing how his per-spective as a reader influenced his response to the narrator and her husband in "The Yellow Wall-Paper." I hope you will notice also that in his revision Tom maintained control of his own paper. That is, he didn't revise merely by reacting to what his reviewers had said or by just plugging in some statements to "answer" the questions his reviewers had raised. Nor did his revisions con-sist only of changing words here and there to make his paper "sound better." Tom kept his sights on the purpose he had defined for himself as a writer in his first draft and made substantial revisions as well as some necessarily more superficial ones. He also cited the story itself in several places and provided correct Modern Language Association (MLA) documentation style. His revised draft appears below. His more major changes are bracketed and accompanied by my marginal comments on them.

STUDENT WRITING
Tom Karabinus: Revised Draft

"The Yellow Wall-Paper" is a short story that I would like to deal with from a sociological perspective. Trying to understand the story from this perspective entails applying my social beliefs along with some knowledge of sociological history. The dates in which the author of the story, Charlotte Perkins Gilman, was alive were during the Progressive Era. During this period in American history, social reform was at somewhat of a standstill in its dealing with mental illness. There was no cure and no study, just blame. The blame was placed on the individual and his or her morality instead of dealing with it as an illness. [In reading "The Yellow Wall-Paper," I sympathize with the narrator as a victim of unenlightened attitudes toward the treatment of mental illness.] I cannot believe that the narrator could feel so trapped by society and at the same time so aware of her environment through her writing. [At the same time, I have mixed feelings toward her husband, John, who I see as both perpetuating unhelpful attitudes toward mental illness and genuinely caring for his wife.]

Because mental illness tended to be blamed on the person who had it, not much could be done for the insane. Treating the mentally ill was considered to be as simple as sitting the person in a room, alone with her thoughts with nothing but time and boredom to heal her. This concept is portrayed in the story. The narrator sits in a room generally alone except for a few occasions when her husband, a doctor, stays with her.

[John, her husband, was the classic example of a doctor who did not understand mental illness during the Progressive Era. John

He added two sentences to express his thesis about how this perspective affected his sympathy for characters.

kept his wife locked away because he had the money to remove her from her normal surroundings. If he had not had the money he would probably have had no choice but to institutionalize her in a facility that would not have given her proper treatment. John does not try to understand the illness at all, he simply wishes his wife was well; however, as a doctor of the time he thought that there was little he could do but wait. Today institutions are care centers and not the prisons that they were during the Progressive Era. For this reason I sympathize with John as a caring husband, but I also do not care for the character because of the broader negligence of the mentally ill that he symbolizes in the story.]

He added a paragraph explaining the difference between his own perspective of treatment of mental illness and that of the Progressive Era.

This treatment to me is immoral. Living in the late twentieth century, I like to feel as though I have a better understanding of the mentally ill. It is not some sociopathic behavior that the victim can control, but the contrary. I believe that mentally ill people feel trapped inside their bodies that will not do their mind's bidding. Because of this, the mentally ill become preoccupied with thoughts that would not enter the average person's mind. I use this belief to understand the narrator's feelings because her thoughts seemed to be trapped in the wall-paper.

Even though her husband was a doctor, he never seemed to know what to do for her. The reason for this is that "insanity" was not looked upon as being treatable by a doctor in those days because psychiatry was a budding science that was not widely known of or accepted. Someone wise in the ways of medicine like her husband would more than likely have heard of better treatments if they had existed. I do not feel that keeping her out in the country, away from the public, and bedridden should be construed as negligence on her husband's part because this was the accepted treatment of the time. [I find myself sympathizing with John again because he does want to help his wife, but I find that the means were unavailable to him. Although John resembles a villain, I believe his caring attitude as a husband led to the modern ways of dealing with the mentally ill.]

I sympathize with the narrator because she knows that there is something wrong with her. Her husband tells her that it is simply nerves. [He says it is "temporary nervous depression—a slight hysterical tendency" (286); however, that is just a cover because by telling someone that they are going crazy just hurries the process.] She feels compelled to do more than just lie there and let her overactive imagination run wild. I believe her mind is telling her that something is wrong. [Her sane side drives her to write: "I don't know why I should write this. I don't want to. I don't feel able" (291).] While she is writing, I believe that she is trying to figure out what her mind is telling her. [I often do this to figure things out; if I am having trouble with something I will write a letter to myself to try to figure out what the problem is and it seems to satisfy me.] The narrator imagines these odd things that I believe are the symbols of her problems. She feels as though a woman is trapped in the pattern of the wall-paper. This is a symbol of how the mentally ill were trapped in the pattern that society has set for them at that time. Just locking them away with no help or treatment was the easiest thing to do. She feels as though she wants to get out but once labelled as disturbed, she cannot escape from the pattern.

Separating a person from a common environment probably was not the best treatment. I can not understand the purpose of putting a person in a strange and therefore stressful environment. I think it would be better if she would have stayed with her family and friends who could talk to her and help her deal with her problems. [I believe this because it is the closest thing to counseling that she could have had in the Progressive Era. I know that even her friends couldn't talk to her because the mentally ill were looked at as dirty, different, and dangerous.] Her husband shouldn't have separated

These sentences clarified his mixed feelings toward John, as stated in his thesis.

Tom cited the story twice to demonstrate the source in the text of his responses.

He cited himself as another source of his response

He again referred to his knowledge about Progressive Era treatment of mental illness.

her in such a manner just to keep her from public view. He has removed the restraints that society places on individuals that act along with her conscience to make a person act in a socially acceptable way. Removing these societal restraints and her being in the state of mind that she is allow her to act in a way that encourages the behavior that would normally be repressed by social expectations. [Even through her narration, I can see that her thoughts aren't being restrained by society. Eventually, she prefers to be alone with the wall-paper, away from people: "I don't want to go out, and I don't want to have anybody come in. . . . It is so pleasant to be out in this great room and creep around as I please!" (297).]

He cited the text again, showing what in it made him conclude the narrator's isolation drove her insane.

[I find myself swaying back and forth, sympathizing with John and the narrator. I feel as though all doctors want to help people, but then again I sympathize with the narrator because I don't feel he is doing enough for her. I guess I try to believe that the world is a nice place to live and I try to look at the positive side. In this story, I can not find any positive. The story truly is a look at the pathetic history of our society. I am glad society has made substantial steps away from this, but this story does not let me forget the harsh past no matter where my sympathies lie.]

He added a concluding paragraph summarizing his response and the role of his perspective as a reader in producing it.

Tom's paper had come a long way from his initial response to this close-to-final draft. In the process, Tom had both demonstrated and achieved considerable awareness of himself as a reader and the role of the perspective from which he read in making meaning of the text. Furthermore, Tom's writing not only explained his unique reading, it also expressed his personal voice. It was *his* paper; he owned it. This is certainly a credit to Tom as a student, but I hope it also suggests that you can do the same if you practice self-consciousness as a goal and a method as you read fiction and write about it, both for yourself and for another reader.

Editing

All that remained at this point in the writing process was for Tom to do some editing and polishing. A couple of days before his final draft was due, Tom took a copy of his revised draft to the campus Writing Center, where he worked with a peer tutor to identify areas of his writing that could be edited to comply with standard practices in grammar, punctuation, and spelling. Altogether, Tom made nearly 20 changes to smooth out his sentence structure, clarify pronoun references, and tighten his prose style. In the interest of the efficient use of space, Tom's edited final draft is not reprinted here. Instead, you may look at the revised draft of one of Tom's classmates who also developed a formal paper on her response to "The Yellow Wall-Paper."

Before you do that, however, take a moment to reflect on how Tom developed his original response statement to "The Yellow Wall-Paper" into a strong reading by analyzing the interaction of an element of his ideology with that of the text. Doing this can also be regarded as a **cultural analysis:** It is Tom's situation within ideology and history that produces his beliefs, not only about how mental illness should be treated but also about how it was *mis*-treated during the Progressive Era. Other kinds of cultural analyses are possible. A feminist reading of "The Yellow Wall-Paper," for instance, might examine how, from a late-twentieth-century perspective, the narrator's supposed "madness" may be read as a metaphor for the oppression of women at the turn of the century.

Collaborating

I hope you can see from reading Tom's revised draft how he benefited from the input he received from both his teacher and a classmate, both of whom read his draft and offered constructive suggestions. Now take a look at the work of another student, Melissa Dugan, whose paper also benefited from her collaboration with a classmate, but in a different way from Tom's.

Melissa's first response statement focused on the unreliability of the narrator and how that text strategy caused Melissa to disbelieve some of the statements the narrator made about her situation. When Melissa decided to try to develop that response statement into a paper, she did some more exploratory writing and went back and reread "The Yellow Wall-Paper." In the process, she discovered that her initial disbelief, though not transformed into belief of the narrator's statements, was not as simple and pervasive as she had first experienced. When she shared her first draft with a classmate, Derrick Wright, in a peer workshop, her response became problematized further because Derrick had not been as skeptical about the narrator's reliability. Derrick had one explanation for the gaps introduced by the narrator's unreliability; Melissa had another. As a result of hearing a different perspective on the text, Melissa revised her first draft in the direction of explaining how the text opened up multiple interpretive options. As you read Melissa's revised draft below, notice how she credits her classmate with complicating her reading.

STUDENT WRITING
Melissa Dugan: Revised Draft

Whatever form a text takes, whether it be fiction, poetry, drama, etc., every individual reader's interpretation depends greatly on the interaction of both the text and reader. Because readers are different, various text interpretations may be quite diverse. Some text strategies, such as gaps/blanks, may also influence the reader to come to his/her own conclusions as to what might have happened. Again, each reader does not necessarily come to the same conclusion. For these reasons, it is possible for a text to yield multiple interpretive options.

In the case of Charlotte Perkins Gilman's short story entitled "The Yellow Wall-Paper," I, as the reader, did not recognize the different interpretive options right away. It was not until I read deeper into the text and certain things were revealed that I changed my original viewpoint. This wandering viewpoint provoked me to look back at what I had read so far and revise, even perhaps disregard, my preconceptions. The majority of my thought reconsideration was due to the usual view of the narrator as unreliable. The unreliability arose because of my uncertainty on whether or not to believe what the narrator said. Another problem surfaced since this unreliable narrator was in the first person. I was provided with only one side of the story, and who's to say it was the truth?

The narrator started off by telling about how she and her husband, John, had just rented a mansion for the summer, while their home was being repaired. At this point, I did not find any reason to disbelieve her. However, as the narration continued, she described many aspects of the room which triggered something in my mind. It seemed strange that there were bars on the windows. The bed was nailed to the floor, and there was a gate at the head of the stairs. Looking out a window from that same room she seemed to spend all of her time in, the narrator told the reader the house was set apart from the village and had hedges, walls and gates that locked. I remembered back to the beginning of the story where I read that the narrator had a nervous condition. Could there be more to this nervous condition than what the narrator wrote? After some consideration, I changed my mind against what I had originally thought. This was not, in fact, a summer house that the narrator was living in; it was a mental institution, and she was a patient.

From the discussion we had in class about "The Yellow Wall-Paper," I was introduced to a different interpretation offered by a classmate. He argued that there was a very good reason for the bars and locks the narrator mentioned. As a matter of fact, that reason was even provided by the narrator herself. She explained the room used to be a nursery and the barred windows and such were at one time there to protect the children. He also used in his defense what the narrator said about how her husband planned to repaper the room and could ask why he would repaper a room in an institution. As a rebuttal to that comment, I would ask why anyone would repaper a room in a house which he/she arranged to stay in only three months.

There were other things I read in the story that I believe supported my interpretation. The narrator claimed her husband was a physician and he spent all day and many nights away "when his cases [were] serious" (paragraph 42). I wondered if John was even her husband and I decided he was simply one of her doctors that she had fantasies about. I also inferred that the woman, Jennie, who supposedly visited and helped John by keeping an eye on the narrator was a doctor, too. The narrator mentioned she lay down and was exceptionally tired a lot, which I believe was caused by the medication she probably had to take for her illness. I assumed she took medication because most patients in a mental hospital are required to do so. Unfortunately, her illness became progressively worse. Early on in the story the narrator remarked that she took "pains . . . before [John], at least" (paragraph 26). That led me to believe her worsening condition was caused because she only took her medication when the doctor was watching.

My classmate disputed my interpretation with the belief that the husband actually caused the narrator's condition to continue downhill. In the beginning of the story, the narrator said her husband did not believe she was sick and convinced her friends and relatives the same. Basically, John did not care about his wife and avoided the hassle of dealing with her by trying to assure his wife her problem was all in her head. That John buried himself in his work and frequently left his wife alone intensified her condition. Isolated by herself for such long periods of time in the room, the narrator was left with nothing else to do but to let her imagination run wild. Her imagination clouded her reality and she therefore began to see a figure moving behind the wallpaper.

I was not surprised when the narrator first started seeing shapes in the wallpaper and did not blame it on her mental condition. I, too, would start envisioning things if I were in a room that long. However, as time went on, the narrator actually classified the figure as a woman and wanted to catch her when she crept around at night. This illusion seemed quite typical of a patient in a mental institution. In fact, I think the actions of the woman portrayed the narrator's frustrations. The woman wanted to get out and tried to take "hold of the bars and shake them" (paragraph 190), just as the narrator probably wanted to shake loose the bars on her windows to escape.

The ending of the story was the hardest part for me to interpret without it conflicting with my viewpoint so far. But, after reading it about a dozen times, I felt confident that I had come up with a plausible rendition. According to the narrator, she had a rope in the room that no one knew about. Since it was improbable that a patient could get a hold of a rope, I think she used the sheets from her bed to twist and tie in knots which resembled a rope. She utilized these sheets to tie around the door knob and bed leg to secure the door shut. That was the reason that John asked for an axe and I believe that was what he used to get into the room, even though she said he recovered the key she threw out the window.

The narrator wrote that John fainted when he walked into the room and she had to step over him every time because he was blocking her path to the wall. If he only fainted, why would she have to step over him "every time"? I think that when the doctor barged into the room the narrator felt as if he ruined her whole plan to escape. In her deranged mind, she got revenge by thinking that her actions killed him.

The other reader, my classmate, who believed most of what the narrator said, disagreed again with my interpretation. He presented the argument that the narrator had been counting down to the day she and her husband moved back into their home. If they were not going back, she would not have looked forward to it. As for the end, he accepted what the narrator said to be what happened. And he blamed the husband's fainting on his having the thought that since he ignored his wife's problem he did not realize the extent of her illness. Because of his ignorance, he was caught by extreme surprise at what his wife was doing in the room.

Throughout this paper I have presented my interpretation of a text along the interpretation of one of my classmates that conflicted with mine. Although the interpretations are opposites, neither should be considered wrong. In reality, both are correct and they are not the only possible interpretations. Considering that the text introduces an unreliable narrator, the extent to which readers believe her is solely up to each individual. Readers who trust the word of the narrator may assume that the readers who label the narrator as unreliable take the easy way out. This thought process could be reversed to assume that it is easy to just read a text and accept it for what it is, without digging deeper to reveal its meaning. Whichever way a reader chooses to interpret this text, he/she must realize that it could be described in different ways because each reader brings a part of himself/herself to the story, allowing for endless possibilities in interpretation.

Like Tom, Melissa still had to edit this draft of her paper to smooth out her prose style and tighten her writing. You shouldn't take this version of her paper as a model of polished expository writing. But it does illustrate how an academic paper can reflect the contributions of more than one reader of a text. Melissa's draft still focuses on her response to "The Yellow Wall-Paper," but she has been flexible enough to do some **cognitive analysis** of her reading of the text and of her reading laid alongside someone else's. Instead of trying to argue that her interpretation is correct and her classmate's incorrect, Melissa has gained the larger perspective, through collaboration, to see that differing interpretations can coexist.

Self-conscious analyses such as Melissa's and Tom's, with their equal emphasis on the reader and the text, are different from the traditional kind of literary analysis, which emphasizes the text in isolation. The intellectual discipline of analysis is a common one and an important one in academic life. It is a discipline you are likely to have to practice as you develop a response statement into a formal paper. Tom's and Melissa's papers are good models for this practice, even though the kinds of analysis each writer undertakes is different. Tom's work is also a good model for the entire writing process from note-taking, through prewriting and drafting, to revising and final editing. If you are as careful and thorough as Tom was through his writing process, and as self-conscious as he and Melissa were about their reading, you should be able to achieve two valuable goals of academic writing: learning something for yourself and communicating that learning to others.

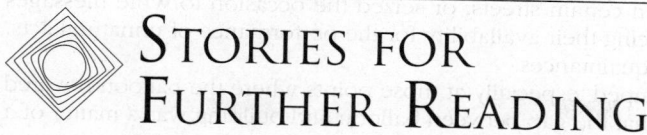

STORIES FOR FURTHER READING

Donald Barthelme   1931–1989

The Balloon

1967

The balloon, beginning at a point on Fourteenth Street, the exact location of which I cannot reveal, expanded northward all one night, while people were sleeping, until it reached the Park.[1] There, I stopped it; at dawn the northernmost edges lay over the Plaza[2]; the free-hanging motion was frivolous and gentle. But experiencing a faint irritation at stopping, even to protect the trees, and seeing no reason the balloon should not be allowed to expand upward, over the parts of the city it was already covering, into the "air space" to be found there, I asked the engineers to see to it. This expansion took place throughout the morning, soft imperceptible sighing of gas through the valves. The balloon then covered forty-five blocks north-south on either side of the Avenue in some places. That was the situation, then.

But it is wrong to speak of "situations," implying sets of circumstances leading to some resolution, some escape of tension; there were no situations, simply the balloon hanging there—muted heavy grays and browns for the most part, contrasting with walnut and soft yellows. A deliberate lack of finish, enhanced by skillful installation, gave the surface a rough, forgotten quality; sliding weights on the inside, carefully adjusted, anchored the great, vari-shaped mass at a number of points. Now we have had a flood of original ideas in all media, works of singular beauty as well as significant milestones in the history of inflation, but at that moment there was only *this balloon,* concrete particular, hanging there.

There were reactions. Some people found the balloon "interesting." As a response this seemed inadequate to the immensity of the balloon, the suddenness of its appearance over the city; on the other hand, in the absence of hysteria or other societally induced anxiety, it must be judged a calm, "mature" one. There was a certain amount of initial argumentation about the "meaning" of the balloon; this subsided, because we have learned not to insist on meanings, and they are rarely even looked for now, except in cases involving the simplest, safest phenomena. It was agreed that since the meaning of the balloon could never be known absolutely, extended discussion was pointless, or at least less purposeful than the activities of those who, for example, hung green and blue paper lanterns from the

[1]the Park—Central Park, Manhattan, New York City.
[2]the Plaza—hotel along the south edge of Central Park.

warm gray underside, in certain streets, or seized the occasion to write messages on the surface, announcing their availability for the performance of unnatural acts, or the availability of acquaintances.

Daring children jumped, especially at those points where the balloon hovered close to a building, so that the gap between balloon and building was a matter of a few inches, or points where the balloon actually made contact, exerting an ever-so-slight pressure against the side of a building, so that balloon and building seemed a unity. The upper surface was so structured that a "landscape" was presented, small valleys as well as slight knolls, or mounds; once atop the balloon, a stroll was possible, or even a trip, from one place to another. There was pleasure in being able to run down an incline, then up the opposing slope, both gently graded, or in making a leap from one side to the other. Bouncing was possible, because of the pneumaticity of the surface, and even falling, if that was your wish. That all these varied motions, as well as others, were within one's possibilities, in experiencing the "up" side of the balloon, was extremely exciting for children, accustomed to the city's flat, hard skin. But the purpose of the balloon was not to amuse children.

Too, the number of people, children and adults, who took advantage of the opportunities described was not so large as it might have been: a certain timidity, lack of trust in the balloon, was seen. There was, furthermore, some hostility. Because we had hidden the pumps, which fed helium to the interior, and because the surface was so vast that the authorities could not determine the point of entry—that is, the point at which the gas was injected—a degree of frustration was evidenced by those city officers into whose province such manifestations normally fell. The apparent purposelessness of the balloon was vexing (as was the fact that it was "there" at all). Had we painted, in great letters, "LABORATORY TESTS PROVE" or "18% MORE EFFECTIVE!" on the sides of the balloon, this difficulty would have been circumvented. But I could not bear to do so. On the whole, these officers were remarkably tolerant, considering the dimensions of the anomaly, this tolerance being the result of, first, secret tests conducted by night that convinced them that little or nothing could be done in the way of removing or destroying the balloon, and, secondly, a public warmth that arose (not uncolored by touches of the aforementioned hostility) toward the balloon, from ordinary citizens.

As a single balloon must stand for a lifetime of thinking about balloons, so each citizen expressed, in the attitude he chose, a complex of attitudes. One man might consider that the balloon had to do with the notion *sullied,* as in the sentence *The big balloon sullied the otherwise clear and radiant Manhattan sky.* That is, the balloon was, in this man's view, an imposture, something inferior to the sky that had formerly been there, something interposed between the people and their "sky." But in fact it was January, the sky was dark and ugly; it was not a sky you could look up into, lying on your back in the street, with pleasure, unless pleasure, for you, proceeded from having been threatened, from having been misused. And the underside of the balloon was a pleasure to look up into, we had seen to that, muted grays and browns for the most part, contrasted with walnut and soft, forgotten yellows. And so, while this man was thinking *sullied,* still there was an admixture of pleasurable cognition in his thinking, struggling with the original perception.

Another man, on the other hand, might view the balloon as if it were part of a system of unanticipated rewards, as when one's employer walks in and says, "Here, Henry, take this package of money I have wrapped for you, because we have been doing so well in the business here, and I admire the way you bruise the tulips, without which bruising your department would not be a success, or at least not the success that it is." For this man the balloon might be a brilliantly heroic "muscle and pluck" experience, even if an experience poorly understood.

Another man might say, "Without the example of——, it is doubtful that—— would exist today in its present form," and find many to agree with him, or to argue with him. Ideas of "bloat" and "float" were introduced, as well as concepts of dream and responsibility. Others engaged in remarkably detailed fantasies having to do with a wish either to lose themselves in the balloon, or to engorge it. The private character of these wishes, of their origins, deeply buried and unknown, was such that they were not much spoken of; yet there is evidence that they were widespread. It was also argued that what was important was what you felt when you stood under the balloon; some people claimed that they felt sheltered, warmed, as never before, while enemies of the balloon felt, or reported feeling, constrained, a "heavy" feeling.

Critical opinion was divided:

"monstrous pourings"

"harp"

xxxxxxx *"certain contrasts with darker portions"*
"inner joy"
"large, square corners"
"conservative eclecticism that has so far governed modern balloon design"
:::::::*"abnormal vigor"*
"warm, soft, lazy passages"
The Balloon
"Has unity been sacrificed for a sprawling quality?"
"Quelle catastrophe!"
"munching"

People began, in a curious way, to locate themselves in relation to aspects of the balloon: I'll be at that place where it dips down into Forty-seventh Street almost to the sidewalk, near the Alamo Chile House," or, "Why don't we go stand on top, and take the air, and maybe walk about a bit, where it forms a tight, curving line with the façade of the Gallery of Modern Art—" Marginal intersections offered entrances with a given time duration, as well as "warm, soft, lazy passages" in which ... But it is wrong to speak of "marginal intersections," each intersection was crucial, none could be ignored (as if, walking there, you might not find someone capable of turning your attention, in a flash, from old exercises to new exercises, risks and escalations). Each intersection was crucial, meeting of balloon and building, meeting of balloon and man, meeting of balloon and balloon. 10

It was suggested that what was admired about the balloon was finally this: that it was not limited, or defined. Sometimes a bulge, blister, or sub-section would carry all the way east to the river on its own initiative, in the manner of an army's movements on a map, as seen in a headquarters remote from the fighting. Then that part would be, as it were, thrown back again, or would withdraw into new dispositions: the next morning, that part would have made another sortie, or disappeared altogether. This ability of the balloon to shift its shape, to change, was very pleasing, especially to people whose lives were rather rigidly patterned, persons to whom change, although desired, was not available. The balloon, for the twenty-two days of its existence, offered the possibility, in its randomness, of mislocation of the self, in contradistinction to the grid of precise, rectangular pathways under our feet. The amount of specialized training currently needed, and the consequent desirability of long-term commitments, has been occasioned by the steadily growing importance of complex machinery, in virtually all kinds of operations; as this tendency increases, more and more people will turn, in bewildered inadequacy, to solutions for which the balloon may stand as a prototype, or "rough draft."

I met you under the balloon, on the occasion of your return from Norway; you asked if it was mine; I said it was. The balloon, I said, is a spontaneous autobiographical disclosure, having to do with the unease I felt at your absence, and with sexual deprivation, but now that your visit to Bergen has been terminated, it is no longer necessary or appropriate. Removal of the balloon was easy; trailer trucks carried away the depleted fabric, which is now stored in West Virginia, awaiting some other time of unhappiness, sometime, perhaps, when we are angry with one another.

Ambrose Bierce   1842–1914

An Occurrence at Owl Creek Bridge   1891

A man stood upon a railroad bridge in Northern Alabama, looking down into the swift waters twenty feet below. The man's hands were behind his back, the wrists bound with a cord. A rope loosely encircled his neck. It was attached to a stout cross-timber above his head, and the slack fell to the level of his knees. Some loose boards laid upon the sleepers supporting the metals of the railway supplied a footing for him and his executioners—two private soldiers of the Federal army, directed by a sergeant, who in civil life may have been a deputy sheriff. At a short remove upon the same temporary platform was an officer in the uniform of his rank, armed. He was a captain. A sentinel at each end of the bridge stood with his rifle in the position known as "support," that is to say, vertical in front of the left shoulder, the hammer resting on the forearm thrown straight across the chest—a formal and unnatural position, enforcing an erect carriage of the body. It did not appear to be the duty of these two men to know what was occurring at the centre of the bridge; they merely blockaded the two ends of the foot plank which traversed it.

Beyond one of the sentinels nobody was in sight; the railroad ran straight away into a forest for a hundred yards, then, curving, was lost to view. Doubtless there was an outpost further along. The other bank of the stream was open ground—a gentle acclivity crowned with a stockade of vertical tree trunks, loopholed for rifles, with a single embrasure through which protruded the muzzle of a brass cannon commanding the bridge. Midway of the slope between bridge and fort were the spectators—a single company of infantry in line, at "parade rest," the butts of the rifles on the ground, the barrels inclining slightly backward against the right shoulder, the hands crossed upon the stock. A lieutenant stood at the right of the line, the point of his sword upon the ground, his left hand resting upon his right. Excepting the group of four at the centre of the bridge not a man moved. The company faced the bridge, staring stonily, motionless. The sentinels, facing the banks of the stream, might have been statues to adorn the bridge. The captain stood with folded arms, silent, observing the work of his subordinates but making no sign. Death is a dignitary who, when he comes announced, is to be received with formal manifestations of respect, even by those most familiar with him. In the code of military etiquette silence and fixity are forms of deference.

The man who was engaged in being hanged was apparently about thirty-five years of age. He was a civilian, if one might judge from his dress, which was that of a planter. His features were good—a straight nose, firm mouth, broad forehead, from which his long, dark hair was combed straight back, falling behind his ears to the collar of his well-fitting frock coat. He wore a moustache and pointed beard, but no whiskers; his eyes were large and dark grey and had a kindly expression which one would hardly have expected in one whose neck was in the hemp. Evidently this was no vulgar assassin. The liberal military code makes provision for hanging many kinds of people, and gentlemen are not excluded.

The preparations being complete, the two private soldiers stepped aside and each drew away the plank upon which he had been standing. The sergeant turned to the captain, saluted and placed himself immediately behind that officer, who in turn moved apart one pace. These movements left the condemned man and the sergeant standing on the two ends of the same plank, which spanned three of the cross-ties of the bridge. The end upon which the civilian stood almost, but not quite, reached a fourth. This plank had been held in place by the weight of the captain; it was now held by that of the sergeant. At a signal from the former, the latter would step aside, the plank would tilt and the condemned man go down between two ties. The arrangement commended itself to his judgment as simple and effective. His face had not been covered nor his eyes bandaged. He looked a moment at his "unsteadfast footing," then let his gaze wander to the swirling water of the stream racing madly beneath his feet. A piece of dancing driftwood caught his attention and his eyes followed it down the current. How slowly it appeared to move! What a sluggish stream!

He closed his eyes in order to fix his last thoughts upon his wife and children. 5 The water, touched to gold by the early sun, the brooding mists under the banks at some distance down the stream, the fort, the soldiers, the piece of drift—all had distracted him. And now he became conscious of a new disturbance. Striking through the thought of his dear ones was a sound which he could neither ignore nor understand, a sharp, distinct, metallic percussion like the stroke of a blacksmith's hammer upon the anvil; it had the same ringing quality. He wondered what it was, and whether immeasurably distant or near by—it seemed both. Its recurrence was regular, but as slow as the tolling of a death knell. He awaited each stroke with impatience and—he knew not why—apprehension. The intervals of silence grew progressively longer; the delays became maddening. With their greater infrequency the sounds increased in strength and sharpness. They hurt his ear like the thrust of a knife; he feared he would shriek. What he heard was the ticking of his watch.

He unclosed his eyes and saw again the water below him. "If I could free my hands," he thought, "I might throw off the noose and spring into the stream. By diving I could evade the bullets, and, swimming vigorously, reach the bank, take to the woods, and get away home. My home, thank God, is as yet outside their lines; my wife and little ones are still beyond the invader's farthest advance."

As these thoughts, which have here to be set down in words, were flashed into the doomed man's brain rather than evolved from it, the captain nodded to the sergeant. The sergeant stepped aside.

II

Peyton Farquhar was a well-to-do planter, of an old and highly-respected Alabama family. Being a slave owner, and, like other slave owners, a politician, he was naturally an original secessionist and ardently devoted to the Southern cause. Circumstances of an imperious nature which it is unnecessary to relate here, had prevented him from taking service with the gallant army which had fought the disastrous campaigns ending with the fall of Corinth, and he chafed under the inglorious restraint, longing for the release of his energies, the larger life of the soldier, the opportunity for distinction. That opportunity, he felt, would come, as it comes to all in war time. Meanwhile he did what he could. No service was too humble for him to perform in aid of the South, no adventure too perilous for him to undertake if consistent with the character of a civilian who was at heart a soldier, and who in good faith and without too much qualification assented to at least a part of the frankly villainous dictum that all is fair in love and war.

One evening while Farquhar and his wife were sitting on a rustic bench near the entrance to his grounds, a grey-clad soldier rode up to the gate and asked for a drink of water. Mrs. Farquhar was only too happy to serve him with her own white hands. While she was gone to fetch the water, her husband approached the dusty horseman and inquired eagerly for news from the front.

"The Yanks are repairing the railroads," said the man, "and are getting ready   10
for another advance. They have reached the Owl Creek bridge, put it in order, and built a stockade on the other bank. The commandant has issued an order, which is posted everywhere, declaring that any civilian caught interfering with the railroad, its bridges, tunnels, or trains, will be summarily hanged. I saw the order."

"How far is it to the Owl Creek bridge?" Farquhar asked.

"About thirty miles."

"Is there no force on this side the creek?"

"Only a picket post half a mile out, on the railroad, and a single sentinel at this end of the bridge."

"Suppose a man—a civilian and student of hanging—should elude the picket   15
post and perhaps get the better of the sentinel," said Farquhar, smiling, "what could he accomplish?"

The soldier reflected. "I was there a month ago," he replied. "I observed that the flood of last winter had lodged a great quantity of driftwood against the wooden pier at this end of the bridge. It is now dry and would burn like tow."

The lady had now brought the water, which the soldier drank. He thanked her ceremoniously, bowed to her husband, and rode away. An hour later, after nightfall, he repassed the plantation, going northward in the direction from which he had come. He was a Federal scout.

III

As Peyton Farquhar fell straight downward through the bridge, he lost consciousness and was as one already dead. From this state he was awakened—ages later, it seemed to him—by the pain of a sharp pressure upon his throat, followed by a sense of suffocation. Keen, poignant agonies seemed to shoot from his neck downward through every fibre of his body and limbs. These pains appeared to flash along well-defined lines of ramification, and to beat with a inconceivably rapid periodicity. They seemed like streams of pulsating fire heating him to an intolerable temperature. As to his head, he was conscious of nothing but a feeling of fullness—of congestion. These sensations were unaccompanied by thought. The intellectual part of his nature was already effaced; he had power only to feel, and feeling was torment. He was conscious of motion. Encompassed in a luminous cloud, of which he was now merely the fiery heart, without material substance, he swung through unthinkable arcs of oscillation, like a vast pendulum. Then all at once, with terrible suddenness, the light about him shot upward with the noise of a loud plash; a frightful roaring was in his ears, and all was cold and dark. The power of thought was restored; he knew that the rope had broken and he had fallen into the stream. There was no additional strangulation; the noose about his neck was already suffocating him, and kept the water from his lungs. To die of hanging at the bottom of a river!—the idea seemed to him ludicrous. He opened his eyes in the blackness and saw above him a gleam of light, but how distant, how inaccessible! He was still sinking, for the light became fainter and fainter until it was a mere glimmer. Then it began to grow and brighten, and he knew that he was rising toward the surface—knew it with reluctance, for he was now very comfortable. "To be hanged and drowned," he thought, "that is not so bad; but I do not wish to be shot. No; I will not be shot; that is not fair."

He was not conscious of an effort, but a sharp pain in his wrist apprised him that he was trying to free his hands. He gave the struggle his attention, as an idler might observe the feat of a juggler, without interest in the outcome. What splendid effort!— what magnificent, what superhuman strength! Ah, that was a fine endeavor! Bravo! The cord fell away; his arms parted and floated upward, the hands dimly seen on each side in the growing light. He watched them with a new interest as first one and then the other pounced upon the noose at his neck. They tore it away and thrust it fiercely aside, its undulations resembling those of a water-snake. "Put it back, put it back!" He thought he shouted these words to his hands, for the undoing of the noose had been succeeded by the direst pang which he had yet experienced. His neck ached horribly; his brain was on fire; his heart, which had been fluttering faintly, gave a great leap, trying to force itself out at his mouth. His whole body was racked and wrenched with an insupportable anguish! But his disobedient hands gave no heed to the command. They beat the water vigorously with quick, downward strokes, forcing him to the surface. He felt his head emerge; his eyes were blinded by the sunlight; his chest expanded convulsively, and with a supreme and crowning agony his lungs engulfed a great draught of air, which instantly he expelled in a shriek!

He was now in full possession of his physical senses. They were, indeed, preternaturally keen and alert. Something in the awful disturbance of his organic system had so exalted and refined them that they made record of things never before perceived. He felt the ripples upon his face and heard their separate sounds as they struck. He looked at the forest on the bank of the stream, saw the individual trees, the leaves and the veining of each leaf—saw the very insects upon them, the locusts, the brilliant-bodied flies, the grey spiders stretching their webs from twig to twig. He noted the prismatic colors in all the dewdrops upon a million blades of grass. The humming of the gnats that danced above the eddies of the stream, the beating of the dragon flies' wings, the strokes of the water spiders' legs, like oars which had lifted their boat—all these made audible music. A fish slid along beneath his eyes and he heard the rush of its body parting the water.

He had come to the surface facing down the stream; in a moment the visible world seemed to wheel slowly round, himself the pivotal point, and he saw the bridge, the fort, the soldiers upon the bridge, the captain, the sergeant, the two privates, his executioners. They were in silhouette against the blue sky. They shouted and gesticulated, pointing at him; the captain had drawn his pistol, but did not fire; the others were unarmed. Their movements were grotesque and horrible, their forms gigantic.

Suddenly he heard a sharp report and something struck the water smartly within a few inches of his head, spattering his face with spray. He heard a second report, and saw one of the sentinels with his rifle at his shoulder, a light cloud of blue smoke rising from the muzzle. The man in the water saw the eye of the man on the bridge gazing into his own through the sights of the rife. He observed that it was a grey eye, and remembered having read that grey eyes were keenest and that all famous marksmen had them. Nevertheless, this one had missed.

A counter swirl had caught Farquhar and turned him half round; he was again looking into the forest on the bank opposite the fort. The sound of a clear, high voice in a monotonous singsong now rang out behind him and came across the water with a distinctness that pierced and subdued all other sounds, even the beating of the ripples in his ears. Although no soldier, he had frequented camps enough to know the dread significance of that deliberate, drawling, aspirated chant; the lieutenant on shore was taking a part in the morning's work. How coldly and pitilessly—with what an even, calm intonation, presaging and enforcing tranquillity in the men—with what accurately-measured intervals fell those cruel words:

"Attention, company.... Shoulder arms.... Ready.... Aim.... Fire."

Farquhar dived—dived as deeply as he could. The water roared in his ears   25
like the voice of Niagara, yet he heard the dulled thunder of the volley, and rising again toward the surface, met shining bits of metal, singularly flattened, oscillating slowly downward. Some of them touched him on the face and hands, then fell away, continuing their descent. One lodged between his collar and neck; it was uncomfortably warm, and he snatched it out.

As he rose to the surface, gasping for breath, he saw that he had been a long time under water; he was perceptibly farther down stream—nearer to safety. The soldiers had almost finished reloading; the metal ramrods flashed all at once in the sunshine as they were drawn from the barrels, turned in the air, and thrust into their sockets. The two sentinels fired again, independently and ineffectually.

The hunted man saw all this over his shoulder; he was now swimming vigorously with the current. His brain was as energetic as his arms and legs; he thought with the rapidity of lightning.

"The officer," he reasoned, "will not make that martinet's error a second time. It is as easy to dodge a volley as a single shot. He has probably already given the command to fire at will. God help me, I cannot dodge them all!"

An appalling plash within two yards of him, followed by a loud rushing sound, *diminuendo,* which seemed to travel back through the air to the fort and died in an explosion which stirred the very river to its deeps! A rising sheet of water, which curved over him, fell down upon him, blinded him, strangled him! The cannon had taken a hand in the game. As he shook his head free from the commotion of the smitten water, he heard the deflected shot humming through the air ahead, and in an instant it was cracking and smashing the branches in the forest beyond.

"They will not do that again," he thought; "the next time they will use a charge   30
of grape. I must keep my eye upon the gun; the smoke will apprise me—the report arrives too late; it lags behind the missile. It is a good gun."

Suddenly he felt himself whirled round and round—spinning like a top. The water, the banks, the forest, the now distant bridge, fort and men—all were commingled and blurred. Objects were represented by their colors only, circular horizontal streaks of color—that was all he saw. He had been caught in a vortex and was being whirled on with a velocity of advance and gyration which made him giddy and sick. In a few moments he was flung upon the gravel at the foot of the left bank of the stream—the southern bank—and behind a projecting point which concealed him from his enemies. The sudden arrest of his motion, the abrasion of one of his hands on the gravel, restored him and he wept with delight. He dug his fingers into the sand, threw it over himself in handfuls and audibly blessed it. It looked like gold, like diamonds, rubies, emeralds; he could think of nothing beautiful which it did not resemble. The trees upon the bank were giant garden plants; he noted a definite order in their arrangement, inhaled the fragrance of their blooms. A strange, roseate light shone through the spaces among their trucks, and the wind made in their branches the music of aeolian harps. He had no wish to perfect his escape, was content to remain in that enchanting spot until retaken.

A whizz and rattle of grapeshot among the branches high above his head roused him from his dream. The baffled cannoneer had fired him a random farewell. He sprang to his feet, rushed up the sloping bank, and plunged into the forest.

All that day he travelled, laying his course by the rounding sun. The forest seemed interminable; nowhere did he discover a break in it, not even a woodman's road. He had not known that he lived in so wild a region. There was something uncanny in the revelation.

By nightfall he was fatigued, footsore, famishing. The thought of his wife and children urged him on. At last he found a road which led him in what he knew to be the right direction. It was as wide and straight as a city street, yet it seemed untravelled. No fields bordered it, no dwelling anywhere. Not so much as the barking of a dog suggested human habitation. The black bodies of the great trees formed a straight wall on both sides, terminating on the horizon in a point, like a diagram in a lesson in perspective. Overhead, as he looked up through this rift in the wood, shone great golden stars looking unfamiliar and grouped in strange constellations. He was sure they were arranged in some order which had a secret and malign significance. The wood on either side was full of singular noises, among which—once, twice, and again—he distinctly heard whispers in an unknown tongue.

His neck was in pain, and, lifting his hand to it, he found it horribly swollen. He knew that it had a circle of black where the rope had bruised it. His eyes felt congested; he could no longer close them. His tongue was swollen with thirst; he relieved its fever by thrusting it forward from between his teeth into the cool air. How softly the turf had carpeted the untravelled avenue! He could no longer feel the roadway beneath his feet!

Doubtless, despite his suffering, he fell asleep while walking, for now he sees another scene—perhaps he has merely recovered from a delirium. He stands at the gate of his own home. All is as he left it, and all bright and beautiful in the morning sunshine. He must have travelled the entire night. As he pushes open the gate and passes up the wide white walk, he sees a flutter of female garments; his wife, looking fresh and cool and sweet, steps down from the verandah to meet him. At the bottom of the steps she stands waiting, with a smile of ineffable joy, an attitude of matchless grace and dignity. Ah, how beautiful she is! He springs forward with extended arms. As he is about to clasp her, he feels a stunning blow upon the back of the neck; a blinding white light blazes all about him, with a sound like the shock of a cannon—then all is darkness and silence!

Peyton Farquhar was dead; his body, with a broken neck, swung gently from side to side beneath the timbers of the Owl Creek bridge.

35

Angela Carter   1940–1986

The Snow Child   1979

Midwinter—invincible, immaculate. The Count and his wife go riding, he on a grey mare and she on a black one, she wrapped in the glittering pelts of black foxes; and she wore high, black, shining boots with scarlet heels, and spurs. Fresh snow fell on snow already fallen; when it ceased, the whole world was white. "I wish I had a girl as white as snow," says the Count. They ride on. They come to a hole in the snow; this hole is filled with blood. He says: "I wish I had a girl as red as blood." So they ride on again; here is a raven, perched on a bare bough. "I wish I had a girl as black as that bird's feather."

As soon as he completed her description, there she stood, beside the road, white skin, red mouth, black hair and stark naked; she was the child of his desire and the Countess hated her. The Count lifted her up and sat her in front of him on his saddle but the Countess had only one thought: how shall I be rid of her?

The Countess dropped her glove in the snow and told the girl to get down to look for it; she meant to gallop off and leave her there but the Count said: "I'll buy you new gloves." At that, the furs sprang off the Countess's shoulders and twined round the naked girl. Then the Countess threw her diamond brooch through the ice of a frozen pond: "Dive in and fetch it for me," she said; she thought the girl would drown. But the Count said: "Is she a fish, to swim in such cold weather?" Then her boots leapt off the Countess's feet and on to the girl's legs. Now the Countess was bare as a bone and the girl furred and booted; the Count felt sorry for his wife. They came to a bush of roses, all in flower. "Pick me one," said the Countess to the girl. "I can't deny you that," said the Count.

So the girl picks a rose; pricks her finger on the thorn; bleeds; screams; falls.

Weeping, the Count got off his horse, unfastened his breeches and thrust his virile member into the dead girl. The Countess reined in her stamping mare and watched him narrowly; he was soon finished.   5

Then the girl began to melt. Soon there was nothing left of her but a feather a bird might have dropped; a bloodstain, like the trace of a fox's kill on the snow; and the rose she had pulled off the bush. Now the Countess had all her clothes on again. With her long hand, she stroked her furs. The Count picked up the rose, bowed and handed it to his wife; when she touched it, she dropped it.

"It bites!" she said.

John Cheever   1912–1982

The Swimmer   1964

It was one of those midsummer Sundays when everyone sits around saying, "I *drank* too much last night." You might have heard it whispered by the parishioners leaving church, heard it from the lips of the priest himself, struggling with his cassock in the *vestiarium,* heard it from the golf links and the tennis courts, heard it from the wildlife preserve where the leader of the Audubon group was suffering from a terrible hangover. "I *drank* too much," said Donald Westerhazy. "We all *drank* too much," said Lucinda Merrill. "It must have been the wine," said Helen Westerhazy. "I *drank* too much of that claret."

This was at the edge of the Westerhazys' pool. The pool, fed by an artesian well with a high iron content, was a pale shade of green. It was a fine day. In the west there was a massive stand of cumulus clouds so like a city seen from a distance—from the bow of an approaching ship—that it might have had a name. Lisbon. Hackensack. The sun was hot. Neddy Merrill sat by the green water, one hand in it, one around a glass of gin. He was a slender man—he seemed to have the especial slenderness of youth—and while he was far from young he had slid down his banister that morning and given the bronze backside of Aphrodite on the hall table a smack, as he jogged toward the smell of coffee in his dining room. He might have been compared to a summer's day, particularly the last hours of one, and while he lacked a tennis racket or a sail bag the impression was definitely one of youth, sport, and clement weather. He had been swimming and now he was breathing deeply, stertorously as if he could gulp into his lungs the components of that moment, the heat of the sun, the intenseness of his pleasure. It all seemed to flow into his chest. His own house stood in Bullet Park, eight miles to the south, where his four beautiful daughters would have had their lunch and might be playing tennis. Then it occurred to him that by taking a dogleg to the southwest he could reach his home by water.

His life was not confining and the delight he took in this observation could not be explained by its suggestion of escape. He seemed to see, with a cartographer's eye, that string of swimming pools, that quasi-subterranean stream that curved across the county. He had made a discovery, a contribution to modern geography; he would name the stream Lucinda after his wife. He was not a practical joker nor was he a fool but he was determinedly original and had a vague and modest idea of himself as a legendary figure. The day was beautiful and it seemed to him that a long swim might enlarge and celebrate its beauty.

He took off a sweater that was hung over his shoulders and dove in. He had an inexplicable contempt for men who did not hurl themselves into pools. He swam a choppy crawl, breathing either with every stroke or every fourth stroke and counting somewhere well in the back of his mind the one-two one-two of a flutter kick. It was not a serviceable stoke for long distances but the domestication of swimming had saddled the sport with some customs and in his part of the world a crawl was customary. To be embraced and sustained by the light green water was less a pleasure, it seemed, than the resumption of a natural condition, and he would have liked to swim without trunks, but this was not possible, considering his project. He hoisted himself up on the far curb—he never used the ladder—and started across the lawn. When Lucinda asked where he was going he said he was going to swim home.

The only maps and charts he had to go by were remembered or imaginary but these were clear enough. First there were the Grahams, the Hammers, the Lears, the Howlands, and the Crosscups. He would cross Ditmar Street to the Bunkers and come, after a short portage, to the Levys, the Welchers, and the public pool in Lancaster. Then there were the Hallorans, the Sachses, the Biswangers, Shirley Adams, the Gilmartins, and the Clydes. The day was lovely, and that he lived in a world so generously supplied with water seemed like a clemency, a beneficence. His heart was high and he ran across the grass. Making his way home by an uncommon route gave him the feeling that he was a pilgrim, an explorer, a man with a destiny, and he knew that he would find friends all along the way; friends would line the banks of the Lucinda River.

He went through a hedge that separated the Westerhazy's land from the Grahams', walked under some flowering apple trees, passed the shed that housed their pump and filter, and came out at the Grahams' pool. "Why, Neddy," Mrs. Graham said, "what a marvelous surprise. I've been trying to get you on the phone all morning. Here, let me get you a drink." He saw then, like any explorer, that the hospitable customs and traditions of the natives would have to be handled with diplomacy if he was ever going to reach his destination. He did not want to mystify or seem rude to the Grahams nor did he have the time to linger there. He swam the length of their pool and joined them in the sun and was rescued, a few minutes later, by the arrival of two carloads of friends from Connecticut. During the uproarious reunions he was able to slip away. He went down by the front of the Grahams' house, stepped over a thorny hedge, and crossed a vacant lot to the Hammers'. Mrs. Hammer, looking up from her roses, saw him swim by although she wasn't quite sure who it was. The Lears heard him splashing past the open windows of their living room. The Howlands and the Crosscups were away. After leaving the Howlands' he crossed Ditmar Street and started for the Bunkers', where he could hear, even at that distance, the noise of a party.

The water refracted the sound of voices and laughter and seemed to suspend it in midair. The Bunkers' pool was on a rise and he climbed some stairs to a terrace where twenty-five or thirty men and women were drinking. The only person in the water was Rusty Towers, who floated there on a rubber raft. Oh, how bonny and lush were the banks of the Lucinda River! Prosperous men and women gathered by the sapphire-colored water while caterer's men in white coats passed them cold gin. Overhead a red de Haviland trainer was circling around and around and around in the sky with something like the glee of a child in a swing. Ned felt a passing affection for the scene, a tenderness for the gathering, as if it was something he might touch. In the distance he heard thunder. As soon as Enid Bunker saw him she began to scream: "Oh, look who's here! What a marvelous surprise! When Lucinda said that you couldn't come I thought I'd *die*." She made her way to him through the crowd, and when they had finished kissing she led him to the bar, a progress that was slowed by the fact that he stopped to kiss eight or ten other women and shake the hands of as many men. A smiling bartender he had seen at a hundred parties gave him a gin and tonic and he stood by the bar for a moment, anxious not to get stuck in any conversation that would delay his voyage. When he seemed about to be surrounded he dove in and swam close to the side to avoid colliding with Rusty's raft. At the far end of the pool he bypassed the Tomlinsons with a broad smile and jogged up the garden path. The gravel cut his feet but this was the only unpleasantness. The party was confined to the pool, and as he went toward the house he heard the brilliant, watery sound of voices fade, heard the noise of a radio from the Bunkers' kitchen, where someone was listening to a ball game. Sunday afternoon. He made his way through the parked cars and down the grassy border of their driveway to Alewives Lane. He did not want to be seen on the road in his bathing trunks but there was no traffic and he made the short distance to the Levys' driveway, marked with a PRIVATE PROPERTY sign and a green tube for *The New York Times*. All the doors and windows of the big house were open but there were no signs of life; not even a dog barked. He went around the side of the house to the pool and saw that the Levys had only recently left. Glasses and bottles and dishes of nuts were on a table at the deep end, where there was a bathhouse or gazebo, hung with Japanese lanterns. After swimming the pool he got himself a glass and poured a drink. It was his fourth or fifth drink and he had swum nearly half the length of the Lucinda River. He felt tired, clean, and pleased at that moment to be alone; pleased with everything.

It would storm. The stand of cumulus cloud—that city—had risen and darkened, and while he sat there he heard the percussiveness of thunder again. The de Haviland trainer was still circling overhead and it seemed to Ned that he could almost hear the pilot laugh with pleasure in the afternoon; but when there was another peal of thunder he took off for home. A train whistle blew and he wondered what time it had gotten to be. Four? Five? He thought of the provincial station at that hour, where a waiter, his tuxedo concealed by a raincoat, a dwarf with some flowers wrapped in newspaper, and a woman who had been crying would be waiting for the local. It was suddenly growing dark; it was that moment when the pinheaded birds seem to organize their song into some acute and knowledgeable recognition of the storm's approach. Then there was a fine noise of rushing water from the crown of an oak at his back, as if a spigot there had been turned. Then the noise of fountains came from the crowns of all the tall trees. Why did he love storms, what was the meaning of his excitement when the door sprang open and the rain wind fled rudely up the stairs, why had the simple task of shutting the windows of an old house seemed fitting and urgent, why did the first watery notes of a storm wind have for him the unmistakable sound of good news, cheer, glad tidings? Then there was an explosion, a smell of cordite, and rain lashed the Japanese lanterns that Mrs. Levy had bought in Kyoto the year before last, or was it the year before that?

He stayed in the Levys' gazebo until the storm had passed. The rain had cooled the air and he shivered. The force of the wind had stripped a maple of its red and yellow leaves and scattered them over the grass and the water. Since it was midsummer the trees must be blighted, and yet he felt a peculiar sadness at this sign of autumn. He braced his shoulders, emptied his glass, and started for the Welchers' pool. This meant crossing the Lindleys' riding ring and he was surprised to find it overgrown with grass and all the jumps dismantled. He wondered if the Lindleys had sold their horses or gone away for the summer and put them out to board. He seemed to remember having heard something about the Lindleys and their horses but the memory was unclear. On he went, barefoot through the wet grass, to the Welchers', where he found their pool was dry.

This breach in his chain of water disappointed him absurdly, and he felt like some explorer who seeks a torrential headwater and finds a dead stream. He was disappointed and mystified. It was common enough to go away for the summer but no one ever drained his pool. The Welchers had definitely gone away. The pool furniture was folded, stacked, and covered with a tarpaulin. The bathhouse was locked. All the windows of the house were shut, and when he went around to the driveway in front he saw a FOR SALE sign nailed to a tree. When had he last heard from the Welchers—when, that is, had he and Lucinda last regretted an invitation to dine with them? It seemed only a week or so ago. Was his memory failing or had he so disciplined it in the repression of unpleasant facts that he had damaged his sense of the truth? Then in the distance he heard the sound of a tennis game. This cheered him, cleared away all his apprehensions and let him regard the overcast sky and the cold air with indifference. This was the day that Neddy Merrill swam across the county. That was the day! He started off then for his most difficult portage. 10

Had you gone for a Sunday afternoon ride that day you might have seen him, close to naked, standing on the shoulders of Route 424, waiting for a chance to cross. You might have wondered if he was the victim of foul play, had his car broken down, or was he merely a fool. Standing barefoot in the deposits of the highway—beer cans, rags, and blowout patches—exposed to all kinds of ridicule, he seemed pitiful. He had known when he started that this was a part of his journey—it had been on his maps—but confronted with the lines of traffic, worming through the summery light, he found himself unprepared. He was laughed at, jeered at, a beer can was thrown at him, and he had no dignity or humor to bring to the situation. He could have gone back, back to the Westerhazys', where Lucinda would still be sitting in the sun. He had signed nothing, vowed nothing, pledged nothing, not even to himself. Why, believing as he did, that all human obduracy was susceptible to common sense, was he unable to turn back? Why was he determined to complete his journey even if it meant putting his life in danger? At what point had this prank, this joke, this piece of horseplay become serious? He could not go back, he could not even recall with any clearness the green water at the Westerhazys', the sense of inhaling the day's components, the friendly and relaxed voices saying that they had *drunk* too much. In the space of an hour, more or less, he had covered a distance that made his return impossible.

An old man, tooling down the highway at fifteen miles an hour, let him get to the middle of the road, where there was a grass divider. Here he was exposed to the ridicule of the northbound traffic, but after ten or fifteen minutes he was able to cross. From here he had only a short walk to the Recreation Center at the edge of the village of Lancaster, where there were some handball courts and a public pool.

The effect of the water on voices, the illusion of brilliance and suspense, was the same here as it had been at the Bunkers' but the sounds here were louder, harsher, and more shrill, and as soon as he entered the crowded enclosure he was confronted with regimentation. "ALL SWIMMERS MUST TAKE A SHOWER BEFORE USING THE POOL. ALL SWIMMERS MUST USE THE FOOTBATH. ALL SWIMMERS MUST WEAR THEIR IDENTIFICATION DISKS." He took a shower, washed his feet in a cloudy and bitter solution, and made his way to the edge of the water. It stank of chlorine and looked to him like a sink. A pair of lifeguards in a pair of towers blew police whistles at what seemed to be regular intervals and abused the swimmers through a public address system. Neddy remembered the sapphire water at the Bunkers' with longing and thought that he might contaminate himself—damage his own prosperousness and charm—by swimming in this murk, but he reminded himself that he was an explorer, a pilgrim, and that this was merely a stagnant bend in the Lucinda River. He dove, scowling with distaste, into the chlorine and had to swim with his head above water to avoid collisions, but even so he was bumped into, splashed, and jostled. When he got to the shallow end both lifeguards were shouting at him: "Hey you, you without the identification disk, get outa the water." He did, but they had no way of pursuing him and he went through the reek of suntan oil and chlorine out through the hurricane fence and passed the handball courts. By crossing the road he entered the wooded part of the Halloran estate. The woods were not cleared and the footing was treacherous and difficult until he reached the lawn and the clipped beech hedge that encircled their pool.

The Hallorans were friends, an elderly couple of enormous wealth who seemed to bask in the suspicion that they might be Communists. They were zealous reformers but they were not Communists, and yet when they were accused, as they sometimes were, of subversion, it seemed to gratify and excite them. Their beech hedge was yellow and he guessed this had been blighted like the Levys' maple. He called hullo, hullo, to warn the Hallorans of his approach, to palliate his invasion of their privacy. The Hallorans, for reasons that had never been explained to him, did not wear bathing suits. No explanations were in order, really. Their nakedness was a detail in the uncompromising zeal for reform and he stepped politely out of his trunks before he went through the opening in the hedge.

Mrs. Halloran, a stout woman with white hair and a serene face, was reading the *Times*. Mr. Halloran was taking beech leaves out of the water with a scoop. They seemed not surprised or displeased to see him. Their pool was perhaps the oldest in the county, a fieldstone rectangle, fed by a brook. It had no filter or pump and its waters were the opaque gold of the stream.

"I'm swimming across the county," Ned said.

"Why, I didn't know one could," exclaimed Mrs. Halloran.

"Well, I've made it from the Westerhazys'," Ned said. "That must be about four miles."

He left his trunks at the deep end, walked to the shallow end, and swam this stretch. As he was pulling himself out of the water he heard Mrs. Halloran say, "We've been *terribly* sorry to hear about all your misfortunes, Neddy."

"My misfortunes?" Ned asked. "I don't know what you mean."

"Why, we heard that you'd sold the house and that your poor children ..."

"I don't recall having sold the house," Ned said, "and the girls are at home."

"Yes," Mrs. Halloran sighed. "Yes ..." Her voice filled the air with an unseasonable melancholy and Ned spoke briskly. "Thank you for the swim."

"Well, have a nice trip," said Mrs. Halloran.

Beyond the hedge he pulled on his trunks and fastened them. They were loose and he wondered if, during the space of an afternoon, he could have lost some weight. He was cold and he was tired and the naked Hallorans and their dark water had depressed him. The swim was too much for his strength but how could he have guessed this, sliding down the banister that morning and sitting in the Westerhazys' sun? His arms were lame. His legs felt rubbery and ached at the joints. The worst of it was the cold in his bones and the feeling that he might never be warm again. Leaves were falling down around him and he smelled wood smoke on the wind. Who would be burning wood at this time of year?

He needed a drink. Whiskey would warm him, pick him up, carry him through the last of his journey, refresh his feeling that it was original and valorous to swim across the county. Channel swimmers took brandy. He needed a stimulant. He crossed the lawn in front of the Hallorans' house and went down a little path to where they had built a house for their only daughter, Helen, and her husband, Eric Sachs. The Sachses' pool was small and he found Helen and her husband there.

"Oh, *Neddy*," Helen said. "Did you lunch at Mother's?"

"Not *really*," Ned said. "I *did* stop to see your parents." This seemed to be explanation enough. "I'm terribly sorry to break in on you like this but I've taken a chill and I wonder if you'd give me a drink."

"Why, I'd *love* to," Helen said, "but there hasn't been anything in this house to drink since Eric's operation. That was three years ago."

Was he losing his memory, had his gift for concealing painful facts let him forget that he had sold his house, that his children were in trouble, and that his friend had been ill? His eyes slipped from Eric's face to his abdomen, where he saw three pale, sutured scars, two of them at least a foot long. Gone was his navel, and what, Neddy thought, would the roving hand, bed-checking one's gifts at 3 A.M., make of a belly with no navel, no link to birth, this breach in the succession?

"I'm sure you can get a drink at the Biswangers'," Helen said. "They're having an enormous do. You can hear it from here. Listen!"

She raised her head and from across the road, the lawns, the gardens, the woods, the fields, he heard again the brilliant noise of voices over water. "Well, I'll get wet," he said, still feeling that he had no freedom of choice about his means of travel. He dove into the Sachses' cold water and, gasping, close to drowning, made his way from one end of the pool to the other. "Lucinda and I want *terribly* to see you," he said over his shoulder, his face set toward the Biswangers'. "We're sorry it's been so long and we'll call you *very* soon."

He crossed some fields to the Biswangers' and the sounds of revelry there. They would be honored to give him a drink, they would be happy to give him a drink. The Biswangers invited him and Lucinda for dinner four times a year, six weeks in advance. They were always rebuffed and yet they continued to send out their invitations, unwilling to comprehend the rigid and undemocratic realities of their society. They were the sort of people who discussed the price of things at cocktails, exchanged market tips during dinner, and after dinner told dirty stories to mixed company. They did not belong to Neddy's set—they were not even on Lucinda's Christmas card list. He went toward their pool with feelings of indifference, charity, and some unease, since it seemed to be getting dark and these were the longest days of the year. The party when he joined it was noisy and large. Grace Biswanger was the kind of hostess who asked the optometrist, the veterinarian, the real-estate dealer, and the dentist. No one was swimming and the twilight, reflected on the water of the pool, had a wintry gleam. There was a bar and he started for this. When Grace Biswanger saw him she came toward him, not affectionately as he had every right to expect, but bellicosely.

"Why, this party has everything," she said loudly, "including a gate crasher."

She could not deal him a social blow—there was no question about this and he did not flinch. "As a gate crasher," he asked politely, "do I rate a drink?" 35

"Suit yourself," she said. "You don't seem to pay much attention to invitations."

She turned her back on him and joined some guests, and he went to the bar and ordered a whiskey. The bartender served him but he served him rudely. His was a world in which the caterer's men kept the social score, and to be rebuffed by a part-time barkeep meant that he had suffered some loss of social esteem. Or perhaps the man was new and uninformed. Then he heard Grace at his back say: "They went for broke overnight—nothing but income—and he showed up drunk one Sunday and asked us to loan him five thousand dollars...." She was always talking about money. It was worse than eating your peas off a knife. He dove into the pool, swam its length and went away.

The next pool on his list, the last but two, belonged to his old mistress, Shirley Adams. If he had suffered any injuries at the Biswangers' they would be cured here. Love—sexual roughhouse in fact—was the supreme elixir, the pain killer, the brightly colored pill that would put the spring back into his step, the joy of life in his heart. They had had an affair last week, last month, last year. He couldn't remember. It was he who had broken it off, his was the upper hand, and he stepped through the gate of the wall that surrounded her pool with nothing so considered as self-confidence. It seemed in a way to be his pool, as the lover, particularly the illicit lover, enjoys the possessions of his mistress with an authority unknown to holy matrimony. She was there, her hair the color of brass, but her figure, at the edge of the lighted, cerulean water, excited in him no profound memories. It had been, he thought, a lighthearted affair, although she had wept when he broke it off. She seemed confused to see him and he wondered if she was still wounded. Would she, God forbid, weep again?

"What do you want?" she asked.

"I'm swimming across the county."   40

"Good Christ. Will you ever grow up?"

"What's the matter?"

"If you've come here for money," she said, "I won't give you another cent."

"You could give me a drink."

"I could but I won't. I'm not alone."   45

"Well, I'm on my way."

He dove in and swam the pool, but when he tried to haul himself up onto the curb he found that the strength in his arms and shoulders had gone, and he paddled to the ladder and climbed out. Looking over his shoulder he saw, in the lighted bathhouse, a young man. Going out onto the dark lawn he smelled chrysanthemums or marigolds—some stubborn autumnal fragrance—on the night air, strong as gas. Looking overhead he saw that the stars had come out, but why should he seem to see Andromeda, Cepheus, and Cassiopeia? What had become of the constellations of midsummer? He began to cry.

It was probably the first time in his adult life that he had ever cried, certainly the first time in his life that he had ever felt so miserable, cold, tired, and bewildered. He could not understand the rudeness of the caterer's barkeep or the rudeness of a mistress who had come to him on her knees and showered his trousers with tears. He had swum too long, he had been immersed too long, and his nose and his throat were sore from the water. What he needed then was a drink, some company, and some clean, dry clothes, and while he could have cut directly across the road to his home he went on to the Gilmartins' pool. Here, for the first time in his life, he did not dive but went down the steps into the icy water and swam a hobbled sidestroke that he might have learned as a youth. He staggered with fatigue on his way to the Clydes' and paddled the length of their pool, stopping again and again with his hand on the curb to rest. He climbed up the ladder and wondered if he had the strength to get home. He had done what he wanted, he had swum the county, but he was so stupefied with exhaustion that his triumph seemed vague. Stooped, holding on to the gateposts for support, he turned up the driveway of his own house.

The place was dark. Was it so late that they had all gone to bed? Had Lucinda stayed at the Westerhazys' for supper? Had the girls joined her there or gone someplace else? Hadn't they agreed, as they usually did on Sunday, to regret all their invitations and stay at home? He tried the garage doors to see what cars were in but the doors were locked and rust came off the handles onto his hands. Going toward the house, he saw that the force of the thunderstorm had knocked one of the rain gutters loose. It hung down over the front door like an umbrella rib, but it could be fixed in the morning. The house was locked, and he thought that the stupid cook or the stupid maid must have locked the place up until he remembered that it had been some time since they had employed a maid or a cook. He shouted, pounded on the door, tried to force it with his shoulder, and then, looking in at the windows, saw the place was empty.

Kate Chopin   1851–1904

The Storm   c. 1899

1

The leaves were so still that even Bibi thought it was going to rain. Bobinôt, who was accustomed to converse on terms of perfect equality with his little son, called the child's attention to certain sombre clouds that were rolling with sinister intention from the west, accompanied by a sullen, threatening roar. They were at Friedheimer's store and decided to remain there till the storm had passed. They sat within the door on two empty kegs. Bibi was four years old and looked very wise.

"Mama'll be 'fraid, yes," he suggested with blinking eyes.

"She'll shut the house. Maybe she got Sylvie helpin' her this evenin'," Bobinôt responded reassuringly.

"No, she ent got Sylvie. Sylvie was helpin' her yistiday," piped Bibi.

Bobinôt arose and going across to the counter purchased a can of shrimps, of   5
which Calixta was very fond. Then he returned to his perch on the keg and sat stolidly holding the can of shrimps while the storm burst. It shook the wooden store and seemed to be ripping great furrows in the distant field. Bibi laid his little hand on his father's knee and was not afraid.

2

Calixta, at home, felt no uneasiness for their safety. She sat at a side window sewing furiously on a sewing machine. She was greatly occupied and did not notice the approaching storm. But she felt very warm and often stopped to mop her face on which the perspiration gathered in beads. She unfastened her white sacque at the throat. It began to grow dark, and suddenly realizing the situation she got up hurriedly and went about closing windows and doors.

Out on the small front gallery she had hung Bobinôt's Sunday clothes to air and she hastened out to gather them before the rain fell. As she stepped outside, Alcée Laballière rode in at the gate. She had not seen him very often since her marriage, and never alone. She stood there with Bobinôt's coat in her hands, and the big rain drops began to fall. Alcée rode his horse under the shelter of a side projection where the chickens had huddled and there were plows and a harrow piled up in the corner.

"May I come and wait on your gallery till the storm is over, Calixta?" he asked.

"Come 'long in, M'sieur Alcée."

His voice and her own startled her as if from a trance, and she seized   10
Bobinôt's vest. Alcée, mounting to the porch, grabbed the trousers and snatched Bibi's braided jacket that was about to be carried away by a sudden gust of wind. He expressed an intention to remain outside, but it was soon apparent that he might as well have been out in the open: the water beat in upon the boards in driving sheets, and he went inside, closing the door after him. It was even necessary to put something beneath the door to keep the water out.

"My! what a rain! It's good two years sence it rain' like that," exclaimed Calixta as she rolled up a piece of bagging and Alcée helped her to thrust it beneath the crack.

She was a little fuller of figure than five years before when she married; but she had lost nothing of her vivacity. Her blue eyes still retained their melting quality; and her yellow hair, dishevelled by the wind and rain, kinked more stubbornly than ever about her ears and temples.

The rain beat upon the low, shingled roof with a force and clatter that threatened to break an entrance and deluge them there. They were in the dining room—the sitting room—the general utility room. Adjoining was her bed room, with Bibi's couch along side her own. The door stood open, and the room with its white, monumental bed, its closed shutters, looked dim and mysterious.

Alcée flung himself into a rocker and Calixta nervously began to gather up from the floor the lengths of a cotton sheet which she had been sewing.

"If this keeps up, *Dieu sait*[1] if the levees goin' to stan' it!" she exclaimed.   15

"What have you got to do with the levees?"

"I got enough to do! An' there's Bobinôt with Bibi out in that storm—if he only didn' left Friedheimer's!"

"Let us hope, Calixta, that Bobinôt's got sense enough to come in out of a cyclone."

She went and stood at the window with a greatly disturbed look on her face. She wiped the frame that was clouded with moisture. It was stiflingly hot. Alcée got up and joined her at the window, looking over her shoulder. The rain was coming down in sheets obscuring the view of far-off cabins and enveloping the distant wood in a gray mist. The playing of the lightning was incessant. A bolt stuck a tall chinaberry tree at the edge of the field. It filled all visible space with a blinding glare and the crash seemed to invade the very boards they stood upon.

Calixta put her hands to her eyes, and with a cry, staggered backward. Alcée's   20
arm encircled her, and for an instant he drew her close and spasmodically to him.

"*Bonte!*" she cried, releasing herself from his encircling arm and retreating from the window, "the house'll go next! If I only knew w'ere Bibi was!" She would not compose herself; she would not be seated. Alcée clasped her shoulders and looked into her face. The contact of her warm, palpitating body when he had unthinkingly drawn her into his arms, had aroused all the old-time infatuation and desire for her flesh.

"Calixta," he said, "don't be frightened. Nothing can happen. The house is too low to be stuck, with so many tall trees standing about. There! aren't you going to be quiet? say, aren't you?" He pushed her hair back from her face that was warm and steaming. Her lips were as red and moist as pomegranate seed. Her white neck and a glimpse of her full, firm bosom disturbed him powerfully. As she glanced up at him the fear in her liquid blue eyes had given place to a drowsy gleam that unconsciously betrayed a sensuous desire. He looked down into her eyes and there was nothing for him to do but to gather her lips in a kiss. It reminded him of Assumption.

"Do you remember—in Assumption. Calixta?" he asked in a low voice broken by passion. Oh! she remembered; for in Assumption he had kissed her and kissed and kissed her; until his senses would well nigh fail, and to save her he would resort to a desperate flight. If she was not an immaculate dove in those days, she was still inviolate; a passionate creature whose very defenselessness had made her defense, against which his honor forbade him to prevail. Now—well, now—her lips seemed in a manner free to be tasted, as well as her round, white throat and her whiter breasts.

---

[1] *Dieu sait*—French: Gods knows.

They did not heed the crashing torrents, and the roar of the elements made her laugh as she lay in his arms. She was a revelation in that dim, mysterious chamber; as white as the couch she lay upon. Her firm, elastic flesh that was knowing for the first time its birthright, was like a creamy lily that the sun invites to contribute its breath and perfume to the undying life of the world.

The generous abundance of her passion, without guile or trickery, was like a   25
white flame which penetrated and found response in depths of his own sensuous nature that had never yet been reached.

When he touched her breasts they gave themselves up in quivering ecstasy, inviting his lips. Her mouth was a fountain of delight. And when he possessed her, they seemed to swoon together at the very borderland of life's mystery.

He stayed cushioned upon her, breathless, dazed, enervated, with his heart beating like a hammer upon her. With one hand she clasped his head, her lips lightly touching his forehead. The other hand stroked with a soothing rhythm his muscular shoulders.

The growl of the thunder was distant and passing away. The rain beat softly upon the shingles, inviting them to drowsiness and sleep. But they dared not yield.

The rain was over; and the sun was turning the glistening green world into a palace of gems. Calixta, on the gallery, watched Alcée ride away. He turned and smiled at her with a beaming face; and she lifted her pretty chin in the air and laughed aloud.

3

Bobinôt and Bibi, trudging home, stopped without at the cistern to make them-   30
selves presentable.

"My! Bibi, w'at will yo' mama say! You ought to be ashame'. You oughtn' put on those good pants. Look at 'em! An' that mud on yo' collar! How you got that mud on yo' collar, Bibi? I never saw such a boy!" Bibi was the picture of pathetic resignation. Bobinôt was the embodiment of serious solicitude as he strove to remove from his own person and his son's the signs of their tramp over heavy roads and through wet fields. He scraped the mud off Bibi's bare legs and feet with a stick and carefully removed all traces from his heavy brogans. Then, prepared for the worst—the meeting with an over-scrupulous housewife, they entered cautiously at the back door.

Calixta was preparing supper. She had set the table and was dripping coffee at the hearth. She sprang up as they came in.

"Oh, Bobinôt! You back! My! but I was uneasy. W'ere you been during the rain? An' Bibi? he ain't wet? he ain't hurt?" She had clasped Bibi and was kissing him effusively. Bobinôt's explanations and apologies which he had been composing all along the way, died on his lips as Calixta felt him to see if he were dry, and seemed to express nothing but satisfaction at their safe return.

"I brought you some shrimps, Calixta," offered Bobinôt, hauling the can from his ample side pocket and laying it on the table.

"Shrimps! Oh, Bobinôt! you too good fo' anything!" and she gave him a   35
smacking kiss on the cheek that resounded. "*J'vous responds,*[2] we'll have a feas' tonight! umph-umph!"

---

[2]*J'vous responds*—French: I assure you.

Bobinôt and Bibi began to relax and enjoy themselves, and when the three seated themselves at table they laughed much and so loud that anyone might have heard them as far away as Laballière's.

4

Alcée Laballière wrote to his wife, Clarisse, that night. It was a loving letter, full of tender solicitude. He told her not to hurry back, but if she and the babies liked it at Biloxi, to stay a month longer. He was getting on nicely; and though he missed them, he was willing to bear the separation a while longer—realizing that their health and pleasure were the first things to be considered.

5

As for Clarisse, she was charmed upon receiving her husband's letter. She and the babies were doing well. The society was agreeable; many of her old friends and acquaintances were at the bay. And the first free breath since her marriage seemed to restore the pleasant liberty of her maiden days. Devoted as she was to her husband, their intimate conjugal life was something which she was more than willing to forego for a while.

So the storm passed and everyone was happy.

Kate Chopin   1851–1904

The Story of an Hour   1891

Knowing that Mrs. Mallard was afflicted with a heart trouble, great care was taken to break to her as gently as possible the news of her husband's death.

It was her sister Josephine who told her, in broken sentences; veiled hints that revealed in half concealing. Her husband's friend Richards was there, too, near her. It was he who had been in the newspaper office when intelligence of the railroad disaster was received, with Brently Mallard's name leading the list of "killed." He had only taken the time to assure himself of its truth by a second telegram, and had hastened to forestall any less careful, less tender friend in bearing the sad message.

She did not hear the story as many women have heard the same, with a paralyzed inability to accept its significance. She wept at once, with sudden, wild abandonment, in her sister's arms. When the storm of grief had spent itself she went away to her room alone. She would have no one follow her.

There stood, facing the open window, a comfortable, roomy armchair. Into this she sank, pressed down by a physical exhaustion that haunted her body and seemed to reach into her soul.

She could see in the open square before her house the tops of trees that were all aquiver with the new spring life. The delicious breath of rain was in the air. In the street below a peddler was crying his wares. The notes of a distant song which some one was singing reached her faintly, and countless sparrows were twittering in the eaves.

There were patches of blue sky showing here and there through the clouds that had met and piled one above the other in the west facing her window.

She sat with her head thrown back upon the cushion of the chair, quite motionless, except when a sob came up into her throat and shook her, as a child who had cried itself to sleep continues to sob in its dreams.

She was young, with a fair, calm face, whose lines bespoke repression and even a certain strength. But now there was a dull stare in her eyes, whose gaze was fixed away off yonder on one of those patches of blue sky. It was not a glance of reflection, but rather indicated a suspension of intelligent thought.

There was something coming to her and she was waiting for it, fearfully. What was it? She did not know; it was too subtle and elusive to name. But she felt it, creeping out of the sky, reaching toward her through the sounds, the scents, the color that filled the air.

Now her bosom rose and fell tumultuously. She was beginning to recognize   10
this thing that was approaching to possess her, and she was striving to beat it back with her will—as powerless as her two white slender hands would have been.

When she abandoned herself a little whispered word escaped her slightly parted lips. She said it over and over under her breath: "free, free, free!" The vacant stare and the look of terror that had followed it went from her eyes. They stayed keen and bright. Her pulses beat fast, and the coursing blood warmed and relaxed every inch of her body.

She did not stop to ask if it were or were not a monstrous joy that held her. A clear and exalted perception enabled her to dismiss the suggestion as trivial.

She knew that she would weep again when she saw the kind, tender hands folded in death; the face that had never looked save with love upon her, fixed and gray and dead. But she saw beyond that bitter moment a long procession of years to come that would belong to her absolutely. And she opened and spread her arms out to them in welcome.

There would be no one to live for her during those coming years: she would live for herself. There would be no powerful will bending hers in that blind persistence with which men and women believe they have a right to impose a private will upon a fellow-creature. A kind intention or a cruel intention made the act seem no less a crime as she looked upon it in that brief moment of illumination.

And yet she had loved him—sometimes. Often she had not. What did it matter!   15
What could love, the unsolved mystery, count for in face of this possession of self-assertion which she suddenly recognized as the strongest impulse of her being!

"Free! Body and soul free!" she kept whispering.

Josephine was kneeling before the closed door with her lips to the keyhole, imploring for admission. "Louise, open the door! I beg; open the door—you will make yourself ill. What are you doing, Louise? For heaven's sake open the door."

"Go away. I am not making myself ill." No; she was drinking in a very elixir of life through that open window.

Her fancy was running riot along those days ahead of her. Spring days, and summer days, and all sorts of days that would be her own. She breathed a quick prayer that life might be long. It was only yesterday she had thought with a shudder that life might be long.

She arose at length and opened the door to her sister's importunities. There   20
was a feverish triumph in her eyes, and she carried herself unwittingly like a goddess of Victory. She clasped her sister's waist, and together they descended the stairs. Richards stood waiting for them at the bottom.

Some one was opening the front door with a latchkey. It was Brently Mallard who entered, a little travel-stained, composedly carrying his gripsack and umbrella. He had been far from the scene of accident, and did not even know there had been one. He stood amazed at Josephine's piercing cry; at Richards' quick motion to screen him from the view of his wife.

But Richards was too late.

When the doctors came they said she had died of heart disease—of joy that kills.

Sandra Cisneros   b. 1954

The House on Mango Street   1983

We didn't always live on Mango Street. Before that we lived on Loomis on the third floor, and before that we lived on Keeler. Before Keeler it was Paulina, and before that I can't remember. But what I remember most is moving a lot. Each time it seemed there'd be one more of us. By the time we got to Mango Street we were six—Mama, Papa, Carlos, Kiki, my sister Nenny and me.

The house on Mango Street is ours and we don't have to pay rent to anybody or share the yard with the people downstairs or be careful not to make too much noise and there isn't a landlord banging on the ceiling with a broom. But even so, it's not the house we'd thought we'd get.

We had to leave the flat on Loomis quick. The water pipes broke and the landlord wouldn't fix them because the house was too old. We had to leave fast. We were using the washroom next door and carrying water over in empty milk gallons. That's why Mama and Papa looked for a house, and that's why we moved into the house on Mango Street, far away, on the other side of town.

They always told us that one day we would move into a house, a real house that would be ours for always so we wouldn't have to move each year. And our house would have running water and pipes that worked. And inside it would have real stairs, not hallway stairs, but stairs inside like the houses on T.V. And we'd have a basement and at least three washrooms so when we took a bath we didn't have to tell everybody. Our house would be white with trees around it, a great big yard and grass growing without a fence. This was the house Papa talked about when he held a lottery ticket and this was the house Mama dreamed up in the stories she told us before we went to bed.

But the house on Mango Street is not the way they told it at all. It's small and red with tight little steps in front and windows so small you'd think they were holding their breath. Bricks are crumbling in places, and the front door is so swollen you have to push hard to get in. There is no front yard, only four little elms the city planted by the curb. Out back is a small garage for the car we don't own yet and a small yard that looks smaller between the two buildings on either side. There are stairs in our house, but they're ordinary hallway stairs, and the house has only one washroom, very small. Everybody has to share a bedroom— Mama and Papa, Carlos and Kiki, me and Nenny.

Once when we were living on Loomis, a nun from my school passed by and saw me playing out front. The laundromat downstairs had been boarded up because it had been robbed two days before and the owner had painted on the wood YES WE'RE OPEN so as not to lose business.

Where do you live? she asked.

There, I said pointing up to the third floor.

You live *there?*

There. I had to look to where she pointed—the third floor, the paint peeling,   10
wooden bars Papa had nailed on the windows so we wouldn't fall out. You live
there? The way she said it made me feel like nothing. *There.* I lived *there.* I nodded.

I knew then I had to have a house. A real house. One I could point to. But
this isn't it. The house on Mango Street isn't it. For the time being, Mama says.
Temporary, says Papa. But I know how those things go.

Stephen Crane   1871–1900

The Blue Hotel   *1898*

The Palace Hotel at Fort Romper was painted a light blue, a shade that is on
the legs of a kind of heron, causing the bird to declare its position against any
background. The Palace Hotel, then, was always screaming and howling in a way
that made the dazzling winter landscape of Nebraska seem only a grey swampish
hush. It stood alone on the prairie, and when the snow was falling the town two
hundreds yards away was not visible. But when the traveller alighted at the railway station he was obliged to pass the Palace Hotel before he could come upon
the company of low clapboard houses which composed Fort Romper, and it was
not to be thought that any traveller could pass the Palace Hotel without looking at
it. Pat Scully, the proprietor, had proved himself a master of strategy when he
chose his paints. It is true that on clear days, when the great transcontinental expresses, long lines of swaying Pullmans, swept through Fort Romper, passengers
were overcome at the sight, and the cult that knows the brown-reds and the subdivisions of the dark greens of the East expressed shame, pity, horror, in a laugh.
But the citizens of this prairie town and to the people who would naturally stop
there, Pat Scully had performed a feat. With this opulence and splendour, these
creeds, classes, egotisms, that streamed through Romper on the rails day after day,
they had no colour in common.

As if the displayed delights of such a blue hotel were not sufficiently enticing,
it was Scully's habit to go every morning and evening to meet the leisurely trains
that stopped at Romper and work his seductions upon any man that he might see
wavering, gripsack in hand.

One morning, when a snow-crusted engine dragged its long string of freight
cars and its one passenger coach to the station, Scully performed the marvel of
catching three men. One was a shaky and quick-eyed Swede, with a great shining
cheap valise; one was a tall bronzed cowboy, who was on his way to a ranch near
the Dakota line; one was a little silent man from the East, who didn't look it, and
didn't announce it. Scully practically made them prisoners. He was so nimble and
merry and kindly that each probably felt it would be the height of brutality to try
to escape. They trudged off over the creaking board sidewalks in the wake of the
eager little Irishman. He wore a heavy fur cap squeezed tightly down on his head.
It caused his two red ears to stick out stiffly, as if they were made of tin.

At last, Scully, elaborately, with boisterous hospitality, conducted them
through the portals of the blue hotel. The room which they entered was small. It
seemed to be merely a proper temple for an enormous stove, which, in the centre,
was humming with godlike violence. At various points on its surface the iron had

become luminous and glowed yellow from the heat. Beside the stove Scully's son Johnnie was playing High-Five with an old farmer who had whiskers both grey and sandy. They were quarrelling. Frequently the old farmer turned his face toward a box of sawdust—coloured brown from tobacco juice—that was behind the stove, and spat with an air of great impatience and irritation. With a loud flourish of words Scully destroyed the game of cards, and bustled his son upstairs with part of the baggage of the new guests. He himself conducted them to three basins of the coldest water in the world. The cowboy and the Easterner burnished themselves fiery red with this water, until it seemed to be some kind of metal-polish. The Swede, however, merely dipped his fingers gingerly and with trepidation. It was notable that throughout this series of small ceremonies the three travellers were made to feel that Scully was very benevolent. He was conferring great favours upon them. He handed the towel from one to another with an air of philanthropic impulse.

Afterward they went to the first room, and sitting about the stove, listened to   5
Scully's officious clamour at his daughters, who were preparing the midday meal. They reflected in the silence of experienced men who tread carefully amid new people. Nevertheless, the old farmer, stationary, invincible in his chair near the warmest part of the stove, turned his face from the sawdust-box frequently and addressed a glowing commonplace to the strangers. Usually he was answered in short but adequate sentences by either the cowboy or the Easterner. The Swede said nothing. He seemed to be occupied in making furtive estimates of each man in the room. One might have thought that he had the sense of silly suspicion which comes to guilt. He resembled a badly frightened man.

Later, at dinner, he spoke a little, addressing his conversation entirely to Scully. He volunteered that he had come from New York, where for ten years he had worked as a tailor. These facts seemed to strike Scully as fascinating, and afterward he volunteered that he had lived at Romper for fourteen years. The Swede asked about the crops and the price of labour. He seemed barely to listen to Scully's extended replies. His eyes continued to rove from man to man.

Finally, with a laugh and a wink, he said that some of these Western communities were very dangerous; and after his statement he straightened his legs under the table, tilted his head, and laughed again, loudly. It was plain that the demonstration had no meaning to the others. They looked at him wondering and in silence.

II

As the men trooped heavily back into the front room, the two little windows presented views of a turmoiling sea of snow. The huge arms of the wind were making attempts—mighty, circular, futile—to embrace the flakes as they sped. A gate-post like a still man with a blanched face stood aghast amid this profligate fury. In a hearty voice Scully announced the presence of a blizzard. The guests of the blue hotel, lighting their pipes, assented with grunts of lazy masculine contentment. No island of the sea could be exempt in the degree of this little room with its humming stove. Johnnie, son of Scully, in a tone which defined his opinion of his ability as a card-player, challenged the old farmer of both grey and sandy whiskers to a game of High-Five. The farmer agreed with a contemptuous and bitter scoff. They sat close to the stove, and squared their knees under a wide board. The cowboy and the Easterner watched the game with interest. The Swede remained near the window, aloof, but with a countenance that showed signs of an inexplicable excitement.

The play of Johnnie and the grey-beard was suddenly ended by another quarrel. The old man arose while casting a look of heated scorn at his adversary. He slowly buttoned his coat, and then stalked with fabulous dignity from the room. In the discreet silence of all other men the Swede laughed. His laughter rang somehow childish. Men by this time had begun to look at him askance, as if they wished to inquire what ailed him.

A new game was formed jocosely. The cowboy volunteered to become the   10
partner of Johnnie, and they all then turned to ask the Swede to throw in his lot with the little Easterner. He asked some questions about the game, and, learning that it wore many names, and that he had played it when it was under an alias, he accepted the invitation. He strode toward the men nervously, as if he expected to be assaulted. Finally, seated, he gazed from face to face and laughed shrilly. This laugh was so strange that the Easterner looked up quickly, the cowboy sat intent and with his mouth open, and Johnnie paused, holding the cards with still fingers.

Afterward there was a short silence. Then Johnnie said, "Well, let's get at it. Come on now!" They pulled their chairs forward until their knees were bunched under the board. They began to play, and their interest in the game caused the others to forget the manner of the Swede.

The cowboy was a board-whacker. Each time that he held superior cards he whanged them, one by one, with exceeding force, down upon the improvised table, and took the tricks with a glowing air of prowess and pride that sent thrills of indignation into the hearts of his opponents. A game with a board-whacker in it is sure to become intense. The countenances of the Easterner and the Swede were miserable whenever the cowboy thundered down his aces and kings, while Johnnie, his eyes gleaming with joy, chuckled and chuckled.

Because of the absorbing play none considered the strange ways of the Swede. They paid strict heed to the game. Finally, during a lull caused by a new deal, the Swede suddenly addressed Johnnie: "I suppose there have been a good many men killed in this room." The jaws of the others dropped and they looked at him.

"What in hell are you talking about?" said Johnnie.

The Swede laughed again his blatant laugh, full of a kind of false courage and   15
defiance. "Oh, you know what I mean all right," he answered.

"I'm a liar if I do!" Johnnie protested. The card was halted, and the men stared at the Swede. Johnnie evidently felt that as the son of the proprietor he should make a direct inquiry. "Now, what might you be drivin' at, mister?" he asked. The Swede winked at him. It was a wink full of cunning. His fingers shook on the edge of the board. "Oh, maybe you think I have been to nowheres. Maybe you think I'm a tenderfoot?"

"I don't know nothin' about you," answered Johnnie, "and I don't give a damn where you've been. All I got to say is that I don't know what you're driving at. There hain't never been nobody killed in this room."

The cowboy, who had been steadily gazing at the Swede, then spoke: "What's wrong with you, mister?"

Apparently it seemed to the Swede that he was formidably menaced. He shivered and turned white near the corners of his mouth. He sent an appealing glance in the direction of the little Easterner. During these moments he did not forget to wear his air of advanced pot-valour. "They say they don't know what I mean," he remarked mockingly to the Easterner.

The latter answered after prolonged and cautious reflection. "I don't under-   20
stand you," he said, impassively.

The Swede made movement then which announced that he thought he had encountered treachery from the only quarter where he had expected sympathy, if not help. "Oh, I see you are all against me. I see——"

The cowboy was in a state of deep stupefaction. "Say," he cried, as he tumbled the deck violently down upon the board, "say, what are you gittin' at, hey?"

The Swede sprang up with the celerity of a man escaping from a snake on the floor. "I don't want to fight!" he shouted. "I don't want to fight!"

The cowboy stretched his long legs indolently and deliberately. His hands were in his pockets. He spat into the sawdust-box. "Well, who the hell thought you did?" he inquired.

The Swede backed rapidly toward a corner of the room. His hands were out protecting in front of his chest, but he was making an obvious struggle to control his fright. "Gentlemen," he quavered, "I suppose I am going to be killed before I can leave this house! I suppose I am going to be killed before I can leave this house!" In his eyes was the dying-swan look. Through the windows could be seen the snow turning blue in the shadow of dusk. The wind tore at the house, and some loose thing beat regularly against the clapboards like a spirit tapping.   25

A door opened, and Scully himself entered. He paused in surprise as he noted the tragic attitude of the Swede. Then he said, "What's the matter here?"

The Swede answered him swiftly and eagerly: "These men are going to kill me."

"Kill you!" ejaculated Scully. "Kill you! What are you talkin'?"

The Swede made the gesture of a martyr.

Scully wheeled sternly upon his son. "What is this, Johnnie?"   30

The lad had grown sullen. "Damned if I know," he answered. "I can't make no sense to it." He began to shuffle the cards, fluttering them together with an angry snap. "He says a good many men have been killed in this room, or something like that. And he says he's goin' to be killed here too. I don't know what ails him. He's crazy, I shouldn't wonder."

Scully then looked for explanation to the cowboy, but the cowboy simply shrugged his shoulders.

"Kill you?" said Scully again to the Swede. "Kill you? Man, you're off your nut."

"Oh, I know," burst out the Swede. "I know what will happen. Yes, I'm crazy—yes. Yes, of course, I'm crazy—yes. But I know one thing——" There was a sort of sweat of misery and terror upon his face. "I know I won't get out of here alive."

The cowboy drew a deep breath, as if his mind was passing into the last stages of dissolution. "Well, I'm doggoned," he whispered to himself.   35

Scully wheeled suddenly and faced his son. "You've been troublin' this man!"

Johnnie's voice was loud with its burden of grievance. "Why, good Gawd, I ain't done nothin' to 'im."

The Swede broke in. "Gentlemen, do not disturb yourselves. I will leave this house. I will go away, because"—he accused them dramatically with his glance—"because I do not want to be killed."

Scully was furious with his son. "Will you tell me what is the matter, you young divil? What's the matter, anyhow? Speak out!"

"Blame it!" cried Johnnie in despair, "don't I tell you I don't know? He—he says we want to kill him, and that's all I know. I can't tell what ails him."   40

The Swede continued to repeat: "Never mind, Mr. Scully; never mind. I will leave this house. I will go away, because I do not wish to be killed. Yes, of course,

I am crazy—yes. But I know one thing! I will go away. I will leave this house. Never mind, Mr. Scully; never mind. I will go away."

"You will not go 'way," said Scully. "You will not go 'way until I hear the reason of this business. If anybody has troubled you I will take care of him. This is my house. You are under my roof, and I will not allow any peaceable man to be troubled here." He cast a terrible eye upon Johnnie, the cowboy, and the Easterner.

"Never mind, Mr. Scully; never mind. I will go away. I do not wish to be killed." The Swede moved toward the door which opened upon the stairs. It was evidently his intention to go at once for his baggage.

"No, no," shouted Scully peremptorily; but the white-faced man slid by him and disappeared. "Now," said Scully severely, "what does this mean?"

Johnnie and the cowboy cried together: "Why, we didn't do nothin' to 'im!"   45

Scully's eyes were cold. "No," he said, "you didn't?"

Johnnie swore a deep oath. "Why, this is the wildest loon I ever see. We didn't do nothin' at all. We were jest sittin' here playin' cards, and he——"

The father suddenly spoke to the Easterner. "Mr. Blanc," he asked, "what has these boys been doin'?"

The Easterner reflected again. "I didn't see anything wrong at all," he said at last, slowly.

Scully began to howl. "But what does it mane?" He stared ferociously at his   50
son. "I have a mind to lather you for this, me boy."

Johnnie was frantic. "Well, what have I done?" he bawled at his father.

III

"I think you are tongued-tied," said Scully finally to his son, the cowboy, and the Easterner; and at the end of this scornful sentence he left the room.

Upstairs the Swede was swiftly fastening the straps of his great valise. Once his back happened to be half turned toward the door, and, hearing a noise there, he wheeled and sprang up, uttering a loud cry. Scully's wrinkled visage showed grimly in the light of the small lamp he carried. This yellow effulgence, streaming upward, coloured only his prominent features, and left his eyes, for instance, in mysterious shadow. He resembled a murderer.

"Man! man!" he exclaimed, "have you gone daffy?"

"Oh, no! Oh, no!" rejoined the other. "There are people in this world who   55
know pretty nearly as much as you do—understand?"

For a moment they stood gazing at each other. Upon the Swede's deathly pale cheeks were two spots brightly crimson and sharply edged, as if they had been carefully painted. Scully placed the light on the table and sat himself on the edge of the bed. He spoke ruminatively. "By cracky, I never heard of such a thing in my life. It's a complete muddle. I can't, for the soul of me, think how you ever got this idea into your head." Presently, he lifted his eyes and asked: "And did you sure think they were going to kill you?"

The Swede scanned the old man as if he wished to see into his mind. "I did," he said at last. He obviously suspected that this answer might precipitate an outbreak. As he pulled on a strap his whole arm shook, the elbow wavering like a bit of paper.

Scully banged his hand impressively on the footboard of the bed. "Why, man, we're goin' to have a line of ilictric streetcars in this town next spring."

"A line of electric street cars," repeated the Swede, stupidly.

"And," said Scully, "there's a new railroad goin' to be built down from Bro- 60
ken Arm to here. Not to mintion the four churches and the smashin' big brick
schoolhouse. Then there's the big factory, too. Why, in two years Romper'll be a
met-tro-*pol*-is."

Having finished the preparation of his baggage, the Swede straightened himself. "Mr. Scully," he said, with sudden hardihood "how much do I owe you?"

"You don't owe me anythin'," said the old man, angrily.

"Yes, I do," retorted the Swede. He took seventy-five cents from his pocket
and tendered it to Scully; but the latter snapped his fingers in disdainful refusal.
However, it happened that they both stood gazing in a strange fashion at three silver pieces on the Swede's open palm.

"I'll not take your money," said Scully at last. "Not after what's been goin' on
here." Then a plan seemed to strike him. "Here," he cried, picking up his lamp and
moving toward the door. "Here! Come with me a minute."

"No," said the Swede, in overwhelming alarm.

"Yes," urged the old man. "Come on! I want you to come and see a picter— 65
just across the hall—in my room."

The Swede must have concluded that his hour was come. His jaw dropped
and his teeth showed like a dead man's. He ultimately followed Scully across the
corridor, but he had the step of one hung in chains.

Scully flashed the light high on the wall of his own chamber. There was revealed a ridiculous photograph of a little girl. She was leaning against a balustrade
of gorgeous decoration, and the formidable bang to her hair was prominent. The
figure was as graceful as an upright sledstake, and, withal, it was of the hue of lead.
"There," said Scully, tenderly, "that's the picter of my little girl that died. Her name
was Carrie. She had the purtiest hair you ever saw! I was that fond of her, she——"

Turning then, he saw that the Swede was not contemplating the picture at all,
but, instead, was keeping keen watch on the gloom in the rear.

"Look man!" cried Scully, heartily. "That's the picter of my little gal that died. 70
Her name was Carrie. And then here's the picter of my oldest boy, Michael. He's a
lawyer in Lincoln, an' doin' well. I gave that boy a grand eddication, and I'm glad
for it now. He's a fine boy. Look at 'im now. Ain't he bold as blazes, him there in
Lincoln, an honoured an' respicted gintleman! An honoured and respicted gintleman," concluded Scully with a flourish. And, so saying, he smote the Swede
jovially on the back.

The Swede faintly smiled.

"Now," said the old man, "there's only one more thing." He dropped suddenly
to the floor and thrust his head beneath the bed. The Swede could hear his muffled voice. "I'd keep it under me piller if it wasn't for that boy Johnnie. Then
there's the old woman——Where is it now? I never put it twice in the same place.
Ah, now come out with you!"

Presently he backed clumsily from under the bed, dragging with him an old
coat rolled into a bundle. "I've fetched him," he muttered. Kneeling on the floor, he
unrolled the coat and extracted from its heart a large yellow-brown whisky-bottle.

His first manoeuvre was to hold the bottle up to the light. Reassured, apparently, that nobody had been tampering with it, he thrust it with a generous movement toward the Swede.

The weak-kneed Swede was about to eagerly clutch this element of strength, 75
but he suddenly jerked his hand away and cast a look of horror upon Scully.

"Drink," said the old man affectionately. He had risen to his feet, and now stood facing the Swede.

There was a silence. Then again Scully said: "Drink!"

The Swede laughed wildly. He grabbed the bottle, put it to his mouth; and as his lips curled absurdly around the opening and his throat worked, he kept his glance, burning with hatred, upon the old man's face.

IV

After the departure of Scully the three men, with the cardboard still upon their knees, preserved for a long time an astounded silence. Then Johnnie said: "That's the dod-dangedest Swede I ever see."

"He ain't no Swede," said the cowboy scornfully.   80

"Well, what is he then?" cried Johnnie. "What is he then?"

"It's my opinion," replied the cowboy deliberately, "he's some kind of a Dutchman." It was a venerable custom of the country to entitle as Swedes all light-haired men who spoke with a heavy tongue. In consequence the idea of the cowboy was not without its daring. "Yes, sir," he repeated. "It's my opinion this feller is some kind of a Dutchman."

"Well, he says he's a Swede, anyhow," muttered Johnnie, sulkily. He turned to the Easterner: "What do you think, Mr. Blanc?"

"Oh, I don't know," replied the Easterner.

"Well, what do you think makes him act that way?" asked the cowboy.   85

"Why, he's frightened." The Easterner knocked his pipe against a rim of the stove. "He's clear frightened out of his boots."

"What at?" cried Johnnie and the cowboy together.

The Easterner reflected over his answer.

"What at?" cried the others again.

"Oh, I don't know, but it seems to me this man has been reading dime novels,   90
and he thinks he's right out in the middle of it—the shootin' and stabbin' and all."

"But," said the cowboy, deeply scandalized, "this ain't Wyoming, ner none of them places. This is Nebrasker."

"Yes," added Johnnie, "an' why don't he wait til he gits *out West?*"

The travelled Easterner laughed. "It isn't different there even—not in these days. But he thinks he's right in the middle of hell."

Johnnie and the cowboy mused along.

"It's awful funny," remarked Johnnie at last.   95

"Yes," said the cowboy. "This is a queer game. I hope we don't git snowed in, because then we'd have to stand this here man bein' around with us all the time. That wouldn't be no good."

"I wish pop would throw him out," said Johnnie.

Presently they heard a loud stamping on the stairs, accompanied by ringing jokes in the voice of old Scully, and laughter, evidently from the Swede. The men around the stove stared vacantly at each other. "Gosh!" said the cowboy. The door flew open, and old Scully, flushed and anecdotal, came into the room. He was jabbering at the Swede, who followed him, laughing bravely. It was the entry of two roisterers from a banquet hall.

"Come now," said Scully sharply to the three seated men, "move up and give us a chance at the stove." The cowboy and the Easterner obediently sidled their chairs to make room for the newcomers. Johnnie, however, simply arranged himself in a more indolent attitude, and then remained motionless.

"Come! Git over, there," said Scully.

"Plenty of room on the other side of the stove," said Johnnie.

"Do you think we want to sit in the draught?" roared the father.

But the Swede had interposed with a grandeur of confidence. "No, no. Let the boy sit where he likes," he cried in a bullying voice to the father.

"All right! All right!" said Scully, deferentially. The cowboy and the Easterner exchanged glances of wonder.

The five chairs were formed in a crescent about one side of the stove. The Swede began to talk; he talked arrogantly, profanely, angrily. Johnnie, the cowboy, and the Easterner maintained a morose silence, while old Scully appeared to be receptive and eager, breaking in constantly with sympathetic ejaculations.

Finally the Swede announced that he was thirsty. He moved in his chair, and said that he would go for a drink of water.

"I'll git it for you," cried Scully at once.

"No," said the Swede, contemptuously. "I'll get it for myself." He arose and stalked with the air of an owner off into the executive parts of the hotel.

As soon as the Swede was out of hearing Scully sprang to his feet and whispered intensely to the others: "Upstairs he thought I was tryin' to poison 'im."

"Say," said Johnnie, "this makes me sick. Why don't you throw 'im out in the snow?"

"Why, he's all right now," declared Scully. "It was only that he was from the East, and he thought this was a tough place. That's all. He's all right now."

The cowboy looked with admiration upon the Easterner. "You were straight," he said. "You were on to that there Dutchman."

"Well," said Johnnie to his father, "he may be all right now, but I don't see it. Other time he was scared, but now he's too fresh."

Scully's speech was always a combination of Irish brogue and idiom, Western twang and idiom, and scraps of curiously formal diction taken from the story-books and newspapers. He now hurled a strange mass of language at the head of his son. "What do I keep? What do I keep? What do I keep?" he demanded, in a voice of thunder. He slapped his knee impressively, to indicate that he himself was going to make reply, and that all should heed. "I keep a hotel," he shouted. "A hotel, do you mind? A guest under my roof has sacred privileges. He is to be intimidated by none. Not one word shall he hear that would prijudice him in favour of goin' away. I'll not have it. There's no place in this here town where they can say they iver took in a guest of mine because he was afraid to stay here." He wheeled suddenly upon the cowboy and the Easterner. "Am I right?"

"Yes, Mr. Scully," said the cowboy, "I think you're right."

"Yes, Mr. Scully," said the Easterner, "I think you're right."

V

At six-o'clock supper, the Swede fizzed like a fire-wheel. He sometimes seemed on the point of bursting into riotous song, and in all his madness he was encouraged by old Scully. The Easterner was encased in reserve; the cowboy sat in wide-mouthed amazement, forgetting to eat, while Johnnie wrathily demolished great plates of food. The daughters of the house, when they were obliged to replenish the biscuits, approached as warily as Indians, and, having succeeded in their purpose, fled with ill-concealed trepidation. The Swede domineered the whole feast, and he gave it the appearance of a cruel bacchanal. He seemed to have grown suddenly taller; he gazed, brutally disdainful, into every face. His voice rang through the room. Once when he jabbed out harpoon-fashion with his fork to pinion a biscuit, the weapon nearly impaled the hand of the Easterner, which had been stretched quietly out for the same biscuit.

After supper, as the men filed toward the other room, the Swede smote Scully ruthlessly on the shoulder. "Well, old boy, that was a good, square meal." Johnnie looked hopefully at his father; he knew that shoulder was tender from an old fall; and, indeed, it appeared for a moment as if Scully was going to flame out over the matter, but in the end he smiled a sickly smile and remained silent. The others understood from his manner that he was admitting his responsibility for the Swede's new view-point.

Johnnie, however, addressed his parent in an aside. "Why don't you license somebody to kick you downstairs?" Scully scowled darkly by way of reply.

When they were gathered about the stove, the Swede insisted on another   120 game of High-Five. Scully gently deprecated the plan at first, but the Swede turned a wolfish glare upon him. The old man subsided, and the Swede canvassed the others. In his tone there was always a great threat. The cowboy and the Easterner both remarked indifferently that they would play. Scully said that he would presently have to go to meet the 6.58 train, and so the Swede turned menacingly upon Johnnie. For a moment their glances crossed like blades, and then Johnnie smiled and said, "Yes, I'll play."

They formed a square, with the little board on their knees. The Easterner and the Swede were again partners. As the play went on, it was noticeable that the cowboy was not board-whacking as usual. Meanwhile, Scully, near the lamp, had put on his spectacles and, with an appearance curiously like an old priest, was reading a newspaper. In time he went out to meet the 6.58 train, and, despite his precautions, a gust of polar wind whirled into the room as he opened the door. Besides scattering the cards, it chilled the players to the marrow. The Swede cursed frightfully. When Scully returned, his entrance disturbed a cosy and friendly scene. The Swede again cursed. But presently they were once more intent, their heads bent forward and their hands moving swiftly. The Swede had adopted the fashion of board-whacking.

Scully took up his paper and for a long time remained immersed in matters which were extraordinarily remote from him. The lamp burned badly, and once he stopped to adjust the wick. The newspaper, as he turned from page to page, rustled with a slow and comfortable sound. Then suddenly he heard three terrible words: "You are cheatin'!"

Such scenes often prove that there can be little of dramatic import in environment. Any room can present a tragic front; any room can be comic. This little den was now hideous as a torture-chamber. The new faces of the men themselves had changed it upon the instant. The Swede held a huge fist in front of Johnnie's face, while the latter looked steadily over it into the blazing orbs of his accuser. The Easterner had grown pallid; the cowboy's jaw had dropped in that expression of bovine amazement which was one of his important mannerisms. After the three words, the first sound in the room was made by Scully's paper as it floated forgotten to his feet. His spectacles had also fallen from his nose, but by a clutch he had saved them in air. His hand, grasping the spectacles, now remained poised awkwardly and near his shoulder. He stared at the cardplayers.

Probably the silence was while a second elapsed. Then, if the floor had been suddenly twitched out from under the men they could not have moved quicker. The five had projected themselves head-long toward a common point. It happened that Johnnie, in rising to hurl himself upon the Swede, had stumbled slightly because of his curiously instinctive care for the cards and the board. The loss of the moment allowed time for the arrival of Scully, and also allowed the cowboy time to give the Swede a great push which sent him staggering back. The men found tongue together, and hoarse shouts of rage, appeal, or fear burst from every throat. The cowboy pushed and jostled feverishly at the Swede, and the Easterner and Scully clung wildly to Johnnie; but through the smoky air, above the swaying bodies of the peace-compellers, the eyes of the two warriors ever sought each other in glances of challenge that were at once hot and steely.

Of course the board had been over-turned, and now the whole company of cards was scattered over the floor, where the boots of the men trampled the fat and painted kings and queens as they gazed with their silly eyes at the war that was waging above them.

Scully's voice was dominating the yells. "Stop now! Stop, I say! Stop, now——"

Johnnie, as he struggled to burst through the rank formed by Scully and the Easterner, was crying, "Well, he says I cheated! He says I cheated! I won't allow no man to say I cheated! If he says I cheated, he's a —— ——!"

The cowboy was telling the Swede, "Quit, now! Quit, d'ye hear——"

The screams of the Swede never ceased: "He did cheat! I saw him! I saw him——"

As for the Easterner, he was importuning in a voice that was not heeded: "Wait a moment, can't you? Oh, wait a moment. What's the good of a fight over a game of cards? Wait a moment——"

In this tumult no complete sentences were clear: "Cheat"—"Quit"—"He says"—these fragments pierced the uproar and rang out sharply. It was remarkable that, whereas Scully undoubtedly made the most noise, he was the least heard of any of the riotous band.

Then suddenly there was a great cessation. It was as if each man had paused for breath; and although the room was still lighted with the anger of men, it could be seen that there was no danger of immediate conflict, and at once Johnnie, shouldering his way forward, almost succeeded in confronting the Swede. "What did you say I cheated for? What did you say I cheated for? I don't cheat, and I won't let no man say I do!"

The Swede said, "I saw you! I saw you!"

"Well," cried Johnnie, "I'll fight any man what says I cheat!"

"No, you won't," said the cowboy. "Not here."

"Ah, be still, can't you?" said Scully, coming between them.

The quiet was sufficient to allow the Easterner's voice to be heard. He was repeating, "Oh, wait a moment, can't you? What's the good of a fight over a game of cards? Wait a moment!"

Johnnie, his red face appearing above his father's shoulder, hailed the Swede again. "Did you say I cheated?"

The Swede showed his teeth. "Yes."

"Then," said Johnnie, "we must fight."

"Yes, fight," roared the Swede. He was like a demoniac. "Yes, fight! I'll show you what kind of a man I am! I'll show you who you want to fight! Maybe you think I can't fight! Maybe you think I can't! I'll show you, you skin, you card-sharp! Yes, you cheated! You cheated! You cheated!"

"Well, let's go at it, then, mister," said Johnnie, coolly.

The cowboy's brow was beaded with sweat from his efforts in intercepting all sorts of raids. He turned in despair to Scully. "What are you goin' to do now?"

A change had come over the Celtic visage of the old man. He now seemed all eagerness; his eyes glowed.

"We'll let them fight," he answered, stalwartly. "I can't put up with it any longer. I've stood this damned Swede till I'm sick. We'll let them fight."   145

VI

The men prepared to go out of doors. The Easterner was so nervous that he had great difficulty in getting his arms into the sleeves of his new leather coat. As the cowboy drew his fur cap down over his ears his hands trembled. In fact, Johnnie and old Scully were the only ones who displayed no agitation. These preliminaries were conducted without words.

Scully threw open the door. "Well, come on," he said. Instantly a terrific wind caused the flame of the lamp to struggle at its wick, while a puff of black smoke sprang from the chimney-top. The stove was in mid-current of the blast, and its voice swelled to equal the roar of the storm. Some of the scarred and bedabbled cards were caught up from the floor and dashed helplessly against the farther wall. The men lowered their heads and plunged into the tempest as into a sea.

No snow was falling, but great whirls and clouds of flakes, swept up from the ground by the frantic winds, were streaming southward with the speed of bullets. The covered land was blue with the sheen of an unearthly satin, and there was no other hue save where, at the low, black railway station—which seemed incredibly distant—one light gleamed like a tiny jewel. As the men floundered into a thigh-deep drift, it was known that the Swede was bawling out something. Scully went to him, put a hand on his shoulder, and projected an ear. "What's that you say?" he shouted.

"I say," bawled the Swede again, "I won't stand much show against this gang. I know you'll all pitch on me."

Scully smote him reproachfully on the arm. "Tut, man!" he yelled. The wind tore the words from Scully's lips and scattered them far alee.   150

"You are all a gang of——" boomed the Swede, but the storm also seized the remainder of this sentence.

Immediately turning their backs upon the wind, the men had swung around a corner to the sheltered side of the hotel. It was the function of the little house to preserve here, amid this great devastation of snow, an irregular V-shape of heavily encrusted grass, which crackled beneath the feet. One could imagine the great drifts piled against the windward side. When the party reached the comparative peace of this spot it was found that the Swede was still bellowing.

"Oh, I know what kind of a thing this is! I know you'll all pitch on me. I can't lick you all!"

Scully turned upon him panther-fashion. "You'll not have to whip all of us. You'll have to whip my son Johnnie. An' the man what troubles you durin' that time will have me to dale with."

The arrangements were swiftly made. The two men faced each other, obedient to the harsh commands of Scully, whose face, in the subtly luminous gloom, could be seen set in the austere impersonal lines that are pictured on the countenances of the Roman veterans. The Easterner's teeth were chattering, and he was hopping up and down like a mechanical toy. The cowboy stood rock-like.   155

The contestants had not stripped off any clothing. Each was in his ordinary attire. Their fists were up, and they eyed each other in a calm that had the elements of leonine cruelty in it.

During this pause, the Easterner's mind, like a film, took lasting impressions of three men—the iron-nerved master of the ceremony; the Swede, pale, motionless, terrible; and Johnnie, serene yet ferocious, brutish yet heroic. The entire prelude had in it a tragedy greater than the tragedy of action, and this aspect was accentuated by the long, mellow cry of the blizzard, as it sped the tumbling and wailing flakes into the black abyss of the south.

"Now!" said Scully.

The two combatants leaped forward and crashed together like bullocks. There was heard the cushioned sounds of blows, and of a curse squeezing out from between the tight teeth of one.

As for the spectators, the Easterner's pent-up breath exploded from him   160
with a pop of relief, absolute relief from the tension of the preliminaries. The cowboy bounded into the air with a yowl. Scully was immovable as from supreme amazement and fear at the fury of the fight which he himself had permitted and arranged.

For a time the encounter in the darkness was such a perplexity of flying arms that it presented no more detail than would a swiftly revolving wheel. Occasionally a face, as if illumined by a flash of light, would shine out, ghastly and marked with pink spots. A moment later, the men might have been known as shadows, if it were not for the involuntary utterance of oaths that came from them in whispers.

Suddenly a holocaust of warlike desire caught the cowboy, and he bolted forward with the speed of a broncho. "Go it, Johnnie! Go it! Kill him! Kill him!"

Scully confronted him. "Kape back," he said; and by his glance the cowboy could tell that this man was Johnnie's father.

To the Easterner there was a monotony of unchangeable fighting that was an abomination. This confused mingling was eternal to his sense, which was concentrated in a longing for the end, the priceless end. Once the fighters lurched near him, and as he scrambled hastily backward he heard them breathe like men on the rack.

"Kill him, Johnnie! Kill him! Kill him! Kill him!" The cowboy's face was con-   165
torted like one of those agony masks in museums.

"Keep still," said Scully, icily.

Then there was a sudden loud grunt, incomplete, cut short, and Johnnie's body swung away from the Swede and fell with sickening heaviness to the grass. The cowboy was barely in time to prevent the mad Swede from flinging himself upon his prone adversary. "No, you don't," said the cowboy, interposing an arm. "Wait a second."

Scully was at his son's side. "Johnnie! Johnnie, me boy!" His voice had a quality of melancholy tenderness. "Johnnie! Can you go on with it?" He looked anxiously down into the bloody, pulpy face of his son.

There was a moment of silence, and then Johnnie answered in his ordinary voice, "Yes, I—it—yes."

Assisted by his father he struggled to his feet. "Wait a bit now till you git your   170
wind," said the old man.

A few paces away the cowboy was lecturing the Swede. "No, you don't! Wait a second!"

The Easterner was plucking at Scully's sleeve. "Oh, this is enough," he pleaded. "This is enough! Let it go as it stands. This is enough!"

"Bill," said Scully, "git out of the road." The cowboy stepped aside. "Now." The combatants were actuated by a new caution as they advanced toward collision. They glared at each other, and then the Swede aimed a lightning blow that carried with it his entire weight. Johnnie was evidently half stupid from weakness, but he miraculously dodged, and his fist sent the over-balanced Swede sprawling.

The cowboy, Scully and the Easterner burst into a cheer that was like a chorus of triumphant soldiery, but before its conclusion the Swede had scuffled agilely to his feet and come in berserk abandon at his foe. There was another perplexity of flying arms, and Johnnie's body again swung away and fell, even as a bundle might fall from a roof. The Swede instantly staggered to a little wind-waved tree and leaned upon it, breathing like an engine, while his savage and flamelit eyes roamed from face to face as the men bent over Johnnie. There was a splendour of isolation in his situation at this time which the Easterner felt once when, lifting his eyes from the man on the ground, he beheld that mysterious and lonely figure, waiting.

"Are you any good yet, Johnnie?" asked Scully in a broken voice.   175

The son gasped and opened his eyes languidly. After a moment he answered, "No—I ain't—any good—any—more." Then, from shame and bodily ill, he began to weep, the tears furrowing down through the bloodstains on his face. "He was too—too—too heavy for me."

Scully straightened and addressed the waiting figure. "Stranger," he said, evenly, "it's all up with our side." Then his voice changed into that vibrant huskiness which is commonly the tone of the most simple and deadly announcements. "Johnnie is whipped."

Without replying, the victor moved off on the route to the front door of the hotel. The cowboy was formulating new and unspellable blasphemies. The Easterner was startled to find that they were out in a wind that seemed to come direct from the shadowed arctic floes. He heard again the wail of the snow as it was flung to its grave in the south. He knew now that all this time the cold had been sinking into him deeper and deeper, and he wondered that he had not perished. He felt indifferent to the condition of the vanquished man.

"Johnnie, can you walk?" asked Scully.   180

"Did I hurt—hurt him any?" asked the son.

"Can you walk, boy? Can you walk?"

Johnnie's voice was suddenly strong. There was a robust impatience in it. "I asked you whether I hurt him any!"

"Yes, yes, Johnnie," answered the cowboy, consolingly; "he's hurt a good deal."

They raised him from the ground, and as soon as he was on his feet he went   185 tottering off, rebuffing all attempts at assistance. When the party rounded the corner they were fairly blinded by the pelting of the snow. It burned their faces like fire. The cowboy carried Johnnie through the drift to the door. As they entered, some cards again rose from the floor and beat against the wall.

The Easterner rushed to the stove. He was so profoundly chilled that he almost dared to embrace the glowing iron. The Swede was not in the room. Johnnie sank into a chair and, folding his arms on his knees, buried his face in them. Scully, warming one foot and then the other at a rim of the stove, muttered to himself with Celtic mournfulness. The cowboy had removed his fur cap, and with a dazed and rueful air he was running one hand through his tousled locks. From overhead they could hear the creaking of boards, as the Swede tramped here and there in his room.

The sad quiet was broken by the sudden flinging open of a door that led toward the kitchen. It was instantly followed by an inrush of women. They precipitated themselves upon Johnnie amid a chorus of lamentation. Before they carried their prey off to the kitchen, there to be bathed and harangued with that mixture of sympathy and abuse which is a feat of their sex, the mother straightened herself and fixed old Scully with an eye of stern reproach. "Shame be upon you, Patrick Scully!" she cried. "Your own son, too. Shame be upon you!"

"There, now! Be quiet, now!" said the old man, weakly.

"Shame be upon you, Patrick Scully!" The girls, rallying to this slogan, sniffed disdainfully in the direction of those trembling accomplices, the cowboy and the Easterner. Presently they bore Johnnie away, and left the three men to dismal reflection.

VII

I'd like to fight this here Dutchman myself," said the cowboy, breaking a long silence.

Scully wagged his head sadly. "No, that wouldn't do. It wouldn't be right. It wouldn't be right."

"Well, why wouldn't it?" argued the cowboy, "I don't see no harm in it."

"No," answered Scully, with mournful heroism. "It wouldn't be right. It was Johnnie's fight, and now we mustn't whip the man just because he whipped Johnnie."

"Yes, that's true enough," said the cowboy; "but—he better not get fresh with me, because I couldn't stand no more of it."

"You'll not say a word to him," commanded Scully, and even then they heard the tread of the Swede on the stairs. His entrance was made theatric. He swept the door back with a bang and swaggered to the middle of the room. No one looked at him. "Well," he cried, insolently, at Scully, "I s'pose you'll tell me now how much I owe you?"

The old man remained stolid. "You don't owe me nothin'."

"Huh!" said the Swede, "huh! Don't owe 'im nothin'."

The cowboy addressed the Swede. "Stranger, I don't see how you come to be so gay around here."

Old Scully was instantly alert. "Stop!" he shouted, holding his hand forth, fingers upward. "Bill, you shut up!"

The cowboy spat carelessly into the sawdust-box. "I didn't say a word, did I?" he asked.

"Mr. Scully," called the Swede, "how much do I owe you?" It was seen that he was attired for departure, and that he had his valise in his hand.

"You don't owe me nothin'," repeated Scully in the same imperturbable way.

"Huh!" said the Swede. "I guess you're right. I guess if it was any way at all, you'd owe me somethin'. That's what I guess." He turned to the cowboy. "'Kill him! Kill him! Kill him!'" He mimicked, and then guffawed victoriously. "'Kill him!'" He was convulsed with ironical humour.

But he might have been jeering the dead. The three men were immovable and silent, staring with glassy eyes at the stove.

The Swede opened the door and passed into the storm, giving one derisive glance backward at the still group.

As soon as the door was closed, Scully and the cowboy leaped to their feet and began to curse. They trampled to and fro, waving their arms and smashing into the air with their fists. "Oh, but that was a hard minute!" wailed Scully. "That was a hard minute! Him there leerin' and scoffin'! One bang at his nose was worth forty dollars to me that minute! How did you stand it, Bill?'

"How did I stand it?" cried the cowboy in a quivering voice. "How did I stand it? Oh!"

The old man burst into sudden brogue. "I'd loike to take that Swade," he wailed, "and hould 'im down on a shtone flure and bate 'im to a jelly wid a shtick!"

The cowboy groaned in sympathy. "I'd like to git him by the neck and ha-ammer him"—he brought his hand down on a chair with a noise like a pistol-shot— "hammer that there Dutchman until he couldn't tell himself from a dead coyote!"

"I'd bat 'im until he——"   210

"I'd show *him* some things——"

And then together they raised a yearning, fanatic cry— "Oh-o-oh! if we only could——"

"Yes!"

"Yes!"

"And then I'd——"   215

"O-o-oh!"

VIII

The Swede, tightly gripping his valise, tacked across the face of the storm as if he carried sails. He was following a line of little naked, gasping trees which, he knew, must mark the way of the road. His face, fresh from the pounding of Johnnie's fists, felt more pleasure than pain in the wind and the driving snow. A number of square shapes loomed upon him finally, and he knew them as the houses of the main body of the town. He found a street and made travel along it, leaning heavily upon the wind whenever, at a corner, a terrific blast caught him.

He might have been in a deserted village. We picture the world as thick with conquering and elate humanity, but here, with the bugles of the tempest pealing, it was hard to imagine a peopled earth. One viewed the existence of man then as a marvel, and conceded a glamour of wonder to these lice which were caused to cling to a whirling, fire-smitten, ice-locked, disease-stricken, space-lost bulb. The conceit of man was explained by this storm to be the very engine of life. One was a coxcomb not to die in it. However, the Swede found a saloon.

In front of it an indomitable red light was burning, and the snowflakes were made blood-colour as they flew through the circumscribed territory of the lamp's shining. The Swede pushed open the door of the saloon and entered. A sanded expanse was before him, and at the end of it four men sat about a table drinking. Down one side of the room extended a radiant bar, and its guardian was leaning upon his elbows listening to the talk of the men at the table. The Swede dropped his valise upon the floor and, smiling fraternally upon the barkeeper, said, "Gimme some whisky, will you?" The man placed a bottle, a whisky-glass, and a glass of ice-thick water upon the bar. The Swede poured himself an abnormal portion of whisky and drank it in three gulps. "Pretty bad night," remarked the bartender, in-differently. He was making the pretension of blindness which is usually a distinc-tion of his class; but it could have been seen that he was furtively studying the half-erased blood-stains on the face of the Swede. "Bad night," he said again.

"Oh, it's good enough for me," replied the Swede, hardily, as he poured him-   220
self some more whisky. The barkeeper took his coin and manoeuvred it through

its reception by the highly nickelled cash-machine. A bell rang; a card labelled "20 cts." had appeared.

"No," continued the Swede, "this isn't too bad weather. It's good enough for me."

"So?" murmured the barkeeper, languidly.

The copious drams made the Swede's eyes swim, and he breathed a trifle heavier. "Yes, I like this weather. I like it. It suits me." It was apparently his design to impart a deep significance to these words.

"So?" murmured the bartender again. He turned to gaze dreamily at the scroll-like birds and bird-like scrolls which had been drawn with soap upon the mirrors in back of the bar.

"Well, I guess I'll take another drink," said the Swede, presently. "Having something?"   225

"No, thanks; I'm not drinkin'," answered the bartender. Afterwards he asked, "How did you hurt your face?"

The Swede immediately began to boast loudly. "Why, in a fight. I thumped the soul out of a man down here at Scully's hotel."

The interest of the four men at the table was at last aroused.

"Who was it?" said one.

"Johnnie Scully," blustered the Swede. "Son of the man what runs it. He will   230 be pretty near dead for some weeks, I can tell you. I made a nice thing of him, I did. He couldn't get up. They carried him in the house. Have a drink?"

Instantly the men in some subtle way encased themselves in reserve. "No, thanks," said one. The group was of curious formation. Two were prominent local business men; one was the district attorney; and one was a professional gambler of the kind known as "square." But a scrutiny of the group would not have enabled an observer to pick the gambler from the men of more reputable pursuits. He was, in fact, a man so delicate in manner, when among people of fair class, and so judicious in his choice of victims, that in the strictly masculine part of the town's life he had come to be explicitly trusted and admired. People called him a thoroughbred. The fear and contempt with which his craft was regarded were undoubtedly the reason why his quiet dignity shone conspicuous above the quiet dignity of men who might be merely hatters, billiard-markers, or grocery clerks. Beyond an occasional unwary traveller who came by rail, this gambler was supposed to prey solely upon reckless and senile farmers, who, when flush with good crops, drove into town in all the pride and confidence of an absolutely invulnerable stupidity. Hearing at times in circuitous fashion of the despoilment of such a farmer, the important men of Romper invariably laughed in contempt of the victim, and if they thought of the wolf at all, it was with a kind of pride at the knowledge that he would never dare think of attacking their wisdom and courage. Besides, it was popular that this gambler had a real wife and two children in a neat cottage in a suburb, where he led an exemplary home life; and when any one even suggested a discrepancy in his character, the crowd immediately vociferated descriptions of this virtuous family circle. Then men who led exemplary home lives, and men who did not lead exemplary home lives, all subsided in a bunch, remarking that there was nothing more to be said.

However, when a restriction was placed upon him—as, for instance, when a strong clique of members of the new Pollywog Club refused to permit him, even as a spectator, to appear in the rooms of the organization—the candour and gentleness with which he accepted the judgment disarmed many of his foes and made his friends more desperately partisan. He invariably distinguished between himself and a respectable Romper man so quickly and frankly that his manner actually appeared to be a continual broadcast compliment.

And one must not forget to declare the fundamental fact of his entire position in Romper. It is irrefutable that in all affairs outside his business, in all matters that occur eternally and commonly between man and man, this thieving card-player was so generous, so just, so moral, that, in a contest, he could have put to flight the consciences of nine tenths of the citizens of Romper.

And so it happened that he was seated in this saloon with the two prominent local merchants and the district attorney.

The Swede continued to drink raw whisky, meanwhile babbling at the bar-   235
keeper and trying to induce him to indulge in potations. "Come on. Have a drink. Come on. What—no? Well, have a little one, then. By gawd, I've whipped a man to-night, and I want to celebrate. I whipped him good, too. Gentlemen," the Swede cried to the men at the table, "have a drink?"

"Ssh!" said the barkeeper.

The group at the table, although furtively attentive, had been pretending to be deep in talk, but now a man lifted his eyes toward the Swede and said, shortly, "Thanks. We don't want any more."

At this reply the Swede ruffled out his chest like a rooster. "Well," he exploded, "it seems I can't get anybody to drink with me in this town. Seems so, don't it? Well!"

"Ssh!" said the barkeeper.

"Say," snarled the Swede, "don't you try to shut me up. I won't have it. I'm a   240
gentleman, and I want people to drink with me. And I want 'em to drink with me now. *Now*—do you understand?" He rapped the bar with his knuckles.

Years of experience had calloused the bartender. He merely grew sulky. "I hear you," he answered.

"Well," cried the Swede, "listen hard then. See those men over there? Well, they're going to drink with me, and don't you forget it. Now you watch."

"Hi!" yelled the barkeeper, "this won't do!"

"Why won't it?" demanded the Swede. He stalked over to the table, and by chance laid his hand upon the shoulder of the gambler. "How about this?" he asked wrathfully. "I asked you to drink with me."

The gambler simply twisted his head and spoke over his shoulder. "My friend,   245
I don't know you."

"Oh, hell!" answered the Swede, "come and have a drink."

"Now, my boy," advised the gambler, kindly, "take you hand off my shoulder and go 'way and mind your own business." He was a little, slim man, and it seemed strange to hear him use this tone of heroic patronage to the burly Swede. The other men at the table said nothing.

"What! You won't drink with me, you little dude? I'll make you, then! I'll make you!" The Swede had grasped the gambler frenziedly at the throat, and was dragging him from his chair. The other men sprang up. The barkeeper dashed around the corner of his bar. There was a great tumult, and then was seen a long blade in the hand of the gambler. It shot forward, and a human body, this citadel of virtue, wisdom, power, was pierced as easily as if it had been a melon. The Swede fell with a cry of supreme astonishment.

The prominent merchants and the district attorney must have at once tumbled out of the place backward. The bartender found himself hanging limply to the arm of a chair and gazing into the eyes of a murderer.

"Henry," said the latter, as he wiped his knife on one of the towels that hung 250
beneath the bar rail, "you tell 'em where to find me. I'll be home, waiting for 'em."
Then he vanished. A moment afterward the barkeeper was in the street dinning
through the storm for help and, moreover, companionship.

The corpse of the Swede, alone in the saloon, had its eyes fixed upon a
dreadful legend that dwelt atop the cash-machine: "This registers the amount of
your purchase."

IX

Months later, the cowboy was frying pork over the stove of a little ranch near the
Dakota line, when there was a quick thud of hoofs outside, and presently the Easterner entered with the letters and the papers.

"Well," said the Easterner at once, "the chap that killed the Swede has got
three years. Wasn't much, was it?"

"He has? Three years?" The cowboy poised his pan of pork, while he rumi-
nated upon the news. "Three years. That ain't much."

"No. It was a light sentence," replied the Easterner as he unbuckled his spurs. 255
"Seems there was a good deal of sympathy for him in Romper."

"If the bartender had been any good," observed the cowboy, thoughtfully, "he
would have gone in and cracked that there Dutchman on the head with a bottle in
the beginnin' of it and stopped all this here murderin'."

"Yes, a thousand things might have happened," said the Easterner, tartly.

The cowboy returned his pan of pork to the fire, but his philosophy continued.
"It's funny, ain't it? If he hadn't said Johnnie was cheatin' he'd be alive this minute. He
was an awful fool. Game played for fun, too. Not for money. I believe he was crazy."

"I feel sorry for that gambler," said the Easterner.

"Oh, so do I," said the cowboy. "He don't deserve none of it for killin' who he 260
did."

"The Swede might not have been killed if everything had been square."

"Might not have been killed?" exclaimed the cowboy. "Everythin' square?
Why, when he said that Johnnie was cheatin' and acted like such a jackass? And
then in the saloon he fairly walked up to git hurt?" With these arguments the cowboy browbeat the Easterner and reduced him to rage.

"You're a fool!" cried the Easterner, viciously, "You're a bigger jackass than the
Swede by a million majority. Now let me tell you one thing. Let me tell you something. Listen! Johnnie *was* cheating!"

"'Johnnie,'" said the cowboy, blankly. There was a minute of silence, and then
he said, robustly, "Why no. The game was only for fun."

"Fun or not," said the Easterner, "Johnnie was cheating. I saw him. I know it. 265
I saw him. And I refused to stand up and be a man. I let the Swede fight it out
alone. And you—you were simply puffing around the place and wanting to fight.
And then old Scully himself! We are all in it! This poor gambler isn't even a noun.
He is kind of an adverb. Every sin is the result of a collaboration. We, five of us,
have collaborated in the murder of this Swede. Usually there are from a dozen to
forty women really involved in every murder, but in this case it seems to be only
five men—you, I, Johnnie, old Scully; and that fool of an unfortunate gambler
came merely as a culmination, the apex of a human movement, and gets all the
punishment."

The cowboy, injured and rebellious, cried out blindly into this fog of mysterious theory: "Well, I didn't do anythin', did I?"

Ralph Ellison   b. 1914

Battle Royal   *1947*

It goes a long way back, some twenty years. All my life I had been looking for something, and everywhere I turned someone tried to tell me what it was. I accepted their answers too, though they were often in contradiction and even self-contradictory. I was naive. I was looking for myself and asking everyone except myself questions which I, and only I, could answer. It took me a long time and much painful boomeranging of my expectations to achieve a realization everyone else appears to have been born with: That I am nobody but myself. But first I had to discover that I am an invisible man!

And yet I am no freak of nature, nor of history. I was in the cards, other things having been equal (or unequal) eighty-five years ago. I am not ashamed of my grandparents for having been slaves. I am only ashamed of myself for having at one time been ashamed. About eight-five years ago they were told that they were free, united with others of our country in everything pertaining to the common good, and, in everything social, separate like the fingers of the hand. And they believed it. They exulted in it. They stayed in their place, worked hard, and brought up my father to do the same. But my grandfather is the one. He was an odd old guy, my grandfather, and I am told I take after him. It was he who caused the trouble. On his deathbed he called my father to him and said, "Son, after I'm gone I want you to keep up the fight. I never told you, but our life is a war and I have been a traitor all my born days, a spy in the enemy's country ever since I give up my gun back in the Reconstruction.[1] Live with your head in the lion's mouth. I want you to overcome 'em with yeses, undermine 'em with grins, agree 'em to death and destruction, let 'em swoller you till they vomit or bust wide open." They thought the old man had gone out of his mind. He had been the meekest of men. The younger children were rushed from the room, the shades drawn and the flame of the lamp turned so low that it sputtered on the wick like the old man's breathing. "Learn it to the younguns," he whispered fiercely; then he died.

But my folks were more alarmed over his last words than over his dying. It was as though he had not died at all, his words caused so much anxiety. I was warned emphatically to forget what he had said and, indeed, this is the first time it has been mentioned outside the family circle. It had a tremendous effect upon me, however. I could never be sure of what he meant. Grandfather had been a quiet old man who never made any trouble, yet on his deathbed he had called himself a traitor and a spy, and he had spoken of his meekness as a dangerous activity. It became a constant puzzle which lay unanswered in the back of my mind. And whenever things went well for me I remembered my grandfather and felt guilty and uncomfortable. It was as though I was carrying out his advice in spite of myself. And to make it worse, everyone loved me for it. I was praised by the most

---

[1]Reconstruction—post-Civil War reorganization of the former Confederate states.

lily-white men of the town. I was considered an example of desirable conduct—
just as my grandfather had been. And what puzzled me was that the old man had
defined it as *treachery*. When I was praised for my conduct I felt a guilt that in
some way I was doing something that was really against the wishes of the white
folks, that if they had understood they would have desired me to act just the opposite, that I should have been sulky and mean, and that that really would have
been what they wanted, even though they were fooled and thought they wanted
me to act as I did. It made me afraid that some day they would look upon me as
a traitor and I would be lost. Still I was more afraid to act any other way because
they didn't like that at all. The old man's words were like a curse. On my graduation day I delivered an oration in which I showed that humility was the secret,
indeed, the very essence of progress. (Not that I believed this—how could I,
remembering my grandfather?—I only believed that it worked.) It was a great success. Everyone praised me and I was invited to give the speech at a gathering of
the town's leading white citizens. It was a triumph for our whole community.

It was in the main ballroom of the leading hotel. When I got there I discovered that it was on the occasion of a smoker, and I was told that since I was to be
there anyway I might as well take part in the battle royal to be fought by some of
my schoolmates as part of the entertainment. The battle royal came first.

All of the town's big shots were there in their tuxedos, wolfing down the buf-   5
fet foods, drinking beer and whiskey and smoking black cigars. It was a large
room with a high ceiling. Chairs were arranged in neat rows around three sides of
a portable boxing ring. The fourth side was clear, revealing a gleaming space of
polished floor. I had some misgivings over the battle royal, by the way. Not from
a distaste for fighting, but because I didn't care too much for the other fellows
who were to take part. They were tough guys who seemed to have no grandfather's curse worrying their minds. No one could mistake their toughness. And besides, I suspected that fighting a battle royal might detract from the dignity of my
speech. In those pre-invisible days I visualized myself as a potential Booker T.
Washington.[2] But the other fellows didn't care too much for me either, and there
were nine of them. I felt superior to them in my way, and I didn't like the manner
in which we were all crowded together into the servants' elevator. Nor did they
like my being there. In fact, as the warmly lighted floors flashed past the elevator
we had words over the fact that I, by taking part in the fight, had knocked one of
their friends out of a night's work.

We were led out of the elevator through a rococo hall into an anteroom and
told to get into our fighting togs. Each of us was issued a pair of boxing gloves and
ushered out into the big mirrored hall, which we entered looking cautiously about
us and whispering, lest we might accidentally be heard above the noise of the
room. It was foggy with cigar smoke. And already the whiskey was taking effect. I
was shocked to see some of the most important men of the town quite tipsy. They
were all there—bankers, lawyers, judges, doctors, fire chiefs, teachers, merchants.
Even one of the more fashionable pastors. Something we could not see was going
on up front. A clarinet was vibrating sensuously and the men were standing up
and moving eagerly forward. We were a small tight group, clustered together, our
bare upper bodies touching and shining with anticipatory sweat; while up front
the big shots were becoming increasingly excited over something we still could

---

[2]Booker T. Washington—(1856–1915): African-American educator.

not see. Suddenly I heard the school superintendent, who had told me to come, yell, "Bring up the shines,[3] gentlemen! Bring up the little shines!"

We were rushed up to the front of the ballroom, where it smelled even more strongly of tobacco and whiskey. Then we were pushed into place. I almost wet my pants. A sea of faces, some hostile, some amused, ringed around us, and in the center, facing us, stood a magnificent blonde—stark naked. There was a dead silence. I felt a blast of cold air chill me. I tried to back away, but they were behind me and around me. Some of the boys stood with lowered heads, trembling. I felt a wave of irrational guilt and fear. My teeth chattered, my skin turned to goose flesh, my knees knocked. Yet I was strongly attracted and looked in spite of myself. Had the price of looking been blindness, I would have looked. The hair was yellow like that of a circus kewpie doll, the face heavily powdered and rouged, as though to form an abstract mask, the eyes hollow and smeared a cool blue, the color of a baboon's butt. I felt a desire to spit upon her as my eyes brushed slowly over her body. Her breasts were firm and round as the domes of East Indian temples, and I stood so close as to see the fine skin texture and beads of pearly perspiration glistening like dew around the pink and erected buds of her nipples. I wanted at one and the same time to run from the room, to sink through the floor, or go to her and cover her from my eyes and the eyes of the others with my body; to feel the soft thighs, to caress her and destroy her, to love her and murder her, to hide from her, and yet to stoke where below the small American flag tattooed upon her belly her thighs formed a capital V. I had a notion that of all in the room she saw only me with her impersonal eyes.

And then she began to dance, a slow sensuous movement; the smoke of a hundred cigars clinging to her like the thinnest of veils. She seemed like a fair bird-girl girdled in veils calling to me from the angry surface of some gray and threatening sea. I was transported. Then I became aware of the clarinet playing and the big shots yelling at us. Some threatened us if we looked and others if we did not. On my right I saw one boy faint. And now a man grabbed a silver pitcher from a table and stepped close as he dashed ice water upon him and stood him up and forced two of us to support him as his head hung and moans issued from his thick bluish lips. Another boy began to plead to go home. He was the largest of the group, wearing dark red fighting trunks much too small to conceal the erection which projected from him as though in answer to the insinuating low-registered moaning of the clarinet. He tried to hide himself with his boxing gloves.

And all the while the blonde continued dancing, smiling faintly at the big shots who watched her with fascination, and faintly smiling at our fear. I noticed a certain merchant who followed her hungrily, his lips loose and drooling. He was a large man who wore diamond studs in a shirtfront which swelled with the ample paunch underneath, and each time the blonde swayed her undulating hips he ran his hand through the thin hair of his bald head and, with his arms upheld, his posture clumsy like that of an intoxicated panda, wound his belly in a slow and obscene grind. This creature was completely hypnotized. The music had quickened. As the dancer flung herself about with a detached expression on her face, the men began reaching out to touch her. I could see their beefy fingers sink into the soft flesh. Some of the others tried to stop them and she began to move around the

---

[3]Shines—derogatory term for black people.

floor in graceful circles, as they gave chase, slipping and sliding over the polished floor. It was mad. Chairs went crashing, drinks were spilt, as they ran laughing and howling after her. They caught her just as she reached a door, raised her from the floor, and tossed her as college boys are tossed at a hazing, and above her red, fixed-smiling lips I saw the terror and disgust in her eyes, almost like my own terror and that which I saw in some of the other boys. As I watched, they tossed her twice and her soft breasts seemed to flatten against the air and her legs flung wildly as she spun. Some of the more sober ones helped her to escape. And I started off the floor, heading for the anteroom with the rest of the boys.

Some were still crying and in hysteria. But as we tried to leave we were stopped and ordered to get into the ring. There was nothing to do but what we were told. All ten of us climbed under the ropes and allowed ourselves to be blindfolded with broad bands of white cloth. One of the men seemed to feel a bit sympathetic and tried to cheer us up as we stood with our backs against the ropes. Some of us tried to grin. "See that boy over there?" one of the men said. "I want you to run across at the bell and give it to him right in the belly. If you don't get him, I'm going to get you. I don't like his looks." Each of us was told the same. The blindfolds were put on. Yet even then I had been going over my speech. In my mind each word was as bright as flame. I felt the cloth pressed into place, and frowned so that it would be loosened when I relaxed.

But now I felt a sudden fit of blind terror. I was unused to darkness. It was as though I had suddenly found myself in a dark room filled with poisonous cottonmouths. I could hear the bleary voices yelling insistently for the battle royal to begin.

"Get going in there!"

"Let me at the big nigger!"

I strained to pick up the school superintendent's voice, as though to squeeze some security out of that slightly more familiar sound.

"Let me at those black sonsabitches!" someone yelled.

"No, Jackson, no!" another voice yelled. "Here, somebody, help me hold Jack."

"I want to get at that ginger-colored nigger. Tear him limb from limb," the first voice yelled.

I stood against the ropes trembling. For in those days I was what they called ginger-colored, and he sounded as though he might crunch me between his teeth like a crisp ginger cookie.

Quite a struggle was going on. Chairs were being kicked about and I could hear voices grunting as with a terrific effort. I wanted to see, to see more desperately than ever before. But the blindfold was as tight as a thick skin-puckering scab and when I raised my gloved hands to push the layers of white aside a voice yelled, "Oh, no you don't, black bastard! Leave that alone!"

"Ring the bell before Jackson kills him a coon!" someone boomed in the sudden silence. And I heard the bell clang and the sound of feet scuffling forward.

A glove smacked against my head. I pivoted, striking out stiffly as someone went past, and felt the jar ripple along the length of my arm to my shoulder. Then it seemed as though all nine of the boys had turned upon me at once. Blows pounded me from all sides while I struck out as best I could. So many blows landed upon me that I wondered if I were not the only blindfolded fighter in the ring, or if the man called Jackson hadn't succeeded in getting me after all.

Blindfolded, I could no longer control my motions. I had no dignity. I stumbled about like a baby or a drunken man. The smoke had become thicker and with each new blow it seemed to sear and further restrict my lungs. My saliva became like hot bitter glue. A glove connected with my head, filling my mouth with warm blood. It was everywhere. I could not tell if the moisture I felt upon my body was sweat or blood. A blow landed hard against the nape of my neck. I felt myself going over, my head hitting the floor. Streaks of blue light filled the black world behind the blindfold. I lay prone, pretending that I was knocked-out, but felt myself seized by hands and yanked to my feet. "Get going, black boy! Mix it up!" My arms were like lead, my head smarting from blows. I managed to feel my way to the ropes and held on, trying to catch my breath. A glove landed in my midsection and I went over again, feeling as though the smoke had become a knife jabbed into my guts. Pushed this way and that by the legs milling around me, I finally pulled erect and discovered that I could see the black, sweatwashed forms weaving in the smoky-blue atmosphere like drunken dancers weaving to the rapid drumlike thuds of blows.

Everyone fought hysterically. It was complete anarchy. Everybody fought everybody else. No group fought together for long. Two, three, four, fought one, then turned to fight each other, were themselves attacked. Blows landed below the belt and in the kidney, with the gloves open as well as closed, and with my eye partly opened now there was not so much terror. I moved carefully, avoiding blows, although not too many to attract attention, fighting from group to group. The boys groped about like blind, cautious crabs crouching to protect their mid-sections, their heads pulled in short against their shoulders, their arms stretched nervously before them, with their fists testing the smoke-filled air like the knobbed feelers of hyper-sensitive snails. In the corner I glimpsed a boy violently punching the air and heard him scream in pain as he smashed his hand against a ring post. For a second I saw him bent over holding his hand, then going down as a blow caught his unprotected head. I played one group against the other, slipping in and throwing a punch then stepped out of range while pushing the others into the melee to take the blows blindly aimed at me. The smoke was agonizing and there were no rounds, no bells at three minute intervals to relieve our exhaustion. The room spun around me, a swirl of lights, smoke, sweating bodies surrounded by tense white faces. I bled from both nose and mouth, the blood spattering upon my chest.

The men kept yelling, "Slug him, black boy! Knock his guts out!"

"Uppercut him! Kill him! Kill that big boy!"   25

Taking a fake fall, I saw a boy going down heavily beside me as though we were felled by a single blow, saw a sneaker-clad foot shoot into his groin as the two who had knocked him down stumbled upon him. I rolled out of range, feeling a twinge of nausea.

The harder we fought the more threatening the men became. And yet, I had begun to worry about my speech again. How would it go? Would they recognize my ability? What would they give me?

I was fighting automatically when suddenly I noticed that one after another of the boys was leaving the ring. I was surprised, filled with panic, as though I had been left alone with an unknown danger. Then I understood. The boys had arranged it among themselves. It was custom for the two men left in the ring to slug it out for the winner's prize. I discovered this too late. When the bell sounded two men in tuxedos leaped into the ring and removed the blindfold. I found myself facing Tatlock, the biggest of the gang. I felt sick at my stomach. Hardly had the bell stopped ringing in my ears than it clanged again and I saw him moving swiftly toward me. Thinking of nothing else to do I hit him smash on the nose. He kept coming, bringing the rank sharp violence of stale sweat. His face was a black blank of a face, only his eyes alive—with hate of me and aglow with a feverish terror from what had happened to us all. I became anxious. I wanted to deliver my speech and he came at me as though he meant to beat it out of me. I smashed him again and again, taking his blows as they came. Then on a sudden impulse I struck him lightly and as we clinched, I whispered, "Fake like I knocked you out, you can have the prize."

"I'll break your behind," he whispered hoarsely.

"For *them?*"

"For *me,* sonofabitch."

They were yelling for us to break it up and Tatlock spun me half around with a blow, and as a joggled camera sweeps in a reeling scene, I saw the howling red faces crouching tense beneath the cloud of blue-gray smoke. For a moment the world wavered, unraveled, flowed, then my head cleared and Tatlock bounced before me. The fluttering shadow before my eyes was his jabbing left hand. Then falling forward, my head against his damp shoulder, I whispered.

"I'll make it five dollars more."

"Go to hell!"

But his muscles relaxed a trifle beneath my pressure and I breathed. "Seven?"

"Give it to your ma," he said, ripping me beneath the heart.

And while I still held him I butted him and moved away. I felt myself bombarded with punches. I fought back with hopeless desperation. I wanted to deliver my speech more than anything else in the world, because I felt only these men could judge truly my ability, and now this stupid clown was ruining my chances. I began fighting carefully now, moving in to punch him and out again with my greater speed. A lucky blow to his chin and I had him going too—until I heard a loud voice yell, "I got my money on the big boy."

Hearing this, I almost dropped my guard. I was confused: Should I try to win against the voice out there? Would not this go against my speech, and was not this a moment for humility, for nonresistance? A blow to my head as I danced about sent my right eye popping like a jack-in-the-box and settled my dilemma. The room went red as I fell. It was a dream fall, my body languid and fastidious as to where to land, until the floor became impatient and smashed up to meet me. A moment later I came to. An hypnotic voice said FIVE emphatically. And I lay there, hazily watching a dark red spot of my own blood shaping itself into a butterfly, glistening and soaking into the soiled gray world of the canvas.

When the voice drawled TEN I was lifted up and dragged to a chair. I sat dazed. My eye pained and swelled with each throb of my pounding heart and I wondered if now I would be allowed to speak. I was wringing wet, my mouth still bleeding. We were grouped along the wall now. The other boys ignored me as they congratulated Tatlock and speculated as to how much they would be paid. One boy whimpered over his smashed hand. Looking up front, I saw attendants in white jackets rolling the portable ring away and placing a small square rug in the vacant space surrounded by chairs. Perhaps, I thought, I will stand on the rug to deliver my speech.

Then the M.C. called to us, "Come on up here boys and get your money."

We ran forward to where the men laughed and talked in their chairs, waiting. Everyone seemed friendly now.

"There it is on the rug," the man said. I saw the rug covered with coins of all dimensions and a few crumpled bills. But what excited me, scattered here and there, were the gold pieces.

"Boys, it's all yours," the man said. "You get all you grab."

"That's right, Sambo," a blond man said, winking at me confidentially.

I trembled with excitement, forgetting my pain. I would get the gold and the   45
bills, I thought. I would use both hands. I would throw my body against the boys nearest me to block them from the gold.

"Get down around the rug now," the man commanded, "and don't anyone touch it until I give the signal."

"This ought to be good," I heard.

As told, we got around the square rug on our knees. Slowly the man raised his freckled hand as we followed it upward with our eyes.

I heard, "These niggers look like they're about to pray!"

Then, "Ready," the man said. "Go!"   50

I lunged for a yellow coin lying on the blue design on the carpet, touching it and sending a surprised shriek to join those rising around me. I tried frantically to remove my hand but could not let go. A hot, violent force tore through my body, shaking me like a wet rat. The rug was electrified. The hair bristled up on my head as I shook myself free. My muscles jumped, my nerves jangled, writhed. But I saw that this was not stopping the other boys. Laughing in fear and embarrassment, some were holding back and scooping up the coins knocked off by the painful contortions of the others. The men roared above us as we struggled.

"Pick it up, goddammit, pick it up!" someone called like a bass-voiced parrot. "Go on, get it!"

I crawled rapidly around the floor, picking up the coins, trying to avoid the coppers and to get greenbacks and the gold. Ignoring the shock by laughing, as I brushed the coins off quickly, I discovered that I could contain the electricity—a contradiction, but it works. Then the men began to push us onto the rug. Laughing embarrassedly, we struggled out of their hands and kept after the coins. We were all wet and slippery and hard to hold. Suddenly I saw a boy lifted into the air, glistening with sweat like a circus seal, and dropped, his wet back landing flush upon the charged rug, heard him yell and saw him literally dance upon his back, his elbows beating a frenzied tattoo upon the floor, his muscles twitching like the flesh of a horse stung by many flies. When he finally rolled off, his face was gray and no one stopped him when he ran from the floor amid booming laughter.

"Get the money," the M.C. called "That's good hard American cash!"

And we snatched and grabbed, snatched and grabbed. I was careful not to   55
come too close to the rug now, and when I felt the hot whiskey breath descend upon me like a cloud of foul air I reached out and grabbed the leg of a chair. It was occupied and I held on desperately.

"Leggo nigger! Leggo!"

The huge face wavered down to mine as he tried to push me free. But my body was slippery and he was too drunk. It was Mr. Colcord, who owned a chain of movie houses and "entertainment palaces." Each time he grabbed me I slipped out of his hands. It became a real struggle. I feared the rug more than I did the drunk, so I held on, surprising myself for a moment by trying to topple *him* upon the rug. It was such an enormous idea that I found myself actually carrying it out. I tried not to be obvious, yet when I grabbed his leg, trying to tumble him out of the chair, he raised up roaring with laughter, and, looking at me with soberness dead in the eye, kicked me viciously in the chest. The chair leg flew out of my hand and I felt myself going and rolled. It was as though I had rolled through a bed of hot coals. It seemed a whole century would pass before I would roll free, a century in which I was seared through the deepest levels of my body to the fearful breath within me and the breath seared and heated to the point of explosion. It'll all be over in a flash, I thought as I rolled clear. It'll all be over in a flash.

But not yet, the men on the other side were waiting, red faces swollen as though from apoplexy as they bent forward in their chairs. Seeing their fingers coming toward me I rolled away as a fumbled football rolls off the receiver's fingertips, back into the coals. That time I luckily sent the rug sliding out of place and heard the coins ringing against the floor and the boys scuffling to pick them up and the M.C. calling, "All right, boys, that's all. Go get dressed and get your money."

I was limp as a dish rag. My back felt as though it had been beaten with wires.

When we had dressed the M.C. came in and gave us each five dollars, except 60 Tatlock, who got ten for being last in the ring. Then he told us to leave. I was not to get a chance to deliver my speech, I thought. I was going out into the dim alley in despair when I was stopped and told to go back. I returned to the ballroom, where the men were pushing back their chairs and gathering in groups to talk.

The M.C. knocked on a table for quiet. "Gentlemen," he said, "we almost forgot an important part of the program. A most serious part, gentlemen. This boy was brought here to deliver a speech which he made at his graduation yesterday. . . ."

"Bravo!"

"I'm told that he is the smartest boy we've got out there in Greenwood. I'm told that he knows more big words than a pocket-sized dictionary."

Much applause and laughter.

"So now, gentlemen, I want you to give him your attention."   65

There was still laughter as I faced them, my mouth dry, my eye throbbing. I began slowly, but evidently my throat was tense, because they began shouting, "Louder! Louder!"

"We of the younger generation extol the wisdom of that great leader and educator," I shouted, "who first spoke these flaming words of wisdom. 'A ship lost at sea for many days suddenly sighted a friendly vessel. From the mast of the unfortunate vessel was seen a signal: "Water, water; we die of thirst!" The answer from the friendly vessel came back: "Cast down your bucket where you are." The captain of the distressed vessel, at last heeding the injunction, cast down his bucket, and it came up full of fresh sparkling water from the mouth of the Amazon River.' And like him I say, and in his words, 'To those of my race who depend upon bettering their condition in a foreign land, or who underestimate the importance of cultivating friendly relations with the Southern white man, who is his next-door neighbor, I would say: "Cast down your bucket where you are"—cast it down in making friends in every manly way of the people of all races by whom we are surrounded....'"

I spoke automatically and with such fervor that I did not realize that the men were still talking and laughing until my dry mouth, filling up with blood from the cut, almost strangled me. I coughed, wanting to stop and go to one of the tall brass, sand-filled spittoons to relieve myself, but a few of the men, especially the superintendent, were listening and I was afraid. So I gulped it down, blood, saliva, and all, and continued. (What powers of endurance I had during those days! What enthusiasm! What a belief in the rightness of things!) I spoke even louder in spite

of the pain. But still they talked and still they laughed, as though deaf with cotton
in dirty ears. So I spoke with greater emotional emphasis. I closed my ears and
swallowed blood until I was nauseated. The speech seemed a hundred times as
long as before, but I could not leave out a single word. All had to be said, each
memorized nuance considered, rendered. Nor was that all. Whenever I uttered a
word of three or more syllables a group of voices would yell for me to repeat it. I
used the phrase "social responsibility" and they yelled:

"What's that word you say, boy?"

"Social responsibility," I said.   70

"What?"

"Social . . ."

"Louder."

". . . responsibility."

"More!"   75

"Respon—"

"Repeat!"

"—sibility."

The room filled with the uproar of laughter until, no doubt, distracted by having to gulp down my blood, I made a mistake and yelled a phrase I had often seen
denounced with newspaper editorials, heard debated in private.

"Social . . ."   80

"What?" they yelled.

". . . equality—"

The laughter hung smokelike in the sudden stillness. I opened my eyes puzzled. Sounds of displeasure filled the room. The M.C. rushed forward. They
shouted hostile phrases at me. But I did not understand.

A small dry mustached man in the front row blared out, "Say that slowly, son!"

"What sir?"   85

"What you just said!"

"Social responsibility, sir," I said.

"You weren't being smart, were you, boy?" he said, not unkindly.

"No, sir!"

"You sure that about 'equality' was a mistake?"   90

"Oh, yes, sir," I said. "I was swallowing blood."

"Well, you had better speak more slowly so we can understand. We mean to
do right by you, but you've got to know your place at all times. All right, now, go
on with your speech."

I was afraid. I wanted to leave but I wanted also to speak and I was afraid
they'd snatch me down.

"Thank you, sir," I said, beginning where I had left off, and having them ignore me as before.

Yet when I finished there was a thunderous applause. I was surprised to see   95
the superintendent come forth with a package wrapped in white tissue paper, and,
gesturing for quiet, address the men.

"Gentlemen, you see that I did not overpraise this boy. He makes a good
speech and some day he'll lead his people in the proper paths. And I don't have
to tell you that that is important in these days and times. This is a good, smart boy,
and so to encourage him in the right direction, in the name of the Board of Education I wish to present him a prize in the form of this ..."

He paused, removing the tissue paper and revealing a gleaming calfskin briefcase.

". . . in the form of this first-class article from Shad Whitmore's shop."

"Boy," he said, addressing me, "take this prize and keep it well. Consider it a badge of office. Prize it. Keep developing as you are and some day it will be filled with important papers that will help shape the destiny of your people."

I was so moved that I could hardly express my thanks. A rope of bloody saliva forming a shape like an undiscovered continent drooled upon the leather and I wiped it quickly away. I felt an importance that I had never dreamed.   100

"Open it and see what's inside," I was told.

My fingers a-tremble, I complied, smelling the fresh leather and finding an official-looking document inside. It was a scholarship to the state college for Negroes. My eyes filled with tears and I ran awkwardly off the floor.

I was so overjoyed; I did not even mind when I discovered that the gold pieces I had scrambled for were brass pocket tokens advertising a certain make of automobile.

When I reached home everyone was excited. Next day the neighbors came to congratulate me. I even felt safe from grandfather, whose deathbed curse usually spoiled my triumphs. I stood beneath his photograph with my briefcase in hand and smiled triumphantly into his stolid black peasant's face. It was a face that fascinated me. The eyes seemed to follow everywhere I went.

That night I dreamed I was at a circus with him and that he refused to laugh   105
at the clowns no matter what they did. Then later he told me to open my briefcase and read what was inside and I did, finding an official envelope stamped with the state seal; and inside the envelope I found another and another, endlessly, and I thought I would fall of weariness. "Them's years," he said. "Now open that one." And I did and in it I found an engraved document containing a short message in letters of gold. "Read it," my grandfather said. "Out loud."

"To Whom It May Concern," I intoned. "Keep This Nigger-Boy Running."

I awoke with the old man's laughter ringing in my ears.

(It was a dream I was to remember and dream again for many years after. But at that time I had no insight into its meaning. First I had to attend college.)

Louise Erdrich   b. 1954

Fleur   1986

The first time she drowned in the cold and glassy waters of Lake Turcot, Fleur Pillager was only a girl. Two men saw the boat tip, saw her struggle in the waves. They rowed over to the place she went down, and jumped in. When they dragged her over the gunwales, she was cold to the touch and stiff, so they slapped her face, shook her by the heels, worked her arms back and forth, and pounded her back until she coughed up lake water. She shivered all over like a dog, then took a breath. But it wasn't long afterward that those two men disappeared. The first wandered off, and the other, Jean Hat, got himself run over by a cart.

It went to show, my grandma said. It figured to her, all right. By saving Fleur Pillager, those two men had lost themselves.

The next time she fell in the lake, Fleur Pillager was twenty years old and no one touched her. She washed onshore, her skin a dull dead gray, but when George Many Women bent to look closer, he saw her chest move. Then her eyes spun open, sharp black riprock, and she looked at him. "You'll take my place," she hissed. Everybody scattered and left her there, so no one knows how she dragged herself home. Soon after that we noticed Many Women changed, grew afraid, wouldn't leave his house, and would not be forced to go near water. For his caution, he lived until the day that his sons brought him a new tin bathtub. Then the first time he used the tub he slipped, got knocked out, and breathed water while his wife stood in the other room frying breakfast.

Men stayed clear of Fleur Pillager after the second drowning. Even though she was good-looking, nobody dared to court her because it was clear that Misshepeshu, the waterman, the monster, wanted her for himself. He's a devil, that one, love-hungry with desire and maddened for the touch of young girls, the strong and daring especially, the ones like Fleur.

Our mothers warn us that we'll think he's handsome, for he appears with green eyes, copper skin, a mouth tender as a child's. But if you fall into his arms, he sprouts horns, fangs, claws, fins. His feet are joined as one and his skin, brass scales, rings to the touch. You're fascinated, cannot move. He casts a shell necklace at your feet, weeps gleaming chips that harden into mica on your breasts. He holds you under. Then he takes the body of a lion or a fat brown worm. He's made of gold. He's made of beach moss. He's a thing of dry foam, a thing of death by drowning, the death a Chippewa cannot survive.

Unless you are Fleur Pillager. We all knew she couldn't swim. After the first time, we thought she'd never go back to Lake Turcot. We thought she'd keep to herself, live quiet, stop killing men off by drowning in the lake. After the first time, we thought she'd keep the good ways. But then, after the second drowning, we knew that we were dealing with something much more serious. She was haywire, out of control. She messed with evil, laughed at the old women's advice, and dressed like a man. She got herself into some half-forgotten medicine, studied ways we shouldn't talk about. Some say she kept the finger of a child in her pocket and a powder of unborn rabbits in a leather thong around her neck. She laid the heart of an owl on her tongue so she could see at night, and went out, hunting, not even in her own body. We know for sure because the next morning, in the snow or dust, we followed the tracks of her bare feet and saw where they changed, where the claws sprang out, the pad broadened and pressed into the dirt. By night we heard her chuffing cough, the bear cough. By day her silence and the wide grin she threw to bring down our guard made us frightened. Some thought that Fleur Pillager should be driven off the reservation, but not a single person who spoke like this had the nerve. And finally, when people were just about to get together and throw her out, she left on her own and didn't come back all summer. That's what this story is about.

During that summer, when she lived a few miles south in Argus, things happened. She almost destroyed that town.

When she got down to Argus in the year of 1920, it was just a small grid of six streets on either side of the railroad depot. There were two elevators, one central, the other a few miles west. Two stores competed for the trade of the three hundred citizens, and three churches quarreled with one another for their souls. There was a frame building for Lutherans, a heavy brick one for Episcopalians, and a long narrow shingled Catholic church. This last had a tall slender steeple, twice as high as any building or tree.

No doubt, across the low, flat wheat, watching from the road as she came near Argus on foot, Fleur saw that steeple rise, a shadow thin as a needle. Maybe in that raw space it drew her the way a lone tree draws lightning. Maybe, in the end, the Catholics are to blame. For if she hadn't seen that sign of pride, that slim prayer, that marker, maybe she would have kept walking.

But Fleur Pillager turned, and the first place she went once she came into town was to the back door of the priest's residence attached to the landmark church. She didn't go there for a handout, although she got that, but to ask for work. She got that too, or the town got her. It's hard to tell which came out worse, her or the men or the town, although the upshot of it all was that Fleur lived.

The four men who worked at the butcher's had carved up about a thousand carcasses between them, maybe half of that steers and the other half pigs, sheep, and game animals like deer, elk, and bear. That's not even mentioning the chickens, which were beyond counting. Pete Kozka owned the place, and employed Lily Veddar, Tor Grunewald, and my stepfather, Dutch James, who had brought my mother down from the reservation the year before she disappointed him by dying. Dutch took me out of school to take her place. I kept house half the time and worked the other in the butcher shop, sweeping floors, putting sawdust down, running a hambone across the street to a customer's bean pot or a package of sausage to the corner. I was a good one to have around because until they needed me, I was invisible. I blended into the stained brown walls, a skinny, big-nosed girl with staring eyes. Because I could fade into a corner or squeeze beneath a shelf, I knew everything, what the men said when no one was around, and what they did to Fleur.

Kozka's Meats served farmers for a fifty-mile area, both to slaughter, for it had a stock pen and chute, and to cure the meat by smoking it or spicing it in sausage. The storage locker was a marvel, made of many thicknesses of brick, earth insulation, and Minnesota timber, lined inside with sawdust and vast blocks of ice cut from Lake Turcot, hauled down from home each winter by horse and sledge.

A ramshackle board building, part slaughterhouse, part store, was fixed to the low, thick square of the lockers. That's where Fleur worked. Kozka hired her for her strength. She could lift a haunch or carry a pole of sausages without stumbling, and she soon learned cutting from Pete's wife, a string-thin blonde who chain-smoked and handled the razor-sharp knives with nerveless precision, slicing close to her stained fingers. Fleur and Fritzie Kozka worked afternoons, wrapping their cuts in paper, and Fleur hauled the packages to the lockers. The meat was left outside the heavy oak doors that were only opened at 5:00 each afternoon, before the men ate supper.

Sometimes Dutch, Tor, and Lily ate at the lockers, and when they did I stayed too, cleaned floors, restoked the fires in the front smokehouses, while the men sat around the squat cast-iron stove spearing slats of herring onto hardtack bread. They played long games of poker or cribbage on a board made from the planed end of a salt crate. They talked and I listened, although there wasn't much to hear since almost nothing ever happened in Argus. Tor was married, Dutch had lost my mother, and Lily read circulars. They mainly discussed about the auctions to come, equipment, or women.

10

Every so often, Pete Kozka came out front to make a whist, leaving Fritzie to   15
smoke cigarettes and fry raised doughnuts in the back room. He sat and played a
few rounds but kept his thoughts to himself. Fritzie did not tolerate him talking behind her back, and the one book he read was the New Testament. If he said something, it concerned weather or a surplus of sheep stomachs, a ham that smoked
green or the markets for corn and wheat. He had a good-luck talisman, the opal-
white lens of a cow's eye. Playing cards, he rubbed it between his fingers. That
soft sound and the slap of cards was about the only conversation.

Fleur finally gave them a subject.

Her cheeks were wide and flat, her hands large, chapped, muscular. Fleur's
shoulders were broad as beams, her hips fishlike, slippery, narrow. An old green
dress clung to her waist, worn thin where she sat. Her braids were thick like the
tails of animals, and swung against her when she moved, deliberately, slowly in her
work, held in and half-tamed, but only half. I could tell, but the others never saw.
They never looked into her sly brown eyes or noticed her teeth, strong and curved
and very white. Her legs were bare, and since she padded around in beadwork
moccasins they never saw that her fifth toes were missing. They never knew she'd
drowned. They were blinded, they were stupid, they only saw her in the flesh.

And yet it wasn't just that she was a Chippewa, or even that she was a
woman, it wasn't that she was good-looking or even that she was alone that made
their brains hum. It was how she played cards.

Women didn't usually play with men, so the evening that Fleur drew a chair up
to the men's table without being so much as asked, there was a shock of surprise.

"What's this," said Lily. He was fat, with a snake's cold pale eyes and precious   20
skin, smooth and lily-white, which is how he got his name. Lily had a dog, a
stumpy mean little bull of a thing with a belly drum-tight from eating pork rinds.
The dog liked to play cards just like Lily, and straddled his barrel thighs through
games of stud, rum poker, vingt-un. The dog snapped at Fleur's arm that first
night, but cringed back, its snarl frozen, when she took her place.

"I thought," she said, her voice soft and stroking, "you might deal me in."

There was a space between the heavy bin of spiced flour and the wall where
I just fit. I hunkered down there, kept my eyes open, saw her black hair swing
over the chair, her feet solid on the wood floor. I couldn't see up on the table
where the cards slapped down, so after they were deep in their game I raised myself up in the shadows, and crouched on a sill of wood.

I watched Fleur's hands stack and ruffle, divide the cards, spill them to each
player in a blur, rake them up and shuffle again. Tor, short and scrappy, shut one
eye and squinted the other at Fleur. Dutch screwed his lips around a wet cigar.

"Gotta see a man," he mumbled, getting up to go out back to the privy. The
others broke, put their cards down, and Fleur sat alone in the lamplight that glowed
in a sheen across the push of her breasts. I watched her closely, then she paid me
a beam of notice for the first time. She turned, looked straight at me, and grinned
the white wolf grin a Pillager turns on its victims, except that she wasn't after me.

"Pauline there," she said, "how much money you got?"   25

We'd all been paid for the week that day. Eight cents was in my pocket.

"Stake me," she said, holding out her long fingers. I put the coins in her palm
and then I melted back to nothing, part of the walls and tables. It was a long time
before I understood that the men would not have seen me no matter what I did,
how I moved. I wasn't anything like Fleur. My dress hung loose and my back was

already curved, an old woman's. Work had roughened me, reading made my eyes sore, caring for my mother before she died had hardened my face. I was not much to look at, so they never saw me.

When the men came back and sat around the table, they had drawn together. They shot each other small glances, stuck their tongues in their cheeks, burst out laughing at odd moments, to rattle Fleur. But she never minded. They played their vingt-un, staying even as Fleur slowly gained. Those pennies I had given her drew nickels and attracted dimes until there was a small pile in front of her.

Then she hooked them with five-card draw, nothing wild. She dealt, discarded, drew, and then she sighed and her cards gave a little shiver. Tor's eye gleamed, and Dutch straightened in his seat.

"I'll pay to see that hand," said Lily Veddar.   30

Fleur showed, and she had nothing there, nothing at all.

Tor's thin smile cracked open, and he threw his hand in too.

"Well, we know one thing," he said, leaning back in his chair, "the squaw can't bluff."

With that I lowered myself into a mound of swept sawdust and slept. I woke up during the night, but none of them had moved yet, so I couldn't either. Still later, the men must have gone out again, or Fritzie come out to break the game, because I was lifted, soothed, cradled in a woman's arms and rocked so quiet that I kept my eyes shut while Fleur rolled me into a closet of grimy ledgers, oiled paper, balls of string, and thick files that fit beneath me like a mattress.

The game went on after work the next evening. I got my eight cents back five   35 times over, and Fleur kept the rest of the dollar she'd won for a stake. This time they didn't play so late, but they played regular, and then kept going at it night after night. They played poker now, or variations, for one week straight, and each time Fleur won exactly one dollar, no more and no less, too consistent for luck.

By this time, Lily and the other men were so lit with suspense that they got Pete to join the game with them. They concentrated, the fat dog sitting tense in Lily Veddar's lap, Tor suspicious, Dutch stroking his huge square brow, Pete steady. It wasn't that Fleur won that hooked them in so, because she lost hands too. It was rather that she never had a freak hand or even anything above a straight. She only took on her low cards, which didn't sit right. By chance, Fleur should have gotten a full or flush by now. The irritating thing was she beat with pairs and never bluffed, because she couldn't, and still she ended up each night with exactly one dollar. Lily couldn't believe, first of all, that a woman could be smart enough to play cards, but even if she was, that she would then be stupid enough to cheat for a dollar a night. By day I watched him turn the problem over, his hard white face dull, small fingers probing at his knuckles, until he finally thought he had Fleur figured out as a bit-time player, caution her game. Raising the stakes would throw her.

More than anything now, he wanted Fleur to come away with something but a dollar. Two bits less or ten more, the sum didn't matter, just so he broke her streak.

Night after night she played, won her dollar, and left to stay in a place that just Fritzie and I knew about. Fleur bathed in the slaughtering tub, then slept in the unused brick smokehouse behind the lockers, a windowless place tarred on the inside with scorched fats. When I brushed against her skin I noticed that she smelled of the walls, rich and woody, slightly burnt. Since that night she put me in the closet I was no longer afraid of her, but followed her close, stayed with her, became her moving shadow that the men never noticed, the shadow that could have saved her.

August, the month that bears fruit, closed around the shop, and Pete and Fritzie left for Minnesota to escape the heat. Night by night, running, Fleur had won thirty dollars, and only Pete's presence had kept Lily at bay. But Pete was gone now, and one payday, with the heat so bad no one could move but Fleur, the men sat and played and waited while she finished work. The cards sweat, limp in their fingers, the table was slick with grease, and even the walls were warm to the touch. The air was motionless. Fleur was in the next room boiling heads.

Her green dress, drenched, wrapped her like a transparent sheet. A skin of   40
lakeweed. Black snarls of veining clung to her arms. Her braids were loose, half-unraveled, tied behind her neck in a thick loop. She stood in steam, turning skulls through a vat with a wooden paddle. When scraps boiled to the surface, she bent with a round tin sieve and scooped them out. She'd filled two dishpans.

"Ain't that enough now?" called Lily. "We're waiting." The stump of a dog trembled in his lap, alive with rage. It never smelled me or noticed me above Fleur's smoky skin. The air was heavy in my corner, and pressed me down. Fleur sat with them.

"Now what do you say?" Lily asked the dog. It barked. That was the signal for the real game to start.

"Let's up the ante," said Lily, who had been stalking this night all month. He had a roll of money in his pocket. Fleur had five bills in her dress. The men had each saved their full pay.

"Ante a dollar then," said Fleur, and pitched hers in. She lost, but they let her scrape along, cent by cent. And then she won some. She played unevenly, as if chance was all she had. She reeled them in. The game went on. The dog was stiff now, poised on Lily's knees, a ball of vicious muscle with its yellow eyes slit in concentration. It gave advice, seemed to sniff the lay of Fleur's cards, twitched and nudged. Fleur was up, then down, saved by a scratch. Tor dealt seven cards, three down. The pot grew, round by round, until it held all the money. Nobody folded. Then it all rode on one last card and they went silent. Fleur picked hers up and blew a long breath. The heat lowered like a bell. Her card shook, but she stayed in.

Lily smiled and took the dog's head tenderly between his palms.   45

"Say, Fatso," he said, crooning the words, "you reckon that girl's bluffing?"

The dog whined and Lily laughed. "Me too," he said, "let's show." He swept his bills and coins into the pot and then they turned their cards over.

Lily looked once, looked again, then he squeezed the dog up like a fist of dough and slammed it on the table.

Fleur threw her arms out and drew the money over, grinning that same wolf grin that she'd used on me, the grin that had them. She jammed the bills in her dress, scooped the coins up in waxed white paper that she tied with string.

"Let's go another round," said Lily, his voice choked with burrs. But Fleur   50
opened her mouth and yawned, then walked out back to gather slops for the one big hog that was waiting in the stock pen to be killed.

The men sat still as rocks, their hands spread on the oiled wood table. Dutch had chewed his cigar to damp shreds, Tor's eye was dull. Lily's gaze was the only one to follow Fleur. I didn't move. I felt them gathering, saw my stepfather's veins, the ones in his forehead that stood out in anger. The dog had rolled off the table and curled in a knot below the counter, where none of the men could touch it.

Lily rose and stepped out back to the closet of ledgers where Pete kept his private stock. He brought back a bottle, uncorked and tipped it between his fingers. The lump in his throat moved, then he passed it on. They drank, quickly felt the whiskey's fire, and planned with their eyes things they couldn't say out loud.

When they left, I followed. I hid out back in the clutter of broken boards and chicken crates beside the stock pen, where they waited. Fleur could not be seen at first, and then the moon broke and showed her, slipping cautiously along the rough board chute with a bucket in her hand. Her hair fell, wild and coarse, to her waist, and her dress was a floating patch in the dark. She made a pig-calling sound, rang the tin pail lightly against the wood, froze suspiciously. But too late. In the sound of the ring Lily moved, fat and nimble, stepped right behind Fleur and put out his creamy hands. At his first touch, she whirled and doused him with the bucket of sour slops. He pushed her against the big fence and the package of coins split, went clinking and jumping, winked against the wood. Fleur rolled over once and vanished in the yard.

The moon fell behind a curtain of ragged clouds, and Lily followed into the dark muck. But he tripped, pitched over the huge flank of the pig, who lay mired to the snout, heavily snoring. I sprang out of the weeds and climbed the side of the pen, stuck like glue. I saw the sow rise to her neat, knobby knees, gain her balance, and sway, curious, as Lily stumbled forward. Fleur had backed into the angle of rough wood just beyond, and when Lily tried to jostle past, the sow tipped up on her hind legs and struck, quick and hard as a snake. She plunged her head into Lily's thick side and snatched a mouthful of his shirt. She lunged again, caught him lower, so that he grunted in pained surprise. He seemed to ponder, breathing deep. Then he launched his huge body in a swimmer's dive.

The sow screamed as his body smacked over hers. She rolled, striking out   55
with her knife-sharp hooves, and Lily gathered himself upon her, took her foot-long face by the ears and scraped her snout and cheeks against the trestles of the pen. He hurled the sow's tight skull against an iron post, but instead of knocking her dead, he merely woke her from her dream.

She reared, shrieked, drew him with her so that they posed standing upright. They bowed jerkily to each other, as if to begin. Then his arms swung and flailed. She sank her black fangs into his shoulder, clasping him, dancing him forward and backward through the pen. Their steps picked up pace, went wild. The two dipped as one, box-stepped, tripped each other. She ran her split foot through his hair. He grabbed her kinked tail. They went down and came up, the same shape and then the same color, until the men couldn't tell one from the other in that light and Fleur was able to launch herself over the gates, swing down, hit gravel.

The men saw, yelled, and chased her at a dead run to the smokehouse. And Lily too, once the sow gave up in disgust and freed him. That is where I should have gone to Fleur, saved her, thrown myself on Dutch. But I went stiff with fear and couldn't unlatch myself from the trestles or move at all. I closed my eyes and put my head in my arms, tried to hide, so there is nothing to describe but what I couldn't block out, Fleur's hoarse breath, so loud it filled me, her cry in the old language, and my name repeated over and over among the words.

The heat was still dense the next morning when I came back to work. Fleur was gone but the men were there, slack-faced, hung over. Lily was paler and softer than ever, as if his flesh had steamed on his bones. They smoked, took pulls off a bottle. It wasn't noon yet. I worked awhile, waiting shop and sharpening steel. But I was sick, I was smothered, I was sweating so hard that my hands slipped on the knives, and I wiped my fingers clean of the greasy touch of the customers' coins. Lily opened his mouth and roared once, not in anger. There was no meaning to the sound. His boxer dog, sprawled limp beside his foot, never lifted its head. Nor did the other men.

They didn't notice when I stepped outside, hoping for a clear breath. And then I forgot them because I knew that we were all balanced, ready to tip, to fly, to be crushed as soon as the weather broke. The sky was so low that I felt the weight of it like a yoke. Clouds hung down, witch teats, a tornado's green-brown cones, and as I watched one flicked out and became a delicate probing thumb. Even as I picked up my heels and ran back inside, the wind blew suddenly, cold, and then came rain.

Inside, the men had disappeared already and the whole place was trembling 60 as if a huge hand was pinched at the rafters, shaking it. I ran straight through, screaming for Dutch or for any of them, and then I stopped at the heavy doors of the lockers, where they had surely taken shelter. I stood there a moment. Everything went still. Then I heard a cry building in the wind, faint at first, a whistle and then a shrill scream that tore through the walls and gathered around me, spoke plain so I understood that I should move, put my arms out, and slam down the great iron bar that fit across the hasp and lock.

Outside, the wind was stronger, like a hand held against me. I struggled forward. The bushes tossed, the awnings flapped off storefronts, the rails of porches rattled. The odd cloud became a fat snout that nosed along the earth and sniffled, jabbed, picked at things, sucked them up, blew them apart, rooted around as if it was following a certain scent, then stopped behind me at the butcher shop and bored down like a drill.

I went flying, landed somewhere in a ball. When I opened my eyes and looked, stranger things were happening.

A herd of cattle flew through the air like giant birds, dropping dung, their mouths opened in stunned bellows. A candle, still lighted, blew past, and tables, napkins, garden tools, a whole school of drifting eyeglasses, jackets on hangers, hams, a checkerboard, a lampshade, and at last the sow from behind the lockers, on the run, her hooves a blur, set free, swooping, diving, screaming as everything in Argus fell apart and got turned upside down, smashed, and thoroughly wrecked.

Days passed before the town went looking for the men. They were bachelors, after all, except for Tor, whose wife had suffered a blow to the head that made her forgetful. Everyone was occupied with digging out, in high relief because even though the Catholic steeple had been torn off like a peaked cap and sent across five fields, those huddled in the cellar were unhurt. Walls had fallen, windows were demolished, but the stores were intact and so were the bankers and shop owners who had taken refuge in their safes or beneath their cash registers. It was a fair-minded disaster, no one could be said to have suffered much more than the next, at least not until Fritzie and Pete came home.

Of all the businesses in Argus, Kozka's Meats had suffered worst. The boards 65 of the front building had been split to kindling, piled in a huge pyramid, and the shop equipment was blasted far and wide. Pete paced off the distance the iron bathtub had been flung—a hundred feet. The glass candy case went fifty, and landed without so much as a cracked pane. There were other surprises as well, for the back rooms where Fritzie and Pete lived were undisturbed. Fritzie said the dust still coated her china figures, and upon her kitchen table, in the ashtray, perched the last cigarette she'd put out in haste. She lit it up and finished it, looking through the window. From there, she could see that the old smokehouse Fleur had slept in was crushed to a reddish sand and the stockpens were completely torn apart, the rails stacked helter-skelter. Fritzie asked for Fleur. People shrugged. Then she asked about the others, and, suddenly, the town understood that three men were missing.

There was a rally of help, a gathering of shovels and volunteers. We passed boards from hand to hand, stacked them, uncovered what lay beneath the pile of jagged splinters. The lockers, full of the meat that was Pete and Fritzie's investment, slowly came into sight, still intact. When enough room was made for a man to stand on the roof, there were calls, a general urge to hack through and see what lay below. But Fritzie shouted that she wouldn't allow it because the meat would spoil. And so the work continued, board by board, until at last the heavy oak doors of the freezer were revealed and people pressed to the entry. Everyone wanted to be the first, but since it was my stepfather lost, I was let go in when Pete and Fritzie wedged through into the sudden icy air.

Pete scraped a match on his boot, lit the lamp Fritzie held, and then the three of us stood still in its circle. Light glared off the skinned and hanging carcasses, the crates of wrapped sausages, the bright and cloudy blocks of lake ice, pure as winter. The cold bit into us, pleasant at first, then numbing. We must have stood there a couple of minutes before we saw the men, or more rightly, the humps of fur, the iced and shaggy hides they wore, the bearskins they had taken down and wrapped around themselves. We stepped closer and tilted the lantern beneath the flaps of fur into their faces. The dog was there, perched among them, heavy as a doorstop. The three had hunched around a barrel where the game was still laid out, and a dead lantern and an empty bottle, too. But they had thrown down their last hands and hunkered tight, clutching one another, knuckles raw from beating at the door they had also attacked with hooks. Frost stars gleamed off their eyelashes and the stubble of their beards. Their faces were set in concentration, mouths open as if to speak some careful thought, some agreement they'd come to in each other's arms.

*   *   *

Power travels in the bloodlines, handed out before birth. It comes down through the hands, which in the Pillagers were strong and knotted, big, spidery, and rough, with sensitive fingertips good at dealing cards. It comes through the eyes, too, belligerent, darkest brown, the eyes of those in the bear clan, impolite as they gaze directly at a person.

In my dreams, I look straight back at Fleur, at the men. I am no longer the watcher on the dark sill, the skinny girl.

The blood draws us back, as if it runs through a vein of earth. I've come home and, except for talking to my cousins, live a quiet life. Fleur lives quiet too, down on Lake Turcot with her boat. Some say she's married to the waterman, Misshepeshu, or that she's living in shame with white men or windigos, or that she's killed them all. I'm about the only one here who ever goes to visit her. Last winter, I went to help out in her cabin when she bore the child, whose green eyes and skin the color of an old penny made more talk, as no one could decide if the child was mixed blood or what, fathered in a smokehouse, or by a man with brass scales, or by the lake. The girl is bold, smiling in her sleep, as if she knows what people wonder, as if she hears the old men talk, turning the story over. It comes up different every time and has no ending, no beginning. They get the middle wrong too. They only know that they don't know anything.

Louise Erdrich   b. 1954

The Red Convertible   *1974*

Lyman Lamartine

I was the first one to drive a convertible on my reservation. And of course it was red, a red Olds. I owned that car along with my brother Henry Junior. We owned it together until his boots filled with water on a windy night and he bought out my share. Now Henry owns the whole car, and his younger brother Lyman (that's my-self), Lyman walks everywhere he goes.

How did I earn enough money to buy my share in the first place? My one talent was I could always make money. I had a touch for it, unusual in a Chippewa. From the first I was different that way, and everyone recognized it. I was the only kid they let in the American Legion Hall to shine shoes, for example, and one Christmas I sold spiritual bouquets for the mission door to door. The nuns let me keep a percentage. Once I started, it seemed the more money I made the easier the money came. Everyone encouraged it. When I was fifteen I got a job washing dishes at the Joliet Café, and that was where my first big break happened.

It wasn't long before I was promoted to busing tables, and then the short-order cook quit and I was hired to take her place. No sooner than you know it I was managing the Joliet. The rest is history. I went on managing. I soon became part owner, and of course there was no stopping me then. It wasn't long before the whole thing was mine.

After I'd owned the Joliet for one year, it blew over in the worst tornado ever seen around here. The whole operation was smashed to bits. A total loss. The fryalator was up in a tree, the grill torn in half like it was paper. I was only sixteen. I had it all in my mother's name, and I lost it quick, but before I lost it I had every one of my relatives, and their relatives, to dinner, and I also bought that red Olds I mentioned, along with Henry.

The first time we saw it! I'll tell you when we first saw it. We had gotten a ride up   5
to Winnipeg, and both of us had money. Don't ask me why, because we never mentioned a car or anything, we just had all our money. Mine was cash, a big bankroll from the Joliet's insurance. Henry had two checks—a week's extra pay for being laid off, and his regular check from the Jewel Bearing Plant.

We were walking down Portage anyway, seeing the sights, when we saw it. There it was, parked, large as life. Really as *if* it was alive. I thought of the word *repose,* because the car wasn't simply stopped, parked, or whatever. That car re-posed, calm and gleaming, a FOR SALE sign in its left front window. Then, before we had thought it over at all, the car belonged to us and our pockets were empty. We had just enough money for gas back home.

We went places in that car, me and Henry. We took off driving all one whole summer. We started off toward the Little Knife River and Mandaree in Fort Berthold and then we found ourselves down in Wakpala somehow, and then sud-denly we were over in Montana on the Rocky Boy, and yet the summer was not even half over. Some people hang on to details when they travel, but we didn't let them bother us and just lived our everyday lives here to there.

I do remember this one place with willows. I remember I laid under those trees and it was comfortable. So comfortable. The branches bent down all around me like a tent or a stable. And quiet, it was quiet, even though there was a powwow close enough so I could see it going on. The air was not too still, not too windy either. When the dust rises up and hangs in the air around the dancers like that, I feel good. Henry was asleep with his arms thrown wide. Later on, he woke up and we started driving again. We were somewhere in Montana, or maybe on the Blood Reserve—it could have been anywhere. Anyway it was where we met the girl.

All her hair was in buns around her ears, that's the first thing I noticed about her. She was posed alongside the road with her arm out, so we stopped. That girl was short, so short her lumber shirt looked comical on her, like a nightgown. She had jeans on and fancy moccasins and she carried a little suitcase.

"Hop on in," says Henry. So she climbs in between us.   10

"We'll take you home," I says. "Where do you live?"

"Chicken," she says.

"Where the hell's that?" I ask her.

"Alaska."

"Okay," says Henry, and we drive.   15

We got up there and never wanted to leave. The sun doesn't truly set there in summer, and the night is more a soft dusk. You might doze off, sometimes, but before you know it you're up again, like an animal in nature. You never feel like you have to sleep hard or put away the world. And things would grow up there. One day just dirt or moss, the next day flowers and long grass. The girl's name was Susy. Her family really took to us. They fed us and put us up. We had our own tent to live in by their house, and the kids would be in and out of there all day and night. They couldn't get over me and Henry being brothers, we looked so different. We told them we knew we had the same mother, anyway.

One night Susy came in to visit us. We sat around in the tent talking of this and that. The season was changing. It was getting darker by that time, and the cold was even getting just a little mean. I told her it was time for us to go. She stood up on a chair.

"You never seen my hair," Susy said.

That was true. She was standing on a chair, but still, when she unclipped her buns the hair reached all the way to the ground. Our eyes opened. You couldn't tell how much hair she had when it was rolled up so neatly. Then my brother Henry did something funny. He went up to the chair and said, "Jump on my shoulders." So she did that, and her hair reached down past his waist, and he started twirling, this way and that, so her hair was flung out from side to side.

"I always wondered what it was like to have long pretty hair," Henry says.   20
Well we laughed. It was a funny sight, the way he did it. The next morning we got up and took leave of those people.

On to greener pastures, as they say. It was down through Spokane and across Idaho then Montana and very soon we were racing the weather right along under the Canadian border through Columbus, Des Lacs, and then we were in Botineau County and soon home. We'd made most of the trip, that summer, without putting up the car hood at all. We got home just in time, it turned out, for the army to remember Henry had signed up to join it.

I don't wonder that the army was so glad to get my brother that they turned him into a Marine. He was built like a brick outhouse anyway. We liked to tease him that they really wanted him for his Indian nose. He had a nose big and sharp as a hatchet, like the nose on Red Tomahawk, the Indian who killed Sitting Bull, whose profile is on signs all along the North Dakota highways. Henry went off to training camp, came home once during Christmas, then the next thing you know we got an overseas letter from him. It was 1970, and he said he was stationed up in the northern hill country. Whereabouts I did not know. He wasn't such a hot letter writer, and only got off two before the enemy caught him. I could never keep it straight, which direction those good Vietnam soldiers were from.

I wrote him back several times, even though I didn't know if those letters would get through. I kept him informed all about the car. Most of the time I had it up on blocks in the yard or half taken apart, because that long trip did a hard job on it under the hood.

I always had good luck with numbers, and never worried about the draft myself. I never even had to think about what my number was. But Henry was never lucky in the same way as me. It was at least three years before Henry came home. By then I guess the whole war was solved in the government's mind, but for him it would keep on going. In those years I'd put his car into almost perfect shape. I always thought of it as his car while he was gone, even though when he left he said, "Now it's yours," and threw me his key.

"Thanks for the extra key," I'd said. "I'll put it up in your drawer just in case I   25
need it." He laughed.

When he came home, though, Henry was very different, and I'll say this: the change was no good. You could hardly expect him to change for the better, I know. But he was quiet, so quiet, and never comfortable sitting still anywhere but always up and moving around. I thought back to times we'd sat still for whole afternoons, never moving a muscle, just shifting our weight along the ground, talking to whoever sat with us, watching things. He'd always had a joke, then, too, and now you couldn't get him to laugh, or when he did it was more the sound of a man choking, a sound that stopped up the throats of other people around him. They got to leaving him alone most of the time, and I didn't blame them. It was a fact: Henry was jumpy and mean.

I'd bought a color TV set for my mom and the rest of us while Henry was away. Money still came very easy. I was sorry I'd ever bought it though, because of Henry. I was also sorry I'd bought color, because with black-and-white the pictures seem older and farther away. But what are you going to do? He sat in front of it, watching it, and that was the only time he was completely still. But it was the kind of stillness that you see in a rabbit when it freezes and before it will bolt. He was not easy. He sat in his chair gripping the armrests with all his might, as if the chair itself was moving at a high speed and if he let go at all he would rocket forward and maybe crash right through the set.

Once I was in the room watching TV with Henry and I heard his teeth click at something. I looked over, and he'd bitten through his lip. Blood was going down his chin. I tell you right then I wanted to smash that tube to pieces. I went over to it but Henry must have known what I was up to. He rushed from his chair and shoved me out of the way, against the wall. I told myself he didn't know what he was doing.

My mom came in, turned the set off real quiet, and told us she had made something for supper. So we went and sat down. There was still blood going down Henry's chin, but he didn't notice it and no one said anything, even though every time he took a bite of his bread his blood fell onto it until he was eating his own blood mixed in with the food.

While Henry was not around we talked about what was going to happen to him. There were no Indian doctors on the reservation, and my mom couldn't come around to trusting the old man, Moses Pillager, because he courted her long ago and was jealous of her husbands. He might take revenge through her son. We were afraid that if we brought Henry to a regular hospital they would keep him.

"They don't fix them in those places," Mom said; "they just give them drugs."

"We wouldn't get him there in the first place," I agreed, "so let's just forget about it."

Then I thought about the car.

Henry had not even looked at the car since he'd gotten home, though like I said, it was in tip-top condition and ready to drive. I thought the car might bring the old Henry back somehow. So I bided my time and waited for my chance to interest him in the vehicle.

One night Henry was off somewhere. I took myself a hammer. I went out to that car and I did a number on its underside. Whacked it up. Bent the tail pipe double. Ripped the muffler loose. By the time I was done with the car it looked worse than any typical Indian car that has been driven all its life on reservation roads, which they always say are like government promises—full of holes. It just about hurt me, I'll tell you that! I threw dirt in the carburetor and I ripped all the electric tape off the seats. I made it look just as beat up as I could. Then I sat back and waited for Henry to find it.

Still, it took him over a month. That was all right, because it was just getting warm enough, not melting, but warm enough to work outside.

"Lyman," he says, walking in one day, "that red car looks like shit."

"Well it's old," I says. "You got to expect that."

"No way!" says Henry. "That car's a classic! But you went and ran the piss right out of it, Lyman, and you know it don't deserve that. I kept that car in A-one shape. You don't remember. You're too young. But when I left, that car was running like a watch. Now I don't even know if I can get it to start again, let alone get it anywhere near its old condition."

"Well you try," I said, like I was getting mad, "but I say it's a piece of junk."

Then I walked out before he could realize I knew he'd strung together more than six words at once.

After that I thought he'd freeze himself to death working on that car. He was out there all day, and at night he rigged up a little lamp, ran a cord out the window, and had himself some light to see by while he worked. He was better than he had been before, but that's still not saying much. It was easier for him to do the things the rest of us did. He ate more slowly and didn't jump up and down during the meal to get this or that or look out the window. I put my hand in the back of the TV set, I admit, and fiddled around with it good, so that it was almost impossible now to get a clear picture. He didn't look at it very often anyway. He was always out with that car or going off to get parts for it. By the time it was really melting outside, he had it fixed.

I had been feeling down in the dumps about Henry around this time. We had always been together before. Henry and Lyman. But he was such a loner now that I didn't know how to take it. So I jumped at the chance one day when Henry seemed friendly. It's not that he smiled or anything. He just said, "Let's take that old shitbox for a spin." Just the way he said it made me think he could be coming around.

30

35

40

We went out to the car. It was spring. The sun was shining very bright. My only sister, Bonita, who was just eleven years old, came out and made us stand together for a picture. Henry leaned his elbow on the red car's windshield, and he took his other arm and put it over my shoulder, very carefully, as though it was heavy for him to lift and he didn't want to bring the weight down all at once.

"Smile," Bonita said, and he did.   45

That picture. I never look at it anymore. A few months ago, I don't know why, I got his picture out and tacked it on the wall. I felt good about Henry at the time, close to him. I felt good having his picture on the wall, until one night when I was looking at television. I was a little drunk and stoned. I looked up at the wall and Henry was staring at me. I don't know what it was, but his smile had changed, or maybe it was gone. All I know is I couldn't stay in the same room with that picture. I was shaking. I got up, closed the door, and went into the kitchen. A little later my friend Ray came over and we both went back into that room. We put the picture in a brown bag, folded the bag over and over tightly, then put it way back in a closet.

I still see that picture now, as if it tugs at me, whenever I pass that closet door. The picture is very clear in my mind. It was so sunny that day Henry had to squint against the glare. Or maybe the camera Bonita held flashed like a mirror, blinding him, before she snapped the picture. My face is right out in the sun, big and round. But he might have drawn back, because the shadows on his face are deep as holes. There are two shadows curved like little hooks around the ends of his smile, as if to frame it and try to keep it there—that one, first smile that looked like it might have hurt his face. He has his field jacket on and the worn-in clothes he'd come back in and kept wearing ever since. After Bonita took the picture, she went into the house and we got into the car. There was a full cooler in the trunk. We started off, east, toward Pembina and the Red River because Henry said he wanted to see the high water.

The trip over there was beautiful. When everything starts changing, drying up, clearing off, you feel like your whole life is starting. Henry felt it, too. The top was down and the car hummed like a top. He'd really put it back in shape, even the tape on the seats was very carefully put down and glued back in layers. It's not that he smiled again or even joked, but his face looked to me as if it was clear, more peaceful. It looked as though he wasn't thinking of anything in particular except the bare fields and windbreaks and houses we were passing.

The river was high and full of winter trash when we got there. The sun was still out, but it was colder by the river. There were still little clumps of dirty snow here and there on the banks. The water hadn't gone over the banks yet, but it would, you could tell. It was just at its limit, hard swollen, glossy like an old gray scar. We made ourselves a fire, and we sat down and watched the current go. As I watched it I felt something squeezing inside me and tightening and trying to let go all at the same time. I knew I was not just feeling it myself; I knew I was feeling what Henry was going through at that moment. Except that I couldn't stand it, the closing and opening. I jumped to my feet. I took Henry by the shoulders and I started shaking him. "Wake up," I says, "wake up, wake up, wake up!" I didn't know what had come over me. I sat down beside him again.

His face was totally white and hard. Then it broke, like stones break all of a   50
sudden when water boils up inside them.

"I know it," he says. "I know it. I can't help it. It's no use."

We start talking. He said he knew what I'd done with the car. It was obvious it had been whacked out of shape and not just neglected. He said he wanted to give the car to me for good now, it was no use. He said he'd fixed it just to give it back and I should take it.

"No way," I says. "I don't want it."

"That's okay," he says, "you take it."

"I don't want it, though," I says back to him, and then to emphasize, just to emphasize, you understand, I touch his shoulder. He slaps my hand off.

"Take that car," he says.

"No," I say. "Make me," I say, and then he grabs my jacket and rips the arm loose. That jacket is a class act, suede with tags and zippers. I push Henry backwards, off the log. He jumps up and bowls me over. We go down in a clinch and come up swinging hard, for all we're worth, with our fists. He socks my jaw so hard I feel like it swings loose. Then I'm at his rib cage and land a good one under his chin so his head snaps back. He's dazzled. He looks at me and I look at him and then his eyes are full of tears and blood and at first I think he's crying. But no, he's laughing. "Ha! Ha!" he says. "Ha! Ha! Take good care of it."

"Okay," I says. "Okay, no problem. Ha! Ha!"

I can't help it, and I start laughing, too. My face feels fat and strange, and after a while I get a beer from the cooler in the trunk, and when I hand it to Henry he takes his shirt and wipes my germs off. "Hoof-and-mouth disease," he says. For some reason this cracks me up, and so we're really laughing for a while, and then we drink all the rest of the beers one by one and throw them in the river and see how far, how fast, the current takes them before they fill up and sink.

"You want to go on back?" I ask after a while. "Maybe we could snag a couple nice Kashpaw girls."

He says nothing. But I can tell his mood is turning again.

"They're all crazy, the girls up here, every damn one of them."

"You're crazy, too," I say, to jolly him up. "Crazy Lamartine boys!"

He looks as though he will take this wrong at first. His face twists, then clears, and he jumps up on his feet. "That's right!" he says. "Crazier 'n hell. Crazy Indians!"

I think it's the old Henry again. He throws off his jacket and starts springing his legs up from the knees like a fancy dancer. He's down doing something between a grass dance and a bunny hop, no kind of dance I ever saw before, but neither has anyone else on all this green growing earth. He's wild. He wants to pitch whoopee! He's up and at me and all over. All this time I'm laughing so hard, so hard my belly is getting tied up in a knot.

"Got to cool me off!" he shouts all of a sudden. Then he runs over to the river and jumps in.

There's boards and other things in the current. It's so high. No sound comes from the river after the splash he makes, so I run right over. I look around. It's getting dark. I see he's halfway across the water already, and I know he didn't swim there but the current took him. It's far. I hear his voice, though, very clearly across it.

"My boots are filling," he says.

He says this in a normal voice, like he just noticed and he doesn't know what to think of it. Then he's gone. A branch comes by. Another branch. And I go in.

By the time I get out of the river, off the snag I pulled myself onto, the sun is down. I walk back to the car, turn on the high beams, and drive it up the bank. I put it in first gear and then I take my foot off the clutch. I get out, close the door, and watch it plow softly into the water. The headlights reach in as they go down, searching, still lighted even after the water swirls over the back end. I wait. The wires short out. It is all finally dark. An then there is only the water, the sound of it going and running and going and running and running.

William Faulkner   1897–1962

Barn Burning   1939

The store in which the Justice of the Peace's court was sitting smelled of cheese. The boy, crouched on his nail keg at the back of the crowded room, knew he smelled cheese, and more: from where he sat he could see the ranked shelves close-packed with the solid, squat, dynamic shapes of tin cans whose labels his stomach read, not from the lettering which meant nothing to his mind but from the scarlet devils and the silver curve of fish—this, the cheese which he knew he smelled and the hermetic meat which his intestines believed he smelled coming in intermittent gusts momentary and brief between the other constant one, the smell and sense just a little of fear because mostly of despair and grief, the old fierce pull of blood. He could not see the table where the Justice sat and before which his father and his father's enemy (*our enemy* he thought in that despair: *ourn! mine and hisn both! He's my father!*) stood, but he could hear them, the two of them that is, because his father had said no word yet:

"But what proof have you, Mr. Harris?"

"I told you. The hog got into my corn. I caught it up and sent it back to him. He had no fence that would hold it. I told him so, warned him. The next time I put the hog in my pen. When he came to get it I gave him enough wire to patch up his pen. The next time I put the hog up and kept it. I rode down to his house and saw the wire I gave him still rolled on to the spool in his yard. I told him he could have the hog when he paid me a dollar pound fee. That evening a nigger came with the dollar and got the hog. He was a strange nigger. He said. 'He say to tell you wood and hay kin burn.' I said. 'What?' 'That whut he say to tell you,' the nigger said. 'Wood and hay kin burn.' That night my barn burned. I got the stock out but I lost the barn."

"Where is the nigger? Have you got him?"

"He was a strange nigger, I tell you. I don't know what became of him."

"But that's not proof. Don't you see that's not proof?"

"Get that boy up here. He knows." For a moment the boy thought too that the man meant his older brother until Harris said, "Not him. The little one. The boy," and, crouching, small for his age, small and wiry like his father, in patched and faded jeans even too small for him, with straight, uncombed, brown hair and eyes gray and wild as storm scud, he saw the men between himself and the table part and become a lane of grim faces, at the end of which he saw the Justice, a shabby, collarless, graying man in spectacles, beckoning him. He felt no floor under his bare feet; he seemed to walk beneath the palpable weight of the grim turning faces. His father, stiff in his black Sunday coat donned not for the trial but for the moving, did not even look at him. *He aims for me to lie,* he thought, again with that frantic grief and despair. *And I will have to do hit.*

"What's your name, boy?" the Justice said.

"Colonel Sartoris Snopes," the boy whispered.

"Hey?" the Justice said. "Talk louder. Colonel Sartoris? I reckon anybody named for Colonel Sartoris in this country can't help but tell the truth, can they?" The boy said nothing. *Enemy! Enemy!* he thought; for a moment he could not even see, could not see that the Justice's face was kindly not discern that his voice was troubled when he spoke to the man named Harris: "Do you want me to question this boy?" But he could hear, and during those subsequent long seconds while there was absolutely no sound in the crowded little room save that of quiet and intent breathing it was as if he had swung outward at the end of a grape vine, over a ravine, and at the top of the swing had been caught in a prolonged instant of mesmerized gravity, weightless in time.

"No!" Harris said violently, explosively. "Damnation! Send him out of here!" Now time, the fluid world, rushed beneath him again, the voices coming to him again through the smell of cheese and sealed meat, the fear and despair and the old grief of blood.

"This case is closed. I can't find against you, Snopes, but I can give you advice. Leave this country and don't come back to it."

His father spoke for the first time, his voice cold and harsh, level, without emphasis: "I aim to. I don't figure to stay in a country among people who . . ." he said something unprintable and vile, addressed to no one.

"That'll do," the Justice said. "Take your wagon and get out of this country before dark. Case dismissed."

His father turned, and he followed the stiff black coat, the wiry figure walking a little stiffly from where a Confederate provost's man's musket ball had taken him in the heel on a stolen horse thirty years ago, followed the two backs now; since his older brother had appeared from somewhere in the crowd, no taller than the father but thicker, chewing tobacco steadily, between the two lines of grim-faced men and out of the store and across the worn gallery and down the sagging steps and among the dogs and half-grown boys in the mild May dust, where as he passed a voice hissed:

"Barn burner!"

Again he could not see, whirling; there was a face in a red haze, moonlike, bigger than the full moon, the owner of it half again his size, he leaping in the red haze toward the face, feeling no blow, feeling no shock when his head struck the earth, scrabbling up and leaping again, feeling no blow this time either and tasting no blood, scrabbling up to see the other boy in full flight and himself already leaping into pursuit as his father's hand jerked him back, the harsh, cold voice speaking above him: "Go get in the wagon."

It stood in a grove of locusts and mulberries across the road. His two hulking sisters in their Sunday dresses and his mother and her sister in calico and sunbonnets were already in it, sitting on or among the sorry residue of the dozen and more movings which even the boy could remember—the battered stove, the broken beds and chairs, the clock inlaid with mother-of-pearl, which would not run, stopped at some fourteen minutes past two o'clock of a dead and forgotten day and time, which had been his mother's dowry. She was crying, though when she saw him she drew her sleeve across her face and began to descend from the wagon. "Get back," the father said.

"He's hurt. I got to get some water and wash his. . . ."

"Get back in the wagon," his father said. He got in too, over the tail-gate. His father mounted to the seat where the older brother already sat and struck the gaunt mules two savage blows with the peeled willow, but without heat. It was not even sadistic, it was exactly that same quality which in later years would cause his descendants to over-run the engine before putting a motor car in motion, striking and reining back in the same movement. The wagon went on, the store with its quiet crowd of grimly watching men dropped behind; a curve in the road hid it. *Forever* he thought. *Maybe he's done satisfied now, now that he has* ... stopping himself, not to say it aloud even to himself. His mother's hand touched his shoulder.

"Does hit hurt?" she said.

"Naw," he said. "Hit don't hurt. Lemme be."

"Can't you wipe some of the blood off before hit dries?"

"I'll wash to-night," he said. "Lemme be, I tell you."

The wagon went on. He did not know where they were going. None of them ever did or ever asked, because it was always somewhere, always a house of sorts waiting for them a day or two days or even three days away. Likely his father had already arranged to make a crop on another farm before he ... Again he had to stop himself. He (the father) always did. There was something about his wolflike independence and even courage when the advantage was at least neutral which impressed strangers, as if they got from his latent ravening ferocity not so much a sense of dependability as a feeling that his ferocious conviction in the rightness of his own actions would be of advantage to all whose interest lay with his.

That night they camped, in a grove of oaks and beeches where a spring ran. The nights were still cool and they had a fire against it, of a rail lifted from a nearby fence and cut into lengths—a small fire, neat, niggard almost, a shrewd fire; such fires were his father's habit and custom always, even in freezing weather. Older, the boy might have remarked this and wondered why not a big one; why should not a man who had not only seen the waste and extravagance of war, but who had in his blood an inherent voracious prodigality with material not his own, have burned everything in sight? Then he might have gone a step farther and thought that that was the reason: that niggard blaze was the living fruit of nights passed during those four years in the woods hiding from all men, blue or gray, with his strings of horses (captured horses, he called them). And older still, he might have divined the true reason: that the element of fire spoke to some deep mainspring of his father's being, as the element of steel or of powder spoke to other men, as the one weapon for the preservation of integrity, else breath were not worth the breathing, and hence to be regarded with respect and used with discretion.

But he did not think this now and he had seen those same niggard blazes all his life. He merely ate his supper beside it and was already half asleep over his iron plate when his father called him, and once more he followed the stiff back, the stiff and ruthless limp, up the slope and on to the starlit road where, turning, he could see his father against the stars but without face or depth—a shape black, flat, and bloodless as though cut from tin in the iron folds of the frockcoat which had not been made for him, the voice harsh like tin and without heat like tin:

"You were fixing to tell them. You would have told him."

He didn't answer. His father struck him with the flat of his hand on the side of the head, hard but without heat, exactly as he had struck the two mules at the store, exactly as he would strike either of them with any stick in order to kill a horse fly, his voice still without heat or anger. "You're getting to be a man. You got to learn. You got to learn to stick to your own blood or you ain't going to have any blood to stick to you. Do you think either of them, any man there this morning, would? Don't you know all they wanted was a chance to get at me because they knew I had them beat? Eh?" Later, twenty years later, he was to tell himself, "If I had said they wanted only truth, justice, he would have hit me again." But now he said nothing. He was not crying. He just stood there. "Answer me," his father said.

"Yes," he whispered. His father turned.

"Get on to bed. We'll be there tomorrow."   30

Tomorrow they were there. In the early afternoon the wagon stopped before a paintless two-room house identical almost with the dozen others it had stopped before even in the boy's ten years, and again, as on the other dozen occasions, his mother and aunt got down and began to unload the wagon, although his two sisters and his father and brother had not moved.

"Likely hit ain't fitten for hawgs," one of the sisters said.

"Nevertheless, fit it will and you'll hog it and like it," his father said. "Get out of them chairs and help your Ma unload."

The two sisters got down, big, bovine, in a flutter of cheap ribbons; one of   35
them drew from the jumbled wagon bed a battered lantern, the other a worn broom. His father handed the reins to the older son and began to climb stiffly over the wheel. "When they get unloaded, take the team to the barn and feed them." Then he said, and at first the boy thought he was still speaking to his brother. "Come with me."

"Me?" he said.

"Yes," his father said. "You."

"Abner," his mother said. His father paused and looked back—the harsh level stare beneath the shaggy, graying, irascible brows.

"I reckon I'll have a word with the man that aims to begin tomorrow owning me body and soul for the next eight months."

They went back up the road. A week ago—or before last night, that is—he   40
would have asked where they were going, but not now. His father had struck him before last night but never before had he paused afterward to explain why, it was as if the blow and the following calm, outrageous voice still rang, repercussed, divulging nothing to him save the terrible handicap of being young, the light weight of his few years, just heavy enough to prevent his soaring free of the world as it seemed to be ordered but not heavy enough to keep him footed solid in it, to resist it and try to change the course of events.

Presently he could see the grove of oaks and cedars and the other flowering trees and shrubs where the house would be, though not the house yet. They walked beside a fence massed with honeysuckle and Cherokee roses and came to a gate swinging open between two brick pillars, and now, beyond a sweep of drive, he saw the house for the first time and at that instant he forgot his father and the terror and despair both, and even when he remembered his father again (who had not stopped) the terror and despair did not return. Because, for all the twelve movings, they had sojourned until now in a poor country, a land of small farms and fields and houses, and he had never seen a house like this before. *Hit's big as a courthouse* he thought quietly, with a surge of peace and joy whose reason he could not have thought into words, being too young for that: *They are safe from him. People whose lives are a part of this peace and dignity are beyond his touch, he no more to them than a buzzing wasp: capable of stinging for a little moment but that's all; the spell of this peace and dignity rendering even the barns and stable and cribs which belong to it impervious to the puny flames he might contrive* ... this, the peace and joy, ebbing for an instant as he looked again at the stiff black back, the stiff and implacable limp of the figure which was not dwarfed by the house, for the reason that it had never looked big anywhere and which now,

against the serene columned backdrop, had more than ever that impervious quality of something cut ruthlessly from tin, depthless, as though, sidewise to the sun,
it would cast no shadow. Watching him, the boy remarked the absolutely undeviating course which his father held and saw the stiff foot come squarely down in a
pile of fresh droppings where a horse had stood in the drive and which his father
could have avoided by a simple change of stride. But it ebbed only for a moment,
though he could not have thought this into words either, walking on in the spell
of the house, which he could even want but without envy, without sorrow, certainly never with that ravening and jealous rage which unknown to him walked in
the ironlike black coat before him: *Maybe he will feel it too. Maybe it will even
change him now from what maybe he couldn't help but be.*

They crossed the portico. Now he could hear his father's stiff foot as it came
down on the boards with clocklike finality, a sound out of all proportion to the
displacement of the body it bore and which was not dwarfed either by the white
door before it, as though it had attained to a sort of vicious and ravening minimum
not to be dwarfed by anything—the flat, wide, black hat, the formal coat of broad-
cloth which had once been black but which had now that friction-glazed greenish
cast of the bodies of old house flies, the lifted sleeve which was too large, the
lifted hand like a curled claw. The door opened so promptly that the boy knew
the Negro must have been watching them all the time, an old man with neat grizzled hair, in a linen jacket, who stood barring the door with his body, saying,
"Wipe yo foots, white man, fo you come in here. Major ain't home nohow."

"Get out of my way, nigger," his father said, without heat too, flinging the
door back and the Negro also and entering, his hat still on his head. And now the
boy saw the prints of the stiff foot on the doorjamb and saw them appear on the
pale rug behind the machinelike deliberation of the foot which seemed to bear (or
transmit) twice the weight which the body compassed. The Negro was shouting
"Miss Lula! Miss Lula!" somewhere behind them, then the boy, deluged as though
by a warm wave by a suave turn of the carpeted stair and a pendant glitter of
chandeliers and a mute gleam of gold frames, heard the swift feet and saw her too,
a lady—perhaps he had never seen her like before either—in a gray, smooth
gown with lace at the throat and an apron tied at the waist and the sleeves turned
back, wiping cake or biscuit dough from her hands with a towel as she came up
the hall, looking not at his father at all but at the tracks on the blond rug with an
expression of incredulous amazement.

"I tried," the Negro cried. "I tole him to . . ."

"Will you please go away?" she said in a shaking voice. "Major de Spain is not   45
at home. Will you please go away?"

His father had not spoken again. He did not speak again. He did not even
look at her. He just stood stiff in the center of the rug, in his hat, the shaggy iron-
gray brows twitching slightly above the pebble-colored eyes as he appeared to examine the house with brief deliberation. Then with the same deliberation he
turned; the boy watched him pivot on the good leg and saw the stiff foot drag
round the arc of the turning, leaving a final long and fading smear. His father
never looked at it, he never once looked down at the rug. The Negro held the
door. It closed behind them, upon the hysteric and indistinguishable woman-wail.
His father stopped at the top of the steps and scraped his boot clean on the edge
of it. At the gate he stopped again. He stood for a moment, planted stiffly on the
stiff foot, looking back at the house. "Pretty and white, ain't it?" he said. "That's

sweat. Nigger sweat. Maybe it ain't white enough yet to suit him. Maybe he wants to mix some white sweat with it."

Two hours later the boy was chopping wood behind the house within which his mother and aunt and the two sisters (the mother and aunt, not the two girls, he knew that; even at this distance and muffled by walls the flat loud voices of the two girls emanated an incorrigible idle inertia) were setting up the stove to prepare a meal; when he heard the hooves and saw the linen-clad man on a fine sorrel mare, whom he recognized even before he saw the rolled rug in front of the Negro youth following on a fat bay carriage horse—a suffused, angry face vanishing, still at full gallop, beyond the corner of the house where his father and brother were sitting in the two tilted chairs; and a moment later, almost before he could have put the axe down, he heard the hooves again and watched the sorrel mare go back out of the yard, already galloping again. Then his father began to shout one of the sisters' names, who presently emerged backward from the kitchen door dragging the rolled rug along the ground by one end while the other sister walked behind it.

"If you ain't going to tote, go on and set up the wash pot," the first said.

"You, Sarty!" the second shouted. "Set up the wash pot!" His father appeared at the door, framed against that shabbiness, as he had been against that other bland perfection, impervious to either, the mother's anxious face at his shoulder.

"Go on," the father said. "Pick it up." The two sisters stopped, broad, lethargic; stooping, they presented an incredible expanse of pale cloth and a flutter of tawdry ribbons. 50

"If I thought enough of a rug to have to git hit all the way from France I wouldn't keep hit where folks coming in would have to tromp on hit," the first said. They raised the rug.

"Abner," the mother said. "Let me do it."

"You go back and git dinner," his father said. "I'll tend to this."

From the woodpile through the rest of the afternoon the boy watched them, the rug spread flat in the dust beside the bubbling wash pot, the two sisters stooping over it with that profound and lethargic reluctance, while the father stood over them in turn, implacable and grim, driving them though never raising his voice again. He could smell the harsh homemade lye they were using; he saw his mother come to the door once and look toward them with an expression not anxious now but very like despair; he saw his father turn, and he fell to with the axe and saw from the corner of his eye his father raise from the ground a flattish fragment of field stone and examine it and return to the pot, and this time his mother actually spoke: "Abner, Abner. Please don't. Please, Abner."

Then he was done too. It was dusk; the whippoorwills had already begun. He could smell coffee from the room where they would presently eat the cold food remaining from the midafternoon meal, though when he entered the house he realized they were having coffee again probably because there was a fire on the hearth, before which the rug now lay spread over the backs of the two chairs. The tracks of his father's foot were gone. Where they had been were now long, water-cloudy scoriations resembling the sporadic course of a lilliputian mowing machine. 55

It still hung there while they ate the cold food and then went to bed, scattered without order or claim up and down the two rooms, his mother in one bed, where his father would later lie, the older brother in the other, himself, the aunt, and the two sisters on pallets on the floor. But his father was not in bed yet. The last thing

the boy remembered was the depthless, harsh silhouette of the hat and coat bending over the rug and it seemed to him that he had not even closed his eyes when
the silhouette was standing over him, the fire almost dead behind it, the stiff foot
prodding him awake. "Catch up the mule," his father said.

When he returned with the mule his father was standing in the black door, the
rolled rug over his shoulder. "Ain't you going to ride?" he said.

"No. Give me your foot."

He bent his knee into his father's hand, the wiry, surprising power flowed
smoothly, rising, he rising with it, on to the mule's bare back (they had owned a
saddle once; the boy could remember it though not when or where) and with the
same effortlessness his father swung the rug up in front of him. Now in the starlight
they retraced the afternoon's path, up the dusty road rife with honeysuckle, through
the gate and up the black tunnel of the drive to the lightless house, where he sat
on the mule and felt the rough warp of the rug drag across his thighs and vanish.

"Don't you want me to help?" he whispered. His father did not answer and   60
now he heard again that stiff foot striking the hollow portico with that wooden
and clocklike deliberation, that outrageous overstatement of the weight it carried.
The rug, hunched, not flung (the boy could tell that even in the darkness) from his
father's shoulder struck the angle of wall and floor with a sound unbelievably
loud, thunderous, then the foot again, unhurried and enormous; a light came on
in the house and the boy sat, tense, breathing steadily and quietly and just a little
fast, though the foot itself did not increase its beat at all, descending the steps
now; now the boy could see him.

"Don't you want to ride now?" he whispered. "We kin both ride now," the
light within the house altering now, flaring up and sinking. *He's coming down the
stairs now,* he thought. He had already ridden the mule up beside the horse block;
presently his father was up behind him and he doubled the reins over and slashed
the mule across the neck, but before the animal could begin to trot the hard, thin
arm came around him, the hard, knotted hand jerking the mule back to a walk.

In the first red rays of the sun they were in the lot, putting plow gear on the
mules. This time the sorrel mare was in the lot before he heard it at all, the rider collarless and even bareheaded, trembling, speaking in a shaking voice as the woman
in the house had done, his father merely looking up once before stooping again to
the hame he was buckling, so that the man on the mare spoke to his stooping back:

"You must realize you have ruined that rug. Wasn't there anybody here, any of
your women . . ." he ceased, shaking, the boy watching him, the older brother
leaning now in the stable door, chewing, blinking slowly and steadily at nothing
apparently. "It cost a hundred dollars. But you never had a hundred dollars. You
never will. So I'm going to charge you twenty bushels of corn against your crop.
I'll add it in your contract and when you come to the commissary you can sign it.
That won't keep Mrs. de Spain quiet but maybe it will teach you to wipe your feet
before you enter her house again."

Then he was gone. The boy looked at his father, who still had not spoken or
even looked up again, who was now adjusting the logger-head in the hame.

"Pap," he said. His father looked at him—the inscrutable face, the shaggy   65
brows beneath which the gray eyes glinted coldly. Suddenly the boy went toward
him, fast, stopping as suddenly. "You done the best you could!" he cried. "If he
wanted hit done different why didn't he wait and tell you how? He won't git no
twenty bushels! He won't get none! We'll gether hit and hide it! I kin watch. . . ."

"Did you put the cutter back in that straight stock like I told you?"

"No, sir," he said.

"Then go do it."

That was Wednesday. During the rest of that week he worked steadily, at what was within his scope and some which was beyond it, with an industry that did not need to be driven nor even commanded twice, he had this from his mother, with the difference that some at least of what he did he liked to do, such as splitting wood with the half-size axe which his mother and aunt had earned, or saved money somehow, to present him with at Christmas. In company with the two older women (and on one afternoon, even one of the sisters), he built pens for the shoat and the cow which were part of his father's contract with the landlord, and one afternoon, his father being absent, gone somewhere on one of the mules, he went to the field.

They were running a middle buster now, his brother holding the plow straight while he handled the reins, and walking beside the straining mule, the rich black soil shearing cool and damp against his bare ankles, he thought *Maybe this is the end of it. Maybe even that twenty bushels that seems hard to have to pay for just a rug will be a cheap price for him to stop forever and always from being what he used to be;* thinking, dreaming now, so that his brother had to speak sharply to him to mind the mule. *Maybe he even won't collect the twenty bushels. Maybe it will all add up and balance and vanish—corn, rug, fire; the terror and grief; the being pulled two ways like between two teams of horses—gone, done with for ever and ever.*

Then it was Saturday; he looked up from beneath the mule he was harnessing and saw his father in the black coat and hat. "Not that," his father said. "The wagon gear." And then, two hours later, sitting in the wagon bed behind his father and brother on the seat, the wagon accomplished a final curve, and he saw the weathered paintless store with its tattered tobacco- and patent-medicine posters and the tethered wagons and saddle animals below the gallery. He mounted the gnawed steps behind his father and brother, and there again was the lane of quiet, watching faces for the three of them to walk through. He saw the man in spectacles sitting at the plank table and he did not need to be told this was a Justice of the Peace; he sent one glare of fierce, exultant, partisan defiance at the man in collar and cravat now, whom he had seen but twice before in his life, and that on a galloping horse, who now wore on his face an expression not of rage but of amazed unbelief which the boy could not have known was at the incredible circumstance of being sued by one of his own tenants, and came and stood against his father and cried at the Justice: "He ain't done it! He ain't burnt. . . ."

"Go back to the wagon," his father said.

"Burnt!" the Justice said "Do I understand this rug was burned too?"

"Does anybody here claim it was?" his father said. "Go back to the wagon." But he did not, he merely retreated to the rear of the room, crowded as that other had been, but not to sit down this time, instead, to stand pressing among the motionless bodies, listening to the voices:

"And you claim twenty bushels of corn is too high for the damage you did to the rug?"

"He brought the rug to me and said he wanted the tracks washed out of it. I washed the tracks out and took the rug back to him."

"But you didn't carry the rug back to him in the same condition it was in before you made the tracks on it."

His father did not answer, and now for perhaps half a minute there was no sound at all save that of breathing, the faint, steady suspiration of complete and intent listening.

"You decline to answer that, Mr. Snopes?" Again his father did not answer. "I'm going to find against you, Mr. Snopes. I'm going to find that you were responsible for the injury to Major de Spain's rug and hold you liable for it. But twenty bushels of corn seems a little high for a man in your circumstances to have to pay. Major de Spain claims it cost a hundred dollars. October corn will be worth about fifty cents. I figure that if Major de Spain can stand a ninety-five dollar loss on something he paid cash for, you can stand a five-dollar loss you haven't earned yet. I hold you in damages to Major de Spain to the amount of ten bushels of corn over and above your contract with him, to be paid to him out of your crop at gathering time. Court adjourned."

It had taken no time hardly, the morning was but half begun. He thought they would return home and perhaps back to the field, since they were late, for behind all other farmers. But instead his father passed on behind the wagon, merely indicating with his hand for the older brother to follow with it, and crossed the road toward the blacksmith shop opposite, pressing on after his father, overtaking him, speaking, whispering up at the harsh, calm face beneath the weathered hat: "He won't git no ten bushels either. He won't git one. We'll . . ." until his father glanced for an instant down at him, the face absolutely calm, the grizzled eyebrows tangled above the cold eyes, the voice almost pleasant, almost gentle:

"You think so? Well, we'll wait till October anyway."

The matter of the wagon—the setting of a spoke or two and the tightening of the tires—did not take long either, the business of the tires accomplished by driving the wagon into the spring branch behind the shop and letting it stand there, the mules nuzzling into the water from time to time, and the boy on the seat with the idle reins, looking up the slope and through the sooty tunnel of the shed where the slow hammer rang and where his father sat on an upended cypress bolt, easily, either talking or listening, still sitting there when the boy brought the dripping wagon up out of the branch and halted it before the door.

"Take them on to the shade and hitch," his father said. He did so and returned. His father and the smith and a third man squatting on his heels inside the door were talking, about crops and animals; the boy, squatting too in the ammoniac dust and hoof-parings and scales of rust, heard his father tell a long and unhurried story out of the time before the birth of the older brother even when he had been a professional horsetrader. And then his father came up beside him where he stood before a tattered last year's circus poster on the other side of the store, gazing rapt and quiet at the scarlet horses, the incredible poisings and convulsions of tulle and tights and the painted leers of comedians, and said, "It's time to eat."

But not at home. Squatting beside his brother against the front wall, he watched his father emerge from the store and produce from a paper sack a segment of cheese and divide it carefully and deliberately into three with his pocket knife and produce crackers from the same sack. They all three squatted on the gallery and ate, slowly, without talking; then in the store again, they drank from a tin dipper tepid water smelling of the cedar bucket and of living beech trees. And still they did not go home. It was a horse lot this time, a tall rail fence upon and along which men stood and sat and out of which one by one horses were led, to be walked and trotted and then cantered back and forth along the road while the slow swapping and buying went on and the sun began to slant westward, they—the three of them—watching and listening, the older brother with his muddy eyes and his steady, inevitable tobacco, the father commenting now and then on certain of the animals, to no one in particular.

It was after sundown when they reached home. They ate supper by lamplight, then, sitting on the doorstep, the boy watched the night fully accomplish, listening to the whippoorwills and the frogs, when he heard his mother's voice: "Abner! No! No! Oh, God. Oh, God. Abner!" and he rose, whirled, and saw the altered light through the door where a candle stub now burned in a bottle neck on the table and his father, still in the hat and coat, at once formal and burlesque as though dressed carefully for some shabby and ceremonial violence, emptying the reservoir of the lamp back into the five-gallon kerosene can from which it had been filled, while the mother tugged at his arm until he shifted the lamp to the other hand and flung her back, not savagely or viciously, just hard, into the wall, her hands flung out against the wall for balance, her mouth open and in her face the same quality of hopeless despair as had been in her voice. Then his father saw him standing in the door.

"Go to the barn and get that can of oil we were oiling the wagon with," he said. The boy did not move. Then he could speak.

"What . . ." he cried. "What are you . . ."

"Go get that oil," his father said. "Go."

Then he was moving, running, outside the house, toward the stable; this the old habit, the old blood which he had not been permitted to choose for himself, which had been bequeathed him willy nilly and which had run for so long (and who knew where, battening on what of outrage and savagery and lust) before it came to him. *I could keep on,* he thought. *I could run on and on and never look back, never need to see his face again. Only I can't. I can't,* the rusted can in his hand now, the liquid sploshing in it as he ran back to the house and into it, into the sound of his mother's weeping in the next room, and handed the can to his father.

"Ain't you going to even send a nigger?" he cried. "At least you sent a nigger before?"   90

This time his father didn't strike him. The hand came even faster than the blow had, the same hand which had set the can on the table with almost excruciating care flashing from the can toward him too quick for him to follow it, gripping him by the back of his shirt and on to tiptoe before he had seen it quit the can, the face stooping at him in breathless and frozen ferocity, the cold, dead voice speaking over him to the older brother who leaned against the table, chewing with that steady, curious, sidewise motion of cows:

"Empty the can into the big one and go on. I'll catch up with you."

"Better tie him up to the bedpost," the brother said.

"Do like I told you," the father said. Then the boy was moving, his bunched shirt and the hard, bony hand between his shoulder-blades, his toes just touching the floor, across the room and into the other one, past the sisters sitting with spread heavy thighs in the two chairs over the cold hearth, and to where his mother and aunt sat side by side on the bed, the aunt's arms about his mother's shoulders.

"Hold him," the father said. The aunt made a startled movement. "Not you,"   95
the father said. "Lennie. Take hold of him. I want to see you do it." His mother took him by the wrist. "You'll hold him better than that. If he gets loose don't you know what he is going to do? He will go up yonder." He jerked his head toward the road. "Maybe I'd better tie him."

"I'll hold him," his mother whispered.

"See you do then." Then his father was gone, the stiff foot heavy and measured upon the boards, ceasing at last.

Then he began to struggle. His mother caught him in both arms, he jerking and wrenching at them. He would be stronger in the end, he knew that. But he had no time to wait for it. "Lemme go!" he cried. "I don't want to have to hit you!"

"Let him go!" the aunt said. "If he don't go, before God, I am going up there myself!"

"Don't you see I can't?" his mother cried. "Sarty! Sarty! No! No! Help me, Lizzie!"   100

Then he was free. His aunt grasped at him but it was too late. He whirled, running, his mother stumbled forward on to her knees behind him, crying to the nearest sister. "Catch him. Net! Catch him!" But that was too late too, the sister (the sisters were twins, born at the same time, yet either of them now gave the impression of being, encompassing as much living meat and volume and weight as any other two of the family) not yet having begun to rise from the chair, her head, face, alone merely turned, presenting to him in the flying instant an astonishing expanse of young female features untroubled by any surprise even, wearing only an expression of bovine interest. Then he was out of the room, out of the house, in the mild dust of the starlit road and the heavy rifeness of honeysuckle, the pale ribbon unspooling with terrific slowness under his running feet, reaching the gate at last and turning in, running his heart and lungs drumming, on up the drive toward the lighted house, the lighted door. He did not knock, he burst in, sobbing for breath, incapable for the moment of speech; he saw the astonished face of the Negro in the linen jacket without knowing when the Negro had appeared.

"De Spain!" he cried, panted. "Where's . . ." then he saw the white man too emerging from a white door down the hall. "Barn!" he cried. "Barn!"

"What?" the white man said. "Barn?"

"Yes!" the boy cried. "Barn!"

"Catch him!" the white man shouted.   105

But it was too late this time too. The Negro grasped his shirt, but the entire sleeve, rotten with washing, carried away, and he was out that door too and in the drive again, and had actually never ceased to run even while he was screaming into the white man's face.

Behind him the white man was shouting, "My horse! Fetch my horse!" and he thought for an instant of cutting across the park and climbing the fence into the road, but he did not know the park nor how high the vine-massed fence might be and he dared not risk it. So he ran on down the drive, blood and breath roaring; presently he was in the road again though he could not see it. He could not hear either: the galloping mare was almost upon him before he heard her, and even then he held his course, as if the very urgency of his wild grief and need must in a moment more find him wings, waiting until the ultimate instant to hurl himself aside and into the weed-choked roadside ditch as the horse thundered past and on, for an instant in furious silhouette against the stars, the tranquil early summer night sky which, even before the shape of the horse and rider vanished, strained abruptly and violently upward; a long, swirling roar incredible and soundless, blotting the stars, and he springing up and into the road again, running again, knowing it was too late yet still running even after he heard the shot and, an instant later, two shots, pausing now without knowing he had ceased to run, crying "Pap! Pap!," running again before he knew he had begun to run, stumbling, tripping over something and scrabbling up again without ceasing to run, looking backward over his shoulder at the glare as he got up, running on among the invisible trees, panting, sobbing, "Father! Father!"

At midnight he was sitting on the crest of a hill. He did not know it was midnight and he did not know how far he had come. But there was no glare behind him now and he sat now, his back toward what he had called home for four days anyhow, his face toward the dark woods which he would enter when breath was strong again, small, shaking steadily in the chill darkness, hugging himself into the remainder of his thin, rotten shirt, the grief and despair now no longer terror and fear but just grief and despair. *Father. My father,* he thought. "He was brave!" he cried suddenly, aloud but not loud, no more than a whisper. "He was! He was in the war! He was in Colonel Sartoris' cav'ry!" not knowing that his father had gone to that war a private in the fine old European sense, wearing no uniform, admitting the authority of and giving fidelity to no man or army or flag, going to war as Malbrouck* himself did: for booty—it meant nothing and less than nothing to him if it were enemy booty or his own.

The slow constellations wheeled on. It would be dawn and then sun-up after a while and he would be hungry. But that would be tomorrow and now he was only cold, and walking would cure that. His breathing was easier now and he decided to get up and go on, and then he found that he had been asleep because he knew it was almost dawn, the night almost over. He could tell that from the whippoorwills. They were everywhere now among the dark trees below him, constant and inflectioned and ceaseless, so that, as the instant for giving over to the day birds drew nearer and nearer, there was no interval at all between them. He got up. He was a little stiff, but walking would cure that too as it would the cold, and soon there would be the sun. He went on down the hill, toward the dark woods within which the liquid silver voices of the birds called unceasing—the rapid and urgent beating of the urgent and quiring heart of the late spring night. He did not look back.

William Faulkner   1897–1962

A Rose for Emily   1931

When Miss Emily Grierson died, our whole town went to her funeral: the men through a sort of respectful affection for a fallen monument, the women mostly out of curiosity to see the inside of her house, which no one save an old manservant—a combined gardener and cook—had seen in at least ten years.

It was a big, squarish frame house that had once been white, decorated with cupolas and spires and scrolled balconies in the heavily lightsome style of the seventies, set on what had once been our most select street. But garages and cotton gins had encroached and obliterated even the august names of that neighborhood; only Miss Emily's house was left, lifting its stubborn and coquettish decay above the cotton wagons and the gasoline pumps—an eyesore among eyesores. And now Miss Emily had gone to join the representatives of those august names where they lay in the cedar-bemused cemetery among the ranked and anonymous graves of Union and Confederate soldiers who fell at the battle of Jefferson.

Alive, Miss Emily had been a tradition, a duty, and a care; a sort of hereditary obligation upon the town, dating from that day in 1894 when Colonel Sartoris, the mayor—he who fathered the edict that no Negro woman should appear on the streets without an apron—remitted her taxes, the dispensation dating from the death of her father on into perpetuity. Not that Miss Emily would have accepted charity. Colonel Sartoris invented an involved tale to the effect that Miss Emily's father had loaned money to the town, which the town, as a matter of business, preferred this way of repaying. Only a man of Colonel Sartoris' generation and thought could have invented it, and only a woman could have believed it.

---

*Malbrouck—eighteenth-century English mercenary soldier.

When the next generation, with its more modern ideas, became mayors and aldermen, this arrangement created some little dissatisfaction. On the first of the year they mailed her a tax notice. February came, and there was no reply. They wrote her a formal letter, asking her to call at the sheriff's office at her convenience. A week later the mayor wrote her himself, offering to call or to send his car for her, and received in reply a note on paper of an archaic shape, in a thin, flowing calligraphy in faded ink, to the effect that she no longer went out at all. The tax notice was also enclosed, without comment.

They called a special meeting of the Board of Aldermen. A deputation waited   5
upon her, knocked at the door through which no visitor had passed since she ceased giving china-painting lessons eight or ten years earlier. They were admitted by the old Negro into a dim hall from which a stairway mounted into still more shadow. It smelled of dust and disuse—a close, dank smell. The Negro led them into the parlor. It was furnished in heavy, leather-covered furniture. When the Negro opened the blinds of one window, they could see that the leather was cracked; and when they sat down, a faint dust rose sluggishly about their thighs, spinning with slow motes in the single sun-ray. On a tarnished gilt easel before the fireplace stood a crayon portrait of Miss Emily's father.

They rose when she entered—a small, fat woman in black, with a thin gold chain descending to her waist and vanishing into her belt, leaning on an ebony cane with a tarnished gold head. Her skeleton was small and spare; perhaps that was why what would have been merely plumpness in another was obesity in her. She looked bloated, like a body long submerged in motionless water, and of that pallid hue. Her eyes, lost in the fatty ridges of her face, looked like two small pieces of coal pressed into a lump of dough as they moved from one face to another while the visitors stated their errand.

She did not ask them to sit. She just stood in the door and listened quietly until the spokesman came to a stumbling halt. Then they could hear the invisible watch ticking at the end of the gold chain.

Her voice was dry and cold. "I have no taxes in Jefferson. Colonel Sartoris explained it to me. Perhaps one of you can gain access to the city records and satisfy yourselves."

"But we have. We are the city authorities, Miss Emily. Didn't you get a notice from the sheriff, signed by him?"

"I received a paper, yes," Miss Emily said. "Perhaps he considers himself the   10
sheriff. . . . I have no taxes in Jefferson."

"But there is nothing on the books to show that, you see. We must go by the—"

"See Colonel Sartoris. I have no taxes in Jefferson."

"But, Miss Emily—"

"See Colonel Sartoris." (Colonel Sartoris had been dead almost ten years.) "I have no taxes in Jefferson. Tobe!" The Negro appeared. "Show these gentlemen out."

II

So she vanquished them, horse and foot, just as she had vanquished their fa-   15
thers thirty years before about the smell. That was two years after her father's death and a short time after her sweetheart—the one we believed would marry her—had deserted her. After her father's death she went out very little; after her sweetheart went away, people hardly saw her at all. A few of the ladies had the temerity to call, but were not received, and the only sign of life about the place was the Negro man—a young man then—going in and out with a market basket.

"Just as if a man—any man—could keep a kitchen properly," the ladies said; so they were not surprised when the smell developed. It was another link between the gross, teeming world and the high and mighty Griersons.

A neighbor, a woman, complained to the mayor, Judge Stevens, eighty years old. "But what will you have me do about it, madam?" he said.

"Why, send her word to stop it," the woman said. "Isn't there a law?"

"I'm sure that won't be necessary," Judge Stevens said. "It's probably just a snake or a rat that nigger of hers killed in the yard. I'll speak to him about it." 20

The next day he received two more complaints, one from a man who came in diffident deprecation. "We really must do something about it, Judge. I'd be the last one in the world to bother Miss Emily, but we've got to do something." That night the Board of Alderman met—three graybeards and one younger man, a member of the rising generation.

"It's simple enough," he said. "Send her word to have her place cleaned up. Give her a certain time to do it in, and if she don't . . ."

"Dammit, sir," Judge Stevens said, "will you accuse a lady to her face of smelling bad?"

So the next night, after midnight, four men crossed Miss Emily's lawn and slunk about the house like burglars, sniffing along the base of the brickwork and at the cellar openings while one of them performed a regular sowing motion with his hand out of a sack slung from his shoulder. They broke open the cellar door and sprinkled lime there, and in all the outbuildings. As they recrossed the lawn, a window that had been dark was lighted and Miss Emily sat in it, the light behind her, and her upright torso motionless as that of an idol. They crept quietly across the lawn and into the shadow of the locusts that lined the street. After a week or two the smell went away.

That was when people had begun to feel really sorry for her. People in our town, remembering how old lady Wyatt, her great-aunt, had gone completely crazy at last, believed that the Griersons held themselves a little too high for what they really were. None of the young men were quite good enough for Miss Emily and such. We had long thought of them as a tableau, Miss Emily a slender figure in white in the background, her father a spraddled silhouette in the foreground, his back to her and clutching a horsewhip, the two of them framed by the back-flung front door. So when she got to be thirty and was still single, we were not pleased exactly, but vindicated; even with insanity in the family she wouldn't have turned down all of her chances if they had really materialized. 25

When her father died, it got about that the house was all that was left to her; and in a way, people were glad. At last they could pity Miss Emily. Being left alone, and a pauper, she had become humanized. Now she too would know the old thrill and the old despair of a penny more or less.

The day after his death all the ladies prepared to call at the house and offer condolence and aid, as is our custom. Miss Emily met them at the door, dressed as usual and with no trace of grief on her face. She told them that her father was not dead. She did that for three days, with the ministers calling on her, and the doctors, trying to persuade her to let them dispose of the body. Just as they were about to resort to law and force, she broke down, and they buried her father quickly.

We did not say she was crazy then. We believed she had to do that. We remembered all the young men her father had driven away, and we knew that with nothing left, she would have to cling to that which had robbed her, as people will.

III

She was sick for a long time. When we saw her again, her hair was cut short, making her look like a girl, with a vague resemblance to those angels in colored church windows—sort of tragic and serene.

The town had just let the contracts for paving the sidewalks, and in the sum- 30 mer after her father's death they began the work. The construction company came with niggers and mules and machinery, and a foreman named Homer Barron, a Yankee—a big, dark, ready man, with a big voice and eyes lighter than his face. The little boys would follow in groups to hear him cuss the niggers, and the niggers singing in time to the rise and fall of picks. Pretty soon he knew everybody in town. Whenever you heard a lot of laughing anywhere about the square, Homer Barron would be in the center of the group. Presently we began to see him and Miss Emily on Sunday afternoons driving in that yellow-wheeled buggy and the matched team of bays from the livery stable.

At first we were glad that Miss Emily would have an interest, because the ladies all said, "Of course a Grierson would not think seriously of a Northerner, a day laborer." But there were still others, older people, who said that even grief could not cause a real lady to forget *noblesse oblige**—without calling it *noblesse oblige*. They just said, "Poor Emily. Her kinsfolk should come to her." She had some kin in Alabama; but years ago her father had fallen out with them over the estate of old lady Wyatt, the crazy woman, and there was no communication between the two families. They had not even been represented at the funeral.

And as soon as the old people said, "Poor Emily," the whispering began. "Do you suppose it's really so?" they said to one another. "Of course it is. What else could . . ." This behind their hands; rustling of craned silk and satin behind jalousies closed upon the sun of Sunday afternoon as the thin, swift clop-clop-clop of the matched team passed: "Poor Emily."

She carried her head high enough—even when we believed that she was fallen. It was as if she demanded more than ever the recognition of her dignity as the last Grierson; as if it had wanted that touch of earthiness to reaffirm her imperviousness. Like when she bought the rat poison, the arsenic. That was over a year after they had begun to say "Poor Emily," and while the two female cousins were visiting her.

"I want some poison," she said to the druggist. She was over thirty then, still a slight woman, though thinner than usual, with cold, haughty black eyes in a face the flesh of which was strained across the temples and about the eyesockets as you imagine a lighthouse-keeper's face ought to look. "I want some poison," she said.

"Yes, Miss Emily. What kind? For rats and such? I'd recom—" 35

"I want the best you have. I don't care what kind."

The druggist named several. "They'll kill anything up to an elephant. But what you want is—"

"Arsenic," Miss Emily said. "Is that a good one?"

"Is . . . arsenic? Yes, ma'am. But what you want—"

"I want arsenic."

40

The druggist looked down at her. She looked back at him, erect, her face like a strained flag. "Why, of course," the druggist said. "If that's what you want. But the law requires you to tell what you are going to use it for."

---

noblesse oblige—the idea that persons of noble birth have an obligation of honor and responsibility to their social inferiors.

Miss Emily just stared at him, her head tilted back in order to look him eye for eye, until he looked away and went and got the arsenic and wrapped it up. The Negro delivery boy brought her the package; the druggist didn't come back. When she opened the package at home there was written on the box, under the skull and bones: "For rats."

IV

So the next day we all said, "She will kill herself"; and we said it would be the best thing. When she had first begun to be seen with Homer Barron, we had said, "She will marry him." Then we said, "She will persuade him yet," because Homer himself had remarked—he liked men, and it was known that he drank with the younger men in the Elks' Club—that he was not a marrying man. Later we said, "Poor Emily" behind the jalousies as they passed on Sunday afternoon in the glittering buggy, Miss Emily with her head high and Homer Barron with his hat cocked and a cigar in his teeth, reins and whip in a yellow glove.

Then some of the ladies began to say that it was a disgrace to the town and a bad example to the young people. The men did not want to interfere, but at last the ladies forced the Baptist minister—Miss Emily's people were Episcopal—to call upon her. He would never divulge what happened during that interview, but he refused to go back again. The next Sunday they again drove about the streets, and the following day the minister's wife wrote to Miss Emily's relations in Alabama.

So she had blood-kin under her roof again and we sat back to watch developments. At first nothing happened. Then we were sure that they were to be married. We learned that Miss Emily had been to the jeweler's and ordered a man's toilet set in silver, with the letters H.B. on each piece. Two days later we learned that she had bought a complete outfit of men's clothing, including a nightshirt, and we said, "They are married." We were really glad. We were glad because the two female cousins were even more Grierson than Miss Emily had ever been.

So we were not surprised when Homer Barron—the streets had been finished some time since—was gone. We were a little disappointed that there was not a public blowing-off, but we believed that he had gone on to prepare for Miss Emily's coming, or to give her a chance to get rid of the cousins. (By that time it was a cabal, and we were all Miss Emily's allies to help circumvent the cousins.) Sure enough, after another week they departed. And, as we had expected all along, within three days Homer Barron was back in town. A neighbor saw the Negro man admit him at the kitchen door at dusk one evening.

And that was the last we saw of Homer Barron. And of Miss Emily for some time. The Negro man went in and out with the market basket, but the front door remained closed. Now and then we would see her at a window for a moment, as the men did that night when they sprinkled the lime, but for almost six months she did not appear on the streets. Then we knew that this was to be expected too; as if that quality of her father which had thwarted her woman's life so many times had been too virulent and too furious to die.

When we next saw Miss Emily, she had grown fat and her hair was turning gray. During the next few years it grew grayer and grayer until it attained an even pepper-and-salt iron-gray, when it ceased turning. Up to the day of her death at seventy-four it was still that vigorous iron-gray, like the hair of an active man.

From that time on her front door remained closed, save for a period of six or seven years, when she was about forty, during which she gave lessons in china-painting. She fitted up a studio in one of the downstairs rooms, where the

45

daughters and grand-daughters of Colonel Sartoris' contemporaries were sent to her with the same regularity and in the same spirit that they were sent on Sundays with a twenty-five cent piece for the collection plate. Meanwhile her taxes had been remitted.

The newer generation became the backbone and the spirit of the town, and   50
the painting pupils grew up and fell away and did not send their children to her with boxes of color and tedious brushes and pictures cut from the ladies' magazines. The front door closed upon the last one and remained closed for good. When the town got free postal delivery, Miss Emily alone refused to let them fasten the metal numbers above her door and attach a mailbox to it. She would not listen to them.

Daily, monthly, yearly we watched the Negro grow grayer and more stooped, going in and out with the market basket. Each December we sent her a tax notice, which would be returned by the post office a week later, unclaimed. Now and then we would see her in one of the downstairs windows—she had evidently shut up the top floor of the house—like the carven torso of an idol in a niche, looking or not looking at us, we could never tell which. Thus she passed from generation to generation—dear, inescapable, impervious, tranquil, and perverse.

And so she died. Fell ill in the house filled with dust and shadows, with only a doddering Negro man to wait on her. We did not even know she was sick; we had long since given up trying to get any information from the Negro. He talked to no one, probably not even to her, for his voice had grown harsh and rusty, as if from disuse.

She died in one of the downstairs rooms, in a heavy walnut bed with a curtain, her gray head propped on a pillow yellow and moldy with age and lack of sunlight.

V

The Negro met the first of the ladies at the front door and let them in, with their hushed, sibilant voices and their quick, curious glances, and then he disappeared. He walked right through the house and out the back and was not seen again.

The two female cousins came at once. The held the funeral on the second   55
day, with the town coming to look at Miss Emily beneath a mass of bought flowers, with the crayon face of her father musing profoundly above the bier and the ladies sibilant and macabre; and the very old men—some in their brushed Confederate uniforms—on the porch and the lawn, talking of Miss Emily as if she had been a contemporary of theirs, believing that they had danced with her and courted her perhaps, confusing time with its mathematical progression, as the old do, to whom all the past is not a diminishing road, but, instead, a hugh meadow which no winter ever quite touches, divided from them now by the narrow bottleneck of the most recent decade of years.

Already we knew that there was one room in that region above stairs which no one had seen in forty years, and which would have to be forced. They waited until Miss Emily was decently in the ground before they opened it.

The violence of breaking down the door seemed to fill this room with pervading dust. A thin, acrid pall as of the tomb seemed to lie everywhere upon this room decked and furnished as for a bridal: upon the valance curtains of faded rose color, upon the rose-shaded lights, upon the dressing table, upon the delicate array of crystal and the man's toilet things backed with tarnished silver, silver so tarnished that the monogram was obscured. Among them lay a collar and tie, as if they had just been removed, which, lifted, left upon the surface a pale crescent in the dust. Upon the chair hung the suit, carefully folded; beneath it the two mute shoes and the discarded socks.

The man himself lay in the bed.

For a long while we just stood there, looking down at the profound and flesh-less grin. The body had apparently once lain in the attitude of an embrace, but now the long sleep that outlasts love, that conquers even the grimace of love, had cuckolded him. What was left of him, rotted beneath what was left of the night-shirt, had become inextricable from the bed in which he lay; and upon him and upon the pillow beside him lay that even coating of the patient and biding dust.

Then we noticed that in the second pillow was the indentation of a head. One   60
of us lifted something from it, and leaning forward, that faint and invisible dust dry and acrid in the nostrils, we saw a long strand of iron-gray hair.

F. Scott Fitzgerald   1896–1940

Basil and Cleopatra   1929

Wherever she was, became a beautiful and enchanted place to Basil, but he did not think of it that way. He thought the fascination was inherent in the local-ity, and long afterward a commonplace street or the mere name of a city would exude a peculiar glow, a sustained sound, that struck his soul alert with delight. In her presence he was too absorbed to notice his surroundings; so that her absence never made them empty, but, rather, sent him seeking for her through haunted rooms and gardens that he had never really seen before.

This time, as usual, he saw only the expression of her face, the mouth that gave an attractive interpretation of any emotion she felt or pretended to feel—oh, invaluable mouth—and the rest of her, new as a peach and old as sixteen. He was almost unconscious that they stood in a railroad station and entirely unconscious that she had just glanced over his shoulder and fallen in love with another young man. Turning to walk with the rest to the car, she was already acting for the stranger; no less so because her voice was pitched for Basil and she clung to him, squeezing his arm.

Had Basil noticed this other young man that the train discharged he would merely have been sorry for him—as he had been sorry for the wretched people in the villages along the railroad and for his fellow travelers—they were not entering Yale in a fortnight nor were they about to spend three days in the same town with Miss Erminie Gilbert Labouisse Bibble. There was something dense, hopeless and a little contemptible about them all.

Basil had come to visit here because Erminie Bibble was visiting here. On the sad eve of her departure from his native Western city a month before, she had said, with all the promise one could ask in her urgent voice:

"If you know a boy in Mobile, why don't you make him invite you down   5
when I'll be there?"

He had followed this suggestion. And now with the soft, unfamiliar Southern city actually flowing around him, his excitement led him to believe that Fat Gaspar's car floated off immediately they entered it. A voice from the curb came as a surprise:

"Hi, Bessie Belle. Hi, William. How you all?"

The newcomer was tall and lean and a year or so older than Basil. He wore a white linen suit and a panama hat, under which burned fierce, undefeated Southern eyes.

"Why, Littleboy Le Moyne!" exclaimed Miss Cheever. "When did you get home?"

"Jus' now, Bessie Belle. Saw you lookin' so fine and pretty, had to come and   10
see closer."

He was introduced to Minnie and Basil.

"Drop you somewhere, Littleboy?" asked Fat—on his native heath, William.

"Why—" Le Moyne hesitated. "You're very kind, but the man ought to be here
with the car."

"Jump in."

Le Moyne swung his bag on top of Basil's and with courteous formality got in   15
the back seat beside them. Basil caught Minnie's eye and she smiled quickly back,
as if to say, "This is too bad, but it'll soon be over."

"Do you happen to come from New Orleans, Miss Bibble?" asked Le Moyne.
"Sure do."

"'Cause I just came from there and they told me one of their mos' celebrated
heartbreakers was visiting up here, and meanwhile her suitors were shooting
themselves all over the city. That's the truth. I used to help pick 'em up myself
sometimes when they got littering the streets."

This must be Mobile Bay on the left, Basil thought; "Down Mobile," and the
Dixie moonlight and darky stevedores singing. The houses on either side of the
street were gently faded behind proud, protecting vines; there had been crinolines
on these balconies, and guitars by night in these broken gardens.

It was so warm; the voices were so sure they had time to say everything—   20
even Minnie's voice, answering the banter of the youth with the odd nickname,
seemed slower and lazier—he had scarcely ever thought of her as a Southern girl
before. They stopped at a large gate where flickers of a yellow house showed
through luscious trees. Le Moyne got out.

"I certainly hope you both enjoy your visit here. If you'll permit me I'll call
around and see if there's anything I can do to add to your pleasure." He swooped
his panama. "I bid you good day."

As they started off, Bessie Belle turned around and smiled at Minnie.

"Didn't I tell you?" she demanded.

"I guessed it in the station, before he came up to the car," said Minnie. "Something told me that was him."

"Did you think he was good looking?"   25

"He was divine," Minnie said.

"Of course he's always gone with an older crowd."

To Basil, this prolonged discussion seemed a little out of place. After all, the
young man was simply a local Southerner who lived here; add to that, that he
went with an older crowd, and it seemed that his existence was being unnecessarily insisted upon.

But now Minnie turned to him, said, "Basil," wriggled invitingly and folded her
hands in a humble, expectant way that invariably caused disturbances in his heart.

"I loved your letters," she said.   30

"You might have answered them."

"I haven't had a minute, Basil. I visited in Chicago and then in Nashville. I
haven't even been home." She lowered her voice. "Father and mother are getting
a divorce, Basil. Isn't that awful?"

He was startled; then, after a moment, he adjusted the idea to her and she became doubly poignant; because of its romantic connection with her, the thought of
divorce would never shock him again.

"That's why I didn't write. But I've thought of you so much. You're the best friend I have, Basil. You always understand."

This was decidedly not the note upon which they had parted in St. Paul. A dreadful rumor that he hadn't intended to mention rose to his lips.

"Who is this fellow Bailey you met at Lake Forest?" he inquired lightly.

"Buzz Bailey!" Her big eyes opened in surprise. "He's very attractive and a divine dancer, but we're just friends." She frowned. "I bet Connie Davies has been telling tales in St. Paul. Honestly, I'm so sick of girls that, just out of jealousy or nothing better to do, sit around and criticize you if you have a good time."

He was convinced now that something had occurred in Lake Forest, but he concealed the momentary pang from Minnie.

"Anyhow, you're a fine one to talk." She smiled suddenly. "I guess everybody knows how fickle you are, Mr. Basil Duke Lee."

Generally such an implication is considered flattering, but the lightness, almost the indifference, with which she spoke increased his alarm—and then suddenly the bomb exploded.

"You needn't worry about Buzz Bailey. At present I'm absolutely heartwhole and fancy free."

Before he could even comprehend the enormity of what she had said, they stopped at Bessie Belle Cheever's door and the two girls ran up the steps, calling back, "We'll see you this afternoon."

Mechanically Basil climbed into the front seat beside his host.

"Going out for freshman football, Basil?" William asked.

"What? Oh, sure. If I can get off my two conditions." There was no if in his heart; it was the greatest ambition of his life.

"You'll probably make the freshman team easy. That fellow Littleboy Le Moyne you just met is going to Princeton this fall. He played end at V. M. I."

"Where'd he get that crazy name?"

"Why, his family always called him that and everybody picked it up." After a moment he added, "He asked them to the country-club dance with him tonight."

"When did he?" Basil demanded in surprise.

"Right then. That's what they were talking about. I meant to ask them and I was just leading up to it gradually, but he stepped in before I could get a chance." He sighed, blaming himself. "Well, anyhow, we'll see them there."

"Sure; it doesn't matter," said Basil. But was it Fat's mistake? Couldn't Minnie have said right out: "But Basil came all this way to see me and I ought to go with him on his first night here."

What had happened? One month ago, in the dim, thunderous Union Station at St. Paul, they had gone behind a baggage truck and he had kissed her, and her eyes had said: Again. Up to the very end, when she disappeared in a swirl of vapor at the car window, she had been his—those weren't things you thought; they were things you knew. He was bewildered. It wasn't like Minnie, who, for all her glittering popularity, was invariably kind. He tried to think of something in his letters that might have offended her, and searched himself for shortcomings. Perhaps she didn't like him the way he was in the morning. The joyous mood in which he had arrived was vanishing into air.

She was her familiar self when they played tennis that afternoon; she admired his strokes and once, when they were close at the net, she suddenly patted his hand. But later, as they drank lemonade on the Cheevers' wide, shady porch, he couldn't seem to be alone with her even for a minute. Was it by accident that, coming back from the courts, she had sat in front with Fat? Last summer she had made opportunities to be alone with him—made them out of nothing. It was in a state that seemed to border on some terrible realization that he dressed for the country-club dance.

The club lay in a little valley, almost roofed over by willows, and down through their black silhouettes, in irregular blobs and patches, dripped the light of a huge harvest moon. As they parked the car, Basil's tune of tunes, Chinatown, drifted from the windows and dissolved into its notes which thronged like elves through the glade. His heart quickened, suffocating him; the throbbing tropical darkness held a promise of such romance as he had dreamed of; but faced with it, he felt himself too small and impotent to seize the felicity he desired. When he danced with Minnie he was ashamed of inflicting his merely mortal presence on her in this fairyland whose unfamiliar figures reached towering proportions of magnificence and beauty. To make him king here, she would have to reach forth and draw him close to her with soft words; but she only said, "Isn't it wonderful, Basil? Did you ever have a better time?"

Talking for a moment with Le Moyne in the stag line, Basil was hesitantly jealous and oddly shy. He resented the tall form that stooped down so fiercely over Minnie as they danced, but he found it impossible to dislike him or not to be amused by the line of sober-faced banter he kept up with passing girls. He and William Gaspar were the youngest boys here, as Bessie Belle and Minnie were the youngest girls, and for the first time in his life he wanted passionately to be older, less impressionable, less impressed. Quivering at every scent, sigh or tune, he wanted to be blasé and calm. Wretchedly he felt the whole world of beauty pour down upon him like moonlight, pressing on him, making his breath now sighing, now short, as he wallowed helplessly in a superabundance of youth for which a hundred adults present would have given years of life.

Next day, meeting her in a world that had shrunk back to reality, things were more natural, but something was gone and he could not bring himself to be amusing and gay. It would be like being brave after the battle. He should have been all that the night before. They went downtown in an unpaired foursome and called at a photographer's for some pictures of Minnie. Basil liked one proof that no one else liked—somehow, it reminded him of her as she had been in St. Paul—so he ordered two—one for her to keep and one to send after him to Yale. All afternoon she was distracted and vaguely singing, but back at the Cheevers' she sprang up the steps at the sound of the phone inside. Ten minutes later she appeared, sulky and lowering, and Basil heard a quick exchange between the two girls:

"He can't get out of it."

"—a pity."

"—back Friday."

It could only be Le Moyne who had gone away, and to Minnie it mattered. Presently, unable to endure her disappointment, he got up wretchedly and suggested to William that they go home. To his surprise, Minnie's hand on his arm arrested him.

"Don't go, Basil. It doesn't seem as if I've seen you a minute since you've been here."

He laughed unhappily.

"As if it mattered to you."

"Basil, don't be silly." She bit her lip as if she were hurt. "Let's go out to the swing."

He was suddenly radiant with hope and happiness. Her tender smile, which   65
seemed to come from the heart of freshness, soothed him and he drank down her
lies in grateful gulps like cool water. The last sunshine touched her cheeks with
the unearthly radiance he had seen there before, as she told him how she hadn't
wanted to accept Le Moyne's invitation, and how surprised and hurt she had been
when he hadn't come near her last night.

"Then do one thing, Minnie," he pleaded: "Won't you let me kiss you just
once?"

"But not here," she exclaimed, "you silly!"

"Let's go in the summerhouse, for just a minute."

"Basil, I can't. Bessie Belle and William are on the porch. Maybe some other
time."

He looked at her distraught, unable to believe or disbelieve in her, and she   70
changed the subject quickly:

"I'm going to Miss Beecher's school, Basil. It's only a few hours from New
Haven. You can come up and see me this fall. The only thing is, they say you have
to sit in glass parlors. Isn't that terrible?"

"Awful," he agreed fervently.

William and Bessie Belle had left the veranda and were out in front, talking to
some people in a car.

"Minnie, come into the summerhouse now—for just a minute. They're so far
away."

Her face set unwillingly.   75

"I can't, Basil. Don't you see I can't?"

"Why not? I've got to leave tommorrow."

"Oh, no."

"I have to. I only have four days to get ready for my exams. Minnie—"

He took her hand. It rested calmly enough in his, but when he tried to pull   80
her to her feet she plucked it sharply away. The swing moved with the little struggle and Basil put out his foot and made it stop. It was terrible to swing when one
was at a disadvantage.

She laid the recovered hand on his knee.

"I've stopped kissing people, Basil. Really. I'm too old; I'll be seventeen
next May."

"I'll bet you kissed Le Moyne," he said bitterly.

"Well, you're pretty fresh—"

Basil got out of the swing.   85

"I think I'll go."

Looking up, she judged him dispassionately, as she never had before—his
sturdy, graceful figure; the high, warm color through his tanned skin; his black,
shining hair that she had once thought so romantic. She felt, too—as even those
who disliked him felt—that there was something else in his face—a mark, a hint
of destiny, a persistence that was more than will, that was rather a necessity of
pressing its own pattern on the world, of having its way. That he would most
probably succeed at Yale, that it would be nice to go there this year as his girl,
meant nothing to her. She had never needed to be calculating. Hesitating, she al-
ternatingly drew him toward her in her mind and let him go. There were so many
men and they wanted her so much. If Le Moyne had been here at hand she
wouldn't have hesitated, for nothing must interfere with the mysterious opening

glory of that affair; but he was gone for three days and she couldn't decide quite
yet to let Basil go.

"Stay over till Wednesday and I'll—I'll do what you want," she said.

"But I can't. I've got these exams to study for. I ought to have left this afternoon."

"Study on the train."   90

She wriggled, dropped her hands in her lap and smiled at him. Taking her
hand suddenly, he pulled her to her feet and toward the summerhouse and the
cool darkness behind its vines.

The following Friday Basil arrived in New Haven and set about crowding five
days' work into two. He had done no studying on the train; instead he sat in a
trance and concentrated upon Minnie, wondering what was happening now that
Le Moyne was there. She had kept her promise to him, but only literally—kissed
him once in the playhouse, once, grudgingly, the second evening; but the day of
his departure there had been a telegram from Le Moyne, and in front of Bessie
Belle she had not even dared to kiss him good-bye. As a sort of amend she had
given him permission to call on the first day permitted by Miss Beecher's school.

The opening of college found him rooming with Brick Wales and George
Dorsey in a suite of two bedrooms and a study in Wright Hall. Until the result of
his trigonometry examination was published he was ineligible to play football, but
watching the freshmen practice on Yale field, he saw that the quarterback position
lay between Cullum, last year's Andover captain, and a man named Danziger from
a New Bedford high school. There was a rumor that Cullum would be moved to
halfback. The other quarterbacks did not appear formidable and Basil felt a great
impatience to be out there with a team in his hands to move over the springy turf.
He was sure he could at least get in some of the games.

Behind everything, as a light showing through, was the image of Minnie; he
would see her in a week, three days, tomorrow. On the eve of the occasion he ran
into Fat Gaspar, who was in Sheff, in the oval by Haughton Hall. In the first busy
weeks they had scarcely met; now they walked along for a little way together.

"We all came North together," Fat said. "You ought to have been along. We
had some excitement. Minnie got in a jam with Littleboy Le Moyne."

Basil's blood ran cold.   95

"It was funny afterward, but she was pretty scared for a while," continued Fat.
"She had a compartment with Bessie Belle, but she and Littleboy wanted to be
alone; so in the afternoon Bessie Belle came and played cards in ours. Well, after
about two hours Bessie Belle and I went back, and there were Minnie and Littleboy
standing in the vestibule arguing with the conductor; Minnie white as a sheet.
Seems they locked the door and pulled down the blinds, and I guess there was a little petting going on. When he came along after the tickets and knocked on the
door, they thought it was us kidding them, and wouldn't let him in at first, and
when they did, he was pretty upset. He asked Littleboy if that was his compartment,
and whether he and Minnie were married that they locked the door, and Littleboy
lost his temper trying to explain that there was nothing wrong. He said the conductor had insulted Minnie and he wanted him to fight. But that conductor could have
made trouble, and believe me, I had an awful time smoothing it all over."

With every detail imagined, with every refinement of jealousy beating in his
mind, including even envy for their community of misfortune as they stood together in the vestibule, Basil went up to Miss Beecher's next day. Radiant and
glowing, more mysteriously desirable than ever, wearing her very sins like stars,

she came down to him in her plain white uniform dress, and his heart turned over at the kindness of her eyes.

"You were wonderful to come up, Basil. I'm so excited having a beau so soon. Everybody's jealous of me."

The glass doors hinged like French windows, shutting them in on all sides. It was hot. Down through three more compartments he could see another couple—a girl and her brother, Minnie said—and from time to time they moved and gestured soundlessly, as unreal in these tiny human conservatories as the vase of paper flowers on the table. Basil walked up and down nervously. 100

"Minnie, I want to be a great man some day and I want to do everything for you. I understand you're tired of me now. I don't know how it happened, but somebody else came along—it doesn't matter. There isn't any hurry. But I just want you to—oh, remember me in some different way—try to think of me as you used to, not as if I was just another one you threw over. Maybe you'd better not see me for a while—I mean at the dance this fall. Wait till I've accomplished some big scene or deed, you know, and I can show it to you and say I did that all for you."

It was very futile and young and sad. Once, carried away by the tragedy of it all, he was on the verge of tears, but he controlled himself to that extent. There was sweat on his forehead. He sat across the room from her, and Minnie sat on the couch, looking at the floor, and said several times: "Can't we be friends, Basil? I always think of you as one of my best friends."

Toward the end she rose patiently.

"Don't you want to see the chapel?"

They walked upstairs and he glanced dismally into a small dark space, with 105 her living, sweet-smelling presence half a yard from his shoulder. He was almost glad when the funereal business was over and he walked out of the school into the fresh autumn air.

Back in New Haven he found two pieces of mail on his desk. One was a notice from the registrar telling him that he had failed his trigonometry examination and would be ineligible for football. The second was a photograph of Minnie—the picture that he had liked and ordered two of in Mobile. At first the inscription puzzled him: "L. L. from E. G. L. B. Trains are bad for the heart." Then suddenly he realized what had happened, and threw himself on his bed, shaken with wild laughter.

Three weeks later, having requested and passed a special examination in trigonometry, Basil began to look around him gloomily to see if there was anything left in life. Not since his miserable first year at school had he passed through such a period of misery; only now did he begin for the first time to be aware of Yale. The quality of romantic speculation reawoke, and, listlessly at first, then with growing determination, he set about merging himself into this spirit which had fed his dreams so long.

I want to be chairman of the News or the Record, thought his old self one October morning, and I want to get my letter in football, and I want to be in Skull and Bones.

Whenever the vision of Minnie and Le Moyne on the train occurred to him, he repeated this phrase like an incantation. Already he thought with shame of having stayed over in Mobile, and there began to be long strings of hours when he scarcely brooded about her at all.

He had missed half of the freshman football season, and it was with scant 110 hope that he joined the squad on Yale field. Dressed in his black and white St.

Regis jersey, amid the motley of forty schools, he looked enviously at the proud two dozen in Yale blue. At the end of four days he was reconciling himself to obscurity for the rest of the season when the voice of Carson, assistant coach, singled him suddenly out of a crowd of scrub backs.

"Who was throwing those passes just now?"

"I was, sir."

"I haven't seen you before, have I?"

"I just got eligible."

"Know the signals?"   115

"Yes, sir."

"Well, you take this team down the field—ends, Krutch and Bispam; tackles—"

A moment later he heard his own voice snapping out on the crisp air: "Thirty-two, sixty-five, sixty-seven, twenty-two—"

There was a ripple of laughter.

"Wait a minute!" Where'd you learn to call signals like that?" said Carson.   120

"Why, we had a Harvard coach, sir."

"Well, just drop the Haughton emphasis. You'll get everybody too excited."

After a few minutes they were called in and told to put on headgears.

"Where's Waite?" Carson asked. "Test, eh? Well, you then—what's your name?—in the black and white sweater?"

"Lee."   125

"You call signals. And let's see you get some life into this outfit. Some of you guards and tackles are big enough for the varsity. Keep them on their toes, you—what's your name?"

"Lee."

They lined up with possession of the ball on the freshmen's twenty-yard line. They were allowed unlimited downs, but when, after a dozen plays, they were in approximately that same place, the ball was given to the first team.

That's that! thought Basil. That finishes me.

But an hour later, as they got out of the bus, Carson spoke to him: 130

"Did you weigh this afternoon?"

"Yes. Hundred and fifty-eight."

"Let me give you a tip—you're still playing prep-school football. You're still satisfied with stopping them. The idea here is that if you lay them down hard enough you wear them out. Can you kick?"

"No, sir."

"Well, its too bad you didn't get out sooner."   135

A week later his name was read out as one of those to go to Andover. Two quarterbacks ranked ahead of him, Danziger and a little hard rubber ball of a man, named Appleton, and Basil watched the game from the sidelines, but when, the following Tuesday, Danziger splintered his arm in practice, Basil was ordered to report to training table.

On the eve of the game with the Princeton freshmen, the egress of the student body to Princeton for the Varsity encounter left the campus almost deserted. Deep autumn had set in, with a crackling wind from the west, and walking back to his room after final skull practice, Basil felt the old lust for glory sweep over him. Le Moyne was playing end on the Princeton freshmen and it was probable that Minnie would be in the stands, but now, as he ran along the springy grass in front of Osborne, swaying to elude imaginary tacklers, the fact seemed of less importance than the game. Like most Americans, he was seldom able really to grasp the moment, to say: "This, for me, is the great equation by which everything else will be measured; this is the golden time," but for once the present was sufficient. He was going to spend two hours in a country where life ran at the pace he demanded of it.

The day was fair and cool; an unimpassioned crowd, mostly townsmen, was scattered through the stands. The Princeton freshmen looked sturdy and solid in their diagonal stripes, and Basil picked out Le Moyne, noting coldly that he was exceptionally fast, and bigger than he had seemed in his clothes. On an impulse Basil turned and searched for Minnie in the crowd, but he could not find her. A minute later the whistle blew; sitting at the coach's side, he concentrated all his faculties on the play.

The first half was played between the thirty-yard lines. The main principles of Yale's offense seemed to Basil too simple; less effective than the fragments of the Haughton system he had learned at school, while the Princeton tactics, still evolved in Sam White's long shadow, were built around a punter and the hope of a break. When the break came, it was Yale's. At the start of the second half Princeton fumbled and Appleton sent over a drop kick from the thirty-yard line.

It was his last act of the day. He was hurt on the next kick-off and, to a burst of freshmen cheering, assisted from the game.   140

With his heart in a riot, Basil sprinted out on the field. He felt an overpowering strangeness, and it was someone else in his skin who called the first signals and sent an unsuccessful play through the line. As he forced his eyes to take in the field slowly, they met Le Moyne's, and Le Moyne grinned at him. Basil called for a short pass over the line, throwing it himself for a gain of seven yards. He sent Cullum off tackle for three more and a first down. At the forty, with more latitude, his mind began to function smoothly and surely. His short passes worried the Princeton fullback, and, in consequence, the running gains through the line were averaging four yards instead of two.

At the Princeton forty he dropped back to kick formation and tried Le Moyne's end, but Le Moyne went under the interfering halfback and caught Basil by a foot. Savagely Basil tugged himself free, but too late—the halfback bowled him over. Again Le Moyne's face grinned at him, and Basil hated it. He called the same end and, with Cullum carrying the ball, they rolled over Le Moyne six yards, to Princeton's thirty-two. He was slowing down, was he? Then run him ragged! System counseled a pass, but he heard himself calling the end again. He ran parallel to the line, saw his interference melt away and Le Moyne, his jaw set, coming for him. Instead of cutting in, Basil turned full about and tried to reverse his field. When he was trapped he had lost fifteen yards.

A few minutes later the ball changed hands and he ran back to the safety position thinking: They'd yank me if they had anybody to put in my place.

The Princeton team suddenly woke up. A long pass gained thirty yards. A fast new back dazzled his way through the line for another first down. Yale was on the defensive, but even before they had realized the fact, the disaster had happened. Basil was drawn on an apparently developed play; too late he saw the ball shoot out of scrimmage to a loose end; saw, as he was neatly blocked, that the Princeton substitutes were jumping around wildly, waving their blankets. They had scored.

He got up with his heart black, but his brain cool. Blunders could be atoned for—if they only wouldn't take him out. The whistle blew for the quarter, and squatting on the turf with the exhausted team, he made himself believe that he hadn't lost their confidence, kept his face intent and rigid, refusing no man's eye. He had made his errors for today.   145

On the kick-off he ran the ball back to the thirty-five, and a steady rolling progress began. The short passes, a weak spot inside tackle, Le Moyne's end. Le Moyne was tired now. His face was drawn and dogged as he smashed blindly into the interference; the ball carrier eluded him—Basil or another.

Thirty more to go—twenty—over Le Moyne again. Disentangling himself from the pile, Basil met the Southerner's weary glance and insulted him in a crisp voice: "You've quit, Littleboy. They better take you out."

He started the next play at him and, as Le Moyne charged in furiously, tossed a pass over his head for the score. Yale 10, Princeton 7. Up and down the field again, with Basil fresher every minute and another score in sight, and suddenly the game was over.

Trudging off the field, Basil's eye ranged over the stands, but he could not see her.   150

I wonder if she knows I was pretty bad, he thought, and then bitterly: If I don't, he'll tell her.

He could hear him telling her in that soft Southern voice—the voice that had wooed her so persuasively that afternoon on the train. As he emerged from the dressing room an hour later he ran into Le Moyne coming out of the visitors' quarters next door. He looked at Basil with an expression at once uncertain and angry.

"Hello, Lee." After a momentary hesitation he added: "Good work."

"Hello, Le Moyne," said Basil, clipping his words.   155

Le Moyne turned away, turned back again.

"What's the matter?" he demanded. "Do you want to carry this any further?"

Basil didn't answer. The bruised face and the bandaged hand assuaged his hatred a little, but he couldn't bring himself to speak. The game was over, and now Le Moyne would meet Minnie somewhere, make the defeat negligible in the victory of the night.

"If it's about Minnie, you're wasting your time being sore," Le Moyne exploded suddenly. "I asked her to the game, but she didn't come."

"Didn't she?" Basil was startled.

"That was it, eh? I wasn't sure. I thought you were just trying to get my goat in   160
there." His eyes narrowed. "The young lady kicked me about a month ago."

"Kicked you?"

"Threw me over. Got a little weary of me. She runs through things quickly."

Basil perceived that his face was miserable.

"Who is it now?" he asked in more civil tone.

"It seems to be a classmate of yours named Jubal—and a mighty sad bird, if   165
you ask me. She met him in New York the day before her school opened, and I hear it's pretty heavy. She'll be at the Lawn Club Dance tonight."

Basil had dinner at the Taft with Jobena Dorsey and her brother George. The Varsity had won at Princeton and the college was jubilant and enthusiastic; as they came in, a table of freshmen by the door gave Basil a hand.

"You're getting very important," Jobena said.

A year ago Basil had thought for a few weeks that he was in love with Jobena; when they next met he knew immediately that he was not.

"And why was that?" he asked her now, as they danced. "Why did it all go so quick?"

"Do you really want to know?"   170

"Yes."

"Because I let it go."

"You let it go?" he repeated. "I like that!"

"I decided you were too young."

"Didn't I have anything to do with it?"

She shook her head.

"That's what Bernard Shaw says," Basil admitted thoughtfully. "But I thought 175
it was just about older people. So you go after the men."

"Well, I should say not!" Her body stiffened indignantly in his arms. "The men
are usually there, and the girl blinks at them or something. It's just instinct."

"Can't a man make a girl fall for him?"

"Some men can—the ones who really don't care." 180

He pondered this awful fact for a moment and stowed it away for future examination. On the way to the Lawn Club he brought forth more questions. If a girl
who had been "crazy about a boy" became suddenly infatuated with another, what
ought the first boy to do?

"Let her go," said Jobena.

"Supposing he wasn't willing to do that. What ought he to do?"

"There isn't anything to do."

"Well, what's the best thing?" 185

Laughing, Jobena laid her head on his shoulder.

"Poor Basil," she said, "I'll be Laura Jean Libbey and you tell me the whole
story."

He summarized the affair. "You see," he concluded, "if she was just anybody I
could get over it, no matter how much I loved her. But she isn't—she's the most
popular, most beautiful girl I've ever seen. I mean she's like Messalina and Cleopatra and Salome and all that."

"Louder," requested George from the front seat.

"She's sort of an immortal woman," continued Basil in a lower voice. "You 190
know, like Madame du Barry and all that sort of thing. She's not just—"

"Not just like me."

"No. That is, you're sort of like her—all the girls I've cared about are sort of
the same. Oh, Jobena, you know what I mean."

As the lights of the New Haven Lawn Club loomed up she became oblig-
ingly serious:

"There's nothing to do. I can see that. She's more sophisticated than you. She
staged the whole thing from the beginning, even when you thought it was you. I
don't know why she got tired, but evidently she is, and she couldn't create it
again, even if she wanted to, and you couldn't because you're—"

"Go on. What?"

"You're too much in love. All that's left for you to do is to show her you don't 195
care. Any girl hates to lose an old beau; so she may even smile at you—but don't
go back. It's all over."

In the dressing room Basil stood thoughtfully brushing his hair. It was all over.
Jobena's words had taken away his last faint hope, and after the strain of the afternoon the realization brought tears to his eyes. Hurriedly filling the bowl, he
washed his face. Someone came in and slapped him on the back.

"You played a nice game, Lee."

"Thanks, but I was rotten."

"You were great. That last quarter—" 200

He went into the dance. Immediately he saw her, and in the same breath he was dizzy and confused with excitement. A little dribble of stags pursued her wherever she went, and she looked up at each one of them with the bright-eyed, passionate smile he knew so well. Presently he located her escort and indignantly discovered it was a flip, blatant boy from Hill School he had already noticed and set down as impossible. What quality lurked behind those watery eyes that drew her? How could that raw temperament appreciate that she was one of the immortal sirens of the world?

Having examined Mr. Jubal desperately and in vain for the answers to these questions, he cut in and danced all of twenty feet with her, smiling with cynical melancholy when she said:

"I'm so proud to know you, Basil. Everybody says you were wonderful this afternoon."

But the phrase was precious to him and he stood against the wall repeating it over to himself, separating it into its component parts and trying to suck out any lurking meaning. If enough people praised him it might influence her. "I'm proud to know you, Basil. Everybody says you were wonderful this afternoon."

There was a commotion near the door and someone said, "By golly, they got   205
in after all!"

"Who?" another asked.

"Some Princeton freshmen. Their football season's over and three or four of them broke training at the Hofbrau."

And now suddenly the curious specter of a young man burst out of the commotion, as a back breaks through a line, and neatly straight-arming a member of the dance committee, rushed unsteadily onto the floor. He wore no collar with his dinner coat, his shirt front had long expelled its studs, his hair and eyes were wild. For a moment he glanced around as if blinded by the lights; then his glance fell on Minnie Bibble and an unmistakable love light came into his face. Even before he reached her he began to call her name aloud in a strained, poignant Southern voice.

Basil sprang forward, but others were before him, and Littleboy Le Moyne, fighting hard, disappeared into the coatroom in a flurry of legs and arms, many of which were not his own. Standing in the doorway, Basil found his disgust tempered with a monstrous sympathy; for Le Moyne, each time his head emerged from under the faucet, spoke desperately of his rejected love.

But when Basil danced with Minnie again, he found her frightened and angry;   210
so much so that she seemed to appeal to Basil for support, made him sit down.

"Wasn't he a fool?" she cried feelingly. "That sort of thing gives a girl a terrible reputation. They ought to have put him in jail."

"He didn't know what he was doing. He played a hard game and he's all in, that's all."

But her eyes filled with tears.

"Oh, Basil," she pleaded, "am I just perfectly terrible? I never want to be mean to anybody; things just happen."

He wanted to put his arm around her and tell her she was the most romantic   215
person in the world, but he saw in her eyes that she scarcely perceived him; he was a lay figure—she might have been talking to another girl. He remembered what Jobena had said—there was nothing left except to escape with his pride.

"You've got more sense." Her soft voice flowed around him like an enchanted river. "You know that when two people aren't—aren't crazy about each other any more, the thing is to be sensible."

"Of course," he said, and forced himself to add lightly: "When a thing's over, it's over."

"Oh, Basil, you're so satisfactory. You always understand." And now suddenly, for the first time in months, she was actually thinking of him. He would be an invaluable person in any girl's life, she thought, if that brain of his, which was so annoying sometimes, was really used "to sort of understand."

He was watching Jobena dance, and Minnie followed his eyes.

"You brought a girl, didn't you? She's awfully pretty."

"Not as pretty as you."   220

"Basil."

Resolutely he refused to look at her, guessing that she had wriggled slightly and folded her hands in her lap. And as he held on to himself an extraordinary thing happened—the world around, outside of her, brightened a little. Presently more freshmen would approach him to congratulate him on the game, and he would like it—the words and the tribute in their eyes. There was a good chance he would start against Harvard next week.

"Basil!"

His heart made a dizzy tour of his chest. Around the corner of his eyes he felt   225
her eyes waiting. Was she really sorry? Should he seize the opportunity to turn to her and say: "Minnie, tell this crazy nut to go jump in the river, and come back to me." He wavered, but a thought that had helped him this afternoon returned: He had made all his mistakes for this time. Deep inside of him the plea expired slowly.

Jubal the impossible came up with an air of possession, and Basil's heart went bobbing off around the ballroom in a pink silk dress. Lost again in a fog of indecision, he walked out on the veranda. There was a flurry of premature snow in the air and the stars looked cold. Staring up at them he saw that they were his stars as always—symbols of ambition, struggle and glory. The wind blew through them, trumpeting that high white note for which he always listened, and the thin-blown clouds, stripped for battle, passed in review. The scene was of an unparalleled brightness and magnificence, and only the practiced eye of the commander saw that one star was no longer there.

Mary E. Wilkins Freeman   1852–1930

The Revolt of "Mother"   1891

"Father!"

"What is it?"

"What are them men diggin' over there in the field for?"

There was a sudden dropping and enlarging of the lower part of the old man's face, as if some heavy weight had settled therein; he shut his mouth tight, and went on harnessing the great bay mare. He hustled the collar on to her neck with a jerk.

"Father!"   5

The old man slapped the saddle upon the mare's back.

"Look here, father, I want to know what them men are diggin' over in the field for, an' I'm goin' to know."

"I wish you'd go into the house, mother, an' 'tend to your own affairs," the old man said then. He ran his words together, and his speech was almost as inarticulate as a growl.

But the woman understood; it was her most native tongue. "I ain't goin' into the house till you tell me what them men are doin' over there in the field," said she.

Then she stood waiting. She was a small woman, short and straight-waisted   10
like a child in her brown cotton gown. Her forehead was mild and benevolent between the smooth curves of gray hair; there were meek downward lines about her nose and mouth; but her eyes, fixed upon the old man, looked as if the meekness had been the result of her own will, never of the will of another.

They were in the barn, standing before the wide open doors. The spring air, full of the smell of growing grass and unseen blossoms, came in their faces. The deep yard in front was littered with farm wagons and piles of wood; on the edges, close to the fence and the house, the grass was a vivid green, and there were some dandelions.

The old man glanced doggedly at his wife as he tightened the last buckles on the harness. She looked as immovable to him as one of the rocks in his pastureland, bound to the earth with generations of blackberry vines. He slapped the reins over the horse, and started forth from the barn.

"*Father!*" said she.

The old man pulled up. "What is it?"

"I want to know what them men are diggin' over there in that field for."   15

"They're diggin' a cellar, I s'pose, if you've got to know."

"A cellar for what?"

"A barn."

"A barn? You ain't goin' to build a barn over there where we was goin' to have a house, father?"

The old man said not another word. He hurried the horse into the farm   20
wagon, and clattered out of the yard, jouncing as sturdily on his seat as a boy.

The woman stood a moment looking after him, then she went out of the barn across a corner of the yard to the house. The house, standing at right angles with the great barn and a long reach of sheds and out-buildings, was infinitesimal compared with them. It was scarcely as commodious for people as the little boxes under the barn eaves were for doves.

A pretty girl's face, pink and delicate as a flower, was looking out of one of the house windows. She was watching three men who were digging over in the field which bounded the yard near the road line. She turned quietly when the woman entered.

"What are they digging for, mother?" said she. "Did he tell you?"

"They're diggin' for—a cellar for a new barn."

"Oh, mother, he ain't going to build another barn?"   25

"That's what he says."

A boy stood before the kitchen glass combing his hair. He combed slowly and painstakingly, arranging his brown hair in a smooth hillock over his forehead. He did not seem to pay any attention to the conversation.

"Sammy, did you know father was going to build a new barn?" asked the girl.

The boy combed assiduously.

"Sammy!"

He turned, and showed a face like his father's under his smooth crest of hair. "Yes, I s'pose I did," he said, reluctantly.

"How long have you known it?" asked his mother.

"'Bout three months, I guess."

"Why didn't you tell of it?"

"Didn't think 'twould do no good."

"I don't see what father wants another barn for," said the girl, in her sweet, slow voice. She turned again to the window, and stared out at the digging men in the field. Her tender, sweet face was full of a gentle distress. Her forehead was as bald and innocent as a baby's, with the light hair strained back from it in a row of curl-papers. She was quite large, but her soft curves did not look as if they covered muscles.

Her mother looked sternly at the boy. "Is he goin' to buy more cows?" said she.

The boy did not reply; he was tying his shoes.

"Sammy, I want you to tell me if he's goin' to buy more cows."

"I s'pose he is."

"How many?"

"Four, I guess."

His mother said nothing more. She went into the pantry, and there was a clatter of dishes. The boy got his cap from a nail behind the door, took an old arithmetic from the shelf, and started for school. He was lightly built, but clumsy. He went out of the yard with a curious spring in his hips, that made his loose home-made jacket tilt up in the rear.

The girl went to the sink, and began to wash the dishes that were piled up there. Her mother came promptly out of the pantry, and shoved her aside. "You wipe 'em," said she; "I'll wash. There's a good many this mornin'."

The mother plunged her hands vigorously into the water, the girl wiped the plates slowly and dreamily. "Mother," said she, "don't you think it's too bad father's going to build that new barn, much as we need a decent house to live in?"

Her mother scrubbed a dish fiercely. "You ain't found out yet we're women-folks, Nanny Penn," said she. "You ain't seen enough of men-folks yet to. One of these days you'll find it out, an' then you'll know that we know only what men-folks think we do, so far as any use of it goes, an' how we'd ought to reckon men-folks in with Providence, an' not complain of what they do any more than we do of the weather."

"I don't care; I don't believe George is anything like that, anyhow," said Nanny. Her delicate face flushed pink, her lips pouted softly, as if she were going to cry.

"You wait an' see. I guess George Eastman ain't no better than other men. You hadn't ought to judge father, though. He can't help it, 'cause he don't look at things jest the way we do. An' we've been pretty comfortable here, after all. The roof don't leak—ain't never but once—that's one thing. Father's kept it shingled right up."

"I do wish we had a parlor."

"I guess it won't hurt George Eastman any to come to see you in a nice clean kitchen. I guess a good many girls don't have as good a place as this. Nobody's ever heard me complain."

"I ain't complained either, mother."

"Well, I don't think you'd better, a good father an' a good home as you've got. S'pose your father made you go out an' work for your livin'? Lots of girls have to that ain't no stronger an' better able to than you be."

Sarah Penn washed the frying pan with a conclusive air. She scrubbed the outside of it as faithfully as the inside. She was a masterly keeper of her box of a house. Her one living room never seemed to have in it any of the dust which the friction of life with inanimate matter produces. She swept, and there seemed to be no dirt to go before the broom; she cleaned, and one could see no difference. She was like an artist so perfect that he has apparently no art. To-day she got out a mixing bowl and a board, and rolled some pies, and there was no more flour upon her than upon her daughter who was doing finer work. Nanny was to be married in the fall, and she was sewing on some white cambric and embroidery. She sewed industriously while her mother cooked, her soft milk-white hands and wrists showed whiter than her delicate work.

"We must have the stove moved out in the shed before long," said Mrs. Penn. "Talk about not havin' things, it's been a real blessin' to be able to put a stove up in that shed in hot weather. Father did one good thing when he fixed that stovepipe out there."

Sarah Penn's face as she rolled her pies had that expression of meek vigor   55
which might have characterized one of the New Testament saints. She was making mince-pies. Her husband, Adoniram Penn, liked them better than any other kind. She baked twice a week. Adoniram often liked a piece of pie between meals. She hurried this morning. It had been later than usual when she began, and she wanted to have a pie baked for dinner. However deep a resentment she might be forced to hold against her husband, she would never fail in sedulous attention to his wants.

Nobility of character manifests itself at loop-holes when it is not provided with large doors. Sarah Penn's showed itself to-day in flaky dishes of pastry. So she made the pies faithfully, while across the table she could see, when she glanced up from her work, the sight that rankled in her patient and steadfast soul—the digging of the cellar of the new barn in the place where Adoniram forty years ago had promised her their new house should stand.

The pies were done for dinner. Adoniram and Sammy were home a few minutes after twelve o'clock. The dinner was eaten with serious haste. There was never much conversation at the table in the Penn family. Adoniram asked a blessing, and they ate promptly, then rose up and went about their work.

Sammy went back to school, taking soft sly lopes out of the yard like a rabbit. He wanted a game of marbles before school, and feared his father would give him some chores to do. Adoniram hastened to the door and called after him, but he was out of sight.

"I don't see what you let him go for, mother," said he. "I wanted him to help me unload that wood."

Adoniram went to work out in the yard unloading wood from the wagon. Sarah   60
put away the dinner dishes, while Nanny took down her curl-papers and changed her dress. She was going down to the store to buy some more embroidery and thread.

When Nanny was gone, Mrs. Penn went to the door. "Father!" she called.

"Well, what is it!"

"I want to see you jest a minute, father."

"I can't leave this wood nohow. I've got to git it unloaded an' go for a load of gravel afore two o'clock. Sammy had ought to helped me. You hadn't ought to let him go to school so early."

"I want to see you jest a minute."   65

"I tell ye I can't, nohow, mother."

"Father, you come here." Sarah Penn stood in the door like a queen; she held her head as if it bore a crown; there was that patience which makes authority royal in her voice. Adoniram went.

Mrs. Penn led the way into the kitchen, and pointed to a chair. "Sit down, father," said she: "I've got somethin' I want to say to you."

He sat down heavily; his face was quite stolid, but he looked at her with restive eyes. "Well, what is it, mother?"

"I want to know what you're buildin' that new barn for, father?"   70

"I ain't got nothin' to say about it."

"It can't be you think you need another barn?"

"I tell ye I ain't got nothin' to say about it, mother; an' I ain't goin' to say nothin'."

"Be you goin' to buy more cows?"

Adoniram did not reply; he shut his mouth tight.   75

"I know you be, as well as I want to. Now, father, look here"—Sarah Penn had not sat down; she stood before her husband in the humble fashion of a Scripture woman—"I'm goin' to talk real plain to you; I never have sence I married you, but I'm goin' to now. I ain't never complained, an' I ain't goin' to complain now, but I'm goin' to talk plain. You see this room here, father; you look at it well. You see there ain't no carpet on the floor, an' you see the paper is all dirty, an' droppin' off the walls. We ain't had no new paper on it for ten year, an' then I put it on myself, an' it didn't cost but ninepence a roll. You see this room, father; it's all the one I've had to work in an' eat in an' sit in sence we was married. There ain't another woman in the whole town whose husband ain't got half the means you have but what's got better. It's all the room Nanny's got to have her company in; an' there ain't one of her mates but what's got better, an' their fathers not so able as hers is. It's all the room she'll have to be married in. What would you have thought, father, if we had had our weddin' in a room no better than this? I was married in my mother's parlor, with a carpet on the floor, an' stuffed furniture, an' a mahogany card-table. An' this is all the room my daughter will have to be married in. Look here, father!"

Sarah Penn went across the room as though it were a tragic stage. She flung open a door and disclosed a tiny bedroom, only large enough for a bed and bureau, with a path between. "There, father," said she—"there's all the room I've had to sleep in forty year. All my children were born there—the two that died, an' the two that's livin'. I was sick with a fever there."

She stepped to another door and opened it. It led into the small, ill-lighted pantry. "Here," said she, "is all the buttery I've got—every place I've got for my dishes, to set away my victuals in, an' to keep my milk-pans in. Father, I've been takin' care of the milk of six cows in this place, an' now you're goin' to build a new barn, an' keep more cows, an' give me more to do in it."

She threw open another door. A narrow crooked flight of stairs wound upward from it. "There, father," said she, "I want you to look at the stairs that go up to them two unfinished chambers that are all the places our son an' daughter have had to sleep in all their lives. There ain't a prettier girl in town nor a more ladylike one than Nanny, an' that's the place she has to sleep in. It ain't so good as your horse's stall; it ain't so warm an' tight."

Sarah Penn went back and stood before her husband. "Now, father," said she,   80
"I want to know if you think you're doin' right an' accordin' to what you profess. Here, when we was married, forty year ago, you promised me faithful that we

should have a new house built in that lot over in the field before the year was out. You said you had money enough, an' you wouldn't ask me to live in no such place as this. It is forty year now, an' you've been makin' more money, an' I've been savin' of it for you ever since, an' you ain't built no house yet. You've built sheds an' cowhouses an' one new barn, an' now you're goin' to build another. Father, I want to know if you think it's right. You're lodgin' your dumb beasts better than you are your own flesh an' blood. I want to know if you think it's right."

"I ain't got nothin' to say."

"You can't say nothin' without ownin' it ain't right, father. An' there's another thing—I ain't complained; I've got along forty year, an' I s'pose I should forty more, if it wa'n't for that—if we don't have another house. Nanny she can't live with us after she's married. She'll have to go somewheres else to live away from us, an' it don't seem as if I could have it so, noways, father. She wa'n't ever strong. She's got considerable color, but there wa'n't ever any backbone to her. I've always took the heft of everything off her, an' she ain't fit to keep house an' do everything herself. She'll be all worn out inside of a year. Think of her doin' all the washin' an' ironin' an' bakin' with them soft white hands an' arms, an' sweepin'! I can't have it so, noways, father."

Mrs. Penn's face was burning; her mild eyes gleamed. She had pleaded her little cause like a Webster; she had ranged from severity to pathos; but her opponent employed that obstinate silence which makes eloquence futile with mocking echoes. Adoniram arose clumsily.

"Father, ain't you got nothin' to say?" said Mrs. Penn.

"I've got to go off after that load of gravel. I can't stan' here talkin' all day."   85

"Father, won't you think it over, an' have a house built there instead of a barn?"

"I ain't got nothin' to say."

Adoniram shuffled out. Mrs. Penn went into her bedroom. When she came out, her eyes were red. She had a roll of unbleached cotton cloth. She spread it out on the kitchen table, and began cutting out some shirts for her husband. The men over in the field had a team to help them this afternoon; she could hear their halloos. She had a scanty pattern for the shirts; she had to plan and piece the sleeves.

Nanny came home with her embroidery, and sat down with her needlework. She had taken down her curl-papers, and there was a soft roll of fair hair like an auerole over her forehead; her face was as delicately fine and clear as porcelain. Suddenly she looked up, and the tender red flamed all over her face and neck. "Mother," said she.

"What say?"   90

"I've been thinking—I don't see how we're goin' to have any—wedding in this room. I'd be ashamed to have his folks come if we didn't have anybody else."

"Mebbe we can have some new paper before then; I can put it on. I guess you won't have no call to be ashamed of your belongin's."

"We might have the wedding in the new barn," said Nanny, with gentle pettishness. "Why, mother, what makes you look so?"

Mrs. Penn had started, and was staring at her with a curious expression. She turned again to her work, and spread out a pattern carefully on the cloth. "Nothin'," said she.

Presently Adoniram clattered out of the yard in his two-wheeled dump cart,   95
standing as proudly upright as a Roman charioteer. Mrs. Penn opened the door and stood there a minute looking out; the halloos of the men sounded louder.

It seemed to her all through the spring months that she heard nothing but the halloos and the noises of saws and hammers. The new barn grew fast. It was a fine edifice for this little village. Men came on pleasant Sundays, in their meeting suits and clean shirt bosoms, and stood around it admiringly. Mrs. Penn did not speak of it, and Adoniram did not mention it to her, although sometimes, upon a return from inspecting it, he bore himself with injured dignity.

"It's a strange thing how your mother feels about the new barn," he said, confidentially, to Sammy one day.

Sammy only grunted after an odd fashion for a boy; he had learned it from his father.

The barn was all completed ready for use by the third week in July. Adoniram had planned to move his stock in on Wednesday; on Tuesday he received a letter which changed his plans. He came in with it early in the morning. "Sammy's been to the post-office," said he, "an' I've got a letter from Hiram." Hiram was Mrs. Penn's brother, who lived in Vermont.

"Well," said Mrs. Penn, "what does he say about the folks?"

"I guess they're all right. He says he thinks if I come up country right off there's a chance to buy jest the kind of a horse I want." He stared reflectively out of the window at the new barn.

Mrs. Penn was making pies. She went on clapping the rolling-pin into the crust, although she was very pale, and her heart beat loudly.

"I dun' know but what I'd better go," said Adoniram. "I hate to go off just now, right in the midst of hayin', but the ten-acre lot's cut, an' I guess Rufus an' the others can git along without me three or four days. I can't get a horse round here to suit me, nohow, an' I've got to have another for all that wood-haulin' in the fall. I told Hiram to watch out, an' if he got wind of a good horse to let me know. I guess I'd better go."

"I'll get out your clean shirt an' collar," said Mrs. Penn calmly.

She laid out Adoniram's Sunday suit and his clean clothes on the bed in the little bedroom. She got his shaving-water and razor ready. At last she buttoned on his collar and fastened his black cravat.

Adoniram never wore his collar and cravat except on extra occasions. He held his head high, with a rasped dignity. When he was all ready, with his coat and hat brushed, and a lunch of pie and cheese in a paper bag, he hesitated on the threshold of the door. He looked at his wife, and his manner was defiantly apologetic. "*If* them cows come to-day, Sammy can drive 'em into the new barn," said he; "an' when they bring the hay up, they can pitch it in there."

"Well," replied Mrs. Penn.

Adoniram set his shaven face ahead and started. When he had cleared the door-step, he turned and looked back with a kind of nervous solemnity. "I shall be back by Saturday if nothin' happens," said he.

"Do be careful, father," returned his wife.

She stood in the door with Nanny at her elbow and watched him out of sight. Her eyes had a strange, doubtful expression in them; her peaceful forehead was contracted. She went in, and about her baking again. Nanny sat sewing. Her wedding-day was drawing nearer, and she was getting pale and thin with her steady sewing. Her mother kept glancing at her.

"Have you got that pain in your side this mornin'?" she asked.

"A little."

Mrs. Penn's face, as she worked, changed, her perplexed forehead smoothed, her eyes were steady, her lips firmly set. She formed a maxim for herself, although incoherently with her unlettered thoughts. "Unsolicited opportunities are the guide-posts of the Lord to the new roads of life," she repeated in effect and she made up her mind to her course of action.

"S'posin' I *had* wrote to Hiram," she muttered once, when she was in the pantry—"s'posin' I had wrote, an' asked him if he knew of any horse? But I didn't, an' father's goin' wa'n't none of my doin'. It looks like a providence." Her voice rang out quite loud at the last.

"What you talkin' about, mother?" called Nanny.   115

"Nothin'."

Mrs. Penn hurried her baking; at eleven o'clock it was all done. The load of hay from the west field came slowly down the cart track, and drew up at the new barn. Mrs. Penn ran out. "Stop!" she screamed—"stop!"

The men stopped and looked; Sammy upreared from the top of the load, and stared at his mother.

"Stop!" she cried out again. "Don't you put the hay in that barn; put it in the old one."

"Why, he said to put it in here," returned one of the hay-makers, wonderingly.   120
He was a young man, a neighbor's son, whom Adoniram hired by the year to help on the farm.

"Don't you put the hay in the new barn; there's room enough in the old one, ain't there?" said Mrs. Penn.

"Room enough," returned the hired man, in his thick, rustic tones. "Didn't need the new barn, nohow, far as room's concerned. Well, I s'pose he changed his mind." He took hold of the horses' bridles.

Mrs. Penn went back to the house. Soon the kitchen windows were darkened, and a fragrance like warm honey came into the room.

Nanny laid down her work. "I thought father wanted them to put the hay into the new barn?" she said, wonderingly.

"It's all right," replied her mother.   125

Sammy slid down from the load of hay, and came in to see if dinner was ready.

"I ain't goin' to get a regular dinner to-day, as long as father's gone," said his mother. "I've let the fire go out. You can have some bread an' milk an' pie. I thought we could get along." She set out some bowls of milk, some bread and a pie on the kitchen table. "You'd better eat your dinner now," said she. "You might jest as well get through with it. I want you to help me afterward."

Nanny and Sammy stared at each other. There was something strange in their mother's manner. Mrs. Penn did not eat anything herself. She went into the pantry, and they heard her moving dishes while they ate. Presently she came out with a pile of plates. She got the clothes-basket out of the shed, and packed them in it. Nanny and Sammy watched. She brought out cups and saucers, and put them in with the plates.

"What you goin' to do, mother?" inquired Nanny, in a timid voice. A sense of something unusual made her tremble, as if it were a ghost. Sammy rolled his eyes over his pie.

"You'll see what I'm goin' to do," replied Mrs. Penn. "If you're through Nanny,   130
I want you to go up-stairs an' pack up your things; an' I want you, Sammy, to help me take down the bed in the bedroom."

"Oh, mother, what for?" gasped Nanny.

"You'll see."

During the next few hours a feat was performed by this simple, pious New England mother which was equal in its way to Wolfe's[1] storming of the Heights of Abraham. It took no more genius and audacity of bravery for Wolfe to cheer his wondering soldiers up those steep precipices, under the sleeping eyes of the enemy, than for Sarah Penn, at the head of her children, to move all their little household goods into the new barn while her husband was away.

Nanny and Sammy followed their mother's instructions without a murmur; indeed, they were overawed. There is a certain uncanny and superhuman quality about all such purely original undertakings as their mother's was to them. Nanny went back and forth with her light loads, and Sammy tugged with sober energy.

At five o'clock in the afternoon the little house in which the Penns had lived 135
for forty years had emptied itself into the new barn.

Every builder builds somewhat for unknown purposes, and is in a measure a prophet. The architect of Adoniram Penn's barn, while he designed it for the comfort of four-footed animals, had planned better than he knew for the comfort of humans. Sarah Penn saw at a glance its possibilities. These great box-stalls, with quilts hung before them, would make better bedrooms than the one she had occupied for forty years, and there was a tight carriage-room. The harness-room, with its chimney and shelves, would make a kitchen of her dreams. The great middle space would make a parlor, by-and-by, fit for a palace. Up-stairs there was as much room as down. With partitions and windows, what a house would there be! Sarah looked at the row of stanchions before the allotted space for cows, and reflected that she would have her front entry there.

At six o'clock the stove was up in the harness-room, the kettle was boiling, and the table set for tea. It looked almost as home-like as the abandoned house across the yard had ever done. The young hired man milked, and Sarah directed him calmly to bring the milk to the new barn. He came gaping, dropping little blots of foam from the brimming pails on the grass. Before the next morning he had spread the story of Adoniram Penn's wife moving into the new barn all over the little village. Men assembled in the store and talked it over, women with shawls over their heads scuttled into each other's houses before their work was done. Any deviation from the ordinary course of life in this quiet town was enough to stop all progress in it. Everybody paused to look at the staid, independent figure on the side track. There was a difference of opinion with regard to her. Some held her to be insane; some, of a lawless and rebellious spirit.

Friday the minister went to see her. It was in the forenoon, and she was at the barn door shelling pease for dinner. She looked up and returned his salutation with dignity, then she went on with her work. She did not invite him in. The saintly expression of her face remained fixed, but there was an angry flush over it.

The minister stood awkwardly before her, and talked. She handled the pease as if they were bullets. At last she looked up, and her eyes showed the spirit that her meek front had covered for a lifetime.

"There ain't no use talkin', Mr. Hersey," said she. "I've thought it all over an' 140
over, an' I believe I'm doin' what's right. I've made it the subject of prayer, an' it's betwixt me an' the Lord an' Adoniram. There ain't no call for nobody else to worry about it."

---

[1]Wolfe-James (1727–1759): English general who led an army up steep cliffs in the Battle of Quebec.

"Well, of course, if you have brought it to the Lord in prayer, and feel satisfied that you are doing right, Mrs. Penn," said the minister, helplessly. His thin gray-bearded face was pathetic. He was a sickly man; his youthful confidence had cooled; he had to scourge himself up to some of his pastoral duties as relentlessly as a Catholic ascetic, and then he was prostrated by the smart.

"I think it's right jest as much as I think it was right for our forefathers to come over from the old country 'cause they didn't have what belonged to 'em," said Mrs. Penn. She arose. The barn threshold might have been Plymouth Rock from her bearing. "I don't doubt you mean well, Mr. Hersey," said she, "but there are things people hadn't ought to interfere with. I've been a member of the church for over forty year. I've got my own mind an' my own feet, an' I'm goin' to think my own thoughts an' go my own ways, an' nobody but the Lord is goin' to dictate to me unless I've a mind to have him. Won't you come in an' set down? How is Mis' Hersey?"

"She is well, I thank you," replied the minister. He added some more perplexed apologetic remarks; then he retreated.

He could expound the intricacies of every character study in the Scriptures, he was competent to grasp the Pilgrim Fathers and all historical innovators, but Sarah Penn was beyond him. He could deal with primal cases, but parallel ones worsted him. But, after all, although it was aside from his province, he wondered more how Adoniram Penn would deal with his wife than how the Lord would. Everybody shared the wonder. When Adoniram's four new cows arrived, Sarah ordered three to be put in the old barn, the other in the house shed where the cooking-stove had stood. That added to the excitement. It was whispered that all four cows were domiciled in the house.

Towards sunset on Saturday, when Adoniram was expected home, there was a knot of men in the road near the new barn. The hired man had milked, but he still hung around the premises. Sarah Penn had supper all ready. There were brown bread and baked beans and a custard pie; it was the supper Adoniram loved on a Saturday night. She had a clean calico, and she bore herself imperturbably. Nanny and Sammy kept close at her heels. Their eyes were large, and Nanny was full of nervous tremors. Still there was to them more pleasant excitement than anything else. An inborn confidence in their mother over their father asserted itself.

Sammy looked out of the harness-room window. "There he is," he announced, in an awed whisper. He and Nanny peeped around the casing. Mrs. Penn kept on about her work. The children watched Adoniram leave the new horse standing in the drive while he went to the house door. It was fastened. Then he went around to the shed. That door was seldom locked, even when the family was away. The thought how her father would be confronted by the cow flashed upon Nanny. There was a hysterical sob in her throat. Adoniram emerged from the shed and stood looking about in a dazed fashion. His lips moved; he was saying something, but they could not hear what it was. The hired man was peeping around a corner of the old barn, but nobody saw him.

Adoniram took the new horse by the bridle and led him across the yard to the new barn. Nanny and Sammy slunk close to their mother. The barn doors rolled back, and there stood Adoniram, with the long mild face of the great Canadian farm horse looking over his shoulder.

Nanny kept behind her mother, but Sammy stepped suddenly forward, and stood in front of her.

145

Adoniram stared at the group. "What on airth you all down here for?" said he. "What's the matter over to the house?"

"We've come here to live, father," said Sammy. His shrill voice quavered out 150 bravely.

"What"—Adoniram sniffed—"what is it smells like cookin'?" said he. He stepped forward and looked in the open door of the harness-room. Then he turned to his wife. His old bristling face was pale and frightened. "What on airth does this mean, mother?" he gasped.

"You come in here, father," said Sarah. She led the way into the harness-room and shut the door. "Now, father," said she, "you needn't be scared. I ain't crazy. There ain't nothin' to be upset over. But we've come here to live, an' we're goin' to live here. We've got jest as good a right here as new horses an' cows. The house wa'n't fit for us to live in any longer, an' I made up my mind I wa'n't goin' to stay there. I've done my duty by you forty year, an' I'm goin' to do it now; but I'm goin' to live here. You've got to put in some windows and partitions; an' you'll have to buy some furniture."

"Why, mother!" the old man gasped.

"You'd better take your coat off an' get washed—there's the wash-basin—an' then we'll have supper."

"Why, mother!" 155

Sammy went past the window, leading the new horse to the old barn. The old man saw him, and shook his head speechlessly. He tried to take off his coat, but his arms seemed to lack the power. His wife helped him. She poured some water into the tin basin, and put in a piece of soap. She got the comb and brush, and smoothed his thin gray hair after he had washed. Then she put the beans, hot bread, and tea on the table. Sammy came in, and the family drew up. Adoniram sat looking dazedly at his plate, and they waited.

"Ain't you goin' to ask a blessin', father?" said Sarah.

And the old man bent his head and mumbled.

All through the meal he stopped eating at intervals, and stared furtively at his wife; but he ate well. The home food tasted good to him, and his old frame was too sturdily healthy to be affected by his mind. But after supper he went out, and sat down on the step of the smaller door at the right of the barn, through which he had meant his Jerseys to pass in stately file, but which Sarah designed for her front house door, and he leaned his head on his hands.

After the supper dishes were cleared away and the milk-pans washed, Sarah 160 went out to him. The twilight was deepening. There was a clear green glow in the sky. Before them stretched the smooth level of field; in the distance was a cluster of hay-stacks like the huts of a village; the air was very cool and calm and sweet. The landscape might have been an ideal one of peace.

Sarah bent over and touched her husband on one of his thin, sinewy shoulders. "Father!"

The old man's shoulders heaved: he was weeping.

"Why, don't do so, father," said Sarah.

"I'll—put up the—partitions, an'—everything you—want, mother."

Sarah put her apron up to her face; she was overcome by her own triumph. 165

Adoniram was like a fortress whose walls had no active resistance, and went down the instant the right besieging tools were used. "Why, mother," he said, hoarsely, "I hadn't no idee you was so set on't as all this comes to."

Nathaniel Hawthorne   1804–1864

Young Goodman Brown   *1835*

Young Goodman Brown came forth at sunset into the street at Salem village; but put his head back, after crossing the threshold, to exchange a parting kiss with his young wife. And Faith, as the wife was aptly named, thrust her own pretty head into the street, letting the wind play with the pink ribbons of her cap while she called to Goodman Brown.

"Dearest heart," whispered she, softly and rather sadly, when her lips were close to his ear, "prithee put off your journey until sunrise and sleep in your own bed to-night. A lone woman is troubled with such dreams and such thoughts that she's afeared of herself sometimes. Pray tarry with me this night, dear husband, of all nights in the year."

"My love and my Faith," replied young Goodman Brown, "of all nights in the year, this one night must I tarry away from thee. My journey, as thou callest it, forth and back again, must needs be done 'twixt now and sunrise. What, my sweet, pretty wife, dost thou doubt me already, and we but three months married?"

"Then God bless you!" said Faith, with the pink ribbons; "and may you find all well when you come back."

"Amen!" cried Goodman Brown. "Say thy prayers, dear Faith, and go to bed at dusk, and no harm will come to thee."   5

So they parted; and the young man pursued his way until, being about to turn the corner by the meeting-house, he looked back and saw the head of Faith still peeping after him with a melancholy air, in spite of her pink ribbons.

"Poor little Faith!" thought he, for his heart smote him. "What a wretch am I to leave her on such an errand! She talks of dreams, too. Methought as she spoke there was trouble in her face, as if a dream had warned her what work is to be done tonight. But no, no; 't would kill her to think it. Well, she's a blessed angel on earth; and after this one night I'll cling to her skirts and follow her to heaven."

With this excellent resolve for the future, Goodman Brown felt himself justified in making more haste on his present evil purpose. He had taken a dreary road, darkened by all the gloomiest trees of the forest, which barely stood aside to let the narrow path creep through, and closed immediately behind. It was all as lonely as could be; and there is this peculiarity in such a solitude, that the traveller knows not who may be concealed by the innumerable trunks and the thick boughs overhead; so that with lonely footsteps he may yet be passing through an unseen multitude.

"There may be a devilish Indian behind every tree," said Goodman Brown to himself; and he glanced fearfully behind him as he added, "What if the devil himself should be at my very elbow!"

His head being turned back, he passed a crook of the road, and, looking forward again, beheld the figure of a man, in grave and decent attire, seated at the foot of an old tree. He arose at Goodman Brown's approach and walked onward side by side with him.   10

"You are late, Goodman Brown," said he. "The clock of the Old South was striking as I came through Boston, and that is full fifteen minutes agone."

"Faith kept me back awhile," replied the young man, with a tremor in his voice, caused by the sudden appearance of his companion, though not wholly unexpected.

It was now deep dusk in the forest, and deepest in that part of it where these two were journeying. As nearly as could be discerned, the second traveller was about fifty years old, apparently in the same rank of life as Goodman Brown, and bearing a considerable resemblance to him, though perhaps more in expression than features. Still they might have been taken for father and son. And yet, though the elder person was as simply clad as the younger, and as simple in manner too, he had an indescribable air of one who knew the world, and who would not have felt abashed at the governor's dinner table or in King William's court, were it possible that his affairs should call him thither. But the only thing about him that could be fixed upon as remarkable was his staff, which bore the likeness of a great black snake, so curiously wrought that it might almost be seen to twist and wriggle itself like a living serpent. This, of course, must have been an ocular deception, assisted by the uncertain light.

"Come, Goodman Brown," cried his fellow-traveller, "this is a dull pace for the beginning of a journey. Take my staff, if you are so soon weary."

"Friend," said the other, exchanging his slow pace for a full stop, "having kept   15 covenant by meeting thee here, it is my purpose now to return whence I came. I have scruples touching the matter thou wot'st of."

"Sayest thou so?" replied he of the serpent, smiling apart. "Let us walk on, nevertheless, reasoning as we go; and if I convince thee not thou shalt turn back. We are but a little way in the forest yet."

"Too far! too far!" exclaimed the goodman, unconsciously resuming his walk. "My father never went into the woods on such an errand, nor his father before him. We have been a race of honest men and good Christians since the days of the martyrs; and shall I be the first of the name of Brown that ever took this path and kept"—

"Such company, thou wouldst say," observed the elder person, interpreting his pause. "Well said, Goodman Brown! I have been as well acquainted with your family as with ever a one among the Puritans; and that's no trifle to say. I helped your grandfather, the constable, when he lashed the Quaker woman so smartly through the streets of Salem; and it was I that brought your father a pitch-pine knot, kindled at my own hearth, to set fire to an Indian village, in King Philip's war. They were my good friends, both; and many a pleasant walk have we had along this path, and returned merrily after midnight. I would fain be friends with you for their sake."

"If it be as thou sayest," replied Goodman Brown, "I marvel they never spoke of these matters; or, verily, I marvel not, seeing that the least rumor of the sort would have driven them from New England. We are a people of prayer, and good works to boot, and abide no such wickedness."

"Wickedness or not," said the traveller with the twisted staff, "I have a very   20 general acquaintance here in New England. The deacons of many a church have drunk the communion wine with me; the selectmen of divers towns make me their chairman; and a majority of the Great and General Court are firm supporters of my interest. The governor and I, too— But these are state secrets."

"Can this be so?" cried Goodman Brown, with a stare of amazement at his undisturbed companion. "Howbeit, I have nothing to do with the governor and council; they have their own ways, and are no rule for a simple husbandman like me. But, were I to go on with thee, how should I meet the eye of that good old man, our minister, at Salem village? Oh, his voice would make me tremble both Sabbath day and lecture day."

Thus far the elder traveller had listened with due gravity; but now burst into a fit of irrepressible mirth, shaking himself so violently that his snake-like staff actually seemed to wriggle in sympathy.

"Ha! ha! ha!" shouted he again and again; then composing himself, "Well, go on, Goodman Brown, go on; but, prithee, don't kill me with laughing."

"Well, then, to end the matter at once," said Goodman Brown, considerably nettled, "there is my wife, Faith. It would break her dear little heart; and I'd rather break my own."

"Nay, if that be the case," answered the other, "e'en go thy ways, Goodman Brown. I would not for twenty old women like the one hobbling before us that Faith should come to any harm."   25

As he spoke he pointed his staff at a female figure on the path, in whom Goodman Brown recognized a very pious and exemplary dame, who had taught him his catechism in youth, and was still his moral and spiritual adviser, jointly with the minister and Deacon Gookin.

"A marvel, truly that Goody Cloyse should be so far in the wilderness at nightfall," said he. "But with your leave, friend, I shall take a cut through the woods until we have left this Christian woman behind. Being a stranger to you, she might ask whom I was consorting with and whither I was going."

"Be it so," said his fellow-traveller. "Betake you to the woods, and let me keep the path."

Accordingly the young man turned aside, but took care to watch his companion, who advanced softly along the road until he had come within a staff's length of the old dame. She, meanwhile, was making the best of her way, with singular speed for so aged a woman, and mumbling some indistinct words—a prayer, doubtless—as she went. The traveller put forth his staff and touched her withered neck with what seemed the serpent's tail.

"The devil!" screamed the pious old lady.   30

"Then Goody Cloyse knows her old friend?" observed the traveller, confronting her and leaning on his writhing stick.

"Ah, forsooth, and is it your worship indeed?" cried the good dame. "Yea, truly is it, and in the very image of my old gossip, Goodman Brown, the grandfather of the silly fellow that now is. But—would your worship believe it? —my broomstick hath strangely disappeared, stolen, as I suspect, by that unhanged witch, Goody Cory, and that, too, when I was all anointed with the juice of smallage, and cinquefoil, and wolf's bane"—

"Mingled with fine wheat and the fat of a new-born babe," said the shape of old Goodman Brown.

"Ah, your worship knows the recipe," cried the old lady, cackling aloud. "So, as I was saying, being all ready for the meeting, and no horse to ride on, I made up my mind to foot it; for they tell me there is a nice young man to be taken into communion to-night. But now your good worship will lend me your arm, and we shall be there in a twinkling."

"That can hardly be," answered her friend. "I may not spare you my arm,   35
Goody Cloyse; but here is my staff, if you will."

So saying, he threw it down at her feet, where, perhaps, it assumed life, being one of the rods which its owner had formerly lent to the Egyptian magi. Of this fact, however, Goodman Brown could not take cognizance. He had cast up his eyes in astonishment, and, looking down again, beheld neither Goody Cloyse nor the serpentine staff, but his fellow-traveller alone, who waited for him as calmly as if nothing had happened.

"That old woman taught me my catechism," said the young man; and there was a world of meaning in this simple comment.

They continued to walk onward, while the elder traveller exhorted his companion to make good speed and persevere in the path, discoursing so aptly that his arguments seemed rather to spring up in the bosom of his auditor than to be suggested by himself. As they went, he plucked a branch of maple to serve for a walking stick, and began to strip it of the twigs and little boughs, which were wet with evening dew. The moment his fingers touched them they became strangely withered and dried up as with a week's sunshine. Thus the pair proceeded, at a good free pace, until suddenly, in a gloomy hollow of the road, Goodman Brown sat himself down on the stump of a tree and refused to go any farther.

"Friend," he said, stubbornly, "my mind is made up. Not another step will I budge on this errand. What if a wretched old woman do choose to go to the devil when I thought she was going to heaven: is that any reason why I should quit my dear Faith and go after her?"

"You will think better of this by and by," said his acquaintance, composedly. 40 "Sit here and rest yourself a while; and when you feel like moving again, there is my staff to help you along."

Without more words, he threw his companion the maple stick, and was as speedily out of sight as if he had vanished into the deepening gloom. The young man sat a few moments by the roadside, applauding himself greatly, and thinking with how clear a conscience he should meet the minister in his morning walk, nor shrink from the eye of good old Deacon Gookin. And what calm sleep would be his that very night, which was to have been spent so wickedly, but so purely and sweetly now, in the arms of Faith! Amidst these pleasant and praiseworthy meditations, Goodman Brown heard the tramp of horses along the road, and deemed it advisable to conceal himself within the verge of the forest, conscious of the guilty purpose that had brought him thither, though now so happily turned from it.

On came the hoof tramps and the voices of the riders, two grave old voices, conversing soberly as they drew near. These mingled sounds appeared to pass along the road, within a few yards of the young man's hiding-place; but, owing doubtless to the depth of the gloom at that particular spot, neither the travellers nor their steeds were visible. Though their figures brushed the small boughs by the wayside, it could not be seen that they intercepted, even for a moment, the faint gleam from the strip of bright sky athwart which they must have passed. Goodman Brown alternately crouched and stood on tiptoe, pulling aside the branches and thrusting forth his head as far as he durst without discerning so much as a shadow. It vexed him the more, because he could have sworn, were such a thing possible, that he recognized the voices of the minister and Deacon Gookin, jogging along quietly, as they were wont to do, when bound to some ordination or ecclesiastical council. While yet within hearing, one of the riders stopped to pluck a switch.

"Of the two, reverend sir," said the voice like the deacon's, "I had rather miss an ordination dinner than to-night's meeting. They tell me that some of our community are to be here from Falmouth and beyond, and others from Connecticut and Rhode Island, besides several of the Indian powwows, who, after their fashion, know almost as much deviltry as the best of us. Moreover, there is a goodly young woman to be taken into communion."

"Mighty well, Deacon Gookin!" replied the solemn old tones of the minister. "Spur up, or we shall be late. Nothing can be done, you know, until I get on the ground."

The hoofs clattered again; and the voices, talking so strangely in the empty air,   45
passed on through the forest, where no church had ever been gathered or solitary
Christian prayed. Whither, then, could these holy men be journeying so deep into
the heathen wilderness? Young Goodman Brown caught hold of a tree for support,
being ready to sink down on the ground, faint and overburdened with the heavy
sickness of his heart. He looked up to the sky, doubting whether there really was
a heaven above him. Yet there was the blue arch, and the stars brightening in it.

"With heaven above and Faith below, I will yet stand firm against the devil!"
cried Goodman Brown.

While he still gazed upward into the deep arch of the firmament and had
lifted his hands to pray, a cloud, though no wind was stirring, hurried across the
zenith and hid the brightening stars. The blue sky was still visible, except directly
overhead, where this black mass of cloud was sweeping swiftly northward. Aloft
in the air, as if from the depths of the cloud, came a confused and doubtful sound
of voices. Once the listener fancied that he could distinguish the accents of towns-
people of his own, men and women, both pious and ungodly, many of whom he
had met at the communion table, and had seen others rioting at the tavern. The
next moment, so indistinct were the sounds, he doubted whether he had heard
aught but the murmur of the old forest, whispering without a wind. Then came a
stronger swell of those familiar tones, heard daily in the sunshine at Salem village,
but never until now from a cloud of night. There was one voice, of a young
woman, uttering lamentations, yet with an uncertain sorrow, and entreating for
some favor, which, perhaps, it would grieve her to obtain; and all the unseen multitude, both saints and sinners, seemed to encourage her onward.

"Faith!" shouted Goodman Brown, in a voice of agony and desperation; and
the echoes of the forest mocked him, crying, "Faith! Faith!" as if bewildered
wretches were seeking her all through the wilderness.

The cry of grief, rage, and terror was yet piercing the night, when the unhappy husband held his breath for a response. There was a scream, drowned immediately in a louder murmur of voices, fading into far-off laughter, as the dark
cloud swept away, leaving the clear and silent sky above Goodman Brown. But
something fluttered lightly down through the air and caught on the branch of a
tree. The young man seized it, and beheld a pink ribbon.

"My Faith is gone!" cried he after one stupefied moment. "There is no good on   50
earth; and sin is but a name. Come, devil; for to thee is this world given."

And, maddened with despair, so that he laughed loud and long, did Goodman
Brown grasp his staff and set forth again, at such a rate that he seemed to fly along
the forest path rather than to walk or run. The road grew wilder and drearier and
more faintly traced, and vanished at length, leaving him in the heart of the dark
wilderness, still rushing onward with the instinct that guides mortal man to evil.
The whole forest was peopled with frightful sounds—the creaking of the trees, the
howling of wild beasts, and the yell of Indians; while sometimes the wind tolled
like a distant church bell, and sometimes gave a broad roar around the traveller, as
if all Nature were laughing him to scorn. But he was himself the chief horror of the
scene, and shrank not from its other horrors.

"Ha! ha! ha!" roared Goodman Brown when the wind laughed at him. "Let us
hear which will laugh loudest. Think not to frighten me with your deviltry. Come
witch, come wizard, come Indian powwow, come devil himself, and here comes
Goodman Brown. You may as well fear him as he fear you."

In truth, all through the haunted forest there could be nothing more frightful than the figure of Goodman Brown. On he flew among the black pines, brandishing his staff with frenzied gestures, now giving vent to an inspiration of horrid blasphemy, and now shouting forth such laughter as set all the echoes of the forest laughing like demons around him. The fiend in his own shape is less hideous than when he rages in the breast of man. Thus sped the demoniac on his course, until, quivering among the trees, he saw a red light before him, as when the felled trunks and branches of a clearing have been set on fire, and throw up their lurid blaze against the sky, at the hour of midnight. He paused, in a lull of the tempest that had driven him onward, and heard the swell of what seemed a hymn, rolling solemnly from a distance with the weight of many voices. He knew the tune; it was a familiar one in the choir of the village meeting-house. The verse died heavily away, and was lengthened by a chorus, not of human voices, but of all the sounds of the benighted wilderness pealing in awful harmony together. Goodman Brown cried out, and his cry was lost to his own ear by its unison with the cry of the desert.

In the interval of silence he stole forward until the light glared full upon his eyes. At one extremity of an open space, hemmed in by the dark wall of the forest, arose a rock, bearing some rude, natural resemblance either to an altar or a pulpit, and surrounded by four blazing pines, their tops aflame, their stems untouched, like candles at an evening meeting. The mass of foliage that had overgrown the summit of the rock was all on fire, blazing high into the night and fitfully illuminating the whole field. Each pendent twig and leafy festoon was in a blaze. As the red light arose and fell, a numerous congregation alternately shone forth, then disappeared in shadow, and again grew, as it were, out of the darkness, peopling the heart of the solitary woods at once.

"A grave and dark-clad company," quoth Goodman Brown.   55

In truth they were such. Among them, quivering to and fro between gloom and splendor, appeared faces that would be seen next day at the council board of the province, and others which, Sabbath after Sabbath, looked devoutly heavenward, and benignantly over the crowded pews, from the holiest pulpits in the land. Some affirm that the lady of the governor was there. At least there were high dames well known to her, and wives of honored husbands, and widows, a great multitude, and ancient maidens, all of excellent repute, and fair young girls, who trembled lest their mothers should espy them. Either the sudden gleams of light flashing over the obscure field bedazzled Goodman Brown, or he recognized a score of the church members of Salem village famous for their especial sanctity. Good old Deacon Gookin had arrived, and waited at the skirts of that venerable saint, his revered pastor. But, irreverently consorting with these grave, reputable, and pious people, these elders of the church, these chaste dames and dewy virgins, there were men of dissolute lives and women of spotted fame, wretches given over to all mean and filthy vice, and suspected even of horrid crimes. It was strange to see that the good shrank not from the wicked, nor were the sinners abashed by the saints. Scattered also among their pale-faced enemies were the Indian priests, or powwows, who had often scared their native forest with more hideous incantations than any known to English witchcraft.

"But where is Faith?" thought Goodman Brown; and, as hope came into his heart, he trembled.

Another verse of the hymn arose, a slow and mournful strain, such as the pious love, but joined to words which expressed all that our nature can conceive

of sin, and darkly hinted at far more. Unfathomable to mere mortals is the lore of
fiends. Verse after verse was sung; and still the chorus of the desert swelled between like the deepest tone of a mighty organ; and with the final peal of that
dreadful anthem there came a sound, as if the roaring wind, the rushing streams,
the howling beasts, and every other voice of the unconcerted wilderness were
mingling and according with the voice of guilty man in homage to the prince of
all. The four blazing pines threw up a loftier flame, and obscurely discovered
shapes and visages of horror on the smoke wreaths above the impious assembly.
At the same moment the fire on the rock shot redly forth and formed a glowing
arch above its base, where now appeared a figure. With reverence be it spoken,
the figure bore no slight similitude, both in garb and manner, to some grave divine
of the New England churches.

"Bring forth the converts!" cried a voice that echoed through the field and
rolled into the forest.

At the word, Goodman Brown stepped forth from the shadow of the trees and 60
approached the congregation, with whom he felt a loathful brotherhood by the
sympathy of all that was wicked in his heart. He could have well-nigh sworn that
the shape of his own dead father beckoned him to advance, looking downward
from a smoke wreath, while a woman, with dim features of despair, threw out her
hand to warn him back. Was it his mother? But he had no power to retreat one
step, nor to resist, even in thought, when the minister and good old Deacon
Gookin seized his arms and led him to the blazing rock. Thither came also the
slender form of a veiled female, led between Goody Cloyse, that pious teacher of
the catechism, and Martha Carrier, who had received the devil's promise to be
queen of hell. A rampant hag was she. And there stood the proselytes beneath the
canopy of fire.

"Welcome, my children," said the dark figure, "to the communion of your
race. Ye have found thus young your nature and your destiny. My children, look
behind you!"

They turned; and flashing forth, as it were, in a sheet of flame, the fiend worshippers were seen; the smile of welcome gleamed darkly on every visage.

"There," resumed the sable form, "are all whom ye have reverenced from
youth. Ye deemed them holier than yourselves and shrank from your own sin, contrasting it with their lives of righteousness and prayerful aspirations heavenward.
Yet here are they all in my worshipping assembly. This night it shall be granted you
to know their secret deeds: how hoary-bearded elders of the church have whispered wanton words to the young maids of their households; how many a woman,
eager for widows' weeds, has given her husband a drink at bedtime and let him
sleep his last sleep in her bosom; how beardless youths have made haste to inherit
their fathers' wealth; and how fair damsels—blush not, sweet ones—have dug little
graves in the garden, and bidden me, the sole guest, to an infant's funeral. By the
sympathy of your human hearts for sin ye shall scent out all the places—whether in
church, bedchamber, street, field, or forest—where crime has been committed, and
shall exult to behold the whole earth one stain of guilt, one mighty blood spot. Far
more than this. It shall be yours to penetrate, in every bosom, the deep mystery of
sin, the fountain of all wicked arts, and which inexhaustibly supplies more evil im-
pulses than human power—than my power at its utmost—can make manifest in
deeds. And now, my children, look upon each other."

They did so; and, by the blaze of the hell-kindled torches, the wretched man
beheld his Faith, and the wife her husband, trembling before that unhallowed altar.

"Lo, there ye stand, my children," said the figure, in a deep and solemn tone, 65
almost sad with its despairing awfulness, as if his once angelic nature could yet
mourn for our miserable race. "Depending upon one another's hearts, ye had still
hoped that virtue were not all a dream. Now are ye undeceived. Evil is the nature
of mankind. Evil must be your only happiness. Welcome again, my children, to the
communion of your race."

"Welcome," repeated the fiend worshippers in one cry of despair and
triumph.

And there they stood, the only pair, as it seemed, who were yet hesitating on
the verge of wickedness in this dark world. A basin was hollowed, naturally, in the
rock. Did it contain water, reddened by the lurid light? or was it blood? or, perchance, a liquid flame? Herein did the shape of evil dip his hand and prepare to
lay the mark of baptism upon their foreheads, that they might be partakers of the
mystery of sin, more conscious of the secret guilt of others, both in deed and
thought, than they could now be of their own. The husband cast one look at his
pale wife, and Faith at him. What polluted wretches would the next glance show
them to each other, shuddering alike at what they disclosed and what they saw!

"Faith! Faith!" cried the husband, "look up to heaven, and resist the wicked one."

Whether Faith obeyed he knew not. Hardly had he spoken when he found
himself amid calm night and solitude, listening to a roar of the wind which died
heavily away through the forest. He staggered against the rock, and felt it chill and
damp; while a hanging twig, that had been all on fire, besprinkled his cheek with
the coldest dew.

The next morning young Goodman Brown came slowly into the street of   70
Salem village, staring around him like a bewildered man. The good old minister
was taking a walk along the graveyard to get an appetite for breakfast and meditate his sermon, and bestowed a blessing, as he passed, on Goodman Brown. He
shrank from the venerable saint as if to avoid an anathema. Old Deacon Gookin
was at domestic worship, and the holy words of his prayer were heard through the
open window. "What God doth the wizard pray to?" quoth Goodman Brown.
Goody Cloyse, that excellent old Christian, stood in the early sunshine at her own
lattice, catechizing a little girl who had brought her a pint of morning's milk.
Goodman Brown snatched away the child as from the grasp of the fiend himself.
Turning the corner by the meeting-house, he spied the head of Faith, with the
pink ribbons, gazing anxiously forth, and bursting into such joy at sight of him that
she skipped along the street and almost kissed her husband before the whole village. But Goodman Brown looked sternly and sadly into her face, and passed on
without a greeting.

Had Goodman Brown fallen asleep in the forest and only dreamed a wild
dream of a witch-meeting?

Be it so if you will; but, alas! it was a dream of evil omen for young Goodman
Brown. A stern, a sad, a darkly meditative, a distrustful, if not a desperate man did
he become from the night of that fearful dream. On the Sabbath day, when the
congregation were singing a holy psalm, he could not listen because an anthem of
sin rushed loudly upon his ear and drowned all the blessed strain. When the minister spoke from the pulpit with power and fervid eloquence, and, with his hand
on the open Bible, of the sacred truths of our religion, and of saint-like lives and
triumphant deaths, and of future bliss or misery unutterable, then did Goodman
Brown turn pale, dreading lest the roof should thunder down upon the gray blasphemer and his hearers. Often, awaking suddenly at midnight, he shrank from the

bosom of Faith; and at morning or eventide, when the family knelt down at prayer, he scowled and muttered to himself, and gazed sternly at his wife, and turned away. And when he had lived long, and was borne to his grave a hoary corpse, followed by Faith, an aged woman, and children and grandchildren, a goodly procession, besides neighbors not a few, they carved no hopeful verse upon his tombstone, for his dying hour was gloom.

James Joyce   1882–1941

Araby   *1914*

North Richmond Street, being blind,[1] was a quiet street except at the hour when the Christian Brothers' School set the boys free. An uninhabited house of two stories stood at the blind end, detached from its neighbors in a square ground. The other houses of the street, conscious of decent lives within them, gazed at one another with brown imperturbable faces.

The former tenant of our house, a priest, had died in the back drawing room. Air, musty from having long been enclosed, hung in all the rooms, and the waste room behind the kitchen was littered with old useless papers. Among these I found a few paper-covered books, the pages of which were curled and damp: *The Abbot,* by Walter Scott, *The Devout Communicant,* and *The Memoirs of Vidocq.* I liked the last best because its leaves were yellow. The wild garden behind the house contained a central apple-tree and a few straggling bushes under one of which I found the late tenant's rusty bicycle pump. He had been a very charitable priest; in his will he had left all his money to institutions and the furniture of his house to his sister.

When the short days of winter came dusk fell before we had well eaten our dinners. When we met in the street the houses had grown somber. The space of sky above us was the color of ever-changing violet and towards it the lamps of the street lifted their feeble lanterns. The cold air stung us and we played till our bodies glowed. Our shouts echoed in the silent street. The career of our play brought us through the dark muddy lanes behind the houses where we ran the gantlet of the rough tribes from the cottages, to the back doors of the dark dripping gardens where odors arose from the ashpits, to the dark odorous stables where a coachman smoothed and combed the horse or shook music from the buckled harness. When we returned to the street light from the kitchen windows had filled the areas. If my uncle was seen turning the corner we hid in the shadow until we had seen him safely housed. Or if Mangan's sister came out on the doorstep to call her brother in to his tea we watched her from our shadow peer up and down the street. We waited to see whether she would remain or go in and, if she remained, we left our shadow and walked up to Mangan's steps resignedly. She was waiting for us, her figure defined by the light from the half-opened door. Her brother always teased her before he obeyed and I stood by the railings looking at her. Her dress swung as she moved her body and the soft rope of her hair tossed from side to side.

Every morning I lay on the floor in the front parlor watching her door. The blind was pulled down within an inch of the sash so that I could not be seen. When she came out on the doorstep my heart leaped. I ran to the hall, seized my books, and followed her. I kept her brown figure always in my eye and, when we

---

[1] blind—dead-end.

came near the point at which our ways diverged, I quickened my pace and passed her. This happened morning after morning. I had never spoken to her, except for a few casual words, and yet her name was like a summons to all my foolish blood.

Her image accompanied me even in places the most hostile to romance. On Saturday evenings when my aunt went marketing I had to go to carry some of the parcels. We walked through the flaring streets, jostled by drunken men and bargaining women, amid the curses of laborers, the shrill litanies of shopboys who stood on guard by the barrels of pigs' cheeks, the nasal chanting of street singers, who sang a *come-all-you* about O'Donovan Rossa,[2] or a ballad about the troubles in our native land. These noises converged in a single sensation of life for me: I imagined that I bore my chalice safely through the throng of foes. Her name sprang to my lips at moments in strange prayers and praises which I myself did not understand. My eyes were often full of tears (I could not tell why) and at times a flood from my heart seemed to pour itself out into my bosom. I thought little of the future. I did not know whether I would ever speak to her or not or, if I spoke to her, how I could tell her of my confused adoration. But my body was like a harp and her words and gestures were like fingers running upon the wires.

One evening I went into the back drawing room in which the priest had died. It was a dark rainy evening and there was no sound in the house. Through one of the broken panes I heard the rain impinge upon the earth, the fine incessant needles of water playing in the sodden beds. Some distant lamp or lighted window gleamed below me. I was thankful that I could see so little. All my senses seemed to desire to veil themselves and, feeling that I was about to slip from them, I pressed the palms of my hands together until they trembled, murmuring: *O love! O love!* many times.

At last she spoke to me. When she addressed the first words to me I was so confused that I did not know what to answer. She asked me was I going to *Araby*. I forget whether I answered yes or no. It would be a splendid bazaar, she said; she would love to go.

—And why can't you? I asked.

While she spoke she turned a silver bracelet round and round her wrist. She could not go, she said, because there would be a retreat that week in her convent. Her brother and two other boys were fighting for their caps and I was alone at the railings. She held one of the spikes, bowing her head towards me. The light from the lamp opposite our door caught the white curve of her neck, lit up her hair that rested there, and, falling, lit up the hand upon the railing. It fell over one side of her dress and caught the white border of a petticoat, just visible as she stood at ease.

—It's well for you, she said.

—If I go, I said, I will bring you something.

What innumerable follies laid waste my waking and sleeping thoughts after that evening! I wished to annihilate the tedious intervening days. I chafed against the work of school. At night in my bedroom and by day in the classroom her image came between me and the page I strove to read. The syllables of the word *Araby* were called to me through the silence in which my soul luxuriated and cast an Eastern enchantment over me. I asked for leave to go to the bazaar on Saturday night. My aunt was surprised and hoped it was not some Freemason affair. I answered few questions in class. I watched my master's face pass from amiability to sternness; he hoped I was not beginning to idle. I could not call my wandering thoughts together. I had hardly any patience with the serious work of life which,

---

[2]O'Donovan Rossa—Irish Nationalist leader.

now that it stood between me and my desire, seemed to me child's play, ugly monotonous child's play.

On Saturday morning I reminded my uncle that I wished to go to the bazaar in the evening. He was fussing at the hallstand, looking for the hat-brush, and answered me curtly:

—Yes, boy, I know.

As he was in the hall I could not go into the front parlor and lie at the window. I left the house in bad humor and walked slowly towards the school. The air was pitilessly raw and already my heart misgave me.

When I came home to dinner my uncle had not yet been home. Still it was early. I sat staring at the clock for some time and, when its ticking began to irritate me, I left the room. I mounted the staircase and gained the upper part of the house. The high cold empty gloomy rooms liberated me and I went from room to room singing. From the front window I saw my companions playing below in the street. Their cries reached me weakened and indistinct and, leaning my forehead against the cool glass, I looked over at the dark house where she lived. I may have stood there for an hour, seeing nothing but the brown-clad figure cast by my imagination, touched discreetly by the lamplight at the curved neck, at the hand upon the railings, and at the border below the dress.

When I came downstairs again I found Mrs. Mercer sitting at the fire. She was an old garrulous woman, a pawnbroker's widow, who collected used stamps for some pious purpose. I had to endure the gossip of the tea-table. The meal was prolonged beyond an hour and still my uncle did not come. Mrs. Mercer stood up to go; she was sorry she couldn't wait any longer, but it was after eight o'clock and she did not like to be out late, as the night air was bad for her. When she had gone I began to walk up and down the room, clenching my fists. My aunt said:

—I'm afraid you may put off your bazaar for this night of Our Lord.

At nine o'clock I heard my uncle's latchkey in the hall door. I heard him talking to himself and heard the hallstand rocking when it had received the weight of his overcoat. I could interpret these signs. When he was midway through his dinner I asked him to give me the money to go to the bazaar. He had forgotten.

—The people are in bed and after their first sleep now, he said.

I did not smile. My aunt said to him energetically:

—Can't you give him the money and let him go? You've kept him late enough as it is.

My uncle said he was very sorry he had forgotten. He said he believed in the old saying: *All work and no play makes Jack a dull boy*. He asked me where I was going and, when I had told him a second time he asked me did I know *The Arab's Farewell to His Steed*. When I left the kitchen he was about to recite the opening lines of the piece to my aunt.

I held a florin tightly in my hand as I strode down Buckingham Street towards the station. The sight of the streets thronged with buyers and glaring with gas recalled to me the purpose of my journey. I took my seat in a third-class carriage of a deserted train. After an intolerable delay the train moved out of the station slowly. It crept onward among ruinous houses and over the twinkling river. At Westland Row Station a crowd of people pressed to the carriage doors; but the porters moved them back saying it was a special train for the bazaar. I remained alone in the bare carriage. In a few minutes the train drew up beside an improvised wooden platform. I passed out on to the road and saw by the lighted dial of a clock that it was ten minutes to ten. In front of me was a large building which displayed the magical name.

I could not find any sixpenny entrance and, fearing that the bazaar would be closed, I passed in quickly through a turnstile, handing a shilling to a weary-looking man. I found myself in a big hall girdled at half its height by a gallery. Nearly all the stalls were closed and the greater part of the hall was in darkness. I recognized a silence like that which pervades a church after a service. I walked into the center of the bazaar timidly. A few people were gathered about the stalls which were still open. Before a curtain, over which the words *Café Chantant*[3] were written in colored lamps, two men were counting money on a salver. I listened to the fall of the coins.

Remembering with difficulty why I had come I went over to one of the stalls and examined porcelain vases and flowered tea-sets. At the door of the stall a young lady was talking and laughing with two young gentlemen. I remarked their English accents and listened vaguely to their conversation.

—O, I never said such a thing!

—O, but you did!

—O, but I didn't!

—Didn't she say that?

—Yes. I heard her.

—O, there's a . . . fib!

Observing me the young lady came over and asked me did I wish to buy anything. The tone of her voice was not encouraging; she seemed to have spoken to me out of a sense of duty. I looked humbly at the great jars that stood like eastern guards at either side of the dark entrance to the stall and murmured:

—No, thank you.

The young lady changed the position of one of the vases and went back to the two young men. They began to talk of the same subject. Once or twice the young lady glanced at me over her shoulder.

I lingered before her stall, though I knew my stay was useless, to make my interest in her wares seem the more real. Then I turned away slowly and walked down the middle of the bazaar. I allowed the two pennies to fall against the sixpence in my pocket. I heard a voice call from one end of the gallery that the light was out. The upper part of the hall was now completely dark.

Gazing into the darkness I saw myself as a creature driven and derided by vanity; and my eyes burned with anguish and anger.

Jamaica Kincaid   b. 1949

Girl   *1984*

Wash the white clothes on Monday and put them on the stone heap; wash the color clothes on Tuesday and put them on the clothesline to dry; don't walk barehead in the hot sun; cook pumpkin fritters in very hot sweet oil; soak your little clothes right after you take them off; when buying cotton to make yourself a nice blouse, be sure that it doesn't have gum on it, because that way it won't hold up well after a wash; soak salt fish overnight before you cook it; is it true that you sing benna[1] in Sunday school?; always eat your food in such a way that it won't

---

[3]*Café Chantant*—coffeehouse with musical entertainment.
[1]benna—calypso music.

turn someone else's stomach; on Sundays try to walk like a lady and not like the slut you are so bent on becoming; don't sing benna in Sunday school; you mustn't speak to wharf-rat boys, not even to give directions; don't eat fruits on the street— flies will follow you; *but I don't sing benna on Sundays at all and never in Sunday school;* this is how to sew on a button; this is how to make a buttonhole for the button you have just sewed on; this is how to hem a dress when you see the hem coming down and so to prevent yourself from looking like the slut I know you are so bent on becoming; this is how you iron your father's khaki shirt so that it doesn't have a crease; this is how you iron your father's khaki pants so that they don't have a crease; this is how you grow okra—far from the house, because okra tree harbors red ants; when you are growing dasheen, make sure it gets plenty of water or else it makes your throat itch when you are eating it; this is how you sweep a corner; this is how you sweep a whole house; this is how you sweep a yard; this is how you smile to someone you don't like too much; this is how you smile to someone you don't like at all; this is how you smile to someone you like completely; this is how you set a table for tea; this is how you set a table for dinner; this is how you set a table for dinner with an important guest; this is how you set a table for lunch; this is how you set a table for breakfast; this is how to behave in the presence of men who don't know you very well, and this way they won't recognize immediately the slut I have warned you against becoming; be sure to wash every day, even if it is with your own spit; don't squat down to play marbles—you are not a boy, you know; don't pick people's flowers—you might catch something; don't throw stones at blackbirds, because it might not be a blackbird at all; this is how to make a bread pudding; this is how to make doukona[2]; this is how to make pepper pot; this is how to make a good medicine for a cold; this is how to make a good medicine to throw away a child before it even becomes a child; this is how to catch a fish; this is how to throw back a fish you don't like, and that way something bad won't fall on you; this is how to bully a man; this is how a man bullies you; this is how to love a man, and if this doesn't work there are other ways, and if they don't work don't feel too bad about giving up; this is how to spit up in the air if you feel like it, and this is how to move quickly so that it doesn't fall on you; this is how to make ends meet; always squeeze bread to make sure it's fresh; *but what if the baker won't let me feel the bread?;* you mean to say that after all you are really going to be the kind of woman who the baker won't let near the bread?

Bobbie Ann Mason   b. 1940

Shiloh   *1982*

Leroy Moffitt's wife, Norma Jean, is working on her pectorals. She lifts three-pound dumbbells to warm up, then progresses to a twenty-pound barbell. Standing with her legs apart, she reminds Leroy of Wonder Woman.

"I'd give anything if I could just get these muscles to where they're real hard," says Norma Jean. "Feel this arm. It's not as hard as the other one."

"That's 'cause you're right-handed," says Leroy, dodging as she swings the barbell in an arc.

---

[2]doukona—a spicy pudding made from plantain.

"Do you think so?"

"Sure."   5

Leroy is a truckdriver. He injured his leg in a highway accident four months ago, and his physical therapy, which involves weights and a pulley, prompted Norma Jean to try building herself up. Now she is attending a body-building class. Leroy has been collecting temporary disability since his tractor-trailer jackknifed in Missouri, badly twisting his left leg in its socket. He has a steel pin in his hip. He will probably not be able to drive his rig again. It sits in the backyard, like a gigantic bird that has flown home to roost. Leroy has been home in Kentucky for three months, and his leg is almost healed, but the accident frightened him and he does not want to drive any more long hauls. He is not sure what to do next. In the meantime, he makes things from craft kits. He started by building a miniature log cabin from notched Popsicle sticks. He varnished it and placed it on the TV set, where it remains. It reminds him of a rustic Nativity scene. Then he tried string art (sailing ships on black velvet), a macramé owl kit, a snap-together B–17 Flying Fortress, and a lamp made out of a model truck, with a light fixture screwed in the top of the cab. At first the kits were diversions, something to kill time, but now he is thinking about building a full-scale log house from a kit. It would be considerably cheaper than building a regular house, and besides, Leroy has grown to appreciate how things are put together. He has begun to realize that in all the years he was on the road he never took time to examine anything. He was always flying past scenery.

"They won't let you build a log cabin in any of the new subdivisions," Norma Jean tells him.

"They will if I tell them it's for you," he says, teasing her. Ever since they were married, he has promised Norma Jean he would build her a new home one day. They have always rented, and the house they live in is small and nondescript. It does not even feel like a home, Leroy realizes now.

Norma Jean works at the Rexall drugstore, and she has acquired an amazing amount of information about cosmetics. When she explains to Leroy the three stages of complexion care, involving creams, toners, and moisturizers, he thinks happily of other petroleum products—axle grease, diesel fuel. This is a connection between him and Norma Jean. Since he has been home, he has felt unusually tender about his wife and guilty over his long absences. But he can't tell what she feels about him. Norma Jean has never complained about his traveling; she has never made hurt remarks, like calling his truck a "widow-maker." He is reasonably certain she has been faithful to him, but he wishes she would celebrate his permanent homecoming more happily. Norma Jean is often startled to find Leroy at home, and he thinks she seems a little disappointed about it. Perhaps he reminds her too much of the early days of their marriage, before he went on the road. They had a child who died as an infant, years ago. They never speak about their memories of Randy, which have almost faded, but now that Leroy is home all the time, they sometimes feel awkward around each other, and Leroy wonders if one of them should mention the child. He has the feeling that they are waking up out of a dream together—that they must create a new marriage, start afresh. They are lucky they are still married. Leroy has read that for most people losing a child destroys the marriage—or else he heard this on *Donahue*. He can't always remember where he learns things anymore.

At Christmas, Leroy bought an electric organ for Norma Jean. She used to play   10 the piano when she was in high school. "It don't leave you," she told him once. "It's like riding a bicycle."

The new instrument had so many keys and buttons that she was bewildered by it at first. She touched the keys tentatively, pushed some buttons, then pecked out "Chopsticks." It came out in an amplified fox-trot rhythm, with marimba sounds.

"It's an orchestra!" she cried.

The organ had a pecan-look finish and eighteen preset chords, with optional flute, violin, trumpet, clarinet, and banjo accompaniments. Norma Jean mastered the organ almost immediately. At first she played Christmas songs. Then she bought *The Sixties Songbook* and learned every tune in it, adding variations to each with the rows of brightly colored buttons.

"I didn't like these old songs back then," she said. "But I have this crazy feeling I missed something."

"You didn't miss a thing," said Leroy.   15

Leroy likes to lie on the couch and smoke a joint and listen to Norma Jean play "Can't Take My Eyes Off You" and "I'll Be Back." He is back again. After fifteen years on the road, he is finally settling down with the woman he loves. She is still pretty. Her skin is flawless. Her frosted curls resemble pencil trimmings.

Now that Leroy has come home to stay, he notices how much the town has changed. Subdivisions are spreading across western Kentucky like an oil slick. The sign at the edge of town says "Pop: 11,500"—only seven hundred more than it said twenty years before. Leroy can't figure out who is living in all the new houses. The farmers who used to gather around the courthouse square on Saturday afternoons to play checkers and spit tobacco juice have gone. It has been years since Leroy has thought about the farmers, and they have disappeared without his noticing.

Leroy meets a kid named Stevie Hamilton in the parking lot at the new shopping center. While they pretend to be strangers meeting over a stalled car, Stevie tosses an ounce of marijuana under the front seat of Leroy's car. Stevie is wearing orange jogging shoes and a T-shirt that says CHATTAHOOCHEE SUPER-RAT. His father is a prominent doctor who lives in one of the expensive subdivisions in a new white-columned brick house that looks like a funeral parlor. In the phone book under his name there is a separate number, with the listing "Teenagers."

"Where do you get this stuff?" asks Leroy. "From your pappy?"

"That's for me to know and you to find out," Stevie says. He is slit-eyed and   20
skinny.

"What else you got?"

"What you interested in?"

"Nothing special. Just wondered."

Leroy used to take speed on the road. Now he has to go slowly. He needs to be mellow. He leans back against the car and says, "I'm aiming to build me a log house, soon as I get time. My wife, though, I don't think she likes the idea."

"Well, let me know when you want me again," Stevie says. He has a cigarette   25
in his cupped palm, as though sheltering it from the wind. He takes a long drag, then stomps it on the asphalt and slouches away.

Stevie's father was two years ahead of Leroy in high school. Leroy is thirty-four. He married Norma Jean when they were both eighteen, and their child Randy was born a few months later, but he died at the age of four months and three days. He would be about Stevie's age now. Norma Jean and Leroy were at the drive-in, watching a double feature (*Dr. Strangelove* and *Lover Come Back*), and the baby was sleeping in the back seat. When the first movie ended, the baby was dead. It was the sudden infant death syndrome. Leroy remembers handing Randy to a nurse at the emergency room, as though he were offering her a large doll as a present. A dead baby feels like a sack of flour. "It just happens sometimes," said the doctor, in what Leroy always recalls as a nonchalant tone. Leroy can hardly remember the child anymore, but he still sees vividly a scene from *Dr. Strangelove* in which the President of the United States was talking in a folksy voice on the hot line to the Soviet premier about the bomber accidentally headed toward Russia. He was in the War Room, and the world map was lit up. Leroy remembers Norma Jean standing catatonically beside him in the hospital and himself thinking: Who is this strange girl? He had forgotten who she was. Now scientists are saying that crib death is caused by a virus. Nobody knows anything, Leroy thinks. The answers are always changing.

When Leroy gets home from the shopping center, Norma Jean's mother, Mabel Beasley, is there. Until this year, Leroy has not realized how much time she spends with Norma Jean. When she visits, she inspects the closets and then the plants, informing Norma Jean when a plant is droopy or yellow. Mabel calls the plants "flowers," although there are never any blooms. She always notices if Norma Jean's laundry is piling up. Mabel is a short, overweight woman whose tight, brown-dyed curls look more like a wig than the actual wig she sometimes wears. Today she has brought Norma Jean an off-white dust ruffle she made for the bed; Mabel works in a custom-upholstery shop.

"This is the tenth one I made this year," Mabel says. "I got started and couldn't stop."

"It's real pretty," says Norma Jean.

"Now we can hide things under the bed," says Leroy, who gets along with his mother-in-law primarily by joking with her. Mabel has never really forgiven him for disgracing her by getting Norma Jean pregnant. When the baby died, she said that fate was mocking her.   30

"What's that thing?" Mabel says to Leroy in a loud voice, pointing to a tangle of yarn on a piece of canvas.

Leroy holds it up for Mabel to see. "It's my needlepoint," he explains. "This is a *Star Trek* pillow cover."

"That's what a woman would do," says Mabel. "Great day in the morning!"

"All the big football players on TV do it," he says.

"Why, Leroy, you're always trying to fool me. I don't believe you for one minute. You don't know what to do with yourself—that's the whole trouble. Sewing!"   35

"I'm aiming to build a log house," says Leroy. "Soon as my plans come."

"Like *heck* you are," says Norma Jean. She takes Leroy's needlepoint and shoves it into a drawer. "You have to find a job first. Nobody can afford to build now anyway."

Mabel straightens her girdle and says, "I still think before you get tied down y'all ought to take a little run to Shiloh."

"One of these days, Mama," Norma Jean says impatiently.

Mabel is talking about Shiloh, Tennessee. For the past few years, she has been urging Leroy and Norma Jean to visit the Civil War battleground there. Mabel went there on her honeymoon—the only real trip she ever took. Her husband died of a perforated ulcer when Norma Jean was ten, but Mabel, who was accepted into the United Daughters of the Confederacy in 1975, is still preoccupied with going back to Shiloh.   40

"I've been to kingdom come and back in that truck out yonder," Leroy says to Mabel, "but we never yet set foot in that battleground. Ain't that something? How did I miss it?"

"It's not even that far," Mabel says.

After Mabel leaves, Norma Jean reads to Leroy from a list she has made. "Things you could do," she announces. "You could get a job as a guard at Union Carbide, where they'd let you set on a stool. You could get on at the lumberyard. You could do a little carpenter work, if you want to build so bad. You could—"

"I can't do something where I'd have to stand up all day."

"You ought to try standing up all day behind a cosmetics counter. It's amazing   45
that I have strong feet, coming from two parents that never had strong feet at all."
At the moment Norma Jean is holding on to the kitchen counter, raising her knees one at a time as she talks. She is wearing two-pound ankle weights.

"Don't worry," says Leroy. "I'll do something."

"You could truck calves to slaughter for somebody. You wouldn't have to drive any big old truck for that."

"I'm going to build you this house," says Leroy. "I want to make you a real home."

"I don't want to live in any log cabin."

"It's not a cabin. It's a house."   50

"I don't care. It looks like a cabin."

"You and me together could lift those logs. It's just like lifting weights."

Norma Jean doesn't answer. Under her breath, she is counting. Now she is marching through the kitchen. She is doing goose steps.

Before his accident, when Leroy came home he used to stay in the house with Norma Jean, watching TV in bed and playing cards. She would cook fried chicken, picnic ham, chocolate pie—all his favorites. Now he is home alone much of the time. In the mornings, Norma Jean disappears, leaving a cooling place in the bed. She eats a cereal called Body Buddies, and she leaves the bowl on the table, with the soggy tan balls floating in a milk puddle. He sees things about Norma Jean that he never realized before. When she chops onions, she stares off into a corner, as if she can't bear to look. She puts on her house slippers almost precisely at nine o'clock every evening and nudges her jogging shoes under the couch. She saves bread heels for the birds. Leroy watches the birds at the feeder. He notices the peculiar way goldfinches fly past the window. They close their wings, then fall, then spread their wings to catch and lift themselves. He wonders if they close their eyes when they fall. Norma Jean closes her eyes when they are in bed. She wants the lights turned out. Even then, he is sure she closes her eyes.

He goes for long drives around town. He tends to drive a car rather carelessly.   55
Power steering and an automatic shift make a car feel so small and inconsequential that his body is hardly involved in the driving process. His injured leg stretches out comfortably. Once or twice he has almost hit something, but even the prospect of an accident seems minor in a car. He cruises the new subdivisions, feeling like a criminal rehearsing for a robbery. Norma Jean is probably right about a log house being inappropriate here in the new subdivisions. All the houses look grand and complicated. They depress him.

One day when Leroy comes home from a drive he finds Norma Jean in tears. She is in the kitchen making a potato and mushroom-soup casserole, with grated-cheese topping. She is crying because her mother caught her smoking.

"I didn't hear her coming. I was standing here puffing away pretty as you please," Norma Jean says, wiping her eyes.

"I knew it would happen sooner or later," says Leroy, putting his arm around her.

"She don't know the meaning of the word 'knock,'" says Norma Jean. "It's a wonder she hadn't caught me years ago."

"Think of it this way," Leroy says. "What if she caught me with a joint?"   60

"You better not let her!" Norma Jean shrieks. "I'm warning you, Leroy Moffitt!"

"I'm just kidding. Here, play me a tune. That'll help you relax."

Norma Jean puts the casserole in the oven and sets the timer. Then she plays a ragtime tune, with horns and banjo, as Leroy lights up a joint and lies on the couch, laughing to himself about Mabel's catching him at it. He thinks of Stevie Hamilton—a doctor's son pushing grass. Everything is funny. The whole town seems crazy and small. He is reminded of Virgil Mathis, a boastful policeman Leroy used to shoot pool with. Virgil recently led a drug bust in a back room at a bowling alley, where he seized ten thousand dollars' worth of marijuana. The newspaper had a picture of him holding up the bags of grass and grinning widely. Right now, Leroy can imagine Virgil breaking down the door and arresting him with a lungful of smoke. Virgil would probably have been alerted to the scene because of all the racket Norma Jean is making. Now she sounds like a hard-rock band. Norma Jean is terrific. When she switches to a Latin-rhythm version of "Sunshine Superman," Leroy hums along. Norma Jean's foot goes up and down, up and down.

"Well, what do you think?" Leroy says, when Norma Jean pauses to search through her music.

"What do I think about what?"   65

His mind has gone blank. Then he says, "I'll sell my rig and build a house." That wasn't what he wanted to say. He wanted to know what she thought—what she *really* thought—about them.

"Don't start in on that again," says Norma Jean. She begins playing "Who'll Be the Next in Line?"

Leroy used to tell hitchhikers his whole life story—about his travels, his hometown, the baby. He would end with a question: "Well, what do you think?" It was just a rhetorical question. In time, he had the feeling that he'd been telling the same story over and over to the same hitchhikers. He quit talking to hitchhikers when he realized how his voice sounded—whining and self-pitying, like some teenage-tragedy song. Now Leroy has the sudden impulse to tell Norma Jean about himself, as if he had just met her. They have known each other so long they have forgotten a lot about each other. They could become reacquainted. But when the oven timer goes off and she runs to the kitchen, he forgets why he wants to do this.

The next day, Mabel drops by. It is Saturday and Norma Jean is cleaning. Leroy is studying the plans of his log house, which have finally come in the mail. He has them spread out on the table—big sheets of stiff blue paper, with diagrams and numbers printed in white. While Norma Jean runs the vacuum, Mabel drinks coffee. She sets her coffee cup on a blueprint.

"I'm just waiting for time to pass," she says to Leroy, drumming her fingers on the table.   70

As soon as Norma Jean switches off the vacuum, Mabel says in a loud voice, "Did you hear about the datsun dog that killed the baby?"

Norma Jean says, "The word is 'dachshund.'"

"They put the dog on trial. It chewed the baby's legs off. The mother was in the next room all the time." She raises her voice. "They thought it was neglect."

Norma Jean is holding her ears. Leroy manages to open the refrigerator and get some Diet Pepsi to offer Mabel. Mabel still has some coffee and she waves away the Pepsi.

"Datsuns are like that," Mabel says. "They're jealous dogs. They'll tear a place   75
to pieces if you don't keep an eye on them."

"You better watch out what you're saying, Mabel," says Leroy.

"Well, facts is facts."

Leroy looks out the window at his rig. It is like a huge piece of furniture gathering dust in the backyard. Pretty soon it will be an antique. He hears the vacuum cleaner. Norma Jean seems to be cleaning the living room rug again.

Later, she says to Leroy. "She just said that about the baby because she caught me smoking. She's trying to pay me back."

"What are you talking about?" Leroy says, nervously shuffling blueprints.   80

"You know good and well," Norma Jean says. She is sitting in a kitchen chair with her feet up and her arms wrapped around her knees. She looks small and helpless. She says, "The very idea, her bringing up a subject like that! Saying it was neglect."

"She didn't mean that," Leroy says.

"She might not have *thought* she meant it. She always says things like that. You don't know how she goes on."

"But she didn't really mean it. She was just talking."

Leroy opens a king-sized bottle of beer and pours it into two glasses, dividing   85
it carefully. He hands a glass to Norma Jean and she takes it from him mechanically. For a long time, they sit by the kitchen window watching the birds at the feeder.

Something is happening. Norma Jean is going to night school. She has graduated from her six-week body-building course and now she is taking an adult-education course in composition at Paducah Community College. She spends her evenings outlining paragraphs.

"First you have a topic sentence," she explains to Leroy. "Then you divide it up. Your secondary topic has to be connected to your primary topic."

To Leroy, this sounds intimidating. "I never was any good in English," he says.

"It makes a lot of sense."

"What are you doing this for, anyhow?"   90

She shrugs. "It's something to do." She stands up and lifts her dumbbells a few times.

"Driving a rig, nobody cared about my English."

"I'm not criticizing your English."

Norma Jean used to say, "If I lose ten minutes' sleep, I just drag all day." Now she stays up late, writing compositions. She got a B on her first paper—a how-to theme on soup-based casseroles. Recently Norma Jean has been cooking unusual foods—tacos, lasagna, Bombay chicken. She doesn't play the organ anymore, though her second paper was called "Why Music Is Important to Me." She sits at the kitchen table, concentrating on her outlines, while Leroy plays with his log house plans, practicing with a set of Lincoln Logs. The thought of getting a truckload of notched, numbered logs scares him, and he wants to be prepared. As he and Norma Jean work together at the kitchen table, Leroy has the hopeful thought that they are sharing something, but he knows he is a fool to think this. Norma Jean is miles away. He knows he is going to lose her. Like Mabel, he is just waiting for time to pass.

One day, Mabel is there before Norma Jean gets home from work, and Leroy ⁣⁣95
finds himself confiding in her. Mabel, he realizes, must know Norma Jean better
than he does.

"I don't know what's got into that girl," Mabel says. "She used to go to bed with
the chickens. Now you say she's up all hours. Plus her a-smoking. I like to died."

"I want to make her this beautiful home," Leroy says, indicating the Lincoln
Logs. "I don't think she even wants it. Maybe she was happier with me gone."

"She don't know what to make of you, coming home like this."

"Is that it?"

Mabel takes the roof off his Lincoln Log cabin. "You couldn't get *me* in a log ⁣⁣100
cabin," she says. "I was raised in one. It's no picnic, let me tell you."

"They're different now," says Leroy.

"I tell you what," Mabel says, smiling oddly at Leroy.

"What?"

"Take her on down to Shiloh. Y'all need to get out together, stir a little. Her
brain's all balled up over them books."

Leroy can see traces of Norma Jean's features in her mother's face. Mabel's ⁣⁣105
worn face has the texture of crinkled cotton, but suddenly she looks pretty. It occurs to Leroy that Mabel has been hinting all along that she wants them to take her
with them to Shiloh.

"Let's all go to Shiloh," he says. "You and me and her. Some Sunday."

Mabel throws up her hands in protest. "Oh, no, not me. Young folks want to
be by theirselves."

When Norma Jean comes in with groceries, Leroy says excitedly, "Your mama
here's been dying to go to Shiloh for forty-five years. It's about time we went,
don't you think?"

"I'm not going to butt in on anybody's second honeymoon," Mabel says.

"Who's going on a honeymoon, for Christ's sake?" Norma Jean says loudly. ⁣⁣110

"I never raised no daughter of mine to talk that-a-way," Mabel says.

"You ain't seen nothing yet," says Norma Jean. She starts putting away boxes
and cans, slamming cabinet doors.

"There's a log cabin at Shiloh," Mabel says. "It was there during the battle.
There's bullet holes in it."

"When are you going to *shut up* about Shiloh, Mama?" asks Norma Jean.

"I always thought Shiloh was the prettiest place, so full of history," Mabel goes ⁣⁣115
on. "I just hoped y'all could see it once before I die, so you could tell me about it."
Later, she whispers to Leroy, "You do what I said. A little change is what she needs."

"Your name means 'the king,'" Norma Jean says to Leroy that evening. He is
trying to get her to go to Shiloh, and she is reading a book about another century.

"Well, I reckon I ought to be right proud."

"I guess so."

"Am I still king around here?"

Norma Jean flexes her biceps and feels them for hardness. "I'm not fooling ⁣⁣120
around with anybody, if that's what you mean," she says.

"Would you tell me if you were?"

"I don't know."

"What does *your* name mean?"

"It was Marilyn Monroe's real name."

"No kidding!" ⁣⁣125

"Norma comes from the Normans. They were invaders," she says. She closes her book and looks hard at Leroy. "I'll go to Shiloh with you if you'll stop staring at me."

On Sunday, Norma Jean packs a picnic and they go to Shiloh. To Leroy's relief, Mabel says she does not want to come with them. Norma Jean drives, and Leroy, sitting beside her, feels like some boring hitchhiker she has picked up. He tries some conversation, but she answers him in monosyllables. At Shiloh, she drives aimlessly through the park, past bluffs and trails and steep ravines. Shiloh is an immense place, and Leroy cannot see it as a battleground. It is not what he expected. He thought it would look like a golf course. Monuments are everywhere, showing through the thick clusters of trees. Norma Jean passes the log cabin Mabel mentioned. It is surrounded by tourists looking for bullet holes.

"That's not the kind of log house I've got in mind," says Leroy apologetically.

"I know *that*."

"This is a pretty place. Your mama was right."   130

"It's O.K.," says Norma Jean. "Well, we've seen it. I hope she's satisfied."

They burst out laughing together.

At the park museum, a movie on Shiloh is shown every half hour, but they decide that they don't want to see it. They buy a souvenir Confederate flag for Mabel, and then they find a picnic spot near the cemetery. Norma Jean has brought a picnic cooler, with pimiento sandwiches, soft drinks, and Yodels. Leroy eats a sandwich and then smokes a joint, hiding it behind the picnic cooler. Norma Jean has quit smoking altogether. She is picking cake crumbs from the cellophane wrapper, like a fussy bird.

Leroy says, "So the boys in gray ended up in Corinth. The Union soldiers zapped 'em finally, April 7, 1862."

They both know that he doesn't know any history. He is just talking about   135
some of the historical plaques they have read. He feels awkward, like a boy on a date with an older girl. They are still just making conversation.

"Corinth is where Mama eloped to," says Norma Jean.

They sit in silence and stare at the cemetery for the Union dead and, beyond, at a tall cluster of trees. Campers are parked nearby, bumper to bumper, and small children in bright clothing are cavorting and squealing. Norma Jean wads up the cake wrapper and squeezes it tightly in her hand. Without looking at Leroy, she says, "I want to leave you."

Leroy takes a bottle of Coke out of the cooler and flips off the cap. He holds the bottle poised near his mouth but cannot remember to take a drink. Finally he says, "No, you don't."

"Yes, I do."

"I won't let you."   140

"You can't stop me."

"Don't do me that way."

Leroy knows Norma Jean will have her own way. "Didn't I promise to be home from now on?" he says.

"In some ways, a woman prefers a man who wanders," says Norma Jean. "That sounds crazy, I know."

"You're not crazy."   145

Leroy remembers to drink from his Coke. Then he says, "Yes, you *are* crazy. You and me could start all over again. Right back at the beginning."

"We *have* started all over again," says Norma Jean. "And this is how it turned out."

"What did I do wrong?"

"Nothing."

"Is this one of those women's lib things?" Leroy asks.   150

"Don't be funny."

The cemetery, a green slope dotted with white markers, looks like a subdivision site. Leroy is trying to comprehend that his marriage is breaking up, but for some reason he is wondering about white slabs in a graveyard.

"Everything was fine till Mama caught me smoking," says Norma Jean, standing up. "That set something off."

"What are you talking about?"

"She won't leave me alone—*you* won't leave me alone." Norma Jean seems to   155
be crying, but she is looking away from him. "I feel eighteen again. I can't face that all over again." She starts walking away. "No, it *wasn't* fine. I don't know what I'm saying. Forget it."

Leroy takes a lungful of smoke and closes his eyes as Norma Jean's words sink in. He tries to focus on the fact that thirty-five hundred soldiers died on the grounds around him. He can only think of that war as a board game with plastic soldiers. Leroy almost smiles, as he compares the Confederates' daring attack on the Union camps and Virgil Mathis's raid on the bowling alley. General Grant, drunk and furious, shoved the Southerners back to Corinth, where Mabel and Jet Beasley were married years later, when Mabel was still thin and good-looking. The next day, Mabel and Jet visited the battleground, and then Norma Jean was born, and then she married Leroy and they had a baby, which they lost, and now Leroy and Norma Jean are here at the same battleground. Leroy knows he is leaving out a lot. He is leaving out the insides of history. History was always just names and dates to him. It occurs to him that building a house out of logs is similarly empty— too simple. And the real inner workings of a marriage, like most of history, have escaped him. Now he sees that building a log house is the dumbest idea he could have had. It was clumsy of him to think Norma Jean would want a log house. It was a crazy idea. He'll have to think of something else, quickly. He will wad the blueprints into tight balls and fling them into the lake. Then he'll get moving again. He opens his eyes. Norma Jean has moved away and is walking through the cemetery, following a serpentine brick path.

Leroy gets up to follow his wife, but his good leg is asleep and his bad leg still hurts him. Norma Jean is far away, walking rapidly toward the bluff by the river, and he tries to hobble toward her. Some children run past him, screaming noisily. Norma Jean has reached the bluff, and she is looking out over the Tennessee River. Now she turns toward Leroy and waves her arms. Is she beckoning to him? She seems to be doing an exercise for her chest muscles. The sky is unusually pale—the color of the dust ruffle Mabel made for their bed.

Alice Munro   b. 1931

Spelling   *1978*

In the store, in the old days, Flo used to say she could tell when some woman was going off the track. Special headgear or footwear were often the first give-aways. Galoshes flopping open on a summer day. Rubber boots they slopped around in, or men's workboots. They might say it was on account of corns, but Flo knew better. It was deliberate, it was meant to tell. Next might come the old felt hat, the torn raincoat worn in all weathers, the trousers held up at the waist with twine, the dim shredded scarves, the layers of ravelling sweaters.

Mothers and daughters often the same way. It was always in them. Waves of craziness, always rising, irresistible as giggles, from some place deep inside, gradually getting the better of them.

They used to come telling Flo their stories. Flo would string them along. "Is that so?" she would say. "Isn't that a shame?"

My vegetable grater is gone and I know who took it.

There is a man comes and looks at me when I take my clothes off at night. I pull   5
the blind down and he looks through the crack.

Two hills of new potatoes stolen. A jar of whole peaches. Some nice ducks' eggs.

One of those women they took to the County Home at last. The first thing they did, Flo said, was give her a bath. The next thing they did was cut off her hair, which had grown out like a haystack. They expected to find anything in it, a dead bird or maybe a nest of baby mouse skeletons. They did find burrs and leaves and a bee that must have got caught and buzzed itself to death. When they had cut down far enough they found a cloth hat. It had rotted on her head and the hair had just pushed up through it, like grass through wire.

Flo had got into the habit of keeping the table set for the next meal, to save trouble. The plastic cloth was gummy, the outline of the plate and saucer plain on it as the outline of pictures on a greasy wall. The refrigerator was full of sulfurous scraps, dark crusts, furry oddments. Rose got to work cleaning, scraping, scalding. Sometimes Flo came lumbering through on her two canes. She might ignore Rose's presence altogether, she might tip the jug of maple syrup up against her mouth and drink it like wine. She loved sweet things now, craved them. Brown sugar by the spoonful, maple syrup, tinned puddings, jelly, globs of sweetness to slide down her throat. She had given up smoking, probably for fear of fire.

Another time she said, "What are you doing in there behind the counter? You ask me what you want, and I'll get it." She thought the kitchen was the store.

"I'm *Rose*," Rose said in a loud, slow voice. "We're in the *kitchen*. I'm cleaning   10
up the *kitchen*."

The old arrangement of the kitchen: mysterious, personal, eccentric. Big pan in the oven, medium-sized pan under the potato pot on the corner shelf, little pan hanging on the nail by the sink. Colander under the sink. Dishrags, newspaper clippings, scissors, muffin tins, hanging on various nails. Piles of bills and letters on the sewing machine, on the telephone shelf. You would think someone had set them down a day or two ago, but they were years old. Rose had come across some letters written by herself, in a forced and spritely style. False messengers; false connections, with a lost period of her life.

"Rose is away," Flo said. She had a habit now of sticking her bottom lip out, when she was displeased or perplexed. "Rose got married."

The second morning Rose got up and found that a gigantic stirring-up had occurred in the kitchen, as if someone had wielded a big shaky spoon. The big pan was lodged behind the refrigerator; the egg lifter was in with the towels, the bread knife was in the flour bin and the roasting pan wedged in the pipes under the sink. Rose made Flo's breakfast porridge and Flo said, "You're that woman they were sending to look after me."

"Yes."

"You aren't from around here?"

"No."

"I haven't got money to pay you. They sent you, they can pay you."

Flo spread brown sugar over her porridge until the porridge was entirely covered, then patted the sugar smooth with her spoon.

After breakfast she spied the cutting board, which Rose had been using when she cut bread for her own toast. "What is this thing doing here getting in our road?" said Flo authoritatively, picking it up and marching off—as well as anybody with two canes could march—to hide it somewhere, in the piano bench or under the back steps.

Years ago, Flo had had a little glassed-in side porch built on to the house. From there she could watch the road just as she used to watch from behind the counter of the store (the store window was now boarded up, the old advertising signs painted over). The road wasn't the main road out of Hanratty through West Hanratty to the Lake anymore; there was a highway bypass. And it was paved, now, with wide gutters, new mercury vapor street lights. The old bridge was gone and a new, wide bridge, much less emphatic, had taken its place. The change from Hanratty to West Hanratty was hardly noticeable. West Hanratty had got itself spruced up with paint and aluminum siding; Flo's place was about the only eyesore left.

What were the things Flo put up to look at, in her little porch, where she had been sitting for years now with her joints and arteries hardening?

A calendar with a picture of a puppy and a kitten on it. Faces turned toward each other so that the noses touched, and the space between the two bodies made a heart.

A photograph, in color, of Princess Anne as a child.

A Blue Mountain pottery vase, gift from Brian and Phoebe, with three yellow plastic roses in it, vase and roses bearing several seasons' sifting of dust.

Six shells from the Pacific coast, sent home by Rose but not gathered by her, as Flo believed, or had once believed. Bought on a vacation in the state of Washington. They were an impulse item in a plastic bag by the cashier's desk in a tourist restaurant.

THE LORD IS MY SHEPHERD, in black cutout scroll with a sprinkling of glitter. Free gift from a dairy.

Newspaper photograph of seven coffins in a row. Two large and five small. Parents and children, all shot by the father in the middle of the night, for reasons nobody knew, in a farmhouse out in the country. That house was not easy to find but Flo had seen it. Neighbors took her, on a Sunday drive, in the days when she was using only one cane. They had to ask directions at a gas station on the highway, and again at a crossroads store. They were told that many people had asked the same questions, had been equally determined. Though Flo had to admit there was nothing much to see. A house like any other. The chimney, the windows, the shingles, the door. Something that could have been a dish towel, or a diaper, that nobody had felt like taking in, left to rot on the line.

Rose had not been back to see Flo for nearly two years. She had been busy, she had been traveling with small companies, financed by grants, putting on plays or scenes from plays, or giving readings, in high school auditoriums and community halls, all over the country. It was part of her job to go on local television chatting about these productions, trying to drum up interest, telling amusing stories about things that had happened during the tour. There was nothing shameful about any of this, but sometimes Rose was deeply, unaccountably ashamed. She did not let her confusion show. When she talked in public she was frank and charming; she had a puzzled, diffident way of leading into her anecdotes, as if she were just now remembering, had not told them a hundred times already. Back in her hotel room, she often shivered and moaned, as if she were having an attack of fever. She blamed it on exhaustion, or her approaching menopause. She couldn't remember any of the people she had met, the charming, interesting people who had invited her to dinner and to whom, over drinks in various cities, she had told intimate things about her life.

Neglect in Flo's house had turned a final corner, since Rose saw it last. The rooms were plugged up with rags and papers and dirt. Pull a blind to let some light in, and the blind comes apart in your hand. Shake a curtain and the curtain falls to rags, letting loose a choking dust. Put a hand into a drawer and it sinks into something soft and dark and rubbishy.

We hate to write bad news but it looks like she has got past where she can look   30
after herself. We try to look in on her but we are not so young ourselves anymore so
it looks like maybe the time has come.

The same letter, more or less, had been written to Rose and to her half brother, Brian, who was an engineer, living in Toronto. Rose had just come back from her tour. She had assumed that Brian and his wife, Phoebe, whom she saw seldom, were keeping in touch with Flo. After all, Flo was Brian's mother, Rose's stepmother. And it turned out that they had been keeping in touch, or so they thought. Brian had recently been in South America but Phoebe had been phoning Flo every Sunday night. Flo had little to say but she had never talked to Phoebe anyway; she had said she was fine, everything was fine, she had offered some information about the weather. Rose had observed Flo on the telephone, since she came home, and she saw how Phoebe could have been deceived. Flo spoke normally, she said hello, fine, that was a big storm we had last night, yes, the lights were out here for hours. If you didn't live in the neighborhood you wouldn't realize there hadn't been any storm.

It wasn't that Rose had entirely forgotten Flo in those two years. She had fits of worry about her. It was just that for some time now she had been between fits. One time the fit had come over her in the middle of a January storm, she had driven two hundred miles through blizzards, past ditched cars, and when she finally parked on Flo's street, finally tramped up the walk Flo had not been able to shovel, she was full of relief for herself and concern for Flo, a general turmoil of feelings both anxious and pleasurable. Flo opened the door and gave a bark of warning.

"You can't park there!"

"What?"

"Can't park there!"   35

Flo said there was a new bylaw; no parking on the streets during the winter months.

"You'll have to shovel out a place."

Of course Rose had an explosion.

"If you say one more word right now I'll get in the car and drive back."

"Well you can't park—"   40

"One more word!"

"Why do you have to stand here and argue with the cold blasting into the house?"

Rose stepped inside. Home.

That was one of the stories she told about Flo. She did it well; her own exhaustion and sense of virtue; Flo's bark, her waving cane, her fierce unwillingness to be the object of anybody's rescue.

After she read the letter Rose had phoned Phoebe, and Phoebe had asked her to come to dinner, so they could talk. Rose resolved to behave well. She had an idea that Brian and Phoebe moved in a permanent cloud of disapproval of her. She thought that they disapproved of her success, limited and precarious and provincial though it might be, and that they disapproved of her even more when she failed. She also knew it was not likely they would have her on their minds so much, or feel anything so definite. 45

She put on a plain skirt and an old blouse, but at the last minute changed into a long dress, made of thin red and gold cotton from India, the very thing that would justify their saying that Rose was always so theatrical.

Nevertheless she made up her mind as she usually did that she would speak in a low voice, stick to facts, not get into any stale and silly arguments with Brian. And as usual most of the sense seemed to fly out of her head as soon as she entered their house, was subjected to their calm routines, felt the flow of satisfaction, self-satisfaction, perfectly justified self-satisfaction, that emanated from the very bowls and draperies. She was nervous, when Phoebe asked her about her tour, and Phoebe was a bit nervous too, because Brian sat silent, not exactly frowning but indicating that the frivolity of the subject did not please him. In Rose's presence Brian had said more than once that he had no use for people in her line of work. But he had no use for a good many people. Actors, artists, journalists, rich people (he would never admit to being one himself), the entire Arts faculty of universities. Whole classes and categories, down the drain. Convicted of woolly-mindedness, and showy behavior; inaccurate talk, many excesses. Rose did not know if he spoke the truth or if this was something he had to say in front of her. He offered the bait of his low-voiced contempt; she rose to it; they had fights, she had left his house in tears. And underneath all this, Rose felt, they loved each other. But they could never stop the old, old competition; who is the better person, who has chosen the better work? What were they looking for? Each other's good opinion, which perhaps they meant to grant, in full, but not yet. Phoebe, who was a calm and dutiful woman with a great talent for normalizing things (the very opposite of their family talent for blowing things up) would serve food and pour coffee and regard them with a polite puzzlement; their contest, their vulnerability, their hurt, perhaps seemed as odd to her as the antics of comic-strip characters who stick their fingers into light sockets.

"I always wished Flo could have come back for another visit with us," Phoebe said. Flo had come once, and asked to be taken home after three days. But afterward it seemed to be a pleasure to her, to sit and list the things Brian and Phoebe owned, the features of their house. Brian and Phoebe lived quite unostentatiously, in Don Mills, and the things Flo dwelt on—the door chimes, the automatic garage doors, the swimming pool—were among the ordinary suburban acquisitions. Rose had said as much to Flo who believed that she, Rose, was jealous.

"You wouldn't turn them down if you was offered."

"Yes I would." 50

That was true, Rose believed it was true, but how could she ever explain it to Flo or anybody in Hanratty? If you stay in Hanratty and do not get rich it is all right because you are living out your life as was intended, but if you go away and do not get rich, or, like Rose, do not remain rich, then what was the point?

After dinner Rose and Brian and Phoebe sat in the backyard beside the pool, where the youngest of Brian and Phoebe's four daughters was riding an inflated dragon. Everything had gone amicably, so far. It had been decided that Rose would go to Hanratty, that she would make arrangements to get Flo into the Wawanash County Home. Brian had already made inquiries about it, or his secretary had, and he said that it seemed not only cheaper but better run, with more facilities, than any private nursing home.

"She'll probably meet old friends there," Phoebe said.

Rose's docility, her good behavior, was partly based on a vision she had been building up all evening, and would never reveal to Brian and Phoebe. She pictured herself going to Hanratty and looking after Flo, living with her, taking care of her for as long as was necessary. She thought how she would clean and paint Flo's kitchen, patch the shingles over the leaky spots (that was one of the things the letter had mentioned), plant flowers in the pots, and make nourishing soup. She wasn't so far gone as to imagine Flo fitting comfortably into this picture, settling down to a life of gratitude. But the crankier Flo got, the milder and more patient Rose would become, and who, then, could accuse her of egotism and frivolity?

This vision did not survive the first two days of being home.   55

"Would you like a pudding?" Rose said.

"Oh, I don't care."

The elaborate carelessness some people will show, the gleam of hope, on being offered a drink.

Rose made a trifle. Berries, peaches, custard, cake, whipped cream and sweet sherry.

Flo ate half the bowlful. She dipped in greedily, not bothering to transfer a   60
portion to a smaller bowl.

"That was lovely," she said. Rose had never heard such an admission of grateful pleasure from her. "Lovely," said Flo and sat remembering, appreciating, belching a little. The suave dreamy custard, the nipping berries, robust peaches, luxury of sherry-soaked cake, munificence of whipped cream.

Rose thought that she had never done anything in her life that came as near pleasing Flo as this did.

"I'll make another soon."

Flo recovered herself. "Oh well. You do what you like."
                                                                                 65
Rose drove out to the County Home. She was conducted through it. She tried to tell Flo about it when she came back.

"Whose home?" said Flo.

"No, the *County* Home."

Rose mentioned some people she had seen there. Flo would not admit to knowing any of them. Rose spoke of the view and the pleasant rooms. Flo looked angry; her face darkened and she stuck out her lip. Rose handed her a mobile she had bought for fifty cents in the County Home Crafts Center. Cutout birds of blue and yellow paper were bobbing and dancing, on undetectable currents of air.

"Stick it up your arse," said Flo.

Rose put the mobile up in the porch and said she had seen the trays coming   70
up, with supper on them.

"They go to the dining room if they're able, and if they're not they have trays in their rooms. I saw what they were having.

"Roast beef, well done, mashed potatoes and green beans, the frozen not the canned kind. Or an omelette. You could have a mushroom omelette or a chicken omelette or a plain omelette, if you liked."

"What was for dessert?"

"Ice cream. You could have sauce on it."

"What kind of sauce was there?"   75

"Chocolate. Butterscotch. Walnut."

"I can't eat walnuts."

"There was marshmallow too."

Out at the Home the old people were arranged in tiers. On the first floor were the bright and tidy ones. They walked around, usually with the help of canes. They visited each other, played cards. They had singsongs and hobbies. In the Crafts Center they painted pictures, hooked rugs, made quilts. If they were not able to do things like that they could make rag dolls, mobiles like the one Rose bought, poodles and snowmen which were constructed of Styrofoam balls, with sequins for eyes; they also made silhouette pictures by placing thumbtacks on traced outlines: knights on horseback, battleships, airplanes, castles.

They organized concerts; they held dances; they had checker tournaments.   80

"Some of them say they are the happiest here they have ever been in their lives."

Up one floor there was more television watching, there were more wheelchairs. There were those whose heads drooped, whose tongues lolled, whose limbs shook uncontrollably. Nevertheless sociability was still flourishing, also rationality, with occasional blanks and absences.

On the third floor you might get some surprises.

Some of them up there had given up speaking.

Some had given up moving, except for odd jerks and tosses of the head, flail-   85
ing of the arms, that seemed to be without purpose or control.

Nearly all had given up worrying about whether they were wet or dry.

Bodies were fed and wiped, taken up and tied in chairs, untied and put to bed. Taking in oxygen, giving out carbon dioxide, they continued to participate in the life of the world.

Crouched in her crib, diapered, dark as a nut, with three tufts of hair like dandelion floss sprouting from her head, an old woman was making loud shaky noises.

"Hello Aunty," the nurse said. "You're spelling today. It's lovely weather outside." She bent to the old woman's ear. "Can you spell weather?"

This nurse showed her gums when she smiled, which was all the time; she   90
had an air of nearly demented hilarity.

"Weather," said the old woman. She strained forward, grunting, to get the word. Rose thought she might be going to have a bowel movement. "W-E-A-T-H-E-R."

That reminded her.

"Whether. W-H-E-T-H-E-R."

So far so good.

"Now you say something to her," the nurse said to Rose.   95

The words in Rose's mind were for a moment all obscene or despairing.

But without prompting came another.

"Forest. F-O-R-E-S-T."

"Celebrate," said Rose suddenly.

"C-E-L-E-B-R-A-T-E."   100

You had to listen very hard to make out what the old woman was saying, because she had lost much of the power to shape sounds. What she said seemed to come not from her mouth or her throat, but from deep in her lungs and belly.

"Isn't she a wonder," the nurse said. "She can't see and that's the only way we can tell she can hear. Like if you say, 'Here's your dinner,' she won't pay any attention to it, but she might start spelling *dinner*."

"Dinner," she said, to illustrate, and the old woman picked it up. "D-I-N-N ..." Sometimes a long wait, a long wait between letters. It seemed she had only the thinnest thread to follow, meandering through that emptiness or confusion that nobody on this side can do more than guess at. But she didn't lose it, she followed it through to the end, however tricky the word might be, or cumbersome. Finished. Then she was sitting waiting; waiting, in the middle of her sightless eventless day, till up from somewhere popped another word. She would encompass it, bend all her energy to master it. Rose wondered what the words were like, when she held them in her mind. Did they carry their usual meaning, or any meaning at all? Were they like words in dreams or in the minds of young children, each one marvelous and distinct and alive as a new animal? This one limp and clear, like a jellyfish, that one hard and mean and secretive, like a horned snail. They could be austere and comical as top hats, or smooth and lively and flattering as ribbons. A parade of private visitors, not over yet.

Something woke Rose early the next morning. She was sleeping in the little porch, the only place in Flo's house where the smell was bearable. The sky was milky and brightening. The trees across the river—due to be cut down soon, to make room for a trailer park—were hunched against the dawn sky like shaggy dark animals, like buffalo. Rose had been dreaming. She had been having a dream obviously connected with her tour of the Home the day before.

Someone was taking her through a large building where there were people in cages. Everything was dim and cobwebby at first, and Rose was protesting that this seemed a poor arrangement. But as she went on the cages got larger and more elaborate, they were like enormous wicker birdcages, Victorian birdcages, fancifully shaped and decorated. Food was being offered to the people in the cages and Rose examined it, saw that it was choice; chocolate mousse, trifle, Black Forest cake. Then in one of the cages Rose spotted Flo, who was handsomely seated on a thronelike chair, spelling out words in a clear authoritative voice (what the words were, Rose, wakening, could not remember) and looking pleased with herself, for showing powers she had kept secret till now.

Rose listened to hear Flo breathing, stirring, in her rubble-lined room. She heard nothing. What if Flo had died? Suppose she had died at the very moment she was making her radiant, satisfied appearance in Rose's dream? Rose hurried out of bed, ran barefoot to Flo's room. The bed there was empty. She went into the kitchen and found Flo sitting at the table, dressed to go out, wearing the navy blue summer coat and matching turban hat she had worn to Brian's and Phoebe's wedding. The coat was rumpled and in need of cleaning, the turban was crooked.

"Now I'm ready for to go," Flo said.

"Go where?"

"Out there," said Flo, jerking her head. "Out to the whattayacallit. The Poorhouse."

"The Home," said Rose. "You don't have to go today."

"They hired you to take me, now you get a move on and take me," Flo said.
"I'm not hired. I'm Rose. I'll make you a cup of tea."

"You can make it. I won't drink it."

She made Rose think of a woman who had started in labor. Such was her concentration, her determination, her urgency. Rose thought Flo felt her death moving in her like a child, getting ready to tear her. So she gave up arguing, she got dressed, hastily packed a bag for Flo, got her to the car and drove her out to the Home, but in the matter of Flo's quickly tearing and relieving death she was mistaken.

Some time before this, Rose had been in a play, on national television. *The Trojan Women*. She had no lines, and in fact she was in the play simply to do a favor for a friend, who had got a better part elsewhere. The director thought to liven all the weeping and mourning by having the Trojan women go barebreasted. One breast apiece, they showed, the right in the case of royal personages such as Hecuba and Helen; the left, in the case of ordinary virgins or wives, such as Rose. Rose didn't think herself enhanced by this exposure—she was getting on, after all, her bosom tended to flop—but she got used to the idea. She didn't count on the sensation they would create. She didn't think many people would be watching. She forgot about those parts of the country where people can't exercise their preference for quiz shows, police-car chases, American situation comedies, and are compelled to put up with talks on public affairs and tours of art galleries and ambitious offerings of drama. She did not think they would be so amazed, either, now that every magazine rack in every town was serving up slices and cutlets of bare flesh. How could such outrage fasten on the Trojan ladies' sad-eyed collection, puckered with cold then running with sweat under the lights, badly and chalkily made-up, all looking rather foolish without their mates, rather pitiful and unnatural, like tumors?

Flo took to pen and paper over that, forced her still swollen fingers, crippled almost out of use with arthritis, to write the word *Shame*. She wrote that if Rose's father had not been dead long ago he would now wish that he was. That was true. Rose read the letter, or part of it, out loud to some friends she was having for dinner. She read it for comic effect, and dramatic effect, to show the gulf that lay behind her, though she did realize, if she thought about it, that such a gulf was nothing special. Most of her friends, who seemed to her ordinarily hardworking, anxious, and hopeful people, could lay claim to being disowned or prayed for, in some disappointed home.

Halfway through she had to stop reading. It wasn't that she thought how shabby it was, to be exposing and making fun of Flo this way. She had done it often enough before; it was no news to her that it was shabby. What stopped her was, in fact, that gulf; she had a fresh and overwhelming realization of it, and it was nothing to laugh about. These reproaches of Flo's made as much sense as a protest about raising umbrellas, a warning against eating raisins. But they were painfully, truly, meant; they were all a hard life had to offer. Shame on a bare breast.

Another time, Rose was getting an award. So were several other people. A reception was being held, in a Toronto hotel. Flo had been sent an invitation, but Rose had never thought that she would come. She had thought she should give someone's name, when the organizers asked about relatives, and she could hardly name Brian and Phoebe. Of course it was possible that she did, secretly, want Flo to come, wanted to show Flo, intimidate her, finally remove herself from Flo's shade. That would be a natural thing to want to do.

Flo came down on the train, unannounced. She got to the hotel. She was arthritic then, but still moving without a cane. She had always been decently, soberly, cheaply, dressed, but now it seemed she had spent money and asked advice. She was wearing a mauve and purple checked pants suit, and beads like strings of white and yellow popcorn. Her hair was covered by a thick gray-blue wig, pulled low on her forehead like a woollen cap. From the vee of the jacket, and its too-short sleeves, her neck and wrists stuck out brown and warty as if covered with bark. When she saw Rose she stood still. She seemed to be waiting—not just for Rose to go over to her but for her feelings about the scene in front of her to crystallize.

Soon they did.   120

"Look at the nigger!" said Flo in a loud voice, before Rose was anywhere near her. Her tone was one of simple, gratified astonishment, as if she had been peering down the Grand Canyon or seen oranges growing on a tree.

She meant George, who was getting one of the awards. He turned around, to see if someone was feeding him a comic line. And Flo did look like a comic character, except that her bewilderment, her authenticity, were quite daunting. Did she note the stir she had caused? Possibly. After that one outburst she clammed up, would not speak again except in the most grudging monosyllables, would not eat any food or drink any drink offered her, would not sit down, but stood astonished and unflinching in the middle of that gathering of the bearded and beaded, the unisexual and the unashamedly un-Anglo-Saxon, until it was time for her to be taken to her train and sent home.

Rose found that wig under the bed, during the horrifying cleanup that followed Flo's removal. She took it out to the Home, along with some clothes she had washed or had dry-cleaned, and some stockings, talcum powder, cologne, that she had bought. Sometimes Flo seemed to think Rose was a doctor, and she said, "I don't want no woman doctor, you can just clear out." But when she saw Rose carrying the wig she said, "Rose! What is that you got in your hands, is it a dead gray squirrel?"

"No," said Rose, "it's a wig."

"What?"   125

"A wig," said Rose, and Flo began to laugh. Rose laughed too. The wig did look like a dead cat or squirrel, even though she had washed and brushed it; it was a disturbing-looking object.

"My God, Rose, I thought what is she doing bringing me a dead squirrel! If I put it on somebody'd be sure to take a shot at me."

Rose stuck it on her own head, to continue the comedy, and Flo laughed so that she rocked back and forth in her crib.

When she got her breath Flo said, "What am I doing with these damn sides up on my bed? Are you and Brian behaving yourselves? Don't fight, it gets on your father's nerves. Do you know how many gallstones they took out of me? Fifteen! One as big as a pullet's egg. I got them somewhere. I'm going to take them home." She pulled at the sheets searching. "They were in a bottle."

"I've got them already," said Rose. "I took them home."   130

"Did you? Did you show your father?"

"Yes."

"Oh, well, that's where they are then," said Flo, and she lay down and closed her eyes.

Tim O'Brien   b. 1946

The Things They Carried   1990

First Lieutenant Jimmy Cross carried letters from a girl named Martha, a junior at Mount Sebastian College in New Jersey. They were not love letters, but Lieutenant Cross was hoping, so he kept them folded in plastic at the bottom of his rucksack. In the late afternoon, after a day's march, he would dig his foxhole, wash his hands under a canteen, unwrap the letters, hold them with the tips of his fingers, and spend the last hour of light pretending. He would imagine romantic camping trips into the White Mountains in New Hampshire. He would sometimes taste the envelope flaps, knowing her tongue had been there. More than anything, he wanted Martha to love him as he loved her, but the letters were mostly chatty, elusive on the matter of love. She was a virgin, he was almost sure. She was an English major at Mount Sebastian, and she wrote beautifully about her professors and roommates and midterm exams, about her respect for Chaucer and her great affection for Virginia Woolf. She often quoted lines of poetry; she never mentioned the war, except to say, Jimmy, take care of yourself. The letters weighed ten ounces. They were signed "Love, Martha," but Lieutenant Cross understood that "Love" was only a way of signing and did not mean what he sometimes pretended it meant. At dusk, he would carefully return the letters to his rucksack. Slowly, a bit distracted, he would get up and move among his men, checking the perimeter, then at full dark he would return to his hole and watch the night and wonder if Martha was a virgin.

The things they carried were largely determined by necessity. Among the necessities or near necessities were P–38 can openers, pocketknives, heat tabs, wristwatches, dog tags, mosquito repellent, chewing gum, candy, cigarettes, salt tablets, packets of Kool-Aid, lighters, matches, sewing kits, Military Payment Certificates, C rations, and two or three canteens of water. Together, these items weighed between fifteen and twenty pounds, depending upon a man's habits or rate of metabolism. Henry Dobbins, who was a big man, carried extra rations; he was especially fond of canned peaches in heavy syrup over pound cake. Dave Jensen, who practiced field hygiene, carried a toothbrush, dental floss, and several hotel-size bars of soap he'd stolen on R&R in Sydney, Australia. Ted Lavender, who was scared, carried tranquilizers until he was shot in the head outside the village of Than Khe in mid-April. By necessity, and because it was SOP,[1] they all carried steel helmets that weighed five pounds including the liner and camouflage cover. They carried the standard fatigue jackets and trousers. Very few carried underwear. On their feet they carried jungle boots—2.1 pounds—and Dave Jensen carried three pairs of socks and a can of Dr. Scholl's foot powder as a precaution against trench foot. Until he was shot, Ted Lavender carried six or seven ounces of premium dope, which for him was a necessity. Mitchell Sanders, the RTO,[2] carried condoms. Norman Bowker carried a diary. Rat Kiley carried comic books. Kiowa, a devout Baptist, carried an illustrated New Testament that had been presented to him by his father, who taught Sunday school in Oklahoma City, Oklahoma. As a hedge against bad times, however, Kiowa also carried his grandmother's distrust of the white man, his grandfather's old hunting hatchet. Necessity dictated. Because

---

[1]SOP—standard operating procedure.
[2]RTO—radio telephone operator.

the land was mined and booby-trapped, it was SOP for each man to carry a steel-centered, nylon-covered flak jacket, which weighed 6.7 pounds, but which on hot days seemed much heavier. Because you could die so quickly, each man carried at least one large compress bandage, usually in the helmet band for easy access. Because the nights were cold, and because the monsoons were wet, each carried a green plastic poncho that could be used as a raincoat or ground sheet or makeshift tent. With its quilted liner, the poncho weighed almost two pounds, but it was worth every ounce. In April, for instance, when Ted Lavender was shot, they used his poncho to wrap him up, then to carry him across the paddy, then to lift him into the chopper that took him away.

They were called legs or grunts.

To carry something was to "hump" it, as when Lieutenant Jimmy Cross humped his love for Martha up the hills and through the swamps. In its intransitive form, "to hump" meant "to walk," or "to march," but it implied burdens far beyond the intransitive.

Almost everyone humped photographs. In his wallet, Lieutenant Cross carried two photographs of Martha. The first was a Kodachrome snapshot signed "Love," though he knew better. She stood against a brick wall. Her eyes were gray and neutral, her lips slightly open as she stared straight-on at the camera. At night, sometimes, Lieutenant Cross wondered who had taken the picture, because he knew she had boyfriends, because he loved her so much, and because he could see the shadow of the picture taker spreading out against the brick wall. The second photograph had been clipped from the 1968 Mount Sebastian yearbook. It was an action shot—women's volleyball—and Martha was bent horizontal to the floor, reaching, the palms of her hands in sharp focus, the tongue taut, the expression frank and competitive. There was no visible sweat. She wore white gym shorts. Her legs, he thought, were almost certainly the legs of a virgin, dry and without hair, the left knee cocked and carrying her entire weight, which was just over one hundred pounds. Lieutenant Cross remembered touching that left knee. A dark theater, he remembered, and the movie was *Bonnie and Clyde,* and Martha wore a tweed skirt, and during the final scene, when he touched her knee, she turned and looked at him in a sad, sober way that made him pull his hand back, but he would always remember the feel of the tweed skirt and the knee beneath it and the sound of the gunfire that killed Bonnie and Clyde, how embarrassing it was, how slow and oppressive. He remembered kissing her good night at the dorm door. Right then, he thought, he should've done something brave. He should've carried her up the stairs to her room and tied her to the bed and touched that left knee all night long. He should've risked it. Whenever he looked at the photographs, he thought of new things he should've done.

What they carried was partly a function of rank, partly of field speciality.

As a first lieutenant and platoon leader, Jimmy Cross carried a compass, maps, code books, binoculars, and a .45-caliber pistol that weighed 2.9 pounds fully loaded. He carried a strobe light and the responsibility for the lives of his men.

As an RTO, Mitchell Sanders carried the PRC–25 radio, a killer, twenty-six pounds with its battery.

As a medic, Rat Kiley carried a canvas satchel filled with morphine and plasma and malaria tablets and surgical tape and comic books and all the things a medic must carry, including M&Ms for especially bad wounds, for a total weight of nearly twenty pounds.

As a big man, therefore a machine gunner, Henry Dobbins carried the M–60, which weighed twenty-three pounds unloaded, but which was almost always loaded. In addition, Dobbins carried between ten and fifteen pounds of ammunition draped in belts across his chest and shoulders.

As PFCs or Spec 4s, most of them were common grunts and carried the standard M–16 gas-operated assault rifle. The weapon weighed 7.5 pounds unloaded, 8.2 pounds with its full twenty-round magazine. Depending on numerous factors, such as topography and psychology, the riflemen carried anywhere from twelve to twenty magazines, usually in cloth bandoliers, adding on another 8.4 pounds at minimum, fourteen pounds at maximum. When it was available, they also carried M–16 maintenance gear—rods and steel brushes and swabs and tubes of LSA oil— all of which weighed about a pound. Among the grunts, some carried the M–79 grenade launcher, 5.9 pounds unloaded, a reasonably light weapon except for the ammunition, which was heavy. A single round weighed ten ounces. The typical load was twenty-five rounds. But Ted Lavender, who was scared, carried thirty-four rounds when he was shot and killed outside Than Khe, and he went down under an exceptional burden, more than twenty pounds of ammunition, plus the flak jacket and helmet and rations and water and toilet paper and tranquilizers and all the rest, plus the unweighed fear. He was dead weight. There was no twitching or flopping. Kiowa, who saw it happen, said it was like watching a rock fall, or a big sandbag or something—just boom, then down—not like the movies where the dead guy rolls around and does fancy spins and goes ass-over-teakettle—not like that, Kiowa said, the poor bastard just flat-fuck fell. Boom. Down. Nothing else. It was a bright morning in mid-April. Lieutenant Cross felt the pain. He blamed himself. They stripped off Lavender's canteens and ammo, all the heavy things, and Rat Kiley said the obvious, the guy's dead, and Mitchell Sanders used his radio to report one U.S. KIA and to request a chopper. Then they wrapped Lavender in his poncho. They carried him out to a dry paddy, established security, and sat smoking the dead man's dope until the chopper came. Lieutenant Cross kept to himself. He pictured Martha's smooth young face, thinking he loved her more than anything, more than his men, and now Ted Lavender was dead because he loved her so much and could not stop thinking about her. When the dust-off arrived, they carried Lavender aboard. Afterward they burned Than Khe. They marched until dusk, then dug their holes, and that night Kiowa kept explaining how you had to be there, how fast it was, how the poor guy just dropped like so much concrete. Boom-down, he said. Like cement.

In addition to the three standard weapons—the M–60, M–16, and M–79—they carried whatever presented itself, or whatever seemed appropriate as a means of killing or staying alive. They carried catch-as-catch-can. At various times, in various situations, they carried M–14s and CAR–15s and Swedish Ks and grease guns and captured AK–47s and Chi-Coms and RPGs and Simonov carbines and black-market Uzis and .38-caliber Smith & Wesson handguns and 66-mm LAWs and shotguns and silencers and blackjacks and bayonets and C–4 plastic explosives. Lee Strunk carried a slingshot; a weapon of last resort, he called it. Mitchell Sanders carried brass knuckles. Kiowa carried his grandfather's feathered hatchet. Every third or fourth man carried a Claymore antipersonnel mine—3.5 pounds with its firing device. They all carried fragmentation grenades—fourteen ounces each.

They all carried at least one M-18 colored smoke grenade—twenty-four ounces. Some carried CS or tear-gas grenades. Some carried white-phosphorus grenades. They carried all they could bear, and then some, including a silent awe for the terrible power of the things they carried.

In the first week of April, before Lavender died, Lieutenant Jimmy Cross received a good-luck charm from Martha. It was a simple pebble, an ounce at most. Smooth to the touch, it was a milky-white color with flecks of orange and violet, oval-shaped, like a miniature egg. In the accompanying letter, Martha wrote that she had found the pebble on the Jersey shoreline, precisely where the land touched the water at high tide, where things came together but also separated. It was this separate-but-together quality, she wrote, that had inspired her to pick up the pebble and to carry it in her breast pocket for several days; where it seemed weightless, and then to send it through the mail, by air, as a token of her truest feelings for him. Lieutenant Cross found this romantic. But he wondered what her truest feelings were, exactly, and what she meant by separate-but-together. He wondered how the tides and waves had come into play on that afternoon along the Jersey shoreline when Martha saw the pebble and bent down to rescue it from geology. He imagined bare feet. Martha was a poet, with the poet's sensibilities, and her feet would be brown and bare, the toenails unpainted, the eyes chilly and somber like the ocean in March, and though it was painful, he wondered who had been with her that afternoon. He imagined a pair of shadows moving along the strip of sand where things came together but also separated. It was phantom jealousy, he knew, but he couldn't help himself. He loved her so much. On the march, through the hot days of early April, he carried the pebble in his mouth, turning it with his tongue, tasting sea salts and moisture. His mind wandered. He had difficulty keeping his attention on the war. On occasion he would yell at his men to spread out the column, to keep their eyes open, but then he would slip away into daydreams, just pretending, walking barefoot along the Jersey shore, with Martha, carrying nothing. He would feel himself rising. Sun and waves and gentle winds, all love and lightness.

What they carried varied by mission.

When a mission took them to the mountains, they carried mosquito netting, machetes, canvas tarps, and extra bug juice.   15

If a mission seemed especially hazardous, or if it involved a place they knew to be bad, they carried everything they could. In certain heavily mined AOs,[3] where the land was dense with Toe Poppers and Bouncing Betties, they took turns humping a twenty-eight pound mine detector. With its headphones and big sensing plate, the equipment was a stress on the lower back and shoulders, awkward to handle, often useless because of the shrapnel in the earth, but they carried it anyway, partly for safety, partly for the illusion of safety.

On ambush, or other night missions, they carried peculiar little odds and ends. Kiowa always took along his New Testament and a pair of moccasins for silence. Dave Jensen carried night-sight vitamins high in carotin. Lee Strunk carried his slingshot; ammo, he claimed, would never be a problem. Rat Kiley carried brandy and M&Ms. Until he was shot, Ted Lavender carried the starlight scope,

---

[3]AOs—areas of operation.

which weighed 6.3 pounds with its aluminum carrying case. Henry Dobbins carried his girlfriend's pantyhose wrapped around his neck as a comforter. They all carried ghosts. When dark came, they would move out single file across the meadows and paddies to their ambush coordinates, where they would quietly set up the Claymores and lie down and spend the night waiting.

Other missions were more complicated and required special equipment. In mid-April, it was their mission to search out and destroy the elaborate tunnel complexes in the Than Khe area south of Chu Lai. To blow the tunnels, they carried one-pound blocks of pentrite high explosives, four blocks to a man, sixty-eight pounds in all. They carried wiring, detonators, and battery-powered clackers. Dave Jensen carried earplugs. Most often, before blowing the tunnels, they were ordered by higher command to search them, which was considered bad news, but by and large they just shrugged and carried out orders. Because he was a big man, Henry Dobbins was excused from tunnel duty. The others would draw numbers. Before Lavender died there were seventeen men in the platoon, and whoever drew the number seventeen would strip off his gear and crawl in head first with a flashlight and Lieutenant Cross's .45-caliber pistol. The rest of them would fan out as security. They would sit down or kneel, not facing the hole, listening to the ground beneath them, imagining cobwebs and ghosts, whatever was down there—the tunnel walls squeezing in—how the flashlight seemed impossibly heavy in the hand and how it was tunnel vision in the very strictest sense, compression in all ways, even time, and how you had to wriggle in—ass and elbows— a swallowed-up feeling—and how you found yourself worrying about odd things—will your flashlight go dead? Do rats carry rabies? If you screamed, how far would the sound carry? Would your buddies hear it? Would they have the courage to drag you out? In some respects, though not many, the waiting was worse than the tunnel itself. Imagination was a killer.

On April 16, when Lee Strunk drew the number seventeen, he laughed and muttered something and went down quickly. The morning was hot and very still. Not good, Kiowa said. He looked at the tunnel opening, then out across a dry paddy toward the village of Than Khe. Nothing moved. No clouds or birds or people. As they waited, the men smoked and drank Kool-Aid, not talking much, feeling sympathy for Lee Strunk but also feeling the luck of the draw. You win some, you lose some, said Mitchell Sanders, and sometimes you settle for a rain check. It was a tired line and no one laughed.

Henry Dobbins ate a tropical chocolate bar. Ted Lavender popped a tranquilizer and went off to pee.   20

After five minutes, Lieutenant Jimmy Cross moved to the tunnel, leaned down, and examined the darkness. Trouble, he thought—a cave-in maybe. And then suddenly, without willing it, he was thinking about Martha. The stresses and fractures, the quick collapse, the two of them buried alive under all that weight. Dense, crushing love. Kneeling, watching the hole, he tried to concentrate on Lee Strunk and the war, all the dangers, but his love was too much for him, he felt paralyzed, he wanted to sleep inside her lungs and breathe her blood and be smothered. He wanted her to be a virgin and not a virgin, all at once. He wanted to know her. Intimate secrets—why poetry? Why so sad? Why that grayness in her eyes? Why so alone? Not lonely, just alone—riding her bike across campus or sitting off by herself in the cafeteria. Even dancing, she danced alone—and it was the aloneness that filled him with love. He remembered telling her that one evening. How she nodded and looked away. And how, later, when he kissed her, she received the kiss without returning it, her eyes wide open, not afraid, not a virgin's eyes, just flat and uninvolved.

Lieutenant Cross gazed at the tunnel. But he was not there. He was buried with Martha under the white sand at the Jersey shore. They were pressed together, and the pebble in his mouth was her tongue. He was smiling. Vaguely, he was aware of how quiet the day was, the sullen paddies, yet he could not bring himself to worry about matters of security. He was beyond that. He was just a kid at war, in love. He was twenty-two years old. He couldn't help it.

A few moments later Lee Strunk crawled out of the tunnel. He came up grinning, filthy but alive. Lieutenant Cross nodded and closed his eyes while the others clapped Strunk on the back and made jokes about rising from the dead.

Worms, Rat Kiley said. Right out of the grave. Fuckin' zombie.

The men laughed. They all felt great relief.   25

Spook City, said Mitchell Sanders.

Lee Strunk made a funny ghost sound, a kind of moaning, yet very happy, and right then, when Strunk made that high happy moaning sound, when he went *Ahhooooo,* right then Ted Lavender was shot in the head on his way back from peeing. He lay with his mouth open. The teeth were broken. There was a swollen black bruise under his left eye. The cheekbone was gone. Oh shit, Rat Kiley said, the guy's dead. The guy's dead, he kept saying, which seemed profound—the guy's dead. I mean really.

The things they carried were determined to some extent by superstition. Lieutenant Cross carried his good-luck pebble. Dave Jensen carried a rabbit's foot. Norman Bowker, otherwise a very gentle person, carried a thumb that had been presented to him as a gift by Mitchell Sanders. The thumb was dark brown, rubbery to the touch, and weighed four ounces at most. It had been cut from a VC corpse, a boy of fifteen or sixteen. They'd found him at the bottom of an irrigation ditch, badly burned, flies in his mouth and eyes. The boy wore black shorts and sandals. At the time of his death he had been carrying a pouch of rice, a rifle, and three magazines of ammunition.

You want my opinion, Mitchell Sanders said, there's a definite moral here.

He put his hand on the dead boy's wrist. He was quiet for a time, as if counting a pulse, then he patted the stomach, almost affectionately, and used Kiowa's hunting hatchet to remove the thumb.   30

Henry Dobbins asked what the moral was.

Moral?

You know. *Moral.*

Sanders wrapped the thumb in toilet paper and handed it across to Norman Bowker. There was no blood. Smiling, he kicked the boy's head, watched the flies scatter, and said, It's like with that old TV show—Paladin. Have gun, will travel.

Henry Dobbins thought about it.   35

Yeah, well, he finally said. I don't see no moral.

There it *is*, man.

Fuck off.

They carried USO stationery and pencils and pens. They carried Sterno, safety pins, trip flares, signal flares, spools of wire, razor blades, chewing tobacco, liberated joss sticks and statuettes of the smiling Buddha, candles, grease pencils, *The Stars and Stripes,* fingernail clippers, Psy Ops[4] leaflets, bush hats, bolos, and much more. Twice a week, when the resupply choppers came in, they carried hot chow in green Mermite cans and large canvas bags filled with iced beer and soda pop. They carried plastic water containers, each with a two-gallon capacity. Mitchell Sanders carried a set of starched tiger fatigues for special occasions. Henry Dobbins carried Black Flag insecticide. Dave Jensen carried empty sandbags that could be filled at night for added protection. Lee Strunk carried tanning lotion. Some things they carried in common. Taking turns, they carried the big PRC–77 scrambler radio, which weighed thirty pounds with its battery. They shared the weight of memory. They took up what others could no longer bear. Often, they carried each other, the wounded or weak. They carried infections. They carried chess sets, basketballs, Vietnamese-English dictionaries, insignia of rank, Bronze Stars and Purple Hearts, plastic cards imprinted with the Code of Conduct. They carried diseases, among them malaria and dysentery. They carried lice and ringworm and leeches and paddy algae and various rots and molds. They carried the land itself—Vietnam, the place, the soil—a powdery orange-red dust that covered their boots and fatigues and faces. They carried the sky. The whole atmosphere, they carried it, the humidity, the monsoons, the stink of fungus and decay, all of it, they carried gravity. They moved like mules. By daylight they took sniper fire, at night they were mortared, but it was not battle, it was just the endless march, village to village, without purpose, nothing won or lost. They marched for the sake of the march. They plodded along slowly, dumbly, leaning forward against the heat, unthinking, all blood and bone, simple grunts, soldiering with their legs, toiling up the hills and down into the paddies and across the rivers and up again and down, just humping, one step and then the next and then another, but no volition, no will, because it was automatic, it was anatomy, and the war was entirely a matter of posture and carriage, the hump was everything, a kind of inertia, a kind of emptiness, a dullness of desire and intellect and conscience and hope and human sensibility. Their principles were in their feet. Their calculations were biological. They had no sense of strategy or mission. They searched the villages without knowing what to look for, not caring, kicking over jars of rice, frisking children and old men, blowing tunnels, sometimes setting fires and sometimes not, then forming up and moving on to the next village, then other villages, where it would always be the same. They carried their own lives. The pressures were enormous. In the heat of early afternoon, they would remove their helmets and flak jackets, walking bare, which was dangerous but which helped ease the strain. They would often discard things along the route of march. Purely for comfort, they would throw away rations, blow their Claymores and grenades, no matter, because by nightfall the resupply choppers would arrive with more of the same, then a day or two later still more, fresh watermelons and crates of ammunition and sunglasses and woolen sweaters—the resources were stunning—sparklers for the Fourth of July, colored eggs for Easter. It was the great American war chest—the fruits of science, the smokestacks, the canneries, the arsenals at Hartford, the Minnesota forests, the machine shops, the vast fields of corn and wheat—they carried like freight trains; they carried it on their backs and shoulders—and for all the

---

[4]Psy Ops—Psychological Operations

ambiguities of Vietnam, all the mysteries and unknowns, there was at least the single abiding certainty that they would never be at a loss for things to carry.   40

After the chopper took Lavender away, Lieutenant Jimmy Cross led his men into the village of Than Khe. They burned everything. They shot chickens and dogs, they trashed the village well, they called in artillery and watched the wreckage, then they marched for several hours through the hot afternoon, and then at dusk, while Kiowa explained how Lavender died, Lieutenant Cross found himself trembling.

He tried not to cry. With his entrenching tool, which weighed five pounds, he began digging a hole in the earth.

He felt shame. He hated himself. He had loved Martha more than his men, and as a consequence Lavender was now dead, and this was something he would have to carry like a stone in his stomach for the rest of the war.

All he could do was dig. He used his entrenching tool like an ax, slashing, feeling both love and hate, and then later, when it was full dark, he sat at the bottom of his foxhole and wept. It went on for a long while. In part, he was grieving for Ted Lavender, but mostly it was for Martha, and for himself, because she belonged to another world, which was not quite real, and because she was a junior at Mount Sebastian College in New Jersey, a poet and a virgin and uninvolved, and because he realized she did not love him and never would.

Like cement, Kiowa whispered in the dark. I swear to God—boom-down. Not a word.

I've heard this, said Norman Bowker.   45

A pisser, you know? Still zipping himself up. Zapped while zipping.

All right, fine. That's enough.

Yeah, but you had to see it, the guy just—

I *heard*, man. Cement. So why not shut the fuck *up?*

Kiowa shook his head sadly and glanced over at the hole where Lieutenant   50
Jimmy Cross sat watching the night. The air was thick and wet. A warm, dense fog had settled over the paddies and there was the stillness that precedes rain.

After a time Kiowa sighed.

One thing for sure, he said. The Lieutenant's in some deep hurt. I mean that crying jag—the way he was carrying on—it wasn't fake or anything, it was real heavy-duty hurt. The man cares.

Sure, Norman Bowker said.

Say what you want, the man does care.

We all got problems.   55

Not Lavender.

No, I guess not, Bowker said. Do me a favor, though.

Shut up?

That's a smart Indian. Shut up.

Shrugging, Kiowa pulled off his boots. He wanted to say more, just to lighten   60
up his sleep, but instead he opened his New Testament and arranged it beneath his head as a pillow. The fog made things seem hollow and unattached. He tried not to think about Ted Lavender, but then he was thinking how fast it was, no drama, down and dead, and how it was hard to feel anything except surprise. It seemed un-Christian. He wished he could find some great sadness, or even anger, but the emotion wasn't there and he couldn't make it happen. Mostly he felt pleased to be alive. He liked the smell of the New Testament under his cheek, the

leather and ink and paper and glue, whatever the chemicals were. He liked hearing the sounds of night. Even his fatigue, it felt fine, the stiff muscles and the prickly awareness of his own body, a floating feeling. He enjoyed not being dead. Lying there, Kiowa admired Lieutenant Jimmy Cross's capacity for grief. He wanted to share the man's pain, he wanted to care as Jimmy Cross cared. And yet when he closed his eyes, all he could think was Boom-down, and all he could feel was the pleasure of having his boots off and the fog curling in around him and the damp soil and the Bible smells and the plush comfort of night.

After a moment Norman Bowker sat up in the dark.

What the hell, he said. You want to talk, *talk*. Tell it to me.

Forget it.

No, man, go on. One thing I hate, it's a silent Indian.

For the most part they carried themselves with poise, a kind of dignity. Now and then, however, there were times of panic, when they squealed or wanted to squeal but couldn't, when they twitched and made moaning sounds and covered their heads and said Dear Jesus and flopped around on the earth and fired their weapons blindly and cringed and sobbed and begged for the noise to stop and went wild and made stupid promises to themselves and to God and to their mothers and fathers, hoping not to die. In different ways, it happened to all of them. Afterward, when the firing ended, they would blink and peek up. They would touch their bodies, feeling shame, then quickly hiding it. They would force themselves to stand. As if in slow motion, frame by frame, the world would take on the old logic—absolute silence, then the wind, then sunlight, then voices. It was the burden of being alive. Awkwardly, the men would reassemble themselves, first in private, then in groups, becoming soldiers again. They would repair the leaks in their eyes. They would check for casualties, call in dust-offs, light cigarettes, try to smile, clear their throats and spit, and begin cleaning their weapons. After a time someone would shake his head and say, No lie, I almost shit my pants, and someone else would laugh, which meant it was bad, yes, but the guy had obviously not shit his pants, it wasn't that bad, and in any case nobody would ever do such a thing and then go ahead and talk about it. They would squint into the dense, oppressive sunlight. For a few moments, perhaps, they would fall silent, lighting a joint and tracking its passage from man to man, inhaling, holding in the humiliation. Scary stuff, one of them might say. But then someone else would grin or flick his eyebrows and say, Rodger-dodger, almost cut me a new asshole, *almost*.

There were numerous such poses. Some carried themselves with a sort of wistful resignation, others with pride or stiff soldierly discipline or good humor or macho zeal. They were afraid of dying but they were even more afraid to show it.

They found jokes to tell.

They used a hard vocabulary to contain the terrible softness. *Greased,* they'd say. *Offed, lit up, zapped while zipping*. It wasn't cruelty, just stage presence. They were actors and the war came at them in 3-D. When someone died, it wasn't quite dying, because in a curious way it seemed scripted, and because they had their lines mostly memorized, irony mixed with tragedy, and because they called it by other names, as if to encyst and destroy the reality of death itself. They kicked corpses. They cut off thumbs. They talked grunt lingo. They told stories about Ted Lavender's supply of tranquilizers, how the poor guy didn't feel a thing, how incredibly tranquil he was.

There's a moral here, said Mitchell Sanders.

They were waiting for Lavender's chopper, smoking the dead man's dope.

The moral's pretty obvious, Sanders said, and winked. Stay away from drugs. No joke, they'll ruin your day every time.

Cute, said Henry Dobbins.

Mind-blower, get it? Talk about wiggy—nothing left, just blood and brains.

They made themselves laugh.

There it is, they'd say, over and over, as if the repetition itself were an act of poise, a balance between crazy and almost crazy, knowing without going. There it is, which meant be cool, let it ride, because oh yeah, man, you can't change what can't be changed, there it is, there it absolutely and positively and fucking well *is*. 75

They were tough.

They carried all the emotional baggage of men who might die. Grief, terror, love, longing—these were intangibles, but the intangibles had their own mass and specific gravity, they had tangible weight. They carried shameful memories. They carried the common secret of cowardice barely restrained, the instinct to run or freeze or hide, and in many respects this was the heaviest burden of all, for it could never be put down, it required perfect balance and perfect posture. They carried their reputations. They carried the soldier's greatest fear, which was the fear of blushing. Men killed, and died, because they were embarrassed not to. It was what had brought them to the war in the first place, nothing positive, no dreams of glory or honor, just to avoid the blush of dishonor. They died so as not to die of embarrassment. They crawled into tunnels and walked point and advanced under fire. Each morning, despite the unknowns, they made their legs move. They endured. They kept humping. They did not submit to the obvious alternative, which was simply to close the eyes and fall. So easy, really. Go limp and tumble to the ground and let the muscles unwind and not speak and not budge until your buddies picked you up and lifted you into the chopper that would roar and dip its nose and carry you off to the world. A mere matter of falling, yet no one ever fell. It was not courage, exactly; the object was not valor. Rather, they were too frightened to be cowards.

By and large they carried these things inside, maintaining the masks of composure. They sneered at sick call. They spoke bitterly about guys who had found release by shooting off their own toes or fingers. Pussies, they'd say. Candy-asses. It was fierce, mocking talk, with only a trace of envy or awe, but even so, the image played itself out behind their eyes.

They imagined the muzzle against flesh. They imagined the quick, sweet pain, then the evacuation to Japan, then a hospital with warm beds and cute geisha nurses.

They dreamed of freedom birds.

At night, on guard, staring into the dark, they were carried away by jumbo jets. They felt the rush of takeoff. *Gone!* they yelled. And then velocity, wings and engines, a smiling stewardess—but it was more than a plane, it was a real bird, a big sleek silver bird with feathers and talons and high screeching. They were flying. The weights fell off, there was nothing to bear. They laughed and held on tight, feeling the cold slap of wind and altitude, soaring, thinking *It's over, I'm gone!*—they were naked, they were light and free—it was all lightness, bright and fast and buoyant, light as light, a helium buzz in the brain, a giddy bubbling in the lungs as they were taken up over the clouds and the war, beyond duty, beyond gravity and mortification and global entanglements—*Sin loi!*[5] they yelled, *I'm* 80

---

[5]*Sin loi!*—Vietnamese: Sorry about that!

sorry, motherfuckers, but I'm out of it, I'm goofed, I'm on a space cruise, I'm gone!— and it was a restful, disencumbered sensation, just riding the light waves, sailing that big silver freedom bird over the mountains and oceans, over America, over the farms and great sleeping cities and cemeteries and highways and the golden arches of McDonald's. It was flight, a kind of fleeing, a kind of falling, falling higher and higher, spinning off the edge of the earth and beyond the sun and through the vast, silent vacuum where there were no burdens and where everything weighed exactly nothing. *Gone!* they screamed, *I'm sorry but I'm gone!* And so at night, not quite dreaming, they gave themselves over to lightness, they were carried, they were purely borne.

On the morning after Ted Lavender died, First Lieutenant Jimmy Cross crouched at the bottom of his foxhole and burned Martha's letters. Then he burned the two photographs. There was a steady rain falling, which made it difficult, but he used heat tabs and Sterno to build a small fire, screening it with his body, holding the photographs over the tight blue flame with the tips of his fingers.

He realized it was only a gesture. Stupid, he thought. Sentimental, too, but mostly just stupid.

Lavender was dead. You couldn't burn the blame.

Besides, the letters were in his head. And even now, without photographs, Lieutenant Cross could see Martha playing volleyball in her white gym shorts and yellow T-shirt. He could see her moving in the rain.

When the fire died out, Lieutenant Cross pulled his poncho over his shoulders and ate breakfast from a can.

There was no great mystery, he decided.

In those burned letters Martha had never mentioned the war, except to say, Jimmy, take care of yourself. She wasn't involved. She signed the letters "Love," but it wasn't love, and all the fine lines and technicalities did not matter.

The morning came up wet and blurry. Everything seemed part of everything else, the fog and Martha and the deepening rain.

It was a war, after all.

Half smiling, Lieutenant Jimmy Cross took out his maps. He shook his head hard, as if to clear it, then bent forward and began planning the day's march. In ten minutes, or maybe twenty, he would rouse the men and they would pack up and head west, where the maps showed the country to be green and inviting. They would do what they had always done. The rain might add some weight, but otherwise it would be one more day layered upon all the other days.

He was realistic about it. There was that new hardness in his stomach.

No more fantasies, he told himself.

Henceforth, when he thought about Martha, it would be only to think that she belonged elsewhere. He would shut down the daydreams. This was not Mount Sebastian, it was another world, where there were no pretty poems or midterm exams, a place where men died because of carelessness and gross stupidity. Kiowa was right. Boom-down, and you were dead, never partly dead.

Briefly, in the rain, Lieutenant Cross saw Martha's gray eyes gazing back at him.

He understood.

It was very sad, he thought. The things men carried inside. The things men did or felt they had to do.

He almost nodded at her, but didn't.

Instead he went back to his maps. He was now determined to perform his duties firmly and without negligence. It wouldn't help Lavender, he knew that, but from this point on he would comport himself as a soldier. He would dispose of his good-luck pebble. Swallow it, maybe, or use Lee Strunk's slingshot, or just drop it along the trail. On the march he would impose strict field discipline. He would be careful to send out flank security, to prevent straggling or bunching up, to keep his troops moving at the proper pace and at the proper interval. He would insist on clean weapons. He would confiscate the remainder of Lavender's dope. Later in the day, perhaps, he would call the men together and speak to them plainly. He would accept the blame for what had happened to Ted Lavender. He would be a man about it. He would look them in the eyes, keeping his chin level, and he would issue the new SOPs in a calm, impersonal tone of voice, an officer's voice, leaving no room for argument or discussion. Commencing immediately, he'd tell them, they would no longer abandon equipment along the route of march. They would police up their acts. They would get their shit together, and keep it together, and maintain it neatly and in good working order.

He would not tolerate laxity. He would show strength, distancing himself.   100

Among the men there would be grumbling, of course, and maybe worse, because their days would seem longer and their loads heavier, but Lieutenant Cross reminded himself that his obligation was not to be loved but to lead. He would dispense with love; it was not now a factor. And if anyone quarreled or complained, he would simply tighten his lips and arrange his shoulders in the correct command posture. He might give a curt little nod. Or he might not. He might just shrug and say Carry on, then they would saddle up and form into a column and move out toward the villages of Than Khe.

Flannery O'Connor   1925–1964

A Good Man Is Hard to Find   1955

The grandmother didn't want to go to Florida. She wanted to visit some of her connections in east Tennessee and she was seizing every chance to change Bailey's mind. Bailey was the son she lived with, her only boy. He was sitting on the edge of his chair at the table, bent over the orange sports section of the *Journal*. "Now look here, Bailey," she said, "see here, read this," and she stood with one hand on her thin hip and the other rattling the newspaper at his bald head. "Here this fellow that calls himself The Misfit is aloose from the Federal Pen and headed toward Florida and you read here what it says he did to these people. Just you read it. I wouldn't take my children in any direction with a criminal like that aloose in it. I couldn't answer to my conscience if I did."

Bailey didn't look up from his reading so she wheeled around then and faced the children's mother; a young woman in slacks, whose face was as broad and innocent as a cabbage and was tied around with a green headkerchief that had two points on the top like rabbit's ears. She was sitting on the sofa, feeding the baby his apricots out of a jar. "The children have been to Florida before," the old lady said. "You all ought to take them somewhere else for a change so they would see different parts of the world and be broad. They never have been to east Tennessee."

The children's mother didn't seem to hear her, but the eight-year-old boy, John Wesley, a stocky child with glasses, said, "If you don't want to go to Florida, why dontcha stay at home?" He and the little girl, June Star, were reading the funny papers on the floor.

"She wouldn't stay at home to be queen for a day," June Star said without raising her yellow head.

"Yes, and what would you do if this fellow, The Misfit, caught you?" the grandmother asked.

"I'd smack his face," John Wesley said.

"She wouldn't stay at home for a million bucks," June Star said. "Afraid she'd miss something. She has to go everywhere we go."

"All right, Miss," the grandmother said. "Just remember that the next time you want me to curl your hair."

June Star said her hair was naturally curly.

The next morning the grandmother was the first one in the car, ready to go. She had her big black valise that looked like the head of a hippopotamus in one corner, and underneath it she was hiding a basket with Pitty Sing, the cat, in it. She didn't intend for the cat to be left alone in the house for three days because he would miss her too much and she was afraid he might brush against one of the gas burners and accidentally asphyxiate himself. Her son, Bailey, didn't like to arrive at a motel with a cat.

She sat in the middle of the back seat with John Wesley and June Star on either side of her. Bailey and the children's mother and the baby sat in the front and they left Atlanta at eight forty-five with the mileage on the car at 55890. The grandmother wrote this down because she thought it would be interesting to say how many miles they had been when they got back. It took them twenty minutes to reach the outskirts of the city.

The old lady settled herself comfortably, removing her white cotton gloves and putting them up with her purse on the shelf in front of the back window. The children's mother still had on slacks and still had her head tied up in a green kerchief, but the grandmother had on a navy blue straw sailor hat with a bunch of white violets on the brim and a navy blue dress with a small white dot in the print. Her collar and cuffs were white organdy trimmed with lace and at her neckline she had pinned a purple spray of cloth violets containing a sachet. In case of an accident, anyone seeing her dead on the highway would know at once that she was a lady.

She said she thought it was going to be a good day for driving, neither too hot nor too cold, and she cautioned Bailey that the speed limit was fifty-five miles an hour and that the patrolmen hid themselves behind billboards and small clumps of trees and sped out after you before you had a chance to slow down. She pointed out interesting details of the scenery: Stone Mountain; the blue granite that in some places came up to both sides of the highway; the brilliant red clay banks slightly streaked with purple; and the various crops that made rows of green lace-work on the ground. The trees were full of silver-white sunlights and the meanest of them sparkled. The children were reading comic magazines and their mother had gone back to sleep.

"Let's go through Georgia fast so we won't have to look at it much," John Wesley said.

"If I were a little boy," said the grandmother, "I wouldn't talk about my native state that way. Tennessee has the mountains and Georgia has the hills."

"Tennessee is just a hillbilly dumping ground," John Wesley said, "and Georgia is a lousy state too."

"You said it," June Star said.

"In my time," said the grandmother, folding her thin veined fingers, "children were more respectful of their native states and their parents and everything else. People did right then. Oh look at the cute little pickaninny!" she said and pointed to a Negro child standing in the door of a shack. "Wouldn't that make a picture, now?" she asked and they all turned and looked at the little Negro out of the back window. He waved.

"He didn't have any britches on," June Star said.

"He probably didn't have any," the grandmother explained. "Little niggers in the   20
country don't have things like we do. If I could paint, I'd paint that picture," she said.

The children exchanged comic books.

The grandmother offered to hold the baby and the children's mother passed him over the front seat to her. She set him on her knee and bounced him and told him about the things they were passing. She rolled her eyes and screwed up her mouth and stuck her leathery thin face into his smooth bland one. Occasionally he gave her a faraway smile. They passed a large cotton field with five or six graves fenced in the middle of it, like a small island. "Look at the graveyard!" the grandmother said, pointing it out. "That was the old family burying ground. That belonged to the plantation."

"Where's the plantation?" John Wesley asked.

"Gone With the Wind," said the grandmother. "Ha. Ha."

When the children finished all the comic books they had brought, they   25
opened the lunch and ate it. The grandmother ate a peanut butter sandwich and an olive and would not let the children throw the box and the paper napkins out the window. When there was nothing else to do they played a game by choosing a cloud and making the other two guess what shape it suggested. John Wesley took one the shape of a cow and June Star guessed a cow and John Wesley said, no, an automobile, and June Star said he didn't play fair, and they began to slap each other over the grandmother.

The grandmother said she would tell them a story if they would keep quiet. When she told a story, she rolled her eyes and waved her head and was very dramatic. She said once when she was a maiden lady she had been courted by a Mr. Edgar Atkins Teagarden from Jasper, Georgia. She said he was a very good-looking man and a gentleman and that he brought her a watermelon every Saturday afternoon with his initials cut in it, E.A.T. Well, one Saturday, she said, Mr. Teagarden brought the watermelon and there was nobody at home and he left it on the front porch and returned in his buggy to Jasper, but she never got the watermelon, she said, because a nigger boy ate it when he saw the initials, E.A.T.! This story tickled John Wesley's funny bone and he giggled and giggled but June Star didn't think it was any good. She said she wouldn't marry a man that just brought her a watermelon on Saturday. The grandmother said she would have done well to marry Mr. Teagarden because he was a gentleman and had bought Coca-Cola stock when it first came out and that he had died only a few years ago, a very wealthy man.

They stopped at The Tower for barbecued sandwiches. The Tower was a part-stucco and part-wood filling station and dance hall set in a clearing outside of Timothy. A fat man named Red Sammy Butts ran it and there were signs stuck here and there on the building and for miles up and down the highway saying, TRY RED

SAMMY'S FAMOUS BARBECUE. NONE LIKE FAMOUS RED SAMMY'S! RED SAM! THE FAT BOY WITH THE
HAPPY LAUGH. A VETERAN! RED SAMMY'S YOUR MAN!

Red Sammy was lying on the bare ground outside The Tower with his head
under a truck while a gray monkey about a foot high, chained to a small chinaberry
tree, chattered nearby. The monkey sprang back into the tree and got on the highest limb as soon as he saw the children jump out of the car and run toward him.

Inside, The Tower was a long dark room with a counter at one end and tables
at the other and dancing space in the middle. They all sat down at a broad table
next to the nickelodeon and Red Sam's wife, a tall burnt-brown woman with hair
and eyes lighter than her skin, came and took their order. The children's mother put
a dime in the machine and played "The Tennessee Waltz," and the grandmother
said that tune always made her want to dance. She asked Bailey if he would like to
dance but he only glared at her. He didn't have a naturally sunny disposition like
she did and trips made him nervous. The grandmother's brown eyes were very
bright. She swayed her head from side to side and pretended she was dancing in
her chair. June Star said play something she could tap to so the children's mother
put in another dime and played a fast number and June Star stepped out onto the
dance floor and did her tap routine.

"Ain't she cute?" Red Sam's wife said, leaning over the counter. "Would you   30
like to come be my little girl?"

"No, I certainly wouldn't," June Star said. "I wouldn't live in a broken-down
place like this for a million bucks!" and she ran back to the table.

"Ain't she cute?" the woman repeated, stretching her mouth politely.

"Aren't you ashamed?" hissed the grandmother.

Red Sam came in and told his wife to quit lounging on the counter and hurry
up with these people's order. His khaki trousers reached just to his hip bones and
his stomach hung over them like a sack of meal swaying under his shirt. He came
over and sat down at a table nearby and let out a combination sigh and yodel.
"You can't win," he said. "You can't win," and he wiped his sweating red face off
with a gray handkerchief. "These days you don't know who to trust," he said.
"Ain't that the truth?"

"People are certainly not nice like they used to be," said the grandmother.   35

"Two fellers come in here last week," Red Sammy said, "driving a Chrysler. It
was an old beat-up car but it was a good one and these boys looked all right to
me. Said they worked at the mill and you know I let them fellers charge the gas
they bought? Now why did I do that?"

"Because you're a good man!" the grandmother said at once.

"Yes'm, I suppose so," Red Sam said as if he were struck with this answer.

His wife brought the orders, carrying the five plates all at once without a tray,
two in each hand and one balanced on her arm. "It isn't a soul in this green world
of God's that you can trust," she said. "And I don't count nobody out of that, not
nobody," she repeated, looking at Red Sammy.

"Did you read about that criminal, The Misfit, that's escaped?" asked the   40
grandmother.

"I wouldn't be a bit surprised if he didn't attack this place right here," said the
woman. "If he hears about it being here, I wouldn't be none surprised to see him.
If he hears it's two cent in the cash register, I wouldn't be a tall surprised if he ..."

"That'll do," Red Sam said. "Go bring these people their Co'-Colas," and the
woman went off to get the rest of the order.

"A good man is hard to find," Red Sammy said. "Everything is getting terrible. I remember the day you could go off and leave your screen door unlatched. Not no more."

He and the grandmother discussed better times. The old lady said that in her opinion Europe was entirely to blame for the way things were now. She said the way Europe acted you would think we were made of money and Red Sam said it was no use talking about it, she was exactly right. The children ran outside into the white sunlight and looked at the monkey in the lacy chinaberry tree. He was busy catching fleas on himself and biting each one carefully between his teeth as if it were a delicacy.

They drove off again into the hot afternoon. The grandmother took cat naps   45
and woke up every few minutes with her own snoring. Outside of Toombsboro she woke up and recalled an old plantation that she had visited in this neighborhood once when she was a young lady. She said the house had six white columns across the front and that there was an avenue of oaks leading up to it and two little wooden trellis arbors on either side in front where you sat down with your suitor after a stroll in the garden. She recalled exactly which road to turn off to get to it. She knew that Bailey would not be willing to lose any time looking at an old house, but the more she talked about it, the more she wanted to see it once again and find out if the little twin arbors were still standing. "There was a secret panel in this house," she said craftily, not telling the truth but wishing that she were, "and the story went that all the family silver was hidden in it when Sherman came through but it was never found …"

"Hey!" John Wesley said. "Let's go see it! We'll find it! We'll poke all the woodwork and find it! Who lives there? Where do you turn off at? Hey Pop, can't we turn off there?"

"We never have seen a house with a secret panel!" June Star shrieked. "Let's go to the house with the secret panel! Hey Pop, can't we go see the house with the secret panel!"

"It's not far from here, I know," the grandmother said. "It wouldn't take over twenty minutes."

Bailey was looking straight ahead. His jaw was as rigid as a horseshoe. "No," he said.

The children began to yell and scream that they wanted to see the house with   50
the secret panel. John Wesley kicked the back of the front seat and June Star hung over her mother's shoulder and whined desperately into her ear that they never had any fun even on their vacation, that they could never do what THEY wanted to do. The baby began to scream and John Wesley kicked the back of the seat so hard that his father could feel the blows in his kidneys.

"All right!" he shouted and drew the car to a stop at the side of the road. "Will you all shut up? Will you all just shut up for one second? If you don't shut up, we won't go anywhere."

"It would be very educational for them," the grandmother murmured.

"All right," Bailey said, "but get this. This is the only time we're going to stop for anything like this. This is the one and only time."

"The dirt road that you have to turn down is about a mile back," the grandmother directed. "I marked it when we passed."

"A dirt road," Bailey groaned.   55

After they had turned around and were headed toward the dirt road, the grandmother recalled other points about the house, the beautiful glass over the front doorway and the candle lamp in the hall. John Wesley said that the secret panel was probably in the fireplace.

"You can't go inside this house," Bailey said. "You don't know who lives there."

"While you all talk to the people in front, I'll run around behind and get in a window," John Wesley suggested.

"We'll all stay in the car," his mother said.

They turned onto the dirt road and the car raced roughly along in a swirl of pink dust. The grandmother recalled the times when there were no paved roads and thirty miles was a day's journey. The dirt road was hilly and there were sudden washes in it and sharp curves on dangerous embankments. All at once they would be on a hill, looking down over the blue tops of trees for miles around, then the next minute, they would be in a red depression with the dust-coated trees looking down on them.

"This place had better turn up in a minute," Bailey said, "or I'm going to turn around."

The road looked as if no one had traveled on it in months.

"It's not much farther," the grandmother said and just as she said it, a horrible thought came to her. The thought was so embarrassing that she turned red in the face and her eyes dilated and her feet jumped up, upsetting her valise in the corner. The instant the valise moved, the newspaper top she had over the basket under it rose with a snarl and Pitty Sing, the cat, sprang onto Bailey's shoulder.

The children were thrown to the floor and their mother, clutching the baby, was thrown out the door onto the ground; the old lady was thrown into the front seat. The car turned over once and landed right-side-up in a gulch on the side of the road. Bailey remained in the driver's seat with the cat—gray-striped with a broad white face and an orange nose—clinging to his neck like a caterpillar.

As soon as the children saw they could move their arms and legs, they scrambled out of the car, shouting, "We've had an ACCIDENT!" The grandmother was curled up under the dashboard, hoping she was injured so that Bailey's wrath would not come down on her all at once. The horrible thought she had had before the accident was that the house she had remembered so vividly was not in Georgia but in Tennessee.

Bailey removed the cat from his neck with both hands and flung it out the window against the side of a pine tree. Then he got out of the car and started looking for the children's mother. She was sitting against the side of the red gutted ditch, holding the screaming baby, but she only had a cut down her face and a broken shoulder. "We've had an ACCIDENT!" the children screamed in a frenzy of delight.

"But nobody's killed," June Star said with disappointment as the grandmother limped out of the car, her hat still pinned to her head but the broken front brim standing up at a jaunty angle and the violet spray hanging off the side. They all sat down in the ditch, except the children, to recover from the shock. They were all shaking.

"Maybe a car will come along," said the children's mother hoarsely.

"I believe I have injured an organ," said the grandmother, pressing her side, but no one answered her. Bailey's teeth were clattering. He had on a yellow sport shirt with bright blue parrots designed in it and his face was as yellow as the shirt. The grandmother decided that she would not mention that the house was in Tennessee.

The road was about ten feet above and they could see only the tops of the trees on the other side of it. Behind the ditch they were sitting in there were more woods, tall and dark and deep. In a few minutes they saw a car some distance away on top of a hill, coming slowly as if the occupants were watching them. The grandmother stood up and waved both arms dramatically to attract their attention. The car continued to come on slowly, disappeared around a bend and appeared again, moving even slower, on top of the hill they had gone over. It was a big black battered hearselike automobile. There were three men in it.

It came to a stop over them and for some minutes, the driver looked down with a steady expressionless gaze to where they were sitting, and didn't speak. Then he turned his head and muttered something to the other two and they got out. One was a fat boy in black trousers and a red sweat shirt with a silver stallion embossed on the front of it. He moved around on the right side of them and stood staring, his mouth partly open in a kind of loose grin. The other had on khaki pants and a blue striped coat and a gray hat pulled down very low, hiding most of his face. He came around slowly on the left side. Neither spoke.

The driver got out of the car and stood by the side of it, looking down at them. He was an older man than the other two. His hair was just beginning to gray and he wore silver-rimmed spectacles that gave him a scholarly look. He had a long creased face and didn't have on any shirt or undershirt. He had on blue jeans that were too tight for him and was holding a black hat and a gun. The two boys also had guns.

"We've had an ACCIDENT!" the children screamed.

The grandmother had the peculiar feeling that the bespectacled man was someone she knew. His face was as familiar to her as if she had known him all her life but she could not recall who he was. He moved away from the car and began to come down the embankment, placing his feet carefully so that he wouldn't slip. He had on tan and white shoes and no socks, and his ankles were red and thin. "Good afternoon," he said. "I see you all had you a little spill."

"We turned over twice!" said the grandmother.   75

"Oncet," he corrected. "We seen it happen. Try their car and see will it run, Hiram," he said quietly to the boy with the gray hat.

"What you got that gun for?" John Wesley asked. "Whatcha gonna do with that gun?"

"Lady," the man said to the children's mother, "would you mind calling them children to sit down by you? Children make me nervous. I want all you all to sit down right together there were you're at."

"What are you telling us what to do for?" June Star asked.

Behind them the line of woods gaped like a dark open mouth. "Come here,"   80
said their mother.

"Look here now," Bailey began suddenly, "we're in a predicament! We're in ..."
The grandmother shrieked. She scrambled to her feet and stood staring.

"You're The Misfit!" she said. "I recognized you at once!"

"Yes'm," the man said, smiling slightly as if he were pleased in spite of himself to be known, "but it would have been better for all of you, lady, if you hadn't of reckernized me."

Bailey turned his head sharply and said something to his mother that shocked   85
even the children. The old lady began to cry and The Misfit reddened.

"Lady," he said, "don't you get upset. Sometimes a man says things he don't mean. I don't reckon he meant to talk to you thataway."

"You wouldn't shoot a lady, would you?" the grandmother said and removed a clean handkerchief from her cuff and began to slap at her eyes with it.

The Misfit pointed the toe of his shoe into the ground and made a little hole and then covered it up again. "I would hate to have to," he said.

"Listen," the grandmother almost screamed, "I know you're a good man. You don't look a bit like you have common blood. I know you must have come from nice people!"

"Yes mam," he said, "finest people in the world." When he smiled he showed 90 a row of strong white teeth. "God never made a finer woman than my mother and my daddy's heart was pure gold," he said. The boy with the red sweat shirt had come around behind them and was standing with his gun at his hip. The Misfit squatted down on the ground. "Watch them children, Bobby Lee," he said. "You know they make me nervous." He looked at the six of them huddled together in front of him and he seemed to be embarrassed as if he couldn't think of anything to say. "Ain't a cloud in the sky," he remarked, looking up at it. "Don't see no sun but don't see no cloud neither."

"Yes, it's a beautiful day," said the grandmother. "Listen," she said, "you shouldn't call yourself The Misfit because I know you're a good man at heart. I can just look at you and tell."

"Hush!" Bailey yelled. "Hush! Everybody shut up and let me handle this!" He was squatting in the position of a runner about to spring forward but he didn't move.

"I pre-chate that, lady," The Misfit said and drew a little circle in the ground with the butt of his gun.

"It'll take a half a hour to fix this here car," Hiram called, looking over the raised hood of it.

"Well, first you and Bobby Lee get him and that little boy to step over yonder 95 with you," The Misfit said, pointing to Bailey and John Wesley. "The boys want to ask you something," he said to Bailey. "Would you mind stepping back in them woods there with them?"

"Listen," Bailey began, "we're in a terrible predicament! Nobody realizes what this is," and his voice cracked. His eyes were as blue and intense as the parrots in his shirt and he remained perfectly still.

The grandmother reached up to adjust her hat brim as if she were going to the woods with him but it came off in her hand. She stood staring at it and after a second she let it fall on the ground. Hiram pulled Bailey up by the arm as if he were assisting an old man. John Wesley caught hold of his father's hand and Bobby Lee followed. They went off toward the woods and just as they reached the dark edge, Bailey turned and supporting himself against a gray naked pine trunk, he shouted, "I'll be back in a minute, Mamma, wait on me!"

"Come back this instant!" his mother shrilled but they all disappeared into the woods.

"Bailey Boy!" the grandmother called in a tragic voice but she found she was looking at The Misfit squatting on the ground in front of her. "I just know you're a good man," she said desperately. "You're not a bit common!"

"Nome, I ain't a good man," The Misfit said after a second as if he had consid- 100 ered her statement carefully, "but I ain't the worst in the world neither. My daddy said I was a different breed of dog from my brothers and sisters. 'You know,' Daddy said, 'it's some that can live their whole life out without asking about it and it's others has to know why it is, and this boy is one of the latters. He's going to be into everything!" He put on his black hat and looked up suddenly and then away deep into the woods as if he were embarrassed again. "I'm sorry I don't have on a shirt before you ladies," he said, hunching his shoulders slightly. "We buried our clothes that we had on when we escaped and we're just making do until we can get better. We borrowed these from some folks we met," he explained.

"That's perfectly all right," the grandmother said. "Maybe Bailey has an extra shirt in his suitcase."

"I'll look and see terrectly," The Misfit said.

"Where are they taking him?" the children's mother screamed.

"Daddy was a card himself," The Misfit said. "You couldn't put anything over on him. He never got in trouble with the Authorities though. Just had the knack of handling them."

"You could be honest too if you'd only try," said the grandmother. "Think   105
how wonderful it would be to settle down and live a comfortable life and not have to think about somebody chasing you all the time."

The Misfit kept scratching in the ground with the butt of his gun as if he were thinking about it. "Yes'm, somebody is always after you," he murmured.

The grandmother noticed how thin his shoulder blades were just behind his hat because she was standing up looking down on him. "Do you ever pray?" she asked.

He shook his head. All she saw was the black hat wiggle between his shoulder blades. "Nome," he said.

There was a pistol shot from the woods, followed closely by another. Then silence. The old lady's head jerked around. She could hear the wind move through the tree tops like a long satisfied insuck of breath. "Bailey Boy!" she called.

"I was a gospel singer for a while," The Misfit said. "I been most everything.   110
Been in the arm service, both land and sea, at home and abroad, been twict married, been an undertaker, been with the railroads, plowed Mother Earth, been in a tornado, seen a man burnt alive oncet," and he looked up at the children's mother and the little girl who were sitting close together, their faces white and their eyes glassy; "I even seen a woman flogged," he said.

"Pray, pray," the grandmother began, "pray, pray ..."

"I never was a bad boy that I remember of," The Misfit said in an almost dreamy voice, "but somewheres along the line I done something wrong and got sent to the penitentiary. I was buried alive," and he looked up and held her attention to him by a steady stare.

"That's when you should have started to pray," she said. "What did you do to get sent to the penitentiary that first time?"

"Turn to the right, it was a wall," The Misfit said, looking up again at the cloudless sky. "Turn to the left, it was a wall. Look up it was a ceiling, look down it was a floor. I forget what I done, lady. I set there and set there, trying to remember what it was I done and I ain't recalled it to this day. Oncet in a while, I would think it was coming to me, but it never come."

"Maybe they put you in by mistake," the old lady said vaguely.   115

"Nome," he said. "It wasn't no mistake. They had the papers on me."

"You must have stolen something," she said.

The Misfit sneered slightly. "Nobody had nothing I wanted," he said. "It was a head-doctor at the penitentiary said what I had done was kill my daddy but I known that for a lie. My daddy died in nineteen ought nineteen of the epidemic flu and I never had a thing to do with it. He was buried in the Mount Hopewell Baptist churchyard and you can go there and see for yourself."

"If you would pray," the old lady said, "Jesus would help you."

"That's right," The Misfit said.   120

"Well then, why don't you pray?" she asked trembling with delight suddenly.

"I don't want no hep," he said. "I'm doing all right by myself."

Bobby Lee and Hiram came ambling back from the woods. Bobby Lee was dragging a yellow shirt with bright blue parrots in it.

"Throw me that shirt, Bobby Lee," The Misfit said. The shirt came flying at him and landed on his shoulder and he put it on. The grandmother couldn't name what the shirt reminded her of. "No, lady," The Misfit said while he was buttoning up, "I found out the crime don't matter. You can do one thing or you can do another, kill a man or take a tire off his car, because sooner or later you're going to forget what it was you done and just be punished for it."

The children's mother had begun to make heaving noises as if she couldn't get her breath. "Lady," he asked, "would you and that little girl like to step off yonder with Bobby Lee and Hiram and join your husband?"   125

"Yes, thank you," the mother said faintly. Her left arm dangled helplessly and she was holding the baby, who had gone to sleep, in the other. "Hep that lady up, Hiram," The Misfit said as she struggled to climb out of the ditch, "and Bobby Lee, you hold onto that little girl's hand."

"I don't want to hold hands with him," June Star said. "He reminds me of a pig."

The fat boy blushed and laughed and caught her by the arm and pulled her off into the woods after Hiram and her mother.

Alone with The Misfit, the grandmother found that she had lost her voice. There was not a cloud in the sky nor any sun. There was nothing around her but woods. She wanted to tell him that he must pray. She opened and closed her mouth several times before anything came out. Finally she found herself saying, "Jesus, Jesus," meaning, Jesus will help you, but the way she was saying it, it sounded as if she might be cursing.

"Yes'm," The Misfit said as if he agreed. "Jesus thrown everything off balance. It was the same case with Him as with me except He hadn't committed any crime and they could prove I had committed one because they had the papers on me. Of course," he said, "they never shown me my papers. That's why I sign myself now. I said long ago, you get you a signature and sign everything you do and keep a copy of it. Then you'll know what you done and you can hold up the crime to the punishment and see do they match and in the end you'll have something to prove you ain't been treated right. I call myself The Misfit," he said, "because I can't make what all I done wrong fit what all I gone through in punishment."   130

There was a piercing scream from the woods, followed closely by a pistol report. "Does it seem right to you, lady, that one is punished a heap and another ain't punished at all?"

"Jesus!" the old lady cried. "You've got good blood! I know you wouldn't shoot a lady! I know you come from nice people! Pray! Jesus, you ought not to shoot a lady. I'll give you all the money I've got!"

"Lady," The Misfit said, looking beyond her far into the woods, "there never was a body that give the undertaker a tip."

There were two more pistol reports and the grandmother raised her head like a parched old turkey hen crying for water and called, "Bailey Boy, Bailey Boy!" as if her heart would break.

"Jesus was the only One that ever raised the dead," The Misfit continued, "and He shouldn't have done it. He thrown everything off balance. If He did what He said, then it's nothing for you to do but throw away everything and follow Him, and if He didn't then it's nothing for you to do but enjoy the few minutes you got   135 left the best way you can—by killing somebody or burning down his house or doing some other meanness to him. No pleasure but meanness," he said and his voice had become almost a snarl.

"Maybe He didn't raise the dead," the old lady mumbled, not knowing what she was saying and feeling so dizzy that she sank down in the ditch with her legs twisted under her.

"I wasn't there so I can't say He didn't," The Misfit said. "I wisht I had of been there," he said, hitting the ground with his fist. "It ain't right I wasn't there because if I had of been there I would of known. Listen lady," he said in a high voice, "if I had of been there I would of known and I wouldn't be like I am now." His voice seemed about to crack and the grandmother's head cleared for an instant. She saw the man's face twisted close to her own as if he were going to cry and she murmured, "Why, you're one of my babies. You're one of my own children!" She reached out and touched him on the shoulder. The Misfit sprang back as if a snake had bitten him and shot her three times through the chest. Then he put his gun down on the ground and took off his glasses and began to clean them.

Hiram and Bobby Lee returned from the woods and stood over the ditch, looking down at the grandmother who half sat and half lay in a puddle of blood with her legs crossed under her like a child's and her face smiling up at the cloudless sky.

Without his glasses, The Misfit's eyes were red-rimmed and pale and defenseless-looking. "Take her off and throw her where you thrown the others," he said, picking up the cat that was rubbing itself against his leg.

"She was a talker, wasn't she?" Bobby Lee said, sliding down the ditch with a   140 yodel.

"She would of been a good woman," The Misfit said, "if it had been somebody there to shoot her every minute of her life."

"Some fun!" Bobby Lee said.

"Shut up, Bobby Lee," The Misfit said. "It's no real pleasure in life."

Katherine Anne Porter   1890–1980

The Grave   1945

The grandfather, dead for more than thirty years, had been twice disturbed in his long repose by the constancy and possessiveness of his widow. She removed his bones first to Louisiana and then to Texas as if she had set out to find her own burial place, knowing well she would never return to the places she had left. In Texas she set up a small cemetery in a corner of her first farm, and as the family connection grew, and oddments of relations came over from Kentucky to settle, it contained at last about twenty graves. After the grandmother's death, part of her land was to be sold for the benefit of certain of her children, and the cemetery happened to lie in the part set aside for sale. It was necessary to take up the bodies and bury them again in the family plot in the big new public cemetery, where the grandmother had been buried. At last her husband was to lie beside her for eternity, as she had planned.

The family cemetery had been a pleasant small neglected garden of tangled rose bushes and ragged cedar trees and cypress, the simple flat stones rising out of uncropped sweet-smelling wild grass. The graves were lying open and empty one burning day when Miranda and her brother Paul, who often went together to hunt rabbits and doves, propped their twenty-two Winchester rifles carefully against the rail fence, climbed over and explored among the graves. She was nine years old and he was twelve.

They peered into the pits all shaped alike with such purposeful accuracy, and looking at each other with pleased adventurous eyes, they said in solemn tones: "These were graves!" trying by words to shape a special, suitable emotion in their minds, but they felt nothing except an agreeable thrill of wonder: they were see-ing a new sight, doing something they had not done before. In them both there was also a small disappointment at the entire commonplaceness of the actual spectacle. Even if it had once contained a coffin for years upon years, when the coffin was gone a grave was just a hole in the ground. Miranda leaped into the pit that had held her grandfather's bones. Scratching around aimlessly and pleasur-ably as any young animal, she scooped up a lump of earth and weighed it in her palm. It had a pleasantly sweet, corrupt smell, being mixed with cedar needles and small leaves, and as the crumbs fell apart, she saw a silver dove no larger than a hazel nut, with spread wings and a neat fan-shaped tail. The breast had a deep round hollow in it. Turning it up to the fierce sunlight, she saw that the inside of the hollow was cut in little whorls. She scrambled out, over the pile of loose earth that had fallen back into one end of the grave, calling to Paul that she had found something, he must guess what.... His head appeared smiling over the rim of an-other grave. He waved a closed hand at her. "I've got something too!" They ran to compare treasures, making a game of it, so many guesses each, all wrong, and a final showdown with opened palms. Paul had found a thin wide gold ring carved with intricate flowers and leaves. Miranda was smitten at sight of the ring and wished to have it. Paul seemed more impressed by the dove. They made a trade, with some little bickering. After he had got the dove in his hand, Paul said, "Don't you know what this is? This is a screw head for a *coffin!* ... I'll bet nobody else in the world has one like this!"

Miranda glanced at it without covetousness. She had the gold ring on her thumb; it fitted perfectly. "Maybe we ought to go now," she said, "maybe one of the niggers'll see us and tell somebody." They knew the land had been sold, the ceme-tery was no longer theirs, and they felt like trespassers. They climbed back over the fence, slung their rifles loosely under their arms—they had been shooting at targets with various kinds of firearms since they were seven years old—and set out to look for the rabbits and doves or whatever small game might happen along. On these ex-peditions Miranda always followed at Paul's heels along the path, obeying instruc-tions about handling her gun when going through fences; learning how to stand it up properly so it would not slip and fire unexpectedly; how to wait her time for a shot and not just bang away in the air without looking, spoiling shots for Paul, who really could hit things if given a chance. Now and then, in her excitement at seeing birds whizz up suddenly before her face, or a rabbit leap across her very toes, she lost her head, and almost without sighting she flung her rifle up and pulled the trig-ger. She hardly ever hit any sort of mark. She had no proper sense of hunting at all. Her brother would be often completely disgusted with her. "You don't care whether you get your bird or not," he said. "That's no way to hunt." Miranda could not un-derstand his indignation. She had seen him smash his hat and yell with fury when he had missed his aim. "What I like about shooting," said Miranda, with exasperat-ing inconsequence, "is pulling the trigger and hearing the noise."

"Then, by golly," said Paul, "whyn't you go back to the range and shoot at bulls-eyes?"   5

"I'd just as soon," said Miranda, "only like this, we walk around more."

"Well, you just stay behind and stop spoiling my shots," said Paul, who, when he made a kill, wanted to be certain he had made it. Miranda, who alone brought down a bird once in twenty rounds, always claimed as her own any game they got when they fired at the same moment. It was tiresome and unfair and her brother was sick of it.

"Now, the first dove we see, or the first rabbit, is mine," he told her. "And the next will be yours. Remember that and don't get smarty."

"What about snakes?" asked Miranda idly. "Can I have the first snake?"

Waving her thumb gently and watching her gold ring glitter, Miranda lost inter-est in shooting. She was wearing her summer roughing outfit: dark blue overalls, a light blue shirt, a hired-man's straw hat, and thick brown sandals. Her brother had the same outfit except his was a sober hickory-nut color. Ordinarily Miranda pre-ferred her overalls to any other dress, though it was making rather a scandal in the countryside, for the year was 1903, and in the back country the law of female deco-rum had teeth in it. Her father had been criticized for letting his girls dress like boys and go careering around astride barebacked horses. Big sister Maria, the really in-dependent and fearless one, in spite of her rather affected ways, rode at a dead run with only a rope knotted around her horse's nose. It was said the motherless fam-ily was running down, with the Grandmother no longer there to hold it together. It was known that she had discriminated against her son Harry in her will, and that he was in straits about money. Some of his neighbors reflected with vicious satisfac-tion that now he would probably not be so stiffnecked, nor have any more high-stepping horses either. Miranda knew this, though she could not say how. She had met along the road old women of the kind who smoked corn-cob pipes, who had treated her grandmother with most sincere respect. They slanted their gummy old eyes side-ways at the granddaughter and said, "Ain't you ashamed of yoself, Missy? It's aginst the Scriptures to dress like that. Whut yo Pappy thinkin about?" Miranda, with her powerful social sense, which was like a fine set of antennae radiating from every pore of her skin, would feel ashamed because she knew well it was rude and ill-bred to shock anybody, even bad-tempered old crones, though she had faith in her father's judgment and was perfectly comfortable in the clothes. Her father had said, "They're just what you need, and they'll save your dresses for school...." This sounded quite simple and natural to her. She had been brought up in rigorous economy. Wastefulness was vulgar. It was also a sin. These were truths; she had heard them repeated many times and never once disputed.

Now the ring, shining with the serene purity of fine gold on her rather grubby thumb, turned her feelings against her overalls and sockless feet, toes sticking through the thick brown leather straps. She wanted to go back to the farmhouse, take a good cold bath, dust herself with plenty of Maria's violet talcum powder—provided Maria was not present to object, of course—put on the thinnest, most be-coming dress she owned, with a big sash, and sit in a wicker chair under the trees.... These things were not all she wanted, of course; she had vague stirrings of desire for luxury and a grand way of living which could not take precise form in her imagination but were founded on family legend of past wealth and leisure. These immediate comforts were what she could have, and she wanted them at once. She lagged rather far behind Paul, and once she thought of just turning back without a word and going home. She stopped, thinking that Paul would never do that to her, and so she would have to tell him. When a rabbit leaped, she let Paul have it without dispute. He killed it with one shot.

When she came up with him, he was already kneeling, examining the wound, the rabbit trailing from his hands, "Right through the head," he said complacently, as if he had aimed for it. He took out his sharp, competent bowie knife and started to skin the body. He did it very cleanly and quickly. Uncle Jimbilly knew how to prepare the skins so that Miranda always had fur coats for her dolls, for though she never cared much for her dolls she liked seeing them in fur coats. The children knelt facing each other over the dead animal. Miranda watched admiringly while her brother stripped the skin away as if he were taking off a glove. The flayed flesh emerged dark scarlet, sleek, firm; Miranda with thumb and finger felt the long fine muscles with the silvery flat strips binding them to the joints. Brother lifted the oddly bloated belly. "Look," he said, in a low amazed voice. "It was going to have young ones."

Very carefully he slit the thin flesh from the center ribs to the flanks, and a scarlet bag appeared. He slit again and pulled the bag open, and there lay a bundle of tiny rabbits, each wrapped in a thin scarlet veil. The brother pulled these off and there they were, dark gray, their sleek wet down lying in minute even ripples, like a baby's head just washed, their unbelievably small delicate ears folded close, their little blind faces almost featureless.

Miranda said, "Oh, I want to *see*," under her breath. She looked and looked—excited but not frightened, for she was accustomed to the sight of animals killed in hunting—filled with pity and astonishment and a kind of shocked delight in the wonderful little creatures for their own sakes, they were so pretty. She touched one of them ever so carefully, "Ah, there's blood running over them," she said and began to tremble without knowing why. Yet she wanted most deeply to see and to know. Having seen, she felt at once as if she had known all along. The very memory of her former ignorance faded, she had always known just this. No one had ever told her anything outright, she had been rather unobservant of the animal life around her because she was accustomed to animals. They seemed simply disorderly and unaccountably rude in their habits, but altogether natural and not very interesting. Her brother had spoken as if he had known about everything all along. He may have seen all this before. He had never said a word to her, but she knew now a part at least of what he knew. She understood a little of the secret formless intuitions in her own mind and body, which had been clearing up, taking form, so gradually and so steadily she had not realized that she was learning what she had to know. Paul said cautiously, as if he were talking about something forbidden: "They were just about ready to be born." His voice dropped on the last word. "I know," said Miranda, "like kittens. I know, like babies." She was quietly and terribly agitated, standing again with her rifle under her arm, looking down at the bloody heap. "I don't want the skin," she said, "I won't have it." Paul buried the young rabbits again in their mother's body, wrapped the skin around her, carried her to a clump of sage bushes, and hid her away. He came out again at once and said to Miranda, with an eager friendliness, a confidential tone quite unusual in him, as if her were taking her into an important secret on equal terms: "Listen now. Now you listen to me, and don't ever forget. Don't you ever tell a living soul that you saw this. Don't tell a soul. Don't tell Dad because I'll get into trouble. He'll say I'm leading you into things you ought not to do. He's always saying that. So now don't go and forget and blab out something the way you're always doing.... Now, that's a secret. Don't you tell."

Miranda never told, she did not even wish to tell anybody. She thought about the whole worrisome affair with confused unhappiness for a few days. Then it sank quietly into her mind and was heaped over by accumulated thousands of impressions, for nearly twenty years. One day she was picking her path among the puddles and crushed refuse of a market street in a strange city of a strange country, when without warning, plain and clear in its true colors as if she looked through a frame upon a scene that had not stirred nor changed since the moment it happened, the episode of that far-off day leaped from its burial place before her mind's eye. She was so reasonably horrified she halted suddenly staring, the scene before her eyes dimmed by the vision back of them. An Indian vendor had held up before her a tray of dyed sugar sweets, in the shapes of all kinds of small creatures: birds, baby chicks, baby rabbits, lambs, baby pigs. They were in gay colors and smelled of vanilla, maybe.... It was a very hot day and the smell in the market, with its piles of raw flesh and wilting flowers, was like the mingled sweetness and corruption she had smelled that other day in the empty cemetery at home: the day she had remembered always until now vaguely as the time she and her brother had found treasure in the opened graves. Instantly upon this thought the dreadful vision faded, and she saw clearly her brother, whose childhood face she had forgotten, standing again in the blazing sunshine, again twelve years old, a pleased sober smile in his eyes, turning the silver dove over and over in his hands.

Alice Walker   b. 1944

To Hell with Dying   1967

"To hell with dying," my father would say. "These children want Mr. Sweet!"

Mr. Sweet was a diabetic and an alcoholic and a guitar player and lived down the road from us on a neglected cotton farm. My older brothers and sisters got the most benefit from Mr. Sweet, for when they were growing up he had quite a few years ahead of him and so was capable of being called back from the brink of death any number of times—whenever the voice of my father reached him as he lay expiring. "To hell with dying, man," my father would say, pushing his wife away from the bedside (in tears although she knew the death was not necessarily the last one unless Mr. Sweet really wanted it to be). "These children want Mr. Sweet!" And they did want him, for at a signal from Father they would come crowding around the bed and throw themselves on the covers, and whoever was the smallest at the time would kiss him all over his wrinkled brown face and tickle him so that he would laugh all down in his stomach, and his mustache, which was long and sort of straggly, would shake like Spanish moss and was also that color.

Mr. Sweet had been ambitious as a boy, wanted to be a doctor or lawyer or sailor, only to find that black men fare better if they are not. Since he could become none of these things he turned to fishing as his only earnest career and playing the guitar as his only claim to doing anything extraordinarily well. His son, the only one that he and his wife, Miss Mary, had, was shiftless as the day is long and spent money as if he were trying to see the bottom of the mint, which Mr. Sweet would tell him was the clean brown palm of his hand. Miss Mary loved her "baby," however, and worked hard to get him the "li'l necessaries" of life, which turned out mostly to be women.

Mr. Sweet was a tall, thinnish man with thick kinky hair going dead white. He was dark brown, his eyes were squinty and sort of bluish, and he chewed Brown Mule tobacco. He was constantly on the verge of being blind drunk, for he brewed his own liquor and was not in the least a stingy sort of man, and was always very melancholy and sad, though frequently when he was "feelin' good" he'd dance around the yard with us, usually keeling over just as my mother came to see what the commotion was.

Toward all of us children he was very kind, and had the grace to be shy with us, which is unusual in grown-ups. He had great respect for my mother for she never held his drunkenness against him and would let us play with him even when he was about to fall in the fireplace from drink. Although Mr. Sweet would sometimes lose complete or nearly complete control of his head and neck so that he would loll in his chair, his mind remained strangely acute and his speech not too affected. His ability to be drunk and sober at the same time made him an ideal playmate, for he was as weak as we were and we could usually best him in wrestling, all the while keeping a fairly coherent conversation going.

We never felt anything of Mr. Sweet's age when we played with him. We loved his wrinkles and would draw some on our brows to be like him, and his white hair was my special treasure and he knew it and would never come to visit us just after he had had his hair cut off at the barbershop. Once he came to our house for something, probably to see my father about fertilizer for his crops because, although he never paid the slightest attention to his crops, he liked to know what things would be best to use on them if he ever did. Anyhow, he had not come with his hair since he had just had it shaved off at the barbershop. He wore a huge straw hat to keep off the sun and also to keep his head away from me. But as soon as I saw him I ran up and demanded that he take me up and kiss me with his funny beard which smelled so strongly of tobacco. Looking forward to burying my small fingers into his woolly hair I threw away his hat only to find he had done something to his hair, that it was no longer there! I let out a squall which made my mother think that Mr. Sweet had finally dropped me in the well or something and from that day I've been wary of men in hats. However, not long after, Mr. Sweet showed up with his hair grown out and just as white and kinky and impenetrable as it ever was.

Mr. Sweet used to call me his princess, and I believed it. He made me feel pretty at five and six, and simply outrageously devastating at the blazing age of eight and a half. When he came to our house with his guitar the whole family would stop whatever they were doing to sit around him and listen to him play. He liked to play "Sweet Georgia Brown," that was what he called me sometimes, and also he liked to play "Caldonia" and all sorts of sweet, sad, wonderful songs which he sometimes made up. It was from one of these songs that I heard that he had had to marry Miss Mary when he had in fact loved somebody else (now living in Chica-go, or De-stroy, Michigan). He was not sure that Joe Lee, her "baby," was also his baby. Sometimes he would cry and that was an indication that he was about to die again. And so we would all get prepared, for we were sure to be called upon.

I was seven the first time I remember actually participating in one of Mr. Sweet's "revivals"—my parents told me I had participated before, I had been the one chosen to kiss him and tickle him long before I knew the rite of Mr. Sweet's rehabilitation. He had come to our house, it was a few years after his wife's death, and was very sad, and also, typically, very drunk. He sat on the floor next to me and my older brother, the rest of the children were grown up and lived elsewhere, and began to play his guitar and cry. I held his woolly head in my arms and wished I could have been old enough to have been the woman he loved so much and that I had not been lost years and years ago.

When he was leaving, my mother said to us that we'd better sleep light that night for we'd probably have to go over to Mr. Sweet's before daylight. And we did. For soon after we had gone to bed one of the neighbors knocked on our door and called my father and said that Mr. Sweet was sinking fast and if he wanted to get in a word before the crossover he'd better shake a leg and get over to Mr. Sweet's house. All the neighbors knew to come to our house if something was wrong with Mr. Sweet, but they did not know how we always managed to make him well, or at least stop him from dying, when he was so often near death. As soon as we heard the cry we got up, by brother and I and my mother and father, and put on our clothes. We hurried out of the house and down the road for we were always afraid that we might someday be too late and Mr. Sweet would get tired of dallying.

When we got to the house, a very poor shack really, we found the front room   10
full of neighbors and relatives and someone met us at the door and said it was all very sad that old Mr. Sweet Little (for Little was his family name, although we mostly ignored it) was about to kick the bucket. My parents were advised not to take my brother and me into the "death room," seeing we were so young and all, but we were so much more accustomed to the death room than he that we ignored him and dashed in without giving his warning a second thought. I was almost in tears, for these deaths upset me fearfully, and the thought of how much depended on me and my brother (who was such a ham most of the time) made me very nervous.

The doctor was bending over the bed and turned back to tell us for at least the tenth time in the history of my family that, alas, old Mr. Sweet Little was dying and that the children had best not see the face of implacable death (I didn't know what "implacable" was, but whatever it was, Mr. Sweet was not!). My father pushed him rather abruptly out of the way saying, as he always did and very loudly for he was saying it to Mr. Sweet, "To hell with dying, man, these children want Mr. Sweet"—which was my cue to throw myself upon the bed and kiss Mr. Sweet all around the whiskers and under the eyes and around the collar of his nightshirt where he smelled so strongly of all sorts of things, mostly liniment.

I was very good at bringing him around, for as soon as I saw that he was struggling to open his eyes I knew he was going to be all right, and so could finish my revival sure of success. As soon as his eyes were open he would begin to smile and that way I knew that I had surely won. Once, though, I got a tremendous scare, for he could not open his eyes and later I learned that he had had a stroke and that one side of his face was stiff and hard to get into motion. When he began to smile I could tickle him in earnest because I was sure that nothing would get in the way of his laughter, although once he began to cough so hard that he almost threw me off his stomach, but that was when I was very small, little more than a baby, and my bushy hair had gotten in his nose.

When we were sure he would listen to us we would ask him why he was in bed and when he was coming to see us again and could we play his guitar, which more than likely would be leaning against the bed. His eyes would get all misty and he would sometimes cry out loud, but we never let it embarrass us, for he knew that we loved him and that we sometimes cried too for no reason. My parents would leave the room to just the three of us; Mr. Sweet, by that time, would be propped up in bed with a number of pillows behind his head and with me sitting and lying on his shoulder and along his chest. Even when he had trouble breathing he would not ask me to get down. Looking into my eyes he would shake his white head and run a scratchy old finger all around my hairline, which was rather low down, nearly to my eyebrows, and made some people say I looked like a baby monkey.

My brother was very generous in all this, he let me do all the revivaling—he had done it for years before I was born and so was glad to be able to pass it on to someone new. What he would do while I talked to Mr. Sweet was pretend to play the guitar, in fact pretend that he was a young version of Mr. Sweet, and it always made Mr. Sweet glad to think that someone wanted to be like him—of course, we did not know this then, we played the thing by ear, and whatever he seemed to like, we did. We were desperately afraid that he was just going to take off one day and leave us.

It did not occur to us that we were doing anything special; we had not learned that death was final when it did come. We thought nothing of triumphing over it so many times, and in fact became a trifle contemptuous of people who let themselves be carried away. It did not occur to us that if our father had been dying we could not have stopped it, that Mr. Sweet was the only person over whom we had power.   15

When Mr. Sweet was in his eighties I was studying in the university many miles from home. I saw him whenever I went home, but he was never on the verge of dying that I could tell and I began to feel that my anxiety for his health and psychological well-being was unnecessary. By this time he not only had a mustache but a long flowing snow-white beard, which I loved and combed and braided for hours. He was very peaceful, fragile, gentle, and the only jarring note about him was his old steel guitar, which he still played in the old sad, sweet, down-home blues way.

On Mr. Sweet's ninetieth birthday I was finishing my doctorate in Massachusetts and had been making arrangements to go home for several weeks' rest. That morning I got a telegram telling me that Mr. Sweet was dying again and could I please drop everything and come home. Of course I could. My dissertation could wait and my teachers would understand when I explained to them when I got back. I ran to the phone, called the airport, and within four hours I was speeding along the dusty road to Mr. Sweet's.

The house was more dilapidated than when I was last there, barely a shack, but it was overgrown with yellow roses which my family had planted many years ago. The air was heavy and sweet and very peaceful. I felt strange walking through the gate and up the old rickety steps. But the strangeness left me as I caught sight of the long white beard I loved so well flowing down the thin body over the familiar quilt coverlet. Mr. Sweet!

His eyes were closed tight and his hands, crossed over his stomach, were thin and delicate, no longer scratchy. I remembered how always before I had run and jumped up on him just anywhere; now I knew he would not be able to support my weight. I looked around at my parents, and was surprised to see that my father and mother also looked old and frail. My father, his own hair very gray, leaned over the quietly sleeping old man, who, incidentally, smelled still of wine and to-bacco, and said, as he'd done so many times, "To hell with dying, man! My daughter is home to see Mr. Sweet!" My brother had not been able to come as he was in the war in Asia. I bent down and gently stroked the closed eyes and gradually they began to open. The closed, wine-stained lips twitched a little, then parted in a warm, slightly embarrassed smile. Mr. Sweet could see me and he recognized me and his eyes looked very spry and twinkly for a moment. I put my head down on the pillow next to his and we just looked at each other for a long time. Then he began to trace my peculiar hairline with a thin, smooth finger. I closed my eyes when his finger halted above my ear (he used to rejoice at the dirt in my ears when I was little), his hand stayed cupped around my cheek. When I opened my eyes, sure that I had reached him in time, his were closed.

Even at twenty-four how could I believe that I had failed? that Mr. Sweet was   20
really gone? He had never gone before. But when I looked at my parents I saw that they were holding back tears. They had loved him dearly. He was like a piece of rare and delicate china which was always being saved from breaking and which finally fell. I looked long at the old face, the wrinkled forehead, the red lips, the hands that still reached out to me. Soon I felt my father pushing something cool into my hands. It was Mr. Sweet's guitar. He had asked them months before to give it to me; he had known that even if I came next time he would not be able to respond in the old way. He did not want me to feel that my trip had been for nothing.

The old guitar! I plucked the strings, hummed "Sweet Georgia Brown." The magic of Mr. Sweet lingered still in the cool steel box. Through the window I could catch the fragrant delicate scent of tender yellow roses. The man on the high old-fashioned bed with the quilt coverlet and the flowing white beard had been my first love.

Eudora Welty   b. 1909

A Worn Path   *1941*

It was December—a bright frozen day in the early morning. Far out in the country there was an old Negro woman with her head tied in a red rag, coming along a path through the pinewoods. Her name was Phoenix Jackson. She was very old and small and she walked slowly in the dark pine shadows, moving a little from side to side in her steps, with the balanced heaviness and lightness of a pendulum in a grandfather clock. She carried a thin, small cane made from an umbrella, and with this she kept tapping the frozen earth in front of her. This made a grave and persistent noise in the still air, that seemed meditative like the chirping of a solitary little bird.

She wore a dark striped dress reaching down to her shoe tops, and an equally long apron of bleached sugar sacks, with a full pocket: all neat and tidy, but every time she took a step she might have fallen over her shoelaces, which dragged from her unlaced shoes. She looked straight ahead. Her eyes were blue with age. Her skin had a pattern all its own of numberless branching wrinkles and as though a whole little tree stood in the middle of her forehead, but a golden color ran underneath, and the two knobs of her cheeks were illumined by a yellow burning under the dark. Under the red rag her hair came down on her neck in the frailest of ringlets, still black, and with an odor like copper.

Now and then there was a quivering in the thicket. Old Phoenix said, "Out of my way, all you foxes, owls, beetles, jack rabbits, coons, and wild animals! ... Keep out from under these feet, little bobwhites.... Keep the big wild hogs out of my path. Don't let none of those come running my direction. I got a long way."

Under her small black-freckled hand her cane, limber as a buggy whip, would switch at the brush as if to rouse up any hiding things.

On she went. The woods were deep and still. The sun made the pine needles almost too bright to look at, up where the wind rocked. The cones dropped as light as feathers. Down in the hollow was the mourning dove—it was not too late for him.

The path ran up a hill. "Seem like there is chains about my feet, time I get this far," she said, in the voice of argument old people keep to use with themselves. "Something always take a hold of me on this hill—pleads I should stay."

After she got to the top she turned and gave a full, severe look behind her where she had come. "Up through pines," she said at length. "Now down through oaks."

Her eyes opened their widest, and she started down gently. But before she got to the bottom of the hill a bush caught her dress.

Her fingers were busy and intent, but her skirts were full and long, so that before she could pull them free in one place they were caught in another. It was not possible to allow the dress to tear. "I in the thorny bush," she said. "Thorns, you doing your appointed work. Never want to let folks pass, no air. Old eyes thought you was a pretty little *green* bush."

Finally, trembling all over, she stood free, and after a moment dared to stoop for her cane.

"Sun so high!" she cried, leaning back and looking, while the thick tears went over her eyes. "The time getting all gone here."

At the foot of this hill was a place where a log was laid across the creek. "Now comes the trial," said Phoenix.

Putting her right foot out, she mounted the log and shut her eyes. Lifting her skirt, leveling her cane fiercely before her, like a festival figure in some parade, she began to march across. Then she opened her eyes and she was safe on the other side.

"I wasn't as old as I thought," she said.

But she sat down to rest. She spread her skirts on the bank around her and folded her hands over her knees. Up above her was a tree in a pearly cloud of mistletoe. She did not dare to close her eyes, and when a little boy brought her a plate with a slice of marble-cake on it she spoke to him. "That would be acceptable," she said. But when she went to take it there was just her own hand in the air.

So she left that tree, and had to go through a barbed-wire fence. There she had to creep and crawl, spreading her knees and stretching her fingers like a baby trying to climb the steps. But she talked loudly to herself: she could not let her dress be torn now, so late in the day, and she could not pay for having her arm or her leg sawed off if she got caught fast where she was.

At last she was safe through the fence and risen up out in the clearing. Big dead trees, like black men with one arm, were standing in the purple stalks of the withered cotton field. There sat a buzzard.

"Who you watching?"

In the furrow she made her way along.

"Glad this not the season for bulls," she said, looking sideways, "and the good Lord made his snakes to curl up and sleep in the winter. A pleasure I don't see no two-headed snake coming around that tree, where it come once. It took a while to get by him, back in the summer."

She passed through the old cotton and went into a field of dead corn. It whispered and shook and was taller than her head. "Through the maze now," she said, for there was no path.

Then there was something tall, black, and skinny there, moving before her.

At first she took it for a man. It could have been a man dancing in the field. But she stood still and listened, and it did not make a sound. It was as silent as a ghost.

"Ghost," she said sharply, "who be you the ghost of? For I have heard of nary death close by."

But there was no answer—only the ragged dancing in the wind.

She shut her eyes, reached out her hand, and touched a sleeve. She found a   25
coat and inside that an emptiness, cold as ice.

"You scarecrow," she said. Her face lighted. "I ought to be shut up for good," she said with laughter. "My senses is gone. I too old. I the oldest people I ever know. Dance, old scarecrow," she said, "while I dancing with you."

She kicked her foot over the furrow, and with mouth drawn down, shook her head once or twice in a little strutting way. Some husks blew down and whirled in streamers about her skirts.

Then she went on, parting her way from side to side with the cane, through the whispering field. At last she came to the end, to a wagon track where the silver grass blew between the red ruts. The quail were walking around like pullets, seeming all dainty and unseen.

"Walk pretty," she said. "This the easy place. This the easy going."

She followed the track, swaying through the quiet bare fields, through the lit-   30
tle strings of trees silver in their dead leaves, past cabins silver from weather, with the doors and windows boarded shut, all like old women under a spell sitting there. "I walking in their sleep," she said, nodding her head vigorously.

In a ravine she went where a spring was silently flowing through a hollow log. Old Phoenix bent and drank. "Sweet-gum makes the water sweet," she said, and drank more. "Nobody know who made this well, for it was here when I was born."

The track crossed a swampy part where the moss hung as white as lace from every limb. "Sleep on, alligators, and blow your bubbles." Then the track went into the road.

Deep, deep the road went down between the high green-colored banks. Overhead the live-oaks met, and it was as dark as a cave.

A black dog with a lolling tongue came up out of the weeds by the ditch. She was meditating, and not ready, and when he came at her she only hit him a little with her cane. Over she went in the ditch, like a little puff of milkweed.

Down there, her senses drifted away. A dream visited her, and she reached   35
her hand up, but nothing reached down and gave her a pull. So she lay there and presently went to talking. "Old woman," she said to herself, "that black dog come up out of the weeds to stall you off, and now there he sitting on his fine tail, smiling at you."

A white man finally came along and found her—a hunter, a young man, with his dog on a chain.

"Well, Granny!" he laughed. "What are you doing there?"

"Lying on my back like a June-bug waiting to be turned over, mister," she said, reaching up her hand.

He lifted her up, gave her a swing in the air, and set her down. "Anything broken, Granny?"

"No sir, them old dead weeds is springy enough," said Phoenix, when she had   40
got her breath. "I thank you for your trouble."

"Where do you live, Granny?" he asked, while the two dogs were growling at each other.

"Away back yonder, sir, behind the ridge. You can't even see it from here."

"On your way home?"

"No sir, going to town."

"Why, that's too far! That's as far as I walk when I come out myself, and I get something for my trouble." He patted the stuffed bag he carried, and there hung down a little closed claw. It was one of the bobwhites, with its beak hooked bitterly to show it was dead. "Now you go on home, Granny!"

"I bound to go to town, Mister," said Phoenix. "The time come around."

He gave another laugh, filling the whole landscape. "I know you old colored people! Wouldn't miss going to town to see Santa Claus!"

But something held old Phoenix very still. The deep lines in her face went into a fierce and different radiation. Without warning, she had seen with her own eyes a flashing nickel fall out of the man's pocket onto the ground.

"How old are you, Granny?" he was saying.

"There is no telling, mister," she said, "no telling."

Then she gave a little cry and clapped her hands and said, "Git on away from here, dog! Look! Look at that dog!" She laughed as if in admiration. "He ain't scared of nobody. He a big black dog." She whispered, "Sic him!"

"Watch me get rid of that cur," said the man. "Sic him, Pete! Sic him!"

Phoenix heard the dogs fighting, and heard the man running and throwing sticks. She even heard a gunshot. But she was slowly bending forward by that time, further and further forward, the lids stretched down over her eyes, as if she were doing this in her sleep. Her chin was lowered almost to her knees. The yellow palm of her hand came out from the fold of her apron. Her fingers slid down and along the ground under the piece of money with the grace and care they would have in lifting an egg from under a setting hen. Then she slowly straightened up, she stood erect, and the nickel was in her apron pocket. A bird flew by. Her lips moved. "God watching me the whole time. I come to stealing."

The man came back, and his own dog panted about them. "Well, I scared him off that time," he said, and then he laughed and lifted his gun and pointed it at Phoenix.

She stood straight and faced him.

"Doesn't the gun scare you?" he said, still pointing it.

"No, sir, I seen plenty go off closer by, in my day, and for less than what I done," she said, holding utterly still.

He smiled, and shouldered the gun. "Well, Granny," he said, "you must be a hundred years old, and scared of nothing. I'd give you a dime if I had any money with me. But you take my advice and stay home, and nothing will happen to you."

"I bound to go on my way, mister," said Phoenix. She inclined her head in the red rag. Then they went in different directions, but she could hear the gun shooting again and again over the hill.

She walked on. The shadows hung from the oak trees to the road like curtains. Then she smelled wood-smoke, and smelled the river, and she saw a steeple and the cabins on their steep steps. Dozens of little black children whirled around her. There ahead was Natchez shining. Bells were ringing. She walked on.

In the paved city it was Christmas time. There were red and green electric lights strung and crisscrossed everywhere, and all turned on in the daytime. Old Phoenix would have been lost if she had not distrusted her eyesight and depended on her feet to know where to take her.

She paused quietly on the sidewalk where people were passing by. A lady came along in the crowd, carrying an armful of red-, green-, and silver-wrapped presents; she gave off perfume like the red roses in hot summer, and Phoenix stopped her.

"Please, missy, will you lace up my shoe?" She held up her foot.

"What do you want, Grandma?"

"See my shoe," said Phoenix. "Do all right for out in the country, but wouldn't   65
look right to go in a big building."

"Stand still then, Grandma," said the lady. She put her packages down on the sidewalk beside her and laced and tied both shoes tightly.

"Can't lace 'em with a cane," said Phoenix. "Thank you, missy. I doesn't mind asking a nice lady to tie up my shoe, when I gets out on the street."

Moving slowly and from side to side, she went into the big building, and into a tower of steps, where she walked up and around and around until her feet knew to stop.

She entered a door, and there she saw nailed up on the wall the document that had been stamped with the gold seal and framed in the gold frame, which matched the dream that was hung in her head.

"Here I be," she said. The was a fixed and ceremonial stiffness over her body.   70

"A charity case, I suppose," said an attendant who sat at the desk before her.

But Phoenix only looked above her head. There was sweat on her face, the wrinkles in her skin shone like a bright net.

"Speak up, Grandma," the woman said. "What's your name? We must have your history, you know. Have you been here before? What seems to be the trouble with you?

Old Phoenix only gave a twitch to her face as if a fly were bothering her.

"Are you deaf?" cried the attendant.   75

But then the nurse came in.

"Oh, that's just old Aunt Phoenix," she said. "She doesn't come for herself—she has a little grandson. She makes these trips just as regular as clockwork. She lives away back off the Old Natchez Trace." She bent down. "Well, Aunt Phoenix, why don't you just take a seat? We won't keep you standing after your long trip." She pointed.

The old woman sat down, bolt upright in the chair.

"Now, how is the boy?" asked the nurse.

Old Phoenix did not speak.   80

"I said, how is the boy?"

But Phoenix only waited and stared straight ahead, her face very solemn and withdrawn into rigidity.

"Is his throat any better?" asked the nurse. "Aunt Phoenix, don't you hear me? Is your grandson's throat any better since the last time you came for the medicine?"

With her hands on her knees, the old woman waited, silent, erect and motionless, just as if she were in armor.

"You mustn't take up our time this way, Aunt Phoenix," the nurse said. "Tell   85
us quickly about your grandson, and get it over. He isn't dead, is he?"

At last there came a flicker and then a flame of comprehension across her face, and she spoke.

"My grandson. It was my memory had left me. There I sat and forgot why I made my long trip."

"Forgot?" The nurse frowned. "After you came so far?"

Then Phoenix was like an old woman begging a dignified forgiveness for waking up frightened in the night. "I never did go to school, I was too old at the

Surrender," she said in a soft voice. "I'm an old woman without an education. It was my memory fail me. My little grandson, he is just the same, and I forgot it in the coming."

"Throat never heals, does it?" said the nurse, speaking in a loud, sure voice to old Phoenix. By now she had a card with something written on it, a little list. "Yes. Swallowed lye. When was it?—January—two, three years ago—?"

Phoenix spoke unasked now. "No, missy, he is not dead, he just the same. Every little while his throat begin to close up again, and he not able to swallow. He not get his breath. He not able to help himself. So the time come around, and I go on another trip for the soothing medicine."

"All right. The doctor said as long as you came to get it, you could have it," said the nurse. "But it's an obstinate case."

"My little grandson, he sit up there in the house all wrapped up, waiting by himself," Phoenix went on. "We is the only two left in the world. He suffer and it don't seem to put him back at all. He got a sweet look. He going to last. He wear a little patch quilt and peep out holding his mouth open like a little bird. I remembers so plain now. I not going to forget him again, no, the whole enduring time. I could tell him from all the others in creation."

"All right." The nurse was trying to hush her now. She brought her a bottle of medicine. "Charity," she said, making a check mark in a book.

Old Phoenix held the bottle close to her eyes, and then carefully put it into her pocket.

"I thank you," she said.

"It's Christmas time, Grandma," said the attendant. "Could I give you a few pennies out of my purse?"

"Five pennies is a nickel," said Phoenix stiffly.

"Here's a nickel," said the attendant.

Phoenix rose carefully and held out her hand. She received the nickel and then fished the other nickel out of her pocket and laid it beside the new one. She stared at her palm closely, with her head on one side.

Then she gave a tap with her cane on the floor.

"This is what come to me to do," she said. "I going to the store and buy my child a little windmill they sells, made out of paper. He going to find it hard to believe there such a thing in the world. I'll march myself back where he waiting, holding it straight up in this hand."

She lifted her free hand, gave a little nod, turned around, and walked out of the doctor's office. Then her slow step began on the stairs, going down.

Richard Wright   1908–1960

The Man Who Was Almost a Man   *1940*

Dave struck out across the fields, looking homeward through paling light. Whuts the usa talkin wid em niggers in the field? Anyhow, his mother was putting supper on the table. Them niggers can't understand *nothing*. One of these days he was going to get a gun and practice shooting, then they can't talk to him as though he were a little boy. He slowed, looking at the ground. Shucks, Ah ain scareda them even ef they are biggern me! Aw, Ah know whut Ahma do. . . . Ahm going by ol Joe's sto n git that Sears Roebuck catlog n look at them guns. Mabbe Ma will

lemme buy one when she gits mah pay from ol man Hawkins. Ahma beg her t
gimme some money. Ahm ol enough to hava gun. Ahm seventeen. Almost a man.
He strode, feeling his long, loose-jointed limbs. Shucks, a man oughta hava little
gun aftah he done worked hard all day. . . .'

He came in sight of Joe's store. A yellow lantern glowed on the front porch.
He mounted steps and went through the screen door, hearing it bang behind him.
There was a strong smell of coal oil and mackerel fish. He felt very confident until
he saw fat Joe walk in through the rear door, then his courage began to ooze.

'Howdy, Dave! Whutcha want?'

'How yuh, Mistah Joe? Aw, Ah don wanna buy nothing. Ah jus wanted t see ef
yuhd lemme look at tha ol catlog erwhile.'

'Sure! You wanna see it here?'   5

'Nawsuh. Ah wats t take it home wid me. Ahll bring it back termorrow when
Ah come in from the fiels.'

'You plannin on buyin something?'

'Yessuh.'

'Your ma letting you have your own money now?'

'Shucks. Mistah Joe, Ahm gittin t be a man like anybody else!'   10

Joe laughed and wiped his greasy white face with a red bandanna.

'Whut you plannin on buyin?'

Dave looked at the floor, scratched his head, scratched his thigh, and smiled.
Then he looked up shyly.

'Ah'll tell yuh, Mistah Joe, ef yuh promise yuh won't tell.'

'I promise.'   15

'Waal, Ahma buy a gun.'

'A gun? Whut you want with a gun?'

'Ah wanna keep it.'

'You ain't nothing but a boy. You don't need a gun.'

'Aw, lemme have the catalog, Mistah Joe. Ahll bring it back.'   20

Joe walked through the rear door. Dave was elated. He looked around at barrels of sugar and flour. He heard Joe coming back. He craned his neck to see if he
were bringing the book. Yeah, he's got it! Gawddog, he's got it!

'Here; but be sure you bring it back. It's the only one I got.'

'Sho, Mistah Joe.'

'Say, if you wanna buy a gun, why don't you buy one from me. I gotta gun to
sell.'

'Will it shoot?'   25

'Sure it'll shoot.'

'Whut kind is it?'

'Oh, it's kinda old. . . . A Lefthand Wheeler. A pistol. A big one.'

'Is it got bullets in it?'

'It's loaded.'

'Kin Ah see it?'   30

'Where's your money?'

'Whut yuh wan fer it?'

'I'll let you have it for two dollars.'

'Just *two* dollahs? Shucks, 'Ah could buy tha when Ah git mah pay.'   35

'I'll have it here when you want it.'

'Awright, suh. Ah be in fer it.'

He went through the door, hearing it slam again behind him. Ahma git some money from Ma n buy me a gun! Only *two* dollahs! He tucked the thick catalogue under his arm and hurried.

'Where yuh been, boy?' His mother held a steaming dish of black-eyed peas.

'Aw, Ma, Ah jus stopped down the road t talk wid th boys.'   40

'Yuh know bettah than t keep suppah waitin.'

He sat down, resting the catalogue on the edge of the table.

'Yuh git up from there and git to the well n wash yosef! Ah ain feedin no hogs in mah house!'

She grabbed his shoulder and pushed him. He stumbled out of the room, then came back to get the catalogue.

'Whut this?'   45

'Aw, Ma, it's jusa catlog.'

'Who yuh git it from?'

'From Joe, down at the sto.'

'Waal, thas good. We kin use it around the house.'

'Naw, Ma.' He grabbed for it. 'Gimme mah catlog, Ma.'   50

She held onto it and glared at him.

'Quit hollerin at me! Whuts wrong wid yuh? Yuh crazy?'

'But Ma, please. It ain mine! It's Joe's! He tol me t bring it back t im termorrow.'

She gave up the book. He stumbled down the back steps, hugging the thick book under his arm. When he had splashed water on his face and hands, he groped back to the kitchen and fumbled in a corner for the towel. He bumped into a chair; it clattered to the floor. The catalogue sprawled at his feet. When he had dried his eyes he snatched up the book and held it again under his arm. His mother stood watching him.

'Now, ef yuh gonna acka fool over that ol book, Ahll take it n burn it up.'   55

'Naw, Ma, please.'

'Waal, set down n be still!'

He sat and drew the oil lamp close. He thumbed page after page, unaware of the food his mother set on the table. His father came in. Then his small brother.

'Whutcha got there, Dave?' his father asked.

'Jusa catlog,' he answered, not looking up.   60

'Ywah, here they is!' His eyes glowed at blue and black revolvers. He glanced up, feeling sudden guilt. His father was watching him. He eased the book under the table and rested it on his knees. After the blessing was asked, he ate. He scooped up peas and swallowed fat meat without chewing. Buttermilk helped to wash it down. He did not want to mention money before his father. He would do much better by cornering his mother when she was alone. He looked at his father uneasily out of the edge of his eye.

'Boy, how come yuh don quit foolin wid that book n eat yo suppah?'

'Yessuh.'

'How yuh n ol man Hawkins gittin erlong?'

'Suh?'   65

'Can't yuh hear? Why don yuh lissen? Ah ast yuh how wuz yuh n ol man Hawkins gittin erlong?'

'Oh, swell, Pa. Ah plows mo lan than anybody over there.'

'Waal, yuh oughta keep yo min on whut yuh doin.'

'Yessuh.'

He poured his plate full of molasses and sopped at it slowly with a chunk of   70
cornbread. When all but his mother had left the kitchen, he still sat and looked again
at the guns in the catalogue. Lawd, ef Ah only had tha pretty one! He could almost
feel the slickness of the weapon with his fingers. If he had a gun like that he would
polish it and keep it shining so it would never rust. N Ahd keep it loaded, by Gawd!

'Ma?'

'Hunh?'

'Ol man Hawkins give yuh mah money yit?'

'Yeah, but ain't no usa thinkin bout throwin nona it erway. Ahm keepin tha
money sos yuh kin have cloes t go to school this winter.'

He rose and went to her side with the open catalogue in his palms. She was   75
washing dishes, her head bent low over a pan. Shyly he raised the open book.
When he spoke his voice was husky, faint.

'Ma, Gawd knows Ah wans one of these.'

'One of whut?' she asked, not raising her eyes.

'One of *these*,' he said again, not daring even to point. She glanced up at the
page, then at him with wide eyes.

'Nigger, is yuh gone plum crazy?'

'Ah, Ma—'   80

'Git outta here! Don yuh talk t me bout no gun? Yuh a fool!'

'Ma, Ah kin buy one fer *two* dollahs.'

'Not ef Ah knows it yuh ain!'

'But yuh promised me one—'

'Ah don care whut Ah promised! Yuh ain nothing but a boy yit!'   85

'Ma, ef yuh lemme buy one Ahll *never* ast yuh fer nothing no mo.'

'Ah tol yuh t git outta here! Yuh ain gonna toucha penny of tha money fer no
gun! Thas how come Ah has Mistah Hawkins t pay yo wages t me, cause Ah
knows yuh ain got no sense.'

'But Ma, we needa gun. Pa ain got no gun. We needa gun in the house. Yuh
kin never tell whut might happen.'

'Now don yuh try to maka fool outta me, boy! Ef we did hava gun yuh
wouldn't have it!'

He laid the catalogue down and slipped his arm around her waist.   90

'Aw, Ma, Ah done worked hard alla summer n ain ast yuh fer nothin, is Ah, now?'

'Thas whut yuh spose t do!'

'But Ma, Ah wans a gun. Yuh kin lemme have two dollahs outta mah money.
Please, Ma. I kin give it to Pa . . . Please, Ma! Ah loves yuh, Ma.'

When she spoke her voice came soft and low.

'Whut yuh wan wida gun, Dave? Yuh don need no gun. Yuhll git in trouble. N   95
ef yo Pa jus *thought* Ah let yuh have money t buy a gun he'd hava fit.'

'Ahll hide it, Ma, it ain but two dollahs.'

'Lawd, chil, whuts wrong wid yuh?'

'Ain nothing wrong, Ma. Ahm almos a man now. Ah wans a gun.'

'Who gonna sell yuh a gun?'

'Ol Joe at the sto.'   100

'N it don cos but two dollahs?'

'Thas all, Ma. Just two dollahs. Please, Ma.'

She was stacking the plates away; her hands moved slowly, reflectively. Dave
kept an anxious silence. Finally, she turned to him.

'Ahll let yuh git tha gun ef yuh promise me one thing.'

'Whuts tha, Ma?'   105

'Yuh bring it straight back t *me*, yuh hear? Itll be fer Pa.'

'Yessum! Lemme go now, Ma.'

She stooped, turned slightly to one side, raised the hem of her dress, rolled down the top of her stocking, and came up with a slender wad of bills.

'Here,' she said. 'Lawd knows yuh don need no gun. But yer Pa does. Yuh bring it right back t *me*, yuh hear? Ahma put it up. Now ef yuh don, Ahma have yuh Pa lick yuh so hard yuh won ferget it.'

'Yessum.'   110

He took the money, ran down the steps, and across the yard.

'Dave! Yuuuuuh Daaaaave!'

He heard, but he was not going to stop now. "Naw, Lawd!"

The first movement he made the following morning was to reach under his pillow for the gun. In the gray light of dawn he held it loosely, feeling a sense of power. Could killa man wida gun like this. Kill anybody, black er white. And if he were holding his gun in his hand nobody could run over him; they would have to respect him. It was a big gun, with a long barrel and a heavy handle. He raised and lowered it in his hand, marveling at it weight.

He had not come straight home with it as his mother had asked; instead he   115
had stayed out in the fields, holding the weapon in his hand, aiming it now and then at some imaginary foe. But he had not fired it; he had been afraid that his father might hear. Also he was not sure he knew how to fire it.

To avoid surrendering the pistol he had not come into the house until he knew that all were asleep. When his mother had tiptoed to his bedside late that night and demanded the gun, he had first played 'possum; then he had told her that the gun was hidden outdoors, that he would bring it to her in the morning. Now he lay turning it slowly in his hands. He broke it, took out the cartridges, felt them, and then put them back.

He slid out of bed, got a long strip of old flannel from a trunk, wrapped the gun in it, and tied it to his naked thigh while it was still loaded. He did not go in to breakfast. Even though it was not yet daylight, he started for Jim Hawkins' plantation. Just as the sun was rising he reached the barns where the mules and plows were kept.

'Hey! That you, Dave?'

He turned. Jim Hawkins stood eying him suspiciously.

'Whatre yuh doing here so early?'   120

'Ah didn't know Ah wuz gittin up so early, Mistah Hawkins. Ah wuz fixin t hitch up ol Jenny n take her t the fiels.'

'Good. Since you're here so early, how about plowing that stretch down by the woods?'

'Suits me, Mistah Hawkins.'

'O.K. Go to it!'   125

He hitched Jenny to a plow and started across the fields. Hot dog! This was just what he wanted. If he could get down by the woods, he could shoot his gun and nobody would hear. He walked behind the plow, hearing the traces creaking, feeling the gun tied tight to his thigh.

When he reached the woods, he plowed two whole rows before he decided to take out the gun. Finally, he stopped, looked in all directions, then untied the gun and held it in his hand. He turned to the mule and smiled.

'Know whut this is, Jenny? Naw, yuh wouldn't know! Yuhs jusa ol mule! Anyhow, this is a gun, n it kin shoot, by Gawd!'

He held the gun at arm's length. Whut t hell, Ahma shoot this thing! He looked at Jenny again.

'Lissen here, Jenny! When Ah pull this ol trigger Ah don wan yuh t run n acka fool now.'

Jenny stood with her head down, her short ears pricked straight. Dave walked   130
off about twenty feet, held the gun far out from him, at arm's length, and turned his head. Hell, he told himself, Ah ain afraid. The gun felt loose in his fingers; he waved it wildly for a moment. Then he shut his eyes and tightened his forefinger. *Blooom!* A report half-deafened him and he thought his right hand was torn from his arm. He heard Jenny whinnying and galloping over the field, and he found himself on his knees, squeezing his fingers hard between his legs. His hand was numb; he jammed it into his mouth, trying to warm it, trying to stop the pain. The gun lay at his feet. He did not quite know what had happened. He stood up and stared at the gun as though it were a live thing. He gritted his teeth and kicked the gun. Yuh almos broke mah arm! He turned to look for Jenny; she was far over the fields, tossing her head and kicking wildly.

'Hol on there, ol mule!'

When he caught up with her she stood trembling, walling her big white eyes at him. The plow was far away; the traces had broken. Then Dave stopped short, looking, not believing. Jenny was bleeding. Her left side was red and wet with blood. He went closer. Lawd have mercy! Wondah did Ah shoot this mule? He grabbed for Jenny's mane. She flinched, snorted, whirled, tossing her head.

'Hol on now! Hol on.'

Then he saw the hole in Jenny's side, right between the ribs. It was round, wet, red. A crimson stream streaked down the front leg, flowing fast. Good Gawd! Ah wuznt shootin at tha mule. . . . He felt panic. He knew he had to stop that blood, or Jenny would bleed to death. He had never seen so much blood in all his life. He ran the mule for half a mile, trying to catch her. Finally she stopped, breathing hard, stumpy tail half arched. He caught her mane and led her back to where the plow and gun lay. Then he stopped and grabbed handfuls of damp black earth and tried to plug the bullet hole. Jenny shuddered, whinnied, and broke from him.

'Hol on! Hol on now!'   135

He tried to plug it again, but blood came anyhow. His fingers were hot and sticky. He rubbed dirt hard into his palms, trying to dry them. Then again he attempted to plug the bullet hole, but Jenny shied away, kicking her heels high. He stood helpless. He had to do something. He ran at Jenny; she dodged him. He watched a red stream of blood flow down Jenny's leg and form a bright pool at her feet.

'Jenny . . . Jenny . . .' he called weakly.

His lips trembled. She's bleeding t death! He looked in the direction of home, wanting to go back, wanting to get help. But he saw the pistol lying in the damp black clay. He had a queer feeling that if he only did something, this would not be; Jenny would not be there bleeding to death.

When he went to her this time, she did not move. She stood with sleepy, dreamy eyes; and when he touched her she gave a low-pitched whinny and knelt to the ground, her front knees slopping in blood.

'Jenny . . . Jenny . . .' he whispered.   140

For a long time she held her neck erect; then her head sank, slowly. Her ribs swelled with a mighty heave and she went over.

Dave's stomach felt empty, very empty. He picked up the gun and held it gingerly between his thumb and forefinger. He buried it at the foot of a tree. He took a stick and tried to cover the pool of blood with dirt—but what was the use? There was Jenny lying with her mouth open and her eyes walled and glassy. He could not tell Jim Hawkins he had shot his mule. But he had to tell something. Yeah, Ahll tell em Jenny started gittin wil n fell on the joint of the plow.... But that would hardly happen to a mule. He walked across the field slowly, head down.

It was sunset. Two of Jim Hawkins' men were over near the edge of the woods digging a hole in which to bury Jenny. Dave was surrounded by a knot of people; all of them were looking down at the dead mule.

'I don't see how in the world it happened,' said Jim Hawkins for the tenth time.

The crowd parted and Dave's mother, father, and small brother pushed into   145
the center.

'Where Dave?' his mother called.

'There he is,' said Jim Hawkins.

His mother grabbed him.

'Whut happened, Dave? Whut yuh done?'

'Nothing.'   150

'C'mon, boy, talk,' his father said.

Dave took a deep breath and told the story he knew nobody believed.

'Waal,' he drawled, 'Ah brung ol Jenny down here sos Ah could do mah plowin. Ah plowed bout two rows, just like yuh see.' He stopped and pointed at the long rows of upturned earth. 'Then something musta been wrong wid ol Jenny. She wouldn't ack right atall. She started snortin n kickin her heels. Ah tried to hol her, but she pulled erway, rearin n goin on. Then when the point of the plow was stickin up in the air, she swung erroun n twisted hersef back on it. . . . She stuck hersef n started t bleed. N fo Ah could do anything, she wuz dead.'

'Did you ever hear anything like that in all your life?' asked Jim Hawkins.

There were white and black standing in the crowd. They murmured. Dave's   155
mother came close to him and looked hard into his face.

'Tell the truth, Dave,' she said.

'Looks like a bullet hole ter me,' said one man.

'Dave, whut yuh do wid tha gun?' his mother asked.

The crowd surged in, looking at him. He jammed his hands into his pockets, shook his head slowly from left to right, and backed away. His eyes were wide and painful.

'Did he hava gun?' asked Jim Hawkins.   160

'By Gawd, Ah tol yuh tha wuz a *gun* wound,' said a man, slapping his thigh.

His father caught his shoulders and shook him till his teeth rattled.

'Tell whut happened, yuh rascal? Tell whut . . .'

Dave looked at Jenny's stiff legs and began to cry.

'Whut yuh do wid tha gun?' his mother asked.   165

'Whut wuz he doin wida gun?' his father asked.

'Come on and tell the truth,' said Hawkins. 'Ain't nobody going to hurt you...'

His mother crowded close to him.

'Did yuh shoot tha mule, Dave?'

Dave cried, seeing blurred white and black faces.   170

'Ahh ddinnt gggo tt sshoooot hher. . . . Ah sssswear off Gawd Ahh ddint. . . . Ah wuz a-tryin t sssee ef the ol gggun would sshoot—'

'Where yuh git the gun from?' his father asked.

'Ah got it from Joe, at the sto.'

Where yuh git the money?'

'Ma give it t me.'   175

'He kept worryin me, Bob. . . . Ah hat t. . . . Ah tol im t bring the gun right back t me. . . . It was fer yuh, the gun.'

'But how yuh happen to shoot that mule?' asked Jim Hawkins.

'Ah wuznt shootin at the mule, Mistah Hawkins. The gun jumped when Ah pulled the trigger . . . N fo Ah knowed anything Jenny wuz there a-bleedin.'

Somebody in the crowd laughed. Jim Hawkins walked close to Dave and looked into his face.

'Well, looks like you have bought you a mule, Dave.'   180

'Ah swear fo Gawd, Ah didn't go t kill the mule, Mistah Hawkins!'

'But you killed her!'

All the crowd was laughing now. They stood on tiptoe and poked heads over one another's shoulders.

'Well, boy, looks like yuh done bought a dead mule! Hahaha!'

'Ain tha ershame.'   185

'Hohohohoho.'

Dave stood head down, twisting his feet in the dirt.

'Well, you needn't worry about it, Bob,' said Jim Hawkins to Dave's father. 'Just let the boy keep on working and pay me two dollars a month.'

'Whut yuh wan fer yo mule, Mistah Hawkins?'

Jim Hawkins screwed up his eyes.   190

'Fifty dollars.'

'Whut yuh do wid tha gun?' Dave's father demanded.

Dave said nothing.

'Yuh wan me t take a tree lim n beat yuh till yuh talk!'

'Nawsuh!'   195

'Whut yuh do wid it?'

'Ah throwed it erway.'

'Where?'

'Ah . . . Ah throwed it in the creek.'

'Waal, c'mon home. N firs thing in the mawnin git to tha creek n fin tha gun.' 200

'Yessuh.'

'Whut yuh pay fer it?'

'Two dollahs.'

'Take tha gun n git yo money back n carry it t Mistah Hawkins, yuh hear? N don fergit Ahma lam yo black bottom good fer this! Now march yosef on home, suh!'

Dave turned and walked slowly. He heard people laughing. Dave glared, his 205
eyes welling with tears. Hot anger bubbled in him. Then he swallowed and stumbled on.

That night Dave did not sleep. He was glad that he had gotten out of killing the mule so easily, but he was hurt. Something hot seemed to turn over inside him each time he remembered how they had laughed. He tossed on his bed, feeling his hard pillow. *N Pa says he's gonna beat me.* . . . He remembered other beatings, and his back quivered. *Naw, naw, Ah sho don wan im t beat me tha way no mo....* *Dam em* all! Nobody ever gave him anything. All he did was work. *They treat me like a mule....* *N then they beat me....* He gritted his teeth. *N Ma had t tell on me.*

Well, if he had to, he would take old man Hawkins that two dollars. But that meant selling the gun. And he wanted to keep that gun. *Fifty dollahs fer a dead mule.*

He turned over, thinking of how he had fired the gun. He had an itch to fire it again. *Ef other men kin shoota gun, by Gawd, Ah kin!* He was still listening. *Mebbe they all sleepin now.* . . . The house was still. He heard the soft breathing of his brother. *Yes, now!* He would go down and get that gun and see if he could fire it! He eased out of bed and slipped into overalls.

The moon was bright. He ran almost all the way to the edge of the woods. He stumbled over the ground, looking for the spot where he had buried the gun. *Yeah, here it is.* Like a hungry dog scratching for a bone he pawed it up. He puffed his black cheeks and blew dirt from the trigger and barrel. He broke it and found four cartridges unshot. He looked around; the fields were filled with silence and moonlight. He clutched the gun stiff and hard in his fingers. But as soon as he wanted to pull the trigger, he shut his eyes and turned his head. *Naw, Ah can't shoot wid mah eyes closed n mah head turned.* With effort he held his eyes open; then he squeezed. *Blooooom!* He was stiff, not breathing. The gun was still in his hands. Dammit, he'd done it! He fired again. *Blooooom!* He smiled. *Blooooom! Blooooom! Click, click.* There! It was empty. If anybody could shoot a gun, he could. He put the gun into his hip pocket and started across the fields.

When he reached the top of a ridge he stood straight and proud in the moon-light, looking at Jim Hawkins' big white house, feeling the gun sagging in his pocket. *Lawd, ef Ah had jus one mo bullet Ahd taka shot at tha house. Ahd like t scare ol man Hawkins jusa little.* . . . *Jussa enough t let im know Dave Sanders is a man.*   210

To his left the road curved, running to the tracks of the Illinois Central. He jerked his head, listening. From far off came a faint *hoooof-hoooof; hoooof-hoooof; hoooof-hoooof* . . . *Tha's number eight.* He took a swift look at Jim Hawkins' white house; he thought of pa, of ma, of his little brother, and the boys. He thought of the dead mule and heard *hoooof-hoooof; hoooof-hoooof; hoooof-hoooof* . . . He stood rigid. *Two dollahs a mont. Les see now* . . . *Tha means itll take bout two years. Shucks! Ahll be dam!*

He started down the road, toward the tracks. *Yeah, here she comes!* He stood beside the track and held himself stiffly. *Here she comes, erroun the ben.* . . . *C'mon, yuh slow poke! C mon!* He had his hand on his gun; something quivered in his stomach. Then the train thundered past, the gray and brown box cars rum-bling and clinking. He gripped the gun tightly; then he jerked his hand out of his pocket. *Ah betcha Bill wouldn't do it! Ah betcha* . . . The cars slid past, steel grind-ing upon steel. *Ahm riding yuh ternight so hep me Gawd!* He was hot all over. He hesitated just a moment; then he grabbed, pulled atop of a car, and lay flat. He felt his pocket; the gun was still there. Ahead the long rails were glinting in the moon-light, stretching away, away to somewhere, somewhere where he could be a man . . .

READING
AND
RESPONDING
TO
POETRY

PART
THREE

READING
AND
RESPONDING
TO
POETRY

10 ◆ What Is Poetry?

You are probably familiar with "math anxiety." You may suffer from it yourself, or you may know someone who does. Math anxiety comprises a variety of reactions, emotions, and attitudes that are precipitated by any math situation. A person may freeze up at the prospect of trying to solve math problems, especially in the more complex areas of algebra, trigonometry, or calculus; he or she may feel uncomfortable when reading or studying a math textbook or dread math courses in school, perhaps delaying taking them for as long as possible or avoiding them altogether if possible. People with math anxiety may even believe that they are inept when it comes to math and may prove it to themselves repeatedly with things like balancing their checkbooks.

But are you familiar with "poetry anxiety"? That is a "condition" not as high profile as "math anxiety" but perhaps just as prevalent. With just some slight adjustments, you could substitute "poetry" for "math" in the preceding paragraph and have a fair description of this "condition." If you suffer from it, you may freeze up in the face of reading ("trying to solve"?) poetry "problems"; you may feel uncomfortable when you read about or study poetry in a textbook; perhaps you dread or avoid taking literature courses because you know studying poetry will be involved. There may be nothing poetically analogous to a checkbook, but your experience with poetry in school may have made you vow never to read poetry by choice.

If you are someone with "poetry anxiety," you know that this description is not entirely facetious, even if it is tongue-in-cheek. As you are about to begin reading and studying some poems, you will have a more enriching and enjoyable educational experience if you confront your "poetry anxiety." If you face your anxiety, you can take some steps toward attacking and overcoming it. In turn, I believe you will find that poems aren't necessarily as alien and confusing as you may have thought them to be. Over the longer term, you will strengthen your critical thinking skills (both analytical and associational), which will help you in other academic areas and beyond. Finally, by extending your attack on "poetry anxiety" into other areas, you may see that other things you have anxiety about can be successfully dealt with in a conscious manner.

On the other hand, perhaps you don't have poetry anxiety; maybe you already are comfortable with or even an avid reader of poetry. Perhaps you write poetry yourself—lots of people do—or enjoy hearing it read or recited. If that's the case, perhaps you wouldn't mind testifying to your anxiety-ridden classmates. In turn, they could unload their anxieties on you and use your help toward ultimately reducing their fear of reading poetry.

Attitude Inventory

The two brief exercises that follow should promote some dialogue (with yourself and with other readers) on the issue of poetry anxiety. The first exercise may be done privately; it is just an attempt to talk to yourself on paper. The second exercise may be started on your own and then brought to class for sharing in discussion. The first exercise asks you to try to trace your general attitude toward poetry in terms of your personal history as a reader of poetry. The second asks you to list some specific "positive" and "negative" things about some particular poems, offered as concrete instances of the abstraction "poetry."

POETRY AND YOU: Use this space or a page in your notebook to write a brief history of yourself as a reader of poetry. Consider your experience with poems in school, at home, or anywhere else you may have encountered them. What attitudes toward poetry have you been encouraged to take? By whom? How have you responded? How have these experiences contributed to your present attitude toward reading poetry?

Before you begin the next exercise, read the three short poems that follow. The first is by an English poet writing about 100 years ago; the second is by a contemporary American poet; and the third is by a Japanese poet, recently deceased.

A. E. Housman   1859–1936

Loveliest of Trees   *1896*

Loveliest of trees, the cherry now
Is hung with bloom along the bough,
And stands about the woodland ride
Wearing white for Eastertide.

Now, of my threescore years and ten,   5
Twenty will not come again,
And take from seventy springs a score,
It only leaves me fifty more.

And since to look at things in bloom
Fifty springs are little room,   10
About the woodlands I will go
To see the cherry hung with snow.

Gwendolyn Brooks   b. 1917

First Fight. Then Fiddle   1949

First fight. Then fiddle. Ply the slipping string
With feathery sorcery; muzzle the note
With hurting love; the music that they wrote
Bewitch, bewilder. Qualify to sing
Threadwise. Devise no salt, no hempen thing   5
For the dear instrument to bear. Devote
The bow to silks and honey. Be remote
A while from malice and from murdering.
But first to arms, to armor. Carry hate
In front of you and harmony behind.   10
Be deaf to music and to beauty blind.
Win war. Rise bloody, maybe not too late
For having first to civilize a space
Wherein to play your violin with grace.

Shinkichi Takahashi   1901–1987

Explosion   1973

Translated by Lucien Stryk and Takashi Ikemoto

I'm an unthinking dog,
a good-for-nothing cat,
a fog over gutter,
a blossom-swiping rain.

I close my eyes, breathe—   5
radioactive air! A billion years
and I'll be shrunk to half,
pollution strikes my marrow.

So what—I'll whoop at what
remains. Yet scant blood left,
reduced to emptiness by nuclear
fission, I'm running very fast.

10

SHARE AND COMPARE: Based on the poems by Housman, Brooks, and
Takahashi, take a few minutes to jot down some of what you like or understand about poetry in general and/or some of what bothers you or
you don't understand. Share your notes with your classmates.

Likes   Dislikes

1.   1.

2.   2.

3.   3.

4.   4.

5.   5.

The purpose of these activities is not to polarize your classroom between
pro- or anti-poetry factions or isolate any student as someone who loves or
fears reading poetry. It is to encourage some debate, in a playful spirit, on the
merits or demerits of poetry (or of reading poetry). If you suffer from "poetry
anxiety" and if you can participate in such a debate in such a spirit, perhaps
this exercise will be a first step to confronting and reducing your anxiety. If
you enjoy reading poetry, perhaps a brief debate will confirm your beliefs and
attitudes as well as help others see the good side of something they don't like
as well.

The Texture of Poetic Language

Taking the poems by Housman, Brooks, and Takahashi as examples, we can
try to generalize a few things more or less objectively about poetry, to reveal
some differences between poetic language and the language of prose.

Brevity and Density

First of all, a poem is likely to be relatively short. Each of the poems you have
just read has fewer than 15 lines; the longest of them has approximately 100
words. There are longer poems, of course, but though 1,000 words may be
short for a piece of prose (a short story or an essay), it is long for a poem. But
a poem is not just short; it's also dense. That is, its relatively few words pack
in a lot of sense and associations; each word or phrase bears considerable
weight; each word or phrase counts more heavily than in prose.

Imagery

The density of poetry also typically means that whatever ideas a poem may be concerned with are suggested, implied, connoted, or referred to indirectly instead of presented explicitly. Often those suggestions or implications come through **imagery**—concrete language that recalls specific sensations from the wider world and in the process associates an abstract idea with those sensations. The word "snow" in "Loveliest of Trees," for instance, refers to the white blooms on the cherry trees in spring; in this way it recalls the specific sensation of seeing those white blossoms. At the same time, the word "snow" may suggest winter and, by a chain of association, the abstractions "coldness" and "death." The second stanza of "Loveliest of Trees" refers to the typical human life span of 70 years, and the **voice** in the poem seems sensitive to the shortness of life, so an indirect reference to death in the word "snow" in the last line is consistent with an idea the poem brings up elsewhere.

Connotation

Consider the phrase "Ply the slipping string / With feathery sorcery" in "First Fight. Then Fiddle." The "string" seems to be that of a fiddle, but the word "slipping" may suggest some unusual quality of a fiddle string, which, to my knowledge anyway, is more nearly taut, firm, or vibrating than "slipping." If the string is indeed that of a fiddle, that is a word roughly synonymous with "violin" but one that carries very different **connotations**. To mention just one, the infamous emperor Nero supposedly *fiddled* while Rome burned; he didn't *play the violin*. And the phrase in the poem says "Ply [not "Play"] the slipping string." "Ply" seems to suggest a kind of conscious or strategic action different from "play," a sense perhaps deepened by the word "sorcery" in the next line, which connotes magic, especially "black" or "evil" magic. These words make me suspect the poem is not talking about the usual or literal kind of fiddle playing. Other ideas, an attitude of trickery or subterfuge, seem to arise from the words "ply" and "slipping" in this phrase. This kind of verbal density may contribute to the anxiety that poetry produces in some people, or it may contribute to other people's enjoyment. In any case, it is a characteristic of the poetic use of language.

Figurative Language

Another way to speak of the indirectness of language in these examples drawn from the Housman and Brooks poems is to call it **figurative**; words appear to be used in other-than-usual ways. Perhaps my brief discussion of the "fiddling" referred to in Brooks' poem suggests that the "string," the "bow," and the "instrument" there do not refer to a literal fiddle but a figurative one; that the language points not to a violin but to something else that is being likened to a violin. A **metaphor**—an implied analogy between two things or ideas that are not normally thought of as similar—is one kind of figure of speech that you may be familiar with as especially prevalent in poetry. The first stanza of "Explosion," if you don't take it literally, has a metaphor per line.

In the seventh and tenth lines of "Loveliest of Trees," you may recognize another verbal figure in the word "springs," which seems to mean both the time of year when trees first bloom and years of life. Referring to the whole of something ("year") in terms of a part of it ("spring") is an instance of **synecdoche**. Whether you are aware of the more common figure of speech, metaphor, or the less common one, synecdoche, you may be conscious of the presence of figurative language as a feature that distinguishes poetry from prose.

Syntax and Sentence Construction

Poetry is also written in **verse**—lines having, usually, some discernible **rhythm** or **meter** and, as in the case of two of these poems, **rhyme**. The metrical or rhyme requirements of verse contribute to poetry's verbal density because they set relatively close limits on the number of syllables or words a line may consist of or the kinds of words that can fall at the ends of lines. In turn, the construction of poetic sentences may be different from that of ordinary prose sentences. Take, for instance, the third clause in the third sentence in the Brooks poem: "the music that they wrote / Bewitch, bewilder." The **syntax** or word order of this sentence is inverted: As an imperative sentence, "you" is an implied subject, not stated at all. Normally in English imperative and declarative prose sentences the direct object follows the verb, and the subject, whether stated or implied, precedes the verb. Here, the direct object, "music," precedes the verb(s). To rearrange this clause in normal English word order, it would read, "[you] bewitch, bewilder the music that they wrote." But if the clause were in that order, the rhyming word "wrote" (rhyming with "note," line 2, and "devote" and "remote," lines 6 and 7) would fall in the middle of line 4 instead of at the end of line 3.

Similarly, in "Explosion" the last sentence has the main clause—"I'm running very fast"—at the end, preceded by two phrases that modify "I." The first of those phrases is elliptical; it leaves out words that, presumably, the immediate context will allow a reader to understand: "[I have] scant blood left." Inverted and elliptical constructions are not unknown in English prose sentences, but they occur much more frequently in poetic sentences, as in these two from the poems by Brooks and Takahashi.

Sound

The rhyme and meter that are characteristic of poetry make it sound different from prose. If you read a poem on a printed page with your eyes, you don't hear this sound component, although you may be aware of it when you see accented syllables that you know sound alike: "now" and "bough," "string" and "sing." But if you read a poem with your voice or hear someone else read it, you do notice the repetition of sounds in accented syllables (rhyme) and the regular pattern of accented and unaccented syllables (meter). Not all verse is rhymed, of course, and not all of it is written in a regularly repeating meter, as further examples will show. But poetry does feature sound qualities of one kind or another, not necessarily limited to rhyme or meter. In both "Loveliest of Trees" and "First Fight. Then Fiddle." **alliteration**—the repetition of initial consonant sounds or vowel sounds in words near to one another—contributes to the sound quality too. You can see this in the *w* sounds in lines 3 and 4 of "Loveliest of Trees" and in the *s* sounds in line 7. In "First Fight. Then Fiddle." four of the first ten words begin with *f* sounds. All these **text strategies** and other uses of the sound qualities of English are surely part of poetry's appeal, from nursery rhymes on up. But to appreciate this aspect of poetry you have to hear it vocalized—by yourself or another reader.

The Vitality of Poetry

Perhaps the most anxiety-producing aspect of poetry is having to approach poetry in terms of the technicalities of meter, versification, figures of speech, and so forth, and the occasional difficulty presented by such a relatively unusual and often consciously **aesthetic** use of language. But if you stop and think for a minute, you may realize that poetry in one form or another is all around you. You encounter different kinds of it almost daily in various media—greeting card verse, advertising slogans or jingles, popular song lyrics, bumper-sticker or T-shirt messages, and even graffiti. Poetry's presence in these forms is testimony to the broad appeal of the same aesthetic features that otherwise may cause difficulty, and to the pleasures poetry affords in terms of sound quality, wordplay, and the imaginative use of language.

At the other end of the spectrum lies the "serious" or high-art poetry represented here by the poems of Housman, Brooks, and Takahashi that you have just read. In the Western literary **canon**, the Englishman Housman has a secure place, and Brooks is well-established among contemporary American poets. Poems by the Japanese Takahashi are not usually found in the Western canon, but as the introduction to this book mentioned, that canon is broadening and changing as readers' appreciation for texts produced in many world cultures expands. That expansion is one way in which the variety of poems you might read in the academic context is also increasing, and that variety means that the poetry at the "high-art" end of the spectrum is not all the same. Even within the relatively narrow range of poems you are likely to study in school—in this book and in other literature courses—there are differences in form, ideas, levels of language, and cultural perspective.

The distinction made in Chapter 2 between texts and literary works can be helpful here too. "Serious" poetry, the kind mostly read and studied in school, seems to have a corner on "literature," leaving all the other kinds out of consideration for classroom study. At the same time, the mass culture accords a rather low status to "high-art" poetry—at least as measured by book sales and publishers advances for poets as compared to novelists. But if you use the concept of textuality to broaden the scope of what you study in the academic context as well as to take more seriously what you encounter in other contexts, you may find some common ground in which poems from all across the spectrum can converse with one another.

Perhaps also, if you have "poetry anxiety," you can gain some perspective on the study of poetry in college by keeping the broad spectrum of poetic texts in mind. Yes, "serious" poetry can be hard to read, but like any demanding or challenging activity, reading poetry—reading it carefully, conscientiously—can be enormously rewarding. Poetry is surely the most consciously artistic use of language, whether any particular poem is at the "high-art" or the "low-art" end of the spectrum. It calls attention to itself; it says, "Look! This is different!" In so doing, it offers aesthetic pleasures analogous to those that may be derived from music, painting, dance, sculpture, photography, or any art form that invites you to step, however briefly, out of your ordinary world. Or the poetic use of language—as we have considered it very briefly in terms of the poems by Housman, Brooks, and Takahashi—affords you the chance to see the world differently, even if for just a few moments. It allows your mind and emotions to interact with other people's—poets' *and* other readers'.

Through the years, college teachers and students have tended to find "serious" poems to be strong texts—instances of language that reciprocate readers' active approaches to them. But a self-conscious approach to reading any kind of text nominated as a poem can promote strength in a reader and help to reveal strength in that text. The poetry you encounter in mass media and popular culture does not seem to call for technical analysis and **close reading**, although readers are certainly free to apply those ways of reading to those kinds of texts, and thus to transform them from "trivial" cultural products to something more serious and meaningful. As you will see, even readers who experience "poetry anxiety" in the face of "high-art" poems already have **reading strategies** (though they might not be aware that they do) for poetic texts that fall elsewhere on the spectrum. Those reading strategies can be adapted to encounters with the more demanding kinds of poems, and other reading strategies can be learned and practiced to make you a stronger reader of poems of any kind. The benefits of reading poetry are available to anyone who will put some interest and conscience into the effort, whether the poems he or she reads are canonical or popular texts.

Found Poetry

One kind of text that is usually excluded from the canon of "serious" or "high-art" poetry is **found poetry**. It can be usefully considered in several ways. For one thing, because it is not of the kind that alienates some readers, it shows that not all poetry has to be anxiety producing. For another, it introduces an element of **play** into the reading of poetry that can be carried over to encounters with those other, more "serious" or "academic" kinds. It also reveals something crucial about poems in general: that they may be considered as the creations of *readers* just as much as poets. This idea of play goes a long way toward restoring to the reader much of the power in the reading transaction, and no doubt part of the anxiety-producing capacity of some poems is their nearly total power over some readers.

Found poetry developed on the model of the *objet trouvé*—the "found object"—that French painter Marcel Duchamp put forward as art earlier in this century. Perhaps you are more familiar with Andy Warhol's paintings of Campbell's Soup® cans, which may be considered a further development of the *objet trouvé*. Found poetry doesn't need an elaborate definition: it is simply any text a person might find somewhere—the telephone book, an instruction manual, road signs—and rearrange on the page to resemble a poem. The only "rule" is that the text not be originally intended as a poem. (Advertising copy is disqualified because it is often written in and arranged on the page in poetic form.) Here is one example of published found poetry.

Bernard Phillips   b. 1931

JFK   1967

The body
is that
of a muscular
well-developed
and well-nourished
adult   5
Caucasian male
measuring seventy-two
and a half
inches
and weighing approximately   10
one hundred
and seventy
pounds.

Phillips found this poem in the Warren Commission Report on the assassination of President John F. Kennedy. His creativity lay in finding the text in the first place and then rearranging it in poetic form on the page. This poem doesn't rhyme, but does it share other poetic qualities with any of the poems you read on pages 506–507? What is its effect on you? Can you accept it as a poem, either in terms of its poetic qualities or its effect? Why or why not?

Here's a found poem of mine:

Rumble
strips
ahead

This was taken from a road sign I saw nearly 20 years ago. At the time, I had no idea what "rumble strips" were. Now, I know; but this found poem illustrates the point about poetry as *playing* with language—or language at play. Usually, highway signs are read as **monovalent**, that is, as having only one meaning. It is customary to read poems, however, as **polyvalent**—as having several meanings. This text at first presented itself to me—I must have been in a playful frame of mind at the time—as ambiguous or polyvalent: Was it announcing, for instance, the proximity of narrow areas where gang fights ("rumbles") were taking place? Or zones where thunder was audible? Was it describing the actions of someone named Rumble? I could picture "him" ripping the leaves off a head of lettuce.

Here is another found poem. It takes a little **poetic license** with the found material, which was in an Associated Press news story about the 1966 marriage of singer Frank Sinatra and actress Mia Farrow. The finder or poet, Ronald Gross, not only rearranged the words on the page, he repeated certain phrases to form a **refrain**.

Ronald Gross   b. 1935

Miss Farrow Just Smiled   *1967*

Singer Frank Sinatra
honeymooned, somewhere,
with his third wife,
Mia Farrow, today
after a Las Vegas   5
wedding performed
between plane flights.

Exactly where they went
hasn't been determined.

After the ceremony   10
the couple walked out
on the apartment's patio
and Sinatra beamed:
"How are you, baby?"

Miss Farrow just smiled.   15

After the ceremony
the couple walked out
on the apartment's patio
and Sinatra beamed:
"How are you, baby?"   20

Exactly where they went
hasn't been determined.

Singer Frank Sinatra
honeymooned, somewhere,
with his third wife,   25

Mia Farrow, today
after a Las Vegas
wedding performed
between plane flights.

Exactly where they went   30
hasn't been determined.

After the ceremony
the couple walked out
on the apartment's patio
and Sinatra beamed: 35
"How are you, baby?"
Miss Farrow just smiled.

    The title phrase in this poem gets additional emphasis from its placement in the poem. The first occurrence of "Miss Farrow just smiled" is in the center of the poem, and the second half repeats the first three stanzas in roughly reverse order, allowing the poem to end with the title phrase again. You might consider the effect of this repetition—what difference it makes that the poem has 22 lines after line 15.

    The next page has is a space for you to create your own found poem. Look around you, not in especially "poetic" or "inspirational" places, for instances of language already written that you can remake, through arrangement or repetition or both, into a poem. Try a textbook from another course, your college or university catalog, an official notice displayed around your campus or elsewhere, or a letter from home. One student, Heather Colgan, created this found poem from fragments of text in a newspaper and in her dormitory.

H.R. Colgan   b. 1974

To Eric: A Dedication   *1994*

Death
causes feelings of
isolation,
loneliness
Celtic Classic draws thousands
ten dead in Haiti
Pull ring pin
start from eight feet
back
To restore current
press handle to reset,
then on
WARNING!!!
these doors must be kept closed at all times.

In the box below, the blank line at the top is for a title. If this box isn't big enough, you could also use a page in your notebook to write a found poem.

FOUND POEM

The Reader at Play

Found poems are exercises in "creative writing" because of the work (or play) the "finding poet" must do. The theory behind this book holds that reading texts is a creative operation itself, so "writing" a found poem is merely that process made most obvious. Taking this idea a step further, consider that these texts presented as poems reveal that poetry is a *way of reading*, not merely a kind of writing. Based on that idea, perhaps you can see that all poetry—even the difficult or "serious" kind—can be manipulated or played with. Any close reading of a text is a kind of play with its language, and the principles of that manipulation—the reading strategies that not only apply *to* poems but make texts *into* poems—can be systematically studied and brought under your conscious control.

The key notion here is play. Generally, to read or write a poem is to play with language, or to put language in play—allowing its polyvalent tendencies to come to the surface. To do that—from either side of the transaction—is to **poeticize** a text. I would invite you to think about and to read poems in a spirit of play. To do so may mean resisting the atmosphere of the academic setting, where generally you "work" and are "serious," not an easy task. But to do so is also, I suggest, in keeping with the poetic use of language. To get a better sense of this, try the following exercise, which requires you to do a little digging inside a good college-level dictionary.

EXERCISE—"PLAY": Look up the word *play* in your dictionary, both its noun and verb senses. You may be surprised at how many definitions are given. In the space below or in your journal, list the definitions that seem to apply to the reading or the writing of poetry. You can be a little playful as you do so.

1.   7.

2.   8.

3.   9.

4.   10.

5.   11.

6.   12.

Besides creating found poems, another example of creatively playing with a text comes from an older or "nontraditional" student who is an amateur jazz musician. This student, Tim Blangger, incorporated Gary Snyder's poem "Riprap" into the weekly sessions he has with two friends and fellow musicians. In his journal, Tim wrote an account of how he—a flute and percussion player—and his friends Randy, who plays saxophone, clarinet, and percussion, and Bob, a guitarist, play with Snyder's poem, making it into their own text. Some of that account appears below, but first here is the original poem.

Gary Snyder   b. 1930

Riprap   *1959*

Lay down these words
Before your mind like rocks.
        placed solid, by hands
In choice of place, set
Before the body of the mind   5
        in space and time:
Solidity of bark, leaf, or wall
        riprap of things:
Cobble of milky way,
        straying planets,   10
These poems, people,
        lost ponies with

Dragging saddles—
    and rocky sure-foot trails.
The worlds like an endless
    four-dimensional
Game of *Go*.
    ants and pebbles
In the thin loam, each rock a word
    a creek-washed stone
Granite: ingrained
    with torment of fire and weight
Crystal and sediment linked hot
    all change, in thoughts,
As well as things.

    15

    20

    25

STUDENT WRITING
Tim Blangger: Reading Journal Entry

> We've been playing together, each Wednesday evening, for about two and a
> half years. Bob and Randy began a musical conversation years ago; once I heard it,
> I wanted to add something to it, not because I felt it needed something "else," but
> because what I heard inspired me to action. This is a common theme that comes up
> when we talk about what we do. One player plays a line, or simply creates a sound,
> and the emotions, the feelings expressed, inspire the others. This is, in many ways,
> the same spirit in which we use poems, as a framework for musical development
> and expression. In general, we work around individual lines, not words, and de-
> velop free-form, momentary elements that in some way relate—rhythmically or
> sonically—to the original theme.

Tim wrote that when his trio first started using poems, they tried several
by Gary Snyder but none offered "any window into them, some place where
we could add music without interrupting the poem's flow." That "idea of
flow," he wrote, brought to mind "Riprap":

> . . . with its suggestions of a mountain stream . . . [and] its connections to a
> higher order of nature. "Disorder in order" is how I try to think of it when we play
> to and around the words. Like that mountain stream, each time down, each season,
> the path of our play changes in ways small and large.
>
> In working with the poem as a soloist, I start out in middle D, . . . [playing] a
> triplet pattern that moves up and down the flute with a deliberate, even pace, end-

ing on a trilled A. I play it twice, . . . with the second run-through of a slower pace than the first. The [vocal] reader begins, with the guitar quietly strumming in the background, until the first colon [line 6]. Here, a sound plate, a sort of gong, is struck, twice again, and again with differing lengths, and the guitar takes a solo, using A and D as some basis. The reader resumes, slowly building up the power and force of his voice until . . . [line 8]. Again, there is a strike of the sound plate and a brief, explosive flute solo that suggests a pentatonic (five-note) scale, from D up. The reader resumes, somewhat calmer, until . . . [line 17]. Here, the flute and guitar perform a conversational phrase for between two and five minutes. The last section is read as if it were one line, because reading it that way seems to highlight the dynamic forces in the poem. At the end, the sound plate is struck once, and the flute trills a high D.

> This framework serves as a good starting point, but . . . it also has its limitations, and we've found that playing the music and reading the poem several times, with each version a little looser than the previous one, produces different ideas and different ways for us, as musicians, to react. . . . By varying the delivery and the space between parts of the poem, we can emphasize different aspects without changing the text or the meaning. "Riprap" is a wonderful poem for many reasons, but one of my favorites is the way words like "sediment," "crystal," and "granite" are at the bottom of the poem, a sort of cross-section of nature and the Earth and a schematic of how a riprap would be on a mountain side, with the heavier stones at the bottom. The flow of the words allows us to fit our playing in and around the lines so we can preserve the integrity of the poem itself and still have some sort of meaningful, interactive experience.

The way Tim and his friends play (in several senses of the word) with "Riprap" illustrates the possibilities of playing with a text to emphasize or realize some of its special poetic qualities. Although it is not the usual kind, what Tim and his friends do is also a conscientious reading, an interpretation, of a poem. You have the chance to perform in analogous fashion whenever you read a poem, any poem. Read it aloud. Without changing the words around, you can create your own reading. Your voice can emphasize certain words or phrases, and pauses of varying duration can add to your oral interpretation. Try it with "Riprap." In your classroom, it can be interesting and fun to hear different readers' oral interpretations of the same poem. Even subtle differences are examples of readers playing with a text.

Your excursion into the dictionary for different senses of "play" should have revealed that not all of the word's meanings have to do with fun; some senses of "play" are serious, for instance "to exploit or manipulate" (from my dictionary, *Webster's Ninth New Collegiate*). Tim and his friends seemed to be having fun with "Riprap" in their play with it, but they are also serious about what they're doing as musicians to "manipulate" the written text. Another, more traditional way in which poems are "manipulated" by readers is in **parody**—a close imitation, usually of a poetic style, that concerns a "lower" poetic subject. Parodies are a way of having fun with a text, but they can also serve a more serious purpose. For one thing, they can be a kind of tribute to an original text because they emphasize some outstanding quality of the original—along the lines of "imitation is the sincerest form of flattery." They can also serve a serious cultural function by calling into question the "high" status generally accorded to certain writers, subjects, or styles. Examples of poetic parodies may be found in each of the next three chapters. To acquaint yourself with the concept here, however, read the following poem by Robert Frost and the parody of it by Firman Houghton.

Robert Frost   1874–1963

Birches   *1915*

When I see birches bend to the left and right
Across the lines of straighter darker trees,
I like to think some boy's been swinging them.
But swinging doesn't bend them down to stay
As ice-storms do. Often you must have seen them   5
Loaded with ice a sunny winter morning
After a rain. They click upon themselves
As the breeze rises, and turn many-colored
As the stir cracks and crazes their enamel.
Soon the sun's warmth makes them shed crystal shells   10
Shattering and avalanching on the snow-crust—
Such heaps of broken glass to sweep away
You'd think the inner dome of heaven had fallen.
They are dragged to the withered bracken by the load,
And they seem not to break; though once they are bowed   15
So low for long, they never right themselves:
You may see their trunks arching in the woods
Years afterwards, trailing their leaves on the ground
Like girls on hands and knees that throw their hair
Before them over their heads to dry in the sun.   20
But I was going to say when Truth broke in

With all her matter-of-fact about the ice-storm
I should prefer to have some boy bend them
As he went out and in to fetch the cows—
Some boy too far from town to learn baseball,   25
Whose only play was what he found himself,
Summer or winter, and could play alone.
One by one he subdued his father's trees
By riding them down over and over again
Until he took the stiffness out of them,   30
And not one but hung limp, not one was left
For him to conquer. He learned all there was
To learn about not launching out too soon
And so not carrying the tree away
Clear to the ground. He always kept his poise   35
To the top branches, climbing carefully
With the same pains you use to fill a cup
Up to the brim, and even above the brim.
Then he flung outward, feet first, with a swish,
Kicking his way down through the air to the ground.   40
So was I once myself a swinger of birches.
And so I dream of going back to be.
It's when I'm weary of considerations,
And life is too much like a pathless wood
Where your face burns and tickles with the cobwebs   45
Broken across it, and one eye is weeping
From a twig's having lashed across it open.
I'd like to get away from earth a while
And then come back to it and begin over.
May no fate willfully misunderstand me   50
And half grant what I wish and snatch me away
Not to return. Earth's the right place for love:
I don't know where it's likely to go better.
I'd like to go by climbing a birch tree,
And climb black branches up a snow-white trunk   55
Toward Heaven, till the tree could bear no more,
But dipped its top and set me down again.
That would be good both going and coming back.
One could do worse than be a swinger of birches.

Firman Houghton

Mr. Frost Goes South to Boston

WHEN I SEE buildings in a town together,
Stretching all around to touch the sky,
I like to know that they come down again

And so I go around the block to see,
And, sure enough, there is the downward side.   5
I say to myself these buildings never quite
Arrive at heaven although they went that way.
That's the way with buildings and with people.
The same applies to colts and cats and chickens
And cattle of all breeds and dogs and horses.   10
I think the buildings Boston has are high
Enough. I like to ride the elevator
Up to the top and then back I come again.
Now, don't get me wrong. I wouldn't want
A ticket to New York to ride up higher.   15
These buildings come as close to heaven now
As I myself would ever want to go.

Houghton's poem is a good deal shorter than Frost's—parodies don't have
to match the original text in length—but it does imitate the language of the
original. Houghton's phrases "When I see buildings" in line 1 and "I like to
know" in line 3 echo "When I see birches" and "I like to think" in the corresponding lines of Frost's poem. And Houghton's poem "lowers" the subject of
Frost's by substituting buildings—an ordinary or dull feature of the urban
landscape—for birches, which Frost's poem seems to treat as wonderful, not
ordinary, parts of the rural scene.

Do you see a contrast in the perspectives of the speakers in the two
poems—one being attuned to the solitary activities of a boy in the woods, the
other perhaps poking fun at the "country bumpkin come to town" to gaze in
wonder at the tall buildings? Frost's first three books of poems—entitled *A
Boy's Will, North of Boston,* and *Mountain Interval*—including many poems
set in the rural landscape of New Hampshire where Frost had lived for 10
years as a young man in the early years of the twentieth century. Later, Frost
lived in Vermont, and that residence plus the setting and subjects of his earlier
poems earned him the reputation of a "poet of New England." From the perspective of a sophisticated Bostonian, however, Frost may appear to be a
backwoods Yankee, puzzled or awestruck by tall city buildings "Stretching all
around to touch the sky." To imagine him in that way is to play with the persona that he developed through such poems as "Birches," and to carry that
sense of play over to an imitation of a particular text is to engage in parody.

READING CULTURE The Experience of Song

Let's return for a moment to the sense of play involved in Tim Blangger's reading of "Riprap." Perhaps you don't perform a reading of a poem the way Tim
and his friends did; all the same, you can borrow other reading strategies from
your encounters with texts that are performed for you: popular songs. Using
these strategies can help you see that the distance between texts at the popular and the academic ends of the poetry spectrum may not really be all that
enormous. And if you have "poetry anxiety," drawing on the reading strategies

you use for popular songs can help you reduce that anxiety when you read more "serious" poems.

Like found poems, popular songs share with high-art poems several essential qualities of poetry. They are written in verse; the lines typically rhyme in some pattern and are written in some kind of meter; and the language is dense and often indirect and connotative. The sound quality of these texts is enhanced by the music to which they are set, which, like the other qualities, is a **convention** or regularly occurring practice of the genre. Whether you are aware of it or not, you have certain strategies, I suspect, for reading a popular song. To help you heighten your consciousness of this process, here are the lyrics from a fairly recent rock song.

Michelle Shocked   c. 1962

Anchorage   *1988*

I took the time to write to my old friend
I walked across that burning bridge
I mailed my letter off to Dallas but
Her reply came from Anchorage, Alaska

She said Hey Girl it's about time you wrote   5
It's been over two years now my old friend
Take me back to the days of the foreign telegrams
And the all night rock 'n rollin' hey Chel
We was wild then

Hey Chel you know it's kinda funny   10
Texas always seems so big
But you know you're in the largest state in the Union
When you're anchored down in Anchorage

Hey girl I think the last time I saw you
Was on me and Leroy's wedding day   15
What was the name of that
Love song you played

I forget how it goes
I don't recall how it goes

Leroy got a better job so we moved   20
Kevin lost a tooth, he's starting school
I got a brand new eight month old baby girl
I sound like a housewife
I think I'm a housewife

Hey girl what's it like to be in New York   25
New York City imagine that
What's it like to be skateboard punk rocker

Leroy says send a picture
Leroy says hello
Leroy says keep on rocking girl
Yeh keep on rocking

Take a few minutes here to jot down what you do—what reading strategies you use—when you listen to a popular song, especially one you like. Keep in mind that the lyrics of "Anchorage" or any song constitute only part of the text.

READING STRATEGIES FOR POPULAR SONGS

1.

2.

3.

4.

5.

6.

Compare your list with the one below, a kind of composite of what I do myself and what I suppose most people do.

READING STRATEGIES FOR POPULAR SONGS

1. Listen to it over and over again.

2. "Say" or sing it aloud, at least in part.

3. Memorize phrases, lines, verses.

4. Create themes or meanings according to my own life experience.

5. Share it with other "readers"; discuss it.

I don't suppose your list is too terribly different from this one. If your strategies are like these, would you say they are "successful" ones for reading these texts? Do these strategies *play with* these texts more than *work on* them? And would you say these texts are a good deal more complex, polyvalent, and dense than the examples of found poetry we were considering just a minute ago? Assuming you do agree, why not carry those strategies over to the perhaps slightly more complex, polyvalent, and dense texts that you typically encounter in your classroom studies?

It's not that simple, of course. There's the matter of difference in motivation, for one thing, and the differences between the classroom and your leisure time in the kinds of pressures you're under or what's at stake. But let's look at that a little more closely. Try this exercise, making two lists: one of what's at stake reading a poem for class and one of what's at stake listening to a popular song.

WHAT'S AT STAKE?

Poem for Class	Popular Song
1.	1.
2.	2.
3.	3.
4.	4.
5.	5.
6.	6.

Again, I will compose two lists for comparison purposes. Here's what I suppose a hypothetical reader might say.

WHAT'S AT STAKE?

Poem for Class	Popular Song
1. Might be called on to analyze or interpret.	1. No such pressures.
2. Have to know "what it means."	2. This is up to me.
3. Test, quiz, or paper: grades.	3. No such pressures: enjoyment only.
4. My "reputation" with teacher, fellow students: don't want to appear "stupid."	4. My "reputation" with friends, peers; don't want to appear "uncool."
5. Degree of tension, anxiety.	5. Fun.
6. My tastes, what I like, self-discovery.	6. My tastes, what I like, self-discovery.

Here, I suppose, there may be greater difference between your list and mine; I suppose there are more variables in what's at stake for different students/readers. But if your list has much at all in common with mine, here's the point: What's at stake goes a long way toward determining the kinds of reading strategies you use with each kind of poetic text. It may seem that the academic and the leisure reading situations are widely different. But the concept of textuality helps to bring what you read in each situation together for consideration, and the notion of play helps to permit similarities in how you read. At the least, it should be useful to you, if you have poetry anxiety, to bring some of the reading strategies you use with popular songs into the classroom for application to the kinds of poetic texts you are likely to encounter there.

CONNECT: Read another poem titled "Anchorage," this one by Joy Harjo, in the Poems for Further Reading. Try the same reading strategies for Harjo's poem as you did for Shocked's. Are there any important similarities, beyond the common title? What different aspects of or attitudes toward that title subject do these two texts suggest to you? To what uses, similar or different, do the two texts put the name of the city in Alaska?

I hope the variety of poetic texts reprinted in this chapter and what you have seen about some different ways to approach any poetic text will help break down "poetry anxiety," if you have it, and will enhance your enjoyment of reading poetry. The next chapter will look more closely at some reading strategies you can use for poetry, but here are a few more poems for you to read playfully now.

Poems for Exploration

Christina Rossetti   1830–1894

Uphill   1858

Does the road wind uphill all the way?
    Yes, to the very end.
Will the day's journey take the whole long day?
    From morn to night, my friend.

But is there for the night a resting place?
    A roof for when the slow dark hours begin.

5

May not the darkness hide it from my face?
    You cannot miss that inn.

Shall I meet other wayfarers at night?
    Those who have gone before.
Then must I knock, or call when just in sight?
    They will not keep you standing at that door.

Shall I find comfort, travel-sore and weak?
    Of labor you shall find the sum.
Will there be beds for me and all who seek?
    Yea, beds for all who come.

10

15

Robert Frost   1874–1963

Nothing Gold Can Stay   *1923*

Nature's first green is gold,
Her hardest hue to hold.
Her early leaf's a flower;
But only so an hour.
Then leaf subsides to leaf.
So Eden sank to grief,
So dawn goes down to day.
Nothing gold can stay.

5

Louise Bogan   1897–1970

The Dream   *1941*

O God, in the dream the terrible horse began
To paw at the air, and make for me with his blows.
Fear kept for thirty-five years poured through his mane,
And retribution equally old, or nearly, breathed through his nose.

5

Coward complete, I lay and wept on the ground
When some strong creature appeared, and leapt for the rein.
Another woman, as I lay half in a swound°   *fainting fit*
Leapt in the air, and clutched at the leather and chain.

Give him, she said, something of yours as a charm.
Throw him, she said, some poor thing you alone claim.
No, no, I cried, he hates me; he's out for harm,
And whether I yield or not, it is all the same.

10

But, like a lion in a legend, when I flung the glove
Pulled from my sweating, my cold right hand,

The terrible beast, that no one may understand,   15
Came to my side, and put down his head in love.

Luis Cabalquinto   b. 1935

Hometown   *1984*

After a supper of mountain rice
And wood-roasted river crab
I sit on a long bench outside
The old house, looking at a river

Alone, myself, again away   5
From that other self in the city
On this piece of ancestor land
My pulses slowed, I am at peace

I have no wish but this place
To remain here in a stopped time   10
With stars moving on that water
And in the sky a brightness

Answering: I want nothing else
But this stillness filling me
From a pure darkness over the land   15
That smells ever freshly of trees

The night and I are quiet now
But for small laughter from a neighbor
The quick sweep of a winged creature
And a warm dog, snuggled by my feet   20

Mahmoud Darwish   b. 1942

Psalm 4   *1989*

Translated by Lena Jayyusi and Anselm Hollo

I left my face on my mother's handkerchief,
packed the mountains in my memory
and departed . . .
The city was slamming its doors
and moving onto ships, multiplying   5
the way weeds multiply in receding gardens . . .
I lean against the wind.
You, unbreakable figure—
why am I staggering? When you are my wall?

The distance hones me, the way   10
fresh death hones the faces of lovers.
The closer I get to the psalms,
the leaner I grow . . .
Oh, passageways busy with emptiness:
when will I arrive?   15

Blessed is he who cloaks himself in his own skin!
Blessed is he who remembers his first name without a mistake!
Blessed is he who eats an apple and does not become a tree!
Blessed is he who drinks from the waters of distant rivers
and does not turn into a cloud!   20
Blessed is the rock that worships its own captivity;
and does not choose the freedom of the wind!

READING AND WRITING PROJECTS

FOR CREATIVE AND CRITICAL THINKING

A major goal of this book is to help you learn about yourself as a reader—
both what you do cognitively when you read and how culture impinges on
the kind of reader you are when you interact with any particular text. Writing
in all its manifestations is an important means to that goal because performing
the actions of writing causes you to focus on the actions you take and the
situation you are in as a reader. In addition to the kinds of writing already
discussed and exemplified in this book, there are other ways to use writing
to learn.

The following writing suggestions are intended to help you integrate your
reading of and writing about literary texts in various ways. These suggestions
include exploratory writing, playing with texts and language, creative efforts
in various genres, and other writing exercises designed to strengthen your
awareness of the cognitive and cultural processes involved in your reading.

▶ Pick a poem from the Poems for Further Reading section (beginning on
page 651) that you have not read before to do a "segmented" reading.
First, glance at it to see where you can divide it into segments—for instance, breaks between stanzas, periods that fall at the end of lines, and
lines that close out rhymes (abba, etc.). Then draw a line beneath each
line that ends a "segment." Cover the entire poem with a piece of paper.
By sliding the piece of paper slowly down over the poem, you can reveal
one segment at a time. As you read each segment, write a few sentences
or a paragraph of response. Try to include your expectations for the next
segment and, for segments after the first, what happened to those expectations. After you have read the last segment and written your brief response, read the entire poem through from beginning to end and write a
brief response to the whole.

A segmented reading can later be developed into a paper of self-conscious analysis in which you trace through time your process of reading a poem.

▶ In similar fashion to doing a segmented reading, write a **narrative account** of how you read each of three or four poems. Pay attention to what you do as a reader, what happens to you as you read, where and why you get "hung up" as you read, where and why you are able to move past any obstacles, and what decisions you make and questions you have as a reader. Then look back over your narratives and construct a portrait of yourself as a poetry reader. From your carefully charted experience reading several poems, what can you conclude about your specific problems and successes as a reader of poetry?

▶ Choose one poem that you consider the best or the worst of those you have read in this chapter. Write an explanation of why this poem is so good or so bad. What can you conclude about "goodness" or "badness" in poetry in general, based on what you particularly admire or detest about the poem you have chosen?

▶ Select a text from mass or popular culture that you wish to nominate as a poem. This text should not be a found poem as described in this chapter; that is, it should already be written in verse. A popular song lyric, a greeting card verse, or an advertising slogan or jingle would be eligible. Treat the text seriously, as you would a poem from the high-culture tradition. Write a **response statement** in which you emphasize the features or characteristics of this text that resemble those of academic poetry.

▶ Find several volunteers to read aloud a poem you have selected. Record their readings on audiotape. (It would probably be best to tape each reader separately, apart from the other readers.) Write an analysis of these three or four oral readings, concentrating on the different interpretations suggested by the various readers. You don't have to evaluate them, just take a look at how different readers use their voices to change the text however subtly.

▶ Identify three to five people who say they like to read poetry and three to five people who say they have "poetry anxiety." Interview these people. Summarize your interviewees' comments, both "pro" and "con." Then write a brief discussion of the conclusions you can draw from these interviews of why people like or fear poetry. How do these conclusions affect your own general attitude toward reading poetry?

▶ Write a letter to a poet, telling or asking him or her anything you wish about a poem or poems you have read. This exercise is a way to articulate your thoughts about a poem without having to come up with "all the answers." It doesn't matter if the poet to whom you write is dead or alive. If she or he is alive, you could send your letter to the poet care of her or his publisher. Regardless of the poet's status, any questions you have could become the basis for a research assignment in which library materials provide some "answers."

Below is an example of a letter written by a student to Emily Dickinson after the student had read several of Dickinson's poems.*

October 23, 1991

Dear Miss Dickinson,

I am writing to you because I found your descriptions of your mental illness so moving. I am unsure of the exact nature of that illness, whether it was a depression or a manic-depressive disorder or some other type of malady, but it doesn't really matter to the reading of your poetry. Ten and a half years ago, after the birth of my first child, I started a slide into depression that intensified after the birth of my second child two years later. Having children was more a catalyst than a cause; other circumstances in my life had also changed and I was unable to cope with everything. I spent the next two years trying to make it from one day to the next and then went into therapy. The next four and a half years contained some of the most painful and difficult and liberating experiences I have ever had, and reading your poems about pain and depression brings them back to me very vividly.

There are three poems that speak to me of the depression itself, while others speak more to the pain involved in the process of breaking out of it. "[It was not Death, for I stood up]," which tries to tell what depression feels like; "[Pain—has an element of Blank]," about pain being the only thing that one comprehends; and "[The Heart Asks Pleasure—First]," in which the heart asks to die rather than keep on keeping on—these describe for me that period of two years prior to my entering therapy. I saw no hope for ever escaping the unhappiness that weighed down my soul.

Therapy is a slow process; it takes a long time to break down the structures that a psyche builds to protect itself. My progress seemed to come in increments too small to measure, but that there was progress was proved when I had a "breakthrough." It feels more accurate to say that I survived a breakthrough. It was so in-

---

*I am indebted to Professor Louise Todd Taylor of Meredith College, Raleigh, North Carolina, for the idea for this assignment, and to Laurie Buck, one of Professor Taylor's students, for this letter.

credibly painful (and I had to go through it alone) that for five days afterwards, until I finally saw my therapist again, I thought I had had a break*down*. I walked through my daily life like a zombie. I tried to verbalize my feelings at the time, and it seemed that I felt simultaneously as if every nerve had been stripped from my body, while I also felt surrounded by some kind of invisible bubble that kept me from any contact with other human beings. And so I believe I know what your poem "[After great pain, a formal feeling comes]" means and I am unable to rid my brain of the image of "nerves sit[ting] ceremonious, like Tombs." I have never written poetry, I have trouble understanding it, but "[After great pain]" is a poem that speaks so directly to my anguish that I cannot read it and hold back my tears.

I have not been able to assign "[I felt a Funeral, in my Brain]" a specific place in the time frame of my depression, but I know that although it may refer to a measure of loss that I have not experienced, I have been close enough to it to understand what it is that you are writing about.

I finished therapy more than a year and a half ago and am happy, and as safe as I suppose most of us ever can be.

Thank you.

Laurie J. Buck

11 ◈ READING POEMS ACTIVELY

Chapter 10 introduced a very general reading strategy for poetry—*playing with a text*. It may be equally useful to think of that strategy as an *attitude* with which to approach a poem, especially considering two other ideas from Chapter 10: (1) that a poem is an instance of language at play and (2) that poetry is as much a way of reading as a form of writing. Keep those principles in mind as you read about some more particular reading strategies to apply to individual poems.

These reading strategies are not new and different; they are all implied by the attitudes toward poetry discussed in Chapter 10 and the interactive model of reading, as described in Chapter 2. These strategies are really a set of eight practical reading strategies that will improve the quality of your interaction with poetry. Each will be explained briefly, with occasional reference to the following poem.

Anne Sexton   1928–1974

Her Kind   1960

I have gone out, a possessed witch,
haunting the black air, braver at night;
dreaming evil, I have done my hitch
over the plain houses, light by light:
lonely thing, twelve-fingered, out of mind.   5
A woman like that is not a woman, quite.
I have been her kind.

I have found the warm caves in the woods,
filled them with skillets, carvings, shelves,
closets, silks, innumerable goods;   10
fixed the suppers for the worms and the elves:
whining, rearranging the disaligned.
A woman like that is misunderstood.
I have been her kind.

533

I have ridden in your cart, driver,   15
waved my nude arms at villages going by,
learning the last bright routes, survivor
where your flames still bite my thigh
and my ribs crack where your wheels wind.
A woman like that is not ashamed to die.   20
I have been her kind.

Practical Reading Strategies

1. Read a poem several times. Perhaps the first reading should be done fairly quickly just to get a sense of it, but then read it again and again—to get the feel of it, to let it work on you, to give yourself a chance to play with it. At least one of your readings should be aloud. Like popular songs, other kinds of poems have sound qualities that can be appreciated only if you use your voice and ears. Try to memorize a line or phrase in the poem that really strikes you. The refrain line of "Her Kind" may be tempting, but too easy, to seize onto so perhaps there's another line or phrase that you can add to your treasury: "fixed the suppers for the worms and the elves," for instance.

2. Read the sentences in the poem, if it's written and punctuated like prose sentences. Many, though not all, poems have sentences, and you can use the same visual cues you rely on in reading prose sentences to see where thoughts start and stop and where pauses of different kinds occur. This strategy is often more helpful than letting line breaks indicate thought breaks, especially in poems with a regular end-of-line rhyme pattern, in which it is tempting to take the recurrence of rhyming sounds for the end of a thought pattern. Each stanza in "Her Kind" consists of three sentences, the first of which occupies five lines of a stanza.

3. Read the grammar of the sentences, phrases, stanzas, etc. I don't mean "diagram" the sentences, but pay attention to such things as which grammatical subjects go with which verbs and what pronouns refer to. In the first sentence of the first stanza of "Her Kind," for instance, "a possessed witch" is an appositive phrase modifying "I." So are "lonely thing," "twelve-fingered," and "out of mind" in line 5. You might mentally make a complete sentence out of the grammatical subject "I" and the phrases in line 5 as follows: "I have [been a] lonely thing, twelve-fingered, out of [my] mind."

4. Use your dictionary as you read. Look up words you aren't familiar with, or words that seem to be used in an unfamiliar way. And when you do this, don't just latch on to one dictionary meaning for the word in question. Here's an excellent opportunity to begin to play with the text by considering different meanings of a given word, its connotations (its emotional shadings or suggestions) as well as its **denotations** (its surface or "objective" meanings).

The word "witch" in "Her Kind" is a good example. It's not the kind you have to look up in a dictionary to find out what it means in the first place. But do look it up in a good desk dictionary. Consider the **etymology**—the historical origins of the word, usually provided in brackets right after the phonetic spelling of the entry term. Compare the different senses listed (and determine whether your dictionary lists senses in order of preference or in historical order). My dictionary (*Webster's Ninth New Collegiate*, © 1990) lists, consecutively, these apparently contradictory senses of "witch" as a noun: "an ugly old woman: hag" and "a charming or alluring girl or woman." These entries are interesting because it suggests to me the contradictory ways in which women are viewed in our culture, and that idea, in turn, enriches the first stanza of the poem for me because it makes me think of "a woman like that" in more ways than just the typical sense of "witch" as a woman flying around on a broom.

5. Read with a pen or pencil in your hand, and *use* it. Write with it, both as you read and after you read. (And sometimes even before you read; see the discussion in Chapter 3, pages 38–43.) Underline words, phrases, and lines that strike you in any way, good or bad. Scribble brief notes in the margins. Draw question marks, exclamation points, or stars wherever you have those kinds of quick responses.[1]

6. Jot down some other notes, either in your book or elsewhere. As you do so, try to get a grasp on such things as:

- the **speaker** in the poem, if there is one: What kind of "person" is saying the words of the poem? (In "Her Kind," it seems that "I" is a woman herself, one sympathetic to the different kinds of women she describes.)

- the **spoken-to** in the poem, if there is one: Is there another "character" to whom the speaker addresses his or her words? (There is no one like this in "Her Kind.")

- the **setting** of the poem, if there is one: Where or when is the speaker saying the words she or he says? What is the situation in which the words are being said? (There really is no setting *per se* in "Her Kind," although the descriptive language in the first sentence of each stanza does suggest a certain "scene" or "place" or perhaps a situation that may account for why these words are being spoken.)

- the gist of the poem, expressed in a prose sentence or two, sometimes called a **paraphrase**. (You may use the space on the next page to draft a tentative paraphrase of "Her Kind," although that may not be easily done.)

---

[1]Ask your instructor what she or he does while reading a poem; what kind of marking and note-jotting does he or she do in the book? I'll bet you it's the kind of things I've just mentioned. If you think teachers have a "secret" for understanding poems, this reading strategy is a big part of it. So why not use it yourself?!

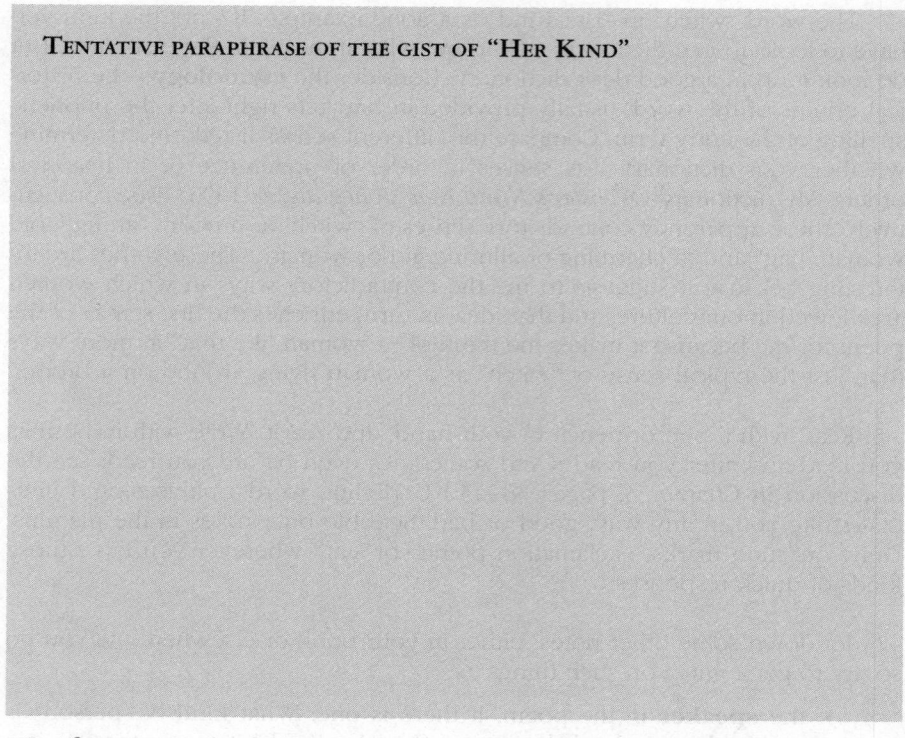

TENTATIVE PARAPHRASE OF THE GIST OF "HER KIND"

7. After you read, of course, you can write a response statement, which is an exploratory exercise, not a definitive interpretation. I will not offer an example of a response statement for "Her Kind" here, but I will invite you to write your own in your notebook or journal. You can use the basic questions first presented in Chapter 3 (pages 47–54):

- What is my response to this text?

- What accounts for that response, in terms of . . .
  the text?
  myself as a reader?

- What does my response tell me about myself or my culture?

8. Talk about your emerging reading. Listen to the responses of other readers. Class discussion should provide this opportunity. Class discussion should not be a time and place where fully articulated readings of poems are aired. It should be a time and place where a community of readers explore the process of their readings of texts.

Two Readers Reading: Caroline Smith and Jack Dudley

Let's take a look now at two poems read by two readers and see how some of these reading strategies play out. Reproduced with the first poem below are some notes made by a student, Caroline Smith, in an early reading of this poem. She applied the other practical reading strategies as well.

Gerard Manley Hopkins   1844–1889

The Windhover   1877

To Christ Our Lord

I caught this morning morning's minion°, king   *favorite*
   dom of daylight's dauphin,° dapple-dawn-drawn Falcon, in his riding   *prince*
   Of the rolling level underneath him steady air, and striding

High there, how he rung upon the rein of a wimpling° wing   *rippling*
In his ecstasy! then off, off forth on swing,   5
   As a skate's heel sweeps smooth on a bow-bend: the hurl and gliding
   Rebuffed the big wind. My heart in hiding
Stirred for a bird,—the achieve of, the mastery of the thing!

Brute beauty and valor and act, oh, air, pride, plume, here
   Buckle! AND the fire that breaks from thee then, a billion   10
Times told lovelier, more dangerous, O my chevalier!°   *knight*
   No wonder of it: shéer plód makes plow down sillion°   *furrow*
Shine, and blue-black embers, ah my dear,
   Fall, gall themselves, and gash gold-vermilion.

The (Windhover)?
To Christ our Lord   (1877)

— minor "idol"

Windhover is bird? Dictionary: kestral-a small European falcon

I caught this morning morning's minion, king-
dom of daylight's dauphin, dapple-dawn-drawn   *alliteration*
Falcon, in his riding   *eldest son of King of France=prince*
Of the rolling level underneath him steady air,
   and striding

High there, how he rung upon the rein of a
   wimpling wing   *fervent attitude*
In his ecstasy() then off, off forth on swing,   *intense!*   5
As a skate's heel sweeps smooth on a bow-bend: the
   hurl and gliding
Rebuffed the big wind. My heart in hiding
Stirred for a bird, – – the achieve of, the mastery   *} feelings of awe for bird-and for God*
   of the thing()   *Holy Spirit?*

Brute beauty and valor and act, oh, air, pride,
   plume, here
Buckle() AND the fire that breaks from thee then,
   a billion   10
Times told lovelier, more dangerous, O my   *uplifting*
   chevalier()
No wonder of it: shéer plód makes plow down   *} ?*
   sillion
Shine, and blue-bleak embers, ah my dear,   *What is this last part about?*
Fall, gall themselves, and gash gold-vermilion. ?

magnificence of God thru bird?

After she made these notes, Caroline wrote in a journal entry that her first response was "Huh?!?" and that she "just wanted to forget the poem and move on." So if you found this poem difficult, you're not alone. But Caroline stuck with it, rereading the poem a number of times and consulting her dictionary for especially troublesome words such as "windhover." In discussion, a classmate mentioned the idea of nature as a cathedral, bearing witness to the wonder of creation in a Christian sense, and Caroline said that comment summed up beautifully her sense that the speaker in the poem was having a religious experience in contemplating the bird. She also said that another of her reading strategies was attempting to connect the dedication "To Christ Our Lord" with the text's apparent subject matter of a person's response to a bird seen in the morning. In a response statement, she acknowledged how her background as someone who had spent a lot of time going to Sunday school and church also contributed to her reading of the poem in religious terms (whereas a classmate who called herself "not religious" said she actively tried to avoid a religious reading of the poem).

"The Windhover" *is* a complex and demanding poem. It uses words in an unusual way, some of them contrary to grammatical convention ("achieve," for instance, in line 8: a verb form used as a noun). The thoughts of the speaker leap quickly from one idea to another. (In fact, when I asked a class to rate "The Windhover" 1 to 10 on a scale of difficulty, with 10 being the most difficult, most of the class called it an 8.) Caroline, the student who made the notes to it, did not claim to have fully understood it even after several readings, and neither will you. But no mountain climber gets better just by scaling sand dunes.

Now read another poem, one that you probably won't find as difficult as "The Windhover," but one that will also bear fruit from a careful reading. This text also is accompanied by annotations made by a reader, Jack Dudley, an older, "nontraditional" student. Following it is a response statement this reader wrote.

Mark De Foe   b. 1942

Hoop League   1986

Few can one at the buzzer here.
Yet some hands recall that last caress,
the wrist snap, the fingers' sweet goodbye
when once they launched the one that won it all.

But no crowd bellowing for points tonight.   5
Just the squeal of shoes, the banter,
slap and grunt and wheeze, and always
the pounding heartbeat of the ball—

the arcing ball—the netcords flouncing
like the skirts of a girl who laughs,   10
taunting men who won't admit
they've lost a step or two to life.

Of course, some cannot shake the vision.
Cool, they glide, spin, and drive. They play
to find the rightness, rhythm, zone,   15
hurtle up into that other

element, where again, again
they pop it, rip it, nothing but net.
Where they sky, double-pumping joy.
Where they in-your-face the world.   20

Become a comet, a crazy copter,
windmilling over mortal earth—
suspended forever, lightning
flashing in the slam-dunk's thunder.

Hoop League

*Awkward verb—
main vb., not
aux.*

Few can one at the buzzer here.
Yet some hands recall that last caress,
the wrist snap, the fingers' sweet goodbye | *Yes!*
when once they launched the one that won it all.

*Noises, but
quiet ones*
{
But no crowd bellowing for points tonight.   5
Just the squeal of shoes, the banter,
slap and grunt and wheeze, and always
the pounding heartbeat of the ball – –

*What's involved
here? sex.
attractiveness?*

the arching ball – – the netcords flouncing
like the skirts of a girl who laughs,   10
taunting men who won't admit
they've lost a step or two to life. *Not just to b'ball*

Of course, some cannot shake the vision.
Cool, they glide, spin and drive. They play
to find the rightness, rhythm, zone,   15
hurtle up into that other *zen*

element, where again, again
they pop it, rip it, nothing but net.
Where they sky, double-pumping joy. *Trash talk*

*Now it's
imagination*

Where they in-your-face the world. *verb*   20

Become a comet, a crazy copter,
windmilling over mortal earth – –
suspended forever, lightning
flashing in the slam-dunk's thunder. *Pow!*

STUDENT WRITING
Jack Dudley: Response Statement

I think this is a *great* poem! It expresses a lot of my feelings, both about basketball and growing old.

I like the sounds in it, and the rhythm—not so much the technical meter of it but how it sort of builds from something kind of quiet at the beginning, reflective, contemplative, through the "squeal of shoes, the banter,/slap and grunt and wheeze" to the climax in the last six or seven lines. *Great* last word: thunder (although I am bothered by the verb "can" in the first line, which I continually misread as an auxiliary verb. I'd have changed it to "nail" or "drop" to avoid that).

A lot of those words and the images they convey of an amateur basketball league or pick-up games are just right also in suggesting the sensuality of the game. I've played lots of sports, especially baseball and football, and while baseball too is a very sensual game—partly because it's played outdoors in nice weather—basketball has its own special sensuality too. Football does too, I suppose, but so much of it is buried under the heavy layers of macho that are involved in that game. But basketball is sensual in more subtle ways: the "wrist snap" and "the fingers' sweet goodbye" to *any* shot that feels good when you let it go. You hear pro and college basketball players all the time describing the experience of a particular shot they sensed was going in in those terms: "It felt good when I released it." (Maybe this isn't so subtle after all!) And this poem is also authentic in some of the lingo of the game—not its rules, but the way players say things: "pop it, rip it, nothing but net" and "in-your-face" used as a verb. Of course a lot of that *is* exaggeration, but basketball is a lot about exaggeration and boasting—trash-talking, jaw-jacking. And players do this whether they are really "good" or not. The players in this poem seem to play just for the love of the game, which describes me and the guys I play with. And most of them/us can't do the stuff that's mentioned in the last two stanzas. Or we can't do it anymore, if we once could. But we *remember* it. Or we *imagine* it, so I know just where the poem is coming from in that way when it talks about finding that "zone," "that other element" where these kind of spectacular "in-your-face" feats can still happen for us older guys. It's Zen basketball, really.

When I read through the poem again a few times, I begin to notice the sensuality working on another level: the theme of sexual attraction begins to emerge. The netcords flounce "like the skirts of a girl who laughs, / taunting men who won't admit/they've lost a step or two to life." Oh, that's good! She's taunting the men playing, but in a friendly, teasing way, I think, just like the men are taunting each other. But she's a girl—eternally young, while these men are losing "a step or two to life." It makes me aware that part of playing these "kids' games" at my age (40 something) is maintaining sexual attractiveness. Not that any women or girls (unless they're the players' daughters, whom they are babysitting) are watching. But we "jocks" or ex-jocks, most of us, have our own images of our sexual attractiveness all tied up with our athletic prowess. We don't want to admit we've "lost a step or two" in *either* area!

Jack's response pretty plainly comes from a *gendered* perspective: He wrote it, as he read the poem, from the specific point of view of a male, and a certain kind of male at that—"40 something," an "ex-jock," a man who is apparently nervous about losing his attractiveness to women. That point of view is certainly only one of many perspectives that could contribute to a reading of "Hoop League"; by no means is it the "right" or the "best" reading of this poem. A reading from a consciously female perspective might make "Hoop League" seem to say something entirely different, whether a female reader is a basketball player or not. But perhaps the response recorded here does suggest a playful attitude on the part of this reader, as well as his close attention to the language of the poem and his willingness to read the poem several times, to make it his own in the process.

From the notes readers made to these two poems, from the comments in class discussion about "The Windhover," and from the response statement to "Hoop League," I hope you can begin to see how reading poems—whether they are "difficult" or "easy" poems—in a spirit of play can be rewarding. Without necessarily thinking of what they do as "play," many readers of poetry do, I am confident, approach a poem with that attitude, which is also nearly the opposite of anxiety. So readers who do feel "poetry anxiety" can take a big step toward allaying that feeling by reading playfully.

One form of playing with a poetic text is to write a parody of it, a playful imitation. There is a long tradition in English poetry of poems that play with other poems in this way. Here is a parody of Gerard Manley Hopkins' poem

"The Windhover" in which the parodist, Anthony Brode, imitates Hopkins' individual style of "sprung rhythm."

Anthony Brode

Breakfast with Gerard Manley Hopkins

"Delicious heart-of-the-corn, fresh-from-the-oven flakes are sparkled and spangled with sugar for a can't-be-resisted flavor."

— Legend on a packet of breakfast cereal.

Serious over my cereals I broke one breakfast
  my fast
 With something-to-read-searching retinas
  retained by print on a packet;
Sprung rhythm sprang, and I found (the mind   5
  fact-mining at last)
 An influence Father-Hopkins-fathered on the
  copy-writing racket.

Parenthesis-proud, bracket-bold, happiest
  with hyphens   10
 The writers stagger intoxicated by terms,
  adjective-unsteadied—
Describing in graceless phrases fizzling like
  soda syphons
 All things crisp, crunchy, malted, tangy,   15
  sugared and shredded.

Far too, yes, too early we are urged to be
  purged, to savor   20
 Salt, malt and phosphates in English
  twisted and torn,
As, sparkled and spangled with sugar for a
  can't-be-resisted flavor,
 Come fresh-from-the-oven flakes direct from
  the heart of the corn.

Broadening Your Literary Experience

A playful reader is a stronger reader of poetry. In the interest of building strength as a reader of poetic texts, refer again to the reading model discussed in Chapter 2. There and in Chapter 3, you were invited to pursue the goal of becoming a stronger reader of all forms of literature and of all cultural texts as well. Here again is a sketch of the interactive model of reading.

The Reading Interaction

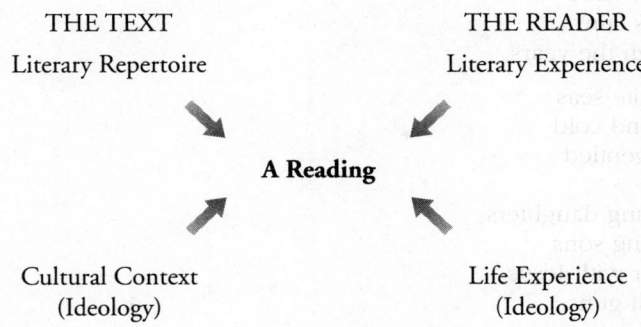

THE TEXT
Literary Repertoire

THE READER
Literary Experience

A Reading

Cultural Context
(Ideology)

Life Experience
(Ideology)

If you do have poetry anxiety, this model locates it in the interaction of the text's **literary repertoire** (the particular features that make a poem what it is and not some other kind of text) and your **literary experience**, including your strategies for reading poems. The causes of poetry anxiety lie not with the poem alone but are shared by the text and the anxious reader. To make this statement is not to blame the reader, but to give anxious readers a foundation from which to build strength and so overcome that anxiety.

The reading and writing you have done in Chapter 10 and so far in this chapter have probably made you more aware of your reading strategies; therefore, now is a good time to look further into the literary repertoire of poetry. An understanding of that, including a consideration of how some of the text strategies of a poem may contribute to the interaction, will be another important step in strengthening yourself as a reader because it will serve to broaden your literary experience. Furthermore, if poetry is playing with language, studying the literary repertoire of poetry can help you appreciate some of the tricks of the game.

In the case of poetry as a genre, looking at the literary repertoire of the text can get complicated. Rather than launch into a detailed discussion of the literary elements of poetry, I will ask you now to list or brainstorm what you already know to be part of the literary repertoire of a "typical" poem. Take a few minutes now to do that, referring to the short poem that follows. I'll start you off with a couple of elements; you can fill in some more, either by yourself or by a group effort in class.

Maya Angelou   b. 1928

Africa   1975

Thus she had lain
sugar cane sweet
deserts her hair

golden her feet
mountains her breasts   5
two Niles her tears
Thus she has lain
Black through the years.

Over the white seas
rime white and cold   10
brigands ungentled
icicle bold
took her young daughters
sold her strong sons
churched her with Jesus   15
bled her with guns.
Thus she has lain.

Now she is rising
remember her pain
remember the losses   20
her screams loud and vain
remember her riches
her history slain
now she is striding
although she had lain.   25

SHARE AND COMPARE: Text strategies of a poem

1. words	7.
2. rhyme	8.
3.	9.
4.	10.
5.	11.
6.	12.

The elements I contributed to the list are perhaps the easiest ones to notice. Any poem is written in words. Not all poems rhyme, but in "Africa," the second and fourth and sixth and eighth lines in each stanza do rhyme. Did you also notice a rhythmical pattern? Most of the lines have two stressed syllables, the first and the last.

Perhaps you also identified instances of figurative language (whether or not you could name the particular figures), such as the comparison of "brigands" to "icicle[s]" and the **personification** of Africa. You may have noticed the arrangement of words in unusual order ("her screams loud and vain," where the modifiers follow the noun) and omitted words ("deserts [*are(?)*] her hair").

If you followed my lead and listed the kinds of features you are likely to find in a "typical" poem, you listed about a dozen poetic conventions—the text strategies of any genre that have come to be accepted as the usual practices, even some of the *defining* practices, of that genre. Any group of literature students is likely to have different degrees of awareness of the conventions of poetry and of the appropriate terminology. The exploration of poetic text strategies in this chapter and the next will broaden your literary experience by introducing you to some of these terms, if you don't know them already. What matters most now, however, is not that you memorize these terms, or that you are able to cite examples of these conventions, but that you work toward an understanding of how any or many of them contribute to the interaction you have in the case of a particular reading experience.

Narrative and Lyric Poems

Chapter 10 mentioned the great variety of poetry that spans the cultural spectrum. Poems at the "high-art" end of the spectrum also demonstrate that variety. As a move toward understanding how the literary repertoire of poetry contributes to the reading interaction, consider the subgenres or categories into which poetry may be divided. To an extent, conventional or textual practices vary according to the specific category of poetry. A very basic yet useful division of poetry is into the categories **narrative** and **lyric**.

Narrative may be roughly defined as poetry that tells a story. As such, it shares an essential quality with texts in the genre of prose fiction. Indeed, narrative poems may be seen to use such "fiction-like" text strategies as **plot**, **setting**, and **character**. In narrative poetry usually the feelings of the speaker or voice aren't as important or essential as the story that speaker is relating.

What are some examples of narrative poetry? **Epic** poems are narratives. Homer's *Iliad* and *Odyssey*, Virgil's *Aeneid*, Dante's *The Divine Comedy*, and Milton's *Paradise Lost* may be familiar to you. All are very long poems that relate the adventures of a hero. However, all are too long (even their individual "Books" or "Cantos" are hundreds or thousands of lines in length) to reproduce for quick reading in the context of this discussion. Something a little shorter in the way of narrative poetry are **ballads**, which often recount a single episode in a character's life and perhaps mention some of the deeds for which someone is famous or infamous.

It's interesting to note that both epics and ballads were originally oral types of poetry. In part, at least, they came about because they fit the needs—aesthetic, practical, and psychological—of preliterate societies. People liked to hear stories, especially those about great cultural heroes. If those stories were cast into rhyming verse with occasional repeated refrains, they carried a certain incantatory or chanting power that suggested mystery or magic. At the same time, the structure of verse stanzas, with or without refrains, made those narratives relatively easy to recite and remember. Later, in the folk tradition of many cultures and nations, ballads continued to have a healthy oral life as a sung form of poetry. For purposes of illustrating narrative poetry, consider the following traditional Scottish ballad from the thirteenth century.

Anonymous (traditional Scottish ballad)

Sir Patrick Spence

The king sits in Dumferling toune,
  Drinking the blude-reid wine:
"O whar will I get guid sailor
  To sail this schip of mine?"

Up and spak an eldern knicht,   5
  Sat at the kings richt kne:
"Sir Patrick Spence is the best sailor
  That sails upon the se."

The king has written a braid letter,
  And signed it wi' his hand,   10
And sent it to Sir Patrick Spence,
  Was walking on the sand.

The first line that Sir Patrick red,
  A loud lauch laucèd he;
The next line that Sir Patrick red,   15
  The teir blinded his ee.

"O wha° is this has don this deid,   who
  This ill deid don to me,
To send me out this time o' the yeir,
  To sail upon the se!   20

"Mak haste, mak haste, my mirry men all,
  Our guid schip sails the morne."
"O say na sae°, my master deir,   so
  For I feir a deadlie storme.

"Late late yestreen I saw the new moone,   25
  Wi' the auld moone in hir arme,
And I feir, I feir, my deir master,
  That we will cum to harme."

O our Scots nobles wer richt laith°   loath
  To weet° their cork-heild schoone;°   wet; shoes 30
Bot lang owre° a' the play wer playd,   before
  Their hats they swam aboone°.   above

O lang, lang may their ladies sit,
  Wi' their fans into their hand,
Or ere' they se Sir Patrick Spence   35
  Cum sailing to the land.

O lang, lang may the ladies stand,
  Wi' their gold kems° in their hair,   combs

Waiting for their ain° deir lords, own
   For they'll se thame na mair. 40

Haf owre°, haf owre to Aberdour, halfway over
   It's fiftie fadom deip,
And thair lies guid Sir Patrick Spence,
   Wi' the Scots lords at his feit.

This poem tells, briefly, the story of the doomed voyage of Sir Patrick Spence and the "Scots lords." While they are not developed, the "characters" of Sir Patrick and others do populate the poem and their spoken words are related. There is, however, no speaker to offer particular insights about or individual perception of the events of the story. If it is possible to conceive of a narrator of this story—whoever knows these events and relates them in language—that narrator certainly takes a back seat to the account of what happened. Also, Sir Patrick's reaction to the king's letter (a presumably emotional moment with potential for exploration or dramatization) is rendered in third person, keeping Sir Patrick at a bit of a distance from the reader or listener.

Reading "Sir Patrick Spence" aloud should help you appreciate the relation of sound to form. The rhythmical pattern in which a line with four stressed syllables alternates with a line of three stresses and the end rhymes in the second and fourth lines of each stanza provide a basic structure that a balladeer could remember, interchanging improvised stanzas or lines if he had not actually memorized the entire ballad. Even today, many ballads that have existed for the most part in the oral tradition of a culture have numerous variants, indicating the improvisational nature of their recitation by balladeers.

CONNECT: For other, more recent, narrative poems, see Martín Espada's "Federico's Ghost," Woody Guthrie's "Pretty Boy Floyd," and Dudley Randall's "Ballad of Birmingham" in the Poems for Further Reading. Guthrie's poem is a ballad written originally to be recited or sung, not to be published on paper.

Lyric poetry may be defined, negatively, as poetry that is not narrative. A more positive definition is that lyric poetry is the expression of a single speaker on a specific subject and on a particular occasion, as opposed to the story of a character extended through some period of time. A *lyric* treatment of the situation of Sir Patrick Spence might concentrate solely on Sir Patrick's feelings, expressing them in his own voice, at, say, the moment he reads the letter from the king.

Partly because lyric poetry does not have a story to relate, it tends to rely more heavily on the sound quality of verse and to say whatever it has to say through several of the text strategies we have looked at briefly in connection with the poems in this chapter and Chapter 10: figurative language, wordplay, and imagery. Lyric poems are also characteristically briefer and denser than narrative poems. "Her Kind," "The Windhover," "Hoop League," and "Africa" are all examples of lyric poems.

In terms of the historical origin of lyric poetry, it too was originally a pre-literate and sung form; in fact the word "lyric" itself derives from the stringed instrument, the lyre, on which early poets, especially in ancient Greece, accompanied themselves as they sang their verses. Today, that sense of the word "lyric" echoes in the common reference to the verbal part of songs as "the lyrics." Lyric poetry is the more commonly written kind today, a trend that may be traced to ancient societies both Eastern and Western and to poets such as the Greek Sappho from the sixth century B.C., the Roman Catullus from the first century B.C., and the Chinese Li Po from the eighth century A.D. In the modern European tradition, lyric poetry was written throughout the Middle Ages and, like other fine arts, enjoyed a surge in popularity in the Renaissance, when one of the marks of the ideal courtier was his ability to write verse. With the European development of printing in the fifteenth century, lyric poetry became more exclusively a written form, a factor that has greatly affected many of the conventions of the genre ever since. By way of contrast with narrative poetry, consider the following as an example of a lyric poem.

Pat Mora   b. 1942

Elena   1984

My Spanish isn't enough.
I remember how I'd smile
listening to my little ones,
understanding every word they'd say,
their jokes, their songs, their plots.   5
   Vamos a pedirle dulces a mamá. Vamos.
But that was in Mexico.
Now my children go to American high schools.
They speak English. At night they sit around
the kitchen table, laugh with one another.   10
I stand by the stove and feel dumb, alone.
I bought a book to learn English.
My husband frowned, drank more beer.
My oldest said, "*Mamá,* he doesn't want you
to be smarter than he is." I'm forty,   15
embarrassed at mispronouncing words,
embarrassed at the laughter of my children,
the grocer, the mailman. Sometimes I take
my English book and lock myself in the bathroom,
say the thick words softly,   20
for if I stop trying, I will be deaf
when my children need my help.

This poem offers the expression of a single speaker—presumably the "Elena" of the title—on a specific subject—her struggles to learn English, her family relationships—on a specific occasion—whenever it is she says these words, perhaps one time when she is reflecting on her family life. Please note that the first-person speaker in a lyric poem is not necessarily the poet. "Elena" illustrates this because if the speaker is a woman named Elena and the poet's name is Pat, Elena must be an imaginative creation. Also, while there may be a story embedded in Elena's words, her feelings take precedence over an account of events. In "Sir Patrick Spence," the opposite is true. The sound qualities of "Elena" are also much more subtle than in "Sir Patrick Spence," as befits a text that in the late twentieth century exists first as a written form. "Elena" does not rhyme, and there is no regular metrical pattern: It is written in **free verse**, which is verse that neither rhymes nor follows a set meter.

You might also consider the relation to external reality in narrative and lyric poetry, as exemplified by "Sir Patrick Spence" and "Elena." The former poem presumably retells, albeit in summary form, events that happened elsewhere, at another time, to other people. The latter poem presumably renders, makes immediate, the feelings of one person. Reality, for the narrative poem, is external; it is "out there," separate from the language of the poem, which merely recapitulates it. For the lyric poem, reality is more nearly in the language of the poem, a factor that tends to make lyrics more susceptible to interpretation. Playing with a lyric poem may typically involve a reader's mind and feelings; with a narrative poem, play more often involves performing it as a recitation or as music.

Dramatic Qualities in Poems

The division of poetry into narrative and lyric is a dichotomy—a complete division into two mutually exclusive categories. This division is useful because, as the foregoing discussion has tried to show, there are some marked differences between narrative and lyric poems. At the same time, however, the two categories may not really be mutually exclusive; there is some overlap. You may have observed some lyric qualities in "Sir Patrick Spence," for instance, that are present in ballads in general. They are short enough, and many of them have been set to music and sung in the folk tradition. More recently, ballads have been written specifically to be sung, as song lyrics. (Examples abound in the work of the Americans Woody Guthrie and Bob Dylan.) By the same token, lyric poems often have a narrative element to them, as you can see in "Elena," wherein the sequence of certain events in the speaker's life, beyond her immediate feelings, is implied. (She used to live in Mexico when her children were small; later they moved to the United States.)

Furthermore, most narrative poems have a dramatic quality to them. As "Sir Patrick Spence" illustrates, they present an action to the reader or listener, and they create then resolve suspense. Many lyric poems are dramatic also: They emphasize the situation in which a speaker says his or her words, and if a reader feels that he or she is being spoken to directly, a lyric poem may provide an even stronger sense of immediacy than a narrative poem does. In

"Elena," perhaps you found that the scene the speaker describes while she is situated in it lends an air of dramatized life.

> **CONNECT:**   Think back to Christina Rossetti's poem "Uphill" in Chapter 10, pages 526–527. The "dialogue" between two speakers in that poem suggests the dramatic quality that lyric poems can sometimes have.

The presence of a dramatic quality in both narrative and lyric poems blurs the clear distinction between the two kinds. Nevertheless, if you have the categories "narrative" and "lyric" poems in your literary experience, you do have a useful, if less-than-perfect, distinction. Knowing something about the characteristics of one kind allows you to observe the presence of those qualities in a poem of the other kind. You can build on this knowledge to broaden your literary experience. There is, for instance, a kind of lyric poetry that draws on the story-telling nature of narrative poetry. That kind is the **dramatic monologue**.

The Dramatic Monologue

According to the definition offered earlier, most lyric poems may be considered monologues—that is, the words of a single speaker. Those words become more obviously *dramatic* monologues, however, when a listener or *spoken-to* is part of the situation. The presence of another person and an enlarged sense of situation—a specific place and time—lend the poem a dramatic quality, like that of a stage drama, hence the dramatic monologue. In addition, although the speaker in a dramatic monologue may not be primarily concerned with relating a plot to his or her listener, what he or she says often does suggest a "story" in terms of background to the present situation or a larger situation or condition. The speaker's words often reveal him or her in some depth as a character, too. In both those senses, dramatic monologues borrow qualities of narrative for use in lyric poems.

The poems in Chapter 2, Matthew Arnold's "Dover Beach" and Bruce Springsteen's "Cover Me," may now be reconsidered as dramatic monologues. The speaker in "Dover Beach" addresses another person who is presumably in the room at the same time. ("Come to the window, sweet is the night air!" the speaker says at one point.) The couple are together in that room in a specific place and time: on the coast of England, near Dover, on a night sometime in the late nineteenth century. This situational specificity in "Dover Beach" makes reading that poem as a dramatic monologue fairly easy. With Bruce Springsteen's "Cover Me," on the other hand, a reader's activity in constructing a dramatic situation may be required to realize the text as a dramatic monologue. It may not be hard to understand the speaker's words as addressed to another person who is present to hear them, but the reader may have to supply the location or specific situation in which those words are spoken. The couple in "Cover Me" apparently are in a room somewhere because the speaker asks his or her listener to "Turn out the light [and] / Bolt the door" because "Outside's the rain, the driving snow / . . . [and] the wild wind blowing."

Whether this room is in New Jersey or Oregon or some other North American location is left as a **gap** for the active reader to fill in. Although neither "Dover Beach" nor "Cover Me" recounts a series of events the way "Sir Patrick Spence" does, each text may be seen to imply a story of two people's relationship within a larger situation, historical or cultural. In that sense, each implies a narrative element. If these larger situations or stories are not made explicit, they too constitute gaps that the reader may fill in from his or her own life experience. In reading any dramatic monologue, your ability to construct, picture, or imagine the situation will depend partly on the aspects of your life experience that you bring to the text to fill in these gaps.

Reading a Dramatic Monologue

Following is one of the best-known dramatic monologues from the high-culture tradition of Anglo-American poetry, Robert Browning's "My Last Duchess." Even more so than "Dover Beach" or "Cover Me," it is a text in which the words of the dramatic speaker reveal his character and provide an account of some of the events of his recent past. To practice some of the reading strategies suggested in Chapter 10, read "My Last Duchess" and write a response statement or journal entry, using the questions that follow the poem. But first, a quick review of those reading strategies.

Basic Reading Strategies for a Poem

- Read the poem several times, at least once aloud. Try to memorize part of the poem if there's a line or phrase that really strikes you.
- Read the *sentences* in the poem and read the *grammar* of the sentences, phrases, stanzas, etc., paying attention to such things as which grammatical subjects go with which verbs and what pronouns refer to.
- Use your dictionary as you read. Look up words you aren't familiar with, or words that seem to be used in an unfamiliar way. Begin to *play* with the text by considering different meanings of a given word, its connotations as well as its denotations.
- Read with a pen or pencil in your hand. Underline words, phrases, lines that strike you in any way, good or bad. Scribble brief notes in the margins. Draw question marks or exclamation points or stars wherever you have those kinds of quick responses.
- Try to get a grasp on the *setting*, the *speaker* and the *spoken-to*, and the *gist* of the poem.

Robert Browning   1812–1889

My Last Duchess   1842

Ferrara

That's my last duchess painted on the wall,
Looking as if she were alive. I call
That piece a wonder, now: Frà Pandolf's° hands   Brother Pandolf (a monk or friar)

Worked busily a day, and there she stands.
Will 't please you sit and look at her? I said   5
"Frà Pandolf" by design,° for never read   on purpose
Strangers like you that pictured countenance,°   face
The depth and passion of its earnest glance,
But to myself they turned (since none puts by
The curtain I have drawn for you, but I)   10
And seemed as they would ask me, if they durst,°   dared
How such a glance came there; so, not the first
Are you to turn and ask thus. Sir, 't was not
Her husband's presence only, called° that spot   that called
Of joy into the Duchess' cheek: perhaps   15
Frà Pandolf chanced to say "Her mantle laps
Over my lady's wrist too much," or "Paint
Must never hope to reproduce the faint
Half-flush that dies along her throat": such stuff
Was courtesy, she thought, and cause enough   20
For calling up that spot of joy. She had
A heart—how shall I say?—too soon made glad,
Too easily impressed; she liked whate'er
She looked on, and her looks went everywhere.
Sir, 't was all one! My favor° at her breast,   love token   25
The dropping of the daylight in the west,
The bough of cherries some officious fool
Broke in the orchard for her, the white mule
She rode with round the terrace—all and each
Would draw from her alike the approving speech,   30
Or blush, at least. She thanked men—good! but thanked
Somehow—I know not how—as if she ranked
My gift of a nine-hundred-years-old name
With anybody's gift. Who'd stoop to blame
This sort of trifling? Even had you skill   35
In speech—which I have not—to make your will
Quite clear to such an one, and say, "Just this
Or that in you disgusts me; here you miss,
Or there exceed the mark"—and if she let
Herself be lessoned so, nor plainly set   40
Her wit to yours, forsooth,° and made excuse   in truth
—E'en then would be some stooping; and I choose
Never to stoop. Oh sir, she smiled, no doubt,
Whene'er I passed her, but who passed without
Much the same smile? This grew; I gave commands;   45
Then all smiles stopped together. There she stands
As if alive. Will 't please you rise? We'll meet
The company below, then. I repeat,
The Count your master's known munificence
Is ample warrant that no just pretense   50

Of mine for dowry will be disallowed;
Though his fair daughter's self, as I avowed
At starting, is my object. Nay, we'll go
Together down, sir. Notice Neptune, though,
Taming a sea-horse, thought a rarity,
Which Claus of Innsbruck cast in bronze for me.

Response Statement Questions

- What is your construction of the dramatic situation here? Who is speaking to whom, where, on what occasion?
- What words or phrases help you to make that construction?
- What kind of person do you imagine the speaker to be? Do you get a sense of anything about him being revealed through his words, in contrast perhaps to what his words are superficially about?
- What is your response to the kind of person "the Duke" seems to be? What values or beliefs of yours are involved in this response?
- *Share and Compare* Exchange your response statement with other readers in your class. What different constructions of the dramatic situation and the character of the speaker emerge from this sharing? What different responses to the kind of person "the Duke" seems to be come out? How are these responses related to the values or beliefs of different readers?

The Dramatic Situation

"My Last Duchess" is a good text with which to practice the basic strategies for reading a poem because, as a dramatic monologue, it presents text strategies that emphasize speaker, spoken-to, and setting. The following discussion is an example of how a response to the first four response statement questions might look.

The speaker is a Duke, the husband of the late Duchess whose portrait hangs on the wall. He is speaking to someone, as is plain from his invitation in line 5 to "sit and look at her [portrait]." The spoken-to could be just anyone at this point, but in line 49, his identity is revealed as a servant of "The Count your master." "Emissary" or "representative" might be a better word than "servant" because the Duke is more courteous toward him than a nobleman would be toward a mere servant. The Duke invites him to sit, he doesn't order him, and when he says, "Nay, we'll go / together down, sir" (lines 53–54), he appears to be declining this person's gesture offering to follow the Duke down the stairs. At one point, the Duke's words suggest his listener's role at the same time as they reveal something of the situation in which the Duke speaks:

> The Count your master's known munificence
> Is ample warrant that no just pretense
> Of mine for dowry will be disallowed;
> Though his fair daughter's self, as I avowed
> At starting, is my object.

The Duke's listener must be an important, trusted member of the Count's household because the Duke and he have been discussing the Duke's intention to marry the Count's daughter. That, in turn, would help explain why the Duke is showing a painting of his *last* (his previous) Duchess to this man and why the Duke drops the names of the painter, "Frà Pandolf," and the sculptor, "Claus of Innsbruck," who "cast in bronze" the "Neptune . . . Taming a sea-horse."

A dramatic monologue like "My Last Duchess" can be fun to read aloud too, for the subtle but definite rhyme pattern and for the dramatic rendering you can do of the Duke's personality as he speaks. "My Last Duchess" is written in **couplets**, pairs of rhyming lines. I call the rhyme pattern subtle because if you read the *sentences* the Duke speaks, letting their punctuation instead of the verse lines determine your pauses, the end rhymes are not so obvious. If you did not do so before, read the poem again, aloud, according to the sentence punctuation, as if the text were prose, not verse. Listen to a classmate's oral reading of the poem, too, to get a sense of how differences in vocal emphasis and phrasing affect the dramatic quality of the poem.[2]

You may also see a dramatic quality in "My Last Duchess" in another way besides someone speaking to someone else about something on some particular occasion. Perhaps you may see this poem as dramatic in that, like in a stage drama, something of the moral character of the speaker is revealed through his words. Besides being a name-dropper, what other judgments can you make of the kind of person the Duke is? Is he self-assured? Suave? Proud? What does he think of his late duchess—as a person, as opposed to the subject of a painting? What account does he give of her while she was alive? Many readers have found the Duke's comment in lines 45–46 especially revealing, even shocking, about the kind of man the Duke is. (He says, "I gave commands; / Then all smiles stopped together.")

Is it possible to reconstruct the Duke's **ideology**, with respect to people, marriage, and property, for instance, from his words? What are his values, beliefs, assumptions, or attitudes toward any of these matters? If you sense a difference between the kind of person the Duke presents himself to be to his listener and the kind of person his words reveal him to be underneath that surface, you are reading the Duke's words as **ironic**. If so, what inferences might be made about Robert Browning's ideology? How distant does he seem to be from the Duke, how morally close to or far from him? These are matters for interpretation of "My Last Duchess" or any dramatic monologue, and they involve play too: the play of ideology among created character, poet, and reader. The literal difference between the poet and the speaker in a dramatic monologue, like that between author and character in fiction or drama, makes irony in the speaker's words possible because it also allows the possibility that the poet's ideology is different from the speaker's.

---

[2]To take playing with the text a little further, consider dramatizing "My Last Duchess" even more by acting it out. The scene here could be staged, and the roles of the Duke and the Count's emissary could be cast. The latter has no lines to say, but he could do physical acting as he listens to the Duke and reacts to his words. Both characters' movements could be *blocked* (their movements within the set and in relation to one another planned out). Doing these things might reveal even more plainly the *dramatic* quality of the poem. (See the Reading and Writing Projects for Creative and Critical Thinking section at the end of this chapter.)

Sharing Your Reading

After trying to get a grasp on the speaker, the spoken-to, the setting, and the gist of "My Last Duchess," your next step should be to share some of the results of your reading with other readers in class or small-group discussions. That sharing should reveal some differences in:

- the kind of picture readers are constructing of the dramatic elements of "My Last Duchess";
- what different readers are focusing on as important words and phrases, how they are playing with connotations, for instance;
- interpretations of and responses to the Duke as a character; and
- the values and beliefs that readers are bringing to the text to make these decisions.

Your own careful, active reading of "My Last Duchess" and your class's sharing of readings should also show something about the interactive nature of the reading process: Both the text and the reader are contributing to the construction of meaning and to the reading experience with "My Last Duchess" or any poem.

Different responses to the moral character of the Duke and to the Duke's values or implied opposing values that may render the Duke's words ironic show interaction occurring in an ideological dimension. Your awareness of the interaction in a literary dimension will be enhanced if you know something about what the text brings to the reading situation from its literary repertoire as a dramatic monologue and if you have consciously applied the practical reading strategies for poems.

With the strength and awareness you have gained from the reading you've done in this chapter, you are now ready to tackle some more lyric poems, as presented in the next chapter. But first, to illustrate something of the variety of the dramatic monologue, here are some more poems for you to read and respond to. Some of them may be more obviously dramatic monologues than others, just as "Dover Beach" is more immediately recognizable as a dramatic monologue than "Cover Me." But your activity as a reader in any of these poems will help to emphasize their dramatic qualities, and the similarity or difference of aspects of your life experience to the dramatic situation in any of these poems will make that poem come more or less "alive" for you as you read.

Poems for Exploration

John Donne   1572–1631

The Flea   *1633*

Mark° but this flea, and mark in this   notice
How little that which thou deny'st me is;
It sucked me first, and now sucks thee,
And in this flea our two bloods mingled be;

Thou know'st that this cannot be said
A sin, nor shame, nor loss of maidenhead;
   Yet this enjoys before it woo,
    And pampered swells with one blood made of two,
    And this, alas, is more than we would do.   5

Oh stay,° three lives in one flea spare,   wait   10
Where we almost, yea, more than married are.
This flea is you and I, and this
Our marriage bed and marriage temple is;
Though parents grudge, and you, we are met
And cloistered in these living walls of jet.°   black   15
   Though use° make you apt to kill me,   custom
    Let not to that, self-murder added be,
    And sacrilege, three sins in killing three.

Cruel and sudden, hast thou since
Purpled thy nail in blood of innocence?   20
Wherein could this flea guilty be,
Except in that drop which it sucked from thee?
Yet thou triumph'st and say'st that thou
Find'st not thyself, nor me the weaker now.
   'Tis true. Then learn how false fears be: 25
    Just so much honor, when thou yield'st to me,
    Will waste, as this flea's death took life from thee.

Alfred, Lord Tennyson   1809–1892

Ulysses   *1833*

It little profits that an idle king,
By this still hearth, among these barren crags,
Matched with an agèd wife, I mete and dole
Unequal laws unto a savage race,
That hoard, and sleep, and feed, and know not me.   5
I cannot rest from travel; I will drain
Life to the lees. All times I have enjoy'd
Greatly, have suffer'd greatly, both with those
That love me, and alone; on shore, and when
Thro' scudding drifts the rainy Hyades   10
Vexed the dim sea. I am become a name;
For always roaming with a hungry heart
Much have I seen and known,—cities of men
And manners, climates, councils, governments,
Myself not least, but honored of them all,—   15
And drunk delight of battle with my peers,
Far on the ringing plains of windy Troy.

I am a part of all that I have met;
Yet all experience is an arch wherethrough
Gleams that untravelled world whose margin fades   20
For ever and for ever when I move.
How dull it is to pause, to make an end,
To rust unburnished, not to shine in use!
As though to breathe were life! Life piled on life
Were all too little, and of one to me   25
Little remains; but every hour is saved
From that eternal silence, something more,
A bringer of new things; and vile it were
For some three suns to store and hoard myself,
And this gray spirit yearning in desire   30
To follow knowledge like a sinking star,
Beyond the utmost bound of human thought.

     This is my son, mine own Telemachus,
To whom I leave the scepter and the isle,—
Well-loved of me, discerning to fulfill   35
This labor, by slow prudence to make mild
A rugged people, and through soft degrees
Subdue them to the useful and the good.
Most blameless is he, centered in the sphere
Of common duties, decent not to fail   40
In offices of tenderness, and pay
Meet adoration to my household gods,
When I am gone. He works his work, I mine.

     There lies the port; the vessel puffs her sail;
There gloom the dark, broad seas. My mariners,
Souls that have toiled, and wrought, and thought with me,—   45
That ever with a frolic° welcome took   cheerful
The thunder and the sunshine, and opposed
Free hearts, free foreheads,—you and I are old;
Old age hath yet his honor and his toil.
Death closes all; but something ere the end,   50
Some work of noble note, may yet be done,
Not unbecoming men that strove with Gods.
The lights begin to twinkle from the rocks;
The long day wanes; the slow moon climbs; the deep
Moans round with many voices. Come, friends,   55
'Tis not too late to seek a newer world.
Push off, and sitting well in order smite
The sounding furrows; for my purpose holds
To sail beyond the sunset, and the baths
Of all the western stars, until I die.   60
It may be that the gulfs will wash us down;
It may be we shall touch the Happy Isles,
And see the great Achilles, whom we knew.

Though much is taken, much abides; and though   65
We are not now that strength which in old days
Moved earth and heaven, that which we are, we are,—
One equal temper of heroic hearts,
Made weak by time and fate, but strong in will
To strive, to seek, to find, and not to yield.   70

Dwight Okita   b. 1958

IN RESPONSE TO EXECUTIVE ORDER 9066:
ALL AMERICANS OF JAPANESE DESCENT
MUST REPORT TO RELOCATION CENTERS   1983

Dear Sirs:
Of course I'll come. I've packed my galoshes
and three packets of tomato seeds. Janet calls them
"love apples." My father says where we're going
they won't grow.

I am a fourteen-year-old girl with bad spelling   5
and a messy room. If it helps any, I will tell you
I have always felt funny using chopsticks
and my favorite food is hot dogs.
My best friend is a white girl named Denise—
we look at boys together. She sat in front of me   10
all through grade school because of our names:
O'Connor, Ozawa. I know the back of Denise's head very well.
I tell her she's going bald. She tells me I copy on tests.
We're best friends.

I saw Denise today in Geography class.   15
She was sitting on the other side of the room.
"You're trying to start a war," she said, "giving secrets away
to the Enemy. Why can't you keep your big mouth shut?"
I didn't know what to say.
I gave her a packet of tomato seeds   20
and asked her to plant them for me, told her
when the first tomato ripens
she'd miss me.

Louise Erdrich   b. 1954

Windigo   1984

For Angela

> *The Windigo is a flesh-eating, wintry demon with a man buried deep inside of
> it. In some Chippewa stories, a young girl vanquishes this monster by forcing
> boiling lard down its throat, thereby releasing the human at the core of ice.*

You knew I was coming for you, little one,
when the kettle jumped into the fire.
Towels flapped on the hooks,
and the dog crept off, groaning,
to the deepest part of the woods.   5

In the hackles of dry brush a thin laughter started up.
Mother scolded the food warm and smooth in the pot
and called you to eat.
But I spoke in the cold trees:
New one, I have come for you, child hide and lie still.   10

The sumac pushed sour red cones through the air.
Copper burned in the raw wood.
You saw me drag toward you.
Oh touch me. I murmured, and licked the soles of your feet.
You dug your hands into my pale, melting fur.   15

I stole you off, a huge thing in my bristling armor.
Steam rolled from my wintry arms, each leaf shivered
from the bushes we passed
until they stood, naked, spread like the cleaned spines of fish.

Then your warm hands hummed over and shoveled themselves full   20
of the ice and the snow. I would darken and spill
all night running, until at last morning broke the cold earth
and I carried you home,
a river shaking in the sun.

Tracy Chapman   b. 1964

Fast Car   *1987*

You got a fast car
I want a ticket to anywhere
Maybe we make a deal
Maybe together we can get somewhere
Anyplace is better   5
Starting from zero got nothing to lose
Maybe we'll make something
But me myself I got nothing to prove

You got a fast car
And I got a plan to get us out of here   10
I been working at the convenience store
Managed to save just a little bit of money
We won't have to drive too far
Just 'cross the border and into the city
You and I can both get jobs   15
And finally see what it means to be living

You see my old man's got a problem
He live with the bottle that's the way it is
He says his body's too old for working
I say his body's too young to look like his   20
My mama went off and left him
She wanted more from life than he could give
I said somebody's got to take care of him
So I quit school and that's what I did

You got a fast car   25
But is it fast enough so we can fly away
We gotta make a decision
We leave tonight or live and die this way

I remember we were driving driving in your car
The speed so fast I felt like I was drunk   30
City lights lay out before us
And your arm felt nice wrapped 'round my shoulder
And I had a feeling that I belonged
And I had feeling I could be someone, be someone, be someone

You got a fast car   35
And we go cruising to entertain ourselves
You still ain't got a job
And I work in a market as a checkout girl
I know things will get better
You'll find work and I'll get promoted   40
We'll move out of the shelter
Buy a big house and live in the suburbs

You got a fast car
And I got a job that pays all our bills
You stay out drinking late at the bar   45
See more of your friends than you do of your kids
I'd always hoped for better
Thought maybe together you and me would find it
I got no plans I ain't going nowhere
So take your fast car and keep on driving   50

You got a fast car
But is it fast enough so you can fly away
You gotta make a decision
You leave tonight or live and die this way

 # READING AND WRITING PROJECTS

FOR CREATIVE AND CRITICAL THINKING

A major goal of this book is to help you learn about yourself as a reader—both
what you do cognitively when you read and how culture impinges on the kind

of reader you are when you interact with any particular text. Writing in all its manifestations is an important means to that goal because performing the actions of writing causes you to focus on the actions you take and the situation you are in as a reader. In addition to the kinds of writing already discussed and exemplified in this book, there are other ways to use writing to learn.

The following writing suggestions are intended to help you integrate your reading of and writing about literary texts in various ways. These suggestions include exploratory writing, playing with texts and language, creative efforts in various genres, and other writing exercises designed to strengthen your awareness of the cognitive and cultural processes involved in your reading.

▶ Assume the role of the person who is *spoken to* in a dramatic monologue. Write a prose account, to a specific reader, of that person's reaction to the words she or he heard spoken by the speaker in the dramatic monologue. For example, take the role of the Count's emissary in "My Last Duchess" and write a report to "your master the Count" about your visit to the Duke of Ferrara. (After all, the Duke is seeking to marry the Count's daughter, and the Count has sent you to hear the Duke's proposal.) You could also write an account of one of Ulysses' men in Tennyson's poem of that name. How might he react to his leader's decision to "Push off" and "sail beyond the sunset"?

▶ As suggested in this chapter, rewrite a dramatic monologue as a **script** for stage, television, or film production. Think of it as a scene, rather than as a complete act or play. Following the conventions of realistic drama, write a set description, brief descriptions of characters (appearance, age, costume, etc.), dialogue (some of which you may take from the words of the speaker in the poem), and stage directions for the characters' movements and actions. As a follow-up to this, "stage" or enact your dramatization of the poem. It could be performed live for your class or another class, or it could be videotaped for presentation at another time.

▶ Rewrite a lyric poem as an expository essay. Assume the point of view of the voice in the poem and rewrite in prose what he or she has to say. Try to capture the poetic speaker's tone as you do so, but don't lean too heavily on his or her actual language. At the same time, don't just transcribe the poetry into prose sentences. If a poem is a condensed expression of someone's thoughts or feelings, a prose rewrite should be more discursive—longer, if not rambling.

▶ Write a lyric poem in the voice of a character in a narrative poem. For example, assume the point of view of Sir Patrick Spence and express his thoughts and feelings at some particular moment—for instance, when he first reads the letter from the king telling him to make his voyage.

▶ Write an imaginary journal entry for a character in a narrative poem. This assignment is more or less a prose version of the poetry writing assignment above. Writing a journal entry for, say, Sir Patrick Spence, expressing his reaction to the king's letter, would give you a chance to reveal a character's thoughts and feelings, which the narrative genre conceals.

▶ Write a background account, in prose, of the situation and feelings of the speaker in a lyric poem. What circumstances led this person to say what he or she says on the occasion in which he or she is speaking in this poem?

12 ◈ TYPES OF POETRY

Chapter 11 offered a brief look at some of the most general kinds of poetry—narrative and lyric—and then considered the dramatic monologue in more detail as one category of lyric poetry. Your ability to categorize a poem like "My Last Duchess" as a dramatic monologue or "Sir Patrick Spence" as a ballad depends on being able to see how the poem practices the conventions of the genre. If you were to try to write your own dramatic monologue or ballad, you would have to work within a certain set of conventions. Therefore, discrete kinds of poems may be regarded as sets of organized text strategies: certain ways of arranging or playing with language according to established practices. In saying this, I don't mean to reduce something as lively as "My Last Duchess," an actual poem, to a mere formula, but rather I mean to suggest that there is a degree of formal regularity to poems that belong to certain recognized categories. Furthermore, a reader who is aware of the regular text strategies or conventions of a genre can enrich his or her interaction with poems of that genre. He or she will bring more *to* the poem in terms of literary experience and know more of what the text brings in terms of its literary repertoire.

Fixed and Open Forms

Besides the division of poems into the general types of narrative and lyric, there is another division according to formal considerations. A poem may be written or read as a **fixed-form** poem or an **open-form** poem. There are many fixed forms—that is, regular, set arrangements of numbers of lines and stanzas, rhyme patterns, and meter—and all kinds of open-form poems that are not arranged in any of the fixed ways. This chapter will examine six fixed forms—the **sonnet**, the **haiku**, the **epigram**, the **sestina**, the **villanelle**, and the **pantoum**—and then take a look at some open-form poems.

Fixed-Form Poems

The form of a poem relates to its content in several ways. Form shapes content, in a sense, because of the limitations the form presents. This should be evident in even the most basic ways, irrespective of any specific genre: Formal requirements of rhyme or meter or even brevity affect what may be said in the language of a poem. (You can demonstrate this for yourself by writing within strict formal limits of number of lines, a rhyme scheme, and a regular meter.) In addition, the tradition of certain fixed forms has been to focus on certain subjects or treat them in certain ways, one reason being that some forms lend themselves better to light or serious treatment of a subject. Because of this relationship between form and content, your interactions with poems can be enriched if you broaden your experience with formal categories as well as with open forms.

The Sonnet

Because it is perhaps the most widely known and practiced of the fixed forms, the sonnet perhaps deserves more attention here than the other fixed forms. To define this category of lyric in basic formal terms, a sonnet (originally "little song") in the English poetic tradition is 14 lines of iambic pentameter verse. *Iambic pentameter* is a metrical pattern in which each line has five stressed syllables (*pent*ameter) and the syllables alternate unstressed, stressed. Most sonnets rhyme, but there is a variation: the **blank verse** sonnet, which is 14 lines of unrhymed iambic pentameter. Within sonnets that do rhyme, the rhyming pattern may vary, but the 14-line limit is virtually absolute.

The sonnet came into fashion in English poetry in the sixteenth century, through the influence of Thomas Wyatt and Henry Howard, Earl of Surrey. Wyatt translated the fourteenth-century sonnets of the Italian Francesco Petrarca (Petrarch, in English), who had developed and popularized the form and established certain subjects—devotion to a "lost" lover, religious piety—as conventional to the form. Slightly later than the time of Wyatt and Surrey, William Shakespeare wrote so many sonnets so competently and powerfully that his name is often given to one variation of the basic sonnet form: the Shakespearean, or English, sonnet. (Another form is known as the Petrarchan, or Italian, sonnet.) These early practices established the conventions of the sonnet form, which has been practiced by many poets in the Anglo-American tradition. Many of those poems are firmly ensconced in the canon, but the sonnet is certainly not merely a "historical" form, because sonnets are still being written by poets today.

Within the sonnet's 14 lines, poets usually adopt one of several **rhyme schemes** and organizational patterns or strategies. The Italian sonnet is conventionally organized into eight-line and six-line stanzas, an **octave** and a **sestet**. Sometimes there's a visual break on the page after the eighth line; sometimes there isn't. Conventionally, the octave presents a topic, a problem, or a situation, and the sestet comments on it, extends its implications, or ponders it. The rhyme scheme often parallels this organization: The pattern of rhyming sounds at the ends of lines in the octave is *abbaabba*; in the sestet it may be *cdecde, cdcdcd,* or *cdedce*. Five rhyming vowel sounds are involved.

The English sonnet does things a little differently than the Italian, sometimes dividing the octave into two four-line stanzas or **quatrains,** including another quatrain as part of the sestet, and closing with a couplet, or two rhyming lines. In addition to making the sound quality of the poem a bit more complex, this arrangement affords some flexibility as far as the "thematic" division of the sonnet is concerned. It allows the poet the chance to use the closing couplet as, for instance, a "commentary" on whatever has been presented in the preceding 12 lines. A typical rhyme scheme for an English sonnet is *abab cdcd efef gg*: for example, be*hold, hang, cold, sang; day, west,* a*way, rest; fire, lie,* ex*pire, by; strong, long.*

As with the dramatic monologue, it is also true of the sonnet that a reader doesn't *have* to know all this technical information to have a meaningful interaction with a text written in that form. But a reader who is aware of some of the text strategies that are at work in a sonnet and in effect define a poem as a sonnet will have more to interact with.

As to content, it may interest you to know, if you don't already, that Petrarch wrote hundreds of sonnets to and about "Laura," a woman he "loved from afar." Following his practice, early poets working in the sonnet form wrote mostly about "love" in some way or another, or at least about relations between men and women. Of course, when the sonnet was first becoming popular, the poets who wrote them—and the perspective they wrote from—were mostly male, and the "poetic objects" they wrote to and about were female. So it might be more correct to say that originally sonnets were mostly about love from the man's point of view. In many *Elizabethan* sonnets (a historical, not a formal, designation: sonnets written in England generally during the reign of Elizabeth I—1558–1603), the poet or speaker often adopted an attitude toward the poetic object, such as quasi-religious adoration or wistful recollection of the missing or departed lover. Often these ideas were expressed figuratively in an intellectually elaborate comparison—a **conceit** or an extended metaphor or **simile**—between the speaker and something else: the seasons of the year, for instance.

This feature of the sonnet illustrates one of the essential qualities of lyric, as opposed to narrative poetry: the expression of the feelings or thoughts of a single speaker on a specific subject. When the sonnet form was first being established in the Western literary canon, those feelings and that subject usually had to do with love or romantic relations, as seen from the man's perspective, but later practitioners of the form broadened the range of subjects to include tributes to people of either gender, politics, the natural scene, and so forth.

Reading Sonnets Actively   With this short discussion as background, either adding something to your literary experience that was not already there or reinforcing something that was, turn now to a couple of examples for reading and responding. The first is an early instance, the second more recent. Read each according to the method outlined in Chapter 11 (pages 534–536) and write a response statement, using the questions that follow each poem.

William Shakespeare   1564–1616

Sonnet 73   *1609*

That time of year thou mayst in me behold
When yellow leaves, or none, or few, do hang
Upon those boughs which shake against the cold,
Bare ruined choirs, where late the sweet birds sang.

In me thou seest the twilight of such day   5
As after sunset fadeth in the west;
Which by and by black night doth take away,
Death's second self, that seals up all in rest.
In me thou seest the glowing of such fire
That on the ashes of his youth doth lie,   10
As the deathbed whereon it must expire,
Consumed with that which it was nourished by,
This thou perceivest, which makes thy love more strong,
To love that well which thou must leave ere long.

Response Statement Questions

- How do any of the text strategies of the sonnet in Shakespeare's poem affect the way you read it?
- What particular reading strategies did you adopt, knowing this poem to be a sonnet?
- Can you write a prose paraphrase of what the speaker seems to be "saying"? Where, if anywhere, do you have any trouble doing this: Is any part of the poem more difficult to understand conceptually than other parts? Are you able to "outline" a logical organization to the thought in this poem?
- What one word would you use to name the speaker's attitude or **tone** here?
- What is your response to what the speaker seems to be saying or his tone? What aspects of your ideology contribute to your response here?
- *Share and Compare*   Discuss your responses to the above questions with your classmates. What similarities and differences emerge from that discussion?

Edna St. Vincent Millay   1892–1950

What Lips My Lips Have Kissed, and Where,   1923
and Why

What lips my lips have kissed, and where, and why,
I have forgotten, and what arms have lain
Under my head till morning; but the rain
Is full of ghosts tonight, that tap and sigh
Upon the glass and listen for reply,   5
And in my heart there stirs a quiet pain
For unremembered lads that not again
Will turn to me at midnight with a cry.
Thus in the winter stands the lonely tree,
Nor knows what birds have vanished one by one,   10
Yet knows its boughs more silent than before:
I cannot say what loves have come and gone,

I only know that summer sang in me
A little while, that in me sings no more.

Response Statement Questions

- How do any of the text strategies of the sonnet in Millay's poem affect the way you read it?
- What particular reading strategies did you adopt, knowing this poem to be a sonnet?
- Can you write a prose paraphrase of what the speaker seems to be "saying"? Where, if anywhere, do you have any trouble doing this: Is any part of the poem more difficult to understand conceptually than other parts?
- What one word would you use to name the speaker's attitude or tone here?
- What is your response to what the speaker seems to be saying or her tone? What aspects of your ideology contribute to your response here?
- *Share and Compare*   Discuss your responses to the above questions with your classmates. What similarities and differences emerge from that discussion? Compare your class's responses to the Millay sonnet to the one by Shakespeare: What seems to account for any differences in the way readers responded to the two texts?

Convention and Variety   Reading these poems as sonnets should help you have a more harmonious interaction with them at the literary level: You know "what to look for" in terms of their organization of ideas, rhyme patterns, meter, and so on; you know "how to read them" in terms of seeing the division of thought into blocks of lines. In the Shakespeare sonnet, for instance, each group of four lines is a single sentence, and the rhyme pattern in each group closes with the final period in the sentence. The final couplet is another sentence. In terms of division of thought, the poem could be said to present three statements about the age (or ag*ing*) of the speaker, then one about the speaker's lover.

The Millay poem follows the rhyme pattern of the Italian sonnet (*abab, baab, cde, dce*). The octave (first eight lines) constitutes one sentence, with the fourth instance of the *b* sound closing the sentence and the octave. The sestet (final six lines) is another sentence, again with the repetition of a sound (*e*) at the close.

In Shakespeare's sonnet, were you able to see any of the attitudes of the speaker as conventional, typical, or "poetic"? Were you surprised by anything the speaker "said" or any turns in his logic? Were you able to paraphrase it reasonably well? Was the subject matter close to what you might expect of a Shakespearean sonnet? Did the ideas or attitude you saw in the poem seem especially masculine? Did they seem old, historically? Romantic?

How did your (and your classmates') experience reading and responding to Millay's sonnet compare to your (and their) experience with Shakespeare's? Was it any easier or harder to paraphrase? to follow the turns in the speaker's logic? to establish a sense of the speaker's tone? Did the ideas or the attitude you saw in this poem seem especially feminine or modern, in comparison to the Shakespeare poem?

Now consider some other text strategies of these poems, ones that may or may not be peculiar to the sonnet form. If you were able to "outline" the thought structure in Sonnet 73, perhaps you were aided by or noticed the figurative language, specifically the metaphors, in the poem. A metaphor is an implied comparison of two superficially unlike things, the point of which is to suggest an underlying, perhaps startling, similarity between them. In each of the first three sentences/four-line groups, the speaker compares his condition to an example of age and decay: a tree in late autumn, the twilight of a day, a fire reduced to embers. These comparisons set up the idea in the final couplet that, if the speaker's lover recognizes his aging, she loves him all the more strongly because of that recognition.

In the first eight lines of Millay's poem, the speaker presents her thoughts more directly than Shakespeare's speaker. These lines could be paraphrased as, "I've forgotten the individual lovers I've had, but I remember having them and I miss them now." The sestet introduces a metaphor similar to the first one in Sonnet 73: The speaker describes a tree in winter, deserted by birds that once perched there and somehow aware that its "boughs" are "silent." The colon at the end of line 11 is a punctuation sign indicating that the rest of the sentence (lines 12–14) will complete the thought in the first part, in this case by comparing the speaker to the tree and her former lovers to the birds, her present situation to winter and her past to summer.

Perhaps you found, as I did, that this metaphor offers a striking instance of **intertextuality** between these two poems. Shakespeare's poem is well known, a highly canonical text. Millay's poem is not so well known; she is considered a "minor" twentieth-century poet. The speakers in both poems invoke the image of the empty tree in winter in a metaphor for an aging lover. Is Millay's handling of this image any less effective than Shakespeare's, for all the difference in the two poets' canonical status? Does either treatment of the figure strike you more powerfully? If so, behind your answer may lie something you bring to the poem in terms of your ideology regarding romance, loneliness, aging, or the effect of historical situation or gender on any of those topics.

As is usually the case in lyric poetry, the linguistic figures in these two poems are not so much ornaments or embellishments on the structure of thought as they are the vehicle through which the thought is carried—or, more to the point, both vehicle *and* the thought itself. If Shakespeare or Millay were to select different metaphors to carry the thought, it would change the thought itself, perhaps not basically but subtly and definitely nonetheless. This fact is worth noting because it means that in poetry, form and content are often inseparable, even though our language, by having one word for one and another for the other, suggests they are separable. Perhaps the metaphors in these two poems also suggest something about the voice in each poem: They don't merely tell you what the speaker is thinking, but the "kind of person" the speaker is who would think in these particular figures.

Roughly synonymous with "figurative language" is the term imagery, a collective noun comprising such particular figures as metaphor and simile (an explicit comparison signaled by such words as *like* or *as*). An individual image, however, while it is a figure of speech, may be understood as involving something "outside" the poem that is "recalled" by the language of the text. Of course, in the interactive model of reading, the mind or imagination of the reader is also involved in this "recollection," as it is in completing the circuit with any figurative language. The three metaphors in Sonnet 73, therefore, can be understood as images (assuming, of course, that a reader is able to "picture" or "see" a tree in late fall with "yellow leaves, or none, or few" hanging "Upon those boughs," for instance). And all the metaphors in the poem can be regarded as constituting its imagery. To dwell on the first of these for just a moment, the comparison of the speaker to a tree contains another metaphor in which the branches of the tree are compared to a part of a church ("choirs," as in choirlofts) that are now "bare [and] ruined." In this figure, the "sweet birds" become church singers. This metaphor-within-a-metaphor seems to connote or suggest a religious level of meaning to the speaker's aging process, a connotation that increases the seriousness of the speaker's attitude.

Millay's sonnet does not seem to use metaphor as an organizing device the way Sonnet 73 does, but it does have one metaphor in the sestet and it is not devoid of images elsewhere. Do the concrete language and sensory detail of the octave—"lips," "arms," "head," "rain," "glass," "heart," "cry"—help you see and hear what the speaker is talking about? Do they help you experience her feelings? Does your own experience with recollections of lovers past come into play to help you complete the circuit here? The gist of the octave may be paraphrasable the way I have done it, but to say "I've forgotten the individual lovers I've had, but I remember having them and I miss them now" is to put abstractly what Millay's lines put concretely and sensuously. And those images are surely more effective in making a connection with an individual reader's experience than the abstract language of the paraphrase would be.

CONNECT: Look again at the two poems in Chapter 2—Matthew Arnold's "Dover Beach" and Bruce Springsteen's "Cover Me." How are any implied attitudes toward romantic love in those poems like or unlike the attitudes in the sonnets by Shakespeare and Millay? Of all four poems, which one or two are closest to your own attitude toward or experience with romantic love?

Reading Gwendolyn Brooks' "First Fight. Then Fiddle." as a Sonnet   I hope this discussion of the sonnet and these examples help you see something about the relationship of form and content as it exists in one category of poetry. Knowing about the text strategies of that category broadens your literary experience, so that any other time you encounter a 14-line lyric you'll have some basis for a harmonious interaction with it in literary terms.

Now look again at the poem by Gwendolyn Brooks, "First Fight. Then Fiddle." in Chapter 10 (pages 506–507). When you encountered it there the first time, no mention was made of it being a sonnet. Now, however, with a broadened literary experience regarding this poetic form, you should be able to see that it is. Written even more recently than Millay's sonnet, "First Fight. Then Fiddle." shows that the content of the sonnet form does not have to be limited to romantic love. Although the word "love" is mentioned in the poem, it is qualified by the seemingly contrary adjective "hurting," and the speaker seems to be neither reminiscing about her youth, as in the Millay sonnet, nor commenting on her own status as a love object, as in Shakespeare's.

This speaker is addressing someone (the reader?) directly, as indicated by the imperative mood of the verbs in the poem, and is apparently urging that person to action. Neither Millay's nor Shakespeare's speaker directly addresses the reader or advocates taking actions. In rereading Brooks' poem, perhaps you did see much of the language as figurative, which would indicate a text strategy common among the three sonnets. Maybe you read the "violin" as a symbol, not as a literal stringed instrument. A symbol differs from a metaphor in that the latter suggests a relatively explicit comparison between two things (a person and a tree, for instance), whereas the former offers only one of the things being compared and leaves the other at least initially indeterminate. In Brooks' poem, something—some idea, some value, some condition—seems to be likened to a violin or to playing a violin, but the identity of that something is not made explicit. This indeterminacy, of course, leaves "First Fight. Then Fiddle." open to interpretation in a way that neither of the other two sonnets is, requiring a reader to be more active if he or she is to make sense of the text.

Parody   One form of playing with a poetic text is to write a parody of it, a playful imitation. There is a long tradition in English poetry of poems that play with other poems in this way. Here is an example of a well-known sonnet by Shakespeare that was parodied by a twentieth-century American writer, Howard Moss. Moss's poem might also be considered a verse paraphrase of Shakespeare's original.

William Shakespeare   1564–1616

Sonnet 18   *1609*

Shall I compare thee to a summer's day?
Thou art more lovely and more temperate.
Rough winds do shake the darling buds of May,
And summer's lease hath all too short a date.
Sometime too hot the eye of heaven shines,   5
And often is his gold complexion dimmed;
And every fair from fair sometimes declines,
By chance, or nature's changing course untrimmed;
But thy eternal summer shall not fade,
Nor lose possession of that fair thou ows't;   10

Nor shall death brag thou wand'rest in his shade,
When in eternal lines to time thou grow'st.
So long as men can breathe or eyes can see,
So long lives this, and this gives life to thee.

Howard Moss   1922–1987

Shall I Compare Thee to a Summer's Day?   1976

Who says you're like one of the dog days?
You're nicer. And better.
Even in May, the weather can be gray,
And a summer sub-let doesn't last forever.
Sometimes the sun's too hot;
Sometimes it is not.   5
Who can stay young forever?
People break their necks or just drop dead!
But you? Never!

If there's just one condensed reader left
Who can figure out the abridged alphabet,   10
    After you're dead and gone,
    In this poem you'll live on!

Other Fixed Forms

In addition to the sonnet, knowing other sets of organized text strategies and the conventions those categories observe will broaden your literary experience still further. Because it is always 14-lines long, whether Italian or English, the sonnet is one of several types of fixed-form lyric poetry. Other types further illustrate the great variety of poetry, both "serious" and "light." Following are five more fixed forms, each briefly defined and illustrated with an example. In order to understand these forms, however, it may first be necessary to know something about metrics, the system of regular rhythm, or meter, in English poetry.

A poetic or metric foot is a pattern of syllables containing one *accent* or *stress* and one or two unaccented or unstressed syllables. For example, an anapestic foot is two unaccented syllables followed by an accented syllable, as in the word *contradíct* or the phrase *on the phóne*. The other most common English metric feet are the iamb (one unaccented, one accented: *Kathleén*), the trochee (one accented, one unaccented: *Gáry*), and the dactyl (one accented, two unaccented: *Nícholas*).

Poetic meter is a term for a more or less regular pattern of rhythm in verse lines. Much poetry written in English can be described or **scanned** in terms of the kind of feet that predominate and the number of such feet per line of verse; hence *iambic pentameter* (five iambic feet per line), or *anapestic hexameter* (six anapestic feet per line), and so on. Iambic pentameter is the dominant meter in the sonnets by Shakespeare, Millay, and Brooks. Here is the first line of Sonnet 73, with the stresses shown:

$$\breve{\text{That}} \acute{\text{time}} \breve{\text{of}} \acute{\text{year}} \breve{\text{thou}} \acute{\text{mayst}} \breve{\text{in}} \acute{\text{me}} \breve{\text{be}} \acute{\text{hold}}$$

When you read that line aloud, of course, the accents will fall naturally, making the line sound like regular English speech, not something artificially rhythmical. Here is a newspaper headline that scans as *dactylic tetramater*. I have placed the accents. ("A-B-E" is an airport financed in part by two counties.)

$$\acute{\text{A}}\text{-}\breve{\text{B}}\text{-}\breve{\text{E}}, \acute{\text{counties}} \breve{} \breve{} \acute{\text{to}} \breve{\text{settle}} \breve{} \acute{\text{dispute}}$$

Depending on your literary experience with such matters, you may have spent time in class scanning lines of verse to determine their meter or the meter an entire poem is written in. I will not encourage you to do that here, although you may find it enjoyable. But knowing about metrics may add to your awareness of the sound quality or music of some English poetry (or of the English language in general), and it may enlarge your literary experience with respect to some of the formal aspects of English verse.

The Haiku

The haiku is originally a Japanese form consisting of three lines totaling 17 syllables broken down into lines of five, seven, and five syllables. However, translations from the Japanese, as in the first example below, and many English originals do not follow the syllable count strictly.

Kawai Chigetsu-Ni   1632–1736

Grasshoppers

Translated by Kenneth Rexroth and Ikuko Atsumi

Grasshoppers
Chirping in the sleeves
Of a scarecrow.

Etheridge Knight   1931–1991

Eastern Guard Tower   1968

Eastern guard tower
glints in sunset; convicts rest
like lizards on rocks.

The Epigram

The epigram is a short poem—of unspecified number of lines but usually fewer than six—that ends in a clever turn of thought. The first example that follows both defines and illustrates the form.

Samuel Taylor Coleridge   1772–1834

What Is an Epigram?   *1802*

What is an epigram? A dwarfish whole;
Its body brevity, and wit its soul.

Paul Laurence Dunbar   1872–1906

Theology   *1896*

There is a heaven, for ever, day by day,
The upward longing of my soul doth tell me so.
There is a hell, I'm quite as sure; for pray,
If there were not, where would my neighbors go?

It's fun to try your hand at writing haiku or epigrams. It's also good discipline to make yourself work within the formal limits—line numbers, syllables, meter—of either of these types. Some longer fixed forms, usually devoted to more serious subjects or more serious treatment of subject, are the sestina, the villanelle, and the pantoum.

The Sestina

The sestina, originally a French form from the twelfth century, is usually unrhymed. It consists of 39 lines of any length, divided into six six-line stanzas and a final three-line stanza (or tercet) known as an *envoy*. What makes the sestina an especially difficult form to write is the requirement that the six words that end the lines of the first stanza be repeated at the ends of the lines of the other five stanzas. Those six words must also appear in the envoy. Furthermore, there is a conventional order that those six words follow, both in the stanzas and in the envoy. In the stanzas the order is *abcdef, faebdc, cfdabe, ecbfad, deacfb, bdfeca.* If you look at the sestina that follows, you can see that it observes this conventional pattern for repeating the end words in the opening stanza: *house, grandmother, child, stove, almanac, tears.* In the envoy, one of the six end words occurs within each line and one at the end of each line; the conventional order here is *be, dc, fa.*

Elizabeth Bishop   1911–1979

Sestina   *1965*

September rain falls on the house.
In the failing light, the old grandmother
sits in the kitchen with the child
beside the Little Marvel Stove,

reading the jokes from the almanac,   5
laughing and talking to hide her tears.

She thinks that her equinoctial tears
and the rain that beats on the roof of the house
were both foretold by the almanac,
but only known to a grandmother.   10
The iron kettle sings on the stove.
She cuts some bread and says to the child,

It's time for tea now; but the child
is watching the teakettle's small hard tears
dance like mad on the hot black stove,   15
the way the rain must dance on the house.
Tidying up, the old grandmother
hangs up the clever almanac

on its string. Birdlike, the almanac
hovers half open above the child,   20
hovers above the old grandmother
and her teacup full of dark brown tears.
She shivers and says she thinks the house
feels chilly, and puts more wood in the stove.

It was to be, says the Marvel Stove.   25
I know what I know, says the almanac.
With crayons the child draws a rigid house
and a winding pathway. Then the child
puts in a man with buttons like tears
and shows it proudly to the grandmother.   30

But secretly, while the grandmother
busies herself about the stove,
the little moons fall down like tears
from between the pages of the almanac
into the flower bed the child   35
has carefully placed in the front of the house.

Time to plant tears, says the almanac.
The grandmother sings to the marvelous stove
and the child draws another inscrutable house.

The Villanelle

The villanelle, another French form, dates to the Renaissance. It is a 19-line
poem consisting of five tercets and a final quatrain with only two rhyming
sounds in the entire poem. The first and third lines of the first tercet rhyme,
and these sounds are repeated in each subsequent tercet and in the quatrain,

which may be regarded as a tercet with an extra rhyming line added. One of the best-known villanelles in the English tradition follows.

Dylan Thomas   1914–1953

Do Not Go Gentle into That Good Night   1952

Do not go gentle into that good night,
Old age should burn and rave at close of day;
Rage, rage against the dying of the light.

Though wise men at their end know dark is right,
Because their words had forked no lightning they   5
Do not go gentle into that good night.

Good men, the last wave by, crying how bright
Their frail deeds might have danced in a green bay,
Rage, rage against the dying of the light.

Wild men who caught and sang the sun in flight,   10
And learn too late, they grieved it on its way,
Do not go gentle into that good night.

Grave men, near death, who see with blinding sight
Blind eyes could blaze like meteors and be gay,
Rage, rage against the dying of the light.   15

And you, my father, there on the sad height,
Curse, bless, me now with your fierce tears, I pray.
Do not go gentle into that good night.
Rage, rage against the dying of the light.

Parody   Forms can be parodied or played with in verse just as a particular poem or a poet's style can be. Here is one student's playful attempt at writing a villanelle.

STUDENT WRITING

Catherine Bachochin   b. 1971

Can You Write a Villanelle? I Certainly Cannot.   1993

Can you write a villanelle? I certainly cannot.
Restrictive is the form, it's just too hard to do.
Try though I may, I can't write a jot!

Good poets can rhyme and rhyme, yes, that's their lot.
Still others sing lyrics, and now how 'bout you?   5
Can you write a villanelle? I certainly cannot.

I'm vexed, for very few words end with "ot,"
And still less with "oo" in the books I've been through.
Try though I may, I *can't* write a jot.

O Dylan, "Do not go gentle . . . "—is his poem forgot?   10
Study his poem and I shall then ask you,
"Can you write a villanelle?" I certainly cannot.

I, the earnest, sober writer; he, the drunken sot.
How did he expound on subjects tried and true?
Try though I may, *I* can't write a jot!   15

Here it is, a villanelle—If you weren't pleased, I care not.
Think it was easy? Oh, and answer me this one, too:
Can *you* write a villanelle? I certainly cannot.
Try though I may, I can't write a jot!

The Pantoum

The pantoum originated in Malaya and entered the Western tradition via France in the nineteenth century. It consists of any number of quatrains, with the end words in two lines of one quatrain repeating, but at the ends of different lines, in the next quatrain. The final quatrain usually consists of the initial repeated lines or end words from the first quatrain and two lines or end words from the next-to-last quatrain. Here is an example.

Donald Justice   b. 1925

In the Attic   1979

There's a half hour towards dusk when flies,
Trapped by the summer screens, expire
Musically in the dust of sills;
And ceilings slope towards remembrance.

The same crimson afternoons expire   5
Over the same few rooftops repeatedly;
Only, being stored up for remembrance,
They somehow escape the ordinary.

Childhood is like that, repeatedly
Lost in the very longueurs it redeems.   10
One forgets how small and ordinary
The world looked once by dusklight from above ...

But not the moment which redeems
The drowsy arias of the flies—

And the chin settles onto palms above
Numbed elbows propped on rotting sills.

> CONNECT: Among the Poems for Exploration near the end of this chapter is Lewis Carroll's "Jabberwocky," a *formal* poem—written in four-line stanzas rhymed *abab, cdcd,* etc. Consider, however, the relationship of form to content that seems to be at least partly "nonsense." For instance, does the formal structure help you to understand the "nonsense" content?

Open-Form Poems

In addition to poems written according to fixed forms, there is another kind of lyric poetry: open-form. These poems do not follow any established metrical or rhyming pattern. Poets who write in this style, which is also known as free verse, try to let each poem create or discover its own right form; they do not rely on regular meter or rhyme.

History and Variety

Historically, although free verse has antecedents in the Biblical *Song of Solomon* and in some of John Milton's poetry from the seventeenth century, it didn't really see widespread use until the nineteenth century. In the United States, Walt Whitman wrote his long poem "Song of Myself" and other poems in *Leaves of Grass* in open form, and in France such poets as Arthur Rimbaud and Jules Laforgue wrote free verse that later appealed to such influential Modernist poets as Ezra Pound, T. S. Eliot, William Carlos Williams, and Hilda Doolittle (H. D.).

For examples of the variety of open-form poetry, you could also look at Ezra Pound's "In a Station of the Metro" and Walt Whitman's "Crossing Brooklyn Ferry" among the Poems for Further Reading. Pound's poem, a minimalist attempt to capture an image in very concrete language, is just two lines long. Whitman's is 130 lines divided into nine sections of varying lengths. In his longer poems like "Crossing Brooklyn Ferry," Whitman characteristically started with his own perception and expanded outward through space and time. Doing this produces a longer poem. Thus form and content are also related in open-form poetry; generally, the content shapes the form, whereas in fixed-form poetry the form more nearly shapes the content.

Constraints on Open-Form Poetry

Although Robert Frost is reported to have likened writing free verse to playing tennis with the net down, it is really not that easy. Open-form does not mean form*less*. The absence of rhyme pattern in open-form poetry should free the poet from having to invert normal word order, as we saw Brooks doing in "First Fight. Then Fiddle." But the lines of an open-form poem still have rhythm, even if it is not regular, and the rhythm should both sound like normal speech and provide emphasis for key words. Line length can vary greatly from one poem to another. In the examples below, William Carlos Williams' "This Is Just to Say" has very short lines, partly because one consideration Williams had was the visual arrangement of a poem on the page. The poems by H. D. and Cathy Song, on the other hand, have longer lines. As you can see from those examples, open-form poems may still be divided into stanzas, and the subject of the poem or its treatment determine such formal matters as stanza length and the length of the entire poem.

H. D. (Hilda Doolittle)   1886–1961

Heat   1916

O wind, rend open the heat,
cut apart the heat,
rend it to tatters.

Fruit cannot drop   5
through this thick air—
that presses up and blunts
the points of pears
and rounds the grapes.

Cut the heat—   10
plow through it,
turning it on either side
of your path.

William Carlos Williams   1883–1963

This Is Just to Say   1934

I have eaten
the plums
that were in
the icebox

and which   5
you were probably
saving
for breakfast

Forgive me
they were delicious   10

so sweet
and so cold.

Cathy Song   b. 1955

The White Porch   *1983*

I wrap the blue towel
after washing,
around the damp
weight of hair, bulky
as a sleeping cat,   5
and sit out on the porch.
Still dripping water,
it'll be dry by supper,
by the time the dust
settles off your shoes,   10
though it's only five
past noon. Think
of the luxury: how to use
the afternoon like the stretch
of lawn spread before me.   15
There's the laundry,
sun-warm clothes at twilight,
and the mountain of beans
in my lap. Each one,
I'll break and snap   20
thoughtfully in half.

But there is this slow arousal.
The small buttons
of my cotton blouse
are pulling away from my body.   25
I feel the strain of threads,
the swollen magnolias
heavy as a flock of birds
in the tree. Already,
the orange sponge cake   30
is rising in the oven.
I know you'll say it makes
your mouth dry
and I'll watch you
drench your slice of it   35
in canned peaches
and lick the plate clean.

So much hair, my mother
used to say; grabbing

the thick braided rope   40
in her hands while we washed
the breakfast dishes, discussing
dresses and pastries.
My mind often elsewhere
as we did the morning chores together.   45
Sometimes, a few strands
would catch in her gold ring.
I worked hard then,
anticipating the hour
when I would let the rope down   50
at night, strips of sheets,
knotted and tied,
while she slept in tight blankets.
My hair, freshly washed
like a measure of wealth,   55
like a bridal veil.
Crouching in the grass,
you would wait for the signal,
for the movement of curtains
before releasing yourself   60
from the shadow of moths.
Cloth, hair and hands,
smuggling you in.

Response Statement Questions

- "Heat," "This Is Just to Say," and "The White Porch" may be open-form poems, but are they formless? Can you see any formal patterns in lines, stanzas, or throughout the whole poem?
- These three poems do not rhyme, but consider their use of sounds of words. Does any of them seem to you to manage or shape sound in an especially pleasing way?
- How do these poems employ any of the other text strategies—irony, imagery, voice, setting, thought—that we have considered in fixed-form poems such as "My Last Duchess," Sonnet 73, or "What Lips My Lips Have Kissed, and Where, and Why"?
- Based on the poems you have read so far in this chapter, can you state a preference for fixed- or open-form poetry? If so, why? If not, why not?
- *Share and Compare*   What are your preferences for open- or fixed-form poetry in general or any of the three open-form poems above? What are the preferences of classmates?

Poetic License

In the seventeenth century, English poet and critic John Dryden wrote of "the liberty . . . poets have assumed . . . of speaking things in verse which are beyond the severity of prose." The term poetic license usually applies to the variations in diction or syntax—word choice or word order—that poets may practice, but it also applies more broadly to any of the things poets may do with language that ordinary prose writers do not do: poets' habit of *playing* with language, in short. The term is also a useful way of getting at some of "the libert[ies] … poets have assumed" to make some poems different not only from "the severity of prose" but from other poems as well. The conventions of poetry that were considered in Chapters 10 and 11 contribute to poetry's being different from prose, but they are not absolute rules that all poems must follow.

In all three chapters in this section, you have seen examples of poems that do not rhyme. The free-verse poems by H. D., Williams, and Song are not metrically regular. Not all poems are written or punctuated to resemble prose sentences. Cabalquinto's "Hometown" (Chapter 10, page 528) has no periods to indicate ends of sentences. Angelou's "Africa" (Chapter 11, page 543) has periods at the end of some "sentences," but it also seems to have other "sentences" that lack end punctuation. Those two poems also show variety in capitalization: "Hometown" capitalizes the first word of every line; "Africa" does not. Here is a poem by a Hispanic-American writer that dispenses with capitalization and sentence-ending punctuation entirely, although it does include some internal punctuation. It is also unconventional in its mixture of languages.

Evangelina Vigil   b. 1952

warm heart contains life   *1982*

to our amás

warm heart contains life
heart's warmth
which penetrates through pen
lifeblood that reveals inner thoughts
subtly
like rustling leaves would secrets   5
to the winter wind

secrets collected
pressed between pages
to be kissed by lips red
protruding with warmth, desire   10
sometimes hurt, pain:
recuerdos
like that autumn leaf you singled out
and saved
pressed in-between the memories of your mind   15
diary never written
but always remembered, felt
scripted en tu mente—
your daughters will never read it   20

but they'll inherit it
and they'll know it
when they look into your eyes
shining luz de amor, corazón
unspoken, untold   25
keepsake for our treasure chests
que cargamos aquí adentro
radiant with jewels
sculpted by sentimientos y penas
y bastante amor: 30

> intuition tells us
> better having lived through pain
> than never having felt
> life's full intensity

Response Statement Questions

- What is the effect on your reading of the poem's lack of capitalization and punctuation? For instance, does that text strategy make the poem harder to read, or does it open the poem up to more active reading on your part?
- What is the role of your literary experience concerning the conventions of punctuation and capitalization on your response to the question above?
- What is the effect on your response of the poem's mixture of Spanish and English? How is this effect related to your own ability to speak and read different languages? How is it related to your cultural situation?
- *Share and Compare* In small-group or class discussion, what differences emerge in terms of how different readers read a poem that takes liberties with the conventions of punctuation and capitalization?

> CONNECT: Pat Mora's poem "Elena" (Chapter 11, page 548) is another that includes phrases from Spanish in an English poem. What is the effect on you of this text strategy? How is that effect related to your own degree of familiarity with Spanish?

Another American poet whose style was thoroughly unconventional is e. e. cummings. (He even preferred that his own name not be capitalized!) One way to approach his poems is to regard them as instances of playing with the conventions of language in numerous ways: not only punctuation and capitalization, but word division and spatial arrangement as well. Some of cummings' poems, like the one that follows, show another way in which form and content relate—in this case the physical form of the poem on the page. Such poetry is also known as **concrete poetry.**

e. e. cummings   1894–1962

l(a

1923

```
l(a

le
af
fa

ll

s)
one
l

iness
```

5

Response Statement Questions

- What reading strategies does this text seem to require if it is to be read "successfully" or understood? What reading strategies that you may usually apply to a poem do not seem to work with this one?
- What is the effect on you of the physical arrangement of the words on the page? Would a more conventional arrangement and more conventional capitalization and punctuation practices improve the poem? Why or why not?
- Despite its unconventionality, is this poem unconventional in *all* ways? If not, what poetic conventions does it observe and how do these contribute to your response?
- *Share and Compare*   In small-group or class discussion, if different readers report varying degrees of "success" in reading this poem, to what may that "success" (or "failure") be attributed?

CONNECT: For other examples of concrete poetry, see George Herbert's "Easter Wings" and May Swenson's "Women" in the Poems for Further Readings. Those poems and cummings' "l(a" show that concrete poetry can be written in both open and fixed form.

The Artificiality of Poems

I hope this brief survey of some of the forms and genres of poetry has helped you see something of the great variety of poems, so that you might not have quite so uniform a view of "poetry." One thing all poems have in common, though—whether they are lyric or narrative, fixed form or open, serious or light—is their *artificiality*. Even found poems assume an artistic shape when they are transferred from their original context to the page. Poetry is the most artificial, the most consciously made or shaped, literary genre. One feature or result of that artificiality is the density of language in poems, as we considered briefly in Chapter 10. The literary repertoire of poetry contains all the technical or formal matters, all the text strategies, mentioned in the preceding pages, as well as some common to other genres: irony and symbol, for instance, and, sometimes, setting and character. But especially because of those text strategies peculiar to poetry and its dense and highly artificial character, the genre seems to require certain reading strategies that don't seem quite so necessary with a short story, novel, or drama. You have already looked at some of the most practical of those strategies, offered primarily as basic ways to approach a poem in conscientious fashion. In the next chapter, I will ask you to consider some other reading strategies that, while they are also applicable to texts in other genres, have special worth with regard to poems.

Parody

Verse parody may be considered an instance of poetic license at work (or play). And just as fixed-form poems may be parodied, open-form poems may be also. An open-form "imagist" poem by Ezra Pound has been parodied by Svetlana among the Reading and Writing Projects for Creative and Critical Thinking at the end of Chapter 13. Notice that unlike Howard Moss's parody of Shakespeare's Sonnet 18, Svetlana's imitation of Pound's poem extends the original rather than paraphrases it.

Poems for Exploration

Lewis Carroll   1832–1898

Jabberwocky   1871

'Twas brillig, and the slithy toves
    Did gyre and gimble in the wabe:
All mimsy were the borogoves,
    And the mome raths outgrabe.

"Beware the Jabberwock, my son!   5
    The jaws that bite, the claws that catch!
Beware the Jubjub bird, and shun
    The frumious Bandersnatch!"

He took his vorpal sword in hand;
    Long time the manxome foe he sought—   10
So rested he by the Tumtum tree
    And stood awhile in thought.

And, as in uffish thought he stood,
    The Jabberwock, with eyes of flame,
Came whiffling through the tulgey wood,   15
    And burbled as it came!

One, two! One, two! And through and through
    The vorpal blade went snicker-snack!
He left it dead, and with its head
    He went galumphing back.   20

"And hast thou slain the Jabberwock?
    Come to my arms, my beamish boy!
O frabjous day! Callooh, Callay!"
    He chortled in his joy.

'Twas brillig, and the slithy toves   25
    Did gyre and gimble in the wabe:
All mimsy were the borogoves,
    And the mome raths outgrabe.

Kamala Das   b. 1934

An Introduction   *1962*

I don't know politics but I know the names
Of those in power, and can repeat them like
Days of the week, or names of months, beginning with
Nehru.° I am Indian, very brown, born in   India's first prime minister, after
                                   the country's independence in 1948
Malabar, I speak three languages, write in   5
Two, dream in one. Don't write in English, they said,
English is not your mother-tongue. Why not leave
Me alone, critics, friends, visiting cousins,
Every one of you? Why not let me speak in
Any language I like? The language I speak   10
Becomes mine, its distortions, its queernesses
All mine, mine alone. It is half English, half
Indian, funny perhaps, but it is honest,
It is as human as I am human, don't
You see? It voices my joys, my longings, my   15
Hopes, and it is useful to me as cawing
Is to crows or roaring to the lions, it
Is human speech, the speech of the mind that is
Here and not there, a mind that sees and hears and
Is aware. Not the deaf, blind speech   20
Of trees in storm or of monsoon clouds or of rain or the
Incoherent mutterings of the blazing
Funeral pyre. I was child, and later they
Told me I grew, for I became tall, my limbs
Swelled and one or two places sprouted hair. When   25
I asked for love, not knowing what else to ask
For, he drew a youth of sixteen to the
Bedroom and closed the door. He did not beat me
But my sad woman-body felt so beaten.

The weight of my breasts and womb crushed me. I shrank   30
Pitifully. Then . . . I wore a shirt and my
Brother's trousers, cut my hair short and ignored
My womanliness. Dress in saris,° be girl,   traditional dress of Indian women
Be wife, they said. Be embroiderer, be cook,
Be a quarreller with servants. Fit in. Oh,   35
Belong, cried the categorizers. Don't sit
On walls or peep in through our lace-draped windows.
Be Amy, or be Kamala. Or, better
Still, be Madhavikutty.° It is time to   pseudonym Das uses for stories she
Choose a name, a role. Don't play pretending games.   writes in the Malayalam language
Don't play at schizophrenia or be a
Nympho. Don't cry embarrassingly loud when
Jilted in love . . . I met a man, loved him. Call
Him not by any name, he is every man
Who wants a woman, just as I am every   45
Woman who seeks love. In him . . . the hungry haste
Of rivers, in me . . . the ocean's tireless
Waiting. Who are you, I ask each and everyone,
The answer is, it is I. Anywhere and
Everywhere, I see the one who calls himself   50
I; in this world, he is tightly packed like the
Sword in its sheath. It is I who drink lonely
Drinks at twelve, midnight, in hotels of strange towns,
It is I who laugh, it is I who make love
And then feel shame, it is I who lie dying   55
With a rattle in my throat. I am sinner,
I am saint. I am the beloved and the
Betrayed. I have no joys which are not yours, no
Aches which are not yours. I too call myself I.

Gary Snyder   b. 1930

"They Didn't Hire Him"   *1967*

They didn't hire him
      so he ate his lunch alone:
the noon whistle

Lucille Clifton   b. 1936

My Mama Moved among the Days   *1969*

My Mama moved among the days
like a dreamwalker in a field;
seemed like what she touched was hers

seemed like what touched her couldn't hold,
she got us almost through the high grass
then seemed like she turned around and ran
right back in
right back on in

5

Mazisi Kunene   b. 1930

On the Nature of Truth   1982

'People do not follow the same direction, like water'
Zulu saying

Those who claim the monopoly of truth
Blinded by their own discoveries of power,
Curb the thrust of their own fierce vision.
For there is not one eye over the universe
But a seething nest of rays ever dividing and ever linking.
The multiple creations do not invite disorder,
Nor are the many languages the enemies of humankind.
But the little tyrant must mould things into one body
To control them and give them his single vision.
Yet those who are truly great
On whom time has bequeathed the gift of wisdom
Know all truth must be born of seeing
And all the various dances of humankind are beautiful
They are enriched by the great songs of our planet.

5
10

READING AND WRITING PROJECTS

FOR CREATIVE AND CRITICAL THINKING

A major goal of this book is to help you learn about yourself as a reader—
both what you do cognitively when you read and how culture impinges on
the kind of reader you are when you interact with any particular text. Writing in all its manifestations is an important means to that goal because performing the actions of writing causes you to focus on the actions you take
and the situation you are in as a reader. In addition to the kinds of writing already discussed and exemplified in this book, there are other ways to use
writing to learn.

The following writing suggestions are intended to help you integrate your
reading of and writing about literary texts in various ways. These suggestions
include exploratory writing, playing with texts and language, creative efforts
in various genres, and other writing exercises designed to strengthen your
awareness of the cognitive and cultural processes involved in your reading.

▶ "Answer back," in verse, to any particular poem. As a model, read Christopher Marlowe's "The Passionate Shepherd to His Love" (page 733) and Walter Raleigh's "The Nymph's Reply to the Shepherd" (pages 762–763). Raleigh's poem "answers back" to Marlowe's. You can do something similar with just about any poem in which a speaker addresses someone.

   As an additional option for this assignment, write a piece of expository prose in which you explain your choices and decisions as a verse writer.

▶ Try your hand at writing a poem in any of the fixed forms illustrated in this chapter (sonnet, haiku, epigram, sestina, villanelle, pantoum). These kinds of poems can be written collaboratively as well as individually. If most or all of your classmates do this kind of writing, whether as individuals or in collaborative groups, your class could publish its own anthology of verse for distribution to other classes or to a local elementary or high school. As an option and as an experience in condensation, rewrite another, longer poem as one of the shorter fixed forms (sonnet, haiku, or epigram).

▶ Write a bad poem, an intentionally *not* good one. Then write a prose piece describing or analyzing the poem's badness. What specific moves might make this bad poem better (besides crumbling it into a wad and heaving it into the wastebasket)? Based on this experience, what conclusions can you reach about your criteria for goodness in poetry?

▶ Generate a list of questions to a poem you read. These questions can be very specific and literal, or they can be more interpretive and inferential. You don't have to answer your questions, but you could share them with classmates in a small group in which everyone has read the same poem. Your classmates could write "answers" to whichever questions you or they choose, and you could do the same with theirs.

▶ Write an explanation of a poem from the point of view of its author. That is, assume the position of the author and have him or her tell his or her readers what he or she was trying to do in this poem and why he or she did it that way and not some other way. As an additional option, write an account in your *own* voice of why you said what you said in the *poet's* voice.

13 ◈ SPECIAL FOCUS IN POETRY: ADDITIONAL READING STRATEGIES

The preceding chapters presented ways to begin to overcome poetry anxiety or to strengthen poetry appreciation. Those ways consisted, generally, of recognizing some of the features of the literary repertoire of poems: certain genres or formal conventional patterns of poetry, something of the history of those patterns, and some of the text strategies you are likely to encounter in an interaction with a poem. In the process, those chapters also considered some aspects of your literary experience as a reader: your experiences with and attitudes toward reading poetry, your expectations for any particular interaction with a poetic text, and your reading strategies—for all kinds of texts that the genre "poetry" might comprise. In short, we have been concentrating on the *literary* interaction in the transactional model of the reading process. That seems appropriate because of the special nature of poems as literary texts.

Interactions Between Readers and Poems

We have yet to consider, however, the other level of interaction in our reading model: the *ideological*. At some point, it is possible and even desirable to separate those two kinds of interactions: literary and ideological. A formal paper on a reader's response to a text might have to narrow its focus to one of the two kinds of interactions. But in the reading dynamic itself, while a reading is under way, such separation is not always possible; your interaction with a poem can be looked at in terms of four sectors at once, not just two, as this graphic representation of the model shows.

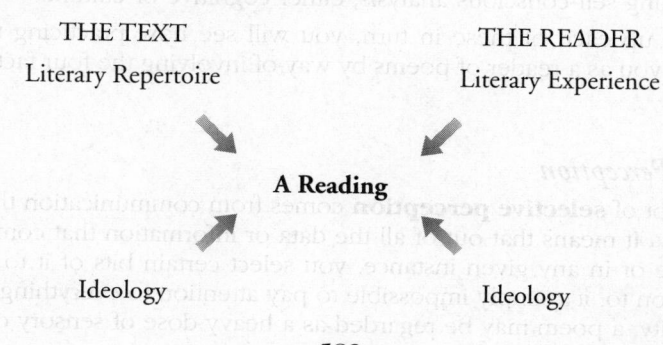

THE TEXT · THE READER
Literary Repertoire · · · · · · · · · · · · · · · · Literary Experience

A Reading

Ideology · Ideology

Becoming a stronger reader of poetry—whether you start from a position of anxiety or of appreciation—requires an awareness of the interaction of both literary and ideological matters in the reading dynamic. Ideology, remember, involves the values, beliefs, memories, ideas, associations, and so forth that both a text and a reader bring to the reading interaction. Your own ideology affects both what you emphasize and what you downplay from the text's ideology as you read. (Some ideological interactions have already been suggested in the preceding chapters in this section: in the discussions of responding to "The Windhover," "Hoop League," and "My Last Duchess" in Chapter 11 and Sonnet 73 and "What Lips My Lips Have Kissed, and Where, and Why" in Chapter 12.) Sometimes, however, it may be hard to negotiate your way through the literary repertoire of a poem to interact with its ideology. With that in mind, consider now some additional reading strategies. These strategies are worth consideration in at least four ways:

- They are produced by or are effects of aspects of your ideology.
- They activate or respond to aspects of the text's ideology.
- They are especially well suited to some of the text strategies of poems.
- They involve the spirit of play or playfulness that the preceding chapters recommended as an approach to poetry in general.

If you have much experience with reading poems, these strategies are not really new. You already have them in your literary experience, I suggest, although you might not call them what I am about to call them. If you have relatively little experience with reading poems, these strategies may be new to you. If so, don't be afraid of them! They will help you begin a meaningful ideological interaction with a poem.

Reading Strategies for Poetry

- Reading with selective perception: noticing some things and downplaying others.
- Identifying or creating gaps, indeterminacies, or **sites of struggle.**
- Creating themes, or generalizing meaning beyond the surface level of the text.
- Deciding to read literally or figuratively.
- Reading against the grain.
- Beginning self-conscious analysis, either cognitive or cultural.

Taking up each of these in turn, you will see how practicing them can strengthen you as a reader of poems by way of involving the four factors listed above.

Selective Perception

The concept of **selective perception** comes from communication theory and psychology. It means that out of all the data or information that comes at you all the time or in any given instance, you select certain bits of it to notice or pay attention to; it's simply impossible to pay attention to everything. Because of its density, a poem may be regarded as a heavy dose of sensory data or intellectual and emotional information in concentrated form. As a reader, you probably already read a poem using selective perception, whether you call it that or not, but certainly you can heighten your awareness of how you do that. With any text, you notice, pay attention to, or focus on certain aspects more than others. As a consequence, you tend to downplay, ignore, or over-look other aspects. It's important to realize this is not a flaw in your reading strategies or a wrong way to read; it's simply a description of part of the read-ing process.

You read with selective perception partly because of certain strategies de-ployed by the text; a poem can try to get you to notice or emphasize certain words, phrases, lines, or images. But you do this because of aspects of your ideology as well. And if you can recognize when and why you are doing this in reading any poem, you can take an important step toward becoming a stronger, more self-aware reader. You can do something else too, once you make this recognition: You can *re*read the text and try to change or adjust what you emphasize and what you de-emphasize. Then you can see the effect such decisions have on your overall reading and response.

Take the following poem as an example. Read it carefully, applying some of the reading strategies already reviewed in previous chapters. Underlining, highlighting, circling, starring, or similar active reading strategies are ways of exercising selective perception as you read, so be sure to do that here. Then write a response statement.

Robert Frost   1874–1963

The Road Not Taken   1915

Two roads diverged in a yellow wood,
And sorry I could not travel both
And be one traveler, long I stood
And looked down one as far as I could
To where it bent in the undergrowth;   5

Then took the other, as just as fair,
And having perhaps the better claim,
Because it was grassy and wanted wear;
Though as for that the passing there
Had worn them really about the same,   10

And both that morning equally lay
In leaves no step had trodden black.
Oh, I kept the first for another day!
Yet knowing how way leads on to way,
I doubted if I should ever come back.   15

I shall be telling this with a sigh
Somewhere ages and ages hence:
Two roads diverged in a wood, and I—

I took the one less traveled by,
And that has made all the difference.   20

Response Statement Questions

- What words, phrases, lines, or images did you especially notice and mark? Why these?
- What paraphrase can you make of the thought of this poem? How is that paraphrase related to or produced by the words, etc. you noticed and marked?
- In general, do you take the speaker's tone in this text to be positive or negative, optimistic or pessimistic, confident or doubtful?
- *Share and Compare*   In small groups or as a whole class, see what different words and phrases each reader emphasized in responding to the second and third questions.

Sharing Your Reading   Sharing responses will give you the opportunity to see how selective perception works in your reading and the readings of your classmates. Sharing also allows you to realize that what you noticed is what someone else overlooked or downplayed, and vice versa. These diverging experiences indicate that the "same" text is really different for different readers, all because of different choices they make, perhaps unconsciously, in response to the "data" they perceive as "present" in their interactions with the text. Your next move could take you in one of two ways (although in this case you probably *can* come back to where the ways diverged): You can reread the poem trying to adopt the perspective of another reader who noticed or emphasized things differently from the way you did—and see how taking that perspective changes the way you respond to the second and third questions above. Or you can further explore your own answers to all the response statement questions, trying to move in the direction of a **cognitive** or **cultural analysis** of your reading. Because your selective perceptions are at least partly the result of your ideology, this kind of analysis is possible as well as enlightening.

In "The Road Not Taken," places such as lines 16 and 20 and words such as "sigh" and "difference" in those lines and the word "Not" in the title are especially likely to be emphasized or downplayed differently by different readers. And the choices readers make with regard to those lines and words are likely to affect their overall interpretation of the poem or how they read the ideology of the text. As I trust your small-group or class discussion has shown you, this text can be, in fact *is*, read with pretty nearly opposite interpretations: Some readers see it as a positive affirmation of a person's individual choice; others see it as a reflection on a crucial moment that perhaps didn't turn out so well. Your discussion may even have gotten quite heated as different readers argued their interpretations, which has happened with my students. In any case, I hope you are able to be "objective" enough to see that the text is quite open on this matter, open to interpretation.

Another way of expressing this openness is to say the text is **indeterminate** on the question of an optimistic or pessimistic tone: it's virtually impossible to decide—based on the text alone—which ideology is speaking through the text. So any reader may identify particular lines or words as indeterminate or, if you look at it in terms of competing ideologies, as sites of struggle. A "site" is a place, a location; "struggle" expresses the competition that seems to be going on between ideologies or aspects of someone's—in this case the dramatic speaker's—ideology. If you haven't already, discuss this with your whole class or a small group: How do especially the words "sigh" and "difference" and the lines in which they appear in "The Road Not Taken" signal different, even competing ideological positions on the consequences of individual choice?

Focus on Reading with Selective Perception   Read the following two poems carefully, paying attention to what words, phrases, or lines "stand out" for you—or which ones your selective perception allows to stand out. In a response statement or in class discussion, consider how what you bring to the reading in terms of ideology—what values, beliefs, memories, ideas—affects both what you emphasize and what you downplay as you read.

Theodore Roethke   1908–1963

My Papa's Waltz   1948

The whiskey on your breath
Could make a small boy dizzy;
But I hung on like death:
Such waltzing was not easy.

We romped until the pans   5
Slid from the kitchen shelf;
My mother's countenance
Could not unfrown itself.

The hand that held my wrist
Was battered on one knuckle;   10
At every step you missed
My right ear scraped a buckle.

You beat time on my head
With a palm caked hard by dirt,
Then waltzed me off to bed   15
Still clinging to your shirt.

Denise Levertov   b. 1923

The Ache of Marriage   1964

The ache of marriage:

thigh and tongue, beloved,
are heavy with it,
it throbs in the teeth

We look for communion   5
and are turned away, beloved,
each and each
It is leviathan° and we   a whale
in its belly
looking for joy, some joy
not to be known outside it   10

two by two in the ark of
the ache of it.

Interpretive Moments

What you did with a couple of pivotal words or lines in "The Road Not Taken"
was a matter of identifying indeterminacies or sites of struggle. That is, they already seemed to "be there," even if every reader didn't notice them equally or
at the same time. But you can also create an indeterminacy or a site of struggle by virtue of your ideology acting upon a text. This is a way of reading poetically or playfully. As an example of this, consider again the poem by
William Carlos Williams that you read in Chapter 12.

This Is Just to Say

I have eaten
the plums
that were in
the icebox

and which   5
you were probably
saving
for breakfast

Forgive me
they were delicious   10
so sweet
and so cold

Here's what one student, Elaine Kaplowe, wrote in her journal in response to reading this poem:

> "This Is Just to Say" is a pleasant enough poem to read and understand. No
>
> problems anywhere, as long as I continue to think of it as a pleasant enough poem.
>
> But that's too easy. . . . So now I'm suspicious of W.C.W. I want to accuse him of
>
> burying fascinating meanings under a casual title and the delicious taste of ice-cold
>
> plums. What if the title of the poem were something like "Forgive Me" or "A

Stolen Indulgence"? Then readers might be urged to examine the poem more closely.

Without naming it as such, Elaine is creating indeterminacy out of this whole poem by playing with its title. And she does that because her ideology contains an element of mischievousness that will not allow her to rest content with an "easy" or "pleasant enough" reading of a text, even though that may seem to be all there is to it.

Similarly, a reader may either identify or create gaps in a text. Like an indeterminacy or a site of struggle, a gap or a blank is a place in a text where something—some information, some meaning—is "missing" or where some logical connection is not completed. In "This Is Just to Say," for instance, the referent of the pronoun "you" may be identified as a gap: Who is that? The speaker's wife? Husband? Roommate? Lover? A homeowner who has been robbed by the speaker, who is a witty burglar? The speaker may be identified as another gap: Is the speaker male or female? how old? when, where, and why is she or he speaking these words? Still another gap is how many plums did the speaker eat? How many "were in the icebox" to begin with? Another indeterminacy, of course, as the snippet of response journal quoted above may suggest, is what does it mean? Does this text mean just what it seems to say on the surface, or does it mean something at a deeper level?

Some gaps, such as these, perhaps, are easy to identify, to put your finger on. They seem to exist "in" the text. However, because the interactive model of reading emphasizes the reader's contributions to making a text what it is for that reader, keep in mind that you can also create gaps in a text. Doing this is related to the process of selective perception in that you decide what sites you want to read as gaps. Then you can pry into them with your mental or imaginative crowbar, so to speak. Having done that, whether you have created a gap or merely noticed one that already seems to be there, your literary experience and your ideology provide the material with which you can build a bridge over the gap or fill it in—to imagine what's missing, complete the thought, or begin to produce an interpretation.

For example, if in reading "This Is Just to Say," you decide to concentrate on the speaker as a gap, you may begin to construct that text as a dramatic monologue (if you can call that genre up from your literary experience), albeit a very short one. Creating that monologue may lead to a reading of the kind of person this speaker is, in terms of the categories I offered just above and of the qualities of his or her personality. In turn, that might lead to a reading of the poem more in terms of what it—or you interacting with it—might reveal about this speaker both through his or her words and *in spite* of them, if you choose to fill the gap with irony. Thus you might construct a speaker who, beneath the apparent forthrightness of confessing to having eaten the plums and the contrition of asking for forgiveness, is actually arrogant, mocking whomever she or he is addressing.

Demonstration: A Student Reading "The Urine Speciman" Here's a demonstration of another reader using selective perception to identify or create a gap in a text, then filling it in from his ideology. As you read the poem that follows, try to be aware of the picture you are constructing in your mind, and think especially about the kind of person you construct as its speaker, through or behind the voice you hear.

Ted Kooser   b. 1939

The Urine Specimen   1985

In the clinic, a sun-bleached shell of stone
on the shore of the city, you enter
the last small chamber, a little closet
chastened with pearl, cool, white, and glistening,
and over the chilly well of the toilet   5
you trickle your precious sum in a cup.
It's as simple as that. But the heat
of this gold your body's melted and poured out
into a form begins to enthrall you,
warming your hand with your flesh's fevers   10
in a terrible way. It's like holding
an organ—spleen or fatty pancreas,
a lobe from your foamy brain still steaming
with worry. You know that just outside
a nurse is waiting to cool it into a gel   15
and slice it onto a microscope slide
for the doctor, who in it will read your future,
wringing his hands. You lift the chalice and toast
the long life of your friend there in the mirror,
who wanly smiles, but does not drink to you.   20

One student who read and responded to this poem created a gap as he tried to construct the speaker. Even though most readers in this student's class tended to see the speaker as a male (did you? why?), this reader wrote in a response statement:

> I found the voice to be very worrisome and the tone of this voice seemed to be
>
> very hesitant and unsure. I felt this way because all I could think of as I read this
>
> poem was a young teen-age[d] girl at a clinic, giving a urine sample to see if she
>
> was pregnant or not. I pictured the girl standing in front of a mirror with a cup of
>
> urine symbolizing her future. What a relief if the results are negative, but what if
>
> the results are positive? . . . "The Urine Specimen"—what a silly name but what a
>
> serious subject it talks about!

This student's instructor asked him why he pictured the speaker as female and why he thought she would be relieved if the results of a pregnancy test were negative. It would seem to be just as easy to read the speaker as a male, or just as easy to read a female speaker as hopeful, not worried, that she is pregnant. As it turned out, when this student developed his response statement into a formal paper on his reading of "The Urine Specimen," the reason for his prying open this particular gap and immediately supplying from his ideology what was "missing" became apparent:

> Growing up in my latter years of high school and my first two years of college, I had a serious girlfriend. As our . . . relationship grew, sex became a part of . . . [it]. Along with sex comes the possibility of pregnancy. At most times pregnancy is a cause for celebration, but for two teen-agers pregnancy is justification for suicide. . . . [T]here were a few occasions during our relationship where my girlfriend had to get a pregnancy test. As I read further and further into the poem all I could picture was my girlfriend in the bathroom of the pregnancy clinic giving a urine sample and me in the waiting room ready to throw up and faint because I was so worried about what was going on. In her urine sample was the future of our lives. If the results of the test were positive, we were both unwillingly thrust into the position of parents-to-be. All the plans of college and living the life of a normal college student were down the drain. . . . [T]his poem put me in those exact same shoes again. As I read the poem, I honestly felt like I was back in that waiting room again.

As you can see, this reader was serious to the point of having his palms sweat. That may not seem like *playing* with the text, but it is, because the reader was identifying or creating a gap and bridging it over or filling it in from his ideology; he was *making* it say something other ("what a serious subject") than what it appeared to say on the surface ("what a silly name").

Focus on Identifying Interpretive Moments   In the process of identifying and filling in a gap in "The Urine Specimen," this reader was also engaging in the next reading strategy I will ask you to consider. But first, here are some more poems that you may read to identify or create gaps, indeterminacies, or sites of struggle. Read them closely, and write a response statement or discuss with your classmates the causes for and effects of your reading decisions.

William Blake   1757–1827

The Tyger   *1794*

Tyger! Tyger! burning bright
In the forests of the night,
What immortal hand or eye
Could frame thy fearful symmetry?

In what distant deeps or skies   5
Burnt the fire of thine eyes?
On what wings dare he aspire?
What the hand, dare seize the fire?

And what shoulder, & what art,
Could twist the sinews of thy heart?   10
And when thy heart began to beat,
What dread hand? & what dread feet?

What the hammer? what the chain?
In what furnace was thy brain?
What the anvil? what dread grasp   15
Dare its deadly terrors clasp?

When the stars threw down their spears,
And water'd heaven with their tears,
Did he smile his work to see?
Did he who made the lamb make thee?   20

Tyger! Tyger! burning bright
In the forests of the night
What immortal hand or eye
Dare frame thy fearful symmetry?

Emily Dickinson   1830–1886

The Soul selects her own Society   *c. 1862*

The Soul selects her own Society—
Then—shuts the Door—
To her divine Majority—
Present no more—

Unmoved—she notes the Chariots—pausing   5
At her low Gate—
Unmoved—an Emperor be kneeling
Upon her Mat—

I've known her—from an ample nation—
Choose One—
Then—close the Valves of her attention—   10
Like Stone—

Creating Themes

For many students, reading for **theme** is the main purpose in reading poetry.
The dominant ideology with respect to poetry in our culture—and especially
in the culture of the literature classroom—holds that poems contain or convey
themes. The reader's task is to dig beneath the surface of the text to find a

theme that is hidden there: the "buried treasure" model of reading. Or else the reader's purpose is to analyze the complex relationships among such elements as imagery, structure, meter, and rhyme to decipher the underlying meaning: the "code-cracking" model of reading. In any case, such models lead to if not assume the idea that there is *a* meaning or theme, buried or encoded by the poet, that can be pulled out of the text by a reader who interprets the surface clues or signs correctly. Are you familiar with models like these? Do you assume them as governing the reading process with poetry?

Contesting those models, however, is the idea that interpretation is an interactive process, in which theme or meaning is not assumed to be hidden in a text by an author and pulled out by a reader, but negotiated or *created* by a reader as she or he brings her or his literary experience and ideology into play. Themes may be further negotiated, modified, revised, clarified, or extended through interactions with other readers, as in classroom discussion. Like the other models, the interactive one assumes that meaning or theme may lie elsewhere than on the surface of a text, but instead of locating it beneath or behind the surface, the interactive model prefers the word *beyond* because that orientation allows for the interaction of the reader's ideology with the text's, both of which extend beyond the text, which is a site of their interaction. As a reader you are thus permitted to do something you probably actually do already but are forced to deny in other reading models: read meaning *into* a text from your ideology.

Does this model mean, then, that any reading is as valid as any other? Does emphasizing the role of the reader's ideology in making meaning out of his or her encounters with texts mean giving complete license to eccentric or idiosyncratic readings? If so, should those readings be considered as legitimate as one that sticks closely to the words on the page? If so, is the author discounted as the person who supposedly "put" meaning "into" the text in the first place?

The answer to most of these questions is yes. I would qualify the license or freedom a reader has in producing an eccentric or idiosyncratic reading by saying that, for practical purposes, such as writing in an academic setting, any reading has to be plausible or persuasive to other readers—especially if they would not produce it themselves. This plausibility or persuasiveness comes from the reader's ability to explain his or her reading, to trace an interpretation to its bases in logic or evidence, whether those bases lie in the text, in the reader, or in the interaction between them. In the interactive model of reading, the bases for an interpretation do not lie entirely within the text, its author, or the cultural situation in which the text was produced. While all of these are *part* of the bases for interpretation and so are worth study, investigation, and research, they constitute only one pole in the circuit of reading.

Another pole is the reader, who is both constrained and free. The reader is constrained to some extent by the text in that it provides certain cues for response and interpretation. These cues activate or are activated by aspects of the reader's literary experience and ideology, which in turn are "written" by larger cultural and ideological discourses. People are "sites of struggle" themselves, not just between competing desires, but between conflicting ideologies and contradictory discourses that influence their beliefs, emotions, and behaviors. Yet within these limits, any reader is a free agent, able to make certain choices and not make others, and to be conscious of why she or he does so and what is going on as she or he does so.

Many readers feel or assume that they are constrained by the author's intentions. They assume or have been consistently taught that the "true" or "real" meaning of a text is what the author intended it to mean. For such readers, theme in a text is nearly identical with the author's intention, purpose, or point. Such readers assume a model of reading in which theme is put into a text by an author and the reader's job is to get that theme out of the text. Assumptions like these are powerful at least partly because of Western culture's ideological emphasis on the importance of and respect for authority. Applying this idea to literary texts, many readers believe in the author as the ultimate author*ity* where meaning or theme are concerned. Chapter 2 challenged the dominance of the author's intentions in the ideology of reading, so I won't rehash that argument here other than to acknowledge that poetry's reputation for difficulty or obscurity and some readers' sense of helplessness seem to make the author's intentions an attractive solution to reading problems.

To return to the practical application of this reading strategy, you can see readers at least beginning to create themes as they interact with poems if you look again at the excerpts from responses to "This Is Just to Say" and "The Urine Specimen" on pages 594–595 and 596–597. In each instance, the reader's ideology—his or her beliefs, memories, associations, or habits of mind— played important roles in making meaning of the encounter with a text. For you, a response statement or journal provides an excellent opportunity to practice this reading strategy because that kind of nongraded situation facilitates writing to discover something you didn't know you knew; you can take some intellectual and interpretive risks; you can follow or pursue those creative ideas to see where they will lead you—beyond the text of a poem to something in your own life or in your culture.

In exercising the playfulness involved in creating a theme, it may help you to keep in mind something else that was considered in Chapter 2: intertextuality. As texts, poems exist in a network of relations to other texts, both literary and otherwise. The text strategy of allusion, also discussed in Chapter 2, is a gesture toward intertextuality in that one text—usually literary in the case of an allusion—is invoked in another. Intertextuality as a reading strategy is different from allusion as a text strategy, however, in several ways: a text is invoked *by* another text (or, more to the point, by a reader in reading another); the text invoked may not be strictly a literary one; the text invoked and whether one is invoked at all will depend on a reader's storehouse of texts; and the intertextual relation will reveal something about the reader's culture more than it will about the author's. Deciding on intertextuality is a creative, interpretive move. It happens when a circuit is established between text and reader, both bringing their storehouses of and experiences with other texts to the reading situation.

Look back at Matthew Arnold's "Dover Beach" and Bruce Springsteen's "Cover Me" in Chapter 2, pages 24–25 and 31 respectively. The brief discussion of "Dover Beach" there pointed to that poem's apparent ideology that in light of the recession of the "Sea of Faith" people's recourse was to be "true to one another," presumably in some love relationship. It seems fairly easy to generalize such a theme in reading "Dover Beach," and if so that theme does not seem to extend far beyond the surface ideology of the text, as expressed by its speaker. At the same time, to say that "Dover Beach" is about loss of religious or philosophical certainty and taking refuge in romantic or sexual pleasure is to generalize a meaning beyond the particular dramatic situation of the speaker in the poem. Furthermore, to see intertextuality between "Dover Beach" and "Cover Me" is to read *both* texts—one from the canon of English poetry, the other from popular culture—in terms of this larger theme. As a reader whose ideology contains the belief that the world is an uncertain and confusing place, I am able to establish an intertextual thematic connection between the two texts, and I can do so without any knowledge of Springsteen's intentions or his awareness of Arnold's poem.

As another example of an active reader generalizing a meaning beyond the surface level of the text, some excerpts from a student's response to a contemporary American poem follow. Read the poem yourself here, and then read the student's writing.

Marge Piercy   b. 1936

Barbie Doll   *1969*

This girlchild was born as usual
and presented dolls that did pee-pee
and miniature GE stoves and irons
and wee lipsticks the color of cherry candy.
Then in the magic of puberty, a classmate said: 5
You have a great big nose and fat legs.

She was healthy, tested intelligent,
possessed strong arms and back,
abundant sexual drive and manual dexterity.
She went to and fro apologizing.   10
Everyone saw a fat nose on thick legs.

She was advised to play coy,
exhorted to come on hearty,
exercise, diet, smile and wheedle.
Her good nature wore out   15
like a fan belt.
So she cut off her nose and her legs
and offered them up.

In the casket displayed on satin she lay
with the undertaker's cosmetics painted on,   20
a turned-up putty nose,
dressed in a pink and white nightie.
Doesn't she look pretty? everyone said.
Consummation at last.
To every woman a happy ending.   25

STUDENT WRITING
Katerina Minakakis: Response Statement

Reading . . . ["Barbie Doll"] made me both angry and sad . . . because it deals with two topics that I have strong opinions and beliefs about, namely pressures by society to look perfect and male and female roles in society. . . .

This poem angered me because I hate the fact that little girls and boys can only play with toys that are considered proper for their gender. Little girls can only play with dolls, household appliances, make-up, and so on. Little boys can only play with rough and tumble toys, such as . . . trucks, . . . cars, guns, etc. This society forces male and female stereotypes on people from the time they are little children, and many people don't realize this. I personally see nothing wrong with a little girl play-ing with trucks, guns, or G.I. Joe dolls, because playing with stoves and doing dolls' hair aren't the only things little girls like to do. They only do these things because they are taught that those are the only things they can play with. And there is ab-solutely nothing wrong with little boys playing with stoves, dolls, or any other type of "female" toys. Most people would probably frown on a little boy who played with a doll, or a little girl who played with trucks, and possibly become worried that they were homosexual. Yet I see it as a healthy thing because it would help to break the prominent stereotypical roles of males and females in this society. As a child, I played with the typical female toys, yet I also played with my brothers' toys as well, maybe even more so than with mine. My parents didn't push me to play with my toys, so I grew up with the idea that girls and boys could play with whatever they chose to. This view broadened as I got older and led to my belief that men and women should have the same choices in life and should be treated equally.

Another thing that angered me is the fact that looks play such an important role in how someone is seen as a person. A great deal of emphasis is put on physi-cal appearance in this society, and it is a great hindrance to those who don't fit into the norms of physical attractiveness. Those who are good-looking, have excellent bodies, and dress stylishly are . . . usually accepted, even if they have the worst per-sonalities or no brains. . . . The girl in this poem was made fun of because of her "im-perfections," even though she had a head on her shoulders and was probably an extremely sweet person. People couldn't see past her "big nose and fat legs" (line 6), which is the case for many special people who contribute a lot to this society mentally, not physically. The fact that the main character in this poem is female emphasizes . . . that looks are important, because I believe that more stress is put on women to look perfect physically. I believe this because every time I open a magazine or turn on the television I am constantly bombarded with women who have perfect facial features, perfect bodies, and perfect wardrobes....Of course there are male models, but they aren't as emphasized as female models are. There are no male "super" models, and if there are male models in magazines, no one knows their names. But just about everyone knows at least one female model's name. I know a few, not by choice but because my friends make it a point to tell me....

In the response statement from which these excerpts are taken, Katerina's interpretation of "Barbie Doll" is emerging from what the text says on the surface. At the same time, the beliefs and experiences she brings to her encounter with the text allow her to extend its implications beyond the situation of "This girlchild" to American women in general. Your own ideology may confirm what Katerina says, or it may prompt you to say that Katerina is *overgeneralizing* from the text to a larger issue. Whether Katerina is "right" or "wrong" in what she says about gender stereotypes in American society or the pressures on women to be physically "perfect" doesn't really matter. She probably could stand to refine and qualify some of the statements she has made, but the point is that by acknowledging some of the ideology she brings to her interaction with "Barbie Doll" she is able to actively *create* themes as she reads the poem and to make the poem her own in the process.

Focus on Creating Themes   As an opportunity to practice a similar kind of active reading and creative theme making yourself, read either or both of the following poems. Each poem is followed by response statement questions that focus on some of the ideological issues in the text and that may enable you to see how your ideology is involved in your response.

Rosemary Catacalos   b. 1944

La Casa   *1984*

The house by the acequia,°   irrigation canal
its front porch dark and
cool with begonias,
an old house, always there,
always of the same adobe,   5
always full of the same lessons.
We would like to stop.

We know we belonged there once.
Our mothers are inside.
All the mothers are inside,   10
lighting candles, swaying
back and forth on their knees,
begging The Virgin's forgiveness
for having reeled us out
on such very weak string.   15
They are afraid for us.
They know we will not stop.
We will only wave as we pass by.
They will go on praying
that we might be simple again.   20

Response Statement Questions

- What ideas does this poem seem to put forward in its description of "The house by the *acequia*"? What paraphrases can you write to make those ideas explicit?
- What is your response to any of those ideas? In broad terms, is your response positive or negative?
- In terms of your own ideology, what ideas, beliefs, or experiences clash or harmonize with ideas that the poem suggests? As you explore this interaction, what larger theme(s) seem to emerge? (Specific issues that you might consider include houses, homes, mothers, children who have gone out on their own.)
- *Share and Compare*   If differences among your classmates emerge in discussion of this poem, that should lead you to a consideration of the role of different ideologies in constructing interpretation of this text.

Mitsuye Yamada   b. 1923

A Bedtime Story   1976

Once upon a time,
an old Japanese legend
goes as told
by Papa,
an old woman traveled through   5
many small villages
seeking refuge
for the night.
Each door opened
a sliver   10
in answer to her knock
then closed.
Unable to walk

any further
she wearily climbed a hill   15
found a clearing
and there lay down to rest
a few moments to catch
her breath.

The village town below   20
lay asleep except
for a few starlike lights.
Suddenly the clouds opened
and a full moon came into view
over the town.   25

The old woman sat up
turned toward
the village town
and in supplication
called out   30
Thank you people
of the village,
If it had not been for your
kindness
in refusing me a bed   35
for the night
these humble eyes would never
have seen this
memorable sight.

Papa paused, I waited.   40
In the comfort of our
hilltop home in Seattle
overlooking the valley,
I shouted
"That's the *end?*"   45

Response Statement Questions

- What ideas does this poem seem to put forward in its description of the "old Japanese legend" and of the speaker's description of hearing this story as a child? What paraphrases can you write to make those ideas explicit?
- What is your response to any of those ideas? In broad terms, is your response positive or negative?
- In terms of your own ideology, what ideas, beliefs, or experiences clash or harmonize with ideas that the poem suggests? As you explore this interaction, what larger theme(s) seem to emerge? (Specific issues that you might consider include hospitality, gratitude, unexpected pleasures, comfort, childhood versus adult understanding, the purposes of bedtime stories.)

- *Share and Compare* If differences among your classmates emerge in discussion of this poem, that should lead you to a consideration of the role of different ideologies in constructing interpretation of this text.

Deciding to Read Literally or Figuratively

One move toward creating an interpretation of a poem involves your decision to take the language you find in the poem literally or figuratively. In Chapter 12, when we considered figurative language as one of the text strategies of poetry, we considered also the reader's role in completing the circuit between words and phrases of a poem and the extratextual reality those images recall. We can now emphasize the reader's role even more by considering his or her decision to read certain words or phrases literally or figuratively.

It is true that some texts practically invite you to understand them on an extraliteral level: Some texts "mean" consistently in other terms than the literal meaning of the language. In this section, poems such as Brooks' "First Fight. Then Fiddle." and Blake's "The Tyger" seem to make little sense at the literal level, therefore inviting a figurative reading. But if you accept the premise of the polyvalency of language, especially in poetry, and if you practice the strategy of reading poetically, you can read *any* text in other-than-literal terms at any time. It's simply a matter of choosing to do so, although you will find that some texts more than others seem to lend themselves to, if not require, this reading strategy.

Take, for instance, the following poem. Read it and write a response statement using the questions that follow it.

Margaret Atwood   b. 1939

This Is a Photograph of Me   *1967*

It was taken some time ago.
At first it seems to be
a smeared
print: blurred lines and grey flecks
blended with the paper;   5

then, as you scan
it, you see in the left-hand corner
a thing that is like a branch: part of a tree
(balsam or spruce) emerging
and, to the right, halfway up   10
what ought to be a gentle
slope, a small frame house.

In the background there is a lake,
and beyond that, some low hills.

(The photograph was taken   15
the day after I drowned.

I am in the lake, in the center
of the picture, just under the surface.

It is difficult to say where
precisely, or to say   20
how large or small I am:
the effect of water
on light is a distortion

but if you look long enough,
eventually   25
you will be able to see me.)

Response Statement Questions

- Summarize the scene described by the speaker in this poem. Who or what does this speaker seem to be? What is the speaker's vantage point on what she or he is describing?
- What kind of problems of logic or understanding does reading this poem literally present you with?
- In your reading of this poem, did you adopt any strategies to help you overcome problems in logic or understanding that might arise from a literal reading? If so, what were they?
- *Share and Compare* Does small-group or class discussion reveal that more than one reader was confused in trying to make sense of the text at a literal level? Did any reader report success by reading figuratively?

In responding to "This Is a Photograph of Me," many students find themselves surprised and baffled by the turn in lines 15–16. Those lines, most readers find, constitute a gap that presents a challenge to a literal reading: Unless you believe in ghosts or voices from beyond the grave, it seems logically absurd for the speaker to be dead. Many readers persist, though, in reading this text literally, partly because the first 14 lines seem so literal, partly because the voice in the poem seems so matter-of-fact throughout, and partly because they are not used to exercising their own choice to read such a straightforward-seeming poem in any way other than the literal. And so the poem is a puzzle or a dilemma for many readers, perhaps annoying them because it "doesn't make sense" (in literal terms). Was your response anything like this?

Here is part of a response statement of one reader who not only read the poem figuratively but also was aware of her decision to do so, and its effects.

STUDENT WRITING

Stephanie Beacher: Response Statement

My initial response to Margaret Atwood's "This Is a Photograph of Me" was inquiry and sympathy. I was disoriented in lines 15 and 16, when the mood of the poem made a complete turn around. At this point I began to question just what exactly I was reading about. I was, however, able to redirect my reading by seeing this poem as a metaphor. In using this strategy, I was able to make sense of the piece as well as personally identify with it.

I was able to shift my reading to a figurative one due to my past experience with poetry and visual art. Although my experience in poetry has been limited, I have been exposed to a great deal of visual art. Visual art, like poetry, can be seen metaphorically.... When the poet in line[s] 15 [and 16] stated, "(This photograph was taken / the day after I drowned)" I began to question how she could be dead yet write a poem of her death. Obviously a reading strategy would be needed to make sense of the text. I came to the conclusion that the poem would make the most sense to me if I read it metaphorically. In doing so my response shifted from inquiry to sympathy.

I believe my response to the poem was influenced by my own experience with feeling isolated and misunderstood. The poem reminded me of a time in high school when I felt this way. I was fifteen years old, my parents were getting divorced and my mother was moving out of state with my six-year-old brother. Despite the hurt and feelings of desertion I felt, no one seemed to see past the forced smile and distortions that high school image-making creates.

This parallels the poem in the first and second stanzas when the reader is only aware of the narration of the photograph. The reader at this point has not yet been alerted to the eerie reality of the photograph, that someone is dead in the water. The beginning of the poem distracts the reader in order to create a sense of shock when the tragedy is discovered. To me this structure of the poem demonstrates how perceptions change and how perceptions may not be correct.

My experience in high school went unnoticed for a long time. People could not perceive the true me, nor was I confident enough to ask for help in coping with my feelings. As a result, I felt lonely and isolated. These feelings could very well be described as a drowned feeling as Atwood wrote in her poem. I fell deeper into depression. Drinking alcohol became a problem, yet even this was perceived with distortions. Drinking became attributed to me as a "party" asset. Nobody seemed to be perceptive enough to realize that drinking was a reaction to the hurt I was feeling.

Many times in our society serious issues such as drinking or depression can be overlooked or distorted. Atwood describes a picture that is blurred and hard to

make out. In high school alcohol is hard to make out and the reality of the substance is distorted. It is treated as a social aspect that contributes to popularity. On
the surface a person may be well dressed, popular and attending all the parties.
These three elements distract others from seeing the destructive reality of alcohol,
just as the smeared landscape hid the tragic reality of the photograph in Atwood's
poem. In making these comparisons between my life and observations of society I
was able to make sense of Atwood's poem.

As this response statement indicates, Stephanie was able to work toward a
logical interpretation of this poem by reading it figuratively instead of literally.
Doing so also allowed her to put her ideology into play as an active force in
building an interpretation. That action shows the reader's power in completing
the circuit left open by certain instances of language in a poem, so it's not necessary to figure out what Atwood intends with this logically strange poem in
order to arrive at a satisfying and strong reading.

Focus on Deciding to Read Literally or Figuratively   Below are two
poems by twentieth-century American writers. To develop your own strength
as a reader, read either or both poems and write a response statement or journal entry using the questions that follow each poem.

Wallace Stevens   1879–1955

Anecdote of the Jar   1923

I placed a jar in Tennessee,
And round it was, upon a hill.
It made the slovenly wilderness
Surround that hill.

The wilderness rose up to it,
And sprawled around, no longer wild.
The jar was round upon the ground
And tall and of a port in air.

It took dominion everywhere.
The jar was gray and bare.
It did not give of bird or bush,
Like nothing else in Tennessee.

5

10

Response Statement Questions

- How might you paraphrase what this poem seems to be saying at a literal
  level? How easy or difficult is it to write this paraphrase? Does this text
  seem to make literal sense?

- What word, phrase, line, or image in this poem, if any, seems to suggest a figurative level of meaning for the whole text? If you read the poem figuratively, how is its meaning different from that produced through a literal reading?
- If you read this poem figuratively, how do you decide what the figurative language means? What aspects of your ideology come in to play to supply this meaning?
- Are you more satisfied with a literal or a figurative reading of this poem? Why?
- *Share and Compare*   In small-group or class discussion, what differences arise as readers attempt to interpret this poem? How might those differences be traced to readers' reading strategies and ideologies?

Maxine Kumin   b. 1925

Morning Swim   *1965*

Into my empty head there come
a cotton beach, a dock wherefrom

I set out, oily and nude
through mist, in chilly solitude.

There was no line, no roof or floor   5
to tell the water from the air.

Night fog thick as terry cloth
closed me in its fuzzy growth.

I hung my bathrobe on two pegs.
I took the lake between my legs.   10

Invaded and invader, I
went overhand on that flat sky.

Fish twitched beneath me, quick and tame.
In their green zone they sang my name

and in the rhythm of the swim   15
I hummed a two-four-time slow hymn.

I hummed *Abide with Me.*° The beat   a hymn
rose in the fine thrash of my feet,

rose in the bubbles I put out
slantwise, trailing through my mouth.   20

My bones drank water; water fell
through all my doors. I was the well

that fed the lake that met my sea
in which I sang *Abide with Me.*

Response Statement Questions

- How might you paraphrase what this poem seems to be saying at a literal level? How easy or difficult is it to write this paraphrase? Does this text seem to make literal sense?
- What word, phrase, line, or image in this poem, if any, seems to suggest a figurative level of meaning for the whole text? If you read the poem figuratively, how is its meaning different from that produced through a literal reading?
- If you read this poem figuratively, how do you decide what the figurative language means? What aspects of your ideology come in to play to supply this meaning?
- Are you more satisfied with a literal or a figurative reading of this poem? Why?
- *Share and Compare*   In small-group or class discussion, what differences arise as readers attempt to interpret this poem? How might those differences be traced to readers' reading strategies and ideologies?

Reading Against the Grain

Still another strategy for becoming a strong reader of poetry is to problematize your reading or read a text **against the grain**. This strategy is also a variety of a creative reading. One expression of it may be found in the earlier statement from the student who resisted a "too easy" reading of "This Is Just to Say."

As that statement indicated, however, this kind of reading strategy probably comes into play only after you have done a careful initial reading, using the strategies outlined in Chapter 11. An initial reading should actually be several readings—to get a feel for its language and rhythms; to note its play of language through connotations, denotations, and imagery; to try to construct its setting, speaker, and spoken-to; to try to state its logical thought in a paraphrase. At that point—or perhaps later, after you have written a first response statement or while you are writing a first response—you can try to problematize your initial reading. To do this you can draw on some of the reading strategies already mentioned in this chapter. For instance, you can look for and pry open gaps in the text. If, say, your initial reading was fairly smooth, if you read the text as logically coherent or if you saw its text strategies and ideology meshing, you could now look for problem areas (gaps) where you could disrupt that smoothness or coherence.

Why would you want to do such a perverse thing, you may ask. *Play* is the answer. Play with the text. Treat it as a malleable object, subject to your decisions as a reader. Consider this strategy an exercise in strengthening yourself as a reader, just practice. Try it. You may find that you see not only differently but more clearly; you may create a reading that is more convincing to you than an initial "smooth" one, or a reading that tells you more about yourself and the text than you had seen before.

Identifying or creating gaps is a way to change the text. You can also problematize your reading by changing yourself. Remind yourself that you are not a unified self, and the "you" who reads the text initially doesn't have to be the one who reads it *every* time. You can consciously adopt a different perspective. Did you read initially as a female? Read again from a male perspective. You read initially as a young person? Read again from the perspective of an old person. You read initially as a middle-class American? Read again as a member of the underclass, as someone from the Third World. And so on. You can be arbitrary about this, or a given text may suggest some way it "wants" to be read, and you can adopt a perspective different from that.

PROFESSIONAL WRITING Jon Mukand Reading "The Urine Specimen"   To get a better sense of this, go back to the poem "The Urine Specimen" on page 596. I'm not asking you to read it now from a different perspective than that from which you read it initially, but do try to be conscious of the perspective you adopted the first time you read it. I will assume you read it from the perspective of the patient giving the urine specimen. That's easy enough because the speaker seems to adopt that perspective "himself." But that poem was once reprinted in the *Journal of the American Medical Association*, where it was accompanied by a reading from a medical doctor. The physician, Jon Mukand, wrote:

> *Tests, whether academic or medical, have acquired negative con-
> notations: anxiety, difficulty, pain, failure. In medicine, the inverted
> logic of testing causes a "positive" result to have negative consequences
> because pathology is discovered. But it is better to have a "false positive"
> than a "false negative," since the latter means that the diagnosis was
> missed! Medical tests can vary in the level of discomfort they involve. We
> physicians, so used to ordering various studies, usually do not consider
> the emotional responses that even minor procedures can generate in
> patients. Some of the language we use—such as "routine" bloodwork
> and "routine" X-ray views—suggests our attitude. For the patient this
> may translate into the trauma of a needle, which can be mild, involve
> multiple attempts, or cause a painful hematoma [blood clot].*
>
> *But surely, we might say, something as noninvasive as "the urine
> specimen" can hardly provoke emotional turbulence. The poet Ted
> Kooser convinces us otherwise. Through the careful choice of words
> and phrases such as "last small chamber," "chastened," and "chalice,"
> he creates an austere, almost religious mood. "The last small cham-
> ber" seems like the successful conclusion of a quest that has led the
> speaker all the way to "the shore of the city." Just as in mythology and
> folklore wells are associated with supernatural creatures, here a toilet
> is "the chilly well." The inflated language used for the urine itself—
> "gold," "precious sum"—makes us realize that this is no ordinary visit
> to the bathroom. By saying that the physician-priest can "read your
> future," the poet suggests that the urine test is similar to an oracle, with
> its attendant rituals that carry symbolic value. The juxtaposition cre-
> ates an ironic effect, since one hardly associates the act of urination
> with religious rites. The daring conclusion, an attempt to minimize the
> implications of the test, is a rare literary example of deadpan bedpan
> humor.[1]*

---

[1]Jon Mukand, "Poetry and Medicine," *JAMA* 261 (1989):1130.

Mukand reveals his perspective at one or two places in his first paragraph. We might narrow that perspective even further from "physician" to "physician especially sensitive to patients' feelings" as he addresses colleagues who "usually do not consider the emotional responses that even minor procedures can generate in patients." Elsewhere in this text, Mukand adopts a different, perhaps more typical, physician's role: that of the scientific observer who can see "objectively" what's in the data he analyzes. So he makes the kinds of statements he does about "the poet" and the "choice of words" in his second paragraph. But overall, it seems, he is trying to get *his* readers—other doctors—to adopt the patient's perspective on texts such as "routine" medical tests, which, he suggests, are read differently by physicians and patients. At the same time, Mukand's statements indicate his reading of "the grain" of "The Urine Specimen."

The grain of any text—in other words, the ideology of the text with respect to whatever issue it appears to be concerned with—must first be constructed before you can read against it. Then, either "easily" out of your ideology or more self-consciously by adopting a different perspective, you can read against the grain, argue with the text, dispute it, quibble with it, disagree with it.[2] Or just play with it; you don't have to be angry to be a strong reader.

Focus on Reading Against the Grain   As an exercise—not a fully worked out reading against the grain but perhaps the beginning of one—go back to any of the poems you have read and responded to in the chapters in this unit. Look again at your written response, especially for indications of your interpretation of the ideology of the text. Then do some preliminary writing—perhaps brainstorming notes, making lists, or freewriting—*against* that idea, drawing on your ideology to do so.

> **CONNECT:**   Strong readings don't always have to be in prose. Look back to the parody of Robert Frost's "Birches" in Chapter 10, pages 521–522—the poem called "Mr. Frost Goes South to Boston," by Firman Houghton. Consider how Houghton's poem goes beyond imitating Frost's style and having fun with his subject, to making its own statement about Frost as a person or a poet.

Here are four other poems in which ideology—of a speaker if not of the poet—regarding the subject "America" may be constructed as you read. With any one or more of these poems, first try to write a paraphrase of the ideological "statement" the speaker or the text is making; what is being said about what issue, idea, or topic related to "America"? Then try to take an ideological position of your own *against* the text or its speaker. This contesting or **resisting reading** does not limit you to a position you already believe; any of several ideological positions may be adopted, especially in relation to different cultural situations from which you could read and write.

---

[2]Or, as discussed in Chapter 8 with respect to fiction, adopt a *resisting* reading.

Claude McKay   1889–1948

America   1922

Although she feeds me bread of bitterness,
And sinks into my throat her tiger's tooth,
Stealing my breath of life, I will confess
I love this cultured hell that tests my youth!
Her vigor flows like tides into my blood,   5
Giving me strength erect against her hate.
Her bigness sweeps my being like a flood.
Yet as a rebel fronts a king in state,
I stand within her walls with not a shred
Of terror, malice, not a word of jeer.   10
Darkly I gaze into the days ahead,
And see her might and granite wonders there,
Beneath the touch of Time's unerring hand,
Like priceless treasures sinking in the sand.

Robert Creeley   b. 1926

America   1969

America, you ode for reality!
Give back the people you took.

Let the sun shine again
on the four corners of the world

you thought of first but do not   5
own, or keep like a convenience.

People are your own word, you
invented that locus and term.

Here, you said and say, is
where we are. Give back   10

what we are, these people you made,
us, and nowhere but you to be.

Abelardo Delgado   b. 1931

stupid america   1969

stupid america, see that chicano
with a big knife
in his steady hand
he doesn't want to knife you

he wants to sit on a bench   5
and carve christ figures
but you won't let him.
stupid america, hear that chicano
shouting curses on the street
he is a poet   10
without paper and pencil
and since he cannot write
he will explode.
stupid america, remember that chicanito
flunking math and english   15
he is the picasso
of your western states
but he will die
with one thousand masterpieces
hanging only from his mind.   20

Aurora Levins Morales   b. 1954

Child of the Americas   *1986*

I am a child of the Americas,
a light-skinned mestiza of the Caribbean,
a child of many diaspora, born into this continent at a crossroads.

I am a U.S. Puerto Rican Jew,
a product of the ghettos of New York I have never known.   5
An immigrant and the daughter and granddaughter of immigrants.
I speak English with passion: it's the tongue of my consciousness.
a flashing knife blade of crystal, my tool, my craft.

I am Caribeña, island grown. Spanish is in my flesh,
ripples from my tongue, lodges in my hips: 10
the language of garlic and mangoes,
the singing in my poetry, the flying gestures of my hands.
I am of Latinoamerica, rooted in the history of my continent:

I speak from that body.
I am not african. Africa is in me, but I cannot return.   15
I am not taína. Taíno is in me, but there is no way back.
I am not european. Europe lives in me, but I have no home there.

I am new. History made me. My first language was spanglish.
I was born at the crossroads
and I am whole.   20

Thinking Critically About Poetry: Analytical Approaches

If you recall from Chapter 2, self-consciousness has been suggested as a goal for reading and a way of reading all along. As you move in the direction of becoming a stronger reader of poetry, you would do well to recall this suggestion now. All the reading strategies recommended in this chapter have, to one degree or another, involved self-consciousness as a way and a goal. If you have practiced any of those methods in exercises or response statements throughout this chapter, you have already begun a self-conscious analysis of your interaction with a poem. Additional response statements or journal writing or more formally developed response essays will give you a chance to pursue self-conscious analysis further.

In general, self-conscious analysis may be divided into two kinds, according to the orientation of the analysis. The first kind, *cognitive analysis,* looks at some of the things you do as a reader in a given situation, why you do them, and the effects they have. This analysis would include examining your reading strategies, considering what aspects of your literary experience or ideology cause you to read, think, and interpret as you do (or did on a particular occasion). In the time-flow of reading, you can look at how your reading strategies or interpretations change in the course of a reading or over several successive readings, and what was involved in those changes. You can do a comparative cognitive analysis of different effects produced by different reading strategies or the adoption of different perspectives in successive readings. Chapter 14 will illustrate this kind of self-conscious analysis.

A *cultural analysis* looks at the cultural factors that produce your literary experience and ideology or that are responsible for the kind of interaction you had with a text. This analysis may lead you in the direction of library research, if you want to find out more about the literary repertoire or ideology of a text in order to analyze its similarities with or differences from your own. Or it could lead you to explore some of the larger cultural issues in your ideology that are involved in your response. The excerpts from response statements to "Barbie Doll" and "This Is a Photograph of Me" in this chapter reflect the beginnings of a cultural analysis. A cultural analysis could also lead you to examine or develop intertextual connections, like those between a poem and nonliterary texts, especially those from popular culture that may have a profound effect on shaping your response to a particular poem.

In any case, self-conscious analysis carries you away from textual analysis. Because it doesn't privilege the text as much as the traditional kind of textual analysis or interpretation, self-conscious analysis can be another way for a reader to overcome poetry anxiety. But because it does use the text as the occasion for the analysis, it can also be a way to stay in touch with what a reader loves about poetry.

Texts produced from cultures that are in some or many ways markedly different from your own are particularly active sites for the interaction of ideologies. A distinct difference between the cultural situation of a text and your own cultural situation allows you to gain some perspective on how many things, large and small, are culture-bound. At the same time, reading texts from cultures other than your own offers you the chance to discover what is universal.

The poems below, for instance, were produced by various cultural and historical situations—of Central and South American nations, of Mexican-American and Native American lives, of people marginalized for their race, ethnicity, or nationality. Reading these poems provides an excellent opportunity for you to heighten your consciousness of the role your own ethnic, national, or racial circumstances play in shaping you as a reader. Your differences or similarities in terms of race, ethnicity, nationality, or social class with the poets themselves or the speakers or other people in the poems should play a definite role in your responses. Awareness of those differences or similarities should also allow you to do the kind of cultural analysis of your responses that strengthens your awareness of yourself as a socially constructed reader.

At the same time, these texts offer further opportunities for you to engage in a cognitive analysis of the literary interaction that happens when you read them, just as any strong or challenging poem would do.

Poems for Exploration

Pablo Neruda   1904–1973

*The United Fruit Co.** 1950

Translated by Robert Bly

When the trumpet sounded, it was
all prepared on the earth,
and Jehovah parceled out the earth
to Coca-Cola, Inc., Anaconda,
Ford Motors, and other entities:
The Fruit Company, Inc.
reserved for itself the most succulent,
the central coast of my own land,
the delicate waist of America.
It rechristened its territories
as the "Banana Republics"
and over the sleeping dead,
over the restless heroes
who brought about the greatness,

5

10

---

*In the first half of the twentieth century, United Fruit, a United States company, became a major grower, shipper, and wholesaler of Latin American fruit, particularly bananas. The company's involvement in Latin American politics made it for many Latinos a symbol of "Yankee" imperialism.

the liberty and the flags,   15
it established the comic opera:
abolished the independencies,
presented crowns of Caesar,
unsheathed envy, attracted
the dictatorship of the flies,   20
Trujillo flies, Tacho flies,
Carias flies, Martinez flies,
Ubico flies,° damp flies   Trujillo, Tacho, Carias, Martinez, Ubico—all Latin American dictators
of modest blood and marmalade,
drunken flies who zoom   25
over the ordinary graves,
circus flies, wise flies
well trained in tyranny.

Among the bloodthirsty flies
the Fruit Company lands its ships,   30
taking off the coffee and the fruit;
the treasure of our submerged
territories flows as though
on plates into the ships.

Meanwhile Indians are falling
into the sugared chasms
of the harbors, wrapped
for burial in the mist of the dawn:
a body rolls, a thing
that has no name, a fallen cipher,   40
a cluster of dead fruit
thrown down on the dump.

Claribel Alegria   b. 1924

I, Mirror   1978

*Translated by Electa Arenal and Keitha Sapsin**

Water sparkles
on my skin
I don't feel it
water streams
down my back
I don't feel it   5

---

*An earlier version was co-translated by Marsha Gabriela Dreyer.

I rub myself with a towel
I pinch myself in the arm
I feel nothing
I begin to get dressed
stumbling   10
from the corners
like lightning bolts
shouts burst forth
tortured eyes
rats run   15
teeth
still I feel nothing
I wander through the streets:
children with dirty faces
ask me for money   20
child prostitutes
not yet fifteen
wound-filled streets
tanks approach
bayonets raised   25
bodies fall
weeping
at last I feel my arm
I am no longer a phantom
I hurt   30
therefore I exist
again I watch the scene:
children run
streaming blood
women with panic   35
on their faces
this time it hurts me less
I pinch myself again
and can feel nothing
I simply reflect   40
what is happening next to me
the tanks
are not tanks
nor the shouts
shouts   45
I am a blank mirror
that nothing penetrates
my surface
is hard
is brilliant   50
is polished
I became the mirror

I am fleshless
barely keeping
a vague memory
of pain.

N. Scott Momaday   b. 1934

New World   *1976*

1.
First Man,
behold:
the earth
glitters
with leaves;
the sky
glistens
with rain.   5
Pollen
is borne   10
on winds
that low
and lean
upon
mountains.
Cedars
blacken
the slopes—
and pines.

2.
At dawn
eagles
hie and
hover
above
the plain   15
where light
gathers
in pools.
Grasses
shimmer
and shine.
Shadows
withdraw
and lie
away
like smoke.

3.
At noon
turtles
enter
slowly
into
the warm   20
dark loam.
Bees hold
the swarm.
Meadows
recede
through planes
of heat
and pure
distance.

4.
At dusk
the gray   20
foxes
stiffen
in cold;
blackbirds   25
are fixed
in the
branches.
Rivers
follow   30
the moon,
the long
white track
of the
full moon.   35

Lorna Dee Cervantes   b. 1954

Poem for the Young White Man Who Asked Me How I, an Intelligent, Well-Read Person Could Believe in the War Between Races   1981

In my land there are no distinctions.
The barbed wire politics of oppression
have been torn down long ago. The only reminder
of past battles, lost or won, is a slight
rutting in the fertile fields.   5

In my land
people write poems about love,
full of nothing but contented childlike syllables.
Everyone reads Russian short stories and weeps.
There are no boundaries.   10
There is no hunger, no
complicated famine or greed.

I am not revolutionary.
I don't even like political poems.
Do you think I can believe in a war between races?   15
I can deny it. I can forget about it
when I'm safe,
living on my own continent of harmony
and home, but I am not
there.   20

I believe in revolution
because everywhere the crosses are burning,
sharp-shooting goose-steppers round every corner,
there are snipers in schools ...
(I know you don't believe this.   25
You think this is nothing
but faddish exaggeration. But they
are not shooting at you.)

I'm marked by the color of my skin.
The bullets are discrete and designed to kill slowly.   30
They are aiming at my children.
These are facts.
Let me show you my wounds: my stumbling mind, my
"excuse me" tongue, and this
nagging preoccupation   35
with the feeling of not being good enough.

These bullets bury deeper than logic.
Racism is not intellectual.
I can not reason these scars away.

Outside my door   40
there is a real enemy
who hates me.
I am a poet
who yearns to dance on rooftops,
to whisper delicate lines about joy   45
and the blessings of human understanding.
I try. I go to my land, my tower of words and
bolt the door, but the typewriter doesn't fade out
the sounds of blasting and muffled outrage.
My own days bring me slaps on the face.   50
Every day I am deluged with reminders
that this is not
my land
and this is my land.

I do not believe in the war between races.   55

but in this country
there is war.

Roberto Sosa   b. 1930

The Poor   *1969*

Translated by Jim Lindsey

The poor are many.
That's why
we cannot forget them.

Surely   5
they see
in the morning light
many buildings
they would like
to live in with their children.

They can   10
shoulder
the coffin of a star.
They can
rip up the air like furious birds,
blot out the sun.   15

But now knowing their treasures
they enter and leave by mirrors of blood;
they walk, and die, slowly.   20

That's why
we cannot forget them.

READING AND WRITING PROJECTS
FOR CREATIVE AND CRITICAL THINKING

A major goal of this book is to help you learn about yourself as a reader—both what you do cognitively when you read and how culture impinges on the kind of reader you are when you interact with any particular text. Writing in all its manifestations is an important means to that goal because performing the actions of writing causes you to focus on the actions you take and the situation you are in as a reader. In addition to the kinds of writing already discussed and exemplified in this book, there are other ways to use writing to learn.

The following suggestions are intended to help you integrate your reading of and writing about literary texts in various ways. These suggestions include exploratory writing, playing with texts and language, creative efforts in various genres, and other writing exercises designed to strengthen your awareness of the cognitive and cultural processes involved in your reading.

▶ Having seen some examples of poetic parodies (by Houghton, Brode, and Moss), try your hand at writing your own verse parody. You could choose either of two options: (1) Parody a poet's *style*, with the subject of your poem being anything you choose. To do this, you might have to read several poems by a particular poet to get a grasp of that poet's style. In this book, e. e. cummings, Emily Dickinson, Gerard Manley Hopkins, and Ishmael Reed are some poets with distinctive styles that may lend themselves to parody. Anthony Brode's "Breakfast with Gerard Manley Hopkins" (page 542) is an example of a stylistic parody. (2) Parody any poem's *treatment of subject*, in any verse style you can work with. The poem by Howard Moss (page 571) is an example of a subject parody. An additional option for this assignment is to write a piece of expository prose in which you explain your choices and decisions as a parodist. An example of a student's parody of a poem and some "critical" prose she wrote about her parody follow this section.

▶ Construct the "ideal" reader for a particular poem. What attitudes, values, beliefs, knowledge, etc. should this person have to best "understand" or "appreciate" this poem? Would this reader's gender, race, age, ethnicity, or nationality be a factor? Compare yourself to this ideal reader. How similar to or different from him or her are you?

▶ As a variation on the above assignment, construct the *"un-*ideal" reader for a particular poem. What attitudes, values, beliefs, knowledge, etc. would most alienate someone from this poem? Would this reader's gender, race, age, ethnicity, or nationality be a factor? Compare yourself to this un-ideal reader. How similar to or different from him or her are you?

▶ Go back to a poem you have read and responded to in any of the chapters in this unit. Consider the perspective—in terms of gender, race, class, age, ethnicity, or any other cultural category—from which you read it the first time. Then consciously adopt a different perspective and try reading the poem again from that angle. In a piece of expository prose, describe the effect of changing your perspective. (As examples, Chapter 11 offered a reading of "Hoop League" from the perspective of a male ex-athlete, and Chapter 13 offered a reading of "Barbie Doll" from a feminist perspective. Either of those poems could be read from other perspectives, in which case different ideological issues would emerge.)

Under the name "Svetlana," student Catherine Bachochin writes poetry for her own amusement and for that of a friend who is away at medical school. Catherine/Svetlana's poem "L'art, 1993" is a parody of modern open-form poetry in general, but the text that triggered it was the following poem by Ezra Pound:

Ezra Pound   1885–1972

L'art, 1910   1916

Green arsenic smeared on an egg-white cloth,
Crushed strawberries! Come, let us feast our eyes.

Here is "Svetlana's" take on Pound's poem. Following it is Catherine's prose commentary on the poem, which is itself a parody of critical prose.

Svetlana

L'art, 1993
Or, My First Modern Poem
Or still further, Eat Yo' Heart Out Ezra   1993

"la la"
—T. S. Eliot, line 306, Ill. The Fire Sermon,
The Wasteland

Modern poetry.
What is
it.
Is it

trying to represent a lyrical thought   5
by using
lines
       and
    spaces as your
canvas?   10

Or is it
veiled emotional *regurgitation*
of words for the *satisfaction*
and wild megalomaniac *gratification*
of its   15
author?

Let's make the POET, or his emotions,
reign freely over his verse.
Why not, it's so easy, just make
your phrases short.   20
And terse.

Sometimeswhenitgetssoemotional(iunderstanditissodifficulttoexistiknow)and
thereisnotimetostopthelineandtakeabreatherbutthenoutofthebluethecrazypoet
getsacataclysmicideaandallofasuddenit
stops
and takes a dramatic
pause.

Only to make you think.

Yet, is modern poetry
redeeming in some way?
"i like keats," some, "no, *shelley*,"
others would say.
But can modern poets
matter to our lives today?

Who knows, who cares
when my life's full of woe:
taxation, death, war,
Larry, Curly, and Moe

Larry
    Curly
        and
Moe.

They're dead, don't you understand?   "Hey leave me alone, you know that
How can you sit there complacently?   only *Matlock* is the one for me."

Modern poets use
metaphors for they

are the scribes of mankind
And
as they bend over their
pieces d'art and conjure up
similes because, you know, they are like those really really good poets of let's
say the Romantic age or like even earlier like that Avon english guy who wrote
West Side Story or something—who can think up juicy, extra fruity, shake yo'
booty similes . . .
LIKE THIS ONE

Now, let's forgo meter
and not make the words rhyme,
it's so *passe*, come on, i can't
afford to waste time.

And verse—(hello, what was that, excuse me, nurse?)
What a curse, what a curse, to write in verse.
Modern poets move forward, not in reverse—
Remember, those who use it only end up in a hearse.

Trochaic, Dactyllic, those SKEEMS are for the boids:
i'm flying my own crazy plane, what matters is *woids*.
Words and mo' words only matter to me,
who cares whether you understand or even *dig* me?

i can be obscure as
pink concrete jello
which seeps to my bones
or throw in a
flaming crusty armadillo
whose last name is . . . jones.

You See
Those Things
Mean More
To Me.
(. . . iambic dimeter, like *yeah*, man)

You know, it seems to me
(I'd know Dylan would agree)
that I sincerely think
that reading modern poetry only
drives one, well, to *drink*.

STUDENT WRITING

Catherine Bachochin: A Critical Commentary on "L'art, 1993"

Svetlana, let it be said, is arguably one of the finest, if not entirely enigmatic,

poetesses of the twentieth century. In her poetry, Svetlana shows us her penchant for the off-beat, her desire to shock her readers, and of course, her whimsy for the bizarre. Her poetry has a certain *je ne sais quoi* of which she herself has said to be at times totally unaware. As a contemporary of Svetlana, who wishes not to be named, has even been quoted as saying, "Svetlana . . . Svetlana . . . give me a minute, it'll come to me . . . wait, who did you say again?" Svetlana wields that much power and influence over her contemporaries.

As a little girl growing up in a Siberian suburb, Svetlana knew at an early age what course her life was to take. She herself has said, "My impetus to create reams and reams of poetry I guess you could say started when I realized that they could move people, make them feel something, give them something to get excited about, oh, and also provide them with an extra source of fuel." Indeed, the Siberian winters were arduous for the young Siberian poetess and it was not long before the Siberian people were reading (and burning) her manuscripts. At the urging of her closest friend Natasha, Svetlana chose to leave Siberia and assume her new appellation, "astute young Russian exile." The Siberians were sorry to see her manuscripts go, but happy to have a Siberian attain the level of greatness that is Svetlana's.

Our focus of this essay, however, is not to provide the reader with an overview of Svetlana's biographical trials and tribulations. Instead, this essay attempts to analyze the deep poetic recesses of Svetlana's mind, the charred poetic sensibility that she possesses, and ultimately, her astounding poem of self-mockery of the profession she holds dear, "L'art, 1993."

Percy Bysshe Shelley once said of poetry in his 1821 essay *A Defence of Poetry*, "the finest passages of poetry are produced by labour and study." Such is not the case with Svetlana, though. Svetlana, instead, writes out of sheer instinct and raw talent, "winging it" as it were, to produce her verse. Although Svetlana denies vehemently any incidence of forethought in her poetry, she does concede that she has had many poets and their poems inspire her works. It is certainly no mistake then that "L'art, 1993" is quasi-dedicated to Ezra Pound and contains a very revealing quote of *The Wasteland* by T.S. Eliot. It is commonly known among poetical pundits that Svetlana admired the works of Ezra Pound to the point of obsession. The almost mocking tone of "Eat Yo' Heart Out Ezra" suggests a departure from the usual psychotic phrases and declamations of other dedications devoted to Pound in previous poems. Critics who endeavor to explain this change of sentiment in Svetlana theorize that Svetlana grew and matured as a poet or point to the fact that the therapeutic drugs finally kicked in. In any case, there is no argument that Pound has had a profound influence on the poetry of Svetlana via the verse and stanza formation, the epigrammatic stylings of her diction, and of course her perky and almost whimsical attitude of neglect and abject indifference for the reader's feelings. T.S. Eliot, another poet who has shaped and warped Svetlana's formative poetic years, is often extensively quoted in the works of Svetlana. Svetlana has been known to borrow large chunks of Eliot's verse and not credit the verse as belonging to him. And it is also a well known fact that Svetlana's *The Lunchroom* is a stunning but lack-luster tribute to Eliot's *The Wasteland*. One does not have to wrack their brains for long in order to discover the reason for Svetlana's particular affinity with *The Wasteland*. *The Wasteland*, in particular *The Fire Sermon*, is a poem which reminds Svetlana of her Siberian homeland and recalls the simple yet daily strife to which Svetlana was subjected during her childhood. The poetical atmosphere, or *milieu*, if you will, that Pound and Eliot conjure up in the mind of Svetlana is then the starting point for the critic in an analysis of "L'art, 1993."

Svetlana begins her poem by introducing the gripping and haunting statement, "Modern poetry." Indeed, Modern poetry. Svetlana, by means of reduction methods which even Jacques Derrida would be proud, creates a sentence that has well occupied the modern intellectual mind of today. Svetlana invites and slyly coerces the reader to consider the whole sordid mess that is the Modern poem. She continues by further suggesting to the reader two rhetorical questions which answer yet answer not the nature of the Modern poem. Having subjected the reader to this agonizing conundrum, Svetlana skillfully resolves the question for us in stanza three: "Let's make the POET, or his emotions / reign freely over his verse." This revelation is nothing short of commonplace: Svetlana echoes the sentiments of Wordsworth when the great Romantic poet said, "Poetry is the spontaneous overflow of powerful feelings...."

However, there is a somewhat darker, meatier purpose behind the statement in the third stanza. Svetlana writes stanza three as well as the following stanzas in a markedly incriminatory tone, as if she repudiates the role of the Modern Poet writing the Modern Poem. Svetlana mercilessly mocks such modern poetical conventions as the small "i" pronoun, the run-on line, intra-verse dialogue, the arcane reference, colloquial speech, and other poetical subject motifs.

One of the more significant established motifs on which Svetlana picks is the tripartite soul or state. Tripartite symbolism has been utilized in a religious context to make reference to the trinity or, the tripartite division of power of God. In the Platonic scheme of things, the tripartite symbolism has been used to describe a well-functioning state (one of the philosopher-king, the protectors, and the workers) as well as the functioning of the soul (reason, passion, and appetite). With the inclusion of The Three Stooges reference, "Larry, Curly, and Moe," Svetlana breathes new life into the tripartite symbolism of yore. Because Svetlana breaks all orthodox rules with this startling reconfiguration of the tripartite soul/state, its meaning can only fall under the realm of conjecture. One can say with a certain amount of probity that Svetlana means to turn the critical world upside down with this reference to a popular trinity of comedians; however, beyond that, one must make one's own conclusions about Svetlana's recondite meaning.

Are Larry, Curly, and Moe the new divisions for our modern souls? If so, what are the parameters for deciding who plays which role? Who makes these decisions? And what about Shemp, the sometime-Stooge? Is he yet another division of our souls? Is he the "modern" counterpart to man's basic alienation in the world today? And what of The Three Stooges' proclivity for slapstick and physical humor? Do we devise a tripartite soul replete with all bodily and physical desires but void of any spiritual or rational guidance? Or do we abandon the tripartite system altogether and formulate a whole new set of symbols, complete with a new mythology, based on the gifted trinity of comedy? Indeed, these are all questions which Svetlana wants us to ask. And unfortunately for us, these are also questions which Svetlana has declined to answer definitively.

At the risk of becoming prolix, this essay would not be complete without a discussion of the imagery in "L'art, 1993." Svetlana's use of tactile and visual imagery in stanza thirteen is a feast for the senses for it is resplendent with color, motion, and life. Who else but Svetlana would dare to consider the seeming anomalous images of "pink concrete jello," and "flaming crusty armadillo"? Svetlana, with her iron mental constitution, tackles and welcomes the opposite, the contrasts, ergo, the yin and yang inherent within all of us. Svetlana adeptly manipulates the impenetrable nature of concrete with the more than pliant and malleable texture of jello. But this is not enough for Svetlana: she further describes an armadillo which has crusted over yet is engulfed with flames. This incongruity that Svetlana forces us to consider may be too much for the sensitive reader, and perhaps even Svetlana realizes this, for she quickly and decisively ends her poem soon after this stanza.

And what is left for us to piece together from this jigsaw of a modern poem? It is difficult to say: one cannot use standard poetical devices such as meter, rhyme, and imagery to judge the aesthetic value of this poem. Svetlana effectively mocks, lampoons, and deconstructs the entire conventional basis for modern poetry today: the use and misuse of meter, the inclusion and exclusion of rhyme, the playful but menacing exchange of dialogue (reminiscent of Frost's "Home Burial"), the reduction of the significance of the poet ("i" pronoun), and the *bouleversement* and rejection of standard and accepted symbols and myths. Svetlana's poem does not conform to any rules—instead, she makes us consider a poem not subject to the limitations of standard poetical conventions.

Svetlana creates then, in "L'art, 1993," an environment in which she is free of the poetic shackles which once enchained her lyrical and metrical brethren. She submits to no higher poetical authority but herself, and therein lies one of the most gripping discoveries the reader can make for himself: Svetlana's propinquity to the basic tenets of existentialism. Svetlana is "engaged" then in the business of poetry: she writes poetry because she exists, and, paradoxically, she exists because she is the product of her poetry. Even though Svetlana writes "L'art, 1993" in this world of certain incertitude, she leaves the reader with a significant concrete statement, one which includes her use of iambic dimeter and the return to the capital "I" pronoun. Svetlana's deliberate reversion to a formal metrical line and the capital "I" indicates that the modern poet, in his cyclic poetical maturity, will indeed return to those same poetic conventions, but will reinvigorate, reconfigure, and reassemble them into an entirely dynamic "other entity."

The exact definition of the "other entity" that modern poetry is to become as well as its precise trajectory is still largely unknown amongst the most erudite scholars of today. Svetlana, who claims she knows what path the "other entity" will take, will not comment on its essential nature. To assuage the critics who study the "other entity" in abject futility, Svetlana has offered little if any help to them in discovering its true meaning. She has been quoted as saying, "I just wanted to have my own set of objects or my own ambiguous formula for finding the true emotional meaning in poetry. I was really getting sick of that pompous T.S. Eliot's abstruse 'objective correlative' and I thought that it was high time that there should be another equally as annoying term to explain and mean absolutely nothing."

Despite the fact that Svetlana may not be yet willing to shed some light on the "other entity," she does offer us an inkling of its meaning and application in "L'art, 1993." To be sure, critics and readers alike will have to wait patiently for the exciting new developments to surface concerning this new literary terminology from the talented Russian exile, Svetlana.

14 ◆ WRITING ABOUT POETRY

Space doesn't permit showing examples of all of the different options for self-conscious analysis that can be explored in extended pieces of writing. However, this chapter will demonstrate a self-conscious analysis, developed from a response statement, that displays a number of strong reading strategies in one paper. Before looking at what this student wrote, though, you should read the text she responded to and respond to it yourself.

Robert Buck   b. 1958
Natalie Merchant   b. 1964

Hey Jack Kerouac   1987

Hey Jack Kerouac, I think of your
mother and the tears she cried, she cried
for none other than her little boy lost in
our little world that hated and dared
to drag him down. Her little boy cour-   5
ageous who chose his words from
mouths of babes got lost in the wood.
Hip flask slinging madmen, steaming
cafe flirts, they all spoke through you.
Hey Jack, now for the tricky part,   10
when you were the brightest star who
were the shadows? Of the San Francisco
beat boys you were the favorite. Now
they sit and rattle their bones and think
of their blood stoned days. You chose   15
your words from mouths of babes got
lost in the wood. The hip flask slinging
madmen, steaming cafe flirts, in Chinatown howling at night.
Allen baby, why so jaded? Have the   20
boys all grown up and their beauty faded?
Billy, what a saint they've made you, just
like Mary down in Mexico on All Souls'
Day.
You chose your words from mouths   25
of babes got lost in the wood. Cool junk

booting madmen, street minded girls in
Harlem howling at night. What a tear
stained shock of the world, you've gone
away without saying goodbye.

30

Response Statement Questions

- Does this text seem like a poem to you? If not, what genre of writing does it seem to be? If so, what makes it a poem?
- What do you think this text is "about"? Are there references in it that you don't understand or "get"? Even if this is so, are you able to construct a line of thought or a theme?
- What seems to be the attitude of the voice in this text toward what it is talking about? How would you characterize it: Adoring? Praising? Blaming? Negative? Ironic? Sarcastic? Sympathetic? Something else? How are you able to construct this voice with this attitude?
- If you are familiar with this text in another context, how would you characterize any additional text strategies you know about? How or what do they contribute to the text in that context?
- *Share and Compare* What reading strategies do other readers use with this text? Why do they use those? What knowledge of or attitudes toward any of the people referred to in the text do your classmates have?

From Response Statement to Formal Paper

"Hey Jack Kerouac" is unconventional in at least two ways: first, it's a popular song, not a canonized poem; second, on the page it appears to be prose, not verse. I would invite you, however, to listen to a performance of it by 10,000 Maniacs on their album *In My Tribe* (Elektra Records, 1987), in which the phrases are vocalized by Natalie Merchant to sound like verse lines, even though most of the "lines" are unrhymed. Both that performance and the reading below *poeticize* the prose in which the lyrics are written. This strategy illustrates a point made in Chapter 10: that poetry is a way of *reading*, not just of writing.

Here is a response statement that a student wrote to her initial reading of "Hey Jack Kerouac."

STUDENT WRITING
Elaine Kaplowe: Response Statement

Before ever reading this song, I'd heard it many times. I was accustomed to its melody and the sound of the singer's voice. The song always seemed very positive to me. I didn't know who Jack Kerouac was at the time, but I assumed he was somebody relatively famous who had lived a tragic life and possibly died a tragic death.

I didn't actually read the lyrics of the song until a few years later, when I decided to do a paper on Jack Kerouac and his novel *On the Road*. Since at the time I was working on the paper I really admired Kerouac, I suppose I assumed everyone else did, also—especially if they had written and sung a song about him.

But on a subsequent reading of the song, a few things began to bother me. There were some words and phrases in the lyrics that didn't seem to be praising Kerouac. Once I picked up on these negative sections, the entire song took on a whole new meaning. It seemed as though the writer didn't admire Kerouac. The text was putting pressure on my original response to the song.

The first portion of the first paragraph seems to be the writer's interpretation of Kerouac's mother's feelings toward her son. It almost seems as if the writer is trying to make Kerouac feel guilty for the way he treated his mother. Further into the song, the writer is attempting to place even more blame on Kerouac. All the "hip flask slinging madmen, steaming cafe flirts" spoke through Kerouac. Yet when Kerouac was the "brightest star," these others were "the shadows." I get the impression from these phrases that Kerouac took all the claim to fame of the Beat Generation.

However, I don't agree with that. From what I know of Kerouac, he didn't even want the fame that was thrust upon him. He wrote because he felt writing was his duty on earth, and he wrote for money, not for fame. Other members of the Beat Generation were also writers. Some of them made it, some of them didn't. It was like any writing market. Those who are the most talented and most widely read make it to the top.

Kerouac did choose his words from "mouths of babes got lost in the wood," but how else could he capture the essence of his generation? I think all the Beats were babes lost in the wood, even Kerouac. And someone had to be the responsible note-taker. Someone had to carry a little notebook with him wherever he went. Someone had to make certain that their small circle didn't go unnoticed in the hands of time.

Besides picking on Kerouac, the writer also belittles two of his contemporaries. By using only their first names, she robs them of their standing as well known writers, just as she did with Kerouac. I admire all three of these men, but I don't refer to them by their first names only. To me, that's an action of disrespect. Allen Ginsberg and Bill Burroughs were friends with Kerouac and fellow members of the Beat Generation. Is the writer picking on them because they're Kerouac's buddies, or is she cutting them down because they're related to the Beat Generation?

It's difficult for me to respond to the song, because I don't think it has a very strong central theme. Is the song about how selfish Jack Kerouac was, or is it about the poor babes who lost their souls during this generation? I know that Kerouac is considered the Spokesperson and the Father of the Beat Generation. So maybe the writer feels the need to contact Kerouac and lay all these problems and concerns on him, especially since he's remembered as the one who was in charge.

The ideology of this text seems to include many negative views of Kerouac and his generation. If that's the case, then my ideology completely clashes with the text's. I'm a supporter of Kerouac and the literary period of which he was a part. I think he's a wonderful, innovative writer whose words came directly from his soul, not from the people around him. His works are largely autobiographical, so he did use his friends as characters, but I don't see anything wrong with that. Most writers are advised to write what they know, and that's exactly what Kerouac was doing.

This response statement illustrates some of the reading strategies discussed in Chapters 10–13. First, notice how Elaine got used to this text—or at least one version, the performed version, of it—for a while before she did an initial reading. As discussed in Chapter 10, that is a common strategy for popular songs, but there's no reason it cannot be applied to other, more conventionally literary, texts. Second, notice how her response shifts direction, from a smooth to a problematized interaction and then to resisting the text. Elaine recognized the clashing interaction of ideologies that was occurring as she did an initial reading. Third, and no doubt related to the second strategy, notice how Elaine maintained a questioning attitude as she read and responded, how she questioned both the text and her own responses. She wasn't trying to "find" or invent a theme just to get closure on the text, as she indicates in her next-to-last paragraph. She was able to maintain a playful attitude toward both the text and her response to it.

Prewriting

Elaine's response statement and several readings of "Hey Jack Kerouac" became, in effect, **prewriting** when she decided to develop her first response into a paper of self-conscious analysis. At that point in her writing process, she asked her instructor to reread her response statement and make some suggestions as she began to revise and expand it into a more formal paper. Elaine's instructor gave her some feedback in the form of questions rather than suggestions or directions. This was her paper, after all, not his, so he tried to leave the responsibility for its development in her hands. He asked her the following questions, which emerged from what she had already written in her response statement.

- Could she say more about particular text strategies she responded to?

- Could she say more about the reading strategies she employed and their effects on her response?
- Could she explore the cultural factors behind the negative criticism of Jack Kerouac?
- Could she say more about the cognitive and cultural factors involved in her desire to defend Kerouac against this negative criticism?

As she considered how to address these questions, Elaine went back and reread her response statement herself and did some **freewriting** to brainstorm ideas. Those efforts led her to a tentative **thesis** for a first draft of a paper and a scratch **outline** or rough plan for the organization of that draft. Rather than reproduce Elaine's entire first draft here, look at her tentative thesis and scratch outline.

Tentative Thesis

Reading "Hey Jack Kerouac" was both a confusing and an enlightening experience for me. My reading strategies and what I brought to the text in the way of beliefs and knowledge about Kerouac and the Beats alternately clashed and harmonized with the text, but eventually I decided on a way to read it that resolved my dilemmas.

Scratch Outline

Background—my first acquaintance with the song.

- my assumptions about 10,000 Maniacs' view of K.
- my decision to use the lyrics in a paper praising K. and the Beats.
- why I went back to the text again.

My next reading: disturbing

- it seemed to be criticizing K. for taking advantage of people around him: "chose his words from mouths of babes."
- it seemed to accuse him of failing to give credit to others: he was "the brightest star"; others were "the shadows."
- it seemed to satirize Ginsberg and Burroughs and the Beats in general: "Allen baby," Billy "a saint."

My disharmonious response to this negativity: I was resisting these negative attitudes b/c of my admiration for K.

My desire to dispel this disharmony:

- I reread the text, looking for positives.

- In this reading, I emphasized evidence of sympathy for K.:

"little boy lost in a little world that hated"; he no longer stole his words, he chose them: "they all spoke through you"; he's giving voice to anonymous others;

now that K. is gone and G. and B. are "faded," something's been lost, the tone is sad.

But the negatives lingered. Was there a third way to read this text, neither positive *nor* negative?

How I wanted a more definite conclusion, so I read it again as *neutral*, mentioning both positive and negative aspects of K.'s life and career but neither praising nor blaming him completely.

Now, K. is realistic:

- "hated" by the world b/c he's chosen to be a marginalized figure.
- to do what he wanted as an author, he had to stay out of the mainstream.
- his and other Beats' subjects were just what they were, neither villains nor heroes.
- text strategies that imitate K.'s style are just a representation, neither praise nor mockery.

Revising

The draft that Elaine wrote from this scratch outline did try to address the questions her instructor asked about her first response statement. This draft was moving in the direction of a strong self-conscious analysis because Elaine was acknowledging what she did as a reader, why she did those things, and the effect her reading strategies and ideology had in her successive readings. But Elaine herself was not satisfied with the direction her paper was taking after the first draft. After having done a lot of work, she was understandably frustrated that her first draft hadn't turned out quite like she'd wanted. Her instructor helped her to see, however, that sometimes a "false start" is necessary in order to find a better way of solving a writing problem. Looking at her work in that light, Elaine saw that the work she had done in planning and composing her first draft was not wasted. So as she revised, she went back "behind" her first draft and produced another scratch outline and revised her thesis. Here is her new plan for her paper.

Scratch Outline with New Thesis

Intro:

By reading "Hey Jack Kerouac" as a literary text rather than simply regarding it as a musical experience, I was able to trace my reading process and responses as I became more deeply involved with and committed to the text. The choices and ac-

tions I made as a reader blended together with my knowledge of Jack Kerouac and

the Beat Generation to form a solid response to the song.

my first reaction to hearing the song

Background to this literary reading of the song:

- my Kerouac course

- my renewed interest in the song

What happened when I listened again:

- some difficult words, so I read the printed lyrics

- the odd arrangement of the lyrics and the differences between the printed

  words and the sung version

- the result of this reading: an interpretation of the song as negative toward K.

  "The tricky part" as the crucial phrase.

How my experience w/ other negative criticism of K. and my desire to "de-

fend" him led to my next reading of the text:

- I reviewed K.'s life.

- went back to "the tricky part," tried to go against the grain.

- how rereading the text in a more positive light opened more doors into the

  text; saw text strategies that now seemed friendlier to K.

- how I was able to harmonize the lyrics with what I knew of K's life.

- how I saw grammar and diction of the text as a tribute to K.'s prose style.

  Conclusion: how I felt like a collaborator with the text in honoring K.

- what this reading process showed me about myself

Elaine dropped her previous plan to discuss three readings of the text:
one as "negative," one as "positive," and a third as more "realistic" or "neutral."
In her revised version, Elaine saw her second reading as a strong one on behalf of Kerouac, and the satisfaction this reading brought meant that she did
not have to resolve the dilemma between "positive" and "negative" readings in
some third way, as she had been trying to do in the previous draft.

Elaine wrote out a new draft based on the above plan, went over it with a
peer tutor in her college's writing center, and edited it to produce the version
that follows. When you read it, please notice the technical matter of citing
lines of verse parenthetically in the text of the paper. Even though "Hey Jack
Kerouac" looks like prose on the page, as a poem it is cited in the conven-

tional way according to line number. Elaine's first parenthetical citation of the text of "Hey Jack Kerouac" includes the word "lines." After that, her parenthetical citations have only the line numbers. Her paper includes a Works Cited entry to the Elektra Records recording, following MLA style.

STUDENT WRITING

Elaine Kaplowe: "Now for the tricky part": A Cognitive Analysis of My Reading Process

The song "Hey Jack Kerouac" by 10,000 Maniacs taught me many things about my reading process. By responding to the song as a literary text rather than simply as a musical experience, I was able to trace my reading process and responses as I became more deeply involved with and committed to the text. The choices and actions I made as a reader blended together with my knowledge of Jack Kerouac and the Beat Generation to form a solid response to the song. But in order to form that solid response I had to overcome some frustrating and confusing obstacles. I was forced to work harder than usual to form an interpretation which satisfied my wants and needs as a reader and as a person.

The first time I heard the song "Hey Jack Kerouac" I liked it immediately. I didn't know much about Jack Kerouac at that time, so what originally attracted me to the song was its upbeat musical quality. As with most songs that I hear for the first time, I didn't pay much attention to the lyrics as an actual text. I did pick up on a few of the words, however, and something about the way they were sung and the order in which they were arranged stuck in my mind.

A few years later, when I "discovered" Kerouac and the Beat Generation in a college course, the song "Hey Jack Kerouac" resurfaced in my mind. Remembering that it had been about Kerouac, I decided to listen to it again, more closely this time, becoming more accustomed to its melody and lyrics, as well as attempting to apply those lyrics to what I knew of Kerouac's life and times. I thought very highly of him, and I assumed that 10,000 Maniacs, an off-beat, slightly progressive musical group, would also think highly of a counterculture figure such as Kerouac. As a result of this assumption, I believed, upon listening to the song again, that the lyrics portrayed Kerouac in a positive light.

There were a few words I had trouble understanding, so I decided finally to read the lyrics. At first it was difficult to read the song because it turned out that the song was sung much differently from the way it was arranged on the page. The written text was grouped in sentences and paragraphs, not at all the typical poetic format I expected for song lyrics. Also, the singer paused at places where in the actual text there were no line breaks or marks of punctuation. Because of these discrepancies, I was forced to concentrate on reading the song as if I had encountered it for the first time on paper rather than through a musical medium.

After I read the song as a written text, its words and theme began to bother me. The song didn't seem so upbeat and positive anymore. It seemed more of a critical accusation toward Kerouac than a composition of praise and admiration for him, as I'd first assumed it to be. In attempting to identify the source of these negative feelings, I was drawn to perhaps the most crucial lines in the song: "Hey Jack, now for the tricky part, / when you were the brightest star who / were the shadows?" (lines 10–12). To me, "tricky" is the most important word in the song because it has the power to spark different themes in the mind of the reader. Because I read "tricky" to mean cunning or sly, my response to the entire song was affected. By reading those lines as an attack on Kerouac, I ended up restructuring the lyrics to echo my negative interpretation of what exactly the "tricky part" was.

I interpreted the song like this: Kerouac had become the brightest star by stealing words from the "mouths of babes," the "shadows." He was the "favorite," while the others went unnoticed. The following paragraph about Allen Ginsberg and William Burroughs, prominent members of the Beat Generation who are alive today, seemed to be the writer's idea of a joke. I know, for example, that Allen Ginsberg is a homosexual. So I read these lines—"Have the / boys all grown up and their beauty faded?"—to be a teasing remark (20–21). And the final line of the song seemed to be yet another sarcastic remark, as if it really weren't such a shock that Kerouac had died without saying goodbye.

My negative response caused tension to come between the text and me as a reader. I was used to reading negative criticism on Kerouac, so I responded immediately to the first word which didn't seem to be written in praise of him: "tricky." But I didn't want to read the song as an unfavorable depiction of Kerouac, so I took a moment to reflect on some of the finer points of his life and writing. After "regaining" my positive feelings for him, I read the text again.

Since I hadn't encountered problems with the beginning paragraph of the text, I immediately jumped to the "tricky part." And this time when I read that line I noticed something new: the words "Hey Jack," which were an echo of the title. The title and the near repetition of it in the second paragraph were text strategies that gave me a sense of casual teamwork. The writer/singer was addressing the song to Kerouac, calling out to him, in the title. And then in the second paragraph she seemed to be engaged in conversation with him, especially since she expressed an air of informality by using his first name only. She wasn't demanding that Kerouac answer this question on his own; she was offering to help him with it. She wasn't accusing him of overshadowing his contemporaries and friends; she was simply asking him who the shadows were.

So the writer/singer and Kerouac answered this question together—in a figurative sense, of course, since Kerouac isn't alive. The question served as a transition from Kerouac to some other members of the Beat Generation who may not have received the recognition they deserved, the ones who in 1987, when the song was written, "rattle their bones and think / of their blood stoned days" (14–15). These men were the "shadows" (12) when Kerouac was the "brightest star" (11).

Responding to the song in a positive light opened up more reading options for me. Since I wasn't struggling with conflicting emotions anymore, I was more comfortable with the text. I decided to read the text closely, relying upon my knowledge of Kerouac and the Beat Generation to interpret the words I was examining.

As a whole, I read the text as a portrait of Kerouac's life. But there were several individual "moments" of his life depicted within the lyrics. The song began with his mother, the only woman to whom Kerouac continually returned. The first few lines seemed to be "told" from his mother's point of view: "she cried / for none other than her little boy lost in / our little world that hated and that dared / to drag him

down" (2–5). But I could see these lines from other points of view as well. Any Kerouac fan would have made that observation. Because even now, even after he's
been dead for 24 years, Kerouac is still lost in this society which for the most part
doesn't admire him and doesn't hesitate to drag him down: "little boy cour- /
ageous who . . . / got lost in the wood" (5–7). (When I first heard the song, I thought
it was "world" rather than "wood." That may be why I formed that response.)

The next few lines of the song described Kerouac's inspiration as a writer. He
"chose his words from / mouths of babes" (6–7). From the research I had done on
Kerouac, I knew something about his writing and thought processes. Kerouac believed that writing was his duty on earth. That's why he devoted his life to writing.
During his lifetime he spent a lot of time writing in solitude, but he also spent a
good amount of time studying the habits and recording the conversations of the
people around him—the other members of the Beat Generation. He wrote in his
novel On the Road that he "shambled" after the "mad" people, because they were
the most interesting. And since Kerouac was considered the spokesman of the Beat
Generation, the rest of the members seemed to use him as a responsible note-taker
who could pin their generation on the literary map: "Hip flask slinging madmen,
steaming / cafe flirts, they all spoke through you" (8–9).

The "tricky part" of the song, as I mentioned earlier, dealt with the other
members of the Beat Generation. When Kerouac was alive, the Beats spoke
through him—he was "the brightest star" and the "favorite." But now the surviving Beats simply "sit and rattle their bones and think / of their blood stoned days."
All they have left are memories—memories of their younger days. Their voices, for
the most part, aren't being heard today. The Beat Generation is a past period. So
the song is, in some senses, a tribute to Kerouac and the Beats. Some of the lyrics
seemed to be written in an attempt to ingrain the images of these "shadows,"
along with the image of Kerouac, in the minds of the current generation, especially
these lines, which are the repeated "chorus" of the song:

You chose
your words from mouths of babes got
lost in the wood. The hip flask slinging

madmen, steaming cafe flirts, in Chinatown howling at night. (15–19)

The new paragraph beginning immediately after this repetition includes Allen Ginsberg and William Burroughs, the two prominent surviving members of the Beat Generation. They're not only surviving members in the sense that they're still alive, they're also surviving in the sense of being relatively famous. Both of these men have published a significant amount of work and are sometimes even anthologized. But when I read the song, I got a sense that they were feeling a bit wistful, as if their fame wasn't as satisfying as their younger days as members of the Beat Generation were. I pictured the Beats as young men racing around the country, trying to experience at one time everything that life had to offer. And now that the surviving Beats are older and their generation has "faded," their lives aren't the same anymore. They didn't die young, so they're alive to see their beliefs and friends slowly disappear. They have outlived their generation: "Have the / boys all grown up and their beauty faded?" Yet because they're still living, they have the power to make sure that their generation is remembered. The Beat Generation has not yet faded out entirely.

The last paragraph of the song contains yet another repetition of this line: "You chose your words from mouths / of babes got lost in the wood" (25–26). But the next line further describes the members of the Beat Generation: "Cool junk / booting madmen, street minded girls in / Harlem howling at night" (26–28). These repetitions and further descriptions serve to strengthen Kerouac's ties to his contemporaries and friends. They also stress the importance of those people who were considered the "shadows."

The final lines of the song—"What a tear / stained shock of the world, you've gone / away without saying goodbye"—had the most impact on me (28–30). (Again, this response probably stemmed from hearing the song—the final lines are sung with powerful emotion.) As part of the printed text, these lines served as the final knot in Kerouac's life. The preceding words and sentences built up sympathy for him and his contemporaries, but this line made his death real. He left without saying goodbye; he faded away, leaving disheartened shadows in his wake. The last line also seemed as though it was a method of wrapping up the song, of tying it together. The song began with the personal tears of Kerouac's mother, but finished with the collective tears of the world.

Besides the meanings of the words and phrases, however, there was the grammar and diction of these words and phrases. Some lines and some words appeared to be a deliberate imitation of Kerouac's writing style. For the most part, he wrote in a style he called "Spontaneous Prose." This style gave him the freedom to let the words spill from his mind right onto the page, without using the usual grammatical and structural conventions. This sentence in particular sounded like something that Kerouac would have written: "You chose your words from mouths / of babes got lost in the wood." It sounded strange to me at first because it was missing the word "who" or "and" between "babes" and "got." But Kerouac was in the habit of leaving "unnecessary" words out. His writing also consisted of words piled on top of one another without any punctuation barriers. The words "babes got lost" were piled together in the text, seemingly in imitation of Kerouac's style.

Some individual words in the song—"hip," "madmen," "howling," "cool," and "junk"—also reminded me of Kerouac. These five words were used quite frequently in Kerouac's books and in the everyday language of the Beats. "Hip" and "cool" were popular adjectives; "madmen" was what Kerouac termed most of the Beats; "junk" was a word for the drugs they used; and "howling" was what they did in the streets at night, as the song said. This "Kerouacean" language in the text seemed to be a collaboration between Kerouac and the singer/writer.

This close reading of the song allowed me to test my favorable response to the text and my feelings toward Kerouac. And both my response and my feelings passed the test—I read the song positively and I still loved Kerouac. Now only one complication lingers in my mind. I fear that my "final" response to this text is not stable. I know that my reading, like all opinions and ideas, is subject to change. Two months, or even two days from now, I might pick up this song again and interpret it differently. The words on the page will always remain the same, but I will grow and learn. And the next time I read this song, my expanded mind will bring new ideas to the text.

Works Cited

Buck, Robert, and Natalie Merchant. "Hey Jack Kerouac." 10,000 Maniacs. *In My Tribe*. Elektra, 1987.

This paper is an excellent example of a self-conscious analysis achieved by a strong reader who, as she herself says, didn't start out particularly strong with respect to this text. It also shows the reader's contribution to poeticizing a text, as well as to creating an interpretation. It indicates something of the recursive nature of the reading process: that is, how a reading moves through time in circular fashion, covering the same territory again and again but differently, and how a reader builds response and interpretation through successive readings. And finally it shows, in the last paragraph, an aware reader's sense that *no* reading is, in a sense, final because readers change, and as they do so they may change the texts they read.

If you compare this version of Elaine's paper with her plan for the previous draft, I hope you will see that the changes she made concerned the content of her paper in terms of what she wanted to say about her reading of "Hey Jack Kerouac." But perhaps more importantly, her change in direction from the first plan to the second concerned the structure of her paper—its organization, the order in which she wanted to say things. Basically, Elaine's decision to restructure her paper affected its content; it made what she wanted to say come clearer to her as she worked through the revision process. All these aspects of Elaine's reading and writing process and the features of her paper itself indicate what you or anyone can do by way of becoming a strong, conscientious, self-conscious reader of poetry.

The Perils of Free Associating

Elaine's work shows what an aware and conscientious reader can do in developing a response statement toward a formal paper. She explained her reading by reference to both parties to the interaction: herself and the text. In the process, while she engaged in some close reading of the text, she avoided turning her paper into an "objective" analysis of the text alone. On the other hand, she also steered clear of a paper that had more to do with herself as a person than with that person interacting with the text.

As an example of what can go wrong in moving from response statement to formal paper, consider the case of Steve, who wrote a response statement to "The Urine Specimen." His first response was very interesting in the way that it drew on an element of his personal experience, but the paper he eventually drafted based on that response statement took a decidedly wrong turn in terms of giving *his* reader insight into Steve's interaction with the text. In the hope that you can avoid a similar misstep by seeing the pitfall that caught this student, I offer the following response statement and draft of a paper, accompanied by some brief comments. Before you read Steve's response, you may want to reacquaint yourself with "The Urine Specimen," which appears on page 596.

STUDENT WRITING
Steve T.: Response Statement

Reading this poem, it brought back many memories of my six years spent in the USMC. About every four months we had to take a piss test. (That's what we called them.) The Marine Corps was looking for people who used drugs. Taking a piss test was very strange because you had someone looking over your shoulder while you were pissing to make sure that the urine was coming out of your penis and not something else. One Marine hid a squeeze bottle filled with colored water and a long tube taped to his dick and when he was pissing in the cup (not really) he just squeezed the bottle and filled it up with the colored water and that's why we had people looking over our shoulders. One time during a piss test a staff sergeant told me if I didn't piss in two minutes he would punch me in the bladder to make me piss. Another time I could not piss and I was told that if I didn't piss by 4 o'clock they would take me to medical and stuff a catheter tube up me to make me piss. Luckily I pissed at 3:58. One thing funny we used to do is piss on the side of the cup and hand it to the person in charge. (Well, we thought it was funny.)

In the M.C., piss tests were looked upon with grave importance as it seems to this man in the poem. He seems to be worried about the piss test, and people in the M.C. who did drugs before a piss test were worried too. This poem had a very powerful impact on me and I think any subject matter is appropriate for poetry. As far as what the poem is about, it is in the mind of the reader and as I stated before I believe that it is test anxiety. The voice I hear in the poem is one of worry and fright.

Later, when Steve's class was assigned to write a formal paper developing an initial response statement, Steve chose this response to "The Urine Sample" to work with. His instructor endorsed his decision. The sentence in the response statement that the poem had a "very powerful" impact on Steve and his apparently harmonious ideological interaction with the text's suggestion of the pressure and anxiety of giving a urine sample seemed to indicate that Steve had some good material to work with and would produce an interesting self-conscious analysis.

That's not what happened, though, because instead of staying in touch with the text as he tried to analyze the role of his experience and ideology in his reading, Steve indulged in some uncontrolled *free association*, writing almost exclusively about part of his experience and virtually ignoring the *interaction* of that experience with the text. Here is a draft of his formal paper.

STUDENT WRITING
Steve T.: Response Paper

In reading and re-reading the poem "The Urine Specimen," I have come to two conclusions. The author, Ted Kooser, is trying to get the message of test anxiety across to his readers. The other message that I got out of this poem is the power the person who is testing your urine specimen has and what your future will be like after he gives back the results.

Reading the poem brought back many memories of the six years I spent in the United State Marine Corps. I would like to share some of those memories with you in this paper.

I would like to start my trip down memory lane by breaking the poem up into sections, and telling you what they mean to me, and their connections with my time spent in the Marine Corps. The first three words of the poem, "In the clinic" (line 1), brought back many memories. Although most of our urine specimens—we called them "piss tests"—were taken in the squad bay, some of them were taken, or should I say given, in the clinic. The urine specimens that were taken in the clinic were done for different reasons than the ones taken in the squad bay. The difference between the tests taken in the clinic and in the squad bay were medical and drugs, respectively. The second part of the first sentence in the poem talks about the "last small chamber, a little closet / chastened with pearl, cool, white, and glistening (3–4). This is an eccentric way to describe the bathroom, or as we called it in the Marine Corps, "The Head." This is the place where we would "trickle our precious sum in a cup" (6). Trickling our precious sum: some people might consider urine a precious sum, but in the Marine Corps, we just called it piss. The next line of the poem says, "It's as simple as that" (7). I'm not quite sure what Kooser means by this. What is "simple"? Does he mean that the art of pissing into a cup is simple, or does he mean it in a general way? The reason why I ask this question of the poem is the fact that all our piss tests were not so simple. I can remember two stories about the piss test that made them certainly less than simple. I would like to share those two stories with you. Both stories involve Marines doing drugs just prior, say a few weeks, to the piss test.

The first story is quite neat. The Marine that did the drugs was in the "chamber," the head, with another Marine. He simply asked his friend if he would piss in his cup. Even though he knew it was wrong to ask his friend to do that, he did so anyway. His friend obliged without any questions. During his extended cup-filling, a staff sergeant walked in on the two Marines, and witnessed the violation. Needless to say, they both suffered the consequences of their actions.

The second story is a bit more eccentric and imaginative. The Marine in this story had everything planned out in his head. Due to the fact that he used drugs before the piss test, he needed help also. Instead of asking a friend to piss in his cup, he devised the ultimate plan. He simply filled a squeezable ketchup bottle with colored water and taped a long tube to his body. The ketchup bottle was held under his arm pit, and the tube went down the front of his body to the end of his "precious sum" shooter. Needless to say, the Marine was caught in this blatant act of defiance. From that moment on, the words "piss test" loomed like shreds of black clouds over every Marine's head.

After those two Marines were caught, the words "piss test" took on a whole new meaning, and as I stated before, it loomed over all Marines. This I feel is the best way to describe the new way of taking a piss test. Now a Staff NCO (non-commissioned officer) would look over your shoulder to make sure that your "precious sum" was indeed coming out of your penis and nowhere else. I don't know about you, but I do not like someone staring at my penis to make sure the urine is coming from it. Let's just say I have stage fright! The statement "stage fright" brings to my mind two stories about myself taking "piss tests."

The first one happened in my unit called BSSG–1 (Brigade Service Support Group–1). We had a mandatory "piss test" for the whole unit, and when it came time for me to fill the cup, I could not go. Staff Sergeant Smith was standing behind me telling me, "You have five minutes to fill the cup or I will help you." I said,

"What do you mean, help me?" He stated, "I will punch you in the bladder to make you piss." Seconds before the blow to my bladder, my "precious sum" began to "trickle" into the cup.

My second memory was a "piss test" at the air wing. When I was on station guard duty, upon entering "the head," we had to sign a roster, and we had to piss on the date of the roster. I don't know what was wrong, but I could not piss. I had to piss by 4 o'clock. The CO (commanding officer) told me they would sign a release to have a catheter stuck in me to make me piss. The story ended on a relieving note. I filled the cup at 3:58, and I do mean a relieving note.

I would like now to talk about the lines in the poem,

> But the heat
> of this gold your body's melted and poured out
> into a form begins to enthrall you,
> warming your hand with your flesh's fevers
> in a terrible way. (7–11)

As far as my own, or anyone else's, urine enthralling me is beyond my imagi- nation. The only way I think that your own urine could "enthrall" you is if you hold in your hand a cup of urine that was bound to get you in trouble.

On the lighter side of the whole subject, a funny thing comes to mind about the "piss test." I mean a few Marines liked to piss on the side of the bottle and hand it to the person in charge, waiting to collect your "precious sum." The Staff NCOIC (non-commissioned officer in charge) would always say the same thing: "Take this in the head and wipe it off." But no matter what his attitude towards the situation was, we always thought it was funny.

I would like to add one more story about a certain piss test I had in the Marine Corps, three months before my discharge. I had an accident. I don't think the acci- dent is important, but I was hit by a car while driving a motorcycle. I spent two weeks in the Tripler Army Medical Center, where I received many types of medica- tion. My last piss test came back positive for heroin, morphine, and cocaine. This was due to the drugs I was given in the hospital. I don't know if you know anything about the military, but paperwork moves very slowly. Needless to say, I was facing some serious trouble until the paperwork came from the hospital stating the medication I was given. The weight of the world was lifted off my back with the acquiring of this information. Except for this near close call, I am proud to say that I never had a urine specimen in my hand that was anything but pure.

I have shared with you many memories of six wonderful years spent protecting this great country, and if it wasn't for my accident, I would still be. I hope this paper is as enjoyable for you to read as it was for me to recall and write down.

As I hope you can see, the potential in Steve's first response statement for a deeper response and some self-conscious analysis went unrealized in this draft. While he did indicate some responses to certain parts of the text of "The Urine Specimen," for the most part he indulged in, as he put it, a "trip down memory lane" recounting some of his Marine Corps experiences. Although memories are an important part of any reader's ideology and so can be legitimately talked about in a self-conscious analysis, in this case they *took over* the paper, which had little to offer its reader in terms of analyzing Steve's interaction with the text.

Paragraph # 9 of this draft is particularly illustrative of Steve's tendency to get off the track. There, he said he would like to talk about certain lines in the poem, but after quoting them he just headed off into two more stories of his Marines days and never really talked about the lines after all.

Practice in Peer Review

As a final exercise in your study of writing about reading poems, pretend you are a peer reviewer of Steve's first draft. In the margins of the draft above or in your notebook, point out some specific places where Steve's free association goes astray from an analysis of his interaction with "The Urine Specimen." As if you were sitting down with him face to face, suggest some alternate moves he could make to get his writing back on track, some suggestions that would help him in revision. It may be too late now to actually help Steve get back on track with this paper, but your own writing efforts may profit from an effort to study where and how he went wrong and to put into your own words some active suggestions for recuperation. Doing this may help you and avoid the perils of free association in your own work.

POEMS FOR FURTHER READING

Maya Angelou   b. 1928

My Arkansas   1978

There is a deep brooding
in Arkansas.
Old crimes like moss pend
from poplar trees.
The sullen earth
is much too
red for comfort.

Sunrise seems to hesitate
and in that second
lose its
incandescent aim, and
dusk no more shadows
than the noon.
The past is brighter yet.

Old hates and
ante-bellum lace are rent
but not discarded.
Today is yet to come
in Arkansas.
It writhes. It writhes in awful
waves of brooding.

Margaret Atwood   b. 1939

you fit into me   1971

you fit into me
like a hook into an eye

a fish hook
an open eye

W. H. Auden   1907–1973

Musée des Beaux Arts   *1940*

About suffering they were never wrong,
The Old Masters: how well they understood
Its human position; how it takes place
While someone else is eating or opening a window or just walking dully along;
How, when the aged are reverently, passionately waiting   5
For the miraculous birth, there always must be
Children who did not specially want it to happen, skating
On a pond at the edge of the wood:
They never forgot
That even the dreadful martyrdom must run its course   10
Anyhow in a corner, some untidy spot
Where the dogs go on with their doggy life and the torturer's horse
Scratches its innocent behind on a tree.

In Brueghel's *Icarus*, for instance: how everything turns away
Quite leisurely from the disaster; the ploughman may   15
Have heard the splash, the forsaken cry,
But for him it was not an important failure; the sun shone
As it had to on the white legs disappearing into the green
Water; and the expensive delicate ship that must have seen
Something amazing, a boy falling out of the sky,   20
Had somewhere to get to and sailed calmly on.

The Unknown Citizen   *1940*

(To JS/07/M/378
This Marble Monument
Is Erected by the State)

He was found by the Bureau of Statistics to be
One against whom there was no official complaint,
And all the reports of his conduct agree
That in the modern sense of an old-fashioned word, he was a saint,
For in everything he did he served the Greater Community.   5
Except for the War till the day he retired
He worked in a factory and never got fired,
But satisfied his employers, Fudge Motors Inc.
Yet he wasn't a scab° or odd in his views,   strikebreaker
For his Union reports that he paid his dues,   10
(Our report on his Union shows it was sound)
And our Social Psychology workers found
That he was popular with his mates° and liked a drink.   his friends
The Press are convinced that he bought a paper every day
And that his reactions to advertisements were normal in every way.   15
Policies taken out in his name prove that he was fully insured,

And his Health-card shows he was once in a hospital but left it cured.
Both Producers Research and High-Grade Living declare
He was fully sensible to the advantages of the Installment Plan
And had everything necessary to the Modern Man,   20
A phonograph, a radio, a car and a frigidaire.
Our researchers into Public Opinion are content
That he held the proper opinions for the time of year;
When there was peace, he was for peace; when there was war he went.
He was married and added five children to the population,   25
Which our Eugenist° says was the right number for a parent of his generation,   population
And our teachers report that he never interfered with their education.   planner
Was he free? Was he happy? The question is absurd:
Had anything been wrong, we should certainly have heard.

Jimmy Santiago Baca   b. 1952

Ancestor   *1979*

It was a time when they were afraid of him.
My father, a bare man, a gypsy, a horse
with broken knees no one would shoot.
Then again, he was like the orange tree,
and young women plucked from him sweet fruit.   5
To meet him, you must be in the right place,
even his sons and daughter, we wondered
where was papa now and what was he doing.
He held the mystique of travelers
that pass your backyard and disappear into the trees.   10
Then, when you follow, you find nothing,
not a stir, not a twig displaced from its bough.
And then he would appear one night.
Half covered in shadows and half in light,
his voice quiet, absorbing our unspoken thoughts.   15
When his hands lay on the table at breakfast,
they were hands that had not fixed our crumbling home,
hands that had not taken us into them
and the fingers did not gently rub along our lips.
They were hands of a gypsy that filled our home   20
with love and safety, for a moment;
with all the shambles of boards and empty stomachs,
they filled us because of the love in them.
Beyond the ordinary love, beyond the coordinated life,
beyond the sponging of broken hearts,
came the untimely word, the fallen smile, the quiet tear,   25
that made us grow up quick and romantic.
Papa gave us something: when we paused from work,
my sister fourteen years old working the cotton fields,
my brother and I running like deer,
we would pause, because we had a papa no one could catch,   30

who spoke when he spoke and bragged and drank,
he bragged about us: he did not say we were smart,
nor did he say we were strong and were going to be rich someday.
He said we were good. He held us up to the world for it to see,   35
three children that were good, who understood love in a quiet way,
who owned nothing but calloused hands and true freedom,
and that is how he made us: he offered us to the wind,
to the mountains, to the skies of autumn and spring.
He said, "Here are my children! Care for them!"   40
And he left again, going somewhere like a child
with a warrior's heart, nothing could stop him.
My grandmother would look at him for a long time,
and then she would say nothing.
She chose to remain silent, praying each night,   45
guiding down like a root in the heart of earth,
clutching sunlight and rains to her ancient breast.

And I am the blossom of many nights.
A threefold blossom: my sister is as she is,
my brother is as he is, and I am as I am.   50
Through sacred ceremony of living, daily living,
arose three distinct hopes, three loves,
out of the long felt nights and days of yesterday.

T. M. Baker   b. 1946

Turtle Considers Plato   *1988*

Barrelling down the
Bertha Parker Bypass
In my orange '76
Silverado pickup truck
Tuned, of course,   5
To the local AM
Band belting out
Songs of sorrow
Beer and betrayal—
I hear Dolly   10
Sweetly singing
That love is like a butterfly
And that
A many colored coat
Sewn with love   15
Will keep you warm—
Heart, soul, body, and brains—
In a culture that
Like Plato
Hates tits   20
And cannot, by God,
Live without them.
Ain't it the truth!

Amiri Baraka   b. 1934

An Agony. As now.   *1964*

I am inside someone
who hates me. I look
out from his eyes. Smell
what fouled tunes come in
to his breath. Love his   5
wretched women.

Slits in the metal, for sun. Where
my eyes sit turning, at the cool air
the glance of light, or hard flesh
rubbed against me, a woman, a man,   10
without shadow, or voice, or meaning.

This is the enclosure (flesh,
where innocence is a weapon. An
abstraction. Touch. (Not mine.
Or yours, if you are the soul I had   15
and abandoned when I was blind and had
my enemies carry me as a dead man
(if he is beautiful, or pitied.

It can be pain. (As now, as all his
flesh hurts me.) It can be that. Or   20
pain. As when she ran from me into
that forest.

             Or pain, the mind
silver spiraled whirled against the
sun, higher than even old men thought
God would be. Or pain. And the other. The   25
yes. (Inside his books, his fingers. They
are withered yellow flowers and were never
beautiful.) The yes. You will, lost soul, say
"beauty." Beauty, practiced, as the tree. The
slow river. A white sun in its wet sentences.   30

Or, the cold men in their gale. Ecstasy. Flesh
or souls. The yes. (Their robes blown. Their bowls
empty. They chant at my heels, not at yours.) Flesh
or soul, as corrupt. Where the answer moves too quickly.
Where the God is a self, after all.)   35

Cold air blown through narrow blind eyes. Flesh,
white hot metal. Glows as the day with its sun.
It is a human love, I live inside. A bony skeleton
you recognize as words or simple feeling.

But it has no feeling. As the metal, is hot, it is not,   40
given to love.

It burns the thing
inside it. And that thing
screams.

Black People: This Is Our Destiny   1969

The road runs straight with no turning, the circle
runs complete as it is in the storm of peace, the all
embraced embracing in the circle complete turning road
straight like a burning straight with the circle complete
as in a peaceful storm, the elements, the niggers' voices   5
harmonized with creation on a peak in the holy black man's
eyes that we rise, whose race is only direction up, where
we go to meet the realization of makers knowing who we are
and the war in our hearts but the purity of the holy world
that we long for, knowing how to live, and what life is, and   10
who God is, and the many revolutions we must spin through in our
seven adventures in the endlessness of all existing feeling, all
existing forms of life, the gases, the plants, the ghost minerals
the spirits the souls the light in the stillness where the storm
the glow the nothing in God is complete except there is nothing   15
to be incomplete the pulse and change of rhythm, blown flight
to be anything at all ... vibration holy nuance beating against
itself, a rhythm a playing re-understood now by one of the 1st race
the primitives the first men who evolve again to civilize the
world.   20

Elizabeth Bishop   1911–1979

The Fish   1946

I caught a tremendous fish
and held him beside the boat
half out of water, with my hook
fast in a corner of his mouth.
He didn't fight.   5
He hadn't fought at all.
He hung a grunting weight,
battered and venerable
and homely. Here and there
his brown skin hung in strips   10
like ancient wallpaper,
and its pattern of darker brown
was like wallpaper:
shapes like full-blown roses
stained and lost through age.   15
He was speckled with barnacles,
fine rosettes of lime,
and infested

with tiny white sea-lice,
and underneath two or three
rags of green weed hung down.
While his gills were breathing in
the terrible oxygen
—the frightening gills,
fresh and crisp with blood,
that can cut so badly—
I thought of the coarse white flesh
packed in like feathers,
the big bones and the little bones,
the dramatic reds and blacks
of his shiny entrails,
and the pink swim-bladder
like a big peony.
I looked into his eyes
which were far larger than mine
but shallower, and yellowed,
the irises backed and packed
with tarnished tinfoil
seen through the lenses
of old scratched isinglass.
They shifted a little, but not
to return my stare.
—It was more like a tipping
of an object toward the light.
I admired his sullen face,
the mechanism of his jaw,
and then I saw
that from his lower lip
—if you could call it a lip—
grim, wet, and weaponlike,
hung five old pieces of fish-line,
or four and a wire leader
with the swivel still attached,
with all their five big hooks
grown firmly in his mouth.
A green line, frayed at the end
where he broke it, two heavier lines,
and a fine black thread
still crimped from the strain and snap
when it broke and he got away.
Like medals with their ribbons
frayed and wavering,
a five-haired beard of wisdom
trailing from his aching jaw.
I stared and stared
and victory filled up
the little rented boat,
from the pool of bilge
where oil had spread a rainbow
around the rusted engine

to the bailer rusted orange,
the sun-cracked thwarts,
the oarlocks on their strings,
the gunnels—until everything
was rainbow, rainbow, rainbow!   75
And I let the fish go.

William Blake   1757–1827

The Chimney Sweeper   *1789*

When my mother died I was very young,
And my father sold me while yet my tongue
Could scarcely cry weep weep weep weep.
So your chimneys I sweep & in soot I sleep.

Theres little Tom Dacre, who cried when his head   5
That curl'd like a lambs back, was shav'd, so I said
Hush Tom never mind it, for when your head's bare,
You know that the soot cannot spoil your white hair.

And so he was quiet, & that very night,
As Tom was a sleeping he had such a sight,   10
That thousands of sweepers Dick, Joe Ned & Jack
Were all of them lock'd up in coffins of black.

And by came an Angel who had a bright key,
And he open'd the coffins & set them all free.
Then down a green plain leaping laughing they run   15
And wash in a river and shine in the Sun.

Then naked & white, all their bags left behind,
They rise upon clouds, and sport in the wind.
And the Angel told Tom if he'd be a good boy,
He'd have God for his father & never want joy.   20

And so Tom awoke and we rose in the dark
And got with our bags & our brushes to work.
Tho' the morning was cold, Tom was happy & warm,
So if all do their duty, they need not fear harm.

The Garden of Love   *1794*

I went to the Garden of Love,
And saw what I never had seen:
A Chapel was built in the midst,
Where I used to play on the green.

And the gates of this Chapel were shut,   5
And "Thou shalt not" writ over the door;
So I turned to the Garden of Love
That so many sweet flowers bore;

And I saw it was filled with graves,
And tomb-stones where flowers should be;   10
And Priests in black gowns were walking their rounds,
And binding with briars my joys and desires.

The Lamb   *1789*

    Little Lamb, who made thee?
    Dost thou know who made thee?
Gave thee life & bid thee feed,
By the stream & o'er the mead;
Gave the clothing of delight,   5
Softest clothing wooly bright;
Gave thee such a tender voice,
Making all the vales rejoice!
    Little Lamb who made thee?
    Dost thou know who made thee?   10

    Little Lamb I'll tell thee,
    Little Lamb I'll tell thee!
He is calléd by thy name,
For he calls himself a Lamb:
He is meek & he is mild: 15
He became a little child:
I a child & thou a lamb,
We are calléd by his name.
    Little Lamb God bless thee.
    Little Lamb God bless thee.   20

The Sick Rose   *1794*

O rose, thou art sick!
The invisible worm
That flies in the night
In the howling storm

Has found out thy bed
Of crimson joy,
And his dark secret love
Does thy life destroy.

Louise Bogan   1897–1970

Women   *1923*

Women have no wilderness in them,
They are provident instead,
Content in the tight hot cell of their hearts
To eat dusty bread.

They do not see cattle cropping red winter grass,
They do not hear
Snow water going down under culverts
Shallow and clear.

They wait, when they should turn to journeys,
They stiffen, when they should bend.
They use against themselves that benevolence
To which no man is friend.

They cannot think of so many crops to a field
Or of clean wood cleft by an axe.
Their love is an eager meaninglessness
Too tense, or too lax.

They hear in every whisper that speaks to them
A shout and a cry.
As like as not, when they take life over their door-sills
They should let it go by.

Anne Bradstreet   1612–1672

Before the Birth of One of Her Children   *1678*

All things within this fading world hath end,
Adversity doth still our joys attend;
No ties so strong, no friends so dear and sweet,
But with death's parting blow is sure to meet.
The sentence past is most irrevocable,
A common thing, yet oh, inevitable.
How soon, my Dear, death may my steps attend,
How soon't may be thy lot to lose thy friend,
We both are ignorant, yet love bids me
These farewell lines to recommend to thee,
That when that knot's untied that made us one,
I may seem thine, who in effect am none.
And if I see not half my days that's due,
What nature would, God grant to yours and you;
The many faults that well you know I have
Let be interred in my oblivious grave;
If any worth or virtue were in me,
Let that live freshly in thy memory
And when thou feel'st no grief, as I no harms,
Yet love thy dead, who long lay in thine arms.
And when thy loss shall be repaid with gains
Look to my little babes, my dear remains.
And if chance to thine eyes shall bring this verse,
With some sad sighs honor my absent hearse;
And kiss this paper for thy love's dear sake,
Who with salt tears this last farewell did take.

A Letter to Her Husband, Absent upon Public Employment

1678

My head, my heart, mine eyes, my life, nay, more,
My joy, my magazine of earthly store,
If two be one, as surely thou and I,
How stayest thou there, whilst I at Ipswich lie?
So many steps, head from the heart to sever,   5
If but a neck, soon should we be together.
I, like the Earth this season, mourn in black,
My Sun is gone so far in's zodiac,
Whom whilst I 'joyed, nor storms, nor frost I felt,
His warmth such frigid colds did cause to melt,   10
My chilled limbs now numbed lie forlorn;
Return, return, sweet Sol,° from Capricorn;°   *sun/winter*
In this dead time, alas, what can I more
Than view those fruits which through thy heat I bore?
Which sweet contentment yield me for a space,   15
True living pictures of their father's face.
O strange effect! now thou art southward gone,
I weary grow the tedious day so long;
But when thou northward to me shalt return,
I wish my Sun may never set, but burn   20
Within the Cancer° of my glowing breast,   *summer*
The welcome house of him my dearest guest.
Where ever, ever stay, and go not thence,
Till nature's sad decree shall call thee hence;
Flesh of thy flesh, bone of thy bone,   25
I here, thou there, yet both but one.

Gwendolyn Brooks   b. 1917

The Boy Died in My Alley

1975

Without my having known.
Policeman said, next morning,
"Apparently died Alone."
"You heard a shot?" Policeman said.
Shots I hear and Shots I hear.   5
I never see the dead.

The Shot that killed him yes I heard
as I heard the Thousand shots before;
careening tinnily down the nights
across my years and arteries.   10

Policeman pounded on my door.
"Who is it?" "POLICE!" Policeman yelled.
"A boy was dying in your alley.

A boy is dead, and in your alley.
And have you known this Boy before?"   15

I have known this Boy before.
I have known this Boy before, who

ornaments my alley.
I never saw his face at all.
I never saw his futurefall.   20
But I have known this Boy.

I have always heard him deal with death.
I have always heard the shout, the volley.
I have closed my heart-ears late and early.
And I have killed him ever.   25
I joined the Wild and killed him
with knowledgeable unknowing.
I saw where he was going.
I saw him Crossed. And seeing,
I did not take him down.   30

He cried not only "Father!"
but "Mother!"
Sister!
Brother!"
The cry climbed up the alley.   35
It went up to the wind.
It hung upon the heaven
for a long
stretch-strain of Moment.

The red floor of my alley   40
is a special speech to me.

We Real Cool   *1960*

The Pool Players.
Seven at the Golden Shovel.

We real cool. We
Left school. We

Lurk late. We
Strike straight. We

Sing sin. We
Thin gin. We   5

Jazz June. We
Die soon.

Elizabeth Barrett Browning   1806–1861

How do I love thee? Let me count the ways   *1845*

How do I love thee? Let me count the ways.
I love thee to the depth and breadth and height
My soul can reach, when feeling out of sight
For the ends of Being and ideal Grace.
I love thee to the level of every day's   5
Most quiet need, by sun and candle-light.
I love thee freely, as men strive for right;
I love thee purely, as they turn from Praise.
I love thee with the passion put to use
In my old griefs, and with my childhood's faith.   10
I love thee with a love I seemed to lose
With my lost saints—I love thee with the breath,
Smiles, tears, of all my life!—and, if God choose,
I shall but love thee better after death.

Robert Burns   1759–1796

A Red, Red Rose   *1796*

O my Luve's like a red, red rose,
    That's newly sprung in June:
O my Luve's like the melodie
    That's sweetly play'd in tune.

As fair art thou, my bonnie lass,   5
    So deep in luve am I;
And I will luve thee still, my Dear,
    Till a'° the seas gang° dry.   all; go

Till a' the seas gang dry, my Dear,
    And the rocks melt wi'° the sun: with   10
And I will luve thee still, my Dear,
    While the sands o' life shall run.

And fare thee weel, my only Luve!
    And fare thee weel, awhile!
And I will come again, my Luve,   15
    Tho' it were ten thousand mile!

Lorna Dee Cervantes   b. 1954

Refugee Ship   *1981*

Like wet cornstarch, I slide
past my grandmother's eyes. Bible
at her side, she removes her glasses.

The pudding thickens.
Mama raised me without language,   5

I'm orphaned from my Spanish name.
The words are foreign, stumbling
on my tongue. I see in the mirror
My reflection: bronzed skin, black hair.

I feel I am a captive   10
aboard the refugee ship.
The ship that will never dock.
El barco que nunca atraca.

Samuel Taylor Coleridge   1772–1834

Kubla Khan   *1816*

In Xanadu did Kubla Khan
A stately pleasure dome decree:
Where Alph, the sacred river, ran
Through caverns measureless to man
    Down to a sunless sea.
So twice five miles of fertile ground   5
With walls and towers were girdled round:
And there were gardens bright with sinuous rills,
Where blossomed many an incense-bearing tree;
And here were forest ancient as the hills,
Enfolding sunny spots of greenery.   10

But oh! that deep romantic chasm which slanted
Down the green hill athwart a cedarn cover!
A savage place! as holy and enchanted
As e'er beneath a waning moon was haunted
By woman wailing for her demon lover!   15
And from this chasm, with ceaseless turmoil seething,
As if this earth in fast thick pants were breathing,
A mighty fountain momently was forced:
Amid whose swift half-intermitted burst
Huge fragments vaulted like rebounding hail,   20
Or chaffy grain beneath the thresher's flail:
And 'mid these dancing rocks at once and ever
It flung up momently the sacred river.
Five miles meandering with a mazy motion
Through wood and dale the sacred river ran,   25
Then reached the caverns measureless to man,
And sank in tumult to a lifeless ocean:
And 'mid this tumult Kubla heard from far
Ancestral voices prophesying war!
    The shadow of the dome of pleasure   30
    Floated midway on the waves;
    Where was heard the mingled measure

From the fountain and the caves.
It was a miracle of rare device,
A sunny pleasure dome with caves of ice!   35

        A damsel with a dulcimer
        In a vision once I saw:
        It was an Abyssinian maid,
        And on her dulcimer she played
        Singing of Mount Abora.   40
Could I revive within me
Her symphony and song,
To such a deep delight 'twould win me,
That with music loud and long,
I would build that dome in air,   45
That sunny dome! those caves of ice!
And all who heard should see them there,
And all should cry, Beware! Beware!
His flashing eyes, his floating hair!
Weave a circle round him thrice,   50
And close your eyes with holy dread,
For he on honeydew hath fed,
And drunk the milk of Paradise.

Steve Crow   b. 1949

Louisiana

1975

I can't say our garden is a delight
because the patch in our backyard
is the shape of Louisiana by accident.
Weeds the shape of brown pelicans
by reincarnation, and a small swamp,
unsafe to be around after dark.   5

Each time I drain the garden
a swamp water bubbles to the surface
with gar minnows and water moccasins
the size of earthworms. When I set
the weeds afire they begin mouthing   10
the air, wingless, pulling at their
roots to take seed elsewhere.

And tonight, magic in the wind,
rain the color of ashes.
I expect Lafitte° to come poling   15
his pirogue across the yard,
whistling for his pirates   Jean LaFitte—a French pirate
to follow him out of the cypress
with my head on a flambeau.
I never trusted Louisiana.   20
I should have stayed there.

Countee Cullen   1903–1946

Yet Do I Marvel   1925

I doubt not God is good, well-meaning, kind,
And did He stoop to quibble could tell why
The little buried mole continues blind,
Why flesh that mirrors Him must some day die,
Make plain the reason tortured Tantalus   5
Is baited by the fickle fruit, declare
If merely brute caprice dooms Sisyphus
To struggle up a never-ending stair.
Inscrutable His ways are, and immune
To catechism by a mind too strewn   10
With petty cares to slightly understand
What awful brain compels His awful hand.
Yet do I marvel at this curious thing:
To make a poet black, and bid him sing!

e. e. cummings   1894–1962

anyone lived in a pretty how town   1940

anyone lived in a pretty how town
(with up so floating many bells down)
spring summer autumn winter
he sang his didn't he danced his did.

Women and men (both little and small)   5
cared for anyone not at all
they sowed their isn't they reaped their same
sun moon stars rain

children guessed (but only a few
and down they forget as up they grew   10
autumn winter spring summer)
that noone loved him more by more

when by now and tree by leaf
she laughed his joy she cried his grief
bird by snow and stir by still   15
anyone's any was all to her

someones married their everyones
laughed their cryings and did their dance
(sleep wake hope and then) they
said their nevers they slept their dream   20

stars rain sun moon
(and only the snow can begin to explain
how children are apt to forget to remember
with up so floating many bells down)

one day anyone died i guess
(and noone stooped to kiss his face)
busy folk buried them side by side
little by little and was by was

all by all and deep by deep
and more by more they dream their sleep
noone and anyone earth by april
wish by spirit and if by yes.

Women and men (both dong and ding)
summer autumn winter spring
reaped their sowing and went their came
sun moon stars rain

25

30

35

Buffalo Bill's

1923

Buffalo Bill's
defunct
            who used to
            ride a watersmooth-silver
                        stallion
and break onetwothreefourfive pigeonsjustlikethat
                                    Jesus
he was a handsome man
                    and what i want to know is
how do you like your blueeyed boy
Mister Death

5

10

r-p-o-p-h-e-s-s-a-g-r

1935

                        r-p-o-p-h-e-s-s-a-g-r
                who
a)s w(e loo)k
upnowgath

                            PPEGORHRASS
                                eringint(o-
aThe):l
        eA
            p:
S
                        (r   a
rIvInG
                                    .gRrEaPsPhOs)
                                        to
rea(be)rran(com)gi(e)ngly
,grasshopper;

somewhere i have never travelled   *1959*

somewhere i have never travelled,gladly beyond
any experience your eyes have their silence:
in your most frail gesture are things which enclose me,
or which i cannot touch because they are too near

your slightest look easily will unclose me
though i have closed myself as fingers,
you open always petal by petal myself as Spring opens
(touching skilfully,mysteriously)her first rose

or if your wish be to close me,i and
my life will shut very beautifully,suddenly,   10
as when the heart of this flower imagines
the snow carefully everywhere descending;

nothing which we are to perceive in this world equals
the power of your intense fragility:whose texture
compels me with the colour of its countries,   15
rendering death and forever with each breathing

(i do not know what it is about you that closes
and opens; only something in me understands
the voice of your eyes is deeper than all roses)
nobody,not even the rain,has such small hands   20

Emily Dickinson   1830–1886

After great pain, a formal feeling comes—   *c. 1862*

After great pain, a formal feeling comes—
The Nerves sit ceremonious, like Tombs—
The still Heart questions was it He, that bore,
And Yesterday, or Centuries before?

The Feet, mechanical, go round—   5
Of Ground, or Air, or Ought—
A Wooden way
Regardless grown,
A Quartz contentment, like a stone—

This is the Hour of Lead—   10
Remembered, if outlived,
As Freezing persons, recollect the Snow—
First—Chill—then Stupor—then the letting go—

A narrow Fellow in the Grass   *c. 1865*

A narrow Fellow in the Grass
Occasionally rides—
You may have met Him—did you not
His notice sudden is—

The Grass divides as with a Comb—
A spotted shaft is seen—
And then it closes at your feet
And opens further on—

He likes a Boggy Acre
A Floor too cool for Corn—
Yet when a Boy, and Barefoot—
I more than once at Noon
Have passed, I thought, a Whip lash
Unbraiding in the Sun
When stopping to secure it
It wrinkled, and was gone—

Several of Nature's People
I know, and they know me—
I feel for them a transport
Of cordiality—

But never met this Fellow
Attended, or alone
Without a tighter breathing
And Zero at the Bone—

Because I could not stop for Death   *c. 1863*

Because I could not stop for Death—
He kindly stopped for me—
The Carriage held but just Ourselves—
and Immortality.

We slowly drove—He knew no haste
And I had put away
My labor and my leisure too,
For His Civility—

We passed the School, where Children strove
At Recess—in the Ring—
We passed the Fields of Gazing Grain—
We passed the Setting Sun—

Or rather—He passed Us—
The Dews drew quivering and chill—
For only Gossamer, my Gown—
My Tippet°—only Tulle—   scarf

We paused before a House that seemed
A Swelling of the Ground—
The Roof was scarely visible—
The Cornice—in the Ground—

Since then—'tis Centuries—and yet
Feels shorter than the Day
I first surmised the Horses' Heads
Were toward Eternity—

I heard a Fly buzz—when I died

c. 1862

I heard a Fly buzz—when I died—
The Stillness in the Room
Was like the Stillness in the Air—
Between the Heaves of Storm—

The Eyes around—had wrung them dry—   5
And Breaths were gathering firm
For that last Onset—when the King
Be witnessed—in the Room—

I willed my Keepsakes—Signed away
What portion of me be   10
Assignable—and then it was
There interposed a Fly—

With Blue—uncertain stumbling Buzz—
Between the light—and me—
And then the Windows failed—and then   15
I could not see to see—

I taste a liquor never brewed—

c. 1860

I taste a liquor never brewed—
From Tankards scooped in Pearl—
Not all the Vats upon the Rhine
Yield such an Alcohol!

Inebriate of Air—am I—   5
And Debauchee of Dew—
Reeling—thro endless summer days—
From inns of Molten Blue—

When "Landlords" turn the drunken Bee
Out of the Foxglove's door—   10
When Butterflies—renounce their "drams"—
I shall but drink the more!

Till Seraphs swing their snowy Hats—
And Saints—to windows run—
To see the little Tippler   15
Leaning against the—Sun—

Some keep the Sabbath going to Church

c. 1860

Some keep the Sabbath going to Church—
I keep it, staying at Home—
With a Bobolink for a Chorister—
And an Orchard, for a Dome—

Some keep the Sabbath in Surplice—   5
I just wear my Wings—

And instead of tolling the Bell, for Church,
Our little Sexton—sings.

God preaches, a noted Clergyman—
And the sermon is never long,
So instead of getting to Heaven, at last—
I'm going, all along.

10

Success is counted sweetest

c. 1859

Success is counted sweetest
By those who ne'er succeed
To comprehend a nectar
Requires sorest need.

Not one of all the purple Host
Who took the Flag today
Can tell the definition
So clear of Victory

5

As he defeated—dying—
One whose forbidden ear
The distant strains of triumph
Burst agonized and clear!

10

John Donne   1572–1631

The Apparition

1633

When by thy scorn, O murderess, I am dead,
        And that thou thinkst thee free
From all solicitatïon from me,
Then shall my ghost come to thy bed,
And thee, feigned vestal, in worse arms shall see;   5
Then thy sick taper° will begin to wink,   candle
And he, whose thou art then, being tired before,
Will, if thou stir, or pinch to wake him, think
        Thou call'st for more,
And in false sleep will from thee shrink.
And then, poor aspen wretch, neglected, thou,   10
Bathed in a cold quicksilver sweat, wilt lie
        A verier° ghost than I.   truer
What I will say, I will not tell thee now,
Lest that preserve thee; and since my love is spent,
I had rather thou shouldst painfully repent,   15
Than by my threatenings rest still innocent.

Holy Sonnet 10   c. 1609

Death, be not proud, though some have callèd thee
Mighty and dreadful, for thou are not so;
For those whom thou thinkst thou dost overthrow
Die not, poor Death, nor yet canst thou kill me.
From rest and sleep, which but thy pictures be,   5
Much pleasure—then from thee much more must flow,
And soonest our best men with thee do go,
Rest of their bones, and soul's delivery.
Thou art slave to fate, chance, kings, and desperate men,
And dost with poison, war, and sickness dwell,   10
And poppy or charm can make us sleep as well
And better than thy stroke; why swellst thou then?
One short sleep past, we wake eternally
And death shall be no more; Death, thou shalt die.

A Valediction: Forbidding Mourning   1611

As virtuous men pass mildly away,
And whisper to their souls to go,
Whilst some of their sad friends do say
The breath goes now, and some say no:

So let us melt, and make no noise,   5
No tear floods, nor sigh-tempests move;
'Twere profanation° of our joys   it would make profane
To tell the laity° our love.   common people

Moving of the earth brings harms and fears;
Men reckon what it did and meant;   10
But trepidation of the spheres,
Though greater far, is innocent.

Dull sublunary lovers' love
(Whose soul is sense) cannot admit
Absence, because it doth remove   15
Those things which elemented it.

But we, by a love so much refined
That ourselves know not what it is,
Inter-assurèd of the mind,
Care less eyes, lips, and hands to miss.   20

Our two souls, therefore, which are one,
Though I must go, endure not yet
A breach, but an expansion,
Like gold to airy thinness beat.

If they be two, they are two so   25
As stiff twin compasses are two:
Thy soul, the fixed foot, makes no show
To move, but doth if the other do.

And though it in the center sit,
Yet when the other far doth roam,
It leans and harkens after it,   30
And grows erect as that comes home.

Such wilt thou be to me, who must,
Like the other foot, obliquely run;
Thy firmness makes my circle just,
And makes me end where I begun.   35

H. D. (Hilda Doolittle)   1886–1961

Helen   *1924*

All Greece hates
the still eyes in the white face,
the luster as of olives
where she stands,
And the white hands.

All Greece reviles   5
the wan face when she smiles,
hating it deeper still
when it grows wan and white,
remembering past enchantments
And past ills.   10

Greece sees unmoved,
God's daughter, born of love,
the beauty of cool feet
and slenderest knees,
could love indeed the maid,   15
only if she were laid,
white ash amid funereal cypresses.

Sea Rose   *1916*

Rose, harsh rose,
marred and with stint of petals,
meagre flower, thin,
sparse of leaf,

more precious   5
than a wet rose
single on a stem—
you are caught in the drift.

Stunted, with small leaf,
you are flung on the sand,
you are lifted   10
in the crisp sand
that drives in the wind.

Can the spice-rose
drip such acrid fragrance   15
hardened in a leaf?

Rita Dove   b. 1952

Daystar   *1986*

She wanted a little room for thinking:
but she saw diapers steaming on the line,
a doll slumped behind the door.
So she lugged a chair behind the garage
to sit out the children's naps.   5

Sometimes there were things to watch—
the pinched armor of a vanished cricket,
a floating maple leaf. Other days
she stared until she was assured
when she closed her eyes   10
she'd see only her own vivid blood.

She had an hour, at best, before Liza appeared
pouting from the top of the stairs.
And just *what* was mother doing
out back with the field mice? Why,   15

building a palace. Later
that night when Thomas rolled over and
lurched into her, she would open her eyes
and think of the place that was hers
for an hour—where   20
she was nothing,
pure nothing, in the middle of the day.

Ö*   *1980*

Shape the lips to an *o*, say *a*.
That's *island*.

One word of Swedish has changed the whole neighborhood.
When I look up, the yellow house on the corner
is a galleon stranded in flowers. Around it   5
the wind. Even the high roar of a leaf-mulcher
could be the horn-blast from a ship
as it skirts the misted shoals.

We don't need much more to keep things going.
Families complete themselves   10
and refuse to budge from the present,

————
*Ö: the Swedish word for "island."

the present extends its glass forehead to sea
(backyard breezes, scattered cardinals

and if, one evening, the house on the corner
took off over the marshland,   15
neither I nor my neighbor
would be amazed. Sometimes

a word is found so right it trembles
at the slightest explanation.
You start out with one thing, end   20
up with another, and nothing's
like it used to be, not even the future.

Richard Eberhart   b. 1904

The Groundhog   1936

In June, amid the golden fields,
I saw a groundhog lying dead.
Dead lay he; my senses shook,
And mind outshot our naked frailty.
There lowly in the vigorous summer   5
His form began its senseless change,
And made my senses waver dim
Seeing nature ferocious in him.
Inspecting close his maggots' might
And seething cauldron of his being,   10
Half with loathing, half with a strange love,
I poked him with an angry stick.
The fever arose, became a flame
And Vigour circumscribed the skies,
Immense energy in the sun,   15
And through my frame a sunless trembling.
My stick had done nor good nor harm.
Then stood I silent in the day
Watching the object, as before;
And kept my reverence for knowledge   20
Trying for control, to be still,
To quell the passion of the blood;
Until I had bent down on my knees
Praying for joy in the sight of decay.
And so I left; and I returned   25
In Autumn strict of eye, to see
The sap gone out of the groundhog,
But the bony sodden hulk remained.
But the year had lost its meaning,
And in intellectual chains   30
I lost both love and loathing,
Mured up in the wall of wisdom.
Another summer took the fields again

Massive and burning, full of life,
But when I chanced upon the spot
There was only a little hair left,
And bones bleaching in the sunlight
Beautiful as architecture;
I watched them like a geometer,
And cut a walking stick from a birch.
It has been three years, now.
There is no sign of the groundhog.
I stood there in the whirling summer,
My hand capped a withered heart,
And thought of China and of Greece,
Of Alexander in his tent;
Of Montaigne in his tower,
Of Saint Theresa in her wild lament.

35

40

45

T. S. Eliot   1888–1965

The Love Song of J. Alfred Prufrock   1917

> *S'io credesse che mia risposta fosse*
> *A persona che mai tornasse al mondo,*
> *Questa fiamma staria senza piu scosse.*
> *Ma perciocche giammai di questo fondo*
> *Non torno vivo alcun, s'i'odo il vero,*
> *Senza tema d'infamia ti rispondo.*

[From Dante's *Inferno:* "If I thought my answer were given / to anyone who would ever return to the world, / this flame would stand still without moving any further. / But since never from this abyss has anyone ever returned alive, if what I hear is true, / without fear of infamy I answer thee."]

Let us go then, you and I,
When the evening is spread out against the sky
Like a patient etherized upon a table;
Let us go, through certain half-deserted streets,
The muttering retreats
Of restless nights in one-night cheap hotels
And sawdust restaurants with oyster-shells:
Streets that follow like a tedious argument
Of insidious intent
To lead you to an overwhelming question . . .
Oh, do not ask, "What is it?"
Let us go and make our visit.

In the room the women come and go
Talking of Michelangelo.

The yellow fog that rubs its back upon the window-panes
The yellow smoke that rubs its muzzle on the window-panes
Licked its tongue into the corners of the evening,

5

10

15

Lingered upon the pools that stand in drains,
Let fall upon its back the soot that falls from chimneys,
Slipped by the terrace, made a sudden leap,   20
And seeing that it was a soft October night,
Curled once about the house, and fell asleep.

And indeed there will be time
For the yellow smoke that slides along the street,
Rubbing its back upon the window-panes;   25
There will be time, there will be time
To prepare a face to meet the faces that you meet;
There will be time to murder and create,
And time for all the works and days of hands
That lift and drop a question on your plate;   30
Time for you and time for me,
And time yet for a hundred indecisions,
And for a hundred visions and revisions,
Before the taking of a toast and tea.

In the room the women come and go   35
Talking of Michelangelo.

And indeed there will be time
To wonder, "Do I dare?" and, "Do I dare?"
Time to turn back and descend the stair,
With a bald spot in the middle of my hair—   40
[They will say: "How his hair is growing thin!"]
My morning coat, my collar mounting firmly to the chin,
My necktie rich and modest, but asserted by a simple pin—
[They will say: "But how his arms and legs are thin!"]
Do I dare   45
Disturb the universe?
In a minute there is time
For decisions and revisions which a minute will reverse.

For I have known them all already, known them all:
Have known the evenings, mornings, afternoons,   50
I have measured out my life with coffee spoons;
I know the voices dying with a dying fall
Beneath the music from a farther room.
        So how should I presume?

And I have known the eyes already, known them all—   55
The eyes that fix you in a formulated phrase,
And when I am formulated, sprawling on a pin,
When I am pinned and wriggling on the wall,
Then how should I begin
To spit out all the butt-ends of my days and ways?   60
        And how should I presume?

And I have known the arms already, known them all—
Arms that are braceleted and white and bare
[But in the lamplight, downed with light brown hair!]
Is it perfume from a dress   65

That makes me so digress?
Arms that lie along a table, or wrap about a shawl.
    And should I then presume?
    And how should I begin?
        . . . .

Shall I say, I have gone at dusk through narrow streets   70
And watched the smoke that rises from the pipes
Of lonely men in shirt-sleeves, leaning out of windows? . . .

I should have been a pair of ragged claws
Scuttling across the floors of silent seas.
        . . . .

And the afternoon, the evening, sleeps so peacefully!   75
Smoothed by long fingers,
Asleep . . . tired . . . or it malingers,
Stretched on the floor, here beside you and me.
Should I, after tea and cakes and ices,
Have the strength to force the moment to its crisis?   80
But though I have wept and fasted, wept and prayed,
Though I have seen my head [grown slightly bald] brought in upon a platter,
I am no prophet—and here's no great matter;
I have seen the moment of my greatness flicker,
And I have seen the eternal Footman hold my coat, and snicker,   85
And in short, I was afraid.

And would it have been worth it, after all,
After the cups, the marmalade, the tea,
Among the porcelain, among some talk of you and me,
Would it have been worth while,
To have bitten off the matter with a smile,   90
To have squeezed the universe into a ball
To roll it toward some overwhelming question,
To say: "I am Lazarus,° come from the dead,   raised from the dead by Jesus
Come back to tell you all, I shall tell you all"—
If one, settling a pillow by her head,   95
    Should say: "That is not what I meant at all.
    That is not it, at all."

And would it have been worth it, after all,
Would it have worth while,
After the sunsets and the dooryards and the sprinkled streets,   100
After the novels, after the teacups, after the skirts that trail along the floor—
And this, and so much more?—
It is impossible to say just what I mean!
But as if a magic lantern threw the nerves in patterns on a screen: 105
Would it have been worth while
If one, settling a pillow or throwing off a shawl,
And turning toward the window, should say:
    "That is not it at all,
    That is not what I meant, at all."   110
        . . . .

No! I am not Prince Hamlet, nor was meant to be;
Am an attendant lord, one that will do
To swell a progress, start a scene or two,
Advise the prince; no doubt, an easy tool,
Deferential, glad to be of use,   115
Politic, cautious, and meticulous;
Full of high sentence, but a bit obtuse;
At times, indeed, almost ridiculous—
Almost, at times, the Fool.

I grow old . . . I grow old . . .   120
I shall wear the bottoms of my trousers rolled.

Shall I part my hair behind? Do I dare to eat a peach?
I shall wear white flannel trousers, and walk upon the beach.
I have heard the mermaids singing, each to each.

I do not think that they will sing to me.   125

I have seen them riding seaward on the waves
Combing the white hair of the waves blown back
When the wind blows the water white and black.

We have lingered in the chambers of the sea
By sea-girls wreathed with seaweed red and brown   130
Till human voices wake us, and we drown.

Rhapsody on a Windy Night   1911

Twelve o'clock.
Along the reaches of the street
Held in a lunar synthesis,
Whispering lunar incantations
Dissolve the floors of memory   5
And all its clear relations,
Its divisions and precisions,
Every street lamp that I pass
Beats like a fatalistic drum,
And through the spaces of the dark   10
Midnight shakes the memory
As a madman shakes a dead geranium.

Half-past one,
The street-lamp sputtered,
The street-lamp muttered,   15
The street-lamp said, 'Regard that woman
Who hesitates toward you in the light of the door
Which opens on her like a grin.
You see the border of her dress
Is torn and stained with sand,   20
And you see the corner of her eye
Twists like a crooked pin.'

The memory throws up high and dry
A crowd of twisted things;
A twisted branch upon the beach   25
Eaten smooth, and polished
As if the world gave up
The secret of its skeleton,
Stiff and white.
A broken spring in a factory yard,   30
Rust that clings to the form that the strength has left
Hard and curled and ready to snap.

Half-past two,
The street-lamp said,
'Remark the cat which flattens itself in the gutter,   35
Slips out its tongue
And devours a morsel of rancid butter.'
So the hand of the child, automatic,
Slipped out and pocketed a toy that was running along the quay.

I could see nothing behind that child's eye.   40
I have seen eyes in the street
Trying to peer through lighted shutters,
And a crab one afternoon in a pool,
An old crab with barnacles on his back,
Gripped the end of a stick which I held him.   45

Half-past three,
The lamp sputtered,
The lamp muttered in the dark.
The lamp hummed:
'Regard the moon,   50
La lune ne garde aucune rancune,°   the moon looks on without malice
She winks a feeble eye,
She smiles into corners.
She smooths the hair of the grass.
The moon has lost her memory.   55
A washed-out smallpox cracks her face,
Her hand twists a paper rose,
That smells of dust and eau de Cologne,
She is alone
With all the old nocturnal smells   60
That cross and cross across her brain.'
The reminiscence comes
Of sunless dry geraniums
And dust in crevices,
Smells of chestnuts in the streets,   65
And female smells in shuttered rooms,
And cigarettes in corridors
And cocktail smells in bars.

The lamp said,
'Four o'clock,
Here is the number on the door.   70

Memory!
You have the key,
The little lamp spreads a ring on the stair.
Mount.
The bed is open; the tooth-brush hangs on the wall, 75
Put your shoes at the door, sleep, prepare for life.'

The last twist of the knife.

Martín Espada   b. 1957

Federico's Ghost   *1990*

The story is
that whole families of fruitpickers
still crept between the furrows
of the field at dusk,
when for reasons of whiskey or whatever 5
the cropduster plane sprayed anyway,
floating a pesticide drizzle
over the pickers
who thrashed like dark birds
in a glistening white net, 10
except for Federico,
a skinny boy who stood apart
in his own green row,
and, knowing the pilot
would not understand in Spanish 15
that he was the son of a whore,
instead jerked his arm
and thrust an obscene finger.

The pilot understood
He circled the plane and sprayed again, 20
watching a fine gauze of poison
drift over the brown bodies
that cowered and scurried on the ground,
and aiming for Federico,
leaving the skin beneath his shirt
wet and blistered, 25
but still pumping his finger at the sky.

After Federico died,
rumors at the labor camp
told of tomatoes picked and smashed at night,
growers muttering of vandal children 30
or communists in camp,
first threatening to call Immigration,
then promising every Sunday off
if only the smashing of tomatoes would stop. 35

Still tomatoes were picked and squashed
in the dark,
and the old women in camp
said it was Federico,
laboring after sundown   40
to cool the burns on his arms,
flinging tomatoes
at the cropduster
that hummed like a mosquito
lost in his ear,   45
and kept his soul awake.

Latin Night at the Pawnshop   1987
Chelsea, Massachusetts
Christmas, 1987

The apparition of a salsa band
gleaming in the Liberty Loan
pawnshop window:

Golden trumpet.
silver trombone,
congas, maracas, tambourine,   5
all with price tags dangling
like the city morgue ticket
on a dead man's toe.

Mari Evans

Black jam for dr. negro   1970

Pullin me in off the corner to wash my face an
cut my fro off turn
my collar
down
when that aint my   5
thang I
walk heels first
nose round an tilted
up
my ancient   10
eyes
see your thang
baby
an it aint
shit   15
your thang
puts my eyes out baby
turns my seeking fingers

into splintering fists
messes up my head
an I scream you out   20
your thang
is what's wrong
        an' you keep
        pilin it on rubbin it
        in   25
        smoothly
        doin it
        to death
what you sweatin
baby   30
                        your guts
puked an rotten
waitin'

to be defended   35

I Am a Black Woman   *1970*

I am a black woman
the music of my song
some sweet arpeggio of tears
is written in a minor key
and I
can be heard humming in the night   5
Can be heard
                humming
in the night

I saw my mate leap screaming to the sea   10
and I/with these hands/cupped the lifebreath
from my issue in the canebrake
I lost Nat's swinging body in a rain of tears
and heard my son scream all the way from Anzio°   site of World War II battle in Italy
for Peace he never knew. . . . I
learned Da Nang and Pork Chop Hill°   15
in anguish   sites of battles in Vietnam

Now my nostrils know the gas
and these trigger tire/d fingers
seek the softness in my warrior's beard   20

I
am a black woman
tall as a cypress
strong
beyond all definition still   25
defying place
and time
and circumstance

assailed
    impervious
        indestructible   30
Look
   on me and be
renewed

Faiz Ahmed Faiz   1911–1984

Prison Daybreak   1952

Translated by Naomi Lazard

Though it was still night
the moon stood beside my pillow and said:
                   "Wake up,
the wine of sleep that was your portion
is finished. The wineglass is empty.   5
Morning is here."
             I said good-bye to my beloved's image
in the black satin waters of the night
that hung still and stagnant on the world.
                Here and there   10
moonlight whirled, the lotus dance commenced;
silver nebulas of stars dropped from the moon's white hand.
They went under, rose again to float, faded and opened.
For a long time night and daybreak swayed,
locked together in each other's arms.   15
           In the prison yard
my comrades' faces, incandescent as candlelight,
flickered through the gloom. Sleep had washed them
with its dew, turned them into gold.
              For that moment   20
these faces were rinsed clean of grief for our people,
absolved from the pain of separation from their dear ones.
In the distance a gong struck the hour;
wretched footsteps stumbled forward on their rounds,
wasted by near starvation, *maestros* of the morning shuffle,   25
lockstepped, arm in arm with their own terrible laments.
Mutilated voices, broken on the rack, awakened.
           Somewhere a door opened,
another one closed; a chain muttered, grumbled,
shrieked out loud. Somewhere a knife plunged   30
into the gizzard of a lock; a window went mad
and began to beat its own head.

This is the way the enemies of life,
shaken from sleep, showed themselves.
These daemons, hacked from stone and steel,   35
use their great hands to grind down the spirit,

slim as a feather now, of my useless days and nights.
They make it cry out in despair.
                      The prisoners,
all of us, keep watch for our savior
who is on his way in the form of a storybook prince,
arrows of hope burning in his quiver,
              ready to let them fly.
                                           40

Lawrence Ferlinghetti   b. 1919

The Pennycandystore Beyond The El   *1958*

The pennycandystore beyond the El
is where I first
            fell in love
                  with unreality
Jellybeans glowed in the semi-gloom   5
of that september afternoon
A cat upon the counter moved among
                     the licorice sticks
            and tootsie rolls
     and Oh Boy Gum   10

Outside the leaves were falling as they died

A wind had blown away the sun

A girl ran in
Her hair was rainy
Her breasts were breathless in the little room   15

Outside the leaves were falling
                and they cried
                      Too soon! too soon!

John Finlay   1941–1991

The Bog Sacrifice   *1992*

The iron and acid water of the bog,
Rising and falling with the winter rains,
Two thousand years, preserved him as he died,
Pinned naked to the floor by wooden crooks.
No fire had cut and cleaned the clotted soul.
Runic stakes, washed white as salt, were laid   5
Over his narrow breast, sunk in the peat.

The sacrificial rope they hanged him from,
Of woven skins, still cut into his throat,
Tight as when death came. His gentle face,
Forced upward by the torsion of the noose,   10

Bore with monstrous discipline his bane,
As loose ends, like serpents, meandered down
His naked length, pressed into his flesh.

A cap of wolfskin hived his shaven head.   15
Descended from a line of conscript priests,
He died in youth, still delicate and whole.
When he was lifted from the pit, the earth
Itself then sweating like an ancient beast,
He looked as if alive. Faint cries of snipes   20
Brought sunlight piercing to his closing eyes.

Before Christ reached this isolated north,
A chthonic goddess, holding iron breasts,
Each year in early spring exacted death.
In winter when the winds blew keen off ice,   25
Or summer with its rippling swarm of weeds,
The bog seemed never raised above the sea,
But underneath, out of whose depths she came.

Carolyn Forché   b. 1950

Because One Is Always Forgotten   *1981*

IN MEMORIAM, JOSÉ RUDOLFO VIERA
1939–1981: EL SALVADOR

When Viera was buried we knew it had come to an end,
his coffin rocking into the ground like a boat or a cradle.

I could take my heart, he said, and give it to a *campesino*
and he would cut it up and give it back:

you can't eat heart in those four dark   5
chambers where a man can be kept years.

A boy soldier in the bone-hot sun works his knife
to peel the face from a dead man

and hang it from the branch of a tree
flowering with such faces.   10

The heart is the toughest part of the body.
Tenderness is in the hands.

Selective Service   *1981*

We rise from the snow where we've
lain on our backs and flown like children,
from the imprint of perfect wings and cold gowns,
and we stagger together wine-breathed into town
where our people are building
their armies again, short years after   5

body bags, after burnings. There is a man
I've come to love after thirty, and we have
our rituals of coffee, of airports, regret.
After love we smoke and sleep   10
with magazines, two shot glasses
and the black and white collapse of hours.
In what time do we live that it is too late
to have children? In what place
that we consider the various ways to leave?   15
There is no list long enough
for a selective service card shriveling
under a match, the prison that comes of it,
a flag in the wind eaten from its pole
and boys sent back in trash bags.   20
We'll tell you. You were at that time
learning fractions. We'll tell you
about fractions. Half of us are dead or quiet
or lost. Let them speak for themselves
We lie down in the fields and leave behind   25
the corpses of angels.

Robert Frost   1874–1963

Design   *1936*

I found a dimpled spider, fat and white,
On a white heal-all, holding up a moth
Like a white piece of rigid satin cloth—
Assorted characters of death and blight
Mixed ready to begin the morning right,   5
Like the ingredients of a witches' broth—
A snow-drop spider, a flower like a froth,
And dead wings carried like a paper kite.

What had that flower to do with being white,
The wayside blue and innocent heal-all?   10
What brought the kindred spider to that height,
Then steered the white moth thither in the night?
What but design of darkness to appall?—
If design govern in a thing so small.

Mending Wall   *1914*

Something there is that doesn't love a wall,
That sends the frozen-ground-swell under it
And spills the upper boulders in the sun,
And makes gaps even two can pass abreast.
The work of hunters is another thing: 5
I have come after them and made repair

Where they have left not one stone on a stone,
But they would have the rabbit out of hiding,
To please the yelping dogs. The gaps I mean,
No one has seen them made or heard them made,
But at spring mending-time we find them there.   10
I let my neighbor know beyond the hill;
And on a day we meet to walk the line
And set the wall between us once again.
We keep the wall between us as we go.
To each the boulders that have fallen to each.   15
And some are loaves and some so nearly balls
We have to use a spell to make them balance:
"Stay where you are until our backs are turned!"
We wear our fingers rough with handling them.
Oh, just another kind of outdoor game,   20
One on a side. It comes to little more:
There where it is we do not need the wall:
He is all pine and I am apple orchard.
My apple trees will never get across
And eat the cones under his pines, I tell him.   25
He only says, "Good fences make good neighbors."
Spring is the mischief in me, and I wonder
If I could put a notion in his head:
"Why do they make good neighbors? Isn't it   30
Where there are cows? But here there are no cows.
Before I built a wall I'd ask to know
What I was walling in or walling out,
And to whom I was like to give offense.
Something there is that doesn't love a wall,   35
That wants it down." I could say "Elves" to him,
But it's not elves exactly, and I'd rather
He said it for himself. I see him there,
Bringing a stone grasped firmly by the top
In each hand, like an old-stone savage armed.   40
He moves in darkness as it seems to me,
Not of woods only and the shade of trees.
He will not go behind his father's saying,
And he likes having thought of it so well
He says again, "Good fences make good neighbors."   45

Once by the Pacific   1928

The shattered water made a misty din.
Great waves looked over others coming in,
And thought of doing something to the shore
That water never did to land before.
The clouds were low and hairy in the skies,
Like locks blown forward in the gleam of eyes.   5
You could not tell, and yet it looked as if

The shore was lucky in being backed by cliff,
The cliff in being backed by continent;
It looked as if a night of dark intent   10
Was coming, and not only a night, an age.
Someone had better be prepared for rage.
There would be more than ocean-water broken
Before God's last *Put out the Light* was spoken.

Stopping by Woods on a Snowy Evening   1923

Whose woods these are I think I know.
His house is in the village though;
He will not see me stopping here
To watch his woods fill up with snow.

My little horse must think it queer   5
To stop without a farmhouse near
Between the woods and frozen lake
The darkest evening of the year.

He gives his harness bells a shake
To ask if there is some mistake.   10
The only other sound's the sweep
Of easy wind and downy flake.

The woods are lovely, dark and deep,
But I have promises to keep,
And miles to go before I sleep,   15
And miles to go before I sleep.

Allen Ginsberg   b. 1926

First Party at Ken Kesey's with Hell's Angels   1965

Cool black night thru the redwoods
cars parked outside in shade
behind the gate, stars dim above
the ravine, a fire burning by the side
porch and a few tired souls hunched over   5
in black leather jackets. In the huge
wooden house, a yellow chandelier
at 3 A.M. the blast of loudspeakers
hi-fi Rolling Stones Ray Charles Beatles
Jumping Joe Jackson and twenty youths   10
dancing to the vibration thru the floor,
a little weed in the bathroom, girls in scarlet
tights, one muscular smooth skinned man
sweating dancing for hours, beer cans
bent littering the yard, a hanged man   15
sculpture dangling from a high creek branch,
children sleeping softly in their bedroom bunks.

And 4 police cars parked outside the painted
gate, red lights revolving in the leaves.

A Supermarket in California   1956

What thoughts I have of you tonight, Walt Whitman, for I walked down the
sidestreets under the trees with a headache self-conscious looking at the full moon.

In my hungry fatigue, and shopping for images, I went into the neon fruit supermarket, dreaming of your enumerations!

What peaches and what penumbras!° Whole families shopping at night! Aisles   parital
full of husbands! Wives in the avocados, babies in the tomatoes—and you, Garcia   shadows
Lorca,° what were you doing down by the watermelons?   Spanish
                                                                                  poet
I saw you, Walt Whitman, childless, lonely old grubber, poking among the
meats in the refrigerator and eyeing the grocery boys.

I heard you asking questions of each: Who killed the pork chops? What price   5
bananas? Are you my Angel?

I wandered in and out of the brilliant stacks of cans following you, and followed in my imagination by the store detective.

We strode down the open corridors together in our solitary fancy tasting arti-
chokes, possessing every frozen delicacy, and never passing the cashier.

Where are we going, Walt Whitman? The doors close in an hour. Which way
does your beard point tonight?

(I touch your book and dream of our odyssey in the supermarket and feel absurd.)

Will we walk all night through solitary streets? The trees add shade to shade,   10
lights out in the houses, we'll both be lonely.

Will we stroll dreaming of the lost America of love past blue automobiles in
driveways, home to our silent cottage?

Ah, dear father, graybeard, lonely old courage-teacher, what America did you
have when Charon° quit poling his ferry and you got out on a smoking bank and
stood watching the boat disappear on the black waters of Lethe?°   ferryman of Hell/river of
                                                                           forgetfulness

Nikki Giovanni   b. 1943

Nikki-Rosa   1968

childhood remembrances are always a drag
if you're Black
you always remember things like living in Woodlawn°   district of Cincinnati
with no inside toilet
and if you become famous or something   5
they never talk about how happy you were to have your mother
all to yourself and
how good the water felt when you got your bath from one of those
big tubs that folk in chicago barbecue in
and somehow when you talk about home
it never gets across how much you   10
understood their feelings
as the whole family attended meetings about Hollydale

and even though you remember
your biographers never understand
your father's pain as he sells his stock
and another dream goes
and though you're poor it isn't poverty that
concerns you
and though they fought a lot
it isn't your father's drinking that makes any difference
but only that everybody is together and you
and your sister have happy birthdays and very good christmasses
and I really hope no white person ever has cause to write about me
because they never understand Black love is Black wealth and they'll
probably talk about my hard childhood and never understand that
all the while I was quite happy

15

20

25

Woman   1978

she wanted to be a blade
of grass amid the fields
but he wouldn't agree
to be the dandelion

she wanted to be a robin singing
through the leaves   5

but he refused to be
her tree

she spun herself into a web
    and looking for a place to rest
turned to him   10
but he stood straight
declining to be her corner

she tried to be a book
but he wouldn't read
she turned herself into a bulb   15
but he wouldn't let her grow

she decided to become
a woman
and though he still refused
to be a man   20
she decided it was all
right

Rafael Jesús González   b. 1935

Sestina: Santa Prisca   1969

One would think that these
Dry standards of pink stone
Would whip the wind with iron

Tongues and speak the word
Kept by their chiseled, gesticulating saints
Weeping dust tears upon the courtyard floor.   5

From the chequered, knee-rubbed floor
Rise supplications cast with wings of iron
To perch with gentle claws upon the word
"God" carved with gold upon the pimpled stone.
Futile as this chasuble of rock, these   10
Prayers can never tame the gestures of the saints.

Now the sun strikes with glory the cold saints
Forcing their lips to simulate a word
Voiced in silver by the bells of iron.
Each note a silver globule floats to crack these   15
Shallow crystals of the morning hours lying on the floor
And scatter their potions of tranquility on the stone.

It is not time for winds to ruffle the starched stone
Which clothes the rock-ribbed bosoms of the saints
And checks the pulses of the word.   20
It will never be time to resuscitate these
Dead theologies groveling on the vestry floor
Rehearsing one-time truths from vellums bound in iron.

The lace work of the sun-forced iron   25
Is not wide enough to let the saints
Escape wearing their still phylacteries of stone.
The bougainvillaea climbs its progress from the floor
To leave its purple kisses on the saints' lips; these
Let the bits of passion drop, but keep the precious word.   30

But it is there, the tongue-tied word
Encapsuled in its throats of iron,
To shake to truth the rock hinged saints
Hanging like dead murmurs above the ocean floor.
The matutinal orations will rise on plumes of stone   35
And the loud tongues of candles whisper: "Listen to these."

The bells of iron will testify their love and these
Flowers on the floor become testaments from which the saints
Will preach the golden word and the green life-stone.

Woody Guthrie   1912–1967

Pretty Boy Floyd   *1958*

If you'll gather 'round me, children,
A story I will tell,
About Pretty Boy Floyd, an outlaw,
Oklahoma knew him well.

It was in the town of Shawnee on a Saturday afternoon   5
His wife beside him in the wagon as into town they rode.
There a deputy sheriff reproached him in a manner rather rude
Using vulgar words of anger, and his wife she overheard.

Pretty Boy grabbed a log chain, the deputy grabbed his gun,
And in the fight that followed, he laid that deputy down.   10
Then he took to the trees and timber and lived a life of shame,
Every crime in Oklahoma was added to his name.

Yes, he took to the river bottom along the river shore,
And Pretty Boy found a welcome at every farmer's door.
The papers said that Pretty Boy had robbed a bank each day,   15
While he was setting in some farmhouse 300 miles away.

There's many a starving farmer the same old story told
How the outlaw paid their mortgage and saved their little home.
Others tell you 'bout a stranger that come to beg a meal
And when the meal was finished left a thousand dollar bill.   20

It was in Oklahoma City, it was on Christmas Day,
There come a whole carload of groceries with a note to say:
"You say that I'm an outlaw, you say that I'm a thief.
Here's a Christmas dinner for the families on relief."

Yes, as through this world I ramble, I see lots of funny men.   25
Some will rob you with a 6 gun, and some with a fountain pen.
But as through your life you'll travel, wherever you may roam.
You won't never see an Outlaw drive a family from their home.

Donald Hall   b. 1928

My Son, My Executioner   *1955*

My son, my executioner,
    I take you in my arms,

Quiet and small and just astir,
    And whom my body warms.

Sweet death, small son, our instrument   5
    Of immortality,
Your cries and hungers document
    Our bodily decay.

We twenty-five and twenty-two,
    Who seemed to live forever,   10
Observe enduring life in you
    and start to die together.

Thomas Hardy   1840–1928

Ah, Are You Digging on My Grave?   *1914*

"Ah, are you digging on my grave,
   My loved one?—planting rue?"
—   "No: yesterday he went to wed
One of the brightest wealth has bred.
'It cannot hurt her now,' he said,   5
   'That I should not be true.'"

"Then who is digging on my grave?
   My nearest dearest kin?"
—   "Ah, no: they sit and think, 'What use!
What good will planting flowers produce?   10
No tendance of her mound can loose
   Her spirit from Death's gin.'"

"But some one digs upon my grave?
   My enemy?—prodding sly?"
—   "Nay: When she heard you had passed the Gate   15
That shuts on all flesh soon or late,
She thought you no more worth her hate,
   And cares not where you lie."

"Then, who is digging on my grave?
   Say—since I have not guessed!"   20
—   "O it is I, my mistress dear,
Your little dog, who still lives near,
And much I hope my movements here
   Have not disturbed your rest?"

"Ah, yes! *You* dig upon my grave . . .P   25
   Why flashed it not on me
That one true heart was left behind!
What feeling do we ever find
To equal among human kind
   A dog's fidelity!"   30

"Mistress, I dug upon your grave
   To bury a bone, in case
I should be hungry near this spot
When passing on my daily trot.
I am sorry, but I quite forgot   35
   It was your resting-place."

The Man He Killed   *1902*

"Had he and I but met
   By some old ancient inn,
We should have sat us down to wet
   Right many a nipperkin!

"But ranged as infantry,
   And staring face to face,   5

I shot at him as he at me,
    And killed him in his place.

"I shot him dead because—
Because he was my foe,
Just so: my foe of course he was;
    That's clear enough; although   10

"He thought he'd 'list, perhaps,
Off-hand like—just as I—
Was out of work—had sold his traps—   15
    No other reason why.

"Yes; quaint and curious war is!
You shoot a fellow down
You'd treat if met where any bar is,
    Or help to half-a-crown."   20

Neutral Tones   *1898*

We stood by a pond that winter day,
And the sun was white, as though chidden of God,
And a few leaves lay on the starving sod;
    —They had fallen from an ash, and were gray.

Your eyes on me were as eyes that rove   5
Over tedious riddles of years ago;
And some words played between us to and fro
    On which lost the more by our love.

The smile on your mouth was the deadest thing
Alive enough to have strength to die;   10
And a grin of bitterness swept thereby
    Like an omnious bird a-wing....

Since then, keen lessons that love deceives.
And wrings with wrong, have shaped to me
Your face, and the God-cursed sun, and a tree,   15
    And a pond edged with grayish leaves.

Joy Harjo   b. 1951

Anchorage   *1983*

for Audre Lorde

This city is made of stone, of blood, and fish.
There are Chugatch Mountains to the east
and whale and seal to the west.
It hasn't always been this way, because glaciers
who are ice ghosts create oceans, carve earth   5
and shape this city here, by the sound.
They swim backwards in time.

Once a storm of boiling earth cracked open
the streets, threw open the town.
It's quiet now, but underneath the concrete   10
is the cooking earth,
                    and above that, air
which is another ocean, where spirits we can't see
are dancing   joking   getting full
on roasted caribou, and the praying   15
goes on, extends out.

Nora and I go walking down 4th Avenue
and know it is all happening.
On a park bench we see someone's Athabascan
grandmother, folded up, smelling like 200 years   20
of blood and piss, her eyes closed against some
unimagined darkness, where she is buried in an ache
in which nothing makes
                                sense.

We keep on breathing, walking, but softer now,   25
the clouds whirling in the air above us.
What can we say that would make us understand
better than we do already?
Except to speak of her home and claim her
as our own history, and know that our dreams   30
don't end here, two blocks away from the ocean
where our hearts still batter away at the muddy shore.

And I think of the 6th Avenue jail, of mostly Native
and Black men, where Henry told about being shot at
eight times outside a liquor store in L.A., but when   35
the car sped away he was surprised he was alive,
no bullet holes, man, and eight cartridges strewn
on the sidewalk
                all around him.

Everyone laughed at the impossibility of it,   40
but also the truth. Because who would believe
the fantastic and terrible story of all of our survival
those who were never meant
                        to survive?

The Woman Hanging
from the Thirteenth Floor Window   *1983*

She is the woman hanging from the 13th floor
window. Her hands are pressed white against the
concrete molding of the tenement building. She
hangs from the 13th floor window in east Chicago,
with a swirl of birds over her head. They could   5
be a halo, or a storm of glass waiting to crush her.

She thinks she will be set free.

The woman hanging from the 13th floor window
on the east side of Chicago is not alone.
She is a woman of children, of the baby, Carlos,
and of Margaret, and of Jimmy who is the oldest.   10
She is her mother's daughter and her father's son.
She is several pieces between the two husbands
she has had. She is all the women of the apartment
building who stand watching her, watching themselves.   15

When she was young she ate wild rice on scraped down
plates in warm wood rooms. It was in the farther
north and she was the baby then. They rocked her.
She sees Lake Michigan lapping at the shores of
herself. It is a dizzy hole of water and the rich   20
live in tall glass houses at the edge of it. In some
places Lake Michigan speaks softly, here, it just sputters
and butts itself against the asphalt. She sees
other buildings just like hers. She sees other
women hanging from many-floored windows   25
counting their lives in the palms of their hands
and in the palms of their children's hands.

She is the woman hanging from the 13th floor window
on the Indian side of town. Her belly is soft from
her children's births, her worn levis swing down below   30
her waist, and then her feet, and then her heart.
She is dangling.

The woman hanging from the 13th floor hears voices.
They come to her in the night when the lights have gone
dim. Sometimes they are little cats mewing and scratching 35
at the door, sometimes they are her grandmother's voice,
and sometimes they are gigantic men of light whispering
to her to get up, to get up, to get up. That's when she wants
to have another child to hold onto in the night, to be able
to fall back into dreams.   40

And the woman hanging from the 13th floor window
hears other voices. Some of them scream out from below
for her to jump, they would push her over. Others cry softly
from the sidewalks, pull their children up like flowers and gather
them into their arms. They would help her, like themselves. 45

But she is the woman hanging from the 13th floor window,
and she knows she is hanging by her own fingers, her
own skin, her own thread of indecision.

She thinks of Carlos, of Margaret, of Jimmy.
She thinks of her father, and of her mother.
She thinks of all the women she has been, of all   50
the men. She thinks of the color of her skin, and
of Chicago streets, and of waterfalls and pines.
She thinks of moonlight nights, and of cool spring storms.
Her mind chatters like neon and northside bars.
She thinks of the 4 a.m. lonelinesses that have folded   55

her up like death, discordant, without logical and
beautiful conclusion. Her teeth break off at the edges.
She would speak.

The woman hangs from the 13th floor window crying for   60
the lost beauty of her own life. She sees the
sun falling west over the grey plane of Chicago.
She thinks she remembers listening to her own life
break loose, as she falls from the 13th floor
window on the east side of Chicago, or as she   65
climbs back up to claim herself again.

Michael Harper   b. 1938

Here Where Coltrane Is*   *1977*

Soul and race
are private dominions,
memories and modal
songs, a tenor blossoming,
which would paint suffering   5
a clear color but is not in
this Victorian house
without oil in zero degree
weather and a forty-mile-an-hour wind;
it is all a well-knit family: 10
a love supreme.
Oak leaves pile up on walkway
and steps, catholic as apples
in a special mist of clear white
children who love my children.   15
I play "Alabama"
on a warped record player
skipping the scratches
on your faces over the fibrous
conical hairs of plastic   20
under the wooden floors.

Dreaming on a train from New York
to Philly, you hand out six
notes which become an anthem
to our memories of you: 25
oak, birch, maple,
apple, cocoa, rubber.
For this reason Martin° is dead;   Martin Luther King, Jr. (1929–1968)—African-American civil rights leader
for this reason Malcolm° is dead;   Malcolm X (1925–1965)—African-American leader
for this reason Coltrane is dead;   30
in the eyes of my first son are the browns
of these men and their music.

---

*John Coltrane (1926–1967)—jazz saxophonist

Nightmare Begins Responsibility   *1975*

I place these numbed wrists to the pane
watching white uniforms whisk over
him in the tube-kept
prison
fear what they will do in experiment   5
watch my gloved stickshifting gasolined hands
breathe *boxcar-information-please* infirmary tubes
distrusting white-pink mending paperthin
silkened end hairs, distrusting tubes
shrunk in his *trunk-skincapped*   10
shaven head, in thighs
distrusting-white-hands-picking-baboon-light
on this son who will not make his second night
of this wardstrewn intensive airpocket
where his father's asthmatic   15
hymns of *night-train,* train done gone
his mother can only know that he has flown
up into essential calm unseen corridor
going boxscarred home, *mamaborn, sweetsonchild*
gonedowntown into *researchtestingwarehousebatteryacid*   20
mama-son-done-gone/me telling her 'nother
train tonight, no music, no breathstroked
heartbeat in my infinite distrust of them:
and of my distrusting self
white-doctor-who-breathed-for-him-all-night   25
say it for two sons gone,
say nightmare, say it loud
panebreaking heartmadness:
nightmare begins responsibility.

Robery Hayden   1913–1980

Those Winter Sundays   *1962*

Sundays too my father got up early,
and put his clothes on in the blueblack cold,
then with cracked hands that ached
from labor in the weekday weather made
banked fires blaze. No one ever thanked him.   5

I'd wake and hear the cold splintering, breaking.
When the rooms were warm, he'd call,
and slowly I would rise and dress,
fearing the chronic angers of that house.

Speaking indifferently to him,   10
who had driven out the cold
and polished my good shoes as well.

What did I know, what did I know
of love's austere and lonely offices?

Seamus Heaney   b. 1939

Bog Queen   1975

I lay waiting
between turf-face and demesne wall,
between heathery levels
and glass-toothed stone.

My body was braille   5
for the creeping influences:
dawn suns groped over my head
and cooled at my feet,

through my fabrics and skins
the seeps of winter
digested me,   10
the illiterate roots

pondered and died
in the cavings
of stomach and socket.   15
I lay waiting

on the gravel bottom,
my brain darkening,
a jar of spawn
fermenting underground   20

dreams of Baltic amber.
Bruised berries under my nails,
the vital hoard reducing
in the crock of the pelvis.

My diadem grew carious,   25
gemstones dropped
in the peat floe
like the bearings of history.

My sash was a black glacier
wrinkling, dyed weaves   30
and phoenician stitchwork
retted on my breasts'

soft moraines.
I knew winter cold
like the nuzzle of fjords   35
at my thighs—

the soaked fledge, the heavy
swaddle of hides.

My skull hibernated
in the wet nest of my hair.   40

Which they robbed.
I was barbered
and stripped
by a turfcutter's spade

who veiled me again   45
and packed coomb softly
between the stone jambs
at my head and my feet.

Till a peer's wife bribed him.
The plait of my hair,   50
a slimy birth-cord
of bog, had been cut

and I rose from the dark,
hacked bone, skull-ware,
frayed stitches, tufts,   55
small gleams on the bank.

Digging   *1966*

Between my finger and my thumb
The squat pen rests; snug as a gun.

Under my window, a clean rasping sound
When the spade sinks into gravelly ground:
My father, digging. I look down   5

Till his straining rump among the flowerbeds
Bends low, comes up twenty years away
Stooping in rhythm through potato drills
Where he was digging.

The coarse boot nestled on the lug, the shaft   10
Against the inside knee was levered firmly.
He rooted out tall tops, buried the bright edge deep
To scatter new potatoes that we picked
Loving their cool hardness in our hands.

By God, the old man could handle a spade.   15
Just like his old man.

My grandfather cut more turf in a day
Than any other man on Toner's bog.
Once I carried him milk in a bottle
Corked sloppily with paper. He straightened up   20
To drink it, then fell to right away

Nicking and slicing neatly, heaving sods
Over his shoulder, going down and down
For the good turf. Digging.

The cold smell of potato mould, the squelch and slap   25
Of soggy peat, the curt cuts of an edge
Through living roots awaken in my head.
But I've no spade to follow men like them.

Between my finger and my thumb
The squat pen rests.   30
I'll dig with it.

Anthony Hecht   b. 1923

The Dover Bitch   *1967*

A Criticism of Life
For Andrews Wanning

So there stood Matthew Arnold and this girl
With the cliffs of England crumbling away behind them,
And he said to her, "Try to be true to me,
And I'll do the same for you, for things are bad
All over, etc., etc."   5
Well now, I knew this girl. It's true she had read
Sophocles in a fairly good translation
And caught that bitter allusion to the sea,
But all the time he was talking she had in mind
The notion of what his whiskers would feel like   10
On the back of her neck. She told me later on
That after a while she got to looking out
At the lights across the channel, and really felt sad,
Thinking of all the wine and enormous beds
And blandishments in French and the perfumes.   15
And then she got really angry. To have been brought
All the way down from London, and then be addressed
As sort of a mournful cosmic last resort
Is really tough on a girl, and she was pretty.
Anyway, she watched him pace the room   20
And finger his watch-chain and seem to sweat a bit,
And then she said one or two unprintable things.
But you mustn't judge her by that. What I mean to say is,
She's really all right. I still see her once in a while
And she always treats me right.   25
We have a drink
And I give her a good time, and perhaps it's a year
Before I see her again, but there she is,
Running to fat, but dependable as they come,
And sometimes I bring her a bottle of *Nuit d'Amour*.   30

George Herbert   1593–1633

Easter Wings   *1633*

Lord, who createdst man in wealth and store,°   plenty
   Though foolishly he lost the same,
      Decaying more and more
         Till he became
           Most poor.   5
           With thee
         O let me rise
      As larks, harmoniously,
   And sing this day thy victories:
Then shall the fall further the flight in me.   10

My tender age in sorrow did begin:
   And still with sicknesses and shame
      Thou didst so punish sin,
         That I became
           Most thin.   15
           With thee
         Let me combine,
      And feel this day thy victory;
   For, if I imp° my wing on thine,   graft
Affliction shall advance the flight in me.   20

Robert Herrick   1591–1674

To the Virgins, to Make Much of Time   *1648*

Gather ye rosebuds while ye may,
   Old time is still a-flying,
And this same flower that smiles today
   Tomorrow will be dying.

The glorious lamp of heaven, the sun,   5
   The higher he's a-getting,
The sooner will his race be run,
   And nearer he's to setting.

That age is best which is the first,
   When youth and blood are warmer;   10
But being spent, the worse, and worst
   Times still succeed the former.

Then be not coy, but use your time,
   And while ye may go marry,
For, having lost once your prime,   15
   You may forever tarry.

Nazim Hikmet   1902–1963

Life, Friends, Enemies, You and the Earth   *1939*

Translated by Taner Baybars

I am so happy to be alive!
I love the Earth, the Sun

    fighting for my bread.
Although I know the Earth's measurements
    down to the last centimetre,   5
although it looks tiny next to the Sun,
the Earth is incomprehensibly
        large for me.

I long to travel and see
fishes I have not seen   10
      fruits and stars.
But only through reading
have I made my journey across Europe,
and all my life I have waited
    for a letter with a blue stamp   15
      franked in Asia.
My local grocer and I
are physically unknown in America
but all the same
I have friends and enemies   20
    all the way
      from China to Spain,
from the Cape of Good Hope
        to Alaska,
at every knot at every kilometre.   25
Friends whose hands I have not shaken
but for whom and with whom
      I am ready to die
in our struggle for Freedom.
And enemies whose blood I could drain   30
and who could drain my own blood.
My greatest point of strength
    is to know
      that I am not alone
        in this world.   35
The world and its multitudes
are not obscurities in my heart
nor mysteries in scientific books.

In our great struggle
I have chosen my rank   40
    openly, fearlessly.
And outside this rank
    neither the soil nor you

can be my completion.
And yet you are so incredibly beautiful
   the soil so warm

          so lovable . . .

                            45

Garrett Kaoru Hongo   b. 1951

Off from Swing Shift   *1982*

Late, just past midnight,
freeway noise from the Harbor
and San Diego leaking in
from the vent over the stove,
and he's off from swing shift at Lear's.
Eight hours of twisting circuitry,   5
charting ohms and maximum gains
while transformers hum
and helicopters swirl
on the roofs above the small factory.
He hails me with a head-fake,   10
then the bob and weave
of a weekend middleweight
learned at the Y on Kapiolani
ten years before I was born.

                            15

The shoes and gold London Fogger
come off first, then the easy grin
saying he's lucky as they come.
He gets into the slippers
my brother gives him every Christmas,
carries his Thermos over to the sink,   20
and slides into the one chair at the table
that's made of wood and not yellow plastic.
He pushes aside stacks
of *Sporting News* and *Outdoor Life,*
big round tins of Holland butter cookies,   25
and clears a space for his elbows, his pens,
and the *Racing Form's* Late Evening Final.

His left hand reaches out,
flicks on the Sony transistor
we bought for his birthday   30
when I was fifteen.
The right ferries in the earphone,
a small, flesh-colored star,
like a tiny miracle of hearing,
and fits it into place.   35
I see him plot black constellations
of figures and calculations
on the magazine's margins,

alternately squint and frown
as he fingers the knob of the tuner
searching for the one band
that will call out today's results.

There are whole cosmologies
in a single handicap,
a lifetime of two-dollar losing
in one pick of the Daily Double.
Maybe tonight is his night
for winning, his night
for beating the odds
of going deaf from a shell
at Anzio still echoing
in the cave of his inner ear,
his night for cashing in
the blue chips of shrapnel still grinding
at the thickening joints of his legs.

But no one calls
the horse's name, no one

says Shackles, Rebate, or Pouring Rain.
No one speaks a word.

40

45

50

55

60

Who Among You Knows the Essence of Garlic?   1982

Can your foreigner's nose smell mullets
roasting in a glaze of brown bean paste
and sprinkled with novas of sea salt?

Can you hear my grandmother
chant the mushroom's sutra?°   in Buddhism, a spiritual narrative   5

Can you hear the papayas crying
as they bleed in porcelain plates?

I'm telling you that the bamboo
slips the long pliant shoots
of its myriad soft tongues
into your mouth that is full of oranges.   10

I'm saying that the silver waterfalls
of bean threads will burst in hot oil
and stain your lips like zinc.

The marbled skin of the blue mackerel
works good for men. The purple oils   15
from its flesh perfume the tongues of women.

If you swallow them whole, the rice cakes
soaking in a broth of coconut milk and brown sugar
will never leave the bottom of your stomach.   20

Flukes of giant black mushrooms
leap from their murky tubs
and strangle the toes of young carrots.

Broiling chickens ooze grease,   25
yellow tears of fat collect
and spatter in the smoking pot.

Soft ripe pears, blushing
on the kitchen window sill,
kneel like plump women   30
taking a long luxurious shampoo,
and invite you to bite their hips.

Why not grab basketfuls of steaming noodles,
lush and slick as the hair of a fine lady,
and squeeze?   35

The shrimps, big as Portuguese thumbs,
stew among cut guavas, red onions,
ginger root, and rosemary in lemon juice,
the palm oil bubbling to the top,
breaking through layers and layers   40
of shredded coconut and sliced cashews.

Who among you knows the essence
of garlic and black lotus root,
of red and green peppers sizzling
among squads of oysters in the skillet,   45
of crushed ginger, fresh green onions,
and pale-blue rice wine simmering
in the stomach of a big red fish?

Gerard Manley Hopkins   1844–1889

Pied Beauty   *1877*

Glory be to God for dappled things—
    For skies of couple-color as a brinded cow;
        For rose-moles all in stipple upon trout that swim;
Fresh firecoal chestnut-falls; finches' wings;
    Landscape plotted and pieced—fold, fallow, and plow;   5
        And áll trádes, their gear and tackle and trim.
All things counter, original, spare, strange;
    Whatever is fickle, freckled (who knows how?)
        With swift, slow; sweet, sour; adazzle, dim;
He fathers-forth whose beauty is past change: 10
            Praise him.

A. E. Housman   1859–1936

To an Athlete Dying Young   *1896*

The time you won your town the race
We chaired you through the market-place;
Man and boy stood cheering by,
And home we brought you shoulder-high.

Today, the road all runners come,   5
Shoulder-high we bring you home,
And set you at your threshold down,
Townsman of a stiller town.

Smart lad, to slip betimes away
From fields where glory does not stay   10
And early though the laurel grows
It withers quicker than the rose.

Eyes the shady night has shut
Cannot see the record cut,
And silence sounds no worse than cheers   15
After earth has stopped the ears:

Now you will not swell the rout
Of lads that wore their honors out,
Runners whom renown outran
And the name died before the man.   20

So set, before its echoes fade,
The fleet foot on the sill of shade,
And hold to the low lintel° up   support beam on a door or window
The still-defended challenge-cup.

And round that early-laureled head   25
Will flock to gaze the strengthless dead,
And find unwithered on its curls
The garland briefer than a girl's.

Langston Hughes   1902–1967

Dream Deferred   *1951*

What happens to a dream deferred?
Does it dry up
Like a raisin in the sun?
Or fester like a sore—
And then run?   5
Does it stink like rotten meat?
Or crust and sugar over—
like a syrupy sweet?

Maybe it just sags
Like a heavy load.

Or does it explode?

10

The Negro Speaks of Rivers

1921

I've known rivers:
I've known rivers ancient as the world and older than the flow of
  human blood in human veins.

My soul has grown deep like the rivers.

I bathed in the Euphrates when dawns were young.
I built my hut near the Congo and it lulled me to sleep.
I looked upon the Nile and raised the pyramids above it.

5

I heard the singing of the Mississippi when Abe Lincoln
  went down to New Orleans, and I've seen its muddy
  bosom turn all golden in the sunset.

I've known rivers:
Ancient, dusky rivers.

10

My soul has grown deep like the rivers.

Theme for English B

1951

The instructor said,

> *Go home and write*
> *a page tonight.*
> *And let that page come out of you—*
> *Then, it will be true.*

5

I wonder if it's that simple?
I am twenty-two, colored, born in Winston-Salem.
I went to school there, then Durham, then here
to this college on the hill above Harlem.
I am the only colored student in my class.
The steps from the hill lead down into Harlem,
through a park, then I cross St. Nicholas,
Eighth Avenue, Seventh, and I come to the Y,
the Harlem Branch Y, where I take the elevator
up to my room, sit down, and write this page:

10

15

It's not easy to know what is true for you or me
at twenty-two, my age. But I guess I'm what
I feel and see and hear, Harlem, I hear you:
hear you, hear me—we two—you, me, talk on this page.
(I hear New York, too.) Me—who?

20

Well, I like to eat, sleep, drink, and be in love.
I like to work, read, learn and understand life.
I like a pipe for a Christmas present,
or records—Bessie,° bop, or Bach.   Smith (1894–1937), blues singer
I guess being colored doesn't make me *not* like   25
the same things other folks like who are other races.
So will my page be colored that I write?

Being me, it will not be white.
But it will be
a part of you, instructor.   30
You are white—
yet a part of me, as I am a part of you.
That's American.
Sometimes perhaps you don't want to be part of me.
Nor do I often want to be a part of you.   35
But we are, that's true!
As I learn from you,
I guess you learn from me—

although you're older—and white—
and somewhat more free.   40

This is my page for English B.

Ben Jonson   1573?–1637

On My First Daughter   *1616*

Here lies, to each her parents' ruth,
Mary, the daughter of their youth;
Yet all heaven's gifts being heaven's due,
It makes the father less to rue.
At six months' end she parted hence   5
With safety of her innocence;
Whose soul heaven's queen, whose name she bears,
In comfort of her mother's tears,
Hath placed amongst her virgin-train:
Where, while that severed doth remain,   10
This grave partakes the fleshly birth;
Which cover lightly, gentle earth!

On My First Son   *1603*

Farewell, thou child of my right hand,° and joy.   "Benjamin" in Hebrew means
My sin was too much hope of thee, loved boy;   "child of my right hand"
Seven years thou wert lent to me, and I thee pay,
Exacted by thy fate, on the just° day.
Oh, could I lose all father now. For why   exact, precise
Will man lament the state he should envy?—   5

To have so soon 'scaped world's and flesh's rage,
And, if no other misery, yet age.
Rest in soft peace, and asked, say, "Here doth lie
Ben Jonson his best piece of poetry,"
For whose sake henceforth all his vows be such   10
As what he loves may never like too much.

To Celia   *1616*

Drink to me only with thine eyes,
    And I will pledge with mine;
Or leave a kiss but in the cup,
    And I'll not ask for wine.
The thirst that from the soul doth rise
    Doth ask a drink divine;   5
But might I of Jove's nectar sup,
    I would not change for thine.
I sent thee late a rosy wreath,
    Not so much honoring thee
As giving it a hope that there   10
    It could not withered be.
But thou thereon didst only breathe,
    And sent'st it back to me;
Since when it grows, and smells, I swear,
    Not of itself but thee.   15

Donald Justice   b. 1925

On the Death of Friends in Childhood   *1960*

We shall not ever meet them bearded in heaven,
Nor sunning themselves among the bald of hell;
If anywhere, in the deserted schoolyard at twilight,
Forming a ring, perhaps, or joining hands
In games whose very names we have forgotten.
Come, memory, let us seek them there in the shadows.

John Keats   1795–1821

Ode to a Nightingale   *1819*

1

My heart aches, and a drowsy numbness pains
    My sense, as though of hemlock° I had drunk,   *a poisonous herb*
Or emptied some dull opiate to the drains

One minute past, and Lethe-wards° had sunk: underworld river of forgetfulness
Tis not through envy of thy happy lot, 5
   But being too happy in thine happiness,—
      That thou, light-winged Dryad° of the trees, wood nymph
         In some melodious plot
Of beechen green, and shadows numberless,
      Singest of summer in full-throated ease. 10

2

O, for a draught of vintage! that hath been
   Cool'd a long age in the deep-delved earth,
Tasting of Flora° and the country green, Roman goddess of flowers
   Dance, and Provençal° song, and sunburnt mirth! region in the South of France
O for a beaker full of the warm South, 15
   Full of the true, the blushful Hippocrene,° mythical fountain of the muses; poetic inspirations
      With beaded bubbles winking at the brim,
         And purple-stained mouth;
That I might drink, and leave the world unseen,
      And with thee fade away into the forest dim: 20

3

Fade far away, dissolve, and quite forget
   What thou among the leaves hast never known,
The weariness, the fever, and the fret
   Here, where men sit and hear each other groan;
Where palsy shakes a few, sad, last gray hairs, 25
   Where youth grows pale, and spectre-thin, and dies;
      Where but to think is to be full of sorrow
         And leaden-eyed despairs,
Where Beauty cannot keep her lustrous eyes,
      Or new Love pine at them beyond to-morrow. 30

4

Away! away! for I will fly to thee,
   Not charioted by Bacchus° and his pards, Roman god of wine, whose chariot
But on the viewless wings of Poesy, was pulled by leopards
   Though the dull brain perplexes and regards:
Already with thee! tender is the night, 35
   And haply° the Queen-Moon is on her throne, perchance
      Cluster'd around by all her starry Fays;° fairies
         But here there is no light,
Save what from heaven is with the breezes blown
   Through verdurous glooms and winding mossy ways. 40

5

I cannot see what flowers are at my feet,
   Nor what soft incense hangs upon the boughs,
But, in embalmed° darkness, guess each sweet perfumed
   Wherewith the seasonable month endows
The grass, the thicket, and the fruit-tree wild; 45
   White hawthorn, and the pastoral eglantine;° honeysuckle
      Fast fading violets cover'd up in leaves;
         And mid-May's eldest child,

The coming musk-rose, full of dewy wine,
   The murmurous haunt of flies on summer eves.   50

6

Darkling° I listen; and, for many a time   *in the dark*
   I have been half in love with easeful Death,
Call'd him soft names in many a mused° rhyme,   *contemplated*
   To take into the air my quiet breath;
Now more than ever seems it rich to die,   55
   To cease upon the midnight with no pain,
     While thou art pouring forth thy soul abroad
      In such an ecstasy!
Still wouldst thou sing, and I have ears in vain—
   To thy high requiem become a sod.   60

7

Thou wast not born for death, immortal Bird!
   No hungry generations tread thee down;
The voice I hear this passing night was heard
   In ancient days by emperor and clown:
Perhaps the self-same song that found a path   65
   Through the sad heart of Ruth,° when, sick for home,   *young widow in the biblical*
     She stood in tears amid the alien corn;   *book of Ruth who left her*
      The same that oft-times hath   *homeland to live with her mother-in-law*
Charm'd magic casements, opening on the foam
   Of perilous seas, in faery lands forlorn.   70

8

Forlorn! the very word is like a bell
   To toll me back from thee to my sole self!
Adieu! the fancy° cannot cheat so well   *imagination*
   As she is fam'd to do, deceiving elf.
Adieu! adieu! thy plaintive anthem fades   75
   Past the near meadows, over the still stream,
     Up the hill-side; and now 'tis buried deep
      In the next valley-glades:
Was it a vision, or a waking dream?
   Fled is that music:—Do I wake or sleep?   80

On First Looking into Chapman's Homer   *1816*

Much have I traveled in the realms of gold,
   And many goodly states and kingdoms seen;
   Round many western islands have I been
Which bards in fealty to Apollo° hold.   *Greek god of poetry*
Oft of one wide expanse had I been told
   That deep-browed Homer ruled as his demesne;   5
   Yet did I never breathe its pure serene
Till I heard Chapman° speak out loud and bold: *George Chapman (1558?–1634), poet who had*
Then felt I like some watcher of the skies   *published an English translation of The Iliad*
   When a new planet swims into his ken;   *and The Odyssey of Homer*

                                               10

Or like stout Cortez when with eagle eyes
    He stared at the Pacific—and all his men
Looked at each other with a wild surmise—
    Silent, upon a peak in Darien.°

                                        in Panama, where the Spanish explorer Balboa,
                                        not Cortez, first saw the Pacific Ocean

To Autumn   *1819*

Season of mists and mellow fruitfulness,
    Close bosom-friend of the maturing sun;
Conspiring with him how to load and bless
    With fruit the vines that round the thatch-eaves run;
To bend with apples the mossed cottage-trees,   5
    And fill all fruit with ripeness to the core;
        To swell the gourd, and plump the hazel shells
With a sweet kernel; to set budding more,
    And still more, later flowers for the bees,
    Until they think warm days will never cease,   10
        For summer has o'er-brimmed their clammy cells.

Who hath not seen thee oft amid thy store?
    Sometimes whoever seeks abroad may find
Thee sitting careless on a granary floor,
    Thy hair soft-lifted by the winnowing wind;   15
Or on a half-reaped furrow half asleep,
    Drowsed with the fume of poppies, while thy hook
        Spares the next swath and all its twinèd flowers:
And sometimes like a gleaner thou dost keep
    Steady thy laden head across a brook;   20
    Or by a cider-press with patient look
        Thou watchest the last oozings hours by hours.

Where are the songs of Spring? Aye, where are they?
    Think not of them, thou hast thy music too—
While barrèd clouds bloom the soft-dying day,   25
    And touch the stubble-plains with rosy hue;
Then in a wailful choir the small gnats mourn
    Among the river sallows, borne aloft
        Or sinking as the light wind lives or dies;
And full-grown lambs loud bleat from hilly bourn;   30
    Hedge crickets sing; and now with treble soft
    The redbreast whistles from a garden-croft;
        And gathering swallows twitter in the skies.

When I Have Fears   *1818*

When I have fears that I may cease to be
    Before my pen has gleaned my teeming brain,
Before high-pilèd books, in charact'ry,°   *written characters, letters*
    Hold like rich garners the full-ripened grain;

When I behold, upon the night's starred face,
    Huge cloudy symbols of a high romance,
And think that I may never live to trace
    Their shadows, with the magic hand of chance;
And when I feel, fair creature of an hour,
    That I shall never look upon thee more,
Never have relish in the faery power
    Of unreflecting love!—then on the shore
Of the wide world I stand alone, and think
Till Love and Fame to nothingness do sink.

          5

          10

Etheridge Knight   1931–1991

The Idea of Ancestry   *1968*

I

Taped to the wall of my cell are 47 pictures: 47 black
faces: my father, mother, grandmothers (1 dead), grand
fathers (both dead), brothers, sisters, uncles, aunts,
cousins (1st & 2nd), nieces, and nephews. They stare
across the space at my sprawling on my bunk. I know
their dark eyes, they know mine. I know their style,
they know mine. I am all of them, they are all of me;
they are farmers, I am a thief, I am me, they are thee.

I have at one time or another been in love with my mother,
1 grandmother, 2 sisters, 2 aunts (1 went to the asylum),
and 5 cousins. I am now in love with a 7 yr old niece
(she sends me letters written in large block print, and
her picture is the only one that smiles at me).

I have the same name as 1 grandfather, 3 cousins, 3 nephews,
and 1 uncle. The uncle disappeared when he was 15, just took
off and caught a freight (they say). He's discussed each year
when the family has a reunion, he causes uneasiness in
the clan, he is an empty space. My father's mother, who is 93
and who keeps the Family Bible with everybody's birth dates
(and death dates) in it, always mentions him. There is no
place in her Bible for "whereabouts unknown."

     5

     10

     15

     20

II

Each Fall the graves of my grandfathers call me, the brown
hills and red gullies of mississippi send out their electric
messages, galvanizing my genes. Last yr/like a salmon quitting
the cold ocean—leaping and bucking up his birthstream/I
hitchhiked my way from L.A. with 16 caps° in my pocket and a
monkey on my back, and I almost kicked it with the kinfolks.
I walked barefooted in my grandmother's backyard/I smelled the old
land and the woods/I sipped cornwhiskey from fruit jars with the men/
I flirted with the women/I had a ball till the caps ran out

     25

doses of heroin

     30

and my habit came down. That night I looked at my grandmother
and split/my guts were screaming for junk/but I was almost
contented/I had almost caught up with me.
The next day in Memphis I cracked a croaker's crib°/for a fix.   doctor's house

This yr there is a gray stone wall damming my stream, and when   35
the falling leaves stir my genes, I pace my cell or flop on my bunk
and stare at 47 black faces across the space. I am all of them,
they are all of me, I am me, they are thee, and I have no sons
to float in the space between.

Joan Larkin   b. 1939

Notations—The F Train   1975

Kool I
Bruce
Head 155
Steam One
Chino   5
Gonzo 22

What is scrawled on the subway walls
is a certain notion of strength.

                there is also the strength of water
                that flows (around the rock)   10
                that flows (over the stone)
                that carries with itself
                leaf and leaf and leaf
                the letters of green lives

The station at West 4th Street   15
smells of smoke; I notice it tonight.

It is 2 o'clock.

There are two women with dyed, worried faces
and hard hair, the color of dolls' wigs
standing together in coats that mimic fur.   20

They are the only other women
in this night station of men—
men lounging and watching, chewing gum,
reading their Sunday paper,
some with thumbs in their trousers,   25
with keys, with umbrellas
striding the platform.
One man stands by a post and vomits
and vomits and vomits.

No one seems to be taking   30
notice of anyone,

except a few whose eyes
let me see that I am alone here.
At this hour, women do not travel.

        water   35
        travels
        without stopping
        falls, both hitting the stone
        and flowing over the stone
        making the unstopped   40
        music of water
        its continuous going
        over the earth and through it
        wearing the rock
        the rock the rock   45
        softening
        everything on earth that is hard
        a certain notion of strength

I may not let my eyes meet
their eyes, on the train to Brooklyn
That is a sort of invitation.   50

There is a joke the cops in my neighborhood
shared with certain women
during the most recent rape scare.
It was that the victims
had found the rapist desirable   55
and had asked for it anyway
by being out on the street at night.

Where were you going anyway?
they asked my sister,
who was—and this is a fact—   60
on her way to a meeting about the survival of earth,
but who, between 9 and 11,
was walked to the park at gunpoint,
raped,
then told to turn her back at the fence   65
where she clung, waiting
maybe to be murdered,
while the man who had just raped her
ran
into the darkness.   70

        water
        runs
        it is a certain notion of strength
        a woman has revealed in a film
        which she made by allowing the time   75
        to look at water
        moving
        to listen to the sound of water
        hour after hour after hour
                                                    80

keeping her eyes on the water
and holding it with her camera

They were asking my sister
the tour guide
Where can I find a woman?
My home, so far away.   85
I have need for a woman.
What are you doing tonight?
I have need, have need, have need.
Where can I find a woman?   90

On the subway wall, I see the sentence
I doin' it to death!
In a red-yellow rainbow of spray-paint

I,
I,
I,   95

doin' it,
doin' it,
doin' it,

to death,   100
to death,
to death.

I am waiting for the F train.
My wombs throbs
when the train thunders   105
The smoke-stench fills my nostrils.
I am on my way home from the city
late at night, in a station
where there is probably nothing
to be afraid of.   110

there is a notion of strength
that is without impact

energy that is still like water
energy that keeps going like water
energy that is sustained motion like water   115

turbulences and falls
flats deep

and slow dark passages

go down to the water and look

go down to the water and look   120

go down to the water and look

go down to the water and look

go down to the water and look

Philip Larkin   1922–1985

Church Going   1955

Once I am sure there's nothing going on
I step inside, letting the door thud shut.
Another church: matting, seats, and stone,
And little books; sprawlings of flowers, cut
For Sunday, brownish now; some brass and stuff   5
Up at the holy end; the small neat organ;
And a tense, musty, unignorable silence,
Brewed God knows how long. Hatless, I take off
My cycle-clips in awkward reverence,

Move forward, run my hand around the font.   10
From where I stand, the roof looks almost new—
Cleaned, or restored? Someone would know: I don't.
Mounting the lectern, I peruse a few
Hectoring large-scale verses, and pronounce
"Here endeth" much more loudly than I'd meant.
The echoes snigger briefly. Back at the door   15
I sign the book, donate an Irish sixpence,
Reflect the place was not worth stopping for.

Yet stop I did: in fact I often do,
And always end much at a loss like this,
Wondering what to look for, wondering, too,   20
When churches fall completely out of use
What we shall turn them into, if we shall keep
A few cathedrals chronically on show,
Their parchment, plate and pyx° in locked cases,   *box for keeping communion wafers*   25
And let the rest rent-free to rain and sheep.
Shall we avoid them as unlucky places?

Or, after dark, will dubious women come
To make their children touch a particular stone;
Pick simples° for a cancer; or on some   *medicinal herbs*   30
Advised night see walking a dead one?
Power of some sort or other will go on
In games, in riddles, seemingly at random;
But superstition, like belief, must die,
And what remains when disbelief has gone?
Grass, weedy pavement, brambles, buttress, sky,   35

A shape less recognizable each week,
A purpose more obscure. I wonder who
Will be the last, the very last, to seek
This place for what it was; one of the crew
That tap and jot and know what rood-lofts were?   40
Some ruin-bibber, randy for antique,
Or Christmas-addict, counting on a whiff

Of gown-and-bands and organ-pipes and myrrh?
Or will he be my representative,   45

Bored, uninformed, knowing the ghostly silt
Dispersed, yet tending to this cross of ground
Through suburb scrub because it held unspilt
So long and equably what since is found
Only in separation—marriage, and birth,   50
And death, and thoughts of these—for whom was built
This special shell? For though I've no idea
What this accoutered frowsty barn is worth,
It pleases me to stand in silence here;

A serious house on serious earth it is,   55
In whose blent air all our compulsions meet,
Are recognized, and robed as destinies.
And that much never can be obsolete,
Since someone will forever be surprising
A hunger in himself to be more serious,   60
And gravitating with it to this ground,
Which, he once heard, was proper to grow wise in,
If only that so many dead lie round.

D. H. Lawrence   1885–1930

Piano   1918

Softly, in the dusk, a woman is singing to me;
Taking me back down the vista of years, till I see
A child sitting under the piano, in the boom of the tingling strings
And pressing the small, poised feet of a mother who smiles as she sings.

In spite of myself, the insidious mastery of song   5
Betrays me back, till the heart of me weeps to belong
To the old Sunday evenings at home, with winter outside
And hymns in the cozy parlor, the tinkling piano our guide.

So now it is vain for the singer to burst into clamor
With the great black piano appassionato. The glamor   10
Of childish days is upon me, my manhood is cast
Down in the flood of remembrance, I weep like a child for the past.

Snake   1923

A snake came to my water-trough
On a hot, hot day, and I in pajamas for the heat,
To drink there.

In the deep, strange-scented shade of the great dark carob-tree
I came down the steps with my pitcher
And must wait, must stand and wait, for there he was at the trough before me.   5

He reached down from a fissure in the earth-wall in the gloom
And trailed his yellow-brown slackness soft-bellied down, over the edge of the
    stone trough
And rested his throat upon the stone bottom,
And where the water had dripped from the tap, in a small clearness,
He sipped with his straight mouth,   10
Softly drank through his straight gums, into his slack long body,
Silently.

Someone was before me at my water-trough.
And I, like a second comer, waiting.

He lifted his head from his drinking, as cattle do,   15
And looked at me vaguely, as drinking cattle do,
And flickered his two-forked tongue from his lips, and mused a moment,
And stooped and drank a little more,
Being earth-brown, earth-golden from the burning bowels of the earth   20
On the day of Sicilian July, with Etna° smoking.   volcano in Sicily

The voice of my education said to me
He must be killed,
For in Sicily the black, black snakes are innocent, the gold are venomous.

And voices in me said, If you were a man   25
You would take a stick and break him now, and finish him off.

But must I confess how I liked him,
How glad I was he had come like a guest in quiet, to drink at my water-trough
And depart peaceful, pacified, and thankless,
Into the burning bowels of this earth?   30

Was it cowardice, that I dared not kill him?
Was it perversity, that I longed to talk to him?
Was it humility, to feel so honored?
I felt so honored.

And yet those voices: 35
If you were not afraid, you would kill him!

And truly I was afraid, I was most afraid,
But even so, honored still more
That he should seek my hospitality
From out the dark door of the secret earth.   40

He drank enough
And lifted his head, dreamily, as one who has drunken,
And flickered his tongue like a forked night on the air, so black,
Seeming to lick his lips,
And looked around like a god, unseeing, into the air,   45
And slowly turned his head,
And slowly, very slowly, as if thrice adream,
Proceeded to draw his slow length curving round
And climb again the broken bank of my wall-face.

And as he put his head into that dreadful hole,   50
And as he slowly drew up, snake-easing his shoulders, and entered farther,

A sort of horror, a sort of protest against his withdrawing into that horrid black
   hole,
Deliberately going into the blackness, and slowly drawing himself after,
Overcame me now his back was turned.

I looked round, I put down my pitcher,   55
I picked up a clumsy log
And threw it at the water-trough with a clatter.

I think it did not hit him,
But suddenly that part of him that was left behind convulsed in undignified haste,
Writhed like lightning, and was gone   60
Into the black hole, the earth-lipped fissure in the wall-front,
At which, in the intense still noon, I stared with fascination.

And immediately I regretted it.
I thought how paltry, how vulgar, what a mean act!
I despised myself and the voices of my accursed human education.   65
And I thought of the albatross,
And I wished he would come back, my snake.

For he seemed to me again like a king,
Like a king in exile, uncrowned in the underworld,
Now due to be crowned again.   70

And so, I missed my chance with one of the lords
Of life.
And I have something to expiate:
A pettiness.

Li-Young Lee   b. 1957

The Gift   1986

To pull the metal splinter from my palm
my father recited a story in a low voice.
I watched his lovely face and not the blade.
Before the story ended he'd removed
the iron sliver I thought I'd die from.   5

I can't remember the tale
but hear his voice still, a well
of dark water, a prayer.
And I recall his hands,
two measures of tenderness
he laid against my face,   10
the flames of discipline
he raised above my head.

Had you entered that afternoon
you would have thought you saw a man
planting something in a boy's palm,   15

a silver tear, a tiny flame.
Had you followed that boy
you would have arrived here,
where I bend over my wife's right hand.   20

Look how I shave her thumbnail down
so carefully she feels no pain.
Watch as I lift the splinter out.
I was seven when my father
took my hand like this,   25
and I did not hold that shard
between my fingers and think,
Metal that will bury me,
christen it Little Assassin,
Ore Going Deep for My Heart.   30
And I did not lift up my wound and cry,
Death visited here!
I did what a child does
when he's given something to keep.
I kissed my father.   35

Persimmons   *1986*

In sixth grade Mrs. Walker
slapped the back of my head
and made me stand in the corner
for not knowing the difference
between *persimmon* and *precision*.   5
How to choose

persimmons. This is precision.
Ripe ones are soft and brown-spotted.
Sniff the bottoms. The sweet one
will be fragrant. How to eat: 10
put the knife away, lay down newspaper.
Peel the skin tenderly, not to tear the meat.
Chew the skin, suck it,
and swallow. Now, eat

the meat of the fruit,   15
so sweet,
all of it, to the heart.

Donna undresses, her stomach is white.
In the yard, dewy and shivering
with crickets, we lie naked,   20
face-up, face-down.
I teach her Chinese.
Crickets: *chiu chiu.* Dew: I've forgotten.
Naked: I've forgotten.
Ni, wo: you and me.   25

I part her legs,
remember to tell her
she is beautiful as the moon.

Other words
that got me into trouble were
fight and *fright*, *wren* and *yarn*.   30
Fight was what I did when I was frightened,
fright was what I felt when I was fighting.
Wrens are small, plain birds,
yarn is what one knits with.   35
Wrens are soft as yarn.
My mother made birds out of yarn.
I loved to watch her tie the stuff;
a bird, a rabbit, a wee man.

Mrs. Walker brought a persimmon to class   40
and cut it up
so everyone could taste
a *Chinese apple*. Knowing
it wasn't ripe or sweet, I didn't eat
but watched the other faces.

                                                                            45

My mother said every persimmon has a sun
inside, something golden, glowing,
warm as my face.

Once, in the cellar, I found two wrapped in newspaper,
forgotten and not yet ripe.   50
I took them and set both on my bedroom windowsill,
where each morning a cardinal
sang, *The sun, the sun.*

Finally understanding
he was going blind,   55
my father sat up all one night
waiting for a song, a ghost.
I gave him the persimmons,
swelled, heavy as sadness,
and sweet as love.   60

This year, in the muddy lighting
of my parents' cellar, I rummage, looking
for something I lost.
My father sits on the tired, wooden stairs,
black cane between his knees,   65
hand over hand, gripping the handle.

He's so happy that I've come home.
I ask how his eyes are, a stupid question.
All gone, he answers.

Under some blankets, I find a box.   70
Inside the box I find three scrolls.
I sit beside him and untie

three paintings by my father:
Hibiscus leaf and a white flower.
Two cats preening.
Two persimmons, so full they want to drop from the cloth. 75

He raises both hands to touch the cloth,
asks, *Which is this?*

This is persimmons, Father.

Oh, the feel of the wolftail on the silk,
the strength, the tense 80
precision in the wrist.
I painted them hundreds of times
eyes closed. These I painted blind.
Some things never leave a person:
scent of the hair of one you love, 85
the texture of persimmons,
in your palm, the ripe weight.

Denise Levertov   b. 1923

A Woman Alone   *1978*

When she cannot be sure
which of two lovers it was with whom she felt
this or that moment of pleasure, of something fiery
streaking from head to heels, the way the white
flame of a cascade streaks a mountainside 5
seen from a car across a valley, the car
changing gear, skirting a precipice,
climbing . . .
When she can sit or walk for hours after a movie
talking earnestly and with bursts of laughter 10
with friends, without worrying
that it's late, dinner at midnight, her time
spent without counting the change . . .
When half her bed is covered with books
and no one is kept awake by the reading light 15
and she disconnects the phone, to sleep till noon . . .
Then
selfpity dries up, a joy
untainted by guilt lifts her.
She has fears, but not about loneliness;
fears about how to deal with the aging 20
of her body—how to deal
with photographs and the mirror. She feels
so much younger and more beautiful
than she looks. At her happiest
—or even in the midst of 25
some less than joyful hour, sweating

patiently through a heatwave in the city
or hearing the sparrows at daybreak, dully gray,
toneless, the sound of fatigue—
a kind of sober euphoria makes her believe   30
in her future as an old woman, a wanderer,
seamed and brown,
little luxuries of the middle of life all gone,
watching cities and rivers, people and mountains,   35
without being watched; not grim nor sad,
an old winedrinking woman, who knows
the old roads, grass-grown, and laughs to herself ...
She knows it can't be:
that's Mrs. Doasyouwouldbedoneby from   40
                               The Water-Babies.

no one can walk the world any more,
a world of fumes and decibels.
But she thinks maybe
she could get to be tough and wise, some way,
anyway. Now at least   45
she is past the time of mourning,
now she can say without shame or deceit,
O blessed Solitude.

Stephen Shu-Ning Liu   b. 1930

My Father's Martial Art   1982

When he came home Mother said he looked
like a monk and stank of green fungus.
At the fireside he told us about life
at the monastery: his rock pillow,
his cold bath, his steel-bar lifting   5
and his wood-chopping. He didn't see
a woman for three winters, on Mountain O Mei.

"My Master was both light and heavy.
He skipped over treetops like a squirrel.
Once he stood on a chair, one foot tied
to a rope. We four pulled; we couldn't   10
move him a bit. His kicks could split
a cedar's trunk."

I saw Father break into a pumpkin
with his fingers. I saw him drop a hawk
with bamboo arrows. He rose before dawn, filled   15
our backyard with a harsh sound *hah, hah, hah:*
there was his Black Dragon Sweep, his Crane Stand,
his Mantis Walk, his Tiger Leap, his Cobra Coil ...
Infrequently he taught me tricks and made me
fight the best of all the village boys.   20

From a busy street I brood over high cliffs
on O Mei, where my father and his Master sit:
shadows spread across their faces as the smog
between us deepens into a funeral pyre.   25
But don't retreat into night, my father.
Come down from the cliffs. Come
with a single Black Dragon Sweep and hush
this oncoming traffic with your *hah, hah, hah*.

Audre Lorde   1934–1992

The Art of Response   1986

The first answer was incorrect
the second was
sorry   the third trimmed its toenails
on the Vatican steps
the fourth went mad
the fifth   5
nursed a grudge until it bore twins
that drank poisoned grape juice in Jonestown
the sixth   wrote a book about it
the seventh   10
argued a case before the Supreme Court
against taxation on Girl Scout Cookies
the eighth held a news conference
while four Black babies
and one other   picketed New York City   15
for a hospital bed to die in
the ninth and tenth swore
Revenge on the Opposition
and the eleventh dug their graves
next to Eternal Truth   20
the twelfth
processed funds from a Third World country
that provides doctors for Central Harlem
the thirteenth
refused   25
the fourteenth sold cocaine and shamrocks
near a toilet in the Big Apple circus
the fifteenth
changed the question.

To My Daughter the Junkie on a Train   1972

Children we have not borne
bedevil us by becoming
themselves

painfully sharp   unavoidable
like a needle in our flesh.

Coming home on the subway from a PTA meeting
of minds committed to murder   or suicide
in their own private struggle
a long-legged girl with a horse in her brain
slumps down beside me
begging to be ridden asleep
for the price of a midnight train
free from desire.

Little girl   on the nod
if we are measured by dreams we avoid
then you are the nightmare
of all sleeping mothers
rocking back and forth
the dead weight of your arms
locked about our necks
heavier than our habit
of looking for reasons.

My corrupt concern will not replace
what you once needed
but I am locked into my own addiction
and offer you my help   one eye
out for my own station.

Roused and deprived
your costly dream explodes
in terrible technicolored laughter
at my failure
up and down   across the aisle
women avert their eyes
as other mothers who became useless
curse our children   who became junk.

Robert Lowell   1917–1977

Skunk Hour   *1959*

(*for Elizabeth Bishop*)

Nautilus Island's° hermit   *in Maine*
heiress still lives through winter in her Spartan cottage;
her sheep still graze above the sea.
Her son's a bishop. Her farmer
is first selectman° in our village;   *elected official*   5
she's in her dotage.

Thirsting for
the hierarchic privacy
of Queen Victoria's century,

she buys up all
the eyesores facing her shore,
and lets them fall.

The season's ill—
we've lost our summer millionaire,
who seemed to leap from an L. L. Bean
catalogue. His nine-knot yawl°   boat
was auctioned off to lobstermen.
A red fox stain covers Blue Hill.

And now our fairy
decorator brightens his shop for fall;
his fishnet's filled with orange cork,
orange, his cobbler's bench and awl;
there is no money in his work,
he'd rather marry.

One dark night,
my Tudor Ford climbed the hill's skull;
I watched for love-cars. Lights turned down,
they lay together, hull to hull,
where the graveyard shelves on the town....
My mind's not right.

A car radio bleats,
"Love, O careless Love...." I hear
my ill-spirit sob in each blood cell,
as if my hand were at its throat....
I myself am hell;
nobody's here—

only skunks, that search
in the moonlight for a bite to eat.
They march on their soles up Main Street:
white stripes, moonstruck eyes' red fire
under the chalk-dry and spar spire
of the Trinitarian Church.

I stand on top
of our back steps and breathe the rich air—
a mother skunk with her column of kittens swills the garbage pail.
She jabs her wedge-head in a cup
of sour cream, drops her ostrich tail,
and will not scare.

Wing Tek Lum   b. 1946

It's Something Our Family Has Always Done   1987

On every trip away from these islands
on the day of departure and on the day of return
we go to the graves, all seven of them,

but for one the sum total of all of our ancestors
who died in this place we call home.   5

The drive to the cemetery is only five minutes long.
Stopping by a florist adds maybe ten minutes more.
Yet my wife and I on the day of our flight
are so rushed with packing and last minute chores.
Why do we still make the time to go?   10

The concrete road is one lane wide.
We turn around at the circle up at the top,
always to park just to the side of the large banyan tree
as the road begins its slope back down.
I turn the wheels; we now lock our car.   15

As if by rote, we bring anthuriums,
at least two flowers for each of our dead.
On our way we stop to pay our respects to the "Old Man"
—that first one lain here, all wind and water before him—
who watches over this graveyard, and our island home.   20

Approaching my grandparents, we divide up our offering,
placing their long stems into the holes filled with sand.
Squatting in front of each marble tablet,
I make it a point to read off their names in Chinese.
My hands pull out crabgrass running over stone.   25

I stand erect, clutching palm around fist,
swinging the air three times up and down.
My wife from the waist bows once, arms at her sides.
I manage to whisper a few phrases out loud,
conversing like my father would, as if all could hear.   30

We do Grandfather, Grandmother, and my parents below them.
Following the same path we always take,
we make our way through the tombstones and mounds,
skirting their concrete borders, to the other two Lums
and to our Granduncle on the Chang side.   35

Back up the hill, we spend a few moments by the curb
picking off black, thin burrs from our cuffs and socks.
We talk about what errands we must do next.
I glance around us at these man-made gardens,
thrust upon a slope of earth, spirit houses rising to the sky.   40

As I get into our car, and look out at the sea,
I am struck with the same thought as always.
We spend so little time in front of these graves
asking each in turn to protect us when we are far away.
I question them all: what good does it really do?   45

I have read ancient poets who parted with sorrow
from family and friends, fearing never to return.
Our oral histories celebrate brave peasants
daring oceans and the lonely beds: they looked even more
to blessings at long distance from their spirit dead.   50

My father superstitious, even to the jet age,
still averred: but every little bit helps.
These sentiments I know, but I confess I do not feel.
Maybe it's for this loss that I still come here.
They are family, and I respect them so.   55

Archibald MacLeish   1892–1982

Ars Poetica   1926

A poem should be palpable and mute
As a globed fruit,

Dumb
As old medallions to the thumb,

Silent as the sleeve-worn stone   5
Of casement ledges where the moss has grown—

A poem should be wordless
As the flight of birds.

A poem should be motionless in time
As the moon climbs,   10

Leaving, as the moon releases
Twig by twig the night-entangled trees,

Leaving, as the moon behind the winter leaves,
Memory by memory the mind—

A poem should be motionless in time   15
As the moon climbs.

A poem should be equal to:
Not true.

For all the history of grief
An empty doorway and a maple leaf.   20

For love
The leaning grasses and two lights above the sea—

A poem should not mean
But be.

Claude McKay   1889–1948

The Harlem Dancer   1917

Applauding youths laughed with young prostitutes
And watched her perfect, half-clothed body sway;
Her voice was like the sound of blended flutes
Blown by black players upon a picnic day.

She sang and danced on gracefully and calm,
The light gauze hanging loose about her form;
To me she seemed a proudly-swaying palm
Grown lovelier for passing through a storm.
Upon her swarthy neck black shiny curls
Luxuriant fell; and tossing coins in praise,
The wine-flushed, bold-eyed boys, and even the girls,
Devoured her shape with eager, passionate gaze;
But looking at her falsely-smiling face,
I knew her self was not in that strange place.

Nazik Al-Mala'ika   b. 1923

I Am   *1949*

Translated by Kamal Boullata

The night asks me who I am
    Its impenetrable black, its unquiet secret
                    I am
    Its lull rebellious.
    I veil myself with silence
    Wrapping my heart with doubt
    Solemnly, I gaze
    While ages ask me
        who I am.

The wind asks me who I am
    Its bedevilled spirit I am
    Denied by Time, going nowhere
    I journey on and on
    Passing without a pause
    And when reaching an edge
    I think it may be the end
    Of suffering, but then:
        the void.

Time asks me who I am
    A giant enfolding centuries I am
    Later to give new births
    I have created the dim past
    From the bliss of unbound hope
    I push it back into its grave
    To make a new yesterday, its tomorrow
    is ice.

The self asks me who I am
    Baffled, I stare into the dark
    Nothing brings me peace
    I ask, but the answer

Remains hooded in mirage
I keep thinking it is near
Upon reaching it, it dissolves.

Christopher Marlowe   1564–1593

The Passionate Shepherd to His Love   *1600*

Come live with me and be my love,
And we will all the pleasures prove°   try
That valleys, groves, hills, and fields,
Woods, or steepy mountain yields.

And we will sit upon the rocks,   5
Seeing the shepherds feed their flocks,
By shallow rivers to whose falls
Melodious birds sing madrigals.°   harmonic songs

And I will make thee beds of roses
And a thousand fragrant posies,
A cap of flowers, and a kirtle°   10
Embroidered all with leaves of myrtle;   skirt

A gown made of the finest wool
Which from our pretty lambs we pull;
Fair lined slippers for the cold,
With buckles of the purest gold;   15

A belt of straw and ivy buds,
With coral clasps and amber studs:
And if these pleasures may thee move,
Come live with me, and be my love.

The shepherds' swains° shall dance and sing   20
For thy delight each May morning: helpers
If these delights thy mind may move,
Then live with me and be my love.

Andrew Marvell   1621–1678

To His Coy Mistress   *c. 1678*

Had we but world enough, and time,
This coyness, lady, were° no crime.   would be
We would sit down and think which way
To walk and pass our long love's day.
Thou by the Indian Ganges'° side   river in India   5
Shouldst rubies find; I by the tide
Of Humber° would complain.° I would   river in England; write plaintive love songs
Love you ten years before the flood,

And you should, if you please, refuse
Till the conversion of the Jews.
My vegetable love should grow   10
Vaster than empires and more slow;
An hundred years should go to praise
Thine eyes and on thy forehead gaze,
Two hundred to adore each breast,   15
But thirty thousand to the rest,
An age at least to every part,
And the last age should show your heart.
For, lady, you deserve this state,°   high station
Nor would I love at lower rate.   20
      But at my back I always hear
Time's wingèd chariot hurrying near,
And yonder all before us lie
Deserts of vast eternity.
Thy beauty shall no more be found,   25
Nor, in thy marble vault, shall sound
My echoing song; then worms shall try
That long-preserved virginity,
And your quaint honor° turn to dust,   deliberate virtue
And into ashes all my lust.   30
The grave's a fine and private place,
But none, I think, do there embrace.
      Now therefore, while the youthful hue
Sits on thy skin like morning dew,
And while thy willing soul transpires°   breathes forth   35
At every pore with instant fires,
Now let us sport us while we may,
And now, like amorous birds of prey,
Rather at once our time devour
Than languish in his slow-chapped° power.   slowly chewing   40
Let us roll all our strength and all
Our sweetness up into one ball,
And tear our pleasures with rough strife
Thorough° the iron gates of life.   through
Thus, though we cannot make our sun   45
Stand still, yet we will make him run.

Edna St. Vincent Millay   1892–1950

Elegy before Death   *1921*

There will be rose and rhododendron
      When you are dead and under ground;
Still will be heard from white syringas
      Heavy with bees, a sunny sound;

Still will the tamaracks be raining   5
      After the rain has ceased, and still

Will there be robins in the stubble,
    Grey sheep upon the warm green hill.

Spring will not ail nor autumn falter;
    Nothing will know that you are gone,—   10
Saving alone some sullen plough-land
    None but yourself sets foot upon;

Saving the may-weed and the pig-weed
    Nothing will know that you are dead,—
These, and perhaps a useless wagon   15
    Standing beside some tumbled shed.

Oh, there will pass with your great passing
    Little of beauty not your own,—
Only the light from common water,
    Only the grace from simple stone!   20

I, being born a woman and distressed   1923

I, being born a woman and distressed
By all the needs and notions of my kind,
Am urged by your propinquity° to find   nearness
Your person fair, and feel a certain zest
To bear your body's weight upon my breast: 5
So subtly is the fume of life designed
To clarify the pulse and cloud the mind,
And leave me once again undone, possessed.
Think not for this, however, the poor treason
Of my stout blood against my staggering brain,   10
I shall remember you with love, or season
My scorn with pity,—let me make it plain:
I find this frenzy insufficient reason
For conversation when we meet again.

John Milton   1608–1674

When I consider how my light is spent   1655

When I consider how my light is spent
Ere half my days, in this dark world and wide,
And that one talent which is death to hide
Lodged with me useless, though my soul more bent
To serve therewith my Maker, and present   5
My true account, lest he returning chide;
"Doth God exact day-labor, light denied?"
I fondly° ask; but Patience to prevent   foolishly
That murmur, soon replies, "God doth not need
Either man's work or his own gifts; who best   10

Bear his mild yoke, they serve him best. His state
Is kingly. Thousands at his bidding speed
And post o'er land and ocean without rest:
They also serve who only stand and wait."

How Soon Hath Time   1631

How soon hath Time, the subtle thief of youth,
   Stoln on his wing my three and twentieth year!
   My hasting days fly on with full career,
   But my late spring no bud or blossom shew'th.°   shows
Perhaps my semblance might deceive the truth,   5
   That I to manhood am arrived so near,
   And inward ripeness doth much less appear,
   That some more timely-happy spirits endu'th.°   endow
Yet be it less or more, or soon or slow,
   It shall be still in strictest measure even   10
   To that same lot, however mean or high,
Toward which Time leads me, and the will of Heaven;
   All is, if I have grace to use it so,
   As ever in my great Taskmaster's eye.

Janice Mirikitani   b. 1942

Desert Flowers   1978

Flowers
faded
in the desert wind.
No flowers grow
where dust winds blow   5
and rain is like
a dry heave moan.

        Mama, did you dream about that
        beau who would take you
        away from it all,
        who would show you   10
        in his '41 ford
        and tell you how soft
        your hands
        like the silk kimono
        you folded for the wedding?   15
        Make you forget
        about That place,
        the back bending
        wind that fell like a wall.
        drowned all your geraniums   20
        and flooded the shed
        where you tried to sleep

away hyenas?
And mama,
bending in the candlelight,   25
after lights out in barracks.
an ageless shadow
grows victory flowers
made from crepe paper,   30
shaping those petals
like the tears
your eyes bled.
Your fingers
knotted at knuckles
wounded, winding around wire stems   35
the tiny, sloganed banner:

        "america for americans".

Did you dream
of the shiny ford
(only always a dream)   40
ride your youth
like the wind
in the headless night?

Flowers
2 ¢ a dozen,   45
flowers for American Legions
worn like a badge
on america's lapel
made in post-concentration camps
by candlelight.   50
Flowers
watered
by the spit
of "no japs wanted here",
planted in poverty   55
of postwar relocations,
plucked by
victory's veterans.

Mama, do you dream   60
of the wall of wind
that falls
on your limbless desert.
on stems
brimming with petals crushed
crepepaper   65
growing
from the crippled
mouth of your hand?

Your tears, mama,
have nourished us.   70

Your children
like pollen
scatter in the wind.

For My Father   1978

He came over the ocean
carrying Mt. Fuji
on his back/Tule Lake on his chest
hacked through the brush
of deserts   5
and made them grow
strawberries

            we stole berries
            from the stem
            we could not afford them   10
            for breakfast

his eyes held
nothing
as he whipped us
for stealing.   15

the desert had dried
his soul.

wordless
he sold
the rich,   20
full berries
to hakujines
whose children
pointed at our eyes

            they ate fresh   25
            strawberries
            with cream.

Father,
I wanted to scream
at your silence.   30
Your strength
was a stranger
I could never touch.
iron
in your eyes   35
to shield
the pain
to shield desert-like wind
from patches
of strawberries   40

grown
from
tears.

Gabriela Mistral   1889–1957

To Drink   *1938*

Translated by Gunda Kaiser

I remember gestures of infants
and they were gestures of giving me water.

In the valley of Rio Blanco
where the Aconcagua° has its beginning,   mountain in the Andes
I came to drink, I rushed to drink   5
in the fountain of a cascade,
which fell long and hard
and broke up rigid and white.
I held my mouth to the boiling spring
and the blessed water burned me,   10
and my mouth bled three days
from that sip from the valley of Aconcagua.

In the fields of Mitla,° a day   village in southern Mexico
of harvest flies, of sun, of motion,
I bent down to a well and a native came   15
to hold me over the water,
and my head, like a fruit,
was within his palms.
I drank what he drank,
for his face was with my face,   20
and in a lightning flash I realized
I, too, was of the race of Mitla.

On the Island of Puerto Rico,
During the slumber of full blue,
my body calm, the waves wild,   25
and the palms like a hundred mothers,
a child broke through skill
close to my mouth a coconut for water,
and I drank, like a daughter,
water from a mother, water from a palm.   30
And I have not partaken greater sweetness
with my body nor with my soul.

At the house of my childhood
my mother brought me water.
From one sip to another sip   35
I saw her over the jug.

The more her head rose up
the more the jug was lowered.
I still have my valley,
    I have my thirst and her vision.
This will be eternity
for we still are as we were.   40

I remember gestures of infants
    and they were gestures of giving me water.

Marianne Moore   1887–1972

Poetry   *1921*

I, too, dislike it: there are things that are important beyond all this fiddle.
Reading it, however, with a perfect contempt for it, one discovers in it
    after all, a place for the genuine.

        Hands that can grasp, eyes
          that can dilate, hair that can rise
             if it must, these things are important not because a   5

high-sounding interpretation can be put upon them but because they are
    useful. When they become so derivative as to become unintelligible,
    the same thing may be said for all of us, that we
        do not admire what
        we cannot understand: the bat   10
          holding on upside down or in quest of something to

eat, elephants pushing, a wild horse taking a roll, a tireless wolf under
    a tree, the immovable critic twitching his skin like a horse that
    feels a
        flea, the base-
        ball fan, the statistician—   15
          nor is it valid
             to discriminate against "business documents and

school-books"; all these phenomena are important. One must make a
    distinction   20
    however: when dragged into prominence by half poets, the result is
        not poetry,
    nor till the poets among us can be
        "literalists of
        the imagination"—above   25
          insolence and triviality and can present

for inspection, "imaginary gardens with real toads in them," shall
    we have
    it. In the meantime, if you demand on the one hand,
    the raw material of poetry in
        all its rawness and   30
        that which is on the other hand
          genuine, you are interested in poetry.

Pat Mora   b. 1942

Borders

1986

> *My research suggests that men and women may*
> *speak different languages that they*
> *assume are the same.*—Carol Gilligan

If we're so bright,
why didn't we notice?

I

The side-by-side translations
were the easy ones.
Our tongues tasted *luna*
chanting, chanting to the words   5
it touched; our lips circled
moon sighing its longing.
We knew: similar but different.

II

And we knew of grown-up talk,
how even in our own home   10
like became unlike,
how the child's singsong
                   I want, I want
burned our mouth
when we whispered in the dark.   15

III

But us? You and I
who've talked for years
tossing words back and forth
                 success, happiness
back and forth   20
over coffee, over wine
at parties, in bed
and I was sure you heard,
    understood,
though now I think of it   25
I can remember screaming
to be sure.

So who can hear
the words we speak
you and I, like but unlike,   30
and translate us to us
side by side

Paul Muldoon   b. 1951

Ireland   *1980*

The Volkswagen parked in the gap,
But gently ticking over.
You wonder if it's lovers
And not men hurrying back
Across two fields and a river.

The Sightseers   *1983*

My father and mother, my brother and sister
and I, with uncle Pat, our dour best-loved uncle,
had set out that Sunday afternoon in July
in his broken-down Ford

not to visit some graveyard—one died of shingles,   5
one of fever, another's knees turned to jelly—
but the brand-new roundabout at Ballygawley,
the first in mid-Ulster.

Uncle Pat was telling us how the B-Specials°   British military police
had stopped him one night somewhere near Ballygawley   10
and smashed his bicycle

and made him sing the Sash° and curse the Pope of Rome.   Ulster Protestant song
They held a pistol so hard against his forehead
there was still the mark of an O when he got home.

Elías Miguel Muñoz   b. 1954

Little Sister Born In This Land   *1989*

When you slip
slowly and lovingly
through my fingers
I cannot hold you
and explain a thousand things   5
Each time you smile
and show me your shoes with buckles
or tell me a story
of space flights
(I low you would love to be a princess   10
in those absurd and bloody wars)
Each time you intrigue me
with your riddles
with your words
that will always be foreign   15
to our experience

It isn't a reproach
sister
Little sister born in this land
It's just that you will never know
of hens nesting   20
(Is there anywhere in your childhood
a similar feeling?)
Once upon a time
there was a boy
on paving stones so white   25
and excursions on foot
toys made of tin
There was also mystery
in the ravines
There were evil pirates   30
and brave corsairs
There were lessons
for carving men
out of stone
There was caramel candy   35
and sweet potato pudding

It isn't a reproach
sister
Little sister born in this land
It's just that you have only   40
the joy of Disney heroes
Because you will smile
when the ingenious man
behind the cartoons
makes of you   45
of every child
a little clown
plastic and ridiculous

When you slip away
slowly and lovingly   50
I cannot invent
another childhood for you
cannot offer you mine
also nourished by heroes
but tasting of palm leaf   55
and *mamoncillo*
It did not suffer the mockery
of expensive toys
that the deceptive
ghost of December   60
brings to you

When you slip away
slowly and lovingly
we cannot bury together
in the backyard   65

(That warm and always
open earth)
the models
that will take hold of you   70
that already stalk you
from their cardboard boxes
and their printed letters
on a glass of milk
or Coca Cola   75

It isn't a reproach
Sister
Little Sister born in this land

Howard Nemerov   1920–1991

The Goose Fish   *1955*

On the long shore, lit by the moon
To show them properly alone,
Two lovers suddenly embraced
So that their shadows were as one.
The ordinary night was graced   5
For them by the swift tide of blood
That silently they took at flood,
And for a little time they prized
    Themselves emparadised.

Then, as if shaken by stage-fright   10
Beneath the hard moon's bony light,
They stood together on the sand—
Embarrassed in each other's sight
But still conspiring hand in hand,
Until they saw, there underfoot,   15
As though the world had found them out,
The goose fish turning up, though dead,
    His hugely grinning head.

There in the china light he lay,
Most ancient and corrupt and grey   20
They hesitated at his smile.
Wondering what it seemed to say
To lovers who a little while
Before had thought to understand,
By violence upon the sand,   25

The only way that could be known
    To make a world their own.

It was a wide and moony grin
Together peaceful and obscene;
They knew not what he would express,   30
So finished a comedian

He might mean failure or success,
But took it for an emblem of
Their sudden, new and guilty love
To be observed by, when they kissed,
    That rigid optimist.   35

So he became their patriarch,
Dreadfully mild in the half-dark.
His throat that the sand seemed to choke,
His picket teeth, these left their mark
But never did explain the joke   40
That so amused him, lying there
While the moon went down to disappear
Along the still and tilted track
    That bears the zodiac.   45

The Town Dump   1958

"The art of our necessities is strange
That can make vile things precious."

A mile out in the marshes, under a sky
Which seems to be always going away
In a hurry, on that Venetian land threaded
With hidden canals, you will find the city
Which seconds ours (so cemeteries, too,   5
Reflect a town from hillsides out of town),
Where Being most Becomingly ends up
Becoming some more. From cardboard tenements,
Windowed with cellophane, or simply tenting
In paper bags, the angry mackerel eyes
Glare at you out of stove-in, sunken heads   10
Far from the sea; the lobster, also, lifts
An empty claw in his most minatory
Of gestures; oyster, crab, and mussel shells
Lie here in heaps, savage as money hurled
Away at the gate of hell. If you want results,   15
These are results.
            Objects of value or virtue,
However, are also to be picked up here,
Though rarely, lying with bones and rotten meat,
Eggshells and mouldy bread, banana peels   20
No one will skid on, apple cores that caused
Neither the fall of man nor a theory
Of gravitation. People do throw out
The family pearls by accident, sometimes,
Not often; I've known dealers in antiques   25
To prowl this place by night, with flashlights, on
The off-chance of somebody's having left
Derelict chairs which will turn out to be
By Hepplewhite°, a perfect set of six   30

°18th-century English furniture maker

Going to show, I guess, that in any sty
Someone's heaven may open and shower down
Riches responsive to the right dream; though
It is a small chance, certainly, that sends
The ghostly dealer, heavy with fly-netting   35
Over his head, across these hills in darkness,
Stumbling in cut-glass goblets, lacquered cups,
And other products of his dreamy midden
Pencilled with light and guarded by the flies.

For there are flies, of course. A dynamo   40
Composed, by thousands, of our ancient black
Retainers, hums here day and night, steady
As someone telling beads, the hum becoming
A high whine at any disturbance; then,
Settled again, they shine under the sun   45
Like oil-drops, or are invisible as night,
By night.
          All this continually smoulders,
Crackles, and smokes with mostly invisible fires
Which, working deep, rarely flash out and flare,   50
And never finish. Nothing finishes;
The flies, feeling the heat, keep on the move.
Among the flies, the purifying fires,
The hunters by night, acquainted with the art
Of our necessities, and the new deposits   55
That each day wastes with treasure, you may say
There should be ratios. You may sum up
The results, if you want results. But I will add
That wild birds, drawn to the carrion and flies,
Assemble in some numbers here, their wings   60
Shining with light, their flight enviably free,
Their music marvelous, though sad, and strange.

Sharon Olds   b. 1942

The Death of Marilyn Monroe   1983

The ambulance men touched her cold
body, lifted it, heavy as iron,
onto the stretcher, tried to close the
mouth, closed the eyes, tied the
arms to the sides, moved a caught   5
strand of hair, as if it mattered,
saw the shape of her breasts, flattened by
gravity, under the sheet,
carried her, as if it were she,
down the steps.   10

These men were never the same. They went out
afterwards, as they always did,
for a drink or two, but they could not meet
each other's eyes.

          Their lives took   15
a turn—one had nightmares, strange
pains, impotence, depression. One did not
like his work, his wife looked
different, his kids. Even death
seemed different to him—a place where she   20
would be waiting.

And one found himself standing at night
in the doorway to a room of sleep, listening to
a woman breathing, just an ordinary
woman   25
breathing.

35/10   *1984*

Brushing out my daughter's dark
silken hair before the mirror
I see the grey gleaming on my head,
the silver-haired servant behind her. Why is it
just as we begin to go   5
they begin to arrive, the fold in my neck
clarifying as the fine bones of her
hips sharpen? As my skin shows
its dry pitting, she opens like a small
pale flower on the tip of a cactus;   10
as my last chances to bear a child
are falling through my body, the duds among them,
her full purse of eggs, round and
firm as hard-boiled yolks, is about
to snap its clasp. I brush her tangled
fragrant hair at bedtime. It's an old   15
story—the oldest we have on our planet—
the story of replacement.

Simon J. Ortiz   b. 1941

My Father's Song   *1976*

Wanting to say things,
I miss my father tonight.
His voice, the slight catch,
the depth from his thin chest,

the tremble of emotion
in something he has just said
to his son, his song:

We planted corn one Spring at Acu—
we planted several times
but this one particular time
I remember the soft damp sand
in my hand.

My father had stopped at one point
to show me an overturned furrow;
the plowshare had unearthed
the burrow nest of a mouse
in the soft moist sand.

Very gently, he scooped tiny pink animals
into the palm of his hand
and told me to touch them.
We took them to the edge
of the field and put them in the shade
of a sand moist clod.

I remember the very softness
of cool and warm sand and tiny alive mice
and my father saying things.

Speaking   1977

I take him outside
under the trees,
have him stand on the ground.
We listen to the crickets,
cicadas, million years old sound.
Ants come by us.
I tell them,
"This is he, my son.
This boy is looking at you.
I am speaking for him."

The crickets, cicadas,
the ants, the millions of years
are watching us,
hear us.
My son murmurs infant words,
speaking, small laughter
bubbles from him.
Tree leaves tremble.
They listen to this boy
speaking for me.

Wilfred Owen   1893–1918

Anthem for Doomed Youth   1920

What passing-bells for these who die as cattle?
    Only the monstrous anger of the guns.
    Only the stuttering rifles' rapid rattle
Can patter out their hasty orisons.°   *prayers*
No mockeries now for them; no prayers nor bells,
    Nor any voice of mourning save the choirs—   5
The shrill, demented choirs of wailing shells;
    And bugles calling for them from sad shires.°   *counties*

What candles may be held to speed them all?
    Not in the hands of boys, but in their eyes
Shall shine the holy glimmers of good-byes.
    The pallor of girls' brows shall be their pall;   10
Their flowers the tenderness of patient minds,
And each slow dusk a drawing-down of blinds.

Linda Pastan   b. 1932

Anger   1985

You tell me
that it's all right
to let it out of its cage,
though it may claw someone,
even bite.
You say that letting it out   5
may tame it somehow.
But loose it may
turn on me, maul
my face, draw blood.
Ah, you think you know so much,   10
you whose anger is a pet dog,
its canines dull with disuse.
But mine is a rabid thing, sharpening its teeth
on my very bones,
and I will never let it go.   15

Ethics   1980

In ethics class so many years ago
our teacher asked this question every fall:
if there were a fire in a museum
which would you save, a Rembrandt painting

or an old woman who hadn't many
years left anyhow? Restless on hard chairs   5
caring little for pictures or old age
we'd opt one year for life, the next for art
and always half-heartedly. Sometimes
the woman borrowed my grandmother's face   10
leaving her usual kitchen to wander
some drafty, half imagined museum.
One year, feeling clever, I replied
why not let the woman decide herself?
Linda, the teacher would report, eschews   15
the burdens of responsibility.
This fall in a real museum I stand
before a real Rembrandt, old woman,
or nearly so, myself. The colors
within this frame are darker than autumn,   20
darker even than winter—the browns of earth,
though earth's most radiant elements burn
through the canvas. I know now that woman
and painting and season are almost one
and all beyond saving by children.   25

Marge Piercy   b. 1936

The woman in the ordinary   1970

The woman in the ordinary pudgy downcast girl
is crouching with eyes and muscles clenched.
Round and pebble smooth she effaces herself
under ripples of conversation and debate.
The woman in the block of ivory soap   5
has massive thighs that neigh,
great breasts that blare and strong arms that trumpet.

The woman of the golden fleece
laughs uproariously from the belly
inside the girl who imitates   10
a Christmas card virgin with glued hands,
who fishes for herself in other's eyes,
who stoops and creeps to make herself smaller.
In her bottled up is a woman peppery as curry,
a yam of a woman of butter and brass,   15
compounded of acid and sweet like a pineapple,
like a handgrenade set to explode,
like goldenrod ready to bloom.

Pedro Pietri   b. 1944

Traffic Violations   *1983*

you go into chicken delight
and order dinosaurs
because you are hungry
and want something different
now that you no longer   5
eat meat or fish or vegetables
you are told politely
is against company policies
to be that different
so you remove a button off   10
your absentminded overcoat
the scenery changes
you are waiting in line
to take a mean leak
at one of those public toilets   15
in the times square area
the line is 3 weeks long

many waited with their lunch
inside brown paper bags
singing the battle hymn   20
of the republic to keep warm

you remove another button off
your absentminded overcoat
all you can see now are
high heels and low quarter shoes   25
coming at your eyeballs
disappearing when they come
close enough to make contact

you try to get up off the floor
but you forgot how to move
umbrellas open up inside your head   30
you start screaming backwards
your legs behave like flat tires
your mind melts in slow motion

you remove another button off   35
your absentminded overcoat
is late in the evening
according to everybody
who keeps track of time
you are about to jump off the roof   40
emergency sirens are heard

A crowd of skilled & unskilled
Laborers on their mental lunch break

congregate on the street below
the roof you are about to jump from
they are laughing hysterically   45
nobody tries to talk you out of it
everybody wants you to jump
so they can get some sleep tonight—
should you change your mind about jumping   50
All the spectators will get uptight

red white and blue representatives
from the suicide prevention bureau
order you to jump immediately
you refuse to obey their orders   55
they sendout a helicopter to push you
off the roof into the morning headlines
the laughter from the crowd
on the street breaks the sound barrier

you try removing another button off   60
your absentminded overcoat
but that button is reported missing
the helicopter pushes you off the roof
everybody is feeling much better
you are losing your memory real fast   65
the clouds put on black arm bands
it starts raining needles and thread

a few seconds before having breakfast
at a cafeteria in the hereafter
you remove your absentminded overcoat   70

you are on the front and back seat
of a bi-lingo spaceship
smoking grass with your friends
from the past present and future
nothing unusual is happening   75
you are all speeding
without moving an inch
making sure nobody does the driving

Chin Woon Ping   b. 1945

Seven Vietnamese Boys   *1987*

crossing the road at 46th and walnut
where the 7–11 parking lot meets sunoco station
and the watutsi pub meets the gothic complex
apartment's arched balconies from where sullen
cambodian men scan lines of traffic: 5
their skin-tight jeans and denim jackets
hightops and one tall dude's hair slashed
diagonally with orange dye, blue shadow

dolling his eyes gorgeous as Prince's
a slick overcoat falling to his skins billowing   10
in the wind, they waited at the spot
where someone split open john cooper's head
to clean his pockets one summer night.
almost adoring i wanted to run up to ask,
when you get to where you are going   15
what do you do for thrills?
do your mothers sit with bare light bulbs
hanging overhead when they keep your rice
warm waiting? do your fathers watch miami vice
and drink rolling rock to unwind?   20
do you lie awake at night remembering the skyscraper
waves off the indian ocean, the stinging
sands of pulau bidong?
when the snow melts into clumps peppered with black soot
does it bother you the way it bothers me?   25
does the smell of lemon grass give you a pang?
do you dream of moving to the suburbs
with cars as long as alligators
and refrigerators full of spring rolls?
are you fooled by the wasp
world of michael j. fox?   30
have you noticed how the sun
setting over the end of chester avenue
leaves a hue as fiery as dragons?

Sylvia Plath   1932–1963

Daddy   *1965*

You do not do, you do not do
Any more, black shoe
In which I have lived like a foot
For thirty years, poor and white,
Barely daring to breathe or Achoo.   5

Daddy, I have had to kill you.
You died before I had time—
Marble-heavy, a bag full of God,
Ghastly statue with one gray toe
Big as a Frisco seal   10

And a head in the freakish Atlantic
Where it pours bean green over blue
In the waters off beautiful Nauset.°   on Cape Cod Bay
I used to pray to recover you.
Ach, du.   15

In the German tongue, in the Polish town
Scraped flat by the roller

Of wars, wars, wars.
But the name of the town is common.
My Polack friend

Says there are a dozen or two.   20
So I never could tell where you
Put your foot, your root,
I never could talk to you.
The tongue stuck in my jaw.
                                                                        25
It stuck in a barb wire snare.
Ich, ich, ich, ich,
I could hardly speak.
I thought every German was you.
And the language obscene
                                                                        30
An engine, an engine
Chuffing me off like a Jew.
A Jew to Dachau, Auschwitz, Belsen.°   Nazi concentration camps
I began to talk like a Jew.
I think I may well be a Jew.
                                                                        35
The snows of the Tyrol, the clear beer of Vienna
Are not very pure or true.
With my gipsy ancestress and my weird luck
And my Taroc pack and my Taroc pack°   Tarot cards
I may be a bit of a Jew.
                                                                        40
I have always been scared of *you,*
With your Luftwaffe, your gobbledygoo.
And your neat mustache
And your Aryan eye, bright blue.
Panzer-man, panzer-man, O You—
                                                                        45
Not God but a swastika
So black no sky could squeak through.
Every woman adores a Fascist,
The boot in the face, the brute
Brute heart of a brute like you.
                                                                        50
You stand at the blackboard, daddy,
In the picture I have of you,
A cleft in your chin instead of your foot
But no less a devil for that, no not
Any less the black man who
                                                                        55
Bit my pretty red heart in two.
I was ten when they buried you.
At twenty I tried to die
and get back, back, back to you.
I thought even the bones would do.
                                                                        60
But they pulled me out of the sack,
And they stuck me together with glue.
And then I knew what to do.

I made a model of you,
A man in black with a Meinkampf look   65

And a love of the rack and the screw.
And I said I do, I do.
So daddy, I'm finally through.
The black telephone's off at the root,   70
The voices just can't worm through.

If I've killed one man, I've killed two—
The vampire who said he was you
And drank my blood for a year,
Seven years, if you want to know.   75
Daddy, you can lie back now.

There's a stake in your fat black heart
And the villagers never liked you.
They are dancing and stamping on you.
They always *knew* it was you.   80
Daddy, daddy, you bastard, I'm through.

Metaphors   *1960*

I'm a riddle in nine syllables,
An elephant, a ponderous house,
A melon strolling on two tendrils.
O red fruit, ivory, fine timbers!
This loaf's big with its yeasty rising.   5
Money's new-minted in this fat purse.
I'm a means, a stage, a cow in calf.
I've eaten a bag of green apples,
Boarded the train there's no getting off.

Edgar Allan Poe   1809–1849

The Sleeper   *1831*

At midnight, in the month of June,
I stand beneath the mystic moon.
An opiate vapour, dewy, dim,
Exhales from out her golden rim,
And, softly dripping, drop by drop,   5
Upon the quiet mountain top,
Steals drowsily and musically
Into the universal valley.
The rosemary nods upon the grave;
The lily lolls upon the wave;   10
Wrapping the fog about its breast,
The ruin moulders into rest;

Looking like Lethe,° see! the lake   mythical underworld river of forgetfulness
A conscious slumber seems to take,
And would not, for the world, awake.
All Beauty sleeps!—and lo! where lies   15
Irene, with her Destinies!

Oh, lady bright! can it be right—
This window open to the night?
The wanton airs, from the tree-top,
Laughingly through the lattice drop—   20
The bodiless airs, a wizard rout,
Flit through thy chamber in and out,
And wave the curtain canopy
So fitfully—so fearfully—
Above the closed and fringéd lid   25
'Neath which thy slumb'ring soul lies hid,
That, o'er the floor and down the wall,
Like ghosts the shadows rise and fall!
Oh, lady dear, hast thou no fear?
Why and what art thou dreaming here?   30
Sure thou art come o'er far-off seas,
A wonder to these garden trees!
Strange is thy pallor! strange thy dress!
Strange, above all, thy length of tress,
And this all solemn silentness!   35

The lady sleeps! Oh, may her sleep,
Which is enduring, so be deep!
Heaven have her in its sacred keep!
This chamber changed for one more holy,
This bed for one more melancholy,   40
I pray to God that she may lie
Forever with unopened eye,
While the pale sheeted ghosts go by!

    45

My love, she sleeps! Oh, may her sleep,
As it is lasting, so be deep!
Soft may the worms about her creep!
Far in the forest, dim and old,
For her may some tall vault unfold—
Some vault that oft hath flung its black   50
And wingéd panels fluttering back,
Triumphant, o'er the crested palls,
Of her grand family funerals—
Some sepulchre, remote, alone,
Against whose portal she hath thrown,   55
In childhood, many an idle stone—
Some tomb from out whose sounding door
She ne'er shall force an echo more,
Thrilling to think, poor child of sin!
It was the dead who groaned within.   60

Ezra Pound   1885–1972

In a Station of the Metro   1916

The apparition of these faces in the crowd;
Petals on a wet, black bough.

The River-Merchant's Wife: A Letter   1915

*(after Rihaku)**

While my hair was still cut straight across my forehead
I played about the front gate, pulling flowers.
You came by on bamboo stilts, playing horse,
You walked about my seat, playing with blue plums.
And we went on living in the village of Chokan: 5
Two small people, without dislike or suspicion.

At fourteen I married My Lord you.
I never laughed, being bashful.
Lowering my head, I looked at the wall.
Called to, a thousand times, I never looked back.   10

At fifteen I stopped scowling,
I desired my dust to be mingled with yours
For ever and for ever and for ever.
Why should I climb the look out?

At sixteen you departed,   15
You went into far Ku-to-yen, by river of swirling eddies,
And you have been gone five months.
The monkeys make sorrowful noise overhead.

You dragged your feet when you went out.
By the gate now, the moss is grown, the different mosses,   20
Too deep to clear them away!
The leaves fall early this autumn, in wind.
The paired butterflies are already yellow with August
Over the grass in the West garden;
They hurt me. I grow older,   25
If you are coming down through the narrows of the river Kiang,
Please let me know beforehand,
And I will come out to meet you
        As far as Cho-fu-Sa.

---

*Japanese name for the eighth-century Chinese poet Li Po

Wyatt Prunty   b. 1947

The Kite   1982

Away from playground games and fights,
He sings to himself, dancing in the grass,
Steps trailing, a single figure
Intent on the private craft of kites.

It flies because he will not let it go,   5
Because he wraps the twine around his hand
So tight that blood collects, darkening
Under the wind's insistent tug.

From liquid wrist the string dissolves into its length,
Its curve rising from the ground,   10
An anchored flight of immobility
And fragile parts strung taut to give them strength.

Vivid for the sky's emptiness,
A bright red patch against the haze and blue,
It soars along a shortened line, but falls   15
When given run before the wind;

Or like a solitary song's release,
The kite unreels along a spool of thread,
An outward surge over the wind
Flying by the force of being held.   20

The single master of a vacant lot,
By pulling down it rises up,
This craft of putting fragile things aloft,
Of letting go and holding on at once.

Rooms Without Walls   1986

Late sunlight breaking through the room
And a boy's round face against the glass,
Breath clouding, eyes narrowed to the sun.
Outside, snow falls through the light;
The sky is granular and close,   5
All pattern of the wind's white slant,
That wind about the house, and branches'
Snow-muffled scrapes against the eaves.

Later, the power lines will fail,
And, twelve years old, I will stand outside   10
Counting the coal oil lamps that float
From room to room as though our house
Did not have walls inside but was
One space through which my family sent
Their liquid light without effort,   15
Like quiet conversation.

All this before the heart disease,
Cancers, and little suicides
Of cigarettes and whiskey turned
Events into a daguerreotype 20
Fading and slightly out of focus.
The snow, deeper than ever before,
Was in a frame I took outside
But never brought back in again.

Instead, with power lines knocked down 25
All over town, I stamped in the street,
My feet so cold they hurt, and gazed
Until I turned my family's warm house
Inside out, the snow's unfolding linen
And pillows deep as a child's gathering 30
Unconsciousness that sleeps through any sound
Made for the mind's stark furnishings.

Two blocks past where I stood, small shacks began,
Unpainted shotguns shouldered together
Into a row of narrow facings 35
I studied from the school bus window
Or counted as our car drove past—
Ten to a block, identical,
Each with its small front yard
Of bright red clay, as hard as pavement. 40

From that direction, over the stillness
The snow had brought, I heard the blows
And the high voice of a small girl
Who could not beg but only gasp
"Daddy, Daddy" between the cracking sounds 45
Made by whatever he'd picked up.
I stood more still than I had ever thought.
He beat her until there was silence.

And I think that action took forever.
More than the snow's cold multiplicity 50
Or all the lights that failed to work
In our small town, or hands that rested
In laps, in pockets, near telephones,
The hands of those who waited for
The power, thinking the novelty 55
Of such a deep snow, and that far south.

And later that night, beyond crying,
I began to shake for that small child,
For both of us; not in the arms and legs
But in the chest and gut. And I felt 60
As though I had a fishing line
In my head, drawn to the point of breaking.
And when I closed my eyes a light
Would flash, then run like iodine.

What I know now is that the frame   65
Made by the window where I stood
One afternoon was cold and arbitrary.
If anything, the snow's white sifting
Down my glass meant anonymity
Far past the best or worst we ever do,   70
Beyond all melting at our touch
Which like regret arrives past tense.

What I know is that our meanings work
Like games thought up by children in a street;
The space, number of players, goals   75
And objects moved are arbitrary.
And yet our games are serious,
As players go beyond themselves
Into a violence that wins,
And lets us say they were responsible.   80

The house I saw outside that night
Was covered by a heavy snow
That rounded all its borders; no hedge
Or wall could separate its space
From a smaller space two blocks away,   85
The place of one small girl's great pain,
Which still echoes in the stillness that we are.

Public Enemy   c. 1960

Air Hoodlum   *1991*

Risen up in the 'velt
Strong island New York
The 'hood in case
You did not know my base
There was a ballplayer   5
Who had all the skillz
Wit' the pill
To pay the piper
Plus all the bills
Mick his first name   10
Mack the awesome game
Practiced in the heat
In the rain or in pain
Mick so quick 6 foot 6
Down to be picked   15
By anyone but the Celtics
Oh what a handle
Could score from the floor
Wit' people hangin' on 'em
PR even hangin' on 'em   20
But what he did best above all the rest was . . .

Grades 9 & 10
Mickey Mack was all dat
But in class his ass
Sat way in the back
How I know 'cause I know   25
I used to flow wit' the bro
He didn't mind I used
To read him his own headlines
'Cause he could not read 'em
His school wouldn't need 'em   30
If the lines wouldn't've went like dis
Mickey Mack
Jumped over the candlestick
And stacked
Was his stats   35
But his D was still wack
Grades 11 & 12
He found the wrong clientele
And all

During class he would dribble   40
In the hall
But he got in trouble
In school but the trouble was
It was cool
If your brain was just another bubble   45
As long as he could
Score fiddy 2
Get 33 re-bounds
Fuckin' around
Teams lost to 'em   50
He went right thru 'em
Division, county, state
That's 3 count 'em
Championships
For a small town bro   55
That's bound to go pro

S.A.T.'s didn't matter
'Cause he waz
All dat
You know the fat on the back   60
He was always in da news
You gotta know what it means
It means revenue
And I'm tellin' you
I saw cars and geez   65
Come to our school pleaze approach
Hell wit' the principal
Where is da coach
Went to college four years
Wit' a scholarship   70
And came back wit' a championship

But when it came to his life
He didn't care
'Cause he took it to the air

The fall began
When Mickey Mack fell
Hell ripped his knee
Drafted last by personnel
Oh how he loved the game
It was fantastic
Until he was cut 'n' couldn't stick
Times got tighter & tighter
He had an attitude
Was rude so he turned
Into a fighter

School wouldn't give
Him a job that he needed
Assistant to the assistant coach
They didn't need it
Then he resorted to a
Stick up kid—ski mask & gatt
But this game he wasn't good at
And the drugs on the side
Police ambushed his ride
Bang it was
Another homicide
He was ghost you know
Hometown hero
But now he's a zero
To those hypocrites
Who ripped him blind
For his skills
Without the will to develop his mind
Forever in the news
The community views
Him only as air hoodlum

Sir Walter Raleigh   1552–1618

The Nymph's Reply to the Shepherd   1600

(A reply to Marlowe's "The Passionate Shepherd to His Love")

If all the world and love were young,
And truth in every shepherd's tongue,
These pretty pleasures might me move
To live with thee and be thy love.

Time drives the flocks from field to fold   5
When rivers rage and rocks grow cold,
And Philomel° becometh dumb;   the nightingale

The rest complains of cares to come.

The flowers do fade, and wanton fields
To wayward winter reckoning yields;
A honey tongue, a heart of gall,°   bitterness   10
Is fancy's spring, but sorrow's fall.

Thy gowns, thy shoes, thy beds of roses,
Thy cap, thy kirtle,° and thy posies   skirt
Soon break, soon wither, soon forgotten—   15
In folly ripe, in reason rotten.

Thy belt of straw and ivy buds,
Thy coral clasps and amber studs,
All these in me no means can move
To come to thee and be thy love.   20

But could youth last and love still breed,
Had joys no date° nor age no need,   end
Then these delights my mind might move
To live with thee and be thy love.

Dudley Randall   b. 1914

Ballad of Birmingham   *1966*

(On the bombing of a church in Birmingham, Alabama, 1963)

"Mother dear, may I go downtown
Instead of out to play,
And march the streets of Birmingham
In a Freedom March today?"

"No, baby, no, you may not go,   5
For the dogs are fierce and wild,
And clubs and hoses, guns and jails
Aren't good for a little child."

"But, mother, I won't be alone.
Other children will go with me,
And march the streets of Birmingham   10
To make our country free."

"No, baby, no, you may not go,
For I fear those guns will fire.
But you may go to church instead
And sing in the children's choir."   15

She has combed and brushed her night-dark hair,
And bathed rose petal sweet,
And drawn white gloves on her small brown hands,
And white shoes on her feet.

The mother smiled to know her child   20
Was in the sacred place,

But that smile was the last smile
To come upon her face.

For when she heard the explosion,   25
Her eyes grew wet and wild.
She raced through the streets of Birmingham
Calling for her child.

She clawed through bits of glass and brick,
Then lifted out a shoe.   30
"O, here's the shoe my baby wore,
But, baby, where are you?"

John Crowe Ransom   1888–1974

Bells for John Whiteside's Daughter   1924

There was such speed in her little body,
And such lightness in her footfall,
It is no wonder her brown study
Astonishes us all.

Her wars were bruited in our high window,   5
We looked among orchard trees and beyond
Where she took arms against her shadow,
Or harried unto the pond

The lazy geese like a snow cloud
Dripping their snow on the green grass,   10
Tricking and stopping, sleepy and proud,
Who cried in goose, Alas,

For the tireless heart within the little
Lady with rod that made them rise
From their noon apple-dreams and scuttle   15
Goose-fashion under the skies!

But now go the bells, and we are ready,
In one house we are sternly stopped
To say we are vexed at her brown study,
Lying so primly propped.   20

Henry Reed   b. 1914

Naming of Parts   1946

To-day we have naming of parts. Yesterday,
We had daily cleaning. And to-morrow morning,
We shall have what to do after firing. But to-day
To-day we have naming of parts. Japonica

Glistens like coral in all of the neighboring gardens,
    And to-day we have naming of parts.

This is the lower sling swivel. And this
Is the upper sling swivel, whose use you will see,
When you are given your slings. And this is the piling swivel,
Which in your case you have not got. The branches
Hold in the gardens their silent, eloquent gestures,
    Which in our case we have not got.

This is the safety-catch, which is always released
With an easy flick of the thumb. And please do not let me
See anyone using his finger. You can do it quite easy
If you have any strength in your thumb. The blossoms
Are fragile and motionless, never letting anyone see
    Any of them using their finger.

And this you can see is the bolt. The purpose of this
Is to open the breech, as you see. We can slide it
Rapidly backwards and forwards: we call this
Easing the spring. And rapidly backwards and forwards
The early bees are assaulting and fumbling the flowers:
    They call it easing the Spring.

They call it easing the Spring: it is perfectly easy
If you have any strength in your thumb: like the bolt,
And the breech, and the cocking-piece, and the point of balance,
Which in our case we have not got: and the almond-blossom
Silent in all of the gardens and the bees going backwards and forwards,
    For to-day we have naming of parts.

Ishmael Reed   b. 1938

beware : do not read this poem   1972

tonite , thriller was
abt an ol woman , so vain she
surrounded herself w/
    many mirrors

it got so bad that finally she
locked herself indoors & her
whole life became the
    mirrors

one day the villagers broke
into her house   ,   but she was too
swift for them   .   she disappeared
    into a mirror

each tenant who bought the house
after that   ,   lost a loved one to

the ol woman in the mirror   :   15
first a little girl
then a young woman
then the young woman/s husband

the hunger of this poem is legendary
it has taken in many victims   20

back off from this poem
it has drawn in yr feet
back off from this poem
it has drawn in yr legs

back off from this poem   25
it is a greedy mirror
you are into this poem   .   from
    the waist down
nobody can hear you can they   ?
this poem has had you up to here   30
    belch
this poem aint got no manners
you cant call out frm this poem
relax now & go w/ this poem
move & roll on to this poem   35
do not resist this poem
this poem has yr eyes
this poem has his head
this poem has his arms
this poem has his fingers   40
this poem has his fingertips

this poem is the reader & the
reader this poem

statistic   :   the us bureau of missing persons reports
                that in 1968 over 100,000 people disappeared   45
                leaving no solid clues
                    nor trace   only
    a space   in the lives of their friends

I Am a Cowboy in the Boat of Ra   1972

*The devil must be forced to reveal any such physical evil (potions, charms, fetishes,
etc.) still outside the body and these must be burned.*
    —Rituale Romanum, *published 1947, endorsed by the coat of arms and intro-
    duction letter from Francis Cardinal Spellman*

I am a cowboy in the boat of Ra,°   Egyptian sun god
sidewinders in the saloons of fools
bit my forehead   like   O
the untrustworthiness of Egyptologists

Who do not know their trips. Who was that
dog-faced man? they asked, the day I rode
from town.

School marms with halitosis cannot see
the Nefertiti° fake chipped on the run by slick   Egyptian queen of the 14th century B.C.
germans, the hawk behind Sonny Rollins'° head or   jazz saxophonist   10
the ritual beard of his axe, a longhorn winding
its bells thru the Field of Reeds.

I am a cowboy in the boat of Ra. I bedded
down with Isis,° Lady of the Boogaloo, dove   Egyptian goddess of nature
down deep in her horny, stuck up her Wells-Far-ago   15
in daring midday get away. "Start grabbing the
blue," i said from top of my double crown.

I am a cowboy in the boat of Ra. Ezzard Charles°   heavyweight boxing champion
of the Chisholm Trail. Took up the bass but they
blew off my thumb. Alchemist in ringmanship but a   20
sucker for the right cross.

I am a cowboy in the boat of Ra. Vamoosed from
the temple i bide my time. The price on the wanted
poster was a-going down, outlaw alias copped my stance
and moody greenhorns were making me dance; while my mouth's   25
shooting iron got its chambers jammed.

I am a cowboy in the boat of Ra. Boning-up in
the ol West i bide my time. You should see
me pick off these tin cans whippersnappers. I
write the motown long plays for the comeback of   30
Osiris.° Make them up when stars stare at sleeping   Egyptian god of the dead
steer out here near the campfire. Women arrive
on the backs of goats and throw themselves on
my Bowie.°   hunting knife

I am a cowboy in the boat of Ra. Lord of the lash,   35
the Loup Garou° Kid. Half breed son of Pisces and   werewolf
Aquarius. I hold the souls of men in my pot. I do
the dirty boogie with scorpions. I make the bulls
keep still and was the first swinger to grape the taste.

I am a cowboy in his boat. Pope Joan of the   40
Ptah Ra. C/mere a minute willya doll?
Be a good girl and
Bring me my Buffalo horn of black powder
Bring me my headdress of black feathers
Bring me my bones of Ju-Ju snake   45
Go get my eyelids of red paint.
Hand me my shadow
I'm going into town after Set

I am a cowboy in the boat of Ra
look out Set   here i come Set   50

to get Set   to sunset Set
to unseat Set   to Set down Set
                 usurper of the Royal couch
                 imposter RAdio of Moses' bush
                 party pooper O hater of dance   55
                 vampire outlaw of the milky way

Adrienne Rich   b. 1929

Aunt Jennifer's Tigers   *1951*

Aunt Jennifer's tigers prance across a screen,
Bright topaz denizens of a world of green.
They do not fear the men beneath the tree;
They pace in sleek chivalric certainty.

Aunt Jennifer's fingers fluttering through her wool   5
Find even the ivory needle hard to pull.
The massive weight of Uncle's wedding band
Sits heavily upon Aunt Jennifer's hand.

When Aunt is dead, her terrified hands will lie
Still ringed with ordeals she was mastered by.   10
The tigers in the panel that she made
Will go on prancing, proud and unafraid.

Living in Sin   *1955*

She had thought the studio would keep itself,
no dust upon the furniture of love.
Half heresy, to wish the taps less vocal,
the panes relieved of grime. A plate of pears,
a piano with a Persian shawl, a cat   5
stalking the picturesque amusing mouse
had risen at his urging.
Not that at five each separate stair would writhe
under the milkman's tramp; that morning light
so coldly would delineate the scraps   10
of last night's cheese and three sepulchral bottles;
that on the kitchen shelf among the saucers
a pair of beetle-eyes would fix her own—
envoy from some black village in the mouldings ...
Meanwhile, he, with a yawn,   15
sounded a dozen notes upon the keyboard,
declared it out of tune, shrugged at the mirror,
rubbed at his beard, went out for cigarettes;
while she, jeered by the minor demons,
pulled back the sheets and made the bed and found   20
a towel to dust the table-top,
and let the coffee-pot boil over on the stove.

By evening she was back in love again,
though not so wholly but throughout the night
she woke sometimes to feel the daylight coming
like a relentless milkman up the stairs.   25

Edwin Arlington Robinson   1869–1935

Richard Cory

1897

Whenever Richard Cory went down town,
We people on the pavement looked at him:
He was a gentleman from sole to crown,
Clean favored, and imperially slim.

And he was always quietly arrayed,
And he was always human when he talked;   5
But still he fluttered pulses when he said,
"Good-morning," and he glittered when he walked.

And he was rich—yes, richer than a king—
And admirably schooled in every grace:
In fine, we thought that he was everything   10
To make us wish that we were in his place.

So on we worked, and waited for the light,
And went without the meat, and cursed the bread;
And Richard Cory, one calm summer night,
Went home and put a bullet through his head.   15

Wendy Rose   b. 1948

If I am too brown or too white for you

1985

remember I am a garnet woman
whirling into precision
as a crystal arithmetic
or a cluster and so

why the dream
in my mouth,   5
the flutter of blackbirds
at my wrists?

In the morning
there you are
at the edge of the river   10
on one knee

and you are selecting me
from among polished stones
more definitely red or white
between which tiny serpents swim   15

and you see
that my body is blood
frozen into giving birth
over and over, a single motion,   20

and you touch the matrix
shattered in winter
and begin to piece together
the shape of me

wanting the curl in your palm   25
to be perfect
and the image less clouded,
less mixed

but you always see
just in time   30
working me around
the last hour of the day

there is a small light
in the smoke, a tiny sun
in the blood, so deep   35
it is there and not there,

so pure
it is singing.

Three Thousand Dollar Death Song   *1980*

Nineteen American Indian Skeletons from Nevada . . . valued at $3000 . . .
                                —Museum invoice, 1975

Is it in cold hard cash? the kind
that dusts the insides of men's pockets
lying silver-polished surface along the cloth.
Or in bills? papering the wallets of they
who thread the night with dark words. Or   5
checks? paper promises weighing the same
as words spoken once on the other side
of the grown grass and damned rivers
of history. However it goes, it goes
Through my body it goes assessing each nerve, running its edges   10
along my arteries, planning ahead
for whose hands will rip me
into pieces of dusty red paper,
whose hands will smooth or smatter me
into traces of rubble. Invoiced now,   15
it's official how our bones are valued
that stretch out pointing to sunrise
or are flexed into one last foetal bend,
that are removed and tossed about,
catalogued, numbered with black ink   20

on newly-white foreheads.
As we were formed to the white soldier's voice,
so we explode under white students' hands.
Death is a long trail of days
in our fleshless prison.

From this distant point we watch our bones   25
auctioned with our careful beadwork,
our quilled medicine bundles, even the bridles
of our shot-down horses. You: who have
priced us, you who have removed us: at what cost?
What price the pits where our bones share   30
a single bit of memory, how one century
turns our dead into specimens, our history
into dust, our survivors into clowns.
Our memory might be catching, you know;
picture the mortars, the arrowheads, the labrets°   35
shaking off their labels like bears
suddenly awake to find the seasons have ended
while they slept. Watch them touch each other,
measure reality, march out the museum door!
Watch as they lift their faces   40
and smell about for us; watch our bones rise
to meet them and mount the horses once again!
The cost, then, will be paid
for our sweetgrass-smelling having-been
in clam shell beads and steatite,°   45
dentalia° and woodpecker scalp, turquoise
and copper, blood and oil, coal
and uranium, children, a universe
of stolen things.   50

ornaments worn in pierced lips (line 35)

soapstone (line 45)

shellfish (line 46)

Isaac Rosenberg   1890–1918

Break of Day in the Trenches   *1922*

The darkness crumbles away.
It is the same old druid° Time as ever,
Only a live thing leaps my hand,
A queer sardonic rat,

As I pull the parapet's° poppy   5
To stick behind my ear.
Droll rat, they would shoot you if they knew
Your cosmopolitan sympathies.
Now you have touched this English hand
You will do the same to a German   10
Soon, no doubt, if it be your pleasure
To cross the sleeping green between.
It seems you inwardly grin as you pass
Strong eyes, fine limbs, haughty athletes,   15

ancient (line 2)

wall protecting a trench (line 5)

Less chanced than you for life,
Bonds to the whims of murder,
Sprawled in the bowels of the earth,
The torn fields of France.
What do you see in our eyes   20
At the shrieking iron and flame
Hurled through still heavens?
What quaver—what heart aghast?
Poppies whose roots are in man's veins
Drop, and are ever dropping;   25
But mine in my ear is safe—
Just a little white with the dust.

Christina Rossetti   1830–1894

Remember   *1862*

Remember me when I am gone away,
    Gone far away into the silent land;
    When you can no more hold me by the hand,
Nor I half turn to go yet turning stay.
Remember me when no more day by day   5
    You tell me of our future that you planned:
    Only remember me: you understand
It will be late to counsel then or pray.
Yet if you should forget me for a while
    And afterwards remember, do not grieve: 10
    For if the darkness and corruption leave
    A vestige of the thoughts that once I had,
Better by far you should forget and smile
    Than that you should remember and be sad.

Sonia Sanchez   b. 1934

a poem for my father   *1970*

how sad it must be
to love so many women
to need so many black
perfumed bodies weeping
underneath you.   5
                    when i remember all those nights
i filled my mind with
long wars between short
sighted trojans & greeks
while you slapped some
wide hips about in   10
your pvt dungeon,
when i remember your

deformity   i want to
do something about your
makeshift manhood.   15
i guess
          that is why
on meeting your sixth
wife, i cross myself   20
with her confessionals.

to blk/record/buyers   1969

don't play me no
righteous bros.
                    white people
ain't rt bout nothing
no mo.
             don't tell me bout   5
foreign dudes
          cuz no blk/
people are grooving on a
sunday afternoon.
          they either   10
making out/
          signifying/
                    drinking/
making molotov cocktails/
                    stealing   15
or rather more taking their goods
from the honky thieves who
ain't hung up
          on no pacifist/jesus/
                    cross/   but.   20
play blk/songs
          to drown out the
shit/screams of honkies.   AAAH.
AAAH   AAAH   yeah.   brothers.   25
          andmanymoretogo.

Yvonne Sapia   b. 1946

Grandmother, a Caribbean Indian,
Described by My Father   1987

Nearly a hundred when she died,
mi viejita
was an open boat,
and I had no map
to show her the safe places.   5
There was much to grieve.

Her shoulders were stooped.
Her hands were never young.
They broke jars
at the watering holes,
like bones, like hearts.   10

When she was a girl,
she was given the island
but no wings.
She wanted wings,   15
though she bruised
like a persimmon.
She was not ruined
before her marriage.
But after the first baby died,   20
she disappeared in the middle
of days to worship
her black saint,
after the second,
to sleep with a hand towel   25
across her eyes.

I had to take care
not to exhume
from the mound of memory
these myths, these lost ones.   30
Born sleek as swans
on her river, my brother,
the man you have met
who has one arm,
and I glided into the sun.   35
Other children poured forth,
and by the time I was sixteen
I lost my place
in her thatched house.

She let me go,   40
and she did not come to the pier
the day the banana boat
pushed away from her shore
towards Nueva York
where I had heard   45
there would be room for me.

Anne Sexton   1928–1974

Cinderella   *1970*

You always read about it:
the plumber with twelve children
who wins the Irish Sweepstakes.

From toilets to riches.
That story.

Or the nursemaid,
some luscious sweet from Denmark
who captures the oldest son's heart.
From diapers to Dior.°
That story.

high fashion (by designer Christian Dior)

Or a milkman who serves the wealthy,
eggs, cream, butter, yogurt, milk,
the white truck like an ambulance
who goes into real estate
and makes a pile.
From homogenized to martinis at lunch.

Or the charwoman
who is on the bus when it cracks up
and collects enough from the insurance.
From mops to Bonwit Teller.°
That story.

exclusive store

Once
the wife of a rich man was on her deathbed
and she said to her daughter Cinderella:
Be devout. Be good. Then I will smile
down from heaven in the seam of a cloud.
The man took another wife who had
two daughters, pretty enough
but with hearts like blackjacks.
Cinderella was their maid.
She slept on the sooty hearth each night
and walked around looking like Al Jolson.°
Her father brought presents home from town,
jewels and gowns for the other women
but the twig of a tree for Cinderella.
She planted that twig on her mother's grave
and it grew to a tree where a white dove sat.
Whenever she wished for anything the dove
would drop it like an egg upon the ground.
The bird is important, my dears, so heed him.

white singer known for his black-face
minstrel performances

Next came the ball, as you all know.
It was a marriage market.
The prince was looking for a wife.
All but Cinderella were preparing
and gussying up for the big event.
Cinderella begged to go too.
Her stepmother threw a dish of lentils
into the cinders and said: Pick them
up in an hour and you shall go.
The white dove brought all his friends;
all the warm wings of the fatherland came,
and picked up the lentils in a jiffy.

5

10

15

20

25

30

35

40

45

50

No, Cinderella, said the stepmother,
you have no clothes and cannot dance.
That's the way with stepmothers.   55

Cinderella went to the tree at the grave
and cried forth like a gospel singer:
Mama! Mama! My turtledove,
send me to the prince's ball!
The bird dropped down a golden dress   60
and delicate little gold slippers.
Rather a large package for a simple bird.
So she went. Which is no surprise.
Her stepmother and sisters didn't
recognize her without her cinder face   65
and the prince took her hand on the spot
and danced with no other the whole day.

As nightfall came she thought she'd better
get home. The prince walked her home
and she disappeared into the pigeon house   70
and although the prince took an axe and broke
it open she was gone. Back to her cinders.
These events repeated themselves for three days.
However on the third day the prince
covered the palace steps with cobbler's wax   75
and Cinderella's gold shoe stuck upon it.
Now he would find whom the shoe fit
and find his strange dancing girl for keeps.
He went to their house and the two sisters
were delighted because they had lovely feet.   80
The eldest went into a room to try the slipper on
but her big toe got in the way so she simply
sliced it off and put on the slipper.
The prince rode away with her until the white dove
told him to look at the blood pouring forth.   85
That is the way with amputations.
They don't just heal up like a wish.
The other sister cut off her heel
but the blood told as blood will.
The prince was getting tired.   90
He began to feel like a shoe salesman.
But he gave it one last try.
This time Cinderella fit into the shoe
like a love letter into its envelope.
At the wedding ceremony   95
the two sisters came to curry favor
and the white dove pecked their eyes out.
Two hollow spots were left
like soup spoons.

Cinderella and the prince   100
lived, they say, happily ever after,
like two dolls in a museum case
never bothered by diapers or dust,

never arguing over the timing of an egg,
never telling the same story twice,
never getting a middle-aged spread,   105
their darling smiles pasted on for eternity
Regular Bobbsey Twins.°   two sets of twins in a popular series of early twentieth-century
That story.   children's books; they led carefree, happy lives

William Shakespeare   1564–1616

Sonnet 29   *1604*

When, in disgrace with Fortune and men's eyes,
I all alone beweep my outcast state,
And trouble deaf heaven with my bootless cries,
And look upon myself and curse my fate,
Wishing me like to one more rich in hope,   5
Featured like him, like him with friends possessed,
Desiring this man's art and that man's scope,
With what I most enjoy contented least;
Yet in these thoughts myself almost despising,
Haply I think on thee, and then my state   10
(Like to the lark at break of day arising
From sullen earth) sings hymns at heaven's gate;
For thy sweet love remembered such wealth brings
That then I scorn to change my state with kings.

Sonnet 55   *1609*

Not marble, nor the gilded monuments
Of princes, shall outlive this powerful rhyme;
But you shall shine more bright in these conténts
Than unswept stone, besmeared with sluttish time.
When wasteful war shall statues overturn,
And broils root out the work of masonry,   5
Nor Mars his sword nor war's quick fire shall burn
The living record of your memory.
'Gainst death and all-oblivious enmity
Shall you pace forth; your praise shall still find room
Even in the eyes of all posterity   10
That wear this world out to the ending doom.
    So, till the judgment that yourself arise,
    You live in this, and dwell in lovers' eyes.

Sonnet 116   *1609*

Let me not to the marriage of true minds
Admit impediments. Love is not love
Which alters when it alteration finds,

Or bends with the remover to remove:
Oh, no! it is an ever-fixèd mark,
That looks on tempests and is never shaken;   5
It is the star to every wandering bark,°   boat
Whose worth's unknown, although his height be taken.°   measured
Love's not Time's fool, though rosy lips and cheeks
Within his bending sickle's compass come;   10
Love alters not with his brief hours and weeks,
But bears it out even to the edge of doom.
If this be error and upon me proved,
I never writ, nor no man ever loved.

Sonnet 130   1609

My mistress' eyes are nothing like the sun;
Coral is far more red than her lips' red;
If snow be white, why then her breasts are dun;°   gray-brown
If hairs be wires, black wires grow on her head.
I have seen roses damasked,° red and white,   multicolored   5
But no such roses see I in her cheeks;
And in some perfumes there is more delight
Than in the breath that from my mistress reeks.
I love to hear her speak, yet well I know
That music hath a far more pleasing sound;   10
I grant I never saw a goddess go;
My mistress, when she walks, treads on the ground.
And yet, by heaven, I think my love as rare
As any she belied° with false compare.   misrepresented

Percy Bysshe Shelley   1792–1822

Ode to the West Wind   1820

I

O wild West Wind, thou breath of Autumn's being,
Thou, from whose unseen presence the leaves dead
Are driven, like ghosts from an enchanter fleeing,

Yellow, and black, and pale, and hectic red,
Pestilence-stricken multitudes: O Thou,   5
Who chariotest to their dark wintry bed

The winged seeds, where they lie cold and low,
Each like a corpse within its grave, until
Thine azure sister of the Spring shall blow

Her clarion o'er the dreaming earth, and fill   10
(Driving sweet buds like flocks to feed in air)
With living hues and odours plain and hill:

Wild Spirit, which art moving everywhere;
Destroyer and Preserver; hear, O hear!

II

Thou on whose stream, mid the steep sky's commotion,
Loose clouds like Earth's decaying leaves are shed,   15
Shook from the tangled boughs of Heaven and Ocean,

Angels of rain and lightning: there are spread
On the blue surface of thine aery surge,
Like the bright hair uplifted from the head   20

Of some fierce Maenad,° even from the dim verge   *devotee of Dionysus*
Of the horizon to the zenith's height,
The locks of the approaching storm. Thou Dirge

Of the dying year, to which this closing night
Will be the dome of a vast sepulchre,   25
Vaulted with all thy congregated might

Of vapours, from whose solid atmosphere
Black rain and fire and hail will burst: O hear!

III

Thou who didst waken from his summer dreams
The blue Mediterranean, where he lay,   30
Lulled by the coil of his crystalline streams,

Beside a pumice isle in Baiae's bay,°   *near Naples, Italy*
And saw in sleep old palaces and towers
Quivering within the wave's intenser day,

All overgrown with azure moss and flowers   35
So sweet, the sense faints picturing them! Thou
For whose path the Atlantic's level powers

Cleave themselves into chasms, while far below
The sea-blooms and the oozy woods which wear
The sapless foliage of the ocean, know   40

Thy voice, and suddenly grow grey with fear,
And tremble and despoil themselves: O hear!

IV

If I were a dead leaf thou mightest bear;
If I were a swift cloud to fly with thee;
A wave to pant beneath thy power, and share   45

The impulse of thy strength, only less free
Than thou, O Uncontrollable! If even
I were as in my boyhood, and could be

The comrade of thy wanderings over Heaven,
As then, when to outstrip thy skiey speed   50
Scarce seemed a vision; I would ne'er have striven

As thus with thee in prayer in my sore need,
Oh! lift me as a wave, a leaf, a cloud!
I fall upon thorns of life! I bleed!

A heavy weight of hours has chained and bowed   55
One too like thee: tameless, and swift, and proud.

V

Make me thy lyre,° even as the forest is: wind-harp
What if my leaves are falling like its own!
The tumult of thy mighty harmonies

Will take from both a deep, autumnal tone,   60
Sweet though in sadness. Be thou, Spirit fierce,
My spirit! Be thou me, impetuous one!

Drive my dead thoughts over the universe
Like withered leaves to quicken a new birth!
And, by the incantation of this verse,   65

Scatter, as from an unextinguished hearth
Ashes and sparks, my words among mankind!
Be through my lips to unawakened Earth

The trumpet of a prophecy! O Wind,
If Winter comes, can Spring be far behind?   70

Ozymandias   1818

I met a traveler from an antique land
Who said: "Two vast and trunkless legs of stone
Stand in the desert ... Near them on the sand,
Half-sunk, a shattered visage lies, whose frown,
And wrinkled lip, and sneer of cold command,   5
Tell that its sculptor well those passions read
Which yet survive, stamped on these lifeless things,
The hand that mocked them, and the heart that fed:
And on the pedestal these words appear:
'My name is Ozymandias, king of kings: 10
Look on my works, ye Mighty, and despair.'
Nothing beside remains. Round the decay
Of that colossal wreck, boundless and bare
The lone and level sands stretch far away."

Cathy Song   b. 1955

Lost Sister   1983

1

In China,
even the peasants
named their first daughters
Jade—
the stone that in the far fields   5
could moisten the dry season,
could make men move mountains
for the healing green of the inner hills
glistening like slices of winter melon.

And the daughters were grateful:
they never left home.
To move freely was a luxury
stolen from them at birth.
Instead, they gathered patience,
learning to walk in shoes
the size of teacups,
without breaking—
the arc of their movements
as dormant as the rooted willow,
as redundant as the farmyard hens.
But they traveled far
in surviving,
learning to stretch the family rice,
to quiet the demons,
the noisy stomachs.

2

There is a sister
across the ocean,
who relinquished her name,
diluting jade green
with the blue of the Pacific.
Rising with a tide of locusts,
she swarmed with others
to inundate another shore.
In America,
there are many roads
and women can stride along with men.

But in another wilderness,
the possibilities,
the loneliness,
can strangulate like jungle vines.
The meager provisions and sentiments
of once belonging—
fermented roots, Mah-Jongg tiles and firecrackers—
set but a flimsy household
in a forest of nightless cities.
A giant snake rattles above,
spewing black clouds into your kitchen.
Dough-faced landlords
slip in and out of your keyholes,
making claims you don't understand,
tapping into your communication systems
of laundry lines and restaurant chains.

You find you need China:
your one fragile identification,
a jade link
handcuffed to your wrist.
You remember your mother
who walked for centuries,

footless—
and like her,
you have left no footprints,   60
but only because
there is an ocean in between,
the unremitting space of your rebellion.

Gary Soto   b. 1952

Mexicans Begin Jogging   1981

At the factory I worked
In the fleck of rubber, under the press
Of an oven yellow with flame,
Until the border patrol opened
Their vans and my boss waved for us to run.   5
"Over the fence, Soto," he shouted,
And I shouted that I was American.
"No time for lies," he said, and pressed
A dollar in my palm, hurrying me
Through the back door.   10

Since I was on his time, I ran
And became the wag to a short tail of Mexicans—
Ran past the amazed crowds that lined
The street and blurred like photographs, in rain.
I ran from that industrial road to the soft   15
Houses where people paled at the turn of an autumn sky.
What could I do but yell vivas
To baseball, milkshakes, and those sociologists
Who would clock me
As I jog into the next century   20
On the power of a great, silly grin.

Oranges   1985

The first time I talked
With a girl, I was twelve,
Cold, and weighted down
With two oranges in my jacket.
December. Frost cracking   5
Beneath my steps, my breath
Before me, then gone,
As I walked toward
Her house, the one whose
Porch light burned yellow   10
Night and day, in any weather.
A dog barked at me, until
She came out pulling
At her gloves, face bright

With rouge. I smiled,
Touched her shoulder, and led
Her down the street, across
A used car lot and a line
Of newly planted trees,
Until we were breathing
Before a drugstore. We
Entered, the tiny bell
Bringing a saleslady
Down a narrow aisle of goods.
I turned to the candies
Tiered like bleachers
And asked what she wanted—
Light in her eyes, a smile
Starting at the corners
Of her mouth. I fingered
A nickel in my pocket,
And when she lifted a chocolate
That cost a dime,
I didn't say anything.
I took the nickel from
My pocket, then an orange,
And set them quietly on
The counter. When I looked up,
The lady's eyes met mine,
And held them, knowing
Very well what it was all
About.

      Outside,
A few cars hissing past,
Fog hanging like old
Coats between the trees.
I took my girl's hand
In mine for two blocks,
Then released it to let
Her unwrap the chocolate
That was so bright against
The grey of December
That, from some distance,
Someone might have thought
I was making a fire in my hands.

       15

       20

       25

       30

       35

       40

       45

       50

       55

Bruce Springsteen   b. 1949

4th of July, Asbury Park (Sandy)   *1973*

Sandy, the fireworks are hailin'
Over little Eden tonight
Forcing a light into all those stony faces

Left stranded on this warm July
Down in the town the circuit's full of switchblade lovers   5
So fast, so shiny, and so sharp
As the wizards play down on pinball way
On the boardwalk way past dark
And the boys from the casino dance with their shirts open
Like Latin lovers on the shore   10
Chasing all them silly New York virgins by the score

And Sandy, the aurora is rising behind us
Its pale lights our carnival life forever
Oh, love me tonight for I may never see you again
Hey Sandy girl, my my baby   15

Now the greasers, they tramp the streets
Or get busted for sleeping on the beach all night
Them boys in their high heels, ah, Sandy,
Their skins are so white
And me, I just got tired of hanging in them dusty arcades   20
Banging them pleasure machines
Chasing the factory girls underneath the boardwalk
Where they all promise to unsnap their jeans
And you know that tilt-a-whirl down on the south beach drag
I got on it last night and my shirt got caught   25
And it kept me spinning
Didn't think I'd ever get off

Oh Sandy, the aurora is rising behind us
Its pale lights our carnival life on the water
Running, laughing 'neath the boardwalk   3
With the voices, darling . . .
I remember Sandy girl, now now now now baby

Sandy, that waitress I was seeing lost her desire for me
I spoke with her last night
She said she won't set herself on fire for me anymore   35
She worked that joint under the boardwalk
She was always the girl you saw boppin' down the beach with the radio
The kids say last night she was dressed like a star
In one of them cheap little seaside bars
And I saw her parked with lover boy out on the kokomo   40
Did you hear the cops finally busted Madame Marie
For tellin' fortunes better than they do?
For me this boardwalk life's through, babe
You oughta quit this scene too

Sandy, the aurora is rising behind us   45
Its pale lights our carnival life forever
Oh love me tonight and I promise I'll love you forever
Oh I mean it, Sandy girl
My my my my baby
Yeah, promise Sandy girl   50
Shalalala baby

William Stafford   b. 1914

Traveling through the Dark   *1960*

Traveling through the dark I found a deer
dead on the edge of the Wilson River road.
It is usually best to roll them into the canyon:
that road is narrow; to swerve might make more dead.

By glow of the tail-light I stumbled back of the car   5
and stood by the heap, a doe, a recent killing;
she had stiffened already, almost cold.
I dragged her off; she was large in the belly.

My fingers touching the side brought me the reason—
her side was warm; her fawn lay there waiting,   10
alive, still, never to be born.
Beside that mountain road I hesitated.

The car aimed ahead its lowered parking lights;
under the hood purred the steady engine.
I stood in the glare of the warm exhaust turning red;   15
around our group I could hear the wilderness listen.

I thought hard for us all—my only swerving—
then pushed her over the edge into the river.

Wallace Stevens   1879–1955

The Emperor of Ice-Cream   *1923*

Call the roller of big cigars,
The muscular one, and bid him whip
In kitchen cups concupiscent curds.
Let the wenches dawdle in such dress
As they are used to wear, and let the boys   5
Bring flowers in last month's newspapers.
Let be be finale of seem.
The only emperor is the emperor of ice-cream.

Take from the dresser of deal,
Lacking the three glass knobs, that sheet   10
On which she embroidered fantails once
And spread it so as to cover her face.
If her horny feet protrude, they come
To show how cold she is, and dumb.
Let the lamp affix its beam.   15
The only emperor is the emperor of ice-cream.

The Snow Man   *1923*

One must have a mind of winter
To regard the frost and the boughs
Of the pine-trees crusted with snow;

And have been cold a long time
To behold the junipers shagged with ice,   5
The spruces rough in the distant glitter

Of the January sun; and not to think
Of any misery in the sound of the wind,
In the sound of a few leaves,

Which is the sound of the land   10
Full of the same wind
That is blowing in the same bare place

For the listener, who listens in the snow,
And, nothing himself, beholds
Nothing that is not there and the nothing that is.   15

Mark Strand   b. 1934

Eating Poetry   *1967*

Ink runs from the corners of my mouth.
There is no happiness like mine.
I have been eating poetry.

The librarian does not believe what she sees.
Her eyes are sad   5
and she walks with her hands in her dress.

The poems are gone.
The light is dim.
The dogs are on the basement stairs and coming up.

Their eyeballs roll,   10
their blond legs burn like brush.
The poor librarian begins to stamp her feet and weep.

She does not understand.
When I get on my knees and lick her hand,
she screams.   15

I am a new man.
I snarl at her and bark.
I romp with joy in the bookish dark.

May Swenson   1919–1989

Women   *1970*

Women
  should be
    pedestals
      moving
        pedestals
          moving
        to the
      motions
    of men

Or they
  should be
    little horses
      those wooden
        sweet   5
          oldfashioned
        painted
      rocking
    horses

the gladdest things in the toyroom   10

The
pegs
of their
ears
so familiar
and dear
to the trusting
fists
To be chafed

feelingly
and then
unfeelingly
To be
joyfully   15
ridden
rockingly
ridden until
the restored

egos dismount and the legs stride away   20

Immobile
  sweetlipped
    sturdy
      and smiling
        women
          should always
        be waiting

willing
  to be set
    into motion
      Women   25
      should be
    pedestals
      to men

Mary Tallmountain   1918–1994

There Is No Word for Goodbye   *1981*

Sokoya,° I said, looking through   aunt
  the net of wrinkles into
  wise black pools
  of her eyes.

What do you say in Athabaskan
  when you leave each other?   5
  What is the word
  for goodbye?

A shade of feeling rippled
  the wind-tanned skin.
  Ah, nothing, she said,
  watching the river flash.   10

She looked at me close.
  We just say, Tlaa. That means,
  See you.
  We never leave each other.   15
  When does your mouth
  say goodbye to your heart?

She touched me light
  as a bluebell.
  You forget when you leave us;   20
  you're so small then.
  We don't use that word.

We always think you're coming back,
  but if you don't,
  we'll see you someplace else.   25
  You understand.
  There is no word for goodbye.

Dylan Thomas   1914–1953

Fern Hill   *1946*

Now as I was young and easy under the apple boughs
About the lilting house and happy as the grass was green,
    The night above the dingle° starry,   *wooded valley*
      Time let me hail and climb
    Golden in the heydays of his eyes,   5
And honored among wagons I was prince of the apple towns
And once below a time I lordly had the trees and leaves
        Trail with daisies and barley
      Down the rivers of the windfall light.

And as I was green and carefree, famous among the barns   10
About the happy yard and singing as the farm was home,
    In the sun that is young once only,
        Time let me play and be
    Golden in the mercy of his means,
And green and golden I was huntsman and herdsman, the calves 15
Sang to my horn, the foxes on the hills barked clear and cold,
        And the sabbath rang slowly
      In the pebbles of the holy streams.

All the sun long it was running, it was lovely, the hay
Fields high as the house, the tunes from the chimneys, it was air 20
      And playing, lovely and watery

And fire green as grass.
And nightly under the simple stars
As I rode to sleep the owls were bearing the farm away,
All the moon long I heard, blessed among stables, the night-jars°   nightingales   25
Flying with the ricks,° and the horses   haystacks
    Flashing into the dark.

And then to awake, and the farm, like a wanderer white
With the dew, come back, the cock on his shoulder: it was all
    Shining, it was Adam and maiden,
        The sky gathered again   30
    And the sun grew round that very day.
So it must have been after the birth of the simple light
In the first, spinning place, the spellbound horses walking warm
    Out of the whinnying green stable
        On to the fields of praise.   35

And honored among foxes and pheasants by the gay house
Under the new made clouds and happy as the heart was long,
    In the sun born over and over,
        I ran my heedless ways,
    My wishes raced through the house high hay   40
And nothing I cared, at my sky blue trades, that time allows
In all his tuneful turning so few and such morning songs
    Before the children green and golden
        Follow him out of grace,

Nothing I cared, in the lamb white days, that time would take me   45
Up to the swallow thronged loft by the shadow of my hand,
    In the moon that is always rising,
        Nor that riding to sleep
    I should hear him fly with the high fields
And wake to the farm forever fled from the childless land.   50
Oh as I was young and easy in the mercy of his means,
        Time held me green and dying
    Though I sang in my chains like the sea.

The Force That through the
Green Fuse Drives the Flower   *1934*

The force that through the green fuse drives the flower
Drives my green age; that blasts the roots of trees
Is my destroyer.
And I am dumb° to tell the crooked rose   unable to speak
My youth is bent by the same wintry fever.   5

The force that drives the water through the rocks
Drives my red blood; that dries the mouthing streams
Turns mine to wax.

And I am dumb to mouth unto my veins
How at the mountain spring the same mouth sucks.   10

The hand that whirls the water in the pool
Stirs the quicksand; that ropes the blowing wind
Hauls my shroud sail.
And I am dumb to tell the hanging man
How of my clay is made the hangman's lime.°   tree   15

The lips of time leech to the fountain head;
Love drips and gathers, but the fallen blood
Shall calm her sores.
And I am dumb to tell a weather's wind
How time has ticked a heaven round the stars.   20

And I am dumb to tell the lover's tomb
How at my sheet goes the same crooked worm.

Derek Walcott   b. 1930

A Far Cry From Africa   1962

A wind is ruffling the tawny pelt
Of Africa. Kikuyu,° quick as flies,   East African people
Batten upon the bloodstreams of the veldt.°   prairie
Corpses are scattered through a paradise.
Only the worm, colonel of carrion, cries: 5
"Waste no compassion on these separate dead!"
Statistics justify and scholars seize
The salients of colonial policy.
What is that to the white child hacked in bed?
To savages, expendable as Jews?   10

Threshed out by beaters,° the long rushes break   men who chase game out of hiding for hunters
In a white dust of ibises whose cries
Have wheeled since civilization's dawn
From the parched river or beast-teeming plain.
The violence of beast on beast is read   15
As natural law, but upright man
Seeks his divinity by inflicting pain.
Delirious as these worried beasts, his wars
Dance to the tightened carcass of a drum,
While he calls courage still that native dread   20
Of the white peace contracted by the dead.

Again brutish necessity wipes its hands
Upon the napkin of a dirty cause, again
A waste of our compassion, as with Spain,°   in the Spanish Civil War, 1936–1939
The gorilla wrestles with the superman.   25
I who am poisoned with the blood of both,
Where shall I turn, divided to the vein?
I who have cursed

The drunken officer of British rule, how choose
Between this Africa and the English tongue I love?   30
Betray them both, or give back what they give?
How can I face such slaughter and be cool?
How can I turn from Africa and live?

The Glory Trumpeter   *1964*

Old Eddie's face, wrinkled with river lights,
Looked like a Mississippi man's. The eyes,
Derisive and avuncular at once,
Swivelling, fixed me. They'd seen
Too many wakes, too many cathouse nights.   5
The bony, idle fingers on the valves
Of his knee-cradled horn could tear
Through "Georgia on My Mind" or "Jesus Saves"
With the same fury of indifference
If what propelled such frenzy was despair.   10

Now, as the eyes sealed in the ashen flesh,
And Eddie, like a deacon at his prayer,
Rose, tilting the bright horn, I saw a flash
Of gulls and pigeons from the dunes of coal
Near my grandmother's barracks on the wharves,   15
I saw the sallow faces of those men
Who sighed as if they spoke into their graves
About the Negro in America. That was when
The Sunday comics, sprawled out on her floor,
Sent from the States, had a particular odour;   20
Dry smell of money mingled with man's sweat.

And yet, if Eddie's features held our fate,
Secure in childhood I did not know then
A jesus-ragtime or gut-bucket blues
To the bowed heads of lean, compliant men
Back from the States in their funereal serge,   25
Black, rusty homburgs° and limp waiters' ties,   *men's hats*
Slow, honey accents and lard-coloured eyes,
Was Joshua's ram's horn wailing for the Jews°   *Joshua blew a trumpet at the siege of Jericho*
Of patient bitterness or bitter siege.   30

Now it was that, as Eddie turned his back
On our young crowd out fêteing, swilling liquor,
And blew, eyes closed, one foot up, out to sea,
His horn aimed at those cities of the Gulf,
Mobile and Galveston, and sweetly meted
Their horn of plenty through his bitter cup,   35
In lonely exaltation blaming me
For all whom race and exile have defeated,
For my own uncle in America,
That living there I never could look up.   40

Margaret Walker   b. 1915

Lineage   1942

My grandmothers were strong.
They followed plows and bent to toil.
They moved through fields sowing seed.
They touched earth and grain grew.
They were full of sturdiness and singing.   5
My grandmothers were strong.

My grandmothers are full of memories
Smelling of soap and onions and wet clay
With veins rolling roughly over quick hands
They have many clean words to say.   10
My grandmothers were strong.
Why am I not as they?

Robert Penn Warren   b. 1905

You Sort Old Letters

Some are pure business, land deals, receipts, a contract,
Bank statements, dead policies, demand for some payment.
But a beach-party invite!—yes, yes, that tease
Of a hostess and you, withdrawn beyond dunes, lay,
The laughter far off, and for contact   5
Of tongue and teeth, she let you first loosen a breast.
You left town soon after—and now wonder what
Might that day have meant.

Suppose you hadn't left town—well, she's dead anyway.
Three divorces, three children, all born for the sludge of the pit.   10
It was Number One, nice fellow, when she took you to the dunes,
And gasped: "Harder, bite harder!" And you did
In the glare of day. When she scrambled up,

She cried: "Oh, don't you hate me!" And wept
Like a child. You patted, caressed her.   15
Cuddled and kissed her. She said: "I'm a shit."

Do you seem to remember that, for a moment,
Your heart stirred? But you shrug now, remembering
How, in the end, she shacked up
With a likker-head plumber, who, now and then,   20
Would give her a jolt to the jaw, or with heel of a palm
Would flatten lips to the teeth, then slam
Her the works, blood
On her swollen lips—as was common gossip.

You married a little late—and now in this mess   25
Of old papers the words at you stare:
You were smart to blow town. Keep your pecker up!

Signed only: *Yours, maybe.*

Of course, she had everything—money, looks,
Wit, breeding, a charm
Of defenseless appeal—the last what trapped, no doubt,   30
The three near middle-aged fall guys, who got only
Horns for their pains. Yes, she threw all away.
And as you've guessed, by struggling
Sank deeper and deeper into
A slough of self-hate. However, you   35
Are no psychiatrist, and couldn't say
What or why, as you, far away, lay

By the warm and delicious body you loved
So well, in the dark ashamed of
Recurring speculations, as though this   40
Betrayed your love. Years passed. The end, you heard,
Was sleeping pills. You felt some confusion, or guilt—
But how could you be blamed?—Even if
Knees once were grinding sand as sun once smote
Your bare back, or, in a dream, lips,   45
Bloody, lifted for your kiss.

Walt Whitman   1819–1892

Crossing Brooklyn Ferry.   *1881*

1

Flood-tide below me! I see you face to face!
Clouds of the west—sun there half an hour high—I see you also face to face.

Crowds of men and women attired in the usual costumes, how curious you are to
    me!
On the ferry-boats the hundreds and hundreds that cross, returning home, are
    more curious to me than you suppose,
And you that shall cross from shore to shore years hence are more to me, and
    more in my meditations, than you might suppose.   5

2

The impalpable sustenance of me from all things at all hours of the day,
The simple, compact, well-join'd scheme, myself disintegrated, every one
    disintegrated yet part of the scheme,
The similitudes of the past and those of the future,
The glories strung like beads on my smallest sights and hearings, on the walk in
    the street and the passage over the river,
The current rushing so swiftly and swimming with me far away,
The others that are to follow me, the ties between me and them,   10
The certainty of others, the life, love, sight, hearing of others.

Others will enter the gates of the ferry and cross from shore to shore,
Others will watch the run of the flood-tide,
Others will see the shipping of Manhattan north and west, and the heights of

Brooklyn to the south and east,   15
Others will see the islands large and small;
Fifty years hence, others will see them as they cross, the sun half an hour high,
A hundred years hence, or ever so many hundred years hence, others will see
    them,
Will enjoy the sunset, the pouring-in of the flood-tide, the falling-back to the sea
    of the ebb-tide.

3

It avails not, time nor place—distance avails not,   20
I am with you, you men and women of a generation, or ever so many generations
    hence,
Just as you feel when you look on the river and sky, so I felt,
Just as any of you is one of a living crowd, I was one of a crowd,
Just as you are refresh'd by the gladness of the river and the bright flow, I was
    refresh'd,
Just as you stand and lean on the rail, yet hurry with the swift current, I stood
    yet was hurried,   25
Just as you look on the numberless masts of ships and the thick-stemm'd pipes of
    steamboats, I look'd.
I too many and many a time cross'd the river of old,
Watched the Twelfth-month° sea-gulls, saw them high in the air floating with   December
    motionless wings, oscillating their bodies,
Saw how the glistening yellow lit up parts of their bodies and left the rest in strong
    shadow,
Saw the slow-wheeling circles and the gradual edging toward the south,   30
Saw the reflection of the summer sky in the water,
Had my eyes dazzled by the shimmering track of beams,
Look'd at the fine centrifugal spokes of light round the shape of my head in the
    sunlit water,
Look'd on the haze on the hills southward and south-westward,
Look'd on the vapor as it flew in fleeces tinged with violet,   35
Look'd toward the lower bay to notice the vessels arriving,
Saw their approach, saw aboard those that were near me,
Saw the white sails of schooners and sloops, saw the ships at anchor,
The sailors at work in the rigging or out astride the spars,
The round masts, the swinging motion of the hulls, the slender serpentine
    pennants,   40
The large and small steamers in motion, the pilots in their pilot-houses,
The white wake left by the passage, the quick tremulous whirl of the wheels,
The flags of all nations, the falling of them at sunset,
The scallop-edged waves in the twilight, the ladled cups, the frolicsome crests and
    glistening,
The stretch afar growing dimmer and dimmer, the gray walls of the granite
    storehouses by the docks,   45
On the river the shadowy group, the big steam-tug closely flank'd on each side by
    the barges, the hay-boat, the belated lighter,°   barge
On the neighboring shore the fires from the foundry chimneys burning high and
    glaringly into the night,

Casting their flicker of black contrasted with wild red and yellow light over the
    tops of houses, and down into the clefts of streets.

4

These and all else were to me the same as they are to you,
I loved well those cities, loved well the stately and rapid river,
The men and women I saw were all near to me,   50
Others the same—others who look back on me because I look'd forward to them,
(The time will come, though I stop here to-day and to-night.)

5

What is it then between us?
What is the count of the scores or hundreds of years between us?   55

Whatever it is, it avails not—distance avails not, and place avails not,
I too lived, Brooklyn of ample hills was mine,
I too walk'd the streets of Manhattan island, and bathed in the waters around it,
I too felt the curious abrupt questionings stir within me,
In the day among crowds of people sometimes they came upon me,   60
In my walks home late at night or as I lay in my bed they came upon me,
I too had been struck from the float forever held in solution,
I too had receiv'd identity by my body,
That I was I knew was of my body, and what I should be I knew I should be of
    my body.

6

It is not upon you alone the dark patches fall,
The dark threw its patches down upon me also,   65
The best I had done seem'd to me blank and suspicious,
My great thoughts as I supposed them, were they not in reality meagre?
Nor is it you alone who know what it is to be evil,
I am he who knew what it was to be evil,
I too knitted the old knot of contrariety,   70
Blabb'd, blush'd, resented, lied, stole, grudg'd,
Had guile, anger, lust, hot wishes I dared not speak,
Was wayward, vain, greedy, shallow, sly, cowardly, malignant,
The wolf, the snake, the hog, not wanting in me,
The cheating look, the frivolous word, the adulterous wish, not wanting,   75
Refusals, hates, postponements, meanness, laziness, none of these wanting,
Was one with the rest, the days and haps of the rest,
Was call'd by my nightest name by clear loud voices of young men as they saw me
    approaching or passing,
Felt their arms on my neck as I stood, or the negligent leaning of their flesh
    against me as I sat,
Saw many I loved in the street or ferry-boat or public assembly, yet never told   80
    them a word,
Lived the same life with the rest, the same old laughing, gnawing, sleeping,
Play'd the part that still looks back on the actor or actress,
The same old role, the role that is what we make it, as great as we like,
Or as small as we like, or both great and small.   85

7

Closer yet I approach you,
What thought you have of me now, I had as much of you—I laid in my stores in
    advance,
I consider'd long and seriously of you before you were born.

Who was to know what should come home to me?
Who knows but I am enjoying this?   90
Who knows, for all the distance, but I am as good as looking at you now, for all
    you cannot see me?

8

Ah, what can ever be more stately and admirable to me than mast-hemm'd
    Manhattan?
River and sunset and scallop-edg'd waves of flood-tide?
The sea-gulls oscillating their bodies, the hay-boat in the twilight, and the belated
    lighter?
What gods can exceed these that clasp me by the hand, and with voices I love
    call me promptly and loudly by my nighest name as I approach?   95
What is more subtle than this which ties me to the woman or man that looks in my
    face?
Which fuses me into you now, and pours my meaning into you?

We understand then do we not?
What I promis'd without mentioning it, have you not accepted?
What the study could not teach—what the preaching could not accomplish is
    accomplish'd, is it not?   100

9

Flow on, river! flow with the flood-tide, and ebb with the ebb-tide!
Frolic on, crested and scallop-edg'd waves!
Gorgeous clouds of the sunset! drench with your splendor me, or the men and
    women generations after me!
Cross from shore to shore, countless crowds of passengers!
Stand up, tall masts of Mannahatta!° stand up, beautiful hills of Brooklyn!   Manhattan   105
Throb, baffled and curious brain! throw out questions and answers!
Suspend here and everywhere, eternal float of solution!
Gaze, loving and thirsting eyes, in the house or street or public assembly!
Sound out, voices of young men! loudly and musically call me by my nighest
    name!
Live, old life! play the part that looks back on the actor or actress!   110
Play the old role, the role that is great or small according as one makes it!
Consider, you who peruse me, whether I may not in unknown ways be looking
    upon you;
Be firm, rail over the river, to support those who lean idly, yet haste with the
    hasting current;
Fly on, sea-birds! fly sideways, or wheel in large circles high in the air;
Receive the summer sky, you water, and faithfully hold it till all downcast eyes

have time to take it from you!
Diverge, fine spokes of light, from the shape of my head, or any one's head, in the
  sunlit water!   115
Come on, ships from the lower bay! pass up or down, white-sail'd schooners,
  sloops, lighters!
Flaunt away, flags of all nations! be duly lower'd at sunset!
Burn high your fires, foundry chimneys! cast black shadows at nightfall! cast red
  and yellow light over the tops of the houses!
Appearances, now or henceforth, indicate what you are,
You necessary film, continue to envelop the soul,   120
About my body for me, and your body for you, be hung our divinest aromas,
Thrive, cities—bring your freight, bring your shows, ample and sufficient rivers,
Expand, being than which none else is perhaps more spiritual,
Keep your places, objects than which none else is more lasting.   125

You have waited, you always wait, you dumb, beautiful ministers,
We receive you with free sense at last, and are insatiate henceforward,
Not you any more shall be able to foil us, or withhold yourselves from us,
We use you, and do not cast you aside—we plant you permanently within us,
We fathom you not—we love you—there is perfection in you also,   130
You furnish your parts toward eternity,
Great or small, you furnish your parts toward the soul.

There Was a Child Went Forth   1855

There was a child went forth every day,
And the first object he looked upon, that object he became,
And that object became part of him for the day or a certain part of the day,
Or for many years or stretching cycles of years.

The early lilacs became part of this child,   5
And grass and white and red morning-glories, and white and red clover, and the
  song of the phoebe-bird,
And the Third-month lambs and the sow's pink-faint litter, and the mare's foal and
  the cow's calf,
And the noisy brood of the barnyard or by the mire of the pond-side,
And the fish suspending themselves so curiously below there, and the beautiful
  curious liquid,
And the water-plants with their graceful flat heads, all became part of him.   10

The field-sprouts of Fourth-month and Fifth-month became part of him,
Winter-grain sprouts and those of the light-yellow corn, and the esculent°   edible
  roots of the garden,
And the apple-trees covered with blossoms and the fruit afterward, and wood-
  berries, and the commonest weeds by the road,
And the old drunkard staggering home from the outhouse of the tavern whence
  he had lately risen,
And the schoolmistress that passed on her way to the school,   15

And the friendly boys that passed, and the quarrelsome boys,
And the tidy and fresh-cheeked girls, and the barefoot negro boy and girl,
And all the changes of city and country wherever he went.

His own parents, he that had fathered him and she that had conceived him in her
    womb and birthed him,
They gave this child more of themselves than that,   20
They gave him afterward every day, they became part of him.

The mother at home quietly placing the dishes on the supper-table,
The mother with mild words, clean her cap and gown, a wholesome odor falling
    off her person and clothes as she walks by,
The father, strong, self-sufficient, manly, mean, angered, unjust,
The blow, the quick loud word, the tight bargain, the crafty lure,   25
The family usages, the language, the company, the furniture, the yearning and
    swelling heart,
Affection that will not be gainsayed, the sense of what is real, the thought if after
    all it should prove unreal,
The doubts of day-time and the doubts of night-time, the curious whether and
    how,
Whether that which appears so is so, or is it all flashes and specks?
Men and women crowding fast in the streets, if they are not
    flashes and specks what are they?   30
The streets themselves and the façades of houses, and goods in the windows,
Vehicles, teams, the heavy-planked wharves, the huge crossing at the ferries,
The village on the highland seen from afar at sunset, the river between,
Shadows, aureola and mist, the light falling on roofs and gables of white or brown
    two miles off,
The schooner near by sleepily dropping down the tide, the
    little boat slack-towed astern,   35
The hurrying tumbling waves, quick-broken crests, slapping,
The strata of colored clouds, the long bar of maroon-tint away solitary by itself, the
    spread of purity it lies motionless in,
The horizon's edge, the flying sea-crow, the fragrance of salt marsh and shore
    mud,
These became part of that child who went forth every day, and who now goes,
    and will always go forth every day.

When I Heard the Learn'd Astronomer   1865

When I heard the learn'd astronomer,
When the proofs, the figures, were ranged in columns before me,
When I was shown the charts and diagrams, to add, divide, and measure them,
When I sitting heard the astronomer where he lectured with much applause in the
    lecture room,
How soon unaccountable I became tired and sick,   5
Till rising and gliding out I wandered off by myself,
In the mystical moist night air, and from time to time,
Looked up in perfect silence at the stars.

Richard Wilbur   b. 1921

The Writer   *1976*

In her room at the prow of the house
Where light breaks, and the windows are tossed with linden,°   shade tree
My daughter is writing a story.

I pause in the stairwell, hearing
From her shut door a commotion of typewriter-keys
Like a chain hauled over a gunwale.°   5
         boat's rail

Young as she is, the stuff
Of her life is a great cargo, and some of it heavy:
I wish her a lucky passage.

But now it is she who pauses,   10
As if to reject my thought and its easy figure.
A stillness greatens, in which

The whole house seems to be thinking,
And then she is at it again with a bunched clamor
Of strokes, and again is silent.   15

I remember the dazed starling°   bird
Which was trapped in that very room, two years ago,
How we stole in, lifted a sash

And retreated, not to affright it;
And how for a helpless hour, through the crack of the door,   20
We watched the sleek, wild, dark

And iridescent creature
Batter against the brilliance, drop like a glove
To the hard floor, or the desk-top,

And wait then, humped and bloody,   25
For the wits to try it again; and how our spirits
Rose when, suddenly sure,

It lifted off from a chair-back,
Beating a smooth course for the right window
And clearing the sill of the world.   30

It is always a matter, my darling,
Of life or death, as I had forgotten. I wish
What I wished you before, but harder.

William Carlos Williams   1883–1963

Raleigh Was Right   1941

We cannot go to the country
for the country will bring us no peace
What can the small violets tell us
that grow on furry stems in
the long grass among lance shaped leaves?   5

Though you praise us
and call to mind the poets
who sung of our loveliness
it was long ago!
long ago! when country people   10
would plow and sow with
flowering minds and pockets at ease—
if ever this were true.

Not now. Love itself a flower
with roots in a parched ground.   15
Empty pockets make empty heads.
Cure it if you can but
do not believe that we can live
today in the country
for the country will bring us no peace.   20

The Red Wheelbarrow   1923

so much depends
upon

a red wheel
barrow

glazed with rain
water

beside the white
chickens.

William Wordsworth   1770–1850

She Dwelt among the Untrodden Ways   1800

She dwelt among the untrodden ways
    Beside the springs of Dove,°   a stream in the north of England
A Maid whom there were none to praise
    And very few to love:

A violet by a mossy stone   5
    Half hidden from the eye!

—Fair as a star, when only one
    Is shining in the sky.

She lived unknown, and few could know
    When Lucy ceased to be;
But she is in her grave, and, oh,   10
    The difference to me!

Lines Composed a Few Miles Above Tintern Abbey on Revisiting the Banks of the Wye During a Tour, June 13, 1798

1798

Five years have past; five summers, with the length
Of five long winters! and again I hear
These waters, rolling from their mountain-springs
With a soft inland murmur.—Once again
Do I behold these steep and lofty cliffs,   5
That on a wild secluded scene impress
Thoughts of more deep seclusion, and connect
The landscape with the quiet of the sky.
The day is come when I again repose
Here, under this dark sycamore, and view   10
These plots of cottage-ground, these orchard-tufts,
Which at this season, with their unripe fruits,
Are clad in one green hue, and lose themselves
'Mid groves and copses. Once again I see
These hedge-rows, hardly hedge-rows, little lines   15
Of sportive wood run wild; these pastoral farms,
Green to the very door; and wreaths of smoke
Sent up, in silence, from among the trees!
With some uncertain notice, as might seem
Of vagrant dwellers in the houseless woods,   20
Or of some Hermit's cave, where by his fire
The Hermit sits alone.
                These beauteous forms,
Through a long absence, have not been to me
As is a landscape to a blind man's eye:
But oft, in lonely rooms, and 'mid the din   25
Of towns and cities, I have owed to them
In hours of weariness, sensations sweet,
Felt in the blood, and felt along the heart;
And passing even into my purer mind,
With tranquil restoration:—feelings too   30
Of unremembered pleasure: such, perhaps,
As have no slight or trivial influence
On that best portion of a good man's life,
His little, nameless, unremembered acts
Of kindness and of love. Nor less, I trust,   35
To them I may have owed another gift,
Of aspect more sublime; that blessed mood,

In which the burden of the mystery,
In which the heavy and the weary weight
Of all this unintelligible world,   40
Is lightened:—that serene and blessed mood,
In which the affections gently lead us on,—
Until, the breath of this corporeal frame
And even the motion of our human blood
Almost suspended, we are laid asleep   45
In body, and become a living soul:
While with an eye made quiet by the power
Of harmony, and the deep power of joy,
We see into the life of things.
                                   If this
Be but a vain belief, yet, oh!—how oft—   50
In darkness and amid the many shapes
Of joyless daylight; when the fretful stir
Unprofitable, and the fever of the world,
Have hung upon the beatings of my heart—
How oft, in spirit, have I turned to thee,   55
O sylvan Wye! thou wanderer thro' the woods,
How often has my spirit turned to thee!
And now, with gleams of half extinguished thought,
With many recognitions dim and faint,
And somewhat of a sad perplexity,   60
The picture of the mind revives again:
While here I stand, not only with the sense
Of present pleasure, but with pleasing thoughts
That in this moment there is life and food
For future years. And so I dare to hope,   65
Though changed, no doubt, from what I was when first
I came among these hills; when like a roe
I bounded o'er the mountains, by the sides
Of the deep rivers, and the lonely streams,
Wherever nature led: more like a man   70
Flying from something that he dreads, than one
Who sought the thing he loved. For nature then
(The coarser pleasures of my boyish days,
And their glad animal movements all gone by)
To me was all in all.—I cannot paint   75
What then I was. The sounding cataract
Haunted me like a passion: the tall rock,
The mountain, and the deep and gloomy wood,
Their colours, and their forms, were then to me
An appetite; a feeling and a love,   80
That had no need of a remoter charm,
By thought supplied, nor any interest
Unborrowed from the eye.—That time is past,
And all its aching joys are now no more,
And all its dizzy raptures. Not for this   85
Faint° I, nor mourn nor murmur; other gifts   lose heart
Have followed; for such loss, I would believe,

Abundant recompense. For I have learned
To look on nature, not as in the hour
Of thoughtless youth; but hearing oftentimes
The still, sad music of humanity,   90
Nor harsh nor grating, though of ample power
To chasten and subdue. And I have felt
A presence that disturbs me with the joy
Of elevated thoughts; a sense sublime
Of something far more deeply interfused,   95
Whose dwelling is the light of setting suns,
And the round ocean, and the living air,
And the blue sky, and in the mind of man;
A motion and a spirit, that impels
All thinking things, all objects of all thought,   100
And rolls through all things. Therefore am I still
A lover of the meadows and the woods,
And mountains; and of all that we behold
From this green earth; of all the mighty world
Of eye, and ear,—both what they half create,   105
And what perceive; well pleased to recognize
In nature and the language of the sense,
The anchor of my purest thoughts, the nurse,
The guide, the guardian of my heart, and soul
Of all my mortal being.   110
                        Nor perchance,
If I were not thus taught, should I the more
Suffer my genial spirits° to decay: creative powers
For thou art with me here upon the banks
Of this fair river; thou my dearest Friend,°   Wordsworth's sister, Dorothy 115
My dear, dear Friend; and in thy voice I catch
The language of my former heart, and read
My former pleasures in the shooting lights
Of thy wild eyes. Oh! yet a little while
May I behold in thee what I was once,
My dear, dear Sister! and this prayer I make,   120
Knowing that Nature never did betray
The heart that loved her; 'tis her privilege,
Through all the years of this our life, to lead
From joy to joy: for she can so inform
The mind that is within us, so impress   125
With quietness and beauty, and so feed
With lofty thoughts, that neither evil tongues,
Rash judgments, nor the sneers of selfish men,
Nor greetings where no kindness is, nor all
The dreary intercourse of daily life,   130
Shall e'er prevail against us, or disturb
Our cheerful faith that all which we behold
Is full of blessings. Therefore let the moon
Shine on thee in thy solitary walk;
And let the misty mountain-winds be free   135

To blow against thee: and, in after years,
When these wild ecstasies shall be matured
Into a sober pleasure; when thy mind
Shall be a mansion for all lovely forms,   140
Thy memory be as a dwelling-place
For all sweet sounds and harmonies; oh! then,
If solitude, or fear, or pain, or grief,
Should be thy portion, with what healing thoughts
Of tender joy wilt thou remember me,   145
And these my exhortations! Nor, perchance—
If I should be where I no more can hear
Thy voice, nor catch from thy wild eyes these gleams
Of past existence—wilt thou then forget
That on the banks of this delightful stream   150
We stood together; and that I, so long
A worshipper of Nature, hither came
Unwearied in that service: rather say
With warmer love—oh! with far deeper zeal
Of holier love. Nor wilt thou then forget,   155
That after many wanderings, many years
Of absence, these steep woods and lofty cliffs,
And this green pastoral landscape, were to me
More dear, both for themselves and for thy sake!

The World Is Too Much with Us   1807

The world is too much with us; late and soon,
Getting and spending, we lay waste our powers;
Little we see in Nature that is ours;
We have given our hearts away, a sordid boon.
This Sea that bares her bosom to the moon,   5
The winds that will be howling at all hours,
And are up-gathered now like sleeping flowers,
For this, for everything, we are out of tune;
It moves us not.—Great God! I'd rather be
A Pagan suckled in a creed outworn;   10
So might I, standing on this pleasant lea,°   meadow
Have glimpses that would make me less forlorn;
Have sight of Proteus° rising from the sea;   old man of the sea who was able to change his shape
Or hear old Triton° blow his wreathèd horn.   sea deity who blew on a conch shell

James Wright   1927–1980

A Blessing   1961

Just off the highway to Rochester, Minnesota,
Twilight bounds softly forth on the grass.
And the eyes of those two Indian ponies
Darken with kindness.

They have come gladly out of the willows
To welcome my friend and me.   5
We step over the barbed wire into the pasture
Where they have been grazing all day, alone.
They ripple tensely, they can hardly contain their happiness
That we have come.
They bow shyly as wet swans. They love each other.   10
There is no loneliness like theirs.
At home once more,
They begin munching the young tufts of spring in the darkness.
I would like to hold the slenderer one in my arms,
For she has walked over to me   15
And nuzzled my left hand.
She is black and white,
Her mane falls wild on her forehead,
And the light breeze moves me to caress her long ear
That is delicate as the skin over a girl's wrist.   20
Suddenly I realize
That if I stepped out of my body I would break
Into blossom.

Mitsuye Yamada   b. 1923

The Question Of Loyalty   1976

I met the deadline
for alien registration
once before
was numbered fingerprinted
and ordered not to travel
without permit.   5

But alien still they said I must
forswear allegiance to the emperor.
for me that was easy
I didn't even know him
but my mother who did cried out   10
    If I sign this
    What will I be?
    I am doubly loyal
    to my American children
    also to my own people.   15
    How can double mean nothing?
    I wish no one to lose this war.
    Everyone does.

I was poor
at math.   20
I signed
my only ticket out.

William Butler Yeats 1865–1939

Crazy Jane Talks with the Bishop 1933

I met the Bishop on the road
And much said he and I.
"Those breasts are flat and fallen now,
Those veins must soon be dry;
Live in a heavenly mansion,   5
Not in some foul sty."

"Fair and foul are near of kin,
And fair needs foul," I cried.
"My friends are gone, but that's a truth
Nor grave nor bed denied,   10
Learned in bodily lowliness
And in the heart's pride.

"A woman can be proud and stiff
When on love intent;
But Love has pitched his mansion in   15
The place of excrement;
For nothing can be sole or whole
That has not been rent.°"   torn

The Lake Isle of Innisfree 1892

I will arise and go now, and go to Innisfree,°   island in Lough Gill, County Sligo, Ireland
And a small cabin build there, of clay and wattles° made: twigs
Nine bean-rows will I have there, a hive for the honey-bee,
And live alone in the bee-loud glade.

And I shall have some peace there, for peace comes dropping slow,   5
Dropping from the veils of the morning to where the cricket sings;
There midnight's all a glimmer, and noon a purple glow,
And evening full of the linnet's wings.

I will arise and go now, for always night and day
I hear lake water lapping with low sounds by the shore;   10
While I stand on the roadway, or on the pavements grey,
I hear it in the deep heart's core.

Leda and the Swan 1923

A sudden blow: the great wings beating still
Above the staggering girl, her thighs caressed
By the dark webs, her nape caught in his bill,
He holds her helpless breast upon his breast.

How can those terrified vague fingers push   5
The feathered glory from her loosening thighs?
And how can body, laid in that white rush,
But feel the strange heart beating where it lies?

A shudder in the loins engenders there
The broken wall, the burning roof and tower
And Agamemnon° dead.   10
                    Being so caught up,
So mastered by the brute blood of the air,
Did she put on his knowledge with his power
Before the indifferent beak could let her drop?   15

> Greek king, brother-in-law of Helen of Troy, killed by his wife, Clytemnestra who, along with her sister Helen, were Leda's children by the god Zeus, who, in the form of a swan, raped Leda

The Second Coming   *1921*

Turning and turning in the widening gyre°   spiral
The falcon cannot hear the falconer;
Things fall apart; the center cannot hold;
Mere anarchy is loosed upon the world,
The blood-dimmed tide is loosed, and everywhere   5
The ceremony of innocence is drowned;
The best lack all conviction, while the worst
Are full of passionate intensity.

Surely some revelation is at hand;
Surely the Second Coming is at hand;
The Second Coming! Hardly are those words out   10
When a vast image out of *Spiritus Mundi*°   world spirit
Troubles my sight: somewhere in sands of the desert
A shape with lion body and the head of a man,
A gaze blank and pitiless as the sun,
Is moving its slow thighs, while all about it   15
Reel shadows of the indignant desert birds.
The darkness drops again; but now I know
That twenty centuries of stony sleep
Were vexed to nightmare by a rocking cradle,
And what rough beast, its hour come round at last,   20
Slouches towards Bethlehem to be born?

When You Are Old   *1892*

When you are old and grey and full of sleep,
And nodding by the fire, take down this book,
And slowly read, and dream of the soft look
Your eyes had once, and of their shadows deep;

How many loved your moments of glad grace,   5
And loved your beauty with love false or true,
But one man loved the pilgrim soul in you,
And loved the sorrows of your changing face;

And bending down beside the glowing bars,
Murmur, a little sadly, how Love fled
And paced upon the mountains overhead   10
And hid his face amid a crowd of stars.

Cyn. Zarco   b. 1950

Flipochinos   *1986*

when a brown person
gets together
with a yellow person
it is something like
the mating of a chico and a banana   5
the brown meat of the chico
plus the yellow skin of the banana
take the seed of the chico for eyes
peel the banana for sex appeal
lick the juice from your fingers   10
and watch your step

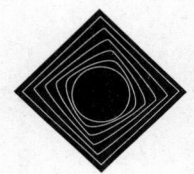

READING
AND
RESPONDING
TO
DRAMA

READING

AND

RESPONDING

TO

DRAMA

15 ◈ What is Drama?

In what is called real life, certain events assume a kind of shape that leads people to call them dramatic: the rescue of hikers stranded by an avalanche in the mountains; the hijacking of an airplane, a kidnapping, or a hostage situation; a basketball team coming back from a 20-point deficit in the second half of an important game. You could probably supply your own examples from whatever is in the news at the time you are reading this chapter.

Drama and Real Life

The above mentioned events are not instances of drama in the literary or artistic sense, of course, but in certain respects they resemble some of the characteristics of theatrical drama. These events, like theatrical drama, involve some kind of conflict of opposing forces or desires; the conflict works itself out through a sequence of actions that assume something of the shape of a plot. The situation is highly emotional for both the participants and the "audience" (who usually "watch" the dramatic event unfold through the media). Things people do or say may involve irony because of important differences in levels of knowing (or unknowing) between the participants and those who watch. The participants take on roles, almost acting as characters, and the events and people may even seem to be following a script in that what they are doing or are involved in bears resemblance to similar previous events.

You may have participated in or observed "live" social events that also resemble drama in that they are highly structured and require you to assume a role. Think of your high school graduation—a staged ceremony, "performed" before an audience, in which the participants wear special costumes, assume certain definite roles, and (at least some of them) have more or less set speeches to deliver. Wedding ceremonies and some church services are also staged ceremonies. You also play different roles from time to time and in different areas of your life; you change in and out of different costumes for different occasions and roles. For example, you may have roles as student, employee, athlete, dancer, son, daughter, parent, friend, lover, tutor, or date. These roles require different costumes: uniforms, sweats, jeans, suits, caps, and hairstyles.

Of course, in several important ways real-life events such as those that make news are different from theatrical drama. They occur more spontaneously and informally and can happen almost anywhere; they are not planned, rehearsed, and performed in a space devoted to the presentation of

811

such events. Unlike a **play**, they turn out differently, and often unpredictably, each time. But they do share with theatrical drama something that seems to be essential: people in action.

In the fifth century B.C., the Greek philosopher Aristotle called drama "an imitation of an action," and this definition still applies today. In this context, real-life dramatic events are "action," and plays imitate real life, giving it artistic shape. For people in the theater audience, the immediacy and emotional authenticity of performance is often so strong that they are moved to laughter or to tears just as they might be by real-life events. Perhaps you have had the experience of leaving a movie theater, for instance, and having the sensation that the world outside the theater, the so-called real world, is somehow colored by or seems almost identical with the fictitious world on the screen in front of which you have just spent a couple of hours.

I invite you now to think about some of the important similarities and differences between dramatic events that play out in real life and theatrical presentations of drama. You may use the box below or a page in your notebook to list some of those similarities and differences. Mark what you consider to be the most important similarity and difference between real-life events and theatrical drama.

Real-life Dramatic Events	Theatrical Drama	
1.		
2.		
3.		
4.		
5.		
6.		

In terms of what has come to be understood over the centuries as dramatic literature, the question "What is drama?" can be answered in two general ways: Drama is texts or a text that may be *read* on the page, and drama is texts or a text that may be *seen* on the stage. It's a virtual certainty that you have some familiarity with drama in the artistic sense. If you are 18 or older and have spent any time at all in North American or Western society, it's hard to imagine your escaping exposure to some form of drama, at the very least in television shows or movies. "Groundhog Day," "Forrest Gump," "Fried Green Tomatoes," "Robocop," "Friends," "Melrose Place," "Cheers," "ER"—all are dramas.

READING CULTURE Drama in the Mass Media: A Television Script

As an example of drama in the context of the mass media, here is part of the script for an episode of a currently popular television show, "Seinfeld." You may have seen this episode when it was originally broadcast (January 8, 1992) or as a rerun sometime in the past few years. Read it now, then do another brief exercise.

Written by Larry Charles
Directed by Tom Cherones

SEINFELD   *"The Subway"*

AS BROADCAST
January 8, 1992
ALL RIGHTS RESERVED
COPYRIGHT © 1991, CASTLE ROCK ENTERTAINMENT

SHOW OPEN

STAND-UP #1

INT. COMEDY CLUB – NIGHT

JERRY: When I was a kid my favorite ride was the bumper car ride, remember that   5
ride? Go around in a circle. There were cars that could not do it. Remember this
kid? As soon as the ride gets started he'd be like stuck in a pack of empty cars
just ... "Excuse me. Excuse me, it won't go. Come on. It's almost over." And he always ends up with the attendant hanging off that big pole helping him steer it,
you know. "Stop crying." Then there's always that other really bad car—the   10
hopeless father and son team. This is another car, just not going anywhere.
They're never organized. Who's on the wheel, who's pressing on the gas.
They're just, "Whoa Son, turn the wheel."

CUT TO:

ACT ONE, SCENE A

INT. COFFEE SHOP—MORNING

*JERRY, GEORGE, ELAINE, KRAMER, IN NECK BRACE. GEORGE IS WRITING
IN A MEMO PAD. KRAMER HAS A SUBWAY MAP SPREAD OUT ON TABLE. HE
IS EXPLAINING A ROUTE TO JERRY.*

KRAMER: Alright, Coney Island. Okay, you can take the 'B' or the 'F' and switch for the   15
'N' at Broadway-Lafayette, or you can go over the bridge to DeKalb and catch
the 'Q' to Atlantic Avenue and then switch to the 'IRT,' '2, 3, 4 or 5'. But don't get
on the 'G'. See that's very tempting, but you'll wind up on Smith and 9th street,
then you gotta get on the 'R.'
ELAINE: Couldn't he just take the 'D' straight to Coney Island?
KRAMER: Well, yeah ...
ELAINE: Okay ... What time's your job interview, George?   20

GEORGE: Nine forty-five.

JERRY: Remember don't whistle on the elevator.

GEORGE: Why not?

JERRY: That's what Willy Loman told Biff before his interview in "Death of a Salesman."   25

GEORGE: What, you're comparing me to Biff Loman? Very encouraging. The biggest loser in the history of American Literature.

ELAINE: Alright, I'm gonna get going.

JERRY: What time's the lesbian wedding?

ELAINE: Nine-thirty.

GEORGE: Lesbian Wedding. How do they work the bride and groom on that? What   30 do they flip a coin?

ELAINE: Yeah, they flip a coin.

GEORGE: What, was that not politically correct? It's a, it's a legitimate question.

JERRY: I'm so tired. I'm gonna fall asleep on the train.

GEORGE: I always get the feeling when lesbians are looking at me, they're thinking,   35 "That's why I'm not a heterosexual."

KRAMER: (IMPATIENT) Alright Jerry, come on. Let's go. Pick up the check so we can go.

JERRY: Oh I'm paying for breakfast?

KRAMER: Yeah.

ELAINE: Yeah.   40

GEORGE: Yeah.

JERRY: Why do I always pay? What am I, made of money? You bunch of deadbeats.

HE THROWS DOWN MONEY AND EXITS.

CUT TO:

ACT ONE, SCENE B

INT. SUBWAY CAR—MORNING

JERRY, GEORGE, KRAMER AND ELAINE CARRYING A GIFT. JERRY YAWNS.

JERRY: (TO KRAMER) How many tickets you paying today?   45

KRAMER: Uh let's see . . . (HE USES HIS FINGERS) Speeding, running a red light, no license, no registration, no plates, no brake lights, no rear view mirror . . . Look at that one.

GEORGE: No doors?

KRAMER: Yeah, I'm fighting that one. You know this is gonna cost me over six-hun-   50 dred bucks.

A BLIND MUSICIAN, HERB, PLAYING A VIOLIN WITH A TIN CUP ATTACHED, STAGGERS BY. JERRY, ELAINE, AND KRAMER DROP CHANGE IN THE CUP.

GEORGE: Oh I, I can't carry change in these pants. It falls out.

KRAMER LITERALLY FILLS HIS CUP WITH CHANGE.

HERB: Thank you.

GEORGE: That guy's not blind.   55

ELAINE: Ugh.

JERRY: So, can I convince anybody to come down to Coney Island with me? I gotta pick up my car at the pound. George?

GEORGE: I can't believe they actually found your stolen car.   60

JERRY: Not only did they find it, it was Simonized and the front end was aligned.

GEORGE: It's amazing.

JERRY: So whatdya say? Ride on the Cyclone, hot dog at Nathan's on me.

GEORGE: Who are you, Satan? I'm close to a job here. It's my second interview.

JERRY: Alright Biff . . . Elaine, merry-go-round?   65

ELAINE: I can't. I'm the best man.

JERRY: Kramer. Bumper cars?

KRAMER: I gotta go to court. I'll get in trouble. What's the matter with you?

JERRY: It could be years 'til I get back to Coney Island. I can't go on rides alone.

P.A. #1 (O.S.)   42nd St. Change for the D, N, the double RR, the 2, 3, 4, 5, 7, the C, E,   70
and F train.

*THE DOOR OPENS. THEY PAUSE AS IF TRYING TO SAY GOODBYE, THINK
BETTER OF IT AND GO THEIR SEPARATE WAYS, ELAINE IS THE LAST ONE
TO GO.*

ELAINE: (CALLING) See ya.   75

CUT TO:

ACT ONE, SCENE C

INT. JERRY'S SUBWAY CAR—MORNING

DOORS OPEN. JERRY, ALONG WITH A FEW SCATTERED PASSENGERS
ENTER. *HE FINDS A SEAT AND TAKES IT. HE NODS TO THE MAN OPPO-
SITE HIM, A MIDDLE AGED MAN, IN CONSERVATIVE SUIT, WITH NEWSPA-
PER AND BRIEFCASE. HE IS IRWIN, THE SORT OF ANONYMOUS COM-
MUTER THAT FILLS THESE TRAINS DAY IN AND DAY OUT. THERE IS NO
TENSION. IF ANY WORD COULD CHARACTERIZE THE MOOD, IT WOULD
BE WEARINESS.*

CUT TO:

ACT ONE, SCENE D

INT. ELAINE'S SUBWAY CAR—MORNING

DOORS OPEN. ELAINE ENTERS. *SHE IS SMILING, HAPPY. LIKE AUDREY
HEPBURN IN "BREAKFAST AT TIFFANY'S." A SINGLE WOMAN IN NEW
YORK CITY, FILLED WITH THE POSSIBILITIES OF LIFE THAT THE BIG
APPLE HAS TO OFFER.*

CUT TO:

ACT ONE, SCENE E

INT. GEORGE'S SUBWAY CAR—MORNING

DOORS OPEN. GEORGE ENTERS, *CARRYING THE NEW YORK TIMES. HE IS
NATTY. HE LOOKS GOOD. IF YOU DIDN'T KNOW IT WAS GEORGE, YOU*

WOULDN'T KNOW IT WAS GEORGE. HE FINDS A SEAT NEXT TO AN AT-
TRACTIVE, EVEN SEDUCTIVE LOOKING WOMAN, LUANNE. THEY EX-
CHANGE A SILENT, BUT SIGNIFICANT GLANCE. ON GEORGE'S SURPRISED
REACTION WE . . .

CUT TO:

ACT ONE, SCENE F

INT. KRAMER'S SUBWAY CAR—MORNING

DOORS OPEN. THERE'S A STAMPEDE OF PEOPLE PLUNGING THRU THE
DOORS LIKE WATER THROUGH A BURST DAM. HURTLING ALONG IN THE
CROWD LIKE AN ASTEROID THRU SPACE LIKE PIECES OF DEBRIS WHIP-
PING IN THE WIND, IS KRAMER. JOSTLED, ELBOWED, SHOVED, POKED,
PUNCHED, TWISTED AND TOSSED. HE IS CAUGHT IN A HUMAN HURRI-
CANE. PEOPLE RUSH TO GRAB SEATS LIKE SOME SORT OF LIFE AND
DEATH VERSION OF MUSICAL CHAIRS. KRAMER TRIES TO COMPETE,
DASHING MADLY FOR EVERY EMPTY SPACE, RICOCHETING TO THE NEXT
ONE LIKE A PINBALL, AS HE GETS BURNED AND THWARTED AT EVERY AT-
TEMPT. HE IS EVEN BEATEN OUT BY A VERY AGGRESSIVE OLD LADY AND
PREGNANT WOMAN. KRAMER FINDS HIMSELF THE ONLY ONE IN THE
SUBWAY CAR, LEFT STANDING. HE STEPS FORWARD, THEN PIVOTS
AROUND, LOOKING FOR A SPOT. FINALLY, HE FINDS A SMALL SPACE
NEXT TO A VERY OBESE TEENAGER. HE GIVES HIM NO SILENT SIGN OF
COOPERATION. IN FACT, HE IGNORES HIS LOOMING PRESENCE ABOVE
THEM. HE MAKES NO EFFORT TO MOVE, OR MAKE ROOM. FINALLY
KRAMER DECIDES TO SIT. HE SQUEEZES INTO THE SPACE THAT DOESN'T
FIT HIM, LIKE A FAT MAN TRYING ON PANTS THREE SIZES TOO SMALL.
WE REMAIN ON HIM FOR ONE LONG UNCOMFORTABLE BEAT. THEN . . .

CUT TO:

ACT ONE, SCENE G

INT. JERRY'S SUBWAY CAR—MORNING

JERRY, HEAVY LIDDED, IS HAVING TROUBLE KEEPING HIS EYES OPEN. HE
DRIFTS OFF, THEN JERKS HIMSELF AWAKE. THEN, DRIFTS OFF, ONLY TO
JERK AWAKE ONCE AGAIN. FINALLY, HE SWITCHES POSITIONS, AND BE-
GINS TO NOD OFF AGAIN. HE LEANS, RESTING HIS HEAD ON AN OLDER
UNAPPRECIATIVE WOMAN. SHE SNAPS HIS HEAD BACK. HE LEANS OVER
AGAIN. THIS TIME, SHE GETS UP, AND HIS HEAD FALLS ONTO SEAT, WAK-
ING HIM WITH A START. HE LOOKS AROUND, THEN CHANGES POSITIONS,
GETS COMFORTABLE AND CLOSES HIS EYES AGAIN.

CUT TO:

ACT ONE, SCENE H

INT. GEORGE'S SUBWAY CAR—MORNING

*GEORGE AND LUANNE READ THEIR PAPERS, OCCASIONALLY GLANCING
AT EACH OTHER. FINALLY . . .*

LUANNE: You looking for a job?
GEORGE: Me? Why?   80
LUANNE: Well, you're reading the classifieds.
GEORGE: (QUICKLY SHUFFLES THE PAPER) Oh uh, no, no, no. I uh, I was just look-
ing for the stock page . . . Ah, here it is . . . Looking for the quotes. Gotta check
the quotes. Love a good quote. Oh, IBM up a quarter. Whatdya know?
LUANNE: You didn't look like someone who needed a job.   85
GEORGE: Me? No, no, I don't. I don't. I'm doing very well. Very well. Yep.
LUANNE: So, you're in the market?
GEORGE: Oh yeah, yeah. I'm uh, in the market.
LUANNE: Which market?
GEORGE: Which market? The uh, the big one. The, uh, big market with the big board. 90
Bull market, bear market, you name the market, I'm there.
LUANNE: So, do you work for one of the big brokerage houses?
GEORGE: They wish. I hate the big brokerage houses. Hate them with a passion. Big
brokerage houses killed my father.
LUANNE: Really?   95
GEORGE: Well, they hurt him bad. Really hurt his feelings. It's a long story, I, I don't
like to talk about it. But uh, I swore there and then that I would never work for
a big brokerage house. Y'see, all they care about is money. I'm about more than
money. I'm about uh . . . people. So, I've always gone my own way. And uh, I've
never looked back.

A LOUD HORN SOUNDS AND GEORGE NERVOUSLY LOOKS AROUND.

CUT TO:

ACT ONE, SCENE I

INT. ELAINE'S SUBWAY CAR—MORNING

*TWO MEN BEAT ELAINE AND A MIDDLE AGED WOMAN, ADELE, TO TWO
SEATS . . .*

ADELE: I started riding these trains in the forties. Those days, a man'd give up his   100
seat for a woman. Now we're liberated. We have to stand.
ELAINE: It's ironic.
ADELE: What's ironic?
ELAINE: This. That we've come all this way. We made all this progress, but, y'know,
we lost the little things, the niceties.
ADELE: No. I, I mean what does ironic *mean*? Where're you off to with such a nice   105
present, huh? A birthday party?
ELAINE: A wedding.
ADELE: A wedding.
ELAINE: Yeah.

ADELE: Ha! I didn't think people still get married. It's hard today with the men and
women.

ELAINE: You're telling me.   110

ADELE: So, uh, they're a nice couple?

ELAINE: Oh very nice.

ADELE: What does he do, if you don't mind my asking?

ELAINE: She.

ADELE: She. She, she works. He doesn't work. He sounds like my son.   115

ELAINE: There is no he.

ADELE: There's no he? So, uh, who's gettin' married?

ELAINE: Um, two women. It's a (SWALLOWS HARD), a lesbian wedding.

ADELE: A lesbian wedding?

ELAINE: Uh-huh. Yep. Yep. I'm the uh (COUGHS) . . . the best man.   120

ADELE: Great. My luck, I don't talk to a soul in the subway for thirty-five years, I get
the best man at a lesbian wedding.

SHE EXITS.

ELAINE: No, no, no, you don't understand. I'm not a lesbian! I hate men but I'm not   125
a lesbian!

CUT TO:

ACT ONE, SCENE J

INT. KRAMER'S SUBWAY—MORNING

*THE PASSENGER CRUSH HAS THINNED, A BIT, AND KRAMER HAS NOW
FOUND A SEAT. FURTHER DOWN THE BENCH, A MAN READS A NEWSPA-
PER. EQUIDISTANT FROM HIM, IN THE OTHER DIRECTION SITS AN-
OTHER MAN, HIS ARM IS IN A SLING. THE TRAIN COMES TO A STOP. THE
MAN WITH THE NEWSPAPER RISES AND EXITS LEAVING THE NEWSPA-
PER BEHIND. THE TRAIN STARTS UP AGAIN AS KRAMER AND MAN EYE
NEWSPAPER HUNGRILY, AND EACH OTHER, SUSPICIOUSLY. AFTER A FEW
MOMENTS OF FEELING EACH OTHER OUT, THEY BOTH MAKE A QUICK
MOVE FOR THE PAPER. THEY EACH GET A GRIP ON IT AND SNARL AND
PULL AT IT LIKE RABID DOGS. THE MAN MANAGES TO SECURE MOST OF
IT AND STORMS AWAY, LEAVING KRAMER WITH A TORN PAGE. HE SITS
DOWN AND READS.*

CUT TO:

ACT ONE, SCENE K

INT. JERRY'S SUBWAY CAR—MORNING

*JERRY, SLUMPED ACROSS SEAT. HEAD BACK. MOUTH OPEN. SNORING. WE
SEE IRWIN ACROSS AISLE GLANCE AT HIM.*

CUT TO:

ACT ONE, SCENE L

INT. ELAINE'S SUBWAY CAR—MORNING

ELAINE, HOLDING HER GIFT. SHE IS CRUSHED AMIDST BURLY COM-MUTERS. TRAIN IS TOOLING ALONG. SHE GLANCES AROUND.

ELAINE: (V.O.)   I'm really looking forward to this. I love weddings. Maybe I'll meet   130
somebody ... Mm maybe not.

SUDDENLY THE TRAIN LURCHES TO A HALT. AS ELAINE LOOKS AROUND:

ELAINE: (V.O.) (CONT'D)   Oh man, we're stopping? ...

CUT TO:

ACT ONE, SCENE M

INT. GEORGE'S SUBWAY—MORNING

THE TRAIN IS PULLING INTO THE STATION. LUANNE RISES.

LUANNE: Well um, this is where I get off.
GEORGE: Oh you do? Um ...   135
LUANNE: Yeah ... Hey, why don't you ... Oh, nothing ...
LUANNE: No, no, no, what ... what?
LUANNE: Well, I was going to say, why don't you get off with me. But you're obvi-
ously very busy, on your way to some important meeting or something.

TRAIN STOPS. GEORGE GLANCES AT WATCH.

GEORGE: Yeah, well ...   140
LUANNE: See. I, I knew it was a bad idea ...

DOORS OPEN, LUANNE AND THE CROWD START TO HEAD OUT. GEORGE STANDS.

GEORGE: Hey! What's another million, give or take. I get off when and where I want
to get off.

GEORGE HESITATES. THE TRAIN DOORS CLOSE. GEORGE LEAPS TO GET OUT AND GETS CAUGHT BETWEEN THE DOORS.

GEORGE: (CONT'D)   I'm stuck, could you just give me a little, just give me a second...   145

SHE BEGINS TO YANK HIM, TRYING TO FREE HIM FROM THE DOORS.

GEORGE: (CONT'D)   (YELLING DOWN PLATFORM) Don't start the train! Don't
start the train!

AS SHE CONTINUES TO TUG, WE:

CUT TO:

ACT ONE, SCENE N

INT. KRAMER'S SUBWAY—MORNING

KRAMER IS READING THE SMALL REMNANT OF THE PAPER. TWO MEN,
LOUIS AND LES, SIT NEAR HIM, DRESSED NEATLY, WITH SHIRTS AND TIES.
ONE CARRIES THE "RACING TELEGRAM" OBVIOUSLY TRYING TO FIND
SOMETHING.

LOUIS: Here it is. Here it is. The four horse in the first race. "Pappanick."   150
LES: How do you know he's gonna win?
LOUIS: My UPS guy, Lance, the guys who own the horse are his regular customers.
          Every horse he's ever given me has won.
LES: Yeah?

KRAMER'S EYES LIGHT UP BEHIND HIS FRAGMENT OF NEWSPAPER.

LOUIS: Yeah, see, they've been sandbagging, looking for a good spot. He's been get-   155
          ting in light cause they're using a bug boy on him and the workouts have been
          unpublished.

KRAMER TRIES TO FOLLOW THIS.

LOUIS: (CONT'D)   Now, they're ready to run with him. They're gonna break his
          maiden. He's gonna go off at a great price. Maybe thirty to one.

KRAMER FRANTICALLY DOES THE MATH IN HIS HEAD.

LOUIS: (CONT'D)   I'm telling you, it's a lock.   160

KRAMER PULLS HIS CASH OUT AND BEGINS TO COUNT.

LES: But it rained last night.
LOUIS: Exactly. This horse loves the slop. It's in his bloodlines. His father was a mud-
          der, his mother was a mudder.

KRAMER LOOKS PUZZLED.

LES: His mother was a mudder?   165
LOUIS: What did I just say? . . . Come on. Let's go up to the office, I want to call my
          bookie . . . and, hey, don't tell anybody.

THEY LOOK AT KRAMER. KRAMER COVERS UP HIS FACE WITH NEWSPAPER
FRAGMENT. THEY EXIT.

CUT TO:

ACT ONE, SCENE O

INT. JERRY'S SUBWAY CAR—MORNING

JERRY IS STILL OPEN MOUTHED, HEAD BACK, SNORING, ASLEEP. TRAIN
JERKS, WAKING HIM UP WITH A START. AS HE SHAKES THE COBWEBS, HE
AND WE SEE THAT EVERYONE THAT HAS BEEN SITTING AROUND HIM
ARE NOW ALL CROWDED TOGETHER AT THE FAR END OF THE TRAIN—
WITH ONE EXCEPTION. ACROSS FROM JERRY SITS IRWIN. THE MAN WHO
HAS BEEN THERE ALL ALONG. WE PAN UP HIS BODY AND NOTICE ONE,
MAJOR, SIGNIFICANT CHANGE. EXCEPT FOR HIS SHOES AND SOCKS AND

HAT AND A BRIEFCASE ACROSS HIS LAP, HE IS COMPLETELY AND UT-
TERLY BUCK NAKED. ON JERRY'S TAKE WE:

JERRY: Okay.

FADE OUT

END OF ACT ONE

170

Take a few minutes now, using the box below or a page in your notebook, to list some to the characteristics of drama in general that you can identify from this portion of a script.

> **Characteristics of Drama in a Television Script**
> 1.
> 2.
> 3.
> 4.
> 5.
> 6.

    In part, you can identify some characteristics of drama in the "Seinfeld" script because of the drama you've seen on television or in movies, even though you may have less experience reading a script like this one. If you have seen this or any episode of "Seinfeld," you are able to use that experience to fill in many of the numerous **gaps** in this text: You can picture Jerry, Elaine, George, and Kramer; you can visualize the sets in which the action takes place; in your mind, you can hear the characters speaking the dialogue and you can see their reactions to what other characters say and do. Of course, you can do that because the actors who play these characters, the director of the **production**, the set designers, and the costumers have filled in many of the gaps that exist in this printed version of "The Subway" episode.

    If you have seen "The Subway" or any episode of "Seinfeld" on television, I would ask you to consider the difference between that production and this script. The televised production is so "complete," the characters are so "real" compared with this "bare bones" script. In this way, "Seinfeld" is no different from any television drama and little different from the **screenplay** of any movie. In this way also, "The Subway" is analogous to almost any printed play: what you encounter on the page is a script, waiting to be brought to life—in the mind, on the stage, or before the cameras—by the imaginative action of a reader.

The Variety of Live Drama

Although you are familiar with televised and filmed dramas, you may have relatively little experience with drama in live theater. In the United States today, live drama is presented in school productions, in dinner-theaters, in community playhouses, on Broadway, off-Broadway, off-off-Broadway. Many cities in the United States and Canada have resident theater companies that present plays from the **canon** of Western drama as well as new plays by contemporary authors. Some communities have theater workshops or collectives that concentrate on more experimental forms of drama or performance art. What is *your* experience with live drama at any level? Take a few minutes here to inventory your theatergoing repertoire. List some of the plays you have seen and the kinds of theaters you have seen in them in.

Theater Experiences

	Play	*Theater*
1.		
2.		
3.		
4.		
5.		
6.		

Audience and Actors in the Theater

I will emphasize live theater, as opposed to television and film, because in most literature courses the plays you read are examples of "serious" drama—whether tragedy or comedy—written for performance in live theater. I also want to emphasize the theatergoer's interaction with drama on the stage, because it is that aspect that distinguishes drama from the other literary genres.

The dynamic interaction between actors and audience in live theater is unique to drama among the literary genres. Through such overt gestures as laughter or applause and subtler ones such as restlessness or attentive silence, the audience responds immediately to **text strategies** it notices in a performance, and that response is immediately returned to the actors. These responses may affect the pace, volume, or manner with which the actors deliver their lines, which affects the audience, who react accordingly in turn—and so on in reciprocal fashion. You may know, for instance, that some television shows, like "Seinfeld," are filmed in front of an audience. For those audiences, the experience of watching and responding to the action would more closely resemble the experience of seeing live theater, whereas your experience watching "Seinfeld" on television does not allow for the same kind of immediate feedback to the actors of an audience's reaction. But because of the relationship between audience and actors that can and does happen in live theater, drama exemplifies especially well the interactive model of reading that we have been working with throughout this book.

The nature of this interaction is complicated by the differences in audience response and actors' performances from one evening to the next in any given production of a play: Lines or scenes that one audience may find hysterical will get only a subdued reaction from another audience. Actors will be right on their cues and crisp in their movements for one performance and just a little off another time. There may be nothing empirically demonstrable about cause and effect here, but if you talk to actors—professional or amateur—or if you have acting experience yourself, you will find at least anecdotal confirmation of this. For instance, the Irish actor Kenneth Branagh told an interviewer what happened in one performance while he was playing Hamlet with the Royal Shakespeare Company in Stratford, England. "The night before," Branagh said, "I had had a few drinks—it was the Heineken Hamlet, the hungover Hamlet—and the sword fell apart [during the sword-fight scene in Act V] in my hands and I started to laugh. . . . Someone said later, 'You were so emotional.' I was crying—but they weren't the right tears.[1] Spontaneity like this cannot happen when the dramatic performance is captured and packaged on film or videotape for the consumption of movie or television audiences.

To return to the basic question, or to the first way of answering the question "What is drama?" you can begin your consideration by looking at drama as texts or a text that may be read on the page. In doing this, you may apply the interactive model of reading just as you have done with fiction and poetry. That model, you will recall, emphasizes a reading as an event produced by the contributions of both the text and the reader.

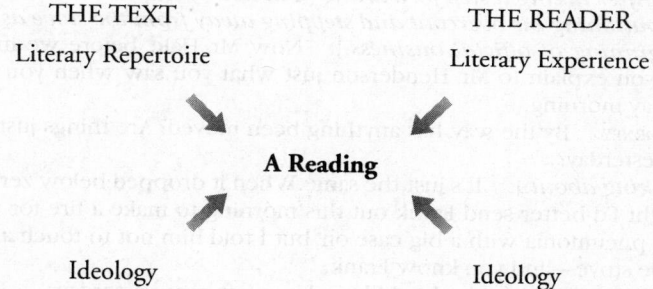

THE TEXT — Literary Repertoire — Ideology

THE READER — Literary Experience — Ideology

A Reading

Readers and Plays in Print

Let's look first at the **literary repertoire** of dramatic texts. Many of the text strategies you encounter when you read drama on the page exist because plays are written to be performed on the stage. Because of this, drama offers some text strategies that are unique among literary genres. Probably the best way to proceed is for you to have at least a portion of a play before you to refer to. As with the genres of fiction and poetry, there is a great deal of variety within drama, so it's not easy to pick one play as "typical" or "representative" of the genre as a class. But to see something about text strategies of drama, you can start with a play that's fairly short—a **one-act**—and fairly

---

[1]Dinitia Smith, "Much Ado About Branagh," *New York Magazine* 24 May 1993: 38.

conventional. Read this scene from Susan Glaspell's play *Trifles*, first performed in 1916.

Susan Glaspell   1882–1948

Trifles   *1916*

(Part One)

SCENE: The kitchen in the now abandoned farmhouse of John Wright, a gloomy kitchen, and left without having been put in order—unwashed pans under the table—other signs of uncompleted work. At the rear the outer door opens and the Sheriff comes in followed by the County Attorney and Hale. The Sheriff and Hale are men in middle life, the County Attorney is a young man; all are bundled up and go at once to the stove. They are followed by the two women—the Sheriff's wife first; she is a slight wiry woman, a thin nervous face. Mrs. Hale is larger and would ordinarily be called more comfortable looking, but she is disturbed now and looks fearfully about as she enters. The women have come in slowly, and stand close together near the door.

COUNTY ATTORNEY [*Rubbing his hands.*]:   This feels good. Come up to the fire, ladies.

MRS. PETERS [*After taking a step forward.*]:   I'm not—cold.

SHERIFF [*Unbuttoning his overcoat and stepping away from the stove as if to mark the beginning of official business.*]:   Now, Mr. Hale, before we move things about, you explain to Mr. Henderson just what you saw when you came here yesterday morning.

COUNTY ATTORNEY: By the way, has anything been moved? Are things just as you left them yesterday?

SHERIFF [*Looking about.*]:   It's just the same. When it dropped below zero last night   5
I thought I'd better send Frank out this morning to make a fire for us—no use getting pneumonia with a big case on, but I told him not to touch anything except the stove—and you know Frank.

COUNTY ATTORNEY: Somebody should have been left here yesterday.

SHERIFF: Oh—yesterday. When I had to send Frank to Morris Center for that man who went crazy—I want you to know I had my hands full yesterday. I knew you could get back from Omaha by today and as long as I went over everything here myself—

COUNTY ATTORNEY: Well, Mr. Hale, tell just what happened when you came here yesterday morning.

HALE: Harry and I had started to town with a load of potatoes. We came along the road from my place and as I got here I said, "I'm going to see if I can't get John Wright to go in with me on a party telephone." I spoke to Wright about it once before and he put me off, saying folks talked too much anyway, and all he asked was peace and quiet—I guess you know about how much he talked himself; but I thought maybe if I went to the house and talked about it before his wife, though I said to Harry that I didn't know as what his wife wanted made much difference to John—

COUNTY ATTORNEY: Let's talk about that later, Mr. Hale. I do want to talk about that,   10
but tell now just what happened when you got to the house.

HALE: I didn't hear or see anything; I knocked at the door, and still it was all quiet inside. I knew they must be up, it was past eight o'clock. So I knocked again, and I thought I heard somebody say, "Come in." I wasn't sure, I'm not sure yet, but I opened the door—this door [*indicating the door by which the two women are still standing*] and there in that rocker—[*pointing to it*] sat Mrs. Wright.

[*They all look at the rocker.*]

COUNTY ATTORNEY: What—was she doing?

HALE: She was rockin' back and forth. She had her apron in her hand and was kind of—pleating it.

COUNTY ATTORNEY: And how did she—look?

HALE: Well, she looked queer.

COUNTY ATTORNEY: How do you mean—queer?

HALE: Well, as if she didn't know what she was going to do next. And kind of done up.

COUNTY ATTORNEY: How did she seem to feel about your coming?

HALE: Why, I don't think she minded—one way or other. She didn't pay much attention. I said, "How do, Mrs. Wright, it's cold, ain't it?" And she said, "Is it?"—and went on kind of pleating at her apron. Well, I was surprised; she didn't ask me to come up to the stove, or to set down, but just sat there, not even looking at me, so I said, "I want to see John." And then she—laughed. I guess you would call it a laugh. I thought of Harry and the team outside, so I said a little sharp: "Can't I see John?" "No," she says, kind o' dull like. "Ain't he home?" says I. "Yes," says she, "he's home." "Then why can't I see him?" I asked her out of patience. "'Cause he's dead," says she. "*Dead?*" says I. She just nodded her head, not getting a bit excited, but rockin' back and forth. "Why—where is he?" says I, not knowing what to say. She just pointed upstairs—like that [*himself pointing to the room above*]. I got up, with the idea of going up there. I walked from there to here— then I says, "Why, what did he die of?" "He died of a rope around his neck," says she, and just went on pleatin' at her apron. Well, I went out and called Harry. I thought I might—need help. We went upstairs and there he was lyin'—

COUNTY ATTORNEY: I think I'd rather have you go into that upstairs, where you can point it all out. Just go on now with the rest of the story.

HALE: Well, my first thought was to get that rope off. It looked . . . [*Stops, his face twitches.*] . . . but Harry, he went up to him, and he said, "No, he's dead all right and we'd better not touch anything." So we went back downstairs. She was still sitting that same way. "Has anybody been notified?" I asked. "No," says she, unconcerned. "Who did this, Mrs. Wright?" said Harry. He said it business-like—and she stopped pleatin' of her apron. "I don't know," she says. "You don't *know*?" says Harry. "No," says she. "Weren't you sleepin' in the bed with him?" says Harry. "Yes," says she, "but I was on the inside." "Somebody slipped a rope round his neck and strangled him and you didn't wake up?" says Harry. "I didn't wake up," she said after him. We must 'a looked as if we didn't see how that could be, for after a minute she said, "I sleep sound." Harry was going to ask her more questions but I said maybe we ought to let her tell her story first to the coroner, or the sheriff, so Harry went fast as he could to Rivers' place, where there's a telephone.

COUNTY ATTORNEY: And what did Mrs. Wright do when she knew that you had gone for the coroner?

HALE: She moved from that chair to this one over here [*Pointing to a small chair in the corner.*] and just sat there with her hands held together and looking down. I got a feeling that I ought to make some conversation, so I said I had come in to see if John wanted to put in a telephone, and at that she started to laugh, and then she stopped and looked at me—scared. [*The County Attorney, who has had his notebook out, makes a note.*] I dunno, maybe it wasn't scared. I wouldn't like to say it was. Soon Harry got back, and then Dr. Lloyd came, and you, Mr. Peters, and so I guess that's all I know that you don't.

COUNTY ATTORNEY [*Looking around*]:   I guess we'll go upstairs first—and then out to the barn and around there. [*To the Sheriff*]: You're convinced that there was nothing important here—nothing that would point to any motive.

SHERIFF: Nothing here but kitchen things.   25

[*The County Attorney, after again looking around the kitchen, opens the door of a cupboard closet. He gets up on a chair and looks on a shelf. Pulls his hand away, sticky.*]

COUNTY ATTORNEY: Here's a nice mess.

[*The women draw nearer.*]

MRS. PETERS [*To the other woman.*]:   Oh, her fruit; it did freeze. [*To the Lawyer*]: She worried about that when it turned so cold. She said the fire'd go out and her jars would break.

SHERIFF: Well, can you beat the women! Held for murder and worryin' about her preserves.

COUNTY ATTORNEY: I guess before we're through she may have something more seri-   ous than preserves to worry about.

HALE: Well, women are used to worrying over trifles.   30

[*The two women move a little closer together.*]

COUNTY ATTORNEY [*With the gallantry of a young politician.*]:   And yet, for all their worries, what would we do without the ladies? [*The women do not unbend. He goes to the sink, takes a dipperful of water from the pail and pouring it into a basin, washes his hands. Starts to wipe them on the roller-towel, turns it for a cleaner place.*] Dirty towels! [*Kicks his foot against the pans under the sink.*] Not much of a housekeeper, would you say, ladies?

MRS. HALE [*Stiffly.*]:   There's a great deal of work to be done on a farm.

COUNTY ATTORNEY: To be sure. And yet [*With a little bow to her.*] I know there are some Dickson County farmhouses which do not have such roller towels.

[*He gives it a pull to expose its full length again.*]

MRS. HALE: Those towels get dirty awful quick. Men's hands aren't always as clean as they might be.

COUNTY ATTORNEY: Ah, loyal to your sex, I see. But you and Mrs. Wright were neigh-   35   bors. I suppose you were friends, too.

MRS. HALE [*Shaking her head.*]:   I've not seen much of her of late years. I've not been in this house—it's more than a year.

COUNTY ATTORNEY: And why was that? You didn't like her?

MRS. HALE: I liked her all well enough. Farmers' wives have their hands full, Mr. Henderson. And then—

COUNTY ATTORNEY: Yes—?

MRS. HALE [*Looking about.*]:   It never seemed a very cheerful place.   40

COUNTY ATTORNEY: No—it's not cheerful. I shouldn't say she had the homemaking instinct.

MRS. HALE: Well, I don't know as Wright had, either.

COUNTY ATTORNEY: You mean that they didn't get on very well?

MRS. HALE: No, I don't mean anything. But I don't think a place'd be any cheerfuller for John Wright's being in it.

COUNTY ATTORNEY: I'd like to talk more of that a little later. I want to get the lay of things upstairs now.

[He goes to the left, where three steps lead to a stair door.]

SHERIFF: I suppose anything Mrs. Peters does'll be all right. She was to take in some clothes for her, you know, and a few little things. We left in such a hurry yesterday.

COUNTY ATTORNEY: Yes, but I would like to see what you take, Mrs. Peters, and keep an eye out for anything that might be of use to us.

MRS. PETERS: Yes, Mr. Henderson.

[The women listen to the men's steps on the stairs, then look about the kitchen.]

MRS. HALE: I'd hate to have men coming into my kitchen, snooping around and criticizing.

This excerpt is about one-third of Glaspell's play. Looking at it, what text strategies can you identify? List them in the box below.

> **Text Strategies of Drama in *Trifles***
>
> 1.
> 2.
> 3.
> 4.
> 5.
> 6.

Are any of the text strategies you listed similar to those you are familiar with from reading fiction? Which ones are peculiar to drama? Go back to the box and mark any text strategies you listed that are peculiar to drama.

Here is another list, not necessarily the "correct" one, but one that will provide the basis for the discussion to follow. In the interest of helping you to a clear understanding of these text strategies, this discussion will consider the listed points separately, but in any play you read on the page and especially any you see on the stage these text strategies are interconnected, not separate.

> **Text Strategies of Drama in *Trifles***
>
> 1. Begins with brief description of set and characters.
>
> 2. It's all dialogue, with only brief stage directions occasionally accompanying what characters say; virtually no narrative.
>
> 3. No background to the action is provided; we have to figure out what has happened through the characters' words.
>
> 4. A plot or conflict situation begins to take shape as we realize this is a murder investigation. Several questions arise: Why did Mrs. Wright act so strangely when Mr. Hale found her? Did she kill her husband? If so, why? Does the condition of the kitchen suggest any motive for Mrs. Wright's killing her husband?

Set and Character Descriptions

When you read many plays written from the late nineteenth century on, and certainly any **realistic** play, you find a **set description** like the one that opens *Trifles*. There may or may not be a formal list of characters preceding that description, but there usually is some brief phrase or sentence describing how each character is supposed to look. The action of *Trifles* is set in a farmhouse kitchen. The opening description states this location, mentions some of the furniture in the room, and indicates what lies on the other side of the doors that lead into it.

The opening descriptions of set and characters are among the conventions of realistic drama. These conventions are in place mostly because of the constraints and practices of the theater circa 1916, although they have not changed much over the rest of the century. *Trifles* was probably written to be performed on a **proscenium** stage with a **box set**. A proscenium stage is the kind you are most probably familiar with from your high school auditorium or most theaters where you have seen live drama performed. Strictly speaking, the word "proscenium" refers to the relatively small area of the entire stage that lies between the curtain and the audience, often curving slightly outward toward the audience in the center. Over the years this term has come to refer to the entire stage in such theaters where the audience sits facing the stage on one side, even if fanned out in an arc.

A set is what the audience first sees on the stage upon entering the theater or when the curtain is raised. A *box* set has three walls to a room, a floor and a ceiling, just like an actual room from whatever era the play is set in. The *fourth wall* is presumably transparent or "removed" so that the audience can look "through" it at the action. The set of *Trifles* is just such a room; the opening set description actually makes no reference to the stage where the set would be, instead treating it as "really" the "kitchen in the now abandoned farmhouse of JOHN WRIGHT." As becomes apparent from Hale's account of what he saw when he came to the house "yesterday," there is a ceiling to this room, above which is the bedroom where John Wright was found dead.

Gaps

In a typical brief set and character description, a little is said, but a lot is unsaid. In other words, the written text leaves several rather large gaps regarding set and character, gaps that fiction may or may not leave gaping so widely. If you would see a production of *Trifles* on stage, the director along with one or more designers—set designer, costume designer, production designer, lighting designer—will have filled in these gaps in various ways. They may furnish the set more completely than what the set description provides for, and they may paint the walls of the set and light it in such a way as to make it look "gloomy," as per the set description's word. They may also cast certain actors for the character roles and costume them to "look the part." In the case of a play like *Trifles*, there actually may be relatively fewer gaps for director and designers to fill because the time and place in which the play is set provide guidelines and constraints as to those decisions.

In contrast, a Shakespearean play, for instance, which provides even less in the way of set descriptions and stage directions, offers wide gaps for director and designers to fill. It is not uncommon to see productions of Shakespearean plays set and costumed in different historical eras. I personally have seen a production of Shakespeare's *Twelfth Night* set in the 1920s era of "flappers" and jazz and one of *Hamlet* that was set in really no time at all, using a mostly bare stage and nondescript costumes. The 1993 film production of *Much Ado About Nothing*, directed by Kenneth Branagh, was set in some nonspecific time that could be anywhere from the seventeenth to the nineteenth century.

In reading a play on the page, you would do well to remember a point made in the introductory chapters of this book that is especially applicable to drama. That point is the idea that any written text is *potential*: It awaits actualization by the action of a reader. In the case of staged drama, the director, the various designers, and the actors are readers whose readings constitute the live production that the audience sees. In that situation, no narrative description of anything is needed; the audience can see for themselves what the set and characters look like, where and how characters move, to whom they address certain comments, and in what tone of voice.

Dialogue

In your listing exercise, you may have noted some similarity between the opening set description, and perhaps some of the other **stage directions** in this excerpt, and **narration** in fiction. It is conventional for written drama to enclose such descriptive bits in brackets and/or to italicize them, so as to differentiate them from the **dialogue**, which is the actual spoken words of the characters. If there is a similarity between written drama and prose fiction in this regard, there are also a couple of notable differences. Short stories and novels do not usually separate narrative from dialogue by means of brackets or italics, but short stories and novels usually do mark off dialogue by means of quotation marks. This "reversal" of text strategies from the one genre to the other indicates a fundamental strategy of drama: its reliance on dialogue (and the corresponding virtual absence of narrative) to present action to the audience.

Because a play that you read on the page is a version of a script written to be performed on a stage, dialogue predominates and anything resembling narrative is relatively absent. As acting styles have evolved, especially under the influence of realistic drama from the late nineteenth century on, the dialogue is spoken in the context of movements and gestures directed from character to character. All of what they say is dialogue; there are no **soliloquies** or **asides**—lines spoken for the audience's benefit only, unheard by other characters. As a realistic play, *Trifles* follows the convention of pretending that what happens onstage is an actual episode from real life that the audience just happens to be "looking in" on. The action goes on as it would in real life, as if the audience weren't there. For its part, the audience is asked to engage in what the English poet and critic Samuel Taylor Coleridge called a "willing suspension of disbelief": its contribution to the illusion of reality that much live drama seeks to establish.

At the same time, when you read a play on the page you may be especially aware, perhaps more so than with reading fiction, that what you are reading is an artificial linguistic construct. The presence of stage directions and speaker tags in the written text may serve as constant reminders of this artificiality, making a willing suspension of disbelief a little harder to achieve for the reader of drama than for the reader of a short story or novel. The reader of fiction often feels swept away into the created world of the text because the conventions of its literary repertoire are simultaneously more familiar and less visible.

CONNECT: Recall the description of the man reading a novel in Julio Cortázar's story "Continuity of Parks," reprinted in Chapter 5. It was said that the man "tasted the almost perverse pleasure of disengaging himself line by line from the things around him" and that as he read "word by word . . . [he let] himself be absorbed to the point where the images settled down and took on color and movement. . . ."

The third and fourth points on my list of text strategies above—the absence of background to the action being presented and the beginnings of a plot or conflict taking shape—might be thought of as proceeding from the importance of dialogue as a text strategy. Let's consider those points next.

The Absence of Background Information

Because a printed play is almost all dialogue, there is no narrative **voice** to explain characters' personalities, motives, or thoughts or to tell readers what has happened prior to the presented action. Again, in terms of the conventions of realistic drama, this is like life, which also lacks a narrative voice to tell us what's going on and what it may mean. It's true that in the first part of *Trifles* some background to the present situation is given through Mr. Hale's descriptions of what he saw "yesterday." But this information comes through dialogue, not through narration, and it is realistic given the just-beginning investigation by the Sheriff and the County Attorney. Speeches like those given by Mr. Hale in response to the County Attorney's questions are known as **exposition** in drama: information provided very early in a play to orient the audience/reader, in the absence of narration, to the situation that is being presented.

As you read on in the scene from *Trifles*, you may begin to learn more than just what Mr. Hale saw "yesterday": You may begin to put together some ideas about the relationship of John Wright to his wife, of the Wrights to other people in their community, of the County Attorney—a "gallant . . . young politician"—to the older characters, of Mrs. Hale and Mrs. Peters to Mrs. Wright, and of the women to the men. Even without narrative, if you were to see a performance of *Trifles* you would have a little more to go on because these relationships, like those you observe and draw conclusions about in real life, are suggested through the actions and words of people in social intercourse. But in reading *Trifles* on the page, you have very little in the way of text strategies besides the characters' speeches on which to base your inferences and conclusions.

One of my students who read *Trifles* reported he was able to feel "sympathy with Mrs. Wright's plight from the outset" because of Mr. Hale's description of Mr. Wright as reclusive. This student cited Mr. Hale's comment that "I guess you know how much he [John Wright] talked himself" and Mrs. Hale's statements that "I don't think a place'd be any cheerfuller for John Wright's being in it" and that she didn't visit the Wrights' house because "It never seemed a very cheerful place." He went on to say that

> As the women discover that the disorderliness of the house is not a permanent condition but rather just the result of a hasty departure, I realize that the gloominess of the house is apparently due more to the gloominess of the husband than to its situation in a hollow hidden from the road.

This student is beginning to draw some conclusions about the relationship between John and Minnie Wright by way of background to the situation with which the play opens.

Plot and Conflict

As you read through roughly the first third of *Trifles* earlier, you probably got far enough along to start to see something of a plot or conflict situation developing. In some ways, this conflict may involve the relationships among the characters considered briefly just above. It may also involve several apparent conflicts implied in the questions I identified on my list or in other questions you may have formulated. For instance, if Mrs. Wright did kill her husband, will her reasons for doing so be discovered in the official investigation? The plot probably also involves a degree of **suspense** because you do not know at this point how these questions will be resolved, even if in formulating the questions you are beginning to suspect some answers. This text strategy of building suspense as the plot "thickens" is essential to much drama, and not just realistic drama or "whodunits." It gets to the heart of the reader's or audience member's involvement in plays that have plots: what is known versus what is unknown.

Knowing and Unknowing

What does the audience know and not know about what has happened, what is happening, what will happen? In *Trifles*, Mr. Hale's account of what he saw "yesterday" in the Wrights' kitchen is realistic as part of the way the County Attorney conducts his investigation. But Mr. Hale's speeches also provide important information that a reader/audience member can use, not only to learn about the background to the present action, but to understand the relationships among the characters and to begin to wonder about or guess some specific directions the plot might take. Another of my students who read *Trifles* wrote in her journal that readers "never see the murder or meet the people [the Wrights], but they are characterized by what the women say." This student wrote that her "initial response [to the murder] is to be horrified, but through the gradual relation of information" she was able to "understand why Minnie might have done it." As you read on through *Trifles* or any play in which plot is an important text strategy, what the characters do and say allows you to gradually find out more and more, although you do not find out "everything" until the final resolution or **denouement**.

This matter of knowing and unknowing may work in different directions in different plays or subgenres of drama. In some cases, the reader or audience member knows *more* than a character, perhaps because other characters have imparted this information while a particular character is off-stage. This allows **dramatic irony** to operate as a text strategy. A good example of this occurs in Shakespeare's *Hamlet* when, after the play within the play provides Hamlet with apparent confirmation of King Claudius' guilt in the death of Hamlet's father (and Claudius' brother), Hamlet comes upon Claudius praying alone in the chapel and realizes it is an opportunity to kill Claudius and exact the revenge the ghost of Hamlet's father has implored Hamlet to get. But Hamlet stops himself from committing the act because he thinks that if he kills Claudius at his prayers, his soul will go to heaven and Hamlet's revenge will be thwarted; he wants Claudius' soul to go to hell, so he vows to wait to kill Claudius until he can catch the king in the throes of sin. As soon as Hamlet exits in this scene, Claudius confesses in a brief soliloquy that because of his guilt he is unable to pray. Hamlet doesn't know this, but the audience does, and so may see the scene as ironic.

A character's knowing or unknowing about himself or his circumstances may also be a central issue in the plot itself. This is often the case in **classical tragedy**, where a character's gradual enlightenment as to his situation constitutes the tragedy. This is ironic because the good—an increase in the character's self-knowledge—is inseparable from the bad—a moral flaw in the character and a reversal of the character's good fortune. Even in some **comedies**, knowing and unknowing are crucial. An important character's well-being, or even the well-being of a community, may be threatened by some lack of knowledge on the character's part. Much of the suspense of the plot of such plays depends on the character's unknowing and the question of whether he will "wake up" in time to avoid disaster. An example is in Molière's *Tartuffe*, where every "sensible" character in Orgon's household—as well as, presumably, the audience—knows that Tartuffe is a scheming hypocrite, but unless and until Orgon becomes aware of this, social and domestic disaster is a distinct possibility.

As they are raised by what the text of a play says and does not say, questions of knowing and unknowing are text strategies that are crucial to a reader's interaction with a play. As that reader—or audience member—becomes involved with the text, the text allows her or him to know certain things and not to know others. All the text strategies of drama that have been presented so far contribute to both the reader's knowledge and his or her lack of knowledge about the total situation in the play—where it is set, who is involved, how those characters relate to one another, what is happening in the present action and what has happened in the background, and why any of it is happening. This integration of dramatic text strategies is especially potent in a stage (or film) production of a play, as a later chapter will consider. In the next chapter, however, I will ask you to look a little more closely at what a reader might do in building up his or her knowledge as she or he reads.

 ## READING AND WRITING PROJECTS

FOR CREATIVE AND CRITICAL THINKING

Your own writing is important as you try to learn more about yourself as a reader—both what you do cognitively when you read and how culture impinges on the kind of reader you are when you interact with any particular text. In addition to response statements and the formal expository paper that may grow out of them, there are other ways to use writing to learn.

The following suggestions are intended to help you integrate your reading of and writing about literary texts in various ways. These suggestions include exploratory writing, playing with texts and language, creative efforts in various genres, and other writing exercises designed to strengthen your awareness of the cognitive and cultural processes involved in your reading.

▶ Take any short story (or a scene from a short story) and transform it into a dramatic script. Provide descriptions of characters and set as appropriate to whether your script is realistic or not. Provide stage directions where needed, but write mainly dialogue for the characters. As an optional additional exercise, you could write a prose comment on which genre—fiction or drama—this particular story works best in, or on the effects of transforming a story from fiction to drama.

▶ Write a scene for a play—or a one-act play—based on either of these options: (1) continuing, updating, or providing an alternative to the action from a play you have read; (2) turning some experience in your own life into a script. With the first option, you should use characters from a play you have read and put them into a different situation—perhaps "after" the original play ends (either immediately after or some time later)—or "instead" of what happens in a scene from the original. Working with *Trifles*, for instance, you might write a scene involving Minnie Wright meeting with Mrs. Hale and Mrs. Peters at the jail, when the latter two women take Minnie's things to her. Or you might write a scene in which the County Attorney and the Sheriff finally do figure out who killed John Wright. An additional option for this project could be to write an explanation, in your own voice, of why you created the new scene you wrote.

▶ Write a biopoem about any character in a play. This is an 11-line poem, not necessarily rhymed or in regular meter, that takes the following form:

Line 1: First name of character
Line 2: Four traits that describe the character
Line 3: [Relative] _____ of _____
Line 4: Who loves _____ (list several people or things)
Line 5: Who feels _____ (several things)
Line 6: Who needs _____ (several things)
Line 7: Who fears _____ (several things)
Line 8: Who gives _____ (several things)
Line 9: Who would like to see _____ (several things)
Line 10: Resident of _____
Line 11: Last name of character

This can turn into a group project in several ways: the poem can be composed by a group, for instance with different members writing different lines; poems written about the same character can be exchanged and commented upon, either in writing or in discussion; poems written about different characters can be used as ways to introduce a play that one person has in his or her storehouse of texts to classmates who have not yet read that play.

▶ Imagine you work for a toy manufacturing company. Looking for a new product line, you hit upon the idea of designing a series of "action figures" for young children. As a variation on the "Teenage Mutant Ninja Turtles"® or the "Mighty Morphin Power Rangers,"® you think a collection of action figures (or dolls) based on famous dramatic characters might be successful. Design such figures or dolls based on any play of your choosing. How might they be dressed? What props or equipment might they carry or have available as accessories? You don't have to actually make the figures or dolls, but you should at least describe them verbally and make some sketches of what they might look like. This project lends itself to collaborative work, especially if one person is better at verbalizing and another at drawing.

16 ◈ READING DRAMA ACTIVELY

Printed drama may be enough like prose fiction that you may tend to apply the reading strategies you use for fiction when you read a play. To the extent that the two genres share some text strategies, those reading strategies should help produce a harmonious literary interaction. Most printed drama—at least most printed drama written since the eighteenth century—does not require the more specialized reading strategies that the section on poetry recommends. You can use some of your fiction-reading strategies successfully. But because printed drama does exhibit some text strategies different from those of prose fiction, it stands to reason that those text strategies either stimulate or require certain reading strategies in order for a harmonious interaction to occur. In the interest of becoming a self-conscious reader, you should heighten your awareness of the strategies you already use as well as try to be a more active reader by using some that you may not have used before.

Reading Strategies for Printed Drama

To begin this consideration of reading strategies for drama on the page, take a few moments now to list the reading strategies you already use. Refer to your experience reading the first part of *Trifles* as you think of items for your list.

Reading Strategies for Printed Drama

1.
2.
3.
4.
5.
6.

Which of these strategies is like any you use for reading fiction? Is any of them peculiar to drama?

Now I am going to offer you another list of reading strategies. You may notice that some of them bear similarities to strategies for reading fiction, but there is also an emphasis here on applications to drama on the page. As was done with text strategies earlier, I will ask you to consider these reading strategies one at a time. As with text strategies also, I will ask you to keep in mind that these reading strategies are interconnected too; no reader uses any of them in isolation from any of the others, nor would I suggest you do so. A clear understanding of these reading strategies seems to require looking at them individually, but at the end of this chapter you can read a journal entry that shows the integration of reading strategies in one student's response.

Some Reading Strategies for Printed Drama

1. Visualize.
2. Narrate.
3. Identify gaps; begin to decide how to fill them in.
4. Make plot predictions.
5. Build consistency.

Visualizing

As you have seen in looking at the first part of *Trifles* and at the portion of the "Seinfeld" episode reprinted in Chapter 15, drama on the page leaves much unsaid or unnarrated. That seems to require, if not almost automatically stimulate, the first of the reading strategies listed here: **visualizing**. When you visualize you see in your mind's eye everything that your literal eyes would see if you were watching a production of the play you're reading. This visualization includes the characters—what they look like, how they're dressed, how and where they move, their gestures and other physical actions, their facial expressions, how they speak (which might be thought of as "audializing": hearing with "your mind's ear"). It would also include the set—furniture, windows, doors, what's *beyond* those windows and doors, or walls of a box set, lighting, shadows, background. As *Trifles* shows, the set and character descriptions in a realistic play will help you begin this visualization, but you can work consciously on doing this on your own. As you have with the other genres in this book, with printed drama you should practice writing while you read. In the case of drama, one special way of doing this is to make notes of what and how you visualize as you read, which brings me to the second reading strategy on the list: **narrating**.

Narrating

Because there usually isn't a narrator in printed drama, it may help you as you read to act as a surrogate narrator yourself. If you are seeing and hearing things in your mind as you read a play, and if you write those things down as you read—even if just in brief notes—you are in effect acting as a kind of narrator. It's not really necessary to write any lengthy stretches of narrative prose as you visualize; just notes would do. Those notes will help you actualize the potential of the text of printed drama because writing them will stimulate further visualization on your part; it will not be just the record of what you have already visualized. You should see the truth of this if you try this strategy in conscious fashion.

As a demonstration, go back and reread the opening part of *Trifles*. As you do so—either here in your book, on a separate sheet of paper, or on your computer screen—jot down some of the particulars you find yourself visualizing. You might want to list them in two columns, just for convenience sake, as I have indicated below. Then, in class discussion or by exchanging writing, you could compare the version of set and characters that you are creating in your mind with those of your classmates.

Visualizations—First Part of *Trifles*

Characters.		*Set*
1.		1.
2.		2.
3.		3.
4.		4.
5.		5.
6.		6.
7.		7.
8.		8.
9.		9.
10.		10.

In beginning this process of visualizing and narrating, you are also beginning to "direct" and "design" your own "mental production" of *Trifles,* and you can and should do something similar whenever you read a printed play. If you have the opportunity to see a live or filmed production of a play you have read, consciously visualizing and making notes of your visualizations will help you be a stronger reader of that production because you will have something more definite in your mind to compare with what you see on the stage or the screen.

Identifying and Filling in Gaps

If you write down what you are visualizing as you read, you are also beginning to practice the third of the reading strategies listed earlier—identifying and filling in gaps. A printed play has numerous gaps. Even in the dialogue, which constitutes most of a play on the page, gaps exist in terms of a character's tone and volume of voice, pace of speech, pauses, emphases—all the variables of spoken utterances. You can keep this third reading strategy distinct from the first two by starring, underlining, or highlighting those items in your notes that indicate your decisions to fill in a gap in the text. When you do this, you may find that almost everything on your list is starred, underlined, or highlighted! That is to be expected, not because you are a weak reader, but because printed plays leave so much *un*said, so many gaps.

To pursue this strategy further, you might try to identify gaps that consist of what you can*not* at first visualize: questions, or unknowns, or matters that are more intellectual or emotional than physical. In the first part of *Trifles*, this exploration might take you into the characters' motives or thoughts or feelings: things they are *not* saying, matters that do not take physical or sensory form. If, for instance, you put into visible words your speculation about what the County Attorney thinks of Mrs. Wright based on the condition of her kitchen, you can begin to see what's involved in your decisions to bridge or fill in these gaps the way you do. One of the students I quoted in the previous chapter did something like this as he wrote in his journal. He said, "The relationship between the three men and the two women . . . mirrors that of the Wrights and by example allows . . . [me] to glimpse the [Wrights'] relationship." The relationship between John and Minnie Wright is a gap early in the play because it is not shown in the action; it can only be "glimpsed," as this student put it, by the reader's active filling in of the gap.

Making Plot Predictions

Related to the strategy of filling in gaps is the fourth one, which is to make some predictions about where the plot of the play is heading. A plot (for the first-time reader certainly) as it is unfolding is a gap that is continually narrowed or filled in as you read along. As with the other reading strategies listed here, this one is probably something you can't help doing as you read, especially as you read a realistic drama. What may be new or different or self-conscious is to write down your plot predictions as you make them.

CONNECT: Guy de Maupassant's story "The Necklace" in Chapter 5 is, like *Trifles*, strongly plot-driven. In terms of making plot predictions, how are your reading strategies for *Trifles* similar to your reading strategies for "The Necklace"? If there are close similarities, can you draw any conclusions about realism in both fiction and drama?

Earlier, when I suggested some text strategies in *Trifles*, I listed some questions that may arise out of the developing plot of that play: Why did Mrs. Wright act so strangely when Mr. Hale found her? Did she kill her husband? If so, why? Does the condition of the kitchen suggest a motive for Mrs. Wright's killing her husband? The action in the first part of the play seems to give rise to these questions about plot and suggests the reciprocity of text strategies and reading strategies: As you get some information about plot, for instance, you begin to formulate questions and make predictions based on that information, questions and predictions that will be answered, confirmed, or denied by further information you get from reading on. This process is closely related to the last suggested reading strategy.

Building Consistency

The Reading and Responding to Fiction section discussed the reading strategy of **consistency building**, which is the tendency of readers to formulate and then answer questions about any aspect of a text where logical or thematic consistency may be seen to operate: plot, character, imagery, symbolism. In the case of reading drama—or seeing it performed live—it is quite likely that consistency building will be one of your reading strategies. This is so for three reasons. First, if you have experience reading fiction, you are likely to carry your reading strategies over from one genre to the other. Second, it is in the nature of realistic drama to create suspense, to raise questions for readers/viewers, and to focus their attention on matters of knowing and unknowing. Third, if you have experience watching drama in movies or on television, you have probably practiced consistency building there, even if you weren't self-conscious about your reading strategies. Because the particular questions raised and the predictions made in answering them will vary from one reader to another, it is the *process* of reading a play that I am outlining here, not so much the actual questions and answers.

As an exercise, go back to the excerpt from *Trifles* once more and see what plot predictions, questions, and answers you have. What do you think will happen as the play goes on? What do you find yourself wondering about or asking about or wanting to know, in terms of the action of the play? What guesses do you have as to how these matters might be answered?

If you are building consistency as you read, what direction does that take? Do you begin to interpret the play in a certain way or create a **theme** as you read? Take a few minutes to list some of those predictions here.

Plot Predictions and Consistency Building for *Trifles*

1.

2.

3.

4.

5.

6.

Doing a Cognitive Analysis

Now that you've done some self-conscious interactive reading with *Trifles*, it seems an opportune time to point out how these reading strategies lay the groundwork for a **strong reading** along the lines of a **cognitive analysis**. What you have been demonstrating for yourself through these exercises is how your reading strategies interact with certain text strategies and what happens in that interaction, particularly in the matter of your degree of knowledge as a reader. You are really looking at what you know, how you know it, and how well you know it (or what you don't know and why you don't). If you keep this up as you read the rest of *Trifles* or if you practice it systematically with any play you read, you are not far from having the material to draft a paper in which you analyze cognitively your response to a text. And doing that once, perhaps for the first time in your experience as a reader of drama, will strengthen you as a reader of drama on future occasions. You will begin to understand how you process a play in your mind as you read it. That understanding, in turn, will help you control your reading strategies, so that you can use them when you want to and how you want to. If you do that, you'll be a stronger reader, aware and in command of your contributions to the reading interaction.

Now, however, it's probably high time you got some closure on *Trifles*, so here is the rest of that play. We left it just when Mrs. Hale was saying to Mrs. Peters:

I'd hate to have men coming into my kitchen, snooping around and criticizing.

[She arranges the pans under the sink which the County Attorney has shoved out of place.]

Mrs. Peters: Of course it's no more than their duty.   50

Mrs. Hale: Duty's all right, but I guess that deputy sheriff that came out to make the fire might have got a little of this on. [*Gives the roller towel a pull.*] Wish I'd thought of that sooner. Seems mean to talk about her for not having things slicked up when she had to come away in such a hurry.

Mrs. Peters [*Who has gone to a small table in the left rear corner of the room, and lifted one end of a towel that covers a pan.*]:   She had bread set.

[Stands still.]

Mrs. Hale [*Eyes fixed on a loaf of bread beside the breadbox, which is on a low shelf at the other side of the room. Moves slowly toward it.*]:   She was going to put this in there. [*Picks up loaf, then abruptly drops it. In a manner of returning to familiar things.*] It's a shame about her fruit. I wonder if it's all gone. [*Gets up on the chair and looks.*] I think there's some here that's all right, Mrs. Peters. Yes—here: believe that's the only one. [*Gets down, bottle in her hand. Goes to the sink and wipes it off on the outside.*] She'll feel awful bad after all her hard work in the hot weather. I remember the afternoon I put up my cherries last summer.

[She puts the bottle on the big kitchen table, center of the room. With a sigh, is about to sit down in the rocking-chair. Before she is seated realizes what chair it is; with a slow look at it, steps back. The chair which she has touched rocks back and forth.]

Mrs. Peters: Well, I must get those things from the front room closet. [*She goes to the door at the right, but after looking into the other room, steps back.*] You coming with me, Mrs. Hale? You could help me carry them.

[They go into the other room; reappear, Mrs. Peters carrying a dress and skirt, Mrs. Hale following with a pair of shoes.]

Mrs. Peters: My, it's cold in there.   55

[She puts the clothes on the big table, and hurries to the stove.]

MRS. HALE [*Examining the skirt.*]:   Wright was close. I think maybe that's why she kept so much to herself. She didn't even belong to the Ladies Aid. I suppose she felt she couldn't do her part, and then you don't enjoy things when you feel shabby. She used to wear pretty clothes and be lively, when she was Minnie Foster, one of the town girls singing in the choir. But that—oh, that was thirty years ago. This all you was to take in?

MRS. PETERS: She said she wanted an apron. Funny thing to want, for there isn't much to get you dirty in jail, goodness knows. But I suppose just to make her feel more natural. She said they was in the top drawer in this cupboard. Yes, here. And then her little shawl that always hung behind the door. [*Opens stair door and looks.*] Yes, here it is.

[*Quickly shuts door leading upstairs.*]

MRS. HALE [*Abruptly moving toward her.*]:   Mrs. Peters?
MRS. PETERS: Yes, Mrs. Hale?
MRS. HALE: Do you think she did it?
MRS. PETERS [*In a frightened voice.*]:   Oh, I don't know.   60
MRS. HALE: Well, I don't think she did. Asking for an apron and her little shawl. Worrying about her fruit.
MRS. PETERS [*Starts to speak, glances up, where footsteps are heard in the room above. In a low voice.*]:   Mr. Peters says it looks bad for her. Mr. Henderson is awful sarcastic in a speech and he'll make fun of her sayin' she didn't wake up.
MRS. HALE: Well, I guess John Wright didn't wake when they was slipping that rope under his neck.
MRS. PETERS: No, it's strange. It must have been done awful crafty and still. They say it was such a—funny way to kill a man, rigging it all up like that.   65
MRS. HALE: That's just what Mr. Hale said. There was a gun in the house. He says that's what he can't understand.
MRS. PETERS: Mr. Henderson said coming out that what was needed for the case was a motive; something to show anger, or—sudden feeling.
MRS. HALE [*Who is standing by the table.*]:   Well, I don't see any signs of anger around here. [*She puts her hand on the dish towel which lies on the table, stands looking down at table, one half of which is clean, the other half messy.*] It's wiped to here. [*Makes a move as if to finish work, then turns and looks at loaf of bread outside the breadbox. Drops towel. In that voice of coming back to familiar things.*] Wonder how they are finding things upstairs. I hope she had it a little more red-up up there. You know, it seems kind of *sneaking*. Locking her up in town and then coming out here and trying to get her own house to run against her!
MRS. PETERS: But Mrs. Hale, the law is the law.
MRS. HALE: I s'pose 'tis. [*Unbuttoning her coat.*] Better loosen up your things, Mrs. Peters. You won't feel them when you go out.   70

[*Mrs. Peters takes off her fur tippet, goes to hang it on hook at back of room, stands looking at the under part of the small corner table.*]

MRS. PETERS: She was piecing a quilt.

[*She brings the large sewing basket and they look at the bright pieces.*]

MRS. HALE: It's log cabin pattern. Pretty, isn't it? I wonder if she was goin' to quilt it or just knot it?

[*Footsteps are heard coming down the stairs. The Sheriff enters followed by Hale and the County Attorney.*]

SHERIFF: They wonder if she was going to quilt it or just knot it!

[The men laugh; the women look abashed.]

COUNTY ATTORNEY [*Rubbing his hands over the stove.*]:   Frank's fire didn't do much up there, did it? Well, let's go out to the barn and get that cleared up.

[The men go outside.]

MRS. HALE [*Resentfully.*]:   I don't know as there's anything so strange, our takin' up   75
our time with little things while we're waiting for them to get the evidence.
[*She sits down at the big table, smoothing out a block with decision.*] I don't
see as it's anything to laugh about.

MRS. PETERS [*Apologetically.*]:   Of course they've got awful important things on
their minds.

[Pulls up a chair and joins Mrs. Hale at the table.]

MRS. HALE [*Examining another block.*]:   Mrs. Peters, look at this one. Here, this is
the one she was working on, and look at the sewing! It's all over the place! Why,
it looks as if she didn't know what she was about!

[After she has said this they look at each other, then start to glance back at the door. After an instant Mrs. Hale has pulled at a knot and ripped the sewing.]

MRS. PETERS: Oh, what are you doing, Mrs. Hale?

MRS. HALE [*Mildly.*]:   Just pulling out a stitch or two that's not sewed very good.
[*Threading a needle.*] Bad sewing always made me fidgety.

MRS. PETERS [*Nervously.*]:   I don't think we ought to touch things.

MRS. HALE: I'll just finish up this end. [*Suddenly stopping and leaning forward.*]   80
Mrs. Peters?

MRS. PETERS: Yes, Mrs. Hale?

MRS. HALE: What do you suppose she was so nervous about?

MRS. PETERS: Oh—I don't know. I don't know as she was nervous. I sometimes sew
awful queer when I'm just tired. [*Mrs. Hale starts to say something, looks at
Mrs. Peters, then goes on sewing.*] Well I must get these things wrapped up.
They may be through sooner than we think. [*Putting apron and other things
together.*] I wonder where I can find a piece of paper, and string.

MRS. HALE: In that cupboard, maybe.   85

MRS. PETERS [*Looking in cupboard.*]:   Why, here's a bird-cage. [*Holds it up.*] Did she
have a bird, Mrs. Hale?

MRS. HALE: Why, I don't know whether she did or not—I've not been here for so
long. There was a man around last year selling canaries cheap, but I don't know
as she took one; maybe she did. She used to sing real pretty herself.

MRS. PETERS [*Glancing around.*]:   Seems funny to think of a bird here. But she must
have had one, or why would she have a cage? I wonder what happened to it.

MRS. HALE: I s'pose maybe the cat got it.

MRS. PETERS: No, she didn't have a cat. She's got that feeling some people have   90
about cats—being afraid of them. My cat got in her room and she was real upset
and asked me to take it out.

MRS. HALE: My sister Bessie was like that. Queer, ain't it?

MRS. PETERS [*Examining the cage.*]:   Why, look at this door. It's broke. One hinge is
pulled apart.

MRS. HALE [*Looking too.*]:   Looks as if someone must have been rough with it.

MRS. PETERS: Why, yes.

[She brings the cage forward and puts it on the table.]

MRS. HALE: I wish if they're going to find any evidence they'd be about it. I don't like this place.   95

MRS. PETERS: But I'm awful glad you came with me, Mrs. Hale. It would be lonesome for me sitting here alone.

MRS. HALE: It would, wouldn't it? [*Dropping her sewing.*] But I tell you what I do wish, Mrs. Peters. I wish I had come over sometimes when *she* was here. I— [*Looking around the room.*]—wish I had.

MRS. PETERS: But of course you were awful busy, Mrs. Hale—your house and your children.

MRS. HALE: I could've come. I stayed away because it weren't cheerful—and that's why I ought to have come. I—I've never liked this place. Maybe because it's down in a hollow and you don't see the road. I dunno what it is, but it's a lonesome place and always was. I wish I had come over to see Minnie Foster sometimes. I can see now—

[Shakes her head.]

MRS. PETERS: Well, you mustn't reproach yourself, Mrs. Hale. Somehow we just don't see how it is with other folks until—something comes up.   100

MRS. HALE: Not having children makes less work—but it makes a quiet house, and Wright out to work all day, and no company when he did come in. Did you know John Wright, Mrs. Peters?

MRS. PETERS: Not to know him; I've seen him in town. They say he was a good man.

MRS. HALE: Yes—good: he didn't drink, and kept his word as well as most, I guess, and paid his debts. But he was a hard man, Mrs. Peters. Just to pass the time of day with him—[*Shivers.*] Like a raw wind that gets to the bone. [*Pauses, her eye falling on the cage.*] I should think she would 'a wanted a bird. But what do you suppose went with it?

MRS. PETERS: I don't know, unless it got sick and died.

[She reaches over and swings the broken door, swings it again, both women watch it.]

MRS. HALE: You weren't raised round here, were you? [*Mrs. Peters shakes her head.*] You didn't know—her?   105

MRS. PETERS: Not till they brought her yesterday.

MRS. HALE: She—come to think of it, she was kind of like a bird herself—real sweet and pretty, but kind of timid and—fluttery. How—she—did—change. [*Silence; then as if struck by a happy thought and relieved to get back to everyday things.*] Tell you what, Mrs. Peters, why don't you take the quilt in with you? It might take up her mind.

MRS. PETERS: Why, I think that's a real nice idea, Mrs. Hale. There couldn't possibly be any objection to it, could there? Now, just what would I take? I wonder if her patches are in here—and her things.

[They look in sewing basket.]

MRS. HALE: Here's some red. I expect this has got sewing things in it. [*Brings out a fancy box.*] What a pretty box. Looks like something somebody would give you. Maybe her scissors are in here. [*Opens box. Suddenly puts her hand to her nose.*] Why—[*Mrs. Peters bends nearer, then turns her face away.*] There's something wrapped up in this piece of silk.

MRS. PETERS: Why, this isn't her scissors.   110

MRS. HALE [*Lifting the silk*.]:   Oh, Mrs. Peters—it's—

[*Mrs. Peters bends closer.*]

MRS. PETERS: It's the bird.

MRS. HALE [*Jumping up*.]:   But, Mrs. Peters—look at it! Its neck! Look at its neck! It's all—other side *to*.

MRS. PETERS: Somebody—wrung—its—neck.

[*Their eyes meet. A look of growing comprehension, of horror. Steps are heard outside. Mrs. Hale slips box under quilt pieces, and sinks into her chair. Enter Sheriff and County Attorney. Mrs. Peters rises.*]

COUNTY ATTORNEY [*As one turning from serious things to little pleasantries*.]:   115
Well, ladies, have you decided whether she was going to quilt it or knot it?

MRS. PETERS: We think she was going to—knot it.

COUNTY ATTORNEY: Well, that's interesting, I'm sure. [*Seeing the birdcage.*] Has the bird flown?

MRS. HALE [*Putting more quilt over the box*.]:   We think the—cat got it.

COUNTY ATTORNEY [*Preoccupied*.]:   Is there a cat?

[*Mrs. Hale glances a quick covert way at Mrs. Peters.*]

MRS. PETERS: Well, not *now*. They're superstitious, you know. They leave.   120

COUNTY ATTORNEY [*To Sheriff Peters, continuing an interrupted conversation*.]:
No sign at all of anyone having come from the outside. Their own rope. Now let's go up again and go over it piece by piece. [*They start upstairs.*] It would have to have been someone who knew just the—

[*Mrs. Peters sits down. The two women sit there not looking at one another, but as if peering into something and at the same time holding back. When they talk now it is in the manner of feeling their way over strange ground, as if afraid of what they are saying, but as if they can not help saying it.*]

MRS. HALE: She liked the bird. She was going to bury it in that pretty box.

MRS. PETERS [*In a whisper*.]:   When I was a girl—my kitten—there was a boy took a hatchet, and before my eyes—and before I could get there—[*Covers her face an instant.*] If they hadn't held me back I would have—[*Catches herself, looks upstairs where steps are heard, falters weakly.*]—hurt him.

MRS. HALE [*With a slow look around her*.]:   I wonder how it would seem never to have had any children around. [*Pause.*] No, Wright wouldn't like the bird—a thing that sang. She used to sing. He killed that, too.

MRS. PETERS [*Moving uneasily*.]:   We don't know who killed the bird.   125

MRS. HALE: I knew John Wright.

MRS. PETERS: It was an awful thing was done in this house that night, Mrs. Hale. Killing a man while he slept, slipping a rope around his neck that choked the life out of him.

MRS. HALE: His neck. Choked the life out of him.

[*Her hand goes out and rests on the bird cage.*]

MRS. PETERS [*With rising voice*.]:   We don't know who killed him. We don't *know*.

MRS. HALE [*Her own feeling not interrupted*.]:   If there'd been years and years of   130
nothing, then a bird sang to you, it would be awful—still, after the bird was still.

MRS. PETERS [*Something within her speaking*.]:   I know what stillness is. When we homesteaded in Dakota, and my first baby died—after he was two years old, and me with no other then—

MRS. HALE [*Moving.*]:   How soon do you suppose they'll be through, looking for the evidence?

MRS. PETERS: I know what stillness is. [*Pulling herself back.*] The law has got to punish crime, Mrs. Hale.

MRS. HALE [*Not as if answering that.*]:   I wish you'd seen Minnie Foster when she wore a white dress with blue ribbons and stood up there in the choir and sang. [*A look around the room.*] Oh, I *wish* I'd come over here once in a while! That was a crime! Who's going to punish that?

MRS. PETERS [*Looking upstairs.*]:   We mustn't—take on.   135

MRS. HALE: I might have known she needed help! I know how things can be—for women. I tell you, it's queer, Mrs. Peters. We live close together and we live far apart. We all go through the same things—it's all just a different kind of the same thing. [*Brushes her eyes, noticing the bottle of fruit, reaches out for it.*] If I was you I wouldn't tell her her fruit was gone. Tell her it *ain't.* Tell her it's all right. Take this in to prove it to her. She—she may never know whether it was broke or not.

MRS. PETERS [*Takes the bottle, looks about for something to wrap it in; takes petticoat from the clothes brought from the other room, very nervously begins winding this around the bottle. In a false voice.*]:   My, it's a good thing the men couldn't hear us. Wouldn't they just laugh? Getting all stirred up over a little thing like a—dead canary. As if that could have anything to do with—with— wouldn't they *laugh!*

[*The men are heard coming downstairs.*]

MRS. HALE [*Under her breath.*]:   Maybe they would—maybe they wouldn't.

COUNTY ATTORNEY: No, Peters, it's all perfectly clear except a reason for doing it. But you know juries when it comes to women. If there was some definite thing. Something to show—something to make a story about—a thing that would connect up with this strange way of doing it—

[*The women's eyes meet for an instant. Enter Hale from outer door.*]

HALE: Well, I've got the team around. Pretty cold out there.   140

COUNTY ATTORNEY: I'm going to stay here a while by myself. [*To the Sheriff.*] You can send Frank out for me, can't you? I want to go over everything. I'm not satisfied that we can't do better.

SHERIFF: Do you want to see what Mrs. Peters is going to take in?

[*The Lawyer goes to the table, picks up the apron, laughs.*]

COUNTY ATTORNEY: Oh, I guess they're not very dangerous things the ladies have picked out. [*Moves a few things about, disturbing the quilt pieces which cover the box. Steps back.*] No, Mrs. Peters doesn't need supervising. For that matter, a sheriff's wife is married to the law. Ever think of it that way, Mrs. Peters?

MRS. PETERS: Not—just that way.

SHERIFF [*Chuckling.*]:   Married to the law. [*Moves toward the other room.*] I just want   145
you to come in here a minute, George. We ought to take a look at these windows.

COUNTY ATTORNEY [*Scoffingly.*]:   Oh, windows!

SHERIFF: We'll be right out, Mrs. Hale.

[*Hale goes outside. The Sheriff follows the County Attorney into the other room. Then Mrs. Hale rises, hands tight together, looking intensely at Mrs. Peters, whose eyes make a slow turn, finally meeting Mrs. Hale's. A moment Mrs. Hale holds her, then her own eyes point the way to where the box is concealed. Suddenly Mrs. Peters throws back quilt pieces and tries to put the box in the bag she is wearing. It is too big. She opens box, starts to take bird out, cannot touch it, goes to pieces, stands there helpless. Sound of a knob turning in the other room. Mrs. Hale snatches the box and puts it in the pocket of her big coat. Enter County Attorney and Sheriff.]*

COUNTY ATTORNEY [*Facetiously*.]:   Well, Henry, at least we found out that she was not going to quilt it. She was going to—what is it you call it, ladies?

MRS. HALE [*Her hand against her pocket*.]:   We call it—knot it, Mr. Henderson.
(CURTAIN)

Additional Text Strategies of Drama

Having read to the end of this play, presumably your questions concerning the direction and outcome of its plot are now answered. Did the action move in the direction you thought it would, or did it surprise you?

Looking back over the course of the plot, are you now able to chart it in terms of an initial conflict, **rising action** toward a **climax**, and then **falling action** to **resolution** or a denouement? How about something like this?

Plot Development in *Trifles*

Initial conflict: The unsolved strangulation of John Wright.

Rising action: The County Attorney and the Sheriff investigate, finding no clues as to a motive. Mrs. Hale and Mrs. Peters do find clues. Will they tell the County Attorney and the Sheriff of the motive they have inferred?

Climax: When the men re-enter the kitchen, still searching for a motive, and the women know they have one.

Falling action: The men's decision that the women remain "clueless" and don't "need supervising."

Resolution/Denouement: Mrs. Hale's concealment of the dead canary in her coat pocket, with the implication that she and Mrs. Peters will continue to conceal what they know.

This scheme is merely an estimation: Some readers may identify the climax as a different point in the action, perhaps as late as the point where Mrs. Hale takes the canary's "coffin" from Mrs. Peters and hides it in her coat pocket. In that case, the falling action would consist only of the County Attorney's comment about the quilt and Mrs. Hale's reply. And the resolution would be the implication that the women are going to continue keeping silent about what they know. Even stages of plot development are subject to individual readers' interpretations!

Whether or not you assent to this analysis of plot development in *Trifles*, I hope you are able to recognize some kind of plot structure in this play. You should be able to see how your questions that arose about the action of the play as you were reading it are related to the plot structure: How the initial conflict and rising action kept those questions alive, and how the climax and falling action answered them. Also, you should recognize how closely involved your own knowledge or the lack of it is with the developing plot:

How as the plot moved ahead, you knew certain things, didn't know others, gradually came to know more, but still didn't know what was going to happen until it did. As a one-act play, and as a short one at that, *Trifles* is probably too brief and has too few characters to involve a **subplot**, but in longer and more complex plays with more characters, a second or even a third line of action may be defined. A subplot may parallel the main plot, pose an ironic contrast to it, or relate to the main plot in any number of ways.

In addition to plot, there are some other text strategies of drama you could consider in *Trifles*. For the purpose of this discussion, I will ask you to take a look at four of these: **character**, **symbol**, **irony**, and **theme**.

Characters

In addition to plot, there are some other text strategies of drama you could consider in *Trifles*. Obviously, this play employs the usual text strategies of characters in a particular setting or situation. Mr. Hale, it turns out, is a relatively *minor* character, while the other two men and the two women are *major* characters. That is, Mr. Hale is there mostly to provide the audience with some necessary background information, whereas the other characters hold more interest as people. A further distinction might be made between *static* and *dynamic* characters in this play: The County Attorney and the Sheriff don't really grow or change, but Mrs. Hale and Mrs. Peters do as they seem to recognize a bond with Minnie Wright.

This character distinction is related to the crucial matter of knowledge: The two women characters know more to start with about women's "trifles" than the men do, but they also come to know more about Minnie Wright—and her motive for strangling her husband—than the men do. Not only that, but they come to know something about themselves that they probably didn't know before: that they could assume and act on a bond with another woman whose experiences were enough like their own that they could see themselves in her place. Mrs. Hale and Mrs. Peters leave the Wrights' house different people from who they were when they came in. The Sheriff and the County Attorney could also be considered **foils**—or contrasting characters—to Mrs. Hale and Mrs. Peters. The men's lack of understanding about Mrs. Wright's motives stands in sharp contrast to the women's insight. In this way, the two men may help you as a reader gain a better understanding of the two women.

Symbols

Perhaps you identified some things in the setting as **symbols**, things that make literal sense within the realistic context of the action but that seem to have *figurative* meaning of another sort. How about the cold that the characters comment on and complain about? That makes realistic sense in terms of winter on the American Great Plains, which is the apparent geographical and seasonal setting of the play. But you might also take the cold air as symbolic of the atmosphere in the Wrights' home. The text seems to invite this association when Mrs. Hale, with a shiver, likens John Wright to "a raw wind." Minnie Wright's dead canary also seems to have symbolic value; certainly Mrs. Hale and Mrs. Peters see it that way as they construct from it a fairly elaborate scenario of John Wright's emotional cruelty to his wife and Minnie's consequent motive for strangling her husband.

It doesn't seem to stretch matters too far to observe that these symbolic associations involve a change in knowledge on the part of both the women characters and readers of the play: Both the cold air and the dead bird seem natural enough when you first encounter them in the play, but if you come to regard them as symbols, you know about or understand them in a different way.

Irony

Finally, you might consider some irony in *Trifles*. Irony depends on the issue of knowing and unknowing for its impact. For instance, when the County Attorney re-enters the kitchen from upstairs just after Mrs. Hale first hides the bird under some quilt pieces, he asks the women if they have "decided whether [Minnie Wright] was going to quilt it or knot it," as if such a decision is the limit of what the women could arrive at. Of course the audience knows what the County Attorney does not know at this point—that Mrs. Peters and Mrs. Hale are beginning to reach a far more profound decision—and so his question and his condescending air are ironic. You may also have observed that the entire action of the play is ironic, in that the criminal investigators are unable to learn what the housewives figure out pretty easily, and which is the central question that those two men are trying to solve.

Theme

Reaching conclusions such as these about irony in *Trifles* probably also involves your construction of a theme as you read the play. Perhaps you see the title as ironic because the "trifles" with which the female characters are concerned are actually the important facts the male characters are searching for but are unable to see. Perhaps also you see irony in the attitude, expressed by the County Attorney, that women cannot know anything important because all they are concerned with is "trifles." These ironies, involving an opposition between men and women, as well as what Mrs. Hale and Mrs. Peters come to realize—that Minnie Wright apparently did strangle her husband because of his emotional and psychological abuse of her—may lead you to some conclusions about theme in *Trifles*.

Plays such as *Trifles*, with its careful plot construction, relatively consistent characters, specific locality of setting, and verbal and physical symbols, may seem to have underlying themes that account for and arrange all these other text strategies. In realistic drama in general, it may seem that theme is a text strategy, an element *of* or *in* the text. However, as the sections of this book on reading fiction and reading poetry argue, theme is something that a reader *creates* in his or her interaction with a literary text. A reader makes this creative or interpretative move because of text strategies he or she encounters in reading drama on the page, but also because of beliefs, values, opinions, feelings, and experiences she or he brings to the encounter with the text from her or his **ideology**.

If you consider *Trifles* in terms of its ideology interacting with yours, what do you think it is about in terms of theme? Is it primarily a murder mystery, a whodunit (or perhaps more accurately a "whydunit")? Is it about the process of figuring out someone's guilt and motive for a guilty act? Does it reveal the lengths to which a woman will go to protect herself from an emotionally and possibly physically abusive man? Does it track the dawning consciousness on the part of two women that they have solidarity with a third against the world of men? Or is it about the relation of gender to *epistemology,* or ways of knowing: Who we are in gender terms affects what we know and how we know it? Or is it about something else that I haven't mentioned? In any case, can you locate your interpretation in the interaction of the text's ideology and your own? Because you've already read the play once—and the first part of it more than once—I will not ask you to read it again now and write a response statement in terms of the ideological interaction, but I would suggest you and your class discuss these questions and especially try to identify the sources (in the text and in different readers' ideologies) for the decisions about theme in *Trifles* that emerge.

Interactions Between the Reader and the Play

In the preceding chapter, I pointed out how interconnected the text strategies of a play are. I hope your experience reading *Trifles* has shown you how the same is true of reading strategies for drama: none of them is applied in isolation from the others. Furthermore, it may seem that the text strategies of *Trifles* reveal that play's ideology, and your response to the play may involve your own ideology. To try to bring this all together in concrete fashion, I will ask you to read the following response journal entry written by a student. Her name is Gail Nagy; she read *Trifles* for the first time as a 45-year-old woman. Gail was able to build some consistency of theme as she read because of her gender and her personal experience with a marriage, and she was aware of her own reading strategies interacting with text strategies as she read. As they read *Trifles,* Gail's class was asked to focus on the following questions.

- In terms of what the text contributes to your response, what is the role of any text strategies peculiar to drama? That is, how does the text as a play "do" anything that affects your response?
- As you are reading through this play, how do you piece together the information you get? Do you, for instance, begin to build a logically consistent picture of the relationship between John and Minnie Wright? Do you start to put together some solutions to the puzzle that the investigators are confronted with? As you read along, do you make guesses or predictions about what is going to happen or be revealed? If you do any of these or similar things as a reader, can you trace your process of doing so? When, why, and how do you put things together the way you do?
- With whom do you find yourself identifying or sympathizing as you read? Is there any change in your sympathies as you read on? To what extent does your sympathy relate to your own age or gender, relative to the characters?
- Can you identify a theme in your reading of *Trifles?* What allows you to decide what this is?

STUDENT WRITING
Gail Nagy: Journal Entry

First, all drama involves human beings engaged in some type of action. These human actions result in some type of conflict. It is this conflict that ... all plays deal [with]. Drama is not like narrative literature, where lengthy, detailed descriptions are necessary. Instead, drama is a portrayal of different aspects of human life (and death) dealt with in a succinct manner.... That means there is a lot happening in a short time within the text of a play. The playwright is trying to directly touch the reader or the audience, and he wants to touch them quickly and intensely. There isn't a lot of time to set up lengthy descriptions and summaries of the "before" moments in a play.

In *Trifles*, it takes less than a second to find out that something terrible is happening. The first character we meet is the County Attorney and his stage directions call for him to be "rubbing his hands." That's the first clue. There's got to be a big problem if the County Attorney is involved. Then, three lines into the dialogue, the Sheriff is speaking.... The play is starting to unfold with detail after detail. And these details unveil situations in which we can all relate. Curiosity is another tool used by playwrights. We are curious creatures. We want to know what's going on and what is happening to our neighbors, friends and relatives. So, naturally, drama contributes to our curiosity. You know, "inquiring minds want to know!"

Regarding *Trifles* and how I logically piece together the plot, I can only say that I usually read like a detective would search for clues in a case. I look for important words and phrases that offer a tip. For instance, when it's mentioned that Minnie Wright is despondent when talked to and is sitting in her rocker pleating her apron, I mentally take note. My wheels start to turn and I ask myself, why is she acting this way? The next clue was the laugh. That was my tip that she is guilty of something. It is a revenge laugh.... She is probably sitting in that rocker thinking about what happened and is still in a state of shock. But also, she is commending herself for actually following through with this act, whatever it is at this point in the action.

Eventually, as the text reveals more details about the couple's relationship, I make a decision that she indeed must be the murderer or has put someone else up to the murder. However, when the two women discover the bird, then I scream to myself, "motive, motive!"

Another tactic I use while reading is placing myself in the character role. I envision myself in the situation and try to decide what I would do. Would I run away and hide? Or would I just sit there in my rocking chair, like Minnie, boldly pleating and laughing? I was able to relate to Minnie because, you see, I lived with "John Wright" for three years and two babies. I didn't own a bird, like Minnie, instead I owned two babies. Abuse is abuse and it doesn't have any other description. Whether physical or mental, it is always devastating, humiliating and debilitating. No, it isn't right to take another person's life, but Minnie's life was already taken from her. She is already dead. True, her physical being exists, but everything else she is and possesses (even the bird) is gone. I actually chuckled out loud when I read about her love for singing. Here's a bit of irony. My "John Wright" threatened to push me down the steps (I was pregnant) if he heard me sing one more lullaby to our son. I wasn't even allowed to sing along with the radio. Why? Because he said so!

Yes, I can relate to gender in *Trifles*. Glaspell is showing me the repression of women. Some of the dialogue sickened me, to think that these "good ol' boys" would make fun of women so blatantly. I knew sexism was bad in that era, but I guess I never realized just how bad. I'm only glad that I didn't live then, or my name probably could have been Minnie Wright.

The theme that Gail produces from her interaction with the text may not be very unusual. Probably someone in your class responded along similar lines, especially if that reader's ideology included experiences similar to Gail's as a married woman. But I hope you can see, from reading Gail's journal entry or from discussion in your own classroom, how numerous text strategies, certain reading strategies, and elements of ideology of both text and reader combine to produce an interpretation.

SHARE AND COMPARE: Even though Gail is not your classmate, you can interact with her response to *Trifles*. Use this space or a page in your notebook to respond to her response. One option is to reply to her in terms of your reading of the play. Another is to analyze her journal entry in terms of the literary and ideological interactions it reveals: Where or how does she respond on the literary level (matching her reading strategies with text strategies of the play)? Where or how does she respond on the ideological level (matching her life experiences or beliefs with the apparent ideological concerns of the text)?

Drama for Exploration

Wole Soyinka   b. 1934

The Strong Breed   *1963*

Characters

Eman, a stranger
Sunma, Jaguna's daughter
Ifada, an idiot
A Girl
Jaguna
Oroge
Attendant Stalwarts, the villagers from Eman's past—
Old Man, his father
Omae, his betrothed
Tutor
Priest
Attendants, the villagers

The scenes are described briefly, but very often a darkened stage with lit area will not only suffice but is necessary. Except for the one indicated place, there can be no break in the action. A distracting scene-change would be ruinous. A mud house with space in front of it. Eman, in light buba and trousers, stands at the window looking out. Inside, Sunma is clearing the table of what looks like a modest clinic, putting the things away in a cupboard. Another rough table in the room is piled with exercise books, two or three worn textbooks, etc. Sunma appears agitated. Outside, just beyond the window, crouches Ifada. He looks up with a shy smile from time to time, waiting for Eman to notice him.

SUNMA *(hesitant):*   You will have to make up your mind soon, Eman. The lorry[1] leaves very shortly.

As Eman does not answer, Sunma continues her work, more nervously: Two villagers, obvious travelers, pass hurriedly in front the house, the man has a small raffia sack, the woman a cloth-covered basket, the man enters first, turns, and urges the woman who is just emerging to hurry.

SUNMA *(seeing them, her tone is more intense):*   Eman, are we going or aren't we? You will leave it till too late.

EMAN *(quietly):*   There is still time—if you want to go.

SUNMA: If I want to go . . . and you?

Eman makes no reply.

SUNMA *(bitterly):*   You don't really want to leave here. You never want to go away—   5
even for a minute.

Ifada continues his antics. Eman eventually pats him on the head and the boy grins happily. Leaps up suddenly and returns with a basket of oranges, which he offers Eman.

EMAN: My gift for today's festival enh?

Ifada nods, grinning.

EMAN: They look ripe—that's a change.

SUNMA *(she has gone inside the room. Looks round the door):*   Did you call me?

EMAN: No. *(She goes back.)* And what will you do tonight, Ifada? Will you take part   10
in the dancing? Or perhaps you will mount your own masquerade?

Ifada shakes his head, regretfully.

EMAN: You won't? So you haven't any? But you would like to own one.

Ifada nods eagerly.

EMAN: Then why don't you make your own?

Ifada stares, puzzled by this idea.

EMAN: Sunma will let you have some cloth you know. And bits of wool . . .

SUNMA *(coming out):*   Who are you talking to, Eman?

EMAN: Ifada. I am trying to persuade him to join the young maskers.   15

SUNMA *(losing control):*   What does he want here? Why is he hanging round us?

EMAN *(amazed):*   What . . . ? I said Ifada, Ifada.

SUNMA: Just tell him to go away. Let him go and play somewhere else!

EMAN: What is this? Hasn't he always played here?

SUNMA: I don't want him here. *(Rushes to the window.)* Get away, idiot. Don't bring   20
your foolish face here any more, do you hear? Go on, go away from here . . .

EMAN *(restraining her):*   Control yourself, Sunma. What on earth has got into you?

Ifada, hurt and bewildered, backs slowly away.

[1]lorry—truck

SUNMA: He comes crawling round here like some horrible insect. I never want to lay my eyes on him again.

EMAN: I don't understand. It *is* Ifada you know, Ifada! The unfortunate one who runs errands for you and doesn't hurt a soul.

SUNMA: I cannot bear the sight of him.

EMAN: You can't do what? It can't be two days since he last fetched water for you.   25

SUNMA: What else can he do except that? He is useless. Just because we have been kind to him. . . . Others would have put him in an asylum.

EMAN: You are not making sense. He is not a madman, he is just a little more un-lucky than other children. *(Looks keenly at her.)* But what is the matter?

SUNMA: It's nothing. I only wish we had sent him off to one of those places for crea-tures like him.

EMAN: He is quite happy here. He doesn't bother anyone and he makes himself useful.

SUNMA: Useful! Is that one of any use to anybody? Boys of his age are already earn-   30
ing a living but all he can do is hang around and drool at the mouth.

EMAN: But he does work. You know he does a lot for you.

SUNMA: Does he? And what about the farm you started for him! Does he ever work on it? Or have you forgotten that it was really for Ifada you cleared the brush. Now you have to go and work it yourself. You spend all your time on it and you have no room for anything else.

EMAN: That wasn't his fault. I should first have asked him if he was fond of farming.

SUNMA: Oh, so he can choose? As if he shouldn't be thankful for being allowed to live.

EMAN: Sunma!   35

SUNMA: He does not like farming but he knows how to feast his dumb mouth on the fruits.

EMAN: But I want him to. I encourage him.

SUNMA: Well keep him. I don't want to see him any more.

EMAN *(after some moments):*   But why? You cannot be telling all the truth. What has he done?

SUNMA: The sight of him fills me with revulsion.   40

EMAN *(goes to her and holds her):*   What really is it? *(Sunma avoids his eyes.)* It is almost as if you are forcing yourself to hate him. Why?

SUNMA: That is not true. Why should I?

EMAN: Then what is the secret? You've even played with him before.

SUNMA: I have always merely tolerated him. But I cannot any more. Suddenly my dis-gust won't take him any more. Perhaps . . . perhaps it is the new year. Yes, yes, it must be the new year.

EMAN: I don't believe that.   45

SUNMA: It must be. I am a woman, and these things matter. I don't want a misshape near me. Surely for one day in the year, I may demand some wholesomeness.

EMAN: I do not understand you.

Sunma is silent.

It was cruel of you. And to Ifada who is so helpless and alone. We are the only friends he has.

SUNMA: No, just you. I have told you, with me it has always been only an act of kind-ness. And now I haven't any pity left for him.

EMAN: No. He is not a wholesome being.

He turns back to looking through the window.

SUNMA *(half-pleading):*   Ifada can rouse your pity. And yet if anything, I need more   50
kindness from you. Every time my weakness betrays me, you close your mind
against me ... Eman ... Eman ...

*A Girl comes in view, dragging an effigy by a rope attached to one of its legs. She stands for a
while gazing at Eman. Ifada, who has crept back shyly to his accustomed position, becomes
somewhat excited when he sees the effigy. The Girl is unsmiling. She possesses, in fact, a kind of
inscrutability which does not make her hard but is unsettling.*

GIRL: Is the teacher in?
EMAN *(smiling):*   No.
GIRL: Where is he gone?
EMAN: I don't really know. Shall I ask?
GIRL: Yes, do.
EMAN *(turning slightly):*   Sunma, a girl outside wants to know ...   55

Sunma turns away, goes into the inside room.

EMAN: Oh. *(Returns to the girl, but his slight gaiety is lost.)* There is no one at
home who can tell me.
GIRL: Why are you not in?
EMAN: I don't really know. Maybe I went somewhere.
GIRL: All right. I will wait until you get back.   60

She pulls the effigy to her, sits down.

EMAN *(slowly regaining his amusement):*   So you are ready for the new year.
GIRL *(without turning round):*   I am not going to the festival.
EMAN: Then why have you got that?
GIRL: Do you mean my carrier? I am unwell you know. My mother says it will take
away my sickness with the old year.
EMAN: Won't you share the carrier with your playmates?   65
GIRL: Oh, no. Don't you know I play alone? The other children won't come near
me. Their mothers would beat them.
EMAN: But I have never seen you here. Why don't you come to the clinic?
GIRL: My mother said No.

Gets up, begins to move off.

EMAN: You are not going away?
GIRL: I must not stay talking to you. If my mother caught me ...   70
EMAN: All right, tell me what you want before you go.
GIRL *(stops. For some moments she remains silent):*   I must have some clothes for
my carrier.
EMAN: Is that all? You wait a moment.

*Sunma comes out as he takes down a buba from the wall. She goes to the window and glares al-
most with hatred at the Girl. The Girl retreats hastily, still impassive.*

By the way, Sunma, do you know who that girl is?

SUNMA: I hope you don't really mean to give her that.
EMAN: Why not? I hardly ever use it.   75
SUNMA: Just the same don't give it to her. She is not a child. She is as evil as the
rest of them.
EMAN: What has got into you today?

SUNMA: All right, all right. Do what you wish.

She withdraws. Baffled, Eman returns to the window.

EMAN: Here . . . will this do? Come and look at it.
GIRL: Throw it.
EMAN: What is the matter? I am not going to eat you.   80
GIRL: No one lets me come near them.
EMAN: But I am not afraid of catching your disease.
GIRL: Throw it.

Eman shrugs and tosses the buba. She takes it without a word and slips it on the effigy, completely absorbed in the task. Eman watches for a while, then joins Sunma in the inner room.

GIRL: *(after a long, cool survey of Ifada):*   You have a head like a spider's egg, and   85
   your mouth dribbles like a roof. But there is no one else. Would you like to play?

Ifada nods eagerly, quite excited.

GIRL: You will have to get a stick.

Ifada rushes around, finds a big stick, and whirls it aloft, bearing down on the carrier.

GIRL: Wait. I don't want you to spoil it. If it gets torn I shall drive you away. Now,
   let me see how you are going to beat it.

Ifada hits it gently.

GIRL: You may hit harder than that. As long as there is something left to hang at the
   end.

She appraises him up and down.

   You are not very tall . . . will you be able to hang it from a tree?

Ifada nods, grinning happily.

GIRL: You will hang it up and I will set fire to it. *(Then, with surprising venom.)*
   But just because you are helping me, don't think it is going to cure you. I am the
   one who will get well at midnight, do you understand? It is my carrier and it is
   for me alone. *(She pulls at the rope to make sure that it is well attached to the
   leg.)* Well don't stand there drooling. Let's go.

She begins to walk off, dragging the effigy in the dust. Ifada remains where he is for some moments, seemingly puzzled. Then his face breaks into a large grin and he leaps after the procession, belaboring the effigy with all his strength. The stage remains empty for some moments. Then the horn of a lorry is sounded and Sunma rushes out. The hooting continues for some time with a rhythmic pattern. Eman comes out.

EMAN: I am going to the village . . . I shan't be back before nightfall.   90
SUNMA *(blankly):*   Yes.
EMAN *(hesitates):*   Well what do you want me to do?
SUNMA: The lorry was hooting just now.
EMAN: I didn't hear it.
SUNMA: It will leave in a few minutes. And you did promise we could go away.   95
EMAN: I promised nothing. Will you go home by yourself or shall I come back for you?
SUNMA: You don't even want me here?
EMAN: But you have to go home, haven't you?
SUNMA: I had hoped we would watch the new year together—in some other place.
EMAN: Why do you continue to distress yourself?   100

SUNMA: Because you will not listen to me. Why do you continue to stay where nobody wants you?

EMAN: That is not true.

SUNMA: It is. You are wasting your life on people who really want you out of their way.

EMAN: You don't know what you are saying.

SUNMA: You think they love you? Do you think they care at all for what you—or I—do for them?   105

EMAN: *Them?* These are your own people. Sometimes you talk as if you were a stranger too.

SUNMA: I wonder if I really sprang from here. I know they are evil and I am not. From the oldest to the smallest child, they are nourished in evil and unwholesomeness in which I have no part.

EMAN: You knew this when you returned?

SUNMA: You reproach me then for trying at all?

EMAN: I reproach you with nothing? But you must leave me out of your plans. I can have no part in them.   110

SUNMA *(nearly pleading):*   Once I could have run away. I would have gone and never looked back.

EMAN: I cannot listen when you talk like that.

SUNMA: I swear to you, I do not mind what happens afterwards. But you must help me tear myself away from here. I can no longer do it by myself. . . . It is only a little thing. And we have worked so hard this past year . . . surely we can go away for a week . . . even a few days would be enough.

EMAN: I have told you, Sunma . . .

SUNMA *(desperately):*   Two days, Eman. Only two days.   115

EMAN *(distressed):*   But I tell you I have no wish to go.

SUNMA *(suddenly angry):*   Are you so afraid then?

EMAN: Me? Afraid of what?

SUNMA: You think you will not want to come back.

EMAN *(pitying):*   You cannot dare me that way.   120

SUNMA: Then why won't you leave here, even for an hour? If you are so sure that your life is settled here, why are you afraid to do this thing for me? What is so wrong that you will not go into the next town for a day or two?

EMAN: I don't want to. I do not have to persuade you, or myself about anything. I simply have no desire to go away.

SUNMA *(his quiet confidence appears to incense her):*   You are afraid. You accuse me of losing my sense of mission, but you are afraid to put yours to the test.

EMAN: You are wrong, Sunma. I have no sense of mission. But I have found peace here and I am content with that.

SUNMA: I haven't. For a while I thought that too, but I found there could be no peace in the midst of so much cruelty. Eman, tonight at least, the last night of the old year . . .   125

EMAN: No, Sunma. I find this too distressing; you should go home now.

SUNMA: It is the time for making changes in one's life, Eman. Let's breathe in the new year away from here.

EMAN: You are hurting yourself.

SUNMA: Tonight. Only tonight. We will come back tomorrow, as early as you like. But let us go away for this one night. Don't let another year break on me in this place . . . you don't know how important it is to me, but I will tell you, I will tell you on the way . . . but we must not be here today, Eman, do this one thing for me.

EMAN *(sadly):*   I cannot.

130

SUNMA (*suddenly calm*):   I was a fool to think it would be otherwise. The whole village may use you as they will but for me there is nothing. Sometimes I think you believe that doing anything for me makes you unfaithful to some part of your life. If it was a woman then I pity her for what she must have suffered.

Eman winces and hardens slowly. Sunma notices nothing.

Keeping faith with so much is slowly making you inhuman. (*Seeing the change in Eman.*) Eman. Eman. What is it?

As she goes towards him, Eman goes into the house.

SUNMA (*apprehensive, follows him*):   What did I say? Eman, forgive me, forgive me please.

Eman remains facing into the slow darkness of the room. Sunma, distressed, cannot decide what to do.

I swear I didn't know. . . . I would not have said it for all the world.

A lorry is heard taking off somewhere nearby. The sound comes up and slowly fades away into the distance. Sunma starts visibly, goes slowly to the window.

SUNMA (*as the sound dies off, to herself*):   What happens now?
EMAN (*joining her at the window*):   What did you say?
SUNMA: Nothing.   135
EMAN: Was that not the lorry going off?
SUNMA: It was.
EMAN: I am sorry I couldn't help you.

Sunma, about to speak, changes her mind.

EMAN: I think you ought to go home now.
SUNMA: No, don't send me away. It's the least you can do for me. Let me stay here   140
until all the noise is over.
EMAN: But are you not needed at home? You have a part in the festival.
SUNMA: I have renounced it; I am Jaguna's eldest daughter only in name.
EMAN: Renouncing one's self is not so easy—surely you know that.
SUNMA: I don't want to talk about it. Will you at least let us be together tonight?
EMAN: But . . .   145
SUNMA: Unless you are afraid my father will accuse you of harboring me.
EMAN: All right, we will go out together.
SUNMA: Go out? I want us to stay here.
EMAN: When there is so much going on outside?
SUNMA: Some day you will wish that you went away when I tried to make you.   150
EMAN: Are we going back to that?
SUNMA: No, I promise you I will not recall it again. But you must know that it was
also for your sake that I tried to get us away.
EMAN: For me? How?
SUNMA: By yourself you can do nothing here. Have you not noticed now tightly
we shut out strangers? Even if you lived here for a lifetime, you would remain
a stranger.
EMAN: Perhaps that is what I like. There is peace in being a stranger.   155
SUNMA: For a while perhaps. But they would reject you in the end. I tell you it is
only I who stand between you and contempt. And because of this you have
earned their hatred. I don't know why I say this now, except that somehow, I

feel that it no longer matters. It is only I who have stood between you and much humiliation.

EMAN: Think carefully before you say any more. I am incapable of feeling indebted to you. This will make no difference at all.

SUNMA: I ask for nothing. But you must know it all the same. It is true I hadn't the strength to go by myself. And I must confess this now, if you had come with me, I would have done everything to keep you from returning.

EMAN: I know that.

SUNMA: You see, I bare myself to you. For days I had thought it over, this was to be a new beginning for us. And I placed my fate wholly in your hands. Now the thought will not leave me, I have a feeling which will not be shaken off, that in some way, you have tonight totally destroyed my life.   160

EMAN: You are depressed, you don't know what you are saying.

SUNMA: Don't think I am accusing you. I say all this only because I cannot help it.

EMAN: We must not remain shut up here. Let us go and be part of the living.

SUNMA: No. Leave them alone.

EMAN: Surely you don't want to stay indoors when the whole town is alive with rejoicing.   165

SUNMA: Rejoicing! Is that what it seems to you? No, let us remain here. Whatever happens I must not go out until all this is over.

There is silence. It has grown much darker.

EMAN: I shall light the lamp.

SUNMA *(eager to do something):*   No, let me do it.

She goes into the inner room. Eman paces the room, stops by a shelf, and toys with the seeds in an "ayo" board, takes down the whole board and places it on a table, playing by himself.

The Girl is now seen coming back, still dragging her "carrier." Ifada brings up the rear as before. As he comes round the corner of the house two men emerge from the shadows. A sack is thrown over Ifada's head, the rope is pulled tight rendering him instantly helpless. The Girl has reached the front of the house before she turns round at the sound of scuffle. She is in time to see Ifada thrown over the shoulders and borne away. Her face betraying no emotion at all, the Girl backs slowly away, turns, and flees, leaving the "carrier" behind. Sunma enters, carrying two kerosene lamps. She hangs one up from the wall.

EMAN: One is enough.

SUNMA: I want to leave one outside.   170

She goes out, hangs the lamp from a nail just above the door. As she turns she sees the effigy and gasps. Eman rushes out.

EMAN: What is it? Oh, is that what frighted you?

SUNMA: I thought ... I didn't really see it properly.

Eman goes towards the object, stoops to pick it up.

EMAN: It must belong to that sick girl.

SUNMA: Don't touch it.

EMAN: Let's keep it for her.   175

SUNMA: Leave it alone. Don't touch it, Eman.

EMAN *(shrugs and goes back):*   You are very nervous.

SUNMA: Let's go in.

EMAN: Wait. *(He detains her by the door, under the lamp.)* I know there is something more than you've told me. What are you afraid of tonight?

SUNMA: I was only scared by that thing. There is nothing else.   180

EMAN: I am not blind, Sunma. It is true I would not run away when you wanted me to, but that doesn't mean I do not feel things. What does tonight really mean that it makes you so helpless?

SUNMA: It is only a mood. And your indifference to me . . . let's go in.

Eman moves aside and she enters; he remains there for a moment and then follows. She fiddles with the lamp, looks vaguely round the room, then goes and shuts the door, bolting it. When she turns, it is to meet Eman's eyes, questioning.

SUNMA: There is a cold wind coming in.

Eman keeps his gaze on her.

SUNMA: It *was* getting cold.

She moves guiltily to the table and stands by the ayo board, rearranging the seeds. Eman remains where he is for a few moments, then brings a stool and sits opposite her. She sits down also and they begin to play in silence.

SUNMA: What brought you here at all, Eman? And what makes you stay?   185
    There is another silence.

SUNMA: I am not trying to share your life. I know you too well by now. But at least we have worked together since you came. Is there nothing at all I deserve to know?

EMAN: Let me continue a stranger—especially to you. Those who have much to give fulfill themselves only in total loneliness.

SUNMA: Then there is no love in what you do.

EMAN: There is. Love comes to me more easily with strangers.

SUNMA: That is unnatural.   190

EMAN: Not for me. I know I find consummation only when I have spent myself for a total stranger.

SUNMA: It seems unnatural to me. But then I am a woman. I have a woman's longings and weaknesses. And the ties of blood are very strong in me.

EMAN *(smiling)*:   You think I have cut loose from all these—ties of blood.

SUNMA: Sometimes you are so inhuman.

EMAN: I don't know what that means. But I am very much my father's son.   195

They play in silence. Suddenly Eman pauses, listening.

EMAN: Did you hear that?

SUNMA *(quickly)*:   I heard nothing . . . it's your turn.

EMAN: Perhaps some of the mummers are coming this way.

Eman, about to play, leaps up suddenly.

SUNMA: What is it? Don't you want to play any more?

Eman moves to the door.

SUNMA: No. Don't go out, Eman.   200

EMAN: If it's the dancers I want to ask them to stay. At least we won't have to miss everything.

SUNMA: No, no. Don't open the door. Let us keep out everyone tonight.

A terrified and disordered figure bursts suddenly round the corner, past the window and begins hammering at the door. It is Ifada. Desperate with terror, he pounds madly at the door, dumb-moaning all the while.

EMAN: Isn't that Ifada?

SUNMA: They are only fooling about. Don't pay any attention.

EMAN *(looks round the window):*   That is Ifada. *(Begins to unbolt the door.)*   205

SUNMA *(pulling at his hands):*   It is only a trick they are playing on you. Don't take any notice, Eman.

EMAN: What are you saying? The boy is out of his sense with fear.

SUNMA: No, no. Don't interfere, Eman. For God's sake don't interfere.

EMAN: Do you know something of this then?

SUNMA: You are a stranger here, Eman. Just leave us alone and go your own way.   210
There is nothing you can do.

EMAN *(he tries to push her out of the way but she clings fiercely to him):*   Have you gone mad? I tell you the boy must come in.

SUNMA: Why won't you listen to me, Eman? I tell you it's none of your business. For your own sake do as I say.

Eman pushes her off, unbolts the door. Ifada rushes in, clasps Eman round the knees, dumb-moaning against his legs.

EMAN *(manages to rebolt the door):*   What is it, Ifada? What is the matter?

Shouts and voices are heard coming nearer the house.

SUNMA: Before it's too late, let him go. For once, Eman, believe what I tell you. Don't harbor him or you will regret it all your life.

Eman tries to calm Ifada, who becomes more and more abject as the outside voices get nearer.

EMAN: What have they done to him? At least tell me that. What is going on, Sunma?   215

SUNMA *(with sudden venom):*   Monster! Could you not take yourself somewhere else?

EMAN: Stop talking like that.

SUNMA: He could have run into the bush couldn't he? Toad! Why must he follow us with his own disasters!

VOICES OUTSIDE: It's here. . . . Round the back. . . . Spread, spread . . . this way . . . no, head him off . . . use the bush path and head him off . . . get some more lights . . .

Eman listens. Lifts Ifada bodily and carries him into the inner room. Returns at once, shutting the door behind him.

SUNMA *(slumps into a chair, resigned):*   You always follow your own way.

JAGUNA *(comes round the corner followed by Oroge and three men, one bearing a*   220
torch):   I knew he would come here.

OROGE: I hope our friend won't make trouble.

JAGUNA: He had better not. You, recall all the men and tell them to surround the house.

OROGE: But he may not be in the house after all.

JAGUNA: I know he is here . . . *(To the men.)* . . . go on, do as I say.

He bangs on the door.

Teacher, open your door . . . you two stay by the door. If I need you I will call you.

Eman opens the door.

JAGUNA *(speaks as he enters):*   We know he is here.   225

EMAN: Who?

JAGUNA: Don't let us waste time. We are grown men, teacher. You understand me and I understand you. But we must take back the boy.

EMAN: This is my house.

JAGUNA: Daughter, you'd better tell your friend. I don't think he quite knows our ways. Tell him why he must give up the boy.

SUNMA: Father, I . . .   230

JAGUNA: Are you going to tell him or aren't you?

SUNMA: Father, I beg you, leave us alone tonight . . .

JAGUNA: I thought you might be a hindrance. Go home then if you will not use your
sense.

SUNMA: But there are other ways . . .

JAGUNA *(turning to the men):*   See that she gets home. I no longer trust her. If she   235
gives trouble carry her. And see that the women stay with her until all this is over.

Sunma departs, accompanied by one of the men.

JAGUNA: Now, teacher . . .

OROGE *(restrains him):*   You see, Mister Eman, it is like this. Right now, nobody
knows that Ifada has taken refuge here. No one except us and our men—and
they know how to keep their mouths shut. We don't want to have to burn down
the house, you see, but if the word gets around, we would have no choice.

JAGUNA: In fact, it may be too late already. A carrier should end up in the bush, not a
house. Anyone who doesn't guard his door when the carrier goes by has himself to blame. A contaminated house should be burnt down.

OROGE: But we are willing to let it pass. Only, you must bring him out quickly.

EMAN: All right. But at least you will let me ask you something.   240

JAGUNA: What is there to ask? Don't you understand what we have told you?

EMAN: Yes. But why did you pick on a helpless boy? Obviously he is not willing.

JAGUNA: What is the man talking about? Ifada is a godsend. Does he have to be willing?

EMAN: In my home, we believe that a man should be willing.

OROGE: Mister Eman, I don't think you quite understand. This is not a simple matter   245
at all. I don't know what you do, but here, it is not a cheap task for anybody. No
one in his senses would do such a job. Why do you think we give refuge to idiots like him? We don't know where he came from. One morning, he is simply
there, just like that. From nowhere at all. You see, there is a purpose in that.

JAGUNA: We only waste time.

OROGE: Jaguna, be patient. After all, the man has been with us for some time now and
deserves to know. The evil of the old year is no light thing to load on any man's head.

EMAN: I know something about that.

OROGE: You do? *(Turns to Jaguna, who snorts impatiently.)* You see I told you so,
didn't I? From the moment you came I saw you were one of the knowing ones.

JAGUNA: Then let him behave like a man and give back the boy.   250

EMAN: It is you who are not behaving like men.

JAGUNA *(advances aggressively):*   That is a quick mouth you have . . .

OROGE: Patience, Jaguna . . . if you want the new year to cushion the land there
must be no deeds of anger. What did you mean, my friend?

EMAN: It is a simple thing. A village which cannot produce its own carrier contains no men.

JAGUNA: Enough. Let there be no more talk or this business will be ruined by some   255
rashness. You . . . come inside. Bring the boy out, he must be in the room there.

EMAN: Wait.

The men hesitate.

JAGUNA *(hitting the nearer one and propelling him forward):*   Go on. Have you
changed masters now that you listen to what he says?

OROGE *(sadly):*   I am sorry you would not understand, Mister Eman. But you ought
to know that no carrier may return to the village. If he does, the people will
stone him to death. It has happened before. Surely it is too much to ask a man
to give up his own soil.

EMAN: I know others who have done more.

Ifada is brought out, abjectly dumb-moaning.

EMAN: You can see him with your own eyes. Does it really have meaning to use one 260
as unwilling as that?

OROGE *(smiling):*   He shall be willing. Not only willing but actually joyous. I am the
one who prepares them all, and I have seen worse. This one escaped before I
began to prepare him for the event. But you will see him later tonight, the most
joyous creature in the festival. Then perhaps you will understand.

EMAN: Then it is only a deceit. Do you believe the spirit of a new year is so easily
fooled?

JAGUNA: Take him out. *(The men carry out Ifada.)* You see, it is so easy to talk. You
say there are no men in this village because they cannot provide a willing carrier. And yet I heard Oroge tell you we only use strangers. There is only one
other stranger in the village, but I have not heard him offer himself. *(Spits.)* It is
so easy to talk is it not?

*He turns his back on him. They go off, taking Ifada with them, limp and silent. The only sign
of life is that he strains his neck to keep his eyes on Eman till the very moment that he disappears
from sight. Eman remains where they left him, staring after the group.*

*A blackout lasting no more than a minute. The lights come up slowly, and Ifada is seen return-
ing to the house. He stops at the window and looks in. Seeing no one, he bangs on the sill. Appears surprised that there is no response. He slithers down on his favorite spot, then sees the effigy
still lying where the Girl had dropped it in her flight. After some hesitation, he goes towards it,
begins to strip it of the clothing. Just then the Girl comes in.*

GIRL: Hey, leave that alone. You know it's mine.

Ifada pauses, then speeds up his action.

GIRL: I said it is mine. Leave it where you found it. *(She rushes at him and begins* 265
to struggle for possession of the carrier.) Thief! Thief! Let it go, it is mine. Let it
go. You animal, just because I let you play with it. Idiot! Idiot!

*The struggle becomes quite violent. The Girl is hanging to the effigy and Ifada lifts her with it,
flinging her all about. The Girl hangs on grimly.*

GIRL: You are spoiling it . . . why don't you get your own? Thief! Let it go, you thief!

*Sunma comes in walking very fast, throwing apprehensive glances over her shoulder. Seeing the
two children, she becomes immediately angry. Advances on them.*

SUNMA: So you've made this place your playground. Get away, you untrained pigs.
Get out of here.

Ifada flees at once, the Girl retreats also, retaining possession of the carrier.

*Sunma goes to the door. She has her hand on the door when the significance of Ifada's presence
strikes her for the first time. She stands rooted to the spot, then turns slowly round.*

SUNMA: Ifada! What are you doing here?

*Ifada is bewildered. Sunma turns suddenly and rushes into the house, flying into the inner room
and out again.*

Eman! Eman! Eman!

She rushes outside.

Where did he go? Where did they take him?

Ifada distressed, points. Sunma seizes him by the arm, drags him off.

> Take me there at once. God help you if we are too late. You loathsome thing, if you have let him suffer . . .

Her voice fades into other shouts, running footsteps, banged tins, bells, dogs, etc., rising in volume.

It is a narrow passageway between two mudhouses. At the far end one man after another is seen running across the entry, the noise dying off gradually.

About halfway down the passage, Eman is crouching against the wall, tense with apprehension. As the noise dies off, he seems to relax, but the alert, hunted look is still in his eyes, which are ringed in a reddish color. The rest of his body has been whitened with a floury substance. He is naked down to the waist, wears a baggy pair of trousers, calf-length, and around both feet are bangles.

EMAN: I will simply stay here till dawn. I have done enough.

A window is thrown open and a woman empties some slop from a pail. With a startled cry Eman leaps aside to avoid it and the woman puts out her head.

WOMAN: Oh, my head. What have I done! Forgive me, neighbor . . . Eh, it's the carrier! *(Very rapidly she clears her throat and spits on him, flings the pail at him and runs off, shouting)* He's here. The carrier is hiding in the passage. Quickly, I have found the carrier!   270

The cry is taken up and Eman flees down the passage. Shortly afterwards his pursuers come pouring down the passage in full cry. After the last of them come Jaguna and Oroge.

OROGE: Wait, wait. I cannot go so fast.

JAGUNA: We will rest a little then. We can do nothing anyway.

OROGE: If only he had let me prepare him.

JAGUNA: They are the ones who break first, these fools who think they were born to carry suffering like a hat. What are we to do now?

OROGE: When they catch him I must prepare him.   275

JAGUNA: He? It will be impossible now. There can be no joy left in that one.

OROGE: Still, it took him by surprise. He was not expecting what he met.

JAGUNA: Why then did he refuse to listen? Did he think he was coming to sit down to a feast? He had not even gone through one compound before he bolted. Did he think he was taken round the people to be blessed? A woman, that is all he is.

OROGE: No, no. He took the beating well enough. I think he is the kind who would let himself be beaten from night till dawn and not utter a sound. He would let himself be stoned until he dropped dead.

JAGUNA: Then what made him run like a coward?   280

OROGE: I don't know. I don't really know. It is a night of curses, Jaguna. It is not many unprepared minds will remain unhinged under the load.

JAGUNA: We must find him. It is a poor beginning for a new year when our own curses remain hovering over our homes because the carrier refused to take them.

They go. The scene changes. Eman is crouching beside some shrubs, torn and bleeding.

EMAN: They are even guarding my house . . . as if I would go there, but I need water . . . they could at least grant me that . . . I can be thirsty too . . . *(He pricks his ears.)* . . . there must be a stream nearby . . . *(As he looks round him, his eyes widen at a scene he encounters.)*

An Old Man, short and vigorous looking, is seated on a stool. He also is wearing calf-length baggy trousers, white. On his head, a white cap. An attendant is engaged in rubbing his body with oil. Round his eyes, two white rings have already been marked.

OLD MAN: Have they prepared the boat?

ATTENDANT: They are making the last sacrifice.   285

OLD MAN: Good. Did you send for my son?

ATTENDANT: He's on his way.

OLD MAN: I have never met the carrying of the boat with such a heavy heart. I hope nothing comes of it.

ATTENDANT: The gods will not desert us on that account.

OLD MAN: A man should be at his strongest when he takes the boat, my friend. To   290 be weighed down inside and out is not a wise thing. I hope when the moment comes I shall have found my strength.

Enter Eman, a wrapper round his waist and a danski [2] *over it.*

OLD MAN: I meant to wait until after my journey to the river, but my mind is so burdened with my own grief and yours I could not delay it. You know I must have all my strength. But I sit here, feeling it all eaten slowly away by my unspoken grief. It helps to say it out. It even helps to cry sometimes.

He signals to the attendant to leave them.

Come nearer . . . we will never meet again, son. Not on this side of the flesh. What I do not know is whether you will return to take my place.

EMAN: I will never come back.

OLD MAN: Do you know what you are saying? Ours is a strong breed, my son. It is only a strong breed that can take this boat to the river year after year and wax stronger on it. I have taken down each year's evils for over twenty years. I hoped you would follow me.

EMAN: My life here died with Omae.

OLD MAN: Omae died giving birth to your child and you think the world is ended.   295 Eman, my pain did not begin when Omae died. Since you sent her to stay with me, son, I lived with the burden of knowing that this child would die bearing your son.

EMAN: Father . . .

OLD MAN: Don't you know it was the same with you? And me? No woman survives the bearing of the strong ones. Son, it is not the mouth of the boaster that says he belongs to the strong breed. It is the tongue that is red with pain and black with sorrow. Twelve years you were away, my son, and for those twelve years I knew the love of an old man for his daughter and the pain of a man helplessly awaiting his loss.

EMAN: I wish I had stayed away. I wish I never came back to meet her.

OLD MAN: It had to be. But you know now what slowly ate away my strength. I awaited your return with love and fear. Forgive me then if I say that your grief is light. It will pass. This grief may drive you now from home. But you must return.

EMAN: You do not understand. It is not grief alone.   300

OLD MAN: What is it then? Tell me, I can still learn.

EMAN: I was away twelve years. I changed much in that time.

OLD MAN: I am listening.

EMAN: I am unfitted for your work, father. I wish to say no more. But I am totally unfitted for your call.

OLD MAN: It is only time you need, son. Stay longer and you will answer the urge of   305 your blood.

EMAN: That I stayed at all was because of Omae. I did not expect to find her waiting. I would have taken her away, but hard as you claim to be, it would have killed you. And I was a tired man. I needed peace. Because Omae was peace, I stayed. Now nothing holds me here.

---

[2]*danski*—A garment

Old Man: Other men would rot and die doing this task year after year. It is strong medicine which only we can take. Our blood is strong like no other. Anything you do in life must be less than this, son.

Eman: That is not true, father.

Old Man: I tell you it is true. Your own blood will betray you, son, because you cannot hold it back. If you make it do less than this, it will rush to your head and burst it open. I say what I know, my son.

Eman: There are other tasks in life, father. This one is not for me. There are even   310
greater things you know nothing of.

Old Man: I am very sad. You only go to give to others what rightly belongs to us. You will use your strength among thieves. They are thieves because they take what is ours, they have no claim of blood to it. They will even lack the knowledge to use it wisely. Truth is my companion at this moment, my son. I know everything I say will surely bring the sadness of truth.

Eman: I am going, father.

Old Man: Call my attendant. And be with me in your strength for this last journey. A-ah, did you hear that? It came out without my knowing it; this is indeed my last journey. But I am not afraid.

Eman goes out. A few moments later, the attendant enters.

Attendant: The boat is ready.

Old Man: So am I.   315

He sits perfectly still for several moments. Drumming begins somewhere in the distance, and the Old Man sways his head almost imperceptibly. Two men come in bearing a miniature boat, containing an indefinable mound. They rush it in and set it briskly down near the Old Man, and stand well back. The Old Man gets up slowly, the attendant watching him keenly. He signs to the men, who lift the boat quickly onto the Old Man's head. As soon as it touches his head, he holds it down with both hands and runs off, the men give him a start, then follow at a trot. As the last man disappears Oroge limps in and comes face to face with Eman—as carrier—who is now seen still standing beside the shrubs, staring into the scene he has just witnessed. Oroge, struck by the look on Eman's face, looks anxiously behind him to see what has engaged Eman's attention. Eman notices him then, and the pair stare at each other. Jaguna enters, sees him and shouts, "Here he is," rushes at Eman, who is whipped back to the immediate and flees, Jaguna in pursuit. Three or four others enter and follow them. Oroge remains where he is, thoughtful.

Jaguna *(re-enters)*:   They have closed in on him now, we'll get him this time.

Oroge: It is nearly midnight.

Jaguna: You were standing there looking at him as if he was some strange spirit. Why didn't you shout?

Oroge: You shouted didn't you? Did that catch him?

Jaguna: Don't worry. We have him now. But things have taken a bad turn. It is no   320
longer enough to drive him past every house. There is too much contamination about already.

Oroge *(not listening)*:   He saw something. Why may I not know what it was?

Jaguna: What are you talking about?

Oroge: Hm. What is it?

Jaguna: I said there is too much harm done already. The year will demand more from this carrier than we thought.

Oroge: What do you mean?   325

Jaguna: Do we have to talk with the full mouth?

Oroge: S-sh . . . look!

Jaguna turns just in time to see Sunma fly at him, clawing at his face like a crazed tigress.

SUNMA: Murderer! What are you doing to him. Murderer! Murderer!

Jaguna finds himself struggling really hard to keep off his daughter, he succeeds in pushing her off and striking her so hard on the face that she falls to her knees. He moves on her to hit her again.

OROGE *(comes between):*   Think what you are doing, Jaguna, she is your daughter.

JAGUNA: My daughter! Does this one look like my daughter? Let me cripple the har-   330
lot for life.

OROGE: That is a wicked thought, Jaguna.

JAGUNA: Don't come between me and her.

OROGE: Nothing in anger —do you forget what tonight is?

JAGUNA: Can you blame me for forgetting?

Draws his hand across his cheek—it is covered with blood.

OROGE: This is an unhappy night for us all. I fear what is to come of it.   335

JAGUNA: Let's go. I cannot restrain myself in this creature's presence. My own
daughter ... and for a stranger ...

They go off, Ifada, who came in with Sunma and had stood apart, horror-stricken, comes shyly forward. He helps Sunma up. They go off, he holding Sunma bent and sobbing.

Enter Eman—as carrier. He is physically present in the bounds of this next scene, a side of a round thatched hut. A young girl, about fourteen, runs in, stops beside the hut. She looks carefully to see that she is not observed, puts her mouth to a little hole in the wall.

OMAE: Eman ... Eman ...

Eman—as carrier—responds, as he does throughout the scene, but they are unaware of him.

EMAN *(from inside):*   Who is it?

OMAE: It is me, Omae.

EMAN: How dare you come here!

*Two hands appear at the hole and, pushing outwards, create a much larger hole through which   340
Eman puts out his head. It is Eman as a boy, the same age as the girl.*

Go away at once. Are you trying to get me into trouble!

OMAE: What is the matter?

EMAN: You. Go away.

OMAE: But I came to see you.

EMAN: Are you deaf? I say I don't want to see you. Now go before my tutor
catches you.

OMAE: All right. Come out.

EMAN: You must be mad.   345

OMAE *(sits on the ground):*   All right, if you don't come out I shall simply stay here
until your tutor arrives.

EMAN *(about to explode, thinks better of it and the head disappears. A moment   350
later he emerges from behind the hut):*   What sort of a devil has got into you?

OMAE: None. I just wanted to see you.

EMAN *(his mimicry is nearly hysterical):*   "None. I just wanted to see you." Do you
think this place is the stream where you can go and molest innocent people?

OMAE *(coyly):*   Aren't you glad to see me?

EMAN: I am not.

OMAE: Why?

EMAN: Why? Do you really ask me why? Because you are a woman and a most trou-   355
blesome woman. Don't you know anything about this at all? We are not meant
to see any woman. So go away before more harm is done.

OMAE *(flirtatious):*   What is so secret about it anyway? What do they teach you?

EMAN: Nothing any woman can understand.

OMAE: Ha ha. You think we don't know eh? You've all come to be circumcised.

EMAN: Shut up. You don't know anything.

OMAE: Just think, all this time you haven't been circumcised, and you dared make eyes at us women.   360

EMAN: Thank you—woman. Now go.

OMAE: Do they give you enough to eat?

EMAN *(testily):*   No. We are so hungry that when silly girls like you turn up, we eat them.

OMAE *(feigning tears):*   Oh, oh, oh, he's abusing me. He's abusing me.   365

EMAN *(alarmed):*   Don't try that here. Go quickly if you are going to cry.

OMAE: All right, I won't cry.

EMAN: Cry or no cry, go away and leave me alone. What do you think will happen if my tutor turns up now?

OMAE: He won't.

EMAN *(mimicking):*   "He won't." I suppose you are his wife and he tells you where he goes. In fact this is just the time he comes round to our huts. He could be at the next hut this very moment.   370

OMAE: Ha-ha. You're lying. I left him by the stream, pinching the girls' bottoms. Is that the sort of thing he teaches you?

EMAN: Don't say anything against him or I shall beat you. Isn't it you loose girls who tease him, wiggling your bottoms under his nose?

OMAE *(going tearful again):*   A-ah, so I am one of the loose girls eh?

EMAN: Now don't start accusing me of things I didn't say.

OMAE: But you said it. You said it.

EMAN: I didn't. Look, Omae, someone will hear you and I'll be in disgrace. Why don't you go before anything happens.   375

OMAE: It's all right. My friends have promised to hold your old rascal tutor till I get back.

EMAN: Then go back right now. I have work to do. *(Going in.)*

OMAE *(runs after and tries to hold him. Eman leaps back, genuinely scared):* What is the matter? I was not going to bite you.

EMAN: Do you know what you nearly did? You almost touched me!

OMAE: Well?   380

EMAN: Well! Isn't it enough that you let me set my eyes on you? Must you now totally pollute me with your touch? Don't you understand anything?

OMAE: Oh, that.

EMAN *(nearly screaming):*   It is not "oh that." Do you think this is only a joke or a little visit like spending the night with your grandmother? This is an important period of my life. Look, these huts, we built them with our own hands. Every boy builds his own. We learn things, do you understand? And we spend much time just thinking. At least, I do. It is the first time I have had nothing to do except think. Don't you see, I am becoming a man. For the first time, I understand that I have a life to fulfill. Has that thought ever worried you?

OMAE: You are frightening me.

EMAN: There. That is all you can say. And what use will that be when a man finds   385
himself alone—like that? *(Points to the hut.)* A man must go on his own, go where no one can help him, and test his strength. Because he may find himself one day sitting alone in a wall as round as that. In there, my mind could hold no other thought. I may never have such moments again to myself. Don't dare to come and steal any more of it.

OMAE (*this time, genuinely tearful*):   Oh, I know you hate me. You only want to
   drive me away.

EMAN: Yes, yes, I know I hate you—but go.

OMAE (*going, all tears. Wipes her eyes, suddenly all mischief*):   Eman.

EMAN: What now?

OMAE: I only want to ask one thing . . . do you promise to tell me?

EMAN: Well, what is it?   390

OMAE (*gleefully*):   Does it hurt?

She turns instantly and flees, landing straight into the arms of the returning tutor.

TUTOR: Te-he-he . . . what have we here? What little mouse leaps straight into the
   beak of the wise old owl eh?

Omae struggles to free herself, flies to the opposite side, grimacing with distaste.

TUTOR: I suppose you merely came to pick some fruits eh? You did not sneak here
   to see any of my children.

OMAE: Yes, I came to steal your fruits.

TUTOR: Te-he-he . . . I thought so. And that dutiful son of mine over there. He saw   395
   you and came to chase you off my fruit trees didn't he? Te-he-he . . . I'm sure he
   did, isn't that so, my young Eman?

EMAN: I was talking to her.

TUTOR: Indeed you were. Now be good enough to go into your hut until I decide
   your punishment. (*Eman withdraws.*) Te-he-he . . . now now, my little daughter,
   you need not be afraid of me.

OMAE (*spiritedly*):   I am not.

TUTOR: Good. Very good. We ought to be friendly. (*His voice becomes leering.*)   400
   Now this is nothing to worry you, my daughter . . . a very small thing indeed.
   Although of course if I were to let it slip that your young Eman had broken a
   strong taboo, it might go hard on him, you know. I am sure you would not like
   that to happen, would you?

OMAE: No.

TUTOR: Good. You are sensible, my girl. Can you wash clothes?

OMAE: Yes.

TUTOR: Good. If you will come with me now to my hut, I shall give you some
   clothes to wash, and then we will forget all about this matter eh? Well, come on.

OMAE: I shall wait here. You go and bring the clothes.

TUTOR: Eh? What is that? Now now, don't make me angry. You should know better   405
   than to talk back at your elders. Come now.

He takes her by the arm, and tries to drag her off.

OMAE: No, no, I won't come to your hut. Leave me. Leave me alone, you shameless
   old man.

TUTOR: If you don't come I shall disgrace the whole family of Eman, and yours too.

Eman reenters with a small bundle.

EMAN: Leave her alone. Let us go, Omae.

TUTOR: And where do you think you are going?

EMAN: Home.   410

TUTOR: Te-he-he . . . As easy as that eh? You think you can leave here any time you
   please? Get right back inside that hut!

Eman takes Omae by the arm and begins to walk off.

TUTOR: Come back at once.

He goes after him and raises his stick. Eman catches it, wrenches it from him, and throws it away.

OMAE *(hopping delightedly):*   Kill him. Beat him to death.

TUTOR: Help! Help! He is killing me! Help!   415

Alarmed, Eman clamps his hand over his mouth.

EMAN: Old tutor, I don't mean you any harm, but you mustn't try to harm me either. *(He removes his hand.)*

TUTOR: You think you can get away with your crime. My report shall reach the elders before you ever get into town.

EMAN: You are afraid of what I will say about you? Don't worry. Only if you try to shame me, then I will speak. I am not going back to the village anyway. Just tell them I have gone, no more. If you say one word more than that I shall hear of it the same day and I shall come back.

TUTOR: You are telling me what to do? But don't think to come back next year because I will drive you away. Don't think to come back here even ten years from now. And don't send your children. *(Goes off with threatening gestures.)*

EMAN: I won't come back.   420

OMAE: Smoked vulture! But Eman, he says you cannot return next year. What will you do?

EMAN: It is a small thing one can do in the big towns.

OMAE: I thought you were going to beat him that time. Why didn't you crack his dirty hide?

EMAN: Listen carefully, Omae . . . I am going on a journey.

OMAE: Come on. Tell me about it on the way.   425

EMAN: No, I go that way. I cannot return to the village.

OMAE: Because of that wretched man? Anyway you will first talk to your father.

EMAN: Go and see him for me. Tell him I have gone away for some time. I think he will know.

OMAE: But, Eman . . .

EMAN: I haven't finished. You will go and live with him till I get back. I have spoken   430
to him about you. Look after him!

OMAE: But what is this journey? When will you come back?

EMAN: I don't know. But this is a good moment to go. Nothing ties me down.

OMAE: But, Eman, you want to leave me.

EMAN: Don't forget all I said. I don't know how long I will be. Stay in my father's house as long as you remember me. When you become tired of waiting, you must do as you please. You understand? You must do as you please.

OMAE: I cannot understand anything, Eman. I don't know where you are going or   435
why. Suppose you never come back! Don't go, Eman. Don't leave me by myself.

EMAN: I must go. Now let me see you on your way.

OMAE: I shall come with you.

EMAN: Come with me! And who will look after you? Me? You will only be in my way, you know that! You will hold me back and I shall desert you in a strange place. Go home and do as I say. Take care of my father and let him take care of you. *(He starts going but Omae clings to him.)*

OMAE: But, Eman, stay the night at least. You will only lose your way. Your father, Eman, what will he say? I won't remember what you said . . . come back to the village . . . I cannot return alone, Eman . . . come with me as far as the crossroads.

His face set, Eman strides off and Omae loses balance as he increases his pace. Falling, she quickly wraps her arms around his ankle, but Eman continues unchecked, dragging her along.

OMAE: Don't go, Eman . . . Eman, don't leave me, don't leave me . . . don't leave your
           Omae . . . don't go, Eman . . . don't leave your Omae . . .   440

*Eman—as carrier—makes a nervous move as if he intends to go after the vanished pair. He
stops but continues to stare at the point where he last saw them. There is stillness for a while.
Then the Girl enters from the same place and remains looking at Eman. Startled, Eman looks
apprehensively round him. The Girl goes nearer but keeps beyond arm's length.*

GIRL: Are you the carrier?
EMAN: Yes, I am Eman.
GIRL: Why are you hiding?
EMAN: I really came for a drink of water . . . er . . . is there anyone in front of the house?
GIRL: No.
EMAN: But there might be people in the house. Did you hear voices?   445
GIRL: There is no one here.
EMAN: Good. Thank you. *(He is about to go, stops suddenly.)* Er . . . would you . . .
           you will find a cup on the table. Could you bring me the water out here? The
           water pot is in a corner.

The Girl goes. She enters the house, then, watching Eman carefully, slips out and runs off.

EMAN *(sitting):*   Perhaps they have all gone home. It will be good to rest. *(He hears
           voices and listens hard.)* Too late. *(Moves cautiously nearer the house.)*
           Quickly, Girl, I can hear people coming. Hurry up. *(Looks through the win-
           dow.)* Where are you? Where is she? *(The truth dawns on him suddenly and
           he moves off, sadly.)*

Enter Jaguna and Oroge, led by the Girl.

GIRL *(pointing):*   He was there.
JAGUNA: Ay, he's gone now. He is a sly one is your friend. But it won't save him forever.   450
OROGE: What was he doing when you saw him?
GIRL: He asked me for a drink of water.
JAGUNA: } Ah! *(They look at each other.)*
OROGE:
OROGE: We should have thought of that.
JAGUNA: He is surely finished now. If only we had thought of it earlier.   455
OROGE: It is not too late. There is still an hour before midnight.
JAGUNA: We must call back all the men. Now we need only wait for him—in the
           right place.
OROGE: Everyone must be told. We don't want anyone heading him off again.
JAGUNA: And it works so well. This is surely the help of the gods themselves, Oroge.   460
           Don't you know at once what is on the path to the stream?
OROGE: The sacred trees.
JAGUNA: I tell you it is the very hand of the gods. Let us go.

*An overgrown part of the village. Eman wanders in, aimlessly, seemingly uncaring of discovery.
Beyond him, an area lights up, revealing a group of people clustered round a spot, all the heads
are bowed. One figure stands away and separate from them. Even as Eman looks, the group
breaks up and the people disperse, coming down and past him. Only three people are left, a man
(Eman) whose back is turned, the village Priest, and the isolated one. They stand on opposite
sides of the grave, the man on the mound of earth. The Priest walks round to the man's side and
lays a hand on his shoulder.*

PRIEST: Come.
EMAN: I will. Give me a few moments here alone.
PRIEST: Be comforted.
                                                                                          465

They fall silent.

EMAN: I was gone twelve years but she waited. She whom I thought had too much of the laughing child in her. Twelve years I was a pilgrim, seeking the vain shrine of secret strength. And all the time, strange knowledge, this silent strength of my child-woman.

PRIEST: We all saw it. It was a lesson to us; we did not know that such goodness could be found among us.

EMAN: Then why? Why the wasted years if she had to perish giving birth to my child? *(They are both silent.)* I do not really know for what great meaning I searched. When I returned home, I could not be certain I had found it. Until I reached my home and I found her a full-grown woman, still a child at heart. When I grew to believe it, I thought, this, after all, is what I sought. It was here all the time. And I threw away my new-gained knowledge. I buried the part of me that was formed in strange places. I made a home in my birthplace.

PRIEST: That was as it should be.

EMAN: Any truth of that was killed in the cruelty of her brief happiness.   470

PRIEST *(looks up and sees the figure standing away from them, the child in his arms. He is totally still):*   Your father—he is over there.

EMAN: I knew he would come. Has he my son with him?

PRIEST: Yes.

EMAN: He will let no one take the child. Go and comfort him, priest. He loved Omae like a daughter, and you all know how well she looked after him. You see how strong we really are. In his heart of hearts the old man's love really awaited a daughter. Go and comfort him. His grief is more than mine.

The Priest goes. The Old Man has stood well away from the burial group. His face is hard and his gaze unswerving from the grave. The Priest goes to him, pauses, but sees that he can make no dent in the man's grief. Bowed, he goes on his way.

Eman, as carrier, walks towards the graveside, the other Eman having gone. His feet sink into the mound and he breaks slowly on to his knees, scooping up the sand in his hands and pouring it on his head. The scene blacks out slowly.

Enter Jaguna and Oroge.

OROGE: We have only a little time.

JAGUNA: He will come. All the wells are guarded. There is only the stream left him.   475
The animal must come to drink.

OROGE: You are sure it will not fail—the trap, I mean.

JAGUNA: When Jaguna sets the trap, even elephants pay homage—their trunks downwards and one leg up in the sky. When the carrier steps on the fallen twigs, it is up in the sacred trees with him.

OROGE: I shall breathe again when this long night is over.

They go out.

Enter Eman—as carrier—from the same direction as the last two entered. In front of him is a still figure, the Old Man as he was, carrying the dwarf boat.

EMAN *(joyfully):*   Father.

The figure does not turn around.

EMAN: It is your son, Eman. *(He moves nearer.)* Don't you want to look at me? It is   480
I, Eman. *(He moves nearer still.)*

OLD MAN: You are coming too close. Don't you know what I carry on my head?

EMAN: But, father, I am your son.

OLD MAN: Then go back. We cannot give the two of us.

EMAN: Tell me first where you are going.

OLD MAN: Do *you* ask that? Where else but to the river?

EMAN (*visibly relieved*):   I only wanted to be sure. My throat is burning. I have been   485
looking for the stream all night.

OLD MAN: It is the other way.

EMAN: But you said . . .

OLD MAN: I take the longer way, you know how I must do this. It is quicker if you
take the other way. Go now.

EMAN: No, I will only get lost again. I shall go with you.   490

OLD MAN: Go back, my son. Go back.

EMAN: Why? Won't you even look at me?

OLD MAN: Listen to your father. Go back.

EMAN: But, father!

*He makes to hold him. Instantly the Old Man breaks into a rapid trot. Eman hesitates, then
follows, his strength nearly gone.*

EMAN: Wait, father. I am coming with you . . . wait . . . wait for me, father . . .   500

There is a sound of twigs breaking, of a sudden trembling in the branches. Then silence.

*The front of Eman's house. The effigy is hanging from the sheaves. Enter Sunma. Still supported
by Ifada, she stands transfixed as she sees the hanging figure. Ifada appears to go mad, rushes at
the object, and tears it down. Sunma, her last bit of will gone, crumbles against the wall. Some
distance away from them, partly hidden, stands the Girl, impassively watching. Ifada hugs the
effigy to him, stands above Sunma. The Girl remains where she is, observing. Almost at once,
the villagers begin to return, subdued and guilty. They walk across the front, skirting the house
as widely as they can. No word is exchanged. Jaguna and Oroge eventually appear. Jaguna, who
is leading, sees Sunma as soon as he comes in view. He stops at once, retreating slightly.*

OROGE (*almost whispering*):   What is it?

JAGUNA: The viper.

Oroge looks cautiously at the woman.

OROGE: I don't think she will even see you.

JAGUNA: Are you sure? I am in no frame of mind for another meeting with her.

OROGE: Let's go home.

JAGUNA: I am sick to the heart of the cowardice I have seen tonight.   505

OROGE: That is the nature of men.

JAGUNA: Then it is a sorry world to live in. We did it for them. It was all for their own
common good. What did it benefit me whether the man lived or died? But did you
see them? One and all they looked up at the man and words died in their throats.

OROGE: It was no common sight.

JAGUNA: Women could not have behaved so shamefully. One by one they crept off   510
like sick dogs. Not one could raise a curse.

OROGE: It was not only him they fled. Do you see how unattended we are?

JAGUNA: There are those who will pay for this night's work!

OROGE: Ay, let us go home.

They go off. Sunma, Ifada, and the Girl remain as they are, the light fading slowly on them.

Response Statement Questions

- How does *The Strong Breed* exhibit any of the text strategies of drama that
were discussed in this chapter and illustrated in *Trifles?* Does *The Strong*

Breed deviate from those text strategies in any way? What is your response to its adherence to or deviation from the conventional text strategies of drama?

- How does *The Strong Breed* involve matters of knowing and unknowing as you read it? Do any of the characters experience an increase in knowledge as the action unfolds? Do you experience any such increase in knowledge? Whether you do or not, how is your knowing or unknowing affected by text strategies of the play? How is it affected by your reading strategies?

- To what extent is this play realistic? To what extent is your determination of its realism related to the difference between your cultural situation and the cultural situation in which the play is set?

- What is your response to the cultural practice of the "carrier" as it is depicted in *The Strong Breed?* Does it make any sense to you? Do you see any value in it? Does your culture have any similar practices or beliefs? How does your cultural ideology influence your response to this text strategy?

- What is the effect of your gender on your response to this text? Does it affect your sympathy for Sunma or Eman? Does it affect your response to the different roles assigned to boys/men and to girls/women in the cultural setting of the play? Does your gender, interacting with the cultural values of the play, raise issues of the different roles assigned to boys/men and to girls/women in *your* culture?

- Who is "strong" in this play? Why? What is the nature of their strength? Who is "weak"? Why? What is the nature of their weakness? What is the contribution of your ideology to the way you answer these questions?

- *Share and Compare*   What does discussion in your class or in small groups reveal about differences in the ways readers respond to *The Strong Breed?* Did different readers use different reading strategies, and with what varying degrees of success? What different text strategies did different readers emphasize, and how were those decisions related to the ideologies that different readers brought to this text?

READING AND WRITING PROJECTS

FOR CREATIVE AND CRITICAL THINKING

Your own writing is important as you try to learn more about yourself as a reader—both what you do cognitively when you read and how culture impinges on the kind of reader you are when you interact with any particular text. In addition to response statements and the formal expository paper that may grow out of them, there are other ways to use writing to learn.

The following suggestions are intended to help you integrate your reading of and writing about literary texts in various ways. These suggestions include exploratory writing, playing with texts and language, creative efforts in various genres, and other writing exercises designed to strengthen your awareness of the cognitive and cultural processes involved in your reading.

▶ Select a character from any play and write a letter to or from him or her discussing any problem that character may have. If you write *to* the character, perhaps you could offer some advice. If you want to write a letter *as* the character, try having him or her address you, trying to explain things as he or she sees them. Other variations of this project are possible; for instance, you could have one character write a letter to another, or you could write to an author, or have the author write to you. You could also work with a classmate: One of you writes a letter from one person to another; the other replies in the role of the person addressed by the first letter.

▶ Select a character from any play and create an advertisement in which this character endorses a product or service. Write some copy for this character to "say" or be quoted as saying. (For example, Minnie Wright might be a good choice to endorse a certain brand of rope.) This project could be extended or modified by writing an explanation of why you chose this character for this product or service. This project could also be done in a small group; advertising agencies often assign a team to a campaign: some members work in words, others in visual elements.

▶ Assume the point of view of a minor character in any play and write a prose account of that character's thoughts on the actions and conflicts of the play's major characters. For example, what might Berte, the Tesmans' maid in *Hedda Gabler*, think of what's going on in that household? Or (though she is not exactly "minor") what might Ophelia say about her relationship with Hamlet?

▶ As a variation on the preceding project, write a narrative account, in the voice of any character in any play, of his or her situation, personality, or actions. What factors in the character's life or background—especially those factors that antedate the action of the play itself—have caused the character to turn out as she or he has when you encounter him or her in the text of the play?

17 ◆ EXAMINING DRAMATIC CONVENTIONS

You may or may not have much theatergoing experience. You may or may not have much play-reading experience either. But you probably do have a fair amount of "drama-seeing" experience from watching television and movies. Dramas in both those genres—whether they are comedies, tragedies, both, or neither—exhibit many of the conventions we observed in the printed version of *Trifles* in the previous chapter. In reading a play like *Trifles*, you may also be able to use your experience with reading fiction. That experience, including an awareness of the conventions of fiction, should help you toward a successful interaction with a text like *Trifles*. That play probably meets your expectations for written or printed drama, and that, in turn, affects or reinforces your expectations for reading other plays on the page.

The Reader's Expectations

As a kind of self-review at this point, please take a few minutes to inventory your literary experience with respect to plays. What do you expect to find when you read a play? What do you think will happen, in terms of your experience with such a text?

My Expectations for Reading a Play

1.
2.
3.
4.
5.
6.

Armed with those expectations from your literary experience and with some of the reading strategies suggested in the previous chapter, turn now to another printed play, Edward Albee's *The Sandbox*. Read it and write a response statement or journal entry. Some questions to prompt your writing follow the play on page 881.

Edward Albee   b. 1928

The Sandbox   1959

Players

The Young Man, 25, a good-looking, well-built boy in a bathing suit
Mommy, 55, a well-dressed, imposing woman
Daddy, 60, a small man; gray, thin
Grandma, 86, a tiny, wizened woman with bright eyes
The Musician, no particular age, but young would be nice

NOTE. When, in the course of the play, Mommy and Daddy call each other by these names, there should be no suggestion of regionalism. These names are of empty affection and point up the presenility and vacuity of their characters.

The Scene. A bare stage, with only the following: Near the footlights, far stage-right, two simple chairs set side by side, facing the audience; near the footlights, far stage-left, a chair facing stage-right with a music stand before it; farther back, and stage center, slightly elevated and raked, a large child's sandbox with a toy pail and shovel; the background is the sky, which alters from brightest day to deepest night.

At the beginning, it is brightest day; the Young Man is alone on stage to the rear of the sandbox, and to one side. He is doing calisthenics; he does calisthenics until quite at the very end of the play. These calisthenics, employing the arms only, should suggest the beating and fluttering of wings. The Young Man is, after all, the Angel of Death.

Mommy and Daddy enter from stage-left, Mommy first.

MOMMY [*Motioning to Daddy*]:   Well, here we are; this is the beach.
DADDY [*Whining*]:   I'm cold.
MOMMY [*Dismissing him with a little laugh*]:   Don't be silly; it's as warm as toast. Look at that nice young man over there; *he* doesn't think it's cold. [*Waves to the Young Man*] Hello.
YOUNG MAN [*With an endearing smile*]:   Hi!
MOMMY [*Looking about*]:   This will do perfectly . . . don't you think so, Daddy? There's sand there . . . and the water beyond. What do you think, Daddy?   5
DADDY [*Vaguely*]:   Whatever you say, Mommy.
MOMMY [*With the same little laugh*]:   Well, of course . . . whatever I say. Then, it's settled, is it?
DADDY [*Shrugs*]:   She's *your* mother, not mine.
MOMMY: *I* know she's my mother. What do you take me for? [*A pause*] All right, now; let's get on with it. [*She shouts into the wings, stage-left*] You! Out there! You can come in now. [*The Musician enters, seats himself in the chair, stage left, places music on the music stand, is ready to play. Mommy nods approvingly.*] Very nice; very nice. Are you ready, Daddy? Let's go get Grandma.
DADDY: Whatever you say, Mommy.
MOMMY [*Leading the way out, stage-left*]:   Of course, whatever I say. [*To the Musician*] You can begin now. [*The Musician begins playing; Mommy and Daddy exit; the Musician, all the while playing, nods to the Young Man.*]   10

YOUNG MAN [*With the same endearing smile*]:   Hi! [*After a moment, Mommy and Daddy re-enter, carrying Grandma. She is borne in by their hands under her armpits; she is quite rigid; her legs are drawn up; her feet do not touch the ground; the expression on her ancient face is that of puzzlement and fear.*]

DADDY: Where do we put her?

MOMMY [*With the same little laugh*]:   Wherever I say, of course. Let me see ... well ... all right, over there ... in the sandbox. [*Pause*] Well, what are you waiting for, Daddy? ... The sandbox! [*Together they carry Grandma over to the sandbox and more or less dump her in.*]

GRANDMA [*Righting herself to a sitting position; her voice a cross between a baby's laugh and cry*]:   Ahhhhhh! Graaaaa!   15

DADDY [*Dusting himself*]:   What do we do now?

MOMMY [*To the Musician*]:   You can stop now. [*The Musician stops.*] [*Back to Daddy*] What do you mean, what do we do now? We go over there and sit down, of course. [*To the Young Man*] Hello there.

YOUNG MAN [*Again smiling*]:   Hi! [*Mommy and Daddy move to the chairs, stage-right, and sit down. A pause.*]

GRANDMA [*Same as before*]:   Ahhhhhh! Ah-haaaaaa! Graaaaaa!

DADDY: Do you think ... do you think she's ... comfortable?   20

MOMMY [*Impatiently*]:   How would I know?

DADDY [*Pause*]:   What do we do now?

MOMMY [*As if remembering*]:   We ... wait. We ... sit here ... and we wait ... that's what we do.

DADDY [*After a pause*]:   Shall we talk to each other?

MOMMY [*With that little laugh; picking something off her dress*]:   Well, *you* can talk, if you want to ... if you can think of anything to say ... if you can think of anything *new*.   25

DADDY [*Thinks*]:   No ... I suppose not.

MOMMY [*With a triumphant laugh*]:   Of course not!

GRANDMA [*Banging the toy shovel against the pail*]:   Haaaaaa! Ah-haaaaaa!

MOMMY [*Out over the audience*]:   Be quiet, Grandma ... just be quiet, and wait. [*Grandma throws a shovelful of sand at Mommy. Still out over the audience*] She's throwing sand at me! You stop that, Grandma; you stop throwing sand at Mommy! [*To Daddy*] She's throwing sand at me. [*Daddy looks around at Grandma, who screams at him.*]

GRANDMA: GRAAAAA!   30

MOMMY: Don't look at her. Just ... sit here ... be very still ... and wait. [*To the Musician*] You ... uh ... you go ahead and do whatever it is you do. [*The Musician plays. Mommy and Daddy are fixed, staring out beyond the audience. Grandma looks at them, looks at the Musician, looks at the sandbox, throws down the shovel.*]

GRANDMA: Ah-haaaaaa! Graaaaaa! [*Looks for reaction; gets none. Now ... directly to the audience*] Honestly! What a way to treat an old woman! Drag her out of the house ... stick her in a car ... bring her out here from the city ... dump her in a pile of sand ... and leave her here to set. I'm eighty-six years old! I was married when I was seventeen. To a farmer. He died when I was thirty. [*To the Musician*] Will you stop that, please? [*The Musician stops playing.*] I'm a feeble old woman ... how do you expect anybody to hear me over that peep! peep! peep! [*To herself*] There's no respect around here. [*To the Young Man*] There's no respect around here!

YOUNG MAN [*Same smile*]:   Hi!

GRANDMA [*After a pause, a mild double-take, continues, to the audience*]:   My husband died when I was thirty [*Indicates Mommy*], and I had to raise that big cow over there all by my lonesome. You can imagine what *that* was like. Lordy! [*To the Young Man*] Where'd they get *you*?

YOUNG MAN: Oh ... I've been around for a while.

GRANDMA: I'll bet you have! Heh, heh, heh. Will you look at you!   35

YOUNG MAN [*Flexing his muscles*]:   Isn't that something?

    [*Continues his calisthenics*]

GRANDMA: Boy, oh boy; I'll say. Pretty good.

YOUNG MAN [*Sweetly*]:   I'll say.

GRANDMA: Where ya from?

YOUNG MAN: Southern California.   40

GRANDMA [*Nodding*]:   Figgers; figgers. What's your name, honey?

YOUNG MAN: I don't know ...

GRANDMA [*To the audience*]:   Bright, too!

YOUNG MAN: I mean ... I mean, they haven't given me one yet ... the studio ...   45

GRANDMA [*Giving him the once over*]:   You don't say ... you don't say. Well ... uh, I've got to talk some more ... don't you go 'way.

YOUNG MAN: Oh, no.

GRANDMA [*Turning her attention back to the audience*]:   Fine; fine. [*Then, once more, back to the Young Man*] You're ... you're an actor, hunh?

YOUNG MAN [*Beaming*]:   Yes, I am.

GRANDMA [*To the audience again; shrugs*]:   I'm smart that way. *Anyhow*, I had to   50 raise ... *that* over there all by my lonesome; and what's next to her there ... that's what she married. Rich? I tell you ... money, money, money. They took me off the *farm* ... which was real decent of them ... fixed a nice place for me under the stove ... gave me an army blanket ... and my own dish ... my very own dish! So, what have I got to complain about? Nothing, of course. I'm not complaining. [*She looks up at the sky, shouts to someone offstage.*] Shouldn't it be getting dark now, dear? [*The lights dim; night comes on. The Musician begins to play; it becomes deepest night. There are spots on all the players, including the Young Man, who is, of course, continuing his calisthenics.*]

DADDY [*Stirring*]:   It's nighttime.

MOMMY: Shhhh. Be still ... wait.

DADDY [*Whining*]:   It's so hot.

MOMMY: Shhhhhh. Be still ... wait.

GRANDMA [*To herself*]:   That's better. Night. [*To the Musician*] Honey, do you play all   55 through this part? [*The Musician nods.*] Well, keep it nice and soft; that's a good boy. [*The Musician nods again; plays softly.*] That's nice. [*There is an off-stage rumble.*]

DADDY [*Stirring*]:   What was that?

MOMMY [*Beginning to weep*]:   It was nothing.

DADDY: It was ... it was ... thunder ... or a wave breaking ... or something.

MOMMY [*Whispering, through her tears*]:   It was an off-stage rumble ... and you know what *that* means ...

DADDY: I forget ...

MOMMY [*Barely able to talk*]:   It means the time has come for poor Grandma ... and   60 I can't bear it!

DADDY [*Vacantly*]:   I ... I suppose you've got to be brave.

GRANDMA [*Mockingly*]:   That's right, kid; be brave. You'll bear up, you'll get over it. [*Another off-stage rumble ... louder*]

MOMMY: Ohhhhhhhh ... poor Grandma ... poor Grandma ...

GRANDMA [*To Mommy*]:   I'm fine! I'm all right! It hasn't happened yet! [*A violent*   65
*off-stage rumble. All the lights go out, save the spot on the Young Man; the
Musician stops playing.*]

MOMMY: Ohhhhhhhhh ... Ohhhhhhhhhh ... [*Silence*]

GRANDMA: Don't put the lights up yet ... I'm not ready; I'm not quite ready. [*Silence*]
All right, dear ... I'm about done. [*The lights come up again, to brightest day;
the Musician begins to play. Grandma is discovered, still in the sandbox,
lying on her side, propped up on an elbow, half covered, busily shoveling
sand over herself.*]

GRANDMA [*Muttering*]:   I don't know how I'm supposed to do anything with this
goddamn toy shovel ...

DADDY: Mommy! It's daylight!

MOMMY [*Brightly*]:   So it is! Well! Our long night is over. We must put away our   70
tears, take off our mourning ... and face the future. It's our duty.

GRANDMA [*Still shoveling; mimicking*]:   ... take off our mourning ... face the future ...
Lordy! [*Mommy and Daddy rise, stretch. Mommy waves to the Young Man.*]

YOUNG MAN [*With that smile*]:   Hi! [*Grandma plays dead. (!) Mommy and Daddy
go over to look at her; she is a little more than half buried in the sand; the toy
shovel is in her hands, which are crossed on her breast.*]

MOMMY [*Before the sandbox; shaking her head*]:   Lovely! It's ... it's hard to be sad
... she looks ... so happy. [*With pride and conviction*] It pays to do things well.
[*To the Musician*] All right, you can stop now, if you want to. I mean, stay
around for a swim, or something; it's all right with us. [*She sighs heavily.*] Well,
Daddy ... off we go.

DADDY: Brave Mommy!

MOMMY: Brave Daddy! [*They exit, stage left.*]   75

GRANDMA [*After they leave; lying quite still*]:   It pays to do things well ... Boy, oh
boy! [*She tries to sit up.*] ... well, kids ... [*But she finds she can't.*] ... I ... I can't
get up. I ... I can't move ... [*The Young Man stops his calisthenics, nods to the
Musician, walks over to Grandma, kneels down by the sandbox.*]

GRANDMA: I ... can't move ...

YOUNG MAN: Shhhhh ... be very still ...

GRANDMA: I ... I can't move ...

YOUNG MAN: Uh ... ma'am; I ... I have a line here.   80

GRANDMA: Oh, I'm sorry, sweetie; you go right ahead.

YOUNG MAN: I am ... uh ...

GRANDMA: Take your time, dear.

YOUNG MAN [*Prepares; delivers the line like a real amateur*]:   I am the Angel of
Death. I am ... uh ... I am come for you.

GRANDMA: What ... wha ... [*Then, with resignation*] ... ohhhhh ... ohhhhh, I see.   85
[*The Young Man bends over, kisses Grandma gently on the forehead.*]

GRANDMA [*Her eyes closed, her hands folded on her breast again, the shovel between
her hands, a sweet smile on her face*]:   Well ... that was very nice, dear ...

YOUNG MAN [*Still kneeling*]:   Shhhhh ... be still ...

GRANDMA: What I meant was ... you did that very well, dear ...

YOUNG MAN [*Blushing*]:   ... oh ...

GRANDMA: No; I mean it. You've got that ... you've got a quality.   90

YOUNG MAN [*With his endearing smile*]:   Oh ... thank you; thank you very much ...
ma'am.

GRANDMA [*Slowly; softly—as the Young Man puts his hands on top of Grandma's*]:
You're ... you're welcome ... dear.

[Tableau. The Musician continues to play as the curtain slowly comes down.]

Response Statement Questions

- What is your response to any one or more of the following text strategies of *The Sandbox?*

    the opening set and character descriptions

    the dialogue, the kind of "conversation" that goes on among the characters

    the characters' behavior, the development of any or all of them from the opening curtain onward

    the plot, both structure and issues

- How easy or difficult is it to construct a theme as you read this text?
- In what way or ways did this text meet or defy your expectations and/or your reading strategies for printed drama?
- Is *The Sandbox* a drama at all? In what way or ways?
- *Share and Compare* In your class or discussion group, what kinds of harmonious or clashing literary interactions did different readers experience with *The Sandbox?* What do different readers report as contributing to such interactions, in terms of their reading strategies?

Unconventional, Antirealistic Text Strategies of *The Sandbox*

I imagine you noticed several obvious differences between *The Sandbox* and *Trifles*, probably right from the beginning of your reading experience with Albee's play. The set description, for one thing, indicates a bare stage with only a few pieces of furniture and other props. There is no box set to help create the illusion of a real place on the stage. The opening description refers to locations on the stage (stage-right, stage-left, which are those parts of the stage looking toward the audience) instead of to parts of a room, as was the case in *Trifles.*

Perhaps you found the characters not as persuasively realistic as those in *Trifles.* Two of them are anonymous, and the other three have only familiar names. You probably know people who are called Mommy, Daddy, and Grandma, but those familiar names don't seem to make the characters as true-to-life as full names would. There are gaps here: the rest of the characters' identities, their occupations (except for the Musician's and, as is revealed later in the play, the Young Man's), where they came from, why they have come to wherever it is they are. Their behavior is odd too, isn't it? It's not completely unrecognizable in terms of human behavior, but, except perhaps in an abstract way, not exactly imitative of the larger world of experience. Is it realistic to have an apparently mature, middle-aged married couple dump the woman's mother into a sandbox and leave her there, pretty much ignoring her?

In responding to this play, two of my students used the word "strange" to describe the set and character descriptions:

I thought the description of the players was extremely strange because I was not used to the descriptions being based on age, appearance, and clothing. . . . I also found it odd that the players didn't have real names. . . . The scene was described as bare, [so] I was automatically turned off by the play. *(Carl Hill)*

Wow! This play did not match my expectations at all! When I started reading the character descriptions, I wrinkled my brow in confusion. . . . I would not naturally assume that a young man exercising would be an angel of death. . . . [The character descriptions] did not seem to be traditional at all. The set description seemed different, too. In most plays, there is an elaborate description, but this was extremely simple. *(Sharon DiBiagio)*

What about the dialogue? If you took anything any of the characters says out of context, it might seem real enough. What they say is intelligible on the literal level. But none of the conversations among the characters reveals antecedent action, or suggests relationships that you might believe are realistic, or does anything that dramatic dialogue usually does—such as provide exposition and advance the plot. As another of my students put it, "The dialogue is certainly not the kind that one is used to, of the sort where a dramatic conflict happens between people and they respond to it realistically." Still another said, "The dialogue between the grandmother and the young man confused me."

And is there a plot? The play does have a beginning, a middle, and an end, but what kind of structure does it have in terms of conflict, rising action, and resolution? How much and what kind of suspense is there? What kinds of questions of knowing or unknowing are involved in the action?

As a reader, perhaps even as a reader who has used the reading strategies of visualizing and narrating recommended in Chapter 16 and that may have proven successful with *Trifles*, how easily could you suspend your disbelief and enter the created world of the play? Did you find yourself confronted with your disbelief throughout the reading experience? Perhaps you found yourself reminded several times—and not just through the usual means such as speech tags and stage directions—that you were reading a play. Perhaps you noticed that some of the characters refer to themselves as being in a play and that Grandma, at least, addresses a couple of lines to the audience. The student whom I quoted about dialogue also said,

The Sandbox is . . . not a normal play; . . . it parodies theater, and points out that it is nothing more than a play, the characters are only actors, not real people to sympathize with. Therefore, we can't be moved by it, only amused and confused.

(Barbara Nelson)

The unconventional text strategies in *The Sandbox* make consistency building problematical. The characters may display little in the way of logical motivation for their actions and feelings within the world of the play. The plot may be elusive at best or almost nonexistent at worst, offering little in the way of conflict and leading to no resolution. The text's unconventionality may increase the difficulty in constructing a theme for this text or in trying to interpret it by reference to the real world of experience. Certainly some of my students felt that way.

> I had trouble finding a message in the play. (*Carl Hill*)

> I had a difficult time constructing a theme. . . . Perhaps this is because I found little realism in the text. Because there wasn't a great deal of realism, I had a difficult time relating the characters' actions to anything remotely close to my experience. (*Gina Koonce*)

> It is difficult to construct a theme for this play. . . . One can never pin down the theme. . . . It could . . . represent the chaos of the modern world, as there are no clear answers anymore; likewise, there are no clear themes, nothing is clear to anyone, everything is uncertain. (*Barbara Nelson*)

Perhaps *The Sandbox* leaves you with a sense of artificiality. If you were to see it performed, chances are you would be well aware that it was a theatrical production and not an episode from "real life" or the "imitation of an action." It would be interesting to see how many in the audience of a production of *The Sandbox* would categorize it as a play and how many would be reluctant to do so because of the way it challenges some of the conventions of the genre. Among the conventions spurned is the idea that a play should avoid any reference to the theatricality of what is being presented.

Because of the unconventional text strategies of *The Sandbox* and its apparent willingness to regard itself *as* something artificial and to have the audience do the same, this text seems most definitely to be a play and not something else. To see this play performed is an aesthetic experience; the self-awareness of the way it is crafted and shaped leaves you in no doubt that it is not an episode from real life the audience just happens to have come across. At the same time, despite its unconventionality in some ways, *The Sandbox* does bear the stamp of conventional drama in several others, ways that may seem so natural that you may tend to forget that they too are artificial, conventional. It has a title, it has an author, it is a written text that appears in a book under the heading "drama," it apparently is intended for presentation on stage, and it may have an actual history of performance. For reasons such as these, you may have written in response to reading *The Sandbox* that it is a play and not something else, even though it may challenge your expectations and some of your reading strategies.

CONNECT: In Chapter 6, you read Ronald Sukenick's unconventional story "The Birds." At some points it, like *The Sandbox*, destroys the reader's illusions of experiencing reality by referring to itself as a story.

Here is a longer excerpt from a student's response journal entry on *The Sandbox*. This writer, Barbara Nelson, is the same student whom I quoted earlier to the effect that "*The Sandbox* is . . . not a normal play." At the end of her journal entry, she wrote:

The Sandbox is a drama, because it deals with the conflict between Grandma and Mommy, and that conflict is somewhat resolved, because Mommy and Daddy leave Grandma to die: Grandma goes off with the young man, whom we think is the Angel of Death, though we don't know. Admittedly, it's not a clear resolution, but it is a resolution. The characters have dialogue with one another, although it is stilted and trite.

This play says more about the world of drama than about the characters, because it deals with stepping in and out of their parts, how long people have to be in the play, all the technical details of a drama. I like the fact that it is not afraid to mock the theater, which lessens the other conflict in the play, which is fine with me. I like plays that admit that they are ones, where they stop the action and say, before you get too attached to these people, they're not real, they're only acting. This especially works here, because we're not attached to the characters as their dialogue is asinine, so the result is we don't pay as close attention to them. Though I think that this play is hard to read, it is worthwhile, because its absurdist notions create an interesting, albeit strange, drama.

I have not presented *The Sandbox* to you here just to be annoying. Asking you to read *Trifles* first and to think about some reading strategies for processing a printed play was not just to set you up to seemingly fail with *The Sandbox*. If you did find your expectations and reading strategies confounded by this text, I hope you will take a minute to consider that confusion analogous to what may happen in any genre (literary or otherwise). In many ways, your experience with any kind of a text depends heavily on the expectations you bring to the reading situation. Experience with a variety of texts within a genre, those that stretch conventions and challenge expectations as well as those that conform and confirm, broadens your literary experience and expands your horizon of expectations so that you can become more flexible and stronger as a reader.

Deciding to Read Figuratively

Chapter 16 offered a brief look at the process of creating theme from the interaction of a reader's ideology and the text strategies and ideology that a realistic play such as *Trifles* may present. But as the student comments quoted earlier indicate, the unconventional text strategies of a play like *The Sandbox* may make creating theme difficult, inasmuch as those text strategies seem to inhibit consistency building.

Then again, if theme is something that readers create, how much does the lack of the usual kind of dramatic coherence really matter? Perhaps you are able to use a different reading strategy, one that was suggested in the section on reading poetry: deciding to **read figuratively**. Perhaps approaching *The Sandbox* with this strategy allows you to disregard the variations from ordinary realism or reality and see the whole play as a metaphor: It doesn't attempt to represent ordinary reality on the stage or the page; it doesn't try to be "an imitation of an action"; the whole text *stands for* something else, something in the way of an idea. If you read that way, you are probably close to creating a theme for that play, perhaps about the treatment of old people in American culture; perhaps about the condition of the family in American culture; perhaps about the emptiness of certain American traditions, such as beach vacations or funerals.

Literary and Ideological Interactions

Here is the complete response statement of one student, Shirin Arastu, who read *The Sandbox* for the first time as a freshman in an introductory literature course. For Shirin, theme in *The Sandbox* was "pretty evident." She reported that it was "easy" for her to discover a theme as she read because the text "reflected [her] ideas." Her response statement mentions some of the ideas she brought to the text, as you will see. But it also indicates that she was reading figuratively, and that because of this reading strategy she was not befuddled by the failure of the text to "make sense" on the literal level.

STUDENT WRITING
Shirin Arastu: Response Statement

I liked the text strategies used in this play. The dialogue and the characters' behavior had the most impact. The whole attitude created towards the very solemn issue of death was one of a superficial staged performance. The message I got was that life itself is a drama and this earth the stage. I guess God could be the director. In the beginning, before I could make this interpretation, the play seemed like a play about the rehearsal of another play due to the conversation of the characters where they told each other what to do next. For example, Mommy gets scared of the off-stage rumble and Daddy forgets what that means—she tells him as a part of her dialogue.

The theme, which I think is the issue of death and the rituals of mourning and burial, seemed pretty evident. I often think of death as an ironic happening and every time someone I know has died—life itself begins to seem like a staged performance. I guess it was easy for me to see a theme because the text reflected my ideas. However, without the stage direction and character descriptions it could be hard to figure out a theme till the end if one cannot pick up the hints through the conversation, for example, when Mommy says there is so much peace on Grandma's face. Actually, if I was not told that the Young Man was the Angel of Death, I would not have ever guessed a young well-built boy in a bathing suit was the Angel of Death, because it is contrary to popular belief of an angel with wings in a long white gown of purity. Yet this picturization and the playful conversation is what I liked the most. It made me think, what is all this death and mourning? Isn't it all a staged performance that will be over very soon? Am I an actor in someone else's play—a play unrehearsed?

As far as mourning goes, I don't understand it. I remember I tried very hard to cry when my grandfather died, but totally in vain. At last after praying very hard to be able to mourn, I was able to let out a hard sob without tears at the viewing. I know I was sad, but the ritualistic mourning was just another staged direction. In the play this ritual is symbolized by them just sitting there, and the playful remark by Daddy of whether they could talk just emphasizes the superficiality. Finally, when the symbolic night is over and Mommy and Daddy comment, "Brave Mommy," "Brave Daddy," it was the epitome of this customary performance.

I hope you can see how Shirin's ideology about death and the cultural conventions of dealing with death contributed to her construction of theme as she read *The Sandbox*. I hope you can also see how, although she doesn't acknowledge it as such, her decision or ability to read certain text strategies as figurative or symbolic rather than literal contributed to her harmonious interaction. When Shirin's class discussed their responses to *The Sandbox*, however, Shirin found that her interpretation of the text in terms of a critique of mourning rituals was inconsistent with the interpretation of a number of her classmates. They tended to read the play more in terms of a critique of the treatment of the elderly in our society. Neither reading was "correct," of course, but the difference Shirin felt between the themes some of her classmates constructed prompted her to broaden her literary experience, through some library research, regarding *The Sandbox*. The results of that effort will be demonstrated in Chapter 23.

SHARE AND COMPARE: Even though Shirin is not your classmate, you can interact with her response to *The Sandbox*. Use this space or a page in your notebook to respond to her response. One option is to *reply* to her in terms of your reading of the play. Another is to *analyze* her journal entry in terms of the literary and ideological interactions it reveals: Where or how does she respond on the *literary* level (matching her reading strategies with text strategies of the play)? Where or how does she respond on the ideological level (matching her life experiences or beliefs with the apparent ideological concerns of the text)?

Drama on the Stage: Text Strategies and Ideology

In addition to the text strategies discussed in this chapter and in Chapter 16, there are, of course, others that are merely latent in the printed version of any play. In *Trifles*, for instance, despite the many stage directions the text includes as to, for instance, the two women's movements and reactions and the way in which they deliver some of their lines, the text strategies of action and speech cannot assume their full dimensions on the page. It would take a live or a filmed performance of *Trifles* for these elements to be fully realized. The same is true with the set, lighting, costumes, and perhaps even the music. You can and should practice the reading strategy of visualizing these elements as you read, but it takes a live or filmed performance to make them concrete. When *Trifles*, *The Sandbox*, a "Seinfeld" episode, or any play is produced on stage or on film, the audience sees, in effect, the results of the director's, the set designer's, and the costume designer's visualizations, for they too have at one point been readers of the drama on the page.

Ideology of the Theater

A production of a play also involves ideology in a more complicated way than does a printed version. In the theater, the ideology of the text includes the author and the historical/cultural situation in which the text was written. That, in turn, includes some ideology of theater, perhaps the dominant one of a certain historical moment, perhaps a counter-dominant one, and some ideological position toward subject matter.

One way you might understand this is in terms of what may or may not be depicted in drama. For example in the theater of Athens in the fifth century B.C., physical violence was never depicted onstage, although the results of such violence were directly referred to in front of the audience. In Sophocles' *Oedipus the King*, the title character puts his eyes out in the climactic moment, but this "happens" offstage and only a report of it is given to the audience by a "witness" to the deed. In contrast, violence could be depicted onstage in the theater of seventeenth-century London. In the climactic scene in Shakespeare' *Hamlet*, four people die "before the audience's eyes."

Seeing a play performed, live or on film, involves yet another layer of ideology, at times more obvious than at others but always present. In performance, the ideology of the text includes everything mentioned above plus the ideology of the director and the historical/cultural situation in which the play is produced.

The presence of this last factor is especially evident when older plays are "revived" for performance or when such plays are set in a different time period from that in which they were originally set or in which they were written. Productions of Shakespeare's *Macbeth*, for instance, were more frequent in North America and Britain during the early 1970s, when the Watergate hearings were focusing attention on an apparently power-obsessed U.S. president, Richard Nixon. A common reading of *Macbeth* focuses on the power obsessions of the title character and his wife, Lady Macbeth. At a time when the issue of women in positions of power had emerged as a topic of public concern, a production of *King Lear*—retitled just *Lear*—in New York in 1990 set the play in the southern United States in the 1950s and reversed the gender roles in the script. The plot of *King Lear*, in case the play is not in your storehouse of texts, involves an aging monarch who divides his kingdom among his three daughters; two of them scheme against him with their conspiring husbands, while the third remains loyal but is mistaken as disloyal by Lear. A subplot involves the loyal and disloyal sons of Lear's advisor. The reversal of the gender roles and the resetting of the play in time and locality presumably allowed gender issues in American culture to come to the surface.

The Audience and the Director

With both printed and performed drama, the reader or viewer brings his or her ideology to the reading or viewing. And the ideological interaction that happens between a viewer of live drama and the performed text may be complicated by the viewer's having read or seen the play previously. Some theatergoers object to productions of Shakespeare's plays that change the time setting. Neither their literary experience nor their ideology can accommodate such a change. They may have seen—or visualized—a particular play done in more "traditional" costumes and staging, and their ideology may prefer the traditional stay traditional, which is to say "authentic."

Such theatergoers are unable to recognize, however, that "authentic" stagings of Shakespeare plays are themselves an ideological construction, not what the Elizabethan theater actually put on. The large "Shakespeare industry" that has a financial stake in the plays as a kind of literary tourism to the English Renaissance perpetuates a taste for a version of "authentic" productions of Shakespeare, costumed and set, supposedly, in Shakespeare's own time. That Shakespeare's own theater used boy actors to play female roles, paid very little attention to geographical or historical accuracy in the setting of many of the plays, and did not attempt "realistic" costuming and sets is conveniently ignored by an ideology that prefers its version of the "timeless" plays of "the Bard of Avon." So productions that update the setting of a Shakespearean play or make other interpretive changes in the way certain scenes are staged or played are often controversial. For example, in an otherwise fairly "traditional" production, director Franco Zeffirelli's 1991 film version of *Hamlet* suggested in a number of scenes a sexual attraction if not an incestuous relationship between Hamlet and his mother, Queen Gertrude. This suggestion drew the objection of several reviewers and moviegoers. And the 1990 gender-reversed *Lear* was poorly received by most New York reviewers as "loony," "sophomoric," or "trendy claptrap."[1]

When an older play is produced with these kinds of adaptations in setting or interpretations of the relationships between characters, presumably it is because a director's strong reading of the printed text is behind the production. Because such a reading imbues the production with a certain ideology, the ideology of individual viewers may be engaged in a more obvious way than with more traditional productions. Zeffirelli, perhaps, emphasized in his reading of *Hamlet* something like an incest theme between Hamlet and his mother. If so, Zeffirelli may have been influenced by an earlier and well-known strong reading of *Hamlet*, by the psychoanalytic critic Ernest Jones, that saw Hamlet's relationship with his mother, as well as his alleged inability

---

[1]See reviews by Melanie Kirkpatrick in *The Wall Street Journal*, 6 February 1990; Frank Rich in *The New York Times*, 26 January 1990; and Howard Kissel in *The Daily News*, 29 January 1990, respectively.

or hesitation to exact the revenge sought by the ghost of his father, in Freudian terms.

Freud had defined an "Oedipal stage" in childhood in which the child feels a latent sexual attraction to the parent of the opposite sex and a corresponding rivalry with the parent of the same sex for the other parent's affection. In Jones' reading of *Hamlet*, the prince's behavior could be understood in those terms, the death of his father kindling in Hamlet a subconscious guilt for his equally subconscious attraction to his mother.[2] Both subconscious feelings could show up in outward behavior: the guilt in Hamlet's apparent paralysis in the face of what he "must do"; the attraction in, at least, Act 3, Scene 4, where Hamlet berates his mother for quickly forgetting her dead first husband and taking up with his brother, Claudius. In this scene in Zeffirelli's film, Hamlet (played by Mel Gibson) pushes Gertrude (played by Glenn Close) down on her bed and kisses her full on the mouth, in a manner suggestive of a sexual assault.

In the printed version of *Hamlet*, there are no stage directions indicating such actions on the part of Hamlet, so it is only in a performed version of the play—or in a strong reading of the printed version—that such actions can be carried out or visualized. But in many printed plays, readers may—through such reading strategies as consistency building, narrating, or predicting plot— create themes as they read. Seeing such a play performed (live or on film) is often so powerful compared to reading it on the page that a strong reading of the text is much harder to accomplish. In the theater, you most likely sit in a darkened and hushed environment watching actors conduct themselves in larger-than-life fashion. You can see a film repeatedly (although most Americans do not employ that particular reading strategy) but that's a little harder to do with a stage play (although I know, and so may you, people who have seen *Cats* or *Les Misérables* or *Nunsense* over and over again). Unless you are watching a play on a video at home, you can't stop the action to study it or think about it or write about it. All these factors make reading **against the grain** of a live or filmed production of a play difficult, but because the situation in which you read the printed version of a play is different, perhaps a strong reading is more likely. I certainly encourage you to develop your own strong readings—acknowledging the role of your ideology in creating an interpretation of a text—with the printed versions of plays you read.

Reality and Ideology in the Theater

Suppose, as was suggested earlier as a reading strategy, you read *The Sandbox* figuratively instead of literally. And suppose you came up with a theme for the play. Maybe establishing a theme settles one major problem you may have had with *The Sandbox:* Is it "about" anything at all? Still, you may feel one big question is still unresolved: Why not just write the play "straight" if the author wants to "make a point"? Why trick it out in so many unconventional ways? After all, *Trifles* seems concerned with making a point, and that play seems to

---

[2]See Jones' book, *Hamlet and Oedipus.* 1949. New York: Norton, 1976.

arrange its text strategies in order to do that. The answer to that question may lie partly in the capacity of drama as a genre—and especially live drama—to challenge and disturb audiences.

Drama, perhaps alone among genres, can do this because it *is* dramatic in the ways that we considered real-life events to be at the beginning of this section: It is live; it is performance; it involves people in action, displaying and eliciting emotion; it is *unmediated*, more *immediate* than other literary genres. Both of those italicized words mean, at the root level, "with nothing in between." This is not of course literally true of drama; whether you are at the theater or reading a play in a book, there are signs all around you that say "aesthetic experience." Yet of all the arts, live drama has the greatest ability to cut through the mediating aesthetic structures that usually provide a buffer from emotions in action. No doubt, realistic plays like *Trifles* can do this if audiences perceive a challenge to the ideologies they bring to the theater. Certainly the Western world's first drama critic, Aristotle, saw this potential of any drama when he observed the capacity of Sophoclean tragedy to move audiences to pity and terror.

However, you may still be left with the question that if a play like *The Sandbox* is supposed to challenge an audience's values, to make them think about some issue or issues, not just about the strangeness of the play they are seeing, how can that challenge succeed if an audience is distracted by trying to figure out literally what's going on on stage? This question raises another about the relationship between text and reality and what that relationship suggests in terms of ideology.

In challenging the usual comfortable relationship between performers and audience and between theater and "reality," plays like *The Sandbox* are ideological about reality and about how we construct reality in our minds. By challenging the assumption that drama represents or imitates reality, this subgenre of theater calls reality into question. The audience's experience in the theater where *The Sandbox* is performed is a reality also, and the belief remains that there is some connection, parallel, or symbolic relationship between that reality and the one that people in the audience live through when they are not in the theater. In the case of realistic drama, the relationship is close, obvious, unproblematical. Deciding what a realistic play like *Trifles* means is probably no more difficult than deciding what it is about on a literal level. When the relationship is problematized as it is in a nonrealistic play, we may be tempted to ask questions like "What's the difference, anyway, between theater and life?" Or "What is real life anyway, if it's in some way nonreal as such plays suggest?"

The whole matter of whether you can "figure out" a "meaning" or a "message" in a play relates to larger philosophical questions of whether meaning can be found in anything, life or art. As one of the students I quoted earlier reported, she struggled to find or create a theme as she read *The Sandbox*. However, that student did seem to be on to the connection between the play's anti-realistic text strategies and a larger ideological issue when she wrote that *The Sandbox* "could . . . represent the chaos of the modern world, as there are no clear answers anymore; likewise, there are no clear themes, nothing is clear to anyone, everything is uncertain."

These, I suggest to you, are radical matters indeed of knowing and un-knowing. They go further or deeper than questions such as those raised by re-alistic plays. They may leave an audience questioning, without the final knowledge that comes with the resolution of a conventional dramatic plot, without even the healing catharsis that Aristotle spoke about in the theater of his day. If they do, they reveal yet another way in which drama has the ca-pacity to disturb an audience.

Drama for Exploration

Milcha Sanchez-Scott   b. 1949

The Cuban Swimmer   *1984*

Characters

Margarita Suárez, the swimmer	**Abuela**, her grandmother
Eduardo Suárez, her father, the coach	*Voice of Mel Munson*
Simón Suárez, her brother	*Voice of Mary Beth White*
Aída Suárez, her mother	*Voice of Radio Operator*

Setting
The Pacific Ocean between San Pedro and Catalina Island.

Time
Summer.
Live conga drums can be used to punctuate the action of the play.

Scene 1
Pacific Ocean. Midday. On the horizon, in perspective, a small boat enters upstage left, crosses to upstage right, and exits. Pause. Lower on the horizon, the same boat, in larger perspective, enters upstage right, crosses and exits upstage left. Blackout.

Scene 2
Pacific Ocean. Midday. The swimmer, Margarita Suárez, is swimming. On the boat following behind her are her father, Eduardo Suárez, holding a megaphone, and Simón, her brother, sitting on top of the cabin with his shirt off, punk sunglasses on, binoculars hanging on his chest.

EDUARDO (*Leaning forward, shouting in time to Margarita's swimming.*):   Uno, dos, uno, dos. Y uno, dos . . . keep your shoulders parallel to the water.

SIMÓN: I'm gonna take these glasses off and look straight into the sun.

EDUARDO (*Through megaphone.*):   Muy bien, muy bien . . . but punch those arms in, baby.

SIMÓN (*Looking directly at the sun through binoculars.*):   Come on, come on, zap me. Show me something. (*He looks behind at the shoreline and ahead at the sea.*) Stop! Stop, *Papi!* Stop!

(Aída Suárez and Abuela, the swimmer's mother and grandmother, enter running from the back of the boat.)

AÍDA AND ABUELA: *Qué? Qué es?*

AÍDA: *Es un* shark?

EDUARDO: Eh?

ABUELA: *Que es un* shark *dicen?*

(Eduardo blows whistle. Margarita looks up at the boat.)

SIMÓN: No, *Papi*, no shark, no shark. We've reached the halfway mark.

ABUELA *(Looking into the water.)*:   *A dónde está?*

AÍDA: It's not in the water.

ABUELA: Oh, no? Oh, no?

AÍDA: No! *A poco* do you think they're gonna have signs in the water to say you are halfway to Santa Catalina? No. It's done very scientific. A *ver, hijo,* explain it to your grandma.

SIMÓN: Well, you see, Abuela—*(He points behind.)* There's San Pedro. *(He points ahead.)* And there's Santa Catalina. Looks halfway to me.

(Abuela shakes her head and is looking back and forth, trying to make the decision, when suddenly the sound of a helicopter is heard.)

ABUELA *(Looking up.)*:   Virgencita de la Caridad del Cobre. *Qué es eso?*

(Sound of helicopter gets closer. Margarita looks up.)

MARGARITA: Papi, Papi!

(A small commotion on the boat, with Everybody pointing at the helicopter above. Shadows of the helicopter fall on the boat. Simón looks up at it through binoculars.)

Papi—qué es? What is it?

EDUARDO *(Through megaphone.)*:   Uh . . . uh . . . uh, *un momentico . . . mi hija. . . .* Your *papi's* got everything under control, understand? Uh . . . you just keep stroking. And stay . . . uh . . . close to the boat.

SIMÓN: Wow, *Papi!* We're on TV, man! Holy Christ, we're all over the fucking U.S.A.! It's Mel Munson and Mary Beth White!

AÍDA: *Por Dios!* Simón, don't swear. And put on your shirt.

(Aída fluffs her hair, puts on her sunglasses and waves to the helicopter. Simón leans over the side of the boat and yells to Margarita.)

SIMÓN: Yo, Margo! You're on TV, man.

EDUARDO: Leave your sister alone. Turn on the radio.

MARGARITA: *Papi! Qué está pasando?*

ABUELA: *Que es la televisión dicen?* (She shakes her head.) *Porque como yo no puedo ver nada sin mis espejuelos.*

(Abuela rummages through the boat, looking for her glasses. Voices of Mel Munson and Mary Beth White are heard over the boat's radio.)

MEL'S VOICE: As we take a closer look at the gallant crew of *La Havana* . . . and there . . . yes, there she is . . . the little Cuban swimmer from Long Beach, California, nineteen-year-old Margarita Suárez. The unknown swimmer is our Cinderella entry . . . a bundle of tenacity, battling her way through the choppy, murky waters of the cold Pacific to reach the Island of Romance . . . Santa Catalina . . . where should she be the first to arrive, two thousand dollars and a gold cup will be waiting for her.

AÍDA: Doesn't even cover our expenses.

ABUELA: *Qué dice?*

EDUARDO: Shhhh!

MARY BETH'S VOICE: This is really a family effort, Mel, and—

MEL'S VOICE: Indeed it is. Her trainer, her coach, her mentor, is her father, Eduardo Suárez. Not a swimmer himself, it says here, Mr. Suárez is head usher of the Holy Name Society and the owner-operator of Suárez Treasures of the Sea and Salvage Yard. I guess it's one of those places—

MARY BETH'S VOICE: If I might interject a fact here, Mel, assisting in this swim is Mrs. Suárez, who is a former Miss Cuba.   30

MEL'S VOICE: And a beautiful woman in her own right. Let's try and get a closer look.

(Helicopter sound gets louder. Margarita, frightened, looks up again.)

MARGARITA: *Papi!*

EDUARDO *(Through megaphone.):   Mi hija,* don't get nervous . . . it's the press. I'm handling it.

AÍDA: I see how you're handling it.

EDUARDO *(Through megaphone.):*   Do you hear? Everything is under control. Get back into your rhythm. Keep your elbows high and kick and kick and kick and kick . . .   35

ABUELA *(Finds her glasses and puts them on.):   Ay sí, es la televisión* . . . *(She points to helicopter.) Qué lindo mira* . . . *(She fluffs her hair, gives a big wave.) Aló América! Viva mi Margarita, viva todo los Cubanos en los Estados Unidos!*

AÍDA: *Ay por Dios,* Cecilia, the man didn't come all this way in his helicopter to look at you jumping up and down, making a fool of yourself.

ABUELA: I don't care. I'm proud.

AÍDA: He can't understand you anyway.

ABUELA: *Viva* . . . *(She stops.) Simón, comó se dice viva?*

SIMÓN: Hurray.   40

ABUELA: Hurray for *mi Margarita y* for all the Cubans living *en* the United States, *y un abrazo* . . . *Simón, abrazo* . . .

SIMÓN: A big hug.

ABUELA: *Sí,* a big hug to all my friends in Miami, Long Beach, Union City, except for my son Carlos, who lives in New York in sin! He lives . . . *(She crosses herself.)* in Brooklyn with a Puerto Rican woman in sin! *No decente* . . .

SIMÓN: Decent.   45

ABUELA: Carlos, *no decente.* This family, *decente.*

AÍDA: Cecilia, *por Dios.*

MEL'S VOICE: Look at that enthusiasm. The whole family has turned out to cheer little Margarita on to victory! I hope they won't be too disappointed.

MARY BETH'S VOICE: She seems to be making good time, Mel.

MEL'S VOICE: Yes, it takes all kinds to make a race. And it's a testimonial to the all-encompassing fairness . . . the greatness of this, the Wrigley Invitational Women's Swim to Catalina, where among all the professionals there is still room for the amateurs . . . like these, the simple people we see below us on the ragtag *La Havana,* taking their long-shot chance to victory. *Vaya con Dios!*   50

(Helicopter sound fading as family, including Margarita, watch silently. Static as Simón turns radio off. Eduardo walks to bow of boat, looks out on the horizon.)

EDUARDO *(To himself.):*   Amateurs.

AÍDA: Eduardo, that person insulted us. Did you hear, Eduardo? That he called us a simple people in a ragtag boat? Did you hear . . . ?

ABUELA *(Clenching her fist at departing helicopter.):*   *Mal-Rayo los parta!*

SIMÓN *(Same gesture.):*   Asshole!

(Aída follows Eduardo as he goes to side of boat and stares at Margarita.)

AÍDA: This person comes in his helicopter to insult your wife, your family, your   55
   daughter . . .
MARGARITA *(Pops her head out of the water.)*:   Papi?
AÍDA: Do you hear me, Eduardo? I am not simple.
ABUELA: *Sí.*
AÍDA: I am complicated.
ABUELA: *Sí, demasiada complicada.*
AÍDA: Me and my family are not so simple.   60
SIMÓN: Mom, the guy's an asshole.
ABUELA *(Shaking her fist at helicopter.)*:   Asshole!
AÍDA: If my daughter was simple, she would not be in that water swimming.
MARGARITA: Simple? *Papi* . . . ?   65
AÍDA: *Ahora,* Eduardo, this is what I want you to do. When we get to Santa Catalina,
   I want you to call the TV station and demand an apology.
EDUARDO: *Cállete mujer! Aquí mando yo.* I will decide what is to be done.
MARGARITA: *Papi,* tell me what's going on.
EDUARDO: Do you understand what I am saying to you, Aída?
SIMÓN *(Leaning over side of boat, to Margarita.)*:   Yo Margo! You know that Mel   70
   Munson guy on TV? He called you a simple amateur and said you didn't have a
   chance.
ABUELA *(Leaning directly behind Simón.)*:   *Mi hija, insultó a la familia. Desgraciado!*
AÍDA *(Leaning in behind Abuela.)*:   He called us peasants! And your father is not
   doing anything about it. He just knows how to yell at me.
EDUARDO *(Through megaphone.)*:   Shut up! All of you! Do you want to break her
   concentration? Is that what you are after? Eh?

(Abuela, Aída, and Simón shrink back. Eduardo paces before them.)

Swimming is rhythm and concentration. You win a race *aquí. (Pointing to his
head.)* Now . . . *(To Simón.)* you, take care of the boat, Aída *y Mama* . . . do
something. Anything. Something practical.

(Abuela and Aída get on knees and pray in Spanish.)

Hija, give it everything, eh? . . . *por la familia. Uno . . . dos. . . .* You must win.

*(Simón goes into cabin. The prayers continue as lights change to indicate bright sunlight, later in
the afternoon.)*

Scene 3

*Tableau for a couple of beats. Eduardo on bow with timer in one hand as he counts strokes
per minute. Simón is in the cabin steering, wearing his sunglasses, baseball cap on backward.
Abuela and Aída are at the side of the boat, heads down, hands folded, still muttering prayers
in Spanish.*

AÍDA AND ABUELA *(Crossing themselves.)*:   *En el nombre del Padre, del Hijo y del
   Espíritu Santo amén.*
EDUARDO *(Through megaphone.)*:   You're stroking seventy-two!   75
SIMÓN *(Singing.)*:   Mama's stroking, Mama's stroking seventy-two. . . .
EDUARDO *(Through megaphone.)*:   You comfortable with it?
SIMÓN *(Singing.)*:   Seventy-two, seventy-two, seventy-two for you.
AÍDA *(Looking at the heavens.)*:   *Ay,* Eduardo, *ven acá,* we should be grateful that
   Nuestro Señor gave us such a beautiful day.

ABUELA *(Crosses herself.):*   Sí, gracias a Dios.   80

EDUARDO: She's stroking seventy-two, with no problem *(He throws a kiss to the sky.)* It's a beautiful day to win.

AÍDA: *Qué hermoso!* So clear and bright. Not a cloud in the sky. *Mira! Mira!* Even rainbows on the water . . . a sign from God.

SIMÓN *(Singing.):*   Rainbows on the water . . . you in my arms . . .

ABUELA AND EDUARDO *(Looking the wrong way.):*   Dónde?

AÍDA *(Pointing toward Margarita.):*   There, dancing in front of Margarita, leading   85
her on . . .

EDUARDO: Rainbows on . . . *Ay coño!* It's an oil slick! You . . . you . . . *(To Simón.)* Stop the boat. *(Runs to bow, yelling.)* Margarita! Margarita!

(On the next stroke, Margarita comes up all covered in black oil.)

MARGARITA: *Papi! Papi . . . !*

(Everybody goes to the side and stares at Margarita, who stares back. Eduardo freezes.)

AÍDA: *Apúrate,* Eduardo, move . . . what's wrong with you . . . *no me oíste,* get my daughter out of the water.

EDUARDO *(Softly.):*   We can't touch her. If we touch her, she's disqualified.

AÍDA: But I'm her mother.   90

EDUARDO: Not even by her own mother. Especially by her own mother. . . . You always want the rules to be different for you, you always want to be the exception. *(To Simón.)* And you . . . you didn't see it, eh? You were playing again?

SIMÓN: *Papi,* I was watching . . .

AÍDA *(Interrupting.):*   *Pues,* do something Eduardo. You are the big coach, the monitor.

SIMÓN: Mentor! Mentor!

EDUARDO: How can a person think around you? *(He walks off to bow, puts head   95
in hands.)*

ABUELA *(Looking over side.):*   *Mira como todos los* little birds are dead. *(She crosses herself.)*

AÍDA: Their little wings are glued to their sides.

SIMÓN: Christ, this is like the La Brea tar pits.

AÍDA: They can't move their little wings.

ABUELA: *Esa niña tiene que moverse.*   100

SIMÓN: Yeah, Margo, you gotta move, man.

(Abuela and Simón gesture for Margarita to move. Aída gestures for her to swim.)

ABUELA: *Anda niña, muévete.*

AÍDA: Swim, *hija,* swim or the *aceite* will stick to your wings.

MARGARITA: *Papi?*

ABUELA *(Taking megaphone.):*   Your *papi* say "move it!"   105

(Margarita with difficulty starts moving.)

ABUELA, AÍDA AND SIMÓN: *(Laboriously counting.) Uno, dos . . . uno, dos . . . anda . . . uno, dos.*

EDUARDO *(Running to take megaphone from Abuela.):*   *Uno, dos . . .*

(Simón races into cabin and starts the engine. Abuela, Aída and Eduardo count together.)

SIMÓN *(Looking ahead.):*   *Papi,* it's over there!

EDUARDO: Eh?

SIMÓN *(Pointing ahead and to the right.):*   It's getting clearer over there.   110

EDUARDO *(Through megaphone.):*   Now pay attention to me. Go to the right.

(Simón, Abuela, Aída and Eduardo all lean over side. They point ahead and to the right, except Abuela, who points to the left.)

FAMILY *(Shouting together.):*   *Para yá! Para yá!*

(Lights go down on boat. A special light on Margarita, swimming through the oil, and on Abuela, watching her.)

ABUELA: *Sangre de mi sangre,* you will be another to save us. En Bolondron, where your great-grandmother Luz Suárez was born, they say one day it rained blood. All the people, they run into their houses. They cry, they pray, *pero* your great-grandmother Luz she had *cojones* like a man. She run outside. She look straight at the sky. She shake her fist. And she say to the evil one, "*Mira ... (Beating her chest.) coño, Diablo, aquí estoy si me quieres.*" And she open her mouth, and she drunk the blood.

Blackout.

Scene 4

Lights up on boat. Aída and Eduardo are on deck watching Margarita swim. We hear the gentle, rhythmic lap, lap, lap of the water, then the sound of inhaling and exhaling as Margarita's breathing becomes louder. Then Margarita's heartbeat is heard, and the lapping of the water and the breathing under it. These sounds continue beneath the dialogue to the end of the scene.

AÍDA: *Dios mío.* Look how she moves through the water. . . .

EDUARDO: You see, it's very simple. It is a matter of concentration.

AÍDA: The first time I put her in water she came to life, she grew before my eyes. She moved, she smiled, she loved it more than me. She didn't want my breast any longer. She wanted the water.   115

EDUARDO: And of course, the rhythm. The rhythm takes away the pain and helps the concentration.

(Pause. Aída and Eduardo watch Margarita.)

AÍDA: Is that my child or a seal. . . .

EDUARDO: Ah, a seal, the reason for that is that she's keeping her arms very close to her body. She cups her hands, and then she reaches and digs, reaches and digs.

AÍDA: To think that a daughter of mine . . .

EDUARDO: It's the training, the hours in the water. I used to tie weights around her little wrists and ankles.   120

AÍDA: A spirit, an ocean spirit, must have entered my body when I was carrying her.

EDUARDO *(To Margarita.):*   Your stroke is slowing down.

(Pause. We hear Margarita's heartbeat with the breathing under, faster now.)

AÍDA: Eduardo, that night, the night on the boat . . .

EDUARDO: Ah, the night on the boat again . . . the moon was . . .

AÍDA: The moon was full. We were coming to America. . . . *Qué romantico.*   125

(Heartbeat and breathing continue.)

EDUARDO: We were cold, afraid, with no money, and on top of everything, you were hysterical, yelling at me, tearing at me with your nails. *(Opens his shirt, points to the base of his neck.)* Look, I still bear the scars . . . telling me that I didn't know what I was doing . . . saying that we were going to die. . . .

AÍDA: You took me, you stole me from my home . . . you didn't give me a chance to prepare. You just said we have to go now, now! Now, you said. You didn't let me take anything. I left everything behind. . . . I left everything behind.

EDUARDO: Saying that I wasn't good enough, that your father didn't raise you so that I could drown you in the sea.

AÍDA: You didn't let me say even a good-bye. You took me, you stole me, you tore   130
me from my home.

EDUARDO: I took you so we could be married.

AÍDA: That was in Miami. But that night on the boat, Eduardo. . . . We were not married, that night on the boat.

EDUARDO: *No pasó nada!* Once and for all get it out of your head, it was cold, you hated me, and we were afraid. . . .

AÍDA: *Mentiroso!*

EDUARDO: A man can't do it when he is afraid.   135

AÍDA: Liar! You did it very well.

EDUARDO: I did?

AÍDA: *Sí.* Gentle. You were so gentle and then strong . . . my passion for you so deep. Standing next to you . . . I would ache . . . . . . looking at your hands I would forget to breathe, you were irresistible.

EDUARDO: I was?

AÍDA: You took me into your arms, you touched my face with your fingertips . . .   140
you kissed my eyes . . . *la esquina de la boca y* . . .

EDUARDO: *Sí, sí,* and then . . .

AÍDA: I look at your face on top of mine, and I see the lights of Havana in your eyes. That's when you seduced me.

EDUARDO: Shhh, they're gonna hear you.

(Lights go down. Special on Aída.)

AÍDA: That was the night. A woman doesn't forget those things . . . and later that night was the dream . . . the dream of a big country with fields of fertile land and big, giant things growing. And there by a green, slimy pond I found a giant pea pod and when I opened it, it was full of little, tiny baby frogs.

(Aída crosses herself as she watches Margarita. We hear louder breathing and heartbeat.)

MARGARITA: Santa Teresa. Little Flower of God, pray for me. San Martín de Porres,   145
pray for me. Santa Rosa de Lima, *Virgencita de la Caridad del Cobre,* pray for me. . . . Mother pray for me.

Scene 5

Loud howling of wind is heard, as lights change to indicate unstable weather, fog and mist. Family on deck, braced and huddled against the wind. Simón is at the helm.

AÍDA: *Ay Dios mío, qué viento.*

EDUARDO *(Through megaphone.):*   Don't drift out . . . that wind is pushing you out. *(To Simón.)* You! Slow down. Can't you see your sister is drifting out?

SIMÓN: It's the wind, *Papi.*

AÍDA: Baby, don't go so far. . . .

ABUELA *(To heaven.):*   *Ay Gran Poder de Dios, quita este maldito viento.*   150

SIMÓN: Margo! Margo! Stay close to the boat.

EDUARDO: Dig in. Dig in hard. . . . Reach down from your guts and dig in.

ABUELA *(To heaven.):*   *Ay Virgen de la Caridad del Cobre, por lo más tú quieres a pararla.*

AÍDA *(Putting her hand out, reaching for Margarita.):*   Baby, don't go far.

(Abuela crosses herself. Action freezes. Lights get dimmer, special on Margarita. She keeps swimming, stops, starts again, stops, then, finally exhausted, stops altogether. The boat stops moving.)

EDUARDO: What's going on here? Why are we stopping?

SIMÓN: *Papi,* she's not moving! Yo Margo!   155

(The family all run to the side.)

EDUARDO: *Hija! . . . Hijita!* You're tired, eh?

AÍDA: *Por supuesto* she's tired. I like to see you get in the water, waving your arms and legs from San Pedro to Santa Catalina. A person isn't a machine, a person has to rest.

SIMÓN: Yo, Mama! Cool out, it ain't fucking brain surgery.

EDUARDO *(To Simón.):*   Shut up, you. *(Louder to Margarita.)* I guess your mother's right for once, huh? . . . I guess you had to stop, eh? . . . Give your brother, the idiot . . . a chance to catch up with you.   160

SIMÓN *(Clowning like Mortimer Snerd.):*   Dum dee dum dee dum ooops, ah shucks . . .

EDUARDO: I don't think he's Cuban.

SIMÓN *(Like Ricky Ricardo.):*   *Oye,* Lucy! I'm home! Ba ba lu!

EDUARDO *(Joins in clowning, grabbing Simón in a headlock.):*   What am I gonna do with this idiot, eh? I don't understand this idiot. He's not like us, Margarita. *(Laughing.)* You think if we put him into your bathing suit with a cap on his head . . . *(He laughs hysterically.)* You think anyone would know . . . huh? Do you think anyone would know? *(Laughs.)*

SIMÓN *(Vamping.):*   *Ay, mi amor.* Anybody looking for tits would know.   165

(Eduardo slaps Simón across the face, knocking him down. Aída runs to Simón's aid. Abuela holds Eduardo back.)

MARGARITA: *Mía culpa! Mía culpa!*

ABUELA: *Qué dices hija?*

MARGARITA: *Papi,* it's my fault, it's all my fault. . . . I'm so cold, I can't move. . . . I put my face in the water . . . and I hear them whispering . . . laughing at me. . . .

AÍDA: Who is laughing at you?

MARGARITA: The fish are all biting me . . . they hate me . . . they whisper about me. She can't swim, they say. She can't glide. She has no grace. . . . Yellowtails, bonita, tuna, man-o'-war, snubnose sharks, *los baracudas* . . . they all hate me . . . only the dolphins care . . . and sometimes I hear the whales crying . . . she is lost, she is dead. I'm so numb, I can't feel. *Papi! Papi!* Am I dead?   170

EDUARDO: *Vamos,* baby, punch those arms in. Come on . . . do you hear me?

MARGARITA: *Papi . . . Papi . . .* forgive me. . . .

(All is silent on the boat. Eduardo drops his megaphone, his head bent down in dejection. Abuela, Aída, Simón, all leaning over the side of the boat. Simón slowly walks away.)

AÍDA: *Mi hija, qué tienes?*

SIMÓN: Oh, Christ, don't make her say it. Please don't make her say it.

ABUELA: Say what? *Qué cosa?*

SIMÓN: She wants to quit, can't you see she's had enough?   175

ABUELA: *Mira, para eso. Esta niña* is turning blue.

AÍDA: *Oyeme, mi hija.* Do you want to come out of the water?

MARGARITA: *Papi?*

SIMÓN *(To Eduardo.):*   She won't come out until *you* tell her.

AÍDA: Eduardo . . . answer your daughter.

EDUARDO: *Le dije* to concentrate . . . concentrate on your rhythm. Then the rhythm would carry her . . . ay, it's a beautiful thing, Aída. It's like yoga, like meditation, the mind over matter . . . the mind controlling the body . . . that's how the great things in the world have been done. I wish you . . . I wish my wife could understand.

MARGARITA: *Papi?*

SIMÓN *(To Margarita.):*   Forget him.

AÍDA *(Imploring.):*   Eduardo, *por favor.*   185

EDUARDO *(Walking in circles.):*   Why didn't you let her concentrate? Don't you understand, the concentration, the rhythm is everything. But no, you wouldn't listen. *(Screaming to the ocean.)* Goddamn Cubans, why, God, why do you make us go everywhere with our families? *(He goes to back of boat.)*

AÍDA *(Opening her arms.):*   *Mi hija, ven,* come to *Mami. (Rocking.)* Your *mami* knows.

(Abuela has taken the training bottle, puts it in a net. She and Simón lower it to Margarita.)

SIMÓN: Take this. Drink it. *(As Margarita drinks, Abuela crosses herself.)*

ABUELA: *Sangre de mi sangre.*

(Music comes up softly. Margarita drinks, gives the bottle back, stretches out her arms, as if on a cross. Floats on her back. She begins a graceful backstroke. Lights fade on boat as special lights come up on Margarita. She stops. Slowly turns over and starts to swim, gradually picking up speed. Suddenly as if in pain she stops, tries again, then stops in pain again. She becomes disoriented and falls to the bottom of the sea. Special on Margarita at the bottom of the sea.)

MARGARITA: *Ya no puedo* . . . I can't. . . . A person isn't a machine . . . *es mi culpa* . . .   190
Father forgive me . . . *Papi! Papi!* One, two. *Uno, dos (Pause.) Papi! A dónde estás? (Pause.)* One, two, one, two. *Papi! Ay, Papi!* Where are you . . . ? Don't leave me. . . . Why don't you answer me? *(Pause. She starts to swim, slowly.) Uno, dos, uno, dos.* Dig in, dig in. *(Stops swimming.) Por favor, Papi! (Starts to swim again.)* One, two, one, two. Kick from your hip, kick from your hip. *(Stops swimming. Starts to cry.)* Oh God, please. . . . *(Pause.)* Hail Mary, full of grace . . . dig in, dig in . . . the Lord is with thee. . . . *(She swims to the rhythm of her Hail Mary.)* Hail Mary, full of grace . . . dig in, dig in . . . the Lord is with thee . . . dig in, dig in. . . . Blessed art thou among women. . . . *Mami,* it hurts. You let go of my hand. I'm lost. . . . And blessed is the fruit of thy womb, now and at the hour of our death. Amen. I don't want to die, I don't want to die.

(Margarita is still swimming. Blackout. She is gone.)

Scene 6

Lights up on boat, we hear radio static. There is a heavy mist. On deck we see only black outline of Abuela with shawl over her head. We hear the voices of Eduardo, Aída, and Radio Operator.

EDUARDO'S VOICE: La Havana! Coming from San Pedro. Over.

RADIO OPERATOR'S VOICE: Right, DT6–6, you say you've lost a swimmer.

AÍDA'S VOICE: Our child, our only daughter . . . listen to me. Her name is Margarita Inez Suárez, she is wearing a black one-piece bathing suit cut high in the legs with a white racing stripe down the sides, a white bathing cap with goggles and her whole body is covered with a . . . with a . . .

EDUARDO'S VOICE: With lanolin and paraffin.

AÍDA'S VOICE: *Sí . . . con lanolin and paraffin.*

(More radio static. Special on Simón, on the edge of the boat.)

SIMÓN: Margo! Yo Margo! *(Pause.)* Man don't do this. *(Pause.)* Come on. . . . Come on. . . . *(Pause.)* God, why does everything have to be so hard? *(Pause.)* Stupid. You know you're not supposed to die for this. Stupid. It's his dream and he can't even swim. *(Pause.)* Punch those arms in. Come home. Come home. I'm your little brother. Don't forget what Mama said. You're not supposed to leave me behind. *Vamos,* Margarita, take your little brother, hold his hand tight when you cross the street. He's so little. *(Pause.)* Oh, Christ, give us a sign. . . . I know! I know! Margo, I'll send you a message . . . like mental telepathy. I'll hold my breath, close my eyes, and I'll bring you home. *(He takes a deep breath; a few beats.)* This time I'll beep . . . I'll send out sonar signals like a dolphin. *(He imitates dolphin sounds.)*

(The sound of real dolphins takes over from Simón, then fades into sound of Abuela saying the Hail Mary in Spanish, as full lights come up slowly.)

Scene 7

Eduardo coming out of cabin, sobbing, Aída holding him. Simón anxiously scanning the horizon. Abuela looking calmly ahead.

EDUARDO: *Es mi culpa, sí, es mi culpa. (He hits his chest.)*

AÍDA: *Ya, ya viejo . . .* it was my sin . . . I left my home.

EDUARDO: Forgive me, forgive me. I've lost our daughter, our sister, our granddaughter, *mi carne, mi sangre, mis ilusiones. (To heaven.) Dios mío,* take me . . . take me, I say. . . . Goddammit, take me!

SIMÓN: I'm going in.

AÍDA AND EDUARDO: No!

EDUARDO *(Grabbing and holding Simón, speaking to heaven.):*   God, take me, not my children. They are my dreams, my illusions . . . and not this one, this one is my mystery . . . he has my secret dreams. In him are the parts of me I cannot see.

(Eduardo embraces Simón. Radio static becomes louder.)

AÍDA: I . . . I think I see her.

SIMÓN: No, it's just a seal.

ABUELA *(Looking out with binoculars.):*   *Mi nietacita, dónde estás? (She feels her heart.)* I don't feel the knife in my heart . . . my little fish is not lost.

(Radio crackles with static. As lights dim on boat, Voices of Mel and Mary Beth are heard over the radio.)

MEL'S VOICE: Tragedy has marred the face of the Wrigley Invitational Women's Race to Catalina. The Cuban swimmer, little Margarita Suárez, has reportedly been lost at sea. Coast Guard and divers are looking for her as we speak. Yet in spite of this tragedy the race must go on because . . .

MARY BETH'S VOICE *(Interrupting loudly.):*   Mel!

MEL'S VOICE *(Startled.):*   What!

MARY BETH'S VOICE: Ah . . . excuse me, Mel . . . we have a winner. We've just received word from Catalina that one of the swimmers is just fifty yards from the breakers . . . it's, oh, it's . . . Margarita Suárez!

(Special on family in cabin listening to radio.)

Mel's Voice: What? I thought she died!

(Special on Margarita, taking off bathing cap, trophy in hand, walking on the water.)

Mary Beth's Voice: Ahh ... unless ... unless this is a tragic ... No ... there she is, Mel. Margarita Suárez! The only one in the race wearing a black bathing suit cut high in the legs with a racing stripe down the side.

(Family cheering, embracing.)

Simón *(Screaming.):*   Way to go, Margo!

Mel's Voice: This is indeed a miracle! It's a resurrection! Margarita Suárez, with a flotilla of boats to meet her, is now walking on the waters, through the breakers ... onto the beach, with crowds of people cheering her on. What a jubilation! This is a miracle!

(Sound of crowds cheering. Lights and cheering sounds fade.)
Blackout.

Response Statement Questions

- What success or difficulty do you have with visualizing the setting and action of this play? What is the effect on you of such text strategies as the descriptions of lighting and sound effects?

- What is your response to the text strategy of mixing Spanish and English in the dialogue? Does that mixture contribute to the realism of the play? Does it make it more enjoyable for you to read? Does it present difficulties for you as a reader? Does it annoy you? How are your answers to any of these questions related to the ideology you bring to the reading?

- What do you know about your own family's history as residents of the United States? When did they come to this country? Where did they come from? To what extent does your situation or that of your family influence your response to this play?

- To what extent is this play realistic? To what extent do you read it figuratively? What reading strategies do you adopt in response to the text strategies of realism or symbolism you detect in the play?

- Who is the main character in *The Cuban Swimmer?* Why do you say it is that person? To what extent does the text influence your answer? To what extent does your ideology influence your answer? If you say the main character is Margarita, what about her small speaking part? What does it mean that the "main character" has such a small speaking part?

- *Share and Compare*   In the context of your class or discussion group, what differences exist among readers according to their gender, native language, and family history of immigration to the United States or Canada? How do readers who are situated differently with respect to any of these factors respond differently to *The Cuban Swimmer?*

READING AND WRITING PROJECTS

FOR CREATIVE AND CRITICAL THINKING

Your own writing is important as you try to learn more about yourself as a reader—both what you do cognitively when you read and how culture impinges on the kind of reader you are when you interact with any particular text. In addition to response statements and the formal expository paper that may grow out of them, there are other ways to use writing to learn.

The following suggestions are intended to help you integrate your reading of and writing about literary texts in various ways. These suggestions include exploratory writing, playing with texts and language, creative efforts in various genres, and other writing exercises designed to strengthen your awareness of the cognitive and cultural processes involved in your reading.

▶ Imagine you are producer/director for a small independent film company, trying to make a film that a Hollywood studio will buy for distribution and promotion in movie theaters across the country. How would you "stage" your company's production of any play in this book to both entertain your audience and challenge them on some deeper intellectual or emotional level? At your disposal for interpretation are set design, location, lighting, music, costumes, camera shots, special effects, acting styles, types of actors, even the script itself. What would you do with any of these plays, and why would you do it that way? Trace your staging decisions to your ideology about drama in general, your interpretation of whichever play you choose to produce/direct, and your assumptions about audiences who might come to see this film. Remember, you want to both entertain them and challenge them to respond intellectually and emotionally.

▶ Pick a scene from any play and block it. That is, plan the characters' movements relative to one another within the scene and decide what the characters will do with any props involved in the action in the scene. These blocking plans are detailed *stage directions* that a director would use to arrange physical acting in a scene. Write out your blocking notes, keying them to specific lines of dialogue. Then write an account of why you made these blocking decisions. How are they related to the interpretation you are trying to get across in your stage production?

▶ As a group project, take any character from any play in this book and put him or her "on trial" for actions they took in the play. Characters such as Oedipus, Hamlet, or Hedda Gabler are perhaps obvious choices to be put on trial for their "crimes," but this project need not be limited to tragic protagonists. Your group will need to research applicable state or federal laws to see how a character may be charged.

Then your group can split into a prosecution team and a defense team. Classmates can be subpoenaed as witnesses—either role-playing as other characters in the play from which the "defendant" comes or as readers who have, in effect, witnessed the character's alleged crime. Classmates can also be seated as jurors, and someone can be chosen as judge.

▶ Create a nonverbal text or display that expresses your response to or understanding of any play. This could take the form of a collage, a drawing or painting, a sculpture, a diorama, a dance, or a musical composition; it could be literal or representational, or symbolic or abstract. Perhaps a brief prose note or introduction would be helpful in orienting viewers of your display to its contents. This project also lends itself well to small-group efforts.

18 ◆ CLASSICAL TRAGEDY

Often the kind of serious drama that is performed, especially in an academic context, will be from the canon of dramatic literature. Even outside the class-room, a significant portion of what is available in the way of live theater con-sists of older plays. Productions of plays by nineteenth-century social realist playwrights such as Henrik Ibsen, Anton Chekhov, and George Bernard Shaw are fairly common. Performances of Neoclassical plays by Racine and Molière or of Restoration drama by William Congreve or William Wycherly show up every so often. Even more common, of course, are productions of plays by William Shakespeare from the Elizabethan era. And Classical drama from an-cient Greek writers like Sophocles is still standard theater fare. Plays from these eras and by these authors are often required reading in literature survey courses as well. Most of these texts are full-length plays rather than the one-acts you have read and responded to in the preceding chapters.

Such plays are staged so frequently not just because they are canonical or full-length, but for at least two other good reasons. For one thing, they are powerful texts in their own right. As such they offer potentially rewarding ex-periences for actors because of the strong parts they contain and for directors and production designers because of the rich possibilities for interpretation they offer. People go to the theater to be entertained, of course, but the par-ticular kind of entertainment offered by serious theater involves seeing the technical and emotional efforts of actors, directors, and others played out for the audience. And this experience is enriched when what is being per-formed—or how it is performed—offers the kinds of challenges to audiences' expectations and ideologies that the previous chapters mentioned.

Drama in History: The Ideology of Theater

The other reason such plays continue to be produced is that serious theater in the Western world is very conscious of its own history as a cultural institution. Fiction and poetry also have histories, and many writers in those genres are aware of those histories and how they relate to the work of the individual fic-tion writer or poet. But because drama is first and foremost a *public* genre, with the power to affect many people together and simultaneously, it involves a greater awareness of history and tradition than do the other genres. Outside the classroom, readers of fiction operate pretty much as individuals. Yes, you may read a novel or short story and discuss it with a friend, but if that happens it is usually very informal. Your reading experience is mostly carried out in solitude, even if what you are reading is a best-seller that millions of people have read.

With poems, the case is similar. They too are made available to the public in books or in magazines, two forms that seem to presuppose an individual reader applying his or her own time to the reading. Public poetry readings are held now and then, but these are a relatively new phenomenon in the long history of poetry, and they are not organized and institutionalized in the same manner as drama. Attendance at poetry readings cannot compare to theater attendance. But plays, as we have considered, are generally written to be performed before a public audience, as they always have been since the earliest days of drama; the publication of plays in book form is relatively recent, and the print medium is not the primary one for drama. Performed in a theater, a play is a communal experience, shared by people in the audience with each other and between the audience and the people who produce the play. It has been this way from the earliest days of theater in the Western world.

All this means that the literary repertoire of a play, as it is produced for the theater, includes the history of drama with all its earlier theater practices and conventions, whether the particular play being produced is conventional or not. There is a continuity in a cultural institution that people have been involved in for a long time. Revivals of old plays remind everyone of that at some level: This play was acted before an audience 40 or 400 or 2,400 years ago. Even new plays, even *avant-garde* (experimental, cutting edge) plays, have a connection with all theater; the "normal" or conventional (as practiced for hundreds of years) is the background against which these newer practices stand out. What you are seeing (or reading) and responding to in drama includes in its literary repertoire all that history of drama and performance. One implication of this cultural continuity for reading drama is that your interaction with a play will be more complex and rewarding if your literary experience contains at least some of what's in the text's literary repertoire.

In the area of the ideological interaction between you and a dramatic production, consider that because of the public nature of theater, the ideology of a play is closer to the surface than the ideology of most poems or pieces of fiction. The presentation of dramatic characters and dramatic action through human actors before an audience inevitably carries with it a strong quotient of ideas, values, and attitudes—involving both the text and the audience—so that an ideological interaction is a prominent feature of the theater experience and facilitates self-consciousness. The truth of this is indicated in Aristotle's observation that the spectacle of a good person's fall from good fortune to bad through the combination of circumstances and his own moral character effected a catharsis of pity and fear in ancient Athenian audiences: basically a harmonious ideological interaction, of which the audience was aware.

For these reasons, it may be more useful with drama than with other genres to know more about the ideology and the literary repertoire of any play you see or read. If you are just reading a play on the page, you may need to be aware only of the cultural and historical situation of its composition. When you see a play produced for the stage, its literary repertoire and ideology are complicated by the cultural situation of its performance, which includes the theater space in which the performance is presented. When plays are produced, they may conform to the constraints of the theater that the author originally wrote for, or they may transcend those constraints. A Shakespearean play, for instance, may be produced much as it was in Elizabethan England, with a relatively bare stage, "authentic" costumes, and little in the way of modern technical effects, or it may be "updated" in setting, costumes, and the use of the impressive technical arsenal modern directors have at their command.

In any case, theater is certainly self-conscious. Because of that, this book's aim to help you become a stronger, more self-conscious reader will be served if you increase your awareness of the literary repertoire and the ideology that any play brings to the reading interaction.

Interacting with Canonical Plays

In the chapters that follow, you will be embarking on a project of learning more about the literary repertoire and ideology of drama in general and of certain canonical plays in particular. As you do so, you will be broadening *your* experience. Before you read a play in these chapters, you will read some introductory material that will tell you a few things about the ideology and the literary repertoire of that text. When you read the one-act plays in Chapters 15–17, you didn't have this kind of background. You will also have the chance, in Chapter 23, to read some student writing on one play, Edward Albee's *The Sandbox*. That writing should demonstrate the application of a self-conscious reading to drama. The draft of the formal paper should also serve as a model for the general process of broadening your experience through library research, then rereading a text in light of that wider or deeper knowledge. Later, when you read a play or see one performed, you will know more about the history of Western drama and some of the ideologies that have shaped it over the years. The focus in these chapters will be on some of the conceptions of tragedy and comedy that constitute the literary repertoire and ideology of drama.

To begin with, it's a good idea for you to take an inventory of thoughts on tragedy and comedy. What do you know, think, or believe about tragedy, for instance? First, consider tragedy, both in the more general sense and in the more specific literary sense. Jot down some of your ideas about what tragedy is, in the general sense of the word. What is involved in it? Can you offer an example, real or hypothetical, of a tragic situation? Are there different levels or degrees of tragedy? Can different situations or events be tragic in greater or lesser degrees? Make your own lists, then compare yours to the ones I offer below.

Qualities of Tragedy

1.

2.

3.

4.

5.

Examples of Tragedy

1.

2.

3.

Here are some of my ideas about tragedy in general—not the "official" or "authoritative" definitions, but from my ideology.

Qualities of Tragedy

1. A reversal of fortune, from good to bad.

2. Often someone dies, undeservedly.

3. There can be lesser degrees of tragedy, such as a loss of happiness or the failure to achieve something desired that was within reach.

4. You can relate, more or less, to the feelings of people affected, or your own feelings are affected.

5. People are left unhappy, at least for a while.

Examples of Tragedy

1. An airplane crash, with loss of life.

2. A debilitating or fatal illness striking someone.

3. War.

Now, if you think about tragedy in an aesthetic or literary sense, how are your ideas modified, if at all? Is it tragic if any character suffers or is subjected to any of the qualities of tragedy that you listed? Does the character have to be a "good" or "noble" person? Does the situation have to be inevitable, or does tragedy derive from the unhappy events being avoidable? Does the character have to die, or is some other kind of physical or emotional suffering sufficient? How much self-awareness must the character have, and does he or she experience anything like moral growth in the process of physical or emotional destruction? Take a few minutes now to list some of your ideas about tragedy in the more literary, especially *dramatic* sense, as well as any examples of tragic characters you can think of or plays that you know or believe to be tragedies.

Qualities of Dramatic Tragedy

1.

2.

3.

4.

5.

Examples

1.

2.

3.

I won't supply my own list here. I don't want anyone thinking she or he is "wrong" in what he or she listed. The purpose of this exercise at this point is just to inventory your experience before you undertake to broaden it. After you work your way through the following chapters, you can come back to these lists and compare them with your broadened experience. You can also compare your ideology on this question with those of different dramatists and theorists through the ages of Western literary history.

Classical Greek Drama

The Irish playwright George Bernard Shaw once said that "The drama was born of old from the union of two desires: the desire to have a dance and the desire to hear a story." Shaw was referring to the origins of drama in the Western world in Greece in the sixth century B.C. During religious festivals in the spring celebrating the god Dionysus, who was associated with fertility and creativity, a goat was sacrificed as part of the ritual. The modern word "tragedy" has its origins in the Greek word *tragoidia*, meaning "goat-song." In these festivals, priests of Dionysus dressed as goats danced and recited chants, while one priest—who took the first "acting" part—spoke some lines as interludes in the chorus's dance.

In the fifth century B.C., the Greek playwright Aeschylus added a second "actor," reduced the size of the chorus and made it more a part of the dramatic action, developed costuming in the form of larger-than-life masks and *buskins* or special high-soled boots, and wrote the first memorable tragedies (*Seven Against Thebes*, produced in 467 B.C.; *Prometheus Bound*, 465 B.C.; and the *Oresteia* trilogy, 458 B.C.). Aeschylus' successors included Euripides and Sophocles, who added a third major actor to the mix and created some uniquely individual heroic parts for tragedies such as *Antigone* (first performed in 441 B.C.) and *Oedipus the King* (430 B.C.).

Drama held a different, more important, cultural place in ancient Athens than it does today. Because it took place in the context of religious festivals, it was both performed and experienced as part of a larger sense of community, neither a private commercial enterprise as it often is today nor attended by a relatively small and select audience.

The theater spaces in which the drama was performed and watched indicate something of its cultural status. (An example of an early Greek theater is illustrated below.)

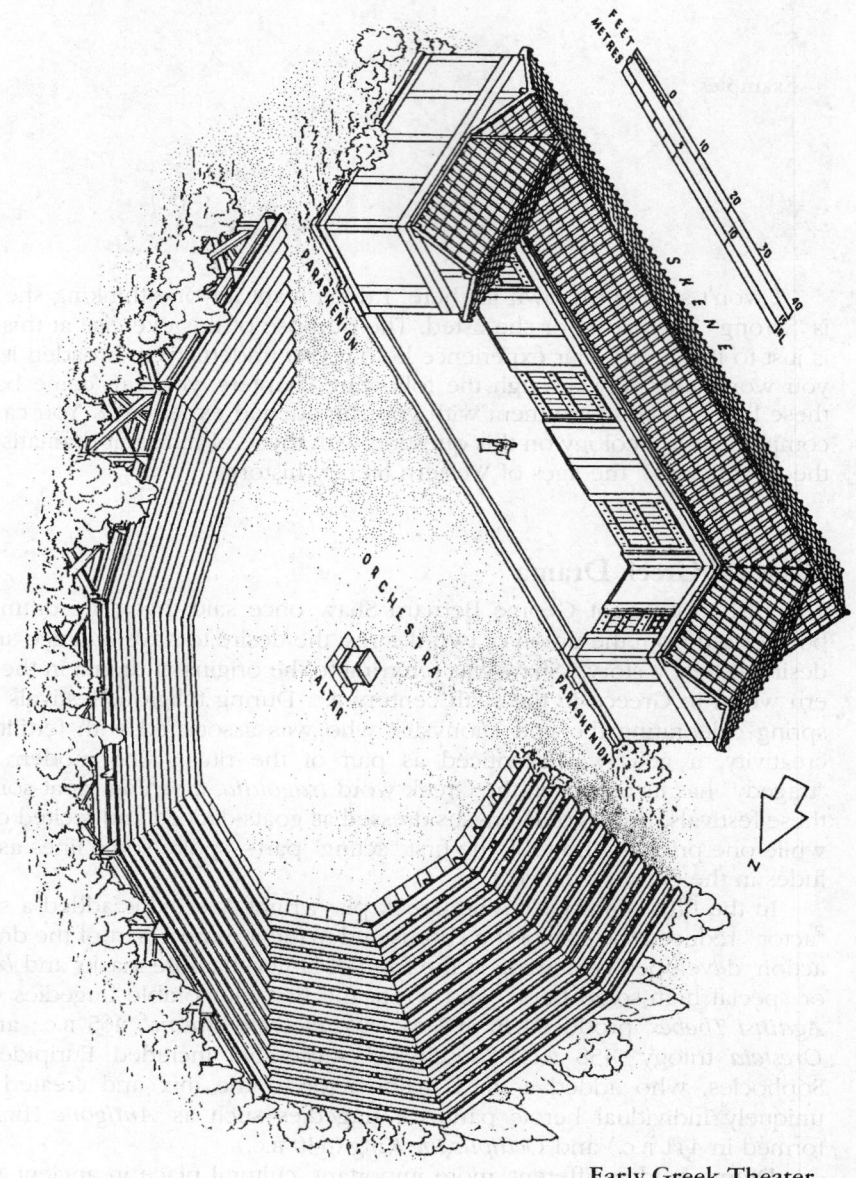

Early Greek Theater

The stories that were dramatized in these ancient plays were based on even older legends; the audience already knew the outcome of the action, so suspense as we know it was not as important for that audience. The plays were more nearly dramatic reminders of aspects of the dominant ideology of the culture, somewhat in the way that religious services or public holiday pageants are today.

Yet some of the Classical plays remain in the performance repertoire of theater companies today, even though those plays may not have the same cultural function they once did. These plays have a continued appeal for at least three reasons: They are assumed to have a "universal" appeal; they present people struggling with destiny and invoke large philosophical issues; and some of the text strategies of those ancient plays established the basis for dramatic practice. For instance, the five-part structure of ancient Greek tragedies was the basis for the conventional division of full-length plays into acts. Having significant action either precede the conflict situation in the play or occur offstage and be reported by a minor character is another practice that has become conventional because it tends to focus attention on the psychological action of the main characters—what goes on in their minds and how they react to it.

CONNECT: You have seen antecedent action in a comparatively contemporary play—Susan Glaspell's *Trifles*—in Chapters 15–16. That play is both conventional and economical in having the antecedent action— the discovery of John Wright's body and the information about Minnie Wright's behavior—be reported by a minor character, Mr. Hale, as the play opens. This move is economical on Glaspell's part because it allows her to focus attention immediately where she wants it: on the reactions to this information by the male and female characters.

Also, our word "theater" comes from an ancient Greek word *theatron,* which means "seeing place." Perhaps this word serves to emphasize the visual and performative nature of drama from earliest times; reading drama from a page is a relatively new phenomenon.

The Theater of Dionysus

If you visit Athens today, at the foot of the Acropolis, atop which stand the ruins of the Parthenon and other religious buildings from ancient times, you can see on the original site a reconstruction of the Theater of Dionysus. On the following page is a sketch of the ground plan of the original theater.

Here, more than 2,000 years ago, up to 20,000 people sitting on raised bleachers could view a play by Sophocles or Euripides. In part, the buskins and masks that the actors wore were adapted so that people seated far from the stage could recognize the characters. The stage itself—or the *proskenion*— was a narrow raised area facing the audience. Directly behind it was a small

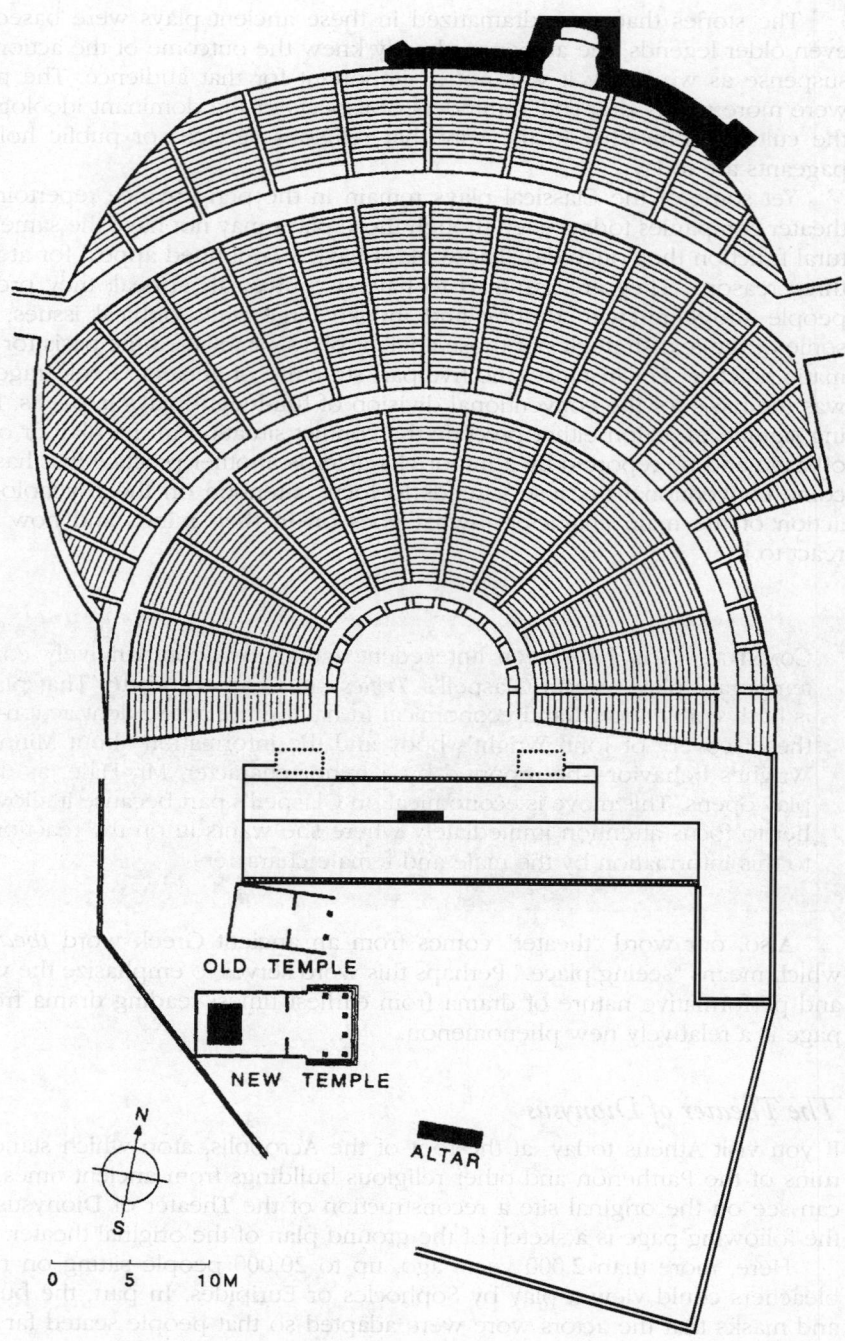

OLD TEMPLE

NEW TEMPLE

ALTAR

N

S

0   5   10M

Original Ground Plan for Theater of Dionysus

building called the *skene* where props were stored and where actors could change costumes. These areas of the ancient Athenian theater are the sources of the modern concept of the *proscenium* stage and the word *scene*.

Between the *proskenion* and the audience was a low circular area, called the orchestra, with an altar to Dionysus in its center. The orchestra was where the *chorus* chanted and danced. Its position was significant because the chorus often represented the public in classical plays, that fact being emphasized by the physical positioning of the chorus in the theater. One of the functions of the chorus was to comment on the action from the public point of view, sometimes in unison, sometimes in the words of a single speaker, the *choragos* or leader. Another function of the chorus was to mark divisions in the action, in the days before a curtain could be lowered or lighting changed to indicate this, by their chants and their dancing movements from one side of the orchestra to the other.

Aisles leading into and out of the orchestra were called *parados*, and this name was given to the first of the choric songs in ancient Greek plays. The choric songs in general were called *stasima* (singular: *stasimon*), and the portions of the drama consisting of dialogue between characters were called *episodia* (the source of the modern word *episode*). A *prologue* handled exposition before the first stasimon, and a play closed with an *exodus* resolving the action and allowing for the formal exit of characters and chorus.

All actors and chorus members, but not all characters, in the ancient Greek theater were men. If you could travel back in time and attend a performance of a tragedy in ancient Greece, you would probably find the acting style strange, not what you are used to today. There was little attempt to make the characters seem like real people that the audience could relate to on a personal level. The actors tended to stay in one place and orate or declaim their lines with great solemnity, rather than have conversations with one another, except when they engaged in *stichtomythy*—a rapid exchange of one-line taunts or insults between two characters. This acting style and the actors' wearing of larger-than-life masks and elevated shoes tended to distance the characters from the audience, to present them as mythic types rather than as individual humans with idiosyncratic personalities. A modern reviewer of a film version of an "authentic" production of *Oedipus* wrote that "watching a movie for an hour and a half in which the characters wear masks continuously can get quite tiresome, and the effect is more like that of an exercise or a ritual than a personal tragedy," but surely Sophocles' contemporary audience would not have had that problem because they would not be expecting a "personal tragedy."[*]

The Ideology of Classical Tragedy

Perhaps this discussion of some of the physical features and performance practices of the ancient Greek theater suggests a connection to the dominant ideology of the culture. Such a connection always exists between ideology

---

[*]Hartung, Philip T. "The Screen: Is It True What They Say About Oedipus?" *The Commonweal* 8 (Feb, 1957): 488–89.

and cultural forms, but it is usually easier to see in cultures that are different from your own in time or place. With a little practice at cultural analysis, you can begin to see not just individual plays but the whole institution of theater in any time or place as a text, with strategies that reveal the ideological presuppositions of whatever culture produces it. Keeping that idea in mind should help you see connections between the literary repertoire and the ideology of Classical tragedy.

Chapter 15 considered a connection between text strategies of drama and the cognitive processes of readers or audience members in terms of knowing and unknowing: The text allows the audience to know some things but not know others, at least not all at once; or it keeps a character in greater relative ignorance than the audience with respect to certain information. In Classical Greek tragedy, matters of knowing and unknowing constitute a site at which the literary repertoire and the ideology of the text converge. For instance, the kind of dramatic suspense we are accustomed to today was not a text strategy of ancient Greek tragedy. The plot was not structured to lead the audience to some new knowledge about the situation or the characters; the audience already had this knowledge because the characters and plots came from legendary material that people living in a homogeneous culture already had in their ideology. (Ideology, not literary experience, because as *myths* these stories expressed deeply held beliefs; they were much more than entertainment.) Instead, the plays served to reinforce ideological beliefs concerning the relationship of human beings to the cosmos.

Put simply, these beliefs stressed the overwhelming power of the gods and the role of destiny in the lives of human beings. The source of dramatic conflict was the clash between strong-willed people and the even stronger supernatural forces. In terms of plot, there was a thoroughgoing sense of inevitability, with a resolution that reminded the audience of the relative unimportance of human desires and moral qualities in a universe governed by fate and divine decree. Ideology also accounts for the reliance on *oracles*, both shrines and priests through which or whom the divine will might be made known to humans, as plot devices in these plays.

CONNECT: In the twentieth-century play *Trifles*, influenced by a different ideology, the plot involves discovery of what was *not* known before.

Furthermore, the Athenian audience knew more than the **protagonist**, or central character, did about his situation and how it would come out. Another way of looking at the plot structure of a Greek tragedy is to see it as the protagonist's psychological movement from unknowing to knowing; this movement involves a turning point or reversal leading to moral insight in a moment of self-knowledge. At the same time, the protagonist moves from knowing less than the audience to knowing the same as the audience—or perhaps even more if his moral insight illuminates his situation more clearly to himself than it does to the audience. He also moves from a superior to an inferior social position, and presumably from having the audience's admiration to eliciting its pity.

This complex pattern also involves dramatic irony to the highest degree. Irony turns upon a difference in levels of awareness or knowledge. If the audience knows, for instance, that the protagonist's moral character and actions are leading him to his own destruction and if the protagonist himself is blind to this fact, the situation is ironic. If the audience knows that the qualities that helped make the protagonist the social and moral superior he is are now also working to bring about his downfall, that too is ironic. And the irony may reach a crescendo when and if the protagonist recognizes it for himself—at the moment when he sees clearly for the first time what the audience has known or suspected all along.

Aristotle observed that this pattern of movement from success to destruction, the sense that it is inevitable given the interaction of the protagonist's moral character with the divine will, and its peaking at the moment of the protagonist's recognition and reversal had a specific effect on the audience. This pattern, he said, aroused the emotions of pity and fear in the audience and allowed for a *catharsis*, or purging, of those emotions. For Aristotle as for his culture, this catharsis was spiritually and psychological healthy. Numerous other observers have remarked that the double movement the protagonist undergoes—simultaneously down in terms of life circumstances and up in terms of moral insight—lends nobility to the tragic hero, making him, at least in the moment of his self-awareness, morally great. But of course concepts such as nobility and moral greatness are ideological and may be more highly valued in one culture than another or by one person than another. As values within the ideology of a reader or even a large population of readers, such concepts may be part of what that reader or those readers bring to the interaction with a text. In the case of Classical tragedies, which tend to rank high in the canon of Western literature, it may be especially difficult to acknowledge the reader's contributions to that interaction, but they are part of it nonetheless.

Reading and Responding: A Classical Tragedy

I trust the foregoing discussion has broadened your **literary experience** somewhat with respect to the theater of ancient Greece, the kind of tragedy that was written for it, and some of the defining qualities of tragedy as they have been understood both in the fifth century B.C. and later. Now might be a good time to return to the lists you made on pages 908–909 and see if you would change anything you wrote there in any way.

Whether you made any changes or not, as you begin to read the play that follows, try to be aware of your literary experience and your ideology concerning tragedy. The response statement questions that follow the text may help focus these thoughts. Also, try to use the reading strategies for a printed play listed on page 836.

Sophocles

Oedipus the King[1]

Characters

Oedipus, king of Thebes
A Priest of Zeus
Creon, brother of Jocasta
A chorus of Theban citizens and their leader
Tiresias, a blind prophet
Jocasta, the queen, wife of Oedipus
A Messenger from Corinth
A Shepherd
A Messenger from inside the palace
Antigone, Ismene, daughters of Oedipus and Jocasta
Guards and attendants
Priests of Thebes

[*Time and Scene: The royal house of Thebes. Double doors dominate the façade; a stone altar stands at the center of the stage.*

Many years have passed since Oedipus solved the riddle of the Sphinx and ascended the throne of Thebes, and now a plague has struck the city. A procession of priests enters; suppliants, broken and despondent, they carry branches wound in wool and lay them on the altar.

The doors open. Guards assemble. Oedipus comes forward, majestic but for a telltale limp, and slowly views the condition of his people.]

OEDIPUS: Oh my children, the new blood of ancient Thebes,
    why are you here? Huddling at my altar,
    praying before me, your branches wound in wool.[2]
    Our city reeks with the smoke of burning incense,
    rings with cries for the Healer[3] and wailing for the dead.   5
    I thought it wrong, my children, to hear the truth
    from others, messengers. Here I am myself—
    you all know me, the world knows my fame:
    I am Oedipus.
        [*Helping a Priest to his feet.*]
                    Speak up, old man. Your years,
    your dignity—you should speak for the others.   10
    Why here and kneeling, what preys upon you so?
    Some sudden fear? some strong desire?
    You can trust me. I am ready to help,
    I'll do anything. I would be blind to misery
    not to pity my people kneeling at my feet.
PRIEST: Oh Oedipus, king of the land, our greatest power!   15
    You see us before you now, men of all ages
    clinging to your altars. Here are boys,

---

[1] Translated by Robert Fagles.
[2] The insignia of suppliants, laid on the altar and left there until the suppliant's request was granted. At the end of the scene, when Oedipus promises action, he will tell them to take the branches away.
[3] A title of Apollo.

still too weak to fly from the nest,
and here the old, bowed down with the years,
the holy ones—a priest of Zeus myself—and here   20
the picked, unmarried men, the young hope of Thebes.
And all the rest, your great family gathers now,
branches wreathed, massing in the squares,
kneeling before the two temples of queen Athena   25
or the river-shrine where the embers glow and die
and Apollo sees the future in the ashes.⁴
                                    Our city—
look around you, see with your own eyes—
our ship pitches wildly, cannot lift her head
from the depths, the red waves of death . . .   30
Thebes is dying. A blight on the fresh crops
and the rich pastures, cattle sicken and die,
and the women die in labor, children stillborn,
and the plague, the fiery god of fever hurls down
on the city, his lightning slashing through us—   35
raging plague in all its vengeance, devastating
the house of Cadmus!⁵ And black Death luxuriates
in the raw, wailing miseries of Thebes.
Now we pray to you. You cannot equal the gods,
your children know that, bending at your altar.   40
But we do rate you first of men,
both in the common crises of our lives
and face-to-face encounters with the gods.
You freed us from the Sphinx,⁶ you came to Thebes
and cut us loose from the bloody tribute⁷ we had paid   45
that harsh, brutal singer. We taught you nothing,
no skill, no extra knowledge, still you triumphed.
A god was with you, so they say, and we believe it—
you lifted up our lives.
                            So now again,
Oedipus, king, we bend to you, your power—   50
we implore you, all of us on our knees:
find us strength, rescue! Perhaps you've heard
the voice of a god or something from other men,
Oedipus . . . what do you know?
The man of experience—you see it every day—   55
his plans will work in a crisis, his first of all.

Act now—we beg you, best of men, raise up our city!
Act, defend yourself, your former glory!

---

⁴ At a temple of Apollo in Thebes the priests foretold the future according to patterns they saw in the ashes of the burned flesh of sacrificial victims.
⁵ Mythical founder of Thebes and its first king.
⁶ The winged female monster that terrorized the city of Thebes until her riddle was finally answered by Oedipus. The riddle was: "What is it that walks on four feet and two feet and three feet and has only one voice; when it walks on most feet, it is weakest?" Oedipus's answer was Man. (He has four feet as a child crawling on "all fours," and three feet in old age when he walks with the aid of a stick.)
⁷ Many young men of Thebes had tried to answer the riddle, failed, and been killed.

Your country calls you savior now
for your zeal, your action years ago.   60
Never let us remember of your reign:
you helped us stand, only to fall once more.
Oh raise up our city, set us on our feet.
The omens were good that day you brought us joy—
be the same man today!   65
Rule our land, you know you have the power,
but rule a land of the living, not a wasteland.
Ship and towered city are nothing, stripped of men
alive within it, living all as one.

OEDIPUS: My children,
I pity you. I see—how could I fail to see   70
what longings bring you here? Well I know
you are sick to death, all of you,
but sick as you are, not one is sick as I.
Your pain strikes each of you alone, each
in the confines of himself, no other. But my spirit   75
grieves for the city, for myself and all of you.
I wasn't asleep, dreaming. You haven't wakened me—
I've wept through the nights, you must know that,
groping, laboring over many paths of thought.
After a painful search I found one cure: 80
I acted at once. I sent Creon,
my wife's own brother, to Delphi[8]—
Apollo the Prophet's oracle—to learn
what I might do or say to save our city.

Today's the day. When I count the days gone by   85
it torments me ... what is he doing?
Strange, he's late, he's gone too long.
But once he returns, then, then I'll be a traitor
if I do not do all the god makes clear.

PRIEST: Timely words. The men over there
are signaling—Creon's just arriving.   90

OEDIPUS [*Sighting Creon, then turning to the altar.*]:
                                Lord Apollo,
let him come with a lucky word of rescue,
shining like his eyes!

PRIEST: Welcome news, I think—he's crowned, look,
and the laurel wreath is bright with berries.[9]   95

OEDIPUS: We'll soon see. He's close enough to hear—
      [*Enter Creon from the side; his face is shaded with a wreath.*]
Creon, prince, my kinsman, what do you bring us?
What message from the god?

CREON: Good news.
I tell you even the hardest things to bear,
if they should turn out well, all would be well.   100

---

[8] The oracular shrine of Apollo at Delphi, below Mount Parnassus in central Greece.
[9] Creon is wearing a crown of laurel as a sign that he brings good news.

OEDIPUS: Of course, but what were the god's *words?* There's no hope
and nothing to fear in what you've said so far.
CREON: If you want my report in the presence of these ...
    [Pointing to the priests while drawing Oedipus toward the palace.]
I'm ready now, or we might go inside.
OEDIPUS: Speak out,
speak to us all. I grieve for these, my people,   105
far more than I fear for my own life.
CREON: Very well,
I will tell you what I heard from the god.
Apollo commands us—he was quite clear—
"Drive the corruption from the land,
don't harbor it any longer, past all cure,   110
don't nurse it in your soil—root it out!"
OEDIPUS: How can we cleanse ourselves—what rites?
What's the source of the trouble?
CREON: Banish the man, or pay back blood with blood.
Murder sets the plague-storm on the city.
OEDIPUS: Whose murder?
Whose fate does Apollo bring to light?   115
CREON: Our leader,
my lord, was once a man named Laius,
before you came and put us straight on course.
OEDIPUS: I know—
or so I've heard. I never saw the man myself.
CREON: Well, he was killed, and Apollo commands us now—
he could not be more clear,   120
"Pay the killers back—whoever is responsible."
OEDIPUS: Where on earth are they? Where to find it now,
the trail of the ancient guilt so hard to trace?
CREON: "Here in Thebes," he said.
Whatever is sought for can be caught, you know,   125
whatever is neglected slips away.
OEDIPUS: But where,
in the palace, the fields or foreign soil,
where did Laius meet his bloody death?
CREON: He went to consult an oracle, Apollo said,
and he set out and never came home again.   130
OEDIPUS: No messenger, no fellow-traveler saw what happened?
Someone to cross-examine?
CREON: No,
they were all killed but one. He escaped,
terrified, he could tell us nothing clearly,
nothing of what he saw—just one thing.   135
OEDIPUS: What's that?
one thing could hold the key to it all,
a small beginning give us grounds for hope.
CREON: He said thieves attacked them—a whole band,
not single-handed, cut King Laius down.
OEDIPUS: A thief, so daring,
so wild, he'd kill a king? Impossible, unless conspirators paid   140
him off in Thebes.

CREON: We suspected as much. But with Laius dead
no leader appeared to help us in our troubles.

OEDIPUS: Trouble? Your *king* was murdered—royal blood!   145
What stopped you from tracking down the killer
then and there?

CREON: The singing, riddling Sphinx.
She ... persuaded us to let the mystery go
and concentrate on what lay at our feet.

OEDIPUS: No,
I'll start again—I'll bring it all to light myself!   150
Apollo is right, and so are you, Creon,
to turn our attention back to the murdered man.
Now you have *me* to fight for you, you'll see:
I am the land's avenger by all rights,
and Apollo's champion too.   155
But not to assist some distant kinsman, no,
for my own sake I'll rid us of this corruption.
Whoever killed the king may decide to kill me too,
with the same violent hand—by avenging Laius
I defend myself.

        [*To the priests.*]
                        Quickly, my children.
Up from the steps, take up your branches now.   160
        [*To the guards.*]
One of you summon the city[10] here before us,
tell them I'll do everything. God help us,
we will see our triumph—or our fall.
        [*Oedipus and Creon enter the palace, followed by the guards.*]

PRIEST: Rise, my sons. The kindness we came for   165
Oedipus volunteers himself.
Apollo has sent his word, his oracle—
Come down, Apollo, save us, stop the plague.
        [*The priests rise, remove their branches and exit to the side. Enter a Chorus, the citizens of Thebes, who have not heard the news that Creon brings. They march around the altar, chanting.*]

CHROUS: Zeus!
Great welcome voice of Zeus,[11] what do you bring?
What word from the gold vaults of Delphi   170
comes to brilliant Thebes? Racked with terror—
        terror shakes my heart
and I cry your wild cries, Apollo, Healer of Delos[12]
I worship you in dread ... what now, what is your price?
some new sacrifice? some ancient rite from the past   175
come round again each spring?—
        what will you bring to birth?
Tell me, child of golden Hope
warm voice that never dies!

---

[10] Represented by the Chorus which comes on to the circular dancing floor immediately after this scene.

[11] Apollo was his son, and spoke for him.

[12] Apollo was born on the sacred island of Delos.

You are the first I call, daughter of Zeus
deathless Athena—I call your sister Artemis,[13]
heart of the market place enthroned in glory,
      guardian of our earth—
I call Apollo, Archer astride the thunderheads of heaven—
O triple shield against death, shine before me now!
If ever, once in the past, you stopped some ruin
launched against our walls
      you hurled the flame of pain
far, far from Thebes—you gods
      come now, come down once more!

                     No, no
the miseries numberless, grief on grief, no end—
too much to bear, we are all dying
O my people ...
    Thebes like a great army dying
and there is no sword of thought to save us, no
and the fruits of our famous earth, they will not ripen
no and the women cannot scream their pangs to birth—
screams for the Healer, children dead in the womb
      and life on life goes down
        you can watch them go
like seabirds winging west, outracing the day's fire
down the horizon, irresistibly
      streaking on to the shores of Evening
                        Death
so many deaths, numberless deaths on deaths, no end—
Thebes is dying, look, her children
stripped of pity ...
    generations strewn on the ground
unburied, unwept, the dead spreading death
and the young wives and gray-haired mothers with them
cling to the altars, trailing in from all over the city—
Thebes, city of death, one long cortege
      and the suffering rises
        wails for mercy rise
and the wild hymn for the Healer blazes out
clashing with our sobs our cries of mourning—
    O golden daughter of god,[14] send rescue
radiant as the kindness in your eyes!

Drive him back!—the fever, the god of death
    that raging god of war[15]
not armored in bronze, not shielded now, he burns me,
battle cries in the onslaught burning on—

180

185

190

195

200

205

210

215

220

---

[13] Sister of Apollo: a goddess associated with hunting, and also a protector of women in childbirth.
[14] Athena, daughter of Zeus.
[15] The plague is identified with Ares, the war god, though he comes now without armor and shield. Ares is not elsewhere connected with plague; this passage may be an allusion to the ea years of the Peloponnesian War, when Spartan troops threatened the city from outside and the plague raged inside the walls.

O rout him from our borders!
Sail him, blast him out to the Sea-queen's chamber
          the black Atlantic gulfs
    or the northern harbor, death to all   225
where the Thracian surf[16] comes crashing.
Now what the night spares he comes by day and kills—
the god of death.

                    O lord of the stormcloud,
you who twirl the lightning, Zeus, Father,
thunder Death to nothing!   230

Apollo, lord of the light, I beg you—
    whip your longbow's golden cord
showering arrows on our enemies—shafts of power
champions strong before us rushing on!

Artemis, Huntress,   235
torches flaring over the eastern ridges—
ride Death down in pain!

God of the headdress gleaming gold, I cry to you—
your name and ours are one, Dionysus—
    come with your face aflame with wine   240
        your raving women's[17] cries
your army on the march! Come with the lightning
come with torches blazing, eyes ablaze with glory!
Burn that god of death that all gods hate!

[*Oedipus enters from the palace to address the Chorus, as if addressing the
entire city of Thebes.*]

OEDIPUS: You pray to the gods? Let me grant your prayers.   245
Come, listen to me—do what the plague demands:
you'll find relief and lift your head from the depths.
I will speak out now as a stranger to the story,
a stranger to the crime. If I'd been present then,
there would have been no mystery, no long hunt   250
without a clue in hand. So now, counted
a native Theban years after the murder,
to all of Thebes I make this proclamation:
if any one of you knows who murdered Laius,
the son of Labdacus, I order him to reveal   255
the whole truth to me. Nothing to fear,
even if he must denounce himself,
let him speak up
and so escape the brunt of the charge—
he will suffer no unbearable punishment,   260
nothing worse than exile, totally unharmed.

[*Oedipus pauses, waiting for a reply.*]
                                              Next,
if anyone knows the murderer is a stranger,

---

16 Ares was thought to be at home among the savages of Thrace, to the northeast of Greece
proper.
17 The Bacchanals, nymphs or human female votaries of the god Dionysus (Bacchus) who celebrated him with wild dancing rites.

a man from alien soil, come, speak up.
I will give him a handsome reward, and lay up
gratitude in my heart for him besides.
    [*Silence again, no reply.*]   265
But if you keep silent, if anyone panicking,
trying to shield himself or friend or kin,
rejects my offer, then hear what I will do.
I order you, every citizen of the state
where I hold throne and power: banish this man—   270
whoever he may be—never shelter him, never
speak a word to him, never make him partner
to your prayers, your victims burned to the gods.
Never let the holy water touch his hands
Drive him out, each of you, from every home.   275
He is the plague, the heart of our corruption,
as Apollo's oracle has just revealed to me.
So I honor my obligations:
I fight for the god and for the murdered man.

Now my curse on the murderer. Whoever he is,   280
a lone man unknown in his crime
or one among many, let that man drag out
his life in agony, step by painful step—
I curse myself as well . . . if by any chance
he proves to be an intimate of our house,   285
here at my hearth, with my full knowledge,
may the curse I just called down on him strike me!

These are your orders: perform them to the last.
I command you, for my sake, for Apollo's, for this country
blasted root and branch by the angry heavens.   290
Even if god had never urged you on to act,
how could you leave the crime uncleansed so long?
A man so noble—your king, brought down in blood—
you should have searched. But I am the king now,
I hold the throne that he held then, possess his bed   295
and a wife who shares our seed . . . why, our seed
might be the same, children born of the same mother
might have created blood-bonds between us
if his hope of offspring hadn't met disaster—
but fate swooped at his head and cut him short.   300
So I will fight for him as if he were my father,
stop at nothing, search the world
to lay my hands on the man who shed his blood,
the son of Labdacus descended of Polydorus,
Cadmus of old and Agenor, founder of the line: 305
their power and mine are one.
                Oh dear gods,
my curse on those who disobey these orders!
Let no crops grow out of the earth for them—
shrivel their women, kill their sons,
burn them to nothing in this plague   310
that hits us now, or something even worse.

But you, loyal men of Thebes who approve my actions,
may our champion, Justice, may all the gods
be with us, fight beside us to the end!

LEADER: In the grip of your curse, my king, I swear   315
I'm not the murderer, I cannot point him out.
As for the search, Apollo pressed it on us—
he should name the killer.

OEDIPUS: Quite right,
but to force the gods to act against their will—
no man has the power.

LEADER: Then if I might mention   320
the next best thing . . .

OEDIPUS: The third best too—
don't hold back, say it.

LEADER: I still believe . . .
Lord Tiresias[18] sees with the eyes of Lord Apollo.
Anyone searching for the truth, my king,
might learn it from the prophet, clear as day.   325

OEDIPUS: I've not been slow with that. On Creon's cue
I sent the escorts, twice, within the hour.
I'm surprised he isn't here.

LEADER: We need him—
without him we have nothing but old, useless rumors.

OEDIPUS: Which rumors? I'll search out every word.

LEADER: Laius was killed, they say, by certain travelers.   330

OEDIPUS: I know—but no one can find the murderer.

LEADER: If the man has a trace of fear in him
he won't stay silent long,
not with your curses ringing in his ears.   335

OEDIPUS: He didn't flinch at murder,
he'll never flinch at words.

          [*Enter Tiresias, the blind prophet, led by a boy with escorts in attendance.
          He remains at a distance.*]

LEADER: Here is the one who will convict him, look,
they bring him on at last, the seer, the man of god.
The truth lives inside him, him alone.

OEDIPUS: O Tiresias,   340
master of all the mysteries of our life,
all you teach and all you dare not tell,
signs in the heavens, signs that walk the earth!
Blind as you are, you can feel all the more
what sickness haunts our city. You, my lord,   345
are the one shield, the one savior we can find.

We asked Apollo—perhaps the messengers
haven't told you—he sent his answer back:
"Relief from the plague can only come one way.
Uncover the murderers of Laius,
put them to death or drive them into exile."   350
So I beg you, grudge us nothing now, no voice,

---

18 The blind prophet of Thebes (whose ghost Odysseus goes to consult in Hades in *Odyssey* XI).

no message plucked from the birds, the embers
or the other mantic ways within your grasp.
Rescue yourself, your city, rescue me—
rescue everything infected by the dead.   355
We are in your hands. For a man to help others
with all his gifts and native strength:
that is the noblest work.

TIRESIAS: How terrible—to see the truth
when the truth is only pain to him who sees!
I knew it well, but I put it from my mind,   360
else I never would have come.

OEDIPUS: What's this? Why so grim, so dire?

TIRESIAS: Just send me home. You bear your burdens,
I'll bear mine. It's better that way,
please believe me.   365

OEDIPUS: Strange response . . . unlawful,
unfriendly too to the state that bred and reared you—
you withhold the word of god.

TIRESIAS: I fail to see
that your own words are so well-timed.
I'd rather not have the same thing said of me . . .

OEDIPUS: For the love of god, don't turn away,   370
not if you know something. We beg you,
all of us on our knees.

TIRESIAS: None of you knows—
and I will never reveal my dreadful secrets,
not to say your own.

OEDIPUS: What? You know and you won't tell?   375
You're bent on betraying us, destroying Thebes?

TIRESIAS: I'd rather not cause pain for you or me.
So why this . . . useless interrogation?
You'll get nothing from me.

OEDIPUS: Nothing! You,
you scum of the earth, you'd enrage a heart of stone!   380
You won't talk? Nothing moves you?
Out with it, once and for all!

TIRESIAS: You criticize my temper . . . unaware
of the one[19] *you* live with, you revile me.

OEDIPUS: Who could restrain his anger hearing you?   385
What outrage—you spurn the city!

TIRESIAS: What will come will come.
Even if I shroud it all in silence.

OEDIPUS: What will come? You're bound to *tell* me that.

TIRESIAS: I'll say no more. Do as you like, build your anger   390
to whatever pitch you please, rage your worst—

OEDIPUS: Oh I'll let loose, I have such fury in me—
now I see it all. You helped hatch the plot,
you did the work, yes, short of killing him
                                                                            395

_____

[19] In the Greek the veiled reference to Jocasta is more forceful, since the word translated "the one"
has a feminine ending (agreeing with the feminine noun *orgê*—"temper").

with your own hands—and given eyes I'd say
you did the killing single-handed!
TIRESIAS: Is that so!
I charge you, then, submit to that decree
you just laid down: from this day onward
speak to no one, not these citizens, not myself.
You are the curse, the corruption of the land!   400
OEDIPUS: You, shameless—
aren't you appalled to start up such a story?
You think you can get away with this?
TIRESIAS: I have already.
The truth with all its power lives inside me.   405
OEDIPUS: Who primed you for this? Not your prophet's trade.
TIRESIAS: You did, you forced me, twisted it out of me.
OEDIPUS: What? Say it again—I'll understand it better.
TIRESIAS: Didn't you understand, just now?
Or are you tempting me to talk?   410
OEDIPUS: No, I can't say I grasped your meaning.
Out with it, again!
TIRESIAS: I say you are the murderer you hunt.
OEDIPUS: That obscenity, twice—by god, you'll pay.
TIRESIAS: Shall I say more, so you can really rage?   415
OEDIPUS: Much as you want. Your words are nothing—futile.
TIRESIAS: You cannot imagine . . . I tell you,
you and your loved ones live together in infamy,
you cannot see how far you've gone in guilt.
OEDIPUS: You think you can keep this up and never suffer?   420
TIRESIAS: Indeed, if the truth has any power.
OEDIPUS: It does
but not for you, old man. You've lost your power,
stone-blind, stone-deaf—senses, eyes blind as stone!
TIRESIAS: I pity you, flinging at me the very insults
each man here will fling at you so soon.
OEDIPUS: Blind,   425
lost in the night, endless night that cursed you!
You can't hurt me or anyone else who sees the light—
you can never touch me.
TIRESIAS: True, it is not your fate
to fall at my hands. Apollo is quite enough,
and he will take some pains to work this out.   430
OEDIPUS: Creon! Is this conspiracy his or yours?
TIRESIAS: Creon is not your downfall, no, you are your own.
OEDIPUS: O power—
wealth and empire, skill outstripping skill
in the heady rivalries of life,
what envy lurks inside you! Just for this,   435
the crown the city gave me—I never sought it,
they laid it in my hands—for this alone, Creon,
the soul of trust, my loyal friend from the start
steals against me . . . so hungry to overthrow me
he sets this wizard on me, this scheming quack,   440

this fortune-teller peddling lies, eyes peeled
for his own profit—seer blind in his craft!

Come here, you pious fraud. Tell me,
when did you ever prove yourself a prophet?
When the Sphinx, that chanting Fury kept her deathwatch here,
why silent then, not a word to set our people free?   445
There was a riddle, not for some passer-by to solve—
it cried out for a prophet. Where were you?
Did you rise to the crisis? Not a word,
you and your birds, your gods—nothing.
No, but I came by, Oedipus the ignorant,   450
I stopped the Sphinx! With no help from the birds,
the flight of my own intelligence hit the mark.

And this is the man you'd try to overthrow?
You think you'll stand by Creon when he's king?
You and the great mastermind—   455
you'll pay in tears, I promise you, for this,
this witch-hunt. If you didn't look so senile
the lash would teach you what your scheming means!
LEADER: I would suggest his words were spoken in anger,
Oedipus . . . yours too, and it isn't what we need.   460
The best solution to the oracle, the riddle
posed by god—we should look for that.
TIRESIAS: You are the king no doubt, but in one respect,
at least, I am your equal: the right to reply.
I claim that privilege too.   465
I am not your slave. I serve Apollo.
I don't need Creon to speak for me in public.
                                                             So,
you mock my blindness? Let me tell you this.
You with your precious eyes,
you're blind to the corruption of your life,   470
to the house you live in, those you live with—
who *are* your parents? Do you know? All unknowing
you are the scourge of your own flesh and blood,
the dead below the earth and the living here above,
and the double lash of your mother and your father's curse   475
will whip you from this land one day, their footfall
treading you down in terror, darkness shrouding
your eyes that now can see the light!
                                   Soon, soon
you'll scream aloud—what haven won't reverberate?
What rock of Cithaeron[20] won't scream back in echo?   480
That day you learn the truth about your marriage,
the wedding-march that sang you into your halls,
the lusty voyage home to the fatal harbor!
And a crowd of other horrors you'd never dream
will level you with yourself and all your children.   485

---

[20] The mountain range near Thebes, on which Oedipus was left to die when an infant.

There. Now smear us with insults—Creon, myself,
and every word I've said. No man will ever
be rooted from the earth as brutally as you.
OEDIPUS: Enough! Such filth from him? Insufferable—   490
what, still alive? Get out—
faster, back where you came from—vanish!
TIRESIAS: I would never have come if you hadn't called me here.
OEDIPUS: If I thought you would blurt out such absurdities,
you'd have died waiting before I'd had you summoned.   495
TIRESIAS: Absurd, am I! To you, not to your parents:
the ones who bore you found me sane enough.
OEDIPUS: Parents—who? Wait . . . who is my father?
TIRESIAS: This day will bring your birth and your destruction.
OEDIPUS: Riddles—all you can say are riddles, murk and darkness.   500
TIRESIAS: Ah, but aren't you the best man alive at solving riddles?
OEDIPUS: Mock me for that, go on, and you'll reveal my greatness.
TIRESIAS: Your great good fortune, true, it was your ruin.
OEDIPUS: Not if I saved the city—what do I care?
TIRESIAS: Well then, I'll be going.

[*To his attendant.*]

                                                   Take me home, boy.   505
OEDIPUS: Yes, take him away. You're a nuisance here.
Out of the way, the irritation's gone.

[*Turning his back on Tiresias, moving toward the palace.*[21]]

TIRESIAS: I will go,
once I have said what I came here to say.
I'll never shrink from the anger in your eyes—
you can't destroy me. Listen to me closely: 510
the man you've sought so long, proclaiming,
cursing up and down, the murderer of Laius—
he is here. A stranger,
you may think, who lives among you,
he soon will be revealed a native Theban   515
but he will take no joy in the revelation.
Blind who now has eyes, beggar who now is rich,
he will grope his way toward a foreign soil,
a stick tapping before him step by step.

[*Oedipus enters the palace.*]

Revealed at last, brother and father both   520
to the children he embraces, to his mother
son and husband both—he sowed the loins
his father sowed, he spilled his father's blood!

Go in and reflect on that, solve that.
And if you find I've lied   525
from this day onward call the prophet blind,

[*Tiresias and the boy exit to the side.*]

CHORUS: Who—
who is the man the voice of god denounces

---

[21] There are no stage directions in our texts. It is suggested here that Oedipus moves off stage and does not hear the critical section of Tiresias's speech (11. 520ff) which he could hardly fail to connect with the prophecy made to him by Apollo many years ago.

resounding out of the rocky gorge of Delphi?
    The horror too dark to tell,
whose ruthless bloody hands have done the work?
His time has come to fly   530
     to outrace the stallions of the storm
        his feet a streak of speed—
Cased in armor, Apollo son of the Father
lunges on him, lightning-bolts afire!
And the grim unerring Furies[22]   535
       closing for the kill.
                       Look,
the word of god has just come blazing
flashing off Parnassus'[23] snowy heights!
    That man who left no trace—
after him, hunt him down with all our strength!   540
Now under bristling timber
    up through rocks and caves he stalks
        like the wild mountain bull—
cut off from men, each step an agony, frenzied, racing blind
but he cannot outrace the dread voices of Delphi   545
ringing out of the heart of Earth,
    the dark wings beating around him shrieking doom
        the doom that never dies, the terror—

The skilled prophet scans the birds and shatters me with terror! 550
I can't accept him, can't deny him, don't know what to say,
I'm lost, and the wings of dark foreboding beating—
I cannot see what's come, what's still to come . . .
and what could breed a blood feud between
    Laius' house and the son of Polybus?[24]
I know of nothing, not in the past and not now,   555
no charge to bring against our king, no cause
to attack his fame that rings throughout Thebes—
    not without proof—not for the ghost of Laius,
    not to avenge a murder gone without a trace.

Zeus and Apollo know, they know, the great masters 560
    of all the dark and depth of human life.
But whether a mere man can know the truth,
whether a seer can fathom more than I—
there is no test, no certain proof
    though matching skill for skill   565
a man can outstrip a rival. No, not till I see
these charges proved will I side with his accusers.
We saw him then, when the she-hawk[25] swept against him,
saw with our own eyes his skill, his brilliant triumph— 570
    there was the test—he was the joy of Thebes!

---

[22] Avenging spirits who pursued a murderer when no earthly avenger was at hand.
[23] A mountain range in central Greece. The great oracular shrine of Apollo at Delphi was on its lower slopes.
[24] King of Corinth and, so far as anyone except Tiresias knows, the father of Oedipus.
[25] The Sphinx.

Never will I convict my king, never in my heart.
[*Enter Creon from the side.*]

CREON: My fellow-citizens, I hear King Oedipus
levels terrible charges at me. I had to come.
I resent it deeply. If, in the present crisis   575
he thinks he suffers any abuse from me,
anything I've done or said that offers him
the slightest injury, why, I've no desire
to linger out this life, my reputation in ruins.
The damage I'd face from such an accusation   580
is nothing simple. No, there's nothing worse:
branded a traitor in the city, a traitor
to all of you and my good friends.

LEADER: True,
but a slur might have been forced out of him,
by anger perhaps, not any firm conviction.   585

CREON: The charge was made in public, wasn't it?
I put the prophet up to spreading lies?

LEADER: Such things were said . . .
I don't know with what intent, if any.

CREON: Was his glance steady, his mind right   590
when the charge was brought against me?

LEADER: I really couldn't say. I never look
to judge the ones in power.
[*The doors open. Oedipus enters.*]
                                  Wait,
here's Oedipus now.

OEDIPUS: You—here? You have the gall
to show your face before the palace gates?
You, plotting to kill me, kill the king—   595
I see it all, the marauding thief himself
scheming to steal my crown and power!
                                  Tell me,
in god's name, what did you take me for,
coward or fool, when you spun out your plot?
Your treachery—you think I'd never detect it   600
creeping against me in the dark? Or sensing it,
not defend myself? Aren't you the fool,
you and your high adventure. Lacking numbers,
powerful friends, out for the big game of empire—
you need riches, armies to bring that quarry down!   605

CREON: Are you quite finished? It's your turn to listen
for just as long as you've . . . instructed me.
Hear me out, then judge me on the facts.

OEDIPUS: You've a wicked way with words, Creon,
but I'll be slow to learn—from you.   610
I find you a menace, a great burden to me.

CREON: Just one thing, hear me out in this.

OEDIPUS: Just one thing,
don't tell *me* you're not the enemy, the traitor.

CREON: Look, if you think crude, mindless stubbornness
such a gift, you've lost your sense of balance.   615

OEDIPUS: If you think you can abuse a kinsman,
    then escape the penalty, you're insane.
CREON: Fair enough, I grant you. But this injury
    you say I've done you, what is it?
OEDIPUS: Did you induce me, yes or no,   620
    to send for that sanctimonious prophet?
CREON: I did. And I'd do the same again.
OEDIPUS: All right then, tell me, how long is it now
    since Laius . . .
CREON: Laius—what did *he* do?
OEDIPUS: Vanished,   625
    swept from sight, murdered in his tracks.
CREON: The count of the years would run you far back . . .
OEDIPUS: And that far back, was the prophet at his trade?
CREON: Skilled as he is today, and just as honored.
OEDIPUS: Did he ever refer to me then, at that time?
CREON: No,   630
    never, at least, when I was in his presence.
OEDIPUS: But you did investigate the murder, didn't you?
CREON: We did our best, of course, discovered nothing.
OEDIPUS: But the great seer never accused me then—why not?
CREON: I don't know. And when I don't, *I* keep quiet.
OEDIPUS: You do know this, you'd tell it too—   635
    if you had a shred of decency.
CREON: What?
    If I know, I won't hold back.
OEDIPUS: Simply this:
    if the two of you had never put heads together,
    we would never have heard about *my* killing Laius.
CREON: If that's what he says . . . well, you know best.   640
    But now I have a right to learn from you
    as you just learned from me.
OEDIPUS: Learn your fill,
    you never will convict me of the murder.
CREON: Tell me, you're married to my sister, aren't you?
OEDIPUS: A genuine discovery—there's no denying that.   645
CREON: And you rule the land with her, with equal power?
OEDIPUS: She receives from me whatever she desires.
CREON: And I am the third, all of us are equals?
OEDIPUS: Yes, and it's there you show your stripes—
    you betray a kinsman.
CREON: Not at all.   650
    Not if you see things calmly, rationally,
    as I do. Look at it this way first:
    who in his right mind would rather rule
    and live in anxiety than sleep in peace?
    Particularly if he enjoys the same authority.   655
    Not I, I'm not the man to yearn for kingship,
    not with a king's power in my hands. Who would?
    Now, as it is, you offer me all I need,
    not a fear in the world. But if I wore the crown . . .   660

there'd be many painful duties to perform,
hardly to my taste.
                    How could kingship
please me more than influence, power
without a qualm? I'm not that deluded yet,   665
to reach for anything but privilege outright,
profit free and clear.
Now all men sing my praises, all salute me,
now all who request your favors curry mine.
I am their best hope: success rests in me.   670
Why give up that, I ask you, and borrow trouble?
A man of sense, someone who sees things clearly
would never resort to treason.
No, I've no lust for conspiracy in me,
nor could I ever suffer one who does.   675

Do you want proof? Go to Delphi yourself,
examine the oracle and see if I've reported
the message word-for-word. This too:
if you detect that I and the clairvoyant
have plotted anything in common, arrest me,   680
execute me. Not on the strength of one vote,
two in this case, mine as well as yours.
But don't convict me on sheer unverified surmise.
How wrong it is to take the good for bad,
purely at random, or take the bad for good.   685
But reject a friend, a kinsman? I would as soon
tear out the life within us, priceless life itself.
You'll learn this well, without fail, in time.
Time alone can bring the just man to light—
the criminal you can spot in one short day.   690

LEADER: Good advice,
    my lord, for anyone who wants to avoid disaster.
    Those who jump to conclusions may go wrong.
OEDIPUS: When my enemy moves against me quickly,
    plots in secret, I move quickly too, I must,
    I plot and pay him back. Relax my guard a moment,   695
    waiting his next move—he wins his objective,
    I lose mine.
CREON: What do you want?
    You want me banished?
OEDIPUS: No, I want you dead.
CREON: Just to show how ugly a grudge can . . .
OEDIPUS: So,
    still stubborn? you don't think I'm serious?   700
CREON: I think you're insane.
OEDIPUS: Quite sane—in my behalf.
CREON: Not just as much in mine?
OEDIPUS: You—my mortal enemy?
CREON: What if you're wholly wrong?
OEDIPUS: No matter—I must rule.
CREON: Not if you rule unjustly.
OEDIPUS: Hear him, Thebes, my city!   705

CREON: My city too, not yours alone!
LEADER: Please, my lords.
          [*Enter Jocasta from the palace.*]
                              Look, Jocasta's coming,
          and just in time too. With her help
          you must put this fighting of yours to rest.
JOCASTA: Have you no sense? Poor misguided men,
          such shouting—why this public outburst?
          Aren't you ashamed, with the land so sick,   710
          to stir up private quarrels?
          [*To Oedipus.*]
          Into the palace now. And Creon, you go home.
          Why make such a furor over nothing?
CREON: My sister, it's dreadful ... Oedipus, your husband,
          he's bent on a choice of punishments for me,   715
          banishment from the fatherland or death.
OEDIPUS: Precisely. I caught him in the act, Jocasta,
          plotting, about to stab me in the back.
CREON: Never—curse me, let me die and be damned
          if I've done you any wrong you charge me with.   720
JOCASTA: Oh god, believe it, Oedipus,
          honor the solemn oath he swears to heaven.
          Do it for me, for the sake of all your people.
          [*The Chorus begins to chant.*]
CHORUS: Believe it, be sensible
          give way, my king, I beg you!   725
OEDIPUS: What do you want from me, concessions?
CHORUS: Respect him—he's been no fool in the past
          and now he's strong with the oath he swears to god.
OEDIPUS: You know what you're asking?
CHORUS: I do.
OEDIPUS: Then out with it!
CHORUS: The man's your friend, your kin, he's under oath—   730
          don't cast him out, disgraced
          branded with guilt on the strength of hearsay only.
OEDIPUS: Know full well, if that is what you want
          you want me dead or banished from the land.
CHORUS: Never—   735
          no, by the blazing Sun, first god of the heavens!
          Stripped of the gods, stripped of loved ones,
          let me die by inches if that ever crossed my mind.
          But the heart inside me sickens, dies as the land dies
          and now on top of the old griefs you pile this,
          your fury—both of you!   740
OEDIPUS: Then let him go,
          even if it does lead to my ruin, my death
          or my disgrace, driven from Thebes for life.
          It's you, not him I pity—your words move me.
          He, wherever he goes, my hate goes with him.
CREON: Look at you, sullen in yielding, brutal in your rage—   745
          you'll go too far. It's perfect justice:
          natures like yours are hardest on themselves.

OEDIPUS: Then leave me alone—get out!

CREON: I'm going.
You're wrong, so wrong. These men know I'm right.   750
    [*Exit to the side. The Chorus turns to Jocasta.*]

CHORUS: Why do you hesitate, my lady
why not help him in?

JOCASTA: Tell me what's happened first.

CHORUS: Loose, ignorant talk started dark suspicions
and a sense of injustice cut deeply too.   755

JOCASTA: On both sides?

CHORUS: Oh yes.

JOCASTA: What did they say?

CHORUS: Enough, please, enough! The land's so racked already
or so it seems to me . . .
End the trouble here, just where they left it.

OEDIPUS: You see what comes of your good intentions now?   760
And all because you tried to blunt my anger.

CHORUS: My king,
I've said it once, I'll say it time and again—
    I'd be insane, you know it,
senseless, ever to turn my back on you.
You who set our beloved land—storm-tossed, shattered—   765
straight on course. Now again, good helmsman,
steer us through the storm!
    [*The Chorus draws away, leaving Oedipus and Jocasta side by side.*]

JOCASTA: For the love of god,
Oedipus, tell me too, what is it?
Why this rage? You're so unbending.

OEDIPUS: I will tell you. I respect you, Jocasta,   770
much more than these . . .
    [*Glancing at the Chorus.*]
Creon's to blame, Creon schemes against me.

JOCASTA: Tell me clearly, how did the quarrel start?

OEDIPUS: He says *I* murdered Laius—I am guilty.

JOCASTA: How does he know? Some secret knowledge   775
or simple hearsay?

OEDIPUS: Oh, he sent his prophet in
to do his dirty work. You know Creon,
Creon keeps his own lips clean.

JOCASTA: A prophet?
Well then, free yourself of every charge!
Listen to me and learn some peace of mind: 780
no skill in the world,
nothing human can penetrate the future.
Here is proof, quick and to the point.

An oracle came to Laius one fine day
(I won't say from Apollo himself   785
but his underlings, his priests) and it said
that doom would strike him down at the hands of a son,
our son, to be born of our own flesh and blood. But Laius,
so the report goes at least, was killed by strangers,
thieves, at a place where three roads meet . . . my son—   790

he wasn't three days old and the boy's father
fastened his ankles, had a henchman fling him away
on a barren, trackless mountain.

There, you see?
Apollo brought neither thing to pass. My baby
no more murdered his father than Laius suffered—
his wildest fear—death at his own son's hands.
That's how the seers and all their revelations
mapped out the future. Brush them from your mind.
Whatever the god needs and seeks
he'll bring to light himself, with ease.

OEDIPUS: Strange,
    hearing you just now . . . my mind wandered,
    my thoughts racing back and forth.
JOCASTA: What do you mean? Why so anxious, startled?
OEDIPUS: I thought I heard you say that Laius
    was cut down at a place where three roads meet.
JOCASTA: That was the story. It hasn't died out yet.
OEDIPUS: Where did this thing happen? Be precise.
JOCASTA: A place called Phocis, where two branching roads,
    one from Daulia, one from Delphi,
    come together—a crossroads.
OEDIPUS: When? How long ago?
JOCASTA: The heralds no sooner reported Laius dead
    than you appeared and they hailed you king of Thebes.
OEDIPUS: My god, my god—what have you planned to do to me?
JOCASTA: What, Oedipus? What haunts you so?
OEDIPUS: Not yet.
    Laius—how did he look? Describe him.
    Had he reached his prime?
JOCASTA: He was swarthy,
    and the gray had just begun to streak his temples,
    and his build . . . wasn't far from yours.
OEDIPUS: Oh no no,
    I think I've just called down a dreadful curse
    upon myself—I simply didn't know!
JOCASTA: What are you saying? I shudder to look at you.
OEDIPUS: I have a terrible fear the blind seer can see.
    I'll know in a moment. One thing more—
JOCASTA: Anything,
    afraid as I am—ask, I'll answer, all I can.
OEDIPUS: Did he go with a light or heavy escort,
    several men-at-arms, like a lord, a king?
JOCASTA: There were five in the party, a herald among them,
    and a single wagon carrying Laius.
OEDIPUS: Ai—
    now I can see it all, clear as day.
    Who told you all this at the time, Jocasta?
JOCASTA: A servant who reached home, the lone survivor.
OEDIPUS: So, could he still be in the palace—even now?
JOCASTA: No indeed. Soon as he returned from the scene
    and saw you on the throne with Laius dead and gone,

795

800

805

810

815

820

825

830

835

he knelt and clutched my hand, pleading with me
to send him into the hinterlands, to pasture,
far as possible, out of sight of Thebes.
I sent him away. Slave though he was,
he'd earned that favor—and much more.   840

OEDIPUS: Can we bring him back, quickly?

JOCASTA: Easily. Why do you want him so?

OEDIPUS: I'm afraid,
Jocasta, I have said too much already.
That man—I've got to see him.

JOCASTA: Then he'll come.
But even I have a right, I'd like to think,   845
to know what's torturing you, my lord.

OEDIPUS: And so you shall—I can hold nothing back from you,
now I've reached this pitch of dark foreboding.
Who means more to me than you? Tell me,
whom would I turn toward but you   850
as I go through all this?

My father was Polybus, king of Corinth.
My mother, a Dorian, Merope. And I was held
the prince of the realm among the people there,
till something struck me out of nowhere,   855
something strange . . . worth remarking perhaps,
hardly worth the anxiety I gave it.
Some man at a banquet who had drunk too much
shouted out—he was far gone, mind you—
that I am not my father's son. Fighting words!   860
I barely restrained myself that day
but early the next I went to mother and father,
questioned them closely, and they were enraged
at the accusation and the fool who let it fly.
So as for my parents I was satisfied,   865
but still this thing kept gnawing at me,
the slander spread—I had to make my move.

                                              And so,
unknown to mother and father I set out for Delphi,
and the god Apollo spurned me, sent me away
denied the facts I came for,   870
but first he flashed before my eyes a future
great with pain, terror, disaster—I can hear him cry,
"You are fated to couple with your mother, you will bring
a breed of children into the light no man can bear to see—
you will kill your father, the one who gave you life!"   875
I heard all that and ran. I abandoned Corinth,
from that day on I gauged its landfall only
by the stars, running, always running
toward some place where I would never see
the shame of all those oracles come true.   880
And as I fled I reached that very spot
where the great king, you say, met his death.

Now, Jocasta, I will tell you all.
Making my way toward this triple crossroad
I began to see a herald, then a brace of colts
drawing a wagon, and mounted on the bench ... a man,   885
just as you've described him, coming face-to-face,
and the one in the lead and the old man himself
were about to thrust me off the road—brute force—
and the one shouldering me aside, the driver,
I strike him in anger!—and the old man, watching me   890
coming up along his wheels—he brings down
his prod, two prongs straight at my head!
I paid him back with interest!
Short work, by god—with one blow of the staff
in this right hand I knock him out of his high seat,   895
roll him out of the wagon, sprawling headlong—
I killed them all—every mother's son!

Oh, but if there is any blood-tie
between Laius and this stranger ...
what man alive more miserable than I?   900
More hated by the gods? *I* am the man
no alien, no citizen welcomes to his house,
law forbids it—not a word to me in public,
driven out of every hearth and home.
And all these curses I—no one but I   905
brought down these piling curses on myself!
And you, his wife, I've touched your body with these,
the hands that killed your husband cover you with blood.

Wasn't I born for torment? Look me in the eyes!   910
I am abomination—heart and soul!
I must be exiled, and even in exile
never see my parents, never set foot
on native ground again. Else I am doomed
to couple with my mother and cut my father down ...   915
Polybus who reared me, gave me life.

                              But why, why?
Wouldn't a man of judgment say—and wouldn't he be right—
some savage power has brought this down upon my head?

Oh no, not that, you pure and awesome gods,
never let me see that day! Let me slip
from the world of men, vanish without a trace   920
before I see myself stained with such corruption,
stained to the heart.
LEADER: My lord, you fill our hearts with fear.
But at least until you question the witness,
do take hope.   925
OEDIPUS: Exactly. He is my last hope—
I am waiting for the shepherd. He is crucial.
JOCASTA: And once he appears, what then? Why so urgent?
OEDIPUS: I will tell you. If it turns out that his story
matches yours, I've escaped the worst.

                                                               930

Jocasta: What did I say? What struck you so?
Oedipus: You said *thieves*—
he told you a whole band of them murdered Laius.
So, if he still holds to the same number,
I cannot be the killer. One can't equal many.
But if he refers to one man, one alone,   935
clearly the scales come down on me:
I am guilty.
Jocasta: Impossible. Trust me,
I told you precisely what he said,
and he can't retract it now;
the whole city heard it, not just I.   940
And even if he should vary his first report
by one man more or less, still, my lord,
he could never make the murder of Laius
truly fit the prophecy. Apollo was explicit:
my son was doomed to kill my husband . . . my son,   945
poor defenseless thing, he never had a chance
to kill his father. They destroyed him first.

So much for prophecy. It's neither here nor there.
From this day on, I wouldn't look right or left.
Oedipus: True, true. Still, that shepherd,   950
someone fetch him—now!
Jocasta: I'll send at once. But do let's go inside.
I'd never displease you, least of all in this.
    [*Oedipus and Jocasta enter the palace.*]
Chorus: Destiny guide me always
Destiny find me filled with reverence   955
    pure in word and deed.
Great laws tower above us, reared on high
born for the brilliant vault of heaven—
    Olympian Sky their only father,
nothing mortal, no man gave them birth,   960
their memory deathless, never lost in sleep:
within them lives a mighty god, the god does not grow old.

Pride breeds the tyrant
violent pride, gorging, crammed to bursting
    with all that is overripe and rich with ruin—   965
clawing up to the heights, headlong pride
crashes down the abyss—sheer doom!
    No footing helps, all foothold lost and gone.
But the healthy strife that makes the city strong—
I pray that god will never end that wrestling: 970
god, my champion, I will never let you go.

But if any man comes striding, high and mighty
    in all he says and does,
no fear of justice, no reverence
for the temples of the gods—   975
    let a rough doom tear him down,
repay his pride, breakneck, ruinous pride!

If he cannot reap his profits fairly
    cannot restrain himself from outrage—
mad, laying hands on the holy things untouchable!

      Can such a man, so desperate, still boast
      he can save his life from the flashing bolts of god?
        If all such violence goes with honor now
          why join the sacred dance?

Never again will I go reverent to Delphi,
    the inviolate heart of Earth
or Apollo's ancient oracle at Abae
or Olympia[26] of the fires—
    unless these prophecies all come true
for all mankind to point toward in wonder.
King of kings, if you deserve your titles
Zeus, remember, never forget!
You and your deathless, everlasting reign.

      They are dying, the old oracles sent to Laius,
      now our masters strike them off the rolls.
        Nowhere Apollo's golden glory now—
          the gods, the gods go down.

[*Enter Jocasta from the palace, carrying a suppliant's branch wound in wool.*]

JOCASTA: Lords of the realm,[27] it occurred to me,
just now, to visit the temples of the gods,
so I have my branch in my hand and incense too.

Oedipus is beside himself. Racked with anguish,
no longer a man of sense, he won't admit
the latest prophecies are hollow as the old—
he's at the mercy of every passing voice
if the voice tells of terror.
I urge him gently, nothing seems to help,
so I turn to you, Apollo, you are nearest.

    [*Placing her branch on the altar, while an old herdsman enters from the side, not the one just summoned by the King but an unexpected Messenger from Corinth.*]

I come with prayers and offerings . . . I beg you,
cleanse us, set us free of defilement!
Look at us, passengers in the grip of fear,
watching the pilot of the vessel go to pieces.

MESSENGER: [*Approaching Jocasta and the Chorus.*]
Strangers, please, I wonder if you could lead us
to the palace of the king . . . I think it's Oedipus.
Better, the man himself—you know where he is?

LEADER: This is his palace, stranger. He's inside.
But here is his queen, his wife and mother
of his children.

980

985

990

995

1000

1005

1010

1015

---

[26] Abae was a city in central Greece, and Olympia a site in the western Peloponnese, where there were important oracles of Apollo and Zeus, respectively.
[27] She is addressing the Chorus.

MESSENGER: Blessings on you, noble queen,
    queen of Oedipus crowned with all your family—
    blessings on you always!
JOCASTA: And the same to you, stranger, you deserve it . . .   1020
    such a greeting. But what have you come for?
    Have you brought us news?
MESSENGER: Wonderful news—
    for the house, my lady, for your husband too.
JOCASTA: Really, what? Who sent you?
MESSENGER: Corinth.
    I'll give you the message in a moment.   1025
    You'll be glad of it—how could you help it?—
    though it costs a little sorrow in the bargain.
JOCASTA: What can it be, with such a double edge?
MESSENGER: The people there, they want to make your Oedipus
    king of Corinth, so they're saying now.   1030
JOCASTA: Why? Isn't old Polybus still in power?
MESSENGER: No more. Death has got him in the tomb.
JOCASTA: What are you saying? Polybus, dead?—dead?
MESSENGER: If not,
    if I'm not telling the truth, strike me dead too.
JOCASTA: [*To a servant.*]
    Quickly, go to your master, tell him this!   1035
    You prophecies of the gods, where are you now?
    This is the man that Oedipus feared for years,
    he fled him, not to kill him—and now he's dead,
    quite by chance, a normal, natural death,
    not murdered by his son.   1040
OEDIPUS: [*Emerging from the palace.*]
                        Dearest,
    what now? Why call me from the palace?
JOCASTA: [*Bringing the Messenger closer.*]
    Listen to *him*, see for yourself what all
    those awful prophecies of god have come to.
OEDIPUS: And who is he? What can he have for me?
JOCASTA: He's from Corinth, he's come to tell you   1045
    your father is no more—Polybus—he's dead!
OEDIPUS: [*Wheeling on the Messenger.*]
    What? Let me have it from your lips.
MESSENGER: Well,
    if that's what you want first, then here it is:
    make no mistake, Polybus is dead and gone.
OEDIPUS: How—murder? sickness?—what? what killed him?   1050
MESSENGER: A light tip of the scales put old bones to rest.
OEDIPUS: Sickness then—poor man, it wore him down.
MESSENGER: That,
    and the long count of years he'd measured out.
OEDIPUS: So!
    Jocasta, why, why look to the Prophet's hearth,
    the fires of the future? Why scan the birds   1055
    that scream above our heads? They winged me on
    to the murder of my father, did they? That was my doom?

Well look, he's dead and buried, hidden under the earth,
and here I am in Thebes, I never put hand to sword—
unless some longing for me wasted him away,
then in a sense you'd say I caused his death.   1060
But now, all those prophecies I feared—Polybus
packs them off to sleep with him in hell!
They're nothing, worthless.

JOCASTA: There.
Didn't I tell you from the start?

OEDIPUS: So you did. I was lost in fear.   1065

JOCASTA: No more, sweep it from your mind forever.

OEDIPUS: But my mother's bed, surely I must fear—

JOCASTA: Fear?
What should a man fear? It's all chance,
chance rules our lives. Not a man on earth   1070
can see a day ahead, groping through the dark.
Better to live at random, best we can.
And as for this marriage with your mother—
have no fear. Many a man before you,
in his dreams, has shared his mother's bed.   1075
Take such things for shadows, nothing at all—
Live, Oedipus,
as if there's no tomorrow!

OEDIPUS: Brave words,
and you'd persuade me if mother weren't alive.
But mother lives, so for all your reassurances   1080
I live in fear, I must.

JOCASTA: But your father's death,
that, at least, is a great blessing, joy to the eyes!

OEDIPUS: Great, I know ... but I fear *her*—she's still alive.

MESSENGER: Wait, who is this woman, makes you so afraid?

OEDIPUS: Merope, old man. The wife of Polybus.   1085

MESSENGER: The queen? What's there to fear in her?

OEDIPUS: A dreadful prophecy, stranger, sent by the gods.

MESSENGER: Tell me, could you? Unless it's forbidden
other ears to hear.

OEDIPUS: Not at all.
Apollo told me once—it is my fate—
I must make love with my own mother,   1090
shed my father's blood with my own hands.
So for years I've given Corinth a wide berth,
and it's been my good fortune too. But still,
to see one's parents and look into their eyes
is the greatest joy I know.   1095

MESSENGER: You're afraid of that?
That kept you out of Corinth?

OEDIPUS: My *father*, old man—
so I wouldn't kill my father.

MESSENGER: So that's it.
Well then, seeing I came with such good will, my king,
why don't I rid you of that old worry now?

OEDIPUS: What a rich reward you'd have for that!   1100

MESSENGER: What do you think I came for, majesty?
  So you'd come home and I'd be better off.
OEDIPUS: Never, I will never go near my parents.
MESSENGER: My boy, it's clear, you don't know what you're doing.   1105
OEDIPUS: What do you mean, old man? For god's sake, explain.
MESSENGER: If you ran from *them*, always dodging home ...
OEDIPUS: Always, terrified Apollo's oracle might come true—
MESSENGER: And you'd be covered with guilt, from both your parents.
OEDIPUS: That's right, old man, that fear is always with me.   1110
MESSENGER: Don't you know? You've really nothing to fear.
OEDIPUS: But why? If I'm their son—Merope, Polybus?
MESSENGER: Polybus was nothing to you, that's why, not in blood.
OEDIPUS: What are you saying—Polybus was not my father?
MESSENGER: No more than I am. He and I are equals.
OEDIPUS: My father—   1115
  how can my father equal nothing? You're nothing to me!
MESSENGER: Neither was he, no more your father than I am.
OEDIPUS: Then why did he call me his son?
MESSENGER: You were a gift,
  years ago—know for a fact he took you
  from my hands.
OEDIPUS: No, from another's hands?
  Then how could he love me so? He loved me, deeply ...   1120
MESSENGER: True, and his early years without a child
  made him love you all the more.
OEDIPUS: And you, did you ...
  buy me? find me by accident?
MESSENGER: I stumbled on you,
  down the woody flanks of Mount Cithaeron.
OEDIPUS: So close,   1125
  what were you doing here, just passing through?
MESSENGER: Watching over my flocks, grazing them on the slopes.
OEDIPUS: A herdsman, were you? A vagabond, scraping for wages?
MESSENGER: Your savior too, my son, in your worst hour.
OEDIPUS: Oh—
  when you picked me up, was I in pain? What exactly?   1130
MESSENGER: Your ankles ... they tell the story. Look at them.
OEDIPUS: Why remind me of that, that old affliction?
MESSENGER: Your ankles were pinned together. I set you free.
OEDIPUS: That dreadful mark—I've had it from the cradle.
MESSENGER: And you got your name[28] from that misfortune too,   1135
  the name's still with you.
OEDIPUS: Dear god, who did it?—
  mother? father? Tell me.
MESSENGER: I don't know.
  The one who gave you to me, he'd know more.
OEDIPUS: What? You took me from someone else?
  You didn't find me yourself?
MESSENGER: No sir,   1140
  another shepherd passed you on to me.

---

[28] In Greek the name *Oidipous* suggests "swollen foot."

OEDIPUS: Who? Do you know? Describe him.

MESSENGER: He called himself a servant of . . .
    if I remember rightly—Laius.
    [*Jocasta turns sharply.*]

OEDIPUS: The king of the land who ruled here long ago?

MESSENGER: That's the one. That herdsman was *his* man.

OEDIPUS: Is he still alive? Can I see him?

MESSENGER: They'd know best, the people of these parts.
    [*Oedipus and the Messenger turn to the Chorus.*]

OEDIPUS: Does anyone know that herdsman,
    the one he mentioned? Anyone seen him
    in the fields, in the city? Out with it!
    The time has come to reveal this once for all.

LEADER: I think he's the very shepherd you wanted to see,
    a moment ago. But the queen, Jocasta,
    she's the one to say.

OEDIPUS: Jocasta,
    you remember the man we just sent for?
    Is *that* the one he means?

JOCASTA: That man . . .
    why ask? Old shepherd, talk, empty nonsense,
    don't give it another thought, don't even think—

OEDIPUS: What—give up now, with a clue like this?
    Fail to solve the mystery of my birth?
    Not for all the world!

JOCASTA: Stop—in the name of god,
    if you love your own life, call off this search!
    My suffering is enough.

OEDIPUS: Courage!
    Even if my mother turns out to be a slave,
    and I a slave, three generations back,
    you would not seem common.

JOCASTA: Oh no,
    listen to me, I beg you, don't do this.

OEDIPUS: Listen to you? No more. I must know it all,
    must see the truth at last.

JOCASTA: No, please—
    for your sake—I want the best for you!

OEDIPUS: Your best is more than I can bear.

JOCASTA: You're doomed—
    may you never fathom who you are!

OEDIPUS: [*To a servant.*] Hurry, fetch me the herdsman, now!
    Leave her to glory in her royal birth.

JOCASTA: Aieeeeee—
            man of agony—
    that is the only name I have for you,
    that, no other—ever, ever, ever!
    [*Flinging through the palace doors. A long, tense silence follows.*]

LEADER: Where's she gone, Oedipus?
    Rushing off, such wild grief . . .
    I'm afraid that from this silence
    something monstrous may come bursting forth.

1145

1150

1155

1160

1165

1170

1175

1180

OEDIPUS: Let it burst! Whatever will, whatever must!
    I must know my birth, no matter how common
    it may be—I must see my origins face-to-face.
    She perhaps, she with her woman's pride   1185
    may well be mortified by my birth,
    but I, I count myself the son of Chance,
    the great goddess, giver of all good things—
    I'll never see myself disgraced. She is my mother!
    And the moons have marked me out, my blood-brothers,   1190
    one moon on the wane, the next moon great with power.
    That is my blood, my nature—I will never betray it,
    never fail to search and learn my birth!
CHORUS: Yes—if I am a true prophet   1195
      if I can grasp the truth,
      by the boundless skies of Olympus,
    at the full moon of tomorrow, Mount Cithaeron
    you will know how Oedipus glories in you—
    you, his birthplace, nurse, his mountain-mother!   1200
    And we will sing you, dancing out your praise—
    you lift our monarch's heart!
      Apollo, Apollo, god of the wild cry
        may our dancing please you!
                        Oedipus—
      son, dear child, who bore you?
    Who of the nymphs who seem to live forever[29]   1205
    mated with Pan,[30] the mountain-striding Father?
    Who was your mother? who, some bride of Apollo
    the god who loves the pastures spreading toward the sun?
      Or was it Hermes, king of the lightning ridges?
    Or Dionysus,[31] lord of frenzy, lord of the barren peaks—   1210
    did he seize you in his hands, dearest of all his lucky finds?—
    found by the nymphs, their warm eyes dancing, gift
    to the lord who loves them dancing out his joy!
    [*Oedipus strains to see a figure coming from the distance. Attended by
    palace guards, an old Shepherd enters slowly, reluctant to approach the
    king.*]
OEDIPUS: I never met the man, my friends . . . still,   1215
    if I had to guess, I'd say that's the shepherd,
    the very one we've looked for all along.
    Brothers in old age, two of a kind,
    he and our guest here. At any rate
    the ones who bring him in are my own men,   1220
    I recognize them.
    [*Turning to the Leader.*]
                  But you know more than I,
    you should, you've seen the man before.
LEADER: I know him, definitely. One of Laius' men,
    a trusty shepherd, if there ever was one.

---

[29] Nymphs were not immortal, like the gods, but lived much longer than mortals.
[30] A woodland god; patron of shepherds and flocks.
[31] Dionysus like Pan and Hermes haunted the wild country, woods and mountains. Hermes was
born on Mount Kyllene in Arcadia.

OEDIPUS: You, I ask you first, stranger,
you from Corinth—is this the one you mean?   1225

MESSENGER: You're looking at him. He's your man.

OEDIPUS: [*To the Shepherd.*]
You, old man, come over here—
look at me. Answer all my questions.
Did you ever serve King Laius?

SHEPHERD: So I did ...   1230
a slave, not bought on the block though,
born and reared in the palace.

OEDIPUS: Your duties, your kind of work?

SHEPHERD: Herding the flocks, the better part of my life.

OEDIPUS: Where, mostly? Where did you do your grazing?   1235

SHEPHERD: Well,
Cithaeron sometimes, or the foothills round about.

OEDIPUS: This man—you know him? ever see him there?

SHEPHERD: [*Confused, glancing from the Messenger to the King.*]
Doing what?—what man do you mean?

OEDIPUS: [*Pointing to the Messenger.*]
This one here—ever have dealings with him?

SHEPHERD: Not so I could say, but give me a chance,   1240
my memory's bad ...

MESSENGER: No wonder he doesn't know me, master.
But let me refresh his memory for him.
I'm sure he recalls old times we had
on the slopes of Mount Cithaeron;   1245
he and I, grazing our flocks, he with two
and I with one—we both struck up together,
three whole seasons, six months at a stretch
from spring to the rising of Arcturus in the fall,[32]
then with winter coming on I'd drive my herds   1250
to my own pens, and back he'd go with his
to Laius' folds.
[*To the Shepherd.*]
                       Now that's how it was,
wasn't it—yes or no?

SHEPHERD: Yes, I suppose ...
it's all so long ago.

MESSENGER: Come, tell me,
you gave me a child back then, a boy, remember?   1255
A little fellow to rear, my very own.

SHEPHERD: What? Why rake up that again?

MESSENGER: Look, here he is, my fine old friend—
the same man who was just a baby then.

SHEPHERD: Damn you, shut your mouth—quiet!   1260

OEDIPUS: Don't lash out at him, old man—
you need lashing more than he does.

SHEPHERD: Why,
master, majesty—what have I done wrong?

---

[32] Arcturus is the principal star in the constellation Bootes. Its "rising" (i.e., its reappearance in the
night sky just before dawn in September) signaled the end of summer.

OEDIPUS: You won't answer his question about the boy.
SHEPHERD: He's talking nonsense, wasting his breath.   1265
OEDIPUS: So, you won't talk willingly—
   then you'll talk with pain.
      [*The guards seize the Shepherd.*]
SHEPHERD: No, dear god, don't torture an old man!
OEDIPUS: Twist his arms back, quickly!
SHEPHERD: God help us, why?—   1270
   what more do you need to know?
OEDIPUS: Did you give him that child? He's asking.
SHEPHERD: I did ... I wish to god I'd died that day.
OEDIPUS: You've got your wish if you don't tell the truth.
SHEPHERD: The more I tell, the worse the death I'll die.
OEDIPUS: Our friend here wants to stretch things out, does he?   1275
      [*Motioning to his men for torture.*]
SHEPHERD: No, no, I gave it to him—I just said so.
OEDIPUS: Where did you get it? Your house? Someone else's?
SHEPHERD: It wasn't mine, no. I got it from ... someone.
OEDIPUS: Which one of them?
      [*Looking at the citizens.*]
                           Whose house?
SHEPHERD: No—
   god's sake, master, no more questions!
OEDIPUS: You're a dead man if I have to ask again.   1280
SHEPHERD: Then—the child came from the house ... of Laius.
OEDIPUS: A slave? or born of his own blood?
SHEPHERD: Oh no,
   I'm right at the edge, the horrible truth—I've got to say it!
OEDIPUS: And I'm at the edge of hearing horrors, yes, but I must hear!
SHEPHERD: All right! His son, they said it was—his son!   1285
   But the one inside, your wife,
   she'd tell it best.
OEDIPUS: My wife—
   she gave it to you?
SHEPHERD: Yes, yes, my king.   1290
OEDIPUS: Why, what for?
SHEPHERD: To kill it.
OEDIPUS: Her own child,
   how could she?
SHEPHERD: She was afraid—   1295
   frightening prophecies.
OEDIPUS: What?
SHEPHERD: They said—
   he'd kill his parents.
OEDIPUS: But you gave him to this old man—why?
SHEPHERD: I pitied the little baby, master,   1300
   hoped he'd take him off to his own country,
   far away, but he saved him for this, his fate.
   If you are the man he says you are, believe me,
   you were born for pain.
OEDIPUS: O god—   1305
   all come true, all burst to light!

O light—now let me look my last on you!
I stand revealed at last—
cursed in my birth, cursed in marriage,
cursed in the lives I cut down with these hands!
[*Rushing through the doors with a great cry. The Corinthian Messenger, the* 1310
Shepherd and attendants exit slowly to the side.]
CHORUS: O the generations of men
     the dying generations—adding the total
     of all your lives I find they come to nothing ...
          does there exist, is there a man on earth
     who seizes more joy than just a dream, a vision? 1315
     And the vision no sooner dawns than dies
     blazing into oblivion.

     You are my great example, you, your life
     your destiny, Oedipus, man of misery—
     I count no man blest.

               You outranged all men! 1320
          Bending your bow to the breaking-point
     you captured priceless glory, O dear god,
     and the Sphinx came crashing down,
          the virgin, claws hooked
     like a bird of omen singing, shrieking death— 1325
     like a fortress reared in the face of death
     you rose and saved our land.

     From that day on we called you king
     we crowned you with honors, Oedipus, towering over all—
     mighty king of the seven gates of Thebes. 1330

     But now to hear your story—is there a man more agonized?
     More wed to pain and frenzy? Not a man on earth,
     the joy of your life ground down to nothing
     O Oedipus, name for the ages—
          one and the same wide harbor served you 1335
               son and father both
     son and father came to rest in the same bridal chamber.
     How, how could the furrows your father plowed
     bear you, your agony, harrowing on
     in silence O so long?

               But now for all your power 1340
     Time, all-seeing Time has dragged you to the light,
     judged your marriage monstrous from the start—
     the son and the father tangling, both one—
     O child of Laius, would to god
          I'd never seen you, never never! 1345
          Now I weep like a man who wails the dead
     and the dirge comes pouring forth with all my heart!
     I tell you the truth, you gave me life
     my breath leapt up in you
     and now you bring down the night upon my eyes.
     [*Enter a Messenger from the palace.*] 1350

MESSENGER: Men of Thebes, always first in honor,
            what horrors you will hear, what you will see,
            what a heavy weight of sorrow you will shoulder . . .
            if you are true to your birth, if you still have
            some feeling for the royal house of Thebes.   1355
            I tell you neither the waters of the Danube
            nor the Nile[33] can wash this palace clean.
            Such things it hides, it soon will bring to light—
            terrible things, and none done blindly now,
            all done with a will. The pains   1360
            we inflict upon ourselves hurt most of all.
LEADER: God knows we have pains enough already.
            What can you add to them?
MESSENGER: The queen is dead.
LEADER: Poor lady—how?
MESSENGER: By her own hand. But you are spared the worst,   1365
            you never had to watch . . . I saw it all,
            and with all the memory that's in me
            you will learn what that poor woman suffered.

            Once she'd broken in through the gates,
            dashing past us, frantic, whipped to fury,   1370
            ripping her hair out with both hands—
            straight to her rooms she rushed, flinging herself
            across the bridal-bed, doors slamming behind her—
            once inside, she wailed for Laius, dead so long,
            remembering how she bore his child long ago,   1375
            the life that rose up to destroy him, leaving
            its mother to mother living creatures
            with the very son she'd borne.
            Oh how she wept, mourning the marriage-bed
            where she let loose that double brood—monsters—   1380
            husband by her husband, children by her child.
                                            And then—
            but how she died is more than I can say. Suddenly
            Oedipus burst in, screaming, he stunned us so
            we couldn't watch her agony to the end,
            our eyes were fixed on him. Circling   1385
            like a maddened beast, stalking, here, there,
            crying out to us—
                        Give him a sword![34] His wife,
            no wife, his mother, where can he find the mother earth
            that cropped two crops at once, himself and all his children?
            He was raging—one of the dark powers pointing the way, 1390
            none of us mortals crowding around him, no,
            with a great shattering cry—someone, something leading him on—
            he hurled at the twin doors and bending the bolts back
            out of their sockets, crashed through the chamber.

---

[33] The Greek says Phasis—a river in Asia Minor. The translator has substituted a big river more familiar to modern readers.
[34] Presumably so that he could kill himself.

And there we saw the woman hanging by the neck,   1395
cradled high in a woven noose, spinning,
swinging back and forth. And when he saw her,
giving a low, wrenching sob that broke our hearts,
slipping the halter from her throat, he eased her down,
in a slow embrace he laid her down, poor thing . . .   1400
then, what came next, what horror we beheld!

He rips off her brooches, the long gold pins
holding her robes—and lifting them high,
looking straight up into the points,
he digs them down the sockets of his eyes, crying, "You,   1405
you'll see no more the pain I suffered, all the pain I caused!
Too long you looked on the ones you never should have seen,
blind to the ones you longed to see, to know! Blind
from this hour on! Blind in the darkness—blind!"
His voice like a dirge, rising, over and over   1410
raising the pins, raking them down his eyes.
And at each stroke blood spurts from the roots,
splashing his beard, a swirl of it, nerves and clots—
black hail of blood pulsing, gushing down.

These are the griefs that burst upon them both,   1415
coupling man and woman. The joy they had so lately,
the fortune of their old ancestral house
was deep joy indeed. Now, in this one day,
wailing, madness and doom, death, disgrace,
all the griefs in the world that you can name,   1420
all are theirs forever.

LEADER: Oh poor man, the misery—
has he any rest from pain now?
[*A voice within, in torment.*]

MESSENGER: He's shouting,
"Loose the bolts, someone, show me to all of Thebes!
My father's murderer, my mother's—"
No, I can't repeat it, it's unholy.   1425
Now he'll tear himself from his native earth,
not linger, curse the house with his own curse.
But he needs strength, and a guide to lead him on.
This is sickness more than he can bear.
[*The palace doors open.*]

                                  Look,
he'll show you himself. The great doors are opening—   1430
you are about to see a sight, a horror
even his mortal enemy would pity.
[*Enter Oedipus, blinded, led by a boy. He stands at the palace steps, as if surveying his people once again.*]

CHORUS: O the terror—
the suffering, for all the world to see,
the worst terror that ever met my eyes.
What madness swept over you? What god,   1435
what dark power leapt beyond all bounds,

beyond belief, to crush your wretched life?—
godforsaken, cursed by the gods!
I pity you but I can't bear to look.
I've much to ask, so much to learn,   1440
so much fascinates my eyes,
but you . . . I shudder at the sight.

OEDIPUS: Oh, Ohh—
the agony! I am agony—
where am I going? where on earth?   1445
where does all this agony hurl me?
where's my voice?—
winging, swept away on a dark tide—
My destiny, my dark power, what a leap you made!

CHORUS: To the depths of terror, too dark to hear, to see.

OEDIPUS: Dark, horror of darkness   1450
my darkness, drowning, swirling around me
crashing wave on wave—unspeakable, irresistible
headwind, fatal harbor! Oh again,
the misery, all at once, over and over
the stabbing daggers, stab of memory   1455
raking me insane.

CHORUS: No wonder you suffer
twice over, the pain of your wounds,
the lasting grief of pain.

OEDIPUS: Dear friend, still here?
Standing by me, still with a care for me,
the blind man? Such compassion,
loyal to the last. Oh it's you,   1460
I know you're here, dark as it is
I'd know you anywhere, your voice—
it's yours, clearly yours.

CHORUS: Dreadful, what you've done . . .
how could you bear it, gouging out your eyes?
What superhuman power drove you on?   1465

OEDIPUS: Apollo, friends, Apollo—
he ordained my agonies—these, my pains on pains!
But the hand that struck my eyes was mine,
mine alone—no one else—
I did it all myself!   1470
What good were eyes to me?
Nothing I could see could bring me joy.

CHORUS: No, no, exactly as you say.

OEDIPUS: What can I ever see?
What love, what call of the heart
can touch my ears with joy? Nothing, friends.   1475
Take me away, far, far from Thebes,
quickly, cast me away, my friends—
this great murderous ruin, this man cursed to heaven,
the man the deathless gods hate most of all!   1480

CHORUS: Pitiful, you suffer so, you understand so much . . .
I wish you'd never known.

OEDIPUS: Die, die—
    whoever he was that day in the wilds
  who cut my ankles free of the ruthless pins,
    he pulled me clear of death, he saved my life
    for this, this kindness—
        Curse him, kill him!
    If I'd died then, I'd never have dragged myself,
  my loved ones through such hell.   1485

CHORUS: Oh if only . . . would to god.

OEDIPUS: I'd never have come to this,   1490
    my father's murderer—never been branded
  mother's husband, all men see me now! Now,
    loathed by the gods, son of the mother I defiled
    coupling in my father's bed, spawning lives in the loins
  that spawned my wretched life. What grief can crown this grief?
    It's mine alone, my destiny—I am Oedipus!   1495

CHORUS: How can I say you've chosen for the best?
  Better to die than be alive and blind.

OEDIPUS: What I did was best—don't lecture me,
  no more advice. I, with *my* eyes,
  how could I look my father in the eyes   1500
  when I go down to death? Or mother, so abused . . .
  I have done such things to the two of them,
  crimes too huge for hanging.
                Worse yet,
  the sight of my children, born as they were born,
  how could I long to look into their eyes?   1505
  No, not with these eyes of mine, never.
  Not this city either, her high towers,
  the sacred glittering images of her gods—
  I am misery! I, her best son, reared
  as no other son of Thebes was ever reared,   1510
  I've stripped myself, I gave the command myself.
  All men must cast away the great blasphemer,
  the curse now brought to light by the gods,
  the son of Laius—I, my father's son!   1515

Now I've exposed my guilt, horrendous guilt,
could I train a level glance on you, my countrymen?
Impossible! No, if I could just block off my ears,
the springs of hearing, I would stop at nothing—
I'd wall up my loathsome body like a prison,   1520
blind to the sound of life, not just the sight:
Oblivion—what a blessing . . .
for the mind to dwell a world away from pain.

O Cithaeron, why did you give me shelter?
Why didn't you take me, crush my life out on the spot?   1525
I'd never have revealed my birth to all mankind.

O Polybus, Corinth, the old house of my fathers,
so I believed—what a handsome prince you raised—
under the skin, what sickness to the core.

Look at me! Born of outrage, outrage to the core.   1530
O triple roads—it all comes back, the secret,
dark ravine, and the oaks closing in
where the three roads join . . .
You drank my father's blood, my own blood
spilled by my own hands—you still remember me?   1535
What things you saw me do? Then I came here
and did them all once more!

            Marriages! O marriage,
you gave me birth, and once you brought me into the world
you brought my sperm rising back, springing to light
fathers, brothers, sons—one murderous breed—   1540
brides, wives, mothers. The blackest things
a man can do, I have done them all!

                  No more—
it's wrong to name what's wrong to do. Quickly,
for the love of god, hide me somewhere,
kill me, hurl me into the sea   1545
where you can never look on me again.
    [*Beckoning to the Chorus as they shrink away.*]
                   Closer,
it's all right. Touch the man of grief.
Do. Don't be afraid. My troubles are mine
and I am the only man alive who can sustain them.
    [*Enter Creon from the palace, attended by palace guards.*]
LEADER: Put your requests to Creon. Here he is,   1550
just when we need him. He'll have a plan, he'll act.
Now that he's the sole defense of the country
in your place.
OEDIPUS: Oh no, what can I say to him?
How can I ever hope to win his trust?
I wronged him so, just now, in every way.   1555
You must see that—I was so wrong, so wrong.
CREON: I haven't come to mock you, Oedipus,
or to criticize your former failings.
    [*Turning to the guards.*]
                You there,
have you lost all respect for human feelings?
At least revere the Sun, the holy fire   1560
that keeps us all alive. Never expose a thing
of guilt and holy dread so great it appalls
the earth, the rain from heaven, the light of day!
Get him into the halls—quickly as you can.
Piety demands no less. Kindred alone   1565
should see a kinsman's shame. This is obscene.
OEDIPUS: Please, in god's name . . . you wipe my fears away,
coming so generously to me, the worst of men.
Do one thing more, for your sake, not mine.
CREON: What do you want? Why so insistent?
OEDIPUS: Drive me out of the land at once, far from sight,   1570
where I can never hear a human voice.

CREON: I'd have done that already, I promise you.
     First I wanted the god to clarify my duties.
OEDIPUS: The god? His command was clear, every word: 1575
     death for the father-killer, the curse—
     he said destroy me!
CREON: So he did. Still, in such a crisis
     it's better to ask precisely what to do.
OEDIPUS: So miserable—
     you'd consult the god about a man like me?
CREON: By all means. And this time, I assume,   1580
     even you will obey the god's decrees.
OEDIPUS: I will,
     I will. And you, I command you—I beg you . . .
     the woman inside, bury her as you see fit.
     It's the only decent thing,
     to give your own the last rites. As for me,   1585
     never condemn the city of my fathers
     to house my body, not while I'm alive, no,
     let me live on the mountains, on Cithaeron,
     my favorite haunt, I have made it famous.
     Mother and father marked out that rock   1590
     to be my everlasting tomb—buried alive.
     Let me die there, where they tried to kill me.
     Oh but this I know: no sickness can destroy me,
     nothing can. I would never have been saved
     from death—I have been saved   1595
     for something great and terrible, something strange.
     Well let my destiny come and take me on its way!
     About my children, Creon, the boys at least,
     don't burden yourself. They're men,
     wherever they go, they'll find the means to live.   1600
     But my two daughters, my poor helpless girls,
     clustering at our table, never without me
     hovering near them . . . whatever I touched,
     they always had their share. Take care of them,
     I beg you. Wait, better—permit me, would you?   1605
     Just to touch them with my hands and take
     our fill of tears. Please . . . my king.
     Grant it, with all your noble heart.
     If I could hold them, just once, I'd think
     I had them with me, like the early days   1610
     when I could see their eyes.

          [Antigone and Ismene, two small children, are led in from the palace by a
          nurse.]
                              What's that
     O god! Do I really hear you sobbing?—
     my two children. Creon, you've pitied me?
     Sent me my darling girls, my own flesh and blood!
     Am I right?   1615
CREON: Yes, it's my doing.
     I know the joy they gave you all these years,
     the joy you must feel now.

OEDIPUS: Bless you, Creon!
      May god watch over you for this kindness,
      better than he ever guarded me.
                              Children, where are you?   1620
      Here, come quickly—
          [*Groping for Antigone and Ismene, who approach their father cautiously,
          then embrace him.*]
                              Come to these hands of mine,
      your brother's hands, your own father's hands
      that served his once bright eyes so well—
      that made them blind. Seeing nothing, children,
      knowing nothing, I became your father,   1625
      I fathered you in the soil that gave me life.

      How I weep for you—I cannot see you now . . .
      just thinking of all your days to come, the bitterness,
      the life that rough mankind will thrust upon you.
      Where are the public gatherings you can join,
      the banquets of the clans? Home you'll come,   1630
      in tears, cut off from the sight of it all,
      the brilliant rites unfinished.
      And when you reach perfection, ripe for marriage,
      who will he be, my dear ones? Risking all
      to shoulder the curse that weighs down my parents,   1635
      yes and you too—that wounds us all together.
      What more misery could you want?
      Your father killed his father, sowed his mother,
      one, one and the selfsame womb sprang you—
      he cropped the very roots of his existence.   1640

      Such disgrace, and you must bear it all!
      Who will marry you then? Not a man on earth.
      Your doom is clear: you'll wither away to nothing,
      single, without a child.
          [*Turning to Creon.*]
                              Oh Creon,   1645
      you are the only father they have now . . .
      we who brought them into the world
      are gone, both gone at a stroke—
      Don't let them go begging, abandoned,
      women without men. Your own flesh and blood!
      Never bring them down to the level of my pains.   1650
      Pity them. Look at them, so young, so vulnerable,
      shorn of everything—you're their only hope.
      Promise me, noble Creon, touch my hand!
          [*Reaching toward Creon, who draws back.*]
      You, little ones, if you were old enough   1655
      to understand, there is much I'd tell you.
      Now, as it is, I'd have you say a prayer.
      Pray for life, my children,
      live where you are free to grow and season.
      Pray god you find a better life than mine,   1660
      the father who begot you.

CREON: Enough.
    You've wept enough. Into the palace now.
OEDIPUS: I must, but I find it very hard.
CREON: Time is the great healer, you will see.
OEDIPUS: I am going—you know on what condition?
CREON: Tell me. I'm listening.   1665
OEDIPUS: Drive me out of Thebes, in exile.
CREON: Not I. Only the gods can give you that.
OEDIPUS: Surely the gods hate me so much—
CREON: You'll get your wish at once.
OEDIPUS: You consent?
CREON: I try to say what I mean; it's my habit.   1670
OEDIPUS: Then take me away. It's time.
CREON: Come along, let go of the children.
OEDIPUS: No—
    don't take them away from me, not now! No no no!
    [*Clutching his daughters as the guards wrench them loose and take them
    through the palace doors.*]
CREON: Still the king, the master of all things?   1675
    No more: here your power ends.
    None of your power follows you through life.
    [*Exit Oedipus and Creon to the palace. The Chorus comes forward to ad-
    dress the audience directly.*]
CHORUS: People of Thebes, my countrymen, look on Oedipus.
    He solved the famous riddle with his brilliance,
    he rose to power, a man beyond all power.
    Who could behold his greatness without envy?   1680
    Now what a black sea of terror has overwhelmed him.
    Now as we keep our watch and wait the final day,
    count no man happy till he dies, free of pain at last.
    [*Exit in procession.*]

Response Statement Questions

• What reading strategies did you use for this text? If you applied the reading strategies suggested in Chapter 16, what happened? To what extent
  did they help you process the text successfully? Did any problems in your
  reading arise? If so, was it because the reading strategies were inadequate
  or because certain text strategies defied those reading strategies? If you
  did encounter problems in reading, were you able to adopt any new
  strategies for processing the text?

• Do you experience this play as a tragedy? If so, in what terms? Is it tragic
  only in relatively limited artistic terms for a 2,500-year-old Mediterranean
  culture, or is it still relevant as tragedy today? Does it conform to ideas of
  tragedy you brought to the reading, or does it challenge those ideas?

• Aristotle wrote that "pity is induced by undeserved misfortune, and fear
  by the misfortunes of normal people" so that the **tragic hero** must be
  "the kind of man who neither is distinguished for excellence and virtue,
  nor comes to grief on account of baseness and vice, but on account of
  some error." Do you see "some error" in Oedipus' moral character that

causes his downfall? Is it the same fault that he identifies in himself? Does he otherwise, for you, meet Aristotle's criteria for a tragic hero?

- What is your response to what Oedipus does after he learns the truth about himself and his past? Are his actions realistic? overly dramatic? symbolically appropriate? horrifying? aesthetically appropriate? ironic? Would the play be any more or less tragic if Oedipus had killed himself? Would he be better off dead?

- In the larger sense, is human fate the result of fateful human choices or of mysterious divine will? How does the text seem to answer this question? How would you answer it according to your ideology? Does your ideology clash or harmonize with the text's on this issue?

- Sigmund Freud wrote the following about *Oedipus the King*. What is your response to his strong reading? What accounts for your response, in terms of your ideology?

> There must be something which makes a voice within us ready to recognize the compelling force of destiny in the Oedipus. . . . His destiny moves us only because it might have been ours—because the oracle laid the same curse upon us before our birth as upon him. It is the fate of all of us [males] ... to direct our first sexual impulse toward our mother and our first hatred and our first murderous wish against our father. Our dreams convince us that that is so. King Oedipus, who slew his father Laius and married his mother Jocasta, merely shows us the fulfillment of our own childhood wishes. But, more fortunate than he, we have meanwhile succeeded, insofar as we have not become psychoneurotics, in detaching our sexual impulses from our mothers and in forgetting our jealousy of our fathers. Here is one [Oedipus] in whom these primeval wishes of our childhood have been fulfilled, and we shrink back from him with the whole force of the repression by which those wishes have since that time been held down within us. While the poet, as he unravels the past, brings to light the guilt of Oedipus, he is at the same time compelling us to recognize our own inner minds, in which those same impulses, though suppressed, are still to be found.
>
> —*The Interpretation of Dreams,*   *1900*

- What is your response to the text strategy of the choral *stasima*? Do the choral songs help you get a perspective on the action involving Oedipus and the other characters, or do they merely "decorate" the play without adding anything substantial to it? Do the opinions of the chorus carry much weight with you? How does your ideology interact with theirs?

- Another text strategy of *Oedipus the King* is that violent acts such as the suicide of Jocasta and Oedipus' blinding occur offstage and are reported rather than shown. What is your response to this? Do you think it weakens the dramatic effect? Does it strengthen it? How is your response affected by your literary experience with respect to displayed violence in television dramas or in films?

- *Share and Compare* What different senses of "tragedy" do readers in your class or discussion group bring to *Oedipus the King* (perhaps with reference to the exercise earlier in this chapter, pages 907–909)? How do those differences affect the ideological interaction different readers had with this play?

BROADENING YOUR LITERARY EXPERIENCE THROUGH RESEARCH

Presumably, what you have read in this chapter and the writing you have done have shown you more than you knew before about the literary repertoire and ideology of *Oedipus the King*, including the features and practices of the Classical Athenian theater and the ideology of the Athenian culture in the fifth century B.C. If you want to further broaden your knowledge with respect to *Oedipus the King*, Sophoclean tragedy, Classical Greek drama in general, Greek religion and philosophy, or any aspect of the ideology behind *Oedipus the King*, the best way to do that is through library research. The reading and writing you have done in this chapter may have raised questions for you that only further research can answer. That's good: Remember that it's questions and questioning that keep learning alive, and that answers are only provisional and temporary. The QAQ method promoted in Chapter 3 applies here too.

Here are some additional questions that you could pursue through library research, followed by a brief bibliography of sources for broadening your repertoire of knowledge in the area of Classical Greek drama. Think of both the sources and the questions as just starting points for further investigation. Even a researched reading, however, should not be considered final. "The truth" about a text does not lie under a rock, waiting to be discovered, or in the library, or in history; it may be pursued, but never possessed. Reading, learning, knowing are processes, of which research is a part. Whenever you read a text, whether you know a lot about it or just a little, you should try to be conscious of the dynamic interaction between you and the text.

Suggestions for Research

- Investigate the source of the Oedipus legend. How or from where did Sophocles know it? What other contemporary literary texts referred to it? What was its larger meaning for Athenians in the mid-fifth century B.C.?
- Investigate the traditions and rituals of religious oracles in ancient Greek culture. Did the belief in and practice of them remain constant, or were they subject to challenge, particularly in Sophocles' day? What was the dominant religious ideology concerning the question of individual freedom versus divine will?

- Inquire into Athenian political philosophy in the mid-fifth century B.C., particularly regarding personal liberty versus the welfare of the state. What was the ideal of or standard for political leadership? Was social exile a worse sentence than death for a political criminal and, if so, why?

- Find out the circumstances of the first production of *Oedipus the King*. How was the play "reviewed" or received in its own day? Was it popular? Was it produced elsewhere in Greece? Did it have much of an effect on subsequent tragedies or on stagecraft in the Classical Greek theater?

- Research the production history of *Oedipus the King* through the ages since the fifth century B.C. Has it been staged pretty continuously since then, or has it come in and gone out of theater fashion? What changes or interpretations have different productions made to Sophocles' text? How have different acting spaces affected the production and reception of the play?

- Investigate how the text has been read in recent centuries, say from the Renaissance (sixteenth century) onward. What strong readings of it are there? Have readers and critics generally accepted it as a tragedy in the same terms that Aristotle or the play's contemporary audience did? Or have any readers challenged its status as a "timeless" or "universal" tragedy?

Selected Bibliography

A good place to begin your search for further information on any of these topics is in the reference section of your library. For any of the above topics, you can find background information and get an overview of related issues and ideas by consulting specialized encyclopedias, handbooks, and readers' guides to particular areas of literature, defined by genre or historical period. Often these kinds of reference works include their own bibliographies of relevant books and periodical articles. Here are some standard reference works for the study of Classical drama.

Coleman, Arthur. *Drama Criticism*, Vol. 2. Denver: Alan Swallow, 1966–71.

Easterling, P. E., and B. M. W. Knox, eds. *The Cambridge History of Classical Literature*. Cambridge: Cambridge UP, 1985.

Feder, Lillian. *Crowell's Handbook of Classical Literature*. New York: Crowell, 1964.

Grant, Michael. *Greek and Latin Authors, 800 B.C.–A.D. 1000*. New York: H. W. Wilson, 1980.

——— and Rachel Kitzinger. *Civilization of the Ancient Mediterranean: Greece and Rome*. 3 vols. New York: Scribner's, 1988.

Luce, T. James. *Ancient Writers: Greece and Rome*. New York: Scribner's, 1982.

The Oxford Classical Dictionary, 2nd ed. Oxford: Clarendon Press, 1970.

Periodicals, such as magazines and scholarly journals, are another good source of information for broadening your literary knowledge. The bibliographies in the above reference sources may list periodical articles, but you can extend your search by consulting any of the following periodical indexes. All are available in both bound volumes and electronic form, as indicated by the note in parentheses following each title.

Arts and Humanities Citation Index. (on line)

Humanities Index. (on line)

MLA International Bibliography. (CD-ROM)

Here is a list of *books* that contain useful information for broadening your knowledge of any of the topics listed earlier.

Baldry, H. C. *The Greek Tragic Theatre.* London: Chatto & Windus, 1971.

Bloom, Harold, ed. *Sophocles' "Oedipus Rex."* New York: Chelsea House, 1987.

Hathorn, Richmond Y. *Tragedy, Myth and Mystery.* Bloomington, Ind.: Indiana UP, 1962.

Jaeger, Werner. *Paedeia: The Ideals of Greek Culture.* Vol. I. Trans. Gilbert Highet. New York: Oxford UP, 1965.

Onians, John. *Art and Thought in the Hellenistic Age.* London: Thames and Hudson, 1979.

Simon, Erika. *The Ancient Theatre.* Trans. C.E. Vafopoulou-Richardson. London: Methuen, 1972.

Walton, J. Michael. *The Greek Sense of Theatre.* London: Methuen, 1984.

19 ◈ THE ELIZABETHAN THEATER

Athens in the fifth and fourth centuries B.C. was the site of the high point of Classical drama. Drama and theater in Western Europe experienced a number of ups and downs in cultural status in the years that followed, but it wasn't until 1,900 years later in Elizabethan and Jacobean England (roughly the years 1560 to 1625, under Queen Elizabeth I and King James I) that another peak was reached.

From Classical Greece to Renaissance England

In ancient Rome drama was presented in the context of larger public events: in religious and secular festivals, alongside gladiatorial matches and other entertainments. An important Roman writer of tragedies was Seneca, who lived in the first century A.D. His plays, or **closet dramas**, were written in verse and intended to be read rather than acted out in a theater (an early and exceptional instance of this type of drama). Written according to a five-act structure that seems to have been the model for later plays, they featured such elements as ghosts, revenge, mayhem, and sensational crimes such as adultery, incest, and murder.

Following the collapse of the Roman Empire in the fifth century A.D., drama suffered a long period of inactivity and suppression by the Catholic Church. Church authorities believed drama encouraged the pursuit of earthly pleasures rather than concern for the salvation of one's eternal soul. Ironically, a revival of drama in the later Middle Ages (the fourteenth and fifteenth centuries) in Europe was brought about by the Church, which used short plays or skits to illustrate biblical stories and sponsored dramatic festivals in which plays depicting the lives of saints or attempting to explain matters of Church doctrine were produced. Acting spaces in this era were again public, as in Classical times, but much more impromptu and informal than ancient Greek and Roman theaters. Plays were often performed on church steps, in town squares, or on platforms atop wagons that rolled like modern parade floats along a public route. Some plays from that era—the anonymously written *Everyman* and *The Second Shepherd's Play*, both from the fifteenth century—are still studied today. However, it was not until the European Renaissance took widespread hold in the sixteenth century that many aspects of the theater and drama that we associate with them today began to be established.

Shakespeare's Theater

As life in post-medieval Europe became more secular and commercial, it brought with it the establishment of relatively small commercial theaters, professional acting companies (sometimes supported by a wealthy, even royal, patron, sometimes by a paying audience), and the reappearance of individual authors writing original plays. William Shakespeare is certainly the best known of these, but during his career he had plenty of company and competition in the persons of Christopher Marlowe, Ben Jonson, Thomas Kyd, John Webster, and others. Drama written by such authors began to be taken seriously as a literary art form, whereas in medieval Europe it had been either trivial entertainment or religious propaganda, more or less. Theaters such as London's famous Globe were commercial enterprises, vying with other attractions for people's "entertainment dollar": bearbaiting and cockfighting matches, athletic contests, public executions and preaching, jugglers and singers. In this way, the cultural situation of the theater began to approach that of today, where live theater competes with an even broader array of entertainment options.

Similarly, the acting spaces of Elizabethan theaters began to assume the characteristics of most theaters today; that is, a relatively intimate venue with covered seating areas and an elevated stage on which the play was performed. The physical relationship between actors and audience was closer than that experienced by most modern theatergoers. The **thrust stage** protruded from one side of the theater, with the audience surrounding it on three sides. In the case of London theaters like The Globe, built in 1599 by the Lord Chamberlain's Men (the acting company to which Shakespeare belonged at the time and for which he wrote plays), the stage was immediately surrounded by an open area—called the yard or the pit—where customers who, for a lower price than for the more expensive covered seats or boxes, could stand to watch the performance. These people were referred to as *groundlings* because they stood on the ground. Behind the yard in semicircular fashion and on three levels were the covered seating areas.

The stage itself was relatively plain, although more complex than the *proskenion* in the typical ancient Greek theater. A commercial theater from Elizabethan England is illustrated on the following page.

Above the stage was a closed structure, known as the "heavens," containing machinery that could be used to raise and lower actors portraying gods and goddesses. This structure was supported by two pillars that could become part of a set if, for instance, a character had to hide and observe another character. On the second level at the back of the stage was a *gallery* where musicians could play and that could be used as a balcony or castle parapet if a script called for such a set. At the back of the stage was an enclosed area called the *tiring house* that was used as a waiting and changing area for actors and as a storage place for props. The stage itself, which was elevated, had a trapdoor in it providing access to the "hell" below the stage. Exits and entrances of characters such as ghosts, devils, or monsters could be made through this trapdoor. There was no curtain at the front of the stage, so changes in scenes were indicated by a character ending a speech in a rhymed *couplet* or by one group of characters leaving the stage and another entering.

An Elizabethan Theater

At theaters like The Globe or The Swan, plays were performed in the daytime, and verbal cues in the dialogue indicated time of day or locality of setting, or characters might carry torches to indicate a night scene. Costumes were elaborate, with kings being instantly recognizable by the crowns they wore and scepters they carried, although they were mostly contemporary dress, not "period" costumes of, say, ancient Rome or ancient Britain that you may be familiar with in modern theaters or in films. Actors—still all males, with young boys often used to play female roles—did not wear masks as they did in the ancient Greek theater, but they did develop a set of stylized and conventional expressions and gestures to indicate certain emotions.

Besides the disappearance of masks for actors, another difference between the Greek and the Elizabethan drama was the elimination of the chorus. In *Oedipus the King*, for instance, the chorus was supposed to be made up of citizens of Thebes, and, as a public group that reacted to the main action of the play, it functioned as a kind of surrogate audience. The Greek chorus probably offered a more overt reaction than the actual audience because the chorus's role assumed they were just finding out what the actual audience already knew.

With the absence of a chorus in the Elizabethan drama, the characters sometimes had to impart information directly to the theater audience. Two conventional and perhaps more personal means of doing this without breaking the spell created by the action onstage were established. Spectators could find out a character's thoughts through a soliloquy, a relatively long, philosophical or reflective speech by a character, alone onstage, who talks not directly to the audience but to himself. Or a character could deliver an aside, in which he or she thinks (and speaks) for the audience but not for the other characters to hear.

For example, even if you have not read *Hamlet*, you may be familiar with one of Hamlet's soliloquies (from Act 3, Scene 1) that begins "To be or not to be, that is the question." In the same scene, just before other characters leave the stage and Hamlet enters, Polonius, the king's adviser, tells his daughter, Ophelia, to pretend she is reading a book. He tells her—and Claudius, the king, hears the remark—that "with devotion's visage / And pious action we do sugar oe'r / The devil himself." Claudius then delivers an aside that presumably informs the audience as to the king's guilty conscience: "O, 'tis too true! / How smart a lash that speech doth give my conscience!"

Elizabethan plays also tended to be more complex than Classical Greek ones in terms of length, number of characters, and plots and subplots. This complexity and the presence of a more heterogenous audience in the theater meant that strategies other than dialogue were needed to maintain interest in the action onstage. One of these strategies was *stage business*—physical as opposed to verbal acting. The surviving printed versions of Shakespeare's plays contain very little in the way of stage directions, which, when you read a play on the page, are often what indicate stage business at a particular point in the action. But in *Hamlet* Act 5, Scene 1, a well-known scene even by those who have not read or seen the entire play, there are some stage directions that indicate stage business. This is the graveyard scene, and the printed text directs one of the grave diggers to dig and sing and to throw up from the ground skulls, one of which Hamlet is directed to take up as he delivers his famous lines "Alas, poor Yorick! I knew him, Horatio. A fellow of infinite jest, of most excellent fancy."

Text Strategies of Shakespearean Drama

There are other text strategies of Shakespearean drama that may need a bit of introduction so you can broaden your literary experience in preparation for reading one or two of his plays. Shakespeare's work as a playwright, actor, and theater company manager and the kind of theater he wrote for—one that was more poetic than realistic and that drew a huge range of viewers, from illiterate London workers to the royal court—affected the plays he wrote in many ways. It affected his choice of subject matter, the kind of humor often included even in his tragedies, the language in which he wrote, and the presence of many and large gaps in the printed versions of his plays. In Shakespeare's day, it was not customary to publish plays in printed form, even though the theater was flourishing. The first publication of his collected plays occurred after his death, when two of his friends and professional associates gathered together copies of *prompt scripts* (versions kept handy for reference during live performances in case an actor forgot a line). Because Shakespeare worked in the theater and because he didn't think of his scripts as permanent written documents, the printed texts of his plays present special problems for readers and editors alike.

Language

Perhaps the biggest problem beginning readers have with Shakespeare's plays concerns the language in which they are written. Elizabethan English was different in many respects from the English spoken today—in vocabulary, in grammar, and in syntax or word order. Also, most of the lines in any of Shakespeare's plays are written in **blank verse**—unrhymed iambic pentameter—with only occasional sections of prose.

Vocabulary or lexical differences have to do with words being used in different senses in Shakespeare's time from the way they are used today or with words being used that are not used today. To cite just two specific examples, Hamlet refers to the ghost of his father as a "worthy pioner" (Act 2, Scene 5. Line 172), meaning a digger or a miner (because the ghost seems to be moving rapidly from place to place beneath Hamlet's feet) and in the same scene the ghost tells Hamlet not to let "the royal bed of Denmark be / A couch for luxury and damnéd incest" (Act 2, Scene 5, Lines 82–83). "Pioner" may be a variant spelling of the word "pioneer," which entered English in the sixteenth century from French, where it had to do with foot soldiers who dig trenches. The idea of digging was the basis for the word's broadening out in meaning to include the first person to go somewhere or embark on some new project, a sense that the word still carries today. "Luxury," on the other hand, carries a usage label *archaic* in *Webster's Ninth New Collegiate Dictionary*, indicating the word is used in that sense "only sporadically or in specific contexts." The word "luxury" is still in use in modern English, but not in the sense of "lust" or "licentiousness," as Hamlet's father's ghost uses it.

Modern editions of any Shakespearean play will provide synonyms for words like these in footnotes or marginal glosses. Other, more commonly used words in Shakespeare's English may not be so translated: "Forsooth," for instance, meaning "truly," or "fie" for "shame," or "methinks" for "I think." Reading a Shakespearean play, you will soon get accustomed to the presence of such words; besides, they aren't as crucial to understanding the sense of the dialogue as more substantive words are.

Grammar

In terms of grammar, the biggest difference between Elizabethan English and our own lies in pronoun forms. Modern English uses only one form for second person, singular and plural, familiar and formal: you. But the English of 400 years ago employed forms of "thee" ("thou" and "thine") for the singular familiar. If your own repertoire of languages includes knowledge of Spanish or German, you are familiar with differences in familiar and formal forms of "you." In addition, the familiar "thou" was used with different verb endings (-t or -st) than we have today; hence, "thou art" or "canst thou." Elizabethan English also sometimes dropped auxiliary verbs that modern English would employ. Our expression "did you come" might be "camest thou," and our "let's get ready" might be "make we ready."

This last example also indicates one of the differences in syntax or word order from the English of Shakespeare's time to our own: While we place a direct object *after* the verb, the Elizabethans often put it *before* the verb; for example, in *Hamlet*, Horatio, having just seen the ghost of Hamlet's father, says "*I might not this believe* / Without the sensible and true avouch [confirmation] / Of mine own eyes." If Horatio were speaking modern English, the italicized phrase might read "*I might not believe this*," with the direct object following the verb.

These matters of grammar and syntax, like certain vocabulary features of Elizabethan English, are not routinely footnoted or glossed in modern editions of Shakespeare's plays, and they may take a little getting used to as you read. To resort to a cliché here, forewarned is forearmed. A reading strategy that should prove helpful with a Shakespeare play is to be aware of some of these linguistic differences and to be confident that, with a little help, you can process the language successfully. At the same time, it's worth remembering that when you see a play produced for stage or film, the context of action and speech will reduce if not eliminate many of the difficulties with language you may encounter with Shakespeare on the page (yet another good reason to *see* his plays produced).

Tragedy in Shakespeare's Ideology

In similar fashion to what you did before reading *Oedipus the King*, spend a few moments now to consider the concept of tragedy in Shakespeare's drama or the kind of tragic drama Shakespeare wrote. If you have read the preceding chapter on Classical tragedy, you bring that sense of tragedy with you as part of your literary experience. But of course Shakespeare's plays were written in different cultural circumstances than Sophocles's, so it would be reasonable to expect some differences in the conception of tragedy held by Shakespeare and his age.

Shakespeare lived and worked in the late Renaissance, a period of about three or four hundred years in Western Europe when appreciation of Classical cultures was relatively widespread and at a height after centuries of relative neglect. For the Elizabethan theater, that meant two things (at least). Generally, it meant that interest in writing, producing, and seeing drama that involved a hero struggling with his fate or with his own moral being—or both—was high. One of the most popular and sensational plays on the English stage when Shakespeare began making his living there in the 1580s was Christopher Marlowe's *Tamburlaine the Great*, the story of a shepherd whose colossal ambition drives him to become emperor of the Mediterranean world before he collapses to a tragic end.

More particularly, the revived interest in the Classical world meant that a certain type of tragedy modeled after Seneca, the Roman playwright, was popular. This was the **revenge tragedy** or, in the variation made fashionable in sixteenth-century English drama, the **tragedy of blood**. It appealed, partly, because contemporary legal and religious prohibitions against blood revenge made the depiction of a protagonist's pursuit of that end daring and sensational. Those same cultural prohibitions also doomed such a protagonist to a tragic end. Seneca's plays, like Greek tragedies before his, had left the violence offstage, to be reported by messengers or other witnesses. Elizabethan audiences, perhaps influenced by violent spectacles available in other forms of popular entertainment such as bearbaitings and public executions, expected to see violence and bloodshed depicted on the stage. Those audiences found what they were looking for in another of the most popular English plays of the late sixteenth century—Thomas Kyd's *The Spanish Tragedy*, a story of murder, revenge, and intrigue.

The Renaissance was also an era that emphasized individual accomplishment and professional reputation to a degree not seen before in Western history. In the contexts of a commercial theater with its appeal to popular taste and a private theater subsidized by influential royal courtiers (both of which Shakespeare was involved with), a playwright had a large stake in putting his individual stamp on older dramatic forms and in presenting distinctively individual dramatic heroes. So you might consider a play like *Hamlet* to be in the mold of the Senecan revenge tragedy, adapted to appeal to contemporary taste, and given a particular spin by its author.

> **CONNECT:**   How much, if at all, has the conception of dramatic tragedy changed from the sixteenth century to the twentieth? Writing in 1966, the English critic Raymond Williams said, "Tragedy, for us, has been mainly the conflict between an individual and the forces that destroy him."

Another part of Shakespeare's literary repertoire was the contemporary adaptation of Classical tragedy into **tragicomedy**—a subgenre that includes comic elements or interludes in a play that conforms to the tragic pattern in other respects. *Hamlet* is not, strictly speaking, a tragicomedy, but neither is it purely a tragedy of the kind his Classical predecessors wrote and that you have read in *Oedipus the King*. It does include what are usually considered comic characters and interludes, and these may at least slightly disturb the unity of effect that a Classical tragedy may be seen to have. Furthermore, in its subplots it may not observe the strict unity of action or single plot conflict that Aristotle observed in *Oedipus* and recommended for tragedy in general. The disunity of *Hamlet* is at least debatable, although some modern literary criticism attempts to find a *thematic* unity that accounts for the presence of virtually all text strategies in the play.

> **CONNECT:**   The play *Six Characters in Search of an Author*, by Luigi Pirandello, in Chapter 22 also mixes tragic and comic elements. If you read that play and *Hamlet*, in which is the mixture of elements most pronounced?

The political context in which Shakespeare wrote is another aspect of the literary repertoire of his plays. Athens in the fifth century B.C. and London in the late sixteenth century A.D. saw cultures that had a strong concern for the relationship of the individual to the state and vice versa. Ancient Athens had an early form of political democracy in which individual and social well-being were interdependent. *Oedipus* is set in the legendary past and in Thebes, not Athens, but these fifth-century Athenian concerns may be seen in the play. Oedipus' fate has political as well as religious dimensions; what happens to the man at the top of the social hierarchy has implications for the entire society. At the same time, even though he is king he is presumably enough like the people in the audience that they can relate to his situation on an individual level. Recall Aristotle's description of the ideal tragic hero, quoted earlier; Aristotle went on to describe tragedy as the fall to grief of "a man of great reputation and prosperity." When those qualities include high social and political standing, the political dimension of the tragedy comes into play.

Although *Hamlet* was written in 1600 and 1601, it is set in an earlier feudal world where the political situation was highly unstable, knowledge of which was part of the ideology of Shakespeare's audience. Issues of royal succession and challenges to the monarch were likely to be on the minds of Shakespeare's audience too. In late sixteenth-century England, such challenges had occurred in the recent past, and lately a strong monarch—Elizabeth I—had consolidated power and raised national pride to a high point through her sponsorship of New World exploration and her navy's defeat of an invading Spanish fleet in 1588. In the 1991 film of *Hamlet*, director Franco Zeffirelli eliminated the character of Fortinbras, the prince of Norway, to whom Hamlet compares himself unfavorably and who returns at the end to restore political order in a kingdom racked with turmoil. As one commentator noted about those cuts in the play, Zeffirelli "acknowledges that the modern audience (unlike the audience of 1600) makes no intimate connections between the body of the state and the body of the ruler"; the dominant ideology about kings and kingship has changed considerably in the ensuing 400 years, so a modern audience may feel nothing substantial is lost by the elimination of what to Shakespeare's audience was a crucial issue.[1]

Reading and Responding: A Shakespearean Tragedy

These political circumstances as well as the literary tradition of the tragic hero inherited from the Classics mean that the basic pattern of Shakespearean tragedy and the social status of its protagonist should be similar to what you have seen in Sophoclean tragedy. Within that broad outline, however, there is still room for considerable variation, as the revenge tragedy subgenre indicates. So now let me just pose some questions for your consideration as you read *Hamlet* in the context of tragedy in general: To what extent is Hamlet the man a mixture of virtues and faults? And to what extent is his downfall (1) inevitable? (2) caused by his own choices or by divine or supernatural will or other powerful forces beyond his control? (3) accompanied by self-recognition or moral insight on Hamlet's part? (4) evocative of pity and fear in the audience, or in you as an individual reader?

In Chapter 15 and in the discussion of *Oedipus the King* in Chapter 18, you were asked to consider the matter of knowing versus unknowing as

---

[1]Joss Lutz Marsh, *Magill's Cinema Annual*, 1991: 143.

essential to drama on numerous levels. If you have not read *Hamlet* before, you probably don't want to know too much about it before you start (and perhaps you think I've given too much away already!). But allow me to sketch out just a few issues of knowing and unknowing regarding some of the major characters in the play. If you have read *Hamlet* before, this should refresh your memory a bit and perhaps frame some issues for reading that you had not considered previously.

Hamlet "knows" something about Claudius that Claudius doesn't know he knows, at least not at first. Hamlet isn't sure what he knows regarding the involvement of Gertrude, his mother, in what Claudius is alleged to have done. You could read the play as the story of Hamlet trying to find out more, or to confirm what he knows. You could also read it as the story of Hamlet in the process of coming to terms with his knowledge: understanding its implications for his own life. Also, Claudius knows something with respect to his guilt or innocence in what Hamlet knows about, and he undergoes a process of coming to know more about what Hamlet knows. Polonius, Claudius' adviser, is involved in trying to know about Hamlet, and that effort has serious consequences for him. His daughter, Ophelia, has a problem with knowledge too: Does she know Hamlet or not? He keeps her in radical uncertainty. When she does come to know one thing for sure about him, that knowledge is apparently too much for her. What her brother, Laertes, knows determines what he does, or tries to do, which affects Hamlet. And even the minor characters Rosencrantz and Guildenstern are given an assignment to find out information but are continually baffled in their efforts, at least partly because Hamlet knows more than they do.[2]

There is one other important thing that all these characters have in common. If you have read *Hamlet* before, perhaps you know or remember what that is. If you have not, you will find out.

Hamlet is a long play, one of Shakespeare's longest in terms of lines and scenes (though all his plays are five acts). Like any play on the page and like Shakespeare's especially, it is riddled with gaps. Many of these gaps, as suggested by the questions above, involve the reader's knowing or unknowing. As you read on through the text, you will fill in some of these gaps easily enough as you find out more through the characters' words and actions. Others will remain open; some that have been identified over the years are still open and always will be, even if one strong reading or another has proposed a way to close them.

One consequence of a reader's identification of gaps in the text is the opportunity to apply consistency building as a reading strategy. As you read, or as you watch a production, you may find yourself trying to explain in some kind of logical or consistent terms why Hamlet does what he does, or why he doesn't do what he's supposed to do—get revenge on Claudius—right away. Indeed the question of Hamlet's "delay" or why he delays exacting revenge has been a significant gap in the text for many readers for the past couple of hundred years, a gap filled in differently by various readers. Many readers also

---

[2]Tom Stoppard's 1967 play *Rosencrantz and Guildenstern Are Dead*—an excellent example of intertextuality—takes off from the lack of knowledge of these two "old friends" of Hamlet. Their unknowing is a source of both comedy and tragedy in Stoppard's play.

have pondered the question of Hamlet's "madness." After he hears his father's ghost's story in Act 1, Hamlet tells his friend Horatio that he will "put an antic disposition on" in order to disguise his inquiry into what the ghost has told him; in other words, he'll act crazy. But over the years, readers have debated the extent to which Hamlet is in control of his insanity act or whether he goes at least temporarily insane as he plays it out. A reader's decision that Hamlet really *is* mad, for instance, based on the way he behaves in Acts 2–4 and on what other characters say about him—is an instance of consistency building to fill in this gap.

The play affords many opportunities for you to use this reading strategy, but you should also remember before you start to read that consistency building has a complementary reading strategy: what the critic Wolfgang Iser calls **wandering viewpoint**. This strategy isn't exactly what it sounds like, so it would probably help if you think of it in contrast to consistency building. If consistency building is filling in gaps or closing down interpretive options as you read (Hamlet delays because he goes insane, for instance), adopting a wandering viewpoint means keeping those gaps or options open, not making up your mind as to, for instance, what makes Hamlet tick.

In an academic context, you are used to engaging in consistency building as you read, even if the term itself is new to you, and you are encouraged to practice it for the sake of writing about literature in papers where you have to argue an interpretation. Reading to come up with a consistent interpretation of a complex character or text seems to be the "natural" way of doing things, but of course it is really a learned procedure. If you find *Hamlet* difficult, apart from the language, it may be because you have trouble building a consistent interpretation with such a contradictory character in such a complex play. So it may just take some of that pressure off you to remember that consistency building is an *optional* reading strategy and that you can also read with a wandering viewpoint and leave your interpretive options open.

Because *Hamlet* is such a long and complex play, you may have an easier time with it if you read and respond to it in segments rather than all at once. For that reason, response statement questions follow each act below, with more comprehensive questions at the end.

William Shakespeare   1564–1616

The Tragedy of Hamlet, Prince of Denmark   1601

[*Dramatis Personae*

Ghost of Hamlet, the former King of Denmark
Claudius, King of Denmark, the former King's brother
Gertrude, Queen of Denmark, widow of the former King and now wife of Claudius
Hamlet, Prince of Denmark, son of the late King and of Gertrude

Polonius, councillor to the King
Laertes, his son
Ophelia, his daughter
Reynaldo, his servant

Horatio, Hamlet's friend and fellow student

Voltimand, Cornelius, Rosencrantz, Guildenstern, Osric, a Gentleman, a Lord,
    members of the Danish court

Bernardo, Francisco, Marcellus, officers and soldiers on watch

Fortinbras, Prince of Norway
Captain in his army

Three or Four *Players,* taking the roles of *Prologue, Player King, Player Queen,* and
    Lucianus
Two *Messengers*
First Sailor
Two *Clowns,* a gravedigger and his companion
Priest
First Ambassador from England
Lords, Soldiers, Attendants, Guards, other Players, Followers of Laertes, other Sailors,
another Ambassador or Ambassadors from England

Scene: *Denmark*]

Act 1, Scene 1

Enter Bernardo and Francisco, two sentinels, [meeting].

BERNARDO:	Who's there?
FRANCISCO:	Nay, answer me. Stand and unfold yourself.
BERNARDO:	Long live the King!
FRANCISCO:	Bernardo?
BERNARDO:	He.
FRANCISCO:	You come most carefully upon your hour.
BERNARDO:	'Tis now struck twelve. Get thee to bed, Francisco.
FRANCISCO:	For this relief much thanks. 'Tis bitter cold,
	And I am sick at heart.
BERNARDO:	Have you had quiet guard?
FRANCISCO:	Not a mouse stirring.
BERNARDO:	Well, good night.
	If you do meet Horatio and Marcellus,
	The rivals of my watch, bid them make haste.

Enter Horatio and Marcellus.

FRANCISCO:	I think I hear them.—Stand, ho! Who is there?
HORATIO:	Friends to this ground.
MARCELLUS:	And liegemen to the Dane.
FRANCISCO:	Give you good night.
MARCELLUS:	O, farewell, honest soldier. Who hath relieved you?
FRANCISCO:	Bernardo hath my place. Give you good night.

2

14

16
17
18

1.1 Location: Elsinore castle. A guard platform.
  2 me (Francisco emphasizes that *he* is the sentry currently on watch.)   **unfold yourself** reveal
    your identity
14 rivals partners   **16 ground** country, land
17 liegeman to the Dane men sworn to serve the Danish king
18 Give i.e., may God give

Exit Francisco.

MARCELLUS: Holla! Bernardo!

BERNARDO: Say, what, is Horatio there?

HORATIO: A piece of him.

BERNARDO: Welcome, Horatio. Welcome, good Marcellus.

HORATIO: What, has this thing appeared again tonight?

BERNARDO: I have seen nothing.

MARCELLUS: Horatio says 'tis but our fantasy,   27
    And will not let belief take hold of him
    Touching this dreaded sight twice seen of us.
    Therefore I have entreated him along   30
    With us to watch the minutes of this night,   31
    That if again this apparition come
    He may approve our eyes and speak to it.   33

HORATIO: Tush, tush, 'twill not appear.

BERNARDO: Sit down awhile,
    And let us once again assail your ears,
    That are so fortified against our story,
    What we have two nights seen.   38

HORATIO: Well, sit we down,
    And let us hear Bernardo speak of this.

BERNARDO: Last night of all,   41
    When yond same star that's westward from the pole
    Had made his course t' illume that part of heaven   42
    Where now it burns, Marcellus and myself,   43
    The bell then beating one—

Enter Ghost.

MARCELLUS: Peace, break thee off! Look where it comes again!

BERNARDO: In the same figure like the King that's dead.

MARCELLUS: Thou art a scholar. Speak to it, Horatio.   48

BERNARDO: Looks 'a not like the King? Mark it, Horatio.   49

HORATIO: Most like. It harrows me with fear and wonder.

BERNARDO: It would be spoke to.   51

MARCELLUS: Speak to it, Horatio.

HORATIO: What art thou that usurp'st this time of night,   53
    Together with that fair and warlike form
    In which the majesty of buried Denmark   55
    Did sometime march? By heaven, I charge thee, speak!   56

MARCELLUS: It is offended.

BERNARDO: See, it stalks away.

HORATIO: Stay! Speak, speak! I charge thee, speak!   *Exit Ghost.*

---

27 fantasy imagination
31 watch keep watch during
38 What with what
42 pole polestar, north star
48 scholar one learned enough to know how to question a ghost properly
49 'a he
51 It . . . to (It was commonly believed that a ghost could not speak until spoken to.)
53 usurp'st wrongfully takes over
56 sometime formerly

30 along to come along
33 approve corroborate
41 Last . . . all i.e., this *very* last night. (Emphatic.)
43 his its.   **illume** illuminate
55 buried Denmark the buried King of Denmark

MARCELLUS: 'Tis gone and will not answer.

BERNARDO: How now, Horatio? You tremble and look pale.
Is not this something more than fantasy?
What think you on 't?   63

HORATIO: Before my God, I might not this believe
Without the sensible and true avouch   65
Of mine own eyes.

MARCELLUS: Is it not like the King?

HORATIO: As thou art to thyself.
Such was the very armor he had on
When he the ambitious Norway combated.   70
So frowned he once when, in an angry parle,   71
He smote the sledded Polacks on the ice.   72
'Tis strange.

MARCELLUS: Thus twice before, and jump at this dead hour,   74
With martial stalk hath he gone by our watch.   75

HORATIO: In what particular thought to work I know not,   76
But in the gross and scope of mine opinion   77
This bodes some strange eruption to our state.

MARCELLUS: Good now, sit down, and tell me, he that knows,   79
Why this same strict and most observant watch
So nightly toils the subject of the land,   81
And why such daily cast of brazen cannon   82
And foreign mart for implements of war,   83
Why such impress of shipwrights, whose sore task   84
Does not divide the Sunday from the week.
What might be toward, that this sweaty haste   86
Doth make the night joint-laborer with the day?
Who is 't that can inform me?

HORATIO: That can I;
At least, the whisper goes so. Our last king,
Whose image even but now appeared to us,
Was, as you know, by Fortinbras of Norway,
Thereto pricked on by a most emulate pride,
Dared to the combat; in which our valiant Hamlet—   93
For so this side of our known world esteemed him—   95
Did slay this Fortinbras; who by a sealed compact   96
Well ratified by law and heraldry

---

63 on 't of it
65 sensible confirmed by the senses   **avouch** warrant, evidence
70 Norway King of Norway   **71 parle** parley
72 sledded traveling on sleds   **Polacks** Poles   **74 jump** exactly
75 stalk stride
76 to work i.e., to collect my thoughts and try to understand this
77 gross and scope general drift
79 Good now (An expression denoting entreaty or expostulation.)
81 toils causes to toil   **subject** subjects   **82 cast** casting
83 mart buying and selling   **84 impress** impressment, conscription
86 toward in preparation
93 Thereto . . . pride (Refers to old Fortinbras, not the Danish King.)   **pricked on** incited.
   emulate emulous, ambitious
95 this . . . world i.e., all Europe, the Western world   **96 sealed** certified, confirmed

Did forfeit, with his life, all those his lands
Which he stood seized of, to the conqueror;   99
Against the which a moiety competent   100
Was gagèd by our king, which had returned   101
To the inheritance of Fortinbras   102
Had he been vanquisher, as, by the same cov'nant   103
And carriage of the article designed,   104
His fell to Hamlet. Now, sir, young Fortinbras,
Of unimprovèd mettle hot and full,   106
Hath in the skirts of Norway here and there   107
Sharked up a list of lawless resolutes   108
For food and diet to some enterprise   109
That hath a stomach in 't, which is no other—   110
As it doth well appear unto our state—
But to recover of us, by strong hand
And terms compulsatory, those foresaid lands
So by his father lost. And this, I take it,
Is the main motive of our preparations,
The source of this our watch, and the chief head   116
Of this posthaste and rummage in the land.   117
BERNARDO: I think it be no other but e'en so.
Well may it sort that this portentous figure   119
Comes armèd through our watch so like the King
That was and is the question of these wars.   121
HORATIO: A mote it is to trouble the mind's eye.   122
In the most high and palmy state of Rome,   123
A little ere the mightiest Julius fell,
The graves stood tenantless, and the sheeted dead   125
Did squeak and gibber in the Roman streets;
As stars with trains of fire and dews of blood,   127
Disasters in the sun; and the moist star   128
Upon whose influence Neptune's empire stands   129
Was sick almost to doomsday with eclipse.   130

---

99 seized possessed
100 Against the in return for   **moiety competent** corresponding portion
101 gagèd engaged, pledged   **had returned** would have passed
102 inheritance possession   **103 cov'nant** i.e., the *sealed compact* of line 96
104 carriage . . . designed carrying out of the article or clause drawn up to cover the point
106 unimprovèd mettle untried, undisciplined spirits
107 skirts outlying regions, outskirts
108 Sharked up gathered up, as a shark takes fish   **list** i.e., troop   **resolutes** desperados
109 For food and diet i.e., they are to serve as *food*, or "means," *to some enterprise; also they
serve in return for the rations they get
110 stomach (1) a spirit of daring (2) an appetite that is fed by the *lawless resolutes*
116 head source   **117 rummage** bustle, commotion
119 sort suit   **121 question** focus of contention
122 mote speck of dust   **123 palmy** flourishing
125 sheeted shrouded
127 As (This abrupt transition suggests that matter is possibly omitted between lines 120 and
121.)   **trains** trails
128 Disasters unfavorable signs or aspects   **moist star** i.e., moon, governing tides
129 Neptune god of the sea   **stands** depends
130 sick . . . doomsday (See Matthew 24:29 and Revelation 6:12.)

And even the like precurse of feared events,   131
As harbingers preceding still the fates   132
And prologue to the omen coming on,   133
Have heaven and earth together demonstrated
Unto our climatures and countrymen.   135

Enter Ghost.

But soft, behold! Lo, where it comes again!   136
I'll cross it, though it blast me. (*It spreads his arms.*)   137
Stay, illusion!
If thou hast any sound or use of voice,
Speak to me!
If there be any good thing to be done
That may to thee do ease and grace to me,
Speak to me!
If thou art privy to the country's fate,
Which, happily, foreknowing may avoid,   144
O, speak!   145
Or if thou hast uphoarded in thy life
Extorted treasure in the womb of earth,
For which, they say, you spirits oft walk in death,
Speak of it! (*The cock crows.*) Stay and speak!—
Stop it, Marcellus.

MARCELLUS: Shall I strike at it with my partisan?   152
HORATIO: Do, if it will not stand.   [*They strike at it.*]
BERNARDO: 'Tis here!
HORATIO: 'Tis here!   [*Exit Ghost.*]
MARCELLUS: 'Tis gone.

We do it wrong, being so majestical,
To offer it the show of violence,
For it is as the air invulnerable,
And our vain blows malicious mockery.

BERNARDO: It was about to speak when the cock crew.
HORATIO: And then it started like a guilty thing
Upon a fearful summons. I have heard
The cock, that is the trumpet to the morn,   164
Doth with his lofty and shrill-sounding throat
Awake the god of day, and at his warning,
Whether in sea or fire, in earth or air,
Th' extravagant and erring spirit hies   168
To his confine; and of the truth herein
This present object made probation.   170

---

131 **precurse** heralding, foreshadowing   132 **harbingers** forerunners   **still** continually
133 **omen** calamitous event   135 **climatures** regions
136 **soft** i.e., enough, break off
137 **cross** stand in its path, confront   **blast** wither, strike with a curse   **s.d. his** its
144 **privy to** in on the secret of   145 **happily** haply, perchance
152 **partisan** long-handled spear   164 **trumpet** trumpeter
168 **extravagant and erring** wandering beyond bounds. (The words have similar meaning.)
    hies hastens
170 **probation** proof

MARCELLUS: It faded on the crowing of the cock.
    Some say that ever 'gainst that season comes   172
    Wherein our Savior's birth is celebrated,
    This bird of dawning singeth all night long,
    And then, they say, no spirit dare stir abroad;
    The nights are wholesome, then no planets strike,   176
    No fairy takes, nor witch hath power to charm,   177
    So hallowed and so gracious is that time.   178
HORATIO: So have I heard and do in part believe it.
    But, look, the morn in russet mantle clad
    Walks o'er the dew of yon high eastward hill.
    Break we our watch up, and by my advice
    Let us impart what we have seen tonight
    Unto young Hamlet; for upon my life,
    This spirit, dumb to us, will speak to him.
    Do you consent we shall acquaint him with it,
    As needful in our loves, fitting our duty?
MARCELLUS: Let's do 't, I pray, and I this morning know
    Where we shall find him most conveniently.

Exeunt.

Act 1, Scene 2

Flourish. Enter Claudius, King of Denmark, Gertrude the Queen, [the] Council, as Polonius and his son Laertes, Hamlet, cum aliis [including Voltimand and Cornelius].

KING: Though yet of Hamlet our dear brother's death   1
    The memory be green, and that is us befitted
    To bear our hearts in grief and our whole kingdom
    To be contracted in one brow of woe,
    Yet so far hath discretion fought with nature
    That we with wisest sorrow think on him
    Together with remembrance of ourselves.
    Therefore our sometime sister, now our queen,   8
    Th' imperial jointress to this warlike state,   9
    Have we, as 'twere with a defeated joy—
    With an auspicious and a dropping eye,   11
    With mirth in funeral and with dirge in marriage,
    In equal scale weighing delight and dole—   13
    Taken to wife. Nor have we herein barred
    Your better wisdoms, which have freely gone
    With this affair along. For all, our thanks.

---

172 'gainst just before
177 takes bewitches
1.2. Location: The castle. s.d. as i.e., such as, including   **cum aliis** with others
 1 our my. (The royal "we"; also in the following lines.)
 8 sometime former
 9 jointress woman possessing property with her husband
11 With . . . eye with one eye smiling and the other weeping
13 dole grief

176 strike destroy by evil influence
178 gracious full of grace

Now follows that you know young Fortinbras,   17
Holding a weak supposal of our worth,   18
Or thinking by our late dear brother's death
Our state to be disjoint and out of frame,
Co-leaguèd with this dream of his advantage,   21
He hath not failed to pester us with message
Importing the surrender of those lands   23
Lost by his father, with all bonds of law,
To our most valiant brother. So much for him.
Now for ourself and for this time of meeting.
Thus much the business is: we have here writ
To Norway, uncle of young Fortinbras—
Who, impotent and bed-rid, scarcely hears   29
Of this his nephew's purpose—to suppress
His further gait herein, in that the levies,   31
The lists, and full proportions are all made   32
Out of his subject; and we here dispatch   33
You, good Cornelius, and you, Voltimand,
For bearers of this greeting to old Norway,
Giving to you no further personal power
To business with the King more than the scope
Of these dilated articles allow.   [*He gives a paper.*]   38
Farewell, and let your haste commend your duty.   39
CORNELIUS, VOLTIMAND: In that, and all things, will we show our duty.
KING: We doubt it nothing. Heartily farewell.   41

[Exeunt Voltimand and Cornelius.]

And now, Laertes, what's the news with you?
You told us of some suit; what is 't, Laertes?
You cannot speak of reason to the Dane   44
And lose your voice. What wouldst thou beg, Laertes,   45
That shall not be my offer, not thy asking?
The head is not more native to the heart,   47
The hand more instrumental to the mouth,   48
Than is the throne of Denmark to thy father.
What wouldst thou have, Laertes?
LAERTES: My dread lord,
Your leave and favor to return to France,   52

---

17 **that you know** what you know already, that; or, that you be informed as follows
18 **weak supposal** low estimate
21 **Co-leaguèd with** joined to, allied with   **dream . . . advantage** illusory hope of having the
  advantage (His only ally is his hope.)
23 **Importing** pertaining to   24 **bonds** contracts
29 **impotent** helpless   31 **His** i.e., Fortinbras'   **gait** proceeding
31–33 **in that . . . subject** since the levying of troops and supplies is drawn entirely from the
  King of Norway's own subjects
38 **dilated** set out at length
39 **let . . . duty** let your swift obeying of orders, rather than mere words, express your dutifulness
41 **nothing** not at all   44 **the Dane** the Danish King
45 **lose your voice** waste your speech   47 **native** closely connected, related
48 **instrumental** serviceable   52 **leave and favor** kind permission

From whence though willingly I came to Denmark
To show my duty in your coronation,
Yet now I must confess, that duty done,
My thoughts and wishes bend again toward France
And bow them to your gracious leave and pardon.   57
KING: Have you your father's leave? What says Polonius?
POLONIUS: H'ath, my lord, wrung from me my slow leave   59
By laborsome petition, and at last
Upon his will I sealed my hard consent.   61
I do beseech you, give him leave to go.
KING: Take thy fair hour, Laertes. Time be thine,   63
And thy best graces spend it at thy will!   64
But now, my cousin Hamlet, and my son—   65
HAMLET: A little more than kin, and less than kind.   66
KING: How is it that the clouds still hang on you?
HAMLET: Not so, my lord. I am too much in the sun.   68
QUEEN: Good Hamlet, cast thy nighted color off,   69
And let thine eye look like a friend on Denmark.   70
Do not forever with thy vailèd lids   71
Seek for thy noble father in the dust.
Thou know'st 'tis common, all that lives must die,   73
Passing through nature to eternity.
HAMLET: Ay, madam, it is common.
QUEEN: If it be,
Why seems it so particular with thee?   77
HAMLET: Seems, madam? Nay, it is. I know not "seems."
'Tis not alone my inky cloak, good Mother,
Nor customary suits of solemn black,   80
Nor windy suspiration of forced breath,   81
No, nor the fruitful river in the eye,   82
Nor the dejected havior of the visage,   83
Together with all forms, moods, shapes of grief,   84
That can denote me truly. These indeed seem,

---

57 bow . . . pardon entreatingly make a deep bow, asking your permission to depart
59 H'ath he has
61 sealed (as if sealing a legal document)   **hard** reluctant
63 Take thy fair hour enjoy your time of youth
64 And . . . will and may your finest qualities guide the way you choose to spend your time
65 cousin any kin not of the immediate family
66 A little . . . kind i.e., closer than an ordinary nephew (since I am stepson), and yet more separated in natural feeling (with pun on *kind* meaning "affectionate" and "natural," "lawful." This line is often read as an aside, but it need not be. The King chooses perhaps not to respond to Hamlet's cryptic and bitter remark.)
68 the sun i.e., the sunshine of the King's royal favor (with pun on *son*)
69 nighted color (1) mourning garments of black (2) dark melancholy
70 Denmark the King of Denmark   **71 vailèd lids** lowered eyes
73 common of universal occurrence (But Hamlet plays on the sense of "vulgar" in line 75.)
77 particular personal
80 customary (1) socially conventional (2) habitual with me
81 suspiration sighing   **82 fruitful** abundant
83 havior expression   **84 moods** outward expression of feeling

For they are actions that a man might play.
But I have that within which passes show;
These but the trappings and the suits of woe.

KING: 'Tis sweet and commendable in your nature, Hamlet,
To give these mourning duties to your father.
But you must know your father lost a father,
That father lost, lost his, and the survivor bound
In filial obligation for some term
To do obsequious sorrow. But to persever   94
In obstinate condolement is a course   95
Of impious stubbornness. 'Tis unmanly grief.
It shows a will most incorrect to heaven,
A heart unfortified, a mind impatient,   98
An understanding simple and unschooled.   99
For what we know must be and is as common
As any the most vulgar thing to sense,   101
Why should we in our peevish opposition
Take it to heart? Fie, 'tis a fault to heaven,
A fault against the dead, a fault to nature,
To reason most absurd, whose common theme
Is death of fathers, and who still hath cried,   106
From the first corpse till he that died today,   107
"This must be so." We pray you, throw to earth
This unprevailing woe and think of us   109
As of a father; for let the world take note,
You are the most immediate to our throne,   111
And with no less nobility of love
Than that which dearest father bears his son
Do I impart toward you. For your intent   114
In going back to school in Wittenberg,   115
It is most retrograde to our desire,   116
And we beseech you bend you to remain   117
Here in the cheer and comfort of our eye,
Our chiefest courtier, cousin, and our son.

QUEEN: Let not thy mother lose her prayers, Hamlet.
I pray thee, stay with us, go not to Wittenberg.

HAMLET: I shall in all my best obey you, madam.   122

KING: Why, 'tis a loving and a fair reply.
Be as ourself in Denmark. Madam, come.
This gentle and unforced accord of Hamlet
Sits smiling to my heart, in grace whereof   126

---

94 obsequious suited to obsequies or funerals   persever persevere
95 condolement sorrowing   98 unfortified i.e., against adversity
99 simple ignorant   101 As . . . sense as the most ordinary experience
106 still always   107 the first corpse (Abel's)
109 unprevailing unavailing, useless   111 most immediate next in succession
114 impart toward i.e., bestow my affection on   For as for
115 to school i.e., to your studies   Wittenburg famous German university founded in 1502
116 retrograde contrary   117 bend you incline yourself
122 in all my best to the best of my ability   126 to i.e., at   grace thanksgiving

No jocund health that Denmark drinks today   127
But the great cannon to the clouds shall tell,
And the King's rouse the heaven shall bruit again,   129
Respeaking earthly thunder. Come away.   130

Flourish. Exeunt all but Hamlet.

HAMLET: O, that this too too sullied flesh would melt,   131
Thaw, and resolve itself into a dew!
Or that the Everlasting had not fixed
His canon 'gainst self-slaughter! O God, God,   134
How weary, stale, flat, and unprofitable
Seem to me all the uses of this world!   136
Fie on 't, ah fie! 'Tis an unweeded garden
That grows to seed. Things rank and gross in nature
Possess it merely. That it should come to this!   139
But two months dead—nay, not so much, not two.
So excellent a king, that was to this   141
Hyperion to a satyr, so loving to my mother   142
That he might not beteem the winds of heaven   143
Visit her face too roughly. Heaven and earth,
Must I remember? Why, she would hang on him
As if increase of appetite had grown
By what it fed on, and yet within a month—
Let me not think on 't; frailty, thy name is woman!—
A little month, or ere those shoes were old   149
With which she followed my poor father's body,
Like Niobe, all tears, why she, even she—   151
O God, a beast, that wants discourse of reason,   152
Would have mourned longer—married with my uncle,
My father's brother, but no more like my father
Than I to Hercules. Within a month,
Ere yet the salt of most unrighteous tears
Had left the flushing in her gallèd eyes,   157
She married. O, most wicked speed, to post   158
With such dexterity to incestuous sheets!   159

---

127 jocund merry
129 rouse drinking of a draft of liquor   **bruit again** loudly echo
130 thunder i.e., of trumpet and kettledrum, sounded when the King drinks; see 1.4.8–12
131 sullied defiled. (The early quartos read *sallied*; the Folio, *solid*.)

134 canon law   **136 all the uses** the whole routine
139 merely completely   **141 to** in comparison to
142 Hyperion Titan sun-god, father of Helios   **satyr** a lecherous creature of classical mythology,
half-human but with a goat's legs, tail, ears, and horns
143 beteem allow   **149 or ere** even before
151 Niobe Tantalus' daughter, Queen of Thebes, who boasted that she had more sons and
daughters than Leto; for this, Apollo and Artemis, children of Leto, slew her fourteen childre
She was turned by Zeus into a stone that continually dropped tears.
152 wants . . . reason lacks the faculty of reason
157 gallèd irritated, inflamed   **158 post** hasten
159 incestuous (In Shakespeare's day, the marriage of a man like Claudius to his deceased
brother's wife was considered incestuous.)

It is not, nor it cannot come to good.
But break, my heart, for I must hold my tongue.

Enter Horatio, Marcellus, and Bernardo.

HORATIO: Hail to your lordship!
HAMLET: I am glad to see you well.
  Horatio!—or I do forget myself.
HORATIO: The same, my lord, and your poor servant ever.
HAMLET: Sir, my good friend; I'll change that name with you.   166
  And what make you from Wittenberg, Horatio?   167
  Marcellus.
MARCELLUS: My good lord.
HAMLET: I am very glad to see you. [*To Bernardo.*] Good even, sir.—
  But what in faith make you from Wittenberg?
HORATIO: A truant disposition, good my lord.
HAMLET: I would not hear your enemy say so,
  Nor shall you do my ear that violence
  To make it truster of your own report
  Against yourself. I know you are no truant.
  But what is your affair in Elsinore?
  We'll teach you to drink deep ere you depart.
HORATIO: My lord, I came to see your father's funeral.
HAMLET: I prithee, do not mock me, fellow student;
  I think it was to see my mother's wedding.
HORATIO: Indeed, my lord, it followed hard upon.
HAMLET: Thrift, thrift, Horatio! The funeral baked meats   182
  Did coldly furnish forth the marriage tables.   183
  Would I had met my dearest foe in heaven   184
  Or ever I had seen that day, Horatio!   185
  My father!—Methinks I see my father.   186
HORATIO: Where, my lord?
HAMLET: In my mind's eye, Horatio.
HORATIO: I saw him once. 'A was a goodly king.
HAMLET: 'A was a man. Take him for all in all,   190
  I shall not look upon his like again.
HORATIO: My lord, I think I saw him yesternight.
HAMLET: Saw? Who?
HORATIO: My lord, the King your father.
HAMLET: The King my father?
HORATIO: Season your admiration for a while   197
  With an attent ear till I may deliver,   198
  Upon the witness of these gentlemen,
  This marvel to you.

---

166 change that name i.e., give and receive reciprocally the name of "friend" (rather than talk of
  "servant")
167 make you from are you doing away from   **182 hard** close
183 baked meats meat pies   **184 coldly** i.e., as cold leftovers
185 dearest closest (and therefore deadliest   **186 Or ever** before
190 'A he
197 Season your admiration restrain your astonishment
198 attent attentive

HAMLET: For God's love, let me hear!
HORATIO: Two nights together had these gentlemen,
      Marcellus and Bernardo, on their watch,
      In the dead waste and middle of the night,   204
      Been thus encountered. A figure like your father,
      Armèd at point exactly, cap-à-pie,   206
      Appears before them, and with solemn march
      Goes slow and stately by them. Thrice he walked
      By their oppressed and fear-surprisèd eyes
      Within his truncheon's length, whilst they, distilled   210
      Almost to jelly with the act of fear,   211
      Stand dumb and speak not to him. This to me
      In dreadful secrecy impart they did,   213
      And I with them the third night kept the watch,
      Where, as they had delivered, both in time,
      Form of the thing, each word made true and good,
      The apparition comes. I knew your father;
      These hands are not more like.
HAMLET: But where was this?
MARCELLUS: My lord, upon the platform where we watch.
HAMLET: Did you speak to it?
HORATIO: My lord, I did,
      But answer made it none. Yet once methought
      It lifted up its head and did address   224
      Itself to motion, like as it would speak;   225
      But even then the morning cock crew loud,   226
      And at the sound it shrunk in haste away
      And vanished from our sight.
HAMLET: 'Tis very strange.
HORATIO: As I do live, my honored lord, 'tis true,
      And we did think it writ down in our duty
      To let you know of it.
HAMLET: Indeed, indeed, sirs. But this troubles me.
      Hold you the watch tonight?
ALL: We do, my lord.
HAMLET: Armed, say you?
ALL: Armed, my lord.
HAMLET: From top to toe?
ALL: My lord, from head to foot.
HAMLET: Then saw you not his face?
HORATIO: O, yes, my lord, he wore his beaver up.   241
HAMLET: What looked he, frowningly?   242
HORATIO: A countenance more in sorrow than in anger.

---

204 dead waste desolate stillness
206 at point correctly in every detail   **cap-à-pie** from head to foot
210 truncheon officer's staff   **distilled** dissolved
211 act action, operation   **213 dreadful** full of dread
224–225 did . . . speak began to move as though it were about to speak
226 even then at that very instant   **241 beaver** visor on the helmet
242 What how

HAMLET: Pale or red?
HORATIO: Nay, very pale.
HAMLET: And fixed his eyes upon you?
HORATIO: Most constantly.
HAMLET: I would I had been there.
HORATIO: It would have much amazed you.
HAMLET: Very like, very like. Stayed it long?
HORATIO: While one with moderate haste might tell a hundred.   251
MARCELLUS, BERNARDO: Longer, longer.
HORATIO: Not when I saw 't.
HAMLET: His beard was grizzled—no?   254
HORATIO: It was, as I have seen it in his life,
     A sable silvered.   256
HAMLET: I will watch tonight.
     Perchance 'twill walk again.
HORATIO: I warrant it will.   259
HAMLET: If it assume my noble father's person,
     I'll speak to it though hell itself should gape
     And bid me hold my peace. I pray you all,
     If you have hitherto concealed this sight,
     Let it be tenable in your silence still,   264
     And whatsoever else shall hap tonight,
     Give it an understanding but no tongue.
     I will requite your loves. So, fare you well.
     Upon the platform twixt eleven and twelve
     I'll visit you.
ALL: Our duty to your honor.
HAMLET: Your loves, as mine to you. Farewell.

Exeunt [all but Hamlet].

     My father's spirit in arms! All is not well.
     I doubt some foul play. Would the night were come!   273
     Till then sit still, my soul. Foul deeds will rise,
     Though all the earth o'erwhelm them, to men's eyes.

Exit

Act 1, Scene 3

Enter Laertes and Ophelia, his sister.

LAERTES: My necessaries are embarked. Farewell.
     And, sister, as the winds give benefit
     And convoy is assistant, do not sleep   3
     But let me hear from you.
OPHELIA: Do you doubt that?
LAERTES: For Hamlet, and the trifling of his favor,
     Hold it a fashion and a toy in blood,   7

---

251 **tell** count
256 **sable silvered** black mixed with white
264 **tenable** held
1.3. **Location: Polonius' chambers.**
3 **convoy is assistant** means of conveyance are available
7 **toy in blood** passing amorous fancy

254 **grizzled** gray
259 **warrant** assure you
273 **doubt** suspect

A violet in the youth of primy nature, 8
Forward, not permanent, sweet, not lasting, 9
The perfume and suppliance of a minute— 10
No more.

OPHELIA: No more but so?

LAERTES: Think it no more.
For nature crescent does not grow alone 14
In thews and bulk, but as this temple waxes 15
The inward service of the mind and soul
Grows wide withal. Perhaps he loves you now, 17
And now no soil nor cautel doth besmirch 18
The virtue of his will; but you must fear, 19
His greatness weighed, his will is not his own. 20
For he himself is subject to his birth.
He may not, as unvalued persons do,
Carve for himself, for on his choice depends 23
The safety and health of this whole state,
And therefore must his choice be circumscribed
Unto the voice and yielding of that body
Whereof he is the head. Then if he says he loves you, 26
It fits your wisdom so far to believe it
As he in his particular act and place
May give his saying deed, which is no further 29
Than the main voice of Denmark goes withal.
Then weigh what loss your honor may sustain 31
If with too credent ear you list his songs,
Or lose your heart, or your chaste treasure open 33
To his unmastered importunity.
Fear it, Ophelia, fear it, my dear sister,
And keep you in the rear of your affection,
Out of the shot and danger of desire. 37
The chariest maid is prodigal enough
If she unmask her beauty to the moon. 39
Virtue itself scapes not calumnious strokes. 40
The canker galls the infants of the spring
Too oft before their buttons be disclosed, 42
And in the morn and liquid dew of youth 43
Contagious blastments are most imminent. 44
                                                                                    45

---

8 primy in its prime, springtime   **9 Forward** precocious
10 suppliance supply, filler   **14 crescent** growing, waxing
15 thews bodily strength   **temple** i.e., body   **17 Grows wide withal** grows along with it
18 soil blemish   **cautel** deceit   **19 will** desire
20 His greatness weighed if you take into account his high position
23 Carve i.e., choose   **26 voice and yielding** assent, approval
29 in . . . place in his particular restricted circumstances
31 main voice general assent   **withal** along with   **33 credent** credulous   **list** listen to
37 keep . . . affection don't advance as far as your affection might lead you (A military metaphor.)
39 chariest most scrupulously modest
40 If she unmask if she does no more than show her beauty   **moon** (Symbol of chastity)
42 canker galls cankerworm destroys   **43 buttons** buds   **disclosed** opened
44 liquid dew i.e., time when dew is fresh and bright
45 blastments blights

Be wary then; best safety lies in fear.
Youth to itself rebels, though none else near.   47
OPHELIA: I shall the effect of this good lesson keep
As watchman to my heart. But, good my brother,
Do not, as some ungracious pastors do,   50
Show me the steep and thorny way to heaven,
Whiles like a puffed and reckless libertine   52
Himself the primrose path of dalliance treads,
And recks not his own rede.   54

Enter Polonius.

LAERTES: O, fear me not.   55
I stay too long. But here my father comes.
A double blessing is a double grace;   57
Occasion smiles upon a second leave.   58
POLONIUS: Yet here, Laertes? Aboard, aboard, for shame!
The wind sits in the shoulder of your sail,
And you are stayed for. There—my blessing with thee!
And these few precepts in thy memory
Look thou character. Give thy thoughts no tongue,   63
Nor any unproportioned thought his act.   64
Be thou familiar, but by no means vulgar.   65
Those friends thou hast, and their adoption tried,   66
Grapple them unto thy soul with hoops of steel,
But do not dull thy palm with entertainment   68
Of each new-hatched, unfledged courage. Beware   69
Of entrance to a quarrel, but being in,
Bear 't that th' opposèd may beware of thee.   71
Give every man thy ear, but few thy voice;
Take each man's censure, but reserve thy judgment.   73
Costly thy habit as thy purse can buy,   74
But not expressed in fancy; rich, not gaudy,   75
For the apparel oft proclaims the man,
And they in France of the best rank and station
Are of a most select and generous chief in that.   78
Neither a borrower nor a lender be,
For loan oft loses both itself and friend,
And borrowing dulleth edge of husbandry.   81

---

47 Youth . . . rebels youth is inherently rebellious   **50 ungracious** ungodly
52 puffed bloated, or swollen with pride
54 recks heeds   **rede** counsel   **55 fear me not** don't worry on my account
57 double (Laertes has already bid his father good-bye.)
58 Occasion . . . leave happy is the circumstance that provides a second leave-taking (The goddess Occasion, or Opportunity, smiles.)
63 Look be sure that   **character** inscribe
64 unproportioned badly calculated, intemperate   **his** its
65 familiar sociable   **vulgar** common
66 and their adoption tried and also their suitability for adoption as friends having been tested
68 dull thy palm i.e., shake hands so often as to make the gesture meaningless
69 courage young man of spirit   **71 Bear 't that** manage it so that
73 censure opinion, judgment   **74 habit** clothing
75 fancy excessive ornament, decadent fashion
78 Are . . . that are of a most refined and well-bred preeminence in choosing what to wear
81 husbandry thrift

This above all: to thine own self be true,
And it must follow, as the night the day,
Thou canst not then be false to any man.
Farewell. My blessing season this in thee!

LAERTES: Most humbly do I take my leave, my lord. 85

POLONIUS: The time invests you. Go, your servants tend. 87

LAERTES: Farewell, Ophelia, and remember well
What I have said to you.

OPHELIA: 'Tis in my memory locked,
And you yourself shall keep the key of it.

LAERTES: Farewell. *Exit Laertes.*

POLONIUS: What is 't, Ophelia, he hath said to you?

OPHELIA: So please you, something touching the Lord Hamlet.

POLONIUS: Marry, well bethought. 95
'Tis told me he hath very oft of late
Given private time to you, and you yourself
Have of your audience been most free and bounteous.
If it be so—as so 'tis put on me, 99
And that in way of caution—I must tell you
You do not understand yourself so clearly
As it behooves my daughter and your honor. 102
What is between you? Give me up the truth.

OPHELIA: He hath, my lord, of late made many tenders 104
Of his affection to me.

POLONIUS: Affection? Pooh! You speak like a green girl,
Unsifted in such perilous circumstance. 107
Do you believe his tenders, as you call them?

OPHELIA: I do not know, my lord, what I should think.

POLONIUS: Marry, I will teach you. Think yourself a baby
That you have ta'en these tenders for true pay
Which are not sterling. Tender yourself more dearly, 112
Or—not to crack the wind of the poor phrase, 113
Running it thus—you'll tender me a fool. 114

OPHELIA: My lord, he hath importuned me with love
In honorable fashion.

POLONIUS: Ay, fashion you may call it. Go to, go to. 117

OPHELIA: And hath given countenance to his speech, my lord, 118
With almost all the holy vows of heaven.

POLONIUS: Ay, springes to catch woodcocks. I do know, 120
When the blood burns, how prodigal the soul 121

---

85 season mature
87 invests besieges, presses upon **tend** attend, wait
95 Marry i.e., by the Virgin Mary (A mild oath.)
99 put on impressed on, told to **102 behooves** befits
104 tenders offers **107 Unsifted** i.e., untried
112 sterling legal currency **Tender** hold, look after, offer
113 crack the wind i.e., run it until it is broken-winded
114 tender me a fool (1) show yourself to me as a fool (2) show me up as a fool (3) present me
with a grandchild (*Fool* was a term of endearment for a child.)
117 fashion mere form, pretense **Go to** (An expression of impatience.)
118 countenance credit, confirmation
120 springes snares **woodcocks** birds easily caught; here used to connote gullibility
121 prodigal prodigally

Lends the tongue vows. These blazes, daughter,
Giving more light than heat, extinct in both
Even in their promise as it is a-making,
You must not take for fire. From this time   124
Be something scanter of your maiden presence.   126
Set your entreatments at a higher rate   127
Than a command to parle. For Lord Hamlet,   128
Believe so much in him that he is young,   129
And with a larger tether may he walk
Than may be given you. In few, Ophelia,   131
Do not believe his vows, for they are brokers,   132
Not of that dye which their investments show,   133
But mere implorators of unholy suits,   134
Breathing like sanctified and pious bawds,   135
The better to beguile. This is for all: 136
I would not, in plain terms, from this time forth
Have you so slander any moment leisure   138
As to give words or talk with the Lord Hamlet.
Look to 't, I charge you. Come your ways.   140

OPHELIA: I shall obey, my lord.   *Exeunt.*

Act 1, Scene 4

Enter Hamlet, Horatio, and Marcellus.

HAMLET: The air bites shrewdly; it is very cold.   1
HORATIO: It is a nipping and an eager air.   2
HAMLET: What hour now?
HORATIO: I think it lacks of twelve.
MARCELLUS: No, it is struck.   4
HORATIO: Indeed? I heard it not.
        It then draws near the season   7
        Wherein the spirit held his wont to walk.   8

A flourish of trumpets, and two pieces go off [within].

        What does this mean, my lord?
HAMLET: The King doth wake tonight and takes his rouse,   10
        Keeps wassail, and the swaggering upspring reels;   11

---

124 it i.e., the promise   **126 something** somewhat
127 entreatments negotiations for surrender (A military term.)
128 parle discuss terms with the enemy (Polonius urges his daughter, in the metaphor of military
   language, not to meet with Hamlet and consider giving in to him merely because he requests
   an interview.)
129 so . . . him this much concerning him   **131 In few** briefly
132 brokers go betweens, procurers
133 dye color or sort   **investments** clothes (The vows are not what they seem.)
134 mere implorators out and out solicitors   **135 Breathing** speaking
136 for all once for all, in sum   **138 slander** abuse, misuse   **moment** moment's
140 Come your ways come along
1.4. Location: The guard platform.
1 shrewdly keenly, sharply   **2 eager** biting
4 lacks of is just short of   **7 season** time
8 held his wont was accustomed   **s.d. pieces** i.e., of ordnance, cannon
10 wake stay awake and hold revel   **takes his rouse** carouses
11 wassail carousal   **upspring** wild German dance   **reels** dances

And as he drains his drafts of Rhenish down,   12
The kettledrum and trumpet thus bray out
The triumph of his pledge   14

HORATIO: Is it a custom?

HAMLET: Ay, marry, is 't,
But to my mind, though I am native here
And to the manner born, it is a custom   18
More honored in the breach than the observance.   19
This heavy-headed revel east and west   20
Makes us traduced and taxed of other nations.   21
They clepe us drunkards, and with swinish phrase   22
Soil our addition; and indeed it takes   23
From our achievements, though performed at height,   24
The pith and marrow of our attribute.   25
So, oft it chances in particular men,
That for some vicious mole of nature in them,
As in their birth—wherein they are not guilty,   27
Since nature cannot choose his origin—
By their o'ergrowth of some complexion,   29
Oft breaking down the pales and forts of reason,   30
Or by some habit that too much o'erleavens   31
The form of plausive manners, that these men,   32
Carrying, I say, the stamp of one defect,   33
Being nature's livery or fortune's star,
His virtues else, be they as pure as grace,   35
As infinite as man may undergo,   36
Shall in the general censure take corruption   37
From that particular fault. The dram of evil   38
Doth all the noble substance often dout   39
To his own scandal.   40
                                                                               41

Enter Ghost.

HORATIO: Look, my lord, it comes!

---

12 Rhenish Rhine wine
14 The triumph . . . pledge i.e., his feat in draining the wine in a single draft
18 manner custom (of drinking)
19 More . . . observance better neglected than followed
20 east and west i.e., everywhere   **21 taxed of** censured by
22 clepe call   **with swinish phrase** i.e., by calling us swine
23 addition reputation   **24 at height** outstandingly
25 The pith . . . attribute the essence of the reputation that others attribute to us
27 for on account of   **mole of nature** natural blemish in one's constitution
29 his its
30 their o'ergrowth . . . complexion the excessive growth in individuals of some natural trait
31 pales palings, fences (as of a fortification)
32 o'erleavens induces a change throughout (as yeast works in dough)
33 plausive pleasing
35 nature's livery sign of one's servitude to nature   **fortune's star** the destiny that chance brings
36 His virtues else i.e., the other qualities of *these* men (line 33)
37 may undergo can sustain
38 general censure general opinion that people have of him
39–41 The dram . . . scandal i.e., the small drop of evil blots out or works against the noble substance of the whole and brings it into disrepute To *dout* is to blot out. (A famous crux.)

HAMLET: Angels and ministers of grace defend us!   43
    Be thou a spirit of health or goblin damned,   44
    Bring with thee airs from heaven or blasts from hell,   45
    Be thy intents wicked or charitable,   46
    Thou com'st in such a questionable shape   47
    That I will speak to thee. I'll call thee Hamlet,
    King, father, royal Dane. O, answer me!
    Let me not burst in ignorance, but tell
    Why thy canonized bones, hearsèd in death,   51
    Have burst their cerements; why the sepulcher   52
    Wherein we saw thee quietly inurned   53
    Hath oped his ponderous and marble jaws
    To cast thee up again. What may this mean,
    That thou, dead corpse, again in complete steel,   56
    Revisits thus the glimpses of the moon,   57
    Making night hideous, and we fools of nature   58
    So horridly to shake our disposition   59
    With thoughts beyond the reaches of our souls?
    Say, why is this? Wherefore? What should we do?

[The Ghost] beckons [Hamlet].

HORATIO: It beckons you to go away with it,
    As if it some impartment did desire   63
    To you alone.
MARCELLUS: Look with what courteous action
    It wafts you to a more removèd ground.
    But do not go with it.
HORATIO: No, by no means.
HAMLET: It will not speak. Then I will follow it.
HORATIO: Do not, my lord!
HAMLET: Why, what should be the fear?
    I do not set my life at a pin's fee,   72
    And for my soul, what can it do to that,
    Being a thing immortal as itself?
    It waves me forth again. I'll follow it.
HORATIO: What if it tempt you toward the flood, my lord,   76
    Or to the dreadful summit of the cliff
    That beetles o'er his base into the sea,   78
    And there assume some other horrible form

---

43 ministers of grace messengers of God
44 Be thou whether you are   **spirit of health** good angel
45 Bring whether you bring   **46 Be thy intents** whether your intentions are
47 questionable inviting question
51 canonized buried according to the canons of the church   **hearsèd** coffined
52 cerements grave clothes   **53 inurned** entombed
56 complete steel full armor
57 glimpses of the moon pale and uncertain moonlight
58 fools of nature mere men, limited to natural knowledge and subject to nature
59 So . . . disposition to distress our mental composure so violently
63 impartment communication   **72 fee** value
76 flood sea
78 beetles o'er overhangs threateningly (like bushy eyebrows)   **his** its

Which might deprive your sovereignty of reason   80
And draw you into madness? Think of it.
The very place puts toys of desperation,   82
Without more motive, into every brain
That looks so many fathoms to the sea
And hears it roar beneath.

HAMLET: It wafts me still.—Go on, I'll follow thee.
MARCELLUS: You shall not go, my lord.   [*They try to stop him.*]
HAMLET: Hold off your hands!
HORATIO: Be ruled. You shall not go.
HAMLET: My fate cries out,   90
And makes each petty artery in this body   91
As hardy as the Nemean lion's nerve.   92
Still am I called. Unhand me, gentlemen.
By heaven, I'll make a ghost of him that lets me!   94
I say, away!—Go on, I'll follow thee.

Exeunt Ghost and Hamlet.

HORATIO: He waxes desperate with imagination.
MARCELLUS: Let's follow. 'Tis not fit thus to obey him.
HORATIO: Have after. To what issue will this come?
MARCELLUS: Something is rotten in the state of Denmark.   98
HORATIO: Heaven will direct it.
MARCELLUS: Nay, let's follow him.   *Exeunt.*   100

Act 1, Scene 5

Enter Ghost and Hamlet.

HAMLET: Whither wilt thou lead me? Speak. I'll go no further.
GHOST: Mark me.
HAMLET: I will.
GHOST: My hour is almost come,
When I to sulfurous and tormenting flames
Must render up myself.
HAMLET: Alas, poor ghost!
GHOST: Pity me not, but lend thy serious hearing
To what I shall unfold.
HAMLET: Speak. I am bound to hear.
GHOST: So art to revenge, when thou shalt hear.   10
HAMLET: What?
GHOST: I am thy father's spirit,
Doomed for a certain term to walk the night,

---

80 deprive . . . reason take away the rule of reason over your mind
82 toys of desperation fancies of desperate acts, i.e., suicide
90 My fate cries out my destiny summons me
91 petty weak   **artery** (through which the vital spirits were thought to have been conveyed)
92 Nemean lion one of the monsters slain by Hercules in his twelve labors   **nerve** sinew
94 lets hinders   **98 Have after** let's go after him   **issue** outcome
100 it i.e., the outcome
1.5. Location: The battlements of the castle.
10 bound (1) ready (2) obligated by duty and fate. (The Ghost, in line 11, answers in the second sense.)

And for the day confined to fast in fires,   15
Till the foul crimes done in my days of nature   16
Are burnt and purged away. But that I am forbid   17
To tell the secrets of my prison house,
I could a tale unfold whose lightest word
Would harrow up thy soul, freeze thy young blood,   20
Make thy two eyes like stars start from their spheres,   21
Thy knotted and combinèd locks to part,   22
And each particular hair to stand on end
Like quills upon the fretful porcupine.
But this eternal blazon must not be   25
To ears of flesh and blood. List, list, O, list!
If thou didst ever thy dear father love—

HAMLET: O God!

GHOST: Revenge his foul and most unnatural murder.

HAMLET: Murder?

GHOST: Murder most foul, as in the best it is,   31
But this most foul, strange, and unnatural.

HAMLET: Haste me to know 't, that I, with wings as swift
As meditation or the thoughts of love,
May sweep to my revenge.

GHOST: I find thee apt;
And duller shouldst thou be than the fat weed   37
That roots itself in ease on Lethe wharf,   38
Wouldst thou not stir in this. Now, Hamlet, hear.
'Tis given out that, sleeping in my orchard,   40
A serpent stung me. So the whole ear of Denmark
Is by a forgèd process of my death   42
Rankly abused. But know, thou noble youth,   43
The serpent that did sting thy father's life
Now wears his crown.

HAMLET: O, my prophetic soul! My uncle!

GHOST: Ay, that incestuous, that adulterate beast,   47
With witchcraft of his wit, with traitorous gifts—   48
O wicked wit and gifts, that have the power
So to seduce!—won to his shameful lust
The will of my most seeming-virtuous queen.
O Hamlet, what a falling off was there!
From me, whose love was of that dignity
That it went hand in hand even with the vow   54

---

15 **fast** do penance by fasting   16 **crimes** sins   **of nature** as a mortal
17 **But that** were it not that   20 **harrow up** lacerate, tear
21 **spheres** i.e., eye-sockets, here compared to the orbits or transparent revolving spheres in
   which, according to Ptolemaic astronomy, the heavenly bodies were fixed
22 **knotted . . . locks** hair neatly arranged and confined
25 **eternal blazon** revelation of the secrets of eternity
31 **in the best** even at best
37 **shouldst thou be** you would have to be   **fat** torpid, lethargic
38 **Lethe** the river of forgetfulness in Hades   40 **orchard** garden
42 **forgèd process** falsified account   43 **abused** deceived
47 **adulterate** adulterous   48 **gifts** (1) talents (2) presents
54 **even with the vow** with the very vow

I made to her in marriage, and to decline
Upon a wretch whose natural gifts were poor
To those of mine!   57
But virtue, as it never will be moved,   58
Though lewdness court it in a shape of heaven,   59
So lust, though to a radiant angel linked,
Will sate itself in a celestial bed   61
And prey on garbage.
But soft, methinks I scent the morning air.
Brief let me be. Sleeping within my orchard,
My custom always of the afternoon,
Upon my secure hour thy uncle stole,   66
With juice of cursèd hebona in a vial,   67
And in the porches of my ears did pour   68
The leprous distillment, whose effect   69
Holds such an enmity with blood of man
That swift as quicksilver it courses through
The natural gates and alleys of the body,
And with a sudden vigor it doth posset   73
And curd, like eager droppings into milk,   74
The thin and wholesome blood. So did it mine,
And a most instant tetter barked about,   76
Most lazar-like, with vile and loathsome crust,   77
All my smooth body.
Thus was I, sleeping, by a brother's hand
Of life, of crown, of queen at once dispatched,   80
Cut off even in the blossoms of my sin,
Unhouseled, disappointed, unaneled,   82
No reckoning made, but sent to my account   83
With all my imperfections on my head.
O, horrible! O, horrible, most horrible!
If thou hast nature in thee, bear it not.   86
Let not the royal bed of Denmark be
A couch for luxury and damnèd incest.   88
But, howsoever thou pursues this act,
Taint not thy mind nor let thy soul contrive
Against thy mother aught. Leave her to heaven

---

57 To compared to   **58 virtue, as it** as virtue
59 shape of heaven heavenly form
61 sate . . . bed cease to find sexual pleasure in a virtuously lawful marriage
66 secure confident, unsuspicious
67 hebona a poison (The word seems to be a form of *ebony*, though it is thought perhaps to be
   related to *henbane*, a poison, or to *ebenus*, "yew.")
68 porches of my ears ears as a porch or entrance of the body
69 leprous distillment distillation causing leprosylike disfigurement
73 posset coagulate, curdle   **74 eager** sour, acid
76 tetter eruption of scabs   **barked** covered with a rough covering, like bark on a tree
77 lazar-like leperlike   **80 dispatched** suddenly deprived
82 Unhouseled without having received the Sacrament   **disappointed** unready (spiritually) for
   the last journey   **unaneled** without having received extreme unction
83 reckoning settling of accounts   **86 nature** i.e., the promptings of a son
88 luxury lechery

And to those thorns that in her bosom lodge,
To prick and sting her. Fare thee well at once.
The glowworm shows the matin to be near,   94
And 'gins to pale his uneffectual fire.   95
Adieu, adieu, adieu! Remember me.   [*Exit.*]
HAMLET: O all you host of heaven! O earth! What else?
And shall I couple hell? O, fie! Hold, hold, my heart,   98
And you, my sinews, grow not instant old,   99
But bear me stiffly up. Remember thee?
Ay, thou poor ghost, whiles memory holds a seat
In this distracted globe. Remember thee?   102
Yea, from the table of my memory   103
I'll wipe away all trivial fond records,   104
All saws of books, all forms, all pressures past   105
That youth and observation copied there,
And thy commandment all alone shall live
Within the book and volume of my brain,
Unmixed with baser matter. Yes, by heaven!
O most pernicious woman!
O villain, villain, smiling, damnèd villain!
My tables—meet it is I set it down   112
That one may smile, and smile, and be a villain.
At least I am sure it may be so in Denmark.

[Writing.]

So, uncle, there you are. Now to my word: 115
It is "Adieu, adieu! Remember me."
I have sworn 't.

Enter Horatio and Marcellus.

HORATIO: My lord, my lord!
MARCELLUS: Lord Hamlet!
HORATIO: Heavens secure him!
HAMLET: So be it.   120
MARCELLUS: Hilo, ho, ho, my lord!
HAMLET: Hillo, ho, ho, boy! Come, bird, come.   123
MARCELLUS: How is 't, my noble lord?
HORATIO: What news, my lord?
HAMLET: O, wonderful!
HORATIO: Good my lord, tell it.

---

94 matin morning
98 couple add   **Hold** hold together
102 globe (1) head (2) world
104 fond foolish
95 his its
99 instant instantly
103 table tablet, slate

105 saws wise sayings   **forms** shapes or images copied onto the slate; general ideas   **pressures** impressions stamped
112 tables writing tablets   **meet it is** it is fitting
115 there you are i.e., there, I've written that down against you
120 secure him keep him safe
123 Hillo . . . come (A falconer's call to a hawk in air. Hamlet mocks the hallooing as though it were a part of hawking.)

HAMLET: No, you will reveal it.

HORATIO: Not I, my lord, by heaven.

MARCELLUS: Nor I, my lord.

HAMLET: How say you, then, would heart of man once think it?   **131**
But you'll be secret?

HORATIO, MARCELLUS: Ay, by heaven, my lord.

HAMLET: There's never a villain dwelling in all Denmark
But he's an arrant knave.   **135**

HORATIO: There needs no ghost, my lord, come from the grave
To tell us this.

HAMLET: Why, right, you are in the right.
And so, without more circumstance at all,   **139**
I hold it fit that we shake hands and part,
You as your business and desire shall point you—
For every man hath business and desire,
Such as it is—and for my own poor part,
Look you, I'll go pray.

HORATIO: These are but wild and whirling words, my lord.

HAMLET: I am sorry they offend you, heartily;
Yes, faith, heartily.

HORATIO: There's no offense, my lord.

HAMLET: Yes, by Saint Patrick, but there is, Horatio,
And much offense too. Touching this vision here,   **149**
It is an honest ghost, that let me tell you.   **150**
For your desire to know what is between us,   **151**
O'ermaster 't as you may. And now, good friends,
As you are friends, scholars, and soldiers,
Give me one poor request.

HORATIO: What it 't, my lord? We will.

HAMLET: Never make known what you have seen tonight.

HORATIO, MARCELLUS   My lord, we will not.

HAMLET: Nay, but swear 't.

HORATIO: In faith, my lord, not I.

MARCELLUS: Nor I, my lord, in faith.   **160**

HAMLET: Upon my sword.   [*He holds out his sword.*]

MARCELLUS: We have sworn, my lord, already.   **162**

HAMLET: Indeed, upon my sword, indeed.   **163**

GHOST: (*cries under the stage*)   Swear.

HAMLET: Ha, ha, boy, sayst thou so? Art thou there, truepenny?   **166**
Come on, you hear this fellow in the cellarage.
Consent to swear.

---

131 once ever   **135 arrant** thoroughgoing

139 circumstance ceremony, elaboration

149 Saint Patrick (The keeper of Purgatory and patron saint of all blunders and confusion.)

150 offense (Hamlet deliberately changes Horatio's "no offense taken" to "an offense against all decency.")

151 an honest ghost i.e., a real ghost and not an evil spirit

160 In faith . . . I i.e., I swear not to tell what I have seen. (Horatio is not refusing to swear.)

162 sword i.e., the hilt in the form of a cross   **163 We . . . already** i.e., we swore *in faith*

166 truepenny honest old fellow

HORATIO:	Propose the oath, my lord.
HAMLET:	Never to speak of this that you have seen,
	Swear by my sword.
GHOST:	[*beneath*] Swear. [*They swear.*]
HAMLET:	*Hic et ubique?* Then we'll shift our ground.

[He moves to another spot.]

Come hither, gentlemen,
And lay your hands again upon my sword.
Swear by my sword.
Never to speak of this that you have heard.

GHOST:	[*beneath*] Swear by his sword. [*They swear.*]
HAMLET:	Well said, old mole. Canst work i' th' earth so fast?
	A worthy pioner!—Once more remove, good friends.

[He moves again.]

HORATIO:	O day and night, but this is wondrous strange!
HAMLET:	And therefore as a stranger give it welcome.

There are more things in heaven and earth, Horatio,
Than are dreamt of in your philosophy.
But come;
Here, as before, never, so help you mercy,
How strange or odd soe'er I bear myself—
As I perchance hereafter shall think meet
To put an antic disposition on—
That you, at such times seeing me, never shall,
With arms encumbered thus, or this headshake,
Or by pronouncing of some doubtful phrase
As "Well, we know," or "We could, an if we would,"
Or "If we list to speak," or "There be, an if they might,"
Or such ambiguous giving out, to note
That you know aught of me—this do swear,
So grace and mercy at your most need help you.

GHOST:	[*beneath*] Swear. [*They swear.*]
HAMLET:	Rest, rest, perturbèd spirit! So, gentlemen,
	With all my love I do commend me to you;
	And what so poor a man as Hamlet is

Line numbers: 172, 173, 180, 182, 184, 186, 189, 191, 193, 194, 195, 196, 200

---

172 s.d. They swear (Seemingly they swear here, and at lines 178 and 197, as they lay their hands on Hamlet's sword. Triple oaths would have particular force; these three oaths deal with what they have seen, what they have heard, and what they promise about Hamlet's *antic disposition*.)
173 *Hic et ubique* here and everywhere (Latin.)
180 pioner foot soldier assigned to dig tunnels and excavations
182 as a stranger i.e., needing your hospitality
184 your philosophy this subject is called "natural philosophy" or "science" that people talk about
186 so help you mercy as you hope for God's mercy when you are judged
189 antic fantastic   **191 encumbered** folded
193 an if if
194 list wished   **There . . . might** i.e., there are people here (we, in fact) who could tell news if we were at liberty to do so
195 giving out intimation   **note** draw attention to the fact
196 aught i.e., something secret   **200 do . . . you** entrust myself to you

May do t' express his love and friending to you, 202
God willing, shall not lack. Let us go in together, 203
And still your fingers on your lips, I pray. 204
The time is out of joint. O cursèd spite 205
That ever I was born to set it right!

[They wait for him to leave first.]
Nay, come, let's go together.   *Exeunt.* 207

Act 1 Response Statement Questions

- How do you respond to the poetry? Is it pleasant to read a play written in verse, or does the poetry give you trouble as a reader? Are there serious gaps in your understanding of the play's language? If so, does Shakespeare's reputation in your mind ease or excuse any of the difficulties his language might present?
- What is your response to the mood with which the play opens and the rumors concerning a ghost? If you don't believe in ghosts in general, how are you able to accept its presence here? Are you able to draw on your literary experience to help you? Do you trust the ghost or view it with skepticism and suspicion? In a production of *Hamlet*, what different interpretations might be suggested according to how the ghost is presented to the audience?
- What is your response to Claudius on his first appearance in Scene 2? Does he seem like a reasonable man? Fit to be a king? A loving husband and uncle? Suspicious or villainous?
- How do you respond to Hamlet when he first appears in Scene 2 and talks with Claudius, Gertrude, and Horatio? How do you fill in various gaps concerning him at this point, for example his age, his intelligence, his emotional makeup? Do you identify with him? Why or why not? What is the role of your gender, class, or cultural situation in your responses?
- In Scene 3, what are your responses to Polonius, Laertes, and Ophelia? How do you feel about the way Polonius and Laertes treat Ophelia and how she responds? What is the role of your gender, class, or cultural situation in your responses?

Act 2, Scene 1

Enter old Polonius with his man [Reynaldo].
POLONIUS: Give his this money and these notes, Reynaldo.

[He gives money and papers.]
REYNALDO: I will, my lord.

---

202 friending friendliness
204 still always
205 The time the state of affairs   **spite** i.e., the spite of Fortune
206 let's go together (Probably they wait for him to leave first, but he refuses this ceremoniousness.)
2.1. Location: Polonius' chambers.

203 lack be lacking

POLONIUS: You shall do marvelous wisely, good Reynaldo,   3
    Before you visit him, to make inquire   4
    Of his behavior.
REYNALDO: My lord, I did intend it.
POLONIUS: Marry, well said, very well said. Look you, sir,
    Inquire me first what Danskers are in Paris,   8
    And how, and who, what means, and where they keep,   9
    What company, at what expense; and finding
    By this encompassment and drift of question   11
    That they do know my son, come you more nearer   12
    Than your particular demands will touch it.   13
    Take you, as 'twere, some distant knowledge of him,   14
    As thus, "I know his father and his friends,
    And in part him." Do you mark this, Reynaldo?
REYNALDO: Ay, very well, my lord.
POLONIUS: "And in part him, but," you may say, "not well.
    But if 't be he I mean, he's very wild,
    Addicted so and so," and there put on him   20
    What forgeries you please—marry, none so rank   21
    As may dishonor him, take heed of that,
    But, sir, such wanton, wild, and usual slips   23
    As are companions noted and most known
    To youth and liberty.
REYNALDO: As gaming, my lord.
POLONIUS: Ay, or drinking, fencing, swearing,
    Quarreling, drabbing—you may go so far.   28
REYNALDO: My lord, that would dishonor him.
POLONIUS: Faith, no, as you may season it in the charge.   30
    You must not put another scandal on him
    That he is open to incontinency;   32
    That's not my meaning. But breathe his faults so quaintly   33
    That they may seem the taints of liberty,   34
    The flash and outbreak of a fiery mind,
    A savageness in unreclaimèd blood,   36
    Of general assault.   37
REYNALDO: But, my good lord—
POLONIUS: Wherefore should you do this?
REYNALDO: Ay, my lord, I would know that.

---

3 **marvelous** marvelously

4 inquire inquiry

8 Danskers Danes

9 what means what wealth (they have)   **keep** dwell

11 encompassment roundabout talking   **drift** gradual approach or course

12–13 come . . . it you will find out more this way than by asking pointed questions (*particular demands*)

14 Take you assume, pretend

20 put on impute to

21 forgeries invented tales   **rank** gross

23 wanton sportive, unrestrained

28 drabbing whoring

30 season temper, soften

32 incontinency habitual sexual excess

33 quaintly artfully, subtly

34 taints of liberty faults resulting from free living

36–37 A savageness . . . assault a wildness in untamed youth that assails all indiscriminately

POLONIUS: Marry, sir, here's my drift,
  And I believe it is a fetch of warrant.
  You laying these slight sullies on my son,   42
  As 'twere a thing a little soiled wi' the working,
  Mark you,   44
  Your party in converse, him you would sound,
  Having ever seen in the prenominate crimes   46
  The youth you breathe of guilty, be assured   47
  He closes with you in this consequence: 48
  "Good sir," or so, or "friend," or "gentleman,"   49
  According to the phrase or the addition
  Of man and country.   51
REYNALDO: Very good, my lord.
POLONIUS: And then, sir, does 'a this—'a does—what was I about to say? By the
  Mass, I was about to say something. Where did I leave?
REYNALDO: At "closes in the consequence."
POLONIUS: At "closes in the consequence," ay, marry.
  He closes thus: "I know the gentleman,
  I saw him yesterday," or "th' other day,"
  Or then, or then, with such or such, "and as you say,
  There was 'a gaming," "there o'ertook in 's rouse,"
  "There falling out at tennis," or perchance   61
  "I saw him enter such a house of sale,"   62
  Videlicet a brothel, or so forth. See you now,
  Your bait of falsehood takes this carp of truth;   64
  And thus do we of wisdom and of reach,   65
  With windlasses and with assays of bias,   66
  By indirections find directions out.   67
  So by my former lecture and advice   68
  Shall you my son. You have me, have you not?
REYNALDO: My lord, I have.   70
POLONIUS: God b'wi' ye; fare ye well.
REYNALDO: Good my lord.   72
POLONIUS: Observe his inclination in yourself.
REYNALDO: I shall, my lord.   74

---

42 fetch of warrant legitimate trick
44 soiled wi' the working soiled by handling while it is being made, i.e., by involvement in the ways of the world
46 converse conversation   **sound** i.e., sound out
47 Having ever if he has ever   **prenominate crimes** before-mentioned offenses
48 breathe speak
49 closes . . . consequence takes you into his confidence in some fashion, as follows
51 addition title

61 o'ertook in 's rouse overcome by drink
62 falling out quarreling   **64 Videlicet** namely
65 carp a fish   **66 reach** capacity, ability
67 windlasses i.e., circuitous paths. (Literally, circuits made to head off the game in hunting.) **assays of bias** attempts through indirection (like the curving path of the bowling ball, which is biased or weighted to one side)
68 directions i.e., the way things really are   **70 have** understand
72 b' wi' be with
74 in yourself in your own person (as well as by asking questions)

POLONIUS: And let him ply his music.
REYNALDO: Well, my lord.
POLONIUS: Farewell. *Exit Reynaldo.*

Enter Ophelia.

      How now, Ophelia, what's the matter?
OPHELIA: O my lord, my lord, I have been so affrighted!
POLONIUS: With what, i' the name of God?
OPHELIA: My lord, as I was sewing in my closet,   82
      Lord Hamlet, with his doublet all unbraced,   83
      No hat upon his head, his stockings fouled,
      Ungartered, and down-gyvèd to his ankle,   85
      Pale as his shirt, his knees knocking each other,
      And with a look so piteous in purport   87
      As if he had been loosèd out of hell
      To speak of horrors—he comes before me.
POLONIUS: Mad for thy love?
OPHELIA: My lord, I do not know,
      But truly I do fear it.
POLONIUS: What said he?
OPHELIA: He took me by the wrist and held me hard.
      Then goes he to the length of all his arm,
      And, with his other hand thus o'er his brow
      He falls to such perusal of my face
      As 'a would draw it. Long stayed he so.   98
      At last, a little shaking of mine arm
      And thrice his head thus waving up and down,
      He raised a sigh so piteous and profound
      As it did seem to shatter all his bulk   102
      And end his being. That done, he lets me go,
      And with his head over his shoulder turned
      He seemed to find his way without his eyes,
      For out o' doors he went without their helps,
      And to the last bended their light on me.
POLONIUS: Come, go with me. I will go seek the King.
      This is the very ecstasy of love,   109
      Whose violent property fordoes itself   110
      And leads the will to desperate undertakings
      As oft as any passion under heaven
      That does afflict our natures. I am sorry.
      What, have you given him any hard words of late?
OPHELIA: No, my good lord, but as you did command
      I did repel his letters and denied
      His access to me.

---

82 closet private chamber
83 doublet close-fitting jacket   **unbraced** unfastened
85 down-gyvèd fallen to the ankles (like gyves or fetters)
87 in purport in what it expressed   **98 As** as if (also in line 102)
102 bulk body   **109 ectasy** madness
110 property nature   **fordoes** destroys

POLONIUS: That hath made him mad.
    I am sorry that with the better heed and judgment
    I had not quoted him. I feared he did but trifle   120
    And meant to wrack thee. But beshrew my jealousy!   121
    By heaven, it is as proper to our age   122
    To cast beyond ourselves in our opinions   123
    As it is common for the younger sort
    To lack discretion. Come, go we to the King.
    This must be known, which, being kept close, might move   126
    More grief to hide than hate to utter love.   127
    Come.   *Exeunt.*

Act 2, Scene 2

Flourish. Enter King and Queen, Rosencrantz, and Guildenstern [with others].

KING: Welcome, dear Rosencrantz and Guildenstern.
    Morever, that we much did long to see you.
    The need we have to use you did provoke   2
    Our hasty sending. Something have you heard
    Of Hamlet's transformation—so call it,
    Sith nor th' exterior nor the inward man   6
    Resembles that it was. What it should be,   7
    More than his father's death, that thus hath put him
    So much from th' understanding of himself,
    I cannot dream of. I entreat you both
    That, being of so young days brought up with him,   11
    And sith so neighbored to his youth and havior,   12
    That you vouchsafe your rest here in our court   13
    Some little time, so by your companies
    To draw him on to pleasures, and to gather
    So much as from occasion you may glean,   16
    Whether aught to us unknown afflicts him thus
    That, opened, lies within our remedy.   18
QUEEN: Good gentlemen, he hath much talked of you,
    And sure I am two men there is not living
    To whom he more adheres. If it will please you

---

120 quoted observed
121 wrack ruin, seduce **beshrew my jealousy** a plague upon my suspicious nature
122 proper . . . age characteristic of us (old) men
123 cast beyond overshoot, miscalculate (A metaphor from hunting.)
126 known made known (to the King) **close** secret
126–127 might . . . love i.e., might cause more grief (because of what Hamlet might do) by hiding the knowledge of Hamlet's strange behavior to Ophelia than unpleasantness by telling it
2.2. Location: The castle.
 2 Moreover that besides the fact that   **6 Sith nor** since neither
 7 that what   **11 of . . . days** from such early youth
12 And sith so neighbored to and since you are (or, and since that time you are) intimately acquainted with **havior** demeanor
13 vouchsafe your rest please to stay   **16 occasion** opportunity
18 opened being revealed

To show us so much gentry and good will   22
As to expend your time with us awhile
For the supply and profit of our hope,   24
Your visitation shall receive such thanks
As fits a king's remembrance.   26
ROSENCRANTZ: Both Your Majesties
Might, by the sovereign power you have of us,   28
Put your dread pleasures more into command   29
Than to entreaty.
GUILDENSTERN: But we both obey,
And here give up ourselves in the full bent   32
To lay our service freely at your feet,
To be commanded.
KING: Thanks, Rosencrantz and gentle Guildenstern.
QUEEN: Thanks, Guildenstern and gentle Rosencrantz.
And I beseech you instantly to visit
My too much changèd son. Go, some of you,
And bring these gentlemen where Hamlet is.
GUILDENSTERN: Heavens make our presence and our practices   40
Pleasant and helpful to him!
QUEEN: Ay, amen!

Exeunt Rosencrantz and Guildenstern [with some attendants].

Enter Polonius.

POLONIUS: Th' ambassadors from Norway, my good lord,
Are joyfully returned.
KING: Thou still hast been the father of good news.   45
POLONIUS: Have I, my lord? I assure my good liege
I hold my duty, as I hold my soul,   47
Both to my God and to my gracious king;
And I do think, or else this brain of mine
Hunts not the trail of policy so sure   50
As it hath used to do, that I have found
The very cause of Hamlet's lunacy.
KING: O, speak of that! That do I long to hear.
POLONIUS: Give first admittance to th' ambassadors.
My news shall be the fruit to that great feast.   55
KING: Thyself do grace to them and bring them in.   56

[Exit Polonius.]

He tells me, my dear Gertrude, he hath found
The head and source of all your son's distemper.

---

22 gentry courtesy
24 supply . . . hope aid and furtherance of what we hope for
26 As fits . . . remembrance as would be a fitting gift of a king who rewards true service
28 of over   **29 dread** inspiring awe
32 in . . . bent to the utmost degree of our capacity. (An archery metaphor.)
40 practices doings   **45 still** always
47 hold maintain   **as** as firmly as **50 policy** sagacity
55 fruit dessert
56 grace honor (punning on grace said before a *feast*, line 52)

QUEEN: I doubt it is no other but the main, 59
    His father's death and our o'erhasty marriage.

Enter Ambassadors [Voltimand and Cornelius, with Polonius].

KING: Well, we shall sift him.—Welcome, my good friends!
    Say, Voltimand, what from our brother Norway? 61
VOLTIMAND: Most fair return of greetings and desires. 62
    Upon our first, he sent out to suppress 63
    His nephew's levies, which to him appeared 64
    To be a preparation 'gainst the Polack,
    But, better looked into, he truly found
    It was against Your Highness. Whereat grieved
    That so his sickness, age, and impotence
    Was falsely borne in hand, sends out arrests 69
    On Fortinbras, which he, in brief, obeys, 70
    Receives rebuke from Norway, and in fine
    Makes vow before his uncle never more 72
    To give th' assay of arms against Your Majesty.
    Whereon old Norway, overcome with joy, 74
    Gives him three thousand crowns in annual fee
    And his commission to employ those soldiers,
    So levied as before, against the Polack,
    With an entreaty, herein further shown,

[giving a paper]

    That it might please you to give quiet pass
    Through your dominions for this enterprise
    On such regards of safety and allowance
    As therein are set down. 82
KING: It likes us well, 84
    And at our more considered time we'll read, 85
    Answer, and think upon this business.
    Meantime we thank you for your well-took labor.
    Go to your rest; at night we'll feast together.
    Most welcome home!   *Exeunt Ambassadors.*
POLONIUS: This business is well ended.
    My liege, and madam, to expostulate
    What majesty should be, what duty is, 91
    Why day is day, night night, and time is time,
    Were nothing but to waste night, day, and time.
    Therefore, since brevity is the soul of wit, 95

---

59 doubt fear, suspect   **main** chief point, principal concern
61 sift him question Polonius closely   **62 brother** fellow king
63 desires good wishes
64 Upon our first at our first words on the business
69 impotence helplessness
70 borne in hand deluded, taken advantage of   **arrests** orders to desist
72 in fine in conclusion   **74 give th' assay** make trial of strength, challenge
82 On . . . allowance i.e., with such considerations for the safety of Denmark and permission for Fortinbras
84 likes pleases   **85 considered** suitable for deliberation
91 expostulate expound, inquire into   **95 wit** sense or judgment

And tediousness the limbs and outward flourishes,
I will be brief. Your noble son is mad.
Mad call I it, for, to define true madness,
What is 't but to be nothing else but mad?
But let that go.

QUEEN: More matter, with less art.

POLONIUS: Madam, I swear I use no art at all.
That he's mad, 'tis true; 'tis true 'tis pity,
And pity 'tis 'tis true—a foolish figure,   104
But farewell it, for I will use no art.
Mad let us grant him, then, and now remains
That we find out the cause of this effect,
Or rather say, the cause of this defect,
For this effect defective comes by cause.   109
Thus it remains, and the remainder thus.
Perpend.   111
I have a daughter—have while she is mine—
Who, in her duty and obedience, mark,
Hath given me this. Now gather and surmise.   114
[*He reads the letter.*] "To the celestial and my soul's idol,
the most beautified Ophelia"—
That's an ill phrase, a vile phrase; "beautifed" is a vile phrase.
But you shall hear. Thus: [*He reads.*]
"In her excellent white bosom, these, etc."   119

QUEEN: Came this from Hamlet to her?

POLONIUS: Good madam, stay awhile, I will be faithful.   121

[*He reads.*]

        "Doubt thou the stars are fire,
            Doubt that the sun doth move,
        Doubt truth to be a liar,   124
            But never doubt I love.
O dear Ophelia, I am ill at these numbers. I have not art to reckon my groans.   126
But that I love thee best, O most best, believe it. Adieu.
                    Thine evermore, most dear lady, whilst this machine is to him, Hamlet."   128
This in obedience hath my daughter shown me,
And, more above, hath his solicitings,   130
As they fell out by time, by means, and place,   131
All given to mine ear.   132

KING: But how hath she
Received his love?

---

104 **figure** figure of speech
109 **For . . . cause** i.e., for this defective behavior, this madness, has a cause
111 **Perpend** consider
114 **gather and surmise** draw your own conclusions
119 **In . . . bosom** (The letter is poetically addressed to her heart.)   **these** i.e., the letter
121 **stay** wait   **faithful** i.e., in reading the letter accurately
124 **Doubt** suspect
126 **ill . . . numbers** unskilled at writing verses   **reckon** (1) count (2) number metrically, scan
128 **machine** i.e., body   130 **more above** moreover
131 **fell out** occurred   **by** according to   132 **given . . . ear** i.e., told me about

POLONIUS:	What do you think of me?	
KING:	As of a man faithful and honorable.	

POLONIUS: I would fain prove so. But what might you think,   137
When I had seen this hot love on the wing—
As I perceived it, I must tell you that,
Before my daughter told me—what might you,
Or my dear Majesty your Queen here, think,
If I had played the desk or table book,   142
Or given my heart a winking, mute and dumb,   143
Or looked upon this love with idle sight?   144
What might you think? No, I went round to work,   145
And my young mistress thus I did bespeak: 146
"Lord Hamlet is a prince out of thy star;   147
This must not be." And then I prescripts gave her,   148
That she should lock herself from his resort,   149
Admit no messengers, receive no tokens.
Which done, she took the fruits of my advice;
And he, repellèd—a short tale to make—
Fell into a sadness, then into a fast,
Thence to a watch, thence into a weakness,   154
Thence to a lightness, and by this declension   155
Into the madness wherein now he raves,
And all we mourn for.   157

KING: [to the Queen]   Do you think 'tis this?

QUEEN: It may be, very like.

POLONIUS: Hath there been such a time—I would fain know that—
That I have positively said "'Tis so,"
When it proved otherwise?

KING: Not that I know.

POLONIUS: Take this from this, if this be otherwise.   164
If circumstances lead me, I will find
Where truth is hid, though it were hid indeed
Within the center.   167

KING: How may we try it further?   168

POLONIUS: You know sometimes he walks four hours together
Here in the lobby.

QUEEN: So he does indeed.

---

137 fain gladly
142 played . . . table book i.e., remained shut up, concealing the information
143 given . . . winking closed the eyes of my heart to this
144 with idle sight complacently or incomprehendingly
145 round roundly, plainly   **146 bespeak** address
147 out of thy star above your sphere, position   **148 prescripts** orders
149 his resort his visits   **154 watch** state of sleeplessness
155 lightness lightheadedness   **declension** decline, deterioration (with a pun on the grammatical sense)
157 all we all of us, or, into everything that we
164 Take this from this (The actor probably gestures, indicating that he means his head from his shoulders, or his staff of office or chain from his hands or neck, or something similar.)
167 center middle point of the earth (which is also the center of the Ptolemaic universe).
168 try test, judge

POLONIUS: At such a time I'll loose my daughter to him.   172
            Be you and I behind an arras then.   173
            Mark the encounter. If he love her not
            And be not from his reason fall'n thereon,   175
            Let me be no assistant for a state,
            But keep a farm and carters.   177
KING: We will try it.

Enter Hamlet [reading a book].

QUEEN: But look where sadly the poor wretch comes reading.   179
POLONIUS: Away, I do beseech you both, away.
            I'll board him presently. O, give me leave.   181

Exeunt King and Queen [with attendants].

            How does my good Lord Hamlet?
HAMLET: Well, God-a-mercy.   183
POLONIUS: Do you know me, my lord?
HAMLET: Excellent well. You are a fishmonger.   185
POLONIUS: Not I, my lord.
HAMLET: Then I would you were so honest a man.
POLONIUS: Honest, my lord?
HAMLET: Ay, sir. To be honest, as this world goes, is to be one man picked out of ten
            thousand.
POLONIUS: That's very true, my lord.
HAMLET: For if the sun breed maggots in a dead dog, being a good kissing carrion—   192
            Have you a daughter?
POLONIUS: I have, my lord.
HAMLET: Let her not walk i' the sun. Conception is a blessing, but as your daughter   195
            may conceive, friend, look to 't.
POLONIUS: [*aside*] How say you by that? Still harping on my daughter. Yet he knew
            me not at first; 'a said I was a fishmonger. 'A is far gone. And truly in my youth I   198
            suffered much extremity for love, very near this. I'll speak to him again.—What
            do you read, my lord?
HAMLET: Words, words, words.
POLONIUS: What is the matter, my lord?   202
HAMLET: Between who?
POLONIUS: I mean, the matter that you read, my lord.
HAMLET: Slanders, sir; for the satirical rogue says here that old men have gray
            beards, that their faces are wrinkled, their eyes purging thick amber and plum-   206

---

172 **loose** (as one might release an animal that is being mated)
173 **arras** hanging, tapestry   175 **thereon** on that account
177 **carters** wagon drivers   179 **sadly** seriously
181 **board** accost   **presently** at once   **give me leave** i.e., excuse me, leave me alone. (Said to
those he hurries offstage, including the King and Queen.)
183 **God-a-mercy** God have mercy, i.e., thank you   185 **fishmonger** fish merchant
192 **a good kissing carrion** i.e., a good piece of flesh for kissing, or for the sun to kiss
195 **i' the sun** in public (with additional implication of the sunshine of princely favors)   **Con-**
ception (1) understanding (2) pregnancy
198 **'a** he
202 **matter** substance. (But Hamlet plays on the sense of "basis for a dispute.")
206 **purging** discharging   **amber** i.e., resin, like the resinous *plumtree gum*

tree gum, and that they have a plentiful lack of wit, together with most weak 207
hams. All which, sir, though I most powerfully and potently believe, yet I hold it
not honesty to have it thus set down, for yourself, sir, shall grow old as I am, if 209
like a crab you could go backward.

POLONIUS: [*aside*] Though this be madness, yet there is method in 't.—Will you
walk out of the air, my lord? 212

HAMLET: Into my grave.

POLONIUS: Indeed, that's out of the air. [*Aside.*] How pregnant sometimes his replies 214
are! A happiness that often madness hits on, which reason and sanity could not 215
so prosperously be delivered of. I will leave him and suddenly contrive the 216
means of meeting between him and my daughter.—My honorable lord, I will
most humbly take my leave of you.

HAMLET: You cannot, sir, take from me anything that I will more willingly part with- 219
al—except my life, except my life, except my life. 220

Enter Guildenstern and Rosencrantz.

POLONIUS: Fare you well, my lord.

HAMLET: These tedious old fools!

POLONIUS: You go to seek the Lord Hamlet. There he is. 222

ROSENCRANTZ: [*to Polonius*] God save you, sir!

[*Exit Polonius.*]

GUILDENSTERN: My honored lord!

ROSENCRANTZ: My most dear lord!

HAMLET: My excellent good friends! How dost thou, Guildenstern? Ah, Rosencrantz!
Good lads, how do you both?

ROSENCRANTZ: As the indifferent children of the earth. 229

GUILDENSTERN: Happy in that we are not overhappy.
On Fortune's cap we are not the very button.

HAMLET: Nor the soles of her shoe?

ROSENCRANTZ: Neither, my lord.

HAMLET: Then you live about her waist, or in the middle of her favors? 234

GUILDENSTERN: Faith, her privates we. 235

HAMLET: In the secret parts of Fortune? O, most true, she is a strumpet. What news? 236

ROSENCRANTZ: None, my lord, but the world's grown honest.

HAMLET: Then is doomsday near. But your news is not true. Let me question more
in particular. What have you, my good friends, deserved at the hands of
Fortune that she sends you to prison hither?

GUILDENSTERN: Prison, my lord?

HAMLET: Denmark's a prison.

---

207 wit understanding   **209 honesty** decency, decorum   **old** as old
212 out of the air (The open air was considered dangerous for sick people.)
214 pregnant quick-witted, full of meaning   **215 happiness** felicity of expression
216 prosperously successfully   **suddenly** immediately
219–220 withal with   **222 old fools** i.e., old men like Polonius
229 indifferent ordinary, at neither extreme of fortune or misfortune
234 favors i.e., sexual favors
235 her privates we i.e., (1) we are sexually intimate with Fortune, the fickle goddess who
bestows her favors indiscriminately (2) we are her private citizens
236 strumpet prostitute. (A common epithet for indiscriminate Fortune.)

ROSENCRANTZ: Then is the world one.

HAMLET: A goodly one, in which there are many confines, wards, and dungeons,   244
Denmark being one o' the worst.

ROSENCRANTZ: We think not so, my lord.

HAMLET: Why then 'tis none to you, for there is nothing either good or bad but
thinking makes it so. To me it is a prison.

ROSENCRANTZ: Why then, your ambition makes it one. 'Tis too narrow for your mind.

HAMLET: O God, I could be bounded in a nutshell and count myself a king of infinite
space, were it not that I have bad dreams.

GUILDENSTERN: Which dreams indeed are ambition, for the very substance of the   252
ambitious is merely the shadow of a dream.   253

HAMLET: A dream itself is but a shadow.

ROSENCRANTZ: Truly, and I hold ambition of so airy and light a quality that it is but a
shadow's shadow.

HAMLET: Then are our beggars bodies, and our monarchs and outstretched heroes   257
the beggars' shadows. Shall we to the court? For, by my fay, I cannot reason.   258

ROSENCRANTZ, GUILDENSTERN: We'll wait upon you.   259

HAMLET: No such matter. I will not sort you with the rest of my servants, for, to   260
speak to you like an honest man, I am most dreadfully attended. But, in the   261
beaten way of friendship, what make you at Elsinore?   262

ROSENCRANTZ: To visit you, my lord, no other occasion.

HAMLET: Beggar that I am, I am even poor in thanks; but I thank you, and sure, dear
friends, my thanks are too dear a halfpenny. Were you not sent for? Is it your   265
own inclining? Is it a free visitation? Come, come, deal justly with me. Come,   266
come. Nay, speak.

GUILDENSTERN: What should we say, my lord?

HAMLET: Anything but to the purpose. You were sent for, and there is a kind of con-   269
fession in your looks which your modesties have not craft enough to color. I   270
know the good King and Queen have sent for you.

ROSENCRANTZ: To what end, my lord?

HAMLET: That you must teach me. But let me conjure you, by the rights of our   273
fellowship, by the consonancy of our youth, by the obligation of our ever-   274
preserved love, and by what more dear a better proposer could charge you   275
withal, be even and direct with me whether you were sent for or no.   276

ROSENCRANTZ: [aside to Guildenstern]   What say you?

---

244 **confines** places of confinement   **wards** cells
252–253 **the very . . . ambitious** that seemingly very substantial thing that the ambitious pursue
257 **bodies** i.e., solid substances rather than shadows (since beggars are not ambitious)   **out-stretched** (1) far-reaching in their ambition (2) elongated as shadows
258 **fay** faith
259 **wait upon** accompany, attend. (But Hamlet uses the phrase in the sense of providing menial service.)
260 **sort** class, categorize
261 **dreadfully attended** waited upon in slovenly fashion
262 **beaten way** familiar path, tried-and-true course   **make** do
265 **too dear a halfpenny** (1) too expensive at even a halfpenny, i.e., of little worth (2) too expensive *by* a halfpenny in return for worthless kindness
266 **free** voluntary
269 **Anything but to the purpose** anything except a straightforward answer. (Said ironically.)
270 **modesties** sense of shame   **color** disguise   **273 conjure** adjure, entreat
274 **the consonancy of our youth** our closeness in our younger days
275 **better** more skillful   **charge** urge   **276 even** straight, honest

HAMLET: [*aside*] Nay, then, I have an eye of you.—If you love me, hold not off.   278

GUILDENSTERN: My lord, we were sent for.

HAMLET: I will tell you why; so shall my anticipation prevent your discovery, and   280
your secrecy to the King and Queen molt no feather. I have of late—but where-   281
fore I know not—lost all my mirth, forgone all custom of exercises; and indeed
it goes so heavily with my disposition that this goodly frame, the earth, seems to
me a sterile promontory; this most excellent canopy, the air, look you, this brave   284
o'erhanging firmament, this majestical roof fretted with golden fire, why, it ap-   285
peareth nothing to me but a foul and pestilent congregation of vapors. What a   286
piece of work is a man! How noble in reason, how infinite in faculties, in form   287
and moving how express and admirable, in action how like an angel, in appre-   288
hension how like a god! The beauty of the world, the paragon of animals! And   289
yet, to me, what is this quintessence of dust? Man delights not me—no, nor   290
woman neither, though by your smiling you seem to say so.

ROSENCRANTZ: My lord, there was no such stuff in my thoughts.

HAMLET: Why did you laugh, then, when I said man delights not me?

ROSENCRANTZ: To think, my lord, if you delight not in man, what Lenten entertain-   294
ment the players shall receive from you. We coted them on the way, and hither   295
are they coming to offer you service.

HAMLET: He that plays the king shall be welcome; His Majesty shall have tribute of   297
me. The adventurous knight shall use his foil and target, the lover shall not sigh   298
gratis, the humorous man shall end his part in peace, the clown shall make   299
those laugh whose lungs are tickle o' the sear, and the lady shall say her mind   300
freely, or the blank verse shall halt for 't. What players are they?   301

ROSENCRANTZ: Even those you were wont to take such delight in, the tragedians of   302
the city.

HAMLET: How chances it they travel? Their residence, both in reputation and profit,   304
was better both ways.

ROSENCRANTZ: I think their inhibition comes by the means of the late innovation.   306

HAMLET: Do they hold the same estimation they did when I was in the city? Are
they so followed?

---

278 of on   **hold not off** don't hold back
280 so . . . discovery in that way my saying first will spare you from revealing the truth
281 molt no feather i.e., not diminish in the least   **284 brave** splendid
285 fretted adorned (with fretwork, as in a vaulted ceiling)
286 congregation mass   **287 piece of work** masterpiece
288 express well-framed, exact, expressive
288–289 apprehension power of comprehending
290 quintessence the fifth essence of ancient philosophy, beyond earth, water, air, and fire, supposed to be the substance of the heavenly bodies and to be latent in all things
294–295 Lenten entertainment meager reception (appropriate to Lent)
295 coted overtook and passed by
297 tribute (1) applause (2) homage paid in money   **of** from
298 foil and target sword and shield
299 gratis for nothing   **humorous man** eccentric character, dominated by one trait or "humor"
in peace i.e., with full license
300 tickle o' the sear easy on the trigger, ready to laugh easily. (A *sear* is part of a gunlock.)
301 halt limp   **302 tragedians** actors
304 residence remaining in their usual place, i.e., in the city
306 inhibition formal prohibition (from acting plays in the city)   **late** recent   **innovation** i.e.,
the new fashion in satirical plays performed by boy actors in the "private" theaters; or possibly a political uprising; or the strict limitations set on the theaters in London in 1600

ROSENCRANTZ: No, indeed are they not.

HAMLET: How comes it? Do they grow rusty?   310

ROSENCRANTZ: Nay, their endeavor keeps in the wonted pace. But there is, sir, an   311
aerie of children, little eyases, that cry out on the top of question and are most   312
tyrannically clapped for 't. These are now the fashion, and so berattle the com-   313
mon stages—so they call them—that many wearing rapiers are afraid of goose   314
quills and dare scarce come thither.   315

HAMLET: What, are they children? Who maintains 'em?
How are they escoted? Will they pursue the quality no longer than they can   317
sing? Will they not say afterwards, if they should grow themselves to common   318
players—as it is most like, if their means are no better—their writers do them   319
wrong to make them exclaim against their own succession?   320

ROSENCRANTZ: Faith, there has been much to-do on both sides, and the nation holds   321
it no sin to tar them to controversy. There was for a while no money bid for   322
argument unless the poet and the player went to cuffs in the question.   323

HAMLET: Is 't possible?

GUILDENSTERN: O, there has been much throwing about of brains.

HAMLET: Do the boys carry it away?   326

ROSENCRANTZ: Ay, that they do, my lord—Hercules and his load too.   327

HAMLET: It is not very strange; for my uncle is King of Denmark, and those that
would make mouths at him while my father lived give twenty, forty, fifty, a hun-   329
dred ducats apiece for his picture in little. 'Sblood, there is something in this   330
more than natural, if philosophy could find it out.   331

A flourish [of trumpets within].

GUILDENSTERN: There are the players.

HAMLET: Gentlemen, you are welcome to Elsinore. Your hands, come then. Th' ap-   333
purtenance of welcome is fashion and ceremony. Let me comply with you in   334

310–327 How . . . load too (The passage, omitted from the early quartos, alludes to the so-called
War of the Theaters, 1599–1602, the rivalry between the children's companies and the adult
actors.)
311 keeps continues   **wonted** usual
312 aerie next   **eyases** young hawks   **cry . . . question** speak shrilly, dominating the controversy (in decrying the public theaters)
313 tyrannically outrageously   **berattle** berate, clamor against.
313–314 common stages public theaters
314 many wearing rapiers i.e., many men of fashion, afraid to patronize the common players
for fear of being satirized by the poets writing for the boy actors.
314–315 goose quills i.e., pens of satirists
317 escoted maintained   **quality** (acting) profession
317–318 no longer . . . sing i.e., only until their voices change
318 common regular, adult
319 like likely   **if . . . better** if they find no better way to support themselves
320 succession i.e., future careers   **321 to-do** ado
322 tar set on (as dogs)
322–323 There . . . question i.e., for a while, no money was offered by the acting companies to
playwrights for the plot to a play unless the satirical poets who wrote for the boys and the
adult actors came to blows in the play itself
326 carry it away i.e., win the day
327 Hercules . . . load (Thought to be an allusion to the sign of the Globe Theatre, which was
Hercules bearing the world on his shoulders.)
329 mouths faces
330 ducats gold coins   **in little** in miniature   **'Sblood** by God's (Christ's) blood
331 philosophy i.e., scientific inquiry   **333–334 appurtenance** proper accompaniment
334 comply observe the formalities of courtesy

this garb, lest my extent to the players, which, I tell you, must show fairly out- 335
wards, should more appear like entertainment than yours. You are welcome. 336
But my uncle-father and aunt-mother are deceived.

GUILDENSTERN: In what, my dear lord?

HAMLET: I am but mad north-north-west. When the wind is southerly I know a 339
hawk from a handsaw. 340

Enter Polonius.

POLONIUS: Well be with you, gentlemen!

HAMLET: Hark you, Guildenstern, and you too; at each ear a hearer. That great baby
you see there is not yet out of his swaddling clouts. 343

ROSENCRANTZ: Haply he is the second time come to them, for they say an old man is 344
twice a child.

HAMLET: I will prophesy he comes to tell me of the players. Mark it.—You say right,
sir, o' Monday morning, 'twas then indeed.

POLONIUS: My lord, I have news to tell you.

HAMLET: My lord, I have news to tell you. When Roscius was an actor in Rome— 349

POLONIUS: The actors are come hither, my lord.

HAMLET: Buzz, buzz! 351

POLONIUS: Upon my honor—

HAMLET: Then came each actor on his ass.

POLONIUS: The best actors in the world, either for tragedy, comedy, history, pastoral,
pastoral-comical, historical-pastoral, tragical-historical, tragical-comical-historical-
pastoral, scene individable, or poem unlimited. Seneca cannot be too heavy, nor 356
Platus too light. For the law of writ and the liberty, these are the only men. 357

HAMLET: O Jephthah, judge of Israel, what a treasure hadst thou! 358

POLONIUS: What a treasure had he, my lord?

HAMLET: Why,
"One fair daughter, and no more,
The which he lovèd passing well." 362

POLONIUS: [*aside*] Still on my daughter.

HAMLET: Am I not i' the right, old Jephthah?

POLONIUS: If you call me Jephthah, my lord, I have a daughter that I love passing well.

HAMLET: Nay, that follows not.

---

335 garb i.e., manner   **my extent** that which I extend, i.e., my polite behavior
335–336 show fairly outwards show every evidence of cordiality   **entertainment** a (warm)
reception
339 north-north-west just off true north, only partly
340 hawk, handsaw i.e., two very different things, though also perhaps meaning a mattock (or
back) and a carpenter's cutting tool, respectively; also birds, with a play on *hernshaw*, or
heron
343 swaddling clouts cloths in which to wrap a newborn baby
344 Haply perhaps
349 Roscius a famous Roman actor who died in 62 B.C.
351 Buzz (An interjection used to denote stale news.)
356 scene individable a play observing the unity of place; or perhaps one that is unclassifiable,
or performed without intermission   **poem unlimited** a play disregarding the unities of time
and place; one that is all-inclusive   **Seneca** writer of Latin tragedies
357 Plautus writer of Latin comedy   **law . . . liberty** dramatic composition both according to the
rules and disregarding the rules   **these** i.e., the actors
358 Jephthah . . . Israel (Jephthah had to sacrifice his daughter; see Judges 11. Hamlet goes on
to quote from a ballad on the theme.)
362 passing surpassingly

POLONIUS: What follows, then, my lord?
HAMLET: Why,
>   "As by lot, God wot,"   369
>   and then, you know,
>   "It came to pass, as most like it was"—   371
>   the first row of the pious chanson will show you more,   372
>   for look where my abridgement comes.   373

Enter the Players.

>   You are welcome, masters; welcome, all. I am glad to see thee well. Welcome,
>   good friends. O, old friend! Why, thy face is valanced since I saw thee last.   375
>   Com'st thou to beard me in Denmark? What, my young lady and mistress! By 'r   376
>   Lady, your ladyship is nearer to heaven than when I saw you last, by the altitude   377
>   of a chopine. Pray God your voice, like a piece of uncurrent gold, be not   378
>   cracked within the ring. Masters, you are all welcome. We'll e'en to 't like   379
>   French falconers, fly at anything we see. We'll have a speech straight. Come, give   380
>   us a taste of your quality. Come, a passionate speech.   381

FIRST PLAYER: What speech, my good lord?

HAMLET: I heard thee speak me a speech once, but it was never acted, or if it was,
>   not above once, for the play, I remember, pleased not the million; 'twas caviar to   384
>   the general. But it was—as I received it, and others, whose judgments in such   385
>   matters cried in the top of mine—an excellent play, well digested in the scenes,   386
>   set down with as much modesty as cunning. I remember one said there were   387
>   no sallets in the lines to make the matter savory, nor no matter in the phrase   388
>   that might indict the author of affectation, but called it an honest method, as   389
>   wholesome as sweet, and by very much more handsome than fine. One speech   390
>   in 't I chiefly loved: 'twas Aeneas' tale to Dido, and thereabout of it especially
>   when he speaks of Priam's slaughter. If it live in your memory, begin at this line: 392
>   let me see, let me see—
>   "The rugged Pyrrhus, like th' Hyrcanian beast"—   394

---

369 lot chance   **wot** knows
372 row stanza   **chanson** ballad, song
373 my abridgment something that cuts short my conversation; also, a diversion
375 valanced fringed (with a beard)
376 beard confront, challenge (with obvious pun)   **young lady** i.e., boy playing women's parts
376–377 By 'r Lady by Our Lady
378 chopine thick-soled shoe of Italian fashion   **uncurrent** not passable as lawful coinage
379 cracked . . . ring i.e., changed from adolescent to male voice, no longer suitable for women's roles. (Coins featured rings enclosing the sovereign's head; if the coin was cracked within this ring, it was unfit for currency.)   **e'en to 't** go at it
380 straight at once   **381 quality** professional skill
384–385 caviar to the general caviar to the multitude, i.e., a choice dish too elegant for coarse tastes
386 cried in the top of i.e., spoke with greater authority than   **digested** arranged, ordered
387 modesty moderation, restraint   **cunning** skill
388 sallets i.e., something savory, spicy improprieties
389 indict convict
390 handsome well-proportioned   **fine** elaborately ornamented, showy
392 Priam's slaughter the slaying of the ruler of Troy, when the Greeks finally took the city
394 Pyrrhus a Greek hero in the Trojan War, also known as Neoptolemus, son of Achilles— another avenging son   **Hyrcanian beast** i.e., tiger (On the death of Priam, see Virgil, *Aeneid,* 2.506 ff.; compare the whole speech with Marlowe's *Dido Queen of Carthage,* 2 ff. On the *Hyrcanian* tiger, see *Aeneid,* 4.366–367. Hyrcania is on the Caspian Sea.)

'Tis not so. It begins with Pyrrhus:
"The rugged Pyrrhus, he whose sable arms,   396
Black as his purpose, did the night resemble
When he lay couchèd in the ominous horse,   398
Hath now this dread and black complexion smeared
With heraldry more dismal. Head to foot   400
Now is he total gules, horridly tricked   401
With blood of fathers, mothers, daughters, sons,
Baked and impasted with the parching streets,   403
That lend a tyrannous and a damnèd light   404
To their lord's murder. Roasted in wrath and fire,   405
And thus o'ersizèd with coagulate gore,   406
With eyes like carbuncles, the hellish Pyrrhus   407
Old grandsire Priam seeks."
So proceed you.

POLONIUS: 'Fore God, my lord, well spoken, with good accent and good discretion.

FIRST PLAYER: 'Anon he finds him
Striking too short at Greeks. His antique sword,   412
Rebellious to his arm, lies where it falls,
Repugnant to command. Unequal matched,   414
Pyrrhus at Priam drives, in rage strikes wide,
But with the whiff and wind of his fell sword   416
Th' unnervèd father falls. Then senseless Ilium,   417
Seeming to feel this blow, with flaming top
Stoops to his base, and with a hideous crash   419
Takes prisoner Pyrrhus' ear. For, lo! His sword,
Which was declining on the milky head   421
Of reverend Priam, seemed i' th' air to stick.
So as a painted tyrant Pyrrhus stood,   423
And, like a neutral to his will and matter,   424
Did nothing.
But as we often see against some storm
A silence in the heavens, the rack stand still,   426
The bold winds speechless, and the orb below   427
                              428

---

396 rugged shaggy, savage   **sable** black (for reasons of camouflage during the episode of the Trojan horse)

398 couchèd concealed   **ominous horse** fateful Trojan horse, by which the Greeks gained access to Troy

400 dismal ill-omened

401 total gules entirely red (A heraldic term)   **tricked** spotted and smeared (Heraldic)

403 impasted crusted, like a thick paste   **with . . . streets** by the parching heat of the streets (because of the fires everywhere)

404 tyrannous cruel   **405 their lord's** i.e., Priam's

406 o'ersizèd covered as with size or glue

407 carbuncles large fiery-red precious stones thought to emit their own light

412 antique ancient, long-used   **414 Repugnant** disobedient, resistant

416 fell cruel

417 unnervèd strengthless   **senseless Ilium** inanimate citadel of Troy

419 his its   **421 declining** descending   **milky** white-haired

423 painted i.e., painted in a picture

424 like . . . matter i.e., as though suspended between his intention and its fulfillment

426 against just before   **427 rack** mass of clouds

428 orb globe, earth

As hush as death, anon the dreadful thunder
Doth rend the region, so, after Pyrrhus' pause,   430
A rousèd vengeance sets him new a-work,
And never did the Cyclops' hammers fall   432
On Mars's armor forged for proof eterne   433
With less remorse than Pyrrhus' bleeding sword   434
Now falls on Priam.
Out, out, thou strumpet Fortune! All you gods
In general synod take away her power!   437
Break all the spokes and fellies from her wheel,   438
And bowl the round nave down the hill of heaven   439
As low as to the fiends!"

POLONIUS: This is too long.

HAMLET: It shall to the barber's with your beard.—Prithee, say on. He's for a jig or a   442
tale of bawdry, or he sleeps. Say on; come to Hecuba.   443

FIRST PLAYER: "But who, ah woe! had seen the moblèd queen"—   444

HAMLET: "The moblèd queen?"

POLONIUS: That's good. "Moblèd queen" is good.

FIRST PLAYER: "Run barefoot up and down, threat'ning the flames   447
With bisson rheum, a clout upon that head   448
Where late the diadem stood, and, for a robe,   449
About her lank and all o'erteemèd loins   450
A blanket, in the alarm of fear caught up—
Who this had seen, with tongue in venom steeped,
'Gainst Fortune's state would treason have pronounced.   453
But if the gods themselves did see her then
When she saw Pyrrhus make malicious sport
In mincing with his sword her husband's limbs,
The instant burst of clamor that she made,
Unless things mortal move them not at all,
Would have made milch the burning eyes of heaven,   459
And passion in the gods."   460

POLONIUS: Look whe'er he has not turned his color and has tears in 's eyes.   461
Prithee, no more.

HAMLET: 'Tis well; I'll have thee speak out the rest of this soon.—Good my lord, will
you see the players well bestowed? Do you hear, let them be well used, for they   464

---

430 region sky
432 Cyclops giant armor makers in the smithy of Vulcan
433 proof eterne eternal resistance to assault   434 remorse pity
437 synod assembly
438 fellies pieces of wood forming the rim of a wheel
439 nave hub   hill of heaven Mount Olympus
442 jig comic song and dance often given at the end of a play
443 Hecuba wife of Priam
444 who . . . had anyone who had (also in line 510)   moblèd muffled
447 threat'ning the flames i.e., weeping hard enough to dampen the flames
448 bisson rheum blinding tears   clout cloth   449 late lately
450 all o'erteemèd utterly worn out with bearing children
453 state rule, managing   pronounced proclaimed
459 milch milky, moist with tears   burning eyes of heaven i.e., heavenly bodies
460 passion overpowering emotion   461 whe'er whether
464 bestowed lodged

are the abstract and brief chronicles of the time. After your death you were bet- 465
ter have a bad epitaph than their ill report while you live.

POLONIUS: My lord, I will use them according to their desert.

HAMLET: God's bodikin, man, much better. Use every man after his desert, and who 468
shall scape whipping? Use them after your own honor and dignity. The less they
deserve, the more merit is in your bounty. Take them in.

POLONIUS: Come, sirs.   [*Exit.*]

HAMLET: Follow him, friends. We'll hear a play tomorrow. *[As they start to leave, Hamlet detains the First Player.]* Dost thou hear me, old friend? Can you play *The Murder of Gonzago?*

FIRST PLAYER: Ay, my lord.

HAMLET: We'll ha 't tomorrow night. You could, for a need, study a speech of some 476
dozen or sixteen lines which I would set down and insert in 't, could you not?

FIRST PLAYER: Ay, my lord.

HAMLET: Very well. Follow that lord, and look you mock him not. (*Exeunt Players.*) My
good friends, I'll leave you till night. You are welcome to Elsinore.

ROSENCRANTZ: Good my lord!

Exeunt [Rosencrantz and Guildenstern].

HAMLET: Ay, so, goodbye to you.—Now I am alone.
O, what a rogue and peasant slave am I!
Is it not monstrous that this player here,
But in a fiction, in a dream of passion,
Could force his soul so to his own conceit   485
That from her working all his visage wanned,   486
Tears in his eyes, distraction in his aspect,   487
A broken voice, and his whole function suiting   488
With forms to his conceit? And all for nothing!   489
For Hecuba!   490
What's Hecuba to him, or he to Hecuba,
That he should weep for her? What would he do
Had he the motive and the cue for passion
That I have? He would drown the stage with tears
And cleave the general ear with horrid speech,
Make mad the guilty and appall the free,   496
Confound the ignorant, and amaze indeed   497
The very faculties of eyes and ears. Yet I,   498

---

465 abstract summary account
468 God's bodikin by God's (Christ's) little body, *bodykin*. (Not to be confused with *bodkin*,
   "dagger.")   **after** according to
476 ha 't have it   **study** memorize
485 But merely
486 force . . . conceit bring his innermost being so entirely into accord with his conception (of
   the role)
487 from her working as a result of, or in response to, his soul's activity   **wanned** grew pale
488 aspect look, glance
489–490 his whole . . . conceit all his bodily powers responding with actions to suit his thought
496 the general ear everyone's ear   **horrid** horrible
497 appall (Literally, make pale.)   **free** innocent
498 Confound the ignorant i.e., dumbfound those who know nothing of the crime that has
   been committed   **amaze** stun

A dull and muddy-mettled rascal, peak 500
Like John-a-dreams, unpregnant of my cause, 501
And can say nothing—no, not for a king
Upon whose property and most dear life 503
A damned defeat was made. Am I a coward? 504
Who calls me villain? Breaks my pate across? 505
Plucks off my beard and blows it in my face?
Tweaks me by the nose? Gives me the lie i' the throat 507
As deep as to the lungs? Who does me this?
Ha, 'swounds, I should take it; for it cannot be 509
But I am pigeon-livered and lack gall 510
To make oppression bitter, or ere this 511
I should ha' fatted all the region kites 512
With this slave's offal. Bloody, bawdy villain! 513
Remorseless, treacherous, lecherous, kindless villain! 514
O, vengeance!
Why, what an ass am I! This is most brave, 516
That I, the son of a dear father murdered,
Prompted to my revenge by heaven and hell,
Must like a whore unpack my heart with words
And fall a-cursing, like a very drab, 520
A scullion! Fie upon 't, foh! About, my brains! 521
Hum, I have heard
That guilty creatures sitting at a play
Have by the very cunning of the scene 524
Been struck so to the soul that presently 525
They have proclaimed their malefactions;
For murder, though it have no tongue, will speak
With most miraculous organ. I'll have these players
Play something like the murder of my father
Before mine uncle. I'll observe his looks;
I'll tent him to the quick. If 'a do blench, 531
I know my course. The spirit that I have seen
May be the devil, and the devil hath power
T' assume a pleasing shape; yea, and perhaps,
Out of my weakness and my melancholy,
As he is very potent with such spirits, 536

---

500 muddy-mettled dull-spirited   **peak** mope, pine
501 John-a-dreams a sleepy, dreaming idler   **unpregnant of** not quickened by
503 property i.e., the crown; also character, quality
504 damned defeat damnable act of destruction
505 pate head   **507 Gives . . . throat** calls me an out-and-out liar
509 'swounds by his (Christ's) wounds
510 pigeon-livered (The pigeon or dove was popularly supposed to be mild because it secreted
no gall.)
511 bitter i.e., bitter to me   **512 region kites** kites (birds of prey) of the air
513 offal entrails   **514 Remorseless** pitiless   **kindless** unnatural
516 brave fine, admirable (Said ironically.)   **520 drab** whore
521 scullion menial kitchen servant (apt to be foul-mouthed)   **About** about it, to work
524 cunning art, skill   **scene** dramatic presentation   **525 presently** at once
531 tent probe   **the quick** the tender part of a wound, the core   **blench** quail, flinch
536 spirits humors (of melancholy)

Abuses me to damn me. I'll have grounds   537
More relative than this. The play's the thing   538
Wherein I'll catch the conscience of the King.   *Exit.*

Act 2 Response Statement Questions

- How do you respond to Hamlet's behavior in Act 2? Do you see him, for instance, as a clever dissembler who merely feigns madness, or do you think he's actually "gone over the edge" of sanity? Or do you interpret his behavior in some other way? If you do see him as a clever dissembler, can you see any purpose in his behavior? Can you begin to draw any larger interpretive conclusions from it (in terms of important issues or themes in the play)?
- How does your response to Claudius develop through Act 2? Do you find your opinion of him changing in light of what you see of his relationships with Polonius and Rosencrantz and Guildenstern?

Act 3, Scene 1

Enter King, Queen, Polonius, Ophelia, Rosencrantz, Guildenstern, lords.

KING: And can you by no drift of conference   1
   Get from him why he puts on this confusion,
   Grating so harshly all his days of quiet
   With turbulent and dangerous lunacy?
ROSENCRANTZ: He does confess he feels himself distracted,
   But from what cause 'a will by no means speak.
GUILDENSTERN: Nor do we find him forward to be sounded,   7
   But with a crafty madness keeps aloof
   When we would bring him on to some confession
   Of his true state.
QUEEN: Did he receive you well?
ROSENCRANTZ: Most like a gentleman.
GUILDENSTERN: But with much forcing of his disposition.   13
ROSENCRANTZ: Niggard of question, but of our demands   14
   Most free in his reply.
QUEEN: Did you assay him   16
   To any pastime?
ROSENCRANTZ: Madam, it so fell out that certain players
   We o'erraught on the way. Of these we told him,   19
   And there did seem in him a kind of joy
   To hear of it. They are here about the court,
   And, as I think, they have already order
   This night to play before him.

---

537 Abuses deludes
3.1. Location: The castle.
 1 drift of conference directing of conversation
 7 forward willing **sounded** questioned
14 Niggard stingy **question** conversation
19 o'erraught overtook

538 relative cogent, pertinent

13 disposition inclination

16 assay try to win

POLONIUS: 'Tis most true,
    And he beseeched me to entreat Your Majesties
    To hear and see the matter.
KING: With all my heart, and it doth much content me
    To hear him so inclined.
    Good gentlemen, give him a further edge   29
    And drive his purpose into these delights.
ROSENCRANTZ: We shall, my lord.

Exeunt Rosencrantz and Guildenstern.

KING: Sweet Gertrude, leave us too,
    For we have closely sent for Hamlet hither,   33
    That he, as 'twere by accident, may here
    Affront Ophelia.   35
    Her father and myself, lawful espials,   36
    Will so bestow ourselves that seeing, unseen,
    We may of their encounter frankly judge,
    And gather by him, as he is behaved,
    If 't be th' affliction of his love or no
    That thus he suffers for.
QUEEN: I shall obey you.
    And for your part, Ophelia, I do wish
    That your good beauties be the happy cause
    Of Hamlet's wildness. So shall I hope your virtues
    Will bring him to his wonted way again,   46
    To both your honors.
OPHELIA: Madam, I wish it may.

[Exit Queen.]

POLONIUS: Ophelia, walk you here.—Gracious, so please you, 49
    We will bestow ourselves. [*To Ophelia.*] Read on this book, [*giving her a book*]   50
    That show of such an exercise may color   51
    Your loneliness. We are oft to blame in this—   52
    'Tis too much proved—that with devotion's visage   53
    And pious action we do sugar o'er
    The devil himself.
KING: [*aside*]:   O, 'tis too true!
    How smart a lash that speech doth give my conscience!
    The harlot's cheek, beautied with plastering art,
    Is not more ugly to the thing that helps it   59
    Than is my deed to my most painted word.
    O heavy burden!

---

29 edge incitement   **33 closely** privately
35 Affront confront, meet   **36 espials** spies
46 wonted accustomed   **49 Gracious** Your Grace (i.e., the King)
50 bestow conceal
51 exercise religious exercise (The book she reads is one of devotion.)   **color** give a plausible
    appearance to
52 loneliness being alone
53 too much proved too often shown to be true, too often practiced
59 to compared to   **the thing** i.e., the cosmetic

POLONIUS: I hear him coming. Let's withdraw, my lord.

[The King and Polonius withdraw.]
Enter Hamlet. [Ophelia pretends to read a book.]

HAMLET: To be, or not to be, that is the question:
Whether 'tis nobler in the mind to suffer
The slings and arrows of outrageous fortune,
Or to take arms against a sea of troubles   65
And by opposing end them. To die, to sleep—
No more—and by a sleep to say we end
The heartache and the thousand natural shocks
That flesh is heir to. 'Tis a consummation
Devoutly to be wished. To die, to sleep;
To sleep, perchance to dream. Ay, there's the rub,   72
For in that sleep of death what dreams may come,
When we have shuffled off this mortal coil,   74
Must give us pause. There's the respect   75
That makes calamity of so long life.   76
For who would bear the whips and scorns of time,
Th' oppressor's wrong, the proud man's contumely,   78
The pangs of disprized love, the law's delay,   79
The insolence of office, and the spurns   80
That patient merit of th' unworthy takes,   81
When he himself might his quietus make   82
With a bare bodkin? Who would fardels bear,   83
To grunt and sweat under a weary life,
But that the dread of something after death,
The undiscovered country from whose bourn
No traveler returns, puzzles the will,   86
And makes us rather bear those ills we have
Than fly to others that we know not of?
Thus conscience does make cowards of us all;
And thus the native hue of resolution
Is sicklied o'er with the pale cast of thought,   91
And enterprises of great pitch and moment   92
With this regard their currents turn awry   93
And lose the name of action.—Soft you now,   94
          95

---

s.d. withdraw (The King and Polonius may retire behind an arras. The stage directions specify that they "enter" again near the end of the scene.)

65 slings missiles

72 rub (Literally, an obstacle in the game of bowls.)

74 shuffled sloughed, cast   **coil** turmoil   **75 respect** consideration

76 of . . . life so long-lived, something we willingly endure for so long (also suggesting that long life is itself a calamity)

78 contumely insolent abuse   **79 disprized** unvalued

80 office officialdom   **spurns** insults   **81 of . . . takes** receives from unworthy persons

82 quietus acquitance; here, death

83 a bare bodkin a mere dagger, unsheathed   **fardels** burdens

86 bourn frontier, boundary   **91 native hue** natural color, complexion

92 cast tinge, shade of color

93 pitch height (as of a falcon's flight)   **moment** importance

94 regard respect, consideration   **currents** courses

95 Soft you i.e., wait a minute, gently

The fair Ophelia. Nymph, in thy orisons   96
Be all my sins remembered.

OPHELIA: Good my lord,
How does your honor for this many a day?

HAMLET: I humbly thank you; well, well, well.

OPHELIA: My lord, I have remembrances of yours,
That I have longèd long to redeliver.
I pray you, now receive them.   [*She offers tokens.*]

HAMLET: No, not I, I never gave you aught.

OPHELIA: My honored lord, you know right well you did,
And with them words of so sweet breath composed
As made the things more rich. Their perfume lost,
Take these again, for to the noble mind
Rich gifts wax poor when givers prove unkind.
There, my lord.   [*She gives tokens.*]

HAMLET: Ha, ha! Are you honest?   111

OPHELIA: My lord?

HAMLET: Are you fair?   113

OPHELIA: What means your lordship?

HAMLET: That if you be honest and fair, your honesty should admit no discourse to   115
your beauty.

OPHELIA: Could beauty, my lord, have better commence than with honesty?   117

HAMLET: Ay, truly, for the power of beauty will sooner transform honesty from what it   119
is to a bawd than the force of honesty can translate beauty into his likeness. This   120
was sometime a paradox, but now the time gives it proof. I did love you once.

OPHELIA: Indeed, my lord, you made me believe so.

HAMLET: You should not have believed me, for virtue cannot so inoculate our old   122
stock but we shall relish of it. I loved you not.   123

OPHELIA: I was the more deceived.

HAMLET: Get thee to a nunnery. Why wouldst thou be a breeder of sinners? I am   125
myself indifferent honest, but yet I could accuse me of such things that it were   126
better my mother had not borne me: I am very proud, revengeful, ambitious,
with more offenses at my beck than I have thoughts to put them in, imagination   128
to give them shape, or time to act them in. What should such fellows as I do
crawling between earth and heaven? We are arrant knaves all; believe none of
us. Go thy ways to a nunnery. Where's your father?

OPHELIA: At home, my lord.

HAMLET: Let the doors be shut upon him, that he may play the fool nowhere but in
's own house. Farewell.

---

96 orisons prayers   **111 honest** (truthful) (2) chaste
113 fair (1) beautiful (2) just, honorable
115 your honesty your chastity   **discourse to** familiar dealings with
117 commerce dealings, intercourse   **119 his** its
120 sometime formerly   **a paradox** a view opposite to commonly held opinion   **the time** the
    present age
122 inoculate graft, be engrafted to
123 but . . . it that we do not still have about us a taste of the old stock, i.e., retain our sinfulness
125 nunnery convent (with possibly an awareness that the word was also used derisively to
    denote a brothel)
126 indifferent honest reasonably virtuous   **128 beck** command

OPHELIA: O, help him, you sweet heavens!

HAMLET: If thou dost marry, I'll give thee this plague for thy dowry: be thou as chaste as ice, as pure as snow, thou shalt not escape calumny. Get thee to a nunnery, farewell. Or, if thou wilt needs marry, marry a fool, for wise men know well enough what monsters you make of them. To a nunnery, go, and quickly too. Farewell.   139

OPHELIA: Heavenly powers, restore him!

HAMLET: I have heard of your paintings too, well enough. God hath given you one face, and you make yourselves another. You jig, you amble, and you lisp, you   142
nickname God's creatures, and make your wantonness your ignorance. Go to,   143
I'll no more on 't; it hath made me mad. I say we will have no more marriage.   144
Those that are married already—all but one—shall live. The rest shall keep as they are. To a nunnery, go.   *Exit.*

OPHELIA: O, what a noble mind is here o'erthrown!
The courtier's, soldier's, scholar's, eye, tongue, sword,
Th' expectancy and rose of the fair state,   149
The glass of fashion and the mold of form,   150
Th' observed of all observers, quite, quite down!   151
And I, of ladies most deject and wretched,
That sucked the honey of his music vows,   153
Now see that noble and most sovereign reason
Like sweet bells jangled out of tune and harsh,
That unmatched form and feature of blown youth   156
Blasted with ecstasy. O woe is me,   157
T' have seen what I have seen, see what I see!

Enter King and Polonius.

KING: Love? His affections do not that way tend;   159
Nor what he spake, though it lacked form a little,
Was not like madness. There's something in his soul
O'er which his melancholy sits on brood,
And I do doubt the hatch and the disclose   162
Will be some danger; which for to prevent,   163
I have in quick determination
Thus set it down: he shall with speed to England   166
For the demand of our neglected tribute.   167
Haply the seas and countries different
With variable objects shall expel   169

---

139 monsters (An illusion to the horns of a cuckold.)   **you** i.e., you women
142 jig dance   **amble** move coyly
143 you nickname . . . creatures i.e., you give trendy names to things in place of their God-given names   **make . . . ignorance** i.e., excuse your affectation on the grounds of pretended ignorance
144 on 't of it   **149 expectancy** hope   **rose** ornament
150 The glass . . . form the mirror of true self-fashioning and the pattern of courtly behavior
151 Th' observed . . . observers i.e., the center of attention and honor in the court
153 music musical, sweetly uttered   **156 blown** blooming
157 Blasted withered   **ecstasy** madness   **159 affections** emotions, feelings
162 sits on brood sits like a bird on a nest, about to *hatch* mischief (line 163)
163 doubt fear   **disclose** disclosure, hatching   **166 set it down** resolved
167 For . . . of to demand
169 variable objects various sights and surroundings to divert him

This something-settled matter in his heart,   170
Whereon his brains still beating puts him thus   171
From fashion of himself. What think you on 't?   172
POLONIUS: It shall do well. But yet do I believe
The origin and commencement of his grief
Sprung from neglected love.—How now, Ophelia?
You need not tell us what Lord Hamlet said;
We heard it all.—My lord, do as you please,
But, if you hold it fit, after the play
Let his queen-mother all alone entreat him   179
To show his grief. Let her be round with him;   180
And I'll be placed, so please you, in the ear
Of all their conference. If she find him not,   182
To England send him, or confine him where
Your wisdom best shall think
KING: It shall be so.
Madness in great ones must not unwatched go.

Exeunt.

Act 3, Scene 2

Enter Hamlet and three of the Players.

HAMLET: Speak the speech, I pray you, as I pronounced it to you, trippingly on the
tongue. But if you mouth it, as many of our players do, I had as lief the town   2
crier spoke my lines. Nor do not saw the air too much with your hand, thus, but
use all gently; for in the very torrent, tempest, and, as I may say, whirlwind of
your passion, you must acquire and beget a temperance that may give it
smoothness. O, it offends me to the soul to hear a robustious periwig-pated fel-   6
low tear a passion to tatters, to very rags, to split the ears of the groundlings,   7
who for the most part are capable of nothing but inexplicable dumb shows and   8
noise. I would have such a fellow whipped for o'erdoing Termagant. It out-   9
Herods Herod. Pray you, avoid it.   10
FIRST PLAYER: I warrant your honor.
HAMLET: Be not too tame neither, but let your own discretion be your tutor. Suit the
action to the word, the word to the action, with this special observance, that
you o'erstep not the modesty of nature. For anything so o'erdone is from the   14
purpose of playing, whose end, both at the first and now, was and is to hold as

---

170 **This something . . . heart** the strange matter settled in his heart
171 **still** continually   172 **From . . . himself** out of his natural manner
179 **queen-mother** queen and mother   180 **round** blunt
182 **find him not** fails to discover what is troubling him
3.2. Location: The castle.
2 **our players** players nowadays   **had as lief** I would just as soon
6 **robustious** violent, boisterous   **periwig-pated** wearing a wig
7 **groundlings** spectators who paid least and stood in the yard of the theater
8 **capable of** able to understand   **dumb shows** mimed performances, often used before Shakespeare's time to precede a play or each act
9 **Termagant** a supposed deity of the Mohammedans, not found in any English medieval play
but elsewhere portrayed as violent and blustering
10 **Herod** Herod of Jewry. (A character in *The Slaughter of the Innocents* and other cycle plays.
The part was played with great noise and fury.)
14 **modesty** restraint, moderation   **from** contrary to

't were the mirror up to nature, to show virtue her feature, scorn her own   16
image, and the very age and body of the time his form and pressure. Now this   17
overdone or come tardy off, though it makes the unskillful laugh, cannot but   18
make the judicious grieve, the censure of the which one must in your al-   19
lowance o'erweigh a whole theater of others. O, there be players that I have   20
seen play, and heard others praise, and that highly, not to speak it profanely,   21
that, neither having th' accent of Christians nor the gait of Christian, pagan, nor   22
man, have so strutted and bellowed that I have thought some of nature's jour-   23
neymen had made men and not made them well, they imitated humanity so   24
abominably.   25

FIRST PLAYER: I hope we have reformed that indifferently with us, sir.   26

HAMLET: O, reform it altogether. And let those that play your clowns speak no more
than is set down for them; for there be of them that will themselves laugh, to set   28
on some quantity of barren spectators to laugh too, though in the meantime   29
some necessary question of the play be then to be considered. That's villainous,
and shows a most pitiful ambition in the fool that uses it. Go make you ready.
[Exeunt Players.]

Enter Polonius, Guildenstern, and Rosencrantz.

How now, my lord, will the King hear this piece of work?

POLONIUS: And the Queen too, and that presently.   33

HAMLET: Bid the players make haste.   [Exit Polonius.]
Will you two help to hasten them?

ROSENCRANTZ: Ay, my lord.   Exeunt they two.

HAMLET: What ho, Horatio!

Enter Horatio.

HORATIO: Here, sweet lord, at your service.

HAMLET: Horatio, thou art e'en as just a man
As e'er my conversation coped withal.

HORATIO: O, my dear lord—   40

HAMLET: Nay, do not think I flatter,
For what advancement may I hope from thee
That no revenue hast but thy good spirits
To feed and clothe thee? Why should the poor be flattered?
No, let the candied tongue lick absurd pomp,
And crook the pregnant hinges of the knee   46
Where thrift may follow fawning. Dost thou hear?   47
                                                                                     48

---

16 scorn i.e., something foolish and deserving of scorn
17 the very . . . time i.e., the present state of affairs   **his** its   **pressure** stamp, impressed character
18 come tardy off inadequately done   **the unskillful** those lacking in judgment
19 the censure . . . one the judgment of even one of whom.
19–20 your allowance your scale of values
21 not . . . profanely (Hamlet anticipates his idea in lines 23–24 that some men were not made
by God at all.)
22 Christians i.e., ordinary decent folk
22–23 nor man i.e., nor any human being at all
23–24 journeymen laborers who are not yet masters in their trade
25 abominably (Shakespeare's usual spelling, *abhominably*, suggests a literal though etymolog-
ically incorrect meaning, "removed from human nature.")

26 indifferently tolerably
29 barren i.e., of wit
40 my . . . withal my dealings encountered
47 pregnant compliant

28 of them some among them
33 presently at once
46 candied sugared, flattering
48 thrift profit

Since my dear soul was mistress of her choice
And could of men distinguish her election,   50
Sh' hath sealed thee for herself, for thou hast been   51
As one, in suffering all, that suffers nothing,
A man that Fortune's buffets and rewards
Hast ta'en with equal thanks; and blest are those
Whose blood and judgment are so well commeddled   55
That they are not a pipe for Fortune's finger
To sound what stop she please. Give me that man   57
That is not passion's slave, and I will wear him
In my heart's core, ay, in my heart of heart,
As I do thee.—Something too much of this.—
There is a play tonight before the King.
One scene of it comes near the circumstance
Which I have told thee of my father's death.
I prithee, when thou seest that act afoot,
Even with the very comment of thy soul   65
Observe my uncle. If his occulted guilt   66
Do not itself unkennel in one speech,   67
It is a damnèd ghost that we have seen,   68
And my imaginations are as foul
As Vulcan's stithy. Give him heedful note,   70
For I mine eyes will rivet to his face,
And after we will both our judgments join
In censure of his seeming.   73
HORATIO: Well, my lord.
If 'a steal aught the whilst this play is playing   75
And scape detecting, I will pay the theft.

[Flourish.] Enter trumpets and kettledrums, King, Queen, Polonius, Ophelia, [Rosencrantz, Guildenstern, and other lords, with guards carrying torches].

HAMLET: They are coming to the play. I must be idle.   77
           Get you a place. [*The King, Queen, and courtiers sit.*]
KING: How fares our cousin Hamlet?   79
HAMLET: Excellent, i' faith, of the chameleon's dish: I eat the air, promise-crammed. 80
           You cannot feed capons so.   81
KING: I have nothing with this answer, Hamlet. These words are not mine. 82

---

50 could . . . election could make distinguishing choices among persons
51 sealed thee (Literally, as one would seal a legal document to mark possession.)
55 blood passion   **commeddled** commingled
57 stop hole in a wind instrument for controlling the sound
65 very . . . soul your most penetrating observation and consideration
66 occulted hidden
67 unkennel (As one would say of a fox driven from its lair.)
68 damnèd in league with Satan   **70 stithy** smithy, place of stiths (anvils)
73 censure of his seeming judgment of his appearance or behavior
75 If 'a steal aught if he gets away with anything   **77 idle** (1) unoccupied (2) mad
79 cousin i.e., close relative
80 chameleon's dish (Chameleons were supposed to feed on air. Hamlet deliberately misinterprets the King's *fares* as "feeds." By his phrase *eat the air* he also plays on the idea of feeding himself with the promise of succession, of being the *heir.*)
81 capons roosters castrated and *crammed* with feed to make them succulent
82 have . . . with make nothing of, or gain nothing from   **are not mine** do not respond to what I asked

HAMLET: No, nor mine now. [*To Polonius.*] My lord, you played once i' th' university,   83
you say?

POLONIUS: That did I, my lord, and was accounted a good actor.

HAMLET: What did you enact?

POLONIUS: I did enact Julius Caesar. I was killed i' the Capitol; Brutus killed me.

HAMLET: It was a brute part of him to kill so capital a calf there.—Be the players ready?   88

ROSENCRANTZ: Ay, my lord. They stay upon your patience.   89

QUEEN: Come hither, my dear Hamlet, sit by me.

HAMLET: No, good Mother, here's metal more attractive.   91

POLONIUS: [*to the King*]   O, ho, do you mark that?

HAMLET: Lady, shall I lie in your lap?

[*Lying down at Ophelia's feet.*]

OPHELIA: No, my lord.

HAMLET: I mean, my head upon your lap?

OPHELIA: Ay, my lord.

HAMLET: Do you think I meant country matters?   97

OPHELIA: I think nothing, my lord.

HAMLET: That's a fair thought to lie between maids' legs.

OPHELIA: What is, my lord?

HAMLET: Nothing.

OPHELIA: You are merry, my lord.   101

HAMLET: Who, I?

OPHELIA: Ay, my lord.

HAMLET: O God, your only jig maker. What should a man do but be merry? For look   105
you how cheerfully my mother looks, and my father died within 's two hours.   106

OPHELIA: Nay, 'tis twice two months, my lord.

HAMLET: So long? Nay then, let the devil wear black, for I'll have a suit of sables. O   108
heavens! Die two months ago, and not forgotten yet? Then there's hope a great
man's memory may outlive his life half a year. But, by 'r Lady, 'a must build
churches, then, or else shall 'a suffer not thinking on, with the hobbyhorse,   111
whose epitaph is "For O, for O, the hobbyhorse is forgot."   112

The trumpets sound. Dumb show follows.

---

83 nor mine now (Once spoken, words are proverbially no longer the speaker's own—and
hence should be uttered warily.)

88 brute (The Latin meaning of *brutus*, "stupid," was often used punningly with the name
Brutus.)   **part** (1) deed (2) role   **calf** fool

89 stay upon await

91 metal substance that is *attractive*, i.e., magnetic, but with suggestion also of *mettle*, "disposition"

97 country matters sexual intercourse (making a bawdy pun on the first syllable of *country*)

101 Nothing the figure zero or naught, suggesting the female sexual anatomy (*Thing* not infrequently has a bawdy connotation of male or female anatomy, and the reference here could
be male.)

105 only jig maker very best composer of jigs, i.e., pointless merriment (Hamlet replies sardon-
ically to Ophelia's observation that he is merry by saying, "If you're looking for someone who
is really merry, you've come to the right person.")

106 within 's within this (i.e., these)

108 suit of sables garments trimmed with the fur of the sable and hence suited for a wealthy person, not a mourner (but with a pun on *sable*, "black," ironically suggesting mourning once
again)

111 suffer . . . on undergo oblivion

112 For . . . forgot (Verse of a song occurring also in *Love's Labor's Lost*, 3.1.27–28. The hobbyhorse was a character made to resemble a horse and rider, appearing in the morris dance and
such May-game sports. This song laments the disappearance of such customs under pressure
from the Puritans.)

Enter a King and a Queen [very lovingly]; the Queen embracing him, and he her. [She kneels, and makes show of protestation unto him.] He takes her up, and declines his head upon her neck. He lies him down upon a bank of flowers. She, seeing him asleep, leaves him. Anon comes in another man, takes off his crown, kisses it, pours poison in the sleeper's ears, and leaves him. The Queen returns, finds the King dead, makes passionate action. The Poisoner with some three or four come in again, seem to condole with her. The dead body is carried away. The Poisoner woos the Queen with gifts; she seems harsh awhile, but in the end accepts love.

[Exeunt players.]

OPHELIA:	What means this, my lord?	
HAMLET:	Marry, this' miching mallico; it means mischief.	114
OPHELIA:	Belike this show imports the argument of the play.	115

Enter Prologue.

HAMLET:	We shall know by this fellow. The players cannot keep counsel; they'll tell all.	116
OPHELIA:	Will 'a tell us what this show meant?	
HAMLET:	Ay, or any show that you will show him. Be not you ashamed to show, he'll not shame to tell you what it means.	118
OPHELIA:	You are naught, you are naught. I'll mark the play.	120
PROLOGUE:	For us, and for our tragedy,	
	Here stooping to your clemency,	122
	We beg your hearing patiently. *[Exit.]*	
HAMLET:	Is this a prologue, or the posy of a ring?	124
OPHELIA:	'Tis brief, my lord.	
HAMLET:	As woman's love.	

Enter [two Players as] King and Queen.

PLAYER KING:	Full thirty times hath Phoebus' cart gone round	127
	Neptune's salt wash and Tellus' orbèd ground,	128
	And thirty dozen moons with borrowed sheen	129
	About the world have times twelve thirties been,	
	Since love our hearts and Hymen did our hands	131
	Unite commutual in most sacred bands.	132
PLAYER QUEEN:	So many journeys may the sun and moon	
	Make us again count o'er love be done!	
	But, woe is me, you are so sick of late,	
	So far from cheer and from your former state,	
	That I distrust you. Yet, though I distrust,	137
	Discomfort you, my lord, it nothing must.	138
	For women's fear and love hold quantity;	139

---

114 **this'miching mallico** this is sneaking mischief   115 **Belike** probably   **argument** plot
116 **counsel** secret   118 **Be not you** provided you are not
120 **naught** indecent (Ophelia is reacting to Hamlet's pointed remarks about not being ashamed to show all.)
122 **stooping** bowing
124 **posy . . . ring** brief motto in verse inscribed in a ring
127 **Pheobus' cart** the sun-god's chariot, making its yearly cycle
128 **salt wash** the sea   **Tellus** goddess of the earth, of the *orbèd ground*
129 **borrowed** i.e., reflected   131 **Hymen** god of matrimony
132 **commutual** mutually   **bands** bonds   137 **distrust** am anxious about
138 **Discomfort** distress   **nothing** not at all
139 **hold quantity** keep proportion with one another

In neither aught, or in extremity.   140
Now, what my love is, proof hath made you know,   141
And as my love is sized, my fear is so.   142
Where love is great, the littlest doubts are fear;
Where little fears grow great, great love grows there.

PLAYER KING: Faith, I must leave thee, love, and shortly too;
My operant powers their functions leave to do.
And thou shalt live in this fair world behind,   146
Honored, beloved; and haply one as kind   147
For husband shalt thou—

PLAYER QUEEN: O, confound the rest!
Such love must needs be treason in my breast.
In second husband let me be accurst!
None wed the second but who killed the first.

HAMLET: Wormwood, wormwood.   153

PLAYER QUEEN: The instances that second marriage move   154
Are base respects of thrift, but none of love.   155
A second time I kill my husband dead   156
When second husband kisses me in bed.

PLAYER KING: I do believe you think what now you speak,
But what we do determine oft we break.
Purpose is but the slave to memory,
Of violent birth, but poor validity,   161
Which now, like fruit unripe, sticks on the tree,   162
But fall unshaken when they mellow be.   163
Most necessary 'tis that we forget
To pay ourselves what to ourselves is debt.   165
What to ourselves in passion we propose,   166
The passion ending, doth the purpose lose.
The violence of either grief or joy
Their own enactures with themselves destroy.
Where joy most revels, grief doth most lament;   170
Grief joys, joy grieves, on slender accident.   171
This world is not for aye, nor 'tis not strange   172
That even our loves should with our fortunes change;   173

---

140 In . . . extremity i.e., women fear and love either too little or too much, but the two, fear and love, are equal in either case
141 proof experience   **142 sized** in size
146 operant powers vital functions   **leave to do** cease to perform
147 behind after I have gone
153 None i.e., let no woman   **but who** except the one who
154 Wormwood i.e., how bitter (Literally, a bitter-tasting plant.)
155 instances motives   **move** motivate
156 base . . . thrift ignoble considerations of material prosperity
161 Purpose . . . memory our good intentions are subject to forgetfulness
162 validity strength, durability   **163 Which** i.e., purpose
165–166 Most . . . debt it's inevitable that in time we forget the obligations we have imposed on ourselves
170 enactures fulfillments
171–172 Where . . . accident the capacity for extreme joy and grief go together, and often one extreme is instantly changed into its opposite on the slightest provocation
173 aye ever

For 'tis a question left us yet to prove,
Whether love lead fortune, or else fortune love.
The great man down, you mark his favorite flies;   177
The poor advanced makes friends of enemies.   178
And hitherto doth love on fortune tend;   179
For who not needs shall never lack a friend,   180
And who in want a hollow friend doth try   181
Directly seasons him his enemy.   182
But, orderly to end where I begun,
Our wills and fates do so contrary run   184
That our devices still are overthrown;   185
Our thoughts are ours, their ends none of our own.   186
So think thou wilt no second husband wed,
But die thy thoughts when thy first lord is dead.
PLAYER QUEEN: Nor earth to me give food, nor heaven light,   189
Sport and repose lock from me day and night,   190
To desperation turn my trust and hope,
An anchor's cheer in prison be my scope!   192
Each opposite that blanks the face of joy   193
Meet what I would have well and it destroy!   194
Both here and hence pursue me lasting strife   195
If, once a widow, ever I be wife!
HAMLET: If she should break it now!
PLAYER KING: 'Tis deeply sworn. Sweet, leave me here awhile;
My spirits grow dull, and fain I would beguile   199
The tedious day with sleep.
PLAYER QUEEN: Sleep rock thy brain,
And never come mischance between us twain!

[He sleeps.] Exit [Player Queen].

HAMLET: Madam, how like you this play?
QUEEN: The lady doth protest too much, methinks.   204
HAMLET: O, but she'll keep her word.
KING: Have you heard the argument? Is there no offense in 't?   206
HAMLET: No, no, they do but jest, poison in jest. No offense i' the world. 207

---

177 down fallen in fortune
178 The poor . . . enemies when one of humble station is promoted, you see his enemies suddenly becoming his friends
179 hitherto up to this point in the argument, or, to this extent   **tend** attend
180 who not needs he who is not in need (of wealth)
181 who in want he who, being in need   **try** test (his generosity)
182 seasons him ripens him into
184 Our . . . run what we want and what we get go so contrarily
185 devices still intentions continually   **186 ends** results
189 Nor let neither
190 Sport . . . night may day deny me its pastimes and night its repose
192 anchor's cheer anchorite's or hermit's fare   **my scope** the extent of my happiness
193–194 Each . . . destroy may every adverse thing that causes the face of joy to turn pale meet
and destroy everything that I desire to see prosper   **blanks** causes to blanch or grow pale
195 hence in the life hereafter   **199 spirits** vital spirits
204 doth . . . much makes to many promises and protestations
206 argument plot
206–207 offense . . . offense cause for objection . . . actual injury, crime
207 jest make believe

KING: What do you call the play?

HAMLET: *The Mousetrap.* Marry, how? Tropically. This play is the image of a murder done   209
in Vienna. Gonzago is the Duke's name, his wife, Baptista. You shall see anon. 'Tis a   210
knavish piece of work, but what of that? Your Majesty, and we that have free souls,   211
it touches us not. Let the galled jade wince, our withers are unwrung.   212

Enter Lucianus.

This is one Lucianus, nephew to the King.

OPHELIA: You are as good as a chorus, my lord.   214

HAMLET: I could interpret between you and your love, if I could see the puppets   215
dallying.   216

OPHELIA: You are keen, my lord, you are keen.   217

HAMLET: It would cost you a groaning to take off mine edge.

OPHELIA: Still better, and worse.   219

HAMLET: So you mis-take your husbands. Begin, murderer; leave thy damnable faces   220
and begin. Come, the croaking raven doth bellow for revenge.

LUCIANUS: Thoughts black, hands apt, drugs fit, and time agreeing,
Confederate season, else no creature seeing,   223
Thou mixture rank, of midnight weeds collected,
With Hecate's ban thrice blasted, thrice infected,   225
Thy natural magic and dire property   226
On wholesome life usurp immediately.

[He pours the poison into the sleeper's ear.]

HAMLET: 'A poisons him i' the garden for his estate. His name's Gonzago. The story   228
is extant, and written in very choice Italian. You shall see anon how the murderer gets the love of Gonzago's wife.

[Claudius rises.]

OPHELIA: The King rises.

HAMLET: What, frighted with false fire?   232

QUEEN: How fares my lord?

---

209 Tropically figuratively (The first Quarto reading, *trapically,* suggests a pun on *trap* in
Mousetrap.)

210 Duke's i.e., King's (A slip that may be due to Shakespeare's possible source, the alleged murder of the Duke of Urbino by Luigi Gonzaga in 1538.)

211 free guiltless

212 galled jade horse whose hide is rubbed by saddle or harness   **withers** the part between the
horse's shoulder blades   **unwrung** not wrung sore

214 chorus (In many Elizabethan plays, the forthcoming action was explained by an actor
known as the "chorus"; at a puppet show, the actor who spoke the dialogue was known as
an "interpreter," as indicated by the lines following.)

215 interpret (1) ventriloquize the dialogue, as in puppet show (2) act as pander

215–216 puppets dallying (With suggestion of sexual play, continued in *keen,* "sexually
aroused," *groaning,* "moaning in pregnancy," and *edge,* "sexual desire" or "impetuosity.")

217 keen sharp, bitter

219 Still . . . worse more keen, always *bettering* what other people say with witty wordplay, but
at the same time more offensive

220 So even thus (in marriage)   **mis-take** take falseheartedly and cheat on. (The marriage
vows say "for better, for worse.")

223 Confederate season the time and occasion conspiring (to assist the murderer)   **else** otherwise   **seeing** seeing me

225 Hecate's ban the curse of Hecate, the goddess of witchcraft

226 dire property baleful quality   **228 estate** i.e., the kingship   **His** i.e., the King's

232 false fire the blank discharge of a gun loaded with powder but no shot

POLONIUS: Give o'er the play.
KING: Give me some light. Away!
POLONIUS: Lights, lights, lights!

Exeunt all but Hamlet and Horatio.

HAMLET: "Why, let the strucken deer go weep,   237
  The hart ungallèd play.   238
 For some must watch, while some must sleep;   239
  Thus runs the world away."   240

Would not this, sir, and a forest of feathers—if the rest of my fortunes turn Turk   241
with me—with two Provincial roses on my razed shoes, get me a fellowship in   242
a cry of players?   243
HORATIO: Half a share.
HAMLET: A whole one, I.
"For thou dost know, O Damon dear,   246
 This realm dismantled was   247
Of Jove himself, and now reigns here
 A very, very—pajock."   249
HORATIO: You might have rhymed.
HAMLET: O good Horatio, I'll take the ghost's word for a thousand pound. Didst perceive?
HORATIO: Very well, my lord.
HAMLET: Upon the talk of the poisoning?
HORATIO: I did very well note him.

Enter Rosencrantz and Guildenstern.

HAMLET: Aha! Come, some music! Come, the recorders.   256
"For if the King like not the comedy,
 Why then, belike, he likes it not, perdy."   258
Come, some music.
GUILDENSTERN: Good my lord, vouchsafe me a word with you.
HAMLET: Sir, a whole history.
GUILDENSTERN: The King, sir—
HAMLET: Ay, sir, what of him?

237–240 Why . . . away (Probably from an old ballad, with allusion to the popular belief that a wounded deer retires to weep and die; compare with *As You Like It*, 2.1.33–66.)
238 ungallèd unafflicted   **239 watch** remain awake
240 Thus . . . away thus the world goes
241 this i.e., the play **feathers** (Allusion to the plumes that Elizabethan actors were fond of wearing.)
241–242 turn Turk with turn renegade against, go back on
242 Provincial roses rosettes of ribbon, named for roses grown in a part of France **razed** with ornamental slashing
242–243 fellowship . . . players partnership in a theatrical company
243 cry pack (of hounds)
246 Damon the friend of Pythias, as Horatio is friend of Hamlet; or, a traditional pastoral name
247–249 This realm . . . pajock i.e., Jove, representing divine authority and justice, has abandoned this realm to its own devices, leaving in his stead only a peacock or vain pretender to virtue (though the rhyme-word expected in place of *pajock* or "peacock" suggests that the realm is now ruled over by an "ass").
247 dismantled stripped, divested
256 recorders wind instruments of the flute kind
258 perdy (A corruption of the French *par dieu*, "by God.")

GUILDENSTERN: Is in his retirement marvelous distempered. 264

HAMLET: With drink, sir?

GUILDENSTERN: No, my lord, with choler. 266

HAMLET: Your wisdom should show itself more richer to signify this to the doctor, for for me to put him to his purgation would perhaps plunge him into more choler. 268

GUILDENSTERN: Good my lord, put your discourse into some frame and start not so 269 wildly from my affair.

HAMLET: I am tame, sir. Pronounce.

GUILDENSTERN: The Queen, your mother, in most great affliction of spirit, hath sent me to you.

HAMLET: You are welcome.

GUILDENSTERN: Nay, good my lord, this courtesy is not of the right breed. If it shall 275 please you to make me a wholesome answer, I will do your mother's commandment; if not, your pardon and my return shall be the end of my business. 277

HAMLET: Sir, I cannot.

ROSENCRANTZ: What, my lord?

HAMLET: Make you a wholesome answer; my wit's diseased. But, sir, such answer as I can make, you shall command, or rather, as you say, my mother. Therefore no more, but to the matter. My mother, you say—

ROSENCRANTZ: Then thus she says: your behavior hath struck her into amazement and admiration.

HAMLET: O wonderful son, that can so stonish a mother! But is there no sequel at 284 the heels of this mother's admiration? Impart.

ROSENCRANTZ: She desires to speak with you in her closet ere you go to bed. 287

HAMLET: We shall obey, were she ten times our mother. Have you any further trade with us?

ROSENCRANTZ: My lord, you once did love me.

HAMLET: And do still, by these pickers and stealers. 291

ROSENCRANTZ: Good my lord, what is your cause of distemper? You do surely bar the door upon your own liberty if you deny your griefs to your friend. 293

HAMLET: Sir, I lack advancement.

ROSENCRANTZ: How can that be, when you have the voice of the King himself for your succession in Denmark?

HAMLET: Ay, sir, but "While the grass grows"—the proverb is something musty. 297

Enter the Players with recorders.

---

264 retirement withdrawal to his chambers **distempered** out of humor (But Hamlet deliberately plays on the wider application to any illness of mind or body, as in lines 292–293 especially to drunkenness.)

268 choler anger (But Hamlet takes the word in its more basic humoral sense of "bilious disorder.") **purgation** (Hamlet hints at something going beyond medical treatment to blood-letting and the extraction of confession.)

269 frame order **start** shy or jump away (like a horse; the opposite of *tame* in line 271)

275 breed (1) kind (2) breeding, manners **277 pardon** permission to depart

284 admiration bewilderment **287 closet** private chamber

291 pickers and stealers i.e., hands (So called from the catechism, "to keep my hands from picking and stealing.")

293 liberty i.e., being freed from *distemper,* line 292; but perhaps with a veiled threat as well **deny** refuse to share

297 While . . . grows (The rest of the proverb is "the silly horse starves"; Hamlet may not live long enough to succeed to the kingdom.) **something** somewhat **s.d. Players** actors

O, the recorders. Let me see one. [*He takes a recorder.*]

HAMLET: To withdraw with you: why do you go about to recover the wind of me, as if   299
you would drive me into a toil?   300

GUILDENSTERN: O, my lord, if my duty be too bold, my love is too unmannerly.   301

HAMLET: I do not well understand that. Will you play upon this pipe?   302

GUILDENSTERN: My lord, I cannot.

HAMLET: I pray you.

GUILDENSTERN: Believe me, I cannot.

HAMLET: I do beseech you.

GUILDENSTERN: I know no touch of it, my lord.

HAMLET: It is as easy as lying. Govern these ventages with your fingers and thumb,   308
give it breath with your mouth, and it will discourse most eloquent music. Look
you, these are the stops.

GUILDENSTERN: But these cannot I command to any utterance of harmony. I have not
the skill.

HAMLET: Why, look you now, how unworthy a thing you make of me! You would
play upon me, you would seem to know my stops, you would pluck out the
heart of my mystery, you would sound me from my lowest note to the top of my   315
compass, and there is much music, excellent voice, in this little organ, yet can-   316
not you make it speak. 'Sblood, do you think I am easier to be played on than a
pipe? Call me what instrument you will, though you can fret me, you cannot   318
play upon me.

Enter Polonius.

God bless you, sir!

POLONIUS: My lord, the Queen would speak with you, and presently.   321

HAMLET: Do you see yonder cloud that's almost in shape of a camel?

POLONIUS: By the Mass and 'tis, like a camel indeed.

HAMLET: Methinks it is like a weasel.

POLONIUS: It is backed like a weasel.

HAMLET: Or like a whale.

POLONIUS: Very like a whale.

HAMLET: Then I will come to my mother by and by. [*Aside.*] They fool me to the top   328
of my bent.—I will come by and by.   329

POLONIUS: I will say so.   [*Exit.*]

HAMLET: "By and by" is easily said. Leave me, friends.

[*Exeunt all but Hamlet.*]

'Tis now the very witching time of night,   332

---

299 withdraw speak privately   **recover the wind** get to the windward side (thus driving the
game into the *toil,* or "net")

300 toil snare

301 if . . . unmannerly if I am using an unmannerly boldness, it is my love that occasions it

302 I . . . that i.e., I don't understand how genuine love can be unmannerly

308 ventages finger-holes or *stops* (line 310) of the recorder

315 sound (1) fathom (2) produce sound in

316 compass range (of voice)   **organ** musical instrument

318 fret irritate (with a quibble on *fret,* meaning the piece of wood, gut, or metal that regulates
the fingering on an instrument)

321 presently at once

328 by and by quite soon   **fool me** trifle with me, humor my fooling

328–329 top of my bent limit of my ability or endurance (Literally, the extent to which a bow
may be bent.)

332 witching time time when spells are cast and evil is abroad

When churchyards yawn and hell itself breathes out
Contagion to this world. Now could I drink hot blood
And do such bitter business as the day
Would quake to look on. Soft, now to my mother.
O heart, lose not thy nature! Let not ever 337
The soul of Nero enter this firm bosom. 338
Let me be cruel, not unnatural;
I will speak daggers to her, but use none.
My tongue and soul in this be hypocrites:
How in my words soever she be shent, 342
To give them seals never my soul consent! *Exit.* 343

Act 3, Scene 3

Enter King, Rosencrantz, and Guildenstern.

KING: I like him not, nor stands it safe with us 1
          To let his madness range. Therefore prepare you.
          I your commission will forthwith dispatch, 3
          And he to England shall along with you.
          The terms of our estate may not endure 5
          Hazard so near 's as doth hourly grow
          Out of his brows. 7

GUILDENSTERN: We will ourselves provide.
          Most holy and religious fear it is
          To keep those many many bodies safe 9
          That live and feed upon Your Majesty.

ROSENCRANTZ: The single and peculiar life is bound 12
          With all the strength and armor of the mind
          To keep itself from noyance, but much more 14
          That spirit upon whose weal depends and rests
          The lives of many. The cess of majesty 16
          Dies not alone, but like a gulf doth draw 17
          What's near it with it; or it is a massy wheel 18
          Fixed on the summit of the highest mount,
          To whose huge spokes ten thousand lesser things
          Are mortised and adjoined, which, when it falls, 21
          Each small annexment, petty consequence, 22
          Attends the boisterous ruin. Never alone 23
          Did the King sigh, but with a general groan.

---

337 nature natural feeling   **338 Nero** murderer of his mother, Agrippina
342 How . . . soever however much by my words   **shent** rebuked
343 give them seals i.e., confirm them with deeds
3.3 Location: The castle.
1 him i.e., his behavior   **3 dispatch** prepare, cause to be drawn up
5 terms of our estate circumstances of my royal position
7 Out of his brows i.e., from his brain, in the form of plots and threats
9 religious fear sacred concern   **12 single and peculiar** individual and private
14 noyance harm   **16 cess** decease, cessation
17 gulf whirlpool   **18 massy** massive
21 mortised fastened (as with a fitted joint)   **when it falls** i.e., when it descends, like the wheel
  of Fortune, bringing a king down with it
22 Each . . . consequence i.e., every hanger-on and unimportant person or thing connected with
  the King
23 Attends participates in

KING: Arm you, I pray you, to this speedy voyage,   25
          For we will fetters put about this fear,
          Which now goes too free-footed.

ROSENCRANTZ: We will haste us.

Exeunt gentlemen [Rosencrantz and Guildenstern]. Enter Polonius.

POLONIUS: My lord, he's going to his mother's closet.
          Behind the arras I'll convey myself   30
          To hear the process. I'll warrant she'll tax him home,   31
          And, as you said—and wisely was it said—
          'Tis meet that some more audience than a mother,   33
          Since nature makes them partial, should o'erhear
          The speech, of vantage. Fare you well, my liege.   35
          I'll call upon you ere you go to bed
          And tell you what I know.

KING: Thanks, dear my lord.

Exit [Polonius].

          O, my offense is rank! It smells to heaven.
          It hath the primal eldest curse upon 't,   40
          A brother's murder. Pray can I not,
          Though inclination be as sharp as will;   42
          My stronger guilt defeats my strong intent,
          And like a man to double business bound   44
          I stand in pause where I shall first begin,
          And both neglect. What if this cursèd hand
          Were thicker than itself with brother's blood,
          Is there not rain enough in the sweet heavens
          To wash it white as snow? Whereto serves mercy   49
          But to confront the visage of offense?   50
          And what's in prayer but this twofold force,
          To be forestallèd ere we come to fall,   52
          Or pardoned being down? Then I'll look up.
          My fault is past. But O, what form of prayer
          Can serve my turn? "Forgive me my foul murder"?
          That cannot be, since I am still possessed
          Of those effects for which I did the murder:
          My crown, mine own ambition, and my queen.
          May one be pardoned and retain th' offense?   59
          In the corrupted currents of this world   60

---

25 Arm prepare

30 arras screen of tapestry placed around the walls of household apartments. (On the Elizabethan stage, the arras was presumably over a door or discovery space in the tiring-house facade.)

31 process proceedings   **tax him home** reprove him severely

33 meet fitting

35 of vantage from an advantageous place, or, in addition

40 the primal eldest curse the curse of Cain, the first murderer; he killed his brother Abel

42 Though . . . will though my desire is as strong as my determination

44 bound (1) destined (2) obliged. (The King wants to repent and still enjoy what he has gained.)

49–50 Whereto . . . offense what function does mercy serve other than to meet sin face to face?

52 forestallèd prevented (from sinning)   **59 th' offense** the thing for which one offended

60 currents courses

Offense's gilded hand may shove by justice,   61
And oft 'tis seen the wicked prize itself   62
Buys out the law. But 'tis not so above.
There is no shuffling, there the action lies   64
In his true nature, and we ourselves compelled,   65
Even to the teeth and forehead of our faults,   66
To give in evidence. What then? What rests?   67
Try what repentance can. What can it not?
Yet what can it, when one cannot repent?
O wretched state, O bosom black as death,
O limèd soul that, struggling to be free,   71
Art more engaged! Help, angels! Make assay.   72
Bow, stubborn knees, and heart with strings of steel,
Be soft as sinews of the newborn babe!
All may be well.   [*He kneels.*]

Enter Hamlet.

HAMLET: Now might I do it pat, now 'a is a-praying;
And now I'll do 't. [*He draws his sword.*] And so 'a goes to heaven,   76
And so am I revenged. That would be scanned:
A villain kills my father, and for that,   78
I, his sole son, do this same villain send
To heaven.
Why, this is hire and salary, not revenge.
'A took my father grossly, full of bread,   83
With all his crimes broad blown, as flush as May;   84
And how his audit stands who knows save heaven?   85
But in our circumstance and course of thought   86
'Tis heavy with him. And am I then revenged,
To take him in the purging of his soul,
When he is fit and seasoned for his passage?   89
No!
Up, sword, and know thou a more horrid hent.   91

[*He puts up his sword.*]

---

61 gilded hand hand offering gold as a bribe   **shove by** thrust aside
62 wicked prize prize won by wickedness
64 There i.e., in heaven   **shuffling** escape by trickery   **the action lies** the accusation is made manifest (A legal metaphor.)
65 his its
66 to the teeth and forehead face to face, concealing nothing
67 give in provide   **rests** remains
71 limèd caught as with birdlime, a sticky substance used to ensnare birds
72 engaged entangled   **assay** trial (Said to himself.)
76 pat opportunely
78 would be scanned needs to be looked into, or, would be interpreted as follows
83 grossly, full of bread i.e., enjoying his worldly pleasures rather than fasting (See Ezekiel 16:49.)
84 crimes broad blown sins in full bloom   **flush** vigorous
85 audit account   **save** except for
86 in . . . thought as we see it from our mortal perspective
89 seasoned matured, readied
91 know . . . hent await to be grasped by me on a more horrid occasion   **hent** act of seizing

When he is drunk asleep, or in his rage,   92
Or in th' incestuous pleasure of his bed,
At game, a-swearing, or about some act   94
That has no relish of salvation in 't—   95
Then trip him, that his heels may kick at heaven,
And that his soul may be as damned and black
As hell, whereto it goes. My mother stays.   98
This physic but prolongs thy sickly days.   *Exit.*   99

KING: My words fly up, my thoughts remain below.
Words without thoughts never to heaven go.   *Exit.*

Act 3, Scene 4

Enter [Queen] Gertrude and Polonius.

POLONIUS: 'A will come straight. Look you lay home to him.   1
Tell him his pranks have been too broad to bear with,   2
And that Your Grace hath screened and stood between
Much heat and him. I'll shroud me even here.   4
Pray you, be round with him.   5
HAMLET: *(within)*   Mother, Mother, Mother!
QUEEN: I'll warrant you, fear me not.
Withdraw, I hear him coming.

[Polonius hides behind the arras.] Enter Hamlet.

HAMLET: Now, Mother, what's the matter?
QUEEN: Hamlet, thou hast thy father much offended.
HAMLET: Mother, you have my father much offended.
QUEEN: Come, come, you answer with an idle tongue.   10
HAMLET: Go, go, you question with a wicked tongue.
QUEEN: Why, how now, Hamlet?   12
HAMLET: What's the matter now?
QUEEN: Have you forgot me?   16
HAMLET: No, by the rood, not so: 17
You are the Queen, your husband's brother's wife,
And—would it were not so!—you are my mother.
QUEEN: Nay, then, I'll set those to you that can speak.   20
HAMLET: Come, come, and sit you down; you shall not budge.
You go not till I set you up a glass
Where you may see the inmost part of you.
QUEEN: What wilt thou do? Thou wilt not murder me?

---

92 drunk . . . rage dead drunk, or in a fit of sexual passion
94 game gambling   **95 relish** trace, savor
98 stays awaits (me)
99 physic purging (by prayer), or, Hamlet's postponement of the killing
3.4 Location: The Queen's private chamber.
  1 lay home thrust to the heart, reprove him soundly
  2 broad unrestrained
  4 Much heat i.e., the King's anger   **shroud** conceal (with ironic fitness to Polonius' imminent
    death. The word is only in the First Quarto; the Second Quarto and the Folio read "silence.")
  5 round blunt   **10 thy father** i.e., your stepfather, Claudius
12 idle foolish
16 forgot me i.e., forgotten that I am your mother.
17 rood cross of Christ
                                                           20 speak i.e., to someone so rude

Help, ho!

POLONIUS: *[behind the arras]*   What ho! Help!

HAMLET: *[drawing]*   How now? A rat? Dead for a ducat, dead!   27

[He thrusts his rapier through the arras.]

POLONIUS: *[behind the arras]*   O, I am slain!   *[He falls and dies.]*

QUEEN: O me, what hast thou done?

HAMLET: Nay, I know not. Is it the King?

QUEEN: O, what a rash and bloody deed is this!

HAMLET: A bloody deed—almost as bad, good Mother,
    As kill a king, and marry with his brother.

QUEEN: As kill a king!

HAMLET: Ay, lady, it was my word.

[He parts the arras and discovers Polonius.]

    Thou wretched, rash, intruding fool, farewell!
    I took thee for thy better. Take thy fortune.
    Thou find'st to be too busy is some danger.—
    Leave wringing of your hands. Peace, sit you down,   38
    And let me wring your heart, for so I shall,
    If it be made of penetrable stuff,
    If damnèd custom have not brazed it so   42
    That it be proof and bulwark against sense.   43

QUEEN: What have I done, that thou dar'st wag thy tongue
    In noise so rude against me?

HAMLET: Such an act
    That blurs the grace and blush of modesty,
    Calls virtue hypocrite, takes off the rose
    From the fair forehead of an innocent love
    And sets a blister there, makes marriage vows
    As false as dicers' oaths. O, such a deed   50
    As from the body of contraction plucks   52
    The very soul, and sweet religion makes   53
    A rhapsody of words. Heaven's face does glow   54
    O'er this solidity and compound mass
    With tristful visage, as against the doom,
    Is thought-sick at the act.   57

QUEEN: Ay me, what act,
    That roars so loud and thunders in the index?   59

HAMLET: *[showing her two likenesses]*
    Look here upon this picture, and on this,
    The counterfeit presentment of two brothers.   61

---

27 Dead for a ducat i.e., I bet a ducat he's dead; or, a ducat is his life's fee
38 busy nosey
42 damnèd custom habitual wickedness   **brazed** brazened, hardened
43 proof armor   **sense** feeling   **50 sets a blister** i.e., brands as a harlot
52 contraction the marriage contract
53 sweet religion makes i.e., makes marriage vows
54 rhapsody senseless string
54–57 Heaven's . . . act heaven's face blushes at this solid world compounded of the various
    elements, with sorrowful face as though the day of doom were near, and is sick with horror at
    the deed (i.e., Gertrude's marriage)
59 index table of contents, prelude or preface
61 counterfeit presentment portrayed representation

See what a grace was seated on this brow:
Hyperion's curls, the front of Jove himself,　63
An eye like Mars to threaten and command,　64
A station like the herald Mercury　65
New-lighted on a heaven-kissing hill—　66
A combination and a form indeed
Where every god did seem to set his seal　68
To give the world assurance of a man.
This was your husband. Look you now what follows:
Here is your husband, like a mildewed ear,　71
Blasting his wholesome brother. Have you eyes?　72
Could you on this fair mountain leave to feed　73
And batten on this moor? Ha, have you eyes?　74
You cannot call it love, for at your age
The heyday in the blood is tame, it's humble,　76
And waits upon the judgment, and what judgment
Would step from this to this? Sense, sure, you have,　78
Else could you not have motion, but sure that sense
Is apoplexed, for madness would not err,　80
Nor sense to ecstasy was ne'er so thralled,
But it reserved some quantity of choice　82
To serve in such a difference. What devil was 't　83
That thus hath cozened you at hoodman-blind?　84
Eyes without feeling, feeling without sight,
Ears without hands or eyes, smelling sans all,　86
Or but a sickly part of one true sense
Could not so mope. O shame, where is thy blush?　88
Rebellious hell,
If thou canst mutine in a matron's bones,　90
To flaming youth let virtue be as wax　91
And melt in her own fire. Proclaim no shame　92

---

63 Hyperion's the sun-god's　**front** brow　**64 Mars** god of war
65 station manner of standing　**Mercury** winged messenger of the gods
66 New-lighted newly alighted　**68 set his seal** i.e., affix his approval
71 ear i.e., of grain　**72 Blasting** blighting
73 leave cease
74 batten gorge　**moor** barren or marshy ground (suggesting also "dark skinned")
76 heyday state of excitement　**blood** passion
78 Sense perception through the five senses (the functions of the middle or sensible soul)
80 apoplexed paralyzed (Hamlet goes on to explain that, without such a paralysis of will, mere madness would not so err, nor would the five senses so enthrall themselves to *ecstasy* or lunacy; even such deranged states of mind would be able to make the obvious choice between Hamlet Senior and Claudius.)　**err** so err
82 But but that
83 To . . . difference to help in making a choice between two such men
84 cozened cheated　**hoodman-blind** blindman's buff (In this game, says Hamlet, the devil must have pushed Claudius toward Gertrude while she was blindfolded.)
86 sans without　　**88 mope** be dazed, act aimlessly
90 mutine incite mutiny
91–92 be as wax . . . fire melt like a candle or stick of sealing wax held over the candle flame
92–95 Proclaim . . . will call it no shameful business when the compelling ardor of youth delivers the attack, i.e., commits lechery, since the *frost* of advanced age burns with as active a fire of lust and reason perverts itself by fomenting lust rather than restraining it

When the compulsive ardor gives the charge,
Since frost itself as actively doth burn,
And reason panders will.
QUEEN: O Hamlet, speak no more!   95
Thou turn'st mine eyes into my very soul,
And there I see such black and grainèd spots   98
As will not leave their tinct.   99
HAMLET: Nay, but to live
In the rank sweat of an enseamèd bed,   101
Stewed in corruption, honeying and making love   102
Over the nasty sty!
QUEEN: O, speak to me no more!
These words like daggers enter in my ears.
No more, sweet Hamlet!
HAMLET: A murderer and a villain,
A slave that is not twentieth part the tithe   108
Of your precedent lord, a vice of kings,   109
A cutpurse of the empire and the rule,
That from a shelf the precious diadem stole
And put it in his pocket!
QUEEN: No more!

Enter Ghost [in his nightgown].

HAMLET: A king of shreds and patches—
Save me, and hover o'er me with your wings,
You heavenly guards! What would your gracious figure?   114
QUEEN: Alas, he's mad!
HAMLET: Do you not come your tardy son to chide,
That, lapsed in time and passion, lets go by   119
Th' important acting of your dread command?   120
O, say!
GHOST: Do not forget. This visitation
Is but to whet thy almost blunted purpose.
But look, amazement on thy mother sits.   124
O, step between her and her fighting soul!
Conceit in weakest bodies strongest works.   126
Speak to her, Hamlet.
HAMLET: How is it with you, lady?
QUEEN: Alas, how is 't with you,
That you do bend your eye on vacancy,
And with th' incorporal air do hold discourse?   131
Forth at your eyes your spirits wildly peep,

---

98 grainèd dyed in grain, indelible   **99 leave their tinct** surrender their color
101 enseamèd saturated in the grease and filth of passionate lovemaking
102 Stewed soaked, bathed (with a suggestion of "stew," brothel)
108 tithe tenth part
109 precedent lord former husband   **vice** buffoon (A reference to the Vice of the morality
plays.)
114 shreds and patches i.e., motley, the traditional costume of the clown or fool
119 lapsed delaying   **120 important** importunate, urgent
124 amazement distraction   **126 Conceit** imagination
131 incorporal immaterial

And, as the sleeping soldiers in th' alarm,   133
Your bedded hair, like life in excrements,   134
Start up and stand on end. O gentle son,
Upon the heat and flame of thy distemper   136
Sprinkle cool patience. Whereon do you look?

HAMLET: On him, on him! Look you how pale he glares!
His form and cause conjoined, preaching to stones,   139
Would make them capable.—Do not look upon me,   140
Lest with this piteous action you convert   141
My stern effects. Then what I have to do   142
Will want true color—tears perchance for blood.   143

QUEEN: To whom do you speak this?
HAMLET: Do you see nothing there?
QUEEN: Nothing at all, yet all that is I see.
HAMLET: Nor did you nothing hear?
QUEEN: No, nothing but ourselves.
HAMLET: Why, look you there, look how it steals away!
My father, in his habit as he lived!   150
Look where he goes even now out at the portal!

Exit Ghost.

QUEEN: This is the very coinage of your brain.   152
This bodiless creation ecstasy   153
Is very cunning in.   154
HAMLET: Ecstasy?
My pulse as yours doth temperately keep time,
And makes as healthful music. It is not madness
That I have uttered. Bring me to the test,
And I the matter will reword, which madness   159
Would gambol from. Mother, for love of grace,   160
Lay not that flattering unction to your soul   161
That not your trespass but my madness speaks.
It will but skin and film the ulcerous place,   163
Whiles rank corruption, mining all within,   164
Infects unseen. Confess yourself to heaven,
Repent what's past, avoid what is to come,
And do not spread the compost on the weeds   167

---

133 as . . . alarm like soldiers called out of sleep by an alarm
134 bedded laid flat   **like life in excrements** i.e., as though hair, an outgrowth of the body, had a life of its own (Hair was thought to be lifeless because it lacks sensation, and so its standing on end would be unnatural and ominous.)
136 distemper disorder
139 His . . . conjoined his appearance joined to his cause for speaking
140 capable receptive
141–142 convert. . . effects divert me from my stern duty
143 want . . . blood lack plausibility so that (with a play on the normal sense of *color*) I shall shed colorless tears instead of blood
150 habit clothes   **as** as when   **152 very** mere
153–154 This . . . in madness is skillful in creating this kind of hallucination
159 reword repeat word for word   **160 gambol** skip away
161 unction ointment   **163 skin** grow a skin for
164 mining working under the surface   **167 compost** manure

To make them ranker. Forgive me this my virtue;	168
For in the fatness of these pursy times	169
Virtue itself of vice must pardon beg,	
Yea, curb and woo for leave to do him good.	171

QUEEN: O Hamlet, thou hast cleft my heart in twain.

HAMLET: O, throw away the worser part of it,
And live the purer with the other half.
Good night. But go not to my uncle's bed;
Assume a virtue, if you have it not.
That monster, custom, who all sense doth eat,   177
Of habits devil, is angel yet in this,   178
That to the use of actions fair and good
He likewise gives a frock or livery   180
That aptly is put on. Refrain tonight,   181
And that shall lend a kind of easiness
To the next abstinence; the next more easy;
For use almost can change the stamp of nature,   184
And either ... the devil, or throw him out   185
With wondrous potency. Once more, good night;
And when you are desirous to be blest,   187
I'll blessing beg of you. For this same lord,   188

[pointing to Polonius]

I do repent; but heaven hath pleased it so
To punish me with this, and this with me,
That I must be their scourge and minister.
I will bestow him, and will answer well   191
The death I gave him. So, again, good night.   192
I must be cruel only to be kind.
This bad begins, and worse remains behind.
One word more, good lady.   195

QUEEN: What shall I do?

HAMLET: Not this by no means that I bid you do:
Let the bloat king tempt you again to bed,   199

---

168 this my virtue my virtuous talk in reproving you
169 fatness grossness **pursy** flabby, out of shape
171 curb bow, bend the knee **leave** permission
177 who . . . eat which consumes all proper or natural feeling, all sensibility
178 Of habits devil devil-like in prompting evil habits
180 livery an outer appearance, a customary garb (and hence a predisposition easily assumed in time of stress)
181 aptly readily   **184 use** habit **stamp of nature** our inborn traits
185 And either (A defective line, usually emended by inserting the word *master* after *either*, following the Fourth Quarto and early editors.)
187–188 when . . . you i.e., when you are ready to be penitent and seek God's blessing, I will ask your blessing as a dutiful son should
191 their scourge and minister i.e., agent of heavenly retribution (By *scourge*, Hamlet also suggests that he himself will eventually suffer punishment in the process of fulfilling heaven's will.)
192 bestow stow, dispose of **answer** account or pay for
195 This i.e., the killing of Polonius **behind** to come
199 bloat bloated

Pinch wanton on your cheek, call you his mouse,	200
And let him, for a pair of reechy kisses,	201
Or paddling in your neck with his damned fingers,	202
Make you to ravel all this matter out	203
That I essentially am not in madness,	
But mad in craft. 'Twere good you let him know,	205
For who that's but a queen, fair, sober, wise,	
Would from a paddock, from a bat, a gib,	207
Such dear concernings hide? Who would do so?	208
No, in despite of sense and secrecy,	209
Unpeg the basket on the house's top,	210
Let the birds fly, and like the famous ape,	211
To try conclusions, in the basket creep	212
And break your own neck down.	213

QUEEN: Be thou assured, if words be made of breath,
And breath of life, I have no life to breathe
What thou hast said to me.

HAMLET: I must to England. You know that?

QUEEN: Alack,
I had forgot. 'Tis so concluded on.

HAMLET: There's letters sealed, and my two schoolfellows,	
Whom I will trust as I will adders fanged,	
They bear the mandate; they must sweep my way	222
And marshal me to knavery. Let it work.	223
For 'tis the sport to have the enginer	224
Hoist with his own petard, and 't shall go hard	225
But I will delve one yard below their mines	226
And blow them at the moon. O, 'tis most sweet	
When in one line two crafts directly meet.	228
This man shall set me packing.	229
I'll lug the guts into the neighbor room.	

---

200 Pinch wanton i.e., leave his love pinches on your cheeks, branding you as wanton
201 reechy dirty, filthy   **202 paddling** fingering amorously
203 ravel . . . out unravel, disclose
205 in craft by cunning   **good** (Said sarcastically; also the following eight lines.)
207 paddock toad   **gib** tomcat   **208 dear concernings** important affairs
209 sense and secrecy that common sense requires
210 Unpeg the basket open the cage, i.e., let out the secret
211 famous ape (In a story now lost.)
212 try conclusions test the outcome (in which the ape apparently enters a cage from which birds have been released and then tries to fly out of the cage as they have done, falling to death)
213 down in the fall; utterly
222–223 sweep . . . knavery sweep a path before me and conduct me to some *knavery* or treachery prepared for me
223 work proceed   **224 enginer** maker of military contrivances
225 Hoist with blown up by   **petard** an explosive used to blow in a door or make a breach
225–226 't shall . . . will unless luck is against me, I will
226 mines tunnels used in warfare to undermine the enemy's emplacements; Hamlet will countermine by going under their mines
228 in one line i.e., mines and countermines on a collision course, or the countermines directly below the mines   **crafts** acts of guile, plots
229 set me packing set me to making schemes, and set me to lugging (him), and, also, send me off in a hurry

Mother, good night indeed. This counselor
Is now most still, most secret, and most grave,
Who was in life a foolish prating knave. —
Come, sir, to draw toward an end with you. —
Good night, Mother.

234

Exeunt [separately, Hamlet dragging in Polonius].

Act 3 Response Statement Questions

- What do you think is going on between Hamlet and Ophelia, both in Scene 1 and in offstage action? What is your response to her and to the situation she's in? Does your response to her affect your feelings about Hamlet? How does your age or gender influence your response?
- Through Acts 2 and 3, do you think Hamlet is working toward doing what the ghost told him to do? Or is he procrastinating? If your answer is the latter, what reasons do you see for his delaying? What would you do if you were in his place? If you would act differently from the way he does, why can't he do what you would do?
- How do you think the "Mousetrap" scene (Act 3, Scene 2) should be played in performance, especially in terms of Claudius' reaction to the Players' presentation? What different ways are there to fill in this gap? How would different ways of filling this gap correspond to what different interpretations of the play as a whole at this point?
- Scenes 3 and 4 are often seen as crucial turning points in the action of the play. What is your response to: Claudius in Scene 3? Hamlet's decision not to kill Claudius when he has the chance, and his stated reasons for this decision? Hamlet's interaction with his mother in Scene 4? Hamlet's killing Polonius in Scene 4?
- By the end of Act 3, what is your opinion of Hamlet? Is he, for instance, insane? corrupted by the evil atmosphere surrounding him at Elsinore? ruthless and merciless in pursuing his revenge? a noble prince cleansing his world of villains and evil-doers?
- What do you expect to happen or what do you predict will happen next (in Acts 4 and 5)? What do you base this prediction on?

Act 4, Scene 1

Enter King and Queen, with Rosencrantz and Guildenstern.

KING: There's matter in these sighs, these profound heaves.
         You must translate; 'tis fit we understand them.
         Where is your son?

QUEEN: Bestow this place on us a little while.

1

---

234 draw ... end finish up (with a pun on *draw*, "pull")
4.1. Location: The castle.:   s.d. Enter ... Queen (Some editors argue that Gertrude never exits in 3.4 and that the scene is continuous here, as suggested in the Folio, but the Second Quarto marks an entrance for her and at line 36 Claudius speaks of Gertrude's *closet* as though it were elsewhere. A short time has elapsed, during which the King has become aware of her highly wrought emotional state.)
1 matter significance   **heaves** heavy sighs

[Exeunt Rosencrantz and Guildenstern.]

    Ah, mine own lord, what have I seen tonight!
KING: What, Gertrude? How does Hamlet?
QUEEN: Mad as the sea and wind when both contend
    Which is the mightier. In his lawless fit,
    Behind the arras hearing something stir,
    Whips out his rapier, cries, "A rat, a rat!"
    And in this brainish apprehension kills   11
    The unseen good old man.
KING: O heavy deed!   13
    It had been so with us, had we been there.   14
    His liberty is full of threats to all—
    To you yourself, to us, to everyone.
    Alas, how shall this bloody deed be answered?   17
    It will be laid to us, whose providence   18
    Should have kept short, restrained, and out of haunt   19
    This mad young man. But so much was our love,
    We would not understand what was most fit,
    But, like the owner of a foul disease,
    To keep it from divulging, let it feed   23
    Even on the pith of life. Where is he gone?
QUEEN: To draw apart the body he hath killed,
    O'er whom his very madness, like some ore   26
    Among a mineral of metals base,   27
    Shows itself pure: 'a weeps for what is done.
KING: O Gertrude, come away!
    The sun no sooner shall the mountains touch
    But we will ship him hence, and this vile deed
    We must with all our majesty and skill
    Both countenance and excuse.—Ho, Guildenstern!   33

[Enter Rosencrantz and Guildenstern.]

    Friends both, go join you with some further aid.
    Hamlet in madness hath Polonius slain,
    And from his mother's closet hath he dragged him.
    Go seek him out, speak fair, and bring the body
    Into the chapel. I pray you, haste in this.

[Exeunt Rosencrantz and Guildenstern.]

    Come, Gertrude, we'll call up our wisest friends
    And let them know both what we mean to do
    And what's untimely done   41
    Whose whisper o'er the world's diameter,   42

---

11 brainish apprehension headstrong conception   **13 heavy** grievous
14 us i.e., me (The royal "we"; also in line 16.)   **17 answered** explained
18 providence foresight
19 short i.e., on a short tether   **out of haunt** secluded
23 divulging becoming evident   **26 ore** vein of gold
27 mineral mine   **33 countenance** put the best face on
41 And . . . done (A defective line; conjectures as to the missing words include *So, haply, slander*
[Capell and others]; *For, haply, slander* [Theobald and others]; and *So envious slander*
[Jenkins].)
42 diameter extent from side to side

As level as the cannon to his blank, 43
Transports his poisoned shot, may miss our name
And hit the woundless air. O, come away! 45
My soul is full of discord and dismay. *Exeunt.*

Act 4, Scene 2

Enter Hamlet.

HAMLET: Safely stowed.

ROSENCRANTZ, GUILDENSTERN: (*within*) Hamlet! Lord Hamlet!

HAMLET: But soft, what noise? Who calls on Hamlet? O, here they come.

[Enter Rosencrantz and Guildenstern.]

ROSENCRANTZ: What have you done, my lord, with the dead body?

HAMLET: Compounded it with dust, whereto 'tis kin.

ROSENCRANTZ: Tell us where 'tis, that we may take it thence
And bear it to the chapel.

HAMLET: Do not believe it.

ROSENCRANTZ: Believe what?

HAMLET: That I can keep your counsel and not mine own. Besides, to be demanded 10
of a sponge, what replication should be made by the son of a king? 11

ROSENCRANTZ: Take you me for a sponge, my lord?

HAMLET: Ay, sir, that soaks up the King's countenance, his rewards, his authorities. 13
But such officers do the King best service in the end. He keeps them, like an
ape, an apple, in the corner of his jaw, first mouthed to be last swallowed. When
he needs what you have gleaned, it is but squeezing you, and, sponge, you shall
be dry again.

ROSENCRANTZ: I understand you not, my lord.

HAMLET: I am glad of it. A knavish speech sleeps in a foolish ear. 19

ROSENCRANTZ: My lord, you must tell us where the body is and go with us to the King.

HAMLET: The body is with the King, but the King is not with the body. The King is a 21
thing—

GUILDENSTERN: A thing, my lord?

HAMLET: Of nothing. Bring me to him. Hide fox, and all after! *Exeunt* [*running*]. 24

Act 4, Scene 3

Enter King, and two or three.

---

43 As level with as direct aim   **his blank** its target a point-blank range
45 woundless invulnerable
4.2. Location: The castle.
10 That . . . own i.e., that I can follow your advice (by telling where the body is) and still keep
my own secret   **demanded of** questioned by
11 replication reply   **13 countenance** favor   **authorities** delegated power, influence
19 sleeps in has no meaning to
21 The . . . body (Perhaps alludes to the legal commonplace of "the king's two bodies," which
drew a distinction between the sacred office of kingship and the particular mortal who possessed it at any given time. Hence, although Claudius' body is necessarily a part of him, true
kingship is not contained in it. Similarly, Claudius will have Polonius' body when it is found,
but there is no kingship in this business either.)
24 Of nothing (1) of no account (2) lacking the essence of kingship, as in lines 21–22 and note
Hide . . . after (An old signal cry in the game of hide-and-seek, suggesting that Hamlet now
runs away from them.)
4.3. Location: The castle.

KING: I have sent to seek him, and to find the body.
How dangerous is it that this man goes loose!
Yet must not we put the strong law on him.
He's loved of the distracted multitude,   4
Who like not in their judgment, but their eyes,   5
And where 'tis so, th' offender's scourge is weighed,   6
But never the offense. To bear all smooth and even,   7
This sudden sending him away must seem
Deliberate pause. Diseases desperate grown   9
By desperate appliance are relieved,   10
Or not at all.

Enter Rosencrantz, [Guildenstern,] and all the rest.
How now, what hath befall'n?
ROSENCRANTZ: Where the dead body is bestowed, my lord,
We cannot get from him.
KING: But where is he?
ROSENCRANTZ: Without, my lord; guarded, to know your pleasure.
KING: Bring him before us.
ROSENCRANTZ: Ho! Bring in the lord.

They enter [with Hamlet].
KING: Now, Hamlet, where's Polonius?
HAMLET: At supper.
KING: At supper? Where?
HAMLET: Not where he eats, but where 'a is eaten. A certain convocation of politic   22
worms are e'en at him. Your worm is your only emperor for diet. We fat all crea-   23
tures else to fat us, and we fat ourselves for maggots. Your fat king and your lean
beggar is but variable service—two dishes, but to one table. That's the end.   25
KING: Alas, alas!
HAMLET: A man may fish with the worm that hath eat of a king, and eat of the fish   27
that hath fed of that worm.
KING: What dost thou mean by this?
HAMLET: Nothing but to show you how a king may go a progress through the guts   30
of a beggar.
KING: Where is Polonius?
HAMLET: In heaven. Send thither to see. If your messenger find him not there, seek
him i' th' other place yourself. But if indeed you find him not within this month,
you shall nose him as you go up the stairs into the lobby.
KING: [*to some attendants*]   Go seek him there.
HAMLET: 'A will stay till you come. [*Exeunt attendants.*]

---

4 of by   **distracted** fickle, unstable
5 Who . . . eyes who choose not by judgment but by appearance
6 scourge punishment. (Literally, blow with a whip.)   **weighed** sympathetically considered
7 To . . . even to manage the business in an unprovocative way
9 Deliberate pause carefully considered action   **10 appliance** remedies
22–23 politic worms crafty worms (suited to a master spy like Polonius).
23 e'en even now   **Your worm** your average worm. Compare *your fat king and your lean beg-gar* in line 24.)   **diet** food, eating (with a punning reference to the Diet of Worms, a famous *convocation* held in 1521)
25 variable service different courses of a single meal
27 eat eaten (Pronounced *et.*)   **30 progress** royal journey of state

KING: Hamlet, this deed, for thine especial safety—
    Which we do tender, as we dearly grieve
    For that which thou hast done—must send thee hence   39
    With fiery quickness. Therefore prepare thyself.
    The bark is ready, and the wind at help,   42
    Th' associates tend, and everything is bent   43
    For England.
HAMLET: For England!
KING: Ay, Hamlet.
HAMLET: Good.
KING: So is it, if thou knew'st our purposes.
HAMLET: I see a cherub that sees them. But come, for England! Farewell, dear mother.   49
KING: Thy loving father, Hamlet.
HAMLET: My mother. Father and mother is man and wife, man and wife is one flesh,
    and so, my mother. Come, for England!   *Exit.*
KING: Follow him at foot; tempt him with speed aboard.   53
    Delay it not. I'll have him hence tonight.
    Away! For everything is sealed and done
    That else leans on th' affair. Pray you, make haste.   56

[Exeunt all but the King.]

    And, England, if my love thou hold'st at aught—   57
    As my great power thereof may give thee sense,   58
    Since yet thy cicatrice looks raw and red   59
    After the Danish sword, and thy free awe   60
    Pays homage to us—thou mayst not coldly set   61
    Our sovereign process, which imports at full,   62
    By letters congruing to that effect,   63
    The present death of Hamlet. Do it, England,   64
    For like the hectic in my blood he rages,   65
    And thou must cure me. Till I know 'tis done,
    Howe'er my haps, my joys were ne'er begun.   *Exit.*   67

Act 4, Scene 4

Enter Fortinbras with his army over the stage.

FORTINBRAS: Go, Captain, from me greet the Danish king.
    Tell him that by his license Fortinbras   2

---

39 tender regard, hold dear   **dearly** intensely   **42 bark** sailing vessel
43 tend wait   **bent** in readiness
49 cherub (Cherubim are angels of knowledge. Hamlet hints that both he and heaven are onto
Claudius' tricks.)
53 at foot close behind, at heel   **56 leans on** bears upon, is related to
57 England i.e., King of England   **at aught** at any value
58 As . . . sense for so my great power may give you a just appreciation of the importance of
valuing my love
59 cicatrice scar   **60 free awe** voluntary show of respect
61 coldly set regard with indifference
62 process command   **imports at full** conveys specific directions for
63 congruing agreeing   **64 present** immediate
65 hectic persistent fever   **67 haps** fortunes
4.4. Location: The coast of Denmark.
2 license permission

Craves the conveyance of a promised march   3
Over his kingdom. You know the rendezvous.
If that His Majesty would aught with us,
We shall express our duty in his eye;   6
And let him know so.
CAPTAIN: I will do 't, my lord.
FORTINBRAS: Go softly on.   [*Exeunt all but the Captain.*]   9

Enter Hamlet, Rosencrantz, [Guildenstern,] etc.

HAMLET: Good sir, whose powers are these?   10
CAPTAIN: They are of Norway, sir.
HAMLET: How purposed, sir, I pray you?
CAPTAIN: Against some part of Poland.
HAMLET: Who commands them, sir?
CAPTAIN: The nephew to old Norway, Fortinbras.
HAMLET: Goes it against the main of Poland, sir,   16
Or for some frontier?
CAPTAIN: Truly to speak, and with no addition,   18
We go to gain a little patch of ground
That hath in it no profit but the name.
To pay five ducats, five, I would not farm it;   21
Nor will it yield to Norway or the Pole
A ranker rate, should it be sold in fee.   23
HAMLET: Why, then the Polack never will defend it.
CAPTAIN: Yes, it is already garrisoned.
HAMLET: Two thousand souls and twenty thousand ducats
Will not debate the question of this straw.   27
This is th' impostume of much wealth and peace,   28
That inward breaks, and shows no cause without
Why the man dies. I humbly thank you, sir.
CAPTAIN: God b' wi' you, sir.   [*Exit.*]
ROSENCRANTZ: Will 't please you go, my lord?
HAMLET: I'll be with you straight. Go a little before.

[*Exeunt all except Hamlet.*]

How all occasions do inform against me   34
And spur my dull revenge! What is a man,
If his chief good and market of his time   36
Be but to sleep and feed? A beast, no more.
Sure he that made us with such large discourse,   38
Looking before and after, gave us not   39
That capability and godlike reason
To fust in us unused. Now, whether it be   41

---

3 **the conveyance of** escort during   6 **duty** respect   **eye** presence
9 **softly** slowly, circumspectly   10 **powers** forces
16 **main** main part   18 **addition** exaggeration
21 **To pay** i.e., for a yearly rental of   **farm it** take a lease of it
23 **ranker** higher   **in fee** fee simple, outright
27 **debate . . . straw** settle this trifling matter   28 **impostume** abscess
34 **inform against** denounce, betray; take shape against
36 **market of** profit of, compensation for
38 **discourse** power of reasoning
39 **Looking before and after** able to review past events and anticipate the future
41 **fust** grow moldy

Bestial oblivion, or some craven scruple 42
Of thinking too precisely on th' event— 43
A thought which, quartered, hath but one part wisdom
And ever three parts coward—I do not know
Why yet I live to say "This thing's to do,"
Sith I have cause, and will, and strength, and means 47
To do 't. Examples gross as earth exhort me: 48
Witness this army of such mass and charge, 49
Led by a delicate and tender prince, 50
Whose spirit with divine ambition puffed
Makes mouths at the invisible event, 52
Exposing what is mortal and unsure
To all that fortune, death, and danger dare, 54
Even for an eggshell. Rightly to be great 55
Is not to stir without great argument,
But greatly to find quarrel in a straw
When honor's at the stake. How stand I, then, 58
That have a father killed, a mother stained,
Excitements of my reason and my blood,
And let all sleep, while to my shame I see 60
The imminent death of twenty thousand men
That for a fantasy and trick of fame 63
Go to their graves like beds, fight for a plot 64
Whereon the numbers cannot try the cause, 65
Which is not tomb enough and continent 66
To hide the slain? O, from this time forth
My thoughts be bloody or be nothing worth! *Exit.*

Act 4, Scene 5

Enter Horatio, [Queen] Gertrude, and a Gentleman.

QUEEN: I will not speak with her.
GENTLEMAN: She is importunate,
    Indeed distract. Her mood will needs be pities.
QUEEN: What would she have? 3
GENTLEMAN: She speaks much of her father, says she hears
    There's tricks i' the world, and hems, and beats her heart, 6

---

42 oblivion forgetfulness   **craven** cowardly
43 precisely scrupulously   **event** outcome
48 gross obvious
50 delicate and tender of fine and youthful qualities
52 Makes mouths makes scornful faces   **invisible event** unforeseeable outcome
54 dare could do (to him)
55–58 Rightly . . . stake   true greatness does not normally consist of rushing into action over some trivial provocation; however, when one's honor is involved, even a trifling insult requires that one respond greatly (?)
58 at the stake (A metaphor from gambling or bearbaiting.)
60 Excitements of promptings by
63 fantasy fanciful caprice, illusion   **trick** trifle, deceit   **64 plot** plot of ground
65 Whereon . . . cause on which there is insufficient room for the soldiers needed to engage in a military contest
66 continent receptacle, container
4.5. Location: The castle.
  3 distract distracted   **6 tricks** deceptions   **hems** makes "hmm" sounds   **heart** i.e., breast

47 Sith since
49 charge expense

Spurns enviously at straws, speaks things in doubt   7
That carry but half sense. Her speech is nothing,
Yet the unshapèd use of it doth move   9
The hearers to collection; they yawn at it,   10
And botch the words up fit to their own thoughts,   11
Which, as her winks and nods and gestures yield them,   12
Indeed would make one think there might be thought,   13
Though nothing sure, yet much unhappily.   14

HORATIO: 'Twere good she were spoken with, for she may strew
Dangerous conjectures in ill-breeding minds.   16

QUEEN: Let her come in.   [*Exit Gentleman.*]
[*Aside.*] To my sick soul, as sin's true nature is,
Each toy seems prologue to some great amiss.   19
So full of artless jealousy is guilt,   20
It spills itself in fearing to be spilt.   21

Enter Ophelia [distracted].

OPHELIA: Where is the beauteous majesty of Denmark?

QUEEN: How now, Ophelia?

OPHELIA: (*she sings*):
"How should I your true love know
   From another one?
By his cockle hat and staff,
   And his sandal shoon."   26
                                                                      27

QUEEN: Alas, sweet lady, what imports this song?

OPHELIA: Say you? Nay, pray you, mark.
"He is dead and gone, lady,   (*Song.*)
   He is dead and gone;
At his head a grass-green turf,
   At his heels a stone."
O, ho!

QUEEN: Nay, but Ophelia—

OPHELIA: Pray you, mark.
[*Sings.*] "White his shroud as the mountain snow"—

Enter King.

QUEEN: Alas, look here, my lord.

---

7 **Spurns . . . straws** kicks spitefully, takes offense at trifles   **in doubt** obscurely
9 **unshapèd use** incoherent manner
10 **collection** inference, a guess at some sort of meaning   **yawn** gape, wonder; grasp (The Folio reading, *aim*, is possible.)
11 **botch** patch   12 **Which** which words   **yield** deliver, represent
13 **thought** intended
14 **unhappily** unpleasantly near the truth, shrewdly
16 **ill-breeding** prone to suspect the worst and to make mischief
19 **toy** trifle   **amiss** calamity
20–21 **So . . . spilt** guilt is so full of suspicion that it unskillfully betrays itself in fearing betrayal
s.d. Enter Ophelia (In the First Quarto, Ophelia enters, "playing on a lute, and her hair down, singing.")
26 **cockle hat** hat with cockle-shell stuck in it as a sign that the wearer had been a pilgrim to the shrine of Saint James of Compostella in Spain
27 **shoon** shoes

OPHELIA: "Larded with sweet flowers; (*Song.*)   39
         Which bewept to the ground did not go
            With true-love showers."

KING: How do you, pretty lady?   41

OPHELIA: Well, God 'ild you! They say the owl was a baker's daughter. Lord, we 43
    know what we are, but know not what we may be. God be at your table!

KING: Conceit upon her father.   45

OPHELIA: Pray let's have no words of this; but when they ask you what it means, say
    you this:
       "Tomorrow is Saint Valentine's day, (*Song.*)
         All in the morning betime,   49
       And I a maid at your window,
         To be your Valentine.
       Then up he rose, and donned his clothes,
         And dupped the chamber door,
       Let in the maid, that out a maid   53
         Never departed more."

KING: Pretty Ophelia—

OPHELIA: Indeed, la, without an oath, I'll make an end on 't: [*Sings.*]
       "By Gis and by Saint Charity,
         Alack, and fie for shame!   58
       Young men will do 't, if they come to 't;
         By Cock, they are to blame.
       Quoth she, 'Before you tumbled me,   61
         You promised me to wed.'"
    He answers:
      "'So would I ha' done, by yonder sun,
         An thou hadst not come to my bed.'"

KING: How long hath she been thus?   66

OPHELIA: I hope all will be well. We must be patient, but I cannot choose but weep
    to think they would lay him i' the cold ground. My brother shall know of it. And
    so I thank you for your good counsel. Come, my coach! Good night, ladies, good
    night, sweet ladies, good night, good night.   [*Exit.*]

KING: [*to Horatio*]   Follow her close. Give her good watch, I pray you.

[*Exit Horatio.*]

    O, this is the poison of deep grief; it springs
    All from her father's death—and now behold!
    O Gertrude, Gertrude,
    When sorrows come, they come not single spies,
    But in battalions. First, her father slain;   76
    Next, your son gone, and he most violent author
    Of his own just remove; the people muddied,   79

---

39 Larded decorated   **41 showers** i.e., tears
43 God 'ild God yield or reward   **owl** (Refers to a legend about a baker's daughter who was turned into an owl for being ungenerous when Jesus begged a loaf of bread.)
45 Conceit brooding   **49 betime** early
53 dupped did up, opened   **58 Gis** Jesus
61 Cock (A perversion of "God" in oaths; here also with a quibble on the slang word for penis.)
66 An if   **76 spies** scouts sent in advance of the main force
79 remove removal   **muddied** stirred up, confused

Thick and unwholesome in their thoughts and whispers
For good Polonius' death—and we have done but greenly, 81
In hugger-mugger to inter him; poor Ophelia 82
Divided from herself and her fair judgment,
Without the which we are pictures or mere beasts;
Last, and as much containing as all these, 85
Her brother is in secret come from France,
Feeds on this wonder, keeps himself in clouds, 87
And wants not buzzers to infect his ear 88
With pestilent speeches of his father's death,
Wherein necessity, of matter beggared, 90
Will nothing stick our person to arraign 91
In ear and ear. O my dear Gertrude, this, 92
Like to a murdering piece, in many places 93
Gives me a superfluous death.   *A noise within.* 94

QUEEN: Alack, what noise is this?

KING: Attend! 96
Where is my Switzers? Let them guard the door. 97

Enter a Messenger.

What is the matter?

MESSENGER: Save yourself, my lord!
The ocean, overpeering of his list, 100
Eats not the flats with more impetuous haste 101
Than young Laertes, in a riotous head, 102
O'erbears your officers. The rabble call him lord,
And, as the world were now but to begin, 104
Antiquity forgot, custom not known,
The ratifiers and props of every word, 106
They cry, "Choose we! Laertes shall be king!"
Caps, hands, and tongues applaud it to the clouds, 108
"Laertes shall be king, Laertes king!"

QUEEN: How cheerfully on the false trail they cry!

A noise within.

---

81 greenly in an inexperienced way, foolishly   **82 hugger-mugger** secret haste
85 as much containing as full of serious matter
87 Feeds . . . clouds feeds his resentment or shocked grievance, holds himself inscrutable and
aloof amid all this rumor
88 wants lacks   **buzzers** gossipers, informers
90 necessity i.e., the need to invent some plausible explanation   **of matter beggared** unprovided with facts
91–92 Will . . . ear will not hesitate to accuse my (royal) person in everybody's ears
93 murdering piece cannon loaded so as to scatter its shot
94 Gives . . . death kills me over and over   **96 Attend** i.e., guard me
97 Switzers Swiss guards, mercenaries
100 overpeering of his list overflowing its shore, boundary
101 flats i.e., flatlands near shore   **impetuous** violent (perhaps also with the meaning of *impiteous* [*impitious*, Q2], "pitiless")
102 head insurrection   **104 as** as if
106 The ratifiers . . . word i.e., *antiquity* (or tradition) and *custom* ought to confirm (*ratify*) and
underprop our every word or promise
108 Caps (The caps are thrown in the air.)

O, this is counter, you false Danish dogs!   111

Enter Laertes with others.

KING: The doors are broke.

LAERTES: Where is this King?—Sirs, stand you all without.

ALL: No, let's come in.

LAERTES: I pray you, give me leave.

ALL: We will, we will.

LAERTES: I thank you. Keep the door. [*Exeunt followers.*] O thou vile king,
  Give me my father!

QUEEN: [*restraining him*]   Calmly, good Laertes.

LAERTES: That drop of blood that's calm proclaims me bastard,
  Cries cuckold to my father, brands the harlot
  Even here, between the chaste unsmirchèd brow   122
  Of my true mother.

KING: What is the cause, Laertes,
  That thy rebellion looks so giantlike?
  Let him go, Gertrude. Do not fear our person.   126
  There's such divinity doth hedge a king   127
  That treason can but peep to what it would,   128
  Acts little of his will. Tell me, Laertes,   129
  Why thou art thus incensed. Let him go, Gertrude.
  Speak, man.

LAERTES: Where is my father?

KING: Dead.

QUEEN: But not by him.

KING: Let him demand his fill.

LAERTES: How came he dead? I'll not be juggled with.   136
  To hell, allegiance! Vows, to the blackest devil!
  Conscience and grace, to the profoundest pit!
  I dare damnation. To this point I stand,   139
  That both the worlds I give to negligence,   140
  Let come what comes, only I'll be revenged
  Most thoroughly for my father.   142

KING: Who shall stay you?

LAERTES: My will, not all the world's.   144
  And for my means, I'lll husband them so well   145
  They shall go far with little.

KING: Good Laertes,
  If you desire to know the certainty

---

111 counter (A hunting term, meaning to follow the trail in a direction opposite to that which the game has taken.)

122 between in the middle of   **126 fear our** fear for my

127 hedge protect, as with a surrounding barrier

128 can . . . would can only peep furtively, as through a barrier, at what it would intend

129 Acts . . . will (but) performs little of what it intends

136 juggled with cheated, deceived   **139 To . . . stand** I am resolved in this

140 both . . . negligence i.e., both this world and the next are of no consequence to me

142 throughly thoroughly

144 My will . . . world's I'll stop (*stay*) when my will is accomplished, not for anyone else's.

145 for as for

Of your dear father, is't writ in your revenge
That, swoopstake, you will draw both friend and foe,   150
Winner and loser?

LAERTES: None but his enemies.

KING: Will you know them, then?

LAERTES: To his good friends thus wide I'll ope my arms,
And like the kind life-rendering pelican   155
Repast them with my blood.   156

KING: Why, now you speak
Like a good child and a true gentleman.
That I am guiltless of your father's death,
And am most sensibly in grief for it,   160
It shall as level to your judgment 'pear   161
As day does to your eye.   *A noise within.*

LAERTES: How now, what noise is that?

Enter Ophelia.

KING: Let her come in.

LAERTES: O heat, dry up my brains! Tears seven times salt
Burn out the sense and virtue of mine eye!   166
By heaven, thy madness shall be paid with weight   167
Till our scale turn the beam. O rose of May!   168
Dear maid, kind sister, sweet Ophelia!
O heavens, is 't possible a young maid's wits
Should be as mortal as an old man's life?
Nature is fine in love, and where 'tis fine   172
It sends some precious instance of itself   173
After the thing it loves.   174

OPHELIA: "They bore him barefaced on the bier,   *(Song.)*
        Hey non nonny, nonny, hey nonny,
        And in his grave rained many a tear—"
Fare you well, my dove!

LAERTES: Hadst thou thy wits and didst persuade revenge,   179
It could not move thus.

OPHELIA: You must sing "A-down a-down," and you   181
"call him a-down-a." O, how the wheel becomes it! It is the false steward that   182
stole his master's daughter.

---

150 swoopstake i.e., indiscriminately (Literally, taking all stakes on the gambling table at once. *Draw* is also a gambling term, meaning "take from.")

155 pelican (Refers to the belief that the female pelican fed its young with its own blood.)

156 Repast feed   **160 sensibly** feelingly

161 level plain   **166 virtue** faculty, power

167 paid with weight repaid, avenged equally or more

168 beam crossbar of a balance   **172 fine in** refined by

173 instance token

174 After . . . loves i.e., into the grave, along with Polonius

179 persuade argue cogently for

181–182 You . . . a-down-a (Ophelia assigns the singing of refrains, like her own "Hey non nonny," to others present.)

182 wheel spinning wheel as accompaniment to the song, or refrain   **false steward** (The story is unknown.)

LAERTES: This nothing's more than matter. 184

OPHELIA: There's rosemary, that's for remembrance; pray you, love, remember. And 185
there is pansies; that's for thoughts. 186

LAERTES: A document in madness, thoughts and remembrance fitted. 187

OPHELIA: There's fennel for you, and columbines. There's rue for you, and here's 188
some for me; we may call it herb of grace o' Sundays. You must wear your rue
with a difference. There's a daisy. I would give you some violets, but they with- 190
ered all when my father died. They say 'a made a good end—
[*Sings.*] "For bonny sweet Robin is all my joy."

LAERTES: Thought and affliction, passion, hell itself, 193
She turns to favor and to prettiness. 194

OPHELIA: "And will 'a not come again? *(Song.)*
And will 'a not come again?
No, no, he is dead.
Go to thy deathbed.
He never will come again.

"His beard was as white as show,
All flaxen was his poll.
He is gone, he is gone, 201
And we cast away moan.
God ha' mercy on his soul!"
And of all Christian souls, I pray God. God b' wi' you.

[Exit, followed by Gertrude.]

LAERTES: Do you see this, O God?

KING: Laertes, I must commune with your grief,
Or you deny me right. Go but apart,
Make choice of whom your wisest friends you will, 209
And they shall hear and judge twixt you and me.
If by direct or by collateral hand 211
They find us touched, we will our kingdom give, 212
Our crown, our life, and all that we call ours
To you in satisfaction; but if not,
Be you content to lend your patience to us,
And we shall jointly labor with your soul
To give it due content.

---

184 This . . . matter this seeming nonsense is more eloquent than sane utterance
185 rosemary (Used as a symbol of remembrance both at weddings and at funerals.)
186 pansies (Emblems of love and courtship; perhaps from French *pensées*, "thoughts.")
187 document instruction, lesson
188 fennel (Emblem of flattery.) **columbines** (Emblems of unchastity or ingratitude **rue**
(Emblem of repentance—a signification that is evident in its popular name, *herb of grace*.)
190 with a difference (A device used in heraldry to distinguish one family from another on the
coat of arms, here suggesting that Ophelia and the others have different causes of sorrow and
repentance; perhaps with a play on *rue* in the sense of "rush," "pity.") **daisy** (Emblem of
dissembling, faithlessness.) **violets** (Emblems of faithfulness.)
193 Thought melancholy **passion** suffering
194 favor grace, beauty
209 whom whichever of
212 us touched me implicated

201 poll head
211 collateral hand indirect agency

LAERTES:	Let this be so.

His means of death, his obscure funeral—
No trophy, sword, not hatchment o'er his bones,   220
No noble rite, nor formal ostentation—   221
Cry to be heard, as 'twere from heaven to earth,
That I must call 't in question.   223

KING:	So you shall,

And where th' offense is, let the great ax fall.
I pray you, go with me.   *Exeunt.*

Act 4, Scene 6

Enter Horatio and others.

HORATIO: What are they that would speak with me?
GENTLEMAN: Seafaring men, sir. They say they have letters for you.
HORATIO: Let them come in.   [*Exit Gentleman.*]
 I do not know from what part of the world
 I should be greeted, if not from Lord Hamlet.

Enter Sailors.

FIRST SAILOR: God bless you, sir.
HORATIO: Let him bless thee too.
FIRST SAILOR: 'A shall, sir, an 't please him. There's a letter for you, sir—it came from   8
 th' ambassador that was bound for England—if your name be Horatio, as I am   9
 let to know it is.   [*He gives a letter.*]
HORATIO: [*reads*] "Horatio, when thou shalt have overlooked this, give these fel-   11
 lows some means to the King; they have letters for him. Ere we were two day   12
 old at sea, a pirate of very warlike appointment gave us chase. Finding ourselves   13
 too slow of sail, we put on a compelled valor, and in the grapple I boarded them.
 On the instant they got clear of our ship, so I alone became their prisoner. They
 have dealt with me like thieves of mercy, but they knew what they did: I am to   16
 do a good turn for them. Let the King have the letters I have sent, and repair   17
 thou to me with as much speed as thou wouldst fly death. I have words to speak
 in thine ear will make thee dumb, yet are they much too light for the bore of the   19
 matter. These good fellows will bring thee where I am. Rosencrantz and Guildenstern hold their course for England. Of them I have much to tell thee. Farewell.
                    He that thou knowest thine, Hamlet."
 Come, I will give you way for these your letters,   23
 And do 't the speedier that you may direct me
 To him from whom you brought them.   *Exeunt.*

---

220 trophy memorial   **hatchment** tablet displaying the armorial bearings of a deceased person
221 ostentation ceremony
223 That so that   **call 't in question** demand an explanation
4.6. Location: The castle.
  8 an 't if it
  9 th' ambassador (Evidently Hamlet. The sailor is being circumspect.)
11 overlooked looked over   **12 means** means of access
13 appointment equipage   **16 thieves of mercy** merciful thieves
17 repair come   **19 bore** caliper, i.e., importance
23 way means of access

Act 4, Scene 7

Enter King and Laertes.

KING: Now must your conscience my acquittance seal,   1
         And you must put me in your heart for friend,
         Sith you have heard, and with a knowing ear,   3
         That he which hath your noble father slain
         Pursued my life.

LAERTES: It well appears. But tell me
         Why you proceeded not against these feats   7
         So crimeful and so capital in nature,   8
         As by your safety, greatness, wisdom, all things else,
         You mainly were stirred up.   10

KING: O, for two special reasons,
         Which may to you perhaps seem much unsinewed,   12
         But yet to me they're strong. The Queen his mother
         Lives almost by his looks, and for myself—
         My virtue or my plague, be it either which—
         She is so conjunctive to my life and soul   16
         That, as the star moves not but in his sphere,   17
         I could not but by her. The other motive
         Why to a public count I might not go   19
         Is the great love the general gender bear him,   20
         Who, dipping all his faults in their affection,
         Work like the spring that turneth wood to stone,   22
         Convert his gyves to graces, so that my arrows,   23
         Too slightly timbered for so loud a wind,   24
         Would have reverted to my bow again   25
         But not where I had aimed them.

LAERTES: And so have I a noble father lost,
         A sister driven into desperate terms,
         Whose worth, if praises may go back again,   28
         Stood challenger on mount of all the age   29
         For her perfections. But my revenge will come.   30

KING: Break not your sleeps for that. You must not think
         That we are made of stuff so flat and dull

4.7. Location: The castle.
1 my acquittance seal confirm or acknowledge my innocence
3 Sith since
8 capital punishable by death   **7 feats** acts
12 unsinewed weak   **10 mainly** greatly
16 conjunctive closely united (An astronomical metaphor.)
17 his its   **sphere** one of the hollow spheres in which, according to Ptolemaic astronomy, the planets were supposed to move
19 count account, reckoning, indictment   **20 general gender** common people
22 Work operate, act   **spring** i.e., a spring with such a concentration of lime that it coats a piece of wood with limestone, in effect gilding and petrifying it
23 gyves fetters (which, gilded by the people's praise, would look like badges of honor)
24 slightly timbered light   **loud** (suggesting public outcry on Hamlet's behalf)
25 reverted returned
29 go back i.e., recall what she was   **28 terms** state, condition
                                                        30 on mount set up on high

That we can let our beard be shook with danger
And think it pastime. You shortly shall hear more.
I loved your father, and we love ourself;
And that, I hope, will teach you to imagine—

Enter a Messenger with letters.

How now? What news?
MESSENGER: Letters, my lord, from Hamlet:
This to Your Majesty, this to the Queen.
[*He gives letters.*]
KING: From Hamlet? Who brought them?
MESSENGER: Sailors, my lord, they say. I saw them not.
They were given me by Claudio. He received them
Of him that brought them.
KING: Laertes, you shall hear them.—
Leave us.   [*Exit Messenger.*]
[*He reads.*] "High and mighty, you shall know I am set naked on your kingdom.   46
Tomorrow shall I beg leave to see your kingly eyes, when I shall, first asking
your pardon, thereunto recount the occasion of my sudden and more strange   48
return.   Hamlet."
What should this mean? Are all the rest come back?
Or is it some abuse, and no such thing?   51
LAERTES: Know you the hand?
KING: 'Tis Hamlet's character. "Naked!"   53
And in a postscript here he says "alone."
Can you devise me?   55
LAERTES: I am lost in it, my lord. But let him come.
It warms the very sickness in my heart
That I shall live and tell him to his teeth,
"Thus didst thou."   59
KING: If it be so, Laertes—
As how should it be so? How otherwise?—   61
Will you be ruled by me?
LAERTES: Ay, my lord,
So you will not o'errule me to a peace.   64
KING: To thine own peace. If he be now returned,
As checking at his voyage, and that he means   66
No more to undertake it, I will work him
To an exploit, now ripe in my device,   68
Under the which he shall not choose but fall;

---

46 **naked** destitute, unarmed, without following   48 **pardon** permission
51 **abuse** deceit   **no such thing** not what it appears
53 **character** handwriting   55 **devise** explain to
59 **Thus didst thou** i.e., here's for what you did to my father
61 **As . . . otherwise** how can this (Hamlet's return) be true? Yet how otherwise that true (since
    we have the evidence of his letter)?
64 **So** provided that
66 **checking at** i.e., turning aside from (like a falcon leaving the quarry to fly at a chance bird)
    that if
68 **device** devising, invention

And for his death no wind of blame shall breathe,
But even his mother shall uncharge the practice   71
And call it accident.

LAERTES: My lord, I will be ruled,
The rather if you could devise it so
That I might be the organ.

KING: It falls right.   75
You have been talked of since your travel much,
And that in Hamlet's hearing, for a quality
Wherein they say you shine. Your sum of parts   79
Did not together pluck such envy from him
As did that one, and that, in my regard,
Of the unworthiest siege.

LAERTES: What part is that, my lord?   82

KING: A very ribbon in the cap of youth,
Yet needful too, for youth no less becomes
The light and careless livery that it wears   85
Than settled age his sables and his weeds
Importing health and graveness. Two months since   87
Here was a gentleman of Normandy.   88
I have seen myself, and served against, the French,
And they can well on horseback, but this gallant
Had witchcraft in 't; he grew unto his seat,   91
And to such wondrous doing brought his horse
As had he been incorpsed and demi-natured
With the brave beast. So far he topped my thought   94
That I in forgery of shapes and tricks   95
Come short of what he did.   96

LAERTES: A Norman was 't?

KING: A Norman.

LAERTES: Upon my life, Lamord.

KING: The very same.

LAERTES: I know him well. He is the brooch indeed
And gem of all the nation.   102

KING: He made confession of you,
And gave you such a masterly report   104
For art and exercise in your defense,
And for your rapier most especial,   106

---

71 uncharge the practice acquit the stratagem of being a plot
75 organ agent, instrument
82 unworthiest siege least important rank   **79 Your . . . parts** i.e., all your other virtues
87 his sables its rich robes furred with sable   **85 no less becomes** is no less suited by
weeds garments
88 Importing . . . graveness signifying a concern for health and dignified prosperity; also,
giving an impression of comfortable prosperity
91 can well are skilled
94 As . . . demi-natured as if he had been of one body and nearly of one nature (like the
centaur)
95 topped surpassed   **96 forgery** imagining
102 brooch ornament
104 confession testimonial, admission of superiority
106 For . . . defense with respect to your skill and practice with your weapon

That he cried out 'twould be a sight indeed
If one could match you. Th' escrimers of their nation,   109
He swore, had neither motion, guard, nor eye
If you opposed them. Sir, this report of his
Did Hamlet so envenom with his envy
That he could nothing do but wish and beg
Your sudden coming o'er, to play with you.   114
Now, out of this—
LAERTES: What out of this, my lord?
KING: Laertes, was your father dear to you?
    Or are you like the painting of a sorrow,
    A face without a heart?
LAERTES: Why ask you this?
KING: Not that I think you did not love your father,
    But that I know love is begun by time,   122
    And that I see, in passages of proof,   123
    Time qualifies the spark and fire of it.   124
    There lives within the very flame of love
    A kind of wick or snuff that will abate it,   126
    And nothing is at a like goodness still,   127
    For goodness, growing to a pleurisy,   128
    Dies in his own too much. That we would do,   129
    We should do when we would; for this "would" changes
    And hath abatements and delays as many   131
    As there are tongues, are hands, are accidents,   132
    And then this "should" is like a spendthrift sigh,   133
    That hurts by easing. But, to the quick o' th' ulcer: 134
    Hamlet comes back. What would you undertake
    To show yourself in deed your father's son
    More than in words?
LAERTES: To cut his throat i' the church.
KING: No place, indeed, should murder sanctuarize;   139
    Revenge should have no bounds. But good Laertes,
    Will you do this, keep close within your chamber.   141
    Hamlet returned shall know you are come home.
    We'll put on those shall praise your excellence   143
    And set a double varnish on the fame

---

109 escrimers fencers   **114 sudden** immediate   **play** fence
122 begun by time i.e., created by the right circumstance and hence subject to change
123 passages of proof actual instances that prove it
124 qualifies weakens, moderates   **126 snuff** the charred part of a candlewick
127 nothing . . . still nothing remains at a constant level of perfection
128 pleurisy excess, plethora (Literally, a chest inflammation.)
129 in . . . much of its own excess   **That** that which
131 abatements diminutions
132 As . . . accidents as there are tongues to dissuade, hands to prevent, and chance events to
    intervene
133 spendthrift sigh (An allusion to the belief that sighs draw blood from the heart.)
134 hurts by easing i.e., costs the heart blood and wastes precious opportunity even while it
    affords emotional relief   **quick o' th' ulcer** i.e., heart of the matter
139 sanctuarize protect from punishment (Alludes to the right of sanctuary with which certain
    religious places were invested.)
141 Will you do this if you wish to do this   **143 put on those shall** arrange for some to

The Frenchman gave you, bring you in fine together,   145
And wager on your heads. He, being remiss,   146
Most generous, and free from all contriving,   147
Will not peruse the foils, so that with ease,
Or with a little shuffling, you may choose
A sword unbated, and in a pass of practice   150
Requite him for your father.

LAERTES: I will do 't,
And for that purpose I'll anoint my sword.
I bought an unction of a mountebank
So mortal that, but dip a knife in it,   154
Where it draws blood no cataplasm so rare,   156
Collected from all simples that have virtue   157
Under the moon, can save the thing from death   158
That is but scratched withal. I'll touch my point
With this contagion, that if I gall him slightly,   160
It may be death.

KING: Let's further think of this,
Weigh what convenience both of time and means
May fit us to our shape. If this should fail,
And that our drift look through our bad performance,   164
'Twere better not assayed. Therefore this project   165
Should have a back or second, that might hold
If this did blast in proof. Soft, let me see.   168
We'll make a solemn wager on your cunnings—   169
I ha 't!
When in your motion you are hot and dry—
As make your bouts more violent to that end—   172
And that he calls for drink, I'll have prepared him
A chalice for the nonce, whereon but sipping,   174
If he by chance escape your venomed stuck,   175
Our purpose may hold there. [*A cry within.*] But stay, what noise?

Enter Queen.

QUEEN: One woe doth tread upon another's heel.
So fast they follow. Your sister's drowned, Laertes.

LAERTES: Drowned! O, where?

QUEEN: There is a willow grows askant the brook,   180
That shows his hoar leaves in the glassy stream;   181

---

145 **in fine** finally   146 **remiss** negligently unsuspicious
147 **generous** noble-minded
150 **unbated** not blunted, having no button   **pass of practice** treacherous thrust
154 **unction** ointment   **mountebank** quack doctor   156 **cataplasm** plaster or poultice
157 **simples** herbs   **virtue** potency
158 **Under the moon** i.e., anywhere (with reference perhaps to the belief that herbs gathered at
   night had a special power)
160 **gall** graze, wound   164 **shape** part we propose to act
165 **drift . . . performance** intention should be made visible by our bungling
168 **blast in proof** burst in the test (like a cannon)   169 **cunnings** respective skills
172 **As** i.e., and you should   174 **nonce** occasion
175 **stuck** thrust (From *stoccado,* a fencing term.)   180 **askant** aslant
181 **hoar leaves** white or gray undersides of the leaves

Therewith fantastic garlands did she make
Of crowflowers, nettles, daisies, and long purples,   183
That liberal shepherds give a grosser name,   184
But our cold maids do dead men's fingers call them.   185
There on the pendent boughs her crownet weeds   186
Clamb'ring to hang, an envious sliver broke,   187
When down her weedy trophies and herself   188
Fell in the weeping brook. Her clothes spread wide,
And mermaidlike awhile they bore her up,
Which time she chanted snatches of old lauds,   191
As one incapable of her own distress,   192
Or like a creature native and endued   193
Unto that element. But long it could not be
Till that her garments, heavy with their drink,
Pulled the poor wretch from her melodious lay
To muddy death.
LAERTES: Alas, then she is drowned?
QUEEN: Drowned, drowned.
LAERTES: Too much of water hast thou, poor Ophelia,
And therefore I forbid my tears. But yet
It is our trick; nature her custom holds,   202
Let shame say what it will. [*He weeps.*] When these are gone,   203
The woman will be out. Adieu, my lord.   204
I have a speech of fire that fain would blaze,
But that this folly douts it.   *Exit.*   206
KING: Let's follow, Gertrude.
How much I had to do to calm his rage!
Now fear I this will give it start again;
Therefore let's follow.   *Exeunt.*

Act 4 Response Statement Questions

- What is your response to Laertes' desire to avenge his father's murder? How would you compare it to Hamlet's similar desire? What are the implications, for your interpretation of the entire play, of your seeing Hamlet and Laertes as alike or different in this regard?
- What is your response to Ophelia's madness (Scene 5) and the subsequent report of her death (Scene 7)? Does what happens to her affect your opinion of Hamlet? Are you able to "fit" her insanity and death into a

---

183 long purples early purple orchids
184 liberal free-spoken   **a grosser name** (The testicle-resembling tubers of the orchid, which also in some cases resemble *dead men's fingers,* have earned various slang names like "dog-stones" and "cullions.")
185 cold chaste
186 pendent overhanging   **crownet** made into a chaplet or coronet
187 envious sliver malicious branch   **188 weedy** i.e., of plants
191 lauds hymns   **192 incapable of** lacking capacity to apprehend
193 endued adapted by nature
202 It is our trick i.e., weeping is our natural way (when sad)
203–204 When . . . out when my tears are all shed, the woman in me will be expended, satisfied
206 douts extinguishes (The Second Quarto reads "drowns.")

developing interpretation of the text, not see it as just something that advances the plot by motivating Laertes' desire for revenge?

- Has your opinion of Claudius changed from what it was earlier in the play? If so, is it a case of his "true nature" emerging, or is he merely reacting out of fear and a desire for self-preservation to the presence of a "loose cannon" in the kingdom in the person of Hamlet?

Act 5, Scene 1

Enter two Clowns [with spades and mattocks].

FIRST CLOWN: Is she to be buried in Christian burial, when she willfully seeks her own salvation?

SECOND CLOWN: I tell thee she is; therefore make her grave straight. The crowner hath sat on her, and finds it Christian burial.

FIRST CLOWN: How can that be, unless she drowned herself in her own defense?

SECOND CLOWN: Why, 'tis found so.

FIRST CLOWN: It must be *se offendendo,* it cannot be else. For here lies the point: if I drown myself wittingly, it argues an act, and an act hath three branches—it is to act, to do, and to perform. Argal, she drowned herself wittingly.

SECOND CLOWN: Nay, but hear you, goodman delver—

FIRST CLOWN: Give me leave. Here lies the water; good. Here stands the man; good. If the man go to this water and drown himself, it is, will he, nill he, he goes, mark you that. But if the water come to him and drown him, he drowns not himself. Argal, he that is not guilty of his own death shortens not his own life.

SECOND CLOWN: But is this law?

FIRST CLOWN: Ay, marry, is 't—crowner's quest law.

SECOND CLOWN: Will you ha' the truth on 't? If this had not been a gentlewoman, she should have been buried out o' Christian burial.

FIRST CLOWN: Why, there thou sayst. And the more pity that great folk should have countenance in this world to drown or hang themselves, more than their even-Christian. Come, my spade. There is no ancient gentlemen but gardeners, ditchers, and grave makers. They hold up Adam's profession.

SECOND CLOWN: Was he a gentleman?

FIRST CLOWN: 'A was the first that ever bore arms.

2
3
4

6
7

9
10

12

16

19
20
21
22

24

5.1. Location: A churchyard. s.d. Clowns rustics
2 salvation (A blunder for "damnation," or perhaps a suggestion that Ophelia was taking her own shortcut to heaven.)
3 straight straightway, immediately (But with a pun on *strait,* "narrow.") **crowner** coroner
4 sat on her conducted an inquest on her case **finds it** gives his official verdict that her means of death was consistent with
6 found so determined so in the coroner's verdict
7 se offendendo (A comic mistake for *se defendendo,* a term used in verdicts of justifiable homicide.)
9 Argal (Corruption of ergo, "therefore.")
10 goodman (An honorific title often used with the name of a profession or craft.)
12 will he, nill he whether he will or no, willy-nilly
16 quest inquest   **19 there thou sayst** i.e., that's right
20 countenance privilege   **20–21 even-Christian** fellow Christians
21 ancient going back to ancient times   **22 hold up** maintain
24 bore arms (To be entitled to bear a coat of arms would make Adam a gentleman, but as one who bore a spade, our common ancestor was an ordinary delver in the earth.)

SECOND CLOWN: Why, he had none.

FIRST CLOWN: What, art a heathen? How dost thou understand the Scripture? The
Scripture says Adam digged. Could he dig without arms? I'll put another ques-   27
tion to thee. If thou answerest me not to the purpose, confess thyself—   28

SECOND CLOWN: Go to.

FIRST CLOWN: What is he that builds stronger than either the mason, the shipwright,
or the carpenter?

SECOND CLOWN: The gallows maker, for that frame outlives a thousand tenants.   32

FIRST CLOWN: I like thy wit well, in good faith. The gallows does well. But how does   33
it well? It does well to those that do ill. Now thou dost ill to say the gallows is
built stronger than the church. Argal, the gallows may do well to thee. To 't
again, come.

SECOND CLOWN: "Who builds stronger than a mason, a shipwright, or a carpenter?"

FIRST CLOWN: Ay, tell me that, and unyoke.   38

SECOND CLOWN: Marry, now I can tell.

FIRST CLOWN: To 't.

SECOND CLOWN: Mass, I cannot tell.   41

Enter Hamlet and Horatio [at a distance].

FIRST CLOWN: Cudgel thy brains no more about it, for your dull ass will not mend his
pace with beating; and when you are asked this question next, say "a grave
maker." The houses he makes lasts till doomsday. Go get thee in and fetch me a
stoup of liquor.   45

[Exit Second Clown. First Clown digs.] Song.

"In youth, when I did love, did love,   46
    Methought it was very sweet,
To contract—O—the time for—a—my behove,   48
    O, methought there—a—was nothing—a—meet."   49

HAMLET: Has this fellow no feeling of his business, 'a sings in grave-making?   50

HORATIO: Custom hath made it in him a property of easiness.   51

HAMLET: 'Tis e'en so. The hand of little employment hath the daintier sense.   52

FIRST CLOWN: *Song.*

"But age with his stealing steps
    Hath clawed me in his clutch,
And hath shipped me into the land,   55
    As if I had never been such."

[He throws up a skull.]

---

27 arms i.e., the arms of the body
28 confess thyself (The saying continues, "and be hanged.")
32 frame (1) gallows (2) structure
33 does well (1) is an apt answer (2) does a good turn
38 unyoke i.e., after this great effort, you may unharness the team of your wits
41 Mass by the Mass   **45 stoup** two-quart measure
46 In . . . love (This and the two following stanzas, with nonsensical variations, are from a poem
attributed to Lord Vaux and printed in *Tottel's Miscellany,* 1557. The *O* and *a* [for "ah"] seemingly are the grunts of the digger.)
48 To contract . . . behove i.e., to shorten the time for my own advantage. (Perhaps he means to
prolong it.)
49 meet suitable i.e., more suitable   **50 'a** that he
51 property of easiness something he can do easily and indifferently
52 daintier sense more delicate sense of feeling
55 into the land i.e., toward my grave (?) (But note the lack of rhyme in *steps, land.*)

HAMLET: That skull had a tongue in it and could sing once. How the knave jowls it   57
to the ground, as if 'twere Cain's jawbone, that did the first murder! This might
be the pate of a politician, which this ass now o'erreaches, one that would cir-   59
cumvent God, might it not?

HORATIO: It might, my lord.

HAMLET: Or of a courtier, which could say, "Good morrow, sweet lord? How dost
thou, sweet lord?" This might be my Lord Such-a-one, that praised my Lord Such-
a-one's horse when 'a meant to beg it, might it not?

HORATIO: Ay, my lord.

HAMLET: Why, e'en so, and now my Lady Worm's, chapless, and knocked about the   66
mazard with a sexton's spade. Here's fine revolution, an we had the trick to see   67
't. Did these bones cost no more the breeding but to play at loggets with them?   68
Mine ache to think on 't.

FIRST CLOWN: *Song.*
"A pickax and a spade, a spade,
For and a shrouding sheet;
O, a pit of clay for to be made   71
For such a guest is meet."

[He throws up another skull.]

HAMLET: There's another. Why may not that be the skull of a lawyer? Where be his
quiddities now, his quillities, his cases, his tenures, and his tricks? Why does he   75
suffer this mad knave now to knock him about the sconce with a dirty shovel,   76
and will not tell him of his action of battery? Hum, this fellow might be in 's   77
time a great buyer of land, with his statutes, his recognizances, his fines, his dou-   78
ble vouchers, his recoveries. Is this the fine of his fines and the recovery of his   79
recoveries, to have his fine pate full of fine dirt? Will his vouchers vouch him no   80
more of his purchases, and double ones too, than the length and breadth of a
pair of indentures? The very conveyances of his lands will scarcely lie in this   82
box, and must th' inheritor himself have no more, ha?   83

---

57 jowls dashes (with a pun on *jowl,* "jawbone")
59 politician schemer, plotter   **o'erreaches** circumvents, gets the better of (with a quibble on
the literal sense)
66 chapless having no lower jaw
67 mazard i.e., head (Literally, a drinking vessel.)   **revolution** turn of Fortune's wheel, change
an if   **trick to see** knack of seeing
68 cost . . . but involve so little expense and care in upbringing that we may   **loggets** a game in
which pieces of hard wood shaped like Indian clubs or bowling pins are thrown to lie as near
as possible to a stake
71 For and and moreover
75 quiddities subtleties, quibbles (From Latin *quid,* "a thing.")   **quillities** verbal niceties, subtle
distinctions (Variation of *quiddities.*)   **tenures** the holding of a piece of property or office, or
the conditions or period of such holding
76 sconce head   **77 action of battery** lawsuit about physical assault
78 statutes, recognizances legal documents guaranteeing a debt by attaching land and property
78–79 fines, recoveries ways of converting entailed estates into "fee simple" or freehold.
double signed by two signatories.
79 vouchers guarantees of the legality of a title to real estate
79–80 fine of his fines . . . fine pate . . . fine dirt end of his legal maneuvers . . . elegant head
. . . minutely sifted dirt
82 pair of indentures legal document drawn up in duplicate on a single sheet and then cut apart
on a zigzag line so that each pair was uniquely matched. (Hamlet may refer to two rows of
teeth or dentures.)   **conveyances** deeds
83 box (1) deed box (2) coffin ("Skull" has been suggested.)   **inheritor** possessor, owner

HORATIO: Not a jot more, my lord.

HAMLET: Is not parchment made of sheepskins?

HORATIO: Ay, my lord, and of calves' skins too.

HAMLET: They are sheep and calves which seek out assurance in that. I will speak   87
to this fellow.—Whose grave's this, sirrah?   88

FIRST CLOWN: Mine, sir.

[Sings.] "O, pit of clay for to be made
    For such a guest is meet."

HAMLET: I think it be thine, indeed, for thou liest in 't.

FIRST CLOWN: You lie out on 't, sir, and therefore 'tis not yours. For my part, I do not
lie in 't, yet it is mine.

HAMLET: Thou dost lie in 't, to be in 't and say it is thine. 'Tis for the dead, not for the   96
quick; therefore thou liest.

FIRST CLOWN: 'Tis a quick lie, sir; 'twill away again from me to you.

HAMLET: What man dost thou dig it for?

FIRST CLOWN: For no man, sir.

HAMLET: What woman, then?

FIRST CLOWN: For none, neither.

HAMLET: Who is to be buried in 't?

FIRST CLOWN: One that was a woman, sir, but, rest her soul, she's dead.

HAMLET: How absolute the knave is! We must speak by the card, or equivocation   104
will undo us. By the Lord, Horatio, this three years I have took note of it: the age   105
is grown so picked that the toe of the peasant comes so near the heel of the   106
courtier, he galls his kibe.—How long hast thou been grave maker?   107

FIRST CLOWN: Of all the days i' the year, I came to 't that day that our last king Hamlet overcame Fortinbras.

HAMLET: How long is that since?

FIRST CLOWN: Cannot you tell that? Every fool can tell that. It was that very day that
young Hamlet was born—he that is mad and sent into England?

FIRST CLOWN: Ay, marry, why was he sent into England?

FIRST CLOWN: Why, because 'a was mad. 'A shall recover his wits there, or if 'a do
not, 'tis no great matter there.

HAMLET: Why?

FIRST CLOWN: 'Twill not be seen in him there. There the men are as mad as he.

HAMLET: How came he mad?

FIRST CLOWN: Very strangely, they say.

HAMLET: How strangely?

FIRST CLOWN: Faith, e'en with losing his wits.

HAMLET: Upon what ground?   122

FIRST CLOWN: Why, here in Denmark. I have been sexton here, man and boy, thirty years.

HAMLET: How long will a man lie i' th' earth ere he rot?

---

87 assurance in that safety in legal parchments
88 sirrah (A term of address to inferiors.)   **96 quick** living
104 absolute strict, precise   **by the card** i.e., with precision. (Literally, by the mariner's
compass-card, on which the points of the compass were marked.)   **equivocation** ambiguity
in the use of terms
105 took taken   **106 picked** refined, fastidious
107 galls his kibe chafes the courtier's chilblain
122 ground cause (But, in the next line, the gravedigger takes the word in the sense of "land,"
"country.")

FIRST CLOWN: Faith, if 'a be not rotten before 'a die—as we have many pocky   126
corpses nowadays, that will scarce hold the laying in—'a will last you some   127
eight year or nine year. A tanner will last you nine year.

HAMLET: Why he more than another?

FIRST CLOWN: Why, sir, his hide is so tanned with his trade that 'a will keep out water
a great while, and your water is a sore decayer of your whoreson dead body. *[He*   130
picks up a skull.] Here's a skull now hath lien you i' th' earth three-and-twenty years.   131

HAMLET: Whose was it?

FIRST CLOWN: A whoreson mad fellow's it was. Whose do you think it was?

HAMLET: Nay, I know not.

FIRST CLOWN: A pestilence on him for a mad rogue! 'A poured a flagon of Rhenish   135
on my head once. This same skull, sir, was, sir, Yorick's skull, the King's jester.

HAMLET: This?

FIRST CLOWN: E'en that.

HAMLET: Let me see. *[He takes the skull.]* Alas, poor Yorick! I knew him, Horatio, a fellow of infinite jest, of most excellent fancy. He hath bore me on his back a thou-   140
sand times, and now how abhorred in my imagination it is! My gorge rises at it.   141
Here hung those lips that I have kissed I know not how oft. Where be your
gibes now? Your gambols, your songs, your flashes of merriment that were wont   143
to set the table on a roar? Not one now, to mock your own grinning? Quite   144
chopfallen? Now get you to my lady's chamber and tell her, let her paint an inch   145
thick, to this favor she must come. Make her laugh at that. Prithee, Horatio, tell   146
me one thing.

HORATIO: What's that, my lord?

HAMLET: Dost thou think Alexander looked o' this fashion i' th' earth?

HORATIO: E'en so.

HAMLET: And smelt so? Pah! *[He throws down the skull.]*

HORATIO: E'en so, my lord.

HAMLET: To what base uses we may return, Horatio! Why may imagination trace the
noble dust of Alexander till 'a find its stopping a bunghole?   154

HORATIO: 'Twere to consider too curiously to consider so.   155

HAMLET: No, faith, not a jot, but to follow him thither with modesty enough, and   156
likelihood to lead it. As thus: Alexander died, Alexander was buried, Alexander
returneth to dust, the dust is earth, of earth we make loam, and why of that loam   158
whereto he was converted might they not stop a beer barrel?
Imperious Caesar, dead and turned to clay,   160
Might stop a hole to keep the wind away.

---

125 pocky rotten, diseased (Literally, with the pox, or syphilis.)
126 hold the laying in hold together long enough to be interred   **last you** last (*You* is used
colloquially here and in the following lines.)
130 sore i.e., terrible, great   **whoreson** i.e., vile, scurvy
131 lien you lain (See the note at line 126.)
135 Rhenish Rhine wine | **140 bore** borne
141 My gorge rises i.e., I feel nauseated | **143 were wont** used
144 mock your own grinning mock at the way your skull seems to be grinning (just as you
used to mock at yourself and those who grinned at you)
145 chopfallen (1) lacking the lower jaw (2) dejected
146 favor aspect, appearance | **154 bunghole** hole for filling or emptying a cask
155 curiously minutely | **156 modesty** plausible moderation
158 loam mortar consisting chiefly of moistened clay and straw
160 Imperious imperial

O, that that earth which kept the world in awe
Should patch a wall t' expel the winter's flaw!   163

Enter King, Queen, Laertes, and the corpse [of Ophelia, in procession, with Priest, lords, etc.].

But soft, but soft awhile! Here comes the King,   164
The Queen, the courtiers. Who is this they follow?
And with such maimèd rites? This doth betoken   166
The corpse they follow did with desperate hand
Fordo its own life. 'Twas of some estate.   168
Couch we awhile and mark.   169

[He and Horatio conceal themselves. Ophelia's body is taken to the grave.]

LAERTES: What ceremony else?
HAMLET: *[to Horatio]*   That is Laertes, a very noble youth. Mark.
LAERTES: What ceremony else?
PRIEST: Her obsequies have been as far enlarged
As we have warranty. Her death was doubtful,   174
And but that great command o'ersways the order   175
She should in ground unsanctified been lodged   176
Till the last trumpet. For charitable prayers,   177
Shards, flints, and pebbles should be thrown on her.   178
Yet here she is allowed her virgin crants,   179
Her maiden strewments, and the bringing home   180
Of bell and burial.   181
LAERTES: Must there no more be done?
PRIEST: No more be done.
We should profane the service of the dead
To sing a requiem and such rest to her   185
As to peace-parted souls.   186
LAERTES: Lay her i' th'earth,
And from her fair and unpolluted flesh
May violets spring! I tell thee, churlish priest,   189
A ministering angel shall my sister be
When thou liest howling.   191
HAMLET: *[to Horatio]*   What, the fair Ophelia!
QUEEN: *[scattering flowers]* Sweets to the sweet! Farewell.
I hoped thou shouldst have been my Hamlet's wife.
I thought thy bride-bed to have decked, sweet maid,
And not t' have strewed thy grave.
LAERTES: O, treble woe
Fall ten times treble on that cursèd head

---

163 flaw gust of wind
166 maimèd mutilated, incomplete
169 Couch we let's hide, lie low
175 great . . . order orders from on high overrule the prescribed procedures
176 She should . . . lodged she should have been buried in unsanctified ground
177 For in place of
179 crants garlands betokening maidenhood
180–181 bringing . . . burial laying the body to rest, to the sound of the bell
185 such rest i.e., to pray for such rest
186 peace-parted souls those who have died at peace with God
189 violets (See 4.5.190 and note.)

164 soft i.e., wait, be careful
168 Fordo destroy   **estate** rank
174 warranty i.e., ecclesiastical authority

178 Shards broken bits of pottery

180 strewments flowers strewn on a coffin

191 howling i.e., in hell

Whose wicked deed thy most ingenious sense 199
Deprived thee of! Hold off the earth awhile,
Till I have caught her once more in mine arms.

[He leaps into the grave and embraces Ophelia.]

Now pile your dust upon the quick and dead,
Till of this flat a mountain you have made
T' o'ertop old Pelion or the skyish head 204
Of blue Olympus. 205

HAMLET: *[coming forward]* What is he whose grief
Bears such an emphasis, whose phrase of sorrow 207
Conjures the wandering stars and makes them stand 208
Like wonder-wounded hearers? This is I, 209
Hamlet the Dane. 210

LAERTES: *[grappling with him]* The devil take thy soul!

HAMLET: Thou pray'st not well.
I prithee, take thy fingers from my throat,
For though I am not splenitive and rash,
Yet have I in me something dangerous, 214
Which let thy wisdom fear. Hold off thy hand.

KING: Pluck them asunder.

QUEEN: Hamlet, Hamlet!

ALL: Gentlemen!

HORATIO: Good my lord, be quiet.

[Hamlet and Laertes are parted.]

HAMLET: Why, I will fight with him upon this theme
Until my eyelids will no longer wag. 222

QUEEN: O my son, what theme?

HAMLET: I loved Ophelia. Forty thousand brothers
Could not with all their quantity of love
Make up my sum. What wilt thou do for her?

KING: O, he is mad, Laertes.

QUEEN: For love of God, forbear him. 228

HAMLET: 'Swounds, show me what thou'lt do. 229
Woo't weep? Woo't fight? Woo't fast? Woo't tear thyself? 230

---

199 ingenious sense a mind that is quick, alert, of fine qualities
204–205 Pelion, Olympus sacred mountains in the north of Thessaly; see also Ossa, below, at line 238
207 emphasis i.e., rhetorical and florid emphasis (*Phrase* has a similar rhetorical connotation.)
208 wandering stars planets   **209 wonder-wounded** struck with amazement
210 the Dane (This title normally signifies the King; see 1.1.17 and note.)
s.d. grappling with him The testimony of the First Quarto that "*Hamlet leaps in after Laertes*" and the "Elegy on Burbage" ("Oft have I seen him leap into the grave") seem to indicate one way in which this fight was staged; however, the difficulty of fitting two contenders and Ophelia's body into a confined space (probably the trapdoor) suggests to many editors the alternative, tha Laertes jumps out of the grave to attack Hamlet.)
214 splenitive quick-tempered
222 wag move (A fluttering eyelid is a conventional sign that life has not yet gone.)
228 forbear him leave him alone   **229 'Swounds** by His (Christ's) wounds
230 Woo't wilt thou

Woo't drink up eisel? Eat a crocodile?   231
I'll do 't. Dost come here to whine?
To outface me with leaping in her grave?
Be buried quick with her, and so will I.   234
And if thou prate of mountains, let them throw
Millions of acres on us, till our ground,
Singeing his pate against the burning zone,   237
Make Ossa like a wart! Nay, an thou'lt mouth,   238
I'll rant as well as thou.

QUEEN: This is mere madness,   240
And thus awhile the fit will work on him;
Anon, as patient as the female dove
When that her golden couplets are disclosed,   243
His silence will sit drooping.

HAMLET: Hear you, sir.
What is the reason that you use me thus?
I loved you ever. But it is no matter.
Let Hercules himself do what he may,   248
The cat will mew, and dog will have his day.   249

Exit Hamlet.

KING: I pray thee, good Horatio, wait upon him.
         [Exit] Horatio.
         [To Laertes.] Strengthen your patience in our last night's speech;   252
         We'll put the matter to the present push.—   253
         Good Gertrude, set some watch over your son.—
         This grave shall have a living monument.   255
         An hour of quiet shortly shall we see;   256
         Till then, in patience our proceeding be.   *Exeunt.*

Act 5, Scene 2

Enter Hamlet and Horatio.

HAMLET: So much for this, sir; now shall you see the other.   1
           You do remember all the circumstance?

---

231 drink up drink deeply **eisel** vinegar **crocodile** (Crocodiles were tough and dangerous, and were supposed to shed hypocritical tears.)
234 quick alive
237 his pate its head, i.e., top **burning zone** zone in the celestial sphere containing the sun's orbit, between the tropics of Cancer and Capricorn
238 Ossa another mountain in Thessaly (In their war against the Olympian gods, the giants attempted to heap Ossa on Pelion to scale Olympus.) **an** if **mouth** i.e., rant
240 mere utter
243 golden couplets two baby pigeons, covered with yellow down **disclosed** hatched
248–249 Let . . . day i.e., (1) even Hercules couldn't stop Laertes' theatrical rant (2) I, too, will have my turn, i.e., despite any blustering attempts at interference, every person will sooner or later do what he or she must do
252 in i.e., by recalling   **253 present push** immediate test
255 living lasting (For Laertes' private understanding, Claudius also hints that Hamlet's death will serve as such a monument.)
256 hour of quiet time free of conflict
5.2. Location: The castle.
1 see the other hear the other news

HORATIO: Remember it, my lord!

HAMLET: Sir, in my heart there was a kind of fighting
That would not let me sleep. Methought I lay
Worse than the mutines in the bilboes. Rashly,   6
And praised be rashness for it—let us know   7
Our indiscretion sometimes serves us well   8
When our deep plots do pall, and that should learn us   9
There's a divinity that shapes our ends,
Rough-hew them how we will—   11

HORATIO: That is most certain.

HAMLET: Up from my cabin,
My sea-gown scarfed about me, in the dark   14
Groped I to find out them, had my desire,   15
Fingered their packet, and in fine withdrew   16
To mine own room again, making so bold,
My fears forgetting manners, to unseal
Their grand commission; where I found, Horatio—
Ah, royal knavery!—an exact command,
Larded with many several sorts of reasons   21
Importing Denmark's health and England's too,   22
With, ho! such bugs and goblins in my life,   23
That on the supervise, no leisure bated,   24
No, not to stay the grinding of the ax,   25
My head should be struck off.

HORATIO: Is 't possible?

HAMLET: [giving a document]
Here's the commission. Read it at more leisure.
But wilt thou hear now how I did proceed?

HORATIO: I beseech you.

HAMLET: Being thus benetted round with villainies—
Ere I could make a prologue to my brains,   32
They had begun the play—I sat me down,   33
Devised a new commission, wrote it fair.   34
I once did hold it, as our statists do,   35
A baseness to write fair, and labored much   36

---

6 mutines mutineers   **bilboes** shackles   **Rashly** on impulse. This adverb goes with lines 13 ff.

7 know acknowledge

8 indiscretion lack of foresight and judgment (not an indiscreet act)

9 pall fail, falter, go stale   **learn** teach   **11 Rough-hew** shape roughly

14 sea-gown seaman's coat   **scarfed** loosely wrapped

15 them i.e., Rosencrantz and Guildenstern

16 Fingered pilfered, pinched   **in fine** finally, in conclusion

21 Larded garnished   **several** different   **22 Importing** relating to

23 bugs bugbears, hobgoblins   **in my life** i.e., to be feared if I were allowed to live

24 supervise reading   **leisure bated** delay allowed

25 stay await

32–33 Ere . . . play before I could consciously turn my brain to the matter, it had started working on a plan

34 fair in a clear hand   **35 statists** statesmen

36 baseness i.e., lower-class trait

How to forget that learning, but, sir, now
It did me yeoman's service. Wilt thou know   38
Th' effect of what I wrote?   39

HORATIO: Ay, good my lord.

HAMLET: An earnest conjuration from the King,   41
As England was his faithful tributary,
As love between them like the palm might flourish,   43
As peace should still her wheaten garland wear   44
And stand a comma 'tween their amities,   45
And many suchlike "as"es of great charge,   46
That on the view and knowing of these contents,
Without debatement further more or less,
He should those bearers put to sudden death,
Not shriving time allowed.   50

HORATIO: How was this sealed?

HAMLET: Why, even in that was heaven ordinant.   52
I had my father's signet in my purse,   53
Which was the model of that Danish seal;   54
Folded the writ up in the form of th' other,   55
Subscribed it, gave 't th' impression, placed it safely,   56
The changeling never known. Now, the next day   57
Was our sea fight, and what to this was sequent   58
Thou knowest already.

HORATIO: So Guildenstern and Rosencrantz go to 't.

HAMLET: Why, man, they did make love to this employment.
They are not near my conscience. Their defeat   62
Does by their own insinuation grow.   63
'Tis dangerous when the baser nature comes   64
Between the pass and fell incensèd points   65
Of mighty opposites.   66

HORATIO: Why, what a king is this!

HAMLET: Does it not, think thee, stand me now upon—   68
He that hath killed my king and whored my mother,
Popped in between th' election and my hopes,   70
Thrown out his angle for my proper life,   71

---

38 yeoman's i.e., substantial, faithful, loyal   **39 effect** purport
41 conjuration entreaty   **43 palm** (An image of health; see Psalm 92:12.)
44 still always   **wheaten garland** (Symbolic of fruitful agriculture, of peace and plenty.)
45 comma (Indicating continuity, link.)
46 "as"es (1) the "whereases" of a formal document (2) asses   **charge** (1) import (2) burden
  (appropriate to asses)
50 shriving time time for confession and absolution
52 ordinant directing   **53 signet** small seal
54 model replica   **55 writ** writing
56 Subscribed signed (with forged signature)   **impression** i.e., with a wax seal
57 changeling i.e., substituted letter. (Literally, a fairy child substituted for a human one.)
58 was sequent followed   **62 defeat** destruction
63 insinuation intrusive intervention, sticking their noses in my business
64 baser of lower social station   **65 pass** thrust   **fell** fierce
66 opposites antagonists
68 stand me now upon become incumbent on me now
70 election (The Danish monarch was "elected" by a small number of high-ranking electors.)
71 angle fishhook   **proper** very

And with such cozenage—it 't not perfect conscience	72
To quit him with this arm? And it 't not to be damned	73
To let this canker of our nature come	74
In further evil?	75

HORATIO: It must be shortly known to him from England
    What is the issue of the business there.

HAMLET: It will be short. The interim is mine,
    And a man's life's no more than to say "one."   79
    But I am very sorry, good Horatio,
    That to Laertes I forgot myself,
    For by the image of my cause I see
    The portraiture of his. I'll court his favors.
    But, sure, the bravery of his grief did put me   84
    Into a tow'ring passion.

HORATIO: Peace, who comes here?

Enter a Courtier [Osric].

OSRIC: Your lordship is right welcome back to Denmark.

HAMLET: I humbly thank you, sir. *[To Horatio.]* Dost know this water fly?

HORATIO: No, my good lord.

HAMLET: Thy state is the more gracious, for 'tis a vice to know him. He hath much
    land, and fertile. Let a beast be lord of beasts, and his crib shall stand at the   91
    King's mess. 'Tis a chuff, but, as I say, spacious in the possession of dirt.   92

OSRIC: Sweet lord, if your lordship were at leisure, I should impart a thing to you
    from His Majesty.

HAMLET: I will receive it, sir, with all diligence of spirit.
    Put your bonnet to his right use; 'tis for the head.   96

OSRIC: I thank your lordship, it is very hot.

HAMLET: No, believe me, 'tis very cold. The wind is northerly.

OSRIC: It is indifferent cold, my lord, indeed.   99

HAMLET: But yet methinks it is very sultry and hot for my complexion.   100

OSRIC: Exceedingly, my lord. It is very sultry, as 'twere—I cannot tell how. My lord,
    His Majesty bade me signify to you that 'a has laid a great wager on your head.
    Sir, this is the matter—

HAMLET: I beseech you, remember.

[Hamlet moves him to put on his hat.]

OSRIC: Nay, good my lord; for my ease, in good faith. Sir, here is newly come to court   105
    Laertes—believe me, an absolute gentleman, full of most excellent differences,   106

---

72 cozenage trickery
73 quit requite, pay back
74 canker ulcer
74–75 come In grow into
79 a man's . . . "one" one's whole life occupies such a short time, only as long as it takes to count to 1
84 bravery bravado
91–92 Let . . . mess i.e., if a man, no matter how beastlike, is as rich in livestock and possessions as Osric, he may eat at the King's table
91 crib manger
92 chuff boor, churl (The Second Quarto spelling, *chough,* is a variant spelling that also suggests the meaning here of "chattering jackdaw.")
96 bonnet any kind of cap or hat   **his** its   **99 indifferent** somewhat
100 complexion temperament
105 for my ease (A conventional reply declining the invitation to put his hat back on.)
106 absolute perfect   **differences** special qualities

of very soft society and great showing. Indeed, to speak feelingly of him, he is   107
the card or calendar of gentry, for you shall find in him the continent of what   108
part a gentleman would see.

HAMLET: Sir, his definement suffers no perdition in you, though I know to divide   110
him inventorially would dozy th' arithmetic of memory, and yet but yaw neither   111
in respect of his quick sail. But, in the verity of extolment, I take him to be a soul   112
of great article, and his infusion of such dearth and rareness as, to make true   113
diction of him, his semblable is his mirror and who else would trace him his   114
umbrage, nothing more.   115

OSRIC: Your lordship speaks most infallibly of him.

HAMLET: The concernancy, sir? Why do we wrap the gentleman in our more rawer   117
breath?   118

OSRIC: Sir?

HORATIO: Is 't not possible to understand in another tongue? You will do 't, sir, really.   120

HAMLET: What imports the nomination of this gentleman?   121

OSRIC: Of Laertes?

HORATIO: *[to Hamlet]*   His purse is empty already; all 's golden words are spent.

HAMLET: Of him, sir.

OSRIC: I know you are not ignorant—

HAMLET: I would you did, sir. Yet in faith if you did, it would not much approve me.   126
Well, sir?

OSRIC: You are not ignorant of what excellence Laertes is—

HAMLET: I dare not confess that, lest I should compare with him in excellence. But   129
to know a man well were to know himself.   130

OSRIC: I mean, sir, for his weapon; but in the imputation laid on him by them, in his   131
meed he's unfellowed.   132

---

107 soft society agreeable manners   **great showing** distinguished appearance   **feelingly** with
just perception

108 card chart, map   **calendar** guide   **gentry** good breeding

108–109 the continent . . . see one who contains in him all the qualities a gentleman would like
to see (A *continent* is that which contains.)

110 definement definition (Hamlet proceeds to mock Osric by throwing his lofty diction back at
him.)   **perdition** loss, diminution   **you** your description

110–111 divide him inventorially enumerate his graces

111 dozy dizzy   **yaw** swing unsteadily off course (Said of a ship.)   **neither** for all that

112 in respect of in comparison with   **in . . . extolment** in true praise (of him)

113 of great article one with many articles in his inventory   **infusion** essence, character in-
fused into him by nature   **dearth and rareness** rarity

113–114 make true diction speak truly   **semblable** only true likeness   **who . . . trace** any
other person who would wish to follow.

115 umbrage shadow   **117 concernancy** import, relevance

117–118 rawer breath unrefined speech that can only come short in praising him

120 to understand . . . tongue i.e., for you, Osric, to understand when someone else speaks
your language (Horatio twits Osric for not being able to understand the kind of flowery
speech he himself uses, when Hamlet speaks in such a vein. Alternatively, all this could be
said to Hamlet.)   **You will do 't** i.e., you can if you try, or, you may well have to try (to
speak plainly)

121 nomination naming   **126 approve** commend

129–130 I dare . . . himself I dare not boast of knowing Laertes' excellence lest I seem to imply
a comparable excellence in myself. Certainly, to know another person well, one must know
oneself.

131 for i.e., with   **imputation . . . them** reputation given him by others

132 meed merit   **unfellowed** unmatched

HAMLET: What's his weapon?
OSRIC: Rapier and dagger.
HAMLET: That's two of his weapons—but well.   135
OSRIC: The King, sir, hath wagered with him six Barbary horses, against the which
   he has impawned, as I take it, six French rapiers and poniards, with their as-   137
   signs, as girdle, hangers, and so. Three of the carriages, in faith, are very dear to   138
   fancy, very responsive to the hilts, most delicate carriages, and of very liberal   139
   conceit.   140
HAMLET: What call you the carriages?
HORATIO: *[to Hamlet]* I knew you must be edified by the margent ere you had done.   142
OSRIC: The carriages, sir, are the hangers.
HAMLET: The phrase would be more germane to the matter if we could carry a
   cannon by our sides; I would it might be hangers till then. But, on: six Barbary
   horses against six French swords, their assigns, and three liberal-conceited car-
   riages; that's the French bet against the Danish. Why is this impawned, as you
   call it?
OSRIC: The King, sir, hath laid, sir, that in a dozen passes between yourself and him,   149
   he shall not exceed you three hits. He hath laid on twelve for nine, and it would
   come to immediate trial, if your lordship would vouchsafe the answer.   151
HAMLET: How if I answer no?
OSRIC: I mean, my lord, the opposition of your person in trial.
HAMLET: Sir, I will walk here in the hall. If it please His Majesty, it is the breathing   154
   time of day with me. Let the foils be brought, the gentleman willing, and the   155
   King hold his purpose, I will win for him an I can; if not, I will gain nothing but
   my shame and the odd hits.
OSRIC: Shall I deliver you so?   158
HAMLET: To this effect, sir—after what flourish your nature will.
OSRIC: I commend my duty to your lordship.   160
HAMLET: Yours, yours. *[Exit Osric.]* 'A does well to commend it himself; there are no
   tongues else for 's turn.   162
HORATIO: This lapwing runs away with the shell on his head.   163

---

135 but well but never mind
137 he i.e., Laertes   **impawned** staked wagered   **poniards** daggers
137–138 assigns appurtenances
138 hangers straps on the sword belt (*girdle*), from which the sword hung   **and so** and so on
   carriages (An affected way of saying *hangers;* literally, gun carriages.)
138–139 dear to fancy delightful to the fancy
139 responsive corresponding closely, matching or well adjusted   **delicate** (i.e., in workmanship)
139–140 liberal conceit elaborate design
142 margent margin of a book, place for explanatory notes
149 laid wagered   **passes** bouts (The odds of the betting are hard to explain. Possibly the King
   bets that Hamlet will win at least five out of twelve, at which point Laertes raises the odds
   against himself by betting he will win nine.)
151 vouchsafe the answer be so good as to accept the challenge (Hamlet deliberately takes the
   phrase in its literal sense of replying.)
154–155 breathing time exercise period   **Let** i.e., if
158 deliver you report what you say
160 commend commit to your favor (A conventional salutation, but Hamlet wryly uses a more
   literal meaning, "recommend," "praise," in line 161.)
162 for 's turn for his purposes, i.e., to do it for him
163 lapwing (A proverbial type of youthful forwardness. Also, a bird that draws intruders away
   from its nest and was thought to run about with its head in the shell when newly hatched; a
   seeming reference to Osric's hat.)

HAMLET: 'A did comply with his dug before 'a sucked it. Thus has he—and many   164
more of the same breed that I know the drossy age dotes on—only got the tune   165
of the time and, out of an habit of encounter, a kind of yeasty collection, which   166
carries them through and through the most fanned and winnowed opinions;   167
and do but blow them to their trial, the bubbles are out.   168

Enter a Lord.

LORD: My lord, His Majesty commended him to you by young Osric, who brings
back to him that you attend him in the hall. He sends to know if your pleasure   170
hold to play with Laertes, or that you will take longer time.

HAMLET: I am constant to my purposes; they follow the King's pleasure. If his fitness   172
speaks, mine is ready; now or whensoever, provided I be so able as now.   173

LORD: The King and Queen and all are coming down.

HAMLET: In happy time.   175

LORD: The Queen desires you to use some gentle entertainment to Laertes before   176
you fall to play.

HAMLET: She well instructs me.   *[Exit Lord.]*

HORATIO: You will lose, my lord.

HAMLET: I do not think so. Since he went into France, I have been in continual practice; I shall win at the odds. But thou wouldst not think how ill all's here about
my heart; but it is no matter.

HORATIO: Nay, good my lord—

HAMLET: It is but foolery, but it is such a kind of gain-giving as would perhaps trou-   184
ble a woman.

HORATIO: If your mind dislike anything, obey it. I will forestall their repair hither   186
and say you are not fit.

HAMLET: Not a whit, we defy augury. There is special providence in the fall of a
sparrow. If it be now, 'tis not to come; if it be not to come, it will be now; if it be
not now; yet it will come. The readiness is all. Since no man of aught he leaves   190
knows, what is 't to leave betimes. Let be.   191

*A table prepared. [Enter] trumpets, drums, and officers with cushions; King, Queen, [Osric,]
and all the state; foils, daggers, [and wine borne in;] and Laertes.*

KING: Come, Hamlet, come and take this hand from me.

[The King puts Laertes' hand into Hamlet's.]

HAMLET: *[to Laertes]*   Give me your pardon, sir. I have done you wrong,
But pardon 't as you are a gentleman.

---

164 comply . . . dug observe ceremonious formality toward his nurse's or mother's teat
165 drossy laden with scum and impurities, frivolous   **tune** temper, mood, manner of speech
166 an habit of encounter   a demeanor in conversing (with courtiers of his own kind)   **yeasty**
frothy   **collection** i.e., of current phrases
167 carries . . . opinions sustains them right through the scrutiny of persons whose opinions are
select and refined (Literally, like grain separated from its chaff. Osric is both the chaff and the
bubbly froth on the surface of the liquor that is soon blown away.)
168 and do yet do   **blow . . . out** test them by merely blowing on them, and their bubbles burst
170 that if
172–173 If . . . ready if he declares his readiness, my convenience waits on his
175 In happy time (A phrase of courtesy indicating that the time is convenient.)
176 entertainment greeting   **184 gaingiving** misgiving
186 repair coming
190–191 Since . . . Let be since no one has knowledge of what he is leaving behind, what does
an early death matter after all? Enough; don't struggle against it.

This presence knows, 195
And you must needs have heard, how I am punished 196
With a sore distraction. What I have done
That might be your nature, honor, and exception 198
Roughly awake, I here proclaim was madness.
Was 't Hamlet wronged Laertes? Never Hamlet.
If Hamlet from himself be ta'en away,
And when he's not himself does wrong Laertes,
Then Hamlet does it not, Hamlet denies it.
Who does it, then? His madness. If 't be so,
Hamlet is of the faction that is wronged; 205
His madness is poor Hamlet's enemy.
Sir, in this audience
Let my disclaiming from a purposed evil
Free me so far in your most generous thoughts
That I have shot my arrow o'er the house 210
And hurt my brother.

LAERTES: I am satisfied in nature, 212
Whose motive in this case should stir me most 213
To my revenge. But in terms of honor
I stand aloof, and will no reconcilement
Till by some elder masters of known honor
I have a voice and precedent of peace 217
To keep my name ungored. But till that time 218
I do receive your offered love like love,
And will not wrong it.

HAMLET: I embrace it freely,
And will this brothers' wager frankly play.— 222
Give us the foils. Come on.

LAERTES: Come, one for me.

HAMLET: I'll be your foil, Laertes. In mine ignorance 225
Your skill shall, like a star i' the darkest night,
Stick fiery off indeed. 227

LAERTES: You mock me, sir.

HAMLET: No, by this hand.

KING: Give them the foils, young Osric. Cousin Hamlet,
You know the wager?

HAMLET: Very well, my lord.
Your Grace has laid the odds o' the weaker side. 233

KING: I do not fear it; I have seen you both.
But since he is bettered, we have therefore odds. 235

---

195 presence royal assembly
196 punished afflicted
198 exception disapproval
205 faction party
210 That I have as if I had
212 in nature i.e., as to my personal feelings
213 motive prompting
217 voice authoritative pronouncement **of peace** for reconciliation
218 name ungored reputation unwounded
222 frankly without ill feeling or the burden of rancor
225 foil thin metal background which sets a jewel off (with pun on the blunted rapier for fencing)
227 Stick fiery off stand out brilliantly **233 laid the odds o'** bet on, backed
235 is bettered has improved; is the odds-on favorite. (Laertes' handicap is the "three hits" specified in line 150.)

LAERTES: This is too heavy. Let me see another.

[He exchanges his foil for another.]

HAMLET: This likes me well. These foils have all a length?   237

[They prepare to play.]

OSRIC: Ay, my good lord.

KING: Set me the stoups of wine upon that table.
    If Hamlet give the first or second hit,
    Or quit in answer of the third exchange,   241
    Let all the battlements their ordnance fire.
    The King shall drink to Hamlet's better breath,   243
    And in the cup an union shall he throw   244
    Richer than that which four successive kings
    In Denmark's crown have worn. Give me the cups,
    And let the kettle to the trumpet speak,   247
    The trumpet to the cannoneer without,
    The cannons to the heavens, the heaven to earth,
    "Now the King drinks to Hamlet." Come, begin.

Trumpets the while.

    And you, the judges, bear a wary eye.

HAMLET: Come on, sir.

LAERTES: Come, my lord. *[They play. Hamlet scores a hit.]*

HAMLET: One.

LAERTES: No.

HAMLET: Judgment.

OSRIC: A hit, a very palpable hit.

Drum, trumpets, and shot. Flourish.   A piece goes off.

LAERTES: Well, again.

KING: Stay, give me drink. Hamlet, this pearl is thine.

[He drinks, and throws a pearl in Hamlet's cup.]

    Here's to thy health. Give him the cup.

HAMLET: I'll play this bout first. Set it by awhile.
    Come. *[They play.]* Another hit; what say you?

LAERTES: A touch, a touch, I do confess 't.

KING: Our son shall win.

QUEEN: He's fat and scant of breath.   265
    Here, Hamlet, take my napkin, rub thy brows.   266
    The Queen carouses to thy fortune, Hamlet.   267

HAMLET: Good madam!

KING: Gertrude, do not drink.

QUEEN: I will, my lord, I pray you pardon me.   *[She drinks.]*

KING: *[aside]* It is the poisoned cup. It is too late.

---

237 likes me pleases me
241 Or . . . exchange i.e., or requites Laertes in the third bout for having won the first two
243 better breath improved vigor
244 union pearl (So called, according to Pliny's *Natural History,* 9, because pearls are *unique,* never identical.)
247 kettle kettledrum   **265 fat** not physically fit, out of training
266 napkin handkerchief   **267 carouses** drinks a toast

HAMLET: I dare not drink yet, madam; by and by.

QUEEN: Come, let me wipe thy face.

LAERTES: *[to King]* My lord, I'll hit him now.

KING: I do not think 't.

LAERTES: *[aside]* And yet it is almost against my conscience.

HAMLET: Come, for the third, Laertes. You do but dally.
   I pray you, pass with your best violence;   278
   I am afeard you make a wanton of me.   279

LAERTES: Say you so? Come on.   *[They play.]*

OSRIC: Nothing neither way.

LAERTES: Have at you now!

[Laertes wounds Hamlet; then, in scuffling, they change rapiers, and Hamlet wounds Laertes.]

KING: Part them! They are incensed.

HAMLET: Nay, come, again.   *[The Queen falls.]*

OSRIC: Look to the Queen there, ho!

HORATIO: They bleed on both sides. How is it, my lord?

OSRIC: How is 't, Laertes?

LAERTES: Why, as a woodcock to mine own springe, Osric;   288
   I am justly killed with mine own treachery.

HAMLET: How does the Queen?

KING: She swoons to see them bleed.

QUEEN: No, no, the drink, the drink—O my dear Hamlet—
   The drink, the drink! I am poisoned.   *[She dies.]*

HAMLET: O villainy! Ho, let the door be locked!
   Treachery! Seek it out.   *[Laertes falls. Exit Osric.]*

LAERTES: It is here, Hamlet. Hamlet, thou art slain.
   No med'cine in the world can do thee good;
   In thee there is not half an hour's life.
   The treacherous instrument is in thy hand,
   Unbated and envenomed. The foul practice   300
   Hath turned itself on me. Lo, here I lie,
   Never to rise again. Thy mother's poisoned.
   I can no more. The King, the King's to blame.

HAMLET: The point envenomed too? Then, venom, to thy work.   *[He stabs the King.]*

ALL: Treason! Treason!

KING: O, yet defend me, friends! I am but hurt.

HAMLET: *[forcing the King to drink]* Here, thou incestuous,
   murderous, damnèd Dane, Drink off this potion.
   Is thy union here?   308
   Follow my mother.   *[The King dies.]*

---

278 pass thrust
279 make . . . me i.e., treat me like a spoiled child, trifle with me
s.d. in scuffling, they change rapiers (This stage direction occurs in the Folio. According to a widespread stage tradition, Hamlet receives a scratch, realizes that Laertes' sword is unbated, and accordingly forces an exchange.)
288 woodcock a bird, a type of stupidity of as a decoy   **springe** trap, snare
300 Unbated not blunted with a button   **practice** plot
308 union pearl (See line 244; with grim puns on the word's other meanings: marriage, shared death.)

LAERTES: He is justly served.
   It is a poison tempered by himself.   311
   Exchange forgiveness with me, noble Hamlet.
   Mine and my father's death come not upon thee,
   Nor thine on me!   [He dies.]
HAMLET: Heaven make thee free of it! I follow thee.
   I am dead, Horatio. Wretched Queen, adieu!
   You that look pale and tremble at this chance,   317
   That are but mutes or audience to this act,   318
   Had I but time—as this fell sergeant, Death,   319
   Is strict in his arrest—O, I could tell you—   320
   But let it be. Horatio, I am dead;
   Thou livest. Report me and my cause aright
   To the unsatisfied.
HORATIO: Never believe it.
   I am more an antique Roman than a Dane.   325
   Here's yet some liquor left.

[He attempts to drink from the poisoned cup. Hamlet prevents him.]
HAMLET: As thou'rt a man,
   Give me the cup! Let go! By heaven, I'll ha 't.
   O God, Horatio, what a wounded name,
   Things standing thus unknown, shall I leave behind me!
   If thou didst ever hold me in thy heart,
   Absent thee from felicity awhile,
   And in this harsh world draw thy breath in pain
   To tell my story. *A march afar off [and a volley within].*
   What warlike noise is this?

Enter Osric.
OSRIC: Young Fortinbras, with conquest come from Poland,
   To th' ambassadors of England gives
   This warlike volley.
HAMLET: O, I die, Horatio!
   The potent poison quite o'ercrows my spirit.   339
   I cannot live to hear the news from England,
   But I do prophesy th' election lights
   On Fortinbras. He has my dying voice.   342
   So tell him, with th' occurrents more and less   343
   Which have solicited—the rest is silence.   [He dies.]   344
HORATIO: Now cracks a noble heart. Good night, sweet prince,
   And flights of angels sing thee to thy rest!

---

311 tempered mixed   **317 chance** mischance
318 mutes silent observers (Literally, actors with nonspeaking parts.)
319 fell cruel   **sergeant** sheriff's officer
320 strict (1) severely just (2) unavoidable   **arrest** (1) taking into custody (2) stopping my speech
325 Roman (Suicide was an honorable choice for many Romans as an alternative to a dishonorable life.)
339 o'ercrows triumphs over (like the winner in a cockfight)
342 voice vote   **343 occurrents** events, incidents
344 solicited moved, urged (Hamlet doesn't finish saying what the events have prompted—presumably, his acts of vengeance, or his reporting of those events to Fortinbras.)

[March within.]
    Why does the drum come hither?

Enter Fortinbras, with the [English] Ambassadors [with drum, colors, and attendants].

FORTINBRAS: Where is this sight?
HORATIO: What is it you would see?
    If aught of woe or wonder, cease your search.
FORTINBRAS: This quarry cries on havoc. O proud Death,   351
    What feast is toward in thine eternal cell,   352
    That thou so many princes at a shot
    So bloodily hast struck?
FIRST AMBASSADOR: The sight is dismal,
    And our affairs from England come too late.
    The ears are senseless that should give us hearing,
    To tell him his commandment is fulfilled,
    That Rosencrantz and Guildenstern are dead.
    Where should we have our thanks?
HORATIO: Not from his mouth,
    Had it th' ability of life to thank you.
    He never gave commandment for their death.
    But since, so jump upon this bloody question,   364
    You from the Polack wars, and you from England,
    Are here arrived, give order that these bodies
    High on a stage be placèd to the view,   367
    And let me speak to th' yet unknowing world
    How these things came about. So shall you hear
    Of carnal, bloody, and unnatural acts,
    Of accidental judgments, casual slaughters,   371
    Of deaths put on by cunning and forced cause,   372
    And, in this upshot, purposes mistook
    Fall'n on on th' inventors' heads. All this can I
    Truly deliver.
FORTINBRAS: Let us haste to hear it,
    And call the noblest to the audience.
    For me, with sorrow I embrace my fortune.
    I have some rights of memory in this kingdom,
    Which now to claim my vantage doth invite me.   379
HORATIO: Of that I shall have also to speak,   380
    And from his mouth whose voice will draw on more.
    But let this same be presently performed,   382
    Even while men's minds are wild, lest more mischance   383
    On plots and errors happen.   385

---

351 quarry heap of dead   **cries on havoc** proclaims a general slaughter
352 feast i.e., Claudius'
364 jump precisely, immediately   **question** dispute, affair
367 stage platform
371 judgments retributions   **casual** occurring by chance
372 put on instigated   **forced cause** contrivance
379 of memory traditional, remembered, unforgotten
380 vantage favorable opportunity   **382 voice . . . more** vote will influence still others
383 presently immediately   **385 On** on the basis of; on top of

FORTINBRAS: Let four captains
      Bear Hamlet, like a soldier, to the stage,
      For he was likely, had he been put on,   388
      To have proved most royal; and for his passage,   389
      The soldiers' music and the rite of war
      Speak loudly for him.   391
      Take up the bodies. Such a sight as this
      Becomes the field, but here shows much amiss.   393
      Go bid the soldiers shoot.

Exeunt [marching, bearing off the dead bodies; a peal of ordnance is shot off].

Act 5 Response Statement Questions

- Hamlet is offstage for most of Act 4. When he reappears in Act 5, does he
  seem different? If so, in what way or ways? Can you see any cause for a
  change in him, or does this change seem arbitrary? How does any change
  you see in him now affect your opinion of him?
- What is your response to the ending or denouement of the action? Does it
  seem a matter of chaotic events that render the characters' plotting ironic?
  Does it seem a case of poetic justice, with all the plotters getting what they
  deserve at last? Are there any innocent victims here?
- What feeling are you left with at the end of the play? Assuming you do
  feel the events are tragic, are they so because they were inevitable? because of some human error that might have been avoided? because of the
  operation of powers beyond human control?
- Is Denmark better off at the end of the play than at the beginning? What
  makes you say so, either way? Can you relate your response to beliefs in
  your ideology about what should be done about political corruption?

Overall Response Questions

- What is your opinion of Hamlet as a tragic hero? How is your answer to
  this question influenced by ideas of that concept you may have brought to
  the reading? Does the story of Hamlet cause you to modify any of those
  ideas, enlarging or revising your sense of what a tragic hero is?
- How does your historical and cultural situation affect your response to the
  whole play? How much does it matter, for instance, that your situation is
  different from Hamlet's in time, circumstances, social class, political responsibilities, and so on? How much does it matter that your situation is
  different from that of Shakespeare's original audience?
- What reading strategies did you use with this text? Which ones, if any, had
  to be discarded as unworkable? Which ones, if any, proved to be more
  successful? Were you able to adopt any new ones that you had not used
  much before? Did you find yourself becoming any more successful as a
  reader of the text as you went along?

---

388 put on i.e., invested in royal office and so put to the test
389 passage i.e., from life to death   **391 Speak** (let them) speak
393 Becomes the field suits the field of battle

- *Hamlet* and *Oedipus the King* are widely considered two of the greatest tragic dramas in the Western canon. Both involve men of high social and political standing as protagonists. Does that status and the male gender seem necessary for a tragic protagonist? Can there be tragedy in the same sense if the protagonist is either female or of low social status or both? If not, what are the implications for Western ideology?
- *Share and Compare*   Considering the lack of consensus about the theme or meaning of *Hamlet* over the years, you should not be surprised if different interpretations emerge from readers in your class. Discussion of these differing readings can become quite lively, with readers citing different scenes or lines from the text as the bases for their interpretations. In your class, however, can differing interpretations of the play be traced, at least partly, to the differing ideologies of readers?

BROADENING YOUR LITERARY EXPERIENCE THROUGH RESEARCH

Presumably, what you have read in this chapter and the writing you have done have shown you more than you knew before about the literary repertoire and ideology of *Hamlet*, including the features and practices of the Elizabethan theater and the ideology of English culture in the sixteenth century. If you want to further broaden your knowledge with respect to *Hamlet*, Shakespearean tragedy, Elizabethan drama in general, Renaissance English politics and philosophy, or any aspect of the ideology behind *Hamlet*, the best way to do that is through library research. The reading and writing you have done in this chapter may have raised questions for you that only further research can answer. That's good: Remember that it's questions and questioning that keep learning alive, and that answers are only provisional and temporary. The QAQ method promoted in Chapter 3 applies here too.

Here are some additional questions that you could pursue through library research, followed by a brief bibliography of sources for broadening your repertoire of knowledge in the area of Elizabethan tragedy. Think of both the sources and the questions as just starting points for further investigation. Even a researched reading, however, should not be considered final. "The truth" about a text does not lie under a rock, waiting to be discovered, or in the library or in history; it may be pursued, but never possessed. Reading, learning, knowing are processes, of which research is a part. Whenever you read a text, whether you know a lot about it or just a little, you should try to be conscious of the dynamic interaction between you and the text.

Suggestions for Research

- Investigate the history of productions of *Hamlet*. What notable productions are you able to find described or reviewed? What cuts or other changes were made in the original text? What emphases and interpretations have directors and actors made? To what extent is *Hamlet* a stable or timeless text and to what extent is it subject to changing local or cultural conditions?

- Investigate some critical interpretations of *Hamlet*, especially some strong readings. (The brief bibliography below may provide a starting point.) What have different influential readers said about the text? How does your interpretation compare with any of these readings? How is your interpretation affected by any of these? What makes you agree or disagree with any interpretation you find?

- Investigate the issue of individual action and initiative in Renaissance England. What were the larger implications of this issue (something that we take for granted as "natural" and good in our culture) in Shakespeare's time? Did the meaning that individual initiative had in the Elizabethan cultural ideology affect the way *Hamlet* might have been understood back then?

- Read the article by Laura Bohannan called "Shakespeare in the Bush" in the Essays for Further Reading, page 1545. How is the Tiv's reading of *Hamlet* culture-bound? Does it suggest any ways in which your own reading of *Hamlet* is culture-bound? What are the implications of the Tiv's reading for the idea that *Hamlet* (or any great work of literature) is "timeless" or has "universal meaning"?

Selected Bibliography

A good place to begin your search for further information on any of these topics is in the reference section of your library. For any of the above topics, you can find background information and get an overview of related issues and ideas by consulting specialized encyclopedias, handbooks, and readers' guides to particular areas of literature, defined by genre or historical period. Often these kinds of reference works include their own bibliographies of relevant books and periodical articles. Here are some standard reference works for the study of Shakespearean tragedy.

Cahn, Victor L., ed. *Shakespeare the Playwright: A Companion to the Complete Tragedies, Histories, Comedies, and Romances.* New York: Greenwood Press, 1991.

Champion, Larry S. *The Essential Shakespeare: An Annotated Bibilography of Major Modern Studies.* New York: G. K. Hall, 1993.

Hackman, Stanley, ed. *McGraw-Hill Encyclopedia of World Drama.* 5 vols. New York: McGraw-Hill, 1984.

Wills, Stanley, ed. *Shakespeare: A Bibliographic Guide.* Oxford: Clarendon Press, 1990.

Periodicals, such as magazines and scholarly journals, are another good source of information for broadening your literary knowledge. The bibliographies in the above reference sources may list periodical articles, but you can extend your search by consulting any of the following periodical indexes. All are available in both bound volumes and electronic form, as indicated by the note in parentheses following each title.

Arts and Humanities Citation Index. (on-line)
Humanities Index. (on-line)
MLA International Bibliography. (CD-ROM)

Here is a list of books that contain useful information for broadening your knowledge of any of the topics listed earlier.

Bevington, David, ed. *Twentieth-Century Interpretations of "Hamlet": A Collection of Critical Essays.* Englewood Cliffs, N. J.: Prentice-Hall, 1968.

Bradley, A. C. *Shakespearean Tragedy.* New York: Meridian, 1955.

David, Richard. *Shakespeare in the Theatre.* New York: Cambridge UP, 1978.

Greenblatt, Stephen. *Renaissance Self-Fashioning.* Chicago: University of Chicago Press, 1980.

———. *Shakespearean Negotiations.* Berkeley: University of California Press, 1988.

Gurr, Andrew. *The Shakespearean Stage: 1574–1642.* New York: Cambridge UP, 1980.

Kermode, Frank, ed. *Four Centuries of Shakespearian Criticism.* New York: Avon, 1965.

Mills, John L. *Hamlet on Stage: The Great Tradition.* Westport, Connecticut: Greenwood Press, 1985.

Rabkin, Norman. *Shakespeare and the Common Understanding.* New York: Free Press, 1967.

Weitz, Morris, ed. *Hamlet and the Philosophy of Literary Criticism.* Chicago: University of Chicago Press, 1964.

20 ◈ COMEDY

In the drama festivals put on during the annual celebrations of Dionysus in ancient Athens, tragedy predominated. A playwright would submit three tragedies to be performed on successive days. He would also submit a comedy to follow the tragedies; the celebrations marked the life-giving powers of the god, after all, and presumably the audience needed a psychological break from the intensely cathartic experience of watching tragedy. You may also be familiar with the idea of **comic relief** in Shakespearean tragedy and other serious drama—brief interludes of comedy that momentarily break the tension that has built up as an audience watches a tragedy unfold. As you have now read two of the great tragedies in the canon of Western drama, you too are probably ready for a break. Therefore, this chapter is devoted to broadening your experience with respect to comedy.

What Is Comedy?

Start by taking an inventory of your ideology on the subject of comedy. What do you know, think, or believe about what is comic in general? Take a few minutes to jot down some of your ideas about what comedy is, in the general sense of the word. What creates comic effects, and can you offer an example, real or hypothetical, of a comic situation? Are there different levels or degrees of comedy, allowing for different situations or events to be comic in greater or lesser degrees? Make your own lists, then compare yours to the ones I offer below.

Qualities of Comedy

1.

2.

3.

4.

5.

Examples of Comedy

1.

2.

3.

Here are some of my ideas about comedy.

Qualities of Comedy

1. It makes you laugh, or at least smile or feel happy.

2. Things turn out well for people for whom you want things to turn out well.

3. Something silly or unusual happens.

4. Nobody is really hurt badly; maybe just their pride or ego is bruised a little.

5. Words are used in a clever or amusing way.

Examples of Comedy

1. Cliché—somebody slips on a banana peel.

2. A joke, a witticism, a pun.

3. The "Seinfeld" episode reprinted in Chapter 15.

Now, if you think about comedy in an aesthetic or literary sense, how are your ideas modified, if at all? What does your literary experience contain about comedy? Is it comic if any character experiences any of the qualities of comedy that you listed? Or does the character have to be a "good" person, one that you find yourself rooting for? Does the situation have to involve some obstacle to a character's happiness, which he or she overcomes in the end? If so, how serious a threat to the character's happiness does this obstacle have to be? How serious can the situation be and still be comic? Does the character have to succeed? Does there have to be a happy ending, or can a character "fail" and the situation still be comic? If he or she does fail, does she or he have to be someone you laugh *at* rather than *with*?

Take a few minutes now to list some of your ideas about comedy in the more literary, especially *dramatic* sense, as well as any examples of comic characters you can think of or plays that you know or believe to be comedies.

Qualities of Dramatic Comedy

1.

2.

3.

4.

5.

Examples

1.

2.

3.

The purpose of this exercise is for you to inventory your experience and ideology before you undertake to broaden them. After you work your way through the following discussion and read a comedy, you can come back to these lists and compare them with your broadened knowledge. You can also compare your beliefs on this question with those of different dramatists and theorists through the ages of Western literary history.

A Brief History of Dramatic Comedy

The modern word "comedy" derives from ancient Greek words meaning "revel" and "singer," indicating the genre's festive origins in very loosely structured celebrations (revels) that included songs. In the fifth and early fourth centuries B.C., ancient Athens saw the production of comedies written by Aristophanes. These comedies were typically **satires** on contemporary political and cultural issues in Athens—plays that tried to provoke laughter toward some actual or typical people or their beliefs. Perhaps the best known of his plays—and the one you may find performed even today—is *Lysistrata*, the story of Athenian women who decide to withhold sex from their husbands as a war protest.

Plays like *Lysistrata* later came to be called *old comedy*, as distinguished from *new comedy*, which was less satirical and more **romantic**. The leading author of new comedies in ancient Greece was Menander (342–291 B.C.). "Romantic" in this sense means that young lovers were involved as major characters and that the primary interest in the play was whether they could overcome some kind of obstacle that was put in the way of their happiness. The new comedy also established conventions of setting, such as enchanted woods or faraway lands, and of **stock characters**, such as the meddling parent, the scheming servant, and the wealthy older rival for the young woman's affection. Menander's plays were the model for the comedies written by the early Romans Plautus and Terence, which in turn influenced the romantic comedy written in Renaissance England.

The terms *old comedy* and *new comedy* are specialized bits of literary information (though you might as well file them in your literary repertoire). But the basic distinction between satire and romance that parallels the distinction between old comedy and new is worth hanging onto because those two strains of comedy have continued throughout Western literary history.

In addition to romantic comedy (one of which will be considered in more detail shortly), the English Renaissance saw the revival of satiric comedy, especially in the **comedy of humours** popularized by writers such as Ben Jonson. Medicine and psychology of the sixteenth century held that personality was determined by traits related to four bodily humours or fluids—blood, phlegm, and yellow and black bile. A person was psychologically balanced (normal) when the humours were in balance. Abnormal behavior could be traced to an imbalance in the humours. Such imbalanced people were characters—with names like Kno'well, Down-right, Well-bred, and Formal—in plays such as Jonson's *Every Man in His Humour* (1598). In the late seventeenth century, the French Neoclassical playwright Molière satirized similar character types in his comedies about misers, hypochondriacs, social climbers, and religious hypocrites. Molière's play *Tartuffe* is in the Plays for Further Reading in this section.

In the Restoration and eighteenth-century English theater, satiric comedy took the form of the **comedy of manners**, which critically examined social behavior among the more refined classes, mocking characters who were excessive in their pursuits of love, for instance, or in other social habits, or characters who were would-be sophisticates. Plays such as William Congreve's *The Way of the World* (1700) and Richard Sheridan's *School for Scandal* (1777) are leading examples of the comedy of manners. In the Anglo-American tradition, writers such as Oscar Wilde, George Bernard Shaw, Noel Coward, Neil Simon, Beth Henley, and Wendy Wasserstein have continued to develop the comedy of manners in the nineteenth and twentieth centuries.

In the late nineteenth century, the English novelist and critic George Meredith published an essay in which he distinguished between *high* and *low* comedy. The former, he said, appealed primarily to the intellect of the audience through its use of witty language, clever characters, and sophisticated social situations. The latter relied more on physical humor, broad or bawdy language, and outrageous or improbable situations. Some plays, such as those in the comedy of manners tradition, may be regarded as primarily high comedy in these terms.

On the other hand, by the time Meredith drew this distinction there had been a long tradition of plays that involved healthy doses of low comedy in the interest of satire. The sixteenth-century Italian *commedia dell'arte* featured a type of **farce** or broad comedy involving stock characters in wildly improbable situations doing silly things such as tripping and falling, bashing each other over the head, and making bawdy jokes. (If this sounds a bit like what you know today as slapstick, that's because it derived from earlier Roman comedies in which clownish characters slapped each other with sticks, an early piece of **stage business**.) The audience's laughter, likely to be louder and heartier than what high comedy provokes, is directed at the bumbling of stock characters. Low comedy has not developed into subgenres of serious drama the way that high comedy has, but elements of it may be seen in Renaissance English comedy—including the plays of Shakespeare—in Molière's plays, and in twentieth-century **absurdist** drama such as plays written by Samuel Beckett and Tom Stoppard. And of course it coexists with high comedy in mass media forms today—television sit-coms, movies, and cartoons.

CONNECT: A portion of a script from an episode of "Seinfeld" is reprinted in Chapter 15. To what degree does it mix high and low comedy? If you have seen that episode on television, to what degree do the actors' gestures and expressions add low comedy elements to the script?

Romantic comedy, meanwhile, has its own history from the sixteenth century on down to the present. Less concerned with poking fun, subtly or broadly, at human follies or vices, it treats its generally attractive characters with more sympathy. After yielding dominance on the English stage to the satiric comedies of manners in the late seventeenth century, it returned to popularity in the **sentimental comedy** developed especially by Richard Steele in the eighteenth century. Plays like Steele's *The Conscious Lovers* (1722) offer outstandingly virtuous characters who appeal to the audience's feelings or sentiments more than to their intellect. The audience presumably finds pleasure in watching such characters survive their domestic problems and end up "happily ever after." This kind of comedy remained popular through the nineteenth century in England and the United States, even to the extent that *Romeo and Juliet* was produced with a happy ending in which the doomed lovers' "deaths" were revealed to be mere fainting spells. Some elements of romantic comedy remain staples of modern popular television soap operas, where clearly defined "villains," "heroes," and "heroines" are easy to root for or against. In serious drama, the two threads of romantic and satiric comedy have been woven together in the same play by some of the nineteenth- and twentieth-century authors of comedies of manners listed above: Wilde (*The Importance of Being Earnest*), Shaw (*Pygmalion*), and Henley (*Am I Blue?*), for instance.

Some Ideologies of Comedy

Let's now consider some of the qualities of dramatic comedy that have predominated in the literary repertoire of the theater in the Western world—as opposed to the types or subgenres of comedies that have been written.

The tradition of satiric comedy pretty clearly has a purpose of identifying some personality type or behavior to be made the object of ridicule and the audience's laughter. If you think about that for a minute, you might realize that some ideology is involved as well: Some standards of correct or incorrect behavior, some definition of foolish people are implicitly the basis for satiric humor. This could be the ideology of an individual playwright, but because drama is a social art form, the ideology of the audience is also important if satire is to succeed. The audience has to be at least willing to see certain things the same way the playwright does; the audience and the playwright have to agree, more or less, that a certain behavior or personality is foolish and deserving of laughter. This agreement, or harmonious ideological interaction, suggests that satiric comedy tries to perform a social function by singling out personality types and behaviors that clash with some part of the dominant ideology. In one age, this might be the religious hypocrite who subverts a man's reason; in another, it might be the crude *nouveau riche* social climber who lacks the grace and *savoir faire* of sophisticated society; in another, the tightwad who doesn't realize that his miserliness keeps him from enjoying the simple pleasures of life.

As one indication of this ideology, the seventeenth-century French comic dramatist Molière wrote that the purpose of comedy is to "correct men's vices by holding them up to laughter." The play tries to enlist the audience's agreement that some behavior is a vice and that it and the person who exhibits it should be laughed at. If people in the audience are concerned with social conformity, they will presumably have an interest in correcting these vices in themselves and others. Of course there's no guarantee this will happen. Readers and theatergoers are always free to read against the grain of any text, but that can be especially hard to do in the case of theater. What is presented on stage, or even on film, has a powerful persuasive effect, and the circumstances of viewing drama in an auditorium full of people laughing heartily at the folly of a character on the stage or screen make it hard to resist the ideology that is being promoted.

Text Strategies of Satiric Comedy

What text strategies of drama does satiric comedy use to accomplish its purposes? For simplicity's sake, I will divide these into language and plot. With language, satiric comedy can have characters say humorous things to or about the satirized character, provoking the audience's laughter. Or the satirized character himself (or herself) can say things that make other characters or the audience laugh at him. In the latter case, **verbal irony** is involved since, presumably, the satirized character doesn't understand his or her words as funny in the way the audience or other characters do. In both cases, knowing and unknowing are involved: The audience and the playwright or the audience and some characters together know that the satirized character is talking foolishly; the satirized character of course does not know this—and often the more she or he doesn't know it, the funnier the comedy is.

Satiric comedy can also use plot structure to accomplish its purpose. A basic text strategy of comedy is a plot that turns out happily for the audience and for those characters who are identified as deserving happiness. For characters who are being satirized, however, things turn out unhappily. Not that they die or are mutilated; they usually suffer some social punishment within the world of the play—having their plans foiled, being laughed out of town or hauled off to jail, being exposed for the fools they are. Presumably the audience leaves the theater feeling good for the characters they like and feeling better than the characters they don't like.

Text Strategies and Ideology in Romantic Comedy

Plays in the tradition of romantic comedy may have a less obvious social purpose, and their ideology may not seem so close to the surface. The general concern of romantic comedies with the trials and tribulations and eventual happiness of young lovers reveals the presence of ideology nonetheless. In a romantic comedy, the audience presumably wants to see things work out for the young lovers, for them to overcome the obstacles that stand in their way. By posing and then banishing a threat to attractive characters like these, romantic comedy ultimately reassures its audience that love will conquer all and that the world really loves lovers.

Furthermore, romantic comedies typically end with a marriage, perhaps more than one if two characters who didn't realize they were in love get caught up in the general air of good feeling radiated by the successful young lovers and decide they too should be married. Marriage is an important institution in our culture because it signifies not only individual happiness but domestic and social order and continuity. Thus plot structure is the main text strategy to reinforce ideology in romantic comedies.

The importance of plot structure in both satiric and romantic comedies suggests something essential about comedy: that it is a *pattern* analogous to tragedy. A character or characters move from misfortune (though of a relatively mild kind) to happiness. The experience for the audience or reader might be a movement from anxiety to satisfaction. Within this pattern, there may be and probably are humorous elements—in language, situation, or physical action. However, it's worth distinguishing between the *humorous* in these terms and the *comic* in terms of the overall pattern. Some plays (as you have seen in *Hamlet*) include humorous elements within the overall tragic pattern.

Shakespearean Comedy

If your literary experience has been broadened before you read a play, your interaction with the text will be both more complex and more satisfying than if you brought less in the way of literary experience to the reading situation. The reading you have done in this and the previous chapter has, presumably, broadened your literary experience with respect to Shakespeare's theater and dramatic comedy. In addition, if you have read Shakespeare's *Hamlet*, your literary experience has broadened. (See Chapter 19, pages 964–965, if you need a refresher on the language and grammar of Shakespearean English.) Chapter 19 also reminded you of the many gaps in any play and particularly in any Shakespearean play, and it suggested you be conscious of the reading strategies of consistency building and maintaining a wandering viewpoint as you attempt to process a Shakespearean tragedy. Those same things apply when you read a Shakespearean comedy.

I will try to broaden your repertoire just a bit further by briefly mentioning some of the popular conventions of dramatic comedy in Shakespeare's culture and by asking you to consider anew how issues of knowing versus unknowing may be involved in a Shakespearean comedy, as they are in all drama.

Reading and Responding: A Shakespearean Comedy

This chapter has already mentioned how Renaissance English drama rediscovered the plays of Roman comedians such as Plautus. Conventions such as characters in disguise and the inevitable cases of mistaken identity that result were established in these ancient plays and were repopularized in Shakespeare's time. Shakespeare's first play, *The Comedy of Errors* (1588), reworks a situation derived from Plautus concerning the adventures of identical twins lost in a shipwreck. *As You Like It* (1599) involves aristocratic characters lost in a wood and assuming disguised identities. One of Shakespeare's best known comic characters, Falstaff (in *Henry IV* Part 1, 1597; Part 2, 1598) is modeled after the "braggart soldier" in one of Plautus' plays. Because Italy was both fashionable and slightly exotic to London audiences, Italian settings were also popular in Elizabethan plays: Several of Shakespeare's early plays—*The Taming of the Shrew* (1593), *Two Gentlemen of Verona* (1593), *Romeo and Juliet* (1594), *The Merchant of Venice* (1596), and *Much Ado About Nothing* (1598)— are set in Italy. These kinds of situations, characters, and settings were likely ingredients for a play originally written to be performed before London law students as part of their annual Christmas season revels, as scholars believe Shakespeare's *Twelfth Night* was, in 1602.

The conventions of lost twins, disguise, and mistaken identity also easily involve questions of knowing and unknowing. Just to cite a few of these, characters in disguise know their own identities, and so does the audience, but other characters either don't know the truth about who these characters are or they mistake them for other people. There are great possibilities for humor here, and the confusion that results lends itself nicely to the comic pattern.

Characters can also conspire with other characters in a disguise game played at the expense of other characters who mistake the disguise for someone's true identity. The audience can enjoy this subterfuge and scheming as well. If the comic pattern holds, the disguises will be dropped, the mistaken identities cleared up, and whoever is "lost" will be found somehow at the end of the play. All, presumably, will come out of unknowing into full knowing, and the audience will also know this has happened. In a more serious vein (if a reader chooses to look for this in comedy, or if a director chooses to emphasize it in production), the issue of a person's ability or inability to know his or her own identity may be raised. Characters may have the chance to come to know themselves better or differently from the way they knew themselves when lost or disguised.

At the beginning of this chapter you were promised some comic relief. By now, you may be wondering if that is ever going to come. You've waited long enough! Now I invite you to enjoy some comedy. As with *Hamlet*, however, you may find it easier and more enjoyable to break the reading of the following play up into smaller segments. For that reason, each act of the play reprinted below is followed by response statement questions for that act alone. Response statement questions for the entire play follow Act 5.

William Shakespeare   1564–1616

Twelfth Night; or, What You Will   1600

[*Dramatis Personae*

Orsino,   Duke (or Count) of Illyria
Valentine,   gentleman attending on Orsino
Curio,   gentleman attending on Orsino

Viola, a shipwrecked lady, later disguised as Cesario
Sebastian, twin brother of Viola
Antonio, a sea captain, friend to Sebastian
Captain of the shipwrecked vessel

Olivia, a rich countess of Illyria
Maria, gentlewoman in Olivia's household
Sir Toby Belch, Olivia's uncle
Sir Andrew Aguecheek, a companion of Sir Toby
Malvolio, steward of Olivia's household
Fabian, a member of Olivia's household
Feste, a clown, also called *Fool,* Olivia's jester

A Priest
First Officer
Second Officer
Lords, Sailors, Musicians, and other Attendants
Scene: A city in Illyria, and the seacoast near it]

Act 1, Scene 1

Enter Orsino Duke of Illyria, Curio, and other lords [with musicians].

ORSINO: If music be the food of love, play on;
  Give me excess of it, that surfeiting,
  The appetite may sicken and so die.
  That strain again! It had a dying fall;   4
  O, it came o'er my ear like the sweet sound
  That breathes upon a bank of violets,
  Stealing and giving odor. Enough, no more.
  'Tis not so sweet now as it was before.
  O spirit of love, how quick and fresh art thou,   9
  That, notwithstanding thy capacity
  Receiveth as the sea, naught enters there,
  Of what validity and pitch soe'er,   12
  But falls into abatement and low price   13
  Even in a minute! So full of shapes is fancy   14
  That it alone is high fantastical.   15
CURIO: Will you go hunt, my lord?
ORSINO: What, Curio?
CURIO: The hart.
ORSINO: Why, so I do, the noblest that I have.   19
  O, when mine eyes did see Olivia first,
  Methought she purged the air of pestilence.

1.1. Location: Orsino's court. s.d. Illyria An imaginary place, nominally on the east coast of
the Adriatic Sea, but with a suggestion also of "illusion" and "delirium."
  4 fall cadence   **9 quick and fresh** keen and hungry
  12 validity value **pitch** superiority (Literally, the highest point of a falcon's flight.)
  13 abatement depreciation. (The lover's brain entertains innumerable fantasies but soon tires of
  them all.)
  14 shapes imagined forms **fancy** love
  15 it . . . fantastical it surpasses everything else in imaginative power
  19 the noblest . . . have i.e., my noblest part, my heart (punning on *hart*)

That instant was I turned into a hart,
And my desires, like fell and cruel hounds,   23
E'er since pursue me.   24

Enter Valentine.

How now, what news from her?
VALENTINE: So please my lord, I might not be admitted,
But from her handmaid do return this answer:
The element itself, till seven years' heat,   28
Shall not behold her face at ample view;
But like a cloistress she will vèilèd walk,   30
And water once a day her chamber round
With eye-offending brine—all this to season   32
A brother's dead love, which she would keep fresh   33
And lasting in her sad remembrance.
ORSINO: O, she that hath a heart of that fine frame   35
To pay this debt of love but to a brother,
How will she love, when the rich golden shaft   37
Hath killed the flock of all affections else   38
That live in her; when liver, brain, and heart,   39
These sovereign thrones, are all supplied, and filled   40
Her sweet perfections, with one self king!   41
Away before me to sweet beds of flowers.
Love-thoughts lie rich when canopied with bowers.

Exeunt.

Act 1, Scene 2

Enter Viola, a Captain, and sailors.

VIOLA: What country, friends, is this?
CAPTAIN: This is Illyria, lady.
VIOLA: And what should I do in Illyria?
My brother he is in Elysium.   4
Perchance he is not drowned. What think you, sailors?   5
CAPTAIN: It is perchance that you yourself were saved.   6

---

23 fell fierce
24 pursue me (Alludes to the story in Ovid of Actaeon, who, having seen Diana bathing, was transformed into a stag and killed by his own hounds.)
28 element sky   **seven years' heat** seven summers
30 cloistress nun secluded in a religious community
32 season keep fresh (playing on the idea of the salt in her tears)
33 A brother's dead love her love for her dead brother and the memory of his love for her
35 frame construction
37 golden shaft Cupid's golden-tipped arrow, causing love. (His lead-tipped arrow causes aversion.)
38 affections else other feelings
39 liver, brain, and heart (in medieval and Elizabethan psychology, these organs were the seats of the passions, of thought, and of feeling.)
40 supplied filled
40–41 and . . . perfections and her sweet perfections filled
41 self king single lord (the object of her entire affection)
1.2. Location: The seacoast.
 4 Elysium classical abode of the blessed dead
 5–6 Perchance . . . perchance perhaps . . . by mere chance

VIOLA: O, my poor brother! And so perchance may he be.
CAPTAIN: True, madam, and to comfort you with chance,   8
    Assure yourself, after our ship did split,
    When you and those poor number saved with you
    Hung on our driving boat, I saw your brother,   11
    Most provident in peril, bind himself,
    Courage and hope both teaching him the practice,
    To a strong mast that lived upon the sea;   14
    Where, like Arion on the dolphin's back,   15
    I saw him hold acquaintance with the waves
    So long as I could see.
VIOLA: For saying so, there's gold. [*She gives money.*]
    Mine own escape unfoldeth to my hope,   19
    Whereto thy speech serves for authority,   20
    The like of him. Know'st thou this country?   21
CAPTAIN: Ay, madam, well, for I was bred and born
    Not three hours' travel from this very place.
VIOLA: Who governs here?
CAPTAIN: A noble duke, in nature as in name.
VIOLA: What is his name?
CAPTAIN: Orsino.
VIOLA: Orsino! I have heard my father name him.
    He was a bachelor then.
CAPTAIN: And so is now, or was so very late;
    For but a month ago I went from hence,
    And then 'twas fresh in murmur—as, you know,   32
    What great ones do the less will prattle of—   33
    That he did seek the love of fair Olivia.
VIOLA: What's she?
CAPTAIN: A virtuous maid, the daughter of a count
    That died some twelvemonth since, then leaving her
    In the protection of his son, her brother,
    Who shortly also died; for whose dear love,
    They say, she hath abjured the sight
    And company of men.
VIOLA: O, that I served that lady,
    And might not be delivered to the world   43
    Till I had made mine own occasion mellow,   44
    What my estate is!   45
CAPTAIN: That were hard to compass,   46
    Because she will admit no kind of suit,
    No, not the Duke's.   48

---

8 chance i.e., what one may hope that chance will bring about
11 driving drifting, driven by the seas   **14 lived** i.e., kept afloat
15 Arion a Greek poet who so charmed the dolphins with his lyre that they saved him when he
   leaped into the sea to escape murderous sailors
19–21 unfoldeth . . . him offers a hopeful example that he may have escaped similarly, to which
   hope your speech provides support
32 murmur rumor   **33 less** social inferiors
43 delivered revealed, made known (with suggestion of "born")
44 mellow ready or convenient (to be made known)
45 estate position in society   **46 compass** bring about, encompass
48 not not even

VIOLA: There is a fair behavior in thee, Captain,
And though that nature with a beauteous wall
Doth oft close in pollution, yet of thee   50
I will believe thou hast a mind that suits
With this thy fair and outward character.   53
I prithee, and I'll pay thee bounteously,
Conceal me what I am, and be my aid
For such disguise as haply shall become   56
The form of my intent. I'll serve this duke.   57
Thou shalt present me as an eunuch to him.   58
It may be worth thy pains, for I can sing
And speak to him in many sorts of music
That will allow me very worth his service.   61
What else may hap, to time I will commit;
Only shape thou thy silence to my wit.   63
CAPTAIN: Be you his eunuch, and your mute I'll be;   64
When my tongue blabs, then let mine eyes not see.
VIOLA: I thank thee. Lead me on.   *Exeunt.*

Act 1, Scene 3

Enter Sir Toby [Belch] and Maria.

SIR TOBY: What a plague means my niece to take the death of her brother thus? I am
sure care's an enemy to life.
MARIA: By my troth, Sir Toby, you must come in earlier o' nights. Your cousin, my   3
lady, takes great exceptions to your ill hours.
SIR TOBY: Why, let her except before excepted.   5
MARIA: Ay, but you must confine yourself within the modest limits of order.   6
SIR TOBY: Confine? I'll confine myself no finer than I am. These clothes are good   7
enough to drink in, and so be these boots too. An they be not, let them hang   8
themselves in their own straps.
MARIA: That quaffing and drinking will undo you. I heard my lady talk of it yester-
day, and of a foolish knight that you brought in one night here to be her wooer.
SIR TOBY: Who, Sir Andrew Aguecheek?
MARIA: Ay, he.
SIR TOBY: He's as tall a man as any's in Illyria.
MARIA: What's that to the purpose?   14
SIR TOBY: Why, he has three thousand ducats a year.
MARIA: Ay, but he'll have but a year in all these ducats. He's a very fool and a prodigal.   16
                                                                                          17

---

50 though that though
53 character face or features as indicating moral qualities
56–57 as haply . . . intent as may suit the nature of my purpose
58 eunuch castrato, high-voiced singer   **61 allow** prove
63 wit plan, invention
64 mute silent attendant (sometimes used of nonspeaking actors)
1.3. Location: Olivia's house.   **3 cousin** kinswoman
 5 let . . . excepted i.e., let her take exception to my conduct all she wants; I don't care. (Plays
    on the legal phrase *exceptis excipiendis,* "with the exceptions before named.")
 6 modest moderate
 7 I'll . . . finer (1) I'll constrain myself no more rigorously (2) I'll dress myself no more finely
 8 An if
14 tall brave (But Maria pretends to take the word in the common sense.)
16 ducats coins worth about four or five shillings
17 he'll . . . ducats he'll spend all his money within a year

Sir Toby: Fie, that you'll say so! He plays o' the viol-de-gamboys, and speaks three or   18
four languages word for word without book, and hath all the good gifts of nature.   19

Maria: He hath indeed, almost natural, for, besides that he's a fool, he's a great quar-   20
reler, and but that he hath the gift of a coward to allay the gust he hath in quar-   21
reling, 'tis thought among the prudent he would quickly have the gift of a grave.

Sir Toby: By this hand, they are scoundrels and substractors that say so of him.   23
Who are they?

Maria: They that add, moreover, he's drunk nightly in your company.

Sir Toby: With drinking healths to my niece. I'll drink to her as long as there is a
passage in my throat and drink in Illyria. He's a coward and a coistrel that will   27
not drink to my niece till his brains turn o' the toe like a parish top. What,   28
wench? *Castiliano vulgo!* For here comes Sir Andrew Agueface.   29

Enter Sir Andrew [Aguecheek].

Sir Andrew: Sir Toby Belch! How now, Sir Toby Belch?

Sir Toby: Sweet Sir Andrew!

Sir Andrew: [*to Maria*]   Bless you, fair shrew.   32

Maria: And you too, sir.

Sir Toby: Accost, Sir Andrew, accost.   34

Sir Andrew: What's that?

Sir Toby: My niece's chambermaid.   36

Sir Tndrew: Good Mistress Accost, I desire better acquaintance.

Maria: My name is Mary, sir.

Sir Andrew: Good Mistress Mary Accost—

Sir Toby: You mistake, night. "Accost" is front her, board her, woo her, assail her.   40

Sir Andrew: By my troth, I would not undertake her in this company. Is that the   41
meaning of "accost"?

Maria: Fare you well, gentlemen.   [*Going.*]

Sir Toby: An thou let part so, Sir Andrew, would thou mightst never draw sword again.   44

Sir Andrew: An you part so, mistress, I would I might never draw sword again. Fair
lady, do you think you have fools in hand?

Maria: Sir, I have not you by the hand.   47

Sir Andrew: Marry, but you shall have, and here's my hand.   [*He gives   48
her his hand.*]

---

18 viol-de-gamboys viola da gamba, leg-viol, bass viol
19 without book by heart   **20 natural** (with a play on the sense "born idiot")
21 gift natural ability (But shifted to mean "present" in line 22.) **allay the gust** moderate the taste
23 substractors i.e., detractors   **27 coistrel** horse-groom, base fellow
28 parish top a large top provided by the parish to be spun by whipping, apparently for exercise
29 Castiliano vulgo (Of uncertain meaning. Possibly Sir Toby is saying "Speak of the devil!"
Castiliano is the name adopted by a devil in Haughton's *Grim the Collier of Croydon.*) **Agueface** (Like *Aguecheek*, this name betokens the thin, pale countenance of one suffering from
an ague.)
32 shrew i.e., diminutive creature (but with probably unintended suggestion of shrewishness)
34 Accost go alongside (a nautical term), i.e., greet her, address her
36 chambermaid lady-in-waiting (a gentlewoman, not one who would do menial tasks)
40 front confront, come alongside   **board** greet, approach (as though preparing to board in a
naval encounter)
41 undertake have to do with (here with unintended sexual suggestion, to which Maria mirth-
fully replies with her jokes about *dry jests, barren,* and *buttery-bar*)
44 an . . . part if you let her leave
47 have . . . hand i.e., have to deal with fools (But Maria puns on the literal sense.)
48 Marry i.e., indeed (Originally, "By the Virgin Mary.")

MARIA: Now, sir, thought is free. I pray you, bring your hand to the buttery-bar, and 49
let it drink.

SIR ANDREW: Wherefore, sweetheart? What's your metaphor?

MARIA: It's dry, sir.

SIR ANDREW: Why, I think so. I am not such an ass but I can keep my hand dry. But 52
what's your jest?

MARIA: A dry jest, sir.

SIR ANDREW: Are you full of them? 55

MARIA: Ay, sir, I have them at my fingers' ends. Marry, now I let go your hand, I am 57
barren. 58

[*She let go his hand.*] *Exit Maria.*

SIR TOBY: O knight, thou lack'st a cop of canary? When did I see thee so put down? 59

SIR ANDREW: Never in your life, I think, unless you see canary put me down. Me- 60
thinks sometimes I have no more wit than a Christian or an ordinary man has.
But I am a great eater of beef, and I believe that does harm to my wit.

SIR TOBY: No question.

SIR ANDREW: An I thought that, I'd forswear it. I'll ride home tomorrow, Sir Toby.

SIR TOBY: *Pourquoi,* my dear knight?

SIR ANDREW: What is "*pourquoi*"? Do or not do? I would I had bestowed that time in 65
the tongues that I have in fencing, dancing, and bearbaiting. O, had I but fol- 67
lowed the arts! 68

SIR TOBY: Then hadst thou had an excellent head of hair.

SIR ANDREW: Why, would that have mended my hair? 70

SIR TOBY: Past question, for thou seest it will not curl by nature.

SIR ANDREW: But it becomes me well enough, does 't not?

SIR TOBY: Excellent. It hangs like flax on a distaff; and I hope to see a huswife take 73
thee between her legs and spin it off. 74

SIR ANDREW: Faith, I'll home tomorrow, Sir Toby. Your niece will not be seen, or if she
be, it's four to one she'll none of me. The Count himself here hard by woos her. 76

SIR TOBY: She'll none o' the Count. She'll not match above her degree, neither in es- 77
tate, years, nor wit; I have heard her swear 't. Tut, there's life in 't, man. 78

SIR ANDREW: I'll stay a month longer. I am a fellow o' the strangest mind i' the world;
I delight in masques and revels sometimes altogether.

---

49 thought is free i.e., I may think what I like. (Proverbial; replying to *do you think . . . in hand,*
above.)   **buttery-bar** ledge on top of the half-door to the buttery or the wine cellar
52 dry thirsty; also dried up, a sign of age and sexual debility
55 dry (1) ironic (2) dull, barren (referring to Sir Andrew)
57 at my fingers' ends (1) at the ready (2) by the hand
58 barren i.e., empty of jests and of Sir Andrew's hand
59 thou . . . canary i.e., you look as if you need a drink (*Canary* is sweet wine from the Canary
Islands.)
60 put me down (1) baffle my wits (2) lay me out flat
65 Pourquoi why
67 tongues languages (Sir Toby then puns on "tongs," curling irons.)
68 the arts the liberal arts, learning (But Sir Toby plays on the phrase as meaning "artifice," the
antithesis of *nature.*)
70 mended improved
73 distaff a staff for holding the flax, tow, or wool in spinning
74 spin it off i.e., (1) treat your flaxen hair as though it were flax on a distaff to be spun (2) cause
you to lose hair as a result of venereal disease. (*Huswife* suggests "hussy," "whore.")
76 Count i.e., Duke Orsino, sometimes referred to as Count   **hard** near
77 degree social position   **estate** fortune, social position
78 there's life in 't i.e., while there's life there's hope

SIR TOBY: Art thou good at these kickshawses, knight?   81

SIR ANDREW: As any man in Illyria, whatsoever he be, under the degree of my betters,   82
and yet I will not compare with an old man.   83

SIR TOBY: What is thy excellence in a galliard, knight?   84

SIR ANDREW: Faith, I can cut a caper.   85

SIR TOBY: And I can cut the mutton to 't.

SIR ANDREW: And I think I have the back-trick simply as strong as any man in Illyria.   87

SIR TOBY: Wherefore are these things hid? Wherefore have these gifts a curtain before 'em? Are they like to take dust, like Mistress Mall's picture? Why dost thou   89
not go to church in a galliard and come home in a coranto? My very walk   90
should be a jig; I would not so much as make water but in a sink-a-pace. What   91
dost thou mean? Is it a world to hide virtues in? I did think, by the excellent   92
constitution of thy leg, it was formed under the star of a galliard.   93

SIR ANDREW: Ay, 'tis strong, and it does indifferent well in a dun-colored stock. Shall   94
we set about some revels?

SIR TOBY: What shall we do else? Were we not born under Taurus?   96

SIR ANDREW: Taurus? That's sides and heart.

SIR TOBY: No, sir, it is legs and thighs. Let me see thee caper. [*Sir Andrew capers.*]
Ha, higher! Ha, ha, excellent!   *Exeunt.*

Act 1, Scene 4

Enter Valentine, and Viola in man's attire.

VALENTINE: If the Duke continue these favors towards you, Cesario, you are like to
be much advanced. He hath known you but three days, and already you are no
stranger.

VIOLA: You either fear his humor or my negligence, that you call in question the   4
continuance of his love. Is he inconstant, sir, in his favors?

VALENTINE: No, believe me.

Enter Duke [Orsino], Curio, and attendants.

VIOLA: I thank you. Here comes the Count.

ORSINO: Who saw Cesario, ho?

VIOLA: On your attendance, my lord, here.   9

---

81 kickshawses delicacies, fancy trifles (From the French *quelque chose*.)
82 under . . . betters excepting those who are above me
83 old man i.e., one experienced through age   **84 galliard** lively dance in triple time
85 cut a caper make a lively leap (But Sir Toby puns on the *caper* used to make a sauce served
with mutton. *Mutton*, in turn, suggests "whore.")
87 back-trick backward step in the galliard
89 like to take likely to collect   **Mistress Mall's picture** i.e., perhaps the portrait of some
woman protected from light and dust, as many pictures were, by curtain
90 coranto lively running dance
91 sink-a-pace dance like the galliard. (French *cinquepace*.)
92 virtues talents
93 under . . . galliard i.e., under a star favorable to dancing
94 indifferent well well enough (Said complacently.)   **dun-colored stock** mouse-colored
stocking
96 Taurus zodiacal sign (Sir Andrew is mistaken, since Leo governed sides and hearts in medical
astrology. Taurus governed legs and thighs, or, more commonly, neck and throat.)
1.4. Location: Orsino's court.
 4 humor changeableness
 9 On your attendance ready to do you service

ORSINO: Stand you awhile aloof. [*The others stand aside.*] Cesario,
             Thou know'st no less but all. I have unclasped
             To thee the book even of my secret soul.
             Therefore, good youth, address thy gait unto her;
             Be not denied access, stand at her doors,   13
             And tell them, there thy fixèd foot shall grow
             Till thou have audience.   15
VIOLA: Sure, my noble lord,
             If she be so abandoned to her sorrow
             As it is spoke, she never will admit me.
ORSINO: Be clamorous and leap all civil bounds   20
             Rather than make unprofited return.
VIOLA: Say I do speak with her, my lord, what then?
ORSINO: O, then unfold the passion of my love;
             Surprise her with discourse of my dear faith.   24
             It shall become thee well to act my woes;   25
             She will attend it better in thy youth
             Than in a nuncio's of more grave aspect.   27
VIOLA: I think not so, my lord.
ORSINO: Dear lad, believe it;
             For they shall yet belie thy happy years
             That say thou art a man. Diana's lip
             Is not more smooth and rubious; thy small pipe   32
             Is as the maiden's organ, shrill and sound,   33
             And all is semblative a woman's part.   34
             I know thy constellation is right apt   35
             For this affair.—Some four or five attend him.
             All, if you will, for I myself am best
             When least in company.—Prosper well in this,
             And thou shalt live as freely as thy lord,
             To call his fortunes thine.
VIOLA: I'll do my best
             To woo your lady. [*Aside.*] Yet a barful strife!
             Who'er I woo, myself would be his wife.   *Exeunt.*   42

Act 1, Scene 5

Enter Maria and Clown [Feste].

MARIA: Nay, either tell me where thou hast been, or I will not open my lips so wide as
             a bristle may enter in way of thy excuse. My lady will hang thee for thy absence.
FESTE: Let her hang me. He that is well hanged in this world needs to fear no colors.   3

---

13 **address thy gait** go
20 **civil bounds** bounds of civility   15 **them** i.e., Olivia's servants
24 **Surprise** take by storm (A military term.)   **dear** heartfelt
25 **become** suit   27 **nuncio's** messenger's
32 **rubious** ruby red   **pipe** voice, throat   33 **shrill and sound** high and clear, uncracked
34 **semblative** resembling, like
35 **constellation** i.e., nature as determined by your horoscope
42 **barful strife** endeavor full of impediments
1.5. Location: Olivia's house.
 3 **fear no colors** i.e., fear no foe, fear nothing (with pun on *colors,* worldly deceptions, and
   "collars," halters or nooses)

MARIA: Make that good.   4
FESTE: He shall see none to fear.   5
MARIA: A good Lenten answer. I can tell thee where that saying was born, of "I fear   6
  no colors."
FESTE: Where, good Mistress Mary?
MARIA: In the wars, and that may you be bold to say in your foolery.   9
FESTE: Well, God give them wisdom that have it; and those that are fools, let them
  use their talents.   11
MARIA: Yet you will be hanged for being so long absent; or to be turned away, is not   12
  that as good as a hanging to you?
FESTE: Many a good hanging prevents a bad marriage; and for turning away, let sum-   14
  mer bear it out.   15
MARIA: You are resolute, then?
FESTE: Not so, neither, but I am resolved on two points.   17
MARIA: That if one break, the other will hold; or if both break, your gaskins fall.   18
FESTE: Apt, in good faith, very apt. Well, go thy way. If Sir Toby would leave drinking,
  thou wert as witty a piece of Eve's flesh as any in Illyria.   20
MARIA: Peace, you rogue, no more o' that. Here comes my lady. Make your excuse
  wisely, you were best.   [Exit.]   22

Enter Lady Olivia with Malvolio, [and attendants].

FESTE: [aside] Wit, an 't be thy will, put me into good fooling! Those wits that   23
  think they have thee do very oft prove fools, and I that am sure I lack thee may
  pass for a wise man. For what says Quinapalus? "Better a witty fool than a fool-   25
  ish wit."—God bless thee, lady!
OLIVIA: [to attendants]   Take the fool away.
FESTE: Do you not hear, fellows? Take away the lady.
OLIVIA: Go to, you're a dry fool. I'll no more of you. Besides, you grow dishonest.   29
FESTE: Two faults, madonna, that drink and good counsel will amend. For give the   30
  dry fool drink, then is the fool not dry. Bid the dishonest man mend himself; if
  he mend, he is no longer dishonest; if he cannot, let the botcher mend him. Any-   32
  thing that's mended is but patched; virtue that transgresses is but patched with   33

---

4 Make that good explain that
5 He . . . fear i.e., he'll be dead and unable to see anything
6 Lenten meager, scanty (like Lenten fare), and morbid
9 In the wars (where *colors* would mean "military standards, enemy flags"—the literal meaning
  of the proverb)   **that . . . foolery** that's an answer you may be bold to use in your fool's
  conundrums
11 talents abilities (also alluding to the parable of the talents, Matthew 25:14–29, and to "talons,"
  claws)
12 turned away dismissed (possibly also meaning "turned off," "hanged")
14 good hanging (with possible bawdy pun on "being well hung")   **for** as for
14–15 let . . . out i.e., let mild weather make dismissal endurable
17 points (Maria plays on the meaning "laces used to hold up hose or breeches.")
18 gaskins wide breeches
20 thou . . . Illyria (Feste may be observing ironically that Maria is as likely to prove witty as Sir
  Toby is to give up drinking; or he may hint at a match between the two.)
22 you were best it would be best for you   **23 an 't** if it
25 Quinapalus (Feste's invented authority.)
29 Go to (An expression of annoyance or expostulation.)   **dry** dull
30 madonna my lady
32 botcher mender of old clothes and shoes (playing on two senses of *mend*: "reform" and
  "repair")
32–33 Anything . . . patched i.e., life is patched or parti-colored like the Fool's garment, a mix
  of good and bad

sin, and sin that amends is but patched with virtue. If that this simple syllogism will serve, so; if it will not, what remedy? As there is no true cuckold but calamity, so beauty's a flower. The lady bade take away the fool; therefore I say again, take her away. 35 36

OLIVIA: Sir, I bade them take away you.

FESTE: Misprision in the highest degree! Lady, *cucullus non facit monachum;* that's as much to say as I wear not motley in my brain. Good madonna, give me leave to prove you a fool. 39 40

OLIVIA: Can you do it?

FESTE: Dexterously, good madonna.

OLIVIA: Make your proof.

FESTE: I must catechize you for it, madonna. Good my mouse of virtue, answer me. 45

OLIVIA: Well, sir, for want of other idleness, I'll bide your proof. 46

FESTE: Good madonna, why mourn'st thou?

OLIVIA: Good fool, for my brother's death.

FESTE: I think his soul is in hell, madonna.

OLIVIA: I know his soul is in heaven, fool.

FESTE: The more fool, madonna, to mourn for your brother's soul, being in heaven. Take away the fool, gentlemen.

OLIVIA: What think you of this fool, Malvolio? Doth he not mend? 53

MALVOLIO: Yes, and shall do till the pangs of death shake him. Infirmity, that decays the wise, doth ever make the better fool.

FESTE: God send you, sir, a speedy infirmity for the better increasing your folly! Sir Toby will be sworn that I am no fox, but he will not pass his word for twopence that you are no fool. 57

OLIVIA: How say you to that, Malvolio?

MALVOLIO: I marvel your ladyship takes delight in such a barren rascal. I saw him put down the other day with an ordinary fool that has no more brain than a stone. Look you now, he's out of his guard already. Unless you laugh and minister occasion to him, he is gagged. I protest I take these wise men that crow so at these set kind of fools no better than the fools' zanies. 61 62 63 64

OLIVIA: O, you are sick of self-love, Malvolio, and taste with a distempered appetite. To be generous, guiltless, and of free disposition is to take those things for birdbolts that you deem cannon bullets. There is no slander in an allowed fool, 65 66 67

---

35 so well and good
35–36 As . . . flower i.e., Olivia has wedded calamity but will not be faithful to it, for the natural course is to seize the moment of youth and beauty before we lose it
39 Misprision mistake, misunderstanding (A legal term meaning a wrongful action or misdemeanor.) **cucullus . . . monachum** the cowl does not make the monk
40 motley the many-colored garments of jesters
45 Good . . . virtue my good, virtuous mouse (A term of endearment.)
46 idleness pastime **bide** endure
53 mend i.e., improve, grow more amusing (But Malvolio uses the word to mean "grow more like a fool.")
57 pass give
61 with by
62 out of his guard defenseless, unprovided with a witty answer
62–63 minister occasion provide opportunity (for his fooling) **protest** avow, declare **crow** laugh stridently
64 set artificial, stereotyped **zanies** assistants, aping attendants
65 distempered diseased
66 generous noble-minded **free** magnanimous
66–67 bird-bolts blunt arrows for shooting small birds
67 allowed licensed (to speak freely)

though he do nothing but rail; nor no railing in a known discreet man, though   68
he do nothing but reprove.   69

FESTE: Now Mercury endue thee with leasing, for thou speak'st well of fools!   70

Enter Maria.

MARIA: Madam, there is at the gate a young gentleman much desires to speak with you.

OLIVIA: From the Count Orsino, is it?

MARIA: I know not, madam. 'Tis a fair young man, and well attended.

OLIVIA: Who of my people hold him in delay?

MARIA: Sir Toby, madam, your kinsman.

OLIVIA: Fetch him off, I pray you. He speaks nothing but madman. Fie on him! [*Exit*   76
Maria.] Go you, Malvolio. If it be a suit from the Count, I am sick, or not at
home; what you will, to dismiss it. *(Exit Malvolio.)* Now you see, sir, how your
fooling grows old, and people dislike it.

FESTE: Thou hast spoke for us, madonna, as if thy eldest son should be a fool; whose
skull Jove cram with brains, for—here he comes—

Enter Sir Toby.

one of thy kin has a most weak *pia mater.*   82

OLIVIA: By mine honor, half drunk. What is he at the gate, cousin?

SIR TOBY: A gentleman.

OLIVIA: A gentleman? What gentleman?

SIR TOBY: 'Tis a gentleman here—[*He belches.*] A plague o' these pickle-herring! [*To
Feste.*] How now, sot?   87

FESTE: Good Sir Toby.

OLIVIA: Cousin, cousin, how have you come so early by this lethargy?   89

SIR TOBY: Lechery? I defy lechery. There's one at the gate.

OLIVIA: Ay, marry, what is he?

SIR TOBY: Let him be the devil an he will, I care not. Give me faith, say I. Well, it's all   92
one.   *Exit*   93

OLIVIA: What's a drunken man like, Fool?

FESTE: Like a drowned man, a fool, and a madman. One draft above heat makes him   95
a fool, the second mads him, and a third drowns him.

OLIVIA: Go thou and seek the crowner, and let him sit o' my coz; for he's in the third   97
degree of drink, he's drowned. Go, look after him.

FESTE: He is but mad yet, madonna; and the fool shall look to the madman.   [*Exit.*]

Enter Malvolio.

MALVOLIO: Madam, yond young fellow swears he will speak with you. I told him you
were sick; he takes on him to understand so much, and therefore comes to
speak with you. I told him you were asleep; he seems to have a foreknowledge
of that too, and therefore comes to speak with you. What is to be said to him,
lady? He's fortified against any denial.

68–69 nor . . . reprove (Olivia gently chides Malvolio for not reproving more civilly, while at the
same time tactfully complimenting his sobriety.)
70 Now . . . leasing i.e., may Mercury, the god of deception, make you a skillful liar
76 madman i.e., the words of madness
82 pia mater i.e., brain (actually the soft membrane enclosing the brain)
87 sot (1) fool (2) drunkard   **89 Cousin** kinsman (here, uncle)
92 Give me faith i.e., to resist the devil   **92–93 it's all one** it doesn't matter
95 draft drinking portion   **above heat** above the point needed to make him normally warm
97 crowner coroner   **sit o' my coz** hold an inquest on my kinsman (Sir Toby)

OLIVIA: Tell him he shall not speak with me.

MALVOLIO: He's been told so; and he says he'll stand at your door like a sheriff's post, and be the supporter to a bench, but he'll speak with you.   106

OLIVIA: What kind o' man is he?

MALVOLIO: Why, of mankind.

OLIVIA: What manner of man?

MALVOLIO: Of very ill manner. He'll speak with you, will you or no.

OLIVIA: Of what personage and years is he?

MALVOLIO: Not yet old enough for a man, nor young enough for a boy; as a squash is before 'tis a peascod, or a codling when 'tis almost an apple. 'Tis with him in standing water between boy and man. He is very well-favored, and he speaks very shrewishly. One would think his mother's milk were scarce out of him.   113   114   115   116

OLIVIA: Let him approach. Call in my gentlewoman.

MALVOLIO: Gentlewoman, my lady calls.   *Exit.*

Enter Maria.

OLIVIA: Give me my veil. Come, throw it o'er my face. We'll once more hear Orsino's embassy. [*Olivia veils.*]

Enter Viola.

VIOLA: The honorable lady of the house, which is she?

OLIVIA: Speak to me; I shall answer for her. Your will?

VIOLA: Most radiant, exquisite, and unmatchable beauty—I pray you, tell me if this be the lady of the house, for I never saw her. I would be loath to cast away my speech; for besides that it is excellently well penned, I have taken great pains to con it. Good beauties, let me sustain no scorn; I am very comptible, even to the least sinister usage.   126   127

OLIVIA: Whence came you, sir?

VIOLA: I can say little more than I have studied, and that question's out of my part. Good gentle one, give me modest assurance if you be the lady of the house, that I may proceed in my speech.   130

OLIVIA: Are you a comedian?   132

VIOLA: No, my profound heart; and yet, by the very fangs of malice, I swear I am not that I play. Are you the lady of the house?   133   134

OLIVIA: If I do not usurp myself, I am.   135

VIOLA: Most certain, if you are she, you do usurp yourself; for what is yours to bestow is not yours to reserve. But this is from my commission. I will on with my speech in your praise, and then show you the heart of my message.   136   137

OLIVIA: Come to what is important in 't. I forgive you the praise.   139

---

106 sheriff's post post before the sheriff's door to mark a residence of authority
113 squash unripe pea pod   **114 peascod** pea pod   **codling** unripe apple
114–115 in standing water at the turn of the tide   **well-favored** good-looking
116 shrewishly sharply
126 con learn by heart   **comptible** susceptible, sensitive
127 least sinister slightest discourteous   **130 modest** reasonable
132 comedian actor
133 my profound heart my most wise lady; or, in all sincerity
133–134 by . . . I play i.e., I swear, whatever people may maliciously suppose, I am not what I impersonate
135 do . . . myself am not an imposter
136 usurp yourself i.e., misappropriate yourself, by withholding yourself from love and marriage
137 from outside of
                139 forgive you excuse you from repeating

Viola: Alas, I took great pains to study it, and 'tis poetical.

Olivia: It is the more like to be feigned. I pray you, keep it in. I heard you were saucy at my gates, and allowed your approach rather to wonder at you than to hear you. If you be not mad, begone; if you have reason, be brief. 'Tis not that time of moon with me to make one in so skipping a dialogue.   143 144

Maria: Will you hoist sail, sir? Here lies your way.

Viola: No, good swabber, I am to hull here a little longer.—Some mollification for your giant, sweet lady. Tell me your mind; I am a messenger.   146 147

Olivia: Sure you have some hideous matter to deliver, when the courtesy of it is so fearful. Speak your office.   148 149

Viola: It alone concerns your ear. I bring no overture of war, no taxation of homage. I hold the olive in my hand; my words are as full of peace as matter.   150 151

Olivia: Yet you began rudely. What are you? What would you?   152

Viola: The rudeness that hath appeared in me have I learned from my entertainment. What I am and what I would are as secret as maidenhead—to your ears, divinity; to any other's, profanation.   153

155

Olivia: Give us the place alone. We will hear this divinity. [*Exeunt Maria and attendants.*] Now, sir, what is your text?

Viola: Most sweet lady—

Olivia: A comfortable doctrine, and much may be said of it. Where lies your text?   159

Viola: In Orsino's bosom.

Olivia: In his bosom? In what chapter of his bosom?

Viola: To answer by the method, in the first of his heart.   162

Olivia: O, I have read it. It is heresy. Have you no more to say?

Viola: Good madam, let me see your face.

Olivia: Have you any commission from your lord to negotiate with my face? You are now out of your text. But we will draw the curtain and show you the picture. [*Unveiling.*] Look you, sir, such a one I was this present. Is 't not well done?   166 167

Viola: Excellently done, if God did all.

Olivia: 'Tis in grain, sir; 'twill endure wind and weather.   169

---

143 If . . . mad i.e., if you don't have madness to excuse your saucy behavior, or, if you be not altogether mad(?) Possibly an error for *if . . . but mad* (?)   **reason** sanity
144 moon (The moon was thought to affect lunatics according to its changing phases.)   **make one** take part
146 swabber one in charge of washing the decks (A nautical retort to *hoist sail*.)   **hull** lie with sails furled   **Some . . . for** i.e., please mollify, pacify.
147 giant i.e., the diminutive Maria who, like many giants in medieval romances, is guarding the lady
148 courtesy i.e., complimentary, "poetical" introduction (Or Olivia may refer to Cesario's importunate manner at her gate, as reported by Malvolio.)
149 office commission, business
150 overture declaration (Literally, opening.)   **taxation** demand for the payment.
151 olive olive-branch (signifying peace)
152 Yet . . . rudely i.e., yet you were saucy at my gates
153–154 entertainment reception   **155 divinity** sacred discourse
159 comfortable comforting
162 To . . . method i.e., to continue the metaphor (of delivering a sermon, begun with *divinity* and *what is your text* and continued in *doctrine, heresy,* etc.)
166 out of straying from
167 such . . . present this is a recent portrait of me (Since it was customary to hang curtains in front of pictures, Olivia in unveiling speaks as if she were displaying a picture of herself.)
169 in grain fast dyed

VIOLA: 'Tis beauty truly blent, whose red and white   170
    Nature's own sweet and cunning hand laid on.   171
    Lady, you are the cruel'st she alive
    If you will lead these graces to the grave
    And leave the world no copy.   174

OLIVIA: O, sir, I will not be so hardhearted. I will give out divers schedules of my   175
    beauty. It shall be inventoried, and every particle and utensil labeled to my will: 176
    as, item, two lips, indifferent red; item, two gray eyes, with lids to them; item, one   177
    neck, one chin, and so forth. Were you sent hither to praise me?   178

VIOLA: I see you what you are: you are too proud.
    But, if you were the devil, you are fair.
    My lord and master loves you. O, such love   180
    Could be but recompensed, though you were crowned   182
    The nonpareil of beauty!

OLIVIA: How does he love me?

VIOLA: With adorations, fertile tears,
    With groans that thunder love, with sighs of fire.

OLIVIA: Your lord does know my mind; I cannot love him.
    Yet I suppose him virtuous, know him noble,
    Of great estate, of fresh and stainless youth,
    In voices well divulged, free, learned, and valiant,   190
    And in dimension and the shape of nature   191
    A gracious person. But yet I cannot love him.   192
    He might have took his answer long ago.

VIOLA: If I did love you in my master's flame,   194
    With such a suffering, such a deadly life,   195
    In your denial I would find no sense;
    I would not understand it.

OLIVIA: Why, what would you?

VIOLA: Make me a willow cabin at your gate   199
    And call upon my soul within the house;   200
    Write loyal cantons of contemnèd love   201
    And sing them loud even in the dead of night;
    Hallow your name to the reverberate hills,   203
    And make the babbling gossip of the air   204
    Cry out "Olivia!" O, you should not rest
    Between the elements of air and earth
    But you should pity me!

---

170 blent blended   **171 cunning** skillful

174 copy i.e., a child (But Olivia uses the word to mean "transcript.")

175 schedules inventories   **176 utensil** article, item   **labeled** added as a codicil

177 indifferent somewhat   **178 praise** (with pun on "appraise")

180 if even if

182 but . . . though no more than evenly repaid even though

185 fertile copious   **190 In . . . divulged** well spoken of   **free** generous

191 in . . . nature in his physical form   **192 gracious** graceful, attractive

194 flame passion   **195 deadly** deathlike

199 willow cabin shelter, hut (Willow was a symbol of unrequited love.)

200 my soul i.e., Olivia   **201 cantons** songs   **contemnèd** rejected

203 Hallow (1) halloo (2) bless   **204 babbling . . . air** echo

OLIVIA: You might do much.
        What is your parentage?
VIOLA: Above my fortunes, yet my state is well: 210
        I am a gentleman.
OLIVIA: Get you to your lord.
        I cannot love him. Let him send no more—
        Unless, perchance, you come to me again
        To tell me how he takes it. Fare you well.
        I thank you for your pains. Spend this for me.   [She offers a purse.]
VIOLA: I am no fee'd post, lady. Keep your purse.   217
        My master, not myself, lacks recompense.
        Love make his heart of flint that you shall love,   219
        And let your fervor, like my master's, be
        Placed in contempt! Farewell, fair cruelty.   Exit.
OLIVIA: "What is your parentage?"
        "Above my fortunes, yet my state is well:
        I am a gentleman." I'll be sworn thou art!
        Thy tongue, thy face, thy limbs, actions, and spirit
        Do give thee fivefold blazon. Not too fast! Soft, soft!   226
        Unless the master were the man. How now?   227
        Even so quickly may one catch the plague?
        Methinks I feel this youth's perfections
        With an invisible and subtle stealth
        To creep in at mine eyes. Well, let it be.
        What ho, Malvolio!

Enter Malvolio.

MALVOLIO: Here, madam, at your service.
OLIVIA: Run after that same peevish messenger,
        The County's man. He left this ring behind him,   [giving a ring]   235
        Would I or not. Tell him I'll none of it.   236
        Desire him not to flatter with his lord,   237
        Nor hold him up with hopes; I am not for him.
        If that the youth will come this way tomorrow,
        I'll give him reasons for 't. Hie thee, Malvolio.
MALVOLIO: Madam, I will.   Exit
OLIVIA: I do I know not what, and fear to find
        Mine eye too great a flatterer for my mind.   243
        Fate, show thy force. Ourselves we do not owe.   244
        What is decreed must be; and be this so.   [Exit.]

---

210 state social standing   **217 fee'd post** messenger to be tipped
219 Love . . . love may Love make the heart of the man you love as hard as flint
226 blazon heraldic description   **Soft** wait a minute
227 Unless . . . man i.e., unless Cesario and Orsino changed places
235 County's Count's, i.e., Duke's   **236 Would I or not** whether I wanted it or not
237 flatter with encourage
243 Mine . . . mind i.e., that my eyes (through which love enters the soul) have betrayed my
    reason by giving a flattering view of Cesario
244 owe own, control

Act 1 Response Statement Questions

- What were your expectations before you began to read? What previous experience with reading drama, Shakespearean drama, or Shakespearean comedy affected these expectations? What happened when your expectations met the actuality of the text?
- What reading strategies did you adopt? Did you find yourself changing or modifying your reading strategies in light of what you actually encountered with this text? What was the effect of your reading strategies?
- What is your initial response to any of these characters: Duke Orsino, Olivia, Viola? Or to these characters as a group involved with one another? How do any attitudes you have about romantic love and courtship in your ideology influence your response? How do any similarities or differences between their place in society and yours or between their problems and yours influence your response?
- What is your initial response to any of these characters: Sir Toby? Sir Andrew? Maria? Feste (the Clown)? Malvolio? Or to these characters as a group involved with one another?
- What plot lines can you begin to identify in Act 1? If there are more than one, does that bother you as a reader? Are you most interested in one plot line over the others, and if so why? What conflicts do you see being set up in Act 1? Do you find yourself taking sides in any of these conflicts? If so, why in terms of what you bring to the text from your ideology?
- What expectations for the rest of the play did Act 1 set up for you? Can you predict the direction of the plot or plots, for instance? Do you have questions that you think the rest of the play will answer? Are you beginning to build consistency of theme at this point?

Act 2, Scene 1

Enter Antonio and Sebastian

ANTONIO: Will you stay no longer? Nor will you not that I go with you?   1

SEBASTIAN: By your patience, no. My stars shine darkly over me. The malignancy of   2
my fate might perhaps distemper yours; therefore I shall crave of you your leave   3
that I may bear my evils alone. It were a bad recompense for your love to lay any
of them on you.

ANTONIO: Let me yet know of you whither you are bound.

SEBASTIAN: No, sooth, sir; my determinate voyage is mere extravagancy. But I per-   7
ceive in you so excellent a touch of modesty that you will not extort from me
what I am willing to keep in; therefore it charges me in manners the rather to   9

2.1. Location: Somewhere in Illyria.
1 Nor will you not do you not wish
2 patience leave   **malignancy** malevolence (of the stars; also in a medical sense)
3 distemper infect
7 sooth truly   **determinate** intended, determined upon   **extravagancy** aimless wandering
9 am willing ... in wish to keep secret   **it ... manners** it is incumbent upon me in all courtesy

express myself. You must know of me then, Antonio, my name is Sebastian, 10
which I called Roderigo. My father was that Sebastian of Messaline whom I 11
know you have heard of. He left behind him myself and a sister, both born in an 12
hour. If the heavens had been pleased, would we had so ended! But you, sir, al- 13
tered that, for some hour before you took me from the breach of the sea was my 14
sister drowned.

ANTONIO: Alas the day!

SEBASTIAN: A lady, sir, though it was said she much resembled me, was yet of many
accounted beautiful. But though I could not with such estimable wonder over- 18
far believe that, yet thus far I will boldly publish her: she bore a mind that envy 19
could not but call fair. She is drowned already, sir, with salt water, though I seem
to drown her remembrance again with more.

ANTONIO: Pardon me, sir, your bad entertainment. 22

SEBASTIAN: O good Antonio, forgive me your trouble. 23

ANTONIO: If you will not murder me for my love, let me be your servant. 24

SEBASTIAN: If you will not undo what you have done, that is, kill him whom you have
recovered, desire it not. Fare ye well at once. My bosom is full of kindness, and 26
I am yet so near the manners of my mother that upon the least occasion more 27
mine eyes will tell tales of me. I am bound to the Count Orsino's court. Farewell.

Exit.

ANTONIO: The gentleness of all the gods go with thee!
I have many enemies in Orsino's court,
Else would I very shortly see thee there.
But come what may, I do adore thee so
That danger shall seem sport, and I will go.   *Exit.*

Act 2, Scene 2

Enter Viola and Malvolio, at several doors.

MALVOLIO: Were not you even now with the Countess Olivia?

VIOLA: Even now, sir. On a moderate pace I have since arrived but hither.

MALVOLIO: She returns this ring to you, sir. You might have saved me my pains, to 3
have taken it away yourself. She adds, moreover, that you should put your lord 4
into a desperate assurance she will none of him. And one thing more: that you 5
be never so hardy to come again in his affairs, unless it be to report your lord's 6
taking of this. Receive it so.

VIOLA: She took the ring of me. I'll none of it. 8

---

10 express reveal
11 Messaline possibly Messina, or, more likely, Massila (the modern Marseilles). In Plautus'
Menaechmi, Massilians and Illyrians are mentioned together.
12–13 in an hour in the same hour
14 some hour about an hour   **breach of the sea** surf
18 estimable wonder admiring judgment   **19 publish** proclaim   **envy** even malice
22 entertainment reception, hospitality   **23 your trouble** the trouble I put you to
24 murder me for i.e., be the cause of my death in return for
26 recovered rescued, restored   **kindness** tenderness, natural emotion (of grief)
27 manners of my mother i.e., womanly inclination to weep
2.2. Location: Outside Olivia's house.   s.d. several different
3–4 to have taken by taking   **5 desperate** without hope
6 hardy to come bold as to come
8 She . . . it (Viola tells a quick and friendly lie to shield Olivia.)

MALVOLIO: Come, sir, you peevishly threw it to her, and her will is it should be so re- 10
turned. [*He throws down the ring.*] If it be worth stooping for, there it lies, in
your eye; if not, be it his that finds it.   *Exit.* 11

VIOLA: [*picking up the ring*]
I left no ring with her. What means this lady?
Fortune forbid my outside have not charmed her! 13
She made good view of me, indeed so much
That sure methought her eyes had lost her tongue, 15
For she did speak in starts, distractedly.
She loves me, sure! The cunning of her passion
Invites me in this churlish messenger.
None of my lord's ring? Why, he sent her none. 18
I am the man. If it be so—as 'tis—
Poor lady, she were better love a dream. 20
Disguise, I see, thou art a wickedness
Wherein the pregnant enemy does much.
How easy is it for the proper false 23
In women's waxen hearts to set their forms! 24
Alas, our frailty is the cause, not we, 25
For such as we are made of, such we be.
How will this fadge? My master loves her dearly, 27
And I, poor monster, fond as much on him; 28
And she, mistaken, seems to dote on me. 29
What will become of this? As I am man,
My state is desperate for my master's love;
As I am woman—now, alas the day!—
What thriftless sighs shall poor Olivia breathe! 34
O Time, thou must untangle this, not I;
It is too hard a knot for me t' untie.   [*Exit.*]

Act 2, Scene 3

Enter Sir Toby and Sir Andrew.

SIR TOBY: Approach, Sir Andrew. Not to be abed after midnight is to be up betimes; 1
and *diluculo surgere,* thou know'st— 2
SIR ANDREW: Nay, by my troth, I know not, but I know to be up late is to be up late.

10–11 in your eye in plain sight
15 lost caused her to lose
20 the man the man of her choice
23 pregnant quick, resourceful   **enemy** i.e., Satan
24 proper false men who are handsome and deceitful
25 waxen i.e., malleable, impressionable   **set their forms** stamp their images (as of a seal)
27 such as . . . be being made of frail material, we are frail
28 fadge turn out
29 monster i.e., being both man and woman   **fond** dote
34 thriftless unprofitable
2.3. Location: Olivia's house.
1 betimes early
2 *diluculo surgere [saluberrimum est]* to rise early is most healthful. (A sentence from Lilly's *Latin Grammar.*)

13 charmed enchanted
18 in in the person of

SIR TOBY: A false conclusion. I hate it as an unfilled can. To be up after midnight and   4
    to go to bed then, is early; so that to go to bed after midnight is to go to bed be-
    times. Does not our lives consist of the four elements?   6
SIR ANDREW: Faith, so they say, but I think it rather consists of eating and drinking.
SIR TOBY: Thou'rt a scholar; let us therefore eat and drink. Marian, I say, a stoup of wine!   8
    Enter Clown [Feste].
SIR ANDREW: Here comes the Fool, i' faith.
FESTE: How now, my hearts! Did you never see the picture of "we three"?   10
SIR TOBY: Welcome, ass. Now let's have a catch.   11
SIR ANDREW: By my troth, the Fool has an excellent breast. I had rather than forty   12
    shillings I had such a leg, and so sweet a breath to sing, as the fool has. In sooth,
    thou wast in very gracious fooling last night, when thou spok'st of Pigrogromi-   14
    tus, of the Vapians passing the equinoctial of Queubus. 'Twas very good, i' faith.   15
    I sent thee sixpence for thy leman. Hadst it?   16
FESTE: I did impeticos thy gratillity; for Malvolio's nose is no whipstock. My lady   17
    as a white hand, and the Myrmidons are no bottle-ale houses.   18
SIR AANDREW: Excellent! Why, this is the best fooling, when all is done. Now, a song.
SIR TOBY: Come on, there is sixpence for you. [*He gives money.*] Let's have a song.
SIR ANDREW: There's a testril of me too. [*He gives money.*] If one knight give a—   21
FESTE: Would you have a love song, or a song of good life?   22
SIR TOBY: A love song, a love song.
SIR ANDREW: Ay, ay, I care not for good life.
FESTE: *(sings)*
        O mistress mine, where are you roaming?
        O, stay and hear, your true love 's coming,
            That can sing both high and low.
        Trip no further, pretty sweeting;
        Journeys end in lovers' meeting,
            Every wise man's son doth know.
SIR ANDREW: Excellent good, i' faith.
SIR TOBY: Good, good.
FESTE: [*sings*]
        What is love? 'tis not hereafter;
        Present mirth hath present laughter;

---

4 **can** tankard
6 **four elements** i.e., fire, air, water, and earth, the elements that were thought to make up all matter
8 **stoup** drinking vessel
10 **picture of "we three"** picture of two fools or asses inscribed "we three," the spectator being the third
11 **catch** round   12 **breast** voice
14–15 **Pigrogromitus . . . Queubus** (Feste's mock erudition.)
16 **leman** sweetheart
17 **impeticos thy gratillity** (Suggests "impetticoat, or pocket up, thy gratuity.") **whipstock** whip handle (Possibly suggests that Malvolio can't be led by the nose; or, just nonsense.)
18 **has a white hand** i.e., is ladylike (But Feste's speech may be mere nonsense.) **Myrmidons** followers of Achilles **bottle-ale houses** (Used contemptuously of taverns because they sold low-class drink.)
21 **testril** tester, a coin worth sixpence
22 **good life** virtuous living (Or perhaps Feste means simply "life's pleasures," but is misunderstood by Sir Andrew to mean "virtuous living.")

What's to come is still unsure.   35
In delay there lies no plenty.
Then come kiss me, sweet and twenty;   37
Youth's a stuff will not endure.

SIR ANDREW: A mellifluous voice, as I am true knight.

SIR TOBY: A contagious breath.   40

SIR ANDREW: Very sweet and contagious, i' faith.

SIR TOBY: To hear by the nose, it is dulcet in contagion. But shall we make the   42
welkin dance indeed? Shall we rouse the night owl in a catch that will draw   43
three souls out of one weaver? Shall we do that?   44

SIR ANDREW: An you love me, let's do 't. I am dog at a catch.   45

FESTE: By 'r Lady, sir, and some dogs will catch well.   46

SIR ANDREW: Most certain. Let our catch be "Thou knave."   47

FESTE: "Hold thy peace, thou knave," knight? I shall be constrained in 't to call thee
knave, knight.

SIR ANDREW: 'Tis not the first time I have constrained one to call me knave. Begin,
Fool. It begins, "Hold thy peace."

FESTE: I shall never begin if I hold my peace.

SIR ANDREW: Good, i' faith. Come, begin.   *Catch sung.*

Enter Maria.

MARIA: What a caterwauling do you keep here! If my lady have not called up her
steward Malvolio and bid him turn you out of doors, never trust me.

SIR TOBY: My lady's a Cataian, we are politicians, Malvolio's a Peg-o'-Ramsey, and [*he*   56
sings] "Three merry men be we." Am not I consanguineous? Am I not of her   57
blood? Tillyvally! Lady! [*He sings.*] "There dwelt a man in Babylon, lady, lady."   58

FESTE: Beshrew me, the knight's in admirable fooling.   59

SIR ANDREW: Ay, he does well enough if he be disposed, and so do I too. He does it
with a better grace, but I do it more natural.   61

---

35 still always
37 sweet and twenty i.e., sweet and twenty times sweet
40 A contagious breath (1) a catchy voice (2) an infected or contagious breath
42 To . . . contagion i.e., if we were to describe hearing in olfactory terms, we could say it is
sweet in stench. (Sir Toby may be mocking Sir Andrew's uncritical acceptance of the word
contagious, missing the pun.)
42–43 make . . . dance i.e., drink till the sky seems to turn around
43–44 draw three souls (Refers to the threefold nature of the soul—vegetal, sensible, and intellectual—or to the three singers of the three-part catch; or, just a comic exaggeration.)
44 weaver (Weavers were often associated with psalm singing.)
45 dog at very clever at (But Feste uses the word literally.)   **catch** round (But Feste uses it to
mean "seize.")
46 By 'r Lady (An oath, originally, "by the Virgin Mary.")
47 Thou knave (This popular round is arranged so that the three singers repeatedly sing to one
another, "Thou knave." "Knight and knave" is a common antithesis, like "rich and poor.")
56 Cataian Cathayan, i.e., Chinese, a trickster or inscrutable; or, just nonsense   **politicians**
schemers, intriguers   **Peg-o'-Ramsey** character in a popular song. (Used here contemptuously.)
57 Three . . . we (A snatch of an old song.)   **consanguineous** i.e., a blood relative of Olivia
58 Tillyvally nonsense, fiddle-faddle   **There . . . lady** (The first line of a ballad, "The Constancy
of Susanna," together with the refrain, "Lady, lady.")
59 Beshrew i.e., devil take (A mild curse.)
61 natural naturally (but unconsciously suggesting idiocy)

SIR TOBY: [*sings*]   "O' the twelfth day of December"—   62
MARIA: For the love o' God, peace!

Enter Malvolio.

MALVOLIO: My masters, are you mad? Or what are you? Have you no wit, manners, nor   64
honesty but to gabble like tinkers at this time of night? Do ye make an ale-house   65
of my lady's house, that ye squeak out your coziers' catches without any mitiga-   66
tion or remorse of voice? Is there no respect of place, persons, nor time in you?   67
SIR TOBY: We did keep time, sir, in our catches. Sneck up!   68
MALVOLIO: Sir Toby, I must be round with you. My lady bade me tell you that though   69
she harbors you as her kinsman, she's nothing allied to your disorders. If you can
separate yourself and your misdemeanors, you are welcome to the house; if not,
an it would please you to take leave of her, she is very willing to bid you farewell.
SIR TOBY: [*sings*]   "Farewell, dear heart, since I must needs be gone."   73
MARIA: Nay, good Sir Toby.
FESTE: [*sings*]   "His eyes do show his days are almost done."
MALVOLIO: Is 't even so?
SIR TOBY: [*sings*]   "But I will never die."
FESTE: "Sir Toby, there you lie."
MALVOLIO: This is much credit to you.
SIR TOBY: [*sings*]   "Shall I bid him go?"
FESTE: [*sings*]   "What an if you do?"
SIR TOBY: [*sings*]   "Shall I bid him go, and spare not?"
FESTE: [*sings*]   "O, no, no, no, no, you dare not."
SIR TOBY: Out o' tune, sir? Ye lie. Art any more than a steward? Dost thou think, be-   84
cause thou art virtuous, there shall be no more cakes and ale?
FESTE: Yes, by Saint Anne, and ginger shall be hot i' the mouth, too.   86
SIR TOBY: Thou'rt i' the right.—Go, sir, rub your chain with crumbs.—A stoup of
wine, Maria!
MALVOLIO: Mistress Mary, if you prized my lady's favor at anything more than con-
tempt, you would not give means for this uncivil rule. She shall know of it, by   90
this hand.   *Exit.*
MARIA: Go shake your ears.   92
SIR ANDREW: 'Twere as good a deed as to drink when a man's a-hungry to challenge
him the field and then to break promise with him and make a fool of him.   94
SIR TOBY: Do 't, knight. I'll write thee a challenge, or I'll deliver thy indignation to
him by word of mouth.

---

62 O' . . . December (Possibly part of a ballad about the Battle of Musselburgh Field, or Toby's error for the "twelfth day of Christmas," i.e., Twelfth Night.)
64 wit common sense   **65 honesty** decency
66 coziers' cobblers'
66–67 mitigation or remorse i.e., considerate lowering
68 Sneck up go hang   **69 round** blunt
73 Farewell . . . gone (From the ballad "Corydon's Farewell to Phyllis.")
84 Out o' tune (Perhaps a quibbling reply—"We did too keep time in our tune"—to Malvolio's accusation of having no respect for place or time, line 68. Often emended to *Out o' time*, easily misread in secretary hand.)
86 Saint Anne mother of the Virgin Mary (Her cult was derided in the Reformation, much as Puritan reformers also derided the tradition of *cakes and ale* at church feasts.)   **ginger** (Commonly used to spice ale.)
87 Go . . . crumbs i.e., scour or polish your steward's chain; attend to your own business and remember your station
90 give means i.e., supply drink   **rule** conduct   **92 your ears** i.e., your ass's ears
94 the field i.e., to a duel

MARIA: Sweet Sir Toby, be patient for tonight. Since the youth of the Count's was today with my lady, she is much out of quiet. For Monsieur Malvolio, let me alone with him. If I do not gull him into a nayword and make him a common recreation, do not think I have wit enough to lie straight in my bed. I know I can do it. `98` `99` `100`

SIR TOBY: Possess us, possess us. Tell us something of him. `102`

MARIA: Marry, sir, sometimes he is a kind of puritan. `103`

SIR ANDREW: O, if I thought that, I'd beat him like a dog.

SIR TOBY: What, for being a puritan? Thy exquisite reason, dear knight?

SIR ANDREW: I have no exquisite reason for 't, but I have reason good enough.

MARIA: The devil a puritan that he is, or anything constantly, but a time-pleaser; an affectioned ass, that cons state without book and utters it by great swaths; the best persuaded of himself, so crammed, as he thinks, with excellencies, that it is his grounds of faith that all that look on him love him; and on that vice in him will my revenge find notable cause to work. `107` `108` `109` `110`

SIR TOBY: What wilt thou do?

MARIA: I will drop in his way some obscure epistles of love, wherein by the color of his beard, the shape of his leg, the manner of his gait, the expressure of his eye, forehead, and complexion, he shall find himself most feelingly personated. I can write very like my lady your niece; on a forgotten matter we can hardly make distinction of our hands. `114` `115` `116`

SIR TOBY: Excellent! I smell a device.

SIR ANDREW: I have 't in my nose too.

SIR TOBY: He shall think, by the letters that thou wilt drop, that they come from my niece, and that she's in love with him.

MARIA: My purpose is indeed a horse of that color.

SIR ANDREW: And your horse now would make him an ass.

MARIA: Ass, I doubt not.

SIR ANDREW: O, 'twill be admirable! `124`

MARIA: Sport royal, I warrant you. I know my physic will work with him. I will plant you two, and let the Fool make a third, where he shall find the letter. Observe his construction of it. For this night, to bed, and dream on the event. Farewell.   *Exit.* `126` `128`

SIR TOBY: Good night, Penthesilea. `130`

---

98 For as for

99 gull trick   **nayword** byword (His name will be synonymous with "dupe.")

98-99 let . . . him leave him to me

100 recreation sport   **102 Possess** inform

103 puritan (Maria's point is that Malvolio is sometimes a *kind* of Puritan, insofar as he is precise about moral conduct and censorious of others for immoral conduct, but that he is nothing consistently except a time-server. He is not, then, simply a satirical type of the Puritan sect. The extent of the resemblance is left unstated.)

107 constantly consistently   **time-pleaser** time-server, sycophant

108 affectioned affected   **cons . . . book** learns by heart the phrases and mannerisms of the great   **by great swaths** in great sweeps, like rows of mown grain

109 best persuaded having the best opinion   **110 grounds of faith** creed, belief

114 expressure expression

115 complexion countenance   **personated** represented

116 on a forgotten matter when we've forgotten which of us wrote something or what it was about

124 Ass, I (with a pun on "as I")   **126 physic** medicine

128 construction interpretation   **event** outcome

130 Penthesilea Queen of the Amazons (Another ironical allusion to Maria's diminutive stature.)

SIR ANDREW: Before me, she's a good wench.   131
SIR TOBY: She's a beagle true-bred and one that adores me. What o' that?   132
SIR ANDREW: I was adored once, too.
SIR TOBY: Let's to bed, knight. Thou hadst need send for more money.
SIR ANDREW: If I cannot recover your niece, I am a foul way out.   135
SIR TOBY: Send for money, knight. If thou hast her not i' the end, call me cut. 136
SIR ANDREW: If I do not, never trust me, take it how you will.
SIR TOBY: Come, come, I'll go burn some sack. 'Tis too late to go to bed now. Come, 138
  knight; come, knight.   139

Exeunt.

Act 2, Scene 4

Enter Duke [Orsino] Viola, Curio, and others.

ORSINO: Give me some music. Now, good morrow, friends.   1
  Now, good Cesario, but that piece of song,   2
  That old and antique song we heard last night.   3
  Methought it did relieve my passion much,
  More than light airs and recollected terms   5
  Of these most brisk and giddy-pacèd times.
  Come, but one verse.
CURIO: He is not here, so please your lordship, that should sing it.
ORSINO: Who was it?
CURIO: Feste the jester, my lord, a fool that the Lady Olivia's father took much de-
  light in. He is about the house.
ORSINO: Seek him out, and play the tune the while.   *[Exit Curio.] Music plays.*
  [*To Viola.*] Come hither, boy. If ever thou shalt love,
  In the sweet pangs of it remember me;
  For such as I am, all true lovers are,
  Unstaid and skittish in all motions else   16
  Save in the constant image of the creature
  That is beloved. How dost thou like this tune?
VIOLA: It gives a very echo to the seat   19
  Where Love is throned.
ORSINO: Thou dost speak masterly.
  My life upon 't, young though thou art, thine eye
  Hath stayed upon some favor that it loves.   23
  Hath it not, boy?
VIOLA: A little, by your favor.   25

---

131 Before me i.e., on my soul   **132 beagle** a small, intelligent hunting dog
135 recover win **foul way out** i.e., miserably out of pocket (Literally, out of my way and in the
  mire.)
136 cut a horse with a docked tail; also, a gelding, or the female genital organ
138 burn some sack warm some Spanish wine
139 s.d. Exeunt (Feste may have left earlier; he says nothing after line 86 and is perhaps referred
  to without his being present at 126–127.)
2.4. Location: Orsino's court.
  1 morrow morning   **2 but** i.e., I ask only
  3 antique old, quaint, fantastic
  5 recollected terms studied and artificial expressions
16 motions else other thoughts and emotions   **19 the seat** i.e., the heart
23 stayed . . . favor rested upon some face
25 by your favor if you please (but also hinting at "like you in feature")

ORSINO: What kind of woman is 't?

VIOLA: Of your complexion.

ORSINO: She is not worth thee, then. What years, i' faith?

VIOLA: About your years, my lord.

ORSINO: Too old, by heaven. Let still the woman take   30
    An elder than herself. So wears she to him;   31
    So sways she level in her husband's heart.   32
    For, boy, however we do praise ourselves,
    Our fancies are more giddy and unfirm,
    More longing, wavering, sooner lost and worn,   35
    Than women's are.

VIOLA: I think it well, my lord.

ORSINO: Then let thy love be younger than thyself,
    Or thy affection cannot hold the bent;
    For women are as roses, whose fair flower   39
    Being once displayed, doth fall that very hour.

VIOLA: And so they are. Alas that they are so,   41
    To die even when they to perfection grow!   43

Enter Curio and Clown [Feste].

ORSINO: O fellow, come, the song we had last night.
    Mark it, Cesario, it is old and plain;
    The spinsters and the knitters in the sun,
    And the free maids that weave their thread with bones,   46
    Do use to chant it. It is silly sooth,   47
    And dallies with the innocence of love,   48
    Like the old age.   49
        50

FESTE: Are you ready, sir?

ORSINO: Ay, prithee, sing.   *Music.*

The Song.

FESTE: [*sings*]
    Come away, come away, death,
        And in sad cypress let me be laid.   53
    Fly away, fly away, breath;   54
        I am slain by a fair cruel maid.

    My shroud of white, stuck all with yew,
        O, prepare it!   57
    My part of death, no one so true
        Did share it.   59
        60

---

30 still always   **31 wears she** she adapts herself
32 sways she level she keeps a perfect equipoise and steady affection
35 worn exhausted (Sometimes emended to *won*.)
39 hold the bent hold steady, stand the strain (like the tension of a bow)
41 displayed full blown   **43 even when** just as
46 spinsters spinners
47 free carefree, innocent   **bones** bobbins on which bone-lace was made
48 Do use are accustomed   **silly sooth** simple truth
49 dallies with dwells lovingly on, sports with
50 Like . . . age as in the good old times   **53 Come away** come hither
54 cypress i.e., a coffin of cypress wood, or bier strewn with sprigs of cypress
57 yew yew sprigs (Emblematic of mourning, like cypress.)
59–60 My . . . it no one died for love so true to love as I

Not a flower, not a flower sweet
   On my black coffin let there be strown;   62
Not a friend, not a friend greet
   My poor corpse, where my bones shall be thrown.
A thousand thousand sighs to save,
   Lay me, O, where
Sad true lover never find my grave,
   To weep there!

ORSINO: [*offering money*]   There's for thy pains.

FESTE: No pains, sir. I take pleasure in singing, sir.

ORSINO: I'll pay thy pleasure then.

FESTE: Truly, sir, and pleasure will be paid, one time or another.   72

ORSINO: Give me now leave to leave thee.   73

FESTE: Now, the melancholy god protect thee, and the tailor make thy doublet of   74
changeable taffeta, for thy mind is a very opal. I would have men of such con-   75
stancy put to sea, that their business might be everything and their intent every-   76
where, for that's it that always makes a good voyage of nothing. Farewell.   77

Exit.

ORSINO: Let all the rest give place. [*Curio and attendants withdraw.*]   78
   Once more, Cesario,
Get thee to yond same sovereign cruelty.
Tell her, my love, more noble than the world,
Prizes not quantity of dirty lands;
The parts that fortune hath bestowed upon her,   83
Tell her, I hold as giddily as fortune;   84
But 'tis that miracle and queen of gems   85
That nature pranks her in attracts my soul.   86

VIOLA: But if she cannot love you, sir?

ORSINO: I cannot be so answered.

VIOLA: Sooth, but you must.   89
Say that some lady, as perhaps there is,
Hath for your love as great a pang of heart
As you have for Olivia. You cannot love her;
You tell her so. Must she not then be answered?   93

---

62 strown strewn
72 pleasure . . . another sooner or later one must pay for indulgence
73 leave to leave permission to take leave of, dismiss
74 the melancholy god i.e., Saturn, whose planet was thought to control the melancholy temperament   **doublet** close-fitting jacket.
75 changeable taffeta a silk so woven of various-colored threads that its color shifts with changing perspective   **opal** an iridescent precious stone that changes color when seen from various
angles or in different lights
76–77 that . . . everywhere i.e., so that in the changeableness of the sea their inconstancy could
always be exercised
76 intent destination
77 for . . . nothing because that's the quality that succeeds in making a "good" voyage come to
nothing
78 give place withdraw   **83 parts** attributes such as wealth or rank
84 I . . . fortune I esteem as carelessly as I do fortune, that fickle goddess
85 that miracle . . . gems i.e., her beauty   **86 pranks** adorns   **attracts** that attracts
89 Sooth in truth   **93 be answered** accept your answer

ORSINO: There is no woman's sides
      Can bide the beating of so strong a passion
      As love doth give my heart; no woman's heart   95
      So big, to hold so much. They lack retention.   97
      Alas, their love may be called appetite,
      No motion of the liver, but the palate,   99
      That suffer surfeit, cloyment, and revolt;
      But mine is all as hungry as the sea,
      And can digest as much. Make no compare   102
      Between that love a woman can bear me
      And that I owe Olivia.   104
VIOLA: Ay, but I know—
ORSINO: What dost thou know?
VIOLA: Too well what love women to men may owe.
      In faith, they are as true of heart as we.
      My father had a daughter loved a man
      As it might be, perhaps, were I a woman,
      I should your lordship.
ORSINO: And what's her history?
VIOLA: A blank, my lord. She never told her love,
      But let concealment, like a worm i' the bud,
      Feed on her damask cheek. She pined in thought,
      And with a green and yellow melancholy   115
      She sat like Patience on a monument,   116
      Smiling at grief. What not this love indeed?   117
      We men may say more, swear more, but indeed
      Our shows are more than will; for still we prove   120
      Much in our vows, but little in our love.
ORSINO: But died thy sister of her love, my boy?
VIOLA: I am all the daughters of my father's house,
      And all the brothers too—and yet I know not.
      Sir, shall I to this lady?
ORSINO: Ay, that's the theme.
      To her in haste; give her this jewel. [*He gives a jewel.*]   Say
      My love can give no place, bide no denay.   128

Exeunt [separately].

---

95 bide withstand
97 to hold as to contain   **retention** constancy, the power of retaining
99 motion impulse   **liver . . . palate** (Real love is a passion of the liver, whereas fancy, light love, is born in the eye and nourished in the palate.)
100 cloyment satiety   **revolt** sickness, revulsion
102 compare comparison
104 owe have for
115 damask pink and white like the damask rose
116 green and yellow pale and sallow
117 on a monument carved in statuary on a tomb
120 shows displays of passion   **more than will** greater than our feelings   **still** always
128 can . . . denay cannot yield or endure denial

Act 2, Scene 5

Enter Sir Toby, Sir Andrew, and Fabian

SIR TOBY: Come thy ways, Signor Fabian.   1

FABIAN: Nay, I'll come. If I lose a scruple of this sport, let me be boiled to death with   2
melancholy.

SIR TOBY: Wouldst thou not be glad to have the niggardly rascally sheep-biter come   4
by some notable shame?

FABIAN: I would exult, man. You know he brought me out o' favor with my lady   7
about a bearbaiting here.

SIR TOBY: To anger him we'll have the bear again, and we will fool him black and   8
blue. Shall we not, Sir Andrew?   9

SIR ANDREW: An we do not, it is pity of our lives.   10

Enter Maria [with a letter].

SIR TOBY: Here comes the little villain.—How now, my metal of India!   11

MARIA: Get ye all three into the boxtree. Malvolio's coming down this walk. He has   12
been yonder i' the sun practicing behavior to his own shadow this half hour.
Observe him, for the love of mockery, for I know this letter will make a con-   14
templative idiot of him. Close, in the name of jesting! [*The others hide.*] Lie   15
thou there [*throwing down a letter*]; for here comes the trout that must be
caught with tickling.   *Exit.*   17

Enter Malvolio.

MALVOLIO: 'Tis but fortune; all is fortune. Maria once told me she did affect me; and   18
I have heard herself come thus near, that should she fancy, it should be one of   19
my complexion. Besides, she uses me with a more exalted respect than anyone
else that follows her. What should I think on 't?   21

SIR TOBY: Here's an overweening rogue!

FABIAN: O, peace! Contemplation makes a rare turkeycock of him. How he jets   23
under his advanced plumes!   24

SIR ANDREW: 'Slight, I could so beat the rogue!   25

SIR TOBY: Peace, I say.

MALVOLIO: To be Count Malvolio.

SIR TOBY: Ah, rogue!

SIR ANDREW: Pistol him, pistol him.

SIR TOBY: Peace, peace!

2.5. Location: Olivia's garden.
 1 Come thy ways come along
 2 scruple the least bit   **boiled** (with a pun on "biled"; black bile was the "humor" of melancholy and was thought to be a cold humor)
 4 sheep-biter a dog that bites sheep, i.e., a sneak and a censorious fellow
 7 bearbaiting (A special target of Puritan disapproval.)
 8–9 fool . . . blue mock him until he is figuratively black and blue
 10 An if   **pity of our lives** a pity we should live
 11 villain (Here, a term of endearment.)   **metal** gold, i.e., priceless one
 12 boxtree an evergreen shrub
 14–15 contemplative i.e., from his musings   **15 Close** i.e., keep close, stay hidden
 17 tickling (1) stroking gently about the gills—an actual method of fishing (2) flattery
 18 she Olivia   **affect** have fondness for   **19 fancy** fall in love
 21 follows serves   **23 rare** excellent   **jets** struts
 24 advanced raised   **25 'Slight** by His (God's) light

MALVOLIO: There is example for 't. The lady of the Strachy married the yeoman of   31
the wardrobe.

SIR ANDREW: Fie on him, Jezebel!   33

FABIAN: O, peace! Now he's deeply in. Look how imagination blows him.   34

MALVOLIO: Having been three months married to her, sitting in my state—   35

SIR TOBY: O, for a stone-bow, to hit him in the eye!   36

MALVOLIO: Calling my officers about me, in my branched velvet gown; having come   37
from a daybed, where I have left Olivia sleeping—   38

SIR TOBY: Fire and brimstone!

FABIAN: O, peace, peace!

MALVOLIO: And then to have the humor of state; and after a demure travel of regard,   41
telling them I know my place as I would they should do theirs, to ask for my   42
kinsman Toby.   43

SIR TOBY: Bolts and shackles!

FABIAN: O, peace, peace, peace! Now, now.

MALVOLIO: Seven of my people, with an obedient start, make out for him. I frown
the while, and perchance wind up my watch, or play with my—some rich   47
jewel. Toby approaches; curtsies there to me—

SIR TOBY: Shall this fellow live?

FABIAN: Though our silence be drawn from us with cars, yet peace.   50

MALVOLIO: I extend my hand to him thus, quenching my familiar smile with an aus-   51
tere regard of control—   52

SIR TOBY: And does not Toby take you a blow o' the lips then?   53

MALVOLIO: Saying, "Cousin Toby, my fortunes having cast me on your niece give me
this prerogative of speech—"

SIR TOBY: What, what?

MALVOLIO: "You must amend your drunkenness."

SIR TOBY: Out, scab!

FABIAN: Nay, patience, or we break the sinews of our plot.   58   59

MALVOLIO: "Besides, you waste the treasure of your time with a foolish knight—"

SIR ANDREW: That's me, I warrant you.

MALVOLIO: "One Sir Andrew."

SIR ANDREW: I knew 'twas I, for many do call me fool.

---

31 example precedent **lady of the Strachy** (Apparently a lady who had married below her
station; no certain identification.)
33 Jezebel the proud queen of Ahab, King of Israel
34 blows puffs up   **35 state** chair of state
36 stone-bow crossbow that shoots stones
37 branched adorned with a figured pattern suggesting branched leaves or flowers
38 daybed sofa, couch
41 have . . . state adopt the imperious manner of authority **demure . . . regard** grave survey of
the company
42 telling indicating to   **43 Toby** (Malvolio omits the title *Sir.*)
47 play with my (Malvolio perhaps means his steward's chain but checks himself in time; as
"Count Malvolio," he would not be wearing it. A bawdy meaning of playing with himself is
also suggested.)
48 curtsies bows   **50 with cars** with chariots, i.e., by force
51 familiar friendly   **52 regard of control** look of authority
53 take deliver   **58 scab** scurvy fellow
59 break . . . of hamstring, disable

MALVOLIO:	What employment have we here? [*Taking up the letter.*]
FABIAN:	Now is the woodcock near the gin.
SIR TOBY:	O, peace, and the spirit of humors intimate reading aloud to him!
MALVOLIO:	By my life, this is my lady's hand. These be her very c's, her u's, and her t's; and thus makes she her great P's. It is in contempt of question her hand.
SIR ANDREW:	Her c's, her u's, and her t's. Why that?
MALVOLIO:	[*reads*] "To the unknown beloved, this, and my good wishes."—Her very phrases! By your leave, wax. Soft! And the impressure her Lucrece, with which she uses to seal. 'Tis my lady. To whom should this be? [*He opens the letter.*]
FABIAN:	This wins him, liver and all.
MALVOLIO:	[*reads*]

"Jove knows I love,
    But who?
Lips, do not move;
    No man must know."

"No man must know." What follows? The numbers altered! "No man must know." If this should be thee, Malvolio?

SIR TOBY:	Marry, hang thee, brock!
MALVOLIO:	[*reads*]

"I may command where I adore,
    But silence, like a Lucrece knife,
With bloodless stroke my heart doth gore;
    M.O.A.I. doth sway my life."

FABIAN:	A fustian riddle!
SIR TOBY:	Excellent wench, say I.
MALVOLIO:	"M.O.A.I. doth sway my life." Nay, but first, let me see, let me see, let me see.
FABIAN:	What dish o' poison has she dressed him!
SIR TOBY:	And with what wing the staniel checks at it!
MALVOLIO:	"I may command where I adore." Why, she may command me; I serve her, she is my lady. Why, this is evident to any formal capacity. There is no obstruction in this. And the end—what should that alphabetical position portend? If I could make that resemble something in me! Softly! M.O.A.I.—
SIR TOBY:	O, ay, make up that. He is now at a cold scent.
FABIAN:	Sowter will cry upon 't for all this, though it be as rank as a fox.

Line numbers: 64, 65, 66, 67, 68, 71, 72, 73, 78, 80, 85, 88, 89, 91, 92, 94, 95

---

64 employment business
65 woodcock (A bird proverbial for its stupidity.)   **gin** snare
66 humors whim, caprice
67–68 c's . . . t's i.e., cut, slang for the female pudenda
68 great (1) uppercase (2) copious (*P* suggests "pee.")   **in contempt of** beyond
71 By . . . wax (Addressed to the seal on the letter.)   **Soft** softly, not so fast   **impressure** device imprinted on the seal   **Lucrece** Lucretia, chaste matron who, ravished by Tarquin, committed suicide
72 uses is accustomed   **73 liver** i.e., the seat of passion
78 The numbers altered more verses, in a different meter
80 brock badger (Used contemptuously.)   **85 fustian** bombastic, ridiculously pompous
88 What what a   **dressed** prepared for
89 wing i.e., speed   **staniel** kestrel, a sparrow hawk (The word is used contemptuously because of the uselessness of the staniel for falconry.)   **checks at it** turns to fly at it
91 formal capacity normal understanding   **92 position** arrangement
94 O, ay (playing on O.I. of M.O.A.I.)   **make up** work out
95 Sowter . . . fox i.e., the hound, having lost the *cold scent* of the hare, will "give tongue" in picking up the rank new scent of the fox and will dash away on this false trail   **Sowter** cobbler. (Here, the name for a hound.)

MALVOLIO: M—Malvolio. M! Why, that begins my name!

FABIAN: Did not I say he would work it out? The cur is excellent at faults. 97

MALVOLIO: M—But then there is no consonancy in the sequel that suffers under 98
probation: A should follow, but O does. 99

FABIAN: And O shall end, I hope.

SIR TOBY: Ay, or I'll cudgel him, and make him cry "O!"

MALVOLIO: And then I comes behind.

FABIAN: Ay, an you had any eye behind you, you might see more detraction at your 103
heels than fortunes before you. 104

MALVOLIO: M.O.A.I. This simulation is not as the former. And yet, to crush this a little, 105
it would bow to me, for every one of these letters are in my name. Soft! Here follows prose.

[*He reads.*] "If this fall into thy hand, revolve. In my stars I am above thee, but be 108
not afraid of greatness. Some are born great, some achieve greatness, and some
have greatness thrust upon 'em. Thy Fates open their hands; let thy blood and 110
spirit embrace them; and, to inure thyself to what thou art like to be, cast thy 111
humble slough and appear fresh. Be opposite with a kinsman, surly with ser- 112
vants. Let thy tongue tang arguments of state; put thyself into the trick of singu- 113
larity. She thus advises thee that sighs for thee. Remember who commended thy 114
yellow stockings, and wished to see thee ever cross-gartered. I say, remember. 115
Go to, thou art made, if thou desir'st to be so. If not, let me see thee a steward 116
still, the fellow of servants, and not worthy to touch Fortune's fingers. Farewell.
She that would alter services with thee, 118

The Fortunate-Unhappy."

Daylight and champaign discovers not more! This is open. I will be proud, I will 120
read politic authors, I will baffle Sir Toby, I will wash off gross acquaintance, I 121
will be point-devise the very man. I do not now fool myself, to let imagination 122
jade me; for every reason excites to this, that my lady loves me. She did com- 123
mend my yellow stockings of late, she did praise my leg being cross-gartered;

---

97 at faults i.e., at maneuvering his way past breaks in the line of scent—in this case, on a false trail

98–99 consonancy . . . probation pattern in the following letters that stands up under examination. (In fact, the letters "M.O.A.I." represents the first, last, second, and next to last letters of Malvolio's name.)

100 O shall end (1) O ends Malvolio's name (2) a noose shall end his life (3) *omega* ends the Greek alphabet (4) his cry of pain will end the joke

103 eye (punning on the "I" of "O, ay" and "M.O.A.I.")   **detraction** defamation

103–104 at your heels pursuing you

105 simulation disguise, puzzle

108 revolve consider   **stars** fortune

110 open their hands offer their bounty

111 inure accustom   **like** likely   **cast** cast off

112 slough skin of a snake; hence, former demeanor of humbleness   **opposite** contradictory

113 tang sound loud with   **state** politics, statecraft

113–114 trick of singularity eccentricity of manner

115 cross-gartered wearing garters above and below the knee so as to cross behind it

116 Go to (An expression of remonstrance.)

118 alter services i.e., exchange place of mistress and servant

120 champaign open country   **discovers** discloses

121 politic dealing with state affairs   **baffle** deride, degrade (A technical chivalric term used to describe the disgrace of a perjured knight.)   **gross** base

122 point-devise correct to the letter   **to let** by letting

123 jade trick (as an unruly horse does)   **excites to this** prompts this conclusion

and in this she manifests herself to my love, and with a kind of injunction drive 125
me to these habits of her liking. I thank my stars, I am happy. I will be strange, 126
stout, in yellow stockings and cross-gartered, even with the swiftness of putting 127
on. Jove and my stars be praised! Here is yet a postscript. [*He reads.*] "Thou
canst not choose but know who I am. If thou entertain'st my love, let it appear 129
in thy smiling; thy smiles become thee well. Therefore in my presence still 130
smile, dear my sweet, I prithee."
Jove, I thank thee. I will smile; I will do everything that thou wilt have me.   *Exit.*

[*Sir Toby, Sir Andrew, and Fabian come from hiding.*]

FABIAN: I will not give my part of this sport for a pension of thousands to be paid
from the Sophy.   134

SIR TOBY: I could marry this wench for this device.

SIR ANDREW: So could I too.

SIR TOBY: And ask no other dowry with her but such another jest.

Enter Maria.

SIR ANDREW: Nor I neither.

FABIAN: Here comes my noble gull-catcher.   139

SIR TOBY: Wilt thou set thy foot o' my neck?

SIR ANDREW: Or o' mine either?

SIR TOBY: Shall I play my freedom at tray-trip, and become thy bondslave?   142

SIR ANDREW: I' faith, or I either?

SIR TOBY: Why, thou hast put him in such a dream that when the image of it leaves
him he must run mad.

MARIA: Nay, but say true, does it work upon him?

SIR TOBY: Like aqua vitae with a midwife.   147

MARIA: If you will then see the fruits of the sport, mark his first approach before my
lady. He will come to her in yellow stockings, and 'tis a color she abhors, and
cross-gartered, a fashion she detests; and he will smile upon her, which will now
be so unsuitable to her disposition, being addicted to a melancholy as she is,
that it cannot but turn him into a notable contempt. If you will see it, follow me.   152

SIR TOBY: To the gates of Tartar, thou most excellent devil of wit!   153

SIR ANDREW: I'll make one too.   *Exeunt.*   154

Act 2 Response Statement Questions

- New characters are introduced in Act 2: Sebastian and Antonio. Do you
  enjoy this possible plot complication or not? Why, in terms of your reading strategies for this text or your literary experience with respect to plays
  in general or comedy in particular?

---

125 this this letter
126 these habits this attire   **happy** fortunate   **strange** aloof
127 stout haughty   **129 thou entertain'st** you accept
130 still continually   **134 Sophy** Shah of Persia
139 gull-catcher tricker of *gulls* or dupes
142 play gamble   **tray-trip** a game of dice, success in which depended on throwing a three
(*tray*)
147 aqua vitae brandy or other distilled liquors
152 notable contempt notorious object of contempt
153 Tartar Tartarus, the infernal regions   **154 make one** i.e., tag along

- What is your response to the general situation of confusion and disguised identities that is established by now? Do you find it humorous? enjoyable? bothersome? How is your response related to your reading strategies for this text or your literary experience with respect to plays in general or comedy in particular?
- What is your response to the scheming against Malvolio that develops in Act 2? Is it merely a humorous bit, or does it have a point to make? Do you feel allied with Sirs Andrew and Toby, Maria, and Feste against Malvolio? Is he being satirized, and if so for what?
- Can you identify any different styles of romantic love or ways of loving established or discussed in the text through Act 2? Are these gender-specific? Does Viola's cross-dressing provide any perspective for you or for any characters on the social conventions of love and courtship?

Act 3, Scene 1

Enter Viola, and Clown [Feste, playing his pipe and tabor].

VIOLA: Save thee, friend, and thy music. Dost thou live by thy tabor? 1

FESTE: No, sir, I live by the church.

VIOLA: Art thou a churchman?

FESTE: No such matter, sir. I do live by the church, for I do live at my house, and my house doth stand by the church.

VIOLA: So thou mayst say the king lies by a beggar if a beggar dwell near him, or the 6
church stands by thy tabor if thy tabor stand by the church. 7

FESTE: You have said, sir. To see this age! A sentence is but a cheveril glove to a good 8
wit. How quickly the wrong side may be turned outward!

VIOLA: Nay, that's certain. They that dally nicely with words may quickly make them 10
wanton.

FESTE: I would therefore my sister had had no name, sir. 11

VIOLA: Why, man?

FESTE: Why, sir, her name's a word, and to dally with that word might make my sister wanton. But indeed, words are very rascals since bonds disgraced them. 15

VIOLA: Thy reason, man?

FESTE: Troth, sir, I can yield you none without words, and words are grown so false I am loath to prove reason with them.

VIOLA: I warrant thou art a merry fellow and car'st for nothing. 19

FESTE: Not so, sir, I do care for something; but in my conscience, sir, I do not care for you. If that be to care for nothing sir, I would it would make you invisible. 21

3.1. Location: Olivia's garden.
1 Save God save   **live by** earn your living with (But Feste uses the phrase to mean "dwell near.")   **tabor** small drum
6 lies by (1) lies sexually with (2) dwells near
7 stands by . . . stand by (1) is maintained by (2) is placed near
8 You have said you've expressed your opinion   **sentence** maxim, judgment opinion   **cheveril** kidskin
10 dally nicely (1) play subtly (2) toy amorously
11 wanton (1) equivocal (2) licentious, unchaste (Feste then "dallies" with the word in its sexual sense; see line 20.)
15 since . . . them i.e., since sworn statements have been needed to make them good
19 car'st for nothing are without any worries. (But Feste puns on *care for* in line 20 in the sense of "like.")
21 invisible i.e., nothing; absent

VIOLA: Art not thou the Lady Olivia's fool?

FESTE: No indeed, sir. The Lady Olivia has no folly. She will keep no fool, sir, till she
be married, and fools are as like husbands as pilchers are to herrings—the hus-   24
band's the bigger. I am indeed not her fool but her corrupter of words.

VIOLA: I saw thee late at the Count Orsino's.   26

FESTE: Foolery, sir, does walk about the orb like the sun; it shines everywhere. I   27
would be sorry, sir, but the fool should be as oft with your master as with my   28
mistress. I think I saw your wisdom there.   29

VIOLA: Nay, an thou pass upon me, I'll no more with thee. Hold, there's expenses   30
for thee.   [*She gives a coin.*]

FESTE: Now Jove, in his next commodity of hair, send thee a beard!   32

VIOLA: By my troth, I'll tell thee, I am almost sick for one—[*aside*] though I would   33
not have it grow on my chin.—Is thy lady within?

FESTE: Would not a pair of these have bred, sir?

VIOLA: Yes, being kept together and put to use.   36

FESTE: I would play Lord Pandarus of Phrygia, sir, to bring a Cressida to this Troilus.   37

VIOLA: I understand you, sir. 'Tis well begged.   [*She gives another coin.*]

FESTE: The matter, I hope, is not great, sir, begging but a beggar; Cressida was a beg-   39
gar. My lady is within, sir. I will conster to them whence you come. Who you are   40
and what you would are out of my welkin—I might say "element," but the word   41
is overworn.   *Exit.*

VIOLA: This fellow is wise enough to play the fool,
And to do that well craves a kind of wit.
He must observe their mood on whom he jests,
The quality of persons, and the time,   46
And, like the haggard, check at every feather   47
That comes before his eye. This is a practice   48
As full of labor as a wise man's art;
For folly that he wisely shows is fit,   50
But wise men, folly-fall'n, quite taint their wit.   51

Enter Sir Toby and [Sir] Andrew.

---

24 pilchers pilchards, fish resembling herring   **26 late** recently
27 orb earth
27–29 I would . . . mistress (1) I should be sorry not to visit Orsino's house often (2) it would
be a shame if folly were no less common there than in Olivia's household
28 but unless
29 your wisdom i.e., you (A title of mock courtesy.)
30 an . . . me if you fence (verbally) with me, pass judgment on me
32 commodity supply
33 sick for one (1) eager to have a beard (2) in love with a bearded man
36 put to use put out at interest
37 Pandarus the go-between in the love story of Troilus and Cressida; uncle to Cressida
39 begging . . . beggar (A reference to Henryson's *Testament of Cresseid* in which Cressida
became a leper and a beggar. Feste desires another coin to be the mate of the one he has, as
Cressida, the beggar, was mate to Troilus.)
40 conster construe, explain
41 welkin sky   **element** (The word can be synonymous with *welkin,* but the common phrase
out of my element means "beyond my scope.")
46 quality character, rank
47 haggard untrained adult hawk, hence unmanageable
47–48 check . . . eye strike at every bird it sees, i.e., dart adroitly from subject to subject
48 practice exercise of skill
50 folly . . . fit the folly he displays is a proper skill
51 folly-fall'n having fallen into folly   **taint their wit** infect and impugn their own intelligence

SIR TOBY: Save you, gentleman.

VIOLA: And you, sir.

SIR ANDREW: *Dieu vous garde, monsieur.*   54

VIOLA: *Et vous aussi; votre serviteur.*   55

SIR ANDREW: I hope, sir, you are, and I am yours.

SIR TOBY: Will you encounter the house? My niece is desirous you should enter, if   57
your trade be to her.

VIOLA: I am bound to your niece, sir; I mean, she is the list of my voyage.   58

SIR TOBY: Taste your legs, sir. Put them to motion.   59

VIOLA: My legs do better understand me, sir, than I understand what you mean by   60
bidding me taste my legs.   61

SIR TOBY: I mean, to go, sir, to enter.

VIOLA: I will answer you with gait and entrance.—But we are prevented.   64

Enter Olivia and gentlewoman [Maria].

    Most excellent accomplished lady, the heavens rain odors on you!

SIR ANDREW: That youth's a rare courtier. "Rain odors"—well.

VIOLA: My matter hath no voice, lady, but to your own most pregnant and vouch-   67
safed ear.   68

SIR ANDREW: "Odors," "pregnant," and "vouchsafed." I'll get 'em all three all ready.   69

OLIVIA: Let the garden door be shut, and leave me to my hearing. [*Exeunt Sir Toby,
Sir Andrew, and Maria.*] Give me your hand, sir.

VIOLA: My duty, madam, and most humble service.

OLIVIA: What is your name?

VIOLA: Cesario is your servant's name, fair princess.

OLIVIA: My servant, sir? 'Twas never merry world
Since lowly feigning was called compliment.   75
You're servant to the Count Orsino, youth.   76

VIOLA: And he is yours, and his must needs be yours;
Your servant's servant is your servant, madam.   78

OLIVIA: For him, I think not on him. For his thoughts,
Would they were blanks, rather than filled with me!   80
    81

VIOLA: Madam, I come to whet your gentle thoughts
On his behalf.

OLIVIA: O, by your leave, I pray you.
I bade you never speak again of him.   84

---

54 Dieu ... monsieur God keep you, sir
55 Et ... serviteur and you, too; (I am) your servant. (Sir Andrew is not quite up to a reply in
    French.)
57 encounter (High-sounding word to express "approach.")
58 trade business (suggesting also a commercial venture)
59 I am bound (1) I am on a journey. (Continuing Sir Toby's metaphor in *trade*.) (2) I am obliged
    list limit, destination
60 Taste try   **61 understand** stand under, support
64 gait and entrance going and entering (with a pun on *gate:* [1] stride [2] entryway)   **pre-
    vented** anticipated
67 hath no voice cannot be uttered   **pregnant** receptive
67–68 vouchsafed proffered, i.e., attentive
69 all ready committed to memory for future use
75–76 'Twas ... compliment things have never been the same since affected humility (like call-
    ing oneself another's servant) began to be mistaken for courtesy
78 yours your servant   **his** those belonging to him   **80 For** as for
81 blanks blank coins ready to be stamped or empty sheets of paper
84 by your leave i.e., allow me to interrupt

But, would you undertake another suit,
I had rather hear you to solicit that
Than music from the spheres.   88
VIOLA: Dear lady—
OLIVIA: Give me leave, beseech you. I did send,
After the last enchantment you did here,
A ring in chase of you; so did I abuse   92
Myself, my servant, and, I fear me, you.
Under your hard construction must I sit,   94
To force that on you in a shameful cunning   95
Which you knew none of yours. What might you think?
Have you not set mine honor at the stake   97
And baited it with all th' unmuzzled thoughts   98
That tyrannous heart can think? To one of your receiving   99
Enough is shown; a cypress, not a bosom,   100
Hides my heart. So, let me hear you speak.
VIOLA: I pity you.
OLIVIA: That's a degree to love.
VIOLA: No, not a grece; for 'tis a vulgar proof   104
That very oft we pity enemies.
OLIVIA: Why then, methinks 'tis time to smile again.   106
O world, how apt the poor are to be proud!   107
If one should be a prey, how much the better
To fall before the lion than the wolf!   *Clock strikes.*   109
The clock upbraids me with the waste of time.
Be not afraid, good youth, I will not have you;
And yet, when wit and youth is come to harvest
Your wife is like to reap a proper man.   113
There lies your way, due west.
VIOLA: Then westward ho!
Grace and good disposition attend your ladyship.   116
You'll nothing, madam, to my lord by me?
OLIVIA: Stay.
I prithee, tell me what thou think'st of me.
VIOLA: That you do think you are not what you are.   120

---

88 music from the spheres (The heavenly bodies were thought to be fixed in hollow concentric spheres that revolved one about the other, producing a harmony too exquisite to be heard by human ears.)

92 abuse wrong, mislead   **94 hard construction** harsh interpretation
95 To force for forcing
97 at the stake (The figure is from bearbaiting.)
98 baited harassed (Literally, set the dogs on to bite the bear.)
99 receiving capacity, intelligence   **100 cypress** a thin, gauzelike, black material
104 grece step (Synonymous with *degree* in the preceding line.) **vulgar proof** common experience
106 smile i.e., cast off love's melancholy
107 how . . . proud how ready the unfortunate and rejected (like myself) are to find something to be proud of in their distress
109 To fall . . . wolf i.e., to fall before a noble adversary
113 like likely   **proper** handsome, worthy
116 Grace . . . ladyship may you enjoy God's blessing and a happy frame of mind
120 That . . . are i.e., that you think you are in love with a man, and you are mistaken

OLIVIA: If I think so, I think the same of you.
VIOLA: Then think you right. I am not what I am.   121
OLIVIA: I would you were as I would have you be!
VIOLA: Would it be better, madam, than I am?
        I wish it might, for now I am your fool.   125
OLIVIA: [*aside*]
        O, what a deal of scorn looks beautiful
        In the contempt and anger of his lip!
        A murderous guilt shows not itself more soon
        Than love that would seem hid; love's night is noon.—   129
        Cesario, by the roses of the spring,
        By maidhood, honor, truth, and everything,
        I love thee so that, maugre all thy pride,   132
        Nor wit nor reason can my passion hide.   133
        Do not extort thy reasons from this clause,   134
        For that I woo, thou therefore hast no cause.   135
        But rather reason thus with reason fetter: 136
        Love sought is good, but given unsought is better.
VIOLA: By innocence I swear, and by my youth,
        I have one heart, one bosom, and one truth,
        And that no woman has, nor never none
        Shall mistress be of it save I alone.
        And so adieu, good madam. Nevermore
        Will I my master's tears to you deplore.   143
OLIVIA: Yet come again, for thou perhaps mayst move
        That heart, which now abhors, to like his love.

Exeunt [separately].

Act 3, Scene 2

Enter Sir Toby, Sir Andrew, and Fabian

SIR ANDREW: No, faith, I'll not stay a jot longer.
SIR TOBY: Thy reason, dear venom, give thy reason.
FABIAN: You must needs yield your reason, Sir Andrew.   2
SIR ANDREW: Marry, I saw your niece do more favors to the Count's servingman than
        ever she bestowed upon me. I saw 't i' the orchard.
SIR TOBY: Did she see thee the while, old boy? Tell me that.   5
SIR ANDREW: As plain as I see you now.
FABIAN: This was a great argument of love in her toward you.   8

---

121 If . . . you (Olivia may interpret Viola's cryptic statement as suggesting that Olivia "does not
    know herself," i.e., is distracted with passion; she may also hint at her suspicion that
    "Cesario" is higher born that he admits.)
125 fool butt
129 love's . . . noon i.e., love, despite its attempt to be secret, reveals itself as plain as day
132 maugre in spite of   **133 Nor** neither
134–135 Do . . . cause do not rationalize your indifference along these lines, that because I am
    the wooer you have no cause to reciprocate
136 But . . . fetter but instead control your reasoning with the following reason
143 deplore beweep
3.2. Location: Olivia's house.
2 venom i.e., person filled with venom (Sir Andrew professes to be angry.)
5 orchard garden   **8 argument** proof

SIR ANDREW:	'Slight, will you make an ass o' me?	9
FABIAN:	I will prove it legitimate, sir, upon the oaths of judgment and reason.	10
SIR TOBY:	And they have been grand-jurymen since before Noah was a sailor.	

FABIAN: She did show favor to the youth in your sight only to exasperate you, to awake your dormouse valor, to put fire in your heart and brimstone in your 13 liver. You should then have accosted her, and with some excellent jests, fire-new from the mint, you should have banged the youth into dumbness. This was 15 looked for at your hand, and this was balked. The double gilt of this opportunity 16 you let time wash off, and you are now sailed into the north of my lady's opin- 17 ion, where you will hang like an icicle on a Dutchman's beard unless you do 18 redeem it by some laudable attempt either of valor or policy. 19

SIR ANDREW: An 't be any way, it must be with valor, for policy I hate. I had as lief be a Brownist as a politician. 21

SIR TOBY: Why, then, build me thy fortunes upon the basis of valor. Challenge me the 22 Count's youth to fight with him; hurt him in eleven places. My niece shall take note of it; and assure thyself, there is no love-broker in the world can more pre- 24 vail in man's commendation with woman than report of valor.

FABIAN: There is no way but this, Sir Andrew.

SIR ANDREW: Will either of you bear me a challenge to him?

SIR TOBY: Go, write it in a martial hand. Be curst and brief; it is no matter how witty, 28 so it be eloquent and full of invention. Taunt him with the license of ink. If thou 29 "thou"-est him some thrice, it shall not be amiss; and as many lies as will lie in 30 thy sheet of paper, although the sheet were big enough for the bed of Ware in 31 England, set 'em down. Go, about it. Let there be gall enough in thy ink, though 32 thou write with a goose pen, no matter. About it. 33

SIR ANDREW: Where shall I find you?

SIR TOBY: We'll call thee at the cubiculo. Go. 35

Exit Sir Andrew.

FABIAN: This is a dear manikin to you, Sir Toby. 36

SIR TOBY: I have been dear to him, lad, some two thousand strong or so. 37

FABIAN: We shall have a rare letter from him; but you'll not deliver 't?

---

9 'Slight by his (God's) light
10 it my contention   **oaths** i.e., testimony under oath
13 dormouse i.e., sleepy and timid   **15 banged** struck
16 balked missed, neglected   **double gilt** thick layer of gold, i.e., rare worth
17 north i.e., out of the warmth and sunshine of her favor
18 icicle . . . beard (Alludes to the arctic voyage of William Barentz in 1596–1597.)
19 policy stratagem
21 Brownist (An early name of the Congregationalists, from the name of the founder, Robert Browne.)   **politician** intriguer (Sir Andrew misinterprets Sir Toby's more neutral use of *policy,* "clever strategem.")
22 build me i.e., build   **24 love-broker** agent between lovers
28 curst fierce
29 with . . . ink i.e., with the freedom that may be risked in writing but not in conversation
30 "thou"-est ("Thou" was used only between friends or to inferiors.)   **lies** charges of lying
31 bed of Ware A famous bedstead capable of holding twelve persons, about eleven feet square, said to have been at the Stag Inn in Ware, Hertfordshire.
32 gall (1) bitterness, rancor (2) a growth found on certain oaks, used as an ingredient of ink
33 goose pen (1) goose quill (2) foolish style
35 call thee call for you   **cubiculo** little chamber
36 manikin puppet
37 dear expensive (playing on *dear,* "a source of pleasure," in the previous speech)

SIR TOBY: Never trust me, then; and by all means stir on the youth to an answer. I think oxen and wainropes cannot hale them together. For Andrew, if he were opened and you find so much blood in his liver as will clog the foot of a flea, I'll eat the rest of th' anatomy. 40 41 42

FABIAN: And his opposite, the youth, bears in his visage no great presage of cruelty. 43

Enter Maria.

SIR TOBY: Look where the youngest wren of nine comes. 44

MARIA: If you desire the spleen, and will laugh yourselves into stitches, follow me. Yond gull Malvolio is turned heathen, a very renegado; for there is no Christian that means to be saved by believing rightly can ever believe such impossible passages of grossness. He's in yellow stockings. 45 46 47

SIR TOBY: And cross-gartered? 48

MARIA: Most villainously, like a pedant that keeps a school i' the church. I have dogged him like his murderer. He does obey every point of the letter that I dropped to betray him. He does smile his face into more lines than is in the new map with the augmentation of the Indies. You have not seen such a thing as 'tis. I can hardly forbear hurling things at him. I know my lady will strike him. If she do, he'll smile and take 't for a great favor. 50 52 53

SIR TOBY: Come, bring us, bring us where he is.

Exeunt omnes.

Act 3, Scene 3

Enter Sebastian and Antonio.

SEBASTIAN: I would not by my will have troubled you,
But since you make your pleasure of your pains,
I will no further chide you.

ANTONIO: I could not stay behind you. My desire,
More sharp than filèd steel, did spur me forth,
And not all love to see you—though so much
As might have drawn one to a longer voyage— 6
But jealousy what might befall your travel,
Being skilless in these parts, which to a stranger, 8
Unguided and unfriended, often prove 9
Rough and unhospitable. My willing love,
The rather by these arguments of fear,
Set forth in your pursuit. 12

---

40 wainropes wagon ropes   **hale** haul   **For** as for
41 liver (A pale and bloodless liver was a sign of cowardice.)
42 anatomy cadaver   **43 opposite** adversary
44 youngest . . . nine the last hatched and smallest of a nest of wrens
45 the spleen a laughing fit (The spleen was thought to be the seat of immoderate laughter.)
46 renegado renegade, deserter of his religion
47–48 impossible passages of grossness gross impossibilities (i.e., in the letter)
50 villainously i.e., abominably   **pedant** schoolmaster
52–53 new map (Probably a reference to a map made by Emmeric Mollineux in 1599 for the purchasers of Hakluyt's *Voyages,* showing more of the East Indies, including Japan, than had ever been mapped before.)
3.3. Location: A street.
 6 all only, merely   **so much** i.e., that was great enough
 8 jealousy anxiety   **9 skilless in** unacquainted with
12 The rather made all the more willing

SEBASTIAN: My kind Antonio,
  I can no other answer make but thanks,
  And thanks; and ever oft good turns   16
  Are shuffled off with such uncurrent pay.   17
  But were my worth, as is my conscience, firm,   18
  You should find better dealing. What's to do?   19
  Shall we go see the relics of this town?   20

ANTONIO: Tomorrow, sir. Best first go see your lodging.

SEBASTIAN: I am not weary, and 'tis long to night.
  I pray you, let us satisfy our eyes
  With the memorials and the things of fame
  That do renown this city.   25

ANTONIO: Would you'd pardon me.
  I do not without danger walk these streets.
  Once in a sea fight 'gainst the Count his galleys   28
  I did some service, of such note indeed
  That were I ta'en here it would scarce be answered.   30

SEBASTIAN: Belike you slew great number of his people?   31

ANTONIO: Th' offense is not of such a bloody nature,
  Albeit the quality of the time and quarrel
  Might well have given us bloody argument.   34
  It might have since been answered in repaying   35
  What we took from them, which for traffic's sake   36
  Most of our city did. Only myself stood out,
  For which, if I be lapsèd in this place,   38
  I shall pay dear.

SEBASTIAN: Do not then walk too open.

ANTONIO: It doth not fit me. Hold, sir, here's my purse.   *[He gives his purse.]*
  In the south suburbs, at the Elephant,   42
  Is best to lodge. I will bespeak our diet,   43
  Whiles you beguile the time and feed your knowledge
  With viewing of the town. There shall you have me.

SEBASTIAN: Why I your purse?

ANTONIO: Haply your eye shall light upon some toy   47
  You have desire to purchase; and your store   48
  I think is not for idle markets, sir.   49

---

16 And . . . turns (This probably corrupt line is usually made to read, "And thanks and ever thanks; and oft good turns.")
17 shuffled off turned aside **uncurrent** worthless (such as mere thanks)
18 worth wealth **conscience** i.e., moral inclination to assist
19 dealing treatment, payment
20 relics antiquities
25 renown make famous
28 Count his Count's, i.e., Duke's
30 it . . . answered I'd be hard put to offer a defense
31 Belike perhaps
34 bloody argument cause for bloodshed   **35 answered** compensated
36 traffic's trade's   **38 lapsèd** caught off guard, surprised
42 Elephant the name of an inn   **43 bespeak our diet** order our food
47 Haply perhaps **toy** trifle   **48 store** store of money
49 idle markets unnecessary purchases, luxuries

SEBASTIAN: I'll be your purse-bearer and leave you
> For an hour.
ANTONIO: To th' Elephant.
SEBASTIAN: I do remember.

Exeunt [separately].

Act 3, Scene 4

Enter Olivia and Maria.

OLIVIA: [*aside*]
> I have sent after him; he says he'll come.   1
> How shall I feast him? What bestow of him?   2
> For youth is bought more oft than begged or borrowed.
> I speak too loud.—
> Where's Malvolio? He is sad and civil,   5
> And suits well for a servant with my fortunes.
> Where is Malvolio?

MARIA: He's coming, madam, but in very strange manner. He is, sure, possessed,   8
madam.

OLIVIA: Why, what's the matter? Does he rave?

MARIA: No, madam, he does nothing but smile. Your ladyship were best to have
some guard about you if he come, for sure the man is tainted in 's wits.   12

OLIVIA: Go call him hither. [*Maria summons Malvolio.*] I am as mad as he,
If sad and merry madness equal be.

Enter Malvolio, [cross-gartered and in yellow stockings].

> How now, Malvolio?

MALVOLIO: Sweet lady, ho, ho!

OLIVIA: Smil'st thou? I sent for thee upon a sad occasion.   17

MALVOLIO: Sad, lady? I could be sad. This does make some obstruction in the blood,   18
this cross-gartering, but what of that? If it please the eye of one, it is with me as
the very true sonnet is, "Please one and please all."   20

OLIVIA: Why, how dost thou, man? What is the matter with thee?

MALVOLIO: Not black in my mind, though yellow in my legs. It did come to his   22
hands, and commands shall be executed. I think we do know the sweet roman   23
hand.

OLIVIA: Wilt thou go to bed, Malvolio?   24

MALVOLIO: To bed! "Ay, sweetheart, and I'll come to thee."   25   26

OLIVIA: God comfort thee! Why dost thou smile so and kiss thy hand so oft?

MARIA: How do you, Malvolio?

3.4. Location: Olivia's garden.
1 he . . . come i.e., suppose he says he'll come
2 of on
8 possessed i.e., possessed with an evil spirit
17 sad serious
20 sonnet song, ballad   **Please . . . all** to please one special person is as good as to please
everybody. (*The refrain of a ballad.*)
22 black i.e., melancholic   **It** i.e., the letter   **his** Malvolio's
23–24 roman hand fashionable italic style of handwriting
25 go to bed i.e., try to sleep off your mental distress
26 Ay . . . thee (Malvolio quotes from a popular song of the day.)

5 sad and civil sober and decorous
12 in 's in his
18 sad (1) serious (2) melancholy

MALVOLIO: At your request? Yes, nightingales answer daws.   29
MARIA: Why appear you with this ridiculous boldness before my lady?
MALVOLIO: "Be not afraid of greatness." 'Twas well writ.
OLIVIA: What mean'st thou by that, Malvolio?
MALVOLIO: "Some are born great—"
OLIVIA: Ha?
MALVOLIO: "Some achieve greatness—"
OLIVIA: What sayst thou?
MALVOLIO: "And some have greatness thrust upon them."
OLIVIA: Heaven restore thee!
MALVOLIO: "Remember who commended thy yellow stockings—"
OLIVIA: Thy yellow stockings?
MALVOLIO: "And wished to see thee cross-gartered."
OLIVIA: Cross-gartered?
MALVOLIO: "Go to, thou art made, if thou desir'st to be so—"
OLIVIA: Am I made?
MALVOLIO: "If not, let me see thee a servant still."
OLIVIA: Why, this is very midsummer madness.   46

Enter Servant.

SERVANT: Madam, the young gentleman of the Count Orsino's is returned. I could
hardly entreat him back. He attends your ladyship's pleasure.
OLIVIA: I'll come to him. [*Exit Servant.*] Good Maria, let this fellow be looked to.
Where's my cousin Toby? Let some of my people have a special care of him. I
would not have him miscarry for the half of my dowry.   51

Exeunt [Olivia and Maria, different ways].

MALVOLIO: Oho, do you come near me now? No worse man than Sir Toby to look to   52
me! This concurs directly with the letter. She sends him on purpose that I may
appear stubborn to him, for she incites me to that in the letter. "Cast thy humble
slough," says she; "be opposite with a kinsman, surly with servants; let thy
tongue tang with arguments of state; put thyself into the trick of singularity."
And consequently sets down the manner how: as, a sad face, a reverend car-   57
riage, a slow tongue, in the habit of some sir of note, and so forth. I have limed   58
her, but it is Jove's doing, and Jove make me thankful! And when she went away
now, "Let this fellow be looked to." "Fellow!" Not "Malvolio," nor after my degree,   60
but "fellow." Why, everything adheres together, that no dram of a scruple, no   61
scruple of a scruple, no obstacle, no incredulous or unsafe circumstance—what   62
can be said?—nothing that can be can come between me and the full prospect
of my hopes. Well, Jove, not I, is the doer of this, and he is to be thanked.

---

29 nightingales answer daws i.e., (to Maria), do you suppose a fine fellow like me would
answer a lowly creature (a *daw,* a "crow") like you
46 midsummer madness (A proverbial phrase; the midsummer moon was supposed to cause
madness.)
51 miscarry come to harm
52 come near understand, appreciate
57 consequently thereafter   **sad** serious
58 habit . . . note attire suited to a man of distinction   **limed** caught like a bird with birdlime
(a sticky substance spread on branches)
60 Fellow (Malvolio takes the original meaning, "companion.")   **after my degree** according to
my position
61 dram (Literally, one-eighth of a fluid ounce.)   **scruple** (Literally, one-third of a dram.)
62 incredulous incredible   **unsafe** uncertain, unreliable

Enter [Sir] Toby, Fabian, and Maria.

SIR TOBY: Which way is he, in the name of sanctity? If all the devils of hell be drawn   65
in little, and Legion himself possessed him, yet I'll speak to him.   66

FABIAN: Here he is, here he is.—How is 't with you, sir? How is 't with you, man?

MALVOLIO: Go off. I discard you. Let me enjoy my private. Go off.   68

MARIA: Lo, how hollow the fiend speaks within him! Did not I tell you? Sir Toby, my
lady prays you to have a care of him.

MALVOLIO: Aha, does she so?

SIR TOBY: Go to, go to! Peace, peace, we must deal gently with him. Let me alone.—   72
How do you, Malvolio? How is 't with you? What, man, defy the devil! Consider,   73
he's an enemy to mankind.

MALVOLIO: Do you know what you say?

MARIA: La you, an you speak ill of the devil, how he takes it at heart! Pray God he   76
be not bewitched!

FABIAN: Carry his water to the wisewoman.

MARIA: Marry, and it shall be done tomorrow morning, if I live. My lady would not
lose him for more than I'll say.

MALVOLIO: How now, mistress?

MARIA: O Lord!

SIR TOBY: Prithee, hold thy peace; this is not the way. Do you not see you move him?   83
Let me alone with him.

FABIAN: No way but gentleness, gently, gently. The fiend is rough, and will not be
roughly used.

SIR TOBY: Why, how now, my bawcock! How dost thou, chuck?   87

MALVOLIO: Sir!

SIR TOBY: Ay, biddy, come with me. What, man, 'tis not for gravity to play at cherry-   89
pit with Satan. Hang him, foul collier!

MARIA: Get him to say his prayers, good Sir Toby, get him to pray.

MALVOLIO: My prayers, minx?

MARIA: No, I warrant you, he will not hear of godliness.

MALVOLIO: Go hang yourselves all! You are idle, shallow things; I am not of your ele-   94
ment. You shall know more hereafter.   *Exit.*   95

SIR TOBY: Is 't possible?

FABIAN: If this were played upon a stage, now, I could condemn it as an improbable fiction.

SIR TOBY: His very genius hath taken the infection of the device, man.   99

MARIA: Nay, pursue him now, lest the device take air and taint.   100

FABIAN: Why, we shall make him mad indeed.

65–66 drawn in little (1) portrayed in miniature (2) gathered into a small space, i.e., in Malvolio's heart
66 Legion an unclean spirit ("My name is Legion, for we are many," Mark 5:9.)
68 private privacy   **72 Let me alone** leave him to me
73 defy renounce   **76 La you** look you
78 water urine (for medical analysis)   **83 move** upset, excite
87 bawcock fine fellow (From the French *beau-coq*.)   **chuck** (A form of "chick," term of endearment.)
89 biddy chicken   **for gravity** suitable for a man of your dignity   **cherry-pit** a children's game consisting of throwing cherry stones into a little hole
90 collier i.e., Satan (Literally, a coal vendor.)   **94 idle** foolish
94–95 element sphere of existence   **95 know more** i.e., hear about this
99 genius i.e., soul, spirit
100 take . . . taint become exposed to air (i.e., become known) and thus spoil

MARIA: The house will be the quieter.

SIR TOBY: Come, we'll have him in a dark room and bound. My niece is already in   103
the belief that he's mad. We may carry it thus for our pleasure and his penance   104
till our very pastime, tired out of breath, prompt us to have mercy on him, at
which time we will bring the device to the bar and crown thee for a finder of   106
madmen. But see, but see!   107

Enter Sir Andrew [with a letter].

FABIAN: More matter for a May morning.   108

SIR ANDREW: Here's the challenge. Read it. I warrant there's vinegar and pepper in 't.

FABIAN: Is 't so saucy?   110

SIR ANDREW: Ay, is 't, I warrant him. Do but read.

SIR TOBY: Give me. [*He reads.*] "Youth, whatsoever thou art, thou art but a scurvy
fellow."

FABIAN: Good, and valiant.

SIR TOBY: [*reads*]   "Wonder not, nor admire not in thy mind, why I do call thee   115
so, for I will show thee no reason for 't."

FABIAN: A good note, that keeps you from the blow of the law.   117

SIR TOBY: [*reads*]   "Thou com'st to the Lady Olivia, and in my sight she uses thee
kindly. But thou liest in thy throat; that is not the matter I challenge thee for."

FABIAN: Very brief, and to exceeding good sense—less.

SIR TOBY: [*reads*]   "I will waylay thee going home, where if it be thy chance to
kill me—"

FABIAN: Good.

SIR TOBY: [*reads*]   "Thou kill'st me like a rogue and a villain."

FABIAN: Still you keep o' the windy side of the law. Good.   125

SIR TOBY: [*reads*]   "Fare thee well, and God have mercy upon one of our souls!
He may have mercy upon mine, but my hope is better, and so look to thyself.   127
Thy friend, as thou usest him, and thy sworn enemy,

                                                    Andrew Aguecheek."

If this letter move him not, his legs cannot. I'll give 't him.   130

MARIA: You may have very fit occasion for 't. He is now in some commerce with my   131
lady, and will by and by depart.

SIR TOBY: Go, Sir Andrew. Scout me for him at the corner of the orchard like a bum-   133
baily. So soon as ever thou seest him, draw, and as thou draw'st, swear horrible;   134
for it comes to pass oft that a terrible oath, with a swaggering accent sharply
twanged off, gives manhood more approbation than ever proof itself would   136
have earned him. Away!

---

103 in . . . bound (The standard treatment for insanity at this time.)
104 carry manage   **106 bar** i.e., bar of judgment
106–107 finder of madmen member of a jury charged with "finding" if the accused is insane
108 matter . . . morning sport for Mayday plays or games
110 saucy (1) spicy (2) insolent   **115 admire** marvel
117 note observation, remark
125 windy windward, i.e., safe, where one is less likely to be driven onto legal rocks and shoals
127 my hope is better (Sir Andrew's comically inept way of saying he hopes to be the survivor;
instead, he seems to say, "May I be damned.")
130 move (1) stir up (2) set in motion   **131 commerce** transaction
133 Scout me keep watch
133–134 bum-baily minor sheriff's officer employed in making arrests   **horrible** horribly
136 approbation reputation (for courage)   **proof** performance

SIR ANDREW: Nay, let me alone for swearing.   *Exit.*   138

SIR TOBY: Now will not I deliver his letter, for the behavior of the young gentleman gives him out to be of good capacity and breeding; his employment between his lord and my niece confirms no less. Therefore this letter, being so excellently ignorant, will breed no terror in the youth. He will find it comes from a clod-   142 poll. But, sir, I will deliver his challenge by word of mouth, set upon Aguecheek   143 a notable report of valor, and drive the gentleman—as I know his youth will   144 aptly receive it—into a most hideous opinion of his rage, skill, fury, and impetu-   145 osity. This will so fright them both that they will kill one another by the look, like cockatrices.   147

Enter Olivia and Viola.

FABIAN: Here he comes with your niece. Give them way till he take leave, and   148 presently after him.   149

SIR TOBY: I will meditate the while upon some horrid message for a challenge.   150

[Exeunt Sir Toby, Fabian, and Maria.]

OLIVIA: I have said too much unto a heart of stone
    And laid mine honor too unchary on 't.
    There's something in me that reproves my fault,   152
    But such a headstrong potent fault it is
    That it but mocks reproof.

VIOLA: With the same havior that your passion bears
    Goes on my master's griefs.

OLIVIA: [*giving a locket*]
    Here, wear this jewel for me. 'Tis my picture.
    Refuse it not; it hath no tongue to vex you.   158
    And I beseech you come again tomorrow.
    What shall you ask of me that I'll deny,
    That honor, saved, may upon asking give?   162

VIOLA: Nothing but this: your true love for my master.

OLIVIA: How with mine honor may I give him that
    Which I have given to you?

VIOLA: I will acquit you.   166

OLIVIA: Well, come again tomorrow. Fare thee well.
    A fiend like thee might bear my soul to hell.   [*Exit.*]   168

Enter [Sir] Toby and Fabian.

SIR TOBY: Gentleman, God save thee.

VIOLA: And you, sir.

SIR TOBY: That defense thou hast, betake thee to 't. Of what nature the wrongs are thou hast done him, I know not, but thy intercepter, full of despite, bloody as   172

---

138 let . . . swearing don't worry about my ability in swearing
142–143 clodpoll blockhead
144–145 his . . . it his inexperience will make him all the more ready to believe it
147 cockatrices basilisks, fabulous serpents reputed to be able to kill by a mere look
148 Give them way stay out of their way   **149 presently** immediately
150 horrid terrifying (Literally, "bristling.")
152 laid hazarded   **unchary on 't** recklessly on it
158 jewel (Any piece of jewelry; here, seemingly, a locket.)
162 That . . . give that can be granted without compromising any honor
166 acquit you release you of your promise   **168 like** resembling
172 intercepter he who lies in wait   **despite** defiance

the hunter, attends thee at the orchard end. Dismount thy tuck, be yare in thy   173
preparation, for thy assailant is quick, skillful, and deadly.

VIOLA: You mistake sir. I am sure no man hath any quarrel to me. My remembrance   175
is very free and clear from any image of offense done to any man.

SIR TOBY: You'll find it otherwise, I assure you. Therefore, if you hold your life at any
price, betake you to your guard, for your opposite hath in him what youth,   178
strength, skill, and wrath can furnish man withal.   179

VIOLA: I pray you, sir, what is he?

SIR TOBY: He is knight, dubbed with unhatched rapier and on carpet consideration,   181
but he is a devil in private brawl. Souls and bodies hath he divorced three, and
his incensement at this moment is so implacable that satisfaction can be none
but by pangs of death and sepulcher. Hob, nob is his word; give 't or take 't.   184

VIOLA: I will return again into the house and desire some conduct of the lady. I am   185
no fighter. I have heard of some kind of men that put quarrels purposely on others, to taste their valor. Belike this is a man of that quirk.   187

SIR TOBY: Sir, no. His indignation derives itself out of a very competent injury; there-   188
fore, get you on and give him his desire. Back you shall not to the house unless
you undertake that with me which with as much safety you might answer him.   190
Therefore, on, or strip your sword stark naked; for meddle you must, that's cer-   191
tain, or forswear to wear iron about you.   192

VIOLA: This is as uncivil as strange. I beseech you, do me this courteous office, as to
know of the knight what my offense to him is. It is something of my negligence,   194
nothing of my purpose.

SIR TOBY: I will do so.—Signor Fabian, stay you by this gentleman till my return.

Exit [Sir] Toby.

VIOLA: Pray you, sir, do you know of this matter?

FABIAN: I know the knight is incensed against you, even to a mortal arbitrament,   198
but nothing of the circumstance more.

VIOLA: I beseech you, what manner of man is he?

FABIAN: Nothing of that wonderful promise, to read him by his form, as you are like   201
to find him in the proof of his valor. He is, indeed, sir, the most skillful, bloody,
and fatal opposite that you could possibly have found in any part of Illyria. Will   203
you walk towards him, I will make your peace with him if I can.   204

VIOLA: I shall be much bound to you for 't. I am one that had rather go with Sir Priest   205
than Sir Knight. I care not who knows so much of my mettle. *Exeunt.*

Enter [Sir] Toby and [Sir] Andrew.

172–173 bloody as the hunter bloodthirsty as a hunting dog
173 Dismount thy tuck draw your rapier   **yare** ready, nimble
175 to with   **178 opposite** opponent   **what** whatsoever
179 withal with
181 unhatched unhacked, unused in battle   **carpet consideration** (A carpet knight was one
whose title was obtained, not in battle, but through connections at court.)
184 Hob, nob have or have not, i.e., give it or take it, kill or be killed   **word** motto
185 conduct escort
187 taste test   **Belike** probably   **quirk** peculiar humor
188 competent sufficient   **190 that** i.e., to give satisfaction in a duel
191 meddle engage (in conflict)
192 forswear . . . iron give up your right to wear a sword
194 know of inquire from   **198 mortal arbitrament** trial to the death
201 read . . . form judge him by his appearance   **like** likely
203–204 Will you if you will
205 go with associate with   **Sir Priest** (*Sir* was a courtesy title for priests.)

SIR TOBY: Why, man, he's a very devil; I have not seen such a firago. I had a pass with him, rapier, scabbard, and all, and he gives me the stuck in with such a mortal motion that it is inevitable; and on the answer, he pays you as surely as your feet hits the ground they step on. They say he has been fencer to the Sophy. 207 208 209 210

SIR ANDREW: Pox on 't, I'll not meddle with him.

SIR TOBY: Ay, but he will not now be pacified. Fabian can scarce hold him yonder.

SIR ANDREW: Plague on 't, an I thought he had been valiant and so cunning in fence, I'd have seen him damned ere I'd have challenged him. Let him let the matter slip and I'll give him my horse, gray Capilet. 215

SIR TOBY: I'll make the motion. Stand here, make a good show on 't. This shall end without the perdition of souls. [*Aside, as he crosses to meet Fabian.*] Marry, I'll ride your horse as well as I ride you. 216 217

Enter Fabian and Viola.

[*Aside to Fabian.*] I have his horse to take up the quarrel. I have persuaded him the youth's a devil. 219

FABIAN: He is as horribly conceited of him, and pants and looks pale as if a bear were at his heels. 221

SIR TOBY: [*to Viola*] There's no remedy, sir, he will fight with you for 's oath's sake. Marry, he hath better bethought him of his quarrel, and he finds that now scarce to be worth talking of. Therefore draw, for the supportance of his vow; he protests he will not hurt you. 225

VIOLA: [*aside*] Pray God defend me! A little thing would make me tell them how much I lack of a man.

FABIAN: Give ground, if you see him furious.

SIR TOBY: [*crossing to Sir Andrew*] Come, Sir Andrew, there's no remedy. The gentleman will, for his honor's sake, have one bout with you. He cannot by the *duello* avoid it. But he has promised me, as he is a gentleman and a soldier, he will not hurt you. Come on, to 't. 232

SIR ANDREW: Pray God he keep his oath!

Enter Antonio.

VIOLA: I do assure you, 'tis against my will. [*They draw.*]

ANTONIO: [*drawing, to Sir Andrew*]
Put up your sword. If this young gentleman
Have done offense, I take the fault on me;
If you offend him, I for him defy you.

SIR TOBY: You, sir? Why, what are you?

ANTONIO: One, sir, that for his love dares yet do more
Than you have heard him brag to you he will.

SIR TOBY: [*drawing*] Nay, if you be an undertaker, I am for you. 242

Enter Officers.

FABIAN: O good Sir Toby, hold! Here come the officers.

---

207 firago virago **pass** bout
209 answer return hit
215 Capilet i.e., "little horse." (From "capel," a nag.)
216 motion offer
219 take up settle, make up
221 He . . . him i.e., Cesario has as horrible a conception of Sir Andrew
225 supportance upholding

208 stuck in stoccado, a thrust in fencing
210 to in the service of

217 perdition of souls i.e., loss of lives

232 *duello* dueling code
242 undertaker one who takes upon himself a task or business; here, a challenger **for you** ready for you

SIR TOBY: [*to Antonio*]   I'll be with you anon.

VIOLA: [*to Sir Andrew*]   Pray, sir, put your sword up, if you please.

SIR ANDREW: Marry, will I, sir; and for that I promised you, I'll be as good as my word.   246
    He will bear you easily, and reins well.   247

FIRST OFFICER: This is the man. Do thy office.

SECOND OFFICER: Antonio, I arrest thee at the suit
    Of Count Orsino.

ANTONIO: You do mistake me, sir.

FIRST OFFICER: No, sir, no jot. I know your favor well,   252
    Though now you have no sea-cap on your head.—
    Take him away. He knows I know him well.

ANTONIO: I must obey. [*To Viola.*] This comes with seeking you.
    But there's no remedy; I shall answer it.   256
    What will you do, now my necessity
    Makes me to ask you for my purse? It grieves me
    Much more for what I cannot do for you
    Than what befalls myself. You stand amazed,
    But be of comfort.

SECOND OFFICER: Come, sir, away.

ANTONIO: [*to Viola*]   I must entreat of you some of that money.

VIOLA: What money, sir?
    For the fair kindness you have showed me here,
    And part being prompted by your present trouble,   266
    Out of my lean and low ability
    I'll lend you something. My having is not much;   268
    I'll make division of my present with you.   269
    Hold, there's half my coffer.   [*She offers money.*]   270

ANTONIO: Will you deny me now?
    Is 't possible that my deserts to you   272
    Can lack persuasion? Do not tempt my misery,   273
    Lest that it make me so unsound a man   274
    As to upbraid you with those kindnesses
    That I have done for you.

VIOLA: I know of none,
    Nor know I you by voice or any feature.
    I hate ingratitude more in a man
    Than lying, vainness, babbling drunkenness,   280
    Or any taint of vice whose strong corruption
    Inhabits our frail blood.

ANTONIO: O heavens themselves!

SECOND OFFICER: Come, sir, I pray you, go.

ANTONIO: Let me speak a little. This youth that you see here
    I snatched one half out of the jaws of death,
    Relieved him with such sanctity of love,   287

---

246 for that as for what
252 favor face
256 answer it stand trial and make reparation for it
266 part partly
269 present present store
272–273 deserts . . . persuasion claims on you can fail to persuade you to help me
273 tempt try too severely
280 vainness vaingloriousness

247 He i.e., the horse

268 having wealth
270 coffer purse (Literally, strongbox.)

274 unsound morally weak, lacking in self-control
287 such much

And to his image, which methought did promise   288
Most venerable worth, did I devotion.   289

FIRST OFFICER: What's that to us? The time goes by. Away!

ANTONIO: But, O, how vile an idol proves this god!
Thou hast, Sebastian, done good feature shame.   292
In nature there's no blemish but the mind;
None can be called deformed but the unkind.   294
Virtue is beauty, but the beauteous evil   295
Are empty trunks o'erflourished by the devil.   296

FIRST OFFICER: The man grows mad. Away with him! Come, come, sir.

ANTONIO: Lead me on.   *Exit [with Officers].*

VIOLA: [*aside*]
Methinks his words do from such passion fly
That he believes himself. So do not I.
Prove true, imagination, O, prove true,   300
That I, dear brother, be now ta'en for you!

SIR TOBY: Come hither, knight. Come hither, Fabian.
We'll whisper o'er a couplet or two of most sage saws.   304

[*They gather apart from Viola.*]

VIOLA: He named Sebastian. I my brother know   305
Yet living in my glass; even such and so   306
In favor was my brother, and he went
Still in this fashion, color, ornament,   308
For him I imitate. O, if it prove,   309
Tempests are kind, and salt waves fresh in love!   [*Exit.*]

SIR TOBY: A very dishonest paltry boy, and more a coward than a hare. His dishon-   311
esty appears in leaving his friend here in necessity and denying him; and for his   312
cowardship, ask Fabian.

FABIAN: A coward, a most devout coward, religious in it.   314

SIR ANDREW: 'Slid, I'll after him again and beat him.   315

SIR TOBY: Do, cuff him soundly, but never draw thy sword.

SIR ANDREW: An I do not—   [*Exit.*]

FABIAN: Come, let's see the event.   318

SIR TOBY: I dare lay any money 'twill be nothing yet.   319

Exeunt.

---

288 image what he appeared to be (playing on the idea of a religious icon to be venerated)
289 venerable worth worthiness of being venerated
292 Thou . . . shame i.e., you have shamed physical beauty by showing that it does not always reflect inner beauty
294 unkind ungrateful, unnatural
295 beauteous evil those who are outwardly beautiful but evil within
296 trunks (1) chests (2) bodies   **o'erflourished** (1) covered with ornamental carvings (2) made outwardly beautiful
300 So . . . I i.e., I do not believe myself (in the hope that has arisen in me)
304 saws sayings
305–306 I . . . glass i.e., I know my brother is virtually alive every time I look in a mirror, because we looked so much alike
308 Still always   **309 prove** prove true
311 dishonest dishonorable   **311–312 dishonesty** dishonor
312 denying refusing to acknowledge   **314 religious in it** making a religion of cowardice
315 'Slid by his (God's) eyelid   **318 event** outcome
319 lay wager   **yet** nevertheless, after all

Act 3 Response Statement Questions

- In Scene 2, Sir Toby and Fabian hatch a plan for Sir Andrew to challenge "Cesario" to a fight to impress Olivia and win her love. Do you find their thinking logical or conventional within the patterns of courtship in your culture? If so, can you identify any ideology that lies behind it?
- Can you list all the confusions and cases of mistaking the truth that have been established through Act 3? What potential does each of these have for turning out happily or causing trouble? Is any of these problems potentially more dangerous than the others?
- How would you describe the progress of the plot or plots at the end of Act 3? Has there been a turning point or a major climax in the main plot? Where do you anticipate the main or secondary plots heading through Acts 4 and 5?

Act 4, Scene 1

Enter Sebastian and Clown [Feste]

FESTE: Will you make be believe that I am not sent for you?

SEBASTIAN: Go to, go to, thou art a foolish fellow. Let me be clear of thee.

FESTE: Well held out, i' faith! No, I do not know you, nor I am not sent to you by my   3
lady to bid you come speak with her, nor your name is not Master Cesario, nor
this is not my nose, neither. Nothing that is so is so.

SEBASTIAN: I prithee, vent thy folly somewhere else. Thou know'st not me.   6

FESTE: Vent my folly! He has heard that word of some great man, and now applies it   7
to a fool. Vent my folly! I am afraid this great lubber, the world, will prove a cock-   8
ney. I prithee now, ungird thy strangeness and tell me what I shall vent to my   9
lady. Shall I vent to her that thou art coming?

SEBASTIAN: I prithee, foolish Greek, depart from me. There's money for thee. [*He*   11
gives money.] If you tarry longer, I shall give worse payment.

FESTE: By my troth, thou hast an open hand. These wise men that give fools money   13
get themselves a good report—after fourteen years' purchase.   14

Enter [Sir] Andrew, [Sir] Toby, and Fabian.

SIR ANDREW: Now, sir, have I met you again? There's for you!

[He strikes Sebastian.]

SEBASTIAN: Why, there's for thee, and there, and there!

[He beats Sir Andrew with the hilt of his dagger.]

4.1. Location: Before Olivia's house.

3 held out kept up

6 vent (1) give vent to (2) void, excrete

7 of from, suited to the diction of; or, with reference to

8 lubber lout

8–9 cockney effeminate or foppish fellow (Feste comically despairs of finding common sense anywhere if people start using affected phrases like those Sebastian uses.)

9 ungird thy strangeness put off your affectation of being a stranger (Feste apes the kind of high-flown speech he has just deplored.)

11 Greek (1) one who speaks gibberish (as in "It's all Greek to me") (2) buffoon (as in "merry Greek")

13 open generous (with money or with blows)

14 report reputation   **after . . . purchase** i.e., at great cost and after long delays. (Land was ordinarily valued at the price of twelve years' rental; the Fool adds two years to this figure.)

Are all the people mad?

SIR TOBY: Hold, sir, or I'll throw your dagger o'er the house.

FESTE: This will I tell my lady straight. I would not be in some of your coats for   19
twopence.   [*Exit.*]

SIR TOBY: Come on, sir, hold!   [*He grips Sebastian.*]

SIR ANDREW: Nay, let him alone. I'll go another way to work with him. I'll have an   22
action of battery against him, if there be any law in Illyria. Though I struck him   23
first, yet it's no matter for that.

SEBASTIAN: Let go thy hand!

SIR TOBY: Come, sir, I will not let you go. Come, my young soldier, put up your iron.
You are well fleshed. Come on.   27

SEBASTIAN: I will be free from thee. [*He breaks free and draws his sword.*]
What wouldst thou now?
If thou dar'st tempt me further, draw thy sword.   30

SIR TOBY: What, what? Nay, then I must have an ounce or two of this malapert blood   31
from you.   [*He draws.*]
Enter Olivia.

OLIVIA: Hold, Toby! On thy life I charge thee, hold!

SIR TOBY: Madam—

OLIVIA: Will it be ever thus? Ungracious wretch,
Fit for the mountains and the barbarous caves,
Where manners ne'er were preached! Out of my sight!—
Be not offended, dear Cesario.—
Rudesby, begone!   39

[*Exeunt Sir Toby, Sir Andrew, and Fabian.*]

I prithee, gentle friend,
Let thy fair wisdom, not thy passion, sway
In this uncivil and unjust extent   42
Against thy peace. Go with me to my house,   43
And hear thou there how many fruitless pranks   44
This ruffian hath botched up, that thou thereby   45
Mayst smile at this. Thou shalt not choose but go.   46
Do not deny. Beshrew his soul for me!   47
He started one poor heart of mine, in thee.   48

SEBASTIAN: [*aside*]   What relish is in this? How runs the stream?   49
Or I am mad, or else this is a dream.   50
Let fancy still my sense in Lethe steep;
If it be thus to dream, still let me sleep!   51

OLIVIA: Nay, come, I prithee. Would thou'dst be ruled by me!

---

19 straight at once
27 fleshed initiated into battle
31 malapert saucy, impudent
42 extent attack
46 Thou . . . go I insist on your going with me
47 deny refuse   **Beshrew** curse. (A mild oath.)   **for me** on my account
48 He . . . thee i.e., he alarmed half of my heart, which lies in your bosom (To *start* is also to drive an animal such as a *hart* [*heart*] from its cover, though the term is more usually applied to rabbits.)
49 What . . . this? i.e., what am I to make of this? (*Relish* means "taste.")
50 Or either
51 fancy imagination   **still** ever   **Lethe** the river of forgetfulness in the underworld; i.e., forgetfulness

22–23 action of battery lawsuit for physical assault
30 tempt make trial of
39 Rudesby ruffian
45 botched up clumsily contrived

SEBASTIAN: Madam, I will.
OLIVIA: O, say so, and so be!
Exeunt.

Act 4, Scene 2

Enter Maria [with a gown and a false beard], and Clown [Feste]

MARIA: Nay, I prithee, put on this gown and this beard; make him believe thou art
Sir Topas the curate. Do it quickly. I'll call Sir Toby the whilst.   [*Exit.*]   2

FESTE: Well, I'll put it on, and I will dissemble myself in 't, and I would I were the first   3
that ever dissembled in such a gown. [*He disguises himself in gown and
beard.*] I am not tall enough to become the function well, nor lean enough to be   5
thought a good student; but to be said an honest man and a good housekeeper   6
goes as fairly as to say a careful man and a great scholar. The competitors enter.   7

Enter [Sir] Toby [and Maria].

SIR TOBY: Jove bless thee, Master Parson.

FESTE: *Bonos dies,* Sir Toby. For, as the old hermit of Prague, that never saw pen and   9
ink, very wittily said to a niece of King Gorboduc, "That that is, is"; so I, being   10
Master Parson, am Master Parson; for what is "that" but "that," and "is" but "is"?

SIR TOBY: To him, Sir Topas.

FESTE: What, ho, I say! Peace in this prison!

[He approaches the door behind which Malvolio is confined.]

SIR TOBY: The knave counterfeits well; a good knave.

MALVOLIO: *(within)*   Who calls there?

FESTE: Sir Topas the curate, who comes to visit Malvolio the lunatic.

MALVOLIO: Sir Topas, Sir Topas, good Sir Topas, go to my lady—

FESTE: Out, hyperbolical fiend! How vexest thou this man! Talkest thou nothing but   18
of ladies?

SIR TOBY: Well said, Master Parson.

MALVOLIO: Sir Topas, never was man thus wronged. Good Sir Topas, do not think I
am mad. They have laid me here in hideous darkness.

FESTE: Fie, thou dishonest Satan! I call thee by the most modest terms, for I am one   23
of those gentle ones that will use the devil himself with courtesy. Sayst thou
that house is dark?   25

4.2. Location: Olivia's house.

2 Sir (An honorific title for priests.)   **Topas** (A name perhaps derived from Chaucer's comic
knight in the "Rime of Sir Thopas" or from a similar character in Lyly's *Endymion.* Topaz, a
semiprecious stone, was believed to be a cure for lunacy.)   **the whilst** in the meantime
3 dissemble disguise (with a play on "feign")
5 become grace, adorn   **function** priestly office   **lean** (Scholars were proverbially sparing of
diet.)
6 student scholar (in divinity)   **said** called, known as   **housekeeper** household manager,
hospitable person
7 goes as fairly as sounds just as honorable as   **careful** painstaking in studies (Feste suggests
that honesty and charity are found as often in ordinary men as in clerics.)   **competitors**
associates, partners (in this plot)
9 *Bonos dies* good day   **hermit of Prague** (Probably another invented authority.)
10 King Gorboduc a legendary king of ancient Britain, protagonist in the English tragedy
Gorboduc (1562)
18 hyperbolical vehement, boisterous   **fiend** i.e., the devil supposedly possessing Malvolio
23 modest terms mild terms (such as "dishonest" instead of "lying")
25 house i.e., room

MALVOLIO: As hell, Sir Topas.

FESTE: Why, it hath bay windows transparent as barricadoes, and the clerestories   27
toward the south north are as lustrous as ebony; and yet complainest thou of
obstruction?

MALVOLIO: I am not mad, Sir Topas. I say to you this house is dark.

FESTE: Madman, thou errest. I say there is no darkness but ignorance, in which thou
art more puzzled than the Egyptians in their fog.   32

MALVOLIO: I say this house is as dark as ignorance, though ignorance were as dark as
hell; and I say there was never man thus abused. I am no more mad than you
are. Make the trial of it in any constant question.   35

FESTE: What is the opinion of Pythagoras concerning wildfowl?   36

MALVOLIO: That the soul of our grandam might haply inhabit a bird.   37

FESTE: What think'st thou of his opinion?

MALVOLIO: I think nobly of the soul, and no way approve his opinion.

FESTE: Fare thee well. Remain thou still in darkness. Thou shalt hold th' opinion of
Pythagoras ere I will allow of thy wits, and fear to kill a woodcock lest thou dis-   41
possess the soul of thy grandam. Fare thee well.

[He moves away from Malvolio's prison.]

MALVOLIO: Sir Topas, Sir Topas!

SIR TOBY: My most exquisite Sir Topas!

FESTE: Nay, I am for all waters.   45

MARIA: Thou mightst have done this without thy beard and gown. He sees thee not.

SIR TOBY: To him in thine own voice, and bring me word how thou find'st him. I
would we were well rid of this knavery. If he may be conveniently delivered, I   48
would he were, for I am now so far in offense with my niece that I cannot pursue with any safety this sport to the upshot. Come by and by to my chamber.   50

Exit [with Maria].

FESTE: *[singing as he approaches Malvolio's prison]*
"Hey, Robin, jolly Robin,   51
Tell me how thy lady does."   52

MALVOLIO: Fool!

FESTE: "My lady is unkind, pardie."   54

MALVOLIO: Fool!

FESTE: "Alas, why is she so?"

MALVOLIO: Fool, I say!

FESTE: "She loves another—"Who calls, ha?

---

27 barricadoes barricades (which are opaque. Feste speaks comically in impossible paradoxes,
but Malvolio seems not to notice.)   **clerestories** windows in an upper wall

32 Egyptians . . . fog (Alluding to the darkness brought upon Egypt by Moses; see Exodus
10:21–23.)

35 constant question problem that requires consecutive reasoning

36 Pythagoras . . . wildfowl (An opening for the discussion of transmigration of souls, a doctrine
held by Pythagoras.)

37 haply perhaps

41 allow of thy wits certify your sanity   **woodcock** (A proverbially stupid bird, easily caught.)

45 Nay . . . waters i.e., indeed, I can turn my hand to anything

48 delivered i.e., delivered from prison

50 upshot conclusion

51–52 Hey, Robin . . . does (Another fragment of an old song, a version of which is attributed to
Sir Thomas Wyatt.)

54 pardie i.e., by God, certainly

MALVOLIO: Good Fool, as ever thou wilt deserve well at my hand, help me to a candle, and pen, ink, and paper. As I am a gentleman, I will live to be thankful to thee for 't.

FESTE: Master Malvolio?

MALVOLIO: Ay, good Fool.

FESTE: Alas, sir, how fell you beside your five wits?   64

MALVOLIO: Fool, there was never man so notoriously abused. I am as well in my   65
wits, Fool, as thou art.

FESTE: But as well? Then you are mad indeed, if you be no better in your wits than a   67
fool.

MALVOLIO: They have here propertied me, keep me in darkness, send ministers to   69
me—asses—and do all they can to face me out of my wits.   70

FESTE: Advise you what you say. The minister is here. [*He speaks as Sir Topas.*]   71
Malvolio, Malvolio, thy wits the heavens restore! Endeavor thyself to sleep, and
leave thy vain bibble-babble.

MALVOLIO: Sir Topas!

FESTE: [*in Sir Topas' voice*]   Maintain no words with him, good fellow. [*In his
own voice.*] Who, I, sir? Not I, sir. God b' wi' you, good Sir Topas. [*In Sir Topas'*   76
voice.] Marry, amen. [*In his own voice.*] I will, sir, I will.

MALVOLIO: Fool! Fool! Fool, I say!

FESTE: Alas, sir, be patient. What say you, sir? I am shent for speaking to you.   79

MALVOLIO: Good Fool, help me to some light and some paper. I tell thee I am as well
in my wits as any man in Illyria.

FESTE: Welladay that you were, sir!   82

MALVOLIO: By this hand, I am. Good Fool, some ink, paper, and light; and convey
what I will set down to my lady. It shall advantage thee more than ever the bearing of letter did.

FESTE: I will help you to 't. But tell me true, are you not mad indeed, or do you but
counterfeit?

MALVOLIO: Believe me, I am not. I tell thee true.

FESTE: Nay, I'll ne'er believe a madman till I see his brains. I will fetch you light and
paper and ink.

MALVOLIO: Fool, I'll requite it in the highest degree. I prithee, begone.

FESTE: [*sings*]
                    I am gone, sir,
                    And anon, sir,
                 I'll be with you again,
                    In a trice,
                    Like to the old Vice,
               Your need to sustain;   96

                    Who, with dagger of lath,
                    In his rage and his wrath,   98

---

64 beside out of   **five wits** The intellectual faculties, usually listed as common wit, imagination, fantasy, judgment, and memory
65 notoriously abused egregiously ill treated   **67 But** only
69 propertied me i.e., treated me as property and thrown me into the lumber-room
70 face . . . wits brazenly represent me as having lost my wits
71 Advise you take care   **76 God b' wi' you** God be with you
79 shent scolded, rebuked   **82 Welladay** alas, would that
96 Vice comic tempter of the "old" morality plays
98 dagger of lath comic weapon of the Vice in at least some morality plays

Cries, "Aha!" to the devil;
    Like a mad lad,
    "Pare thy nails, dad?
    Adieu, goodman devil!" *Exit.*   102
    103

Act 4, Scene 3

Enter Sebastian [with a pearl].

SEBASTIAN: This is the air; that is the glorious sun;
    This pearl she gave me, I do feel 't and see 't;
    And though 'tis wonder that enwraps me thus,
    Yet 'tis not madness. Where's Antonio, then?
    I could not find him at the Elephant;
    Yet there he was, and there I found this credit,   6
    That he did range the town to seek me out.
    His counsel now might do me golden service;
    For though my soul disputes well with my sense   9
    That this may be some error, but no madness,
    Yet doth this accident and flood of fortune   11
    So far exceed all instance, all discourse,   12
    That I am ready to distrust mine eyes
    And wrangle with my reason that persuades me
    To any other trust but that I am mad,
    Or else the lady's mad. Yet if 'twere so,   15
    She could not sway her house, command her followers,
    Take and give back affairs and their dispatch   17
    With such a smooth, discreet, and stable bearing   18
    As I perceive she does. There's something in 't
    That is deceivable. But here the lady comes.   21

Enter Olivia and Priest.

OLIVIA: Blame not this haste of mine. If you mean well,
    Now go with me and with this holy man
    Into the chantry by. There, before him,   24
    And underneath that consecrated roof,
    Plight me the full assurance of your faith,
    That my most jealous and too doubtful soul   27
    May live at peace. He shall conceal it
    Whiles you are willing it shall come to note,   29

---

102 Pare thy nails (Evidently a comic routine in Tudor morality drama, though no samples survive.)
103 goodman title for a person of substance but not of gentle birth (This line could be Feste's farewell to Malvolio and his "devil.")
4.3. Location: Olivia's garden.
6 was was previously   **credit** report
9 my soul . . . sense i.e., both my rational faculties and my physical senses come to the conclusion
11 accident unexpected event   **12 instance** precedent   **discourse** reason
15 trust belief   **17 sway** rule
18 Take . . . dispatch receive reports on matters of household business and see to their execution
21 deceivable deceptive   **24 chantry by** privately endowed chapel nearby
27 jealous anxious, mistrustful   **doubtful** full of doubts
29 Whiles until   **come to note** become known

What time we will our celebration keep   30
    According to my birth. What do you say?   31
SEBASTIAN: I'll follow this good man, and go with you,
    And having sworn truth, ever will be true.
OLIVIA: Then lead the way, good Father, and heavens so shine
    That they may fairly note this act of mine!   35

Exeunt.

Act 4 Response Statement Questions

- What is your response to what happens to Malvolio in Scene 2? Does he deserve what happens to him? Why or why not? Do you find yourself enjoying his predicament or feeling sympathy for him? In either case, what aspects of your ideology influence your response? Do you feel the text is successful as comedy in its treatment of the Malvolio plot?
- Are you surprised by Olivia's decision to marry Sebastian? Do you think it will cause problems if and when Olivia finds out she hasn't married "Cesario"? If so, does her decision please or disturb you?

Act 5, Scene 1

Enter Clown [Feste] and Fabian.

FABIAN: Now, as thou lov'st me, let me see his letter.
FESTE: Good Master Fabian, grant me another request.
FABIAN: Anything.
FESTE: Do not desire to see this letter.
FABIAN: This is to give a dog and in recompense desire my dog again.   5

Enter Duke [Orsino], Viola, Curio, and lords.

ORSINO: Belong you to the Lady Olivia, friends?
FESTE: Ay, sir, we are some of her trappings.
ORSINO: I know thee well. How dost thou, my good fellow?   7
FESTE: Truly, sir, the better for my foes and the worse for my friends.
ORSINO: Just the contrary—the better for thy friends.   9
FESTE: No, sir, the worse.
ORSINO: How can that be?
FESTE: Marry, sir, they praise me, and make an ass of me. Now my foes tell me plainly   13
    I am an ass, so that by my foes, sir, I profit in the knowledge of myself, and by my
    friends I am abused; so that, conclusions to be as kisses, if your four negatives   15

---

30 What time at which time   **our celebration** i.e., the actual marriage (What they are about to perform is a binding betrothal.)
31 birth social position   **35 fairly note** look upon with favor
5.1. Location: Before Olivia's house.
  5 This . . . again (Apparently a reference to a well-known reply of Dr. Bulleyn when Queen Elizabeth asked for his dog and promised a gift of his choosing in return; he asked to have h dog back.)
7 trappings ornaments, decorations   **9 for** because of
13 make as ass of me i.e., flatter me into foolishly thinking well of myself
15 abused flatteringly deceived
15–16 conclusions . . . affirmatives i.e., as when a young lady, asked for a kiss, says "no, no" really meaning "yes"; or, as in grammar, two negatives make an affirmative
15 your four negatives the four negatives that people talk about

make your two affirmatives, why then the worse for my friends and the better   16
for my foes.

ORSINO: Why, this is excellent.

FESTE: By my troth, sir, no, though it please you to be one of my friends.   19

ORSINO: Thou shalt not be the worse for me. There's gold.   [*He gives a coin.*]

FESTE: But that it would be double-dealing, sir, I would you could make it another.   21

ORSINO: O, you give me ill counsel.

FESTE: Put your grace in your pocket, sir, for this once, and let your flesh and blood   23
obey it.   24

ORSINO: Well, I will be so much a sinner to be a double-dealer. There's another. [*He   25
gives another coin.*]

FESTE: *Primo, secundo, tertio,* is a good play, and the old saying is, the third pays for   26
all. The triplex, sir, is a good tripping measure; or the bells of Saint Bennet, sir,   27
may put you in mind—one, two, three.

ORSINO: You can fool no more money out of me at this throw. If you will let your   29
lady know I am here to speak with her, and bring her along with you, it may
awake my bounty further.

FESTE: Marry, sir, lullaby to your bounty till I come again. I go, sir, but I would not
have you to think that my desire of having is the sin of covetousness. But as you
say, sir, let your bounty take a nap. I will awake it anon.   *Exit.*

Enter Antonio and Officers.

VIOLA: Here comes the man, sir, that did rescue me.

ORSINO: That face of his I do remember well,
Yet when I saw it last it was besmeared
As black as Vulcan in the smoke of war.
A baubling vessel was he captain of,   38
For shallow draft and bulk unprizable,   39
With which such scatheful grapple did he make   40
With the most noble bottom of our fleet   41
That very envy and the tongue of loss   42
Cried fame and honor on him. What's the matter?   43

FIRST OFFICER: Orsino, this is that Antonio
That took the *Phoenix* and her freight from Candy,
And this is he that did the *Tiger* board   46

---

19 though even though   **friends** i.e., those who, according to Feste's syllogism, flatter him
21 But except for the fact   **double-dealing** (1) giving twice (2) deceit, duplicity
23 Put . . . pocket (1) pocket up your virtue, your grace before God (2) reach in your pocket or
purse and show your customary grace or munificence. (*Your Grace* is also the formal way of
addressing a duke.)
24 it i.e., my "ill counsel"   **25 to be** as to be
26 play (Perhaps a mathematical game or game of dice.)
26–27 the third . . . all the third time is lucky (Proverbial.)
27 triplex triple time in music   **Saint Bennet** church of St. Benedict
29 throw (1) time (2) throw of the dice
38 Vulcan Roman god of fire and smith to the other gods; his face was blackened by the fire.
39 baubling insignificant, trifling
40 For because of   **draft** depth of water a ship draws   **unprizable** of value too slight to be estimated, not worth taking as a "prize"
41 scatheful destructive   **42 bottom** ship
43 very envy i.e., even those who had most reason to hate him, his enemies   **loss** i.e., the losers
46 from Candy on her return from Candia, or Crete

When your young nephew Titus lost his leg.
Here in the streets, desperate of shame and state,   49
In private brabble did we apprehend him.   50

VIOLA: He did me kindness, sir, drew on my side,
But in conclusion put strange speech upon me.   52
I know not what 'twas but distraction.   53

ORSINO: Notable pirate, thou saltwater thief,   54
What foolish boldness brought thee to their mercies
Whom thou in terms so bloody and so dear   56
Hast made thine enemies?

ANTONIO: Orsino, noble sir,
Be pleased that I shake off these names you give me.   59
Antonio never yet was thief or pirate,
Though, I confess, on base and ground enough   61
Orsino's enemy. A witchcraft drew me hither.
That most ingrateful boy there by your side
From the rude sea's enraged and foamy mouth
Did I redeem; a wreck past hope he was.   65
His life I gave him, and did thereto add
My love, without retention or restraint,
All his in dedication. For his sake   67
Did I expose myself—pure for his love—   68
Into the danger of this adverse town,   69
Drew to defend him when he was beset;   70
Where being apprehended, his false cunning,
Not meaning to partake with me in danger,
Taught him to face me out of his acquaintance   74
And grew a twenty years' removèd thing   75
While one would wink; denied me mine own purse,   76
Which I had recommended to his use   77
Not half an hour before.

VIOLA: How can this be?

ORSINO: When came he to this town?

ANTONIO: Today, my lord; and for three months before,   81
No interim, not a minute's vacancy,
Both day and night did we keep company.

Enter Olivia and attendants.

ORSINO: Here comes the Countess. Now heaven walks on earth.
But for thee, fellow—fellow, thy words are madness.

---

49 desperate . . . state recklessly disregarding the disgrace that public quarreling would bring on him and his dangerous status as a wanted man
50 brabble brawl
53 but distraction unless (it was) madness
56 in terms so bloody in so bloodthirsty a manner **dear** costly, grievous
59 Be pleased that I allow me to
65 wreck person cast ashore from a wrecked vessel
67 retention reservation
69 pure entirely, purely
74 face . . . acquaintance brazenly deny he knew me
75–76 grew . . . wink in the twinkling of an eye acted as though we had been estranged for twenty years
77 recommended consigned

52 put . . . me spoke to me strangely
54 Notable notorious
61 base and ground solid grounds
68 All . . . dedication devoted wholly to him
70 Into unto **adverse** hostile

81 for as for

Three months this youth hath tended upon me;
But more of that anon. Take him aside.

OLIVIA: [*to Orsino*]   What would my lord—but that he may not have— 88
Wherein Olivia may seem serviceable?—
Cesario, you do not keep promise with me.

VIOLA: Madam?

ORSINO: Gracious Olivia—

OLIVIA: What do you say, Cesario?—Good my lord— 93

VIOLA: My lord would speak. My duty hushes me.

OLIVIA: If it be aught to the old tune, my lord,
It is as fat and fulsome to mine ear 96
As howling after music.

ORSINO: Still so cruel?

OLIVIA: Still so constant, lord.

ORSINO: What, to perverseness? You uncivil lady,
To whose ingrate and unauspicious altars
My soul the faithfull'st offerings have breathed out 101
That e'er devotion tendered! What shall I do?

OLIVIA: Even what it please my lord that shall become him. 104

ORSINO: Why should I not, had I the heart to do it,
Like to th' Egyptian thief at point of death
Kill what I love?—a savage jealousy 106
That sometimes savors nobly. But hear me this: 108
Since you to nonregardance cast my faith, 109
And that I partly know the instrument 110
That screws me from my true place in your favor, 111
Live you the marble-breasted tyrant still.
But this your minion, whom I know you love, 113
And whom, by heaven I swear, I tender dearly, 114
Him will I tear out of that cruel eye
Where he sits crownèd in his master's spite.— 116
Come, boy, with me. My thoughts are ripe in mischief.
I'll sacrifice the lamb that I do love, 118
To spite a raven's heart within a dove.   [*Going.*] 119

VIOLA: And I, most jocund, apt, and willingly, 120
To do you rest, a thousand deaths would die.   [*Going.*] 121

------

88 but . . . have except that which he may not have—i.e., my love
93 Good my lord (Olivia urges Orsino to listen to Cesario.)
96 fat and fulsome gross and offensive
101 ingrate ungrateful   **unauspicious** unpropitious, not disposed to be favorable
104 become suit
106 Egyptian thief (An allusion to the story of Theagenes and Chariclea in the *Ethiopica,* a Greek romance by Heliodorus. The robber chief, Thyamis of Memphis, having captured Chariclea and fallen in love with her, is attacked by a larger band of robbers; threatened w death, he attempts to slay her first.)
108 savors nobly is not without nobility   **109 nonregardance** neglect
110 that since   **111 screws** pries, forces
113 minion darling, favorite   **114 tender** regard
116 in . . . spite to the vexation of his master
118–119 I'll . . . dove i.e., I'll kill Cesario, whom I love, to revenge myself on this beautiful but black-hearted lady
120 apt readily
121 do you rest give you ease   **die** (with possible suggestion of "have an orgasm")

OLIVIA: Where goes Cesario?
VIOLA: After him I love
    More than I love these eyes, more than my life,
    More by all mores than e'er I shall love wife.   125
    If I do feign, you witnesses above
    Punish my life for tainting of my love!   127
OLIVIA: Ay me, detested! How am I beguiled!   128
VIOLA: Who does beguile you? Who does do you wrong?
OLIVIA: Hast thou forgot thyself? Is it so long?
    Call forth the holy father.   [*Exit an attendant.*]
ORSINO: [*to Viola*]   Come, away!
OLIVIA: Whither, my lord? Cesario, husband, stay.
ORSINO: Husband?
OLIVIA: Ay, husband. Can he that deny?
ORSINO: [*to Viola*]   Her husband, sirrah?   136
VIOLA: No, my lord, not I.
OLIVIA: Alas, it is the baseness of thy fear
    That makes thee strangle thy propriety.   139
    Fear not, Cesario, take thy fortunes up;
    Be that thou know'st thou art, and then thou art   141
    As great as that thou fear'st.   142

Enter Priest

                         O, welcome, Father!
    Father, I charge thee by thy reverence
    Here to unfold—though lately we intended
    To keep in darkness what occasion now
    Reveals before 'tis ripe—what thou dost know
    Hath newly passed between this youth and me.
PRIEST: A contract of eternal bond of love,
    Confirmed by mutual joinder of your hands,   150
    Attested by the holy close of lips,   151
    Strengthened by interchangement of your rings,
    And all the ceremony of this compact
    Sealed in my function, by my testimony;   154
    Since when, my watch hath told me, toward my grave
    I have traveled but two hours.
ORSINO: [*to Viola*]   O thou dissembling cub! What wilt thou be
    When time hath sowed a grizzle on thy case?   158
    Or will not else thy craft so quickly grow
    That thine own trip shall be thine overthrow?   160
    Farewell, and take her, but direct thy feet
    Where thou and I henceforth may never meet.

---

125 by all mores by all such comparisons
127 Punish . . . love punish me with death for being disloyal to the love I feel
128 detested hated and denounced by another
136 sirrah (The normal way of addressing an inferior.)
139 strangle thy propriety i.e., deny what you are   **141 that** that which
142 that thou fear'st him you fear, i.e., Orsino   **150 joinder** joining
151 close meeting
154 Sealed in my function ratified through my carrying out of my priestly office
158 a grizzle scattering of gray hair   **case** skin
160 trip wrestling trick used to throw an opponent (You'll get overclever and trip yourself up.)

VIOLA: My Lord, I do protest—
OLIVIA: O, do not swear!
Hold little faith, though thou hast too much fear.   165

Enter Sir Andrew.

SIR ANDREW: For the love of God, a surgeon! Send one presently to Sir Toby.   166
OLIVIA: What's the matter?
SIR ANDREW: He's broke my head across, and has given Sir Toby a bloody coxcomb   168
too. For the love of God, your help! I had rather than forty pound I were at home.
OLIVIA: Who has done this, Sir Andrew?
SIR ANDREW: The Count's gentleman, one Cesario. We took him for a coward, but he's
the very devil incardinate.   172
ORSINO: My gentleman, Cesario?
SIR ANDREW: 'Od's lifelings, here he is!—You broke my head for nothing, and that 174
that I did I was set on to do 't by Sir Toby.
VIOLA: Why do you speak to me? I never hurt you.
You drew your sword upon me without cause,
But I bespake you fair, and hurt you not.   178
SIR ANDREW: If a bloody coxcomb be a hurt, you have hurt me. I think you set noth- 179
ing by a bloody coxcomb.   180

Enter [Sir] Toby and Clown [Feste].

Here comes Sir Toby, halting. You shall hear more.   181
But if he had not been in drink, he would have tickled you othergates than he did.   182
ORSINO: How now, gentleman? How is 't with you?
SIR TOBY: That's all one. He's hurt me, and there's th' end on 't.—Sot, didst see Dick 184
surgeon, sot?
FESTE: O, he's drunk, Sir Toby, an hour agone; his eyes were set at eight i' the morning. 186
SIR TOBY: Then he's a rogue, and a passy measures pavane. I hate a drunken rogue. 187
OLIVIA: Away with him! Who hath made this havoc with them?
SIR ANDREW: I'll help you, Sir Toby, because we'll be dressed together.   189
SIR TOBY: Will you help? An ass-head and a coxcomb and a knave, a thin-faced
knave, a gull!
OLIVIA: Get him to bed, and let his hurt be looked to.

[Exeunt Feste, Fabian, Sir Toby, and Sir Andrew.] Enter Sebastian.

SEBASTIAN: I am sorry, madam, I have hurt your kinsman;
But, had it been the brother of my blood,
I must have done no less with wit and safety.—   194
You throw a strange regard upon me, and by that   195
                                                                                     196

---

165 Hold little faith keep at least a little part of what you promised
166 presently immediately
168 broke broken the skin, cut   **coxcomb** fool's cap resembling the crest of a cock; here, head
172 incardinate (For "incarnate.")   **174 'Od's lifelings** by God's little lives
178 bespake you fair addressed you courteously
179–180 set nothing by regard as insignificant
181 halting limping   **182 othergates** otherwise
184 That's all one it doesn't matter; never mind   **there's . . . on 't** that's all there is to it   **Sot** (1)
food (2) drunkard
186 agone ago   **set** fixed or closed
187 passy measures pavane passe-measure pavane, a slow-moving, stately dance (suggesting
Sir Toby's impatience to have his wounds dressed)
189 be dressed have our wounds surgically dressed   **194 the brother of my blood** my own brother
195 with wit and safety with intelligent concern for my own safety
196 strange regard look such as one directs at a stranger

I do perceive it hath offended you.
Pardon me, sweet one, even for the vows
We made each other but so late ago.

ORSINO: One face, one voice, one habit, and two persons,   200
A natural perspective, that is and is not!   201

SEBASTIAN: Antonio, O my dear Antonio!
How have the hours racked and tortured me   203
Since I have lost thee!

ANTONIO: Sebastian are you?

SEBASTIAN: Fear'st thou that, Antonio?   206

ANTONIO: How have you made division of yourself?
An apple cleft in two is not more twin
Than these two creatures. Which is Sebastian?

OLIVIA: Most wonderful!

SEBASTIAN: [seeing Viola] Do I stand there? I never had a brother;
Nor can there be that deity in my nature
Of here and everywhere. I had a sister,   213
Whom the blind waves and surges have devoured.   214
Of charity, what kin are you to me?   215
What countryman? What name? What parentage?

VIOLA: Of Messaline. Sebastian was my father.
Such a Sebastian was my brother, too.
So went he suited to his watery tomb.   219
If spirits can assume both form and suit,   220
You come to fright us.

SEBASTIAN: A spirit I am indeed,
But am in that dimension grossly clad   223
Which from the womb I did participate.   224
Were you a woman, as the rest goes even,   225
I should my tears let fall upon your cheek
And say, "Thrice welcome, drownèd Viola!"

VIOLA: My father had a mole upon his brow.

SEBASTIAN: And so had mine.

VIOLA: And died that day when Viola from her birth
Had numbered thirteen years.

SEBASTIAN: O, that record is lively in my soul!   232
He finishèd indeed his mortal act
That day that made my sister thirteen years.

VIOLA: If nothing lets to make us happy both   235
But this my masculine usurped attire,
Do not embrace me till each circumstance
Of place, time, fortune, do cohere and jump   238
That I am Viola—which to confirm

---

200 habit dress
201 A natural perspective an optical device or illusion created in this instance by nature
203 racked tortured
213 here and everywhere omnipresence
215 Of charity (tell me) in kindness
219 suited dressed; clad in human form
220 form and suit physical appearance and dress
223 in . . . clad clothed in that fleshly shape
224 participate possess in common with all humanity
225 as . . . even since everything else agrees
235 lets hinders

206 Fear'st thou that do you doubt that
214 blind heedless, indiscriminating

232 record recollection
238 jump coincide, fit exactly

I'll bring you to a captain in this town
Where lie my maiden weeds, by whose gentle help
I was preserved to serve this noble count.   241
All the occurrence of my fortune since
Hath been between this lady and this lord.

SEBASTIAN: [*to Olivia*] So comes it, lady, you have been mistook.
But nature to her bias drew in that.
You would have been contracted to a maid,   246
Nor are you therein, by my life, deceived.
You are betrothed both to a maid and man.   249

ORSINO: [*to Olivia*] Be not amazed; right noble is his blood.
If this be so, as yet the glass seems true,   251
I shall have share in this most happy wreck.   252
[*To Viola.*] Boy, thou hast said to me a thousand times
Thou never shouldst love woman like to me.   254

VIOLA: And all those sayings will I over swear,   254
And all those swearings keep as true in soul   255
As doth that orbèd continent the fire
That severs day from night.   257

ORSINO: Give me thy hand,
And let me see thee in thy woman's weeds.

VIOLA: The captain that did bring me first on shore
Hath my maid's garments. He upon some action
Is now in durance, at Malvolio's suit,   262
A gentleman and follower of my lady's.   263

OLIVIA: He shall enlarge him. Fetch Malvolio hither.
And yet, alas, now I remember me,   265
They say, poor gentleman, he's much distract.

Enter Clown [Feste] with a letter, and Fabian.

A most extracting frenzy of mine own
From my remembrance clearly banished his.   268
How does he, sirrah?   269

FESTE: Truly, madam, he holds Beelzebub at the stave's end as well as a man in his   271
case may do. He's here writ a letter to you; I should have given 't you today
morning. But as a madman's epistles are no gospels, so it skills not much when   273
they are delivered.   274

---

241 weeds clothes
246 nature . . . that nature followed her bent in that (The metaphor is from the game of bowls.)
249 a maid i.e., a virgin man
251 the glass i.e., the *natural perspective* of line 201
252 wreck shipwreck, accident   **254 like to me** as well as you love me
255 over swear swear again
257 As . . . fire i.e., as the sphere of the sun keeps the fire
262 action legal charge   **263 durance** imprisonment
265 enlarge release
268 extracting i.e., that obsessed me and drew all thoughts except of Cesario from my mind
269 his i.e., his madness
271 holds . . . end i.e., keeps the devil at a safe distance (The metaphor is of fighting with quar-
    terstaffs of long poles.)
273 a madman's . . . gospels i.e., there is no truth in a madman's letters (An allusion to readings
    in the church service of selected passages from the epistles and the gospels.)   **skills** matters
274 delivered (1) delivered to their recipient (2) read aloud

OLIVIA: Open 't and read it.

FESTE: Look then to be well edified when the fool delivers the madman. [*He reads*   276
loudly.] "By the Lord, madam—"

OLIVIA: How now, art thou mad?

FESTE: No, madam, I do but read madness. An your ladyship will have it as it ought   280
to be, you must allow *vox*.   281

OLIVIA: Prithee, read i' thy right wits.   281

FESTE: So I do, madonna; but to read his right wits is to read thus. Therefore per-   282
pend, my princess, and give ear.   283

OLIVIA: [*to Fabian*] Read it you, sirrah.

FABIAN: [*reads*] "By the Lord, madam, you wrong me, and the world shall know it.
Though you have put me into darkness and given your drunken cousin rule
over me, yet have I the benefit of my senses as well as your ladyship. I have your
own letter that induced me to the semblance I put on, with the which I doubt   288
not but to do myself much right or you much shame. Think of me as you please.
I leave my duty a little unthought of, and speak out of my injury.   290

THE madly used Malvolio."

OLIVIA: Did he write this?

FESTE: Ay, madam.

ORSINO: This savors not much of distraction.

OLIVIA: See him delivered, Fabian. Bring him hither.   295

[*Exit Fabian.*]

My lord, so please you, these things further thought on,   296
To think me as well a sister as a wife,   297
One day shall crown th' alliance on 't, so please you,   298
Here at my house and at my proper cost.   299

ORSINO: Madam, I am most apt t' embrace your offer.   300

[*To Viola.*] Your master quits you; and for your service done him,   301
So much against the mettle of your sex,   302
So far beneath your soft and tender breeding,
And since you called me master for so long,
Here is my hand. You shall from this time be
Your master's mistress.

OLIVIA: A sister! You are she.

Enter [Fabian, with] Malvolio.

ORSINO: Is this the madman?

OLIVIA: Ay, my lord, this same.
How now, Malvolio?

---

276 delivers speaks the words of   **280 *vox*** voice, i.e., an appropriately loud voice
281 to read . . . wits to express his true state of mind
282–283 perpend consider, attend (A deliberately lofty word.)
288 the which i.e., the letter
290 I leave . . . injury i.e., in saying this, I speak for the moment not as your steward should, but
as an injured party
295 delivered released
296 so . . . on if you are pleased on further consideration of all that has happened
297 To . . . wife to regard me as favorably as a sister-in-law as you had hoped to regard me as a
wife
298 crown . . . on 't i.e., serve as occasion for two marriages confirming our new relationship
299 proper own   **300 apt** ready
301 quits releases   **302 mettle** natural disposition

MALVOLIO: Madam, you have done me wrong,
 Notorious wrong.
OLIVIA: Have I, Malvolio? No.
MALVOLIO: [*showing a letter*] Lady, you have. Pray you, peruse that letter.
 You must not now deny it is your hand.
 Write from it, if you can, in hand or phrase,
 Or say 'tis not your seal, not your invention.   316
 You can say none of this. Well, grant it then,   317
 And tell me, in the modesty of honor,
 Why you have given me such clear lights of favor,   319
 Bade me come smiling and cross-gartered to you,   320
 To put on yellow stockings, and to frown
 Upon Sir Toby and the lighter people?
 And, acting this in an obedient hope,   323
 Why have you suffered me to be imprisoned,   324
 Kept in a dark house, visited by the priest,
 And made the most notorious geck and gull   326
 That e'er invention played on? Tell me why?   327
OLIVIA: Alas, Malvolio, this is not my writing,   328
 Though, I confess, much like the character;
 But out of question 'tis Maria's hand.   330
 And now I do bethink me, it was she   331
 First told me thou wast mad; then cam'st in smiling,
 And in such forms which here were presupposed   333
 Upon thee in the letter. Prithee, be content.   334
 This practice hath most shrewdly passed upon thee;
 But when we know the grounds and authors of it,   336
 Thou shalt be both the plaintiff and the judge
 Of thine own cause.
FABIAN: Good madam, hear me speak,
 And let no quarrel nor no brawl to come
 Taint the condition of this present hour,   341
 Which I have wondered at. In hope it shall not,   342
 Most freely I confess, myself and Toby
 Set this device against Malvolio here,
 Upon some stubborn and uncourteous parts
 We had conceived against him. Maria writ   346
 The letter at Sir Toby's great importance,   347
 In recompense whereof he hath married her.   348

316 from it differently   **317 invention** composition
319 in . . . honor in the name of all that is decent and honorable
320 clear lights evident signs   **323 lighter** lesser
324 acting . . . hope when I acted thus out of obedience to you and in hope of your favor
326 priest i.e., Feste   **327 geck** dupe
328 invention played on contrivance sported with **330 the character** my handwriting
331 out of beyond   **333 cam'st** you came
334 presupposed specified beforehand
336 practice plot **shrewdly** mischievously **passed** been perpetrated
341 to come in the future   **342 condition** (happy) nature
346 Upon on account of **parts** qualities, deeds
347 conceived against him seen and resented in him
348 importance importunity

How with a sportful malice it was followed　　　　　349
May rather pluck on laughter than revenge,　　　　　350
If that the injuries be justly weighed　　　　　351
That have on both sides passed.

OLIVIA:　[to Malvolio]　Alas, poor fool, how have they baffled thee!　　　353

FESTE:　Why, "Some are born great, some achieve greatness, and some have greatness
thrown upon them." I was one, sir, in this interlude, one Sir Topas, sir, but that's　　355
all one. "By the Lord, fool, I am not mad." But do you remember? "Madam, why　　356
laugh you at such a barren rascal? An you smile not, he's gagged." And thus the
whirligig of time brings in his revenges.　　358

MALVOLIO:　I'll be revenged on the whole pack of you!　　　　　[Exit.]

OLIVIA:　He hath been most notoriously abused.

ORSINO:　Pursue him, and entreat him to a peace.
He hath not told us of the captain yet.
When that is known, and golden time convents,　　　　　363
A solemn combination shall be made
Of our dear souls. Meantime, sweet sister,
We will not part from hence. Cesario, come—
For so you shall be, while you are a man;
But when in other habits you are seen,　　　　　368
Orsino's mistress and his fancy's queen.　　　　　369

Exeunt [all, except Feste].

FESTE:　(sings)
When that I was and a little tiny boy,　　　　　370
　　With hey, ho, the wind and the rain,
A foolish thing was but a toy,　　　　　372
　　For the rain it raineth every day.

But when I came to man's estate,
　　With hey, ho, the wind and the rain,
'Gainst knaves and thieves men shut their gate,
　　For the rain it raineth every day.

But when I came, alas, to wive,
　　With hey, ho, the wind and the rain,
By swaggering could I never thrive,
　　For the rain it raineth every day.

But when I came unto my beds,　　　　　382
　　With hey, ho, the wind and the rain,
With tosspots still had drunken heads,　　　　　384
　　For the rain it raineth every day.

A great while ago the world begun,
　　With hey, ho, the wind and the rain,

---

349 **followed** carried out
351 **If that** if
355 **interlude** little play
358 **whirligig** spinning top
368 **habits** attire
370 **and a little** a little
382 **unto my beds** i.e., (1) drunk to bed, or, perhaps, (2) in the evening of life
384 **tosspots** drunkards

350 **pluck on** induce
353 **baffled** disgraced, quelled
355–356 **that's all one** no matter for that
363 **convents** (1) summons, calls together (2) suits
369 **fancy's** love's
372 **toy** trifle

But that's all one, our play is done,
And we'll strive to please you every day.

[Exit.]

Act 5 Response Statement Questions

- How close to danger does the action veer in Act 5? Does this serve to heighten the comic pleasure when the "truth" is brought to light concerning who is who, or does it annoy you? How thin or wide is the line between comedy and tragedy in this play? in your literary experience otherwise?
- Does the action of the play resolve itself in the way you thought it would earlier? Are you satisfied with the resolution (whether it was what you predicted or not)? What does your response tell you about what you like about and expect from drama?

Overall Response Statement Questions

- Does any character learn anything through his or her experience in this play? If so, who is it and what kind of lesson does she or he learn? Will any lesson learned make the character a better person in the future? To what extent was your satisfaction with the way the play turned out related to your sense that any character was improving?
- Do you learn anything through your experience of reading this play, especially in the way of a moral lesson? Does the text have any applicability to "real life" or is it just a playful romp?
- In terms of the discussion of satiric and romantic comedy that preceded the text of the play, how would you characterize *Twelfth Night?*
- What is your assessment of Shakespeare's technical skill in this play? Does he try to manage more in the way of plots, characters, issues than he really can? Or does he "tie it all together" in aesthetically pleasing fashion?
- Does the text finally answer all the questions it raised for you along the way or are there loose ends? In either case, to what extent is that positive or negative in terms of your literary experience?
- *Share and Compare* How does the gender of different readers in your class or discussion group affect their responses to this play? Can you see in readers' responses any pattern according to gender? Are there such things as male and female "ideologies of love" that affect readers' responses?

BROADENING YOUR LITERARY EXPERIENCE THROUGH RESEARCH

Presumably, what you have read in this chapter and the writing you have done have shown you more than you knew before about the literary repertoire and ideology of *Twelfth Night*, including the features and practices of the Elizabethan theater and the ideology of the English culture in the sixteenth century. If you want to further broaden your knowledge with respect to

Twelfth Night, Shakespearean comedy, Elizabethan drama in general, English politics or philosophy, or any aspect of the ideology behind *Twelfth Night*, the best way to do that is through library research. The reading and writing you have done in this chapter may have raised questions for you that only further research can answer. That's good: Remember that it's questions and questioning that keep learning alive, and that answers are only provisional and temporary. The QAQ method promoted in Chapter 3 applies here too.

Here are some additional questions that you could pursue through library research, followed by a brief bibliography of sources for broadening your repertoire of knowledge in the area of Elizabethan comedy. Think of both the sources and the questions as just starting points for further investigation. Even a researched reading, however, should not be considered final. "The truth" about a text does not lie under a rock, waiting to be discovered, or in the library or in history; it may be pursued, but never possessed. Reading, learning, knowing are processes, of which research is a part. Whenever you read a text, whether you know a lot about it or just a little, you should try to be conscious of the dynamic interaction between you and the text.

Suggestions for Research

- Investigate the performance history of *Twelfth Night*. What different kinds of interpretations and emphases have directors or actors lent to the text over the years? Have directors left out certain scenes or parts or otherwise rewritten the text? How can you relate these decisions to changes in ideology over the years?
- Investigate some of the responses to Malvolio that readers have had over the years. Compare your own response to theirs. What differences in ideology are suggested by different responses to this character and his role in the text?
- Investigate feminist criticism of *Twelfth Night*—or any criticism that reads the text in terms of gender issues. What is your response to these readings? Are such critics "reading too much into" the text, or are their ideological perspectives allowing them to see things in the text that a different critical orientation would not?
- Investigate the text strategies of lost aristocrats, disguises, or mistaken identity in Shakespeare's comedies in general. What patterns or effects do critics see in these text strategies? How might you relate any such general pattern or effect to the particular text strategies in *Twelfth Night*?

Selected Bibliography

A good place to begin your search for further information on any of these topics is in the reference section of your library. For any of the above topics, you can find background information and get an overview of related issues and ideas by consulting specialized encyclopedias, handbooks, and readers' guides to particular areas of literature, defined by genre or historical period.

Often these kinds of reference works include their own bibliographies of relevant books and periodical articles. Here are some standard reference works for the study of Shakespearean comedy.

Cahn, Victor L., ed. *Shakespeare the Playwright: A Companion to the Complete Tragedies, Histories, Comedies, and Romances.* New York: Greenwood Press, 1991.

Champion, Larry S. *The Essential Shakespeare: An Annotated Bibilography of Major Modern Studies.* New York: G. K. Hall, 1993.

Hackman, Stanley, ed. *McGraw-Hill Encyclopedia of World Drama.* 5 vols. New York: McGraw-Hill, 1984.

Wills, Stanley, ed. *Shakespeare: A Bibliographic Guide.* Oxford: Clarendon Press, 1990.

Periodicals, such as magazines and scholarly journals, are another good source of information for broadening your literary knowledge. The bibliographies in the above reference sources may list periodical articles, but you can extend your search by consulting any of the following periodical indexes. All are available in both bound volumes and electronic form, as indicated by the note in parentheses following each title.

Arts and Humanities Citation Index. (on-line)

Humanities Index. (on-line)

MLA International Bibliography. (CD-ROM)

Here is a list of books that contain useful information for broadening your knowledge of any of the topics listed earlier.

Barber, C. L. *Shakespeare's Festive Comedy.* Princeton: Princeton UP, 1959.

Bloom, Harold. *Shakespeare's "Twelfth Night."* New York: Chelsea House, 1987.

Bush, Geoffrey. *Shakespeare and the Natural Condition.* Cambridge: Harvard UP, 1956.

Byrne, M. St. Clare. *Elizabethan Life in Town and Country.* Rev. ed. New York: Barnes and Noble, 1961.

Chambers, E. K. *The Elizabethan Stage,* 4 vols. New York: Oxford UP, 1945.

Kalin, Philip C. *Shakespeare and Feminist Criticism.* New York: Garland, 1991.

King, Walter, ed. *Twentieth Century Interpretations of "Twelfth Night."* Englewood Cliffs, N.J.: Prentice-Hall, 1968.

Novy, Marianne. *Love's Argument: Gender Relations in Shakespeare.* Chapel Hill: University of North Carolina Press, 1984.

Schoenbaum, S. *Shakespeare: The Globe and the World.* New York: Oxford UP, 1979.

Thomson, Peter. *Shakespeare's Theatre.* London: Routledge and Kegan Paul, 1983.

Westlund, Joseph. *Shakespeare's Reparative Comedies.* Chicago: University of Chicago Press, 1984.

Wilson, John Dover. *Shakespeare's Happy Comedies.* Evanston, Ill.: Northwestern UP, 1962.

21 ◈ The Beginnings of the Modern Theater

In its broad outlines, the history of Western drama since the Renaissance has been one of action and reaction. This chapter will look at some of the ideological forces that affected drama from the seventeenth to the nineteenth centuries and at the major ways in which drama reacted to those forces.

From the Seventeenth Century to the Nineteenth

In England in the mid-seventeenth century, the Puritans and their allies gained effective political and cultural control for a time, deposing and executing King Charles I. They also closed the theaters and suppressed the publication of plays, acting on a long-held belief that plays and theatergoing were sinful. As you will recall from the preceding chapter, performances of plays had also been suppressed in early Medieval Europe. In France, by contrast, a secular theater, featuring the Neoclassical tragedies of Jean Racine and the satiric comedies of Molière, flourished at the court of King Louis XIV in the seventeenth century. The son of the deposed English king spent a period of exile in France, where he developed a taste for the theater. When he was restored to the English throne in 1660 as Charles II, he had the London theaters reopened, and a new wave of original English drama peaked.

In the satiric comedy of seventeenth-century France and Restoration England, drama served the social and cultural function of ridiculing behavior considered foolish or extreme by the dominant ideology by holding that behavior up to public laughter, even if the "public" was a narrow segment of the total population. Among the targets of satire was the sense of propriety and appropriate public conduct (an overdeveloped sense, as some playwrights and their supporters saw it) that was part of the counter-dominant ideology of the Puritans and some clergy in other denominations. But that ideology had its influence nonetheless, and by the eighteenth century a reaction to the "immoral excesses" of Restoration drama had set in. Although plays weren't suppressed and the theaters weren't closed, playwrights did tend to tone down the sexual innuendo that had permeated the language of Restoration plays and to soften the satire of social conservatives to avoid incurring their wrath. Romantic comedies, lacking the hard edge of satire, became more common, and some productions of Shakespeare's tragedies altered the plays' most shocking or painful aspects.

In the nineteenth century, a burgeoning middle class with increasing amounts of leisure time and more discretionary income contributed to the growth of the commercial theater. In that theater, **melodramas** became popular, continuing theater's tendency from the eighteenth century to appeal to a broad audience and avoid challenging it. Similar to the sentimental comedies discussed in Chapter 20, these plays typically featured one-dimensional, good or wicked characters who appealed to the most easily evoked emotions of the audience, and dramatic conflicts were resolved in simplistically happy or sad endings.

In England, interestingly enough, the appearance of melodrama was also at least partly a response to the monopolization of "serious" drama by two or three London theater companies. In the Restoration era these companies had secured government patents granting them exclusive control of play productions and the right to censor new plays, privileges that these companies continued to enjoy until the 1840s. In the meantime, the same licensing laws that granted monopolies to these theater companies permitted others to stage musical entertainments. Melodramas—originally plays with music—developed in early nineteenth-century England as a way of circumventing the licensing laws and also as a dramatic form that appealed to a wide audience. Today, melodramas occupy a large portion of popular drama in film and on television. Melodramas have been serious drama, too, not just "brain candy" for the masses.

Dramatic Realism and Ideology

In reaction to melodrama both as popular theater and as the only original drama being written for the stage at the time, realism arose in the later nineteenth-century theater. This too can be connected to the ideology and the literary repertoire of the nineteenth-century theater. The rise of industrial capitalism in Europe and the United States brought with it an urban middle class that became increasingly large and powerful—politically, economically, and culturally. The monarchies that had developed out of feudalism in the Middle Ages and had been so powerful for three or four hundred years had now been replaced by generally democratic forms of government in much of Europe. These changes were accompanied by increasing literacy and education, which contributed to the development of a new mass culture. The production and delivery of art was less and less controlled by a relatively few interests at or near the top of a hierarchical social structure, and the consumption of art had spread to a much wider spectrum of people. In literature, consequently, the second half of the nineteenth century in Western Europe saw the rise of fiction as a serious art form, a phenomenon caused in part by the growth of a large, educated bourgeois audience and in part by writers and critics (Charles Dickens, for instance) who were themselves part of this class.

The strongest movements in fiction were **Realism** and **Naturalism**. Realism emphasized the treatment of everyday, mostly middle-class, life and characters in novels and short stories; Naturalism, influenced by the writings of Charles Darwin, Karl Marx, and others, portrayed human beings as subject to large "natural" forces—biological, social, economic—beyond their conscious control. Both of these movements in fiction, as well as the increased popularity of fiction itself, affected the drama of the late nineteenth century. While melodrama had been one response to a changing audience, some playwrights—notably Henrik Ibsen in Norway, Anton Chekhov in Russia, and George Bernard Shaw in England—were developing a drama that took middle-class life more seriously by putting representations of it on the stage. Their plays sometimes challenged the values and beliefs of their audiences. Ibsen's 1881 play *Ghosts*, for instance, was shocking in its presentation of the consequences for a respectable middle-class family of sexually transmitted disease. A definite social problem then as now, it was generally ignored by the dominant bourgeois ideology that forbade frankness on sexual subjects. This play and others were also symptomatic of a basic contradiction in bourgeois ideology: the simultaneous stress on social conformity and the belief in individual expression.

Some Text Strategies of Realistic Drama

In terms of text strategies, these authors' plays were often published in book form before they were produced in a theater. To some extent the inclusion of detailed, realistic set descriptions and stage directions provided something like the narrative links between scenes or speeches that a fiction-reading public had come to expect. These details, along with the writers' concern with issues of contemporary domestic or social life, also led serious theater to use more realistic set designs and costumes. From the 1880s on, people entering a theater like the one shown on page 1163 were likely to find the curtain lifted on a box set that very closely resembled the parlor of a middle class urban home. Women were now accepted as actors too, having been first introduced on stage in continental Europe in the sixteenth century and in England in the Restoration era (post-1660).

Under the influence of Constantin Stanislavsky, who produced some of Chekhov's plays for the Moscow Art Theatre, a more realistic acting style developed, with actors adopting more natural movements and expressions of the kinds of characters they were portraying. The presence of the theater audience was conventionally ignored; they were assumed to be witnessing the action through an invisible fourth wall of the stage set, and so earlier text strategies for communicating important information to the audience, such as asides and soliloquies, disappeared from the literary repertoire of the Realistic theater. In their place, dialogue—no longer in verse but in everyday informal speech—and exposition carried more of the load of informing the audience about antecedent action and characters' thoughts. Because the dialogue consisted mostly of true-to-life conversation among characters, considerable skill on the part of the author was required to present important information to the audience in seemingly natural fashion.

Consequently, other text strategies assumed greater importance in conveying some information symbolically. Elements of the set decor or props, for

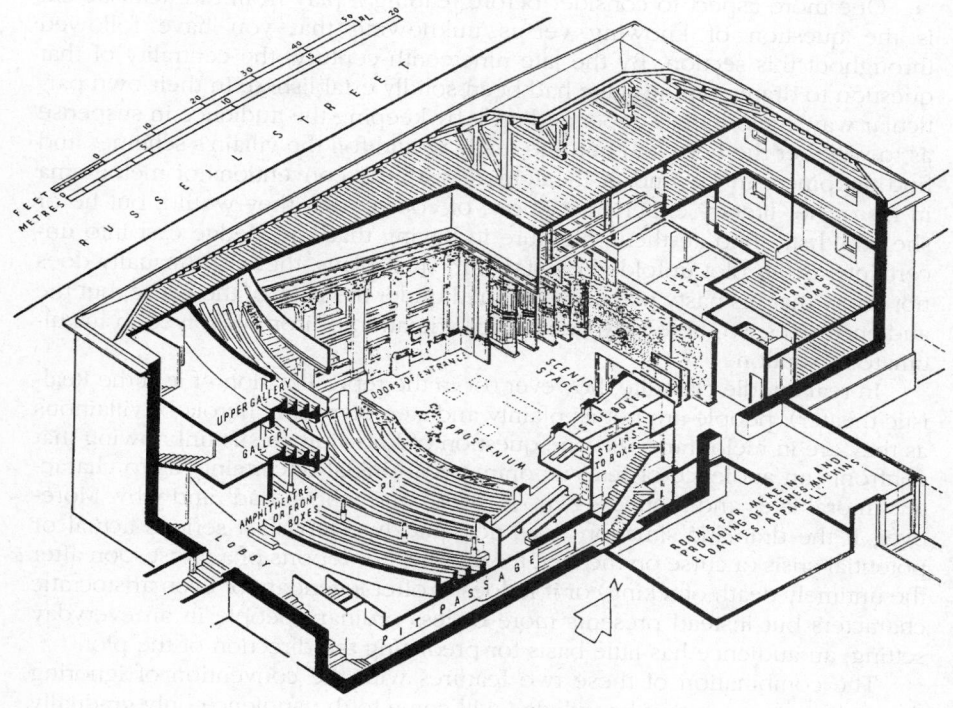

The Modern Theater

instance, might not only be believable as the kind of thing a certain sort of middle-class family would have in their home but also significant of characters' emotional or psychological conditions. So might costumes—not obvious signs of characters' inner states like dressing in black for mourning, but more subtle ones: a tight collar or dress perhaps indicating some kind of psychological or emotional pressure. Similarly, the greater sophistication in technical areas could be brought to bear in symbolic ways. Lighting, for instance, could indicate changing times of day or seasons, both of which could suggest changes in characters' fortunes or emotional conditions in the absence of soliloquies or highly declamatory speeches. You may be familiar with such theatrical conventions yourself because this kind of realism is still very strong in theater today, although not as dominant as it was a century ago.

CONNECT: How many of the text strategies described here apply to the 1916 play *Trifles* you read in Chapters 15–16?

One more aspect to consider before reading a play from the Realistic era is the question of knowing versus unknowing that you have followed throughout this section. By the late nineteenth century, the centrality of that question to drama on the stage had been solidly established. In their own particular way, melodramas depended on it by keeping the audience in suspense as to whether the hero and heroine really would foil the villain's schemes and find happiness in the end. A theatergoer with the conventions of melodrama in his or her literary experience knew, of course, that they would, but he or she could still find aesthetic pleasure in having that knowledge cast into uncertainty as the plot unfolded on stage. In such plays, the villain usually does not know that his nasty plans are doomed under the laws of the genre, but the audience does, so there may be an approximation of irony involved in his ultimate frustration.

In real middle-class life, however (or in the representation of it in the Realistic theater), people are not as plainly and stereotypically heroic or villainous as they are in melodrama. So one question of knowing versus unknowing that confronts an audience of realistic drama is an initial uncertainty as to characters' moral lives and motives—who's "good" and who's "bad" and why. Moreover, if the dramatic situation does not quickly establish a serious actual or potential crisis (a curse on the city, for instance, or reports of a ghost soon after the untimely death of a king) or if it doesn't offer legendary or even aristocratic characters but instead presents more or less ordinary people in an everyday setting, an audience has little basis for predicting the direction of the plot.

The combination of these two features with the convention of ignoring the audience means that knowledge will come to the audience only gradually as it watches and listens to the characters interact. There must be something to know about, however, if what the audience is seeing is a drama, some conflict that will move a plot forward and have consequences for the characters. And if this conflict is not provided by extraordinary circumstances but comes instead "naturally" out of the lives of the characters, the audience has to pay close attention to signs—often symbolic ones—in the language or movements of characters to find out what the conflict may be.

In the interest of aesthetic economy and according to the ideology of realism that dramatic conflicts exist in ordinary lives, realistic plays adopt the convention of presenting only the critical or final episode in an action that has begun in the past, before the situation the audience sees as the curtain goes up. Consequently, the exposition of a realistic play must ensure that the audience knows what it needs to know about the characters' past, yet this information must come out "naturally," without destroying **verisimilitude**, or "trueness-to-life." As the audience is gaining this knowledge, it sees the consequences or complications of the past situation in the present, which, in combination with the moral qualities of the main characters, drives the plot toward its climax. This climax, finally, must be believable within the framework of characters, situation, and air of real life that the play has established for itself. This framework may create a climax that is comparatively anticlimactic, in contrast to melodrama, Classical or Shakespearean tragedy, or romantic or satiric comedy.

Reading and Responding: A Realistic Play

If you are familiar with the conventional practices of realistic drama, perhaps the foregoing discussion has not broadened your experience to the extent that the discussions of ancient Greek theater and Shakespearean theater in Chapters 18 and 19 did. Perhaps this discussion was mostly a "refresher" for you after learning about those earlier and more alien eras. All the same, however, you should go into your reading of *Hedda Gabler* with a heightened awareness of the ideology and literary repertoire of that 1890 play so you can be better prepared to analyze your interaction with the text in cognitive or cultural terms.

Another aspect of that repertoire as well as the ideology of *Hedda Gabler* is the contemporary understanding of tragedy and the tragic hero. The ideology and the literary repertoire of the nineteenth-century theater contained the tradition of tragedy, with its continuity and its changes, from the earlier notable eras of Western drama. But because *Hedda Gabler* also appeared originally in the context of a newly dominant bourgeois ideology, as sketched out earlier, that sense of tragedy differed in important ways from the ideologies of fifth-century B.C. Greece and sixteenth-century England. The focus of life and art had changed considerably in 300 years, and as the French playwright and novelist Emile Zola said in 1878, the challenge for the realistic dramatist or novelist was "to do great things with the subjects and characters that our eyes, accustomed to the spectacle of the daily round, have come to see as small."

> **CONNECT:** *Trifles* involves questions of the audience's knowing and unknowing much in the way they are involved for realistic drama in general. It is a play whose climax involves not great dramatic action but certain characters and the audience coming to know or realize something at the same time.

As you read *Hedda Gabler*, I am sure you will notice differences between the social status and practices of the main characters and your own; the play is after all more than 100 years old. But I suppose these differences will be relatively minor compared to those that exist between you and the worlds of *Hamlet* or *Oedipus the King*. Assuming then, some basic similarities, both between your world and the genteel bourgeois society of late nineteenth-century Norway and between your literary experience concerning drama and that of the late nineteenth-century Realistic theater, there should be a smaller gap in knowledge to span by further discussion. Instead, I will just ask you, as you begin to read, to think about some of the questions regarding tragedy that you were asked to consider earlier with reference to *Oedipus the King* and *Hamlet*.

- What is the relation of a character's social status to his or her being tragic? Does a character have to be aristocratic or a political and social leader, for instance, to be a tragic hero?

- What is the relationship between a character's own "flaws" or actions and the operation of powerful outside forces in producing tragedy? Can internal or external factors alone produce a tragic outcome, or is some kind of combination of these factors necessary?
- How is a character's recognition of himself or herself as either fatally flawed or trapped in fateful circumstances related to that character being tragic? How do knowing and unknowing contribute to a tragic or melodramatic situation—for any character or for you as a reader?
- Must a character be male to be a tragic hero? Can a female character have whatever degree of high social status it takes to be potentially tragic?

As with the plays in the previous three chapters, each act of *Hedda Gabler* will be followed by response statement questions.

Henrik Ibsen   1828–1906

Hedda Gabler[1]   *1890*

Charactors

George Tesman, research graduate in cultural history	*Judge Brack*
Hedda, his wife	*Eilert Loevborg*
Miss Juliana Tesman, his aunt	*Bertha*, a maid
Mrs. Elvsted	

The action takes place in Tesman's villa in the fashionable quarter of town.

Act 1

Scene: A large drawing room, handsomely and tastefully furnished; decorated in dark colors. In the rear wall is a broad open doorway, with curtains drawn back to either side. It leads to a smaller room, decorated in the same style as the drawing room. In the right-hand wall of the drawing room, a folding door leads out to the hall. The opposite wall, on the left, contains french windows, also with curtains drawn back on either side. Through the glass we can see part of a verandah, and trees in autumn colors. Downstage stands an oval table, covered by a cloth and surrounded by chairs. Downstage right, against the wall is a broad stove tiled with dark porcelain; in front of it stand a high-backed armchair, a cushioned footrest, and two footstools. Upstage right, in an alcove, is a corner sofa, with a small, round table. Downstage left, a little away from the wall, is another sofa. Upstage of the french windows, a piano. On either side of the open doorway in the rear wall stand what-nots holding ornaments of terra cotta and majolica. Against the rear wall of the smaller room can be seen a sofa, a table, and a couple of chairs. Above this sofa hangs the portrait of a handsome old man in general's uniform. Above the table a lamp hangs from the ceiling, with a shade of opalescent, milky glass. All round the drawing room bunches of flowers stand in vases and glasses. More bunches lie on the tables. The floors of both rooms are covered with thick carpets. Morning light. The sun shines in through the french windows.

Miss Juliana Tesman, wearing a hat and carrying a parasol, enters from the hall, followed by Bertha, who is carrying a bunch of flowers wrapped in paper. Miss Tesman is about sixty-five, of pleasant and kindly appearance. She is neatly but simply dressed in grey outdoor clothes. Bertha, the maid, is rather simple and rustic-looking. She is getting on in years.

---

[1]Translated by Michael Meyer.

MISS TESMAN: [*Stops just inside the door, listens, and says in a hushed voice.*] No, bless my soul! They're not up yet.

BERTHA: [*Also in hushed tones.*] What did I tell you, miss? The boat didn't get in till midnight. And when they did turn up—Jesus, miss, you should have seen all the things Madam made me unpack before she'd go to bed!

MISS TESMAN: Ah, well. Let them have a good lie in. But let's have some nice fresh air waiting for them when they do come down. [*Goes to the french windows and throws them wide open.*]

BERTHA: [*Bewildered at the table, the bunch of flowers in her hand.*] I'm blessed if there's a square inch left to put anything. I'll have to let it lie here, miss. [*Puts it on the piano.*]

MISS TESMAN: Well, Bertha dear, so now you have a new mistress. Heaven knows it nearly broke my heart to have to part with you.   5

BERTHA: [*Snivels*] What about me, Miss Juju? How do you suppose I felt? After all the happy years I've spent with you and Miss Rena?

MISS TESMAN: We must accept it bravely, Bertha. It was the only way. George needs you to take care of him. He could never manage without you. You've looked after him ever since he was a tiny boy.

BERTHA: Oh, but Miss Juju, I can't help thinking about Miss Rena, lying there all helpless, poor dear. And that new girl? She'll never learn the proper way to handle an invalid.

MISS TESMAN: Oh, I'll manage to train her. I'll do most of the work myself, you know. You needn't worry about my poor sister, Bertha dear.

BERTHA: But Miss Juju, there's another thing. I'm frightened Madam may not find me suitable.   10

MISS TESMAN: Oh, nonsense, Bertha. There may be one or two little things to begin with——

BERTHA: She's a real lady. Wants everything just so.

MISS TESMAN: But of course she does! General Gabler's daughter! Think of what she was accustomed to when the General was alive. You remember how we used to see her out riding with her father? In that long black skirt? With the feather in her hat?

BERTHA: Oh, yes, miss. As if I could forget! But, Lord! I never dreamed I'd live to see a match between her and Master Georgie.

MISS TESMAN: Neither did I. By the way, Bertha, from now on you must stop calling him Master Georgie. You must say: Dr. Tesman.   15

BERTHA: Yes, Madam said something about that too. Last night—the moment they'd set foot inside the door. It is true, then, miss?

MISS TESMAN: Indeed it is. Just imagine, Bertha, some foreigners have made him a doctor.[2] It happened while they were away. I had no idea till he told me when they got off the boat.

BERTHA: Well, I suppose there's no limit to what he won't become. He's that clever. I never thought he'd go in for hospital work, though.

MISS TESMAN: No, he's not that kind of doctor. [*Nods impressively.*] In any case, you may soon have to address him by an even grander title.

BERTHA: You don't say! What might that be, miss?   20

MISS TESMAN: [*Smiles*] Ah! If you only knew! [*Moved*] Dear God, if only poor dear Joachim could rise out of his grave and see what his little son has grown into! [*Looks round.*] But Bertha, why have you done this? Taken the chintz covers off all the furniture!

---

[2]Awarded him a doctoral degree.

BERTHA: Madam said I was to. Can't stand chintz covers on chairs, she said.

MISS TESMAN: But surely they're not going to use this room as a parlor?

BERTHA: So I gathered, miss. From what Madam said. He didn't say anything. The Doctor.

[George Tesman comes into the rear room, from the right, humming, with an open, empty traveling bag in his hand. He is about thirty-three, of medium height and youthful appearance, rather plump, with an open, round, contented face, and fair hair and beard. He wears spectacles, and is dressed in comfortable, indoor clothes.]

MISS TESMAN: Good morning! Good morning, George!   25

TESMAN: *[In open doorway.]* Auntie Juju! Dear Auntie Juju! *[Comes forward and shakes her hand.]* You've come all the way out here! And so early! What?

MISS TESMAN: Well, I had to make sure you'd settled in comfortably.

TESMAN: But you can't have had a proper night's sleep.

MISS TESMAN: Oh, never mind that.

TESMAN: We were so sorry we couldn't give you a lift. But you saw how it was—   30
Hedda had so much luggage—and she insisted on having it all with her.

MISS TESMAN: Yes, I've never seen so much luggage.

BERTHA: *[To Tesman.]* Shall I go and ask Madam if there's anything I can lend her a hand with?

TESMAN: Er—thank you, Bertha; no, you needn't bother. She says if she wants you for anything she'll ring.

BERTHA: *[Over to right.]* Oh. Very good.   35

TESMAN: Oh, Bertha—take this bag, will you?

BERTHA: *[Takes it.]* I'll put it in the attic. *[Goes out into the hall.]*

TESMAN: Just fancy, Auntie Juju, I filled that whole bag with notes for my book. You know, it's really incredible what I've managed to find rooting through those archives. By Jove! Wonderful old things no one even knew existed——

MISS TESMAN: I'm sure you didn't waste a single moment of your honeymoon, George dear.

TESMAN: No, I think I can truthfully claim that. But, Auntie Juju, do take your hat off. Here. Let me untie it for you. What?

MISS TESMAN: *[As he does so.]* Oh dear, oh dear! It's just as if you were still living at   40
home with us.

TESMAN: *[Turns the hat in his hand and looks at it.]* I say! What a splendid new hat!

MISS TESMAN: I bought it for Hedda's sake.

TESMAN: For Hedda's sake? What?

MISS TESMAN: So that Hedda needn't be ashamed of me, in case we ever go for a walk together.

TESMAN: *[Pats her cheek.]* You still think of everything, don't you, Auntie Juju? *[Puts*   45
the hat down on a chair by the table.] Come on, let's sit down here on the sofa. And have a little chat while we wait for Hedda.

[They sit. She puts her parasol on the corner of the sofa.]

MISS TESMAN: *[Clasps both his hands and looks at him.]* Oh, George, it's so wonderful to have you back, and be able to see you with my own eyes again! Poor dear Joachim's own son!

TESMAN: What about me! It's wonderful for me to see you again, Auntie Juju. You've been a mother to me. And a father, too.

MISS TESMAN: You'll always keep a soft spot in your heart for your old aunties, won't you, George dear?

TESMAN: I suppose Auntie Rena's no better? What?

MISS TESMAN: Alas, no. I'm afraid she'll never get better, poor dear. She's lying there   50
just as she has for all these years. Please God I may be allowed to keep her for a
little longer. If I lost her I don't know what I'd do. Especially now I haven't you
to look after.

TESMAN: [*Pats her on the back.*] There, there, there!

MISS TESMAN: [*With a sudden change of mood.*] Oh but George, fancy you being a
married man! And to think it's you who've won Hedda Gabler! Fancy! The beautiful Hedda Gabler! She was always so surrounded by admirers.

TESMAN: [*Hums a little and smiles contentedly.*] Yes, I suppose there are quite a
few people in this town who wouldn't mind being in my shoes. What?

MISS TESMAN: And what a honeymoon! Five months! Nearly six.

TESMAN: Well, I've done a lot of work, you know. All those archives to go through.   55
And I've had to read lots of books.

MISS TESMAN: Yes, dear, of course. [*Lowers her voice confidentially.*] But tell me,
George—haven't you any—any extra little piece of news to give me?

TESMAN: You mean, arising out of the honeymoon?

MISS TESMAN: Yes.

TESMAN: No, I don't think there's anything I didn't tell you in my letters. My doctorate, of course—but I told you about that last night, didn't I?

MISS TESMAN: Yes, yes, I didn't mean that kind of thing. I was just wondering—are   60
you—are you expecting——?

TESMAN: Expecting what?

MISS TESMAN: Oh, come on George, I'm your old aunt!

TESMAN: Well actually—yes, I am expecting something.

MISS TESMAN: I knew it!

TESMAN: You'll be happy to hear that before very long I expect to become a   65
professor.

MISS TESMAN: Professor?

TESMAN: I think I may say that the matter has been decided. But, Auntie Juju, you
know about this.

MISS TESMAN: [*Gives a little laugh.*] Yes, of course. I'd forgotten. [*Changes her tone.*]
But we were talking about your honeymoon. It must have cost a dreadful
amount of money, George?

TESMAN: Oh well, you know, that big research grant I got helped a good deal.

MISS TESMAN: But how on earth did you manage to make it do for two?   70

TESMAN: Well, to tell the truth it was a bit tricky. What?

MISS TESMAN: Especially when one's traveling with a lady. A little bird tells me that
makes things very much more expensive.

TESMAN: Well, yes, of course it does make things a little more expensive. But Hedda
has to do things in style, Auntie Juju. I mean, she has to. Anything less grand
wouldn't have suited her.

MISS TESMAN: No, no, I suppose not. A honeymoon abroad seems to be the vogue
nowadays. But tell me, have you had time to look round the house?

TESMAN: You bet. I've been up since the crack of dawn.   75

MISS TESMAN: Well, what do you think of it?

TESMAN: Splendid. Absolutely splendid. I'm only wondering what we're going to do
with those two empty rooms between that little one and Hedda's bedroom.

MISS TESMAN: [*Laughs slyly.*] Ah, George dear, I'm sure you'll manage to find some
use for them—in time.

TESMAN: Yes, of course, Auntie Juju, how stupid of me. You're thinking of my
books. What?

MISS TTESMAN: Yes, yes, dear boy. I was thinking of your books.   80

TESMAN: You know, I'm so happy for Hedda's sake that we've managed to get this house. Before we became engaged she often used to say this was the only house in town she felt she could really bear to live in. It used to belong to Mrs. Falk— you know, the Prime Minister's widow.

MISS TESMAN: Fancy that! And what a stroke of luck it happened to come into the market. Just as you'd left on your honeymoon.

TESMAN: Yes, Auntie Juju, we've certainly had all the luck with us. What?

MISS TESMAN: But, George dear, the expense! It's going to make a dreadful hole in your pocket, all this.

TESMAN: [A little downcast.] Yes, I—I suppose it will, won't it?   85

MISS TESMAN: Oh, George, really!

TESMAN: How much do you think it'll cost? Roughly, I mean? What?

MISS TESMAN: I can't possibly say till I see the bills.

TESMAN: Well, luckily Judge Brack's managed to get it on very favorable terms. He wrote and told Hedda so.

MISS TESMAN: Don't you worry, George dear. Anyway I've stood security for all the   90
furniture and carpets.

TESMAN: Security? But dear, sweet Auntie Juju, how could you possibly stand security?

MISS TESMAN: I've arranged a mortgage on our annuity.

TESMAN: [Jumps up.] What? On your annuity? And—Auntie Rena's?

MISS TESMAN: Yes. Well, I couldn't think of any other way.

TESMAN: [Stands in front of her.] Auntie Juju, have you gone completely out of your   95
mind? That annuity's all you and Auntie Rena have.

MISS TESMAN: All right, there's no need to get so excited about it. It's a pure formality, you know. Judge Brack told me so. He was so kind as to arrange it all for me. A pure formality; those were his very words.

TESMAN: I dare say. All the same——

MISS TESMAN: Anyway, you'll have a salary of your own now. And, good heavens, even if we did have to fork out a little—tighten our belts for a week or two—why, we'd be happy to do so for your sake.

TESMAN: Oh, Auntie Juju! Will you ever stop sacrificing yourself for me?

MISS TESMAN: [Gets up and puts her hands on his shoulders.] What else have I to   100
live for but to smooth your road a little, my dear boy? You've never had any mother or father to turn to. And now at last we've achieved our goal. I won't deny we've had our little difficulties now and then. But now, thank the good Lord, George dear, all your worries are past.

TESMAN: Yes, it's wonderful really how everything's gone just right for me.

MISS TESMAN: Yes! And the enemies who tried to bar your way have been struck down. They have been made to bite the dust. The man who was your most dangerous rival has had the mightiest fall. And now he's lying there in the pit he dug for himself, poor misguided creature.

TESMAN: Have you heard any news of Eilert? Since I went away?

MISS TESMAN: Only that he's said to have published a new book.

TESMAN: What! Eilert Loevborg? You mean—just recently? What?   105

MISS TESMAN: So they say. I don't imagine it can be of any value, do you? When your new book comes out, that'll be another story. What's it going to be about?

TESMAN: The domestic industries of Brabant[3] in the Middle Ages.

---

[3]Prosperous duchy (1190–1477), now divided between Belgium and the Netherlands.

MISS TESMAN: Oh, George! The things you know about!

TESMAN: Mind you, it may be some time before I actually get down to writing it. I've made these very extensive notes, and I've got to file and index them first.

MISS TESMAN: Ah, yes! Making notes; filing and indexing; you've always been won-   110
derful at that. Poor dear Joachim was just the same.

TESMAN: I'm looking forward so much to getting down to that. Especially now I've a home of my own to work in.

MISS TESMAN: And above all, now that you have the girl you set your heart on, George dear.

TESMAN: [Embraces her.] Oh, yes, Auntie Juju, yes! Hedda's the loveliest thing of all! [Looks towards the doorway.] I think I hear her coming. What?

[Hedda enters the rear room from the left, and comes into the drawing room. She is a woman of twenty-nine. Distinguished, aristocratic face and figure. Her complexion is pale and opalescent. Her eyes are steel-grey, with an expression of cold, calm serenity. Her hair is of a handsome auburn color, but it is not especially abundant. She is dressed in an elegant, somewhat loose-fitting morning gown.]

MISS TESMAN: [Goes to greet her.] Good morning, Hedda dear! Good morning!   115

HEDDA: [Holds out her hand.] Good morning, dear Miss Tesman. What an early hour to call. So kind of you.

MISS TESMAN: [Seems somewhat embarrassed.] And the young bride slept well in her new home?

HEDDA: Oh—thank you, yes. Passably well.

TESMAN: [Laughs.] Passably. I say, Hedda, that's good! When I jumped out of bed, you were sleeping like a top.

HEDDA: Yes. Fortunately. One has to accustom oneself to anything new, Miss Tes-man. It takes time. [Looks left.] Oh, that maid's left the french windows open. This room's flooded with sun.

MISS TESMAN: [Goes towards the windows.] Oh—let me close them.   120

HEDDA: No, no, don't do that. Tesman dear, draw the curtains. This light's blinding me.

TESMAN: [At the windows.] Yes, yes, dear. There, Hedda, now you've got shade and fresh air.

HEDDA: This room needs fresh air. All these flowers—But my dear Miss Tesman, won't you take a seat?

MISS TESMAN: No, really not, thank you. I just wanted to make sure you have every-thing you need. I must see about getting back home. My poor dear sister will be waiting for me.

TESMAN: Be sure to give her my love, won't you? Tell her I'll run over and see her   125
later today.

MISS TESMAN: Oh yes, I'll tell her that. Oh, George—— [Fumbles in the pocket of her skirt.] I almost forgot. I've brought something for you.

TESMAN: What's that, Auntie Juju? What?

MISS TESMAN: [Pulls out a flat package wrapped in newspaper and gives it to him.] Open and see, dear boy.

TESMAN: [Opens the package.] Good heavens! Auntie Juju, you've kept them! Hedda, this is really very touching. What?

HEDDA: [By the what-nots, on the right.] What is it, Tesman?   130

TESMAN: My old shoes! My slippers, Hedda!

HEDDA: Oh, them. I remember you kept talking about them on our honeymoon.

TESMAN: Yes, I missed them dreadfully. [Goes over to her.] Here, Hedda, take a look.

HEDDA: [Goes away towards the stove.] Thanks, I won't bother.   135

TESMAN: [Follows her.] Fancy, Hedda, Auntie Rena's embroidered them for me. De-spite her being so ill. Oh, you can't imagine what memories they have for me.

HEDDA: [*By the table.*] Not for me.
MISS TESMAN: No, Hedda's right there, George.
TESMAN: Yes, but I thought since she's one of the family now——
HEDDA: [*Interrupts.*] Tesman, we really can't go on keeping this maid.
MISS TESMAN: Not keep Bertha?   140
TESMAN: What makes you say that, dear? What?
HEDDA: [*Points.*] Look at that! She's left her old hat lying on the chair.
TESMAN: [*Appalled, drops his slippers on the floor.*] But, Hedda——!
HEDDA: Suppose someone came in and saw it?   145
TESMAN: But Hedda—that's Auntie Juju's hat.
HEDDA: Oh?
MISS TESMAN: [*Picks up the hat.*] Indeed it's mine. And it doesn't happen to be old,
            Hedda dear.
HEDDA: I didn't look at it very closely, Miss Tesman.
MISS TTESMAN: [*Tying on the hat.*] As a matter of fact, it's the first time I've worn it.
            As the good Lord is my witness.
TESMAN: It's very pretty, too. Really smart.   150
MISS TESMAN: Oh, I'm afraid it's nothing much really. [*Looks around.*] My parasol?
            Ah, here it is. [*Takes it.*] This is mine, too. [*Murmurs.*] Not Bertha's.
TESMAN: A new hat and a new parasol! I say, Hedda, fancy that!
HEDDA: Very pretty and charming.
TESMAN: Yes, isn't it? What? But Auntie Juju, take a good look at Hedda before you
            go. Isn't she pretty and charming?
MISS TESMAN: Dear boy, there's nothing new in that. Hedda's been a beauty ever   155
            since the day she was born. [*Nods and goes right.*]
TESMAN: [*Follows her.*] Yes, but have you noticed how strong and healthy she's look-
            ing? And how she's filled out since we went away?
MISS TESMAN: [*Stops and turns.*] Filled out?
HEDDA: [*Walks across the room.*] Oh, can't we forget it?
TESMAN: Yes, Auntie Juju—you can't see it so clearly with that dress on. But I've
            good reason to know——
HEDDA: [*By the french windows, impatiently.*] You haven't good reason to know   160
            anything.
TESMAN: It must have been the mountain air up there in the Tyrol——
HEDDA: [*Curtly, interrupts him.*] I'm exactly the same as when I went away.
TESMAN: You keep on saying so. But you're not. I'm right, aren't I, Auntie Juju?
MISS TESMAN: [*Has folded her hands and is gazing at her.*] She's beautiful—beauti-
            ful. Hedda is beautiful. [*Goes over to Hedda, takes her head between her
            hands, draws it down and kisses her hair.*] God bless and keep you, Hedda Tes-
            man. For George's sake.
HEDDA: [*Frees herself politely.*] Oh—let me go, please.   165
MISS TESMAN: [*Quietly, emotionally.*] I shall come see you both every day.
TESMAN: Yes, Auntie Juju, please do. What?
MISS TESMAN: Good-bye! Good-bye!

*[She goes out into the hall. Tesman follows her. The door remains open. Tesman is heard sending
his love to Aunt Rena and thanking Miss Tesman for his slippers. Meanwhile Hedda walks up
and down the room raising her arms and clenching her fists as though in desperation. Then she
throws aside the curtains from the french windows and stands there, looking out. A few moments
later, Tesman returns and closes the door behind him.]*

TESMAN: [*Picks up his slippers from the floor.*] What are you looking at, Hedda?

HEDDA: [*Calm and controlled again.*] Only the leaves. They're so golden. And   170
withered.

TESMAN: [*Wraps up the slippers and lays them on the table.*] Well, we're in September now.

HEDDA: [*Restless again.*] Yes. We're already into September.

TESMAN: Auntie Juju was behaving rather oddly, I thought, didn't you? Almost as
though she was in church or something. I wonder what came over her. Any idea?

HEDDA: I hardly know her. Does she often act like that?

TESMAN: Not to the extent she did today.   175

HEDDA: [*Goes away from the french windows.*] Do you think she was hurt by
what I said about the hat?

TESMAN: Oh, I don't think so. A little at first, perhaps——

HEDDA: But what a thing to do, throw her hat down in someone's drawing room.
People don't do such things.

TESMAN: I'm sure Auntie Juju doesn't do it very often.

HEDDA: oh well, I'll make it up with her.   180

TESMAN: Oh Hedda, would you?

HEDDA: When you see them this afternoon invite her to come out here this evening.

TESMAN: You bet I will! I say, there's another thing which would please her enormously.

HEDDA: Oh?   185

TESMAN: If you could bring yourself to call her Auntie Juju. For my sake, Hedda? What?

HEDDA: Oh no, really Tesman, you mustn't ask me to do that. I've told you so once
before. I'll try to call her Aunt Juliana. That's as far as I'll go.

TESMAN: [*After a moment.*] I say, Hedda, is anything wrong? What?

HEDDA: I'm just looking at my old piano. It doesn't really go with all this.

TESMAN: As soon as I start getting my salary we'll see about changing it.

HEDDA: No, no, don't let's change it. I don't want to part with it. We can move it into   190
that little room and get another one to put in here.

TESMAN: [*A little downcast.*] Yes, we—might do that.

HEDDA: [*Picks up the bunch of flowers from the piano.*] These flowers weren't
here when we arrived last night.

TESMAN: I expect Auntie Juju brought them.

HEDDA: Here's a card. [*Takes it out and reads.*] "Will come back later today." Guess
who it's from?

TESMAN: No idea. Who? What?   195

HEDDA: It says: "Mrs. Elvsted."

TESMAN: No, really? Mrs. Elvsted! She used to be Miss Rysing, didn't she?

HEDDA: Yes. She was the one with that irritating hair she was always showing off. I
hear she used to be an old flame of yours.

TESMAN: [*Laughs.*] That didn't last long. Anyway, that was before I got to know you,
Hedda. By Jove, fancy her being in town!

HEDDA: Strange she should call. I only knew her at school.   200

TESMAN: Yes, I haven't seen her for—oh, heaven knows how long. I don't know
how she manages to stick it out up there in the north. What?

HEDDA: [*Thinks for a moment, then says suddenly.*] Tell me, Tesman, doesn't he
live somewhere up in those parts? You know—Eilert Loevborg?

TESMAN: Yes, that's right. So he does. [*Bertha enters from the hall.*]

BERTHA: She's here again, madam. The lady who came and left the flowers. [*Points.*]
The ones you're holding.

HEDDA: Oh, is she? Well, show her in.   205

[*Bertha opens the door for Mrs. Elvsted and goes out. Mrs. Elvsted is a delicately built woman with gentle, attractive features. Her eyes are light blue, large, and somewhat prominent, with a frightened, questioning expression. Her hair is extremely fair, almost flaxen, and it is exceptionally wavy and abundant. She is two or three years younger than Hedda. She is wearing a dark visiting dress, in good taste but not quite in the latest fashion.*]

HEDDA: [*Goes cordially to greet her.*] Dear Mrs. Elvsted, good morning. How delightful to see you again after all this time.

MRS. ELVSTED: [*Nervously, trying to control herself.*] Yes, it's many years since we met.

TESMAN: And since *we* met. What?

HEDDA: Thank you for your lovely flowers.

MRS. ELVSTED: Oh, please—I wanted to come yesterday afternoon. But they told me   210
  you were away——

TESMAN: You've only just arrived in town, then? What?

MRS. ELVSTED: I got here yesterday, around midday. Oh, I became almost desperate
  when I heard you weren't here.

HEDDA: Desperate? Why?

TESMAN: My dear Mrs. Rysing—Elvsted——

HEDDA: There's nothing wrong, I hope?   215

MRS. ELVSTED: Yes, there is. And I don't know anyone else here whom I can
  turn to.

HEDDA: [*Puts the flowers down on the table.*] Come and sit with me on the sofa——

MRS. ELVSTED: Oh, I feel too restless to sit down.

HEDDA: You must. Come along, now. [*She pulls Mrs. Elvsted down on to the sofa
  and sits beside her.*]

TESMAN: Well? Tell us, Mrs.—er——   220

HEDDA: Has something happened at home?

MRS. ELVSTED: Yes—that is, yes and no. Oh, I do hope you won't misunderstand me——

HEDDA: Then you'd better tell us the whole story, Mrs. Elvsted.

TESMAN: That's why you've come. What?

MRS. ELVSTED: Yes—yes, it is. Well, then—in case you don't already know—Eilert   225
  Loevborg is in town.

HEDDA: Loevborg here?

TESMAN: Eilert back in town? By Jove, Hedda, did you hear that?

HEDDA: Yes, of course I heard.

MRS. ELVSTED: He's been here a week. A whole week! In this city. Alone. With all
  those dreadful people——

HEDDA: But my dear Mrs. Elvsted, what concern is he of yours?   230

MRS. ELVSTED: [*Gives her a frightened look and says quickly.*] He's been tutoring
  the children.

HEDDA: Your children?

MRS. ELVSTED: My husband's. I have none.

HEDDA: Oh, you mean your stepchildren.

MRS. ELVSTED: Yes.   225

TESMAN: [*Gropingly.*] But was he sufficiently—I don't know how to put it—sufficiently regular in his habits to be suited to such a post? What?

MRS. ELVSTED: For the past two to three years he has been living irreproachably.

TESMAN: You don't say! By Jove, Hedda, hear that?

HEDDA: I hear.

MRS. ELVSTED: Quite irreproachably, I assure you. In every respect. All the same—in   240
this big city—with money in his pockets—I'm so dreadfully frightened something may happen to him.

TESMAN: But why didn't he stay up there with you and your husband?

MRS. ELVSTED: Once his book had come out, he became restless.

TESMAN: Oh, yes—Auntie Juju said he's brought out a new book.

MRS. ELVSTED: Yes, a big new book about the history of civilization. A kind of general
survey. It came out a fortnight ago. Everyone's been buying it and reading it—
it's created a tremendous stir——

TESMAN: Has it really? It must be something he's dug up, then.   245

MRS. ELVSTED: You mean from the old days?

TESMAN: Yes.

MRS. ELVSTED: No, he's written it all since he came to live with us.

TESMAN: Well, that's splendid news, Hedda. Fancy that!

MRS. ELVSTED: Oh, yes! If only he can go on like this!   250

HEDDA: Have you met him since you came here?

MRS. ELVSTED: No, not yet, I had such dreadful difficulty finding his address. But this
morning I managed to track him down at last.

HEDDA: [*Looks searchingly at her.*] I must say I find it a little strange that your
husband—hm——

MRS. ELVSTED: [*Starts nervously.*] My husband! What do you mean?

HEDDA: That he should send you all the way here on an errand of this kind. I'm sur-   255
prised he didn't come himself to keep an eye on his friend.

MRS. ELVSTED: Oh, no, no—my husband hasn't the time. Besides, I—er—wanted to
do some shopping here.

HEDDA: [*With a slight smile.*] Ah. Well, that's different.

MRS. ELVSTED: [*Gets up quickly, restlessly.*] Please, Mr. Tesman, I beg you—be kind to
Eilert Loevborg if he comes here. I'm sure he will. I mean, you used to be such
good friends in the old days. And you're both studying the same subject, as far as
I can understand. You're in the same field, aren't you?

TESMAN: Well, we used to be, anyway.

MRS. ELVSTED: Yes—so I beg you earnestly, do please, please, keep an eye on him.   260
Oh, Mr. Tesman, do promise me you will.

TESMAN: I shall be only too happy to do so, Mrs. Rysing.

HEDDA: Elvsted.

TESMAN: I'll do everything for Eilert that lies in my power. You can rely on that.

MRS. ELVSTED: Oh, how good and kind you are! [*Presses his hands.*] Thank you,
thank you, thank you. [*Frightened.*] My husband's so fond of him, you see.

HEDDA: [*Gets up.*] You'd better send him a note, Tesman. He may not come to you of   265
his own accord.

TESMAN: Yes, that'd probably be the best plan, Hedda. What?

HEDDA: The sooner the better. Why not do it now?

MRS. ELVSTED: [*Pleadingly.*] Oh yes, if only you would!

TESMAN: I'll do it this very moment. Do you have his address, Mrs.—er—Elvsted?

MRS. ELVSTED: Yes. [*Takes a small piece of paper from her pocket and gives it to   270
him.*]

TESMAN: Good, good. Right, well I'll go inside and——[*Looks round.*] Where are my
slippers. Oh yes, here. [*Picks up the package and is about to go.*]

HEDDA: Try to sound friendly. Make it a nice long letter.

TESMAN: Right, I will.

MRS. ELVSTED: Please don't say anything about my having seen you.

TESMAN: Good heavens no, of course not. What? [*Goes out through the rear room*   275
to the right.]

HEDDA: [*Goes over to Mrs. Elvsted, smiles and says softly.*] Well! Now we've killed
two birds with one stone.

MRS. ELVSTED: What do you mean?

HEDDA: Didn't you realize I wanted to get him out of the room?

MRS. ELVSTED: So that he could write the letter?

HEDDA: And so that I could talk to you alone.   280

MRS. ELVSTED: [*Confused*] About this?

HEDDA: Yes, about this.

MRS. ELVSTED: [*In alarm.*] But there's nothing more to tell, Mrs. Tesman. Really
there isn't.

HEDDA: Oh, yes there is. There's a lot more. I can see that. Come along, let's sit down
and have a little chat.

[*She pushes Mrs. Elvsted down into the armchair by the stove and seats herself on one of the
footstools.*]

MRS. ELVSTED: [*Looks anxiously at her watch.*] Really, Mrs. Tesman, I think I ought   285
to be going now.

HEDDA: There's no hurry. Well? How are things at home?

MRS. ELVSTED: I'd rather not speak about that.

HEDDA: But my dear, you can tell me. Good heavens, we were at school together.

MRS. ELVSTED: Yes, but you were a year senior to me. Oh, I used to be terribly frightened of you in those days.

HEDDA: Frightened of me?   290

MRS. ELVSTED: Yes, terribly frightened. Whenever you met me on the staircase you
used to pull my hair.

HEDDA: No, did I?

MRS. ELVSTED: Yes. And once you said you'd burn it all off.

HEDDA: Oh, that was only in fun.

MRS. ELVSTED: Yes, but I was so silly in those days. And then afterwards—I mean,   295
we've drifted so far apart. Our backgrounds were so different.

HEDDA: Well, now we must try to drift together again. Now listen. When we were at
school we used to call each other by our Christian names——

MRS. ELVSTED: No, I'm sure you're mistaken.

HEDDA: I'm sure I'm not. I remember it quite clearly. Let's tell each other our secrets, as we used to in the old days. [*Moves closer on her footstool.*] There, now.
[*Kisses her on the cheek.*] You must call me Hedda.

MRS. ELVSTED: [*Squeezes her hands and pats them.*] Oh, you're so kind. I'm not
used to people being so nice to me.

HEDDA: Now, now, now. And I shall call you Tora, the way I used to.   300

MRS. ELVSTED: My name is Thea.

HEDDA: Yes, of course. Of course. I meant Thea. [*Looks at her sympathetically.*] So
you're not used to kindness, Thea? In your own home?

MRS. ELVSTED: Oh, if only I had a home! But I haven't. I've never had one.

HEDDA: [*Looks at her for a moment.*] I thought that was it.

MRS. ELVSTED: [*Stares blankly and helplessly.*] Yes—yes—yes.   305

HEDDA: I can't remember exactly now, but didn't you first go to Mr. Elvsted as a
housekeeper?

MRS. ELVSTED: Governess, actually. But his wife—at the time, I mean—she was an invalid, and had to spend most of her time in bed. So I had to look after the house too.

HEDDA: But in the end, you became mistress of the house.

MRS. ELVSTED: [*Sadly.*] Yes, I did.

HEDDA: Let me see. Roughly how long ago was that?   310

MRS. ELVSTED: When I got married, you mean?

HEDDA: Yes.

MRS. ELVSTED: About five years.

HEDDA: Yes, it must be about that.

MRS. ELVSTED: Oh, those five years! Especially that last two or three. Oh, Mrs. Tesman,   315
if you only knew——

HEDDA: [*Slaps her hand gently.*] Mrs. Tesman? Oh, Thea!

MRS. ELVSTED: I'm sorry, I'll try to remember. Yes—if you had any idea——

HEDDA: [*Casually.*] Eilert Loevborg's been up here too, for about three years, hasn't
he?

MRS. ELVSTED: [*Looks at her uncertainly.*] Eilert Loevborg? Yes, he has.

HEDDA: Did you know him before? When you were here?   320

MRS. ELVSTED: No, not really. That is—I knew him by name, of course.

HEDDA: But up there, he used to visit you?

MRS. ELVSTED: Yes, he used to come and see us every day. To give the children
lessons. I found I couldn't do that as well as manage the house.

HEDDA: I'm sure you couldn't. And your husband——? I suppose being a magistrate
he has to be away from home a good deal?

MRS. ELVSTED: Yes. You see, Mrs.—— you see, Hedda, he has to cover the whole district.   325

HEDDA: [*Leans against the arm of Mrs. Elvsted's chair.*] Poor, pretty little Thea!
Now you must tell me the whole story. From beginning to end.

MRS. ELVSTED: Well—what do you want to know?

HEDDA: What kind of a man is your husband, Thea? I mean, as a person. Is he kind to
you?

MRS. ELVSTED: [*Evasively.*] I'm sure he does his best to be.

HEDDA: I only wonder if he isn't too old for you. There's more than twenty years be-   330
tween you, isn't there?

MRS. ELVSTED: [*Irritably.*] Yes, there's that too. Oh, there are so many things. We're
different in every way. We've nothing in common. Nothing whatever.

HEDDA: But he loves you, surely? In his own way?

MRS. ELVSTED: Oh, I don't know. I think he just finds me useful. And then I don't cost
much to keep. I'm cheap.

HEDDA: Now you're being stupid.

MRS. ELVSTED: [*Shakes her head*] It can't be any different. With him. He doesn't love   335
anyone except himself. And perhaps the children—a little.

HEDDA: He must be fond of Eilert Loevborg, Thea.

MRS. ELVSTED: [*Looks at her.*] Eilert Loevborg? What makes you think that?

HEDDA: Well, if he sends you all the way down here to look for him——[*Smiles
almost imperceptibly.*] Besides, you said so yourself to Tesman.

MRS. ELVSTED: [*With a nervous twitch.*] Did I? Oh yes, I suppose I did. [*Impulsively,
but keeping her voice low.*] Well, I might as well tell you the whole story. It's
bound to come out sooner or later.

HEDDA: But my dear Thea——?

MRS. ELVSTED: My husband had no idea I was coming here.   340

HEDDA: What? Your husband didn't know?

MRS. ELVSTED: No, of course not. As a matter of fact, he wasn't even there. He was away at the assizes. Oh, I couldn't stand it any longer, Hedda! I just couldn't. I'd be so dreadfully lonely up there now.

HEDDA: Go on.

MRS. ELVSTED: So I packed a few things. Secretly. And went.   345

HEDDA: Without telling anyone?

MRS. ELVSTED: Yes. I caught the train and came straight here.

HEDDA: But my dear Thea! How brave of you!

MRS. ELVSTED: [*Gets up and walks across the room.*] Well, what else could I do?

HEDDA: But what do you suppose your husband will say when you get back?   350

MRS. ELVSTED: [*By the table, looks at her.*] Back there? To him?

HEDDA: Yes. Surely——?

MRS. ELVSTED: I shall never go back to him.

HEDDA: [*Gets up and goes closer.*] You mean you've left your home for good?

MRS. ELVSTED: Yes. I didn't see what else I could do.   355

HEDDA: But to do it so openly!

MRS. ELVSTED: Oh, it's no use trying to keep a thing like that secret.

HEDDA: But what do you suppose people will say?

MRS. ELVSTED: They can say what they like. [*Sits sadly, wearily on the sofa.*] I had to do it.

HEDDA: [*After a short silence.*] What do you intend to do now? How are you   360 going to live?

MRS. ELVSTED: I don't know. I only know that I must live wherever Eilert Loevborg is. If I am to go on living.

HEDDA: [*Moves a chair from the table, sits on it near Mrs. Elvsted and strokes her hands.*] Tell me, Thea, how did this—friendship between you and Eilert Loevborg begin?

MRS. ELVSTED: Oh, it came about gradually. I developed a kind of—power over him.

HEDDA: Oh?

MRS. ELVSTED: He gave up his old habits. Not because I asked him to. I'd never have   365 dared to do that. I suppose he just noticed I didn't like that kind of thing. So he gave it up.

HEDDA: [*Hides a smile.*] So you've made a new man of him. Clever little Thea!

MRS. ELVSTED: Yes—anyway, he says I have. And he's made a—sort of—real person of me. Taught me to think—and to understand all kinds of things.

HEDDA: Did he give you lessons too?

MRS. ELVSTED: Not exactly lessons. But he talked to me. About—oh, you've no idea— so many things! And then he let me work with him. Oh, it was wonderful. I was so happy to be allowed to help him.

HEDDA: Did he allow you to help him!   370

MRS. ELVSTED: Yes. Whenever he wrote anything we always—did it together.

HEDDA: Like good pals?

MRS. ELVSTED: [*Eagerly.*] Pals! Yes—why, Hedda, that's exactly the word he used! Oh, I ought to feel so happy. But I can't. I don't know if it will last.

HEDDA: You don't seem very sure of him.

MRS. ELVSTED: [*Sadly.*] Something stands between Eilert Loevberg and me. The   375 shadow of another woman.

HEDDA: Who can that be?

MRS. ELVSTED: I don't know. Someone he used to be friendly with in—in the old days. Someone he's never been able to forget.

HEDDA: What has he told you about her?

MRS. ELVSTED: Oh, he only mentioned her once, casually.

HEDDA: Well! What did he say?

MRS. ELVSTED: He said when he left her she tried to shoot him with a pistol.   380

HEDDA: [*Cold, controlled.*] What nonsense. People don't do such things. The kind of people we know.

MRS. ELVSTED: No, I think it must have been that red-haired singer he used to——

HEDDA: Ah yes, very probably.

MRS. ELVSTED: I remember they used to say she always carried a loaded pistol.   385

HEDDA: Well then, it must be her.

MRS. ELVSTED: But Hedda, I hear she's come back, and is living here. Oh, I'm so desperate——!

HEDDA: [*Glances toward the rear room.*] Ssh! Tesman's coming. [*Gets up and whispers.*] Thea, we mustn't breathe a word about this to anyone.

MRS. ELVSTED: [*Jumps up.*] Oh, no, no! Please don't!

[*George Tesman appears from the right in the rear room with a letter in his hand, and comes into the drawing room.*]

TESMAN: Well, here's my little epistle all signed and sealed.   390

HEDDA: Good. I think Mrs. Elvsted wants to go now. Wait a moment—I'll see you as far as the garden gate.

TESMAN: Er—Hedda, do you think Bertha could deal with this?

HEDDA: [*Takes the letter.*] I'll give her instructions.

[*Bertha enters from the hall.*]

BERTHA: Judge Brack is here and asks if he may pay his respects to Madam and the Doctor.

HEDDA: Yes, ask him to be so good as to come in. And—wait a moment—drop this   395
letter in the post box.

BERTHA: [*Takes the letter.*] Very good, madam.

[*She opens the door for Judge Brack, and goes out. Judge Brack is forty-five; rather short, but well-built, and elastic in his movements. He has a roundish face with an aristocratic profile. His hair, cut short, is still almost black, and is carefully barbered. Eyes lively and humorous. Thick eyebrows. His moustache is also thick, and is trimmed square at the ends. He is wearing outdoor clothes which are elegant but a little too youthful for him. He has a monocle in one eye; now and then he lets it drop.*]

BRACK: [*Hat in hand, bows.*] May one presume to call so early?

HEDDA: One may presume.

TESMAN: [*Shakes his hand.*] You're welcome here any time. Judge Brack—Mrs. Rysing.

[*Hedda sighs.*]

BRACK: [*Bows.*] Ah—charmed——

HEDDA: [*Looks at him and laughs.*] What fun to be able to see you by daylight for   400
once, Judge.

BRACK: Do I look—different?

HEDDA: Yes. A little younger, I think.

BRACK: Obliged.

TESMAN: Well, what do you think of Hedda? What? Doesn't she look well? Hasn't   405
she filled out——?

HEDDA: Oh, do stop it. You ought to be thanking Judge Brack for all the inconvenience he's put himself to——

BRACK: Nonsense, it was a pleasure——

HEDDA: You're a loyal friend. But my other friend is pining to get away. Au revoir, Judge. I won't be a minute.

[Mutual salutations. Mrs. Elvsted and Hedda go out through the hall.]

BRACK: Well, is your wife satisfied with everything?

TESMAN: Yes, we can't thank you enough. That is—we may have to shift one or two   410
things around, she tells me. And we're short of one or two little items we'll have
to purchase.

BRACK: Oh? Really?

TESMAN: But you mustn't worry your head about that. Hedda says she'll get what's
needed. I say, why don't we sit down? What?

BRACK: Thanks, just for a moment. *[Sits at the table.]* There's something I'd like to
talk to you about, my dear Tesman.

TESMAN: Oh? Ah yes, of course. *[Sits.]* After the feast comes the reckoning. What?

BRACK: Oh, never mind about the financial side—there's no hurry about that.   415
Though I could wish we'd arranged things a little less palatially.

TESMAN: Good heavens, that'd never have done. Think of Hedda, my dear chap. You
know her. I couldn't possibly ask her to live like a suburban housewife.

BRACK: No, no—that's just the problem.

TESMAN: Anyway, it can't be long now before my nomination[4] comes through.

BRACK: Well, you know, these things often take time.

TESMAN: Have you heard any more news? What?   420

BRACK: Nothing definite. *[Changing the subject.]* Oh, by the way, I have one piece
of news for you.

TESMAN: What?

BRACK: Your old friend Eilert Loevborg is back in town.

TESMAN: I know that already.

BRACK: Oh? How did you hear that?

TESMAN: She told me. That lady who went out with Hedda.

BRACK: I see. What was her name? I didn't catch it.

TESMAN: Mrs. Elvsted.

BRACK: Oh, the magistrate's wife. Yes, Loevborg's been living up near them, hasn't he?

TESMAN: I'm delighted to hear he's become a decent human being again.   430

BRACK: Yes, so they say.

TESMAN: I gather he's published a new book, too. What?

BRACK: Indeed he has.

TESMAN: I hear it's created rather a stir.

BRACK: Quite an unusual stir.   435

TESMAN: I say, isn't that splendid news! He's such a gifted chap—and I was afraid
he'd gone to the dogs for good.

BRACK: Most people thought he had.

TESMAN: But I can't think what he'll do now. How on earth will he manage to make
ends meet? What?

[As he speaks his last words, Hedda enters from the hall.]

HEDDA: *[To Brack, laughs slightly scornfully.]* Tesman is always worrying about
making ends meet.

TESMAN: We were talking about poor Eilert Loevborg, Hedda dear.   440

HEDDA: *[Gives him a quick look.]* Oh, were you? *[Sits in the armchair by the
stove and asks casually.]* Is he in trouble?

----

[4]To a professorship at the university.

TESMAN: Well, he must have run through his inheritance long ago by now. And he
can't write a new book every year. What? So I'm wondering what's going to become of him.

BRACK: I may be able to enlighten you there.

TESMAN: Oh?

BRACK: You mustn't forget he has relatives who wield a good deal of influence.   445

TESMAN: Relatives? Oh, they've quite washed their hands of him, I'm afraid.

BRACK: They used to regard him as the hope of the family.

TESMAN: Used to, yes. But he's put an end to that.

HEDDA: Who knows? [*With a little smile.*] I hear the Elvsteds have made a new
man of him.

BRACK: And then this book he's just published——   450

TESMAN: Well, let's hope they find something for him. I've just written him a note.
Oh, by the way, Hedda, I asked him to come over and see us this evening.

BRACK: But my dear chap, you're coming to me this evening. My bachelor party. You
promised me last night when I met you at the boat.

HEDDA: Had you forgotten, Tesman?

TESMAN: Good heavens, yes, I'd quite forgotten.

BRACK: Anyway, you can be quite sure he won't turn up here.   455

TESMAN: Why do you think that? What?

BRACK: [*A little unwillingly, gets up and rests his hands on the back of his chair.*]
My dear Tesman—and you, too, Mrs. Tesman—there's something I feel you
ought to know.

TESMAN: Concerning Eilert?

BRACK: Concerning him and you.

TESMAN: Well, my dear Judge, tell us, please!   460

BRACK: You must be prepared for your nomination not to come through quite as
quickly as you hope and expect.

TESMAN: [*Jumps up uneasily.*] Is anything wrong? What?

BRACK: There's a possibility that the appointment may be decided by
competition——

TESMAN: Competition! By Jove, Hedda, fancy that!

HEDDA: [*Leans further back in her chair.*] Ah! How interesting!   465

TESMAN: But who else——? I say, you don't mean——?

BRACK: Exactly. By competition with Eilert Loevborg.

TESMAN: [*Clasps his hands in alarm.*] No, no, but this is inconceivable! It's absolutely impossible! What?

BRACK: Hm. We may find it'll happen, all the same.

TESMAN: No, but—Judge Brack, they couldn't be so inconsiderate toward me!   470
[*Waves his arms.*] I mean, by Jove, I—I'm a married man! It was on the strength
of this that Hedda and I *got* married! We ran up some pretty hefty debts. And
borrowed money from Auntie Juju! I mean, good heavens, they practically
promised me the appointment. What?

BRACK: Well, well, I'm sure you'll get it. But you'll have to go through a competition.

HEDDA: [*Motionless in her armchair.*] How exciting, Tesman. It'll be a kind of
duel, by Jove.

TESMAN: My dear Hedda, how can you take it so lightly?

HEDDA: [*As before.*] I'm not. I can't wait to see who's going to win.

BRACK: In any case, Mrs. Tesman, it's best you should know how things stand. I   475
mean before you commit yourself to these little items I hear you're threatening
to purchase.

HEDDA: I can't allow this to alter my plans.

BRACK: Indeed? Well, that's your business. Good-bye. [*To Tesman.*] I'll come and collect you on the way home from my afternoon walk.

TESMAN: Oh, yes, yes. I'm sorry, I'm all upside down just now.

HEDDA: [*Lying in her chair, holds out her hand.*] Good-bye, Judge. See you this
afternoon.

BRACK: Thank you. Good-bye, good-bye.   480

TESMAN: [*Sees him to the door.*] Good-bye, my dear Judge. You will excuse me,
won't you?

[Judge Brack goes out through the hall.]

TESMAN: [*Pacing up and down.*] Oh, Hedda! One oughtn't to go plunging off on
wild adventures. What?

HEDDA: [*Looks at him and smiles.*] Like you're doing?

TESMAN: Yes. I mean, there's no denying it, it was a pretty big adventure to go off
and get married and set up house merely on expectation.

HEDDA: Perhaps you're right.   485

TESMAN: Well, anyway, we have our home, Hedda. By Jove, yes. The home we
dreamed of. And set our hearts on. What?

HEDDA: [*Gets up slowly, wearily.*] You agreed that we should enter society. And
keep open house. That was the bargain.

TESMAN: Yes. Good heavens, I was looking forward to it all so much. To seeing you
play hostess to a select circle! By Jove! What? Ah, well, for the time being we
shall have to make do with each other's company, Hedda. Perhaps have Auntie
Juju in now and then. Oh dear, this wasn't all what you had in mind——

HEDDA: I won't be able to have a liveried footman. For a start.

TESMAN: Oh no, we couldn't possibly afford a footman.   490

HEDDA: And that thoroughbred horse you promised me——

TESMAN: [*Fearfully.*] Thoroughbred horse!

HEDDA: I mustn't even think of that now.

TESMAN: Heaven forbid!

HEDDA: [*Walks across the room.*] Ah, well. I still have one thing left to amuse my-   495
self with.

TESMAN: [*Joyfully*] Thank goodness for that. What's that, Hedda? What?

HEDDA: [*In the open doorway, looks at him with concealed scorn.*] My pistols,
George darling.

TESMAN: [*Alarmed.*] Pistols!

HEDDA: [*Her eyes cold.*] General Gabler's pistols. [*She goes into the rear room and
disappears.*]

TESMAN: [*Runs to the doorway and calls after her.*] For heaven's sake, Hedda dear,   500
don't touch those things. They're dangerous. Hedda—please—for my sake!
What?

Act 1 Response Statement Questions

- To what extent does the opening set description help you visualize the
setting of the play? Reading it, how able are you to suspend disbelief and
accept this setting as a realistic locale? Do you have experience reading or
seeing other plays that helps you picture the setting here?

- What impressions do you form of Tesman from the conversation between
his aunt and Bertha, the maid? from his first appearance and conversation?
Is he a believable realistic individual? a stereotype?

- What impressions do you form of Hedda from other characters' conversation before she first appears? from her comments and actions when she first appears?
- What impression do you form of Hedda and Tesman's relationship as a married couple? as newlyweds? of each of them in terms of their husband/wife roles? in terms of gender roles? How would you feel if you were married to either one?
- How would you analyze the dynamics of Hedda's relationship to Mrs. Elvsted as it unfolds in Act 1? of their relationship in the past? What is your response to Mrs. Elvsted in Act 1? What is your response to Hedda's reaction to her?
- What impressions do you form of Eilert Loevborg from other characters' conversation about him before he first appears? How does he seem to compare to Tesman?

Act 2

SCENE—*The same as in Act 1 except that the piano has been removed and an elegant little writing table, with a bookcase, stands in its place. By the sofa on the left a smaller table has been placed. Most of the flowers have been removed. Mrs. Elvsted's bouquet stands on the larger table, downstage. It is afternoon.*

Hedda, dressed to receive callers, is alone in the room. She is standing by the open french windows, loading a revolver. The pair to it is lying in an open pistol case on the writing table.

HEDDA: [*Looks down into the garden and calls.*] Good afternoon, Judge.
BRACK: [*In the distance, below.*] Afternoon, Mrs. Tesman.
HEDDA: [*Raises the pistol and takes aim.*] I'm going to shoot you, Judge Brack.
BRACK: [*Shouts from below.*] No no, no! Don't aim that thing at me!
HEDDA: This'll teach you to enter houses by the back door. [*Fires.*]   5
BRACK: [*Below.*] Have you gone completely out of your mind?
HEDDA: Oh dear! Did I hit you.
BRACK: [*Still outside.*] Stop playing these silly tricks.
HEDDA: All right, Judge. Come along in.

[*Judge Brack, dressed for a bachelor party, enters through the french windows. He has a light overcoat on his arm.*]

BRACK: For God's sake! Haven't you stopped fooling around with those things yet?   10
      What are you trying to hit?
HEDDA: Oh, I was just shooting at the sky.
BRACK: [*Takes the pistol gently from her hand.*] By your leave, ma'am. [*Looks at it.*] Ah, yes—I know this old friend well. [*Looks around.*] Where's the case? Oh, yes. [*Puts the pistol in the case and closes it.*] That's enough of that little game for today.
HEDDA: Well, what on earth *am* I to do?
BRACK: You haven't had any visitors?
HEDDA: [*Closes the french windows.*] Not one. I suppose the best people are all   15
      still in the country.
BRACK: Your husband isn't home yet?
HEDDA: [*Locks the pistol case away in a drawer of the writing table.*] No. The moment he'd finished eating he ran off to his aunties. He wasn't expecting you so early.

BRACK: Ah, why didn't I think of that? How stupid of me.
HEDDA: [*Turns her head and looks at him.*] Why stupid?
BRACK: I'd have come a little sooner.   20
HEDDA: [*Walks across the room.*] There'd have been no one to receive you. I've
          been in my room since lunch, dressing.
BRACK: You haven't a tiny crack in the door through which we might have negotiated?
HEDDA: You forgot to arrange one.
BRACK: Another stupidity.
HEDDA: Well, we'll have to sit down here. And wait. Tesman won't be back for   25
          some time.
BRACK: Sad. Well, I'll be patient.

[*Hedda sits on the corner of the sofa. Brack puts his coat over the back of the nearest chair and
seats himself, keeping his hat in his hand. Short pause. They look at each other.*]

HEDDA: Well?
BRACK: [*In the same tone of voice.*] Well?
HEDDA: I asked first.
BRACK: [*Leans forward slightly.*] Yes, well, now we can enjoy a nice, cosy little   30
          chat—Mrs. Hedda.
HEDDA: [*Leans further back in her chair.*] It seems such ages since we had a talk. I
          don't count last night or this morning.
BRACK: You mean: *à deux?*
HEDDA: Mm—yes. That's roughly what I meant.
BRACK: I've been longing so much for you to come home.
HEDDA: So have I.   35
BRACK: You? Really, Mrs. Hedda? And I thought you were having such a wonderful
          honeymoon.
HEDDA: Oh, yes. Wonderful!
BRACK: But your husband wrote such ecstatic letters.
HEDDA: He! Oh, yes! He thinks life has nothing better to offer than rooting around
          in libraries and copying old pieces of parchment, or whatever it is he does.
BRACK: [*A little maliciously.*] Well, that *is* his life. Most of it, anyway.   40
HEDDA: Yes, I know. Well, it's all right for him. But for me! Oh no, my dear Judge. I've
          been bored to death.
BRACK: [*Sympathetically.*] Do you mean that? Seriously?
HEDDA: Yes. Can you imagine? Six whole months without ever meeting a single per-
          son who was one of us, and to whom I could talk about the kind of things we
          talk about.
BRACK: Yes, I can understand. I'd miss that, too.
HEDDA: That wasn't the worst, though.   45
BRACK: What was?
HEDDA: Having to spend every minute of one's life with—with the same person.
BRACK: [*Nods.*] Yes. What a thought! Morning; noon; and——
HEDDA: [*Coldly.*] As I said: every minute of one's life.
BRACK: I stand corrected. But dear Tesman is such a clever fellow, I should have   50
          thought one ought to be able——
HEDDA: Tesman is only interested in one thing, my dear Judge. His special subject.
BRACK: True.
HEDDA: And people who are only interested in one thing don't make the most
          amusing company. Not for long, anyway.
BRACK: Not even when they happen to be the person one loves?

HEDDA: Oh, don't use that sickly, stupid word.

BRACK: [*Starts.*] But, Mrs. Hedda——!

HEDDA: [*Half laughing, half annoyed.*] You just try it, Judge. Listening to the history of civilization morning, noon and——

BRACK: [*Corrects her.*] Every minute of one's life.

HEDDA: All right. Oh, and those domestic industries of Brabant in the Middle Ages! That really is beyond the limit.

BRACK: [*Looks at her searchingly.*] But, tell me—if you feel like this why on earth did you——? Ha——

HEDDA: Why on earth did I marry George Tesman?

BRACK: If you like to put it that way.

HEDDA: Do you think it so very strange?

BRACK: Yes—and no, Mrs. Hedda.

HEDDA: I'd danced myself tired, Judge. I felt my time was up——[*Gives a slight shudder.*] No, I mustn't say that. Or even think it.

BRACK: You've no rational cause to think it.

HEDDA: Oh—cause, cause——[*Looks searchingly at him.*] After all, George Tesman—well, I mean, he's a very respectable man.

BRACK: Very respectable, sound as a rock. No denying that.

HEDDA: And there's nothing exactly ridiculous about him. Is there?

BRACK: Ridiculous? No-no, I wouldn't say that.

HEDDA: Mm. He's very clever at collecting material and all that, isn't he? I mean, he may go quite far in time.

BRACK: [*Looks at her a little uncertainly.*] I thought you believed, like everyone else, that he would become a very prominent man.

HEDDA: [*Looks tired.*] Yes, I did. And when he came and begged me on his bended knees to be allowed to love and to cherish me, I didn't see why I shouldn't let him.

BRACK: No, well—if one looks at it like that——

HEDDA: It was more than my other admirers were prepared to do, Judge dear.

BRACK: [*Laughs.*] Well, I can't answer for the others. As far as I myself am concerned, you know I've always had a considerable respect for the institution of marriage. As an institution.

HEDDA: [*Lightly.*] Oh, I've never entertained any hopes of you.

BRACK: All I want is to have a circle of friends whom I can trust, whom I can help with advice or—or by any other means, and into whose houses I may come and go as a—trusted friend.

HEDDA: Of the husband?

BRACK: [*Bows.*] Preferably, to be frank, of the wife. And of the husband too, of course. Yes, you know, this kind of—triangle is a delightful arrangement for all parties concerned.

HEDDA: Yes, I often longed for a third person while I was away. Oh, those hours we spent alone in railway compartments——

BRACK: Fortunately your honeymoon is now over.

HEDDA: [*Shakes her head.*] There's a long way still to go. I've only reached a stop on the line.

BRACK: Why not jump out and stretch your legs a little, Mrs. Hedda?

HEDDA: I'm not the jumping sort.

BRACK: Aren't you?

HEDDA: No. There's always someone around who——

BRACK: [*Laughs.*] Who looks at one's legs?

HEDDA: Yes. Exactly.
BRACK: Well, but surely——   90
HEDDA: [*With a gesture of rejection.*] I don't like it. I'd rather stay where I am. Sit-
          ting in the compartment. *À deux.*
BRACK: But suppose a third person were to step into the compartment?
HEDDA: That would be different.
BRACK: A trusted friend—someone who understood——
HEDDA: And was lively and amusing——   95
BRACK: And interested in—more subjects than one——
HEDDA: [*Sighs audibly.*] Yes, that'd be a relief.
BRACK: [*Hears the front door open and shut.*] The triangle is completed.
HEDDA: [*Half under breath.*] And the train goes on.

[*George Tesman, in grey walking dress with a soft felt hat, enters from the hall. He has a number
of paper-covered books under his arm and in his pockets.*]

TESMAN: [*Goes over to the table by the corner sofa.*] Phew! It's too hot to be lug-   100
          ging all this around. [*Puts the books down.*] I'm positively sweating, Hedda.
          Why, hullo, hullo! You here already, judge? What? Bertha didn't tell me.
BRACK: [*Gets up.*] I came in through the garden.
HEDDA: What are all those books you've got there?
TESMAN: [*Stands glancing through them.*] Oh, some new publications dealing with
          my special subject. I had to buy them.
HEDDA: Your special subject?
BRACK: His special subject, Mrs. Tesman.   105

[*Brack and Hedda exchange a smile.*]

HEDDA: Haven't you collected enough material on your special subject?
TESMAN: My dear Hedda, one can never have too much. One must keep abreast of
          what other people are writing.
HEDDA: Yes. Of course.
TESMAN: [*Rooting among the books.*] Look—I bought a copy of Eilert Loevborg's
          new book, too. [*Holds it out to her.*] Perhaps you'd like to have a look at it,
          Hedda? What?
HEDDA: No, thank you. Er—yes, perhaps I will, later.   110
TESMAN: I glanced through it on my way home.
BRACK: What's your opinion—as a specialist on the subject?
TESMAN: I'm amazed how sound and balanced it is. He never used to write like that.
          [*Gathers his books together.*] Well, I must get down to these at once. I can
          hardly wait to cut the pages.[5] Oh, I've got to change, too. [*To Brack.*] We don't
          have to be off just yet, do we? What?
BRACK: Heavens, no. We've plenty of time yet.
TESMAN: Good, I needn't hurry, then. [*Goes with his books, but stops and turns in*   115
          the doorway.] Oh, by the way, Hedda, Auntie Juju won't be coming to see you
          this evening.
HEDDA: Won't she? Oh—the hat, I suppose.
TESMAN: Good heavens, no. How could you think such a thing of Auntie Juju?
          Fancy——! No, Auntie Rena's very ill.
HEDDA: She always is.
TESMAN: Yes, but today she's been taken really bad.

---

[5]Books used to be sold with the pages folded but uncut as they came from the printing press; the
owner had to cut the pages in order to read the book.

HEDDA: Oh, then it's quite understandable that the other one should want to stay   120
    with her. Well, I shall have to swallow my disappointment.

TESMAN: You can't imagine how happy Auntie Juju was in spite of everything. At
    your looking so well after the honeymoon!

HEDDA: [*Half beneath her breath, as she rises.*] Oh, these everlasting aunts!

TESMAN: What?

HEDDA: [*Goes over to the french windows.*] Nothing.

TESMAN: Oh. All right. [*Goes into the rear room and out of sight.*]   125

BRACK: What was that about the hat?

HEDDA: Oh, something that happened with Miss Tesman this morning. She'd put
    her hat down on a chair. [*Looks at him and smiles.*] And I pretended to think it
    was the servant's.

BRACK: [*Shakes his head.*] But my dear Mrs. Hedda, how could you do such a thing?
    To that poor old lady?

HEDDA: [*Nervously, walking across the room.*] Sometimes a mood like that hits
    me. And I can't stop myself. [*Throws herself down in the armchair by the
    stove.*] Oh, I don't know how to explain it.

BRACK: [*Behind her chair.*] You're not really happy. That's the answer.   130

HEDDA: [*Stares ahead of her.*] Why on earth should I be happy? Can you give me a
    reason?

BRACK: Yes. For one thing you've got the home you always wanted.

HEDDA: [*Looks at him.*] You really believe that story?

BRACK: You mean it isn't true?

HEDDA: Oh, yes, it's partly true.

BRACK: Well?   135

HEDDA: It's true I got Tesman to see me home from parties last summer——

BRACK: It was a pity my home lay in another direction.

HEDDA: Yes. Your interests lay in another direction, too.

BRACK: [*Laughs.*] That's naughty of you, Mrs. Hedda. But to return to you and   140
    Tesman——

HEDDA: Well, we walked past this house one evening. And poor Tesman was fid-
    geting in his boots trying to find something to talk about. I felt sorry for the
    great scholar——

BRACK: [*Smiles incredulously.*] Did you? Hm.

HEDDA: Yes, honestly I did. Well, to help him out of his misery, I happened to say
    quite frivolously how much I'd love to live in this house.

BRACK: Was that all?

HEDDA: That evening, yes.

BRACK: But—afterwards?   145

HEDDA: Yes. My little frivolity had its consequences, my dear Judge.

BRACK: Our little frivolities do. Much too often, unfortunately.

HEDDA: Thank you. Well, it was our mutual admiration for the late Prime Minister's
    house that brought George Tesman and me together on common ground. So we
    got engaged, and we got married, and we went on our honeymoon, and—ah
    well, Judge, I've—made my bed and I must lie in it, I was about to say.

BRACK: How utterly fantastic! And you didn't really care in the least about the house?   150

HEDDA: God knows I didn't.

BRACK: Yes, but now that we've furnished it so beautifully for you?

HEDDA: Ugh—all the rooms smell of lavender and dried roses. But perhaps Auntie
    Juju brought that in.

BRACK: [*Laughs.*] More likely the Prime Minister's widow, rest her soul.

HEDDA: Yes, it's got the odor of death about it. It reminds me of the flowers one has   155
          worn at a ball—the morning after. [*Clasps her hands behind her neck, leans
          back in the chair and looks up at him.*] Oh, my dear Judge, you've no idea how
          hideously bored I'm going to be out here.

BRACK: Couldn't you find some kind of occupation, Mrs. Hedda? Like your husband?

HEDDA: Occupation? That'd interest me?

BRACK: Well—preferably.

HEDDA: God knows what. I've often thought——[*Breaks off.*] No, that wouldn't
          work either.

BRACK: Who knows? Tell me about it.   160

HEDDA: I was thinking—if I could persuade Tesman to go into politics, for example.

BRACK: [*Laughs.*] Tesman! No, honestly, I don't think he's quite cut out to be a
          politician.

HEDDA: Perhaps not. But if I could persuade him to have a go at it?

BRACK: What satisfaction would that give you? If he turned out to be no good? Why
          do you want to make him do that?

HEDDA: Because I'm bored. [*After a moment.*] You feel there's absolutely no possi-   165
          bility of Tesman becoming Prime Minister, then?

BRACK: Well, you know, Mrs. Hedda, for one thing he'd have to be pretty well off be-
          fore he could become that.

HEDDA: [*Gets up impatiently.*] There you are! [*Walks across the room.*] It's this
          wretched poverty that makes life so hateful. And ludicrous. Well, it is!

BRACK: I don't think that's the real cause.

HEDDA: What is, then?

BRACK: Nothing really exciting has ever happened to you.   170

HEDDA: Nothing serious, you mean?

BRACK: Call it that if you like. But now perhaps it may.

HEDDA: [*Tosses her head.*] Oh, you're thinking of this competition for that
          wretched professorship? That's Tesman's affair. I'm not going to waste my time
          worrying about that.

BRACK: Very well, let's forget about that then. But suppose you were to find yourself
          faced with what people call—to use the conventional phrase—the most solemn
          of human responsibilities? [*Smiles.*] A new responsibility, little Mrs. Hedda.

HEDDA: [*Angrily.*] Be quiet! Nothing like that's going to happen.   175

BRACK: [*Warily.*] We'll talk about it again in a year's time. If not earlier.

HEDDA: [*Curtly.*] I've no leanings in that direction, Judge. I don't want any—re-
          sponsibilities.

BRACK: But surely you must feel some inclination to make use of that—natural tal-
          ent which every woman——

HEDDA: [*Over by the french windows.*] Oh, be quiet, I say! I often think there's only
          one thing for which I have any natural talent.

BRACK: [*Goes closer.*] And what is that, if I may be so bold as to ask?   180

HEDDA: [*Stands looking out.*] For boring myself to death. Now you know. [*Turns,
          looks toward the rear room and laughs.*] Talking of boring, here comes the
          professor.

BRACK: [*Quietly, warningly.*] Now, now, now, Mrs. Hedda!

[*George Tesman, in evening dress, with gloves and hat in his hand, enters through the rear room
from the right.*]

TESMAN: Hedda, hasn't any message come from Eilert? What?

HEDDA: No.

TESMAN: Ah, then we'll have him here presently. You wait and see.   185
BRACK: You really think he'll come?
TESMAN: Yes, I'm almost sure he will. What you were saying about him this morning
is just gossip.
BRACK: Oh?
TESMAN: Yes. Auntie Juju said she didn't believe he'd ever dare to stand in my way
again. Fancy that!
BRACK: Then everything in the garden's lovely.   190
TESMAN: [*Puts his hat, with his gloves in it, on a chair, right.*] Yes, but you really
must let me wait for him as long as possible.
BRACK: We've plenty of time. No one'll be turning up at my place before seven or
half past.
TESMAN: Ah, then we can keep Hedda company a little longer. And see if he turns
up. What?
HEDDA: [*Picks up Brack's coat and hat and carries them over to the corner sofa.*]
And if the worst comes to the worst, Mr. Loevborg can sit here and talk to me.
BRACK: [*Offering to take his things from her.*] No, please. What do you mean by "if   195
the worst comes to the worst"?
HEDDA: If he doesn't want to go with you and Tesman.
TESMAN: [*Looks doubtfully at her.*] I say, Hedda, do you think it'll be all right for
him to stay here with you? What? Remember Auntie Juju isn't coming.
HEDDA: Yes, but Mrs. Elvsted is. The three of us can have a cup of tea together.
TESMAN: Ah, that'll be all right then.
BRACK: [*Smiles.*] It's probably the safest solution as far as he's concerned.   200
HEDDA: Why?
BRACK: My dear Mrs. Tesman, you always say of my little bachelor parties that they
should be attended only by men of the strongest principles.
HEDDA: But Mr. Loevborg is a man of principle now. You know what they say about
a reformed sinner——

[*Bertha enters from the hall.*]

BERTHA: Madam, there's a gentleman here who wants to see you——
HEDDA: Ask him to come in.
TESMAN: [*Quietly.*] I'm sure it's him. By Jove. Fancy that!   205

[*Eilert Loevborg enters from the hall. He is slim and lean, of the same age as Tesman, but looks
older and somewhat haggard. His hair and beard are of a blackish-brown; his face is long and
pale, but with a couple of reddish patches on his cheekbones. He is dressed in an elegant and
fairly new black suit, and carries black gloves and a top hat in his hand. He stops just inside the
door and bows abruptly. He seems somewhat embarrassed.*]

TESMAN: [*Goes over and shakes his hand.*] My dear Eilert! How grand to see you
again after all these years!
EILERT LOEVBORG: [*Speaks softly.*] It was good of you to write, George. [*Goes nearer
to Hedda.*] May I shake hands with you, too, Mrs. Tesman?
HEDDA: [*Accepts his hand.*] Delighted to see you, Mr. Loevborg. [*With a gesture.*] I
don't know if you two gentlemen——
LOEVBORG: [*Bows slightly.*] Judge Brack, I believe.
BRACK: [*Also with a slight bow.*] Correct. We—met some years ago——   210
TESMAN: [*Puts his hands on Loevborg's shoulders.*] Now you're to treat this house
just as though it were your own home, Eilert. Isn't that right, Hedda? I hear
you've decided to settle here again? What?
LOEVBORG: Yes, I have.

TESMAN: Quite understandable. Oh, by the bye—I've just bought your new book. Though to tell the truth I haven't found time to read it yet.

LOEVBORG: You needn't bother.   215

TESMAN: Oh? Why?

LOEVBORG: There's nothing much in it.

TESMAN: By Jove, fancy hearing that from you!

BRACK: But everyone's praising it.

LOEVBORG: That was exactly what I wanted to happen. So I only wrote what I knew   220
everyone would agree with.

BRACK: Very sensible.

TESMAN: Yes, but my dear Eilert——

LOEVBORG: I want to try to re-establish myself. To begin again—from the beginning.

TESMAN: [*A little embarrassed.*] Yes, I—er—suppose you do. What?

LOEVBORG: [*Smiles, puts down his hat and takes a package wrapped in paper*   225
from his coat pocket.] But when this gets published—George Tesman—read it.
This is my real book. The one in which I have spoken with my own voice.

TESMAN: Oh, really? What's it about?

LOEVBORG: It's the sequel.

TESMAN: Sequel? To what?

LOEVBORG: To the other book.

TESMAN: The one that's just come out?   230

LOEVBORG: Yes.

TESMAN: But my dear Eilert, that covers the subject right up to the present day.

LOEVBORG: It does. But this is about the future.

TESMAN: The future! But, I say, we don't know anything about that.

LOEVBORG: No. But there are one or two things that need to be said about it. [*Opens*   235
the package.] Here, have a look.

TESMAN: Surely that's not your handwriting?

LOEVBORG: I dictated it. [*Turns the pages.*] It's in two parts. The first deals with the
forces that will shape our civilization. [*Turns further on towards the end.*] And
the second indicates the direction in which that civilization may develop.

TESMAN: Amazing! I'd never think of writing about anything like that.

HEDDA: [*By the french windows, drumming on the pane.*] No. You wouldn't.

LOEVBORG: [*Puts the pages back into their cover and lays the package on the table.*]   240
I brought it because I thought I might possibly read you a few pages this evening.

TESMAN: I say, what a kind idea! Oh, but this evening——? [*Glances at Brack*] I'm
not quite sure whether——

LOEVBORG: Well, some other time, then. There's no hurry.

BRACK: The truth is, Mr. Loevborg, I'm giving a little dinner this evening. In Tesman's
honor, you know.

LOEVBORG: [*Looks round for his hat.*] Oh—then I mustn't——

BRACK: No, wait a minute. Won't you do me the honor of joining us?   245

LOEVBORG: [*Curtly, with decision.*] No I can't. Thank you so much.

BRACK: Oh, nonsense. Do—please. There'll only be a few of us. And I can promise
you we shall have some good sport, as Mrs. Hed—as Mrs. Tesman puts it.

LOEVBORG: I've no doubt. Nevertheless——

BRACK: You could bring your manuscript along and read it to Tesman at my place.
I could lend you a room.

TESMAN: By Jove, Eilert, that's an idea. What?   250

HEDDA: [*Interposes.*] But Tesman, Mr. Loevborg doesn't want to go. I'm sure Mr.
Loevborg would much rather sit here and have supper with me.

LOEVBORG: [*Looks at her.*] With you, Mrs. Tesman?
HEDDA: And Mrs. Elvsted.
LOEVBORG: Oh. [*Casually.*] I ran into her this afternoon.
HEDDA: Did you? Well, she's coming here this evening. So you really must stay, Mr.   255
   Loevborg. Otherwise she'll have no one to see her home.
LOEVBORG: That's true. Well—thank you, Mrs. Tesman, I'll stay then.
HEDDA: I'll just tell the servant.

[*She goes to the door which leads into the hall, and rings. Bertha enters. Hedda talks softly to her and points towards the rear room. Bertha nods and goes out.*]

TESMAN: [*To Loevborg, as Hedda does this.*] I say, Eilert. This new subject of
   yours—the—er—future—is that the one you're going to lecture about?
LOEVBORG: Yes.
TESMAN: They told me down at the bookshop that you're going to hold a series of   260
   lectures here during the autumn.
LOEVBORG: Yes, I am, I—hope you don't mind, Tesman.
TESMAN: Good heavens, no! But——?
LOEVBORG: I can quite understand it might queer your pitch a little.
TESMAN: [*Dejectedly.*] Oh well, I can't expect you to put them off for my sake.
LOEVBORG: I'll wait till your appointment's been announced.   265
TESMAN: You'll wait! But—but—aren't you going to compete with me for the
   post? What?
LOEVBORG: No. I only want to defeat you in the eyes of the world.
TESMAN: Good heavens! Then Auntie Juju was right after all! Oh, I knew it, I knew it!
   Hear that, Hedda? Fancy! Eilert *doesn't* want to stand in our way.
HEDDA: [*Curtly.*] Our? Leave me out of it, please.

[*She goes toward the rear room, where Bertha is setting a tray with decanters and glasses on the table. Hedda nods approval, and comes back into the drawing room. Bertha goes out.*]

TESMAN: [*While this is happening.*] Judge Brack, what do you think about all this?   270
   What?
BRACK: Oh, I think honor and victory can be very splendid things——
TESMAN: Of course they can. Still——
HEDDA: [*Looks at Tesman with a cold smile.*] You look as if you'd been hit by a
   thunderbolt.
TESMAN: Yes, I feel rather like it.
BRACK: There was a black cloud looming up, Mrs. Tesman. But it seems to have   275
   passed over.
HEDDA: [*Points toward the rear room.*] Well, gentlemen, won't you go in and take
   a glass of cold punch?
BRACK: [*Glances at his watch.*] A stirrup cup? Yes, why not?
TESMAN: An admirable suggestion, Hedda. Admirable! Oh, I feel so relieved!
HEDDA: Won't you have one, too, Mr. Loevborg?
LOEVBORG: No, thank you. I'd rather not.
BRACK: Great heavens, man, cold punch isn't poison. Take my word for it.   280
LOEVBORG: Not for everyone, perhaps.
HEDDA: I'll keep Mr. Loevborg company while you drink.
TESMAN: Yes, Hedda dear, would you?

[*He and Brack go into the rear room, sit down, drink punch, smoke cigarettes and talk cheerfully during the following scene. Eilert Loevborg remains standing by the stove. Hedda goes to the writing table.*]

HEDDA: [*Raising her voice slightly.*] I've some photographs I'd like to show you, if   285
          you'd care to see them. Tesman and I visited the Tyrol[6] on our way home.

[*She comes back with an album, places it on the table by the sofa and sits in the upstage corner of the sofa. Eilert Loevborg comes toward her, stops and looks at her. Then he takes a chair and sits down on her left, with his back toward the rear room.*]

HEDDA: [*Opens the album.*] You see these mountains, Mr. Loevborg? That's the Or-
          tler group. Tesman has written the name underneath. You see: "The Ortler
          Group near Meran."

LOEVBORG: [*Has not taken his eyes from her; says softly, slowly.*] Hedda—Gabler!

HEDDA: [*Gives him a quick glance.*] Ssh!

LOEVBORG: [*Repeats softly.*] Hedda Gabler!

HEDDA: [*Looks at the album.*] Yes, that used to be my name. When we first knew   290
          each other.

LOEVBORG: And from now on—for the rest of my life—I must teach myself never to
          say: Hedda Gabler.

HEDDA: [*Still turning the pages.*] Yes, you must. You'd better start getting into prac-
          tice. The sooner the better.

LOEVBORG: [*Bitterly.*] Hedda Gabler married? And to George Tesman?

HEDDA: Yes. Well—that's life.

LOEVBORG: Oh, Hedda, Hedda! How could you throw yourself away like that?   295

HEDDA: [*Looks sharply at him.*] Stop it.

LOEVBORG: What do you mean?

[*Tesman comes in and goes toward the sofa.*]

HEDDA: [*Hears him coming and says casually.*] And this, Mr. Loevborg, is the view
          from the Ampezzo valley. Look at those mountains. [*Glances affectionately up
          at Tesman.*] What did you say those curious mountains were called, dear?

TESMAN: Let me have a look. Oh, those are the Dolomites.

HEDDA: Of course. Those are the Dolomites, Mr. Loevborg.   300

TESMAN: Hedda, I just wanted to ask you, can't we bring some punch in here? A
          glass for you, anyway. What?

HEDDA: Thank you, yes. And a biscuit or two, perhaps.

TESMAN: You wouldn't like a cigarette?

HEDDA: No.

TESMAN: Right.   305

[*He goes into the rear room and over to the right. Brack is sitting there, glancing occasionally at Hedda and Loevborg.*]

LOEVBORG: [*Softly, as before.*] Answer me, Hedda. How could you do it?

HEDDA: [*Apparently absorbed in the album.*] If you go on calling me Hedda I
          won't talk to you any more.

LOEVBORG: Mayn't I even when we're alone?

HEDDA: No. You can think it. But you mustn't say it.

LOEVBORG: Oh, I see. Because you love George Tesman.   310

HEDDA: [*Glances at him and smiles.*] Love? Don't be funny.

LOEVBORG: You don't love him?

HEDDA: I don't intend to be unfaithful to him. That's not what I want.

LOEVBORG: Hedda—just tell me one thing——

HEDDA: Ssh!   315

[*Tesman enters from the rear room, carrying a tray.*]

---

[6]Region in the Alps, now primarily in Austria, near the Italian border.

TESMAN: Here we are! Here come the goodies! [*Puts the tray down on the table.*]

HEDDA: Why didn't you ask the servant to bring it in?

TESMAN: [*Fills the glasses.*] I like waiting on you, Hedda.

HEDDA: But you've filled both glasses. Mr. Loevborg doesn't want to drink.

TESMAN: Yes, but Mrs. Elvsted'll be here soon.

HEDDA: Oh yes, that's true. Mrs. Elvsted——   320

TESMAN: Had you forgotten her? What?

HEDDA: We're so absorbed with these photographs. [*Shows him one.*] You remember this little village?

TESMAN: Oh, that one down by the Brenner Pass. We spent a night there——

HEDDA: Yes, and met all those amusing people.

TESMAN: Oh yes, it was there, wasn't it? By Jove, if only we could have had you with   325
us, Eilert! Ah, well. [*Goes back into the other room and sits down with Brack.*]

LOEVBORG: Tell me one thing, Hedda.

HEDDA: Yes?

LOEVBORG: Didn't you love me either? Not—just a little?

HEDDA: Well now, I wonder? No, I think we were just good pals—really good pals   330
who could tell each other anything. [*Smiles.*] You certainly poured your heart
out to me.

LOEVBORG: You begged me to.

HEDDA: Looking back on it, there was something beautiful and fascinating—and
brave—about the way we told each other everything. That secret friendship no
one else knew about.

LOEVBORG: Yes, Hedda, yes! Do you remember? How I used to come up to your father's house in the afternoon—and the General sat by the window and read his
newspapers—with his back toward us——

HEDDA: And we sat on the sofa in the corner——

LOEVBORG: Always reading the same illustrated magazine——   335

HEDDA: We hadn't any photograph album.

LOEVBORG: Yes, Hedda. I regarded you as a kind of confessor. Told you things about
myself which no one else knew about—then. Those days and nights of drinking
and—oh, Hedda, what power did you have to make me confess such things?

HEDDA: Power? You think I had some power over you?

LOEVBORG: Yes—I don't know how else to explain it. And all those—oblique questions you asked me——

HEDDA: You knew what they meant.

LOEVBORG: But that you could sit there and ask me such questions! So   340
unashamedly——

HEDDA: I thought you said they were oblique.

LOEVBORG: Yes, but you asked them so unashamedly. That you could question me
about—about that kind of thing!

HEDDA: You answered willingly enough.

LOEVBORG: Yes—that's what I can't understand—looking back on it. But tell me,   345
Hedda—what you felt for me—wasn't that—love? When you asked me those
questions and made me confess my sins to you, wasn't it because you wanted to
wash me clean?

HEDDA: No, not exactly.

LOEVBORG: Why did you do it, then?

HEDDA: Do you find it so incredible that a young girl, given the chance to do so
without anyone knowing, should want to be allowed a glimpse into a forbidden
world of whose existence she is supposed to be ignorant?

LOEVBORG: So that was it?

HEDDA: One reason. One reason—I think.   350

LOEVBORG: You didn't love me, then. You just wanted—knowledge. But if that was so, why did you break it off?

HEDDA: That was your fault.

LOEVBORG: It was you who put an end to it.

HEDDA: Yes, when I realized that our friendship was threatening to develop into something—something else. Shame on you, Eilert Loevborg! How could you abuse the trust of your dearest friend?

LOEVBORG: [*Clenches his fists.*] Oh, why didn't you do it? Why didn't you shoot me   355
dead? As you threatened to?

HEDDA: I was afraid. Of the scandal.

LOEVBORG: Yes, Hedda. You're a coward at heart.

HEDDA: A dreadful coward. [*Changes her tone.*] Luckily for you. Well, now you've found consolation with the Elvsteds.

LOEVBORG: I know what Thea's been telling you.

HEDDA: I dare say you told her about us.   360

LOEVBORG: Not a word. She's too silly to understand that kind of thing.

HEDDA: Silly?

LOEVBORG: She's silly about that kind of thing.

HEDDA: And I am a coward. [*Leans closer to him, without looking him in the eyes, and says quietly.*] But let me tell you something. Something you don't know.

LOEVBORG: [*Tensely.*] Yes?   365

HEDDA: My failure to shoot you wasn't my worst act of cowardice that evening.

LOEVBORG: [*Looks at her for a moment, realizes her meaning and whispers passionately.*] Oh, Hedda! Hedda Gabler! Now I see what was behind those questions. Yes! It wasn't knowledge you wanted! It was life!

HEDDA: [*Flashes a look at him and says quietly.*] Take care! Don't you delude yourself!

[*It has begun to grow dark. Bertha, from outside, opens the door leading to the hall.*]

HEDDA: [*Closes the album with a snap and cries, smiling.*] Ah, at last! Come in, Thea dear!

[*Mrs. Elvsted enters from the hall, in evening dress. The door is closed behind her.*]

HEDDA: [*On the sofa, stretches out her arms toward her.*] Thea darling, I thought   370
you were never coming!

[*Mrs. Elvsted makes a slight bow to the gentlemen in the rear room as she passes the open doorway, and they to her. Then she goes to the table and holds out her hand to Hedda. Eilert Loevborg has risen from his chair. He and Mrs. Elvsted nod silently to each other.*]

MRS. ELVSTED: Perhaps I ought to go in and say a few words to your husband?

HEDDA: Oh, there's no need. They're happy by themselves. They'll be going soon.

MRS. ELVSTED: Going?

HEDDA: Yes, they're off on a spree this evening.

MRS. ELVSTED: [*Quickly, to Loevborg.*] You're not going with them?   375

LOEVBORG: No.

HEDDA: Mr. Loevborg is staying here with us.

MRS. ELVSTED: [*Takes a chair and is about to sit down beside him.*] Oh, how nice it is to be here!

HEDDA: No, Thea darling, not there. Come over here and sit beside me. I want to be in the middle.

MRS. ELVSTED: Yes, just as you wish.   380

[She goes right the table and sits on the sofa, on Hedda's right. Loevborg sits down again in his chair.]

LOEVBORG: *[After a short pause, to Hedda.]* Isn't she lovely to look at?

HEDDA: *[Strokes her hair gently.]* Only to look at?

LOEVBORG: Yes. We're just good pals. We trust each other implicitly. We can talk to each other quite unashamedly.

HEDDA: No need to be oblique?

MRS. ELVSTED: *[Nestles close to Hedda and says quietly.]* Oh, Hedda, I'm so happy. Imagine—he says I've inspired him!   385

HEDDA: *[Looks at her with a smile.]* Dear Thea! Does he really?

LOEVBORG: She has the courage of her convictions, Mrs. Tesman.

MRS. ELVSTED: I? Courage?

LOEVBORG: Absolute courage. Where friendship is concerned.

HEDDA: Yes. Courage. Yes. If only one had that——   390

LOEVBORG: Yes?

HEDDA: One might be able to live. In spite of everything. *[Changes her tone suddenly.]* Well, Thea darling, now you're going to drink a nice glass of cold punch.

MRS. ELVSTED: No, thank you. I never drink anything like that.

HEDDA: Oh. You, Mr. Loevborg?

LOEVBORG: Thank you, I don't either.   395

MRS. ELVSTED: No, he doesn't, either.

HEDDA: *[Looks into his eyes.]* But if I want you to?

LOEVBORG: That doesn't make any difference.

HEDDA: *[Laughs.]* Have I no power over you at all? Poor me!

LOEVBORG: Not where this is concerned.

HEDDA: Seriously, I think you should. For your own sake.   400

MRS. ELVSTED: Hedda!

LOEVBORG: Why?

HEDDA: Or perhaps I should say for other people's sake.

LOEVBORG: What do you mean?   405

HEDDA: People might think you didn't feel absolutely and unashamedly sure of yourself. In your heart of hearts.

MRS. ELVSTED: *[Quietly.]* Oh, Hedda, no!

LOEVBORG: People can think what they like. For the present.

MRS. ELVSTED: *[Happily.]* Yes, that's true.

HEDDA: I saw it so clearly in Judge Brack a few minutes ago.   410

LOEVBORG: Oh. What did you see?

HEDDA: He smiled so scornfully when he saw you were afraid to go in there and drink with them.

LOEVBORG: Afraid! I wanted to stay here and talk to you.

MRS. ELVSTED: That was only natural, Hedda.

HEDDA: But the judge wasn't to know that. I saw him wink at Tesman when you   415
showed you didn't dare to join their wretched little party.

LOEVBORG: Didn't dare! Are you saying I didn't dare?

HEDDA: I'm not saying so. But that was what Judge Brack thought.

LOEVBORG: Well, let him.

HEDDA: You're not going, then?

LOEVBORG: I'm staying here with you and Thea.

MRS. ELVSTED: Yes, Hedda, of course he is.   420

HEDDA: *[Smiles, and nods approvingly to Loevborg.]* Firm as a rock! A man of principle! That's how a man should be! *[Turns to Mrs. Elvsted and strokes her cheek.]* Didn't I tell you so this morning when you came here in such a panic——

LOEVBORG: [*Starts.*] Panic?

MRS. ELVSTED: [*Frightened.*] Hedda! But—Hedda!

HEDDA: Well, now you can see for yourself. There's no earthly need for you to get   425
scared to death just because——[*Stops.*] Well! Let's all three cheer up and enjoy
ourselves.

LOEVBORG: Mrs. Tesman, would you mind explaining to me what this is all about?

MRS. ELVSTED: Oh, my God, my God, Hedda, what are you saying? What are you doing?

HEDDA: Keep calm. That horrid Judge has his eye on you.

LOEVBORG: Scared to death, were you? For my sake?

MRS. ELVSTED: [*Quietly, trembling.*] Oh, Hedda! You've made me so unhappy!   430

LOEVBORG: [*Looks coldly at her for a moment. His face is distorted.*] So that was
how much you trusted me.

MRS. ELVSTED: Eilert dear, please listen to me——

LOEVBORG: [*Takes one of the glasses of punch, raises it and says quietly, hoarsely.*]
Skoal, Thea! [*Empties the glass, puts it down and picks up one of the others.*]

MRS. ELVSTED: [*Quietly.*] Hedda, Hedda! Why did you want this to happen?

HEDDA: I—want it? Are you mad?

LOEVBORG: Skoal to you too, Mrs. Tesman. Thanks for telling me the truth. Here's to
the truth! [*Empties his glass and refills it.*]

HEDDA: [*Puts her hand on his arm.*] Steady. That's enough for now. Don't forget
the party.

MRS. ELVSTED: No, no, no!

HEDDA: Ssh! They're looking at you.

LOEVBORG: [*Puts down his glass.*] Thea, tell me the truth——   440

MRS. ELVSTED: Yes!

LOEVBORG: Did your husband know you were following me?

MRS. ELVSTED: Oh, Hedda!

LOEVBORG: Did you and he have an agreement that you should come here and keep
an eye on me? Perhaps he gave you the idea? After all, he's a magistrate. I suppose he needed me back in his office. Or did he miss my companionship at the
card table?

MRS. ELVSTED: [*Quietly, sobbing.*] Eilert, Eilert!   445

LOEVBORG: [*Seizes a glass and is about to fill it.*] Let's drink to him, too.

HEDDA: No more now. Remember you're going to read your book to Tesman.

LOEVBORG: [*Calm again, puts down his glass.*] That was silly of me, Thea. To take it
like that, I mean. Don't be angry with me, my dear. You'll see—yes, and they'll see,
too—that though I fell, I—I have raised myself up again. With your help, Thea.

MRS. ELVSTED: [*Happily.*] Oh, thank God!

[*Brack has meanwhile glanced at his watch. He and Tesman get up and come into the drawing
room.*]

BRACK: [*Takes his hat and overcoat.*] Well, Mrs. Tesman. It's time for us to go.   450

HEDDA: Yes, I suppose it must be.

LOEVBORG: [*Gets up.*] Time for me too, Judge.

MRS. ELVSTED: [*Quietly, pleadingly.*] Eilert, please don't!

HEDDA: [*Pinches her arm.*] They can hear you.

MRS. ELVSTED: [*Gives a little cry.*] Oh!   455

LOEVBORG: [*To Brack.*] You were kind enough to ask me to join you.

BRACK: Are you coming?

LOEVBORG: If I may.

BRACK: Delighted.

LOEVBORG: [*Puts the paper package in his pocket and says to Tesman.*] I'd like to   460
show you one or two things before I send it off to the printer.

TESMAN: I say, that'll be fun. Fancy——! Oh, but Hedda, how'll Mrs. Elvsted get home? What?

HEDDA: Oh, we'll manage somehow.

LOEVBORG: [*Glances over toward the ladies.*] Mrs. Elvsted? I shall come back and collect her, naturally. [*Goes closer.*] About ten o'clock, Mrs. Tesman? Will that suit you?

HEDDA: Yes. That'll suit me admirably.

TESMAN: Good, that's settled. But you mustn't expect me back so early, Hedda.   465

HEDDA: Stay as long as you c—as long as you like, dear.

MRS. ELVSTED: [*Trying to hide her anxiety.*] Well then, Mr. Loevborg, I'll wait here till you come.

LOEVBORG: [*His hat in his hand.*] Pray do, Mrs. Elvsted.

BRACK: Well, gentlemen, now the party begins. I trust that, in the words of a certain fair lady, we shall enjoy good sport.

HEDDA: What a pity the fair lady can't be there, invisible.   470

BRACK: Why invisible?

HEDDA: So as to be able to hear some of your uncensored witticisms, your honor.

BRACK: [*Laughs.*] Oh, I shouldn't advise the fair lady to do that.

TESMAN: [*Laughs too.*] I say, Hedda, that's good. By Jove! Fancy that!

BRACK: Well, good night, ladies, good night!   475

LOEVBORG: [*Bows farewell.*] About ten o'clock, then.

[*Brack, Loevborg and Tesman go out through the hall. As they do so Bertha enters from the rear room with a lighted lamp. She puts it on the drawing-room table, then goes out the way she came.*]

MRS. ELVSTED: [*Has got up and is walking uneasily to and fro.*] Oh Hedda, Hedda! How is all this going to end?

HEDDA: At ten o'clock, then. He'll be here. I can see him. With a crown of vine-leaves in his hair. Burning and unashamed!

MRS. ELVSTED: Oh, I do hope so!

HEDDA: Can't you see? Then he'll be himself again! He'll be a free man for the rest   480
of his days!

MRS. ELVSTED: Please God you're right.

HEDDA: That's how he'll come! [*Gets up and goes closer.*] You can doubt him as much as you like. I believe in him! Now we'll see which of us——

MRS. ELVSTED: You're after something, Hedda.

HEDDA: Yes, I am. For once in my life I want to have the power to shape a man's destiny.

MRS. ELVSTED: Haven't you that power already?   485

HEDDA: No, I haven't. I've never had it.

MRS. ELVSTED: What about your husband?

HEDDA: Him! Oh, if you could only understand how poor I am. And you're allowed to be so rich, so rich! [*Clasps her passionately.*] I think I'll burn your hair off after all!

MRS. ELVSTED: Let me go! Let me go! You frighten me, Hedda!

BERTHA: [*In the open doorway.*] I've laid tea in the dining room, madam.   490

HEDDA: Good, we're coming.

MRS. ELVSTED: No, no, no! I'd rather go home alone! Now—at once!

HEDDA: Rubbish! First you're going to have some tea, you little idiot. And then—at ten o'clock—Eilert Loevborg will come. With a crown of vine-leaves in his hair![7]
[*She drags Mrs. Elvsted almost forcibly toward the open doorway.*]

---

[7]Worshippers of Dionysus, Greek god of wine, wore garlands of vine leaves as a sign of divine intoxication.

Act 2 Response Statement Questions

- What is your response to Hedda's gunplay? Does it aid you in consistency building about the kind of person she is?
- What are your initials impressions of Judge Brack? Does he seem trust-worthy and loyal? Should he be viewed with suspicion? Is he looking out for his own interests? What makes you respond to him as you do?
- What further impressions do you form of Hedda and Tesman's marriage from the action and dialogue in Act 2? Hedda seems to feel trapped in the marriage, but do you think she is? What options does she have? Would her options be different today than in the 1890s? If you think they would be, does the difference affect your response to her?
- What impressions do you form of Eilert Loevborg from his first appear-ance? In comparison to Tesman, does he seem to match up to what was said about him in Act 1? Can you see what Hedda sees in him?
- How would you analyze the dynamics of Hedda's relationship to Eilert as it unfolds in Act 2? of their relationship in the past?
- What predictions are you able to make for the plot based on the action so far?

Act 3

Scene: The same. The curtains are drawn across the open doorway, and also across the french windows. The lamp, half turned down, with a shade over it, is burning on the table. In the stove, the door of which is open, a fire has been burning, but it is now almost out.

Mrs. Elvsted, wrapped in a large shawl and with her feet resting on a footstool, is sitting near the stove, huddled in the armchair. Hedda is lying asleep on this sofa, fully dressed, with a blan-ket over her.

MRS. ELVSTED: [*After a pause, suddenly sits up in her chair and listens tensely. Then she sinks wearily back again and sighs.*] Not back yet! Oh, God! Oh, God! Not back yet!

[*Bertha tiptoes cautiously in from the hall. She has a letter in her hand.*]

MRS. ELVSTED: [*Turns and whispers.*] What is it? Has someone come?

BERTHA: [*Quietly.*] Yes, a servant's just called with this letter.

MRS. ELVSTED: [*Quickly, holding out her hand.*] A letter! Give it to me!

BERTHA: But it's for the Doctor, madam.   5

MRS. ELVSTED: Oh. I see.

BERTHA: Miss Tesman's maid brought it. I'll leave it here on the table.

MRS. ELVSTED: Yes, do.

BERTHA: [*Puts down the letter.*] I'd better put the lamp out. It's starting to smoke.

MRS. ELVSTED: Yes, put it out. It'll soon be daylight.   10

BERTHA: [*Puts out the lamp.*] It's daylight already, madam.

MRS. ELVSTED: Yes. Broad day. And not home yet.

BERTHA: Oh dear, I was afraid this would happen.

MRS. ELVSTED: Were you?

BERTHA: Yes. When I heard that a certain gentleman had returned to town, and saw   15
him go off with them. I've heard all about him.

MRS. ELVSTED: Don't talk so loud. You'll wake your mistress.

BERTHA: [*Looks at the sofa and sighs.*] Yes. Let her go on sleeping, poor dear. Shall I put some more wood on the fire?

MRS. ELVSTED: Thank you, don't bother on my account.

BERTHA: Very good. [*Goes quietly out through the hall.*]

HEDDA: [*Wakes as the door closes and looks up.*] What's that?

MRS. ELVSTED: It was only the maid.

HEDDA: [*Looks round.*] What am I doing here? Oh, now I remember. [*Sits up on the sofa, stretches herself and rubs her eyes.*] What time is it, Thea?

MRS. ELVSTED: It's gone seven.

HEDDA: When did Tesman get back?

MRS. ELVSTED: He's not back yet.

HEDDA: Not home yet?

MRS. ELVSTED: [*Gets up.*] No one's come.

HEDDA: And we sat up waiting for them till four o'clock.

MRS. ELVSTED: God! How I waited for him!

HEDDA: [*Yawns and says with her hand in front of her mouth.*] Oh, dear. We might have saved ourselves the trouble.

MRS. ELVSTED: Did you manage to sleep?

HEDDA: Oh, yes. Quite well, I think. Didn't you get any?

MRS. ELVSTED: Not a wink. I couldn't, Hedda. I just couldn't.

HEDDA: [*Gets up and comes over to her.*] Now, now, now. There's nothing to worry about. I know what's happened.

MRS. ELVSTED: What? Please tell me.

HEDDA: Well, obviously the party went on very late——

MRS. ELVSTED: Oh dear, I suppose it must have. But——

HEDDA: And Tesman didn't want to come home and wake us all up in the middle of the night. [*Laughs.*] Probably wasn't too keen to show his face either, after a spree like that.

MRS. ELVSTED: But where could he have gone?

HEDDA: I should think he's probably slept at his aunts'. They keep his old room for him.

MRS. ELVSTED: No, he can't be with them. A letter came for him just now from Miss Tesman. It's over there.

HEDDA: Oh? [*Looks at the envelope.*] Yes, it's Auntie Juju's handwriting. Well, he must still be at Judge Brack's, then. And Eilert Loevborg is sitting there, reading to him. With a crown of vine-leaves in his hair.

MRS. ELVSTED: Hedda, you're only saying that. You don't believe it.

HEDDA: Thea, you really are a little fool.

MRS. ELVSTED: Perhaps I am.

HEDDA: You look tired to death.

MRS. ELVSTED: Yes. I am tired to death.

HEDDA: Go to my room and lie down for a little. Do as I say, now; don't argue.

MRS. ELVSTED: No, no. I couldn't possibly sleep.

HEDDA: Of course you can.

MRS. ELVSTED: But your husband'll be home soon. And I must know at once——

HEDDA: I'll tell you when he comes.

MRS. ELVSTED: Promise me, Hedda?

HEDDA: Yes, don't worry. Go and get some sleep.

MRS. ELVSTED: Thank you. All right, I'll try.

[*She goes out through the rear room. Hedda goes to the french windows and draws the curtains. Broad daylight floods into the room. She goes to the writing table, takes a small hand mirror from it and arranges her hair. Then she goes to the door leading into the hall and presses the bell. After a few moments, Bertha enters.*]

BERTHA: Did you want anything, madam?

HEDDA: Yes, put some more wood on the fire. I'm freezing.

BERTHA: Bless you, I'll soon have this room warmed up. [*She rakes the embers together and puts a fresh piece of wood on them. Suddenly she stops and listens.*] There's someone at the front door, madam.

HEDDA: Well, go and open it. I'll see to the fire.

BERTHA: It'll burn up in a moment.   60

[She goes out through the hall. Hedda kneels on the footstool and puts more wood in the stove. After a few seconds, George Tesman enters from the hall. He looks tired, and rather worried. He tiptoes toward the open doorway and is about to slip through the curtains.]

HEDDA: [*At the stove, without looking up.*] Good morning.

TESMAN: [*Turns.*] Hedda! [*Comes nearer.*] Good heavens, are you up already? What?

HEDDA: Yes, I got up very early this morning.

TESMAN: I was sure you'd still be sleeping. Fancy that!

HEDDA: Don't talk so loud. Mrs. Elvsted's asleep in my room.   65

TESMAN: Mrs. Elvsted? Has she stayed the night here?

HEDDA: Yes. No one came to escort her home.

TESMAN: Oh. No, I suppose not.

HEDDA: [*Closes the door of the stove and gets up.*] Well. Was it fun?

TESMAN: Have you been anxious about me? What?   70

HEDDA: Not in the least. I asked if you'd had fun.

TESMAN: Oh yes, rather! Well, I thought, for once in a while—The first part was the best; when Eilert read his book to me. We arrived over an hour too early—what about that, eh? By Jove! Brack had a lot of things to see to, so Eilert read to me.

HEDDA: [*Sits at the right-hand side of the table.*] Well? Tell me about it.

TESMAN: [*Sits on a footstool by the stove.*] Honestly, Hedda, you've no idea what a book that's going to be. It's really one of the most remarkable things that's ever been written. By Jove!

HEDDA: Oh, never mind about the book——   75

TESMAN: I'm going to make a confession to you, Hedda. When he'd finished reading a sort of beastly feeling came over me.

HEDDA: Beastly feeling?

TESMAN: I found myself envying Eilert for being able to write like that. Imagine that, Hedda!

HEDDA: Yes. I can imagine.

TESMAN: What a tragedy that with all those gifts he should be so incorrigible.   80

HEDDA: You mean he's less afraid of life than most men?

TESMAN: Good heavens, no. He just doesn't know the meaning of the word moderation.

HEDDA: What happened afterwards?

TESMAN: Well, looking back on it I suppose you might almost call it an orgy, Hedda.

HEDDA: Had he vine-leaves in his hair?   85

TESMAN: Vine-leaves? No, I didn't see any of them. He made a long, rambling oration in honor of the woman who'd inspired him to write this book. Yes, those were the words he used.

HEDDA: Did he name her?

TESMAN: No. But I suppose it must be Mrs. Elvsted. You wait and see!

HEDDA: Where did you leave him?

TESMAN: On the way home. We left in a bunch—the last of us, that is—and Brack   90
came with us to get a little fresh air. Well, then, you see, we agreed we ought to see Eilert home. He'd had a drop too much.

HEDDA: You don't say?

TESMAN: But now comes the funny part, Hedda. Or I should really say the tragic part. Oh, I'm almost ashamed to tell you. For Eilert's sake, I mean——

HEDDA: Why, what happened?

TESMAN: Well, you see, as we were walking toward town I happened to drop behind for a minute. Only for a minute—er—you understand——

HEDDA: Yes, yes——?   95

TESMAN: Well then, when I ran on to catch them up, what do you think I found by the roadside. What?

HEDDA: How on earth should I know?

TESMAN: You mustn't tell anyone, Hedda. What? Promise me that—for Eilert's sake. [*Takes a package wrapped in paper from his coat pocket.*] Just fancy! I found this.

HEDDA: Isn't this the one he brought here yesterday?

TESMAN: Yes! The whole of that precious, irreplaceable manuscript! And he went   100
and lost it. Didn't even notice! What about that? By Jove! Tragic.

HEDDA: But why didn't you give it back to him?

TESMAN: I didn't dare to, in the state he was in.

HEDDA: Didn't you tell any of the others?

TESMAN: Good heavens, no. I didn't want to do that. For Eilert's sake, you understand.

HEDDA: Then no one else knows you have his manuscript?   105

TESMAN: No. And no one must be allowed to know.

HEDDA: Didn't it come up in the conversation later?

TESMAN: I didn't get a chance to talk to him anymore. As soon as we got into the outskirts of town, he and one or two of the others gave us the slip. Disappeared, by Jove!

HEDDA: Oh? I suppose they took him home.

TESMAN: Yes, I imagine that was the idea. Brack left us, too.   110

HEDDA: And what have you been up to since then?

TESMAN: Well, I and one or two of the others—awfully jolly chaps, they were—went back to where one of them lived, had a cup of morning coffee. Morning-after coffee—what? Ah, well. I'll just lie down for a bit and give Eilert time to sleep it off, poor chap, then I'll run over and give this back to him.

HEDDA: [*Holds out her hand for the package.*] No, don't do that. Not just yet. Let me read it first.

TESMAN: Oh no, really, Hedda dear, honestly, I daren't do that.

HEDDA: Daren't?   115

TESMAN: No—imagine how desperate he'll be when he wakes up and finds his manuscript's missing. He hasn't any copy, you see. He told me so himself.

HEDDA: Can't a thing like that be rewritten?

TESMAN: Oh no, not possibly, I shouldn't think. I mean, the inspiration, you know——

HEDDA: Oh, yes. I'd forgotten that. [*Casually.*] By the way, there's a letter for you.

TESMAN: Is there? Fancy that!   120

HEDDA: [*Holds it out to him.*] It came early this morning.

TESMAN: I say, it's from Auntie Juju! What on earth can it be? [*Puts the package on the other footstool, opens the letter, reads it and jumps up.*] Oh, Hedda! She says poor Auntie Rena's dying.

HEDDA: Well, we've been expecting that.

TESMAN: She says if I want to see her I must go quickly. I'll run over at once.

HEDDA: [*Hides a smile*] Run?   125

TESMAN: Hedda dear, I suppose you wouldn't like to come with me? What about that, eh?

HEDDA: [*Gets up and says wearily and with repulsion.*] No, no, don't ask me to do
          anything like that. I can't bear illness or death. I loathe anything ugly.
TESMAN: Yes, yes. Of course. [*In a dither.*] My hat? My overcoat? Oh yes, in the hall.
          I do hope I won't get there too late, Hedda? What?
HEDDA: You'll be all right if you run.

[*Bertha enters from the hall.*]

BERTHA: Judge Brack's outside and wants to know if he can come in.   130
TESMAN: At this hour? No, I can't possibly receive him now.
HEDDA: I can [*To Bertha.*] Ask his honor to come in.

[*Bertha goes.*]

HEDDA: [*Whispers quickly.*] The manuscript, Tesman. [*She snatches it from the
          footstool.*]
TESMAN: Yes, give it to me.
HEDDA: No, I'll look after it for now.   135

[*She goes over to the writing table and puts it in the bookcase. Tesman stands dithering, unable
to get his gloves on. Judge Brack enters from the hall.*]

HEDDA: [*Nods to him.*] Well, you're an early bird.
BRACK: Yes, aren't I? [*To Tesman.*] Are you up and about, too?
TESMAN: Yes, I've got to go and see my aunts. Poor Auntie Rena's dying.
BRACK: Oh dear, is she? Then you mustn't let me detain you. At so tragic a——
TESMAN: Yes, I really must run. Good bye! Good-bye! [*Runs out through the hall.*]   140
HEDDA: [*Goes nearer.*] You seem to have had excellent sport last night—Judge.
BRACK: Indeed yes, Mrs. Hedda. I haven't even had time to take my clothes off.
HEDDA: *You* haven't either?
BRACK: As you see. What's Tesman told you about last night's escapades?
HEDDA: Oh, only some boring story about having gone and drunk coffee somewhere.   145
BRACK: Yes, I've heard about that coffee party. Eilert Loevborg wasn't with them, I
          gather?
HEDDA: No, they took him home first.
BRACK: Did Tesman go with him?
HEDDA: No, one or two of the others, he said.
BRACK: [*Smiles.*] George Tesman is a credulous man, Mrs. Hedda.   150
HEDDA: God knows. But—has something happened?
BRACK: Well, yes, I'm afraid it has.
HEDDA: I see. Sit down and tell me. [*She sits on the left of the table,* BRACK *at the
          long side of it, near her.*] Well?
BRACK: I had a special reason for keeping track of my guests last night. Or perhaps
          I should say some of my guests.
HEDDA: Including Eilert Loevborg?   155
BRACK: I must confess—yes.
HEDDA: You're beginning to make me curious.
BRACK: Do you know where he and some of my other guests spent the latter half of
          last night, Mrs. Hedda?
HEDDA: Tell me. If it won't shock me.
BRACK: Oh, I don't think it'll shock you. They found themselves participating in an   160
          exceedingly animated *soirée.*
HEDDA: Of a sporting character?
BRACK: Of a highly sporting character.
HEDDA: Tell me more.

BRACK: Loevborg had received an invitation in advance—as had the others. I knew all about that. But he had refused. As you know, he's become a new man.

HEDDA: Up at the Elvsteds', yes. But he went?

BRACK: Well, you see, Mrs. Hedda, last night at my house, unhappily, the spirit moved him.

HEDDA: Yes, I hear he became inspired.

BRACK: Somewhat violently inspired. And as a result, I suppose, his thoughts strayed. We men, alas, don't always stick to our principles as firmly as we should.

HEDDA: I'm sure you're an exception, Judge Brack. But go on about Loevborg.

BRACK: Well, to cut a long story short, he ended up in the establishment of a certain Mademoiselle Danielle.

HEDDA: Mademoiselle Danielle?

BRACK: She was holding the *soirée*. For a selected circle of friends and admirers.

HEDDA: Has she got red hair?

BRACK: She has.

HEDDA: A singer of some kind?

BRACK: Yes—among other accomplishments. She's also a celebrated huntress—of men, Mrs. Hedda. I'm sure you've heard about her. Eilert Loevborg used to be one of her most ardent patrons. In his salad days.

HEDDA: And how did all this end?

BRACK: Not entirely amicably, from all accounts. Mademoiselle Danielle began by receiving him with the utmost tenderness and ended by resorting to her fists.

HEDDA: Against Loevborg?

BRACK: Yes. He accused her, or her friends, of having robbed him. He claimed his pocketbook had been stolen. Among other things. In short, he seems to have made a bloodthirsty scene.

HEDDA: And what did this lead to?

BRACK: It led to a general free-for-all, in which both sexes participated. Fortunately, in the end the police arrived.

HEDDA: The police too?

BRACK: Yes. I'm afraid it may turn out to be rather an expensive joke for Master Eilert. Crazy fool!

HEDDA: Oh?

BRACK: Apparently, he put up a very violent resistance. Hit one of the constables on the ear and tore his uniform. He had to accompany them to the police station.

HEDDA: Where did you learn all this?

BRACK: From the police.

HEDDA: [*To herself.*] So that's what happened. He didn't have a crown of vine-leaves in his hair.

BRACK: Vine-leaves, Mrs. Hedda?

HEDDA: [*In her normal voice again.*] But, tell me, Judge, why do you take such a close interest in Eilert Loevborg?

BRACK: For one thing it'll hardly be a matter of complete indifference to me if it's revealed in court that he came there straight from my house.

HEDDA: Will it come to court?

BRACK: Of course. Well, I don't regard that as particularly serious. Still, I thought it my duty, as a friend of the family, to give you and your husband a full account of his nocturnal adventures.

HEDDA: Why?

BRACK: Because I've a shrewd suspicion that he's hoping to use you as a kind of screen.

HEDDA: What makes you think that?

BRACK: Oh, for heaven's sake, Mrs. Hedda, we're not blind. You wait and see. This Mrs. Elvsted won't be going back to her husband just yet.

HEDDA: Well, if there were anything between those two there are plenty of other places where they could meet.

BRACK: Not in anyone's home. From now on every respectable house will once again be closed to Eilert Loevborg. 200

HEDDA: And mine should be too, you mean?

BRACK: Yes. I confess I should find it more than irksome if this gentleman were to be granted unrestricted access to this house. If he were superfluously to intrude into——

HEDDA: The triangle?

BRACK: Precisely. For me it would be like losing a home.

HEDDA: [Looks at him and smiles.] I see. You want to be the cock of the walk. 205

BRACK: [Nods slowly and lowers his voice.] Yes, that is my aim. And I shall fight for it with—every weapon at my disposal.

HEDDA: [As her smile fades.] You're a dangerous man, aren't you? When you really want something.

BRACK: You think so?

HEDDA: Yes. I'm beginning to think so. I'm deeply thankful you haven't any kind of hold over me.

BRACK: [Laughs equivocally.] Well, well, Mrs. Hedda—perhaps you're right. If I had, 210 who knows what I might not think up?

HEDDA: Come, Judge Brack. That sounds almost like a threat.

BRACK: [Gets up.] Heaven forbid! In the creation of a triangle—and its continuance—the question of compulsion should never arise.

HEDDA: Exactly what I was thinking.

BRACK: Well, I've said what I came to say. I must be getting back. Good-bye, Mrs. Hedda. [Goes toward the french windows.]

HEDDA: [Gets up.] Are you going out through the garden? 215

BRACK: Yes, it's shorter.

HEDDA: Yes. And it's the back door, isn't it?

BRACK: I've nothing against back doors. They can be quite intriguing—sometimes.

HEDDA: When people fire pistols out of them, for example?

BRACK: [In the doorway, laughs.] Oh, people don't shoot tame cocks. 220

HEDDA: [Laughs too.] I suppose not. When they've only got one.

[They nod good-bye, laughing. He goes. She closes the french windows behind him, and stands for a moment, looking out pensively. Then she walks across the room and glances through the curtains in the open doorway. Goes to the writing table, takes Loevborg's package from the bookcase and is about to leaf through the pages when Bertha is heard remonstrating loudly in the hall. Hedda turns and listens. She hastily puts the package back in the drawer, locks it and puts the key in the inkstand. Eilert Loevborg, with his overcoat on and his hat in his hand, throws the door open. He looks somewhat confused and excited.]

LOEVBORG: [Shouts as he enters.] I must come in, I tell you! Let me pass! [He closes the door, turns, sees Hedda, controls himself immediately and bows.]

HEDDA: [At the writing table.] Well, Mr. Loevborg, this is rather a late hour to be collecting Thea.

LOEVBORG: And an early hour to call on you. Please forgive me.

HEDDA: How do you know she's still here? 225

LOEVBORG: They told me at her lodgings that she has been out all night.

HEDDA: [Goes to the table.] Did you notice anything about their behavior when they told you?

LOEVBORG: [*Looks at her, puzzled.*] Notice anything?

HEDDA: Did they sound as if they thought it—strange?

LOEVBORG: [*Suddenly understands.*] Oh, I see what you mean. I'm dragging her 230
down with me. No, as a matter of fact I didn't notice anything. I suppose Tesman
isn't up yet?

HEDDA: No, I don't think so.

LOEVBORG: When did he get home?

HEDDA: Very late.

LOEVBORG: Did he tell you anything?

HEDDA: Yes. I gather you had a merry party at Judge Brack's last night. 235

LOEVBORG: He didn't tell you anything else?

HEDDA: I don't think so. I was so terribly sleepy——

[Mrs. Elvsted comes through the curtains in the open doorway.]

MRS. ELVSTED: [*Runs toward him.*] Oh, Eilert! At last!

LOEVBORG: Yes—at last. And too late.

MRS. ELVSTED: What is too late?

LOEVBORG: Everything—now. I'm finished, Thea. 240

MRS. ELVSTED: Oh, no, no! Don't say that!

LOEVBORG: You'll say it yourself, when you've heard what I——

MRS. ELVSTED: I don't want to hear anything!

HEDDA: Perhaps you'd rather speak to her alone? I'd better go. 245

LOEVBORG: No, stay.

MRS. ELVSTED: But I don't want to hear anything, I tell you!

LOEVBORG: It's not about last night.

MRS. ELVSTED: Then what——?

LOEVBORG: I want to tell you that from now on we must stop seeing each other. 250

MRS. ELVSTED: Stop seeing each other!

HEDDA: [*Involuntarily.*] I knew it!

LOEVBORG: I have no further use for you, Thea.

MRS. ELVSTED: You can stand there and say that! No further use for me! Surely I can
go on helping you? We'll go on working together, won't we?

LOEVBORG: I don't intend to do any more work from now on. 255

MRS. ELVSTED: [*Desperately.*] Then what use have I for my life?

LOEVBORG: You must try to live as if you had never known me.

MRS. ELVSTED: But I can't!

LOEVBORG: Try to, Thea. Go back home——

MRS. ELVSTED: Never! I want to be wherever you are! I won't let myself be driven 260
away like this! I want to stay here—and be with you when the book comes out.

HEDDA: [*Whispers.*] Ah, yes! The book!

LOEVBORG: [*Looks at her.*] Our book; Thea's and mine. It belongs to both of us.

MRS. ELVSTED: Oh, yes! I feel that, too! And I've a right to be with you when it comes
into the world. I want to see people respect and honor you again. And the joy!
The joy! I want to share it with you!

LOEVBORG: Thea—our book will never come into the world.

HEDDA: Ah! 265

MRS. ELVSTED: Not——?

LOEVBORG: It cannot, ever.

MRS. ELVSTED: Eilert—what have you done with the manuscript? Where is it?

LOEVBORG: Oh Thea, please don't ask me that!

MRS. ELVSTED: Yes, yes—I must know. I've a right to know. Now! 270

LOEVBORG: The manuscript. I've torn it up.

MRS. ELVSTED: [*Screams.*] No, no!

HEDDA: [*Involuntarily.*] But that's not——!

LOEVBORG: [*Looks at her.*] Not true, you think?

HEDDA: [*Controls herself.*] Why—yes, of course it is, if you say so. It just sounded so   275
incredible——

LOEVBORG: It's true, nevertheless.

MRS. ELVSTED: Oh, my God, my God, Hedda—he's destroyed his own book!

LOEVBORG: I have destroyed my life. Why not my life's work, too?

MRS. ELVSTED: And you—did this last night?

LOEVBORG: Yes, Thea. I tore it into a thousand pieces. And scattered them out across   280
the fjord. It's good, clean, salt water. Let it carry them away; let them drift in the
current and the wind. And in a little while, they will sink. Deeper and deeper. As
I shall, Thea.

MRS. ELVSTED: Do you know, Eilert—this book—all my life I shall feel as though
you'd killed a little child?

LOEVBORG: You're right. It is like killing a child.

MRS. ELVSTED: But how could you? It was my child, too!

HEDDA: [*Almost inaudibly.*] Oh—the child——!

MRS. ELVSTED: [*Breathes heavily.*] It's all over, then. Well—I'll go now, Hedda.   285

HEDDA: You're not leaving town?

MRS. ELVSTED: I don't know what I'm going to do. I can't see anything except—darkness. [*She goes out through the hall.*]

HEDDA: [*Waits a moment.*] Aren't you going to escort her home, Mr. Loevborg?

LOEVBORG: I? Through the streets? Do you want me to let people see her with me?

HEDDA: Of course I don't know what else may have happened last night. But is it so   290
utterly beyond redress?

LOEVBORG: It isn't just last night. It'll go on happening. I know it. But the curse of it
is, I don't want to live that kind of life. I don't want to start all that again. She's
broken my courage. I can't spit in the eyes of the world any longer.

HEDDA: [*As though to herself.*] That pretty little fool's been trying to shape a man's
destiny. [*Looks at him.*] But how could you be so heartless toward her?

LOEVBORG: Don't call me heartless!

HEDDA: To go and destroy the one thing that's made her life worth living? You don't
call that heartless?

LOEVBORG: Do you want to know the truth, Hedda?   295

HEDDA: The truth?

LOEVBORG: Promise me first—give me your word—that you'll never let Thea know
about this.

HEDDA: I give you my word.

LOEVBORG: Good. Well; what I told her just now was a lie.

HEDDA: About the manuscript?   300

LOEVBORG: Yes. I didn't tear it up. Or throw it in the fjord.

HEDDA: You didn't? But where is it, then?

LOEVBORG: I destroyed it, all the same. I destroyed it, Hedda!

HEDDA: I don't understand

LOEVBORG: Thea said that what I had done was like killing a child.   305

HEDDA: Yes. That's what she said.

LOEVBORG: But to kill a child isn't the worst thing a father can do to it.

HEDDA: What could be worse than that?

LOEVBORG: Hedda—suppose a man came home one morning, after a night of de-
bauchery, and said to the mother of his child: "Look here, I've been wandering
round all night. I've been to—such-and-such a place and such-and-such a place.

And I had our child with me. I took him to—these places. And I've lost him. Just—lost him. God knows where he is or whose hands he's fallen into."

HEDDA: I see. But when all's said and done, this was only a book—— 310

LOEVBORG: Thea's heart and soul were in that book. It was her whole life.

HEDDA: Yes. I understand.

LOEVBORG: Well, then you must also understand that she and I cannot possibly ever see each other again.

HEDDA: Where will you go?

LOEVBORG: Nowhere. I just want to put an end to it all. As soon as possible. 315

HEDDA: [*Takes a step toward him.*] Eilert Loevborg, listen to me. Do it—beautifully!

LOEVBORG: Beautifully? [*Smiles.*] With a crown of vine-leaves in my hair? The way you used to dream of me—in the old days?

HEDDA: No. I don't believe in that crown any longer. But—do it beautifully, all the same. Just this once. Good-bye. You must go now. And don't come back.

LOEVBORG: Adieu, madam. Give my love to George Tesman. [*Turns to go.*]

HEDDA: Wait. I want to give you a souvenir to take with you. 320

[*She goes over to the writing table, opens the drawer and the pistol-case, and comes back to Loevborg with one of the pistols.*]

LOEVBORG: [*Looks at her.*] This? Is this the souvenir?

HEDDA: [*Nods slowly.*] You recognize it? You looked down its barrel once.

LOEVBORG: You should have used it then.

HEDDA: Here! Use it now!

LOEVBORG: [*Puts the pistol in his breast pocket.*] Thank you. 325

HEDDA: Do it beautifully, Eilert Loevborg. Only promise me that!

LOEVBORG: Good-bye, Hedda Gabler.

[*He goes out through the hall. Hedda stands by the door for a moment, listening. Then she goes over to the writing table, takes out the package containing the manuscript, glances inside it, pulls some of the pages half out and looks at them. Then she takes it to the armchair by the stove and sits down with the package in her lap. After a moment, she opens the door of the stove; then she opens the packet.*]

HEDDA: [*Throws one of the pages into the stove and whispers to herself.*] I'm burning your child, Thea! You with your beautiful wavy hair! [*She throws a few more pages into the stove.*] The child Eilert Loevborg gave you. [*Throws the rest of the manuscript in.*] I'm burning it! I'm burning your child!

Act 3 Response Statement Questions

- What is your response to the plot developments in Act 3? Do you see anything like a turning point in the action here? Does the plot seem to be assuming a tragic pattern or not? If so, which character or characters is it tragic for? How and why?
- What is your attitude toward Hedda now? toward Eilert? Do you see them as consistent characters? Does their behavior, motivations, thoughts, or feelings conform to any labels you could attach to them such as "controlling" or "eccentric genius"?

Act 4

Scene: The same. It is evening. The drawing room is in darkness. The small room is illuminated by the hanging lamp over the table. The curtains are drawn across the french windows. Hedda, dressed in black, is walking up and down in the darkened room. Then she goes into the small room and crosses to the left. A few chords are heard from the piano. She comes back into the drawing room.

Bertha comes through the small room from the right with a lighted lamp, which she places on the table in front of the corner sofa in the drawing room. Her eyes are red with crying, and she has black ribbons on her cap. She goes quietly out, right. Hedda goes over to the french windows, draws the curtains slightly to one side and looks out into the darkness.

A few moments later, Miss Tesman enters from the hall. She is dressed in mourning, with a black hat and veil. Hedda goes to meet her and holds out her hand.

MISS TESMAN: Well, Hedda, here I am in the weeds of sorrow. My poor sister has ended her struggles at last.

HEDDA: I've already heard. Tesman sent me a card.

MISS TESMAN: Yes, he promised me he would. But I thought, no, I must go and break the news of death to Hedda myself—here, in the house of life.

HEDDA: It's very kind of you.

MISS TESMAN: Ah, Rena shouldn't have chosen a time like this to pass away. This is no   5
moment for Hedda's house to be a place of mourning.

HEDDA: [*Changing the subject.*] She died peacefully, Miss Tesman?

MISS TESMAN: Oh, it was quite beautiful! The end came so calmly. And she was so happy at being able to see George once again. And say good-bye to him. Hasn't he come home yet?

HEDDA: No. He wrote that I mustn't expect him too soon. But please sit down.

MISS TESMAN: No, thank you, Hedda dear—bless you. I'd like to. But I've so little time. I must dress her and lay her out as well as I can. She shall go to her grave looking really beautiful.

HEDDA: Can't I help with anything?   10

MISS TESMAN: Why, you mustn't think of such a thing! Hedda Tesman mustn't let her hands be soiled by contact with death. Or her thoughts. Not at this time.

HEDDA: One can't always control one's thoughts.

MISS TESMAN: [*Continues.*] Ah, well, that's life. Now we must start to sew poor Rena's shroud. There'll be sewing to be done in this house too before long, I shouldn't wonder. But not for a shroud, praise God.

[George Tesman enters from the hall.]

HEDDA: You've come at last! Thank heavens!

TESMAN: Are you here, Auntie Juju? With Hedda? Fancy that!   15

MISS TESMAN: I was just on the point of leaving, dear boy. Well, have you done everything you promised me?

TESMAN: No, I'm afraid I forgot half of it. I'll have to run over again tomorrow. My head's in a complete whirl today. I can't collect my thoughts.

MISS TESMAN: But George dear, you mustn't take it like this.

TESMAN: Oh? Well—er—how should I?

MISS TESMAN: You must be happy in your grief. Happy for what's happened. As I am.   20

TESMAN: Oh, yes, yes. You're thinking of Aunt Rena.

HEDDA: It'll be lonely for you now, Miss Tesman.

MISS TESMAN: For the first few days, yes. But it won't last long, I hope. Poor dear Rena's little room isn't going to stay empty.

TESMAN: Oh? Whom are you going to move in there? What?

MISS TESMAN: Oh, there's always some poor invalid who needs care and attention.   25

HEDDA: Do you really want another cross like that to bear?

MISS TESMAN: Cross! God forgive you, child. It's been no cross for me.

HEDDA: But now—if a complete stranger comes to live with you——?

MISS TESMAN: Oh, one soon makes friends with invalids. And I need so much to have someone to live for. Like you, my dear. Well, I expect there'll soon be work in this house too for an old aunt, praise God!

HEDDA: Oh—please!

TESMAN: By Jove, yes! What a splendid time the three of us could have together if——   30

HEDDA: If?

TESMAN: [*Uneasily.*] Oh, never mind. It'll all work out. Let's hope so—what?

MISS TESMAN: Yes, yes. Well, I'm sure you two would like to be alone. [*Smiles.*] Perhaps Hedda may have something to tell you, George. Good-bye. I must go home to Rena. [*Turns to the door.*] Dear God, how strange! Now Rena is with me and with poor dear Joachim.

TESMAN: Fancy that. Yes, Auntie Juju! What?   35

[Miss Tesman goes out through the hall.]

HEDDA: [*Follows Tesman coldly and searchingly with her eyes.*] I really believe this death distresses you more than it does her.

TESMAN: Oh, it isn't just Auntie Rena. It's Eilert I'm so worried about.

HEDDA: [*Quickly.*] Is there any news of him?

TESMAN: I ran over to see him this afternoon. I wanted to tell him his manuscript was in safe hands.

HEDDA: Oh? You didn't find him?   40

TESMAN: No. He wasn't at home. But later I met Mrs. Elvsted and she told me he'd been here early this morning.

HEDDA: Yes, just after you'd left.

TESMAN: It seems he said he'd torn the manuscript up. What?

HEDDA: Yes, he claimed to have done so.

TESMAN: You told him we had it, of course?

HEDDA: No. [*Quickly.*] Did you tell Mrs. Elvsted?   45

TESMAN: No, I didn't like to. But you ought to have told him. Think if he should go home and do something desperate! Give me the manuscript, Hedda. I'll run over to him with it right away. Where did you put it?

HEDDA: [*Cold and motionless, leaning against the armchair.*] I haven't got it any longer.

TESMAN: Haven't got it? What on earth do you mean?

HEDDA: I've burned it.

TESMAN: [*Starts, terrified.*] Burned it! Burned Eilert's manuscript!   50

HEDDA: Don't shout. The servant will hear you.

TESMAN: Burned it! But in heaven's name——! Oh, no, no, no! This is impossible!

HEDDA: Well, it's true.

TESMAN: But Hedda, do you realize what you've done? That's appropriating lost property! It's against the law! By Jove! You ask Judge Brack and see if I'm not right.   55

HEDDA: You'd be well advised not to talk about it to Judge Brack or anyone else.

TESMAN: But how could you go and do such a dreadful thing? What on earth put the idea into your head? What came over you? Answer me! What?

HEDDA: [*Represses an almost imperceptible smile.*] I did it for your sake, George.

TESMAN: For my sake?

HEDDA: When you came home this morning and described how he'd read his book to you——   60

TESMAN: Yes, yes?

HEDDA: You admitted you were jealous of him.

TESMAN: But, good heavens, I didn't mean it literally!

HEDDA: No matter. I couldn't bear the thought that anyone else should push you into the background.

TESMAN: [*Torn between doubt and joy.*] Hedda—is this true? But—but—but I never realized you loved me like that! Fancy——   65

HEDDA: Well, I suppose you'd better know. I'm going to have—— [*Breaks off and says violently.*] No, no—you'd better ask your Auntie Juju. She'll tell you.

TESMAN: Hedda! I think I understand what you mean. [*Clasps his hands.*] Good heavens, can it really be true! What?

HEDDA: Don't shout. The servant will hear you.

TESMAN: [*Laughing with joy.*] The servant! I say, that's good! The servant! Why, that's Bertha! I'll run out and tell her at once!

HEDDA: [*Clenches her hands in despair.*] Oh, its destroying me, all this—it's de-   70
stroying me!

TESMAN: I say, Hedda, what's up? What?

HEDDA: [*Cold, controlled.*] Oh, it's all so—absurd—George.

TESMAN: Absurd? That I'm so happy? But surely——? Ah, well—perhaps I won't say anything to Bertha.

HEDDA: No, do. She might as well know too.

TESMAN: No, no, I won't tell her yet. But Auntie Juju—I must let her know! And   75
you—you called me George! For the first time! Fancy that! Oh, it'll make Auntie Juju so happy, all this! So very happy!

HEDDA: Will she be happy when she hears I've burned Eilert Loevborg's manuscript—for your sake?

TESMAN: No, I'd forgotten about that. Of course no one must be allowed to know about the manuscript. But that you're burning with love for me, Hedda, I must certainly let Auntie Juju know that. I say, I wonder if young wives often feel like that toward their husbands? What?

HEDDA: You might ask Auntie Juju about that too.

TESMAN: I will, as soon as I get the chance. [*Looks uneasy and thoughtful again.*] But I say, you know, that manuscript. Dreadful business. Poor Eilert!

[Mrs. Elvsted, dressed as on her first visit, with hat and overcoat, enters from the hall.]

MRS. ELVSTED: [*Greets them hastily and tremulously.*] Oh, Hedda dear, do please   80
forgive me for coming here again.

HEDDA: Why, Thea, what's happened?

TESMAN: Is it anything to do with Eilert Loevborg? What?

MRS. ELVSTED: Yes—I'm so dreadfully afraid he may have met with an accident.

HEDDA: [*Grips her arm.*] You think so?

TESMAN: But, good heavens, Mrs. Elvsted, what makes you think that?   85

MRS. ELVSTED: I heard them talking about him at the boarding-house, as I went in. Oh, there are the most terrible rumors being spread about him in town today.

TESMAN: Fancy. Yes, I heard about them too. But I can testify that he went straight home to bed. Fancy that!

HEDDA: Well—what did they say in the boarding-house?

MRS. ELVSTED: Oh, I couldn't find out anything. Either they didn't know, or else—— they stopped talking when they saw me. And I didn't dare to ask.

TESMAN: [*Fidgets uneasily.*] We must hope—we must hope you misheard them,   90
Mrs. Elvsted.

MRS. ELVSTED: No, no, I'm sure it was he they were talking about. I heard them say something about a hospital——

TESMAN: Hospital!

HEDDA: Oh no, surely that's impossible!

MRS. ELVSTED: Oh, I became so afraid. So I went up to his rooms and asked to see him.

HEDDA: Do you think that was wise, Thea?   95

MRS. ELVSTED: Well, what else could I do? I couldn't bear the uncertainty any longer.

TESMAN: But you didn't manage to find him either? What?

MRS. ELVSTED: No. And they had no idea where he was. They said he hadn't been home since yesterday afternoon.

TESMAN: Since yesterday? Fancy that!

MRS. ELVSTED: I'm sure he must have met with an accident.

TESMAN: Hedda, I wonder if I ought to go into town and make one or two enquiries?   100

HEDDA: No, no, don't you get mixed up in this.

[Judge Brack enters from the hall, hat in hand. Bertha, who has opened the door for him, closes it. He looks serious and greets them silently.]

TESMAN: Hullo, my dear Judge. Fancy seeing you!

BRACK: I had to come and talk to you.

TESMAN: I can see Auntie Juju's told you the news.

BRACK: Yes, I've heard about that too.   105

TESMAN: Tragic, isn't it?

BRACK: Well, my dear chap, that depends how you look at it.

TESMAN: *[Looks uncertainly at him.]* Has something else happened?

BRACK: Yes.

HEDDA: Another tragedy?   110

BRACK: That also depends on how you look at it, Mrs. Tesman.

MRS. ELVSTED: Oh, it's something to do with Eilert Loevborg!

BRACK: *[Looks at her for a moment.]* How did you guess? Perhaps you've heard already——?

MRS. ELVSTED: *[Confused.]* No, no, not at all—I——   115

TESMAN: For heaven's sake, tell us!

BRACK: *[Shrugs his shoulders.]* Well, I'm afraid they've taken him to the hospital. He's dying.

MRS. ELVSTED: *[Screams.]* Oh God, God!

TESMAN: The hospital! Dying!

HEDDA: *[Involuntarily.]* So quickly!   120

MRS. ELVSTED: *[Weeping.]* Oh, Hedda! And we parted enemies!

HEDDA: *[Whispers.]* Thea—Thea!

MRS. ELVSTED: *[ignoring her.]* I must see him! I must see him before he dies!

BRACK: It's no use, Mrs. Elvsted. No one's allowed to see him now.

MRS. ELVSTED: But what's happened to him? You must tell me!   125

TESMAN: He hasn't tried to do anything to himself? What?

HEDDA: Yes, he has. I'm sure of it.

TESMAN: Hedda, how can you——?

BRACK: *[Who has not taken his eyes from her.]* I'm afraid you've guessed correctly, Mrs. Tesman.

MRS. ELVSTED: How dreadful!

TESMAN: Attempted suicide! Fancy that!   130

HEDDA: Shot himself!

BRACK: Right again, Mrs. Tesman.

MRS. ELVSTED: *[Tries to compose herself.]* When did this happen, Judge Brack?

BRACK: This afternoon. Between three and four.

TESMAN: But, good heavens—where? What?   135

BRACK: *[A little hesitantly.]* Where? Why, my dear chap, in his rooms of course.

MRS. ELVSTED: No, that's impossible. I was there soon after six.

BRACK: Well, it must have been somewhere else, then. I don't know exactly. I only know that they found him. He'd shot himself—through the breast.

MRS. ELVSTED: Oh, how horrible! That he should end like that!   140

HEDDA: [*To Brack.*] Through the breast, you said?

BRACK: That is what I said.

HEDDA: Not through the head?

BRACK: Through the breast, Mrs. Tesman.

HEDDA: The breast. Yes; yes. That's good, too.   145

BRACK: Why, Mrs. Tesman?

HEDDA: Oh—no, I didn't mean anything.

TESMAN: And the wound's dangerous you say? What?

BRACK: Mortal. He's probably already dead.

MRS. ELVSTED: Yes, yes—I feel it! It's all over. All over. Oh Hedda——!   150

TESMAN: But, tell me, how did you manage to learn all this?

BRACK: [*Curtly.*] From the police. I spoke to one of them.

HEDDA: [*Loudly, clearly.*] At last! Oh, thank god!

TESMAN: [*Appalled.*] For god's sake, Hedda, what are you saying?

HEDDA: I am saying there's beauty in what he has done.   155

BRACK: Mm—Mrs. Tesman——

TESMAN: Beauty! Oh, but I say!

MRS. ELVSTED: Hedda, how can you talk of beauty in connection with a thing like this?

HEDDA: Eilert Loevborg has settled his account with life. He's had the courage to do
what—what he had to do.

MRS. ELVSTED: No, that's not why it happened. He did it because he was mad.   160

TESMAN: He did it because he was desperate.

HEDDA: You're wrong! I know!

MRS. ELVSTED: He must have been mad. The same as when he tore up the manuscript.

BRACK: [*Starts.*] Manuscript? Did he tear it up?

MRS. ELVSTED: Yes. Last night.   165

TESMAN: [*Whispers.*] Oh, Hedda, we shall never be able to escape from this.

BRACK: Hm. Strange.

TESMAN: [*Wanders round the room.*] To think of Eilert dying like that. And not leaving behind him the thing that would have made his name endure.

MRS. ELVSTED: If only it could be pieced together again!

TESMAN: Yes, fancy! If only it could! I'd give anything——   170

MRS. ELVSTED: Perhaps it can, Mr. Tesman.

TESMAN: What do you mean?

MRS. ELVSTED: [*Searches in the pocket of her dress.*] Look! I kept the notes he dictated it from.

HEDDA: [*Takes a step nearer.*] Ah!

TESMAN: You kept them, Mrs. Elvsted! What?   175

MRS. ELVSTED: Yes, here they are. I brought them with me when I left home. They've
been in my pocket ever since.

TESMAN: Let me have a look.

MRS. ELVSTED: [*Hands him a wad of small sheets of paper.*] They're in a terrible
muddle. All mixed up.

TESMAN: I say, just fancy if we can sort them out! Perhaps if we work on them together——?

MRS. ELVSTED: Oh, yes? Let's try, anyway!   180

TESMAN: We'll manage it. We must! I shall dedicate my life to this.

HEDDA: *You,* George? Your life?

TESMAN: Yes—well, all the time I can spare. My book'll have to wait. Hedda, you do
understand? What? I owe it to Eilert's memory.

HEDDA: Perhaps.

TESMAN: Well, my dear Mrs. Elvsted, you and I'll have to pool our brains. No use cry- 185
ing over spilt milk, what? We must try to approach this matter calmly.

MRS. ELVSTED: Yes, yes, Mr. Tesman. I'll do my best.

TESMAN: Well, come over here and let's start looking at these notes right away.
Where shall we sit? Here? No, the other room. You'll excuse us, won't you,
Judge? Come along with me, Mrs. Elvsted.

MRS. ELVSTED: Oh, God! If only we can manage to do it!

*[Tesman and Mrs. Elvsted go into the rear room. He takes off his hat and overcoat. They sit at a
table beneath the hanging lamp and absorb themselves in the notes. Hedda walks across to the
stove and sits in the armchair. After a moment, Brack goes over to her.]*

HEDDA: [*Half aloud.*] Oh, Judge! This act of Eilert Loevborg's—doesn't it give one a
sense of release!

BRACK: Release, Mrs. Hedda? Well, it's a release for him, of course—— 190

HEDDA: oh, I don't mean him—I mean me! The release of knowing that someone
can do something really brave! Something beautiful!

BRACK: [*Smiles.*] Hm—my dear Mrs. Hedda——

HEDDA: oh, I know what you're going to say. You're a bourgeois at heart too, just
like—ah, well!

BRACK: [*Looks at her.*] Eilert Loevborg has meant more to you than you're willing
to admit to yourself. Or am I wrong?

HEDDA: I'm not answering questions like that from you. I only know that Eilert Lo- 195
evborg has had the courage to live according to his own principles. And now, at
last, he's done something big! Something beautiful! To have the courage and the
will to rise from the feast of life so early!

BRACK: It distresses me deeply, Mrs. Hedda, but I'm afraid I must rob you of that
charming illusion.

HEDDA: Illusion?

BRACK: You wouldn't have been allowed to keep it for long, anyway.

HEDDA: What do you mean?

BRACK: He didn't shoot himself on purpose.

HEDDA: Not on purpose? 200

BRACK: No. It didn't happen quite the way I told you.

HEDDA: Have you been hiding something? What is it?

BRACK: In order to spare poor Mrs. Elvsted's feelings, I permitted myself one or two
small—equivocations.

HEDDA: What? 205

BRACK: To begin with, he is already dead.

HEDDA: He died at the hospital?

BRACK: Yes. Without regaining consciousness.

HEDDA: What else haven't you told us?

BRACK: The incident didn't take place at his lodgings. 210

HEDDA: Well, that's utterly unimportant.

BRACK: Not utterly. The fact is, you see, that Eilert Loevborg was found shot in Mademoiselle Danielle's boudoir.

HEDDA: [*Almost jumps up, but instead sinks back in her chair.*] That's impossible.
He can't have been there today.

BRACK: He was there this afternoon. He went to ask for something he claimed
they'd taken from him. Talked some crazy nonsense about a child which had
got lost——

HEDDA: Oh! So that was the reason!

215

BRACK: I thought at first he might have been referring to his manuscript. But I hear
    he destroyed that himself. So he must have meant his pocketbook—I suppose.

HEDDA: Yes, I suppose so. So they found him there?

BRACK: Yes; there. With a discharged pistol in his breast pocket. The shot had
    wounded him mortally.

HEDDA: Yes. In the breast.

BRACK: No. In the—hm—stomach. The—lower part——   220

HEDDA: [*Looks at him with an expression of repulsion.*] That too! Oh, why does
    everything I touch become mean and ludicrous? It's like a curse!

BRACK: There's something else, Mrs. Hedda. It's rather disagreeable, too.

HEDDA: What?

BRACK: The pistol he had on him——   225

HEDDA: Yes? What about it?

BRACK: He must have stolen it.

HEDDA: [*Jumps up.*] Stolen it! That isn't true! He didn't!

BRACK: It's the only explanation. He must have stolen it. Ssh!

[Tesman and Mrs. Elvsted have got up from the table in the rear room and come into the draw-
ing room.]

TESMAN: [*His hands full of papers.*] Hedda, I can't see properly under that lamp.
    Think!

HEDDA: I am thinking.   230

TESMAN: Do you think we could possibly use your writing table for a little? What?

HEDDA: Yes, of course. [*Quickly.*] No, wait? Let me tidy it up first.

TESMAN: Oh, don't you trouble about that. There's plenty of room.

HEDDA: No, no, let me tidy it up first, I say. I'll take this in and put them on the
    piano. Here.

[She pulls an object, covered with sheets of music, out from under the bookcase, puts some more
sheets on top and carries it all into the rear room and away to the left. Tesman puts his papers
on the writing table and moves the lamp over from the corner table. He and Mrs. Elvsted sit
down and begin working again. Hedda comes back.]

HEDDA: [*Behind Mrs. Elvsted's chair, ruffles her hair gently.*] Well, my pretty Thea!   235
    And how is work progressing on Eilert Loevborg's memorial?

MRS. ELVSTED: [*Looks up at her, dejectedly.*] Oh, it's going to be terribly difficult to
    get these into any order.

TESMAN: We've got to do it. We must! After all, putting other people's papers into
    order is rather my specialty, what?

[Hedda goes over to the stove and sits on one of the footstools. Brack stands over her, leaning
against the armchair.]

HEDDA: [*Whispers.*] What was that you were saying about the pistol?

BRACK: [*softly.*] I said he must have stolen it.

HEDDA: Why do you think that?   240

BRACK: Because any other explanation is unthinkable, Mrs. Hedda, or ought to be.

HEDDA: I see.

BRACK: [*Looks at her for a moment.*] Eilert Loevborg was here this morning.
    Wasn't he?

HEDDA: Yes.

BRACK: Were you alone with him?   245

HEDDA: For a few moments.

BRACK: You didn't leave the room while he was here?

HEDDA: No.

BRACK: Think again. Are you sure you didn't go out for a moment?

HEDDA: Oh—yes, I might have gone into the hall. Just for a few seconds.   250

BRACK: And where was your pistol-case during this time?

HEDDA: I'd locked it in that——

BRACK: Er—Mrs. Hedda?

HEDDA: It was lying over there on my writing table.

BRACK: Have you looked to see of both the pistols are still there?   255

HEDDA: No.

BRACK: You needn't bother. I saw the pistol Loevborg had when they found him. I recognized it at once. From yesterday. And other occasions.

HEDDA: Have you got it?

BRACK: No. The police have it.

HEDDA: What will the police do with this pistol?   260

BRACK: Try to trace the owner.

HEDDA: Do you think they'll succeed?

BRACK: [*Leans down and whispers.*] No, Hedda Gabler. Not as long as I hold my tongue.

HEDDA: [*Looks nervously at him.*] And if you don't?

BRACK: [*Shrugs his shoulders.*] You could always say he'd stolen it.   265

HEDDA: I'd rather die!

BRACK: [*Smiles.*] People say that. They never do it.

HEDDA: [*Not replying.*] And suppose the pistol wasn't stolen? And they trace the owner? What then?

BRACK: There'll be a scandal, Hedda.

HEDDA: A scandal!   270

BRACK: Yes, a scandal. The thing you're so frightened of. You'll have to appear in court. Together with Mademoiselle Danielle. She'll have to explain how it all happened. Was it an accident, or was it—homicide? Was he about to take the pistol from his pocket to threaten her? And did it go off? Or did she snatch the pistol from his hand, shoot him and then put it back in his pocket? She might quite easily have done it. She's a resourceful lady, is Mademoiselle Danielle.

HEDDA: But I had nothing to do with this repulsive business.

BRACK: No. But you'll have to answer one question. Why did you give Eilert Loevborg this pistol? And what conclusions will people draw when it is proved you did give it to him?

HEDDA: [*Bows her head.*] That's true. I hadn't thought of that.

BRACK: Well, luckily there's no danger as long as I hold my tongue.   275

HEDDA: [*Looks up at him.*] In other words, I'm in your power, Judge. From now on, you've got your hold over me.

BRACK: [*Whispers, more slowly*] Hedda, my dearest—believe me—I will not abuse my position.

HEDDA: Nevertheless, I'm in your power. Dependent on your will, and your demands. Not free. Still not free! [*Rises passionately.*] No. I couldn't bear that. No.

BRACK: [*Looks half-derisively at her.*] Most people resign themselves to the inevitable, sooner or later.

HEDDA: [*Returns his gaze.*] Possibly they do. [*She goes across to the writing table.*]   280

HEDDA: [*Represses an involuntary smile and says in Tesman's voice.*] Well, George. Think you'll be able to manage? What?

TESMAN: Heaven knows, dear. This is going to take months and months.

HEDDA: [*In the same tone as before.*] Fancy that, by Jove! [*Runs her hands gently through Mrs. Elvsted's hair.*] Doesn't it feel strange, Thea? Here you are working away with Tesman just the way you used to work with Eilert Loevborg.

MRS. ELVSTED: Oh—if only I can inspire your husband too!

HEDDA: Oh, it'll come. In time.   285

TESMAN: Yes—do you know, Hedda, I really think I'm beginning to feel a bit—well—that way. But you go back and talk to Judge Brack.

HEDDA: Can't I be of any use to you two in any way?

TESMAN: No, none at all. [*Turns his head.*] You'll have to keep Hedda company from now on, Judge, and see she doesn't get bored. If you don't mind.

BRACK: [*Glances at Hedda.*] It'll be a pleasure.

HEDDA: Thank you. But I'm tired this evening. I think I'll lie down on the sofa in   290
there for a little while.

TESMAN: Yes, dear—do. What?

[*Hedda goes into the rear room and draws the curtain behind her. Short pause. Suddenly she begins to play a frenzied dance melody on the piano.*]

MRS. ELVSTED: [*Starts up from her chair.*] Oh, what's that?

TESMAN: [*Runs to the doorway.*] Hedda dear, please! Don't play dance music tonight! Think of Auntie Rena. And Eilert.

HEDDA: [*Puts her head out through the curtains.*] And Auntie Juju. And all the rest of them. From now on I'll be quiet. [*Closes the curtains behind her.*]

TESMAN: [*At the writing table.*] It distresses her to watch us doing this. I say, Mrs.   295
Elvsted, I've an idea. Why don't you move in with Auntie Juju? I'll run over each evening, and we can sit and work there. What?

MRS. ELVSTED: Yes, that might be the best plan.

HEDDA: [*From the rear room.*] I can hear what you're saying, Tesman. But how shall I spend the evenings out here?

TESMAN: [*Looking through his papers.*] Oh, I'm sure Judge Brack'll be kind enough to come over and keep you company. You won't mind my not being here, Judge?

BRACK: [*In the armchair, calls gaily.*] I'll be delighted, Mrs. Tesman. I'll be here every evening. We'll have great fun together, you and I.

HEDDA: [*Loud and clear.*] Yes, that'll suit you, won't it, Judge? The only cock on the   300
dunghill——!

[*A shot is heard from the rear room. Tesman, Mrs. Elvsted and Judge Brack start from their chairs.*]

TESMAN: Oh, she's playing with those pistols again.

[*He pulls the curtains aside and runs in. Mrs. Elvsted follows him. Hedda is lying dead on the sofa. Confusion and shouting. Bertha enters in alarm from the right.*]

TESMAN: [*Screams to Brack.*] She's shot herself! Shot herself in the head! By Jove! Fancy that!

BRACK: [*Half paralyzed in the armchair.*] But, good God! People don't do such things!

Act 4 Response Statement Questions

- What is your response to Tesman in the first part of this Act? Does he seem the same or different from how you saw him earlier?
- What is your response to Eilert now, in light of what he's done while off-stage? Is your response consistent with the way you saw him earlier or has he surprised you in any way?
- Is Hedda complicit in Eilert's actions? Is she an accessory to a crime? Is she guilty or responsible for what's happened to Eilert? Is she "sick"? To what

extent do her gender and her class encourage her to be a manipulator of men?

- What's your response to Hedda's death? Is it tragic, or is poetic justice served? Can you relate your response to your view of what's appropriate for a woman in her situation to feel and do? And can you relate that to your own gender and social class?

Overall Response Statement Questions

- Do you see evidence of moral growth, insight, or self-awareness on the part of any of the characters in this play? If so or if not, what are the implications for them or the world they inhabit? for yours?
- Is this play a tragedy? If so, by what definition? Is it the same kind of tragedy as you saw in plays from earlier eras (*Oedipus the King, Hamlet*)?
- Assuming the play records Hedda's downfall, what are its causes? Does Hedda have a "tragic flaw" at the center of her personality? Are external circumstances or forces responsible for destroying her? Is some combination of moral characteristics and external circumstances the cause of her downfall? In any case, is the cause appropriate to tragedy?
- Is the impact or relevance of this play limited to its own time and place, or does it touch your world somehow? If you think the latter, what kind of harmonious ideological interaction do you have with the text that allows you to see it as relevant to modern concerns?
- *Share and Compare*   If different readers in your class or discussion group express different degrees of sympathy or antipathy for Hedda, to what extent are those differences related to the gender, age, marital status, or social class of those readers?

BROADENING YOUR LITERARY EXPERIENCE THROUGH RESEARCH

Presumably, what you have read in this chapter and the writing you have done have shown you more than you knew before about the literary repertoire and ideology of *Hedda Gabler*, including the features and practices of the Realistic theater and the ideology of the middle-class European culture in the nineteenth century. If you want to further broaden your knowledge with respect to *Hedda Gabler*, Ibsen's plays, Realistic drama in general, or any aspect of the ideology behind *Hedda Gabler*, the best way to do that is through library research. The reading and writing you have done in this chapter may have raised questions for you that only further research can answer. That's good: Remember that it's questions and questioning that keep learning alive, and that answers are only provisional and temporary. The QAQ method promoted in Chapter 3 applies here too.

Here are some additional questions that you could pursue through library research, followed by a brief bibliography of sources for broadening your repertoire of knowledge in the area of Realistic drama. Think of both the sources and the questions as just starting points for further investigation. Even a researched reading, however, should not be considered final. "The truth" about a text does not lie under a rock, waiting to be discovered, or in the library or in history; it may be pursued, but never possessed. Reading, learning, knowing are processes, of which research is a part. Whenever you read a text, whether you know a lot about it or just a little, you should try to be conscious of the dynamic interaction between you and the text.

Suggestions for Research

- The role of Hedda Gabler has been one of the great parts for female actors over the years. Investigate the performance history of major productions (for stage and film) to see how different actors have interpreted the role.

- Find out what Henrik Ibsen's ideology consisted of on the questions of women's rights, female emancipation, or middle-class conformity versus individual expression. Do his views affect your reading of *Hedda Gabler?*

- Research the kinds of responses *Hedda Gabler* received in its own time—in Norway, elsewhere in Europe, in North America. How were productions of it reviewed from 1890 until about 1920? What kind of critical comments did readers of the printed text offer in those same years?

- Investigate the status of middle-class women in Ibsen's Norway, in late-nineteenth- and early-twentieth-century Europe. Based on this investigation, what can you say about how realistic Ibsen's portrayal of Hedda Gabler was for its own place and time?

- Research the history of women actors in Western theater. Why were there none even in Elizabethan England? What was the reputation or social status of women actors from the seventeenth century to the twentieth? What issues of cultural ideology lie behind the relatively late appearance of women on the stage and their social reputation once they did appear?

- Investigate the changing conceptions of tragic drama from Classical through Realistic theater. How has the literary repertoire of the theater in the Western World changed with regard to tragedy? What have some different theorists and playwrights said about it? How have changes in cultural ideology affected the literary repertoire of the theater in this way?

- Read a nineteenth-century English or American melodrama. (Two good candidates are *East Lynne* by Mrs. Henry Wood and *Under the Gaslight* by Augustin Daly.) What text strategies do you see at work in such a play, in contrast with those in a realistic play like *Hedda Gabler?* What is your response to it, in contrast to your response to any of the tragedies you have read?

- Investigate the literary repertoire of theater in Asia or Africa. How has it developed? Is there a pattern comparable to the history of theater in the

West? What is the place of theater in an Asian or African culture and has that place been affected by any of the drama of the West?

Selected Bibliography

A good place to begin your search for further information on any of these topics is in the reference section of your library. For any of the above topics, you can find background information and get an overview of related issues and ideas by consulting specialized encyclopedias, handbooks, and readers' guides to particular areas of literature, defined by genre or historical period. Often these kinds of reference works include their own bibliographies of relevant books and periodical articles. Here are some standard reference works for the study of realistic drama.

Breed, Paul F., and Florence M. Sniderman, eds. *Dramatic Criticism Index: A Bibliography of Commentaries from Ibsen to the Avant-Garde.* Detroit: Gale, 1972.

Carpenter, Charles A. *Modern Drama Scholarship and Criticism, 1966–1980: An International Bibliography.* Toronto: University of Toronto Press, 1986.

Coleman, Arthur. *Drama Criticism,* vol. 2. Denver: Alan Swallow, 1966–1971.

Gassner, John, ed. *Reader's Encyclopedia of World Drama.* New York: Crowell, 1969.

Hochman, Stanley, ed. *McGraw-Hill Encyclopedia of World Drama,* 5 vols. New York: McGraw-Hill, 1984.

Periodicals, such as magazines and scholarly journals, are another good source of information for broadening your literary knowledge. The bibliographies in the above reference sources may list periodical articles, but you can extend your search by consulting any of the following periodical indexes. All are available in both bound volumes and electronic form, as indicated by the note in parentheses following each title.

Arts and Humanities Citation Index. (on-line)

Humanities Index. (on-line)

MLA International Bibliography. (CD-ROM)

Here is a list of books that contain useful information for broadening your knowledge of any of the topics listed earlier.

Bennett, Benjamin. *Theater as Problem: Modern Drama and Its Place in Literature.* Ithaca, N.Y.: Cornell UP, 1990.

Brockett, Oscar. *The History of the Theatre,* 5th ed. Boston: Allyn and Bacon, 1987.

Brustein, Robert. *The Theatre of Revolt.* Boston: Little, Brown, 1962.

Gilman, Richard. *The Making of Modern Drama.* New York: Farrar, Strauss & Giroux, 1974.

Lebovitz, Naomi. *Ibsen and the Great World.* Baton Rouge: Louisiana State UP, 1974.

Lyons, Charles R. *"Hedda Gabler": Gender, Role, and World.* Boston: Twayne, 1990.

Marker, Frederick J., Marker, Lise-Lone. *Ibsen's Lively Art: A Performance Study of the Major Plays.* Cambridge: Cambridge UP, 1989.

Shaw, George Bernard. *The Quintessence of Ibsenism.* New York: Hill and Wang, 1957.

Williams, Raymond. *Modern Tragedy.* Stanford, Calif.: Stanford UP, 1966.

22 ◆ Theater in the Twentieth Century

By the turn of the twentieth century, drama in the Western world had nearly 2,500 years of history. In that time it had gone from a quasi-religious, ritualistic depiction of mythical characters struggling against fate and divine decree to a very close approximation of the tensions of real people struggling with their social roles. In the process, as the preceding chapters have suggested, it reflected or signified the concerns, the worldview, the ideology of not only individual authors but different cultural circumstances as well. The theater had also become well established as a cultural institution—a major form of popular entertainment and a site of serious artistic effort.

Changes in the World, Challenges in Ideology

Like many other cultural institutions and art forms, however, drama and theater have been subject to great changes in the twentieth century. The Western world in general has gone through and is still undergoing enormous upheaval in this century. Starting with the First World War—known then as The Great War because nothing of its geographic scale and loss of life had been experienced or recorded before—the history of the West in this century has been virtually constant political and economic crises. There was the rise of totalitarian fascist and communist states in Europe, the continuing exploitation of the Third World by the industrial and commercial powers of the West and Japan, and the inevitable nationalist revolts against those colonial masters. A Second World War was fought on a scale even more vast than the First, and it ended with the use of atomic weapons of previously unimaginable destructive power.

From the early 1930s on, the most powerful nations of the world have been in a constant state of war-preparedness, and countless "small" wars have erupted continuously all over the world since the late 1940s. There has been at least one widespread economic depression, the rise of huge multinational corporations responsible to no government authority or voting population, an enormous gulf between fabulous wealth and desperate poverty, nearly universal political corruption, a systematic attack on human rights under various dictatorships around the world, real and ever-growing threats to the natural environment, and increasingly powerful and omnipresent communications media to tell everyone everything. These events and conditions have meant continuing challenges to the social and political order—to the point where

1220

many may wonder if there's any such thing as order any more—and to the mental and emotional stability of individual people.

Meanwhile, this century has seen the appearance of a number of challenging ideas and theories that have also contributed to changing the way reality itself is understood. To mention just a few, the work of Sigmund Freud and his followers in psychoanalysis has put an awareness of subconscious motives and causes for behavior into most people's ideology, even if they have never read Freud or even if on one level they dispute his theories. The ideas of the French philosopher Henri Bergson have influenced the way people understand mental time and memory and the mind as a "place" where past, present, and future coexist in the same temporary reality. The thought of existentialists such as Jean-Paul Sartre—who was also a playwright—has affected a sense of individual identity, life, and reality as always being invented and of the outer world as essentially meaningless (which of course makes the value of individual action extremely problematic!). The theories of Albert Einstein, which say the very "laws" that govern the physical universe are relative, have further undermined belief in cosmic permanence.

In the arts, the century has seen revolutions that have obliterated some of the traditional ways that painting and sculpture have tried to relate to or represent external reality. To take just one example, the Cubists early in the century "fractured" the visual planes in their paintings so that a human figure, for example, does not look like it does to the eye of the ordinary person. In turn, these changes in artistic vision have affected the way people view reality and in some cases reality itself! Eventually, architecture, furniture design, automobile design, and other practical areas of modern life show the effects of a new way of seeing "reality."

Western Culture

In the midst of all this change and upheaval, one way to think about drama in the twentieth century is to see it as symptomatic or reflective of the larger world of which it is a part. My approach in the preceding chapters has been to suggest that same kind of relationship between drama and the theater in each earlier historical era, so this viewpoint is no different. But because the *world* is different in the twentieth century from what it had been before, so is drama. This is still a useful way to understand the cultural situation of drama, but I would like to explore briefly two or three other matters that may be equally useful in expanding your repertoire of information about twentieth century plays. These are so closely intertwined that it's hard to separate them for discussion, but let's try.

One issue is the tendency, beginning perhaps with Henrik Ibsen and George Bernard Shaw in the late nineteenth century and influenced by their contemporaries in fiction (Emile Zola, for instance, and Henry James), for twentieth-century playwrights to regard their work as literary art as opposed to theatrical entertainment. I don't mean that these playwrights did not and do not write for the stage, but that drama has been seen to take its place beside fiction and poetry as, one, written texts to be read and studied for their aesthetic values as literature and, two, a self-conscious artistic attempt to respond to the changing sense of reality that has confronted all artists since the early decades of the century. For both of these reasons, twentieth-century playwrights have introduced innovative text strategies that have challenged the conventions of realistic drama and the expectations of audiences alike.

At the same time, the twentieth century has seen a marked split between what is often called "high" and "low" or "serious" and "popular" culture, literature, and theater, accompanied by a similar split in the audience. This split also began in the nineteenth century, and it is implicit in Ibsen's plays to the extent that they may be read as attempts to confront and criticize bourgeois values. In varying degrees other playwrights have felt that creating literary art is incompatible with appealing to a wide audience. A parallel phenomenon may be seen in the other arts—music, painting, and sculpture, for instance—in the twentieth century. Many "average" people seem offended or, at least, challenged by modern art to the extent that it puts greater and different demands on the audience, and not everyone is willing to meet those demands. Furthermore, to the extent that playwrights, like artists in other media, have been aware of a reality that conventional dramatic realism or melodrama was inadequate to treat, and to the extent that that awareness has forced them to introduce text strategies that violate the expectations of theatergoers, an alienation of at least some portion of the audience seems inevitable.

This interpretation emphasizes the actions of authors, but we shouldn't leave out of consideration the situation of the theater itself in capitalist economies and a growing mass culture. In Europe and North America, the nineteenth century had seen the growth of theater entertainment such as melodrama, minstrel shows, and vaudeville that were deliberately light and undemanding intellectually or emotionally for the audiences. Yet such serious drama as Shakespearean plays was also popular and widely staged in the nineteenth century, and not just in Britain.[1] Having become well-established, the theater business had of course an interest in keeping itself financially healthy and profitable. But staging plays that alienate or exclude any significant portion of the audience is antithetical to that interest. The big money, consequently, has tended to go into more popular forms of drama—from lavish musicals produced on Broadway or in London's West End to commercial television drama to big-budget Hollywood movies—that are more or less guaranteed of attracting an audience or substantial financial backing, as well as generating spin-offs such as recordings, T-shirts, and memorabilia of all sorts. In complementary fashion, this state of affairs has tended to keep the

---

[1]In New York in 1849, when competing productions of Macbeth starring two of the big-name actors of the day, Edwin Forrest and William Charles Macready, were staged, theatergoers loyal to one actor or the other rioted and 22 people were killed, so seriously was Shakespearean drama taken.

mass audience more or less contented and unchallenged. People may feel that they have enough discontent and challenge in everyday life, and they turn to various forms of mass entertainment for escape. When that expectation to be entertained is violated, as it is likely to be by serious or art drama today, you may hear the same kinds of objections that people raise to abstract sculpture in public places, politically relevant comic strips, or hard-news stories on the sports pages.

At the same time, there has remained a strong, if smaller, audience for serious drama, so that a "highbrow" theater subsidized by government and corporate grants or university drama schools or operating on small budgets "off-off-Broadway" has been the province of art plays. This split is also evident in television, where serious drama is usually limited to public stations, and in film, where it is produced by independent filmmakers and plays in the "art houses," not the multiscreen mall theaters. Shakespeare's plays were, if you recall, both serious and popular at once, but they had little claim to status as literature in the highbrow sense when they were first written and produced. It was only after Shakespeare's death that his work began to acquire a literary reputation. Today's popular drama may one day acquire a similar high cultural status, but in this chapter I want to focus on the twentieth-century drama regarded as serious by authors, critics, producers, theatergoers, and readers.

Challenge and Diversity

In twentieth-century drama, what seems to stand out is *challenge*—to the conventions and underlying assumptions of realistic drama, to audiences, and to the generally understood relationship between the theater and real life. This challenge constitutes yet another reaction in the historical pattern of action and reaction that may be seen in Western drama since the Elizabethan era.

Modern drama challenges many of the conventional text strategies of realistic drama, but the three I will ask you to consider briefly here are the "basics" of plot, character, and setting. You have experience reading at least one modern play (*The Sandbox* in Chapter 17), so I invite you to recall that as you read on here.

Set

Modern plays may present an audience with a conventionally realistic set, or they may place the action in a specific time and place, but many of them, such as *The Sandbox*, take place at no particular time or locality. The stage may be bare or set with just a few backdrops or pieces of furniture to suggest a mood rather than a specific physical or temporal location. If the action is supposed to *symbolize* mental, spiritual, or social conditions rather than *represent* an episode in the lives of realistic people as they move in linear fashion through time, then such a bare or abstract setting seems appropriate.

Plot

The conventional linear movement of plot structure has also been challenged and disrupted. Perhaps the action does not move forward in strict chronological fashion or proceed logically out of something that had happened in the characters' past. It may move back and forth in time through **flashback** scenes or **flash forwards**. There have been various attempts, using lighting, sets, even mixed media, to enact scenes from characters' memory, which, as you are aware, exists in present time but contains past time. This strategy is one way in which modern drama has attempted to be more realistic than realistic drama—or to more accurately represent a newer sense of what constitutes reality—and to challenge what its ideology sees as artificial rather than realistic theater practices.

Another challenging text strategy is the virtual elimination of plot as it had been understood since the earliest days of Western drama. A play might present scenes and situations that lead nowhere, that have no resolution, or that end up exactly where they started, rendering the ideas of consequential action and motivation meaningless. This text strategy and the accompanying ideology are hallmarks of one variety of modern drama, called the **theater of the absurd**. These plays, reflecting an existentialist ideology, typically present a series of incidents involving bewildered people in an incomprehensible universe, rather than a logical plot that is finally resolved logically, whether to the characters' happiness or misery. The challenge of such plays to prevailing conventions of theater and to audiences may be indicated by this statement from Edward Albee, author of *The Sandbox*:

> *The Theater of the Absurd, in the sense that it is truly the contemporary theater, facing as it does man's condition as it is, is the Realistic theater of our time; and the supposed Realistic theater—the term used here to mean most of what is done on Broadway—in the sense that it panders to the public need for self-congratulation and reassurance and presents a false picture of ourselves to ourselves, is . . . really and truly The Theater of the Absurd.*

Character

Conventional understandings of character have also been challenged in modern drama. The people in action on the stage may not have realistic names or identities, nor even be legendary or archetypal. They may be purposefully flat and anonymous—think of the anonymous characters of *The Sandbox*—or they may be deliberately artificial or fictional.

In concert with the challenge to dramatic characters, some modern playwrights have challenged the assumptions of "method" acting in which the actor's identity is presumably subsumed in the character he or she is portraying. Plays in the epic theater of the German playwright Bertolt Brecht called for actors to "demonstrate" characters rather than impersonate them, stripping away much of the pretense of reality to which audiences and actors alike had become accustomed. Instead of exiting a scene to some "real" place, presumably logically related to the stage set, Brecht's characters/actors would await their next scenes sitting on benches onstage in full view of the audience.

Anti- or nonrealistic text strategies like these have further tended to call into question the relation of or difference between theater and reality, drama and life. In an age when so many actual public events seem unreal—that word, along with expressions like "Incredible!" and "I don't believe it!" now being common in colloquial American speech—it would seem appropriate for drama to have to find new ways of presenting reality, whatever that is.

Genre

In addition to these text strategies, modern drama has also called into question the traditional generic distinction between tragedy and comedy. The discussion of the conventions of Elizabethan drama in Chapter 19 mentioned the mixture of comic elements or interludes in tragedies such as *Hamlet*, and the consideration of *Twelfth Night* in Chapter 20 suggested how closely the plot of romantic comedy might veer toward tragedy. Each of those forms in its own way seems to establish or reinforce some kind of larger order through the pattern it follows: a moral or cosmic order in tragedy, a social order in comedy. But in a world widely understood as having *no* order, logic, rationality, or meaning, clear-cut distinctions between tragedy and comedy have been blurred if not obliterated. The American comedian Tom Lehrer, who in the 1950s and 1960s had established a successful career of nightclub performances and record albums in which he satirized elements of contemporary life, was asked in the 1980s why he had retired early from comedy writing. He replied that after Henry Kissinger (the architect of the American saturation bombing of Cambodia during the Vietnam War) had been awarded the Nobel Peace Prize, there were no possibilities for satire any more. His remark was at once comedic and deadly serious, characteristic of the tragicomic irony that seems to pervade life in the twentieth century. Modern plays may present this kind of **black comedy**—humorous elements with a darkly ironic underside—or they may seem to veer wildly between comedic and tragic emphases. Perhaps you noticed this when you read *The Sandbox*. To what extent would you classify that play as comedy or tragedy?

Acting Spaces

In addition to being different, modern drama has often been presented in different acting spaces. The box set and the proscenium stage are no longer the staples they once were. In some theaters, a variation of the Elizabethan thrust stage has returned, where the audience surrounds the stage on three sides, and others (sometimes called **theater in the round**) feature an **arena stage**, raised or flat, which the audience sits around on all sides. Both of these stages do without a curtain to enforce a visual separation between audience and action, and this distinction may be further broken down if actors' entrances and exits are made through the aisles, as these theaters may encourage, or if some parts of the action are moved off the stage entirely and into the audience.

At the same time, some twentieth-century playwrights and producers have tried to challenge audience's conceptions of what theater is and to break down the sense of elitism attached to serious theater as opposed to popular by moving beyond theaters to other sites. Maria Irene Fornes' 1967 play *A Vietnamese Wedding* was originally put on in a church in New York City. The opening set description of *A Vietnamese Wedding* says the text is "not a play" and calls for 10 members of the audience to participate as "characters" in the action presented. The contemporary Latino playwright Luis Valdez formed *El Teatro Campesino* (The Farmworkers' Theater) in 1965 to present original plays and sketches depicting various aspects of Mexican-American life. These were performed in churches, schools, and community centers throughout the American Southwest—even in the fields where Chicano and Chicana migrants worked.

The diversity of dramatic styles and acting spaces in twentieth-century theater has been matched by a diversity among playwrights. The repertoire of modern Western drama includes not only plays by American and British playwrights like Edward Albee and Tom Stoppard—both of whom are white males—but also plays by men and women with a variety of national, ethnic, and racial backgrounds: the German Brecht; the French Sartre; the Italian Luigi

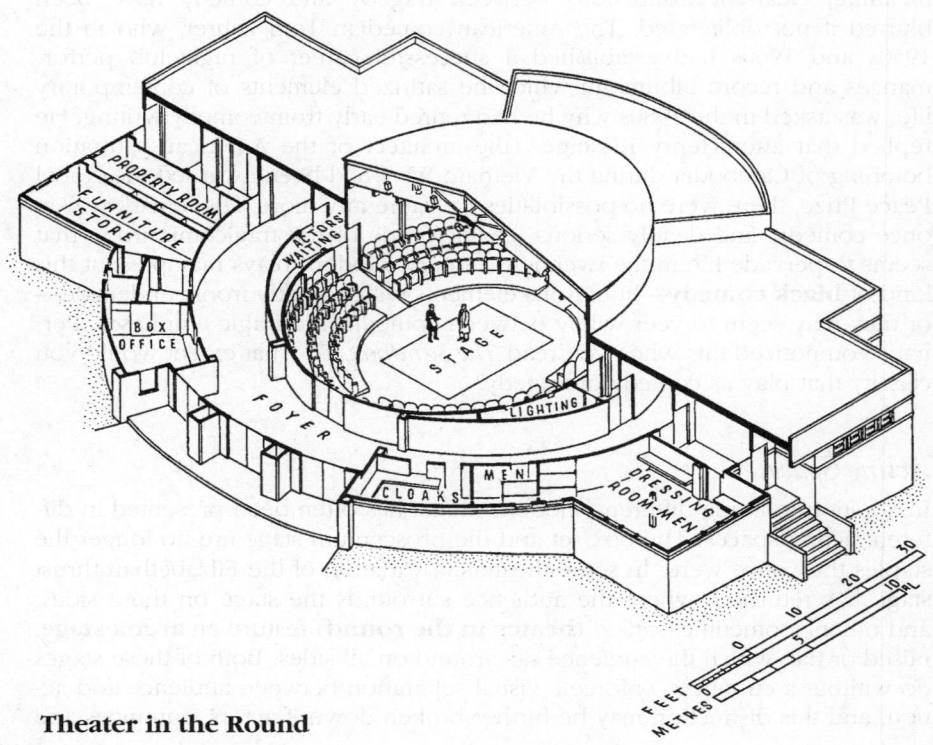

Theater in the Round

Pirandello; the Irish (living in France and writing in French) Samuel Beckett; the English Caryl Churchill; the Nigerian Wole Soyinka; the South African Athol Fugard; the African-Americans Amiri Baraka, Adrienne Kennedy, and August Wilson; the Latino-Americans Fornes and Valdez; the Asian-American David Henry Hwang; the white Americans Beth Henley, Wendy Wasserstein, Eugene O'Neill, Tennessee Williams, and Arthur Miller—just to name a few.

Reading and Responding: A Modern Play

The diversity of twentieth-century drama makes finding a representative full-length modern play difficult. Many offer challenges to the conventions of real-istic drama and the expectations of readers. But the text that you will read in this chapter is worthy of consideration for at least three reasons: (1) it deliber-atly twists several of the conventions of realistic drama; (2) it may be seen to offer a particularly modern version of knowing versus unknowing; and, (3) it may be seen to confuse or mix comedy and tragedy.

The conventional pretense of realistic drama is that the characters are real people or, as actors portray characters on stage, that actors *realize* characters as people, bring them to life. But *Six Characters in Search of an Author*, by the Italian author Luigi Pirandello, presents characters *as* characters. The dra-matic situation interposes fictional beings—Characters with a capital C—who are aware of their status as fictions, and more conventional characters—called "Actors" in the text—who presumably have "real" lives and identities. The Characters, as you will see, interrupt the Actors as they begin to rehearse a play and claim that they need an author to finish their stories. The theater company manager agrees to use his Actors to dramatize the story of the Char-acters, but the Characters object to the portrayals, saying that no one can enact their lives without distortion. From this premise, this text calls into question not only the dramatic convention of character, but also those of plot and the presumed relationship of staged drama and its audience. The Actors become an audience for the Characters' reenactment of episodes in their lives. The Characters become directors, telling the Actors how they should and should not try to realize the Characters. But of course, on another level, both the Characters and the Actors are actors. So the reading or viewing audience seems faced with the question, of these two groups, which "people"—or which "roles"—are more believable, true-to-life, "realistic"?

This unusual text strategy of admitting the fictional status of dramatic char-acters also raises some different questions of knowing and unknowing, or, closely related, matters of believing and disbelieving or degrees or differences in understanding the "same reality." The Characters know their own lives and stories, but they don't all understand their lives and stories in the same way. The Actors come to know or understand the Characters' lives and stories from what they hear the Characters say, but the Actors' attempt at re-presenting the Characters indicates differences in knowledge or understanding between themselves and the Characters.

Then what is the audience to believe? What do they know about the "re-ality-status" of the Characters or the Actors or even about themselves? What would happen to the "truth" of your own life if someone were to try to act your life out on stage? Would it be interpreted? *Re*-interpreted? *Mis*-interpreted? What is the capacity, and what are the limitations, of drama in general to re-present "reality" or "truth"? To the extent that drama presumes and is presumed to re-present reality on stage, it is required to be plausible, believable. But to the extent that drama is a re-presentation, it does not presume and is not presumed to be true. As one of the Characters says, "[L]ife is full of infinite absurdities which, strangely enough, do not even need to appear plausible, since they are true." But realistic drama, which tries "to make seem true that which isn't true," must appear to be plausible exactly because it is *not* true! These questions about the realism and the artificiality of drama are ones that most plays—or at least most plays before the twentieth century—cover over rather than bring to the surface.

> **CONNECT:**   Edward Albee's *The Sandbox*, reprinted in Chapter 17, is another play that challenges the reality status of its characters. Does that play go as far as *Six Characters in Search of an Author* in questioning the reality of individual identity, or does it go farther?

Perhaps what I have said already about *Six Characters in Search of an Author* has confused you about reality versus drama, but this play may be seen to confuse or challenge the generic distinction between comedy and tragedy, too. The Characters occasionally refer to events in their lives (both past and future) as "tragic." (In a sense, because characters are fictions, their past and their future collapse into an eternal present. Hamlet's story, for instance, is never going to turn out differently "this time"; every time it is enacted on stage or read on the page, he will have the same past and the same future.) But they also refer to the reenactment of their story as "comic." At one point, one of the Characters says the stage, in any theater, is "a place ... where people play at being serious, a place where they act comedies. We've got to act a comedy now, dead serious...." These lines perhaps reveal the mixture or confusion of tragedy or comedy—or tragic and comic elements—in *Six Characters in Search of an Author*. In addition, the absurdity of the dramatic situation itself in this play, the implausibility of it, may be implicitly comic because comedy itself in a loose sense has to do with any ridiculous difference between what is and what ought to be. Add to that the "fantastic" quality of the Characters in Pirandello's play, and you may see some resemblances between *Six Characters* and a cartoon: Daffy Duck or Wiley P. Coyote constantly get into situations that leave them humiliated or physically mangled, but because they are fiction and nothing can "really" happen to them, those situations are comic rather than tragic.

At the same time, you may notice some features of *Six Characters in Search of an Author* that bear an intertextual relationship with other, more conventional plays. Like Sophocles' *Oedipus the King* and Shakespeare's *Hamlet*, Pirandello's play presents characters who are concerned with finding out about an event or episode from the past. In all three plays, that event or episode from the past has an important bearing on the present and ultimate situations of central characters. The difference, of course, is that those earlier, more conventional plays resolve the concern with the past in some way: Oedipus learns it is he who is the cause of the curse on Thebes and he acts accordingly by blinding himself; Hamlet finally does carry out the vengeance sought by his father's ghost for his murder at the hands of Claudius. In *Six Characters in Search of an Author*, however, the conventional dramatic resolution is not provided; the Characters' concern with an episode from their past does not result in any definite action on their part or by the company of Actors they intrude upon.

Luigi Pirandello   1867–1936

Six Characters in Search of an Author   1922

An English Version By Edward Storer

Characters of the Comedy in the Making

The Father	Madame Pace
The Mother	The Boy ⎱ (These two do not speak)
The Stepdaughter	The Child ⎰
The Son	

Actors of the Company

The Manager	Other Actors and Actresses
Leading Lady	Property Man
Leading Man	Prompter
Second Lady Lead	Machinist
L'ingénue[1]	Manager's Secretary
Juvenile Lead	Doorkeeper
	Scene-shifters

Daytime: The Stage of a Theatre.

N.B. The Comedy is without acts or scenes. The performance is interrupted once, without the curtain being lowered, when the Manager and the chief characters withdraw to arrange the scenario. A second interruption of the action takes place when, by mistake, the stage hands let the curtain down.

Act 1

The spectators will find the curtain raised and the stage as it usually is during the daytime. It will be half dark, and empty, so that from the beginning the public may have the impression of an impromptu performance.

Prompter's box and a small table and chair for the Manager.

---

[1]L'ingénue—young girl actor.

Two other small tables and several chairs scattered about as during rehearsals. The Actors and Actresses of the company enter from the back of the stage: First one, then another, then two to-gether: nine or ten in all. They are about to rehearse a Pirandello play: Mixing It Up. *Some of the company move off towards their dressing rooms. The Prompter, who has the "book" under his arm, is waiting for the Manager in order to begin the rehearsal.*

The Actors and Actresses, some standing, some sitting, chat and smoke. One perhaps reads a paper; another cons his part.

Finally, the Manager enters and goes to the table prepared for him. His Secretary brings him his mail, through which he glances. The Prompter takes his seat, turns on a light, and opens the "book."

THE MANAGER: *(Throwing a letter down on the table)* I can't see. *(To Property Man)* Let's have a little light, please!

PROPERTY MAN: Yes sir, yes, at once. *(A light comes down on to the stage.)*

THE MANAGER: *(Clapping his hands)*   Come along! Come along! Second act of *Mixing It Up. (Sits down.)*

The Actors and Actresses go from the front of the stage to the wings, all except the three who are to begin the rehearsal.

PROMPTER: *(Reading the "book")*   "Leo Gala's house. A curious room serving as dining-room and study."

THE MANAGER: *(To Property Man)*   Fix up the old red room.   5

PROPERTY MAN: *(Noting it down)*   Red set. All right!

PROMPTER: *(Continuing to read from the "book")* "Table already laid and writing desk with books and papers. Bookshelves. Exit rear to Leo's bedroom. Exit left to kitchen. Principal exit to right."

THE MANAGER: *(Energetically)* Well, you understand: The principal exit over there; here, the kitchen. *(Turning to Actor who is to play the part of Socrates)* You make your entrances and exits here. *(To Property Man)* The baize doors at the rear, and curtains.

PROPERTY MAN: *(Noting it down)*   Right-o!

PROMPTER: *(Reading as before)* "When the curtain rises, Leo Gala, dressed in   10 cook's cap and apron is busy beating an egg in a cup. Philip, also dressed as a cook, is beating another egg. Guido Venanzi is seated and listening."

LEADING MAN: *(To Manager)*   Excuse me, but must I absolutely wear a cook's cap?

THE MANAGER: *(Annoyed)*   I imagine so. It says so there anyway. *(Pointing to the "book")*

LEADING MAN: But it's ridiculous!

THE MANAGER: Ridiculous? Ridiculous? Is it my fault if France won't send us any more good comedies, and we are reduced to putting on Pirandello's work where nobody understands anything, and where the author plays the fool with us all? *(The Actors grin. The Manager goes to Leading Man and shouts)* Yes sir, you put on the cook's cap and beat eggs. Do you suppose that with all this egg-beating business you are on an ordinary stage? Get that out of your head. You represent the shell of the eggs you are beating! *(Laughter and comments among the Actors)* Silence! and listen to my explanations, please! *(To Leading Man)* "The empty form of reason without the fullness of instinct, which is blind"—You stand for reason, your wife is instinct. It's a mixing up of the parts, according to which you who act your own part become the puppet of yourself. Do you understand?

LEADING MAN: I'm hanged if I do.   15

THE MANAGER: Neither do I. But let's get on with it. It's sure to be a glorious failure anyway. (*Confidentially*) But I say, please face three-quarters. Otherwise, what with the abstruseness of the dialogue, and the public that won't be able to hear you, the whole thing will go to hell. Come on! come on!

PROMPTER: Pardon sir, may I get into my box? There's a bit of a draught.

THE MANAGER: Yes, yes, of course!

At this point, the Doorkeeper has entered from the stage door and advances towards the Manager's table, taking off his braided cap. During this maneuver, The Six Characters enter, and stop by the door at back of stage, so that when the Doorkeeper is about to announce their coming to the Manager, they are already on the stage. A tenuous light surrounds them, almost as if irradiated by them—the faint breath of their fantastic reality.

This light will disappear when they come forward towards the actors. They preserve, however, something of the dream lightness in which they seem almost suspended but this does not detract from the essential reality of their forms and expressions.

He who is known as the Father is a man of about 50: hair, reddish in color, thin at the temples; he is not bald, however; thick moustaches, falling over his still fresh mouth, which often opens in a empty and uncertain smile. He is fattish, pale; with an especially wide forehead. He has blue, oval-shaped eyes, very clear and piercing. Wears light trousers and a dark jacket. He is alternatively mellifluous and violent in his manner.

The Mother seems crushed and terrified as if by an intolerable weight of shame and abasement. She is dressed in modest black and wears a thick widow's veil of crêpe. When she lifts this, she reveals a wax-like face. She always keeps her eyes downcast.

The Stepdaughter is dashing, almost impudent, beautiful. She wears mourning too, but with great elegance. She shows contempt for the timid half-frightened manner of the wretched Boy (14 years old, and also dressed in black); on the other hand, she displays a lively tenderness for her little sister, the Child (about four), who is dressed in white, with a black silk sash at the waist.

The Son (22) tall, severe in his attitude of contempt for the Father, supercilious and indifferent to the Mother. He looks as if he had come on the stage against his will.

DOORKEEPER: (*Cap in hand*)   Excuse me, sir....

THE MANAGER: (*Rudely*)   Eh? What is it?

DOORKEEPER: (*Timidly*)   These people are asking for you, sir.   20

THE MANAGER: (*Furious*)   I am rehearsing, and you know perfectly well no one's allowed to come in during rehearsals! (*Turning to the Characters*) Who are you, please? What do you want?

THE FATHER: (*Coming forward a little, followed by the others, who seem embarrassed*)   As a matter of fact . . . We have come here in search of an author....

THE MANAGER: (*Half angry, half amazed*)   An author? What author?

THE FATHER: Any author, sir.   25

THE MANAGER: But there's no author here. We are not rehearsing a new piece.

THE STEPDAUGHTER: (*Vivaciously*)   So much the better, so much the better! We can be your new piece.

AN ACTOR: (*Coming forward from the others*)   Oh, do you hear that?

THE FATHER: (*To Stepdaughter*)   Yes, but if the author isn't here . . . (*To Manager*) ... Unless you would be willing....

THE MANAGER: You are trying to be funny.

THE FATHER: No, for Heaven's sake, what are you saying? We bring you a drama, sir.   30

THE STEPDAUGHTER: We may be your fortune.

THE MANAGER: Will you oblige me by going away? We haven't time to waste with mad people.

THE FATHER: *(Mellifluously)*   Oh sir, you know well that life is full of infinite absurdities, which, strangely enough, do not even need to appear plausible, since
they are true.

THE MANAGER: What the devil is he talking about?   35

THE FATHER: I say that to reverse the ordinary process may well be considered a
madness: that is, to create credible situations, in order that they may appear
true. But permit me to observe that if this be madness, it is the sole *raison
d'être* of your profession, gentlemen. *(The Actors look hurt and perplexed.)*

THE MANAGER: *(Getting up and looking at him)*   So our profession seems to you
one worthy of madmen then?

THE FATHER: Well, to make seem true that which isn't true ...Without any need ...
for a joke as it were ...Isn't that your mission, gentlemen: to give life to fantastic characters on the stage?

THE MANAGER: *(Interpreting the rising anger of the Company)*   But I would beg you
to believe, my dear sir, that the profession of the comedian is a noble one. If today,
as things go, the playwrights give us stupid comedies to play and puppets to represent instead of men, remember we are proud to have given life to immortal
works here on these very boards! *(The Actors, satisfied, applaud their Manager.)*

THE FATHER: *(Interrupting furiously)*   Exactly, perfectly, to living beings more alive   40
than those who breathe and wear clothes: being less real perhaps, but truer! I
agree with you entirely. *(The Actors look at one another in amazement.)*

THE MANAGER: But what do you mean? Before, you said ...

THE FATHER: No, excuse me, I meant it for you, sir, who were crying out that you
had no time to lose with madmen, while no one better than yourself knows
that nature uses the instrument of human fantasy in order to pursue her high
creative purpose.

THE MANAGER: Very well—but where does all this take us?

THE FATHER: Nowhere! It is merely to show you that one is born to life in many
forms, in many shapes, as tree, or as stone, as water, as butterfly, or as woman. So
one may also be born a character in a play.

THE MANAGER: *(With feigned comic dismay)*   So you and these other friends of   45
yours have been born characters?

THE FATHER: Exactly, and alive as you see! *(Manager and Actors burst out laughing.)*

THE FATHER: *(Hurt)*   I am sorry you laugh, because we carry in us a drama, as you
can guess from this woman here, veiled in black.

THE MANAGER: *(Losing patience at last and almost indignant)*   Oh, chuck it! Get away
please! Clear out of here! *(To Property Man)* For Heaven's sake, turn them out!

THE FATHER: *(Resisting)*   No, no, look here, we....

THE MANAGER: *(Roaring)*   We come here to work, you know.   50

LEADING MAN: One cannot let oneself be made such a fool of.

THE FATHER: *(Determined, coming forward)*   I marvel at your incredulity, gentlemen. Are you not accustomed to see the characters created by an author spring
to life in yourselves and face each other? Just because there is no "book" *(Pointing to the Prompter's box)* which contains us, you refuse to believe....

THE STEPDAUGHTER: *(Advances towards Manager, smiling and coquettish)*   Believe me, we are really six most interesting characters, sir; side-tracked however.

THE FATHER: Yes, that is the word! *(To Manager all at once)* In the sense, that is,
that the author who created us alive no longer wished, or was no longer able,
materially to put us into a work of art. And this was a real crime, sir; because he
who has had the luck to be born a character can laugh even at death. He cannot
die. The man, the writer, the instrument of the creation will die, but his creation

does not die. And to live for ever, it does not need to have extraordinary gifts or to be able to work wonders. Who was Sancho Panza? Who was Don Abbondio? Yet they live eternally because—live germs as they were—they had the fortune to find a fecundating matrix, a fantasy which could raise and nourish them; make them live for ever!

THE MANAGER: That is quite all right. But what do you want here, all of you?   55
THE FATHER: We want to live.
THE MANAGER: *(Ironically)* For eternity?
THE FATHER: No, sir, only for a moment . . . In you.
AN ACTOR: Just listen to him!
LEADING LADY: They want to live, in us! . . .   60
JUVENILE LEAD: *(Pointing to the Stepdaughter)*   I've no objection, as far as that one is concerned!
THE FATHER: Look here! Look here! The comedy has to be made. *(To the Manager)* But if you and your actors are willing, we can soon concert it among ourselves.
THE MANAGER: *(Annoyed)*   But what do you want to concert? We don't go in for concerts here. Here we play dramas and comedies!
THE FATHER: Exactly! That is just why we have come to you.
THE MANAGER: And where is the "book"?   65
THE FATHER: It is in us! *(The Actors laugh)* The drama is in us, and we are the drama. We are impatient to play it. Our inner passion drives us on to this.
THE STEPDAUGHTER: *(Disdainful, alluring, treacherous, full of impudence)*   My passion, sir! Ah, if you only knew! My passion for him! *(Points to the Father and makes a pretense of embracing him. Then she breaks out into a loud laugh.)*
THE FATHER: *(Angrily)*   Behave yourself! And please don't laugh in that fashion.
THE STEPDAUGHTER: With your permission, gentlemen, I, who am a two months orphan, will show you how I can dance and sing. *(Sings and then dances Prenez garde à Tchou-Tchin-Tchou.)*

Les chinois sont un peuple malin.
De Shanghaî à Pékin.
Ils ont mis des écriteaux partout:
Prenez garde à Tchou-Tchin-Tchou.

ACTORS AND ACTRESSES: Bravo! Well done! Tip-top!   70
THE MANAGER: Silence! This isn't a café concert, you know! *(Turning to the Father in consternation)* Is she mad?
THE FATHER: Mad? No, she's worse than mad.
THE STEPDAUGHTER: *(To Manager)*   Worse? Worse? Listen! Stage this drama for us at once! Then you will see that at a certain moment I . . . when this little darling here . . . *(Takes the Child by the hand and leads her to the Manager)* Isn't she a dear? *(Takes her up and kisses her)* Darling! Darling! *(Puts her down again and adds feelingly)* Well, when God suddenly takes this dear little Child away from that poor mother there and this imbecile here *(seizing hold of the Boy roughly and pushing him forward)* does the stupidest things, like the fool he is, you will see me run away. Yes, gentlemen, I shall be off. But the moment hasn't arrived yet. After what has taken place between him and me *(indicates the Father with a horrible wink)* I can't remain any longer in this society, to have to witness the anguish of this mother here for that fool . . . *(Indicates the Son)* Look at him! Look at him! See how indifferent, how frigid he is, because he is the legitimate son. He despises me, despises him *(pointing to the Boy)*,

despises this baby here; because . . . we are bastards. *(Goes to the Mother and embraces her)* And he doesn't want to recognize her as his mother—she who is the common mother of us all. He looks down upon her as if she were only the mother of us three bastards. Wretch! *(She says all this very rapidly, excitedly. At the word "bastards" she raises her voice, and almost spits out the final "Wretch!")*

THE MOTHER: *(To the Manager, in anguish)*   On the name of these two little children. I beg you . . . *(She grows faint and is about to fall)* Oh God!

THE FATHER: *(Coming forward to support her as do some of the Actors)*   Quick, a   75
chair, a chair for this poor widow!

THE ACTORS: Is it true? Has she really fainted?

THE MANAGER: Quick. A chair! Here!

One of The Actors brings a chair, the others proffer assistance. The Mother tries to prevent The Father from lifting the veil which covers her face.

THE FATHER: Look at her! Look at her!

THE MOTHER: No, stop; stop it please!

THE FATHER: *(Raising her veil)*   Let them see you!   80

THE MOTHER: *(Rising and covering her face with her hands, in desperation)*   I beg you, sir, to prevent this man from carrying out his plan which is loathsome to me.

THE MANAGER: *(Dumbfounded)*   I don't understand at all.   What is the situation? Is this lady your wife? *(To the Father.)*

THE FATHER: Yes, gentlemen: my wife!

THE MANAGER: But how can she be a widow if you are alive? *(The Actors find relief for their astonishment in a loud laugh.)*

THE FATHER: Don't laugh! Don't laugh like that, for Heaven's sake. Her drama lies   85
just here in this: she has had a lover, a man who ought to be here.

THE MOTHER: *(With a cry)*   No! No!

THE STEPDAUGHTER: Fortunately for her, he is dead. Two months ago as I said. We are mourning, as you see.

THE FATHER: He isn't here you see, not because he is dead. He isn't here—look at her a moment and you will understand—because her drama isn't a drama of the love of two men for whom she was incapable of feeling anything except possibly a little gratitude—gratitude not for me but for the other. She isn't a woman, she is a mother, and her drama—powerful, sir, I assure you—lies, as a matter of fact, all in these four children she has had by two men.

THE MOTHER: I had them? Have you got the courage to say that I wanted them? *(To the Company)* It was his doing. It was he who gave me that other man, who forced me to go away with him.

THE STEPDAUGHTER: It isn't true.

THE MOTHER: *(Startled)*   Not true, isn't it?   90

THE STEPDAUGHTER: No, it isn't true, it just isn't true.

THE MOTHER: And what can you know about it?

THE STEPDAUGHTER: It isn't true. Don't believe it. *(To Manager)* Do you know why she says so? For that fellow there. *(Indicates the Son).* She tortures herself, destroys herself on account of the neglect of that son there; and she wants him to believe that if she abandoned him when he was only two years old, it was because he *(indicates the Father)* made her do so.

THE MOTHER: *(Vigorously)*   He forced me to it, and I call God to witness it. *(To the   95
Manager)* Ask him *(indicates the Father)* if it isn't true. Let him speak. You *(To Daughter)* are not in a position to know anything about it.

THE STEPDAUGHTER: I know you lived in peace and happiness with my father while he lived. Can you deny it?

THE MOTHER: No, I don't deny it . . .

THE STEPDAUGHTER: He was always full of affection and kindness for you. *(To the Boy, angrily)* It's true, isn't it? Tell them! Why don't you speak, you little fool?

THE MOTHER: Leave the poor boy alone. Why do you want to make me appear ungrateful, daughter? I don't want to offend your father. I have answered him that I didn't abandon my house and my son through any fault of mine, nor from any wilful passion.

THE FATHER: It is true. It was my doing.   100

LEADING MAN: *(To the Company)*   What a spectacle!

LEADING LADY: We are the audience this time.

JUVENILE LEAD: For once, in a way.

THE MANAGER: *(Beginning to get really interested)*   Let's hear them out. Listen!

THE SON: Oh yes, you're going to hear a fine bit now. He will talk to you of the   105
Demon of Experiment.

THE FATHER: You are a cynical imbecile. I've told you so already a hundred times. *(To the Manager)* He tries to make fun of me on account of this expression which I have found to excuse myself with.

THE SON: *(With disgust)*   Yes, phrases! phrases!

THE FATHER: Phrases! Isn't everyone consoled when faced with a trouble or fact he doesn't understand, by a word, some simple word, which tells us nothing and yet calms us?

THE STEPDAUGHTER: Even in the case of remorse. In fact, especially then.

THE FATHER: Remorse? No, that isn't true. I've done more than use words to quiet   110
the remorse in me.

THE STEPDAUGHTER: Yes, there was a bit of money too. Yes, yes, a bit of money. There were the hundred lire he was about to offer me in payment, gentlemen. . . . *(Sensation of horror among the Actors.)*

THE SON: *(To the Stepdaughter)*   This is vile.

THE STEPDAUGHTER: Vile? There they were in a pale blue envelope on a little mahogany table in the back of Madame Pace's shop. You know Madame Pace—one of those ladies who attract poor girls of good family into their ateliers,[2] under the pretext of their selling *robes et manteaux.*[3]

THE SON: And he thinks he has bought the right to tyrannize over us all with those hundred lire he was going to pay; but which, fortunately—note this, gentlemen—he had no chance of paying.

THE STEPDAUGHTER: It was a near thing, though, you know! *(Laughs ironically)*   115

THE MOTHER: *(Protesting)*   Shame, my daughter, shame!

THE STEPDAUGHTER: Shame indeed! This is my revenge! I am dying to live that scene. . . . The room . . . I see it . . . Here is the window with the mantles exposed, there the divan, the looking-glass, a screen, there in front of the window the little mahogany table with the blue envelope containing one hundred lire. I see it. I see it. I could take hold of it . . . But you, gentlemen, you ought to turn your backs now: I am almost nude, you know. But I don't blush: I leave that to him. *(Indicating Father.)*

THE MANAGER: I don't understand this at all.

---

[2]ateliers—studios, shops.
[3]*robes et manteaux*—dresses and shawls.

THE FATHER: Naturally enough. I would ask you, sir, to exercise your authority a little here, and let me speak before you believe all she is trying to blame me with. Let me explain.

THE STEPDAUGHTER: Ah yes, explain it in your own way.   120

THE FATHER: But don't you see that the whole trouble lies here. In words, words. Each one of us has within him a whole world of things, each man of us his own special world. And how can we ever come to an understanding if I put in the words I utter the sense and value of things as I see them; while you who listen to me must inevitably translate them according to the conception of things each one of you has within himself. We think we understand each other, but we never really do. Look there! This woman *(indicating the Mother)* takes all my pity for her as a specially ferocious form of cruelty.

THE MOTHER: But you drove me away.

THE FATHER: Do you hear her? I drove her away! She believes I really sent her away.

THE MOTHER: You know how to talk, and I don't; but, believe me sir *(To Manager)*, after he had married me ... who knows why? ... I was a poor insignificant woman....

THE FATHER: But, good Heaven! it was just for your humility that I married you. I   125 loved this simplicity in you. *(He stops when he sees she makes signs to contradict him, opens his arms wide in sign of desperation, seeing how hopeless it is to make himself understood)* You see she denies it. Her mental deafness, believe me, is phenomenal, the limit *(touches his forehead)*: deaf, deaf, mentally deaf! She had plenty of feeling. Oh yes, a good heart for the children; but the brain—deaf, to the point of desperation—!

THE STEPDAUGHTER: Yes, but ask him how his intelligence has helped us.

THE FATHER: If we could see all the evil that may spring from good, what should we do? *(At this point the Leading Lady who is biting her lips with rage at seeing the Leading Man flirting with the Stepdaughter, comes forward and says to the Manager.)*

LEADING LADY: Excuse me, but are we going to rehearse today?

THE MANAGER: Of course, of course; but let's hear them out.

JUVENILE LEAD: This is something quite new.   130

L'INGÉNUE: Most interesting!

LEADING LADY: Yes, for the people who like that kind of thing. *(Casts a glance at Leading Man.)*

THE MANAGER: *(To Father)*   You must please explain yourself quite clearly. *(Sits down.)*

THE FATHER: Very well then: listen! I had in my service a poor man, a clerk, a secretary of mine, full of devotion, who became friends with her. *(Indicating the Mother)* They understood one another, were kindred souls in fact, without, however, the least suspicion of any evil existing. They were incapable even of thinking of it.

THE STEPDAUGHTER: So he thought of it—for them!   135

THE FATHER: That's not true. I meant to do good to them—and to myself, I confess, at the same time. Things had come to the point that I could not say a word to either of them without their making a mute appeal, one to the other, with their eyes. I could see them silently asking each other how I was to be kept in countenance, how I was to be kept quiet. And this, believe me, was just about enough of itself to keep me in a constant rage, to exasperate me beyond measure.

THE MANAGER: And why didn't you send him away then—this secretary of yours?

THE FATHER: Precisely what I did, sir. And then I had to watch this poor woman drifting forlornly about the house like an animal without a master, like an animal one has taken in out of pity.

THE MOTHER: Ah yes! …

THE FATHER: *(Suddenly turning to the Mother)* It's true about the son anyway,   140
isn't it?

THE MOTHER: He took my son away from me first of all.

THE FATHER: But not from cruelty. I did so that he should grow up healthy and
strong by living in the country.

THE STEPDAUGHTER: *(Pointing to him ironically)* As one can see.

THE FATHER: *(Quickly)* Is it my fault if he has grown up like this? I sent him to a
wet nurse in the country, a peasant, as *she* did not seem to me strong enough,
though she is of humble origin. That was, anyway, the reason I married her. Unpleasant all this may be, but how can it be helped? My mistake possibly, but
there we are! All my life I have had these confounded aspirations towards a certain moral sanity. *(At this point the Stepdaughter bursts out into a noisy
laugh.)* Oh, stop it! Stop it! I can't stand it.

THE MANAGER: Yes, please stop it, for Heaven's sake.   145

THE STEPDAUGHTER: But imagine moral sanity from him, if you please—the client of
certain ateliers like that of Madame Pace!

THE FATHER: Fool! That is proof that I am a man! This seeming contradiction, gentlemen, is the strongest proof that I stand here a live man before you. Why, it is just
for this very incongruity in my nature that I have had to suffer what I have. I
could not live by the side of that woman *(indicating the Mother)* any longer, but
not so much for the boredom she inspired me with as for the pity I felt for her.

THE MOTHER: And so he turned me out—.

THE FATHER: —well provided for! Yes, I sent her to that man, gentlemen . . . to let her
go free of me.

THE MOTHER: And to free himself.   150

THE FATHER: Yes, I admit it. It was also a liberation for me. But great evil has come of
it. I meant well when I did it; and I did it more for her sake than mine. I swear it.
(Crosses his arms on his chest; then turns suddenly to the Mother) Did I ever
lose sight of you until that other man carried you off to another town, like the
angry fool he was? And on account of my pure interest in you . . . my pure interest, I repeat, that had no base motive in it . . . I watched with the tenderest concern the new family that grew up around her. She can bear witness to this.
(Points to the Stepdaughter)

THE STEPDAUGHTER: Oh yes, that's true enough. When I was a kiddie, so so high, you
know, with plaits over my shoulders and knickers longer than my skirts, I used
to see him waiting outside the school for me to come out. He came to see how
I was growing up.

THE FATHER: This is infamous, shameful!

THE STEPDAUGHTER: No. Why?

THE FATHER: Infamous! Infamous! *(Then excitedly to Manager, explaining)* After   155
she *(indicating Mother)* went away, my house seemed suddenly empty. She
was my incubus, but she filled my house. I was like a dazed fly alone in the
empty rooms. This boy here *(indicating the Son)* was educated away from
home, and when he came back, he seemed to me to be no more mine. With no
mother to stand between him and me, he grew up entirely for himself, on his
own, apart, with no tie of intellect or affection binding him to me. And then—
strange but true—I was driven, by curiosity at first and then by some tender
sentiment, towards her family, which had come into being through my will. The
thought of her began gradually to fill up the emptiness I felt all around me. I
wanted to know if she were happy in living out the simple daily duties of life. I

wanted to think of her as fortunate and happy because far away from the complicated torments of my spirit. And so, to have proof of this, I used to watch that child coming out of school.

THE STEPDAUGHTER: Yes, yes. True. He used to follow me in the street and smiled at me, waved his hand, like this. I would look at him with interest, wondering who he might be. I told my mother, who guessed at once. *(the Mother agrees with a nod)* Then she didn't want to send me to school for some days; and when I finally went back, there he was again—looking so ridiculous—with a paper parcel in his hands. He came close to me, caressed me, and drew out a fine straw hat from the parcel, with a bouquet of flowers—all for me!

THE MANAGER: A bit discursive this, you know!

THE SON: *(Contemptuously)* Literature! Literature!

THE FATHER: Literature indeed! This is life, this is passion!

THE MANAGER: It may be, but it won't act.   160

THE FATHER: I agree. This is only the part leading up. I don't suggest this should be staged. She *(pointing to the Stepdaughter)*, as you see, is no longer the flapper with plaits down her back—.

THE STEPDAUGHTER: —and the knickers showing below the skirt!

THE FATHER: The drama is coming now, sir; something new, complex, most interesting.

THE STEPDAUGHTER: As soon as my father died....

THE FATHER: —there was absolute misery for them. They came back here, unknown   165
to me. Through her stupidity! *(Pointing to the Mother)* It is true she can barely write her own name; but she could anyhow have got her daughter to write to me that they were in need....

THE MOTHER: And how was I to divine all this sentiment in him?

THE FATHER: That is exactly your mistake, never to have guessed any of my sentiments.

THE MOTHER: After so many years apart, and all that had happened....

THE FATHER: Was it my fault if that fellow carried you away? It happened quite suddenly; for after he had obtained some job or other, I could find no trace of them; and so, not unnaturally, my interest in them dwindled. But the drama culminated unforeseen and violent on their return, when I was impelled by my miserable flesh that still lives.... Ah! what misery, what wretchedness is that of the man who is alone and disdains debasing *liaisons!* Not old enough to do without women, and not young enough to go and look for one without shame. Misery? It's worse than misery; it's a horror; for no woman can any longer give him love; and when a man feels this ... One ought to do without, you say? Yes, yes, I know. Each of us when he appears before his fellows is clothed in a certain dignity. But every man knows what unconfessable things pass within the secrecy of his own heart. One gives way to the temptation, only to rise from it again, afterwards, with a great eagerness to reestablish one's dignity, as if it were a tombstone to place on the grave of one's shame, and a monument to hide and sign the memory of our weaknesses. Everybody's in the same case. Some folks haven't the courage to say certain things, that's all!

THE STEPDAUGHTER: All appear to have the courage to do them though.   170

THE FATHER: Yes, but in secret. Therefore, you want more courage to say these things. Let a man but speak these things out, and folks at once label him a cynic. But it isn't true. He is like all the others, better indeed, because he isn't afraid to reveal with the light of the intelligence the red shame of human bestiality on which most men close their eyes so as not to see it. Woman—for example, look at her case! She turns tantalizing inviting glances on you. You seize her. No sooner does she feel herself in your grasp than she closes her eyes. It is the sign of her mission, the sign by which she says to man: "Blind yourself, for I am blind."

THE STEPDAUGHTER: Sometimes she can close them no more: when she no longer feels the need of hiding her shame to herself, but dry-eyed and dispassionately, sees only that of the man who has blinded himself without love. Oh, all these intellectual complications make me sick, disgust me—all this philosophy that uncovers the beast in man, and then seeks to save him, excuse him . . . I can't stand it, sir. When a man seeks to "simplify" life bestially, throwing aside every relic of humanity, every chaste aspiration, every pure feeling, all sense of ideality, duty, modesty, shame . . . then nothing is more revolting and nauseous than a certain kind of remorse—crocodiles' tears, that's what it is.

THE MANAGER: Let's come to the point. This is only discussion.

THE FATHER: Very good, sir! But a fact is like a sack which won't stand up when it is empty. In order that it may stand up, one has to put into it the reason and sentiment which have caused it to exist. I couldn't possibly know that after the death of that man, they had decided to return here, that they were in misery, and that she *(pointing to the Mother)* had gone to work as a modiste,[4] and at a shop of the type of that of Madame Pace.

THE STEPDAUGHTER: A real high-class modiste, you must know, gentlemen. In appearance, she works for the leaders of the best society; but she arranges matters so that these elegant ladies serve her purpose . . . without prejudice to other ladies who are . . . well . . . only so so.   175

THE MOTHER: You will believe me, gentlemen, that it never entered my mind that the old hag offered me work because she had her eye on my daughter.

THE STEPDAUGHTER: Poor mamma! Do you know, sir, what that woman did when I brought her back the work my mother had finished? She would point out to me that I had torn one of my frocks, and she would give it back to my mother to mend. It was I who paid for it, always I; while this poor creature here believed she was sacrificing herself for me and these two children here, sitting up at night sewing Madame Pace's robes.

THE MANAGER: And one day you met there....

THE STEPDAUGHTER: Him, him. Yes, sir, an old client. There's a scene for you to play! Superb!

THE FATHER: She, the Mother arrived just then....   180

THE STEPDAUGHTER: *(Treacherously)*   Almost in time!

THE FATHER: *(Crying out)*   No, in time! in time! Fortunately I recognized her . . . In time. And I took them back home with me to my house. You can imagine now her position and mine; she, as you see her; and I who cannot look her in the face.

THE STEPDAUGHTER: Absurd! How can I possibly be expected—after that—to be a modest young miss, a fit person to go with his confounded aspirations for "a solid moral sanity"?

THE FATHER: For the drama lies all in this—in the conscience that I have, that each one of us has. We believe this conscience to be a single thing, but it is many-sided. There is one for this person, and another for that. Diverse consciences. So we have this illusion of being one person for all, of having a personality that is unique in all our acts. But it isn't true. We perceive this when, tragically perhaps, in something we do, we are, as it were, suspended, caught up in the air on a kind of hook. Then we perceive that all of us was not in that act, and that it would be an atrocious injustice to judge us by that action alone, as if all our existence were summed up in that one deed. Now do you understand the perfidy of this girl? She surprised me in a place where she ought not to have known

---

[4]modiste—someone who produces, designs, or deals in ladies' fashions.

me, just as I could not exist for her; and she now seeks to attach to me a reality such as I could never suppose I should have to assume for her in a shameful and fleeting moment of my life. I feel this above all else. And the drama, you will see, acquires a tremendous value from this point. Then there is the position of the others . . . his . . . *(Indicating the Son.)*

THE SON: *(Shrugging his shoulders scornfully)*   Leave me alone! I don't come   185
into this.

THE FATHER: What? You don't come into this?

THE SON: I've got nothing to do with it, and don't want to have; because you know well enough I wasn't made to be mixed up in all this with the rest of you.

THE STEPDAUGHTER: We are only vulgar folk! He is the fine gentleman. You may have noticed, Mr. Manager, that I fix him now and again with a look of scorn while he lowers his eyes—for he knows the evil he has done me.

THE SON: *(Scarcely looking at her)*   I?

THE STEPDAUGHTER: You! you! I owe my life on the streets to you. Did you or did you   190
not deny us, with your behavior. I won't say the intimacy of home, but even that mere hospitality which makes guests feel at their ease? We were intruders who had come to disturb the kingdom of your legitimacy. I should like to have you witness, Mr. Manager, certain scenes between him and me. He says I have tyrannized over everyone. But it was just his behavior which made me insist on the reason for which I had come into the house—this reason he calls "vile"—into his house, with my mother, who is his mother too. And I came as mistress of the house.

THE SON: It's easy for them to put me always in the wrong. But imagine, gentlemen, the position of a son, whose fate it is to see arrive one day at his home a young woman of impudent bearing, a young woman who inquires for his father, with whom who knows what business she has. This young man has then to witness her return bolder than ever, accompanied by that child there. He is obliged to watch her treat his father in an equivocal and confidential manner. She asks money of him in a way that lets one suppose he must give it her, *must*, do you understand, because he has every obligation to do so.

THE FATHER: But I have, as a matter of fact, this obligation. I owe it to your mother.

THE SON: How should I know? When had I ever seen or heard of her? One day there arrive with her *(indicating Stepdaughter)* that lad and this baby here. I am told: "This is *your* mother too, you know." I divine from her manner *(indicating Stepdaughter again)* why it is they have come home. I had rather not say what I feel and think about it. I shouldn't even care to confess to myself. No action can therefore be hoped for from me in this affair. Believe me, Mr. Manager, I am an "unrealized" character, dramatically speaking; and I find myself not at all at ease in their company. Leave me out of it. I beg you.

THE FATHER: What? It is just because you are so that . . .

THE SON: How do you know what I am like? When did you ever bother your head   195
about me?

THE FATHER: I admit it. I admit it. But isn't that a situation in itself? This aloofness of yours which is so cruel to me and to your mother, who returns home and sees you almost for the first time grown up, who doesn't recognize you but knows you are her son . . . *(Pointing out the Mother to the Manager)* See, she's crying!

THE STEPDAUGHTER: *(Angrily, stamping her foot)*   Like a fool!

THE FATHER: *(Indicating Stepdaughter)*   She can't stand him, you know. *(Then referring again to the Son)* He says he doesn't come into the affair, whereas he is really the hinge of the whole action. Look at that lad who is always clinging to his mother, frightened and humiliated. It is on account of this fellow here.

Possibly his situation is the most painful of all. He feels himself a stranger more than the others. The poor little chap feels mortified, humiliated at being brought into a home out of charity as it were. *(In confidence)*—He is the image of his father. Hardly talks at all. Humble and quiet.

THE MANAGER: Oh, we'll cut him out. You've no notion what a nuisance boys are on the stage ...

THE FATHER: He disappears soon, you know. And the baby too. She is the first to vanish from the scene. The drama consists finally in this: when that mother re-enters my house, her family born outside of it, and shall we say superimposed on the original, ends with the death of the little girl, the tragedy of the boy and flight of the elder daughter. It cannot go on, because it is foreign to its sur-roundings. So after much torment, we three remain: I, the mother, that son. Then, owing to the disappearance of that extraneous family, we too find our-selves strange to one another. We find we are living in an atmosphere of mor-tal desolation which is the revenge, as he *(indicating Son)* scornfully said of the Demon of Experiment, that unfortunately hides in me. Thus, sir, you see when faith is lacking, it becomes impossible to create certain states of happi-ness, for we lack the necessary humility. Vaingloriously, we try to substitute ourselves for this faith, creating thus for the rest of the world a reality which we believe after their fashion, while, actually, it doesn't exist. For each one of us has his own reality to be respected before God, even when it is harmful to one's very self.

THE MANAGER: There is something in what you say. I assure you all this interests me very much. I begin to think there's the stuff for a drama in all this, and not a bad drama either.

THE STEPDAUGHTER: *(Coming forward)*   When you've got a character like me.

THE FATHER: *(Shutting her up, all excited to learn the decision of the Manager)* You be quiet!

THE MANAGER: *(Reflecting, heedless of interruption)*   It's new ... hem ... yes ...

THE FATHER: Absolutely new!

THE MANAGER: You've got a nerve though, I must say, to come here and fling it at me like this ...

THE FATHER: You will understand, sir, born as we are for the stage ...

THE MANAGER: Are you amateur Actors then?

THE FATHER: No, I say born for the stage, because ...

THE MANAGER: Oh, nonsense. You're an old hand, you know.

THE FATHER: No sir, no. We act that rôle for which we have been cast, that rôle which we are given in life. And in my own case, passion itself, as usually hap-pens, becomes a trifle theatrical when it is exalted.

THE MANAGER: Well, well, that will do. But you see, without an author ... I could give you the address of an author if you like ...

THE FATHER: No, no. Look here! You must be the author.

THE MANAGER: I? What are you talking about?

THE FATHER: Yes, you, you! Why not?

THE MANAGER: Because I have never been an author: that's why.

THE FATHER: Then why not turn author now? Everybody does it. You don't want any special qualities. Your task is made much easier by the fact that we are all here alive before you ...

THE MANAGER: It won't do.

THE FATHER: What? When you see us live our drama ...

THE MANAGER: Yes, that's all right. But you want someone to write it.

THE FATHER: No, no. Someone to take it down, possibly, while we play it, scene by
    scene! It will be enough to sketch it out at first, and then try it over.
THE MANAGER: Well . . . I am almost tempted. It's a bit of an idea. One might have a
    shot at it.
THE FATHER: Of course. You'll see what scenes will come out of it. I can give you
    one, at once . . .
THE MANAGER: By Jove, it tempts me, I'd like to have a go at it. Let's try it out. Come
    with me to my office. *(Turning to the Actors)* You are at liberty for a bit, but
    don't step out of the theatre for long. In a quarter of an hour, twenty minutes, all
    back here again! *(To the Father)* We'll see what can be done. Who knows if we
    can't get something really extraordinary out of it?
THE FATHER: There's no doubt about it. They *(indicating the Characters)* had better   225
    come with us too, hadn't they?
THE MANAGER: Yes, yes. Come on! Come on! *(Moves away and then turning to the
    Actors)* Be punctual, please.

*Manager and the Six Characters cross the stage and go off. The other Actors remain, looking at
one another in astonishment.*

LEADING MAN: Is he serious? What the devil does he want to do?
JUVENILE LEAD: This is rank madness.
THIRD ACTOR: Does he expect to knock up a drama in five minutes?
JUVENILE LEAD: Like the improvisers!   230
LEADING LADY: If he thinks I'm going to take part in a joke like this . . .
JUVENILE LEAD: I'm out of it anyway.
FOURTH ACTOR: I should like to know who they are. *(Alludes to Characters.)*
THIRD ACTOR: What do you suppose? Madmen or rascals!
JUVENILE LEAD: And he takes them seriously!   235
L'INGÉNUE: Vanity! He fancies himself as an author now.
LEADING MAN: It's absolutely unheard of. If the stage has come to this . . . well I'm . . .
FIFTH ACTOR: It's rather a joke.
THIRD ACTOR: Well, we'll see what's going to happen next.

*Thus talking, the Actors leave the stage; some going out by the little door at the back; others re-
tiring to their dressing-rooms.*

The curtain remains up.

The action of the play is suspended for twenty minutes.

Act 1 Response Statement Questions

- Do you "believe" the Characters when they enter and begin to explain
  themselves? Are you able to willingly suspend your disbelief, or are you
  more aware of your disbelief as something that is hard to suspend? In any
  case, how is your response related to your experience with and expectations for characters in a play?
- As information from the Characters' past comes out in the dialogue, what
  sense do you make of it? Is it any harder or easier to make sense of than
  similar revelations about characters' pasts in other plays you have read?
- What is your response to the Father's speech about "Diverse consciences"
  in which he says "[W]e have this illusion of being one person for all, of
  having a personality that is unique in all our acts. But it isn't true"? Do

you agree? Disagree? In either case, how is your response affected by your ideology regarding personality?

Act 2

The stage call-bells ring to warn the company that the play is about to begin again.

THE STEPDAUGHTER: *(comes out of the Manager's office along with the Child and the Boy. As she comes out of the office, she cries)*   Nonsense! Nonsense! Do it yourselves! I'm not going to mix myself up in this mess. *(Turning to the Child and coming quickly with her on to the stage)* Come on, Rosetta, let's run!

The Boy follows them slowly, remaining a little behind and seeming perplexed.

THE STEPDAUGHTER: *(Stops, bends over the Child and takes the latter's face between her hands)*   My little darling! You're frightened, aren't you? You don't know where we are, do you? *(Pretending to reply to a question of the Child)* What is the stage? It's a place, baby, you know, where people play at being serious, a place where they act comedies. We've got to act a comedy now, dead serious, you know and you're in it also, little one. *(Embraces her, pressing the little head to her breast, and rocking the Child for a moment)* Oh darling, darling, what a horrid comedy you've got to play! What a wretched part they've found for you! A garden ... A fountain ... look ... just suppose, kiddie, it's here. Where, you say? Why, right here in the middle. It's all pretense you know. That's the trouble, my pet: it's all make-believe here. It's better to imagine it though, because if they fix it up for you, it'll only be painted cardboard, painted cardboard for the rockery, the water, the plants ... Ah, but I think a baby like this one would sooner have a make-believe fountain than a real one, so she could play with it. What a joke it'll be for the others! But for you, alas! Not quite such a joke: you who are real, baby dear, and really play by a real fountain that is big and green and beautiful, with ever so many bamboos around it that are reflected in the water, and a whole lot of little ducks swimming about ... No, Rosetta, no, your mother doesn't bother about you on account of that wretch of a son there. I'm in the devil of a temper, and as for that lad ... *(Seizes Boy by the arm to force him to take one of his hands out of his pockets)* What have you got there? What are you hiding? *(Pulls his hand out of his pocket. Looks into it and catches the glint of a revolver)* Ah, where did you get this?

The Boy, very pale in the face, looks at her, but does not answer.

Idiot! If I'd been in your place, instead of killing myself, I'd have shot one of those two, or both of them: father and son.

The Father enters from the office, all excited from his work. The Manager follows him.

THE FATHER: Come on, come on, dear! Come here for a minute! We've arranged everything. It's all fixed up.

THE MANAGER: *(Also excited)*   If you please, young lady, there are one or two points to settle still. Will you come along?

THE STEPDAUGHTER: *(Following him towards the office)*   Ouff! what's the good, if you've arranged everything.

The Father, Manager and Stepdaughter go back into the office again [off] for a moment. At the same time, the Son, followed by the Mother, comes out.

THE SON: *(Looking at the three entering office)*   Oh this is fine, fine! And to think I can't even get away!

The Mother attempts to look at him, but lowers her eyes immediately when he turns away from her. She then sits down. The Boy and the Child approach her. She casts a glance at the Son, and speaks with humble tones, trying to draw him into conversation.

THE MOTHER: And isn't my punishment the worst of all? *(Then seeing from the Son's manner that he will not bother himself about her)* My God! Why are you so cruel? Isn't it enough for one person to support all this torment? Must you then insist on others seeing it also?

THE SON: *(Half to himself, meaning the Mother to hear, however)*   And they want to put it on the stage! If there was at least a reason for it! He thinks he has got at the meaning of it all. Just as if each one of us in every circumstance of life couldn't find his own explanation of it! *(Pauses)* He complains he was discovered in a place where he ought not to have been seen, in a moment of his life which ought to have remained hidden and kept out of the reach of that convention which he has to maintain for other people. And what about my case? Haven't I had to reveal what no son ought ever to reveal: how father and mother live and are man and wife for themselves quite apart from that idea of father and mother which we give them? When this idea is revealed, our life is then linked at one point only to that man and that woman; and as such it should shame them, shouldn't it?

The Mother hides her face in her hands. From the dressing-rooms and the little door at the back of the stage the Actors and Stage Manager return, followed by the Property Man, and the Prompter. At the same moment, the Manager comes out of his office, accompanied by the Father and the Stepdaughter.

THE MANAGER: Come on, come on, ladies and gentlemen! Heh! You there, machinist!

MACHINIST: Yes sir?   10

THE MANAGER: Fix up the white parlor with the floral decorations. Two wings and a drop with a door will do. Hurry up!

The Machinist runs off at once to prepare the scene, and arranges it while the Manager talks with the Stage Manager, the Property Man, and the Prompter on matters of detail.

THE MANAGER: *(To Property Man)*   Just have a look, and see if there isn't a sofa or divan in the wardrobe ...

PROPERTY MAN: There's the green one.

THE STEPDAUGHTER: No, no! Green won't do. It was yellow, ornamented with flowers—very large! And most comfortable!

PROPERTY MAN: There isn't one like that.   15

THE MANAGER: It doesn't matter. Use the one we've got.

THE STEPDAUGHTER: Doesn't matter? It's most important!

THE MANAGER: We're only trying it now. Please don't interfere. *(To Property Man)* See if we've got a shop window—long and narrowish.

THE STEPDAUGHTER: And the little table! The little mahogany table for the pale blue envelope!

PROPERTY MAN: *(To Manager)*   There's that little gilt one.   20

THE MANAGER: That'll do fine.

THE FATHER: A mirror.

THE STEPDAUGHTER: And the screen! We must have a screen. Otherwise how can I manage?

PROPERTY MAN: That's all right, Miss. We've got any amount of them.

THE MANAGER: *(To the Stepdaughter)*   We want some clothes pegs too, don't we?   25

THE STEPDAUGHTER: Yes, several, several!

THE MANAGER: See how many we've got and bring them all.

PROPERTY MAN: All right!

The Property Man hurries off to obey his orders. While he is putting the things in their places, the Manager talks to the Prompter and then with the Characters and the Actors.

THE MANAGER: *(To Prompter)* Take your seat. Look here: this is the outline of the scenes, act by act. *(Hands him some sheets of paper)* And now I'm going to ask you to do something out of the ordinary.

PROMPTER: Take it down in shorthand?

THE MANAGER: *(Pleasantly surprised)* Exactly! Can you do shorthand? ₃₀

PROMPTER: Yes, a little.

THE MANAGER: Good! *(Turning to a stage hand)* Go and get some paper from my office, plenty, as much as you can find.

The Stage Hand goes off, and soon returns with a handful of paper which he gives to the Prompter.

THE MANAGER: *(To Prompter)* You follow the scenes as we play them, and try and get the points down, at any rate the most important ones. *(Then addressing the Actors)* Clear the stage, ladies and gentlemen! Come over here *(Pointing to the Left)* and listen attentively.

LEADING LADY: But, excuse me, we ...

THE MANAGER: *(Guessing her thought)* Don't worry! You won't have to improvise. ₃₅

LEADING MAN: What have we to do then?

THE MANAGER: Nothing. For the moment you just watch and listen. Everybody will get his part written out afterwards. At present we're going to try the thing as best we can. They're going to act now.

THE FATHER: *(As if fallen from the clouds into the confusion of the state)* We? What do you mean, if you please, by a rehearsal?

THE MANAGER: A rehearsal for them. *(Points to the Actors.)* ₄₀

THE FATHER: But since we are the characters ...

THE MANAGER: All right: "characters" then, if you insist on calling yourselves such. But here, my dear sir, the characters don't act. Here the Actors do the acting. The characters are there, in the "book" — *(Pointing towards Prompter's box)* when there is a "book"!

THE FATHER: I won't contradict you; but excuse me, the actors aren't the characters. They want to be, they pretend to be, don't they? Now if these gentlemen here are fortunate enough to have us alive before them ...

THE MANAGER: Oh this is grand! You want to come before the public yourselves then?

THE FATHER: As we are ...

THE MANAGER: I can assure you it would be a magnificent spectacle! ₄₅

LEADING MAN: What's the use of us here anyway then?

THE MANAGER: You're not going to pretend that you can act? It makes me laugh! *(The Actors laugh)* There, you see, they are laughing at the notion. But, by the way, I must cast the parts. That won't be difficult. They cast themselves. *(To the Second Lady Lead)* You play the mother. *(To the Father)* We must find her a name.

THE FATHER: Amalia, sir.

THE MANAGER: But that is the real name of your wife. We don't want to call her by ₅₀ her real name.

THE FATHER: Why ever not, if it is her name? ... Still, perhaps, if that lady must ... *(Makes a slight motion of the hand to indicate the Second Lady Lead)* I see this woman here *(means the Mother)* as Amalia. But do as you like. *(Gets more and more confused)* I don't know what to say to you. Already, I begin to hear my own words ring false, as if they had another sound ...

THE MANAGER: Don't you worry about it. It'll be our job to find the right tones. And as for her name, if you want her Amalia, Amalia it shall be; and if you don't like it, we'll find another! For the moment though, we'll call the characters in this way: *(to Juvenile Lead)* You are the Son; *(to the Leading Lady)* You naturally are the Stepdaughter ...

THE STEPDAUGHTER: *(Excitedly)* What? What? I, that woman there? *(Bursts out laughing.)*

THE MANAGER: *(Angry)* What is there to laugh at?

LEADING LADY: *(Indignant)*   Nobody has ever dared to laugh at me. I insist on   55
being treated with respect; otherwise I go away.

THE STEPDAUGHTER: No, no, excuse me ... I am not laughing at you ...

THE MANAGER: *(To Stepdaughter)*   You ought to feel honored to be played by ...

LEADING LADY: *(At once, contemptuously)*   "That woman there" ...

THE STEPDAUGHTER: But I wasn't speaking of you, you know. I was speaking of my-self—whom I can't see at all in you! That is all. I don't know ... but ... you ... aren't in the least like me ...

THE FATHER: True. Here's the point. Look here, sir, our temperaments, our souls ...   60

THE MANAGER: Temperament, soul, be hanged. Do you suppose the spirit of the piece is in you? Nothing of the kind!

THE FATHER: What, haven't we our own temperaments, our own souls?

THE MANAGER: Not at all. Your soul or whatever you like to call it takes shape here. The actors give body and form to it, voice and gesture. And my actors—I may tell you—have given expression to much more lofty material than this little drama of yours, which may or may not hold up on the stage. But if it does, the merit of it, believe me, will be due to my actors.

THE FATHER: I don't dare contradict you, sir; but, believe me, it is a terrible suffering for us who are as we are, with these bodies of ours, these features to see ...

THE MANAGER: *(Cutting him short and out of patience)*   Good heavens! The   65
make-up will remedy all that, man, the make-up ...

THE FATHER: Maybe. But the voice, the gestures ...

THE MANAGER: Now, look here! On the stage, you as yourself, cannot exist. The actor here acts you, and that's an end to it!

THE FATHER: I understand. And now I think I see why our author who conceived us as we are, all alive, didn't want to put us on the stage after all. I haven't the least desire to offend your actors. Far from it! But when I think that I am to be acted by ... I don't know by whom ...

LEADING MAN: *(On his dignity)*   By me, if you've no objection!

THE FATHER: *(Humbly; mellifluously)*   Honored, I assure you, sir. *(Bows)* Still, I   70
must say that try as this gentleman may, with all his good will and wonderful art, to absorb me into himself ...

LEADING MAN: Oh chuck it! "Wonderful art!" Withdraw that, please!

THE FATHER: The performance he will give, even doing his best with make-up to look like me ...

LEADING MAN: It will certainly be a bit difficult! *(The Actors laugh.)*

THE FATHER: Exactly! It will be difficult to act me as I really am. The effect will be rather—apart from the make-up—according as to how he supposes I am, as he senses me—if he does sense me—and not as I inside of myself feel myself to be. It seems to me then that account should be taken of this by everyone whose duty it may become to criticize us ...

THE MANAGER: Heavens! The man's starting to think about the critics now! Let them   75
say what they like. It's up to us to put on the play if we can. *(Looking around)* Come on! come on! Is the stage set? *(To the Actors and Characters)* Stand back—stand back! Let me see, and don't let's lose any more time! *(To the Step-daughter)* Is it all right as it is now?

THE STEPDAUGHTER: Well, to tell the truth, I don't recognize the scene.

THE MANAGER: My dear lady, you can't possibly suppose that we can construct that shop of Madame Pace piece by piece here? *(To the Father)* You said a white room with flowered wall paper, didn't you?

THE FATHER: Yes.

THE MANAGER: Well then. We've got the furniture right, more or less. Bring that little table a bit further forward. *(The Stage Hands obey the order. To Property Man)* You go and find an envelope, if possible, a pale blue one; and give it to that gentleman. *(Indicates Father.)*

PROPERTY MAN: An ordinary envelope?

MANAGER AND FATHER: Yes, yes, an ordinary envelope.

PROPERTY MAN: At once, sir. *(Exit.)*

THE MANAGER: Ready, everyone! First scene—the Young Lady. *(The Leading Lady comes forward)* No, no, you must wait. I meant her. *(Indicating the Stepdaughter)* You just watch—

THE STEPDAUGHTER: *(Adding at once)* How I shall play it, how I shall live it! . . .

LEADING LADY: *(Offended)* I shall live it also, you may be sure, as soon as I begin!

THE MANAGER: *(With his hands to his head)* Ladies and gentlemen, if you please! No more useless discussions! Scene I: the young lady with Madame Pace: Oh! *(Looks around as if lost)* And this Madame Pace, where is she?

THE FATHER: She isn't with us, sir.

THE MANAGER: Then what the devil's to be done?

THE FATHER: But she is alive too.

THE MANAGER: Yes, but where is she?

THE FATHER: One minute. Let me speak! *(Turning to the Actresses)* If these ladies could be so good as to give me their hats for a moment . . .

THE ACTRESSES: *(Half surprised, half laughing, in chorus)* What? Why? Our hats?
What does he say?

THE MANAGER: What are you going to do with the ladies' hats? *(The Actors laugh.)*

THE FATHER: Oh nothing. I just want to put them on these pegs for a moment. And one of the ladies will be so kind as to take off her mantle . . .

THE ACTORS: Oh, what d'you think of that? Only the mantle? He must be mad.

SOME ACTRESSES: But why?
Mantles as well?

THE FATHER: To hang them up there for a moment. Please be so kind, will you?

THE ACTRESSES: *(Taking off their hats, one or two also their cloaks, and going to hang them on the racks)* After all, why not?
There you are!
This is really funny.
We've got to put them on show.

THE FATHER: Exactly; just like that, on show.

THE MANAGER: May we know why?

THE FATHER: I'll tell you. Who knows if, by arranging the stage for her, she does not come here herself, attracted by the very articles of her trade? *(Inviting the Actors to look towards the exit at back of stage)* Look! Look!

The door at the back of stage opens and Madame Pace enters and takes a few steps forward. She is a fat, oldish woman with puffy oxygenated hair. She is rouged and powdered, dressed with a comical elegance in black silk. Round her waist is a long silver chain from which hangs a pair of scissors. The Stepdaughter runs over to her at once amid the stupor of the Actors.

THE STEPDAUGHTER: *(Turning towards her)* There she is! There she is!

THE FATHER: *(Radiant)* It's she! I said so, didn't I? There she is!

THE MANAGER: *(Conquering his surprise, and then becoming indignant)* What sort of a trick is this?

LEADING MAN: *(Almost at the same time)* What's going to happen next?

JUVENILE LEAD: Where does *she* come from?

L'INGÉNUE: They've been holding her in reserve, I guess.

LEADING LADY: A vulgar trick!

THE FATHER: *(Dominating the protests)* Excuse me, all of you! Why are you so anxious to destroy in the name of a vulgar, commonplace sense of truth, this reality which comes to birth attracted and formed by the magic of the stage itself, which has indeed more right to live here than you, since it is much truer than you—if you don't mind my saying so? Which is the actress among you who is to play Madame Pace? Well, here is Madame Pace herself. And you will allow, I fancy, that the actress who acts her will be less true than this woman here, who is herself in person. You see my daughter recognized her and went over to her at once. Now you're going to witness the scene!

But the scene between the Stepdaughter and Madame Pace has already begun despite the protest of the Actors and the reply of the Father. It has begun quietly, naturally, in a manner impossible for the stage. So when the Actors, called to attention by the Father, turn round and see Madame Pace, who has placed on hand under the Stepdaughter's chin to raise her head, they observe her at first with great attention, but hearing her speak in an unintelligible manner their interest begins to wane.

THE MANAGER: Well? well?

LEADING MAN: What does she say?

LEADING LADY: One can't hear a word.

JUVENILE LEAD: Louder! Louder please!

THE STEPDAUGHTER: *(Leaving Madame Pace, who smiles a Sphinxlike smile, and advancing towards the Actors)* Louder? Louder? What are you talking about? These aren't matters which can be shouted at the top of one's voice. If I have spoken them out loud, it was to shame him and have my revenge. *(Indicates Father)* But for Madame it's quite a different matter.

THE MANAGER: Indeed? Indeed? But here, you know, people have got to make themselves heard, my dear. Even we who are on the stage can't hear you. What will it be when the public's in the theater? And anyway, you can very well speak up now among yourselves, since we shan't be present to listen to you as we are now. You've got to pretend to be alone in a room at the back of a shop where no one can hear you.

The Stepdaughter coquettishly and with a touch of malice makes a sign of disagreement two or three times with her finger.

THE MANAGER: What do you mean by no?

THE STEPDAUGHTER: *(Sotto voce,[5] mysteriously)* There's someone who will hear us if she *(indicating Madame Pace)* speaks out loud.

THE MANAGER: *(In consternation)* What? Have you got someone else to spring on us now? *(The Actors burst out laughing.)*

THE FATHER: No, no sir. She is alluding to me. I've got to be here—there behind that door, in waiting; and Madame Pace knows it. In fact, if you will allow me, I'll go there at once, so I can be quite ready. *(Moves away.)*

---

[5]soto voce—quietly, so no one else can hear.

THE MANAGER: *(Stopping him)* No! wait! wait! We must observe the conventions of the theater. Before you are ready . . .

THE STEPDAUGHTER: *(Interrupting him)* No, get on with it at once! I'm just dying, I 120
tell you, to act this scene. If he's ready, I'm more than ready.

THE MANAGER: *(Shouting)* But, my dear young lady, first of all, we must have the scene between you and this lady . . . *(Indicates Madame Pace)* Do you understand? . . .

THE STEPDAUGHTER: Good Heavens! She's been telling me what you know already: that Mamma's work is badly done again, that the material's ruined; and that if I want her to continue to help us in our misery I must be patient . . .

MADAME PACE: *(Coming forward with an air of great importance)* Yes indeed, sir. I no wanta take advantage of her. I no wanta be hard . . .

Note: Madam Pace is supposed to talk in a jargon half Italian, half English.

THE MANAGER: *(Alarmed)* What? What? she talks like that? *(The Actors burst out laughing again.)*

THE STEPDAUGHTER: *(Also laughing)* Yes, yes, that's the way she talks, half English, 125
half Italian! Most comical it is!

MADAME PACE: Itta seem not verra polite gentlemen laugha atta me eef I trya best speaka English.

THE MANAGER: *Diamine!*[6] Of course! Of course! Let her talk like that! Just what we want. Talk just like that, Madame, if you please! The effect will be certain. Exactly what was wanted to put a little comic relief into the crudity of the situation. Of course she talks like that! Magnificent!

THE STEPDAUGHTER: Magnificent? Certainly! When certain suggestions are made to one in a language of that kind, the effect is certain, since it seems almost a joke. One feels inclined to laugh when one hears her talk about an "old signore"[7] "who wanta talka nicely with you." Nice old signore, eh, Madame?

MADAME PACE: Not so old, my dear, not so old! And even if you no lika him, he won't make any scandal!

THE MOTHER: *(Jumping up amid the amazement and consternation of the Actors* 130
who had not been noticing her. They move to restrain her) You old devil! You murderess!

THE STEPDAUGHTER: *(Running over to calm her Mother)* Calm yourself, mother, calm yourself! Please don't . . .

THE FATHER: *(Going to her also at the same time)* Calm yourself! Don't get excited! Sit down now!

THE MOTHER: Well then, take that woman away out of my sight!

THE STEPDAUGHTER: *(To Manager)* It is impossible for my mother to remain here.

THE FATHER: *(To Manager)* They can't be here together. And for this reason, 135
you see: that woman there was not with us when we came . . . If they are on together, the whole thing is given away inevitably, as you see.

THE MANAGER: It doesn't matter. This is only a rough sketch—just to get an idea of the various points of the scene, even confusedly . . . *(Turning to the Mother and leading her to her chair)* Come along, my dear lady, sit down now, and let's get on with the scene . . .

Meanwhile, the Stepdaughter, coming forward again, turns to Madame Pace.

THE STEPDAUGHTER: Come on, Madame, come on!

---

[6]*Diamine*—marvelous.
[7]*signore*—gentleman.

MADAME PACE: *(Offended)*   No, no, *grazie.*[8] I do not do anything witha your mother present.

THE STEPDAUGHTER: Nonsense! Introduce this "old signore" who wants to talk nicely to me. *(Addressing the Company imperiously)* We've got to do this scene one way or another, haven't we? Come on! *(To Madame Pace)* You can go!

MADAME PACE: Ah yes! I go 'way! I go 'way! Certainly! *(Exits furious.)*   140

THE STEPDAUGHTER: *(To the Father)*   Now you make your entry. No, you needn't go over there. Come here. Let's suppose you've already come in. Like that, yes! I'm here with bowed head, modest-like. Come on! Out with your voice! Say "Good morning, Miss" in that peculiar tone, that special tone . . .

THE MANAGER: Excuse me, but are you the Manager, or am I? *(To the Father who looks undecided and perplexed)* Get on with it, man! Go down there to the back of the stage. You needn't go off. Then come right forward here.

The Father does as he is told, looking troubled and perplexed at first. But as soon as he begins to move, the reality of the action affects him, and he begins to smile and to be more natural. The Actors watch intently.

THE MANAGER: *(Sotto voce, quickly to the Prompter in his box)*   Ready! Ready? Get ready to write now.

THE FATHER: *(Coming forward and speaking in a different tone)*   Good afternoon, Miss!

THE STEPDAUGHTER: *(Head bowed down slightly, with restrained disgust)*   Good   145
afternoon!

THE FATHER: *(Looks under her hat which partly covers her face. Perceiving she is very young, he makes an exclamation, partly of surprise, partly of fear lest he compromise himself in a risky adventure)* Ah . . . but . . . ah . . . I say . . . this is not the first time you have come here, is it?

THE STEPDAUGHTER: *(Modestly)*   No sir.

THE FATHER: You've been here before, eh? *(Then seeing her nod agreement)* More than once? *(Waits for her to answer, looks under her hat, smiles, and then says)* Well then, there's no need to be so shy, is there? May I take off your hat?

THE STEPDAUGHTER: *(Anticipating him and with veiled disgust)*   No sir . . . I'll do it myself. *(Takes it off quickly.)*

The Mother, who watches the progress of the scene with the son and the other two Children who cling to her, is on thorns; and follows with varying expressions of sorrow, indignation, anxiety, and horror the words and actions of the other two. From time to time she hides her face in her hands and sobs.

THE MOTHER: Oh, my God, my God!   150

THE FATHER: *(Playing his part with a touch of gallantry)*   Give it to me! I'll put it down. *(Takes hat from her hands)* But a dear little head like yours ought to have a smarter hat. Come and help me choose one from the stock, won't you?

L'INGÉNUE: *(Interrupting)*   I say . . . Those are our hats, you know.

THE MANAGER: *(Furious)*   Silence! silence! Don't try and be funny, if you please . . . We're playing the scene now, I'd have you notice. *(To the Stepdaughter)* Begin again, please!

THE STEPDAUGHTER: *(Continuing)*   No thank you, sir.

THE FATHER: Oh, come now. Don't talk like that. You must take it. I shall be upset if   155
you don't. There are some lovely little hats here; and then—Madame will be pleased. She expects it, anyway, you know.

THE STEPDAUGHTER: No, no! I couldn't wear it!

---

[8]grazie—thank you.

THE FATHER: Oh, you're thinking about what they'd say at home if they saw you come in with a new hat? My dear girl, there's always a way round these little matters, you know.

THE STEPDAUGHTER: *(All keyed up)*   No, it's not that. I couldn't wear it because I am ... as you see ... you might have noticed ... *(Showing her black dress.)*

THE FATHER: ... in mourning! Of course: I beg your pardon; I'm frightfully sorry ...

THE STEPDAUGHTER: *(Forcing herself to conquer her indignation and nausea)*   160
Stop! Stop! It's I who must thank you. There's no need for you to feel mortified or specially sorry. Don't think any more of what I've said. *(Tries to smile)* I must forget that I'm dressed so ...

THE MANAGER: *(Interrupting and turning to the Prompter)* Stop a minute! Stop! Don't write that down. Cut out that last bit. *(Then to the Father and Stepdaughter)* Fine! It's going fine! *(To the Father only)* And now you can go on as we arranged. *(To the Actors)* Pretty good that scene, where he offers her the hat, eh?

THE STEPDAUGHTER: The best's coming now. Why can't we go on?

THE MANAGER: Have a little patience! *(To the Actors)*   Of course, it must be treated rather lightly.

LEADING MAN: Still, with a bit of go in it!

LEADING LADY: Of course! It's easy enough! *(To Leading Man)* Shall you and I try it now?   165

LEADING MAN: Why, yes! I'll prepare my entrance. *(Exit in order to make his entrance.)*

THE MANAGER: *(To Leading Lady)* See here! The scene between you and Madame Pace is finished. I'll have it written out properly after. You remain here ... Oh, where are you going?

LEADING LADY: One minute. I want to put my hat on again. *(Goes over to hat rack and puts her hat on her head.)*

THE MANAGER: Good! You stay here with your head bowed down a bit.

THE STEPDAUGHTER: But she isn't dressed in black.

LEADING LADY: But I shall be, and much more effectively than you.   170

THE MANAGER: *(To Stepdaughter)*   Be quiet please, and watch! You'll be able to learn something. *(Clapping his hands)* Come on! Come on! Entrance, please!

The door at rear of stage opens, and the Leading Man enters with the lively manner of an old gallant. The rendering of the scene by the Actors from the very first words is seen to be quite a different thing, though it has not in any way the air of a parody. Naturally, the Stepdaughter and the Father, not being able to recognize themselves in the Leading Lady and the Leading Man, who deliver their words in different tones and with a different psychology, express, sometimes with smiles, sometimes with gestures, the impression they receive.

LEADING MAN: Good afternoon, Miss ...

THE FATHER: *(At once unable to contain himself)*   No! no!
The Stepdaughter, noticing the way the Leading Man enters, bursts out laughing.

THE MANAGER: *(Furious)*   Silence! And you, please, just stop that laughing. If we go   175
on like this, we shall never finish.

THE STEPDAUGHTER: Forgive me, sir, but it's natural enough. This lady *(indicating Leading Lady)* stands there still; but if she is supposed to be me, I can assure you that if I heard anyone say "Good afternoon" in that manner and in that tone, I should burst out laughing as I did.

THE FATHER: Yes, yes, the manner, the tone ...

THE MANAGER: Nonsense! Rubbish! Stand aside and let me see the action.

LEADING MAN: If I've got to represent an old fellow who's coming into a house of an equivocal character ...

THE MANAGER: Don't listen to them, for Heaven's sake! Do it again! It goes fine.   180
(Waiting for the Actors to begin again) Well?

LEADING MAN: Good afternoon, Miss.

LEADING LADY: Good afternoon.

LEADING MAN: *(Imitating the gesture of the Father when he looked under the hat, and then expressing quite clearly first satisfaction and then fear)*   Ah, but ... I say ... This is not the first time that you have come here, is it?

THE MANAGER: Good, but not quite so heavily. Like this. *(Acts himself)* "This isn't the first time that you have come here" ... *(To Leading Lady)* And you say: "No, sir."

LEADING LADY: No, sir.   185

LEADING MAN: You've been here before, more than once.

THE MANAGER: No, no, stop! Let her nod "yes" first. "You've been here before, eh?"

The Leading Lady lifts up her head slightly and closes her eyes as though in disgust. Then she inclines her head twice.

THE STEPDAUGHTER: *(Unable to contain herself)*   Oh my God! *(Puts a hand to her mouth to prevent herself from laughing.)*

THE MANAGER: *(Turning round)*   What's the matter?   190

THE STEPDAUGHTER: Nothing, nothing!

THE MANAGER: *(To Leading Man)* Go on!

LEADING MAN: You've been here before, eh? Well, then, there's no need to be so shy, is there? May I take off your hat?

The Leading Man says this last speech in such a tone and with such gestures that the Stepdaughter, though she has her hand to her mouth, cannot keep from laughing.

LEADING LADY: *(Indignant)*   I'm not going to stop here to be made a fool of by that woman there.

LEADING MAN: Neither am I! I'm through with it!

THE MANAGER: *(Shouting to Stepdaughter)*   Silence! for once and all, I tell you!   195

STEPDAUGHTER: Forgive me! forgive me!

THE MANAGER: You haven't any manners; that's what it is! You go too far.

THE FATHER: *(Endeavoring to intervene)*   Yes, it's true, but excuse her ...

THE MANAGER: Excuse what? It's absolutely disgusting.

THE FATHER: Yes, sir, but believe me, it has such a strange effect when ...   200

THE MANAGER: Strange? Why strange? Where is it strange?

THE FATHER: No, sir; I admire your actors—this gentleman here, this lady; but they are certainly not us!

THE MANAGER: I should hope not.   Evidently they cannot be you, if they are actors.

THE FATHER: Just so: actors! Both of them act our parts exceedingly well. But, believe me, it produces quite a different effect on us. They want to be us, but they aren't, all the same.

THE MANAGER: What is it then anyway?   205

THE FATHER: Something that is ... that is theirs—and no longer ours ...

THE MANAGER: But naturally, inevitably. I've told you so already.

THE FATHER: Yes, I understand ... I understand ...

THE MANAGER: Well then, let's have no more of it! *(Turning to the Actors)* We'll have the rehearsals by ourselves, afterwards, in the ordinary way. I never could stand rehearsing with the author present. He's never satisfied! *(Turning to Father and Stepdaughter)* Come on! Let's get on with it again; and try and see if you can't keep from laughing.

THE STEPDAUGHTER: Oh. I shan't laugh any more. There's a nice little bit coming from   210
me now; you'll see.

THE MANAGER: Well then: when she says "Don't think anymore of what I've said. I must forget, etc.," you *(addressing the Father)* come in sharp with "I understand, I understand"; and then you ask her ...

THE STEPDAUGHTER: *(Interrupting)* What?

THE MANAGER: Why she is in mourning.

THE STEPDAUGHTER: Not at all! See here: when I told him that it was useless for me to be thinking about my wearing mourning, do you know how he answered me? "Ah well," he said, "then let's take off this little frock."

THE MANAGER: Great! Just what we want, to make a riot in the theater! 215

THE STEPDAUGHTER: But it's the truth!

THE MANAGER: What does that matter? Acting is our business here. Truth up to a certain point, but no further.

THE STEPDAUGHTER: What do you want to do then?

THE MANAGER: You'll see, you'll see! Leave it to me.

THE STEPDAUGHTER: No sir! What you want to do is piece together a little romantic 220 sentimental scene out of my disgust, out of all the reasons, each more cruel and viler than the other, why I am what I am. He is to ask my why I'm in mourning; and I'm to answer with tears in my eyes, that it is just two months since papa died. No sir, no! He's got to say to me; as he did say: "well, let's take off this little dress at once." And I; with my two months' mourning in my heart, went there behind that screen, and with these fingers tingling with shame . . .

THE MANAGER: *(Running his hands through his hair)* For Heaven's sake! What are you saying?

THE STEPDAUGHTER: *(Crying out excitedly)* The truth! The truth!

THE MANAGER: It may be. I don't deny it, and I can understand all your horror; but you must surely see that you can't have this kind of thing on the stage. It won't go.

THE STEPDAUGHTER: Not possible, eh? Very well! I'm much obliged to you—but I'm off!

THE MANAGER: Now be reasonable! Don't lose your temper! 225

THE STEPDAUGHTER: I won't stop here? I won't! I can see you've fixed it all up with him in your office. All this talk about what is possible for the stage . . . I understand! He wants to get at his complicated "cerebral drama," to have his famous remorses and torments acted; but I want to act my part, *my part!*

THE MANAGER: *(Annoyed, shaking his shoulders)* Ah! Just *your* part! But, if you will pardon me, there are other parts than yours: his *(indicating the Father)* and hers! *(Indicating the Mother)* On the stage you can't have a character becoming too prominent and overshadowing all the others. The thing is to pack them all into a neat little framework and then act what is actable. I am aware of the fact that everyone has his own interior life which he wants very much to put forward. But the difficulty lies in this fact: to set out just so much as is necessary for the stage, taking the other characters into consideration, and at the same time hint at the unrevealed interior life of each. I am willing to admit, my dear young lady, that from your point of view it would be a fine idea if each character could tell the public all his troubles in a nice monologue or a regular one-hour lecture. *(Good-humoredly)* You must restrain yourself, my dear, and in your own interest, too; because this fury of yours, this exaggerated disgust you show, may make a bad impression, you know. After you have confessed to me that there were others before him at Madame Pace's and more than once . . .

THE STEPDAUGHTER: *(Bowing her head, impressed)* It's true. But remember those others mean him for me all the same.

THE MANAGER: *(Not understanding)* What? The others? What do you mean?

THE STEPDAUGHTER: For one who has gone wrong, sir, he who was responsible for the 230 first fault is responsible for all that follow. He is responsible for my faults, was, even before I was born. Look at him, and see if it isn't true!

THE MANAGER: Well, well! And does the weight of so much responsibility seem nothing to you? Give him a chance to act it, to get it over!

THE STEPDAUGHTER: How? How can he act all his "noble remorses," all his "moral torments," if you want to spare him the horror of being discovered one day—after he
had asked her what he did ask her—in the arms of her, that already fallen woman,
that child, sir, that child he used to watch come out of school? (*She is moved.*)

*The Mother at this point is overcome with emotion, and breaks out into a fit of crying. All are
touched. A long pause.*

THE STEPDAUGHTER: (*As soon as the Mother becomes a little quieter, adds resolutely
and gravely*) At present, we are unknown to the public. Tomorrow, you will act
us as you wish, treating us in your own manner. But do you really want to see
drama, do you want to see it flash out as it really did?

THE MANAGER: Of course! That's just what I do want, so I can use as much of it as is
possible.

THE STEPDAUGHTER: Well then, ask that Mother there to leave us.   235

THE MOTHER: (*Changing her low plaint into a sharp cry*)   No! No! Don't permit
it, sir, don't permit it!

THE MANAGER: But it's only to try it.

THE MOTHER: I can't bear it. I can't.

THE MANAGER: But since it has happened already . . . I don't understand!

THE MOTHER: It's taking place now. It happens all the time. My torment isn't a pre-   240
tended one. I live and feel every minute of my torture. Those two children
there—have you heard them speak? They can't speak any more. They cling to
me to keep my torment actual and vivid for me. But for themselves, they do not
exist, they aren't any more. And she (*indicating Stepdaughter*) has run away,
she has left me, and is lost. If I now see her here before me, it is only to renew
for me the tortures I have suffered for her too.

THE FATHER: The external moment! She (*indicating the Stepdaughter*) is here to catch
me, fix me, and hold me eternally in the stocks for that one fleeting and shameful
moment of my life. She can't give it up! And you sir, cannot either fairly spare me it.

THE MANAGER: I never said I didn't want to act it. It will form, as a matter of fact, the
nucleus of the whole first act right up to her surprise. (*Indicating the Mother.*)

THE FATHER: Just so! This is my punishment: the passion in all of us that must culmi-
nate in her final cry.

THE STEPDAUGHTER: I can hear it still in my ears. It's driven me mad, that cry—you
can put me on as you like; it doesn't matter. Fully dressed, if you like—provided
I have at least the arm bare; because standing like this (*she goes close to the
Father and leans her head on his breast*) with my head so, and my arms round
his neck, I saw a vein pulsing in my arm here; and then, as if that live vein had
awakened disgust in me, I closed my eyes like this, and let my head sink on his
breast. (*Turning to the Mother*) Cry out, mother! Cry out! (*Buries head in
Father's breast, and with her shoulders raised as if to prevent her hearing the
cry, adds in tones of intense emotion*) Cry out as you did then!

THE MOTHER: (*Coming forward to separate them*)   No! My daughter, my daugh-   245
ter! (*And after having pulled her away from him*) You brute! you brute! She
is my daughter! Don't you see she's my daughter?

THE MANAGER: (*Walking backwards towards footlights*)   Fine! fine! Damned
good! And then, of course—curtain!

THE FATHER: (*Going towards him excitedly*)   Yes, of course, because that's the
way it really happened.

THE MANAGER: (*Convinced and pleased*)   Oh, yes, no doubt about it. Curtain
here. Curtain!

*At the reiterated cry of the Manager, the Machinist lets the curtain down, leaving the Manager
and the Father in front of it before the footlights.*

THE MANAGER: The darned idiot! I said "curtain" to show the act should end there, and he goes and lets it down in earnest. *(To the Father, while he pulls the curtain back to go onto the stage again.)* Yes, yes, it's all right. Effect certain! That's the right ending. I'll guarantee the first act, at any rate.

Act 2 Response Statement Questions

- As the Manager begins to arrange a set for the Characters to rehearse their play, do you regard the situation as different from what it seemed to be in Act I? Is it now more real or more theatrical?
- What is your response to the Characters' negative reaction to the Actors taking their parts in the planned play? Does any dramatic character have a say in who acts his or her part and how that actor acts? How is your response related to your ideas about the relation of characters to actors in drama?
- What is your response to the appearance of Madame Pace? Is it possible or believable? If not, by what standard of theatrical realism are you judging her appearance?

Act 3

When the curtain goes up again, it is seen that the stage hands have shifted the bit of scenery used in the last part, and have rigged up instead at the back of the stage a drop, with some trees, and one or two wings. A portion of a fountain basin is visible. The Mother is sitting on the Right with the two Children by her side. The son is on the same side, but away from the others. He seems bored, angry, and full of shame. The Father and the Stepdaughter are also seated towards the Right front. On the other side (Left) are the Actors, much in the positions they occupied before the curtain was lowered. Only the Manager is standing up in the middle of the stage, with his hand closed over his mouth, in the act of meditating.

THE MANAGER: *(Shaking his shoulders after a brief pause)*   Ah yes: the second act! Leave it to me, leave it all to me as we arranged, and you'll see! It'll go fine!

THE STEPDAUGHTER: Our entry into his house *(indicates Father)* in spite of him ... *(indicates the Son.)*

THE MANAGER: *(Out of patience)*   Leave it to me, I tell you!

THE STEPDAUGHTER: Do let it be clear, at any rate, that it is in spite of my wishes.

THE MOTHER: *(From her corner, shaking her head)*   For all the good that's come   5
of it ...

THE STEPDAUGHTER: *(Turning towards her quickly)*   It doesn't matter. The more harm done to us, the more remorse for him.

THE MANAGER: *(Impatiently)*   I understand! Good Heavens! I understand! I'm taking it into account.

THE MOTHER: *(Supplicatingly)*   I beg you, sir, to let it appear quite plain that for conscience' sake I did try in every way ...

THE STEPDAUGHTER: *(Interrupting indignantly and continuing for the Mother)* ... to pacify me, to dissuade me from spiting him. *(To Manager)* Do as she wants; satisfy her, because it is true! I enjoy it immensely. Anyhow, as you can see, the meeker she is, the more she tries to get at his heart, the more distant and aloof does he become.

THE MANAGER: Are we going to begin this second act or not?   10

THE STEPDAUGHTER: I'm not going to talk any more now. But I must tell you this: you can't have the whole action take place in the garden, as you suggest. It isn't possible!

THE MANAGER: Why not?

THE STEPDAUGHTER: Because he *(indicates the Son again)* is always shut up alone in his room. And then there's all the part of that poor dazed-looking boy there which takes place indoors.

THE MANAGER: Maybe! On the other hand, you will understand—we can't change scenes three or four times in one act.

THE LEADING MAN: They used to once.   15

THE MANAGER: Yes, when the public was up to the level of that child there.

THE LEADING LADY: It makes the illusion easier.

THE FATHER: *(Irritated)*   The illusion! For Heaven's sake, don't say illusion. Please don't use that word, which is particularly painful for us.

THE MANAGER: *(Astounded)*   And why, if you please?

THE FATHER: It's painful, cruel, really cruel; and you ought to understand that.   20

THE MANAGER: But why? What ought we to say then? The illusion, I tell you, sir, which we've got to create for the audience ...

THE LEADING MAN: With our acting.

THE MANAGER: The illusion of a reality.

THE FATHER: I understand you; but you, perhaps, do not understand us. Forgive me! You see ... here for you and your actors, the thing is only—and rightly so ... a kind of game ...

LEADING LADY: *(Interrupting indignantly)*   A game! We're not children here, if you   25
please! We are serious actors.

THE FATHER: I don't deny it. What I mean is the game, or play, of your art, which has to give, as the gentleman says, a perfect illusion of reality.

THE MANAGER: Precisely——!

THE FATHER: Now, if you consider the fact that we *(indicates himself and the other five Characters)*, as we are, have no other reality outside of this illusion ...

THE MANAGER: *(Astonished, looking at his Actors, who are also amazed)*   And what does that mean?

THE FATHER: *(After watching them for a moment with a wan smile)*   As I say, sir,   30
that which is a game of art for you is our sole reality. *(Brief pause. He goes a step or two nearer the Manager and adds)* But not only for us, you know, by the way. Just you think it over well. *(Looks him in the eyes)* Can you tell me who you are?

THE MANAGER: *(Perplexed, half smiling)*   What? Who am I? I am myself.

THE FATHER: And if I were to tell you that that isn't true, because you are I? ...

THE MANAGER: I should say you were mad——! *(The Actors laugh.)*

THE FATHER: You're quite right to laugh; because we are all making believe here. *(To Manager)* And you can therefore object that it's only for a joke that that gentleman there *(indicates the Leading Man)*, who naturally is himself, has to be me, who am on the contrary myself—this thing you see here. You see I've caught you in a trap! *(The Actors laugh.)*

THE MANAGER: *(Annoyed)*   But we've had all this over once before. Do you want to   35
begin again?

THE FATHER: No, no! That wasn't my meaning! In fact, I should like to request you to abandon this game of art *(Looking at the Leading Lady as if anticipating her)* which you are accustomed to play here with your actors, and to ask you seriously once again: who are you?

THE MANAGER: *(Astonished and irritated, turning to his Actors)*   If this fellow here hasn't got a nerve! A man who calls himself a character comes and asks me who I am!

THE FATHER: *(With dignity, but not offended)*   A character, sir, may always ask a man who he is. Because a character has really a life of his own, marked with his especial characteristics; for which reason he is always "somebody." But a man— I'm not speaking of you now—may very well be "nobody."

THE MANAGER: Yes, but you are asking these questions of me, the boss, The Manager! Do you understand?

THE FATHER: But only in order to know if you, as you really are now, see yourself as you   40
once were with all the illusions that were yours then, with all the things both inside and outside of you as they seemed to you—as they were then indeed for you.
Well, sir, if you think of all those illusions that mean nothing to you now, of all
those things which don't even *seem* to you to exist any more, while once they
were for you, don't you feel that—I won't say these boards—but the very earth
under your feet is sinking away from you when you reflect that in the same way
this *you* as you feel it today—all this present reality of yours—is fated to seem a
mere illusion to you tomorrow?

THE MANAGER: *(Without having understood much, but astonished by the specious
argument)*   Well, well! And where does all this take us anyway?

THE FATHER: Oh, nowhere! It's only to show you that if we *(indicating the Characters)* have no other reality beyond illusion, you too must not count overmuch
on your reality as you feel it today, since, like that of yesterday, it may prove an illusion for you tomorrow.

THE MANAGER: *(Determining to make fun of him)*   Ah, excellent! Then you'll be
saying next that you, with this comedy of yours that you brought here to act, are
truer and more real than I am.

THE FATHER: *(With the greatest seriousness)*   But of course; without doubt!

THE MANAGER: Ah, really?

THE FATHER: Why, I thought you'd understand that from the beginning.   45

THE MANAGER: More real than I?

THE FATHER: If your reality can change from one day to another ...

THE MANAGER: But everyone knows it can change. It is always changing, the same as
anyone else's.

THE FATHER: *(With a cry)*   No, sir, not ours! Look here! That is the very difference!   50
Our reality doesn't change: it can't change! It can't be other than what it is, because it is already fixed for ever. It's terrible. Ours is an immutable reality
which should make you shudder when you approach us if you are really conscious of the fact that your reality is a mere transitory and fleeting illusion, taking this form today and that tomorrow, according to the conditions, according
to your will, your sentiments, which in turn are controlled by an intellect that
shows them to you today in one manner and tomorrow ... who knows how?
... Illusions of reality represented in this fatuous comedy of life that never
ends, nor can ever end! Because if tomorrow it were to end ... Then why, all
would be finished.

THE MANAGER: Oh for God's sake, will you *at least* finish with this philosophizing and let
us try and shape this comedy which you yourself have brought me here? You argue
and philosophize a bit too much, my dear sir. You know you seem to me almost,
almost ... *(Stops and looks him over from head to foot)* Ah, by the way, I think
you introduced yourself to me as a—what shall ... we say—a "character," created
by an author who did not afterwards care to make a drama of his own creations.

THE FATHER: It is the simple truth, sir.

THE MANAGER: Nonsense! Cut that out, please! None of us believes it, because it isn't
a thing, as you must recognize yourself, which one can believe seriously. If you
want to know, it seems to me you are trying to imitate the manner of a certain
author whom I heartily detest—I warn you—although I have unfortunately
bound myself to put on one of his works. As a matter of fact, I was just starting
to rehearse it, when you arrived. *(Turning to the Actors)* And this is what we've
gained—out of the frying-pan into the fire!

THE FATHER: I don't know to what author you may be alluding, but believe me I feel
what I think; and I seem to be philosophizing only for those who do not think

what they feel, because they blind themselves with their own sentiment. I know that for many people this self-blinding seems much more "human"; but the contrary is really true. For man never reasons so much and becomes so introspective as when he suffers; since he is anxious to get at the cause of his sufferings, to learn who has produced them, and whether it is just or unjust that he should have to bear them. On the other hand, when he is happy, he takes his happiness as it comes and doesn't analyze it, just as if happiness were his right. The animals suffer without reasoning about their sufferings. But take the case of a man who suffers and begins to reason about it. Oh no! it can't be allowed! Let him suffer like an animal, and then—ah yes, he is "human!"

THE MANAGER: Look here! Look here! You're off again, philosophizing worse than ever.   55

THE FATHER: Because I suffer, sir! I'm not philosophizing: I'm crying aloud the reasons of my sufferings.

THE MANAGER: *(Makes brusque movement as he is taken with a new idea)* I should like to know if anyone has ever heard of a character who gets right out of his part and perorates and speechifies as you do. Have you ever heard of a case? I haven't.

THE FATHER: You have never met such a case, sir, because authors, as a rule, hide the labor of their creations. When the characters are really alive before their author, the latter does nothing but follow them in their action, in their words, in the situations which they suggest to him; and he has to will them the way they will themselves—for there's trouble if he doesn't. When a character is born, he acquires at once such an independence, even of his own author, that he can be imagined by everybody even in many other situations where the author never dreamed of placing him; and so he acquires for himself a meaning which the author never thought of giving him.

THE MANAGER: Yes, yes, I know this.

THE FATHER: What is there then to marvel at in us? Imagine such a misfortune for   60
characters as I have described to you: to be born of an author's fantasy, and be denied life by him; and then answer me if these characters left alive, and yet without life, weren't right in doing what they did do and are doing now, after they have attempted everything in their power to persuade him to give them their stage life. We've all tried him in turn. I, she *(indicating the Stepdaughter)* and she. *(Indicating the Mother.)*

THE STEPDAUGHTER: It's true. I too have sought to tempt him, many, many times, when he had been sitting at his writing table, feeling a bit melancholy, at the twilight hour. He would sit in his armchair too lazy to switch on the light, and all the shadows that crept into his room were full of our presence coming to tempt him. *(As if she saw herself still there by the writing table, and was annoyed by the presence of the Actors)* Oh, if you would only go away, go away and leave us alone—mother here with that son of hers—I with that Child—that boy there always alone—and then I with him—*(just hints at the Father)*—and then I alone, alone . . . in those shadows! *(Makes a sudden movement as if in the vision she has of herself illuminating those shadows she wanted to seize hold of herself)* Ah! my life! my life! Oh, what scenes we proposed to him—and I tempted him more than any of the others!

THE FATHER: Maybe. But perhaps it was your fault that he refused to give us life; because you were too insistent, too troublesome.

THE STEPDAUGHTER: Nonsense! Didn't he make me so himself? *(Goes close to the Manager to tell him as if in confidence)* In my opinion he abandoned us in a fit of depression, of disgust for the ordinary theater as the public knows it and likes it.

THE SON: Exactly what it was, sir; exactly that!

THE FATHER: Not at all! Don't believe it for a minute. Listen to me! You'll be doing quite right to modify, as you suggest, the excesses both of this girl here, who wants to do too much, and of this young man, who won't do anything at all.

THE SON: No, nothing!

THE MANAGER: You too get over the mark occasionally, my dear sir, if I may say so.

THE FATHER: I? When? Where?

THE MANAGER: Always! Continuously! Then there's this insistence of yours in trying to make us believe you are a character. And then too, you must really argue and philosophize less, you know, much less.

THE FATHER: Well, if you want to take away from me the possibility of representing the torment of my spirit which never gives me peace, you will be suppressing me; that's all. Every true man, sir, who is a little above the level of the beasts and plants does not live for the sake of living, without knowing how to live; but he lives so as to give a meaning and a value of his own to life. For me this is *everything*. I cannot give up this, just to represent a mere fact as she *(indicating the Stepdaughter)* wants. It's all very well for her, since her "vendetta" lies in the "fact." I'm not going to do it. It destroys my *raison d'être*.

THE MANAGER: Your *raison d'être!* Oh, we're going ahead fine! First she starts off, and then you jump in. At this rate, we'll never finish.

THE FATHER: Now, don't be offended! Have it your own way—provided, however, that within the limits of the parts you assign us each one's sacrifice isn't too great.

THE MANAGER: You've got to understand that you can't go on arguing at your own pleasure. Drama is action, sir, action and not confounded philosophy.

THE FATHER: All right. I'll do just as much arguing and philosophizing as everybody does when he is considering his own torments.

THE MANAGER: If the drama permits! But for Heaven's sake, man, let's get along and come to the scene.

THE STEPDAUGHTER: It seems to me we've got too much action with our coming into his house. *(Indicating Father)* You said, before, you couldn't change the scene every five minutes.

THE MANAGER: Of course not. What we've got to do is to combine and group up all the facts in one simultaneous, close-knit action. We can't have it as you want, with your little brother wandering like a ghost from room to room, hiding behind doors and meditating a project which—what did you say it did to him?

THE STEPDAUGHTER: Consumes him, sir, wastes him away!

THE MANAGER: Well, it may be. And then at the same time, you want the little girl there to be playing in the garden . . . one in the house, and the other in the garden; isn't that it?

THE STEPDAUGHTER: Yes, in the sun, in the sun! That is my only pleasure: to see her happy and careless in the garden after the misery and squalor of the horrible room where we all four slept together. And I had to sleep with her—I, do you understand?—with my vile contaminated body next to hers; with her folding me fast in her loving little arms. In the garden, whenever she spied me, she would run to take me by the hand. She didn't care for the big flowers, only the little ones; and she loved to show me them and pet me.

THE MANAGER: Well then, we'll have it in the garden. Everything shall happen in the garden; and we'll group the other scenes there. *(Calls a Stage Hand)* Here, a back-cloth with trees and something to do as a fountain basin. *(Turning round to look at the back of the stage)* Ah, you've fixed it up. Good! *(To Stepdaughter)*

This is just to give an idea, of course. The Boy, instead of hiding behind the doors, will wander about here in the garden, hiding behind the trees. But it's going to be rather difficult to find a child to do that scene with you where she shows you the flowers. *(Turning to the Boy)* Come forward a little, will you please? Let's try it now! Come along! come along! *(Then seeing him come shyly forward, full of fear and looking lost)* It's a nice business, this lad here. What's the matter with him? We'll have to give him a word or two to say. *(Goes close to him, puts a hand on his shoulders, and leads him behind the one of the trees)* Come on! come on! Let me see you a little! Hide here ... yes, like that. Try and show your head just a little as if you were looking for someone ... *(Goes back to observe the effect, when the Boy at once goes through the action)* Excellent! fine! *(Turning to Stepdaughter)* Suppose the little girl there were to surprise him as he looks round, and run over to him, so we could give him a word or two to say?

THE STEPDAUGHTER: It's useless to hope he will speak, as long as that fellow there is here ... *(Indicates the Son)* You must send him away first.

THE SON: *(Jumping up)*   Delighted! delighted! I don't ask for anything better. *(Begins to move away.)*

THE MANAGER: *(At once stopping him)*   No! No! Where are you going? Wait a bit!

The Mother gets up, alarmed and terrified at the thought that he is really about to go away. Instinctively she lifts her arms to prevent him, without, however, leaving her seat.

THE SON: *(To Manager, who stops him)*   I've got nothing to do with this affair. Let   85
me go please! Let me go!

THE MANAGER: What do you mean by saying you've got nothing to do with this?

THE STEPDAUGHTER: *(Calmly, with irony)*   Don't bother to stop him; he won't go away.

THE FATHER: He has to act the terrible scene in the garden with his mother.

THE SON: *(Suddenly resolute and with dignity)*   I shall act nothing at all. I've said so from the very beginning. *(To the Manager)* Let me go!

THE STEPDAUGHTER: *(Going over to the Manager)*   Allow me? *(Puts down the Man-*   90
ager's arm which is restraining the Son) Well, go away then, if you want to! *(The Son looks at her with contempt and hatred. She laughs and says)* You see, he can't, he can't go away! He is obliged to stay here, indissolubly bound to the chain. If I, who fly off when that happens which has to happen, because I can't bear him—if I am still here and support that face and expression of his, you can well imagine that he is unable to move. He has to remain here, has to stop with that nice Father of his, and that Mother whose only son he is. *(Turning to the Mother)* Come on, mother, come along! *(Turning to Manager to indicate her)* You see, she was getting up to keep him back. *(To the Mother, beckoning her with her hand)* Come on! Come on! *(Then to Manager)* You can imagine how little she wants to show these actors of yours what she really feels; but so eager is she to get near him that ... There, you see? She is willing to act her part. *(And in fact, the Mother approaches him; and as soon as the Stepdaughter has finished speaking, opens her arms to signify that she consents.)*

THE SON: *(Suddenly)*   No! No! If I can't go away, then I'll stop here; but I repeat: I act nothing!

THE FATHER: *(To Manager excitedly)*   You can force him, sir.

THE SON: Nobody can force me.

THE FATHER: I can.

THE STEPDAUGHTER: Wait a minute, wait ... First of all, the baby has to go to the foun-   95
tain ... *(Runs to take the Child and leads her to the fountain.)*

THE MANAGER: Yes, yes of course; that's it. Both at the same time.

The Second Lady Lead and the Juvenile Lead at this point separate themselves from the group of Actors. One watches the Mother attentively; the other moves about studying the movements and manner of the Son whom he will have to act.

THE SON: *(To Manager)* What do you mean by both at the same time? It isn't right. There was no scene between me and her. *(Indicates the Mother)* Ask her how it was!

THE MOTHER: Yes, its true. I had come into his room ...

THE SON: Into my room, do you understand? Nothing to do with the garden.

THE MANAGER: It doesn't matter. Haven't I told you we've got to group the action? 100

THE SON: *(Observing the Juvenile Lead studying him)* What do you want?

JUVENILE LEAD: Nothing! I was just looking at you.

THE SON: *(Turning towards the Second Lady Lead)* Ah! she's at it too: to re-act her part! *(Indicating the Mother.)*

THE MANAGER: Exactly! And it seems to me that you ought to be grateful to them for their interest.

THE SON: Yes, but haven't you yet perceived that it isn't possible to live in front of a 105 mirror which not only freezes us with the image of ourselves, but throws our likeness back at us with a horrible grimace?

THE FATHER: That is true, absolutely true. You must see that.

THE MANAGER: *(To Second Lady Lead and Juvenile Lead)* He's right! Move away from them!

THE SON: Do as you like. I'm out of this!

THE MANAGER: Be quiet, you, will you? And let me hear your mother! *(To Mother)* You were saying you had entered ...

THE MOTHER: Yes, into his room, because I couldn't stand it any longer. I went to 110 empty my heart to him of all the anguish that tortures me ... But as soon as he saw me come in ...

THE SON: Nothing happened! There was no scene. I went away, that's all! I don't care for scenes!

THE MOTHER: It's true, true. That's how it was.

THE MANAGER: Well now, we've got to do this bit between you and him. It's indispensable.

THE MOTHER: I'm ready ... when you are ready. If you could only find a chance for me to tell him what I feel here in my heart.

THE FATHER: *(Going to Son in a great rage)* You'll do this for your mother, for 115 your mother, do you understand?

THE SON: *(Quite determined)* I do nothing!

THE FATHER: *(Taking hold of him and shaking him)* For God's sake, do as I tell you! Don't you hear your Mother asking you for a favor? Haven't you even got the guts to be a son?

THE SON: *(Taking hold of the Father)* No! No! And for God's sake stop it, or else ... *(General agitation. The Mother, frightened, tries to separate them.)*

THE MOTHER: *(Pleading)* Please! please!

THE FATHER: *(Not leaving hold of the Son)* You've got to obey, do you hear? 120

THE SON: *(Almost crying from rage)* What does it mean, this madness you've got? *(They separate)* Have you no decency, that you insist on showing everyone our shame? I won't do it! I won't! And I stand for the will of our author in this. He didn't want to put us on the stage, after all!

THE MANAGER: Man alive! You came here ...

THE SON: *(Indicating Father)* He did! I didn't!

THE MANAGER: Aren't you here now?

THE SON: It was his wish, and he dragged us along with him. He's told you not only   125
the things that did happen, but also the things that have never happened at all.

THE MANAGER: Well, tell me then what did happen. You went out of your room without
saying a word?

THE SON: Without a word, so as to avoid a scene!

THE MANAGER: And then what did you do?

THE SON: Nothing . . . walking in the garden . . . *(Hesitates for a moment with expression of gloom.)*

THE MANAGER: *(Coming closer to him, interested by his extraordinary reserve)*   130
Well, well . . . walking in the garden . . .

THE SON: *(Exasperated)*   Why on earth do you insist? It's horrible! *(The Mother trembles, sobs, and looks towards the fountain.)*

THE MANAGER: *(Slowly observing the glance and turning towards the Son with increasing apprehension)*   The baby?

THE SON: There in the fountain . . .

THE FATHER: *(Pointing with tender pity to the Mother)*   She was following him at the moment . . .

THE MANAGER: *(To the Son, anxiously)*   And then you . . .   135

THE SON: I ran over to her; I was jumping in to drag her out when I saw something that froze my blood . . . the boy there, standing stock still, with eyes like a madman's, watching his little drowned sister, in the fountain! *(The Stepdaughter bends over the fountain to hide the Child. She sobs)* Then . . . *(A revolver shot rings out behind the trees where the Boy is hidden.)*

THE MOTHER: *(With a cry of terror runs over in that direction together with several of the Actors amid general confusion)*   My son! My son! *(Then amid the cries and exclamations one hears her voice)* Help! Help!

THE MANAGER: *(Pushing the Actors aside while they lift up the Boy and carry him off)*   Is he really wounded?

SOME ACTORS: He's dead, dead!

OTHER ACTORS: No, no, it's only make-believe, it's only pretense!

THE FATHER: *(With a terrible cry)*   Pretense? Reality, sir, reality!

THE MANAGER: Pretense? Reality? To hell with it all! Never in my life has such a thing happened to me. I've lost a whole day over these a people, a whole day!

Curtain

Act 3 Response Statement Questions

- What is your response to the disputes among the characters as to "what really happened" or whose individual story should be emphasized? Is this realistic? Can characters compete with one another for status? Is this impossible, or is it at all like life or like drama?

- Does the father's speech about the reality of characters versus the illusion of "real" people apply beyond the situation in this play? Why or why not? What beliefs of yours about the "roles" people play and people's "true" identity influence your response?

- What is your response to the way the play ends? Is it satisfying, in dramatic terms? Why or why not? Is it fitting, given the nature of this play up to this point? If it is fitting, but at the same time the ending is unsatisfying dramatically, what can you say about the opposition between drama in general and this play in particular?

Overall Response Statement Questions

- Are you able to construct a theme as you read *Six Characters in Search of an Author?* If not, why? How is any inability of yours to construct a theme related to the text? How is it related to you as a reader? If you are able to construct a theme, what aspects of the text do you focus on to do so? How is any ability of yours to construct a theme related to beliefs about life or about theater that you bring to this reading?
- Which expectations of yours about the nature of real life and the nature of drama does this text confirm? Which does it challenge?
- Do you like this play? How is your liking or disliking it related to the questions just above?
- Can *Six Characters in Search of an Author* be staged? What problems, if any, do you see in putting this play on for an audience? For instance, if the Characters are to be played by actors, would the presence of actual people pretending to be fictional characters undercut for the audience the Characters' claims to be just characters? If this is a problem, is it fundamentally different from the problem of actors in any theater bringing any characters to life on the stage?
- *Share and Compare* In your class or discussion group, who is intrigued by this play? Who is annoyed by it? How are those responses related to different readers' ideologies about the relationship between theatrical drama and real life?

BROADENING YOUR LITERARY EXPERIENCE THROUGH RESEARCH

Presumably, what you have read in this chapter and the writing you have done have shown you more than you knew before about the literary repertoire and ideology of *Six Characters in Search of an Author*, including the features and practices of the Modern theater and the ideology of the middle-class European culture in the twentieth century. If you want to further broaden your knowledge with respect to *Six Characters in Search of an Author*, Pirandello's plays, Modern drama in general, or any aspect of the ideology behind *Six Characters in Search of an Author*, the best way to do that is through library research. The reading and writing you have done in this chapter may have raised questions for you that only further research can answer. That's good: Remember that it's questions and questioning that keep learning alive, and that answers are only provisional and temporary. The QAQ method promoted in Chapter 3 applies here too.

Here are some additional questions that you could pursue through library research, followed by a brief bibliography of sources for broadening your repertoire of knowledge in the area of Modern drama. Think of both the sources and the questions as just starting points for further investigation. Even a researched reading, however, should not be considered final. "The truth" about a text does not lie under a rock, waiting to be discovered, or in the library or in history; it may be pursued, but never possessed. Reading, learning, knowing are processes, of which research is a part. Whenever you read a text, whether you know a lot about it or just a little, you should try to be conscious of the dynamic interaction between you and the text.

Suggestions for Research

- Investigate what other readers—critics, reviewers—have said about *Six Characters in Search of an Author,* either the printed text or productions of it. Do any of their responses or interpretations influence the way you think about the play?

- Investigate the Theater of the Absurd. What were its aims and methods? What ideas seem to have gone into its ideology? How does learning more about this set of text strategies affect your response to *Six Characters in Search of an Author?*

- Investigate the production history of *Six Characters in Search of an Author.* How has the play been staged? What text strategies of live drama have any directors employed with this unconventional play? What have reviewers said about these productions?

- Conduct research to learn if there are other twentieth-century plays in which characters are acknowledged as characters, not as real people. If there are such plays, were their authors influenced by Pirandello? What were these authors thinking when they wrote such unconventional plays? Read any play that seems similar in this respect to *Six Characters in Search of an Author,* what is your response to it, and how is that response affected by what you know about the author's theory of drama?

Selected Bibliography

A good place to begin your search for further information on any of these topics is in the reference section of your library. For any of the above topics, you can find background information and get an overview of related issues and ideas by consulting specialized encyclopedias, handbooks, and readers' guides to particular areas of literature, defined by genre or historical period. Often these kinds of reference works include their own bibliographies of relevant books and periodical articles. Here are some standard reference works for the study of realistic drama.

Breed, Paul F., and Florence M. Sniderman, eds. *Dramatic Criticism Index: A Bibliography of Commentaries from Ibsen to the Avant-Garde.* Detroit: Gale, 1972.

Carpenter, Charles A. *Modern Drama Scholarship and Criticism, 1966–1980: An International Bibliography.* Toronto: University of Toronto Press, 1986.

Coleman, Arthur. *Drama Criticism,* 2 vols. Denver: Alan Swallow, 1966–1971.

Fleischmann, Wolfgang B., ed. *Encyclopedia of World Literature in the Twentieth Century,* rev. ed., 5 vols. New York: F. Ungar, 1981–1993.

Gassner, John, ed. *Reader's Encyclopedia of World Drama.* New York: Crowell, 1969.

Hede, Jean-Albert, and William B. Edgerton, eds. *Columbia Dictionary of Modern European Literature*, 2nd. ed. New York: Columbia UP, 1980.

Hochman, Stanley, ed. *McGraw-Hill Encyclopedia of World Drama*, 5 vols. New York: McGraw-Hill, 1984.

Periodicals, such as magazines and scholarly journals, are another good source of information for broadening your literary knowledge. The bibliographies in the above reference sources may list periodical articles, but you can extend your search by consulting any of the following periodical indexes. All are available in both bound volumes and electronic form, as indicated by the note in parentheses following each title.

Arts and Humanities Citation Index. (on-line)

Humanities Index. (on-line)

MLA International Bibliography. (CD-ROM)

Here is a list of books that contain useful information for broadening your knowledge of any of the topics listed earlier.

Artaud, Antonin. *The Theater and Its Double*. Trans. Mary Caroline Richards. New York: Grove Press, 1958.

Brockett, Oscar, and Robert R. Findlay. *Century of Innovations: A History of European and American Theatre and Drama Since 1870*. Englewood Cliffs, N.J.: Prentice-Hall, 1973.

Brook, Peter. *The Empty Space*. New York: Avon Books, 1968.

Cambon, Glauco. *Pirandello: A Collection of Critical Essays*. Englewood Cliffs, N.J.: Prentice-Hall, 1967.

Esslin, Martin. *Theatre of the Absurd*. New York: Doubleday, 1969.

Greenberg, Clement. *Art and Culture*. Boston: Beacon Press, 1961.

Grossvogel, David I. *The Blasphemers: The Theatre of Brecht, Ionesco, Beckett, Genet*. Ithaca, N.Y.: Cornell UP, 1962.

Paolucci, Anne. *Pirandello's Theater: The Recovery of the Modern Stage for Dramatic Art*. Carbondale, IL.: Southern Illinois UP, 1974.

Watson, Jack, and Grant McKernie. *A Cultural History of Theatre*. New York: Longman's, 1993.

23 ◆ Writing About Drama

Each of the preceding chapters on the history of Western drama has ended with the suggestion that your response to any play can be deepened if you find out more about the literary repertoire and the ideology of that play. The literary repertoire of a particular play includes not only the text strategies it employs, but the available text strategies of drama in general at the particular historical moment when the play is written. A play's ideology includes beliefs about the place of drama in society that are current when the play is written. It also includes ideas held by the author and the author's culture about certain subjects—for instance, beliefs about oracles and prophecy in ancient Athens, the concern with the relationship of the health of the monarch and the health of the nation in Elizabethan England, and attitudes toward bourgeois social respectability in nineteenth-century Europe. Many of these matters can be inferred from the text of a play itself, but such inferences may be strengthened or confirmed—or challenged—by *extra*textual material. Because it helps you see the text in *con*text, reading history, biography, or literary criticism can enlarge your understanding of both the literary repertoire and the ideology of any literary text.

The Purpose of Library Research

The way information is organized in Western culture means that, while you are in school at least, library research gives you access to extratextual material. That material is recorded and stored in books and periodicals housed in libraries. Finding such material relevant to a particular text is an academic skill that you will be expected to develop and practice in your college years. This chapter will demonstrate how one student used library sources to broaden her experience about one play and how she then applied the knowledge she gained to a subsequent reading of the play. Her writing about how finding out more about the literary repertoire and ideology of the text affected her reading shows one way in which a broadened literary experience can be put to practical use. In a larger sense, this student's experience reinforces the idea that reading is a process and is never really final. As a reader changes, what he or she brings to a text changes, and so the quality of the reader's interaction with a text changes.

Using a Response Statement to Motivate Research

Previous chapters have stressed how questions and question*ing* energize your efforts as a learner. Applied to the process of broadening your literary experience with respect to a particular text, asking a question is the starting point. Think of your **response statement** writing not only as an attempt to answer questions about your interaction with a text, but also as a source of questions that you may pursue or explore further. That is what happened with Shirin Arastu, whose response statement to Edward Albee's play *The Sandbox* was reproduced in Chapter 17. Shirin's response to her first reading of that play and the responses of her classmates, as shared in class discussion, raised questions for her, questions whose answers she pursued through library research. Here is a bit of what she wrote in her journal after that discussion.

> I was pretty content with my interpretation [of *The Sandbox*] until I came to
> class. The discussion seemed to point towards the abandonment of old people. No
> one seemed to interpret the play the way I did [emphasizing the emptiness of
> mourning rituals; see her response statement, Chapter 17]. That is when I wanted
> to know what was the real purpose. Why did Albee use the writing technique he
> did, and what was the purpose of the characters and the theme? Did anyone inter-
> pret it my way?

When she was given a library research assignment in her literature course, these questions gave Shirin some direction in broadening her literary experi- ence. These questions motivated her to find information, and, because the questions were relatively narrow, Shirin's library search was more efficient than if she had gone in search of virtually any information about Albee or *The Sandbox*.

From Response Statement to Rough Draft

The research assignment Shirin's class was given asked them to broaden their literary experience with respect to any short story, poem, or play they had read in roughly the first three-quarters of a semester. They were to apply that broadened experience to a subsequent reading of that text and discuss the re- sults. The students were told that their responses should still be emphasized, and that their subsequent or more informed reading of a text could still be an- alyzed in terms of interactivity, just as their first reading had been. They were told that they should regard any published criticism or interpretation of a text as the opinions of other readers—professional and experienced readers, to be sure—but readers nonetheless, and that they should think of themselves as participating in a conversation with those other readers, much as they might do in class discussion. In other words, the students' own responses and inter- pretations might be modified, challenged, or confirmed by what they found in published sources, but those responses should not necessarily be superseded merely because they were "only" students and the critics were professionals.

Chapter 28 of this book discusses in greater detail the process of doing library research to broaden your literary experience. So as to emphasize writ- ing, the present discussion will take you rather quickly through Shirin's research process, leading to her first draft of a paper in which she discussed the effect broadening her literary experience had on her subsequent reading of *The Sandbox*. That research process had two stages: developing a **working bibliography** of library sources and doing exploratory reading of those sources. This second stage also consisted of some writing, as Shirin made notes about what she was finding out through her reading. Even at this level, her reading was active.

A bibliography is a list of sources. In literary research, those sources usually consist of books, of course, but also articles in scholarly journals. A *working* bibliography is a list of sources that appear likely to provide you with the information you need to broaden your literary experience. Those sources are potential, because you don't know until you read them just what kind of information they will provide or how applicable that information will be. Given Shirin's questions, you would expect her working bibliography to consist of books and journal articles that talk about Albee's playwriting technique in general and that interpret *The Sandbox* in particular. There may be lots of such sources, but which ones provide information that would affect Shirin's response to *The Sandbox* would not be known until she actually looked at them.

Shirin did a few basic things to develop a working bibliography for her project. She searched the on-line catalog in her college library, using "Albee" as a subject keyword, so as to identify books about him or his plays. She consulted encyclopedias and other reference works to see what bibliographies of sources about Albee or *The Sandbox* they offered. And she searched the *MLA International Bibliography*—a huge and comprehensive list of books and articles on subjects in modern, as opposed to ancient, languages and literature. This bibliography was available in Shirin's college library on CD-ROM. When she ran a search using "Albee, Edward" as a key term, she found more than 100 sources listed in books and periodicals.

Having come up with a list of potentially useful sources in books and scholarly journals, Shirin proceeded to read through them, taking notes on and making photocopies of particular informative discussions. How did Shirin decide which discussions were especially useful? She looked at her sources for answers to her original questions and for support of or challenges to ideas in her first response to *The Sandbox*. She also kept her mind open for new ideas or information, perhaps slightly beyond the scope of her original questions but defined by those questions. This kind of active reading applied to library sources helped Shirin make efficient use of the time she spent in the library.*

Shirin looked for and found interpretations of *The Sandbox* that supported her response statement idea that the action of the play as "staged performance" and the characters' behavior amounted to a critique of the artificiality of mourning rituals. She also found discussions of *The Sandbox* in the contexts of the circumstances of its composition and of Albee's own life. Because Shirin had a strong sense of direction as she undertook her library research, she was able to connect these discussions to her first reading of the play, confirming

---

*Chapter 28 discusses this reading and note-taking process, as it applies to any research project, in more detail.

her initial interpretation. She also found sources that read the play in terms of the issue of abandonment of the elderly that some of her classmates had emphasized, and she read about *The Sandbox* in the context of the ideology of the theater of the absurd.

Shirin had found plenty of information that broadened her literary experience about *The Sandbox*, that told her more than she knew when she first read the play. She then went back and reread the play. In doing so, one way in which she read actively was to mark sections of the text that confirmed her (now reinforced) sense of a link between the stage performance quality of the play and the idea of the artificiality of mourning rituals in American life. Her initial response statement had merely summarized those passages from the text; her paper, reflecting her second reading of the play, would quote such passages in order to substantiate Shirin's interpretation.

In writing a rough draft of her paper, Shirin decided the best way to organize and clarify her thoughts would be to follow a narrative structure. She would describe her entire process of reading–researching–rereading. This broke down into three areas for her rough draft:

I. An account of her first response to *The Sandbox* and the questions that response raised for her;
II. A discussion of the information she found from her library sources;
III. A discussion of her second reading of *The Sandbox*, with an awareness of how the information she found affected that reading.

Using this organizational plan, Shirin wrote a 10-page rough draft. This was almost double what the assignment called for, but Shirin wrote expansively, trying to let the act of writing give expression to her ideas. She didn't restrain or edit herself at this point; that would come later. This approach and organizational plan also allowed Shirin to keep the emphasis on her own ideas and not turn her paper into a summary of critics' ideas.

Shirin's rough draft is too long to be reproduced in its entirety here, but so that you may appreciate some of her revision moves, read this paragraph, from the third part of her outline:

> As I read [*The Sandbox*] the second time, the idea of elderly abandonment was appreciable, but my interpretation did not change. More evident to me was the numbed sensitivity of humans to their own vulnerability, portrayed by Mommy and Daddy. Also, when the reality is conveyed, 90% of the sorrow seems like selfish fear and the other 10% may be the sorrow of losing someone. Maybe the cliché, instead of "I'm sorry you lost someone" should be "I'm sorry you will die one day." I know this sounds harsh, I realize that there do exist honest emotions on this earth, but this play seems to satirize fake, selfish emotions and therefore I am dwelling on this.

You can compare this portion of Shirin's second reading of the play with her handling of it in her revised draft.

From Rough Draft to Final Paper

As the first part of her revision process, Shirin asked a classmate to read her rough draft in an in-class workshop. As part of this entire assignment, Shirin and her classmates were asked to write entries in their journals describing their writing process. Here is part of what Shirin wrote about her rough-draft workshop session:

> My partner was very helpful. He pointed out that my rough draft was going in a lot of different directions, but he couldn't figure out what my purpose was in some places. He suggested that I decide what the most important parts were and go from there.

One reason Shirin's partner thought her rough draft "was going in a lot of different directions" was that Shirin had included in it considerable information from her sources about the circumstances of composition of *The Sandbox* and the theater of the absurd and comments supporting the "abandonment" reading of the play. Another reason for this response was Shirin's narrative approach in the first draft; while that approach was useful to Shirin in getting her ideas down on paper, it caused at least one reader to be uncertain about Shirin's purpose or emphasis.

Shirin might have been able to see her rough draft in these terms on her own, but having a peer partner read it and give feedback helped Shirin get some distance from her writing so that she could reshape it. Getting a peer's comments also helped Shirin think in terms of the effect of her writing on another reader. Part of her revision effort, therefore, was to try to look at her writing in terms of her readers. Her attempts at focusing her discussion and emphasizing her purpose would be undertaken with another reader in mind. As Shirin wrote in her journal,

> When I went to revise my rough draft for readers, I tried to put myself in their shoes. They had read the play, but they didn't all know me. And they didn't know what my ideas or interpretation of the play were.

As Shirin looked again at her rough draft, with her eventual readers and her peer partner's comments in mind, she saw that

> There seemed to be two levels to my ideas about the play. First is the idea that the play seems like a rehearsal. Second is that the play imitates real life. I looked at my rough draft to see if I could rearrange my ideas to make the connection between them obvious. It seemed to me that I would have to change from the order of first reading—research—second reading to a different order based on my two ideas. So first I wrote out my main ideas, and then underneath I listed the sources and page numbers that seemed to fit with them.

As you can see from these notes, Shirin was willing to go back beyond her first draft to reorganize the presentation of her ideas. She didn't feel wedded to her first organizational plan or to the information from library sources that she had used in her rough draft. Here is a bit more from her reflective journal writing.

> I couldn't find a way to fit in a lot of the research I had done. It was interesting, especially the parts that supported my classmates' interpretations of the abandonment of the elderly, but I didn't think it had anything to do with my reading of the play. Actually, I think I could write about three or four different papers based on my research! My working bibliography was much longer than my actual Works Cited page [would be].

A virtue of Shirin's organizational plan for her first draft was that it allowed her to get information from her library sources into her paper easily. She merely devoted the entire middle section of her draft to describing that information. A defect of this same plan was that putting all that library information together in one section kept Shirin from discriminating among more and less useful information, as defined by her purpose as a writer. As she revised, Shirin now faced the problem of how to integrate information from her sources into her discussion, rather than just leaving that information separate in one part of her paper. Furthermore, if Shirin were to keep her own ideas paramount in her revised paper, this integration of source material would have to be handled carefully in individual paragraphs and sentences. When you read Shirin's revised paper you will to see that she smoothly incorporated her sources' ideas into her own discussion. To give you a better idea of what that integration entailed, however, I have reproduced below passages from two of Shirin's sources, each followed by an example of Shirin's handling of these sources in one paragraph of her paper.

From Anne Paolucci, *From Tension to Tonic: The Plays of Edward Albee*, page 27.

> *The sandbox doesn't make us smile, though it is funny; and Grandma's barbs, like so much old-time vaudeville humor, make us wince.... [T]he whole play is a grotesque parody. Grandma herself doesn't seem to mind the sandbox too much, once she settles down in it, and she actually enjoys it after a while, covering herself with sand the way a child might do.... Mommy, in fact, is right there with Daddy beside her, while the horrible masque takes place; and when the rumble in the distance announces that "the time has come," she utters the clichés which cover up the inadequacies of such moments and hurries away. In another context, her insensitivity and the commonplaces she resorts to might produce a smile; but here the best we can do is grimace at her description of the place of death as "warm as toast," at her obvious enjoyment of her role of bereaved, at the tears she sheds as the music—like the music piped in at all funeral parlors—softens her indifference....*

From Shirin's Paper

> The Sandbox seems like a play rehearsal when Mommy gets scared of the off-
> stage rumble and Daddy forgets what the noise means. Mommy tells him that the
> time for Grandma has come, as if this is all part of the script (Albee 61). In her book
> From Tension to Tonic, critic Anne Paolucci says that "when the rumble in the dis-
> tance announces that the 'time has come,' she [Mommy] utters the clichés which
> cover up the inadequacies of such moments and hurries away" (27). Mommy reacts
> to the rumble as if to a stage direction.

From Gerry McCarthy, *Edward Albee,* page 48.

> *The artificiality of performance is highlighted as part of a burlesque process
> which manifests the insincerity of Mommy's attitudes and the absence of
> any initiative at all in the role of Daddy. Mommy's grief at Grandma's
> passing is indicated clearly as stage emotion. When a sound-effect is heard,
> Mommy reminds Daddy tearfully, "It was an off-stage rumble . . . and you
> know what that means . . . It means the time has come for poor Grandma."*

From Shirin's Paper

> [Mommy] only begins crying when the cue to do so is given to her, emphasiz-
> ing her "insincerity" (McCarthy 48).

Shirin's statement that the play "seems like a play rehearsal" is her own interpretation, as first expressed in her initial response statement. In Paolucci
and McCarthy, Shirin has found two critics who read the play in similar terms.
But even though those critics also talk about the artificiality of what is being
done and said in this scene, Shirin does not have to cite them as sources for
an idea she already had. Shirin cites Albee as author of *The Sandbox* here because this paragraph appears very early in her paper, and this summary of this
bit of dialogue is Shirin's first specific reference to the language of the play. In
her book, Paolucci's comment about Mommy's uttering "the clichés which
cover up the inadequacies of such moments" occurs in the context of a discussion of the humor in the play, but Shirin is able to use that comment for
her own purpose to link the ideas of the rehearsal-like nature of the play and
the artificiality of mourning rituals. McCarthy's comment reveals him as a critic
who reads *The Sandbox* much the way Shirin did initially, but in the interest of
a concise discussion, Shirin has to use only one word from his book in support of her reading.

Shirin's paragraph that I have shown you here appeared at the beginning of the body of her paper, which went on for about six more pages to integrate ideas from her library sources with her own ideas as a reader, in like manner. As the note in Shirin's reflective journal entry indicated, the revised version of her paper left out some interesting material from her library sources that her first draft had included. Shirin had to make some hard decisions, based on her purpose as a writer. At the same time, in trying to acknowledge the role of her own ideology and life experience in her response to *The Sandbox*, Shirin decided to include some of what she had written in her first response statement. She used this material as a way to introduce and close her paper. As she described it in her journal,

> When I had the middle part of my paper written, I realized that I hadn't talked about my own feelings after my grandfather died [as she had in her response statement and first draft]. Then I got the idea to introduce my interpretation with my own feelings. Maybe my readers would connect with that experience. But I didn't want my readers to think that I didn't care about my grandfather's death, so I ended my paper in a way that made that point.

Having done this thorough rethinking and reworking of her rough draft, all that remained for Shirin was to edit her revised version to make sure its grammar, spelling, and punctuation were acceptable for an academic paper, to double check her documentation of sources, to create a Works Cited list that gave full bibliographic information for all works *actually cited*—but only those works—in her paper. When she had done all this, Shirin was ready to hand in her paper, which appears in full below. As you read Shirin's paper, please notice how it achieves two goals of research-based writing: It integrates sources smoothly and correctly, according to the conventions of MLA style, and it emphasizes the writer's ideas, as first discovered in her initial response statement.

STUDENT WRITING
Shirin Arastu: The Last Act: A Play Unrehearsed

I tried very hard to cry when my grandfather died, but in vain. I was sad, but I couldn't bring myself to cry at the "appropriate" moments of the mourning period. In fact, every time someone I know has died, life itself has begun to feel to me like a staged performance that will be over very soon. Am I just an actor in someone else's play?—a play unrehearsed? As I read Edward Albee's play *The Sandbox* for the first time, this image of life as playacting helped form my interpretation. The whole attitude created in the play toward how people react to the reality of death is one of a superficial, staged performance. Acting in this performance helps the characters avoid their real fears of their own deaths.

The Sandbox seems like a play rehearsal when Mommy gets scared of the off-stage rumble and Daddy forgets what the noise means. Mommy tells him that the time for Grandma has come, as if this is all part of the script (Albee 61). In her book *From Tension to Tonic* critic Anne Paolucci says that "when the rumble in the distance announces that the 'time has come,' she [Mommy] utters the clichés which cover up the inadequacies of such moments and hurries away" (27). Mommy reacts to the rumble as if to a stage direction. She only begins crying when the cue to do so is given to her, emphasizing her "insincerity" (McCarthy 48).

The lines the Young Man speaks toward the end of the play also make it seem like the rehearsal for another play. For example, when Grandma asks the Young Man his name, he says "they haven't given me one yet . . . the studio . . ." (Albee 45). Later he says "Uh . . . ma'am; I . . . I have a line here" (80). The stage directions say that he speaks his next line "like a real amateur" (84).

The play includes ironic or satiric comments about American clichés of death and mourning. When Grandma plays dead, Mommy within a blink of an eye claims she and Daddy must now move on with their lives. One critic states that the characters only pretend to mourn (Gabbard 29): "The audience is made aware that Mommy and Daddy are staging a performance by the presence of the Musician and by the characters' references to themselves as actors and role players" (30). Throughout the play, characters shout for the light to change or the Musician to enter or stop playing. Once Grandma has been dumped in the sandbox, Mommy and Daddy "sit" and "wait" as though sitting by her deathbed (Albee 22). The following exchange while they are sitting and waiting emphasizes the lifelessness or artificiality of funeral conventions:

DADDY: (after a pause). Shall we talk to each other?

MOMMY: (with that little laugh; picking something off her dress). Well, you can talk, if you want to . . . if you can think of anything to say . . . if you can think of anything new.

DADDY: (thinks). No . . . I suppose not. (28)

Neither Mommy nor Daddy can find anything new, and therefore real, to say. They only care about acting out the conventional roles of mourners, not about what they really feel or think about Grandma's impending death.

Mommy says that Grandma's face "looks . . . so happy" (73), a remark typically made at viewings or funerals, but then she follows her comment with "It pays to do things well" (73), suggesting that she is more concerned about seeming to observe the conventions than about Grandma's death. Finally, the symbolic night is over and Mommy and Daddy reassure each other with "Brave Mommy" and "Brave Daddy," a customary performance after a death (75).

The impression I get is that Albee is saying that American culture cares more about the appearance of mourning than the actual experience. Albee's preface to another play he was writing at the same time as *The Sandbox*, called *The American Dream*, seems to apply equally well to *The Sandbox*. Albee himself said that he put some characters from *The American Dream* in a new, "but related," situation in *The Sandbox* (qtd. in Vos 13). Albee wrote that *The American Dream* was "an examination of the American scene, an attack on the substitution of artificial for real values in our society" (qtd. in Paolucci 25). Although in class discussion I found that many American students interpreted the play to be about the abandonment of old people, I was not aware of this focus in the play, perhaps because in my culture the elderly are kept at home and taken care of. I did have a very emotional experience and a philosophical view of the death of my grandfather; thus the play, and Albee's comments, connect me more with the aspect of the play having to do with rituals of death than its theme of abandonment.

The character of the Grandma seems real in contrast to the superficial nature of Mommy and Daddy. Many critics suggest a connection between the Grandma of the play and Albee's real grandmother, who passed away the year he wrote this play. Albee dedicated the play to his grandmother; one critic, Walter Kerr, calls the play "a soft little elegy" (qtd. in Amacher 165). Albee, an adopted child, and his grandmother were both outsiders to his parents' troubled marriage. To Albee his grandmother seemed to be the only member of his family who sincerely loved him, completely unlike his inauthentic, materialistic mother (Roudané, *Understanding*

58–59). The Grandma in the play seems to me to be a symbol of a longing for honesty or freedom from lifeless conventions.

While Mommy and Daddy seem "content to remain in their somnolence" (Vos 14), Grandma seems to be aware of the true realities of life and death. Mommy and Daddy sit around posing as mourners, but Grandma screams. Grandma talks about her life, but Mommy and Daddy talk about nothing. Martin Esslin says that in the Theater of the Absurd "[T]he dignity of man lies in his ability to face reality in all its senselessness; to accept it freely, without fear, without illusions—and to laugh at it" (qtd. in Vos 13). This is exactly what Grandma does when she buries herself in the sand (Albee 67). She faces the coming of her own death "with resignation" (85)—and she does cultivate a respect in my heart for her.

In my second reading what was more evident to me was the numbed sensitivity of humans to their own vulnerability, portrayed by Mommy and Daddy. Maybe people find it easier to utter clichés than to examine their real feelings because if they did examine them, they might have to face their fear of their own death. In an interview Albee explained he is "very interested in . . . the fact that people avoid thinking about death—and about *living*" (Roudané, "Playwright" 195). When the reality is conveyed 90% of the sorrow seems like selfish fear and the other 10% may be the sorrow of losing someone. Maybe the cliché instead of being "I'm sorry you lost someone" should be "I'm sorry you will die one day."

At my grandfather's viewing, after praying to be able to mourn, I was able to let out one hard sob. Unlike the tears Mommy pretends to shed in *The Sandbox*, my sob was real. But was I mourning his passing, or worrying about my own? When we mourn for others are we actually rehearsing for the final "act" of our life—our death? I'm not sure I'll ever know, but reading *The Sandbox* makes me ask the question.

Works Cited

Albee, Edward, *The Sandbox*. *Literature: Reading and Responding to Fiction, Poetry, Drama, and the Essay*. Ed. Joel Wingard. New York: Harper, 1996. 877–881.

Amacher, Richard E. *Edward Albee*. Twayne's United States Authors Series. New York: Twayne, 1969.

Gabbard, Lucina. "Edward Albee's Triptych on Abandonment." *Twentieth Century Literature*, Spring 1982: 14–33.

McCarthy, Gerry. *Edward Albee*. Macmillan Modern Dramatists' Series. New York: St. Martin's, 1987.

Paolucci, Anne. *From Tension to Tonic: The Plays of Edward Albee*. Crosscurrents. Carbondale: Southern Illinois UP, 1972.

Roudané, Matthew C. *Understanding Edward Albee*. Understanding Contemporary American Literature. Columbia: University of South Carolina Press, 1987.

———. "A Playwright Speaks: An Interview with Edward Albee." *Critical Essays on Edward Albee*. Eds. Philip C. Kolin and J. Madison Davis. Boston: Hall, 1986. 193–199.

Vos, Nelvin. *Eugene Ionesco and Edward Albee: A Critical Essay*. Grand Rapids, MI: Eeerdmans, 1968.

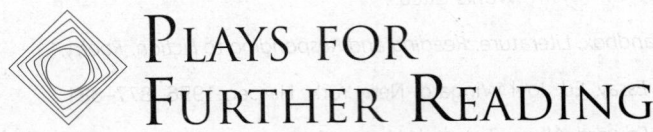

PLAYS FOR FURTHER READING

Sophocles   496?–406 B.C.

Antigone   *c. 441* B.C.

Translated by Robert Fagles

Characters

Antigone, daughter of Oedipus and Jocasta
Ismene, sister of Antigone
A Chorus of old Theban citizens and their *Leader*
Creon, king of Thebes, uncle of Antigone and Ismene
A Sentry
Haemon, son of Creon and Eurydice
Tiresias, a blind prophet
A Messenger
Eurydice, wife of Creon
Guards, Attendants, and a *Boy*

*Time and Scene: The royal house of Thebes. It is still night, and the invading armies of Argos have
just been driven from the city. Fighting on opposite sides, the sons of Oedipus, Eteocles and Polynices,
have killed each other in combat. Their uncle, Creon, is now king of Thebes.*

*Enter Antigone, slipping through the central doors of the palace. She motions to her sister, Ismene,
who follows her cautiously toward an alter at the center of the stage.*

ANTIGONE: My own flesh and blood—dear sister, dear Ismene,
        how many griefs our father Oedipus handed down!
        Do you know one, I ask you, one grief
        that Zeus will not perfect for the two of us
        while we still live and breathe! There's nothing,
        no pain—our lives are pain—no private shame,   5
        no public disgrace, nothing I haven't seen
        in your griefs and mine. And now this:
        an emergency decree, they say, the Commander
        has just declared for all of Thebes.   10
        What, haven't you heard? Don't you see?
        The doom reserved for enemies
        marches on the ones we love the most.
ISMENE: Not I, I haven't heard a word, Antigone.
        Nothing of loved ones,   15
        no joy or pain has come my way, not since
        the two of us were robbed of our two brothers,

1278

the two of us were robbed of our two brothers,
both gone in a day, a double blow—
not since the armies of Argos vanished,
just this very night. I know nothing more,
whether our luck's improved or ruin's still to come.   20

ANTIGONE: I thought so. That's why I brought you out here,
past the gates, so you could hear in private.

ISMENE: What's the matter? Trouble, clearly . . .
you sound so dark, so grim.

ANTIGONE: Why not? Our own brothers' burial!   25
Hasn't Creon graced one with all the rites,
disgraced the other? Eteocles, they say,
has been given full military honors,
rightly so—Creon's laid him in the earth   30
and he goes with glory down among the dead.
But the body of Polynices, who died miserably—
why, a city-wide proclamation, rumor has it,
forbids anyone to bury him, even mourn him.
He's to be left unwept, unburied, a lovely treasure   35
for birds that scan the field and feast to their heart's content.

Such, I hear, is the martial law our good Creon
lays down for you and me—yes, me, I tell you—
and he's coming here to alert the uninformed
in no uncertain terms,   40
and he won't treat the matter lightly. Whoever
disobeys in the least will die, his doom is sealed:
stoning to death inside the city walls!

There you have it. You'll soon show what you are,
worth your breeding, Ismene, or a coward—   45
for all your royal blood.

ISMENE: My poor sister, if things have come to this,
who am I to make or mend them, tell me,
what good am I to you?

ANTIGONE: Decide.
Will you share the labor, share the work?   50

ISMENE: What work, what's the risk? What do you mean?

ANTIGONE: *Raising her hands.*   Will you lift up his body with these bare hands
and lower it with me?

ISMENE: What? You'd bury him—
when a law forbids the city?

ANTIGONE: Yes!
He is my brother and—deny it as you will—   55
your brother too.
No one will ever convict me for a traitor.

ISMENE: So desperate, and Creon has expressly—

ANTIGONE: No,
he has no right to keep me from my own.

ISMENE: Oh my sister, think—   60
think how our own father died, hated,
his reputation in ruins, driven on
by the crimes he brought to light himself
to gouge out his eyes with his own hands—
then mother . . . his mother and wife, both in one,   65
mutilating her life in the twisted noose—

and last, our two brothers dead in a single day,
both shedding their own blood, poor suffering boys,
battling out their common destiny hand-to-hand.

Now look at the two of us, left so alone . . .   70
think what a death we'll die, the worst of all
if we violate the laws and override
the fixed decree of the throne, its power—
we must be sensible. Remember we are women,
we're not born to contend with men. Then too,   75
we're underlings, ruled by much stronger hands,
so we must submit in this, and things still worse.

I, for one, I'll beg the dead to forgive me—
I'm forced, I have no choice—I must obey
the ones who stand in power. Why rush to extremes?   80
It's madness, madness.

ANTIGONE: I won't insist,
no, even if you should have a change of heart,
I'd never welcome you in the labor, not with me.
So, do as you like, whatever suits you best—
I'll bury him myself.   85
And even if I die in the act, that death will be a glory.
I'll lie with the one I love and loved by him—
an outrage sacred to the gods! I have longer
to please the dead than please the living here:
in the kingdom down below I'll lie forever.   90
Do as you like, dishonor the laws
the gods hold in honor.

ISMENE: I'd do them no dishonor . . .
but defy the city? I have no strength for that.

ANTIGONE: You have your excuses. I am on my way,
I'll raise a mound for him, for my dear brother.   95

ISMENE: Oh Antigone, you're so rash—I'm so afraid for you!

ANTIGONE: Don't fear for me. Set your own life in order.

ISMENE: Then don't, at least, blurt this out to anyone.
Keep it a secret. I'll join you in that, I promise.

ANTIGONE: Dear god, shout it from the rooftops. I'll hate you   100
all the more for silence—tell the world!

ISMENE: So fiery—and it ought to chill your heart.

ANTIGONE: I know I please where I must please the most.

ISMENE: Yes, if you can, but you're in love with impossibility.

ANTIGONE: Very well then, once my strength gives out   105
I will be done at last.

ISMENE: You're wrong from the start,
you're off on a hopeless quest.

ANTIGONE: If you say so, you will make me hate you,
and the hatred of the dead, by all rights,
will haunt you night and day.   110
But leave me to my own absurdity, leave me
to suffer this—dreadful thing. I'll suffer
nothing as great as death without glory.   *Exit to the side.*

ISMENE: Then go if you must, but rest assured,
wild, irrational as you are, my sister,   115
you are truly dear to the ones who love you.

Withdrawing to the palace. Enter a Chorus, the old citizens of Thebes, chanting as the sun begins to rise.

CHORUS: Glory!—great beam of sun, brightest of all
    that ever rose on the seven gates of Thebes,
            you burn through night at last!
                Great eye of the golden day,   120
    mounting the Dirce's banks you throw him back—
    the enemy out of Argos, the white shield, the man of bronze—
    he's flying headlong now
            the bridle of fate stampeding him with pain!

    And he had driven against our borders,   125
    launched by the warring claims of Polynices—
    like an eagle screaming, winging havoc
    over the land, wings of armor
    shielded white as snow,
    a huge army massing,
    crested helmets bristling for assault.   130

He hovered above our roofs, his vast maw gaping
closing down around our seven gates,
    his spears thirsting for the kill
            but now he's gone, look,
before he could glut his jaws with Theban blood   13
or the god of fire put our crown of towers to the torch.
He grappled the Dragon none can master—Thebes—
        the clang of our arms like thunder at his back!

    Zeus hates with a vengeance all bravado,   140
    the mighty boasts of men. He watched them
    coming on in a rising flood, the pride
    of their golden armor ringing shrill—
    and brandishing his lightning
    blasted the fighter just at the goal,
    rushing to shout his triumph from our walls.   145

Down from the heights he crashed, pounding down on the earth!
And a moment ago, blazing torch in hand—
        mad for attack, ecstatic
he breathed his rage, the storm
of his fury hurling at our heads!   150
But now his high hopes have laid him low
and down the enemy ranks the iron god of war
        deals his rewards, his stunning blows—Ares
        rapture of battle, our right arm in the crisis.

    Seven captains marshaled at seven gates   155
    seven against their equals, gave
    their brazen trophies up to Zeus,
    god of the breaking rout of battle,
    all but two: those blood brothers,
    one father, one mother—matched in rage,   160
    spears matched for the twin conquest—
    clashed and won the common prize of death.

But now for Victory! Glorious in the morning,
joy in her eyes to meet our joy
    she is winging down to Thebes,
our fleets of chariots wheeling in her wake—
    Now let us win oblivion from the wars,
thronging the temples of the gods
in singing, dancing choirs through the night!
    Lord Dionysus, god of the dance
    that shakes the land of Thebes, now lead the way!   165

  170

Enter Creon from the palace, attended by his guard.

    But look, the king of the realm is coming,
    Creon, the new man for the new day,
    whatever the gods are sending now ...
    what new plan will he launch?
    Why this, this special session?
    Why this sudden call to the old men
    summoned at one command?   175

CREON: My countrymen,
  the ship of state is safe. The gods who rocked her,
after a long, merciless pounding in the storm,
have righted her once more.   180
               Out of the whole city
I have called you here alone. Well I know,
first, your undeviating respect
for the throne and royal power of King Laius.
Next, while Oedipus steered the land of Thebes,
and even after he died, your loyalty was unshakable,   185
you still stood by their children. Now then,
since the two sons are dead—two blows of fate
in the same day, cut down by each other's hands,
both killers, both brothers stained with blood—
as I am next in kin to the dead,   190
I now possess the throne and all its powers.

Of course you cannot know a man completely,
his character, his principles, sense of judgment,
not till he's shown his colors, ruling the people,
making laws. Experience, there's the test.   195
As I see it, whoever assumes the task,
the awesome task of setting the city's course,
and refuses to adopt the soundest policies
but fearing someone, keeps his lips locked tight,
he's utterly worthless. So I rate him now,   200
I always have. And whoever places a friend
above the good of his own country, he is nothing:
I have no use for him. Zeus my witness,
Zeus who sees all things, always—
I could never stand by silent, watching destruction   205
march against our city, putting safety to rout,
nor could I ever make that man a friend of mine
who menaces our country. Remember this:
our country *is* our safety.   210
Only while she voyages true on course
can we establish friendships, truer than blood itself.
Such are my standards. They make our city great.

Closely akin to them I have proclaimed,   215
just now, the following decree to our people
concerning the two sons of Oedipus.
Eteocles, who died fighting for Thebes,
excelling all in arms: he shall be buried,
crowned with a hero's honors, the cups we pour   220
to soak the earth and reach the famous dead.

But as for his blood brother, Polynices,
who returned from exile, home to his father-city
and the gods of his race, consumed with one desire—
to burn them roof to roots—who thirsted to drink   225
his kinsmen's blood and sell the rest to slavery:
that man—a proclamation has forbidden the city
to dignify him with burial, mourn him at all.
No, he must be left unburied, his corpse
carrion for the birds and dogs to tear,   230
an obscenity for the citizens to behold!

These are my principles. Never at my hands
will the traitor be honored above the patriot.
But whoever proves his loyalty to the state:
I'll prize that man in death as well as life.   235
LEADER: If this is your pleasure, Creon, treating
    our city's enemy and our friend this way . . .
    The power is yours, I suppose, to enforce it
    with the laws, both for the dead and all of us,
    the living.
CREON: Follow my orders closely then,   240
    be on your guard.
LEADER: We're too old.
    Lay that burden on younger shoulders.
CREON: No, no,
    I don't mean the body—I've posted guards already.
LEADER: What commands for us then? What other service?
CREON: See that you never side with those who break my orders.   245
LEADER: Never. Only a fool could be in love with death.
CREON: Death is the price—you're right. But all too often
    the mere hope of money has ruined many men.

A Sentry enters from the side.

SENTRY: My lord,
    I can't say I'm winded from running, or set out
    with any spring in my legs either—no sir,   250
    I was lost in thought, and it made me stop, often,
    dead in my tracks, wheeling, turning back,
    and all the time a voice inside me muttering,
    "Idiot, why? You're going straight to your death."
    Then muttering, "Stopped again, poor fool?   255
    If somebody gets the news to Creon first,
    what's to save your neck?"
                        And so,
    mulling it over, on I trudged, dragging my feet,
    you can make a short road take forever . . .
    but at last, look, common sense won out,   260

I'm here, and I'm all yours,
and even though I come empty-handed
I'll tell my story just the same, because
I've come with a good grip on one hope,
what will come will come, whatever fate—   265
CREON: Come to the point!
    What's wrong—why so afraid?
SENTRY: First, myself, I've got to tell you,
    I didn't do it, didn't see who did—
    Be fair, don't take it out on me.   270
CREON: You're playing it safe, soldier,
    barricading yourself from any trouble.
    It's obvious, you've something strange to tell.
SENTRY: Dangerous too, and danger makes you delay
    for all you're worth.   275
CREON: Out with it—then dismiss!
SENTRY: All right, here it comes. The body—
    someone's just buried it, then run off . . .
    sprinkled some dry dust on the flesh,
    given it proper rites.
CREON: What?   280
    What man alive would dare—
SENTRY: I've no idea, I swear it.
    There was no mark of a spade, no pickaxe there,
    no earth turned up, the ground packed hard and dry,
    unbroken, no tracks, no wheelruts, nothing,
    the workman left no trace. Just at sunup   285
    the first watch of the day points it out—
    it was a wonder! We were stunned . . .
    a terrific burden too, for all of us, listen:
    you can't see the corpse, not that it's buried,
    really, just a light cover of road-dust on it,   290
    as if someone meant to lay the dead to rest
    and keep from getting cursed.
    Not a sign in sight that dogs or wild beasts
    had worried the body, even torn the skin.

    But what came next! Rough talk flew thick and fast,   295
    guard grilling guard—we'd have come to blows
    at last, nothing to stop it; each man for himself
    and each the culprit, no one caught red-handed,
    all of us pleading ignorance, dodging the charges,
    ready to take up red-hot iron in our fists,   300
    go through fire, swear oaths to the gods—
    "I didn't do it, I had no hand in it either,
    not in the plotting, not in the work itself!"

    Finally, after all this wrangling came to nothing,
    one man spoke out and made us stare at the ground,   305
    hanging our heads in fear. No way to counter him,
    no way to take his advice and come through
    safe and sound. Here's what he said:
    "Look, we've got to report the facts to Creon,
    we can't keep this hidden." Well, that won out,   310
    and the lot fell on me, condemned me,

unlucky as ever, I got the prize. So here I am,
against my will and yours too, well I know—
no one wants the man who brings bad news.

LEADER: My king,
ever since he began I've been debating in my mind,
could this possibly be the work of the gods?   315

CREON: Stop—
before you make me choke with anger—the gods!
You, you're senile, must you be insane?
You say—why it's intolerable—say the gods
could have the slightest concern for that corpse?   320
Tell me, was it for meritorious service
they proceeded to bury him, prized him so? The hero
who came to burn their temples ringed with pillars,
their golden treasures—scorch their hallowed earth
and fling their laws to the winds.   325
Exactly when did you last see the gods
celebrating traitors? Inconceivable!

No, from the first there were certain citizens
who could hardly stand the spirit of my regime,
grumbling against me in the dark, heads together,   330
tossing wildly, never keeping their necks beneath
the yoke, loyally submitting to their king.
These are the instigators, I'm convinced—
they've perverted by own guard, bribed them
to do their work.

                    Money! Nothing worse   335
in our lives, so current, rampant, so corrupting.
Money—you demolish cities, root men from their homes,
you train and twist good minds and set them on
to the most atrocious schemes. No limit,
you make them adept at every kind of outrage,   340
every godless crime—money!

                              Everyone—
the whole crew bribed to commit this crime,
they've made one thing sure at least:
sooner or later they will pay the price.

Wheeling on the Sentry.

                              You—
I swear to Zeus as I still believe in Zeus,   345
if you don't find the man who buried that corpse,
the very man, and produce him before my eyes,
simple death won't be enough for you,
not till we string you up alive
and wring the immortality out of you.   350
Then you can steal the rest of your days,
better informed about where to make a killing.
You'll have learned, at last, it doesn't pay
to itch for rewards from every hand that beckons.
Filthy profits wreck most men, you'll see—   355
they'll never save your life.

SENTRY: Please,
may I say a word or two, or just turn and go?

CREON: Can't you tell? Everything you say offends me.
SENTRY: Where does it hurt you, in the ears or in the heart?
CREON: And who are you to pinpoint my displeasure?   360
SENTRY: The culprit grates on your feelings,
     I just annoy your ears.
CREON: Still talking?
     You talk too much! A born nuisance—
SENTRY: Maybe so,
     but I never did this thing, so help me!
CREON: Yes you did—
     what's more, you squandered your life for silver!   365
SENTRY: Oh it's terrible when the one who does the judging
     judges things all wrong.
CREON: Well now,
     you just be clever about your judgments—
     if you fail to produce the criminals for me,
     you'll swear your dirty money brought you pain.   370

Turning sharply, reentering the palace.

SENTRY: I hope he's found. Best thing by far.
     But caught or not, that's in the lap of fortune;
     I'll never come back, you've seen the last of me.
     I'm saved, even now, and I never thought,
     I never hoped—   375
     dear gods, I owe you all my thanks!   *Rushing out.*
CHORUS: Numberless wonders
     terrible wonders walk the world but none the match for man—
     that great wonder crossing the heaving gray sea,
              driven on by the blast of winter
     on through breakers crashing left and right,   380
         holds his steady course
     and the oldest of the gods he wears away—
     the Earth, the immortal, the inexhaustible—
     as his plows go back and forth, year in, year out
         with the breed of stallions turning up the furrows.   385

     And the blithe, lightheaded race of birds he snares,
     the tribes of savage beasts, the life that swarms the depths—
              with one fling of his nets
     woven and coiled tight, he takes them all,
         man the skilled, the brilliant!   390
     He conquers all, taming with his techniques
     the prey that roams the cliffs and wild lairs,
     training the stallion, clamping the yoke across
         his shaggy neck, and the tireless mountain bull.

     And speech and thought, quick as the wind   395
     and the mood and mind for law that rules the city—
         all these he has taught himself
     and shelter from the arrows of the frost
     when there's rough lodging under the cold clear sky
     and the shafts of lashing rain—   400
              ready, resourceful man!
                   Never without resources
     never an impasse as he marches on the future—

only Death, from Death alone he will find no rescue
but from desperate plagues he has plotted his escapes.

Man the master, ingenious past all measure
past all dreams, the skills within his grasp—
     he forges on, now to destruction
now again to greatness. When he weaves in
the laws of the land, and the justice of the gods
that binds his oaths together
        he and his city rise high—
           but the city casts out
that man who weds himself to inhumanity
thanks to reckless daring. Never share my hearth
never think my thoughts, whoever does such things.

410

415

Enter Antigone from the side, accompanied by the Sentry.

    Here is a dark sign from the gods—
    what to make of this? I know her,
    how can I deny it? That young girl's Antigone!
    Wretched, child of a wretched father,
    Oedipus. Look, is it possible?
    They bring you in like a prisoner—
    why? did you break the king's laws?
    Did they take you in some act of mad defiance?

420

SENTRY: She's the one, she did it single-handed—
    we caught her burying the body. Where's Creon?

425

Enter Creon from the palace.

LEADER: Back again, just in time when you need him.
CREON: In time for what? What is it?
SENTRY: My king,
    there's nothing you can swear you'll never do—
    second thoughts make liars of us all.
    I could have sworn I wouldn't hurry back
    (what with your threats, the buffeting I just took),
    but a stroke of luck beyond our wildest hopes,
    what a joy, there's nothing like it. So,
    back I've come, breaking my oath, who cares?
    I'm bringing in our prisoner—this young girl—
    we took her giving the dead the last rites.
    But no casting lots this time, this is *my* luck,
    my prize, no one else's.

430

435

                Now, my lord,
    here she is. Take her, question her,
    cross-examine her to your heart's content.
    But set me free, it's only right—
    I'm rid of this dreadful business once for all.

440

CREON: Prisoner! Her? You took her—where, doing what?
SENTRY: Burying the man. That's the whole story.
CREON: What?
    You mean what you say, you're telling me the truth?

445

SENTRY: She's the one. With my own eyes I saw her
    bury the body, just what you've forbidden.
    There. Is that plain and clear?
CREON: What did you see? Did you catch her in the act?

450

SENTRY: Here's what happened. We went back to our post,
    those threats of yours breathing down our necks—
    we brushed the corpse clean of the dust that covered it,
    stripped it bare ... it was slimy, going soft,
    and we took to high ground, backs to the wind   455
    so the stink of him couldn't hit us;
    jostling, baiting each other to keep awake,
    shouting back and forth—no napping on the job,
    not this time. And so the hours dragged by
    until the sun stood dead above our heads,   460
    a huge white ball in the noon sky, beating,
    blazing down, and then it happened—
    suddenly, a whirlwind!
    Twisting a great dust-storm up from the earth,
    a black plague of the heavens, filling the plain,   465
    ripping the leaves off every tree in sight,
    choking the air and sky. We squinted hard
    and took our whipping from the gods.

    And after the storm passed—it seemed endless—
    there, we saw the girl!   470
    And she cried out a sharp, piercing cry,
    like a bird come back to an empty nest,
    peering into its bed, and all the babies gone ...
    Just so, when she sees the corpse bare
    she bursts into a long, shattering wail   475
    and calls down withering curses on the heads
    of all who did the work. And she scoops up dry dust,
    handfuls, quickly, and lifting a fine bronze urn,
    lifting it high and pouring, she crowns the dead
    with three full libations.

                      Soon as we saw   480
    we rushed her, closed on the kill like hunters,
    and she, she didn't flinch. We interrogated her,
    charging her with offenses past and present—
    she stood up to it all, denied nothing. I tell you,
    it made me ache and laugh in the same breath.   485
    It's pure joy to escape the worst yourself,
    it hurts a man to bring down his friends.
    But all that, I'm afraid, means less to me
    than my own skin. That's the way I'm made.
CREON: *Wheeling on Antigone.*   You,
    with your eyes fixed on the ground—speak up.   490
    Do you deny you did this, yes or no?
ANTIGONE: I did it. I don't deny a thing.
CREON: *To the sentry.*   You, get out, wherever you please—
    you're clear of a very heavy charge.
He leaves; Creon turns back to Antigone.
    You, tell me briefly, no long speeches—   495
    were you aware a decree had forbidden this?
ANTIGONE: Well aware. How could I avoid it? It was public.
CREON: And still you had the gall to break this law?
ANTIGONE: Of course I did. It wasn't Zeus, not in the least,
    who made this proclamation—not to me.   500

Nor did that Justice, dwelling with the gods
beneath the earth, ordain such laws for men.
Nor did I think your edict had such force
that you, a mere mortal, could override the gods,
the great unwritten, unshakable traditions.   505
They are alive, not just today or yesterday:
they live forever, from the first of time,
and no one knows when they first saw the light.

These laws—I was not about to break them,
not out of fear of some man's wounded pride,
and face the retribution of the gods.   510
Die I must, I've known it all my life—
how could I keep from knowing?—even without
your death-sentence ringing in my ears.
And if I am to die before my time
I consider that a gain. Who on earth,   515
alive in the midst of so much grief as I,
could fail to find his death a rich reward?
So for me, at least, to meet this doom of yours
is precious little pain. But if I had allowed
my own mother's son to rot, an unburied corpse—   520
that would have been an agony! This is nothing.
And if my present actions strike you as foolish,
let's just say I've been accused of folly
by a fool.
LEADER: Like father like daughter,   525
passionate, wild . . .
she hasn't learned to bend before adversity.
CREON: No? Believe me, the stiffest stubborn wills
fall the hardest; the toughest iron,
tempered strong in the white-hot fire,
you'll see it crack and shatter first of all.   530
And I've known spirited horses you can break
with a light bit—proud, rebellious horses.
There's no room for pride, not in a slave
not with the lord and master standing by.   535

This girl was an old hand at insolence
when she overrode the edicts we made public.
But once she'd done it—the insolence,
twice over—to glory in it, laughing,
mocking us to our face with what she'd done.   540
I'm not the man, not now: she is the man
if this victory goes to her and she goes free.

Never! Sister's child or closer in blood
than all my family clustered at my altar
worshiping Guardian Zeus—she'll never escape,   545
she and her blood sister, the most barbaric death.
Yes, I accuse her sister of an equal part
in scheming this, this burial.

To his attendants.

                    Bring her here!
I just saw her inside, hysterical, gone to pieces.

It never fails: the mind convicts itself   550
in advance, when scoundrels are up to no good,
plotting in the dark. Oh but I hate it more
when a traitor, caught red-handed,
tries to glorify his crimes.

ANTIGONE: Creon, what more do you want   555
than my arrest and execution?

CREON: Nothing. Then I have it all.

ANTIGONE: Then why delay? Your moralizing repels me,
every word you say—pray god it always will.
So naturally all I say repels you too.
                                    Enough.   560
Give me glory! What greater glory could I win
than to give my own brother decent burial?
These citizens here would all agree,

To the Chorus.

they'd praise me too
if their lips weren't locked in fear.   565

Pointing to Creon.

Lucky tyrants—the perquisites of power!
Ruthless power to do and say whatever pleases *them*.

CREON: You alone, of all the people in Thebes,
see things that way.

ANTIGONE: They see it just that way
but defer to you and keep their tongues in leash.   570

CREON: And you, aren't you ashamed to differ so from them?
So disloyal!

ANTIGONE: Not ashamed for a moment,
not to honor my brother, my own flesh and blood.

CREON: Wasn't Eteocles a brother too—cut down, facing him?

ANTIGONE: Brother, yes, by the same mother, the same father.   575

CREON: Then how can you render his enemy such honors,
such impieties in his eyes?

ANTIGONE: He'll never testify to that,
Eteocles dead and buried.

CREON: He will—
if you honor the traitor just as much as him.   580

ANTIGONE: But it was his brother, not some slave that died—

CREON: Ravaging our country!—
but Eteocles died fighting in our behalf.

ANTIGONE: No matter—Death longs for the same rites for all.

CREON: Never the same for the patriot and the traitor.   585

ANTIGONE: Who, Creon, who on earth can say the ones below
don't find this pure and uncorrupt?

CREON: Never. Once an enemy, never a friend,
not even after death.

ANTIGONE: I was born to join in love, not hate—   590
that is my nature.

CREON: Go down below and love,
if love you must—love the dead! While I'm alive,
no woman is going to lord it over me.

Enter Ismene from the palace, under guard.

CHORUS: Look,
    Ismene's coming, weeping a sister's tears,
    loving sister, under a cloud . . .   595
    her face is flushed, her cheeks streaming.
    Sorrow puts her lovely radiance in the dark.
CREON: You—
    in my house, you viper, slinking undetected,
    sucking my life-blood! I never knew
    I was breeding twin disasters, the two of you   600
    rising up against my throne. Come, tell me,
    will you confess your part in the crime or not?
    Answer me. Swear to me.
ISMENE: I did it, yes—
    if only she consents—I share the guilt,
    the consequences too.
ANTIGONE: No,
    Justice will never suffer that—not you,   605
    you were unwilling. I never brought you in.
ISMENE: But now you face such dangers . . . I'm not ashamed
    to sail through trouble with you,
    make your troubles mine.
ANTIGONE: Who did the work?
    Let the dead and the god of death bear witness!   610
    I've no love for a friend who loves in words alone.
ISMENE: Oh no, my sister, don't reject me, please,
    let me die beside you, consecrating
    the dead together.
ANTIGONE: Never share my dying,   615
    don't lay claim to what you never touched.
    My death will be enough.
ISMENE: What do I care for life, cut off from you?
ANTIGONE: Ask Creon. Your concern is all for him.
ISMENE: Why abuse me so? It doesn't help you now.
ANTIGONE: You're right—   620
    if I mock you, I get no pleasure from it,
    only pain.
ISMENE: Tell me, dear one,
    what can I do to help you, even now?
ANTIGONE: Save yourself. I don't grudge you your survival.
ISMENE: Oh no, no, denied my portion in your death?   625
ANTIGONE: You chose to live, I chose to die.
ISMENE: Not, at least,
    without every kind of caution I could voice.
ANTIGONE: Your wisdom appealed to one world—mine, another.
ISMENE: But look, we're both guilty, both condemned to death.
ANTIGONE: Courage! Live your life. I gave myself to death,   630
    long ago, so I might serve the dead.
CREON: They're both mad, I tell you, the two of them.
    One's just shown it, the other's been that way
    since she was born.
ISMENE: True, my king,
    the sense we were born with cannot last forever . . .   635
    commit cruelty on a person long enough
    and the mind begins to go.

CREON: Yours did,
    when you chose to commit your crimes with her.
ISMENE: How can I live alone, without her?
CREON: Her?
    Don't even mention her—she no longer exists.   640
ISMENE: What? You'd kill your own son's bride?
CREON: Absolutely:
    there are other fields for him to plow.
ISMENE: Perhaps,
    but never as true, as close a bond as theirs.
CREON: A worthless woman for my son? It repels me.
ISMENE: Dearest Haemon, your father wrongs you so!   645
CREON: Enough, enough—you and your talk of marriage!
ISMENE: Creon—you're really going to rob your son of Antigone?
CREON: Death will do it for me—break their marriage off.
LEADER: So, it's settled then? Antigone must die?
CREON: Settled, yes—we both know that.   650

To the guards.

    Stop wasting time. Take them in.
    From now on they'll act like women.
    Tie them up, no more running loose;
    even the bravest will cut and run,
    once they see Death coming for their lives.   655

The guards escort Antigone and Ismene into the palace. Creon remains while the old citizens form their chorus.

CHORUS: Blest, they are truly blest who all their lives
    have never tasted devastation. For others, once
    the gods have rocked a house to its foundations
        the ruin will never cease, cresting on and on
    from one generation on throughout the race—   660
    like a great mounting tide
    driven on by savage northern gales,
        surging over the dead black depths
    roiling up from the bottom dark heaves of sand
    and the headlands, taking the storm's onslaught full-force,   665
    roar, and the low moaning
                echoes on and on
                    and now
    as in ancient times I see the sorrows of the house,
    the living heirs of the old ancestral kings,
    piling on the sorrows of the dead
        and one generation cannot free the next—   670
    some god will bring them crashing down,
    the race finds no release.
    And now the light, the hope
        springing up from the late last root
    in the house of Oedipus, that hope's cut down in turn   675
    by the long, bloody knife swung by the gods of death
    by a senseless word
            by fury at the heart.
                      Zeus,
    yours is the power, Zeus, what man on earth
    can override it, who can hold it back?

Power that neither Sleep, the all-ensnaring
    no, nor the tireless months of heaven
can ever overmaster—young through all time,
mighty lord of power, you hold fast
    the dazzling crystal mansions of Olympus.
And throughout the future, late and soon
as through the past, your law prevails:
no towering form of greatness
        enters into the lives of mortals
            free and clear of ruin.

                             True,
our dreams, our high hopes voyaging far and wide
bring sheer delight to many, to many others
    delusion, blithe, mindless lusts
and the fraud steals on one slowly . . . unaware
till he trips and puts his foot into the fire.
    He was a wise old man who coined
the famous saying: "Sooner or later
foul is fair, fair is foul
to the man the gods will ruin"—
    He goes his way for a moment only
            free of blinding ruin.

Enter Haemon from the palace.

    Here's Haemon now, the last of all your sons.
    Does he come in tears for his bride,
    his doomed bride, Antigone—
    bitter at being cheated of their marriage?

CREON: We'll soon know, better than seers could tell us.

Turning to Haemon.

    Son, you've heard the final verdict on your bride?
    Are you coming now, raving against your father?
    Or do you love me, no matter what I do?

HAEMON: Father, I'm your *son* . . . you in your wisdom
    set my bearings for me—I obey you.
    No marriage could ever mean more to me than you,
    whatever good direction you may offer.

CREON: Fine, Haemon.
That's how you ought to feel within your heart,
subordinate to your father's will in every way.
That's what a man prays for: to produce good sons—
households full of them, dutiful and attentive,
so they can pay his enemy back with interest
and match the respect their father shows his friend.
But the man who rears a brood of useless children,
what has he brought into the world, I ask you?
Nothing but trouble for himself, and mockery
from his enemies laughing in his face.
                  Oh Haemon,
never lose your sense of judgment over a woman.
The warmth, the rush of pleasure, it all goes cold
in your arms, I warn you . . . a worthless woman
in your house, a misery in your bed.

680

685

690

695

700

705

710

715

720

725

What wound cuts deeper than a loved one
turned against you? Spit her out,
like a mortal enemy—let the girl go.
Let her find a husband down among the dead.   730

Imagine it: I caught her in naked rebellion,
the traitor, the only one in the whole city.
I'm not about to prove myself a liar,
not to my people, no, I'm going to kill her!
That's right—so let her cry for mercy, sing her hymns   735
to Zeus who defends all bonds of kindred blood.
Why, if I bring up my own kin to be rebels,
think what I'd suffer from the world at large.
Show me the man who rules his household well:
I'll show you someone fit to rule the state.   740
That good man, my son,
I have every confidence he and he alone
can give commands and take them too. Staunch
in the storm of spears he'll stand his ground,
a loyal, unflinching comrade at your side.   745

But whoever steps out of line, violates the laws
or presumes to hand out orders to his superiors,
he'll win no praise from me. But that man
the city places in authority, his orders
must be obeyed, large and small,   750
right and wrong.
                    Anarchy—
show me a greater crime in all the earth!
She, she destroys cities, rips up houses,
breaks the ranks of spearmen into headlong rout.
But the ones who last it out, the great mass of them   755
owe their lives to discipline. Therefore
we must defend the men who live by law,
never let some woman triumph over us.
Better to fall from power, if fall we must,
at the hands of a man—never be rated   760
inferior to a woman, never.

LEADER: To us,
unless old age has robbed us of our wits,
you seem to say what you have to say with sense.

HAEMON: Father, only the gods endow a man with reason,
the finest of all their gifts, a treasure.   765
Far be it from me—I haven't the skill,
and certainly no desire, to tell you when,
if ever, you make a slip in speech . . . though
someone else might have a good suggestion.

Of course it's not for you,   770
in the normal run of things, to watch
whatever men say or do, or find to criticize.
The man in the street, you know, dreads your glance,
he'd never say anything displeasing to your face.
But it's for me to catch the murmurs in the dark,   775
the way the city mourns for this young girl.
"No woman," they say, "ever deserved death less,

and such a brutal death for such a glorious action.
She, with her own dear brother lying in his blood—
she couldn't bear to leave him dead, unburied,   780
food for the wild dogs or wheeling vultures.
Death? She deserves a glowing crown of gold!"
So they say, and the rumor spreads in secret,
darkly . . .
                    I rejoice in your success, father—
nothing more precious to me in the world.   785
What medal of honor brighter to his children
than a father's growing glory? Or a child's
to his proud father? Now don't, please,
be quite so single-minded, self-involved,
or assume the world is wrong and you are right.   790
Whoever thinks that he alone possesses intelligence,
the gift of eloquence, he and no one else,
and character too . . . such men, I tell you,
spread them open—you will find them empty.
                                          No,
it's no disgrace for a man, even a wise man,   795
to learn many things and not to be too rigid.
You've seen trees by a raging winter torrent,
how many sway with the flood and salvage every twig,
but not the stubborn—they're ripped out, roots and all.
Bend or break. The same when a man is sailing: 800
haul your sheets too taut, never give an inch,
you'll capsize, go the rest of the voyage
keel up and the rowing-benches under.

Oh give way. Relax your anger—change!
I'm young, I know, but let me offer this: 805
it would be best by far, I admit,
if a man were born infallible, right by nature.
If not—and things don't often go that way,
it's best to learn from those with good advice.
LEADER: You'd do well, my lord, if he's speaking to the point,   810
          to learn from him.

Turning to Haemon.

                    and you, my boy, from him.
You both are talking sense.
CREON: So,
men our age, we're to be lectured, are we?—
schooled by a boy his age?
HAEMON: Only in what is right. But if I seem young,   815
          look less to my years and more to what I do.
CREON: Do? Is admiring rebels an achievement?
HAEMON: I'd never suggest that you admire treason.
CREON: Oh?—
isn't that just the sickness that's attacked her?
HAEMON: The whole city of Thebes denies it, to a man.
CREON: And is Thebes about to tell me how to rule?   820
HAEMON: Now, you see? Who's talking like a child?
CREON: Am I to rule this land for others—or myself?
HAEMON: It's no city at all, owned by one man alone.

CREON: What? The city *is* the king's—that's the law!   825
HAEMON: What a splendid king you'd make of a desert island—
you and you alone.
CREON: *To the Chorus.*   This boy, I do believe,
is fighting on her side, the woman's side.
HAEMON: If you are a woman, yes;
my concern is all for you.   830
CREON: Why, you degenerate—bandying accusations,
threatening me with justice, your own father!
HAEMON: I see my father offending justice—wrong.
CREON: Wrong?
To protect my royal rights?
HAEMON: Protect your rights?
When you trample down the honors of the gods?   835
CREON: You, you soul of corruption, rotten through—
woman's accomplice!
HAEMON: That may be,
but you'll never find me accomplice to a criminal.
CREON: That's what *she* is,
and every word you say is a blatant appeal for her—   840
HAEMON: And you, and me, and the gods beneath the earth.
CREON: You'll never marry her, not while she's alive.
HAEMON: Then she'll die . . . but her death will kill another.
CREON: What, brazen threats? You go too far!
HAEMON: What threat?
Combating your empty, mindless judgments with a word?   845
CREON: You'll suffer for your sermons, you and your empty wisdom!
HAEMON: If you weren't my father, I'd say you were insane.
CREON: Don't flatter me with Father—you woman's slave!
HAEMON: You really expect to fling abuse at me
and not receive the same?
CREON: Is that so!   850
Now, by heaven, I promise you, you'll pay—
taunting, insulting me! Bring her out,
that hateful—she'll die now, here,
in front of his eyes, beside her groom!
HAEMON: No, no, she will never die beside me—   855
don't delude yourself. And you will never
see me, never set eyes on my face again.
Rage your heart out, rage with friends
who can stand the sight of you.   *Rushing out.*
LEADER: Gone, my king, in a burst of anger.   860
A temper young as his . . . hurt him once,
he may do something violent.
CREON: Let him do—
dream up something desperate, past all human limit!
Good riddance. Rest assured,
he'll never save those two young girls from death.   865
LEADER: Both of them, you really intend to kill them both?
CREON: No, not her, the one whose hands are clean;
you're quite right.
LEADER: But Antigone—
what sort of death do you have in mind for her?

CREON:	I'll take her down some wild, desolate path	870
	never trod by men, and wall her up alive	
	in a rocky vault, and set out short rations,	
	just a gesture of piety	
	to keep the entire city free of defilement.	
	There let her pray to the one god she worships:	875
	Death—who knows?—may just reprieve her from death.	
	Or she may learn at last, better late than never,	
	what a waste of breath it is to worship Death.	

Exit to the palace.

CHORUS:	Love, never conquered in battle	
	Love the plunderer laying waste the rich!	
	Love standing the night-watch	880
	guarding a girl's soft cheek,	
	you range the seas, the shepherds' steadings off in the wilds—	
	not even the deathless gods can flee your onset,	
	nothing human born for a day—	
	whoever feels your grip is driven mad.	885
	Love	
	you wrench the minds of the righteous into outrage,	
	swerve them to their ruin—you have ignited this,	
	this kindred strife, father and son at war	
	and Love alone the victor—	
	warm glance of the bride triumphant, burning with desire!	890
	Throned in power, side-by-side with the mighty laws!	
	Irresistible Aphrodite, never conquered—	
	Love, you mock us for your sport.	

Antigone is brought from the palace under guard.

	But now, even I'd rebel against the king,	895
	I'd break all bounds when I see this—	
	I fill with tears, can't hold them back,	
	not any more . . . I see Antigone make her way	
	to the bridal vault where all are laid to rest.	
ANTIGONE:	Look at me, men of my fatherland,	900
	setting out on the last road	
	looking into the last light of day	
	the last I'll ever see . . .	
	the god of death who puts us all to bed	
	takes me down to the banks of Acheron alive—	905
	denied my part in the wedding-songs,	
	no wedding-song in the dusk has crowned my marriage—	
	I go to wed the lord of the dark waters.	
CHORUS:	Not crowned with glory, crowned with a dirge,	
	you leave for the deep pit of the dead.	910
	No withering illness laid you low,	
	no strokes of the sword—a law to yourself,	
	alone, no mortal like you, ever, you go down	
	to the halls of Death alive and breathing.	
ANTIGONE:	But think of Niobe—well I know her story—	915
	think what a living death she died,	
	Tantalus' daughter, stranger queen from the east:	
	there on the mountain heights, growing stone	

binding as ivy, slowly walled her round
and the rains will never cease, the legends say   920
the snows will never leave her . . .
       wasting away, under her brows the tears
showering down her breasting ridge and slopes—
a rocky death like hers puts me to sleep.

CHORUS: But she was a god, born of gods,   925
and we are only mortals born to die.
And yet, of course, it's a great thing
for a dying girl to hear, just hear
she shares a destiny equal to the gods,
during life and later, once she's dead.

ANTIGONE: O you mock me!   930
Why, in the name of all my fathers' gods
why can't you wait till I am gone—
    must you abuse me to my face?
O my city, all your fine rich sons!
And you, you springs of the Dirce,   935
holy grove of Thebes where the chariots gather,
      you at least, you'll bear me witness, look,
unmourned by friends and forced by such crude laws
I go to my rockbound prison, strange new tomb—
    always a stranger, O dear god,   940
    I have no home on earth and none below,
      not with the living, not with the breathless dead.

CHORUS: You went too far, the last limits of daring—
smashing against the high throne of Justice!
Your life's in ruins, child—I wonder . . .   945
do you pay for your father's terrible ordeal?

ANTIGONE: There—at last you've touched it, the worst pain
the worst anguish! Raking up the grief for father
    three times over, for all the doom
that's struck us down, the brilliant house of Laius.   950
O mother, your marriage-bed
the coiling horrors, the coupling there—
    you with your own son, my father—doomstruck mother!
Such, such were my parents, and I their wretched child.
I go to them now, cursed, unwed, to share their home—   955
    I am a stranger! O dear brother, doomed
    in your marriage—your marriage murders mine,
      your dying drags me down to death alive!

Enter Creon.

CHORUS: Reverence asks some reverence in return—
but attacks on power never go unchecked,   960
    not by the man who holds the reins of power.
Your own blind will, your passion has destroyed you.

ANTIGONE: No one to weep for me, my friends,
no wedding-song—they take me away
in all my pain . . . the road lies open, waiting.   965
Never again, the law forbids me to see
the sacred eye of day. I am agony!
No tears for the destiny that's mine,
no loved one mourns my death.

CREON: Can't you see?
 If a man could wail his own dirge *before* he dies,   970
 he'd never finish.

To the guards.

       Take her away, quickly!
 Wall her up in the tomb, you have your orders.
 Abandon her there, alone, and let her choose—
 death or a buried life with a good roof for shelter.
 As for myself, my hands are clean. This young girl—   975
 dead or alive, she will be stripped of her rights,
 her stranger's rights, here in the world above.

ANTIGONE: O tomb, my bridal-bed—my house, my prison
 cut in the hollow rock, my everlasting watch!
 I'll soon be there, soon embrace my own,   980
 the great growing family of our dead
 Persephone has received among her ghosts.

        I,
 the last of them all, the most reviled by far,
 go down before my destined time's run out.
 But still I go, cherishing one good hope: 985
 my arrival may be dear to father,
 dear to you, my mother,
 dear to you, my loving brother, Eteocles—
 When you died I washed you with my hands,
 I dressed you all, I poured the cups   990
 across your tombs. But now, Polynices,
 because I laid your body out as well,
 this, this is my reward. Nevertheless
 I honored you—the decent will admit it—
 well and wisely too.

       Never, I tell you,   995
 if I had been the mother of children
 or if my husband died, exposed and rotting—
 I'd never have taken this ordeal upon myself,
 never defied our people's will. What law,
 you ask, do I satisfy with what I say?   1000
 A husband dead, there might have been another.
 A child by another too, if I had lost the first.
 But mother and father both lost in the halls of Death,
 no brother could ever spring to light again.

 For this law alone I held you first in honor.   1005
 For this, Creon, the king, judges me a criminal
 guilty of dreadful outrage, my dear brother!
 And now he leads me off, a captive in his hands,
 with no part in the bridal-song, the bridal-bed,
 denied all joy of marriage, raising children—   1010
 deserted so by loved ones, struck by fate,
 I descend alive to the caverns of the dead.

 What law of the mighty gods have I transgressed?
 Why look to the heavens any more, tormented as I am?
 Whom to call, what comrades now? Just think,   1015
 my reverence only brands me for irreverence!

Very well: if this is the pleasure of the gods,
once I suffer I will know that I was wrong.
But if these men are wrong, let them suffer
nothing worse than they mete out to me—
these masters of injustice!   1020

LEADER: Still the same rough winds, the wild passion
raging through the girl.

CREON: *To the guards.*   Take her away.
You're wasting time—you'll pay for it too.

ANTIGONE: Oh god, the voice of death. It's come, it's here.   1025

CREON: True. Not a word of hope—your doom is sealed.

ANTIGONE: Land of Thebes, city of all my fathers—
O you gods, the first gods of the race!
They drag me away, now, no more delay.
Look on me, you noble sons of Thebes—   1030
the last of a great line of kings,
I alone, see what I suffer now
at the hands of what breed of men—
all for reverence, my reverence for the gods!

She leaves under guard; the Chorus gathers.

CHORUS: Danaë, Danaë—
even she endured a fate like yours,   1035
      in all her lovely strength she traded
the light of day for the bolted brazen vault—
buried within her tomb, her bridal-chamber,
wed to the yoke and broken.
      But she was of glorious birth
                        my child, my child   1040
and treasured the seed of Zeus within her womb,
the cloudburst streaming gold!
      The power of fate is a wonder,
      dark, terrible wonder—   1045
neither wealth nor armies
towered walls nor ships
black hulls lashed by the salt
can save us from that force.   1050

The yoke tamed him too
      young Lycurgus flaming in anger
king of Edonia, all for his mad taunts
Dionysus clamped him down, encased
in the chain-mail of rock   1055
      and there his rage
                        his terrible flowering rage burst—
sobbing, dying away . . . at last that madman
came to know his god—
      the power he mocked, the power   1060
      he taunted in all his frenzy
trying to stamp out
      the women strong with the god—
      the torch, the raving sacred cries—
enraging the Muses who adore the flute.   1065

And far north where the Black Rocks
      cut the sea in half

and murderous straits
split the coast of Thrace
    a forbidding city stands
where once, hard by the walls   1070
the savage Ares thrilled to watch
a king's new queen, a Fury rearing in rage
      against his two royal sons—
          her bloody hands, her dagger-shuttle   1075
stabbing out their eyes—cursed, blinding wounds—
their eyes blind sockets screaming for revenge!

They wailed in agony, cries echoing cries
    the princes doomed at birth . . .
and their mother doomed to chains,   1080
    walled off in a tomb of stone—
      but she traced her own birth back
to a proud Athenian line and the high gods
and off in caverns half the world away,
born of the wild North Wind   1085
      she sprang on her father's gales,
        racing stallions up the leaping cliffs—
child of the heavens. But even on her the Fates
the gray everlasting Fates rode hard
my child, my child.

Enter Tiresias, the blind prophet, led by a boy.

TIRESIAS: Lords of Thebes,   1090
I and the boy have come together,
hand in hand. Two see with the eyes of one . . .
so the blind must go, with a guide to lead the way.
CREON: What is it, old Tiresias? What news now?
TIRESIAS: I will teach you. And you obey the seer.
CREON: I will,   1095
I've never wavered from your advice before.
TIRESIAS: And so you kept the city straight on course.
CREON: I owe you a great deal, I swear to that.
TIRESIAS: Then reflect, my son: you are poised,
once more, on the razor-edge of fate.   1100
CREON: What is it? I shudder to hear you.
TIRESIAS: You will learn
when you listen to the warnings of my craft.
As I sat in the ancient seat of augury,
in the sanctuary where every bird I know
will hover at my hands—suddenly I heard it,   1105
a strange voice in the wingbeats, unintelligible,
barbaric, a mad scream! Talons flashing, ripping,
they were killing each other—that much I knew—
the murderous fury whirring in those wings
made that much clear!
                I was afraid,   1110
I turned quickly, tested the burnt-sacrifice,
ignited the altar at all points—but no fire,
the god in the fire never blazed.
Not from those offerings . . . over the embers
slid a heavy ooze from the long thighbones,   1115
smoking, sputtering out, and the bladder

puffed and burst—spraying gall into the air—
and the fat wrapping the bones slithered off
and left them glistening white. No fire!
The rites failed that might have blazed the future   1120
with a sign. So I learned from the boy here;
he is my guide, as I am guide to others.
              And it's you—
your high resolve that sets this plague on Thebes.
The public altars and sacred hearths are fouled,
one and all, by the birds and dogs with carrion   1125
torn from the corpse, the doomstruck son of Oedipus!
And so the gods are deaf to our prayers, they spurn
the offerings in our hands, the flame of holy flesh.
No birds cry out an omen clear and true—
they're gorged with the murdered victim's blood and fat.   1130
Take these things to heart, my son, I warn you.
All men make mistakes, it is only human.
But once the wrong is done, a man
can turn his back on folly, misfortune too,
if he tries to make amends, however low he's fallen,   1135
and stops his bullnecked ways. Stubbornness
brands you for stupidity—pride is a crime.
No, yield to the dead!
Never stab the fighter when he's down.
Where's the glory, killing the dead twice over?   1140

I mean you well. I give you sound advice.
It's best to learn from a good adviser
when he speaks for your own good:
it's pure gain.
CREON: Old man—all of you! So,
you shoot your arrows at my head like archers at the target—   1145
I even have *him* loosed on me, this fortune-teller.
Oh his ilk has tried to sell me short
and ship me off for years. Well,
drive your bargains, traffic—much as you like—
in the gold of India, silver-gold of Sardis.   1150
You'll never bury that body in the grave,
not even if Zeus's eagles rip the corpse
and wing their rotten pickings off to the throne of god!
Never, not even in fear of such defilement
will I tolerate his burial, that traitor.   1155
Well I know, we can't defile the gods—
no mortal has the power.
           No,
reverend old Tiresias, all men fall,
it's only human, but the wisest fall obscenely
when they glorify obscene advice with rhetoric—   1160
all for their own gain.
TIRESIAS: Oh god, is there a man alive
who knows, who actually believes ...
CREON: What now?
What earth-shattering truth are you about to utter?
TIRESIAS: ... just how much a sense of judgment, wisdom   1165
is the greatest gift we have?

CREON: Just as much, I'd say,
    as a twisted mind is the worst affliction going.
TIRESIAS: You are the one who's sick, Creon, sick to death.
CREON: I am in no mood to trade insults with a seer.
TIRESIAS: You have already, calling my prophecies a lie.
CREON: Why not?   1170
    You and the whole breed of seers are mad for money!
TIRESIAS: And the whole race of tyrants lusts to rake it in.
CREON: This slander of yours—
    are you aware you're speaking to the king?
TIRESIAS: Well aware. Who helped you save the city?
CREON: You—   1175
    you have your skills, old seer, but you lust for injustice!
TIRESIAS: You will drive me to utter the dreadful secret in my heart.
CREON: Spit it out! Just don't speak it out for profit.
TIRESIAS: Profit? No, not a bit of profit, not for you.
CREON: Know full well, you'll never buy off my resolve.   1180
TIRESIAS: Then know this too, learn this by heart!
    The chariot of the sun will not race through
    so many circuits more, before you have surrendered
    one born of your own loins, your own flesh and blood,
    a corpse for corpses given in return, since you have thrust   1185
    to the world below a child sprung from the world above,
    ruthlessly lodged a living soul within the grave—
    then you've robbed the gods below the earth,
    keeping a dead body here in the bright air,
    unburied, unsung, unhallowed by the rites.   1190

    You, you have no business with the dead,
    nor do the gods above—this is violence
    you have forced upon the heavens.
    And so the avengers, the dark destroyers late
    but true to the mark, now lie in wait for you,   1195
    the Furies sent by the gods and the god of death
    to strike you down with the pains that you perfected!

    There. Reflect on that, tell me I've been bribed.
    The day comes soon, no long test of time, not now,
    that wakes the wails for men and women in your halls.   1200
    Great hatred rises against you—
    cities in tumult, all whose mutilated sons
    the dogs have graced with burial, or the wild beasts,
    some wheeling crow that wings the ungodly stench of carrion
    back to each city, each warrior's heart and home.   1205

    These arrows for your heart! Since you've raked me
    I loose them like an archer in my anger,
    arrows deadly true. You'll never escape
    their burning, searing force.

Motioning to his escort.

    Come, boy, take me home.   1210
    So he can vent his rage on younger men,
    and learn to keep a gentler tongue in his head
    and better sense than what he carries now.

Exit to the side.

LEADER: The old man's gone, my king—
          terrible prophecies. Well I know,   1215
          since the hair on his old head went gray,
          he's never lied to Thebes.
CREON: I know it myself—I'm shaken, torn.
          It's a dreadful thing to yield . . . but resist now?
          Lay my pride bare to the blows of ruin?   1220
          That's dreadful too.
LEADER: But good advice,
          Creon, take it now, you must.
CREON: What should I do? Tell me . . . I'll obey.
LEADER: Go! Free the girl from the rocky vault
          and raise a mound for the body you exposed.   1225
CREON: That's your advice? You think I should give in?
LEADER: Yes, my king, quickly. Disasters sent by the gods
          cut short our follies in a flash.
CREON: Oh it's hard,
          giving up the heart's desire . . . but I will do it—
          no more fighting a losing battle with necessity.   1230
LEADER: Do it now, go, don't leave it to others.
CREON: Now—I'm on my way! Come, each of you,
          take up axes, make for the high ground,
          over there, quickly! I and my better judgment
          have come round to this—I shackled her,   1235
          I'll set her free myself. I am afraid . . .
          it's best to keep the established laws
          to the very day we die.

Rushing out, followed by his entourage. The Chorus clusters around the altar.

CHORUS: God of a hundred names!
                              Great Dionysus—
                    Son and glory of Semele! Pride of Thebes—
          Child of Zeus whose thunder rocks the clouds—   1240
          Lord of the famous lands of evening—
          King of the Mysteries!
                              King of Eleusis, Demeter's plain
          her breasting hills that welcome in the world—
          Great Dionysus!
                              Bacchus, living in Thebes   1245
          the mother-city of all your frenzied women—
                                        Bacchus
                    living along the Ismenus' rippling waters
          standing over the field sown with the Dragons' teeth!

          You—we have seen you through the flaring smoky fires,
                    your torches blazing over the twin peaks   1250
          where nymphs of the hallowed cave climb onward
                              fired with you, your sacred rage—
          we have seen you at Castalia's running spring
          and down from the heights of Nysa crowned with ivy
          the greening shore rioting vines and grapes   1255
                              down you come in your storm of wild women
          ecstatic, mystic cries—
                                        Dionysus—
          down to watch and ward the roads of Thebes!

First of all cities, Thebes you honor first
you and your mother, bride of the lightning—
come, Dionysus! now your people lie
in the iron grip of plague,
come in your racing, healing stride
                 down Parnassus' slopes
or across the moaning straits.
                    Lord of the dancing—
dance, dance the constellations breathing fire!
Great master of the voices of the night!
Child of Zeus, God's offspring, come, come forth!
Lord, king, dance with your nymphs, swirling, raving
arm-in-arm in frenzy through the night
                 they dance you, Iacchus—
                Dance, Dionysus
giver of all good things!

Enter a Messenger from the side.

MESSENGER: Neighbors,
friends of the house of Cadmus and the kings,
there's not a thing in this life of ours
I'd praise or blame as settled once for all.
Fortune lifts and Fortune fells the lucky
and unlucky every day. No prophet on earth
can tell a man his fate. Take Creon:
there was a man to rouse your envy once,
as I see it. He saved the realm from enemies;
taking power, he alone, the lord of the fatherland,
he set us true on course—flourished like a tree
with the noble line of sons he bred and reared . . .
and now it's lost, all gone.
                   Believe me,
when a man has squandered his true joys,
he's good as dead, I tell you, a living corpse.
Pile up riches in your house, as much as you like—
live like a king with a huge show of pomp,
but if real delight is missing from the lot,
I wouldn't give you a wisp of smoke for it,
not compared with joy.
LEADER: What now?
What new grief do you bring the house of kings?
MESSENGER: Dead, dead—and the living are guilty of their death!
LEADER: Who's the murderer? Who is dead? Tell us.
MESSENGER: Haemon's gone, his blood spilled by the very hand—
LEADER: His father's or his own?
MESSENGER: His own . . .
raging mad with his father for the death—
LEADER: Oh great seer,
you saw it all, you brought your word to birth!
MESSENGER: Those are the facts. Deal with them as you will.

As he turns to go, Eurydice enters from the palace.

LEADER: Look, Eurydice. Poor woman, Creon's wife,
so close at hand. By chance perhaps,
unless she's heard the news about her son.

1260

1265

1270

1275

1280

1285

1290

1295

1300

EURYDICE: My countrymen,
    all of you—I caught the sound of your words
    as I was leaving to do my part,
    to appeal to queen Athena with my prayers.   1305
    I was just loosing the bolts, opening the doors,
    when a voice filled with sorrow, family sorrow,
    struck my ears, and I fell back, terrified,
    into the women's arms—everything went black.
    Tell me the news, again, whatever it is . . .   1310
    sorrow and I are hardly strangers;
    I can bear the worst.
MESSENGER: I—dear lady,
    I'll speak as an eye-witness. I was there.
    And I won't pass over one word of the truth.
    Why should I try to soothe you with a story,   1315
    only to prove a liar in a moment?
    Truth is always best.
              So,
    I escorted your lord, I guided him
    to the edge of the plain where the body lay,
    Polynices, torn by the dogs and still unmourned.   1320
    And saying a prayer to Hecate of the Crossroads,
    Pluto too, to hold their anger and be kind,
    we washed the dead in a bath of holy water
    and plucking some fresh branches, gathering . . .
    what was left of him, we burned them all together   1325
    and raised a high mound of native earth, and then
    we turned and made for that rocky vault of hers,
    the hollow, empty bed of the bride of Death.
    And far off, one of us heard a voice,
    a long wail rising, echoing   1330
    out of that unhallowed wedding-chamber;
    he ran to alert the master and Creon pressed on,
    closer—the strange, inscrutable cry came sharper,
    throbbing around him now, and he let loose
    a cry of his own, enough to wrench the heart,   1335
    "Oh god, am I the prophet now? going down
    the darkest road I've ever gone? My son—
    it's *his* dear voice, he greets me! Go, men,
    closer, quickly! Go through the gap,
    the rocks are dragged back—   1340
    right to the tomb's very mouth—and look,
    see if it's Haemon's voice I think I hear,
    or the gods have robbed me of my senses."

    The king was shattered. We took his orders,
    went and searched, and there in the deepest,   1345
    dark recesses of the tomb we found her . . .
    hanged by the neck in a fine linen noose,
    strangled in her veils—and the boy,
    his arms flung around her waist,
    clinging to her, wailing for his bride,   1350
    dead and down below, for his father's crimes
    and the bed of his marriage blighted by misfortune.
    When Creon saw him, he gave a deep sob,

he ran in, shouting, crying out to him,
"Oh my child—what have you done? what seized you, 1355
what insanity? what disaster drove you mad?
Come out, my son! I beg you on my knees!"
But the boy gave him a wild burning glance,
spat in his face, not a word in reply,
he drew his sword—his father rushed out, 1360
running as Haemon lunged and missed!—
and then, doomed, desperate with himself,
suddenly leaning his full weight on the blade,
he buried it in his body, halfway to the hilt.
And still in his senses, pouring his arms around her, 1365
he embraced the girl and breathing hard,
released a quick rush of blood,
bright red on her cheek glistening white.
And there he lies, body enfolding body . . .
he has won his bride at last, poor boy,
not here but in the houses of the dead. 1370

Creon shows the world that of all the ills
afflicting men the worst is lack of judgment.

Eurydice turns and reenters the palace.

LEADER: What do you make of that? The lady's gone,
    without a word, good or bad.
MESSENGER: I'm alarmed too 1375
    but here's my hope—faced with her son's death,
    she finds it unbecoming to mourn in public.
    Inside, under her roof, she'll set her women
    to the task and wail the sorrow of the house.
    She's too discreet. She won't do something rash. 1380
LEADER: I'm not so sure. To me, at least,
    a long heavy silence promises danger,
    just as much as a lot of empty outcries.
MESSENGER: We'll see if she's holding something back,
    hiding some passion in her heart.
    I'm going in. You may be right—who knows? 1385
    Even too much silence has its dangers.

Exit to the palace. Enter Creon from the side, escorted by attendants carrying Haemon's body on a bier.

LEADER: The king himself! Coming toward us,
    look, holding the boy's head in his hands.
    Clear, damning proof, if it's right to say so—
    proof of his own madness, no one else's, 1390
        no, his own blind wrongs.
CREON: Ohhh,
    so senseless, so insane . . . my crimes,
    my stubborn, deadly—
    Look at us, the killer, the killed,
    father and son, the same blood—the misery! 1395
    My plans, my mad fanatic heart,
    my son, cut off so young!
    Ai, dead, lost to the world,
    not through your stupidity, no, my own.

LEADER: Too late,   1400
  too late, you see what justice means.
CREON: Oh I've learned
  through blood and tears! Then, it was then,
  when the god came down and struck me—a great weight
  shattering, driving me down that wild savage path,
  ruining, trampling down my joy. Oh the agony,   1405
  the heartbreaking agonies of our lives.

Enter the Messenger from the palace.

MESSENGER: Master,
  what a hoard of grief you have, and you'll have more.
  The grief that lies to hand you've brought yourself—

Pointing to Haemon's body.

  the rest, in the house, you'll see it all too soon.
CREON: What now? What's worse than this?
MESSENGER: The queen is dead.   1410
  The mother of this dead boy . . . mother to the end—
  poor thing, her wounds are fresh.
CREON: No, no,
  harbor of Death, so choked, so hard to cleanse!—
  why me? why are you killing me?
  Herald of pain, more words, more grief?   1415
  I died once, you kill me again and again!
  What's the report, boy . . . some news for me?
  My wife dead? O dear god!
  Slaughter heaped on slaughter?

The doors open; the body of Eurydice is brought out on her bier.

MESSENGER: See for yourself:
  now they bring her body from the palace.
CREON: Oh no,   1420
  another, a second loss to break the heart.
  What next, what fate still waits for me?
  I just held my son in my arms and now,
  look, a new corpse rising before my eyes—
  wretched, helpless mother—O my son!   1425
MESSENGER: She stabbed herself at the altar,
  then her eyes went dark, after she'd raised
  a cry for the noble fate of Megareus, the hero
  killed in the first assault, then for Haemon,
  then with her dying breath she called down   1430
  torments on your head—you killed her sons.
CREON: Oh the dread,
  I shudder with dread! Why not kill me too?—
  run me through with a good sharp sword?
  Oh god, the misery, anguish—
  I, I'm churning with it, going under.   1435
MESSENGER: Yes, and the dead, the woman lying there,
  piles the guilt of all their deaths on you.
CREON: How did she end her life, what bloody stroke?
MESSENGER: She drove home to the heart with her own hand,
  once she learned her son was dead . . . that agony.   1440

CREON: And the guilt is all mine—
        can never be fixed on another man,
        no escape for me. I killed you,
        I, god help me, I admit it all!

To his attendants.

        Take me away, quickly, out of sight.   1445
        I don't even exist—I'm no one. Nothing.
LEADER: Good advice, if there's any good in suffering.
        Quickest is best when troubles block the way.
CREON:

Kneeling in prayer.

        Come, let it come!—that best of fates for me
        that brings the final day, best fate of all.   1450
        Oh quickly, now—
        so I never have to see another sunrise.
LEADER: That will come when it comes;
        we must deal with all that lies before us.
        The future rests with the ones who tend the future.   1455
CREON: That prayer—I poured my heart into that prayer!
LEADER: No more prayers now. For mortal men
        there is no escape from the doom we must endure.
CREON: Take me away, I beg you, out of sight.
        A rash, indiscriminate fool!   1460
        I murdered you, my son, against my will—
        you too, my wife . . .
                              Wailing wreck of a man,
        whom to look to? where to lean for support?

Desperately turning from Haemon to Eurydice on their biers.

        Whatever I touch goes wrong—once more
        a crushing fate's come down upon my head.   1465

The Messenger and attendants lead Creon into the palace.

CHORUS: Wisdom is by far the greatest part of joy,
        and reverence toward the gods must be safeguarded.
        The mighty words of the proud are paid in full
        with mighty blows of fate, and at long last
        those blows will teach us wisdom.   1470

The old citizens exit to the side.

Molière   (1622–1673)

Tartuffe   *1664*

Translated by Richard Wilbur

Characters

Madame Pernelle, Orgon's mother
Orgon, Elmire's husband
Elmire, Orgon's wife
Damis, Orgon's son, Elmire's stepson

Mariane, Orgon's daughter, Elmire's stepdaughter, in love with Valère
Valère, in love with Mariane
Cléante, Orgon's brother-in-law
Tartuffe, a hypocrite
Dorine, Mariane's lady's-maid
M. Loyal, a bailiff
A Police Officer
Flipote, Mme Pernelle's maid

The scene throughout: Orgon's house in Paris

Act 1, Scene 1

Madame Pernelle and Flipote, her maid, Elmire, Mariane, Dorine, Damis, Cléante

MADAME PERNELLE: Come, come, Flipote; it's time I left this place.
ELMIRE: I can't keep up, you walk at such a pace.
MADAME PERNELLE: Don't trouble, child; no need to show me out.
    It's not your manners I'm concerned about.
ELMIRE: We merely pay you the respect we owe.   5
    But, Mother, why this hurry? Must you go?
MADAME PERNELLE: I must. This house appals me. No one in it
    Will pay attention for a single minute.
    Children, I take my leave much vexed in spirit.
    I offer good advice, but you won't hear it.   10
    You all break in and chatter on and on.
    It's like a madhouse with the keeper gone.
DORINE: If . . .
MADAME PERNELLE: Girl, you talk too much, and I'm afraid
    You're far too saucy for a lady's-maid.
    You push in everywhere and have your say.   15
DAMIS: But . . .
MADAME PERNELLE: You, boy, grow more foolish every day.
    To think my grandson should be such a dunce!
    I've said a hundred times, if I've said it once,
    That if you keep the course on which you've started,
    You'll leave your worthy father broken-hearted.   20
MARIANE: I think . . .
MADAME PERNELLE: And you, his sister, seem so pure,
    So shy, so innocent, and so demure.
    But you know what they say about still waters.
    I pity parents with secretive daughters.
ELMIRE: Now, Mother . . .
MADAME PERNELLE: And as for you, child, let me add   25
    That your behavior is extremely bad,
    And a poor example for these children, too.
    Their dear, dead mother did far better than you.
    You're much too free with money, and I'm distressed
    To see you so elaborately dressed.   30
    When it's one's husband that one aims to please,
    One has no need of costly fripperies.
CLÉANTE: Oh, Madam, really . . .
MADAME PERNELLE: You are her brother, Sir,
    And I respect and love you; yet if I were
    My son, this lady's good and pious spouse,   35

I wouldn't make you welcome in my house.
You're full of worldly counsels which, I fear,
Aren't suitable for decent folk to hear.
I've spoken bluntly, Sir; but it behooves us
Not to mince words when righteous fervor moves us.   40

DAMIS: Your man Tartuffe is full of holy speeches . . .

MADAME PERNELLE: And practises precisely what he preaches.
He's a fine man, and should be listened to.
I will not hear him mocked by fools like you.

DAMIS: Good God! Do you expect me to submit   45
To the tyranny of that carping hypocrite?
Must we forgo all joys and satisfactions
Because that bigot censures all our actions?

DORINE: To hear him talk—and he talks all the time—
There's nothing one can do that's not a crime.   50
He rails at everything, your dear Tartuffe.

MADAME PERNELLE: Whatever he reproves deserves reproof.
He's out to save your souls, and all of you
Must love him, as my son would have you do.

DAMIS: Ah no, Grandmother, I could never take   55
To such a rascal, even for my father's sake.
That's how I feel, and I shall not dissemble.
His every action makes me seethe and tremble
With helpless anger, and I have no doubt
That he and I will shortly have it out.   60

DORINE: Surely it is a shame and a disgrace
To see this man usurp the master's place—
To see this beggar who, when first he came,
Had not a shoe or shoestring to his name
So far forget himself that he behaves   65
As if the house were his, and we his slaves.

MADAME PERNELLE: Well, mark my words, your souls would fare far better
If you obeyed his precepts to the letter.

DORINE: You see him as a saint. I'm far less awed;
In fact, I see right through him. He's a fraud.   70

MADAME PERNELLE: Nonsense!

DORINE: His man Laurent's the same, or worse;
I'd not trust either with a penny purse.

MADAME PERNELLE: I can't say what his servant's morals may be;
His own great goodness I can guarantee.
You all regard him with distaste and fear   75
Because he tells you what you're loath to hear,
Condemns your sins, points out your moral flaws,
And humbly strives to further Heaven's cause.

DORINE: If sin is all that bothers him, why is it
He's so upset when folk drop in to visit?   80
Is Heaven so outraged by a social call
That he must prophesy against us all?
I'll tell you what I think: if you ask me,
He's jealous of my mistress' company.

MADAME PERNELLE: Rubbish! (To Elmire.) He's not alone, child, in complaining 85
Of all of your promiscuous entertaining.
Why, the whole neighborhood's upset, I know,
By all these carriages that come and go,

With crowds of guests parading in and out
And noisy servants loitering about.   90
In all of this, I'm sure there's nothing vicious;
But why give people cause to be suspicious?

CLÉANTE: They need no cause; they'll talk in any case.
Madam, this world would be a joyless place
If, fearing what malicious tongues might say,   95
We locked our doors and turned our friends away.
And even if one did so dreary a thing,
D'you think those tongues would cease their chattering?
One can't fight slander; it's a losing battle;
Let us instead ignore their tittle-tattle.   100
Let's strive to live by conscience' clear decrees,
And let the gossips gossip as they please.

DORINE: If there is talk against us, I know the source:
It's Daphne and her little husband, of course.
Those who have greatest cause for guilt and shame   105
Are quickest to besmirch a neighbor's name.
When there's a chance for libel, they never miss it;
When something can be made to seem illicit
They're off at once to spread the joyous news,
Adding to fact what fantasies they choose.   110
By talking up their neighbor's indiscretions
They seek to camouflage their own transgressions,
Hoping that others' innocent affairs
Will lend a hue of innocence to theirs.
Or that their own black guilt will come to seem   115
Part of a general shady color-scheme.

MADAME PERNELLE: All that is quite irrelevant. I doubt
That anyone's more virtuous and devout
Than dear Orante; and I'm informed that she
Condemns your mode of life most vehemently.   120

DORINE: Oh, yes, she's strict, devout, and has no taint
Of worldliness; in short, she seems a saint.
But it was time which taught her that disguise;
She's thus because she can't be otherwise.
So long as her attractions could enthrall,   125
She flounced and flirted and enjoyed it all,
But now that they're no longer what they were
She quits a world which fast is quitting her,
And wears a veil of virtue to conceal
Her bankrupt beauty and her lost appeal.   130
That's what becomes of old coquettes today:
Distressed when all their lovers fall away,
They see no recourse but to play the prude,
And so confer a style on solitude.
Thereafter, they're severe with everyone,   135
Condemning all our actions, pardoning none,
And claiming to be pure, austere, and zealous
When, if the truth were known, they're merely jealous,
And cannot bear to see another know
The pleasures time has forced them to forgo.   140

MADAME PERNELLE: *(Initially to Elmire)*   That sort of talk is what you like to hear;
Therefore you'd have us all keep still, my dear,

While Madam rattles on the livelong day.
Nevertheless, I mean to have my say.
I tell you that you're blest to have Tartuffe   145
Dwelling, as my son's guest, beneath this roof;
That Heaven has sent him to forestall its wrath
By leading you, once more, to the true path;
That all he reprehends is reprehensible,
And that you'd better heed him, and be sensible.   150
These visits, balls, and parties in which you revel
Are nothing but inventions of the Devil.
One never hears a word that's edifying:
Nothing but chaff and foolishness and lying,
As well as vicious gossip in which one's neighbor   155
Is cut to bits with epee, foil, and saber.
People of sense are driven half-insane
At such affairs, where noise and folly reign
And reputations perish thick and fast.
As a wise preacher said on Sunday last,   160
Parties are Towers of Babylon, because
The guests all babble on with never a pause;
And then he told a story which, I think . . .

(To Cléante.)

I heard that laugh, Sir, and I saw that wink!
Go find your silly friends and laugh some more!   165
Enough; I'm going; don't show me to the door.
I leave this household much dismayed and vexed;
I cannot say when I shall see you next.

(Slapping Flipote.)

Wake up, don't stand there gaping into space!
I'll slap some sense into that stupid face.   170
Move, move, you slut.

Act 1, Scene 2

Cléante, Dorine

CLÉANTE: I think I'll stay behind;
I want no further pieces of her mind.
How that old lady . . .
DORINE: Oh, what wouldn't she say
If she could hear you speak of her that way!
She'd thank you for the *lady*, but I'm sure   5
She'd find the old a little premature.
CLÉANTE: My, what a scene she made, and what a din!
And how this man Tartuffe has taken her in!
DORINE: Yes, but her son is even worse deceived;
His folly must be seen to be believed.   10
In the late troubles, he played an able part
And served his king with wise and loyal heart,
But he's quite lost his senses since he fell
Beneath Tartuffe's infatuating spell.
He calls him brother, and loves him as his life,
Preferring him to mother, child, or wife.   15
In him and him alone will he confide;

He's made him his confessor and his guide;
He pets and pampers him with love more tender
Than any pretty mistress could engender,   20
Gives him the place of honor when they dine,
Delights to see him gorging like a swine,
Stuffs him with dainties till his guts distend,
And when he belches, cries "God bless you, friend!"
In short, he's mad; he worships him; he dotes;   25
His deeds he marvels at, his words he quotes,
Thinking each act a miracle, each word
Oracular as those that Moses heard.
Tartuffe, much pleased to find so easy a victim,
Has in a hundred ways beguiled and tricked him,   30
Milked him of money, and with his permission
Established here a sort of Inquisition.
Even Laurent, his lackey, dares to give
Us arrogant advice on how to live;
He sermonizes us in thundering tones   35
And confiscates our ribbons and colognes.
Last week he tore a kerchief into pieces
Because he found it pressed in a *Life of Jesus:*
He said it was a sin to juxtapose
Unholy vanities and holy prose.   40

Act 1, Scene 3

Elmire, Mariane, Damis, Cléante, Dorine

ELMIRE: (*To Cléante*)   You did well not to follow; she stood in the door
            And said *verbatim* all she'd said before.
            I saw my husband coming. I think I'd best
            Go upstairs now, and take a little rest.
CLÉANTE: I'll wait and greet him here; then I must go.   5
            I've really only time to say hello.
DAMIS: Sound him about my sister's wedding, please.
            I think Tartuffe's against it, and that he's
            Been urging Father to withdraw his blessing.
            As you well know, I'd find that most distressing.   10
            Unless my sister and Valère can marry,
            My hopes to wed *his* sister will miscarry,
            And I'm determined ...
DORINE: He's coming.

Act 1, Scene 4

Orgon, Cléante, Dorine

ORGON: Ah, Brother, good-day.
CLÉANTE: Well, welcome back. I'm sorry I can't stay.
            How was the country? Blooming, I trust, and green?
ORGON: Excuse me, Brother; just one moment.

(To Dorine.)

                               Dorine ...

(To Cléante.)

To put my mind at rest, I always learn
The household news the moment I return.

(To Dorine)

Has all been well, these two days I've been gone?
How are the family? What's been going on?

DORINE: Your wife, two days ago, had a bad fever,
And a fierce headache which refused to leave her.

ORGON: Ah. And Tartuffe?

DORINE: Tartuffe? Why, he's round and red,
Bursting with health, and excellently fed.

ORGON: Poor fellow!

DORINE: That night, the mistress was unable
To take a single bite at the dinner-table.
Her headache-pains, she said, were simply hellish.

ORGON: Ah. And Tartuffe?

DORINE: He ate his meal with relish,
And zealously devoured in her presence
A leg of mutton and a brace of pheasants.

ORGON: Poor fellow!

DORINE: Well, the pains continued strong,
And so she tossed and tossed the whole night long,
Now icy-cold, now burning like a flame.
We sat beside her bed till morning came.

ORGON: Ah. And Tartuffe?

DORINE: Why, having eaten, he rose
And sought his room, already in a doze,
Got into his warm bed, and snored away
In perfect peace until the break of day.

ORGON: Poor fellow!

DORINE: After much ado, we talked her
Into dispatching someone for the doctor.
He bled her, and the fever quickly fell.

ORGON: Ah. And Tartuffe?

DORINE: He bore it very well.
To keep his cheerfulness at any cost,
And make up for the blood *Madame* had lost,
He drank, at lunch, four beakers full of port.

ORGON: Poor fellow!

DORINE: Both are doing well, in short.
I'll go and tell *Madame* that you've expressed
Keen sympathy and anxious interest.

Act 1, Scene 5

Orgon, Cléante

CLÉANTE: That girl was laughing in your face, and though
I've no wish to offend you, even so
I'm bound to say that she had some excuse.
How can you possibly be such a goose?
Are you so dazed by this man's hocus-pocus
That all the world, save him, is out of focus?
You've given him clothing, shelter, food, and care;
Why must you also ...

ORGON: Brother, stop right there.
   You do not know the man of whom you speak.
CLÉANTE: I grant you that. But my judgment's not so weak   10
   That I can't tell, by his effect on others . . .
ORGON: Ah, when you meet him, you two will be like brothers!
   There's been no loftier soul since time began.
   He is a man who . . . a man who . . . an excellent man.
   To keep his precepts is to be reborn,   15
   And view this dunghill of a world with scorn.
   Yes, thanks to him I'm a changed man indeed.
   Under his tutelage my soul's been freed
   From earthly loves, and every human tie:
   My mother, children, brother, and wife could die,   20
   And I'd not feel a single moment's pain.
CLÉANTE: That's a fine sentiment, Brother; most humane.
ORGON: Oh, had you seen Tartuffe as I first knew him,
   Your heart, like mine, would have surrendered to him.
   He used to come into our church each day   25
   And humbly kneel nearby, and start to pray.
   He'd draw the eyes of everybody there
   By the deep fervor of his heartfelt prayer;
   He'd sigh and weep, and sometimes with a sound
   Of rapture he would bend and kiss the ground;   30
   And when I rose to go, he'd run before
   To offer me holy-water at the door.
   His serving-man, no less devout then he,
   Informed me of his master's poverty;
   I gave him gifts, but in his humbleness   35
   He'd beg me every time to give him less.
   "Oh, that's too much," he'd cry, "too much by twice!
   I don't deserve it. The half, Sir, would suffice."
   And when I wouldn't take it back, he'd share
   Half of it with the poor, right then and there.   40
   At length, Heaven prompted me to take him in
   To dwell with us, and free our souls from sin.
   He guides our lives, and to protect my honor
   Stays by my wife, and keeps an eye upon her;
   He tells me whom she sees, and all she does,   45
   And seems more jealous than I ever was!
   And how austere he is! Why, he can detect
   A mortal sin where you would least suspect;
   In smallest trifles, he's extremely strict.
   Last week, his conscience was severely pricked   50
   Because, while praying, he had caught a flea
   And killed it, so he felt, too wrathfully.
CLÉANTE: Good God, man! Have you lost your common sense—
   Or is this all some joke at my expense?
   How can you stand there and in all sobriety . . .   55
ORGON: Brother, your language savors of impiety.
   Too much free-thinking's made your faith unsteady,
   And as I've warned you many times already,
   'Twill get you into trouble before you're through.
CLÉANTE: So I've been told before by dupes like you;   60
   Being blind, you'd have all others blind as well;

The clear-eyed man you call an infidel,
And he who sees through humbug and pretense
Is charged, by you, with want of reverence.
Spare me your warnings, Brother; I have no fear   65
Of speaking out, for you and Heaven to hear,
Against affected zeal and pious knavery.
There's true and false in piety, as in bravery,
And just as those whose courage shines the most
In battle, are the least inclined to boast,   70
So those whose hearts are truly pure and lowly
Don't make a flashy show of being holy.
There's a vast difference, so it seems to me,
Between true piety and hypocrisy:
How do you fail to see it, may I ask?   75
Is not a face quite different from a mask?
Cannot sincerity and cunning art,
Reality and semblance, be told apart?
Are scarecrows just like men, and do you hold
That a false coin is just as good as gold?   80
Ah, Brother, man's a strangely fashioned creature
Who seldom is content to follow Nature,
But recklessly pursues his inclination
Beyond the narrow bounds of moderation,
And often, by transgressing Reason's laws,   85
Perverts a lofty aim or noble cause.
A passing observation, but it applies.

ORGON: I see, dear Brother, that you're profoundly wise;
You harbor all the insight of the age.
You are our one clear mind, our only sage,   90
The era's oracle, its Cato too,
And all mankind are fools compared to you.

CLÉANTE: Brother, I don't pretend to be a sage,
Nor have I all the wisdom of the age.
There's just one insight I would dare to claim: 95
I know that true and false are not the same;
And just as there is nothing I more revere
Than a soul whose faith is steadfast and sincere,
Nothing that I more cherish and admire
Than honest zeal and true religious fire,   100
So there is nothing that I find more base
Than specious piety's dishonest face—
Than these bold mountebanks, these histrios
Whose impious mummeries and hollow shows
Exploit our love of Heaven, and make a jest   105
Of all that men think holiest and best;
These calculating souls who offer prayers
Not to their Maker, but as public wares,
And seek to buy respect and reputation
With lifted eyes and sighs of exaltation;   110
These charlatans, I say, whose pilgrim souls
Proceed, by way of Heaven, toward earthly goals,
Who weep and pray and swindle and extort,
Who preach the monkish life, but haunt the court,
Who make their zeal the partner of their vice—   115

Such men are vengeful, sly, and cold as ice,
And when there is an enemy to defame
They cloak their spite in fair religion's name,
Their private spleen and malice being made
To seem a high and virtuous crusade,   120
Until, to mankind's reverent applause,
They crucify their foe in Heaven's cause.
Such knaves are all too common; yet, for the wise.
True piety isn't hard to recognize,
And, happily, these present times provide us   125
With bright examples to instruct and guide us.
Consider Ariston and Périandre;
Look at Oronte, Alcidamas, Clitandre;
Their virtue is acknowledged; who could doubt it?
But you won't hear them beat the drum about it.   130
They're never ostentatious, never vain,
And their religion's moderate and humane;
It's not their way to criticize and chide:
They think censoriousness a mark of pride,
And therefore, letting others preach and rave,   135
They show, by deeds, how Christians should behave.
They think no evil of their fellow man,
But judge of him as kindly as they can.
They don't intrigue and wangle and conspire;
To lead a good life is their one desire;   140
The sinner wakes no rancorous hate in them;
It is the sin alone which they condemn;
Nor do they try to show a fiercer zeal
For Heaven's cause then Heaven itself could feel.
These men I honor, these men I advocate   145
As models for us all to emulate.
Your man is not their sort at all, I fear:
And, while your praise of him is quite sincere,
I think that you've been dreadfully deluded.

ORGON: Now then, dear Brother, is your speech concluded?   150
CLÉANTE: Why, yes.
ORGON: Your servant, Sir.   *(He turns to go.)*
CLÉANTE: No, Brother; wait.
        There's one more matter. You agreed of late
        That young Valère might have your daughter's hand.
ORGON: I did.
CLÉANTE: And set the date, I understand.
ORGON: Quite so.
CLÉANTE: You've now postponed it; is that true?   155
ORGON: No doubt.
CLÉANTE: The match no longer pleases you?
ORGON: Who knows?
CLÉANTE: D'you mean to go back on your word?
ORGON: I won't say that.
CLÉANTE: Has anything occurred
        Which might entitle you to break your pledge?
ORGON: Perhaps.
CLÉANTE: Why must you hem, and haw, and hedge?   160
        The boy asked me to sound you in this affair . . .

ORGON: It's been a pleasure.
CLÉANTE: But what shall I tell Valère?
ORGON: Whatever you like.
CLÉANTE: But what have you decided?
    What are your plans?
ORGON: I plan, Sir, to be guided
    By Heaven's will.
CLÉANTE: Come, Brother, don't talk rot.
    You've given Valère your word; will you keep it, or not?   165
ORGON: Good day.
CLÉANTE: This looks like poor Valère's undoing;
    I'll go and warn him that there's trouble brewing.

Act 2, Scene 1

Orgon, Mariane

ORGON: Mariane.
MARIANE: Yes, Father?
ORGON: A word with you; come here.
MARIANE: What are you looking for?
ORGON: *(Peering into a small closet.)*   Eavesdroppers, dear.
    I'm making sure we shan't be overheard.
    Someone in there could catch our every word.
    Ah, good, we're safe. Now, Mariane, my child,   5
    You're a sweet girl who's tractable and mild,
    Whom I hold dear, and think most highly of.
MARIANE: I'm deeply grateful, Father, for your love.
ORGON: That's well said, Daughter; and you can repay me
    If, in all things, you'll cheerfully obey me.   10
MARIANE: To please you, Sir, is what delights me best.
ORGON: Good, good. Now, what d'you think of Tartuffe, our guest?
MARIANE: I, Sir?
ORGON: Yes. Weigh your answer; think it through.
MARIANE: Oh, dear. I'll say whatever you wish me to.
ORGON: That's wisely said, my Daughter. Say of him, then,   15
    That he's the very worthiest of men,
    And that you're fond of him, and would rejoice
    In being his wife, if that should be my choice.
    Well?
MARIANE: What?
ORGON: What's that?
MARIANE: I . . .
ORGON: Well?
MARIANE: Forgive me, pray.
ORGON: Did you not hear me?
MARIANE: Of *whom*, Sir, must I say   20
    That I am fond of him, and would rejoice
    In being his wife, if that should be your choice?
ORGON: Why, of Tartuffe.
MARIANE: But, Father, that's false, you know.
    Why would you have me say what isn't so?
ORGON: Because I am resolved it shall be true.   25
    That it's my wish should be enough for you.
MARIANE: You can't mean, Father . . .

ORGON: Yes, Tartuffe shall be
   Allied by marriage to this family,
   And he's to be your husband, is that clear?
   It's a father's privilege ...

Act 2, Scene 2

Dorine, Orgon, Mariane

ORGON: *(To Dorine.)*   What are you doing in here?
   Is curiosity so fierce a passion
   With you, that you must eavesdrop in this fashion?
DORINE: There's lately been a rumor going about—
   Based on some hunch or chance remark, no doubt—   5
   That you mean Mariane to wed Tartuffe.
   I've laughed it off, of course, as just a spoof.
ORGON: You find it so incredible?
DORINE: Yes, I do.
   I won't accept that story, even from you.
ORGON: Well, you'll believe it when the thing is done.   10
DORINE: Yes, yes, of course. Go on and have your fun.
ORGON: I've never been more serious in my life.
DORINE: Ha!
ORGON: Daughter, I mean it; you're to be his wife.
DORINE: No, don't believe your father; it's all a hoax.
ORGON: See here, young woman ...
DORINE: Come, Sir, no more jokes;   15
   You can't fool us.
ORGON: How dare you talk that way?
DORINE: All right, then: we believe you, sad to say.
   But how a man like you, who looks so wise
   And wears a moustache of such splendid size,
   Can be so foolish as to ...
ORGON: Silence, please!   20
   My girl, you take too many liberties.
   I'm master here, as you must not forget.
DORINE: Do let's discuss this calmly; don't be upset.
   You can't be serious, Sir, about this plan.
   What should that bigot want with Mariane?   25
   Praying and fasting ought to keep him busy.
   And then, in terms of wealth and rank, what is he?
   Why should a man of property like you
   Pick out a beggar son-in-law?
ORGON: That will do.
   Speak of his poverty with reverence.   30
   His is a pure and saintly indigence
   Which far transcends all worldly pride and pelf.
   He lost his fortune, as he says himself,
   Because he cared for Heaven alone, and so
   Was careless of his interests here below.   35
   I mean to get him out of his present straits
   And help him to recover his estates—
   Which, in his part of the world, have no small fame.
   Poor though he is, he's a gentleman just the same.

DORINE: Yes, so he tells us; and, Sir, it seems to me   40
      Such pride goes very ill with piety.
      A man whose spirit spurns this dungy earth
      Ought not to brag of lands and noble birth;
      Such worldly arrogance will hardly square
      With meek devotion and the life of prayer.   45
      . . . But this approach, I see, has drawn a blank;
      Let's speak, then, of his person, not his rank.
      Doesn't it seem to you a trifle grim
      To give a girl like her to a man like him?
      When two are so ill-suited, can't you see   50
      What the sad consequences is bound to be?
      A young girl's virtue is imperilled, Sir,
      When such a marriage is imposed on her;
      For if one's bridegroom isn't to one's taste,
      It's hardly an inducement to be chaste,   55
      And many a man with horns upon his brow
      Has made his wife the thing that she is now.
      It's hard to be a faithful wife, in short,
      To certain husbands of a certain sort,
      And he who gives his daughter to a man she hates   60
      Must answer for her sins at Heaven's gates.
      Think, Sir, before you play so risky a role.
ORGON: This servant-girl presumes to save my soul!
DORINE: You would do well to ponder what I've said.
ORGON: Daughter, we'll disregard this dunderhead.   65
      Just trust your father's judgment. Oh, I'm aware
      That I once promised you to young Valère;
      But now I hear he gambles, which greatly shocks me;
      What's more, I've doubts about his orthodoxy.
      His visits to church, I note, are very few.   70
DORINE: Would you have him go at the same hours as you,
      And kneel nearby, to be sure of being seen?
ORGON: I can dispense with such remarks, Dorine.

(To Mariane.)

      Tartuffe, however, is sure of Heaven's blessing,
      And that's the only treasure worth possessing.   75
      This match will bring you joys beyond all measure;
      Your cup will overflow with every pleasure;
      You two will interchange your faithful loves
      Like two sweet cherubs, or two turtle-doves.
      No harsh word shall be heard, no frown be seen,   80
      And he shall make you happy as a queen.
DORINE: And she'll make him a cuckold, just wait and see.
ORGON: What language!
DORINE: Oh, he's a man of destiny;
      He's *made* for horns, and what the stars demand
      Your daughter's virtue surely can't withstand.
ORGON: Don't interrupt me further. Why can't you learn   85
      That certain things are none of your concern?
DORINE: It's for your own sake that I interfere.

(She repeatedly interrupts Orgon just as he is turning to speak to his daughter.)

ORGON: Most kind of you. Now, hold your tongue, d'you hear?

DORINE: If I didn't love you ...

ORGON: Spare me your affection.   90

DORINE: I'll love you, Sir, in spite of your objection.

ORGON: Blast!

DORINE: I can't bear, Sir, for your honor's sake,
            To let you make this ludicrous mistake.

ORGON: You mean to go on talking?

DORINE: If I didn't protest
            This sinful marriage, my conscience couldn't rest.   95

ORGON: If you don't hold your tongue, you little shrew ...

DORINE: What, lost your temper? A pious man like you?

ORGON: Yes! Yes! You talk and talk. I'm maddened by it.
            Once and for all, I tell you to be quiet.

DORINE: Well, I'll be quiet. But I'll be thinking hard.   100

ORGON: Think all you like, but you had better guard
            That saucy tongue of yours, or I'll ...

(Turning back to Mariane.)

                                     Now, child,
            I've weighed this matter fully.

DORINE: *(Aside.)*   It drives me wild
            That I can't speak.

(Orgon turns his head, and she is silent.)

ORGON: Tartuffe is no young dandy,
            But, still, his person ...

DORINE: *(Aside.)*   Is as sweet as candy.   105

ORGON: Is such that, even if you shouldn't care
            for his other merits ...

(He turns and stands facing Dorine, arms crossed.)

DORINE: *(Aside.)*   They'll make a lovely pair.
            If I were she, no man would marry me
            Against my inclination, and go scot-free.
            He'd learn, before the wedding-day was over,   110
            How readily a wife can find a lover.

ORGON: *(To Dorine.)*   It seems you treat my orders as a joke.

DORINE: Why, what's the matter? 'Twas not to you I spoke.

ORGON: What *were* you doing?

DORINE: Talking to myself, that's all.

ORGON: Ah! *(Aside.)* One more bit of impudence and gall,   115
            And I shall give her a good slap in the face.

(He puts himself in position to slap her; Dorine, whenever he glances at her, stands immobile and silent.)

            Daughter, you shall accept, and with good grace,
            The husband I've selected ...Your wedding-day ...

(To Dorine.)

            Why don't you talk to yourself?

DORINE: I've nothing to say.

ORGON: Come, just one word.

DORINE: No thank you, Sir. I pass.   120

ORGON: Come, speak; I'm waiting.

DORINE: I'd not be such an ass.

ORGON: *(Turning to Mariane.)*
　　　In short, dear Daughter, I mean to be obeyed,
　　　And you must bow to the sound choice I've made.
DORINE: *(Moving away.)*   I'd not wed such a monster, even in jest.

(Orgon attempts to slap her, but misses.)

ORGON: Daughter, that maid of yours is a thorough pest;   125
　　　She makes me sinfully annoyed and nettled.
　　　I can't speak further; my nerves are too unsettled.
　　　She's so upset me by her insolent talk,
　　　I'll calm myself by going for a walk.

Act 2, Scene 3

Dorine, Mariane

DORINE: *(Returning.)*   Well, have you lost your tongue, girl? Must I play
　　　Your part, and say the lines you ought to say?
　　　Faced with a fate so hideous and absurd,
　　　Can you not utter one dissenting word?
MARIANE: What good would it do? A father's power is great.   5
DORINE: Resist him now, or it will be too late.
MARIANE: But . . .
DORINE: Tell him one cannot love at a father's whim;
　　　That you shall marry for yourself, not him;
　　　That since it's you who are to be the bride,
　　　It's you, not he, who must be satisfied;   10
　　　And that if his Tartuffe is so sublime,
　　　He's free to marry him at any time.
MARIANE: I've bowed so long to Father's strict control,
　　　I couldn't oppose him now, to save my soul.
DORINE: Come, come, Mariane. Do listen to reason, won't you?   15
　　　Valère has asked your hand. Do you love him, or don't you?
MARIANE: Oh, how unjust of you! What can you mean
　　　By asking such a question, dear Dorine?
　　　You know the depth of my affection for him;
　　　I've told you a hundred times how I adore him.   20
DORINE: I don't believe in everything I hear;
　　　Who knows if your professions were sincere?
MARIANE: They were, Dorine, and you do me wrong to doubt it;
　　　Heaven knows that I've been all too frank about it.
DORINE: You love him, then?
MARIANE: Oh, more than I can express.   25
DORINE: And he, I take it, cares for you no less?
MARIANE: I think so.
DORINE: And you both, with equal fire,
　　　Burn to be married?
MARIANE: That is our one desire.
DORINE: What of Tartuffe, then? What of your father's plan?
MARIANE: I'll kill myself, if I'm forced to wed that man.   30
DORINE: I hadn't thought of that recourse. How splendid!
　　　Just die, and all your troubles will be ended!
　　　A fine solution. Oh, it maddens me
　　　To hear you talk in that self-pitying key.
MARIANE: Dorine, how harsh you are! It's most unfair.   35
　　　You have no sympathy for my despair.

DORINE: I've none at all for people who talk drivel
    And, faced with difficulties, whine and snivel.
MARIANE: No doubt I'm timid, but it would be wrong . . .
DORINE: True love requires a heart that's firm and strong.   40
MARIANE: I'm strong in my affection for Valère,
    But coping with my father is his affair.
DORINE: But if your father's brain has grown so cracked
    Over his dear Tartuffe that he can retract
    His blessing, though your wedding-day was named,   45
    It's surely not Valère who's to be blamed.
MARIANE: If I defied my father, as you suggest,
    Would it not seem unmaidenly, at best?
    Shall I defend my love at the expense
    Of brazenness and disobedience?   50
    Shall I parade my heart's desires, and flaunt . . .
DORINE: No. I ask nothing of you. Clearly you want
    To be Madame Tartuffe, and I feel bound
    Not to oppose a wish so very sound.
    What right have I to criticize the match?   55
    Indeed, my dear, the man's a brilliant catch.
    Monsieur Tartuffe! Now, there's a man of weight!
    Yet, yes, Monsieur Tartuffe, I'm bound to state,
    Is quite a person; that's not to be denied;
    'Twill be no little thing to be his bride.   60
    The world already rings with his renown;
    He's a great noble—in his native town;
    His ears are red, he has a pink complexion,
    And all in all, he'll suit you to perfection.
MARIANE: Dear God!
DORINE: Oh, how triumphant you will feel   65
    At having caught a husband so ideal!
MARIANE: Oh, do stop teasing, and use your cleverness
    To get me out of this appalling mess.
    Advise me, and I'll do whatever you say.
DORINE: Ah no, a dutiful daughter must obey   70
    Her father, even if he weds her to an ape.
    You've a bright future: why struggle to escape?
    Tartuffe will take you back where his family lives,
    To a small town aswarm with relatives—
    Uncles and cousins whom you'll be charmed to meet.   75
    You'll be received at once by the elite,
    Calling upon the bailiff's wife, no less—
    Even, perhaps, upon the mayoress,
    Who'll sit you down in the *best* kitchen chair.
    Then, once a year, you'll dance at the village fair   80
    To the drone of bagpipes—two of them, in fact—
    And see a puppet-show, or an animal act.
    Your husband . . .
MARIANE: Oh, you turn my blood to ice!
    Stop torturing me, and give me your advice.
DORINE: *(Threatening to go.)*
    Your servant, Madam.
MARIANE: Dorine, I beg of you . . .   85
DORINE: No, you deserve it; this marriage must go through.

MARIANE: Dorine!
DORINE: No.
MARIANE: Not Tartuffe! You know I think him . . .
DORINE: Tartuffe's your cup of tea, and you shall drink him.
MARIANE: I've always told you everything, and relied . . .
DORINE: No. You deserve to be tartuffified.   90
MARIANE: Well, since you mock me and refuse to care,
    I'll henceforth seek my solace in despair:
    Despair shall be my counsellor and friend,
    And help me bring my sorrows to an end.

(She starts to leave.)

DORINE: There now, come back; my anger has subsided.   95
    You do deserve some pity, I've decided.
MARIANE: Dorine, if Father makes me undergo
    This dreadful martyrdom, I'll die, I know.
DORINE: Don't fret; it won't be difficult to discover
    Some plan of action . . . But here's Valère, your lover.   100

Act 2, Scene 4

Valère, Mariane, Dorine

VALÈRE: Madam, I've just received some wondrous news
    Regarding which I'd like to hear your views.
MARIANE: What news?
VALÈRE: You're marrying Tartuffe.
MARIANE: I find
    That Father does have such a match in mind.
VALÈRE: Your father, Madam . . .
MARIANE: . . . has just this minute said   5
    That it's Tartuffe he wishes me to wed.
VALÈRE: Can he be serious?
MARIANE: Oh, indeed he can;
    He's clearly set his heart upon the plan.
VALÈRE: And what position do you propose to take, Madam?
MARIANE: Why—I don't know?
VALÈRE: For heaven's sake—   10
    You don't know?
MARIANE: No.
VALÈRE: Well, well!
MARIANE: Advise me, do.
VALÈRE: Marry the man. That's my advice to you.
MARIANE: That's your advice?
VALÈRE: Yes.
MARIANE: Truly?
VALÈRE: Oh, absolutely.
    You couldn't choose more wisely, more astutely.
MARIANE: Thanks for this counsel; I'll follow it, of course.
VALÈRE: Do, do; I'm sure 'twill cost you no remorse.   15
MARIANE: To give it didn't cause your heart to break.
VALÈRE: I gave it, Madam, only for your sake.
MARIANE: And it's for your sake that I take it, Sir.
DORINE: *(Withdrawing to the rear of the stage.)*
    Let's see which fool will prove the stubborner.   20

VALÈRE: So! I am nothing to you, and it was flat
    Deception when you . . .
MARIANE: Please, enough of that.
    You've told me plainly that I should agree
    To wed the man my father's chosen for me,
    And since you've deigned to counsel me so wisely,   25
    I promise, Sir, to do as you advise me.
VALÈRE: Ah, no, 'twas not by me that you were swayed.
    No, your decision was already made;
    Though now, to save appearances, you protest
    That you're betraying me at my behest.   30
MARIANE: Just as you say.
VALÈRE: Quite so. And I now see
    That you were never truly in love with me.
MARIANE: Alas, you're free to think so if you choose.
VALÈRE: I choose to think so, and here's a bit of news:
    You've spurned by hand, but I know where to turn   35
    For kinder treatment, as you shall quickly learn.
MARIANE: I'm sure you do. Your noble qualities
    Inspire affection . . .
VALÈRE: Forget my qualities, please.
    They don't inspire you overmuch, I find.
    But there's another lady I have in mind   40
    Whose sweet and generous nature will not scorn
    To compensate me for the loss I've borne.
MARIANE: I'm no great loss, and I'm sure that you'll transfer
    Your heart quite painlessly from me to her.
VALÈRE: I'll do my best to take it in my stride.   45
    The pain I feel at being cast aside
    Time and forgetfulness may put an end to.
    Or if I can't forget, I shall pretend to.
    No self-respecting person is expected
    To go on loving once he's been rejected.   50
MARIANE: Now, that's a fine, high-minded sentiment.
VALÈRE: One to which any sane man would assent.
    Would you prefer it if I pined away
    In hopeless passion till my dying day?
    Am I to yield you to a rival's arms   55
    And not console myself with other charms?
MARIANE: Go then: console yourself; don't hesitate.
    I wish you to; indeed, I cannot wait.
VALÈRE: You wish me to?
MARIANE: Yes.
VALÈRE: That's the final straw.
    Madam, farewell. Your wish shall by my law.   6

(He starts to leave, and then returns: this repeatedly.)

MARIANE: Splendid.
VALÈRE: *(Coming back again.)*
        This breach, remember, is of your making;
    It's you who've driven me to the step I'm taking.
MARIANE: Of course.
VALÈRE: *(Coming back again.)*
        Remember, too, that I am merely
    Following your example.

MARIANE: I see that clearly.
VALÈRE: Enough. I'll go and do your bidding, then.   65
MARIANE: Good.
VALÈRE: (Coming back again.)
                    You shall never see my face again.
MARIANE: Excellent.
VALÈRE: (Walking to the door, then turning about.)
                          Yes?
MARIANE: What?
VALÈRE: What's that? What did you say?
MARIANE: Nothing. You're dreaming.
VALÈRE: Ah. Well, I'm on my way.
        Farewell, Madame.   (He moves slowly away.)
MARIANE: Farewell.
DORINE: (To Mariane.)   If you ask me
        Both of you are as mad as mad can be.   70
        Do stop this nonsense, now. I've only let you
        Squabble so long to see where it would get you.
        Whoa there, Monsieure Valère!

(She goes and seizes Valère by the arm; he makes a great show of resistance.)

VALÈRE: What's this, Dorine?
DORINE: Come here.
VALÈRE: No, no, my heart's too full of spleen.
        Don't hold me back; her wish must be obeyed.   75
DORINE: Stop!
VALÈRE: It's too late now; my decision's made.
DORINE: Oh, pooh!
MARIANE: (Aside.)   He hates the sight of me, that's plain.
        I'll go, and so deliver him from pain.
DORINE: (Leaving Valère, running after Mariane.)
        And now you run away! Come back.
MARIANE: No, no.
        Nothing you say will keep me here. Let go!   80
VALÈRE: (Aside.)   She cannot bear my presence, I perceive.
        To spare her further torment, I shall leave.
DORINE: (Leaving Mariane, running after Valère.)
        Again! You'll not escape, Sir; don't you try it.
        Come here, you two. Stop fussing, and be quiet.

(She takes Valère by the hand, then Mariane, and draws them together.)

VALÈRE: (To Dorine.)   What do you want of me?
MARIANE: (To Dorine.)   What is the point of this?   85
DORINE: We're going to have a little armistice.

(To Valère.)

        Now, weren't you silly to get so overheated?
VALÈRE: Didn't you see how badly I was treated?
DORINE: (To Mariane.)   Aren't you a simpleton, to have lost your head?
MARIANE: Didn't you hear the hateful things he said?   90
DORINE: (To Valère.)
        You're both great fools. Her sole desire, Valère,
        Is to be yours in marriage. To that I'll swear.

(To Mariane.)

He loves you only, and he wants no wife
But you, Mariane. On that I'll stake my life.

MARIANE: *(To Valère.)*   Then why you advised me so, I cannot see.
VALÈRE: *(To Mariane.)*   On such a question, why ask advice of *me*?   95
DORINE: Oh, you're impossible. Give me your hands, you two.

(To Valère.)

Yours first.
VALÈRE: *(Giving Dorine his hand.)*
                    But why?
DORINE: *(To Mariane.)*
                         And now a hand from you.
MARIANE: *(Also giving Dorine her hand.)*
     What are you doing?
DORINE: There: a perfect fit.
     You suit each other better than you'll admit.   100

(Valère and Mariane hold hands for some time without looking at each other.)

VALÈRE: *(Turning toward Mariane.)*
     Ah, come, don't be so haughty. Give a man
     A look of kindness, won't you, Mariane?

(Mariane turns toward Valère and smiles.)

DORINE: I tell you, lovers are completely mad!
VALÈRE: *(To Mariane.)*   Now come, confess that you were very bad
     To hurt my feelings as you did just now.   105
     I have a just complaint, you must allow.
MARIANE: *You* must allow that you were most unpleasant ...
DORINE: Let's table that discussion for the present;
     Your father has a plan which must be stopped.
MARIANE: Advise us, then; what means must we adopt?   110
DORINE: We'll use all manner of means, and all at once.

(To Mariane.)

     Your father's addled; he's acting like a dunce.
     Therefore you'd better humor the old fossil.
     Pretend to yield to him, be sweet and docile,
     And then postpone, as often as necessary,   115
     The day on which you have agreed to marry.
     You'll thus gain time, and time will turn the trick.
     Sometimes, for instance, you'll be taken sick,
     And that will seem good reason for delay;
     Or some bad omen will make you change the day—   120
     You'll dream of muddy water, or you'll pass
     A dead man's hearse, or break a looking-glass.
     If all else fails, no man can marry you
     Unless you take his ring and say "I do."
     But now, let's separate. If they should find   125
     Us talking here, our plot might be divined.

(To Valère.)

     Go to your friends, and tell them what's occurred,
     And have them urge her father to keep his word.
     Meanwhile, we'll stir her brother into action,
     And get Elmire, as well, to join our faction.   130
     Good-bye.

VALÈRE: *(To Mariane.)*   Though each of us will do his best,
　　　It's your true heart on which my hopes shall rest.
MARIANE: *(To Valère.)*   Regardless of what Father may decide,
　　　None but Valère shall claim me as his bride.
VALÈRE: Oh, how those words content me! Come what will ...   135
DORINE: Oh, lover, lovers! Their tongues are never still.
　　　Be off, now.
VALÈRE: *(Turning to go, then turning back.)*
　　　　　　　One last word ...
DORINE:　　　　　　　　　No time to chat:
　　　You leave by this door: and *you* leave by that.

(Dorine pushes them, by the shoulders, toward opposing doors.)

Act 3, Scene 1

Damis, Dorine

DAMIS: May lightning strike me even as I speak,
　　　May all men call me cowardly and weak,
　　　If any fear or scruple holds me back
　　　From settling things, at once, with that great quack!
DORINE: Now, don't give way to violent emotion.   5
　　　Your father's merely talked about this notion,
　　　And words and deeds are far from being one.
　　　Much that is talked about is left undone.
DAMIS: No, I must stop that scoundrel's machinations;
　　　I'll go and tell him off; I'm out of patience.   10
DORINE: Do calm down and be practical. I had rather
　　　My mistress dealt with him—and with your father.
　　　She has some influence with Tartuffe, I've noted.
　　　He hangs upon her words, seems most devoted,
　　　And may, indeed, be smitten by her charm.   15
　　　Pray Heaven it's true! 'Twould do our cause no harm.
　　　She sent for him, just now, to sound him out
　　　On this affair you're so incensed about;
　　　She'll find out where he stands, and tell him, too,
　　　What dreadful strife and trouble will ensue   20
　　　If he lends countenance to your father's plan.
　　　I couldn't get in to see him, but his man
　　　Says that he's almost finished with his prayers.
　　　Go, now. I'll catch him when he comes downstairs.
DAMIS: I want to hear this conference, and I will.   25
DORINE: No, they must be alone.
DAMIS:　　　　　　　　Oh, I'll keep still.
DORINE: Not you. I know your temper. You'd start a brawl,
　　　And shout and stamp your foot and spoil it all.
　　　Go on.
DAMIS: I won't; I have a perfect right ...
DORINE: Lord, you're a nuisance! He's coming; get out of sight.   30

(Damis conceals himself in a closet at the rear of the stage.)

Act 3, Scene 2

Tartuffe, Dorine

TARTUFFE: *(Observing Dorine, and calling to his manservant offstage.)*
　　　Hang up my hair-shirt, put my scourge in place,

And pray, Laurent, for Heaven's perpetual grace.
I'm going to the prison now, to share
My last few coins with the poor wretches there.

DORINE: *(Aside.)*   Dear God, what affectation! What a fake!
TARTUFFE: You wished to see me?   5
DORINE: Yes . . .
TARTUFFE: *(Taking a handkerchief from his pocket.)*
                                      For mercy's sake,
Please take this handkerchief, before you speak.
DORINE: What?
TARTUFFE: Cover that bosom, girl. The flesh is weak,
And unclean thoughts are difficult to control.
Such sights as that can undermine the soul.   10
DORINE: Your soul, it seems, has very poor defenses,
And flesh makes quite an impact on your senses.
It's strange that you're so easily excited;
My own desires are not so soon ignited,
And if I saw you naked as a beast,   15
Not all your hide would tempt me in the least.
TARTUFFE: Girl, speak more modestly; unless you do,
I shall be forced to take my leave of you.
DORINE: Oh, no, it's I who must be on my way;
I've just one little message to convey.   20
Madame is coming down, and begs you, Sir,
To wait and have a word or two with her.
TARTUFFE: Gladly.
DORINE: *(Aside.) That* had a softening effect!
I think my guess about him was correct.
TARTUFFE: Will she be long?
DORINE: No; that's her step I hear.   25
Ah, here she is, and I shall disappear.

Act 3, Scene 3

Elmire, Tartuffe

TARTUFFE: May Heaven, whose infinite goodness we adore,
Preserve your body and soul forevermore,
And bless your days, and answer thus the plea
Of one who is its humblest votary.
ELMIRE: I thank you for that pious wish. But please,   5
Do take a chair and let's be more at ease.

(They sit down.)

TARTUFFE: I trust that you are once more well and strong?
ELMIRE: Oh, yes: the fever didn't last for long.
TARTUFFE: My prayers are too unworthy, I am sure,
To have gained from Heaven this most gracious cure;   10
But lately, Madam, my every supplication
Has had for object your recuperation.
ELMIRE: You shouldn't have troubled so. I don't deserve it.
TARTUFFE: Your health is priceless, Madam, and to preserve it
I'd gladly give my own, in all sincerity.   15
ELMIRE: Sir, you outdo us all in Christian charity.
You've been most kind. I count myself your debtor.
TARTUFFE: 'Twas nothing, Madam. I long to serve you better.

ELMIRE: There's a private matter I'm anxious to discuss.
           I'm glad there's no one here to hinder us.   20
TARTUFFE: I too am glad; it floods my heart with bliss
           To find myself alone with you like this.
           For just this chance I've prayed with all my power—
           But prayed in vain, until this happy hour.
ELMIRE: This won't take long, Sir, and I hope you'll be   25
           Entirely frank and unconstrained with me.
TARTUFFE: Indeed, there's nothing I had rather do
           Than bare my inmost heart and soul to you.
           First, let me say that what remarks I've made
           About the constant visits you are paid   30
           Were prompted not by any mean emotion,
           But rather by a pure and deep devotion,
           A fervent zeal . . .
ELMIRE: No need for explanation.
           Your sole concern, I'm sure, was my salvation.
TARTUFFE: *(Taking Elmire's hand and pressing her fingertips.)*
           Quite so; and such great fervor do I feel . . .   35
ELMIRE: Ooh! Please! You're pinching!
TARTUFFE: 'Twas from excess of zeal.
           I never meant to cause you pain, I swear.
           I'd rather . . .

(He places his hand on Elmire's knee.)

ELMIRE: What can your hand be doing there?
TARTUFFE: Feeling your gown; what soft, fine-woven stuff!
ELMIRE: Please, I'm extremely ticklish. That's enough.   40

(She draws her chair away; Tartuffe pulls his after her.)

TARTUFFE: *(Fondling the lace collar of her gown.)*
           My, my, what lovely lacework on your dress!
           The workmanships's miraculous, no less.
           I've not seen anything to equal it.
ELMIRE: Yes, quite. But let's talk business for a bit.   45
           They say my husband means to break his word
           And give his daughter to you, Sir. Had you heard?
TARTUFFE: He did once mention it. But I confess
           I dream of quite a different happiness.
           It's elsewhere, Madam, that my eyes discern
           The promise of that bliss for which I yearn.   50
ELMIRE: I see: you care for nothing here below.
TARTUFFE: Ah, well—my heart's not made of stone, you know.
ELMIRE: All your desires mount heavenward, I'm sure,
           In scorn of all that's earthly and impure.
TARTUFFE: A love of heavenly beauty does not preclude   55
           A proper love for earthly pulchritude;
           Our senses are quite rightly captivated
           By perfect works our Maker has created.
           Some glory clings to all that Heaven has made;
           In you, all Heaven's marvels are displayed.   60
           On that fair face, such beauties have been lavished,
           The eyes are dazzled and the heart is ravished;
           How could I look on you, O flawless creature,
           And not adore the Author of all Nature,

Feeling a love both passionate and pure   65
For you, his triumph of self-portraiture?
At first, I trembled lest that love should be
A subtle snare that Hell had laid for me;
I vowed to flee the sight of you, eschewing
A rapture that might prove my soul's undoing;   70
But soon, fair being, I became aware
That my deep passion could be made to square
With rectitude, and with my bounden duty.
I thereupon surrendered to your beauty.
It is, I know, presumptuous on my part   75
To bring you this poor offering of my heart,
And it is not my merit, Heaven knows,
But your compassion on which my hopes repose.
You are my peace, my solace, my salvation;
On you depends my bliss—or desolation;   80
I bide your judgment and, as you think best,
I shall be either miserable or blest.

ELMIRE: Your declaration is most gallant, Sir,
But don't you think it's out of character?
You'd have done better to restrain your passion   85
And think before you spoke in such a fashion.
It ill becomes a pious man like you ...

TARTUFFE: I may be pious, but I'm human too:
With your celestial charms before his eyes,
A man has not the power to be wise.   90
I know such words sound strangely, coming from me,
But I'm no angel, nor was meant to be,
And if you blame my passion, you must needs
Reproach as well the charms on which it feeds.
Your loveliness I had no sooner seen   95
Than you became my soul's unrivalled queen;
Before your seraph glance, divinely sweet,
My heart's defenses crumbled in defeat,
And nothing fasting, prayer, or tears might do
Could stay my spirit from adoring you.   100
My eyes, my sighs have told you in the past
What now my lips make bold to say at last,
And if, in your great goodness, you will deign
To look upon your slave, and ease his pain,
If, in compassion for my soul's distress,   105
You'll stoop to comfort my unworthiness,
I'll raise to you, in thanks for that sweet manna,
An endless hymn, an infinite hosanna.
With me, of course, there need be no anxiety.
No fear of scandal or of notoriety.   110
These young court gallants, whom all the ladies fancy,
Are vain in speech, in action rash and chancy;
When they succeed in love, the world soon knows it;
No favor's granted them but they disclose it
And by the looseness of their tongues profane   115
The very altar where their hearts have lain.
Men of my sort, however, love discreetly,

And one may trust our reticence completely.
My keen concern for my good name insures
The absolute security of yours;   120
In short, I offer you, my dear Elmire,
Love without scandal, pleasure without fear.

ELMIRE: I've heard your well-turned speeches to the end,
And what you urge I clearly apprehend.
Aren't you afraid that I may take a notion   125
To tell my husband of your warm devotion,
And that, supposing he were duly told,
His feelings toward you might grow rather cold?

TARTUFFE: I know, dear lady, that your exceeding charity
Will lead your heart to pardon my temerity;   130
That you'll excuse my violent affection
As human weakness, human imperfection;
And that—O fairest!—you will bear in mind
That I'm but flesh and blood, and am not blind.

ELMIRE: Some women might do otherwise, perhaps,   135
But I shall be discreet about your lapse;
I'll tell my husband nothing of what's occurred
If, in return, you'll give your solemn word
To advocate as forcefully as you can
The marriage of Valère and Mariane,   140
Renouncing all desire to dispossess
Another of his rightful happiness,
And . . .

Act 3, Scene 4

Damis, Elmire, Tartuffe

DAMIS: *(Emerging from the closet where he has been hiding.)*
No! We'll not hush up this vile affair;
I heard it all inside that closet there,
Where Heaven, in order to confound the pride
Of this great rascal, prompted me to hide.
Ah, now I have my long-awaited chance   5
To punish his deceit and arrogance,
And give my father clear and shocking proof
Of the black character of his dear Tartuffe.

ELMIRE: Ah no, Damis; I'll be content if he
Will study to deserve my leniency.   10
I've promised silence—don't make me break my word;
To make a scandal would be too absurd.
Good wives laugh off such trifles, and forget them;
Why should they tell their husbands, and upset them?

DAMIS: You have your reasons for taking such a course,   15
And I have reasons, too, of equal force.
To spare him now would be insanely wrong.
I've swallowed my just wrath for far too long
And watched this insolent bigot bringing strife
And bitterness into our family life.   20
Too long he's meddled in my father's affairs,
Thwarting my marriage-hopes, and poor Valère's.
It's high time that my father was undeceived,

And now I've proof that can't be disbelieved—
Proof that was furnished me by Heaven above.   25
It's too good not to take advantage of.
This is my chance, and I deserve to lose it
If, for one moment, I hesitate to use it.

ELMIRE: Damis . . .

DAMIS: No, I must do what I think right.
Madam, my heart is bursting with delight,   30
And, say whatever you will, I'll not consent
To lose the sweet revenge on which I'm bent.
I'll settle matters without more ado;
And here, most opportunely, is my cue.

Act 3, Scene 5

Orgon, Damis, Tartuffe, Elmire

DAMIS: Father, I'm glad you've joined us. Let us advise you
Of some fresh news which doubtless will surprise you.
You've just now been repaid with interest
For all your loving-kindness to our guest.
He's proved his warm and grateful feelings toward you;   5
It's with a pair of horns he would reward you.
Yes, I surprised him with your wife, and heard
His whole adulterous offer, every word.
She, with her all too gentle disposition,
Would not have told you of his proposition;   10
But I shall not make terms with brazen lechery,
And feel that not to tell you would be treachery.

ELMIRE: And I hold that one's husband's peace of mind
Should not be spoilt by tattle of this kind.
One's honor doesn't require it: to be proficient   15
In keeping men at bay is quite sufficient.
These are my sentiments, and I wish, Damis,
That you had heeded me and held your peace.

Act 3, Scene 6

Orgon, Damis, Tartuffe

ORGON: Can it be true, this dreadful thing I hear?

TARTUFFE: Yes, Brother, I'm a wicked man, I fear:
A wretched sinner, all depraved and twisted,
The greatest villain that has ever existed.
My life's one heap of crimes, which grows each minute;   5
There's naught but foulness and corruption in it;
And I perceive that Heaven, outraged by me,
Has chosen this occasion to mortify me.
Charge me with any deed you wish to name;
I'll not defend myself, but take the blame.   10
Believe what you are told, and drive Tartuffe
Like some base criminal from beneath your roof;
Yes, drive me hence, and with a parting curse;
I shan't protest, for I deserve far worse.

ORGON: *(To Damis.)* Ah, you deceitful boy, how dare you try
To stain his purity with so foul a lie?   15

DAMIS: What! Are you taken in by such a bluff?
      Did you not hear . . . ?

ORGON: Enough, you rogue, enough!

TARTUFFE: Ah, Brother, let him speak: you're being unjust.
      Believe his story; the boy deserves your trust.   20
      Why, after all, should you have faith in me?
      How can you know what I might do, or be?
      Is it on my good actions that you base
      Your favor? Do you trust my pious face?
      Ah, no, don't be deceived by hollow shows;   25
      I'm far, alas, from being what men suppose;
      Though the world takes me for a man of worth,
      I'm truly the most worthless man on earth.

(To Damis.)

      Yes, my dear son, speak out now: call me the chief
      Of sinners, a wretch, a murderer, a thief;
      Load me with all the names men most abhor;   30
      I'll not complain; I've earned them all, and more;
      I'll kneel here while you pour them on my head
      As a just punishment for the life I've led.

ORGON: *(To Tartuffe.)*   This is too much, dear Brother.

(To Damis.)

                    Have you no heart?   35

DAMIS: Are you so hoodwinked by this rascal's art . . . ?

ORGON: Be still, you monster.

(To Tartuffe.)

                    Brother, I pray you, rise.

(To Damis.)

      Villain!

DAMIS: But . . .

ORGON: Silence!

DAMIS: Can't you realize . . . ?

ORGON: Just one word more, and I'll tear you limb from limb.

TARTUFFE: In God's name, Brother, don't be harsh with him.   40
      I'd rather far be tortured at the stake
      Than see him bear one scratch for my poor sake.

ORGON: *(To Damis.)*   Ingrate!

TARTUFFE: If I must beg you, on bended knee,
      To pardon him . . .

ORGON: *(Falling to his knees, addressing Tartuffe.)*
                    Such goodness cannot be!

(To Damis.)

      Now, *there's* true charity!

DAMIS: What, you . . . ?

ORGON: Villain, be still!   45
      I know your motives; I know you wish him ill:
      Yes, all of you—wife, children, servants, all—
      Conspire against him and desire his fall,
      Employing every shameful trick you can
      To alienate me from this saintly man.
      Ah, but the more you seek to drive him away,   50

The more I'll do to keep him. Without delay,
I'll spite this household and confound its pride
By giving him my daughter as his bride.
DAMIS: You're going to force her to accept his hand?
ORGON: Yes, and this very night, d'you understand?   55
I shall defy you all, and make it clear
That I'm the one who gives the orders here.
Come, wretch, kneel down and clasp his blessed feet,
And ask his pardon for your black deceit.
DAMIS: I ask that swindler's pardon? Why, I'd rather . . .   60
ORGON: So! You insult him, and defy your father!
A stick! A stick! (*To Tartuffe.*) No, no—release me, do.

(*To Damis.*)

Out of my house this minute! Be off with you,
And never dare set foot in it again.   65
DAMIS: Well, I shall go, but . . .
ORGON: Well, go quickly, then.
I disinherit you; an empty purse
Is all you'll get from me—except my curse!

Act 3, Scene 7

Orgon, Tartuffe

ORGON: How he blasphemed your goodness! What a son!
TARTUFFE: Forgive him, Lord, as I've already done.

(*To Orgon.*)

You can't know how it hurts when someone tries
To blacken me in my dear Brother's eyes.
ORGON: Ahh!
TARTUFFE: The mere thought of such ingratitude   5
Plunges my soul into so dark a mood . . .
Such horror grips my heart . . . I gasp for breath,
And cannot speak, and feel myself near death.
ORGON: (*He runs, in tears, to the door through which he has just driven his son.*)
You blackguard! Why did I spare you? Why did I not
Break you in little pieces on the spot?   10
Compose yourself, and don't be hurt, dear friend.
TARTUFFE: These scenes, these dreadful quarrels, have got to end.
I've much upset your household, and I perceive
That the best thing will be for me to leave.
ORGON: What are you saying!
TARTUFFE: They're all against me here;   15
They'd have you think me false and insincere.
ORGON: Ah, what of that? Have I ceased believing in you?
TARTUFFE: Their adverse talk will certainly continue,
And charges which you now repudiate
You may find credible at a later date.   20
ORGON: No, Brother, never.
TARTUFFE: Brother, a wife can sway
Her husband's mind in many a subtle way.
ORGON: No, no.
TARTUFFE: To leave at once is the solution;
Thus only can I end their persecution.

ORGON: No, no, I'll not allow it; you shall remain.   25

TARTUFFE: Ah, well; 'twill mean much martyrdom and pain,
    But if you wish it . . .

ORGON: Ah!

TARTUFFE: Enough; so be it.
    But one thing must be settled, as I see it.
    For your dear honor, and for our friendship's sake,
    There's one precaution I feel bound to take.
    I shall avoid your wife, and keep away . . .   30

ORGON: No, you shall not, whatever they may say.
    It pleases me to vex them, and for spite
    I'd have them see you with her day and night.
    What's more, I'm going to drive them to despair   35
    By making you my only son and heir;
    This very day, I'll give to you alone
    Clear deed and title to everything I own.
    A dear, good friend and son-in-law-to-be
    Is more than wife, or child, or kin to me.
    Will you accept my offer, dearest son?   40

TARTUFFE: In all things, let the will of Heaven be done.

ORGON: Poor fellow! Come, we'll go draw up the deed.
    Then let them burst with disappointed greed!

Act 4, Scene 1

Cléante, Tartuffe

CLÉANTE: Yes, all the town's discussing it, and truly,
    Their comments do not flatter you unduly.
    I'm glad we've met, Sir, and I'll give my view
    Of this sad matter in a word or two.
    As for who's guilty, that I shan't discuss;   5
    Let's say it was Damis who caused the fuss;
    Assuming, then, that you have been ill-used
    By young Damis, and groundlessly accused,
    Ought not a Christian to forgive, and ought
    He not to stifle every vengeful thought?   10
    Should you stand by and watch a father make
    His only son an exile for your sake?
    Again I tell you frankly, be advised:
    The whole town, high and low, is scandalized;
    This quarrel must be mended, and my advice is   15
    Not to push matters to a further crisis.
    No, sacrifice your wrath to God above,
    And help Damis regain his father's love.

TARTUFFE: Alas, for my part I should take great joy
    In doing so. I've nothing against the boy.   20
    I pardon all, I harbor no resentment;
    To serve him would afford me much contentment.
    But Heaven's interest will not have it so;
    If he comes back, then I shall have to go.
    After his conduct—so extreme, so vicious—   25
    Our further intercourse would look suspicious.
    God knows what people would think! Why, they'd describe

My goodness to him as a sort of bribe;
They'd say that out of guilt I made pretense
Of loving-kindness and benevolence—   30
That, fearing my accuser's tongue, I strove
To buy his silence with a show of love.

CLÉANTE: Your reasoning is badly warped and stretched,
And these excuses, Sir, are most far-fetched.
Why put yourself in charge of Heaven's cause?   35
Does Heaven need our help to enforce its laws?
Leave vengeance to the Lord, Sir; while we live,
Our duty's not to punish, but forgive;
And what the Lord commands, we should obey
Without regard to what the world may say.   40
What! Shall the fear of being misunderstood
Prevent our doing what is right and good?
No, no; let's simply do what Heaven ordains,
And let no other thoughts perplex our brains.

TARTUFFE: Again, Sir, let me say that I've forgiven   45
Damis, and thus obeyed the laws of Heaven;
But I am not commanded by the Bible
To live with one who smears my name with libel.

CLÉANTE: Were you commanded, Sir, to indulge the whim
Of poor Orgon, and to encourage him   50
In suddenly transferring to your name
A large estate to which you have no claim?

TARTUFFE: 'Twould never occur to those who know me best
To think I acted from self-interest.
The treasures of this world I quite despise;   55
Their specious glitter does not charm my eyes;
And if I have resigned myself to taking
The gift which my dear Brother insists on making,
I do so only, as he well understands,
Lest so much wealth fall into wicked hands,   60
Lest those to whom it might descend in time
Turn it to purposes of sin and crime,
And not, as I shall do, make use of it.
For Heaven's glory and mankind's benefit.

CLÉANTE: Forget these trumped-up fears. Your argument   65
Is one the rightful heir might well resent;
It *is* a moral burden to inherit
Such wealth, but give Damis a chance to bear it.
And would it not be worse to be accused
Of swindling, than to see that wealth misused?   70
I'm shocked that you allowed Orgon to broach
This matter, and that you feel no self-reproach;
Does true religion teach that lawful heirs
May freely be deprived of what is theirs?
And if the Lord has told you in your heart   75
That you and young Damis must dwell apart,
Would it not be the decent thing to beat
A generous and honorable retreat,
Rather than let the son of the house be sent,
For your convenience, into banishment?   80
Sir, if you wish to prove the honesty
Of your intentions . . .

TARTUFFE: Sir, it is half-past three.
    I've certain pious duties to attend to,
    And hope my prompt departure won't offend you.
CLÉANTE: *(Alone.)*   Damn.

85

Act 4, Scene 2

Elmire, Mariane, Cléante, Dorine

DORINE: Stay, Sir, and help Mariane, for Heaven's sake
    She's suffering so, I fear her heart will break.
    Her father's plan to marry her off tonight
    Has put the poor child in a desperate plight.
    I hear him coming. Let's stand together, now,
    And see if we can't change his mind, somehow,
    About this match we all deplore and fear.

5

Act 4, Scene 3

Orgon, Elmire, Mariane, Cléante, Dorine

ORGON: Hah! Glad to find you all assembled here.

(To Mariane.)

    This contract, child, contains your happiness,
    And what it says I think your heart can guess.
MARIANE: *(Falling to her knees.)*
    Sir, by that Heaven which sees me here distressed,
    And by whatever else can move your breast,
    Do not employ a father's power, I pray you,
    To crush my heart and force it to obey you,
    Nor by your harsh commands oppress me so
    That I'll begrudge the duty which I owe—
    And do not so embitter and enslave me
    That I shall hate the very life you gave me.
    If my sweet hopes must perish, if you refuse
    To give me to the one I've dared to choose,
    Spare me at least—I beg you, I implore—
    The pain of wedding one whom I abhor;
    And do not, by a heartless use of force,
    Drive me to contemplate some desperate course.
ORGON: *(Feeling himself touched by her.)*
    Be firm, my soul. No human weakness, now.
MARIANE: I don't resent your love for him. Allow
    Your heart free rein, Sir; give him your property,
    And if that's not enough, take mine from me;
    He's welcome to my money; take it, do,
    But don't, I pray, include my person too.
    Spare me, I beg you; and let me end the tale
    Of my sad days behind a convent veil.
ORGON: A convent! Hah! When crossed in their amours,
    All lovesick girls have the same thought as yours.
    Get up! The more you loathe the man, and dread him,
    The more ennobling it will be to wed him.
    Marry Tartuffe, and mortify your flesh!
    Enough: don't start that whimpering afresh.

5

10

15

20

25

30

DORINE: But why ...?

ORGON: Be still, there. Speak when you're spoken to.
    Not one more bit of impudence out of you.

CLÉANTE: If I may offer a word of counsel here ...

ORGON: Brother, in counseling you have no peer;   35
    All your advice is forceful, sound, and clever;
    I don't propose to follow it, however.

ELMIRE: *(To Orgon.)*   I am amazed, and don't know what to say;
    Your blindness simply takes my breath away.
    You are indeed bewitched, to take no warning   40
    From our account of what occurred this morning.

ORGON: Madam, I know a few plain facts, and one
    Is that you're partial to my rascal son;
    Hence, when he sought to make Tartuffe the victim
    Of a base lie, you dared not contradict him.   45
    Ah, but you underplayed your part, my pet;
    You should have looked more angry, more upset.

ELMIRE: When men make overtures, must we reply
    With righteous anger and a battle-cry?
    Must we turn back their amorous advances   50
    With sharp reproaches and with fiery glances?
    Myself, I find such offers merely amusing,
    And make no scenes and fusses in refusing;
    My taste is for good-natured rectitude,
    And I dislike the savage sort of prude   55
    Who guards her virtue with her teeth and claws,
    And tears men's eyes out for the slightest cause;
    The Lord preserve me from such honor as that,
    Which bites and scratches like an alley-cat!
    I've found that a polite and cool rebuff   60
    Discourages a lover quite enough.

ORGON: I know the facts, and I shall not be shaken.

ELMIRE: I marvel at your power to be mistaken.
    Would it, I wonder, carry weight with you
    If I could *show* you that our tale was true?   65

ORGON: Show me?

ELMIRE: Yes.

ORGON: Rot.

ELMIRE: Come, what if I found a way
    To make you see the facts as plain as day?

ORGON: Nonsense.

ELMIRE: Do answer me; don't be absurd.
    I'm not now asking you to trust our word.
    Suppose that from some hiding-place in here   70
    You learned the whole sad truth by eye and ear—
    What would you say of your good friend, after that?

ORGON: Why, I'd say ... nothing, by Jehoshaphat!
    It can't be true.

ELMIRE: You've been too long deceived,
    And I'm quite tired of being disbelieved.   75
    Come now; let's put my statements to the test,
    And you shall see the truth made manifest.

ORGON: I'll take that challenge. Now do your uttermost.
    We'll see how you make good your empty boast.

ELMIRE: *(To Dorine.)* Send him to me.

DORINE: He's crafty; it may be hard 80
To catch the cunning scoundrel off his guard.

ELMIRE: No, amorous men are gullible. Their conceit
So blinds them that they're never hard to cheat.
Have him come down *(To Cléante and Mariane)* Please leave us, for a bit.

Act 4, Scene 4

Elmire, Orgon

ELMIRE: Pull up this table, and get under it.

ORGON: What?

ELMIRE: It's essential that you be well-hidden.

ORGON: Why there?

ELMIRE: Oh, Heavens! Just do as you are bidden
I have my plans; we'll soon see how they fare.
Under the table, now; and once you're there, 5
Take care that you are neither seen nor heard.

ORGON: Well, I'll indulge you, since I gave my word
To see you through this infantile charade.

ELMIRE: Once it is over, you'll be glad we played.

(To her husband, who is now under the table.)

I'm going to act quite strangely, now, and you 10
Must not be shocked at anything I do.
Whatever I may say, you must excuse
As part of that deceit I'm forced to use.
I shall employ sweet speeches in the task
Of making that impostor drop his mask; 15
I'll give encouragement to his bold desires,
And furnish fuel to his amorous fires.
Since it's for your sake, and for his destruction,
That I shall seem to yield to his seduction,
I'll gladly stop whenever you decide 20
That all your doubts are fully satisfied.
I'll count on you, as soon as you have seen
What sort of man he is, to intervene,
And not expose me to his odious lust
One moment longer than you feel you must. 25
Remember: you're to save me from my plight
Whenever . . . He's coming! Hush! Keep out of sight!

Act 4, Scene 5

Tartuffe, Elmire, Orgon

TARTUFFE: You wish to have a word with me, I'm told.

ELMIRE: Yes. I've a little secret to unfold.
Before I speak, however, it would be wise
To close that door, and look about for spies.

(Tartuffe goes to the door, closes it, and returns.)

The very last thing that must happen now 5
Is a repetition of this morning's row.

I've never been so badly caught off guard.
Oh, how I feared for you! You saw how hard
I tried to make that troublesome Damis
Control his dreadful temper, and hold his peace.   10
In my confusion, I didn't have the sense
Simply to contradict his evidence;
But as it happened, that was for the best,
And all has worked out in our interest.
This storm has only bettered your position;   15
My husband doesn't have the least suspicion,
And now, in mockery of those who do,
He bids me be continually with you.
And that is why, quite fearless of reproof,
I now can be alone with my Tartuffe,   20
And why my heart—perhaps too quick to yield—
Feels free to let its passion be revealed.

TARTUFFE: Madam, your words confuse me. Not long ago,
You spoke in quite a different style, you know.

ELMIRE: Ah, Sir, if that refusal made you smart,   25
It's little that you know of woman's heart,
Or what that heart is trying to convey
When it resists in such a feeble way!
Always, at first, our modesty prevents
The frank avowal of tender sentiments;   30
However high the passion which inflames us,
Still, to confess its power somehow shames us.
Thus we reluct, at first, yet in a tone
Which tells you that our heart is overthrown,
That what our lips deny, our pulse confesses,   35
And that, in time, all noes will turn to yesses.
I fear my words are all too frank and free,
And a poor proof of woman's modesty;
But since I'm started, tell me, if you will—
Would I have tried to make Damis be still,   40
Would I have listened, calm and unoffended,
Until your lengthy offer of love was ended,
And been so very mild in my reaction,
Had your sweet words not given me satisfaction?
And when I tried to force you to undo   45
The marriage-plans my husband has in view,
What did my urgent pleading signify
If not that I admired you, and that I
Deplored the thought that someone else might own
Part of a heart I wished for mine alone?   50

TARTUFFE: Madam, no happiness is so complete
As when, from lips we love, come words so sweet;
Their nectar floods my every sense, and drains
In honeyed rivulets through all my veins.
To please you is my joy, my only goal;   55
Your love is the restorer of my soul;
And yet I must beg leave, now, to confess
Some lingering doubts as to my happiness
Might this not be a trick? Might not the catch
Be that you wish me to break off the match   60

With Mariane, and so have feigned to love me?
I shan't quite trust your fond opinion of me
Until the feelings you've expressed so sweetly
Are demonstrated somewhat more concretely,
And you have shown, by certain kind concessions,   65
That I may put my faith in your professions.
ELMIRE: *(She coughs, to warn her husband.)*
Why be in such a hurry? Must my heart
Exhaust its bounty at the very start?
To make that sweet admission cost me dear,
But you'll not be content, it would appear,   70
Unless my store of favors is disbursed
To the last farthing, and at the very first.
TARTUFFE: The less we merit, the less we dare to hope,
And with our doubts, mere words can never cope.
We trust no promised bliss till we receive it;   75
Not till a joy is ours can we believe it.
I, who so little merit your esteem,
Can't credit this fulfillment of my dream,
And shan't believe it, Madam, until I savor
Some palpable assurance of your favor.   80
ELMIRE: My, how tyrannical your love can be,
And how it flusters and perplexes me!
How furiously you take one's heart in hand,
And make your every wish a fierce command!
Come, must you hound and harry me to death?   85
Will you not give me time to catch my breath?
Can it be right to press me with such force,
Give me no quarter, show me no remorse,
And take advantage, by your stern insistence,
Of the fond feelings which weaken my resistance?   90
TARTUFFE: Well, if you look with favor upon my love,
Why, then, begrudge me some clear proof thereof?
ELMIRE: But how can I consent without offense
To Heaven, toward which you feel such reverence?
TARTUFFE: If Heaven is all that holds you back, don't worry.   95
I can remove that hindrance in a hurry.
Nothing of that sort need obstruct our path.
ELMIRE: Must one not be afraid of Heaven's wrath?
TARTUFFE: Madam, forget such fears, and be my pupil,
And I shall teach you how to conquer scruple.   100
Some joys, it's true, are wrong in Heaven's eyes;
Yet Heaven is not averse to compromise;
There is a science, lately formulated,
Whereby one's conscience may be liberated,
And any wrongful act you care to mention   105
May be redeemed by purity of intention.
I'll teach you, Madam, the secrets of that science;
Meanwhile, just place on me your full reliance.
Assuage my keen desires, and feel no dread:
The sin, if any, shall be on my head.   110

(Elmire coughs, this time more loudly.)

You've a bad cough.

ELMIRE: Yes, yes. It's bad indeed.
TARTUFFE: *(Producing a little paper bag.)*
     A bit of licorice may be what you need.
ELMIRE: No, I've a stubborn cold, it seems. I'm sure it
     Will take much more than licorice to cure it.
TARTUFFE: How aggravating.
ELMIRE: Oh, more than I can say.   115
TARTUFFE: If you're still troubled, think of things this way:
     No one shall know our joys, save us alone,
     And there's no evil till the act is known;
     It's scandal, Madam, which makes it an offense,
     And it's no sin to sin in confidence.   120
ELMIRE: *(Having coughed once more.)*
     Well, clearly I must do as you require,
     And yield to your importunate desire.
     It is apparent, now, that nothing less
     Will satisfy you, and so I acquiesce.
     To go so far is much against my will;   125
     I'm vexed that it should come to this; but still,
     Since you are so determined on it, since you
     Will not allow mere language to convince you,
     And since you ask for concrete evidence, I
     See nothing for it, now, but to comply.   130
     If this is sinful, if I'm wrong to do it,
     So much the worse for him who drove me to it.
     The fault can surely not be charged to me.
TARTUFFE: Madam, the fault is mine, if fault there be, And . . .
ELMIRE: Open the door a little and peek out;   135
     I wouldn't want my husband poking about.
TARTUFFE: Why worry about the man? Each day he grows
     More gullible; one can lead him by the nose.
     To find us here would fill him with delight,
     And if he saw the worst, he'd doubt his sight.   140
ELMIRE: Nevertheless, do step out for a minute
     Into the hall, and see that no one's in it.

Act 4, Scene 6

Orgon, Elmire

ORGON: *(Coming out from under the table.)*
     That man's a perfect monster, I must admit!
     I'm simply stunned. I can't get over it.
ELMIRE: What, coming out so soon? How premature!
     Get back in hiding, and wait until you're sure.
     Stay till the end, and be convinced completely;   5
     We mustn't stop till things are proved concretely.
ORGON: Hell never harbored anything so vicious!
ELMIRE: Tut, don't be hasty. Try to be judicious.
     Wait, and be certain that there's no mistake.
     No jumping to conclusions, for Heaven's sake!   10

(She places Orgon behind her, as Tartuffe re-enters.)

Act 4, Scene 7

Tartuffe, Elmire, Orgon

TARTUFFE: *(Not seeing Orgon.)*   Madam, all things have worked out to perfection;
 I've given the neighboring rooms a full inspection;
 No one's about; and now I may at last ...
ORGON: *(Intercepting him.)*   Hold on, my passionate fellow, not so fast!   5
 I should advise a little more restraint.
 Well, so you thought you'd fool me, my dear saint!
 How soon you wearied of the saintly life—
 Wedding my daughter, and coveting my wife!
 I've long suspected you, and had a feeling
 That soon I'd catch you at your double-dealing.   10
 Just now, you've given me evidence galore;
 It's quite enough; I have no wish for more.
ELMIRE: *(To Tartuffe.)*   I'm sorry to have treated you so slyly.
 But circumstances forced me to be wily.
TARTUFFE: Brother, you can't think ...
ORGON: No more talk from you;   15
 Just leave this household, without more ado.
TARTUFFE: What I intended ...
ORGON: That seems fairly clear.
 Spare me your falsehoods and get out of here.
TARTUFFE: No, I'm the master, and you're the one to go!
 This house belongs to me, I'll have you know,
 And I shall show you that you can't hurt *me*   20
 By this contemptible conspiracy,
 That those who cross me know not what they do,
 And that I've means to expose and punish you,
 Avenge offended Heaven, and make you grieve
 That ever you dared order me to leave.   25

Act 4, Scene 8

Elmire, Orgon

ELMIRE: What was the point of all that angry chatter?
ORGON: Dear God, I'm worried. This is no laughing matter.
ELMIRE: How so?
ORGON: I fear I understood his drift.
 I'm much disturbed about that deed of gift.
ELMIRE: You gave him ...?
ORGON: Yes, it's all been drawn and signed.   5
 But one thing more is weighing on my mind.
ELMIRE: What's that?
ORGON: I'll tell you; but first let's see if there's
 A certain strong-box in his room upstairs.

Act 5, Scene 1

Orgon, Cléante

CLÉANTE: Where are you going so fast?
ORGON: God knows!

CLÉANTE: Then wait;
    Let's have a conference, and deliberate
    On how this situation's to be met.
ORGON: That strong-box has me utterly upset;
    This is the worst of many, many shocks.   5
CLÉANTE: Is there some fearful mystery in that box?
ORGON: My poor friend Argas brought that box to me
    With his own hands, in utmost secrecy;
    'Twas on the very morning of his flight.
    It's full of papers which, if they came to light,   10
    Would ruin him—or such is my impression.
CLÉANTE: Then why did you let it out of your possession?
ORGON: Those papers vexed my conscience, and it seemed best
    To ask the counsel of my pious guest.
    The cunning scoundrel got me to agree   15
    To leave the strong-box in his custody,
    So that, in case of an investigation,
    I could employ a slight equivocation
    And swear I didn't have it, and thereby,
    At no expense to conscience, tell a lie.   20
CLÉANTE: It looks to me as if you're out on a limb.
    Trusting him with that box, and offering him
    That deed of gift, were actions of a kind
    Which scarcely indicate a prudent mind.
    With two such weapons, he has the upper hand,   25
    And since you're vulnerable, as matters stand,
    You erred once more in bringing him to bay.
    You should have acted in some subtler way.
ORGON: Just think of it: behind that fervent face,
    A heart so wicked, and a soul so base!   30
    I took him in, a hungry beggar, and then . . .
    Enough, by God! I'm through with pious men:
    Henceforth I'll hate the whole false brotherhood.
    And persecute them worse than Satan could.
CLÉANTE: Ah, there you go—extravagant as ever.   35
    Why can you not be rational? You never
    Manage to take the middle course, it seems,
    But jump, instead, between absurd extremes
    You've recognized your recent grave mistake
    In falling victim to a pious fake;   40
    Now, to correct that error, must you embrace
    An even greater error in its place,
    And judge our worthy neighbors as a whole
    By what you've learned of one corrupted soul?
    Come, just because one rascal made you swallow   45
    A show of zeal which turned out to be hollow,
    Shall you conclude that all men are deceivers,
    And that, today, there are no true believers?
    Let atheists make that foolish inference;
    Learn to distinguish virtue from pretense,   50
    Be cautious in bestowing admiration,
    And cultivate a sober moderation.
    Don't humor fraud, but also don't asperse

True piety; the latter fault is worse,
And it is best to err, if err one must,
As you have done, upon the side of trust.

55

Act 5, Scene 2

Damis, Orgon Cléante

DAMIS: Father, I hear that scoundrel's uttered threats
Against you; that he pridefully forgets
How, in his need, he was befriended by you.
And means to use your gifts to crucify you.

ORGON: It's true, my boy. I'm too distressed for tears.

5

DAMIS: Leave it to me, Sir: let me trim his ears.
Faced with such insolence, we must not waver.
I shall rejoice in doing you the favor
Of cutting short his life, and your distress.

CLÉANTE: What a display of young hotheadedness!
Do learn to moderate your fits of rage.
In this just kingdom, this enlightened age,
One does not settle things by violence.

10

Act 5, Scene 3

Madame Pernelle, Mariane, Elmire, Dorine, Damis, Orgon, Cléante

MADAME PERNELLE: I hear strange tales of very strange events.

ORGON: Yes, strange events which these two eyes beheld.
The man's ingratitude is unparalleled.
I save a wretched pauper from starvation.
House him, and treat him like a blood relation,
Shower him every day with my largesse,
Give him my daughter, and all that I possess;
And meanwhile the unconscionable knave
Tries to induce my wife to misbehave;
And not content with such extreme rascality,
Now threatens me with my own liberality,
And aims, by taking base advantage of
The gifts I gave him out of Christian love,
To drive me from my house, a ruined man.
And make me end a pauper, as he began.

5

10

15

DORINE: Poor fellow!

MADAME PERNELLE: No, my son, I'll never bring
Myself to think him guilty of such a thing.

ORGON: How's that?

MADAME PERNELLE: The righteous always were maligned.

ORGON: Speak clearly, Mother. Say what's on your mind.

MADAME PERNELLE: I mean that I can smell a rat, my dear.
You know how everybody hates him, here.

20

ORGON: That has no bearing on the case at all.

MADAME PERNELLE: I told you a hundred times, when you were small,
That virtue in this world is hated ever;
Malicious men may die, but malice never.

25

ORGON: No doubt that's true, but how does it apply?

MADAME PERNELLE: They've turned you against him by a clever lie.

ORGON: I've told you, I was there and saw it done.
MADAME PERNELLE: Ah, slanderers will stop at nothing, Son.
ORGON: Mother, I'll lose my temper . . . For the last time,   30
   I tell you I was witness to the crime.
MADAME PERNELLE: The tongues of spite are busy night and noon
   And to their venom no man is immune.
ORGON: You're talking nonsense. Can't you realize
   I saw it; saw it; saw it with my eyes?   35
   Saw, do you understand me? Must I shout it
   Into your ears before you'll cease to doubt it?
MADAME PERNELLE: Appearances can deceive, my son. Dear me.
   We cannot always judge by what we see.
ORGON: Drat! Drat!
MADAME PERNELLE: One often interprets things awry;   40
   Good can seem evil to a suspicious eye.
ORGON: Was I to see his pawing at Elmire
   As an act of charity?
MADAME PERNELLE: Till his guilt is clear,
   A man deserves the benefit of the doubt.
   You should have waited, to see how things turned out.   45
ORGON: Great God in Heaven, what more proof did I need?
   Was I to sit there, watching, until he'd . . .
   You drive me to the brink of impropriety.
MADAME PERNELLE: No, no, a man of such surpassing piety
   Could not do such a thing. You cannot shake me.   50
   I don't believe it, and you shall not make me.
ORGON: You vex me so that, if you weren't my mother,
   I'd say to you . . . some dreadful thing or other.
DORINE: It's your turn now, Sir, not to be listened to;
   You'd not trust us, and now she won't trust you.   55
CLÉANTE: My friends, we're wasting time which should be spent
   In facing up to our predicament.
   I fear that scoundrel's threats weren't made in sport.
DAMIS: Do you think he'd have the nerve to go to court?
ELMIRE: I'm sure he won't; they'd find it all too crude   60
   A case of swindling and ingratitude.
CLÉANTE: Don't be too sure. He won't be at a loss
   To give his claims a high and righteous gloss;
   And clever rogues with far less valid cause
   Have trapped their victims in a web of laws.   65
   I say again that to antagonize
   A man so strongly armed was most unwise.
ORGON: I know it; but the man's appalling cheek
   Outraged me so, I couldn't control my pique.
CLÉANTE: I wish to Heaven that we could devise   70
   Some truce between you, or some compromise.
ELMIRE: If I had known what cards he held, I'd not
   Have roused his anger by my little plot.
ORGON: (To Dorine, as M. Loyal enters.)
   What is that fellow looking for? Who is he?
   Go talk to him—and tell him that I'm busy.   75

Act 5, Scene 4

Monsieur Loyal, Madame Pernelle, Orgon, Damis, Mariane, Dorine, Elmire, Cléante

MONSIEUR LOYAL: Good day, dear sister. Kindly let me see
    your master.
DORINE: He's involved with company,
    And cannot be disturbed just now I fear.
MONSIEUR LOYAL: I hate to intrude, but what has brought me here
    Will not disturb your master, in any event.
    Indeed, my news will make him most content.   5
DORINE: Your name?
MONSIEUR LOYAL: Just say that I bring greetings from
    Monsieur Tartuffe, on whose behalf I've come.
DORINE: (To Orgon.)   Sir, he's a very gracious man, and bears
    A message from Tartuffe, which, he declares,
    Will make you most content.   10
CLÉANTE: Upon my word.
    I think this man had best be seen, and heard.
ORGON: Perhaps he has some settlement to suggest.
    How shall I treat him? What manner would be best?
CLÉANTE: Control your anger, and if he should mention   15
    Some fair adjustment, give him your full attention.
MONSIEUR LOYAL: Good health to you, good Sir. May Heaven confound
    Your enemies, and may your joys abound.
ORGON: (Aside, to Cléante.)   A gentle salutation: it confirms
    My guess that he is here to offer terms.   20
MONSIEUR LOYAL: I've always held your family most dear;
    I served your father, Sir, for many a year.
ORGON: Sir, I must ask your pardon; to my shame,
    I cannot now recall your face or name.
MONSIEUR LOYAL: Loyal's my name; I come from Normandy,   25
    And I'm a bailiff, in all modesty.
    For forty years, praise God, it's been my boast
    To serve with honor in that vital post,
    And I am here, Sir, if you will permit
    The liberty, to serve you with this writ ...   30
ORGON: To—what?
MONSIEUR LOYAL: Now, please, Sir, let us have no friction:
    It's nothing but an order of eviction.
    You are to move your goods and family out
    And make way for new occupants, without
    Deferment or delay, and give the keys ...   35
ORGON: I? Leave this house?
MONSIEUR LOYAL: Why yes, Sir, if you please.
    This house, Sir, from the cellar to the roof,
    Belongs now to the good Monsieur Tartuffe.
    And he is lord and master of your estate
    By virtue of a deed of present date,
    Drawn in due form, with clearest legal phrasing ...   40
DAMIS: Your insolence is utterly amazing!
MONSIEUR LOYAL: Young man, my business here is not with you,
    But with your wise and temperate father, who,
    Like every worthy citizen, stands in awe
    Of justice, and would never obstruct the law.   45
ORGON: But ...
MONSIEUR LOYAL: Not for a million, Sir, would you rebel
    Against authority; I know that well.

You'll not make trouble, Sir, or interfere
        With the execution of my duties here.   50
DAMIS: Someone may execute a smart tattoo
        On that black jacket of yours, before you're through.
MONSIEUR LOYAL: Sir, bid your son be silent. I'd much regret
        Having to mention such a nasty threat
        Of violence, in writing my report.   55
DORINE: *(Aside.)*   This man Loyal's a most disloyal sort!
MONSIEUR LOYAL: I love all men of upright character,
        And when I agreed to serve these papers, Sir,
        It was your feelings that I had in mind.
        I couldn't bear to see the case assigned
        To someone else, who might esteem you less   60
        And so subject you to unpleasantness.
ORGON: What's more unpleasant than telling a man to leave
        His house and home?
MONSIEUR LOYAL: You'd like a short reprieve?
        If you desire, Sir, I shall not press you,
        But wait until tomorrow to dispossess you.   65
        Splendid. I'll come and spend the night here, then,
        Most quietly, with half a score of men.
        For form's sake, you might bring me, just before
        You go to bed, the keys to the front door.   70
        My men, I promise, will be on their best
        Behavior, and will not disturb your rest.
        But bright and early, Sir, you must be quick
        And move out all your furniture, every stick;
        The men I've chosen are both young and strong,   75
        And with their help it shouldn't take you long.
        In short, I'll make things pleasant and convenient,
        And since I'm being so extremely lenient,
        Please show me, Sir, a like consideration,
        And give me your entire cooperation.   80
ORGON: *(Aside.)*   I may be all but bankrupt, but I vow
        I'd give a hundred louis, here and now,
        Just for the pleasure of landing one good clout
        Right on the end of that complacent snout.
CLÉANTE: Careful; don't make things worse.
DAMIS: My bootsole itches   85
        To give that beggar a good kick in the breeches.
DORINE: Monsieur Loyal, I'd love to hear the whack
        Of a stout stick across your fine broad back.
MONSIEUR LOYAL: Take care: a woman too may go to jail if
        She uses threatening language to a bailiff.   90
CLÉANTE: Enough, enough, Sir. This must not go on.
        Give me that paper, please, and then begone.
MONSIEUR LOYAL: Well, *au revoir.* God give you all good cheer!
ORGON: May God confound you, and him who sent you here!

Act 5, Scene 5

Orgon, Cléante, Mariane, Elmire, Madame Pernelle, Dorine, Damis

ORGON: Now, Mother, was I right or not? This writ
        Should change your notion of Tartuffe a bit.

Do you perceive his villainy at last?

MADAME PERNELLE: I'm thunderstruck. I'm utterly aghast.

DORINE: Oh, come, be fair. You mustn't take offense
At this new proof of his benevolence.   5
He's acting out of selfless love, I know.
Material things enslave the soul, and so
He kindly has arranged your liberation
From all that might endanger your salvation.

ORGON: Will you not ever hold your tongue, you dunce?   10

CLÉANTE: Come, you must take some action, and at once.

ELMIRE: Go tell the world of the low trick he's tried.
The deed of gift is surely nullified
By such behavior, and public rage will not   15
Permit the wretch to carry out his plot.

Act 5, Scene 6

Valère, Orgon, Cléante, Elmire, Mariane, Madame Pernelle, Damis, Dorine

VALÈRE: Sir, though I hate to bring you more bad news,
Such is the danger that I cannot choose.
A friend who is extremely close to me
And knows my interest in your family
Has, for my sake, presumed to violate   5
The secrecy that's due to things of state,
And sends me word that you are in a plight
From which your one salvation lies in flight.
That scoundrel who's imposed upon you so
Denounced you to the King an hour ago   10
And, as supporting evidence, displayed
The strong-box of a certain renegade
Whose secret papers, so he testified,
You had disloyally agreed to hide.
I don't know just what charges may be pressed.   15
But there's a warrant out for your arrest;
Tartuffe has been instructed, furthermore,
To guide the arresting officer to your door.

CLÉANTE: He's clearly done this to facilitate
His seizure of your house and your estate.   20

ORGON: That man, I must say, is a vicious beast!

VALÈRE: Quick, Sir, you mustn't tarry in the least.
My carriage is outside, to take you hence;
This thousand louis should cover all expense.
Let's lose no time, or you shall be undone;   25
The sole defense, in this case, is to run.
I shall go with you all the way, and place you
In a safe refuge to which they'll never trace you.

ORGON: Alas, dear boy, I wish that I could show you
My gratitude for everything I owe you.   30
But now is not the time; I pray the Lord
That I may live to give you your reward.
Farewell, my dears; be careful . . .

CLÉANTE: Brother, hurry.
    We shall take care of things; you needn't worry.

Act 5, Scene 7

The Officer, Tartuffe, Valère, Orgon, Elmire, Mariane, Madame Pernelle, Dorine, Cléante, Damis

TARTUFFE: Gently, Sir, gently; stay right where you are.
    No need for haste; your lodging isn't far.
    You're off to prison, by order of the Prince.
ORGON: This is the crowning blow, you wretch; and since   5
    It means my total ruin and defeat,
    Your villainy is now at last complete.
TARTUFFE: You needn't try to provoke me; it's no use.
    Those who serve Heaven must expect abuse.
CLÉANTE: You are indeed most patient, sweet, and blameless.
DORINE: How he exploits the name of Heaven! It's shameless.   10
TARTUFFE: Your taunts and mockeries are all for naught;
    To do my duty is my only thought.
MARIANE: Your love of duty is more meritorious,
    And what you've done is little short of glorious.
TARTUFFE: All deeds are glorious, Madam, which obey   15
    The sovereign prince who sent me here today.
ORGON: I rescued you when you were destitute,
    Have you forgotten that, you thankless brute?
TARTUFFE: No, no, I well remember everything;
    But my first duty is to serve my King.   20
    That obligation is so paramount
    That other claims, beside it, do not count;
    And for it I would sacrifice my wife,
    My family, my friend, or my own life.
ELMIRE: Hypocrite!
DORINE: All that we most revere, he uses   25
    To cloak his plots and camouflage his ruses.
CLÉANTE: If it is true that you are animated
    By pure and loyal zeal, as you have stated,
    Why was this zeal not roused until you'd sought
    To make Orgon a cuckold, and been caught?   30
    Why weren't you moved to give your evidence
    Until your outraged host had driven you hence?
    I shan't say that the gift of all his treasure
    Ought to have damped your zeal in any measure;
    But if he is a traitor, as you declare,   35
    How could you condescend to be his heir?
TARTUFFE: *(To the Officer.)*   Sir, spare me all this clamor; it's growing shrill.
    Please carry out your orders, if you will.
OFFICER: Yes, I've delayed too long, Sir. Thank you kindly.
    You're just the proper person to remind me.   40
    Come, you are off to join the other boarders
    In the King's prison, according to his orders.
TARTUFFE: Who? I, Sir?
OFFICER: Yes.
TARTUFFE: To prison? This can't be true!
OFFICER: I owe an explanation, but not to you.

(To ORGON.)

Sir, all is well; rest easy, and be grateful. 45
We serve a Prince to whom all sham is hateful,
A Prince who sees into our inmost hearts,
And can't be fooled by any trickster's arts.
His royal soul, though generous and human,
Views all things with discernment and acumen; 50
His sovereign reason is not lightly swayed,
And all his judgments are discreetly weighed.
He honors righteous men of every kind,
And yet his zeal for virtue is not blind,
Nor does his love of piety numb his wits 55
And make him tolerant of hypocrites.
'Twas hardly likely that this man could cozen
A King who's foiled such liars by the dozen.
With one keen glance, the King perceived the whole
Perverseness and corruption of his soul, 60
And thus high Heaven's justice was displayed:
Betraying you, the rogue stood self-betrayed.
The King soon recognized Tartuffe as one
Notorious by another name, who'd done
So many vicious crimes that one could fill 65
Ten volumes with them, and be writing still.
But to be brief: our sovereign was appalled
By this man's treachery toward you, which he called
The last, worst villainy of a vile career.
And bade me follow the impostor here 70
To see how gross his impudence could be,
And force him to restore your property.
Your private papers, by the King's command,
I hereby seize and give into your hand.
The King, by royal order, invalidates 75
The deed which gave this rascal your estates.
And pardons, furthermore, your grave offense
In harboring an exile's documents.
By these decrees, our Prince rewards you for
Your loyal deeds in the late civil war, 80
And shows how heartfelt is his satisfaction
In recompensing any worthy action,
How much he prizes merit, and how he makes
More of men's virtues than of their mistakes.

DORINE: Heaven be praised!

MADAME PERNELLE: I breathe again, at last. 85

ELMIRE: We're safe.

MARIANE: I can't believe the danger's past.

ORGON: *(To Tartuffe.)*   Well, traitor, now you see ...

CLÉANTE: Ah, Brother, please,
Let's not descend to such indignities.
Leave the poor wretch to his unhappy fate.
And don't say anything to aggravate 90
His present woes; but rather hope that he
Will soon embrace an honest piety,
And mend his ways, and by a true repentance
Move our just King to moderate his sentence.

Meanwhile, go kneel before your sovereign's throne   95
And thank him for the mercies he has shown.

ORGON: Well said: let's go at once and, gladly kneeling,
Express the gratitude which all are feeling.
Then, when that first great duty has been done,   100
We'll turn with pleasure to a second one.
And give Valère, whose love has proven so true,
The wedded happiness which is his due.

Arthur Miller   b. 1915

Death of a Salesman   *1949*

Certain Private Conversations in Two Acts and a Requiem

Willy Loman
Linda, his wife
Biff ⎫ his sons
Happy ⎭
Uncle Ben
Charley
Bernard

The Woman
Howard Wagner
Jenny
Stanley
Miss Forsythe
Letta

The action takes place in Willy Loman's house and yard and in various places he visits in the New York and Boston of today.

Throughout the play, in the stage directions, left and right mean stage left and stage right.

Act 1

A melody is heard, played upon a flute. It is small and fine, telling of grass and trees and the horizon. The curtain rises.

Before us is the Salesman's house. We are aware of towering, angular shapes behind it, surrounding it on all sides. Only the blue light of the sky falls upon the house and forestage; the surrounding area shows an angry glow of orange. As more light appears, we see a solid vault of apartment houses around the small, fragile-seeming home. An air of the dream clings to the place, a dream rising out of reality. The kitchen at center seems actual enough, for there is a kitchen table with three chairs, and a refrigerator. But no other fixtures are seen. At the back of the kitchen there is a draped entrance, which leads to the livingroom. To the right of the kitchen, on a level raised two feet, is a bedroom furnished only with a brass bedstead and a straight chair. On a shelf over the bed a silver athletic trophy stands. A window opens onto the apartment house at the side.

Behind the kitchen, on a level raised six and a half feet, is the boys' bedroom, at present barely visible. Two beds are dimly seen, and at the back of the room a dormer window. (This bedroom is above the unseen livingroom.) At the left a stairway curves up to it from the kitchen.

The entire setting is wholly or, in some places, partially transparent. The roofline of the house is one-dimensional; under and over it we see the apartment buildings. Before the house lies an apron, curving beyond the forestage into the orchestra. This forward area serves as the back yard as well as the lo-cale of all Willy's imaginings and of his city scenes. Whenever the action is in the present the actors observe the imaginary wall-lines, entering the house only through the door at the left. But in the scenes of the past these boundaries are broken, and characters enter or leave a room by stepping "through" a wall onto the forestage.

From the right, Willy Loman, the Salesman, enters, carrying two large sample cases. The flute plays on. He hears but is not aware of it. He is past sixty years of age, dressed quietly. Even as he crosses the stage to the doorway of the house, his exhaustion is apparent. He unlocks the door, comes into the kitchen, and thankfully lets his burden down, feeling the soreness of his palms. A word-sigh escapes his lips—it might be "Oh, boy, oh, boy." He closes the door, then carries his cases out into the livingroom, though the draped kitchen doorway.

Linda, his wife, has stirred in her bed at the right. She gets out and puts on a robe, listening. Most often jovial, she has developed an iron repression of her exceptions to Willy's behavior—she more than loves him, she admires him, as though his mercurial nature, his temper, his massive dreams and little cruelties, served her only as sharp reminders of the turbulent longings within him, longings which she shares but lacks the temperament to utter and follow to their end.

LINDA: *(hearing Willy outside the bedroom, calls with some trepidation)* Willy!
WILLY: It's all right. I came back.
LINDA: Why? What happened? *(Slight pause.)* Did something happen, Willy?
WILLY: No, nothing happened.
LINDA: You didn't smash the car, did you?   5
WILLY: *(with casual irritation)* I said nothing happened. Didn't you hear me?
LINDA: Don't you feel well?
WILLY: I am tired to the death. *(The flute has faded away. He sits on the bed beside her, a little numb.)* I couldn't make it. I just couldn't make it, Linda.
LINDA: *(very carefully, delicately)* Where were you all day? You look terrible.
WILLY: I got as far as a little above Yonkers. I stopped for a cup of coffee. Maybe it was   10
        the coffee.
LINDA: What?
WILLY: *(after a pause)* I suddenly couldn't drive any more. The car kept going onto the
        shoulder, y'know?
LINDA: *(helpfully)* Oh. Maybe it was the steering again. I don't think Angelo knows the
        Studebaker.
WILLY: No, it's me, it's me. Suddenly I realize I'm goin' sixty miles an hour and I don't re-
        member the last five minutes. I'm—I can't seem to—keep my mind to it.
LINDA: Maybe it's your glasses. You never went for your new glasses.   15
WILLY: No, I see everything. I came back ten miles an hour. It took me nearly four hours
        from Yonkers.
LINDA: *(resigned)* Well, you'll just have to take a rest, Willy, you can't continue this way.
WILLY: I just got back from Florida.
LINDA: But you didn't rest your mind. Your mind is overactive, and the mind is what
        counts, dear.
WILLY: I'll start out in the morning. Maybe I'll feel better in the morning. *(She is taking*   20
        off his shoes.) These goddam arch supports are killing me.
LINDA: Take an aspirin. Should I get you an aspirin? It'll soothe you.
WILLY: *(with wonder)* I was driving along, you understand? And I was fine. I was even
        observing the scenery. You can imagine, me looking at scenery, on the road every
        week of my life. But it's so beautiful up there, Linda, the trees are so thick, and the
        sun is warm. I opened the windshield and just let the warm air bathe over me. And
        then all of a sudden I'm goin' off the road! I'm tellin' ya, I absolutely forgot I was dri-
        ving. If I'd've gone the other way over the white line I might've killed somebody. So
        I went on again—and five minutes later I'm dreamin' again, and I nearly—*(He
        presses two fingers against his eyes.)* I have such thoughts, I have such strange
        thoughts.
LINDA: Willy, dear. Talk to them again. There's no reason why you can't work in New
        York.
WILLY: They don't need me in New York. I'm the New England man. I'm vital in New
        England.

LINDA: But you're sixty years old. They can't expect you to keep traveling every week.   25
WILLY: I'll have to send a wire to Portland. I'm supposed to see Brown and Morrison tomorrow morning at ten o'clock to show the line. Goddammit, I could sell them! *(He starts putting on his jacket.)*
LINDA: *(taking the jacket from him)* Why don't you go down to the place tomorrow and tell Howard you've simply got to work in New York? You're too accommodating, dear.
WILLY: If old man Wagner was alive I'd a been in charge of New York now! That man was a prince, he was a masterful man. But that boy of his, that Howard, he don't appreciate. When I went north the first time, the Wagner Company didn't know where New England was!
LINDA: Why don't you tell those things to Howard, dear?
WILLY: *(encouraged)* I will, I definitely will. Is there any cheese?   30
LINDA: I'll make you a sandwich.
WILLY: No, go to sleep. I'll take some milk. I'll be up right away. The boys in?
LINDA: They're sleeping. Happy took Biff on a date tonight.
WILLY: *(interested)* That so?
LINDA: It was so nice to see them shaving together, one behind the other, in the bathroom. And going out together. You notice? The whole house smells of shaving lotion.   35
WILLY: Figure it out. Work a lifetime to pay off a house. You finally own it, and there's nobody to live in it.
LINDA: Well, dear, life is a casting off. It's always that way.
WILLY: No, no, some people—some people accomplish something. Did Biff say anything after I went this morning?
LINDA: You shouldn't have criticized him, Willy, especially after he just got off the train. You mustn't lose your temper with him.
WILLY: When the hell did I lose my temper? I simply asked him if he was making any money. Is that a criticism?   40
LINDA: But, dear, how could he make any money?
WILLY: *(worried and angered)* There's such an undercurrent in him. He became a moody man. Did he apologize when I left this morning?
LINDA: He was crestfallen, Willy. You know how he admires you. I think if he finds himself, then you'll both be happier and not fight any more.
WILLY: How can he find himself on a farm? Is that a life? A farmhand? In the beginning, when he was young, I thought, well, a young man, it's good for him to tramp around, take a lot of different jobs. But it's more than ten years now and he has yet to make thirty-five dollars a week!
LINDA: He's finding himself, Willy.   45
WILLY: Not finding yourself at the age of thirty-four is a disgrace!
LINDA: Shh!
WILLY: The trouble is he's lazy, goddammit!
LINDA: Willy, please!
WILLY: Biff is a lazy bum!   50
LINDA: They're sleeping. Get something to eat. Go on down.
WILLY: Why did he come home? I would like to know what brought him home.
LINDA: I don't know. I think he's still lost, Willy. I think he's very lost.
WILLY: Biff Loman is lost. In the greatest country in the world a young man with such—personal attractiveness, gets lost. And such a hard worker. There's one thing about Biff—he's not lazy.
LINDA: Never.   55
WILLY: *(with pity and resolve)* I'll see him in the morning; I'll have a nice talk with him. I'll get him a job selling. He could be big in no time. My God! Remember how they used to follow him around in high school? When he smiled at one of them

their faces lit up. When he walked down the street . . . *(He loses himself in reminiscences.)*

LINDA: *(trying to bring him out of it)* Willy, dear, I got a new kind of American-type cheese today. It's whipped.

WILLY: Why do you get American when I like Swiss?

LINDA: I just thought you'd like a change—

WILLY: I don't want a change! I want Swiss cheese. Why am I always being contradicted? 60

LINDA: *(with a covering laugh)* I thought it would be a surprise.

WILLY: Why don't you open a window in here, for God's sake?

LINDA: *(with infinite patience)* They're all open, dear.

WILLY: The way they boxed us in here. Bricks and windows, windows and bricks.

LINDA: We should've bought the land next door. 65

WILLY: The street is lined with cars. There's not a breath of fresh air in the neighborhood. The grass don't grow any more, you can't raise a carrot in the back yard. They should've had a law against apartment houses. Remember those two beautiful elm trees out there? When I and Biff hung the swing between them?

LINDA: Yeah, like being a million miles from the city.

WILLY: They should've arrested the builder for cutting those down. They massacred the neighborhood. *(Lost.)* More and more I think of those days, Linda. This time of year it was lilac and wisteria. And then the peonies would come out, and the daffodils. What fragrance in this room!

LINDA: Well, after all, people had to move somewhere.

WILLY: No, there's more people now.

LINDA: I don't think there's more people. I think— 70

WILLY: There's more people! That's what's ruining this country! Population is getting out of control. The competition is maddening! Smell the stink from that apartment house! And another on the other side . . . How can they whip cheese?

On Willy's last line, Biff and Happy raise themselves up in their beds, listening.

LINDA: Go down, try it. And be quiet.

WILLY: *(turning to Linda, guiltily)* You're not worried about me, are you, sweetheart?

BIFF: What's the matter? 75

HAPPY: Listen!

LINDA: You're got too much on the ball to worry about.

WILLY: You're my foundation and my support, Linda.

LINDA: Just try to relax, dear. You make mountains out of molehills.

WILLY: I won't fight with him any more. If he wants to go back to Texas, let him go. 80

LINDA: He'll find his way.

WILLY: Sure. Certain men just don't get started till later in life. Like Thomas Edison, I think. Or B. F. Goodrich. One of them was deaf. *(He starts for the bedroom doorway.)* I'll put my money on Biff.

LINDA: And Willy—if it's warm Sunday we'll drive in the country. And we'll open the windshield, and take lunch.

WILLY: No, the windshields don't open on the new cars.

LINDA: But you opened it today.

WILLY: Me? I didn't. *(He stops.)* Now isn't that peculiar! Isn't that remarkable—*(He breaks off in amazement and fright as the flute is heard distantly.)*

LINDA: What, darling?

WILLY: That is the most remarkable thing.

LINDA: What, dear?

WILLY: I was thinking of the Chevvy. *(Slight pause.)* Nineteen twenty-eight . . . when I had that red Chevvy—*(Breaks off.)* That funny? I coulda sworn I was driving that Chevvy today.

LINDA: Well, that's nothing. Something must've reminded you.

WILLY: Remarkable. Ts. Remember those days? The way Biff used to simonize that car?
The dealer refused to believe there was eighty thousand miles on it. *(He shakes his
head.)* Heh! *(To Linda.)* Close your eyes, I'll be right up. *(He walks out of the bedroom.)*

HAPPY: *(to Biff)* Jesus, maybe he smashed up the car again!

LINDA: *(calling after Willy)* Be careful on the stairs, dear! The cheese is on the middle
shelf! *(She turns, goes over to the bed, takes his jacket, and goes out of the bedroom.)*

*Light has risen on the boys' room. Unseen, Willy is heard talking to himself, "Eighty thousand miles,"
and a little laugh. Biff gets out of bed, comes downstage a bit, and stands attentively. Biff is two years
older than his brother Happy, well built, but in these days bears a worn air and seems less self-assured.
He has succeeded less, and his dreams are stronger and less acceptable than Happy's. Happy is tall,
powerfully made. Sexuality is like a visible color on him, or a scent that many women have discovered. He, like his brother, is lost, but in a different way, for he has never allowed himself to turn his
face toward defeat and is thus more confused and hard-skinned, although seemingly more content.*

HAPPY: *(getting out of bed)* He's going to get his license taken away if he keeps that up.   95
I'm getting nervous about him, y'know, Biff?

BIFF: His eyes are going.

HAPPY: No, I've driven with him. He sees all right. He just doesn't keep his mind on it. I
drove into the city with him last week. He stops at a green light and then it turns red
and he goes. *(He laughs.)*

BIFF: Maybe he's color-blind.

HAPPY: Pop? Why he's got the finest eye for color in the business. You know that.

BIFF: *(sitting down on his bed)* I'm going to sleep.   100

HAPPY: You're not still sour on Dad, are you, Biff?

BIFF: He's all right, I guess.

WILLY: *(underneath them, in the livingroom)* Yes, sir, eighty thousand miles—eighty-
two thousand!

BIFF: You smoking?

HAPPY: *(holding out a pack of cigarettes)* Want one?   105

BIFF: *(taking a cigarette)* I can never sleep when I smell it.

WILLY: What a simonizing job, heh!

HAPPY: *(with deep sentiment)* Funny, Biff, y'know? Us sleeping in here again? The old
beds. *(He pats his bed affectionately.)* All the talk that went across those two beds,
huh? Our whole lives.

BIFF: Yeah. Lotta dreams and plans.

HAPPY: *(with a deep and masculine laugh)* About five hundred women would like to   110
know what was said in this room.

They share a soft laugh.

BIFF: Remember that big Betsy something—what the hell was her name—over on
Bushwick Avenue?

HAPPY: *(combing his hair)* With the collie dog!

BIFF: That's the one. I got you in there, remember?

HAPPY: Yeah, that was my first time—I think. Boy, there was a pig! *(They laugh, almost
crudely.)* You taught me everything I know about women. Don't forget that.

BIFF: I bet you forgot how bashful you used to be. Especially with girls.   115

HAPPY: Oh, I still am, Biff.

BIFF: Oh, go on.

HAPPY: I just control it, that's all. I think I got less bashful and you got more so. What happened, Biff? Where's the old humor, the old confidence? *(He shakes Biff's knee. Biff
gets up and moves restlessly about the room.)* What's the matter?

BIFF: Why does Dad mock me all the time?

HAPPY: He's not mocking you, he—   120

BIFF: Everything I say there's a twist of mockery on his face. I can't get near him.

HAPPY: He just wants you to make good, that's all. I wanted to talk to you about Dad for a long time, Biff. Something's—happening to him. He—talks to himself.

BIFF: I noticed that this morning. But he always mumbled.

HAPPY: But not so noticeable. It got so embarrassing I sent him to Florida. And you know something? Most of the time he's talking to you.

BIFF: What's he say about me?   125

HAPPY: I can't make it out.

BIFF: What's he say about me?

HAPPY: I think the fact that you're not settled, that you're still kind of up in the air . . .

BIFF: There's one or two other things depressing him, Happy.

HAPPY: What do you mean?   130

BIFF: Never mind. Just don't lay it all to me.

HAPPY: But I think if you just got started—I mean—is there any future for you out there?

BIFF: I tell ya, Hap, I don't know what the future is. I don't know—what I'm supposed to want.

HAPPY: What do you mean?

BIFF: Well, I spent six or seven years after high school trying to work myself up. Ship-   135
ping clerk, salesman, business of one kind or another. And it's a measly manner of existence. To get on that subway on the hot mornings in summer. To devote your whole life to keeping stock, or making phone calls, or selling or buying. To suffer fifty weeks of the year for the sake of a two-week vacation, when all you really desire is to be outdoors, with your shirt off. And always to have to get ahead of the next fella. And still—that's how you build a future.

HAPPY: Well, you really enjoy it on a farm? Are you content out there?

BIFF: *(with rising agitation)* Hap, I've had twenty or thirty different kinds of jobs since I left home before the war, and it always turns out the same. I just realized it lately. In Nebraska when I herded cattle, and the Dakotas, and Arizona, and now in Texas. It's why I came home now, I guess, because I realized it. This farm I work on, it's spring there now, see? And they've got about fifteen new colts. There's nothing more in-spiring or—beautiful than the sight of a mare and a new colt. And it's cool there now, see? Texas is cool now, and it's spring. And whenever spring comes to where I am, I suddenly get the feeling, my God, I'm not gettin' anywhere! What the hell am I doing, playing around with horses, twenty-eight dollars a week! I'm thirty-four years old, I oughta be makin' my future. That's when I come running home. And now, I get here, and I don't known what to do with myself. *(After a pause.)* I've always made a point of not wasting my life, and everytime I come back here I know that all I've done is to waste my life.

HAPPY: You're a poet, you know that, Biff? You're a —you're an idealist!

BIFF: No, I'm mixed up very bad. Maybe I oughta get married. Maybe I oughta get stuck into something. Maybe that's my trouble. I'm like a boy. I'm not married, I'm not in business, I just—I'm like a boy. Are you content, Hap? You're a success, aren't you? Are you content?

HAPPY: Hell, no!   140

BIFF: Why? You're making money, aren't you?

HAPPY: *(moving about with energy, expressiveness)* All I can do now is wait for the merchandise manager to die. And suppose I get to be merchandise manager? He's a good friend of mine, and he just built a terrific estate on Long Island. And he lived there about two months and sold it, and now he's building another one. He can't enjoy it once it's finished. And I know that's just what I would do. I don't know what the hell I'm workin' for. Sometimes I sit in my apartment—all alone. And I think of the rent I'm paying. And it's crazy. But then, it's what I always wanted. My own apart-ment, a car, and plenty of women. And still, goddammit, I'm lonely.

BIFF: *(with enthusiasm)* Listen, why don't you come out West with me?

HAPPY: You and I, heh?

BIFF: Sure, maybe we could buy a ranch. Raise cattle, use our muscles. Men built like we   145
are should be working out in the open.

HAPPY: *(avidly)* The Loman Brothers, heh?

BIFF: *(with vast affection)* Sure, we'd be known all over the counties!

HAPPY: *(enthralled)* That's what I dream about, Biff. Sometimes I want to just rip my
clothes off in the middle of the store and outbox that goddam merchandise manager. I mean I can outbox, outrun, and outlift anybody in that store, and I have to
take orders from those common, petty sons-of-bitches till I can't stand it any more.

BIFF: I'm telln' you, kid, if you were with me I'd be happy out there.

HAPPY: *(enthused)* See, Biff, everybody around me is so false that I'm constantly lower-   150
ing my ideals . . .

BIFF: Baby, together we'd stand up for one another, we'd have someone to trust.

HAPPY: If I were around you—

BIFF: Hap, the trouble is we weren't brought up to grub for money. I don't know how to
do it.

HAPPY: Neither can I!

BIFF: Then let's go!   155

HAPPY: The only thing is—what can you make out there?

BIFF: But look at your friend. Builds an estate and then hasn't the peace of mind to live
in it.

HAPPY: Yeah, but when he walks into the store the waves part in front of him. That's
fifty-two thousand dollars a year coming through the revolving door, and I got more
in my pinky finger than he's got in his head.

BIFF: Yeah, but you just said—

HAPPY: I gotta show some of those pompous, self-important executives over there that   160
Hap Loman can make the grade. I want to walk into the store the way he walks in.
Then I'll go with you, Biff. We'll be together yet, I swear. But take those two we had
tonight. Now weren't they gorgeous creatures?

BIFF: Yeah, yeah, most gorgeous I've had in years.

HAPPY: I get that any time I want, Biff. Whenever I feel disgusted. The only trouble is, it
gets like bowling or something. I just keep knockin' them over and it doesn't mean
anything. You still run around a lot?

BIFF: Naa. I'd like to find a girl—steady, somebody with substance.

HAPPY: That's what I long for.

BIFF: Go on! You'd never come home.   165

HAPPY: I would! Somebody with character, with resistance! Like Mom, y'know? You're
gonna call me a bastard when I tell you this. That girl Charlotte I was with tonight is
engaged to be married in five weeks. *(He tries on his new hat.)*

BIFF: No kiddin'!

HAPPY: Sure, the guy's in line for the vice-presidency of the store. I don't know what
gets into me, maybe I just have an overdeveloped sense of competition or something, but I went and ruined her, and furthermore I can't get rid of her. And he's the
third executive I've done that to. Isn't that a crummy characteristic? And to top it all,
I go to their weddings! *(Indignantly, but laughing.)* Like I'm not supposed to take
bribes. Manufacturers offer me a hundred-dollar bill now and then to throw an
order their way. You know how honest I am, but it's like this girl, see. I hate myself
for it. Because I don't want the girl, and, still, I take it and—I love it!

BIFF: Let's go to sleep.

HAPPY: I guess we didn't settle anything, heh?   170

BIFF: I just got one idea that I think I'm going to try.

HAPPY: What's that?

BIFF: Remember Bill Oliver?

HAPPY: Sure, Oliver is very big now. You want to work for him again?

BIFF: No, but when I quit he said something to me. He put his arm on my shoulder, and   175
he said, "Biff, if you ever need anything, come to me."

HAPPY: I remember that. That sounds good.

BIFF: I think I'll go to see him. If I could get ten thousand or even seven or eight thousand dollars I could buy a beautiful ranch.

HAPPY: I bet he'd back you. 'Cause he thought highly of you, Biff, I mean, they all do.
You're well liked, Biff. That's why I say to come back here, and we both have the
apartment. And I'm telln' you, Biff, any babe you want . . .

BIFF: No, with a ranch I could do the work I like and still be something. I just wonder
though. I wonder if Oliver still thinks I stole that carton of basketballs.

HAPPY: Oh, he probably forgot that long ago. It's almost ten years. You're too sensitive.   180
Anyway, he didn't really fire you.

BIFF: Well, I think he was going to. I think that's why I quit. I was never sure whether he
knew or not. I know he thought the world of me, though. I was the only one he'd let
lock up the place.

WILLY: *(below)* You gonna wash the engine, Biff?

HAPPY: Shh!

Biff looks at Happy, who is gazing down, listening. Willy is mumbling in the parlor.

HAPPY: You hear that?

They listen. Willy laughs warmly.

BIFF: *(growing angry)* Doesn't he know Mom can hear that?   185

WILLY: Don't get your sweater dirty, Biff!

A look of pain crosses Biff's face.

HAPPY: Isn't that terrible? Don't leave again, will you? You'll find a job here. You gotta
stick around. I don't know what to do about him, it's getting embarrassing.

WILLY: What a simonizing job!

BIFF: Mom's hearing that!

WILLY: No kiddin', Biff, you got a date? Wonderful!   190

HAPPY: Go on to sleep. But talk to him in the morning, will you?

BIFF: *(reluctantly getting into bed)* With her in the house. Brother!

HAPPY: *(getting into bed)* I wish you'd have a good talk with him.
The light on their room begins to fade.

BIFF: *(to himself in bed)* That selfish, stupid . . .

HAPPY: Sh . . . Sleep, Biff.   195

*Their light is out. Well before they have finished speaking, Willy's form is dimly seen below in the
darkened kitchen. He opens the refrigerator, searches in there, and takes out a bottle of milk. The
apartment houses are fading out, and the entire house and surroundings become covered with leaves.
Music insinuates itself as the leaves appear.*

WILLY: Just wanna be careful with those girls, Biff, that's all. Don't make any promises.
No promises of any kind. Because a girl, y'know, they always believe what you tell
'em, and you're very young, Biff, you're too young to be talking seriously to girls.

*Light rises on the kitchen. Willy, talking, shuts the refrigerator door and comes downstage to the
kitchen table. He pours milk into a glass. He is totally immersed in himself, smiling faintly.*

WILLY: Too young entirely, Biff. You want to watch your schooling first. Then when
you're all set, there'll be plenty of girls for a boy like you. *(He smiles broadly at a
kitchen chair.)* That so? The girls pay for you? *(He laughs.)* Boy, you must really be
makin' a hit.

*Willy is gradually addressing—physically—a point offstage, speaking through the wall of the kitchen,
and his voice has been rising in volume to that of a normal conversation.*

WILLY: I been wondering why you polish the car so careful. Ha! Don't leave the hub-caps, boys. Get the chamois to the hubcaps. Happy, use newspaper on the windows, it's the easiest thing. Show him how to do it, Biff! You see, Happy? Pad it up, use it like a pad. That's it, that's it, good work. You're doin' all right, Hap. *(He pauses, then nods in approbation for a few seconds, then looks upward.)* Biff, first thing we gotta do when we get time is clip that big branch over the house. Afraid it's gonna fall in a storm and hit the roof. Tell you what. We get a rope and sling her around, and then we climb up there with a couple of saws and take her down. Soon as you fin-ish the car, boys, I wanna see ya. I got a surprise for you, boys.

BIFF: *(offstage)* Whatta ya got, Dad?

WILLY: No, you finish first. Never leave a job till you're finished—remember that. *(Look-ing toward the "big trees.")* Biff, up in Albany I saw a beautiful hammock. I think I'll buy it next trip, and we'll hang it right between those two elms. Wouldn't that be something? Just swingin' there under those branches. Boy, that would be . . . 200

Young Biff and Young Happy appear from the direction Willy was addressing. Happy carries rags and a pail of water. Biff, wearing a sweater with a block "S," carries a football.

BIFF: *(pointing in the direction of the car offstage)* How's that, Pop, professional?

WILLY: Terrific. Terrific job, boys. Good work, Biff.

HAPPY: Where's the surprise, Pop?

WILLY: In the back seat of the car.

HAPPY: Boy! *(He runs off.)* 205

BIFF: What is it, Dad? Tell me, what'd you buy?

WILLY: *(laughing, cuffs him)* Never mind, something I want you to have.

BIFF: *(turns and starts off)* What is it, Hap?

HAPPY: *(offstage)* It's a punching bag!

BIFF: Oh, Pop! 210

WILLY: It's got Gene Tunney's signature on it!

Happy runs onstage with a punching bag.

BIFF: Gee, how'd you know we wanted a punching bag?

WILLY: Well, it's the finest thing for the timing.

HAPPY: *(lies down on his back and pedals with his feet)* I'm losing weight, you notice, Pop?

WILLY: *(to Happy)* Jumping rope is good too. 215

BIFF: Did you see the new football I got?

WILLY: *(examining the ball)* Where'd you get a new ball?

BIFF: The coach told me to practice my passing.

WILLY: That so? And he gave you the ball, heh?

BIFF: Well, I borrowed it from the locker room. *(He laughs confidentially.)* 220

WILLY: *(laughing with him at the theft)* I want you to return that.

HAPPY: I told you he wouldn't like it!

BIFF: *(angrily)* Well, I'm bringing it back!

WILLY: *(stopping the incipient argument, to Happy)* Sure, he's gotta practice with a regulation ball, doesn't he? *(To Biff.)* Coach'll probably congratulate you on your initiative!

BIFF: Oh, he keeps congratulating my initiative all the time, Pop. 225

WILLY: That's because he likes you. If somebody else took that ball there'd be an uproar. So what's the report, boys, what's the report?

BIFF: Where'd you go this time, Dad? Gee we were lonesome for you.

WILLY: *(pleased, puts an arm around each boy and they come down to the apron)* Lonesome, heh?

BIFF: Missed you every minute.

WILLY: Don't say? Tell you a secret, boys. Don't breathe it to a soul. Someday I'll have my own business, and I'll never have to leave home any more. 230

HAPPY: Like Uncle Charley, heh?

WILLY: Bigger than Uncle Charley! Because Charley is not—liked. He's liked, but he's not—well liked.

BIFF: Where'd you go this time, Dad?

WILLY: Well, I got on the road, and I went north to Providence. Met the Mayor.

BIFF: The Mayor of Providence!   235

WILLY: He was sitting in the hotel lobby.

BIFF: What'd he say?

WILLY: He said, "Morning!" And I said, "You've got a fine city here, Mayor." And then he had coffee with me. And then I went to Waterbury. Waterbury is a fine city. Big clock city, the famous Waterbury clock. Sold a nice bill there. And then Boston—Boston is the cradle of the Revolution. A fine city. And a couple of other towns in Mass., and on to Portland and Bangor and straight home!

BIFF: Gee, I'd love to go with you sometime, Dad.

WILLY: Soon as summer comes.   240

HAPPY: Promise?

WILLY: You and Hap and I, and I'll show you all the towns. America is full of beautiful towns and fine, upstanding people. And they know me, boys, they know me up and down New England. The finest people. And when I bring you fellas up, there'll be open sesame for all of us, 'cause one thing, boys: I have friends. I can park my car in any street in New England, and the cops protect it like their own. This summer, heh?

BIFF AND HAPPY: *(together)* Yeah! You bet!

WILLY: We'll take our bathing suits.

HAPPY: We'll carry your bags, Pop!   245

WILLY: Oh, won't that be something! Me comin' into the Boston store with you boys carryin' my bags. What a sensation!

Biff is prancing around, practicing passing the ball.

WILLY: You nervous, Biff, about the game?

BIFF: Not if you're gonna be there.

WILLY: What do they say about you in school, now that they made you captain?

HAPPY: There's a crowd of girls behind him everytime the classes change.   250

BIFF: *(taking Willy's hand)* This Saturday, Pop, this Saturday—just for you, I'm going to break through for a touchdown.

HAPPY: You're supposed to pass.

BIFF: I'm takin' one play for Pop. You watch me, Pop, and when I take off my helmet, that means I'm breakin' out. Then you watch me crash through that line!

WILLY: *(kisses Biff)* Oh, wait'll I tell this in Boston!

Bernard enters in knickers. He is younger than Biff, earnest and loyal, a worried boy.

BERNARD: Biff, where are you? You're supposed to study with me today.   255

WILLY: Hey, looka Bernard. What're you lookin' so anemic about, Bernard?

BERNARD: He's gotta study, Uncle Willy. He's got Regents next week.

HAPPY: *(tauntingly, spinning Bernard around)* Let's box, Bernard!

BERNARD: Biff! *(He gets away from Happy.)* Listen, Biff, I heard Mr. Birnbaum say that if you don't start studyin' math he's gonna flunk you, and you won't graduate. I heard him!

WILLY: You better study with him, Biff. Go ahead now.   260

BERNARD: I heard him!

BIFF: Oh, Pop, you didn't see my sneakers! *(He holds up a foot for Willy to look at.)*

WILLY: Hey, that's a beautiful job of printing!

BERNARD: *(wiping his glasses)* Just because he printed University of Virginia on his sneakers doesn't mean they've got to graduate him, Uncle Willy!

WILLY: *(angrily)* What're you talking about? With scholarships to three universities   265
they're gonna flunk him?

BERNARD: But I heard Mr. Birnbaum say—
WILLY: Don't be a pest, Bernard! *(To his boys.)* What an anemic!
BERNARD: Okay, I'm waiting for you in my house, Biff.

Bernard goes off. The Lomans laugh.

WILLY: Bernard is not well liked, is he?
BIFF: He's liked, but he's not well liked.   270
HAPPY: That's right, Pop.
WILLY: That's just what I mean. Bernard can get the best marks in school, y'understand,
   but when he gets out in the business world, y'understand, you are going to be five
   times ahead of him. That's why I thank Almighty God you're both built like Adonises.
   Because the man who makes an appearance in the business world, the man who
   creates personal interest, is the man who gets ahead. Be liked and you will never
   want. You take me, for instance. I never have to wait in line to see a buyer. "Willy
   Loman is here!" That's all they have to know, and I go right through.
BIFF: Did you knock them dead, Pop?
WILLY: Knocked 'em cold in Providence, slaughtered 'em in Boston.
HAPPY: *(on his back, pedaling again)* I'm losing weight, you notice, Pop?   275

Linda enters, as of old, a ribbon in her hair, carrying a basket of washing.

LINDA: *(with youthful energy)* Hello, dear!
WILLY: Sweetheart!
LINDA: How'd the Chevvy run?
WILLY: Chevrolet, Linda, is the greatest car ever built. *(To the boys.)* Since when do you
   let your mother carry wash up the stairs?
BIFF: Grab hold there, boy!   280
HAPPY: Where to, Mom?
LINDA: Hang them up on the line. And you better go down to your friends, Biff. The cel-
   lar is full of boys. They don't know what to do with themselves.
BIFF: Ah, when Pop comes home they can wait!
WILLY: *(laughs appreciatively)* You better go down and tell them what to do, Biff.
BIFF: I think I'll have them sweep out the furnace room.   285
WILLY: Good work, Biff.
BIFF: *(goes through wall-line of kitchen to doorway at back and calls down)* Fellas!
   Everybody sweep out the furnace room! I'll be right down!
VOICES: All right! Okay, Biff.
BIFF: George and Sam and Frank, come out back! We're hangin' up the wash! Come on,
   Hap, on the double! *(He and Happy carry out the basket.)*
LINDA: The way they obey him!   290
WILLY: Well, that's training, the training. I'm tellin' you, I was sellin' thousands and thou-
   sands, but I had to come home.
LINDA: Oh, the whole block'll be at that game. Did you sell anything?
WILLY: I did five hundred gross in Providence and seven hundred gross in Boston.
LINDA: No! Wait a minute, I've got a pencil. *(She pulls pencil and paper out of her
   apron pocket,)* That makes your commission . . . Two hundred—my God! Two hun-
   dred and twelve dollars!
WILLY: Well, I didn't figure it yet, but . . .   295
LINDA: How much did you do?
WILLY: Well, I—I did—about a hundred and eighty gross in Providence. Well no—it
   came to—roughly two hundred gross on the whole trip.
LINDA: *(without hesitation)* Two hundred gross. That's . . . *(She figures.)*
WILLY: The trouble was that three of the stores were half closed for inventory in
   Boston. Otherwise I woulda broke records.

LINDA:	Well, it makes seventy dollars and some pennies. That's very good.	300
WILLY:	What do we owe?	
LINDA:	Well, on the first there's sixteen dollars on the refrigerator—	
WILLY:	Why sixteen?	
LINDA:	Well, the fan belt broke, so it was a dollar eighty.	
WILLY:	But it's brand new.	305
LINDA:	Well, the man said that's the way it is. Till they work themselves in, y'know.	

They move through the wall-line into the kitchen.

WILLY:	I hope we didn't get stuck on that machine.
LINDA:	They got the biggest ads of any of them!
WILLY:	I know, it's a fine machine. What else?
LINDA:	Well, there's nine-sixty for the washing machine. And for the vacuum cleaner there's three and a half due on the fifteenth. Then the roof, you got twenty-one dollars remaining.	310
WILLY:	It don't leak, does it?
LINDA:	No, they did a wonderful job. Then you owe Frank for the carburetor.
WILLY:	I'm not going to pay that man! That goddam Chevrolet, they ought to prohibit the manufacture of that car!
LINDA:	Well, you owe him three and a half. And odds and ends, comes to around a hundred and twenty dollars by the fifteenth.
WILLY:	A hundred and twenty dollars! My God, if business don't pick up I don't know what I'm gonna do!	315
LINDA:	Well, next week you'll do better.
WILLY:	Oh, I'll knock them dead next week. I'll go to Hartford. I'm very well liked in Hartford. You know, the trouble is, Linda, people don't seem to take to me.

They move onto the forestage.

LINDA:	Oh, don't be foolish.
WILLY:	I know it when I walk in. They seem to laugh at me.
LINDA:	Why? Why would they laugh at you? Don't talk that way, Willy.	320

Willy moves to the edge of the stage. Linda goes into the kitchen and starts to darn stockings.

WILLY:	I don't know the reason for it, but they just pass me by. I'm not noticed.
LINDA:	But you're doing wonderful, dear. You're making seventy to a hundred dollars a week.
WILLY:	But I gotta be at it ten, twelve hours a day. Other men—I don't know—they do it easier. I don't know why—I can't stop myself—I talk too much. A man oughta come in with a few words. One thing about Charley. He's a man of few words, and they respect him.
LINDA:	You don't talk too much, you're just lively.
WILLY:	*(smiling)* Well, I figure, what the hell, life is short, a couple of jokes. *(To himself.)* I joke too much! *(The smile goes.)*	325
LINDA:	Why? You're—
WILLY:	I'm fat. I'm very—foolish to look at, Linda. I didn't tell you, but Christmas time I happened to be calling on F. H. Stewarts, and a salesman I know, as I was going in to see the buyer I heard him say something about—walrus. And I—I cracked him right across the face. I won't take that. I simply will not take that. But they do laugh at me. I know that.
LINDA:	Darling . . .
WILLY:	I gotta overcome it. I know I gotta overcome it. I'm not dressing to advantage, maybe.
LINDA:	Willy, darling, you're the handsomest man in the world—	330
WILLY:	Oh, no, Linda.

LINDA: To me you are. *(Slight pause.)* The handsomest.

From the darkness is heard the laughter of a woman. Willy doesn't turn to it, but it continues through Linda's lines.

LINDA: And the boys, Willy. Few men are idolized by their children the way you are.

Music is heard as behind a scrim, to the left of the house, The Woman, dimly seen, is dressing.

WILLY: *(with great feeling)* You're the best there is, Linda, you're a pal, you know that? On the road—I want to grab you sometimes and just kiss the life outa you.

The laughter is loud now, and he moves into a brightening area at the left, where The Woman has come from behind the scrim and is standing, putting on her hat, looking into a "mirror" and laughing.

WILLY: 'Cause I get so lonely—especially when business is bad and there's nobody to   335
    talk to. I get the feeling that I'll never sell anything again, that I won't make a living
    for you, or a business, a business for the boys. *(He talks through The Woman's sub-
    siding laughter; The Woman primps at the "mirror.")* There's so much I want to
    make for—

THE WOMAN: Me? You didn't make me, Willy. I picked you.

WILLY: *(pleased)* You picked me?

THE WOMAN: *(who is quite proper-looking, Willy's age)* I did. I've been sitting at that
    desk watching all the salesmen go by, day in, day out. But you've got such a sense of
    humor, and we do have such a good time together, don't we?

WILLY: Sure, sure. *(He takes her in his arms.)* Why do you have to go now?

THE WOMAN: It's two o'clock . . .   340

WILLY: No, come on in! *(He pulls her.)*

THE WOMAN: . . . my sisters'll be scandalized. When'll you be back?

WILLY: Oh, two weeks about. Will you come up again?

THE WOMAN: Sure thing. You do make me laugh. It's good for me. *(She squeezes his arm,
    kisses him.)* And I think you're a wonderful man.

WILLY: You picked me, heh?   345

THE WOMAN: Sure. Because you're so sweet. And such a kidder.

WILLY: Well, I'll see you next time I'm in Boston.

THE WOMAN: I'll put you right through to the buyers.

WILLY: *(slapping her bottom)* Right. Well, bottoms up!

THE WOMAN: *(slaps him gently and laughs)* You just kill me, Willy. *(He suddenly grabs*   350
    her and kisses her roughly.) You kill me. And thanks for the stockings. I love a lot of
    stockings. Well, good night.

WILLY: Good night. And keep your pores open!

THE WOMAN: Oh, Willy!

The Woman bursts out laughing, and Linda's laughter blends in. The Woman disappears into the dark. Now the area at the kitchen table brightens. Linda is sitting where she was at the kitchen table, but now is mending a pair of silk stockings.

LINDA: You are, Willy. The handsomest man. You've got no reason to feel that—

WILLY: *(coming out of the Woman's dimming area and going over to Linda)* I'll make
    it all up to you, Linda, I'll—

LINDA: There's nothing to make up, dear. You're doing fine, better than—   355

WILLY: *(noticing her mending)* What's that?

LINDA: Just mending my stockings. They're so expensive—

WILLY: *(angrily, taking them from her)* I won't have you mending stockings in this
    house! Now throw them out!

Linda puts the stockings in her pocket.

BERNARD: *(entering on the run)* Where is he? If he doesn't study!

WILLY: *(moving to the forestage, with great agitation)* You'll give him the answers!   360
BERNARD: I do, but I can't on a Regents! That's a state exam! They're liable to arrest me!
WILLY: Where is he? I'll whip him, I'll whip him!
LINDA: And he'd better give back that football, Willy, it's not nice.
WILLY: Biff! Where is he? Why is he taking everything?
LINDA: He's too tough with the girls, Willy. All the mothers are afraid of him!   365
WILLY: I'll whip him!
BERNARD: He's driving the car without a license!

The Woman's laugh is heard.

WILLY: Shut up!
LINDA: All the mothers—
WILLY: Shut up!   370
BERNARD: *(backing quietly away and out)* Mr. Birnbaum says he's stuck up.
WILLY: Get outa here!
BERNARD: If he doesn't buckle down he'll flunk math! *(He goes off.)*
LINDA: He's right, Willy, you've gotta—
WILLY: *(exploding at her)* There's nothing the matter with him! You want him to be a   375
worm like Bernard? He's got spirit, personality . . .

As he speaks, Linda, almost in tears, exits into the livingroom. Willy is alone in the kitchen, wilting and staring. The leaves are gone. It is night again, and the apartment houses look down from behind.

WILLY: Loaded with it. Loaded! What is he stealing? He's giving it back, isn't he? Why is
he stealing? What did I tell him? I never in my life told him anything but decent
things.

Happy in pajamas has come down the stairs; Willy suddenly becomes aware of Happy's presence.

HAPPY: Let's go now, come on.
WILLY: *(sitting down at the kitchen table)* Huh! Why did she have to wax the floors
herself? Everytime she waxes the floors she keels over. She knows that!
HAPPY: Shh! Take it easy. What brought you back tonight?
WILLY: I got an awful scare. Nearly hit a kid in Yonkers. God! Why didn't I go to Alaska   380
with my brother Ben that time! Ben! That man was a genius, that man was success
incarnate! What a mistake! He begged me to go.
HAPPY: Well, there's no use in—
WILLY: You guys! There was a man started with the clothes on his back and ended up
with diamond mines!
HAPPY: Boy, someday I'd like to know how he did it.
WILLY: What's the mystery? The man knew what he wanted and went out and got it!
Walked into a jungle, and comes out, the age of twenty-one, and he's rich! The world
is an oyster, but you don't crack it open on a mattress!
HAPPY: Pop, I told you I'm gonna retire you for life.   385
WILLY: You'll retire me for life on seventy goddam dollars a week? And your women and
your car and your apartment, and you'll retire me for life! Christ's sake, I couldn't get
past Yonkers today! Where are you guys, where are you? The woods are burning! I
can't drive a car!

Charley has appeared in the doorway. He is a large man, slow of speech, laconic, immovable. In all he says, despite what he says, there is pity, and now, trepidation. He has a robe over his pajamas, slippers on his feet. He enters the kitchen.

CHARLEY: Everything all right?
HAPPY: Yeah, Charley, everything's . . .
WILLY: What's the matter?
CHARLEY: I heard some noise. I thought something happened. Can't we do something   390
about the walls? You sneeze in here, and in my house hats blow off.

HAPPY: Let's go to bed, Dad. Come on.

Charley signals to Happy to go.

WILLY: You go ahead, I'm not tired at the moment.

HAPPY: *(to Willy)* Take it easy, huh? *(He exits.)*

WILLY: What're you doin' up?

CHARLEY: *(sitting down at the kitchen table opposite Willy)* Couldn't sleep good. I had   395
a heartburn.

WILLY: Well, you don't know how to eat.

CHARLEY: I eat with my mouth.

WILLY: No, you're ignorant. You gotta know about vitamins and things like that.

CHARLEY: Come on, let's shoot. Tire you out a little.

WILLY: *(hesitantly)* All right. You got cards?   400

CHARLEY: *(taking a deck from his pocket)* Yeah, I got them. Someplace. What is it with
those vitamins?

WILLY: *(dealing)* They build up your bones. Chemistry.

CHARLEY: Yeah, but there's no bones in a heartburn.

WILLY: What are you talkin' about? Do you know the first thing about it?

CHARLEY: Don't get insulted.   405

WILLY: Don't talk about something you don't know anything about.

They are playing. Pause.

CHARLEY: What're you doin' home?

WILLY: A little trouble with the car.

CHARLEY: Oh. *(Pause.)* I'd like to take a trip to California.

WILLY: Don't say.   410

CHARLEY: You want a job?

WILLY: I got a job, I told you that. *(After a slight pause.)* What the hell are you offering
me a job for?

CHARLEY: Don't get insulted.

WILLY: Don't insult me.

CHARLEY: I don't see no sense in it. You don't have to go on this way.   415

WILLY: I got a good job. *(Slight pause.)* What do you keep comin' in here for?

CHARLEY: You want me to go?

WILLY: *(after a pause, withering)* I can't understand it. He's going back to Texas again.
What the hell is that?

CHARLEY: Let him go.

WILLY: I got nothin' to give him, Charley, I'm clean, I'm clean.   420

CHARLEY: He won't starve. None a them starve. Forget about him.

WILLY: Then what have I got to remember?

CHARLEY: You take it too hard. To hell with it. When a deposit bottle is broken you don't
get your nickel back.

WILLY: That's easy enough for you to say.

CHARLEY: That ain't easy for me to say.   425

WILLY: Did you see the ceiling I put up in the livingroom?

CHARLEY: Yeah, that's a piece of work. To put up a ceiling is a mystery to me. How do you
do it?

WILLY: What's the difference?

CHARLEY: Well, talk about it.

WILLY: You gonna put up a ceiling?   430

CHARLEY: How could I put up a ceiling?

WILLY: Then what the hell are you bothering me for?

CHARLEY: You're insulted again.

WILLY: A man who can't handle tools is not a man. You're disgusting.

CHARLEY: Don't call me disgusting, Willy.   435

Uncle Ben, carrying a valise and an umbrella, enters the forestage from around the right corner of the house. He is a stolid man, in his sixties, with a mustache and an authoritative air. He is utterly certain of his destiny, and there is an aura of far places about him. He enters exactly as Willy speaks.

WILLY: I'm getting awfully tired, Ben.

Ben's music is heard. Ben looks around at everything.

CHARLEY: Good, keep playing; you'll sleep better. Did you call me Ben?

Ben looks at his watch.

WILLY: That's funny. For a second there you reminded me of my brother Ben.

BEN: I have only a few minutes. *(He strolls, inspecting the place. Willy and Charley continue playing.)*

CHARLEY: You never heard from him again, heh? Since that time?   440

WILLY: Didn't Linda tell you? Couple of weeks ago we got a letter from his wife in Africa. He died.

CHARLEY: That so.

BEN: *(chuckling)* So this is Brooklyn, eh?

CHARLEY: Maybe you're in for some of his money.

WILLY: Naa, he had seven sons. There's just one opportunity I had with that man ...   445

BEN: I must make a train, William. There are several properties I'm looking at in Alaska.

WILLY: Sure, sure! If I'd gone with him to Alaska that time, everything would've been totally different.

CHARLEY: Go on, you'd froze to death up there.

WILLY: What're you talking about?

BEN: Opportunity is tremendous in Alaska, William. Surprised you're not up there.   450

WILLY: Sure, tremendous.

CHARLEY: Heh?

WILLY: There was the only man I ever met who knew the answers.

CHARLEY: Who?

BEN: How are you all?   455

WILLY: *(taking a pot, smiling)* Fine, fine.

CHARLEY: Pretty sharp tonight.

BEN: Is Mother living with you?

WILLY: No, she died a long time ago.

CHARLEY: Who?   460

BEN: That's too bad. Fine specimen of a lady, Mother.

WILLY: *(to Charley)* Heh?

BEN: I'd hoped to see the old girl.

CHARLEY: Who died?

BEN: Heard anything from Father, have you?   465

WILLY: *(unnerved)* What do you mean, who died?

CHARLEY: *(taking a pot)* What're you talkin' about?

BEN: *(looking at his watch)* William, it's half-past eight!

WILLY: *(as though to dispel his confusion he angrily stops Charley's hand)* That's my build!

CHARLEY: I put the ace—   470

WILLY: If you don't know how to play the game I'm not gonna throw my money away on you!

CHARLEY: *(rising)* It was my ace, for God's sake!

WILLY: I'm through, I'm through!

BEN: When did Mother die?

WILLY: Long ago. Since the beginning you never knew how to play cards.   475

CHARLEY: *(picks up the cards and goes to the door)* All right! Next time I'll bring a deck with five aces.

WILLY: I don't play that kind of game!

CHARLEY: *(turning to him)* You should be ashamed of yourself!

WILLY: Yeah?

CHARLEY: Yeah! *(He goes out.)*

WILLY: *(slamming the door after him)* Ignoramus!

BEN: *(as Willy comes toward him through the wall-line of the kitchen)* So you're William.

WILLY: *(shaking Ben's hand)* Ben! I've been waiting for you so long! What's the answer? How did you do it?

BEN: Oh, there's a story in that.

Linda enters the forestage, as of old, carrying the wash basket.

LINDA: Is this Ben?

BEN: *(gallantly)* How do you do, my dear.

LINDA: Where've you been all these years? Willy's always wondered why you—

WILLY: *(pulling Ben away from her impatiently)* Where is Dad? Didn't you follow him? How did you get started?

BEN: Well, I don't know how much you remember.

WILLY: Well, I was just a baby, of course, only three or four years old—

BEN: Three years and eleven months.

WILLY: What a memory, Ben!

BEN: I have many enterprises, William, and I have never kept books.

WILLY: I remember I was sitting under the wagon in—was it Nebraska?

BEN: It was South Dakota, and I gave you a bunch of wild flowers.

WILLY: I remember you walking away down some open road.

BEN: *(laughing)* I was going to find Father in Alaska.

WILLY: Where is he?

BEN: At that age I had a very faulty view of geography, William. I discovered after a few days that I was heading due south, so instead of Alaska, I ended up in Africa.

LINDA: Africa!

WILLY: The Gold Coast!

BEN: Principally, diamond mines.

LINDA: Diamond mines!

BEN: Yes, my dear. But I've only a few minutes—

WILLY: No! Boys! Boys! *(Young Biff and Happy appear.)* Listen to this. This is your Uncle Ben, a great man! Tell my boys, Ben!

BEN: Why, boys, when I was seventeen I walked into the jungle, and when I was twenty-one I walked out. *(He laughs.)* And by God I was rich.

WILLY: *(to the boys)* You see what I have been talking about? The greatest things can happen!

BEN: *(glancing at his watch)* I have an appointment in Ketchikan Tuesday week.

WILLY: No, Ben! Please tell about Dad. I want my boys to hear. I want them to know the kind of stock they spring from. All I remember is a man with a big beard, and I was in Mamma's lap, sitting around a fire, and some kind of high music.

BEN: His flute. He played the flute.

WILLY: Sure, the flute, that's right!

New music is heard, a high, rollicking tune.

BEN: Father was a very great and a very wild-hearted man: We would start in Boston, and he'd toss the whole family into the wagon, and then he'd drive the team right across the country; through Ohio, and Indiana, Michigan, Illinois, and all the Western states. And we'd stop in the towns and sell the flutes that he'd made on the way. Great inventor, Father. With one gadget he made more in a week than a man like you could make in a lifetime.

WILLY: That's just the way I'm bringing them up, Ben—rugged, well liked, all-around.

BEN: Yeah? *(To Biff.)* Hit that, boy—hard as you can. *(He pounds his stomach.)*

480

485

490

495

500

505

510

BIFF: Oh, no, sir!   515
BEN: *(taking boxing stance)* Come on, get to me! *(He laughs.)*
WILLY: Go to it, Biff! Go ahead, show him!
BIFF: Okay! *(He cocks his fist and starts in.)*
LINDA: *(to Willy)* Why must he fight, dear?
BEN: *(sparring with Biff)* Good boy! Good boy!   520
WILLY: How's that, Ben, heh?
HAPPY: Give him the left, Biff!
LINDA: Why are you fighting?
BEN: Good boy! *(Suddenly comes in, trips Biff, and stands over him, the point of his
    umbrella poised over Biff's eye.)*
LINDA: Look out, Biff!
BIFF: Gee!   525
BEN: *(patting Biff's knee)* Never fight fair with a stranger, boy. You'll never get out of
    the jungle that way. *(Taking Linda's hand and bowing.)* It was an honor and a plea-
    sure to meet you, Linda.
LINDA: *(withdrawing her hand coldly, frightened)* Have a nice—trip.
BEN: *(to Willy)* And good luck with your—what do you do?
WILLY: Selling.   530
BEN: Yes. Well . . . *(He raises his hand in farewell to all.)*
WILLY: No, Ben, I don't want you to think . . . *(He takes Ben's arm to show him.)* It's
    Brooklyn, I know, but we hunt too.
BEN: Really, now.
WILLY: Oh, sure, there's snakes and rabbits and—that's why I moved out here. Why, Biff
    can fell any one of these trees in no time! Boys! Go right over to where they're build-
    ing the apartment house and get some sand. We're gonna rebuild the entire front
    stoop right now! Watch this, Ben!
BIFF: Yes, sir! On the double, Hap!   535
HAPPY: *(as he and Biff run off)* I lost weight, Pop, you notice?

Charley enters in knickers, even before the boys are gone.

CHARLEY: Listen, if they steal any more from that building the watchman'll put the cops
    on them!
LINDA: *(to Willy)* Don't let Biff . . .

Ben laughs lustily.

WILLY: You shoulda seen the lumber they brought home last week. At least a dozen six-
    by-tens worth all kinds of money.
CHARLEY: Listen, if that watchman—
WILLY: I gave them hell, understand. But I got a couple of fearless characters there.   540
CHARLEY: Willy, the jails are full of fearless characters.
BEN: *(clapping Willy on the back, with a laugh at Charley)* And the stock exchange,
    friend!
WILLY: *(joining in Ben's laughter)* Where are the rest of your pants?
CHARLEY: My wife bought them.   545
WILLY: Now all you need is a golf club and you can go upstairs and go to sleep. *(To
    Ben.)* Great athlete! Between him and his son Bernard they can't hammer a nail!
BERNARD: *(rushing in)* The watchman's chasing Biff!
WILLY: *(angrily)* Shut up! He's not stealing anything!
LINDA: *(alarmed, hurrying off left)* Where is he? Biff, dear! *(She exits.)*
WILLY: *(moving toward the left, away from Ben)* There's nothing wrong. What's the   550
    matter with you?
BEN: Nervy boy. Good!
WILLY: *(laughing)* Oh, nerves of iron, that Biff!

CHARLEY: Don't know what it is. My New England man comes back and he's bleedin', they murdered him up there.

WILLY: It's contacts, Charley, I got important contacts!

CHARLEY: *(sarcastically)* Glad to hear it, Willy. Come in later, we'll shoot a little casino.   555
I'll take some of your Portland money. *(He laughs at Willy and exits.)*

WILLY: *(turning to Ben)* Business is bad, it's murderous. But not for me, of course.

BEN: I'll stop by on my way back to Africa.

WILLY: *(longingly)* Can't you stay a few days? You're just what I need, Ben, because I—I have a fine position here, but I—well, Dad left when I was such a baby and I never had a chance to talk to him and I still feel—kind of temporary about myself.

BEN: I'll be late for my train.

They are at opposite ends of the stage.

WILLY: Ben, my boys—can't we talk? They'd go into the jaws of hell for me, see, but I—   560

BEN: William, you're being first-rate with your boys. Outstanding, manly chaps!

WILLY: *(hanging on to his words)* Oh, Ben, that's good to hear! Because sometimes I'm afraid that I'm not teaching them the right kind of—Ben, how should I teach them?

BEN: *(giving great weight to each word, and with a certain vicious audacity)* William, when I walked into the jungle, I was seventeen. When I walked out I was twenty-one. And, by God, I was rich! *(He goes off into darkness around the right corner of the house.)*

WILLY: ...was rich! That's just the spirit I want to imbue them with! To walk into a jungle! I was right! I was right! I was right!

Ben is gone, but Willy is still speaking to him as Linda, in nightgown and robe, enters the kitchen, glances around for Willy, then goes to the door of the house, looks out and sees him. Comes down to his left. He looks at her.

LINDA: Willy, dear? Willy?   565

WILLY: I was right!

LINDA: Did you have some cheese? *(He can't answer.)* It's very late, darling. Come to bed, heh?

WILLY: *(looking straight up)* Gotta break your neck to see a star in this yard.

LINDA: You coming in?

WILLY: What ever happened to that diamond watch fob? Remember? When Ben came   570
from Africa that time? Didn't he give me a watch fob with a diamond in it?

LINDA: You pawned it, dear. Twelve, thirteen years ago. For Biff's radio correspondence course.

WILLY: Gee, that was a beautiful thing. I'll take a walk.

LINDA: But you're in your slippers.

WILLY: *(starting to go around the house at the left)* I was right! I was! *(Half to Linda, as he goes, shaking his head.)* What a man! There was a man worth talking to. I was right!

LINDA: *(calling after Willy)* But in your slippers, Willy!   575

Willy is almost gone when Biff, in his pajamas, comes down the stairs and enters the kitchen.

BIFF: What is he doing out there?

LINDA: Sh!

BIFF: God Almighty, Mom, how long has he been doing this?

LINDA: Don't, he'll hear you.

BIFF: What the hell is the matter with him?   580

LINDA: It'll pass by morning.

BIFF: Shouldn't we do anything?

LINDA: Oh, my dear, you should do a lot of things, but there's nothing to do, so go to sleep.

Happy comes down the stairs and sits on the steps.

HAPPY: I never heard him so loud, Mom.

LINDA: Well, come around more often; you'll hear him. *(She sits down at the table and*   585
mends the lining of Willy's jacket.)

BIFF: Why didn't you ever write me about this, Mom?

LINDA: How would I write to you? For over three months you had no address.

BIFF: I was on the move. But you know I thought of you all the time. You know that,
don't you, pal?

LINDA: I know, dear, I know. But he likes to have a letter. Just to know that there's still a
possibility for better things.

BIFF: He's not like this all the time, is he?   590

LINDA: It's when you come home he's always the worst.

BIFF: When I come home?

LINDA: When you write you're coming, he's all smiles, and talks about the future, and—
he's just wonderful. And then the closer you seem to come, the more shaky he gets,
and then, by the time you get here, he's arguing, and he seems angry at you. I think
it's just that maybe he can't bring himself to—to open up to you. Why are you so
hateful to each other? Why is that?

BIFF: *(evasively)* I'm not hateful, Mom.

LINDA: But you no sooner come in the door than you're fighting!   595

BIFF: I don't know why. I mean to change. I'm tryin', Mom, you understand?

LINDA: Are you home to stay now?

BIFF: I don't know. I want to look around, see what's doin'.

LINDA: Biff, you can't look around all your life, can you?

BIFF: I just can't take hold, Mom. I can't take hold of some kind of a life.   600

LINDA: Biff, a man is not a bird, to come and go with the springtime.

BIFF: Your hair . . . *(He touches her hair.)* Your hair got so gray.

LINDA: Oh, it's been gray since you were in high school. I just stopped dyeing it, that's
all.

BIFF: Dye it again, will ya? I don't want my pal looking old. *(He smiles.)*

LINDA: You're such a boy! You think you can go away for a year and . . . You've got to get   605
it into your head now that one day you'll knock on this door and there'll be strange
people here—

BIFF: What are you talking about? You're not even sixty, Mom.

LINDA: But what about your father?

BIFF: *(lamely)* Well, I meant him too.

HAPPY: He admires Pop.

LINDA: Biff, dear, if you don't have any feeling for him, then you can't have any feeling for   610
me.

BIFF: Sure I can, Mom.

LINDA: No. You can't just come to see me, because I love him. *(With a threat, but only a
threat, of tears.)* He's the dearest man in the world to me, and I won't have anyone
making him feel unwanted and low and blue. You're got to make up your mind now,
darling, there's no leeway any more. Either he's your father and you pay him that
respect, or else you're not to come here. I know he's not easy to get along with—
nobody knows that better than me—but . . .

WILLY: *(from the left, with a laugh)* Hey, hey, Biffo!

BIFF: *(starting to go out after Willy)* What the hell is the matter with him? *(Happy stops
him.)*

LINDA: Don't—don't go near him!   615

BIFF: Stop making excuses for him! He always, always wiped the floor with you. Never
had an ounce of respect for you.

HAPPY: He's always had respect for—

BIFF: What the hell do you know about it?

HAPPY: *(surlily)* Just don't call him crazy!

BIFF: He's got no character—Charley wouldn't do this. Not in his own house—spewing   620
out that vomit from his mind.

HAPPY: Charley never had to cope with what he's go to.

BIFF: People are worse off than Willy Loman. Believe me, I've seen them!

LINDA: Then make Charley your father, Biff. You can't do that, can you? I don't say he's a
great man. Willy Loman never made a lot of money. His name was never in the paper.
He's not the finest character that ever lived. But he's a human being, and a terrible
thing is happening to him. So attention must be paid. He's not to be allowed to fall
into his grave like an old dog. Attention, attention must be finally paid to such a person. You called him crazy—

BIFF: I didn't mean—

LINDA: No, a lot of people think he's lost his—balance. But you don't have to be very   625
smart to know what his trouble is. The man is exhausted.

HAPPY: Sure!

LINDA: A small man can be just as exhausted as a great man. He works for a company
thirty-six years this March, opens up unheard-of-territories to their trademark, and
now in his old age they take his salary away.

HAPPY: *(indignantly)* I didn't know that, Mom.

LINDA: You never asked, my dear! Now that you get your spending money someplace
else you don't trouble your mind with him.

HAPPY: But I gave you money last—   630

LINDA: Christmas time, fifty dollars! To fix the hot water it cost ninety-seven fifty! For
five weeks he's been on straight commission, like a beginner, an unknown!

BIFF: Those ungrateful bastards!

LINDA: Are they any worse than his sons? When he brought them business, when he was
young, they were glad to see him. But now his old friends, the old buyers that loved
him so and always found some order to hand him in a pinch—they're all dead, retired. He used to be able to make six, seven calls a day in Boston. Now he takes his
valises out the car and puts them back and takes them out again and he's exhausted.
Instead of walking he talks now. He drives seven hundred miles, and when he gets
there no one knows him any more, no one welcomes him. And what goes through a
man's mind, driving seven hundred miles home without having earned a cent? Why
shouldn't he talk to himself? Why? When he has to go to Charley and borrow fifty
dollars a week and pretend to me that it's his pay? How long can that go on? How
long? You see what I'm sitting here and waiting for? And you tell me he has no character? The man who never worked a day but for your benefit? When does he get the
medal for that? Is this his reward—to turn around at the age of sixty-three and find
his sons, who he loved better than his life, one a philandering bum—

HAPPY: Mom!

LINDA: That's all you are, my baby! *(To Biff.)* And you! What happened to the love you   635
had for him? You were such pals! How you used to talk to him on the phone every
night! How lonely he was till he could come home to you!

BIFF: All right, Mom. I'll live here in my room, and I'll get a job. I'll keep away from him,
that's all.

LINDA: No, Biff. You can't stay here and fight all the time.

BIFF: He threw me out of this house, remember that.

LINDA: Why did he do that? I never knew why.

BIFF: Because I know he's a fake and he doesn't like anybody around who knows!   640

LINDA: Why a fake? In what way? What do you mean?

BIFF: Just don't lay it all at my feet. It's between me and him—that's all I have to say. I'll
chip in from now on. He'll settle for half my pay check. He'll be all right. I'm going to
bed. *(He starts for the stairs.)*

LINDA: He won't be all right.

BIFF: *(turning on the stairs, furiously)* I hate this city and I'll stay here. Now what do you want?

LINDA: He's dying, Biff.

Happy turns quickly to her, shocked.

BIFF: *(after a pause)* Why is he dying?

LINDA: He's been trying to kill himself.

BIFF: *(with great horror)* How?

LINDA: I live from day to day.

BIFF: What're you talking about?

LINDA: Remember I wrote you that he smashed up the car again? In February?

BIFF: Well?

LINDA: The insurance inspector came. He said that they have evidence. That all these accidents in the last year—weren't—weren't—accidents.

HAPPY: How can they tell that? That's a lie.

LINDA: It seems there's a woman . . . *(She takes a breath as—)*

BIFF: *(sharply but contained)* What woman?

LINDA: *(simultaneously)* . . . and this woman . . .

LINDA: What?

BIFF: Nothing. Go ahead.

LINDA: What did you say?

BIFF: Nothing. I just said what woman?

HAPPY: What about her?

LINDA: Well, it seems she was walking down the road and saw his car. She says that he wasn't driving fast at all, and that he didn't skid. She says he came to that little bridge, and then deliberately smashed into the railing, and it was only the shallowness of the water that saved him.

BIFF: Oh, no, he probably just fell asleep again.

LINDA: I don't think he fell asleep.

BIFF: Why not?

LINDA: Last month . . . *(With great difficulty.)* Oh, boys, it's so hard to say a thing like this! He's just a big stupid man to you, but I tell you there's more good in him than in many other people. *(She chokes, wipes her eyes.)* I was looking for a fuse. The lights blew out, and I went down the cellar. And behind the fuse box—it happened to fall out—was a length of rubber pipe—just short.

HAPPY: No kidding?

LINDA: There's a little attachment on the end of it. I knew right away. And sure enough, on the bottom of the water heater there's a new little nipple on the gas pipe.

HAPPY: *(angrily)* That—jerk.

BIFF: Did you have it taken off?

LINDA: I'm—I'm ashamed to. How can I mention it to him? Every day I go down and take away that little rubber pipe. But, when he comes home, I put it back where it was. How can I insult him that way? I don't know what to do. I live from day to day, boys. I tell you, I know every thought in his mind. It sounds so old-fashioned and silly, but I tell you he put his whole life into you and you've turned your backs on him. *(She is bent over in the chair, weeping, her face in her hands.)* Biff, I swear to God! Biff, his life is in your hands!

HAPPY: *(to Biff)* How do you like that damned fool!

BIFF: *(kissing her)* All right, pal, all right. It's all settled now. I've been remiss. I know that, Mom, but now I'll stay, and I swear to you, I'll apply myself. *(Kneeling in front of her, in a fever of self-reproach.)* It's just—you see, Mom, I don't fit in business. Not that I won't try. I'll try, and I'll make good.

HAPPY: Sure you will. The trouble with you in business was you never tried to please people.

BIFF: I know, I—

HAPPY: Like when you worked for Harrison's. Bob Harrison said you were tops, and then you go and do some damn fool thing like whistling whole songs in the elevator like a comedian.

BIFF: *(against Happy)* So what? I like to whistle sometimes.

HAPPY: You don't raise a guy to a responsible job who whistles in the elevator!

LINDA: Well, don't argue about it now.   680

HAPPY: Like when you'd go off and swim in the middle of the day instead of taking the line around.

BIFF: *(his resentment rising)* Well, don't you run off? You take off sometimes, don't you? On a nice summer day?

HAPPY: Yeah, but I cover myself!

LINDA: Boys!

HAPPY: If I'm going to take a fade the boss can call any number where I'm supposed to   685
be and they'll swear to him that I just left. I'll tell you something that I hate to say, Biff, but in the business world some of them think you're crazy.

BIFF: *(angered)* Screw the business world!

HAPPY: All right, screw it! Great, but cover yourself!

LINDA: Hap, Hap!

BIFF: I don't care what they think! They've laughed at Dad for years, and you know why? Because we don't belong in this nut-house of a city! We should be mixing cement on some open plain, or—or carpenters. A carpenter is allowed to whistle!

Willy walks in from the entrance of the house, at left.

WILLY: Even your grandfather was better than a carpenter. *(Pause. They watch him.)*   690
You never grew up. Bernard does not whistle in the elevator, I assure you.

BIFF: *(as though to laugh Willy out of it)* Yeah, but you do, Pop.

WILLY: I never in my life whistled in an elevator! And who in the business world thinks I'm crazy?

BIFF: I didn't mean it like that, Pop. Now don't make a whole thing out of it, will ya?

WILLY: Go back to the West! Be a carpenter, a cowboy, enjoy yourself!

LINDA: Willy, he was just saying—   695

WILLY: I heard what he said!

HAPPY: *(trying to quiet Willy)* Hey, Pop, come on now ...

WILLY: *(continuing over Happy's line)* They laugh at me, heh? Go to Filene's, go to the Hub, go to Slattery's, Boston. Call out the name Willy Loman and see what happens! Big shot!

BIFF: All right, Pop.

WILLY: Big!   700

BIFF: All right!

WILLY: Why do you always insult me?

BIFF: I didn't say a word. *(To Linda.)* Did I say a word?

LINDA: He didn't say anything, Willy.

WILLY: *(going to the doorway of the livingroom)* All right, good night, good night.   705

LINDA: Willy, dear, he just decided ...

WILLY: *(to Biff)* If you get tired hanging around tomorrow, paint the ceiling I put up in the livingroom.

BIFF: I'm leaving early tomorrow.

HAPPY: He's going to see Bill Oliver, Pop.

WILLY: *(interestedly)* Oliver? For what?   710

BIFF: *(with reserve, but trying, trying)* He always said he'd stake me. I'd like to go into business, so maybe I can take him up on it.

LINDA: Isn't that wonderful?

WILLY: Don't interrupt. What's wonderful about it? There's fifty men in the City of New York who'd stake him. *(To Biff.)* Sporting goods?

BIFF: I guess so. I know something about it and—

WILLY: He knows something about it! You know sporting goods better than Spalding,   715
for God's sake! How much is he giving you?

BIFF: I don't know, I didn't even see him yet, but—

WILLY: Then what're you talkin' about?

BIFF: *(getting angry)* Well, all I said was I'm gonna see him, that's all!

WILLY: *(turning away)* Ah, you're counting your chickens again.

BIFF: *(starting left for the stairs)* Oh, Jesus, I'm going to sleep!   720

WILLY: *(calling after him)* Don't curse in this house!

BIFF: *(turning)* Since when did you get so clean!

HAPPY: *(trying to stop them)* Wait a . . .

WILLY: Don't use that language to me! I won't have it!

HAPPY: *(grabbing Biff, shouts)* Wait a minute! I got an idea. I got a feasible idea. Come   725
here, Biff, let's talk this over now, let's talk some sense here. When I was down in
Florida last time, I thought of a great idea to sell sporting goods. It just came back to
me. You and I, Biff—we have a line, the Loman Line. We train a couple of weeks, and
put on a couple of exhibitions, see?

WILLY: That's an idea!

HAPPY: Wait! We form two basketball teams, see. Two water-polo teams. We play each
other. It's a million dollars' worth of publicity. Two brothers, see? The Loman Brothers. Displays in the Royal Palms—all the hotels. And banners over the ring and the
basketball court: "Loman Brothers." Baby, we could sell sporting goods!

WILLY: That is a one-million-dollar idea.

LINDA: Marvelous!

BIFF: I'm in great shape as far as that's concerned.   730

HAPPY: And the beauty of it is, Biff, it wouldn't be like a business. We'd be out playin' ball
again . . .

BIFF: *(enthused)* Yeah, that's . . .

WILLY: Million-dollar . . .

HAPPY: And you wouldn't get fed up with it, Biff. It'd be the family again. There'd be the
old honor, and comradeship, and if you wanted to go off for a swim or somethin'—
well, you'd do it! Without some smart cooky gettin' up ahead of you!

WILLY: Lick the world! You guys together could absolutely lick the civilized world.   735

BIFF: I'll see Oliver tomorrow. Hap, if we could work that out . . .

LINDA: Maybe things are beginning to—

WILLY: *(wildly enthused, to Linda)* Stop interrupting! *(To Biff.)* But don't wear sport
jacket and slacks when you see Oliver.

BIFF: No, I'll—

WILLY: A business suit, and talk as little as possible, and don't crack any jokes.   740

BIFF: He did like me. Always liked me.

LINDA: He loved you!

WILLY: *(to Linda)* Will you stop! *(To Biff.)* Walk in very serious. You are not applying for
a boy's job. Money is to pass. Be quiet, fine, and serious. Everybody likes a kidder, but
nobody lends him money.

HAPPY: I'll try to get some myself, Biff. I'm sure I can.

WILLY: I can see great things for you, kids, I think your troubles are over. But remember,   745
start big and you'll end big. Ask for fifteen. How much you gonna ask for?

BIFF: Gee, I don't know—

WILLY: And don't say "Gee." "Gee" is a boy's word. A man walking in for fifteen thousand
dollars does not say "Gee!"

BIFF: Ten, I think, would be top though.

WILLY: Don't be so modest. You always started too low. Walk in with a big laugh. Don't
look worried. Start off with a couple of your good stories to lighten things up. It's
not what you say, it's how you say it—because personality always wins the day.

LINDA: Oliver always thought the highest of him—   750

WILLY: Will you let me talk?

BIFF: Don't yell at her, Pop, will ya?

WILLY: *(angrily)* I was talking, wasn't I!

BIFF: I don't like you yelling at her all the time, and I'm tellin' you, that's all.

WILLY: What're you, takin' over this house?   755

LINDA: Willy—

WILLY: *(turning on her.)* Don't take his side all the time, goddammit.

BIFF: *(furiously)* Stop yelling at her.

WILLY: *(suddenly pulling on his cheek, breaks down, guilt ridden)* Give my best to Bill
Oliver—he may remember me. *(He exits through the livingroom doorway.)*

LINDA: *(her voice subdued)* What'd you have to start that for? *(Biff turns away.)* You   760
see how sweet he was as soon as you talked hopefully? *(She goes over to Biff.)*
Come up and say good night to him. Don't let him go to bed that way.

HAPPY: Come on, Biff, let's buck him up.

LINDA: Please, dear. Just say good night. It takes so little to make him happy. Come. *(She
goes through the livingroom doorway, calling upstairs from within the livingroom.)* Your pajamas are hanging in the bathroom. Willy!

HAPPY: *(looking toward where Linda went out)* What a woman! They broke the mold
when they made her. You know that, Biff?

BIFF: He's off salary. My God, working on commission!

HAPPY: Well, let's face it: he's no hot-shot selling man. Except that sometimes, you have   765
to admit, he's a sweet personality.

BIFF: *(deciding)* Lend me ten bucks, will ya? I want to buy some new ties.

HAPPY: I'll take you to a place I know. Beautiful stuff. Wear one of my striped shirts tomorrow.

BIFF: She got gray. Mom got awful old. Gee, I'm gonna go in to Oliver tomorrow and
knock him for a—

HAPPY: Come on up. Tell that to Dad. Let's give him a whirl. Come on.

BIFF: *(steamed up)* You know, with ten thousand bucks, boy!   770

HAPPY: *(as they go into the livingroom)* That's the talk, Biff, that's the first time I've
heard the old confidence out of you! *(From within the livingroom, fading off.)*
You're gonna live with me, kid, and any babe you want you just say the word . . . *(The
last lines are hardly heard. They are mounting the stairs to their parents' bedroom.)*

LINDA: *(entering her bedroom and addressing Willy, who is in the bathroom. She is
straightening the bed for him)* Can you do anything about the shower? It drips.

WILLY: *(from the bathroom)* All of a sudden everything falls to pieces! Goddam plumb-
ing, oughta be sued, those people. I hardly finished putting it in and the thing . . . *(His
words rumble off.)*

LINDA: I'm just wondering if Oliver will remember him. You think he might?

WILLY: *(coming out of the bathroom in his pajamas)* Remember him? What's the mat-   775
ter with you, you crazy? If he'd've stayed with Oliver he'd be on top by now! Wait'll
Oliver gets a look at him. You don't know the average caliber any more. The average
young man today—*(he is getting into bed)*—is got a caliber of zero. Greatest thing
in the world for him was to bum around.

Biff and Happy enter the bedroom. Slight pause.

WILLY: *(stops short, looking at Biff)* Glad to hear it, boy.

HAPPY: He wanted to say good night to you, sport.

WILLY: *(to Biff)* Yeah. Knock him dead, boy. What'd you want to tell me?

BIFF: Just take it easy, Pop. Good night. *(He turns to go.)*

WILLY: *(unable to resist)* And if anything falls off the desk while you're talking to him—   780
like a package or something—don't you pick it up. They have office boys for that.

LINDA: I'll make a big breakfast—

WILLY: Will you let me finish? *(To Biff.)* Tell him you were in the business in the West. Not farm work.

BIFF: All right, Dad.

LINDA: I think everything—

WILLY: *(going right through her speech)* And don't undersell yourself. No less than fifteen thousand dollars. 785

BIFF: *(unable to bear him)* Okay. Good night, Mom. *(He starts moving.)*

WILLY: Because you got a greatness in you, Biff, remember that. You got all kinds of greatness . . . *(He lies back, exhausted. Biff walks out.)*

LINDA: *(calling after Biff)* Sleep well, darling!

HAPPY: I'm gonna get married, Mom. I wanted to tell you.

LINDA: Go to sleep, dear.

HAPPY: *(going)* I just wanted to tell you. 790

WILLY: Keep up the good work. *(Happy exits.)* God . . . remember that Ebbets Field game? The championship of the city?

LINDA: Just rest. Should I sing to you?

WILLY: Yeah. Sing to me. *(Linda hums a soft lullaby.)* When that team came out—he was the tallest, remember?

LINDA: Oh, yes. And in gold. 795

Biff enters the darkened kitchen, takes a cigarette, and leaves the house. He comes downstage into a golden pool of light. He smokes, staring at the night.

WILLY: Like a young god. Hercules—something like that. And the sun, the sun all around him. Remember how he waved to me? Right up from the field, with the representatives of three colleges standing by? And the buyers I brought, and the cheers when he came out—Loman, Loman, Loman! God Almighty, he'll be great yet. A star like that, magnificent, can never really fade away!

The light on Willy is fading. The gas heater begins to glow through the kitchen wall, near the stairs, a blue flame beneath red coils.

LINDA: *(timidly)* Willy, dear, what has he got against you?

WILLY: I'm so tired. Don't talk any more.

Biff slowly returns to the kitchen. He stops, stares toward the heater.

LINDA: Will you ask Howard to let you work in New York?

WILLY: First thing in the morning. Everything'll be all right. 800

Biff reaches behind the heater and draws out a length of rubber tubing. He is horrified and turns his head toward Willy's room, still dimly lit, from which the strains of Linda's desperate but monotonous humming rise.

WILLY: *(staring through the window into the moonlight)* Gee, look at the moon moving between the buildings!

Biff wraps the tubing around his hand and quickly goes up the stairs. Curtain.

Act 2

Music is heard, gay and bright. The curtain rises as the music fades away. Willy, in shirt sleeves, is sitting at the kitchen table, sipping coffee, his hat in his lap. Linda is filling his cup when she can.

WILLY: Wonderful coffee. Meal in itself.

LINDA: Can I make you some eggs?

WILLY: No. Take a breath.

LINDA: You look so rested, dear.

WILLY: I slept like a dead one. First time in months. Imagine, sleeping till ten on a Tuesday morning. Boys left nice and early, heh? 5

LINDA: They were out of here by eight o'clock.

WILLY: Good work!

LINDA: It was so thrilling to see them leaving together. I can't get over the shaving lotion
          in this house.
WILLY: *(smiling)* Mmm—
LINDA: Biff was very changed this morning. His whole attitude seemed to be hopeful. He   10
          couldn't wait to get downtown to see Oliver.
WILLY: He's heading for a change. There's no question, there simply are certain men that
          take longer to get—solidified. How did he dress?
LINDA: His blue suit. He's so handsome in that suit. He could be a—anything in that suit!

Willy gets up from the table. Linda holds his jacket for him.

WILLY: There's no question, no question at all. Gee, on the way home tonight I'd like to
          buy some seeds.
LINDA: *(laughing)* That'd be wonderful. But not enough sun gets back there. Nothing'll
          grow any more.
WILLY: You wait, kid, before it's all over we're gonna get a little place out in the country,   15
          and I'll raise some vegetables, a couple of chickens . . .
LINDA: You'll do it yet, dear.

Willy walks out of his jacket. Linda follows him.

WILLY: And they'll get married, and come for a weekend. I'd build a little guest house.
          'Cause I got so many fine tools, all I'd need would be a little lumber and some peace
          of mind.
LINDA: *(joyfully)* I sewed the lining . . .
WILLY: I could build two guest houses, so they'd both come. Did he decide how much
          he's going to ask Oliver for?
LINDA: *(getting him into the jacket)* He didn't mention it, but I imagine ten or fifteen   20
          thousand. You going to talk to Howard today?
WILLY: Yeah. I'll put it to him straight and simple. He'll just have to take me off the road.
LINDA: And Willy, don't forget to ask for a little advance, because we've got the insurance
          premium. It's the grace period now.
WILLY: That's a hundred . . . ?
LINDA: A hundred and eight, sixty-eight. Because we're a little short again.
WILLY: Why are we short?   25
LINDA: Well, you had the motor job on the car . . .
WILLY: That goddam Studebaker!
LINDA: And you got one more payment on the refrigerator . . .
WILLY: But it just broke again!
LINDA: Well, it's old, dear.   30
WILLY: I told you we should've bought a well-advertised machine. Charley bought a
          General Electric and it's twenty years old and it's still good, that son-of-a-bitch.
LINDA: But, Willy—
WILLY: Whoever heard of a Hastings refrigerator? Once in my life I would like to own
          something outright before it's broken! I'm always in a race with the junkyard! I just
          finished paying for the car and it's on its last legs. The refrigerator consumes belts
          like a goddam maniac. They time those things. They time them so when you finally
          paid for them, they're used up.
LINDA: *(buttoning up his jacket as he unbuttons it)* All told, about two hundred dollars
          would carry us, dear. But that includes the last payment on the mortgage. After this
          payment, Willy, the house belongs to us.
WILLY: It's twenty-five years!   35
LINDA: Biff was nine years old when we bought it.
WILLY: Well, that's a great thing. To weather a twenty-five year mortgage is—
LINDA: It's an accomplishment.
WILLY: All the cement, the lumber, the reconstruction I put in this house! There ain't a
          crack to be found in it any more.

LINDA: Well, it served its purpose.   40

WILLY: What purpose? Some stranger'll come along, move in, and that's that. If only Biff
would take this house, and raise a family … *(He starts to go.)* Good-by, I'm late.

LINDA: *(suddenly remembering)* Oh, I forgot! You're supposed to meet them for dinner.

WILLY: Me?

LINDA: At Frank's Chop House on Forty-eighth near Sixth Avenue.

WILLY: Is that so? How about you?   45

LINDA: No, just the three of you. They're gonna blow you to a big meal!

WILLY: Don't say! Who thought of that?

LINDA: Biff came to me this morning, Willy, and he said, "Tell Dad, we want to blow him
to a big meal." Be there six o'clock. You and your two boys are going to have dinner.

WILLY: Gee whiz! That's really somethin'. I'm gonna knock Howard for a loop, kid. I'll
get an advance, and I'll come home with a New York job. Goddammit, now I'm
gonna do it!

LINDA: Oh, that's the spirit, Willy!   50

WILLY: I will never get behind a wheel the rest of my life!

LINDA: It's changing, Willy, I can feel it changing!

WILLY: Beyond a question. G'by, I'm late. *(He starts to go again.)*

LINDA: *(calling after him as she runs to the kitchen table for a handkerchief)* You got
your glasses?

WILLY: *(feels for them, then comes back in)* Yeah, yeah, got my glasses.   55

LINDA: *(giving him the handkerchief)* And a handkerchief.

WILLY: Yeah, handkerchief.

LINDA: And your saccharine?

WILLY: Yeah, my saccharine.

LINDA: Be careful on the subway stairs.   60

She kisses him, and a silk stocking is seen hanging from her hand. Willy notices it.

WILLY: Will you stop mending stockings? At least while I'm in the house. It gets me nervous. I can't tell you. Please.

Linda hides the stocking in her hand as she follows Willy across the forestage in front of the house.

LINDA: Remember, Frank's Chop House.

WILLY: *(passing the apron)* Maybe beets would grow out there.

LINDA: *(laughing)* But you tried so many times.

WILLY: Yeah. Well, don't work hard today. *(He disappears around the right corner of*   65
the house.)

LINDA: Be careful!

*As Willy vanishes, Linda waves to him. Suddenly the phone rings. She runs across the stage and into
the kitchen and lifts it.*

LINDA: Hello? Oh, Biff! I'm so glad you called, I just … Yes, sure, I just told him. Yes, he'll be
there for dinner at six o'clock, I didn't forget. Listen, I was just dying to tell you. You
know that little rubber pipe I told you about? That he connected to the gas heater? I
finally decided to go down the cellar this morning and take it away and destroy it. But
it's gone! Imagine? He took it away himself, it isn't there! *(She listens.)* When? Oh,
then you took it. Oh—nothing, it's just that I'd hoped he'd taken it away himself. Oh,
I'm not worried, darling, because this morning he left in such high spirits, it was like
the old days! I'm not afraid any more. Did Mr. Oliver see you? … Well, you wait there
then. And make a nice impression on him, darling. Just don't perspire too much before you see him. And have a nice time with Dad. He may have big news too! …
That's right, a New York job. And be sweet to him tonight, dear. Be loving to him. Because he's only a little boat looking for a harbor. *(She is trembling with sorrow and
joy.)* Oh, that's wonderful, Biff, you'll save his life. Thanks, darling. Just put

your arm around him when he comes into the restaurant. Give him a smile. That's the boy . . . Good-by, dear. . . . You got your comb? . . . That's fine. Good-by, Biff dear.

In the middle of her speech, Howard Wagner, thirty-six, wheels in a small typewriter table on which is a wire-recording machine and proceeds to plug it in. This is on the left forestage. Light slowly fades on Linda as it rises on Howard. Howard is intent on treading the machine and only glances over his shoulder as Willy appears.

WILLY: Pst! Pst!

HOWARD: Hello, Willy, come in.

WILLY: Like to have a little talk with you, Howard.   70

HOWARD: Sorry to keep you waiting. I'll be with you in a minute.

WILLY: What's that, Howard?

HOWARD: Didn't you ever see one of these? Wire recorder.

WILLY: Oh. Can we talk a minute?

HOWARD: Records things. Just got delivery yesterday. Been driving me crazy, the most ter-   75
    rific machine I ever saw in my life. I was up all night with it.

WILLY: What do you do with it?

HOWARD: I bought it for dictation, but you can do anything with it. Listen to this. I had it
    home last night. Listen to what I picked up. The first one is my daughter. Get this.
    (He flicks the switch and "Roll out the Barrel" is heard being whistled.) Listen to
    that kid whistle.

WILLY: That is lifelike, isn't it?

HOWARD: Seven years old. Get that tone.

WILLY: Ts, ts. Like to ask a little favor if you . . .   80

The whistling breaks off, and the voice of Howard's Daughter is heard.

HIS DAUGHTER: "Now you, Daddy."

HOWARD: She's crazy for me! *(Again the same song is whistled.)* That's me! Ha! *(He
    winks.)*

WILLY: You're very good!

The whistling breaks off again. The machine runs silent for a moment.

HOWARD: Sh! Get this now, this is my son.

HIS SON: "The capital of Alabama is Montgomery; the capital of Arizona is Phoenix; the   85
    capital of Arkansas is Little Rock; the capital of California is Sacramento . . ." *(And on,
    and on.)*

HOWARD: *(Holding up five fingers)* Five years old, Willy!

WILLY: He'll make an announcer some day!

HIS SON: *(continuing)* "The capital . . ."

HOWARD: Get that—alphabetical order! *(The machine breaks off suddenly.)* Wait a
    minute. The maid kicked the plug out.

WILLY: It certainly is a—   90

HOWARD: Sh, for God's sake!

HIS SON: "It's nine o'clock, Bulova watch time. So I have to go to sleep."

WILLY: That really is—

HOWARD: Wait a minute! The next is my wife.

They wait.

HOWARD'S VOICE: "Go on, say something." *(Pause.)* "Well, you gonna talk?"   95

HIS WIFE: "I can't think of anything."

HOWARD'S VOICE: "Well, talk—it's turning."

HIS WIFE: *(shyly, beaten)* "Hello." *(Silence.)* "Oh, Howard, I can't talk into this . . ."

HOWARD: *(snapping the machine off)* That was my wife.

HOWARD: I tell you, Willy, I'm gonna take my camera, and my bandsaw, and all my hob-   100
    bies, and out they go. This is the most fascinating relaxation I ever found.

WILLY: I think I'll get one myself.

HOWARD: Sure, they're only a hundred and a half. You can't do without it. Supposing you wanna hear Jack Benny, see? But you can't be home at that hour. So you tell the maid to turn the radio on when Jack Benny comes on, and this automatically goes on with the radio ...

WILLY: And when you come home you ...

HOWARD: You can come home twelve o'clock, one o'clock, any time you like, and you   105
get yourself a Coke and sit yourself down, throw the switch, and there's Jack Benny's program in the middle of the night!

WILLY: I'm definitely going to get one. Because lots of time I'm on the road, and I think to myself, what I must be missing on the radio!

HOWARD: Don't you have a radio in the car?

WILLY: Well, yeah, but who ever thinks of turning it on?

HOWARD: Say, aren't you supposed to be in Boston?

WILLY: That's what I want to talk to you about, Howard. You got a minute?   110

(He draws a chair in from the wing.)

HOWARD: What happened? What're you doing here?

WILLY: Well ...

HOWARD: You didn't crack up again, did you?

WILLY: Oh, no. No ...

HOWARD: Geez, you had me worried there for a minute. What's the trouble?   115

WILLY: Well, to tell you the truth, Howard, I've come to the decision that I'd rather not travel any more.

HOWARD: Not travel! Well, what'll you do?

WILLY: Remember, Christmas time, when you had the party here? You said you'd try to think of some spot for me here in town.

HOWARD: With us?

WILLY: Well, sure.

HOWARD: Oh, yeah, yeah. I remember. Well, I couldn't think of anything for you, Willy.   120

WILLY: I tell ya, Howard. The kids are all grown up, y'know. I don't need much any more. If I could take home—well, sixty-five dollars a week, I could swing it.

HOWARD: Yeah, but Willy, see I—

WILLY: I tell ya why, Howard. Speaking frankly and between the two of us, y'know—I'm just a little tired.

HOWARD: Oh, I could understand that, Willy. But you're a road man, Willy, and we do a   125
road business. We've only got a half-dozen salesmen on the floor here.

WILLY: God knows, Howard, I never asked a favor of any man. But I was with the firm when your father used to carry you in here in his arms.

HOWARD: I know that, Willy, but—

WILLY: Your father came to me the day you were born and asked me what I thought of the name of Howard, may he rest in peace.

HOWARD: I appreciate that, Willy, but there just is no spot here for you. If I had a spot I'd slam you right in, but I just don't have a single, solitary spot.

He looks for his lighter. Willy has picked it up and gives it to him. Pause.

WILLY: *(with increasing anger)* Howard, all I need to set my table is fifty dollars a   130
week.

HOWARD: But where am I going to put you, kid?

WILLY: Look, it isn't a question of whether I can sell merchandise, is it?

HOWARD: No, but it's a business, kid, and everybody's gotta pull his own weight.

WILLY: *(desperately)* Just let me tell you a story, Howard—

HOWARD: 'Cause you gotta admit, business is business.   135

WILLY: *(angrily)* Business is definitely business, but just listen for a minute. You don't understand this. When I was a boy—eighteen, nineteen—I was already on the road.

And there was a question in my mind as to whether selling had a future for me. Because in those days I had a yearning to go to Alaska. See, there were three gold strikes in one month in Alaska, and I felt like going out. Just for the ride, you might say.

HOWARD: *(barely interested)* Don't say.

WILLY: Oh, yeah, my father lived many years in Alaska. He was an adventurous man. We've got quite a little streak of self-reliance in our family. I thought I'd go out with my older brother and try to locate him, and maybe settle in the North with the old man. And I was almost decided to go, when I met a salesman in the Parker House. His name was Dave Singleman. And he was eighty-four years old, and he'd drummed merchandise in thirty-one states. And old Dave, he'd go up to his room, y'under-stand, put on his green velvet slippers—I'll never forget—and pick up his phone and call the buyers, and without ever leaving his room, at the age of eighty-four, he made his living. And when I saw that, I realized that selling was the greatest career a man could want. 'Cause what could be more satisfying than to be able to go, at the age of eighty-four, into twenty or thirty different cities, and pick up a phone, and be remembered and loved and helped by so many different people? Do you know? when he died—and by the way he died the death of a salesman, in his green velvet slippers in the smoker of the New York, New Haven and Hartford, going into Boston—when he died, hundreds of salesmen and buyers were at his funeral. Things were sad on a lotta trains for months after that. *(He stands up. Howard has not looked at him.)* In those days there was personality in it, Howard. There was re-spect, and comradeship, and gratitude in it. Today, it's all cut and dried, and there's no chance for bringing friendship to bear—or personality. You see what I mean? They don't know me any more.

HOWARD: *(moving away, to the right)* That's just the thing, Willy.

WILLY: If I had forty dollars a week—that's all I'd need. Forty dollars, Howard.   140

HOWARD: Kid, I can't take blood from a stone, I—

WILLY: *(desperation is on him now)* Howard, the year Al Smith was nominated, your fa-ther came to me and—

HOWARD: *(starting to go off)* I've got to see some people, kid.

WILLY: *(stopping him)* I'm talking about your father! There were promises made across this desk! You mustn't tell me you've got people to see—I put thirty-four years into this firm, Howard, and now I can't pay my insurance! You can't eat the orange and throw the peel away—a man is not a piece of fruit! *(After a pause.)* Now pay atten-tion. Your father—in 1928 I had a big year. I averaged a hundred and seventy dollars a week in commissions.

HOWARD: *(impatiently)* Now, Willy, you never averaged—   145

WILLY: *(banging his hand on the desk)* I averaged a hundred and seventy dollars a week in the year of 1928! And your father came to me—or rather, I was in the office here—it was right over this desk—and he put his hand on my shoulder—

HOWARD: *(getting up)* You'll have to excuse me, Willy, I gotta see some people. Pull your-self together. *(Going out.)* I'll be back in a little while.

On Howard's exit, the light on his chair grows very bright and strange.

WILLY: Pull yourself together! What the hell did I say to him? My God, I was yelling at him! How could I! *(Willy breaks off, staring at the light, which occupies the chair, animating it. He approaches this chair, standing across the desk from it.)* Frank, Frank, don't you remember what you told me that time? How you put your hand on my shoulder, and Frank . . . *(He leans on the desk and as he speaks the dead man's name he accidentally switches on the recorder, and instantly—)*

HOWARD'S SON: ". . . of New York is Albany. The capital of Ohio is Cincinnati, the capital of Rhode Island is . . . " *(The recitation continues.)*

WILLY: *(leaping away with fright, shouting)* Ha! Howard! Howard! Howard!   150

HOWARD: *(rushing in)* What happened?

WILLY: *(pointing at the machine, which continues nasally, childishly, with the capital cities)* Shut it off! Shut it off!

HOWARD: *(pulling the plug out)* Look, Willy . . .

WILLY: *(pressing his hands to his eyes)* I gotta get myself some coffee. I'll get some coffee . . .

Willy starts to walk out. Howard stops him.

HOWARD: *(rolling up the cord)* Willy, look . . .   155

WILLY: I'll go to Boston.

HOWARD: Willy, you can't go to Boston for us.

WILLY: Why can't I go?

HOWARD: I don't want you to represent us. I've been meaning to tell you for a long time now.

WILLY: Howard, are you firing me?   160

HOWARD: I think you need a good long rest, Willy.

WILLY: Howard—

HOWARD: And when you feel better, come back, and we'll see if we can work something out.

WILLY: But I gotta earn money, Howard. I'm in no position—

HOWARD: Where are your sons? Why don't your sons give you a hand?   165

WILLY: They're working on a very big deal.

HOWARD: This is no time for false pride, Willy. You go to your sons and tell them that you're tired. You've got two great boys, haven't you?

WILLY: Oh, no question, no question, but in the meantime . . .

HOWARD: Then that's that, heh?

WILLY: All right, I'll go to Boston tomorrow.   170

HOWARD: No, no.

WILLY: I can't throw myself on my sons. I'm not a cripple!

HOWARD: Look, kid, I'm busy this morning.

WILLY: *(grasping Howard's arm)* Howard, you've got to let me go to Boston!

HOWARD: *(hard, keeping himself under control)* I've got a line of people to see this   175
morning. Sit down, take five minutes, and pull yourself together, and then go home, will ya? I need the office, Willy. *(He starts to go, turns, remembering the recorder, starts to push off the table holding the recorder.)* Oh, yeah. Whenever you can this week, stop by and drop off the samples. You'll feel better, Willy, and then come back and we'll talk. Pull yourself together, kid, there's people outside.

Howard exits, pushing the table off left. Willy stares into space, exhausted. Now the music is heard—Ben's music—first distantly, then closer, closer. As Willy speaks, Ben enters from the right. He carries valise and umbrella.

WILLY: Oh, Ben, how did you do it? What is the answer? Did you wind up the Alaska deal already?

BEN: Doesn't take much time if you know what you're doing. Just a short business trip. Boarding ship in an hour. Wanted to say good-by.

WILLY: Ben, I've got to talk to you.

BEN: *(glancing at his watch)* Haven't the time, William.

WILLY: *(crossing the apron to Ben)* Ben, nothing's working out. I don't know what   180
to do.

BEN: Now, look here, William. I've bought timberland in Alaska and I need a man to look after things for me.

WILLY: God, timberland! Me and my boys in those grand outdoors!

BEN: You've a new continent at your doorstep, William. Get out of these cities, they're full of talk and time payments and courts of law. Screw on your fists and you can fight for a fortune up there.

WILLY: Yes, yes! Linda! Linda!

Linda enters as of old, with the wash.

LINDA: Oh, you're back?

BEN: I haven't much time.

WILLY: No, wait! Linda, he's got a proposition for me in Alaska.

LINDA: But you've got—*(To Ben.)* He's got a beautiful job here.

WILLY: But in Alaska, kid, I could—

LINDA: You're doing well enough, Willy!

BEN: *(to Linda)* Enough for what, my dear?

LINDA: *(frightened of Ben and angry at him)* Don't say those things to him! Enough to be happy right here, right now. *(To Willy, while Ben laughs.)* Why must everybody conquer the world? You're well liked, and the boys love you, and someday—*(to Ben)*—why, old man Wagner told him just the other day that if he keeps it up he'll be a member of the firm, didn't he, Willy?

WILLY: Sure, sure. I am building something with this firm, Ben, and if a man is building something he must be on the right track, mustn't he?

BEN: What are you building? Lay your hand on it. Where is it?

WILLY: *(hesitantly)* That's true, Linda, there's nothing.

LINDA: Why? *(To Ben.)* There's a man eighty-four years old—

WILLY: That's right, Ben, that's right. When I look at that man I say, what is there to worry about?

BEN: Bah!

WILLY: It's true, Ben. All he has to do is go into any city, pick up the phone, and he's making his living and you know why?

BEN: *(picking up his valise)* I've got to go.

WILLY: *(holding Ben back)* Look at this boy!

Biff, in his high school sweater, enters carrying suitcase. Happy carries Biff's shoulder guards, gold helmet, and football pants.

WILLY: Without a penny to his name, three great universities are begging for him, and from there the sky's the limit, because it's not what you do, Ben. It's who you know, and the smile on your face! It's contacts, Ben, contacts! The whole wealth of Alaska passes over the lunch table at the Commodore Hotel, and that's the wonder, the wonder of this country, that a man can end with diamonds here on the basis of being liked! *(He turns to Biff.)* And that's why when you get out on that field today it's important. Because thousands of people will be rooting for you and loving you. *(To Ben, who has again begun to leave.)* And Ben! when he walks into a business office his name will sound out like a bell and all the doors will open to him! I've seen it, Ben, I've seen it a thousand times! You can't feel it with your hand like timber, but it's there!

BEN: Good-by, William.

WILLY: Ben, am I right? Don't you think I'm right? I value your advice.

BEN: There's a new continent at your doorstep, William. You could walk out rich. Rich. *(He is gone.)*

WILLY: We'll do it here, Ben! You hear me? We're gonna do it here!

Young Bernard rushes in. The gay music of the boys is heard.

BERNARD: Oh, gee, I was afraid you left already!

WILLY: Why? What time is it?

BERNARD: It's half-past one!

WILLY: Well, come on, everybody! Ebbets Field next stop! Where's the pennants? *(He rushes through the wall-line of the kitchen and out into the livingroom.)*

LINDA: *(to Biff)* Did you pack fresh underwear?

BIFF: *(who has been limbering up)* I want to go!

BERNARD: Biff, I'm carrying your helmet, ain't I?

185

190

195

200

205

210

Happy: No, I'm carrying the helmet.

Bernard: Oh, Biff, you promised me.   215

Happy: I'm carrying the helmet.

Bernard: How am I going to get in the locker room?

Linda: Let him carry the shoulder guards. *(She puts her coat and hat on in the kitchen.)*

Bernard: Can I, Biff? 'Cause I told everybody I'm going to be in the locker room.

Happy: In Ebbets Field it's the clubhouse.   220

Bernard: I meant the clubhouse. Biff!

Happy: Biff!

Biff: *(grandly, after a slight pause)* Let him carry the shoulder guards.

Happy: *(as he gives Bernard the shoulder guards)* Stay close to use now.

Willy rushes in with the pennants.

Willy: *(handling them out)* Everybody wave when Biff comes out on the field. *(Happy   225
and Bernard run off.)* You set now, boy?

The music has died away.

Biff: Ready to go, Pop. Every muscle is ready.

Willy: *(at the edge of the apron)* You realize what this means?

Biff: That's right, Pop.

Willy: *(feeling Biff's muscles)* You're comin' home this afternoon captain of the All-
Scholastic Championship Team of the City of New York.

Biff: I got it, Pop. And remember, pal, when I take off my helmet, that touchdown is for   230
you.

Willy: Let's go! *(He is starting out, with his arm around Biff, when Charley enters, as
of old, in knickers.)* I got no room for you, Charley.

Charley: Room? For what?

Willy: In the car.

Charley: You goin' for a ride? I wanted to shoot some casino.

Willy: *(furiously)* Casino! *(Incredulously.)* Don't you realize what today is?   235

Linda: Oh he knows, Willy. He's just kidding you.

Willy: That's nothing to kid about!

Charley: No, Linda, what's goin' on?

Linda: He's playing in Ebbets Field.

Charley: Baseball in this weather?   240

Willy: Don't talk to him. Come on, come on! *(He is pushing them out.)*

Charley: Wait a minute, didn't you hear the news?

Willy: What?

Charley: Don't you listen to the radio? Ebbets Field just blew up.

Willy: You go to hell! *(Charley laughs. Pushing them out.)* Come on, come on! We're   245
late.

Charley: *(as they go)* Knock a homer, Biff, knock a homer!

Willy: *(the last to leave, turning to Charley)* I don't think that was funny, Charley. This
is the greatest day of his life.

Charley: Willy, when are you going to grow up?

Willy: Yeah, heh? When this game is over, Charley, you'll be laughing out of the other
side of your face. They'll be calling him another Red Grange. Twenty-five thousand
a year.

Charley: *(kidding)* Is that so?   250

Willy: Yeah, that's so.

Charley: Well, then, I'm sorry, Willy. But tell me something.

Willy: What?

Charley: Who is Red Grange?

Willy: Put up your hands. Goddam you, put up your hands!   255

Charley, chuckling, shakes his head and walks away, around the left corner of the stage. Willy follows him. The music rises to a mocking frenzy.

WILLY: Who the hell do you think you are, better than everybody else? You don't know everything, you big, ignorant, stupid . . . Put up your hands!

Light rises, on the right side of the forestage, on a small table in the reception room of Charley's office. Traffic sounds are heard. Bernard, now mature, sits whistling to himself. A pair of tennis rackets and an overnight bag are on the floor beside him.

WILLY: *(offstage)* What are you walking away for? Don't walk away! If you're going to say something say it to my face! I know you laugh at me behind my back. You'll laugh out of the other side of your goddam face after this game. Touchdown! Touchdown! Eighty thousand people! Touchdown! Right between the goal posts.

Bernard is a quiet, earnest, but self-assured young man. Willy's voice is coming from right upstage now. Bernard lowers his feet off the table and listens. Jenny, his father's secretary, enters.

JENNY: *(distressed)* Say, Bernard, will you go out in the hall?
BERNARD: What is that noise? Who is it?
JENNY: Mr. Loman. He just got off the elevator.   260
BERNARD: *(getting up)* Who's he arguing with?
JENNY: Nobody. There's nobody with him. I can't deal with him any more, and your father gets all upset everytime he comes. I've got a lot of typing to do, and your father's waiting to sign it. Will you see him?
WILLY: *(entering)* Touchdown! Touch—*(He sees Jenny.)* Jenny, Jenny, good to see you. How're ya? Workin'? Or still honest?
JENNY: Fine. How've you been feeling?
WILLY: Not much any more, Jenny. Ha, ha! *(He is surprised to see the rackets.)*   265
BERNARD: Hello, Uncle Willy.
WILLY: *(almost shocked)* Bernard! Well, look who's here! *(He comes quickly, guiltily, to Bernard and warmly shakes his hand.)*
BERNARD: How are you? Good to see you.
WILLY: What are you doing here?
BERNARD: Oh, just stopped by to see Pop. Get off my feet till my train leaves. I'm going to   270
Washington in a few minutes.
WILLY: Is he in?
BERNARD: Yes, he's in his office with the accountant. Sit down.
WILLY: *(sitting down)* What're you going to do in Washington?
BERNARD: Oh, just a case I've got there, Willy.
WILLY: That so? *(indicating the rackets)* You going to play tennis there?   275
BERNARD: I'm staying with a friend who's got a court.
WILLY: Don't say. His own tennis court. Must be fine people, I bet.
BERNARD: They are, very nice. Dad tells me Biff's in town.
WILLY: *(with a big smile)* Yeah, Biff's in. Working on a very big deal, Bernard.
BERNARD: What's Biff doing?   280
WILLY: Well, he's been doing very big things in the West. But he decided to establish himself here. Very big. We're having dinner. Did I hear your wife had a boy?
BERNARD: That's right. Our second.
WILLY: Two boys! What do you know!
BERNARD: What kind of a deal has Biff got?
WILLY: Well, Bill Oliver—very big sporting-goods man—he wants Biff very badly. Called   285
him in from the West. Long distance, carte blanche, special deliveries. Your friends have their own private tennis court?
BERNARD: You still with the old firm, Willy?
WILLY: *(after a pause)* I'm—I'm overjoyed to see how you made the grade, Bernard, overjoyed. It's an encouraging thing to see a young man really—really—Looks very

good for Biff—very—*(He breaks off, then.)* Bernard—*(He is so full of emotion, he breaks off again.)*

BERNARD: What is it, Willy?

WILLY: *(small and alone)* What—what's the secret?

BERNARD: What secret?

WILLY: How—how did you? Why didn't he ever catch on?

BERNARD: I wouldn't know that, Willy.

WILLY: *(confidentially, desperately)* You were his friend, his boyhood friend. There's something I don't understand about it. His life ended after that Ebbets Field game. From the age of seventeen nothing good ever happened to him.

BERNARD: He never trained himself for anything.

WILLY: But he did, he did. After high school he took so many correspondence courses. Radio mechanics; television; God knows what, and never made the slightest mark.

BERNARD: *(taking off his glasses)* Willy, do you want to talk candidly?

WILLY: *(rising, faces Bernard)* I regard you as a very brilliant man, Bernard. I value your advice.

BERNARD: Oh, the hell with the advise, Willy. I couldn't advise you. There's just one thing I've always wanted to ask you. When he was supposed to graduate, and the math teacher flunked him—

WILLY: Oh, that son-of-a-bitch ruined his life.

BERNARD: Yeah, but, Willy, all he had to do was go to summer school and make up that subject.

WILLY: That's right, that's right.

BERNARD: Did you tell him not to go to summer school?

WILLY: Me? I begged him to go. I ordered him to go!

BERNARD: Then why wouldn't he go?

WILLY: Why? Why! Bernard, that question has been trailing me like a ghost for the last fifteen years. He flunked the subject, and laid down and died like a hammer hit him!

BERNARD: Take it easy, kid.

WILLY: Let me talk to you—I got nobody to talk to. Bernard, Bernard, was it my fault? Y'see? It keeps going around in my mind, maybe I did something to him. I got nothing to give him.

BERNARD: Don't take it so hard.

WILLY: Why did he lay down? What is the story there? You were his friend!

BERNARD: Willy, I remember, it was June, and our grades came out. And he flunked math.

WILLY: That son-of-a-bitch!

BERNARD: No, it wasn't right then. Biff just got very angry, I remember, and he was ready to enroll in summer school.

WILLY: *(surprised)* He was?

BERNARD: He wasn't beaten by it at all. But then, Willy, he disappeared from the block for almost a month. And I got the idea that he'd gone up to New England to see you. Did he have a talk with you then?

Willy stares in silence.

BERNARD: Willy?

WILLY: *(with a strong edge of resentment in his voice)* Yeah, he came to Boston. What about it?

BERNARD: Well, just that when he came back—I'll never forget this, it always mystifies me. Because I'd thought so well of Biff, even though he'd always taken advantage of me. I loved him, Willy, y'know? And he came back after that month and took his sneakers—remember those sneakers with "University of Virginia" printed on them? He was so proud of those, wore them every day. And he took them down in the cellar, and burned them up in the furnace. We had a fist fight. It lasted at least half an hour. Just the two of us, punching each other down the cellar, and crying right through it. I've often thought of how strange it was that I knew he'd given up his life. What happened in Boston, Willy?

Willy looks at him as at an intruder.

BERNARD: I just bring it up because you asked me.

WILLY: *(angrily)* Nothing. What do you mean, "What happened?" What's that got to do with anything?

BERNARD: Well, don't get sore.   320

WILLY: What are you trying to do, blame it on me? If a boy lays down is that my fault?

BERNARD: Now, Willy, don't get—

WILLY: Well, don't—don't talk to me that way! What does that mean, "What happened?"

Charley enters. He is in his vest, and he carries a bottle of bourbon.

CHARLEY: Hey, you're going to miss that train. *(He waves the bottle.)*

BERNARD: Yeah, I'm going. *(He takes the bottle.)* Thanks, Pop. *(He picks up his rackets*   325
and bag.) Good-by, Willy, and don't worry about it. You know, "If at first you don't succeed . . ."

WILLY: Yes, I believe in that.

BERNARD: But sometimes, Willy, it's better for a man just to walk away.

WILLY: Walk away?

BERNARD: That's right.

WILLY: But if you can't walk away?   330

BERNARD: *(after a slight pause)* I guess that's when it's tough. *(Extending his hand.)* Good-by, Willy.

WILLY: *(shaking Bernard's hand)* Good-by, boy.

CHARLEY: *(an arm on Bernard's shoulder)* How do you like this kid? Gonna argue a case in front of the Supreme Court.

BERNARD: *(protesting)* Pop!

WILLY: *(genuinely, shocked, pained, and happy)* No! The Supreme Court!   335

BERNARD: I gotta run. 'By, Dad!

CHARLEY: Knock 'em dead, Bernard!

Bernard goes off.

WILLY: *(as Charley takes out his wallet)* The Supreme Court! And he didn't even mention it!

CHARLEY: *(counting out money on the desk)* He don't have to—he's gonna do it.

WILLY: And you never told him what to do, did you? You never took any interest in him.   340

CHARLEY: My salvation is that I never took any interest in anything. There's some money—fifty dollars. I got an accountant inside.

WILLY: Charley, look . . . *(With difficulty.)* I got my insurance to pay. If you can manage it—I need a hundred and ten dollars.

Charley doesn't reply for a moment; merely stops moving.

WILLY: I'd draw it from my bank but Linda would know, and I . . .

CHARLEY: Sit down, Willy.

WILLY: *(moving toward the chair)* I'm keeping an account of everything, remember.   345
I'll pay every penny back. *(He sits.)*

CHARLEY: Now listen to me, Willy.

WILLY: I want you to know I appreciate . . .

CHARLEY: *(sitting down on the table)* Willy, what're you doin'? What the hell is goin' on in your head?

WILLY: Why? I'm simply . . .

CHARLEY: I offered you a job. You can make fifty dollars a week. And I won't send you on   350
the road.

WILLY: I've got a job.

CHARLEY: Without pay? What kind of a job is a job without pay? *(He rises.)* Now, look, kid, enough is enough. I'm no genius but I know when I'm being insulted.

WILLY: Insulted!

CHARLEY: Why don't you want to work for me?

WILLY: What's the matter with you? I've got a job.   355

CHARLEY: Then what're you walkin' in here every week for?

WILLY: *(getting up)* Well, if you don't want me to walk in here—

CHARLEY: I am offering you a job.

WILLY: I don't want your goddam job!

CHARLEY: When the hell are you going to grow up?   360

WILLY: *(furiously)* You big ignoramus, if you say that to me again I'll rap you one! I don't
care how big you are! *(He's ready to fight.)*

Pause.

CHARLEY: *(kindly, going to him)* How much do you need, Willy?

WILLY: Charley, I'm strapped. I'm strapped. I don't know what to do. I was just fired.

CHARLEY: Howard fired you?

WILLY: That snotnose. Imagine that? I named him. I named him Howard.   365

CHARLEY: Willy, when're you gonna realize that them things don't mean anything? You
named him Howard, but you can't sell that. The only thing you got in this world is
what you can sell. And the funny thing is that you're a salesman, and you don't know
that.

WILLY: I've always tried to think otherwise, I guess. I always felt that if a man was impressive, and well liked, that nothing—

CHARLEY: Why must everybody like you? Who liked J. P. Morgan? Was he impressive? In a
Turkish bath he'd look like a butcher. But with his pockets on he was very well
liked. Now listen, Willy, I know you don't like me, and nobody can say I'm in love
with you, but I'll give you a job because—just for the hell of it, put it that way. Now
what do you say?

WILLY: I—I just can't work for you, Charley.

CHARLEY: What're you, jealous of me?   370

WILLY: I can't work for you, that's all, don't ask me why.

CHARLEY: *(angered, takes out more bills)* You been jealous of me all your life, you
damned fool! Here, pay your insurance. *(He puts the money in Willy's hand.)*

WILLY: I'm keeping strict accounts.

CHARLEY: I've got some work to do. Take care of yourself. And pay your insurance.

WILLY: *(moving to the right)* Funny, y'know? After all the highways, and the trains, and   375
the appointments, and the years, you end up worth more dead than alive.

CHARLEY: Willy, nobody's worth nothin' dead. *(After a slight pause.)* Did you hear what
I said?

Willy stands still, dreaming.

CHARLEY: Willy!

WILLY: Apologize to Bernard for me when you see him. I didn't mean to argue with him.
He's a fine boy. They're all fine boys, and they'll end up big—all of them. Someday
they'll all play tennis together. Wish me luck, Charley. He saw Bill Oliver today.

CHARLEY: Good luck.

WILLY: *(on the verge of tears)* Charley, you're the only friend I got. Isn't that a remark-   380
able thing? *(He goes out.)*

CHARLEY: Jesus!

*Charley stares after him a moment and follows. All light blacks out. Suddenly raucous music is heard,
and a red glow rises behind the screen at right. Stanley, a young waiter, appears, carrying a table, followed by Happy, who is carrying two chairs.*

STANLEY: *(putting the table down)* That's all right, Mr. Loman, I can handle it myself. *(He
turns and takes the chairs from Happy and places them at the table.)*

HAPPY: *(glancing around)* Oh, this is better.

STANLEY: Sure, in the front there you're in the middle of all kinds a noise. Whenever you
    got a party, Mr. Loman, you just tell me and I'll put you back here. Y'know, there's a
    lotta people they don't like it private, because when they go out they like to see a
    lotta action around them because they're sick and tired to stay in the house by their-
    self. But I know you, you ain't from Hackensack. You know what I mean?

HAPPY: *(sitting down)* So, how's it coming, Stanley?   385

STANLEY: Ah, it's a dog's life. I only wish during the war they'd a took me in the Army. I
    coulda been dead by now.

HAPPY: My brother's back, Stanley.

STANLEY: Oh, he come back, heh? From the Far West.

HAPPY: Yeah, big cattle man, my brother, so treat him right. And my father's coming too.

STANLEY: Oh, your father too!   390

HAPPY: You got a couple of nice lobsters?

STANLEY: Hundred per cent, big.

HAPPY: I want them with the claws.

STANLEY: Don't worry, I don't give you no mice. *(Happy laughs.)* How about some
    wine? It'll put a head on the meal.

HAPPY: No. You remember, Stanley, that recipe I brought you from overseas? With the   395
    champagne in it?

STANLEY: Oh, yeah, sure. I still got it tacked up yet in the kitchen. But that'll have to cost
    a buck apiece anyways.

HAPPY: That's all right.

STANLEY: What'd you, hit a number or somethin'?

HAPPY: No, it's a little celebration. My brother is—I think he pulled off a big deal today.
    I think we're going into business together.

STANLEY: Great! That's the best for you. Because a family business, you know what I   400
    mean?—that's the best.

HAPPY: That's what I think.

STANLEY: 'Cause what's the difference? Somebody steals? It's in the family. Know what I
    mean? *(Sotto voce.)* Like this bartender here. The boss is goin' crazy what kinda leak
    he's got in the cash register. You put it in but it don't come out.

HAPPY: *(raising his head)* Sh!

STANLEY: What?

HAPPY: You notice I wasn't lookin' right or left, was I?   405

STANLEY: No.

HAPPY: And my eyes are closed.

STANLEY: So what's the—

HAPPY: Strudel's comin'.

STANLEY: *(catching on, looks around)* Ah, no, there's no—   410

*He breaks off as a furred, lavishly dressed Girl enters and sits at the next table. Both follow her with
their eyes.*

STANLEY: Geez, how'd ya know?

HAPPY: I got radar or something. *(Staring directly at her profile.)* Oooooooo . . . Stanley.

STANLEY: I think that's for you, Mr. Loman.

HAPPY: Look at that mouth. Oh, God. And the binoculars.

STANLEY: Geez, you got a life, Mr. Loman.   415

HAPPY: Wait on her.

STANLEY: *(going to The Girl's table)* Would you like a menu, ma'am?

GIRL: I'm expecting someone, but I'd like a—

HAPPY: Why don't you bring her—excuse me, miss, do you mind? I sell champagne, and
    I'd like you to try my brand. Bring her a champagne, Stanley.

GIRL: That's awfully nice of you.   420

HAPPY: Don't mention it. It's all company money. *(He laughs.)*

GIRL: That's a charming product to be selling, isn't it?

HAPPY: Oh, gets to be like everything else. Selling is selling, y'know.

GIRL: I suppose.

HAPPY: You don't happen to sell, do you?   425

GIRL: No, I don't sell.

HAPPY: Would you object to a compliment from a stranger? You ought to be on a maga-
          zine cover.

GIRL: *(looking at him a little archly)* I have been.

Stanley comes in with a glass of champagne.

HAPPY: What'd I say before, Stanley? You see? She's a cover girl.

STANLEY: Oh, I could see, I could see.   430

HAPPY: *(to The Girl)* What magazine?

GIRL: Oh, a lot of them. *(She takes the drink.)* Thank you.

HAPPY: You know what they say in France, don't you? "Champagne is the drink of the
          complexion"—Hya, Biff!

Biff has entered and sits with Happy.

BIFF: Hello, kid. Sorry I'm late.

HAPPY: I just got here. Uh, Miss—?   435

GIRL: Forsythe.

HAPPY: Miss Forsythe, this is my bother.

BIFF: Is Dad here?

HAPPY: His name is Biff. You might've heard of him. Great football player.

GIRL: Really? What team?   440

HAPPY: Are you familiar with football?

GIRL: No, I'm afraid I'm not.

HAPPY: Biff is quarterback with the New York Giants.

GIRL: Well, that is nice, isn't it? *(She drinks.)*

HAPPY: Good health.   445

GIRL: I'm happy to meet you.

HAPPY: That's my name. Hap. It's really Harold, but at West Point they called me Happy.

GIRL: *(now really impressed)* Oh, I see. How do you do? *(She turns her profile.)*

BIFF: Isn't Dad coming?

HAPPY: You want her?   450

BIFF: Oh, I could never make that.

HAPPY: I remember the time that idea would never come into your head. Where's the
          old confidence, Biff?

BIFF: I just saw Oliver—

HAPPY: Wait a minute. I've got to see that old confidence again. Do you want her? She's
          on call.

BIFF: Oh, no. *(He turns to look at The Girl.)*   455

HAPPY: I'm telling you. Watch this. *(Turning to The Girl.)* Honey? *(She turns to him.)*
          Are you busy?

GIRL: Well, I am . . . but I could make a phone call.

HAPPY: Do that, will you, honey? And see if you can get a friend. We'll be here for a
          while. Biff is one of the greatest football players in the country.

GIRL: *(standing up)* Well, I'm certainly happy to meet you.

HAPPY: Come back soon.   460

GIRL: I'll try.

HAPPY: Don't try, honey, try hard.

The Girl exits. Stanley follows, shaking his head in bewildered admiration.

HAPPY: Isn't that a shame now? A beautiful girl like that? That's why I can't get married.
          There's not a good woman in a thousand. New York is loaded with them, kid!

BIFF: Hap, look—
HAPPY: I told you she was on call!   465
BIFF: *(strangely unnerved)* Cut it out, will ya? I want to say something to you.
HAPPY: Did you see Oliver?
BIFF: I saw him all right. Now look, I want to tell Dad a couple of things and I want you
         to help me.
HAPPY: What? Is he going to back you?   470
BIFF: Are you crazy? You're out of your goddam head, you know that?
HAPPY: Why? What happened?
BIFF: *(breathlessly)* I did a terrible thing today, Hap. It's been the strangest day I ever
         went through. I'm all numb, I swear.
HAPPY: You mean he wouldn't see you?
BIFF: Well, I waited six hours for him, see? All day. Kept sending my name in. Even tried
         to date his secretary so she'd get me to him, but no soap.
HAPPY: Because you're not showin' the old confidence, Biff. He remembered you, didn't   475
         he?
BIFF: *(stopping Happy with a gesture)* Finally, about five o'clock, he comes out. Didn't
         remember who I was or anything. I felt like such an idiot, Hap.
HAPPY: Did you tell him my Florida idea?
BIFF: He walked away. I saw him for one minute. I got so mad I could've torn the walls
         down! How the hell did I ever get the idea I was a salesman there? I even believed
         myself that I'd been a salesman for him! And then he gave me one look and—I real-
         ized what a ridiculous lie my whole life has been! We've been talking in a dream for
         fifteen years. I was a shipping clerk.
HAPPY: What'd you do?
BIFF: *(with great tension and wonder)* Well, he left, see. And the secretary went out. I   480
         was all alone in the waiting room. I don't know what came over me, Hap. The next
         thing I know I'm in his office—paneled walls, everything. I can't explain it. I—Hap,
         I took his fountain pen.
HAPPY: Geez, did he catch you?
BIFF: I ran out. I ran down all eleven flights. I ran and ran and ran.
HAPPY: That was an awful dumb—what'd you do that for?
BIFF: *(agonized)* I don't know, I just—wanted to take something, I don't know. You
         gotta help me, Hap. I'm gonna tell Pop.
HAPPY: You crazy? What for?   485
BIFF: Hap, he's got to understand that I'm not the man somebody lends that kind of
         money to. He thinks I've been spiting him all these years and it's eating him up.
HAPPY: That's just it. You tell him something nice.
BIFF: I can't.
HAPPY: Say you got a lunch date with Oliver tomorrow.
BIFF: So what do I do tomorrow?   490
HAPPY: You leave the house tomorrow and come back at night and say Oliver is think-
         ing it over. And he thinks it over for a couple of weeks, and gradually it fades away
         and nobody's the worse.
BIFF: But it'll go on forever!
HAPPY: Dad is never so happy as when he's looking forward to something!
Willy enters.
HAPPY: Hello, scout!
WILLY: Gee, I haven't been here in years!   495
Stanley has followed Willy in and sets a chair for him. Stanley starts off but Happy stops him.
HAPPY: Stanley!
Stanley stands by, waiting for an order.
BIFF: *(going to Willy with guilt, as to an invalid)* Sit down, Pop. You want a drink?

WILLY: Sure, I don't mind.
BIFF: Let's get a load on.
WILLY: You look worried.   500
BIFF: N-no. *(To Stanley.)* Scotch all around. Make it doubles.
STANLEY: Doubles, right. *(He goes.)*
WILLY: You had a couple already, didn't you?
BIFF: Just a couple, yeah.
WILLY: Well, what happened, boy? *(Nodding affirmatively, with a smile.)* Everything   505
    go all right?
BIFF: *(takes a breath, then reaches out and grasps Willy's hand)* Pal ... *(He is smiling*
    bravely, and Willy is smiling too.) I had an experience today.
HAPPY: Terrific, Pop.
WILLY: That so? What happened?
BIFF: *(high, slightly alcoholic, above the earth)* I'm going to tell you everything from
    first to last. It's been a strange day. *(Silence. He looks around, composes himself as*
    best he can, but his breath keeps breaking the rhythm of his voice.) I had to wait
    quite a while for him, and—
WILLY: Oliver?   510
BIFF: Yeah, Oliver. All day, as a matter of cold fact. And a lot of—instances—facts, Pop,
    facts about my life came back to me. Who was it, Pop? Who ever said I was a sales-
    man with Oliver?
WILLY: Well, you were.
BIFF: No, Dad, I was a shipping clerk.
WILLY: But you were practically—
BIFF: *(with determination)* Dad, I don't know who said it first, but I was never a sales-   515
    man for Bill Oliver.
WILLY: What're you talking about?
BIFF: Let's hold on to the facts tonight, Pop. We're not going to get anywhere bullin'
    around. I was a shipping clerk.
WILLY: *(angrily)* All right, now listen to me—
BIFF: Why don't you let me finish?
WILLY: I'm not interested in stories about the past or any crap of that kind because the   520
    woods are burning, boys, you understand? There's a big blaze going on all around. I
    was fired today.
BIFF: *(shocked)* How could you be?
WILLY: I was fired, and I'm looking for a little good news to tell your mother, because
    the woman has waited and the woman has suffered. The gist of it is that I haven't got
    a story left in my head, Biff. So don't give me a lecture about facts and aspects. I am
    not interested. Now what've you got to say to me?

Stanley enters with three drinks. They wait until he leaves.

WILLY: Did you see Oliver?
BIFF: Jesus, Dad!
WILLY: You mean you didn't go up there?   525
HAPPY: Sure he went up there.
BIFF: I did. I saw—him. How could they fire you?
WILLY: *(on the edge of his chair)* What kind of a welcome did he give you?
BIFF: He won't even let you work on commission?
WILLY: I'm out! *(Driving.)* So tell me, he gave you a warm welcome?   530
HAPPY: Sure, Pop, sure!
BIFF: *(driven)* Well, it was kind of—
WILLY: I was wondering if he'd remember you. *(To Happy.)* Imagine, man doesn't see
    him for ten, twelve years and gives him that kind of a welcome!
HAPPY: Damn right!

Biff: *(trying to return to the offensive)* Pop, look—   535
Willy: You know why he remembered you, don't you? Because you impressed him in
those days.
Biff: Let's talk quietly and get this down to the facts, huh?
Willy: *(as though Biff had been interrupting)* Well, what happened? It's great news,
Biff. Did he take you into his office or'd you talk in the waiting-room?
Biff: Well, he came in, see, and—
Willy: *(With a big smile)* What'd he say? Betcha he threw his arm around you.   540
Biff: Well, he kinda—
Willy: He's a fine man. *(To Happy.)* Very hard man to see, y'know.
Happy: *(agreeing)* Oh, I know.
Willy: *(to Biff)* Is that where you had the drinks?
Biff: Yeah, he gave me a couple of—no, no!   545
Happy: *(cutting in)* He told him my Florida idea.
Willy: Don't interrupt. *(To Biff.)* How'd he react to the Florida idea?
Biff: Dad, will you give me a minute to explain?
Willy: I've been waiting for you to explain since I sat down here! What happened? He
took you into his office and what?
Biff: Well—I talked. And—and he listened, see.   550
Willy: Famous for the way he listens, y'know. What was his answer?
Biff: His answer was—*(He breaks off, suddenly angry.)* Dad, you're not letting me tell
you what I want to tell you!
Willy: *(accusing, angered)* You didn't see him, did you?
Biff: I did see him!
Willy: What'd you insult him or something? You insulted him, didn't you?   555
Biff: Listen, will you let me out of it, will you just let me out of it!
Happy: What the hell!
Willy: Tell me what happened!
Biff: *(to Happy)* I can't talk to him!

*A single trumpet note jars the ear. The light of green leaves stains the house, which holds the air of
night and a dream. Young Bernard enters and knocks on the door of the house.*

Young Bernard: *(frantically)* Mrs. Loman, Mrs. Loman!   560
Happy: Tell him what happened!
Biff: *(to Happy)* Shut up and leave me alone!
Willy: No, no! You had to go and flunk math!
Biff: What math? What're you talking about?
Young Bernard: Mrs. Loman, Mrs. Loman!   565

Linda appears in the house, as of old.

Willy: *(wildly)* Math, math, math!
Biff: Take it easy, Pop!
Young Bernard: Mrs. Loman!
Willy: *(furiously)* If you hadn't flunked you'd 've been set by now!
Biff: Now, look, I'm gonna tell you what happened, and you're going to listen to me.   570
Young Bernard: Mrs. Loman!
Biff: I waited six hours—
Happy: What the hell are you saying?
Biff: I kept sending in my name but he wouldn't see me. So finally he ... *(He continues
unheard as light fades low on the restaurant.)*
Young Bernard: Biff flunked math!   575
Linda: No!
Young Bernard: Birnbaum flunked him! They won't graduate him!
Linda: But they have to. He's gotta go to the university. Where is he? Biff! Biff!

YOUNG BERNARD: No, he left. He went to Grand Central.
LINDA: Grand—You mean he went to Boston!   580
YOUNG BERNARD: Is Uncle Willy in Boston?
LINDA: Oh, maybe Willy can talk to the teacher. Oh, the poor, poor boy!

Light on house area snaps out.

BIFF: *(at the table, now audible, holding up a gold fountain pen)* ...so I'm washed up
    with Oliver, you understand? Are you listening to me?
WILLY: *(at a loss)* Yeah, sure. If you hadn't flunked—
BIFF: Flunked what? What're you talking about?   585
WILLY: Don't blame everything on me! I didn't flunk math—you did! What pen?
HAPPY: That was awful dumb, Biff, a pen like that is worth—
WILLY: *(seeing the pen for the first time)* You took Oliver's pen?
BIFF: *(weakening)* Dad, I just explained it to you.
WILLY: You stole Bill Oliver's fountain pen!   590
BIFF: I didn't exactly steal it! That's just what I've been explaining to you!
HAPPY: He had it in his hand and just then Oliver walked in, so he got nervous and stuck
    it in his pocket!
WILLY: My God, Biff!
BIFF: I never intended to do it, Dad!
OPERATOR'S VOICE: Standish Arms, good evening!   595
WILLY: *(shouting)* I'm not in my room!
BIFF: *(frightened)* Dad, what's the matter? *(He and Happy stand up.)*
OPERATOR: Ringing Mr. Loman for you!
WILLY: I'm not there, stop it.
BIFF: *(horrified, gets down on one knee before Willy)* Dad, I'll make good, I'll make   600
    good. *(Willy tries to get to his feet. Biff holds him down.)* Sit down now.
WILLY: No, you're no good, you're no good for anything.
BIFF: I am, Dad, I'll find something else, you understand? Now don't worry about any-
    thing. *(He holds up Willy's face.)* Talk to me, Dad.
OPERATOR: Mr. Loman does not answer. Shall I page him?
WILLY: *(attempting to stand, as though to rush and silence the Operator)* No, no, no!
HAPPY: He'll strike something, Pop.   605
WILLY: No, no ...
BIFF: *(desperately, standing over Willy)* Pop, listen! Listen to me! I'm telling you some-
    thing good. Oliver talked to his partner about the Florida idea. You listening? He—he
    talked to his partner and he came to me ... I'm going to be all right, you hear? Dad,
    listen to me, he said it was just a question of the amount!
WILLY: Then you ... got it?
HAPPY: He's gonna be terrific, Pop!
WILLY: *(trying to stand)* Then you got it, haven't you? You got it! You got it!   610
BIFF: *(agonized, holds Willy down)* No, no. Look, Pop. I'm supposed to have lunch with
    them tomorrow. I'm just telling you this so you'll know that I can still make an im-
    pression, Pop. And I'll make good somewhere, but I can't go tomorrow, see?
WILLY: Why not? You simply—
BIFF: But the pen, Pop!
WILLY: You give it to him and tell him it was an oversight!
HAPPY: Sure, have lunch tomorrow!   615
BIFF: I can't say that—
WILLY: You were doing a crossword puzzle and accidentally used his pen!
BIFF: Listen, kid, I took those balls years ago, now I walk in with his fountain pen? That
    clinches it, don't you see? I can't face him like that! I'll try elsewhere.
PAGE'S VOICE: Paging Mr. Loman!
WILLY: Don't you want to be anything?   620

Biff: Pop, how can I go back?

Willy: You don't want to be anything, is that what's behind it?

Biff: *(now angry at Willy for not crediting his sympathy)* Don't take it that way! You
think it was easy walking into that office after what I'd done to him? A team of
horses couldn't have dragged me back to Bill Oliver!

Willy: Then why'd you go?

Biff: Why did I go? Why did I go? Look at you! Look at what's become of you!   625

Off left, The Woman laughs.

Willy: Biff, you're going to go to that lunch tomorrow, or—

Biff: I can't go. I've got no appointment!

Happy: Biff, for . . .!

Willy: Are you spiting me?

Biff: Don't take it that way! Goddammit!   630

Willy: *(strikes Biff and falters away from the table)* You rotten little louse! Are you
spiting me?

The Woman: Someone's at the door, Willy!

Biff: I'm no good, can't you see what I am?

Happy: *(separating them)* Hey, you're in a restaurant! Now cut it out, both of you! *(The
Girls enter.)* Hello, girls, sit down.

The Woman laughs, off left.

Miss Forsythe: I guess we might as well. This is Letta.   635

The Woman: Willy, are you going to wake up?

Biff: *(ignoring Willy)* How're ya, miss, sit down. What do you drink?

Miss Forsythe: Letta might not be able to stay long.

Letta: I gotta get up very early tomorrow. I got jury duty. I'm so excited! Were you fellows ever on a jury?

Biff: No, but I been in front of them! *(The Girls laugh.)* This is my father.   640

Letta: Isn't he cute? Sit down with us, Pop.

Happy: Sit him down, Biff!

Biff: *(going to him)* Come on, slugger, drink us under the table. To hell with it! Come
on, sit down, pal.

On Biff's last insistence, Willy is about to sit.

The Woman: *(now urgently)* Willy, are you going to answer the door!

The Woman's call pulls Willy back. He starts right, befuddled.

Biff: Hey, where are you going?   645

Willy: Open the door.

Biff: The door?

Willy: The washroom . . . the door . . . where's the door?

Biff: *(leading Willy to the left)* Just go straight down.

Willy moves left.

The Woman: Willy, Willy, are you going to get up, get up, get up, get up?   650

Willy exits left.

Letta: I think it's sweet you bring your daddy along.

Miss Forsythe: Oh, he isn't really your father!

Biff: *(at left, turning to her resentfully)* Miss Forsythe, you've just seen a prince walk
by. A fine, troubled prince. A hard-working, unappreciated prince. A pal, you understand? A good companion. Always for his boys.

Letta: That's so sweet.

Happy: Well, girls, what's the program? We're wasting time. Come on, Biff. Gather round.   655
Where would you like to go?

Biff: Why don't you do something for him?

HAPPY: Me!

BIFF: Don't you give a damn for him, Hap?

HAPPY: What're you talking about? I'm the one who—

BIFF: I sense it, you don't give a good goddam about him. *(He takes the rolled-up hose*   660
from his pocket and puts it on the table in front of Happy.) Look what I found in
the cellar, for Christ's sake. How can you bear to let it go on?

HAPPY: Me? Who goes away? Who runs off and—

BIFF: Yeah, but he doesn't mean anything to you. You could help him—I can't! Don't
you understand what I'm talking about? He's going to kill himself, don't you know
that?

HAPPY: Don't I know it! Me!

BIFF: Hap, help him! Jesus . . . help him . . . Help me, help me, I can't bear to look at his
face! *(Ready to weep, he hurries out, up right.)*

HAPPY: *(starting after him)* Where are you going?   665

MISS FORSYTHE: What's he so mad about?

HAPPY: Come on girls, we'll catch up with him.

MISS FORSYTHE: *(as Happy pushes her out)* Say, I don't like that temper of his!

HAPPY: He's just a little overstrung, he'll be all right!

WILLY: *(off left, as The Woman laughs)* Don't answer! Don't answer!   670

LETTA: Don't you want to tell your father—

HAPPY: No, that's not my father. He's just a guy. Come on, we'll catch Biff, and, honey,
we're going to paint this town! Stanley, where's the check! Hey, Stanley!

They exit. Stanley looks toward left.

STANLEY: *(calling to Happy indignantly)* Mr. Loman! Mr. Loman!

Stanley picks up a chair and follows them off. Knocking is heard off left. The Woman enters, laugh-
ing. Willy follows her. She is in a black slip; he is buttoning his shirt. Raw, sensuous music accompa-
nies their speech.

WILLY: Will you stop laughing? Will you stop?

THE WOMAN: Aren't you going to answer the door? He'll wake the whole hotel.   675

WILLY: I'm not expecting anybody.

THE WOMAN: Whyn't you have another drink, honey, and stop being so damn self-centered?

WILLY: I'm so lonely.

THE WOMAN: You know you ruined me, Willy? From now on, whenever you come to the
office, I'll see that you go right through to the buyers. No waiting at my desk any
more, Willy. You ruined me.

WILLY: That's nice of you to say that.   680

THE WOMAN: Gee, you are self-centered! Why so sad? You are the saddest self-centeredest
soul I ever did see-saw. *(She laughs. He kisses her.)* Come on inside, drummer boy.
It's silly to be dressing in the middle of the night. *(As knocking is heard.)* Aren't you
going to answer the door?

WILLY: They're knocking on the wrong door.

THE WOMAN: But I felt the knocking. And he heard us talking in here. Maybe the hotel's
on fire!

WILLY: *(his terror rising)* It's a mistake.

THE WOMAN: Then tell him to go away!   685

WILLY: There's nobody there.

THE WOMAN: It's getting on my nerves, Willy. There's somebody standing out there and
it's getting on my nerves!

WILLY: *(pushing her away from him)* All right, stay in the bathroom here, and don't
come out. I think there's a law in Massachusetts about it, so don't come out. It may
be that new room clerk. He looked very mean. So don't come out. It's a mistake,
there's no fire.

The knocking is heard again. He takes a few steps away from her, and she vanishes into the wing. The light follows him, and now he is facing Young Biff, who carries a suitcase. Biff steps toward him. The music is gone.

BIFF: Why didn't you answer?

WILLY: Biff! What are you doing in Boston?

BIFF: Why didn't you answer? I've been knocking for five minutes. I called you on the phone— 690

WILLY: I just heard you. I was in the bathroom and had the door shut. Did anything happen home?

BIFF: Dad—I let you down.

WILLY: What do you mean?

BIFF: Dad . . . 695

WILLY: Biffo, what's this about? *(Putting his arm around Biff.)* Come on, let's go downstairs and get you a malted.

BIFF: Dad, I flunked math.

WILLY: Not for the term?

BIFF: The term. I haven't got enough credits to graduate.

WILLY: You mean to say Bernard wouldn't give you the answers? 700

BIFF: He did, he tried, but I only got a sixty-one.

WILLY: And they wouldn't give you four points?

BIFF: Birnbaum refused absolutely. I begged him, Pop, but he won't give me those points. You gotta talk to him before they close the school. Because if he saw the kind of man you are, and you just talked to him in your way, I'm sure he'd come through for me. The class came right before practice, see, and I didn't go enough. Would you talk to him? He'd like you, Pop. You know the way you could talk.

WILLY: You're on. We'll drive right back.

BIFF: Oh, Dad, good work! I'm sure he'll change it for you! 705

WILLY: Go downstairs and tell the clerk I'm checkin' out. Go right down.

BIFF: Yes Sir! See, the reason he hates me, Pop—one day he was late for class so I got up at the blackboard and imitated him. I crossed my eyes and talked with a lithp.

WILLY: *(laughing)* You did? The kids like it?

BIFF: They nearly died laughing!

WILLY: Yeah? What'd you do? 710

BIFF: The thquare root of thixthy twee is . . . *(Willy bursts out laughing; Biff joins him.)* And in the middle of it he walked in!

Willy laughs and The Woman joins in offstage.

WILLY: *(without hesitating)* Hurry downstairs and—

BIFF: Somebody in there?

WILLY: No, that was next door.

The Woman laughs offstage.

BIFF: Somebody got in your bathroom!

WILLY: No, it's the next room, there's a party— 715

THE WOMAN: *(enters, laughing. She lisps this)* Can I come in? There's something in the bathtub, Willy, and it's moving!

Willy looks at Biff, who is staring open-mouthed and horrified at The Woman.

WILLY: Ah—you better go back to your room. They must be finished painting by now. They're painting her room so I let her take a shower here. Go back, go back . . . *(He pushes her.)*

THE WOMAN: *(resisting)* But I've got to get dressed, Willy, I can't—

WILLY: Get out of her! Go back, go back . . . *(Suddenly striving for the ordinary.)* This is 720 Miss Francis, Biff, she's a buyer. They're painting her room. Go back, Miss Francis, go back . . .

THE WOMAN: But my clothes, I can't go out naked in the hall!

WILLY: *(pushing her offstage)* Get outa here! Go back, go back!

Biff slowly sits down on his suitcase as the argument continues offstage.

THE WOMAN: Where's my stockings? You promised me stockings, Willy!

WILLY: I have no stockings here!

THE WOMAN: You had two boxes of size nine sheers for me, and I want them!   725

WILLY: Here, for God's sake, will you get outa here!

THE WOMAN: *(enters holding a box of stockings)* I just hope there's nobody in the hall. That's all I hope. *(To Biff.)* Are you football or baseball?

BIFF: Football.

THE WOMAN: *(angry, humiliated)* That's me too. G'night. *(She snatches her clothes from Willy, and walks out.)*

WILLY: *(after a pause)* Well, better get going. I want to get to the school first thing in   730
the morning. Get my suits out of the closet. I'll get my valise. *(Biff doesn't move.)*
What's the matter? *(Biff remains motionless, tears falling.)* She's a buyer. Buys for
J. H. Simmons. She lives down the hall—they're painting. You don't imagine—*(He
breaks off. After a pause.)* Now listen, pal, she's just a buyer. She sees merchandise
in her room and they have to keep it looking just so . . . *(Pause. Assuming command.)* All right, get my suits. *(Biff doesn't move.)* Now stop crying and do as I say.
I gave you an order. Biff, I gave you an order! Is that what you do when I give you an
order? How dare you cry! *(Putting his arm around Biff.)* Now look, Biff, when you
grow up you'll understand about these things. You mustn't—you mustn't overem-
phasize a thing like this. I'll see Birnbaum first thing in the morning.

BIFF: Never mind.

WILLY: *(getting down beside Biff)* Never mind! He's going to give you those points. I'll
see to it.

BIFF: He wouldn't listen to you.

WILLY: He certainly will listen to me. You need those points for the U. of Virginia.

BIFF: I'm not going there.   735

WILLY: Heh? If I can't get him to change that mark you'll make it up in summer school.
You've got all summer to—

BIFF: *(his weeping breaking from him)* Dad . . .

WILLY: *(infected by it)* Oh, my boy . . .

BIFF: Dad . . .

WILLY: She's nothing to me, Biff. I was lonely, I was terribly lonely.   740

BIFF: You—you gave her Mama's stockings! *(His tears break through and he rises to
go.)*

WILLY: *(grabbing for Biff)* I gave you an order!

BIFF: Don't touch me, you—liar!

WILLY: Apologize for that!

BIFF: You fake! You phony little fake! You fake! *(Overcome, he turns quickly and weep-   745
ing fully goes out with his suitcase. Willy is left on the floor on his knees.)*

WILLY: I gave you an order! Biff, come back here or I'll beat you! Come back here! I'll
whip you!

Stanley comes quickly in from the right and stands in front of Willy.

WILLY: *(shouts at Stanley)* I gave you an order . . .

STANLEY: Hey, let's pick it up, pick it up, Mr. Loman. *(He helps Willy to his feet.)* Your boys
left with the chippies. They said they'll see you home.

A second waiter watches some distance away.

WILLY: But we were supposed to have dinner together.

Music is heard, Willy's theme.

STANLEY: Can you make it?   750

WILLY: I'll—sure, I can make it. *(Suddenly concerned about his clothes.)* Do I—I look all right?

STANLEY: Sure, you look all right. *(He flicks a speck off Willy's lapel.)*

WILLY: Here—here's a dollar.

STANLEY: Oh, your son paid me. It's all right.

WILLY: *(putting it in Stanley's hand)* No, take it. You're a good boy.   755

STANLEY: Oh, no, you don't have to . . .

WILLY: Here—here's some more, I don't need it any more. *(After a slight pause.)* Tell me—is there a seed store in the neighborhood?

STANLEY: Seeds? You mean like to plant?

As Willy turns, Stanley slips the money back into his jacket pocket.

WILLY: Yes. Carrots, peas . . .

STANLEY: Well, there's hardware stores on Sixth Avenue, but it may be too late now.   760

WILLY: *(anxiously)* Oh, I'd better hurry. I've got to get some seeds. *(He starts off to the right.)* I've got to get some seeds, right away. Nothing's planted. I don't have a thing in the ground.

Willy hurries out as the light goes down. Stanley moves over to the right after him, watches him off. The other waiter has been staring at Willy.

STANLEY: *(to the waiter)* Well, whatta you looking at?

The waiter picks up the chairs and moves off right. Stanley takes the table and follows him. The light fades on this area. There is a long pause, the sound of the flute coming over. The light gradually rises on the kitchen, which is empty. Happy appears at the door of the house, followed by Biff. Happy is carrying a large bunch of long-stemmed roses. He enters the kitchen, looks around for Linda. Not seeing her, he turns to Biff, who is just outside the house door, and makes a gesture with his hands, indicating "Not here, I guess." He looks into the livingroom and freezes. Inside, Linda, unseen, is seated, Willy's coat on her lap. She rises ominously and quietly and moves toward Happy, who backs up into the kitchen, afraid.

HAPPY: Hey, what're you doing up? *(Linda says nothing but moves toward him implacably.)* Where's Pop? *(He keeps backing to the right, and now Linda is in full view in the doorway to the livingroom.)* Is he sleeping?

LINDA: Where were you?

HAPPY: *(trying to laugh it off)* We met two girls, Mom, very fine types. Here, we brought   765
you some flowers. *(Offering them to her.)* Put them in your room, Ma.

She knocks them to the floor at Biff's feet. He has now come inside and closed the door behind him. She stares at Biff, silent.

HAPPY: Now what'd you do that for? Mom, I want you to have some flowers—

LINDA: *(cutting Happy off, violently to Biff)* Don't you care whether he lives or dies?

HAPPY: *(going to the stairs)* Come upstairs, Biff.

BIFF: *(with a flare of disgust, to Happy)* Go away from me! *(To Linda.)* What do you mean, lives or dies? Nobody's dying around here, pal.

LINDA: Get out of my sight! Get out of here!   770

BIFF: I wanna see the boss.

LINDA: You're not going near him!

BIFF: Where is he? *(He moves into the livingroom and Linda follows.)*

LINDA: *(shouting after Biff)* You invite him for dinner. He looks forward to it all day—
(Biff appears in his parents' bedroom, looks around, and exits)—and then you desert him there. There's no stranger you'd do that to!

HAPPY: Why? He had a swell time with us. Listen, when I—*(Linda comes back into the   775
kitchen)*—desert him I hope I don't outlive the day!

LINDA: Get out of here!

HAPPY: Now look, Mom . . .

LINDA: Did you have to go to women tonight? You and your lousy rotten whores!

Biff re-enters the kitchen.

HAPPY: Mom, all we did was follow Biff around trying to cheer him up! *(To Biff.)* Boy, what a night you gave me!

LINDA: Get out of here, both of you, and don't come back! I don't want you tormenting him any more. Go on now, get your things together! *(To Biff.)* You can sleep in his apartment. *(She starts to pick up the flowers and stops herself.)* Pick up this stuff, I'm not your maid any more. Pick it up, you bum, you!

Happy turns his back to her in refusal. Biff slowly moves over and gets down on his knees, picking up the flowers.

LINDA: You're a pair of animals! Not one, not another living soul would have had the cruelty to walk out on that man in a restaurant!

BIFF: *(not looking at her)* Is that what he said?

LINDA: He didn't have to say anything. He was so humiliated he nearly limped when he came in.

HAPPY: But, Mom he had a great time with us—

BIFF: *(cutting him off violently)* Shut up!

Without another word, Happy goes upstairs.

LINDA: You! You didn't even go in to see if he was all right!

BIFF: *(still on the floor in front of Linda, the flowers in his hand; with self-loathing)* No. Didn't. Didn't do a damned thing. How do you like that, heh? Left him babbling in a toilet.

LINDA: You louse. You . . .

BIFF: Now you hit it on the nose! *(He gets up, throws the flowers in the wastebasket.)* The scum of the earth, and you're looking at him!

LINDA: Get out of here!

BIFF: I gotta talk to the boss, Mom. Where is he?

LINDA: You're not going near him. Get out of this house!

BIFF: *(with absolute assurance, determination)* No. We're gonna have an abrupt conversation, him and me.

LINDA: You're not talking to him!

Hammering is heard from outside the house, off right. Biff turns toward the noise.

LINDA: *(suddenly pleading)* Will you please leave him alone?

BIFF: What's he doing out there?

LINDA: He's planting the garden!

BIFF: *(quietly)* Now? Oh, my God!

Biff moves outside, Linda following. The light dies down on them and comes up on the center of the apron as Willy walks into it. He is carrying a flashlight, a hoe and a handful of seed packets. He raps the top of the hoe sharply to fix it firmly, and then moves to the left, measuring off the distance with his foot. He holds the flashlight to look at the seed packets, reading off the instructions. He is in the blue of night.

WILLY: Carrots . . . quarter-inch apart. Rows . . . one-foot rows. *(He measures it off.)* One foot. *(He puts down a package and measures off.)* Beets. *(He puts down another package and measures again.)* Lettuce. *(He reads the package, puts it down.)* One foot—*(He breaks off as Ben appears at the right and moves slowly down to him.)* What a proposition, ts, ts. Terrific, terrific. 'Cause she's suffered, Ben, the woman has suffered. You understand me? A man can't go out the way he came in, Ben, a man has got to add up to something. You can't, you can't—*(Ben moves toward him as though to interrupt.)* You gotta consider, now. Don't answer so quick. Remember, it's a guaranteed twenty-thousand-dollar proposition. Now look, Ben, I want you to go through the ins and outs of this thing with me. I've got nobody to talk to, Ben, and the woman has suffered, you hear me?

BEN: *(standing still, considering)* What's the proposition?   800

WILLY: It's twenty thousand dollars on the barrelhead. Guaranteed, gilt-edged, you understand?

BEN: You don't want to make a fool of yourself. They might not honor the policy.

WILLY: How can they dare refuse? Didn't I work like a coolie to meet every premium on the nose? And now they don't pay off? Impossible!

BEN: It's called a cowardly thing, William.

WILLY: Why? Does it take more guts to stand here the rest of my life ringing up a zero?   805

BEN: *(yielding)*   That's a point, William. *(He moves, thinking, turns.)* And twenty thousand—that *is* something one can feel with the hand, it is there.

WILLY: *(now assured, with rising power)* Oh, Ben, that's the whole beauty of it! I see it like a diamond, shining in the dark, hard and rough, that I can pick up and touch in my hand. Not like—like an appointment! This would not be another damned-fool appointment, Ben, and it changes all the aspects. Because he thinks I'm nothing, see, and so he spites me. But the funeral—*(Straightening up.)* Ben, that funeral will be massive! They'll come from Maine, Massachusetts, Vermont, New Hampshire! All the old-timers with the strange license plates—that boy will be thunder-struck, Ben, because he never realized—I am known! Rhode Island, New York, New Jersey—I am known, Ben, and he'll see it with his eyes once and for all. He'll see what I am, Ben! He's in for a shock, that boy!

BEN: *(coming down to the edge of the garden)* He'll call you a coward.

WILLY: *(suddenly fearful)* No, that would be terrible.

BEN: Yes, And a damned fool.   810

WILLY: No, no, he mustn't, I won't have that! *(He is broken and desperate.)*

BEN: He'll hate you, William.

The gay music of the boys is heard.

WILLY: Oh, Ben, how do we get back to all the great times? Used to be so full of light, and comradeship, the sleigh-riding in winter, and the ruddiness on his cheeks. And always some kind of good news coming up, always something nice coming up ahead. And never even let me carry the valises in the house, and simonizing, simonizing that little red car! Why, why can't I give him something and not have him hate me?

BEN: Let me think about it. *(He glances at his watch.)* I still have a little time. Remarkable proposition, but you've got to be sure you're not making a fool of yourself.

Ben drifts off upstage and goes out of sight. Biff comes down from the left.

WILLY: *(suddenly conscious of Biff, turns and looks up at him, then begins picking*   815
up the packages of seeds in confusion) Where the hell is that seed? *(Indignantly.)* You can't see nothing out here! They boxed in the whole goddam neighborhood!

BIFF: There are people all around here. Don't you realize that?

WILLY: I'm busy. Don't bother me.

BIFF: *(taking the hoe from Willy)* I'm saying good-by to you, Pop. *(Willy looks at him, silent, unable to move.)* I'm not coming back any more.

WILLY: You're not going to see Oliver tomorrow?

BIFF: I've got no appointment, Dad.   820

WILLY: He put his arm around you, and you've got no appointment?

BIFF: Pop, get this now, will you? Everytime I've left it's been a fight that sent me out of here. Today I realized something about myself and I tried to explain it to you and I— I think I'm just not smart enough to make any sense out of it for you. To hell with whose fault it is or anything like that. *(He takes Willy's arm.)* Let's just wrap it up, heh? Come on in, we'll tell Mom. *(He gently tries to pull Willy to the left.)*

WILLY: *(frozen, immobile, with guilt in his voice)* No, I don't want to see her.

BIFF: Come on! (*He pulls again, and Willy tries to pull away.*)

WILLY: (*highly nervous*) No, no, I don't want to see her.   825

BIFF: (*tries to look into Willy's face, as if to find the answer there*) Why don't you want to see her?

WILLY: (*more harshly now*) Don't bother me, will you?

BIFF: What do you mean, you don't want to see her? You don't want them calling you yellow, do you? This isn't your fault; it's me, I'm a bum. Now come inside! (*Willy strains to get away.*) Did you hear what I said to you?

Willy pulls away and quickly goes by himself into the house. Biff follows.

LINDA: (*to Willy*) Did you plant, dear?

BIFF: (*at the door, to Linda*) All right, we had it out. I'm going and I'm not writing any   830
more.

LINDA: (*going to Willy in the kitchen*) I think that's the best way, dear. 'Cause there's no use drawing it out, you'll just never get along.

Willy doesn't respond.

BIFF: People ask where I am and what I'm doing, you don't know, and you don't care. That way it'll be off your mind and you can start brightening up again. All right? That clears it, doesn't it? (*Willy is silent, and Biff goes to him.*) You gonna wish me luck, scout? (*He extends his hand.*) What do you say?

LINDA: Shake his hand, Willy.

WILLY: (*turning to her, seething with hurt*) There's no necessity to mention the pen at all, y'know.

BIFF: (*gently*) I've got no appointment, Dad.

WILLY: (*erupting fiercely*) He put his arm around ...?   835

BIFF: Dad, you're never going to see what I am, so what's the use of arguing? If I strike oil I'll send you a check. Meantime forget I'm alive.

WILLY: (*to Linda*) Spite, see?

BIFF: Shake hands, Dad.

WILLY: Not my hand.   840

BIFF: I was hoping not to go this way.

WILLY: Well, this is the way you're going. Good-by.

Biff looks at him a moment, then turns sharply and goes to the stairs.

WILLY: (*stops him with*) May you rot in hell if you leave this house!

BIFF: (*turning*) Exactly what is it that you want from me?

WILLY: I want you to know, on the train, in the mountains, in the valleys, wherever you   845
go, that you cut down your life for spite!

BIFF: No, no.

WILLY: Spite, spite, is the word of your undoing! And when you're down and out, remember what did it. When you're rotting somewhere beside the railroad tracks, remember, and don't you dare blame it on me!

BIFF: I'm not blaming it on you!

WILLY: I won't take the rap for this, you hear?

Happy comes down the stairs and stands on the bottom step, watching.

BIFF: That's just what I'm telling you!   850

WILLY: (*sinking into a chair at the table, with full accusation*) You're trying to put a knife in me—don't think I don't know what you're doing!

BIFF: All right, phony! Then let's lay it on the line. (*He whips the rubber tube out of his pocket and puts it on the table.*)

HAPPY: You crazy—

LINDA: Biff! (*She moves to grab the hose, but Biff holds it down with his hand.*)

BIFF: Leave it there! Don't move it!   855

WILLY: (*not looking at it*) What is that?

BIFF: You know goddam well what that is.

WILLY: *(caged, wanting to escape)* I never saw that.

BIFF: You saw it. The mice didn't bring it into the cellar! What is this supposed to do, make a hero out of you? This supposed to make me sorry for you?

WILLY: Never heard of it.   860

BIFF: There'll be no pity for you, you hear it? No pity!

WILLY: *(to Linda)* You hear the spite!

BIFF: No, you're going to hear the truth—what you are and what I am!

LINDA: Stop it!

WILLY: Spite!   865

HAPPY: *(coming down toward Biff)* You cut it now!

BIFF: *(to Happy)* The man don't know who we are! The man is gonna know! *(To Willy.)* We never told the truth for ten minutes in this house!

HAPPY: We always told the truth!

BIFF: *(turning on him)* You big blow, are you the assistant buyer? You're one of the two assistants to the assistant, aren't you?

HAPPY: Well, I'm practically—   870

BIFF: You're practically full of it! We all are! And I'm through with it. *(To Willy.)* Now hear this, Willy, this is me.

WILLY: I know you!

BIFF: You know why I had no address for three months? I stole a suit in Kansas City and I was in jail. *(To Linda, who is sobbing.)* Stop crying. I'm through with it.

Linda turns away from them, her hands covering her face.

WILLY: I suppose that's my fault!

BIFF: I stole myself out of every good job since high school!   875

WILLY: And whose fault is that?

BIFF: And I never got anywhere because you blew me so full of hot air I could never stand taking orders from anybody! That's whose fault it is!

WILLY: I hear that!

LINDA: Don't, Biff!

BIFF: It's goddam time you heard that! I had to be boss big shot in two weeks, and I'm   880
through with it!

WILLY: Then hang yourself! For spite, hang yourself!

BIFF: No! Nobody's hanging himself, Willy! I ran down eleven flights with a pen in my hand today. And suddenly I stopped, you hear me? And in the middle of that office building, do you hear this? I stopped in the middle of that building and I saw—the sky. I saw the things that I love in this world. The work and the food and time to sit and smoke. And I looked at the pen and said to myself, what the hell am I grabbing this for? Why am I trying to become what I don't want to be? What am I doing in an office, making a contemptuous, begging fool of myself, when all I want is out there, waiting for me the minute I say I know who I am! Why can't I say that, Willy? *(He tries to make Willy face him, but Willy pulls away and moves to the left.)*

WILLY: *(with hatred, threateningly)* The door of your life is wide open!

BIFF: Pop! I'm a dime a dozen, and so are you!

WILLY: *(turning on him now in an uncontrolled outburst)* I am not a dime a dozen! I   885
am Willy Loman, and you are Biff Loman!

Biff starts for Willy, but is blocked by Happy. In his fury, Biff seems on the verge of attacking his father.

BIFF: I am not a leader of men, Willy, and neither are you. You were never anything but a hard-working drummer who landed in the ash can like all the rest of them! I'm one dollar an hour, Willy! I tried seven states and couldn't raise it. A buck an hour! Do you gather my meaning? I'm not bringing home any prizes any more, and you're going to stop waiting for me to bring them home!

WILLY: *(directly to Biff)* You vengeful, spiteful mutt!

Biff breaks from Happy. Willy, in fright, starts up the stairs. Biff grabs him.

BIFF: *(at the peak of his fury)* Pop, I'm nothing! I'm nothing, Pop. Can't you understand that? There's no spite in it any more. I'm just what I am, that's all.

Biff's fury has spent itself, and he breaks down, sobbing, holding on to Willy, who dumbly fumbles for Biff's face.

WILLY: *(astonished)* What're you doing? What're you doing? *(To Linda.)* Why is he crying?

BIFF: *(crying, broken)* Will you let me go, for Christ's sake? Will you take that phony   890
dream and burn it before something happens? *(Struggling to contain himself, he pulls away and moves to the stairs.)* I'll go in the morning. Put him—put him to bed. *(Exhausted, Biff moves up the stairs to his room.)*

WILLY: *(after a long pause, astonished, elevated)* Isn't that remarkable? Biff—he likes me!

LINDA: He loves you, Willy!

HAPPY: *(deeply moved)* Always did, Pop.

WILLY: Oh, Biff! *(Staring wildly.)* He cried! Cried to me! *(He is choking with his love, and now cries out his promise.)* That boy—that boy is going to be magnificent!

Ben appears in the light just outside the kitchen.

BEN: Yes, outstanding, with twenty thousand behind him.   895

LINDA: *(sensing the racing of his mind, fearfully, carefully)* Now come to bed, Willy. It's all settled now.

WILLY: *(finding it difficult not to rush out of the house)* Yes, we'll sleep. Come on. Go to sleep, Hap.

BEN: And it does take a great kind of man to crack the jungle.

In accents of dread, Ben's idyllic music starts up.

HAPPY: *(his arm around Linda)* I'm getting married, Pop, don't forget it. I'm changing everything. I'm gonna run that department before the year is up. You'll see, Mom. *(He kisses her.)*

BEN: The jungle is dark but full of diamonds, Willy.   900

Willy turns, moves, listening to Ben.

LINDA: Be good. You're both good boys, just act that way, that's all.

HAPPY: 'Night, Pop. *(He goes upstairs.)*

LINDA: *(to Willy)* Come, dear.

BEN: *(with greater force)* One must go in to fetch a diamond out.

WILLY: *(to Linda, as he moves slowly along the edge of the kitchen, toward the door)*   905
I just want to get settled down, Linda. Let me sit alone for a little.

LINDA: *(almost uttering her fear)* I want you upstairs.

WILLY: *(taking her in his arms)* In a few minutes, Linda. I couldn't sleep right now. Go on, you look awful tired. *(He kisses her.)*

BEN: Not like an appointment at all. A diamond is rough and hard to the touch.

WILLY: Go on now. I'll be right up.

LINDA: I think this is the only way, Willy.   910

WILLY: Sure, it's the best thing.

BEN: Best thing!

WILLY: The only way. Everything is gonna be—go on, kid, get to bed. You look so tired.

LINDA: Come right up.

WILLY: Two minutes.   915

Linda goes into the livingroom, then reappears in her bedroom. Willy moves just outside the kitchen door.

WILLY: Loves me. *(Wonderingly.)* Always loved me. Isn't that a remarkable thing? Ben, he'll worship me for it!

BEN: *(with promise)* It's dark there, but full of diamonds.

WILLY: Can you imagine that magnificence with twenty thousand dollars in his pocket?

LINDA: *(calling from her room)* Willy! Come up!

WILLY: *(calling from the kitchen)* Yes! Yes! Coming! It's very smart, you realize that,   920
don't you, sweetheart? Even Ben sees it. I gotta go, baby. 'By! By! *(Going over to Ben,
almost dancing.)* Imagine? When the mail comes he'll be ahead of Bernard again!

BEN: A perfect proposition all around.

WILLY: Did you see how he cried to me? Oh, if I could kiss him, Ben!

BEN: Time, William, time!

WILLY: Oh, Ben, I always knew one way or another we were gonna make it, Biff and I!

BEN: *(looking at his watch)* The boat. We'll be late. *(He moves slowly off into the dark-*   925
ness.)

WILLY: *(elegiacally, turning to the house)* Now when you kick off, boy, I want a sev-
enty-yard boot, and get right down the field under the ball, and when you hit, hit low
and hit hard, because it's important, boy. *(He swings around and faces the audience.)* There's all kinds of important people in the stands, and the first thing you
know ... *(Suddenly realizing he is alone.)* Ben! Ben, where do I ... *(He makes a
sudden movement of search.)* Ben, how do I ... ?

LINDA: *(calling)* Willy, you coming up?

WILLY: *(uttering a gasp of fear, whirling about as if to quiet her)* Sh! *(He turns
around as if to find his way; sounds, faces, voices, seem to be swarming in upon
him and he flicks at them, crying.)* Sh! Sh! *(Suddenly music, faint and high, stops
him. It rises in intensity, almost to an unbearable scream. He goes up and down
on his toes, and rushes off around the house.)* Shhh!

LINDA: Willy?

*There is no answer. Linda waits. Biff gets up off his bed. He is still in his clothes. Happy sits up. Biff
stands listening.*

LINDA: *(with real fear)* Willy, answer me! Willy!   930

There is the sound of a car starting and moving away at full speed.

LINDA: No!

BIFF: *(rushing down the stairs)* Pop!

*As the car speeds off, the music crashes down in a frenzy of sound, which becomes the soft pulsation of
a single cello string. Biff slowly returns to his bedroom. He and Happy gravely don their jackets.
Linda slowly walks out of her room. The music has developed into a dead march. The leaves of day
are appearing over everything. Charley and Bernard, somberly dressed, appear and knock on the
kitchen door. Biff and Happy slowly descend the stairs to the kitchen as Charley and Bernard enter.
All stop a moment when Linda, in clothes of mourning, bearing a little bunch of roses, comes through
the draped doorway into the kitchen. She goes to Charley and takes his arm. Now all move toward
the audience, through the wall-line of the kitchen. At the limit of the apron, Linda lays down the
flowers, kneels, and sits back on her heels. All stare down at the grave.*

Requiem

CHARLEY: It's getting dark, Linda.

Linda doesn't react. She stares at the grave.

BIFF: How about it, Mom? Better get some rest, heh? They'll be closing the gate soon.

Linda makes no move. Pause.

HAPPY: *(deeply angered)* He had no right to do that! There was no necessity for it. We
would've helped him.

CHARLEY: *(grunting)* Hmmm.

BIFF: Come along, Mom.   5

LINDA: Why didn't anybody come?

CHARLEY: It was a very nice funeral.

LINDA: But where are all the people he knew? Maybe they blame him.

CHARLEY: Naa. It's a rough world, Linda. They wouldn't blame him.

LINDA: I can't understand it. All this time especially. First time in thirty-five years we   10
were just about free and clear. He only needed a little salary. He was even finished
with the dentist.

CHARLEY: No man only needs a little salary.

LINDA: I can't understand it.

BIFF: There were a lot of nice days. When he'd come home from a trip; or on Sundays,
making the stoop; finishing the cellar; putting on the new porch; when he built the
extra bathroom; and put up the garage. You know something, Charley, there's more
of him in that front stoop than in all the sales he ever made.

CHARLEY: Yeah. He was a happy man with a batch of cement.

LINDA: He was so wonderful with his hands.

BIFF: He had the wrong dreams. All, all, wrong.   15

HAPPY: *(almost ready to fight Biff)* Don't say that!

BIFF: He never knew who he was.

CHARLEY: *(stopping Happy's movement and reply. To Biff.)* Nobody dast blame this
man. You don't understand: Willy was a salesman. And for a salesman, there is no
rock bottom to the life. He don't put a bolt on a nut, he don't tell you the law or give
you medicine. He's a man out there in the blue, riding on a smile and a shoeshine.
And when they start not smiling back—that's an earthquake. And then you get yourself a couple of spots on your hat, and you're finished. Nobody dast blame this man.
A salesman is got to dream, boy. It comes with the territory.

BIFF: Charley, the man didn't know who he was.

HAPPY: *(infuriated)* Don't say that!   20

BIFF: Why don't you come with me, Happy?

HAPPY: I'm not licked that easily. I'm staying right in this city, and I'm gonna beat this
racket! *(He looks at Biff, his chin set.)* The Loman Brothers!

BIFF: I know who I am, kid.

HAPPY: All right, boy, I'm gonna show you and everybody else that Willy Loman did not   25
die in vain. He had a good dream. It's the only dream you can have—to come out
number-one man. He fought it out here, and this is where I'm gonna win it for him.

BIFF: *(with a hopeless glance at Happy, bends toward his mother)* Let's go, Mom.

LINDA: I'll be with you in a minute. Go on, Charley. *(He hesitates.)* I want to, just for a
minute. I never had a chance to say good-by.

*Charley moves away, followed by Happy. Biff remains a slight distance up and left of Linda. She sits
there, summoning herself. The flute begins, not far away, playing behind her speech.*

LINDA: Forgive me, dear. I can't cry. I don't know what it is, but I can't cry. I don't understand it. Why did you ever do that? Help me, Willy, I can't cry. It seems to me that
you're just on another trip. I keep expecting you. Willy, dear, I can't cry. Why did you
do it? I search and search and I search, and I can't understand it, Willy. I made the last
payment on the house today. Today, dear. And there'll be nobody home. *(A sob rises
in her throat.)* We're free and clear. *(Sobbing more fully, released.)* We're free. *(Biff
comes slowly toward her.)* We're free . . . We're free . . .

*Biff lifts her to her feet and moves out up right with her in his arms. Linda sobs quietly. Bernard and
Charley come together and follow them, followed by Happy. Only the music of the flute is left on the
darkening stage as over the house the hard towers of the apartment buildings rise into sharp focus,
and—*

THE CURTAIN FALLS

Lorraine Hansberry 1930–1965

A Raisin in the Sun 1959

> What happens to a dream deferred?
> Does it dry up
> Like a raisin in the sun?
> Or fester like a sore—
> and then run?
> Does it stink like rotten meat?
> Or crust and sugar over—
> Like a syrupy sweet?
>
> Maybe it just sags
> Like a heavy load.
>
> Or does it explode?
>
> LANGSTON HUGHES

Characters

Ruth Younger
Travis Younger
Walter Lee Younger (Brother)
Beneatha Younger
Lena Younger (Mama)
Joseph Sasagai
George Murchison
Karl Lindner
Bobo
Moving Men

The action of the play is set in Chicago's Southside, sometime between World War II and the present.

ACT 1
    SCENE 1: *Friday morning.*
    SCENE 2: *The following morning.*

ACT 2
    SCENE 1: *Later, the same day.*
    SCENE 2: *Friday night, a few weeks later.*
    SCENE 3: *Moving day, one week later.*

ACT 3
    An hour later.

Act 1, Scene 1

The Younger living room would be a comfortable and well-ordered room if it were not for a number of indestructible contradictions to this state of being. Its furnishings are typical and undistinguished and their primary feature now is that they have clearly had to accommodate the living of too many people for too many years—and they are tired. Still, we can see that at some time, a time probably no longer remembered by the family (except perhaps for Mama), the furnishings of this room were actually selected with care and love and even hope—and brought to this apartment and arranged with taste and pride.

That was a long time ago. Now the once loved pattern of the couch upholstery has to fight to show itself from under acres of crocheted doilies and couch covers which have themselves finally come to be more important than the upholstery. And here a table or a chair has been moved to disguise the worn places in the carpet; but the carpet has fought back by showing its weariness, with depressing uniformity, elsewhere on its surface.

Weariness has, in fact, won in this room. Everything has been polished, washed, sat on, used, scrubbed too often. All pretenses but living itself have long since vanished from the very atmosphere of this room.

Moreover, a section of this room, for it is not really a room unto itself, though the landlord's lease would make it seem so, slopes backward to provide a small kitchen area, where the family prepares the meals that are eaten in the living room proper, which must also serve as dining room. The single window that has been provided for these "two" rooms is located in this kitchen area. The sole natural light the family may enjoy in the course of a day is only that which fights its way through this little window.

At left, a door leads to a bedroom which is shared by Mama and her daughter, Beneatha. At right, opposite, is a second room (which in the beginning of the life of this apartment was probably a breakfast room) which serves as a bedroom for Walter and his wife, Ruth.

TIME: *Sometime between World War II and the present.*

PLACE: *Chicago's Southside.*

AT RISE: *It is morning dark in the living room. Travis is asleep on the make-down bed at center. An alarm clock sounds from within the bedroom at right, and presently Ruth enters from that room and closes the door behind her. She crosses sleepily toward the window. As she passes her sleeping son she reaches down and shakes him a little. At the window she raises the shade and a dusky Southside morning light comes in feebly. She fills a pot with water and puts it on to boil. She calls to the boy, between yawns, in a slightly muffled voice.*

Ruth is about thirty. We can see that she was a pretty girl, even exceptionally so, but now it is apparent that life has been little that she expected, and disappointment has already begun to hang in her face. In a few years, before thirty-five even, she will be known among her people as a "settled woman."

She crosses to her son and gives him a good, final, rousing shake.

RUTH: Come on now, boy, it's seven thirty! (*Her son sits up at last, in a stupor of sleepiness.*) I say hurry up, Travis! You ain't the only person in the world got to use a bathroom! (*The child, a sturdy handsome little boy of ten or eleven, drags himself out of the bed and almost blindly takes his towels and "today's clothes" from drawers and a closet and goes out to the bathroom, which is in an outside hall and which is shared by another family or families on the same floor.* RUTH *crosses to the bedroom door at right and opens it and calls in to her husband.*) Walter Lee! . . . It's after seven thirty! Lemme see you do some waking up in there now! (*She waits.*) You better get up from there, man! It's after seven thirty I tell you. (*She waits again.*) All right, you just go ahead and lay there and next thing you know Travis be finished and Mr. Johnson'll be in there and you'll be fussing and cussing round here like a madman! And be late too! (*She waits, at the end of patience.*) Walter Lee—it's time for you to GET UP!

She waits another second and then starts to go into the bedroom, but is apparently satisfied that her husband has begun to get up. She stops, pulls the door to, and returns to the kitchen area. She wipes her face with a moist cloth and runs her fingers through her sleep-disheveled hair in a vain effort and ties an apron around her housecoat. The bedroom door at right opens and her husband stands in the doorway in his pajamas, which are rumpled and mismated. He is a lean, intense young man in his middle thirties, inclined to quick nervous movements and erratic speech habits—and always in his voice there is a quality of indictment.

WALTER: Is he out yet?
RUTH: What you mean *out?* He ain't hardly got in there good yet.
WALTER: (*wandering in, still more oriented to sleep than to a new day*)   Well, what was you doing all that yelling for if I can't even get in there yet? (*stopping and thinking*) Check coming today?

RUTH: They *said* Saturday and this is just Friday and I hopes to God you ain't going to   5
get up here first thing this morning and start talking to me 'bout no money—'cause
I 'bout don't want to hear it.

WALTER: Something the matter with you this morning?

RUTH: No—I'm just sleepy as the devil. What kind of eggs you want?

WALTER: Not scrambled. (*Ruth starts to scramble eggs.*) Paper come? (*Ruth points impatiently to the rolled up* Tribune *on the table, and he gets it and spreads it out
and vaguely reads the front page.*) Set off another bomb yesterday.

RUTH: (*maximum indifference*) Did they?

WALTER: (*looking up*) What's the matter with you?   10

RUTH: Ain't nothing the matter with me. And don't keep asking me that this morning.

WALTER: Ain't nobody bothering you. (*reading the news of the day absently again*) Say
Colonel McCormick is sick.

RUTH: (*affecting tea-party interest*) Is he now? Poor thing.

WALTER: (*sighing and looking at his watch*) Oh, me. (*He waits.*) Now what is that
boy doing in that bathroom all this time? He just going to have to start getting up
earlier. I can't be being late to work on account of him fooling around in there.

RUTH: (*turning on him*) Oh, no he ain't going to be getting up no earlier no such   15
thing! It ain't his fault that he can't get to bed no earlier nights 'cause he got a bunch
of crazy good-for-nothing clowns sitting up running their mouths in what is supposed to be his bedroom after ten o'clock at night . . .

WALTER: That's what you mad about, ain't it? The things I want to talk about with my
friends just couldn't be important in your mind, could they?

*He rises and finds a cigarette in her handbag on the table and crosses to the little window and looks
out, smoking and deeply enjoying this first one.*

RUTH: (*almost matter of factly, a complaint too automatic to deserve emphasis*)
Why you always got to smoke before you eat in the morning?

WALTER: (*at the window*) Just look at 'em down there . . . Running and racing to work
. . . (*he turns and faces his wife and watches her a moment at the stove, and then,
suddenly*) You look young this morning, baby.

RUTH: (*indifferently*) Yeah?

WALTER: Just for a second—stirring them eggs. Just for a second it was—you looked real   20
young again. (*He reaches for her; she crosses away. Then, drily.*) It's gone now—you
look like yourself again!

RUTH: Man, if you don't shut up and leave me alone.

WALTER: (*looking out to the street again*) First thing a man ought to learn in life is not
to make love to no colored woman first thing in the morning. You all some eeeevil
people at eight o'clock in the morning.

*Travis appears in the hall doorway, almost fully dressed and quite wide awake now, his towels and
pajamas across his shoulders. He opens the door and signals for his father to make the bathroom in a
hurry.*

TRAVIS: (*watching the bathroom*) Daddy, come on!

Walter gets his bathroom utensils and flies out to the bathroom.

RUTH: Sit down and have your breakfast, Travis.

TRAVIS: Mama, this is Friday. (*gleefully*) Check coming tomorrow, huh?   25

RUTH: You get your mind off money and eat your breakfast.

TRAVIS: (*eating*) This is the morning we supposed to bring the fifty cents to school.

RUTH: Well, I ain't got no fifty cents this morning.

TRAVIS: Teacher say we have to.

RUTH: I don't care what teacher say. I ain't got it. Eat your breakfast, Travis.   30

TRAVIS: I *am* eating.

RUTH: Hush up now and just eat!

The boy gives her an exasperated look for her lack of understanding, and eats grudgingly.

TRAVIS: You think Grandmama would have it?

RUTH: No! And I want you to stop asking your grandmother for money, you hear me?

TRAVIS: *(outraged)*   Gaaaleee! I don't ask her, she just gimme it sometimes!

RUTH: Travis Willard Younger—I got too much on me this morning to be—

TRAVIS: Maybe Daddy—

RUTH: *Travis!*

The boy hushes abruptly. They are both quiet and tense for several seconds.

TRAVIS: *(presently)*   Could I maybe go carry some groceries in front of the supermarket for a little while after school then?

RUTH: Just hush, I said. (*Travis jabs his spoon into his cereal bowl viciously, and rests his head in anger upon his fists.*) If you through eating, you can get over there and make up your bed.

The boy obeys stiffly and crosses the room, almost mechanically, to the bed and more or less folds the bedding into a heap, then angrily gets his books and cap.

TRAVIS: *(sulking and standing apart from her unnaturally)*   I'm gone.

RUTH: *(looking up from the stove to inspect him automatically)*   Come here. (*He crosses to her and she studies his head.*) If you don't take this comb and fix this here head, you better! (*Travis puts down his books with a great sigh of oppression, and crosses to the mirror. His mother mutters under her breath about his "stubbornness."*) 'Bout to march out of here with that head looking just like chickens slept in it! I just don't know where you get your stubborn ways . . . And get your jacket, too. Looks chilly out this morning.

TRAVIS: *(with conspicuously brushed hair and jacket)*   I'm gone.

RUTH: Get carfare and milk money—*(waving one finger)*—and not a single penny for no caps, you hear me?

TRAVIS: *(with sullen politeness)*   Yes'm.

He turns in outrage to leave. His mother watches after him as in his frustration he approaches the door almost comically. When she speaks to him, her voice has became a very gentle tease.

RUTH: *(mocking; as she thinks he would say it)*   Oh, Mama makes me so mad sometimes, I don't know what to do! (*She waits and continues to his back as he stands stock-still in front of the door.*) I wouldn't kiss that woman good-bye for nothing in this world this morning! (*The boy finally turns around and rolls his eyes at her, knowing the mood has changed and he is vindicated; he does not, however, move toward her yet.*) Not for nothing in this world! (*She finally laughs aloud at him and holds out her arms to him and we see that it is a way between them, very old and practiced. He crosses to her and allows her to embrace him warmly but keeps his face fixed with masculine rigidity. She holds him back from her presently and looks at him and runs her fingers over the features of his face. With utter gentleness.*) Now—whose little old angry man are you?

TRAVIS: *(The masculinity and gruffness start to fade at last.)*   Aw gaalee—Mama . . .

RUTH: *(mimicking)*   Aw—gaaaaalleeeee, Mama! (*She pushes him, with rough playfulness and finality, toward the door.*) Get on out of here or you going to be late.

TRAVIS: *(in the face of love, new aggressiveness)*   Mama, could I *please* go carry groceries?

RUTH: Honey, it's starting to get so cold evenings.

WALTER: *(coming in from the bathroom and drawing a make-believe gun from a make-believe holster and shooting at his son)*   What is it he wants to do?

RUTH: Go carry groceries after school at the supermarket.

WALTER: Well, let him go . . .

TRAVIS: *(quickly, to the ally)*   I *have* to—she won't gimme the fifty cents . . .

WALTER: *(to his wife only)*   Why not?

Ruth: (*simply, and with flavor*)   'Cause we don't have it.
Walter: (*to Ruth only*)   What you tell the boy things like that for? (*reaching down into his pants with a rather important gesture*) Here, son—

He hands the boy the coin, but his eyes are directed to his wife's. Travis takes the money happily.

Travis: Thanks, Daddy.

He starts out. Ruth watches both of them with murder in her eyes. Walter stands and stares back at her with defiance, and suddenly reaches into his pocket again on an afterthought.

Walter: (*without even looking at his son, still staring hard at his wife*)   In fact, here's another fifty cents . . . Buy yourself some fruit today—or take a taxicab to school or something!
Travis: Whoopee—   60

He leaps up and clasps his father around the middle with his legs, and they face each other in mutual appreciation; slowly Walter Lee peeks around the boy to catch the violent rays from his wife's eyes and draws his head back as if shot.

Walter: You better get down now—and get to school, man.
Travis: (*at the door*)   O.K. Good-bye.

He exits.

Walter: (*after him, pointing with pride*)   That's *my* boy. (*She looks at him in disgust and turns back to her work.*) You know what I was thinking 'bout in the bathroom this morning?
Ruth: No.
Walter: How come you always try to be so pleasant!   65
Ruth: What is there to be pleasant 'bout!
Walter: You want to know what I was thinking 'bout in the bathroom or not!
Ruth: I know what you thinking 'bout.
Walter: (*ignoring her*)   'Bout what me and Willy Harris was talking about last night.
Ruth: (*immediately—a refrain*)   Willy Harris is a good-for-nothing loudmouth.   70
Walter: Anybody who talks to me has got to be a good-for-nothing loudmouth, ain't he? And what you know about who is just a good-for-nothing loudmouth? Charlie Atkins was just a "good-for-nothing loudmouth" too, wasn't he! When he wanted me to go in the dry-cleaning business with him. And now—he's grossing a hundred thousand a year. A hundred thousand dollars a year! You still call *him* a loudmouth!
Ruth: (*bitterly*)   Oh, Walter Lee . . .

She folds her head on her arms over the table.

Walter: (*rising and coming to her and standing over her*)   You tired, ain't you? Tired of everything. Me, the boy, the way we live—this beat-up hole—everything. Ain't you? (*She doesn't look up, doesn't answer.*) So tired—moaning and groaning all the time, but you wouldn't do nothing to help, would you? You couldn't be on my side that long for nothing, could you?
Ruth: Walter, please leave me alone.
Walter: A man needs for a woman to back him up . . .   75
Ruth: Walter—
Walter: Mama would listen to you. You know she listen to you more than she do me and Bennie. She think more of you. All you have to do is just sit down with her when you drinking your coffee one morning and talking 'bout things like you do and—(*He sits down beside her and demonstrates graphically what he thinks her methods and tone should be.*)—you just sip your coffee, see, and say easy like that you been thinking 'bout that deal Walter Lee is so interested in, 'bout the store and all, and sip some more coffee, like what you saying ain't really that important to you—And the next thing you know, she be listening good and asking you questions

and when I come home—I can tell her the details. This ain't no fly-by-night proposition, baby. I mean we figured it out, me and Willy and Bobo.

RUTH: (*with a frown*)   Bobo?

WALTER: Yeah. You see, this little liquor store we got in mind cost seventy-five thousand and we figured the initial investment on the place be 'bout thirty thousand, see. That be ten thousand each. Course, there's a couple of hundred you got to pay so's you don't spend your life just waiting for them clowns to let your license get approved—

RUTH: You mean graft?

WALTER: (*frowning impatiently*)   Don't call it that. See there, that just goes to show you what women understand about the world. Baby, don't *nothing* happen for you in this world 'less you pay *somebody* off!

RUTH: Walter, leave me alone! (*she raises her head and stares at him vigorously—then says, more quietly*) Eat your eggs, they gonna be cold.

WALTER: (*straightening up from her and looking off*)   That's it. There you are. Man say to his woman: I got me a dream. His woman say: Eat your eggs. (*sadly, but gaining in power*) Man say: I got to take hold of this here world, baby! And a woman will say: Eat your eggs and go to work. (*passionately now*) Man say: I got to change my life, I'm choking to death, baby! And his woman say—(*in utter anguish as he brings his fists down on his thighs*)—Your eggs is getting cold!

RUTH: (*softly*)   Walter, that ain't none of our money.

WALTER: (*not listening at all or even looking at her*)   This morning, I was lookin' in the mirror and thinking about it . . . I'm thirty-five years old; I been married eleven years and I got a boy who sleeps in the living room—(*very, very quietly*)—and all I got to give him is stories about how rich white people live . . .

RUTH: Eat your eggs, Walter.

WALTER: (*slams the table and jumps up*)   DAMN MY EGGS—DAMN ALL THE EGGS THAT EVER WAS!

RUTH: Then go to work.

WALTER: (*looking up at her*)   See—I'm trying to talk to you 'bout myself—(*shaking his head with the repetition*)—and all you can say is eat them eggs and go to work.

RUTH: (*wearily*)   Honey, you never say nothing new. I listen to you every day, every night and every morning, and you never say nothing new. (*shrugging*) So you would rather *be* Mr. Arnold than be his chauffeur. So—I would *rather* be living in Buckingham Palace.

WALTER: That is just what is wrong with the colored woman in this world . . . Don't understand about building their men up and making 'em feel like they somebody. Like they can do something.

RUTH: (*drily, but to hurt*)   There *are* colored men who do things.

WALTER: No thanks to the colored woman.

RUTH: Well, being a colored woman, I guess I can't help myself none.

She rises and gets the ironing board and sets it up and attacks a huge pile of rough-dried clothes, sprinkling them in preparation for the ironing and then rolling them into tight fat balls.

WALTER: (*mumbling*)   We one group of men tied to a race of women with small minds!

His sister Beneatha enters. She is about twenty, as slim and intense as her brother. She is not as pretty as her sister-in-law, but her lean, almost intellectual face has a handsomeness of its own. She wears a bright-red flannel nightie, and her thick hair stands wildly about her head. Her speech is a mixture of many things; it is different from the rest of the family's insofar as education has permeated her sense of English—and perhaps the Midwest rather than the South has finally—at last—won out in her inflection; but not altogether, because over all of it is a soft slurring and transformed use of vowels which is the decided influence of the Southside. She passes through the room without looking at either Ruth or Walter and goes to the outside door and looks, a little blindly, out to the bathroom. She sees that it has been lost to the Johnsons. She closes the door with a sleepy vengeance and crosses to the table and sits down a little defeated.

BENEATHA: I am going to start timing those people.

WALTER: You should get up earlier.

BENEATHA: (*Her face in her hands. She is still fighting the urge to go back to bed.*)   Really—would you suggest dawn? Where's the paper?

WALTER: (*pushing the paper across the table to her as he studies her almost clinically, as though he has never seen her before*)   You a horrible-looking chick at this hour.

BENEATHA: (*drily*)   Good morning, everybody.   100

WALTER: (*senselessly*)   How is school coming?

BENEATHA: (*in the same spirit*)   Lovely. Lovely. And you know, biology is the greatest. (*looking up at him*) I dissected something that looked just like you yesterday.

WALTER: I just wondered if you've made up your mind and everything.

BENEATHA: (*gaining in sharpness and impatience*)   And what did I answer yesterday morning—and the day before that?

RUTH: (*from the ironing board, like someone disinterested and old*)   Don't be so   105
nasty, Bennie.

BENEATHA: (*still to her brother*)   And the day before that and the day before that!

WALTER: (*defensively*)   I'm interested in you. Something wrong with that? Ain't many girls who decide—

WALTER AND BENEATHA: (*in unison*)   —"to be a doctor."

Silence.

WALTER: Have we figured out yet just exactly how much medical school is going to cost?

RUTH: Walter Lee, why don't you leave that girl alone and get out of here to work?   110

BENEATHA: (*exits to the bathroom and bangs on the door*)   Come on out of there, please!

She comes back into the room.

WALTER: (*looking at his sister intently*)   You know the check is coming tomorrow.

BENEATHA: (*turning on him with a sharpness all her own*)   That money belongs to Mama, Walter, and it's for her to decide how she wants to use it. I don't care if she wants to buy a house or a rocket ship or just nail it up somewhere and look at it. It's hers. Not ours—*hers.*

WALTER: (*bitterly*)   Now ain't that fine! You just got your mother's interest at heart, ain't you, girl? You such a nice girl—but if Mama got that money she can always take a few thousand and help you through school too—can't she?

BENEATHA: I have never asked anyone around here to do anything for me!   115

WALTER: No! And the line between asking and just accepting when the time comes is big and wide—ain't it!

BENEATHA: (*with fury*)   What do you want from me, Brother—that I quit school or just drop dead, which!

WALTER: I don't want nothing but for you to stop acting holy 'round here. Me and Ruth done made some sacrifices for you—why can't you do something for the family?

RUTH: Walter, don't be dragging me in it.

WALTER: You are in it—Don't you get up and go work in somebody's kitchen for the last   120
three years to help put clothes on her back?

RUTH: Oh, Walter—that's not fair . . .

WALTER: It ain't that nobody expects you to get on your knees and say thank you, Brother; thank you, Ruth; thank you, Mama—and thank you, Travis, for wearing the same pair of shoes for two semesters—

BENEATHA: (*dropping to her knees*)   Well—I *do*—all right?—thank everybody! And forgive me for ever wanting to be anything at all! (*pursuing him on her knees across the floor*) FORGIVE ME, FORGIVE ME, FORGIVE ME!

RUTH: Please stop it! Your mama'll hear you.

WALTER: Who the hell told you you had to be a doctor? If you so crazy 'bout messing   125
'round with sick people—then go be a nurse like other women—or just get married
and be quiet ...

BENEATHA: Well—you finally got it said ... It took you three years but you finally got it
said. Walter, give up; leave me alone—it's Mama's money.

WALTER: *He was my father, too!*

BENEATHA: So what? He was mine, too—and Travis' grandfather—but the insurance
money belongs to Mama. Picking on me is not going to make her give it to you to invest in any liquor stores—(*underbreath, dropping into a chair*)—and I for one say,
God bless Mama for that!

WALTER: (*to Ruth*)   See—did you hear? Did you hear!

RUTH: Honey, please go to work.   130

WALTER: Nobody in this house is ever going to understand me.

BENEATHA: Because you're a nut.

WALTER: Who's a nut?

BENEATHA: You—you are a nut. Thee is mad, boy.

WALTER: (*looking at his wife and his sister from the door, very sadly*)   The world's   135
most backward race of people, and that's a fact.

BENEATHA: (*turning slowly in her chair*)   And then there are all those prophets who
would lead us out of the wilderness—(*Walter slams out of the house*)—into the
swamps!

RUTH: Bennie, why you always gotta be pickin' on your brother? Can't you be a little
sweeter sometimes? (*Door opens. Walter walks in. He fumbles with his cap, starts
to speak, clears throat, looks everywhere but at Ruth. Finally.*)

WALTER: (*to Ruth*)   I need some money for carfare.

RUTH: (*looks at him, then warms; teasing, but tenderly*)   Fifty cents? (*She goes to her
bag and gets money.*) Here—take a taxi!

*Walter exits. Mama enters. She is a woman in her early sixties, full-bodied and strong. She is one of
those women of a certain grace and beauty who wear it so unobtrusively that it takes a while to notice.
Her dark-brown face is surrounded by the total whiteness of her hair, and, being a woman who has
adjusted to many things in life and overcome many more, her face is full of strength. She has, we can
see, wit and faith of a kind that keep her eyes lit and full of interest and expectancy. She is, in a word,
a beautiful woman. Her bearing is perhaps most like the noble bearing of the women of the Hereros
of Southwest Africa—rather as if she imagines that as she walks she still bears a basket or a vessel
upon her head. Her speech, on the other hand, is as careless as her carriage is precise—she is inclined
to slur everything—but her voice is perhaps not so much quiet as simply soft.*

MAMA: Who that 'round here slamming doors at this hour?   140

*She crosses through the room, goes to the window, opens it, and brings in a feeble little plant growing
doggedly in a small pot on the window sill. She feels the dirt and puts it back out.*

RUTH: That was Walter Lee. He and Bennie was at it again.

MAMA: My children and they tempers. Lord, if this little old plant don't get more sun
than it's been getting it ain't never going to see spring again. (*She turns from the
window.*) What's the matter with you this morning, Ruth? You looks right peaked.
You aiming to iron all them things? Leave some for me. I'll get to 'em this afternoon.
Bennie honey, it's too drafty for you to be sitting 'round half dressed. Where's your
robe?

BENEATHA: In the cleaners.

MAMA: Well, go get mine and put it on.

BENEATHA: I'm not cold, Mama, honest.   145

MAMA: I know—but you so thin ...

BENEATHA: (*irritably*)   Mama, I'm not cold.

MAMA: (*seeing the make-down bed as Travis has left it*)   Lord have mercy, look at that poor bed. Bless his heart—he tries, don't he?

She moves to the bed Travis has sloppily made up.

RUTH: No—he don't half try at all 'cause he knows you going to come along behind him and fix everything. That's just how come he don't know how to do nothing right now—you done spoiled that boy so.

MAMA: (*folding bedding*)   Well—he's a little boy. Ain't supposed to know 'bout house- 150 keeping. My baby, that's what he is. What you fix for his breakfast this morning?

RUTH: (*angrily*)   I feed my son, Lena!

MAMA: I ain't meddling—(*underbreath; busy-bodyish*)   I just noticed all last week he had cold cereal, and when it starts getting this chilly in the fall a child ought to have some hot grits or something when he goes out in the cold—

RUTH: (*furious*)   I gave him hot oats—is that all right!

MAMA: I ain't meddling. (*pause*) Put a lot of nice butter on it? (*Ruth shoots her an angry look and does not reply.*) He likes lots of butter.

RUTH: (*exasperated*)   Lena— 155

MAMA: (*To Beneatha. Mama is inclined to wander conversationally sometimes.*) What was you and your brother fussing 'bout this morning?

BENEATHA: It's not important, Mama.

She gets up and goes to look out at the bathroom, which is apparently free, and she picks up her towels and rushes out.

MAMA: What was they fighting about?

RUTH: Now you know as well as I do.

MAMA: (*shaking her head*)   Brother still worrying hisself sick about that money? 160

RUTH: You know he is.

MAMA: You had breakfast?

RUTH: Some coffee.

MAMA: Girl, you better start eating and looking after yourself better. You almost thin as Travis.

RUTH: Lena— 165

MAMA: Un-hunh?

RUTH: What are you going to do with it?

MAMA: Now don't you start, child. It's too early in the morning to be talking about money. It ain't Christian.

RUTH: It's just that he got his heart set on that store—

MAMA: You mean that liquor store that Willy Harris want him to invest in? 170

RUTH: Yes—

MAMA: We ain't no business people, Ruth. We just plain working folks.

RUTH: Ain't nobody business people till they go into business. Walter Lee say colored people ain't never going to start getting ahead till they start gambling on some dif- ferent kinds of things in the world—investments and things.

MAMA: What done got into you, girl? Walter Lee done finally sold you on investing.

RUTH: No. Mama, something is happening between Walter and me. I don't know what it 175 is—but he needs something—something I can't give him any more. He needs this chance, Lena.

MAMA: (*frowning deeply*)   But liquor, honey—

RUTH: Well—like Walter say—I spec people going to always be drinking themselves some liquor.

MAMA: Well—whether they drinks it or not ain't none of my business. But whether I go into business selling it to 'em *is,* and I don't want that on my ledger this late in life. (*stopping suddenly and studying her daughter-in-law*) Ruth Younger, what's the matter with you today? You look like you could fall over right there.

RUTH: I'm tired.

MAMA: Then you better stay home from work today.   180

RUTH: I can't stay home. She'd be calling up the agency and screaming at them, "My girl
didn't come in today—send me somebody! My girl didn't come in!" Oh, she just
have a fit ...

MAMA: Well, let her have it. I'll just call her up and say you got the flu—

RUTH: (*laughing*) Why the flu?

MAMA: 'Cause it sounds respectable to 'em. Something white people get, too. They know
'bout the flu. Otherwise they think you been cut up or something when you tell 'em
you sick.

RUTH: I got to go in. We need the money.   185

MAMA: Somebody would of thought my children done all but starved to death the
way they talk about money here late. Child, we got a great big old check coming
tomorrow.

RUTH: (*sincerely, but also self-righteously*) Now that's your money. It ain't got nothing to do with me. We all feel like that—Walter and Bennie and me—even Travis.

MAMA: (*thoughtfully, and suddenly very far away*) Ten thousand dollars—

RUTH: Sure is wonderful.

MAMA: Ten thousand dollars.   190

RUTH: You know what you should do, Miss Lena? You should take yourself a trip somewhere. To Europe or South America or someplace—

MAMA: (*throwing up her hands at the thought*) Oh, child!

RUTH: I'm serious. Just pack up and leave! Go on away and enjoy yourself some. Forget
about the family and have yourself a ball for once in your life—

MAMA: (*drily*) You sound like I'm just about ready to die. Who'd go with me? What I
look like wandering 'round Europe by myself?

RUTH: Shoot—these here rich white women do it all the time. They don't think nothing 195
of packing up they suitcases and piling on one of them big steamships and—
swoosh!—they gone, child.

MAMA: Something always told me I wasn't no rich white woman.

RUTH: Well—what are you going to do with it then?

MAMA: I ain't rightly decided. (*Thinking. She speaks now with emphasis.*) Some of it
got to be put away for Beneatha and her schoolin'—and ain't nothing going to
touch that part of it. Nothing. (*She waits several seconds, trying to make up her
mind about something, and looks at Ruth a little tentatively before going on.*)
Been thinking that we maybe could meet the notes on a little old two-story somewhere, with a yard where Travis could play in the summertime, if we use part of the
insurance for a down payment and everybody kind of pitch in. I could maybe take
on a little day work again, few days a week—

RUTH: (*studying her mother-in-law furtively and concentrating on her ironing, anxious to encourage without seeming to*) Well, Lord knows, we've put enough rent
into this here rat trap to pay for four houses by now ...

MAMA: (*looking up at the words "rat trap" and then looking around and leaning*   200
back and sighing—in a suddenly reflective mood) "Rat trap"—yes, that's all it is.
(*smiling*) I remember just as well the day me and Big Walter moved in here. Hadn't
been married but two weeks and wasn't planning on living here no more than a
year. (*She shakes her head at the dissolved dream.*) We was going to set away, little
by little, don't you know, and buy a little place out in Morgan Park. We had even
picked out the house. (*chuckling a little*) Looks right dumpy today. But Lord, child,
you should know all the dreams I had 'bout buying that house and fixing it up and
making me a little garden in the back—(*She waits and stops smiling.*) And didn't
none of it happen.

Dropping her hands in a futile gesture.

RUTH: (*keeps her head down, ironing*)   Yes, life can be a barrel of disappointments, sometimes.

MAMA: Honey, Big Walter would come in here some nights back then and slump down on that couch there and just look at the rug, and look at me and look at the rug and then back at me—and I'd know he was down then . . . really down. (*After a second very long and thoughtful pause; she is seeing back to times that only she can see.*) And then, Lord, when I lost that baby—little Claude—I almost thought I was going to lose Big Walter too. Oh, that man grieved hisself! He was one man to love his children.

RUTH: Ain't nothin' can tear at you like losin' your baby.

MAMA: I guess that's how come that man finally worked hisself to death like he done. Like he was fighting his own war with this here world that took his baby from him.

RUTH: He sure was a fine man, all right. I always liked Mr. Younger.   205

MAMA: Crazy 'bout his children! God knows there was plenty wrong with Walter Younger—hard-headed, mean, kind of wild with women—plenty wrong with him. But he sure loved his children. Always wanted them to have something—be something. That's where Brother gets all these notions, I reckon. Big Walter used to say, he'd get right wet in the eyes sometimes, lean his head back with the water standing in his eyes and say, "Seem like God didn't see fit to give the black man nothing but dreams—but He did give us children to make them dreams seem worth while." (*She smiles.*) He could talk like that, don't you know.

RUTH: Yes, he sure could. He was a good man, Mr. Younger.

MAMA: Yes, a fine man—just couldn't never catch up with his dreams, that's all.

Beneatha comes in, brushing her hair and looking up to the ceiling, where the sound of a vacuum cleaner has started up.

BENEATHA: What could be so dirty on that woman's rugs that she has to vacuum them every single day?

RUTH: I wish certain young women 'round here who I could name would take inspira-   210
tion about certain rugs in a certain apartment I could also mention.

BENEATHA: (*shrugging*)   How much cleaning can a house need, for Christ's sakes.

MAMA: (*not liking the Lord's name used thus*)   Bennie!

RUTH: Just listen to her—just listen!

BENEATHA: Oh, God!

MAMA: If you use the Lord's name just one more time—   215

BENEATHA: (*a bit of a whine*)   Oh, Mama—

RUTH: Fresh—just fresh as salt, this girl!

BENEATHA: (*drily*)   Well—if the salt loses its savor—

MAMA: Now that will do. I just ain't going to have you 'round here reciting the scriptures in vain—you hear me?

BENEATHA: How did I manage to get on everybody's wrong side by just walking into a   220
room?

RUTH: If you weren't so fresh—

BENEATHA: Ruth, I'm twenty years old.

MAMA: What time you be home from school today?

BENEATHA: Kind of late. (*with enthusiasm*) Madeline is going to start my guitar lessons today.

Mama and Ruth look up with the same expression.

MAMA: Your *what* kind of lessons?   225

BENEATHA: Guitar.

RUTH: Oh, Father!

MAMA: How come you done taken it in your mind to learn to play the guitar?

BENEATHA: I just want to, that's all.

MAMA: (*smiling*)   Lord, child, don't you know what to get tired of this now—like you   230
    got tired of that little *do* with yourself? How long it going to be before you play-
    acting group you joined last year? (*looking at Ruth*) And what was it the year before
    that?

RUTH: The horseback-riding club for which she bought that fifty-five-dollar riding habit
    that's been hanging in the closet ever since!

MAMA: (*to Beneatha*)   Why you got to flit so from one thing to another, baby?

BENEATHA: (*sharply*)   I just want to learn to play the guitar. Is there anything wrong
    with that?

MAMA: Ain't nobody trying to stop you. I just wonders sometimes why you has to flit so
    from one thing to another all the time. You ain't never done nothing with all that
    camera equipment you brought home—

BENEATHA: I don't flit! I—I experiment with different forms of expression—   235

RUTH: Like riding a horse?

BENEATHA: —People have to express themselves one way or another.

MAMA: What is it you want to express?

BENEATHA: (*angrily*)   Me! (*Mama and Ruth look at each other and burst into rau-
    cous laughter.*) Don't worry—I don't expect you to understand.

MAMA: (*to change the subject*)   Who you going out with tomorrow night?   240

BENEATHA: (*with displeasure*)   George Murchison again.

MAMA: (*pleased*)   Oh—you getting a little sweet on him?

RUTH: You ask me, this child ain't sweet on nobody but herself—(*underbreath*) Ex-
    press herself!

They laugh.

BENEATHA: Oh—I like George all right, Mama. I mean I like him enough to go out with
    him and stuff, but—

RUTH: (*for devilment*)   What does *and stuff* mean?   245

BENEATHA: Mind your own business.

MAMA: Stop picking at her now, Ruth. (*She chuckles—then a suspicious sudden look at
    her daughter as she turns in her chair for emphasis.*) What DOES it mean?

BENEATHA: (*wearily*)   Oh, I just mean I couldn't ever really be serious about George.
    He's—he's so shallow.

RUTH: Shallow—what do you mean he's shallow? He's *Rich!*

MAMA: Hush, Ruth.   250

BENEATHA: I know he's rich. He knows he's rich, too.

RUTH: Well—what other qualities a man got to have to satisfy you, little girl?

BENEATHA: You wouldn't even begin to understand. Anybody who married Walter could
    not possibly understand.

MAMA: (*outraged*)   What kind of way is that to talk about your brother?

BENEATHA: Brother is a flip—let's face it.   255

MAMA: (*to Ruth, helplessly*)   What's a flip?

RUTH: (*glad to add kindling*)   She's saying he's crazy.

BENEATHA: Not crazy. Brother isn't really crazy yet—he—he's an elaborate neurotic.

MAMA: Hush your mouth!

BENEATHA: As for George. Well. George looks good—he's got a beautiful car and he takes   260
    me to nice places and, as my sister-in-law says, he is probably the richest boy I will
    ever get to know and I even like him sometimes—but if the Youngers are sitting
    around waiting to see if their little Bennie is going to tie up the family with the
    Murchisons, they are wasting their time.

RUTH: You mean you wouldn't marry George Murchison if he asked you someday? That
    pretty, rich thing? Honey, I knew you was odd—

BENEATHA: No I would not marry him if all I felt for him was what I feel now. Besides,
    George's family wouldn't really like it.

MAMA: Why not?

BENEATHA: Oh, Mama—the Murchisons are honest-to-God-real-*live*-rich colored people, and the only people in the world who are more snobbish than rich white people are rich colored people. I thought everybody knew that. I've met Mrs. Murchison. She's a scene!

MAMA: You must not dislike people 'cause they well off, honey.   265

BENEATHA: Why not? It makes just as much sense as disliking people 'cause they are poor, and lots of people do that.

RUTH: (*A wisdom-of-the-ages manner. To Mama*)   Well, she'll get over some of this—

BENEATHA: Get over it? What are you talking about, Ruth? Listen, I'm going to be a doctor. I'm not worried about who I'm going to marry yet—if I ever get married.

MAMA AND RUTH: *If!*

MAMA: Now, Bennie—   270

BENEATHA: Oh, I probably will . . . but first I'm going to be a doctor, and George, for one, still thinks that's pretty funny. I couldn't be bothered with that. I am going to be a doctor and everybody around here better understand that!

MAMA: (*kindly*)   'Course you going to be a doctor, honey, God willing.

BENEATHA: (*drily*)   God hasn't got a thing to do with it.

MAMA: Beneatha—that just wasn't necessary.

BENEATHA: Well—neither is God. I get sick of hearing about God.   275

MAMA: Beneatha!

BENEATHA: I mean it! I'm just tired of hearing about God all the time. What has He got to do with anything? Does he pay tuition?

MAMA: You 'bout to get your fresh little jaw slapped!

RUTH: That's just what she needs, all right!

BENEATHA: Why? Why can't I say what I want to around here, like everybody else?   280

MAMA: It don't sound nice for a young girl to say things like that—you wasn't brought up that way. Me and your father went to trouble to get you and Brother to church every Sunday.

BENEATHA: Mama, you don't understand. It's all a matter of ideas, and God is just one idea I don't accept. It's not important. I am not going out and be immoral or commit crimes because I don't believe in God. I don't even think about it. It's just that I get tired of Him getting credit for all the things the human race achieves through its own stubborn effort. There simply is no blasted God—there is only man and it is *he* who makes miracles!

Mama absorbs this speech, studies her daughter and rises slowly and crosses to Beneatha and slaps her powerfully across the face. After, there is only silence and the daughter drops her eyes from her mother's face, and Mama is very tall before her.

MAMA: Now—you say after me, in my mother's house there is still God. (*There is a long pause and Beneatha stares at the floor wordlessly. Mama repeats the phrase with precision and cool emotion.*) In my mother's house there is still God.

BENEATHA: In my mother's house there is still God.

A long pause.

MAMA: (*Walking away from Beneatha, too disturbed for triumphant posture. Stop-   285
ping and turning back to her daughter.*)   There are some ideas we ain't going to have in this house. Not long as I am at the head of this family.

BENEATHA: Yes, ma'am.

Mama walks out of the room.

RUTH: (*almost gently, with profound understanding*)   You think you a woman, Ben-nie—but you still a little girl. What you did was childish—so you got treated like a child.

BENEATHA: I see. (*quietly*)   I also see that everybody thinks it's all right for Mama to be a tyrant. But all the tyranny in the world will never put a God in the heavens!

She picks up her books and goes out. Pause.

RUTH: (*goes to Mama's door*)   She said she was sorry.

MAMA: (*coming out, going to her plant*)   They frightens me, Ruth. My children.   290

RUTH: You got good children, Lena. They just a little off sometimes—but they're good.

MAMA: No—there's something come down between me and them that don't let us understand each other and I don't know what it is. One done almost lost his mind thinking 'bout money all the time and the other done commence to talk about things I can't seem to understand in no form or fashion. What is it that's changing, Ruth.

RUTH: (*soothingly, older than her years*)   Now . . . you taking it all too seriously. You just got strong-willed children and it takes a strong woman like you to keep 'em in hand.

MAMA: (*looking at her plant and sprinkling a little water on it*)   They spirited all right, my children. Got to admit they got spirit—Bennie and Walter. Like this little old plant that ain't never had enough sunshine or nothing—and look at it . . .

She has her back to Ruth, who has had to stop ironing and lean against something and put the back of her hand to her forehead.

RUTH: (*trying to keep Mama from noticing*)   You . . . sure . . . loves that little old thing,   295
don't you? . . .

MAMA: Well, I always wanted me a garden like I used to see sometimes at the back of the houses down home. This plant is close as I ever got to having one. (*She looks out of the window as she replaces the plant.*) Lord, ain't nothing as dreary as the view from this window on a dreary day, is there? Why ain't you singing this morning, Ruth? Sing that "No Ways Tired." That song always lifts me up so—(*She turns at last to see that Ruth has slipped quietly to the floor, in a state of semiconsciousness.*) Ruth! Ruth honey—what's the matter with you . . . Ruth!

Curtain.

Scene 2

It is the following morning; a Saturday morning, and house cleaning is in progress at the Youngers. Furniture has been shoved hither and yon and Mama is giving the kitchen-area walls a washing down. Beneatha, in dungarees, with a handkerchief tied around her face, is spraying insecticide into the cracks in the walls. As they work, the radio is on and a Southside disk-jockey program is inappropriately filling the house with a rather exotic saxophone blues. Travis, the sole idle one, is leaning on his arms, looking out of the window.

TRAVIS: Grandmama, that stuff Bennie is using smells awful. Can I go downstairs, please?

MAMA: Did you get all them chores done already? I ain't seen you doing much.

TRAVIS: Yes'm—finished early. Where did Mama go this morning?

MAMA: (*looking at Beneatha*)   She had to go on a little errand.   300

The phone rings. Beneatha runs to answer it and reaches it before Walter, who has entered from bedroom.

TRAVIS: Where?

MAMA: To tend to her business.

BENEATHA: Haylo . . . (*disappointed*) Yes, he is. (*She tosses the phone to* WALTER, *who barely catches it.*) It's Willie Harris again.

WALTER: (*as privately as possible under Mama's gaze*)   Hello, Willie. Did you get the papers from the lawyer? . . . No, not yet. I told you the mailman doesn't get here till ten-thirty . . . No, I'll come there . . . Yeah! Right away. (*He hangs up and goes for his coat.*)

BENEATHA: Brother, where did Ruth go?   305

WALTER: (*as he exits*)   How should I know!

TRAVIS: Aw come on, Grandma. Can I go outside?

MAMA: Oh, I guess so. You stay right in front of the house, though, and keep a good lookout for the postman.

TRAVIS: Yes'm. (*He darts into bedroom for stickball and bat, reenters, and sees
Beneatha on her knees spraying under sofa with behind upraised. He edges closer
to the target, takes aim, and lets her have it. She screams.*) Leave them poor little
cockroaches alone, they ain't bothering you none! (*He runs as she swings the
spraygun at him viciously and playfully.*) Grandma! Grandma!

MAMA: Look out there, girl, before you be spilling some of that stuff on that child!   310

TRAVIS: (*safely behind the bastion of Mama*)   That's right—look out, now! (*He exits.*)

BENEATHA: (*drily*)   I can't imagine that it would hurt him—it has never hurt the
roaches.

MAMA: Well, little boys' hides ain't as tough as Southside roaches. You better get over
there behind the bureau. I seen one marching out of there like Napoleon yesterday.

BENEATHA: There's really only one way to get rid of them, Mama—

MAMA: How?   315

BENEATHA: Set fire to this building! Mama, where did Ruth go?

MAMA: (*looking at her with meaning*)   To the doctor, I think.

BENEATHA: The doctor? What's the matter? (*They exchange glances*) You don't think—

MAMA: (*with her sense of drama*)   Now I ain't saying what I think. But I ain't never
been wrong 'bout a woman neither.

The phone rings.

BENEATHA: (*at the phone*)   Hay-lo . . . (*pause, and a moment of recognition.*) Well—   320
when did you get back! . . . And how was it? . . . Of course I've missed you—in my
way . . . This morning? No . . . house cleaning and all that and Mama hates it if I let
people come over when the house is like this . . . You *have?* Well, that's different . . .
What is it— Oh, what the hell, come on over . . . Right, see you then. *Arrividerci.*

She hangs up.

MAMA: (*who has listened vigorously, as is her habit*)   Who is that you inviting over
here with this house looking like this? You ain't got the pride you was born with!

BENEATHA: Asagai doesn't care how houses look, Mama—he's an intellectual.

MAMA: *Who?*

BENEATHA: Asagai—Joseph Asagai. He's an African boy I met on campus. He's been studying in Canada all summer.

MAMA: What's his name?   325

BENEATHA: Asagai, Joseph. Ah—sah—guy . . . He's from Nigeria.

MAMA: Oh, that's the little country that was founded by slaves way back . . .

BENEATHA: No, Mama—that's Liberia.

MAMA: I don't think I never met no African before.

BENEATHA: Well, do me a favor and don't ask him a whole lot of ignorant questions about   330
Africans. I mean, do they wear clothes and all that—

MAMA: Well, now, I guess if you think we so ignorant 'round here maybe you shouldn't
bring your friends here—

BENEATHA: It's just that people ask such crazy things. All anyone seems to know about
when it comes to Africa is Tarzan—

MAMA: (*indignantly*)   Why should I know anything about Africa?

BENEATHA: Why do you give money at church for the missionary work?

MAMA: Well, that's to help save people.   335

BENEATHA: You mean save them from *heathenism*—

MAMA: (*innocently*)   Yes.

BENEATHA: I'm afraid they need more salvation from the British and the French.

Ruth comes in forlornly and pulls off her coat with dejection. They both turn to look at her.

RUTH: (*dispiritedly*)   Well, I guess from all the happy faces—everybody knows.

BENEATHA: You pregnant?   340

MAMA: Lord have mercy, I sure hope it's a little old girl. Travis ought to have a sister.

Beneatha and Ruth give her a hopeless look for this grandmotherly enthusiasm.

BENEATHA: How far along are you?

RUTH: Two months.

BENEATHA: Did you mean to? I mean did you plan it or was it an accident?

MAMA: What do you know about planning or not planning?   345

BENEATHA: Oh, Mama.

RUTH: (*wearily*) She's twenty years old, Lena.

BENEATHA: Did you plan it, Ruth?

RUTH: Mind your own business.

BENEATHA: It is my business—where is he going to live, on the *roof*? (*There is silence fol-*   350
lowing the remark as the three women react to the sense of it.) Gee—I didn't
mean that, Ruth, honest. Gee, I don't feel like that at all. I—I think it is wonderful.

RUTH: (*dully*) Wonderful.

BENEATHA: Yes—really. (*There is a sudden commotion from the street and she goes to
the window to look out.*) What on earth is going on out there? These kids. (*There
are, as she throws open the window, the shouts of children rising up from the
street. She sticks her head out to see better and calls out.*) TRAVIS! TRAVIS! . . .
WHAT ARE YOU DOING DOWN THERE? (*She sees.*) Oh Lord, they're chasing a rat!

Ruth covers her face with hands and turns away.

MAMA: (*angrily*) Tell that youngun to get himself up here, at once!

BENEATHA: TRAVIS . . . YOU COME UPSTAIRS . . . AT ONCE!

RUTH: (*her face twisted*) Chasing a rat . . .   355

MAMA: (*looking at Ruth, worried*) Doctor say everything going to be all right?

RUTH: (*far away*) Yes—she says everything is going to be fine . . .

MAMA: (*immediately suspicious*) "She"— What doctor you went to?

Ruth just looks at Mama meaningfully and Mama opens her mouth to speak as Travis bursts in.

TRAVIS: (*excited and full of narrative, coming directly to his mother*) Mama, you
should of seen the rat . . . Big as a cat, honest! (*He shows an exaggerated size with
his hands.*) Gaaleee, that rat was really cuttin' and Bubber caught him with his heel
and the janitor, Mr. Barnett, got him with a stick—and then they got him in a corner
and BAM! BAM! BAM!—and he was still jumping around and bleeding like everything too—there's rat blood all over the street—

*Ruth reaches out suddenly and grabs her son without even looking at him and clamps her hand over
his mouth and holds him to her. Mama crosses to them rapidly and takes the boy from her.*

MAMA: You hush up now . . . talking all that terrible stuff . . . (*Travis is staring at his*   360
*mother with a stunned expression. Beneatha comes quickly and takes him away
from his grandmother and ushers him to the door.*)

BENEATHA: You go back outside and play . . . but not with any rats. (*She pushes him gently out the door with the boy straining to see what is wrong with his mother.*)

MAMA: (*worriedly hovering over Ruth*) Ruth honey—what's the matter with you—
you sick?

*Ruth has her fists clenched on her thighs and is fighting hard to suppress a scream that seems to be ris-
ing in her.*

BENEATHA: What's the matter with her, Mama?

MAMA: (*working her fingers in Ruth's shoulders to relax her*) She be all right.
Women gets right depressed sometimes when they get her way. (*speaking softly, ex-
pertly, rapidly*) Now you just relax. That's right . . . just lean back, don't think 'bout
nothing at all . . . nothing at all—

RUTH: I'm all right . . .   365

The glassy-eyed look melts and then she collapses into a fit of heavy sobbing. The bell rings.

BENEATHA: Oh, my God—that must be Asagai.

MAMA: (*to Ruth*)   Come on now, honey. You need to lie down and rest awhile . . . then have some nice hot food.

They exit, Ruth's weight on her mother-in-law. Beneatha, herself profoundly disturbed, opens the door to admit a rather dramatic-looking young man with a large package.

ASAGAI: Hello, Alaiyo—

BENEATHA: (*holding the door open and regarding him with pleasure*)   Hello . . . (*long pause*) Well—come in. And please excuse everything. My mother was very upset about my letting anyone come here with the place like this.

ASAGAI: (*coming into the room*)   You look disturbed too . . . Is something wrong?   370

BENEATHA: (*still at the door, absently*)   Yes . . . we've all got acute ghetto-itus. (*She smiles and comes toward him, finding a cigarette and sitting*)   So—sit down! No! Wait! (*She whips the spraygun off sofa where she had left it and puts the cushions back. At last perches on arm of sofa. He sits.*) So, how was Canada?

ASAGAI: (*a sophisticate*)   Canadian.

BENEATHA: (*looking at him*)   Asagai, I'm very glad you are back.

ASAGAI: (*looking back at her in turn*)   Are you really?

BENEATHA: Yes—very.   375

ASAGAI: Why?—you were quite glad when I went away. What happened?

BENEATHA: You went away.

ASAGAI: Ahhhhhhhh.

BENEATHA: Before—you wanted to be so serious before there was time.

ASAGAI: How much time must there be before one knows what one feels?

BENEATHA: (*Stalling this particular conversation. Her hands pressed together, in a de-   380
liberately childish gesture.*)   What did you bring me?

ASAGAI: (*handing her the package*)   Open it and see.

BENEATHA: (*eagerly opening the package and drawing out some records and the colorful robes of a Nigerian woman*)   Oh, Asagai! . . . You got them for me! . . . How beautiful . . . and the records too! (*She lifts out the robes and runs to the mirror with them and holds the drapery up in front of herself.*)

ASAGAI: (*coming to her at the mirror*)   I shall have to teach you how to drape it properly. (*He flings the material about her for the moment and stands back to look at her.*)   Ah—*Oh-pay-gay-day, oh-gbah-mu-shay.* (*a Yoruba exclamation for admiration*) You wear it well . . . very well . . . mutilated hair and all.

BENEATHA: (*turning suddenly*)   My hair—what's wrong with my hair?

ASAGAI: (*shrugging*)   Were you born with it like that?

BENEATHA: (*reaching up to touch it*)   No . . . of course not.

She looks back to the mirror, disturbed.

ASAGAI: (*smiling*)   How then?

BENEATHA: You know perfectly well how . . . as crinkly as yours . . . that's how.

ASAGAI: And it is ugly to you that way?

BENEATHA: (*quickly*)   Oh, no—not ugly . . . (*more slowly, apologetically*)   But it's so   390
hard to manage when it's, well—raw.

ASAGAI: And so to accommodate that—you mutilate it every week?

BENEATHA: It's not mutilation!

ASAGAI: (*laughing aloud at her seriousness*)   Oh . . . please! I am only teasing you because you are so very serious about these things. (*He stands back from her and folds his arms across his chest as he watches her pulling at her hair and frowning in the mirror.*)   Do you remember the first time you met me at school? . . . (*He laughs.*) You came up to me and you said—and I thought you were the most serious little thing I had ever seen—you said: (*He imitates her.*) "Mr. Asagai—I want very much to talk with you. About Africa. You see, Mr. Asagai, I am looking for my *identity*!"

He laughs.

BENEATHA: (*turning to him, not laughing*)   Yes—

Her face is quizzical, profoundly disturbed.

ASAGAI: (*still teasing and reaching out and taking her face in his hands and turning her profile to him*)   Well . . . it is true that this is not so much a profile of a Hollywood queen as perhaps a queen of the Nile—(*a mock dismissal of the importance of the question*) But what does it matter? Assimilationism is so popular in your country.   395

BENEATHA: (*wheeling, passionately, sharply*)   I am not an assimilationist!

ASAGAI: (*The protest hangs in the room for a moment and Asagai studies her, his laughter fading.*)   Such a serious one. (*There is a pause.*) So—you like the robes? You must take excellent care of them—they are from my sister's personal wardrobe.

BENEATHA: (*with incredulity*)   You—you sent all the way home—for me?

ASAGAI: (*with charm*)   For you—I would do much more . . . Well, that is what I came for. I must go.

BENEATHA: Will you call me Monday?   400

ASAGAI: Yes . . . We have a great deal to talk about. I mean about identity and time and all that.

BENEATHA: Time?

ASAGAI: Yes. About how much time one needs to know what one feels.

BENEATHA: You see! You never understood that there is more than one kind of feeling which can exist between a man and a woman—or, at least, there should be.

ASAGAI: (*shaking his head negatively but gently*)   No. Between a man and a woman there need be only one kind of feeling. I have that for you . . . Now even . . . right this moment . . .   405

BENEATHA: I know—and by itself—it won't do. I can find that anywhere.

ASAGAI: For a woman it should be enough.

BENEATHA: I know—because that's what it says in all the novels that men write. But it isn't. Go ahead and laugh—but I'm not interested in being someone's little episode in America or—(*with feminine vengeance*)—one of them! (*Asagai has burst into laughter again.*) That's funny as hell, huh!

ASAGAI: It's just that every American girl I have known has said that to me. White—black—in this you are all the same. And the same speech, too!

BENEATHA: (*angrily*)   Yuk, yuk, yuk!   410

ASAGAI: It's how you can be sure that the world's most liberated women are not liberated at all. You all talk about it too much!

Mama enters and is immediately all social charm because of the presence of a guest.

BENEATHA: Oh—Mama—this is Mr. Asagai.

MAMA: How do you do?

ASAGAI: (*total politeness to an elder*)   How do you do, Mrs. Younger. Please forgive me for coming at such an outrageous hour on a Saturday.

MAMA: Well, you are quite welcome. I just hope you understand that our house don't always look like this. (*chatterish*) You must come again. I would love to hear all about—(*not sure of the name*)—your country. I think it's so sad the way our American Negroes don't know nothing about Africa 'cept Tarzan and all that. And all that money they pour into these churches when they ought to be helping you people over there drive out them French and Englishmen done taken away your land.   415

The mother flashes a slightly superior look at her daughter upon completion of the recitation.

ASAGAI: (*taken aback by this sudden and acutely unrelated expression of sympathy*)   Yes . . . yes . . .

MAMA: (*smiling at him suddenly and relaxing and looking him over*)   How many miles is it from here to where you come from?

ASAGAI: Many thousands.

MAMA: (*looking at him as she would* Walter)   I bet you don't half look after yourself, being away from your mama either. I spec you better come 'round here from time to time to get yourself some decent homecooked meals . . .

ASAGAI: (*moved*)   Thank you. Thank you very much. (*they are all quiet, then*) Well . . . I   420
must go. I will call you Monday, Alaiyo.

MAMA: What's that he call you?

ASAGAI: Oh—"Alaiyo." I hope you don't mind. It is what you would call a nickname, I think. It is a Yoruba word. I am a Yoruba.

MAMA: (*looking at Beneatha*)   I—I thought he was from—(*uncertain*)

ASAGAI: (*understanding*)   Nigeria is my country. Yoruba is my tribal origin—

BENEATHA: You didn't tell us what Alaiyo means . . . for all I know, you might be calling me   425
Little Idiot or something . . .

ASAGAI: Well . . . let me see . . . I do not know how just to explain it . . . The sense of a thing can be so different when it changes languages.

BENEATHA: You're evading.

ASAGAI: No—really it is difficult . . . (*thinking*) It means . . . it means One for Whom Bread—Food—Is Not Enough. (*He looks at her.*) Is that all right?

BENEATHA: (*understanding, softly*)   Thank you.

MAMA: (*looking from one to the other and not understanding any of it*)   Well . . .   430
that's nice . . . You must come see us again—Mr.—

ASAGAI: Ah—sah—guy . . .

MAMA: Yes . . . Do come again.

ASAGAI: Good-bye.

He exits.

MAMA: (*after him*)   Lord, that's a pretty thing just went out here! (*insinuatingly, to her daughter*) Yes, I guess I see why we done commence to get so interested in Africa 'round here. Missionaries my aunt Jenny!

She exits.

BENEATHA: Oh, Mama!   435

She picks up the Nigerian dress and holds it up to her in front of the mirror again. She sets the head-dress on haphazardly and then notices her hair again and clutches at it and then replaces the head-dress and frowns at herself. Then she starts to wriggle in front of the mirror as she thinks a Nigerian woman might. Travis enters and stands regarding her.

TRAVIS: What's the matter, girl, you cracking up?

BENEATHA: Shut up.

She pulls the headdress off and looks at herself in the mirror and clutches at her hair again and squinches her eyes as if trying to imagine something. Then, suddenly, she gets her raincoat and ker-chief and hurriedly prepares for going out.

MAMA: (*coming back into the room*)   She's resting now. Travis, baby, run next door and ask Miss Johnson to please let me have a little kitchen cleanser. This here can is empty as Jacob's kettle.

TRAVIS: I just came in.

MAMA: Do as you told. (*He exits and she looks at her daughter.*) Where you going?   440

BENEATHA: (*halting at the door*)   To become a queen of the Nile!

She exits in a breathless blaze of glory. Ruth appears in the bedroom doorway.

MAMA: Who told you to get up?

RUTH: Ain't nothing wrong with me to be lying in no bed for. Where did Bennie go?

MAMA: (*drumming her fingers*)   Far as I could make out—to Egypt. (*Ruth just looks at her.*) What time is it getting to?

RUTH: Ten twenty. And the mailman going to ring that bell this morning just like he   445
done every morning for the last umpteen years.

Travis comes in with the cleanser can.

TRAVIS: She say to tell you that she don't have much.

MAMA: (*angrily*)   Lord, some people I could name sure is tight-fisted! (*directing her
grandson*) Mark two cans of cleanser down on the list there. If she that hard up for
kitchen cleanser, I sure don't want to forget to get her none!

RUTH: Lena—maybe the woman is just short on cleanser—

MAMA: (*not listening*)   Much baking powder as she done borrowed from me all these
years, she could of done gone into the baking business!

*The bell sounds suddenly and sharply and all three are stunned—serious and silent—mid-speech. In
spite of all the other conversations and distractions of the morning, this is what they have been waiting for, even Travis, who looks helplessly from his mother to his grandmother. Ruth is the first to come
to life again.*

RUTH: (*to Ttravis*)   *Get down them steps, boy!*   450

Travis snaps to life and flies out to get the mail.

MAMA: (*her eyes wide, her hand to her breast*)   You mean it done really come?

RUTH: (*excited*)   Oh, Miss Lena!

MAMA: (*collecting herself*)   Well ... I don't know what we all so excited about 'round
here for. We known it was coming for months.

RUTH: That's a whole lot different from having it come and being able to hold it in your
hands ... a piece of paper worth ten thousand dollars ... (*Travis bursts back into
the room. He holds the envelope high above his head, like a little dancer, his face
is radiant and he is breathless. He moves to his grandmother with sudden slow
ceremony and puts the envelope into her hands. She accepts it, and then merely
holds it and looks at it.*) Come on! Open it ... Lord have mercy, I wish Walter Lee
was here!

TRAVIS: Open it, Grandmama!   455

MAMA: (*staring at it*)   Now you all be quiet. It's just a check.

RUTH: Open it ...

MAMA: (*still staring at it*)   Now don't act silly ... We ain't never been no people to act
silly 'bout no money—

RUTH: (*swiftly*)   We ain't never had none before—OPEN IT!

*Mama finally makes a good strong tear and pulls out the thin blue slice of paper and inspects it
closely. The boy and his mother study it raptly over Mama's shoulders.*

MAMA: Travis! (*She is counting off with doubt.*)   Is that the right number of zeros?   460

TRAVIS: Yes'm ... ten thousand dollars. Gaalee, Grandmama, you rich.

MAMA: (*She holds the check away from her, still looking at it. Slowly her face sobers
into a mask of unhappiness.*)   Ten thousand dollars. (*She hands it to Ruth.*) Put it
away somewhere, Ruth. (*She does not look at Ruth; her eyes seem to be seeing
something somewhere very far off.*) Ten thousand dollars they give you. Ten thousand dollars.

TRAVIS: (*to his mother, sincerely*)   What's the matter with Grandmama—don't she
want to be rich?

RUTH: (*distractedly*)   You go on out and play now, baby. (*Travis exits. Mama starts
wiping dishes absently, humming intently to herself. Ruth turns to her, with kind
exasperation.*) You've gone and got yourself upset.

MAMA: (*not looking at her*)   I spec if it wasn't for you all ... I would just put that   465
money away or give it to the church or something.

RUTH: Now what kind of talk is that. Mr. Younger would just be plain mad if he could
hear you talking foolish like that.

MAMA: (*stopping and staring off*)   Yes . . . he sure would. (*sighing*) We got enough to
do with that money, all right. (*She halts then, and turns and looks at her daughter-in-law hard; Ruth avoids her eyes and Mama wipes her hands with finality and starts to speak firmly to Ruth.*) Where did you go today, girl?

RUTH: To the doctor.

MAMA: (*impatiently*)   Now, Ruth . . . you know better than that. Old Doctor Jones is
strange enough in his way but there ain't nothing 'bout him make somebody slip
and call him "she"—like you done this morning.

RUTH: Well, that's what happened—my tongue slipped.   470

MAMA: You went to see that woman, didn't you?

RUTH: (*defensively, giving herself away*)   What woman you talking about?

MAMA: (*angrily*)   That woman who—

Walter enters in great excitement.

WALTER: Did it come?

MAMA: (*quietly*)   Can't you give people a Christian greeting before you start asking   475
about money?

WALTER: (*to Ruth*)   Did it come? (*Ruth unfolds the check and lays it quietly before
him, watching him intently with thoughts of her own. Walter sits down and
grasps it close and counts off the zeros.*) Ten thousand dollars—(*He turns suddenly, frantically to his mother and draws some papers out of his breast pocket.*)
Mama—look. Old Willy Harris put everything on paper—

MAMA: Son—I think you ought to talk to your wife . . . I'll go on out and leave you alone
if you want—

WALTER: I can talk to her later—Mama, look—

MAMA: Son—

WALTER: WILL SOMEBODY PLEASE LISTEN TO ME TODAY!   480

MAMA: (*quietly*)   I don't 'low no yellin' in this house, Walter Lee, and you know it—
(*Walter stares at them in frustration and starts to speak several times.*) And there
ain't going to be no investing in no liquor stores.

WALTER: But, Mama, you ain't even looked at it.

MAMA: I don't aim to have to speak on that again.

A long pause.

WALTER: You ain't looked at it and you don't aim to have to speak on that again? You
ain't even looked at it and *you* have decided—(*crumpling his papers*) Well, *you* tell
that to my boy tonight when you put him to sleep on the living-room couch . . .
(*turning to Mama and speaking directly to her*) Yeah—and tell it to my wife,
Mama, tomorrow when she has to go out of here to look after somebody else's kids.
And tell it to *me,* Mama, every time we need a new pair of curtains and I have to
watch *you* go out and work in somebody's kitchen. Yeah, you tell me then!

Walter starts out.

RUTH: Where you going?   485

WALTER: I'm going out!

RUTH: Where?

WALTER: Just out of this house somewhere—

RUTH: (*getting her coat*)   I'll come too.

WALTER: I don't want you to come!   490

RUTH: I got something to talk to you about, Walter.

WALTER: That's too bad.

MAMA: (*still quietly*)   Walter Lee—(*She waits and he finally turns and looks at her.*)
Sit down.

WALTER: I'm a grown man, Mama.

MAMA: Ain't nobody said you wasn't grown. But you still in my house and my presence.   495
And as long as you are— you'll talk to your wife civil. Now sit down.

RUTH: (*suddenly*)   Oh, let him go on out and drink himself to death! He makes me sick to my stomach! (*She flings her coat against him and exits to bedroom.*)

WALTER: (*violently flinging the coat after her*)   And you turn mine too, baby! (*The door slams behind her.*) That was my biggest mistake—

MAMA: (*still quietly*)   Walter, what is the matter with you?

WALTER: Matter with me? Ain't nothing the matter with *me*!

MAMA: Yes there is. Something eating you up like a crazy man. Something more than me   500
not giving you this money. The past few years I been watching it happen to you. You get all nervous acting and kind of wild in the eyes—(*Walter jumps up impatiently at her words*) I said sit there now, I'm talking to you!

WALTER: Mama—I don't need no nagging at me today.

MAMA: Seem like you getting to a place where you always tied up in some kind of knot about something. But if anybody ask you 'bout it you just yell at 'em and bust out the house and go out and drink somewheres. Walter Lee, people can't live with that. Ruth's a good, patient girl in her way—but you getting to be too much. Boy, don't make the mistake of driving that girl away from you.

WALTER: Why—what she do for me?

MAMA: She loves you.

WALTER: Mama—I'm going out. I want to go off somewhere and be by myself for a   505
while.

MAMA: I'm sorry 'bout your liquor store, son. It just wasn't the thing for us to do. That's what I want to tell you about—

WALTER: I got to go out, Mama—

He rises.

MAMA: It's dangerous, son.

WALTER: What's dangerous?

MAMA: When a man goes outside his home to look for peace.   510

WALTER: (*beseechingly*)   Then why can't there never be no peace in this house then?

MAMA: You done found it in some other house?

WALTER: No—there ain't no woman! Why do women always think there's a woman somewhere when a man gets restless. (*picks up the check*) Do you know what this money means to me? Do you know what this money can do for us? (*puts it back*) Mama—Mama— I want so many things . . .

MAMA: Yes, son—

WALTER: I want so many things that they are driving me kind of crazy . . . Mama—look at   515
me.

MAMA: I'm looking at you. You a good-looking boy. You got a job, a nice wife, a fine boy and—

WALTER: A job. (*looks at her*) Mama, a job? I open and close car doors all day long. I drive a man around in his limousine and I say, "Yes, sir; no, sir; very good, sir; shall I take the Drive, sir?" Mama, that ain't no kind of job . . . that ain't nothing at all. (*very quietly*) Mama, I don't know if I can make you understand.

MAMA: Understand what, baby?

WALTER: (*quietly*)   Sometimes it's like I can see the future stretched out in front of me—just plain as day. The future, Mama. Hanging over there at the edge of my days. Just waiting for me—a big, looming blank space—full of *nothing*. Just waiting for *me*. But it don't have to be. (*Pause. Kneeling beside her chair.*) Mama—sometimes when I'm downtown and I pass them cool, quiet-looking restaurants where them white boys are sitting back and talking 'bout things . . . sitting there turning deals worth millions of dollars . . . sometimes I see guys don't look much older than me—

MAMA: Son—how come you talk so much 'bout money?   520

WALTER: (*with immense passion*)   Because it is life, Mama!

MAMA: (*quietly*)   Oh—(*very quietly*) So now it's life. Money is life. Once upon a time freedom used to be life—now it's money. I guess the world really do change . . .

WALTER: No—it was always money, Mama. We just didn't know about it.

MAMA: No . . . something has changed. (*She looks at him.*) You something new, boy. In my time we was worried about not being lynched and getting to the North if we could and how to stay alive and still have a pinch of dignity too . . . Now here come you and Beneatha—talking 'bout things we ain't never even thought about hardly, me and your daddy. You ain't satisfied or proud of nothing we done. I mean that you had a home; that we kept you out of trouble till you was grown; that you don't have to ride to work on the back of nobody's streetcar— You my children—but how different we done become.

WALTER: (*A long beat. He pats her hand and gets up.*)   You just don't understand, Mama, you just don't understand.   525

MAMA: Son—do you know your wife is expecting another baby? (*Walter stands, stunned, and absorbs what his mother has said.*) That's what she wanted to talk to you about. (*Walter sinks down into a chair.*) This ain't for me to be telling—but you ought to know. (*She waits.*) I think Ruth is thinking 'bout getting rid of that child.

WALTER: (*slowly understanding*)   No—no—Ruth wouldn't do that.

MAMA: When the world gets ugly enough—a woman will do anything for her family. *The part that's already living.*

WALTER: You don't know Ruth, Mama, if you think she would do that.

Ruth opens the bedroom door and stands there a little limp.

RUTH: (*beaten*)   Yes I would too, Walter. (*pause*) I gave her a five-dollar down payment.   530

There is total silence as the man stares at his wife and the mother stares at her son.

MAMA: (*presently*)   Well—(*tightly*) Well—son, I'm waiting to hear you say something . . . (*She waits.*) I'm waiting to hear how you be your father's son. Be the man he was . . . (*Pause. The silence shouts.*) Your wife say she going to destroy your child. And I'm waiting to hear you talk like him and say we a people who give children life, not who destroys them—(*She rises.*) I'm waiting to see you stand up and look like your daddy and say we done give up one baby to poverty and that we ain't going to give up nary another one . . . I'm waiting.

WALTER: Ruth—(*He can say nothing.*)

MAMA: If you a son of mine, tell her! (*Walter picks up his keys and his coat and walks out. She continues, bitterly.*) You . . . you are a disgrace to your father's memory. Somebody get me my hat!

Curtain.

Act 2, Scene 1

TIME: *Later the same day.*

AT RISE: *Ruth is ironing again. She has the radio going. Presently Beneatha's bedroom door opens and Ruth's mouth falls and she puts down the iron in fascination.*

RUTH: What have we got on tonight!

BENEATHA: (*emerging grandly from the doorway so that we can see her thoroughly robed in the costume Asagai brought*)   You are looking at what a well-dressed Nigerian woman wears—(*She parades for Ruth, her hair completely hidden by the headdress; she is coquettishly fanning herself with an ornate oriental fan, mistakenly more like Butterfly than any Nigerian that ever was.*) Isn't it beautiful? (*She promenades to the radio and, with an arrogant flourish, turns off the good loud blues that is playing.*) Enough of this assimilationist junk! (*Ruth follows her with her eyes as she goes to the phonograph and puts on a record and turns and waits ceremoniously for the music to come up. Then, with a shout—*) OCOMOGOSIAY!

Ruth jumps. The music comes up, a lovely Nigerian melody. Beneatha listens, enraptured, her eyes far away—"back to the past." She begins to dance. Ruth is dumfounded.

RUTH: What kind of dance is that?

BENEATHA: A folk dance.

RUTH: (*Pearl Bailey*)   What kind of folks do that, honey?   5

BENEATHA: It's from Nigeria. It's a dance of welcome.

RUTH: Who you welcoming?

BENEATHA: The men back to the village.

RUTH: Where they been?

BENEATHA: How should I know—out hunting or something. Anyway, they are coming   10
back now . . .

RUTH: Well, that's good.

BENEATHA: (*with the record*)

Alundi, alundi
Alundi alunya
Jop pu a jeepua
Ang gu soooooooooo

Ai yai yae . . .
Ayehaye—alundi . . .

Walter comes in during this performance; he has obviously been drinking. He leans against the door heavily and watches his sister, at first with distaste. Then his eyes look off—"back to the past"—as he lifts both his fists to the roof, screaming.

WALTER: YEAH . . . AND ETHIOPIA STRETCH FORTH HER HANDS AGAIN! . . .

RUTH: (*drily, looking at him*)   Yes—and Africa sure is claiming her own tonight. (*She gives them both up and starts ironing again.*)

WALTER: (*all in a drunken, dramatic shout*)   Shut up! . . . I'm digging them drums . . .   15
them drums move me! . . . (*He makes his weaving way to his wife's face and leans in close to her.*) In my *heart of hearts*—(*He thumps his chest.*)—I am much warrior!

RUTH: (*without even looking up*)   In your heart of hearts you are much drunkard.

WALTER: (*coming away from her and starting to wander around the room, shouting*)   Me and Jomo . . . (*Intently, in his sister's face. She has stopped dancing to watch him in this unknown mood.*) That's my man, Kenyatta. (*shouting and thumping his chest*)   FLAMING SPEAR! HOT DAMN! (*He is suddenly in possession of an imaginary spear and actively spearing enemies all over the room.*) OCOMOGOSIAY . . .

BENEATHA: (*to encourage Walter, thoroughly caught up with this side of him*) OCOMOGOSIAY, FLAMING SPEAR!

WALTER: THE LION IS WAKING . . . OWIMOWEH! (*He pulls his shirt open and leaps up on a table and gestures with his spear.*)

BENEATHA: OWIMOWEH!

WALTER: (*On the table, very far gone, his eyes pure glass sheets. He sees what we can-   20
not, that he is a leader of his people, a great chief, a descendant of Chaka, and that the hour to march has come.*)   Listen, my black brothers—

BENEATHA: OCOMOGOSIAY!

WALTER: —Do you hear the waters rushing against the shores of the coastlands—

BENEATHA: OCOMOGOSIAY!

WALTER: —Do you hear the screeching of the cocks in yonder hills beyond where the   25
chiefs meet in council for the coming of the mighty war—

BENEATHA: OCOMOGOSIAY!

And now the lighting shifts subtly to suggest the world of Walter's imagination, and the mood shifts from pure comedy. It is the inner Walter speaking: the Southside chauffeur has assumed an unexpected majesty.

WALTER: —Do you hear the beating of the wings of the birds flying low over the mountains and the low places of our land—

BENEATHA: OCOMOGOSIAY!

WALTER: —Do you hear the singing of the women, singing the war songs of our fathers
to the babies in the great houses? Singing the sweet war songs? (*The doorbell
rings.*) OH, DO YOU HEAR, MY *BLACK* BROTHERS!

BENEATHA: (*completely gone*)   We hear you, Flaming Spear—   30

Ruth shuts off the phonograph and opens the door. George Murchison enters.

WALTER: Telling us to prepare for the GREATNESS OF THE TIME!—(*Lights back to normal. He turns and sees George.*) Black Brother!

He extends his hand for the fraternal clasp.

GEORGE: Black Brother, hell!

RUTH: (*having had enough, and embarrassed for the family*)   Beneatha, you got
company—what's the matter with you? Walter Lee Younger, get down off that table
and stop acting like a fool ...

Walter comes down off the table suddenly and makes a quick exit to the bathroom.

RUTH: He's had a little to drink ... I don't know what her excuse is.

GEORGE: (*to Beneatha*)   Look honey, we're going *to* the theatre—we're not going to be   35
in it ... so go change, huh?

*Beneatha looks at him and slowly, ceremoniously, lifts her hands and pulls off the headdress. Her hair
is close-cropped and unstraightened. George freezes mid-sentence and Ruth's eyes all but fall out of her
head.*

GEORGE: What in the name of—

RUTH: (*touching Beneatha's hair*)   Girl, you done lost your natural mind!? Look at
your head!

GEORGE: What have you done to your head—I mean your hair!

BENEATHA: Nothing—except cut it off.

RUTH: Now that's the truth—it's what ain't been done to it! You expect this boy to go   40
out with you with your head all nappy like that?

BENEATHA: (*looking at George*)   That's up to George. If he's ashamed of his heritage—

GEORGE: Oh, don't be so proud of yourself, Bennie—just because you look eccentric.

BENEATHA: How can something that's natural be eccentric?

GEORGE: That's what being eccentric means—being natural. Get dressed.

BENEATHA: I don't like that, George.   45

RUTH: Why must you and your brother make an argument out of everything people say?

BENEATHA: Because I hate assimilationist Negroes!

RUTH: Will somebody please tell me what assimila-who-ever means!

GEORGE: Oh, it's just a college girl's way of calling people Uncle Toms—but that isn't
what it means at all.

RUTH: Well, what does it mean?   50

BENEATHA: (*cutting George off and staring at him as she replies to Ruth*)   It means
someone who is willing to give up his own culture and submerge himself completely in the dominant, and in this case, *oppressive* culture!

GEORGE: Oh, dear, dear, dear! Here we go! A lecture on the African past! On our Great
West African Heritage! In one second we will hear all about the great Ashanti empires; the great Songhay civilizations; and the great sculpture of Bénin—and then
some poetry in the Bantu—and the whole monologue will end with the word *heritage!* (*nastily*) Let's face it, baby, your heritage is nothing but a bunch of raggedy-
assed spirituals and some grass huts!

BENEATHA: GRASS HUTS! (*Ruth crosses to her and forcibly pushes her toward the bedroom.*) See there ... you are standing there in your splendid ignorance talking about
people who were the first to smelt iron on the face of the earth! (*Ruth is pushing
her through the door.*) The Ashanti were performing surgical operations when the
English—(*Ruth pulls the door to, with Beneatha on the other side, and smiles*

graciously at George. Beneatha opens the door and shouts the end of the sentence defiantly at George)—were still tatooing themselves with blue dragons! (*She goes back inside.*)

RUTH: Have a seat, George. (*They both sit. Ruth folds her hands rather primly on her lap, determined to demonstrate the civilization of the family.*) Warm, ain't it? I mean for September. (*pause*) Just like they always say about Chicago weather: If it's too hot or cold for you, just wait a minute and it'll change. (*She smiles happily at this cliché of clichés.*) Everybody say it's got to do with them bombs and things they keep setting off. (*pause*) Would you like a nice cold beer?

GEORGE: No, thank you. I don't care for beer. (*He looks at his watch.*) I hope she hurries   55
up.

RUTH: What time is the show?

GEORGE: It's an eight-thirty curtain. That's just Chicago, though. In New York standard curtain time is eight forty.

He is rather proud of this knowledge.

RUTH: (*properly appreciating it*)   You get to New York a lot?

GEORGE: (*offhand*)   Few times a year.

RUTH: Oh—that's nice. I've never been to New York.   60

walter enters. We feel he has relieved himself, but the edge of unreality is still with him.

WALTER: New York ain't got nothing Chicago ain't. Just a bunch of hustling people all squeezed up together—being "Eastern."

He turns his face into a screw of displeasure.

GEORGE: Oh—you've been?

WALTER: *Plenty* of times.

RUTH: (*shocked at the lie*)   Walter Lee Younger!

WALTER: (*staring her down*)   Plenty! (*pause*) What we got to drink in this house? Why   65
don't you offer this man some refreshment. (*to George*) They don't know how to entertain people in this house, man.

GEORGE: Thank you—I don't really care for anything.

WALTER: (*feeling his head; sobriety coming*)   Where's Mama?

RUTH: She ain't come back yet.

WALTER: (*looking Murchison over from head to toe, scrutinizing his carefully casual tweed sports jacket over cashmere V-neck sweater over soft eyelet shirt and tie, and soft slacks, finished off with white buckskin shoes*)   Why all you college boys wear them faggoty-looking white shoes?

RUTH: Walter Lee!   70

George Murchison ignores the remark.

WALTER: (*to Ruth*)   Well, they look crazy as hell—white shoes, cold as it is.

RUTH: (*crushed*)   You have to excuse him—

WALTER: No he don't! Excuse me for what? What you always excusing me for! I'll excuse myself when I needs to be excused! (*a pause*) They look as funny as them black knee socks Beneatha wears out of here all the time.

RUTH: It's the college *style*, Walter.

WALTER: Style, hell. She looks like she got burnt legs or something!   75

RUTH: Oh, Walter—

WALTER: (*an irritable mimic*)   Oh, Walter! Oh, Walter! (*to Murchison*) How's your old man making out? I understand you all going to buy that big hotel on the Drive? (*He finds a beer in the refrigerator, wanders over to Murchison, sipping and wiping his lips with the back of his hand, and straddling a chair backwards to talk to the other man.*) Shrewd move. Your old man is all right, man. (*tapping his head and half winking for emphasis*) I mean he knows how to operate. I mean he thinks *big*, you know what I mean, I mean for a *home,* you know? But I think he's kind of running out of ideas now. I'd like to talk to him. Listen, man, I got some plans that could turn this city upside down. I mean think like he does. *Big.* Invest big, gamble big, hell, lose *big* if you have to, you know what I mean. It's hard to find a man on this whole Southside who understands my kind of thinking—you dig? (*He scrutinizes Murchison again, drinks his beer, squints his eyes and leans in close, confidential, man to man.*) Me and you ought to sit down and talk sometimes, man. Man, I got me some ideas . . .

MURCHISON: (*with boredom*) Yeah—sometimes we'll have to do that, Walter.

WALTER: (*understanding the indifference, and offended*) Yeah—well, when you get the time, man. I know you a busy little boy.

RUTH: Walter, please—   80

WALTER: (*bitterly, hurt*) I know ain't nothing in this world as busy as you colored college boys with your fraternity pins and white shoes . . .

RUTH: (*covering her face with humiliation*) Oh, Walter Lee—

WALTER: I see you all all the time—with the books tucked under your arms—going to your (*British A—a mimic*) "clahsses." And for what! What the hell you learning over there? Filling up your heads—(*counting off on his fingers*)—with the sociology and the psychology—but they teaching you how to be a man? How to take over and run the world? They teaching you how to run a rubber plantation or a steel mill? Naw— just to talk proper and read books and wear them faggoty-looking white shoes . . .

GEORGE: (*looking at him with distaste, a little above it all*) You're all wacked up with bitterness, man.

WALTER: (*intently, almost quietly, between the teeth, glaring at the boy*) And you—   85
ain't you bitter, man? Ain't you just about had it yet? Don't you see no stars gleaming that you can't reach out and grab? You happy?—you contented son-of-a-bitch—you happy? You got it made? Bitter? Man, I'm a volcano. Bitter? Here I am a giant—surrounded by ants! Ants who can't even understand what it is the giant is talking about.

RUTH: (*passionately and suddenly*) Oh Walter—ain't you with nobody!

WALTER: (*violently*) No! 'Cause ain't nobody with me! Not even my own mother!

RUTH: Walter, that's a terrible thing to say!

Beneatha enters, dressed for the evening in a cocktail dress and earrings, hair natural.

GEORGE: Well—hey—(*crosses to Beneatha; thoughtful, with emphasis, since this is a reversal*) You look great!

WALTER: (*seeing his sister's hair for the first time*) What's the matter with your head?   90

BENEATHA: (*tired of the jokes now*) I cut it off, Brother.

WALTER: (*coming close to inspect it and walking around her*) Well, I'll be damned. So that's what they mean by the African bush . . .

BENEATHA: Ha ha. Let's go, George.

GEORGE: (*looking at her*) You know something? I like it. It's sharp. I mean it really is. (*helps her into her wrap*)

RUTH: Yes—I think so, too. (*She goes to the mirror and starts to clutch at her hair.*)   95

WALTER: Oh no! You leave yours alone, baby. You might turn out to have a pin-shaped head or something!

BENEATHA: See you all later.

RUTH: Have a nice time.

GEORGE: Thanks. Good night. (*Half out the door, he reopens it. to Walter.*) Good night, Prometheus!

Beneatha and George exit.

WALTER: (*to Ruth*) Who is Prometheus?   100

RUTH: I don't know. Don't worry about it.

WALTER: (*in fury, pointing after George*)   See there—they get to a point where they can't insult you man to man—they got to go talk about something ain't nobody never heard of!

RUTH: How do you know it was an insult? (*to humor him*) Maybe Prometheus is a nice fellow.

WALTER: Prometheus! I bet there ain't even no such thing! I bet that simple-minded clown—

RUTH: Walter—

She stops what she is doing and looks at him.

WALTER: (*yelling*)   Don't start!

RUTH: Start what?

WALTER: Your nagging! Where was I? Who was I with? How much money did I spend?

RUTH: (*plaintively*)   Walter Lee—why don't we just try to talk about it . . .

WALTER: (*not listening*)   I been out talking with people who understand me. People who care about the things I got on my mind.

RUTH: (*wearily*)   I guess that means people like Willy Harris.

WALTER: Yes, people like Willy Harris.

RUTH: (*with a sudden flash of impatience*) Why don't you all just hurry up and go into the banking business and stop talking about it!

WALTER: Why? You want to know why? 'Cause we all tied up in a race of people that don't know how to do nothing but moan, pray and have babies!

The line is too bitter even for him and he looks at her and sits down.

RUTH: Oh, Walter . . . (*softly*) Honey, why can't you stop fighting me?

WALTER: (*without thinking*)   Who's fighting you? Who even cares about you?

This line begins the retardation of his mood.

RUTH: Well—(*She waits a long time, and then with resignation starts to put away her things.*) I guess I might as well go on to bed . . . (*more or less to herself*) I don't know where we lost it . . . but we have . . . (*then, to him*) I—I'm sorry about this new baby, Walter. I guess maybe I better go on and do what I started . . . I guess I just didn't realize how bad things was with us . . . I guess I just didn't really realize—(*She starts out to the bedroom and stops.*) You want some hot milk?

WALTER: Hot milk?

RUTH: Yes—hot milk.

WALTER: Why hot milk?

RUTH: 'Cause after all that liquor you come home with you ought to have something hot in your stomach.

WALTER: I don't want no milk.

RUTH: You want some coffee then?

WALTER: No, I don't want no coffee. I don't want nothing hot to drink. (*almost plaintively*) Why you always trying to give me something to eat?

RUTH: (*standing and looking at him helplessly*)   What *else* can I give you, Walter Lee Younger?

She stands and looks at him and presently turns to go out again. He lifts his head and watches her going away from him in a new mood which began to emerge when he asked her "Who cares about you?"

WALTER: It's been rough, ain't it, baby? (*She hears and stops but does not turn around and he continues to her back.*) I guess between two people there ain't never as much understood as folks generally thinks there is. I mean like between me and you— (*She turns to face him.*) How we gets to the place where we scared to talk softness to each other. (*He waits, thinking hard himself.*) Why you think it got to be like that? (*He is thoughtful, almost as a child would be.*) Ruth, what is it gets into people ought to be close?

105

110

115

120

125

RUTH: I don't know, honey. I think about it a lot.

WALTER: On account of you and me, you mean? The way things are with us. The way something done come down between us.

RUTH: There ain't so much between us, Walter . . . Not when you come to me and try to talk to me. Try to be with me . . . a little even.

WALTER: (*total honesty*) Sometimes . . . sometimes . . . I don't even know how to try.   130

RUTH: Walter—

WALTER: Yes?

RUTH: (*coming to him, gently and with misgiving, but coming to him*) Honey . . . life don't have to be like this. I mean sometimes people can do things so that things are better . . . You remember how we used to talk when Travis was born . . . about the way we were going to live . . . the kind of house . . . (*She is stroking his head.*) Well, it's all starting to slip away from us . . .

He turns her to him and they look at each other and kiss, tenderly and hungrily. The door opens and Mama enters—Walter breaks away and jumps up. A beat.

WALTER: Mama, where have you been?

MAMA: My—them steps is longer than they used to be. Whew! (*She sits down and ig-   135
nores him.*) How you feeling this evening, Ruth?

Ruth shrugs, disturbed at having been interrupted and watching her husband knowingly.

WALTER: Mama, where have you been all day?

MAMA: (*still ignoring him and leaning on the table and changing to more comfortable shoes*) Where's Travis?

RUTH: I let him go out earlier and he ain't come back yet. Boy, is he going to get it!

WALTER: Mama!

MAMA: (*as if she has heard him for the first time*) Yes, son?   140

WALTER: Where did you go this afternoon?

MAMA: I went downtown to tend to some business that I had to tend to.

WALTER: What kind of business?

MAMA: You know better than to question me like a child, Brother.

WALTER: (*rising and bending over the table*) Where were you, Mama? (*bringing his   145
fists down and shouting*) Mama, you didn't go do something with that insurance money, something crazy?

The front door opens slowly, interrupting him, and Travis peeks his head in, less than hopefully.

TRAVIS: (*to his mother*) Mama, I—

RUTH: "Mama I" nothing! You're going to get it, boy! Get on in that bedroom and get yourself ready!

TRAVIS: But I—

MAMA: Why don't you all never let the child explain hisself.

RUTH: Keep out of it now, Lena.   150

Mama clamps her lips together, and Ruth advances toward her son menacingly.

RUTH: A thousand times I have told you not to go off like that—

MAMA: (*holding out her arms to her grandson*) Well—at least let me tell him something. I want him to be the first one to hear . . . Come here, Travis. (*The boy obeys,
gladly.*) Travis—(*She takes him by the shoulder and looks into his face.*)—you
know that money we got in the mail this morning?

TRAVIS: Yes'm—

MAMA: Well—what you think your grandmama gone and done with that money?

TRAVIS: I don't know, Grandmama.   155

MAMA: (*putting her finger on his nose for emphasis*) She went out and she bought
you a house! (*The explosion comes from Walter at the end of the revelation and he
jumps up and turns away from all of them in a fury. Mama continues, to Travis.*)
You glad about the house? It's going to be yours when you get to be a man.

TRAVIS: Yeah—I always wanted to live in a house.

MAMA: All right, gimme some sugar then—(*Travis puts his arms around her neck as she watches her son over the boy's shoulder. Then, to Travis, after the embrace.*) Now when you say your prayers tonight, you thank God and your grandfather—'cause it was him who give you the house—in his way.

RUTH: (*taking the boy from Mama and pushing him toward the bedroom*) Now you get out of here and get ready for your beating.

TRAVIS: Aw, Mama—

RUTH: Get on in there—(*closing the door behind him and turning radiantly to her mother-in-law*) So you went and did it!

MAMA: (*quietly, looking at her son with pain*) Yes, I did.

RUTH: (*raising both arms classically*) PRAISE GOD! (*Looks at Walter a moment, who says nothing. She crosses rapidly to her husband.*) Please, honey—let me be glad . . . you be glad too. (*She has laid her hands on his shoulders, but he shakes himself free of her roughly, without turning to face her.*) Oh, Walter . . . a home . . . a home. (*She comes back to Mama.*) Well—where is it? How big is it? How much it going to cost?

MAMA: Well—

RUTH: When we moving?

MAMA: (*smiling at her*) First of the month.

RUTH: (*throwing back her head with jubilance*) PRAISE GOD!

MAMA: (*tentatively, still looking at her son's back turned against her and Ruth*) It's—it's a nice house too . . . (*She cannot help speaking directly to him. An imploring quality in her voice, her manner, makes her almost like a girl now.*) Three bedrooms—nice big one for you and Ruth . . . Me and Beneatha still have to share our room, but Travis have one of his own—and (*with difficulty*) I figure if the—new baby—is a boy, we could get one of them double-decker outfits . . . And there's a yard with a little patch of dirt where I could maybe get to grow me a few flowers . . . And a nice big basement . . .

RUTH: Walter honey, be glad—

MAMA: (*still to his back, fingering things on the table*) 'Course I don't want to make it sound fancier than it is . . . It's just a plain little old house—but it's made good and solid—and it will be *ours*. Walter Lee—it makes a difference in a man when he can walk on floors that belong to *him* . . .

RUTH: Where is it?

MAMA: (*frightened at this telling*) Well—well—it's out there in Clybourne Park—

Ruth's radiance fades abruptly, and Walter finally turns slowly to face his mother with incredulity and hostility.

RUTH: Where?

MAMA: (*matter-of-factly*) Four o six Clybourne Street, Clybourne Park.

RUTH: Clybourne Park? Mama, there ain't no colored people living in Clybourne Park.

MAMA: (*almost idiotically*) Well, I guess there's going to be some now.

WALTER: (*bitterly*) So that's the peace and comfort you went out and bought for us today!

MAMA: (*raising her eyes to meet his finally*) Son—I just tried to find the nicest place for the least amount of money for my family.

RUTH: (*trying to recover from the shock*) Well—well—'course I ain't one never been 'fraid of no crackers, mind you—but—well, wasn't there no other houses nowhere?

MAMA: Them houses they put up for colored in them areas way out all seem to cost twice as much as other houses. I did the best I could.

RUTH: (*Struck senseless with the news, in its various degrees of goodness and trouble, she sits a moment, her fists propping her chin in thought, and then she starts to rise, bringing her fists down with vigor, the radiance spreading from cheek to cheek again.*) Well—well!—All I can say is—if this is my time in life—*MY* TIME—to say good-bye—(*And she builds with momentum as she starts to circle the room with an exuberant, almost tearfully happy release.*)—to these Goddamned cracking walls!—(*She pounds the walls.*)—and these marching roaches!—(*She wipes at an imaginary army of marching roaches.*)—and this cramped little closet which ain't now or never was no kitchen! . . . then I say it loud and good, HALLELUJAH! AND GOOD-BYE MISERY . . . I DON'T NEVER WANT TO SEE YOUR UGLY FACE AGAIN! (*She laughs joyously, having practically destroyed the apartment, and flings her arms up and lets them come down happily, slowly, reflectively, over her abdomen, aware for the first time perhaps that the life therein pulses with happiness and not despair.*) Lena?

MAMA: (*moved, watching her happiness*) Yes, honey?

RUTH: (*looking off*) Is there—is there a whole lot of sunlight?

MAMA: (*understanding*) Yes, child, there's a whole lot of sunlight.

Long pause.

RUTH: (*collecting herself and going to the door of the room* TRAVIS *is in*) Well—I 185 guess I better see 'bout Travis. (*to Mama*) Lord, I sure don't feel like whipping nobody today!

She exits.

MAMA: (*The mother and son are left alone now and the mother waits a long time, considering deeply, before she speaks.*) Son—you—you understand what I done, don't you? (*Walter is silent and sullen.*) I—I just seen my family falling apart today . . . just falling to pieces in front of my eyes . . . We couldn't of gone on like we was today. We was going backwards 'stead of forwards—talking 'bout killing babies and wishing each other was dead . . . When it gets like that in life—you just got to do something different, push on out and do something bigger . . . (*She waits.*) I wish you say something, son . . . I wish you'd say how deep inside you think I done the right thing—

WALTER: (*crossing slowly to his bedroom door and finally turning there and speaking measuredly*) What you need me to say you done right for? *You* the head of this family. You run our lives like you want to. It was your money and you did what you wanted with it. So what you need for me to say it was all right for? (*bitterly, to hurt her as deeply as he knows is possible*) So you butchered up a dream of mine—you—who always talking 'bout your children's dreams . . .

MAMA: Walter Lee—

He just closes the door behind him. MAMA *sits alone, thinking heavily.*

Curtain.

Scene 2

TIME: *Friday night. A few weeks later.*

AT RISE: *Packing crates mark the intention of the family to move. Beneatha and George come in, presumably from an evening out again.*

GEORGE: O.K. . . . O.K., whatever you say . . . (*They both sit on the couch. He tries to kiss her. She moves away.*) Look, we've had a nice evening; let's not spoil it, huh? . . .

He again turns her head and tries to nuzzle in and she turns away from him, not with distaste but with momentary lack of interest; in a mood to pursue what they were talking about.

BENEATHA: I'm *trying* to talk to you.   190

GEORGE: We always talk.

BENEATHA: Yes—and I love to talk.

GEORGE: (*exasperated; rising*) I know it and I don't mind it sometimes . . . I want you to cut it out, see—The moody stuff, I mean. I don't like it. You're a nice-looking girl . . . all over. That's all you need, honey, forget the atmosphere. Guys aren't going to go for the atmosphere—they're going to go for what they see. Be glad for that. Drop the Garbo routine. It doesn't go with you. As for myself, I want a nice—(*groping*)—simple (*thoughtfully*)—sophisticated girl . . . not a poet—O.K.?

He starts to kiss her, she rebuffs him again and he jumps up.

BENEATHA: Why are you angry, George?

GEORGE: Because this is stupid! I don't go out with you to discuss the nature of "quiet desperation" or to hear all about your thoughts—because the world will go on thinking what it thinks regardless— 195

BENEATHA: Then why read books? Why go to school?

GEORGE: (*with artificial patience, counting on his fingers*) It's simple. You read books—to learn facts—to get grades—to pass the course—to get a degree. That's all—it has nothing to do with thoughts.

A long pause.

BENEATHA: I see. (*He starts to sit.*) Good night, George.

George looks at her a little oddly, and starts to exit. He meets Mama coming in.

GEORGE: Oh—hello, Mrs. Younger.

MAMA: Hello, George, how you feeling?

GEORGE: Fine—fine, how are you? 200

MAMA: Oh, a little tired. You know them steps can get you after a day's work. You all have a nice time tonight?

GEORGE: Yes—a fine time. A fine time.

MAMA: Well, good night.

GEORGE: Good night. 205

He exits. Mama closes the door behind her.

MAMA: Hello, honey. What you sitting like that for?

BENEATHA: I'm just sitting.

MAMA: Didn't you have a nice time?

BENEATHA: No.

MAMA: No? What's the matter?

BENEATHA: Mama, George is a fool—honest. (*She rises.*) 210

MAMA: (*Hustling around unloading the packages she has entered with. She stops.*) Is he, baby?

BENEATHA: Yes.

Beneatha makes up Travis' bed as she talks.

MAMA: You sure?

BENEATHA: Yes.

MAMA: Well—I guess you better not waste your time with no fools. 215

Beneatha looks up at her mother, watching her put groceries in the refrigerator. Finally she gathers up her things and starts into the bedroom. At the door she stops and looks back at her mother.

BENEATHA: Mama—

MAMA: Yes, baby—

BENEATHA: Thank you.

MAMA: For what? 220

BENEATHA: For understanding me this time.

She exits quickly and the mother stands, smiling a little, looking at the place where Beneatha just stood. Ruth enters.

RUTH: Now don't you fool with any of this stuff, Lena—

MAMA: Oh, I just thought I'd sort a few things out. Is Brother here?

RUTH: Yes.

MAMA: (*with concern*) Is he—

RUTH: (*reading her eyes*) Yes. 225

Mama is silent and someone knocks on the door. Mama and Ruth exchange weary and knowing glances and Ruth opens it to admit the neighbor, Mrs. Johnson, who is a rather squeaky wide-eyed lady of no particular age, with a newspaper under her arm.

MAMA: *(changing her expression to acute delight and a ringing cheerful greeting)* Oh—hello there, Johnson.

JOHNSON: *(This is a woman who decided long ago to be enthusiastic about everything in life and she is inclined to wave her wrist vigorously at the height of her exclamatory comments.)* Hello there, yourself! H'you this evening, Ruth?

RUTH: *(not much of a deceptive type)* Fine, Mis' Johnson, h'you?

JOHNSON: Fine. *(reaching out quickly, playfully, and patting Ruth's stomach)* Ain't you   230
starting to poke out none yet! *(She mugs with delight at the over-familiar remark and her eyes dart around looking at the crates and packing preparation; Mama's face is a cold sheet of endurance.)* Oh, ain't we getting ready round here, though! Yessir! Lookathere! I'm telling you the Youngers is really getting ready to "move on up a little higher!"—Bless God!

MAMA: *(a little drily, doubting the total sincerity of the Blesser)* Bless God.

JOHNSON: He's good, ain't He?

MAMA: Oh yes, He's good.

JOHNSON: I mean sometimes He works in mysterious ways . . . but He works, don't He!

MAMA: *(the same)* Yes, He does.   235

JOHNSON: I'm just soooooo happy for y'all. And this here child—*(about Ruth)* looks like she could just pop open with happiness, don't she. Where's all the rest of the family?

MAMA: Bennie's gone to bed—

JOHNSON: Ain't no . . . *(The implication is pregnancy.)* sickness done hit you—I hope . . . ?

MAMA: No—she just tired. She was out this evening.

JOHNSON: *(All is a coo, an emphatic coo.)* Aw—ain't that lovely. She still going out   240
with the little Murchison boy?

MAMA: *(drily)* Ummmm huh.

JOHNSON: That's lovely. You sure got lovely children, Younger. Me and Isaiah talks all the time 'bout what fine children you was blessed with. We sure do.

MAMA: Ruth, give Mis' Johnson a piece of sweet potato pie and some milk.

JOHNSON: Oh honey, I can't stay hardly a minute—I just dropped in to see if there was anything I could do. *(accepting the food easily)* I guess y'all seen the news what's all over the colored paper this week . . .

MAMA: No—didn't get mine yet this week.   245

JOHNSON: *(lifting her head and blinking with the spirit of catastrophe)* You mean you ain't read 'bout them colored people that was bombed out their place out there?

Ruth straightens with concern and takes the paper and reads it. Johnson notices her and feeds commentary.

JOHNSON: Ain't it something how bad these here white folks is getting here in Chicago! Lord, getting so you think you right down in Mississippi! *(with a tremendous and rather insincere sense of melodrama)* 'Course I thinks it's wonderful how our folks keeps on pushing out. You hear some of these Negroes round here talking 'bout how they don't go where they ain't wanted and all that—but not me, honey! *(This is a lie.)* Wilhemenia Othella Johnson goes anywhere, any time she feels like it! *(with head movement for emphasis)* Yes I do! Why if we left it up to these here crackers, the poor niggers wouldn't have nothing—*(She clasps her hand over her mouth.)* Oh, I always forgets you don't 'low that word in your house.

MAMA: *(quietly, looking at her)* No—I don't 'low it.

JOHNSON: *(vigorously again)* Me neither! I was just telling Isaiah yesterday when he come using it in front of me—I said, "Isaiah, it's just like Mis' Younger says all the time—"

MAMA: Don't you want some more pie?   250

JOHNSON: No—no thank you; this was lovely. I got to get on over home and have my midnight coffee. I hear some people say it don't let them sleep but I finds I can't close
my eyes right lessen I done had that laaaast cup of coffee . . . (*She waits. A beat. Un-
daunted.*) My Goodnight coffee, I calls it!

MAMA: (*with much eye-rolling and communication between herself and Ruth*)
Ruth, why don't you give Mis' Johnson some coffee.

Ruth gives Mama an unpleasant look for her kindness.

JOHNSON: (*accepting the coffee*)   Where's Brother tonight?

MAMA: He's lying down.

JOHNSON: MMmmmmm, he sure gets his beauty rest, don't he? Good-looking man. Sure is   255
a good-looking man! (*reaching out to pat Ruth's stomach again*) I guess that's how
come we keep on having babies around here. (*She winks at Mama.*) One thing
'bout Brother, he always know how to have a *good* time. And sooooo ambitious!
I bet it was his idea y'all moving out to Clybourne Park. Lord—I bet this time next
month y'all's names will have been in the papers plenty—(*holding up her hands
to mark off each word of the headline she can see in front of her*) "NEGROES
INVADE CLYBOURNE PARK—BOMBED!"

MAMA: (*She and Ruth look at the woman in amazement.*)   We ain't exactly moving
out there to get bombed.

JOHNSON: Oh, honey—you know I'm praying to God every day that don't nothing like
that happen! But you have to think of life like it is—and these here Chicago peckerwoods is some baaaad peckerwoods.

MAMA: (*wearily*)   We done thought about all that Mis' Johnson.

*Beneatha comes out of the bedroom in her robe and passes through to the bathroom. Mrs. Johnson
turns.*

JOHNSON: Hello there, Bennie!

BENEATHA: (*crisply*)   Hello, Mrs. Johnson.

JOHNSON: How is school?   260

BENEATHA: (*crisply*)   Fine, thank you. (*She goes out.*)

JOHNSON: (*insulted*)   Getting so she don't have much to say to nobody.

MAMA: The child was on her way to the bathroom.

JOHNSON: I know—but sometimes she act like ain't got time to pass the time of day with   265
nobody ain't been to college. Oh—I ain't criticizing her none. It's just—you know
how some of our young people gets when they get a little education. (*Mama and
Ruth say nothing, just look at her.*) Yes—well. Well, I guess I better get on home.
(*unmoving*) 'Course I can understand how she must be proud and everything—
being the only one in the family to make something of herself. I know just being a
chauffeur ain't never satisfied Brother none. He shouldn't feel like that, though. Ain't
nothing wrong with being a chauffeur.

MAMA: There's plenty wrong with it.

JOHNSON: What?

MAMA: Plenty. My husband always said being any kind of a servant wasn't a fit thing for
a man to have to be. He always said a man's hands was made to make things, or to
turn the earth with—not to drive nobody's car for 'em—or—(*She looks at her own
hands.*) carry they slop jars. And my boy is just like him—he wasn't meant to wait
on nobody.

JOHNSON: (*rising, somewhat offended*)   Mmmmmmmmm. The Youngers is too much
for me! (*She looks around.*) You sure one proud-acting bunch of colored folks.
Well—I always thinks like Booker T. Washington said that time—"Education has
spoiled many a good plow hand"—

MAMA: Is that what old Booker T. said?   270

JOHNSON: He sure did.

MAMA: Well, it sounds just like him. The fool.

JOHNSON: (*indignantly*)   Well—he was one of our great men.

MAMA: Who said so?

JOHNSON: (*nonplussed*)   You know, me and you ain't never agreed about some things,   275
    Lena Younger. I guess I better be going—

RUTH: (*quickly*)   Good night.

JOHNSON: Good night. Oh—(*thrusting it at her*) You can keep the paper! (*with a trill*)
    'Night.

MAMA: Good night, Mis' Johnson.

Mrs. Johnson exits.

RUTH: If ignorance was gold . . .

MAMA: Shush. Don't talk about folks behind their backs.   280

RUTH: You do.

MAMA: I'm old and corrupted. (*Beneatha enters.*) You was rude to Mis' Johnson, Be-
    neatha, and I don't like it at all.

BENEATHA: (*at her door*)   Mama, if there are two things we, as a people, have got to
    overcome, one is the Klu Klux Klan—and the other is Mrs. Johnson. (*She exits.*)

MAMA: Smart aleck.

The phone rings.

RUTH: I'll get it.   285

MAMA: Lord, ain't this a popular place tonight.

RUTH: (*at the phone*)   Hello—Just a minute. (*goes to door*) Walter, it's Mrs. Arnold.
    (*Waits. Goes back to the phone. Tense.*) Hello. Yes, this is his wife speaking . . . He's
    lying down now. Yes . . . well, he'll be in tomorrow. He's been very sick. Yes—I know
    we should have called, but we were so sure he'd be able to come in today. Yes—yes,
    I'm very sorry. Yes . . . Thank you very much. (*She hangs up. Walter is standing in the
    doorway of the bedroom behind her.*) That was Mrs. Arnold.

WALTER: (*indifferently*)   Was it?

RUTH: She said if you don't come in tomorrow that they are getting a new man . . .

WALTER: Ain't that sad—ain't that crying sad.   290

RUTH: She said Mr. Arnold has had to take a cab for three days . . . Walter, you ain't been
    to work for three days! (*This is a revelation to her.*) Where you been, Walter Lee
    Younger? (*Walter looks at her and starts to laugh.*) You're going to lose your job.

WALTER: That's right . . . (*He turns on the radio.*)

RUTH: Oh, Walter, and with your mother working like a dog every day—

A steamy, deep blues pours into the room.

WALTER: That's sad too—Everything is sad.

MAMA: What you been doing for these three days, son?   295

WALTER: Mama—you don't know all the things a man what got leisure can find to do in
    this city . . . What's this—Friday night? Well—Wednesday I borrowed Willy Harris' car
    and I went for a drive . . . just me and myself and I drove and drove . . . Way out . . . way
    past South Chicago, and I parked the car and I sat and looked at the steel mills all
    day long. I just sat in the car and looked at them big black chimneys for hours. Then
    I drove back and I went to the Green Hat. (*pause*) And Thursday—Thursday I bor-
    rowed the car again and I got in it and I pointed it the other way and I drove the
    other way—for hours—way, way up to Wisconsin, and I looked at the farms. I just
    drove and looked at the farms. Then I drove back and I went to the Green Hat.
    (*pause*) And today—today I didn't get the car. Today I just walked. All over the
    Southside. And I looked at the Negroes and they looked at me and finally I just sat
    down on the curb at Thirty-ninth and South Parkway and I just sat there and
    watched the Negroes go by. And then I went to the Green Hat. You all sad? You all
    depressed? And you know where I am going right now—

Ruth goes out quietly.

MAMA: Oh, Big Walter, is this the harvest of our days?

WALTER: You know what I like about the Green Hat? I like this little cat they got there who blows a sax ...He blows. He talks to me. He ain't but 'bout five feet tall and he's got a conked head and his eyes is always closed and he's all music—

MAMA: (*rising and getting some papers out of her handbag*)   Walter—

WALTER: And there's this other guy who plays the piano ...and they got a sound. I mean   300
they can work on some music ...They got the best little combo in the world in the Green Hat ...You can just sit there and drink and listen to them three men play and you realize that don't nothing matter worth a damn, but just being there—

MAMA: I've helped do it to you, haven't I, son? Walter, I been wrong.

WALTER: Naw—you ain't never been wrong about nothing, Mama.

MAMA: Listen to me, now. I say I been wrong, son. That I been doing to you what the rest of the world been doing to you. (*She turns off the radio.*) Walter—(*She stops and he looks up slowly at her and she meets his eyes pleadingly.*) What you ain't never understood is that I ain't got nothing, don't own nothing, ain't never really wanted nothing that wasn't for you. There ain't nothing as precious to me ... There ain't nothing worth holding on to, money, dreams, nothing else—if it means—if it means it's going to destroy my boy. (*She takes an envelope out of her handbag and puts it in front of him and he watches her without speaking or moving.*) I paid the man thirty-five hundred dollars down on the house. That leaves sixty-five hundred dollars. Monday morning I want you to take this money and take three thousand dollars and put it in a savings account for Beneatha's medical schooling. The rest you put in a checking account—with your name on it. And from now on any penny that come out of it or that go in it is for you to look after. For you to decide. (*She drops her hands a little helplessly.*) It ain't much, but it's all I got in the world and I'm putting it in your hands. I'm telling you to be the head of this family from now on like you supposed to be.

WALTER: (*stares at the money*)   You trust me like that, Mama?

MAMA: I ain't never stop trusting you. Like I ain't never stop loving you.   305

She goes out, and Walter sits looking at the money on the table. Finally, in a decisive gesture, he gets up, and, in mingled joy and desperation, picks up the money. At the same moment, Travis enters for bed.

TRAVIS: What's the matter, Daddy? You drunk?

WALTER: (*sweetly, more sweetly than we have ever known him*)   No, Daddy ain't drunk. Daddy ain't going to never be drunk again ...

TRAVIS: Well, good night, Daddy.

The Father has come from behind the couch and leans over, embracing his son.

WALTER: Son, I feel like talking to you tonight.

TRAVIS: About what?

WALTER: Oh, about a lot of things. About you and what kind of man you going to be   310
when you grow up ...Son—son, what do you want to be when you grow up?

TRAVIS: A bus driver.

WALTER: (*laughing a little*)   A what? Man, that ain't nothing to want to be!

TRAVIS: Why not?

WALTER: 'Cause, man—it ain't big enough—you know what I mean.   315

TRAVIS: I don't know then. I can't make up my mind. Sometimes Mama asks me that too. And sometimes when I tell her I just want to be like you—she says she don't want me to be like that and sometimes she says she does ...

WALTER: (*gathering him up in his arms*)   You know what, Travis? In seven years you going to be seventeen years old. And things is going to be very different with us in seven years, Travis ...One day when you are seventeen I'll come home—home from my office downtown somewhere—

TRAVIS: You don't work in no office, Daddy.

WALTER: No—but after tonight. After what your daddy gonna do tonight, there's going
to be offices—a whole lot of offices ...

TRAVIS: What you gonna do tonight, Daddy?   320

WALTER: You wouldn't understand yet, son, but your daddy's gonna make a transaction ...
a business transaction that's going to change our lives ... That's how come one day
when you 'bout seventeen years old I'll come home and I'll be pretty tired, you know
what I mean, after a day of conferences and secretaries getting things wrong the way
they do ... 'cause an executive's life is hell, man—(*The more he talks the farther
away he gets.*) And I'll pull the car up on the driveway ... just a plain black Chrysler, I
think, with white walls—no—black tires. More elegant. Rich people don't have to be
flashy ... though I'll have to get something a little sportier for Ruth —maybe a Cadillac
convertible to do her shopping in ... And I'll come up the steps to the house and the
gardener will be clipping away at the hedges and he'll say, "Good evening, Mr.
Younger." And I'll say, "Hello, Jefferson, how are you this evening?" And I'll go inside
and Ruth will come downstairs and meet me at the door and we'll kiss each other and
she'll take my arm and we'll go up to your room to see you sitting on the floor with
the catalogues of all the great schools in America around you ... All the great schools
in the world! And—and I'll say, all right son—it's your seventeenth birthday, what is it
you've decided? ... Just tell me where you want to go to school and you'll *go*. Just tell
me, what it is you want to be—and you'll *be* it ... Whatever you want to be—Yessir!
(*He holds his arms open for Travis.*) You just name it, son ... (*Travis leaps into them.*)
and I hand you the world!

Walter's voice has risen in pitch and hysterical promise and on the last line he lifts Travis high.

(*Blackout*)

Scene 3

TIME: *Saturday, moving day, one week later.*

Before the curtain rises, Ruth's voice, a strident, dramatic church alto, cuts through the silence.

*It is, in the darkness, a triumphant surge, a penetrating statement of expectation: "Oh, Lord, I don't
feel no ways tired! Children, oh, glory hallelujah!"*

*As the curtain rises we see that Ruth is alone in the living room, finishing up the family's packing. It
is moving day. She is nailing crates and tying cartons. Beneatha enters, carrying a guitar case, and
watches her exuberant sister-in-law.*

RUTH: Hey!

BENEATHA: (*putting away the case*)   Hi.

RUTH: (*pointing at a package*)   Honey—look in that package there and see what I
found on sale this morning at the South Center. (*Ruth gets up and moves to the
package and draws out some curtains.*) Lookahere—hand-turned hems!

BENEATHA: How do you know the window size out there?   325

RUTH: (*who hadn't thought of that*)   Oh—Well, they bound to fit something in the
whole house. Anyhow, they was too good a bargain to pass up. (*Ruth slaps her
head, suddenly remembering something.*) Oh, Bennie—I meant to put a special
note on that carton over there. That's your Mama's good china and she wants 'em to
be very careful with it.

BENEATHA: I'll do it.

Beneatha finds a piece of paper and starts to draw large letters on it.

RUTH: You know what I'm going to do soon as I get in that new house?

BENEATHA: What?

RUTH: Honey—I'm going to run me a tub of water up to here ... (*with her fingers practically up to her nostrils*) And I'm going to get in it—and I am going to sit ... and sit   330

...and sit in that hot water and the first person who knocks to tell *me* to hurry up and come out—

BENEATHA: Gets shot at sunrise.

RUTH: (*laughing happily*)   You said it, sister! (*noticing how large Beneatha is absent-mindedly making the note*) Honey, they ain't going to read that from no airplane.

BENEATHA: (*laughing herself*)   I guess I always think things have more emphasis if they are big, somehow.

RUTH: (*looking up at her and smiling*)   You and your brother seem to have that as a philosophy of life. Lord, that man—done changed so 'round here. You know—you know what we did last night? Me and Walter Lee?

BENEATHA: What?

RUTH: (*smiling to herself*)   We went to the movies. (*looking at Beneatha to see if she understands*) We went to the movies. You know the last time me and Walter went to the movies together?

BENEATHA: No.

RUTH: Me neither. That's how long it been. (*smiling again*) But we went last night. The picture wasn't much good, but that didn't seem to matter. We went—and we held hands.

BENEATHA: Oh, Lord!

RUTH: We held hands—and you know what?

BENEATHA: What?

RUTH: When we come out of the show it was late and dark and all the stores and things was closed up . . . and it was kind of chilly and there wasn't many people on the streets . . . and we was still holding hands, me and Walter.

BENEATHA: You're killing me.

Walter enters with a large package. His happiness is deep in him; he cannot keep still with his new-found exuberance. He is singing and wiggling and snapping his fingers. He puts his package in a corner and puts a phonograph record, which he has brought in with him, on the record player. As the music, soulful and sensuous, comes up he dances over to Ruth and tries to get her to dance with him. She gives in at last to his raunchiness and in a fit of giggling allows herself to be drawn into his mood. They dip and she melts into his arms in a classic, body-melding "slow drag."

BENEATHA: (*regarding them a long time as they dance, then drawing in her breath for a deeply exaggerated comment which she does not particularly mean*)   Talk about—olddddddddddd—fashionedddddddd—Negroes!

WALTER: (*stopping momentarily*)   What kind of Negroes?

He says this in fun. He is not angry with her today, nor with anyone. He starts to dance with his wife again.

BENEATHA: Old-fashioned.

WALTER: (*as he dances with Ruth*)   You know, when these *New Negroes* have their convention—(*pointing at his sister*)—that is going to be the chairman of the Committee on Unending Agitation. (*He goes on dancing, then stops.*) Race, race, race! . . . Girl, I do believe you are the first person in the history of the entire human race to successfully brainwash yourself. (*Beneatha breaks up and he goes on dancing. He stops again, enjoying his tease.*) Damn, even the N double A C P takes a holiday sometimes! (*Beneatha and Ruth laugh. He dances with Ruth some more and starts to laugh and stops and pantomimes someone over an operating table.*) I can just see that chick someday looking down at some poor cat on an operating table and before she starts to slice him, she says . . . (*pulling his sleeves back maliciously*) "By the way, what are your views on civil rights down there? . . ."

He laughs at her again and starts to dance happily. The bell sounds.

BENEATHA: Sticks and stones may break my bones but . . . words will never hurt me!

Beneatha goes to the door and opens it as Walter and Ruth go on with the clowning. Beneatha is somewhat surprised to see a quiet-looking middle-aged white man in a business suit holding his hat and a briefcase in his hand and consulting a small piece of paper.

MAN: Uh—how do you do, miss. I am looking for a Mrs.—(*He looks at the slip of paper.*) Mrs. Lena Younger? (*He stops short, struck dumb at the sight of the oblivious Walter and Ruth.*)

BENEATHA: (*smoothing her hair with slight embarrassment*)   Oh—yes, that's my   350
mother. Excuse me. (*She closes the door and turns to quiet the other two.*) Ruth!
Brother! (*Enunciating precisely but soundlessly: "There's a white man at the door!" They stop dancing, Ruth cuts off the phonograph, Beneatha opens the door. The man casts a curious quick glance at all of them.*) Uh—come in please.

MAN: (*coming in*)   Thank you.

BENEATHA: My mother isn't here just now. Is it business?

MAN: Yes . . . well, of a sort.

WALTER: (*freely, the Man of the House*)   Have a seat. I'm Mrs. Younger's son. I look after
most of her business matters.

Ruth and Beneatha exchange amused glances.

MAN: (*regarding Walter, and sitting*)   Well—My name is Karl Lindner . . .   355

WALTER: (*stretching out his hand*)   Walter Younger. This is my wife—(*Ruth nods
politely*)—and my sister.

LINDNER: How do you do.

WALTER: (*amiably, as he sits himself easily on a chair, leaning forward on his knees
with interest and looking expectantly into the newcomer's face*)   What can we
do for you, Mr. Lindner!

LINDNER: (*some minor shuffling of the hat and briefcase on his knees*)   Well—I am a
representative of the Clybourne Park Improvement Association—

WALTER: (*pointing*)   Why don't you sit your things on the floor?   360

LINDNER: Oh—yes. Thank you. (*He slides the briefcase and hat under the chair.*) And as
I was saying—I am from the Clybourne Park Improvement Association and we have
had it brought to our attention at the last meeting that you people—or at least your
mother—has bought a piece of residential property at—(*He digs for the slip of
paper again.*)—four o six Clybourne Street . . .

WALTER: That's right. Care for something to drink? Ruth, get Mr. Lindner a beer.

LINDNER: (*upset for some reason*)   Oh—no, really. I mean thank you very much, but no
thank you.

RUTH: (*innocently*)   Some coffee?

LINDNER: Thank you, nothing at all.   365

Beneatha is watching the man carefully.

LINDNER: Well, I don't know how much you folks know about our organization. (*He is a
gentle man; thoughtful and somewhat labored in his manner.*) It is one of these
community organizations set up to look after—oh, you know, things like block up-
keep and special projects and we also have what we call our New Neighbors Orientation Committee . . .

BENEATHA: (*drily*)   Yes—and what do they do?

LINDNER: (*turning a little to her and then returning the main force to Walter*)   Well—
it's what you might call a sort of welcoming committee, I guess. I mean they, we—
I'm the chairman of the committee—go around and see the new people who move
into the neighborhood and sort of give them the lowdown on the way we do things
out in Clybourne Park.

BENEATHA: (*with appreciation of the two meanings, which escape Ruth and Walter*)
Uh—huh.

LINDNER: And we also have the category of what the association calls—(*He looks else-*   370
where.)—uh—special community problems . . .

BENEATHA: Yes—and what are some of those?

WALTER: Girl, let the man talk.

LINDNER: (*with understated relief*) Thank you. I would sort of like to explain this
thing in my own way. I mean I want to explain to you in a certain way.

WALTER: Go ahead.

LINDNER: Yes. Well. I'm going to try to get right to the point. I'm sure we'll all appreciate   375
that in the long run.

BENEATHA: Yes.

WALTER: Be still now!

LINDNER: Well—

RUTH: (*still innocently*) Would you like another chair—you don't look comfortable.

LINDNER: (*more frustrated than annoyed*) No, thank you very much. Please. Well—to   380
get right to the point I—(*A great breath, and he is off at last.*) I am sure you people
must be aware of some of the incidents which have happened in various parts of
the city when colored people have moved into certain areas—(*Beneatha exhales
heavily and starts tossing a piece of fruit up and down in the air.*) Well—because
we have what I think is going to be a unique type of organization in American community life—not only do we deplore that kind of thing—but we are trying to do
something about it. (*Beneatha stops tossing and turns with a new and quizzical
interest to the man.*) We feel—(*gaining confidence in his mission because of the
interest in the faces of the people he is talking to*)—we feel that most of the trouble
in this world, when you come right down to it—(*He hits his knee for emphasis.*)—
most of the trouble exists because people just don't sit down and talk to each other.

RUTH: (*nodding as she might in church, pleased with the remark*) You can say that
again, mister.

LINDNER: (*more encouraged by such affirmation*) That we don't try hard enough in
this world to understand the other fellow's problem. The other guy's point of view.

RUTH: Now that's right.

Beneatha and Walter merely watch and listen with genuine interest.

LINDNER: Yes—that's the way we feel out in Clybourne Park. And that's why I was
elected to come here this afternoon and talk to you people. Friendly like, you know,
the way people should talk to each other and see if we couldn't find some way to
work this thing out. As I say, the whole business is a matter of *caring* about the other
fellow. Anybody can see that you are a nice family of folks, hard working and honest
I'm sure. (*Beneatha frowns slightly, quizzically, her head tilted regarding him.*)
Today everybody knows what it means to be on the outside of *something*. And of
course, there is always somebody who is out to take advantage of people who don't
always understand.

WALTER: What do you mean?   385

LINDNER: Well—you see our community is made up of people who've worked hard as
the dickens for years to build up that little community. They're not rich and fancy
people; just hard-working, honest people who don't really have much but those little homes and a dream of the kind of community they want to raise their children
in. Now, I don't say we are perfect and there is a lot wrong in some of the things
they want. But you've got to admit that a man, right or wrong, has the right to want
to have the neighborhood he lives in a certain kind of way. And at the moment the
overwhelming majority of our people out there feel that people get along better,
take more of a common interest in the life of the community, when they share a
common background. I want you to believe me when I tell you that race prejudice
simply doesn't enter into it. It is a matter of the people of Clybourne Park believing,
rightly or wrongly, as I say, that for the happiness of all concerned that our Negro
families are happier when they live in their *own* communities.

BENEATHA: (*with a grand and bitter gesture*) This, friends, is the Welcoming Committee!

WALTER: (*dumfounded, looking at Lindner*)   Is this what you came marching all the way over here to tell us?

LINDNER: Well, now we've been having a fine conversation. I hope you'll hear me all the way through.

WALTER: (*tightly*)   Go ahead, man.   390

LINDNER: You see—in the face of all things I have said, we are prepared to make your family a very generous offer . . .

BENEATHA: Thirty pieces and not a coin less!

WALTER: Yeah?

LINDNER: (*putting on his glasses and drawing a form out of the briefcase*)   Our association is prepared, through the collective effort of our people, to buy the house from you at a financial gain to your family.

RUTH: Lord have mercy, ain't this the living gall!   395

WALTER: All right, you through?

LINDNER: Well, I want to give you the exact terms of the financial arrangement—

WALTER: We don't want to hear no exact terms of no arrangements. I want to know if you got any more to tell us 'bout getting together?

LINDNER: (*taking off his glasses*)   Well—I don't suppose that you feel . . .

WALTER: Never mind how I feel—you got any more to say 'bout how people ought to sit   400
down and talk to each other? . . . Get out of my house, man.

He turns his back and walks to the door.

LINDNER: (*looking around at the hostile faces and reaching and assembling his hat
and briefcase*)   Well—I don't understand why you people are reacting this way.
What do you think you are going to gain by moving into a neighborhood where you
just aren't wanted and where some elements—well—people can get awful worked
up when they feel that their whole way of life and everything they've ever worked
for is threatened.

WALTER: Get out.

LINDNER: (*at the door, holding a small card*)   Well—I'm sorry it went like this.

WALTER: Get out.

LINDNER: (*almost sadly regarding Walter*)   You just can't force people to change their   405
hearts, son.

*He turns and puts his card on a table and exits. Walter pushes the door to with stinging hatred, and
stands looking at it. Ruth just sits and Beneatha just stands. They say nothing. Mama and Travis
enter.*

MAMA: Well—this all the packing got done since I left out of here this morning. I testify
before God that my children got all the energy of the *dead!* What time the moving
men due?

BENEATHA: Four o'clock. You had a caller, Mama.

She is smiling, teasingly.

MAMA: Sure enough—who?

BENEATHA: (*her arms folded saucily*)   The Welcoming Committee.

Walter and Ruth giggle.

MAMA: (*innocently*)   Who?   410

BENEATHA: The Welcoming Committee. They said they're sure going to be glad to see you
when you get there.

WALTER: (*devilishly*)   Yeah, they said they can't hardly wait to see your face.

Laughter.

MAMA: (*sensing their facetiousness*)   What's the matter with you all?

WALTER: Ain't nothing the matter with us. We just telling you 'bout the gentleman who
came to see you this afternoon. From the Clybourne Park Improvement Association.

MAMA: What he want?

RUTH: (*in the same mood as Beneatha and Walter*)   To welcome you, honey.

WALTER: He said they can't hardly wait. He said the one thing they don't have, that they just *dying* to have out there is a fine family of fine colored people! (*To Ruth and Beneatha*) Ain't that right!

RUTH: (*mockingly*)   Yeah! He left his card—

BENEATHA: (*handing card to Mama*)   In case.

Mama reads and throws it on the floor—understanding and looking off as she draws her chair up to the table on which she has put her plant and some sticks and some cord.

MAMA: Father, give us strength. (*knowingly—and without fun*) Did he threaten us?

BENEATHA: Oh—Mama—they don't do it like that any more. He talked Brotherhood. He said everybody ought to learn how to sit down and hate each other with good Christian fellowship.

She and Walter shake hands to ridicule the remark.

MAMA: (*sadly*)   Lord, protect us . . .

RUTH: You should hear the money those folks raised to buy the house from us. All we paid and then some.

BENEATHA: What they think we going to do—eat 'em?

RUTH: No, honey, marry 'em.

MAMA: (*shaking her head*)   Lord, Lord, Lord . . .

RUTH: Well—that's the way the crackers crumble. (*a beat*) Joke.

BENEATHA: (*laughingly noticing what her mother is doing*)   Mama, what are you doing?

MAMA: Fixing my plant so it won't get hurt none on the way . . .

BENEATHA: Mama, you going to take *that* to the new house?

MAMA: Un—huh—

BENEATHA: That raggedy-looking old thing?

MAMA: (*stopping and looking at her*)   It expresses ME!

RUTH: (*with delight, to Beneatha*)   So there, Miss Thing!

Walter comes to Mama suddenly and bends down behind her and squeezes her in his arms with all his strength. She is overwhelmed by the suddenness of it and, though delighted, her manner is like that of Ruth and Travis.

MAMA: Look out now, boy! You make me mess up my thing here!

WALTER: (*His face lit, he slips down on his knees beside her, his arms still about her.*) Mama . . . you know what it means to climb up in the chariot?

MAMA: (*gruffly, very happy*)   Get on away from me now . . .

RUTH: (*near the gift-wrapped package, trying to catch Walter's eye*)   Psst—

WALTER: What the old song say, Mama . . .

RUTH: Walter—Now?

She is pointing at the package.

WALTER: (*speaking the lines, sweetly, playfully, in his mother's face*)
    I got wings . . . you got wings . . .
    All God's children got wings . . .

MAMA: Boy—get out of my face and do some work . . .

WALTER: When I get to heaven gonna put on my wings,
    Gonna fly all over God's heaven . . .

BENEATHA: (*teasingly, from across the room*)   Everybody talking 'bout heaven ain't going there!

WALTER: (*to Ruth, who is carrying the box across to them*)   I don't know, you think we ought to give her that . . . Seems to me she ain't been very appreciative around here.

MAMA: (*eying the box, which is obviously a gift*)   What is that?

WALTER: (*taking it from Ruth and putting it on the table in front of Mama*)   Well—
what you all think? Should we give it to her?

RUTH: Oh—she was pretty good today.

MAMA: I'll good you—

She turns her eyes to the box again.

BENEATHA: Open it, Mama.   450

*She stands up, looks at it, turns and looks at all of them, and then presses her hands together and does
not open the package.*

WALTER: (*sweetly*)   Open it, Mama. It's for you. (*Mama looks in his eyes. It is the first
present in her life without its being Christmas. Slowly she opens her package and
lifts out, one by one, a brand-new sparkling set of gardening tools. Walter continues, prodding.*) Ruth made up the note—read it . . .

MAMA: (*picking up the card and adjusting her glasses*)   "To our own Mrs. Miniver—
Love from Brother, Ruth and Beneatha." Ain't that lovely . . .

TRAVIS: (*tugging at his father's sleeve*)   Daddy, can I give her mine now?

WALTER: All right, son. (*Travis flies to get his gift.*)

MAMA: Now I don't have to use my knives and forks no more . . .   455

WALTER: Travis didn't want to go in with the rest of us, Mama. He got his own. (*somewhat amused*) We don't know what it is . . .

TRAVIS: (*racing back in the room with a large hatbox and putting it in front of his
grandmother*)   Here!

MAMA: Lord have mercy, baby. You done gone and bought your grandmother a hat?

TRAVIS: (*very proud*)   Open it!

*She does and lifts out an elaborate, but very elaborate, wide gardening hat, and all the adults break
up at the sight of it.*

RUTH: Travis, honey, what is that?   460

TRAVIS: (*who thinks it is beautiful and appropriate*)   It's a gardening hat! Like the
ladies always have on in the magazines when they work in their gardens.

BENEATHA: (*giggling fiercely*)   Travis—we were trying to make Mama Mrs. Miniver—
not Scarlett O'Hara!

MAMA: (*indignantly*)   What's the matter with you all! This here is a beautiful hat!
(*absurdly*) I always wanted me one just like it!

*She pops it on her head to prove it to her grandson, and the hat is ludicrous and considerably
oversized.*

RUTH: Hot dog! Go, Mama!

WALTER: (*doubled over with laughter*)   I'm sorry, Mama—but you look like you ready   465
to go out and chop you some cotton sure enough!

They all laugh except Mama, out of deference to Travis's feelings.

MAMA: (*gathering the boy up to her*)   Bless your heart—this is the prettiest hat I ever
owned— (*Walter, Ruth and Beneatha chime in—noisily, festively and insincerely
congratulating Travis on his gift.*) What are we all standing around here for? We
ain't finished packin' yet. Bennie, you ain't packed one book.

The bell rings.

BENEATHA: That couldn't be the movers . . . it's not hardly two good yet—

Beneatha goes into her room. Mama starts for door.

WALTER: (*turning, stiffening*)   Wait—wait—I'll get it.

He stands and looks at the door.

MAMA: You expecting company, son?

WALTER: (*just looking at the door*)   Yeah—yeah ...   470

Mama looks at Ruth, and they exchange innocent and unfrightened glances.

MAMA: (*not understanding*)   Well, let them in, son.

BENEATHA: (*from her room*)   We need some more string.

MAMA: Travis—you run to the hardware and get me some string cord.

Mama goes out and Walter turns and looks at Ruth. Travis goes to a dish for money.

RUTH: Why don't you answer the door, man?

WALTER: (*suddenly bounding across the floor to embrace her*)   'Cause sometimes it   475
hard to let the future begin! (*stooping down in her face*)
   I got wings! You got wings!
   All God's children got wings!

*He crosses to the door and throws it open. Standing there is a very slight little man in a not too pros-
perous business suit and with haunted frightened eyes and a hat pulled down tightly, brim up,
around his forehead. Travis passes between the men and exits. Walter leans deep in the man's face,
still in his jubilance.*

   When I get to heaven gonna put on my wings,
   Gonna fly all over God's heaven ...

The little man just stares at him.

   Heaven—

Suddenly he stops and looks past the little man into the empty hallway.

   Where's Willy, man?

BOBO: He ain't with me.

WALTER: (*not disturbed*)   Oh—come on in. You know my wife.

BOBO: (*dumbly, taking off his hat*)   Yes—h'you, Miss Ruth.

RUTH: (*quietly, a mood apart from her husband already, seeing Bobo*)   Hello, Bobo.

WALTER: You right on time today ... Right on time. That's the way! (*He slaps Bobo on his*   480
back.) Sit down ... lemme hear.

*Ruth stands stiffly and quietly in back of them, as though somehow she senses death, her eyes fixed on
her husband.*

BOBO: (*his frightened eyes on the floor, his hat in his hands*)   Could I please get a
drink of water, before I tell you about it, Walter Lee?

*Walter does not take his eyes off the man. Ruth goes blindly to the tap and gets a glass of water and
brings it to Bobo.*

WALTER: There ain't nothing wrong, is there?

BOBO: Lemme tell you—

WALTER: Man—didn't nothing go wrong?

BOBO: Lemme tell you—Walter Lee. (*looking at Ruth and talking to her more than to*   485
Walter) You know how it was. I got to tell you how it was. I mean first I got to tell
you how it was all the way ... I mean about the money I put in, Walter Lee ...

WALTER: (*with taut agitation now*)   What about the money you put in?

BOBO: Well—it wasn't much as we told you—me and Willy—(*He stops.*) I'm sorry, Walter. I got a bad feeling about it. I got a real bad feeling about it ...

WALTER: Man, what you telling me about all this for? ... Tell me what happened in
Springfield ...

BOBO: Springfield.

RUTH: (*like a dead woman*)   What was supposed to happen in Springfield?   490

BOBO: (*to her*):   This deal that me and Walter went into with Willy—Me and Willy was
going to go down to Springfield and spread some money 'round so's we wouldn't
have to wait so long for the liquor license ... That's what we were going to do. Everybody said that was the way you had to do, you understand, Miss Ruth?

WALTER: Man—what happened down there?

BOBO: (*a pitiful man, near tears*)   I'm trying to tell you, Walter.

WALTER: (*screaming at him suddenly*)   THEN TELL ME, GODDAMMIT ... WHAT'S THE
MATTER WITH YOU?

BOBO: Man ... I didn't go to no Springfield, yesterday.   495

WALTER: (*halted, life hanging in the moment*)   Why not?

BOBO: (*the long way, the hard way to tell*)   'Cause I didn't have no reasons to ...

WALTER: Man, what are you talking about!

BOBO: I'm talking about the fact that when I got to the train station yesterday morning—eight o'clock like we planned ... Man—*Willy didn't never show up.*

WALTER: Why ... where was he ... where is he?   500

BOBO: That's what I'm trying to tell you ... I don't know ... I waited six hours ... I called
his house ... and I waited ... six hours ... I waited in that train station six hours ...
(*breaking into tears*) That was all the extra money I had in the world ... (*looking
up at Walter with the tears running down his face*) Man, *Willy is gone.*

WALTER: Gone, what you mean Willy is gone? Gone where? You mean he went by himself. You mean he went off to Springfield by himself—to take care of getting the license—(*turns and looks anxiously at Ruth*) You mean maybe he didn't want too
many people in on the business down there? (*looks to Ruth again, as before*) You
know Willy got his own ways. (*looks back to Bobo*) Maybe you was late yesterday
and he just went on down there without you. Maybe—maybe—he's been callin' you
at home tryin' to tell you what happened or something. Maybe—maybe—he just got
sick. He's somewhere—he's got to be somewhere. We just got to find him—me and
you got to find him. (*grabs Bobo senselessly by the collar and starts to shake him*)
We got to!

BOBO: (*in sudden angry, frightened agony*)   What's the matter with you, Walter!
When a cat take off with your money he don't leave you no road maps!

WALTER: (*turning madly, as though he is looking for Willy in the very room*)   Willy! ...
Willy ... don't do it ... Please don't do it ... Man, not with that money ... Man, please,
not with that money ... Oh, God ... Don't let it be true ... (*He is wandering around,
crying out for Willy and looking for him or perhaps for help from God.*) Man ... I
trusted you ... Man, I put my life in your hands ... (*He starts to crumple down on the
floor as Ruth just covers her face in horror. Mama opens the door and comes into
the room, with Beneatha behind her.*) Man ... (*He starts to pound the floor with
his fists, sobbing wildly.*) THAT MONEY IS MADE OUT OF MY FATHER'S FLESH—

BOBO: (*standing over him helplessly*)   I'm sorry, Walter ... (*Only Walter's sobs reply.*   505
Bobo puts on his hat.*) I had my life staked on this deal, too ...

He exits.

MAMA: (*to Walter*)   Son—(*She goes to him, bends down to him, talks to his bent
head.*) Son ... Is it gone? Son, I gave you sixty-five hundred dollars. Is it gone? All of
it? Beneatha's money too?

WALTER: (*lifting his head slowly*)   Mama ... I never ... went to the bank at all ...

MAMA: (*not wanting to believe him*)   You mean ... your sister's school money ... you
used that too ... Walter? ...

WALTER: Yessss! All of it ... It's all gone ...

*There is total silence. Ruth stands with her face covered with her hands; Beneatha leans forlornly
against a wall, fingering a piece of red ribbon from the mother's gift. Mama stops and looks at her son
without recognition and then, quite without thinking about it, starts to beat him senselessly in the
face. Beneatha goes to them and stops it.*

BENEATHA: Mama!   510

*Mama stops and looks at both of her children and rises slowly and wanders vaguely, aimlessly away
from them.*

MAMA: I seen . . . him . . . night after night . . . come in . . . and look at that rug . . . and then look at me . . . the red showing in his eyes . . . the veins moving in his head . . . I seen him grow thin and old before he was forty . . . working and working and working like somebody's old horse . . . killing himself . . . and you—you give it all away in a day—(*She raises her arms to strike him again.*)

BENEATHA: Mama—

MAMA: Oh, God . . . (*She looks up to Him.*) Look down here—and show me the strength.

BENEATHA: Mama—

MAMA: (*folding over*)   Strength . . .

BENEATHA: (*plaintively*)   Mama . . .

MAMA: Strength!

Curtain.

Act 3

TIME: *An hour later.*

At curtain, there is a sullen light of gloom in the living room, gray light not unlike that which began the first scene of Act One. At left we can see Walter within his room, alone with himself. He is stretched out on the bed, his shirt out and open, his arms under his head. He does not smoke, he does not cry out, he merely lies there, looking up at the ceiling, much as if he were alone in the world.

In the living room Beneatha sits at the table, still surrounded by the now almost ominous packing crates. She sits looking off. We feel that this is a mood struck perhaps an hour before, and it lingers now, full of the empty sound of profound disappointment. We see on a line from her brother's bedroom the sameness of their attitudes. Presently the bell rings and Beneatha rises without ambition or interest in answering. It is Asagai, smiling broadly, striding into the room with energy and happy expectation and conversation.

ASAGAI: I came over . . . I had some free time. I thought I might help with the packing. Ah, I like the look of packing crates! A household in preparation for a journey! It depresses some people . . . but for me . . . it is another feeling. Something full of the flow of life, do you understand? Movement, progress . . . It makes me think of Africa.

BENEATHA: Africa!

ASAGAI: What kind of a mood is this? Have I told you how deeply you move me?

BENEATHA: He gave away the money, Asagai . . .

ASAGAI: Who gave away what money?

BENEATHA: The insurance money. My brother gave it away.

ASAGAI: Gave it away?

BENEATHA: He made an investment! With a man even Travis wouldn't have trusted with his most worn-out marbles.

ASAGAI: And it's gone?

BENEATHA: Gone!

ASAGAI: I'm very sorry . . . And you, now?

BENEATHA: Me? . . . Me? . . . Me, I'm nothing . . . Me. When I was very small . . . We used to take our sleds out in the wintertime and the only hills we had were the ice-covered stone steps of some houses down the street. And we used to fill them in with snow and make them smooth and slide down them all day . . . and it was very dangerous, you know . . . far too steep . . . and sure enough one day a kid named Rufus came down too fast and hit the sidewalk and we saw his face just split open right there in front of us . . . And I remember standing there looking at his bloody open face thinking that was the end of Rufus. But the ambulance came and they took him to the hospital and they fixed the broken bones and they sewed it all up . . . and the next time I saw Rufus he just had a little line down the middle of his face . . . I never got over that . . .

ASAGAI: What?

Beneatha: That that was what one person could do for another, fix him up—sew up the problem, make him all right again. That was the most marvelous thing in the world ... I wanted to do that. I always thought it was the one concrete thing in the world that a human being could do. Fix up the sick, you know—and make them whole again. This was truly being God ...

Asagai: You wanted to be God?   15

Beneatha: No—I wanted to cure. It used to be so important to me. I wanted to cure. It used to matter. I used to care. I mean about people and how their bodies hurt ...

Asagai: And you've stopped caring?

Beneatha: Yes—I think so.

Asagai: Why?

Beneatha: (*bitterly*)   Because it doesn't seem deep enough, close enough to what ails   20 mankind! It was a child's way of seeing things—or an idealist's.

Asagai: Children see things very well sometimes—and idealists even better.

Beneatha: I know that's what you think. Because you are still where I left off. You with all your talk and dreams about Africa! You still think you can patch up the world. Cure the Great Sore of Colonialism—(*loftily, mocking it*) with the Penicillin of Independence—!

Asagai: Yes!

Beneatha: Independence *and then what?* What about all the crooks and thieves and just plain idiots who will come into power and steal and plunder the same as before—only now they will be black and do it in the name of the new Independence—WHAT ABOUT THEM?!

Asagai: That will be the problem for another time. First we must get there.   25

Beneatha: And where does it end?

Asagai: End? Who even spoke of an end? To life? To living?

Beneatha: An end to misery! To stupidity! Don't you see there isn't any real progress, Asagai, there is only one large circle that we march in, around and around, each of us with our own little picture in front of us—our own little mirage that we think is the future.

Asagai: That is the mistake.

Beneatha: What?   30

Asagai: What you just said—about the circle. It isn't a circle—it is simply a long line—as in geometry, you know, one that reaches into infinity. And because we cannot see the end—we also cannot see how it changes. And it is very odd but those who see the changes—who dream, who will not give up—are called idealists ... and those who see only the circle—we call *them* the "realists"!

Beneatha: Asagai, while I was sleeping in that bed in there, people went out and took the future right out of my hands! And nobody asked me, nobody consulted me—they just went out and changed my life!

Asagai: Was it your money?

Beneatha: What?

Asagai: Was it your money he gave away?   35

Beneatha: It belonged to all of us.

Asagai: But did you earn it? Would you have had it at all if your father had not died?

Beneatha: No.

Asagai: Then isn't there something wrong in a house—in a world—where all dreams, good or bad, must depend on the death of a man? I never thought to see *you* like this, Alaiyo. You! Your brother made a mistake and you are grateful to him so that now you can give up the ailing human race on account of it! You talk about what good is struggle, what good is anything! Where are we all going and why are we bothering!

Beneatha: AND YOU CANNOT ANSWER IT!   40

ASAGAI: (*shouting over her*)   *I LIVE THE ANSWER!* (*pause*) In my village at home it is
the exceptional man who can even read a newspaper ... or who ever sees a book at
all. I will go home and much of what I will have to say will seem strange to the people of my village. But I will teach and work and things will happen, slowly and
swiftly. At times it will seem that nothing changes at all ... and then again the sudden dramatic events which make history leap into the future. And then quiet again.
Retrogression even. Guns, murder, revolution. And I even will have moments when I
wonder if the quiet was not better than all that death and hatred. But I will look
about my village at the illiteracy and disease and ignorance and I will not wonder
long. And perhaps ... perhaps I will be a great man ... I mean perhaps I will hold on
to the substance of truth and find my way always with the right course ... and perhaps for it I will be butchered in my bed some night by the servants of empire ...
BENEATHA: *The martyr!*
ASAGAI: (*He smiles.*)   ... or perhaps I shall live to be a very old man, respected and esteemed in my new nation ... And perhaps I shall hold office and this is what I'm trying to tell you, Alaiyo: Perhaps the things I believe now for my country will be
wrong and outmoded, and I will not understand and do terrible things to have
things my way or merely to keep my power. Don't you see that there will be young
men and women—not British soldiers then, but my own black countrymen—to
step out of the shadows some evening and slit my then useless throat? Don't you
see they have always been there ... that they always will be. And that such a thing as
my own death will be an advance? They who might kill me even ... actually replenish all that I was.
BENEATHA: Oh, Asagai, I know all that.
ASAGAI: Good! Then stop moaning and groaning and tell me what you plan to do.   45
BENEATHA: Do?
ASAGAI: I have a bit of a suggestion.
BENEATHA: What?
ASAGAI: (*rather quietly for him*)   That when it is all over—that you come home with
me—
BENEATHA: (*staring at him and crossing away with exasperation*)   Oh—Asagai—at   50
this moment you decide to be romantic!
ASAGAI: (*quickly understanding the misunderstanding*)   My dear, young creature of
the New World—I do not mean across the city—I mean across the ocean: home—to
Africa.
BENEATHA: (*slowly understanding and turning to him with murmured amazement*)
To Africa?
ASAGAI: Yes! ... (*smiling and lifting his arms playfully*) Three hundred years later the
African Prince rose up out of the seas and swept the maiden back across the middle
passage over which her ancestors had come—
BENEATHA: (*unable to play*)   To—to Nigeria?
ASAGAI: Nigeria. Home. (*coming to her with genuine romantic flippancy*) I will show   55
you our mountains and our stars; and give you cool drinks from gourds and teach
you the old songs and the ways of our people—and, in time, we will pretend that—
(*very softly*)—you have only been away for a day. Say that you'll come—(*He swings
her around and takes her full in his arms in a kiss which proceeds to passion.*)
BENEATHA: (*pulling away suddenly*)   You're getting me all mixed up—
ASAGAI: Why?
BENEATHA: Too many things—too many things have happened today. I must sit down
and think. I don't know what I feel about anything right this minute.

She promptly sits down and props her chin on her fist.

ASAGAI: (*charmed*)   All right, I shall leave you. No—don't get up. (*touching her, gently,
sweetly*) Just sit awhile and think ... Never be afraid to sit awhile and think. (*He goes

to door and looks at her.) How often I have looked at you and said, "Ah—so this is what the New World hath finally wrought . . ."

He exits. Beneatha sits on alone. Presently Walter enters from his room and starts to rummage through things, feverishly looking for something. She looks up and turns in her seat.

BENEATHA: *(hissingly)* Yes—just look at what the New World hath wrought! . . . Just   60
look! *(She gestures with bitter disgust.)* There he is! *Monsieur le petit bourgeois noir*—himself! There he is—Symbol of a Rising Class! Entrepreneur! Titan of the system! *(Walter ignores her completely and continues frantically and destructively looking for something and hurling things to floor and tearing things out of their place in his search. Beneatha ignores the eccentricity of his actions and goes on with the monologue of insult.)* Did you dream of yachts on Lake Michigan, Brother? Did you see yourself on that Great Day sitting down at the Conference Table, surrounded by all the mighty bald-headed men in America? All halted, waiting, breathless, waiting for your pronouncements on industry? Waiting for you—Chairman of the Board! *(Walter finds what he is looking for—a small piece of white paper—and pushes it in his pocket and puts on his coat and rushes out without ever having looked at her. She shouts after him.)* I look at you and I see the final triumph of stupidity in the world!

The door slams and she returns to just sitting again. Ruth comes quickly out of Mama's room.

RUTH: Who was that?
BENEATHA: Your husband.
RUTH: Where did he go?
BENEATHA: Who knows—Maybe he has an appointment at U.S. Steel.
RUTH: *(anxiously, with frightened eyes)* You didn't say nothing bad to him, did you?   65
BENEATHA: Bad? Say anything bad to him? No—I told him he was a sweet boy and full of dreams and everything is strictly peachy keen, as the ofay kids say!

Mama enters from her bedroom. She is lost, vague, trying to catch hold, to make some sense of her former command of the world, but it still eludes her. A sense of waste overwhelms her gait; a measure of apology rides on her shoulders. She goes to her plant, which has remained on the table, looks at it, picks it up and takes it to the window sill and sits it outside, and she stands and looks at it a long moment. Then she closes the window, straightens her body with effort and turns around to her children.

MAMA: Well—ain't it a mess in here, though? *(a false cheerfulness, a beginning of something)* I guess we all better stop moping around and get some work done. All this unpacking and everything we got to do. *(Ruth raises her head slowly in response to the sense of the line; and Beneatha in similar manner turns very slowly to look at her mother.)* One of you all better call the moving people and tell 'em not to come.
RUTH: Tell 'em not to come?
MAMA: Of course, baby. Ain't no need in 'em coming all the way here and having to go back. They charges for that too. *(She sits down, fingers to her brow, thinking.)* Lord, ever since I was a little girl, I always remembers people saying, "Lena—Lena Eggleston, you aims too high all the time. You needs to slow down and see life a little more like it is. Just slow down some." That's what they always used to say down home—"Lord, that Lena Eggleston is a high-minded thing. She'll get her due one day!"
RUTH: No, Lena . . .   70
MAMA: Me and Big Walter just didn't never learn right.
RUTH: Lena, no! We gotta go. Bennie—tell her . . . *(She rises and crosses to Beneatha with her arms outstretched. Beneatha doesn't respond.)* Tell her we can still move . . . the notes ain't but a hundred and twenty-five a month. We got four grown people in this house—we can work . . .
MAMA: *(to herself)* Just aimed too high all the time—

RUTH: (*turning and going to Mama fast—the words pouring out with urgency and desperation*)   Lena—I'll work . . . I'll work twenty hours a day in all the kitchens in Chicago . . . I'll strap my baby on my back if I have to and scrub all the floors in America and wash all the sheets in America if I have to—but we got to MOVE! We got to get OUT OF HERE!!

Mama reaches out absently and pats Ruth's hand.

MAMA: No—I sees things differently now. Been thinking 'bout some of the things we   75
could do to fix this place up some. I seen a second-hand bureau over on Maxwell Street just the other day that could fit right there. (*She points to where the new furniture might go. Ruth wanders away from her.*) Would need some new handles on it and then a little varnish and then it look like something brand-new. And—we can put up them new curtains in the kitchen . . . Why this place be looking fine. Cheer us all up so that we forget trouble ever come . . . (*to Ruth*) And you could get some nice screens to put up in your room round the baby's bassinet . . . (*She looks at both of them, pleadingly.*) Sometimes you just got to know when to give up some things . . . and hold on to what you got . . .

Walter enters from the outside, looking spent and leaning against the door, his coat hanging from him.

MAMA: Where you been, son?
WALTER: (*breathing hard*)   Made a call.
MAMA: To who, son?
WALTER: To The Man. (*He heads for his room.*)
MAMA: What man, baby?   80
WALTER: (*stops in the door*)   The Man, Mama. Don't you know who The Man is?
RUTH: Walter Lee?
WALTER: *The Man.* Like the guys in the streets say—The Man. Captain Boss—Mistuh Charley . . . Old Cap'n Please Mr. Bossman . . .
BENEATHA: (*suddenly*)   Lindner!
WALTER: That's right! That's good. I told him to come right over.   85
BENEATHA: (*fiercely, understanding*)   For what? What do you want to see him for!
WALTER: (*looking at his sister*)   We going to do business with him.
MAMA: What you talking 'bout, son?
WALTER: Talking 'bout life, Mama. You all always telling me to see life like it is. Well—I laid in there on my back today . . . and I figured it out. Life just like it is. Who gets and who don't get. (*He sits down with his coat on and laughs.*) Mama, you know it's all divided up. Life is. Sure enough. Between the takers and the "tooken." (*He laughs.*) I've figured it out finally. (*He looks around at them.*) Yeah. Some of us always getting "tooken." (*He laughs.*) People like Willy Harris, they don't never get "tooken." And you know why the rest of us do? 'Cause we all mixed up. Mixed up bad. We get to looking 'round for the right and the wrong; and we worry about it and cry about it and stay up nights trying to figure out 'bout the wrong and the right of things all the time . . . And all the time, man, them takers is out there operating, just taking and taking. Willy Harris? Shoot—Willy Harris don't even count. He don't even count in the big scheme of things. But I'll say one thing for old Willy Harris . . . he's taught me something. He's taught me to keep my eye on what counts in this world. Yeah— (*shouting out a little*) Thanks, Willy!
RUTH: What did you call that man for, Walter Lee?   90
WALTER: Called him to tell him to come on over to the show. Gonna put on a show for the man. Just what he wants to see. You see, Mama, the man came here today and he told us that them people out there where you want us to move—well they so upset they willing to pay us *not* to move! (*He laughs again.*) And—and oh, Mama—you would of been proud of the way me and Ruth and Bennie acted. We told him to get

out . . . Lord have mercy! We told the man to get out! Oh, we was some proud folks this afternoon, yeah. (*He lights a cigarette.*) We were still full of that old-time stuff . . .

RUTH: (*coming toward him slowly*)　You talking 'bout taking them people's money to keep us from moving into that house?

WALTER: I ain't just talking 'bout it, baby—I'm telling you that's what's going to happen!

BENEATHA: Oh, God! Where is the bottom! Where is the real honest-to-God bottom so he can't go any farther!

WALTER: See—that's the old stuff. You and that boy that was here today. You all want　95 everybody to carry a flag and a spear and sing some marching songs, huh? You wanna spend your life looking into things and trying to find the right and the wrong part, huh? Yeah. You know what's going to happen to that boy someday—he'll find himself sitting in a dungeon, locked in forever—and the takers will have the key! Forget it, baby! There ain't no causes—there ain't nothing but taking in this world, and he who takes most is smartest—and it don't make a damn bit of difference *how*.

MAMA: You making something inside me cry, son. Some awful pain inside me.

WALTER: Don't cry, Mama. Understand. That white man is going to walk in that door able to write checks for more money than we ever had. It's important to him and I'm going to help him . . . I'm going to put on the show, Mama.

MAMA: Son—I come from five generations of people who was slaves and sharecroppers—but ain't nobody in my family never let nobody pay 'em no money that was a way of telling us we wasn't fit to walk the earth. We ain't never been that poor. (*raising her eyes and looking at him*) We ain't never been that—dead inside.

BENEATHA: Well—we are dead now. All the talk about dreams and sunlight that goes on in this house. It's all dead now.

WALTER: What's the matter with you all! I didn't make this world! It was give to me this　100 way! Hell, yes, I want me some yachts someday! Yes, I want to hang some real pearls 'round my wife's neck. Ain't she supposed to wear no pearls? Somebody tell me— tell me, who decides which women is suppose to wear pearls in this world. I tell you I am a *man*—and I think my wife should wear some pearls in this world!

This last line hangs a good while and Walter begins to move about the room. The word "Man" has penetrated his consciousness; he mumbles it to himself repeatedly between strange agitated pauses as he moves about.

MAMA: Baby, how you going to feel on the inside?

WALTER: Fine! . . . Going to feel fine . . . a man . . .

MAMA: You won't have nothing left then, Walter Lee.

WALTER: (*coming to her*)　I'm going to feel fine, Mama. I'm going to look that son-of-a-bitch in the eyes and say—(*He falters.*)—and say, "All right, Mr. Lindner—(*He falters even more.*)—that's *your* neighborhood out there! You got the right to keep it like you want! You got the right to have it like you want. Just write the check and—the house is yours." And—and I am going to say—(*His voice almost breaks.*) "And you— you people just put the money in my hand and you won't have to live next to this bunch of stinking niggers! . . ." (*He straightens up and moves away from his mother, walking around the room.*) And maybe—maybe I'll just get down on my black knees . . . (*He does so; Ruth and Bennie and Mama watch him in frozen horror.*) Captain, Mistuh, Bossman—(*groveling and grinning and wringing his hands in profoundly anguished imitation of the slow-witted movie stereotype*) A-hee-hee-hee! Oh, yassuh boss! Yasssssuh! Great white—(*Voice breaking, he forces himself to go on.*) Father, just gi' ussen de money, fo' God's sake, and we's—we's ain't gwine come out deh and dirty up yo' white folks neighborhood . . ." (*He breaks down completely.*) And I'll feel fine! Fine! FINE! (*He gets up and goes into the bedroom.*)

BENEATHA: That is not a man. That is nothing but a toothless rat.　105

MAMA: Yes—death done come in this here house. (*She is nodding, slowly, reflectively.*) Done come walking in my house on the lips of my children. You what supposed to

be my beginning again. You—what supposed to be my harvest. (*to Beneatha*) You—
you mourning your brother?

BENEATHA: He's no brother of mine.

MAMA: What you say?

BENEATHA: I said that that individual in that room is no brother of mine.

MAMA: That's what I thought you said. You feeling like you better than he is today?   110
(*Beneatha does not answer.*) Yes? What you tell him a minute ago? That he wasn't a
man? Yes? You give him up for me? You done wrote his epitaph too—like the rest of
the world? Well, who give you the privilege?

BENEATHA: Be on my side for once! You saw what he just did, Mama! You saw him—
down on his knees. Wasn't it you who taught me to despise any man who would do
that? Do what he's going to do?

MAMA: Yes—I taught you that. Me and your daddy. But I thought I taught you something
else too . . . I thought I taught you to love him.

BENEATHA: Love him? There is nothing left to love.

MAMA: There is *always* something left to love. And if you ain't learned that, you ain't
learned nothing. (*looking at her*) Have you cried for that boy today? I don't mean
for yourself and for the family 'cause we lost the money. I mean for him; what he
been through and what it done to him. Child, when do you think is the time to love
somebody the most? When they done good and made things easy for everybody?
Well then, you ain't through learning—because that ain't the time at all. It's when
he's at his lowest and can't believe in hisself 'cause the world done whipped him
so! When you starts measuring somebody, measure him right, child, measure him
right. Make sure you done taken into account what hills and valleys he come
through before he got to wherever he is.

Travis bursts into the room at the end of the speech, leaving the door open.

TRAVIS: Grandmama—the moving men are downstairs! The truck just pulled up.   115

MAMA: (*turning and looking at him*) Are they, baby? They downstairs?
*She sighs and sits. Lindner appears in the doorway. He peers in and knocks
lightly, to gain attention, and comes in. All turn to look at him.*

LINDNER: (*hat and briefcase in hand*) Uh—hello . . .

*Ruth crosses mechanically to the bedroom door and opens it and lets it swing open freely and slowly as
the lights come up on Walter within, still in his coat, sitting at the far corner of the room. He looks up
and out through the room to Lindner.*

RUTH: He's here.

A long minute passes and Walter slowly gets up.

LINDNER: (*coming to the table with efficiency, putting his briefcase on the table and
starting to unfold papers and unscrew fountain pens*) Well, I certainly was glad
to hear from you people. (*Walter has begun the trek out of the room, slowly and
awkwardly, rather like a small boy, passing the back of his sleeve across his
mouth from time to time.*) Life can really be so much simpler than people let it be
most of the time. Well—with whom do I negotiate? You, Mrs. Younger, or your son
here? (*Mama sits with her hands folded on her lap and her eyes closed as Walter
advances. Travis goes closer to Lindner and looks at the papers curiously.*) Just
some official papers, sonny.

RUTH: Travis, you go downstairs—   120

MAMA: (*opening her eyes and looking into Walter's*) No. Travis, you stay right here.
And you make him understand what you doing, Walter Lee. You teach him good. Like
Willy Harris taught you. You show where our five generations done come to. (*Walter
looks from her to the boy, who grins at him innocently.*) Go ahead, son—(*She folds
her hands and closes her eyes.*) Go ahead.

WALTER: (*at last crosses to Lindner, who is reviewing the contract*)   Well, Mr. Lindner. (*Beneatha turns away.*) We called you—(*There is a profound, simple groping quality in his speech.*)—because, well, me and my family (*He looks around and shifts from one foot to the other.*) Well—we are very plain people . . .

LINDNER: Yes—

WALTER: I mean—I have worked as a chauffeur most of my life—and my wife here, she does domestic work in people's kitchens. So does my mother. I mean—we are plain people . . .

LINDNER: Yes, Mr. Younger—   125

WALTER: (*really like a small boy, looking down at his shoes and then up at the man*) And—uh—well, my father, well, he was a laborer most of his life . . .

LINDNER: (*absolutely confused*)   Uh, yes—yes, I understand. (*He turns back to the contract.*)

WALTER: (*a beat; staring at him*)   And my father—(*with sudden intensity*) My father almost *beat a man to death* once because this man called him a bad name or something, you know what I mean?

LINDNER: (*looking up, frozen*)   No, no, I'm afraid I don't—

WALTER: (*A beat. The tension hangs; then Walter steps back from it.*)   Yeah. Well—   130
what I mean is that we come from people who had a lot of *pride.* I mean—we are very proud people. And that's my sister over there and she's going to be a doctor—and we are very proud—

LINDNER: Well—I am sure that is very nice, but—

WALTER: What I am telling you is that we called you over here to tell you that we are very proud and that this—(*signaling to Travis*) Travis, come here. (*Travis crosses and Walter draws him before him facing the man.*) This is my son, and he makes the sixth generation our family in this country. And we have all thought about your offer—

LINDNER: Well, good . . . good—

WALTER: And we have decided to move into our house because my father—my father—he earned it for us brick by brick. (*Mama has her eyes closed and is rocking back and forth as though she were in church, with her head nodding the Amen yes.*) We don't want to make no trouble for nobody or fight no causes, and we will try to be good neighbors. And that's *all* we got to say about that. (*He looks the man absolutely in the eyes.*) We don't want your money. (*He turns and walks away.*)

LINDNER: (*looking around at all of them*)   I take it then—that you have decided to   135
occupy . . .

BENEATHA: That's what the man said.

LINDNER: (*to Mama in her reverie*)   Then I would like to appeal to you, Mrs. Younger. You are older and wiser and understand things better I am sure . . .

MAMA: I am afraid you don't understand. My son said we was going to move and there ain't nothing left for me to say. (*briskly*) You know how these young folks is nowadays, mister. Can't do a thing with 'em! (*As he opens his mouth, she rises.*) Goodbye.

LINDNER: (*folding up his materials*)   Well—if you are that final about it . . . there is nothing left for me to say. (*He finishes, almost ignored by the family, who are concentrating on Walter Lee. At the door Lindner halts and looks around.*) I sure hope you people know what you're getting into.

He shakes his head and exits.

RUTH: (*looking around and coming to life*)   Well, for God's sake—if the moving men   140
are here—LET'S GET THE HELL OUT OF HERE!

MAMA: (*into action*)   Ain't it the truth! Look at all this here mess. Ruth, put Travis' good jacket on him . . . Walter Lee, fix your tie and tuck your shirt in, you look like somebody's hoodlum! Lord have mercy, where is my plant? (*She flies to get it amid the general bustling of the family, who are deliberately trying to ignore the nobility of the past moment.*) You all start on down ... Travis child, don't go empty-handed ... Ruth, where did I put that box with my skillets in it? I want to be in charge of it myself ... I'm going to make us the biggest dinner we ever ate tonight ... Beneatha, what's the matter with them stockings? Pull them things up, girl ...

The family starts to file out as two moving men appear and begin to carry out the heavier pieces of furniture, bumping into the family as they move about.

BENEATHA: Mama, Asagai asked me to marry him today and go to Africa—

MAMA: (*in the middle of her getting-ready activity*)   He did? You ain't old enough to marry nobody—(*seeing the moving men lifting one of her chairs precariously*) Darling, that ain't no bale of cotton, please handle it so we can sit in it again! I had that chair twenty-five years ...

The movers sigh with exasperation and go on with their work.

BENEATHA: (*girlishly and unreasonably trying to pursue the conversation*)   To go to Africa, Mama—to be a doctor in Africa ...

MAMA: (*distracted*)   Yes, baby—   145

WALTER: *Africa!* What he want you to go to Africa for?

BENEATHA: To practice there ...

WALTER: Girl, if you don't get all them silly ideas out your head! You better marry yourself a man with some loot ...

BENEATHA: (*angrily, precisely as in the first scene of the play*)   What have you got to do with who I marry!

WALTER: Plenty. Now I think George Murchison—   150

BENEATHA: *George Murchison!* I wouldn't marry him if he was Adam and I was Eve!

Walter and Beneatha go out yelling at each other vigorously and the anger is loud and real till their voices diminish. Ruth stands at the door and turns to Mama and smiles knowingly.

MAMA: (*fixing her hat at last*)   Yeah—they something all right, my children ...

RUTH: Yeah—they're something. Let's go, Lena.

MAMA: (*stalling, starting to look around at the house*)   Yes—I'm coming. Ruth—

RUTH: Yes?   155

MAMA: (*quietly, woman to woman*)   He finally come into his manhood today, didn't he? Kind of like a rainbow after the rain ...

RUTH: (*biting her lip lest her own pride explode in front of* MAMA)   Yes, Lena.

Walter's voice calls for them raucously.

WALTER: (*off stage*)   Y'all come on! These people charges by the hour, you know!

MAMA: (*waving Ruth out vaguely*)   All right, honey—go on down. I be down directly.

Ruth hesitates, then exits. Mama stands, at last alone in the living room, her plant on the table before her as the lights start to come down. She looks around at all the walls and ceilings and suddenly, despite herself, while the children call below, a great heaving thing rises in her and she puts her fist to her mouth to stifle it, takes a final desperate look, pulls her coat about her, pats her hat and goes out. The lights dim down. The door opens and she comes back in, grabs her plant, and goes out for the last time. Curtain.

Adrienne Kennedy   b. 1931

A Movie Star Has to Star in Black and White[1]   1976

NOTES

The movie music throughout is romantic.

———
[1]The text is that of *Word Plays 3* (1984).

The ship, the deck, the railings and the dark boat can all be done with lights and silhouettes.
All the colors are shades of black and white.

These movie stars are romantic and moving, never camp or farcical, and the attitude of the support-
ing players to the movie stars is deadly serious.

The movie music sometimes plays at intervals when Clara's thought is still.

Characters

Clara
"Leading Roles" are played by actors who look exactly like:
Bette Davis
Paul Henreid
Jean Peters
Marlon Brando
Montgomery Clift
Shelly Winters
[they all look exactly like their movie roles]
Supporting Roles by
The Mother
The Father
The Husband
[they all look like photographs *Clara* keeps of them except when they're in the hospital]

SCENES

1   Hospital lobby and Now Voyager
2   Brother's room and Viva Zapata
3   Clara's old room and A Place in the Sun

Dark stage. From darkness center appears the Columbia Pictures Lady in a bright light.

COLUMBIA PICTURES LADY: [*Speaks.*] Summer, New York, 1955. Summer, Ohio, 1963. The
scenes are *Now Voyager, Viva Zapata* and *A Place in the Sun.*
The leading roles are played by Bette Davis, Paul Henreid, Jean Peters, Marlon
Brando, Montgomery Clift and Shelly Winters. Supporting roles are played by the
mother, the father, the husband. A bit role is played by Clara.
Now Voyager takes place in the hospital lobby.
Viva Zapata takes place in the brother's room.
A Place in the Sun takes place in Clara's old room.
June 1963.
My producer is Joel Steinberg. He looks different from what I once thought, not at
all like that picture in *Vogue.* He was in *Vogue* with a group of people who were
going to do a musical about Socrates. In the photograph Joel's hair looked dark and
his skin smooth. In real life his skin is blotched. Everyone says he drinks a lot.
Lately I think often of killing myself. Eddie Jr. plays outside in the playground. I'm
very lonely. . . . Met Lee Strasberg: the members of the playwrights unit were invited
to watch his scene. Geraldine Page, Rip Torn and Norman Mailer were there. . . . I
wonder why I lie so much to my mother about how I feel. . . . My father once said his
life has been nothing but a life of hypocrisy and that's why his photograph smiled.
While Eddie Jr. plays outside I read Edith Wharton, a book on Egypt and Chinua
Achebe. Leroi Jones, Ted Joans and Allen Ginsberg are reading in the Village. Eddie
comes every evening right before dark. He wants to know if I'll go back to him for
the sake of our son.

[She fades. At the back of the stage as in a distance a dim light goes on a large doorway in the hospi-
tal. Visible is the foot of the white hospital bed and a figure lying upon it. Movie music. Clara stands

at the doorway of the room. She is a Negro woman of thirty-three wearing a maternity dress. She does not enter the room but turns away and stands very still. Movie music.]

CLARA: [*Reflective; very still facing away from the room.*] My brother is the same . . . my father is coming . . . very depressed.

Before I left New York I got my typewriter from the pawnshop. I'm terribly tired, trying to do a page a day, yet my play is coming together. Each day I wonder with what or with whom can I co-exist in a true union?

[She turns and stares into her brother's room. Scene fades out; then bright lights that convey an ocean liner in motion.]

Scene 1

Movie music. On the deck of the ocean liner from Now Voyager are Bette Davis and Paul Henreid. They sit at a table slightly off stage center. Bette Davis has on a large white summer hat and Paul Henreid a dark summer suit. The light is romantic and glamorous. Beyond backstage left are deck chairs. It is bright sunlight on the deck.

BETTE DAVIS: [*To Paul.*]
June 1955.
When I have the baby I wonder will I turn into a river of blood and die? My mother almost died when I was born. I've always felt sad that I couldn't have been an angel of mercy to my father and mother and saved them from their torment. I used to hope when I was a little girl that one day I would rise above them, an angel with glowing wings and cover them with peace. But I failed. When I came among them it seems to me I did not bring them peace . . . but made them more disconsolate. The crosses they bore always made me sad.
The one reality I wanted never came true . . . to be their angel of mercy to unite them. I keep remembering the time my mother threatened to kill my father with a shot gun. I keep remembering my father's going away to marry a girl who talked to willow trees.

[Onto the deck wander the mother, the father, and the husband. They are Negroes. The parents are as they were when young in 1929 in Atlanta, Georgia. The mother is small, pale and very beautiful. She has on a white summer dress and white shoes. The father is small and dark skinned. He has on a Morehouse sweater, knickers and a cap. They both are emotional and nervous. In presence both are romanticized. The husband is twenty-eight and handsome. He is dressed as in the summer of 1955 wearing a seersucker suit from Kleins that cost thirteen dollars.]

BETTE DAVIS: In the scrapbook that my father left is a picture of my mother in Savannah, Georgia in 1929.

MOTHER: [*Sitting down in a deck chair takes a cigarette out of a beaded purse and smokes nervously. She speaks bitterly in a voice with a strong Georgia accent.*] In our Georgia town the white people lived on one side. It had pavement on the streets and sidewalks and mail was delivered. The Negroes lived on the other side and the roads were dirt and had no sidewalk and you had to go to the Post Office to pick up your mail. In the center of Main Street was a fountain and white people drank on one side and Negroes drank on the other. When a Negro bought something in a store he couldn't try it on. A Negro couldn't sit down at the soda fountain in the drug store but had to take his drink out. In the movies at Montefore you had to go in the side and up the stairs and sit in the last four rows. When you arrived on the train from Cincinnati the first thing you saw was the WHITE and COLORED signs at the depot. White people had one waiting room and we Negroes had another. We sat in only two cars and white people had the rest of the train.

[She is facing Paul Henreid and Bette Davis. The father and the husband sit in deck chairs that face the other side of the sea. The father also smokes. He sits hunched over with his head down thinking.

The husband takes an old text book out of a battered briefcase and starts to study. He looks exhausted and has dark circles under his eyes. His suit is worn.]

BETTE DAVIS: My father used to say John Hope Franklin, Du Bois and Benjamin Mays were fine men.[2]

[Bright sunlight on father sitting on other side of deck. Father gets up and comes toward them . . . to Bette Davis.]

FATHER: Cleveland is a place for opportunity, leadership, a progressive city, a place for education, a chance to come out of the back woods of Georgia. We Negro leaders dream of leading our people out of the wilderness.

[He passes her and goes along the deck whistling. Movie music. Bette Davis stands up looking after the father . . . then distractedly to Paul Henreid.]

BETTE DAVIS: [*Very passionate.*] I'd give anything in the world if I could just once talk to Jesus.
Sometimes he walks through my room but he doesn't stop long enough for us to talk . . . he has an aureole.[3]

[Then to the father who is almost out of sight on the deck whistling.]

Why did you marry the girl who talked to willow trees?

[To Paul Henreid.]

He left us to marry a girl who talked to willow trees.

[Father is whistling, mother is smoking, then the father vanishes into a door on deck. Bette Davis walks down to railing. Paul Henreid follows her.]

BETTE DAVIS: June 1955.
My mother said when she was a girl in the summers she didn't like to go out. She'd sit in the house and help her grandmother iron or shell peas and sometimes she'd sit on the steps.
My father used to come and sit on the steps. He asked her for her first "date." They went for a walk up the road and had an ice cream at Miss Ida's Icecream Parlor and walked back down the road. She was fifteen.
My mother says that my father was one of the most thought of boys in the town, Negro or white. And he was so friendly. He always had a friendly word for every-body.
He used to tell my mother his dreams how he was going to go up north. There was opportunity for Negroes up north and when he was finished at Morehouse he was going to get a job in someplace like New York.
And she said when she walked down the road with my father people were so friendly.
He organized a colored baseball team in Montefore and he was the Captain. And she used to go and watch him play baseball and everybody called him "Cap."
Seven more months and the baby.
Eddie and I don't talk too much these days.
Very often I try to be in bed by the time he comes home.
Most nights I'm wide awake until at least four. I wake up about eight and then I have a headache.
When I'm wide awake I see Jesus a lot.
My mother is giving us the money for the doctor bill. Eddie told her he will pay it back.

[2]Dr. Benjamin Mays (president of Morehouse College):   W.E.B. Dubois (1868–1963) was a promi-nent black educator, writer, and leader. John Hope Franklin is a preeminent black historian.
[3]Radiance.

Also got a letter from her; it said I hope things work out for you both. And pray, pray sometimes. Love Mother.

We also got a letter from Eddie's mother. Eddie's brother had told her that Eddie and I were having some problems. In her letter which was enclosed in a card she said when Eddie's sister had visited us she noticed that Eddie and I don't go to church. She said we mustn't forget the Lord, because God takes care of everything . . . God gives us peace and no matter what problems Eddie and I were having if we trusted in Him God would help us. It was the only letter from Eddie's mother that I ever saved.

Even though the card was Hallmark.

July 1955.

Eddie doesn't seem like the same person since he came back from Korea. And now I'm pregnant again. When I lost the baby he was thousands of miles away. All that bleeding. I'll never forgive him. The Red Cross let him send me a telegram to say he was sorry. I can't believe we used to be so in love on the campus and park the car and kiss and kiss. Yet I was a virgin when we married. A virgin who was to bleed and bleed . . . when I was in the hospital all I had was a photograph of Eddie in GI clothes standing in a woods in Korea. [*Pause.*] Eddie and I went to the Thalia on 95th and Broadway. There's a film festival this summer. We saw *Double Indemnity, The Red Shoes*[4] and *A Place in the Sun.* Next week *Viva Zapata* is coming. Afterwards we went to Reinzis on Macdougal Street and had Viennese coffee. We forced an enthusiasm we didn't feel. We took the subway back up to 116th Street and walked to Bencroft Hall. In the middle of the night I woke and wrote in my diary.

[*A bright light at hospital doorway. Clara younger, fragile, anxious. Movie music. She leaves hospital doorway and comes onto the deck from the door her father entered. She wears maternity dress, white wedgies,[5] her hair is straightened as in the fifties. She has a passive beauty and is totally preoccupied. She pays no attention to anyone, only writing in a notebook. Her movie stars speak for her. Clara lets her movie stars star in her life. Bette Davis and Paul Henreid are at the railing. The mother is smoking. The husband gets up and comes across the deck carrying his battered briefcase. He speaks to Clara who looks away. Paul Henreid goes on staring at the sea.*]

HUSBAND: Clara, please tell me everything the doctor said about the delivery and how   10
many days you'll be in the hospital.

[*Instead of Clara, Bette Davis replies. Paul Henreid is oblivious of him.*]

BETTE DAVIS: [*Very remote.*] I get very jealous of you Eddie. You're doing something with your life.

[*He tries to kiss Clara. She moves away and walks along the deck and writes in notebook.*]

BETTE DAVIS: [*To Eddie*] Eddie, do you think I have floating anxiety? You said everyone in Korea had floating anxiety. I think I might have it. [*Pause.*] Do you think I'm catatonic?

EDDIE: [*Staring at Clara.*] I'm late to class now. We'll talk when I come home. [*He leaves.*] When I get paid I'm going to take you to Birdland. Dizzy's[6] coming back.

[*Movie music.*]

CLARA: July.
I can't sleep. My head always full of thoughts night and day. I feel so nervous. Sometimes I hardly hear what people are saying. I'm writing a lot of my play. I don't want to show it to anyone though. Suppose it's no good.

[*Reads her play.*]

---

[4]*The Red Shoes* (1948) is a tragic colorful tale of a ballet dancer: *Double Indemnity* (1944) is a cynical film of murder.
[5]Shoes with wedge-shaped heels, popular in the 1940s and 1950s.
[6]i.e., Dizzy Gillespie, prominent jazz musician; Birdland was a legendary jazz spot.

They are dragging his body across the green his white hair hanging down. They are taking off his shoes and he is stiff. I must get into the chapel to see him. I must. He is my blood father. God, let me in to his burial. [*He grabs her down center. She, kneeling.*] I call God and the Owl answers. [*Softer.*] It haunts my Tower calling, its feathers are blowing against the cell wall, speckled in the garden on the fig tree, it comes, feathered, great hollow-eyed with yellow skin and yellow eyes, the flying bastard. From my Tower I keep calling and the only answer is the Owl, God. [*Pause. Stands.*] I am only yearning for our kingdom, God.[7] [*Movie music.*]

BETTE DAVIS: [*At railing.*] My father tried to commit suicide once when I was in High School. It was the afternoon he was presented an award by the Mayor of Cleveland at a banquet celebrating the completion of the New Settlement building. It had taken my father seven years to raise money for the New Settlement which was the center of Negro life in our community. He was given credit for being the one without whom it couldn't have been done. It was his biggest achievement.

 I went upstairs and found him whistling in his room. I asked him what was wrong. I want to see my dead mama and papa he said, that's all I really live for is to see my mama and papa. I stared at him. As I was about to leave the room he said I've been waiting to jump off the roof of the Settlement for a long time. I just had to wait until it was completed . . . and he went on whistling.

 He had tried to jump off the roof but had fallen on a scaffold.

[*Movie music. The deck has grown dark except for the light on Bette Davis and Paul Henreid and Clara.*]

CLARA: I loved the wedding night scene from *Viva Zapata* and the scene where the peasants met Zapata on the road and forced the soldiers to take the rope from his neck . . . when they shot Zapata at the end I cried.

[*Deck darker. She walks along the deck and into door, leaving Paul Henreid and Bette Davis at railing. She arrives at the hospital doorway, then enters her brother's room, standing at the foot of his bed. Her brother is in a coma.*]

CLARA: [*To her brother.*] Once I asked you romantically when you came back to the United States on a short leave, how do you like Europe Wally? You were silent. Finally you said, I get into a lot of fights with the Germans. You stared at me. And got up and went into the dining room to the dark sideboard and got a drink.

[*Darkness. Movie music.*]

Scene 2

Hospital room and Viva Zapata. *The hospital bed is now totally visible. In it lies Wally in a white gown. The light of the room is twilight on a summer evening. Clara's brother is handsome and in his late twenties. Beyond the bed is steel hospital apparatus. Clara stands by her brother's bedside. There is no real separation from the hospital room and* Viva Zapata *and the ship lights as there should have been none in* Now Voyager. *Simultaneously brighter lights come up stage center. Wedding night scene in* Viva Zapata. *Yet it is still the stateroom within the ship. Movie music. Marlon Brando and Jean Peters are sitting on the bed. They are both dressed as in* Viva Zapata.

JEAN PETERS: [*To Brando.*]
 July 11.
 I saw my father today. He's come from Georgia to see my brother. He lives in Savannah with his second wife. He seemed smaller and hunched over. When I was young he seemed energetic, speaking before civic groups and rallying people to give money to the Negro Settlement.

---

[7]The speech Clara has read is from Kennedy's play The *Owl Answers* (1965). She also quotes it later.

In the last years he seems introspective, petty and angry. Today he was wearing a white nylon sports shirt that looked slightly too big . . . his dark arms thin. He had on a little straw sport hat cocked slightly to the side.

We stood together in my brother's room. My father touched my brother's bare foot with his hand. My brother is in a coma.

[Silent.]

Eddie and I were married downstairs in this house. My brother was best man. We went to Colorado, but soon after Eddie was sent to Korea. My mother has always said that she felt if she and my father hadn't been fighting so much maybe I wouldn't have lost the baby. After I lost the baby I stopped writing to Eddie and decided I wanted to get a divorce when he came back from Korea. He hadn't been at Columbia long before I got pregnant again with Eddie Jr.

[Marlon Brando listens. They kiss tenderly. She stands up. She is bleeding. She falls back on her bed. Brando pulls a sheet out from under her. The sheets are black. Movie music.]

JEAN PETERS: The doctor says I have to stay in bed when I'm not at the hospital.

[From now until the end Marlon Brando continuously helps Jean Peters change sheets. He puts the black sheets on the floor around them.]

CLARA: *[To her brother, at the same time.]* Wally, you just have to get well. I know you   20
will, even though you do not move or speak.

[Sits down by his bedside watching him. Her mother enters. She is wearing a rose colored summer dress and small hat. The mother is in her fifties now. She sits down by her son's bedside and holds his hand. Silence in the room. The light of the room is constant twilight. They are in the constant dim twilight while Brando and Peters star in a dazzling wedding night light. Mexican peasant wedding music, Zapata remains throughout compassionate, heroic, tender. While Clara and her mother talk Brando and Peters sit on the bed, then enact the Zapata teach-me-to-read scene in which Brando asks Peters to get him a book and teach-him to read.]

MOTHER: What did I do? What did I do?
CLARA: What do you mean?
MOTHER: I don't know what I did to make my children so unhappy.

[Jean Peters gets book for Brando.]

CLARA: I'm not unhappy mother.
MOTHER: Yes you are.
CLARA: I'm not unhappy. I'm very happy. I just want to be a writer. Please don't think   25
I'm unhappy.
MOTHER: Your family's not together and you don't seem happy. *[They sit and read.]*
CLARA: I'm very happy mother. Very. I've just won an award and I'm going to have a play produced. I'm very happy. *[Silence. The mother straightens the sheet on her son's bed.]*
MOTHER: When you grow up in boarding school like I did, the thing you dream of most is to see your children together with their families.
CLARA: Mother you mustn't think I'm unhappy because I am, I really am, very happy.   30
MOTHER: I just pray you'll get yourself together and make some decisions about your life. I pray for you every night. Shouldn't you go back to Eddie especially since you're pregnant?

[There are shadows of the ships lights as if Now Voyager *is still in motion.]*

CLARA: Mother, Eddie doesn't understand me.

[Silence. Twilight dimmer, mother holds Wally's hand. Movie light bright on Jean Peters and Marlon Brando.]

JEAN PETERS: My brother Wally's still alive.

CLARA: [*To her diary.*] Wally was in an accident. A telegram from my mother. Your brother was in an automobile accident ... has been unconscious since last night in St. Luke's hospital. Love, Mother.

JEAN PETERS: Depressed.

35

CLARA: Came to Cleveland. Eddie came to La Guardia[8] to bring me money for my plane ticket and to say he was sorry about Wally who was best man at our wedding. Eddie looks at me with such sadness. It fills me with hatred for him and myself.

[*Brando is at the window looking down on the peasants. Mexican wedding music.*]

JEAN PETERS: Very depressed, and afraid at night since Eddie and I separated. I try to write a page a day on another play. It's going to be called a Lesson in Dead Language.[9] The main image is a girl in a white organdy dress covered with menstrual blood.

[*Clara is writing in her diary. Her mother sits holding Wally's hand. Brando stares out the window, Jean Peters sits on the bed.* Now Voyager *ship, shadows and light.*]

CLARA: It is twilight outside and very warm. The window faces a lawn, very green, with a fountain beyond. Wally does not speak or move. He is in a coma. [*Twilight dims.*] It bothers me that Eddie had to give me money for the ticket to come home. I don't have any money of my own: the option from my play[10] is gone and I don't know how I will be able to work and take care of Eddie Jr. Maybe Eddie and I should go back together.

[*Father enters the room, stands at the foot of his son's bed. He is in his fifties now and wears a white nylon sports shirt a little too big, his dark arms thin, baggy pants and a little straw sports hat cocked to the side. He has been drinking. The moment he enters the room the mother takes out a cigarette and starts to nervously smoke. They do not look at each other. He speaks to Clara, then glances in the direction of the mother. He then touches his son's bare feet. Wally is lying on his back, his hands to his sides. Clara gets up and goes to the window. Brando comes back and sits on the bed next to Jean Peters. They all remain for a long while silent. Suddenly the mother goes and throws herself into her daughter's arms and cries.*]

MOTHER: The doctor said he doesn't see how Wally has much of a chance of surviving: his brain is damaged.

[*She clings to her daughter and cries. Simultaneously:*]

JEAN PETERS: [*To Brando.*] I'm writing on my play. It's about a girl who turns into an Owl. Ow. [*Recites from her writings.*] He came to me in the outhouse, in the fig tree. He told me, "You are an owl, I am your beginning." I call God and the Owl answers. It haunts my tower, calling.

40

[*Silence. Father slightly drunk goes toward his former wife and his daughter. The mother runs out of the room into the lobby.*]

MOTHER: I did everything to make you happy and still you left me for another woman.

[*Clara stares out of the window. Father follows the mother into the lobby and stares at her. Jean Peters stands up. She is bleeding. She falls back on the bed. Marlon Brando pulls a sheet out from under her. The sheets are black. Movie music.*]

JEAN PETERS: The doctor says I have to stay in bed when I'm not at the hospital.

[*From now until the end Marlon Brando continuously helps Jean Peters change sheets. He puts the black sheets on the floor around them.*]

JEAN PETERS: This reminds me of when Eddie was in Korea and I had the miscarriage. For days there was blood on the sheets. Eddie's letters from Korea were about a green

---

[8]New York airport.
[9]Another play (1970) by Kennedy.
[10]Here, money paid her under a preproduction contract giving a producer exclusive rights in her new play.

hill. He sent me photographs of himself. The Red Cross, the letter said, says I cannot call you and I cannot come.

For a soldier to come home there has to be a death in the family.

MOTHER: [*In the hallway the mother breaks down further.*] I have never wanted to go back to the south to live. I hate it. I suffered nothing but humiliation and why should I have gone back there?

FATHER: You ought to have gone back with me. It's what I wanted to do.   45

MOTHER: I never wanted to go back.

FATHER: You yellow bastard. You're a yellow bastard. That's why you didn't want to go back.

MOTHER: You black nigger.

JEAN PETERS: [*Reciting her play.*] I call God and the Owl answers, it haunts my tower, calling, its feathers are blowing against the cell wall, it comes feathered, great hollow-eyes . . . with yellow skin and yellow eyes, the flying bastard. From my tower I keep calling and the only answer is the Owl.

July 8 I got a telegram from my mother. It said your brother has been in an accident and has been unconscious since last night in St. Luke's hospital. Love, Mother. I came home.

My brother is in a white gown on white sheets.

[*The mother and the father walk away from one another. A sudden bright light on the Hospital Lobby and on Wally's room. Clara has come to the doorway and watches her parents.*]

MOTHER: [*To both her former husband and her daughter.*] I was asleep and the police   50
called and told me Wally didn't feel well and would I please come down to the police station and pick him up. When I arrived at the police station they told me they had just taken him to the hospital because he felt worse and they would drive to the hospital. When I arrived here the doctor told me the truth: Wally's car had crashed into another car at an intersection and Wally had been thrown from the car, his body hitting a mail box and he was close to death.

[*Darkness.*]

Scene 3

Jean Peters and Brando are still sitting in Viva Zapata but now there are photographs above the bed of Clara's parents when they were young, as they were in Now Voyager. Wally's room is dark. Lights of the ship from Now Voyager.

JEAN PETERS: Wally is not expected to live. [*She tries to stand.*] He does not move. He is in a coma. [*Pause*] There are so many memories in this house. The rooms besiege me.

My brother has been living here in his old room with my mother. He is separated from his wife and every night has been driving his car crazily around the street where she now lives. On one of these nights was when he had the accident.

[*Jean Peters and Brando stare at each other. A small dark boat from side opposite Wally's room. In it are Shelly Winters and Montgomery Clift. Clara sits behind Shelly Winters writing in her notebook. Montgomery Clift is rowing. It is A Place in the Sun. Movie music. Brando and Jean Peters continue to change sheets.*]

CLARA: I am bleeding. When I'm not at the hospital I have to stay in bed. I am writing my poems. Eddie's come from New York to see my brother. My brother does not speak or move.

[*Montgomery Clift silently rows dark boat across. Clara has on a nightgown and looks as if she has been very sick, and heartbroken by her brother's accident. Montgomery Clift, as was Henreid and Brando, is mute. If they did speak they would speak lines from their actual movies. As the boat comes across Brando and Peters are still. Movie music. Eddie comes in room with Jean Peters and Brando.*]

He still has his text book and briefcase. Shelly Winters sits opposite Montgomery Clift as in A Place in the Sun. *Clara is writing in her notebook.]*

EDDIE: [*To Jean Peters; simultaneously Clara is writing in her diary.*] Are you sure you want to go on with this?
JEAN PETERS: This?
EDDIE: You know what I mean, this obsession of yours?   55
JEAN PETERS: Obsession?
EDDIE: Yes, this obsession to be a writer?
JEAN PETERS: Of course I'm sure.

[Brando is reading. Clara from the boat.]

CLARA: I think the Steinbergs have lost interest in my play. I got a letter from them that said they have to go to Italy and would be in touch when they came back.
EDDIE: I have enough money for us to live well with my teaching. We could all be so   60
     happy.
CLARA: [*From boat.*] Ever since I was twelve I have secretly dreamed of being a writer. Everyone says it's unrealistic for a Negro to want to write.
     Eddie says I've become shy and secretive and I can't accept the passage of time, and that my diaries consume me and that my diaries make me a spectator watching my life like watching a black and white movie.
     He thinks sometimes . . . to me my life is one of my black and white movies that I love so . . . with me playing a bit part.
EDDIE: [*To Jean Peters looking up at the photographs.*] I wonder about your obsession to write about your parents when they were young. You didn't know them. Your mother's not young, your father's not young and we are not that young couple who came to New York in 1955, yet all you ever say to me is Eddie you don't seem the same since you came back from Korea.

[Eddie leaves. Montgomery Clift rows as Shelly Winters speaks to him. Lights on Brando and Peters start slowly to dim.]

SHELLY WINTERS: [*To Montgomery Clift.*] A Sunday rain . . . our next door neighbor drove me through the empty Sunday streets to see my brother. He's the same. My father came by the house last night for the first time since he left Cleveland and he and my mother got into a fight and my mother started laughing. She just kept saying see I can laugh ha ha nothing can hurt me anymore. Nothing you can ever do, Wallace, will ever hurt me again, no one can hurt me since my baby is lying out there in that Hospital and nobody knows whether he's going to live or die. And very loudly again she said ha ha and started walking in circles in her white shoes. My father said how goddamn crazy she was and they started pushing each other. I begged them to stop. My father looked about crazily.
     I hate this house. But it was my money that helped make a down payment on it and I can come here anytime I want. I can come here and see my daughter and you can't stop me, he said.
CLARA: [*To diary.*] The last week in March I called up my mother and I told her that Eddie and I were getting a divorce and I wanted to come to Cleveland right away. She said I'm coming up there.
     When I said. When?
     It was four o'clock in the afternoon. When can you come I said.
     I'll take the train tonight. I'll call you from the station.
     Should I come and meet you?
     No, I'll call you from the station.
     She called at 10:35 that morning. She said she would take a taxi. I went down to the courtyard and waited. When she got out of the taxi I will never forget the expression on her face. Her face had a hundred lines in it. I'd never seen her look so sad.

CLARA: [*Reciting her play.*] They said: I had lost my mind, read so much, buried myself in   65
my books. They said I should stay and teach summer school. But I went. All the way
to London. Out there in the black taxi my cold hands were colder than ever. No
sooner than I left the taxi and passed down a gray walk through a dark gate and into
a garden where there were black ravens on the grass, when I broke down. Oow . . .
oww.

SHELLY WINTERS: This morning my father came by again. He said Clara I want to talk to
you. I want you to know my side. Now, your mother has always thought she was better than me. You know Mr. Harrison raised her like a white girl, and your mother,
mark my words, thinks she's better than me. (It was then I could smell the whisky
on his breath . . . he had already taken a drink from the bottle in his suitcase.)

[She looks anxiously at Montgomery Clift trying to get him to listen.]

CLARA: [*Reading from her notebook.*] He came to me in the outhouse, in the garden, in
the fig tree. He told me you are an owl, ow, oww, I am your beginning, ow. You belong here with us owls in the fig tree, not to somebody that cooks for your Goddamn Father, oww, and I ran to the outhouse in the night crying oww. Bastard they
say, the people in the town all say Bastard, but I—I belong to God and the owls, ow,
and I sat in the fig tree. My Goddamn Father is the Richest White Man in the Town,
but I belong to the owls.

[Putting down her notebook. Lights shift back to Peters and Brando on the bed.]

JEAN PETERS: When my brother was in the army in Germany, he was involved in a crime
and was court-martialled. He won't talk about it. I went to visit him in the stockade.
It was in a Quonset hut in New Jersey. His head was shaven and he didn't have on
any shoes. He has a vein that runs down his forehead and large brown eyes. When he
was in high school he was in All City track in the two-twenty dash. We all thought he
was going to be a great athlete. His dream was the Olympics. After high school he
went to several colleges and left them; Morehouse (where my father went), Ohio
State (where I went), and Western Reserve. I'm a failure he said. I can't make it in
those schools. I'm tired. He suddenly joined the army.
After Wally left the army he worked nights as an orderly in hospitals; he liked the
mental wards. For a few years every fall he started to school but dropped out after a
few months. He and his wife married right before he was sent to Germany. He met
her at Western Reserve and she graduated cum laude while he was a prisoner in the
stockade.

*[Movie music. Dark boat with Montgomery Clift and Shelly Winters reappears from opposite side.
Montgomery Clift rows. Clara is crying.]*

SHELLY WINTERS AND CLARA: Eddie's come from New York because my brother might die.
He did not speak again today and did not move. We don't really know his condition.
All we know is that his brain is possibly badly damaged. He doesn't speak or move.

JEAN PETERS: I am bleeding.   70

*[Lights suddenly dim on Marlon Brando and Jean Peters. Quite suddenly Shelly Winters stands up
and falls "into the water." She is in the water, only her head is visible, calling silently. Montgomery
Clift only stares at her. She continues to call silently as for help, but Montgomery Clift only stares at
her. Movie music. Clara starts to speak as Shelly Winters continues to cry silently for help.]*

CLARA: The doctor said today that my brother will live; he will be brain damaged and
paralyzed.
After he told us, my mother cried in my arms outside the hospital. We were standing
on the steps, and she shook so that I thought both of us were going to fall headlong
down the steps.

*[Shelly Winters drowns. Light goes down on Montgomery Clift as he stares at Shelly Winters drown-
ing. Lights on Clara. Movie music. Darkness. Brief dazzling image of Columbia Pictures Lady.]*

END

Part FIVE

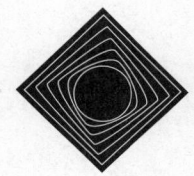

READING AND RESPONDING TO THE ESSAY

24 ◈ What Is The Essay?

You may be more familiar with *writing* essays than with *reading* them. It seems likely that in your educational experience, probably in English classes and quite possibly in other subjects, you have been assigned to write some expository or argumentative prose to explain an idea or try to get a reader to believe the truth of a certain statement. You most certainly have written essays on tests. In English classes, and perhaps others, however, most of the assigned reading consists of stories, poems, and plays, not essays.

The Variety of Essays

But surely you have read and studied essays in other disciplines: history, social studies, psychology, philosophy, religion. You probably have read and studied these texts for their content rather than the **aesthetic** qualities that more "literary" texts (poems, plays, and stories) are supposed to have; you don't study how they use language for the sake of beauty or artistic qualities. By the same token, the essays you write for tests and papers in school are read mostly for their content—to see whether you "understand the material," if you are able to "support or develop a thesis" or "argue a point," if you can "express your ideas clearly in prose." Your essays are not usually read for their aesthetic qualities either.

I may have put the worst face on matters here by concentrating on just one narrow variety of this large and diverse genre: the academic essay, something that many students actively dislike or, at best, consider a necessary evil. Perhaps what should be considered now is the wider variety of the genre—not just academic essays but the many other types of nonfiction prose. To begin to do that, please take a few minutes to list in the box below (or orally with your classmates) some of the different kinds of texts you are familiar with reading, in school or out, that are not poems, plays, stories, or novels.

KINDS OF NONLITERARY WRITING

Now here's my version of the list you just made.

KINDS OF NONLITERARY WRITING

news articles

feature articles

profiles of people in the news

instructions or how-to articles

first-person narratives

historical accounts

reviews

critical essays

editorials

opinion pieces

columns

letters-to-the-editor

speeches

statements to the press

memos

letters

notes

advertising copy

pamphlets

brochures

chapters of textbooks

I don't think mine is an exhaustive list; there must be kinds of writing that I did not list that you did. But maybe the activity of listing the kinds of nonfiction prose will get you started thinking about all the types there are.

Can we call all these kinds of writing essays? Is the term "essay" equivalent in meaning to "nonfiction prose" so that, say, a news article is an essay? Or is an essay a subcategory of nonfiction prose? My list of kinds of nonfiction prose included the "critical essay," a kind of writing that typically analyzes or evaluates literature or any art. The inclusion of this type of writing among "kinds of nonliterary writing" suggests that the essay may indeed be a subcategory of nonfiction prose. Perhaps it is apparent by now that considering the essay as a distinct genre means walking a thin line between categories of writing. Perhaps a brief look at the history of this kind of writing will help steady your steps.

Origins and Development of the Essay

As the first truly literate Western culture, the ancient Greeks developed writing in many genres. One of those genres, the Classical tragedy, was considered in Chapter 18. That chapter also quoted from a Classical text in nonfiction prose: Aristotle's *Poetics*, a book in which the author discussed the effects of drama on the audiences of his day and analyzed the causes of those effects. This book, or the fragments of it that have survived, is sometimes called the first piece of literary criticism in the Western tradition. In that sense, it is close to one of the categories of nonfiction prose I listed above: the critical essay.

The ancient Greeks and the Romans after them wrote nonfiction prose in such subject areas as history, philosophy, and politics. In the early Christian era and into the Middle Ages, books, treatises, and other manuscripts were written on philosophical, theological, and scientific topics. It may be interesting to note here that for centuries the word "science" meant "knowledge," not the relatively specialized branch of knowledge now designated by that word. So from ancient times until relatively recently—the eighteenth century—people who were writing "science" were merely writing about what they knew in various subject areas.

The English word "essay" derives from the French verb *essayer*: to try or attempt. As a noun, *essay* was coined in the sixteenth century by the French writer Michel de Montaigne as a label for a kind of writing in which he discussed a particular topic in an unsystematic way, exploring or trying out his thoughts, rather than presenting them in a formal or systematic way. (See "Of cannibals," page 1597.) Montaigne was consciously trying to differentiate the kind of writing he was doing in these pieces from the scientific or philosophical writing that constituted much of the learned nonfiction prose of his day. Montaigne published a collection of his *Essais* (on such subjects as sadness, liars, smells, and ancient customs) in 1580; a second edition appeared posthumously, in 1595.

In England, Francis Bacon published a collection of his essays in 1597, but the genre was otherwise untapped until the eighteenth century, when literary magazines first appeared in London. The leading magazines—*The Tatler*, which ran from 1709–1711 and was edited by Joseph Addison, and *The Spectator*, edited by Addison and Richard Steele in 1711 and 1712—sought and published short formal pieces on serious issues such as marriage, death, and education or more casual writing on the follies and social customs of the day. A growing urban middle class in the eighteenth century expanded the audience for such periodicals and the kind of writing they published. There were now more people who could read, with the time to read, and they tended to be interested in the kinds of subjects that magazines covered. Modern magazines such as *The New Yorker* that seek a sophisticated audience—and publish essays—are the descendants of these first English-language magazines.

As the middle class increased in numbers and in buying power in the nineteenth-century Western world, more literary magazines appeared. Charles Lamb, Matthew Arnold, Ralph Waldo Emerson, Mark Twain, and Edgar Allan Poe were all writing during this period. Literary magazines—usually with the name "Review" in the title—still exist, although they attract a relatively narrow audience today. But the growth of an even larger middle-class audience through most of this century has contributed to the proliferation of magazines, especially popular magazines. Nonfiction prose, mostly informative articles, is the stock-in-trade of most of these magazines, although some do publish essays in the more informal tradition of Montaigne's writing. Some notable twentieth-century American essayists are Russell Baker, James Baldwin, Joan Didion, Molly Ivins, H. L. Mencken, Alice Walker, and E. B. White.

This brief historical survey may have led right back to where this chapter started—trying to distinguish between the essay and the many other forms of nonfiction prose available today. This distinction may never be made completely clear or final; it may be better to think of it as something to work *toward* rather than something to start out with.

Chapter 2 of this book entertained the notion of a contrast between "literature" and "texts." To recapitulate that discussion very briefly, that distinction was offered as a way of avoiding the tendency to rank certain pieces of writing as superior by labeling them as literature. *All* kinds of writing—from the most solidly canonized poem to such transient and anonymous productions as graffiti—are texts. As such they are all subject to serious analysis in terms of the same kind of cognitive or cultural engagement that readers may experience with essays. If this concept is extended to nonfiction prose texts, the distinction between essays and non-essays may be seen to be as arbitrary as that between literature and non-literature, and so *any* nonfiction prose text may be taken as eligible for study. To illustrate this idea—and to begin to examine essays in terms of their **text strategies**—I will now ask you to look at a text from the contemporary mass media: a magazine advertisement.

READING CULTURE An "Essay" from the Media

In capitalist cultures, advertisements constitute a large part of the mass media texts that people read every day on television and radio, on billboards and placards, and in newspapers and magazines. For the most part, these texts are read passively, not actively, but that doesn't mean that they can't be read and responded to self-consciously. To read them that way is to adopt a **resisting** stance, because ads, like many other texts, don't want to be analyzed.

Strictly speaking, an advertisement is not purely a piece of nonfiction prose because usually it includes pictures (or art) with the words (or copy); the words alone don't convey the ad's message. But as you will see, advertisements have some close **intertextual** connections to essays, which makes them worth considering here. For that matter, advertisements may have intertextual connections to any of the literary genres: to poetry if they involve jingles, for instance; to fiction if they offer an imaginary situation involving a conflict, which is usually resolved satisfactorily for the characters because of their use of whatever product is being advertised; to drama if a situation is presented and acted out. In the present context, however, what is most relevant is advertisements' intertextual connections to essays.

An ad from a mass-circulation popular magazine is shown on page 1482. Look at its combination of art and copy. Then consider it more closely in terms of what I will propose as six basic text strategies of the essay:

- prose
- consciousness of an audience
- voice/tone
- concern with an idea, issue, or topic
- structure
- rhetoric

I have tried to keep this list simple, to limit it to the essential characteristics of the genre. The only text strategies on this list that may need definition or elaboration are **voice** or **tone** and **rhetoric**.

If you recall, voice was also a text strategy of poetry, as discussed in Chapter 11. There, voice was considered as the sense of a person speaking in or through the words of the poem. In this way, voice may also resemble the **narrator** in a piece of fiction, especially if that narrator seems to have a "personality." Tone may be defined as the attitude toward subject matter or audience that the voice seems to take. In an essay, voice and tone are so closely related that they may be regarded as a single text strategy. At the same time, you should recognize that both voice and tone are as much the creations of a reader as they are "objective" features of a text. The term rhetoric comprises a number of text strategies, varying from essay to essay, whose specific purpose is to persuade or move a formal essay's audience. These text strategies involve structure, tone, diction, the kinds of examples or evidence presented, the kind of logic employed—anything calculated to have a specific effect on the audience.

The simplicity of my list of essay text strategies may also serve to underline the point made earlier that the difference between the essay and other types of nonfiction prose may be negligible. An ordinary newspaper article, for instance, may conform to all these characteristics; its tone may be "neutral," so much so that voice seems not to be a factor at all. The subjectivity of these qualities is evident, however, in the reactions of readers of different ideological orientations toward the same news article: different readers may see different biases on the part of the writer, according to the ideological positions from which they read.

Prose; Consciousness of an Audience

The writing in this advertisement is in prose rather than in verse, but typically the medium of a magazine ad like this one is words (or copy) and pictures (or art) working together as a pair of text strategies. Consciousness of an audience is a given of advertisements, which are composed with a specific "target" audience in mind, but the composition of the audience will vary according to the media context any particular ad appears in—what kind of television show or magazine, for instance. I said this ad appeared in a mass-circulation popular magazine, which might suggest that its audience is broad or general. But even popular magazines attract readers of a certain age and demographic group, which narrows the audience for any ad that appears in such a magazine, and some ads may be aimed at readers of one gender rather than the other.

Concern with an Idea, Issue, or Topic; Tone

Concern with an idea, issue, or topic is also a given, in that every ad promotes a particular product, service, or organization—in this case Frangelico liqueur. The attitude(s) this ad seems to take toward its particular audience and topic (its tone) should be something you can construct as you consider how it combines words and images about the topic and about certain qualities or values it tries to associate with the liqueur. Before looking further at the tone of this ad, however, consider its **structure**.

Structure

In most essays, structure is the organization of ideas. In the advertisement, however, structure consists of art elements such as images and type and the relationship of the art to the copy. The dominant art in this Frangelico advertisement is the black-and-white photograph at the top. The sides of the picture look like the edges of a piece of film, which, in turn, suggests the copy superimposed on the picture is a subtitle from a foreign movie. The plain typeface of that copy is consistent with movie subtitles. Apparently this is an Italian film, judging from the name "Vincenzo" and the Italian-seeming word "Frangelico." The names in the copy in parentheses and the tag phrase at the bottom, "Translated directly from the Italian," confirm this. So it appears the ad presents a moment in a scene from an Italian film, perhaps one from the 1950s or early 1960s, judging from the men's dress and appearance. In that sense, the ad offers an implied narrative structure, a plot, if you will: A woman has left the presence of these two men, one of whom, "Vincenzo," appears concerned about this and would go after her except that his friend restrains him with the commonsense advice that "She cannot go far without her shoes" and the invitation to "have a Frangelico." The copy in parentheses below fills in a **gap** by informing readers what happened next.

In terms of tone again, you might construct this ad's attitude toward its audience as follows: It assumes an interest in romance and intrigue, perhaps slightly exotic Italian romance, on the part of that audience. The ad's attitude toward its subject seems to be favorable, specifically calling Frangelico "The Intriguing Liqueur." Because of the references to an Italian film, the ad seems to suggest that Frangelico is intriguing in a romantic Italian sort of way.

Rhetoric

The values associated with "intrigue," "romance," and "Italian men" are elements of the rhetoric of the Frangelico advertisement. The ad seems to try to tap readers' favorable attitudes (part of their **ideologies**) toward the ideas of "romance" and "Italian" through the favorable connotation of a word—"intriguing." There also seems to be an element of playfulness in this ad: It doesn't take itself, its audience, or the product all that seriously; it wants its audience to try Frangelico, of course, but it seems to make that offer in a spirit of fun. Perhaps this too is a rhetorical strategy to get the audience of consumers to drop their defenses and feel receptive toward Frangelico.

What other rhetorical strategies might be identified? How about the implications of the "narrative" in the Italian film from which a scene is glimpsed? There is a story, albeit a fictional one, in the film. A reader enters that story right at a dramatic moment of conflict over Gianna's having left—in a rush, apparently—and Vincenzo's desire to go after her. Because this moment is just a fragment of a larger story or dramatic situation, there are numerous gaps that the reader must fill in—with some careful help from the language of the ad. There are many explanations for a woman having rushed off without her shoes from two men dressed in tuxedos. The context of the Italian film serves to narrow this range of explanations so that the reader seems invited to conclude that the woman is passionate, hot-tempered, impetuous, and very attractive (intriguing?) to Vincenzo. The postscript offered at the bottom of the ad indicates how this moment of conflict was resolved: "Gianna [Now we know her name.] came back. Albert [Now we know Vincenzo's friend's name.] left. Vincenzo and Gianna shared a Frangelico. She never got her shoes back on." This resolution suggests something of the "power" of Frangelico and offers a romantically satisfying happy ending to the story of the film.

Perhaps you noticed another element in the implied narrative in this ad. The woman who rushes off without her shoes and the handsome man who would pursue her seem to be an **allusion** to "Cinderella." A reader might build consistency in this narrative by associating the delicate woman's shoe pictured beside the bottle of Frangelico with the "lost slipper" of the Cinderella story. In terms of rhetorical strategies, it seems that in alluding to the Cinderella story, the ad is attempting to draw on the **literary experience** of readers. In so doing, the ad seems to be tapping readers' ideologies as well, because for most readers the Cinderella story "means" the ultimately desirable man recognizes the intriguing heroine's beauty and must have her. It's a two-way fantasy: for the man because he discovers, loses, then tracks down and wins the heroine; for the woman because her beauty is recognized by the man, who then can't get her out of his mind and must come searching for her.

There's a twist here in that Vincenzo did not go searching for her: "Gianna came back." So this ad is probably more directed to men than to women. It seems to tap the ideology that men in American culture are responsible for directing or controlling the social situation of romance. The situation works out for this man because "Gianna came back. Alberto left.... She never got her shoes back on," which means, apparently, that she was either so intrigued by Vincenzo that she ignored her shoelessness or she took the rest of her clothes off. The reader, especially the male reader, is offered this gap to fill in too, although his options for filling it seem to be narrowed to these two choices.

This advertisement appears to be a fairly simple text: one large picture, some additional uncomplicated art, and a few lines of copy. However, considering it as a text in a genre that has several intertextual connections to the essay, perhaps you can see how this ad is more rhetorically complex than it first appears. Reading the text strategies involved in mass media texts such as advertisements can strengthen you as a reader of all texts and as an aware person in today's consumer culture. This examination of the Frangelico ad should also serve to introduce you to the basic text strategies of the essay genre, whether those strategies are deployed in words and images or in words alone.

In addition to these text strategies, there are two other aspects of the essay that should be looked at briefly in this introduction to the genre. One is the division of essays into two broad categories: **formal** and **informal**. The other aspect, which takes us back to the consideration of the distinctiveness of the essay genre with which this chapter opened, is the relationship of the essay to the other literary genres.

Formal and Informal Essays

The division of essays into the categories formal and informal is a matter of both history and practice. Montaigne's essays were personal, casually organized, and exploratory rather than definitive with respect to their topics; in short, they were informal, in keeping with the notion of "attempts." So were Bacon's essays. The proliferation of magazines in nineteenth-century England (especially intellectual magazines known as critical reviews) allowed writers of nonfiction prose to tackle such serious subjects as political rights, the philosophy of education, and the impact of the new mass culture. These topics and the careful, reasoned approach that writers took toward them gave impetus to a more formal kind of essay writing in which the tone was impersonal and serious and the structure tightly controlled. This distinction is not an absolute one; not every essay is clearly classifiable as either formal or informal. The Frangelico ad, for instance, is formal in its carefully managed structure and in its definite rhetorical purpose, but at least some aspects of its tone are informal. In spite of this lack of sharp distinction, having some knowledge in your literary experience of this loose division of essays in terms of these two types should be useful to you.

Essays and the Conventional Literary Genres

Essays differ from poems primarily because essays are written in prose and poems are written in verse. They differ from plays because few essays consist mainly of dialogue. They are more like short stories than any other literary genre, because they are written in prose and because the voice in an essay may be roughly similar to the narrator in a story—although a qualification is necessary here: the voice in an essay is usually **reliable** as a guide to the author's ideology, whereas the narrator in a short story may well be a character or some kind of fictionalized voice quite different from the author's own. This distance between narrator and author in a short story is, in fact, a gap common to that genre but usually absent from the essay, especially the formal essay. Although there are exceptions, the reliability of an essay's voice or the relative lack of distance between an essay's voice and its author is one of the conventions of the genre.

All the same, however, an informal essay may be a **narrative**—typically a first-person account of some incident or episode from the writer's life. Or it may contain, even consist largely of, **dialogue**, although this is probably presented the way dialogue is handled in a short story—with attribution markers ("he said," for example) and with comments by the essay's voice intervening—rather than the way it is handled in a play, where dialogue stands on its own. Or an essay may be similar to a poem. In fact, the eighteenth-century English poet Alexander Pope wrote two long poems that he called "essays": "An Essay on Criticism" and "An Essay on Man." These texts are written in verse rather than prose, but otherwise they are excellent examples of the other five basic text strategies of the essay, as listed on page 1480. Among those strategies, voice is also considered in the Reading Poetry section of this book. Various forms of **figurative language** may also appear in an essay, which may, for instance, be entirely built around a central **metaphor**.

In addition to all these factors, essays, whether formal or informal, may resemble other kinds of literary writing because they use language aesthetically—for the beauty of it crafted a certain way or for the pleasurable experience it may offer a reader. But even though essays are different from short stories, poems, or plays, the language of essays is not purely utilitarian; therefore, essays are more like literature than some other kinds of nonfiction prose.

Talking about aesthetics, however, moves us again into uncertain territory. According to the theory this book is based on and the model of the reading interaction established in Chapter 2, the aesthetic quality of any text is something to be decided on by the reader at least as much as it is determined by the text itself. A sense of beauty or artistic pleasure in language comes from the reader's literary experience interacting with the text's **literary repertoire**, so that, for some readers, writing as prosaic as that in a news story or a cookbook recipe or directions for assembling a bicycle could be aesthetically pleasing. An extreme form of this phenomenon is the practice of creating **found poetry** from such mundane prose texts as road signs or newspaper articles.*

This uncertainty should just serve to caution you, therefore, against the easy categorization of certain texts as mainly aesthetic or utilitarian, or of essays as purely formal or informal, just as you should be wary of clear-cut divisions of nonfiction prose writing into essays and non-essays.

An Essay For Exploration

So that you may understand these abstract considerations in more concrete terms, I offer the following piece of nonfiction prose. Read it and complete the brief exercises that follow it. Those exercises ask you to consider the aesthetic or the utilitarian nature of the language in the piece and the degree of formality or informality it exhibits.

Guan Keguang   b. 1938

A Chinese Reporter on Cape Cod   1986

Next to the newsroom in the *Cape Cod Times* main office building there is a "lunchroom." My colleagues and I sometimes go there to buy something to eat or drink from the vending machines.

The experience has been quite a novelty for me. I put in some coins, push a button, and out comes what I want.

The machines offer a variety of food and drinks. Many of them are new to me and the labels don't tell me much about what's inside. The operation is simple and automatic. But so many decisions!

Such a process epitomizes what I have experienced while struggling hard to adapt my traditional ways of thinking and doing things to an American environment, which demands constantly considering alternatives and making decisions.

This has been no easy job for me.   5

---

*See Chapter 10, pages 512–516.

For almost half a century I have lived in a culture where choices and decisions are made by authorities and circumstances rather than by individuals and personal preferences.

It's OK for young children to have things arranged for them by their parents, because they are inexperienced in life and not wise enough to make important decisions. But when they reach their late teens they don't like to be treated that way—even in China. They yearn for independence and freedom, as the recent demonstrations have shown. They are frustrated when things don't go their way and they find themselves helpless and unable to do anything about their fate.

When the time comes to enter the work force, however, reality sets in. They are assigned a job, and that's it. Moreover, the job assignment determines where you must live.

If you have completed twelve years' schooling, but you fail in the college entrance examination and are not admitted, the government will assign you a job—perhaps as a factory worker, a store clerk, or a bus driver. Very likely that will be your lifelong job, because you can't freely pick and choose or change your job. Once you are in a job you will have to stick to it, unless the authorities want to transfer you to another job. You could negotiate with the authorities, but the government always has the final say.

Students do have an opportunity to state their preference among university and courses of study—and if you pass your exams with flying colors, with scores much higher than others, you will be admitted into a department of a university of your own choice. But once you get into a university you stay in your major for four or five years without a break. You do not change your major. You take the courses given to you, pass all the exams, behave well and toe the party line, earn your bachelor's degree and graduate. 10

Then, you just wait until a job is assigned to you. During the waiting period, students with "connections" seek to influence the decision. A few succeed. In any event, until the decision is made, you will not know where you will go and what your lifelong career will be.

Your job assignment notice is more than a certificate with which you report for duty. It is also a certificate for your residence registration and your daily necessity rations. If you don't like the job assigned to you and refuse to take it, you are jobless. Because you don't have an official permission to live in any place other than where the job is, you won't get your ration coupons.

Your choice, therefore, is very simple: to eat or not to eat.

Every graduate is guaranteed a job. Each job affords the same starting salary. Engineer, schoolteacher, office clerk, truck driver, scientist—the difference in salary is negligible. That is the socialist way.

No matter if you like it or not, you stay with your job. 15

No matter if you are liked or not, you stay with your job.

If you are not very ambitious, life can be very easy for you. Its pace won't be so maddeningly fast as it is here in America. You don't have to worry about choosing alternatives or making decisions. You don't have to worry about getting laid off.

Since you don't have much to choose from and everything is planned and arranged for you, you will be better off if you take things easy. As an old Chinese saying goes: "Those who are content are forever happy."

People like that—who have been content to let their decisions be made for them—would find it hard to get used to the American lifestyle, to keep their eyes open to opportunities, to be searching constantly for a better job, a better place to live. Such a way of life would be too risky, too precarious, too challenging.

Our old tradition taught us to be humble, modest, unassuming, moderate,   20
and passive. Even when a Chinese host treats a guest to a dinner consisting of twelve courses and costing half of his monthly salary, he still apologizes repeatedly to the guest between the courses for the "inadequate" meal he has prepared for his honorable guest. Meanwhile, the guest politely and humbly refuses to accept the food his host keeps piling up on his dish, because he feels he shouldn't assume that he deserves so much good food and he should leave more good stuff for the host family, even though he is very hungry at the moment and he likes the food immensely.

The other day while I was going through the classified ads in the magazine *Editor & Publisher,* I came across ads placed by publications in search of "aggressive, talented, hungry" reporters.

What could I do if I wanted such a position?

If I were hungry, I would try every face-saving means not to admit it.

If I were talented, I would (or should) be modest enough not to advertise it.

Even if I were desperately in need of the position, I still wouldn't know   25
how to be aggressive.

I wonder if I should take a crash course, teaching me how to be aggressive, talented, and hungry.

To what extent does the language of this piece of writing give you pleasure as a reader? What individual words, phrases, sentences, or images seem to be there for their aesthetic value, rather than for their strict usefulness to explain the writer's point? Are there instances of language in this piece that are both aesthetic and utilitarian?

Use the box below or a page in your journal to note some brief answers to those questions.

LANGUAGE USAGE
Mainly Aesthetic

Mainly Utilitarian

Both

If you compare your lists with those of your classmates, you should see some differences in the selection of words as aesthetic and utilitarian instances of language. These differences should indicate two things: (1) to some extent at least, readers decide whether any instance of language is primarily for pleasure or usefulness, and (2) the distinction between aesthetic and utilitarian is not absolute.

Now try another brief exercise with reference to "A Chinese Reporter on Cape Cod." This time, instead of making lists, write a few sentences in answer to the questions provided.

- To what extent does this piece of writing seem to be personal or subjective? To what extent does it seem to be impersonal or objective?
- To what extent does this piece of writing try to explain or prove a specific point? To what extent does it seem to explore a topic or idea?

Taking personal and impersonal as opposite kinds of tone and taking to explain or prove and to explore as opposite purposes, do you find that "A Chinese Reporter on Cape Cod" lies close to either extreme, or is it somewhere in between? How have other readers in your class answered these questions?

I will not provide any definitive answers to these questions. It's more important at this point for you to consider the possibilities for tone and purpose—and language and structure—of an essay than it is for me to tell you that "A Chinese Reporter on Cape Cod" is formal or informal. In the following chapters (so that you may strengthen your understanding of some of the characteristics of the essay in general) you will be asked to consider particular essays as mainly formal or informal. I want to stress, however, that most essays lie somewhere in between the opposite poles of formal and informal and that the difference between formality and informality in the essay is often a matter of degree, not of kind.

 ## READING AND WRITING PROJECTS

FOR CREATIVE AND CRITICAL THINKING

Your own writing is important as you try to learn more about yourself as a reader—both what you do cognitively and what is done to you culturally—to produce the kind of reader you are when you interact with any particular text. In addition to response statements and the formal expository paper that may grow out of them, there are other ways to use writing to learn. What follows are suggestions for integrating your reading of and writing about literary texts in various ways. These suggestions include exploratory writing, playing with texts and language, creative efforts in various genres, and other writing exercises designed to strengthen your awareness of the cognitive and cultural processes involved in your reading.

▶ Write a **letter** to the author of an essay, making a personal response to his or her essay. It doesn't matter if the writer is dead or alive, but if he or she is alive, you could actually send your letter, care of his or her publisher, which you can find in the Acknowledgments section at the back of this book.

▶ As an alternative to the above assignment, imagine you are an advice columnist (á la "Dear Abby"). Write a letter to your advice column from the author of an essay. Have that letter summarize whatever problem the essay discusses. Then write an advice column in response to that letter-formatted essay.

▶ Adopting the persona of any essay, write a personal classified ad "in search of" some kind of person. Many daily or weekly newspapers carry such ads, which can serve as a model for your own. For example:

Legally separated WF [White Female] — 5'8", dark-haired, loves music, dancing, quiet moments. Seeks honest, caring, S/DWM [Single/Divorced White Male], 25–29. Must enjoy children, family times, laughter.

You could also write a brief prose account of why you wrote the kind of ad you did, considering who you were pretending to be when you wrote it.

▶ Rewrite the Frangelico ad as a formal or informal essay or as a short story. Adopt any point of view, but try to use a narrative structure. Your essay or story can go as far back or forward from the scene in the ad as you wish to go.

25 ◆ READING THE FORMAL ESSAY

As you continue to develop a sense of the essay, it will be a good idea to look more closely at text strategies. More particularly, what does a formal essay do with the basic text strategies of the genre, as they were considered in Chapter 24? To provide a quick review, those text strategies are listed below.

> **BASIC TEXT STRATEGIES OF AN ESSAY**
> - prose
> - consciousness of an audience
> - voice/tone
> - concern with an idea, issue, or topic
> - structure
> - rhetoric

Text Strategies in a Formal Essay

Now consider the following text, which I nominate as an essay on the basis of these six text strategies. As you read it, try to see for yourself how those text strategies are deployed.

Thomas Jefferson *et al.*

The Declaration of Independence

In Congress, July 4, 1776
The unanimous Declaration of the
Thirteen United States of America

When in the Course of human events it becomes necessary for one people to dissolve the political bands which have connected them with another, and to assume among the powers of the earth, the separate and equal station to which the Laws of Nature and of Nature's God entitle them, a decent respect to the opinions of mankind requires that they should declare the causes which impel them to the separation.

We hold these truths to be self evident, that all men are created equal, that they are endowed by their Creator with certain unalienable Rights, that among these are Life, Liberty and the pursuit of Happiness. That to secure these rights, Governments are instituted among Men, deriving their just powers from the consent of the governed. That whenever any Form of Government becomes destructive of these ends, it is the Right of the People to alter or to abolish it, and to institute new Government, laying its foundation on such principles and organizing its powers in such form, as to them shall seem most likely to affect their Safety and Happiness. Prudence, indeed, will dictate that Governments long established should not be changed for light and transient causes; and accordingly all experience hath shewn that mankind are more disposed to suffer, while evils are sufferable, than to right themselves by abolishing the forms to which they are accustomed. But when a long train of abuses and usurpations, pursuing invariably the same Object evinces a design to reduce them under absolute Despotism, it is their right, it is their duty, to throw off such Government, and to provide new Guards for their future security. Such has been the patient sufferance of these Colonies; and such is now the necessity which constrains them to alter their former Systems of Government. The history of the present King of Great Britain is a history of repeated injuries and usurpations, all having in direct object the establishment of an absolute Tyranny over these States. To prove this, let Facts be submitted to a candid world.

He has refused his Assent to Laws, the most wholesome and necessary for the public good.

He has forbidden his Government to pass laws of immediate and pressing importance, unless suspended in their operation till his Assent should be obtained; and when so suspended, he has utterly neglected to attend to them.

He has refused to pass other Laws for the accommodation of large districts   5 of people, unless those people would relinquish the right of Representation in the Legislature, a right inestimable to them and formidable to tyrants only.

He has called together legislative bodies at places unusual, uncomfortable, and distant from the depository of Public Records, for the sole purpose of fatiguing them into compliance with his measures.

He has dissolved Representative Houses repeatedly, for opposing with manly firmness his invasions on the rights of the people.

He has refused for a long time, after such dissolutions, to cause others to be elected; whereby the Legislative Powers, incapable of Annihilation, have returned to the People at large for their exercise; the State remaining in the mean time exposed to all the dangers of invasion from without, and convulsions within.

He has endeavored to prevent the population of these States; for that purpose obstructing the Laws for Naturalization of Foreigners; refusing to pass others to encourage their migration hither, and raising the conditions of new Appropriations of Lands.

He has obstructed the Administration of Justice, by refusing his Assent to   10 Laws for establishing Judiciary Powers.

He has made Judges dependent on his Will alone, for the tenure of their offices, and the amount and payment of their salaries.

He has erected a multitude of New Offices, and sent hither swarms of Officers to harass our people, and eat out their substance.

He has kept among us, in times of peace, Standing Armies without the Consent of our legislatures.

He has affected to render the Military independent of and superior to the Civil Power.

He has combined with others to subject us to a jurisdiction foreign to our constitution, and unacknowledged by our laws; giving his Assent to their Acts of pretended Legislation: For quartering large bodies of armed troops among us: For protecting them, by a mock Trial, from punishment for any Murders which they should commit on the Inhabitants of these States: For cutting off our Trade with all parts of the world: For imposing Taxes on us without our Consent: For depriving us in many cases, of the benefits of Trial by Jury: For transporting us beyond Seas to be tried for pretended offenses: For abolishing the free System of English Laws in a neighboring Province, establishing therein an Arbitrary government, and enlarging its Boundaries so as to render it at once an example and fit instrument for introducing the same absolute rule into these Colonies: For taking away our Charters, abolishing our most valuable Laws and altering fundamentally the Forms of our Governments: For suspending our own Legislatures, and declaring themselves invested with power to legislate for us in all cases whatsoever.

He has abdicated Government here, by declaring us out of his Protection and waging War against us.

He has plundered our seas, ravaged our Coasts, burnt our towns, and destroyed the lives of our people.

He is at this time transporting large Armies of foreign Mercenaries to complete the works of death, desolation and tyranny already begun with circumstances of Cruelty & Perfidy scarcely paralleled in the most barbarous ages, and totally unworthy the Head of a civilized nation.

He has constrained our fellow Citizens taken Captive on the high Seas to bear Arms against their Country, to become the executioners of their friends and Brethren, or to fall themselves by their Hands.

He has excited domestic insurrections amongst us, and has endeavored to bring on the inhabitants of our frontiers, the merciless Indian Savages, whose known rule of warfare, is an undistinguished destruction of all ages, sexes, and conditions.

In every stage of these Oppressions We have Petitioned for Redress in the most humble terms: Our repeated Petitions have been answered only by repeated injury. A Prince, whose character is thus marked by every act which may define a Tyrant, is unfit to be the ruler of a free people.

Nor have We been wanting in attention to our British brethren. We have warned them from time to time of attempts by their legislature to extend an unwarrantable jurisdiction over us. We have reminded them of the circumstances of our emigration and settlement here. We have appealed to their native justice and magnanimity, and we have conjured them by the ties of our common kindred to disavow these usurpations, which would inevitably interrupt our connections and correspondence. They too have been deaf to the voice of justice and of consanguinity. We must, therefore, acquiesce in the necessity, which denounces our Separation, and hold them, as we hold the rest of mankind, Enemies in War, in Peace Friends.

We, therefore the Representatives of the United States of America, in General Congress, Assembled, appealing to the Supreme Judge of the world for the rectitude of our intentions, do, in the Name, and by Authority of the good People of these Colonies, solemnly publish and declare, That these United Colonies are, and of Right ought to be free and independent states; that they are Absolved from all Allegiance to the British Crown, and that all political connection between them and the State of Great Britain, is and ought to be totally dissolved; and that as Free and Independent States, they have full Power to levy War, conclude Peace, contract Alliances, establish Commerce, and to do all other Acts and Things which Independent States may of right do. And for the support of this Declaration, with a firm reliance on the protection of Divine Providence, we mutually pledge to each other our Lives, our Fortunes, and our sacred Honor.

Prose and Concern with an Idea, Issue, or Topic

This text is clearly written in prose; it's not written in verse. Identifying that particular text strategy is easy, even though some of the **conventions** of that prose differ from those of our own time—the punctuation and capitalization rules, for instance. It's also easy to see a concern with an idea, issue, or topic in this text. Of course, if you are a United States citizen (born or naturalized) you are surely aware from your ideology what that idea, issue, or topic is as soon as you see the title. For the sake of our discussion here, though, are you able to put that prior knowledge aside long enough to see the text's concern with an idea, issue, or topic?

Consciousness of an Audience

The text's consciousness of an audience may also be fairly easy to identify. In the first paragraph, it refers to "a decent respect to the opinions of mankind" as a reason for the very existence of the text, and at the end of the second paragraph it refers to "a candid world" to whom it is about to submit "Facts." Even without these particular references, however, as a public document this text is conscious of an audience, a broad one at that.

Voice and Tone

Consider the voice or tone in *The Declaration of Independence*. Are you able to identify any qualities of either the kind of "person" who seems to be uttering these words or the attitude the text seems to take toward its subject or its audience? What adjectives would you use to describe the voice or tone here? My choices would be "confident," "aggrieved," "open," and "bold" for the voice. The attitude toward the subject is a bit harder to settle on because first we have to decide what subject is being addressed. Let's say that in this text there are two subjects: the "repeated injuries and usurpations" of the "present King of Great Britain" and the declared independence of the 13 United States. I find the attitude toward the first to be "anger," "disgust," "bordering on contempt" and toward the second to be "pride" and "self-righteousness."

What about the text's attitude toward its audience? Does that seem to you, as it does to me, to be "respect" (as stated in the first paragraph) and a sense of "equality" with other nations? Or does it seem to you, as it also does to me, to be almost a "disrespect," because it describes the "injuries and usurpations" of the king in general terms only but seems to expect its audience to believe them? Is there a certain amount of "belligerence"? The text seems not to care whether the audience believes them or not, it's going to take this action anyway.

Because this particular text is so revered in our culture, by reputation and custom if not because of what it actually says, it may be difficult to distance yourself sufficiently to read it in any other way than reverentially. But try this: pretend you are George III, king of Great Britain in 1776, or a member of the British Parliament loyal to the king. Would you then detect a different tone in this text from the one you see when you read it as an American? If so, you have evidence of how the position of the reader influences the identification of the quality of voice or tone in an essay.

CONNECT: For an interesting and unique management of tone and voice, see Jonathan Swift's essay "A Modest Proposal" in the Essays for Further Reading section.

Structure

The Declaration of Independence gets right to the point, doesn't it? And a serious point it is. What could be more serious, especially in the context of a culture that still believed in the divine right of kings, than the assertion that a people should declare themselves independent of the rule of a monarch and his government? This independence is necessary and justified, the text says early on, because the king's actions are those of a tyrant. Then it offers a fairly long list of evidence—"Facts," to use its word—in support of its claim that the king is a tyrant whose rule over the colonies should be terminated.

In other words, the structure is that of a logical deductive argument: general principles are laid down first, then particular instances are related to those principles, and conclusions that seem logically inescapable are drawn. A general principle of *The Declaration* is that people should be free of tyranny. Particular instances of what the king has done show him to be a tyrant. Therefore (the second word in the last paragraph of this essay), it must be concluded that these people must declare themselves free of this tyrant. This three-part argumentative structure is a *syllogism,* a specific kind of deductive argument that offers a major premise, a minor premise, and a conclusion that derives logically from the relation of the two premises. Readers of *The Declaration* or of any logically structured formal essay may see or be affected by the logical structure even if they do not have the term syllogism in their vocabulary.

Rhetoric

The formal essay's generally serious attitude toward its topic and its reader seems to necessitate a carefully organized structure. (You may have been taught such principles as these for your own essays in school; traditionally, academic essays are formal ones, even if they are not so named.) These text strategies involve rhetoric, which is really a set of text strategies. A formal essay like *The Declaration of Independence* often has a specific purpose: to persuade its reader to adopt a certain point of view, namely the same attitude toward the essay's topic that the essayist takes; or to move the reader to some kind of action with respect to the subject of the essay. This last aim is the purpose of formal argument.

Looking again at *The Declaration of Independence*, can you identify some of its rhetorical strategies? To do this, you have to enforce some distance between yourself and the text. That may not be so easy with such an honored text as this one, but maybe your ability to read it in these pages instead of in a replica of eighteenth-century script framed and displayed in a public building will help. Use the box below or a page in your journal or notebook to list some of the text strategies *The Declaration of Independence* uses to try to persuade its audience.

Rhetorical Strategies in *The Declaration of Independence*

1.

2.

3.

4.

5.

6.

In the case of a formal persuasive essay like *The Declaration,* some of the rhetorical strategies will be identical with the basic text strategies of an essay. I didn't want to say that as a hint before you made your own list, but perhaps in making your list you discovered that for yourself. At any rate, I would list *The Declaration's* structure as one of its rhetorical strategies. That structure, as noted above, assumes the shape of a deductive logical argument: setting forth general premises first, then offering evidence to support the truth of those premises, then drawing what seems to be an inevitable conclusion. Because this kind of logic has such high status in Western culture, a structure like this for a persuasive essay can be a very effective rhetorical tool.

Connect: Andrew Marvell's poem "To His Coy Mistress" (in the Poems for Further Reading, page 733) may be read as an argument in verse. Can you identify its three-part logical structure?

I see tone as another of *The Declaration*'s rhetorical strategies: It takes itself, its subject, and its audience very seriously. That stance helps to persuade its audience because it gives the text a sense of authority, which is necessary if the audience is to lend assent to what the text is saying.

The tone of this text is related to another of its rhetorical strategies: **diction**, or word choice. Consider this idea from the opening paragraph: If the audience of *The Declaration* is a broad one—not only the general population of the 13 colonies and of Britain, but also the political leaders and opinion-makers in the colonies, Britain, and elsewhere among the European powers—and if what is being proposed in the text is indeed very radical, then there is a real need for the text to assume the kind of authoritative, reasoned tone we have already identified. To help this happen, words and phrases such as "it becomes necessary," "dissolve," and "political bands" are chosen. How gentle a word "dissolve" is, as opposed to synonyms such as "break," "disrupt," "throw off," or "cut"; its **connotations** are so nonthreatening that it's almost a euphemism for what the writers are proposing. And what they are dissolving is nothing stronger than "bands which have connected them" with another people, not "chains which have bound them to" or even "bonds which have tied them to" another people. Also, the dissolution of these bands is not being undertaken rashly; instead it has "become . . . necessary" to do this just "in the Course of human events": it's inevitable. Together with other instances of carefully chosen diction throughout the text, these word choices effectively downplay the radical nature of the action being proposed. This strategy of managing the connotations of key words is similar to the rhetorical move that we observed in the Frangelico ad in Chapter 24.

A final rhetorical strategy that I will mention is a matter of the sentence structure in the long middle portion of the essay. This section is the portion where "Facts" (another instance of rhetorical word choice) supporting the allegation that the king is a tyrant are being listed. Eighteen paragraphs of charges are offered, all but one beginning "He has . . ." This repetitive structure tends to pound home the text's contention that "The history of the present King of Great Britain is a history of repeated injuries and usurpations, all having in direct object the establishment of an absolute Tyranny over these States." Indeed, once this list has been recited comes the statement expressing the logical conclusion that "A Prince, whose character is thus marked by every act which may define a Tyrant, is unfit to be the ruler of a free people."

No doubt this brief discussion has mentioned only a few of the rhetorical strategies at work in *The Declaration of Independence*. You can find numerous other instances of the strategies I have pointed out. In turn, your recognition of the rhetorical strategies in any essay can help you see the writing from the writer's point of view: He or she (or, in the case of *The Declaration,* several writers) made certain strategic decisions for rhetorical effect. "Reading the rhetoric" can also help you understand the position and importance of audience to an essay, because rhetoric works best when it is audience-specific. Building on this understanding, you can consciously adopt a stance toward the essay, responding to its rhetoric and tone harmoniously or resistantly. As a writer of essays yourself, you can begin to see how the text strategies of the genre can be deployed to best effect, considering the specific purpose of and audience for a particular essay.

Reading Strategies for a Formal Essay

The idea of an active reader of a formal essay may be a bit strange, because an apparent convention of the genre (or of reading the genre) is for the reader to be fairly passive. A persuasive essay or any essay that is highly rhetorical is based on the presumption that the writing does something to the reader. The essay is active; the reader is acted upon. But the model of reading as a dynamic emphasizes the activity of the reader, his or her power to act upon a text. Looking at text strategies of formal essays, as illustrated by *The Declaration of Independence* in the foregoing discussion, implies the activity of some **reading strategies** for the formal essay too. To recapitulate here, we could list them as follows.

READING STRATEGIES FOR FORMAL ESSAYS

1. Constructing voice/tone.
2. Identifying audience.
3. Identifying structure.
4. Enforcing distance.
5. Deciding on rhetorical strategies.

Constructing Voice and Tone

As cut-and-dried as a formal essay may seem, you should realize that even something as "objective" as voice or tone is subject to the reader's construction of it. This point was touched on earlier when I asked you to try to identify the voice or tone in *The Declaration of Independence*. If you called it something like "strong," "sincere," or "respectful," think for a minute how those qualities are related to your position reading it as an American citizen (if that's what you are). But if you can imaginatively put yourself in the place of a Colonial American Tory or loyalist to the British crown, perhaps you'd identify the voice or tone in more negative terms: "uppity," "disrespectful," or "haughty," for instance. What may appear at first to be questions of objective identification become on closer examination matters of a reader's construction out of his or her ideology or literary experience.

Identifying Audience and Structure

I have listed the next two reading strategies as more nearly objective matters by using the word "identifying" with each. But to look into this a bit further, I would ask you to consider that the matter of audience isn't really that stable either. In the case of a historic text like *The Declaration of Independence*, whenever you read it there may be multiple audiences involved—not just originally, as we have noted above—but also lately. Inasmuch as you are reading it, you are part of its audience, and you are different from readers of 220 years ago. And while the structure of an essay may seem to be objectively identifiable—you could easily outline the major parts and subparts of *The Declaration of Independence*—speaking of structures may be more accurate. Essays don't usually come with an outline attached, so different readers may identify an essay's parts differently. Furthermore, an essay's logical structure may follow one arrangement while its structure of figures of speech may follow another. In any case, paying attention to a formal essay's structure or structures and considering its audience or audiences are strategies for active reading that you can and should use.

Enforcing Distance

Next on this list of reading strategies is something else that was touched on earlier: enforcing distance between yourself and the text. Put another way, this strategy involves removing yourself (mentally, intellectually, emotionally, aesthetically) from the audience the essay is apparently addressing. In the case of *The Declaration of Independence,* this may be both easy and hard to do. It may be easy because, after all, you are already more than 200 years removed from it, but it may be difficult because if you are an American, you probably have a special reverence for it. In fact, part of the difficulty may be your unwillingness to enforce distance in any way but in time from *The Declaration;* to read it actively may seem "unpatriotic." At the same time, the text may exert such a strong effect that many readers may be unable to pull far enough away to analyze it critically.

Deciding on Rhetorical Strategies

If you are able and willing to distance yourself from the text strategies and effect of an essay in the ways I am suggesting, you should begin to find that its rhetoric, which, like its structure, is otherwise invisible, comes to light. If my brief analysis of some of the rhetorical strategies of *The Declaration of Independence* (or of the Frangelico ad in Chapter 24) made any sense to you or especially if it led you to identify other rhetorical strategies, then you can see what I'm talking about here.

These last two reading strategies may also promote **strong reading** on your part, that being active and self-conscious reading. If you can enforce distance from an essay (especially a persuasive one) and begin to identify its rhetorical strategies, you gain back a kind of power against the text; you're not so passively subject to it, as it wants you to be in order to persuade you. This strategy does not necessarily mean that you have to disagree with what the text is trying to get you to believe; you may have already felt some strength as an active reader of *The Declaration of Independence* without now feeling that the American colonies should not have separated themselves from Britain. At the same time, however, adopting such a distanced and analytical stance toward a persuasive essay—or toward any text that seeks to persuade you in some way—does give you conscious control over which ideas you accept and which you reject.

There are a few other reading strategies for formal essays that our earlier discussion of text strategies did not suggest. Let's take a look at some of those now. For convenience sake, I'll divide them into two categories: practical reading strategies and creative ones. These, by the way, will also prove applicable to reading informal essays, as you will see in the next chapter.

Practical Reading Strategies for Essays

Under this heading, I will simply list three strategies that promote active reading, all of which you have heard before if you have read Chapter 10 on Reading Poems. These are underlining, annotating, and looking up new or unusual words. To do the first two of these, you must read with a pen or pencil in your hand and be willing to scribble in your book. If you are hesitant to do that, think of it as a way in which you can make the book and the texts in it your own, your intellectual property. Instead of losing the resale value of a book, you are gaining something much more important and powerful.

The first of these strategies, underlining (or highlighting, or bracketing, or starring), allows you to mark whatever words or passages you decide are important for whatever reason—in the process of identifying rhetorical strategies of a text, for instance, or of just trying to concentrate on the ideas being presented to you. Writing notes in the margins of an essay (annotating) really helps you make a text your own, intellectually or emotionally, because these are your words and thoughts. You can "talk back" to the text this way, or ask questions of it, begin to enter into dialogue with it. Similarly, referring to a dictionary to look up new words or words apparently used in an unfamiliar sense can be more than just an academic drill or exercise. Not only can it help you improve your cognitive understanding of a text, but it also begins to identify and open up gaps or **sites of struggle** (both to be discussed later) and to further analyze text strategies. Words do constitute text strategies, after all.

To illustrate, part of the entry for "dissolve" from *Webster's Ninth New Collegiate Dictionary* is printed here. The words in small capital letters are synonyms. "Dissolve" is not likely to be a new or unfamiliar word to you, and its use in the context of the first sentence of *The Declaration of Independence* may not seem unusual. But comparing it with its synonyms as listed in the dictionary may shed further light on a rhetorical strategy of that essay.

dis•solve \diz-älv, -'ȯlv *also* -äv or -ȯv\ *vb* [ME *dissolven,* fr. L *dissolvere,* fr. *dis-* + *solvere* to loosen — more at SOLVE] *vt* (14c) **1 a** : to cause to disperse or disappear : DESTROY **b** : to separate into component parts : DISINTE-GRATE **c** : to bring to an end : TERMINATE <~ parliament> **2 a** : to cause to pass into solution <~ sugar in water> **b** : MELT, LIQUEFY **c** : to cause to be emotionally moved **d** : to cause to fade out in a dissolve **3** *archaic* : DETACH, LOOSEN **4** : to clear up <~ a problem> *vi* **1 a** : to become dissipated or decomposed **b** : BREAK UP, DISPERSE **c** : to fade away **2 a** : to become fluid : MELT **b** : to pass into solution **c** : to be overcome emotionally <*dis-solved* into tears> <*dissolved* in laughter> **d** : to resolve itself as if by dissolution <hate *dissolved* into fear> **e** : to change by a dissolve <the scene ~s

to a Victorian parlor>— dis•solv•able \-äl-və-bəl, -'ȯl-\ *adj*— dis-solv-er *n*

Wouldn't the effect of the opening of *The Declaration* be different if "destroy," "disintegrate," or "terminate" had been used instead of "dissolve," even though all four of those words mean roughly the same thing in this context?

I am calling these three reading strategies practical ones not because any others are impractical, but to suggest they can be practiced easily, with basic tools like a pen or a dictionary to aid you as you read. Now let's look at a few more reading strategies that involve a little more reader creativity.

Creative Reading Strategies for Essays

In addition to reading strategies that anyone can practice just by having the basic tools handy and using them when reading, there are two other cognitive activities that can take you a little further toward becoming a stronger reader of essays. These strategies might be thought of as "creative" because by using them you tend to actively make meaning out of your interaction with a text. These strategies, ones we have seen and practiced in earlier chapters, are identifying or creating gaps or sites of struggle, and identifying or creating **theme**.

It may seem that formal essays are not subject to these kind of reading strategies because they use language straightforwardly or directly to make a point, unlike other genres in which language may be more indirect in order to provide aesthetic pleasure. But any use of language is subject to gaps and sites of struggle because writers cannot always control what readers will make of a text, and theme, as earlier chapters have demonstrated, is as much created by readers as it is "put into" a text by its writer.

In your earlier reading of *The Declaration of Independence*, you may have already detected or created some gaps in that text. Something fairly obvious along that line is the lack of specificity in the list of "repeated injuries and usurpations" that the text says demonstrate the king's desire to establish "an absolute Tyranny over these States." Consider the first of these—"He has refused his Assent to Laws, the most wholesome and necessary for the public good." The text does not say just what these laws are or why they are "wholesome and necessary for the public good." The punctuation within that sentence may be read as a gap too: does the comma mean that the king has refused his assent only to those laws that would be wholesome and necessary, or does it mean that he has refused his assent to all laws, all of which are wholesome and necessary?

A later charge against the king is that "he has … endeavored to bring on the inhabitants of our frontiers, the merciless Indian Savages, whose known rule of warfare, is an undistinguished destruction of all ages, sexes, and conditions." Can you detect competing ideological values, on the level of assumptions rather than explicit statements, in this sentence? The reference to the Indians as "Savages" seems to indicate that they are apparently held as less than human or at least less than politically recognizable humans, and their "known rule of warfare, … an undistinguished destruction of all ages, sexes, and conditions" is implicitly decried. Yet this text has already invoked "the

Laws of Nature" as one of the bases for its argument. It would seem to me, anyway, that one of "the Laws of Nature" is "an undistinguished destruction of all ages, sexes, and conditions" since that's what happens in death and disease. Also, if "the Laws of Nature" are to be appealed to as higher than the laws of Britain in constructing an argument for political separation, doesn't it seem that those natural laws would support the similarity of the Indians and the American colonists, not any essential human difference between them? Identifying this or any particular passage as a site of struggle is to call your ideology as a reader into play, and so this reading strategy will be looked at again in a little more detail below.

In a formal essay theme may seem to be definitely not something a reader would create. If an essay has a point to make, if it seeks to get its readers to agree with some idea, then it ought to be direct or straightforward in letting readers know what this point is instead of implying or suggesting it indirectly. A statement of an idea put forward to be believed and whose truth (or falsity) can be proven is a **proposition**. *The Declaration of Independence,* for instance, *declares* its idea that the American colonies should be and are "free and independent states." That proposition is *The Declaration's* most explicit theme. This kind of explicit statement of a proposition or theme in a formal essay would seem to take theme-creation out of readers' hands—or minds—entirely. And so the reading strategy of creating theme may be applied more usefully with informal essays, which will be considered in the next chapter.

At the same time, however, if readers are granted a measure of freedom and creativity, if they are allowed to be strong and to assert themselves as makers of meaning in their encounters with texts, then the possibility that readers will create their own themes no matter how constraining a text seems to be must also be allowed. Without trying to demonstrate this by reaching for some far-out interpretation of *The Declaration,* let me just suggest two different emphases that readers of it might assert. One is the specific historical situation of the British American colonies in 1776; the other is more general. Read the first way, *The Declaration* "is about" the leaders of those colonies establishing their political independence from the British crown; read the second way, it "is about" human political freedom in any place and time. The first reading emphasizes specific historical and political conditions; the second emphasizes more general principles of political philosophy. The first interpretation may be more appropriate to American readers, from the eighteenth century on down to today; the second may be more common to readers not geographically connected to the colonies or Great Britain, whose aspirations to national independence were in part legitimized by the words and thoughts of *The Declaration*. In either case, perhaps the role of a reader's historical and cultural situation in deciding on theme becomes more evident. Thinking about that leads to another consideration with regard to reading and responding to essays.

Cultural Values and Reading

Much of what has already been discussed in this chapter is a matter of the interaction of ideologies between a reader and an essay. For instance, in reading *The Declaration of Independence,* we considered how the ideology of a

United States citizen would allow for almost instantaneous recognition of the idea or issue with which that text is concerned, even before she or he would read it again on this occasion. When we were looking at tone and voice as a text strategy of *The Declaration,* we considered briefly how the ideology of someone loyal to the British king would construct the "speaker" of the text and the speaker's attitude. And in our quick look at some "creative" reading strategies, we entertained the idea that a reader's ideological position or cultural or historical situation could affect the way he or she reads a formal essay.

Now let's consider another way in which readers' ideologies may be engaged by certain text strategies of a formal essay. Earlier, we looked at rhetoric as a set or cluster of text strategies whose aim is to get a reader to believe some idea that a formal essay wishes the reader to believe. Belief in the truth of an idea is not a matter of reading strategies so much as it is one of values. So if the proposition in question is any matter of moral, ethical, legal, political, or social value, rhetoric works on or with the ideology of an essay's readers. In *The Declaration of Independence,* the rhetorical strategy of a tightly constructed deductive logical argument interacts harmoniously with the ideology of most Western readers because Western culture teaches a respect for such logical argument as a way to discover and present, even "prove," philosophical truth. But also the text's concern with such value-laden issues as political independence and despotic tyranny addresses the ideologies of its audience.

It may be that the earlier analysis of the text strategies of a formal essay, as exemplified in *The Declaration of Independence,* allowed you to get a little bit of distance from the text and allowed you to begin to analyze the kind of interaction of ideologies you had with it. Ordinarily, in American culture, such a politically sacred text would be taken for granted, not examined for the interplay of values and beliefs that may be involved when someone reads it. You are probably not used to reading *The Declaration* in a critical way. To do so is not necessarily to look for points of disagreement or to find ways to pick holes in it—although those things may happen—but to try to see how it works, why it works the way it does, and what it works on. If you analyze your response to *The Declaration* culturally, you will look at the elements of your ideology that cause you to accept as true or reject as false the entire text or individual parts of it. For example, supposing your situation as an American citizen and as someone who subscribes to the widely held belief in people's right to political self-determination produces a harmonious ideological interaction with the major premise of The Declaration: that "when a long train of abuses and usurpations . . . evinces a design to . . . [put a people] under absolute Despotism, it is . . . [the people's] right . . . to throw off such Government. . . ." And supposing your ideology inclines you to believe most of the charges attached to the king. You still may discover a clash with the text's assumption that the Native Americans were "merciless . . . Savages." In the culture of the late twentieth century in the United States, the ideological pendulum has swung away from such an assumption about Native Americans, who are now widely seen as a subjugated people, victims of near-genocide practiced against them by Europeans who colonized North America. If you are a Native American yourself, your clashing interaction with that assumption in the text may be so strong as to provoke your resistance to the entire *Declaration.*

Still, for most Americans, *The Declaration of Independence*—at least by reputation if not by actual acquaintance with it—is not a text to be challenged on ideological grounds. To the contrary, it is a very powerful text that, because of its place in American history and culture, has contributed mightily to shaping the political ideology of most Americans. For that reason, as I have said, it may be especially difficult to analyze the ideological interaction you have with this text, let alone to practice a resisting reading of it. Perhaps with a different text you can get the distance necessary for such a self-conscious analysis.

Reading and Responding: A Formal Essay

Read the essay reprinted below. Then write a response statement, using the questions that follow.

W. S. Merwin   b. 1927

Unchopping a Tree   *1969*

Start with the leaves, the small twigs, and the nests that have been shaken, ripped, or broken off by the fall; these must be gathered and attached once again to their respective places. It is not arduous work, unless major limbs have been smashed or mutilated. If the fall was carefully and correctly planned, the chances of anything of the kind happening will have been reduced. Again, much depends upon the size, age, shape, and species of the tree. Still, you will be lucky if you can get through this stage without having to use machinery. Even in the best of circumstances it is a labor that will make you wish often that you had won the favor of the universe of ants, the empire of mice, or at least a local tribe of squirrels, and could enlist their labors and their talents. But no, they leave you to it. They have learned, with time. This is men's work. It goes without saying that if the tree was hollow in whole or in part, and contained old nests of bird or mammal or insect, or hoards of nuts or such structures as wasps or bees build for their survival, the contents will have to be repaired where necessary, and reassembled, insofar as possible, in their original order, including the shells of nuts already opened. With spiders' webs you must simply do the best you can. We do not have the spider's weaving equipment, nor any substitute for the leaf's living bond with its point of attachment and nourishment. It is even harder to simulate the latter when the leaves have once become dry—as they are bound to do, for this is not the labor of a moment. Also it hardly needs saying that this is the time for repairing any neighboring trees or bushes or other growth that may have been damaged by the fall. The same rules apply. Where neighboring trees were of the same species it is difficult not to waste time conveying a detached leaf back to the wrong tree. Practice, practice. Put your hope in that.

Now the tackle must be put into place, or the scaffolding, depending on the surroundings and the dimensions of the tree. It is ticklish work. Almost always it involves, in itself, further damage to the area, which will have to be corrected later. But as you've heard, it can't be helped. And care now is likely to save you considerable trouble later. Be careful to grind nothing into the ground.

At last the time comes for the erecting of the trunk. By now it will scarcely be necessary to remind you of the delicacy of this huge skeleton. Every motion of the tackle, every slight upward heave of the trunk, the branches, their elaborately reassembled panoply of leaves (now dead) will draw from you an involuntary gasp. You will watch for a leaf or a twig to be snapped off yet again. You will listen for the nuts to shift in the hollow limb and you will hear whether they are indeed falling into place or are spilling in disorder—in which case, or in the event of anything else of the kind—operations will have to cease, of course, while you correct the matter. The raising itself is no small enterprise, from the moment when the chains tighten around the old bandages until the bole hangs vertical above the stump, splinter above splinter. Now the final straightening of the splinters themselves can take place (the preliminary work is best done while the wood is still green and soft, but at times when the splinters are not badly twisted most of the straightening is left until now, when the torn ends are face to face with each other). When the splinters are perfectly complementary the appropriate fixative is applied. Again we have no duplicate of the original substance. Ours is extremely strong, but it is rigid. It is limited to surfaces, and there is no play in it. However the core is not the part of the trunk that conducted life from the roots up into the branches and back again. It was relatively inert. The fixative for this part is not the same as the one for the outer layers and the bark, and if either of these is involved in the splintered section they must receive applications of the appropriate adhesives. Apart from being incorrect and probably ineffective, the core fixative would leave a scar on the bark.

When all is ready the splintered trunk is lowered onto the splinters of the stump. This, one might say, is only the skeleton of the resurrection. Now the chips must be gathered, and the sawdust, and returned to their former positions. The fixative for the wood layers will be applied to chips and sawdust consisting only of wood. Chips and sawdust consisting of several substances will receive applications of the correct adhesives. It is as well, where possible, to shelter the materials from the elements while working. Weathering makes it harder to identify the smaller fragments. Bark sawdust in particular the earth lays claim to very quickly. You must find your own ways of coping with this problem. There is a certain beauty, you will notice at moments, in the pattern of the chips as they are fitted back into place. You will wonder to what extent it should be described as natural, to what extent man-made. It will lead you on to speculations about the parentage of beauty itself, to which you will return.

The adhesive for the chips is translucent, and not so rigid as that for the splinters. That for the bark and its subcutaneous layers is transparent and runs into the fibers on either side, partially dissolving them into each other. It does not set the sap flowing again but it does pay a kind of tribute to the preoccupations of the ancient thoroughfares. You could not roll an egg over the joints but some of the mineshafts would still be passable, no doubt, for the first   5 exploring insect who raises its head in the tight echoless passages. The day comes when it is all restored, even to the moss (now dead) over the wound. You will sleep badly, thinking of the removal of the scaffolding that must begin the next morning. How you will hope for sun and a still day!

The removal of the scaffolding or tackle is not so dangerous, perhaps, to the surroundings, as its installation, but it presents problems. It should be taken from the spot piece by piece as it is detached and stored at a distance. You have come to accept it as there, around the tree. The sky begins to look naked as the chains and struts one by one vacate their positions. Finally the moment arrives when the last sustaining piece is removed and the tree stands again on its own. It is as though its weight for a moment stood on your heart. You listen for a thud of settlement, a warning creak deep in the intricate joinery. You cannot believe it will hold. How like something dreamed it is, standing there all by itself. How long will it stand there now? The first breeze that touches its dead leaves all seems to flow into your mouth. You are afraid the motion of the clouds will be enough to push it over. What more can you do? What more can you do?

But there is nothing more you can do.

Others are waiting.

Everything is going to have to be put back.

Response Statement Questions

- How would you describe the text's voice or tone? What text strategies contribute to making voice or tone what it is in this essay?
- What idea(s) does this text seem to be concerned with? Is there a difference between its explicit concerns and any that may be implicit?
- What reading strategies did you use in processing this text? To what extent did they contribute to your sense of the idea(s) the text is concerned with?
- What rhetorical strategies can you identify in this text? How effective are they in persuading you to believe anything the text seems to want you to believe?
- What kind of ideological interaction did you experience in reading this text? What ideological values of yours did the text confirm or challenge?
- *Share and Compare*   Below you will find some response-statement-like writing I wrote about "Unchopping a Tree." How is your own response to this text similar to or different from mine? How do differences between your reading strategies and ideology and mine produce different responses between you and me?

A Reading of "Unchopping a Tree"

Did you find the tone of "Unchopping a Tree" serious? Perhaps the title led you to expect a more fanciful tone than the text seems to adopt. It certainly seems serious to me—earnest, especially in contrast to its fanciful subject; it seems to take a reverent attitude toward trees and the life forms—vegetable and animal—that are affected when a tree is chopped down. Just to mention one text strategy that I think contributes to this tone, the absolute straightforwardness with which the text presents an impossible task, its presumption that this task really is possible (this contrast between subject and attitude) is part of what creates, for me, the essay's serious tone. Put another way, this text, I think, must be serious because it applies the familiar subgenre of the directional or "how-to" essay to an impossible task. And because the task is impossible and the tone so serious, I feel led to decide that the text is concerned with something other than what it appears to be concerned with on the surface. What did you say in response to the second set of response statement questions?

In terms of my reading strategies for "Unchopping a Tree," I started reading it with something like curiosity, given its title, but I took it pretty much as straightforward directions at first. The second clause in the first sentence, though, with its solemn requirement that "these [leaves, small twigs, and nests] must be gathered and attached once again to their respective places," made me begin to suspect that the essay was concerned with something other than these literal directions. And when I got to the sentence beginning "Even in the best of circumstances, . . ." I felt that I should modify my expectations that the essay would merely present directions for performing an impossible task. Here is where I really started to think that the essay was concerned with some other, more philosophical idea. From that point on, I read it on two levels at once: the explicit concern with the impossible task in all its impossible detail, on one level, and what I saw as an implicit concern with the ecological consequences of the seemingly inconsequential act of cutting down a tree, on the second.

I felt that interpretation was confirmed and deepened when I got to the parts in the third and fourth paragraphs that mention "fixative[s]" and "adhesives" to put minute parts of the tree back together. That part reminded me that no matter what "super glues" modern chemistry has provided, we still could never duplicate the living "adhesives" that hold a tree together; that might as well be done by magic. Reading this way, when I got to the last sentence in the fourth paragraph I was receptive to the suggestion that I would be led ". . . on to speculations about the parentage of beauty itself." In fact, I thought I had already begun to speculate on such profound philosophical ideas as that. By the time I got to the end of the essay, I found myself ready to believe that "everything is going to have to be put back."

I have tried to summarize my reading process for "Unchopping a Tree" accurately and honestly here. But I also want to point out how my reading demonstrates a **wandering viewpoint** and **consistency building**. My viewpoint "wandered" or alternated between reading the text as a straightforward directive piece and suspecting it of being really about something more philosophical. Then I started to build consistency in terms of the latter interpretation when I got to the parts about the "fixative" and the "adhesives." From there on, my reading looked for confirmation that the text was really about the ecological consequences that we usually overlook when even a single tree is chopped down.

I think the text does want me to think about such philosophical matters as these. I think it wants me to believe that in terms of our relationship with things in the natural world no act is really simple or without profound ecological consequences. In my discussion to this point, I have probably touched on several rhetorical strategies that the essay seems to use to get me to believe this idea. And you have no doubt identified others. But let me just try to make a couple of these strategies a little more explicit here.

The essay's tone, I think, is a rhetorical strategy. The absolute, dead-on seriousness with which the essay presents an impossible task prompts me not only to look for a more serious, less fanciful idea, but also to take that idea seriously. I also see the minute detail that the description of the "unchopping" process goes into as a rhetorical strategy. References to the wood chips, the splinters, and the "mineshafts" through which insects crawl inside the tree make me think about seemingly insignificant aspects of a tree in a new way, and about just how much is destroyed when a tree is cut down.

Finally, I think the essay's occasional statements about how "you" (or I) will feel during the long "unchopping" process is a rhetorical strategy that contributes to my adopting the same attitude toward its subject that the text has. It's conventional for a how-to essay to address its reader directly, as "you." But this essay often goes beyond ordinary directive statements that have "you" as the grammatical subject or that imply "you" as subject by using the imperative mood ("Be careful to grind nothing into the ground.") or as object by using the passive voice ("Now the tackle must be put into place...."). It makes statements like "You will watch for a leaf or a twig to be snapped off yet again" and "You are afraid the motion of the clouds will be enough to push it over." As I read the essay and imagine myself doing this impossible task, I find myself quite willing to believe I'd have such feelings as these. I would certainly worry about what a fragile thing I was putting back together in a tree, about how easily it could topple over again, and having this feeling sets me up emotionally to believe what the text seems to want me to believe.

With all that I have said here, can you tell that I have had a harmonious ideological interaction with this text? Looking at my response from that point of view, I can say that I brought to the reading a set of attitudes and beliefs about ecology in general and trees in particular that made me receptive to the text's ideas. It was easy for me to have a **consoling reading** of "Unchopping a Tree," not that I was already conscious of all the things "a tree" involves or constitutes, especially when it's chopped down. I take trees for granted probably just as much as the next person. But also in my ideology is a belief in the nobility of trees, a sense that many of the trees I encounter are older than I am, and some are older than any person. I respect trees, if for no other reason than their age. Of course, if my situation were different—if I were a logger in the Northwest, for instance—I suppose I'd have a different set of attitudes—probably less "romantic" or "idealistic"—about trees. And so I would probably have a different kind of ideological interaction with this text. What was yours? And how was it affected by your economic or social or geographical situation?

An Essay For Exploration

Emma Goldman 1869–1940

Marriage and Love *1910*

The popular notion about marriage and love is that they are synonymous, that they spring from the same motives, and cover the same human needs. Like most popular notions this also rests not on actual facts, but on superstition.

Marriage and love have nothing in common; they are as far apart as the poles; are, in fact, antagonistic to each other. No doubt some marriages have been the result of love. Not, however, because love could assert itself only in marriage; much rather is it because few people can completely outgrow a convention. There are today large numbers of men and women to whom marriage is naught but a farce, but who submit to it for the sake of public opinion. At any rate, while it is true that some marriages are based on love, and while it is equally true that in some cases love continues in married life, I maintain that it does so regardless of marriage, and not because of it.

On the other hand, it is utterly false that love results from marriage. On rare occasions one does hear of a miraculous case of a married couple falling in love after marriage, but on close examination it will be found that it is a mere adjustment to the inevitable. Certainly the growing-used to each other is far away from the spontaneity, the intensity, and beauty of love, without which the intimacy of marriage must prove degrading to both the woman and the man.

Marriage is primarily an economic arrangement, an insurance pact. It differs from the ordinary life insurance agreement only in that it is more binding, more exacting. Its returns are insignificantly small compared with the investments. In taking out an insurance policy one pays for it in dollars and cents, always at liberty to discontinue payments. If, however, woman's premium is a husband, she pays for it with her name, her privacy, her self-respect, her very life "until death doth part." Moreover, the marriage insurance condemns her to life-long dependency, to parasitism, to complete uselessness, individual as well as social. Man, too, pays his toll, but as his sphere is wider, marriage does not limit him as much as woman. He feels his chains more in an economic sense.

Thus Dante's motto over Inferno applies with equal force to marriage: "Ye who enter here leave all hope behind." 5

That marriage is a failure none but the very stupid will deny. One has but to glance over the statistics of divorce to realize how bitter a failure marriage really is. Nor will the stereotyped Philistine argument that the laxity of divorce laws and the growing looseness of women account for the fact that: first, every twelfth marriage ends in divorce; second, that since 1870 divorces have increased from 28 to 73 for every hundred thousand population; third, that adultery, since 1867, as ground for divorce, has increased 270.8 per cent.; fourth, that desertion increased 369.8 per cent.

Added to these startling figures is a vast amount of material, dramatic and literary, further elucidating this subject. Robert Herrick, in *Together*; Pinero, in *Mid-Channel*; Eugene Walker, in *Paid in Full*, and scores of other writers are discussing the barrenness, the monotony, the sordidness, the inadequacy of marriage as a factor for harmony and understanding.

The thoughtful social student will not content himself with the popular superficial excuse for this phenomenon. He will have to dig down deeper into the very life of the sexes to know why marriage proves so disastrous.

Edward Carpenter says that behind every marriage stands the life-long environment of the two sexes; an environment so different from each other that man and woman must remain strangers. Separated by an insurmountable wall of superstition, custom, and habit, marriage has not the potentiality of developing knowledge of, and respect for, each other, without which every union is doomed to failure.

Henrik Ibsen, the hater of all social shams, was probably the first to realize   10 this great truth. Nora[1] leaves her husband, not—as the stupid critic would have it—because she is tired of her responsibilities or feels the need of woman's rights, but because she has to come to know that for eight years she had lived with a stranger and borne him children. Can there by anything more humiliating, more degrading than a life-long proximity between two strangers? No need for the woman to know anything of the man, save his income. As to the knowledge of the woman—what is there to know except the she has a pleasing appearance? We have not yet outgrown the theologic myth that woman has no soul, that she is a mere appendix to man, made out of his rib just for the convenience of the gentleman who was so strong that he was afraid of his own shadow.

Perchance the poor quality of the material whence woman comes is responsible for her inferiority. At any rate, woman has no soul—what is there to know about her? Besides, the less soul a woman has the greater her asset as a wife, the more readily will she absorb herself in her husband. It is this slavish acquiescence to man's superiority that has kept the marriage institution seemingly intact for so long a period. Now that woman is coming into her own, now that she is actually growing aware of herself as a being outside of the master's grace, the sacred institution of marriage is gradually being undermined, and no amount of sentimental lamentation can stay it.

From infancy, almost the average girl is told that marriage is her ultimate goal; therefore her training and education must be directed toward that end. Like the mute beast fattened for slaughter, she is prepared for that. Yet, strange to say, she is allowed to know much less about her function as wife and mother than the ordinary artisan of his trade. It is indecent and filthy for a respectable girl to know anything of the marital relation. Oh, for the inconsistency of respectability, that needs the marriage vow to turn something which is filthy into the purest and most sacred arrangement that none dare question or criticize. Yet that is exactly the attitude of the average upholder of marriage. The prospective wife and mother is kept in complete ignorance of her only

---

[1]Nora—In Ibsen's play *A Doll's House*, Nora leaves her husband in the final act.

asset in the competitive field—sex. Thus she enters into life-long relations with a man only to find herself shocked, repelled, outraged beyond measure by the most natural and healthy instinct, sex. It is safe to say that a large percentage of the unhappiness, misery, distress, and physical suffering of matrimony is due to the criminal ignorance in sex matters that is being extolled as a great virtue. Nor is it at all an exaggeration when I say that more than one home has been broken up because of this deplorable fact.

If, however, woman is free and big enough to learn the mystery of sex without the sanction of State or Church, she will stand condemned as utterly unfit to become the wife of a "good" man, his goodness consisting of an empty head and plenty of money. Can there by anything more outrageous than the idea that a healthy, grown woman, full of life and passion, must deny nature's demand, must subdue her most intense craving, undermine her health and break her spirit, must stunt her vision, abstain from the depth and glory of sex experience until a "good" man comes along to take her unto himself as a wife? That is precisely what marriage means. How can such an arrangement end except in failure? This is one, though not the least important, factor of marriage, which differentiates it from love.

Ours is a practical age. The time when Romeo and Juliet risked the wrath of their fathers for love, when Gretchen exposed herself to gossip of her neighbors for love, is no more. If, on rare occasions, young people allow themselves the luxury of romance, they are taken in care by the elders, drilled and pounded until they become "sensible."

The moral lesson instilled in the girl is not whether the man has aroused her love, but rather is it, "How much?" The important and only God of practical American life: Can the man make a living? Can he support a wife? That is the only thing that justifies marriage. Gradually this saturates every thought of the girl; her dreams are not of moonlight and kisses, of laughter and tears; she dreams of shopping tours and bargain counters. This soul-poverty and sordidness are the elements inherent in the marriage institution. The State and the Church approve of no other ideal, simply because it is the one that necessitates the State and Church control of men and women.

Doubtless there are people who continue to consider love above dollars and cents. Particularly is this true of that class whom economic necessity has forced to become self-supporting. The tremendous change in woman's position, wrought by that mighty factor, is indeed phenomenal when we reflect that it is but a short time since she has entered the industrial arena. Six million women wage-earners; six million women, who have the equal right with men to be exploited, to be robbed, to go on strike; aye, to starve even. Anything more, my lord? Yes, six million wage-workers in every walk of life, from the highest brain work to the most difficult menial labor in the mines and on the railroad tracks; yes, even detectives and policemen. Surely the emancipation is complete.

Yet with all that, but a very small number of the vast army of women wage-workers look upon work as a permanent issue, in the same light as does man. No matter how decrepit the latter, he has been taught to be independent, self-supporting. Oh, I know that no one is really independent in our economic

15

treadmill; still, the poorest specimen of a man hates to be a parasite; to be known as such, at any rate.

The woman considers her position as worker transitory, to be thrown aside for the first bidder. That is why it is infinitely harder to organize women than men. "Why should I join a union? I am going to get married, to have a home." Has she not been taught from infancy to look upon that as her ultimate calling? She learns soon enough that the home, though not so large a prison as the factory, has more solid doors and bars. It has a keeper so faithful that naught can escape him. The most tragic part, however, is that the home no longer frees her from wage-slavery; it only increases her task.

According to the latest statistics submitted before a Committee "on labor and wages, and congestion of population," ten per cent of the wage workers in New York City alone are married, yet they must continue to work at the most poorly paid labor in the world. Add to this horrible aspect the drudgery of housework, and what remains of the protection and glory of the home? As a matter of fact, even the middle-class girl in marriage can not speak of her home, since it is the man who creates her sphere. It is not important whether the husband is a brute or a darling. What I wish to prove is that marriage guarantees woman a home only by the grace of her husband. There she moves about in *his* home, year after year, until her aspect of life and human affairs becomes as flat, narrow, and drab as her surroundings. Small wonder if she becomes a nag, petty, quarrelsome, gossipy, unbearable, thus driving the man from the house. She could not go, if she wanted to; there is no place to go. Besides, a short period of married life, of complete surrender of all faculties, absolutely incapacitates the average woman for the outside world. She becomes reckless in appearance, clumsy in her movements, dependent in her decisions, cowardly in her judgment, a weight and a bore, which most men grow to hate and despise. Wonderfully inspiring atmosphere for the bearing of life, is it not?

But the child, how is it be protected, if not for marriage? After all, is not   20
that the most important consideration? The sham, the hypocrisy of it! Marriage protecting the child, yet thousands of children destitute and homeless. Marriage protecting the child, yet orphan asylums and reformatories overcrowded, the Society for the Prevention of Cruelty to Children keeping busy in rescuing the little victims from "loving parents," to place them under more loving care, the Gerry Society. Oh, the mockery of it!

Marriage may have the power to "bring the horse to water," but has it ever made him drink? The law will place the father under arrest, and put him in convict's clothes; but has that ever stilled the hunger of the child? If the parent has no work, or if he hides his identity, what does marriage do then? It invokes the law to bring the man to "justice," to put him safely behind closed doors; his labor, however, goes not to the child, but to the State. The child receives but a blighted memory of its father's stripes.

As to the protection of the woman,—therein lies the curse of marriage. Not that it really protects her, but the very idea is so revolting, such an outrage and insult on life, so degrading to human dignity, as to forever condemn this parasitic institution.

It is like that other parental arrangement—capitalism. It robs man of his birthright, stunts his growth, poisons his body, keeps him in ignorance, in poverty and dependence, and then institutes charities that thrive on the last vestige of man's self-respect.

The institution of marriage makes a parasite of woman, an absolute dependent. It incapacitates her for life's struggle, annihilates her social consciousness, paralyzes her imagination, and then imposes its gracious protection, which is in reality a snare, a travesty on human character.

If motherhood is the highest fulfillment of woman's nature, what other protection does it need save love and freedom? Marriage but defiles, outrages and corrupts her fulfillment. Does it not say to woman, Only when you follow me shall you bring forth life? Does it not condemn her to the block, does it not degrade and shame her if she refuses to buy her right to motherhood by selling herself? Does not marriage only sanction motherhood, even though conceived in hatred, in compulsion? Yet, if motherhood be of free choice, of love, of ecstasy, of defiant passion, does it not place a crown of thorns upon an innocent head and carve in letters or blood the hideous epithet, Bastard? Were marriage to contain all the virtues claimed for it, its crimes against motherhood would exclude it forever from the realm of love.

Love, the strongest and deepest element in life, the harbinger of hope, of joy, of ecstasy; love, the defier of all laws, of all conventions; love, the freest, the most powerful moulder of human destiny; how can such an all-compelling force be synonymous with that poor little State and Church-begotten weed, marriage?

Free love? As if love is anything but free! Man has bought brains, but all the millions in the world have failed to buy love. Man has subdued bodies, but all the power on earth has been unable to subdue love. Man has conquered whole nations, but all his armies could not conquer love. Man has chained and fettered the spirit, but he has been utterly helpless before love. High on a throne, with all the splendor and pomp his gold can command, man is yet poor and desolate, if love passes him by. And if it stays, the poorest hovel is radiant with warmth, with life and color. Thus love has the magic power to make of a beggar a king. Yes, love is free; it can dwell in no other atmosphere. In freedom it gives itself unreservedly, abundantly, completely. All the laws on the statutes, all the courts in the universe, cannot tear it from the soil, once love has taken root. If, however, the soil is sterile, how can marriage make it bear fruit? It is like the last desperate struggle of fleeting life against death.

Love needs no protection; it is its own protection. So long as love begets life no child is deserted, or hungry, or famished for the want of affection. I know this to be true. I know women who became mothers in freedom by the men they loved. Few children in wedlock enjoy the care, the protection, the devotion free motherhood is capable of bestowing.

The defenders of authority dread the advent of a free motherhood, lest it will rob them of their prey. Who would fight wars? Who would create wealth? Who would make the policeman, the jailer, if woman were to refuse the indiscriminate breeding of children? The race, the race! shouts the king, the president, the capitalist, the priest. The race must be preserved, though woman be degraded to a mere machine,—and the marriage institution is our only safety valve against the pernicious sex-awakening of woman. But in vain these frantic efforts to maintain a state of bondage. In vain, too, the edicts of the Church, the mad attacks of rulers, in vain even the arm of the law. Woman no longer wants to be a party to the production of a race of sickly, feeble, decrepit, wretched human beings, who have neither the strength nor moral courage to throw off the yoke of poverty and slavery. Instead she desires fewer and better children, begotten and reared in love and through free choice; not by compulsion, as marriage imposes. Our pseudo-moralists have yet to learn the deep sense of responsibility toward the child, that love in freedom has awakened in the breast of woman. Rather would she forego forever the glory of motherhood than bring forth life in an atmosphere that breathes only destruction and death. And if she does become a mother, it is to give to the child the deepest and best her being can yield. To grow with the child is her motto; she knows that in that manner alone can she help build true manhood and womanhood.

Ibsen must have had a vision of free mother, when, with a master stroke, he portrayed Mrs. Alving.[2] She was the ideal mother because she had outgrown marriage and all its horrors, because she had broken her chains, and set her spirit free to soar until it returned a personality, regenerated and strong. Alas, it was too late to rescue her life's joy, her Oswald; but not too late to realize that love in freedom is the only condition of a beautiful life. Those who, like Mrs. Alving, have paid with blood and tears for their spiritual awakening, repudiate marriage as an imposition, a shallow, empty mockery. They know, whether love last but one brief span of time or for eternity, it is the only creative, inspiring, elevating basis for a new race, a new world.

In our present pygmy state love is indeed a stranger to most people. Misunderstood and shunned, it rarely takes root; or if it does, it soon withers and dies. Its delicate fiber can not endure the stress and strain of the daily grind. Its soul is too complex to adjust itself to the slimy woof of our social fabric. It weeps and moans and suffers with those who have need of it, yet lack the capacity to rise to love's summit.

Some day, some day men and women will rise, they will reach the mountain peak, they will meet big and strong and free, ready to receive, to partake, and to bask in the golden rays of love. What fancy, what imagination, what poetic genius can foresee even approximately the potentialities of such a force in the life of men and women. If the world is ever to give birth to true companionship and oneness, not marriage, but love will be the parent.

Response Statement Questions

- How would you describe the voice or tone of this essay? What seems to be the voice's attitude toward its subject? How do you respond to that text strategy? How is your response to the essay's tone influenced by your own attitude toward "marriage and love"?
- What do you see as the main point or **thesis** this essay is trying to argue? What kind of rhetorical strategies can you identify as being used to try to

---

[2]Mrs. Alving—Principal character in Ibsen's play *Ghosts;* Oswald is her son

persuade the essay's audience to believe this thesis? What—in terms of rhetorical strategies of the text and ideological beliefs of yours—allows you to accept or reject the propositions the text is putting forth?

- This essay was first published in 1910. Does reading it nearly 90 years later allow you to establish distance between you and it? What is your response to the essay's ideas as dated or still relevant? How is your response related to your own ideology?

- Overall, what kind of ideological interaction do you experience with this text? If you would describe that interaction as clashing, whose values do you think are closer to the dominant ideology of American culture regarding "marriage and love"—yours or Goldman's? How is your response to Goldman's essay influenced by your own experience with "marriage and love"?

- Compare the attitudes toward "marriage and love" expressed in Goldman's essay with those presented in Ved Mehta's essay "Pom's Engagement" at the end of Chapter 26. Does the discussion of "marriage and love" in Indian culture as presented in Mehta's essay help you gain perspective on Goldman's arguments?

- *Share and Compare*   What different beliefs concerning the relationship of marriage and love exist among readers in your class? How are these beliefs related to readers' own experiences with marriage (for example, if they are married, divorced, or single; if the latter, whether they are engaged to be married or desire or expect to be married some day)?

READING AND WRITING PROJECTS

FOR CREATIVE AND CRITICAL THINKING

Your own writing is important as you try to learn more about yourself as a reader—both what you do cognitively and what is done to you culturally—to produce the kind of reader you are when you interact with any particular text. In addition to response statements and the formal expository paper that may grow out of them, there are other ways to use writing to learn. What follows are suggestions for integrating your reading of and writing about literary texts in various ways. These suggestions include exploratory writing, playing with texts and language, creative efforts in various genres, and other writing exercises designed to strengthen your awareness of the cognitive and cultural processes involved in your reading.

- ▶ Write some directive discourse, as in "Unchopping a Tree." You can make it real and practical—written exactly for the person who will actually have to perform the task you are describing. Or you can make it metaphorical and philosophical, like "Unchopping a Tree," or humorous or ironic—but in some way rhetorical.

- ▶ Both "Unchopping a Tree" and Jonathan Swift's "A Modest Proposal" (in the Essays for Further Reading, page 1610) conduct discourse on two levels at once: One level is the literal meaning of the statements being made; the other is a "subtext" of rhetorical intent. Try your hand at writing a piece of expository or argumentative prose that, like these, does not mean what it says.

▶ Imagine that there were electronic news media in 1776. Write a 30-second radio or television news story based on *The Declaration of Independence* for broadcast in another country. It might begin like this: "The Continental Congress issued a statement today, declaring the United Colonies of America independent of the Crown and Parliament of Great Britain." It could go on in a few sentences to fill in some of the "background" of that lead sentence. As an option, write several such news spots, each for broadcast in a different country. (You can write them in English or not.) How might these news stories differ according to the country's relationship—ally or enemy—to Britain?

▶ Imagine you are an advance scout from a planet in another solar system (whose language is amazingly similar to English). Based on the evidence about Earth life that you can derive from any essay, file a report to your government back home about the cultural practices of Earthlings.

26 ◆ Reading the Informal Essay

The preceding chapter considered some of the basic text strategies of the essay genre. These strategies—prose; consciousness of an audience; the presence of some kind of voice and tone; and a concern with an idea, issue, or topic—are common to both formal and informal essays. Within that common ground, however, a divergence in actual practice with respect to the last two text strategies may be observed. Some essays may be more serious than others in subject matter and the attitude toward that subject matter. This seriousness, in turn, may contribute to the presence of other text strategies—a tight structure and relatively obvious rhetorical strategies—which may appear plain to a reader who is able to enforce a certain degree of distance from the text she or he is reading. Other essays, by contrast, may be more loosely structured and less plainly rhetorical; may concern themselves with less serious topics; or may take a less serious attitude toward whatever topics they do concern themselves with. Essays using these text strategies may be considered informal.

I would like to add a qualification, however. In Chapter 24 the division of essays into formal and informal was deemed arbitrary and less than clear-cut. I would repeat that point here and add that what was just said about some of the differences between text strategies of formal and informal essays does not mean that informal essays must be light-hearted, humorous, or less than serious in subject and tone. Perhaps a better way of understanding the difference in these two broad subcategories of essay is to consider it a matter of degree rather than one of absolute kind. Looked at that way, formal essays can be said to occupy a narrower portion of the spectrum within the genre; informal essays offer a greater variety of text strategies, including, sometimes, seriousness of topic or attitude toward it.

Approaching an Informal Essay Actively

At this point, perhaps some clarification can be gained by looking at an essay. Read the essay that follows and try to assess it in terms of:

- the seriousness of its subject,
- its attitude toward that subject,
- its structure,
- any other text strategies that you may notice.

1517

Alice Walker   b. 1944

Am I Blue?   *1988*

"Ain't these tears in these eyes tellin' you?"

For about three years my companion and I rented a small house in the country that stood on the edge of a large meadow that appeared to run from the end of our deck straight into the mountains. The mountains, however, were quite far away, and between us and them there was, in fact, a town. It was one of the many pleasant aspects of the house that you never really were aware of this.

It was a house of many windows, low, wide, nearly floor to ceiling in the living room, which faced the meadow, and it was from one of these that I first saw our closest neighbor, a large white horse, cropping grass, flipping its mane, and ambling about—not over the entire meadow, which stretched well out of sight of the house, but over the five or so fenced-in acres that were next to the twenty-odd that we had rented. I soon learned that the horse, whose name was Blue, belonged to a man who lived in another town, but was boarded by our neighbors next door. Occasionally, one of the children, usually a stocky teen-ager, but sometimes a much younger girl or boy, could be seen riding Blue. They would appear in the meadow, climb up on his back, ride furiously for ten or fifteen minutes, then get off, slap Blue on the flanks, and not be seen again for a month or more.

There were many apple trees in our yard, and one by the fence that Blue could almost reach. We were soon in the habit of feeding him apples, which he relished, especially because by the middle of summer the meadow grasses—so green and succulent since January—had dried out from lack of rain, and Blue stumbled about munching the dried stalks half-heartedly. Sometimes he would stand very still just by the apple tree, and when one of us came out he would whinny, snort loudly, or stamp the ground. This meant, of course: I want an apple.

It was quite wonderful to pick a few apples, or collect those that had fallen to the ground overnight, and patiently hold them, one by one, up to his large, toothy mouth. I remained as thrilled as a child by his flexible dark lips, huge, cubelike teeth that crunched the apples, core and all, with such finality, and his high, broad-breasted *enormity*; beside which, I felt small indeed. When I was a child, I used to ride horses, and was especially friendly with one named Nan until the day I was riding and my brother deliberately spooked her and I was thrown, head first, against the trunk of a tree. When I came to, I was in bed and my mother was bending worriedly over me; we silently agreed that perhaps horseback riding was not the safest sport for me. Since then I have walked, and prefer walking to horseback riding—but I had forgotten the depth of feeling one could see in horses' eyes.

I was therefore unprepared for the expression in Blue's. Blue was lonely.   5
Blue was horribly lonely and bored. I was not shocked that this should be the case; five acres to tramp by yourself, endlessly, even in the most beautiful of meadows—and his was—cannot provide many interesting events, and once

rainy season turned to dry that was about it. No, I was shocked that I had forgotten that human animals and nonhuman animals can communicate quite well; if we are brought up around animals as children we take this for granted. By the time we are adults we no longer remember. However, the animals have not changed. They are in fact *completed* creatures (at least they seem to be, so much more than we) who are not likely *to* change; it is their nature to express themselves. What else are they going to express? And they do. And, generally speaking, they are ignored.

After giving Blue the apples, I would wander back to the house, aware that he was observing me. Were more apples not forthcoming then? Was that to be his sole entertainment for the day? My partner's small son had decided he wanted to learn how to piece a quilt; we worked in silence on our respective squares as I thought....

Well, about slavery: about white children, who were raised by black people, who knew their first all-accepting love from black women, and then, when they were twelve or so, were told they must "forget" the deep levels of communication between themselves and "mammy" that they knew. Later they would be able to relate quite calmly, "My old mammy was sold to another good family." "My old mammy was _____." Fill in the blank. Many more years later a white woman would say: "I can't understand these Negroes, these blacks. What do they want? They're so different from us."

And about the Indians, considered to be "like animals" by the "settlers" (a very benign euphemism for what they actually were), who did not understand their description as a compliment.

And about the thousands of American men who marry Japanese, Korean, Filipina, and other non-English-speaking women and of how happy they report they are, "*blissfully,*" until their brides learn to speak English, at which point the marriages tend to fall apart. What then did the men see, when they looked into the eyes of the women they married, before they could speak English? Apparently only their own reflections.

I thought of society's impatience with the young. "Why are they playing the music so loud?" Perhaps the children have listened to much of the music of oppressed people their parents danced to before they were born, with its passionate but soft cries for acceptance and love, and they have wondered why their parents failed to hear.   10

I do not know how long Blue had inhabited his five beautiful, boring acres before we moved into our house; a year after we had arrived—and had also traveled to other valleys, other cities, other worlds—he was still there.

But then, in our second year at the house, something happened in Blue's life. One morning, looking out the window at the fog that lay like a ribbon over the meadow, I saw another horse, a brown one, at the other end of Blue's field. Blue appeared to be afraid of it, and for several days made no attempt to go near. We went away for a week. When we returned, Blue had decided to make friends and the two horses ambled or galloped along together, and Blue did not come nearly as often to the fence underneath the apple tree.

When he did, bringing his new friend with him, there was a different look in his eyes. A look of independence, of self-possession, of inalienable *horse-ness*. His friend eventually became pregnant. For months and months there was, it seemed to me, a mutual feeling between me and the horses of justice, of peace. I fed apples to them both. The look in Blue's eyes was one of unabashed "this is *it*ness."

It did not, however, last forever. One day, after a visit to the city, I went out to give Blue some apples. He stood waiting, or so I thought, though not beneath the tree. When I shook the tree and jumped back from the shower of apples, he made no move. I carried some over to him. He managed to half-crunch one. The rest he let fall to the ground. I dreaded looking into his eyes—because I had of course noticed that Brown, his partner, had gone—but I did look. If I had been born into slavery, and my partner had been sold or killed, my eyes would have looked like that. The children next door explained that Blue's partner had been "put with him" (the same expression that old people used, I had noticed, when speaking of an ancestor during slavery who had been impregnated by her owner) so that they could mate and she conceive. Since that was accomplished, she had been taken back by her owner, who lived somewhere else.

Will she be back? I asked.

They didn't know.   15

Blue was like a crazed person. Blue *was*, to me, a crazed person. He galloped furiously, as if he were being ridden, around and around his five beautiful acres. He whinnied until he couldn't. He tore at the ground with his hooves. He butted himself against his single shade tree. He looked always and always toward the road down which his partner had gone. And then, occasionally, when he came up for apples, or I took apples to him, he looked at me. It was a look so piercing, so full of grief, so *human*, I almost laughed (I felt too sad to cry) to think there are people who do not know that animals suffer. People like me who have forgotten, and daily forget all that animals try to tell us. "Everything you do to us will happen to you; we are your teachers, as you are ours. We are one lesson" is essentially it, I think. There are those who never once have even considered animals' rights: those who have been taught that animals actually want to be used and abused by us, as small children "love" to be frightened, or women "love" to be mutilated and raped.... They are the great-grandchildren of those who honestly thought, because someone taught them this: "Women can't think," and "niggers can't faint." But most disturbing of all, in Blue's large brown eyes was a new look, more painful than the look of despair: the look of disgust with human beings, with life; the look of hatred. And it was odd what the look of hatred did. It gave him, for the first time, the look of a beast. And what that meant was that he had put up a barrier within to protect himself from further violence; all the apples in the world wouldn't change that fact.

And so Blue remained, a beautiful part of our landscape, very peaceful to look at from the window, white against the grass. Once a friend came to visit and said, looking out on the soothing view: "And it *would* have to be a *white* horse; the very image of freedom." And I thought, yes, the animals are forced to become for us merely "images" of what they once so beautifully expressed. And we are used to drinking milk from containers showing "contented" cows, whose real lives we want to hear nothing about, eating eggs and drumsticks from "happy" hens, and munching hamburgers advertised by bulls of integrity who seem to command their fate.

As we talked of freedom and justice one day for all, we sat down to steaks. I am eating misery, I thought, as I took the first bite. And spit it out.

Text Strategies of "Am I Blue?"

Subject   What is the subject of "Am I Blue?" Perhaps before you decide on the seriousness of it, you have to decide on what the subject is. Several possibilities, which do not have to be considered mutually exclusive, seem likely here: Walker's relationship with the horse, Blue; sensitivity toward animals in general; animal rights; concern for any beings, human or animal, subject to oppression because of their relative powerlessness. Perhaps you could name other or different subjects. In any case, the possible subjects I listed here all seem serious in themselves, so if you decide that any one or more of those is the topic of concern in this essay, "Am I Blue?" might be considered a formal essay on the basis of this text strategy.

Attitude Toward its Subject   It is possible that such serious subjects as those proposed above could be treated lightly. However, as you read "Am I Blue?" do you detect a light or humorous tone? At one point, the voice does say "I almost laughed" when she looked into Blue's eyes after Brown had been taken away, but that statement is immediately qualified by the parenthetical remark that "I felt too sad to cry." I will suppose that the tone seems to you, as it does to me, to be serious; this essay does seem to want its audience to think carefully about its subject, whatever that subject may be. In terms of this text strategy too, "Am I Blue?" could be considered a formal essay.

Structure   If the subject of "Am I Blue?" is any of those listed as possibilities above (with the possible exception of Walker's relationship to the horse), when, in reading the text, do you decide what that is? I think I can safely answer my own question by saying it is *not* in the first or second paragraph, or even in the first fourth of the essay. The fifth paragraph does mention the idea that "human animals and nonhuman animals can communicate quite well" and perhaps implies that the kind of communication the voice has in mind is emotionally deep, but the next paragraph returns to an account of something else the writer did after observing the loneliness in Blue's eyes.

In fact, as you may have noticed on your own, the structure of the entire essay is mainly narrative; it is constructed much like a short story, recounting an episode from the past and telling it in a chronological sequence. Something like a climax in this narrative is reached in paragraphs 14 to 16, when it is learned that Blue's partner has been taken away and probably will not return. The seventeenth paragraph continues the narrative in terms of Blue's reactions to his absent partner, but it also diverges from narrative for the voice to make some statements about the relationship of animals to humans. The next-to-last paragraph seems constructed the same way, and the very last paragraph returns to the narrative mode, recounting briefly another "event" in the overall story of the writer's relationship with Blue.

My point in tracing this structure is to say that this text strategy is the major way in which "Am I Blue?" differs from a formal essay. The story of the writer's relationship with Blue seems at least as important as anything else the text has to say. That story provides the structure for the essay, which is not structured by an immediate or early statement about the essay's subject. If you compare "Am I Blue?" to either *The Declaration of Independence* or "Unchopping a Tree" on this point, the difference in structure should be evident.

> **CONNECT:** George Orwell's "Shooting an Elephant," in the Essays for Further Reading, page 1605, also recounts an episode from the writer's experience, an encounter with an animal, in order to make a point. What similarities or differences in text strategies do you see in these two essays?

Other Text Strategies   What other text strategies, of whatever sort, did you notice in "Am I Blue?" The above discussion of structure may have suggested, if you didn't already identify it, that narrative is a text strategy here, one that at least this essay shares with the genre of fiction. So while we're on the subject of text strategies that informal essays might share with other genres, use the space below (or a page in your journal or notebook) to list other text strategies in "Am I Blue?" that might also appear in short stories, poems, or plays. These may be ones you noticed when you first read the text, or they may be ones that occur to you now that I've asked you to think about them.

> **LITERARY TEXT STRATEGIES IN "AM I BLUE?"**
> 1.
> 2.
> 3.
> 4.
> 5.
> 6.

You may have listed setting, character, and symbol, all of which this text has in common with short stories. Setting is involved in the locality in time and space of the events recounted in the narrative—the meadow, the seasons, the view of the meadow from Walker's house. Character or characters are involved in the form of Blue and to a lesser extent Brown, both of whom you might consider personified. Perhaps you see Walker's "I" as a character too. At any rate, she interacts dramatically with Blue; we "see" her feeding him, admiring him, responding to him. Symbol is involved, again through Blue, or Walker's view of Blue. Perhaps you saw Walker seeing Blue as a symbol of oppressed beings, human or animal. Or perhaps you noticed Walker's friend's observation that as a white horse, Blue is "the very image of freedom."*

In addition to those "literary" text strategies, consider the digression from the story of Blue in the seventh through tenth paragraphs. This portion of the text recounts Walker's thoughts as she and her companions work on piecing a quilt. None of these thoughts is about Blue or horses in general, and none of those paragraphs even mentions Blue. As you read, you may have wondered why those paragraphs were even there at all, so unrelated they may at first seem. However, you may later have seen a connection between Walker's thoughts about slavery, Indians, and so forth and her feelings for Blue when you read the fourteenth and seventeenth paragraphs, where those things Walker had earlier been thinking of—especially slavery—and Blue are brought together.

Are there rhetorical strategies in "Am I Blue?" The discussion of formal essays in the preceding chapter considered overall structure, sentence structure, and diction as rhetorical strategies—all geared to convince an audience of the truth of a proposition or to adopt the same attitude toward its subject as the text seems to have. Rather than jump to a conclusion about whether or not informal essays are or may be rhetorical, perhaps we should take a look at "Am I Blue?" in this way and see what we find.

Rhetorical Strategies and Indeterminacy

If you look at the overall structure of this essay, does it seem to be organized in such a way as to reinforce a main idea that it wants you to believe? It is not organized in the tight, easy-to-outline structure that *The Declaration of Independence* is. Instead it seems to illustrate well the loose or casual structure of informal essays in general. But could it be that the narrative structure itself is rhetorical? That structure, if you recall from Chapter 5, is usually to introduce a situation involving a character or characters, complicate it with some kind of conflict, and allow suspense to build as the plot moves toward a climax, wherein the conflict is resolved in some way. When that general structure is used in an essay, which has an interest in some idea, perhaps it is rhetorical.

In "Am I Blue?" the initial situation involves Walker's relationship with Blue; the situation is complicated by Blue's getting then losing a mate, Brown; and that conflict seems to be resolved in Blue's becoming disgusted toward and hateful of humans. That, in turn, seems to lead to another climax in Walker's life when she spits out the bite of steak, apparently realizing—though not explicitly stating—that to eat meat is to engage in the exploitation of animals that she deplored with Blue and saw as analogous to the exploitation of supposedly "inferior" races or classes of people. Because the narrative is presented in "first person" (another text strategy) it may be that you were

---

*In this regard, the 1993 film *Into the West,* directed by Mike Newell and starring Gabriel Byrne and Ellen Barkin, also uses the text strategy of a white horse, which may be read as an image of freedom there too. For me, as perhaps for any of you who may have seen this film, *Into the West* and "Am I Blue?" are intertextual with respect to this symbol.

emotionally drawn to the narrator, feeling what she feels in her relationship with Blue. If so, feeling may get so close to belief as to substitute for it, and you may wind up "agreeing" with an implicit proposition in "Am I Blue?"—something to the effect that eating meat is the same kind of cruel exploitation of animals that Walker deplored in the disregard for or ignorance of Blue's feelings when his mate was taken away from him.

What about sentence structure and diction? The first seems pretty easy to rule out as a rhetorical strategy here. The text does not use the repetition of parallel grammatical structure to drive home a point the way that *The Declaration of Independence* does, nor does it use second-person grammatical constructions or passive-voice constructions to work on your attitude the way "Unchopping a Tree" does. The sentences seem constructed primarily to tell the story of Walker's relationship with Blue. Similarly, word choice seems more nearly to serve the narrative, with its enclosed descriptions, than to produce a calculated effect on the reader. But then you may have noticed strategies such as the words "contented" and "happy" being placed in quotes in the next-to-last paragraph, saying, in effect, that those words are misapplied to dairy cows and mass-production chickens, and thus conveying an attitude.

To see rhetorical strategies at work, however, you have to be able to identify a proposition, a belief from the ideology of the text, that you are being asked to accept as true. In "Am I Blue?" this proposition or belief seems hard to determine. Unlike *The Declaration of Independence,* "Am I Blue?" does not state any such proposition explicitly near the beginning, and unlike "Unchopping a Tree," it does not suggest a proposition implicitly through a consistent tone from beginning to end. As a narrative, "Am I Blue?" seems more nearly to explore a topic rather than present a preconceived attitude toward a topic.

And for that matter, what topic or idea is "Am I Blue?" primarily concerned with? Earlier, we tried to identify its topic, and I named a few different possibilities—Walker's relationship with Blue; sensitivity toward animals in general; animal rights; concern for any beings, human or animal, subject to oppression because of their relative powerlessness. But concern with a topic is not the same thing as holding a belief to be true and trying to persuade a reader that it is true. In its exploratory style, the text seems to ruminate about slavery, Indians, and so forth, for instance, rather than making very definite assertions about them. In paragraphs 7 to 10, when those ideas are first mentioned, the voice's thoughts about them seem inconclusive, and the connection between what she thinks about those topics and what she thinks about Blue, although it is made, is not made explicit in terms of something like a truth that the essay tries to get you to believe.

Aside from those topics, the essay may be about "I" as much as anything else; Walker's personal responses to Blue's situation occupy much of the discourse, and if the text is trying to get you to believe that Walker feels or felt a certain way about Blue, animals, and the oppressed, that's not quite the kind of proposition that can be argued or put forward rhetorically; it's a lot more subjective than that.

The same thing seems the case if you read the essay as an account of how Walker became a vegetarian: You can accept that that happened, how it happened, why it happened, but to do that is not the same thing as to believe a proposition that is put forward rhetorically.

The likeliest conclusion about rhetorical strategies in "Am I Blue?" is that they are **indeterminate**; they constitute or may be seen as a gap in the text. If you enforce some distance from this text, you may be able to see some of its text strategies as rhetorical, but their status as such seems much less certain than do some of the text strategies in the formal essays we looked at in Chapter 25. This degree of indeterminacy is in keeping with the lack of clear-cut certainties about informal essays in general that we considered at the beginning of this chapter.

Reading Strategies for Informal Essays

Despite the indeterminacy of rhetorical strategies in an informal essay, you can still apply the same reading strategies that were suggested for a formal essay in Chapter 25. To consider rhetoric a gap in a text is still to decide something about it, as the fifth of the reading strategies listed earlier said. In addition to those, the "practical" and the "creative" strategies discussed in Chapter 25 may be applied to informal essays just as well as to formal ones. In fact, the "creative" strategies should be even more appropriate given the informal essay's closer resemblance to literary texts in the other genres.

Rather than cover that ground again here, I will just mention one other "creative" reading strategy that seems more applicable to informal than to formal essays: creating theme. Actually, this reading strategy has already been considered (though I did not name it *per se*) in the discussion of text strategies in "Am I Blue?" Because the topic or subject of this essay or any informal essay is not as clear-cut as it is with a formal essay, a reader has more room to create a theme, which might be defined as a combination of attitude and subject, while reading an informal essay.

When you read "Am I Blue?" what did you tentatively decide it was about—the particular horse Blue, horses in general, Walker's relationship to Blue, Walker's relationship to animals in general, Walker herself, Walker's feelings for the oppressed of both animal and human species, or something else altogether? Whatever the case, you should know by now that this interpretation was produced as much by you and what you brought to the text as it was by the text and what it brought to you. In addition to reading strategies, you brought your ideology of attitudes, values, and beliefs to the interaction with the text, and that ideology played a part in your decision as to what the text is about.

Personal Values and Reading

Consider just for a moment how your ideology interacts with the text's through the text strategy of a horse as a "character" in "Am I Blue?" What values, especially, does your ideology hold where horses are concerned? Do you consider them "peaceful," "free," "intelligent," "beautiful," "sensitive," "expressive," or in other approving terms? If so, I would guess that you probably had a generally harmonious ideological interaction with the text, because the voice that speaks to the audience in the essay seems to hold values like those where horses are concerned and to assume them on the part of its audience. The voice *confirms* those values in certain readers. How might your ideology be differently engaged if the animal "character" were a pig, a snake, a spider, a bear, a toad, or a shark? Or what if your ideology regards horses as "stubborn," "stupid," "unimaginative," "high-strung," "dangerous," "servile," or other such negative terms? In that case, do you experience a clashing ideological interaction with the text concerning what the horse stands for? Perhaps the text challenges certain values in some readers.

> CONNECT: D. H. Lawrence's poem "Snake," in the Poems for Further Reading, page 720, deals with an animal "character" that comes burdened with negative cultural connotations. That poem may also be read as rhetorical because of the speaker's discussion of his own culturally influenced attitudes toward the snake.

Similarly, what does your ideology hold concerning such groups of people as African Americans, Native Americans, or Asian women? Do you see them as "oppressed?" What about "American men who marry [Asian women]"? Do you see them as oppress*ing*? Or, just to swing things around to another perspective, do you see those groups of people (or animals) as not really oppressed or victimized at all? Do you see "American men who marry [Asian women]" or American men in general or white Americans as, in effect, victims of guilt laid on them for supposedly oppressing minority groups? And what does your ideology hold with respect to eating or not eating meat? Have you made a conscious dietary decision about that?

Your situation with regard to questions like these, which seem to be implicitly raised by this text, will affect the kind of ideological interaction you have with it. And you may be able to do a strong reading of "Am I Blue?" whether the interaction of ideologies you experience in reading it is harmonious or clashing, as long as you are aware of the values and experiences you bring to it and the role of those values and experiences in your response.

Reading and Responding: An Informal Essay

Read the essay below. Then write a response statement, using the questions that follow the text.

Rosario Morales   b. 1920

I Am What I Am   *1983*

I am what I am and I am U.S. American   I haven't wanted to say it because if I did you'd take away the Puerto Rican but now I say go to hell   I am what I am and you can't take it away with all the words and sneers at your command   I am what I am   I am Puerto Rican   I am U.S. American   I am New

York Manhattan and the Bronx   I am what I am I'm not hiding under no stoop   behind no curtain   I am what I am   I am Boricua[1] as boricuas come from the isle of Manhattan and I croon Carlos Gardel tangoes in my sleep and Afro-Cuban beats in my blood and Xavier Cugat's lukewarm latin is so familiar and dear   sneer dear but he's familiar and dear but not Carmen Miranda who's a joke because I never was a joke   I was a bit of a sensation   See! here's a real true honest-to-god Puerto Rican girl and she's in college   Hey! Mary come here and look she's from right here   a South Bronx girl and she's honest-to-god in college now   Ain't that something   who would believe it Ain't science wonderful or some such thing a wonder a wonder

And someone who did languages for a living stopped me in the subway because how I spoke was a linguist's treat   I mean there it was yiddish and spanish and fine refined college educated english and irish which I mainly keep in my prayers   It's dusty now   I haven't said my prayers in decades but try my Hail Marrrry full of grrrace with the nun's burr with the nun's disdain its all true and its all me   do you know I got an English accent from the BBC I always say   For years in the mountains of Puerto Rico when I was 22 and 24 and 26   all those young years   I listened to the BBC and Radio Moscow's English   english announcers announce and denounce and then I read Dickens all the way thru three or four times at least and then later I read Dickens aloud in voices and when I came back to the U.S. I spoke mockdickens and mockBritish especially when I want to be crisp efficient I know what I am doing and you can't scare me   tough   that's why I am what I am and I'm a bit of a snob too

Shit! why am I calling myself names   I really really dig the funny way the British speak   and it's real it's true   and I love too the singing of yiddish sentences that go with shrugs and hands and arms doing melancholy or lively dances   I love the sound and look of yiddish in the air   in the body   in the streets   in the English language   nooo[2] so what's new   so go by the grocer and buy some fruit   oye vey   gevalt   gefilte fish   raisele oh and those words hundreds of them dotting the english language like raisins in the bread shnook   and schlemiel   suftik   tush   schmata   all those soft sweet Jewish-American wasp is foreign and new but Jewish-American is old show familiar schmata familiar and its me dears its me bagels   blintzes and all   I am what I am   Take it or leave me alone.

Response Statement Questions

- How would you describe the voice or tone here? What text strategies contribute to making voice or tone what it is in this essay?
- What reading strategies did you use in processing this text? To what extent did they contribute to your sense of the voice speaking in the text or to the idea(s) the text seems to be concerned with? How active were you in creating theme as you read this text?

---

[1]Boricua—real Puerto Rican
[2]nooo—so? well?; oye vey—oh, dear!; gevalt—expression of anguish; gefilte fish—fish cake; raisele—raisins; shnook—goof-up; schlemiel—bumbler; suftik—plump; tush—butt; schmata—rag, as in clothes

- What idea(s) does this text seem to be concerned with? Is there a difference between its explicit concerns and any that may be implicit?
- What kind of ideological interaction did you experience in reading this text? What values of yours did the text confirm or challenge? How did your own ethnicity or nationality affect your response?
- *Share and Compare*   What different decisions as to theme were made by different readers in your class or reading group as they read "I Am What I Am"? What accounts for these differences, in terms of the readers and the text?

Reading "I Am What I Am" Actively

Constructing Voice or Tone   Voice seems prominent in this essay because of the title phrase, which is repeated numerous times throughout. How did you describe voice and tone in your response statement? Perhaps you used words such as "proud," "self-confident," "aggressive," "unapologetic," "brash," "enthusiastic," "irreverent," or "playful." (Or maybe those are only my words.) At any rate, such text strategies as the repeated "I" and statements like "go to hell," "I'm not hiding under no stoop," and "I know what I'm doing and you can't scare me" seem to contribute to a voice or tone that may be described in words such as those just listed.

Perhaps also you emphasized the text strategy of "bad grammar" as indicated by the double negative in one of the phrases quoted above; the use of "ain't"; the occasional misspellings ("thru" and "its" for the contraction of "it is"); and the uncapitalized proper nouns "yiddish," "spanish," "english," and "irish." If so, did that help you construct tone in any terms similar to those I listed above? Or did you think of the voice as "ignorant," "illiterate," or "lower-class"?

What about the lack of punctuation throughout? That's a text strategy, isn't it? How did that contribute to your sense of voice or tone here? Did it affect the reading strategies you used? Did it force you to abandon your usual way of reading an essay, and if so were you able to fall back on some other strategy from your literary experience? The strategy of reading aloud (from Chapter 10 on Reading Poetry) may be helpful in this case. Or maybe you found yourself "poeticizing" this text: reading it more or less as a poem, even though it is written in prose; that's another reading strategy discussed in the section of this book on Reading Poetry. On the other hand, perhaps you found that unconventional text strategy frustrating, making reading this essay difficult. If so, did whatever difficulty you had reflect negatively on the voice or the author? (What kind of grade do you think this essay would get in school?)

Creating Theme   Did the unconventional text strategies of this essay help you create a theme as you read, or did they render that reading strategy useless for you? Two options here would seem to be (1) to find the unconventional text strategies to obscure any ideas the text may be concerned with or (2) to decide that those text strategies were the ideas, or one idea at any rate. In the latter way of reading, you may decide that the essay is concerned with the writer's unique or individualistic identity. It does seem plain from the repetition of the title phrase that the essay is concerned with the writer's identity, so maybe the violation of some of the usual essay conventions indicates the writer's sense that her identity is unique.

If she seems pleased with or proud of this uniqueness, you may be led back to the question of voice or tone in this essay. Or you may be led to the question of explicit versus implicit ideas here: Perhaps the explicit concern is with the writer's ethnic or national or personal identity, and the implicit concern is with her individuality within—or across—any of those categories.

Interacting Ideologically   It seems to me that this deceptively simple text is really quite complex in terms of how it might interact with readers' ideologies. That is, it may appear to be a kind of stream-of-consciousness or associative rant about the writer's identity, hardly worthy of the name "essay." Maybe that's how you responded to it. If you did, however, that response should afford you a good opportunity to begin to analyze the ideological issues involved in the essay's unconventionality.

The same would be true if, as suggested above, you constructed the voice here as "ignorant," "illiterate," or "lower-class" because usually in American culture those terms involve value judgments; they are not merely descriptive. Either of these responses seems related to the value you place on correct usage and grammar in writing—or in public nonfiction prose, at any rate—and that is a matter of ideology. To the extent that you emphasized these unconventional or "incorrect" text strategies as you read "I Am What I Am," you may also have de-emphasized or resisted seeing other signs of education, intelligence, and linguistic and cultural sophistication on the part of the voice in this text. Or maybe you did emphasize those qualities of the voice here, and so de-emphasized or downplayed the unconventional or "incorrect" strategies of the text. Either of these responses suggests that grammatical correctness and punctuational conventionality in essay writing are not merely matters of text strategies but may also indicate a site of struggle where competition between ideologies reveals itself or may be detected by an active reader.

Your own situation with respect to ethnicity or nationality may have affected your response to this text as well. Ethnicity and nationality seem to be part of the subject with which this essay is concerned and to have a visible place in the writer's ideology. The last decade or so in the United States has been a time in which multiculturalism has been debated widely, from newspaper columns and letters to the editor to school boards and in academic journals. It's a complex issue, so we should beware of oversimplification, but one of the central questions in the debate is the extent to which ethnic or newly immigrated Americans should hold on to their cultural identity as Latinos, Africans, Asians, and so on, or whether they should assimilate with and identify themselves as just "Americans" with no hyphenated prefix. Put in figurative terms, the question is whether the United States is a "melting pot," as it has so long been regarded, or if some other metaphor is more accurate—perhaps a "patchwork quilt" or a "rainbow" or a "kaleidoscope." Your opinion on this question or your own sense of identity as "American" or "ethnic-American" likely contributes to whether "I Am What I Am" confirms or challenges your ideology. What attitude toward cultural assimilation or ethnic identity do you see on the part of the voice in this essay, and how close to or distant from your own attitude is it? Looking into your ideological interaction with the text on this point may prove very fruitful for an informal cultural analysis essay of your own.

CONNECT: The poems "An Introduction" by Kamala Das in Chapter 12 and "I Am a Black Woman" by Mari Evans and "I Am" by Nazik al-Mala'ika, both in the Poems for Further Reading, may be seen as intertextual with "I Am What I Am" because all four texts establish unique voices who insist upon their own identities.

An Essay For Exploration

Ved Mehta   b. 1934

Pom's Engagement   1984

Before we moved to Lahore, Daddyji had gone to Mussoorie, a hill station in the United Provinces, without telling us why he was going out of the Punjab. Now, several months after he made that trip, he gathered us around him in the drawing room at 11 Temple Road while Mamaji mysteriously hurried Sister Pom upstairs. He started talking as if we were all very small and he were conducting one of our "dinner-table-school" discussions. He said that by right and tradition the oldest daughter had to be given in marriage first, and that the ripe age for marriage was nineteen. He said that when a girl approached that age her parents, who had to take the initiative, made many inquiries and followed many leads. They investigated each young man and his family background, his relatives, his friends, his classmates, because it was important to know what kind of family the girl would be marrying into, what kind of company she would be expected to keep. If the girl's parents decided that a particular young man was suitable, then his people also had to make their investigations, but, however favorable their findings, their decision was unpredictable, because good, well-settled boys were in great demand and could afford to be choosy. All this took a lot of time. "That's why I said nothing to you children about why I went to Mussoorie," he concluded. "I went to see a young man for Pom. She's already nineteen."

We were stunned. We have never really faced the idea that Sister Pom might get married and suddenly leave, I thought.

"We won't lose Pom, we'll get a new family member," Daddyji said, as if reading my thoughts.

Then all of us started talking at once. We wanted to know if Sister Pom had been told; if she'd agreed; whom she'd be marrying.

"Your mother has just taken Pom up to tell her," Daddyji said. "But she's a   5
good girl. She will agree." He added, "The young man in question is twenty-
eight years old. He's a dentist, and so has a profession."

"Did you get a dentist because Sister Pom has bad teeth?" Usha asked. Sister Pom had always been held up to us as an example of someone who, as a
child, had spurned greens and had therefore grown up with a mouthful of
poor teeth.

Daddyji laughed. "I confess I didn't think of anyone's teeth when I chose
the young man in question."

"What is he like?" I asked. "What are we to call him?"

"He's a little bit on the short side, but he has a happy-go-lucky nature, like
Nimi's. He doesn't drink, but, unfortunately, he does smoke. His father died at
an early age of a heart attack, but he has a nice mother, who will not give Pom
any trouble. It seems that everyone calls him Kakaji."

We all laughed. Kakaji, or "youngster," was what very small boys were   10
called.

"That's what he must have been called when he was small, and the name
stuck," Daddyji said.

In spite of myself, I pictured a boy smaller than I was and imagined him
taking Sister Pom away, and then I imagined her having to keep his pocket
money, to arrange his clothes in the cupboards, to comb his hair. My mouth
felt dry.

"What will Kakaji call Sister Pom?" I asked.

"Pom, silly—what else?" Sister Umi said.

Mamaji and Sister Pom walked into the room. Daddyji made a place for Sis-   15
ter Pom next to him and said, "Now, now, now, no reason to cry. Is it to be yes?"

"Whatever you say," Sister Pom said in a small voice, between sobs.

"Pom, how can you say that? You've never seen him," Sister Umi said.

"Kakaji's uncle, Dr. Prakash Mehrotra, himself a dentist, has known our
family from his student days in Lahore," Daddyji said. "As a student dentist, he
used to be welcomed in Babuji's Shahalmi Gate house. He would come and
go as he pleased. He has known for a long time what kind of people we are.
He remembered seeing you, Pom, when we went to Mussoorie on holiday. He
said yes immediately, and his approval seemed to be enough for Kakaji."

"You promised me you wouldn't cry again," Mamaji said to Sister Pom,
patting her on the back, and then, to Daddyji, "She's agreed."

Daddyji said much else, sometimes talking just for the sake of talking,   20
sometimes laughing at us because we were sniffling, and all the time trying to
make us believe that this was a happy occasion. First, Sister Umi took issue
with him: parents had no business arranging marriages; if she were Pom she
would run away. Then Sister Nimi: all her life she had heard him say to us
children, "Think for yourself—be independent," and here he was not allowing
Pom to think for herself. Brother Om took Daddyji's part: girls who didn't get
married became a burden on their parents, and Daddyji had four daughters to
marry off, and would be retiring in a few years. Sisters Nimi and Umi retorted:
they hadn't gone to college to get married off, to have some young man following them around like a leech. Daddyji just laughed. I thought he was so
wise, and right.

"Go and bless your big sister," Mamaji said, pushing me in the direction of Sister Pom.

"I don't want to," I said. "I don't know him."

"What'll happen to Sister Pom's room?" Usha asked. She and Ashok didn't have rooms of their own. They slept in Mamaji's room.

"Pom's room will remain empty, so that any time she likes she can come and stay in her room with Kakaji," Daddyji said.

The thought that a man I never met would sleep in Pom's room with Sister Pom there made my heart race. A sob shook me. I ran outside.   25

The whole house seemed to be in an uproar. Mamaji was shouting at Gian Chand, Gian Chand was shouting at the bearer, the bearer was shouting at the sweeper. There were the sounds of the kitchen fire being stoked, of the drain being washed out, of water running in bathrooms. From behind whichever door I passed came the rustle of saris, salwars, and kemises. The house smelled of fresh flowers, but it had a ghostly chill. I would climb to the landing of Sister Pom's room and thump down the stairs two at a time. Brother Om would shout up at me, "Stop it!" Sister Umi would shout down at me, "Don't you have anything better to do?" Sister Nimi would call to me from somewhere, "You're giving Pom a headache." I wouldn't heed any of them. As soon as I had thumped down, I would clatter to the top and thump my way down again.

Daddyji went past on the back veranda. "Who's coming with Kakaji?" I asked. Kakaji was in Lahore to buy some dental equipment, and in a few minutes he was expected for tea, to meet Sister Pom and the family.

"He's coming alone," Daddyji said, over his shoulder. "He's come from very far away." I had somehow imagined that Kakaji would come with at least as many people as we had in our family, because I had started thinking of the tea as a kind of cricket match—the elevens facing off.

I followed Daddyji into the drawing room. "Will he come alone for his wedding, too?"

"No. Then he'll come with the bridegroom's party."   30

We were joined by everyone except Mamaji and Sister Pom, who from the moment we got the news of Sister Pom's marriage had become inseparable.

Gian Chand came in, the tea things rattling on his tray.

Later, I couldn't remember exactly how Kakaji had arrived, but I remember noticing that his footfall was heavy, that his greeting was affectionate, and that his voice seemed to float up with laughter. I don't know what I'd expected, but I imagined that if I had been in his place I would have skulked in the *gulli,* and perhaps changed my mind and not entered at all.

"Better to have ventured and lost than never to have ventured at all," Daddyji was saying to Kakaji about life's battles.

"Yes, Daddyji, just so," he said, with a little laugh. I had never heard anybody outside our family call my father Daddyji. It sounded odd.   35

Sister Pom was sent for, and she came in with Mamaji. Her footsteps were shy, and the rustle of her sari around her feet was slow, as if she felt too conscious of the noise she was making just in walking. Daddyji made some complimentary remark about the silver border on her sari, and told her to sit next to Kakaji. Kakaji and Sister Pom exchanged a few words about a family group photograph on the mantelpiece, and about her studies. There was the clink of china as Sister Pom served Kakaji tea.

"Won't you have some tea yourself?" Kakaji asked Sister Pom.

Sister Pom's sari rustled over her shoulder as she turned to Daddyji.

"Kakaji, none of my children have ever tasted tea or coffee," Daddyji said. "We consider both to be bad habits. My children have been brought up on hot milk, and lately Pom has been taking a little ghi in her milk at bedtime, for health reasons."

We all protested at Daddyji's broadcasting family matters.   40

Kakaji tactfully turned the conversation to a visit to Mussoorie that our family was planning.

Mamaji offered him onion, potato, and cauliflower pakoras. He accepted, remarking how hot and crisp they were.

"Where will Sister Pom live?" Usha asked.

"In the summer, my practice is in Mussoorie," Kakaji said, "but in the winter it's in Dehra Dun."

It struck me for the first time that after Sister Pom got married people we   45 didn't know, people she didn't know, would become more important to her than we were.

Kakaji had left without formally committing himself. Then, four days later, when we were all sitting in the drawing room, a servant brought a letter to Mamaji. She told us that it was from Kakaji's mother, and that it asked if Sister Pom might be engaged to Kakaji. "She even wants to know if Pom can be married in April or May," Mamaji said excitedly. "How propitious! That'll be the fifth wedding in the family in those two months." Cousins Prakash and Dev, Cousin Pushpa (Bhaji Ganga Ram's adopted daughter), and Auntie Vimla were all due to be married in Lahore then.

"You still have time to change your mind," Daddyji said to Sister Pom. "What do you really think of him?"

Sister Pom wouldn't say anything.

"How do you expect her to know what her mind is when all that the two talked about was a picture and her bachelor's exam in May?" Sister Umi demanded. "Could she have fallen in love already?"

"Love, Umi, means something very different from 'falling in love,'" Dad-   50 dyji said. "It's not an act but a lifelong process. The best we can do as Pom's parents is to give her love every opportunity to grow."

"But doesn't your 'every opportunity' include knowing the person better than over a cup of tea, or whatever?" Sister Umi persisted.

"Yes, of course it does. But what we are discussing here is a simple matter of choice—not love," Daddyji said. "To know a person, to love a person, takes years of living together."

"Do you mean, then, that knowing a person and loving a person are the same thing?" Sister Umi asked.

"Not quite, but understanding and respect are essential to love, and that cannot come from talking together, even over a period of days or months. That can come only in good time, through years of experience. It is only when

Pom and Kakaji learn to consider each other's problems as one and the same that they will find love."

"But, Daddyji, look at the risk you're taking, the risk you're making Pom take," Sister Nimi said.

"We are trying to minimize the risk as much as we can by finding Pom a family that is like ours," Daddyji said. "Kakaji is a dentist, I am a doctor. His life and way of thinking will be similar to mine. We are from the same caste, and Kakaji's family originally came from the Punjab. They eat meat and eggs, and they take religion in their stride, and don't pray every day and go to temples, like Brahmans. Kakaji knows how I walk into a club and how I am greeted there. The atmosphere in Pom's new home will be very much the same as the atmosphere here. Now, if I were to give Pom in marriage to a Brahman he'd expect Pom to live as he did. That would really be gambling."

"Then what you're doing is perpetuating the caste system," Sister Nimi said. She was the political rebel in the family. "You seem to presuppose that a Kshatriya should marry only a Kshatriya, that a Brahman should marry only a Brahman. I would just as soon marry a shopkeeper from the Bania caste or an Untouchable, and help to break down caste barriers."

"That day might come," Daddyji said. "But you will admit, Nimi, that by doing that you'd be increasing the odds."

"But for a cause I believe in," Sister Nimi said.

"Yes, but that's a whole other issue," Daddyji said.

"Daddyji, you say that understanding and respect are necessary for love," Sister Umi said. "I don't see why you would respect a person more because you lived with him and shared his problems."

"In our society, we think of understanding and respect as coming only through sacrifice," Daddyji said.

"Then you're advocating the subservience of women," Sister Nimi said. "because it's not Kakaji who will be expected to sacrifice—it's Pom. That's not fair."

"And why do you think that Pom will learn to respect Kakaji because she sacrifices for him?" Sister Umi said, pressing her point.

"No, Umi, it is the other way around," Daddyji said. "It is Kakaji who will respect Pom because she sacrifices for him."

"But that doesn't mean that Pom will respect Kakaji," Sister Umi persisted.

"But if Kakaji is moved by Pom's sacrifices he will show more consideration for her. He will grow to love her. I know in my own case I was moved to the depths to see Shanti suffer so because she was so ill-prepared to be my wife. It took me long enough—too long, I believe—to reach that understanding, perhaps because I had broken away from the old traditions and had given in to Western influences."

"So you admit that Pom will have to suffer for years," Sister Umi said.

"Perhaps," Daddyji said. "But all that time she will be striving for ultimate happiness and love. Those are precious gifts that can only be cultivated in time."

"You haven't told us what this ultimate happiness is," Sister Umi said. "I don't really understand it."

"It is a uniting of ideals and purposes, and a merging of them. This is the tradition of our society, and it is the means we have adopted to make our marriages successful and beautiful. It works because we believe in the goodness

of the individuals going into the marriage and rely on the strength of the sacred bond."

"But my ideal is to be independent," Sister Nimi said. "As you say, 'Think
for yourself.'"

"But often you have to choose among ideals," Daddyji said. "You may
have to choose between being independent and being married."

"But aren't you struck by the fact that all the suffering is going to be on
Pom's part? Shouldn't Kakaji be required to sacrifice for their happiness, too?"
Sister Nimi said, reverting to the old theme.

"There has to be a start," Daddyji said. "Remember, in our tradition it's her   75
life that is joined with his; it is she who will forsake her past to build a new future with him. If both Pom and Kakaji were to be obstinate, were to compete
with each other about who would sacrifice first, who would sacrifice more,
what hope would there be of their ever getting on together, of their ever finding love?"

"Daddyji, you're evading the issue," Sister Nimi said. "Why shouldn't he
take the initiative in this business of sacrifice?"

"He would perhaps be expected to if Pom were working, too, as in the
West, and, though married, leading a whole different life from his. I suppose
more than this I really can't say, and there may be some injustice in our system,
at that. In the West, they go in for romantic love, which is unknown among us.
I'm not sure that that method works any better than our method does."

Then Daddyji said to Sister Pom, "I have done my best. Even after you
marry Kakaji, my responsibility for you will not be over. I will always be there
in the background if you should need me."

"I respect your judgment, Daddyji," Sister Pom said obediently. "I'll do
what you say."

80

Mamaji consulted Shambu Pandit. He compared the horoscopes of Sister
Pom and Kakaji and set the date of the marriage for the eleventh of May....
"That's just three days after she finishes her B.A. finals!" we cried. "When will
she study? You are sacrificing her education to some silly superstition."

But Shambu Pandit would not be budged from the date. "I am only going by
the horoscopes of the couple," he said. "You might as well protest to the stars."

We appealed to Daddyji, but he said that he didn't want to interfere, because such matters were up to Mamaji. That was as much as to say that
Shambu Pandit's date was a settled thing.

I recall that at about that time there was an engagement ceremony. We
all—Daddyji, Mamaji, Sister Pom, many of our Mehta and Mehra relatives—sat
cross-legged on the floor of the front veranda around Shambu Pandit. He recited the Gayatri Mantra, the simple prayer he used to tell us to say before we
went to sleep, and made a thank offering of incense and ghi to a fire in a bra-
zier, much as Mamaji did—behind Daddyji's back—when one of us was going
on a trip or had recovered from a bout of illness. Servants passed around a
platter heaped up with crumbly sweet balls. I heard Kakaji's sister, Billo, saying something to Sister Pom; she had just come from Dehra Dun bearing a
sari, a veil, and the engagement ring for Sister Pom, after Romesh Chachaji,
one of Daddyji's brothers, had gone to Dehra Dun bearing some money, a

silver platter and silver bowls, and sweetmeats for Kakaji. It was the first time that I was able to think of Kakaji both as a remote and frightening dentist who was going to take Sister Pom away and as someone ordinary like us, who had his own family. At some point, Mamaji prodded me, and I scooted forward, crab fashion, to embrace Sister Pom. I felt her hand on my neck. It had something cold and metallic on it, which sent a shiver through me. I realized that she was wearing her engagement ring, and that until then Mamaji was the only one in our family who had worn a ring.

In the evening, the women relatives closeted themselves in the drawing room with Sister Pom for the engagement singsong. I crouched outside with my ear to the door. The door pulsated with the beat of a barrel drum. The pulse in my forehead throbbed in sympathy with the beat as I caught snatches of songs about bedsheets and henna, along with explosions of laughter, the songs themselves rising and falling like the cooing of the doves that nested under the eaves of the veranda. I thought that a couple of years earlier I would have been playing somewhere outside on such an occasion, without knowing what I was missing, or been in the drawing room clapping and singing, but now I was crouching by the door like a thief, and was feeling ashamed even as I was captivated.

Response Statement Questions

- What is your response to the issue of arranged marriage? When that issue is debated among members of the Mehta family, what side do you take? How is your position related to your own cultural situation?
- Do you believe love develops with time, after a couple has made a commitment, or is it the basis of a commitment? How is your opinion influenced by culture?
- Sister Nimi raises "Think for yourself—be independent'" as a positive value. Where do you stand with respect to that belief? If you endorse it, do you see independent thinking as consistent with or antithetical to a committed relationship?
- One literary text strategy in "Pom's Engagement" is the dialogue that is presented among members of the Mehta family. What is your response to this text strategy? Is it effective to have various positions on the issue of arranged marriage presented that way?
- Do you think "Pom's Engagement" has a point to make? If so, what is that point? How does the essay use rhetorical strategies to make or suggest that point?
- Compare the attitudes toward "marriage and love" presented in Mehta's essay with those expressed in Emma Goldman's "Marriage and Love" in Chapter 25. Do Goldman's opinions about "marriage and love" in Western societies help you gain perspective on the dominant ideology concerning marriage and love in Indian culture?

- *Share and Compare*   Are there different attitudes among your classmates or reading group toward the relationship of commitment and love? If so, can your group or class arrange a dialogue something like the debate that ensues among the Mehta family in "Pom's Engagement"?

READING AND WRITING PROJECTS
FOR CREATIVE AND CRITICAL THINKING

Your own writing is important as you try to learn more about yourself as a reader—both what you do cognitively and what is done to you culturally—to produce the kind of reader you are when you interact with any particular text. In addition to response statements and the formal expository paper that may grow out of them, there are other ways to use writing to learn. What follows are suggestions for integrating your reading of and writing about literary texts in various ways. These suggestions include exploratory writing, playing with texts and language, creative efforts in various genres, and other writing exercises designed to strengthen your awareness of the cognitive and cultural processes involved in your reading.

▶ Using "Am I Blue?" as a rough model, tell a story, with a rhetorical point to it, of your experience with an animal. Try to make what you write something other than an "I love my pet" essay; try to give it a larger point or purpose, something that goes beyond your encounter or relationship with a particular animal, but uses that encounter or relationship as a starting point.

▶ Transform a persuasive essay into an advertisement. Write some ad copy. Put the copy together with some art—a photograph, a sketch, something you've copied from another source ("clip art" is available from a number of computer "shareware" sources; you don't have to be able to draw to use art in an ad design). Make a rhetorically persuasive argument, using connotation and suggestiveness in both verbal and visual images, for a target market at whom your ad is aimed. The *Frangelico* ad in Chapter 24 can serve as a model. This project can be done individually or collaboratively. As an option, you could write some expository prose explaining your decisions to create the kind of ad you did.

▶ Transform an essay—formal or informal—into a lyric poem. Of course a poem will not be as long as an essay, but its relative shortness will also necessitate differences in use of language. You may make your poem didactic—explicitly presenting a point for your reader's belief or improvement—or you may make it aesthetic—providing pleasure through its use of words, images, and sounds. An interesting challenge would be to turn an argumentative essay like *The Declaration of Independence* into an aesthetic poem.

▶ Transform the level of diction or style in an essay, making it either more or less formal. For example, you could rewrite "I Am What I Am" in a formally accepted style. Or you could rewrite *The Declaration of Independence*—or perhaps just its first two paragraphs—as a rap lyric. (That transformation would involve a change in genre as well.) In any case, you could add a prose discussion, in your own voice, of the effects of your linguistic or stylistic changes.

27 ◆ Writing About Essays

At the beginning of Chapter 24, I observed that you may have more experience writing essays than reading them. Now that you have worked your way through three chapters in this section and read at least five essays in the process, the scales may be a bit more balanced. This book has also recommended, in the Introduction and throughout, that reading and writing not be seen as separate activities so much as complementary ones. Your experience in writing response statements, formal papers, and any of the Reading and Writing Projects throughout this book should have helped you see this for yourself. When you write your own essays, if you are conscious enough of your own processes to see what's going on, the complementary and recursive nature of reading and writing becomes clear: Your own writing decisions are based partly on your reading of what you have already written, whether in a first draft stage or in revision.

Reading and Responding: A Student Essay

Sometimes, though, it's hard to get sufficient distance from your own writing to read it as someone else would, which is a key technique for doing productive revision. So, to wrap this consideration of essays back around to where it started, I will ask you now to read and respond to an essay written by a student. This essay develops a first-year student's initial response to Alice Walker's "Am I Blue?" which you read in Chapter 26. In some ways, you may treat it as you would any other text: You may interact with it on the literary and the ideological level. You may also approach it in terms of its attempts to do what you may be trying to do yourself as you develop your responses into pieces of public writing intended for an audience.

The writer of this essay, Jody Strausser, is not physically present in your classroom, but in reading and responding to his essay and discussing it with your classmates, you can simulate the peer critiquing that might happen if he were. A set of response statement questions follows Jody's essay, and you may use those to guide your own response. But here are some other questions that you should attend to as you read his essay. Some of them ask you to look at Jody's essay as a text in the essay genre; others repeat some of the questions suggested in Chapter 4 for peer reviewing sessions.

- Is this a distinctly formal or informal essay, or is it a combination or hybrid of those types?
- What seems to be its purpose—to argue a proposition, to explain an idea, or to explore a topic? What seems to be the main idea? How easy or hard is it for you to identify it?
- What kinds of rhetorical strategies does this essay use?
- What kind of voice or tone does it adopt?
- What parts of this draft are particularly clear? Why are they that way? In what parts of this draft do you need more information to understand the point being made? What kind(s) of information would you like to hear there?
- What do you particularly like about this draft?
- What two or three specific suggestions for revision might you make?

To help you answer these questions as you read, you should annotate this text, or at least keep a set of notes on a separate sheet of paper.

STUDENT WRITING
Jody Strausser: Essay in Response to "Am I Blue?"

The essay "Am I Blue?" discusses some of the most controversial issues today, including animal rights, human rights, and vegetarianism. All of these topics are constantly being argued in society one way or another today. In "Am I Blue?," Alice Walker expresses her thoughts on many of these topics. As I read through the essay, there were some ideas with which I agreed, while others did not acquiesce so readily. Her writing provoked both favorable and unfavorable responses in me, mainly due to some of the methods used to convey her ideas.

At first glance, "Am I Blue?" appears to be just another predictable horse story, where the main character comes upon an abused or neglected animal and his or her life changes completely; this is where I stumbled upon the first topic of Walker's essay—animal rights. These stories normally convey the concept of animal rights by getting the reader to feel pity for the cause. This was one topic that coincided with my ideology. The guilt-free way she chose to express it, in my opinion, is an effective persuading strategy, and I generally agree with this method. I was pleased to see this change in topics because now the essay had a worthwhile idea. I'm sure the essay would have been fine even if it was my so-called predictable horse story, but since I read enough of those type of stories in middle and high school, I was glad the essay took this sort of turn towards serious topics. This topic created harmony with me because throughout my life there has always been either a dog or a cat in my house, and for this reason I grew to love and appreciate all animals. Anytime I saw an abused or neglected animal on the news, I became infuriated and had to change the channel. Because of Walker's respect for the horse and all animals, her essay intrigued me, and up to this point I was ready to totally agree with all of her thoughts.

Suddenly the essay again took a strange turn, and Walker started talking about slavery, racism, and minorities. Although I don't consider myself the most politically correct person, all of the mentioned topics are important to me for a few reasons. First, people in general have to overcome their archaic ideas of racism and they have to learn to deal with minorities before anything can change in this country or the world for that matter. Because now Walker was talking about major problems in society, I came to appreciate the essay even more and was happy that I didn't stop reading after the first paragraph when I jumped to the wrong conclusion about the topic of this essay. The second reason I agreed with Walker was that she was making people more aware of these problems by writing about them. Even if one person became somewhat enlightened after reading the essay, it was well worth writing. Finally, Walker's discussion of slavery is also important because it shows some of the problems in dealing with minorities in history, and hopefully people can learn from these mistakes. Up to this point, the author expressed favorable ideas in talking about animal rights, racism, and minorities, and I was inclined to agree with her because these ideas are also important to me.

Next, Walker told the story about the horse's friend that was only there for breeding purposes, and went on to tell about how the horse felt. At this point, I began to differ in opinion because she was applying human feelings to the horse; I think a better way of expressing this idea would have been to simply express the horse's reactions and let the reader come to his or her own decision. I realize this is a technique used to convey her thoughts on animal rights, but I just don't see animals as having certain human emotions. My theory is that animals don't really have emotions in the same respect as humans, but rather they simply have a sense of what's going on based mainly on instinct.

For example, one of our assigned readings in my senior year English class was Jack London's "To Build A Fire." The main character in this story is traveling on a logging trail in the Yukon. At some point a wolf-dog joins him, and they travel along the trail together. I remember the majority of my class thinking how nice it was that the character had a companion at his side. Well, the man builds a fire under a tree and the snow melts off and wets his matches. Faced with freezing to death, the character continues to walk in the hopes that he won't die of frostbite, the dog still at his side. He falls into a snow-covered spring and gets wet, which immediately causes frostbite. The man realizes he is doomed and becoming frantic tries to kill the dog. Unable to kill the dog because of his frostbitten hands, the man is forced to release the dog and it runs away. The dog later comes back and smells the scent of death in the man's body and continues on the trail where it will be able to find the others and get food and warmth. The point of relating this story is that the dog really didn't care about the main character at all; it was just the dog's way of remaining alive by using the man for the fire and food that he could provide. Many people would have thought that the dog liked the man and his company, but in reality it was just using the man. Because of Walker's over-humanizing of the horse, I couldn't really relate any more, but I continued to read ahead anyway.

At the end of her essay, I became frustrated and annoyed when she started talking about vegetarianism. I feel the author led me on with ideas such as human rights, racism, minorities, and animal rights, and then throws vegetarianism at me. I think this gap between ideas was one of the problems I had. I didn't really see how it related. Her statement, "As we talked of freedom and justice one day for all, we sat down to steaks. I am eating misery, I thought, as I took the first bite. And spit it out." was one idea that annoyed me. I understand the irony in her statement, but it was like she was trying to make me, as a non-vegetarian, feel guilty.

I really dislike when people forcefully push their views on me. I have a few vegetarian friends, but they don't make me feel guilty when we sit down to eat and they have a salad while I have my normal meat and potatoes. I used to have a friend who would constantly tell me about animal torture and how humans are so horrible. Every day, I would hear some tidbit she had just read or heard about; sometimes she would even show me pictures. Even though I felt sorry for the animals, she wasn't helping her cause by making me feel guilty. Why can't people just arrange the facts in an organized manner? I consider myself to be somewhat reasonable and intelligent; therefore, I think I am quite capable of making my own decisions without someone pushing his or her views on me. Perhaps my old friend was correct when she said, "Jody, stop being so defensive. It's just your own conscience getting to you again," or maybe she should see my side of the situation a little more.

Overall, "Am I Blue?" seems to be a reasonable essay with serious and important ideas. With the exception of the vegetarian idea, I think the essay was quite informative. Racism, minorities, and animal rights are all problems in today's society; being aware that these problems exist is winning half the battle and takes us one step closer to a solution.

Response Statement Questions

- What kind of literary interaction do you have with this text? Specifically, how do you respond to whatever text strategies you noticed while reading and annotating it? What reading strategies did you apply? How were these affected by knowing you were reading a piece of student writing?
- What revision suggestions would you offer Jody if you were his peer editing partner? How has your experience as a writer of essays yourself affected your response to Jody's essay?
- What kind of ideological interaction do you have with this text? What kind of ideological position does it seem to come from? Does your own ideological position with respect to the issues Jody says Walker presents in "Am I Blue?" help or hinder your ability to act as a peer reviewer of his essay?
- *Share and Compare* What range of opinion exists in your class about the successes and shortcomings of Jody Strausser's essay? To what extent are

these opinions based on *literary* matters, and to what extent on *ideological* matters?

A Final Word: The Spirit of the Essay

As you do further reading of essays from the selections in the Essays for Further Reading or elsewhere, and as you respond in writing to what you read, you should find the rough categories of formal and informal that these chapters have discussed to be useful. Those two kinds of essay share several basic text strategies, but each kind has text strategies peculiar to it. Accordingly, some reading strategies seem more suited to one kind than to the other. And the particular combination of text strategies and reading strategies that is involved in your reading of any text in the essay genre will engage elements of your ideology in different ways. An awareness of these variations should help you work toward becoming a strong reader (and writer) of essays. As you proceed toward that goal, keep somewhere in mind the derivation of the word "essay"—to try.

ESSAYS FOR FURTHER READING

Laura Bohannan

Shakespeare in the Bush   *1966*

Just before I left Oxford for the Tiv in West Africa, conversation turned to the season at Stratford. "You Americans," said a friend, "often have difficulty with Shakespeare. He was, after all, a very English poet, and one can easily misinterpret the universal by misunderstanding the particular."

I protested that human nature is pretty much the same the whole world over; at least the general plot and motivation of the greater tragedies would always be clear—everywhere—although some details of custom might have to be explained and difficulties of translation might produce other slight changes. To end an argument we could not conclude, my friend gave me a copy of *Hamlet* to study in the African bush: it would, he hoped, lift my mind above its primitive surroundings, and possibly I might, by prolonged meditation, achieve the grace of correct interpretation.

It was my second field trip to that African tribe, and I thought myself ready to live in one of its remote sections—an area difficult to cross even on foot. I eventually settled on the hillock of a very knowledgeable old man, the head of a homestead of some hundred and forty people, all of whom were either his close relatives or their wives and children. Like the other elders of the vicinity, the old man spent most of his time performing ceremonies seldom seen these days in the more accessible parts of the tribe. I was delighted. Soon there would be three months of enforced isolation and leisure, between the harvest that takes place just before the rising of the swamps and the clearing of new farms when the water goes down. Then, I thought, they would have even more time to perform ceremonies and explain them to me.

I was quite mistaken. Most of the ceremonies demanded the presence of elders from several homesteads. As the swamps rose, the old men found it too difficult to walk from one homestead to the next, and the ceremonies gradually ceased. As the swamps rose even higher, all activities but one came to an end. The women brewed beer from maize and millet. Men, women, and children sat on their hillocks and drank it.

People began to drink at dawn. By midmorning the whole homestead was singing, dancing, and drumming. When it rained, people had to sit inside their huts: there they drank and sang or they drank and told stories. In any case, by noon or before, I either had to join the party or retire to my own hut and my books. "One does not discuss serious matters when there is beer. Come, drink with us." Since I lacked their capacity for the thick native beer, I spent more and more time with *Hamlet*. Before the end of the second month, grace descended on me. I was quite sure that *Hamlet* had only one possible interpretation, and that one universally obvious.

5

Early every morning, in the hope of having some serious talk before the beer party, I used to call on the old man at his reception hut—a circle of posts supporting a thatched roof above a low mud wall to keep out wind and rain. One day I crawled through the low doorway and found most of the men of the homestead sitting huddled in their ragged cloths on stools, low plank beds, and reclining chairs, warming themselves against the chill of the rain around a smoky fire. In the center were three pots of beer. The party had started.

The old man greeted me cordially. "Sit down and drink." I accepted a large calabash[1] full of beer, poured some into a small drinking gourd, and tossed it down. Then I poured some more into the same gourd for the man second in seniority to my host before I handed my calabash over to a young man for further distribution. Important people shouldn't ladle beer themselves.

"It is better like this," the old man said, looking at me approvingly and plucking at the thatch that had caught in my hair. "You should sit and drink with us more often. Your servants tell me that when you are not with us, you sit inside your hut looking at a paper."

The old man was acquainted with four kinds of "papers": tax receipts, bride price receipts, court fee receipts, and letters. The messenger who brought him letters from the chief used them mainly as a badge of office, for he always knew what was in them and told the old man. Personal letters for the few who had relatives in the government or mission stations were kept until someone went to a large market where there was a letter writer and reader. Since my arrival, letters were brought to me to be read. A few men also brought me bride price receipts, privately, with requests to change the figures to a higher sum. I found moral arguments were of no avail, since in-laws are fair game, and the technical hazards of forgery difficult to explain to an illiterate people. I did not wish them to think me silly enough to look at any such papers for days on end, and I hastily explained that my "paper" was one of the "things of long ago" of my country.

"Ah," said the old man. "Tell us."

I protested that I was not a storyteller. Storytelling is a skilled art among them; their standards are high, and the audiences critical—and vocal in their criticism. I protested in vain. This morning they wanted to hear a story while they drank. They threatened to tell me no more stories until I told them one of mine. Finally, the old man promised that no one would criticize my style "for we know you are struggling with our language." "But," put in one of the elders, "you must explain what we do not understand, as we do when we tell you our stories." Realizing that here was my chance to prove *Hamlet* universally intelligible, I agreed.

The old man handed me some more beer to help me on with my storytelling. Men filled their long wooden pipes and knocked coals from the fire to place in the pipe bowls; then, puffing contentedly, they sat back to listen. I began in the proper style, "Not yesterday, not yesterday, but long ago, a thing occurred. One night three men were keeping watch outside the homestead of the great chief, when suddenly they saw the former chief approach them."

"Why was he no longer their chief?"

"He was dead," I explained. "That is why they were troubled and afraid when they saw him."

"Impossible," began one of the elders, handing his pipe on to his neighbor, who interrupted, "Of course it wasn't the dead chief. It was an omen sent by a witch. Go on."

---

[1]calabash—a gourd used as a bowl or pitcher.

Slightly shaken, I continued. "One of these three was a man who knew things"—the closest translation for scholar, but unfortunately it also meant witch. The second elder looked triumphantly at the first. "So he spoke to the dead chief saying, 'Tell us what we must do so you may rest in your grave,' but the dead chief did not answer. He vanished, and they could see him no more. Then the man who knew things—his name was Horatio—said this event was the affair of the dead chief's son, Hamlet."

There was a general shaking of heads round the circle. "Had the dead chief no living brothers? Or was this son the chief?"

"No," I replied. "That is, he had one living brother who became the chief when the elder brother died."

The old man muttered: such omens were matters for chiefs and elders, not for youngsters; no good could come of going behind a chief's back; clearly Horatio was not a man who knew things.

"Yes, he was," I insisted, shooing a chicken away from my beer. "In our country the son is next to the father. The dead chief's younger brother had become the great chief. He had also married his elder brother's widow only about a month after the funeral."   20

"He did well," the old man beamed and announced to the others, "I told you that if we knew more about Europeans, we would find they really were very like us. In our country also," he added to me, "the younger brother marries the elder brother's widow and becomes the father of his children. Now, if your uncle, who married your widowed mother, is your father's full brother, then he will be a real father to you. Did Hamlet's father and uncle have one mother?"

His question barely penetrated my mind; I was too upset and thrown too far off balance by having one of the most important elements of *Hamlet* knocked straight out of the picture. Rather uncertainly I said that I thought they had the same mother, but I wasn't sure—the story didn't say. The old man told me severely that these genealogical details made all the difference and that when I got home I must ask the elders about it. He shouted out the door to one of his younger wives to bring his goatskin bag.

Determined to save what I could of the mother motif, I took a deep breath and began again. "The son Hamlet was very sad because his mother had married again so quickly. There was no need for her to do so, and it is our custom for a widow not to go to her next husband until she has mourned for two years."

"Two years is too long," objected the wife, who had appeared with the old man's battered goatskin bag. "Who will hoe your farms for you while you have no husband?"

"Hamlet," I retorted without thinking, "was old enough to hoe his mother's farms himself. There was no need for her to remarry." No one looked convinced.   25
I gave up. "His mother and the great chief told Hamlet not to be sad, for the great chief himself would be a father to Hamlet. Furthermore, Hamlet would be the next chief: therefore he must stay to learn the things of a chief. Hamlet agreed to remain, and all the rest went off to drink beer."

While I paused, perplexed at how to render Hamlet's disgusted soliloquy to an audience convinced that Claudius and Gertrude had behaved in the best possible manner, one of the younger men asked me who had married the other wives of the dead chief.

"He had no other wives," I told him.

"But a chief must have many wives! How else can he brew beer and prepare food for all his guests?"

I said firmly that in our country even chiefs had only one wife, that they had servants to do their work, and that they paid them from tax money.

It was better, they returned, for a chief to have many wives and sons who   30
would help him hoe his farms and feed his people; then everyone loved the chief
who gave much and took nothing—taxes were a bad thing.

I agreed with the last comment, but for the rest fell back on their favorite way
of fobbing off my questions: "That is the way it is done, so that is how we do it."

I decided to skip the soliloquy. Even if Claudius was here thought quite right
to marry his brother's widow, there remained the poison motif, and I knew they
would disapprove of fratricide. More hopefully I resumed, "That night Hamlet kept
watch with the three who had seen his dead father. The dead chief again appeared, and although the others were afraid, Hamlet followed his dead father off
to one side. When they were alone, Hamlet's dead father spoke."

"Omens can't talk!" The old man was emphatic.

"Hamlet's dead father wasn't an omen. Seeing him might have been an omen,
but he was not." My audience looked as confused as I sounded. "It *was* Hamlet's
dead father. It was a thing we call a 'ghost.'" I had to use the English word, for unlike many of the neighboring tribes, these people didn't believe in the survival
after death of any individuating part of the personality.

"What is a 'ghost?' An omen?"   35

"No, a 'ghost' is someone who is dead but who walks around and can talk,
and people can hear him and see him but not touch him."

They objected. "One can touch zombis."

"No, no! It was not a dead body the witches had animated to sacrifice and eat.
No one else made Hamlet's dead father walk. He did it himself."

"Dead men can't walk," protested my audience as one man.

I was quite willing to compromise. "A 'ghost' is the dead man's shadow."   40

But again they objected. "Dead men cast no shadows."

"They do in my country," I snapped.

The old man quelled the babble of disbelief that arose immediately and told
me with that insincere, but courteous, agreement one extends to the fancies of the
young, ignorant, and superstitious, "No doubt in your country the dead can also
walk without being zombis." From the depths of his bag he produced a withered
fragment of kola nut, bit off one end to show it wasn't poisoned, and handed me
the rest as a peace offering.

"Anyhow," I resumed, "Hamlet's dead father said that his own brother, the
one who became chief, had poisoned him. He wanted Hamlet to avenge him.
Hamlet believed this in his heart, for he did not like his father's brother." I took
another swallow of beer. "In the country of the great chief, living in the same
homestead, for it was a very large one, was an important elder who was often with
the chief to advise and help him. His name was Polonius. Hamlet was courting his
daughter, but her father and her brother … [I cast hastily about for some tribal
analogy] warned her not to let Hamlet visit her when she was alone on her farm,
for he would be a great chief and so could not marry her."

"Why not?" asked the wife, who had settled down on the edge of the old   45
man's chair. He frowned at her for asking stupid questions and growled, "They
lived in the same homestead."

"That was not the reason," I informed them. "Polonius was a stranger
who lived in the homestead because he helped the chief, not because he was a
relative."

"Then why couldn't Hamlet marry her?"

"He could have, " I explained, "but Polonius didn't think he would. After all,
Hamlet was a man of great importance who ought to marry a chief's daughter, for

in his country a man could have only one wife. Polonius was afraid that if Hamlet made love to his daughter, then no one else would give a high price for her."

"That might be true," remarked one of the shrewder elders, "but a chief's son would give his mistress's father enough presents and patronage to more than make up the difference. Polonius sounds like a fool to me."

"Many people think he was," I agreed. "Meanwhile Polonius sent his son Laertes off to Paris to learn the things of that country, for it was the homestead of a very great chief indeed. Because he was afraid that Laertes might waste a lot of money on beer and women and gambling, or get into trouble by fighting, he sent one of his servants to Paris secretly, to spy out what Laertes was doing. One day Hamlet came upon Polonius's daughter Ophelia. He behaved so oddly he frightened her. Indeed"—I was fumbling for words to express the dubious quality of Hamlet's madness—"the chief and many others had also noticed that when Hamlet talked one could understand the words but not what they meant. Many people thought that he had become mad." My audience suddenly became much more attentive. "The great chief wanted to know what was wrong with Hamlet, so he sent for two of Hamlet's age mates [school friends would have taken long explanation] to talk to Hamlet and find out what troubled his heart. Hamlet, seeing that they had been bribed by the chief to betray him, told them nothing. Polonius, however, insisted that Hamlet was mad because he had been forbidden to see Ophelia, whom he loved."

"Why," inquired a bewildered voice, "should anyone bewitch Hamlet on that account?"

"Bewitch him?"

"Yes, only witchcraft can make anyone mad, unless, of course, one sees the beings that lurk in the forest."

I stopped being a storyteller, took out my notebook and demanded to be told more about these two causes of madness. Even while they spoke and I jotted notes, I tried to calculate the effect of this new factor on the plot. Hamlet had not been exposed to the beings that lurk in the forests. Only his relatives in the male line could bewitch him. Barring relatives not mentioned by Shakespeare, it had to be Claudius who was attempting to harm him. And, of course, it was.

For the moment I staved off questions by saying that the great chief also refused to believe that Hamlet was mad for the love of Ophelia and nothing else. "He was sure that something much more important was troubling Hamlet's heart."

"Now Hamlet's age mates," I continued, "had brought with them a famous storyteller. Hamlet decided to have this man tell the chief and all his homestead a story about a man who had poisoned his brother because he desired his brother's wife and wished to be chief himself. Hamlet was sure the great chief could not hear the story without making a sign if he was indeed guilty, and then he would discover whether his dead father had told him the truth."

The old man interrupted, with deep cunning, "Why should a father lie to his son?" he asked.

I hedged: "Hamlet wasn't sure that it really was his dead father." It was impossible to say anything, in that language, about devil-inspired visions.

"You mean," he said, "it actually was an omen, and he knew witches sometimes send false ones. Hamlet was a fool not to go to one skilled in reading omens and divining the truth in the first place. A man-who-sees-the-truth could have told him how his father died, if he really had been poisoned, and if there was witchcraft in it; then Hamlet could have called the elders to settle the matter."

The shrewd elder ventured to disagree. "Because his father's brother was a great chief, one-who-sees-the-truth might therefore have been afraid to tell it. I

think it was for that reason that a friend of Hamlet's father—a witch and an elder—
sent an omen so his friend's son would know. Was the omen true?"

"Yes," I said, abandoning ghosts and the devil; a witch-sent omen it would
have to be. "It was true, for when the storyteller was telling his tale before all the
homestead, the great chief rose in fear. Afraid that Hamlet knew his secret he
planned to have him killed."

The stage set of the next bit presented some difficulties of translation. I began
cautiously. "The great chief told Hamlet's mother to find out from her son what he
knew. But because a woman's children are always first in her heart, he had the important elder Polonius hide behind a cloth that hung against the wall of Hamlet's
mother's sleeping hut. Hamlet started to scold his mother for what she had done."

There was a shocked murmur from everyone. A man should never scold his
mother.

"She called out in fear, and Polonius moved behind the cloth. Shouting, 'A rat!'
Hamlet took his machete and slashed through the cloth." I paused for dramatic effect. "He had killed Polonius!"

The old men looked at each other in supreme disgust. "That Polonius truly   65
was a fool and a man who knew nothing! What child would not know enough to
shout, 'It's me!'" With a pang, I remembered that these people are ardent hunters,
always armed with bow, arrow, and machete; at the first rustle in the grass an
arrow is aimed and ready, and the hunter shouts "Game!" If no human voice answers immediately, the arrow speeds on its way. Like a good hunter Hamlet had
shouted, "A rat!"

I rushed in to save Polonius's reputation. "Polonius did speak. Hamlet heard
him. But he thought it was the chief and wished to kill him to avenge his father.
He had meant to kill him earlier that evening...." I broke down, unable to describe
to these pagans, who had no belief in individual afterlife, the difference between
dying at one's prayers and dying "unhousell'd, disappointed, unaneled."[2]

This time I had shocked my audience seriously. "For a man to raise his hand
against his father's brother and the one who has become his father—that is a terrible thing. The elders ought to let such a man be bewitched."

I nibbled at my kola nut in some perplexity, then pointed out that after all the
man had killed Hamlet's father.

"No," pronounced the old man, speaking less to me than to the young men
sitting behind the elders. "If your father' brother has killed your father, you must
appeal to your father's age mates; *they* may avenge him. No man may use violence
against his senior relatives." Another thought stuck him. "But if his father's brother
had indeed been wicked enough to bewitch Hamlet and make him mad that
would be a good story indeed, for it would be his fault that Hamlet, being mad, no
longer had any sense and thus was ready to kill his father's brother."

There was a murmur of applause. *Hamlet* was again a good story to them, but   70
it no longer seemed quite the same story to me. As I thought over the coming
complications of plot and motive, I lost courage and decided to skim over dangerous ground quickly.

"The great chief," I went on, "was not sorry that Hamlet had killed Polonius.
It gave him a reason to send Hamlet away, with his two treacherous age mates,
with letters to a chief of a far country, saying that Hamlet should be killed. But
Hamlet changed the writing on their papers, so that the chief killed his age mates
instead." I encountered a reproachful glare from one of the men whom I had told

---

[2]unhousell'd, disappointed, unaneled—without last rites.

undetectable forgery was not merely immoral but beyond human skill. I looked the other way.

"Before Hamlet could return, Laertes came back for his father's funeral. The great chief told him Hamlet had killed Polonius. Laertes swore to kill Hamlet because of this, and because his sister Ophelia, hearing her father had been killed by the man she loved, went mad and drowned in the river."

"Have you already forgotten what we told you?" The old man was reproachful. "One cannot take vengeance on a madman; Hamlet killed Polonius in his madness. As for the girl, she not only went mad, she was drowned. Only witches can make people drown. Water itself can't hurt anything. It is merely something one drinks and bathes in."

I began to get cross. "If you don't like the story, I'll stop."

The old man made soothing noises and himself poured me some more beer. "You tell the story well, and we are listening. But it is clear that the elders of your country have never told you what the story really means. No, don't interrupt! We believe you when you say your marriage customs are different, or your clothes and weapons. But people are the same everywhere; therefore, there are always witches and it is we, the elders, who know how witches work. We told you it was the great chief who wished to kill Hamlet, and now your own words have proved us right. Who were Ophelia's male relatives?"

"There were only her father and her brother." Hamlet was clearly out of my hands.

"There must have been many more; this also you must ask of your elders when you get back to your country. From what you tell us, since Polonius was dead, it must have been Laertes who killed Ophelia, although I do not see the reason for it."

We had emptied one pot of beer, and the old men argued the point with slightly tipsy interest. Finally one of them demanded of me, "What did the servant of Polonius say on his return?"

With difficulty I recollected Reynaldo and his mission. "I don't think he did return before Polonius was killed."

"Listen," said the elder, "and I will tell you how it was and how your story will go, then you may tell me if I am right. Polonius knew his son would get into trouble, and so he did. He had many fines to pay for fighting, and debts from gambling. But he had only two ways of getting money quickly. One was to marry off his sister at once, but it is difficult to find a man who will marry a woman desired by the son of a chief. For if the chief's heir commits adultery with your wife, what can you do? Only a fool calls a case against a man who will someday be his judge. Therefore Laertes had to take the second way: he killed his sister by witchcraft, drowning her so he could secretly sell her body to the witches."

I raised an objection. "They found her body and buried it. Indeed, Laertes jumped into the grave to see his sister once more—so, you see, the body was truly there. Hamlet, who had just come back, jumped in after him."

"What did I tell you?" The elder appealed to the others. "Laertes was up to no good with his sister's body. Hamlet prevented him, because the chief's heir, like a chief, does not wish any other man to grow rich and powerful. Laertes would be angry, because he would have killed his sister without benefit to himself. In our country he would try to kill Hamlet for that reason. Is this not what happened?"

"More or less," I admitted. "When the great chief found Hamlet was still alive, he encouraged Laertes to try to kill Hamlet and arranged a fight with machetes between them. In the fight both the young men were wounded to death. Hamlet's mother drank the poisoned beer that the chief meant for Hamlet in case he won the fight. When he saw his mother die of poison, Hamlet, dying, managed to kill his father's brother with his machete."

"You see, I was right!" exclaimed the elder.

"That was a very good story," added the old man, "and you told it with very few mistakes. There was just one more error, at the very end. The poison Hamlet's mother drank was obviously meant for the survivor of the fight, whichever it was. If Laertes had won, the great chief would have poisoned him, for no one would know that he arranged Hamlet's death. Then, too, he need not fear Laertes' witchcraft; it takes a strong heart to kill one's only sister by witchcraft.

"Sometime," concluded the old man, gathering his ragged toga about him, "you must tell us some more stories of your country. We, who are elders, will instruct you in their true meaning, so that when you return to your own land your elders will see that you have not been sitting in the bush, but among those who know things and who have taught you wisdom."

85

Michelle Cliff   b. 1946

If I Could Write This In Fire, I Would Write This In Fire   1985

I

We were standing under the waterfall at the top of Orange River. Our chests were just beginning to mound—slight hills on either side. In the center of each were our nipples, which were losing their sideways look and rounding into perceptible buttons of dark flesh. Too fast it seemed. We touched each other, then, quickly and almost simultaneously, raised our arms to examine the hairs growing underneath. Another sign. Mine was wispy and light-brown. My friend Zoe had dark hair curled up tight. In each little patch the riverwater caught the sun so we glistened.

The waterfall had come about when my uncles dammed up the river to bring power to the sugar mill. Usually, when I say "sugar mill" to anyone not familiar with the Jamaican countryside or for that matter my family, I can tell their minds cast an image of tall smokestacks, enormous copper cauldrons, a man in a broad-brimmed hat with a whip, and several dozens of slaves—that is, if they have any idea of how large sugar mills once operated. It's a grandiose expression—like plantation, verandah, out-building. (Try substituting farm, porch, outside toilet.) To some people it even sounds romantic.

Our sugar mill was little more than a round-roofed shed, which contained a wheel and woodfire. We paid an old man to run it, tend the fire, and then either bartered or gave the sugar away, after my grandmother had taken what she needed. Our canefield was about two acres of flat land next to the river. My grandmother had six acres in all—one donkey, a mule, two cows, some chickens, a few pigs, and stray dogs and cats who had taken up residence in the yard.

Her house had four rooms, no electricity, no running water. The kitchen was a shed in the back with a small pot-bellied stove. Across from the stove was a mahogany counter, which had a white enamel basin set into it. The only light source was a window, a small space covered partly by a wooden shutter. We washed our faces and hands in enamel bowls with cold water carried in kerosene tins from the river and poured from enamel pitchers. Our chamber pots were enamel also, and in the morning we carefully placed them on the steps at the side of the house where my grandmother collected them and disposed of their contents. The out-house was about thirty yards from the back door—a "closet" as we called it—in-fested with lizards capable of changing color. When the door was shut it was to-tally dark, and the lizards made their presence known by the noise of their scurry-ing through the torn newspaper, or the soft shudder when they dropped from the walls. I remember most clearly the stench of the toilet, which seemed to hang in the air in that climate.

But because every little piece of reality exists in relation to another little piece, our situation was not that simple. It was to our yard that people came with news first. It was in my grandmother's parlor that the Disciples of Christ held their meet-ings.

Zoe lived with her mother and sister on borrowed ground in a place called Breezy Hill. She and I saw each other almost every day on our school vacations over a period of three years. Each morning early—as I sat on the cement porch with my coffee cut with condensed milk—she appeared: in her straw hat, school tunic faded from blue to gray, white blouse, sneakers hanging around her neck. We had coffee together, and a piece of hard-dough bread with butter and cheese, waited a bit and headed for the river. At first we were shy with each other. We did not start from the same place.

There was land. My grandparents' farm. And there was color.

(My family was called *red*. A term which signified a degree of whiteness. "We's just a flock of red people," a cousin of mine said once.) In the hierarchy of shades I was considered among the lightest. The countrywomen who visited my grandmother commented on my "tall" hair—meaning long. Wavy, not curly.

I had spent the years from three to ten in New York and spoke—at first—like an American. I wore American clothes: shorts, slacks, bathing suit. Because of my American past I was looked upon as the creator of games. Cowboys and Indians. Cops and Robbers. Peter Pan.

(While the primary colonial identification for Jamaicans was English, Ameri-can colonialism was a strong force in my childhood—and of course continues today. We were sent American movies and American music. American aluminum companies had already discovered bauxite on the island and were shipping the ore to their mainland. United Fruit bought our bananas. White Americans came to Montego Bay, Ocho Rios, and Kingston for their vacations and their cruise ships docked in Port Antonio and other places. In some ways America was seen as a better place than England by many Jamaicans. The farm laborers sent to work in American agribusiness came home with dollars and gifts and new clothes; there were few who mentioned American racism. Many of the middle class who emi-grated to Brooklyn or Staten Island or Manhattan were able to pass into the white American world—saving their blackness for other Jamaicans or for trips home; in some cases, forgetting it altogether. Those middle-class Jamaicans who could not pass for white managed differently—not unlike the Bajans in Paule Marshall's *Brown Girl, Brownstones*—saving, working, investing, buying property. Com-pletely separate in most cases from Black Americans.)

I was someone who had experience with the place that sent us triple features of B-grade westerns and gangster movies. And I had tall hair and light skin. And I was the granddaughter of my grandmother. So I had power. I was the cowboy, Zoe was my sidekick, the boys we knew were Indians. I was the detective, Zoe was my "girl," the boys were the robbers. I was Peter Pan, Zoe was Wendy Darling, the boys were the lost boys. And the terrain around the river—jungled and dark green—was Tombstone, or Chicago, or Never-Never Land.

This place and my friendship with Zoe never touched my life in Kingston. We did not correspond with each other when I left my grandmother's home.

I never visited Zoe's home the entire time I knew her. It was a given: never suggested, never raised.

Zoe went to a state school held in a country church in Red Hills. It had been my mother's school. I went to a private all-girls school where I was taught by white Englishwomen and pale Jamaicans. In her school the students were caned as punishment. In mine the harshest punishment I remember was being sent to sit under the *lignum vitae* to "commune with nature." Some of the girls were out-and-out white (English and American), the rest of us were colored—only a few were dark. Our uniforms were blood-red gabardine, heavy and hot. Classes were held in buildings meant to recreate England: damp with stone floors, facing onto a cloister, or quad as they called it. We began each day with the headmistress leading us in English hymns. The entire school stood for an hour in the zinc-roofed gymnasium.

Occasionally a girl fainted, or threw up. Once a girl had a grand mal seizure. To any such disturbance the response was always "keep singing." While she flailed on the stone floor, I wondered what the mistresses would do. We sang "Faith of Our Fathers," and watched our classmate as her eyes rolled back in her head. I thought of people swallowing their tongues. This student was dark—here on a scholarship—and the only woman who came forward to help her was the gamesmistress, the only dark teacher. She kneeled beside the girl and slid the white web belt from her tennis shorts, clamping it between the girl's teeth. When the seizure was over, she carried the girl to a tumbling mat in a corner of the gym and covered her so she wouldn't get chilled.

Were the other women unable to touch this girl because of her darkness? I think that now. Her darkness and her scholarship. She lived on Windward Road with her grandmother; her mother was a maid. But darkness is usually enough for women like those to hold back. Then, we usually excused that kind of behavior by saying they were "ladies." (We were constantly being told we should be ladies also. One teacher went so far as to tell us many people thought Jamaicans lived in trees and we had to show these people they were mistaken.) In short, we felt insufficient to judge the behavior of these women. The English ones (who had the corner on power in the school) had come all this way to teach us. Shouldn't we treat them as the missionaries they were certain they were? The creole Jamaicans had a different role: they were passing on to those of us who were light-skinned the creole heritage of collaboration, assimilation, loyalty to our betters. We were expected to be willing subjects in this outpost of civilization.

The girl left school that day and never returned.

After prayers we filed into our classrooms. After classes we had games: tennis, field hockey, rounders (what the English call baseball), netball (what the English call basketball). For games we were divided into "houses"—groups named for Joan of Arc, Edith Cavell, Florence Nightingale, Jane Austen. Four white heroines. Two martyrs. One saint. Two nurses. (None of us knew then that there were Black women with Nightingale at Scutari.) One novelist. Three involved in whitemen's wars. Two dead in whitemen's wars. *Pride and Prejudice.*

Those of us in Cavell wore red badges and recited her last words before a firing squad in W.W.I: "Patriotism is not enough. I must have no hatred or bitterness toward anyone."

Sorry to say I grew up to have exactly that.   20

Looking back: To try and see when the background changed places with the foreground. To try and locate the vanishing point: where the lines of perspective converge and disappear. Lines of color and class. Lines of history and social context. Lines of denial and rejection. When did *we* (the light-skinned middle-class Jamaicans) take over for *them* as oppressors? I need to see when and how this happened. When what should have been reality was overtaken by what was surely unreality. When the house nigger became master.

"What's the matter with you? You think you're white or something?"

"Child, what you want to know 'bout Garvey[1] for? The man was nothing but a damn fool."

"They not our kind of people."   25

Why did we wear wide-brimmed hats and try to get into Oxford? Why did we not return?

Great Expectations: a novel about origins and denial. about the futility and tragedy of that denial. about attempting assimilation. We learned this novel from a light-skinned Jamaican woman—she concentrated on what she called the "love affair" between Pip and Estella.

Looking back: Through the last page of *Sula*[2] "And the loss pressed down on her chest and came up into her throat. 'We was girls together,' she said as though explaining something." It was Zoe, and Zoe alone, I thought of. She snapped into my mind and I remembered no one else. Through the greens and blues of the riverbank. The flame of red hibiscus in front of my grandmother's house. The cracked grave of a former landowner. The fruit of the ackee which poisons those who don't know how to prepare it.

"What is to become of us?"

We borrowed a baby from a woman and used her as our dolly. Dressed and undressed her. Dipped her in the riverwater. Fed her with the milk her mother had left with us: and giggled because we knew where the milk had come from.

A letter: "I am desperate. I need to get away. I beg you one fifty-dollar."   30

I send the money because this is what she asks for. I visit her on a trip back home. Her front teeth are gone. Her husband beats her and she suffers black-outs. I sit on her chair. She is given birth control pills which aggravate her "condition." We boil up sorrel and ginger. She is being taught by Peace Corps volunteers to embroider linen mats with little lambs on them and gives me one as a keepsake. We cool off the sorrel with a block of ice brought from the shop nearby. The shopkeeper immediately recognizes me as my grandmother's granddaughter and refuses to sell me cigarettes. (I am twenty-seven.) We sit in the doorway of her house, pushing back the colored plastic strands which form a curtain, and talk about Babylon and Dred. About Manley and what he's doing for Jamaica. About how hard it is. We walk along the railway tracks—no longer used—to Crooked River and the post office. Her little daughter walks beside us and we recite a poem for her: "Mornin' buddy/Me no buddy fe wunna/Who den, den I saw?" and on and on.

I can come and go. And I leave. To complete my education in London.

II

Their goddam kings and their goddam queens. Grandmotherly Victoria spreading herself thin across the globe. Elizabeth II on our t.v. screens. We stop what we are doing. We quiet down. We pay our respects.

---

[1]Marcus Garvey (1887–1940) Jamaican nationalist leader.
[2]a novel by Toni Morrison.

1981: In Massachusetts I get up at 5 a.m. to watch the royal wedding. I tell my-self maybe the IRA will intervene. It's got to be better than starving themselves to death. Better to be a kamikaze in St. Paul's Cathedral than a hostage in Ulster. And last week Black and white people smashed storefronts all over the United King-dom. But I really don't believe we'll see royal blood on t.v. I watch because they once ruled us. In the back of the cathedral a Maori woman sings an aria from Han-del, and I notice that she is surrounded by the colored subjects.

To those of us in the commonwealth the royal family was the perfect symbol   35
of hegemony. To those of us who were dark in the dark nations, the prime minis-ter, the parliament barely existed. We believed in royalty—we were convinced in this belief. Maybe it played on some ancestral memories of West Africa—where other kings and queens had been. Altars and castles and magic.

The faces of our new rulers were everywhere in my childhood. Calendars, newsreels, magazines. Their presences were often among us. Attending test matches between the West Indians and South Africans. They were our landlords. Not always absentee. And no matter what Black leader we might elect—were we to choose independence—we would be losing something almost holy in our im-pudence.

WE ARE HERE BECAUSE YOU WERE THERE
BLACK PEOPLE AGAINST STATE BRUTALITY
BLACK WOMEN WILL NOT BE INTIMIDATED
WELCOME TO BRITAIN . . . WELCOME TO SECOND-CLASS CITIZENSHIP
(slogans of the Black movement in Britain)

Indian women cleaning the toilets in Heathrow airport. This is the first thing I notice. Dark women in saris trudging buckets back and forth as other dark women in saris—some covered by loosefitting winter coats—form a line to have their passports stamped.

The triangle trade: molasses/rum/slaves. Robinson Crusoe was on a slave-trading journey. Robert Browning was a mulatto. Holding pens. Jamaica was a sea-soning station. Split tongues. Sliced ears. Whipped bodies. The constant pretense of civility against rape. Still. Iron collars. Tinplate masks. The latter a precaution: to stop the slaves from eating the sugar cane.

A pregnant woman is to be whipped—they dig a hole to accommodate her belly and place her face down on the ground. Many of us became light-skinned very fast. Traced ourselves through bastard lines to reach the duke of Devonshire. The earl of Cornwall. The lord of this and the lord of that. Our mothers' rapes were the thing unspoken.

You say: But Britain freed her slaves in 1833. Yes.   40

Tea plantations in India and Ceylon. Mines in Africa. The Cape-to-Cairo Rail-road. Rhodes scholars. Suez Crisis. The whiteman's bloody burden. Boer War. Ban-tustans. Sitting in a theatre in London in the seventies. A play called West of Suez. A lousy play about British colonials. The finale comes when several well-known white actors are machine-gunned by several lesser-known Black actors. (As Nina Simone says: "This is a show tune but the show hasn't been written for it yet.")

The red empire of geography classes. "The sun never sets on the British em-pire and you can't trust it in the dark." Or with the dark peoples. "Because of the Industrial Revolution European countries went in search of markets and raw ma-terials." Another geography (or was it a history) lesson.

Their bloody kings and their bloody queens. Their bloody peers. Their bloody generals. Admirals. Explorers. Livingstone. Hillary. Kitchener. All the bwanas. And all their beaters, porters, sherpas. Who found the source of the Nile. Victoria Falls. The tops of mountains. Their so-called discoveries reek of untruth. How many dark people died so they could misname the physical features in their blasted gazetteer. A statistic we shall never know. Dr. Livingstone, I presume you are here to rape our land and enslave our people.

There are statues of these dead white men all over London.

An interesting fact: The swearword "bloody" is a contraction of "by my lady"—a reference to the Virgin Mary. They do tend to use their ladies. Name ages for them. Places for them. Use them as screens, inspirations, symbols. And many of the ladies comply. While the national martyr Edith Cavell was being executed by the Germans in 1915 in Belgium (called "poor little Belgium" by the allies in the war), the Belgians were engaged in the exploitation of the land and peoples of the Congo.

And will we ever know how many dark peoples were "imported" to fight in whitemen's wars. Probably not. Just as we will never know how many hearts were cut from African people so that the Christian doctor might be a success—i.e., extend a whiteman's life. Our Sister Killjoy observes this from her blackeyed squint.

Dr. Schweitzer—humanitarian, authority on Bach, winner of the Nobel Peace Prize—on the people of Africa: "The Negro is a child, and with children nothing can be done without the use of authority. We must, therefore, so arrange the circumstances of our daily life that my authority can find expression. With regard to Negroes, then, I have coined the formula: 'I am your brother, it is true, but your elder brother.'" (*On the Edge of the Primeval Forest*, 1961)

They like to pretend we didn't fight back. We did: with obeah, poison, revolution. It simply was not enough.

"Colonies . . . these places where 'niggers' are cheap and the earth is rich." (W.E.B. DuBois, "The Souls of White Folk")

A cousin is visiting me from Cal Tech where he is getting a degree in engineering. I am learning about the Italian Renaissance. My cousin is recognizably Black and speaks with an accent. I am not and I do not—unless I am back home, where the "twang" comes upon me. We sit for some time in a bar in his hotel and are not served. A light-skinned Jamaican comes over to our table. He is an older man—a professor at the University of London. "Don't bother with it, you hear. They don't serve us in this bar." A run-of-the-mill incident for all recognizably Black people in this city. But for me it is not.

Henry's eyes fill up, but he refuses to believe our informant. "No, man, the girl is just busy." (The girl is a fifty-year-old white woman, who may just be following orders. But I do not mention this. I have chosen sides.) All I can manage to say is, "Jesus Christ, I hate the fucking English." Henry looks at me. (In the family I am known as the "lady cousin." It has to do with how I look. And the fact that I am twenty-seven and unmarried—and for all they know, unattached. They do not know that I am really the lesbian cousin.) Our informant says—gently, but with a distinct tone of disappointment—"My dear, is that what you're studying at the university?"

You see—the whole business is very complicated.

Henry and I leave without drinks and go to meet some of his white colleagues at a restaurant I know near Covent Garden Opera House. The restaurant caters to theatre types and so I hope there won't be a repeat of the bar scene—at least they know how to pretend. Besides, I tell myself, the owners are Italian *and* gay; they *must* be halfway decent. Henry and his colleagues work for an American company which is paying their way through Cal Tech. They mine bauxite from the hills in the middle of the island and send it to the United States. A turnaround occurs at dinner: Henry joins the whitemen in a sustained mockery of the waiters: their accents and the way they walk. He whispers to me: "Why you want to bring us to a battyman's den, lady?" (*Battyman* = *faggot* in Jamaican.) I keep quiet.

We put the whitemen in a taxi and Henry walks me to the underground station. He asks me to sleep with him. (It wouldn't be incest. His mother was a maid in the house of an uncle and Henry has not seen her since his birth. He was taken into the family. She was let go.) I say that I can't. I plead exams. I can't say that I don't want to. Because I remember what happened in the bar. But I can't say that I'm a lesbian either—even though I want to believe his alliance with the whitemen at dinner was forced: not really him. He doesn't buy my excuse. "Come on, lady, let's do it. What's the matter, you 'fraid?" I pretend I am back home and start patois to show him somehow I am not afraid, not English, not white. I tell him he's a married man and he tells me he's a ram goat. I take the train to where I am staying and try to forget the whole thing. But I don't. I remember our different skins and our different experiences within them. And I have a hard time realizing that I am angry with Henry. That to him—no use in pretending—a queer is a queer.

1981: I hear on the radio that Bob Marley is dead and I drive over the Mohawk Trail listening to a program of his music and I cry and cry and cry. Someone says: "It wasn't the ganja that killed him, it was poverty and working in a steel foundry when he was young." 55

I flash back to my childhood and a young man who worked for an aunt I lived with once. He taught me to smoke ganja behind the house. And to peel an orange with the tip of a machete without cutting through the skin—"Love" it was called: a necklace of orange rind the result. I think about him because I heard he had become a Rastaman. And then I think about Rastas.

We are sitting on the porch of an uncle's house in Kingston—the family and I—and a Rastaman comes to the gate. We have guns but they are locked behind a false closet. We have dogs but they are tied up. We are Jamaicans and know that Rastas mean no harm. We let him in and he sits on the side of the porch and shows us his brooms and brushes. We buy some to take back to New York. "Peace, missis."

There were many Rastas in my childhood. Walking the roadside with their goods. Sitting outside their shacks in the mountains. The outsides painted bright—sometimes with words. Gathering at Palisadoes Airport to greet the Conquering Lion of Judah.[3] They were considered figures of fun by most middle-class Jamaicans. Harmless—like Marcus Garvey.

Later: white American hippies trying to create the effect of dred in their straight white hair. The ganja joint held between their straight white teeth. "Man, the grass is good." Hanging out by the Sheraton pool. Light-skinned Jamaicans also dred-locked, also assuming the ganja. Both groups moving to the music but not the words. Harmless. "Peace, brother."

III

My grandmother: "Let us thank God for a fruitful place." My grandfather: "Let us rescue the perishing world." 60

This evening on the road in western Massachusetts there are pockets of fog. Then clear spaces. Across from a pond a dog staggers in front of my headlights. I

---

[3]Lion of Judah—Haile Selassie (1892–1975) Rastafari emperor of Ethiopia: 1930–1936; 1941–1974.

look closer and see that his mouth is foaming. He stumbles to the side of the road—I go to call the police.

I drive back to the house, radio playing "difficult" piano pieces. And I think about how I need to say all this. This is who I am. I am not what you allow me to be. Whatever you decide me to be. In a bookstore in London I show the woman at the counter my book and she stares at me for a minute, then says: "You're a Jamaican." "Yes." "You're not at all like our Jamaicans."

Encountering the void is nothing more nor less than understanding invisibility. Of being fogbound.

Then: It was never a question of passing. It was a question of hiding. Behind Black and white perceptions of who we were—who they thought we were. Tropics. Plantations. Calypso. Cricket. We were the people with the musical voices and the coronation mugs on our parlor tables. I would be whatever these foreign imaginations cared for me to be. It would be so simple to let others fill in for me. So easy to startle them with a flash of anger when their visions got out of hand—but never to sustain the anger for myself.

It could become a life lived within myself. A life cut off. I know who I am but you will never know who I am. I may in fact lose touch with who I am.   65

I hid from my real sources. But my real sources were also hidden from me.

Now: It is not a question of relinquishing privilege. It is a question of grasping more of myself. I have found that in the real sources are concealed my survival. My speech. My voice. To be colonized is to be rendered insensitive. To have those parts necessary to sustain life numbed. And this is in some cases—in my case—perceived as privilege. The test of a colonized person is to walk through a shantytown in Kingston and not bat an eye. This I cannot do. Because part of me lives there—and as I grasp more of this part I realize what needs to be done with the rest of my life.

Sometimes I used to think we were like the Marranos—the Sephardic Jews forced to pretend they were Christians. The name was given to them by the Christians, and meant "pigs." But once out of Spain and Portugal, they became Jews openly again. Some settled in Jamaica. They knew who the enemy was and acted for their own survival. But they remained Jews always.

We also knew who the enemy was—I remember jokes about the English. Saying they stank. saying they were stingy. that they drank too much and couldn't hold their liquor. that they had bad teeth. were dirty and dishonest. were limey bastards. and horse-faced bitches. We said the men only wanted to sleep with Jamaican women. And that the women made pigs of themselves with Jamaican men.

But of course this was seen by us—the light-skinned middle class—with a double vision. We learned to cherish that part of us that was them—and to deny the part that was not. Believing in some cases that the latter part had ceased to exist.   70

None of this is as simple as it may sound. We were colorists and we aspired to oppressor status. (Of course, almost any aspiration instilled by western civilization is to oppressor status: success, for example.) Color was the symbol of our potential: color taking in hair "quality," skin tone, freckles, nose-width, eyes. We did not see that color symbolism was a method of keeping us apart: in the society, in the family, between friends. Those of us who were light-skinned, straight-haired, etc., were given to believe that we could actually attain whiteness—or at least those qualities of the colonizer which made him superior. We were convinced of white supremacy. If we failed, we were not really responsible for our failures: we had all the advantages—but it was that one persistent drop of blood, that single rogue gene that made us unable to conceptualize abstract ideas, made us love darkness rather than despise it, which was to be blamed for our failure. Our dark part had taken over: an inherited imbalance in which the doom of the creole was sealed.

I am trying to write this as clearly as possible, but as I write I realize that what I say may sound fabulous, or even mythic. It is. It is insane.

Under this system of colorism—the system which prevailed in my childhood in Jamaica, and which has carried over to the present—rarely will dark and light people co-mingle. Rarely will they achieve between themselves an intimacy informed with identity. (I should say here that I am using the categories light and dark both literally and symbolically. There are dark Jamaicans who have achieved lightness and the "advantages" which go with it by their successful pursuit of oppressor status.)

Under this system light and dark people will meet in those ways in which the light-skinned person imitates the oppressor. But imitation goes only so far: the light-skinned person becomes an oppressor in fact. He/she will have a dark chauffeur, a dark nanny, a dark maid, and a dark gardener. These employees will be paid badly. Because of the slave past, because of their dark skin, the servants of the middle class have been used according to the traditions of the slavocracy. They are not seen as workers for their own sake, but for the sake of the family who has employed them. It was not until Michael Manley became prime minister that a minimum wage for houseworkers was enacted—and the indignation of the middle class was profound.

During Manley's leadership the middle class began to abandon the island in droves. Toronto. Miami. New York. Leaving their houses and businesses behind and sewing cash into the tops of suitcases. Today—with a new regime—they are returning: "Come back to the way things used to be" the tourist advertisement on American t.v. says. "Make it Jamaica again. Make it your own."

But let me return to the situation of houseservants as I remember it: They will be paid badly, but they will be "given" room and board. However, the key to the larder will be kept by the mistress in her dresser drawer. They will spend Christmas with the family of their employers and be given a length of English wool for trousers or a few yards of cotton for dresses. They will see their children on their days off: their extended family will care for the children the rest of the time. When the employers visit their relations in the country, the servants may be asked along—oftentimes the servants of the middle class come from the same part of the countryside their employers have come from. But they will be expected to work while they are there. Back in town, there are parts of the house they are allowed to move freely around; other parts they are not allowed to enter. When the family watches the t.v. the servant is allowed to watch also, but only while standing in a doorway. The servant may have a radio in his/her room, also a dresser and a cot. Perhaps a mirror. There will usually be one ceiling light. And one small square louvered window.

A *true* story: One middle-class Jamaican woman ordered a Persian rug from Harrod's in London. The day it arrived so did her new maid. She was going downtown to have her hair touched up, and she told the maid to vacuum the rug. She told the maid she would find the vacuum cleaner in the same shed as the power mower. And when she returned she found that the fine nap of her new rug had been removed.

75

The reaction of the mistress was to tell her friends that the "girl" was backward. She did not fire her until she found that the maid had scrubbed the teflon from all her new set of pots, saying she thought they were coated with "nastiness."

The houseworker/mistress relationship in which one Black woman is the oppressor of another Black woman is a cornerstone of the experience of many Jamaican women.

I remember another true story: In a middle-class family's home one Christmas, a relation was visiting from New York. This woman had brought gifts for everybody, including the house-maid. The maid had been released from a mental institution recently, where they had "treated" her for depression. This visiting light-skinned woman had brought the dark woman a bright red rayon blouse and presented it to her in the garden one afternoon, while the family was having tea. The maid thanked her softly, and the other woman moved toward her as if to embrace her. Then she stopped, her face suddenly covered with tears, and ran into the house, saying, "My God, I can't, I can't." 80

We are women who come from a place almost incredible in its beauty. It is a beauty which can mask a great deal and which has been used in that way. But that the beauty is there is a fact. I remember what I thought the freedom of my childhood, in which the fruitful place was something I took for granted. Just as I took for granted Zoe's appearance every morning on my school vacations—in the sense that I knew she would be there. That she would always be the one to visit me. The perishing world of my grandfather's graces at the table, if I ever seriously thought about it, was something else.

Our souls were affected by the beauty of Jamaica, as much as they were affected by our fears of darkness.

There is no ending to this piece of writing. There is no way to end it. As I read back over it, I see that we/they/I may become confused in the mind of the reader: but these pronouns have always co-existed in my mind. The Rastas talk of the "I and I"—a pronoun in which they combine themselves with Jah. Jah is a contraction of Jahweh and Jehova, but to me always sounds like the beginning of Jamaica. I and Jamaica is who I am. No matter how far I travel—how deep the ambivalence I feel about ever returning. And Jamaica is a place in which we/they/I connect and disconnect—change place.

Judith Ortiz Cofer b. 1952

Silent Dancing *1990*

We have a home movie of this party. Several times my mother and I have watched it together, and I have asked questions about the silent revelers coming in and out of focus. It is grainy and of short duration, but it's a great visual aid to my memory of life at that time. And it is in color—the only complete scene in color I can recall from those years.

We lived in Puerto Rico until my brother was born in 1954. Soon after, because of economic pressures on our growing family, my father joined the United States Navy. He was assigned to duty on a ship in Brooklyn Yard—a place of cement and steel that was to be his home base in the States until his retirement more than twenty years later. He left the Island first, alone, going to New York City and tracking down his uncle who lived with his family across the Hudson River in Paterson, New Jersey. There my father found a tiny apartment in a huge tenement that had once housed Jewish families but was just being taken over and transformed by Puerto Ricans, overflowing from New York City. In 1955 he sent for us. My mother was only twenty years old, I was not quite three, and my brother was a toddler when we arrived at *El Building*, as the place had been christened by its newest residents.

My memories of life in Paterson during those first few years are all in shades of gray. Maybe I was too young to absorb vivid colors and details, or to discriminate between the slate blue of the winter sky and the darker hues of the snow-bearing clouds, but that single color washes over the whole period. The building we lived in was gray, as were the streets, filled with slush the first few months of my life there. The coat my father had bought for me was similar in color and too big; it sat heavily on my thin frame.

I do remember the way the heater pipes banged and rattled, startling all of us out of sleep until we got so used to the sound that we automatically shut it out or raised our voices above the racket. The hiss from the valve punctuated my sleep (which has always been fitful) like a nonhuman presence in the room—a dragon sleeping at the entrance of my childhood. But the pipes were also a connection to all the other lives being lived around us. Having come from a house designed for a single family back in Puerto Rico—my mother's extended-family home—it was curious to know that strangers lived under our floor and above our heads, and that the heater pipe went through everyone's apartments. (My first spanking in Paterson came as a result of playing tunes on the pipes in my room to see if there would be an answer.) My mother was as new to this concept of beehive life as I was, but she had been given strict orders by my father to keep the doors locked, the noise down, ourselves to ourselves.

It seems that Father had learned some painful lessons about prejudice while   5
searching for an apartment in Paterson. Not until years later did I hear how much resistance he had encountered with landlords who were panicking at the influx of Latinos into a neighborhood that had been Jewish for a couple of generations. It made no difference that it was the American phenomenon of ethnic turnover which was changing the urban core of Paterson, and that the human flood could not be held back with an accusing finger.

"You Cuban?" one man had asked my father, pointing at his name tag on the Navy uniform—even though my father had the fair skin and light-brown hair of his northern Spanish background, and the name Ortiz is as common in Puerto Rico as Johnson is in the United States.

"No," my father had answered, looking past the finger into his adversary's angry eyes. "I'm Puerto Rican."

"Same shit." And the door closed.

My father could have passed as European, but we couldn't. My brother and I both have our mother's black hair and olive skin, and so we lived in El Building and visited our great-uncle and his fair children on the next block. It was their private joke that they were the German branch of the family. Not many years later that area too would be mainly Puerto Rican. It was as if the heart of the city map were being gradually colored brown—*café con leche* brown. Our color.

The movie opens with a sweep of the living room. It is "typical" immigrant   10
Puerto Rican decor for the time: The sofa and chairs are square and hard-looking,
upholstered in bright colors (blue and yellow in this instance), and covered with
the transparent plastic that furniture salesmen then were so adept at convincing
women to buy. The linoleum on the floor is light blue; if it had been subjected to
spike heels (as it was in most places), there were dime-sized indentations all over it

that cannot be seen in this movie. The room is full of people dressed up: dark suits for the men, red dresses for the women. When I have asked my mother why most of the women are in red that night, she has shrugged, "I don't remember. Just a coincidence." She doesn't have my obsession for assigning symbolism to everything.

The three women in red sitting on the couch are my mother, my eighteen-year-old cousin, and her brother's girlfriend. The novia *is just up from the Island, which is apparent in her body language. She sits up formally, her dress pulled over her knees. She is a pretty girl, but her posture makes her look insecure, lost in her full-skirted dress, which she has carefully tucked around her to make room for my gorgeous cousin, her future sister-in-law. My cousin has grown up in Paterson and is in her last year of high school. She doesn't have a trace of what Puerto Ricans call* la mancha *(literally, the stain: the mark of the new immigrant —something about the posture, the voice, or the humble demeanor that makes it obvious to everyone the person has just arrived on the mainland). My cousin is wearing a tight, sequined, cocktail dress. Her brown hair has been lightened with peroxide around the bangs, and she is holding a cigarette expertly between her fingers, bringing it up to her mouth in a sensuous arc of her arm as she talks animatedly. My mother, who has come up to sit between the two women, both only a few years younger than herself, is somewhere between the poles they represent in our culture.*

It became my father's obsession to get out of the barrio, and thus we were never permitted to form bonds with the place or with the people who lived there. Yet El Building was a comfort to my mother, who never got over yearning for *la isla.* She felt surrounded by her language: The walls were thin, and voices speaking and arguing in Spanish could be heard all day. *Salsas* blasted out of radios, turned on early in the morning and left on for company. Women seemed to cook rice and beans perpetually—the strong aroma of boiling red kidney beans permeated the hallways.

Though Father preferred that we do our grocery shopping at the supermarket when he came home on weekend leaves, my mother insisted that she could cook only with products whose labels she could read. Consequently, during the week I accompanied her and my little brother to *La Bodega*—a hole-in-the-wall grocery store across the street from El Building. There we squeezed down three narrow aisles jammed with various products. Goya's and Libby's—those were the trademarks that were trusted by *her mamá,* so my mother bought many cans of Goya beans, soups, and condiments, as well as little cans of Libby's fruit juices for us. And she also bought Colgate toothpaste and Palmolive soap. (The final *e* is pronounced in both these products in Spanish, so for many years I believed that they were manufactured on the Island. I remember my surprise at first hearing a commercial on television in which Colgate rhymed with "ate.") We always lingered at La Bodega, for it was there that Mother breathed best, taking in the familiar aromas of the foods she knew from Mamá's kitchen. It was also there that she got to speak to the other women of El Building without violating outright Father's dictates against fraternizing with our neighbors.

Yet Father did his best to make our "assimilation" painless. I can still see him carrying a real Christmas tree up several flights of stairs to our apartment, leaving a trail of aromatic pine. He carried it formally, as if it were a flag in a parade. We were the only ones in El Building that I knew of who got presents on both Christmas day AND *día de Reyes,* the day when the Three Kings brought gifts to Christ and to Hispanic children.

Our supreme luxury in El Building was having our own television set. It must have been a result of Father's guilt feelings over the isolation he had imposed on

15

us, but we were among the first in the barrio to have one. My brother quickly became an avid watcher of Captain Kangaroo and Jungle Jim, while I loved all the series showing families. By the time I started first grade, I could have drawn a map of Middle America as exemplified by the lives of characters in "Father Knows Best," "The Donna Reed Show," "Leave It to Beaver," "My Three Sons," and (my favorite) "Bachelor Father," where John Forsythe treated his adopted teenage daughter like a princess because he was rich and had a Chinese houseboy to do everything for him. In truth, compared to our neighbors in El Building, *we* were rich. My father's Navy check provided us with financial security and a standard of life that the factory workers envied. The only thing his money could not buy us was a place to live away from the barrio—his greatest wish, Mother's greatest fear.

In the home movie the men are shown next, sitting around a card table set up in one corner of the living room, playing dominoes. The clack of the ivory pieces was a familiar sound. I heard it in many houses on the Island and in many apartments in Paterson. In "Leave It to Beaver," the Cleavers played bridge in every other episode; in my childhood, the men started every social occasion with a hotly debated round of dominoes. The women would sit around and watch, but they never participated in the games.

Here and there you can see a small child. Children were always brought to parties and, whenever they got sleepy, were put to bed in the host's bedroom. Babysitting was a concept unrecognized by the Puerto Rican women I knew: A responsible mother did not leave her children with any stranger. And in a culture where children are not considered intrusive, there was no need to leave the children at home. We went where our mother went.

Of my preschool years I have only impressions: the sharp bite of the wind in December as we walked with our parents towards the brightly lit stores downtown; how I felt like a stuffed doll in my heavy coat, boots, and mittens; how good it was to walk into the five-and-dime and sit at the counter drinking hot chocolate. On Saturdays our whole family would walk downtown to shop at the big department stores on Broadway. Mother bought all our clothes at Penney's and Sears, and she liked to buy her dresses at the women's specialty shops like Lerner's and Diana's. At some point we'd go into Woolworth's and sit at the soda fountain to eat.

We never ran into other Latinos at these stores or when eating out, and it became clear to me only years later that the women from El Building shopped mainly in other places—stores owned by other Puerto Ricans or by Jewish merchants who had philosophically accepted our presence in the city and decided to make us their good customers, if not real neighbors and friends. These establishments were located not downtown but in the blocks around our street, and they were referred to generically as *La Tienda, El Bazar, La Bodega, La Botánica.* Everyone knew what was meant. These were the stores where your face did not turn a clerk to stone, where your money was as green as anyone else's.

One New Year's Eve we were dressed up like child models in the Sears catalogue: my brother in a miniature man's suit and bow tie, and I in black patent-leather shoes and a frilly dress with several layers of crinoline underneath. My mother wore a bright red dress that night, I remember, and spike heels; her long black hair hung to her waist. Father, who usually wore his Navy uniform during his short visits home, had put on a dark civilian suit for the occasion: We had been invited to his uncle's house for a big celebration. Everyone was excited because my mother's brother Herman—a bachelor who could indulge himself with luxuries—had bought a home movie camera, which he would be trying out that night.

Even the home movie cannot fill in the sensory details such a gathering left imprinted in a child's brain. The thick sweetness of women's perfumes mixing with the ever-present smells of food cooking in the kitchen: meat and plantain *pasteles,* as well as the ubiquitous rice dish made special with pigeon peas—*gandules*—and seasoned with precious *sofrito* sent up from the Island by somebody's mother or smuggled in by a recent traveler. *Sofrito* was one of the items that women hoarded, since it was hardly ever in stock at La Bodega. It was the flavor of Puerto Rico.

The men drank Palo Viejo rum, and some of the younger ones got weepy. The first time I saw a grown man cry was at a New Year's Eve party: He had been reminded of his mother by the smells in the kitchen. But what I remember most were the boiled *pasteles* —plantain or yucca rectangles stuffed with corned beef or other meats, olives, and many other savory ingredients, all wrapped in banana leaves. Everybody had to fish one out with a fork. There was always a "trick" pastel—one without stuffing—and whoever got that one was the "New Year's Fool."

There was also the music. Long-playing albums were treated like precious china in these homes. Mexican recordings were popular, but the songs that brought tears to my mother's eyes were sung by the melancholy Daniel Santos, whose life as a drug addict was the stuff of legend. Felipe Rodríguez was a particular favorite of couples, since he sang about faithless women and brokenhearted men. There is a snatch of one lyric that has stuck in my mind like a needle on a worn groove: *De piedra ha de ser mi cama, de piedra la cabezera . . . la mujer que a mi me quiera . . . ha de quererme de veras. Ay, Ay, Ay, corazón, porque no amas. . . .* I must have heard it a thousand times since the idea of a bed made of stone, and its connection to love, first troubled me with its disturbing images.

The five-minute home movie ends with people dancing in a circle—the creative filmmaker must have set it up, so that all of them could file past him. It is both comical and sad to watch silent dancing. Since there is no justification for the absurd movements that music provides for some of us, people appear frantic, their faces embarrassingly intense. It's as if you were watching sex. Yet for years I've had dreams in the form of this home movie. In a recurring scene, familiar faces push themselves forward into my mind's eye, plastering their features into distorted close-ups. And I'm asking them: "Who is *she?* Who is the old woman I don't recognize? Is she an aunt? Somebody's wife? Tell me who she is."

> "See the beauty mark on her cheek as big as a hill on the lunar landscape of her face—well, that runs in the family. The women on your father's side of the family wrinkle early; it's the price they pay for that fair skin. The young girl with the green stain on her wedding dress is *La Novia*—just up from the Island. See, she lowers her eyes when she approaches the camera, as she's supposed to. Decent girls never look at you directly in the face. *Humilde,* humble, a girl should express humility in all her actions. She will make a good wife for your cousin. He should consider himself lucky to have met her only weeks after she arrived here. If he marries her quickly, she will make him a good Puerto Rican-style wife; but if he waits too long, she will be corrupted by the city—just like your cousin there."

> "She means me. I do what I want. This is not some primitive island I live on. Do they expect me to wear a black mantilla on my head and go to mass every day? Not me. I'm an American woman, and I will do as I please. I can type faster than anyone in my senior class at Central High, and I'm going to be a secretary to a lawyer when I graduate. I can pass for an American girl anywhere—I've tried it. At least for Italian, anyway—I never speak Spanish in

public. I hate these parties, but I wanted the dress. I look better than any of these *humildes* here. *My* life is going to be different. I have an American boyfriend. He is older and has a car. My parents don't know it, but I sneak out of the house late at night sometimes to be with him. If I marry him, even my name will be American. I hate rice and beans—that's what makes these women fat."

"Your *prima* is pregnant by that man she's been sneaking around with. Would I lie to you? I'm your *Tiá Política,* you great-uncle's common-law wife—the one he abandoned on the Island to go marry your cousin's mother. *I* was not invited to this party, of course, but I came anyway. I came to tell you that story about your cousin that you've always wanted to hear. Do you remember the comment your mother made to a neighbor that has always haunted you? The only thing you heard was your cousin's name, and then you saw your mother pick up your doll from the couch and say: 'It was as big as this doll when they flushed it down the toilet.' This image has bothered you for years, hasn't it? You had nightmares about babies being flushed down the toilet, and you wondered why anyone would do such a horrible thing. You didn't dare ask your mother about it. She would only tell you that you had not heard her right, and yell at you for listening to adult conversations. But later, when you were old enough to know about abortions, you suspected.

"I am here to tell you that you were right. Your cousin was growing an *Americanito* in her belly when this movie was made. Soon after she put something long and pointy into her pretty self, thinking maybe she could get rid of the problem before breakfast and still make it to her first class at the high school. Well, *Niña,* her screams could be heard downtown. Your aunt, her mamá, who had been a midwife on the Island, managed to pull the little thing out. Yes, they probably flushed it down the toilet. What else could they do with it—give it a Christian burial in a little white casket with blue bows and ribbons? Nobody wanted that baby—least of all the father, a teacher at her school with a house in West Paterson that he was filling with real children, and a wife who was a natural blonde.

"Girl, the scandal sent your uncle back to the bottle. And guess where your cousin ended up? Irony of ironies. She was sent to a village in Puerto Rico to live with a relative on her mother's side: a place so far away from civilization that you have to ride a mule to reach it. A real change in scenery. She found a man there—women like that cannot live without male company—but believe me, the men in Puerto Rico know how to put a saddle on a woman like her. *La Gringa,* they call her. Ha, ha, ha. *La Gringa* is what she always wanted to be. . . ."

The old woman's mouth becomes a cavernous black hole I fall into. And as I fall, I can feel the reverberations of her laughter. I hear the echoes of her last mocking words: *La Gringa, La Gringa!* And the conga line keeps moving silently past me. There is no music in my dream for the dancers.

When Odysseus visits Hades to see the spirit of his mother, he makes an offering of sacrificial blood, but since all the souls crave an audience with the living, he has to listen to many of them before he can ask questions. I, too, have to hear the dead and the forgotten speak in my dream. Those who are still part of my life remain silent, going around and around in their dance. The others keep pressing their faces forward to say things about the past.

My father's uncle is last in line. He is dying of alcoholism, shrunken and shriveled like a monkey, his face a mass of wrinkles and broken arteries. As he comes closer I realize that in his features I can see my whole family. If you were to stretch that rubbery flesh, you could find my father's face, and deep within *that* face—my own. I don't want to look into those eyes ringed in purple. In a few years he will retreat into silence, and take a long, long time to die. *Move back, Tío,* I tell him. *I don't want to hear what you have to say. Give the dancers room to move. Soon it will be midnight. Who is the New Year's Fool this time?*

Annie Dillard   b. 1945

The Deer at Providencia   1982

There were four of us North Americans in the jungle, in the Ecuadorian jungle on the banks of the Napo River in the Amazon watershed. The other three North Americans were metropolitan men. We stayed in tents in one riverside village, and visited others. At the village called Providencia we saw a sight which moved us, and which shocked the men.

The first thing we saw when we climbed the riverbank to the village of Providencia was the deer. It was roped to a tree on the grass clearing near the thatch shelter where we would eat lunch.

The deer was small, about the size of a whitetail fawn, but apparently full-grown. It had a rope around its neck and three feet caught in the rope. Someone said that the dogs had caught it that morning and the villagers were going to cook and eat it that night.

This clearing lay at the edge of the little thatched-hut village. We could see the villagers going about their business, scattering feed corn for hens about their houses, and wandering down paths to the river to bathe. The village headman was our host; he stood beside us as we watched the deer struggle. Several village boys were interested in the deer; they formed part of the circle we made around it in the clearing. So also did four businessmen from Quito who were attempting to guide us around the jungle. Few of the very different people standing in this circle had a common language. We watched the deer, and no one said much.

The deer lay on its side at the rope's very end, so the rope lacked slack to let   5 it rest its head in the dust. It was "pretty," delicate of bone like all deer, and thin-skinned for the tropics. Its skin looked virtually hairless, in fact, and almost translucent, like a membrane. Its neck was no thicker than my wrist; it was rubbed open on the rope, and gashed. Trying to paw itself free of the rope, the deer had scratched its own neck with its hooves. The raw underside of its neck showed red stripes and some bruises bleeding inside the muscles. Now three of its feet were hooked in the rope under its jaw. It could not stand, of course, on one leg, so it could not move to slacken the rope and ease the pull on its throat and enable it to rest its head.

Repeatedly the deer paused, motionless, its eyes veiled, with only its rib cage in motion, and its breaths the only sound. Then, after I would think, "It has given up; now it will die," it would heave. The rope twanged; the tree leaves clattered; the deer's free foot beat the ground. We stepped back and held our breaths. It thrashed, kicking, but only one leg moved; the other three legs tightened inside the rope's loop. Its hip jerked; its spine shook. Its eyes rolled; its tongue, thick with spittle, pushed in and out. Then it would rest again. We watched this for fifteen minutes.

Once three young native boys charged in, released its trapped legs, and jumped back to the circle of people. But instantly the deer scratched up its neck with its hooves and snared its forelegs in the rope again. It was easy to imagine a third and then a fourth leg soon stuck, like Brer Rabbit and the Tar Baby.

We watched the deer from the circle, and then we drifted on to lunch. Our palm-roofed shelter stood on a grassy promontory from which we could see the deer tied to the tree, pigs and hens walking under village houses, and black-and-white cattle standing in the river. There was even a breeze.

Lunch, which was the second and better lunch we had that day, was hot and fried. There was a big fish called *doncella,* a kind of catfish, dipped whole in corn flour and beaten egg, then deep fried. With our fingers we pulled soft fragments of it from its sides to our plates, and ate; it was delicate fish-flesh, fresh and mild. Someone found the roe, and I ate of that too—it was fat and stronger, like egg yolk, naturally enough, and warm.

There was also a stew of meat in shreds with rice and pale brown gravy. I had 10 asked what kind of deer it was tied to the tree; Pepe had answered in Spanish, "*Gama.*" Now they told us this was *gama* too, stewed. I suspect the word means merely game or venison. At any rate, I heard that the village dogs had cornered another deer just yesterday, and it was this deer which we were now eating in full sight of the whole article. It was good. I was surprised at its tenderness. But it is a fact that high levels of lactic acid, which builds up in muscle tissues during exertion, tenderizes.

After the fish and meat we ate bananas fried in chunks and served on a tray; they were sweet and full of flavor. I felt terrific. My shirt was wet and cool from swimming; I had had a night's sleep, two decent walks, three meals, and a swim—everything tasted good. From time to time each of us, separately, would look beyond our shaded roof to the sunny spot where the deer was still convulsing in the dust. Our meal completed, we walked around the deer and back to the boats.

That night I learned that while we were watching the deer, the others were watching me.

We four North Americans grew close in the jungle in a way that was not the usual artificial intimacy of travelers. We liked each other. We stayed up all that night talking, murmuring, as though we rocked on hammocks slung above time. The others were from big cities: New York, Washington, Boston. They all said that I had no expression on my face when I was watching the deer—or at any rate, not the expression they expected.

They had looked to see how I, the only woman, and the youngest, was taking the sight of the deer's struggles. I looked detached, apparently, or hard, or calm, or focused, still. I don't know. I was thinking. I remember feeling very old and energetic. I could say like Thoreau that I have traveled widely in Roanoke, Virginia. I have thought a great deal about carnivorousness; I eat meat. These things are not issues; they are mysteries.

Gentlemen of the city, what surprises you? That there is suffering here, or that 15 I know it?

We lay in the tent and talked. "If it had been my wife," one man said with special vigor, amazed, "she wouldn't have cared *what* was going on; she would have dropped *everything* right at that moment and gone in the village from here to there to there, she would not have *stopped* until that animal was out of its suffering one way or another. She couldn't *bear* to see a creature in agony like that."

I nodded.

Now I am home. When I wake I comb my hair before the mirror above my dresser. Every morning for the past two years I have seen in that mirror, beside my sleep-softened face, the blackened face of a burnt man. It is a wire-service photo-graph clipped from a newspaper and taped to my mirror. The caption reads: "Alan McDonald in Miami hospital bed." All you can see in the photograph is a smudged triangle of face from his eyelids to his lower lip; the rest is bandages. You cannot see the expression in his eyes; the bandages shade them.

The story, headed MAN BURNED FOR SECOND TIME, begins:

> "Why does God hate me?" Alan McDonald asked from his hospital bed.
> "When the gunpowder went off, I couldn't believe it," he said. "I just couldn't believe it. I said, 'No, God couldn't do this to me again.'"

He was in a burn ward in Miami, in serious condition. I do not even know if   20
he lived. I wrote him a letter at the time, cringing.

He had been burned before, thirteen years previously, by flaming gasoline. For years he had been having his body restored and his face remade in dozens of operations. He had been a boy, and then a burnt boy. He had already been stunned by what could happen, by how life could veer.

Once I read that people who survive bad burns tend to go crazy; they have a very high suicide rate. Medicine cannot ease their pain; drugs just leak away, soak-ing the sheets, because there is no skin to hold them in. The people just lie there and weep. Later they kill themselves. They had not known, before they were burned, that the world included such suffering, that life could permit them per-sonally such pain.

This time a bowl of gunpowder had exploded on McDonald.

> "I didn't realize what had happened at first," he recounted. "And then I heard that sound from 13 years ago. I was burning. I rolled to put the fire out and I thought, 'Oh God, not again.'"
> "If my friend hadn't been there, I would have jumped into a canal with a rock around my neck."

His wife concludes the piece, "Man, it just isn't fair."

I read the whole clipping again every morning. This is the Big Time here, every minute of it. Will someone please explain to Alan McDonald in his dignity, to the deer at Providencia in his dignity, what is going on? And mail me the carbon.

When we walked by the deer at Providencia for the last time, I said to Pepe,   25
with a pitying glance at the deer, *"Pobrecito"*—"poor little thing." But I was trying out Spanish. I knew at the time it was a ridiculous thing to say.

Football and Snowballs   1987

Some boys taught me to play football. This was fine sport. You thought up a new strategy for every play and whispered it to the others. You went out for a pass, fooling everyone. Best, you got to throw yourself mightily at someone's run-ning legs. Either you brought him down or you hit the ground flat out on your chin, with your arms empty before you. It was all or nothing. If you hesitated in fear, you would miss and get hurt: you would take a hard fall while the kid got away, or you would get kicked in the face while the kid got away. But if you flung yourself wholeheartedly at the back of his knees—if you gathered and joined body and soul and pointed them diving fearlessly—then you likely wouldn't get hurt, and you'd stop the ball. Your fate, and your team's score, depended on your concentration and courage. Nothing girls did could compare with it.

Boys welcomed me at baseball, too, for I had, through enthusiastic practice, what was weirdly known as a boy's arm. In winter, in the snow, there was neither baseball nor football, so the boys and I threw snowballs at passing cars. I got in trouble throwing snowballs, and have seldom been happier since.

On one weekday morning after Christmas, six inches of new snow had just fallen. We were standing up to our boot tops in snow on a front yard on trafficked Reynolds Street, waiting for cars. The cars traveled Reynolds Street slowly and evenly; they were targets all but wrapped in red ribbons, cream puffs. We couldn't miss.

I was seven; the boys were eight, nine, and ten. The oldest two Fahey boys were there—Mikey and Peter—polite blond boys who lived near me on Lloyd Street, and who already had four brothers and sisters. My parents approved Mikey and Peter Fahey. Chickie McBride was there, a tough kid, and Billy Paul and Mackie Kean too, from across Reynolds, where the boys grew up dark and furious, grew up skinny, knowing, and skilled. We had all drifted from our houses that morning looking for action, and had found it here on Reynolds Street.

It was cloudy but cold. The cars' tires laid behind them on the snowy street a   5
complex trail of beige chunks like crenellated castle walls. I had stepped on some earlier; they squeaked. We could have wished for more traffic. When a car came, we all popped it one. In the intervals between cars we reverted to the natural solitude of children.

I started making an iceball—a perfect iceball, from perfectly white snow, perfectly spherical, and squeezed perfectly translucent so no snow remained all the way through. (The Fahey boys and I considered it unfair actually to throw an iceball at somebody, but it had been known to happen.)

I had just embarked on the iceball project when we heard tire chains come clanking from afar. A black Buick was moving toward us down the street. We all spread out, banged together some regular snowballs, took aim, and, when the Buick drew nigh, fired.

A soft snowball hit the driver's windshield right before the driver's face. It made a smashed star with a hump in the middle.

Often, of course, we hit our target, but this time, the only time in all of life, the car pulled over and stopped. Its wide black door opened; a man got out of it, running. He didn't even close the car door.

He ran after us, and we ran from him, up the snowy Reynolds sidewalk. At   10
the corner, I looked back; incredibly, he was still after us. He was in city clothes: a suit and tie, street shoes. Any normal adult would have quit, having sprung us into flight and made his point. This man was gaining on us. He was a thin man, all action. All of a sudden, we were running for our lives.

Wordless, we split up. We were on our turf; we could lose ourselves in the neighborhood backyards, everyone for himself. I paused and considered. Everyone had vanished except Mikey Fahey, who was just rounding the corner of a yellow brick house. Poor Mikey, I trailed him. The driver of the Buick sensibly picked the two of us to follow. The man apparently had all day.

He chased Mikey and me around the yellow house and up a backyard path we knew by heart: under a low tree, up a bank, through a hedge, down some snowy steps, and across the grocery store's delivery driveway. We smashed through a gap in another hedge, entered a scruffy backyard and ran around its back porch and tight between houses to Edgerton Avenue; we ran across Edgerton to an alley and up our own sliding woodpile to the Halls' front yard; he kept coming. We ran up Lloyd Street and wound through mazy backyards toward the steep hilltop at Willard and Lang.

He chased us silently, block after block. He chased us silently over picket fences, through thorny hedges, between houses, and garbage cans, and across streets. Every time I glanced back, choking for breath, I expected he would have quit. He must have been as breathless as we were. His jacket strained over his body. It was an immense discovery, pounding into my hot head with every sliding, joyous step, that this ordinary adult evidently knew what I thought only children who trained at football knew: that you have to fling yourself at what you're doing, you have to point yourself, forget yourself, aim, dive.

Mikey and I had nowhere to go, in our own neighborhood or out of it, but away from this man who was chasing us. He impelled us forward; we compelled him to follow our route. The air was cold; every breath tore my throat. We kept running, block after block; we kept improvising, backyard after backyard, running a frantic course and choosing it simultaneously, failing always to find small places or hard places to slow him down, and discovering always, exhilarated, dismayed, that only bare speed could save us—for he would never give up, this man—and we were losing speed.

He chased us through the backyard labyrinths of ten blocks before he caught us by our jackets. He caught us and we all stopped.   15

We three stood staggering, half blinded, coughing, in an obscure hilltop backyard: a man in his twenties, a boy, a girl. He had released our jackets, our pursuer, our captor, our hero: he knew we weren't going anywhere. We all played by the rules. Mikey and I unzipped our jackets. I pulled off my sopping mittens. Our tracks multiplied in the backyard's new snow. We had been breaking new snow all morning. We didn't look at each other. I was cherishing my excitement. The man's lower pants legs were wet; his cuffs were full of snow, and there was a prow of snow beneath them on his shoes and socks. Some trees bordered the little flat backyard, some messy winter trees. There was no one around: a clearing in a grove, and we the only players.

It was a long time before he could speak. I had some difficulty at first recalling why we were there. My lips felt swollen; I couldn't see out of the sides of my eyes; I kept coughing.

"You stupid kids," he began perfunctorily.

We listened perfunctorily indeed, if we listened at all, for the chewing out was redundant, a mere formality, and beside the point. The point was that he had chased us passionately without giving up, and so he had caught us. Now he came down to earth. I wanted the glory to last forever.

But how could the glory have lasted forever? We could have run through   20
every backyard in North America until we got to Panama. But when he trapped us at the lip of the Panama Canal, what precisely could he have done to prolong the drama of the chase and cap its glory? I brooded about this for the next few years. He could only have fried Mikey Fahey and me in boiling oil, say, or dismembered us piecemeal, or staked us to anthills. None of which I really wanted, and none of which any adult was likely to do, even in the spirit of fun. He could only chew us out there in the Panamanian jungle, after months or years of exalting pursuit. He could only begin, "You stupid kids," and continue in his ordinary Pittsburgh accent with his normal righteous anger and the usual common sense.

If in that snowy backyard the driver of the black Buick had cut off our heads, Mikey's and mine, I would have died happy, for nothing has required so much of me since as being chased all over Pittsburgh in the middle of winter—running terrified, exhausted—by this sainted, skinny, furious red-headed man who wished to have a word with us. I don't know how he found his way back to his car.

Stanley Elkin   b. 1930

Some Overrated Masterpieces   *1992*

There's nothing so convincing as an opinion, and an odd thing about words is the cockeyed weight they're permitted to bear, so that if I say something as fla- grantly meaningless or flat-out arbitrary as that, oh, "He's the sort of person who parts his hair," I've not only suggested something negative about hair-parting, but have made, too, an aspersion on character. He'll think twice before he parts it next time, I bet. And this goes double for written words. "He uses aftershave," I charge, "and his last three cars have been hardtops." "His wife," I continue mercilessly, "dresses the twins alike and pushes them about the streets in a perambulator like one of those wide-load house trailers!"

This isn't just a haughty aesthetic of the superciliary, it's the astonishing Law of the Unframed Indictment, the critical equivalent of holding political prisoners without bringing charges. We condemn a thing simply by mentioning it.

J. M. W. Turner,[1] I claim, as evenly, uninflectedly as I can, paints elements— water and air—in ratios seldom seen in life and got up in murk and slate fug like a foul mood. What's the difference, then, between a Turner and ordinary mall art? Why, merely the weather, only the sobriety of his colors, as if genius were a ques- tion of the intervention of light, like sunblock, say. This time, though, by having introduced a reason, however spurious, I seem to have taken higher ground. But in questions of taste there *is* no higher ground. In matters of art and cuisine, rea- sons are created equal. It's a perfect *democracy* of reasons and, hey, "I know what I like" isn't only a perfectly respectable argument but an absolutely unanswerable one. There *is* nothing so convincing as an opinion.

Am I philistine? What, with *my* up-front heart? Philistine?[2] *Me?* With my sleeves and my hankies and all the other emotional ready-to-wear in the wardrobe of my attentive sentiments? The sucker *I* am for almost any statuary in the open air, in landscape, or any of the kempt green gardens of the world? *This* pushover for the simple human harmonics of any orchestra at work, *any* orchestra, any symphony or pit band, any string quartet, jazz band, pickup bluegrass rhythm jammers, or even just any saw- or jug- or steel-drum-and-washboard skiffle group! What, *this* soft-souled, *nolo-contendere,*[3] hearts-and-minds pussycat? Anybody's fascist, this nose-led company man, as willing—willing? *anxious*—to be stirred as sugar in tea, this lawn-chair enthusiast for all the brass, fife, and oom-pa-pa of high summer's slam-bang reviewing-stand occasions and gazebo patrioticals.

[1]Turner (1775–1851)—English landscape painter.
[2]Philistine—crass, lacking in taste or sensibility.
[3]*Nolo-contendere*—no contest.

But lesser art forms are all collective, I think. Which pretty much—because I   5
know what I don't like, too—puts opera's hyperbolic charms and vocal circus in
their place. Because art ought to be as one-on-one as intimacy, something if not
actually shades-drawn and pulled-curtain to it, then at least discreet, and the last
thing—saving architecture perhaps, which, like that gazebo from which those
marches occur, is public, communal—the last thing art ought to be is stirring. And
if van Gogh's painted room in Arles can command my tears, all I can tell you is
that those are a different sort of tears, *vintage* tears could be, as unlike my public
performances in the sculpture garden as Ripple[4] from champagne. Speaking of
which, incidentally, with its taste like a mixture of dishwater and sugar substitute,
while not one of the overrated masterpieces I mean to consider here, may not be
a bad instance. It comes down to us through the bubbles' reputation. Of course
that's how everything comes down to us, history working its gravitational will
through word of mouth.

Trust me. What I'm talking about has nothing to do with what's in and what's
out, what's up and what's down—prepositional aesthetics. There ain't any old
Roman pleasure to it, the thumbs-up, thumbs-down joys. I already said I know
what I like. It's strictly personal. Because, for me, there *has* to be something personal or I can't function. And there is. Not envy, I *hope* not envy, or not envy exactly, and not sour grapes, *exactly* not sour grapes, with which I've no patience.
Sour grapes are pathetic. Just something inimical in me to the overrated, the next
guy's hype, a kind of rage like an allergy. It's a myth you don't feel your blood
pressure; I *feel* my blood pressure. And for me, the test of time is simply an adjustment of the systolics and diastolics, a subsidence of the personal. So this shall
chiefly take place within the precincts of the safely historical, where bygones are
bygones (I mean, how long can I reasonably hold a grudge against *The Bonfire of
the Vanities?*)[5] and even subjectivity has cooled to a temperature that can't be felt.

Take Leonardo da Vinci, for example, who, with his polymath imagination
and sci-fi instinctuals, seems to have been to art what Jules Verne and H. G. Wells
were to fiction. Indeed, though many of his designs and sketches seem plausible
even today—his tanks and fortifications, his flying machines, catapults, machine
guns, hoists and gears, all the heavy arsenal of his Armageddon heart—there's
something comic about Leonardo, some after-the-fact humor laid on by perspective and hindsight, the joke, that is, of the primitive, like Fred Flintstone propelling
his car by foot power, some principle of the dated operating here. And if this isn't
fair, isn't, in fact, specious at the root, if it suggests that a principle of the dated is
always operable, chipping away and chipping away like a kind of erosion at what
was once thought true and beautiful, the water, wind, and temperature of age,
why not accept at the outset that *most* things left out in history like the open air
oxidize, tarnish, become, finally, subject to the simple human joke of time? The
moving finger writes, paints, makes, and having writ, painted, or made, moves on
to the next thing. Because a lot of what we talk about when we talk about art is,
well, fashion.

Add to my charge against Leonardo that he was a "visionary," this intellectual
rover and time traveler, and it's possible to see an instability in him, a certain failure of *sitzfleisch,* an inability, that is, to sit still in his talent, almost as if he took too

---

[4]Ripple—cheap wine.
[5]*Bonfire of the Vanities*—novel by Tom Wolfe.

seriously the burden of being a Renaissance man, or was the sort of guy who parted his hair.

Now, about this Mona Lisa.

See her there in her cat-who-ate-the-canaries, her smug repose and babushka   10
of hair like a face on a buck. A study in browns, in muds and all the purplish earthens of her jaundiced, low-level, f-stop light. See her, see her there, this, well, girl of a certain age, with a faint streak of bone structure blowing off her skin like a plume of jet trail all she has for brow. See her, see the leftward glancing of her color-coordinated eyes inside the puffy, horizontal parentheses of her lashless lids. See the long, low-slung nose dropped inches below the painterly rules of thumb. Now see her famous statelies, her upright, comfortable aplomb, her left forearm along the arm of a chair, her fat right hand covering it, as clubby and at ease as one foot crossed over another. Look at the background through the open casement, the queer topography like mounds of green volcanic vegetable, the strange striated water and all the wavy switchback of the road like something carved from earth by one of the maestro's anachronistic machines, a backhoe, say, some plow or grader of the yet-to-be.

Focus. *Focus!*

In and closer in to the central occasion of her odd, asexual face, in where the mystery lives, the secret agenda, in toward her giacondas, her giaconundrums, the hidden mystery of her guarded gingivitis smile! Because I'm changing my mind here, a little I am, and thinking maybe it's Nat King Cole's version I'm not that crazy about, his viscous syrups I'm thinking of, confusing the box-step cliché and sentimentals with the fact of her face. Because what levers our attention is that nose and those lips, and a truth about art is the company it keeps with the slightly askew, the fly in that woodpile of symmetry, mere balance in painting, equilibrium, a stunt of the "beautiful." What commissions the eye is face. No likeness hangs on the wall of hair, hands, breasts, behinds, the soles of one's feet. Faces are the most private part. It's the face that draws the eye in the Mona Lisa, but I was only kidding about the mystery of that smile. There *is* no mystery. No one ever had to solve a face, and the notion of *this* face's enigmatics has always been a kind of anthropomorphism, only paint's pathetic fallacy, facial phrenology, a horoscopics by bone structure, an astrology of the eye, the palmistry of character, wrongheaded, literary, the racism of beauty, unreliable finally as any other pseudoscience, as if to say, oh, as if to say, "Read my lips."

Next slide.

Georgia O'Keeffe was a painter who rarely depicted human beings. Her desert subject matter is, in a way, the flip, parched, only apparently sunnier side of Turner's wet coin—blanched, bleached landscapes of polished, picked-clean death. This hermit—in New Mexico she lived at "Ghost Ranch"—this prospector type whose unpopulated, desiccated paintings, save for the fossils that appear in them, seem studies in an almost relished absence. The bones and white skulls of O'Keeffe's work signify not decay so much as the evidence of a fled, efficient hunger—the art of the buzzard, the art of the scavenger hunt. Even her rather wonderful cityscapes (*East River No. I; Shelton Hotel, New York; New York Night*) are alternative versions of shapes found in the desert paintings—the mesa, canyon, adobe variations—and seem deliberate, even perverse, essays in exclusion, as though both nature and the manmade contain value only to the extent that they not only avoid but actually proscribe the human. (Only in *New York Night*, and only if you look carefully, can you make out, in the lower left-hand corner, any people at all—four stick figures of black paint rather more like exclamation points than human beings.) It's as if O'Keeffe were driven by some wilderness,

Sierra Club will, vaguely snobbish, a restrictive, country-club vision. She's Edward Hopper without people, without even the saving grace of their dignified loneliness. She's interested only in shapes (my favorite O'Keeffe paintings, her *Sky Above Clouds* series, have always seemed rather like *New Yorker* covers), but where there is no "face" there can be no interest. Even her suggestive, almost gynecological and phallic flora (which almost never appear in bunches and are rarely "arranged") seem parodic, sterile, lush enough but in their issueless isolation really only a sort of sexual floor plan.

Like other private artists she became her greatest achievement, a beautiful   15 woman whose bone structure was her fate and who posed, in a literal sense, in her black clothes, white scarves, and black hats, paring herself down and paring herself down into a piece of art quite like sculpture, a leathery, unsmiling woman of manipulated style, editing herself and disappearing at last behind the very image of a collective, hermaphroditic animism, some perfected, deliberated simulacrum somewhere between ancient squaw and old manitou, a final, showy mysticism complete and functional as the bony infrastructure of those skulls she preferred to the faces that covered them. I think narcissism infrastructures the infrastructure here, the dangerous virus she contracted by being both a subject—all those portraits she permitted Alfred Stieglitz to make of her—and an arranger of subjects.

But it's hard to talk about art. Maybe there should be a law against it, some First Amendment gag order like crying fire in a crowded theater. Still and all, if one knows what one likes, well, where's the harm, eh? And anyway, as I'm writing now, it's the war, day thirteen or fourteen into the Mother of Battles, though it seems longer of course, deeper into time than anything I can remember—and I'm sixty if I'm a day—and I've seen, well, not a lot, but my share, more than, and what I haven't seen, like everyone else, I fill in the blanks, make an allowance, do the Kentucky windage adjustments, write off if not to experience then to helplessness and despair this, well, looting of end times everywhere, this breaking and entering the other guy's turf, with wiser heads figuring—this is a big benefit of the doubt I'm giving away here—that damn near no one has led the right life. The Gulf's a floating filling station, Marines have died, civilians on all sides in God knows what apocalyptic positions have fallen on what rubble and hoisted on what shrapnel, and I see that over on the Home Shopping Club, Operation Desert Storm sweatshirts are going for $19.75, over 400 sold and counting, and, jeez, if the world made it, it would have been the millennium in nine years and, in another one and a half, the semimillennium of the discovery of the New World. Some millennium. Some semimillennium. So it's pretty late in the day to be having any Mother of Battles. Ain't going to *study* no war no more! And I take it back about injunctions on art talk, prior restraint. Because maybe that's the only thing we ought to be allowed to talk about, stuff above our station, playing catch-up with culture, sucking up to civilization. And the point is, well, God bless the artists the point is. Here's to those with the paints whether we know whereof we speak or not. Here's to artisans, folks who make violins, cast bells, throw pots, have perfected their pitch. Here's, I mean, to all those whose attentions are engaged in innocent acts, to everyone everywhere who doesn't know where the time has flown. To minders of their own determined business who wouldn't hurt a fly. Here's to occupational therapy even, to doodle and whittle, to whistle and hum and all the preoccupied instrumentals of the head and heart, the *eye-lu-loo-lus* and sweet-dream lullabies of softest yore. And to all those makers of those less-than-masterpieces who lend point to the sermon, and to dilettantes, oh, especially, Lord, to dilettantes, window-shoppers on the artier avenues, friends of the museum, patrons of the symphony, pals of the zoo, to everyone everywhere who's ever tossed a pledge to PBS, NPR, ladies and gentlemen of good will who keep the Sunday. So, waiting for the worst, hoping for the best, it's back I go to my own harmless knitting, an expert self-proclamated but innocent as any.

Now what *I* don't much care for is all the boring, adulatory religious art of dark old early times, the triptychs in their layered gilded frames like great wooden fanfares, I mean; the altarpieces; the madonnas with their malnourished, wizened bundles of infant Jesus in fishbowl, space-helmet halos or under rakish nimbi of beanies (not like Michelangelo's pink, meaty, muscular biblicals so oddly anticipatory of Picasso's great fleshy giants); all the Annunciations running together in our heads like a Pony Express of the holy; all the lugubrious figures making their *there theres* of comfort over the spilled milk and blood of the major players on all that stained glass and shining wood; all that adoration in kings' caucus in the stable like so much political buzz, their baksheesh of gold, frankincense, and myrrh; angels in improbable, heavier-than-air wings; lashed, trussed, hangdog Jesus, pathetic, almost sheepish, shouldering a cross like a T-square, neither a Son of Man to inspire confidence nor a God to reckon with, looking nothing near what he's cracked up to be, looking confused in fact, lost, as if he'd rather be in Philadelphia—all the stupefying *junk* I mean, in Europe raised to the level of an industry, complete with guides yet, scholars of the local (and here's to guides in billed caps, gray creased suits and stuffed pockets), all those panels of unskilled, uninspired piety cartoons which looked at long enough bring on the headache and fog up the mind, and cause, as stated, to run together in the memory this blur of art, this crisis of criticism, this deferential politeness on all sides—*"Bella, bella,"* I assure the guide, *"molti, molti, molti bella"*—in my broken business-as-usual, not only as if no one had ever been afraid of being caught short in church but as if tourists were as anatomically incorrect as all those God-doll altarpieces.

And, God forgive me, *Hamlet* is an overrated play. Well, it's too long, but that ain't it, and too melodramatic of course, *and* familiar, but that ain't it either. For one thing, the premise has always bothered me, or if not the premise then what triggers the play, bothered me, I mean, even back in those old new-critical days of my undergraduate youth when we fastened on the incest thing, or the question of the prince's madness, ruse or consequence, or just plain dug H's brilliant, witty manic depression. He was, for most of us, our first "psychological" hero, more psychological even than Ivan in *The Brothers Karamazov,*[6] which we hadn't read yet anyway. Absolutely, Hamlet was our first interesting guy, a role model even, with his get-thees-to-a-nunnery and all the tortured Ophelia-bashing and secret titillation of the dirty private jokes, his breezy killer instincts, all the full-throated cynicism of his bullying intellect—role model, male bonder, man's man, prince's prince. What puts me off, what *I* can't get past, though, is, quite simply, Hamlet's father's ghost, to me as silly as that cadre of icons in all those triptychs on all those altarpieces, the angels and allegoricals, themselves a band of ghosts, sentimental and sweet-cheeked as zephyrs on maps. I am what I am and cut no slack for the times, the other fellow's world view. Besides, at its core *Hamlet* is a realistic play and having truck with ghosts goes against its grain, botches the unity of its tone, and anyway the ghost's only a device to put the ball in play in the play. In a drama so dependent upon personality, this ghost is a stick figure. It has no character. Nor will it do to write the ghost off as a psychological projection. It comes with too much information for that. A forensic pathologist of a ghost, it fingers Claudius,

---

[6] *The Brothers Karamazov*—novel by Leo Tolstoy.

fine-tunes the terms of its dispatch during its afternoon nap ("Cut off even in the blossoms of my sin, / Unhousel'd, disappointed, unanel'd, / No reck'ning made, but sent to my account / With all my imperfections on my head"), charges Hamlet to avenge it, and even dictates how Hamlet is to treat his mother.

(And like where do *I* get off?)

Some soliloquies bother me—all its vaunted to-be-or-not-to-bes, a speech I've   20 never heard delivered by any actor, *any* actor, who's not managed to make it sound silly.

But finally, it isn't the ghost and it isn't the overblown language which grates so much as the flip side of this "interesting" man, for Hamlet's procrastinations lie as heavily on the belly as bad food. One has the sense that Shakespeare, not Hamlet, is vamping till ready, that Hamlet's frozen will is finally as much a device to stall the play as the ghost is to get it going, because for all the brilliant facets of Hamlet's reckless character, his too-fastidious duty pulls him down and locks up the play like so much left luggage, until, well, until we begin to suspect that will paralysis is itself a device, that Hamlet, for all his thoroughbred, live-wire wit, for all his charm and playfulness, is not so much the Dane as one of those paid professionals at an Irish funeral, a bespoke whiner and keener, the ultimate wailer and scold of fate. Brilliant along the brightest edges of its day, the play naps like the old king during the dead, leaden center of its long, endless afternoon.

And get *these* to a nunnery: *Birth of a Nation, The Cabinet of Dr. Caligari* (well, almost every silent movie ever made, including Buster Keaton's, including Charlie Chaplin's). *Citizen Kane, Gone With the Wind,* that documentary about the '36 Olympics, most "screwball" comedies of the thirties (well, most black-and-white films generally). All the Marx Brothers, all the Ritz Brothers, Judy Garland, Fred Astaire. No more "face" to them than the dry, blanched bones of a Georgia O'Keeffe, mask all they *ever* had for a face, as customized as a clown's patented, painted puss. Garland all pixie/gamine/urchin pout and phony hope, that mask out on a ledge somewhere between outrage and melted love and on a kind of red-alert verge of perpetual tears from the tip of her pigtail in *The Wizard of Oz* to the top of her pompadour in *Meet Me in St. Louis*, a face, like the clown's, made for black velvet, crying out for it like a fix, and not much more face to her voice either if you want to know, decibel for decibel its direct weights-and-measure vocal equivalency, all vibrato and belt but slightly off true, and Fred Astaire's fixed puzzled-bumpkin expression more pleasant, perhaps, but as locked-in as Garland's. (Am I cranky, crotchety, under the weather? Are my shoes too tight, is curmudgeon written all over me? Am I this old fogey, is my bite worse than my bark? Or is this still the war news, something fed-up in my bones with hyperbolicized attachment, the red rant of unearned, misunderstood praise?) So take *that*, Fred Astaire, with your vaunted grace in your top hat your white tie and your tails, in your nightclubs, on your patent-leather, art-deco floors, your decks like the seamless, level tiles of chic beauty parlors, barbershops and men's rooms in the basements of world-class hotels. Take that and *that* on your fey, heel/toe, heel/toe bearings in your smug, *noli-me-tangere* aloofness and look-ma-no-hands gravity denials, your tango indifference and vain, vaguely threatening, predatory swoops and leaned inclinations as if, Ginger Rogers or no Ginger Rogers, elegance were only a narcissistic one-man show, *ur* performance art, removed as the elsewhere-engaged attentions of a juggler. Though maybe all movies, could be, fall short of art with their soft blandishments and easy endowments—sound, closeups, an arch, arranged lushness, perfect and unblemished as a gorgeous bay posed on a postcard. (Are my pants too small, is my hat off plumb? Nah, nah, this from a *lover* of movies, one of their easiest marks, privileged to get out of an evening, watch the coming attractions, the trailers, who, settled in his seat in the auditorium, sighs, re-marks to the wife, "What could be better?") Because the truth about art *is* the com-pany it keeps with the slightly askew, and the real stunt of the beautiful is not to be *too* beautiful.

And Jasper Johns's[7] flag series—*White Flag* like a plank floor, *Two Flags* like a wall of carelessly mortared bricks and, for my money, the best of them, *Three Flags*, like a box on a board game. Well, I say "for my money," but who's kidding whom here? All that dough and no Hawaii or Alaska? Jasper Johns in a fallen world an easier target than Astaire or Garland, than *Citizen Kane*, than *Gone With the Wind*, though richer people take him more seriously—a desecration not of the flag but of money.

(And once—this would have been in the middlish sixties, Baby Jane Holtzer was a Presence, People Are Talking About, Buzz Buzz and et cetera—I found my-self in Frank Stella's[8] East-something brownstone. Uninvited, unintroduced, it being a whimsy intentionally inflicted or a perverse, acceptable usage among cer-tain groups never to make a devoir, as if one's physical, accompanied presence in a place—He's-With-Me understood—were a sort of moral vouchsafe or silent pa-role like an obscure but flashy idiom of behavior redounding not so much to the credit of the *schlepped* as the honor of the *schlepper*, but no crasher either, given carte blanche like any real guest, special roaming privileges like a range chicken, to mosey, take it all in. I've never forgotten my first impression. Which was, there, surrounded by the astonishing furniture in the setlike rooms—chrome and leather, glass and steel—and several hundred thousand bucks' worth of Stella's frames and canvases, the paintings like patterns on bolts of fabric, the strangely shaped frames like exercises in bizarre carpentry, a realization that what I saw was visionary, but misunderstanding the vision, not recognizing in what was still only the sixties that what I saw was basically only your expensive *de rigueur* restaurant decor of the seventies, eighties, and nineties, maybe even a first take on the higher mall motifs.

(And another time, years later, in Paris at the Rodin Museum, Stella con-founded, inverted, in a different mode, on a different scale, some metrics of the monumental, translated really, their differences all there was to run them together in my mind and, miles from the ornamental now, beyond decor or the Wagnerian either, the Tristanic and Isoldic, heroism's warp speeds, into cruel health like bloody organ meats on the redded-up floors of some human abattoir, those mon-umental sitters or loungers or drowners in their own stone, Rodin's more-than-solid-citizens, who can't keep their hands to themselves, whose every pose—think *The Thinker*, think the vats and bone banks in *The Gates of Hell*, think *Adam*, think *Eve, The Crouching Woman, I Am Beautiful, The Prodigal Son, Nymph Kneeling*—suggests, whatever its title, not bodies so much as their functions. Rodin embar-rasses finally. He embarrasses *me*. I get, I swear, the penis envy every time I see one of his improbably hung men, I want to sit in the laps of those ladies. Worse yet, and this *is* the war news, prefiguring, to me prefiguring—think of his statue of Victor Hugo—much of the totalitarian art of the last seventy-five years or so—Hitler's, Stalin's, Mussolini's—the romantic, muscular graffiti of all those death trip-pers.)

And, because a man's got to do what a man's got to do, the *New York Times Book Review*. It puts itself forward, bidding itself up and bidding itself up as the

25

---

[7]Jasper Johns—(1930–   ) American "pop art" painter.
[8]Frank Stella—(1936–   ) American painter.

venue of masterpieces—the bourse of books. (Next slide. *Quickly, quickly,* for God's sake!) Harvard. Grappa. Curries. The Book of the Month, the catch of the day. (Acquired tastes generally.) Rolls-Royce automobiles, Vuitton luggage, airports, the configuration of jet planes, all coach-class seating, and any lavatory on every airplane. Into design now but, like the toilets on those planes or the tourists in those churches, anatomically incorrect. Talkin' the truisms, talkin' areas that ought to be taken for granted by now, basic highway design, say, or form-follows-function footwear—talkin' the abhorrent, cryin'-out-to-be-filled vacuums. Like, why are the backs of TVs lopsided, or VCRs lost in a ganglia of connection? Why are cameras badly designed, unbalanced, weighted with topple and as bristled with inexplicable dials and buttons as a camcorder or a fishing reel? (To my way of thinking, the last beautiful camera was the Speed Graphic.) How do you explain the anomalies? Why is it certain articles of men's clothing (their hats, for example—I'm thinking of the fedora, I'm thinking of the borsalino) make a higher fashion statement than women's? Can anyone here say why cutlery is more handsome than dishes, stamps more agreeable to look at than coins, coins easier on the eye than banknotes? (It's the focus of face, the joy of manageable scale.) Or why almost all jewelry, men's *or* women's is unattractive? (Because it tries to mimic in metals or gems—in dead organics—natural forms, a vaguely frozen machinery of moving parts—insects', the stars'.) And how, this late into time, this far into history, more than two dozen days now into the Mother of Battles (because I can't concentrate, because I'm too old to be a soldier and too far away to be bombed, and because there are no priorities like the priorities of life and death and I can't keep my mind on my business), does one explain the aesthetic downside of furniture?

Compared to many forms that lend themselves to art or craft—drama, the novel, painting, the composition of music, even the *interpretation* of music, like, oh, say, singing the national anthem before the game, infinite other forms that seem to thrive, almost to wallow, in permutation, assuming new content, a mother lode of fresh ideas and differentiated styles as they're taken up by one artist after another—it's extraordinary how furniture is like most other furniture, as if furniture, alone among crafts, not only lived along the perimeters of some Platonic Ideal but had somehow actually managed to colonize it: an imperialism of the conventional. Except for a detail here, a detail there, inlay, marquetry, the pile-on of money, of pharaohs' or artistocracy's royal dispensations, a couch is a couch, an escritoire an escritoire. Beds resemble beds, tables and chairs are like tables and chairs. In domestic arrangements, form, bound to the custom cloth of human shape, really *does* follow function. The height of a table has to do with average lap tolerances. Chairs and beds are the hard aura of a strictly skeletal repose. Even so, something's busted, I think, in the imagination of furniture designers—I except the art directors of certain major pictures set in Manhattan apartments; talkin' environment, the ecology of "life-style," of plot and character, what the principals look like against the bookcase, propped among the furnishings; one must learn the script of one's life and be able to afford it; because only in movies does furniture play well (all lamps and appointments, all cunning, edge-of-the-field doodad and inspired housedower; one has at least the illusion one could live with this stuff, that it won't vanish in a season like a Nehru shirt)—something stuck in the vision, some sorcerer's-apprentice effect, which permits to keep on coming and keep on coming with minimal variation, if any, what has come before. It isn't anything as elegant as highest math happening here, just lump-sum arrangement, ballpark figure, bottom line. It's the fallacy of the assembly line, the notion that only costs get cut in such a wide sweep of swath. No, but really, *isn't* it astonishing that personality, surely as real as the width of one's shoulders or the breadth of one's beam, should be so infinite but attention to body so meager and hand-to-mouth that—chairs, say chairs, I *know* about chairs—there's been less progress in the design of chairs than in the design of luggage? (I speak as a cripple full-fledged, confined to a wheelchair. Chairs are a hang-up with me, but set that aside.) It's as if clothing came in a single size, pants like tube socks, every dress like a muumuu. And a rule of the chair seems to be that if it's beautiful it's rarely comfortable, if comfortable it rarely makes the cut to beauty.

Indeed, there are so few contemporary "museum-quality" chairs one can almost list them: Marcel Breuer's side chairs, his Wassily chair like a leather-and-steel cat's cradle; Jacobsen's Egg chair; Thonet's bentwood rockers; Mies van der Rohe's Barcelona; Saarinen's molded plastic chairs on their round bases and tapered stems like cross sections of parfaits; all Eames's ubiquitous plastic like stackable poker chips or the pounded, hollowed-out centers of catcher's mitts, as locked into a vision of the fifties as pole lamps, his famous lounge chair and ottoman. A spectrum of vernacular chairs—soda-fountain chairs, directors' chairs, black canvas camp chairs, those crushed—almost imploded—white or charcoal leather pillow chairs like soft fortresses or marshmallow thrones, some of the new ergonomic chairs that sit on you as much as you ever manage to sit on them.

So I *know* about chairs and still have my eye out, never mind I'm sixty if I'm a day, for that evasive, lost-chord masterpiece of the genre, which, like love, I'll recognize when I see like a sort of fate.

Though maybe not. Not because I haven't the imagination to cut my losses, or   30
even the courage to finesse my life and choose to sit out the close of my days in desuetudinous splendor, but because it may not exist. The chair, my gorgeous prosthetic of choice, may not have been fashioned yet. Because oddly, strangely, ultimately, chairs are all attitude, molds of the supine or up on pointe, aggressive or submissive as sexual position. Occupied or unoccupied, they are shadows, ghosts, signs of the been-and-gone, some pipe-and-slippers choreography of spiritual disposition, how one chooses to acquit oneself, highly personalized as an arrangement of flowers, and oh, oh, if one but had the body for it one would live out one's days in van Gogh's room at Arles, eating up comfort and beauty and having it, too, there in one last fell binge of boyhood in the cane and wood along those powder-blue walls of the utile, of basin and pitcher, of military brush and drinking glass, of apothecary bottles clear as gin on a crowded corner of the nightstand, to be there on the featherbed, on the oilcloth-looking floor amid one's things. All, as I say, you have to know is the script of your life. You wouldn't even have to worry whether you can afford it. What, this poor Goodwill stuff, these nitty-rubbed-gritty YMCA effects of the weathered and flyblown pastoral? I'd pay my life out there gladly, not so much as a hero as a loving dilettante of idyll, using only the plain equipment of beauty. Substituting the hard work of freedom with the even harder work of contemplation, giving way to quietude, calm, doing the doldrums in study's Sargasso Seas, all the light housekeeping of a stock-still ego laced with awe. There are worse character flaws than sloth. Nationalism, I think, patriotism, the too-forgiving love of tribe, maybe even of family itself. All the flaws of a restrictive loyalty, whatever makes us want to be part of a small idea, whatever makes us dangerous or allows us to entertain, even for a moment, the idea of a Mother of Battles. Much better to wait it out at Arles. Much better never to have seen the flashy dance steps from which we take our marching orders.

And it's the day before yesterday now. Joan and I are at the Shady Oak to see *Mr. and Mrs. Bridge.* And it's five o'clock on Presidents' Day, but that's only irony.

It's the Rush Hour Show. Which is the one we always try to make. It's half price at Rush Hour but that's not the reason. We're old, we're old people, we get senior citizen whatever the hour. In spring and summer and some of the autumn it's still light when the movie lets out. It's important, that last bit of light. And anyway, though we know no one, we recognize everyone. Peers, birds of a feather, comfortable at the core as ourselves. We buy our tickets and go in.

The lights are still up, enough to be able to see what I'm doing when I make the difficult transfer from my wheelchair to the theater seat. Joan folds the chair and parks it by the screen. "What could be better?" I ask automatically, but with absolute sincerity, as she slips in beside me.

The lights go down and something happens that has never happened before. They're playing "The Star-Spangled Banner." It's for the war. An American montage like a little music video. American kids in American suburbs; transparent, billowy, slo-mo flag collages; purple mountains' majesty from one shining sea to the next, fields, fruit—all Ma Nature's starched summer dress whites. And they're standing, they're standing and singing! Card-carrying AARPers.[9] It's like, well, it's like *church* is what it's like. They hold, some of them, their hands over their hearts. I mean there they *are*, singing, or perhaps just lip-synching in the dark in some key of the common denominator, negotiating the difficult leaps and bounds of our national anthem. In the dark, singing to a screen as if it wasn't *Mr. and Mrs. Bridge* they'd come to see but *The Rocky Horror Picture Show*. And not to any orchestra but to a sound track! And the Shady Oak is automated, so not even to a projectionist but to a machine. Which, by default, makes Joan and me the only audience at this odd performance. We're embarrassed, but what embarrasses us, I think, is to be so far out of the loop. Hey, there's *nothing* so convincing as an opinion.

We can't know this yet but G-Day is penciled in. Sunday, February 24, 3:00 A.M. Gulf time—two hours earlier at Arles—a ground war will begin that will last only 100 hours and make a name for this overrated masterpiece of a war. But still Saturday the 23, 7:00 P.M. Shady Oak time. When Rush Hour is winding down and the bigger spenders are lining up for the full-fare show. Who are on the cusp and, when the time comes, may or may not know just what it is they were standing for.

Joy Harjo   b. 1951

Ordinary Spirit   1987

I was born in Tulsa, Oklahoma, on May 9, 1951, after a long, hard labor that occurred sporadically for over a week. My mother didn't know it was labor because I wasn't due until mid-July. I also surprised her because I was a single birth; she had been told to possibly expect twins. The birth was hard on both of us. I was kept alive on a machine for the first few days of my life until I made a decision to live. When I looked around I saw my mother, only nineteen, of mixed Cherokee and French blood, who had already worked hard for her short life. And my father, a few years older, a tall, good-looking Creek man who was then working as a mechanic for American Airlines. I don't think I was ever what they expected, but I am grateful that they made my life possible and honor them for it.

---

[9]AARPers—members of the American Association of Retired Persons.

I was the first of four children who were born evenly spaced over the next eight years or so. And much later had my own children, Phil and Rainy Dawn. We are descended from a long line of tribal speakers and leaders from my father's side. Menawa, who led the Red Stick War against Andrew Jackson, is our great-great (and possibly another great) grandfather. I don't know much about the family on my mother's side except there were many rebels and other characters. They are all part of who I am, the root from which I write, even though I may not always name them.

I began writing around the time I was twenty-two years old. I am now thirty-four and feel that after all this time I am just beginning to learn to write. I am only now beginning to comprehend what poetry is, and what it can mean. Each time I write I am in a different and wild place, and travel toward something I do not know the name of. Each poem is a jumping-off edge and I am not safe, but I take more risks and understand better now how to take them. They do not always work, but when they do it is worth it. I could not live without writing and/or thinking about it. In fact, I don't have to think about it; it's there, some word, concept always being born or, just as easily, dying.

I walk in and out of many worlds. I used to see being born of this mixed-blood/mixed-vision a curse, and hated myself for it. It was too confusing and destructive when I saw the world through that focus. The only message I got was not belonging anywhere, not to any side. I have since decided that being familiar with more than one world, more than one vision, is a blessing, and know that I make my own choices. I also know that it is only an illusion that any of the worlds are separate.

It is around midnight. I often write at this time in my workroom near the front   5 of an old Victorian-style house near downtown Denver. Tonight a thick snow has muffled the sounds of traffic. The world is quiet except for the sound of this typewriter humming, the sometimes dash of metallic keys, and the deep breathing of my dog who is asleep nearby. And then, in the middle of working, the world gives way and I see the old, old Creek one who comes in here and watches over me. He tries to make sense of this world in which his grand-daughter has come to live. And often teases me about my occupation of putting words on paper.

I tell him that it is writng these words down, and entering the world through the structure they make, that has allowed me to see him more clearly, and to speak. And he answers that maybe his prayers, songs, and his belief in them has allowed him to create me.

We both laugh, and continue our work through many seasons.

This summer, during one of those sultry summer evenings when the air hums with a chorus of insects and there's the sound of children playing in the street, I sat, writing. Not actually writing but staring into that space above the typewriter where vision telescopes. I began remembering the way the world was before speech in childhood. A time when I was totally conscious of sound, and conscious of being in a world in which the webbed connections between us all were translucent yet apparent. I remember what it felt like to live within that space, where every live thing had a voice, and each voice/sound an aurora of color. It was sometime during that reminiscence that I began this poem:

SUMMER NIGHT

The moon is nearly full,
> the humid air sweet like melon.
Flowers that have cupped the sun all day
> dream of iridescent wings
under the long dark sleep.
> Children's invisible voices call out

in the glimmering moonlight.
Their parents play wornout records
of the *cumbia*. Behind the screendoor
their soft laughter swells
into the rhythm of a smooth guitar.
I watch the world shimmer
inside this globe of a summer night,
listen to the wobble of her
spin and dive. It happens all the time, waiting for you
to come home.
There is an ache that begins
in the sound of an old blues song.
It becomes a house where all the lights have gone out
but one.
And it burns and burns
until there is only the blue smoke of dawn
and everyone is sleeping in someone's arms
even the flowers
even the sound of a thousand silences.
And the arms of night
in the arms of day.
Everyone except me.
But then the smell of damp honeysuckle twisted on the vine.
And the turn of the shoulder
of the ordinary spirit who keeps watch
over this ordinary street
And there you are, the secret
of your own flower of light
blooming in the miraculous dark.
(from *Furious Light*, Watershed Foundation cassette, 1986)

For years I have wanted to capture that ache of a summer night. This summer in Denver was especially humid, reminded me of Oklahoma. I wanted to feel, in the poem, of a thick, sweet air. And I wanted the voices I remembered, my parents' talking and scratchy, faint music of the radio. In the poem it is my neighbors I hear, and their old records of the *cumbia*. I also wanted to sustain a blues mood, pay homage to the blues because I love the blues. There was the sound of a sensuous tenor saxophone beneath the whole poem. I also added the part of everyone being in someone else's arms, "everyone except me," for the blues effect.

But I did not want to leave the poem there, in the center of the ache; I wanted to resolve it. I looked out the front door into the night and caught a glimpse of someone standing near the streetlight, a protecting spirit who was keeping watch over the street. I could have made that up, but I believe it is true. And I knew the spirit belonged in the poem, and because the spirit lives in the poem, too, helps turn the poem around to a place of tender realization. Hence, "And there you are, the secret / of your own flower of light / blooming in the miraculous dark."

When I first began writing, poetry was simply a way for me to speak. I was amazed that I could write anything down and have it come out a little more than coherently. Over the years the process has grown more complicated, more intricate, and the world within the poem more immense. In another recent poem the process is especially important:

TRANSFORMATIONS

This poem is a letter to tell you that I
have smelled the hatred you have tried
to find me with; you would like to destroy me.
Bone splintered in the eye of one you choose
to name your enemy won't make it better for you
to see. It could take a thousand years if you name it
that way, but then, to see after all that time, never
could anything be so clear. Memory has many forms.
When I think of early winter I think of a blackbird
laughing in the frozen air; guards a piece of light. I
saw the whole world caught in that sound. The sun
stopped for a moment because of tough belief. I don't
know what that has to do with what I am trying to tell you
except that I know you can turn a poem into something
else. This poem could be a bear treading the far northern
tundra, smelling the air for sweet alive meat. Or a piece
of seaweed stumbling in the sea. Or a blackbird, laughing.
What I mean is that hatred can be turned into something
else, if you have the right words, the right meanings
buried in that tender place in your heart where
the most precious animals live. Down the street
an ambulance has come to rescue an old man who is slowly
losing his life. Not many can see that he is already
becoming the backyard tree he has tended for years,
before he moves on. He is not sad, but compassionate
for the fears moving around him.
That's what I mean to tell you. On the other side
of the place you live stands a dark woman.
She has been trying to talk to you for years.
You have called the same name in the middle of a nightmare,
from the center of miracles. She is beautiful.
This is your hatred back. She loves you.

When I began writing the poem, I knew I wanted an actual transformation to be enacted within it. I began with someone's hatred, which was a tangible thing, and wanted to turn it into love by the end of the poem. I was also interested in the process of becoming. I tried to include several states of becoming. The "process of the poem" becoming was one. I entered the poem very consciously with lines such as, "I don't know what that has to do with what I am trying to tell you," and "What I mean is . . ." I also consciously switched tenses partly for that reason, and others. I often change tense within a poem and do so knowing what I am doing. It isn't by accident that it happens. Time doesn't realistically work in a linear fashion.

Within the poem is also the process of the "hater" becoming one who is loved, and who ultimately loves. The "I" is also involved in the process.

Earlier in the day an ambulance came into the neighborhood to pick up an elderly neighbor who had suffered a stroke and was near death. It was a major event. All who witnessed it walked carefully through the rest of the day. I was still thinking of him when I wrote the poem and knew that somehow he, too, belonged in the poem, for he was also part of the transformation.

I was not sure how the poem would end when I began writing it, but looking   15
back I realize the ending must have originated in one of two places. One was a
story I heard from a woman who during times of deep emotional troubles would
be visited by a woman who looked just like her. She herself would never see her,
but anyone passing by her room while she was asleep would see this imaginary
woman, standing next to her bed. I always considered the "imaginary" woman as
her other self, the denied self who wanted back in.

And I was reminded, too, of the woman who had followed me around at an
all-night party in Santa Fe a few years before. We had all drifted around the house,
talking, dancing, filled with music and whatever else we had tasted. She finally
caught up with me around dawn and told me that she was sorry she was white,
and then told me that she believed white people had no souls. I was shocked and
sad. And I saw her soul, starved but thinly beautiful, knocking hard on the wall of
cocaine and self-hatred she was hiding behind.

So the poem becomes a way of speaking to her.

It is now very late and I will let someone else take over this story. Maybe the
cricket who likes to come in here and sing and who probably knows a better way
to write a poem than me.

It is not the last song, but to name anything that, only means that I would continue to be amazed at the creation of any new music.

Martin Luther King, Jr.   1929–1968

I Have a Dream   *1963*

I am happy to join with you today in what will go down in history as the
greatest demonstration for freedom in the history of our nation.

Fivescore years ago, a great American, in whose symbolic shadow we stand
today, signed the Emancipation Proclamation. This momentous decree came as a
great beacon light of hope to millions of Negro slaves who had been seared in the
flames of withering injustice. It came as a joyous daybreak to end the long night of
their captivity.

But one hundred years later, the Negro still is not free; one hundred years
later, the life of the Negro is still sadly crippled by the manacles of segregation and
the chains of discrimination; one hundred years later, the Negro lives on a lonely
island of poverty in the midst of a vast ocean of material prosperity; one hundred
years later, the Negro is still languished in the corners of American society and
finds himself in exile in his own land.

So we've come here today to dramatize a shameful condition. In a sense
we've come to our nation's capital to cash a check. When the architects of our republic wrote the magnificent words of the Constitution and the Declaration of Independence, they were signing a promissory note to which every American was to
fall heir. This note was the promise that all men, yes, black men as well as white
men, would be guaranteed the unalienable rights of life, liberty, and the pursuit of
happiness.

It is obvious today that America has defaulted on this promissory note in so   5
far as her citizens of color are concerned. Instead of honoring this sacred obligation, America has given the Negro people a bad check; a check which has come
back marked "insufficient funds." We refuse to believe that there are insufficient

funds in the great vaults of opportunity of this nation. And so we've come to cash this check, a check that will give us upon demand the riches of freedom and the security of justice.

We have also come to this hallowed spot to remind America of the fierce urgency of now. This is no time to engage in the luxury of cooling off or to take the tranquilizing drug of gradualism. Now is the time to make real the promises of democracy; now is the time to rise from the dark and desolate valley of segregation to the sunlit path of racial justice; now is the time to lift our nation from the quicksands of racial injustice to the solid rock of brotherhood; now is the time to make justice a reality for all God's children. It would be fatal for the nation to overlook the urgency of the moment. This sweltering summer of the Negro's legitimate discontent will not pass until there is an invigorating autumn of freedom and equality.

Nineteen sixty-three is not an end, but a beginning. And those who hope that the Negro needed to blow off steam and will now be content, will have a rude awakening if the nation returns to business as usual.

There will be neither rest nor tranquility in America until the Negro is granted his citizenship rights. The whirlwinds of revolt will continue to shake the foundations of our nation until the bright day of justice emerges.

But there is something that I must say to my people who stand on the warm threshold which leads into the palace of justice. In the process of gaining our rightful place we must not be guilty of wrongful deeds.

Let us not seek to satisfy our thirst for freedom by drinking from the cup of   10
bitterness and hatred. We must forever conduct our struggle on the high plane of dignity and discipline. We must not allow our creative protest to degenerate into physical violence. Again and again we must rise to the majestic heights of meeting physical force with soul force.

The marvelous new militancy which has engulfed the Negro community must not lead us to a distrust of all white people, for many of our white brothers, as evidenced by their presence here today, have come to realize that their destiny is tied up with our destiny and they have come to realize that their freedom is inextricably bound to our freedom. This offense we share mounted to storm the battlements of injustice must be carried forth by a biracial army. We cannot walk alone.

And as we walk, we must make the pledge that we shall always march ahead. We cannot turn back. There are those who are asking the devotees of civil rights, "When will you be satisfied?" We can never be satisfied as long as the Negro is the victim of the unspeakable horrors of police brutality.

We can never be satisfied as long as our bodies, heavy with fatigue of travel, cannot gain lodging in the motels of the highways and the hotels of the cities. We cannot be satisfied as long as the Negro's basic mobility is from a smaller ghetto to a larger one.

We can never be satisfied as long as our children are stripped of their selfhood and robbed of their dignity by signs stating "for whites only." We cannot be satisfied as long as a Negro in Mississippi cannot vote and a Negro in New York believes he has nothing for which to vote. No, we are not satisfied, and we will not be satisfied until justice rolls down like waters and righteousness like a mighty stream.

I am not unmindful that some of you have come here out of excessive trials   15
and tribulation. Some of you have come fresh from narrow jail cells. Some of you have come from areas where your quest for freedom left you battered by the storms of persecution and staggered by the winds of police brutality. You have been the veterans of creative suffering. Continue to work with the faith that unearned suffering is redemptive.

Go back to Mississippi; go back to Alabama; go back to South Carolina; go back to Georgia; go back to Louisiana; go back to the slums and ghettos of the northern cities, knowing that somehow this situation can, and will be changed. Let us not wallow in the valley of despair.

So I say to you, my friends, that even though we must face the difficulties of today and tomorrow, I still have a dream. It is a dream deeply rooted in the American dream that one day this nation will rise up and live out the true meaning of its creed—we hold these truths to be self-evident, that all men are created equal.

I have a dream that one day on the red hills of Georgia, sons of former slaves and sons of former slave-owners will be able to sit down together at the table of brotherhood.

I have a dream that one day, even the state of Mississippi, a state sweltering with the heat of injustice, sweltering with the heat of oppression, will be transformed into an oasis of freedom and justice.

I have a dream my four little children will one day live in a nation where they will not be judged by the color of their skin but by content of their character. I have a dream today! 20

I have a dream that one day, down in Alabama, with its vicious racists, with its governor having his lips dripping with the words of interposition and nullification, that one day, right there in Alabama, little black boys and black girls will be able to join hands with little white boys and white girls as sisters and brothers. I have a dream today!

I have a dream that one day every valley shall be exalted, every hill and mountain shall be made low, the rough places shall be made plain, and the crooked places shall be made straight and the glory of the Lord will be revealed and all flesh shall see it together.

This is our hope. This is the faith that I go back to the South with.

With this faith we will be able to hew out of the mountain of despair a stone of hope. With this faith we will be able to transform the jangling discords of our nation into a beautiful symphony of brotherhood.

With this faith we will be able to work together, to pray together, to struggle to- 25 gether, to go to jail together, to stand up for freedom together, knowing that we will be free one day. This will be the day when all of God's children will be able to sing with new meaning—"my country 'tis of thee; sweet land of liberty; of thee I sing; land where my fathers died, land of the pilgrim's pride; from every mountain side, let freedom ring"—and if America is to be a great nation, this must become true.

So let freedom ring from the prodigious hilltops of New Hampshire.

Let freedom ring from the mighty mountains of New York.

Let freedom ring from the heightening Alleghenies of Pennsylvania.

Let freedom ring from the snow-capped Rockies of Colorado.

Let freedom ring from the curvaceous slopes of California. 30

But not only that.

Let freedom ring from Stone Mountain of Georgia.

Let freedom ring from Lookout Mountain of Tennessee.

Let freedom ring from every hill and molehill of Mississippi, from every mountainside, let freedom ring.

And when we allow freedom to ring, when we let it ring from every village 35 and hamlet, from every state and city, we will be able to speed up that day when all of God's children—black men and white men, Jews and Gentiles, Catholics and Protestants—will be able to join hands and to sing in the words of the old Negro spiritual, "Free at last, free at last; thank God Almighty, we are free at last."

Letter from Birmingham Jail   1963

My Dear Fellow Clergymen:

While confined here in the Birmingham city jail, I came across your recent statement calling my present activities "unwise and untimely." Seldom do I pause to answer criticism of my work and ideas. If I sought to answer all the criticisms that cross my desk, my secretaries would have little time for anything other than such correspondence in the course of the day, and I would have no time for constructive work. But since I feel that you are men of genuine good will and that your criticisms are sincerely set forth, I want to try to answer your statement in what I hope will be patient and reasonable terms.

I think I should indicate why I am here in Birmingham, since you have been influenced by the view which argues against "outsiders coming in." I have the honor of serving as president of the Southern Christian Leadership Conference, an organization operating in every southern state, with headquarters in Atlanta, Georgia. We have some eighty-five affiliated organizations across the South, and one of them is the Alabama Christian Movement for Human Rights. Frequently we share staff, educational, and financial resources with our affiliates. Several months ago the affiliate here in Birmingham asked us to be on call to engage in a nonviolent direct-action program if such were deemed necessary. We readily consented, and when the hour came we lived up to our promise. So I, along with several members of my staff, am here because I was invited here. I am here because I have organizational ties here.

But more basically, I am in Birmingham because injustice is here. Just as the prophets of the eighth century B.C. left their villages and carried their "thus saith the Lord" far beyond the boundaries of their home towns, and just as the Apostle Paul left his village of Tarsus and carried the gospel of Jesus Christ to the far corners of the Greco-Roman world, so am I compelled to carry the gospel of freedom beyond my own home town. Like Paul, I must constantly respond to the Macedonian call for aid.

Moreover, I am cognizant of the interrelatedness of all communities and states. I cannot sit idly by in Atlanta and not be concerned about what happens in Birmingham. Injustice anywhere is a threat to justice everywhere. We are caught in an inescapable network of mutuality, tied in a single garment of destiny. Whatever affects one directly, affects all indirectly. Never again can we afford to live with the narrow, provincial, "outside agitator" idea. Anyone who lives inside the United States can never be considered an outsider anywhere within its bounds.

You deplore the demonstrations taking place in Birmingham. But your statement, I am sorry to say, fails to express a similar concern for the conditions that brought about the demonstrations. I am sure that none of you would want to rest content with the superficial kind of social analysis that deals merely with effects and does not grapple with underlying causes. It is unfortunate that demonstrations are taking place in Birmingham, but it is even more unfortunate that the city's white power structure left the Negro community with no alternative.

In any nonviolent campaign there are four basic steps: collection of the facts to determine whether injustices exist; negotiation; self-purification; and direct action. We have gone through all these steps in Birmingham. There can be no gainsaying the fact that racial injustice engulfs this community. Birmingham is probably the most thoroughly segregated city in the United States. Its ugly record of brutality is widely known. Negroes have experienced grossly unjust treatment

5

in courts. There have been more unsolved bombings of Negro homes and churches in Birmingham than in any other city in the nation. These are the hard, brutal facts of the case. On the basis of these conditions, Negro leaders sought to negotiate with the city fathers. But the latter consistently refused to engage in good-faith negotiation.

Then, last September, came the opportunity to talk with leaders of Birmingham's economic community. In the course of the negotiations, certain promises were made by the merchants—for example, to remove the stores' humiliating racial signs. On the basis of these promises, the Reverend Fred Shuttlesworth and the leaders of the Alabama Christian Movement for Human Rights agreed to a moratorium on all demonstrations. As the weeks and months went by, we realized that we were the victims of a broken promise. A few signs, briefly removed, returned; the others remained.

As in so many past experiences, our hopes had been blasted, and the shadow of deep disappointment settled upon us. We had no alternative except to prepare for direct action, whereby we would present our very bodies as means of laying our case before the conscience of the local and the national community. Mindful of the difficulties involved, we decided to undertake a process of self-purification. We began a series of workshops on nonviolence, and we repeatedly asked ourselves: "Are you able to accept blows without retaliating?" "Are you able to endure the ordeal of jail?" We decided to schedule our direct-action program for the Easter season, realizing that except for Christmas, this is the main shopping period of the year. Knowing that a strong economic-withdrawal program would be the by-product of direct action, we felt that this would be the best time to bring pressure to bear on the merchants for the needed change.

Then it occurred to us that Birmingham's mayoral election was coming up in March, and we speedily decided to postpone action until after election day. When we discovered that the Commissioner of Public Safety, Eugene "Bull" Connor, had piled up enough votes to be in the run-off, we decided again to postpone action until the day after the run-off so that the demonstrations could not be used to cloud the issues. Like many others, we waited to see Mr. Connor defeated, and to this end we endured postponement after postponement. Having aided in this community need, we felt that our direct-action program could be delayed no longer.

You may well ask, "Why direct action? Why sit-ins, marches, and so forth? Isn't negotiation a better path?" You are quite right in calling for negotiation. Indeed, this is the very purpose of direct action. Nonviolent direct action seeks to create such a crisis and foster such a tension that a community which has constantly refused to negotiate is forced to confront the issue. It seeks so to dramatize the issue that it can no longer be ignored. My citing the creation of tension as part of the work of the nonviolent tension may sound rather shocking. But I must confess that I am not afraid of the word "tension." I have earnestly opposed violent tension, but there is a type of constructive, nonviolent tension which is necessary for growth. Just as Socrates felt that it was necessary to create a tension in the mind so that individuals could rise from the bondage of myths and half-truths to the unfettered realm of creative analysis and objective appraisal, so must we see the need for nonviolent gadflies to create the kind of tension in society that will help men rise from the dark depths of prejudice and racism to the majestic heights of understanding and brotherhood.

The purpose of our direct-action program is to create a situation so crisis-packed that it will inevitably open the door to negotiation. I therefore concur with you in your call for negotiation. Too long has our beloved Southland been bogged down in a tragic effort to live in monologue rather than dialogue.

One of the basic points in your statement is that the action that I and my associates have taken in Birmingham is untimely. Some have asked: "Why didn't you

10

give the new city administration time to act?" The only answer that I can give to this query is that the new Birmingham administration must be prodded about as much as the outgoing one, before it will act. We are sadly mistaken if we feel that the election of Albert Boutwell as mayor will bring the millennium to Birmingham. While Mr. Boutwell is a much more gentle person than Mr. Connor, they are both segregationists, dedicated to maintenance of the status quo. I have hoped that Mr. Boutwell will be reasonable enough to see the futility of massive resistance to de-segregation. But he will not see this without pressure from devotees of civil rights. My friends, I must say to you that we have not made a single gain in civil rights without determined legal and nonviolent pressure. Lamentably, it is an historical fact that privileged groups seldom give up their privileges voluntarily. Individuals may see the moral light and voluntarily give up their unjust posture; but, as Rein-hold Niebuhr has reminded us, groups tend to be more immoral than individuals.

We know through painful experience that freedom is never voluntarily given by the oppressor; it must be demanded by the oppressed. Frankly, I have yet to engage in a direct-action campaign that was "well timed" in the view of those who have not suffered unduly from the disease of segregation. For years now I have heard the word "Wait!" It rings in the ear of every Negro with piercing familiarity. This "Wait" has almost always meant "Never." We must come to see, with one of our distinguished jurists, that "justice too long delayed is justice denied."

We have waited for more than 340 years for our constitutional and God-given rights. The nations of Asia and Africa are moving with jetlike speed toward gain-ing political independence, but we still creep at horse-and-buggy pace toward gaining a cup of coffee at a lunch counter. Perhaps it is easy for those who have never felt the stinging darts of segregation to say, "Wait." But when you have seen vicious mobs lynch your mothers and fathers at will and drown your sisters and brothers at whim; when you have seen hate-filled policemen curse, kick, and even kill your black brothers and sisters; when you see the vast majority of your twenty million Negro brothers smothering in an airtight cage of poverty in the midst of an affluent society; when you suddenly find your tongue twisted and your speech stammering as you seek to explain to your six-year-old daughter why she can't go to the public amusement park that has just been advertised on television, and see tears welling up in her eyes when she is told that Funtown is closed to colored children, and see ominous clouds of inferiority beginning to form in her little men-tal sky, and see her beginning to distort her personality by developing an uncon-scious bitterness toward white people; when you have to concoct an answer for a five-year-old son who is asking, "Daddy, why do white people treat colored peo-ple so mean?"; when you take a cross-country drive and find it necessary to sleep night after night in the uncomfortable corners of your automobile because no motel will accept you; when you are humiliated day in and day out by nagging signs reading "white" and "colored"; when your first name becomes "nigger," your middle name becomes "boy" (however old you are) and your last name becomes "John," and your wife and mother are never given the respected title "Mrs."; when you are harried by day and haunted by night by the fact that you are a Negro, liv-ing constantly at tiptoe stance, never quite knowing what to expect next, and are plagued with inner fears and outer resentments; when you are forever fighting a degenerating sense of "nobodiness"—then you will understand why we find it dif-ficult to wait. There comes a time when the cup of endurance runs over, and men are no longer willing to be plunged into the abyss of despair. I hope, sirs, you can understand our legitimate and unavoidable impatience.

You express a great deal of anxiety over our willingness to break laws. This is   15
certainly a legitimate concern. Since we so diligently urge people to obey the

Supreme Court's decision of 1954 outlawing segregation in the public schools, at first glance it may seem rather paradoxical for us consciously to break laws. One may well ask: "How can you advocate breaking some laws and obeying others?" The answer lies in the fact that there are two types of laws: just and unjust. I would be the first to advocate obeying just laws. One has not only a legal but a moral responsibility to obey just laws. Conversely, one has a moral responsibility to disobey unjust laws. I would agree with St. Augustine that "an unjust law is no law at all."

Now, what is the difference between the two? How does one determine whether a law is just or unjust? A just law is a manmade code that squares with the moral law or the law of God. An unjust law is a code that is out of harmony with the moral law. To put it in the terms of St. Thomas Aquinas: An unjust law is a human law that is not rooted in eternal law and natural law. Any law that uplifts human personality is just. Any law that degrades human personality is unjust. All segregation statutes are unjust because segregation distorts the soul and damages the personality. It gives the segregator a false sense of superiority and the segregated a false sense of inferiority. Segregation, to use the terminology of the Jewish philosopher Martin Buber, substitutes an "I-it" relationship for an "I-thou" relationship and ends up relegating persons to the status of things. Hence segregation is not only politically, economically, and sociologically unsound, it is morally wrong and sinful. Paul Tillich has said that sin is separation. Is not segregation an existential expression of man's tragic separation, his awful estrangement, his terrible sinfulness? Thus it is that I can urge them to obey the 1954 decision of the Supreme Court, for it is morally right; and I can urge them to disobey segregation ordinances, for they are morally wrong.

Let us consider a more concrete example of just and unjust laws. An unjust law is a code that a numerical or power majority group compels a minority group to obey but does not make binding on itself. This is *difference* made legal. By the same token, a just law is a code that a majority compels a minority to follow and that it is willing to follow itself. This is *sameness* made legal.

Let me give another explanation. A law is unjust if it is inflicted on a minority that, as a result of being denied the right to vote, had no part in enacting or devising the law. Who can say that the legislature of Alabama which set up that state's segregation laws was democratically elected? Throughout Alabama all sorts of devious methods are used to prevent Negroes from becoming registered voters, and there are some counties in which, even though Negroes constitute a majority of the population, not a single Negro is registered. Can any law enacted under such circumstances be considered democratically structured?

Sometimes a law is just on its face and unjust in its application. For instance, I have been arrested on a charge of parading without a permit. Now, there is nothing wrong in having an ordinance which requires a permit for a parade. But such an ordinance becomes unjust when it is used to maintain segregation and to deny citizens the First Amendment privilege of peaceful assembly and protest.

I hope you are able to see the distinction I am trying to point out. In no sense do I advocate evading or defying the law, as would the rabid segregationist. That would lead to anarchy. One who breaks an unjust law must do so openly, lovingly, and with a willingness to accept the penalty. I submit that an individual who breaks a law that conscience tells him is unjust, and who willingly accepts the penalty of imprisonment in order to arouse the conscience of the community over its injustice, is in reality expressing the highest respect for law.

Of course, there is nothing new about this kind of civil disobedience. It was evidenced sublimely in the refusal of Shadrach, Meshach, and Abednego to obey

20

the laws of Nebuchadnezzar, on the ground that a higher moral law was at stake. It was practiced superbly by the early Christians, who were willing to face hungry lions and the excruciating pain of chopping blocks rather than submit to certain unjust laws of the Roman Empire. To a degree, academic freedom is a reality today because Socrates practiced civil disobedience. In our own nation, the Boston Tea Party represented a massive act of civil disobedience.

We should never forget that everything Adolf Hitler did in Germany was "legal" and everything the Hungarian freedom fighters did in Hungary was "illegal." It was "illegal" to aid and comfort a Jew in Hitler's Germany. Even so, I am sure that, had I lived in Germany at the time, I would have aided and comforted my Jewish brothers. If today I lived in a Communist country where certain principles dear to the Christian faith are suppressed, I would openly advocate disobeying that country's antireligious laws.

I must make two honest confessions to you, my Christian and Jewish brothers. First, I must confess that over the past few years I have been gravely disappointed with the white moderate. I have almost reached the regrettable conclusion that the Negro's great stumbling block in his stride toward freedom is not the White Citizen's Counciler or the Ku Klux Klanner, but the white moderate, who is more devoted to "order" than to justice; who prefers a negative peace which is the absence of tension to a positive peace which is the presence of justice; who constantly says, "I agree with you in the goal you seek, but I cannot agree with your methods of direct action"; who paternalistically believes he can set the timetable for another man's freedom; who lives by a mythical concept of time and who constantly advises the Negro to wait for a "more convenient season." Shallow understanding from people of good will is more frustrating than absolute misunderstanding from people of ill will. Lukewarm acceptance is much more bewildering than outright rejection.

I had hoped that the white moderate would understand that law and order exist for the purpose of establishing justice and that when they fail in this purpose they become the dangerously structured dams that block the flow of social progress. I had hoped that the white moderate would understand that the present tension in the South is a necessary phase of the transition from an obnoxious negative peace, in which the Negro passively accepted his unjust plight, to a substantive and positive peace, in which all men will respect the dignity and worth of human personality. Actually, we who engage in nonviolent direct action are not the creators of tension. We merely bring to the surface the hidden tension that is already alive. We bring it out in the open, where it can be seen and dealt with. Like a boil that can never be cured so long as it is covered up but must be opened with all its ugliness to the natural medicines of air and light, injustice must be exposed, with all the tension its exposure creates, to the light of human conscience and the air of national opinion, before it can be cured.

In your statement you assert that our actions, even though peaceful, must be condemned because they precipitate violence. But is this a logical assertion? Isn't this like condemning a robbed man because his possession of money precipitated the evil act of robbery? Isn't this like condemning Socrates because his unswerving commitment to truth and his philosophical inquiries precipitated the act by the misguided populace in which they made him drink hemlock? Isn't this like condemning Jesus because his unique God-consciousness and never-ceasing devotion to God's will precipitated the evil act of crucifixion? We must come to see that, as the federal courts have consistently affirmed, it is wrong to urge an individual to cease his efforts to gain his basic constitutional rights because the quest may precipitate violence. Society must protect the robbed and punish the robber.

25

I had also hoped that the white moderate would reject the myth concerning time in relation to the struggle for freedom. I have just received a letter from a white brother in Texas. He writes: "All Christians know that the colored people will receive equal rights eventually, but it is possible that you are in too great a religious hurry. It has taken Christianity almost two thousand years to accomplish what it has. The teachings of Christ take time to come to earth." Such an attitude stems from a tragic misconception of time, from the strangely irrational notion that there is something in the very flow of time that will inevitably cure all ills. Actually, time itself is neutral; it can be used either destructively or constructively. More and more I feel that the people of ill will have used time much more effectively than have the people of good will. We will have to repent in this generation not merely for the hateful words and actions of the bad people, but for the appalling silence of the good people. Human progress never rolls in on wheels of inevitability; it comes through the tireless efforts of men willing to be co-workers with God, and without this hard work, time itself becomes an ally of the forces of social stagnation. We must use time creatively, in the knowledge that the time is always ripe to do right. Now is the time to make real the promise of democracy and transform our pending national elegy into a creative psalm of brotherhood. Now is the time to lift our national policy from the quicksand of racial injustice to the solid rock of human dignity.

You speak of our activity in Birmingham as extreme. At first I was rather disappointed that fellow clergymen would see my nonviolent effort as those of an extremist. I began thinking about the fact that I stand in the middle of two opposing forces in the Negro community. One is a force of complacency, made up in part of Negroes who, as a result of long years of oppression, are so drained of self-respect and a sense of "somebodiness" that they have adjusted to segregation; and in part of a few middle-class Negroes who, because of a degree of academic and economic security and because in some ways they profit by segregation, have become insensitive to the problems of the masses. The other force is one of bitterness and hatred, and it comes perilously close to advocating violence. It is expressed in the various black nationalist groups that are springing up across the nation, the largest and best-known being Elijah Muhammad's Muslim movement. Nourished by the Negro's frustration over the continued existence of racial discrimination, this movement is made up of people who have lost faith in America, who have absolutely repudiated Christianity, and who have concluded that the white man is an incorrigible "devil."

I have tried to stand between these two forces, saying that we need emulate neither the "do-nothingism" of the complacent nor the hatred and despair of the black nationalist. For there is the more excellent way of love and nonviolent protest. I am grateful to God that, through the influence of the Negro church, the way of nonviolence became an integral part of our struggle.

If this philosophy had not emerged, by now many streets of the South would, I am convinced, be flowing with blood. And I am further convinced that if our white brothers dismiss as "rabble-rousers" and "outside agitors" those of us who employ nonviolent direct action, and if they refuse to support our nonviolent efforts, millions of Negroes will, out of frustration and despair, seek solace and security in black-nationalist ideologies—a development that would inevitably lead to a frightening racial nightmare.

Oppressed people cannot remain oppressed forever. The yearning for freedom eventually manifests itself, and that is what has happened to the American Negro. Something within has reminded him of his birthright of freedom, and something without has reminded him that it can be gained. Consciously or unconsciously, he has been caught up by the *Zeitgeist*, and with his black brothers

30

of Africa and his brown and yellow brothers of Asia, South America, and the Caribbean, the United States Negro is moving with a sense of great urgency toward the promised land of racial justice. If one recognizes this vital urge that has engulfed the Negro community, one should readily understand why public demonstrations are taking place. The Negro has many pent-up resentments and latent frustrations, and he must release them. So let him march; let him make prayer pilgrimages to the city hall; let him go on freedom rides—and try to understand why he must do so. If his repressed emotions are not released in nonviolent ways, they will seek expression through violence; this is not a threat but a fact of history. So I have not said to my people, "Get rid of your discontent." Rather, I have tried to say that this normal and healthy discontent can be channeled into the creative outlet of nonviolent direct action. And now this approach is being termed extremist.

But though I was initially disappointed at being categorized as an extremist, as I continued to think about the matter I gradually gained a measure of satisfaction from the label. Was not Jesus an extremist for love: "Love your enemies, bless them that curse you, do good to them that hate you, and pray for them which despitefully use you, and persecute you." Was not Amos an extremist for justice: "Let justice roll down like waters and righteousness like an ever-flowing stream." Was not Paul an extremist for the Christian gospel: "I bear in my body the marks of the Lord Jesus." Was not Martin Luther an extremist: "Here I stand; I cannot do otherwise, so help me God." And John Bunyan: "I will stay in jail to the end of my days before I make a butchery of my conscience." And Abraham Lincoln: "This nation cannot survive half slave and half free." And Thomas Jefferson: "We hold these truths to be self-evident, that all men are created equal. . . ." So the question is not whether we will be extremists, but what kind of extremists we will be. Will we be extremists for hate or for love? Will we be extremists for the preservation of injustice or for the extension of justice? In that dramatic scene on Calvary's hill three men were crucified. We must never forget that all three were crucified for the same crime—the crime of extremism. Two were extremists for immorality, and thus fell below their environment. The other, Jesus Christ, was an extremist for love, truth, and goodness, and thereby rose above his environment. Perhaps the South, the nation, and the world are in dire need of creative extremists.

I had hoped that the white moderate would see this need. Perhaps I was too optimistic; perhaps I expected too much. I suppose I should have realized that few members of the oppressor race can understand the deep groans and passionate yearnings of the oppressed race, and still fewer have the vision to see that injustice must be rooted out by strong, persistent, and determined action. I am thankful, however, that some of our white brothers in the South have grasped the meaning of this social revolution and committed themselves to it. They are still all too few in quantity, but they are big in quality. Some—such as Ralph McGill, Lillian Smith, Harry Golden, James McBride Dabbs, Ann Braden, and Sarah Patton Boyle—have written about our struggle in eloquent and prophetic terms. Others have marched with us down nameless streets of the South. They have languished in filthy, roach-infested jails, suffering the abuse and brutality of policemen who view them as "dirty nigger-lovers." Unlike so many of their moderate brothers and sisters, they have recognized the urgency of the moment and sensed the need for powerful "action" antidotes to combat the disease of segregation.

Let me take note of my other major disappointment. I have been so greatly disappointed with the white church and its leadership. Of course, there are some notable exceptions. I am not unmindful of the fact that each of you has taken some significant stands on this issue. I commend you, Reverend Stallings, for your Christian stand on this past Sunday, in welcoming Negroes to your worship service on a nonsegregated basis. I commend the Catholic leaders of this state for integrating Spring Hill College several years ago.

But despite these notable exceptions, I must honestly reiterate that I have been disappointed with the church. I do not say this as one of those negative critics who can always find something wrong with the church. I say this as a minister of the gospel, who loves the church; who was nurtured in its bosom; who has been sustained by its spiritual blessings and who will remain true to it as long as the cord of life shall lengthen.

When I was suddenly catapulted into the leadership of the bus protest in Montgomery, Alabama, a few years ago, I felt we would be supported by the white church. I felt that the white ministers, priests, and rabbis of the South would be among our strongest allies. Instead, some have been outright opponents, refusing to understand the freedom movement and misrepresenting its leaders; all too many others have been more cautious than courageous and have remained silent behind the anesthetizing security of stained-glass windows.

In spite of my shattered dreams, I came to Birmingham with the hope that the white religious leadership of this community would see the justice of our cause and, with deep moral concern, would serve as the channel through which our just grievances could reach the power structure. I had hoped that each of you would understand. But again I have been disappointed. . . .

There was a time when the church was very powerful—in the time when the early Christians rejoiced at being deemed worthy to suffer for what they believed. In those days the church was not merely a thermometer that recorded the ideas and principles of popular opinion; it was a thermostat that transformed the mores of society. Whenever the early Christians entered a town, the people in power became disturbed and immediately sought to convict the Christians for being "disturbers of the peace" and "outside agitators." But the Christians pressed on, in the conviction that they were "a colony of heaven," called to obey God rather than man. Small in number, they were big in commitment. They were too God-intoxicated to be "astronomically intimidated." By their effort and example they brought an end to such ancient evils as infanticide and gladitorial contests.

Things are different now. So often the contemporary church is a weak, ineffectual voice with an uncertain sound. So often it is an arch-defender of the status quo. Far from being disturbed by the presence of the church, the power structure of the average community is consoled by the church's silent—and often even vocal—sanction of things as they are.

But the judgment of God is upon the church as never before. If today's church does not recapture the sacrificial spirit of the early church, it will lose its authenticity, forfeit the loyalty of millions, and be dismissed as an irrelevant social club with no meaning for the twentieth century. Every day I meet young people whose disappointment with the church has turned into outright disgust.

Perhaps I have once again been too optimistic. Is organized religion too inextricably bound to the status quo to save our nation and the world? Perhaps I must turn my faith to the inner spiritual church, the church within the church, as the true *ekklesia* and the hope of the world. But again I am thankful to God that some noble souls from the ranks of organized religion have broken loose from the paralyzing chains of conformity and joined us as active partners in the struggle for freedom. They have left their secure congregations and walked the streets of Albany, Georgia, with us. They have gone down the highways of the South on torturous rides for freedom. Yes, they have gone to jail with us. Some have been dismissed from their churches, have lost the support of their bishops and fellow ministers. But they have acted in the faith that right defeated is stronger than evil triumphant. Their witness has been the spiritual salt that has preserved the true meaning of the gospel in these troubled times. They have carved a tunnel of hope through the dark mountain of disappointment.

I hope the church as a whole will meet the challenge of this decisive hour. But even if the church does not come to the aid of justice, I have no despair about the future. I have no fear about the outcome of our struggle in Birmingham, even if our motives are at present misunderstood. We will reach the goal of freedom in Birmingham and all over the nation, because the goal of America is freedom. Abused and scorned though we may be, our destiny is tied up with America's destiny. Before the pilgrims landed at Plymouth, we were here. Before the pen of Jefferson etched the majestic words of the Declaration of Independence across the pages of history, we were here. For more than two centuries our forebears labored in this country without wages; they made cotton king; they built the homes of their masters while suffering gross injustice and shameful humiliation——and yet out of a bottomless vitality they continued to thrive and develop. If the inexpressible cruelties of slavery could not stop us, the opposition we now face will surely fail. We will win our freedom because the sacred heritage of our nation and the eternal will of God are embodied in our echoing demands.

Before closing I feel impelled to mention one other point in your statement that has troubled me profoundly. You warmly commended the Birmingham police force for keeping "order" and "preventing violence." I doubt that you would have so warmly commended the police force if you had seen its dogs sinking their teeth into unarmed, nonviolent Negroes. I doubt that you would so quickly commend the policemen if you were to observe their ugly and inhumane treatment of Negroes here in the city jail; if you were to watch them push and curse old Negro women and young Negro girls; if you were to see them slap and kick old Negro men and young boys; if you were to observe them, as they did on two occasions, refuse to give us food because we wanted to sing our grace together. I cannot join you in your praise of the Birmingham police department.

It is true that the police have exercised a degree of discipline in handling the demonstrators. In this sense they have conducted themselves rather "nonviolently" in public. But for what purpose? To preserve the evil system of segregation. Over the past few years I have consistently preached that nonviolence demands that the means we use must be as pure as the ends we seek. I have tried to make clear that it is wrong to use immoral means to attain moral ends. But now I must affirm that it is just as wrong, or perhaps even more so, to use moral means to preserve immoral ends. Perhaps Mr. Connor and his policemen have been rather nonviolent in public, as was Chief Pritchett in Albany, Georgia, but they have used the moral means of nonviolence to maintain the immoral end of racial injustice. As T. S. Eliot has said, "The last temptation is the greatest treason: To do the right deed for the wrong reason."

I wish you had commended the Negro sit-inners and demonstrators of Birmingham for their sublime courage, their willingness to suffer, and their amazing discipline in the midst of great provocation. One day the South will recognize its real heroes. They will be the James Merediths, with the noble sense of purpose that enables them to face jeering and hostile mobs, and with the agonizing loneliness that characterizes the life of the pioneer. They will be old, oppressed, bat-

tered Negro women, symbolized in a seventy-two-year-old woman in Montgomery, Alabama, who rose up with a sense of dignity and with her people decided not to ride segregated buses, and who responded with ungrammatical pro-
fundity to one who inquired about her weariness: "My feets is tired, but my soul is
at rest." They will be the young high school and college students, the young ministers of the gospel and a host of their elders, courageously and nonviolently sitting in at lunch counters and willingly going to jail for conscience' sake. One day
the South will know that when these disinherited children of God sat down at
lunch counters, they were in reality standing up for what is best in the American
dream and for the most sacred values in our Judaeo-Christian heritage, thereby
bringing our nation back to those great wells of democracy which were dug deep
by the founding fathers in their formulation of the Constitution and the Declaration of Independence.

Never before have I written so long a letter. I'm afraid it is much too long to   45
take your precious time. I can assure you that it would have been much shorter if
I had been writing from a comfortable desk, but what else can one do when he is
alone in a narrow jail cell, other than write long letters, think long thoughts, and
pray long prayers?

If I have said anything in this letter that overstates the truth and indicates an
unreasonable impatience, I beg you to forgive me. If I have said anything that un-
derstates the truth and indicates my having a patience that allows me to settle for
anything less than brotherhood, I beg God to forgive me.

I hope this letter finds you strong in the faith. I also hope that circumstances
will soon make it possible for me to meet each of you, not as an integrationist or
a civil-rights leader but as a fellow clergyman and a Christian brother. Let us all
hope that the dark clouds of racial prejudice will soon pass away and the deep fog
of misunderstanding will be lifted from our fear-drenched communities, and in
some not too distant tomorrow the radiant stars of love and brotherhood will shine
over our great nation with all their scintillating beauty.

Yours for the cause of Peace and Brotherhood,

MARTIN LUTHER KING, JR.

Michel de Montaigne   1533–1592

Of cannibals   1580

When King Pyrrhus passed over into Italy, after he had reconnoitered the formation of the army that the Romans were sending to meet him, he said: "I do not
know what barbarians these are" (for so the Greeks called all foreign nations),
"but the formation of this army that I see is not at all barbarous." The Greeks said
as much of the army that Flaminius brought into their country, and so did Philip,
seeing from a knoll the order and distribution of the Roman camp, in his kingdom,
under Publius Sulpicius Galba. Thus we should beware of clinging to vulgar opinions, and judge things by reason's way, not by popular say.

I had with me for a long time a man who had lived for ten or twelve years in
that other world which has been discovered in our century, in the place where Vil-
legaignon landed, and which he called Antarctic France.[1] This discovery of a

---
[1] Brazil.

boundless country seems worthy of consideration. I don't know if I can guarantee that some other such discovery will not be made in the future, so many personages greater than ourselves having been mistaken about this one. I am afraid we have eyes bigger than our stomachs, and more curiosity than capacity. We embrace everything, but we clasp only wind.

Plato brings in Solon, telling how he had learned from the priests of the city of Saïs in Egypt that in days of old, before the Flood, there was a great island named Atlantis, right at the mouth of the Strait of Gibraltar, which contained more land than Africa and Asia put together, and that the kings of that country, who not only possessed that island but had stretched out so far on the mainland that they held the breadth of Africa as far as Egypt, and the length of Europe as far as Tuscany, undertook to step over into Asia and subjugate all the nations that border on the Mediterranean, as far as the Black Sea; and for this purpose crossed the Spains, Gaul, Italy, as far as Greece, where the Athenians checked them; but that some time after, both the Athenians and themselves and their island were swallowed up by the Flood.

It is quite likely that extreme devastation of waters made amazing changes in the habitations of the earth, as people maintain that the sea cut off Sicily from Italy—

'Tis said an earthquake once asunder tore
These lands with dreadful havoc, which before
Formed but one land, one coast
VIRGIL

—Cyprus from Syria, the island of Euboea from the mainland of Boeotia; and elsewhere joined lands that were divided, filling the channels between them with sand and mud:

A sterile marsh, long fit for rowing, now
Feeds neighbor towns, and feels the heavy plow.
HORACE

But there is no great likelihood that that island was the new world which we have just discovered; for it almost touched Spain, and it would be an incredible result of a flood to have forced it away as far as it is, more than twelve hundred leagues; besides, the travels of the moderns have already almost revealed that it is not an island, but a mainland connected with the East Indies on one side, and elsewhere with the lands under the two poles; or, if it is separated from them, it is by so narrow a strait and interval that it does not deserve to be called an island on that account.

It seems that there are movements, some natural, others feverish, in these   5
great bodies, just as in our own. When I consider the inroads that my river, the Dordogne, is making in my lifetime into the right bank in its descent, and that in twenty years it has gained so much ground and stolen away the foundations of several buildings, I clearly see that this is an extraordinary disturbance; for if it had always gone at this rate, or was to do so in the future, the face of the world would be turned topsy-turvy. But rivers are subject to changes: now they overflow in one direction, now in another, now they keep to their course. I am not speaking of the sudden inundations whose causes are manifest. In Médoc, along the seashore, my brother, the sieur d'Arsac, can see an estate of his buried under the sands that the sea spews forth; the tops of some buildings are still visible; his farms and domains have changed into very thin pasturage. The inhabitants say that for some time the

sea has been pushing toward them so hard that they have lost four leagues of land. These sands are its harbingers; and we see great dunes of moving sand that march half a league ahead of it and keep conquering land.

The other testimony of antiquity with which some would connect this discovery is in Aristotle, at least if that little book *Of Unheard-of Wonders* is by him. He there relates that certain Carthaginians, after setting out upon the Atlantic Ocean from the Strait of Gibraltar and sailing a long time, at last discovered a great fertile island, all clothed in woods and watered by great deep rivers, far remote from any mainland; and that they, and others since, attracted by the goodness and fertility of the soil, went there with their wives and children, and began to settle there. The lords of Carthage, seeing that their country was gradually becoming depopulated, expressly forbade anyone to go there any more, on pain of death, and drove out these new inhabitants, fearing, it is said, that in course of time they might come to multiply so greatly as to supplant their former masters and ruin their state. This story of Aristotle does not fit our new lands any better than the other.

This man I had was a simple, crude fellow—a character fit to bear true witness; for clever people observe more things and more curiously, but they interpret them; and to lend weight and conviction to their interpretation, they cannot help altering history a little. They never show you things as they are, but bend and disguise them according to the way they have seen them; and to give credence to their judgment and attract you to it, they are prone to add something to their matter, to stretch it out and amplify it. We need a man either very honest, or so simple that he has not the stuff to build up false inventions and give them plausibility; and wedded to no theory. Such was my man; and besides this, he at various times brought sailors and merchants, whom he had known on that trip, to see me. So I content myself with his information, without inquiring what the cosmographers say about it.

We ought to have topographers who would give us an exact account of the places where they have been. But because they have over us the advantage of having seen Palestine, they want to enjoy the privilege of telling us news about all the rest of the world. I would like everyone to write what he knows, and as much as he knows, not only in this, but in all other subjects; for a man may have some special knowledge and experience of the nature of a river or a fountain, who in other matters knows only what everybody knows. However, to circulate this little scrap of knowledge, he will undertake to write the whole of physics. From this vice spring many great abuses.

Now, to return to my subject, I think there is nothing barbarous and savage in that nation, from what I have been told, except that each man calls barbarism whatever is not his own practice; for indeed it seems we have no other test of truth and reason than the example and pattern of the opinions and customs of the country we live in. *There* is always the perfect religion, the perfect government, the perfect and accomplished manners in all things. Those people are wild, just as we call wild the fruits that Nature has produced by herself and in her normal course; whereas really it is those that we have changed artificially and led astray from the common order, that we should rather call wild. The former retain alive and vigorous their genuine, their most useful and natural, virtues and properties, which we have debased in the latter in adapting them to gratify our corrupted taste. And yet for all that, the savor and delicacy of some uncultivated fruits of those countries is quite as excellent, even to our taste, as that of our own. It is not reasonable that art should win the place of honor over our great and powerful mother Nature. We have so overloaded the beauty and richness of her works by our inventions that we have quite smothered her. Yet wherever her purity shines forth, she wonderfully puts to shame our vain and frivolous attempts:

Ivy comes readier without our care;
In lonely caves the arbutus grows more fair;
No art with artless bird song can compare.
PROPERTIUS

All our efforts cannot even succeed in reproducing the nest of the tiniest little bird, its contexture, its beauty and convenience; or even the web of the puny spider. All things, says Plato, are produced by nature, by fortune, or by art; the greatest and most beautiful by one or the other of the first two, the least and most imperfect by the last.

These nations, then, seem to me barbarous in this sense, that they have been   10
fashioned very little by the human mind, and are still very close to their original naturalness. The laws of nature still rule them, very little corrupted by ours; and they are in such a state of purity that I am sometimes vexed that they were unknown earlier, in the days when there were men able to judge them better than we. I am sorry that Lycurgus and Plato did not know of them; for it seems to me that what we actually see in these nations surpasses not only all the pictures in which poets have idealized the golden age and all their inventions in imagining a happy state of man, but also the conceptions and the very desire of philosophy. They could not imagine a naturalness so pure and simple as we see by experience; nor could they believe that our society could be maintained with so little artifice and human solder. This is a nation, I should say to Plato, in which there is no sort of traffic, no knowledge of letters, no science of numbers, no name for a magistrate or for political superiority, no custom of servitude, no riches or poverty, no contracts, no successions, no partitions, no occupations but leisure ones, no care for any but common kinship, no clothes, no agriculture, no metal, no use of wine or wheat. The very words that signify lying, treachery, dissimulation, avarice, envy, belittling, pardon—unheard of. How far from this perfection would he find the republic that he imagined: Men fresh sprung from the gods [Seneca].

These manners nature first ordained.
VIRGIL

For the rest, they live in a country with a very pleasant and temperate climate, so that according to my witnesses it is rare to see a sick man there; and they have assured me that they never saw one palsied, bleary-eyed, toothless, or bent with age. They are settled along the sea and shut in on the land side by great high mountains, with a stretch about a hundred leagues wide in between. They have a great abundance of fish and flesh which bear no resemblance to ours, and they eat them with no other artifice than cooking. The first man who rode a horse there, though he had had dealings with them on several other trips, so horrified them in this posture that they shot him dead with arrows before they could recognize him.

Their buildings are very long, with a capacity of two or three hundred souls; they are covered with the bark of great trees, the strips reaching to the ground at one end and supporting and leaning on one another at the top, in the manner of some of our barns, whose covering hangs down to the ground and acts as a side. They have wood so hard that they cut with it and make of it their swords and grills to cook their food. Their beds are of a cotton weave, hung from the roof like those in our ships, each man having his own; for the wives sleep apart from their husbands.

They get up with the sun, and eat immediately upon rising, to last them through the day; for they take no other meal than that one. Like some other Eastern peoples, of whom Suidas tells us, who drank apart from meals, they do not drink then; but they drink several times a day, and to capacity. Their drink is made of some root, and is of the color of our claret wines. They drink it only lukewarm. This beverage keeps only two or three days; it has a slightly sharp taste, is not at all heady, is good for the stomach, and has a laxative effect upon those who are not used to it; it is a very pleasant drink for anyone who is accustomed to it. In place of bread they use a certain white substance like preserved coriander. I have tried it; it tastes sweet and a little flat.

The whole day is spent in dancing. The younger men go to hunt animals with bows. Some of the women busy themselves meanwhile with warming their drink, which is their chief duty. Some one of the old men, in the morning before they begin to eat, preaches to the whole barnful in common, walking from one end to the other, and repeating one single sentence several times until he has completed the circuit (for the buildings are fully a hundred paces long). He recommends to them only two things: valor against the enemy and love for their wives. And they never fail to point out this obligation, as their refrain, that it is their wives who keep their drink warm and seasoned.

There may be seen in several places, including my own house, specimens of their beds, of their ropes, of their wooden swords and the bracelets with which they cover their wrists in combats, and of the big canes, open at one end, by whose sound they keep time in their dances. They are close shaven all over, and shave themselves much more cleanly than we, with nothing but a wooden or stone razor. They believe that souls are immortal, and that those who have deserved well of the gods are lodged in that part of heaven where the sun rises, and the damned in the west.

They have some sort of priests and prophets, but they rarely appear before the people, having their home in the mountains. On their arrival there is a great feast and solemn assembly of several villages—each barn, as I have described it, makes up a village, and they are about one French league from each other. The prophet speaks to them in public, exhorting them to virtue and their duty; but their whole ethical science contains only these two articles: resoluteness in war and affection for their wives. He prophesies to them things to come and the results they are to expect from their undertakings, and urges them to war or holds them back from it; but this is on the condition that when he fails to prophesy correctly, and if things turn out otherwise than he has predicted, he is cut into a thousand pieces if they catch him, and condemned as a false prophet. For this reason, the prophet who has once been mistaken is never seen again.

Divination is a gift of God; that is why its abuse should be punished as imposture. Among the Scythians, when the soothsayers failed to hit the mark, they were laid, chained hand and foot, on carts full of heather and drawn by oxen, on which they were burned. Those who handle matters subject to the control of human capacity are excusable if they do the best they can. But these others, who come and trick us with assurances of an extraordinary faculty that is beyond our ken, should they not be punished for not making good their promise, and for the temerity of their imposture?

They have their wars with the nations beyond the mountains, further inland, to which they go quite naked, with no other arms than bows or wooden swords ending in a sharp point, in the manner of the tongues of our boar spears. It is astonishing what firmness they show in their combats, which never end but in slaughter and bloodshed; for as to routs and terror, they know nothing of either.

15

Each man brings back as his trophy the head of the enemy he has killed, and sets it up at the entrance to his dwelling. After they have treated their prisoners well for a long time with all the hospitality they can think of, each man who has a prisoner calls a great assembly of his acquaintances. He ties a rope to one of the prisoner's arms, by the end of which he holds him, a few steps away, for fear of being hurt, and gives his dearest friend the other arm to hold in the same way; and these two, in the presence of the whole assembly, kill him with their swords. This done, they roast him and eat him in common and send some pieces to their absent friends. This is not, as people think, for nourishment, as of old the Scythians used to do; it is to betoken an extreme revenge. And the proof of this came when they saw the Portuguese, who had joined forces with their adversaries, inflict a different kind of death on them when they took them prisoner, which was to bury them up to the waist, shoot the rest of their body full of arrows, and afterward hang them. They thought that these people from the other world, being men who had sown the knowledge of many vices among their neighbors and were much greater masters than themselves in every sort of wickedness, did not adopt this sort of vengeance without some reason, and that it must be more painful than their own; so they began to give up their old method and to follow this one.

I am not sorry that we notice the barbarous horror of such acts, but I am heartily sorry that, judging their faults rightly, we should be so blind to our own. I think there is more barbarity in eating a man alive than in eating him dead; and in tearing by tortures and the rack a body still full of feeling, in roasting a man bit by bit, in having him bitten and mangled by dogs and swine (as we have not only read but seen within fresh memory, not among ancient enemies, but among neighbors and fellow citizens, and what is worse, on the pretext of piety and religion), than in roasting and eating him after he is dead. 20

Indeed, Chrysippus and Zeno, heads of the Stoic sect, thought there was nothing wrong in using our carcasses for any purpose in case of need, and getting nourishment from them; just as our ancestors, when besieged by Caesar in the city of Alesia, resolved to relieve their famine by eating old men, women, and other people useless for fighting.

> The Gascons once, 'tis said, their life renewed
> By eating of such food.
>   JUVENAL

And physicians do not fear to use human flesh in all sorts of ways for our health, applying it either inwardly or outwardly. But there never was any opinion so disordered as to excuse treachery, disloyalty, tyranny, and cruelty, which are our ordinary vices.

So we may well call these people barbarians, in respect to the rules of reason, but not in respect to ourselves, who surpass them in every kind of barbarity.

Their warfare is wholly noble and generous, and as excusable and beautiful as this human disease can be; its only basis among them is their rivalry in valor. They are not fighting for the conquest of new lands, for they still enjoy that natural abundance that provides them without toil and trouble with all necessary things in such profusion that they have no wish to enlarge their boundaries. They are still in that happy state of desiring only as much as their natural needs demand; anything beyond that is superfluous to them.

They generally call those of the same age, brothers; those who are younger, children; and the old men are fathers to all the others. These leave to their heirs in common the full possession of their property, without division or any other title at all than just the one that Nature gives to her creatures in bringing them into the world.

If their neighbors cross the mountains to attack them and win a victory, the gain of the victor is glory, and the advantage of having proved the master in valor and virtue; for apart from this they have no use for the goods of the vanquished, and they return to their own country, where they lack neither anything necessary nor that great thing, the knowledge of how to enjoy their condition happily and be content with it. These men of ours do the same in their turn. They demand of their prisoners no other ransom than that they confess and acknowledge their defeat. But there is not one in a whole century who does not choose to die rather than to relax a single bit, by word or look, from the grandeur of an invincible courage; not one who would not rather be killed and eaten than so much as ask not to be. They treat them very freely, so that life may be all the dearer to them, and usually entertain them with threats of their coming death, of the torments they will have to suffer, the preparations that are being made for that purpose, the cutting up of their limbs, and the feast that will be made at their expense. All this is done for the sole purpose of extorting from their lips some weak or base word, or making them want to flee, so as to gain the advantage of having terrified them and broken down their firmness. For indeed, if you take it the right way, it is in this point alone that true victory lies:

> It is no victory
> Unless the vanquished foe admits your mastery.
> CLAUDIAN

The Hungarians, very bellicose fighters, did not in olden times pursue their advantage beyond putting the enemy at their mercy. For having wrung a confession from him to this effect, they let him go unharmed and unransomed, except, at most, for exacting his promise never again to take up arms against them.

We win enough advantages over our enemies that are borrowed advantages, not really our own. It is the quality of a porter, not of valor, to have sturdier arms and legs; agility is a dead and corporeal quality; it is a stroke of luck to make our enemy stumble, or dazzle his eyes by the sunlight; it is a trick of art and technique, which may be found in a worthless coward, to be an able fencer. The worth and value of a man is in his heart and his will; there lies his real honor. Valor is the strength, not of legs and arms, but of heart and soul; it consists not in the worth of our horse or our weapons, but in our own. He who falls obstinate in his courage, *if he has fallen, he fights on his knees* [Seneca]. He who relaxes none of his assurance, no matter how great the danger of imminent death; who, giving up his soul, still looks firmly and scornfully at his enemy—he is beaten not by us, but by fortune; he is killed, not conquered.

The most valiant are sometimes the most unfortunate. Thus there are triumphant defeats that rival victories. Nor did those four sister victories, the fairest that the sun ever set eyes on—Salamis, Plataea, Mycale, and Sicily—ever dare match all their combined glory against the glory of the annihilation of King Leonidas and his men at the pass of Thermopylae.

Who ever hastened with more glorious and ambitious desire to win a battle than Captain Ischolas to lose one? Who ever secured his safety more ingeniously and painstakingly than he did his destruction? He was charged to defend a certain pass in the Peloponnesus against the Arcadians. Finding himself wholly incapable of doing this, in view of the nature of the place and the inequality of the forces, he made up his mind that all who confronted the enemy would necessarily have to remain on the field. On the other hand, deeming it unworthy both of his own virtue and magnanimity and of the Lacedaemonian name to fail in his charge, he took a middle course between these two extremes, in this way. The youngest and fittest of his band he preserved for the defense and service of their country, and sent them home; and with those whose loss was less important, he determined to hold this pass, and by their death to make the enemy buy their entry as dearly as he could. And so it turned out. For he was presently surrounded on all sides by the Arcadians, and after slaughtering a large number of them, he and his men were all put to the sword. Is there a trophy dedicated to victors that would not be more due to these vanquished? The role of true victory is in fighting, not in coming off safely; and the honor of valor consists in combating, not in beating.

To return to our story. These prisoners are so far from giving in, in spite of all   30
that is done to them, that on the contrary, during the two or three months that they are kept, they wear a gay expression; they urge their captors to hurry and put them to the test; they defy them, insult them, reproach them with their cowardice and the number of battles they have lost to the prisoners' own people.

I have a song composed by a prisoner which contains this challenge, that they should all come boldly and gather to dine off him, for they will be eating at the same time their own fathers and grandfathers, who have served to feed and nourish his body. "These muscles," he says, "this flesh and these veins are your own, poor fools that you are. You do not recognize that the substance of your ancestors' limbs is still contained in them. Savor them well; you will find in them the taste of your own flesh." An idea that certainly does not smack of barbarity. Those that paint these people dying, and who show the execution, portray the prisoner spitting in the face of his slayers and scowling at them. Indeed, to the last gasp they never stop braving and defying their enemies by word and look. Truly here are real savages by our standards; for either they must be thoroughly so, or we must be; there is an amazing distance between their character and ours.

The men there have several wives, and the higher their reputation for valor the more wives they have. It is a remarkably beautiful thing about their marriages that the same jealousy our wives have to keep us from the affection and kindness of other women, theirs have to win this for them. Being more concerned for their husbands' honor than for anything else, they strive and scheme to have as many companions as they can, since that is a sign of their husbands' valor.

Our wives will cry "Miracle!" but it is no miracle. It is a properly matrimonial virtue, but one of the highest order. In the Bible, Leah, Rachel, Sarah, and Jacob's wives gave their beautiful handmaids to their husbands; and Livia seconded the appetites of Augustus, to her own disadvantage; and Stratonice, the wife of King Deiotarus, not only lent her husband for his use a very beautiful young chambermaid in her service, but carefully brought up her children, and backed them up to succeed to their father's estates.

And lest it be thought that all this is done through a simple and servile bondage to usage and through the pressure of the authority of their ancient customs, without reasoning or judgment, and because their minds are so stupid that they cannot take any other course, I must cite some examples of their capacity. Besides the warlike song I have just quoted, I have another, a love song, which begins in this vein: "Adder, stay; stay, adder, that from the pattern of your coloring my sister may draw the fashion and the workmanship of a rich girdle that I may give to my love; so may your beauty and your pattern be forever preferred to all other serpents." This first couplet is the refrain of the song. Now I am familiar enough with poetry to be a judge of this: not only is there nothing barbarous in this fancy, but it is altogether Anacreontic. Their language, moreover, is a soft language, with an agreeable sound, somewhat like Greek in its endings.

Three of these men, ignorant of the price they will pay some day, in loss of re-   35
pose and happiness, for gaining knowledge of the corruptions of this side of the
ocean; ignorant also of the fact that of this intercourse will come their ruin (which
I suppose is already well advanced: poor wretches, to let themselves be tricked by
the desire for new things, and to have left the serenity of their own sky to come
and see ours!)—three of these men were at Rouen, at the time the late King
Charles IX[2]—was there. The king talked to them for a long time; they were shown
our ways, our splendor, the aspect of a fine city. After that, someone asked their
opinion, and wanted to know what they had found most amazing. They mentioned three things, of which I have forgotten the third, and I am very sorry for it;
but I still remember two of them. They said that in the first place they thought it
very strange that so many grown men, bearded, strong, and armed, who were
around the king (it is likely that they were talking about the Swiss of his guard)
should submit to obey a child, and that one of them was not chosen to command
instead. Second (they have a way in their language of speaking of men as halves
of one another), they had noticed that there were among us men full and gorged
with all sorts of good things, and that their other halves were beggars at their
doors, emaciated with hunger and poverty; and they thought it strange that these
needy halves could endure such an injustice, and did not take the others by the
throat, or set fire to their houses.

I had a very long talk with one of them; but I had an interpreter who followed
my meaning so badly, and who was so hindered by his stupidity in taking in my
ideas, that I could get hardly any satisfaction from the man. When I asked him
what profit he gained from his superior position among his people (for he was a
captain, and our sailors called him king), he told me that it was to march foremost
in war. How many men followed him? He pointed to a piece of ground, to signify
as many as such a space could hold; it might have been four or five thousand
men. Did all his authority expire with the war? He said that this much remained,
that when he visited the villages dependent on him, they made paths for him
through the underbrush by which he might pass quite comfortably.

All this is not too bad—but what's the use? They don't wear breeches.[3]

George Orwell   1903–1950

Shooting an Elephant   1936

In Moulmein, in Lower Burma, I was hated by large numbers of people—the
only time in my life that I have been important enough for this to happen to me. I
was sub-divisional police officer of the town, and in an aimless, petty kind of way
anti-European feeling was very bitter. No one had the guts to raise a riot, but if a
European woman went through the bazaars alone somebody would probably spit
betel juice over her dress. As a police officer I was an obvious target and was
baited whenever it seemed safe to do so. When a nimble Burman tripped me up
on the football field and the referee (another Burman) looked the other way, the
crowd yelled with hideous laughter. This happened more than once. In the end
the sneering yellow faces of young men that met me everywhere, the insults
hooted after me when I was at a safe distance, got badly on my nerves. The young

---

[2]In 1562.
[3]Breeches—trousers.

Buddhist priests were the worst of all. There were several thousands of them in the town and none of them seemed to have anything to do except stand on street corners and jeer at Europeans.

All this was perplexing and upsetting. For at that time I had already made up my mind that imperialism was an evil thing and the sooner I chucked up my job and got out of it the better. Theoretically—and secretly, of course—I was all for the Burmese and all against their oppressors, the British. As for the job I was doing, I hated it more bitterly than I can perhaps make clear. In a job like that you see the dirty work of Empire at close quarters. The wretched prisoners huddling in the stinking cages of the lock-ups, the grey, cowed faces of the long-term convicts, the scarred buttocks of the men who had been flogged with bamboos—all these oppressed me with an intolerable sense of guilt. But I could get nothing into perspective. I was young and ill-educated and I had had to think out my problems in the utter silence that is imposed on every Englishman in the East. I did not even know that the British Empire is dying, still less did I know that it is a great deal better than the younger empires that are going to supplant it. All I knew was that I was stuck between my hatred of the empire I served and my rage against the evil-spirited little beasts who tried to make my job impossible. With one part of my mind I thought of the British Raj[1] as an unbreakable tyranny, as something clamped down, in *saecula saeculorum*,[2] upon the will of prostrate peoples; with another part I thought that the greatest joy in the world would be to drive a bayonet into a Buddhist priest's guts. Feelings like these are the normal by-products of imperialism; ask any Anglo-Indian official, if you can catch him off duty.

One day something happened which in a roundabout way was enlightening. It was a tiny incident in itself, but it gave me a better glimpse than I had had before of the real nature of imperialism—the real motives for which despotic governments act. Early one morning the sub-inspector at a police station the other end of the town rang me up on the 'phone and said that an elephant was ravaging the bazaar. Would I please come and do something about it? I did not know what I could do, but I wanted to see what was happening and I got on to a pony and started out. I took my rifle, an old .44 Winchester and much too small to kill an elephant, but I thought the noise might be useful *in terrorem*. Various Burmans stopped me on the way and told me about the elephant's doings. It was not, of course, a wild elephant, but a tame one which had gone "must."[3] It had been chained up, as tame elephants always are when their attack of "must" is due, but on the previous night it had broken its chain and escaped. Its mahout, the only person who could manage it when it was in that state, had set out in pursuit, but had taken the wrong direction and was now twelve hours' journey away, and in the morning the elephant had suddenly reappeared in the town. The Burmese population had no weapons and were quite helpless against it. It had already destroyed somebody's bamboo hut, killed a cow and raided some fruit-stalls and devoured the stock; also it had met the municipal rubbish van and, when the driver jumped out and took to his heels, had turned the van over and inflicted violences upon it.

The Burmese sub-inspector and some Indian constables were waiting for me in the quarter where the elephant had been seen. It was a very poor quarter, a labyrinth of squalid bamboo huts, thatched with palm-leaf, winding all over a steep hillside. I remember that it was a cloudy, stuffy morning at the beginning of

---

[1]Raj—The British imperial government in India and Burma.
[2]Forever and ever.
[3]"Must"—into sexual heat.

the rains. We began questioning the people as to where the elephant had gone and, as usual, failed to get any definite information. That is invariably the case in the East; a story always sounds clear enough at a distance, but the nearer you get to the scene of events the vaguer it becomes. Some of the people said that the elephant had gone in one direction, some said that he had gone in another, some professed not even to have heard of any elephant. I had almost made up my mind that the whole story was a pack of lies, when we heard yells a little distance away. There was a loud, scandalized cry of "Go away, child! Go away this instant!" and an old woman with a switch in her hand came round the corner of a hut, violently shooing away a crowd of naked children. Some more women followed, clicking their tongues and exclaiming; evidently there was something that the children ought not to have seen. I rounded the hut and saw a man's dead body sprawling in the mud. He was an Indian, a black Dravidian coolie, almost naked, and he could not have been dead many minutes. The people said that the elephant had come suddenly upon him round the corner of the hut, caught him with its trunk, put its foot on his back and ground him into the earth. This was the rainy season and the ground was soft, and his face had scored a trench a foot deep and a couple of yards long. He was lying on his belly with arms crucified and head sharply twisted to one side. His face was coated with mud, the eyes wide open, the teeth bared and grinning with an expression of unendurable agony. (Never tell me, by the way, that the dead look peaceful. Most of the corpses I have seen looked devilish.) The friction of the great beast's foot had stripped the skin from his back as neatly as one skins a rabbit. As soon as I saw the dead man I sent an orderly to a friend's house nearby to borrow an elephant rifle. I had already sent back the pony, not wanting it to go mad with fright and throw me if it smelt the elephant.

The orderly came back in a few minutes with a rifle and five cartridges, and meanwhile some Burmans had arrived and told us that the elephant was in the paddy field below, only a few hundred yards away. As I started forward practically the whole population of the quarter flocked out of the houses and followed me. They had seen the rifle and were all shouting excitedly that I was going to shoot the elephant. They had not shown much interest in the elephant when he was merely ravaging their homes, but it was different now that he was going to be shot. It was a bit of fun to them, as it would be to an English crowd; besides they wanted the meat. It made me vaguely uneasy. I had no intention of shooting the elephant—I had merely sent for the rifle to defend myself if necessary—and it is always unnerving to have a crowd following you. I marched down the hill, looking and feeling a fool, with the rifle over my shoulder and an ever-growing army of people jostling at my heels. At the bottom, when you got away from the huts, there was a metalled road and beyond that a miry waste of paddy fields a thousands yards across, not yet ploughed but soggy from the first rains and dotted with coarse grass. The elephant was standing eight yards from the road, his left side towards us. He took not the slightest notice of the crowd's approach. He was tearing up bunches of grass, beating them against his knees to clean them and stuffing them into his mouth.

I had halted on the road. As soon as I saw the elephant I knew with perfect certainty that I ought not to shoot him. It is a serious matter to shoot a working elephant—it is comparable to destroying a huge and costly piece of machinery—and obviously one ought not to do it if it can possibly be avoided. And at that distance, peacefully eating, the elephant looked no more dangerous than a cow. I thought then and I think now that his attack of "must" was already passing off; in which case he would merely wander harmlessly about until the mahout came back and caught him. Moreover, I did not in the least want to shoot him. I decided that I would watch him for a little while to make sure that he did not turn savage again, and then go home.

But at that moment I glanced round at the crowd that had followed me. It was an immense crowd, two thousand at the least and growing every minute. It blocked the road for a long distance on either side. I looked at the sea of yellow faces above the garish clothes—faces all happy and excited over this bit of fun, all certain that the elephant was going to be shot. They were watching me as they would watch a conjurer about to perform a trick. They did not like me, but with the magical rifle in my hands I was momentarily worth watching. And suddenly I realized that I should have to shoot the elephant after all. The people expected it of me and I had got to do it; I could feel their two thousand wills pressing me forward, irresistibly. And it was at this moment, as I stood there with the rifle in my hands, that I first grasped the hollowness, the futility of the white man's dominion in the East. Here was I, the white man with his gun, standing in front of the unarmed native crowd—seemingly the leading actor of the piece; but in reality I was only an absurd puppet pushed to and fro by the will of those yellow faces behind. I perceived in this moment that when the white man turns tyrant it is his own freedom that he destroys. He becomes a sort of hollow, posing dummy, the conventionalized figure of a sahib. For it is the condition of his rule that he shall spend his life in trying to impress the "natives," and so in every crisis he has got to do what the "natives" expect of him. He wears a mask, and his face grows to fit it. I had got to shoot the elephant. I had committed myself to doing it when I sent for the rifle. A sahib has got to act like a sahib; he has got to appear resolute, to know his own mind and do definite things. To come all that way, rifle in hand, with two thousand people marching at my heels, and then to trail feebly away, having done nothing—no, that was impossible. The crowd would laugh at me. And my whole life, every white man's life in the East, was one long struggle not to be laughed at.

But I did not want to shoot the elephant. I watched him beating his bunch of grass against his knees, with that preoccupied grandmotherly air that elephants have. It seemed to me that it would be murder to shoot him. At that age I was not squeamish about killing animals, but I had never shot an elephant and never wanted to. (Somehow it always seems worse to kill a *large* animal.) Besides, there was the beast's owner to be considered. Alive, the elephant was worth at least a hundred pounds; dead, he would only be worth the value of his tusks, five pounds, possibly. But I had got to act quickly. I turned to some experienced-looking Burmans who had been there when we arrived, and asked them how the elephant had been behaving. They all said the same thing: he took no notice of you if you left him alone, but he might charge if you went too close to him.

It was perfectly clear to me what I ought to do. I ought to walk up to within, say, twenty-five yards of the elephant and test his behavior. If he charged, I could shoot; if he took no notice of me, it would be safe to leave him until the mahout came back. But also I knew that I was going to do no such thing. I was a poor shot with a rifle and the ground was soft mud into which one would sink at every step. If the elephant charged and I missed him, I should have about as much chance as a toad under a steam-roller. But even then I was not thinking particularly of my own skin, only of the watchful yellow faces behind. For at that moment, with the crowd watching me, I was not afraid in the ordinary sense, as I would have been if I had been alone. A white man mustn't be frightened in front of "natives"; and so, in general, he isn't frightened. The sole thought in my mind was that if anything went wrong those two thousand Burmans would see me pursued, caught, trampled on and reduced to a grinning corpse like that Indian up the hill. And if that happened it was quite probable that some of them would laugh.

That would never do. There was only one alternative. I shoved the cartridges into the magazine and lay down on the road to get a better aim.

The crowd grew very still, and a deep, low, happy sigh, as of people who see the theatre curtain go up at last, breathed from innumerable throats. They were going to have their bit of fun after all. The rifle was a beautiful German thing with cross-hair sights. I did not then know that in shooting an elephant one would shoot to cut an imaginary bar running from ear-hole to ear-hole. I ought, therefore, as the elephant was sideways on, to have aimed straight at his ear-hole; actually I aimed several inches in front of this, thinking the brain would be further forward.

When I pulled the trigger I did not hear the bang or feel the kick—one never does when a shot goes home—but I heard the devilish roar of glee that went up from the crowd. In that instant, in too short a time, one would have thought, even for the bullet to get there, a mysterious, terrible change had come over the elephant. He neither stirred nor fell, but every line of his body had altered. He looked suddenly stricken, shrunken, immensely old, as though the frightful impact of the bullet had paralysed him without knocking him down. At last, after what seemed a long time—it might have been five seconds, I dare say—he sagged flabbily to his knees. His mouth slobbered. An enormous senility seemed to have settled upon him. One could have imagined him thousands of years old. I fired again into the same spot. At the second shot he did not collapse but climbed with desperate slowness to his feet and stood weakly upright, with legs sagging and head drooping. I fired a third time. That was the shot that did for him. You could see the agony of it jolt his whole body and knock the last remnant of strength from his legs. But in falling he seemed for a moment to rise, for as his hind legs collapsed beneath him he seemed to tower upward like a huge rock toppling, his trunk reaching skywards like a tree. He trumpeted, for the first and only time. And then down he came, his belly towards me, with a crash that seemed to shake the ground even where I lay.

I got up. The Burmans were already racing past me across the mud. It was obvious that the elephant would never rise again, but he was not dead. He was breathing very rhythmically with long rattling gasps, his great mound of a side painfully rising and falling. His mouth was wide open—I could see far down into caverns of pale pink throat. I waited a long time for him to die, but his breathing did not weaken. Finally I fired my two remaining shots in the spot where I thought his heart must be. The thick blood welled out of him like red velvet, but still he did not die. His body did not even jerk when the shots hit him, the tortured breathing continued without a pause. He was dying, very slowly and in great agony, but in some world remote from me where not even a bullet could damage him further. I felt that I had got to put an end to that dreadful noise. It seemed dreadful to see the great beast lying there, powerless to move and yet powerless to die, and not even to be able to finish him. I sent back for my small rifle and poured shot after shot into his heart and down his throat. They seemed to make no impression. The tortured gasps continued as steadily as the ticking of a clock.

In the end I could not stand it any longer and went away. I heard later that it took him half an hour to die. Burmans were bringing dahs[4] and baskets even before I left, and I was told they had stripped his body almost to the bones by the afternoon.

Afterwards, of course, there were endless discussions about the shooting of the elephant. The owner was furious, but he was only an Indian and could do

---

[4]Butcher knives.

nothing. Besides, legally I had done the right thing, for a mad elephant has to be killed, like a mad dog, if its owner fails to control it. Among the Europeans opinion was divided. The older men said I was right, the younger men said it was a damn shame to shoot an elephant for killing a coolie, because an elephant was worth more than any damn Coringhee coolie. And afterwards I was very glad that the coolie had been killed; it put me legally in the right and it gave me a sufficient pretext for shooting the elephant. I often wondered whether any of the others grasped that I had done it solely to avoid looking a fool.

Jonathan Swift   1667–1745

A Modest Proposal   1729

It is a melancholy object to those who walk through this great town[1] or travel in the country, when they see the streets, the roads, and cabin doors, crowded with beggars of the female sex, followed by three, four, or six children, all in rags and importuning every passenger for an alms. These mothers, instead of being able to work for their honest livelihood, are forced to employ all their time in strolling to beg sustenance for their helpless infants, who, as they grow up, either turn thieves for want of work, or leave their dear native country to fight for the Pretender[2] in Spain, or sell themselves to the Barbadoes.

I think it is agreed by all parties that this prodigious number of children in the arms, or on the backs, or at the heels of their mothers, and frequently of their fathers, is in the present deplorable state of the kingdom a very great additional grievance; and therefore whoever could find out a fair, cheap, and easy method of making these children sound, useful members of the commonwealth would deserve so well of the public as to have his statue set up for a preserver of the nation.

But my intention is very far from being confined to provide only for the children of professed beggars; it is of a much greater extent, and shall take in the whole number of infants at a certain age who are born of parents in effect as little able to support them as those who demand our charity in the streets.

As to my own part, having turned my thoughts for many years upon this important subject, and maturely weighed the several schemes of other projectors, I have always found them grossly mistaken in their computation. It is true, a child just dropped from its dam may be supported by her milk for a solar year, with little other nourishment; at most not above the value of two shillings, which the mother may certainly get, or the value in scraps, by her lawful occupation of begging; and it is exactly at one year old that I propose to provide for them in such a manner as instead of being a charge upon their parents or the parish, or wanting food and raiment for the rest of their lives, they shall on the contrary contribute to the feeding, and partly to the clothing, of many thousands.

There is likewise another great advantage in my scheme, that it will prevent   5 those involuntary abortions, and that horrid practice of women murdering their bastard children, alas, too frequent among us, sacrificing the poor innocent babes, I doubt, more to avoid the expense than the shame, which would move tears and pity in the most savage and inhuman breast.

---

[1]great town—Dublin.
[2]the Pretender—James, son of James II, king of Britain, 1685–1688, and a Roman Catholic.

The number of souls in this kingdom being usually reckoned one million and a half, of these I calculate there may be about two hundred thousand couples whose wives are breeders, from which number I subtract thirty thousand couples who are able to maintain their own children, although I apprehend there cannot be so many under the present distress of the kingdom; but this being granted, there will remain a hundred and seventy thousand breeders. I again subtract fifty thousand for those women who miscarry, or whose children die by accident or disease within the year. There only remain an hundred and twenty thousand children of poor parents annually born. The question therefore is, how this number shall be reared and provided for, which, as I have already said, under the present situation of affairs, is utterly impossible by all the methods hitherto proposed. For we can neither employ them in handicraft nor agriculture; we neither build houses (I mean in the country) nor cultivate land. They can very seldom pick up livelihood by stealing till they arrive at six years old, except where they are of towardly parts; although I confess they learn the rudiments much earlier, during which time they can however be looked upon only as probationers, as I have been informed by a principal gentleman in the country of Cavan, who protested to me that he never knew above one or two instances under the age of six, even in a part of the kingdom so renowned for the quickest proficiency in that art.

I am assured by our merchants that a boy or girl before twelve years old is no salable commodity; and even when they come to this age, they will not yield above three pounds, or three pounds and half a crown at most on the Exchange; which cannot turn to account either to the parents or the kingdom, the charge of nutriment and rags having been at least four times that value.

I shall now therefore humbly propose my own thoughts, which I hope will not be liable to the least objection.

I have been assured by a very knowing American of my acquaintance in London, that a young healthy child well nursed is at a year old a most delicious, nourishing, and wholesome food, whether stewed, roasted, baked, or boiled; and I make no doubt that it will equally serve in fricassee or a ragout.

I do therefore humbly offer it to public consideration that of the hundred and twenty thousand children, already computed, twenty thousand may be reserved for breed, whereof only one fourth part to be males, which is more than we allow to sheep, black cattle, or swine; and my reason is that these children are seldom the fruits of marriage, a circumstance not much regarded by our savages, therefore one male will be sufficient to serve four females. That the remaining hundred thousand may at a year old be offered in sale to the persons of quality and fortune through the kingdom, always advising the mother to let them suck plentifully in the last month, so as to render them plump and fat for a good table. A child will make two dishes at an entertainment for friends; and when the family dines alone, the fore or hind quarter will make a reasonable dish, and seasoned with a little pepper or salt will be very good boiled on the fourth day, especially in winter.

I have reckoned upon a medium that a child just born will weigh twelve pounds, and in a solar year if tolerably nursed increaseth to twenty-eight pounds.

I grant this food will be somewhat dear, and therefore very proper for landlords, who, as they have already devoured most of the parents, seem to have the best title to the children.

Infant's flesh will be in season throughout the year, but more plentiful in March, and a little before and after. For we are told by a grave author, an eminent French physician, that fish being a prolific diet, there are more children born in Roman Catholic countries about nine months after Lent, than at any other season; therefore, reckoning a year after Lent, the markets will be more glutted than usual,

10

because the number of popish infants is at least three to one in this kingdom; and therefore it will have one other collateral advantage, by lessening the number of Papists[3] among us.

I have already computed the chore of nursing a beggar's child (in which list I reckon all cottagers, laborers, and four fifths of the farmers) to be about two shillings per annum, rags included; and I believe no gentlemen would repine to give ten shillings for the carcass of a good fat child, which, as I have said, will make four dishes of excellent nutritive meat, when he hath only some particular friend or his own family to dine with him. Thus the squire will learn to be a good landlord, and grow popular among the tenants; the mother will have eight shillings net profit, and be fit for work till she produces another child.

Those who are more thrifty (as I must confess the times require) may flay the   15 carcass; the skin of which artificially dressed will make admirable gloves for ladies, and summer boots for fine gentlemen.

As to our city of Dublin, shambles [slaughterhouses] may be appointed for this purpose in the most convenient parts of it, and butchers we may be assured will not be wanting; although I rather recommend buying the children alive, and dressing them hot from the knife as we do roasting pigs.

A very worthy person, a true lover of his country, and whose virtues I highly esteem, was lately pleased in discoursing on this matter to offer a refinement upon my scheme. He said that many gentlemen of his kingdom, having of late destroyed their deer, he conceived that the want of venison might be well supplied by the bodies of young lads and maidens, not exceeding fourteen years of age nor under twelve, so great a number of both sexes in every county being now ready to starve for want of work and service; and these to be disposed of by their parents, if alive, or otherwise by their nearest relations. But with due deference to so excellent a friend and so deserving a patriot, I cannot be altogether in his sentiments; for as to the males, my American acquaintance assured me from frequent experience that their flesh was generally tough and lean, like that of our schoolboys, by continual exercise, and their taste disagreeable; and to fatten them would not answer the charge. Then as to the females, it would, I think with humble submission, be a loss to the public, because they soon would become breeders themselves; and besides, it is not improbable that some scrupulous people might be apt to censure such a practice (although indeed very unjustly) as a little bordering upon cruelty; which, I confess, hath always been with me the strongest objection against any project, how well soever intended.

But in order to justify my friend, he confessed that this expedient was put into his head by the famous Psalmanazar, a native of the island Formosa, who came from thence to London above twenty years ago, and in conversation told my friend that in his country when any young person happened to be put to death, the executioner sold the carcass to the persons of quality as a prime dainty; and that in his time the body of a plump girl of fifteen, who was crucified for an attempt to poison the emperor, was sold to his Imperial Majesty's prime minister of state, and other great mandarins of the court, in joints from the gibbet, at four hundred crowns. Neither indeed can I deny that if the same use were made of several plump young girls in this town, who without one single groat to their fortunes cannot stir abroad without a chair, and appear at the playhouse and assemblies in foreign fineries which they never will pay for, the kingdom would not be the worse.

---

[3]Papists—Roman Catholics

Some persons of a desponding spirit are in great concern about that vast number of poor people who are aged, diseased, or maimed, and I have been desired to employ my thoughts what course may be taken to ease the nation of so grievous an encumbrance. But I am not in the least pain upon that matter, because it is very well known that they are every day dying and rotting by cold and famine, and filth and vermin, as fast as can be reasonably expected. And as to the younger laborers, they are now in almost as hopeful a condition. They cannot get work, and consequently pine away for want of nourishment to a degree that if any time they are accidentally hired to common labor, they have not strength to perform it; and thus the country and themselves are happily delivered from the evils to come.

I have too long digressed, and therefore shall return to my subject. I think the   20
advantages by the proposal which I have made are obvious and many, as well as of the highest importance.

For first, as I have already observed, it would greatly lessen the number of Papists, with whom we are yearly overrun, being the principal breeders of the nation as well as our most dangerous enemies; and who stay at home on purpose to deliver the kingdom to the Pretender, hoping to take their advantage by the absence of so many good Protestants, who have chosen rather to leave their country than to stay at home and pay tithes against their conscience to an Episcopal curate.

Secondly, the poorer tenants will have something valuable of their own, which by law may be made liable to distress, and help to pay their landlord's rent, their corn and cattle being already seized and money a thing unknown.

Thirdly, whereas the maintenance of an hundred thousand children, from two years old and upwards, cannot be computed at less than ten shillings a piece per annum, the nation's stock will be thereby increased fifty thousand pounds per annum, besides the profit of a new dish introduced to the tables of all gentlemen of fortune in the kingdom who have any refinement in taste. And the money will circulate among ourselves, the goods being entirely of our own growth and manufacture.

Fourthly, the constant breeders, besides the gain of eight shillings per annum by the sale of their children, will be rid of the charge for maintaining them after the first year.

Fifthly, this food would likewise bring great custom to taverns, where the vint-   25
ners will certainly be so prudent as to procure the best receipts for dressing it to perfection, and consequently have their houses frequented by all the fine gentlemen, who justly value themselves upon their knowledge in good eating; and a skillful cook, who understands how to oblige his guests, will contrive to make it as expensive as they please.

Sixthly, this would be a great inducement to marriage, which all wise nations have either encouraged by rewards or enforced by laws and penalties. It would increase the care and tenderness of mothers toward their children, when they were sure of a settlement for life to the poor babes, provided in some sort by the public, to their annual profit instead of expense. We should see an honest emulation among the married women, which of them could bring the fattest child to the market. Men would become as fond of their wives during the time of pregnancy as they are now of their mares in foal, their cows in calf, or sows when they are ready to farrow; nor offer to beat or kick them (as is too frequent a practice) for fear of a miscarriage.

Many other advantages might be enumerated. For instance, the addition of some thousand carcasses in our exportation of barreled beef, the propagation of swine's flesh, and improvements in the art of making good bacon, so much wanted among us by the great destruction of pigs, too frequent at our tables, which are no way comparable in taste or magnificence to a well-grown, fat, yearling child, which roasted whole will make a considerable figure at a lord mayor's feast or any other public entertainment. But this and many others I omit, being studious of brevity.

Supposing that one thousand families in this city would be constant customers for infants' flesh, besides others who might have it at merry meetings, particularly weddings and christenings, I compute that Dublin would take off annually about twenty thousand carcasses, and the rest of the kingdom (where probably they will be sold somewhat cheaper) the remaining eighty thousand.

I can think of no one objection that will possibly be raised against this proposal, unless it should be urged that the number of people will be thereby much lessened in the kingdom. This I freely own, and it was indeed one principal design in offering it to the world. I desire the reader will observe; that I calculate my remedy for this one individual kingdom of Ireland and for no other that ever was, is, or I think ever can be upon earth. Therefore, let no man talk to me of other expedients: of taxing our absentees at five shillings a pound: of using neither clothes nor household furniture except what is of our own growth and manufacture: of utterly rejecting the materials and instruments that promote foreign luxury: of curing the expensiveness of pride, vanity, idleness, and gaming in our women: of introducing a vein of parsimony, prudence, and temperance: of learning to love our country, in the want of which we differ even from Laplanders and the inhabitants of Topinamboo: of quitting our animosities and factions, nor acting any longer like the Jews, who were murdering one another at the very moment their city was taken: of being a little cautious not to sell our country and conscience for nothing: of teaching landlords to have at least one degree of mercy toward their tenants: lastly, of putting a spirit of honesty, industry, and skill into our shopkeepers; who, if a resolution could now be taken to buy only our native goods, would immediately unite to cheat and exact upon us in the price, the measure, and the goodness, nor could ever yet be brought to make one fair proposal of just dealing, though often and earnestly invited to it.

Therefore, I repeat, let no man talk to me of these and the like expedients, till he hath at least some glimpse of hope that there will ever be some hearty and sincere attempt to put them in practice.

But as to myself, having been wearied out for many years with offering vain, idle, visionary thoughts, and at length utterly despairing of success, I fortunately fell upon this proposal, which, as it is wholly new, so it hath something solid and real, of no expense and little trouble, full in our own power, and whereby we can incur no danger in disobliging England. For this kind of commodity will not bear exportation, the flesh being of too tender a consistence to admit a long continuance in salt, although perhaps I could name a country which would be glad to eat up our whole nation without it.

After all, I am not so violently bent upon my own opinion as to reject any offer proposed by wise men, which shall be found equally innocent, cheap, easy, and effectual. But before something of that kind shall be advanced in contradiction to my scheme, and offering a better, I desire the author or authors will be pleased maturely to consider two points. First, as things now stand, how they will be able to find food and raiment for an hundred thousand useless mouths and backs. And secondly, there being a round million of creatures in human figure throughout this kingdom, whose sole subsistence put into a common stock would leave them in debt two millions of pounds sterling, adding those who are beggars by profession to the bulk of farmers, cottagers, and laborers, with their wives and children who are beggars in effect; I desire those politicians who dislike my overture, and may perhaps be so bold to attempt an answer, that they will first ask the parents of these mortals whether they would not at this day think it a great happiness to have been sold for food at a year old in this manner I prescribe, and

30

thereby have avoided such a perpetual scene of misfortunes as they have since gone through by the oppression of landlords, the impossibility of paying rent without money or trade, the want of common sustenance, with neither house nor clothes to cover them from the inclemencies of the weather, and the most inevitable prospect of entailing the like or greater miseries upon their breed forever.

I profess, in the sincerity of my heart, that I have not the least personal interest in endeavoring to promote this necessary work, having no other motive than the public good of my country, by advancing our trade, providing for infants, relieving the poor, and giving some pleasure to the rich. I have no children by which I can propose to get a single penny; the youngest being nine years old, and my wife past childbearing.

Henry David Thoreau   1817–1862

Resistance to Civil Government   1849

I heartily accept the motto,—"That government is best which governs least;" and I should like to see it acted up to more rapidly and systematically. Carried out, it finally amounts to this, which also I believe,—"That government is best which governs not at all;" and when men are prepared for it, that will be the kind of government which they will have. Government is at best but an expedient; but most governments are usually, and all governments are sometimes, inexpedient. The objections which have been brought against a standing army, and they are many and weighty, and deserve to prevail, may also at last be brought against a standing government. The standing army is only an arm of the standing government. The government itself, which is only the mode which the people have chosen to execute their will, is equally liable to be abused and perverted before the people can act through it. Witness the present Mexican war, the work of comparatively a few individuals using the standing government as their tool; for, in the outset, the people would not have consented to this measure.

This American government,—what is it but a tradition, though a recent one, endeavoring to transmit itself unimpaired to posterity, but each instant losing some of its integrity? It has not the vitality and force of a single living man; for a single man can bend it to his will. It is a sort of wooden gun to the people themselves; and, if ever they should use it in earnest as a real one against each other, it will surely split. But it is not the less necessary for this; for the people must have some complicated machinery or other, and hear its din, to satisfy that idea of government which they have. Governments show thus how successfully men can be imposed on, even impose on themselves, for their own advantage. It is excellent, we must all allow; yet this government never of itself furthered any enterprise, but by the alacrity with which it got out of its way. *It* does not keep the country free. *It* does not settle the West. *It* does not educate. The character inherent in the American people has done all that has been accomplished; and it would have done somewhat more, if the government had not sometimes got in its way. For government is an expedient by which men would fain succeed in letting one another alone; and, as has been said, when it is most expedient, the governed are most let alone by it. Trade and commerce, if they were not made of India rubber, would never manage to bounce over the obstacles which legislators are continually putting in their way; and, if one were to judge these men wholly by the effects of their actions, and not partly by their intentions, they would deserve to be classed and punished with those mischievous persons who put obstructions on the railroads.

But, to speak practically and as a citizen, unlike those who call themselves no-government men, I ask for, not at once no government, but *at once* a better government. Let every man make known what kind of government would command his respect, and that will be one step toward obtaining it.

After all, the practical reason why, when the power is once in the hands of the people, a majority are permitted, and for a long period continue, to rule, is not because they are most likely to be in the right, not because this seems fairest to the minority, but because they are physically the strongest. But a government in which the majority rule in all cases cannot be based on justice, even as far as men understand it. Can there not be a government in which majorities do not virtually decide right and wrong, but conscience?—in which majorities decide only those questions to which the rule of expediency is applicable? Must the citizen ever for a moment, or in the least degree, resign his conscience to the legislator? Why has every man a conscience, then? I think that we should be men first, and subjects afterward. It is not desirable to cultivate a respect for the law, so much as for the right. The only obligation which I have a right to assume, is to do at any time what I think right. It is truly enough said, that a corporation has no conscience; but a corporation of conscientious men is a corporation *with* a conscience. Law never made men a whit more just; and, by means of their respect for it, even the well-disposed are daily made the agents of injustice. A common and natural result of an undue respect for law is, that you may see a file of soldiers, colonel, captain, corporal, privates, powder-monkeys and all, marching in admirable order over hill and dale to the wars, against their wills, aye, against their common sense and consciences, which makes it very steep marching indeed, and produces a palpitation of the heart. They have no doubt that it is a damnable business in which they are concerned; they are all peaceably inclined. Now, what are they? Men at all? or small moveable forts and magazines, at the service of some unscrupulous man in power? Visit the Navy Yard, and behold a marine, such a man as an American government can make, or such as it can make a man with its black arts, a mere shadow and reminiscence of humanity, a man laid out alive and standing, and already, as one may say, buried under arms with funeral accompaniments, though it may be

> "Not a drum was heard, not a funeral note,
>   As his corse to the rampart we hurried;
> Not a soldier discharged his farewell shot
>   O'er the grave where our hero we buried."

The mass of men serve the State thus, not as men mainly, but as machines, with their bodies. They are the standing army, and the militia, jailers, constables, *posse comitatus*, &c. In most cases there is no free exercise whatever of the judgment or of the moral sense; but they put themselves on a level with wood and earth and stones, and wooden men can perhaps be manufactured that will serve the purpose as well. Such command no more respect than men of straw, or a lump of dirt. They have the same sort of worth only as horses and dogs. Yet such as these even are commonly esteemed good citizens. Others, as most legislators, politicians, lawyers, ministers, and office-holders, serve the State chiefly with their heads; and, as they rarely make any moral distinctions, they are as likely to serve the devil, without intending it, as God. A very few, as heroes, patriots, martyrs, reformers in the great sense, and *men*, serve the State with their consciences also, and so necessarily resist it for the most part; and they are commonly treated by it as enemies. A wise man will only be useful as a man, and will not submit to be "clay," and "stop a hole to keep the wind away," but leave that office to his dust at least:—

5

"I am too high-born to be propertied,
To be a secondary at control,
Or useful serving-man and instrument
To any sovereign state throughout the world."

He who gives himself entirely to his fellow-men appears to them useless and selfish; but he who gives himself partially to them is pronounced a benefactor and philanthropist.

How does it become a man to behave toward this American government today? I answer that he cannot without disgrace be associated with it. I cannot for an instant recognize that political organization as *my* government which is the *slave's* government also.

All men recognize the right of revolution; that is, the right to refuse allegiance to and to resist the government, when its tyranny or its inefficiency are great and unendurable. But almost all say that such is not the case now. But such was the case, they think, in the Revolution of '75. If one were to tell me that this was a bad government because it taxed certain foreign commodities brought to its ports, it is most probable that I should not make an ado about it, for I can do without them: all machines have their friction; and possibly this does enough good to counterbalance the evil. At any rate, it is a great evil to make a stir about it. But when the friction comes to have its machine, and oppression and robbery are organized, I say, let us not have such a machine any longer. In other words, when a sixth of the population of a nation which has undertaken to be the refuge of liberty are slaves, and a whole country is unjustly overrun and conquered by a foreign army, and subjected to military law, I think that it is not too soon for honest men to rebel and revolutionize. What makes this duty the more urgent is the fact, that the country so overrun is not our own, but ours is the invading army.

Paley, a common authority with many on moral questions, in his chapter on the "Duty of Submission to Civil Government," resolves all civil obligation into expediency; and he proceeds to say, "that so long as the interest of the whole society requires it, that is, so long as the established government cannot be resisted or changed without public inconveniency, it is the will of God that the established government be obeyed, and no longer." . . . ."This principle being admitted, the justice of every particular case of resistance is reduced to a computation of the quantity of the danger and grievance on the one side, and of the probability and expense of redressing it on the other." Of this, he says, every man shall judge for himself. But Paley appears never to have contemplated those cases to which the rule of expediency does not apply, in which a people, as well as an individual, must do justice, cost what it may. If I have unjustly wrested a plank from a drowning man, I must restore it to him though I drown myself. This, according to Paley, would be inconvenient. But he that would save his life, in such a case, shall lose it. This people must cease to hold slaves, and to make war on Mexico, though it cost them their existence as a people.

In their practice, nations agree with Paley; but does any one think that Massachusetts does exactly what is right at the present crisis?   10

"A drab of state, a cloth-o'-silver slut,
To have her train borne up, and her soul trail in the dirt."

Practically speaking, the opponents to a reform in Massachusetts are not a hundred thousand politicians at the South, but a hundred thousand merchants and farmers here, who are more interested in commerce and agriculture than they are in humanity, and are not prepared to do justice to the slave and to Mexico, *cost what it may*. I quarrel not with far-off foes, but with those who, near at home, co-operate with, and do the bidding of those far away, and without whom the latter would be harmless. We are accustomed to say, that the mass of men are unprepared; but improvement is slow, because the few are not materially wiser or better than the many. It is not so important that many should be as good as you, as that there be some absolute goodness somewhere; for that will leaven the whole lump. There are thousands who are *in opinion* opposed to slavery and to the war, who yet in effect do nothing to put an end to them; who, esteeming themselves children of Washington and Franklin, sit down with their hands in their pockets, and say that they know not what to do, and do nothing; who even postpone the question of freedom to the question of free-trade, and quietly read the prices-current along with the latest advices from Mexico, after dinner, and, it may be, fall asleep over them both. What is the price-current of an honest man and patriot today? They hesitate, and they regret, and sometimes they petition; but they do nothing in earnest and with effect. They will wait, well-disposed, for others to remedy the evil, that they may no longer have it to regret. At most, they give only a cheap vote, and a feeble countenance and God-speed, to the right, as it goes by them. There are nine hundred and ninety-nine patrons of virtue to one virtuous man; but it is easier to deal with the real possessor of a thing than with the temporary guardian of it.

All voting is a sort of gaming, like chequers or backgammon, with a slight moral tinge to it, a playing with right and wrong, with moral questions; and betting naturally accompanies it. The character of the voters is not staked. I cast my vote, perchance, as I think right; but I am not vitally concerned that that right should prevail. I am willing to leave it to the majority. Its obligation, therefore, never exceeds that of expediency. Even voting *for the right* is *doing* nothing for it. It is only expressing to men feebly your desire that it should prevail. A wise man will not leave the right to the mercy of chance, nor wish it to prevail through the power of the majority. There is but little virtue in the action of masses of men. When the majority shall at length vote for the abolition of slavery, it will be because they are indifferent to slavery, or because there is but little slavery left to be abolished by their vote. *They* will then be the only slaves. Only *his* vote can hasten the abolition of slavery who asserts his own freedom by his vote.

I hear of a convention to be held at Baltimore, or elsewhere, for the selection of a candidate for the Presidency, made up chiefly of editors, and men who are politicians by profession; but I think, what is it to any independent, intelligent, and respectable man what decision they may come to, shall we not have the advantage of his wisdom and honesty, nevertheless? Can we not count upon some independent votes? Are there not many individuals in the country who do not attend conventions? But no: I find that the respectable man, so called, has immediately drifted from his position, and despairs of his country, when his country has more reason to despair of him. He forthwith adopts one of the candidates thus selected as the only *available* one, thus proving that he is himself *available* for any purposes of the demagogue. His vote is of no more use than that of any unprincipled foreigner or hireling native, who may have been bought. Oh for a man who is a *man*, and, as my neighbor says, has a bone in his back which you cannot pass your hand through! Our statistics are at fault: the population has been returned too large. How many *men* are there to a square thousand miles in this country? Hardly one. Does not America offer any inducement for men to settle here? The American has dwindled into an Odd Fellow,—one who may be known by the development of his organ of gregariousness, and a manifest lack of intellect and cheerful self-reliance; whose first and chief concern, on coming into the world, is to see that the alms-houses are in good repair; and, before yet he has lawfully donned the virile garb, to collect a fund for the support of the widows and orphans that may be:

who, in short, ventures to live only by the aid of the mutual insurance company, which has promised to bury him decently.

It is not a man's duty, as a matter of course, to devote himself to the eradication of any, even the most enormous wrong; he may still properly have other concerns to engage him; but it is his duty, at least, to wash his hands of it, and, if he gives it no thought longer, not to give it practically his support. If I devote myself to other pursuits and contemplations, I must first see, at least, that I do not pursue them sitting upon another man's shoulders. I must get off him first, that he may pursue his contemplations too. See what gross inconsistency is tolerated. I have heard some of my townsmen say, "I should like to have them order me out to help put down an insurrection of the slaves, or to march to Mexico,—see if I would go;" and yet these very men have each, directly by their allegiance, and so indirectly, at least, by their money, furnished a substitute. The soldier is applauded who refuses to serve in an unjust war by those who do not refuse to sustain the unjust government which makes the war; is applauded by those whose own act and authority he disregards and sets at nought; as if the State were penitent to that degree that it hired one to scourge it while it sinned, but not to that degree that it left off sinning for a moment. Thus, under the name of order and civil government, we are all made at last to pay homage to and support our own meanness. After the first blush of sin, comes its indifference and from immoral it becomes, as it were, *un*moral, and not quite unnecessary to that life which we have made.

The broadest and most prevalent error requires the most disinterested virtue to sustain it. The slight reproach to which the virtue of patriotism is commonly liable, the noble are most likely to incur. Those who, while they disapprove of the character and measures of a government, yield to it their allegiance and support, are undoubtedly its most conscientious supporters, and so frequently the most serious obstacles to reform. Some are petitioning the State to dissolve the Union, to disregard the requisitions of the President. Why do they not dissolve it themselves,—the union between themselves and the State,—and refuse to pay their quota into its treasury? Do not they stand in the same relation to the State, that the State does to the Union? And have not the same reasons prevented the State from resisting the Union, which have prevented them from resisting the State?

How can a man be satisfied to entertain an opinion merely, and enjoy *it*? Is there any enjoyment in it, if his opinion is that he is aggrieved? If you are cheated out of a single dollar by your neighbor, you do not rest satisfied with knowing that you are cheated, or with saying that you are cheated, or even with petitioning him to pay you your due; but you take effectual steps at once to obtain the full amount, and see that you are never cheated again. Action from principle,—the perception and the performance of right,—changes things and relations; it is essentially revolutionary, and does not consist wholly with any thing which was. It not only divides states and churches, it divides families; aye, it divides the *individual,* separating the diabolical in him from the divine. 15

Unjust laws exist: shall we be content to obey them, or shall we endeavor to amend them, and obey them until we have succeeded, or shall we transgress them at once? Men generally, under such a government as this, think that they ought to wait until they have persuaded the majority to alter them. They think that, if they should resist, the remedy would be worse than the evil. But it is the fault of the government itself that the remedy *is* worse than the evil. *It* makes it worse. Why is it not more apt to anticipate and provide for reform? Why does it not cherish its wise minority? Why does it cry and resist before it is hurt? Why does it not encourage its citizens to be on the alert to point out its faults, and *do* better than it would have them? Why does it always crucify Christ, and excommunicate Copernicus and Luther, and pronounce Washington and Franklin rebels?

One would think, that a deliberate and practical denial of its authority was the only offence never contemplated by government; else, why has it not assigned its definite, its suitable and proportionate penalty? If a man who has no property refuses but once to earn nine shillings for the State, he is put in prison for a period unlimited by any law that I know, and determined only by the discretion of those who placed him there; but if he should steal ninety times nine shillings from the State, he is soon permitted to go at large again.

If the injustice is part of the necessary friction of the machine of government, let it go, let it go: perchance it will wear smooth,—certainly the machine will wear out. If the injustice has a spring, or a pulley, or a rope, or a crank, exclusively for itself, then perhaps you may consider whether the remedy will not be worse than the evil; but if it is of such a nature that it requires you to be the agent of injustice to another, then, I say, break the law. Let your life be a counter friction to stop the machine. What I have to do is to see, at any rate, that I do not lend myself to the wrong which I condemn.

As for adopting the ways which the State has provided for remedying the evil, I know not of such ways. They take too much time, and a man's life will be gone. I have other affairs to attend to. I came into this world, not chiefly to make this a good place to live in, but to live in it, be it good or bad. A man has not every thing to do, but something; and because he cannot do *every thing*, it is not necessary that he should do *something* wrong. It is not my business to be petitioning the governor or the legislature any more than it is theirs to petition me; and, if they should not hear my petition, what should I do then? But in this case the State has provided no way: its very Constitution is the evil. This may seem to be harsh and stubborn and unconciliatory; but it is to treat with the utmost kindness and consideration the only spirit that can appreciate or deserves it. So is all change for the better, like birth and death which convulse the body.

I do not hesitate to say, that those who call themselves abolitionists should at   20
once effectually withdraw their support, both in person and property, from the government of Massachusetts, and not wait till they constitute a majority of one, before they suffer the right to prevail through them. I think that it is enough if they have God on their side, without waiting for that other one. Moreover, any man more right than his neighbors, constitutes a majority of one already.

I meet this American government, or its representative the State government, directly, and face to face, once a year, no more, in the person of its tax-gatherer; this is the only mode in which a man situated as I am necessarily meets it; and it then says distinctly, Recognize me; and the simplest, the most effectual, and, in the present posture of affairs, the indispensablest mode of treating with it on this head, of expressing your little satisfaction with and love for it, is to deny it then. My civil neighbor, the tax-gatherer, is the very man I have to deal with,—for it is, after all, with men and not with parchment that I quarrel,—and he has voluntarily chosen to be an agent of the government. How shall he ever know well what he is and does as an officer of the government, or as a man, until he is obliged to consider whether he shall treat me, his neighbor, for whom he has respect, as a neighbor and well-disposed man, or as a maniac and disturber of the peace, and see if he can get over this obstruction to his neighborliness without a ruder and more impetuous thought or speech corresponding with his action? I know this well, that if one thousand, if one hundred, if ten men whom I could name,—if ten *honest* men only,—aye, if *one* HONEST man, in this State of Massachusetts, *ceasing to hold slaves*, were actually to withdraw from this copartnership, and be locked up in the county jail therefor, it would be the abolition of slavery in America. For it matters not how small the beginning may seem to be: what is once well done is done for ever. But we love better to talk about it: that we say is our mission. Reform keeps many scores of newspapers in its service, but not one man. If my esteemed neighbor, the State's ambassador, who will devote his days to the settlement of the question of human rights in the Council Chamber, instead of being threatened with the prisons of Carolina, were to sit down the prisoner of Massachusetts, that State which is so anxious to foist the sin of slavery upon her sister,—though at present she can discover only an act of inhospitality to be the ground of a quarrel with her,—the Legislature would not wholly waive the subject the following winter.

Under a government which imprisons any unjustly, the true place for a just man is also a prison. The proper place to-day, the only place which Massachusetts has provided for her freer and less desponding spirits, is in her prisons, to be put out and locked out of the State by her own act, as they have already put themselves out by their principles. It is there that the fugitive slave, and the Mexican prisoner on parole, and the Indian come to plead the wrongs of his race, should find them; on that separate, but more free and honorable ground, where the State places those who are not *with* her but *against* her,—the only house in a slave-state in which a free man can abide with honor. If any think that their influence would be lost there, and their voices no longer afflict the ear of the State, that they would not be as an enemy within its walls, they do not know by how much truth is stronger than error, nor how much more eloquently and effectively he can combat injustice who has experienced a little in his own person. Cast your whole vote, not a strip of paper merely, but your whole influence. A minority is powerless while it conforms to the majority; it is not even a minority then; but it is irresistible when it clogs by its whole weight. If the alternative is to keep all just men in prison, or give up war and slavery, the State will not hesitate which to choose. If a thousand men were not to pay their tax-bills this year, that would not be a violent and bloody measure, as it would be to pay them, and enable the State to commit violence and shed innocent blood. This is, in fact, the definition of a peaceable revolution, if any such is possible. If the tax-gatherer, or any other public officer, asks me, as one has done, "But what shall I do?" my answer is, "If you really wish to do any thing, resign your office." When the subject has refused allegiance, and the officer has resigned his office, then the revolution is accomplished. But even suppose blood should flow. Is there not a sort of blood shed when the conscience is wounded? Through this wound a man's real manhood and immortality flow out, and he bleeds to an everlasting death. I see this blood flowing now.

I have contemplated the imprisonment of the offender, rather than the seizure of his goods,—though both will serve the same purpose,—because they who assert the purest right, and consequently are most dangerous to a corrupt State, commonly have not spent much time in accumulating property. To such the State renders comparatively small service, and a slight tax is wont to appear exorbitant, particularly if they are obliged to earn it by special labor with their hands. If there were one who lived wholly without the use of money, the State itself would hesitate to demand it of him. But the rich man—not to make any invidious comparison—is always sold to the institution which makes him rich. Absolutely speaking, the more money, the less virtue; for money comes between a man and his objects, and obtains them for him; and it was certainly no great virtue to obtain it. It puts to rest many questions which he would otherwise be taxed to answer; while the only new question which it puts is the hard but superfluous one, how to spend it. Thus his moral ground is taken from under his feet. The opportunities of living are diminished in proportion as what are called the "means" are increased. The best thing a man can do for his culture when he is rich is to endeavour to carry out those schemes which he entertained when he was poor. Christ answered the Herodians according to their condition. "Show me the tribute-money," said he;—and one took a penny out of his pocket;—If you use money which has the image of Caesar on it, and which he has made current and valuable, that is, *if you are men of the State,* and gladly enjoy the advantages of Caesar's government, then pay him back some of his own when he demands it; "Render therefore to Caesar that which is Caesar's, and to God those things which are God's,"—leaving them no wiser than before as to which was which; for they did not wish to know.

When I converse with the freest of my neighbors, I perceive that, whatever they may say about the magnitude and seriousness of the question, and their regard for the public tranquillity, the long and the short of the matter is, that they cannot spare the protection of the existing government, and they dread the consequences of disobedience to it to their property and families. For my own part, I should not like to think that I ever rely on the protection of the State. But, if I deny the authority of the State when it presents its tax-bill, it will soon take and waste all my property, and so harass me and my children without end. This is hard. This makes it impossible for a man to live honestly and at the same time comfortably in outward respects. It will not be worth the while to accumulate property; that would be sure to go again. You must hire or squat somewhere, and raise but a small crop, and eat that soon. You must live within yourself, and depend upon yourself, always tucked up and ready for a start, and not have many affairs. A man may grow rich in Turkey even, if he will be in all respects a good subject of the Turkish government. Confucius said,—"If a State is governed by the principles of reason, poverty and misery are subjects of shame; if a State is not governed by the principles of reason, riches and honors are the subjects of shame." No: until I want the protection of Massachusetts to be extended to me in some distant southern port, where my liberty is endangered, or until I am bent solely on building up an estate at home by peaceful enterprise, I can afford to refuse allegiance to Massachusetts, and her right to my property and life. It costs me less in every sense to incur the penalty of disobedience to the State, than it would to obey. I should feel as if I were worth less in that case.

Some years ago, the State met me in behalf of the church, and commanded me to pay a certain sum toward the support of a clergyman whose preaching my father attended, but never I myself. "Pay it," it said, "or be locked up in the jail." I declined to pay. But, unfortunately, another man saw fit to pay it. I did not see why the schoolmaster should be taxed to support the priest, and not the priest the schoolmaster; for I was not the State's schoolmaster, but I supported myself by voluntary subscription. I did not see why the lyceum should not present its tax-bill, and have the State to back its demand, as well as the church. However, at the request of the selectmen, I condescended to make some such statement as this in writing:—"Know all men by these presents, that I, Henry Thoreau, do not wish to be regarded as a member of any incorporated society which I have not joined." This I gave to the town-clerk; and he has it. The State, having thus learned that I did not wish to be regarded as a member of that church, has never made a like demand on me since; though it said that it must adhere to its original presumption that time. If I had known how to name them, I should then have signed off in detail from all the societies which I never signed on to; but I did not know where to find a complete list.

I have paid no poll-tax for six years. I was put into jail once on this account, for one night; and, as I stood considering the walls of solid stone, two or three feet thick, the door of wood and iron, a foot thick, and the iron grating which strained the light, I could not help being struck with the foolishness of that institution which treated me as if I were mere flesh and blood and bones, to be locked up. I wondered that it should have concluded at length that this was the best use it could put me to, and had never thought to avail itself of my services in some way. I saw that, if there was a wall of stone between me and my townsmen, there was a still more difficult one to climb or break through, before they could get to be as free as I was. I did not for a moment feel confined, and the walls seemed a great waste of stone and mortar. I felt as if I alone of all my townsmen had paid my tax. They plainly did not know how to treat me, but behaved like persons who are underbred. In every threat and in every compliment there was a blunder; for they thought that my chief desire was to stand the other side of that stone wall. I could not but smile to see how industriously they locked the door on my meditations, which followed them out again without let or hinderance, and *they* were really all that was dangerous. As they could not reach me, they had resolved to punish my body; just as boys, if they cannot come at some person against whom they have a spite, will abuse his dog. I saw that the State was half-witted, that it was timid as a lone woman with her silver spoons, and that it did not know its friends from its foes, and I lost all my remaining respect for it, and pitied it.

Thus the State never intentionally confronts a man's sense, intellectual or moral, but only his body, his senses. It is not armed with superior wit or honesty, but with superior physical strength. I was not born to be forced. I will breathe after my own fashion. Let us see who is the strongest. What force has a multitude? They only can force me who obey a higher law than I. They force me to become like themselves. I do not hear of *men* being *forced* to live this way or that by masses of men. What sort of life were that to live? When I meet a government which says to me, "Your money or your life," why should I be in haste to give it my money? It may be in a great strait, and not know what to do: I cannot help that. It must help itself; do as I do. It is not worth the while to snivel about it. I am not responsible for the successful working of the machinery of society. I am not the son of the engineer. I perceive that, when an acorn and a chestnut fall side by side, the one does not remain inert to make way for the other, but both obey their own laws, and spring and grow and flourish as best they can, till one, perchance, overshadows and destroys the other. If a plant cannot live according to its nature, it dies; and so a man.

The night in prison was novel and interesting enough. The prisoners in their shirt-sleeves were enjoying a chat and the evening air in the door-way, when I entered. But the jailer said, "Come, boys, it is time to lock up;" and so they dispersed, and I heard the sound of their steps returning into the hollow apartments. My roommate was introduced to me by the jailer, as "a first-rate fellow and a clever man." When the door was locked, he showed me where to hang my hat, and how he managed matters there. The rooms were whitewashed once a month; and this one, at least, was the whitest, most simply furnished, and probably the neatest apartment in the town. He naturally wanted to know where I came from, and what brought me there; and, when I had told him, I asked him in turn how he came there, presuming him to be an honest man, of course; and, as the world goes, I believe he was. "Why," said he, "they accused me of burning a barn; but I never did it." As near as I could discover, he had probably gone to bed in a barn when drunk, and smoked his pipe there; and so a barn was burnt. He had the reputation of being a clever man, had been there some three months waiting for his trial to come on, and would have to wait as much longer; but he was quite domesticated and contented, since he got his board for nothing, and thought that he was well treated.

He occupied one window, and I the other; and I saw, that, if one stayed there long, his principal business would be to look out the window. I had soon read all the tracts that were left there, and examined where former prisoners had broken out, and where a grate had been sawed off, and heard the history of the various occupants of that room; for I found that even here there was a history and a gossip which never circulated beyond the walls of the jail. Probably this is the only house in the town where verses are composed, which are afterward printed in a circular form, but not published. I was shown quite a long list of verses which were composed by some young men who had been detected in an attempt to escape, who avenged themselves by singing them.

I pumped my fellow-prisoner as dry as I could, for fear I should never see him again; but at length he showed me which was my bed, and left me to blow out the lamp. 30

It was like travelling into a far country, such as I had never expected to behold, to lie there for one night. It seemed to me that I never had heard the town-clock strike before, nor the evening sounds of the village; for we slept with the windows open, which were inside the grating. It was to see my native village in the light of the middle ages, and our Concord was turned into a Rhine stream, and visions of knights and castles passed before me. They were the voices of old burghers that I heard in the streets. I was an involuntary spectator and auditor of whatever was done and said in the kitchen of the adjacent village-inn,—a wholly new and rare experience to me. It was a closer view of my native town. I was fairly inside of it. I never had seen its institutions before. This is one of its peculiar institutions; for it is a shire town. I began to comprehend what its inhabitants were about.

In the morning, our breakfasts were put through the hole in the door, in small oblong-square tin pans, made to fit, and holding a pint of chocolate, with brown bread, and an iron spoon. When they called for the vessels again, I was green enough to return what bread I had left; but my comrade seized it, and said that I should lay that up for lunch or dinner. Soon after, he was let out to work at haying in a neighboring field, whither he went every day, and would not be back till noon; so he bade me good-day, saying that he doubted if he should see me again.

When I came out of prison,— for some one interfered, and paid the tax,— I did not perceive that great changes had taken place on the common, such as he observed who went in a youth, and emerged a tottering and grayheaded man; and yet a change had to my eyes come over the scene,—the town, and State, and country,—greater than any that mere time could effect. I saw yet more distinctly the State in which I lived. I saw to what extent the people among whom I lived could be trusted as good neighbors and friends; that their friendship was for summer weather only; that they did not greatly purpose to do right; that they were a distinct race from me by their prejudices and superstitions, as the Chinamen and Malays are; that, in their sacrifices to humanity, they ran no risks, not even to their property; that, after all, they were not so noble but they treated the thief as he had treated them, and hoped, by a certain outward observance and a few prayers, and by walking in a particular straight though useless path from time to time, to save their souls. This may be to judge my neighbors harshly; for I believe that most of them are not aware that they have such an institution as the jail in their village.

It was formerly the custom in our village, when a poor debtor came out of jail, for his acquaintances to salute him, looking through their fingers, which were crossed to represent the grating of a jail window, "How do ye do?" My neighbors did not thus salute me, but first looked at me, and then at one an-

other, as if I had returned from a long journey. I was put into jail as I was going to the shoemaker's to get a shoe which was mended. When I was let out the next morning, I proceeded to finish my errand, and, having put on my mended shoe, joined a huckleberry party, who were impatient to put themselves under my conduct; and in half an hour,—for the horse was soon tackled, was in the midst of a huckleberry field, on one of our highest hills, two miles off; and then the State was nowhere to be seen.

This is the whole history of "My Prisons."

35

I have never declined paying the highway tax, because I am as desirous of being a good neighbor as I am of being a bad subject; and, as for supporting schools, I am doing my part to educate my fellow-countrymen now. It is for no particular item in the tax-bill that I refuse to pay it. I simply wish to refuse allegiance to the State, to withdraw and stand aloof from it effectually. I do not care to trace the course of my dollar, if I could, till it buys a man, or a musket to shoot one with,—the dollar is innocent,—but I am concerned to trace the effects of my allegiance. In fact, I quietly declare war with the State, after my fashion, though I will still make what use and get what advantage of her I can, as is usual in such cases.

If others pay the tax which is demanded of me, from a sympathy with the State, they do but what they have already done in their own case, or rather they abet injustice to a greater extent than the State requires. If they pay the tax from a mistaken interest in the individual taxed, to save his property or prevent his going to jail, it is because they have not considered wisely how far they let their private feelings interfere with the public good.

This, then, is my position at present. But one cannot be too much on his guard in such a case, lest his action be biassed by obstinacy, or an undue regard for the opinions of men. Let him see that he does only what belongs to himself and to the hour.

I think sometimes, Why, this people mean well; they are only ignorant; they would do better if they knew how: why give your neighbors this pain to treat you as they are not inclined to? But I think, again, this is no reason why I should do as they do, or permit others to suffer much greater pain of a different kind. Again, I sometimes say to myself, When many millions of men, without heat, without ill-will, without personal feeling of any kind, demand of you a few shillings only, without the possibility, such is their constitution, of retracting or altering their present demand, and without the possibility, on your side, of appeal to any other millions, why expose yourself to this overwhelming brute force? You do not resist cold and hunger, the winds and the waves, thus obstinately; you quietly submit to a thousand similar necessities. You do not put your head into the fire. But just in proportion as I regard this as not wholly a brute force, but partly a human force, and consider that I have relations to those millions as to so many millions of men, and not of mere brute or inanimate things, I see that appeal is possible, first and instantaneously, from them to the Maker of them, and, secondly, from them to themselves. But, if I put my head deliberately into the fire, there is no appeal to fire or to the Maker of fire, and I have only myself to blame. If I could convince myself that I have any right to be satisfied with men as they are, and to treat them accordingly, and not according, in some respects, to my requisitions and expectations of what they and I ought to be, then, like a good Mussulman[1] and fatalist, I

---

[1]Mussulman—Muslim.

should endeavor to be satisfied with things as they are, and say it is the will of God. And, above all, there is this difference between resisting this and a purely brute or natural force, that I can resist this with some effect; but I cannot expect, like Orpheus, to change the nature of the rocks and trees and beasts.

I do not wish to quarrel with any man or nation. I do not wish to split hairs, to make fine distinctions, or set myself up as better than my neighbors. I seek rather, I may say, even an excuse for conforming to the laws of the land. I am but too ready to conform to them. Indeed I have reason to suspect myself on this head; and each year, as the tax-gatherer comes round, I find myself disposed to review the acts and position of the general and state governments, and the spirit of the people, to discover a pretext for conformity. I believe that the State will soon be able to take all my work of this sort out of my hands, and then I shall be no better a patriot than my fellow-countrymen. Seen from a lower point of view, the Constitution, with all its faults, is very good; the law and the courts are very respectable; even this State and this American government are, in many respects, very admirable and rare things, to be thankful for, such as a great many have described them; but seen from a point of view a little higher, they are what I have described them; seen from a higher still, and the highest, who shall say what they are, or that they are worth looking at or thinking of at all?

However, the government does not concern me much, and I shall bestow the fewest possible thoughts on it. It is not many moments that I live under a government, even in this world. If a man is thought-free, fancy-free, imagination-free, that which *is not* never for a long time appearing *to be* to him, unwise rulers or reformers cannot fatally interrupt him.

I know that most men think differently from myself; but those whose lives are by profession devoted to the study of these or kindred subjects, content me as little as any. Statesmen and legislators, standing so completely within the institution, never distinctly and nakedly behold it. They speak of moving society, but have no resting-place without it. They may be men of a certain experience and discrimination, and have no doubt invented ingenious and even useful systems, for which we sincerely thank them; but all their wit and usefulness lie within certain not very wide limits. They are wont to forget that the world is not governed by policy and expediency. Webster never goes behind government, and so cannot speak with authority about it. His words are wisdom to those legislators who contemplate no essential reform in the existing government; but for thinkers, and those who legislate for all time, he never once glances at the subject. I know of those whose serene and wise speculations on this theme would soon reveal the limits of his mind's range and hospitality. Yet, compared with the cheap professions of most reformers, and the still cheaper wisdom and eloquence of politicians in general, his are almost the only sensible and valuable words, and we thank Heaven for him. Comparatively, he is always strong, original, and, above all, practical. Still his quality is not wisdom, but prudence. The lawyer's truth is not Truth, but consistency, or a consistent expediency. Truth is always in harmony with herself, and is not concerned chiefly to reveal the justice that may consist with wrong-doing. He well deserves to be called, as he has been called, the Defender of the Constitution. There are really no blows to be given by him but defensive ones. He is not a leader, but a follower. His leaders are the men of '87. "I have never made an effort," he says, "and never propose to make an effort; I have never countenanced an effort, and never mean to countenance an effort, to disturb the arrangement as originally made, by which the various States came into the Union." Still thinking of the sanction which the Constitution gives to slavery, he says, "Because it was a part of the original compact,—let it stand." Notwithstanding his special acuteness

40

and ability, he is unable to take a fact out of its merely political relations, and be-hold it as it lies absolutely to be disposed of by the intellect,—what, for instance, it behoves a man to do here in America to-day with regard to slavery,—but ven-tures, or is driven, to make some such desperate answer as the following, while professing to speak absolutely, and as a private man,—from which what new and singular code of social duties might be inferred?—"The manner," says he, "in which the governments of those States where slavery exists are to regulate it, is for their own consideration, under their responsibility to their constituents, to the gen-eral laws of propriety, humanity, and justice, and to God. Associations formed elsewhere, springing from a feeling of humanity, or any other cause, have nothing whatever to do with it. They have never received any encouragement from me, and they never will."[2]

They who know of no purer sources of truth, who have traced up its stream no higher, stand, and wisely stand, by the Bible and the Constitution, and drink at it there with reverence and humility; but they who behold where it comes trickling into this lake or that pool, gird up their loins once more, and continue their pil-grimage toward its fountain-head.

No man with a genius for legislation has appeared in America. They are rare in the history of the world. There are orators, politicians, and eloquent men, by the thousand; but the speaker has not yet opened his mouth to speak, who is ca-pable of settling the much-vexed questions of the day. We love eloquence for its own sake, and not for any truth which it may utter, or any heroism it may inspire. Our legislators have not yet learned the comparative value of free-trade and of freedom, of union, and of rectitude, to a nation. They have no genius or talent for comparatively humble questions of taxation and finance, commerce and manufac-tures and agriculture. If we were left solely to the wordy wit of legislators in Con-gress for our guidance, uncorrected by the seasonable experience and the effec-tual complaints of the people, America would not long retain her rank among the nations. For eighteen hundred years, though perchance I have no right to say it, the New Testament has been written; yet where is the legislator who has wisdom and practical talent enough to avail himself of the light which it sheds on the sci-ence of legislation?

The authority of government, even such as I am willing to submit to,—for I will cheerfully obey those who know and can do better than I, and in many things even those who neither know nor can do so well,—is still an impure one: to be strictly just, it must have the sanction and consent of the governed. It can have no pure right over my person and property but what I concede to it. The progress from an absolute to a limited monarchy, from a limited monarchy to a democracy, is a progress toward a true respect for the individual. Is a democracy, such as we know it, the last improvement possible in government? Is it not possible to take a step further towards recognizing and organizing the rights of man? There will never be a really free and enlightened State, until the State comes to recognize the individual as a higher and independent power, from which all its own power and authority are derived, and treats him accordingly. I please myself with imagining a State at last which can afford to be just to all men, and to treat the individual with respect as a neighbor; which even would not think it inconsistent with its own re-pose, if a few were to live aloof from it, not meddling with it, nor embraced by it, who fulfilled all the duties of neighbors and fellow-men. A State which bore this

45

---

[2]These extracts have been added since the Lecture was read. [Thoreau's note.]

kind of fruit, and suffered it to drop off as fast as it ripened, would prepare the way for a still more perfect and glorious State, which also I have imagined, but not yet anywhere seen.

E. B. White   1899–1985

The Decline of Sport   1947

(A Preposterous Parable)

In the third decade of the supersonic age, sport gripped the nation in an ever-tightening grip. The horse tracks, the ballparks, the fight rings, the gridirons, all drew crowds in steadily increasing numbers. Every time a game was played, an attendance record was broken. Usually some other sort of record was broken, too—such as the record for the number of consecutive doubles hit by left-handed batters in a Series game, or some such thing as that. Records fell like ripe apples on a windy day. Customs and manners changed, and the five-day business week was reduced to four days, then to three, to give everyone a better chance to memorize the scores.

Not only did sport proliferate but the demands it made on the spectator became greater. Nobody was content to take in one event at a time, and thanks to the magic of radio and television nobody had to. A Yale alumnus, class of 1962, returning to the Bowl with 197,000 others to see the Yale-Cornell football game would take along his pocket radio and pick up the Yankee Stadium, so that while his eye might be following a fumble on the Cornell twenty-two-yard line, his ear would be following a man going down to second in the top of the fifth, seventy miles away. High in the blue sky above the Bowl, skywriters would be at work writing the scores of other major and minor sporting contests, weaving an interminable record of victory and defeat, and using the new high-visibility pink newssmoke perfected by Pepsi-Cola engineers. And in the frames of the giant video sets, just behind the goalposts, this same alumnus could watch Dejected win the Futurity before a record-breaking crowd of 349,872 at Belmont, each of whom was tuned to the Yale Bowl and following the World Series game in the video and searching the sky for further news of events either under way or just completed. The effect of this vast cyclorama of sport was to divide the spectator's attention, over-subtilize his appreciation, and deaden his passion. As the fourth supersonic decade was ushered in, the picture changed and sport began to wane.

A good many factors contributed to the decline of sport. Substitutions in football had increased to such an extent that there were very few fans in the United States capable of holding the players in mind during play. Each play that was called saw two entirely new elevens lined up, and the players whose names and faces you had familiarized yourself with in the first period were seldom seen or heard of again. The spectacle became as diffuse as the main concourse in Grand Central at the commuting hour.

Express motor highways leading to the parks and stadia had become so wide, so unobstructed, so devoid of all life except automobiles and trees that sport fans had got into the habit of travelling enormous distances to attend events. The normal driving speed had been stepped up to ninety-five miles an hour, and the distance between cars had been decreased to fifteen feet. This put an extraordinary strain on the sport lover's nervous system, and he arrived home from a Saturday game, after a road trip of three hundred and fifty miles, glassy-eyed, dazed, and spent. He hadn't really had any relaxation and he had failed to see Czlika (who had gone in for Trusky) take the pass from Bkeeo (who had gone in for Bjallo) in the third period, because at that moment a youngster named Lavagetto had been put in to pinch-hit for Art Gurlack in the bottom of the ninth with the tying run on second, and the skywriter who was attempting to write "Princeton O—Lafayete 43" had banked the wrong way, muffed the "3," and distracted everyone's attention from the fact that Lavagetto had been whiffed.

Cheering, of course, lost its stimulating effect on players, because cheers were no longer associated necessarily with the immediate scene but might as easily apply to something that was happening somewhere else. This was enough to infuriate even the steadiest performer. A football star, hearing the stands break into a roar before the ball was snapped, would realize that their minds were not on him, and would become dispirited and grumpy. Two or three of the big coaches worried so about this that they considered equipping all players with tiny ear sets, so that they, too, could keep abreast of other sporting events while playing, but the idea was abandoned as impractical, and the coaches put it aside in tickler files, to bring up again later.

I think the event that marked the turning point in sport and started it downhill was the Midwest's classic Dust Bowl game of 1975, when Eastern Reserve's great right end, Ed Pistachio, was shot by a spectator. This man, the one who did the shooting, was seated well down in the stands near the forty-yard line on a bleak October afternoon and was so saturated with sport and with the disappointments of sport that he had clearly become deranged. With a minute and fifteen seconds to play and the score tied, the Eastern Reserve quarterback had whipped a long pass over Army's heads into Pistachio's waiting arms. There was no other player anywhere near him, and all Pistachio had to do was catch the ball and run it across the line. He dropped it. At exactly this moment, the spectator—a man named Homer T. Parkinson, of 35 Edgemere Drive, Toledo, O.—suffered at least three other major disappointments in the realm of sport. His horse, Hiccough, on which he had a five-hundred-dollar bet, fell while getting away from the starting gate at Pimlico and broke its leg (clearly visible in the video); his favorite shortstop, Lucky Frimstitch, struck out and let three men die on base in the final game of the Series (to which Parkinson was tuned); and the Governor Dummer soccer team, on which Parkinson's youngest son played goalie, lost to Kent, 4–3, as recorded in the sky overhead. Before anyone could stop him, he drew a gun and drilled Pistachio, before 954,000 persons, the largest crowd that ever attended a football game and the *second*-largest crowd that had ever assembled for any sporting event in any month except July.

This tragedy, by itself, wouldn't have caused sport to decline, I suppose, but it set in motion a chain of other tragedies, the cumulative effect of which was terrific. Almost as soon as the shot was fired, the news flash was picked up by one of the skywriters directly above the field. He glanced down to see whether he could spot the trouble below, and in doing so failed to see another skywriter approaching. The two planes collided and fell, wings locked, leaving a confusing trail of smoke, which some observers tried to interpret as a late sports score. The planes struck in the middle of the nearby east-bound coast-to-coast Sunlight Parkway, and a motorist driving a convertible coupé stopped so short, to avoid hitting them, that he was bumped from behind. The pileup of cars that ensued involved 1,482 vehicles, a record for eastbound parkways. A total of more than three thousand persons lost their lives in the highway accident, including the two pilots, and when panic broke out in the stadium, it cost another 872 in dead and injured. News of the disaster spread quickly to other sports arenas, and started other panics among the crowds trying to get to the exits, where they could buy a paper and study a list of the dead. All in all the afternoon of sport cost 20,003 lives, a record. And nobody had much to show for it, except one small Midwestern boy who hung around the smoking wrecks of the planes, captured some aero news-smoke in a milk bottle, and took it home as a souvenir.

From that day on, sport waned. Through long, noncompetitive Saturday afternoons, the stadia slumbered. Even the parkways fell into disuse as motorists rediscovered the charms of old, twisty roads that led through main streets and past barnyards, with their mild congestions and pleasant smells.

RESEARCH
AND
WRITING

28 ◇ THE RESEARCH PAPER

A research paper is a common assignment in college literature courses. Knowing how to find relevant information about an author or a text, sifting through that information for ideas that relate to your own reading of a literary text, and presenting the results in an orderly fashion for other readers are important skills for all college students. The library research paper gives you a chance to learn and practice all those skills.

Broadening Your Literary Experience Through Research

In keeping with this book's emphasis on the interaction between reader and text, doing library research will be presented as broadening your literary experience. This idea implies that although your literary experience may be relatively narrow prior to doing research, it is not vacant: You do know, think, or believe something about a literary text. Writing a response statement to your first reading of a text should demonstrate that for you because part of what contributes to your response is the literary experience you bring to the interaction with the text. When you read a text, even for the first time, and write a response statement, you broaden your literary experience somewhat because the acts of reading and writing allow you to identify text strategies and begin to articulate why you respond the way you do. In the process, you establish a base on which you can build by finding out more information through library research. Your academic library houses sources that can tell you more than you knew previously about the literary repertoire and ideology of any text or its author or the genre to which a text may belong.

Search Strategies

When you are assigned a research paper or when you decide to undertake research on your own, you should go about broadening your literary experience in a strategic way. The method recommended here is both efficient and effective: efficient because it approaches library sources in a logical sequence; effective because each step in the sequence will identify sources for you. The list below highlights the steps in this search strategy.

Library Search Strategy

1. Narrow your topic; define keywords.
2. Do background reading; begin to compile a working bibliography.

3. Use reference sources to develop your working bibliography.
4. Look for specific sources in books and periodicals.
5. Read your sources and take notes.

Narrow Your Topic

Writing a response statement or doing freewriting about a text is necessary to finding a topic for research. In those kinds of writing, you have the chance to identify, for instance, text strategies that affect your response or themes you have created in your reading. Think of your broad topic as the literary text you are working with; for example, Edward Albee's *The Sandbox* from Chapter 17. Your narrowed topic might be a text strategy you have noticed in that text or a theme you have created in your first reading. A narrowed topic does not have to deal solely with a text strategy or a theme—those are just two examples—but it does have to carve out a "slice" of the entire text to deal with. For example, something like "the abandonment theme in *The Sandbox*" is preferable to just "*The Sandbox*" or "Albee's plays."

A question that arises for you in your first reading of a text is another good way to define a narrowed topic: You may consider the process of broadening your experience as a way of trying to answer such a question. If you are alive to the QAQ method of writing in your response statements or in your journal, you should regard a research project as an extension of that question- and answer-seeking approach. One student, Shirin Arastu, whose work was shown in Chapter 23, wrote some questions in her journal as she was beginning her research:

> *Why did Albee use the writing technique he did, and what was the purpose of the characters and the theme? Did anyone interpret [the play] my way?*

Those questions arose for Shirin out of her first response to *The Sandbox* and from what she heard in class discussion when other students described their responses to that play. Shirin's reading produced "the emptiness of mourning rituals" as a theme, whereas some of her classmates produced an "abandonment of the elderly" theme. Shirin's first response and the questions she defined gave direction to her research and carried on through to her eventual paper.

Define Keywords

Another aspect of narrowing your topic is defining keywords. As the term implies, keywords can be used to unlock doors behind which information can be found. Certainly, you can conduct a library search by using merely the title of a text or an author's name as a keyword, but that approach is inefficient because your search would identify every source published about the author or that text. If you are working with a fairly well-known text or author, you would likely be confronted with an overwhelming number of potential sources, most of which would not pertain to your narrowed topic. You should be able to define keywords easily enough if you have a narrowed topic. The keywords should emerge from writing you have already done—response statements, journal entries, freewriting—on a literary text. In the case of Shirin's research on *The Sandbox*, the word *character*, used in conjunction with the play's title or with the author's name, was a useful keyword. The word *theme*, on the other hand, was not. That word is not used very widely in published literary criticism, but a related phrase, *criticism and interpretation*—again, when linked with an author's name or the title of a text—does appear routinely as a keyword for books and periodical articles that discuss theme.

In any case, an important early step in the research process is to write down potential keywords. Start with the author's last name and the title of a particular text as two keywords. You can narrow your topic by attaching other words and phrases to these two. *Criticism and interpretation* should be generally helpful. *Biography* might be helpful too, if you want to look into some aspect of an author's life. Words or phrases that name particular text strategies—such as *symbol, imagery, language, style*—should be fruitful. Careful attention to this step will soon pay off as you find your key turning in the locks into which you insert it.

Do Background Reading

Encyclopedias provide general or background information on a variety of topics. You are probably familiar with one of the general encyclopedias such as the *Encyclopedia Americana* or the *Encyclopaedia Britannica*. In researching a literary topic, however, you will work more efficiently if you consult a specialized literary encyclopedia for background information on your topic. Reading an article in an encyclopedia will give you an overview of your subject, introduce you to some of the basic issues and ideas that have come to be identified with the study of your subject, and, therefore, let you place your topic or concern in the context of that study. Encyclopedia articles are not usually cited in research writing, but they are the best starting places for research reading. Some of these are listed on pages 1636–1638, but be sure to check with a reference librarian to see if your school library has any specialized encyclopedia you may wish to consult.

Begin to Compile a Working Bibliography

A bibliography is a list of sources. In literary research, those sources usually consist of books and articles in scholarly journals. Such sources are also known as **secondary sources**, as opposed to a literary text, which is a **primary source**. Think of it this way: the literary text—*The Sandbox*, for instance—or your response to it is your primary concern; books and articles you find in the library that say something about *The Sandbox* are secondary to that literary text. A working bibliography is a list of secondary sources that appear likely to provide you with the information you need to broaden your literary experience. Those sources are potential because until you actually read them you don't know just what kind of information they will provide or whether that information will apply to your interests. In terms of the search strategy I am recommending, writing down the titles, authors, and other publication data of secondary sources that may be helpful is crucial. You can begin to compile this list of potential sources by consulting the brief bibliography that usually accompanies an encyclopedia article. The sources listed there have been chosen by the person who wrote the encyclopedia article, and that person is likely to be an expert on whatever subject the article concerns.

Literary Encyclopedias   Here is an alphabetized list of encyclopedias that are specific to literary topics. These resources are commonly held in the reference section of most academic libraries.

American Women Writers: A Critical Reference Guide from Colonial Times to the Present. New York: F. Ungar, 1979–82.

A comprehensive four-volume reference work devoted to 1,000 American women writers from Colonial times to the present, with critical assessments, a complete list of their works, and a selected list of criticism.

Ancient Writers: Greece and Rome. New York: Charles Scribner's Sons, 1982.

A two-volume reference work that contains long articles on Greek and Roman writers. Critical studies are listed at the end of each article.

Black Literature Criticism. Detroit: Gale Research, 1991.

A three-volume reference work that provides profiles on 125 internationally prominent black authors of the eighteenth, nineteenth, and twentieth centuries, excerpts from criticism of their writing, and sources for further reading.

Chicano Literature: A Reference Guide. Ed. Julio A. Martinez and Francisco A. Lomelí. Westport, Conn.: Greenwood Press, 1985.

A reference work composed of signed articles on individual authors as well as topics of literary and historical significance, critical evaluations, and bibliographies of primary and secondary works.

Columbia Dictionary of Modern European Literature. Eds. Jean-Albert Hede and William B. Edgerton. 2nd ed. New York: Columbia UP, 1980.

The word "Modern" in the title of this reference work means beginning with the end of the nineteenth century. More than 1,800 individual authors are treated, each with at least a brief bibliographical note, some with extended bibliographical information; 33 national literatures are described.

Contemporary Dramatists, 4th ed. Ed. James Vinson and D. L. Kirkpatrick. Chicago: St. James, 1988.

This reference work includes compact personal and critical biographies of more than 300 significant playwrights of the English language. Each entry contains a full bibliography of all published works of a writer, as well as selected listings of critical studies of the author's works. An appendix includes complete entries for important playwrights who have died since the 1950s but whose reputations are considered "contemporary" by the compilers.

Contemporary Novelists, 3rd ed. Ed. James Vinson. New York: St. Martin's, 1982.

This reference work contains information about 564 novelists (living or deceased since the 1950s). Each author entry includes a biography, a bibliography of works by the author, a bibliography of works about the author, comments by the author (for about half of the entries), and a signed critical essay on the author's novels.

Contemporary Poets. 4th ed. Eds. James Vinson and D. L. Kirkpatrick. New York: St. Martin's, 1985.

This reference work contains material on about 800 contemporary poets from all over the world who write in English. Each author entry includes a brief biography, a bibliography of works by the author, a bibliography of works about the author, and a signed critical essay on the author's poetry. An appendix covers 19 poets who have died since 1950 but whose reputations are essentially contemporary.

Dictionary of Literary Biography. Detroit: Gale Research, 1978– .

This series, in progress, covers several periods and movements. Individual volumes include biographical-critical entries, long essays on leading figures, chronologies, photographs, facsimiles, a list of contemporary periodicals, and supplementary readings.

Encyclopedia of British Women Writers. Eds. Paul Schlueter and June Schlueter. New York: Garland, 1988.

This reference work contains 400 entries, mostly from eighteenth, nineteenth, and twentieth centuries, bibliographies, and an index of pen names.

Encyclopedia of Indian Literature. Ed. Amaresh Datta. New Delhi: Sahitya Akademi, 1989– .

A work in progress and now complete from A–S in four volumes, this reference work contains signed articles on authors, epic works, styles, and influences and terms, with bibliographic references.

Encyclopedia of World Literature in the Twentieth Century. Ed. Wolfgang B. Fleischmann. Rev. ed. New York: F. Ungar, 1981–84.

The four volumes in this reference work include articles on movements, genres, and national literatures, as well as on individual authors. Bibliographies include writings by and about the authors.

European Writers. New York: Charles Scribner's Sons, 1983–90.

The eleven volumes in this reference work cover the Middle Ages and the Renaissance, the Age of Reason and the Enlightenment, the Romantic Age, and the Twentieth Century with long essays on authors of the time. Bibliographies of criticism fall at the end of each essay.

Fifty Caribbean Writers: A Bio-bibliographical Critical Sourcebook. Ed. Daryl Cumber Dance. New York: Greenwood Press, 1986.

This reference work lists works by and about the authors, including anthologies, collections, and special issues of journals dedicated to Caribbean literature.

Hispanic Literature Criticism. Detroit: Gale Research, 1994.

A two-volume reference work that provides biographical and critical information on approximately 70 internationally prominent Hispanic writers of the nineteenth and twentieth centuries. Each author entry includes excerpts from criticism of the author's work and sources for further reading.

Kanellos, Nicolás. *Biographical Dictionary of Hispanic Literature in the United States: The Literature of Puerto Ricans, Cuban Americans, and other Hispanic Writers.* New York: Greenwood Press, 1989

This reference work contains signed essays on the literary significance of 50 Hispanic authors, a biographical statement, a survey of criticism, and a bibliography of works by and about the author.

Kolin, Philip C. *American Playwrights Since 1945: A Guide to Scholarship, Criticism, and Performance.* New York: Greenwood Press, 1989.

This reference work offers information on 40 playwrights and their works. At the end of each essay, there is an alphabetical checklist of all sources cited in the essay, including criticism, interviews, biographies, and reviews.

Latin American Writers. New York: Charles Scribner's Sons, 1989.

A three-volume reference work that covers the Colonial period to the present these articles have both biographical and literary material on the authors. Biographical and critical studies are listed at the end of each article.

McGraw-Hill Encyclopedia of World Drama. New York: McGraw-Hill, 1984.

A five-volume reference work that contains articles on playwrights, national and ethnic theater traditions, and performance-related topics. A biographical sketch of an author usually ends with bibliographies of works and of criticism.

Native North American Literature. Detroit: Gale Research, 1994.

This reference work provides biographical and critical information on more than 70 native orators and writers of the United States and Canada from the eighteenth century to the present; includes a list of sources for further reading.

Page, James A. *Selected Black American, African and Caribbean Authors: A Bio-bibliography.* Littleton, Colo.: Libraries Unlimited, 1985.

This reference work provides bio-bibliographical information on 632 authors, emphasizing African-American literature of the United States. Contains a bibliography of sources.

Use Reference Sources to Develop Your Working Bibliography

Reading an article or two in a specialized encyclopedia will give you a start on finding out more about your topic. By now, you should have begun to compile a working bibliography by copying down, in your notebook or on note cards, the author, title, and publication data of sources listed in the bibliographies accompanying those encyclopedia articles. If you consult more than one specialized encyclopedia and if you find the same source listed in more than one bibliography, then that source may be a standard work on the topic. Such works are especially useful.

Subject Bibliographies and Checklists   Another excellent way to identify potentially useful sources is to consult subject bibliographies or checklists related to your topic. These reference tools are especially valuable because they contain more extensive and specialized bibliographies than encyclopedias do. As you did when you consulted an encyclopedia, copy down all the information on any listed source that looks like it might be helpful for your topic. Here is an alphabetized list of some subject bibliographies and checklists. Be sure to confirm with the reference staff your library's particular holdings in this area.

Alexander, Harriet S. *American and British Poetry: A Guide to the Criticism, 1925–78.* Athens: Ohio UP, 1984.

This bibliography indexes American and British poetry criticism found in about 500 books published between 1925 and 1978 and in about 170 journals published between 1959/60 and 1978/79. There are entries for about 10,000 poems by about 700 poets, ranging from medieval to contemporary.

Berrian, Brenda F. *Bibliography of Women Writers from the Caribbean.* Washington: Three Continents Press, 1988.

This bibliography includes criticism on novels, short stories, poetry, folklore, autobiographies, biographies, and children's literature by women writing in English, French, Dutch, Spanish, Creole, and other languages.

Black American Fiction: A Bibliography. Metuchen, N.J.: Scarecrow, 1978.

This bibliography comprises a list of about 600 major and minor black America authors of the nineteenth and twentieth centuries with the titles of their novels, short stories, biographies, criticism, and reviews.

Cheung, King-Kok. *Asian American Literature: An Annotated Bibliography.* New York: Modern Language Association of America, 1988.

This bibliography includes primary and secondary sources pertaining to literature written by Asian American writers in the United States and Canada. Writers may include those of Asian descent who have settled in the United States or Canada, those of mixed descent who have at least one Asian parent, and those who may not have permanent North American residence but who have written specifically on the experiences of Asians in the United States or Canada.

Carpenter, Charles A. *Modern Drama Scholarship and Criticism, 1966–80: An International Bibliography.* Buffalo: Toronto UP, 1986.

Divided by national drama, this international, comprehensive bibliography covers periodical articles and books on plays and playwrights since Ibsen. It is supplemented regularly in the journal *Modern Drama.*

Coleman, Arthur. *Drama Criticism.* Denver: Alan Swallow, 1966–71.

In two volumes, this reference work contains bibliographies of criticism and interpretation published in books and periodicals. Volume I covers interpretations since 1940 of English and American plays; Volume II covers interpretations since 1940 of Classical and Continental plays.

Contemporary Literary Criticism: Excerpts from Criticism of the Works of Today's Novelists, Poets, Playwrights, and Other Creative Writers. Detroit: Gale Research, 1973– .

Nineteenth-Century Literature Criticism: Excerpts from Criticism of the Works of Novelists, Poets, Playwrights, Short Story Writers, and Other Creative Writers Who Lived between 1800 and 1900, from the First Published Critical Appraisals to Current Evaluations. Detroit: Gale Research, 1981– .

Twentieth Century Literary Criticism: Excerpts from Criticism of the Works of Novelists, Poets, Playwrights, Short Story Writers, and Other Creative Writers. Detroit: Gale Research, 1978– .

All three of the above multi-volume series are arranged alphabetically by author. Entries include brief introductory statements about the authors and their works, lists of their principal writings, and excerpts of critical commentary from a variety of sources who review the works. An annotated bibliography appears at the end of each entry.

Contemporary Spanish American Poets: A Bibliography of Primary and Secondary Sources. Compiled by Jacobo Sefamí. Westport, Conn.: Greenwood Press, 1992.

This bibliography focuses on poets born between 1910 and 1952. Each entry covers primary and secondary sources, with the secondary sources consisting of bibliographies and critical studies of that poet.

Dramatic Criticism Index: A Bibliography of Commentaries on Playwrights from Ibsen to the Avant-Garde. Eds. Paul F. Breed and Florence M. Sniderman. Detroit: Gale Research, 1972.

This bibliography is arranged alphabetically by playwright. A general section precedes citations for individual plays.

Glikin, Ronda. *Black American Women in Literature: A Bibliography, 1976–87.* Jefferson, N.C.: McFarland, 1989.

This bibliography lists poetry, short fiction, novels, essays, and plays by and criticism on approximately 300 women whose work has been published between 1976 and 1987.

Kuntz, Joseph M. *Poetry Explication: A Checklist of Interpretations Since 1925 of British and American Poems Past and Present,* 3rd ed. Boston: G. K. Hall, 1980.

This reference work is an index of interpretations, up to 1977, of particular poems from a selection of periodicals and books. It is arranged by poet and then by title of specific poem.

Leo, John R. *Guide to American Poetry Explication: Modern and Contemporary.* Boston: G. K. Hall, 1989.

A companion volume to Kuntz' *Poetry Explication . . . ,* this reference work is a comprehensive index of American poetry explication since 1925. It is arranged by poet and then by title of specific poem.

Lindfors, Bernth. *Black African Literature in English: A Guide to Information Sources.* Detroit: Gale Research, 1979. Supplements—1977–81, New York: Africana Publishing, 1986; 1982–86, New York: Zell, 1989.

This guide attempts to list all the important works produced on black African literature through 1986.

Martinez, Nancy C., and Joseph G. R. Martinez. *Guide to British Poetry Explication, Vol. I: Old English to Medieval.* Boston: G.K. Hall, 1991.

A continuation and expansion of Kuntz's *Poetry Explication* . . . , this reference work is a comprehensive index of British poetry interpretation (of the Old English to Medieval periods) since 1925. Arranged by poet and then title of poem.

Ruppert, James. *Guide to American Poetry Explication: Colonial & Nineteenth Century.* Boston: G. K. Hall, 1989.

A companion volume to Leo, *Guide to American Poetry Explication*, this volume covers pre-twentieth-century American poetry. It is especially comprehensive for Dickinson and Whitman.

Short Story Criticism: Excerpts from Criticism of the Works of Short Fiction Writers. Detroit: Gale Research, 1988–.

This series, which is in progress, will cover major short story writers of all eras and nationalities.

Walker, Warren S. *Twentieth-Century Short Story Explication: Interpretations, 1900–75, of Short Fiction Since 1800.* 3rd ed. Hamden, Conn.: Shoe String Press, 1977. 1st, 2nd, and 3rd Supplements to 3rd ed., 1976–84.

This reference work is an index to critical analyses of short stories concerned with theme, symbol, and structure appearing in books, monographs, and periodicals. It is arranged by authors and by stories.

Weixlmann, Joe, ed. *American Short-Fiction Criticism and Scholarship, 1959–1977: A Checklist.* Chicago: Swallow, 1982.

This reference work locates scholarship in 5,000 books and 325 periodicals on over 500 American writers of short fiction. Includes entries for interviews and bibliographies as well as for criticism and makes a special effort to give good coverage to minority authors.

Bibliographic Index and MLA Bibliography   Another reference source that is worth consulting is the *Bibliographic Index* (New York: H. W. Wilson, 1937–). This reference is a multi-volume work, begun in 1937, that lists bibliographies of at least 50 entries published separately or appearing in books or periodicals. Consulting the *Bibliographic Index* is a good move if you are doing research on any particular author or text. With *The Sandbox*, for instance, you could find out if there are any separate bibliographies of secondary sources on Edward Albee. The *Bibliographic Index* is also worth consulting to identify any bibliographies that may have appeared after the publication date of a relevant subject bibliography. For example, Coleman's *Drama Criticism* may yield a list of secondary sources about Albee's plays in general or *The Sandbox* in particular, but only those published up to about 1970. Checking the *Bibliographic Index* after 1971 (the publication date of *Drama Criticism*) will alert you to any bibliographies on Albee that may have appeared in the past 25 years. If you find any listed there, you can try to locate them and use them to develop your working bibliography of secondary sources.

One more very valuable reference source for any literary research topic is the *MLA International Bibliography of Books and Articles on the Modern Languages and Literatures* (New York: Modern Language Association of America, 1947–). This reference (abbreviated MLAIB) is a bibliography of secondary sources by critics of all nationalities about literary authors of all nationalities (except classical Greece and Rome). Because of that comprehensiveness and the fact that it lists sources published in both books and periodicals, the *MLAIB* is an indispensable reference source. But the *MLAIB* is an annual, noncumulative bibliography, which means that it lists only one year's worth of secondary sources per volume. That, in turn, means that you must consult several volumes in order to leave no stone unturned.

Depending on the technology available to you, that limitation may be overcome, however. Two electronic information services, Dialog and WILSONLINE, allow you to search the *MLAIB* online back to 1964 and 1981, respectively, and the *MLAIB* since 1981 is available on CD-ROM. Accessing the *MLAIB* through either of these methods gives you access to about 15 or 30 years of listed secondary sources instead of just a single year. When Shirin Arastu ran a CD-ROM search of the *MLAIB*, using Albee as a keyword, she found more than 100 books and periodical articles listed. She printed out the list and checked to see if her library had any of the books and periodicals cited. Here is one entry from her print-out:

```
3 MLA
        AUTHOR:  Gabbard, Lucina P.
         TITLE:  Edward Albee's Triptych on Abandonment
        SOURCE:  Twentieth Century Literature: A Scholarly and
                 Critical Journal (ISBN 0041-462X) 1982 Spring
                 v28(1) p14-33

SUBJECTS COVERED:
--(slt) American literature (tim) 1900-1999 (sau) Albee,
Edward (swk) The Sandbox (swk) Zoo Story (swk) The Death of
Bessie Smith (lth) abandonment (lth) separation anxiety (sap)
psychoanalytic approach
```

The *MLAIB* on CD-ROM is, in effect, an annotated bibliography: the list of "subjects covered" for each source amounts to a note or brief description of the contents of the source, making this bibliography more useful than just a list of titles would be. The annotation here, for instance, told Shirin that *The Sandbox* was discussed in the journal article, that the topics of "abandonment" and "separation anxiety" were treated, and that the critic used a "psychoanalytic approach" in reading the plays. At least the first two of those bits of information suggested that Shirin might find this article useful to her project. In fact, she did track it down and read it, and she wound up using it in her paper. (See Chapter 23, pages 1273–1277.)

Look for Specific Sources in Books and Periodicals

Once you have compiled a list of potentially useful sources in the form of a working bibliography, your next step in a basic search strategy is to get your hands on some specific sources in books and periodicals. The way to locate books in your library, of course, is to search the catalog. Some smaller libraries may still use a card system, but most academic libraries these days store their catalogs on-line. There are two approaches you can take to searching for books, and to be thorough you should use both.

Books: Search the Catalog   The first approach is to search by author or title for books you have listed in your working bibliography. The second approach, which cross-checks the first, is to search the catalog by subject. If you do the latter, you can almost always use an author's name (for example, Albee, Edward) as a keyword for a subject search of your library's catalog. That should turn up all books *about* Albee or his plays held in your library. Be alert here: if you use "Albee" as an author search, you will come up with a list of books *by* him, which is probably not what you want for your research. Use the name of the author of your primary source only as a keyword in a subject search of your library's catalog. Do an author search only for those people who have written critical or interpretive books: secondary sources.

When Shirin did a subject search of her library's on-line catalog, using *Albee, Edward,* as a keyword, she was shown a screen listing five books with *Albee* in their titles. Here is what she saw when she asked for more detail on one of those books:

```
Call Number  BOOK STACKS Status : Checked In
 PS3551.L25 Z86 1987

AUTHOR 1) Roudane, Matthew Charles, 1953-

TITLE Understanding Edward Albee /

PUBLISHER Columbia, S.C. : University of South Carolina Press, c1987.
PHYS.DESC. xii, 221 p. ; 18 cm.

BIB.NOTES 1) Bibliography: p. 198-210.

SERIES 1)Understanding contemporary American literature
```

SUBJECTS 1) Albee, Edward, -- 1928- -- Criticism and Interpretation

Ultimately, Shirin did use this book in her paper. (See Chapter 23, pages 1275–1277.) But at this point in the library search strategy, you should notice that this screen shows that Roudané's book includes a bibliography covering some 12 pages. Because this book was published in 1987, that bibliography would probably go up through about 1986. It would be worth checking to identify further secondary sources on Albee's plays, but it should also be supplemented by searching the *MLAIB* to close the gap from 1986 to the present. It's also a good idea to print out on-line catalog records and to save those printouts. If your project involved researching Albee, and if you were to use Roudané's book in your paper, you would need the bibliographic information provided on this record for your Works Cited list.

Books, however, are not the only or even necessarily the best source of information for broadening your experience. For one thing, it usually takes more than a year for a critic to research and write a book and for a publisher to print, bind, and distribute it. Some information gets old fast, and periodicals, with their more frequent publication schedule, tend to offer the latest in research findings, criticism, and interpretation. While your library seems to be mainly a storehouse of books, it also holds numerous scholarly journals that can be of great value in any research project.

Articles: Check the Periodical Indexes   The most efficient way to approach a periodical search is to first consult periodical indexes, which list, by topic, articles published in selected journals and magazines for a certain period of time, usually one year or a portion of a year. The *MLAIB*, mentioned on page 1641, is such a periodical index, and no search for secondary sources on a literary topic should neglect it. But the bound volumes of *MLAIB* can be somewhat difficult to negotiate, so especially if your library does not have the *MLAIB* available online or on CD-ROM, you may need to consult another periodical index. You may be familiar with *The Reader's Guide to Periodical Literature*. Chances are you have used it to locate periodical articles on some topic you have researched in high school or otherwise. Because *The Reader's Guide* indexes popular magazines, as opposed to scholarly journals, it is not very useful for college-level research on a literary topic. However, if you know how to use *The Reader's Guide*, you will be able to use other periodical indexes published by the same company: H.W. Wilson. The Wilson index most applicable to broadening your experience with respect to literature is *The Humanities Index*.

The Humanities Index (New York: H.W. Wilson, 1974/75–) is an author and subject index to about 260 English and North American scholarly journals in the humanities. Author and subject entries are listed in a single alphabet. With each journal article entered under its author and under a number of subject headings, the *Humanities Index* offers extensive subheadings, related headings, and cross-references with full bibliographical information. It appears quarterly with annual cumulations. This periodical index is available in bound volumes from 1974 to the present and from 1984 to the present on CD-ROM and through WILSONLINE.

Once you have found articles listed in the periodical indexes, the next step is to see if your library holds the periodicals you need. If your library has an on-line catalog, you may be able to do a title search using the title of a periodical to see if your library holds it and, if so, what years of publication of that journal your library has. Alternatively, you can ask a reference librarian for a list of the periodical holdings of your library and match any periodical title against this list. If your library does have the periodical, and the specific volume thereof, that you want, go to the shelves in the bound periodical section to find the periodical and the article you need.

If a given periodical is *not* held in your library, don't give up. You may be able to request a photocopy of an article through interlibrary loan. In this way you can have access to periodical collections greater than the one in your school's library. You will, however, be charged a fee for a photocopy of an article, and you must realize that filling an interlibrary loan request takes some time, so a good periodical index search should not be rushed. If you have access to the Internet through a computer network at your school or through a modem on your personal computer, you may be able to copy selected journal articles onto your hard drive or diskette. Check with your reference librarian, however, to see if this procedure is recommended and to find out what it will cost and how long it will take.

Read Your Sources and Take Notes

Once you have found books and periodical articles that appear likely to broaden your experience in a specific area, of course you must read them for relevant information and ideas. Like the reading you do for primary sources, your reading of secondary sources should be active. You should read with a pencil or highlighter in your hand—and use it. You should never mark up the pages of a library book or a periodical, of course, so you have two alternatives: to make photocopies of what you think you want to read and annotate or to keep note cards. The latter is the more traditional method, the former perhaps the more common practice now that photocopiers are widely available in libraries. Each method has its advantages. Making note cards involves active reading because you must select what ideas and passages in a source should be recorded on a card and because writing the card itself is an activity. A stack of note cards—with one note per card—can be neatly stored, and cards can be shuffled around as you consider which notes will go where in your paper as you plan your first draft. Similarly, highlighting and writing marginal notes on photocopies requires you to read actively, and making photocopies enables you to do your notemaking work at home or wherever you wish to carry your copies.

With either method, reading actively also means you should think of yourself as carrying on a conversation with the author of the source you are reading about whatever text or author you are researching. The question(s) that have motivated your research in the first place or your ideas from your reading of your primary source (perhaps expressed as a tentative thesis statement) are important here. Library research at the college level requires you to *synthesize* what you read in secondary sources: to relate it to and evaluate it in terms of your own ideas about a primary source, not merely to passively record and report what you read in secondary sources. Again, having a narrowed topic or focus question will help you in this direction much more than if you go into the research process with merely an author's name or the title of a primary source in mind. A researched paper should grow organically out of writing you have done throughout the semester to the point where you start, by choice or assignment, to broaden your literary experience for a formal paper.

Record Bibliographic Information Whether you make note cards or photocopies, a crucial practical matter is to record all the pertinent bibliographic information for each source. For book sources, this information includes author or editor, title, subtitle, place of publication, publisher, and date of publication. For periodical sources, you need author, title of article, title of journal, volume number, issue number or name (e.g., "Spring"), and inclusive pages of the article. Be sure to record this information completely and accurately the first time you read any source; you will regret not doing so if you find you don't have it when you are putting your Works Cited list together and have to go back to the library to track down such a detail.

Summary, Paraphrase, Direct Quotation   Another important consideration is the use to which you will put something you note from a secondary source, and this use relates to the kind of notes you might make. You might **summarize** a source, you might **paraphrase** it, or you might **quote** it directly. A summary boils a passage in a source down to its essence, reducing, perhaps, a paragraph to a single sentence. A paraphrase restates the passage in your own words but maintains roughly the length of the original. A direct quotation is a word-for-word transcription of the source passage. Direct quotation needs no illustration, but the other kinds of notes do. Here, then, is a passage from a source, Cleanth Brooks' *William Faulkner: The Yoknapatawpha Country* (New Haven: Yale UP, 1963), page 68, followed by sample notes that summarize and paraphrase.

> *In* Light in August, *however, the male-female contrast is stressed in a rather different way. Here, the principal male characters suffer alienation. They are separated from the community and are in rebellion against it—and against nature. But Lena moves serenely into the community and it gathers itself about her with protective gestures. Its response to her, of course, is rooted in a deep and sound instinct: Lena embodies the principle upon which any human community is founded. She is the carrier of life, and she has to be protected and nurtured if there is to be any community at all.*

This 100-word paragraph can be summarized in one 25-word sentence:

> *In* Light in August, *male and female characters are contrasted by the alienation of the males from the community and the community's acceptance of Lena (Brooks 68).*

The paragraph can also be paraphrased in five sentences totaling 80 words:

> *In* Light in August, *the contrast between males and females features the alienation of the major male characters. They are not part of the community; in fact, they resist it—and nature as well. The female Lena, however, is embraced by the community. This is because Lena's pregnancy is a sign of the life principle, which is the basis of any human community. As a pregnant woman, Lena must be "protected and nurtured" for the community itself to continue to live (Brooks 68).*

Avoid Plagiarism   Please note that, while the paraphrase is close in length to the source and while it tries to restate all the passage's ideas, it does not lean too heavily on the language of the original, nor does it merely drop the note-taker's words into the sentence structures of the original. Doing either of those things would constitute **plagiarism**, which is academic dishonesty where sources are concerned. Where this note-taker felt that he could not say something in any words other than the source's, he quoted these words directly. One form of plagiarism is the unacknowledged use of another's words or ideas, but a paraphrase that is too close to the words or the style of a source—even if the source is acknowledged—also constitutes plagiarism. In paraphrasing, "your own words" means "your own *sentences*" too.

Documenting Your Sources—MLA Style

In writing a paper based on research, you must acknowledge the sources of words you quote and ideas you borrow, whether those ideas are paraphrased *or* summarized. The governing documentation style for academic papers in English and other language courses is that of the Modern Language Association of America, or MLA. MLA style provides for a systematic way to cite a source within the body of your paper and to provide complete bibliographic information at the end. Briefly, that system calls for parenthetical citations or references to your sources in the paper itself coupled with a Works Cited list at the end. In MLA style, footnotes or endnotes are not used to cite sources; they are used only for explanatory or informational notes. In most papers you will write for your English courses, you will not likely need these kinds of notes, but you may find an example of one in Chapter 23, page 1274. You will, however, need to know how to handle the citation of several types of sources you are likely to encounter, for references within a paper and for a Works Cited list. The following discussion will look first at references in the body of the paper then at examples of entries on a Works Cited list.

References in the Paper

Probably the most common way to refer to a source within a paper consists of naming the source as you introduce what you have taken from him or her and following the passage with parentheses containing the page number or numbers on which the passage appeared in the original. This is especially helpful to your reader when you paraphrase because, in the absence of quotation marks, the presence of the name of a source sets one "boundary" to the borrowed material, with the parentheses setting the other. For example, in a paper, the earlier paraphrase of Brooks' comment on characters in *Light in August* might look like this:

Page Number Alone in Parentheses

> *Critic Cleanth Brooks says that the contrast between males and females in* Light in August *features the alienation of the major male characters. They are not part of the community; in fact, they resist it—and nature as well. The female Lena, however, is embraced by the community (68).*

If *William Faulkner: The Yoknapatawpha Country* is the only source by Brooks cited in the paper, there is no need to put any form of the title in the parenthetical citation. Because his name was used preceding the paraphrase, there is no need to include it in the parentheses either. Page number alone will do, without any abbreviation for the word *page*.

Title in Parentheses   If, however, a paper cites more than one source by the same author, they must be distinguished from one another in the parenthetical citations. A short version of the title of the source will do the job:

> . . . *by the community.* (Yoknapatawpha 68).

These citation requirements are the same whether the source is paraphrased or quoted directly.

Author's Name in Parentheses   A common variation of this kind of citation occurs in the form of a direct quote from a source that is not preceded by the source's name. In this case, the author's last name must appear in the parentheses:

> *"In* Light in August . . . , *the principal male characters suffer alienation"* (Brooks 68).

The ellipses here—the three spaced dots—indicate material has been omitted from the direct quotation; the comma is retained in this case in accordance with the standard practice of using a comma with an introductory phrase.

Framing a Paraphrase   Naming the author in the parenthetical citation only is permissible with paraphrases as well as quotations, but in such cases an indirect reference to the source should be made so that your reader can tell where the borrowed ideas begin:

> *One critic observes that the contrast between males and females in* Light in August *features the alienation of the major male characters* (Brooks 68).

Multiple Sources by One Author   Similarly, if a paper cites more than one source by the same author, the source being paraphrased or summarized on any particular occasion must be mentioned in the parentheses:

> *One critic says that in* Light in August, *male and female characters are contrasted by the alienation of the males from the community and the community's acceptance of Lena* (Brooks, Yoknapatawpha 68).

Different Sources, Common Name   If your paper were to cite sources written by more than one person with the same last name—say, critic Cleanth Brooks and poet Gwendolyn Brooks—you would have to make clear which person you were citing at any given time. You could do this by giving the person's first and last names in an introductory phrase or by using his or her first initial in the parenthetical citation:

> . . . *acceptance of Lena (C. Brooks 68).*

Indirect Citations   Whenever you can, you should cite someone's words or ideas firsthand, directly from a source in which you found them. This is not always possible, however, especially when one person quotes the spoken words of another, as in interviews, for instance. In that case, your parenthetical citation should include the abbreviation *qtd. in* before the name of the source in which you found the other person's words. Several examples of this kind of indirect citation appear in Shirin Arastu's paper in Chapter 23, pages 1274 and 1276.

Other Mechanical Matters

In addition to the above points about documenting your sources in your paper according to MLA style, you need to know a few basic things about the mechanics of handling citations and quotations. Some of these apply to both primary and secondary sources, some to primary sources only.

Handling Quotations   Probably the most common of these mechanical matters has to do with whether a direct quotation is handled within a sentence of your own or set off on its own as a block of type. The rule of thumb for prose passages, from either a primary or a secondary source, is that four or fewer typed lines of direct quotation may be handled within your own sentence. Those lines would, of course, be enclosed in quotation marks. Whatever punctuation your sentence requires following the quoted passage (period, comma, semicolon) falls *after* the parentheses. For example:

> *In describing the development of W. B. Yeats' poetry in the early twentieth century, Richard Ellmann says, "The word that begins to occur constantly in his writings . . . is 'mask,' a word which lent dignity and a kind of traditional sanction to his theories of the pose" (174).*

Again, the ellipses indicate that some portion of the original passage has been omitted from the quotation. Notice also that the word *mask* is enclosed in single quote marks, indicating that it was in quotes in the passage in Ellman's book.

If a prose quotation runs longer than four typed lines, it must be set off as a block of type; that is, indented ten spaces from the left margin. In handling quotations this way, you must do two other things: put the parenthetical citation *after* the punctuation mark that ends the quoted passage and omit quotation marks around the source passage. For example:

> *In describing the development of W. B. Yeats' poetry, Richard Ellmann says,*
> *The word that begins to occur constantly in his writings during the first decade of the [twentieth] century is "mask," a word which lent dignity and a kind of traditional sanction to his theories of the pose. He first used it prominently in verse in a song he wrote in August 1910, for* The Player Queen. *(174)*

Do not indent on the right; in other words, do not center a block quotation. Do maintain double spacing, whether the quoted passage is prose or verse. Words or phrases that you must add to explain or clarify a quoted passage, like "twentieth" in the above example, must be enclosed in square brackets (not parentheses). If your typewriter or printer doesn't have brackets, use dark ink to draw them in by hand.

Quoting Lines of Poetry   With poetry, if you are quoting more than three lines of verse, the quoted passage should be set off as a block:

> Gwendolyn Brooks' sonnet "First Fight. Then Fiddle" opens with
> the command to
>> First fight. Then fiddle. Ply the slipping string
>> With feathery sorcery; muzzle the note
>> With hurting love; the music that they wrote
>> Bewitch, bewilder. (1–4)

Fewer than four lines of verse may be run in with your typed sentence, but use a slash surrounded by spaces to separate the lines:

> Gwendolyn Brooks' sonnet "First Fight. Then Fiddle" opens with
> the command to "First fight. Then fiddle. Ply the slipping string / With
> feathery sorcery; muzzle the note / with hurting love" (1–3).

As with prose quotations, quotations of fewer than four lines of verse are enclosed in quotation marks; more than three lines, set off as a block, are not. In quoting poetry, MLA style calls for the word *line* or *lines* to appear in the parentheses if there is a chance your reader will not immediately recognize that you are quoting verse.[1] With any quoted poem in a paper, however, once you have established that you are quoting verse, you need not use *line* or *lines* in subsequent parenthetical citations.

Quoting a Play   If you are quoting a play that has numbered acts, scenes, and lines—like one of Shakespeare's, for instance—use Arabic numerals, for act, scene, and line numbers. Separate each numeral with a period. For setting off as a block of type or running a quotation into your sentence, follow the same guidelines as for quoting poetry. Here are two examples:

> In Hamlet, *Polonius' speech to Laertes as the latter is preparing to
> leave for Paris contains the proverbial advice to "Neither a borrower
> nor a lender be, / For loan oft loses both itself and friend, / And bor-
> rowing dulleth th' edge of husbandry." (1.3. 75–77)*

> In Hamlet, *Polonius concludes his speech of advice to Laertes as
> the latter is preparing to leave for Paris by saying:*
>> Neither a borrower nor a lender be,
>> For loan oft loses both itself and friend,
>> And borrowing dulleth th' edge of husbandry.
>> This above all: to thine own self be true,
>> And it must follow, as the night the day,
>> Thou canst not then be false to any man. (1.3. 75–80)

The Works Cited List

The last page or pages of your paper should contain an alphabetized list of all the works whose words or ideas you drew upon in writing your paper—those works you actually cited in the body of your paper. Double space consistently throughout this list. The first line of each Works Cited entry should be flush

---

[1]See, for example, Elaine Kaplowe's paper on reading "Hey Jack Kerouac" in Chapter 14, page 639.

with the left margin; second and subsequent lines of any entry should be indented five spaces. Beyond that, the mechanical conventions for different kinds of sources—for example, books, periodical articles, and nonprint sources—vary according to the kind of source. Below is a list of sample Works Cited entries for some of the most common kinds of sources. For a model Works Cited list for a paper that cites both primary and secondary sources, see Chapter 23, page 1277. For information on references in a paper, the Works Cited list, and other related matters, see *The MLA Style Manual*. Ed. Walter S. Achtert and Joseph Gibaldi. New York: Modern Language Association of America, 1985. A similar guide is available in paperback: the *MLA Handbook for Writers of Research Papers*, 4th. ed. Ed. Joseph Gibaldi. New York: Modern Language Association of America, 1995.

A book with one author:

Simpson, Lewis. *The Fable of the Southern Writer*. Baton Rouge: Louisiana State UP, 1994.

A book with more than one author:

Gilbert, Sandra M., and Susan Gubar. *The Madwoman in the Attic: The Woman Writer and the Nineteenth-Century Literary Imagination*. New Haven: Yale UP, 1985.

If a book has more than three authors or editors, you may name only the first person and use the abbreviation *et al.* (for "and others").

An edition:

Shakespeare, William. *The Complete Works of William Shakespeare*. Ed. David Bevington. 4th ed. New York: Harper, 1992.

A translation:

Todorov, Tzvetan. *The Conquest of America*. Trans. Richard Howard. New York: Harper, 1984.

A book published in multiple volumes:

Yeats, W. B. *The Poems*. Ed. Richard J. Finneran. New York: Macmillan, 1989. Vol. 1 of *The Collected Works of W.B. Yeats*. 14 vols. 1989– .

An essay from a collection:

Prigozy, Ruth. "Fitzgerald's Short Stories and the Depression: An Artistic Crisis." *The Short Stories of F. Scott Fitzgerald: New Approaches in Criticism*. Ed. Jackson R. Bryer. Madison: U of Wisconsin Press, 1982. 111–26.

If the collection reprints essays that originally appeared elsewhere, you must give complete bibliographic data for the original publication, followed by the phrase *Rpt. in* (for "reprinted in") and the information for the collection in which you found the essay. If a collection of essays reprints earlier pieces, acknowledgments will appear, either as a separate section in the collection or as a note to each essay.

Kenner, Hugh. "The Experience of the Eye: Marianne Moore's Tradition." *The Southern Review*. ns 1 (1965): 754–69. Rpt. in *Modern American Poetry: Essays in Criticism*. Ed. Jerome Mazzaro. New York: McKay, 1970. 204–21.[2]

A work in an anthology:

Albee, Edward. *The Sandbox*. *Literature: Reading and Responding to Fiction, Poetry, Drama, and the Essay*. Ed. Joel Wingard. New York: Harper, 1996. 877–81.

An article from a journal that paginates continuously throughout each volume:

McDiarmid, Lucy. "Augusta Gregory, Bernard Shaw, and the Shewing-Up of Dublin Castle." *PMLA*. 109 (1994): 26–44.

An article from a journal that paginates each issue separately:

O'Connor, Gerry. "Bernard Malumud's *The Natural*: 'The Worst There Ever Was in the Game.'" *Arete: The Journal of Sport Literature*. 3.2 (1986): 37–42.

An article from a weekly magazine:

Wiener, Jon. "Free Speech on the Internet." *The Nation*. 13 June 1994: 825–28.

An article from a monthly magazine:

Conniff, Richard. "Ireland On Fast-Forward." *National Geographic*. Sept. 1994: 2–31.

An article from a daily newspaper:

Taylor, Mary B. W. "Beckett's Earliest Play To Be Issued." *New York Times*. 26 Jan. 1995: C17.

A review:

Simon, John. "Stoppard Unstoppered." Rev. of *Rosencrantz and Guildenstern Are Dead*, by Tom Stoppard. Roundabout Theater. New York. *New York*. 1 June 1987: 62.

A recording:

Shocked, Michelle. *Short Sharp Shocked*. Mercury, 1988.

A film:

Into the West. Dir. Mike Newell. Perf. Ellen Barkin and Gabriel Byrne. Miramax, 1993.

A television program:

"The Shoes." Dir. Tom Cherones. Writ. Larry David.

---

[2]"ns" in this entry stands for "new series." Some journals, like this one, cease publication for a time. When they resume, they start again with Volume 1. To prevent confusion where a journal has more than one volume with the same number, the abbreviations "ns" and "os" (for "original series") are used.

Seinfeld. Prod. Larry David, Howard West, George Shapiro. NBC. KYW, Philadelphia. 4 Feb. 1993.

Material from a computer service:

Reuss, Martin, and Gerald W. Hartwig. "Bismarck's Imperialism and the Rohlfs Mission." *South Atlantic Quarterly.* 74.1 (1975): 74–85. Dialog file 39, item 829098.

More than one source by the same person:

Brooks, Cleanth. "Faulkner's Vision of Good and Evil." *Massachusetts Review* 3 (1962): 692–712.

———. *William Faulkner: The Yoknapatawpha Country.* New Haven: Yale UP, 1963.

Notice that three hyphens replace the author's name in the second source and that these sources are put in alphabetical order by title.

Formatting Your Paper

In addition to the requirements for documenting your sources, you will have several formal requirements to observe in preparing the final draft of your paper. MLA style covers such matters as what kind of paper to use and how to format an academic paper. You can read about these requirements in more detail in either *The MLA Style Manual* or the *MLA Handbook.* Shirin Arastu's researched paper in Chapter 23 was formatted according to MLA style, so you can use it as a model for your own. Here, however, is a checklist of formal matters to attend to before you type or print out your final draft.

- Make sure that all the sources you cite in your paper appear on your Works Cited list.
- Make sure that everything on your Works Cited list is cited in your paper.
- Check your quotations and paraphrases against their sources: Are direct quotations word-for-word? Have you handled ellipses and brackets correctly?
- Make sure that all your sources are clearly cited in your paper and that the mechanics of citation conform to MLA style.
- Double space your paper throughout, including block quotations and your Works Cited list.
- Underline all titles of separate publications: books, periodicals, plays.
- Use quotation marks for titles of works included within other titles: short stories, poems, periodical articles.
- Begin your Works Cited list with the heading Works Cited, centered at the top of the page.
- Number your paper consecutively in the upper righthand corner, beginning with the first page of text and continuing through the Works Cited list. Do not number a title page.
- An optional title page should have your name, your professor's name, the course for which you are submitting the paper, and the due date. A title itself is also optional. If you use one, do not enclose it in quotes or underline it.

Research and the Writing Process: A Final Word

This chapter has concentrated on the process of broadening your literary experience through library research and some of the formal requirements of handling sources in a researched paper. It has not discussed the writing process in terms of generating ideas and other prewriting activities, drafting, and revising. A good researched paper, however, is no more a mechanically constructed product than any of the other kinds of formal papers exemplified in this book. Your attention to the full scope of the writing process is just as important in any researched paper assignment as it is in papers that do not involve an inquiry into secondary sources. So without undertaking an extended discussion of the writing process as it applies to a researched paper, I will refer you to several earlier parts of this book.

The overall writing process—from response statement through revised draft of a formal paper—is discussed and illustrated in Chapter 4. Models of students' writing processes and the formal papers those students produced are shown and discussed in each of the genre sections (Chapters 9, 14, 23, and 27, respectively). As this Chapter has mentioned, one of those papers—Shirin Arastu's on *The Sandbox* in Chapter 23—does incorporate secondary sources. In relation to the overall writing process, Shirin's paper merely broadens out her initial response writing to include other texts she read—all written by readers of Albee and written on topics related to those on which she had already been writing. In addition, the other students who have major papers in this book have also written excellent researched papers, each bearing the person's individual stamp, by continuing the writing process described and advocated in this book—QAQ. It's really quite simple if you just start writing things down.

29 ◈ THE COMPARISON-CONTRAST PAPER

The student papers that have appeared in chapters 4, 9, 14, 23, and 27 of this book have one basic thing in common: Each takes as its topic the *interaction* between text and reader. Indeed, because of the model of reading upon which it is based, this book has stressed that interaction as a topic for writing about literature. As these papers show, response-based papers can be formal and analytical; they are not necessarily subjective in any negative sense. In fact, an instance when a student did develop a response statement into a paper that was mostly about himself and that generally excluded the text from consideration was shown in Chapter 14 as an example of "The Perils of Free Associating." However, you may find that some academic writing situations call for you to focus more on the text than on your interaction with it. In view of such situations, this chapter will offer you a look at another student paper, one that exemplifies an emphasis on the text.

Writing about Literature: The Question of Emphasis

Actually, this student paper emphasizes *two* texts. The student who wrote it, Justine Johnson, was given an assignment to compare and contrast two poems. Although an assignment such as this seems to have the written product, a paper, primarily in view, it also involves a certain way of reading and thinking as part of the entire writing process. To compare is to look at two texts in terms of similarities; to contrast is to look at them in terms of differences. Recognizing a similarity in two texts also involves a concept introduced in Chapter 2 (and mentioned elsewhere throughout this book): **intertextuality**. This concept means the connections, established by the reader, between texts are important in understanding both texts. In Chapter 2, I used some of the similarities I see underlying the surface differences between a canonical poem from the high culture tradition—Matthew Arnold's "Dover Beach"—and a text from popular culture—Bruce Springsteen's "Cover Me"—to illustrate the concept of intertextuality. If you are given an assignment to compare and contrast two texts, you may be able to draw upon an intertextuality you have already established in your literary experience. This is what Justine did.

Furthermore, because comparing and contrasting is fundamentally a way of looking at two texts, not just a rationale for producing academic papers, it should result in an emphasis on either similarities or differences. My brief discussion of "Dover Beach" and "Cover Me" in Chapter 2 stressed the similarities between two texts from nearly opposite ends of the cultural spectrum. Justine's paper makes a similar move in discovering similarities in two poems that also have their differences: Langston Hughes' "Theme for English B" and Marge Piercy's "The woman in the ordinary" (both in Poems for Further Reading, pages 709 and 750). Here is a portion of the introductory paragraph of her paper. It shows her thinking in terms of comparing and contrasting and her reference to both similarities and differences in the two poems.

> Langston Hughes and Marge Piercy are two American poets who recognize the difficult task of overturning these [false] identities in order to cultivate the private, individual identities buried beneath the surface. Hughes' "Theme for English B," written a few years before the start of the civil rights movement, reveals the reflective thoughts of an African-American college student as he attempts to write an essay about his true self that his white English instructor can understand. Piercy's "The woman in the ordinary" portrays three women whose true identities have been smothered by society's prescribed gender roles. Despite differences in the way Hughes and Piercy present their ideas, both poems examine the ways in which society's expectations, based on racial and gender stereotypes, influence people's identities.

As this portion of her introductory paragraph suggests, Justine did not allow the compare-and-contrast assignment to lead her into oversimplified thinking about two texts. She did not merely present some similarities and some differences. Instead, by first establishing an intertextual connection between Hughes' and Piercy's poems and then by reading both poems closely and carefully in terms of their common concern with the question of individual identity, Justine was able to see some new and quite complex similarities and differences between them. In turn, the paper that she produced from this way of thinking afforded its readers a new look at the poems and at the cultural issue of individual identity.

Structuring the Paper

Justine's paper follows in its entirety later. It is an excellent model of an academic paper built on comparing and contrasting as a way of thinking. Before you read it, however, I will offer a few words on the organization or **structure** of such a paper. In a paper that discusses two texts, you have those texts to talk about as well as the points of comparison and contrast in terms of which you have considered the texts as you read them. These factors suggest two general ways to structure your paper: one way according to the texts themselves, the other according to the points of comparison or contrast. Knowing you have these structuring plans available to you may help you organize what may sometimes seem to be a chaotic hodgepodge of thoughts about your two texts. In that sense, these plans can be valuable.

At the same time, however, you should consider these structuring plans as devices you can use, subject to your adaptation, not as rigid molds into which you pour your ideas. Justine's paper, which originated in a response journal entry, went through several drafts before assuming the shape in which it appears below. In the process, Justine's careful reading of and thinking about the two poems determined the structure of her paper; she did not decide in advance that she would organize her discussion according to her points of comparison instead of treating each poem in consecutive order. But just to highlight the structure of Justine's paper, here it is in outline form:

I. Introduction—Leading to thesis statement:
   Despite differences in the way Hughes and Piercy present their ideas, both poems examine the ways in which society's expectations, based on racial and gender stereotypes, influence people's identities.

II. Body—Five main points
   A. Physical appearance as a social determiner of individual identity.
      1. Hughes' poem.
      2. Piercy's poem.
   B. The difficulty of realizing individual identities that lie beneath the surface of social expectations.
      1. Hughes.
      2. Piercy.
   C. Society's tendency to emphasize individual differences and ignore inherent likenesses among people.
      1. Hughes.
      2. Piercy.
   D. How Hughes and Piercy use different means to emphasize likeness between people.
      1. Hughes.
      2. Piercy.
      3. Hughes.
      4. Piercy.
   E. The importance of race and gender in establishing individual identity.
      1. Hughes.
      2. Piercy.

III. Conclusion—The two poems remind us that accepting differences and similarities among people is necessary for individual identity to realize itself.

Other Important Considerations

As you read Justine's paper, look at how this plan provides structure. You should take note of a few other features of her paper too.

- Her thesis statement sums up and helps organize what the body of her paper says.
- She cites both poems frequently and effectively to illustrate her points.

- She handles the mechanical matters of quoting the poems, including parenthetical citations of them in MLA style.
- She uses transitional words and phrases to signal changes in her discussion from one poem to the other.
- She acknowledges the role of her own cultural situation in forming her interpretation of the poems.
- In general she uses comparing and contrasting to establish a meaningful connection between one poem and the other and between both poems and a larger issue.

STUDENT WRITING

Justine Johnson: Beneath the Surface:

Who am I? This age-old question is deceptively simple because the search for a complete answer often requires a complex, arduous self-examination. Individuals frequently must unearth their true identities from beneath a superficial surface identity, composed of society's expectations layers deep in history. Since our forefathers drafted the Declaration of Independence over two centuries ago, white males have been the most powerful members of the United States. Women and people of color often have to sprout false identities in order to flourish in American society. Langston Hughes and Marge Piercy are two American poets who recognize the difficult task of overturning these identities in order to cultivate the private, individual identities buried beneath the surface. Hughes' "Theme for English B," written a few years before the start of the civil rights movement, reveals the reflective thoughts of an African-American college student as he attempts to write an essay about his true self that his white English instructor can understand. Piercy's "The woman in the ordinary" portrays three women whose true identities have been smothered by society's prescribed gender roles. Despite differences in the way Hughes and Piercy present their ideas, both poems examine the ways in which society's expectations, based on racial and gender stereotypes, influence people's identities.

Our surface identities are defined by other people's perceptions of us. Physical appearance is one of the most important components of surface identity because it is the most visible. The speaker in Hughes' poem describes himself as "twenty-two . . . the only colored student in my class" (7, 10). His skin color sets him apart from his classmates and affects how others perceive him, particularly his instructor. In his class, Hughes' speaker is known as the colored student; his surface identity is based solely on his outer appearance. Similarly, a woman's value in our society often depends on her beauty, rather than her intelligence or personality. In Piercy's poem, "the woman in the ordinary pudgy downcast girl" (1) does not meet society's standards of a beautiful, and therefore valuable, woman; feeling insignificant, the woman "[crouches] with eyes and muscles clenched" (2). Society's emphasis on physical appearance not only makes people feel unimportant but also tends to categorize them by stereotypes. The stereotypical woman is attractive, innocent, and pure, like Piercy's "woman in the block of ivory soap" (5) and the "Christmas card virgin with glued hands" (11). Media stereotypes of African-American men portray uneducated, uncivilized people who avoid work and cannot have loving, lasting relationships with women. In contrast to these stereotypes, Hughes' speaker lists the things he likes to do: "I like to . . . be in love. / I like to work, read, learn, and understand life" (21–22). Surface identities based on stereotypes that create one-dimensional images of people obscure the underlying differences that make each individual unique.

Beneath each of our surface identities lies another private, individual identity rarely revealed to others—and sometimes not fully realized by us. Hughes' speaker acknowledges the difficulty of finding one's identity: "It's not easy to know what is true for you or me" (16). He questions, "Me—who?" (20), revealing his need for further self-examination in order to discover who he truly is. Instead of searching inward, the speaker seems to be reaching outward to the African-American community to find his real identity: "I guess I'm what / I feel and see and hear, Harlem, I hear you" (17–18). His uncertainty is signaled by his frequent use of the hesitant phrase "I guess." Like Hughes' speaker, Piercy's women also cannot recognize their true identities because women are expected to conform to society's patriarchal structure. These women have been silenced in society for so long that they cannot define themselves as individuals, except in relation to men. Hughes' speaker is able to take part of his identity from his community, but Piercy's women cannot even do that: one "effaces herself / under ripples of conversation and debate" (3–4), while another "fishes for herself in other's eyes" (12). Piercy suggests that a woman must look inward to find her unique identity.

Society not only buries individual identities but also ignores the inherent like-ness of all people, regardless of race or gender. In "Theme for English B," Hughes' speaker refuses to polarize himself and his white instructor, opting instead to focus on their similarities. He tells his instructor that they have much in common, despite their racial differences: "I guess being colored doesn't make me *not* / like the same things other folks like who are other races" (25–26). While Hughes' poem resists the polarization of humans along racial lines, Piercy's poem describes the division of human traits into those traditionally labeled masculine and feminine. Women learn to suppress traditionally masculine qualities such as aggressiveness and boldness. Inside the outwardly shy, dependent girl in Piercy's poem is "a woman peppery as curry, / a yam of a woman of butter and brass, / compounded of acid and sweet like a pineapple" (14–16). Piercy identifies the opposites "butter and brass," which I in-terpret as traditionally feminine and masculine qualities; butter represents the per-ceived softness and malleability of women, while brass stands for masculine firm-ness and boldness. Although many women stifle them, traditionally masculine qual-ities remain a part of their private, individual identities. All people possess both "masculine" and "feminine" personality traits; however, socialization buries certain qualities in some people while allowing them to bloom in others.

Hughes and Piercy both emphasize the sameness of humanity in their poems, but they do so in different ways. While Hughes' poem is a first-person account of the speaker's exploration of his identity, Piercy's is a third-person description of women who have buried their identities beneath their surfaces. I would expect to be drawn into Hughes' poem because I can hear the narrator's voice; however, his use of simple, unadorned language lessens my emotional response to it. Hughes' speaker uses plain verbs like "eat," "sleep," "drink," and "work"—verbs which convey his intended meaning but are not very descriptive. Piercy, on the other hand, uses powerful, sense-oriented imagery to describe the women in her poem. Phrases like "stoops and creeps" (13), "round and pebble smooth" (3), and "massive thighs that neigh" (6) allow me to see, feel, and hear the women. Because Piercy's poem appeals to my senses, and because I am a woman and thus identify more closely with it, my emotional response to Piercy's poem is more intense than my response to Hughes'.

Although all people share basic human characteristics, race and gender cannot be ignored when searching for one's true individual identity, especially in a patriarchal, Eurocentric society like ours. Throughout history, society has placed such importance on these physical factors that they have become integral issues of identity. The speaker in Hughes' poem distinguishes between his own skin color and that of his classmates and instructor: "You are white— / yet a part of me, as I am a part of you…. Sometimes perhaps you don't want to be part of me. / Nor do I often want to be a part of you" (31–35). By repeatedly referring to "you" and "me," the speaker places himself and his white associates into separate categories; therefore, he acknowledges his skin color as a significant component of his identity. Hughes' poem discusses both African Americans and white Americans; however, Piercy's poem does not explicitly mention men and therefore is more open to interpretation. Like "the woman in the block of ivory soap / [who] has massive thighs that neigh, / great breasts that blare and strong arms that trumpet" (5–7), women must carve away their outer "feminine" personae to reveal their hidden inner identities, composed of both "feminine" and "masculine" qualities. The contrast between the women's outer and inner identities is so sharp that Piercy's poem becomes a statement in itself of the significance of gender in one's true identity.

Since the founding of the United States in 1776, many steps have been taken toward social, economic, and political equality for all people, regardless of race or gender; however, the fact remains that white men still hold primary power in the United States. Although all of us must brush some topsoil from our surface identities in order to unearth our private, individual identities, women and people of color must dig through additional layers of social stereotypes. The cultivation of our true identities, hidden beneath our surface identities, depends on our ability to see past these stereotypes and realize our unique individual differences. The speaker in "Theme for English B" writes, "As I learn from you, / I guess you learn from me—" (37–38). In the process of discovering our true identities, we can learn from each other—men from women, white people from people of color, and vice versa. Langston Hughes' and Marge Piercy's poems remind us that we must not only accept each other's differences but also realize our similarities, for only then will we be able to allow our hidden, private identities to blossom.

Thinking Critically About Analysis

In addition to being a fine example of comparing and contrasting at work as a way of thinking about texts, Justine's paper also illustrates another concept that this book has mentioned earlier: **cultural analysis**. On one level, Justine is closely analyzing two literary texts. On another level, she is analyzing her culture: the relationship of social pressures and expectations to individual identity. In the process, Justine's work on this paper helped her see more acutely into the cultural situations of women and people of color in the United States. The paper that she has written helps its readers—immediately in her college but now more broadly through this book—see that too and see how literary texts can be read not in isolation from social reality but in vital connection to it. May your own reading of and writing about literature have similar value!

APPENDIX
LIVES OF THE WRITERS

Chinua Achebe (1930–) Chinua Achebe was born in Nigeria, the son of a mission schoolteacher. He attended London University and the University College of Ibadan, earning a B.A. in 1953. Achebe, who believes that "art is at the service of man," has written novels, short stories, and essays. His works include *Things Fall Apart* (1958), for which he won international recognition, *No Longer at Ease* (1962), *Arrow of God* (1964), *A Man of the People* (1966), *Anthills of the Savannah* (1987), and *Girls at War* (1972), a collection of short stories. Achebe's work as a writer and editor has had a profound influence on other African writers. Currently he divides his time between Nigeria and the United States, teaching at several universities, including Stanford and the University of Massachusetts at Amherst.

Edward Albee (1928–) Edward Albee was expelled from several schools and lasted only one year at Trinity College, Connecticut. He worked many jobs in his teens and early adulthood, including record salesperson, counterperson in a luncheonette, and a messenger for Western Union. During this period, he wrote two novels (unpublished) before turning to drama in his thirties. He made a reputation for himself as an absurdist with the production of *The Zoo Story* in 1958. This production was followed by *The Sandbox* (1960), *The American Dream* (1961), and *Who's Afraid of Virginia Woolf* (1962), a play that some critics termed more traditional than his earlier works. In 1967 and 1975, he received Pulitzer Prizes for *A Delicate Balance* and *Seascape*. He won a third Pulitzer in 1994 for *Three Tall Women*. When asked in an interview about a director's insights, Albee responded, "If it's an intention that I think diminishes the play, than the director is wrong. If it's an insight that makes the play far more interesting than I had intended, I instantly pretend that it was my idea to begin with."

Claribel Alegría (1924–) Claribel Alegría was born in Esteli, Nicaragua, but grew up in exile in Santa Ana, El Salvador. She came to the United States in 1943, where she was educated at George Washington University. She then lived in Mexico, Chile, Uruguay, and Spain before returning to Nicaragua in 1979. A novelist and essayist as well as a poet, Alegrí has published poetry since 1948. Her collections include *Sobrevivo* [I Survive] (1978), *Flores del volcan/ Flowers from the Volcano* (1982), *Mujer del rio / Woman of the River* (1988), and *Fugues* (1993).*

Nazik al-Mala'ika (1923–1992) Born into a family of poets, Nazik al-Mala'ika was educated in her native Iraq at Higher Teachers' College in Baghdad. Though her primary interest was in Arabic studies, she also read French and English, and her early poems included translations and rewritings of the English Romantics. She published seven volumes of her own poetry, several books of criticism on Arabic poetry, and feminist social criticism. She also taught Arabic literature at universities in Iraq and Kuwait.

Maya Angelou (1928–) Maya Angelou, originally Marguerite Johnson, was born in St. Louis, Missouri, and grew up in Stamps, Arkansas. While still in her teens, she was

---

*Titles in Spanish and English separated by a slash indicate a book has parallel texts in both languages.

waitress, cook, streetcar conductor, madam, and unwed mother. Her studies of music, dance, and drama blossomed into a successful career in the theater, which continued even as she became a writer. Known both for and through her autobiographical novels, Angelou is also a poet, playwright, screen producer, director, university teacher, and civil rights activist. Her books of poetry include *Oh Pray My Wings Are Gonna Fit Me Well* (1975), *Shaker, Why Don't You Sing?* (1983), *I Shall Not Be Moved* (1990), and *The Complete Poems of Maya Angelou* (1994).

Margaret Atwood (1939–) Born in Ottawa, Ontario, Margaret Atwood wrote fiction and poetry even as a young child. She was educated at the University of Toronto, Radcliffe, and Harvard, and she has taught and lectured widely, gaining a reputation as a strong champion of Canadian literature. Her own works include short story collections, novels, and many volumes of poetry, among them *Double Persephone* (1961), *Power Politics* (1971), *Marsh Hawk* (1977), and *Selected Poems II* (1987).

W. H. Auden (1907–1973) Wystan Hugh Auden was born in York, England, and educated at Oxford University. Although he was involved in the Marxist left and fought on the loyalist side in the Spanish Civil War as a young man, his political ideologies varied throughout his life. He emigrated to America in 1939 and became a citizen some years later. He taught at many colleges and was poet, playwright, librettist, editor, critic, anthologist, and translator. His works of poetry include *Selected Poems* (1938), the Pulitzer Prize-winning *The Age of Anxiety* (1947), *About the House* (1965), and *Thank You Fog: Last Poems* (1974).

Jimmy Santiago Baca (1952–) Jimmy Santiago Baca was born of Chicano and Apache heritage. Both his parents abandoned him before he was two and had died before he was six. After living in an orphanage, he fled at age 11 to a life on the street, where he came to abuse drugs and alcohol. Later incarcerated in an Arizona prison, he endured isolation and shock treatment but also taught himself to read and write. His first poems were published before he was released. He eventually settled on a small farm in New Mexico. His books of poetry include *Immigrants in Our Own Land* (1979), *Swords of Darkness* (1981), *Poems Taken from My Yard* (1986), and *Black Mesa Poems* (1989).

T. M. Baker (1946–) Of Choctaw, Cherokee, and Irish descent, Terri M. Baker is a member of the Choctaw nation. She was born and grew up in Durant, Oklahoma, where her family owned a cafe—a lively center for talk, storytelling, and laughter. She was educated at Southeastern State College, Oklahoma State University, the University of Utah, and Louisiana State University. She is a professor, a consultant to museums, the originator of video and drama presentations, and the author of both nonfiction and poetry. A mild physical disability and her experiences as a woman and a Native American have also involved her in many advocacy roles. Her poems have been published in literary journals.

Amiri Baraka (1934–) Born Everett Leroi Jones, Baraka was raised in a middle-class family in Newark, New Jersey. He was educated at Rutgers, Howard, and Columbia universities, and the New School for Social Research. He was involved in the Beat movement in poetry in the 1950s; in the 1960s he espoused militant black nationalism and changed his name as part of this conversion to the Muslim faith. Later aligning more with Marxism and calling himself a "Third World socialist," Baraka has remained a social and political leader as well as a prolific poet, playwright, and essayist. His poetry collections include *Preface to a Twenty Volume Suicide Note* (1961), *The Dead Lecturer* (1964), *Black Magic* (1969), and *Reggae or Not!* (1982).

Lynne Barrett (b. 1950s) Lynne Barrett grew up in New Jersey, where many of her stories are set. She was educated at Mount Holyoke College and the University of

North Carolina. Barrett has worked as a journalist, bank clerk, secretary, and singer, and now teaches creative writing at Florida International University. Barrett's short stories have appeared in magazines and several anthologies, including *Mondo Barbie* and *The King is Dead*. She has won the Edgar Award from the Mystery Writers of America and has been a Fellow of the National Endowment for the Arts. The story "Inventory" was published in Barrett's collection of short stories, *The Land of Go*.

Donald Barthelme (1931–1989) Donald Barthelme, who worked as a reporter, university publications writer, editor, art museum director, and professor, said about his work: "I try to avoid saying anything directly and just hope that something emerges from what has been written." By the age of 32 Barthelme had published four stories in the *New Yorker*, which over the years became closely identified with and influenced by his work. His works include *City Life* (1970), a short story collection; *The Dead Father* (1975), a novel; and *Amateurs* (1976). The year 1981 was a turning point in his career and the critical reception of his work with the publication of *Sixty Stories*. A contributor to several periodicals and anthologies, Barthelme was the recipient of a Guggenheim Fellowship and the National Book Award.

Ambrose Bierce (1842–1913) Ambrose Bierce was the last of nine children born into an impoverished, strongly religious farm family in Ohio. His only formal schooling consisted of one year at a military academy in Kentucky, after which he volunteered for the Civil War. Some of his best fiction, for example the stories in *Tales of Soldiers and Civilians* (1891), was based on his war experience. After the war he moved to San Francisco where he wrote for and later edited the *News Letter*. In 1872 he married and moved to England where his satirical attitude earned him the nickname "Bitter Bierce." Bierce regarded the novel as "a short story padded" and preferred shorter lengths for his writing. In 1913, after a series of personal disasters—divorce, the deaths of his two sons—he went to Mexico and disappeared without a trace

Elizabeth Bishop (1911–1979) Born in Worcester, Massachusetts, Elizabeth Bishop was raised by her grandparents after her father's death and her mother's mental breakdown. She was educated at Vassar and planned a medical career, but was convinced by poet Marianne Moore to write poetry instead. Bishop lived for some years in Florida and later in Brazil, but she returned to the United States in 1966. She taught at the University of Washington and then at Harvard. Volumes of her poetry include *Poems: North and South* (1956); *A Cold Spring* (1956), for which she won a Pulitzer Prize; *Questions of Travel* (1965); *The Ballad of the Burglar of Babylon* (1968); and *Geography III, 1976* (1976).

William Blake (1757–1827) William Blake was born in London. He had little formal education, and was apprenticed at age 14 to an engraver. At the age of 25 he married Catherine Boucher, whom he taught to read and write. His first poetry collection was published with the help of friends, but he never made a substantial amount of money from his poetry and endured extreme poverty at times. His poems—mystical and mythical in nature—were often elaborately illustrated with his hand-colored engravings. Among his works are *Poetical Sketches* (1783), *Songs of Innocence* (1789), *The Marriage of Heaven and Hell* (1790), and *Songs of Experience* (1794).

Louise Bogan (1897–1970) Louise Bogan was born in Livermore Falls, Maine, and educated at Boston University. She taught at several universities in the United States and Austria. A poet and critic, she was poetry editor of the *New Yorker* magazine for 38 years. Her volumes of poetry include *Body of This Death* (1923), *The Sleeping Fury* (1937), *Collected Poems* 1923–1953 (1954), and *The Blue Estuaries* (1968).

Jorge Luis Borges (1899–1986) Born in Buenos Aires, Argentina, Borges was educated in Switzerland as a teenager. After living in Switzerland, he moved to Spain, where he joined the Ultraists, a group of experimental poets. He returned to Argentina in 1921, and in the 1940s two collections of his best short fiction were published: *Ficciones* (1944) and *El Aleph* (1949). Also a prolific writer of essays and poems, Borges was awarded the Formentor Prize, an international award, in 1961. This award brought his work to the attention of the larger public and translations of his stories began appearing. He became a popular lecturer and teacher around the world. Considered by some critics to be the father of a strong "magic realist" strain in modern fiction, Borges once likened the writing of fiction to a game of chess.

Anne Bradstreet (c. 1612–1672) Born in England and married at age 16, Anne Bradstreet sailed to America at 18. She wrote her poems while raising eight children in the Massachusetts Bay Colony and hers was the first volume of original poetry ever printed in the colonies. Her works include *The Tenth Muse* (1650) and a posthumous collection published in 1678.

Gwendolyn Brooks (1917–) Born in Topeka, Kansas, Gwendolyn Brooks grew up in Chicago and was educated at Wilson Junior College. As a child she published poems in a children's magazine and a city newspaper. She was the first African American to win the Pulitzer Prize, and she became the poet laureate of Illinois. Also a novelist, she has taught at many colleges and universities and has actively supported young African-American poets and writers. Her many works of poetry include *A Street in Bronzeville* (1945), the Pulitzer winner *Annie Allen* (1949), *The Bean Eaters* (1960), *To Disembark* (1981), and *Winnie* (1991).

Elizabeth Barrett Browning (1806–1861) Born in Durham, England, Elizabeth Barrett was the oldest of 11 children. She was educated at home by her wealthy father and is said to have read Greek by the age of eight. In early adolescence she was partially disabled by a riding accident. At 40, she was already a well-known poet when she met Robert Browning and eloped with him to Italy. Her *Sonnets from the Portuguese* (1850) are love poems to Robert, who called her "the Portuguese" as a nickname. Other collections include *The Seraphim and Other Poems* (1838) and *Poems* (1844).

Robert Browning (1812–1889) Largely self-educated by intensive reading, Robert Browning published his first poetry collection, *Pauline,* in 1833, but was little known until after his love affair and elopement with Elizabeth Barrett. During their years in Italy, he developed fully the poetic form for which he is best known: the dramatic monologue. After Elizabeth's death, he returned to his native England, where his popularity soared. His works include *Dramatic Lyrics* (1842), *Men and Women* (1855), and *The Ring and the Book* (1868), which is one of the longest poems in English literature.

Robert Buck (1958–) Robert Buck was born in Chandlers Valley, Pennsylvania, and raised there by his grandparents. His grandmother, a gospel songwriter, taught him to read by age three and to play piano and guitar by the time he was five. Always an avid reader, Buck was educated at Jamestown Community College and the University of Cincinnati, later working on archaeological digs while playing guitar at night. At Jamestown he formed with friends the band that was to be called 10,000 Maniacs. As a songwriter, Buck often collaborates informally with other band members. Albums by 10,000 Maniacs include *Secrets of the I Ching* (1983), *The Wishing Chair* (1986), *In My Tribe* (1987), and *Our Time In Eden* (1992).

Robert Burns (1759–1796) Robert Burns was born to poor tenant farmers in Alloway, Scotland, and his early life was steeped in traditional ballads and songs. To finance his emigration to Jamaica where he hoped to make a living as an overseer, he published

Poems Chiefly in the Scottish Dialect (1786), and its success enabled him to stay in Scotland. When his popularity waned, he went back to farming, then became a tax official before his death at 37.

Luis Cabalquinto (1935–) Luis Cabalquinto was born in Magarao, Philippines. He attended a Jesuit school, and first learned to write in English, but now also writes in Bikolano and Tagalog. He was educated at the University of the Philippines in Manila, at Cornell University, and at New York University, and taught for many years at the University of the Philippines in Los Baños. He settled in the United States in 1968. He is an editor, short-story writer, and novelist as well as a poet. His volumes of poetry include *The Dog Eater and Other Poems* (1989), *The Ibalon Collection* (1991), and *Dreamwanderer* (1992).

Lewis Carroll (1832–1898) Charles Lutwidge Dodson was the son of an English churchman. The eldest of 11 children, he was recognized early as being extremely intelligent and witty. He was educated at Oxford, and there became a lecturer in mathematics, publishing many scholarly treatises. He was also a deacon of the Church of England, but he never went into the priesthood, possibly due to a stammer. A bachelor who rarely left Oxford but who entertained a great deal, he used the name Lewis Carroll to publish the "nonsense" fiction he'd written for a friend's daughter: *Alice in Wonderland* (1865) and *Through the Looking Glass* (1871).

Angela Carter (1940–1992) Angela Carter was born in London and graduated from the University of Bristol. Her first novel, *Shadow Dance,* appeared in 1965, followed by *Honeybuzzard* (1967), *Love* (1971), *The Bloody Chamber* (1979)—which geared fairy tales toward an adult audience—*Nights at the Circus* (1985), and *Old Wives' Fairy Tale Book* (1990). Carter also wrote juvenile literature, poetry, screenplays, radio scripts, and many types of fiction, ranging from fantasy to realistic. When questioned about the fantasy element in her work, she explained: "I have always felt that one person's fantasy is another person's everyday life. It has its own logic as well. I got more and more into it as I got older, because it's a genre with its own rigorous logic."

Raymond Carver (1938–1988) Raymond Carver was born the son of a laborer in Oregon. Just after high school, he married and became the father of two children. Despite the difficulty of supporting a family while attending school, he received a degree in 1963 from Humboldt State University and a M.F.A. in 1966 from the University of Iowa. *Near Klamath* (1968), a collection of poems, was his first published book. Collections of his short stories, such as *Will You Please be Quiet, Please?* (1977) and *Cathedral* (1984), were published some years later. Carver's stories are mainly set in his native Pacific Northwest and are admired for their understanding of poor working people. But Carver once said, "I never felt the people I was writing about were so bad off." He was inducted into the American Academy and Institute of Arts and Letters in 1988 and was nominated for the Pulitzer Prize for fiction in 1989 for *Where I'm Calling From* (1988), a volume of new and collected stories. Recently, Carver has been described by some critics as a contemporary master of the short story.

Rosario Castellanos (1925–1974) Rosario Castellanos, one of Mexico's leading feminists, was raised by a nursemaid who introduced her to the world of Indian myth and legend. Castellanos later attended the National University of Mexico, from which she graduated in 1950 with a degree in philosophy. While in school she became a member of a group whose goal was to rediscover humanism. Her first book of poems, *Notes for a Declaration of Faith*, appeared in 1948. Her first novel, *The Nine Guardians*, was translated into English in 1959. Castellanos served as director for the state of Chiapas and later taught at several universities. In 1971, she became the Mexican ambassador to Israel. Two of her books have recently been translated into

English: *Another Way to Be: Selected Works of Rosario Castellanos* (1990) and *The City of Kings* (1992).

Rosemary Catacalos (1944–) Born into a Greek-Mexican family, Rosemary Catacalos grew up in San Antonio, Texas. She has worked as a copywriter, arts publicist, and newspaper reporter. Catacalos has also taught bilingual poetry workshops in the Arizona, Arkansas, and Texas schools and edited over 30 anthologies of students' work. Her bilingual poetry includes the collection *Again for the First Time* (1984).

Lorna Dee Cervantes (1954–) Born in San Francisco into a working-class Mexican-American family, Lorna Dee Cervantes began writing poetry by the age of eight. After a childhood made difficult by divorce and poverty, she became active in Chicano/Chicana community affairs—as a member of a theater group, an organizer of a cultural center, and the founder of a small press. Her poetry includes the collection *Emplumada* (1981).

Tracy Chapman (1964–) Tracy Chapman was born in Cleveland and educated at Tufts University, where she majored in anthropology. She is a singer, songwriter, and composer, and plays the ukelele, organ, clarinet, and guitar. She has received Grammy awards for best new artist, best female pop vocal performance, and best contemporary folk performance. Her releases include *Tracy Chapman* (1988), *Crossroads* (1989), and *Matters of the Heart* (1992).

John Cheever (1912–1982) John Cheever was expelled from the Thayer Academy at the age of 17 for smoking and laziness. Shortly after, his first story, "Expelled," was published. His first collection of short stories, *The Way Some People Live*, appeared in 1943. Next came *The Enormous Radio and Other Stories* (1953), a collection containing "Goodbye, My Brother" and "The Enormous Radio," both of which critics rank with the best short fiction of this century. "The Swimmer," a story Cheever claims took him many times longer than his normal three-day gestation period to write, is included in another of his collections, *The Brigadier and the Golf Widow* (1964). Cheever, whose stories examined suburbia, remained a private, professional writer throughout his life, seemingly unaffected by the experiments or trends of the fiction-writing world.

Kawai Chigetsu-Ni (1632–1736) Little is written about Kawai Chigetsu-Ni, except that she was a Japanese writer of the seventeenth century.

Chin Woon Ping (1945–) Born in Malacca, Malaysia, Chin Woon Ping lived in Indonesia, Singapore, and China before settling in the United States, where she has taught at several colleges. She has published a performance piece and translated Malaysian aboriginal myths, as well as writing poetry that includes the collection *The Naturalization of Camellia Song* (1993).

Kate Chopin (1851–1904) Kate Chopin asserted her independence early in life by smoking in company and being seen on the streets without a companion, both daring acts for the time. Her major work, *The Awakening* (1899), created a scandal. Critics described it as "trite and sordid," "essentially vulgar," and "unhealthily introspective and morbid and feeling." But now both the book and the author have an honored place in American literary history, Chopin's sexually frank stories having been rediscovered in the 1960s and 1970s. Some of her other works are *At Fault* (1890), *Bayou Folk* (1894), and over 150 stories and sketches. Chopin wrote on a lapboard, surrounded by her six children, claiming she was "completely at the mercy of unconscious selection."

Carolyn Chute (1947–) As a young girl growing up Maine, Carolyn Chute enjoyed writing stories but never dreamed about becoming a writer: "I didn't think of a writer as something you grew up to be. It wasn't a thing I could aspire to. I didn't know any writers. Folks never had any books in their houses." At 16 she dropped out of school to get married. Three years later she was divorced and struggling to support her first child while working toward a diploma. Eventually, she remarried and began writing her first novel, *The Beans of Egypt, Maine* (1985), after the death of her second child. Her husband, a "mountain man" who'd never learned to read or write, listened to her work as she read it aloud and made suggestions, making the novel a collaborative effort. In 1988, she completed a second novel, *Metal Man.* Several of her short stories have appeared in anthologies and periodicals.

Sandra Cisneros (1954–) Born in Chicago, Sandra Cisneros spent her childhood years traveling back and forth from the United States to her family's home in Mexico City. She began writing at the age of 10 and attended the University of Iowa Workshop in the late 1970s. Later she received her B.A. in English from Loyola University. One of the few Chicana writers trained in a formal creative writing program, Cisneros' first book of poetry, *Bad Boys*, appeared in 1980. In 1983, her young adult novel *The House on Mango Street* was published, earning her the American Book Award from the Before Columbus Foundation in 1985. Some of her other works are *The Rodrigo Poems* (1985), *My Wicked, Wicked Ways* (1987), and *Woman Hollering Creek & Other Stories* (1991), a rare example of a Chicana writer being published by a mainstream press (Random House).

Michelle Cliff (1946–) Born in Kingston, Jamaica, Michelle Cliff attended Wagner College and the Warburg Institute in London. Since college, she has worked as a reporter, researcher, and editor and has taught at several colleges and universities. Her interests include black history and visual art, especially the art of the Italian Renaissance and of African-American women. The recipient of several awards and fellowships, Cliff has written a collection of poems, *Claiming an Identity They Taught Me to Despise* (1980); a collection of poems and prose, *Abeng* (1984); and a novel, *The Land of Look Behind* (1985). Her latest work is *Free Enterprise* (1993). Several of her works have also appeared in anthologies.

Lucille Clifton (1936–) Born in Depew, New York, and educated at Howard University, Lucille Clifton was a claims clerk in the New York state government and literary assistant to the federal Office of Education before her award-winning poetry enabled her to turn to full-time writing and teaching. She was poet laureate of Maryland from 1979–1982; she later settled in California. She has published many children's books as well as her works of poetry, which include *Good Times* (1969), *An Ordinary Woman* (1974), *Next: New Poems* (1987), and *The Book of Light* (1993).

Judith Ortiz Cofer (1952–) Judith Ortiz Cofer was born in Puerto Rico but immigrated to the United States in 1956. She earned degrees from Augusta College and Florida Atlantic University and attended Oxford University in 1977. Her early works, *Latin Women Pray* (1980) and *The Native Dancer* (1981), were distributed in pamphlet form. Her later works include *Peregrina* (1986) and *Terms of Survival* (1987), both books of poems; *The Line of the Sun* (1989), a novel; and *Silent Dancing* (1990), a collection of personal essays. Cofer, who has been a bilingual instructor as well as a teacher of English and a member of several writers' conference staffs, made this remark about language: "The 'infinite variety' and power of language interest me. I never cease to experiment with it." Her most recent work is *The Latin Deli: Prose and Poetry* (1993).

Samuel Taylor Coleridge (1772–1834) Samuel Taylor Coleridge was the thirteenth child of a clergyman. He was born in Devonshire, England, and educated at Cambridge University. An idealist who was fascinated with the supernatural, he once had an abortive plan to start a Utopian community in America. In 1795 he met William Wordsworth, and the two friends collaborated on *Lyrical Ballads* (1798). Coleridge also wrote literary criticism and theory. Prescribed opium for rheumatism, by 1802 he had become thoroughly addicted. From 1816 on, he lived in London under the care of a doctor. *Aids to Reflection* was published in 1848.

Julio Cortázar (1914–1984) Argentinean fiction writer Julio Cortázar was born in Belgium and at the age of four moved with his family to Buenos Aires, where he was brought up by his sister in the suburbs. While attending the Universidad De Buenos Aires, he joined a small group of literary-minded friends and began writing. His first collection of short stories, *Bestiario*, was published in 1951, the same year of his self-exile to France. His novel *The Winners* was translated in 1965 and was followed by *Hopscotch* in 1966. An experimental work, *Hopscotch* not only established his importance as a novelist but also paved the way for the United States acceptance of other Latin American novels. Influenced by Kafka, Cortázar was a writer who was constantly experimenting.

Stephen Crane (1871–1900) Stephen Crane was born the youngest of 14 children into a religious family. After flunking out of Lafayette College and Syracuse University, he moved to New York City in 1891. Shortly after, he began to write for newspapers as a free-lance journalist, a job which inspired the book *Maggie: A Girl of the Streets* (1893). At age 24, he published his best-known work, *The Red Badge of Courage*, which earned him an international reputation. Despite his ill health (he suffered from tuberculosis), Crane traveled widely and was a correspondent in the Greek-Turkish War and the Spanish American War. Crane once said to an editor, "After all, I cannot help vanishing and disappearing and dissolving. It is my foremost trait." Crane succumbed to tuberculosis at age 29.

Robert Creeley (1926–) Robert Creeley was born in Arlington, Massachusetts, and educated at Harvard, Black Mountain College, and the University of New Mexico. He was an ambulance driver in India and Burma during World War II, and then lived for a time in France and Spain. After returning to the United States, he taught at Black Mountain College and founded the *Black Mountain Review*. He has since taught at many American and Canadian colleges. His books of poetry include *Le Fou* (1952), *Words* (1967), *Kitchen* (1973), *Echoes* (1982), and *Have A Heart* (1990).

Steve Crow (1949–) Stephen Monroe Crow was born in Birmingham, Alabama, and educated at Louisiana State University, Bowling Green (Ohio) State University, and the University of Michigan. He has taught at universities in Ohio, Michigan, and Minnesota, and is a speaker on Native American issues and poetry. His own poems have been published in anthologies and journals.

Countee Cullen (1903–1946) Countee (pronounced "countay") Leroy Cullen was born in Louisville, Kentucky. He was educated at New York University and Harvard, and became a major figure in the flowering of African-American arts known as the Harlem Renaissance. He was not only a poet, but also an editor, columnist, novelist, and children's author. Cullen published most of his poetry from 1925 to 1929, after which he turned to teaching high school. Toward the end of his life he also wrote plays. His volumes of poetry include *Color* (1925), *Copper Sun* (1927), *The Black Christ and Other Poems* (1929), and *On These I Stand* (1947).

e. e. cummings (1894–1962) Edward Estlin Cummings was born in Cambridge, Massachusetts, the son of a minister. He decided as a child to become a poet, and began at age eight to write a poem a day, a practice he kept up until he was twenty-two. He was educated at Harvard, drove an ambulance during World War I, was briefly a prisoner of war, and then spent some years in Paris studying art—he was a talented painter. His first poetry was published in 1923, garnering mixed reactions to his unorthodox use of language, punctuation, and capitalization. Cummings also wrote novels, essays, plays, and a ballet. His poetry collections include *Tulips and Chimneys* (1923), *No Thanks* (1935), *1 x 1* (1944), and *Poems, 1923–1954* (1954).

Mahmoud Darwish (1942–) Mahmoud Darwish was born in al-Birwa, Palestine, the son of a wealthy farmer and landowner. When he was six, his village was destroyed during the creation of the state of Israel and his father was put to work in a quarry. From an early age, Darwish wrote poetry that caused confrontations with the Israeli military rule, and from 1965 to 1969 he was jailed several times. From 1972 to 1982 he was an editor in Beirut, and later moved to Paris. He won the Lenin Peace Prize in 1983. He has remained active in the Palestinian cause and published many volumes of poetry, including *Sparrows Without Wings* (1960), *Sparrows Die in Galilee* (1970), *Lesser Roses* (1986), and *From Beirut* (1993).

Kamala Das (1934–) Kamala Das was born in the district of Malabar, India (now part of the state of Kerala). Her mother was a poet; her father, an editor; and Das was educated privately. Besides writing poetry, novels, and stories, she has been involved in forestry, environmental protection, and children's film. In 1984, she ran as an independent candidate for the Indian parliament. Her poetry collections include *Summer in Calcutta: Fifty Poems* (1965), *The Descendants* (1967), *The Old Playhouse and Other Poems* (1973), and *Collected Poems* (1984).

Mark DeFoe (1942–) Mark DeFoe was born in Enid, Oklahoma, and grew up as an "Air Force brat" in Texas, Oklahoma, Kansas, and Colorado. His storytelling mother and his fiddlle-playing grandfather were both strong childhood influences. He was educated at Oklahoma State University and the University of Denver, and settled in the Appalachian town of Buckhannon, West Virginia. DeFoe is a college professor who writes essays and occasional free-lance travel pieces as well as poetry. His poetry collections include *Bringing Home Breakfast* (1982) and *Palmate* (1988).

Abelardo Delgado (1931–) Abelardo Delgado was born in La Boquilla de Conchos, Chihuahua, Mexico, the son of a cattle rancher. He came to the United States as a boy and was educated at the University of Texas and the University of Utah. He held construction and restaurant jobs, and later became involved in both education and migrant affairs. He writes poetry, essays, novels, and short stories, has his own small publishing house, and is known for his dramatic poetry readings. His collections include *Twenty-five Pieces of a Chicano Mind* (1969), *A Thermos Bottle Full of Self-Pity: Twenty-five Bottles of Abelardo* (1975), and *Unos perros con metralla [Some Dogs with a Machine Gun]: Twenty-five Dogs of Abelardo* (1982).

Emily Dickinson (1830–1886) Emily Dickinson was born in Amherst, Massachusetts, and lived there all her life, save for one trip to Washington, D. C., and a brief attempt at college. She grew increasingly reclusive, rarely venturing out or accepting visitors. She wrote nearly 1,800 poems but published only seven. The others were found in an attic trunk after her death. Though several collections were then published, they contained rewritings of Dickinson's work. The definitive edition *Poems,* edited by Thomas H. Johnson, did not appear until 1955.

Annie Dillard (1945–) Annie Dillard grew up in Pittsburgh, Pennsylvania, a member of a wealthy family in a country club and private school milieu. She began writing poetry and fiction in high school and went on to earn B.A. and M.A. degrees in English at Hollins College. Her first publication, a small book of poems titled *Tickets for a Prayer Wheel*, appeared in 1974. But her first significant publication was *Pilgrim at Tinker Creek* (1974), for which she won the Pulitzer Prize (general nonfiction) in 1975, at the age of 29. Dillard teaches and is a member of the usage panel for the American Heritage Dictionary. Her other works include *Holy the Firm* (1978), *Living by Fiction*

(1982), *Teaching a Stone to Talk: Expeditions and Encounters* (1982), *An American Childhood* (1987), and *The Living*, a western novel published in 1992.

John Donne (1572–1631) Born in London and educated at Oxford, John Donne held a secretarial post in the court of Queen Elizabeth I. During those years he wrote love poems, but in 1601 he was dismissed for marrying Anne More without her family's consent and experienced a period of poverty. In 1615, at the urging of King James, Donne entered the Anglican ministry, later serving as dean of St. Paul's Cathedral in London. He wrote his religious poems during this time. His works include *Songs and Sonets* (1609), *The First Anniversary* (1611), *The Second Anniversary* (1612), and *Poems* (1633).

H. D. (1886–1961) Hilda Doolittle was born in Bethlehem, Pennsylvania, the daughter of a professor. She attended Bryn Mawr College for two years but suffered a nervous collapse. In 1911 she moved to London. The poet Ezra Pound was instrumental in getting her first poems published. She married, but her marriage deteriorated during World War I. She later met the wealthy Englishwoman Winifred Ellerman, who became her lover and lifelong friend. H.D. translated Greek literature, wrote several novels, and published many works of poetry, including *Sea Garden* (1916), *Collected Poems* (1925), *The Walls Do Not Fall* (1944), and *Helen in Egypt* (1961).

Rita Dove (1952–) Born in Akron, Ohio, Rita Dove was educated at the University of Ohio and the University of Iowa. She is a novelist, short story writer, and university teacher, as well as a poet. She won the Pulitzer Prize for poetry in 1987, and in 1994 was named poet laureate of the United States, the first African American thus honored. Her poetry collections include *The Yellow House on the Corner* (1980), *Museum* (1983), *Thomas and Beulah* (1986), and *Grace Notes* (1989).

Paul Laurence Dunbar (1872–1906) Paul Laurence Dunbar was born and raised in Dayton, Ohio, the son of former slaves. The lone black in his high school class, he was also class poet and president, and by graduation had published in the city paper and edited a local one. Poverty precluded a law career, and he worked as an elevator operator, editor, and court messenger while he wrote and published poetry. He made a reading tour of England and in 1897 was given a clerkship at the Library of Congress. As his health and his marriage deteriorated, he had a nervous breakdown and drank heavily, dying at the age of 33. His books of poetry include *Oak and Ivy* (1893), *Lyrics of the Hearthside* (1899), *Candle-lightin' Time* (1901), and *Joggin'erlong* (1906).

Richard Eberhart (1904–) Richard Eberhart was born in Austin, Minnesota, and educated at the University of Minnesota, Dartmouth College, Cambridge University in England, and Harvard University. From 1930 to 1931, he served as private tutor to the son of the king of Siam, and he also spent time as a businessman and a naval officer. He published poetry steadily from 1930 on, and taught at colleges and universities all across the United States. He won the Pulitzer Prize in 1966. His poetry collections include *Reading the Spirit* (1936), *Great Praises* (1957), *Poems to Poets* (1976), and *Maine Poems* (1989).

T. S. Eliot (1888–1965) Thomas Stearns Eliot was born in St. Louis, Missouri, and educated at Harvard, but settled in London in 1915. While writing poetry, he worked as a bank clerk, then as an editor. In 1927 he became a British citizen and a member of the Church of England, and his poems increasingly reflected his religious faith. He published his last poetry in 1943, and thereafter wrote verse plays for the London stage. Eliot was awarded a Nobel Prize in 1948. Among his poetic works are *Prufrock and Other Observations* (1917), *The Waste Land* (1922), *Ash Wednesday* (1930), and *Four Quartets* (1943).

Stanley Elkin (1930–) Stanley Elkin, considered by some critics to be a "stand-up literary comedian" and a "black humorist," was born in New York City and earned his

A.B., M.A., and Ph.D. from the University of Illinois. As well as contributing to various anthologies and periodicals, Elkin has written several novels and collections of stories and essays. *The Franchisers*, which was a major breakthrough for Elkin, appeared in 1976. Three of his earlier works—*Boswell: A Modern Comedy* (1964), *Criers and Kibitzers, Kibitzers and Criers* (1966) and *A Bad Man* (1967) were reprinted in 1980. Elkin has taught at several universities and has received many fellowships and grants. He resides in the Midwest, which he considers his true home and to which he always returns.

Ralph Ellison (1914–1994) Ralph Ellison, best known for his novel *Invisible Man* (1952), was born in Oklahoma. He attended the Tuskegee Institute in Alabama from 1933 to 1936 and began to publish short stories in 1939. His early influences included Langston Hughes and Richard Wright. In addition to editing the *Negro Quarterly*, Ellison taught at several colleges and universities. Another of his novels, *Shadows and Acts*, was published in 1964. He won the National Book Award in 1953 and the National Newspaper Publishers' Award Medal of Freedom in 1969. Besides being a writer, Ellison was also an accomplished jazz trumpeter, a free-lance photographer, furniture maker, and an electronic equipment expert.

Louise Erdrich (1954–) Of German-American and Chippewa descent, Louise Erdrich was born in Minnesota but grew up in North Dakota. When she was a child, her father gave her a nickel for every story she wrote, and her mother fashioned book covers from stapled strips of construction paper. Erdrich received degrees from Dartmouth College and Johns Hopkins University, and she has been variously employed as a beet weeder, waitress, psychiatric aide, and construction flag signaler. Her first major work, a collection of poems titled *Jacklight*, was published in 1984. Later her novels *Love Medicine* (1984), for which she received the National Book Critics Circle Award, *The Beet Queen* (1986), *Tracks* (1988), and *The Crown of Columbus* (1991) were published. Her short stories have won two national magazine awards and appear widely in anthologies and several periodicals. She published a second book of poetry, *Baptism of Desire*, in 1989. Erdrich, a member of the Turtle Mountain Band of Chippewa, credits her origin for her success as a storyteller: "People in [Native American] families make everything into a story. I suppose that when you grow up constantly hearing the stories rise, break, and fall, it gets into you somehow." Her latest novel, *The Bingo Palace*, was published in 1994.

Martín Espada (1957–) Martín Espada was born and raised in Brooklyn, New York, of Latino heritage. He was educated at the University of Wisconsin and Northeastern University and held a variety of jobs before becoming a tenant lawyer in Boston. His poetry works include *The Immigrant Iceboy's Bolero* (1982), *Trumpets from the Island of Their Eviction* (1987), *Rebellion Is the Circle of a Lover's Hand* (1990), and *City of Coughing and Dead Radiators* (1993).

Mari Evans Mari Evans was born in Toledo, Ohio, and educated at the University of Toledo. From 1968 to 1973, she was the writer, producer, and director for the Indianapolis TV show *The Black Experience*. Besides writing poetry, she has edited a critical work on black women writers, written plays, and authored books for children and young adults. Her volumes of poetry include *I Am a Black Woman* (1970), *Night Star: 1973–1978* (1980), and *A Dark and Splendid Mass* (1992).

Faiz Ahmed Faiz (1911–1984) Faiz Ahmed Faiz was born in Sialkot, British India, now known as Pakistan. He served in the British Indian Army in World War II, and later helped establish labor unions in his homeland. As editor for the *Pakistani Times* and as a poet writing in Urdu, he became a spokesman for Pakistani and Indian rights. During the turmoil in his country, he spent time in prison but still wrote both lyric and political poetry. Once civilian rule was firmly established, Faiz was asked to create a National Council for the Arts. In 1962 he was awarded the Lenin Peace Prize. English translations of his work, all posthumous, include *The True Subject: Selected Poems of Faiz Ahmed Faiz* (1988) and *The Rebel's Silhouette* (1991).

William Faulkner (1897–1962) William Faulkner dropped out of high school in 1915 and had no formal education beyond a year as a special student at the University of Mississippi. In 1925, he went to New Orleans, where he befriended Sherwood Anderson, another writer, who encouraged him to focus on and develop his own style. Faulkner wrote his first novel, *Soldier's Pay* (1926), while in New Orleans. Faulkner set most of his stories and novels in his fictional Yoknapatawpha County, which was based on the area around his hometown of Oxford, Mississippi. He wrote nearly 100 short stories and 19 novels, which include *The Sound and the Fury* (1929), *As I Lay Dying* (1930), *Light in August* (1932), *Absalom, Absalom!* (1936), and *The Reivers* (1962). Faulkner was awarded the 1949 Nobel Prize for Literature; in 1955 and 1963, he received Pulitzer Prizes for fiction. In an acceptance speech he said, "It is [the poet's, the writer's] privilege to help man endure by lifting his heart, by reminding him of the courage and honor and hope and pride and compassion and pity and sacrifice which have been the glory of his past."

Lawrence Ferlinghetti (1919–) Born in Yonkers, New York, Lawrence Ferling survived his father's death, his mother's collapse, the divorce of his custodial aunt and uncle, four years in France with the aunt, and a stint in an orphanage before he was taken in by a wealthy family. He attended the University of North Carolina, Columbia University, and the Sorbonne, and served in the Navy in World War II. In the 1950s he discovered and resumed the original Italian family name, and as Ferlinghetti was a central figure in the Beat movement, founding the City Lights bookstore and press in San Francisco. His books of poetry include *A Coney Island of the Mind* (1958), *Christ Climbed Down* (1965), *Open Eye, Open Heart* (1973), and *When I Look at Pictures* (1990).

John Finlay (1941–1991) John Finlay was born in Ozark, Alabama, and grew up on his parents' peanut and dairy farm in Enterprise, where he named the cows after Greek goddesses and recited Shakespeare to them. He was educated at the University of Alabama and at Louisiana State University and taught for four years at the University of Montevallo. He converted to Catholicism in 1980 and was aware as early as 1981 that he had the virus that causes AIDS. It was during his final decade, while living again on the family farm, that he wrote most of his essays and his best-known poems. His books of poetry include *The Wide Porch and Other Poems* (1984) and *Mind and Blood: The Collected Poems of John Finlay* (1992).

F. Scott Fitzgerald (1896–1940) F. Scott Fitzerald, born in Minnesota, attended Princeton University, but left before graduating to join the army as a second lieutenant during World War I. His first novel, *This Side of Paradise* (1920), was one of the earliest examples of a novel about college life and became an immediate best-seller, making Fitzgerald a celebrity at age 24. The 1920s brought a rapid rise to fame for him, when in fiction he became the voice of the Jazz Age. In 1921 and 1922, two collections of his short stories appeared, *Flappers & Philosophers* and *Tales of the Jazz Age*. He published *The Great Gatsby* in 1925. *Tender is the Night* appeared in 1934. Fitzgerald married, and he and his wife lived a lavish lifestyle of parties and travel, spending more money than he made. His stories of the recklessness of the 1920s lost their popularity during the Great Depression. Fitzgerald's life slowly unraveled under the strain of his alcoholism and his wife's mental illness. He died of a heart attack at age 44.

Carolyn Forché (1950–) Born in Detroit, Carolyn Forché was writing poems by the age of nine. She was educated at Michigan State University and Bowling Green University in Ohio, and worked as a journalist in El Salvador from 1978 to 1980. She reported on human rights conditions to Amnesty International and became—in her poetry and in her public life—a human rights activist. She has also worked in Lebanon for National Public Radio, and has lectured, read, and taught at many colleges and universities. Her books of poetry include *Gathering the Tribes* (1976), *The Country Between Us* (1981), and *The Angel of History* (1994).

Mary E. Wilkins Freeman (1852–1930) Mary E. Wilkins Freeman, born in a small Massachusetts town, was the daughter of strict orthodox Congregationalist parents. Her siblings died at young ages, and Freeman was a weak child. She attended Mt. Holyoke Female Seminary, where Emily Dickinson had gone, and left after only one year, as Dickinson had. Later her formal education was completed at West Brattleboro Seminary. Her works include two collections of short stories, *A Humble Romance* (1887) and *A New England Nun and Other Stories* (1891) and two novels, *Pembroke* (1894) and *The Shoulders of Atlas* (1908). In 1926 she was awarded the W. D. Howells medal for fiction by the American Academy of Arts and Letters. Freeman is best known for her depiction of New England village life.

Robert Frost (1874–1963) Robert Frost was born in San Francisco and moved to Massachusetts at age 11 when his father died. He briefly attended Harvard and Dartmouth, then married, had four children, and spent 20 years in a variety of nonliterary jobs. His poetry had been rejected by American publishers when he took his family to England and published his first two volumes there in 1913 and 1914. By the time he returned to the United States and settled on a farm in New Hampshire, he was recognized as a poet in America. He later won Pulitzer Prizes in 1924, 1931, 1937, and 1943. His collections include *North of Boston* (1914), *New Hampshire* (1923), *West-Running Brook* (1928), *A Further Range* (1936), and *In the Clearing* (1962).

Charlotte Perkins Gilman (1860–1935) Charlotte Perkins Gilman, a leading feminist theoretician and writer of her time, was born in Connecticut. Her father, a nephew of Harriet Beecher Stowe, abandoned the family when Gilman was a young child. She was raised mostly by her mother, who purposely withheld all affection in order to prepare her children for the thorny life ahead of them. Although Gilman suffered from often extended depressions all her life, she managed to write several nonfiction works concerning women's economic independence and social equality and three Utopian feminist novels, including *Herland* (1915). The publication of *Women and Economics* in 1898 brought her immediate celebrity. In 1935, suffering from breast cancer and mourning the death of her second husband, Gilman committed suicide with chloroform.

Allen Ginsberg (1926–) Allen Ginsberg was born in Newark, New Jersey, and educated at Columbia University. After pleading insanity to avoid prosecution for harboring a friend's stolen goods, he spent eight months in a psychiatric institute. He then worked odd jobs and moved to San Francisco, where he became a central figure in the Beat movement of the 1950s. He was strongly drawn to mystical experiences, first through experimentation with drugs and later through yoga and meditation. A political activist and outspoken homosexual, he was arrested several times during the 1960s. He later settled on a farm in New Jersey. Among his works are *Howl and Other Poems* (1956), *Mind Breaths* (1978), *Many Loves* (1984), and *Snapshot Poetics* (1993).

Nikki Giovanni (1943–) Yolande Cornelia Giovanni was born in Knoxville, Tennessee, the daughter of a probation officer and a social worker. She grew up near Cincinnati but spent several summers with her grandmother in Knoxville. She was educated at Fisk, the University of Pennsylvania, and Columbia, and in the 1960s was a political and literary leader among her peers, advocating revolutionary social change. She has remained active in social causes while establishing her own publishing firm and teaching at several universities. Her poetry includes acclaimed volumes for children. Some of her titles are *Black Feeling, Black Talk/Black Judgement* (1968), *My House* (1972), *Cotton Candy on a Rainy Day* (1978), and *Knoxville, Tennessee* (1994).

Susan Glaspell (1882–1948) Susan Glaspell, founder along with her husband, George Cram Cook, of the Provincetown Playhouse, was born in Iowa. She attended Drake University and the University of Chicago and, after a brief career as a journalist in Des Moines, began writing and producing plays. Some of her works include *Trifles* (1916), which she later rewrote as a short story, "A Jury of Her Peers," *A Woman's Honor* (1918), *The Verge* (1921), and the Pulitzer Prize winning *Allison's House* (1930), which was loosely based on Emily Dickinson and her family. She also wrote two novels: *Fidelity* (1915) and *The Morning Is Near Us* (1939). According to Glaspell, *Trifles* was written in one afternoon, as she stared at the empty stage: "After a time, the stage became a kitchen—a kitchen there all by itself."

Emma Goldman (1869–1940) Emma Goldman emigrated in 1885 from Russia to Rochester, New York. In 1906, she founded the magazine *Mother Earth*, which became an outlet for radical political, philosophical, and literary expression. In 1911, she published *Anarchism and Other Essays*, followed in 1914 by *The Social Significance of Modern Drama*, in which she explored the importance of modern drama through the plays of Ibsen, Strindberg, and Shaw. A Russian socialist, Goldman was arrested several times and in 1917 spent two years in jail for opposing the United States military. Upon her release, she was deported to Russia, where she wrote two controversial books: *My Disillusionment in Russia* (1923) and *My Further Disillusionment in Russia* (1924). H. L. Mencken regarded her as "one of the most notable women now extant upon this planet."

Rafael Jesús González (1935–   ) Born and raised in the bilingual and bicultural community of El Paso, Texas, Rafael Jesús González was educated at the University of Texas, Universidad Nacional Autonoma de Mexico, and the University of Oregon. He later settled in California. He is a painter, sculptor, and installation artist, a college professor, and the author of short stories, essays, and scholarly articles. His poems have been widely published in reviews and anthologies as well as in the collection *El hacedor del juegos/The Maker of Games* (1977).

Nadine Gordimer (1923–   ) Nadine Gordimer, a South African short story writer and novelist, began writing at the age of nine, and just six years later published her first story. She attended private schools and later the University of Witwatersrand. Her first collection of short stories, *Face to Face,* was published in 1949. Her first novel, *The Lying Days*, appeared in 1953. Another novel, *Occasion for Loving*, appeared in 1963, and two years later she published another collection of short stories, *Not for Publication.* Another novel, *Burger's Daughter* (1980), brought her worldwide acclaim. Gordimer has won several awards and is an honorary member of the American Academy of Arts & Letters. She claims her fiction focuses on the lives of white, middle-class people— "a terrified white consciousness in the midst of a mysterious and ominous sea of black humanity." Her latest book is *No One to Accompany Me.*

Ronald Gross (1935–   ) Ronald Gross was born in New York City and educated at Syracuse University, but later renounced his degree, believing that credentials are not reliable marks of accomplishment. He considers himself self-educated. His primary career has been as an independent writer, activist, consultant, and teacher in the field of lifelong learning and noninstitutional education. He published "found" poetry in the collection *Pop Poems* (1967).

Woody Guthrie (1912–1967) Woodrow Wilson Guthrie was born into a pioneer family in Okemah, Oklahoma. He quit high school at age 16 and took to the road. Traveling, singing, and writing songs became his way of life, and he was a vocal supporter of migrant workers, labor unions, and the communist movement. He served in the merchant marine during World War II, and in the late 1940s recorded hundreds of songs for the Folkways label. By the mid–1950s he was seriously ill with Huntington's disease, and spent many years bedridden before his death. He left behind over a thousand songs, including "This Land is Your Land," "This Train is Bound for Glory," and "So Long, It's Been Good to Know You," as well as a collection of poems and prose, *Born to Win* (1965).

Donald Hall (1928–) Born in New Haven, Connecticut, Donald Hall started writing poems at age 14. He was educated at Harvard, Oxford, and Stanford universities. A strong interest in acting has been woven into his career as a poet. He has been a TV broadcaster, lecturer, and editor, and has recorded readings of other poets' works as well as "performing" his own poetry. His published volumes include *Exiles and Marriages* (1955), *A Roof of Tiger Lilies* (1964), *The Toy Bone* (1979), and *Old and New Poems* (1990).

Lorraine Hansberry (1930–1965) Lorraine Hansberry grew up in a Chicago ghetto, though her family was not poor. She attended the University of Wisconsin, the Art Institute of Chicago, Roosevelt College, and the New School for Social Research and studied in Guadalajara, Mexico. *A Raisin In the Sun,* originally staged in 1959, was the first Broadway play to be written by a black woman. In that same year, Hansberry was named "most promising playwright" of the season in a poll done by *Variety.* Some of her other plays include *Brustein's Window* (1964); and *To Be Young, Gifted and Black* (1969) and *Les Blancs* (1970), both of which were produced after her death from cancer in 1965. Hansberry was the first African-American playwright to become well-known in New York theater.

Thomas Hardy (1840–1928) Born in Dorset, England, Thomas Hardy was trained as an architect. He began writing in 1867, and left architecture in 1874, after the success of his novel *Far from the Madding Crowd*. He published 11 novels and three collections of short stories, but in 1896, when critics were hostile to the novel *Jude the Obscure*, Hardy turned to poetry. His works include *The Dynasts* (1904), *Late Lyrics and Earlier* (1922), and the posthumous collection, *Winter Words in Various Moods and Metres*.

Joy Harjo (1951–) Joy Harjo was born in Tulsa, Oklahoma, the daughter of a Creek father and a Cherokee-French mother. She was educated at the University of New Mexico and the University of Iowa. Her collections of poetry include *The Last Song* (1975), *What Moon Drove Me to This?* (1979), *She Had Some Horses* (1983), and *In Mad Love and War* (1990). She has also worked on film scripts and contributes both fiction and nonfiction prose to several literary journals. Harjo, who loves the sounds words make, claims: "Words are not just words but sounds, which are voices, which are connected, growing to others. The world is not static, but shifts, changes."

Michael S. Harper (1938–) Michael S. Harper was born and raised in Brooklyn, New York, then lived in Los Angeles as an adolescent. He was strongly influenced by listening to his parents' records of the great jazz musicians. Educated at California State University and the University of Iowa, Harper traveled in Mexico and Europe before settling into his career as poet and university professor. His books include *Dear John, Dear Coltrane* (1970), *Debridement* (1973), *Nightmare Begins Responsibility* (1977), and *Healing Song for the Inner Ear* (1985).

Nathaniel Hawthorne (1804–1864) Born in Salem, Massachusetts, Hawthorne was a descendant of the judge who presided over the Salem witch trials. When Hawthorne was four years old his sea captain father was killed, leaving the family to live in poverty. Later, while working to put himself through Bowdoin College, Hawthorne proclaimed,

"No Man can be a Poet & a Book-Keeper at the same time." Since the publication of his first novel, *The Scarlet Letter*, in 1850, Hawthorne has been recognized as one of America's most important writers. He wrote several other novels, including *The House of the Seven Gables* (1851), and more than 100 short stories and sketches. His short story collections include *Twice-Told Tales* (1837) and *Mosses from an Old Manse* (1846), which included "Young Goodman Brown." He referred to his own work as "romance," and Melville once claimed "Young Goodman Brown" to be a tale "as deep as Dante."

Robert Hayden (1913–1980) Born in Detroit as Asa Bundy Sheffey, Robert Hayden was educated at Wayne State University and the University of Michigan. He then embarked on an academic career, teaching for 23 years at Fisk University and then at the University of Michigan. He espoused the Baha'i faith, an Eastern religion that advocates a world civilization to come. Though Hayden began publishing poetry in 1940, he was little appreciated until the 1960s, when he became the first African American named Consultant in Poetry to the Library of Congress. His works include *Heart-Shape in the Dust* (1940), *A Ballad of Remembrance* (1962), *Angle of Ascent* (1975), and *American Journal* (1978).

Seamus Heaney (1939–) Seamus Heaney was born and raised in a Catholic farming family in County Derry, Northern Ireland. At age 11, he left the farm for Belfast to study on scholarship at a boarding school. He continued his education at Queen's University and taught for a time in secondary schools. In 1972, after he had already published poetry, he moved to a cottage near Dublin to devote himself to his writing. He has since taught at universities, sometimes dividing his time between his home in Dublin and his professorship in the United States. His works include *Death of a Naturalist* (1966), *North* (1975), *The Haw Lantern* (1987), and *The Midnight Verdict* (1993). Heaney was awarded the Nobel Prize for Literature in 1995.

Anthony Hecht (1923–) Anthony Hecht was born in New York City and educated at Bard College and Columbia University. He then embarked on a career as a university teacher, poet, and translator of Greek classics. His poetry won a Pulitzer Prize in 1968. His collections include *A Summoning of Stones* (1954), *The Hard Hours* (1967), *Millions of Strange Shadows* (1977), and *The Transparent Man* (1990).

Ernest Hemingway (1898–1961) Ernest Hemingway is probably best known for his "stripped down" writing style. He once told an interviewer: "I always try to write on the principle of the ice-berg. There is seven-eighths of it under water for every part that shows." After high school, not wanting to attend college, Hemingway landed a job as a cub reporter on the Kansas City Star. At 18, he volunteered as an ambulance driver in World War I. He moved to Paris in 1922, making important friendships with other writers such as Ezra Pound, Gertrude Stein, F. Scott Fitzgerald, and James Joyce. Fitzgerald and Anderson used their influence to help get Hemingway's book of short stories, *In Our Time*, published in 1925. The publication of other works followed: *The Sun Also Rises* (1926), *A Farewell to Arms* (1929), *For Whom the Bell Tolls* (1940), *The Old Man and the Sea* (1952). Hemingway won the Nobel Prize for Literature in 1954, and his work altered the sound and style of English prose. Suffering from poor health and mental illness, he committed suicide in 1961.

George Herbert (1593–1633) A younger son in a wealthy aristocratic English family, George Herbert was educated at Cambridge University, where he began writing religious verse. A lute player as well as a poet, he participated in court life until the death of King James in 1625. He later became an Anglican priest for three years before he died of tuberculosis at the age of 40. His poems were published after his death in the collection *The Temple* (1633).

Robert Herrick (1591–1674) Born in London into a family of goldsmiths, Robert Herrick was educated at Cambridge University. At 32 he joined the Anglican ministry, serving in a parish in Devonshire until he was ousted by the Puritans. He then moved to London, where in 1648 he published his one collection of 1,200 poems—*Hesperides and Noble Numbers*, of which the first section was secular and the second religious. Herrick's work was little recognized until the nineteenth century.

Nazim Hikmet (1902–1963) Nazim Hikmet was born the son of a Turkish physician in Salonika, Greece, which was then under Turkish rule. He published his first poems at 15, and later went to Moscow to study at the University of the Workers of the East. When he returned to Turkey, he joined the Communist Party. His politics and his poetry precipitated a series of exiles and prison terms. The longest incarceration, 1938–1950, ended only when his poetry brought him international attention. He then lived in several socialist countries, dying in Moscow. Most of his work was published after his death. His collections include *La Gioconda and Si-Ya-U* (1929), *The Moscow Symphony and Other Poems* (1952), *Out of Four Prisons* (1966), and *Human Landscapes* (1967).

Garrett Kaoru Hongo (1951–) Born in Volcano, Hawaii, to Japanese-American parents, Garrett Kaoru Hongo grew up in California, attending a racially mixed high school in a working-class neighborhood of Los Angeles. He was strongly influenced by his father, a man who "refused to hate or … to be afraid of difference." Hongo was educated at Pomona College, the University of Michigan, and the University of California, and was later a founding member of the Asian Exclusion Act, a Seattle theater group. His published poetry includes the collections *Yellow Light* (1982) and *The River of Heaven* (1988).

Gerard Manley Hopkins (1844–1889) Gerard Manley Hopkins was born in Essex, England, and educated at Oxford. At the age of 20, he converted from the Anglican Church to Catholicism. He had written poems but apparently burned them when he was ordained into the Jesuit order. He served as priest and teacher in working-class sections of several large cities, but his sermons were deemed odd, and he was sent to Dublin as a professor of classics at University College. In 1875 he resumed writing poetry but didn't publish it. After his death of typhoid fever, a friend published the collection, *Poems* (1918).

A. E. Housman (1859–1936) Alfred Edward Housman was born into a large middle-class Victorian family in Fockbury, Worcestershire, England. He was headed for a career in the classics but failed his final exams at Oxford in 1881. For the next 10 years, while he worked as a clerk in the patent office, he wrote scholarly articles based on independent research at the British Museum. In 1892, his research won him an appointment as a Latin professor, first at the University of London and then at Cambridge, where he lived an increasingly solitary and aloof existence until his death. His first poetry, *A Shropshire Lad*, was published in 1896, but was slow to gain recognition. *Last Poems* was published in 1922.

Langston Hughes (1902–1967) James Langston Hughes was born in Joplin, Missouri, and grew up in Cleveland, publishing his first poems in a high school literary magazine. He worked as a merchant seaman, truck farmer, and waiter before his poetry won him a scholarship, and he was educated at Lincoln University and Columbia. He also traveled in Europe and Africa. A major figure in the Harlem Renaissance, Hughes was the first African American to make a living from his writing. He published novels, stories, plays, song lyrics, children's books, memoirs, translations, essays, and poetry. His collections of poetry include *Dear Lovely Death* (1931), *Freedom's Plow* (1943),

Montage of a Dream Deferred (1951), and *The Panther and the Lash: Poems of Our Times* (1967).

Henrik Ibsen (1828–1906) Born into a mercantile family in provincial Norway, Henrik Ibsen planned to study medicine, but after being rejected from a university decided to become a writer instead. From 1850 to 1864 he worked at the Nationalist Norwegian Theater in Bergen and later at the Mollergate Theater in Oslo. From these experiences he was able to learn about theater firsthand, much like Shakespeare did. After the Nationalist Theater ran into difficulties and his plea for a grant was denied, Ibsen left Norway to live in Italy and Germany for the next 27 years, eventually returning to Oslo, where his work was finally appreciated. Some of his plays are *A Doll's House* (1879), *Ghosts* (1881), *The Wild Duck* (1885), and *Hedda Gabler* (1890). Ibsen's works united the concept of a "well-made play" with the serious examination of social issues. "Ibsenism" has become a term to describe a variety of social causes.

Thomas Jefferson (1743–1826) Thomas Jefferson, who is considered the "penman of the American Revolution," was born in Virginia and grew up at Tuckahoe on the James River near Richmond. At age 16, he entered William and Mary College and then read law with George Wythe from 1762 to 1767. The publication of a pamphlet called *A Summary View of the Rights of British America* in 1774 marked Jefferson's first contribution to political literature. In 1775, he was elected to the Continental Congress, arriving in Philadelphia with what John Adams described as "a reputation for literature, science and a happy talent of composition." In 1776, as part of a five-man committee, Jefferson was asked to write the first draft of a formal declaration of independence from Great Britain. Most of the writing is his, despite the fact that he worked with others. Near the end of his term as governor of Virginia, he created *Notes on the State of Virginia* (1785), a full-length book. He retired to Monticello in 1809, after completing his second term as president. In 1817, he founded the University of Virginia, and in 1821, at the age of 77, he began writing his autobiography. Upon his death, he requested that only the following words be engraved on his tombstone: "Here lies Thomas Jefferson, Author of the Declaration of American Independence, of the Statute of Virginia for Religious Freedom and Father of the University of Virginia."

Ben Jonson (c. 1573–1637) Ben Jonson was born in London, the posthumous son of a Scottish minister. He was schooled in Latin and Greek, worked as a bricklayer, and served in the army. A contemporary of Shakespeare, he became an actor and playwright in the London theater, and wrote lyrical poems, odes, and epigrams. In various London pubs, he presided over literary discussions among a following of younger poets. He was given to fights and brawls, and once narrowly escaped being hanged. Nonetheless, in 1616 he was named poet laureate. His works include *Jonson's Workes* (1616).

James Joyce (1882–1941) Born in Dublin and educated in Jesuit schools, James Joyce fled his Irish Catholic upbringing in 1902 when he moved to Paris. Best known for his novels and short stories, Joyce also published a collection of poetry, *Chamber Music*, in 1907 and a play, *Exiles*, in 1918. *Dubliners*, a collection of stories, was published in 1914, after an eight-year battle with his publisher and printer, who feared the book would offend the British royal family and citizens of Dublin who might recognize themselves in the work. In 1916, Joyce's novel *A Portrait of the Artist as a Young Man* was published, and *Ulysses* followed in 1922. In *Ulysses*, Joyce used the technique of stream-of-consciousness; in his later novel *Finnegan's Wake* (1939), he completely abandoned the conventions of plot and characterization. Joyce's innovative use of language has had a tremendous impact on later writers.

Donald Justice (1925–   ) Donald Justice was born in Miami, Florida, the son of a carpenter and a cook, and was educated at the University of Miami, the University of

North Carolina, Stanford University, and the University of Iowa. He studied music—piano, clarinet, and especially composition—before deciding at age 18 on a literary career. He has continued to compose, draw, and paint as avocations. He has held professorships at many universities while writing poetry, including the collections *The Summer Anniversaries* (1960), *Night Light* (1967), the Pulitzer Prize-winning *Selected Poems* (1979), and *Tremayne* (1984).

John Keats (1795–1821) John Keats was born in London the son of a stable keeper, but lost both parents by his teens. He began writing poetry at 18, and after preparing for a career as a physician, decided instead to devote himself to poetry. In 1818 he fell in love with 16-year-old Fanny Brawne, but didn't marry because he was already ill with tuberculosis. He went to Italy in 1820, hoping to regain his health, but died soon thereafter at 25. He published three works of poetry: *Poems* (1812), the narrative poem *Endymion* (1818), and *Lamia, Isabella, The Eve of St. Agnes, and Other Poems* (1820).

Guan Keguang (1938–) Guan Keguang was born in China and educated at Shanghai Foreign Languages Institute, where he began to learn English. He taught English and journalism from 1960 to 1986, but was unable to teach for almost half that time because of political persecution. Imprisoned by the Red Guards, he was forced to do hard labor for nearly three years in the early 1970s. He has been a visiting scholar at the University of Pittsburgh and a copyeditor and writer at several newspapers. In 1994, Guan became a U.S. citizen.

Adrienne Kennedy (1931–) Raised in a black middle-class neighborhood in Cleveland, Adrienne Kennedy began keeping a diary at an early age. She attended Ohio State University, intending to major in education, but a literature course prompted her to begin writing stories, after which she changed her major. Her first play, *Funnyhouse of a Negro* (1962), is her best known and longest dramatic work. Some of her other plays include *The Owl Answers* (1963), *Collision Course* (1968), and *Scripts I* (1971). She and five other women founded the Women's Theatre Council in 1971. In 1980, she was recognized in juvenile theater with the production of *A Lancashire Lad*. Kennedy has said of her work as a dramatist: "My plays are meant to be states of mind."

Jamaica Kincaid (1949–) Jamaica Kincaid, who now resides in New York, where she works as a staff writer for the *New Yorker*, was born in the West Indies. Now a naturalized U.S. citizen, she has said about her adopted country: "It's given me a place to be myself—but myself as I was formed somewhere else." Her works include *At the Bottom of the River* (1984), an award-winning collection of short stories: *Annie John*, a short story cycle published in 1985; and a nonfiction memoir *A Small Place* (1988). Her latest book is *Autobiography of My Mother* (1994). "Girl" is taken from *At the Bottom of the River*.

Martin Luther King, Jr. (1929–1968) Civil rights activist Martin Luther King, Jr., was born in Atlanta, the son and grandson of ministers. He attended Morehouse College, Crozier Theological Seminary, and Boston University, where he received his Ph.D. His writings include *The Measure of a Man* (1959), *Letter From Birmingham City Jail* (1963), and *Why We Can't Wait* (1964). His most famous speech, "I Have a Dream," was heard in 1963. In 1964, he was awarded the Nobel Prize for Peace. And the day before his assassination in 1968 in Memphis, Tennessee, in a speech collected in *The Words of Martin Luther King, Jr.* (1983), he spoke these words: "We've got some difficult days ahead but it really doesn't matter to me now, because I've been to the mountaintop. And I've seen the promised land. I may not get there with you. But I want you to know tonight that we as a people will get to the promised land."

Etheridge Knight (1931–1991) Born in Corinth, Mississippi, Etheridge Knight went to high school for two years but was largely self-educated. He served in the army from 1947 to 1951, and served a prison term from 1960 to 1968. In prison, his skill at the African-American custom of "toast-telling"—reciting long poems that narrate racy exploits in crude language—may have set the stage for his writing poetry. His collections include *Poems from Prison* (1968), *Belly Song and Other Poems* (1973), *Born of a Woman: New and Selected Poems* (1980), and *The Essential Etheridge Knight* (1986).

Ted Kooser (1939–) Ted Kooser was born in Ames, Iowa, and educated at Iowa State University and the University of Nebraska. He has combined his writing with a career as an insurance underwriter and marketer. He has lived in and written about the Great Plains, without limiting himself to a regional perspective. His collections include *Official Entry Blank* (1969), *Wallflower* (1971), *Cottonwood County* (1980), and *The Blizzard Voices* (1986).

Maxine Kumin (1925–) Maxine Kumin was born in Philadelphia. As a teenager she produced such flowery romantic verse that a teacher told her not to write poetry, and for six years, she didn't. She was educated at Radcliffe College, became a suburban wife and mother, and did not begin writing seriously and publishing until mid-life. She later settled on a farm in New Hampshire to tend horses, garden, and write. Her collections include *Halfway* (1961), *The Privilege* (1965), the Pulitzer Prize-winning *Up Country: Poems of New England* (1972), and *Looking for Luck* (1992).

Mazisi Kunene (1930–) Mazisi Kunene was born in Durban, South Africa, and educated at Natal University and at the School of Oriental and African Studies in London. He has served as a representative in Europe and the United States for the African National Congress, and has been a professor of African literature at several universities. He writes his poems—usually verse narratives of Zulu history, culture, and religion—in the Zulu language, and translates his own work. Kunene was named Poet Laureate of Africa for 1993–1994 by the Afro-Arab Forum, the only South African to have received the award. Among his collections are *Zulu Poems* (1970), *Emperor Shaka the Great: A Zulu Epic* (1979), and *The Ancestors and the Sacred Mountain* (1982).

Joan Larkin (1939–) Born in Boston, Joan Larkin was educated at Swarthmore College and the University of Arizona. As well as writing poetry, she has taught in universities—primarily in New York City—and edited anthologies, including an award-winning anthology of gay and lesbian poetry. Her own collections include *Housework* (1975) and *A Long Sound* (1986).

Philip Larkin (1922–1985) Philip Larkin was born and raised in Coventry, Warwickshire, England, the son of a city treasurer. He was a solitary child with poor eyesight and a stutter, who read avidly and wrote poetry every night. He was educated at the University of Hull, then worked for over 40 years as a university librarian, writing only in his spare time. He was an expert on jazz, and wrote two collections of criticism and two novels as well as his poetry. He traveled little and rarely read foreign literature; increasing deafness intensified his seclusion. He published just four slim—but widely appreciated—volumes of poetry *The North Ship* (1946), *The Less Deceived* (1955), *The Whitsun Weddings* (1964), and *High Windows* (1974).

D. H. Lawrence (1885–1930) David Herbert Lawrence was born and raised in poverty in Eastwood, Nottinghamshire, England. He was educated at University College, Nottingham, and taught school for some years before moving to London and, in 1911, publishing his first novel. He later eloped with another man's wife, and after the two were suspected of treason (he for his pacifist views; she for her German ancestry), they traveled in Europe and North America for many years. Lawrence wrote novels, poetry, essays, and criticism, often incurring outrage and court cases for the sexual explicitness of his work. He died of tuberculosis at 44. His works of poetry include *Amores* (1916), *New Poems* (1918), *Birds, Beasts, and Flowers* (1923), and *Nettles* (1930).

Li-Young Lee (1957–) Li-Young Lee was born in Jakarta, Indonesia. When he was very young, his father, a minister, was jailed for 19 months as a political prisoner, but escaped. The family fled on a long journey that brought them to the United States in 1962. Lee grew up hearing both the Bible and the ancient Chinese poetry his father had memorized. Educated at the University of Pittsburgh and the University of Arizona, Lee began writing seriously in 1981. He has published a memoir as well as poetry, including the collections *Rose* (1986) and *The City in Which I Love You* (1990).

Denise Levertov (1923–) Denise Levertov was born in Ilford, Essex, England, into a cultured, literary family. Her Russian father had converted from Judaism to Christianity and become an Anglican priest. Her Welsh mother educated her at home. Levertov decided at the age of five to become a poet. In World War II, she served as a civilian nurse in London, and then came to the United States in 1948 with her American husband. Levertov is a poet, essayist, editor, and translator, as well as a political activist, especially in the cause of peace. Among her many books of poetry are *The Double Image* (1946), *O Taste and See* (1964), *Life in the Forest* (1978), and *Black Iris* (1988).

Stephen Shu-Ning Liu (1930–) Stephen Shu-Ning Liu was born in Fu-ling, Sichuan, China. He studied at Nanking University and then taught in Taiwan before coming to the United States in 1952, where he attended Wayland Baptist University, the University of Texas, and the University of North Dakota. He has taught at several colleges and universities, and his poems and short stories have appeared in literary magazines internationally. His works of poetry include the bilingual collection *Dream Journeys to China* (1982), and *My Father's Martial Art* (1986).

Audre Lorde (1934–1992) Audre Lorde was born in New York City to parents from Grenada, West Indies. She first published poetry in *Seventeen* magazine during high school. Educated at the University of Mexico, Hunter College, and Columbia University, she worked as a librarian before turning to writing and teaching full-time. Toward the end of her life, she lived for six years on St. Croix in the Virgin Islands. She was a poet, novelist, and essayist, and an active advocate for racial justice, feminism, and lesbian rights. In 1991, she was named poet laureate of New York State. Her poetry collections include *The First Cities* (1968), *The New York Head Shop and Museum* (1974), *Our Dead Behind Us* (1986), and *The Marvelous Arithmetics of Distance* (1993).

Robert Lowell (1917–1977) Born in Boston into an old literary family, Robert Lowell grew up amid tensions between his parents. He left Harvard after a fight with his father, and later attended Kenyon College and Louisiana State University. During World War II, he was imprisoned for resisting the draft as a conscientious objector. Throughout his adult life, he had bouts of manic-depression, some requiring hospitalization. He wrote plays, criticism, translations, and poetry, including the Pulitzer Prize-winning *Lord Weary's Castle* (1946), *Life Studies* (1959), *Near the Ocean* (1967), and *Day by Day* (1977).

Wing Tek Lum (1946–) Born in Honolulu, Hawaii, Wing Tek Lum was educated at Brown University and the Union Theological Seminary. His primary career is in business, and although his poems have won awards, he considers poetry an avocation. His works include *Expounding the Doubtful Points* (1987).

Archibald MacLeish (1892–1982) Born in Glencoe, Illinois, Archibald MacLeish was educated at Yale University and Harvard Law School. After serving in World War I, he had a law practice until he moved to Paris in 1923 with his wife and two children and devoted himself to writing. Over the decades, he continued to move in and out of public life. Among his many statesman roles was that of assistant Secretary of State during the last two years of World War II. As a poet, he taught at Harvard and Amherst College and garnered two Pulitzer Prizes. His works include *Tower of Ivory* (1917), *Sheets in the Moon* (1926), *Songs for Eve* (1954), and *Collected Poems 1917–1982* (1985).

Claude McKay (1889–1948) Claude McKay was born into a peasant farming family in Jamaica. In 1912, an Englishman he knew had two books of McKay's poetry published in England. McKay came to the United States to study agriculture, but after attending Tuskegee Normal and Industrial Institute and Kansas State College, he worked as woodworker, longshoreman, porter, and waiter. After travels in Europe, he lived in New York City and became a key figure in the Harlem Renaissance, writing poetry, fiction, and an autobiography. He traveled extensively during the 1930s, then in 1940 became a U.S. citizen and converted to Catholicism. His poetic works include *Songs of Jamaica* (1912), *Spring In New Hampshire and Other Poems* (1920), and *Harlem Shadows* (1922).

Christopher Marlowe (1564–1593) Christopher Marlowe was born in Canterbury, England, the son of a shoemaker, and was educated at Cambridge University. He was best known for his plays, and was the first dramatist to use blank verse, but he also wrote lyric and narrative poetry and translated Latin works. He may have been a spy for the government of Queen Elizabeth. At the age of 29, he was scheduled to stand trial for his unconventional religious views when he was killed in a tavern brawl.

Gabriel Garcia Márquez (1928–   ) Born in a small Colombian town, Gabriel Garcia Márquez later attended Universidad Nacional de Colombia and Universidad de Cartageña. In high school, Márquez had a reputation for being a writer even though he never wrote anything. In fact, he didn't really begin writing until he was in college, after a strong reaction to the first line in Kafka's "The Metamorphosis." Márquez said, "When I read that line I thought to myself that I didn't know anyone was allowed to write things like that. If I had known, I would have started writing a long time ago." After college, he worked as a journalist. His first short stories were written at night in the newspaper office, after the other journalists had gone home. His most famous work, *One Hundred Years of Solitude*, was published in 1970. Besides several novels, he has also written nonfiction and short stories. In 1982, he won the Nobel Prize for Literature.

Andrew Marvell (1621–1678) Born in Yorkshire, England, Andrew Marvell entered Oxford University at the age of 12. During the English Civil War, he served in the Cromwell government as John Milton's assistant. After the Restoration, he represented the district of Hull in Parliament. He was known for his satirical political commentary, but his poems weren't published until after his death.

Bobbie Ann Mason (1940–   ) Bobbie Ann Mason was born on a dairy farm in Kentucky and earned degrees from the University of Kentucky, the State University of New York, and the University of Connecticut. Mason worked for years on an unpublished novel while she submitted stories, which were all rejected, to the *New Yorker*. Finally, the editors accepted her twentieth try. Mason claims that her years attempting to break into print were her time to discover her true calling, which was to "write about [her] roots and the kinds of people [she'd] known, but from a contemporary perspective." Mason's works include *The Girl Sleuth: A Feminist Guide to the Bobbsey Twins, Nancy Drew, and Their Sisters* (1975), *Shiloh and Other Stories* (1982), *In Country* (1985), *Love Life* (1989), and *Feather Crowns* (1994).

Guy de Maupassant (1850–1893) French short story writer Guy de Maupassant, now considered a master of the genre, did not begin his literary career until the completion of his military service and subsequent acceptance of a position of clerk in the government. While working for the government, he met Gustave Flaubert, a friend of the family, and began to associate with Flaubert's circle of literary friends. Maupassant's first volume of verse, *Des Vers*, appeared in 1880. During the next 10 years, which were his most productive, Maupassant wrote 300 stories, several plays, and six novels, two of which are *A Life* (1883) and *Good-Friend* (1885). After 1886, Maupassant's physical and mental health took a turn for the worse. He suffered from paralysis, then failing reason, and finally insanity. After trying to cut his throat on New Year's Day, 1892, he was committed to an asylum, where he died a little over a year later.

Ved Mehta (1934–) Ved Mehta, born in India, lost his sight at the age of four. His father, knowing that a blind man without an education would end up begging on the streets, sent Mehta to school early. At the age of 15, Mehta traveled to the United States alone to attend a school for the blind. He then went on to receive degrees from Pomona College, Balliol College, Oxford, and Harvard. In 1961, at the age of 26, he became a staff writer for the *New Yorker*. His first book, *Face to Face: An Autobiography* (1957), touched on his blindness, but in subsequent works his lack of sight was rarely mentioned. Some of these other works are *Walking the Indian Streets* (1960), *Delinquent Chacha* (1976), *The New India* (1978), *Vedi* (1982), *Three Stories of the Raj* (1986), and *Portrait of India* (1993). In an interview, Mehta once claimed: "I don't belong to any single tradition. I am an amalgam of five cultures—Indian, British, American, blind and [the *New Yorker*]."

Natalie Merchant (1964–) Natalie Merchant was born and raised in Jamestown, New York, and educated at Jamestown Community College, where her artist stepfather was a teacher. A visual artist as well as a musician, Merchant was 16 when she and friends formed the band 10,000 Maniacs, and she became lead singer, collaborating informally on writing some of the songs. It was years later that she also started playing the piano. Albums by 10,000 Maniacs include *Human Conflict Number Five* (1983), *In My Tribe* (1987), *Blind Man's Zoo* (1989), and *Our Time in Eden* (1992), as well as a solo album, *Tigerlily* (1995).

W. S. Merwin (1927–) W. S. Merwin was raised in Scranton, Pennsylvania, the son of a Presbyterian minister. He attended Princeton University, where he was exposed to poetry other than hymns. At Princeton, he studied foreign languages and literature and eventually became a tutor abroad and a translator. Merwin is the author of several books of poetry—*A Mask for Janus* (1952), *Animae* (1969), *Carrier of Ladders* (1970), for which he won a Pulitzer Prize; *Opening the Hand* (1983)—as well as a book of prose, *The Miner's Pale Children* (1970). He has also written plays and collaborated with other writers. His work has appeared in numerous periodicals, including *Nation, Harper's,* and the *New Yorker*. Merwin once remarked in an interview: "It makes me angry to feel that the natural world is taken to have so little importance." In 1987, a collection of Merwin's work, *Regions of Memory: Uncollected Prose, 1949—1982*, was published.

Edna St. Vincent Millay (1892–1950) Edna St. Vincent Millay was born in Rockland, Maine, and grew up in Camden with a single mother who emphasized reading and musical training. After attending Barnard and Vassar Colleges, Millay lived in Greenwich Village as an actress and playwright known for her humor, feminism, and political activism. She later traveled widely in Europe and Asia. She won a Pulitzer Prize in 1923, but her acclaim had dwindled by 1944, when she had a nervous breakdown. She died of a heart attack six years later, leaving plays, an opera libretto, translations, and some 20 volumes of poetry, including *Second April* (1917), *The Ballad of the Harp-Weaver* (1922), *Fatal Interview* (1939), and *Mine the Harvest* (1954).

Arthur Miller (1915–) Arthur Miller was born in Harlem and raised in Brooklyn. In order to help support his family, he held a variety of jobs as he was growing up. He later graduated from the University of Michigan, where he studied playwriting, in 1938. His first play failed, but the following ones brought him success. *All My Sons*, which earned him a reputation as a major American dramatist, appeared in 1947, followed by *Death of a Salesman* (1949), for which he won a Pulitzer Prize, *The Crucible* (1953), and *After the Fall* (1964), a play loosely based on his brief and rocky marriage to Marilyn Monroe. Miller's plays are frequently produced even today, and he has become a popular lecturer on the subject of his career and American Theater.

John Milton (1608–1674) John Milton was born into a middle-class family in Cheapside, London. His father was a scrivener who also composed music, and his mother schooled him to be a minister. Milton graduated from Cambridge University in 1629, traveled on the continent, then returned to England before the Civil War. An ardent supporter of the Puritan cause, he narrowly escaped execution after the Restoration. He later went completely blind, and lived his last years in poverty. His works included *Lycidas* (1638), *Paradise Lost* (1667), *Paradise Regained* (1671), and *Samson Agonistes* (1671).

Janice Mirikitani (1942–) Janice Mirikitani is a third-generation Japanese-American. She and her family were incarcerated during World War II in an internment camp in Arkansas. Educated at UCLA and the University of California at Berkeley, Mirikitani then developed her skills as poet, choreographer, teacher, administrator, and community activist. As the head of a multicultural and multiservice urban center in San Francisco, she has directed various programs from the performing arts to crisis intervention. She has edited and helped publish the works of many disadvantaged people, as well as publishing her own poetry in such collections as *Awake in the River* (1982), *Shedding Silence* (1987), and *We, The Dangerous* (1994).

Gabriela Mistral (1889–1957) Gabriela Mistral is the pen name of Lucila Godoy Alcayaga, who was born in Vicuña, Chile, raised in a farming community, and educated at the Pedagogical College in Santiago. She taught primary school at age 15, continuing as teacher and administrator for 12 years. When her fiance committed suicide, her profound grief emerged in poetry published under her pen name. Alcayaga became a diplomat for the Chilean government, and also championed children's welfare and the rights of workers and women. In 1945, as the poet Gabriela Mistral, she won the Nobel Prize for literature. Her works include *Sonetos de la Muerte [Sonnets on Death]* (1914), *Tala [Felling]* (1938), *Lagar [Wine Press]* (1954), and *Canto a San Francisco* (1957).

Molière (1622–1673) Born Jean-Baptiste Poquelin into a prosperous mercantile family who had court connections, Molière was taught by his father, who might have intended a life at court for his young son. In 1643 he joined the Illustre Théatre Company, where he took the stage name Molière. When his brother died in 1660, Molière acquired the position of court upholsterer. At the same time, his reputation as a playwright became more widespread. His plays include *Schools for Husbands* (1661), *Schools for Wives* (1662), *Tartuffe* (1664), *The Misanthrope* (1666), *The Miser* (1668), and *The Imaginary Invalid* (1673). Although in ill health in later years, Molière still managed to write "merry" plays and even take on a few roles himself.

N. Scott Momaday (1934–) N. Scott Momaday was born in Lawton, Oklahoma, and spent his early childhood among the Kiowa tribe on a family farm. His mother was a writer and teacher, his father an artist and art teacher. They later moved to New Mexico, and Momaday was educated at the University of New Mexico and Stanford University. He has taught in universities while writing both poetry and novels. In 1969, he won the Pulitzer Prize for fiction. Momaday also draws and paints. His poetry appears in *Angle of Geese and Other Poems* (1974), *The Gourd Dancer* (1976) and *In the Presence of the Sun* (1992).

Michel de Montaigne (1533–1592) Michel de Montaigne, considered the first essayist, was born and raised in France. His father, believing that children should be exposed to the world at an early age, secured peasant godparents for his son and later sent him to live under the guidance of a tutor who spoke Latin. After attending the Collége de Guyenne, Montaigne worked at the Chambre des Enquétes but did not enjoy his job. When his father died, Montaigne inherited the estate and, after retiring in 1571, began to write his famous work, *Essays*. In 1580, the first two books of *Essays* were published, and in 1588, the first three-book editions of *Essays* appeared. He continued making additions to *Essays* right up until his death in 1592. He once wrote about *Essays*: "I have no more made my book than my book has made me, a book consubstantial with its author, concerned with my own, an integral part of my life."

Marianne Moore (1887–1972) Marianne Moore was born in Kirkwood, Missouri, but when her father abandoned the family in 1894, they moved to Pennsylvania. Moore was educated at Bryn Mawr College and Carlisle Commercial College. She than taught business courses at an Indian School, traveled in Europe, worked as a librarian, edited a literary magazine, and became a baseball enthusiast. Her first book, *Poems* (1921), was published in England through the secret efforts of the poet H. D. and others. Many more collections followed, including *Nevertheless* (1944), the Pulitzer Prize-winning *Collected Poems* (1951), and *Unfinished Poems* (1972).

Pat Mora (1942–) Born in El Paso, Texas, Pat Mora was educated at Texas Western College and the University of Texas at El Paso. She later settled in Cincinnati. She first taught in schools, then in community colleges, then at the university level. Her books of poems, exploring political issues, gender, and Hispanic heritage, include *Chants* (1984), *Borders* (1986), and *Communion* (1991).

Aurora Levins Morales (1954–) Aurora Levins Morales was born in Indiera Baja, Puerto Rico, to a Puerto Rican-American mother (Rosario Morales) and a Jewish-American father. She grew up in several American cities as the family followed her father's professorships. She later settled in California. Morales began writing poetry at seven, and now writes fiction and nonfiction as well. She collaborated with her mother on the volume of poetry *Getting Home Alive* (1986).

Rosario Morales (1930–) Rosario Morales, born and raised in New York City, earned a master's degree in anthropology from the University of Chicago. Married at 20, Morales moved to Puerto Rico, where she farmed for five years, raised three children, and did a variety of political organizing among her neighbors. Morales says her writing reflects her upbringing in New York, where she grew up among children of Irish, European Jewish, Puerto Rican, Southern black, and Afro-Caribbeanian migrants. Morales has published in numerous anthologies, among them *This Bridge Called My Back, Writing by Radical Women of Color* (1981), *An Ear to the Ground: An Anthology of Contemporary American Poetry* (1989), and *City River of Voices* (1991). She also co-authored *Getting Home Alive* (1986) with her daughter, Aurora Levins Morales. Morales is currently writing fiction and an autobiography.

Bharati Mukherjee (1940–) Bharati Mukherjee, born in Calcutta, India, has also lived in Canada and currently makes her home in the United States. She attended the university of Calcutta where she earned a M.A. in English and ancient Indian culture. She moved to London shortly after India gained independence in 1947 and became fluent in English. Later she was awarded a scholarship to University of Iowa Writer's Workshop. In 1963 she earned her M.F.A. and married Clark Blaise, a novelist, during a lunch hour in September. She eventually returned to the university and earned her Ph.D. in 1969. Besides writing books and short stories, such as *The Tiger's Daughter* (1972), *Wife* (1975), *Darkness* (1985), *The Middleman and Other Stories* (1988), and

Jasmine (1989), Mukherjee has taught at the University of Iowa and Skidmore College. Currently she teaches creative writing at Queens College and Columbia University. Her latest novel is *The Holder of the World* (1993).

Paul Muldoon (1951–) Paul Muldoon was born in County Armagh, Northern Ireland, the son of a laborer and a schoolteacher. He began writing poems in adolescence, at least once as a substitute for an assigned essay—for him, poetry was easier to write than prose. At Queen's University in Belfast, he studied with poet Seamus Heaney. Muldoon published his first collection when he was 18. From 1973 to 1986 he was a radio producer for the BBC in Belfast. He has since been a lecturer at Princeton and Columbia universities, and has edited anthologies as well as authoring his own collections. His titles include *Knowing My Place* (1971), *Why Brownlee Left* (1980), *Quoof* (1983), and *The Annals of Chile* (1994).

Elías Miguel Muñoz (1954–) Born in Ciego de Avila, Cuba, Elías Miguel Muñoz moved as an adolescent to Hawthorne, California. He was educated at the University of California at Irvine, and later settled in Kansas, where he has taught Spanish and Latin American literature at the university level. He is not only a poet, but also a novelist, a reviewer and literary critic, and the author of scholarly books. His poetic works include the bilingual collection *En estas tierras/In This Land* (1989).

Alice Munro (1931–) Canadian writer Alice Munro believes that the short story is her medium, because "the story will zero in and give you intense, but not connected, moments of experience." Munro, one of the most admired writers in Canada, was born of farm parents. For two years she attended the University of Western Ontario, pausing in her college career at the age of 20, after her first marriage. Some of her works include *Lives of Girls and Women* (1971), *The Beggar Maid* (1982), *The Progress of Love* (1986), and *Friend of My Youth* (1990). Several of Munro's works have won the Governor General's Literary Award in Canada. She has also written television scripts and is a contributor to anthologies and periodicals. *Open Secrets* is her latest collection of short stories.

Howard Nemerov (1920–1993) Howard Nemerov was born and raised in New York City and educated at Harvard. During War II, he served in a fighter squadron of the British Royal Air Force. His long literary career included teaching at colleges and universities, and writing novels, plays, and Pulitzer Prize-winning poetry. Among his poetry collections are *The Image and the Land* (1947), *The Salt Garden* (1955), *Mirrors and Windows* (1958), and *War Stories: Poems About Long Ago and Now* (1987).

Pablo Neruda (1904–1973) Born Neftali Beltan in a small frontier town in southern Chile, Pablo Neruda chose his pseudonym from an admired Czech writer. He published his first poetry, a volume of love poems, at the age of 19. As he developed a career as activist and diplomat, his poetry became more political. He traveled widely, was a consul in the Far East and Mexico, and served in the Chilean senate. He also spent years in exile during the dictatorship in Chile. Neruda was awarded the Nobel Prize in 1971. His works of poetry include *Twenty Love Poems and a Song of Despair* (1924), *Spain in the Heart* (1937), *Canto General* (1958), and *2000* (1974).

Joyce Carol Oates (1938–) Joyce Carol Oates describes the subject matter of fiction as "real people in a real society." Her fiction echoes this statement, with its high density of murder, rape, and physical distress. Oates was educated at Syracuse University and the University of Wisconsin. Her creative writing teacher at Syracuse claimed she was the most brilliant student he'd ever seen at the university. Oates publishes at an incredible rate, usually a novel, a volume of short stories, or some other work each year. She also publishes in periodicals. Her works include *them* (1969), *Wonderland* (1971), *Where Are You Going, Where Have You Been? Stories of Young America* (1974), *Cross-*

ing the Border (1977), *Black Water* (1992), and *Foxfire* (1993). Oates has been the recipient of the Book Award, a Guggenheim Fellowship, the National Institute of Arts and Letters Rosenthal Foundation Award, and two O. Henry prizes. Her latest novel is called *What I Lived For.*

Tim O'Brien (1946–) Best known for his fictional portrayal of Vietnam, Tim O'Brien graduated summa cum laude from Macalester College in 1968. Immediately after graduation, he was drafted into the U.S. Army and shipped to Vietnam. He was later discharged after receiving a shrapnel wound, for which he was awarded a Purple Heart. In 1970, he studied on the graduate level at Harvard. His first book, a collection of anecdotes reminiscent of his time spent in Vietnam, was titled *If I Die in a Combat Zone, Box Me Up and Take Me Home* (1973). His other works include *Northern Lights* (1975), *Going After Cacciato* (1978), for which he won the National Book Award, and *The Things They Carried: A Work of Fiction* (1990). In an essay O'Brien wrote "You practice all the time, then practice some more. You pay attention to craft. You aim for tension and suspense, a sense of drama, displaying in concrete terms the actions and reactions of human beings contesting problems of the heart. You try to make art."

Flannery O'Connor (1925–1964) Flannery O'Connor, born in Georgia into a prosperous Catholic family, received a degree from Georgia State College for Women in 1945 and an M.F.A. in 1947 from the University of Iowa. Her works include *Wise Blood* (1952), *A Good Man Is Hard to Find* (1955), *The Violent Bear it Away* (1960), *Everything That Rises Must Converge* (1965), *Mystery and Manners* (1969), and *Complete Stories of Flannery O'Connor* (1971). In O'Connor's fictional world, unexpected events, usually tragic, yield human insight and the possibility of redemption. A friend claimed that O'-Connor believed that an artist "should face all the truth down to the worst of it." At the age of 39, O'Connor died of lupus.

Dwight Okita (1958–) Dwight Okita was born and raised in Chicago to Japanese-American parents who had been confined during World War II in relocation camps. He began writing poems at the bottom of his homework pages in grade school, because prose composition was difficult for him. He was educated at the University of Illinois in Chicago, and became resident playwright with the Chicago Dramatists Workshop, expanding his writing from plays into musical theater. He describes himself as a gay Japanese-American man, Buddhist by philosophy. His poems have been published in many anthologies, textbooks, and periodicals, as well as in the collection *Crossing With the Light* (1992).

Sharon Olds (1942–) Sharon Olds was born in San Francisco and educated at Stanford and Columbia universities. She later settled in New York City. As well as teaching at universities, she has been a creative writing teacher at a hospital for people with physical disabilities. Olds did not find her own voice as a poet until she was 30, but since then has produced many collections, including *Satan Says* (1980), *The Dead and the Living* (1984), *The Sign of Saturn* (1991), and *The Father* (1992).

Tillie Olsen (1912–) Born in Omaha, Nebraska, Tillie Olsen spent her early life living with her parents in working-class poverty. In her youth, Olsen was arrested twice for political activities, and her formal schooling ended after high school graduation. Later she claimed, "Public libraries were my college." Her first novel *Yonnondio*, was begun in the early 1930s but was not published until 1974. *Tell Me a Riddle*, the collection of short stories from which "I Stand Here Ironing" is excerpted, was published in 1961. And *Silences*, a collection of essays on writers'—particularly women writers'—difficulties, appeared in 1978. Olsen's short stories appear in more than 70 anthologies, and her short story "Tell Me a Riddle" won the O. Henry Award for best short story in 1961. In 1981, San Francisco, where she resides, designated a Tillie Olsen day.

Simon J. Ortiz (1941–) Born in Albuquerque, New Mexico, into the Alcoma Pueblo tribe, Simon J. Ortiz was educated at Fort Lewis College, the University of New Mexico, and the University of Iowa. He served in the Army in Vietnam from 1963 to 1966. A college and university professor, an editor, and an accomplished short story writer, Ortiz has published several books of poetry, including *Going for the Rain* (1976), *A Good Journey* (1977), *From Sand Creek: Rising in This Heart Which is Our America* (1981), and *Woven Stone* (1992).

George Orwell (1903–1950) George Orwell, who never legally changed his name from Eric Arthur Blair, was born in India but grew up in England. After preparatory school, he decided against further schooling and spent five years (1922–1927) with the Indian Imperial Police in Burma. He then left to experience "subsistence living" in Paris and later London, where he held such positions as tutor, teacher, and bookshop assistant while writing. In the 1940s he became England's most prominent political writer and established his international reputation with the publication of *Animal Farm* in 1945 and *1984* in 1949. Orwell believed that, "To write in plain, vigorous language one has to think fearlessly, and if one thinks fearlessly one cannot be politically orthodox." Many of his works revealed his political nature, such as his most famous essay, "Politics and the English Language," and his collections of essays such as *Shooting an Elephant and Other Essays* (1950). He died of tuberculosis in 1950.

Wilfred Owen (1893–1918) Wilfred Owen was born in Oswestry, Shropshire, England, into a devout and relatively poor family. He graduated from Shrewsbury Technical School, but when he did not get a scholarship to London University, he worked for two years as an unpaid assistant to a vicar, and then taught for Berlitz language schools in France. He enlisted in 1916, and was wounded the next year. In the military hospital, he met Siegfried Sassoon and showed him his poetry. After returning to active service, Owen was killed at the age of 25, one week before the armistice. Most of his poems had been written on the front lines, and only a handful had been published. In 1920, Sassoon had a collection published as *Poems*.

Linda Pastan (1932–) Born Linda Olenik in New York City, Linda Pastan was educated at Radcliffe, Simmons, and Brandeis. She later settled in Maryland. She wrote award-winning poetry in college, but married in 1953, had three children, and abandoned her writing for years until her husband encouraged her to get back to it. Much of her work explores the complexities of domestic life. Her collections include *A Perfect Circle of Sun* (1971), *Setting the Table* (1980), *A Fraction of Darkness* (1985), and *An Early Afterlife* (1995).

Marge Piercy (1936–) Born in Detroit into a working-class family, Marge Piercy grew up in a poor section of the city during the Depression. The first in her family to go to college, she was educated at the University of Michigan and Northwestern University. In the 1960s, she began her political activism in the civil rights movement, then dedicated herself to the women's movement. Piercy's first six novel manuscripts were rejected by editors, but she went on to publish novels, essays, and poetry. She settled on Cape Cod, but has given readings and taught at conferences, colleges, and universities nationwide. Her books of poetry include *Hard Loving* (1969), *Living in the Open* (1976), *Available Light* (1988), and *Mars and Her Children* (1992).

Pedro Pietri (1944–) Pedro Pietri was born in Ponce, Puerto Rico, but came to the United States in 1945 and was educated in the New York City schools. He served in the Army from 1966 to 1968. He has taught creative writing both to preschoolers and university students, and his plays have been produced in New York, California, and Puerto Rico. He reports being a member of the "Latin Insomniacs Motorcycle Club." His poetry collections include *Puerto Rican Obituary* (1971), *Out of Order* (1980), *Traffic Violations* (1983), and *Missing Out of Action* (1991).

Luigi Pirandello (1867–1936) Luigi Pirandello, Italian playwright, novelist, short story writer, essayist, and poet, was born in Sicily and died in Italy. He is best known for his trilogy of "theater-in-the-theater" plays: *Six Characters in Search of an Author* (1921), a play-within-the-play; *Tonight We Improvise* (1932), an improvisation; and *Each in His Own Way* (1923), a play-outside-the-play. He is credited with inventing "grotesco," which investigates the disillusionment of reality that lies beneath social appearances. Along with *Six Characters in Search of an Author, Henry IV* (1922) is considered to be one of his most important plays. After the successes of these two plays, Pirandello went on to found his own acting company and win the Nobel Prize for literature in 1934.

Sylvia Plath (1932–1963) Sylvia Plath was born in Boston, and her father died when she was eight. She wrote poems from childhood and published early in *Seventeen* magazine. She was educated at Smith College and Cambridge University in England; in 1956 she married English poet Ted Hughes and settled in England. They had two children but separated in 1962. Plath had struggled with mental illness from adolescence, and committed suicide in 1963, one month after her novel *The Bell Jar* had been published under a pseudonym. Most of her poetry wasn't published until after her death, and she was awarded a posthumous Pulitzer Prize in 1982. Her collections include *The Colossus* (1960), *Ariel* (1965), *Winter Trees* (1971), and *Collected Poems* (1981).

Edgar Allan Poe (1809–1849) Edgar Allan Poe was born in Boston. His parents, both actors, died when he was two. He was taken in by the wealthy John Allan (hence Poe's middle name), and was educated at Richmond Academy and briefly at the University of Virginia. In his late teens Poe moved back to Boston, where he enlisted in the Army under a pseudonym and published his first volume of poetry, *Tamberlane and Other Poems* (1827), at his own expense. In 1831, he published another collection, *Poems by Edgar A. Poe*. He wrote many stories and poems for magazines, and while his writing was admired it never brought him financial success. He had married his 14-year-old cousin, Virginia Clemm, in 1836, and her death from tuberculosis in 1847 hastened his own physical and mental decline and death at age 40.

Katherine Anne Porter (1890–1980) Katherine Anne Porter was raised by her maternal grandmother in extreme poverty after her mother died in childbirth when Porter was two years old. In 1915, after her first divorce (she was married four times), Porter began a life of travel, activity, and a rapid change of jobs. Her career as a writer of short stories, novellas, and novels was brief, but as a writer she was a perfectionist, receiving the Gold Medal from the National Institute of Arts and Letters, a Pulitzer Prize, and a National Book Award. Some of her short story collections are *Flowering Judas* (1930), *The Leaning Tower* (1944), and *Collected Stories* (1966). A novel, *Ship of Fools*, which didn't appear until she was over 70 years old, earned Porter a permanent place among writers of her generation such as Faulkner, Fitzgerald, and Hemingway.

Ezra Pound (1885–1972) Born Weston Loomis in Hailey, Idaho, Ezra Pound decided early to be a poet. He was educated at Hamilton College and the University of Pennsylvania, and then lived in England and Paris. He founded and edited numerous literary magazines and championed many upcoming and later famous writers. In Italy during World War II, Pound made radio broadcasts for the fascists. In 1945, he was arrested and imprisoned in a cage before being sent to the United States and tried for treason. Judged insane, he spent 12 years in a mental hospital until other poets effected his release and he returned to Italy. His works include *A Lume Spento* (1908); *Hugh Selwyn Mauberly* (1920); *Personae* (1949); and *The Cantos* (1–109), which were collected in 1964, but published from 1917 on in many installments.

Wyatt Prunty (1947–) Wyatt Prunty was born in Humboldt, Tennessee, the son of a geographer. He was educated at the University of the South, Johns Hopkins University, and Louisiana State University and served in the Navy from 1969 to 1972. He now lives in Tennessee as a professor of English, where he directs the annual Sewanee Writers Conference at the University of the South. His volumes of poetry include *Domestic of the Outer Banks* (1980), *The Times Between* (1982), *What Women Know, What Men Believe* (1986), and *The Run of the House* (1993).

Sir Walter Raleigh (c. 1552–1618) Walter Raleigh was born in Hayes Barton, Devonshire, England. He attended Oxford, but left to fight with the Huguenots in France; he then embarked on a career of adventure that included attempts to start colonies in North America and searches for gold in South America. Queen Elizabeth I gave Raleigh a huge estate in Ireland, where he introduced the potato and tobacco. He was knighted in 1584. He later lost the queen's favor by marrying one of her maids-of-honor. After James I took power in 1603, Raleigh's fortunes plummeted. He was imprisoned (comfortably—with family and servants) in the Tower of London for 12 years, and then, after another ill-fated exploit in South America, he was executed for disobeying the king.

Dudley Randall (1914–   ) The son of a minister and a teacher, Dudley Randall was born in Washington, D. C., and moved to Detroit when he was nine. He wrote poems at age four and was first published at thirteen. He was educated at Wayne State University, the University of Michigan, and later the University of Ghana. He worked for years in a foundry, served in the Army, and then became a university librarian. The founder and long-time editor of Broadside Press, he encouraged and published many now-famous African-American poets. In 1981, he was named the first poet laureate of Detroit. Among his works are *Dressed All In Pink* (1965), *Cities Burning* (1968), *After the Killing* (1973), and *A Litany of Friends* (1983).

John Crowe Ransom (1888–1974) John Crowe Ransom was born in Pulaski, Tennessee, and educated at Vanderbilt University and Oxford. After serving in the Army from 1917 to 1919, he became increasingly well-known as both poet and critic. He was a major figure in the agrarian movement in poetry, which championed the rural South and an agricultural economy. Ransom settled in Ohio and taught at Kenyon College for many years. His works of poetry, written primarily before 1937, include *Poems About God* (1919), *Grace After Meat* (1924), *Two Gentlemen in Bonds* (1927), and *Selected Poems* (1945).

Henry Reed (1914–   ) Born in Birmingham, Warwickshire, England, Henry Reed was educated at the University of Birmingham. He spent several years as a teacher and free-lance journalist, served in the British Army, and worked for the British Foreign Office. As a radio broadcaster, he began writing radio plays, many of them satires that lampooned British society. He also gained recognition as a poet, critic, translator, and playwright. His poetry collections include *A Map of Verona* (1946), *Lessons of the War* (1970), and *Collected Poems* (1991).

Ishmael Reed (1938–   ) Ishmael Reed was born in Chattanooga, Tennessee, and educated at the University of Buffalo. He co-founded a publishing company and a video production company and established the Before Columbus Foundation, which produces and distributes the work of emerging ethnic writers. He has been a lecturer at many universities and a juror of many literary awards. His own work includes several well-known novels that explore the hoodoo (or voodoo) folklore of Caribbean culture. Reed's poetry collections include *catechism of d neoamerican hoodoo church* (1970), *Conjure, Selected Poems* (1972), *A Secretary to the Spirits* (1978), and *New and Collected Poems* (1988).

Adrienne Rich (1929–   ) Adrienne Rich was born in Baltimore, Maryland, and home-schooled through the fourth grade in her well-to-do Jewish family. She attended Radcliffe College and published her first book of poems at the time of her graduation, receiving prestigious awards from the start. She married in 1953 and had three children, but had been separated from her husband when he committed suicide in 1970. Rich has taught at many colleges and universities and published not only poetry, but also translations, plays, and several controversial books on feminism and lesbianism. Her poetry collections include *A Change of World* (1951), *The Diamond Cutters and Other Poems* (1955), *Necessities of Life* (1966), and *An Atlas of the Difficult World* (1991).

Carl Ridenhour (c. 1960–) Carlton Ridenhour, better known as Chuck D., was educated at Adelphi University, where he studied graphic arts and published the first comic strip by an African-American student. He also worked as a dee-jay at the Adelphi radio station, broadcasting a program of rap and hip-hop, soon adding his own rap over prerecorded rhythm tracks. In 1980, he formed a rap group called Spectrum, which became Public Enemy in 1986. The group, calling themselves "prophets of rage" and urging African-American political consciousness, has raised and survived much controversy. Their releases include *Yo! Bum Rush the Show* (1987), *Fear of a Black Planet* (1990), and *Apocalypse 91: The Enemy Strikes Back* (1991).

Edward Arlington Robinson (1869–1935) Edward Arlington Robinson was born in Head Tide, Maine, the son of a wealthy merchant. He attended Harvard but left when the family fortunes declined; he then worked as office assistant, subway time-checker, and advertising editor. His poems kept garnering rejection slips, so he paid to publish his first collection. When Theodore Roosevelt read it in 1904, he secured Robinson a job in the New York custom house. Robinson went on to win three Pulitzer Prizes. He worked on the proofs of his last book as he lay dying of cancer. His works include *The Torrent and The Night Before* (1896), *The Man Who Died Twice* (1924), *Tristram* (1927), and *King Jasper* (1935).

Theodore Roethke (1908–1963) Theodore Roethke was born in Saginaw, Michigan, where his family ran a large greenhouse. Educated at the University of Michigan and at Harvard, he went on to a career of writing poetry and teaching, primarily as writer-in-residence at the University of Washington in Seattle. He also taught and coached tennis. Roethke died of a heart attack while swimming. His collections include the Pulitzer Prize-winning *The Waking: Poems 1933–1953* (1954) and *Words for the Wind* (1959).

Wendy Rose (1948–) Born in Oakland, California, Wendy Rose is a member of the Hopi/Miwok tribe. She was educated at the University of California at Berkeley. She is an anthropologist, a university lecturer in Native American Studies, and a visual artist, creating illustrations, exhibits, and graphic designs, usually in connection with Native American organizations. She has edited the *American Indian Quarterly,* and her poems have been published in many anthologies and periodicals as well as in the collections *Hopi Roadrunner Dancing* (1973), *Lost Copper* (1980), *The Halfbreed Chronicle* (1985), and *Bone Dance* (1994).

Isaac Rosenberg (1890–1918) Born in Bristol, England, Isaac Rosenberg published his first collection of poetry at age 22. While fighting in France during World War I, he published a volume of poems about the soldier's life, but he was killed in action that same year; his other war poems were published posthumously. His works include *Night and Day* (1912), *Youth* (1918), and *Poems* (1922).

Christina Rossetti (1830–1894) Christina Rossetti was born in London into a poor family. Her father was a native Italian who had come to England as a political refugee. Taught to read by her mother, Rossetti received no formal education. She remained single and cared for her parents in their old age. Her brother Dante Gabriel Rossetti was a well-known pre-Raphaelite painter. Her books include *The Prince's Progress and*

Other Poems (1861), *Goblin Market* (1862), the nursery-rhyme book *Sing-Song* (1872), and *A Pageant and Other Poems* (1881).

Sonia Sanchez (1934–   ) Born in Birmingham, Alabama, Sonia Sanchez moved to Harlem at age nine. She was educated at Hunter College and New York University, studying poetry and political science. In the 1960s she worked in the civil rights movement; she later joined the Nation of Islam for three years, but left after contesting the lesser role of women. A poet, playwright, short story writer, and children's book author, she has taught English, creative writing, and African-American literature in colleges and universities. She emphasizes the oral tradition in poetry and is known for her dramatic readings. Her collections include *Homecoming* (1969), *We a BaddDDD People* (1970), *homegirls & handgrenades* (1984) and *Under a Soprano Sky* (1987).

Yvonne Sapia (1946–   ) Yvonne Sapia was born in New York City, the daughter of a barber, and later settled in Florida. She was educated at Miami-Dade Community College, Florida Atlantic University, and other Florida universities. She has been a journalist, editor, and English instructor, and has taught elderly people, gifted children, and state prisoners. Her poems have been published in many periodicals and in the collections *The Fertile Crescent* (1983) and *Valentino's Hair* (1987).

Anne Sexton (1928–1974) Anne Sexton was born in Newton, Massachusetts, and educated at Boston and Brandeis universities. A suburban housewife by the age of 28, she had a nervous breakdown; writing poetry was an important part of her recovery. Still she recurrently struggled with mental illness. After teaching high school for a year and winning the 1967 Pulitzer Prize, she taught creative writing at Boston University from 1970 until her death by suicide in 1974. Her books of poetry include *To Bedlam and Part Way Back* (1960), *Live or Die* (1966), *The Death Notebooks* (1974), and *The Awful Rowing Toward God* (1975).

William Shakespeare (1564–1616) Born at Stratford-on-Avon into a family of eight children, Shakespeare did not receive much formal education, although he did learn Latin. He learned the craft of theater from the ground up, his experiences most likely beginning in the 1580s, when he went to London. Soon after, he became part of Lord Chamberlain's Men, a group that would later become the King's Men when James I came to the throne in 1603. By the 1590s, Shakespeare was considered by many Londoners to be an up-and-coming playwright, and in 1598, the famous Globe Theater was built. He retired from the theater in 1613, having written some 35 plays and maintained the same theater company for 19 years. His 154 sonnets, written from 1593 to 1601, were later published without his authorization. He died in Stratford-on-Avon at the age of 52. After Shakespeare's death, several members of the King's Men published his plays in a single volume in 1623, a significant action in a time when plays were not considered "literature." Shakespeare's most popular plays are *Hamlet, Othello, King Lear,* and *Macbeth,* although his history plays, comedies, and romances are also widely read and taught in schools. His poetic works include *Venus and Adonis* (1593), *The Rape of Lucrece* (1594), and *Sonnets* (1609).

Percy Bysshe Shelley (1792–1822) Born at Field Place, Sussex, England, Percy Bysshe Shelley was the eldest son of a country squire. He entered Oxford University but was expelled for authoring an atheistic pamphlet. In 1811, he eloped with Harriet Westbrook, but by 1814 his affections had waned. He had become the disciple of radical John Godwin and fled to France with Godwin's daughter. Shelley married Mary Wollstonecraft Godwin in 1816 after Harriet committed suicide. In 1818 they moved with their children to Italy, where Shelley wrote his best work before drowning in a boating accident at the age of 30. His works of poetry include *Queen Mab* (1813), *Prometheus Unbound* (1820), and *Adonais* (1821).

Michelle Shocked (c. 1962–) Michelle Shocked, who does not reveal her original name, was born into a strict Mormon family in Texas, but ran away at age 16. After wandering in the United States and Europe, she was discovered by Englishman Pete Lawrence during a campfire sing at a folk festival. He recorded her on a portable cassette player and later released her first album. Among her recordings are *Texas Campfire Tapes* (1987) and *Short Sharp Shocked* (1988).

Gary Snyder (1930–) Born in San Francisco and raised in Portland, Oregon, Gary Snyder studied Native American cultures as a teenager and developed skills in mountain climbing and wilderness survival. He was educated at Reed College, Indiana University, and the University of California at Berkeley, where he studied Asian languages and associated with the Beat poets. He also worked as a seaman, logger, trailblazer, and forest lookout. In 1956, he went to Japan to study Buddhism, and traveled and studied in the East for the next 12 years. A translator and essayist as well as a poet, he won the Pulitzer Prize in 1975. His collections include *Riprap* (1959), *The Turtle Island* (1974), *Left Out in the Rain* (1986), and *No Nature* (1992).

Cathy Song (1955–) Cathy Song was born into a Chinese-American family in Honolulu, Hawaii, and grew up on the island of Oahu. She was educated at the University of Hawaii, Wellesley College, and Boston University, and has taught creative writing at the University of Hawaii and other universities. Her poetry collections include *Picture Bride* (1983), *Frameless Windows, Squares of Light* (1988), and *School Figures* (1994).

Sophocles (c. 496–406 B.C.) Sophocles is considered to be one of the most important Greek playwrights, along with Aeschylus and Euripedes. Alive for most of the rise and decline of fifth-century Athens, Sophocles was an active public figure, acting, for example, as treasurer of the Athenian imperial league, but his greatest achievements were in theater. Of the 120 plays attributed to him, only seven survive: *Ajax, Trachiniae, Antigone, Oedipus Rex, Electra, Philoctetes,* and *Oedipus at Colonus*. Sophocles is credited for introducing a third character into dramatic performance and for enlarging the size of the chorus from 12 to 15 men. *Oedipus Rex*, which was first performed in Athens around 430 B.C., was used by Aristotle in his definition of tragedy and later by Freud as an example of the truth behind the "Oedipus Complex."

Roberto Sosa (1930–) Roberto Sosa was born in Yoro, Honduras. Although his work, which addresses both political terror and personal anguish, has sometimes been banned by the Honduran government, he has remained a cultural leader. He has been a university professor, the director of a university press, and a juror in many literary competitions. His poetry collections include *Muros [Walls]* 1966, *Los pobres [The Poor]* (1969), and *Un mundo para todos dividido [A World for All Divided]* (1991).

Gary Soto (1952–) Gary Soto was born and raised in Fresno, California, where his Mexican-American parents were migrant workers in the orchards and vegetable fields. He was educated at the California State University in Fresno and the University of California in Irvine. He has since taught Chicano studies and English at Berkeley. He also writes for children. His many poetry collections include *The Elements of San Joaquin* (1977), *Father Is a Pillow Tied to a Broom* (1980), *Living Up the Street* (1985), and *Home Course in Religion* (1991).

Wole Soyinka (1934–) Nigerian playwright Wole Soyinka attended the Government College in Ibadan and later Leeds University in England, where he earned his degree in English in 1957. After college, he remained in England, where he worked as a playwright but was also known as a political reformer and social critic. In 1959, he returned to Nigeria and began to produce his plays, which include *A Dance of the Forests* (1960), *The Road* (1965), and *Death and the King's Horseman* (1976). He was arrested in 1967 and held as a political prisoner. Upon his release in 1969, he wrote *The Man Died*, a memoir of his time spent in prison. In 1985, *A Play of Giants* was produced, and in 1986, Soyinka received the Nobel Prize for literature. Chinua Achebe once described Soyinka as a celebrant of life, even during tough times.

Bruce Springsteen (1949–) Bruce Springsteen was born and raised in Freehold, New Jersey, the only son of a bus driver and a secretary. Attracted to rock by Elvis Presley, he took up the guitar at age 14. When his parents moved to California in search of work, Springsteen stayed with friends in Freehold and played in local bands. He briefly attended Ocean City Community College, but by 1973 had founded what would be the E Street Band and established a regional reputation as a singer and songwriter. His manager got him a contract with Columbia records, launching his superstar career as "The Boss." Springsteen's albums include *Greetings from Asbury Park, NJ* (1973), *Born to Run* (1975), *Nebraska* (1982), *Tunnel of Love* (1987), and *Lucky Town* (1992).

William Stafford (1914–) Born in Hutchinson, Kansas, William Stafford grew up in small towns and fished, hunted, and camped. He was educated at the University of Kansas and the State University of Iowa. In World War II, he was a conscientious objector and so was assigned to labor camps. Exhausted by daily physical labor, he began rising early to write, a habit he has retained throughout his career. He lectured and taught at several universities and colleges, traveled in Egypt and the Middle East, then settled in Oregon, where he was named the state's poet laureate in 1975. His works include *West of Your City* (1960), *Stories That Could Be True* (1977), *An Oregon Message* (1987), and *The Darkness Around Us Deep* (1993).

Gertrude Stein (1874–1946) Gertrude Stein sought to achieve in writing what she called a "continuous present," relying more on description than on narration. Part of the avant garde movement in literature, Stein began living in Paris with her lover, Alice B. Toklas, in 1909. Stein's work was affected by the Cubist painters Picasso and Matisse. She in turn advised younger writers, such as Fitzgerald and Hemingway. Stein's works include *How To Write* (1931), a book of examples; *Tender Buttons* (1914), poetry; *The Making of Americans* (1925), and *Lectures in America* (1935), which describes her philosophy of composition. Stein is considered one of the most radically experimental of the writers of her time. William Carlos Williams said about her work, "Stein has systematically gone smashing every connotation that words have ever had, in order to get them back clean."

Wallace Stevens (1879–1955) Wallace Stevens was born in Reading, Pennsylvania, the son of a lawyer and a schoolteacher. He was educated at Harvard, but left early because of a shortage of family funds. He was a journalist in New York City for a year, but then decided on a law career and went to New York Law School. In 1916, he joined the legal staff of a Hartford insurance company, where he remained for nearly 40 years, writing poetry alongside his law career. It is said he often wrote poems in his head, then dictated them to his secretary. Stevens won a Pulitzer Prize the year he died. His works include *Harmonium* (1923), *Owl's Clover* (1936), *Transport to Summer* (1947), and *The Collected Poems of Wallace Stevens* (1954).

Mark Strand (1934–) Mark Strand was born in Summerside, Prince Edward Island, Canada, but grew up in various American cities, following his salesman father. As a child, he had no facility with words and wanted to be a painter, but by 20 he had decided to be a poet. He was educated at Antioch, Yale, and the State University of Iowa, and has held several professorships. In personal appearances, he is known for his comic flair. Strand was named to the year-long post of United States Poet Laureate in 1990. He has published short stories, children's books, and translations as well as many volumes of poetry, including *Sleeping With One Eye Open* (1964), *The Story of Our Lives* (1973), *The Continuous Life* (1990), and *Dark Harbor: A Poem* (1993).

Ronald Sukenick (1932–) Born in Brooklyn, Ronald Sukenick received a B.A. from Cornell University in 1955 and a Ph.D. in English from Brandeis University in 1962. Sukenick has been a critic of modern poetry and postmodern fiction, a professor of creative writing and literature, publisher of the American Book Review, and co-founder of the Fiction Collective, a group of writers who publish experimental fiction. He has also written several books, including *The Death of the Novel and Other Stories* (1969), *Out* (1973), and *Long Talking Bad Condition Blues* (1979). A blurring of the nonfictional and the fictional character characterizes much of Sukenick's writing. "The Birds," he says, "is the purest improvisation and I had no idea where it was going until the fragments started coming together pretty much of their own accord towards the end." His most recent work, *Doggy Bag: A Collection of Stories,* appeared in 1994.

May Swenson (1919–1989) May Swenson was born to Swedish immigrants in Logan, Utah. She was educated at Utah State University, then worked as an editor in New York City, where she lived for 40 years, making forays to universities all across the country to lecture and read. Among Swenson's books of poetry are two volumes for children. Some of her titles are *Another Arrival* (1954), *Iconographs* (1970), *In Other Words* (1987), and *Nature: Poems Old and New* (1994).

Jonathan Swift (1667–1745) At the age of 14, Jonathan Swift enrolled in Trinity College, Dublin. Subsequently, he attended Oxford University, earning a doctorate of divinity in 1702. A member of the Whig literary circle, Swift befriended Joseph Addison, Richard Steele, and Matthew Prior. After a change in government in 1710, Swift became a part of a new circle, of which Alexander Pope was also a member. Thought to be the greatest prose satirist in the history of English literature, Swift perfected his satirical techniques with the publication of *A Tale of a Tub* in 1704. In 1720, *A Modest Proposal,* an ironic piece that urged the Irish to raise their children for food, was published. At the age of 58, just before the publication of his satiric masterpiece, *Gulliver's Travels* (1726), he wrote to a friend: "I have finished my Travells, and I am now transcribing them: they are admirable Things, and will wonderfully mend the World." Swift also wrote poetry, such as *Cadenus and Vanessa* (1726), and with the publication of essays on the subject of his poetry, he became well known as a master of satiric verse in addition to satiric prose.

Shinkichi Takahashi (1901–1987) Shinkichi Takahashi was born in Japan in the fishing village of Shikoku. He attended high school but dropped out and was otherwise self-educated. He later settled in Tokyo and became the disciple of a Zen master. He wrote many books on Zen and gained a reputation in Japan as the greatest modern Zen poet. His collections include *Afterimages* (1970) and *Complete Poems* (1972).

Mary Tallmountain (1918–1994) Mary Tallmountain was born of Athabaskan, Russian, and Scots-Irish heritage in the Alaskan bush. She later settled in San Francisco. She was an editor of anthologies as well as the author of several volumes of poetry. Her works include *Nine Poems* (1979), *There is No Word for Goodbye* (1981), *Green March Moons* (1987), and *The Light on the Tent Wall: A Bridging* (1990).

Alfred, Lord Tennyson (1809–1892) Alfred Tennyson was born in Somersby, Lincolnshire, England, one of 12 children of an alcoholic clergyman. He attended Cambridge University, but left early because of family problems. He and his brother jointly published a volume of poetry, but after his next two collections were poorly reviewed and a close friend died, Tennyson was silent for 10 years. In 1842, two new volumes were hailed as great poetry. In 1850, Tennyson married his fiance of 14 years and was named Poet Laureate by Queen Victoria. He was elevated to baron in 1883 and added "Lord" to his name. His works include *Poems, Chiefly Lyrical* (1832), *Poems* (1842), *In Memoriam* (1850), and *Idylls of the King* (1859).

Dylan Thomas (1914–1953) Dylan Thomas was born in Swansea, Wales, where his father taught in the grammar school. He did not attend university but moved to London in 1934 and worked as a reporter, reviewer, and actor. He soon married, then settled in a Welsh fishing village and struggled to support his wife and children. In the 1940s he worked in radio for the BBC, making broadcasts and writing film and radio scripts. He later took reading tours of the United States, gaining a reputation for heavy drinking and womanizing. He died in New York City of complications from alcoholism. His poetry collections include *Eighteen Poems* (1934), *Deaths and Entrances* (1946), *Twenty-six Poems* (1950), and *In Country Sleep and Other Poems* (1952).

Henry David Thoreau (1817–1862) Henry David Thoreau spent nearly his entire life in Concord, Massachusetts. His family was not wealthy but made enough money from their pencil-making business to send Thoreau to Harvard College in 1833. Upon graduation he was asked to teach at the Concord school in the same one-room schoolhouse he'd attended as a child. Later he quit, after refusing to adhere to the school's use of corporal punishment, and established his own private school with his brother in 1838. Around this time he also befriended Ralph Waldo Emerson, who encouraged him to keep a journal. Journal-keeping would become a life-long habit for Thoreau. Eventually the private school closed down and Thoreau set out to build a cabin in the Walden woods, where he lived for two years, two months, and two days on the earnings of only six weeks of work. *Walden* (1854), considered by some to be the preeminent piece of nature writing, includes this experience. "Civil Disobedience," which he wrote in 1849, after a night spent in jail for not paying his taxes, influenced activists such as Mahatma Gandhi and Martin Luther King, Jr.

James Thurber (1894–1961) James Thurber attended Ohio State University, where he did poorly but managed to gain an extensive literary background. After college, Thurber traveled to Paris, where he worked for the U.S. Army, and later he landed a job as a free-lance reporter for newspapers written in English. In 1926, he moved to New York City and began working for the *New Yorker*. His short story "The Secret Life of Walter Mitty" appeared in the *New Yorker* in 1939 and since then has become an American classic. In fact, the character of Walter Mitty is now an entry in most dictionaries. At the *New Yorker*, Thurber shared an office with E. B. White, who was an influential and encouraging friend. Thurber once defined humor as "a kind of emotional chaos told about calmly and quietly in retrospect." Some of his works are *The Middle-Aged Man on the Flying Trapeze* (1935), *My World—and Welcome to It* (1942), *Alarms and Diversions* (1957), and *Credos and Curios* (1962), a posthumous collection of stories and sketches.

Anne Tyler (1941–) Anne Tyler was born in Minnesota and spent her early youth in the South, living on Quaker communes until she was 11 years old. She received a B.A. degree from Duke University in 1961 and continued with Russian studies at Columbia University for another year. Some of her best-known novels are *The Clock Winder* (1972), *Celestial Navigation* (1974), *Earthly Possessions* (1977), *Dinner at the Homesick Restaurant* (1982), *Accidental Tourist* (1985), and *Breathing Lessons* (1988). She is also a contributor to numerous periodicals. Her novel *Accidental Tourist* received the National Book Critics Circle fiction award and a Pulitzer Prize nomination for fiction. Tyler now lives with her husband and two daughters in Baltimore, a city she describes as a "wonderful territory for a writer—so many different things to poke around in."

Evangelina Vigil (1952–) Of Mexican-American descent, Evangelina Vigil grew up in San Antonio, Texas. She has edited an anthology of Hispanic woman writers, and in her own poetry she chronicles the exploitation of Mexican Americans by Anglo Americans, while also celebrating the customs and traditions of everyday life. Her collections include *Thirty an'seen a Lot* (1985), and *The Computer Is Down* (1987).

Derek Walcott (1930–) Derek Walcott was born in Castries, St Lucia, West Indies, the son of a civil servant and a teacher. His heritage was both colonial and Caribbean (both his grandfathers were white; both his grandmothers were black), and this racial and ethnic mix has figured in his work. He learned English as a second language after his native French-English patois. He was educated at St. Mary's College and the University of the West Indies in Jamaica. A poet and playwright, he taught in the West Indies and founded the Trinidad Theatre Workshop before taking visiting professorships at American universities. His works include *Twenty-five Poems* (1948), *In a Green Night* (1962), *Sea Grapes* (1976), and *The Arkansas Testament* (1987). Walcott was awarded a Nobel Prize for literature in 1992.

Alice Walker (1944–) Alice Walker was born in Georgia and attended Spelman College and Sarah Lawrence College in the 1960s. At Sarah Lawrence, Walker became pregnant and chose to have an abortion. After this experience she wrote poetry that made up her first book, *Once*, published in 1968. Her first novel, *The Third Life of Grange Copeland* (1970), was also written while she was attending Sarah Lawrence. In the summer of 1966, she decided to volunteer at the voter registration drive in Mississippi rather than accept a writing fellowship. She claims her decision stemmed from "the realization that I could never live happily in Africa—or anywhere else—until I could live freely in Mississippi." Walker is best known for *The Color Purple* (1982), which was a National Book Award winner. She has also written several books of poetry, short stories, and essays.

Margaret Walker (1915–) Born in Birmingham, Alabama, the daughter of a minister and a music teacher, Margaret Walker grew up in a household where both words and creativity were valued. She was educated at Northwestern University and the University of Iowa and at 27 was the youngest twentieth-century African American to publish a volume of poetry. She was a social worker, reporter, and magazine editor before settling into her literary career. A novelist as well as a poet, she has taught English at universities and developed black studies programs. Among her works of poetry are *For My People* (1942), *Ballad of the Free* (1966), *October Journey* (1973), and *This Is My Country* (1989).

Robert Penn Warren (1905–1994) Born in Guthrie, Kentucky, Robert Penn Warren hoped to be a naval officer, but an accident with his eyes canceled his appointment to Annapolis. He studied instead at Vanderbilt University, the University of California at Berkeley, Yale, and Oxford. He later settled in Tennessee, and in the 1940s was known for his novels. In 1954, after 10 years of "poet's block," he turned primarily to poetry. He was the first writer to win Pulitzers for both fiction and poetry. In 1986, he was named the first Poet Laureate of the United States. His collections include *Thirty-six Poems* (1935), *Promises* (1957), *Now and Then* (1978), and *Chief Joseph of the Nez Perce* (1983).

Eudora Welty (1909–) Eudora Welty was born and raised in comfortable circumstances in Jackson, Mississippi, where she has spent almost her entire life. In 1929, she earned a B.A. from the University of Wisconsin, and in 1930–1931 she studied advertising at Columbia University. *A Curtain of Green*, her first book of short stories, appeared in 1941, followed by *The Robber Bridegroom* (1942), *Delta Wedding* (1946), *The Bride of the Innisfallen and Other Stories* (1955), and *The Optimist's Daughter* (1972), for which she won a Pulitzer Prize. Welty received strong support from Katherine Anne Porter, whose writing she admired. Most of Welty's stories demonstrate an attachment to regionalism, and she has said of her work, "Location is the ground conductor of all the currents of emotion and belief and moral conviction that charge out from the story in its course."

E. B. White (1899–1985) E. B. White knew at the age of eight that he wanted to be a writer. He attended Cornell University, where he was the president of his fraternity and the editor-in-chief of the weekly college newspaper. He graduated in 1921 and in 1926 became a staff member of the *New Yorker*, and it is thought that his work and style of writing helped the magazine become a success. At the *New Yorker* he befriended James Thurber, whose artwork White pulled from the trash and successfully submitted to the magazine when Thurber was hesitant to try himself. White's collections of essays include *Every Day is Saturday* (1935), *One Man's Meat* (1942), *The Second Tree From the Corner* (1954), and *The Points of My Compass* (1962). He is also known for his children's books: *Stuart Little* (1945), *Charlotte's Web* (1952), one of the best-selling children's books of all time, and *The Trumpet of the Swan* (1971). When asked about the difference between writing for children and writing for adults, White claimed: "In my experience, the only difference (save for a very slight modification of vocabulary) is in one's state of mind." In 1978, White received the Pulitzer Prize special citation for the body of his work.

Walt Whitman (1819–1892) Walt Whitman was born the son of a poor farmer in West Hills, Long Island, New York. He worked as a schoolteacher, printer, and newspaper editor and published many articles on education, public health, the status of women, prison reform, and the arts. His fervent antislavery opinions finally cost him his job. In 1855 he self-published the poetry collection *Leaves of Grass*, which was to undergo revisions and additions in at least nine later editions. During the Civil War, Whitman volunteered as a hospital nurse and soon wrote the poems for *Drum-Taps* (1865). He held various government posts before suffering a paralytic stroke in 1873. Partially disabled, he lived in Camden, New Jersey, until his death.

John Edgar Wideman (1941–) John Edgar Wideman was born in Washington, D. C., but later moved with his family to Pittsburgh. He attended the University of Pennsylvania, where he quickly established a reputation as a basketball star. Originally a psychology major, he switched to English when psychology "turned out to be rats." After graduating, he pursued a degree in eighteenth-century studies at Oxford University. At the age of 26, he began teaching at the University of Pennsylvania and celebrated the publication of his first book, *A Glance Away*, in 1967. Other works followed: *The Lynchers* (1973); *Hiding Place* (1981); *Sent for You Yesterday* (1983), for which he received the PEN/Faulkner Award, and *Brothers and Keepers* (1984). In 1992, *The Collected Stories of John Edgar Wideman* was published. In his daily life, Wideman attempts to stand by his grandfather's message: "Give them the benefit of the doubt."

Richard Wilbur (1921–) Born in New York City and educated at Amherst College and Harvard, Richard Wilbur served in World War II and then—as poet, lyricist, and translator of French poetry and plays—taught at many prestigious colleges. He later lived in western Massachusetts and Florida. He has received two Pulitzer Prizes and was named U.S. Poet Laureate for 1987–1988. His works include *The Beautiful Changes* (1947), *Things of This World* (1956), *The Mind Reader* (1976), and *More Opposites* (1991).

William Carlos Williams (1883–1963) Born in Rutherford, New Jersey, William Carlos Williams studied medicine at the University of Pennsylvania and the University of Liepzig and from 1910 to 1951 was a practicing physician in New Jersey, often dashing off poems between patients. He was also a playwright, novelist, and essayist. In the late 1940s he had the first of a series of strokes that plagued his later years, even as he wrote poetry that won a Pulitzer Prize the year he died. His collections include *The*

Tempers (1913), *Spring and All* (1923), *The Pink Church* (1949), and *Pictures from Breughel* (1962).

William Wordsworth (1770–1850) Born in Cockersmouth, Cumberland, England, William Wordsworth had lost both his parents by the time he was 13. He was educated at Cambridge University and traveled in Europe. In 1798, he published *Lyrical Ballads* with his friend Samuel Taylor Coleridge, and wrote a preface that became the defining document of English Romantic poetry. The publication of *The Excursion* in 1814 marked the end of Wordsworth's most productive period, but Queen Victoria still appointed him Poet Laureate in 1843. Wordsworth had married long-time friend Mary Hutchinson in 1802 and he lived in England's Lake District until his death.

James Wright (1927–1980) Born in Martins Ferry, Ohio, James Wright was educated at Kenyon College and the University of Washington, served in World War II, and taught at colleges and universities. He was a translator of poetry and a critic and won the 1972 Pulitzer Prize. He died of cancer, leaving many books of poetry, including *A Green Wall* (1957), *The Branch Will Not Break* (1963), *Collected Poems* (1971), and *The Temple in Nimes* (1982).

Richard Wright (1908–1960) Richard Wright grew up with relatives in Mississippi after his father deserted his family. Later he made his way to Chicago and then to New York City, where he began publishing his early short stories. His first collection of stories, *Uncle Tom's Children*, appeared in 1938. Shortly after, *Native Son* (1940) was published and became a best-seller, making Wright the first black American author of a best-seller. After *Native Son*, Wright turned to autobiographical works, such as *Black Boy* (1945), which describes the violence of his early life. In 1947, he settled permanently in France, where he was perceived as an important experimental modernist prose writer. Ralph Ellison claimed that Wright's example "converted the American Negro impulse toward self-annihilation and 'going underground' into a will to confront the world."

Mitsuye Yamada (1923–) The daughter of an interpreter and a seamstress, Mitsuye Yamada was born in Fukuoka, Japan, but grew up in Seattle, Washington. During World War II, she and her family spent time in an internment camp in Idaho. She was educated at New York University, the University of Chicago, and the University of California at Irvine, and became a U.S. citizen in 1955. She settled in California as a college teacher. Her works include *Camp Notes and Other Poems* (1976) and *Desert Run: Poems and Stories* (1989).

W. B. Yeats (1865–1939) William Butler Yeats was born in Dublin, the son of a noted portrait painter. He went to art school for three years, but then chose a literary career. His first collection of poems was published in London in 1889. He went on to found what was to become the Abbey Theater and wrote plays for many years. After the Irish Free State was established, he served as senator from 1922 to 1928. In 1923, he was awarded the Nobel Prize for literature. His works include *The Wanderings of Oisin* (1889) and *A Vision* (1938).

Cyn. Zarco (1950–) Cyn. Zarco was born in Manila, the Phillipines, of Filipino, Chinese, and Spanish heritage. When she was nine, her father, a microbiologist, moved the family to Miami, where there was no Asian-American community, and she was suddenly an outsider and a loner. Educated at the University of California at Berkeley and at Columbia University, she pursued a career in journalism, specializing in profiles of artists and celebrities, and later becoming an accomplished photographer as well. After many years in San Francisco and New York, she settled in Miami Beach. Her poetry includes the collection *cir'cum.nav'i.ga'tion* (1986).

GLOSSARY

absurd, theater of the   a kind of nonrealistic drama that depicts helpless or ignorant **characters** in meaningless or confusing situations that usually have no logical **resolution**.

aesthetic   having to do with beauty or pleasure, especially in the artistic sense. (See also **didactic**.)

aesthetic distance   a sense of detachment from or noninvolvement with a **character** or a situation depicted in art. This sense of distance does not mean apathy so much as detached contemplation. It depends on a reader's awareness that writing is a representation of reality, not reality itself.

allegory   a **narrative** in which the literal meanings of **characters**, actions, and perhaps **settings** have consistent correspondences on a **symbolic** level. Usually the symbolic meaning involves philosophical, moral, or religious abstractions.

alliteration   repetition of a sound, usually a consonant sound, in a sequence of words in a line of **verse**. Related **text strategies** are **consonance**, the repetition of words having the same consonants but different main vowels, and **assonance**, the repetition of stressed vowels in words having different consonants.

allusion   a brief, indirect or implied reference in a text to something (often literary) outside the text. Because it refers to extratextual matters, allusion assumes a harmonious literary interaction between text and reader. (See also **intertextuality**.)

arena stage   a theater stage that the audience surrounds on all sides, also known as **theater in the round**.

aside   a **convention** of drama in which a **character** speaks words to the audience that other characters in the same scene do not hear. (See also **soliloquy**.)

assonance   See **alliteration**.

ballad   a **narrative** poem, originating in oral poetry, usually recounting a single episode in a character's life or mentioning some of the deeds for which a character is famous or infamous and usually featuring **quatrains** rhyming *abcb* and a repeated **refrain**.

bibliography   a list of sources, in any medium, that provide information about a topic. A **working bibliography** is a list of sources being considered for consultation on a topic. A **works cited list** is a bibliography limited to sources actually cited—whose words are quoted directly or paraphrased or whose ideas are summarized—in a particular paper.

black comedy   See **comedy**, **tragicomedy**.

blank verse   unrhymed iambic pentameter lines.

bourgeois tragedy   See **tragedy**.

box set   See **set**.

1702

branching a **prewriting** technique in which ideas generate other ideas and the relationship between ideas is diagrammed by lines or "branches" connecting them.

canon in literary study, a list of texts, generally agreed upon by cultural authorities such as scholars, critics, and teachers as "major" or "classic" texts and therefore most often read and taught in college courses. Although there is a sense that such texts are "timeless" or "universal" masterpieces, their *canonicity* is more nearly the result of complex ideological values. Because of this, the *canon*, while relatively stable in general, is subject to ideological and historical changes.

character a verbal representation in literature of a person (although animals, non-corporeal beings, and even inanimate objects have been characters too). Characters have been classified as *round*, if they are presented in some depth and complexity; *flat*, if they are one-dimensional; *dynamic*, if they change; *or static*, if they remain the same. (See also **stock character**.)

Classical tragedy See **tragedy**.

climax that moment in the **plot** of a story or play at which tensions are highest or **suspense** reaches its height.

close reading a detailed analysis of a literary work, especially a poem, seeking to demonstrate how various elements work together to produce an effect or convey a **theme**.

closet drama a **play** usually written in verse and intended to be read rather than acted out in a theater.

clustering a **prewriting** technique in which similar ideas or topics are clustered or grouped together to show their relationship to other ideas or topics. An example is shown in Chapter 4.

cognitive analysis a purpose in response-based writing to examine how and why you process a given text the way you do. In cognitive analysis you may study your choice of **reading strategies** and their effects on your response or the causes of those reading strategies in terms of your **literary experience** or **ideology** and the **literary repertoire** and ideology of the text. Undertaking a cognitive analysis of your response to a text is one way to become a stronger reader by pursuing self-consciousness as a goal.

comedy a kind of drama that aims to amuse and that ends happily. In the history of Western drama, several types of comedy have developed: **romantic** comedy, which presents young lovers involved in a difficult situation; **satiric** comedy, which invites laughter at the social or political errors of some **character** or characters; **sentimental** comedy, in which generally flat characters experience the triumph of virtue; **black** comedy, which makes death, disease, or the doomed situation of the characters a subject for humor; and **farce**, which involves exaggerated characters in ludicrous situations and much physical activity. A distinction has also been drawn between *high* comedy, inviting intellectual laughter through mainly verbal humor and wit, and *low* comedy, inviting "belly laughs" through physical humor and clowning. (See also **comedy of humours, comedy of manners, tragicomedy**.)

comedy of humours a type of dramatic **comedy** popular in sixteenth-century England that presents characters with a sort of psychological imbalance deriving from the dominance of one of the supposed bodily humours or dispositions.

comedy of manners a type of dramatic **comedy**, often *satiric*, that invites, through clever **dialogue**, thoughtful laughter at the social behavior of sophisticated **characters**.

comic relief in drama, the interruption of serious or tragic action by humorous incidents, episodes, or characters; for instance, the gravedigger scene in Shakespeare's *Hamlet*, Act 5, Scene 1.

conceit in poetry, especially in European Renaissance and seventeenth-century poetry, an ingenious and elaborate comparison, often implied, between two unlike things.

concrete poetry a type of poetry that attempts graphically to show a relation between form and content; the arrangement of type on the page, the visual form in which the poem is written or laid out, represents some aspect of the intellectual or emotional content of the language of the poem.

conflict as an aspect of **plot** in fiction or drama, any opposition (as between two **characters**, or a single character and his or her environment, or a single character's desires and whatever forces limit or thwart those desires, or between elements within a character's personality) that tends to generate interest and **suspense** on the part of a reader.

connotation the emotional overtones that some words carry, as distinct from their **denotations** or literal meanings. Connotations may be nearly universal among speakers of a language, or words may have certain connotations only for certain groups or communities or even for individual people alone. One widespread connotation of "dog" is a "worthless person." (See also **denotation.)**

consistency building the putting together of separate bits of information and making tentative conclusions while reading, in order to develop a sense of the meaning of a text. Usually, readers engage in consistency building without being aware of it, but a self-conscious reader can observe his or her processes of reading and so take a first step toward a **cognitive analysis**. (See also **wandering viewpoint**.)

consoling reading an interaction of **ideologies** between a reader and a text in which the apparent values of the text confirm those the reader brings to the text. (See also **resisting reading**.)

consonance See **alliteration**.

convention any **text strategy** that, through repeated practice by writers and general acceptance by readers, becomes thought of as a "natural" feature of a literary genre. Readers' familiarity with such text strategies contributes to their using certain **reading strategies** that may also be thought of as conventional. This fact is revealed when a reader encounters an unconventional text and finds that his or her familiar reading strategies seem to fail as she or he tries to process the text.

couplet two adjacent lines of **verse** having the same end **rhyme**. The English or Shakespearean **sonnet** closes with a couplet, and Shakespeare also routinely used couplets to signal the close of a scene to his theater audience. The *heroic* couplet, popular in eighteenth-century English poetry, is two rhyming lines of **iambic pentameter**. The *closed* couplet is a complete grammatical unit or sentence.

cultural analysis an exercise in response-based writing to examine how and why your **ideology** and that of the text interact the way they do. A cultural analysis may study the ways in which your culture influences you to read and respond as you do, the cultural values you bring to a text and their influence on your reading, or, through research, the cultural context of a text that influences its ideology. Undertaking a cultural analysis of your response to a text is one way to become a stronger reader by pursuing self-consciousness as a goal.

denotation the surface, objective, or emotionally neutral meaning of a word; what a word "stands for" as a sign. The *denotation* of "dog" is "a four-legged carnivorous mammal, often domesticated." (See also **connotation**.)

denouement originally a French word for an "untying," it signifies the moment of final **resolution** of the **conflict** in a **plot**.

dialogue in fiction or drama, the spoken words of **characters** in conversation with one another. In fiction, dialogue may be distinguished from narration, which is the words of a **narrator** telling the story.

diction word choice. In literary texts, diction may be a matter of **style**; it is also a **text strategy**, because the use of one word instead of another of the same **denotation** but different **connotation** may affect a reader in a particular way. In essays particularly, diction may be used for **rhetorical** effect.

didactic said of writing whose purpose is to expound a particular belief, especially a moral, philosophical, or religious one. In general, a **formal essay** is didactic. So are some plays, poems, and short stories. (See also **aesthetic**.)

direct quotation the reproduction of the exact words of a source, in the same order in which they appeared in the source. Conventionally, direct quotations are indicated by quotation marks at the beginning and end of the quoted material. In an academic paper, any direct quotation requires the citation of its source.

documentation the systematic supplying of information regarding sources used, especially in a researched paper. In Chapter 28, this book recommends the MLA system of documentation.

drafting the process of putting thoughts into words for a formal paper; writing a version of a paper.

dramatic irony See **irony**.

dramatic monologue a type of **lyric** poem in which the words of the poem are presumably spoken by a specific person or **character** to another person or character in a specific situation or **setting**.

dramatized narrator in fiction, the **voice** that relates the events of the story and is also a **character** in the story. (See also **involved narrator**.)

editing the final stage of the writing process for an academic paper; checking the writing for its adherence to standard practices in terms of grammar, punctuation, and spelling.

epic originally a form of oral **narrative** poetry, although later composed in writing, that presents the deeds and adventures of a hero in numerous episodes that ultimately determine the fate of a nation or race.

epigram a short poem, usually fewer than six lines, that ends in a clever turn of thought.

etymology the linguistic history of a word, including its origin and passage from language to language. Standard dictionaries provide *etymologies* of most words in brackets. Considering a word's *etymology* can be a useful strategy when considering the **play** of meanings—**denotations** and **connotations**—in poetic uses of language.

exposition that part of a **short story** or **play**, usually early, that provides background information on **characters**, on **setting**, and **plot**.

falling action that part of the **plot** of a **short story** or **play**, following the **climax**, in which action and **suspense** decline toward a **resolution**.

farce See **comedy**.

figurative language   departures from the normal or literal way in which words express meaning, used to achieve special effects or emphases. Linguistic *figures* include **metaphor, metonymy, personification, simile, synechdoche**, and others.

fixed-form poetry   types of poems whose form has been set by tradition and convention. Examples include the **haiku**, the **pantoum**, the **sestina**, the **sonnet**, and the **villanelle**. (See also **open-form poetry**.)

flash-forward   in fiction or drama, a leap forward in time to tell or show events that have yet to occur in "present" time in the story or play.

flashback   in fiction or drama, a leap backward in time to tell or show events that have preceded those of "present" time in the story or play.

foil   in drama, a **character** whose qualities are in sharp contrast to those of another character and who, by virtue of this contrast, emphasizes the qualities of the other character.

formal essay   a kind of nonfiction **prose** that takes a serious approach to a topic, presents its ideas in a carefully structured fashion, often making an explicit statement of its **thesis**, and tends to hide the presence of the writer behind an "objective" **voice**.

found poetry   any verbal text a person might find somewhere and rearrange on the page to resemble a poem.

free verse   See **open-form poetry**.

freewriting   a **prewriting** technique whereby the writer writes nonstop for a set period of time on whatever comes to mind in relation to a topic or initial idea and does not stop to consider **diction**, spelling, or grammatical correctness.

gaps   places in a text where something, for example description, explanation, information, is "left out." Some gaps are recognizable by most readers of a text, but other gaps may be identified or created by individual readers. This activity is a **reading strategy**.

genre   a category of writing or of art according to the **text strategies** that a number of similar texts have in common. Poetry is a genre; the **ballad** is a genre.

haiku   a **fixed form** of poetry consisting of three lines of 17 syllables altogether, broken down into lines of 5, 7, and 5 syllables. Because of their shortness, haiku usually are written in very concrete language.

ideology   the accumulated knowledge, beliefs, opinions, values, experiences, and memories (both conscious and unconscious) of a society or culture and its individual members. The term is popularly applied to specifically political orientation, but it should be understood as much broader than that, applying to all social or cultural beliefs and practices and revealing itself in texts of all kinds, literary and otherwise. Within *ideology* in the broad sense, certain ideas and values are dominant at any particular time and others are marginalized.

imagery   language that recalls specific, usually visual, sensations from the wider world and in the process associates a topic with those sensations. By appealing to the reader's senses, *imagery* is concrete, rather than abstract, language.

indeterminacy   a quality of uncertainty, undecidability, or ambiguity perceived by a reader at any place in a text. Indeterminacy is closely associated with **gaps**, but may be differentiated in two ways: one, in being a less precisely and "objectively" definable quality of a text, more a matter of a reader's perceptions; two, in being also a quality of reading or interpretation itself.

informal essay a kind of nonfiction prose that takes an exploratory approach to a topic, which may be the writer himself or herself; usually does not state a **thesis** explicitly; assumes a relatively loose **structure**; and often uses **text strategies** similar to those of fiction, drama, or poetry.

intertextuality the implied reference to one text in another or the implied influence of one text on another. The concept of *intertextuality* enables a reader to make connections between texts in different **genres**, for example those considered "serious" art and those from "popular" or mass culture. (See also **allusion**.)

involved narrator a **character** in a piece of fiction, involved in the action, from whose **point of view** the story is told. Because information is conveyed to the reader through the character, the character is the narrator, if the point of view is first person; or the **narrative focus**, if the point of view is third person. A first-person involved narrator is also called a **dramatized** narrator; a third-person involved narrative focus is also called **limited**. (See also **omniscient narrator**.)

irony broadly construed, a difference between appearance and reality. Irony may take verbal form as words that seem to mean one thing but actually mean something different from or even the opposite of their apparent meaning; this is **verbal** irony. In drama, irony may involve the audience knowing something of which a **character** is unaware and the character acting in a way that is markedly different from the truth of the situation as the audience knows it; this is **dramatic** irony.

limited narration the opposite of **omniscient narration**: the telling of a story from any **point of view** from which knowledge (about characters, actions, consequences, meanings, etc.) could not be complete. Any **dramatized narrator** is necessarily limited. (See also **involved narrator** and **omniscient narration**.)

literary experience everything that a reader brings to the interaction with a text in the way of experience with, knowledge or beliefs about, or expectations for specifically literary matters. Literary experience includes the texts a reader has read previously; knowledge of particular **text strategies** previously encountered; **reading strategies** for a kind of text or a particular reading situation; and expectations for a particular reading interaction or specific text, based on similar interactions in the past.

literary repertoire the set of practices available to a literary text, the text strategies it has available to use, or the beliefs about literary matters that exist in the cultural context in which a text is produced.

lyric a short poem expressing the thoughts or feelings of a single **speaker** on a specific subject and on a particular occasion.

melodrama a kind of **play**, especially popular in nineteenth-century Western theater, in which one-dimensionally good or wicked **characters** appeal to the most easily evoked emotions of the audience and in which dramatic **conflicts** are resolved in simplistically happy or sad endings.

metaphor a type of **figurative language** implying an analogy between two things or ideas that are usually not thought of as similar. Often one is abstract, the other concrete. Typically, one thing is referred to *as* the other: in Shinkichi Takahashi's poem "Explosion," for instance, the (presumably human) speaker says he *is* a dog, a cat, a fog, and a rain.

meter recurrent, structured **rhythm** in poetry; a pattern of alternating stressed and unstressed syllables. Meter is described in terms of poetic **feet**—units consisting of a combination of stressed and unstressed syllables—and the number of such feet in a line of **verse**. The standard metric feet in English verse are the *iamb* (unstressed, stressed), the *trochee* (stressed, unstressed), the *anapest* (unstressed, unstressed, stressed), and the *dactyl* (stressed, unstressed, unstressed). The number of feet per line is expressed in one word, of which *meter* is the root and to which numerical prefixes are attached: *mono*meter (one foot), *di*meter (two feet), *tri*meter (three feet) and so on.

metonymy   a type of **figurative language** in which one thing is referred to in terms of another thing with which it is commonly associated; for instance, "the *White House*" for "the American *president*" or "the *presidential staff.*"

monovalent   having just one, or one dominant, meaning; monovalent language is found, for instance, in road signs and other directional discourse (recipes, instruction manuals). In reading any text, however, a reader may decide whether the language of that text is monovalent or **polyvalent**: whether it has one meaning or several.

narrating   a **reading strategy** for drama that involves writing down notes; or **narrative prose** that recounts the events of the unfolding **plot** of a **play**.

narrative   a story, whether told in verse or in prose. The term narrative emphasizes the *told* quality of the story, not just the sequence of events that constitute the action.

narrative focus   a **character** in a piece of fiction through whose **point of view** the story is told but who does not tell the story himself or herself; a third-person **involved narrator**.

narrator   in fiction, the implied person or **voice** who relates the action and **characters** to the reader. A narrator may be a **character**, in which case the *narration* or **point of view** may be called **involved**. If a narrator is not a character so much as a **voice** that reveals certain information to the reader, with a certain **tone** or attitude, the *narration* is said to be **omniscient** or detached. Depending upon the degree of trust a reader may place in the implied personality of a narrator or the information a narrator provides, *narration* may also be described as **reliable** or **unreliable**. (See also **point of view**.)

naturalism   a tendency in nineteenth-century Western literature to "objectively" portray human beings as subject to large "natural" forces—biological, social, economic—beyond their conscious control.

naturalizing   a **reading strategy** in which a reader ignores or downplays the **conventionality** of **text strategies** or differences between the **ideology** of a text and his or her own and processes those text strategies or that ideology as "natural," "universal," or "logical." Naturalizing to some extent is always involved in the reading interaction, but its presence as a reading strategy may go unnoticed with texts that are conventional or whose ideology seems close to the reader's. Conversely, texts with "strange" text strategies or ideas may reveal naturalizing as a reading strategy, whether it succeeds or fails as a processing technique.

octave   any eight-line **stanza** in poetry, but usually limited to mean the first eight lines of a **sonnet**.

omniscient narration   a **convention** of fiction in which the **point of view** is that of an "all-knowing" observer who narrates from a position outside the world of the **characters**. Such a narrator is free to reveal anything about the characters or the action (including things the characters may not be capable of saying about themselves), to shift in and out of the consciousness of a character, to move freely about in time and place, and to comment on the action or the characters (although not all omniscient narrators exercise this privilege).

open-form poetry   poetry not written according to any of the established verse patterns or forms; poetry that seeks its own form in terms of line length, **stanza** pattern, **rhyme** pattern, and arrangement on the page. (See also **fixed-form poetry**.)

outlining a **prewriting** strategy in which the **structure** of a paper is planned. A *formal* outline uses a system of Roman and Arabic numerals and alphabet letters to indicate levels of ideas and supporting details; the less formal *scratch* outline, illustrated in Chapters 4, 9, and 14, lists ideas and supporting details in the rough order in which the writer intends to present them in a draft of the paper.

pantoum a kind of **fixed-form** poem consisting of any number of **quatrains**, with the end words in two lines of one quatrain repeating, but at the ends of different lines, in the next quatrain. The final quatrain usually consists of the initial repeated lines or end words from the first quatrain and two lines or end words from the next-to-last quatrain.

paraphrase a verbal restatement of the language of a text in words other than those of the original text. A prose statement of a reader's sense of the gist of a poem is one type of paraphrase relevant to reading and responding to poetry. Speeches of **characters** in **drama** and portions of or entire **essays** may also commonly be paraphrased.

parody a close imitation, usually of a literary **style**, but treating a "lower" literary subject. A parody is a way of having fun with a text, but it can also be a tribute to an original text because it emphasizes some outstanding quality of the original; it can also serve a serious cultural function by calling into question the "high" status generally accorded to certain writers or subjects or styles.

peer reviewing a strategy in the writing process whereby a writer asks a classmate, or peer, to read and respond to a draft of the writer's paper. Peer reviewing can help writers because it permits feedback from someone who is working at the same writing task and because it allows writers to see their writing through someone else's eyes.

persona See **speaker** and **voice**.

personification a type of **figurative language** in which an animal, an inanimate object, or a concept or abstraction is given human qualities.

plagiarism unacknowledged use of the published words or ideas of a source.

play a written drama performed before an audience. In pattern or mood, a play may be a **comedy**, a **tragedy**, a **tragicomedy**, a **melodrama**, or none of these. In structure, it may be presented in one to five acts and any number of scenes. Play is also suggested in Chapters 10–13 as a way of reading poetry or as a synonym for poetry: in both of these senses, multiple meanings of language are explored or entertained, emphasizing the **polyvalent** quality of language.

plot in fiction or drama, the structure, order, or logical relationship of events. Plot is a **convention** that, while it may assume many patterns, is often understood as consisting of **exposition**, **conflict**, **rising action**, **climax**, and **falling action**. A subordinate line of action or sequence of events is a **subplot**.

poeticize a way of **playing** with language to make it into a poem, as in **found poetry**, in which texts from ordinary, prosaic, or usually unpoetic discourses are selected and arranged on the page to look like and become poems. Beyond found poetry, however, poeticizing may be thought of as a way of reading any text to emphasize **play** and allow the **polyvalent** character of language to emerge. (See also **play**.)

poetic feet See **meter**.

poetic license the variations in word choice or word order that poets may practice; more broadly, any of the things poets may do with language that **prose** writers do not do; poets' actual or reputed practice of violating the **conventions** of language, including capitalization, spelling, literal or **monovalent** senses of words, and the arrangement of words on a page. (See also **play**.)

point of view   the angle or perspective from which action and **characters** in a **short story** are related to the reader; the mode of **narration**. Narrative conventions allow several varieties of point of view. First- or third-person is one division; within those, first-person point of view may be **involved** or detached, and third-person point of view may be **omniscient** or limited. Point of view may be consistent or shifting within a narrative. (See also **narrator**.)

polyvalent   having more than one meaning, with no one meaning necessarily dominant; literature, especially poetry, is often considered polyvalent, whereas other kinds of discourse—instruction manuals, legal documents—are usually considered **monovalent**. A reader is free, however, to read any text as polyvalent.

predicting plot   a **reading strategy** for drama that involves writing down guesses or predictions of how the **plot** will develop in the parts of the **play** as yet unread. (See also **consistency building, suspense**.)

prewriting   a stage in the writing process or a set of strategies designed to get some ideas down on paper in very rough form and to generate other ideas prior to **drafting**. Specific prewriting techniques recommended in this book include **branching, clustering, freewriting**, and **outlining.**

primary source   an original document such as a story, poem, play, or essay that is cited in a researched paper. (See also **secondary source**.)

production   a particular presentation of a **play** in a theater; a production involves the interpretation of the written text of a play by the director and various designers whose ideas affect the actors' performances and the audience's responses.

proposition   in an essay, the statement of an idea, offered for the reader's belief, that can be shown to be true or false. A **formal essay** expresses a proposition as a **thesis** that it proposes to prove or explain.

proscenium stage   a theater stage in which a slightly curved section extends across the front between the curtain and the audience.

prose   written or spoken language in its ordinary form, arranged in sentences and paragraphs, not arranged in **verse** or with special attention to **rhythm** or **rhyme**.

protagonist   the main character in a piece of fiction or drama, especially when the piece is serious or tragic.

quatrain   a **verse stanza** of four lines.

read against the grain   a **reading strategy**, a form of **strong reading,** in which a reader consciously chooses to defy a text in terms of how it seems to "want" to be read, in terms of either its **literary repertoire** or its **ideology**.

read figuratively   a **reading strategy** in which a reader emphasizes the figurative or other-than-literal meaning of language or an entire text. Deciding to read figuratively is a way of doing a **strong reading**.

read literally   a **reading strategy** in which a reader emphasizes the literal meaning of language or an entire text.

reading strategies   the methods by which a reader processes a text in his or her mind; the techniques of reading. Reading strategies include creating **theme, naturalizing**, identifying with **characters, predicting plot**, identifying **symbols**, noticing **intertextuality**, identifying **gaps** and **indeterminacies, playing** with a text, **reading against the grain**, and others. An awareness of one's own reading strategies and of one's ability to adapt them to different **text strategies** or to suit different reading goals is an important step toward becoming a stronger reader.

realism   in fiction and drama, a kind of writing in which fictional events and people are represented in language to resemble everyday external reality and human experience. *Realistic* **short stories** and **plays** seem to be faithful to lived experience or to "reflect" reality, but they are also a particular set of **conventions**, dominant in a particular period in history, practiced by writers and perhaps unrecognized as such by readers. (See also **verisimilitude**.)

refrain   a phrase, line, or group of lines repeated at several places in a poem, usually at the end of each **stanza**. A refrain is a **convention** of the **ballad genre**.

reliable narrator   a **convention** of fiction in which the **voice** or **character** who relates information to the reader is perceived as believable or trustworthy. **Omniscient** narrators conventionally are reliable. **Involved** narrators may or may not be reliable, although inasmuch as they are characters, their reliability should not be assumed; their degree of reliability is **indeterminate**.

resisting reading   a form of **strong reading** in which a reader is aware of or takes a position that resists the **ideology** of the text. A resisting reading can be consciously adopted, or it can arise out of an initial clashing ideological interaction. (See also **strong reading**, **reading against the grain**, **consoling reading**.)

resolution   that part of the **plot** of a **short story** or **play** in which an initial **conflict** is resolved or brought to a logical conclusion; loosely synonymous with **denouement** or "unraveling" (of the "knot" of conflict).

response statement   a kind of writing that records a reader's initial reaction to a text and attempts to account for that response in terms of the literary and/or ideological interaction between text and reader. Response statements are a means toward becoming a self-conscious reader. They may also begin the process of **cognitive** or **cultural analysis** that further enacts the method and advances the goal of self-conscious reading.

revenge tragedy   See **tragedy**.

revising   a stage in the writing process or a writing strategy in which a writer changes a draft of a paper to suit the needs of its intended reader. **Peer reviewing** can be helpful in revising, but even if the writer gets no feedback from someone else, he or she should be willing to consider a reader's needs for clear organization, sufficient development, and definite focus in a paper.

rhetoric   language used to persuade an audience to accept a particular belief or adopt a certain perspective; also, the application of certain **text strategies**—such as **diction**, **tone**, and **structure**—to a persuasive purpose.

rhyme   a **convention** of **verse** involving the repetition of stressed vowel sounds and following consonant sounds. The most common type is *end rhyme*, in which the rhyming words fall at the ends of lines. *Internal rhyme* involves repeated stressed sounds within a single line of **verse**. *Eye rhyme* is the repetition of syllables that, because of the way they are spelled, look as if they would rhyme but which are not pronounced as rhyming: *prove, love*. *Near* or *slant rhymes* involve similar but not identical sounds: *rocks, wax*.

rhyme scheme   the pattern or recurrence of rhyming sounds at the ends of lines in **verse**, for example *abba, abab,* and *abccba*.

rhythm   in **verse**, the periodic, recurring alternation of stressed and unstressed syllables. A broader term than **meter**, rhythm is a **convention** of virtually all poetry, although meter, a regular rhythmical pattern, is not; **open-form poetry** or **free verse** has rhythm but not meter.

rising action   that part of the **plot** of a **short story** or **play** following the initial **conflict** in which, presumably, interest and suspense build toward a **climax**.

romantic comedy   See **comedy**.

satire   a text that blends humor and a critical attitude to expose what the author sees as the faults of some institution, group, or individual. (See also **comedy**.)

scansion   a method of describing **meter** in a poem by noting the pattern of stressed and unstressed syllables and the number and kind of **poetic feet** in which lines are written. (See also **meter**.)

screenplay   a **script** written for a dramatic performance in film or television; the **stage directions** may include notations of camera shots or other technical matters peculiar to the television or film media.

script   the written text of a play; the basis for a **production** of a play.

secondary source   a document such as a book or periodical article that comments on a literary text and that is cited in a researched paper. (See also **primary source**.)

selective perception   the decision, conscious or unconscious, to notice some elements of a sensory experience and not others. Because human beings cannot notice everything all the time, selective perception is always operating. As a **reading strategy**, however, selective perception involves conscious awareness of the process of or ideological basis for selective perception.

sentimental comedy   See **comedy**.

sestet   any six-line **stanza** in poetry, but usually limited to mean the last six lines of a **sonnet**.

sestina   a complex type of **fixed-form poetry** consisting of 39 lines divided into six 6-line **stanzas** and a final 3-line stanza (or **tercet**) known as an *envoy*. The six words that end the lines of the first stanza are repeated at the ends of the lines of the other five stanzas and in the envoy.

set   the scenery constructed for a particular **production** of a **play**, perhaps resembling the interior of a house or other building, as in a **box** set, perhaps merely suggesting a time and place, or perhaps consisting merely of a few props. In some plays, particularly **realistic** ones, a *set description* appears at the beginning to indicate how the author thinks the stage should look.

setting   a **convention** of the **short story**, **drama**, and some **poetry** denoting the location in place and time in which the action takes place and/or the characters exist or speak.

short story   a form of prose fiction characterized by brevity and, usually, the presence of such **text strategies** as **plot**, **character**, and **setting**. The short story form has its roots in oral **narratives** thousands of years old in the Western tradition. As a self-conscious art form, the short story developed rapidly in nineteenth-century Europe and the United States.

simile   a type of **figurative language** in which a comparison between two seemingly unlike things is explicitly made, signaled by the presence of "like," "as," "as if," or "so."

site of struggle   a place in any text—a word, a phrase, a paragraph, the entire text itself—where conflicting meanings coexist and compete for dominance. This conflict is often caused by competing **ideologies** that emphasize different meanings for the same word, phrase, etc. Identifying sites of struggle is a **reading strategy** that active readers may practice.

soliloquy   a relatively long philosophical or reflective speech by a **character** in a **play**, alone onstage, who is presumably talking to himself but whose words are heard by the audience. Soliloquy is a **convention** of European Renaissance drama.

sonnet   a type of **fixed-form poetry** consisting of 14 lines of (usually) rhymed *iambic pentameter* **verse**. The logical **structure** of the poem may be divided into an **octave** and a **sestet** (as in the Italian or Petrarchan sonnet) or three **quatrains** and a **couplet** (as in the English or Shakespearean sonnet).

speaker   in some **lyric** poetry, the "person" who utters the words that constitute the poem. Signaled by the first-person pronoun, "I," the speaker is nevertheless distinct from the author of the poem, especially in **dramatic monologues** or other poems with a dramatic quality. In nondramatic lyrics, the "I" may lack the defining characteristics of a person—name, occupation, physical situation—and hence may be more accurately described as a **voice** or **persona** rather than as a speaker.

spoken-to   in some **lyric** poetry, the "person" to whom the **speaker** utters the words that constitute the poem. In **dramatic monologues** or other poems with a dramatic quality, the spoken-to is a person presumably present on the occasion on which the speaker utters his or her words but who remains silent, only listening to the speaker's words.

stage business   movements or gestures by actors onstage in a **play**, especially those involving props or elements of scenery, such as Hamlet's handling and examining a human skull while he comments on "poor Yorick" in *Hamlet*, 5.1.

stage directions   words in a **script** that tell actors in a play when and where to exit or enter or how to gesture or move at certain moments. In *Trifles*, for instance, the opening **dialogue** of the **characters** is accompanied by stage directions indicating that the County Attorney is "rubbing his hands" as he speaks his first line and that Mrs. Peters delivers her first line "after taking a step forward."

stanza   a group of **verse** lines in a poem set off by a space between lines. Visually separate on the page, **couplets** (two-line groups), **tercets** (three lines), **quatrains** (four lines), and groups of five, six, seven, eight or more lines may constitute stanzas.

stock character   a **character** of a certain type that has become **conventional** to a particular **genre**; for example, the wicked stepmother in "fairy tales"; the dark, mysterious male hero in popular romance novels; or the young female hero disguised as a man in Shakespearean **romantic comedy**.

strong reading   a response or interpretation in which a reader is consciously aware of the effect of his or her **reading strategies** or **ideology** on how she or he reads a text cognitively or culturally. A strong reading may result from a reader's conscious attempt to discover and explain how or why she or he reads in a particular way or from a particular perspective. It may also result from a reader's conscious decision to adopt a particular reading strategy or strategies or a particular **ideological** perspective for a specific instance of reading.

structure   the principle or principles on which a text in the physical sense is built, its organization.

style   the manner in which language is used in a text and associated **conventions**. Style in this sense comprises **diction**, **syntax**, sentence length and grammatical construction, and **figurative language**. Style may be described in various ways, including "formal," "straightforward," "ironic," "humorous," "colloquial," and so forth.

subplot   See **plot**.

summary   in library research, a note that takes a passage from a source and boils it down to its essence. (See also **paraphrase**.)

suspense   an aspect or effect of **plot** in which a reader is able, based on information already provided, to guess or predict what will happen next or ultimately, but is unable to be certain of this prediction because some information has been withheld. Suspense is akin to a reader's anticipation.

symbol   a word or phrase, usually denoting a concrete object, that "stands for" or refers to something else, often an abstract concept or quality, and allows related and nonliteral meanings to come into play. In most cases, symbols depend on common understandings in the **ideologies** of a text and a reader; a symbol is not, therefore, an "objective" element of a literary text. A reader may read a text symbolically or figuratively, just as she or he may read it literally.

synechdoche   a type of **figurative language** in which a part stands for the whole of something. "Fifty *head* of cattle" is an example from common speech.

syntax   word order.

tercet   a three-line **verse stanza**.

text strategies   the methods by which a text takes shape and works as a text; techniques. Certain text strategies practiced widely become **conventions**, such as **characters**, **plot**, and **setting** in fiction. The interaction of text strategies and **reading strategies** may be harmonious or clashing; that is, if a reader is used to following and anticipating plot in a **short story**, his or her literary interaction with a text will be harmonious if that text has a plot, clashing if it does not.

theater in the round   See **arena stage**.

theme   an idea or concept with which a text seems to be concerned. Theme in a text may be a general principle, a moral point, an ethical point, or the logical or aesthetic resolution of a **conflict**. Traditional ways of reading literary texts hold that theme is "in" the text, a **text strategy**, perhaps functioning as a unifying principle for most if not all other text strategies. The model of the reading process operating in this book, however, says that theme is created by the reader interacting with whatever text strategies he or she emphasizes in a reading.

thesis   in **formal essays** or academic papers, a sentence that expresses the central point or idea that the text intends to explain or argue.

thrust stage   a theater stage that extends or "thrusts" out into the audience, which surrounds it on three sides.

title   a **conventional text strategy** that names a literary text to distinguish it from other texts. While often overlooked or taken for granted as a text strategy, a title often exerts a powerful influence on readers' interpretive efforts, as readers, according to their **literary experience**, may regard a title as an indicator of meaning in a text.

tone   an implied attitude, communicated through language, on the part of a **narrator** (in fiction), a **speaker** or **voice** (in poetry or essay), or a **character** (in drama) toward himself or herself, whomever she or he addresses, or whatever subject he or she is talking about. In the case of a first-person narrator in a **short story**, for example, or the speaker in a **lyric** poem, tone may contribute to a reader's sense of a person behind or expressed through that **voice**.

tragedy   broadly, a literary pattern in which a person of some status undergoes a decline in fortunes and ends in catastrophe, with the actions and their consequences treated seriously; more narrowly, that pattern presented in drama, or a particular kind of **play** that conforms to the tragic pattern. Historically, several types of tragedy may be distinguished: **classical** tragedy presents the decline of a person of high degree from fortune to disaster through a combination of his own actions, his moral character, and the operation of cosmic forces such as fate or divine will; **revenge** tragedy or tragedy **of blood** makes a revenge motive central to the **plot** and depicts bloody and violent actions on stage as that revenge is worked out; **middle-class** or **bourgeois** tragedy centers on a middle-class **character** whose misfortunes result from a situation in ordinary life, not a situation of cosmic or national significance.

tragedy of blood   See **revenge tragedy**, **tragedy**.

tragic hero   the main **character** or **protagonist** of a **tragedy**; typically, the tragic hero is a person of high social standing and/or moral character whose decline in fortune and ultimate disaster are presented as the inevitable result of his or her moral qualities combining with circumstances. The tragic hero is assumed to achieve a moral triumph through the insight that comes with the decline of fortunes he or she undergoes.

tragicomedy   a **play** that presents a serious situation like that of **tragedy** but allows it to end happily, as in **comedy**, or one that mixes comic and tragic elements, as in **black** comedy.

unreliable narrator   a **convention** of fiction in which the **voice** or **character** who relates information to the reader is perceived as untrustworthy. **Involved** narrators may or may not be reliable, although inasmuch as they are characters, their reliability should not be assumed; their degree of reliability is **indeterminate**. **Omniscient** narrators conventionally are reliable. The **text strategy** of unreliable narrator allows **irony** to operate in certain ways because that kind of narration suggests a difference, although often an indeterminate degree of difference, between the narrator's words and "reality" or "truth." (See also **reliable narrator**.)

verbal irony   See **irony**.

verisimilitude   a perceived quality of a short story as "true-to-life" or **realistic**; literally, "true-seeming." A sense of verisimilitude may be conveyed through other **text strategies** such as **character**, **setting**, and **style**. (See also **realism**.)

verse   loosely synonymous with **poetry**, but more specifically the quality of poetry as written in or divided into lines on the page according to requirements of **rhyme scheme**, **meter**, or **rhythm**. Thus, verse is distinct from **prose**.

villanelle   a type of **fixed-form poetry**, a 19-line poem consisting of five **tercets** and a final **quatrain** and a strict **rhyme scheme** in which the sounds at the end of the first and third lines of the first tercet are repeated in each subsequent tercet and in the quatrain.

visualization   a **reading strategy** for drama that involves creating mental pictures from the **script** of **characters**, **set**, and action.

voice   the qualities of personality constructed by a reader through the words and **tone** of what is said in some poems and some short stories. In fiction, the term voice is usually applied in cases of **omniscient** or detached narration, as opposed to instances of **involved** or **limited** narration, in which a reader may construct a more complete person or **character** who is telling the story. In poetry, voice may apply especially to the first-person **speaker** in some **lyrics**, as distinguished from the dramatized speaker in a **dramatic monologue**.

wandering viewpoint   a **reading strategy** complementary to **consistency building**. Wandering viewpoint sets up in a reader's mind a range of possible predictions, guesses, or interpretations from which one may be selected for emphasis; consistency building is the process of selecting information from a text that is consistent with a reader's predictions, guesses, or developing interpretations. "Wandering" in this sense really doesn't mean "without direction"; wandering viewpoint is more nearly explorative, reading with an "open" mind, keeping one's interpretive options open; consistency building thus may be thought of as closing or narrowing down the range of interpretive possibilities within a text. (See also **consistency building**.)

working bibliography   See **bibliography**.

works cited list   See **bibliography**.

ACKNOWLEDGMENTS

Fiction

"Dead Man's Path" from GIRLS AT WAR AND OTHER STORIES by Chinua Achebe. Copyright ©1972, 1973 by Chinua Achebe. Reprinted by permission of Doubleday, a division of Bantam Doubleday Dell Publishing Group, Inc. and Harold Ober Associates Incorporated.

"Inventory" by Lynne Barrett. Copyright ©1983 by Lynne Barrett. First published in THE MINNESOTA REVIEW. Reprinted by permission of the author.

"The Balloon" from UNSPEAKABLE PRACTICES, UNNATURAL ACTS by Donald Barthelme. Copyright ©1968 by Donald Barthelme. Reprinted with the permission of Wylie, Aitken & Stone, Inc.

"Theme of the Traitor and the Hero" by Jorge Luis Borges from LABYRINTHS. Copyright ©1962, 1964 by New Directions Publishing Corporation. Reprinted by permission.

"The Snow Child" from THE BLOODY CHAMBER AND OTHER ADULTS TALES by Angela Carter. Copyright ©1979 by Angela Carter. Reprinted by permission of HarperCollins Publishers, Inc.

"Cathedral" from CATHEDRAL by Raymond Carver. Copyright ©1981, 1982, 1983 by Raymond Carver. Reprinted by permission of Alfred A. Knopf, Inc.

"Cooking Lesson" from A ROSARIO CASTELLANOS READER by Rosario Castellanos, edited by Maureen Ahern and others, translated by Maureen Ahern. Copyright ©1988. Reprinted by permission of the editor, the University of Texas Press and Editorial Joaquin Mortiz.

"The Swimmer" from THE STORIES OF JOHN CHEEVER by John Cheever. Copyright ©1964 by John Cheever. Reprinted by permission of Alfred A. Knopf, Inc.

"Tall Woman Love" from THE BEANS OF EGYPT, MAINE by Carolyn Chute. Copyright ©1985 by Carolyn Chute. Reprinted by permission of Houghton Mifflin Company. All rights reserved.

"The House on Mango Street" from THE HOUSE ON MANGO STREET by Sandra Cisneros. Copyright ©1984 by Sandra Cisneros. Published by Vintage Books, a division of Random House, Inc., 1991. Published in hardcover by Alfred A. Knopf, 1994. Reprinted by permssion of Susan Bergholz Literary Services, New York.

"Continuity of Parks" from END OF THE GAME AND OTHER STORIES by Julio Cortzar, translated by Paul Blackburn. Copyright ©1967 by Random House, Inc. Reprinted by permission of Pantheon Books, a division of Random House, Inc.

"Battle Royal" from INVISIBLE MAN by Ralph Ellison. Copyright ©1948 by Ralph Ellison. Reprinted by permission of Random House, Inc.

"Fleur" from TRACKS by Louise Erdrich. Copyright ©1988 by Louise Erdrich. Reprinted by permission of the author.

"The Red Convertible" from LOVE MEDICINE, NEW AND EXPANDED VERSION by Louise Erdrich. Copyright ©1984, 1993 by Louise Erdrich. Reprinted by permission of Henry Holt and Company, Inc.

"A Rose for Emily" from COLLECTED STORIES by William Faulkner. Copyright 1930 and renewed ©1958 by William Faulkner. Reprinted by permission of Random House, Inc.

"Barn Burning" from COLLECTED STORIES by William Faulkner. Copyright 1950 by Random House, Inc. and renewed ©1977 by Jill Faulkner Summers. Reprinted by permission of the publisher.

"Basil and Cleopatra" from AFTERNOON OF AN AUTHOR by F. Scott Fitzgerald. Copyright ©1957 by Princeton University Library. Reprinted by permission of Department of Rare Books and Special Collections, Princeton University Libraries.

"A Very Old Man With Enormous Wings" from LEAF STORM AND OTHER STORIES by Gabriel Garcia Marquez. Coypright ©1971 by Gabriel Garcia Marquez. Reprinted by permission of HarperCollins Publishers, Inc.

"The Train from Rhodesia" from SELECTED STORIES by Nadine Gordimer. Copyright 1952 by Nadine Gordimer. Reprinted by permission of Viking Penguin, a division of Penguin Books USA Inc.

"Hills Like White Elephants" from MEN WITHOUT WOMEN by Ernest Hemingway. Copyright 1927 by Charles Scribner's Sons. Copyright renewed ©1955 Ernest Hemingway. Reprinted by permission of Scribner's, an imprint of Simon & Schuster.

"Eveline" from DUBLINERS by James Joyce. Copyright 1916 by B.W. Heubsch. Definitive text copyright ©1967 by the Estate of James Joyce. Reprinted by permission of Viking Penguin, a division of Penguin Books USA Inc.

"Araby" from DUBLINERS by James Joyce. Copyright 1916 by B.W. Heubsch. Definitive text copyright ©1967 by the Estate of James Joyce. Reprinted by permission of Viking Penguin, a division of Penguin Books USA Inc.

"Girl" from AT THE BOTTOM OF THE RIVER by Jamaica Kincaid. Copyright ©1978, 1983 by Jamaica Kincaid. Reprinted by permission of Farrar, Straus & Giroux, Inc.

"Shiloh" from SHILOH AND OTHER STORIES by Bobbie Ann Mason. Coyright ©1982 by Bobbie Ann Mason. "Shiloh" originally appeared in THE NEW YORKER. Reprinted by permission of HarperCollins Publishers, Inc.

"The Necklace" by Guy de Maupassant, translated by E.V. Roberts from LITERATURE: AN INTRODUCTION TO READING AND WRITING, 3/E edited by Roberts & Jacobs. Copyright ©1992 by Prentice Hall. Reprinted by permission of Prentice Hall, Englewood Cliff, NJ.

"A Wife's Story" from THE MIDDLEMAN AND OTHER STORIES by Bharati Mukherjee. Copyright ©1988 by Bharati Mukherjee. Reprinted by permission of Grove/Atlantic, Inc.

"Spelling" from THE BEGGAR MAID by Alice Munro. Copyright ©1977, 1978 by Alice Munro. Reprinted by permission of Alfred A. Knopf, Inc. and the Virginia Barber Literary Agency.

"Where Are You Going, Where Have You Been?" by Joyce Carol Oates from THE WHEEL OF LOVE AND OTHER STORIES. Copyright ©1970 by Joyce Carol Oates. Reprinted by permission of John Hawkins & Associates, Inc.

"The Things They Carried" by Tim O'Brien. Copyright ©1986 by Tim O'Brien. Originally published in ESQUIRE. Reprinted by permission of the author.

"A Good Man is Hard to Find" from A GOOD MAN IS HARD TO FIND AND OTHER STORIES by Flannery O'Connor. Copyright 1953 by Flannery O'Connor and renewed ©1981 by Regina O'Connor. Reprinted by permission of Harcourt Brace & Company.

"I Stand Here Ironing" from TELL ME A RIDDLE by Tillie Olsen. Copyright ©1956, 1957, 1960, 1961 by Tillie Olsen. Reprinted by permission of Delacorte Press/Seymour Lawrence, a division of Bantam Doubleday Dell Publishing Group, Inc.

"The Grave" from THE LEANING TOWER AND OTHER STORIES by Katherine Ann Porter. Copyright 1944 and renewed ©1972 by Katherine Ann Porter. Rerpinted by permission of Harcourt Brace & Company.

"The Birds" by Ronald Sukenick. Copyright ©1969 by Ronald Sukenick. Reprinted by permission of the author.

"The Secret Life of Walter Mitty" from MY LIFE AND WELCOME TO IT by James Thurber. Copyright 1942 by James Thurber. Copyright ©1970 Helen Thurber & Rosemary A. Thurber. Published by Harcourt Brace & Co. Reprinted by permission of Rosemary A. Thurber.

"Teenage Wasteland" by Anne Tyler, SEVENTEEN MAGAZINE. Copyright ©1983 by Anne Tyler. Reprinted by permission of Russell & Volkening as agents for the author.

"To Hell With Dying" from IN LOVE & TROUBLE: STORIES OF BLACK WOMEN by Alice Walker. Copyright ©1973 by Alice Walker. Reprinted by permission of Harcourt Brace & Company.

"A Worn Path" from A CURTAIN OF GREEN AND OTHER STORIES by Eudora Welty. Copyright 1941 and renewed ©1969 by Eudora Welty. Reprinted by permission of Harcourt Brace & Company.

"everybody knew bubba riff" from THE STORIES OF JOHN EDGAR WIDEMAN by John Edgar Wideman. Copyright ©1992 by John Edgar Wideman. Reprinted by permission of Pantehon Books, a division of Random House Inc.

"The Man Who Was Almost A Man" from EIGHT MEN by Richard Wright. Copyright ©1961 by Richard Wright. Reprinted by permission of the publisher, Thunder's Mouth Press and John Hawkins & Associates.

Poetry

"I, Mirror" by Claribel Algeria from *Y este poema rio*. Translated by Electa Arenal and Keitha Sapsin. (Managua: Editorial Nueva Nicaragua, 1988.) Reprinted by permission of the author and Curbstone Press.

"Africa" from OH PRAY MY WINGS ARE GONNA FIT WELL by Maya Angelou. Copyright ©1975 by Maya Angelou. Reprinted by permission of Random House Inc.

"My Arkansas" from AND STILL I RISE by Maya Angelou. Copyright ©1978 by Maya Angelou. Reprinted by permission of Random House Inc.

"You Fit Into Me" from POWER POLITICS by Margaret Atwood. Copyright ©1971 by Margaret Atwood (The House of Anansi Press). Reprinted by permission of Stoddart Publishing Co., Ltd., Don Mills, Ontario.

"This Is A Photograph of Me" from THE CIRCLE GAME by Margaret Atwood. Copyright ©1966 by Margaret Atwood (The House of Anansi Press). Reprinted by permission of Stoddart Publishing Co., Ltd., Don Mills, Ontario.

"The Unknown Citizen" from COLLECTED POEMS by W.H. Auden. Copyright 1940 and renewed ©1968 by W.H. Auden. Reprinted by permission of Random House, Inc. and Faber and Faber Ltd.

"Musee des Beaux Arts" from COLLECTED POEMS by W.H. Auden. Copyright 1940 and renewed ©1968 by W.H. Auden. Reprinted by permission of Random House, Inc. and Faber and Faber Ltd.

"Ancestor" from IMMIGRANTS IN OUR OWN LAND by Jimmy Santiago Baca. Copyright ©1982 by Jimmy Santiago Baca. Reprinted by permission of New Directions Publishing Corp.

"Turtle Considers Plato" by Terri M. Baker. Copyright ©1988 by Terri M. Baker. Reprinted by permission of the author.

"Black People: This Is Our Destiny" by Amiri Baraka. Copyright ©1969 by Amiri Baraka. Reprinted by permission of Sterling Lord Literistic, Inc.

"An Agony. As Now." by Amiri Baraka. Copyright ©1964 by Amiri Baraka. Reprinted by permission of Sterling Lord Literistic, Inc.

"Sestina" from THE COMPLETE POEMS 1927–1979 by Elizabeth Bishop. Copyright ©1979, 1983 by Alice Helen Methfessel.

Reprinted by permission of Farrar, Straus & Giroux, Inc.

"The Fish" from THE COMPLETE POEMS 1927-1979 by Elizabeth Bishop. Copyright ©1979, 1983 by Alice Helen Methfessel. Reprinted by permission of Farrar, Straus & Giroux, Inc.

"The Dream" from THE BLUE ESTUARIES by Louise Bogan. Copyright ©1968 by Louise Bogan. Reprinted by permission of Farrar, Straux & Giroux, Inc.

"Women" from THE BLUE ESTUARIES by Louise Bogan. Copyright ©1968 by Louise Bogan. Reprinted by permission of Farrar, Straus & Giroux, Inc.

"Breakfast with Gerard Manley Hopkins" by Anthony Brode. Reprinted by permission of Punch, London.

"The Boy Died in My Alley" from BLACKS by Gwendolyn Brooks. Copyright ©1991 Gwendolyn Brooks. Published by Third World Press, Chicago. Reprinted by permission of the author.

"First Fight. Then Fiddle" from BLACKS by Gwendolyn Brooks. Copyright ©1991 Gwendolyn Brooks. Published by Third World Press, Chicago. Reprinted by permission of the author.

"We Real Cool" from BLACKS by Gwendolyn Brooks. Copyright ©1991 Gwendolyn Brooks. Published by Third World Press, Chicago. Reprinted by permission of the author.

"Hometown" by Luis Cabalquinto. Reprinted by permission of the author.

"La Casa" by Rosemary Catacalos. Reprinted by permission of the author.

"Poem for the Young White Man Who Asked Me How I, an Intelligent, Well-Read Person Could Believe in the War Between Races" is reprinted from EMPLUMADA by Lorna Dee Cervantes. Copyright © by Lorna Dee Cervantes. Reprinted by permission of the University of Pittsburgh Press.

"Refugee Ship" by Lorna Dee Cervantes is reprinted with permission from the publisher of A DECADE OF HISPANIC LITERATURE: AN ANNIVERSARY ANTHOLOGY (Houston: Arte Publico Press-University of Houston, 1982.)

"Fast Car" by Tracy Chapman. Copyright ©1988 EMI April Music Inc. and Purple Rabbit Music. All rights controlled and administered by EMI April Music Inc. Reprinted by permission.

"Grasshoppers" by Kawai Chigetsu-Ni from WOMAN POETS OF JAPAN by Kenneth Rexroth. Copyright ©1977 by Kenneth Rexroth and Ikuko Atsumi. Reprinted by permission of New Directions Publishing Corp.

"Momma Moved among the Days" from GOOD WOMAN: POEMS AND A MEMOIR 1969–1980 by Lucille Clifton. Copyright ©1986 by Lucille Clifton. Reprinted by permission of BOA Editions, Ltd. 92 Park Avenue, Brockport, NY 14420.

"America" from COLLECTED POEMS OF ROBERT CREELEY, 1945–1975 by Robert Creeley. Copyright ©1983 The Regents of the University of California. Reprinted by permission of the University of California Press and the author.

"Louisiana" by Steve Crow from HARPER'S ANTHOLOGY OF TWENTIETH CENTURY NATIVE AMERICAN POETRY by Duane Niatum. Copyright ©1988 by Duane Niatum. Introduction copyright ©1988 by Harper & Row Publishers, Inc. Reprinted by permission of HarperCollins Publishers, Inc.

"Yet Do I Marvel" by Countee Cullen. Copyright held by the Amistad Research Center, Tulane University, New Orleans, LA. Administered by JJRK Associated, New York, NY. Reprinted by permission.

"anyone lived in a pretty how town" from COMPLETE POEMS, 1904–1962 by e.e. cummings, edited by George J. Firmage. Copyright 1923, 1931, 1935, 1940, 1951 ©1958, 1959, 1963, 1968, 1986, 1991 by the Trustees for the e.e. cummings Trust. Reprinted by permission of Liveright Publishing Corporation.

"r-p-o-p-h-e-s-s-a-g-r-" from COMPLETE POEMS, 1904–1962 by e.e. cummings, edited by George J. Firmage. Copyright 1923, 1931, 1935, 1940, 1951 ©1958, 1959, 1963, 1968, 1986, 1991 by the Trustees for the e.e. cummings Trust. Reprinted by permission of Liveright Publishing Corporation.

"1(a" from COMPLETE POEMS, 1904–1962 by e.e. cummings, edited by George J. Firmage. Copyright 1923, 1931, 1935, 1940, 1951 ©1958, 1959, 1963, 1968, 1986, 1991 by the Trustees for the e.e. cummings Trust. Reprinted by permission of Liveright Publishing Corporation.

"Buffalo Bill 's" from COMPLETE POEMS, 1904–1962 by e.e. cummings, edited by George J. Firmage. Copyright 1923, 1931, 1935, 1940, 1951 ©1958, 1959, 1963, 1968, 1986, 1991 by the Trustees for the

e.e. cummings Trust. Reprinted by permission of Liveright Publishing Corporation.

"somewhere i have never travelled, gladly beyond" from COMPLETE POEMS, 1904–1962 by e.e. cummings, edited by George J. Firmage. Copyright 1923, 1931, 1935, 1940, 1951 ©1958, 1959, 1963, 1968, 1986, 1991 by the Trustees for the e.e. cummings Trust. Reprinted by permission of Liveright Publishing Corporation.

"Psalm 4" by Mahmoud Darwish, translated by Lena Jayvusi and Anselm Hollo from POEMS, ESSAYS, DOCUMENTS, Poetry East, #38, Spring 1989. Reprinted by permission of DePaul University

"Helen" by H.D. from COLLECTED POEMS 1912–1944. Copyright ©1982 by The Estate of Hilda Doolittle. Reprinted by permission of New Directions Publishing Corp.

"An Introduction" by Kamala Das. Copyright ©1962 by Kamala Das. Reprinted by permission of the author.

"Hoop League" by Mark DeFoe. Copyright ©1986 Mark DeFoe. Reprinted by permission of the author.

"I taste a liquor never brewed" by Emily Dickinson. Reprinted by permission of the publishers and the Trustees of Amherst College from THE POEMS OF EMILY DICKINSON, Thomas J. Johnson, ed., Cambridge, Mass.: The Belknap Press of Harvard University Press. Copyright 1951, ©1955, 1983 by the President and Fellows of Harvard College.

"Success is counted sweetest" by Emily Dickinson. Reprinted by permission of the publishers and the Trustees of Amherst College from THE POEMS OF EMILY DICKINSON, Thomas J. Johnson, ed., Cambridge, Mass.: The Belknap Press of Harvard University Press. Copyright 1951, ©1955, 1983 by the President and Fellows of Harvard College.

"The Soul selects her own Society" by Emily Dickinson. Reprinted by permission of the publishers and the Trustees of Amherst College from THE POEMS OF EMILY DICKINSON, Thomas J. Johnson, ed., Cambridge, Mass.: The Belknap Press of Harvard University Press. Copyright 1951, ©1955, 1983 by the President and Fellows of Harvard College.

"I heard a Fly buzz-when I died" by Emily Dickinson. Reprinted by permission of the publishers and the Trustees of Amherst

College from THE POEMS OF EMILY DICKINSON, Thomas J. Johnson, ed., Cambridge, Mass.: The Belknap Press of Harvard University Press. Copyright 1951, ©1955, 1983 by the President and Fellows of Harvard College.

"Because I could not stop for Death" by Emily Dickinson. Reprinted by permission of the publishers and the Trustees of Amherst College from THE POEMS OF EMILY DICKINSON, Thomas J. Johnson, ed., Cambridge, Mass.: The Belknap Press of Harvard University Press. Copyright 1951, ©1955, 1983 by the President and Fellows of Harvard College.

"Some keep the Sabbath going to Church" by Emily Dickinson. Reprinted by permission of the publishers and the Trustees of Amherst College from THE POEMS OF EMILY DICKINSON, Thomas J. Johnson, ed., Cambridge, Mass.: The Belknap Press of Harvard University Press. Copyright 1951, ©1955, 1983 by the President and Fellows of Harvard College.

"A narrow Fellow in the Grass" by Emily Dickinson. Reprinted by permission of the publishers and the Trustees of Amherst College from THE POEMS OF EMILY DICKINSON, Thomas J. Johnson, ed., Cambridge, Mass.: The Belknap Press of Harvard University Press. Copyright 1951, ©1955, 1983 by the President and Fellows of Harvard College.

"After great pain - a formal feeling comes" (#341) by Emily Dickinson from THE COMPLETE POEMS OF EMILY DICKINSON edited by Thomas J. Johnson. Copyright 1929 by Martha Dickinson Bianchi. Copyright © renewed 1957 by Mary L. Hampson. Reprinted by permission of Little, Brown and Comapny.

"Daystar" from THOMAS AND BEULAH by Rita Dove. Copyright ©1986 by Rita Dove. Reprinted by permission of the author.

"Ö" from THE YELLOW HOUSE ON THE CORNER by Rita Dove. Copyright ©1980 Rita Dove. Reprinted by permission of the author.

"The Groundhog" from COLLECTED POEMS 1930-1986 by Richard Eberhart. Copyright ©1988 by Richard Eberhart. Reprinted by permission of Oxford University Press.

"Rhapsody on a Windy Night" from COLLECTED POEMS 1909-1962 by T.S. Eliot. Reprinted by permission of Faber and Faber Ltd.

"The Love Song of J. Alfred Prufrock" from COLLECTED POEMS 1909-1962 by T.S. Eliot. Reprinted by permission of Faber and Faber Ltd.

"Windigo" from JACKLIGHT by Louise Erdrich. Copyright ©1984 by Louise Erdrich. Reprinted by permission of Henry Holt & Co., Inc.

"Federico's Ghost" from REBELLION IS THE CIRCLE OF A LOVER'S HANDS by Martín Espada. Copyright ©1990 Martín Espada. Reprinted by permission of Curbstone Press.

"Latin Night at the Pawnshop" from REBELLION IS THE CIRCLE OF A LOVER'S HANDS by Martín Espada. Copyright ©1990 Martín Espada. Reprinted by permission of Curbstone Press.

"Black jam for dr. negro" from I AM A BLACK WOMAN by Mari Evans. Copyright ©1970 by Mari Evans. Published by William Morrow & Co. Reprinted by permission of the author.

"I Am a Black Woman" from I AM A BLACK WOMAN by Mari Evans. Copyright ©1970 by Mari Evans. Published by William Morrow & Co. Reprinted by permission of the author.

"Prison Daybreak" by Faiz Ahmed Faiz, translated by Naomi Lazard from THE TRUE SUBJECT: SELECTED POEMS OF FAIZ AHMED FAIZ. Copyright ©1987 Princeton University Press. Reprinted by permission of Princeton University Press.

"The Pennycandystore Beyond the El" from A CONEY ISLAND OF THE MIND by Lawrence Ferlinghetti. Copyright ©1958 by Lawrence Ferlinghetti. Reprinted by permission of New Directions Publishing Corp.

"The Bog Sacrifice" by John Finlay from MIND AND BLOOD: THE COLLECTED POEMS OF JOHN FINLEY edited by David Middleton. Copyright ©1992 Jean Finley. Reprinted by permission of David Middleton, literary executor.

"Selective Service" from THE COUNTRY BETWEEN US by Carolyn Forché. Copyright ©1981 by Carolyn Forché. Reprinted by permission of HarperCollins Publishers, Inc.

"Because One Is Always Forgotten" from THE COUNTRY BETWEEN US by Carolyn Forché. Copyright ©1981 by Carolyn Forché. Reprinted by permission of HarperCollins Publishers, Inc.

"Speaking" from WOVEN STONE by Simon Ortiz. Copyright ©1976 Simon Ortiz. Reprinted by permission of the author.

"Ethics" from PM/AM: NEW AND SELECTED POEMS by Linda Pastan. Copyright ©1982 by Linda Pastan. Reprinted by permission of W.W. Norton & Company, Inc.

"The Seven Deadly Sins" ("Anger" section only) by Linda Pastan from A FRACTION OF DARKNESS. Copyright ©1985 by Linda Pastan. Reprinted by permission of W.W. Norton & Company, Inc.

"Mary Jane's Last Dance," words and music by Tom Petty. Copyright ©1993 Gone Gator Music (ASCAP) International Copyright Secured. Made in USA. All Rights Reserved. Reprinted by permission of CPP/Belwin, Inc., Miami, FL 33014.

"The Woman in the Ordinary" from CIRCLES ON THE WATER by Marge Piercy. Copyright ©1982 by Marge Piercy. Reprinted by permission of Alfred A. Knopf, Inc.

"Barbie Doll" from CIRCLES ON THE WATER by Marge Piercy. Copyright ©1982 by Marge Piercy. Reprinted by permission of Alfred A. Knopf, Inc.

"Traffic Violations" by Pedro Juan Pietri. Copyright ©1983 by Pedro Juan Pietri. Reprinted by permission of the author.

"Daddy" from ARIEL by Sylvia Plath. Copyright ©1963 by Ted Hughes. Copyright Renewed. Reprinted by permission of HarperCollins Publishers, Inc. and Faber and Faber Ltd.

"Metaphors" from CROSSING THE WATER by Sylvia Plath. Copyright ©1960 by Ted Hughes. Copyright Renewed. Reprinted by permission of HarperCollins Publishers, Inc. and Faber and Faber Ltd.

"Seven Vietnamese Boys" by Chin Woon Pong. Copyright ©1987 by Chin Woon Pong. Reprinted by permission of the author.

"In a Station of the Metro" from PERSONAE by Ezra Pound. Copyright ©1926 by Ezra Pound. Reprinted by permission of New Directions Publishing Corp.

"The River Merchant's Wife: A Letter" from PERSONAE by Ezra Pound. Copyright ©1926 by Ezra Pound. Reprinted by permission of New Directions Publishing Corp.

"The Kite" from THE TIME BETWEEN by Wyatt Prunty. Copyright ©1982 The Johns Hopkins University Press. Reprinted by permission of The Johns Hopkins University Press.

"Rooms Without Walls" from THE RUN OF THE HOUSE by Wyatt Prunty. Copyright ©1993 The Johns Hopkins University Press. Reprinted by permission of The Johns Hopkins University Press.

"Air Hoodlum" by Public Enemy. Copyright ©1992 Def American Songs, Inc./Bring the Noize, Inc. All rights reserved. Reprinted by permission.

"Ballad of Birmingham" by Dudley Randall. Copyright ©1966 by Dudley Randall. Reprinted by permission.

"Bells for John Whiteside's Daughter" from SELECTED POEMS by John Crowe Ransom. Copyright ©1924 Alfred A. Knopf, Inc. and renewed 1952 by John Crowe Ranson. Reprinted by permission of Alfred A. Knopf, Inc.

"Naming of Parts" from COLLECTED POEMS by Henry Reed, edited by Jon Stallworthy. Copyright ©1991 The Executor of Henry Reed's Estate. Reprinted by permission of Oxford University Press.

"I am a Cowboy in the boat of Ra" from NEW AND COLLECTED POEMS by Ishmael Reed. Copyright ©1972 Ishmael Reed. Reprinted by permission of Whitman, Breed, Abbott & Morgan.

"beware: do not read this poem" from NEW AND COLLECTED POEMS by Ishmael Reed. Copyright ©1972 Ishmael Reed. Reprinted by permission of Whitman, Breed, Abbott & Morgan.

"Living in Sin" from THE FACT OF A DOORFRAME, POEMS SELECTED AND NEW, 1950–1984 by Adrienne Rich. Copyright ©1984 by Adrienne Rich. Copyright ©1975, 1978 by W.W. Norton & Company, Inc. Copyright ©1981 by Adrienne Rich. Reprinted by permission of W.W. Norton & Company, Inc.

"Aunt Jennifer's Tigers" from THE FACT OF A DOORFRAME, POEMS SELECTED AND NEW, 1950–1984 by Adrienne Rich. Copyright ©1984 by Adrienne Rich. Copyright ©1975, 1978 by W.W. Norton & Company, Inc. Copyright ©1981 by Adrienne Rich. Reprinted by permission of W.W. Norton & Company, Inc.

"My Papa's Waltz" from THE COLLECTED POEMS OF THEODORE ROETHKE by Theodore Roethke. Copyright 1942 by Hearst Magazines, Inc. Reprinted by permission of Doubleday, a division of Bantam Doubleday Dell Publishing Group, Inc.

"If I am too brown or too white for you" from THE HALFBREED CHRONICLES by Wendy Rose, 1985. Reprinted by permission of the author.

"Three Thousand Dollar Death Song" from LOST COPPER by Wendy Rose, 1980. Reprinted by permission of the author.

"to blk/record/buyers" by Sonia Sanchez. Copyright ©1969 by Sonia Sanchez. Reprinted by permission of the author.

"a poem for my father" by Sonia Sanchez. Copyright ©1979 by Sonia Sanchez. Reprinted by permission of the author.

"Grandmother, a Caribbean Indian, Described by My Father" from VALENTINO'S HAIR by Yvonne Sapia. Copyright ©1987 by Yvonne Sapia. Reprinted with the permission of Northeastern University Press.

"Her Kind" from TO BEDLAM AND PART WAY BACK by Anne Sexton. Copyright ©1960 by Anne Sexton, ©renewed 1988 by Linda Gray Sexton. Reprinted by permission of Houghton Mifflin Co. All rights reserved.

"Cinderella" from TRANSFORMATIONS by Anne Sexton. Copyright ©1971 by Anne Sexton. Reprinted by permission of Houghton Mifflin Co. All rights reserved.

"Anchorage" written by Michelle Shocked. Copyright ©1988 PolyGram Music Publishing, Ltd. Administered in the United State and Canada by Songs of PolyGram International, Inc. All Rights Reserved. Reprinted by permission.

"They Didn't Hire Him" from THE BACK COUNTRY by Gary Snyder. Copyright ©1968 Gary Snyder. Reprinted by permission of New Directions Publishing Corp.

"Riprap" from RIPRAP AND COLD MOUNTAIN POEMS by Gary Snyder. Copyright ©1958, 1959, and 1965 by Gary Snyder. Reprinted by permission of North Point Press, a division of Farrar, Straus & Giroux, Inc.

"The White Porch" from PICTURE BRIDE by Cathy Song. Copyright ©1983 by Cathy Song. Reprinted by permission of Yale University Press.

"Lost Sister" from PICTURE BRIDE by Cathy Song. Copyright ©1983 by Cathy Song. Reprinted by permission of Yale University Press.

"The Poor" by Roberto Sosa, translated by Jim Lindsey from THE DIFFICULT DAYS. Copyright ©1983 Princeton University Press.

Reprinted by permission of Princeton University Press.

"Mexicans Begin Jogging" from NEW AND SELECTED POEMS by Gary Soto. Copyright ©1995 Gary Soto. Reprinted by permission of Chronicle Books.

"Oranges" from NEW AND SELECTED POEMS by Gary Soto. Copyright ©1995 Gary Soto. Reprinted by permission of Chronicle Books.

"Cover Me" by Bruce Springsteen. Copyright ©1984 by Bruce Springsteen. Reprinted by permission of John Landau Management.

"4th of July, Asbury Park" by Bruce Springsteen. Copyright ©1973 by Bruce Springsteen. Reprinted by permission of John Landau Management.

"Traveling through the Dark" by William Stafford. Copyright ©1960 by William Stafford. Reprinted by permission.

"The Snow Man" from COLLECTED POEMS by Wallace Stevens. Copyright 1923 and renewed 1951 by Wallace Stevens. Reprinted by permission of Alfred A. Knopf, Inc.

"The Emperor of Ice-Cream" from COLLECTED POEMS by Wallace Stevens. Copyright 1923 and renewed 1951 by Wallace Stevens. Reprinted by permission of Alfred A. Knopf, Inc.

"Anecdote of the Jar" from COLLECTED POEMS by Wallace Stevens. Copyright 1923 and renewed 1951 by Wallace Stevens. Reprinted by permission of Alfred A. Knopf, Inc.

"Eating Poetry" from SELECTED POEMS by Mark Strand. Copyright ©1979, 1980 by Mark Strand. Reprinted by permission of Alfred A. Knopf, Inc.

"Women" by May Swenson. Copyright ©1968 May Swenson. Reprinted by permission of The Literary Estate of May Swenson.

"Explosion" by Shinkichi Takahishi from THE PENGUIN BOOK OF ZEN POETRY, edited and translated by Lucien Stryk. Copyright ©1978 by Lucien Stryk. Reprinted by permission of Lucien Stryk.

"There Is No Word for Goodbye" by Mary TallMountain. Reprinted by permission of the author.

"Do not go gentle into that good night" by Dylan Thomas from POEMS OF DYLAN THOMAS. Copyright 1939 by New Directions,

Drama

Essays

INDEX